To John

April 2007.

Carry on Supporting
Conservation !

Love David

# CONTENTS

## Part 1. Introduction

## Part 2. Plenary papers

# Part 3. Geographic regions

# Part 4.  Cross-cutting issues

# Part 5.  Integrated approaches to waterbird conservation

# Part 6. Waterbirds and people

# Foreword

They are one of the world's most attractive group of birds — and the most threatened: albatrosses, flamingos, swans, geese, ducks, cranes, waders, gulls, terns and auks and all the rest of the world's waterbirds. They share a dependency on the world's wetlands - seas, coasts, estuaries, lagoons, lochs, rivers, marshlands, swamps, tundra and other peatlands, and they have come to symbolize the changing, fragile nature of planet Earth. With the publication of *Waterbirds around the world*, five years of planning, meetings, fundraising and writing come to fruition. And with the publication of this book, we close one chapter and begin another — to improve research and conservation efforts to secure a healthier environment for waterbirds, building on the body of knowledge gathered together in this volume.

It is an honour for us to have been involved in the production of this book. It is the outcome of a major international conference on waterbirds held in Edinburgh in April 2004, and attended by 456 people from 90 countries. In October 2005 we published an overview of the results of the conference. This included the text of *The Edinburgh Declaration*, which calls for urgent action to halt and reverse wetland loss and degradation, and to extend and strengthen networks of key sites for waterbirds along all flyways. Subsequently, at various inter-governmental meetings there have been discussions to assist waterbird flyway conservation, and formal resolutions calling on countries to implement *The Edinburgh Declaration*.

We hope that readers of this book will enjoy the wealth of material drawn together here from across the globe. We are especially pleased to include the presentations by His Royal Highness The Prince of Wales, Government Ministers and leading authorities on waterbird conservation and global flyways. The publication of this book has been a major undertaking, with the core editorial team working together closely since May 2004. All papers presented as part of the conference symposia have been peer-reviewed by a total of almost 70 experts, to whom we are very grateful. The short notes, based on more than a hundred poster presentations, were refereed by the editorial team. It is a pleasure for us to extend our thanks to the team and, of course, to the authors for their unstinting labours, not least in trying to keep the length of submissions short — something which may not be apparent at first sight given the size of this book!

In looking to the future we sincerely hope, and indeed believe, that this volume of work will improve our collective understanding of the needs of waterbirds, and in so doing will stimulate further international cooperation. We live in a world where the spoken or written word can reach anywhere in seconds. Some waterbirds make global journeys which take considerably longer and where they encounter all manner of perils. When you next make a long distance telephone call, or send an email to a friend in some distant country, or enjoy a comfortable airline meal at 9 000 m, spare a thought for waterbirds in flight facing a multitude of hazards over land and sea, very often across scores of national boundaries: travelling between countries the hard way. Unless we act together, uniting our efforts in research, conservation, management and awareness-raising, we shall fail these birds and the human populations enriched by their presence.

What a challenge lies ahead, not least in the face of global concerns about avian flu, climate change and wholesale losses of natural habitats! Quite simply, we now have no alternative but to deploy our shared knowledge and understanding of waterbirds to provide for a better world. People around the world have a right to marvel at the sight and sound of waterbirds as part of a wider, sustainable ecosystem. The conference has shown us how much we can achieve when we work together to help ensure that the planet becomes healthier for wildlife and for humanity.

**Professor Colin A. Galbraith**
**Chairman**

**Dr. Gerard C. Boere**
**Secretary General**

On behalf of the *Waterbirds around the world* Conference Committee, 14 September 2006

Edinburgh Castle. Photo: Colin Galbraith.

# Part 1.

## Introduction

# Address by the Patrons of 'Waterbirds around the world'

We were pleased to be part of nearly 500 waterbird conservationists from all parts of the world, and honoured to act as patrons of the conference. It was good to see three Ministers presenting their views on the importance of migratory water bird conservation and to hear His Royal Highness The Prince of Wales draw attention to the current major threats to albatrosses, those 'perpetual oceanic migrants'.

Boyd, H., Kuijken, E., Hoffman, L., Matthews, G. & Nelson, H. 2006. Address by the Patrons of 'Waterbirds around the world'. *Waterbirds around the world*. Eds. G.C. Boere, C.A. Galbraith & D.A. Stroud. The Stationery Office, Edinburgh, UK. p. 2.

Since we began to be involved in waterbird research, management and conservation in the late 1940s and 1950s, much has changed. (From 6 x 30 binoculars to magnificent telescopes and digiscoping photography, from simple handwritten notebooks to laptops). Research techniques have developed enormously, with the arrival of video-recording, radio-marking and satellite tracking, geographical data-loggers and automatic electronic data collection in the field. There have been corresponding improvements in the presentation and availability of data, illustrations and text. Coloured illustrations are now no longer prohibitively expensive and 'Power Point presentations' full of sound, light and action are now commonplace. Detailed remote sensing images can now be downloaded for every site, even the most isolated or secret place on Earth. For our own field explorations in so many wetlands reliable maps were hardly available!

Yet perhaps the most important change has been in the numbers of players on the conservation scene. Both professionals and volunteers, especially bird people have founded the base of conservation world wide. Where there were hardly any reserve wardens or researchers there are now hundreds. Professional administrators of conservation programmes have inserted themselves too, as they have in so many areas of government.

Patrons of *Waterbirds around the world*: from left to right: Harvey Nelson (USA), Hugh Boyd (Canada), Geoffrey Matthews (UK) and Eckhart Kuijken (Belgium); Luc Hoffmann could not be present at the conference. Photo: Dougie Barnett.

Waterbird conferences since the 1950s organised by IWRB (now Wetlands International) succeeded to attract specialists from over the world and have convinced participants about their growing power to encourage ecologically sound conservation. In this regard the Ramsar Convention is a real masterpiece that sets the scene for further multilateral treaties, and (in a European context) Directives related to biodiversity to follow in later decades.

The Edinburgh conference heard many accounts of progress in research and the development of management tools. Much remains to be done, especially in broadening out from 'saving threatened species' to bringing about major changes in land use beyond the boundaries of reserves, for the benefit of entire ecosystems, including the people who depend on them.

We saw and listened to many outstanding performers. By definition, they will always be scarce. One of the continuing requirements of wetland and waterbird conservation world-wide is to encourage and enable these talented people to flourish, in a far more complicated world than confronted us at the start of our careers. One major feature of the conservation world is its massive dependence on volunteers and their 'citizen science'. This must surely be healthy and help to ensure that ever-broadening circles of people around the world come to understand the importance of keeping it fit for many forms of life to flourish.

Participants enjoy a conference talk in Edinburgh. Photo: Dougie Barnett.

During the second half of the 20th century, international policy instruments proliferated. Unfortunately, if unsurprisingly, they have not been accompanied by sufficient funding to enable them to be fully effective. In particular, enforcement of laws and regulations has often been feeble and far too little effort has been devoted to following up the effectiveness of the reserve networks that have been created. Communication with the public at large in order to raise awareness still is an essential priority in conservation.

We are very grateful for the opportunity we were given to be symbolically involved in the *Waterbirds around the world* conference on such undemanding terms, just presenting a glimpse of historical facts in the growing movement of conservation that we are happy to be part of as pioneers of the mid 20th century. We especially hope that we were able to encourage those now active in the field to continue to work as hard as they can to create and maintain a better world, where biodiversity conservation is an integrated part of sustainable development.

# Acknowledgements

*Waterbirds around the world* could not have happened without the inputs and support of many people. The conference organisers are grateful to all who have given their support over the last six years.

We are especially grateful to: His Royal Highness The Prince of Wales; Minister Elliot Morley, MP; Minister Cees Veerman; Max Finlayson; John Markland; and Deputy Minister Allan Wilson, MSP.

**Board of Patrons:** Hugh Boyd, Luc Hoffmann, Eckhart Kuijken, Geoffrey Matthews and Harvey Nelson.

**The Conference Team:** Gerard Boere, Colin Galbraith, David Stroud, Les Underhill, George Anderson, Ian Enlander, Jenny Griffin, Saskia Henderikse, Adam Kidson, René Looyen, Jane Madgwick, Angela McTeir, Ash Murray, Simon Nash, Daniëlle Nieuwenhuijse, Colin Robertson, Susan Ross, Evert Rougoor, Paul Schmidt, Jan Willem Sneep, Doug Taylor, Des Thompson, Robert Vagg, Inge Veenstra, Marion Whitelaw and Andy Williams.

**The UK Organising Committee** comprised: Colin Galbraith (Chairman), David Stroud (Secretary), Susan Ross, Robert Vagg, Andy Williams, Angela McTeir, Deborah Gooch, Colin Sheddon, John Doherty, Jo Wilson, Duncan Orr-Ewing, Ian Francis, Bill Gardner and Ashley Murray, with additional inputs from Mark Rehfisch, Catherine Gray and Ian Enlander.

**JNCC and SNH:** Deryck Steer, Ian Jardine, Ian McLean, Helen Baker, Janet Sprent, Heather Pegg, Jean Lambert, Saville Gunn, Kerry Jepson, Zena Bailey, Carl Cilenti, Sandra Groome, Sue Wenlock, Alison Lee, Geoff Beall and Kenny MacLean.

The Conference dinner was held in the main hall of the Royal Museum, part of the National Museum of Scotland, following a reception during which delegates explored the museum's extensive collections.  Photo: Taej Mundkur.

The Conference Team is most grateful to Janet Hunter, David Ness, Orela Deane and all the staff of the James Watt Conference Centre at Heriot-Watt University, Edinburgh for their professional support throughout the planning and execution of the conference.

**Many volunteers** freely gave their time and expertise to help during the conference and to lead excursions. We are grateful to them all: Zul Bhatia, Liz Campbell, Zoe Clelland, Hugh Conner, Neil Cowie, John Doherty and staff of WWT's Caerlaverock Wetlands Centre, Richard Evans, Ian Francis, Adam Kidson, Alan Leitch, Andy McFarlane, Duncan Orr-Ewing, Jack Fleming and staff of RSPB's Mersehead Reserve, Catherine Quigley, Jeremy Roberts, Colin Sheddon, Chris Spelding, Ian Thomson, Winnie Thomson, Lornie Wilkie, Andy Williams, Mike Thornton, Susan Haysom, Ellen Wilson and Simon Zisman.

Many people volunteered to help with the conference excursion programme, including to the Bass Rock – which holds an internationally important colony of Northern Gannets *Morus bassana* breeding on the rock, after which the species is named. Photo: Colin Galbraith.

We are grateful to the following organisations for their in-kind support of the excursions: British Association for Shooting and Conservation; the Wildfowl and Wetlands Trust; the Royal Society for the Protection of Birds; and the Scottish Ornithologists' Club.

The Royal Dutch Natural History Society (KNNV), with Paul Kemmeren, facilitated the free distribution of the recently published book *Shorebirds: an illustrated behavioural ecology* to all the conference delegates.

The European Commission (DG Environment) supported the conference through holding a meeting of the Scientific Working Group of the Birds Directive's Ornis Committee within the framework of the conference. This allowed the support of additional delegates from the EU.

The conference programme was developed by the Conference Scientific Committee, comprising: Les Underhill (Chairman), Gerard Boere (Secretary), Marco Barbieri, Peter Bayliss, Leon Bennum, Bart Ebbinge, Gudmundur Gudmundsson, Noritaka Ichida, Jim Kushlan, Randy Milton, Charles Mlingwa, Mark O'Connell, Theunis Piersma, Robert Schlatter, Paul Schmidt, David Stroud and Pavel Tomkovich.

The production of these proceedings would not have happened without the efforts of: Derek Scott, Linda Bridge, Iain Colquhoun, Des Thompson, Les Underhill, Nick Davidson, Ron Wilson, Karen Pope, Jane McNair, Denise Dalrymple, Chris Dalrymple and Jon Dalrymple.

The Conference Team, in October 2003, wrestling with the complexities of the conference programme! Photo: David Stroud.

We thank all **peer-reviewers** who freely gave their time and expertise to review and improve submitted papers: Åke Andersson, Brad Andres, Anny Anselin, Bruce Batt, Albert Beintema, Bob Blohm, Gerard Boere, Stephen Browne, Kees Camphuys, Nick Davidson, Kees van Dijk, Gary Donaldson, Mennobart van Eerden, Morten Ekker, Meinte Engelmoer, Michael Exo, Yves Ferrand, Bob Gill, Lyle Glowka, Adam Gretton, Antti Haapanen, Barry Hartup, Tom van der Have, Hermann Hötker, Marshall Howe, Verena Keller, Roger Jaensch, Alan Johnson, Torsten Larsson, Konstantin Litvin, Frank Majoor, Randy Milton, Clive Minton, Claire Mirande, Johan Mooij, Mike Moser, Wim van Muiswinkel, Harvey Nelson, Leif Nilsson, Guy-Noel Olivier, Tunde Ojej, Sander van Opstal, Dieter Oschladeus, John O'Sullivan, Mike Pienkowski, Eileen Rees, Mark Rehfisch. Klaus Riede, David Rodrigues, Hans-Ulrich Rosner, Clayton Rubec, Frank Saris, Yara Schaeffer-Novelli, Roberto Schlatter, Humphrey Sitters, Ken Smith. Arie Spaans, Melanie Steinkamp, David Stroud, Kees Swennen, John Swift, Zhenya Syroechskovski, Des Thompson, Christophe Tourenq, Jan Veen, Joost van der Ven and Rinse Wassenaar.

We are indebted to **the many photographers** who have allowed us to enliven the pages of these proceedings with their pictures of waterbirds and their habitats worldwide, as well as all those who helped source these photos and/or provided images that unfortunately were not possible to use: Else Ammentorp, Adrian Azpiroz, Mark Barter, Helen Baker, Dougie Barnett, Daniel Bergmann, Gerard Boere, Adrian Boyle, Andy Brown, Ian Carter, Albert Chipps, Nigel Clark, John Cooper, Peter Cranswick, Ruth Cromie, Alistair Crowle, Danmarks Jægerforbund/Danish Hunters Association, Nick Davidson, Hans Dekkers, Sergey Dereliev, C. Donald, Tim Dodman, Andy Douse, Allan Drewitt, Sergey Eliseev, Meinte Englemoer, Ian Francis, Milton Friend, Colin Galbraith, Niels Gilissen (MIRATIO), Ward Hagemeijer, Doug Harebottle, Gareth Hartford, David Hatton, Richard Hearn, Jemi & John Holmes, Menno Hormman, Dave Humburg, J. Jave, Niels Kanstrup, Florian Keil, Verena Keller, Gary Kramer, John Marchant, Ian Mackenzie, Paul Marshall, Brian McKean, David Melville, Randy Milton, Ian Mitchell, Jean-Yves Mondain Monval, Johan Mooij, Steve Moore, Anders Mosbech, Christian Moullec, Taej Mundkur, Petr Musil, Zuzana Musilová, P.K. Nandi, Steve Newton, Ingar Jostein Oien, Dieter Oschadleus, Matt Parsons, Dwight Peck, Ib Krag Petersen, Margaret Petersen, Nikolai Petkov, Anastasia Popovkina, Crawford Prentice, Press Association, Eileen Rees, Rob Robinson, Paul Schmidt, Michael Samuel, Scottish Natural Heritage, David Sowter, Simon Stirrup, David Stroud, Tom Stroud, Katerina Svadova, Niels Søndergaard, Stan Tekiela, Kai-Michael Thomsen, Les Underhill, US Fish & Wildlife Service, US Geological Survey, Jaap de Vlas, Peter Wakerly, Alyn Walsh, Keith Wearne, Richard Webster, Jennifer Wheeler, the Wildfowl & Wetlands Trust, Chris Wilson, Rebecca Woodward, Niklaus Zbinden, Sama Zefania and Christoph Zöckler. Special thanks, in particular, are due to Paul Marshall for the cover photo and his many other beautiful images of the world's waterbirds.

## Sponsors of the conference

**The Netherlands:**  Ministry of Agriculture, Nature and Food Quality

**United Kingdom:**  Department for Environment, Food and Rural Affairs

Joint Nature Conservation Committee

Scottish Natural Heritage

Scottish Executive

English Nature (Natural England from October 2006)

Northern Ireland Environment and Heritage Service

Countryside Council for Wales

African Eurasian Migratory Waterbird Agreement (UNEP/AEWA)

Australia:                    Environment Australia

                             Ministry for Flemish Affairs;

Belgium:

                             Belgian Institute for Nature Conservation

Canada:                      Canadian Wildlife Service

Convention on Migratory Species (UNEP/CMS)

Denmark:                     Ministry of Foreign Affairs

European Commission

Federation of Associations for Hunting and Conservation of the EU (FACE)

Finland:                     Ministry of Environment

Germany:        Federal Ministry for Environment, Nature Conservation and Nuclear Safety

International Council for Game and Wildlife Management (CIC)

Ireland:                     Duchas

Japan:                       Ministry of Environment

Sweden:                      Environment Agency

Switzerland:                 Environment Agency

United States of America:  U.S. Fish and Wildlife Service

## The Edinburgh Declaration

*An international conference on waterbirds, their conservation and sustainable use was held in Edinburgh, Scotland, from 3-8 April 2004, attended by 456 participants from 90 countries.*

**Conscious that** waterbird flyways are biological systems of migration paths that directly link sites and ecosystems in different countries and continents;

**Recalling that** the conservation and wise-use of waterbirds is a shared responsibility of nations and peoples and a common concern of human-kind;

**Recalling also** the long history of international co-operation for waterbird conservation developed over a hundred years with treaties such as that concerned with migratory birds in 1916 between USA and UK (on behalf of Canada), and that over 40 years ago, the first European Meeting on Wildfowl Conservation held in St. Andrews, Scotland in 1963, started a process leading to the establishment of the Convention on wetlands especially as waterfowl habitat in Ramsar, Iran, in 1971;

**Noting that** major international conferences in Noordwijk aan Zee, The Netherlands (1966), Leningrad, USSR (1968), Ramsar, Iran (1971), Astrakhan, USSR (1989), St. Petersburg Beach, Florida, USA (1992), Kushiro, Japan and Strasbourg, France (1994), have further developed international technical exchanges on waterbird conservation;

**Aware of** the development of further inter-governmental co-operation through the establishment and implementation of further treaties, agreements, strategies and programmes; and of the development of considerable non-governmental national and international co-operation in waterbird conservation and monitoring;

**Conscious that** at the World Summit on Sustainable Development, Johannesburg, South Africa, in 2002, world leaders expressed their desire to achieve *"a significant reduction in the current rate of loss of biological diversity"* by 2010, and that in February 2004 this target was further developed by the Seventh Conference of the Parties to the Biodiversity Convention, and **aware that** achieving this target will require significant investments and highly focused and co-ordinated conservation activity on all continents, and **recognising that** communication, education and public awareness and capacity building will play a key role in achieving this target;

**Further conscious** of the urgent need to strengthen international co-operation and partnerships between governments, inter-governmental and non-government organisations, local communities and the private sector;

**Alarmed at** the perilous state of many populations of water-birds, in both terrestrial and marine ecosystems, and at the continued decline in quality and extent of the world's wetlands;

**Noting** the conclusions and priorities for further action identified by the many technical workshops and presentations made at this conference, and recorded subsequently in this Declaration.

**Welcoming** the joint initiative of Wetlands International, and government authorities in the United Kingdom and The Netherlands, with the support also of Australia, Denmark, USA, Japan, Germany, Sweden, Ireland, Belgium, Switzerland, UNEP/CMS, UNEP/AEWA, FACE, and CIC and with the input of many other organisations and individuals, in convening the conference *Waterbirds Around the World* in Edinburgh so as to review the current status of the world's waterbirds;

### The Conference Participants, assembled together in Edinburgh –

**Consider that** although significant progress has been made to conserve waterbirds and their wetland habitats leading to some major successes, overall there remain important challenges, which, together with uncertainties about implications of future changes, requires further efforts and focused actions;

**Reaffirm that,** in the words of the Ramsar Convention, *"water-birds, in their seasonal migrations may transcend frontiers and so should be regarded as an international resource"* and *"that the conservation of wetlands and their flora and fauna can be ensured by combining far-sighted national policies with co-ordinated international action"* and accordingly **urge that** efforts between countries to conserve waterbird populations and their wetland habitats are extended, not only for the values that water-birds have in sustaining human populations, but also for their own sakes;

**Consider that** flyway conservation should combine species- and ecosystem-based approaches, internationally co-ordinated throughout migratory ranges;

**Acknowledge that** the conservation and sustainable use of waterbirds and wetland resources require co-ordinated action by public and private sectors, dependent local communities and other stakeholders;

**Call in particular** for urgent action to:

- Halt and reverse wetland loss and degradation;
- Complete national and international wetland inventories, and promote the conservation of wetlands of importance to waterbirds in the context of surrounding areas, especially through the participation of local communities;
- Extend and strengthen international networks of key sites for waterbirds along all flyways;
- Establish and extend formal agreements and other co-operation arrangements between countries to conserve species, where possible within the frameworks provided by the Conventions on Migratory Species, Biological Diversity and Wetlands;
- Fund and implement recovery plans for all globally threatened waterbird species;
- Halt and reverse recently revealed declines of long-distance migrant shorebirds through sustainable management by governments and others of human activities at sites of unique importance to them;
- Restore albatross and petrel populations to favourable conservation status through urgent and internationally co-ordinated conservation actions, especially through the framework provided by the Agreement on the Conservation of Albatrosses and Petrels;
- Substantially reduce pollution in the marine environment and establish sustainable harvesting of marine resources;
- Underpin future conservation decisions with high-quality scientific advice drawn from co-ordinated, and adequately funded, research and monitoring programmes notably the International Waterbird Census, and to this end, urge governments and other partners to work together collaboratively and supportively;
- Develop policy-relevant indicators of the status of the world's wetlands, especially in the context of the 2010 target, using waterbird and other data generated from robust and sustainable monitoring schemes;
- Invest in communication, education and public awareness activities as a key element of waterbird and wetlands conservation;
- Assess disease risk, and establish monitoring programmes in relation to migratory waterbird movements, the trade of wild birds, and implications for human health.

**Urge that** particular priority be given to capacity building for flyway conservation in countries and territories with limited institutions and resources, given that the wise-use of waterbirds and wetlands is important for sustainable development and poverty alleviation;

**Strongly encourage** countries to ratify and implement relevant conventions, agreements and treaties so as to encourage further international co-operation, and to make use of available resources including the Global Environment Facility in order to finance action required under this Declaration;

**Consider that**, with the long history of co-operative international assessments, waterbirds provide excellent indicators by which to evaluate progress towards achievement of the 2010 target established by world leaders in 2002, and to this end **Call**

**on** the Conventions on Migratory Species, Biological Diversity and Wetlands, and other international agreements to work together and with other partners on such assessments, and in particular with Wetlands International to further develop the analytical content, of the triennial publication *Waterbird Population Estimates* and its use;

**Stress** the need for wide international dissemination of this Declaration and the technical outcomes of this Conference; and

**Agree** to meet again as a conference in ten years time to review progress.

Edinburgh
7 April 2004

**In support of the recommendations above, the Conference concluded the following:**

- For the Flyways of the Americas, collaboration between North, Central and South America and Caribbean nations is developing, based on conclusions of the conference of nations to consider the status of migratory birds held during the VIII[th] Neotropical Congress in Chile, and in the recent completion of a Waterbird Conservation Plan for the Americas. Despite more than a century of conservation efforts in North America and emergence of a shared vision for biologically-based, landscape orientated partnerships, it is clear that international co-operation amongst Pan-American countries sharing migratory birds should increase.
- In African-Eurasian Flyways, the generally good knowledge of waterbirds is not being effectively transferred into necessary national and local actions. Nor have conservation efforts led to maintaining or restoring the health of many waterbird populations, including globally threatened species. There are urgent needs to integrate waterbird conservation as part of sustainable development, to the greater benefit of local communities and other stakeholders dependent on wetlands as well as benefiting biodiversity. The African-Eurasian Waterbird Agreement (UNEP/AEWA) provides a good basis to achieve this.
- Intra-African Flyways are extremely poorly known and would benefit from greater attention.
- Many of the waterbirds of the Central Asian Flyway appear to be declining, although information on status and trends is generally poor. In most countries there has been little previous investment in conservation and low involvement of local stakeholders in the sustainable management of wetlands. An international framework for the development of conservation initiatives for migratory waterbirds in Central Asia is urgently required to promote co-operative action. Better information is needed to identify priority conservation issues and responses.
- The waterbirds of Asian-Australasian Flyways are the most poorly known, and the greatest number of globally threatened waterbirds occur here. This flyway extends across the most densely populated part of the world, where there are extreme pressures not only on unprotected wetlands but also

on protected sites. Effective protection of wetlands of major importance is a critical need, as in other regions of the world. There are huge, and crucial, challenges in ensuring effective wise-use of key sites, as well as ensuring that consumptive uses of waterbirds are sustainable.

Black-browed Albatross *Diomedea melanophris*. Photo: Chris Wilson.

- Conservation of pelagic waterbirds in the open oceans gives a range of unique challenges. The entry into force of the Agreement on the Conservation of Albatrosses and Petrels is a most welcome development, and its full implementation is an urgent need. Addressing issues of seabird by-catch, especially by illegal and unregulated fisheries remains a critical need to reverse the poor conservation status of many species, as is the general need to achieve sustainable marine fisheries.
- Most of the world's known flyways originate in the Arctic. The recent development of international co-operation between arctic countries is welcome, as is the recognition of the crucial need to involve local communities and their traditional local knowledge in waterbird management. Austro-tropical Flyways also require research.
- Climate changes are already affecting waterbirds. The consequences of climate change for waterbirds will be multiple, and will greatly exacerbate current negative impacts such as habitat loss and degradation. There is a need for wide-scale planning, at landscape and flyway scales, to reduce or mitigate the impacts on waterbird populations and their habitats. Research that explores a range of potential future scenarios will be required to underpin this planning and will need data from long-term monitoring and surveillance.
- The conservation status of non-migrant waterbird populations around the world in many cases is poorer than that of migrants, and these waterbirds generally have less focused international attention than migrants. Addressing conservation requirements of non-migrant waterbirds should also be given national and international priority.
- On a densely populated planet it is crucial that waterbird conservationists focus on their relationships with communities and governments as the means both of reversing the causes of poor conservation status, and of resolving conflicts with protected species. Adequately funded programmes of communication, education and public awareness need to be the core of all waterbird conservation initiatives.

- Science has identified the critical importance of a small number of key sites to long-distance migrant shorebirds and that human activities at some of these are responsible for recent dramatic declines in certain shorebird populations.
- Recent research has highlighted the genetic and demographic risks incurred by species that have small populations. These have implications for the design of species recovery programmes.
- The frequency and magnitude of disease losses among waterbirds (from emerging or re-emerging disease agents) have increased to the extent that they demand attention. These diseases not only affect waterbirds but have impacts on humans. Solutions require a multi-disciplinary approach.
- An integrated approach to the monitoring of waterbirds gives cost-effective identification of the reasons for waterbird population changes. There are good examples of the collection of demographic information and its integration with census data. Further such national and especially international schemes should be strongly encouraged and funded.
- Systematic analyses for atlases confirm the value of ringing studies in assessing the conservation status of breeding, wintering and stop-over sites within flyways. To this end, there should be integration of data from conventional ringing and colour-marking, telemetry, stable isotope analyses and genetic markers.

Colin Galbraith presenting the Edinburgh Declaration to the final session of the Conference. Photo: Dougie Barnett.

## Déclaration d'Edimbourg

*Une conférence internationale sur les oiseaux d'eau, leur conservation et leur utilisation rationnelle, s'est déroulée à Edimbourg, en Ecosse, du 3 au 8 avril 2004. Cette conférence a réuni 456 participants venus de 90 pays.*

**Conscients** que les voies de migration des oiseaux d'eau sont des systèmes biologiques qui relient directement des sites et des écosystèmes de différents pays et continents;

**Rappelant** que la conservation et l'utilisation rationnelle des oiseaux d'eau est une responsabilité commune des nations et des peuples, et une préoccupation de l'ensemble de l'humanité;

**Rappelant en outre** la longue histoire de la coopération internationale pour la conservation des oiseaux d'eau, développée sur une centaine d'années avec des traités comme celui de 1916 entre les Etats-Unis et le Royaume-Uni (au nom du Canada) concernant les oiseaux migrateurs; et que, il y a plus de 40 ans, la première Réunion Européenne sur la Conservation des Oiseaux Sauvages, qui s'est tenue en 1963 à St. Andrews, en Ecosse, a marqué le démarrage d'un processus qui a abouti à la création en 1971 à Ramsar, en Iran, de la Convention sur les Zones Humides, en particulier en tant qu'habitat pour les oiseaux d'eau;

**Notant** que les grandes conférences internationales qui se sont tenues à Noordwijk aan Zee, aux Pays-Bas (1966), à Leningrad, en URSS (1968), à Ramsar, en Iran (1971), à Astrakhan, en URSS (1989), à St. Petersburg Beach, en Floride, aux Etats-Unis (1992), à Kushiro, au Japon et à Strasbourg, en France (1994), ont développé davantage les échanges techniques internationaux sur la conservation des oiseaux d'eau;

**Ayant connaissance** du développement d'une coopération inter-gouvernementale plus poussée, à travers l'élaboration et la mise en oeuvre d'autres traités, accords, stratégies et programmes; ainsi que du développement d'une importante coopération non gouvernementale, nationale et internationale, en matière de conservation et de suivi des oiseaux d'eau;

**Conscients** qu'au Sommet mondial sur le développement durable qui s'est tenu en 2002 à Johannesburg, en Afrique du Sud, les dirigeants du monde ont exprimé leur désir d'atteindre *« une importante réduction du taux actuel de perte de diversité biologique »* d'ici à 2010, et qu'en février 2004, cette cible a été élaborée davantage par la Septième Conférence des Parties à la Convention sur la Biodiversité; **sachant** que l'atteinte de cette cible nécessitera d'importants investissements ainsi qu'une activité de conservation très focalisée et coordonnée sur l'ensemble des continents; et **reconnaissant** que la communication, l'éducation et la sensibilisation du public, ainsi que le renforcement des capacités, joueront un rôle crucial dans l'atteinte de cette cible;

**Conscients en outre** de l'urgente nécessité de renforcer la coopération internationale ainsi que les partenariats entre les organisations gouvernementales, intergouvernementales et non-gouvernementales, les communautés locales et le secteur privé;

**Alarmés** par l'état périlleux dans lequel se trouvent de nombreuses populations d'oiseaux d'eau vivant dans les écosystèmes terrestre et marin, ainsi que par la baisse constante de la qualité et de l'étendue des zones humides partout dans le monde;

**Notant** les conclusions et les priorités pour d'autres actions identifiées par les multiples ateliers et présentations techniques au cours de cette conférence, et rapportées par la suite dans cette Déclaration.

**Saluant** l'initiative conjointe de Wetlands International et des autorités gouvernementales du Royaume-Uni et des Pays-Bas, également appuyée par l'Australie, le Danemark, les Etats-Unis, le Japon, l'Allemagne, la Suède, l'Irelande, la Belgique, la Suisse, le PNUE/CMS, le PNUE/AEWA, FACE et CIC, ainsi que la contribution de nombreux autres individus et organisations qui a consisté à convoquer la conférence sur le thème des *Oiseaux d'Eau du Monde* à Edimbourg, aux fins d'examiner l'état actuel des oiseaux d'eau du monde;

### *Les Participants à la Conférence, réunis à Edimbourg –*

**Considèrent** que, malgré les avancées notables en matière de conservation des oiseaux d'eau et de leurs habitats de zones humides, qui ont débouché sur quelques succès majeurs, il reste dans l'ensemble d'importants défis qui, avec les incertitudes concernant les implications des futurs changements, nécessitent des efforts plus poussés et des actions ciblées;

**Réaffirment** que, selon les termes de la Convention de Ramsar, *« au cours de leurs migrations saisonnières, les oiseaux d'eau peuvent transcender les frontières; par conséquent, ils doivent être considérés comme une ressource internationale »* et que *« la conservation des zones humides, ainsi que de leur flore et de leur faune, peut être assurée par la combinaison de politiques nationales clairvoyantes avec une action internationale coordonnée »*; par conséquent, **recommandent** de multiplier les efforts inter-étatiques de conservation des populations d'oiseaux d'eau et de leurs habitats de zones humides, non seulement pour les valeurs des oiseaux d'eau pour l'alimentation des populations humaines, mais aussi pour leur propre bien;

**Considèrent** que la conservation des voies de migration devrait combiner les approches basées sur les espèces et les écosystèmes, coordonnées au niveau international sur toute l'étendue des aires de migration;

**Reconnaissent** que la conservation et l'utilisation rationnelle des oiseaux d'eau et des ressources des zones humides requièrent une action coordonnée par les secteurs public et privé, les communautés locales ainsi que les autres parties prenantes qui en dépendent;

**Appellent en particulier à** une action urgente pour:

- Faire cesser et inverser les pertes et la dégradation de zones humides;
- Achever les inventaires des zones humides, aux niveaux national et international, et promouvoir la conservation des zones humides d'importance vitale pour les oiseaux d'eau, dans le contexte des aires environnantes, en particulier par la participation des communautés locales;
- Développer et renforcer les réseaux internationaux de sites-clés pour les oiseaux d'eau, le long de toutes les voies de migration;
- Etablir et développer des accords formels et autres accords de coopération entre les pays pour la conservation des espèces, si possible dans les cadres fournis par les Conventions sur les Espèces Migratrices, la Diversité Biologique et les Zones Humides;
- Financer et mettre en oeuvre des plans de rétablissement pour toutes les espèces d'oiseaux d'eau menacées dans le monde;
- Faire cesser et inverser les récentes baisses des effectifs d'oiseaux de plage migrant sur de longues distances, grâce à une gestion durable, par les gouvernements et d'autres, des activités anthropiques dans les sites d'importance unique pour ces oiseaux;
- Restaurer les populations d'albatros et de pétrels pour les amener à un état de conservation satisfaisant, par des actions de conservation coordonnées au niveau international, notamment à travers le cadre offert par l'Accord sur la Conservation des Albatros et des Pétrels;
- Réduire considérablement la pollution en milieu marin et instaurer le prélèvement durable des ressources marines;
- Appuyer les futures décisions en matière de conservation par des conseils scientifiques de haute qualité, tirés des programmes de recherche et de suivi coordonnés et adéquatement financés, notamment le Dénombrement International d'Oiseaux d'Eau, et à cette fin, exhorter les gouvernements et autres partenaires à travailler ensemble, de façon collaborative et positive;
- Développer des indicateurs politiques de l'état des zones humides dans le monde, en particulier dans le contexte du cap 2010, en utilisant les données sur les oiseaux d'eau et d'autres données produites par des programmes de suivi solides et durables;
- Investir dans les activités de communication, d'éducation et de sensibilisation du public, en tant qu'élément clé de la conservation des oiseaux d'eau et des zones humides;
- Evaluer les risques de maladies et mettre en place des programmes de suivi concernant les mouvements migratoires des oiseaux d'eau, le commerce d'oiseaux sauvages et leurs implications pour la santé de l'homme.

**Incitent** à accorder une priorité particulière au renforcement des capacités pour la conservation des voies de migration dans les pays et territoires dotés d'institutions et de ressources limitées, étant donné que l'utilisation rationnelle des oiseaux d'eau et des zones humides est importante pour le développement durable et la réduction de la pauvreté;

**Engagent fortement** les pays à ratifier et à mettre en oeuvre les conventions, accords et traités pertinents, afin de promouvoir une coopération internationale plus poussée, et à utiliser les ressources dont ils disposent, notamment le Fonds mondial pour l'environnement, pour financer les actions requises dans le cadre de cette Déclaration;

**Considèrent** qu'avec la longue histoire des évaluations internationales coopératives, les oiseaux d'eau offrent d'excellents indicateurs qui permettent de mesurer les progrès vers l'atteinte du cap 2010 fixé par les dirigeants mondiaux en 2002, et à cet effet, **Invitent** les Conventions sur les Espèces Migratrices, sur la Diversité Biologique et sur les Zones Humides, ainsi que d'autres accords internationaux, à travailler ensemble et avec d'autres partenaires sur ce genre d'évaluations, en particulier avec Wetlands International, pour élaborer davantage le contenu analytique et l'utilisation de la publication triennale *Estimations des Populations d'Oiseaux d'Eau*;

**Insistent** sur la nécessité d'une large dissémination internationale de cette Déclaration ainsi que des produits techniques de cette Conférence; et

**Conviennent** de convoquer de nouveau la conférence dans dix ans, pour examiner les progrès.

Edimbourg
7 Avril 2004

**En appui aux recommandations ci-dessus, la Conférence a conclu ce qui suit:**

- Pour les voies de migration des Amériques, la collaboration se développe entre l'Amérique du Nord, l'Amérique centrale et l'Amérique du Sud, et les états caribéens, selon les conclusions de la conférence des nations pour examiner l'état des oiseaux migrateurs, qui s'est tenue lors du VIII<sup>ème</sup> Congrès néo-tropical au Chili, et le Plan de conservation des oiseaux d'eau pour les Amériques, récemment achevé. Malgré plus d'un siècle d'efforts de conservation en Amérique du Nord et l'émergence d'une vision partagée pour des partenariats biologiques, axés sur l'environnement, il est évident que la coopération internationale entre les pays panaméricains ayant en commun les oiseaux migrateurs devrait s'intensifier.
- Dans les voies de migration Afrique-Eurasie, les connaissances généralement bonnes des oiseaux d'eau ne sont pas effectivement traduites en des actions nationales et locales

nécessaires. Pas plus que les efforts de conservation n'ont abouti au maintien ou à la restauration de la santé de nombreuses populations d'oiseaux d'eau, y compris les espèces menacées dans le monde. Il urge d'intégrer la conservation des oiseaux d'eau dans le cadre du développement durable, pour le plus grand bien des communautés locales et autres parties prenantes dépendant des zones humides, mais aussi, pour le bien de la biodiversité. L'Accord sur les Oiseaux d'Eau Migrateurs d'Afrique-Eurasie (PNUE/AEWA) offre une base adéquate pour réaliser cet objectif.

- Les voies de migration interafricaines sont fort mal connues et tireraient profit d'une plus grande attention.

- Bon nombre des oiseaux d'eau de la voie de migration de l'Asie centrale semblent en déclin, bien que les informations concernant leur état et leurs tendances soient maigres dans l'ensemble. Dans la plupart des pays, il y a eu très peu d'investissement préalable dans la conservation, et une faible participation des acteurs locaux à la gestion durable des zones humides. Il urge de créer un cadre international pour l'élaboration d'initiatives de conservation des oiseaux migrateurs en Asie centrale, en vue de promouvoir l'action coopérative. De meilleures informations sont requises pour identifier les questions de conservation prioritaires et leurs réponses.

- Les oiseaux d'eau des voies de migration Asie-Australasie sont les plus mal connus, et pourtant, c'est là qu'on trouve le plus grand nombre d'oiseaux d'eau menacés dans le monde. Cette voie de migration s'étend à travers la région du monde la plus densément peuplée, où non seulement les zones humides non protégées, mais aussi les sites protégés, sont soumises à des pressions extrêmes. La protection réelle des zones humides d'importance majeure est un besoin vital, ici comme dans les autres régions du monde. Assurer l'utilisation rationnelle effective des sites-clés, ainsi que la consommation durable des oiseaux d'eau, est une rude bataille.

- La conservation des oiseaux d'eau pélagiques en pleine mer présente un éventail de défis uniques. L'entrée en vigueur de l'Accord sur la Conservation des Albatros et des Pétrels est une évolution à saluer, et sa mise en application un besoin urgent. Traiter les questions de captures accessoires d'oiseaux marins, en particulier par des pêches illégales et non-réglementées, demeure un besoin crucial pour inverser le mauvais état de conservation de nombreuses espèces, comme l'est le besoin général de réaliser des pêches maritimes durables.

- La plupart des voies de migration connues dans le monde ont leur origine dans l'Arctique. Le récent développement de la coopération internationale entre les pays de l'Arctique est à saluer, tout comme la reconnaissance du besoin crucial d'impliquer les communautés locales et leurs connaissances traditionnelles locales dans la gestion des oiseaux d'eau. Les voies de migration austro-tropicales nécessitent, elles aussi, de la recherche.

- Les changements climatiques affectent déjà les oiseaux d'eau. Leurs conséquences pour ces oiseaux seront multiples et vont fortement exacerber les impacts négatifs actuels, tels que la perte d'habitats et la dégradation. Il faut une planification en grand, à l'échelle de l'environnement et de la voie de migration, pour réduire ou modérer les impacts sur les populations d'oiseaux d'eau et leurs habitats. Il faudra de la recherche qui explore toute une gamme de scénarios futurs possibles pour soutenir cette planification, ainsi que des données émanant d'un suivi et d'une surveillance à long terme.

- Les populations d'oiseaux d'eau non-migrants partout dans le monde ont, dans bien des cas, un état de conservation plus mauvais que celui des migrants, et en général, focalisent moins l'attention internationale que ces derniers. Il faudra donc également accorder la priorité au traitement des besoins de conservation des oiseaux d'eau non-migrants, au niveau national comme international.

- Sur une planète à forte densité de population, il est crucial que les partisans de la conservation des oiseaux d'eau se focalisent sur leurs rapports avec les communautés et les gouvernements, comme un moyen à la fois de renverser les causes du mauvais état de conservation et de résoudre les conflits avec les espèces protégées. Des programmes de communication, éducation et sensibilisation du public adéquatement financés doivent être au cœur de toutes les initiatives en matière de conservation des oiseaux d'eau.

- La science a identifié l'importance vitale d'une poignée de sites-clés pour les oiseaux de plage migrant sur de longues distances; elle a également déterminé que dans certains de ces sites, l'activité anthropique est responsable des récentes baisses spectaculaires de certaines populations d'oiseaux de plage.

- Les dernières recherches ont mis en évidence les risques génétiques et démographiques encourus par les espèces à faibles populations. Ces découvertes ont des implications pour la conception des programmes de rétablissement de ces espèces.

- La fréquence et l'ampleur des pertes dues aux maladies chez les oiseaux d'eau (provoquées par des agents pathologiques naissants ou faisant leur réapparition) se sont intensifiées, au point de requérir l'attention. Ces maladies non seulement affectent les oiseaux d'eau, mais ont aussi des impacts sur les êtres humains. Les solutions nécessitent une approche multidisciplinaire.

- Une approche intégrée du suivi des oiseaux d'eau produit une identification économique des raisons des variations des populations d'oiseaux d'eau. Il existe de bons exemples de collecte d'informations démographiques et de leur intégration dans les données des dénombrements. D'autres programmes nationaux et surtout internationaux de ce genre doivent être fortement encouragés et financés.

- Des analyses systématiques des atlas confirment la valeur des études du baguage dans l'évaluation de l'état de conservation des sites de reproduction, des quartiers d'hiver et des aires de repos à l'intérieur des voies de migration. A cette fin, les données provenant des classiques baguages et marquages par teinture, de la télémétrie, des analyses d'isotopes stables et des marqueurs génétiques doivent être intégrées.

## Declaración de Edimburgo

*La conferencia internacional sobre aves acuáticas, su conservación y uso sostenible se celebró en Edimburgo, Escocia, del 3 al 8 de abril de 2004. En ella participaron 456 personas provenientes de 90 países.*

**Conscientes** de que los corredores migratorios de las aves acuáticas son sistemas biológicos de trayectos de migración que relacionan sitios y ecosistemas en distintos países y continentes;

**Recordando** que la conservación y uso racional de las aves acuáticas es una responsabilidad compartida entre distintas naciones y pueblos y es una preocupación común del género humano;

**Recordando también** la larga historia de colaboración internacional para la conservación de aves acuáticas desarrollada hace más de cien años en tratados como aquél relativo a las aves migratorias, firmado en 1916 entre los Estados Unidos de América y el Reino Unido (en nombre de Canadá); y que hace más de cuarenta años, la primera Reunión Europea sobre Conservación de Anátidos llevada a cabo en 1963 en San Andrés, Escocia, empezó un proceso que llevó a la creación de la Convención sobre los Humedales, especialmente como hábitat de aves acuáticas; en Ramsar, Irán, en 1971;

**Tomando en cuenta** que importantes conferencias internacionales en Noordwijk aan Zee, Los Países Bajos (1996), Leningrado, Unión Soviética (1968), Ramsar, Irán (1971), Astracán, Unión Soviética (1989), Playa de San Petersburgo (Estados Unidos de América), Kushiro, Japón y Estrasburgo, Francia (1994) han promovido el desarrollado de intercambios técnicos sobre conservación de aves acuáticas;

**Conscientes** del progreso de la cooperación intergubernamental a través del establecimiento e implementación de más tratados, convenios, estrategias y programas, y del desarrollo de importantes esquemas de cooperación no gubernamental a escala nacional e internacional para el monitoreo y conservación de aves acuáticas;

**Conscientes** de que en la Cumbre Mundial sobre Desarrollo Sostenible llevada a cabo en Johannesburgo, Sudáfrica en 2002, los líderes mundiales expresaron su deseo de alcanzar "una reducción significativa en la tasa de pérdida de biodiversidad" para el 2020, y de que en febrero del 2004 este objetivo se amplió aún más en la Séptima Conferencia de las Partes de la Convención sobre Diversidad Biológica; y **conscientes** de que alcanzar este objetivo requerirá inversiones significativas y actividades específicas de conservación enfocadas en todos los continentes; y **reconociendo** que la comunicación, la educación, la concienciación y la capacitación jugarán un papel importante en lograr este objetivo;

**Conscientes** de que se necesita fortalecer la cooperación internacional y las asociaciones entre los gobiernos, las organizaciones intergubernamentales y no gubernamentales, las comunidades locales, y el sector privado;

**Alarmados** por la delicada situación de muchas de las poblaciones de aves acuáticas tanto en ecosistemas marinos como terrestres, y del continuo descenso en la calidad y extensión de los humedales del mundo;

**Tomando en cuenta** las conclusiones y prioridades para la acción identificadas por la mayoría de los talleres y presentaciones realizadas en esta conferencia y documentadas subsecuentemente en la presente Declaración;

**Recibiendo** la iniciativa conjunta de Wetlands International y de las autoridades de los gobiernos del Reino Unido y de los Países Bajos, con el apoyo de Australia, Dinamarca, Estados Unidos de América, Japón, Alemania, Suecia, Irlanda, Bélgica, Suiza, PNUMA/CMS, PNUMA/AEWA, FACE y CIC, con el aporte de muchas otras organizaciones e individuos, y **acordando** la conferencia "Aves Acuáticas Alrededor del Mundo" en Edimburgo para revisar el estado actual de las aves acuáticas del planeta;

### *Los participantes de la Conferencia reunidos en Edimburgo*

**Consideran** que a pesar de que se ha hecho un progreso significativo para conservar las aves acuáticas y los humedales donde éstas habitan, aún existen desafíos que, junto con las incertidumbres sobre las implicancias de los cambios que puedan ocurrir en el futuro, requieren aún más esfuerzos y acciones específicas;

**Reafirman** que, en palabras de la Convención Ramsar, "*las aves acuáticas, en sus migraciones estacionales trascienden fronteras y deben ser consideradas como un recurso internacional*" y "*que la conservación de los humedales, junto con su flora y su fauna puede lograrse combinando políticas visionarias con acciones coordinadas internacionalmente*", por lo tanto **exigen** que se extiendan los esfuerzos entre los países para conservar las poblaciones de aves acuáticas y los humedales donde éstas habitan, no sólo por el valor que las aves acuáticas tienen para sostener las poblaciones humanas sino también para su propio beneficio;

**Consideran** que la conservación de los corredores migratorios debe encararse con enfoques que combinen tanto las especies como los ecosistemas, y que sean coordinados internacionalmente en todo el rango de migración;

**Reconocen** que la conservación y uso sostenible de las aves acuáticas y los recursos provenientes de los humedales requiere acciones coordinadas de los sectores público y privado, las comunidades locales y otras partes interesadas;

**Hacen un llamado** de acción urgente para:
- Detener y revertir la pérdida y degradación de humedales;
- Completar inventarios de humedales a escala nacional e internacional, y promover la conservación de los humedales de importancia para las aves acuáticas, especialmente a través de la participación de las comunidades locales;
- Extender y fortalecer las redes internacionales de sitios claves para las aves acuáticas a lo largo de los corredores migratorios;
- Establecer y extender los acuerdos formales y otros acuerdos de cooperación entre los países, y de ser posible dentro del esquema provisto por las convenciones sobre Especies Migratorias, de Diversidad Biológica y de los Humedales;
- Implementar y financiar planes de recuperación para todas las especies de aves acuáticas amenazadas;
- Detener y revertir la disminución reciente de las aves playeras migratorias de larga distancia a través de planes de manejo sostenible de los gobiernos y de las actividades humanas que se lleven a cabo en sitios de importancia única para estas especies;
- Restablecer las poblaciones de albatros y petreles a niveles favorables para su conservación a través de acciones urgentes coordinadas internacionalmente especialmente a través del marco establecido por el Acuerdo sobre la Conservación de Albatros y Petreles;
- Reducir la contaminación de los ambientes marinos y establecer un sistema de cosecha sostenible de los mismos;
- Respaldar y fortalecer las decisiones futuras de conservación haciendo uso de asesoría científica altamente calificada y especializada proveniente de programas de investigación y monitoreo coordinados y financiados adecuadamente, en particular, del Censo Internacional de Aves Acuáticas, y para ello insta a los gobiernos y otras partes interesadas a trabajar de forma conjunta;
- Desarrollar indicadores relevantes para las políticas en relación con el estado de los humedales del mundo, en particular en el contexto de la meta para el año 2010, haciendo uso de datos generados por sistemas de monitoreo sostenibles y robustos;
- Invertir en actividades de comunicación, educación y concienciación como un elemento primordial para la conservación de las aves acuáticas y los humedales;
- Estudiar los riesgos de enfermedades y establecer programas de monitoreo de los movimientos de las aves acuáticas y del comercio de aves silvestres y sus implicaciones para la salud humana.

**Exhortan** que se debe dar especial prioridad a la formación de capacidades para la conservación de los corredores migratorios en países y territorios con recursos e instituciones limitadas, dado que el uso racional de los humedales y las aves acuáticas es de suma importancia para el desarrollo sostenible y la reducción de la pobreza;

**Alientan** a los países a ratificar e implementar las convenciones, acuerdos y tratados relevantes para estimular la cooperación internacional y hacer uso de los recursos disponibles en el Fondo para el Medio Ambiente Mundial de forma de financiar las acciones necesarias establecidas en esta Declaración;

**Consideran** que, dada la larga historia de estudios de cooperación internacionales, las aves acuáticas proveen indicadores excelentes para evaluar los progresos para alcanzar las metas del 2010 establecidas por los líderes mundiales en el 2002, y **hacen un llamado** a las Convenciones sobre Especies Migratorias, Diversidad Biológica y de los Humedales y otros acuerdos internacionales a trabajar de manera conjunta y con otras partes en estos estudios, y en particular con Wetlands International, para desarrollar aún más el contenido analítico de la publicación trienal *Estimaciones de las Poblaciones de Aves Acuáticas* y sus utilidades;

**Enfatizan** la necesidad de la diseminación a escala internacional de esta Declaración y de los resultados técnicos de esta Conferencia, y

**Acuerdan** reunirse de nuevo dentro de diez años para revisar los progresos realizados.


Edimburgo
7 de abril de 2004


**En apoyo a las recomendaciones mencionadas anteriormente, la Conferencia concluye lo siguiente:**

- Para los corredores migratorios de las Américas se están desarrollando colaboraciones entre las naciones del Norte, Centro y Suramérica y el Caribe, basadas en las conclusiones de la conferencia de naciones sobre el estado de las aves migratorias que se llevó a cabo durante el Octavo Congreso Neotropical en Chile, y la reciente culminación del Plan de Conservación de Aves Acuáticas para las Américas. A pesar de los esfuerzos de conservación en Norte América llevados a cado hace más de un siglo y del surgimiento de una visión compartida para la cooperación basada en aspectos biológicos y paisajísticos, está claro que la cooperación internacional debe aumentar y mejorar entre los países Pan-Americanos que comparten aves migratorias.
- En los corredores migratorios de África y Eurasia, el conocimiento de las aves acuáticas no está siendo transferido de forma adecuada en acciones a escala local o nacional. De igual manera, los esfuerzos de conservación tampoco han contribuido a mantener o restaurar la salud de muchas de las poblaciones de aves acuáticas, incluyendo especies amenazadas a escala global. Es por ello urgente integrar la conservación de las aves acuáticas como una parte integral del desarrollo sostenible y el beneficio de las comunidades locales y otras partes interesadas o dependientes de los recursos de los humedales y de la biodiversidad. El Acuerdo Afro-Euroasiático sobre Aves Acuáticas (PNUMA/AEWA) provee una base apropiada para alcanzar esta meta.
- Muchas de las poblaciones de aves acuáticas del corredor migratorio del Asia Central parecen estar disminuyendo. En la mayoría de los países ha habido poca inversión en conservación y muy poca participación de los actores locales en el

manejo sostenible de los humedales. Se requiere por lo tanto de un marco internacional que promueva acciones para la cooperación y el desarrollo de iniciativas de conservación de las aves migratorias en Asia Central. Se necesita de mejor información para identificar las prioridades de conservación en esta región.

- Las aves acuáticas del corredor migratorio de Asia y Australasia son las menos conocidas y el mayor número de aves migratorias amenazadas a nivel mundial se encuentran en este grupo. Esta ruta migratoria se extiende a lo largo de las áreas más pobladas del planeta, donde existen presiones muy fuertes no sólo en humedales no protegidos sino también en humedales protegidos legalmente. Se necesita urgentemente una protección efectiva de los humedales de mayor importancia tanto en esta zona, como en otras regiones del mundo. Los desafíos tanto para asegurar el uso racional efectivo de sitios claves como para asegurar el consumo sostenible de aves acuáticas son muy grandes.

- La mayoría de las rutas migratorias conocidas se originan en el Ártico. El reciente desarrollo de cooperación internacional entre los países árticos es bienvenida, al igual que el reconocimiento de la necesidad de involucrar a las comunidades locales y su conocimiento tradicional en el manejo de aves acuáticas. Las vías migratorias Austro-Tropicales requieren mayor investigación.

- La conservación de las aves acuáticas pelágicas en los océanos abiertos ofrece desafíos únicos. La entrada en vigor del Acuerdo sobre Conservación de Albatros y Petreles es bienvenido y su implementación es una necesidad imperiosa. La necesidad de tomar en cuenta el problema de la captura incidental de aves acuáticas debido a la pesca ilegal es un asunto crucial para revertir el estado de conservación de muchas especies, y es una necesidad para lograr pesca marina sostenible.

- Los cambios climáticos han afectado a las aves acuáticas, y sus consecuencias pueden ser múltiples y pueden exacerbar los impactos negativos como la pérdida y degradación de hábitat. Se necesita una amplia planificación a escala paisajística y de las vías migratorias de forma de reducir o mitigar los impactos en las poblaciones de aves acuáticas y sus hábitats. Se requiere de investigaciones que exploren escenarios potenciales a futuro para revertir esta situación y de datos de monitoreo a largo plazo.

- El estado de conservación de las poblaciones de aves acuáticas no migratorias es, en muchos casos, muy pobre, inclusive más que el de las especies migratorias. Estas aves no migratorias reciben menos atención que las migratorias. Se necesita dar prioridad a las necesidades de conservación de las especies no migratorias a nivel nacional e internacional.

- Las acciones de conservación en las áreas más pobladas del planeta necesitan enfocarse en las relaciones entre las comunidades y los gobiernos locales como estrategia para revertir las causas que van en contra de la conservación, y para resolver los conflictos de uso de especies protegidas. La capacitación, educación y concienciación son las actividades clave en las que centrar las iniciativas de conservación en estas zonas.

- La ciencia ha identificado la importancia de un reducido número de sitios claves para las especies de aves playeras migratorias de larga distancia. También ha identificado a las actividades humanas como las responsables del reciente declive en las poblaciones de determinadas especies de aves playeras.

- Investigaciones recientes han enfatizado los riesgos genéticos y demográficos que sufren algunas especies que tienen pequeñas poblaciones. Estos riesgos tienen implicaciones en el diseño de los programas de recuperación de especies.

- La frecuencia y magnitud de muertes por enfermedades entre las aves acuáticas (tanto de agentes infecciosos emergentes como re-emergentes) ha incrementado al punto de requerir especial atención. Estas enfermedades no sólo afectan las aves acuáticas sino también a los humanos y requieren soluciones de orden multidisciplinario.

- Un monitoreo integrado de las poblaciones de aves acuáticas da como resultado una identificación eficiente de las razones que explican los cambios observados en las poblaciones de estas aves. Existen ejemplos magníficos de recolección de información demográfica y su integración en los datos de censos. Se requiere mayor financiamiento para esquemas de integración de este tipo a escala nacional e internacional.

- El análisis sistemático de los atlas confirma el valor de los estudios de anillado de aves para evaluar los corredores migratorios en cuanto al estado de conservación de los sitios de reproducción, de parada y de invernada de aves acuáticas migratorias.

Laysan Albatross *Phoebastria immutabilis* at Midway Atoll in the Pacific. Photo: Helen Baker.

# Address by His Royal Highness The Prince of Wales

*Wednesday 7 April 2004*

His Royal Highness The Prince of Wales. 2006. Address to the Waterbirds around the world conference, 7 April 2004. *Waterbirds around the world.* Eds. G.C. Boere, C.A. Galbraith & D.A. Stroud. The Stationery Office, Edinburgh, UK. pp. 16-18.

Ladies and gentlemen, I am conscious that I am appearing very much at the tail end of your conference and, by the look of the programme, you have clearly had a full and varied few days. So you are probably beginning to calculate how quickly you can join your own personal 'flyway' back home. But I am delighted that so many of you are still here and that, by all accounts, you have had such a successful conference. I am just relieved that I arrived in time to hear Dr John Cooper's riveting presentation.

Now, ladies and gentlemen, I am very far from being an expert on either albatrosses or petrels but, like many other one-time mariners, I have a very special affection for these remarkable birds. I remember so well standing on the deck of a fast-moving warship in one of the Southern oceans, watching an albatross maintaining perfect position alongside for hour after hour, and apparently day after day. It is a sight I will never forget, and I find it hard (no, I find it impossible) to accept that it might one day be lost for ever. Yet that does now seem to be a real possibility – unless we, and others around the world, can make a sufficient fuss to prevent it. In 1996, three of the twenty-one species of albatross were officially listed as threatened. Four years later, when I sat down to write an article expressing my concerns about the decline of these magnificent birds, the total of threatened species had risen to sixteen. Another four years on, and all twenty-one species are threatened. The albatross family is now the biggest single bird family with every one of its members under threat.

I don't need to tell this audience that the most potent force driving the members of the albatross family to extinction is indiscriminate longline fishing, which is estimated to kill 100 000 albatrosses every year. One fishing boat reported more than 300 killed in a single day. But before I talk a bit more about that problem, I just want to say some thoroughly positive things.

First, this seems an entirely appropriate time and place to draw attention to the years of dedicated work by research scientists and their support crews, without whom we would know next to nothing about these most nomadic and elusive of birds. It must be hard and lonely work, carried out in cold, wet and thoroughly difficult conditions, and a very long way from home. But without the knowledge and data you take such pains to obtain there can be no coherent evaluation of either the scale of the problem, or the potential for solutions.

This scientific effort has been matched by BirdLife International and other non-governmental organizations, bringing these issues to the attention of a wider public. That is certainly how I first learnt of the scale of the problem and I suspect the same is true for many other people. There is, of course, a huge amount more to be done in terms of awareness-raising and advocacy.

Gaining awareness of the plight of a group of birds most people have never seen, and probably never will see, is a huge challenge. So I also want to mention the efforts of one remarkable man, who has – in his own inimitable fashion – taken up

His Royal Highness The Prince of Wales. Photo: Dougie Barnett.

that challenge and is drawing attention to the issue of albatrosses and longline fishing. John Ridgway, who may or may not like me to tell you that he is now sixty-five, has sailed with his wife, Marie Christine, and a small crew from their home in northern Scotland to the Southern Ocean, following the circumpolar track of the Wandering Albatross. John and Marie Christine and their crew are having great success in engaging with all sorts of different audiences at each landfall, and generating remarkable publicity, most recently in New Zealand and the Falkland Islands. Their yacht, English Rose VI, is now headed for home. They expect to berth in London in June, where there will be further opportunities to raise the profile of this issue.

In view of all the scientific and voluntary efforts I have just mentioned, I am pleased to be able to say that at least some Governments are also alive to the situation and willing to commit to taking effective action.

An international Agreement on the conservation of albatrosses and petrels (known as ACAP) came into force just two months ago. This was a huge achievement – especially as it has taken a very long time to materialize... ACAP is particularly important because it is legally binding on the countries that ratify it, and its emphasis on international co-operation is an essential first step to tackling the multiple threats to such a wide-ranging group of birds. The UK played a leading role in drawing up this key international treaty and was among the first to sign it. But ratification is the essential step. So I couldn't have been more pleased to hear that Mr Elliot Morley, who has been a passionate fighter for the albatross, had announced, earlier in this conference, that the Government has now ratified the Agreement, without reservations and to a tight timescale. And I also want to draw attention to Elliot Morley's personal leadership on this topic, as someone with a deep understanding and concern for the issues.

Well, that was the good news. The bad news is that many countries with fishing interests in the Southern Ocean still need to ratify the ACAP, and some of the most important appear unlikely to do so – for reasons which can only be guessed at. At the same time, the problem of illegal, unregulated and unreported fishing appears to be getting worse. There are believed to be more than a thousand of these substantial pirate vessels, operating under 'flags of convenience', recognizing no rules and – with few exceptions – evading every sort of sanction and penalty available under international law.

Fishermen operating in responsible and well-regulated fisheries have adopted measures that almost entirely eliminate the deaths of albatrosses from longlining. Setting lines under water, or only at night, trailing a bird-scaring line and prohibiting offal discharge while fishing have all proved effective. Many fisheries also insist on the presence of observers on board to monitor results. The pirate vessels in the illegal fisheries, of course, take none of these measures. No-one knows how many albatrosses and petrels they kill every year, but the best estimate is that they are responsible for about one third of the total of around 100 000 deaths. But that is not the total of the environmental havoc they are causing.

One of the principal targets of the pirate ships is the Patagonian Toothfish. Sold under many 'consumer-friendly' aliases, such as Chilean Sea Bass in the USA and Mero in Japan, this valuable species is also very much under threat from overfishing. Indeed, the Australian government has said that if fishing continues at current levels, the species faces commercial extinction. Living up to fifty years, and taking ten years to reach breeding age, it is a slow-growing creature which is being killed faster than it can reproduce. Just like the albatross, in fact, though even less visible.

Of course, it is much easier to be angry about the awful dual threat posed by the pirate fishing boats than to take effective action against them. I rather think that the Greenpeace report on this subject, which is based on intense investigation, is right when

it concludes that the only way to prevent continued pirate fishing is to close ports to these ships, close markets to the fish they catch and penalize the companies that are their true owners and operators. I know that Elliot Morley now leads an OECD Task Force on Pirate Fishing and I wish him every possible success in finding ways to do all those things. I certainly don't think that any single measure is going to succeed when the economic incentives for illegal action are so high and the chances of being detected and prosecuted are so low. It also has to be said that political willingness to act is notably absent in some countries.

Agreements on vessel monitoring and catch documentation do exist for Patagonian Toothfish, and appear to be having some positive effects. But there always seems to be a hard core of countries that want to do as little as possible and as late as possible – and preferably nothing at all. When an International Plan of Action to tackle the problem of pirate fishing was being negotiated under the auspices of the United Nations, several countries made strenuous efforts to water down the draft provisions. In particular, the opportunity to take effective measures against the use of chartered vessels in illegal, unreported and unregulated fisheries was missed. I just wonder how many of those countries claim to be committed to 'sustainable development' at the same time?

Ladies and gentlemen, it would be hard to find a more direct impact of fisheries, whether legal or illegal, on seabirds than the losses the albatross family suffers at the hands of indiscriminate longlining. But there are many examples of less direct effects all round the world.

Not far from here, in the North Sea, there is a sandeel fishery. It is now by far the largest single-species fishery in the North Sea, though not for human consumption – the sandeels are processed into fishmeal and oil, to feed livestock and farmed fish. Whether this so-called industrial fishing, targeting the bottom of the food chain, represents a sensible use of natural resources or not is a subject for another day. The point for now is that the Total Allowable Catch for sandeels for 2004 is 826 000 tonnes, despite the fact that last year the fleet was only able to catch around 300 000 tonnes (one third of its target). The fishing boat skippers simply couldn't find the fish to catch.

The seabirds evidently had the same problem. Kittiwakes are especially dependent on sandeels and last year the massive colony

His Royal Highness The Prince of Wales viewing Northern Royal Albatross *Diomedea sanfordi* at Taiaroa Head, New Zealand. Photo: Press Association.

at the RSPB reserve at Bempton in Lincolnshire had the worst breeding season in eighteen years of records. Many birds failed to nest at all and adults and chicks were clearly suffering from food shortage. Similar effects have, I know, been seen in the Shetland Isles. Here, seabirds had their worst breeding season for twenty-five years, with some Kittiwake colonies disappearing entirely and Puffins and Razorbills also seriously affected.

It is well known that the sandeel population has good and bad years, but there seem to be many more bad years than good. And there is growing evidence that the ecology of the North Sea is changing dramatically. The Sir Alister Hardy Foundation for Ocean Science, which has been monitoring plankton in the North Sea for more than seventy years, has established that higher sea temperatures have driven cold-water species of plankton much further north. They are being replaced by smaller, warm-water species that are less nutritious. Whether or not this is the cause of the dramatic fall in sandeel populations is not certain, but most recent studies show that rising sea temperatures, as a result of the changing global climate, will directly affect marine productivity – with as yet unknown impacts on fisheries and seabirds.

In the case of the sandeel fishery, there is little evidence of direct competition with seabirds. Indeed, one area where competition might have been a particular problem, known as the Wee Bankie and actually just offshore from here, has been closed to fishing for the last three years, to protect nesting seabirds – and this will clearly have to continue. In general, the fishermen and the birds seem to be suffering equally from the absence of their prey. But the sandeel is part of the food chain for other species too, including cod. I am told that at present cod stocks are so low that they are probably making little impact on the sandeels. But drastic measures are being taken to get cod stocks back to the levels of twenty or thirty years ago, and those measures should surely include ensuring that there will be enough sandeels in the North Sea for a recovered cod stock to eat.

There are plenty of complicating factors, but I find it difficult to believe that the sandeel populations of the North Sea will be able to support recovered stocks of cod and mackerel, a major industrial fishery and thriving seabird populations. In those circumstances it would be hard to argue that the industrial fishery should take precedence over human consumption fisheries and the needs of marine wildlife. Surely an 'ecosystem approach' to fisheries management requires fisheries to adapt to the marine environment, not the other way round?

I think the lesson to be drawn from all of this is that we live in an increasingly inter-connected world, in which actions have consequences – and huge actions have huge consequences. Before you point out that this has always been the case, let me explain what I mean – and I have tried to say this on various occasions in the past. It is simply that we now have unprecedented technological capacity to change ecosystems, very directly and very quickly, but also to monitor many of the detailed consequences of our actions. Man has always been able to change his environment, but has only comparatively recently gained the capacity to do so with such speed and finality. I would argue that this means that the need for wisdom and restraint in our actions has never been greater. I would also argue that the need has never been clearer for all the talk (dare I say "hot air"?!) about sustainability to be translated into action and not just the repetition of "business as usual with little brass, sustainable knobs on".

Our ancestors were able to hunt many species of whales to the edge of extinction and they did make the Great Auk extinct. But they did so over hundreds of years and without a fraction of our capacity to know – simultaneously – precisely what was happening. To give just one example, nylon longlines eighty miles long, containing thousands of baited hooks, are doing unprecedented damage, at unprecedented speed, to albatross populations. And, as Dr Cooper pointed out just now, satellite monitors enable us to know a great deal about what is happening.

In many ways the albatross may be the ultimate test of whether or not, as a species ourselves, we are serious about conservation: capable of co-existing on this planet with other species. Or are we going to sacrifice what's left of wisdom on the altar of short-term gain? None of the short cuts and quick fixes that might help some other species will help the albatross. No nature reserve will ever be big enough to encompass more than a fraction of such a nomadic bird's total requirements. Captive breeding and stock enhancement have no conceivable part to play. No corporate sponsor or private philanthropist can do any more than raise awareness of the problems. And no single nation state can take any effective unilateral action. Nor is there much time left – the clock is ticking very, very fast. Even if mortality from long-lining were, somehow, to be stopped overnight, the rate of decline in the populations and the exceptionally slow rate at which albatross species breed are such that recovery would take many decades.

To me, the plight of the albatross is a symbol of the emptiness of the rhetoric surrounding so-called 'sustainable development'. Will it take the complete dodo-like disappearance of this noble winged creature to bring us to our senses? Or are we to remain blind and deaf to the appalling tragedy unfolding, out of sight and out of mind, in the vast foam-flecked spaces of the Southern Ocean?

Whatever the case, it would be a shameful travesty of our duty as stewards of this increasingly fragile globe if we couldn't find a way of living our lives in such a manner that these magnificent birds can continue to share the same planet with us. Ratification of ACAP is an important step in that process, but the reality is that in the current dangerously critical situation the only effective actions will be those that are implemented immediately, and continued indefinitely.

Ladies and gentlemen, I am sorry to have dwelt so much on a single group of birds, and on just one issue. I know that you have covered a huge range of subjects relating to waterbirds during this week, and that some of you will be experts in species that are just as desperately threatened as the albatross.

If there had been time, I would have welcomed the opportunity to talk about subjects such as the importance of wetland habitats and the many adverse consequences of intensive agriculture around the world. Indeed, some people who have heard me speak before may be surprised at my ability to resist that particular temptation!

Forty years after one of the very first gatherings of waterbird specialists took place at St. Andrews, here in Scotland, your work remains hugely important. Reviewing past efforts, considering key questions for future research and co-ordinating future conservation actions are all essential tasks. I hope you feel this particular conference has been worthwhile. I applaud your efforts and I look forward to seeing the implementation of your thinking in years to come.

# Address by Elliot Morley MP, UK Minister for Environment and Agri-Environment

*Sunday 4 April 2004*

Morley, E. 2006. Address to the Waterbirds around the world conference, 4 April 2004. *Waterbirds around the world.* Eds. G.C. Boere, C.A. Galbraith & D.A. Stroud. The Stationery Office, Edinburgh, UK. pp. 19-20.

Ladies and Gentlemen, it is an enormous pleasure to be here. Thank you to John Markland, Chairman of Scottish Natural Heritage, for extending such a warm welcome to Scotland. On behalf of the UK Government, I'd like to say that we have been delighted to play our part in the organisation of this conference and to welcome you to our shores. I'd like to extend a particular welcome to the Dutch Minister, Professor Cees Veerman.

It is quite extraordinary that this conference has attracted 456 people from 90 different countries round the world - as such it is certainly the largest assemblage of waterbird experts ever seen in the UK. When the first European Meeting on Wildfowl Conservation took place just up the coast from here, in St Andrews in 1963, there were just 81 participants from 17 countries. The increase in numbers, and the representation here from right around the world, is a real measure of how our international concern for waterbirds and their wetland habitats has grown over the last 40 years.

I must also say how especially honoured we are by the presence of some of the participants of that meeting in St. Andrew's, here today, continuing to give their support and expertise.

The UK is critically important for migratory waterbirds in the overall pattern of flyways. This is why we believe that it's vital to participate fully in the Bonn Convention and its African-Eurasian Waterbird Agreement. The potential strength of that Agreement is manifested in the fact that it has no fewer than 117 Range States and is growing fast with already 46 Contracting Parties.

We were honoured to host a meeting of the Technical Committee of the African-Eurasian Waterbirds Agreement in North Berwick last week and are committed to the implementation and review of international action plans for species that are specially important to us in the UK, such as the Bittern, the Corncrake, the Roseate Tern and, - for rather different reasons, - the globally-threatened White-headed Duck which is threatened in Europe by the invasive Ruddy Duck, introduced by accident in the UK many years ago. We are implementing a strategy to deal with the Ruddy Duck, which could be seen as the opposite of conservation!

I am especially pleased that UK expertise is helping to assess the habitat priorities for waterbirds in Africa and South-East Asia, including the identification of sites of international importance, and applying restoration and rehabilitation techniques for waterbird habitats - especially those affected by invasive aquatic weeds, a big problem internationally and in the UK. In addition, funding from the UK's Darwin Initiative has been able to help develop waterbird monitoring in eastern Africa. This project stands to make major contributions to wetland and waterbird conservation in that part of the AEWA region.

The Ramsar Convention is also very dear to our hearts in the UK. We have 243 Ramsar sites covering 6% of the land surface. These sites, and others of European importance, are home to

Elliot Morley MP. Photo: Dougie Barnett.

85% of our breeding seabirds, and about half of all the waterbirds over-wintering in the UK. As you will no doubt hear in some of the presentations to come, the UK has many different types of wetlands, from peatlands to estuaries, and from rivers to artificial reservoirs, and each of these habitats is important for different assemblages of waterbirds. We have examples of most of these wetland types within our national Ramsar network, and the UK is currently undertaking a strategic review to identify gaps in network coverage through a detailed audit of all the wetlands in the UK.

The designation of such sites is, of course, just the first step in ensuring their long-term wise-use. In a densely populated and highly developed country such as ours, protected areas face many habitat management challenges. In common with the Netherlands we find that our wetlands are under a whole range of threats. The precise issues may be slightly different from those in other parts of the world, but they are no less acute. The value of international conferences such as this one is the opportunity to share experiences and solutions, and so to learn from each other. I do urge you all to make the most of the opportunities presented in the next few days for such exchanges. This will undoubtedly help us all to deliver better, and more focused conservation.

Elliot Morley MP counting waterbirds on the Humber Estuary Ramsar site. Photo: Gareth Harford.

Throughout your conference, over the next few days you will hear a great deal about the problems faced by migratory waterbirds and the serious conflicts arising from human activities in many parts of the world. Amongst the most serious are of course the threats to some of our especially extraordinary and spectacular migratory seabirds - the albatrosses and petrels of the southern oceans. Only international action can help to address the issues of longline and illegal fishing, which are the principal threats to them.

So I am delighted to be able to announce today that the UK Government has just become the 6th state to ratify the Bonn Convention's Agreement on the Conservation of Albatrosses and Petrels. Our instrument of ratification was deposited with the Australian Government on Friday 2 April. By happy coincidence the Secretary of State for the Environment, Food and Rural Affairs, Margaret Beckett, was on a visit to Australia at the time and was able, during her visit, to reinforce our commitment to this treaty - the UK having played a key role in drafting the Agreement and was amongst the first to sign it. Our ratification covers the UK and three Overseas Territories - the Falkland Islands, South Georgia and the South Sandwich Islands, and the British Antarctic Territory. We will be working hard to extend the ratification to a fourth Overseas Territory, Tristan da Cunha as soon as possible. We also look forward to participating in the first Conference of the Parties when it is convened in the coming year. Our aim, together, must be to make real changes to the fortunes of these amazing birds.

We must bring more and more people to an understanding of the challenges for biodiversity that we face. The plight of the mythical albatross connects peoples across oceans and between continents and captures the poetic imagination. But it can also generate more down-to-earth instincts! I was very interested to discover that the Conservation Foundation is working with Ladbrokes the bookmakers to help raise money for albatross research through what is called 'The Big Bird Race'. This is a serious scientific satellite tracking project based in Tasmania to find out where the Tasmanian Shy Albatrosses migrate. But it's combined with an innovative approach to betting, in which on-line clients back an albatross to win the migration race. This gives a whole new meaning to 'having a flutter'.

This idea could bring a whole new section of society to an interest in biodiversity and to research and data collection. We have come to call the mass involvement of people in research as

'citizen- science' - and the more of this we can encourage the better! Only by engaging the understanding and involvement of people at large can we hope to make the large-scale changes needed to slow the progressive loss of biodiversity worldwide. There are now many tools that we can use - with the Internet, web cams and satellite tracking - to bring these issues to a wider public.

Many of you will know what a strong tradition we have in the UK of using volunteer effort to collect biodiversity information. I'm pleased to say that I myself am a volunteer and have been involved in making low-tide counts on a monthly basis. This helps me to get out on the first Sunday in the month and talk to other enthusiasts and landowners and makes a contribution to the database. Time-series data is essential to monitor population trends and to try and establish what the influences are - and here we have had volunteers collecting data for over 50 years and there are between three and four thousand of them now who collect regularly. For example, we have discovered through our Wetland Bird Survey (or WeBS) monitoring data an early real manifestation of climate change. With increasingly mild winters, it seems that many waders and other waterbirds are not having to fly so far west to find mild winter feeding conditions. Our volunteers are discovering declines in the numbers of waterbirds on estuaries on the west coast of the UK, and commensurate increases on the east. Perhaps in the future - with climate change - these migrants will increasingly over-winter in Denmark and the Baltic. We can see these changes going on, and must consider their implications for conservation management.

I am sure that every one of you is aware of the immediacy of the challenge we face on global biodiversity loss - potentially as a result of long-term climate change - but also of course from the direct and pervasive influences that are apparent here and now. The global community has set itself the target of substantially reducing the rate of biodiversity loss by 2010. Conferences like this one are vital in exchanging ideas, understanding the problems and galvanising initiatives as we strive to achieve that objective. But we must not deceive ourselves into thinking that conferences themselves are a substitute for real action on the ground. I urge you, as you listen to the speakers this week, to consider how their messages can be translated into new, concerted activity that makes a real difference. It is the task of all of us, politicians, scientists and the research community and NGOs to make sure that our work engenders real conservation activity.

I hope that, - just as we look back on the first European wildfowl conference, 40 years ago, as a key point when Governments and NGOs began to work seriously together in partnership internationally to address the conservation problems of waterbirds and wetlands - so we will reflect on this truly 'Global' Flyway Conference as a defining moment when the 2010 target came clearly into sight and became realisable.

The role of migratory waterbirds as indicators of wider ecological change is clear and important. They can be signals of broader environmental threats. Let us make sure that our data is robust and our actions are effective to serve the wider biodiversity community and, most importantly, the people we represent.

Whilst it is absolutely essential for national governments to make decisions in their own national contexts, they must not forget that action in one country impacts on conservation in another. It is wonderful to see so many countries gathered here, so I wish you a very successful conference - one that will help and guide our decision-making.

# Address by Cees Veerman,
# The Netherlands' Minister for Agriculture, Nature and Food Quality

*Sunday 4 April 2004*

Veerman, C. 2006. Address to the Waterbirds around the world conference, 4 April 2004. *Waterbirds around the world*. Eds. G.C. Boere, C.A. Galbraith & D.A. Stroud. The Stationery Office, Edinburgh, UK. pp. 21-22.

Ladies and gentlemen, recently, on a farm in Southwestern France, I heard the high-pitched wail of dozens of Common Cranes as they made their way, far up in the early spring sky, from their wintering sites in North Africa to their Siberian breeding grounds.

As I watched the birds fly steadily North, I stood once again in awe about the unfathomable phenomenon of bird migration. What makes these birds fly thousands of miles along well-defined routes, using the same wetlands as stop-over points for many decades? What moves the Arctic Tern each year to make the 35 000 kilometer round trip from the Arctic to the South Pole and back?

As we gaze deeper and deeper into the Universe, observing galaxies and stars billions of miles away, we haven't even begun to understand the mechanisms that cause bird migration. That is a humbling thought, teaching us profound respect not only for the tiny Arctic Tern on its epic annual journey, but for nature as a whole.

Over the past decades, we have witnessed a remarkable shift in the relationship between nature and man. Even 40 years ago, mankind was ruling the roost, viewing nature as an inexhaustible wellspring of resources that man could mine as he saw fit.

At the dawn of the 21st century, much of man's self-instilled authority over all things living has evaporated. Mankind has learned to see itself not as nature's supreme ruler, but as part of it. A vulnerable part, for there are limits to the extent that we can exploit our natural resources. If we exceed those limits, we now understand, our very existence on this planet may well be in jeopardy. We have discovered the principle of sustainability.

So we have a duty to take care of nature in all its richness and variety. For in my view, taking care of nature equals taking care of mankind itself. If you think this sounds as if I'm talking about nature conservation as an act of self-interest, you are partly right. But taking care of our natural environment is also an intrinsic duty. We are, after all, responsible for husbanding the resources that have been entrusted to us.

This is where biodiversity kicks in. Preserving and protecting it is of the utmost importance, because it is the measure of the richness and variety I was talking about only a minute ago. And it is well understood these days that the richness and variety of nature is the very cornerstone of it. Without biodiversity, our natural environment would not be functioning, or at least not be functioning that well.

Preserving and protecting biodiversity is the common responsibility of mankind. National governments play an important role, to be sure. They may reflect, in the words of Jean-Jacques Rousseau, the volonté générale, or popular will. But governments also have an important trailblazing role. They must stir up popular support for policies that may seem tough or far-fetched at first sight. This is why governments around the globe have a direct responsibility in the quest to save biodiversity.

Cees Veerman. Photo: Dougie Barnett.

However, governments cannot go it alone. We need the cooperation of international bodies, regional and local authorities, non-governmental organizations, the business world and individual citizens. Only then will we succeed in tackling the global problem of the loss of biodiversity.

The growing effort to protect migratory birds is part of the worldwide struggle to halt the loss of biodiversity. It perfectly illustrates the necessity of cooperation: it makes no sense for one single nation to protect and preserve wetlands and other staging posts if the same is not done in other countries further up and down the line.

Co-operation, I am pleased to say, has become the norm in migratory bird conservation. It is one of the pillars of the 1971 Ramsar Convention. The Bonn Convention, whose 25th anniversary we celebrate this year, is exclusively dedicated to migratory species, birds figuring prominently among them. And then there are the broader frameworks such as the Convention on Biological Diversity and the Millennium Goals we all agreed upon during the 2002 World Summit on Sustainable Development in Johannesburg.

I referred earlier to the mysterious and fascinating forces that trigger bird migration. But all this mystery and fascination should not cause a kind of awestruck paralysis. For despite our lack of understanding, there is a lot we can do to let the Common Crane, the Arctic Tern and many hundreds of other species to travel the skies unhindered.

We know, for instance, that strings of connected sanctuaries, such as wetlands, are of the utmost importance to migratory birds. In the Netherlands, creation of a National Ecological Network is one of our priorities - a long slog indeed, for work on it began in the early 1990s and is due for completion in 2018.

Work on an analogous Global Ecological Network - presumably an even longer slog - is underway. International flyways, the routes that migratory birds follow, are an important part of this network. The Dutch government strongly supports the creation of this global network and its concomitant flyways.

One Dutch initiative has ensured the protection of the East Atlantic Flyway from the vast tundra in northern Siberia to the wetlands in the Netherlands and from there on to Africa. This flyway has official status since the African-Eurasian Waterbird Agreement came into force in November 1999.

But we also support flyways that are far from our doorstep: we are participating in the development of the Central Asian Flyway and the Flyways of the Americas. We do this inspired by the spirit of cooperation and by a strong conviction that we carry a global, if shared, responsibility.

So far, I have been stressing preservation and protection, conspicuously avoiding the words 'sustainable use'. But since one of the objectives of this conference is the presentation of an 'update on the harvest and sustainable use of migratory waterbirds', I feel I must briefly address the issue.

Words like 'harvest' would make any true-blue environmentalist shudder. And indeed, the hunt on most migratory water birds is forever closed in the Netherlands. But I stress that we understand and respect the needs of other peoples, whose livelihoods depend, for instance, on duck and goose hunting. As I

said before, man is part of nature and that implies us making use of its 'products'. The vital point is to emphasize the sustainability of such harvesting activities.

At the outset of this talk, I spoke about the past, when man was lording it over nature. I discussed the relatively recent shift in mankind's attitude towards its fellow creatures. In conclusion, let me give one example of that changed relationship.

As you may know, my country has been seriously hit by Avian Influenza last year. There are strong suspicions of a link between bird migration and outbreaks of the disease. In the past, we might have opened the hunt on migrating birds in order to curb Avian Influenza.

Nowadays, we employ monitoring and early warning systems. Simultaneously, we are studying ways to adapt the management of our chicken and duck farms. The simile is probably inappropriate here, but this way we are killing two birds with one stone: the migratory birds fly on, while our farms are protected from Avian Influenza.

It has been a pleasure speaking to you in Edinburgh, a city 'Crowded with Genius', to quote the title of a recent book on the Scottish Enlightenment of the 18th century.

It has also been a pleasure for my ministry to be involved in the preparation of this important conference, in close cooperation with Her Majesty's Government, the Scottish Executive, and Wetlands International, where the idea of this conference was originally conceived.

I particularly want to thank Professor Colin Galbraith, the chair of the Conference Steering Committee, for his unstinting efforts to make this conference a success.

I wish Professor Galbraith and all other participants a fruitful conference, whose outcomes will help migratory birds, after all our fellow creatures, to continue their age-old journeys along the flyways of the world.

Thank you.

The extensive wetlands and floodplains in the Netherlands are a very important wintering area for millions of waterbirds: floodplains of the IJssel river during high water; March 2006, Gorssel. Photo: Gerard Boere.

# Address by Max Finlayson, President, Wetlands International

*Sunday 4 April 2004*

Finlayson, M. 2006. Address to the Waterbirds around the world conference, 4 April 2004. *Waterbirds around the world*. Eds. G.C. Boere, C.A. Galbraith & D.A. Stroud. The Stationery Office, Edinburgh, UK. pp. 23-26.

Ladies and gentlemen, I am pleased to be welcoming you here on behalf of Wetlands International. It's a pleasure to be in Scotland at this conference and to have the opportunity to make a few comments about why we are here. First let me record my pride at being able to represent Wetlands International – as we have been around for a long time many of you know a lot about us and I am confident that during this conference you will see further evidence of the ongoing value of our work. We have a long history – our first office opened its doors in 1954 – some 50 years ago– and we have developed many long-lasting partnerships that will come to the fore during this Conference.

We have a great interest in this conference. In collaboration with our partners in the organising group we have made a major effort to ensure that you have a successful conference. By this I mean that we have worked to ensure that you have a conference that should both educate and entertain you, and set the scene for ongoing outcomes for the conservation and wise use of wetlands and waterbirds worldwide. Let me record my gratitude to the organisers – they have worked long and hard to make this conference a reality – thank-you for your efforts.

I would now like to focus on the globally important concept of flyways – the networks of sites that support waterbirds around the world. Flyways have for a long time been central to the work of Wetlands International. The term 'flyway' refers to a concept for waterbird conservation that encompasses conservation and wise use of wetlands and waterbirds across multiple sites across very large areas – it is global and it is important.

Max Finlayson. Photo: Dougie Barnett.

Stalwarts of waterbird conservation - Hugh Boyd, Geoffrey Matthews, Harvey Nelson and Eckhart Kuijken. Photo: Dougie Barnett.

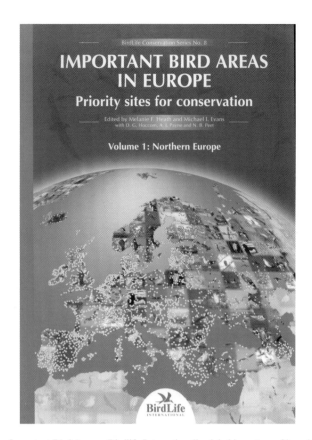

Important Bird Areas – Birdlife International's global inventory of key sites for bird conservation.

Asia-Pacific waterbird counts - Wetlands International's Asian Waterbird Census: part of the International Waterbird Census.

I doubt that any other concept has the same immediate meaning and value for global waterbird conservation and wise use. It can also provide valuable lessons for other conservation planners and managers.

We are keen through the flyway approach to promote concepts and actions that ensure connection between sites, species and the ecological interactions that support these. It is about linkages – both those in the environment and those between people and institutions that support our common goals of conservation and wise use. The concept of linkages is also not new, but recently we have been hearing more and more about interlinkages between conservation efforts globally and locally. Through this conference we can support these efforts – waterbird conservation has long focussed on linkages between sites and between concerned and erudite people. The formation of the Ramsar Convention in 1971 is one example where interlinkages and common purpose came together through the efforts of dedicated and erudite scientists.

This conference presents an opportunity to discuss the science that is needed to conserve our waterbirds – our global waterbirds. Monitoring of waterbirds has been formally undertaken for many decades. The International Waterbird Census was started by Wetlands International (through the component of our organisation that was known as IWRB) in the 1960s and we now have a long time series of data for many species and sites. This dataset and associated products, such as the Waterbird Population Estimates are key resources for the Ramsar Convention. Birdlife International also provides an invaluable data resource through its Important Bird Area program. Many national and international organisations now rely on these datasets. We are pleased to welcome to this conference some of the stalwarts of waterbird conservation and monitoring.

AEWA
UNEP

African-Eurasian Waterbird Agreement

Asia-Pacific Migratory Waterbird Conservation Strategy.

The importance of the datasets that have built up over many years will be well illustrated in this conference. I would also like to draw your attention to the launch of another product from this work, namely, the report of the Asian Wetland Census 1997-2001. This report complements others reporting results from the International Waterbird Census and the *Waterbird Population Estimates*, with the third edition of the latter being launched at the Ramsar Conference (CoP8) in Spain in November 2002, and again demonstrates our commitment to supporting waterbird conservation worldwide.

During this conference we have presentations covering activities across all major waterbird flyways. Through these we will cross the globe and we will enjoy it – it will be fun and exciting, and as we do this we will consider the ecology and future of our waterbirds and their wetland habitats from many important perspectives. Wetlands International sees formal flyway agreements as a powerful way of developing cooperation for the conservation of migratory birds. We strongly support the efforts of the Convention on Migratory Species and others involved in these formal agreements. We would like to see them extended wherever possible.

I am also very aware of major issues that still need to be tackled if we are to conserve our waterbirds. The continued destruction of many important waterbird habitats is well known, as is the decline of many waterbird populations. We are broadly aware of the distribution of wetlands around the globe; however, the global wetland mapping and inventory resource is inadequate for many if not most purposes. The Ramsar Convention has been at the forefront of efforts to close these gaps, but there is a long way to go.

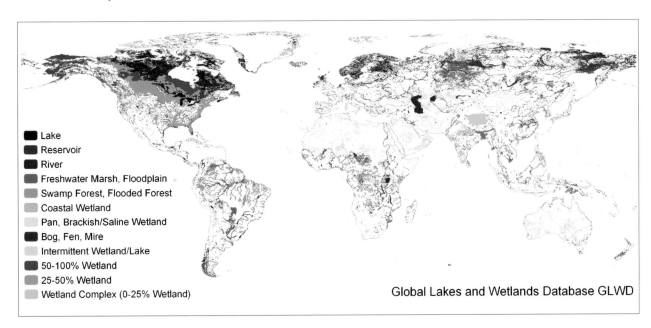

Global distribution of wetlands.

**Percent of species of known status**

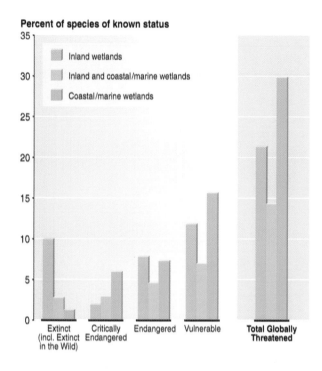

Percentage of Globally Threatened waterbirds, including seabirds, in different threat categories. Each waterbird family is allocated as either depending on only inland wetlands, depending on only coastal/marine systems, or depending on both inland and coastal/marine systems (Millennium Ecosystem Assessment & BirdLife International).

We are also aware that many waterbird populations are in decline with many threatened at a global level by a litany of problems that are all too familiar. We are also aware that our data resources and management both need improving if we are to stop and reverse recent trends. The issue of adequate data is one that recurs regularly. I would like to reinforce Wetlands International's

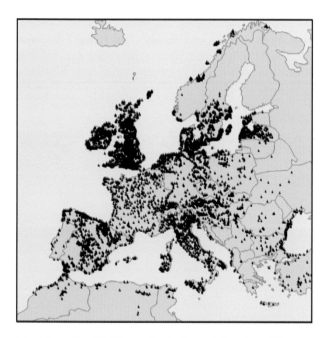

International Waterbird Census sites in Europe and northern Africa.

The Grado Strategy – the forerunner of MedWet.

support for a statement that I first heard at a wetland conference held in Italy in 1991. A now deceased British hydrologist, Dr Ted Hollis, was metaphorically pounding his fist and loudly seeking support for holistic and concerted action to *"halt and reverse wetland loss and degradation"* in the Mediterranean. He did not obtain universal support from the assembled scientists and managers who were stumbling over the concepts of halting and reversing loss and degradation – was it possible?

But times have changed and we recognise that we need to both halt further destruction and to restore or rehabilitate what has already been lost or degraded. To achieve this we need political commitment and support for meaningful outcomes. We need capacity in all parts of the world. We also need science, and we need *quality* science. I cannot emphasise enough the importance of that last point – the rigour of our data is paramount if we are to make our points and be believed and influence managers and policy-makers. Wetlands International is a science-based organisation and our much lauded global monitoring programs must provide the type of data that we require for effective management actions. For this to occur these monitoring programs must be scientifically rigorous and supported fully by the users.

On that closing note – a note that emphasises the importance of basing our work on sound science - I welcome you to this conference and implore you (if this is needed) to enjoy yourselves as you devote your time to this scientific forum. Thank you and welcome on behalf of Wetlands International.

# Address by John Markland, Chairman of Scottish Natural Heritage

*Sunday 4 April 2004*

Markland, J. 2006. Address to the Waterbirds around the world conference, 4 April 2004. *Waterbirds around the world*. Eds. G.C. Boere, C.A. Galbraith & D.A. Stroud. The Stationery Office, Edinburgh, UK. p. 27.

Ladies and gentlemen, welcome to Scotland, and to our capital city, Edinburgh. As the Chairman of Scottish Natural Heritage I am delighted to welcome all of you to Heriot-Watt University to participate in this vitally important, international conference.

Looking across this auditorium I am hugely impressed by the exceptional turnout – I gather we have more than 450 delegates from 90 countries throughout the world. You will be aware of the slogan 'think globally and act locally'. Well, I think it's fair to say that we will be working locally to act globally.

Behind the logos and fliers for this event there has been a huge amount of collaborative work. I congratulate the organising Committee, Government officials of the United Kingdom and the Netherlands, along with the Board and officials of Wetlands International, for working together so brilliantly to bring us here today. In fact, more than thirty organisations and countries have contributed to this event, and I note the leading contributions from the USA, Australia, Denmark and Japan and from global organisations such as the Ramsar Convention, Birdlife International, United Nations Environment Programme, Pacific Seabird Group, The Waterbird Society, and many, many others. We are so pleased to hold this event in Edinburgh, and so proud to be able to point to the splendid partnership approaches being developed in this work.

Effective partnerships are critical if we are to see global impacts from this conference. We have lost vast areas of wetland habitat, and many of our waterbird species now have critically endangered populations in different parts of the world. We are dealing with a unique biological issue, because what brings us here today are the flyways, the connections between where birds nest, rest, feed, stop-off when in transit to moult or over-winter. We get a sense of the vast range of problems facing these birds as they make their way north, south, east and west, some of them travelling immense distances across the globe. We have to find ways of building on the research work, the conservation and management techniques, and the partnership forged between individuals, bodies and countries, to ensure that the globe is a

John Markland. Photo: Dougie Barnett.

safer, better and healthier place for waterbirds, and for the people who love to watch them.

Finally, and on a domestic note, I hope you enjoy the field visits on Tuesday. You have a wonderful choice of locations, including the Clyde, Forth, and Solway Estuaries, Scotland's first recently-established National Park, Loch Lomond & Trossachs, Loch Leven (to be even more local, this is where I live), the River Tay, Blair Atholl and even the Bass Rock. Each of these is a jewel in our nature conservation crown of wetland Scotland. Enjoy these areas and I do hope that you leave the conference with a special memory of your visit to Scotland.

Thank you very much.

Blar nam Faoileag National Nature Reserve (part of the Caithness and Sutherland Peatlands Ramsar site and Special Protection Area) is internationally important for its breeding waterbird populations, and is another "jewel in our nature conservation crown of wetland Scotland". Photo: Steve Moore, NCC.

# Address by Allan Wilson MSP,
# Deputy Minister for Environment and Rural Development, Scotland

*Wednesday 7 April 2004*

Wilson, A. 2006. Address to the Waterbirds around the world conference, 7 April 2004. *Waterbirds around the world.* Eds. G.C. Boere, C.A. Galbraith & D.A. Stroud. The Stationery Office, Edinburgh, UK. p. 28.

Your Royal Highness, Conference Chairman, Delegates, I must open my short address by expressing our gratitude and appreciation to His Royal Highness. Not only for being here today but for sharing with us his expectations as to what this Conference might deliver. In closing this Conference, I offer delegates my two challenges for them to take home, to all parts of the globe.

Everyone here today has been charged with the common duty to care for the natural world. We will do that, not for our benefit but for the generations who will follow us.

We leave here today with the Edinburgh Declaration and the clearest of messages that we all have a common responsibility to protect and conserve our waterbirds. To do that, we must be open with our technical knowledge and expertise. The sharing of knowledge is not an optional extra: information and expertise must be exchanged to help preserve the world's waterbirds.

Ninety countries are represented here today – what of the other countries elsewhere in the world who either couldn't be here or who may not have the resources to take forward the achievements of this Conference? Will you give them the support they need? That is a further challenge laid down by this Conference.

The first challenge I offer is one that only those here can achieve. I ask you to create the opportunity when you go home, and are speaking with your colleagues about your week in Scotland, to consider how YOU are going to make the Declaration work. The Edinburgh Declaration is an important step but at the end of the day, it is only a bit of paper or the text on the screen of a computer monitor. Your task is to turn the words of the Declaration into action.

Conservation is about engaging with others. And not just those who share your views on what nature conservation is and why it is important. Some outside this Conference may see your discussions this week as a threat to them. Don't ignore them. Engage them. Your Conference has focused on the links between people and nature, and has looked at issues such as over-crowding and development and how they can affect both man and species.

We cannot ignore the inter-relationship between man and the other species which inhabit the planet. We need to work with others, many of whom do not share our nature conservation objectives, if we are to ensure that biodiversity is maintained throughout the world. That is the second challenge I set before you and I recognise that it will not be easy to achieve. It is one which we in Scotland have to tackle and we still have much to do to demonstrate the benefits which nature conservation brings, in ecological and in economic terms. That effort must be made and I know that Scotland is not alone in facing that issue.

There has been some very positive press coverage of this Conference. The Scottish Executive too has a positive message to convey in relation to Scotland's contribution to conservation at a national, European and international level, not least through

Allan Wilson MSP. Photo: Dougie Barnett.

our achievements in the Nature Conservation (Scotland) Bill. This Bill is making good progress through our Scottish Parliament and I expect the measures will be law later this year.

The Bill introduces a wide range of initiatives which are good for the natural environment and for water birds. New protective measures for both species and protected habitats are core elements of the Bill. Above all, the Bill recognises the significance of conserving the biodiversity of our planet.

In drawing to a close, I'd like to repeat the pleasure I had to meet you all on Sunday and welcome you to Scotland. I know for many of you it was your first visit to the United Kingdom and I thank you for your contribution to the Conference.

Like the migratory birds you have come to Scotland to discuss, I hope that your flyway route home is safe and secure, and that the habitat to which you are returning is warm and welcoming!

The Conference is now over. Let its ideas, its creativity, its links continue. I wish you all the very best for the future and wish you a safe journey home.

Thank you.

# Waterbird conservation in a new millennium – where from and where to?

*David A. Stroud[1], Gerard C. Boere[2], Colin A. Galbraith[3] & Des Thompson[3]*

*[1] Joint Nature Conservation Conservation Committee, Monkstone House, City Road, Peterborough, PE1 1JY, UK.*
*(email: David.Stroud@jncc.gov.uk)*
*[2] Dorrewold 22, 7213 TG Gorssel, The Netherlands. (email: gcboere@planet.nl)*
*[3] Scottish Natural Heritage, Bonnington Bond, 2 Anderson Place, Edinburgh, EH6 5NP, UK.*

Stroud, D.A., Boere, G.C., Galbraith, C.A., Thompson, D.B.A. 2006. Waterbird conservation in a new millennium – where from and where to? *Waterbirds around the world.* Eds. G.C. Boere, C.A. Galbraith & D.A. Stroud. The Stationery Office, Edinburgh, UK. pp. 29-30.

The *Waterbirds around the world* conference held in Edinburgh in April 2004 was a major milestone for waterbird conservation. There has long been recognition of the need for international perspectives in the conservation of migratory birds, and especially waterbirds. Indeed, 90 years ago the USA and Great Britain, on behalf of Canada, formally agreed the first of the modern international conservation treaties related to migratory birds.

The development of the International Waterfowl Research Bureau (IWRB) in the years following the Second World War is outlined by Kuijken (this volume). On the European continent, IWRB has been highly effective in progressively stimulating a range of collaborative international actions for waterbird and wetland conservation. Major IWRB conferences – more fully described by Kuijken - were held at Noordwijk aan Zee, The Netherlands (1966), Leningrad, USSR (1968), Ramsar, Iran (1971), Astrakhan, USSR (1989), St. Petersburg Beach, Florida, USA (1992), Kushiro, Japan (1994), Strasbourg, France (1994), Kuala Lumpur, Malaysia (1995), and Dakar, Senegal (1998).

Participation in these meetings has grown steeply to the present, in terms of numbers of participants and countries represented, as well as in numbers of represented international organisations (Figs. 1 & 2). It is striking to see such an upsurge of interest since 1989.

In introducing these proceedings and noting that *Waterbirds around the world* was the first major international conference specifically concerning waterbirds of the twenty-first century, we first consider the historical context of international waterbird coferences, and then move on to look beyond the Edinburgh conference. Table 1 summarises the main themes of some of the previous international meetings and conferences on the conservation of waterbirds and their wetland habitats.

## DEVELOPMENT OF MAJOR THEMES IN WATERBIRD CONSERVATION
### Mechanisms and means of international co-operation
The main themes of some of the previous international meetings and conferences on the conservation of waterbirds and their wetland habitats are summarised in Table 1. In North America there has been a very long history of international collaboration in the conservation of waterbirds at continental scales. This was established early through the 1916 Migratory Birds Treaty between the USA and the UK (on behalf of Canada), developed in 1936 through a further treaty between the USA and Mexico (more fully outlined by Schmidt, this volume). The signing of the North American Waterfowl Management Plan in 1985 gave a mechanism for collaboration between governments and a wide range of

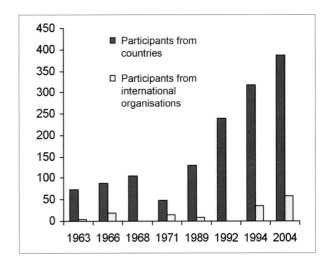

**Fig. 1.** Increasing numbers of participants at international conferences on waterbirds, 1963-2004.

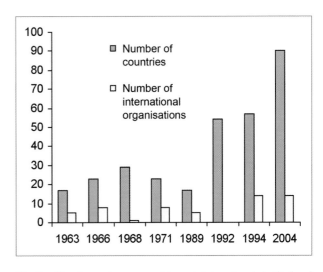

**Fig. 2.** The increasing geographic and international institutional participation in international conferences on waterbirds, 1963-2004.

non-governmental stakeholders and has been particularly effective (Wheeler, this volume). In the 1990s, the Western Hemisphere Shorebird Reserve Network (WHSRN) gave an informal mechanism for site-twinning and thus the building of links between waterbird conservationists in North and South America (Hunter *et al.* 1991). More recently, two international conferences have developed the Western Hemisphere Migratory Species Initiative as a means of promoting international co-operation at continental scales (Schmidt, this volume, Ralph & Rich 2005).

**Fig. 3.** The seventy-eight participants at the First European Meeting on Wildfowl Conservation held in St. Andrews, Scotland, 1963. Photo: Colin Galbraith, from an original by the Nature Conservancy.

The establishment and progressive development of the International Wildfowl Research Bureau (IWRB) by Luc Hoffman and others in the years following the Second World War was a major step forward (see Kuijken, this volume). From the outset, IWRB provided an organisational means of promoting international collaboration and co-operation in wildfowl conservation and research. Its initial activities, however, were largely restricted to NW Europe and parts of North Africa, and largely focussed on understanding the size, distribution and trends of wildfowl populations. However, an important early aim was also to develop a good insight in harvest pressure on species, and the creation of an IWRB Hunting Rationalisation Research Group in 1969 pioneered international assessments of waterbird harvests (Lampio 1974, 1977). Whilst IWRB's initial activity was focussed on Anatidae, the scope of interest and activity progressively broadened to encompass waders (Lippens 1967, Prater 1974) and to other waterbird taxa.

IWRB, in close collaboration with the UK Nature Conservancy, provided the impetus for the convening of a First European Meeting on Wildfowl Conservation in St. Andrews, Scotland. This conference was held in October 1963 and attracted 73 participants from 17 countries (Fig. 3). Much discussion related to the need to create mechanisms of collaboration (Table 1), and one of the key conclusions was that "all delegations [were] unanimously of the opinion that such European meetings should be held at regular intervals in the future..."

A major topic for consideration in St. Andrews was the possibility of establishing an international legal treaty related to the conservation of the wetland habitat of wildfowl. As described in detail by Matthews (1993) and Kuijken (this volume), this was a major theme of the subsequent international conferences leading to the formal agreement of the Convention on Wetlands of International Importance, especially as waterfowl habitat at Ramsar, in Iran 1971 (Carp 1973). The ensuing Ramsar Convention has increasingly broadened its activities and remits from its original focus on wildfowl into a more holistic international instrument concerned with all aspects of wetland conservation, especially in recent years, and now with issues of sustainable development through wetland conservation to the fore.

As the implementation and activities of the Ramsar Convention has developed, other international mechanisms for waterbird conservation and international co-operation have been established. The Convention on Migratory Species (CMS) was established in 1979, in turn leading to the formal agreement of the Agreement on the conservation of Africa-Eurasian migratory waterbirds in 1995 (Boere unpublished; see Lenten, this volume).

The development of formal multilateral treaties in Asia and Oceania have taken somewhat longer to achieve, although a range of formal bilateral agreements on the conservation of migratory waterbirds have been established, mainly between Japan, Russia, USA and Australia (Lane & Parish 1991). The Asia-Pacific Migratory Waterbird Conservation Strategy — more fully described by Mundkur (this volume) has been very influential since 1996 in building not only site-networks but also encouraging informal processes of collaboration research and conservation (Long & Watkins 2005a,b, Straw 1997, 2005). The development in recent decades of a comprehensive environmental protection regime in Antarctica through the 1991 Protocol on Environmental Protection to the Antarctic Treaty has been of huge global significance on constraining potential human impacts on this unspoilt 'continent of science'. Similarly, the adoption in 1982 of the Convention on the Conservation of Antarctic Marine Living Resources (CCAMLR) and its subsequent implementation has been a major step forward in moving, internationally, to regulate man's impact in the marine environment – not withstanding the greatly problematic illegal, unregulated and unreported fishing highlighted by HRH the Prince of Wales in his address to the conference (this volume). Most recently, the coming into force of the Agreement on the Conservation of Albatrosses and Petrels (ACAP) seeks, inter alia, to address the cause of impacts and threats to these species

Fig. 4. The publication of an international species action plan (inset) for Lesser White-fronted Goose *Anser erythropus* (Heredia *et al.* 1996) was an important stimulus for a range of conservation initiatives as reported by several authors elsewhere in this volume. An update of the action plan was discussed at an international conference in Lammi, Finland in April 2005. Photo: Ingar Jostein Øien.

on the international high seas – of crucial importance in reversing current negative population trends. The establishment and implementation of such international regulatory regimes for the environment are a major achievement for proponents of conservation and sustainable use, although they tend often to be overlooked by those whose outlooks are either terrestrial or more orientated to the northern hemisphere.

In the Americas, the Migratory Birds Act 1936 is restricted to Canada, USA and Mexico and does not formally include other Central or South American countries. Potentially the Western Hemisphere Convention could act as multilateral instrument; the recent adopted USA/Neotropical Migratory Bird Conservation Act provides a framework for support to migratory birds projects and programmes, including waterbirds, in the Neotropics, but is not a formal flyway conservation instrument; see also Boere & Rubec (2002) and Boere (2003) for a more detailed overview of relevent bilateral and multilateral instruments.

The Waterbirds around the world Conference in Edinburgh was an opportunity to compare and contrast the different institutional approaches being adopted around the world concerned with the processes of international collaboration for waterbird conservation. One of these, the development of national and international single species action plans for threatened waterbirds, has been an important means of cost-effectively directing conservation activity. Conservation action plans were first discussed at the St. Petersburg conference in 1992, and were an important element of discussions at the Anatidae 2000 Conference in Strasbourg in 1994. In the years since, they have become increasingly adopted as a central means of delivery of conservation actions (e.g. Heredia *et al.* 1996). Whilst early

discussions concentrated on format and structure of action plans, discussions in Edinburgh highlighted that many plans remain largely unimplemented. If action plans are to be effective, they must be adequately resourced, and be sufficiently 'owned' by the interested parties in order for them to be effectively implemented (see Flyway management for species of conservation concern, this volume).

Stroud *et al.* (2004, and this volume) in their review of the status of migratory waders in Africa and Western Eurasia, showed that that area has the greatest number of declining wader populations (12 of 22 populations - 55%). Effectively, this region

Fig. 5. Political changes in the early 1990s aided the undertaking of international research programmes in the Russian arctic. International expedition arriving at the island of Izvestia Tronoy, Taimyr, 1993 to assess numbers of Ivory Gulls *Pagophila eburnea*. Photo: Gerard Boere.

embraces the European Union (EU15), which also has the greatest extent of species-orientated international legislation specifically requiring countries to maintain a favourable conservation status of waders (and other birds). Both the European Union's Directive on the Conservation of Wild Birds (the so called EC Birds Directive) and the Council of Europe's Convention on the Conservation of European Wildlife and Natural Habitats (Bern Convention) have been in force since 1979 suggesting that additional delivery and implementation mechanisms are needed to address the fundamental drivers of population declines. Stroud *et al.* (this volume) stress that whilst national and international strategies and legal conservation instruments have scope to help, they need to be much more penetrating in their implementation so as to address root causes of population declines.

The major political changes in eastern Europe in the late 1980s and early 1990s led to unprecedented new opportunities for international co-operation, not least the organisation of major meetings which brought together waterbird researchers from western Europe with those from the former USSR. A notable example was the International Wader Study Group's conference in Odessa, Ukraine in April 1992, which involved 79 participants from 13 countries, and developed The Odessa Protocol on international co-operation on migratory flyway research and conservation (Hötker *et al.* 1998). The Odessa Proceedings contained a wealth of previously unpublished information on wader research and survey from central and eastern Europe, and Asia. The political changes also facilitated the development of joint research programmes in the Russian arctic, notably through a series of joint expeditions involving, variously, Russian, Dutch and German waterbird researchers (Fig. 5).

### Habitat protection

The need to promote the conservation of wetland habitats in the face of habitat loss and degradation has been a central theme for international conferences. Human impacts on wetlands were clearly the major motivation for initial conservation measure in North America (Schmidt, this volume), and especially the creation of the Ramsar Convention which drew from initial European evaluations in 1962 by Project MAR (Kuijken, this volume, Matthews 1993). Whilst initial conferences focussed on the need to stem habitat loss, more recent conferences (since the 1990s) have increasingly also focussed on the exchange of information regarding means of restoration and rehabilitation of degraded habitats, as well as the appropriate management of wetlands to enhance their carrying capacity (Table 1). The important topic of wetland restoration has increasingly been addressed through targeted meetings (e.g. Moller 1995 in Denmark) and a growing specialist literature has developed especially aimed at practitioners (e.g. Eiseltová 1994, RSPB, NRA & RSNC 1994, Hertzman & Larsson 1999).

Interestingly, as early as the 1968 Leningrad meeting, habitat and predator management as a means of increasing site-carrying capacity was under discussion. Although the impact of non-native species is now recognised as one of the principal causes of biodiversity loss world-wide (Millennium Ecosystem Assessment 2005a), previously there was discussion of the introduction of non-native waterbirds for hunting (most recently at the 1989 Astrakhan conference which heard of proposals to introduce

Canada Geese *Branta canadensis* to the USSR: Gabuzov 1990).

Workshops at Edinburgh considered the need for holistic approaches to conservation which need to include elements related both to site-based protection and wider countryside policies (Building effective ecological networks; and integrating waterbird conservation, populations, habitats and landscapes, this volume).

In spite of modern techniques to analyse habitat losses and the increasingly global coverage of the International Waterfowl Census and other monitoring schemes, it is still almost impossible to determine the consequences of some large scale habitat losses for waterbird populations. Indeed, habitat loss and fragmentation remains a major threat to many waterbird populations. A topical example is the lack of information concerning the fate of the immense waterbird populations formerly present in the Mesopotamian marshes of Iraq (Evans 1994). Although parts of the marshes are now being restored and 're-wetted', the understanding and monitoring of the accompanying ecological changes are limited. Such knowledge limitations typically are the consequence of political instability and/or lack of resources constraining an ability to undertake relevant surveys and monitoring.

### Developing issues

Edinburgh saw substantive discussions on a number of new issues. Climate change has emerged in the last decade as one of the central challenges for the long-term conservation, not only of waterbirds but for the world's biodiversity. It has the potential to further and markedly exacerbate the negative impacts of other current and principal drivers of ecosystem changes such habitat change, the impacts of invasive species, over-exploitation and pollution (Millennium Ecosystem Assessment 2005a, Finlayson *et al.,* this volume; The implications of climate change for waterbirds, this volume). Possible consequences of climate change for the implementation of multilateral treaties in relation to waterbirds are discussed by Boere & Taylor (2004).

Whilst the recent spread of Asian lineage Highly Pathogenic Avian Influenza H5N1 westwards across Eurasia occurred after the Edinburgh Conference, the holding of a workshop on avian disease issues in Edinburgh (Disease emergence and impacts in migratory waterbirds, this volume) underlined the importance of this issue which has not previously been considered as an integral part of any previous international conference on waterbird conservation. The need to better develop links between veterinarians and the ornithological research and conservation communities was emphasised.

Possibly the most significant element in the Edinburgh programme which contrasted with earlier conference programmes, was recognition of the increasing need to promote the 'mainstreaming' of waterbird conservation within other governmental policies. In other words, how to ensure full and effective integration of conservation objectives in the policies and programmes of others – and not just of the traditional conservation 'sector' itself. This was manifest through discussion of the importance of communication, education and public awareness (Let the waterbirds do the talking, this volume); reviews of conflict resolution and reduction (Conflict resolution, this volume); assessments of the opportunities that modification of wider land-use policies provide for the promotion of waterbird conservation (Integrating waterbird conservation, populations,

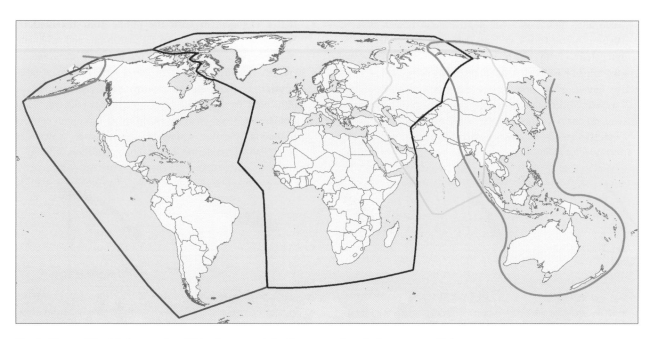

**Fig. 6.** The possible global scope of multilateral agreements for the conservation of migratory waterbirds.

habitats and landscapes, this volume); the need to build human capacity for conservation and research, especially in developing countries (Building and sustaining capacity for waterbird conservation and research, this volume); and finally discussion of a central issue, how to develop sustainable programmes of funding to support conservation initiatives (Financing global conservation: innovation, linkages, options, this volume).

At the beginning of the twenty-first century, and in a world which faces increasing acute pressures not only on ecosystems but also on human communities and societies across most of the less-developed world (Millennium Ecosystem Assessment 2005a,b,c), the cross-sectoral approach to ecosystem conservation and management is taking the centre stage of attention.

### Beyond Edinburgh...

The Conference conclusions were formalised as *The Edinburgh Declaration*. We highlight below several key issues for the future, stressed not only in the Declaration but also in many of the papers included in this volume:

- **Making more effective use of existing legal and policy instruments.** In many parts of the world a wide range of legal and policy instruments relevant to the conservation of waterbirds and their habitats exist, not least, being the Convention on Biological Diversity (CBD) to which 188 countries are currently Contracting Parties. Whilst CBD is essentially a framework Convention, the Ramsar and Bonn Conventions are more specific regarding waterbird and wetland conservation whilst also having global scope and relevance. Such international legislation, supported by national laws and policies already gives considerable opportunity for the promotion of waterbird conservation and the achievement of sustainable use. The immediate challenge is to ensure the effective *implementation* of the provisions of these existing treaties. In doing this the continued sharing of national experiences will continue to be important. However, the development of further multilateral flyway agreements similar in conceptual scope to AEWA could

provide global coverage of migratory flyways and focus for international waterbird conservation (Fig. 6).

- **Enhancing resourcing and human capacity.** There are few, if any, countries where there is adequate capacity to address the multiple challenges posed by the current ever degrading environmental conditions. World leaders at the World Summit on Sustainable Development, Johannesburg, in 2002, established a target of *"a significant reduction in the current rate of loss of biological diversity"* by 2010, but noted that to achieve this target *"will require the provision of new and additional financial and technical resources to developing countries"*. This need remains as urgent as ever, and the Edinburgh workshops on 'Financing global flyway conservation', and 'Building and sustaining capacity for waterbird conservation and research' specifically addressed these issues (Castro, this volume).

- **Responding with urgency.** The planet is currently facing an extinction crisis. The conclusions of the Millennium Ecosystem Assessment (Millennium Ecosystem Assessment 2005a,b,c) have served as a wake-up call to the severity of the issues and the urgency of necessary responses at all levels. The Millennium Ecosystem Assessment found that *"The degradation and loss of wetlands is more rapid than that for other ecosystems. The status of freshwater dependent species (in both inland and coastal areas) is deteriorating faster than those of other ecosystems. Wetland-dependent biodiversity in many parts of the world is in continuing and accelerating decline."* More detailed assessments that re-enforce this conclusion are reported in this volume (Declining waterbirds: problems, processes and sites, this volume). We need to promote early conservation actions: later may be *too* late — patients are typically easier (and certainly cheaper) to treat *before* they reach the Intensive Care Ward!

- **Demonstrating relevance of waterbird conservation in a pressured world.** Governments and others face many priorities in delivering Millennium Development Goals concerning food and water security, sanitation, and poverty reduction. In a world with much extreme human poverty, those concerned for waterbirds will need increasingly to be prepared to justify the relevance of this activity. However, the role of healthy wetlands in providing ecosystem services to human populations across the world (Finlayson, this volume; Millennium Ecosystem Assessment 2005c) provides this rationale. *"Species-focused arguments are unlikely to have significant influence on decision-making on trade-offs between the maintenance of wetland ecosystems and sustain-*

• **Better engagement with the public and stakeholders.** Sustainable development on the one hand, and achieving conservation goals through the resolution of management-conflicts requires close engagement with multiple 'stakeholders' – those people whose lives are affected or influenced by decisions taken or policies adopted. The Conference heard of many examples of successful conflict resolution (Conflict resolution, this volume) as well as specifically considering linked communication, education

Fig. 7. Children celebrating waterbirds dance at the launch of World Migratory Birds Day at Laikipia, Kenya, 9 April 2006. Photo: David Stroud.

*able development, and more potent arguments are likely to involve the importance of maintaining and enhancing ecosystem services so that they continue to support human livelihood. To achieve this requires the maintenance of wetland biodiversity and processes, which in turn will help maintain the ecosystems upon which waterbirds depend. Using waterbirds as flagship indicators of the health of wetland ecosystems can help to secure adequate trade-offs to ensure that these ecosystems can continue to deliver their services. However, more clearly articulating these arguments for continued research and monitoring of waterbirds for the benefit of decision-makers is much needed."* (Davidson & Stroud, this volume). Accordingly, waterbird conservationists will need to become more adept at justifying 'traditional' conservation of biodiversity in the context of human sustainable development. As an example, the role of sustainably managed waterbird populations in providing a valuable source of protein source for human populations in developing countries and elsewhere could be stressed (Kanstrup, this volume).

and public awareness issues (Let the waterbirds do the talking, this volume). These are crucial activities and need to be considered as essential element for any conservation programme to be successful. Initiatives such as the recently established World Migratory Birds Day, on 9 April 2006, provide opportunities to allow the threats faced by migratory waterbirds to be highlighted with a wide range of audiences, as well as giving opportunity to celebrate the cultural importance of waterbirds communication (Fig. 7).

• **Combating negative images of waterbirds.** A consequence of the spread of Asian lineage Highly Pathogenic Avian Influenza H5N1 across Eurasia since the Conference has been that increasingly, the media have portrayed waterbirds in a very negative context and there remains widespread public misunderstanding of the issue in many countries, including circulation of misinformation. Indeed, in the UK, visitor numbers to waterbird conservation centres have fallen in a significant and sustained manner. Such negative portrayal has the potential to undo decades of work by conservation communicators such as Sir Peter Scott and

**Table 1. Main themes of international conferences and meetings related to the conservation of waterbirds and their wetland habitats, 1966-2004.**

| | First European Meeting on Wildfowl Conservation, St. Andrews, Scotland (1963) (Swift 1964) | Noordwijk aan Zee, The Netherlands (1966) (Salverda 1967) | Leningrad, USSR (1968) (Isakov 1970) | Ramsar, Iran (1971) (Carp 1972) | Astrakhan, USSR (1989) (Matthews 1990) | St. Petersburg Beach, Florida, USA (1992) (Moser et al. 1993) | Kushiro, Japan (1994) (Wells & Mundkur 1996) | Anatidae 2000, Strasbourg, France (1994) (Birkan et al. 1996) | International Conference on wetlands and development, Malaysia 1995 (van Vessem 1997) | Second international conference on wetlands and development, Dakar 1998 (Beintema & van Vessem 1999) | Waterbirds around the world, Edinburgh, Scotland (2004) (Boere et al. this volume) |
|---|---|---|---|---|---|---|---|---|---|---|---|
| **Understanding distribution of populations and their sizes** | National status reviews for European countries | Review of status of waders and wader research in Europe, North Africa and Asia Minor | Review of status of main wildfowl populations in western Eurasia | | Reviews on the distribution and status of waterfowl, especially in the USSR and Europe, but also including the Americas and Africa | | National reviews of status for 19 countries or territories Workshops on studies and research for a) shorebirds and b) other waterbirds | Major world-wide status reviews for ducks, geese and swans | | | Regional (flyway-scale) reviews of status and trends of waterbirds especially in the Arctic, Neotropics, North America, intra-African migration systems, Central Asian flyway & the East Asia-Pacific flyway; Global status review for waders |
| **Regional status reviews of species and habitats** | | Review of status of wetlands in countries on the MAR list | Review of results from IWC in western Eurasia | National reports on the status of wetlands and their waterbird populations including those on the MAR list | Reviews of actual or potential international strategies for waterbird conservation under North American Waterfowl Management Plan, and CMS | Workshop on wetland and waterbird conservation in North America | National reviews of status for 19 countries or territories | | | | |
| **Hunting and sustainable use of waterbirds** | Review of hunting legislation in Europe and USA Discussions on the "relationship between conservationists and shooting interests" with case studies | | Presentations on international co-operation, including review of legal options for possible international treaties re shared waterbird resources | Presentations on hunting and other use of waterbirds in Europe, Africa, Middle East and North America | Reviews on: • hunting kill statistics • hunting management, especially in the USSR and North America • lead poisoning | Workshop on hunting and wild use of waterbird populations | Workshop on exploitation of shorebirds | Workshop on management and wise-use of Anatidae populations, including a round-table on lead poisoning in waterfowl | | | Workshops on: • sustainable waterbird harvests • sustainable use of natural resources in the African-Eurasian Flyway |
| **Mechanisms for international collaboration** | Discussions as to improved means of international co-operation in Europe on wildfowl conservation, including the need for regular international meetings | Discussions as to a possible wetlands convention | | Conclusion of the text of the Convention on wetlands of international importance, especially as waterfowl habitat. | | | Workshop on international co-operation | Workshop on scope for enhancing international co-operation, including review of actual and possible legal mechanisms to that end | Workshop on international mechanisms for waterbird conservation | Workshop on implementation priorities for AEWA | |
| **Conservation of wetlands and other waterbird habitats** | | | Review of status of main wildfowl refuges and consideration of possibilities for international site networks | Discussions on criteria for selecting internationally important wetlands | Papers on effects of habitat loss on waterbird populations | Workshop on wetland inventories and measurement of wetland loss | Workshop on domestic policy and legislation for wetland sites and waterbird species | | Workshop on information needs for waterbird and wetland conservation | Case studies from AEWA region presented | Workshop on building effective ecological networks |
| **Management of wetlands and other habitats** | | | Reviews of measures for increasing carrying capacity of wildfowl habitats | | | Workshop on restoration and rehabilitation of degraded wetlands | | | | | Workshop on habitat management and restoration |

**Table 1. Main themes of international conferences and meetings related to the conservation of waterbirds and their wetland habitats, 1966-2004 (continued).**

| | First European Meeting on Wildfowl Conservation, St. Andrews, Scotland (1963) (Swift 1964) | Noordwijk aan Zee, The Netherlands (1966) (Salverda 1967) | Leningrad, USSR (1968) (Isakov 1970) | Ramsar, Iran (1971) (Carp 1972) | Astrakhan, USSR (1989) (Matthews 1990) | St. Petersburg Beach, Florida, USA (1992) (Moser et al. 1993) | Kushiro, Japan (1994) (Wells & Mundkur 1996) | Anatidae 2000, Strasbourg, France (1994) (Birkan et al. 1996) | International Conference on wetlands and development, Malaysia 1995 (van Vessem 1997) | Second international conference on wetlands and development, Dakar 1998 (Beintema & van Vessem 1999) | Waterbirds around the world, Edinburgh, Scotland (2004) (Boere et al. this volume) |
|---|---|---|---|---|---|---|---|---|---|---|---|
| **Species conservation and action planning** | Reviews of various impacts on waterbirds including habitat loss, persistent pesticides and radioactive contamination | Review of legislative status of waders in Europe, North Africa and the Middle East | | | Reviews on: • conservation on threatened species • effects of shooting disturbance | Workshop on international conservation plans for migratory waterbirds | Workshop on domestic policy and legislation for wetland sites and waterbird species | Workshops on: • recovery programmes, including international action plans, for Anatidae • population ecology of threatened species | Workshop on planning, implementation and evaluating conservation actions | Workshop on global waterbird conservation strategies | Workshops on: • flyway management for species of conservation concern • declining waterbirds: problems, processes and sites |
| **Integrated monitoring and conservation for migratory waterbirds** | | | | | | Workshop on integrated monitoring: priorities and needs | | Workshops on: • population dynamics and implications for monitoring and conservation • ecology and implications for conservation | Workshop on information needs for waterbird and wetland conservation | | Workshops on: • flyway-scale monitoring: rising to the challenge • migration and flyway atlases • integrating waterbird conservation: populations, habitats and landscapes |
| **The marine environment** | | | | | | | | Significant inputs related to sea-ducks throughout the conference | | | Workshop on the marine environment: challenges for conservation and implementation |
| **Measuring ecological change in wetlands** | | | | | | | Workshop on ecological change in wetlands and the use of waterbirds as indicators | | | | |
| **Disease processes** | | | | | | | | | | | Workshop on disease emergence and impacts in migratory waterbirds |
| **Waterbirds and people — communication, education and public awareness** | | | | | | | Workshop on training, institutional capacity and public involvement | | | | Workshops on: • conflict resolution • education and public awareness • financing global flyway conservation: innovation, linkages, options • building and sustaining capacity for waterbird conservation and research |
| **Climate change** | | | | | Paper on effects of natural climate cycles on waterbird reproduction | | | | | | Workshop on climate change |

others. Misinformation leading to unnecessary fear creates political pressure for ill-advised and disproportionate policies such as the culling of wild birds and the destruction of wetland habitats. There is an urgent need for conservation scientists and veterinary services to pro-actively work with media to enhance the accuracy of reporting on this issue. As recently stressed by the CMS, AEWA & UNEP International Seminar on avian influenza (2006), this should include the development of much more effective communication strategies to give policy makers, stakeholders and the general public more balanced information on real levels of risk and appropriate responses.

- **Focussing conservation actions where they are most effective.** This volume outlines the wide range of conservation 'tools' that are available in the twenty-first century. However, it is increasingly important that scarce and possibility diminishing resources for waterbird conservation are cost-effectively used to the greatest effect. The development of conservation action plans (Flyway management for species of conservation concern, this volume) provides a means of objectively determining priority actions. These should be informed by integrated population monitoring which identifies critical demographic processes or life-history stages driving population declines (Pienkowski & Galbraith 1993, Piersma, this volume, Blohm *et al.*, this volume).

- **Resourcing monitoring activity.** There is a long history of waterbird monitoring at national and international scales notably through the International Waterbird Census (IWC), yet resourcing for this essential activity remains *ad hoc* and grossly inadequate. Given that monitoring provides us with the most fundamental of information on the status of waterbirds and their trends, it is essential that there is adequate and sustained funding for such monitoring. AEWA (2005) has recently called for an international partnership to support international waterbird monitoring and this should be strongly supported. Compared to the budgets of 'Big Science' projects, the absolute amounts allocated to annually maintain the IWC are tiny – almost trivial. Yet, as stressed throughout this volume, waterbirds are powerful indicators of environmental quality, with birds often integrating environmental information at continental scales (Piersma & Lindström 2004, Piersma, this volume). Data and information derived from the IWC can provide a powerful indication of the status not just directly of waterbirds themselves, but also of many other aspects of wetland biodiversity.

- **Access to data and information for decision makers.** Many governments and others have undertaken risk assessments related to the spread of highly pathogenic avian influenza H5N1. Yet, the process of undertaking these highlighted how poorly organised much data and information on waterbirds is to rapidly inform government and other decision makers. This is no organisational criticism, but is another aspect of the inadequacy of long-term financing for much waterbird conservation. There is an urgent need to synthesize the huge volume of data which exist on individual bird movements into flyway atlases and other information products in order to inform decision makers (Migration and flyway atlases, this volume, Wernham *et al.* 2002, Veen *et al.* 2005). If we are to *really* underpin governmental decisions and policies, our data and information has to be readily and rapidly accessible.

## CONCLUSIONS

We conclude with three reflections on cross-cutting needs highlighted by *Waterbirds around the world*:

- First, we need a **clear understanding of the key issues which are currently affecting waterbird status and trends**. This means establishing and maintaining international monitoring and reporting processes so that we have regularly updated summaries of the status and trends of waterbirds: we need to know what is actually happening out there!

- Second, we need to **establish clear and strategic priorities for action**. There is much, indeed *too* much, to do, and we need to guide actions to where they will be most effective for the greatest good. A sharp focus on the real priorities is paramount.

- Finally, we need to **continue to work co-operatively**, across national borders, both formally and informally, to put in place solutions to the increasingly complex and challenging problems. Working together, we have a chance of tackling these issues; individually, we do not.

Yet we should not end on too pessimistic a note. The *Waterbirds around the world* conference was attended by His Royal Highness, The Prince of Wales and by three Government Ministers with environmental responsibilities. All have demonstrated their commitment to the conservation of wetlands and waterbirds through inspired and spirited presentations – we earnestly hope that such statements will inspire others to act.

## REFERENCES

**AEWA** 2005. Developing an international partnership for support of waterbird population assessments. AEWA/MOP Resolution 3.6. Third Session of the Meeting of the Parties to the Agreement on the Conservation of African-Eurasian Migratory Waterbirds, 23–27 October 2005, Dakar, Senegal. Available at: www.unep-aewa.org/meetings/en/mop/mop3_docs/final_resolutions_pdf/res3_6_partnership_wpa.pdf

**Beintema, A. & van Vessem, J. (eds.)** 1999. Strategies for conserving migratory waterbirds. Proceedings of Workshop 2 of the Second International Conference on Wetlands and Development held in Dakar, Senegal, 8-14 November 1998. Wetlands International Publication No. 55. 71 pp.

**Birkan, M., van Vessem, J., Havet, P., Madsen, J., Trolliet, B. & Moser, M.** (eds.) 1996. Proceedings of the Anatidae 2000 Conference, Strasbourg, France, 5-9 December 1994. Gibier Faune Sauvage, Game and Wildlife 13(1-2). Wetlands International Publication No. 40. 1455 pp.

**Boere, G.C. & Rubec, C.D.A.** 2002. Conservation policies and programmes affecting birds. In: K. Norris & D. Pain (eds) Conserving Bird Biodiversity, general principles and their application. Cambridge University Press: 246-270.

**Boere, G.C.** 2003. Global activities on the conservation, management and sustainable use of migratory waterbirds: an integrated flyway/ecosystem approach. Wader Study Group Bulletin 100: 96-101.

**Boere, G.C. & Taylor, D.R.** 2004. Climate change, waterbird conservation and international treaties. Ibis 146 (Supplement 1): 111-119.

**Boere, G.C.** Unpublished. The African Eurasian Migratory Waterbird Agreement: a review of its history, background, development and implementation. AEWA Secretariat, Bonn.

**Carp, E. (ed.)** 1973. International Conference on the Conservation of Wetlands and Waterfowl, Ramsar, Iran, 30 January - 3 February 1971. IWRB, Slimbridge. 303 pp.

**CMS, AEWA & UNEP** 2006. Seminar on Avian influenza, wild birds and the environment; Gigiri, UNEP HQ Nairobi, Kenya; 10-11 April 2006. Conclusions and recommendations. Available at: www.cms.int/avianflu/conclusions_rec_ai_seminar.pdf.

**Eiseltová, M. (ed.)** 1994. Restoration of lake ecosystems – a holistic approach. IWRB Publication 32. 182 pp.

**Evans, M.I. (ed.)** 1994. Important Bird Areas in the Middle East. BirdLife Conservation Series No. 2. BirdLife International, Cambridge, UK.

**Gabuzov, O.G.** 1990. Prospects for the introduction of *B. canadensis* in the USSR. In: G.V.T. Matthews (ed.) Managing Waterfowl Populations. Proceedings of an IWRB Symposium, Astrakhan, USSR, 2-5 October 1989. IWRB Special Publication No. 12: 152-153.

**Heredia, B., Rose, L. & Painter, M. (eds.).** 1996. Globally threatened birds in Europe: Action plans. Council of Europe Publishing, Strasbourg, France. 408 pp.

**Hertzman, T. & Larsson, T.** 1999. Lake Hornborga, Sweden – the return of a bird lake. Wetlands International Publication 50. 82 pp.

**Hötker, H., Lebedeva, E., Tomkovich, P.S., Gromadzka, J., Davidson, N.C., Evans, J., Stroud, D.A. & West, R.B. (eds.)** 1998. Migration and international conservation of waders. Research and conservation on North Asian, African and European flyways. International Wader Studies 10. 500 pp.

**Hunter, L., Canevari, P., Myers, J. & Payne, L.X.** 1991. Shorebird and wetland conservation in the western Hemisphere. In: Salathé, T. (ed.) Conserving migratory birds. ICBP Technical Publication No. 12. Cambridge: 279-290.

**Isakov, Y.A. (ed.).** 1970. International Regional Meeting on Conservation of Wildfowl Resources (Europe, Western Asia, Northern and Tropical Africa), Leningrad, USSR, 25-30 September 1968. Proceedings. Moscow. 424 pp.

**Lampio, T.** 1974. Hunting rationalization studies. Riistatieteellisiä Julkaisuja (Finnish Game Research) 34: 4-13.

**Lampio, T.** 1977. Changes in the protection of waterfowl in Europe in 1969-75. Riistatieteellisiä Julkaisuja (Finnish Game Research) 36: 1-13.

**Lane, B.A. & Parish, D.** 1991. A review of the Asian-Australasian bird migration system. In: Salathé, T. (ed.) Conserving migratory birds. ICBP Technical Publication No. 12. Cambridge: 291-312.

**Lippens, Count L.** 1967. Evolution of wader numbers during recent years and dangers threatening wading birds in north-western Europe. In: Z. Salverda (ed.). Second European Meeting on Wildfowl Conservation, Noordwijk aan Zee, The Netherlands, 9-14 May 1966. Proceedings. Ministry of Cultural Affairs, Recreation and Social Welfare and RIVON, The Netherlands and International Waterfowl Research Bureau, France: 189-192.

**Long, W.L. & Watkins, D.** 2005a. Shorebird Action Plan for the East Asian-Australasian Flyway - lessons learned. In: Straw, P. (ed.) Status and conservation of shorebirds in the East Asian-Australasian Flyway; Proceedings of the Australasian Shorebirds Conference 13-15 December 2003, Canberra, Australia. Wetlands International Global Series 18; International Wader Studies 17: 190-194.

**Long, W.L. & Watkins, D**. 2005b. Shorebird Action Plan for the East Asian –Australasian Flyway – lessons learnt. In: P. Straw (ed.). Status and conservation of shorebirds in the East Asian-Australasian Flyway. Proceedings of the Australasian Shorebird Conference, 13-15 December 2005, Canberra, Australia. Wetlands International Global Series 18; International Wader Studies 17. Sydney, Australia: 190-194.

**Matthews, G.V.T. (ed.)** 1990. Managing Waterfowl Populations. Proceedings of an IWRB Symposium, Astrakhan, USSR, 2-5 October 1989. IWRB Special Publication No. 12. 230 pp.

**Matthews, G.V.T. (ed.)** 1993. The Ramsar Convention on wetlands: its history and development. Pp. 47-52. Ramsar Convention Bureau, Switzerland. Available at: www.ramsar.org/lib_hist_index.htm

**Millennium Ecosystem Assessment** 2005a. Ecosystems and human well-being: biodiversity synthesis. World Resources Institute, Washington DC. 86 pp. Available at: http://www.millenniumassessment.org/proxy/Document.354.aspx

**Millennium Ecosystem Assessment** 2005b. Ecosystems and human well-being: wetlands and water synthesis. World Resources Institute, Washington DC. 68 pp. Available at: http://www.millenniumassessment.org/proxy/Document.358.aspx

**Millennium Ecosystem Assessment** 2005c. Ecosystems and human well-being: synthesis. World Resources Institute, Washington DC. 137 pp. Available at: http://www.millenniumassessment.org/proxy/Document.356.aspx

**Moller, H.S. (ed.)** 1995. Nature Restoration in the European Union. Proceedings of a seminar 29-31 May, Denmark. Ministry of Environment and Energy, National Forest and Nature Agency, Denmark.

**Moser, M., Prentice, R.C. & van Vessem, J. (eds.)** 1993. Waterfowl and wetland conservation in the 1990s — a global perspective. Proceedings of an IWRB Symposium, St Petersburg Beach, Florida, USA, 12-19 November 1992. IWRB Special Publication No. 26. 263 pp.

**Pienkowski, M.W. & Galbraith, C.A.** 1993. Integrated monitoring: a tool for migratory waterbird conservation. In: M. Moser, R.C. Prentice & J. van Vessem (eds.) Waterfowl and wetland conservation in the 1990s — a global perspective. Proceedings of an IWRB Symposium, St Petersburg Beach, Florida, USA, 12-19 November 1992. IWRB Special Publication No. 26: 1-6.

**Piersma, T. & Lindström, Å.** 2004. Migrating shorebirds as integrative sentinels of global environmental change. Ibis 146 (Supplement 1): 61-69.

**Prater, A.J. (ed.)** 1974. Proceedings of the wader symposium held in Warsaw (Poland) on 13 and 14 September 1973. Polish Group of the IWRB, Zoological Institute of Warsaw University. 113 pp.

**Ralph, C.J. & Rich, T.D. (eds.)** 2005. Bird conservation implementation and integration in the Americas. Proceedings of the Third International Partners in Flight Conference, March 20-24 2002; Asilomar, California. Two volumes. General Technical Report PSW-GTR-191. Albany, CA; Pacific Southwest Research Station, Forest Service, U.S. Department of Agriculture.

**RSPB, NRA & RSNC** 1994. The new rivers and wildlife handbook. RSPB, Sandy, UK. 426 pp.

**Salverda, Z. (ed.).** 1967. Second European Meeting on Wildfowl Conservation, Noordwijk aan Zee, The Netherlands, 9-14 May 1966. Proceedings. Ministry of Cultural Affairs, Recreation and Social Welfare and RIVON, The Netherlands and International Waterfowl Research Bureau, France. 225 pp.

**Straw, P. (ed.)** 1997. Shorebird conservation in the Asia-Pacific Region. Australasian Wader Studies Group. 162 pp.

**Straw, P. (ed.)** 2005. Status and conservation of shorebirds in the East-Asian Flyway. Proceedings of the Australasian Shorebird Conference 13-15 December 2003, Canberra, Australia. Wetlands International Global Series 18, International Wader Studies 17, Sydney, Australia.

**Stroud, D.A., Davidson, N.C., West, R., Scott, D.A., Haanstra, L., Thorup, O., Ganter, B. & Delany, S. (compilers) on behalf of the International Wader Study Group** 2004. Status of migratory wader populations in Africa and Western Eurasia in the 1990s. International Wader Studies 15: 1-259. {www.waderstudygroup.org}

**Swift, J.J. (ed.).** 1964. First European Meeting on Wildfowl Conservation, St. Andrews, Scotland, 16-18 October, 1963. Proceedings. Nature Conservancy London and IWRB, Tour du Valat. 289 pp.

**Veen, J., Yurlov, A.K., Delany, S.N., Mihantiev, A.I., Selinovanova, M.A. & Boere, G.C.** 2005. An atlas of movements of Southwest Siberian waterbirds. Wetlands International, Wageningen, The Netherlands.

**Wells, D.R. & Mundkur, T. (eds.)** 1996. Conservation of migratory waterbirds and their wetland habitats in the East Asian-Australasian Flyway. Proceedings of an International Workshop, Kushiro, Japan, 28 November - 3 December 1994. Wetlands International-Asia-Pacific, Kuala Lumpur, Publication 116 and International Waterfowl and Wetlands Research Bureau-Japan Committee, Tokyo. 304 pp.

**van Vessem, J. (ed.)** 1997. Determining priorities for waterbird and wetland conservation. Proceedings of Workshop 4 of the International Conference on Wetlands and Development held in Kuala Lumpur, Malaysia, 9-13 October 1995. Wetlands International, Kuala Lumpur. 208 pp.

**Wernham, C.V., Toms, M.P., Marchant, J.H., Clark, J.A., Siriwardena, G.M. & Baillie, S.R.** 2002. The Migration Atlas: Movements of the Birds of Britain and Ireland. T. & A.D. Poyser, London, UK.

An international action plan has recently been developed for the globally threatened Sociable Plover *Vanellus gregarius*. This has already stimulated international collaborative research funded under the UK's Darwin Initiative to investigate the causes of decline. Ultimately, the success of international conservation action plans will be judged by their effectiveness in halting and reversing population declines for such threatened waterbirds. Photo: Sergey Dereliev.

# The flyway concept: what it is and what it isn't

*Gerard C. Boere[1] & David A. Stroud[2]*

[1] *Dorrewold 22, 7213 TG Gorssel, The Netherlands. (email: gcboere@planet.nl)*

[2] *Joint Nature Conservation Committee, Monkstone House, City Road, Peterborough, PE1 1JY, UK.*
*(email: David.Stroud@jncc.gov.uk)*

Boere, G.C. & Stroud, D.A. 2006. The flyway concept: what it is and what it isn't. *Waterbirds around the world.* Eds. G.C. Boere, C.A. Galbraith & D.A. Stroud. The Stationery Office, Edinburgh, UK. pp. 40-47.

## INTRODUCTION

Bird migration has always fascinated man although it is only recently that details of international migratory routes have become known. Whilst modern technology such as satellite tracking has given, for some species, huge insights into the details of migration and stopover places used, this has built on a broad body of knowledge derived from over 100 years of bird-ringing using inscribed metal rings and individual colour-marks (Davidson *et al.* 1999) – largely the result of volunteer efforts.

Reviewing this body of information highlights the complexities of migration (Alerstam 1990, Owen 1996, Bairlein *et al.* 2002, Rees *et al.* 2005). Migration routes and schedules can vary by species (and by population within species – Fig. 2) and the extent of any migratory route can vary, both by the total length of flight-path, and the number and duration of stops along the flight-path (Fig. 1). It can also vary according to the age and/or sex of the bird, by season, and with weather (*e.g.* unfavourable headwinds can increase number of stops used). Further, there can be considerable variation between individuals in the same population, reflecting the fact that such variation in migration schedules (timing of migration or routes taken) is adaptive and central to differential evolutionary fitness (Ens *et al.* 1994).

Such individual variation relates to trade-offs between the eco-physiological costs and benefits of arriving earlier or later at different locations along a migratory route (Piersma 1994). A migration strategy that is successful in a season, say, when the arctic summer comes early may be less successful in a year when the arctic thaw on breeding areas comes later. Any population will contain individuals migrating at different times and possibly using different routes, which may in any case vary between years according to a range of environmental conditions such as wind-speed and direction. Indeed, studies of the timing of passerine migration in relation to changing climate provide indications that this variation helps change migratory behaviour at the scale of populations.

Yet despite all this complexity, many waterbird species are highly faithful to the sites they use throughout their annual cycle (both within and between years). Such site fidelity can be explained as a result of various selective pressures that favour individuals which have an intimate knowledge of their environment. Its consequence is that certain locations not only hold large concentrations of waterbirds year after year, but that these sites are repeatedly visited by the same birds. Further, despite variation, migration to breeding areas is often highly synchronised, especially in those species which breed in the high arctic, where the short breeding season makes time a critical commodity.

In terms of the practicalities of implementing conservation policies for migratory species there has been a clear need to simplify the real-world complexities of migration so as to assist consistent international cooperation between governments and non-governmental organisations. This has been successfully achieved through the flyway concept, defined broadly as the biological systems of migration paths that directly link sites and ecosystems in different countries and continents.

This short review provides some background to the flyway concept and the various ways this has been developed over time and has been applied in various parts of the world and for different groups of waterbirds.

## DEFINITION OF A FLYWAY

The *Waterbirds around the world* conference, in many of its sessions, reviewed waterbird migration at many levels of detail: from the long migration routes of many waders to the relative short distance movements of, for example, intra-African migrants such as flamingos (this volume). In almost all cases the word "flyway" has been used to indicate the geographical region along which the species has moved.

In line with the above, a general definition of a flyway, applicable not only for waterbirds, could be:

> "A flyway is the entire range of a migratory bird species (or groups of related species or distinct populations of a single species) through which it moves on an annual basis from the breeding grounds to non-breeding areas, including intermediate resting and feeding places as well as the area within which the birds migrate."

We emphasize that we prefer the term 'non-breeding areas'. The term "wintering areas" is clearly confusing in the case of cross-equatorial migrants as well as being unsuitable for regions were regular migration is the result of unpredictable events such as rainfall in parts of Africa and Australia. Moreover in such cases the movements often do not follow the same route but can be very different from year to year pending the weather conditions.

Flyways can be considered at different scales:

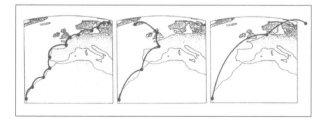

Fig. 1. Different types of migratory strategy shown by waders moving from coastal west Africa to sub-arctic breeding grounds: (from left to right) by Turnstone *Arenaria interpres* ('hop'), Dunlin *Calidris alpina* and Redshank *Tringa totanus* ('skip'); and Red Knot *Calidris canutus* and Bar-tailed Godwit *Limosa lapponica* ('jump'). Source: Piersma 1987.

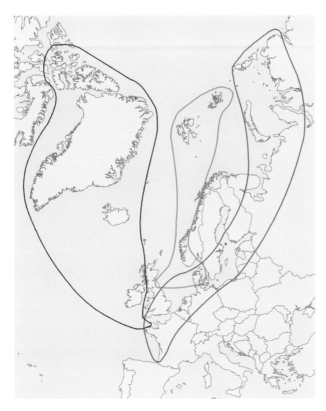

Fig. 2. The migration systems of three populations of Brent Goose *Branta bernicla* occurring in Europe. Source: after Scott & Rose 1996.

- **Single species migration systems.** The distributional extent of the annual migration of a species, or population within a species, encompassing breeding staging and non-breeding areas. Examples are given in Figs. 2 and 3. Whilst often described as the flyways of the species concerned, such annual distributional ranges are better described as the migration system of the species concerned.

- **Multi-species flyway** are defined by the Ramsar Convention (1999) as follows: "A single flyway is composed of many overlapping migration systems of individual waterbird populations and species, each of which has different habitat preferences and migration strategies. From knowledge of these various migration systems it is possible to group the migration routes used by waterbirds into broad flyways, each of which is used by many species, often in a similar way, during their annual migrations. Recent research into the migrations of many wader or shorebird species, for example, indicates that the migrations of waders can broadly be grouped into eight flyways: the East Atlantic Flyway, the Mediterranean/Black Sea Flyway, the West Asia/Africa flyway, the Central Asia/Indian sub-continent Flyway, the East Asia/Australasia Flyway, and three flyways in the Americas and the Neotropics" - (Fig. 4).

- **Global regions for waterbird conservation management.** At a larger scale still are global regions containing species with similar migration systems that are the subject (actual or potential) of shared international conservation activity – what Hagemeijer (this volume) describes as 'political flyways'. Thus, the Agreement area for the African-Eurasian Agreement on the conservation of migratory water-

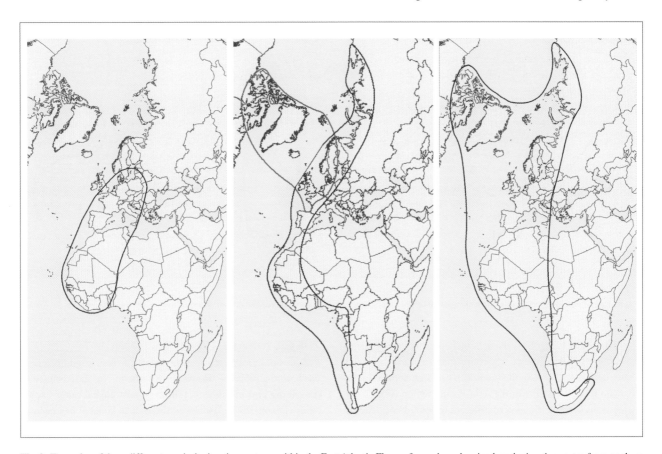

Fig. 3. Examples of three different species' migration systems within the East Atlantic Flyway for waders, showing broad migration routes from northern breeding areas to over-wintering sites in Europe and Africa. Left to right, Kentish Plover *Charadrius alexandrinus*, Red Knot *Calidris canutus* and Sanderling *Calidris alba*. Source: after Smit & Piersma 1998.

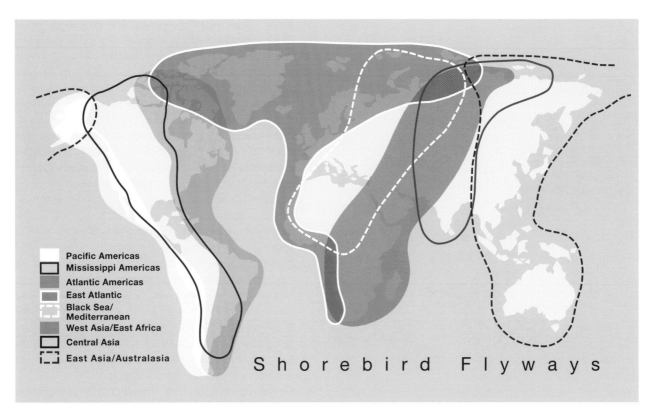

**Fig. 4.** The eight broad flyways of waders/shorebirds. Source: International Wader Study Group. A more detailed evaluation by Brown *et al.* 2001 distinguishes five shorebird flyways in North America: Pacific-Asiatic, Intermountain West, Central, Mississippi, and Atlantic.

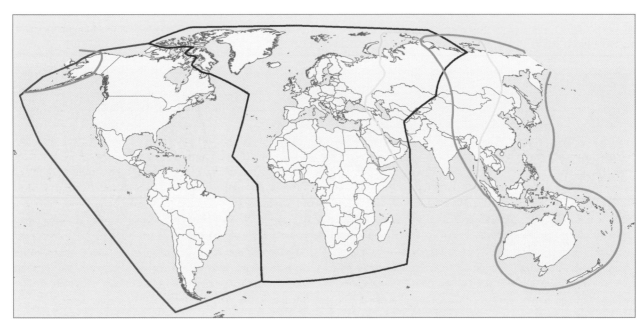

**Fig. 5.** Regions of the world subject to either actual or potential multilateral agreements for the conservation of migratory waterbirds.

birds (AEWA, Fig. 5) is the area that contains the migration systems of all migratory waterbirds that occur in Africa and western Eurasia. A similar approach has been applied to the main flyway systems of the Asia-Pacific region (Fig. 5). It contains multiple flyways of different waterbird taxa, and its value is in terms of the political and governmental processes of international co-operation (e.g. Biber-Klemm 1991). Accordingly, it has rather little descriptive value related to the exact movements of any bird.

## THE HISTORY OF THE FLYWAY CONCEPT

Previous descriptive terminology related to bird migrations have used terms such as 'Route of Migration' in the context of describing bird movements following post glacial range expansions (Dixon 1895). However, the flyway concept has become widely used in the twentieth century because it helps to understand the problems a migratory waterbird encounters throughout its life cycle and identifies those countries that should co-operate to protect and sustainably manage populations.

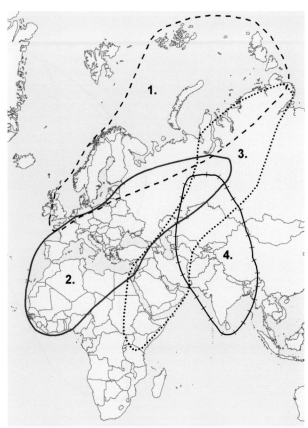

Fig. 6. North American flyways used for the management of migratory waterbirds – especially as related to the regulation of hunting.

The basic multi-species flyway concept was developed in North America in the 1930-40s to provide a spatial management framework for waterbirds (Lincoln 1950, Hochbaum 1955). The system of four flyways, each with its own Council and Technical Committee, was established between 1947-1952 to provide a framework for co-operative management of waterfowl between the federal government, states, provinces and non-governmental organisations (US Department of the Interior 1959, Hawkins *et al.* 1984, Linduska 1964, Nelson & Bartonek 1990, Fig. 6).

Although in Eurasia and northern Africa, a sustained programme of international co-operation for waterbird conservation commenced in post-war years (Kuijken this volume, Stroud *et al.* this volume), coherent planning for the conservation of migratory waterbirds at a flyway level started in the 1960s (Boere 2006). In the Asia-Pacific region, it effectively commenced in the mid-1990s (Wells & Mundkur 1996).

The first flyway maps for waterbirds for western Eurasia were published by the International Waterfowl Research Bureau (IWRB; now Wetlands International) and Prof. Isakov of the USSR Academy of Sciences (Isakov 1970). These maps of the main 'geographical' populations' of Anatidae in the western part of the former USSR and Europe were published against the background of ongoing discussions in the 1960s about an international legal instrument for the conservation of wetlands and migratory waterfowl, which later turned into the Ramsar Convention. Isakov (1967) recognised four major flyways for Anatidae in western Eurasia (Fig. 7). IWRB further developed

Fig. 7. Isakov's (1967) main geographical populations of Anatidae in western Eurasia. Flyway coding: 1. Northern White Sea/North Sea population; 2. European Siberia/Black Sea-Mediterranean population; 3. West Siberian/Caspian/Nile population; and 4. Siberian-Kazakhstan/Pakistan-India population.

the concept, organising a specific symposium in 1976 on the mapping of waterfowl distributions and habitats (Matthews & Isakov 1981).

With the advent of legally binding multilateral treaties such as the Bonn Convention on Migratory Species in 1979 and the African Eurasian Migratory Waterbird Agreement in 1999, as well as the more informal Asia-Pacific Migratory Bird Conservation Strategy in 1996, the concept has proved valuable in focusing attention on strategic needs for waterbirds migrating within defined geographical regions. Similarly, the concept has underpinned the rationale for many bilateral treaties (for example Memoranda of Cooperation) between governments focusing on the conservation of shared migratory species (see Boere & Rubec 2002 and Boere 2003 for more details).

Different groups of waterbirds show broadly similar migration systems, although the extent to which these have all been described – or attempted to be consolidated into broader, multi-

**Table 1. Main published sources of information on the flyways of different taxa of waterbirds.**

| Waterbird taxa | Americas | Europe, Africa and western Eurasia | East Asia - Pacific |
|---|---|---|---|
| Ducks, geese and swans | Fig. 6. | Flyways mapped at species level only e.g. Fig. 2. Scott & Rose 1986 | Fig. 8. Flyways mapped at species level only by Miyabayashi & Mundkur 1999 |
| Waders | Fig. 4. Brown *et al.* 2001 | Fig. 4. Davidson & Pienkowski 1987, Smit & Piersma 1989, Stroud *et al.* 2004; WI/WSG Flyway Atlas in preparation | Fig. 4. Asia-Pacific Migratory Waterbird Conservation Committee 2001; Flyways mapped at species level by Bamford *et al.* in prep. |

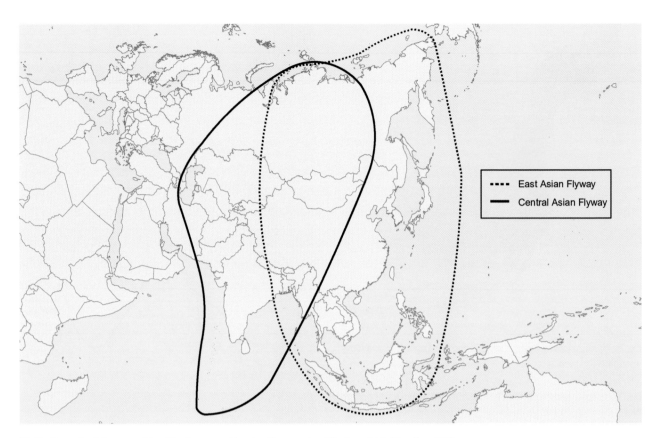

**Fig 8.** Generalised flyways of Anatidae in eastern Eurasia. Source: after Miyabayashi & Mundkur 1999.

species flyways – is quite varied. Table 1 summarizes main information sources related to different flyway systems.

Flyways illustrated on different map projections can appear quite different, and the use of different projections can in themselves give useful messages – thus a polar projection highlights the fact that all the worlds flyways converge in the arctic.

## LIMITATIONS TO THE FLYWAY CONCEPT

The complexity of the migration strategies and systems of individual waterbird species was noted above. Attempts to simplify will, necessarily loose information. For example, whilst in Eurasia (although less so in the Americas), most waterbirds migrate in more or less north-south directions there is an impor-

**Fig. 9.** Ringing recoveries of Pochard *Aythya ferina* showing predominantly east-west movements across Eurasia. Source: Wernham *et al.* 2002.

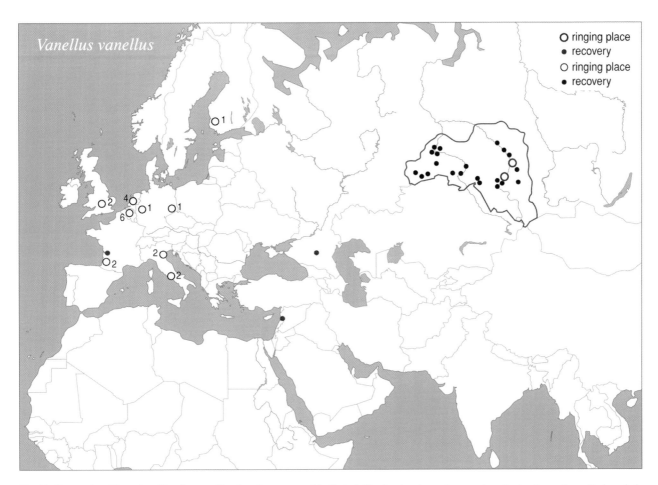

**Fig. 10.** Recoveries of Lapwings *Vanellus vanellus* ringed or recovered in Central Siberia; showing a strong east-west migration pattern. Red symbols refer to birds ringed in Central Siberia. Source: Veen *et al.* 2005.

tant component of east-west migration (see for instance Fig. 9 & 10, (Veen *et al.* 2005 and recovery maps in Fransson & Pettersson 2001, Bakken *et al.* 2003 and Wernham *et al.* 2002). Such elements are not well captured in traditional flyway models.

Further, maps of generalised flyway systems conceal the considerable between-species variation in individual migration systems. Thus Fig. 3 highlights three quite different migration systems for different wader species which all use the East Atlantic Flyway.

Such limitations should not detract from the application of the concept, although they give the scope for considerable confusion, much of which has been apparent in the use of inappropriate flyway maps by the media and others in attempts to describe and predict the possible spread of highly pathogenic avian influenza by migratory waterbirds across Eurasia in late 2005. Thus the global map of wader flyways (Fig. 4) has been widely reproduced as variously relating to all waterbirds, and even more erroneously, as describing the movements of *all* migratory birds (e.g. FAO 2005, Normile 2006, Olsen *et al.* 2006). Such confusion is unhelpful, especially in contexts where potentially important policy formulation can be influenced by such misinformation, although the limitations of the concept are recognised in the EU (Pfeiffer *et al.* 2006).

Thus there needs to be caution in applying the flyway concept to other migratory birds, given that ringing recoveries of passerines indicate widespread broad front migration across continental land-masses (e.g. Wernham *et al.* 2002, Zink 1973, 1975, 1981 & 1985).

## FUTURE DEVELOPMENTS TO THE CONCEPT

The flyway concept directly and valuably supports the 'ecosystem approach' promoted under the Convention on Biological Diversity (CBD) as a framework to help integrate conservation activities and policies.

CBD describes the ecosystem approach as: *"...based on the application of appropriate scientific methodologies focused on levels of biological organization, which encompass the essential structure, processes, functions and interactions among organisms and their environment. ... This focus on structure, processes, functions and interactions is consistent with the definition of "ecosystem" provided in Article 2 of the Convention on Biological Diversity: "'Ecosystem' means a dynamic complex of plant, animal and micro-organism communities and their non-living environment interacting as a functional unit." This definition does not specify any particular spatial unit or scale, in contrast to the Convention definition of "habitat". Thus, the term "ecosystem" does not, necessarily, correspond to the terms "biome" or "ecological zone", but can refer to any functioning unit at any scale. Indeed, the scale of analysis and action should be determined by the problem being addressed. It could, for example, be a grain of soil, a pond, a forest, a biome or the entire biosphere."* (CBD Decision V/6).

A flyway is in fact the totality of the ecological systems that are necessary to enable a migratory waterbird to survive and fulfil its annual cycle. In this sense such bird movements link sites and ecosystem into a single functional unit, the loss of any part of which (for example, a staging area) may jeopardise the long-term viability of the species. Whilst some do not consider that flyways should be seen as ecosystems as defined by CBD (van der Zon pers. communication), we note that the concept has been used within the context of recent decisions of the Global Environment Facility, notably its support for African/Eurasian Migratory Waterbird Flyways project. Further, CBD Decision V/6 (above) explicitly notes the potential inclusion of wide-scale approaches such as are provided by international waterbird flyways.

## ACKNOWLEDGEMENTS

We are very grateful to Greg Conway and the British Trust for Ornithology for the preparation of the flyway maps presented here.

## REFERENCES

**Alerstam, T.** 1990. Bird migration. Cambridge University Press.

**Asia-Pacific Migratory Waterbird Conservation Committee** 2001. Asia-Pacific migratory waterbird conservation strategy: 2001-2005. Wetlands International-Asia Pacific, Kuala Lumpur, Malaysia. Available at: www.wetlands.org/publication.aspx?ID=f45b0a90-3ffe-42f8-9b63-c86da73c23e7

**Bakken, V., Runde, O. & Tjorve, E.** 2003. Norwegian Bird Ringing Atlas. Vol. 1. Stavanger Museum, Stavanger.

**Bamford, M., Watkins, D, Bancroft, W. & Tischler, G.** In prep. Migratory shorebirds of the East Asian–Australasian flyway. Population estimates and key sites. Wetlands International, Oceania.

**Bairlein, F., Elkins, N. & Evans, P.** 2002. Why and how do bird migrate? In: C.V. Wernham, M.P. Toms, J.H. Marchant, J.A. Clark, G.M. Siriwardena & S.R. Baillie (eds.) The Migration Atlas: Movements of the Birds of Britain and Ireland. T. & A.D. Poyser, London, UK: 23-43.

**Biber-Klemm, S**. 1991. International legal protection instruments for the protection of migratory birds: an overview for the West Palearctic-African flyways. In: T. Salathé (ed.). Conserving migratory birds. ICBP Technical Publication No. 12: 315-344.

**Boere, G.C.** 2003. Global activities on the conservation, management and sustainable use of migratory waterbirds: an integrated flyway/ecosystem approach. Wader Study Group Bulletin 100: 96–101.

**Boere, G.C.** 2006. The African Eurasian Migratory Waterbird Agreement: a review. Wetlands International.

**Boere, G.C. & Rubec, C.D.A.** 2002. Conservation policies and programmes affecting birds. In: K. Norris & D. Pain (eds) Conserving Bird Biodiversity, general principles and their application. Cambridge University Press: 246-270.

**Brown, S., Hickey, C., Harrington, B., & Gill, R. (eds.)** 2001. United States Shorebird Conservation Plan. Second edition. Manomet Center for conservation sciences, Massachusetts. 60 pp.

**Davidson, N.C. & Pienkowski, M.W. (eds.)** 1987. The conservation of international flyway populations of waders. Wader Study Group Bulletin 49, Supplement. International Wader Studies 2. 151 pp.

**Davidson, N.C., Bryant, D. & Boere, G.C.** 1999. Conservation uses of ringing data: flyway networks for

waterbirds. Ringing and Migration 19 (supplement.): 83-94.

**Dixon, C.** 1895. The migration of British birds; including their post-glacial emigrations as traced by the application of a new law of dispersal. Chapman and Hall, Ltd., London.

**Ens, B.J., Piersma, T. & Tinbergen, J.M.** 1994. Towards predictive models of bird migration schedules: theoretical and empirical bottlenecks. NIOZ-Rapport 1994-5. 27 pp. Nederlands Instituut voor Onderzoek der Zee, the Netherlands.

**FAO** 2005 Map of H5N1 outbreak in 2005 and major flyways of migratory birds. Situation on 30 August 2005. www.fao.org/ag/againfo/subjects/en/health/diseases-cards/migrationmap.html

**Fransson, T & Pettersson, J.** 2001. Swedish Bird Ringing Atlas. Vol. 1. Stockholm.

**Hawkins, A.S, Hanson, R.C., Nelson, H.K. & Reeves, H.M.** 1984. Flyways. Pioneering waterfowl management in North America. USFWS, Department of Interior, Washington D.C. 517 pp.

**Hochbaum, H.A.** 1955. Travels and traditions of Waterfowl. University of Minnesota Press, USA. 301 pp.

**Isakov, Y.A.** 1967. MAR Project and conservation of waterfowl breeding in the USSR. In: Salverda, Z. (ed.), Proceedings of the Second European Meeting on Wildfowl Conservation, Noordwijk aan Zee, The Netherlands, 9-14 May 1966: 125-138. Ministry of Cultural Affairs, Recreation and Social Welfare, The Netherlands.

**Isakov, Y.A. (ed.).** 1970. International Regional Meeting on Conservation of Wildfowl Resources (Europe, Western Asia, Northern and Tropical Africa), Leningrad, USSR, 25-30 September 1968. Proceedings. Moscow. 424 pp.

**Isakov, Y.A. & Matthews, G.V.T (eds.)** 1981. Studying and management of waterfowl in the USSR. Proceedings of International Symposium on mapping of waterfowl distribution, migration and habitats, Alushta. IWRB and USSR Academy of Sciences, Moscow.

**Lincoln, F.C.** 1950. Migration of birds. US Fish & Wildlife Serrvice Circular 16. 102 pp. United States Government Printing Office, Washington.

**Linduska, J.P. (ed.)** 1964. Waterfowl Tomorrow. U.S. Department of the Interior, Washington D.C.. 769 pp.

**McClure, H.E.** 1974. Migration and survival of the birds of Asia. United States Army Medical Component, South-East Treaty Organisation (SEATO), Bangkok, Thailand.

**Miyabayashi, Y. & Mundkur, T.** 1999. Atlas of Key Sites for Anatidae in the East Asian Flyway. Wetlands International, Kuala Lumpur. Available at: www.jawgp.org/anet/aaa1999/aaaendx.htm

**Nelson, H.K. & Bartonek, J.C.** 1990. History of goose management in North America. Transactions of the 55th North American Wildlife and Natural Resources Conference: 286-292.

**Normile, D.** 2006. Are wild birds to blame? Science 310: 426-428.

**Olsen, B., Munster, V.J., Wallensten, A., Waldenström, J., Osterhaus, A.D.M.E. & Fouchier, R.A.M.** 2006. Global patterns of Influenza A virus in wild birds.

Science 312: 384-388. Available at: www.sciencemag. org/cgi/reprint/312/5772/384.pdf

Owen, M. 1996. Review of the migration strategies of the Anatidae: challenges for conservation. Gibier Faune Sauvage, Game and Wildlife 13: 123-139.

Pfeiffer, D.U., Brown, I., Fouchier, R.A.M., Gaidet, N., Guberti, V., Harder, T., Langston, R., Soares Magalhaes, R.J., Martin, V., Sharp, J.M., Stärk, K., Stroud, D.A., Szewcyk, B., Veen, J. & Waldenström, J. 2006. Scientific Report on migratory birds and their possible role in the spread of highly pathogenic avian influenza. 155 pp + 20 pp figures. [Annex to: Migratory birds and their possible role in the spread of highly pathogenic avian influenza. The European Food Safety Authority Journal 357: 1-46.] Available at: http://www. efsa.eu.int/science/ahaw/ahaw_opinions/1484_en.html

Piersma, T. 1994. Close to the edge: energetic bottlenecks and the evolution of migratory pathways in Knots. Doctoral thesis, Riksuniversiteit Groningen, The Netherlands. 366 pp.

Piersma, T. 1987. Hink, stap of sprong? Reisbeperkingen van arctische steltlopers door voedselzoeken, vetopbouw en vliegsnelheid. [Hop, skip, or jump? Constraints on migration of arctic waders by feeding, fattening and flight speed]. Limosa 60: 185-194.

Rees, E.C., Matthews, G.V.T., Mitchell, C.R. & Owen, M. 2005. Movements and migration. In: J. Kear (ed.) Ducks, geese and swans. Oxford University Press: 112-131.

Scott, D.A. & Rose, P.M. 1996. Atlas of Anatidae populations in Africa and Western Eurasia. Wetlands International Publication, 41. Available at: www.wetlands.org/ publication.aspx?id=792563ec-1b86-4f80-b5f9-170d59f6c406

Smit, C. & Piersma, T. 1989. Numbers, midwinter distribution, and migration of wader populations using the East Atlantic Flyway. In: H. Boyd & J.-Y. Pirot (eds.) Flyways and reserve networks for water birds. IWRB Special Publication No. 9: 24-63.

Stroud, D.A., Davidson, N.C., West, R., Scott, D.A., Hanstra, L., Thorup, O., Ganter, B. & Delany, S. (compilers) on behalf of the International Wader Study Group 2004. Status of migratory wader populations in Africa and Western Eurasia in the 1990s. International Wader Studies 15: 1-259. web.uct.ac.za/depts/stats/adu/wsg/iws15.html

US Department of the Interior 1959. The Waterfowl Councils. A Conservation Partnership. Circular 78. 16 pp. Available at: http://centralflyway.org/pdf/Circular78_Pictures.pdf

Veen, J., Yurlov, A.K., Delany, S.N., Mihantiev, A.I., Selinovanova, M.A. & Boere, G.C. 2005. An atlas of movements of Southwest Siberian waterbirds. Wetlands International, Wageningen, The Netherlands. Available at: www.wetlands.org/getfilefromdb.aspx?ID=9e4c7668-0c40-48be-8cf7-feb2bd3ee5f3

Wells, D.R. & Mundkur, T. (eds.) 1996. Conservation of migratory waterbirds and their wetland habitats in the East Asian-Australasian Flyway. Proceedings of an International Workshop, Kushiro, Japan, 28 November - 3 December 1994. Wetlands International-Asia-Pacific, Kuala Lumpur, Publication 116 and International Waterfowl and Wetlands Research Bureau-Japan Committee, Tokyo. 304 pp.

Wernham, C.V., Toms, M.P., Marchant, J.H., Clark, J.A., Siriwardena, G.M. & Baillie, S.R. (eds.) 2002. The Migration Atlas: Movements of the Birds of Britain and Ireland. T. & A.D. Poyser, London, UK. 884 pp.

Zink, G. 1973–1985. Der Zug Europäischen Singvogel; ein Atlas de Wiederfunde beringter Vogel. Lieferung 1 (1973); Lieferung 2 (1975); Lieferung 3 (1981) & Lieferung 4 (1985). Vogelwarte Radolfzell, Moggingen, Germany.

The East Asian-Australasian Shorebird Reserve Network was launched at Ramsar's sixth Conference of the Parties in 1996 (Brisbane, Australia) and since then has been highly successful in providing a focus for the conservation of important shorebird sites throughout this flyway. Photo: David Stroud.

# Part 2.

## Plenary papers

## Sections

# 2.0 Plenary presentations. Introduction

*David A. Stroud*

*Joint Nature Conservation Committee, Monkstone House, City Road, Peterborough, PE1 1JY, UK. (email: David.Stroud@jncc.gov.uk)*

Stroud, D.A. 2006. Plenary presentations. Introduction. *Waterbirds around the world.* Eds. G.C. Boere, C.A. Galbraith & D.A. Stroud. The Stationery Office, Edinburgh, UK. pp. 50-51.

Throughout the world, much monitoring and surveillance of waterbirds is undertaken by amateur birdwatchers, with financial support of co-ordination provided by governments or state institutions. This has proved to be an extremely cost-effective model. The maintenance of such annual monitoring programmes is of critical importance to give conservation managers the data and information they need to respond to a rapidly changing world. Photo: Meinte Engelmoer.

The plenary presentations gave time to review the major themes that would be touched on throughout the conference programme. The topics covered in the plenaries were all subject to further discussion in the programme of parallel workshops. These gave the opportunity to further discussion of the issues involved.

One strand of the conference programme related to geographical regions and was structured around the world's main waterbird flyway systems. The presentations by Schmidt (2.2, Americas), Davidson & Stroud (2.3, Africa and western Eurasia) and Mundkur (2.5, East Asia and Australasia) provided contrasting reviews of knowledge and conservation activity of these flyways. Of particular note was the contrasting periods during which formal (and informal) international conservation structures have been in place in different parts of the world in order to support and encourage waterbird conservation (a theme further elaborated upon by Kuijken - 2.1). Thus, whilst the 1916 Convention for the Protection of Migratory Birds provided the early and initial stimulus for international co-oper-

ation between the two countries of Canada and USA, structures for international co-operation have only more recently been established in other parts of the world, most recently in the Neotropics through the informal Western Hemisphere Migratory Species Initiative. Whilst formal multilateral intergovernmental conservation treaties have still to be established in some regions, Schmidt and Mundkur both outlined the bilateral treaties involving USA, Russia, Japan and Australia in the East Asia-Australasian flyway. The development of the Agreement on the conservation of migratory African-Eurasian Waterbirds (AEWA) potentially includes 117 countries, and is the most ambitious multilateral treaty related to waterbirds yet to be developed (Lenten, 3.7.1).

Finlayson and colleagues (2.6) gave a stark assessment of the range and complexity of the potential impacts of changing climate on waterbirds and their wetland habitats. Evidence for these impacts is increasingly becoming apparent. Many such effects are predicted first to impact upon arctic environments, and Wohl (2.10) summarised the global significance of this region as the ultimate source of most waterbird flyways, outlining also several recent initiatives to develop pan-arctic environmental co-operation.

The conservation of seabirds, especially whilst they are on the high seas, is an issue of major recent conservation concern. Indeed, nearly all the world's albatross species are now listed as globally threatened. Cooper (2.9) outlined the main approaches being undertaken to address these problems so as to reverse current negative trends.

The impact of fisheries on albatrosses is an example of bycatch or an unintentional harvest. Kanstrup (2.7) reviewed the other deliberate harvests of waterbirds and the basis through which some of these might be made more sustainable.

The critical role of science in understanding and deriving solutions for conservation issues was outlined by Piersma (2.4), and Lank & Nebel (2.8). They stressed the need for evidence-based approaches to the development and implementation of conservation policy.

Considering the wide range of material presented by the plenary speakers, it is clear that recent decades have given waterbird conservationists a wide range of tools with which to address issues and problems. These range from formal inter-governmental treaties, to practical conservation responses such as species action plans (section 4.1), management planning processes to maintain the ecological character of protected areas, as well as wider-scale catchment/water-basin management planning, Integrated Coastal Zone Management and other land-use policies (5.4).

Despite the existence of these tools (notably the wide range of guidances and handbooks developed and published by international conventions such as Ramsar, AEWA and the Convention on Biological Diversity, waterbirds populations and the ecological quality of the wetlands on which they depend continue to decline markedly throughout most of the world. This is a reflection of the massive, unsustainable environmental impacts generated by increasing human populations and their economic demands.

Important though current responses are, the stark findings of the Millennium Ecosystem Assessment in 2005 stress the urgent need for conservation responses to be urgently pro-active in engaging with the primary drivers of environmental degradation. This will take committed waterbird conservationists into increasingly unfamiliar territories.

Seasonal wetlands, such as the floodplain of East Alligator River, Kakadu, Australia are important habitats for many waterbirds. Photo: Nick Davidson.

# A short history of waterbird conservation

*Eckhart Kuijken*

*Institute of Nature Conservation[1], Kliniekstraat 25, B-1070 Brussels, Belgium. (email: eckhart.kuijken@inbo.be)*
*University of Ghent, Biology Department, K.L. Ledeganckstraat 35, B-9000 Ghent, Belgium.*

Kuijken, E. 2006. A short history of waterbird conservation. *Waterbirds around the world.* Eds. G.C. Boere, C.A. Galbraith & D.A. Stroud. The Stationery Office, Edinburgh, UK. pp. 52-59.

## ABSTRACT

For over a century, pioneering naturalists have determined the way in which waterbird conservation has evolved around the world and have been instrumental in the establishment of international organizations such as IUCN. Following declines in North American waterfowl in the 1930s, ICBP launched an International Wildfowl Inquiry and created IWRB, later to become a founding organization of Wetlands International. The inspiring MAR Conference, organized by IUCN, ICBP and IWRB in 1962, was a turning point in the development of conservation strategies. A series of "waterfowl conferences" followed during the 1960s and culminated in the adoption of the Convention on the Conservation of Wetlands of International Importance especially as Waterfowl Habitat in Ramsar, Iran, in 1971. This Convention launched the concept of "wise use". At the United Nations Conference on Environment and Development in Rio de Janeiro in 1992, this concept was translated as "sustainable use". The Convention on Biological Diversity (CBD) was adopted during this world summit and gave wide recognition to the intrinsic value of biodiversity. The recent "Countdown 2010" initiative gives a strong signal to intensify efforts if the CBD conservation goals are to be achieved. Monitoring is a fundamental conservation tool and has remained a central focus of IWRB and subsequently Wetlands International since the 1960s. The International Waterbird Census represents one of the most valuable global data sets. International conservation strategies based on waterbirds as bio-indicators are being developed (e.g. AEWA), but global threats such as climate change are ever-increasing. We should therefore strive to improve land-use policies, increase public awareness and achieve common acceptance of the principles of conservation. Based on an understanding of ecological, economic and social mechanisms including culture, we must now communicate with decision makers and local people about the essentials of "wise use".

## INTRODUCTION

This presentation on the history of waterbird conservation is not a thorough analysis of all existing information, but rather a brief review of some of the relevant initiatives that have served as "stepping stones" in the past. It reflects a mainly personal approach, and has been prepared from a biased point of view, as my own experience is mostly limited to activities in the field of goose research in the Western Palearctic region, inspired to a large extent by the papers of Hugh Boyd at Slimbridge in the early 1950s (e.g. Boyd 1959). Initially based on ornithology, my conservation actions and expertise were subsequently developed within a broader ecological landscape dimension. Active participation at a number of conferences enabled me to have discussions with many of the early pioneers and to witness the changes in views and methods, priorities and actions of research and

*"Waterfowl shall come to you in their thousands"*

Fig. 1. "Waterfowl shall come to you in their thousands" (from a tomb at Thebes, XVIII Dynasty, about BC 1580-1350; now in the British Museum).

conservation. The many meetings also offered me an opportunity to visit some famous wetland habitats in the hosting countries. Finally, my position for the past two decades has trained me to function mainly as an interface between science and policy planning, while at the same time stimulating my growing awareness from local to international level.

The history of waterbird conservation has always been strongly linked with catching and hunting for food or sport, as already illustrated in early Egyptian periods with drawings of wildfowl netting, paintings of goose catching, and many written sources, some of which mention that "Waterfowl shall come to you in their thousands" (Fig. 1). This could be our *leitmotiv* of today, when we consider the Red-breasted Geese *Branta ruficollis* in ancient Egypt and the most recent meeting of Wetlands International's Goose Specialist Group in Odessa in March 2004, which admired the same species along the Black Sea coast.

Throughout history, philosophers, scientists and artists have paid attention to nature, often as a background rather than a subject on its own. Colonialism, following the famous travels of Baerents, Cook, Columbus, Marco Polo and many others, began the exploration – and later exploitation – of the fast shrinking wildernesses, and caused growing interest in exotic species as collectable items or objects for study (from botanical gardens and zoos to Darwin's theory). Natural history books with highly valuable illustrations (Dodonaeus, Buffon and so many others) were well known sources for an increasing scientific approach for half a millennium.

Since the Romanticism at the end of the eighteenth century (J.J. Rousseau: "retour à la nature"), the first concern for nature arose with the industrial revolution, and gradually some real conservation thinking was developed from the mid-1800s

[1] Renamed the Research Institute for Nature and Forest in 2006.

onwards (e.g. the creation of the first National Park at Yellowstone in 1872). This was still a rather elitist movement based on mainly sentimental and aesthetic feelings towards specific plants and animals or scenic landscapes, often combined with hunting activities. When Lenin awarded the status of National Park to the Volga Delta in the early 1900s, this was still an exceptional event, but this prophetic action revealed the Soviet interest in conserving nature.

## FIRST INTERNATIONAL ACTIONS AND ORGANIZATIONS

Stimulated by such isolated initiatives, international dimensions and joint actions for nature protection became organized from the beginning of the last century, with institutions such as the International Council for Bird Preservation (ICBP), International Union for the Conservation of Nature (IUCN), International Wildfowl Research Bureau (IWRB), World Wildlife Fund (WWF) and others eventually taking the lead. The spiritual and social values of conservation were also gradually recognized and received broader public support, especially after World War II.

Ornithological interests have frequently stimulated the first nature protection initiatives, and in this context waterbirds often received special attention. This was a result of the growing concern amongst both wildfowlers and naturalists about the rapid decline in waterfowl populations in the first decades of the twentieth century. Restrictions on hunting seasons, the commercial harvesting of eggs and the use of duck decoys became the subject of much debate. In the USA, the severe drought in the 1930s combined with land reclamation caused a sharp decline in waterfowl populations, and various actions were taken (Linduska 1964, Hawkins *et al.* 1984). This cry of alarm reached Europe, and the Royal Society for the Protection of Birds (RSPB) in the UK and similar bodies in several other countries obtained increasing support to press for the adoption of legal instruments preventing excessive harvesting of waterfowl (Lowe 1941). As in the USA, this was a joint effort of ornithologists and traditional wildfowlers, both with an interest in abundant duck and goose populations and in protecting suitable habitat for breeding and wintering birds.

Gradually, the basic concerns of conservation became separated from hunting considerations. Illustrative of this are the consecutive changes in name and aims of the former IWRB reflecting the newly developing aspirations, needs and opportunities (see Box 1). Concepts and terminology changed from "protection" to "conservation". The International Union for the Conservation of Nature (founded in 1946) was first called the

---

**Box 1. Changes in the name of IWRB to Wetlands International.**

International Committee of Bird Preservation (British Section)
  Wildfowl Inquiry Sub-Committee (1941)
ICBP International Wildfowl Inquiry
International Wildfowl Research Institute
International Wildfowl Research Bureau
International Waterfowl Research Bureau
International Waterfowl & Wetlands Research Bureau
Wetlands International (1995)

---

International Union for the Protection of Nature (IUPN); nowadays it is known as the World Conservation Union, although it has retained the acronym IUCN. The word "wildfowl" became "waterfowl" in the 1980s, and has more recently been replaced by "waterbirds"; in addition, the term "wetlands" appeared in the name of some organizations. These changes were inspired by an increasing ecological awareness that an integrated and scientifically based approach was needed, not only to accommodate hunting interests ("wildfowl" is very much the language of sportsmen), but also to maintain viable populations of endangered species and their often threatened habitats.

In a similar way, the Severn Wildfowl Trust, established in the UK by Sir Peter Scott in 1946, was later (1989) renamed the Wildfowl and Wetlands Trust (WWT). In Belgium, Les Réserves Ornithologiques de Belgique (co-founder Count Léon Lippens, 1951) became Les Réserves Naturelles et Ornithologiques de Belgique and later simply Reserves Naturelles. WWF also changed its name from World Wildlife Fund to Worldwide Fund for Nature, indicating a broader range of interests.

## VISIONARY PIONEERS

The names of some of the pioneers in waterbird conservation have already been mentioned; many more should be added, but this goes beyond the aim of this contribution. Still it is important to remember the efforts of these pioneers, some of whom are still alive today and, in their youth, were active in the period between the two World Wars. Many are remembered from their publications or activities that often represent the very basis of our common conservation goals today. The ornithologists P. Lowe, A. Landsborough Thomson, R. Coombes and C.T. Dalgety were some of the members of the ICBP Wildfowl Inquiry Sub-Committee, while Miss Phyllis Barclay Smith acted as its secretary. She still participated at Executive Board Meetings of IWRB until the early 1970s, ensuring the bridge with the generations to come.

The International Wildfowl Inquiry was organized by ICBP after a meeting in 1937. The results were reported under the title "Factors affecting the general status of wild geese and wild duck" (ICBP 1941). The introductory chapter, "The history of events leading to the formation of the Wildfowl Inquiry subcommittee" by Percy R. Lowe, is worth mentioning as it illustrates how visionary these pioneers were. It also illustrates how conservationists and hunters worked closely together for their common interest. Lowe referred to a report from Sweden presented at the International Ornithological Congress in Copenhagen in 1926, as a result of which "the diminution in the numerical status of wildfowl was brought to the notice of ornithologists and preservationists, followed by official proposals to European Governments which had for their object the establishment of international regulations aimed at a more effective protection of wildfowl on migration". In 1934-36, ICBP received "profoundly shocking news" from the USA (Audubon Society) about the decline of duck and goose populations. This was the combined result of extreme drought in 1930, shrinking wetland habitats due to land claim and large-scale drainage, and excessive shooting. After some political interventions, a temporary shooting ban was declared.

In his personal contribution to the Wildfowl Inquiry, Lowe analysed the situation in European countries and presented the results under the heading "Some Factors Responsible for a

Revolutionary Diminution in the World's Stock of Wildfowl" (Lowe 1941; see Box 2). Many of the factors listed by Lowe have now altered landscapes and nature world-wide, and thus influenced the breeding and wintering of waterbirds in most countries. Furthermore, it is really striking that some problems still need to be solved, despite all the discussions and activities over the past 80 years (e.g. spring shooting, impact of drainage, agriculture, urbanization, etc.). It is certain that ICBP members in the 1930s could not have imagined how incredibly fast "development" would occur, and how natural values in general would suffer from the resulting and ever-increasing environmental pressures at global scale.

In an excellent overview of early pioneering work in North America, Hawkins *et al.* (1984) came to the same alarming conclusions.

## IWRB AND THE SERIES OF WATERFOWL CONFERENCES

The pioneering work of IWRB (in close co-operation with IUCN and ICBP) has been crucial in waterbird and wetland conservation. In western Europe, two groups of dedicated specialists were extremely active: Sir Peter Scott with G.L. Atkinson-Willes, H. Boyd, J. Harrison, J. Kear, G.V.T. Matthews and others at the Wildfowl Trust at Slimbridge (UK); and Dr Luc Hoffmann with his staff (J. Blondel, H. Hafner, A. Johnson and others) at the Station Biologique de la Tour du Valat (founded in 1954) in the Camargue (France). Many of today's leading conservationists obtained their first training and experience at one of these two centres. In addition, specialized groups and field stations were set up by a number of universities and natural history museums, and were active in waterbird research all over Europe and the former USSR. Well-known correspondents from many countries became active members of the early IWRB network of waterbird conservationists.

One particularly significant initiative was the MAR Conference, jointly organized by IUCN, ICBP and IWRB in 1962. Again, it is worthwhile to remember the basic aims and ideals of this conference, as some of the considerations are still extremely relevant today. The introduction to the proceedings of the conference stated that: "Alarmed by the progressive loss of marshes, bogs and other wetlands through drainage and 'improvement', IUCN's Executive Board and scientific advisory body, the Commission on Ecology, proposed early in 1961 that IUCN, in close co-operation with ICBP and IWRB, develop a programme on conservation and management of temperate marshes, bogs and other wetlands, to be called 'Project MAR'...". The main goals of this project are summarized in Box 3.

The MAR Conference was a real turning point in the development of strategies and practices for the conservation of waterbirds and wetlands. Many of the participants in that meeting

---

**Box 2. "Some Factors Responsible for a Revolutionary Diminution in the World's Stock of Wildfowl" (Lowe 1941). The examples given in parenthesis are only a selection of those given by Lowe.**

1. **Increased facilities of travel and transport**
   (steam engines, railways, steamships, internal combustion engine and motor-cars, motor-boats, etc. opening up inaccessible resources, also enabling weekend trips to estuaries; driving ducks together for hunting on the Nile...)

2. **Cold storage and commercialization**
   (commercialization of wildfowl hunting seen as the most serious factor; importation of frozen wildfowl even during the close season...)

3. **Conditions in the far north**
   (depredations by egg collecting in Iceland, Spitsbergen, Greenland)

4. **Ill-considered reclamation of unsuitable areas of land**
   (drainage of marsh lands, swamps and fens destroys breeding haunts and winter quarters of wildfowl and causes a disastrous chain of events, e.g. in USA)

5. **Other agricultural factors**
   (cessation of irrigation of water meadows, new industry of potato farming; growth of villages into towns in Russian Siberia and over-hunting of ducks for commerce)

6. **Siltation in estuaries, inlets and old harbours**
   (caused by the introduction of the exotic *Spartina townsendii* and subsequent spread by swans, and decrease of *Zostera* as a result of disease)

7. **Punt-gunning and shooting from mechanically propelled boats**
   (there is a great need for shortening the open season for punting; ducks becoming shyer, bags becoming smaller, etc.)

8. **Disturbance by aeroplanes**
   (sometimes needless; often deliberate and systematic driving of ducks together for shooting; forbidden from military aeroplanes)

9. **Long hunting seasons**
   (hunting legislation needs scientific background; in most cases, the hunting season opens too early and goes on too long; proposed opening on 1 September; there is an internal dispute in sportsmen's associations on this issue)

---

**Box 3. The main goals of Project MAR, as given in the Introductory Statement in the Proceedings of the MAR Conference, 1964.**

The final goals of the MAR programme are:

1 to prepare a broad statement on the importance of marshes and wetlands to modern mankind and to give the widest publicity to this statement;

2 to assemble all important data on means of conserving wetlands, to keep or improve them for wildlife through proper management, to restore them when debilitated and to make man-made aquatic habitats useful for wildlife: to make this information known and available to all those in a position to take action to advance the conservation of wetlands;

3 to make an inventory and classification of all European and north-west African marshes, bogs and other wetlands of international importance; and

4 to offer technical assistance for establishment of reserves in marshes, bogs and other wetlands classified as of international importance.

remained active until the 1980s or 1990s and supported the fast growing impact of IWRB which became the real engine of waterbird research and conservation. Initially based at the Museum of Natural History in London, IWRB moved its headquarters to the Tour du Valat in the Camargue where it remained until 1968, and then to the Wildfowl Trust in Slimbridge (UK) where it remained until 1995. Since then, its work has been continued by Wetlands International.

From the very beginning, IWRB was responsible for a number of scientific publications as well as booklets on the threatened status of waterbirds and wetlands. One of the first booklets, "Liquid assets", appeared in 1964 with the support of UNESCO (Atkinson-Willes 1964) and was reprinted in 1979. This stressed that wetlands are not wastelands, and drew attention to their importance for recreation, science and education, the costs and dangers of drainage, the problems of pollution, and the desirability of restoring wetlands and managing them wisely.

An impressive amount of knowledge became available thanks to a series of international conferences convened by IWRB and the resulting Proceedings which were published in a similar and recognizable layout (Box 4). In addition to these conferences, IWRB organized most of its Annual Executive Board Meetings in combination with scientific symposia in various parts of the world. This brought national delegates and other active people together on a regular, structured basis, thanks especially to highly professional pioneers working for IWRB, such as E. Carp, G.L. Atkinson-Willes, G.V.T. Matthews, D.A. Scott, M. Smart, M. Moser and many others. The dedicated IWRB secretariat, with M. Moser (successor to G.V.T. Matthews) as Director, moved from Slimbridge to Wageningen (The Netherlands) in 1995. Here, the new headquarters could build up a growing staff with several departments, especially after the XXXVIth Executive Board Meeting in Kuala Lumpur, Malaysia, in 1995 when IWRB merged with Wetlands for the Americas and the Asian Wetland Bureau and became Wetlands International (with Chris Kalden as President).

The first Meeting of the Board of Members of Wetlands International was held during the famous Second Conference on Wetlands and Development in Dakar, Senegal, in 1998, replacing the traditional Executive Board Meetings of IWRB after 36 sessions: quite a change for those of us who had participated in so many earlier meetings.

## THE MASTERPIECE: THE RAMSAR CONVENTION

The above-mentioned meetings during the 1960s were focussed on the development of an international convention specifically related to the conservation of wetlands. This process culminated in a conference held in the Caspian coastal town of Ramsar, Iran, in early 1971. Delegates of 18 countries signed the final text of the Convention on the Conservation of Wetlands of International Importance especially as Waterfowl Habitat on 2 February 1971 (Fig. 2). This date is now known as "World Wetlands Day". The Ramsar Convention is considered to be the first of the modern global environment treaties and is well structured, thanks to a strong secretariat based at IUCN Headquarters in Gland (Switzerland). As part of the evolution of concepts mentioned above, the working title of the Convention (Ramsar Convention on Wetlands) no longer recalls it relationship with waterfowl habitat. There is no need to present the full history of this convention here, as Geoffrey Matthews, former Director of IWRB, has published an excellent overview: "The Ramsar Convention on Wetlands: its History and Development" (Matthews 1993).

Fig. 2. Signing ceremony of the Ramsar Convention, 2 February 1971. From left to right: USSR delegate; E. Firouz (Conference Chair); South African delegate; M.F. Mörzer-Bruijns (The Netherlands, Vice-Chair), G.V.T. Matthews (IWRB Director); and E. Carp (IWRB Secretariat, Conference Rapporteur). Photo: E. Kuijken.

One of the most original and handsome contributions of the Ramsar Convention has been the introduction of the 1% criterion (of waterbird populations at flyway level) for designating internationally important wetland sites. Linked with the water-bird databases of IWRB and its successor Wetlands International, a regular update of 1% thresholds at flyway level has offered an objective and attractive tool. Several sessions at IWRB meetings before 1971 gave considerable attention to the required level of waterbird numbers before a site could be considered as being of "international importance" (Szijj 1972). After studying models with 5% and 2% levels, it was concluded that at these levels the number of outstanding sites would be too low to establish a dense enough network to create a functional series of stepping stones or "fuelling stations" for long-distance migrants. The 1% criterion was therefore adopted and has since become a widely used tool in ecological evaluations, not only in waterbird conservation. Later Conferences of the Parties to the Ramsar Convention have gradually added more criteria for assessing the international importance of wetlands, based on functions, habitats, educational values, importance for fish, etc. In 2005, the ninth Conference of the Parties, formally adopted a

1% criterion for non-avian taxa. This further developed the concept by seeking its application to aquatic fauna for which good population data exist (such as river dolphins, hippos, turtles, crocodiles etc.; Stroud unpublished).

Even more significant during the Ramsar Conference in 1971 was the launch of the "wise use" concept by the pioneering architects of the Ramsar Convention. Although also adopted in the Bern Convention (1979), it was 20 years before this approach became more widespread. The Convention on Biological Diversity (CBD), adopted at the United Nations Conference on Environment and Development in Rio de Janeiro in 1992, included "sustainable development" and "sustainable use" almost as synonyms of "wise use". In its Preamble, the CBD also recognizes the intrinsic value of biodiversity, although this concept remains difficult to explain and even more difficult to bring into practice.

"Wise use", as an anthropocentric approach, gradually became fully respected, especially when appropriate CEPA (communication, education and public awareness) strategies are carried out among local populations dependent on wetlands for their survival. Indeed, the possibilities for balanced use of the vital resources of wetlands are recognized by an increasing number of Ramsar Contracting Parties. This makes a major contribution not only to biodiversity conservation, but also to global strategies to combat poverty and provide security against natural disasters.

Some pessimism may exist as regards achieving the necessary nature conservation goals in the twenty-first century, even if economic development were to turn more to sustainability. Unfortunately, the Rio+10 Conference in Johannesburg in 2002 no longer included "environment" in its title, thus suggesting that qualitative and quantitative needs are considered to be an integral part of development (which, of course, is true in theory). There is a risk, however, that environmental issues may receive less attention. Fortunately, close links have been established between CBD, other environmental treaties and the Ramsar Convention, and must now reinforce the common conservation aims. The recent "Countdown 2010" initiative ("stop the loss of biodiversity by 2010") is giving another strong message for real action before it is too late.

Nowadays, the Ramsar Convention is recognized as a most dynamic and functional treaty, having opened the way for wetland conservation, especially in many developing countries. In the early years, technical support was provided mainly by IWRB, and Wetlands International still plays an important role as one of the Convention's five International Organisation Partners, e.g. in the management of the databases of waterbirds and wetlands, and in the preparation of recommendations in co-operation with the Scientific and Technical Review Panel (STRP).

The increasing efforts made by the growing number of Contracting Parties to designate wetlands of international importance is illustrative of the impact of the Ramsar Convention at global scale (Fig. 3). Since the Eighth Conference of the Parties in Valencia in 2002, a Strategic Work Plan has provided guidelines for the fulfilment of five general and 21 operational objectives. The status of the Convention by 5 July 2006 is impressive: 152 Contracting Parties, and 1 609 Wetlands of International Importance designated for the Ramsar List, covering a total surface area of 145.8 million ha. The triennial Meetings of the Parties are always stimulating and inspiring events, where

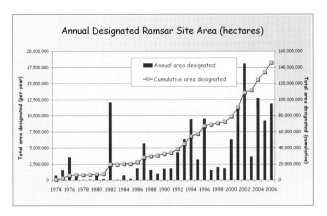

**Fig. 3.** The increase in the area of designated Ramsar sites (from Wetlands International Ramsar Sites Information Service web-site).

criteria are reviewed, results are discussed, and a number of recommendations for further specific actions are developed.

After ratification of the treaty, Ramsar Parties must not only designate at least one wetland, but must also agree to provide compensation when specific Ramsar sites are lost as a consequence of urgent national interest. The very first example of the strength of this Article 4 of the Convention was in relation to the Belgian Ramsar site of Galgenschoor near Antwerp, where 30 ha were lost as a result of the construction of a new container terminal. In compensation, the Flemish government designated 2 500 ha of floodplain along the River IJzer, just at the time of the Regina Conference in 1987.

The "maintenance of the ecological character" of designated wetlands is a permanent obligation. When serious threats exist and are likely to change the characteristics of a designated wetland, this site is to be put on the 'Montreux Record'. Such sites can be the subject of a Ramsar Advisory Mission, with specialists from the Ramsar Secretariat and other Contracting Parties visiting the site and helping the local authorities to develop solutions, adequate management, etc. This controlling system reflects another (moral) impact of the Convention, as the status of sites on the Montreux Record has to be mentioned openly in the National Reports before each of the Conferences of the Parties.

## FROM WATERBIRD MONITORING TO CONSERVATION OF WETLANDS

The need to identify waterfowl species and a curiosity to learn about their fascinating behaviour inspired many authors to publish valuable handbooks, contributing significantly to our knowledge of these species (e.g. Alpheraky 1905, Delacour 1954, Scott 1965). The Wildfowl Inquiry stimulated more concerted action to collect information on the numbers and distribution of ducks, geese and swans. Traditional methods, such as the collection of wings from shot birds, were applied in order to gain better insight of population dynamics. This again illustrated the close co-operation between hunters and conservationists.

The organization of regular international counts of waterbirds (the International Waterbird Census, IWC) has been a key activity of IWRB/Wetlands International for almost four decades. The first mid-winter counts, initiated in 1967, were confined to "wildfowl" (ducks, geese, swans and coots) and were co-ordinated by G.L. Atkinson-Willes at the Wildfowl

Trust in Slimbridge, with the help of dedicated national co-ordinators, specialists and volunteers in the field. Atkinson-Willes had a long history of organizing counts in the British Isles (Atkinson-Willes 1955). The results of the IWC in the period 1967-1983 were published by Rüger *et al.* 1986. The number of co-workers has grown considerably over the years, and now comprises a network of many thousands all over the world. The counts have provided an immense amount of information, not only of scientific value, but also of strategic importance for wetland conservation. These data have enabled the publication at regular intervals of estimates of waterbird populations in each of their different flyways. The first edition of this work was published in 1994 (Rose & Scott 1994). The Specialist Groups of IWRB/Wetlands International play an important role in bringing expert data together. Reports on ducks and geese were among the first to be published (e.g. Mörzer-Bruijns *et al.* 1969), with comprehensive reviews of the status of many other taxa following in the years since. Monitoring the changes in waterbird numbers at specific wetlands of critical importance can also serve as an "early warning system" that can be used to mobilize authorities to take appropriate measures before it is too late.

The development of ecological networks is a present-day priority (e.g. the Natura 2000 networks of Special Protection Areas within the framework of the European Union's Birds and Habitats Directives of 1979 and 1992, respectively). The establishment of a network of protected wetland areas to safeguard populations of waterbirds that migrate over long distances was already a basic goal of the Ramsar Convention, and has since been recognized as an essential functional approach in waterbird conservation, promoting the concepts of corridors and stepping stones to connect larger core areas and enhance the mobility of waterbird populations and their genes.

The African-Eurasian Waterbird Agreement (AEWA) under the Bonn Convention was launched in 1995. The Agreement covers 117 Range States in Europe, western Asia and Africa, as well as parts of Canada. Initiated by Gerard Boere, this is a real IWRB spin-off. The AEWA has been ratified by 57 countries and is currently carrying out its "International Implementation Priorities Plan 2003-2007" which includes many species protection plans and other projects (Lenten, this volume).

In North America, the concept of waterfowl "flyways" was introduced much earlier than in Europe (see "Waterfowl Tomorrow" by Linduska 1964, and "Flyways. Pioneering Waterfowl Management in North America" by Hawkins *et al.* 1984). Both these publications draw attention to the large number of dedicated naturalists who, between the late 1800s and World War II, tried to counteract the negative impacts of the earliest land developments.

In Asia, attention was initially focussed mainly on shorebird (wader) flyways, under the co-ordination of the Asian Wetland Bureau (e.g. Parish & Prentice 1989). International waterbird counts and wetland inventories stimulated many Asian countries into further conservation actions, and this was also the case in Latin America. In many biogeographical regions, specific initiatives relating to wetlands developed into powerful regional organizations (cf. MedWet). Other thematic groups worked on specific wetland types and programmes (peatlands, lakes, riverine systems, dunes and estuaries, etc.). National overviews of waterbird counts and wetlands became available in many countries; in this regard, the states of the former USSR were

Fig. 4. Japanese crane symbol, where waterbirds, wetlands and culture meet. Photo: Eckhart Kuijken.

often well ahead, with famous names such as Yu. Isakov, E. Kumari, E. Rutschke, E. Nowak and many others.

Not only were waterbird population estimates becoming available in a series of publications, but so too were directories of wetlands of international importance (e.g. Olney 1965, Carp 1980, Scott 1980, World Conservation Monitoring Centre 1990 and Frazier 1999, 2002), often on the occasion of the Ramsar Conferences. Such directories are now available for most continents of the world (e.g. Scott & Carbonell 1986, Scott 1989). Again, these provide an immense source of baseline information on the state of the environment in and around wetlands. In addition, interesting discussions on conservation strategies for wetlands have been presented by Moser *et al.* (1993) and Beintema & van Vessem (1999). In general, the number of publications and proceedings has increased tremendously since the 1990s, thanks to the shift in emphasis of IWRB and Wetlands International towards broader scientific disciplines and social sciences, including economics.

Various themes that have been developed in recent years include wetland management and restoration (Erwin 1996), the economics of conservation, the functions and values of wetlands (Hails 1997), and the goods and services of ecosystems in general (Constanza *et al.* 1997). IWRB, WWF and IUCN have also published valuable contributions and handbooks in these fields. Long-lasting debates, e.g. between conservation and agriculture, hunting or other exploitation, have been the subject of inspiring specialist meetings. The increasing concern about water resources is now giving a new impulse to wetland conservation (European Water Framework Directive 2000, World Commission on Dams, etc.). Illustrative of this is a WWF publication (Schuyt & Brander 2004) with a table expressing the economic values of the Dutch Wadden Sea (270 000 ha), a key wetland site in Europe that is still threatened by increasing developments such as gas exploitation, mollusc fisheries and tourism that are probably not sustainable. The economic value of this tidal wetland is estimated at about US$ 2 330 000 000 per year! (For more interesting figures, see Constanza *et al.* 1997).

After the boom in publications, proceedings of wetland meetings, inventories, waterbird atlases, directories, etc., a great variety of web-sites is now joining – if not reducing – traditional printed matter; these web-sites are supported by government offices, international bodies, NGOs or individuals, and often offer a wealth of rapidly updated information. This enables individuals and action groups to make their own conclusions about what is going on within the entire biosphere and how they must react. How far future generations will criticize us for not always storing this short-term electronic information in a useful permanent format remains to be seen. On the other hand, a large amount of knowledge would never have been so widely accessible.

## BIODIVERSITY: THREATS AND THE FUTURE

Wetlands are among the most vulnerable types of habitats. The reasons are well known and do not need to be listed here. Wetland losses have been estimated on several occasions, with alarming figures illustrating the great need to take action (Finlayson & Moser 1991, Millennium Ecosystem Assessment 2005). Hopefully, the Ramsar Convention can help to slow the rate of loss of wetlands significantly. This needs long-term strategies, including research and monitoring, site management, ecologically sound policy planning, education and communication. Without public awareness, most initiatives will fail to achieve any long-term sustainability. This is especially important if national and local authorities are to be convinced to respect wetlands in their physical planning, land-use development plans, education programmes, etc.

As to the needs of wetland and waterbird research and monitoring, the traditional bird counts by volunteers – still of crucial importance – are now increasingly being carried out with specialized equipment, additional research techniques and better financial support. The classic ringing schemes, with most recoveries coming from dead birds, have revealed the major patterns of migrations. However, the use of colour rings and satellite transmitters on individual birds has taught us much more about the various types of movements, habitat use and seasonal patterns in only a couple of decades. Earth observation programmes with satellite imaginary offer ever-increasing opportunities for digital mapping and monitoring of wetland systems world-wide. More new techniques are becoming available, even allowing us to establish new migration routes by using imprinted waterbirds following light aircraft. It is up to this and the next generation to judge if such far-reaching manipulations of natural characteristics are justified. In any event, careful restoration of habitats and ecological networks, enlarging protected areas and improving habitat quality should be our first priorities and duty.

It is not surprising that our knowledge is developing very fast, but at the same time, concerns about the rapid ecological changes must serve as a warning to modern society that it is time for inte-

grated actions and ecologically based economics. Public awareness through education and training must be translated into political pressure at all decision-making levels. The mission of Wetlands International is clear enough: to sustain or restore wetlands, their resources and biodiversity for future generations through research, information exchange and conservation activities world-wide.

Wetlands play a key role in a number of global processes, from climate change to coastal protection, from eco-tourism to food and timber production, from water supply to transportation, and much more, and thus merit the full attention of all sectors in our society. Wetlands are real crossing points where nature and human culture have come together for hundreds of generations, many of whom have used and admired the wealth of waterbirds in their thousands and other living resources. A wide range of traditional skills (often practised by women) and modern techniques are now needed in joint efforts to maintain this worldly heritage, these "liquid assets" of the highest spiritual and aesthetic value.

## ACKNOWLEDGEMENTS

I wish to thank the Ramsar Convention Secretariat (Delmar Blasco, Nick Davidson and Tobias Salaté) and Wetlands International (Doug Taylor) for responding to requests for information, and give special thanks to Gerard Boere for his encouragement to finalize this contribution. I wish to express my sincere appreciation to my colleagues on the "Board of Patrons" of this Conference, H. Boyd, L. Hoffmann, G.V.T. Matthews and H. Nelson, for having accepted me as a "junior" in their stimulating company as real pioneers. I am most grateful to Derek Scott for the final revision of the manuscript.

## REFERENCES

**Alpheraky, S.** 1905. The Geese of Asia and Europe. Rowland Ward, London.

**Atkinson-Willes, G.L.** 1955. Wildfowl counts in the British Isles. Wildfowl Trust Annual Report VII: 29-46.

**Atkinson-Willes, G.L.** 1964. Liquid assets. Wildfowl Trust, IUCN and IWRB, Slimbridge, UK.

**Beintema, A. & van Vessem, J.** 1999. Strategies for Conserving Migratory Waterbirds. Wetlands International Publication No. 55. Wageningen, The Netherlands.

**Boyd, H.** 1959. The composition of goose populations. Ibis 101: 441-445.

**Carp, E.** 1980. Directory of Wetlands of International Importance in the Western Palearctic. IUCN, Gland, Switzerland.

**Constanza, R., d'Arge, R., de Groot, R.S. *et al.*** 1997. The total value of the world's ecosystem services and natural capital. Nature 387: 253-260.

**Delacour, J.** 1954. The Waterfowl of the World. Country Life Ltd., London.

**Erwin, K.L.** 1996. A Bibliography of Wetland Creation and Restoration Literature. Wetlands International, Wageningen, The Netherlands, and the Association of State Wetland Managers, Berne, USA.

**Finlayson, M. & Moser, M.** (eds). 1991. Wetlands. IWRB, Slimbridge, UK.

**Frazier, S.** (ed). 1999. A Directory of Wetlands of International Importance. Compact Disc. Wetlands International, Wageningen, The Netherlands.

**Frazier, S.** (ed). 2002. A Directory of Wetlands of International

Importance. Compact Disc. Wetlands International, Wageningen, The Netherlands.

**Hails, A.J.** 1997. Wetlands, Biodiversity and the Ramsar Convention. The role of the Convention on Wetlands in the Conservation and Wise Use of Biodiversity. Ramsar Convention Bureau, Gland, Switzerland.

**Hawkins, A.S., Hanson, R.C., Nelson, H.K. & Reeves, H.M.** 1984. Flyways. Pioneering Waterfowl Management in North America. U.S. Department of the Interior, Washington, D.C.

**ICBP** 1941. Factors affecting the general status of wild geese and wild duck. Vol. I. Cambridge University Press, Cambridge.

**Lenten, B.** 2006. The Agreement on the conservation of Africa-Eurasian migratory waterbirds. Waterbirds around the world. G.C. Boere, C.A. Galbraith & D.A. Stroud (Eds.), The Stationery Office, Edinburgh, UK. 350-353.

**Linduska, J.P.** 1964. Waterfowl Tomorrow. U.S. Department of the Interior, Washington, D.C. 770 pp.

**Lowe, P.R.** 1941. The history of events leading to the formation of the Wildfowl Inquiry sub-committee. In: ICBP, Factors affecting the general status of wild geese and wild duck. Vol. I. Cambridge University Press, Cambridge.

**Matthews, G.V.T.** 1993. The Ramsar Convention on Wetlands: its history and development. Ramsar Convention Bureau, Gland, Switzerland. Available at: www.ramsar.org/lib_hist_index.htm

**Millennium Ecosystem Assessment** 2005. Ecosystems and human well-being: wetlands and water synthesis. World Resources Institute, Washington DC. 68 pp.

**Mörzer-Bruijns, M.F., Philippona, J. & Timmerman, A.** 1969. Survey of the winter distribution of Palearctic Geese in Europe, Western Asia and North Africa. IWRB Goose Working Group Interim Report. IWRB, Slimbridge, UK.

**Moser, M., Prentice, C. & van Vessem, J.** (eds). 1993. Waterfowl and Wetland Conservation in the 1990s: A Global Perspective. Proceedings of IWRB Workshop, St Petersburg, Florida, 1992. IWRB, Slimbridge, UK.

**Olney, P.J.S.** (ed). 1965. List of European and North African Wetlands of International Importance. IUCN Publication New Series 5, Morges, Switzerland.

**Parish, D. & Prentice, R.C.** (eds). 1989. Wetland and Waterfowl Conservation in Asia. Proceedings of Malacca Conference. Asian Wetland Bureau, Kuala Lumpur, Malaysia, and IWRB, Slimbridge, UK.

**Rose, P.M. & Scott, D.A.** 1994. Waterfowl Population Estimates. IWRB Publication 29, Slimbridge, UK.

**Rüger, A., Prentice, C. & Owen, M.** 1986. Results of IWRB International Waterfowl Census 1967-1983. IWRB Special Publication No. 6, Slimbridge, UK.

**Schuyt, K. & Brander, L.** 2004. Living Waters: Conserving the source of life. The Economic Values of the World's Wetlands. WWF, Zeist, The Netherlands, and Gland, Switzerland.

**Scott, D.A.** (ed). 1980. A Preliminary Inventory of Wetlands of International Importance for Waterfowl in West Europe and Northwest Africa. IWRB Special Publication No. 2, Slimbridge, UK.

**Scott, D.A.** (ed). 1989. A Directory of Asian Wetlands. IUCN, Gland, Switzerland, and Cambridge, UK.

**Scott, D.A. & Carbonell, M.** 1986. A Directory of Neotropical Wetlands. IUCN, Cambridge, & IWRB, Slimbridge, UK.

**Scott, P.** 1965. A coloured key to the wildfowl of the World. Second edition. Country Life Ltd., London.

**Stroud, D.A.** unpublished. Selecting Ramsar sites: the development of criteria from 1971 to 2005. Ramsar Technical Report.

**Szijj, J.** 1972. Some suggested criteria for determining the international importance of wetlands in the Western Palearctic. In: E. Carp (ed) Proceedings of the International Conference on Conservation of Wetlands and Waterfowl, Ramsar, Iran. IWRB, Slimbridge, UK: 101-119.

**World Conservation Monitoring Centre** 1990. Directory of Wetlands of International Importance. Sites designated for the List of Wetlands of International Importance. Ramsar Convention Bureau, Gland, Switzerland.

Part of the Ramsar site of Eqalummiut nunaat – Nassuttuup nunaa, west Greenland, designated in 1987 because of its international importance for breeding waterbirds. Photo: David Stroud.

# North American flyway management: a century of experience in the United States

*Paul R. Schmidt*

*U.S. Fish and Wildlife Service, Migratory Birds and State Programs, 1849 C St. NW, Room 3250, Washington, D.C. 20240, USA.*

Schmidt, P.R. 2006. North American Flyway Management: a century of experience in the United States. *Waterbirds around the world.* Eds. G.C. Boere, C.A. Galbraith & D.A. Stroud. The Stationery Office, Edinburgh, UK. pp. 60-62.

There is a long history of waterbird conservation in the United States of America, with a century of cooperation and legislation. The awakening of the conservation movement dates back to 1900, and the first international agreements for migratory waterbirds were established in 1916. Through the 1920s and 1930s, legal measures for hunting and then habitat protection were introduced; the latter focused on land acquisition and was especially important for wetland conservation. In the 1940s, the first flyway-level cooperation began, incorporating administrative divisions to ensure clarity in approaches. Then in the 1950s, surveys became the focus and, enhanced by technological advances and aerial surveys, became central to understanding waterbird populations in North America. Surveys were conducted on bird populations, habitats and harvesting. Each year, tens of thousands of miles of aerial surveys are carried out. In the 1960s, the roles of management and research came to prominence, and in the 1970s, science was clearly driving management decisions. In the 1980s, the forging of partnerships led to establishment of wider agreements, such as the North American Waterfowl Management Plan, which has also been influential for other species. The 1990s saw the development of other continental partnership efforts to conserve other groups of species, such as Partners in Flight (for landbirds), Waterbird Conservation for the Americas, and the United States Shorebird Plan. Additionally, an effort to integrate population monitoring began to take root. Conservation agreements are living, evolving and dynamic measures, and in 2000 the North American Bird Conservation Initiative was developed between USA, Canada and Mexico with the aim of integrating science and partnerships in management to deliver bird conservation for the benefit of society. The National Wildlife Refuge System was begun in 1903, and birds have been a primary influence on its development. International agreements such as the Western Hemisphere Shorebird Reserve Network (WHSRN) have drawn upon this network. WHSRN is an enormous partnership combining science and voluntary participation in site-based protection. Current initiatives, such as Important Bird Areas of North America, are raising awareness further and identifying critically important sites. Successful conservation demands federal leadership in any country – this has been achieved through the United States Fish and Wildlife Service (USFWS) in the USA. Challenges facing conservation are more complex today than a century ago; there are many continued pressures, of which habitat loss remains the most significant, but there are new pressures such as disease, for example West Nile Virus in North America. The USFWS vision is to combine science and landscape-scale partnerships to deliver the full spectrum of bird conservation and, in doing so, lift human spirit and enrich human lives for generations to come.

*"Propelled by an ancient faith deep within their genes, millions of birds hurdle the globe each season... They are not residents of any single place, but of the whole, and their continued survival rests almost entirely within our hands."* (Scott Weidensaul, author).

*"Many birds are indeed a source of wonder and inspiration. They weave the nations of the globe together as neighbors."* (John Turner, Assistant Secretary of State).

Indeed, the wonder of birds and their migrations have inspired people for generations past. The citizens of the United States of America have connected to this natural resource over the decades, and have demanded a conservation effort that considers birds an international resource not "owned" by anyone. For more than a century now, the United States government has made concerted and organized efforts to ensure that this resource is conserved for future generations of Americans and other people of the world.

Without question, migratory birds are an international shared resource, requiring cooperation among nations. This is evident around the globe with the many international agreements and treaties that have formalized what we all know intuitively. In the case of the United States, there are important and binding international partnerships in this endeavor with Canada, Mexico, Japan, and Russia. Beyond that, the United States has informal arrangements with virtually every country in Central and South America as well.

The milestone for early efforts in the United States to conserve migratory birds was the establishment of the first National Wildlife Refuge in 1903. This refuge, Pelican Island, was, not coincidentally, established for the protection of migratory birds. Federal laws were passed in the early 1900s that established the foundation of a regulatory framework for protection of wildlife. For instance, the Lacey Act in 1900 made it a Federal violation to transport wildlife across state boundaries if that wildlife had been taken in a manner that violated state law. However, without question, the most prominent and important Federal law for the protection of migratory birds was the Migratory Bird Treaty Act of 1918. This domestic legislation implemented a bilateral treaty, signed in 1916, between the United States and Great Britain (on behalf of Canada). This international treaty for the first time clearly established the authority and obligation of the Federal government to protect and conserve migratory birds. Three more bilateral treaties would follow: with Mexico in 1936, with Japan in 1972, and with the Union of Soviet Socialist Republics (later to be Russia) in 1976. The language in these conventions demonstrated the evolution or refinement of conservation science over those decades. Each subsequent treaty was more sophisticated and comprehensive in its language, building on the preceding one(s) and using the state of the art scientific thought. The bottom line is that, in order to be successful, governments must find ways to cooperate in the conservation of shared species and habitats.

The evolution of conservation in the United States over the past century can be characterized by each decade building on the scientific knowledge and customs of the previous decade. Clearly, the twentieth century was an important one for the conservation of migratory birds in the United States and indeed in North America as a whole. Incredible progress was made over that 100 years, such that there is significant hope that birds will be conserved long into the future.

In the early 1900s, there was an awakening of the conservation movement in the United States. It is during this period that governments experimented with laws and regulations as a way of stemming the obvious losses of the robust wildlife populations that the public had taken for granted for so long. Political leaders and conservationists began to realize that unless the commercialization of wildlife was regulated in some fashion, the future of the wildlife resource would be in question. Federal and state laws began to be passed that criminalized abuses that had come to be common practice. The public's interest in conserving wildlife, and in particular birds, was growing. The people were awakened to the need for sustainable use and the idea that there are limits to what the public can do and still have a future blessed with wildlife.

The legal authorities continued to expand in the 1910s, highlighted by the passage of the Weeks-McLean Law in 1913 and the Migratory Bird Treaty Act in 1918. Visionary leaders during this decade realized that this was an international resource that cried out for cooperation and coordination. There was a clear need for Federal authority.

The 1920s brought an emphasis on population management and protection. Individual populations of species of migratory birds were the focus of management efforts throughout the country. The days of unlimited commercial or market hunting were over, as people recognized that some limits had to be established to ensure species survival. The principle of sustainable use was beginning to be understood.

While the efforts in the 1920s were directed at reacting to the influences and effects of human behaviors, the 1930s brought about a response to a natural disaster: continental drought. The "dust bowl era" of the 1930s was exacerbated by poor land use practices and resulted in a significant deterioration of habitat conditions, particularly in the Midwest and West. It was most noticeable in the precipitous drop in populations of waterfowl[1] that relied upon the prairie pothole wetlands for breeding. The wetlands dried up, and the skies, once darkened by flocks of waterfowl, were now clear and silent. Conservationists began to realize that there must be a concerted effort to conserve habitat or these healthy populations would be no more. Conservationists identified key habitats throughout the country that needed to be protected in order to sustain future populations of birds. It was clear that just regulating the public's behavior was not enough. The birds are inextricably linked to the land and water. The passage of the Migratory Bird Hunting and Conservation Stamp Act of 1934 was the first time that a segment of the public (the migratory bird hunters) was willing to be taxed to raise funds to buy lands for wildlife. This Federal law required every hunter of waterfowl over the age of 16 to purchase a Migratory Bird Hunting and Conservation Stamp in order to hunt. The proceeds of the sale of these stamps would be used to buy waterfowl habitat throughout the country for decades to come.

Given the migratory nature of this resource, governments must coordinate their efforts in order to be most effective.

This was certainly realized in the 1940s, when all the states in the United States began acting in concert with each other to best manage the game species that migrated north-south. The "Flyway System" was borne out of this need to coordinate, and the United States was divided into four flyways: Atlantic, Mississippi, Central, and Pacific. The boundaries to these flyways balanced the biological nature of the migration with the geopolitical boundaries of the states. This system allowed for the Federal government U.S. Fish and Wildlife Service to work with the flyway councils to ensure that the biological and public issues could be openly shared and debated. This system has served the birds, the public, the states, and the U.S. Fish and Wildlife Service well.

Visionary biologists and leaders recognized the need to develop systematic surveys in order to gather current data on the status of important bird populations for supporting decisions on the "take" of migratory birds; this was particularly important in establishing hunting seasons. In the 1950s, a few of these visionaries designed the most comprehensive wildlife survey system in the world. With the availability of excess military aircraft after the end of World War II and a few biologists and pilots, the age of aerial surveys began. The waterfowl breeding population survey began in earnest in 1955 and has remained much the same over these past 50 years, providing one of the most widely used databases for migratory birds in the world. Since that time, the Fish and Wildlife Service has added survey components to collect information on habitat conditions and hunter harvest throughout North America. All of these surveys are carried out in cooperation and partnership with Canadian and state biologists. The aerial surveys cover over 80 000 linear miles (128 000 km) each year in the best waterfowl breeding areas in North America.

In the 1960s, there was an emphasis on intensive management to try to improve the status of key populations. Efforts to reduce predation and enhance production were conducted to get the most out of the natural system for the benefit of the public. Biologists experimented with management treatments. These same biologists realized it was incredibly important to use the best available science. Hence, the emphasis in the 1970s was on using science to drive management actions. It was during this decade that much progress was made in understanding the fundamental principles underlying complex biological systems.

The crisis of the decline in waterfowl populations in the 1980s gave rise to the need for a comprehensive effort to secure sufficient habitat to sustain these populations. It was clear that no single organization could make this happen on its own, and therefore formal partnerships were created. In 1986, the Secretary of the Interior for the United States and the Minister of the Environment for Canada signed the North American Waterfowl Management Plan. This Plan would form the rallying point for government and non-governmental organizations to focus work and funds toward a common goal of restoring waterfowl populations to the levels enjoyed in the 1970s. The partnerships were fuelled by new Federal funding in the North American Wetlands Conservation Act of 1989. This new funding would provide matching grants to organizations to protect or restore priority wetland habitats throughout the continent. Private fund-raising efforts were combined with government funding to produce significant results for the protection of wetlands.

The North American Waterfowl Management Plan was used as a model agreement for other partnerships to conserve other

---

[1] The term "waterfowl" is here used in the North American sense, i.e. restricted to ducks, geese and swans (Anatidae).

large groups of migratory birds. In the 1990s, organizations came together for landbirds, waterbirds, and shorebirds. Partners-in-Flight (1991) was formed to bring attention to the decline of many landbirds, particularly neotropical migrants. Waterbirds for Americas was launched in 2001 to focus efforts on waterbirds other than waterfowl. The decline of many shorebird species brought organizations together to develop plans to improve the status of these birds as well. The U.S. Shorebird Conservation Plan was completed in 2000. All of these efforts are built on the principle that science and partnerships can come together to make a significant difference for migratory birds.

As the twentieth century came to a close, partners across the continent formed the North American Bird Conservation Initiative (1999); this effort built on the four bird partnerships that had developed continental plans. The role of the Initiative was to serve as a forum in which partners could share ideas and find efficiencies among the ongoing conservation work. This Initiative includes government and other organizations in Mexico, the United States, and Canada. The hope is that this idea will spread throughout the hemisphere to bring together conservation efforts for the benefit of birds and people.

Regional partnerships called "Joint Ventures" have been formed to plan and implement regional habitat efforts toward the goals of the continental plans. Originally focused on waterfowl, they have all adopted the responsibility of delivering habitat conservation for all migratory birds. The "vision" adopted by all the major partners in bird conservation is "Biologically-based, landscape-oriented regional partnerships delivering the full spectrum of bird conservation." This vision is being realized every day in the dozen or so "joint venture" partnerships that have formed across the USA and Canada, and are beginning to form in Mexico. Each joint venture is responsible for understanding the fundamental needs of the suite of species of migratory birds within its geographic scope, and designing a conservation program that is grounded in the goals of those species. This work entails understanding the gap that exists between a healthy sustainable habitat state and the current state of the landscape. The partners come to the joint venture with ideas and resources to work together on the goals identified.

There are a number of site networks that have been developed in North America over the years that contribute to the overall conservation of migratory birds from a flyway perspective. The National Wildlife Refuge System is a century old and covers almost 100 million acres (40 million hectares) in the United States. There are lands set aside for the conservation of America's wildlife in every one of the 50 States. It is an incredible legacy that will provide lasting benefits to conservation in the flyways forever. The refuges are strategically placed to benefit the many species of migratory birds with which we concern ourselves.

The mission of the Western Hemisphere Shorebird Reserve Network (WHSRN; created in 1985) is to conserve shorebird species and their habitats across the Americas through a network of key sites. The guiding principles of this network are:

- International strategy for local conservation
  - Site-based action
  - Focus on collective actions that individual sites cannot do alone
- Voluntary, non-regulatory
- Science-based

- Community driven (valuing traditional knowledge and customs)
- Integration at national and regional scale

The WHSRN encompasses 57 sites in seven countries and 23 states; it has over 240 partners and affects 20 million acres (8.1 million hectares).

Last but not least, the American Bird Conservancy has been coordinating the Important Bird Areas of North America since 1995. These sites are identified because they are important for threatened, endangered and "watch-list" species, or support large concentrations of birds. The goal of the program is to raise awareness at critical sites on the continent. Over 500 areas have been identified as globally important.

The twenty-first century brings us to a crossroads in the conservation of migratory species. Conservation and management of such a highly mobile group of species requires and demands Federal leadership. The Fish and Wildlife Service is entrusted with this responsibility in the United States, with more than 25 legislative Acts of Congress authorizing the conservation and management of over 800 species. The multiple and expanding constituencies will continue to grow in their demands and expectations on this leadership.

This century will bring a varied and complex set of challenges greater than the century before, including but not limited to:

- Continued habitat loss and degradation
- Pesticides and other contaminants
- Complex harvest program for game species
- Long-line and gillnet fisheries
- Towers and other human-made structures
- Invasive species
- Over-abundant species
- West Nile Virus and other diseases

The Fish and Wildlife Service has recently adopted a new vision and plan to deal with these challenges: "A Blueprint for the Future of Migratory Birds (March 2004)." This strategic plan envisions that: "Through careful management built on solid science and diverse partnerships, the Service and its partners restore and sustain the epic sweep of bird migration and the natural systems on which it depends – fostering a world in which bird populations continue to fulfill their ecological roles while lifting the human spirit and enriching human lives in infinite ways, for generations to come." To these ends, the goals of the Service's Migratory Bird Program are to:

1. maintain and increase healthy migratory bird populations of economic or ecological importance and their associated habitats;

2. improve the status of migratory bird species in decline or listed as threatened or endangered;

3. address concerns regarding over-abundant migratory bird populations; and

4. improve bird-related recreational experiences and opportunities.

These goals will be pursued in a climate that endorses and supports adaptive resource management. For North America, migratory bird conservation, now and in the future, will be biologically-based, landscape-oriented partnerships, delivering the full spectrum of bird conservation.

# African-Western Eurasian Flyways: current knowledge, population status and future challenges

*Nicholas C. Davidson[1] & David A. Stroud[2]*

*[1]Ramsar Convention Secretariat, Rue Mauverney 28, 1196 Gland, Switzerland. (email: davidson@ramsar.org)\**

*[2]Joint Nature Conservation Committee, Monkstone House, City Road, Peterborough, PE1 1JY, UK. (email: David.Stroud@jncc.gov.uk)*

*\* address for correspondence*

Davidson, N.C. & Stroud, D.A. 2006. African-Western Eurasian Flyways: current knowledge, population status and future challenges. *Waterbirds around the world*. Eds. G.C. Boere, C.A. Galbraith & D.A. Stroud. The Stationery Office, Edinburgh, UK. pp. 63-73.

## ABSTRACT

This paper reviews the status of the 762 biogeographical populations of waterbirds (of 307 species in 33 families) which depend upon the African-Western Eurasian region. Fifty-four percent are inter-continental migrants and the remainder are resident or short-distance migrants, the status of which is particularly poorly known. Despite a huge wealth of long-term research and monitoring effort, especially in western Europe, population trends have been estimated for only half of the populations due largely to the dispersed nature of some populations and limited monitoring networks in Africa, the Middle East and western Asia. Many waterbird populations in Africa and Western Eurasia remain in long-term and serious decline: 45% of populations are decreasing and only 16% are increasing. Populations in decline exhibit a variety of characteristics, but it is clear that some waterbird taxa (e.g. rails, cranes, ducks and terns) are particularly threatened, as are populations dependent on some flyways (notably the Black Sea/Mediterranean and West Asian/East African), some regions (e.g. Africa, especially its islands, and West Asia/Middle East) and some key migratory staging areas (notably the Wadden Sea). However, more broad analyses (at the flyway and/or higher taxon levels) are needed to determine at which habitats, regions and key sites our resources and conservation actions should be focused. The main driver of change continues to be wetland loss and degradation, probably now being exacerbated by severe and prolonged droughts and other impacts of climate change. Despite over 30 years of inter-governmental action for waterbirds, notably through the Ramsar Convention on Wetlands and the African-Eurasian Migratory Waterbird Agreement, there remain major gaps, especially in Africa, in the envisaged comprehensive flyway-scale network of sites for waterbirds, with less than one-quarter of key sites having been designated. The future challenges of justifying more waterbird research and monitoring in the context of the African priority for sustainable development to achieve human well-being and elimination of extreme poverty are discussed.

## INTRODUCTION

Waterbirds in Africa and Western Eurasia are amongst the most well-studied animals in the world. Numbers, distributions and status have been extensively monitored and researched for the last 40 years, yielding a wealth of knowledge and understanding of migration movements and phenology, sites and habitats of importance, and leading the way in unravelling the complexities of the eco-physiology of long-distance migrations.

This paper provides a brief overview of the numbers and status of waterbird populations dependent on the African-Western Eurasian region, drawing on examples from studies particularly on waders (shorebirds) and Anatidae (ducks, geese and swans). Whilst focusing on migratory species and populations, it also assesses the status of non-migrant populations and species, which are often less well-known and in poorer status than migratory populations. It assesses their current conservation status, the value of using waterbirds as indicators of global change, and whether the transfer of scientific knowledge to policy-relevant application of conservation measures has been effective in maintaining or restoring the health of waterbird populations. Future challenges are identified, particularly as to how, and if, waterbird science can be shown to be relevant to the key priority issues of securing biodiversity conservation in the context of sustainable development, food and water security and poverty reduction. These issues, set out by the World Summit on Sustainable Development (WSSD; Johannesburg, 2002) and the United Nation's Millennium Development Goals, are the focus of attention in the developing world, and especially Africa.

## THE INTERNATIONAL CONSERVATION FRAMEWORK FOR AFRICAN-WESTERN EURASIAN WATERBIRDS

An international conservation framework for wetlands and waterbirds has now been in place for over 30 years. The importance of maintaining the ecological character of the network of wetlands, both inland and coastal, on which these populations depend was the driving force behind the establishment of the Convention on Wetlands (Ramsar, Iran, 1971), amongst the oldest of the global multilateral environmental agreements (MEAs). More recently, these flyways have become the focus of a further regional MEA, the 1995 Agreement on the Conservation of African-Eurasian Migratory Waterbirds (AEWA). In addition, the 1979 EEC Directive on the Conservation of Wild Birds established a legally-binding instrument for bird conservation throughout the Member States of the European Union (EU). These international intergovernmental agreements for flyway-scale conservation set the international frameworks and context for the many national and local conservation actions designed to safeguard waterbird populations.

The Ramsar Convention delivers its mission of "the conservation and wise use of all wetlands through local, regional and national actions and international co-operation, as a contribution towards achieving sustainable development throughout the world" through three "pillars" of activity:

- the wise use of all wetlands;
- the designation and management of Wetlands of International Importance (Ramsar sites); and
- international co-operation, which includes the establishment of waterbird flyway networks.

The Convention gave an initial priority to the identification and designation of Ramsar sites for waterbirds, and has established quantitative criteria for such designations (see Ramsar Convention 1999). Since the early 1990s, the Convention has been developing so as to address fully its initially-established scope of securing the maintenance of the ecological character of all wetlands and, importantly, through safeguarding the critical role of wetlands in maintaining the global hydrological cycle, securing water supply for current and future generations. The Convention, as at July 2006, has 152 Contracting Parties, including 98 in the African-Western Eurasian region.

The African-Eurasian Migratory Waterbird Agreement (AEWA) is an agreement established in 1995 under the auspices of the Convention on Migratory Species (CMS). The Agreement has now entered into force in 54 countries in the region (as at June 2006), i.e. some 46% of the total number of eligible range states. AEWA has developed an ambitious and comprehensive range of implementation priorities for the period 2003-2007. The CMS itself, established in 1977, aims "to conserve terrestrial, marine and avian migratory species throughout their range" and (as at June 2006) has 98 Contracting Parties, of which 79 are in the African-Western Eurasian region.

In Europe, the 1979 EEC Directive on the Conservation of Wild Birds requires EU Member States to classify a national network of Special Protection Areas (SPAs) for certain listed rare and vulnerable birds, as well as for all migratory species, and urges special priority to be given to wetlands of international importance – an implicit cross-reference to the Ramsar Convention. In addition, Member States are required to maintain the favourable conservation status of bird populations, maintaining their range and distribution. SPAs, together with Special Areas for Conservation established under the subsequent EU Habitats Directive, are intended to form a comprehensive European-wide network of protected areas in the "Natura 2000" network of the European Union.

Non-European Union Contracting Parties to the "Berne" Convention on the Conservation of European Wildlife and Natural Habitats are required to establish national networks of protected sites as a contribution to the European "Emerald Network", which is complementary to the EU's Natura 2000 network.

## STATE OF KNOWLEDGE OF AFRICAN-WESTERN EURASIAN WATERBIRD POPULATIONS
### Number of waterbird species and populations in the African-Western Eurasian region
There is no globally definitive list of "waterbird" species and populations. The Ramsar Convention has defined "waterbirds" as "species of birds which are ecologically dependent on wetlands". The Convention regards "waterbirds" as a term synonymous with "waterfowl" - a treatment followed in this paper - and lists 14 bird orders which especially include waterbirds (Ramsar Convention 1999). Wetlands International's *Waterbird Population Estimates - Third edition* (WPE3; Wetlands International 2002) lists all species and populations of 33 families which have traditionally been considered as "waterbirds", but recognizes that this listing needs expanding to cover wetland-dependent species in other taxa. In the African-Western Eurasian region, there are at least 762 biogeographical populations (including 14 extinct or probably extinct populations) of 307 species (35% of the global total) in the families covered by WPE3.

WPE3 lists 346 populations in Europe and 611 in Africa (but note that some populations occur in both continents). For migratory species, waders (28.9% by species) and Anatidae (ducks, geese and swans; 21.7%) dominate the flyways. In addition, BirdLife International (2001, 2002) has identified at least a further 61 species (including 20 seabirds) in Europe and 217 species (including 77 seabirds) in Africa which can be considered wetland-dependent.

AEWA covers only a subset of these species and populations: 497 populations (65% of African-Western Eurasian populations in these families) of 221 migratory waterbird species in 23 families, since certain migratory species which are not wetland-dependent are excluded, as are resident wetland-dependent species.

Just over half (54%) of the African-Western Eurasian populations listed in WPE3 are inter-continental migrants, with the other 46% being resident or short-distance migrants. Of these, 20% are resident on African islands and many of these are small, declining and/or threatened populations.

### Knowledge of waterbird populations in the region
Waterbirds in the African-Western Eurasian region, especially in western Europe but also increasingly in eastern Europe and Africa, are amongst the most well-studied of anywhere in the world. In some parts of the region, waterbird populations have been monitored regularly for over 50 years, and annual trend analyses for Anatidae in some countries in Western Europe are available since the mid-1950s (e.g. Atkinson-Willes 1963). This wealth of knowledge has been acquired through vast, and often informal, national and international networks of waterbird enthusiasts, usually working on a voluntary basis. The multiple sources upon which this paper is based bear witness to the multi-national, and generously open, collaborations which are essential if migratory species moving along flyways are to be fully understood.

Site and national scale co-ordinated waterbird counts are compiled through Wetlands International's International Waterbird Census (IWC) and regularly summarized for the Western Palearctic and South-west Asia (e.g. Delany *et al.* 1999, Gilissen *et al.* 2002) and Africa (e.g. Dodman *et al.* 1999). This information is supplemented by a large variety of national, regional, key site and taxonomic analyses, such as those for South Africa (Taylor *et al.* 1999), the United Kingdom (e.g. Pollitt *et al.* 2003) and the international Wadden Sea (Meltofte *et al.* 1994), the large number of WIWO (Working Group of International Wader and Waterfowl Research) site reports (summarized in WIWO 1999), and taxonomic reviews of Anatidae (Scott & Rose 1996, Madsen *et al.* 1999) and waders (Stroud *et al.* 2004, International Wader Study Group in prep.).

Underpinning this is a large volume of published research on migration routes and migration phenology (e.g. Piersma & Davidson 1992, Wernham *et al.* 2002), and the eco-physiology of waterbird migrations in the region (e.g. Ens *et al.* 1990 and Piersma 1994 amongst many others). Furthermore, these detailed research findings have been synthesized and, to some extent, have provided source material in support of waterbird conservation decision-making and implementation, at national scale (e.g. Davidson *et al.* 1991), flyway scale (e.g. Davidson & Pienkowski 1987), regional scale (e.g. Hötker *et al.* 1998), and thematically (e.g. Davidson & Rothwell 1993).

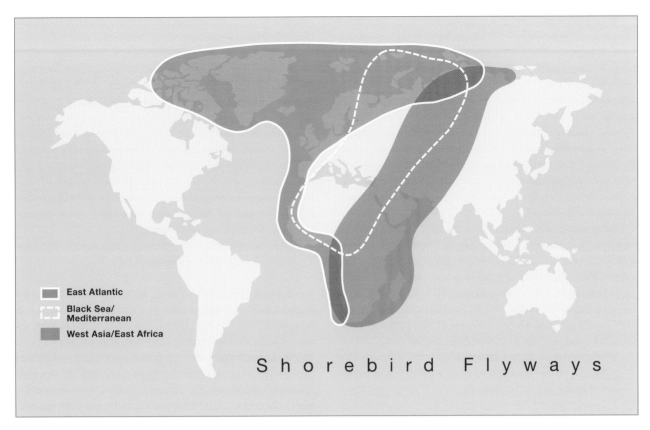

Fig. 1. The three wader flyways which cover the African-Western Eurasian region. Adapted from International Wader Study Group (1992).

Nevertheless, many of the region's waterbird species still remain remarkably poorly known. A recent global analysis of published literature on waders (Thomas *et al.* 2003) found that research has focused on species with large populations, and that one third of all publications are on just five relatively common species in the African-Western Eurasian region: Eurasian Oystercatcher *Haematopus ostralegus*, Northern Lapwing *Vanellus vanellus*, Common Redshank *Tringa totanus*, Red Knot *Calidris canutus* and Dunlin *Calidris alpina*. In contrast, there has been very little, if any, research conducted on many of the scarce and globally threatened wader species, and these should be a focus for better future attention.

### Waterbird flyways in Africa and Western Eurasia

Within the African-Western Eurasian region, several waterbird flyways have been recognized, although it is important to recognize that flyways vary for different waterbird taxa. For example, for waders, three main flyways (East Atlantic, Black Sea/Mediterranean, and West Asian/East African) have been defined, and together these cover the region (Fig. 1). However, for many Anatidae species (especially ducks), population segregation is much less clear, with fewer birds reaching south into Africa, and more moving on a north-east/south-west axis between breeding and wintering areas within Western Eurasia (see, for example, Scott & Rose 1996). In contrast, populations of geese and swans tend to be highly segregated, moving along individual and discrete flyways between traditional breeding and non-breeding areas (Madsen *et al.* 1999). Flyways for most other waterbird taxa in the region have not yet been well established, but are in general likely to be population-specific.

### State of knowledge of waterbird population sizes and trends

Overall, the level of knowledge of waterbird populations in the African-Western Eurasian region is better than in other parts of the world. WPE3 provides a population size estimate for 91% of populations using Africa and 97% of populations using Europe (Table 1). For other global regions, figures range from 59% to 81%. However, it is important to note that these figures include many populations for which there are only rough estimates within a broad size range, and the percentage for which population size is known to greater precision is considerably smaller. For example, for African-Western Eurasian waders (which are better known than many other waterbird taxa), some estimate of population size has been given for 95% of populations, but a more precise estimate is available for only 72% of populations (Stroud *et al.* 2004).

**Table 1. Knowledge of waterbird population sizes and trends. Figures are the percentage of populations with a known population size or trend. Source: Wetlands International (2002).**

| Region[1] | Population size estimate (% of populations) | Population trend estimate (% of populations) |
|---|---|---|
| Europe | 97 | 74 |
| Africa | 91 | 63 |
| North America | 81 | 64 |
| Asia | 79 | 43 |
| Oceania | 66 | 40 |
| Neotropics | 59 | 36 |
| World-wide | 76 | 50 |

[1] Regions are those defined by the Ramsar Convention on Wetlands

Waterbird population trends in the region are less well known than population sizes: WPE3 includes trend information for 63% of African populations and 74% of European populations. However, as for population size, this knowledge base is better than for most other regions of the world (see Table 1). Although knowledge of population trends in the region thus appears good, only for a small number of these populations (largely Anatidae in Europe) is the trend derived from a statistically sound analysis: most remain derived from "best expert assessment" of the available information, which is often derived from only one or two periodic compilations of international population size (see, for example, Stroud *et al*. 2004 for further discussion of this issue).

Furthermore, the regional-scale analysis (Table 1) masks considerable variation in the quality of information between flyways within the African-Western Eurasian region. For waders, for example, there is much better information for coastal populations in the East Atlantic Flyway (93% with trends) than for populations using the Black Sea/Mediterranean Flyway (76%) and West Asia/East Africa Flyway (35%), and particularly for populations confined to Africa (30%) (Stroud *et al*. 2004).

Similarly, there is great variation in the extent of knowledge of population trends between different waterbird taxa in the African-Western Eurasian region (Fig. 2).

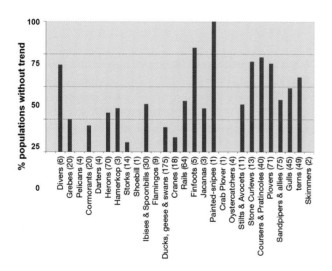

**Fig. 2.** The extent of available information on biogeographic population trends in the waterbird families covered by the 3rd edition of *Waterbird Population Estimates* (Wetlands International 2002). Numbers in parenthesis after family names are the total number of populations in that family in the African-Western Eurasian region.

Information quality is generally better (<20% of populations lacking trend information) for the taxa in which species are large, often localized in distribution and so relatively easier to count, such as pelicans (Pelecanidae), cormorants (Phalacrocoracidae), storks (Ciconiidae), flamingos (Phoeni-copteridae), ducks, geese and swans (Anatidae), cranes (Gruidae) and oystercatchers (Haematopodidae). Conversely, it is particularly poor for taxa in which birds are generally smaller, widely distributed and/or highly cryptic, especially for taxa occurring largely in Africa. Such families, each with >40% of populations without trend information, include divers (Gaviidae), finfoots (Heliornithidae), painted-snipes

(Rostratulidae), stone-curlews (Burhinidae), coursers and pratincoles (Glareolidae), plovers (Charadriidae), gulls (Laridae) and terns (Sternidae).

## INDICATORS OF EFFECTIVENESS OF WATERBIRD CONSERVATION IN AFRICA AND WESTERN EURASIA

Two indicators can provide useful insights into the level of success of conservation efforts to safeguard migratory waterbird populations in this region. These are:

1  A "process-oriented indicator" – progress in the designation of Wetlands of International Importance (Ramsar sites) under the Ramsar Convention; and
2  An "outcome-oriented" indicator - the current status and trends of waterbird populations in the region.

It is important to bear in mind, however, that such outcome-oriented indicators can at best generally provide evidence of correlation between the effectiveness of decision-making and conservation implementation, rather than demonstrating a causal link with specific actions, such as designation and management of Ramsar sites, and species protection and management. Without the existence of a "control" situation, the assessment of such indicators could be interpreted in two ways if, for example, continuing population declines are reported: either that the conservation actions are not effective, or that without such actions the situation would have been far worse.

### Progress in the designation of Ramsar sites

The *Strategic Framework and guidelines for the further development of the List of Wetlands of International Importance*, adopted by the seventh Meeting of the Conference of the Parties to the Ramsar Convention (Ramsar Convention 1999), calls for "*coherent and comprehensive national and international networks*" of Ramsar sites, and for these sites to form the basis of a status and trends monitoring network (Objective 4.1 of the *Strategic Framework*). Such networks are recognized as an essential basis for delivering flyway-scale migratory species conservation.

Two (Criteria 5 and 6) of the nine criteria established for the identification and designation of Ramsar sites are quantitative criteria for waterbirds. The long-term goal and guidance for the application of these criteria indicate that all such wetlands that qualify should be designated as Ramsar sites. In addition, wetlands can be designated for waterbirds under several of the other, qualitative criteria. As the initial emphasis of the Convention focused on a priority for Ramsar site designation for waterbirds (Article 2.2), we can assess how comprehensive an international site network has been created 35 years on.

The application of Criterion 6 for Ramsar site designation depends on two types of information being available: a) knowledge of the population size regularly dependent on the site concerned; and b) sufficient knowledge of the overall size of the biogeographical population to establish a 1% threshold for that population. *Waterbird Population Estimates* has been recognized by the Ramsar Convention as the key authoritative source for these 1% thresholds. For African-Western Eurasian populations, WPE3 has established 1% thresholds for 668 (89%) extant waterbird populations in the region.

As at April 2004, 1 132 Ramsar sites in the African-Western

Eurasian region recognize the value of the wetland for water-birds in one way or another. More specifically, of these, 465 sites had been designated using waterbird Criterion 5 (>20 000 waterbirds) and/or Criterion 6 (>1% biogeographical population). This suite of designations represents almost three-quarters (73%) of sites globally designated under these quantitative Criteria, and overall covered 30.4 million hectares of wetlands in the region. By June 2006, this had increased to 512 such sites covering 38.0 million hectares.

Although this may appear as significant progress towards the "coherent and comprehensive national and international networks" of Ramsar sites called for by the Convention's *Strategic Framework* (Resolution VII.11) (Ramsar Convention 1999), there are major imbalances and gaps in the site network. Of the sites designated by April 2004 specifically for waterbirds, 83% are in Europe, and only 17% in western Asia and Africa. Over half (55%) of all such waterbird sites in the region have been designated by just six countries: United Kingdom (115 sites), The Netherlands (35 sites), Denmark (32 sites), Russia (31 sites), Islamic Republic of Iran (22 sites) and Ukraine (20 sites). At that time no wetlands had been designated under Criterion 5 and/or Criterion 6 in 35 (39%) of the African-Western Eurasian countries which are Party to the Ramsar Convention, and this included almost half (18 countries) of the Ramsar countries in Africa. Many other sites have been recognized as being important for waterbirds, but quantitative data are as yet lacking for the application of Ramsar's numerical criteria.

Despite these major gaps, the Ramsar site network for migratory waterbirds is nevertheless greatly more developed in this region than are the site networks elsewhere. By June 2006, Criteria 5 and/or 6 had been applied to only 55 wetlands in North America, 49 in the Neotropics, 44 in Oceania (almost all in Australia), and 70 in Asia outside the African-Western Eurasian region.

Recent analyses by BirdLife International of Important Bird Areas (IBAs) in relation to Ramsar sites in Europe, the Middle East and Africa found that only 24% of European IBAs, 25% of Middle Eastern IBAs and 14% of African IBAs which appear to qualify for Ramsar designation are wholly or partly Ramsar sites (BirdLife International 2001, 2002, 2004). At least a further 2 176 wetlands appear to qualify for Ramsar designation for waterbirds in these regions. This suggests that fewer than one quarter (22%) of wetlands needed to complete the comprehensive international site network for waterbirds (Ramsar Convention 1999) have as yet been designated by Ramsar Parties in Africa-Western Eurasia. However, this is better progress than elsewhere: only 11% of qualifying IBAs in Asia have part or all of their area designated as Ramsar sites (BirdLife International 2005). At least some of these internationally important sites, although not yet designated as Ramsar sites, are protected through classifications other than Ramsar status; for example, as Natura 2000 sites within the EU or as Emerald network sites elsewhere in Europe. However, it is not possible to readily determine the actual extent of functional protection for internationally important wetlands.

Furthermore, the Ramsar Convention recognizes that such site designations are just the starting point for securing wetland conservation and wise use, and that establishing and implementing management plans for all designated sites is essential. Yet in 2002, it was believed that management plans were being implemented for only 35% of Ramsar sites in Europe and 21%

of Ramsar sites in Africa (Ramsar Convention 2002). There is clearly a long way to go to secure the sustainable management of a comprehensive network of sites for waterbirds at flyway scale in Africa and Western Eurasia.

In addition, very few flyway-scale analyses of the conservation status of site networks for specific biogeographical populations have as yet been made. Exceptions are for the Red Knot *Calidris canutus* (Davidson & Piersma 1992), Greenland White-fronted Geese *Anser albifrons flavirostris* (Stroud 1992), and Lesser White-fronted Goose *Anser erythropus* and Red-breasted Goose *Branta ruficollis* (Dereliev 2006). Such analyses should, however, be a key to identifying action priorities to safeguard sites, since it is from the level of biogeographical populations that coherent flyway networks for migratory species need to be built. Such analyses are also necessary to highlight strategically important locations on flyways, the protection of which is critical in terms of individual migratory and eco-physiological strategies.

## Status and trends of African-Western Eurasian waterbird populations

With over 50 years of geographically extensive monitoring of waterbirds in parts of the region, the waterbird research community has a data set which is of unparalleled importance for biodiversity monitoring. This monitoring information has become of even more relevance in relation to the global biodiversity target established by the WSSD in 2002 of "significantly reducing the rate of loss of biological diversity" by 2010, and the even more challenging EU target of halting the decline of biodiversity by 2010.

From information presented in WPE3, indicators of waterbird population status can be derived to assess current status and trends. It is important to note that a suite of such "sub-indicators" is necessary in order to elucidate taxonomic and geographic patterns of status. It is also important to keep in mind that these analyses include only populations with known trends, and that, as described above, there are significant taxonomic and geographic gaps in this knowledge. Given that quantitative knowledge of waterbirds is best in northern, developed countries, there is the real risk of bias in interpretation of data.

Aggregated indices of status are increasingly attractive in that they can be seen to provide a simple answer understandable to policy-makers and decision-takers. However, accurate understanding and interpretation of such aggregated indices is essential if their results are not to be very misleading. As an example of a simple aggregated trend index at high taxonomic level, the median trend for populations in each of the 33 waterbird families covered by WPE3 suggests that more families are in a "healthy" state (13 families stable or increasing) than are not (eight families decreasing or stable/decreasing). But such analyses need to be treated with caution, since in many of those families that appear to be stable overall, there are many populations in decline as well as an equivalent number which are increasing.

A more detailed status assessment shows that the results are not encouraging. WPE3 reports that, of populations with known trends, 45% are decreasing and only 16% increasing in Africa. The picture is slightly better in Europe, where 39% are decreasing and 32% increasing. Thus, 2.8 times as many populations are decreasing in Africa as are increasing, compared with 1.2 times as many in Europe. More populations are decreasing than increasing in all regions of the world, but overall, waterbirds in Europe appear to be in a relatively more healthy state than in all other regions except North America, where their status is similar. The ratio of decreasing to increasing populations elsewhere is: Asia 3.7 x; Oceania 3.8 x; Neotropics 2.2 x; and North America 1.1 x (Wetlands International 2002).

Recent flyway-scale analyses for African-Western Eurasian waders (International Wader Study Group 2003; Stroud *et al.* 2004, 2006) reveal a similar story. The East Atlantic Flyway is in the healthiest state, with only 37% of populations decreasing. In the Black Sea/Mediterranean Flyway, 65% are decreasing, while in the West Asian/East African Flyway, 53% are decreasing (Fig. 3). Comparison with 1990s population trends indicates that more (eight populations) are in long-term decline than are in long-term increase (three populations). Overall, almost three times as many migratory wader populations are declining as are increasing in the African-Western Eurasian region (Stroud *et al.* 2004, 2006). African resident and island populations have a particularly poor conservation status, yet these populations tend to be ignored with the international focus of attention on migratory populations under, for example, AEWA.

A preliminary analysis for Anatidae suggests that similar declines are widespread across the region. Overall, 43% of the 121 African-Western Eurasian Anatidae populations are decreasing, while only 33% are increasing. Swans (25% decreasing, 75% increasing) and migratory geese (23% decreasing, 50% increasing) have a healthier conservation status than migratory ducks (44% decreasing, 31% increasing) and especially non-migratory populations (45% decreasing and only 14% increasing). Similar analyses for migratory species in other taxa suggest that rails (70% decreasing), cranes (61%), terns (45%), ibises and spoonbills (40%) and herons (40%) have as bad a status as Anatidae and waders, or are in an even worse state. Only grebes and gulls (each 9% decreasing) appear to have a relatively "healthy" status in the region.

Analyses of common characteristics of populations in decline can help point at likely sources of the problem, and can help to focus establishment of priorities for conservation policy and management interventions. For migratory waders, Stroud *et al.* (2004) have identified three groups of populations which are in particular trouble:

i)  populations breeding in the arid and semi-arid zones of western and central Asia and the Mediterranean;

ii) populations breeding in temperate wet grassland in Europe; and

iii) certain long-distance, non-stop migrants in the East Atlantic Flyway.

The likely causes of the declines in coastal wintering populations in the East Atlantic Flyway are not yet wholly clear. These populations breed and overwinter in different geographical areas, and share their wintering and/or breeding areas with other populations that are increasing. It may be that the problems are in the migratory staging areas, since it has been established that, for a number of long-distance migrants, high quality feeding opportunities on spring staging areas are of critical importance for the ability both to reach Arctic breeding areas in adequate nutritional condition and for adult survival (Baker *et al.* 2004, Fox 2003, Piersma 1994, Morrison *et al.* submitted). For waders in the East Atlantic Flyway, Davidson (2003) demonstrated a strong relationship between a high dependency on the

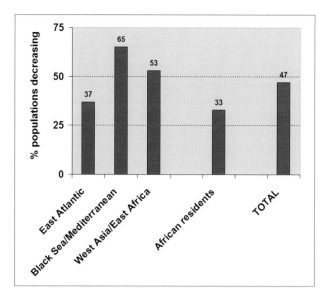

**Fig. 3.** The status (percentage of biogeographic populations of known trend which are in decline) of wader populations on the different flyways in the African-Western Eurasian region. The status of African resident populations is also shown. The number above each bar is the percentage of decreasing populations on that flyway. Data source: Wetlands International (2002).

Wadden Sea for spring staging and population declines, and suggested that this may be a consequence of deteriorating site quality resulting from the well-documented changes to the intertidal ecosystem of the Wadden Sea caused by intensive industrial-scale shell-fisheries (Piersma & Koolhaas 1997). Such findings stress the critical importance of maintaining the ecological character of key staging areas for migratory populations – yet many world-wide continue to be destroyed or degraded.

Few such analyses have as yet been undertaken for other waterbird taxa, although the data to underpin them are readily available in WPE3 and elsewhere. For example, the Anatidae in the African-Western Eurasian region which seem to be in particular trouble are those dependent on the Black Sea/Mediterranean region (25% of the decreasing populations of Anatidae), and Madagascan resident populations (13% of the decreasing populations). Further such regional and synoptic analyses are urgently needed for all waterbird taxa.

Industrial-scale dredging for cockles has severely degraded the intertidal sediments of the Dutch Wadden Sea, with wide ecological impacts. Note the two standing people, indicating scale. Photo: Jaap de Vlas.

Conversely, further insights can be gained from a better understanding of why some populations are increasing, whilst others using similar breeding and/or wintering areas are in decline. More attention to increasing populations is needed to establish whether, for example, these are generally the already widespread and common species. Indications that this may be the case come from an aggregated trend indicator under development for a suite of common, widespread Anatidae and wader species in Europe (Wetlands International *in litt.*), which indicates a long-term stability or increase of such populations, contrary to the findings of more holistic analyses reported above.

## CONCLUSIONS

### Waterbird science is not adequately made available to policy-makers and decision-takers

There is a very extensive science base for waterbird populations in the African-Western Eurasian region. There are unparalleled long-term data sets for waterbirds, and developing a clear status assessment (series of indicators) from these will be invaluable for assessing progress towards the 2010 targets established by the world's governments. However, this science base is still not being fully utilized to produce the key messages for those responsible for making decisions and deciding trade-offs between development and the maintenance of the ecological character of the wetlands on which waterbirds depend.

Most of the analyses reported here had to be undertaken for this paper, rather than being, as they should be, readily available "off-the-shelf". The waterbird science community needs to mine these data more imaginatively to identify likely causes of declines. Essential for this is to provide full access to key data sets, especially Wetlands International's *Waterbird Population Estimates*. The current development by the Ramsar Convention of ecological indicators of the effectiveness of Convention implementation, which will include an indicator of waterbird status and trends, may help to focus, encourage and make available to a wide audience, such information.

In addition to the well-warranted attention being paid to populations and threatened species in decline, and especially those which are globally threatened, more attention also needs to be paid to those populations which are increasing, to establish how and why they have increased whilst others using the same flyway, breeding, staging and wintering areas are in rapid decline.

There also appears to be a tendency to focus research and conservation attention only on migratory species and populations in the region, yet it is clear that many resident waterbird populations, especially those which are endemic to islands, are in serious decline (although many are also very poorly known). Indeed a number are already extinct.

Furthermore, very few broad-scale syntheses of status at the flyway and/or higher taxon scale, such as the International Wader Study Group's 2003 Cadiz Conclusions (International Wader Study Group 2003), seem to have been made, yet these form an essential basis to guide effective use of limited conservation resources: we cannot hope to address all the individual conservation issues on a population by population basis, so this

broader analytical approach is needed to determine at which habitats, regions and key sites our resources and conservation actions should be aimed for maximum effect.

Waterbirds have considerable potential as indicators, acting as surrogates of the overall ecological status of wetlands, since they can be, and often are, more readily and easily surveyed than other features of wetlands. However, care does need to be taken in interpretation of waterbird indicators since, for example, common and ubiquitous species can benefit from wetlands in which the water quality is deteriorating through nutrient enrichment. Simplistic indices which aggregate data for all species may give seriously misleading results.

Whilst continuing research and continued monitoring and status assessment of waterbirds are valuable and necessary in gaining further understanding of whether the 2010 biodiversity targets are being met, and in determining what further conservation action is needed, it is not sufficient only to provide listings of such information. More innovative and focused analyses and better presentation of the messages these convey, in forms suitable for raising public and governmental awareness, are essential to point clearly at what is driving the problems – and what policy and management responses are needed.

### Flyway-scale conservation provision for African-Western Eurasian waterbirds is not yet adequate

Despite there being several well-established and long-standing conservation and wise use frameworks for waterbirds in Africa and Western Eurasia, these have yet to realize their full potential as networks of protected areas for waterbirds. Indeed, international designation of wetlands does not in itself deliver their sustainable management. There remain major gaps in the Ramsar site network for waterbirds in the region, notably in Africa and west Asia, and the ambitious AEWA Action Plan and its associated implementation plan have yet to be substantively funded or implemented. Furthermore, there remain significant gaps in AEWA country membership.

Conservation provision for most of the highly threatened waterbirds is also inconsistent. Of the 17 migratory waterbird species globally threatened with extinction, nine[1] are the subject of international action plans (generally those species occurring in Europe) with most existing plans having been driven by the European Union and/or Council of Europe), whilst eight[2] are not (generally those occurring in Africa and the Middle East). All those species without action plans are still declining, whilst at least some with action plans are either stable or increasing in numbers. Lack of international action planning in Africa and the Middle East is a significant issue to address in the immediate future.

However, there are some indirect indications from the global patterns of waterbird population status that the widespread wetland conservation activity in Europe may have contributed to maintaining waterbirds in a healthier state than would have otherwise been the case, since there are relatively more populations which are increasing in Europe (and similarly in North America) than in other regions of the world. Furthermore, since many

---

[1] Northern Bald Ibis *Geronticus eremita*, Lesser White-fronted Goose *Anser erythropus*, Red-breasted Goose *Branta ruficollis*, Marbled Teal *Marmaronetta angustirostris*, White-headed Duck *Oxyura leucocephala*, Siberian Crane *Grus leucogeranus*, Corncrake *Crex crex*, Sociable Lapwing *Vanellus gregarius* and Slender-billed Curlew *Numenius tenuirostris*.

[2] Socotra Cormorant *Phalacrocorax nigrogularis*, Bank Cormorant *Phalacrocorax neglectus*, Madagascar Pond-Heron *Ardeola idae*, Slaty Egret *Egretta vinaceigula*, Blue Crane *Grus paradisea*, Wattled Crane *Grus carunculatus*, White-winged Flufftail *Sarothrura ayresi*, and Black-tailed Godwit *Limosa limosa*.

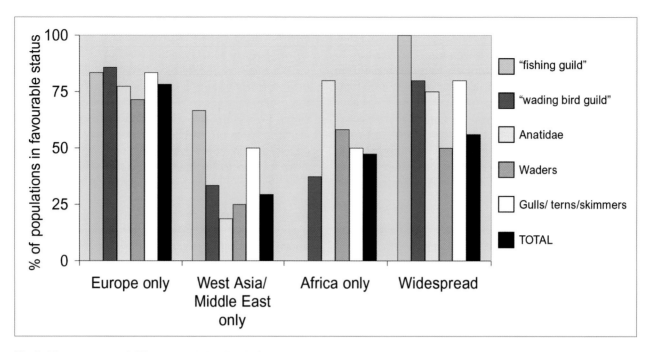

Fig. 4a. The percentages of different waterbird 'guilds' in favourable status (stable or increasing populations) dependent on different African-Western Eurasian sub-regions during the non-breeding season. The category "widespread" is for populations occurring in more than one sub-region. "Fishing guild" is divers, grebes, pelicans and cormorants; "wading bird guild" is herons, storks, ibises and spoonbills, and cranes. No status data is available for "fishing guild" populations in Africa. Data source: Wetlands International (2002).

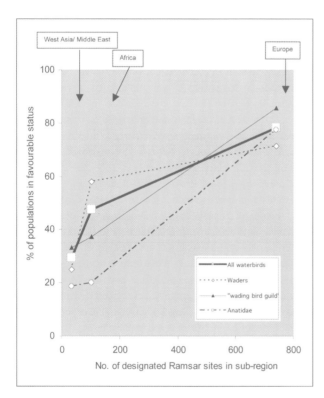

Fig. 4b. The relationship between the number of designated Ramsar sites which are important for waterbirds in each sub-region and the percentage of migratory waterbird populations in favourable status (population trend stable or increasing) which are wholly dependent on that sub-region during the non-breeding season.

waterbirds are more aggregated during their non-breeding seasons than when breeding, it could be predicted that if site safeguard is contributing to securing a favourable conservation status for migratory waterbirds, then those spending their non-breeding seasons wholly in Europe, with its extensive network of Ramsar sites and other protected areas, would have a more favourable status than those depending on other parts of the region. Analysis of the proportion of migratory populations with favourable status (stable and increasing populations) during the non-breeding season in different parts of the African-Western Eurasian region provides some support for this view (Fig. 4). Of populations which spend their non-breeding season wholly within Europe, 78% are in favourable status, compared with only 47% depending on Africa and just 29% depending on West Asia and the Middle East. As might also be expected, populations which are widespread (occurring in more than one of these sub-regions) have a relatively favourable status (56%). This pattern holds for several different groups of waterbirds: fish-eating birds, wading

Populations of Common Snipe *Gallinago gallinago* are in significant decline in many Member States of the European Union as a consequence of agricultural intensification. Photo: Nigel Clark.

birds, duck, geese, swans, waders, gulls, terns and skimmers.

Nevertheless, this is no cause for complacency. Stroud *et al.* (2004) showed that for waders in Africa and Western Eurasia the largest proportion of populations with known status which are declining breed in north-west and western Europe (effectively the European Union - EU15), and consider that, since most of these waders breed in wet grasslands or other low-intensity agricultural land, this is most likely a reflection of Europe-wide agricultural policies which have led to intensification of farming practices (Donald *et al.* 2000). It may therefore be that, whilst broad-scale land-use change is affecting the viability of breeding populations, site-focused conservation action has benefited waterbirds during the period in the non-breeding season when many are more aggregated in their distribution and occur in different habitats. Even if this proves to be the case, it still remains a cause for concern, since to maintain the populations of migratory species, it is pointless to secure their well-being at one stage in their annual cycle whilst other policies lead to their decline at other times of the year. This matter would merit further analysis.

### Many African-Western Eurasian waterbird populations remain in serious decline

Despite the relatively healthy status of waterbirds in Europe in comparison to most other parts of the world, it is clear that many continue to decline; indeed, there are more populations in long-term decline than are increasing, and some populations are in serious long-term decline. For waders, Stroud *et al.* (2004) considered that 45 populations (34% of migratory populations in the Africa-Western Eurasia region) are of significant conservation concern by virtue of their decreasing and/or small populations. Populations in decline exhibit a variety of characteristics, but it is clear that populations dependent on some flyways (notably the Black Sea/Mediterranean and West Asian/East African) and regions (e.g. Africa and especially its islands) are particularly threatened, as are some waterbird taxa (e.g. rails, cranes, ducks and terns) and some populations dependent on West Asia/Middle East or Africa during their non-breeding season.

There are undoubtedly a variety of direct drivers of change to wetlands in Africa and Western Eurasia which are causing these declines, but it seems that broadly it is change in land use leading to loss and deterioration of wetland habitats which remains of major significance. However, in some situations, it is likely that this is being exacerbated by the effects of changing climate; for example, the effects of increasing and prolonged droughts in the Middle East and Central Asia (e.g. Shevckenko 1998). Other aspects of the changing climate may, at least in the short term, benefit some waterbirds. For example, there appears to be a northwards and eastwards shift in the wintering distribution of coastal waders in Britain, which is leading to shorter migration routes to northern breeding grounds (Austin *et al.* 2000, Rehfisch & Austin 2006). However, any benefit gained from reducing migration distances will be counterbalanced if the ecological character of critically important staging areas such as the Wadden Sea continues to deteriorate and/or predicted losses to Arctic breeding habitats occur (Zöckler & Lysenko 2000).

Overall, this assessment of the status of waterbirds in Africa and Western Eurasia indicates that their status is getting worse rather than better, and that much more needs to be done if the 2010 biodiversity targets are to be approached, let alone attained.

### Is waterbird research, monitoring and conservation relevant to human well-being and poverty reduction?

It is clear that securing the health of waterbird populations can make an important contribution to biodiversity conservation, but it is important also to recognize that this can seem largely distant and irrelevant to the governments of developing countries and others charged with addressing the pressing issues of delivering the Millennium Development Goals concerning food and water security, sanitation and poverty reduction. This urgent issue for Africa is reflected in the development and implementation of the New Partnership for African Development, which recognizes that the sustainable management of wetland ecosystems is a key contribution to sustainable development in the continent.

But maintaining the health of ecosystems is fundamentally a matter for societal choice, so it is essential that the science and conservation community gets its message across better to civil society and global governance. However, species-focused arguments are unlikely to have any influence on decision-making on trade-offs between the maintenance of wetland ecosystems and sustainable development, and more potent arguments are likely to involve the importance of maintaining and enhancing ecosystem services so that they continue to support human livelihood. To achieve this requires the maintenance of wetland biodiversity and processes, which in turn will help maintain the ecosystems upon which waterbirds depend. Using waterbirds as flagship indicators of the health of wetland ecosystems can help to secure adequate trade-offs to ensure that these ecosystems can continue to deliver their services. However, more clearly articulating these arguments for continued research and monitoring of waterbirds for the benefit of decision-makers is much needed.

## ACKNOWLEDGEMENTS

We thank Simon Delany and his colleagues at Wetlands International for making available in spreadsheet format data on African-Western Eurasian waterbird populations from *Waterbird Population Estimates - Third edition* (Wetlands International 2002). We also thank Gerard Boere, Peter Bridgewater, Simon Delany, Tony Fox, Lieuwe Haanstra, Bert Lenten, Mike Pienkowski and Theunis Piersma for valuable discussions and information which have helped to develop the ideas addressed in this paper, and Rodney West for preparing Fig. 1. In particular, we thank the many thousands of dedicated waterbird researchers and counters throughout the region who have collected and made available the data and analyses upon which this review paper is based.

## REFERENCES

**Atkinson-Willes, G.L.** (ed.). 1963. Wildfowl in Great Britain. A survey of the winter distribution of the Anatidae and their conservation in England, Scotland and Wales. Monographs of the Nature Conservancy No. 3. HMSO, London.

**Austin, G.E., Peachel, I. & Rehfisch, M.M.** 2000. Regional trends in coastal wintering waders in Britain. Bird Study 47: 352-371.

**Baker, A.J., González, P.M., Piersma, T., Niles, L.J., de Lima Serrano do Nascimento, I., Atkinson, P.W., Clark, N.A., Minton, C.D.T., Peck, M.K. & Aarts, G.** 2004. Rapid decline in red knots: fitness consequences of decreased refueling rates and late arrival in Delaware

Bay. Proceedings of the Royal Society of London B 271: 875-882.

**BirdLife International** 2001. Important Bird Areas and potential Ramsar sites in Europe. BirdLife International, Wageningen, The Netherlands.

**BirdLife International** 2002. Important Bird Areas and potential Ramsar sites in Africa. BirdLife International, Cambridge, UK.

**BirdLife International** 2004. State of the world's birds 2004: indicators for our changing world. BirdLife International, Cambridge, UK.

**BirdLife International** 2005. Important Bird Areas and potential Ramsar sites in Asia. BirdLife International, Cambridge, UK.

**Davidson, N.C.** 2003. Declines in East Atlantic wader populations: Is the Wadden Sea the problem? Wader Study Group Bulletin 101/102: 19-20.

**Davidson, N.C. & Pienkowski, M.W.** (eds). 1987. The conservation of international flyway populations of waders. Wader Study Group Bulletin No. 49, Supplement/IWRB Special Publication No. 7: 1-151.

**Davidson, N.C. & Piersma, T.** 1992. The migration of Knots: conservation needs and implications. Wader Study Group Bulletin 64, Supplement: 198-209.

**Davidson, N.C. & Rothwell, P.** (eds). 1993. Disturbance to waterfowl on estuaries. Wader Study Group Bulletin 68, Special Issue: 1-106.

**Davidson, N.C., Laffoley, D. d'A., Doody, J.P., Way, L.S., Gordon, J., Key, R., Pienkowski, M.W., Mitchell, R. & Duff, K.L.** 1991. Nature conservation and estuaries in Great Britain. Nature Conservancy Council, Peterborough, UK.

**Delany, S., Reyes, C., Hubert, E., Pihl, S., Rees, E., Haanstra, L. & van Strien, A.** 1999. Results from the International Waterbird Census in the Western Palearctic and Southwest Asia, 1995 and 1996. Wetlands International Publication No. 54. Wageningen, The Netherlands.

**Dereliev, S.** 2006. The globally threatened Lesser White-fronted Goose *Anser erythropus* and Red-breasted Goose *Branta ruficollis*: current status and future priorities for the Ramsar sites network in Europe and Asia. Waterbirds around the world. G.C. Boere, C.A. Galbraith & D.A. Stroud (Eds.), The Stationery Office, Edinburgh, UK. 689.

**Dodman, T., Béibro, H.Y., Hubert, E. & Williams, E.** 1999. African Waterbird Census 1998. Wetlands International, Dakar, Senegal.

**Donald, P.F., Green, R.E. & Heath, M.F.** 2000. Agricultural intensification and the collapse of Europe's farmland bird populations. Proceedings of the Royal Society of London B 268: 25-29.

**Ens, B.J., Piersma, T., Wolff, W.J. & Zwarts, L.** (eds). 1990. Homeward bound: problems waders face when migrating from the Banc D'Arguin, Mauritania, to their northern breeding grounds in spring. Ardea 78 (1/2): 1-364.

**Fox, A.D.** 2003. The Greenland White-fronted Goose *Anser albifrons flavirostris*. The Annual Cycle of a Migratory Herbivore on the European Continental Fringe. DSc.

thesis, Natural Environmental Research Institute, Denmark.

**Gilissen, N., Haanstra, L., Delany, S., Boere, G. & Hagemeijer, W.** 2002. Numbers and distribution of wintering waterbirds in the Western Palearctic and Southwest Asia in 1997, 1998 and 1999. Results from the International Waterbird Census. Wetlands International Global Series No. 11. Wageningen, The Netherlands.

**Hötker, H., Lebedeva, E., Tomkovich, P.V., Gromadzka, J., Davidson, N.C., Evans, J., Stroud, D.A. & West, R.B.** (eds). 1998. Migration and international conservation of waders. Research and conservation on north Asian, African and European flyways. International Wader Studies 10: 1-500.

**International Wader Study Group** 1992. The Odessa Protocol on international co-operation on migratory flyway research and conservation. Wader Study Group Bulletin 65: 10-12.

**International Wader Study Group** 2003. Waders are declining worldwide. Conclusions from the 2003 International Wader Study Group Conference, Cádiz, Spain. Wader Study Group Bulletin 101/102: 8-12.

**International Wader Study Group** In prep. Atlas of Wader Populations in Africa and Western Eurasia. Wader Study Group/Wetlands International, Wageningen, The Netherlands.

**Madsen, J., Cracknell, G. & Fox, A.D.** (eds). 1999. Goose populations of the Western Palearctic. A review of status and distribution. Wetlands International Publication No. 48. Wageningen, The Netherlands, & National Environmental Research Institute, Ronde, Denmark.

**Meltofte, H., Blew, J., Frikke, J., Rösner, H.-U. & Smit, C.** 1994. Numbers and distribution of waterbirds in the Wadden Sea. IWRB Publication No. 34/Wader Study Group Bulletin 74, Special Issue.

**Morrison, R.I.G., Davidson, N.C. & Wilson, J.R.** Submitted. Survival of the fattest: body stores on migration and survival in Red Knots *Calidris canutus islandica*. Journal of Avian Biology.

**Piersma, T.** 1994. Close to the edge: energetic bottlenecks and the evolution of migratory pathways in Knots. PhD thesis, University of Groningen, The Netherlands.

**Piersma, T. & Davidson, N.C.** (eds). 1992. The Migration of Knots. Wader Study Group Bulletin 64, Supplement: 1-209.

**Piersma, T. & Koolhaas, A.** 1997. Shorebirds, shellfish(eries) and sediments around Griend, Western Wadden Sea, 1988-1996. Single large-scale exploitative events lead to long-term changes in the intertidal birds-benthos community. NIOZ-Rapport 1997-7. Netherlands Instituut voor Onderzoek der Zee, The Netherlands.

**Pollitt, M.S., Hall, C., Holloway, S.J., Hearn, R.D., Marshall, P.E., Musgrove, A.J., Robinson, J.A. & Cranswick, P.A.** 2003. The Wetland Bird Survey 2000-01: Wildfowl and Wader Counts. BTO/WWT/RSPB/JNCC, Slimbridge, UK.

**Ramsar Convention** 1999. Strategic framework and guidelines for the future development of the List of Wetlands of International Importance. COP7 Resolution VII.11. Available at: http://www.ramsar.org/key_res_vii.11e.htm.

**Ramsar Convention** 2002. Report of the Secretary General on the implementation of the Convention at the global level. Ramsar COP8 DOC. 5. Available at: http://www.ramsar.org/cop8_docs_index_e.htm.

**Rehfisch, M.M. & Austin, G.E.** 2006. Climate change and coastal waterbirds: the United Kingdom reviewed. Waterbirds around the world. G.C. Boere, C.A. Galbraith & D.A. Stroud (Eds.), The Stationery Office, Edinburgh, UK. 398-404.

**Schevchenko, V.L.** 1998. The Sociable Plover *Chettusia gregaria* north of the Caspian Sea. Wader Study Group Bulletin 87: 48-50.

**Scott, D.A. & Rose, P.M.** 1996. Atlas of Anatidae Populations in Africa and Western Eurasia. Wetlands International Publication No. 41. Wetlands International, Wageningen, The Netherlands.

**Stroud, D.A.** 1992. Greenland White-fronted Goose *Anser albifrons flavirostris*: Draft International Conservation Plan. Prepared for NPWS/IWRB by JNCC, Peterborough, UK.

**Stroud, D.A., Davidson, N.C., West, R., Scott, D.A., Haanstra, L., Thorup, O., Ganter, B. & Delany, S.** (compilers, on behalf of the International Wader Study Group). 2004. Status of migratory wader populations in Africa and Western Eurasia in the 1990s. International Wader Studies 15: 1-259.

**Stroud, D.A., Baker, A., Blanco, D., Davidson, N.C., Delany, S., Ganter, B., Gill, R., González, P., Haanstra, L.,**

**Morrison, R.I.G., Piersma, T., Scott, D., Thorup, O., West, R., Wilson, J. & Zöckler, C. (on behalf of the International Wader Study Group).** 2006. The conservation and population status of the world's shorebirds at the turn of the Millennium. Waterbirds around the world. G.C. Boere, C.A. Galbraith & D. Stroud (Eds.), The Stationery Office, Edinburgh, UK. 643-8.

**Taylor, P.B., Navarro, R.A., Wren-Sargent, M., Harrison, J.A. & Kieswetter, S.L.** 1999. TOTAL CWAC Report: Coordinated Waterbird Counts in South Africa, 1992-1997. Avian Demography Unit, Cape Town, South Africa.

**Thomas, G.H., Székely T. & Sutherland, W.J.** 2003. Publication bias in waders. Wader Study Group Bulletin 100: 216-223.

**Wernham, C.V., Toms, M.P., Marchant, J.H., Clark, J.A., Siriwardena, G.M. & Baillie, S.R.** (eds). 2002. The Migration Atlas: movements of the birds of Britain and Ireland. T. & A.D. Poyser, London.

**Wetlands International** 2002. Waterbird Population Estimates – Third edition. Wetlands International Global Series No. 12. Wageningen, The Netherlands.

**WIWO** 1999. Between Taimyr and Table Mountain: Forward Plan 1999-2003. WIWO, Zeist, The Netherlands.

**Zöckler, C. & Lysenko, I.** 2000. Water Birds on the Edge. First circumpolar assessment of climate change impact on Arctic Breeding Water Birds. World Conservation Monitoring Centre, Cambridge, UK.

Arguments for the conservation of wetlands increasingly need to stress their importance in providing wider ecosystem services to human populations. Villagers at a weekly lakeside market: Lake Mburo National Park, Uganda. Photo: David Stroud.

# Migration in the balance: tight ecological margins and the changing fortunes of shorebird populations

*Theunis Piersma*

*Department of Marine Ecology & Evolution, Royal Netherlands Institute for Sea Research (NIOZ), PO Box 59, 1790 AB Den Burg, Texel, The Netherlands; and Animal Ecology Group, Centre for Ecological and Evolutionary Studies, University of Groningen, PO Box 14, 9750 AA Haren, The Netherlands.* (email: theunis@nioz.nl)

Piersma, T. 2006. Migration in the balance: tight ecological margins and the changing fortunes of shorebird populations. *Waterbirds around the world*. Eds. G.C. Boere, C.A. Galbraith & D.A. Stroud. The Stationery Office, Edinburgh, UK. pp. 74-80.

## ABSTRACT

Dependent as they are on rare and remote open habitats for breeding and survival, shorebirds connect continents and hemispheres with their individual movements. Although many of the wetland systems on which shorebirds rely, especially in the rich West, have now some form of protection, two case studies on man-induced declines of Red Knots *Calidris canutus* in The Netherlands and the USA demonstrate that despite the legislation in these countries, the responsible authorities have tragically failed to provide the necessary safeguards. At the same time, these examples indicate how instructive shorebirds can be in elucidating ecosystem changes at local, and at global, scales. I advocate continued close scientific scrutiny of complementary sets of shorebird species so that we can be informed about their fate, and about the fate of ecosystems world-wide that are so effectively connected by their movements.

## INTRODUCTION

Seasonal migration, the phenomenon of birds commuting between parts of the world where they do not reproduce to areas where they do, is a massive phenomenon that has attracted enormous ornithological attention. Shorebirds, or waders, are an important group of truly long-distance migrant waterbirds. These shorebirds connect continents and hemispheres with their individual movements, dependent as they are on rare and remote open habitats for their breeding (mainly in the far north), and on the coastal fringes of the continents or the ephemeral freshwater habitats of continental basins for their survival during the non-breeding season (van de Kam *et al.* 2004, Gill *et al.* 2005). By their very nature, they are particularly susceptible to the effects of human encroachment on coastal habitats, over-exploitation of marine resources, loss of scarce freshwater resources and global climate change (Piersma & Baker 2000,

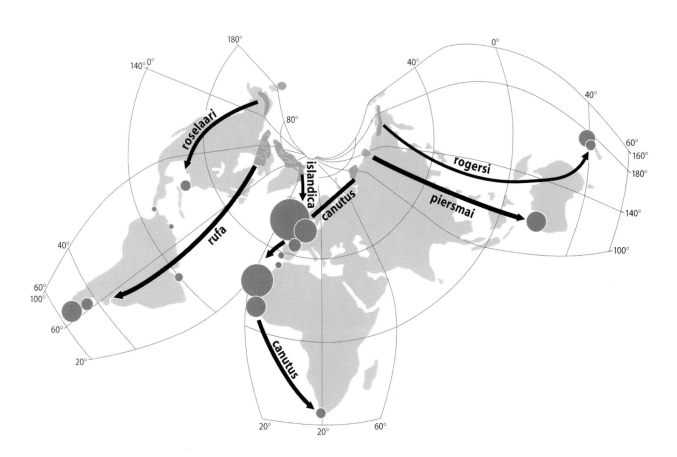

**Fig. 1.** The world-wide network of flyways of the six subspecies of the Red Knot *Calidris canutus*. The dots scale to the approximate size (in 2004) of the respective wintering populations

Piersma & Lindström 2004). A recent survey by the International Wader Study Group has shown that of 207 shorebird populations with known population trends (out of a total of 511), almost half (48%) are now known to be in decline whereas only 16% are increasing (International Wader Study Group 2003, Stroud *et al.* 2006). With three times as many populations in decline as are increasing, shorebirds must be considered as one of the most globally threatened group of the world's long-distance migrants.

In this contribution, I will focus on two case studies that show how human interference at key staging sites can threaten the survival of supposedly large and healthy migrant shorebird populations. The stories emphasize that the human hand is often involved in population declines. My focal species will be the Red Knot *Calidris canutus*. The first case study concerns the recent population history of Red Knots of the *islandica* subspecies trying to establish themselves in the Dutch Wadden Sea after their return from the breeding grounds in Greenland and north-eastern Canada; the second reveals a similar story for the *rufa* subspecies which, at quite some risk, is now dependent on a single stopover site during its northward migration, Delaware Bay in the USA.

Red Knots are a suitable model species because of their highly specialized feeding behaviour and habitat requirements, which restrict their occurrence outside the breeding season to open coastal intertidal wetland habitats, and their diet to hard-shelled molluscs and crustaceans. Red Knots are sandpipers that breed only on high Arctic tundra but move south from their disjunct, circumpolar breeding areas to non-breeding sites on the coasts of all continents (apart from Antarctica), between latitudes 58°N and 53°S (Fig. 1). Due to their specialized sensory capabilities (Piersma *et al.* 1998), Red Knots generally eat hard-shelled prey found on intertidal, mostly soft, substrates (Piersma *et al.* 1995, 2005a). As a consequence, ecologically suitable coastal sites are few and far between, so they must routinely undertake flights of many thousands of kilometres. The six separate tundra breeding areas each host a population with a sufficiently distinct external appearance during the breeding season (body size and plumage) as to have been assigned subspecific status (Piersma & Davidson 1992, Tomkovich 1992, 2001). There appears to be little overlap in occurrence between any combination of subspecies except for the temporary overlap of some *canutus* and *islandica* Knots in the Wadden Sea, an extensive area of intertidal flats share by The Netherlands, Germany and Denmark (Davidson & Wilson 1992, Piersma *et al.* 1995, Nebel *et al.* 2000), and of *roselaari* and *rufa* in Delaware Bay in the eastern USA (Piersma *et al.* 2005a, Atkinson *et al.* 2005). The extant Red Knots shared a common ancestor as recently as within the last 20 000 years or so (Baker *et al.* 1994, Buehler & Baker 2005). As a result of a recent expansion from this severely bottlenecked stock, the subspecies show little genetic divergence across their world-wide range (Buehler & Baker 2005, Buehler *et al.* 2006).

Red Knots are amenable to studies in captivity, and this has enabled us to quantify in great detail the relationships between environmental conditions, time budgets, levels of energy expenditure, prey quality and quantity, and relevant features of the digestive tract (e.g. van Gils *et al.* 2003, 2005a, 2005b, Battley *et al.* 2005). Of particular relevance here is the fact that prey is ingested whole and crushed in a strong muscular stomach, or gizzard (e.g. Piersma *et al.* 1999, Zwarts & Blomert 1992,

Battley & Piersma 2005). This information has turned out to be very important in enabling us to interpret information collected in the field.

## THE DECLINE OF *ISLANDICA* KNOTS IN THE DUTCH WADDEN SEA

The intertidal flats of the Dutch Wadden Sea are a State Nature Monument, and are protected under the Ramsar Convention on Wetlands and the EU Habitats and Birds Directives (Reneerkens *et al.* 2005). Despite this high-level conservation status and the widespread scientific and political concerns about the damaging effects of shellfish-dredging to marine benthic ecosystems (e.g. Hall & Harding 1997, Jackson *et al.* 2001, Coleman & Williams 2002, Dayton 2003), until 2004, three-quarters of the intertidal flats of the Dutch Wadden Sea were open to mechanical dredging for edible cockles *Cerastoderma edule*. A direct, immediate effect of dredging is the complete removal of all organisms larger than 19 mm in the top 5-cm layer. As the dredged sites are usually the most biodiverse (Kraan *et al.* 2006), dredging may also affect smaller cockles, other bivalves such as blue mussels *Mytilus edulis*, Baltic tellins *Macoma balthica* and sandgapers *Mya arenaria*, polychaetes, and crustaceans such as shore crabs *Carcinus maenas*. More indirectly, and over longer time scales, sediments lose fine silts during dredging events, it is this that may lead to long-term reductions in settlement success in both cockles and Baltic tellins (Piersma *et al.* 2001, Hiddink 2003). Between the winters of 1997/1998 and 2002/2003, the numbers of wintering Red Knots in north-west Europe declined by about 25% (from c. 330 000 to c. 250 000; unpubl. data of BTO, SOVON and others), and the numbers in the Dutch Wadden Sea by some 80%, from a level of c. 100 000 to 20 000 or fewer (van Roomen *et al.* 2005). Here we ask whether the decline in the Dutch Wadden Sea can be explained by the short- and long-term effects of suction-dredging, and whether this local decline can then explain what has happened in north-west Europe as a whole. The original analysis is provided by van Gils *et al.* (2006a).

We studied dredging-induced changes in food quantity and quality and their effects on digestive physiology and survival in Red Knots. In an area of roughly 250 km$^2$ in the western Dutch Wadden Sea, we annually sampled the density and quality of knot food in great detail. Each year from early September into December, immediately after completion of our sampling programme, mechanical dredging took place at some of the intertidal flats previously mapped for benthos. Using the black-box GPS data on dredging activity that fishery organizations are obliged to present annually to the Dutch Government (Kamermans & Smaal 2002), we could categorize 1 km$^2$ sample blocks as dredged or undredged. During the years of the study, Red Knots mostly consumed first-year cockles (58%, based on 174 dropping samples of 50-100 droppings), and for this reason we focused our analysis on the effects of dredging on freshly settled, first-year cockles (the so-called "spat"; 16 mm).

It emerged that in dredged areas densities of cockle spat remained stable, whereas densities increased by 2.6% per year in undredged areas (van Gils *et al.* 2006a). This result is consistent with a previous assessment that showed that dredged areas become unattractive for cockles to settle in, perhaps because such sediments lose silt and good structure (Piersma *et al.* 2001). In addition, the quality of cockle spat declined by 11.3% per year in dredged areas and remained stable in undredged areas,

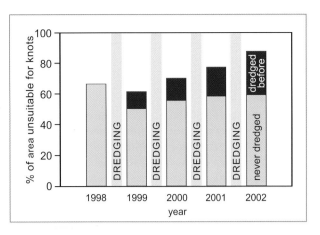

**Fig. 2.** The percentage of intertidal area in the western Dutch Wadden Sea that yielded insufficient intake rates for Red Knots *Calidris canutus* (< 4.8 W) increased between 1998 and 2002 due to an increase in blocks made unsuitable by dredging in previous years (filled bars, as opposed to open bars indicating unsuitable blocks that were never dredged). Based on an analysis of 272 sample blocks of one km$^2$ (van Gils *et al.* 2006b).

something we explain by supposing that coarser sediments lead to worse feeding conditions (Drent *et al.* 2004) and therefore to reduced body condition in deposit-feeding bivalves such as freshly settled cockles (Rossi *et al.* 2004). Thus, both the abundance and the quality of the food of Red Knots decreased in areas where dredging took place. The consequences of these declines were quantified by calculating, for each year, the percentage of the intertidal area that would yield insufficient intake rates for Red Knots to maintain a positive energy balance (Fig. 2). In the Wadden Sea, only a limited part of the available intertidal flats is rich enough in suitable prey to be of any use to foraging Red Knots (Piersma *et al.* 1995, van Gils *et al.* 2006b). From 1988 to 2002, the percentage of 1 km$^2$ blocks that were too poor for Red Knots to obtain a threshold intake rate of 4.8 W increased from 66% to 87% (van Gils *et al.* 2006a). This loss was entirely due to an increase in previously suitable blocks that were dredged; the number of previously unsuitable (and undredged) blocks did not increase.

As a consequence of the widespread dredging in the most biodiverse areas of intertidal flat (Kraan *et al.* 2006), diet quality declined by 11.7% per year and, to compensate for such reductions in prey quality, Red Knots should (Dekinga *et al.* 2001, van Gils *et al.* 2003) and did (van Gils *et al.* 2006a) increase gizzard mass. Nevertheless, re-sightings of individually colour-banded birds of which the gizzards were measured before release demonstrated that birds not seen in our study area within a year after release had undersized gizzards, whereas individuals that we did see again had gizzards that enabled them to achieve a balanced daily energy budget (van Gils *et al.* 2006a). The local annual survival rate (calculated from re-sighting rates of colour-banded birds) increased with year-specific food quality. In summary, this means that birds arriving from the tundra breeding areas with too small a gizzard needed more time to adjust their gizzard than their fat stores allowed them: they faced starvation unless they left the area.

Colour-banded Red Knots that disappeared from our study area may have died or, perhaps more likely for a wide-ranging migrant, emigrated to other areas such as estuaries in the UK. Here they probably paid a mortality cost due to the extra travel

and/or due to uncertainties in the food supply at their new destination. Whatever happened to them, the dramatic decline in numbers of Red Knots wintering in the Dutch Wadden Sea can be satisfactorily explained by these documented population effects of deteriorating feeding conditions (van Gils *et al.* 2006a). The local disappearance can also account for much of the 25% decline of the entire north-west European wintering population over the same period. We must thus conclude that the industrial forms of commercial exploitation allowed by the Dutch Government in one of its best legally protected nature reserves have been directly responsible for the population decline of a long-distance migrant shorebird species which itself is fully protected. Precisely the same conclusion has been reached in studies of the decline of another fully protected shell-fish-eating shorebird, the Eurasian Oystercatcher *Haematopus ostralegus*, in the Dutch Wadden Sea (Verhulst *et al.* 2004) and a nearby estuary (the Wash) in the UK (Atkinson *et al.* 2003).

## THE DECLINE OF *RUFA* KNOTS USING DELAWARE BAY AS A STAGING SITE

Most of the *rufa* subspecies of Red Knots make an enormous annual return migration of 30 000 km between over-wintering sites in Tierra del Fuego and breeding sites in the Canadian Arctic. To achieve this feat, they must make stopovers at a few productive refuelling sites at strategic locations in the flyway. As these Red Knots are moving northwards to their breeding grounds in the central Canadian Arctic, the timing of departure from the stopover sites becomes increasingly synchronized, and at the last stopover site in Delaware Bay, departure for the breeding grounds occurs within a period of a few days (Myers 1986, Clark *et al.* 1993). Here, in Delaware Bay, Red Knots feed almost exclusively on a superabundant supply of eggs of spawning horseshoe crabs *Limulus polyphemus* (Castro & Myers 1993, Tsipoura & Burger 1999). This has traditionally enabled them to approximately double their body mass from 90-120 g on arrival to 180-240 g on departure (Baker *et al.* 2001). At an average rate of mass increase of 4.6 g/day (Piersma *et al.* 2005a), the highest recorded, the birds need to refuel over a period of approximately 17 days. Birds depart from Delaware Bay *en masse* on about 28-30 May each year (Baker *et al.* 2001). Based on an average fat-free mass of 130 g (Piersma 2002), Red Knots need to achieve a departure mass of at least 180-200 g just to cover the costs of the flight to the breeding grounds and to survive an initial few days of snow cover.

Over the past 15 years, there has been a dramatic increase in the commercial fishery of horseshoe crabs by so-called "watermen". This fishery, which provides bait for eel and conch fisheries, began in 1990 and peaked in 1995/96 (Walls *et al.* 2002). There was a six-fold decline in the numbers of horseshoe crabs caught in survey trawls in Delaware Bay by the Delaware Division of Fish and Wildlife (Andres 2003). The analyses by Baker *et al.* (2004) have provided strong evidence that the decline in food resources at this last stopover site during northward migration is negatively impacting the staging *rufa* population. Baker *et al.* (2004) showed that the proportion of well-conditioned Red Knots (200 g or greater) in Delaware Bay near the departure time in late May decreased significantly by 70% between 1997/98 and 2000/02. Within 2-3 days of the mass departure for the Arctic, mean body masses declined from 183 g in 1997 to 162 g in 2002. The annual survival of birds marked and re-sighted in Tierra del

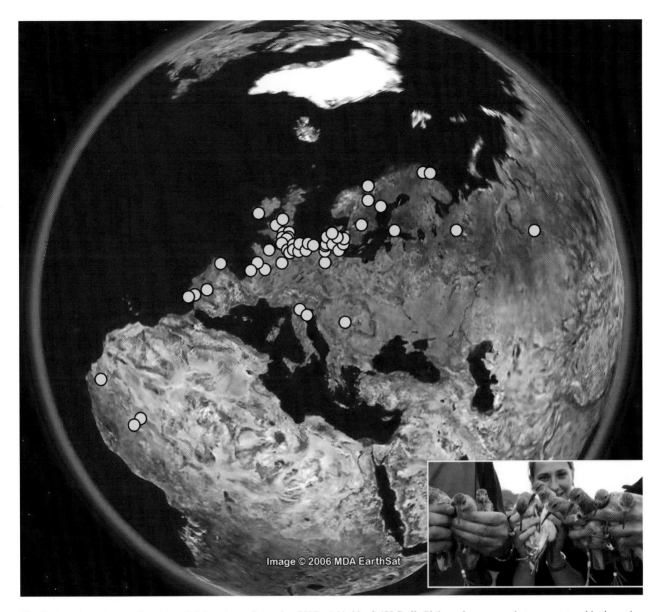

Image © 2006 MDA EarthSat

**Fig. 3.** Locations of recoveries and re-sightings (up to December 2005) yielded by 2 400 Ruffs *Philomachus pugnax* that were captured in the spring of 2004 and 2005 in south-west Fryslân, The Netherlands, and marked with individual colour-ring combinations.

Fuego and Patagonia declined significantly from an average of 87% in the three migration years from 1994/95 to 1997/98 to 55% in the ensuing three year period to 2000/01 (Baker *et al.* 2004). On the basis of a larger mark-recapture data set for the whole flyway (Tierra del Fuego, Patagonia, southern Brazil and Delaware Bay) for the period 1993/94 to 2001/02, Baker *et al.* (2004) detected a similar large decline in annual survival, and pinpointed it to after the birds left Delaware Bay in 2000.

The increases in annual mortality were reflected in the aerial censuses of the non-breeding flocks in Tierra del Fuego: there were 51 000 Red Knots in February 2000, 37 000 in February 2001 and 27 000 in January 2002 (Morrison *et al.* 2004), confirming the large mortality in 2000. The peak count of Red Knots during the stopover in Delaware Bay in May 2000 was only 5 000 lower than the peak count in 1999, again suggesting that the largest loss of birds occurred after departure from this key site. A demographic model suggested that if the 1997/98 to 2000/2001 levels of annual survival were to prevail, *rufa* knots would reach extremely low numbers by 2010 (Baker *et al.* 2004). The aerial census data collected on the non-breeding

grounds in Tierra del Fuego (Morrison *et al.* 2004, pers. comm.) have so far confirmed this doomsday scenario.

The over-harvesting of horseshoe crabs in Delaware Bay has led Red Knots to concentrate their feeding activity on fewer and fewer sites where crab eggs are still abundant. The increasing dependence of birds on so few vulnerable areas and the increasing proportion of birds in poor condition at the time of departure now seem to threaten the viability of the *rufa* subspecies.

## SHOREBIRDS AS INTEGRATIVE SENTINELS OF GLOBAL ENVIRONMENTAL CHANGE

As the two foregoing case studies have shown, even shorebirds that embrace the entire globe within their migration routes provide us with information about local environmental changes. At the same time, they integrate phenomena at larger spatial scales. As proposed by Piersma & Lindström (2004), variations in the number, phenotype and behaviour of particular shorebirds could help provide us with biological "integrators" of global environmental information in ways that no network of observers could realistically ever give us. Weather stations and GIS analyses of land use can tell us about ongoing changes, but bird populations integrate this information in potentially insightful and surprising ways. To illustrate the use of shorebirds as integrative sentinels of our changing world, I will now briefly introduce a third case, involving long-term studies of a species that is doing rather well, the Eurasian Golden Plover *Pluvialis apricaria*. Annual catches of 2 000-3 000 Golden Plovers that make autumn and spring stopovers in The Netherlands have enabled us to monitor their breeding success (a likely function of body condition in spring, summer weather and predator densities) (Jukema *et al.* 2001). We have also been able to follow changes in the degree of stopover site philopatry (a function of the quality of the staging area in terms of food and predation risk), condition and moult in autumn (a function of the food quality at the staging area, that is itself partly weather dependent), timing of southward migration (possibly a function of the quality of the staging area and weather), wintering area (a function of weather, food and predators further south), alternative staging sites in spring (a function of weather and food), condition and moult in spring (a function of weather, food and predation risk), and population size (a demographic function of "everything" listed above) (Jukema *et al.* 2001, Piersma *et al.* 2005b).

Thus, even with relatively simple programmes such as this, we can monitor life cycles that integrate environmental factors from the whole of western and northern Europe. It would be even more informative if sets of complementary species were monitored in similar ways. For example, inclusion of the Northern Lapwing *Vanellus vanellus* and Ruff *Philomachus pugnax* in the comparison would enable us to distinguish between environmental changes on the breeding grounds (the three species breed in different habitats) and on the wintering grounds (the Northern Lapwing and Eurasian Golden Plover winter in Europe, the Ruff in tropical Africa) or en route (they show considerable overlap in the staging areas). Inclusion of shorebird species frequenting intertidal staging areas, such as the Red Knot and Bar-tailed Godwit *Limosa lapponica*, would further increase the scope for relevant comparisons and enable the rejection of more competing explanatory hypotheses. If the Eurasian Golden Plover, Red Knot and Bar-tailed Godwit all showed population declines, but Ruff and Northern Lapwing did not, changes occurring in the northern dry tundra might provide a suitable explanation, especially if the percentage of juveniles in the catches was low. However, if only the Ruff decreased, we would seek changes in the environmental conditions in the Sahel region of Africa, especially if such a decline coincided with reduced survival rates, late arrival in spring, and arriving birds that were lean and showed little development of their nuptial plumage.

Thus, in a comparative framework, the failures and fortunes of migrating shorebirds could be highly informative about the state of their world as well as ours (Piersma & Spaans 2004). In the case of the Ruff, my research team at the University of Groningen recently individually colour-marked as many as 2 400 birds over two spring seasons. All these birds were captured by traditional methods by artisanal bird-catchers (the "wilsternetters"), a group of ringers that also keeps a tally of Eurasian Golden Plovers (Jukema *et al.* 2001). Observers over much of Europe and in West Africa ensured that within a short period of time quite a comprehensive picture of the flyway of Ruffs staging in the west of the province of Fryslân was built up (Fig. 3; Piersma 2006). The fact

that this has been achieved within two years of study also means that we should be able to document changes in flyways in real time; flyway changes that, as we have seen, may often be a consequence of human-induced habitat loss and modification.

## ACKNOWLEDGEMENTS

I am grateful to Gerard Boere and David Stroud for inviting me to contribute to the Edinburgh Conference and to Gerard for being an understanding but persistent compiler of the proceedings. I thank my dear colleagues in the wader world for providing such a congenial social and intellectual environment in which to worry about the future of the earth's biota, and to jointly do as much as we can to turn the tide.

## REFERENCES

**Andres, B.A.** 2003. Delaware Bay Shorebird-Horseshoe Crab Assessment Report – Biological Assessment Shorebird Technical Committee. U.S. Fish and Wildlife Service, Division of Migratory Bird Management, Arlington, Virginia, USA.

**Atkinson, P.W., Clark, N.A., Bell, M.C., Dare, P.J., Clark, J.A. & Ireland, P.L.** 2003. Changes in commercially fished shellfish stocks and shorebird populations in the Wash, England. Biological Conservation 114: 127-141.

**Atkinson, P.W., Baker, A.J., Bevan, R.M., Clark, N.A., Cole, K.B., Gonzalez, P.M., Newton, J., Niles, L.J. & Robinson, R.A.** 2005. Unravelling the migration and moult strategies of a long-distance migrant using stable isotopes: Red Knot *Calidris canutus* movements in the Americas. Ibis 147: 738-749.

**Baker, A.J., Piersma, T. & Rosenmeier, L.** 1994. Unraveling the intraspecific phylogeography of Knots *Calidris canutus*: a progress report on the search for genetic markers. Journal für Ornithologie 135: 599-608.

**Baker, A.J., González, P.M., Minton, C.D.T., Carter, D.B., Niles, L.J., do Nascimiento, I. & Piersma, T.** 2001. Hemispheric problems in the conservation of Red Knots (*Calidris canutus rufa*). In: Proceedings of the VI Neotropical Ornithological Congress, International Shorebird Symposium, Monterrey, Mexico. Western Hemisphere Shorebird Reserve Network, Manomet, Massachusetts, USA: 21-28.

**Baker, A.J., González, P.M., Piersma, T., Niles, L.J., de Lima Serrano do Nascimento, I., Atkinson, P.W., Clark, N.A., Minton, C.D.T., Peck, M.K. & Aarts, G.** 2004. Rapid population decline in red knots: fitness consequences of decreased refuelling rates and late arrival in Delaware Bay. Proceedings of the Royal Society of London B 271: 875-882.

**Battley, P.F. & Piersma, T.** 2005. Adaptive interplay between feeding ecology and features of the digestive tract in birds. In: J.M. Starck & T. Wang (eds) Physiological and Ecological Adaptations to Feeding in Vertebrates. Science Publishers, Enfield, New Hampshire: 201-228.

**Battley, P.F., Rogers, D.I., van Gils, J.A., Piersma, T., Hassell, C.J., Boyle, A. & Hong-Yan, Y.** 2005. How do red knots leave Northwest Australia in May and reach the breeding grounds in June? Predictions of stopover times, fuelling rates and prey quality in the Yellow Sea. Journal of Avian Biology 36: 494-500.

**Buehler, D.M. & Baker, A.J.** 2005. Population divergence times and historical demography in Red Knots and Dunlins. Condor 107: 497-513.

**Buehler, D.M., Baker, A.J. & Piersma, T.** 2006. Reconstructing palaeoflyways of the late Pleistocene and early Holocene Red Knot (*Calidris canutus*). Ardea 94. In press.

**Castro, G. & Myers, J.P.** 1993. Shorebird predation on eggs of horseshoe crabs during spring stopover on Delaware Bay. Auk 110: 927-930.

**Clark, K.E., Niles, L.J. & Burger, J.** 1993. Abundance and distribution of migrant shorebirds in Delaware Bay. Condor 95: 694-705.

**Coleman, F.C. & Williams, S.L.** 2002. Overexploiting marine ecosystem engineers: potential consequences for biodiversity. Trends in Ecology & Evolution 17: 40-44.

**Davidson, N.C. & Wilson, J.R.** 1992. The migration-system of European-wintering Knots *Calidris canutus islandica*. Wader Study Group Bulletin 64, Supplement: 39-51.

**Dayton, P.K.** 2003. The importance of the natural sciences to conservation. American Naturalist 162: 1-13.

**Dekinga, A., Dietz, M.W., Koolhaas, A. & Piersma, T.** 2001. Time course and reversibility of changes in the gizzards of Red Knots alternatively eating hard and soft food. Journal of Experimental Biology 204: 2167-2173.

**Drent, J., Luttikhuizen, P.C. & Piersma, T.** 2004. Morphological dynamics in the foraging apparatus of a deposit feeding marine bivalve: phenotypic plasticity and heritable effects. Functional Ecology 18: 349-356.

**Gill, R.E., Jr., Piersma, T., Hufford, G., Servranckx, R. & Riegen, A.** 2005. Crossing the ultimate ecological barrier: evidence for an 11000-km-long nonstop flight from Alaska to New Zealand and Eastern Australia by bar-tailed godwits. Condor 107: 1-20.

**Hall, S.J. & Harding, M.J.C.** 1997. Physical disturbance and marine benthic communities: The effects of mechanical harvesting of cockles on non-target benthic infauna. Journal of Applied Ecology 34: 497-517.

**Hiddink, J.G.** 2003. Effects of suction-dredging for cockles on non-target fauna in the Wadden Sea. Journal of Sea Research 50: 315-323.

**International Wader Study Group** 2003. Waders are declining worldwide. Wader Study Group Bulletin 101/102: 8-12.

**Jackson, J.B.C. and 19 co-authors.** 2001. Historical over-fishing and the recent collapse of coastal ecosystems. Science 293: 629-638.

**Jukema, J., Piersma, T., Hulscher, J.B., Bunskoeke, E.J., Koolhaas, A. & Veenstra, A.** 2001. Golden Plovers and wilsternetters: a deeply rooted fascination with migrating birds. Fryske Akademy, Ljouwert/KNNV Uitgeverij, Utrecht.

**Kamermans, P. & Smaal, A.C.** 2002. Mussel culture and cockle fisheries in The Netherlands: finding a balance between economy and ecology. Journal of Shellfish Research 21: 509-517.

**Kraan, C., Piersma, T., Dekinga, A., Koolhaas, A. & van der Meer, J.** 2006. Large-scale cockle dredging: short-term consequences of selecting intertidal flats with greatest benthic biodiversity. Submitted MS.

**Morrison, R.I.G., Ross, R.K. & Niles, L.J.** 2004. Declines in wintering populations of Red Knots in southern South America. Condor 109: 60-70.

**Myers, J.P.** 1986. Sex and gluttony on Delaware Bay. Natural History 95: 68-77.

**Nebel, S., Piersma, T., van Gils, J., Dekinga, A. & Spaans, B.** 2000. Length of stopover, fuel storage and a sex-bias in the occurrence of Red Knots *Calidris c. canutus* and *C. c. islandica* in the Wadden Sea during southward migration. Ardea 88: 165-176.

**Piersma, T.** 2002. Energetic bottlenecks and other design constraints in avian annual cycles. Integrative and Comparative Biology 42: 51-67.

**Piersma, T.** 2006. Animal ecology: habitat choice and changing numbers of animals in a changing world. Inaugural Lecture, University of Groningen, The Netherlands.

**Piersma, T. & Baker, A.J.** 2000. Life history characteristics and the conservation of migratory shorebirds. In: L.M. Gosling & W.J. Sutherland (eds) Behaviour and conservation. Cambridge University Press, Cambridge: 105-124.

**Piersma, T. & Davidson, N.C.** (eds). 1992. The Migration of Knots. Wader Study Group Bulletin 64 (Supplement).

**Piersma, T. & Lindström, Å.** 2004. Migrating shorebirds as integrative sentinels of global environmental change. Ibis 146, Supplement 1: 61-69.

**Piersma, T. & Spaans, B.** 2004. Insights from comparisons: ecological research on shorebirds worldwide. Limosa 77: 43-54.

**Piersma, T., van Gils, J., de Goeij, P. & van der Meer, J.** 1995. Holling's functional response model as a tool to link the food-finding mechanism of a probing shorebird with its spatial distribution. Journal of Animal Ecology 64: 493-504.

**Piersma, T., van Aelst, R., Kurk, K., Berkhoudt, H. & Maas, L.R.M.** 1998. A new pressure sensory mechanism for prey detection in birds: the use of principles of seabed dynamics? Proceedings of the Royal Society of London B 265: 1377-1383.

**Piersma, T., Gudmundsson, G.A. & Lilliendahl, K.** 1999. Rapid changes in the size of different functional organ and muscle groups during refueling in a long-distance migrating shorebird. Physiological & Biochemical Zoology 72: 405-415.

**Piersma, T., Koolhaas, A., Dekinga, A., Beukema, J.J., Dekker, R. & Essink, K.** 2001. Long-term indirect effects of mechanical cockle dredging on intertidal bivalve stocks in the Wadden Sea. Journal of Applied Ecology 38: 976-990.

**Piersma, T., Rogers, D.I., González, P.M., Zwarts, L., Niles, L.J., de Lima Serrano do Nascimento, I., Minton, C.D.T. & Baker, A.J.** 2005a. Fuel storage rates before northward flights in red knots worldwide: facing the severest constraint in tropical intertidal environments? In: R. Greenberg & P.P. Marra (eds) Birds of two worlds: the ecology and evolution of migration. Johns Hopkins University Press, Baltimore: 262-273.

**Piersma, T., Rogers, K.G., Boyd, H., Bunskoeke, E.J. & Jukema, J.** 2005b. Demography of Eurasian golden plovers *Pluvialis apricaria* staging in The Netherlands, 1949-2000. Ardea 93: 49-64.

**Reneerkens, J., Piersma, T. & Spaans, B.** 2005. De Waddenzee als kruispunt van vogeltrekwegen. Literatuurstudie naar de kansen en bedreigingen van wadvogels in internationaal perspectief. NIOZ-report 2005-4, Texel.

**Rossi, F., Herman, P.M.J. & Middelburg, J.J.** 2004. Interspecific and intraspecific variation of delta13C and delta15N in deposit- and suspension-feeding bivalves (*Macoma balthica* and *Cerastoderma edule*): evidence of ontogenetic changes in feeding mode of *Macoma balthica*. Limnology & Oceanography 49: 408-414.

**Stroud, D.A., Baker, A., Daniel Blanco, D.E., Davidson, N.C., Delany, S., Ganter, B., Gill, R., González, P., Haanstra, L., Morrison, R.I.G., Piersma, T., Scott, D.A., Thorup, O., West, R., Wilson, J. & Zöckler, C. (on behalf of the International Wader Study Group,** 2006. The conservation and population status of the world's shorebirds at the turn of the millennium. Waterbirds around the world. G.C. Boere, C.A. Galbraith & D.A. Stroud (Eds.), The Stationery Office, Edinburgh, UK. 643-648.

**Tomkovich, P.S.** 1992. An analysis of the geographic variability in Knots *Calidris canutus* based on museum skins. Wader Study Group Bulletin 64, Supplement: 17-23.

**Tomkovich, P.S.** 2001. A new subspecies of Red Knot *Calidris canutus* from the New Siberian islands. Bulletin British Ornithologists' Club 121: 257-263.

**Tsipoura, N. & Burger, J.** 1999. Shorebird diet during spring migration stopover on Delaware Bay. Condor 101: 635-644.

**van de Kam, J., Ens, B.J., Piersma, T. & Zwarts, L.** 2004. Shorebirds: an illustrated behavioural ecology. KNNV Publishers, Utrecht.

**van Gils, J.A., Piersma, T., Dekinga, A. & Dietz, M.W.** 2003. Cost-benefit analysis of mollusc-eating in a shorebird. II.

Optimizing gizzard size in the face of seasonal demands. Journal of Experimental Biology 206: 3369-3380.

**van Gils, J.A., de Rooij, S.R., van Belle, J., van der Meer, J., Dekinga, A., Piersma, T. & Drent, R.** 2005a. Digestive bottleneck affects foraging decisions in Red Knots *Calidris canutus*. I. Prey choice. Journal of Animal Ecology 74: 105-119.

**van Gils, J.A., Battley, P.F., Piersma, T. & Drent, R.** 2005b. Reinterpretation of gizzard sizes of Red Knots worldwide emphasizes overriding importance of prey quality at migratory stopover sites. Proceedings of the Royal Society B 272: 2609-2618.

**van Gils, J.A., Piersma, T., Dekinga, A., Spaans, B. & Kraan, C.** 2006a. Shellfish-dredging pushes a flexible avian top predator out of a protected marine ecosystem. Public Library of Science-Biology (PLOS).

**van Gils, J.A., Spaans, B., Dekinga, A. & Piersma, T.** 2006b. Foraging in a tidally structured environment by Red Knots (*Calidris canutus*): ideal, but not free. Ecology 87: 1189-1202.

**van Roomen, M., van Turnhout, C., van Winden, E., Koks, B., Goedhart, P., Leopold, M. & Smit, C.J.** 2005. Trends in benthivorous waterbirds in the Dutch Wadden Sea 1975-2002: large differences between shellfish-eaters and worm-eaters. Limosa 78: 21-38.

**Verhulst, S., Ens, B.J., Oosterbeek, K. & Rutten, A.L.** 2004. Shellfish fishery severely reduces condition and survival of Oystercatchers despite creation of large marine protected areas. Ecology & Society 9: published online.

**Walls, E.A., Berkson, J. & Smith, S.A.** 2002. The horseshoe crab, *Limulus polyphemus*: 200 million years of existence, 100 years of study. Reviews of Fisheries Science 10: 39-73.

**Zwarts, L. & Blomert, A.-M.** 1992. Why Knots *Calidris canutus* take medium-sized *Macoma balthica* when six prey species are available. Marine Ecology Progress Series 83: 113-128.

Red Knots *Calidris canutus rufa* feeding on the eggs of Horseshoe Crabs *Limulus polyphemus* in Delaware Bay, USA. Photo: Rob Robinson.

# Successes and challenges of promoting conservation of migratory waterbirds and wetlands in the Asia-Pacific region: nine years of a regional strategy

*Taej Mundkur*

*Strategy Coordinator, Wetlands International, 3A39, Block A, Kelana Centre Point, Jalan SS7/19, Petaling Jaya, 47301 Selangor, Malaysia.*
*Present address: Strategy Coordinator, Wetlands International - South Asia, A-25, 2nd Floor, Defence Colony, New Delhi - 110 024, India. (email: taejmundkur.wi@vsnl.net)*

Mundkur, T. 2006. Successes and challenges of promoting conservation of migratory waterbirds and wetlands in the Asia-Pacific region: nine years of a regional strategy. *Waterbirds around the world.* Eds. G.C. Boere, C.A. Galbraith & D.A. Stroud. The Stationery Office, Edinburgh, UK. pp. 81-87.

## ABSTRACT

The Asia-Pacific Migratory Waterbird Conservation Strategy is an international cooperative initiative for the conservation of migratory waterbirds and wetlands, involving governments, conventions, NGOs and local people. Launched in 1996, the Strategy is coordinated by a free-standing international committee, comprising representatives of governments, the Ramsar Convention, CMS, UNDP/GEF, UNEP, NGOs and technical experts. The Strategy provides a framework for the development and implementation of action plans for migratory waterbird species (Anatidae, cranes and shorebirds) in the East Asian-Australasian region, and through it, networks of internationally important sites have been developed. These networks serve as a focus for site-based conservation efforts, including networking, training, awareness raising, research and sound management of wetlands, through international cooperation and resource mobilization. Based on the successes during the period 1996-2000, the Strategy was renewed for a second five-year period (2001-2005). An Action Plan for the Central Asian Flyway is being developed as a framework for this region. The Strategy is recognized by the Ramsar Convention on Wetlands and the Convention on Migratory Species of Wild Animals through a number of Resolutions. This paper presents a review of the approaches used in the initiative, its successes and challenges, in a region dominated by developing countries.

## INTRODUCTION

The Asia-Pacific region is home to over 243 migratory waterbird species, including 49 threatened species. The region also contains over half the world's human population and the highest economic growth rates in the world, creating enormous pressures on wetlands and other natural habitats. Efforts to promote international cooperation have been ongoing through a range of different programmes. However, the outcome of an international meeting organized in Kushiro, Japan, in December 1994 and attended by government representatives, convention representatives and technical experts from across the East Asian-Australasian region was a turning point in the development of an international cooperative framework as outlined in the "Kushiro Statement". The Asia-Pacific Migratory Waterbird Conservation Strategy (Anonymous 1996) was launched in conjunction with the Sixth Conference of the Parties to the Ramsar Convention in Brisbane, Australia, in 1996, as a five-year regional initiative to enhance the long-term conservation of migratory waterbirds and their wetland habitats involving governments, conventions, NGOs and local people. With a primary focus on the East Asian-

Australasian Flyway and on three groups of migratory species (Anatidae, cranes and shorebirds), a wide range of activities were undertaken to promote conservation. Flyway Action Plans served as the main tool in promoting conservation activities in the region, and networks of internationally important waterbird sites (established for shorebirds in 1996, cranes in 1997 and Anatidae in 1999) have provided a framework for site-based management, education and training activities.

Based on the success of the Strategy in its first five years, an international conference held in Okinawa, Japan, in October 2000 called for the continuation of the Strategy (as embodied in the "Okinawa Statement"), and recommended that countries in the region should enhance mechanisms for collaborative action to conserve waterbird species and their habitats, specifically through: (1) action plans for species groups and globally threatened species; and (2) effectively managed networks of sites that are internationally important for migratory waterbirds.

As a consequence, a second five-year Strategy was launched in 2001 and concluded in 2005 (Asia-Pacific Migratory Waterbird Conservation Committee 2001). Discussions are now focused on developing frameworks for post 2005, through the development of a stronger partnership framework linked to a WSSD Type II initiative to conserve migratory waterbirds in the East Asian-Australasian Flyway, and development of an Action Plan for migratory waterbirds and their habitats in the Central Asian Flyway.

The philosophy of the Strategy and the process of its development were first described by Mundkur & Matsui (1997) and Weaver (1997). Reviews of the Strategy and its achievements were presented at the first and second International Conference on Wetlands and Development held in Malaysia in November 1996 and Senegal in November 1998, and reported in Mundkur & Matsui (1998) and Mundkur *et al.* (1999), respectively. This paper is the fifth in the series; it outlines the scope of the current Strategy, and provides a review of the approaches used in the initiative, its successes and challenges, in a region dominated by developing countries.

## SCOPE OF THE STRATEGY

### Geographic area and flyways

The Asia-Pacific region, as defined by the main migratory routes of waterbirds, extends from the Urals across Siberia to Alaska (USA) and southwards across East, Central, South and South-east Asia, Australasia and the Pacific islands, and covers about 57 countries and territories.

Within this region, there are three main migratory waterbird flyways, the Central Asian, East Asian-Australasian and Central Pacific. Some species and species groups have smaller flyway ranges within these broader flyways. In addition, some of the major flyways that extend into Europe, Africa and the Americas also have their origins in the northern latitudes of continental Asia. Here they converge with the flyways of the Asia-Pacific region and overlap in many important breeding, moulting and staging sites.

Conservation of migratory waterbirds in the adjoining flyways is covered by the African-Eurasian Waterbird Agreement (AEWA) under the Convention on Migratory Species of Wild Animals, and the North American Waterfowl Management Plan (NAWMP) and Western Hemisphere Shorebird Reserve Network (WHSRN) in the Americas. The Strategy thus complements these major frameworks to conserve the migratory waterbirds of the world.

## Waterbird species

The Strategy adopts the Ramsar Convention definition of waterbirds, i.e. "birds ecologically dependent on wetlands" (Ramsar Convention Secretariat 2002), with the exception of the wetland-related raptors (Accipitriformes and Falconiformes), coucals (Cuculiformes) and wetland-related owls (Strigiformes), and covers twenty groups of waterbirds (see Table 1 for a list of families). It covers 243 waterbird species, including 49 globally threatened species (BirdLife International 2001, 2003, Wetlands International 2002). Some of these threatened species, such as Oriental White Stork *Ciconia boyciana*, Swan Goose *Anser cygnoides*, Scaly-sided Merganser *Mergus squamatus*, Nordmann's Greenshank *Tringa nordmanni* and Spoon-billed Sandpiper *Eurynorhynchus pygmeus*, are restricted to the Asia-Pacific region.

### Table 1. Waterbird families included in the Asia-Pacific Migratory Waterbird Strategy.

| Taxonomic group | English name |
| --- | --- |
| Gaviidae | Divers (loons) |
| Podicipedidae | Grebes |
| Phalacrocoracidae | Cormorants |
| Pelecanidae | Pelicans |
| Ardeidae | Herons, egrets and bitterns |
| Ciconiidae | Storks |
| Threskiornithidae | Ibises and spoonbills |
| Phoenicopteridae | Flamingos |
| Anatidae | Swans, geese and ducks |
| Gruidae | Cranes |
| Rallidae | Rails, gallinules and coots |
| Heliornithidae | Finfoots |
| Jacanidae | Jacanas |
| Dromadidae | Crab Plover |
| Haematopodidae | Oystercatchers |
| Recurvirostridae | Stilts and avocet |
| Glareolidae | Pratincoles |
| Charadriidae | Plovers |
| Scolopacidae | Sandpipers |
| Laridae | Gulls, terns and skimmers |

Note: Shorebirds (waders) include jacanas, Crab Plover *Dromas ardeola*, oyster-catchers, stilts and Avocet, pratincoles, plovers and sandpipers.

### Table 2. Priority areas of the Asia-Pacific Migratory Waterbird Conservation Strategy: 1996-2000.

**Conservation of habitats**
  Enhancement of site conservation
  Establishment of flyway reserve networks
**Conservation of species**
  Development and implementation of migratory waterbird conservation action plans
  Promotion of the sustainable management of migratory waterbirds
**Research and monitoring**
  Promotion of conservation-oriented monitoring and research activities
  Establishment of advanced migratory waterbird and wetland information storage and retrieval systems
**Education, information and awareness**
  Increased education and public awareness
  Promotion of information flow among waterbird and wetland conservation researchers
  Training of personnel associated with the survey, study and management of waterbirds and their habitats
**Policy and legislation**
  Review and strengthening of waterbird and habitat conservation policies and legislation
  Development of an Asia-Pacific Multilateral Migratory Waterbird Conservation Agreement

The Strategy has taken the approach of promoting the conservation of groups of waterbirds, focussing its efforts primarily on three groups, Anatidae (ducks, geese and swans), shorebirds (or waders) and cranes in the East Asian-Australasian region under three species-group Action Plans. In addition, it has served as a framework to promote conservation of globally threatened species.

## Coordination

The Strategy is coordinated by an international committee, the Asia-Pacific Migratory Waterbird Conservation Committee (MWCC), comprising representatives of governments, the Ramsar Convention on Wetlands, the Convention on Migratory Species of Wild Animals (CMS), UNDP/GEF, UNEP and three international NGOs, as well as the Chairs of the Anatidae, Crane and Shorebird Working Groups and a representative of Wetlands International's Specialist Groups (19 members as at April 2004). The MWCC is currently chaired and co-chaired by Australia and Japan, respectively. The MWCC maintains overall responsibility for coordinating, monitoring and reporting on implementation of the Strategy, fund raising, development of projects, and overseeing activities of the Strategy Coordinator.

A Strategy Coordinator provides secretariat support to the Committee and liaison with the Working Groups. Three Flyway Officers coordinate implementation of the three action plans in the East Asian-Australasian Flyway. A Central Asian Flyway Officer coordinates development of activities in the Central Asian Flyway. Four staff operate from offices of Wetlands International (in Australia, India, Japan and Russia), while the coordinator for cranes is employed by the Wild Bird Society of Japan. Core support has been provided by the Australian Department of the Environment and Heritage, Ministry of the Environment, Japan,

**Table 3.** Overview of actions implemented that contribute to achieving outcomes of the Asia-Pacific Migratory Waterbird Conservation Strategy: 2001-2005.

| Elements | Selected actions undertaken and outcomes achieved |
| --- | --- |
| 1. Action plans for species groups and globally threatened species. | • Action Plans for Anatidae, cranes and shorebirds in the East Asian-Australasian Flyway updated for 2001-2005.<br>• North East Asian Crane Action Plan and Site Network extended to cover conservation action for the globally threatened Oriental White Stork *Ciconia boyciana*.<br>• International task forces established to develop conservation plans for selected globally threatened species:<br> – Swan Goose *Anser cygnoides*<br> – Baikal Teal *Anas formosa*<br> – Spoon-billed Sandpiper *Eurynorhynchus pygmeus*<br>• Synergies developed with the UNEP/GEF/ICF Siberian Crane *Grus leucogeranus* project in two flyways across Asia.<br>• Coordination improved with monitoring and conservation groups for the threatened Black-faced Spoonbill *Platalea minor* in East Asia.<br>• Current status of the threatened White-headed Duck *Oxyura leucocephala* in Central Asia assessed.<br>• Increased marking and study of movements of the threatened Saunders's Gull *Larus saundersi* in East Asia. |
| 2. Effectively managed networks of sites that are internationally important for migratory waterbirds. | • Site Networks for Anatidae, cranes and shorebirds in the East Asian-Australasian Flyway, established during 1996-1999, have been strengthened by the addition of internationally important sites (as at April 2004, the networks covered 80 sites in 13 countries – see table 4).<br>• Increased visibility and recognition of sites at national and international level.<br>• Range of activities undertaken at network sites (and other important sites) including:<br> – Public awareness and information dissemination<br> – Management planning of sites<br> – Training courses for site managers<br> – Field surveys at network sites and other important sites<br> – Monitoring and migration studies of waterbirds<br> – Art exhibitions on nature<br> – Crane Research Handbook of Field Study and Shorebird Study Manual produced and widely used. |
| 3. Raised awareness of waterbirds and their link to wetland values and functions throughout the region and at all levels. | • A range of educational and awareness resources produced in many languages.<br>• Annual awareness-related activities promoted and implemented across the region, at network sites and other important areas, involving a wide range of stakeholders including politicians, government officials, school and college students, and local people at network sites.<br>• Awareness-related activities linked and integrated with national and international events such as World Wetlands Day (2 February).<br>• Wetland centres promoted and facilitated to implement awareness raising activities. |
| 4. Increased capacity of government agencies and non-governmental organizations to implement conservation actions for migratory waterbirds. | • Securing of government and other funding support for conservation, public awareness, education and research activities at the site, national and international level.<br>• Identification of new sites of national and international importance through survey activities.<br>• Strengthening of local capacity to manage wetland and waterbird conservation through organization of training courses.<br>• Study tours and visits organized for network site stakeholders nationally and internationally to build linkages and improve understanding of management and conservation practices.<br>• Increased involvement of community and children in the study and conservation of waterbirds and wetlands. |
| 5. Developed knowledge base and facilitated information exchange for the sound management of migratory waterbirds and their habitats. | • Regional waterbird and habitat monitoring programmes such as the Asian Waterbird Census strengthened through building of national networks (coordinated by Wetlands International).<br>• Improved cooperation on the study of migratory routes of waterbirds through adoption of flyway-wide colour marking schemes, such as through development of the Asia-Pacific Shorebird Colour Flagging Protocol.<br>• Development of a Science Action Plan for the Dunlin *Calidris alpina*.<br>• Up-to-date information on waterbirds, threats and conservation priorities collected and disseminated as technical and non-technical information through a range of media in English and several Asian languages.<br>• Publication of important regional information sources on waterbirds and wetlands including: Threatened Birds of Asia: the BirdLife International Red Data Book (2001) and Saving Asia's threatened Birds: a guide for government and civil society (2003) by BirdLife International, and Waterbird Population Estimates – Third edition (2002) and Numbers and distribution of waterbirds and wetlands in the Asia-Pacific region. Results of the Asian Waterbird Census: 1997-2001 (2004) by Wetlands International[1]. |

---

[1] This publication was formally launched at the Waterbirds around the world Conference.

**Table 3 (cont). Overview of actions implemented that contribute to achieving outcomes of the Asia-Pacific Migratory Waterbird Conservation Strategy: 2001-2005.**

| Elements | Selected actions undertaken and outcomes achieved |
|---|---|
| 5. Developed knowledge base and facilitated information exchange for the sound management of migratory waterbirds and their habitats. (Continued) | • Development of four web-sites dedicated to informing the public about activities and issues relating to waterbird conservation.<br>• Establishment of list servers and e-groups to promote information exchange on waterbird and wetland issues amongst people within the Asia-Pacific region (and globally).<br>• Organization of international and national training courses and meetings to share expertise and information on waterbird and habitat management issues. |
| 6. Harmonized national and state policies and legislation as a foundation for the conservation of migratory waterbirds and their habitats. | • Promotion of increased implementation of policies and legislation in response to resolutions and programmes of global conventions dealing with migratory waterbirds and their habitats:<br>A. Ramsar Convention<br>– Rec. VI.4. The "Brisbane Initiative" on the establishment of a network of listed sites along the East Asian-Australasian Flyway.<br>– Rec. VII.3. Multilateral cooperation on the conservation of migratory waterbirds in the Asia-Pacific region.<br>– Res. VII.21. Enhancing the conservation and wise use of intertidal wetlands.<br>– Res. VIII.37. International cooperation on conservation of migratory waterbirds and their habitats in the Asia-Pacific region.<br>B. Convention on Migratory Species of Wild Animals<br>– Res. 5.4. To take an active role in the development of a conservation initiative for migratory waterbirds of the Central Asian-Indian Flyway.<br>– Res. 6.4. CMS Strategic Action Plan and companion document UNEP/CMS/Conf. 6.12 called on Parties to support and provide input to the Strategy: 1996-2000 and *"future related initiatives that may lead, at an appropriate time, to a formal multilateral Agreement among States of the region, under the auspices of CMS"*.<br>C. Convention on Biological Diversity<br>– Programme of Work on Protected Areas<br>• Increased interaction with regional bodies (e.g. ASEAN and SACEP) to promote regional conservation programmes and action.<br>• Support provided to review and update national policies and legislation on waterbirds and habitats through local and national activities. |
| 7. Enhanced organizational relationships at all levels to increase cooperation and deliver greater conservation benefits. | • Promoting awareness and support for the Strategy at a national and local level.<br>• Seeking greater cooperation of all stakeholders (governments, research institutes, development agencies, business sector, local communities and others).<br>• Implementation of actions outlined in the Strategy and species-group Action Plans through involvement of all stakeholders.<br>• Strengthening the roles of NGOs in implementation of the Strategy.<br>• Reporting on progress on implementation to meetings of the Ramsar Convention, CMS, BirdLife International and Wetlands International. |
| 8. Adequate planning and resources to implement the Strategy. | • Strengthening of international coordination and communication through regular meetings of the MWCC involving a range of stakeholders.<br>• Team of strategy and flyway coordination officers engaged to coordinate implementation of activities.<br>• Resources implemented for activities from an increasing range of government, corporate, non-governmental and private partners and supporters. |

U.S. Fish and Wildlife Service and Government of The Netherlands.

Originally established under the aegis of the Wetlands International – Asia Pacific Council, in 2003 the MWCC became a free-standing committee that reports directly to the Ramsar Convention, CMS, BirdLife International and Wetlands International.

**Focus of the Strategy**

The two Strategies have aimed to respond broadly to the issues of habitat destruction and loss, species declines, low public awareness and support, and limited institutional capacity to manage and monitor waterbirds and their habitats. The Strategy 1996-2000 was structured along six broad and overlapping themes with a total of 11 objectives and a number of priority actions defined for each objective (Table 2). Based on the experience of assessing the progress that had been made during these first five years, the MWCC restructured the Strategy 2001-2005 such that it was presented as eight key elements with a number of expected outcomes for each element (Table 3). In recognition of the challenges and time needed for the development of a formal international agreement without strong interest and commitment from the many governments concerned, no specific action to develop such an agreement was proposed within the timeframe of the second Strategy.

## Achievements to date

The Strategy has called for activities to be undertaken at the international, regional and national level. These activities have primarily been developed separately along the different flyways, although some activities have been more region-wide (such as the monitoring of waterbirds; see Li & Mundkur 2004). A range of activities, including promoting awareness, improving understanding of the migration strategies and conservation needs of waterbirds, and building local capacity to monitor and manage waterbirds and wetlands, have been implemented (Table 3). This work has been achieved largely through encouraging participation of an increasing number and range of stakeholders: governments, NGOs, academe, technical institutions, development agencies, etc. The East Asian-Australasian Flyway has remained the primary region of flyway-wide activities over the last nine years, although during the last few years coordinated work across the Central Asian Flyway has increased.

The three species-group Action Plans prepared during the first Strategy in the East Asian-Australasian Flyway have been reviewed and updated, and have continued to serve as the main tool for implementation of activities (Table 3). The three existing site networks have continued to serve as a focus for site-based conservation efforts for Anatidae, cranes and shorebirds. As at April 2004, thirteen countries, Australia, People's Republic of China, Indonesia, Japan, Democratic People's Republic of Korea, Republic of Korea, Malaysia, Mongolia, New Zealand, Papua New Guinea, Philippines, Russian Federation and Singapore, had nominated eighty sites of international importance for migratory waterbirds to the site networks (Table 4, Fig. 1). Of these, eight sites have been nominated to more than one network in recognition of their importance for multiple waterbird groups. Although the network sites cover both coastal and inland wetland habitats, a slightly larger number are currently coastal wetlands. Fifty-eight percent of the sites are also listed as wetlands of international importance under the Ramsar Convention, enabling a close linkage of many conservation activities under these two frameworks.

To date, many activities in the Central Asian Flyway have focussed on collation of information on waterbird distribution and abundance under the umbrellas of the International Waterbird Census (Gilissen *et al.* 2002) and Asian Waterbird Census (Li & Mundkur 2004), and revitalization of interest and linkages amongst agencies and institutions through rebuilding the capacity of expert networks, especially within the Central Asian countries (see Solokha *et al.*, this volume). The development of a Flyway Action Plan to promote action for all migratory waterbirds was recognized as a priority, and the first major meeting of flyway range states, organized in Tashkent, Uzbekistan, in 2001, has provided an impetus for its development (CMS Secretariat 2001). A follow-up meeting to finalize the Action Plan took place under the aegis of the CMS in New Delhi, India, in 2005.

Over the last few years, new information collected through activities implemented under the Strategy has benefited the production of a number of important global, regional and national reference publications on the status of species and their

**Table 4. Status of the site networks for Anatidae, cranes and shorebirds in the East Asian-Australasian Flyway (as at April 2004).**

| | |
|---|---|
| Total number of sites designated on three networks | 80 |
| • East Asian-Australasian Shorebird Site Network | 35 |
| • North East Asian Crane Site Network | 26 |
| • East Asian Anatidae Site Network | 27 |
| Total number of sites also listed as Ramsar sites | 46 (58%) |
| Number of countries involved in the site networks | 13 |

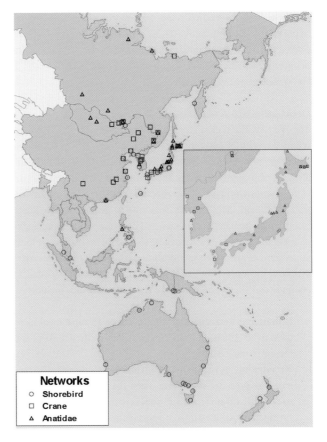

**Fig. 1.** Sites of international importance for migratory waterbirds designated on the Anatidae, Crane and Shorebird Networks in the East Asian-Australasian Flyway (as at April 2004). The inset indicates the network of sites in the Korean Peninsula and Japan.

habitats, such as those by BirdLife International and Wetlands International (Table 3). These references have in turn provided valuable guidance and support for activities and local publications and information resources.

Based on the wide range of activities undertaken during the last nine years, as summarized in Table 3, it is evident that the Strategy has proven to be an important regional initiative with involvement and support from a large number of national and local stakeholders and international partners, including multilateral environmental agreements and non-governmental organizations.

At the international level, the implementation of the Strategy has been widely recognized and supported by two important multilateral environmental agreements, the Ramsar Convention and the CMS. The Conferences of the Parties to these Conventions have passed six resolutions and recommendations at their triennial meetings that support or highlight the main activities of the Strategy (Table 3). In addition, the activities of the Strategy have provided a mechanism for implementing a number of other resolutions of these two Conventions concerning promotion of wetland and species conservation, building local capacity, dissemination of information, monitoring of wetlands and their waterbirds, increasing awareness and public education, etc. The Strategy has also directly contributed to the priorities of the Convention on Biological Diversity, particularly with respect to protected areas, inland wetlands, public awareness and capacity building.

Implementation of the Strategy for migratory waterbirds has benefited resident birds and other wetland species through raised awareness of conservation issues and improved management of important waterbird sites. Thus migratory waterbirds have proved to be an important flagship group that can serve to unite people across the region to promote the conservation of a common heritage and resource.

## CHALLENGES AND PRIORITIES

The Asia-Pacific region is the most populated part of the globe, with a majority of developing countries or countries in transition where the primary focus remains national development, industrialization and improvement of the living standards of the people. Here, the development of conservation initiatives for migratory waterbirds and their habitats is normally given a much lower priority than human development and progress. While implementation of the Strategy has been quite successful in developing local awareness, capacity and interest in waterbird and habitat conservation, a lot more effort, activities and resources are needed to continue and strengthen the work. The main priorities include:

- **Enhancing awareness raising**: Actions to raise awareness need to be enhanced for decision makers, policy makers and the corporate sector.
- **Broadening government involvement**: Government agencies involved to date have been largely limited to the ministries responsible for the environment and forests. Engagement of government agencies responsible for the use and management of wetlands is also needed to enable sustainable development of the wetlands; such agencies include those responsible for water resources, irrigation, agriculture, fisheries, power supply, military, ports, industry, transport, rural development, etc. at the national and sub-national levels.
- **Enhancing species coverage**: The Strategy has focussed on three species groups; additional actions are needed to promote conservation of the ten other species groups covered by the Strategy and the large number of sites of importance for these species. Although good information has been collected on the status and distribution of some species, information across all countries is still lacking and serves as an impediment to quantifying their status and trends.
- **Enhancing site coverage of the networks**: The focus of the Strategy has been to obtain recognition for internationally important sites for migratory waterbirds, especially through the establishment of networks of international important sites in the East Asian-Australasian Flyway. Work undertaken during the Strategy indicates that there are at least 600 sites for migratory shorebirds, cranes and Anatidae (with additional sites for other species). The network of sites

currently includes only 80 sites (13%). Even though new sites are being added to the Site Networks each year, it is unlikely that the targets identified in the Strategy will be achieved unless strategies for site designation are enhanced.

- **Enhancing country coverage**: While the number of national and local partners is increasing, the initiative has not been able to involve all the countries in the region. Particularly in South-east Asia, where the Shorebird Network covers the entire region and the Anatidae Network covers some countries, very few sites have been designated compared to the large number of sites known to be of international importance. Mechanisms need to be developed to involve all countries in the region.
- **Strengthening national networks**: More people capable of collecting information on waterbirds and interested in developing and supporting conservation initiatives are needed.
- **Reporting and publicising the achievements of the initiative**: More effort is needed to publicise the achievements of the initiative to a wide range of audiences both within countries and across the region.
- **Securing a sound financial basis for the initiative**: To date the initiative has been successful in securing resources to develop and support activities on an annual basis. A variety of government, corporate and development agency funds have supported activities at the local and national level. Support for core coordination has been received from only a few government agencies. The lack of funding on a long-term basis has prevented the development of a more extensive regional conservation programme. Broadening of the funding base for coordination and project activities is a priority.

## WHAT OF THE FUTURE?

Despite all these successes over the past nine years of the initiative, the challenges for conservation of migratory waterbirds and wetlands in the Asia-Pacific region are increasing as the destruction and loss of important wetlands continue across the region through human-induced and natural causes. The capacity of local and national agencies and groups to monitor and manage species and their habitats needs to be strengthened in a majority of the countries.

In recognition of the need to ensure sustainable development and the conservation of species and habitats, and to gain support for future activities at flyway and national level in the East Asian-Australasian Flyway, the Governments of Australia and Japan and Wetlands International put forward a proposal to the World Summit on Sustainable Development (WSSD), held in Johannesburg in September 2002, under the Type II Partnership Initiative. The main values of the new initiative are: (a) to provide governments and non-governmental organizations with a formal mechanism for signing up and becoming partners to the broader framework of the initiative; (b) to broaden the work of the Strategy and to place the recognition and effective management of important sites in the international context of sustainable development; and (c) as security for Strategy activities and networks. This framework will be developed to support conservation in the flyway post-2005.

Likewise in the Central Asian Flyway, the Action Plan being developed under the framework of the CMS is being broadened to ensure that the needs of people living at sites used by waterbirds are addressed.

In summary, the prognosis for the conservation of migratory waterbirds and their habitats is brighter through the achievements of the Strategy, but efforts need to be sustained and expanded through improving and broadening the support and participation of all stakeholders to tackle the challenges of the future.

## ACKNOWLEDGEMENTS

The plenary presentation on the Strategy at this Conference was eloquently delivered by Lew Young, and has given a voice to our work. The Strategy has thrived as a cooperative effort, and full acknowledgement is given to all the agencies, organizations, bodies and committed individuals who have participated during the last nine years, even though it is not possible to list them all by name. Members of the MWCC have played an important role in shaping and guiding the development of this initiative. The MWCC Chair Jason Ferris, Vice-Chair Yoshihiro Natori and Alison Russell-French, our previous Chair, have given me strong support, encouragement and guidance. Working closely with my colleagues David Li Zuo Wei, Alexander Solokha, Doug Watkins, Lew Young, Mark Barter, Masuyuki Kurechi, Noritaka Ichida, Simba Chan, Warren Lee Long, Yoshihiko Miyabayashi, Yus Rusila Noor and Yutaka Kanai, we have jointly been able to stimulate our many international, national and local partners to achieve the positive outcomes of this important initiative. Support from Wetlands International has been unflagging and instrumental since 1994; Asae Sayaka, Chen Kelin, C.L. Trisal, Dibjo Sartono, Gerard Boere, Kaori Matsui, Olga Anisimova, Roger Jaensch, Simon Delany, Sundari Ramakrishna and Ward Hagemeijer deserve special mention. Flora George and Khadijah Ahmad have provided strong administrative and financial accountability to our work. My wife Samhita and sons Arnav and Aseem have given me constant support and encouragement to play my part in this work. Financial support from the Australian Department of the Environment and Heritage, Japanese Ministry of the Environment, U.S. Fish and Wildlife Service and Government of The Netherlands has been instrumental in sustaining this initiative. Lastly, funding for my participation in this Conference has been kindly provided by the organizers and many supporters.

## REFERENCES

**Anonymous** 1996. Asia-Pacific migratory waterbird conservation strategy: 1996-2000. Wetlands International – Asia Pacific, Kuala Lumpur, and International Waterfowl and Wetlands Research Bureau, Japan Committee, Tokyo.

**Asia-Pacific Migratory Waterbird Conservation Committee** 2001. Asia-Pacific migratory waterbird conservation strategy: 2001-2005. Wetlands International-Asia Pacific, Kuala Lumpur, Malaysia. Available at: www.wetlands.org

**BirdLife International** 2001. Threatened birds of Asia: the BirdLife International Red Data Book. BirdLife International, Cambridge, UK.

**BirdLife International** 2003. Saving Asia's threatened birds: a guide for government and civil society. BirdLife International, Cambridge, UK.

**CMS Secretariat** 2001. The Central Asian-Indian Flyway: Towards A Strategy For Waterbirds And Wetland Conservation. www.wcmc.org.uk/cms/nw280801 Uzbekistan.htm.

**Gilissen, N., Haanstra, L., Delany, S., Boere, G. & Hagemeijer, W.** 2002. Numbers and distribution of wintering waterbirds in the Western Palearctic and Southwest Asia in 1997, 1998 and 1999. Wetlands International Global Series No 11, Wageningen, The Netherlands.

**Li, Z.W.D. & Mundkur, T.** 2004. Results of the Asian Waterbird Census 1997-2001. Wetlands International Global Series 15, Kuala Lumpur. Available at: www.wetlands.org

**Mundkur, T. & Matsui, K.** 1997. The Asia-Pacific migratory waterbird conservation strategy: 1996-2000. In: J. van Vessem (ed) Determining priorities for waterbird and wetland conservation. Proceedings of Workshop 4 of the International Wetlands and Development Conference, Kuala Lumpur, 9-13 October 1995. Wetlands International, Kuala Lumpur: 57-66.

**Mundkur, T. & Matsui, K.** 1998. Introductory overview of the Asia-Pacific migratory waterbird conservation strategy: 1996-2000. In: Zhen Rende (ed) Wetland and waterbird conservation. Proceedings of an international workshop on wetland and waterbird conservation in North East Asia. Wetlands International – China Programme, China Forestry Publishing House, Beijing: 242-245.

**Mundkur, T., Matsui, K., Chan, S., Miyabayashi, Y. & Watkins, D.** 1999. Promoting migratory waterbird conservation in the Asia-Pacific. In: A. Beintema & J. van Vessem (eds) Strategies for Conserving Migratory Waterbirds. Proceedings of Workshop 2 of the Second International Conference on Wetlands and Development, Dakar, Senegal, 8-14 November 1998. Wetlands International Publication No. 55, Wageningen, The Netherlands: 6-12.

**Ramsar Convention Secretariat** 2002. Strategic Framework and guidelines for the future development of the List of Wetlands of International Importance of the Convention on Wetlands (Ramsar, Iran, 1971). Ramsar Convention Bureau, Gland, Switzerland. Available at: www.ramsar.org/key_guide_list2002_e.htm.

**Weaver, K.** 1997. Conservation planning for migratory waterbirds in the Asia-Pacific flyways: bilateral and multilateral approaches. In: J. van Vessem (ed) Determining priorities for waterbird and wetland conservation. Proceedings of Workshop 4 of the International Conference on Wetlands and Development, Kuala Lumpur, 9-13 October 1995. Wetlands International, Kuala Lumpur: 29-42.

**Wetlands International** 2002. Waterbird Population Estimates – Third edition. Wetlands International Global Series No. 12. Wageningen, The Netherlands.

# Climate variability and change and other pressures on wetlands and waterbirds: impacts and adaptation

*C. Max Finlayson[1,4], Habiba Gitay[2], Maria Bellio[1,4], Rick van Dam[1] & Iain Taylor[3]*

*[1]Environmental Research Institute of the Supervising Scientist, Darwin, NT, Australia.*

*[2]Australian National University, Canberra, ACT, Australia.*

*[3]Charles Sturt University, Albury, NSW, Australia.*

*[4]Present address: International Water Management Institute, PO Box 2075, Colombo, Sri Lanka. (email: M.Finlayson@cgiar.org)*

Finlayson, C.M., Gitay, H., Bellio, M.G., van Dam, R.A. & Taylor, I. 2006. Climate variability and change and other pressures on wetlands and waterbirds: impacts and adaptation. *Waterbirds around the world.* Eds. G.C. Boere, C.A. Galbraith & D.A. Stroud. The Stationery Office, Edinburgh, UK. pp. 88-97.

## ABSTRACT

The atmospheric concentrations of greenhouse gases have increased since the pre-industrial era due to human activities, primarily the combustion of fossil fuels and changes in land use and land cover. These, together with natural forces, have contributed to changes in the Earth's climate (both mean and variability) over the twentieth century; land and ocean surface temperatures have warmed, the spatial and temporal patterns of precipitation have changed, sea level has risen, and the frequency and intensity of El Niño events have increased. These changes have affected wetlands and their biota, especially in coastal and high latitudes, including the timing of reproduction of species, migration of animals, the length of the growing season and the frequency of pest and disease outbreaks. The Earth's mean surface temperature is projected to warm by 1.4 to 5.8°C by the end of the twenty-first century, with land areas warming more than the oceans, and high latitudes warming more than the tropics. Sea level is projected to rise by 0.09 to 0.88 m, and is expected to have further effects on wetlands and their biota either directly (e.g. through changes in sea level and/or increased temperatures) or indirectly (e.g. through changes in hydrology, fire regime and pest outbreaks). These changes will increase the risk of extinction of vulnerable species, and could drastically alter the migration patterns of many others. Populations of some species will decline, whilst some will increase in both size and distribution. The consequences of climate change and variability for waterbirds is likely to be large, but our understanding of the role of climate change versus all the other changes due to human activities (such as changes in land use and land cover, drainage, invasive species etc.) is undermined by the limited extent of our data and existing knowledge. In all but a few cases, the data are totally inadequate. As many wetland habitats and waterbird species are currently under great pressure, we propose that quantitative risk assessments of individual and multiple pressures at multiple sites along flyways and at major wetlands are undertaken as a basis for developing adaptation options for these species and ecosystems.

## INTRODUCTION

We present an overview of the findings of the Intergovernmental Panel on Climate Change (IPCC) Third Assessment Report on climate change and its impacts on wetlands, in particular the information and graphics provided by IPCC (2001 & 2002). We also draw on a paper on climate change and wetlands prepared for the 8th Meeting of the Conference of the Parties of the Ramsar Convention on Wetlands (van Dam *et al.* 2002) and

recent analyses of the observed and projected effects of climate change on waterbirds.

It is well recognized that at the global level, human activities have caused, and will continue to cause, a loss and/or a change in biodiversity in general. More specifically, biodiversity in wetlands has been affected by, *inter alia*, changes in land use and land cover, soil and water pollution and degradation, air pollution, diversion of water to intensively managed ecosystems and urban systems, habitat fragmentation, selective exploitation of species, introduction of non-native species, and stratospheric ozone depletion. It is also well recognized that climate change will constitute an added stress that may act synergistically or cumulatively and further adversely affect biodiversity. In turn, given that wetland biodiversity supports or provides many ecosystem services on which many humans depend (see review by Finlayson & D'Cruz 2005), changes in wetland biodiversity will undoubtedly also affect human well-being.

We therefore consider climate variability and change in the context of global change that encompasses all pressures from human activities. We specifically look at some of the impacts on waterbirds and then look at possible response options (or adaptation options) through a risk assessment framework. The paper covers:

1. climate variability and change, and its impact on wetlands;
2. observed changes in the distribution of specific waterbird species in response to climate variability and change, and changes in land and water use; and
3. a risk analysis framework to develop responses that address the impacts of multiple pressures, including climate change, on wetlands.

## CLIMATE CHANGE AND THE IMPACT ON WETLANDS

We summarize the following:

1. changes that have been observed in the biophysical systems (atmosphere, oceans) and the role of human activities in those changes;
2. the (observed) impacts of these changes on biological systems and especially wetlands; and
3. the role that adaptation can play in responding to these changes.

### Observed changes in biophysical systems

During the period 1750-2000, the concentrations of greenhouse gases in the atmosphere increased (Fig. 1): carbon dioxide by

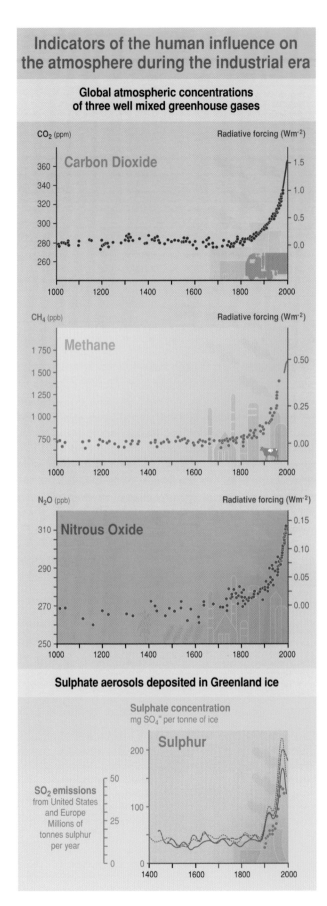

## Indicators of the human influence on the atmosphere during the industrial era

### Global atmospheric concentrations of three well mixed greenhouse gases

**Fig. 1.** Observed changes in atmospheric concentrations of carbon dioxide ($CO_2$), methane ($CH_4$) and nitrous oxide ($N_2O$) over the past 1 000 years and sulphur dioxide ($SO_2$) aerosols over the last 600 years (from IPCC 2001).

about a third (2-35%); methane by about 150% (125-175%); and nitrous oxide by 17% (12-22%). The rates of increase over the past century are unprecedented when compared with the past 40 000 years for which a nearly continuous record exists. The increased concentrations of these gases are attributed to human activities, especially the burning of fossil fuel, leading to a release of 6.3 Gt C $y^{-1}$ on average during the 1990s, and changes in land use and land cover, including deforestation, releasing about 1.7 Gt C $yr^{-1}$. Aerosols, such as sulphur dioxide, that are relatively short-lived and have a cooling effect on the atmosphere, have also increased (Fig. 1).

Due to the increase in the atmospheric concentration of greenhouse gases and natural factors during the twentieth century, the Earth's surface has warmed by 0.4-0.8°C; land areas have warmed more than the oceans, with northern, mid-high latitudes warming more than most other parts ( Fig. 2). The mean annual continental precipitation has increased by 5-10% over the twentieth century in the Northern Hemisphere and parts of Australia, although it has decreased by 3% over much of the subtropical land areas (e.g. in north and west Africa and parts of the Mediterranean). These changes may be partly due to the increasing global mean surface temperature resulting in a change in atmospheric circulation, a more active hydrological cycle, and increases in the water-holding capacity throughout the atmosphere leading to a 2-4% increase in the frequency of heavy precipitation events in the mid- and high latitudes of the Northern Hemisphere over the latter half of the twentieth century (Fig. 3).

The severity of droughts has increased, with summer drying and an associated increased incidence of drought in a few areas. In some regions, such as parts of Asia and Africa, the frequency and intensity of droughts have been observed to increase in recent decades. El Niño events have become more frequent, persistent and intense during the last 20 to 30 years compared to the previous 100 years. This has increased the frequency and intensity of drought and floods in the land-masses around the Pacific, especially in the Southern Hemisphere sub-tropics.

Warming has driven sea-level rise through thermal expansion of seawater and widespread loss of land ice. Based on tide gauge records, and after correcting for land movements, Mean Sea Level increased by an average of 10-20 cm during the twentieth century. A limited number of sites in Europe have nearly continuous records of sea level spanning 300 years and show that the greatest rise in sea level occurred during the twentieth century. Records  from Amsterdam (The Netherlands), Brest (France) and Swinoujscie (Poland), as well as other sites, confirm that there has been an accelerated rise in sea level over the twentieth century as compared to the nineteenth century.

Observed regional changes in temperature have been associated with observed changes in physical and biophysical systems. Examples include: the retreat of non-polar glaciers; a reduction in the extent and thickness of Arctic sea ice in summer; earlier flowering and longer growing and breeding seasons for plants and animals in the Northern Hemisphere (where most long-term studies have been carried out); pole-ward and upward (altitudinal) migration of plants, birds, fish and insects; and earlier spring migration and later departure of birds in the Northern Hemisphere.

Increasing sea surface temperatures were recorded in much of the tropical oceans during the last several decades of the

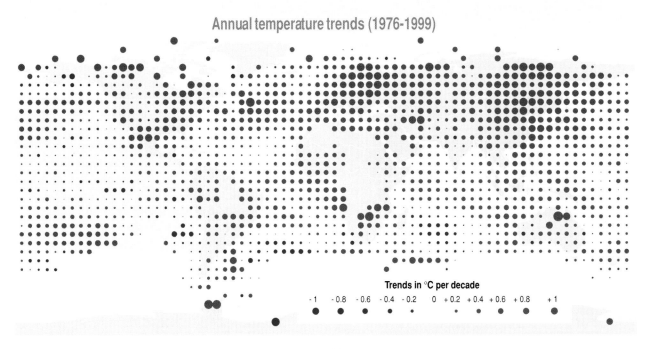

Fig. 2. Observed changes in global-average surface temperature (from IPCC 2001).

twentieth century. Many corals have undergone major, although often partially reversible, bleaching episodes when sea surface temperatures have risen by 1°C above the mean seasonal sea surface temperatures in any one season, and extensive mortality has occurred with a 3°C rise. Bleaching events are also associated with other stresses such as pollution and disease. Changes in the frequency and intensity of precipitation, pH, water temperature, wind, dissolved $CO_2$ and salinity, combined with

anthropogenic pollution by nutrients and toxins, can all affect water quality in estuarine and marine waters. Some marine disease organisms and algal species, including those associated with toxic blooms, are strongly influenced by one or more of these factors. In the last few decades of the twentieth century, there was an increase in reports of diseases affecting coral reefs and sea-grasses, particularly in the Caribbean and temperate oceans.

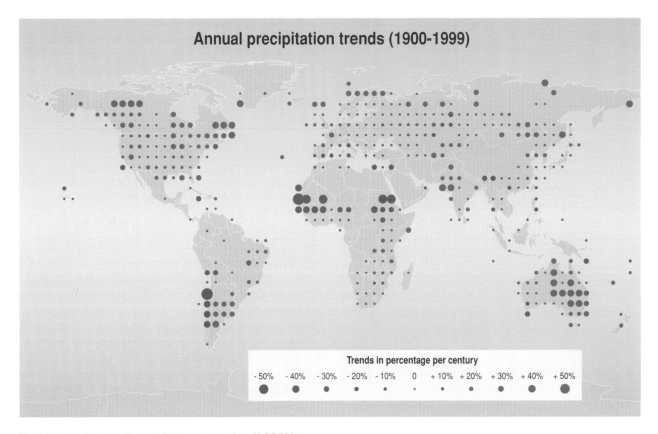

Fig. 3. Observed changes in precipitation patterns (from IPCC 2001).

As mentioned above, most of the warming has been attributed to human activities, particularly the emission of greenhouse gases originating from the burning of fossil fuel, and changes in land use and land cover; the evidence for this attribution has become stronger over time from the first assessment report of the IPCC in 1990 to the second in 1995 and the third in 2000. Specific conclusions from these assessments were:

1   First Assessment Report 1990: *"...the observed increased [warming] could be largely due to ... natural variability; alternatively this variability and other human factors could have offset a still larger human-induced greenhouse warming"*;
2   Second Assessment Report 1995: *"The balance of evidence suggests a discernible human influence on global climate"*; and
3   Third Assessment Report 2000: *"Most of the observed warming in the past 50 years is attributable to human activities"*.

**Projected changes in the climate system and sea level**
Future emissions of greenhouse gases and aerosols are determined by driving forces such as changes in human population (total number and structure), socio-economic development and technological change. The IPCC Special Report on Emission Scenarios presents six groups of scenarios or plausible futures (so called "SRES scenarios") which are based on narrative storylines and span a wide range of driving forces. The scenarios are used to project the future emissions of the greenhouse gases carbon dioxide, methane and nitrous oxide and the aerosol sulphur dioxide. For gases that stay in the atmosphere for a long period, such as carbon dioxide, the atmospheric concentration responds to changes in emissions relatively slowly, whereas for short-lived gases and aerosols, such as sulphate aerosols, the atmospheric concentration responds much more quickly.

Using the SRES scenarios, the IPCC has projected that carbon dioxide concentrations, temperatures and sea levels will continue to rise long after emissions of greenhouse gases are reduced. This is due to the length of the half-life of carbon dioxide in the atmosphere as well as "inertia" in the system. Even if the emissions were to be stopped today, the Earth's surface temperature could continue to rise for a few centuries, and sea level, due to thermal expansion and melting of ice, could continue to increase for several millennia.

Projected changes for surface temperatures, precipitation and sea level are:

1   The globally-averaged surface temperature is projected to increase by 1.4 to 5.8°C over the period 1990-2100. This is about two to ten times larger than the central value of observed warming over the twentieth century. The projected rate of warming is very likely to be without precedent during at least the last 10 000 years, based on long-term data on climate. For the periods 1990-2025 and 1990-2050, the projected increases are 0.4 to 1.1°C and 0.8 to 2.6°C, respectively. These results are for the full range of SRES scenarios, based on a number of climate models.
2   Some areas are projected to become wetter and others drier, with an overall increase in precipitation projected.
3   Global mean sea level is projected to rise by 0.09 to 0.88 m

between the years 1990 and 2100. For the periods 1990-2025 and 1990-2050, the projected rises are 0.03 to 0.14 m and 0.05 to 0.32 m, respectively. This is due primarily to thermal expansion and loss of mass from glaciers and ice-caps.

Projections for climate-related extreme events (e.g. floods, heat waves etc.) include:

1   Higher maximum temperatures; more hot days and heat waves over nearly all land areas;
2   Higher minimum temperatures; fewer cold days, frost days and cold spells over nearly all land areas;
3   More intense precipitation events over many areas;
4   Increased summer drying over most mid-latitude continental interiors and associated risk of drought; and
5   Increase in peak wind intensity and mean and peak precipitation intensities in tropical cyclones.

These projections could lead to increased heat stress in humans and livestock and decreased productivity in some regions, but could also provide some relief from extreme cold events, especially in mid-high latitudes of the Northern Hemisphere.

**Impacts on wetlands**
Climate change is likely to affect wetlands and their biodiversity directly (e.g. through changes in temperature) and indirectly (e.g. through affecting the hydrology). Impacts will depend on the coastal morphology and the balance between sea-level rise, deposition and erosion within catchments and the coastal zone. Wetlands play important roles in the global cycling of water and chemicals, including greenhouse gases; cycles that will be affected by climate change. The risk of impacts of climate change increases with the rate and magnitude of climate change. Specific impacts are projected to include:

1   Initially increased productivity in some mid-latitude regions and a reduction in the tropics and sub-tropics, even with warming of a few degrees;
2   Adverse affects on coastal wetlands and coastal fisheries, e.g. coral bleaching events are expected to increase and mangroves are expected to decline in many coastal zones;
3   Decreased water availability in many arid- and semi-arid regions; and
4   Increased forest productivity, including that of forested wetlands, although forest management will become more difficult because of an increase in disturbances (pest outbreaks and forest fires).

Overall, it is projected that there will be more adverse than beneficial impacts on wetlands. Inland and coastal systems are likely to experience large and early impacts. These include:

1   Increased levels of inundation, storm flooding, accelerated coastal erosion, seawater intrusion into fresh groundwater, encroachment of tidal waters into estuaries and river systems, and elevated sea surface temperatures and ground temperatures; and
2   Adverse impacts on marine mammal and bird species, especially migratory and nomadic bird populations that depend on coastal habitats.

Developing countries are projected to be the most vulnerable to climate change; many are already more prone to floods and droughts. Large portions of the economies of these countries are in "climate sensitive sectors", and they have a lower capacity to adapt because of a lack of financial, institutional and technological capacity and access to knowledge. Traditional indigenous societies that depend on inland and coastal wetlands are already vulnerable (see also McDonald *et al.* 1997), and would become more vulnerable as a result of these projected impacts.

Changes in climate will exert additional pressure on ecological systems. Furthermore, processes such as habitat loss, modification and fragmentation, and the introduction and spread of non-native species will affect the impacts of climate change. A realistic projection of the future state of the Earth's ecosystems needs to take into account patterns of human land use and water use that will greatly affect the ability of organisms to respond to climate change via migration. The composition of most current ecosystems is likely to change, as the species that make up an ecosystem are unlikely to shift together. The most rapid changes are expected where they are accelerated by changes in natural and anthropogenic, non-climatic disturbance patterns.

The risk of extinction will increase for many species that are already vulnerable. Species with limited climatic ranges and/or restricted habitat requirements and/or small populations are typically the most vulnerable to extinction, such as endemic species and biota restricted to islands, peninsulas or coastal areas. In contrast, species with extensive, non-patchy ranges, long-range dispersal mechanisms and large populations are at less risk of extinction. While there is little evidence to suggest that climate change will slow species' losses, there is evidence that it may increase species' losses.

### Impacts on waterbirds

The general nature of the impacts of climate change on waterbirds can be identified, but the exact extent, intensity and time frames are difficult to project with certainty, as all models of global climate change are at too large a scale and the ecology of most waterbirds is insufficiently understood. Potentially, almost all aspects of their ecology could be affected, either directly or indirectly. However, the most severe effects and those most likely to occur earliest (some have already been detected) include the loss of inter-tidal habitats and increased salinity of coastal freshwater habitats caused by rising sea levels, a reduction in the extent of wetlands and duration of flooding in arid and semi-arid areas resulting from changes in climate variability, and the loss of wetland breeding habitats in Arctic and sub-Arctic areas caused by increasing temperatures, expanding boreal forests and forest fires.

The extent of loss of inter-tidal habitats and its effects on coastal waterbirds will depend on the ability of coastal environments to move inland as sea level rises. Where this is possible, either because of a lack of artificial coastal defences or by their removal, inter-tidal areas might expand and some changes in sediment characteristics, especially an increase in coarser sandy sediments, might be expected. This would benefit some species such as the Eurasian Oystercatcher *Haematopus ostralegus*. However, it is more likely that coastal defences around many areas will be strengthened, resulting in a compression of inter-tidal habitats and loss of total inter-tidal area. For the United States, Galbraith *et al.* (2002) have predicted losses of between

20% and 70% of current inter-tidal areas by 2100. This will have serious implications for the total numbers of shorebirds that can be supported (Norris & Atkinson 2000). Critically, the length of time that remaining inter-tidal areas are exposed during each tidal cycle will be reduced. The time shorebirds spend feeding during low tide depends on their body size and ambient temperatures, and is also increased when accumulating reserves prior to migration (Zwarts *et al.* 1990, Piersma & Jukema 1990). Smaller species spend almost all of the time feeding (Dann 1999) and potentially could be the most seriously affected. A reduction in the expenditure of metabolic energy through rising temperatures is unlikely to offset the loss of feeding time. Some inter-tidal areas will probably become unusable by the smaller species. In other areas, reductions in survival during winter and subsequently during migration might be expected, and lower body condition on arrival at Arctic breeding areas might reduce breeding success of migratory waders and other species such as wildfowl (Newton 1998, Pettifor *et al.* 2000).

Changes in immersion periods, sediment characteristics and also rising temperatures will cause changes in the distribution, abundance and growth of the inter-tidal invertebrate populations which constitute the prey of shorebirds (Decker & Beukema 1999, Beukema 2002), and in some cases, this might increase the availability of food. However, this relationship is not clear, as increased temperatures can also lead to a decrease in body condition of some invertebrates during winter, reducing the food value of individual prey items (Honkoop & Beukema 1997).

The effects of rising temperatures on plant communities will be particularly strong in the Arctic (Neilson & Drapek 1998), and this will lead, among other changes, to an expansion of boreal forest into current tundra areas where two thirds of all goose species and 95% of all Calidrid sandpipers breed. Losses in the breeding ranges of these tundra breeding waterbirds of between 5% and 93%, depending on the species and the degree of warming, have been predicted as a result of this forest expansion by 2070/2099 (Zöckler & Lysenko 2000). The annual breeding success of some species is correlated with spring temperatures (Zöckler & Lysenko 2000), so rising temperatures could increase productivity, which might compensate to some extent for habitat loss. Set against this, however, is a likely increase in loss of nests and chicks to predation as temperate climate predators such as the Red Fox *Vulpes vulpes* expand their range (Parmesan & Yohe 2003).

Changes in global circulation patterns will result in alterations to rainfall patterns, with some areas experiencing increases and others decreases. Included in the latter are some currently dry areas, such as Australia and parts of Asia and Africa. Wetlands and waterbird populations in these areas are already highly stressed from habitat loss to agriculture, reduced water flows caused by water abstraction for irrigation, pollution and increasing salinization (Kingsford & Johnson 1998, Kingsford 2000, Kingsford & Norman 2002). Waterbird populations in the drier continents are characterized by unpredictable and relatively infrequent breeding, high adult survival and high mobility. Successful breeding often requires exceptional flooding events that last long enough for completion of the breeding cycle (Leslie 2001, Kingsford & Norman 2002). Reduced rainfall will increase the intervals between flooding events and shorten their duration. Reduced breeding success and recruitment should be expected as a first response, followed by reduced survival of adults and then widespread population declines. Some indication of the sensitivity of such systems is provided by an analysis of the survival rates of the Sedge Warbler *Acrocephalus schoenobaenus*, a wetland passerine, breeding in Britain and wintering in West Africa. Annual survival rates are strongly correlated with rainfall in West Africa, and have varied from 2.5% to 55% (Peach *et al.* 1991).

Changes to waterbird populations should also be expected in less severely affected areas. Increased temperatures will advance breeding seasons and possibly reduce winter mortality (Crick & Sparks 1999, Winkler *et al.* 2002). The vegetation structure of wetlands can be expected to change, altering the physical aspects of habitats and plant productivity. There will almost certainly be great regional variation, with some areas experiencing increases in waterbird populations and others, decreases (Smart & Gill 2003).

## THE ROLE OF ADAPTATION

Adaptation has the potential to reduce the adverse effects of climate change, but cannot prevent all impacts. Numerous adaptation options (projects and processes designed to reduce the impact of climate change) have been identified that can reduce adverse and enhance beneficial impacts of climate change, but will incur costs (see van Dam *et al.* 2002, Gitay *et al.* 2002). Adaptation is a necessary strategy to complement efforts to mitigate climate change (deliberate actions to reduce the sources or enhance the sinks of greenhouse gases). Adaptation and mitigation can contribute to sustainable development objectives for wetlands.

Adaptation activities can promote conservation and sustainable use of biodiversity and reduce the impact of changes in climate and climatic extremes on biodiversity. These activities include the establishment of a mosaic of interconnected multiple-use reserves designed to take into account projected changes in climate, and integrated land and water management activities that reduce non-climate pressures on biodiversity and hence make the systems less vulnerable to changes in climate. Some of these adaptation activities can also make people less vulnerable to climatic extremes. The effectiveness of adaptation and mitigation activities can be enhanced when they are integrated within broader strategies designed to make development paths more sustainable.

The way in which different species respond to changes caused by global warming will be determined by their individual inherent adaptive capacity and the time necessary for those adaptations to take effect. In particular, patterns of bird migration will change and be very different across species, for different latitudes and different regions of the biosphere. The most general definition of animal migration is given by Baker (1978): "Migration: the act of moving from one spatial unit to another". The classic form of bird migration is the regular seasonal movement from the breeding areas to the resting grounds (often called wintering quarters) and back (Schüz *et al.* 1971), but bird movements occur in an abundance of different forms: dispersal, irruption, partial migration, differential migration etc. (Berthold 1993).

Many studies have shown that all the main morphological, physiological and behavioural prerequisites for bird migration are under direct genetic control (Seebohm 1901, Butler & Woakes 1990, Mönkkönen 1992). Therefore, endogenous migratory patterns may not change in a time frame sufficient to adapt to global warming, and as a consequence the species will

be forced to change the extent of their migratory patterns. There is evidence that some species of migratory birds in the Mediterranean region have reduced their migratory behaviour in relation to global warming (Berthold 1988, Berthold & Terrill 1988). The predicted increased incidence of drought in sub-tropical regions could lead to an increase in dry-season migration amongst resident species causing direct competition for food between resident and migratory species. At higher latitudes, mild winters could increase the survival of resident and partially migratory species, with the consequence that long-distant migrants would find themselves at a disadvantage on their arrival on breeding grounds occupied by larger numbers of residents. On the other hand, climatic changes may also have positive effects, such as the expansion of subtropical populations to higher latitudes (Berthold 1988), and result in an unprecedented gene flow and thus a multitude of micro-evolutionary processes.

From the above considerations, it is implicit that, in the next decades, global change (including climate change) in general will play a major role in favouring the survival of certain species and will pose a disadvantage to others, if not threaten their survival. It is likely that partially migratory or less markedly migratory species would succeed in developing resident populations, but it is not clear how quickly long-distance migrants would succeed in reducing their migratory behaviour to such an extent that they would be able to stay on the breeding grounds throughout the year in the event of severe climatic changes (Berthold 1993). Migratory species with restricted ranges, restricted foraging niches (in their breeding and non-breeding ranges), or under threats from other pressures such as loss and modification of habitat, pollution and weed invasion, are likely to be the most affected.

For migratory species, and in particular long-distance migrants, scientists need to devote more research effort to determine:

1. the effects of habitat alteration at stopover points and wintering areas;
2. the amounts and locations of major habitat types, through inventories, as well as the carrying capacities of these habitats; and
3. the behaviour, home range and resource needs of species most likely to be vulnerable to global warming.

On the management and conservation fronts, efforts should be devoted to:

1. maintaining population inventories of migratory birds. These inventories should form the basis for determining and designating critical habitat under various management responses, and hence encourage specific known adaptations;
2. identifying, obtaining and protecting critical stopover and wintering sites, particularly for those species whose populations tend to concentrate at few sites; and
3. addressing policies and legislation at a continental scale, or better flyway scale where possible.

## RISK ASSESSMENT

Ecological risk assessment is not a new tool, but in recent years the usefulness of its application to wetland management has been promoted and accepted formally through the Ramsar

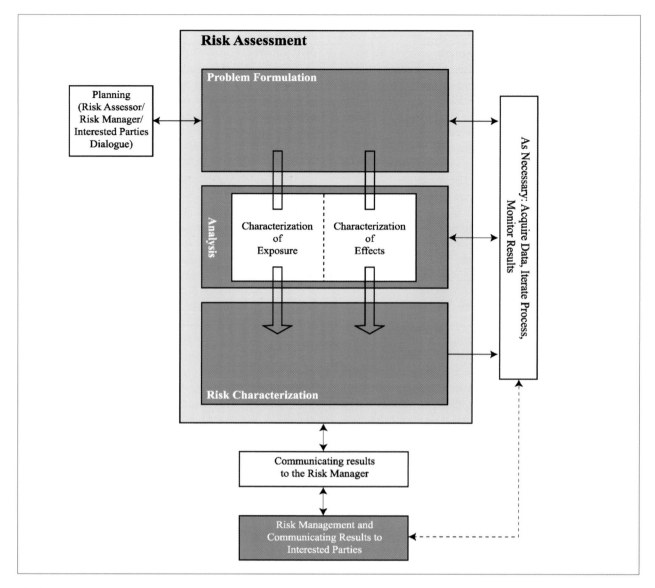

**Fig. 4.** Generalized framework for ecological risk assessment (modified from US EPA 1998).

Convention on Wetlands (van Dam *et al.* 2002). Ecological risk can be described as the likelihood of the occurrence of an adverse ecological effect of specific magnitude. Thus, ecological risk assessment attempts to quantify both the magnitude of an ecological effect and the likelihood of the effect occurring (US EPA 1998). It provides a structured, iterative approach for making rational and transparent decisions based on the best available knowledge and recognition of the associated uncertainties.

Risk assessment frameworks exist in a variety of forms (US EPA 1998, AS/NZS 1999, van Dam *et al.* 1999, US EPA 2003, Hart 2004), although they generally encompass similar steps, most commonly *problem formulation/hazard identification*, *effects assessment*, *exposure (likelihood) assessment* and *risk characterization* (Fig. 4). Additional steps, such as risk communication, risk reduction and monitoring, are also critical in the overall decision-making process, and are necessary to complete the risk management cycle (Burgman 2004). Moreover, identification (and quantification) of the key uncertainties and gaps in knowledge enables prioritization of research and data acquisition, which, through iteration of the risk assessment, decreases uncertainty in the risk predictions and outcomes.

Applications of ecological risk assessment are numerous and include assessments that range from: screening-level (qualitative) to detailed (quantitative) or a combination of both (i.e. tiered ecological risk assessment); predictive to retrospective in temporal scale; local to global in spatial scale; and single stressor to multiple stressors (US EPA 1998, Burgman 2004). Increasingly, risk assessment is being used in a catchment or basin context to assess, prioritize and manage multiple stressors, pathways, ecological resources/assets and competing social values (Serveiss 2001, Hart *et al.* 2003). For example, catchment (or watershed) scale risk assessments have been undertaken in North America (see summaries by Serveiss 2001) and Australia (eg. Begg *et al.* 2001, Pollino *et al.* 2005) estimating relative and/or cumulative risks to aquatic ecosystems of multiple stressors including toxicants, nutrients, sediments and altered flow regimes. Further, the development of a decision support tool to prioritize and protect or restore wetlands of importance to the water quality of Australia's Great Barrier Reef includes a process that assesses and compares ecological risks across multiple wetland sites and from multiple threats (Finlayson *et al.* 2004).

Although climate change poses one of the greatest threats to wetland ecosystems (see van Dam *et al.* 2002), to date there appear to have been few, if any, applications of ecological risk assessment to this issue. Generally, vulnerability assessment has been used to help identify potential impacts of climate change and sea-level rise (IPCC & Coastal Zone Management Subgroup 1991, Waterman 1996). The vulnerability assessment process requires identification of both climatic and non-climatic (e.g. deforestation, water pollution, water extraction, over-fishing) pressures, but does not specifically involve a structured assessment of the relative risks of these pressures or the interactions between them. There are many similarities between ecological risk assessment and vulnerability assessment – a topic that is currently being addressed by the Scientific and Technical Review Panel of the Ramsar Convention on Wetlands (Gitay 2006).

It is anticipated that utilizing existing and emerging methodologies for ecological risk assessment (e.g. Bayesian and frequentist approaches; see Burgman 2004) should enhance vulnerability assessments of the impacts of climate change on wetlands by:

1   including ecological risks of existing pressures as well as projected climate change;
2   comparing ecological risks of existing and predicted/forecast pressures, including climate change;
3   assessing the impact of climate change on risks of existing/forecast pressures (e.g. invasive species, water extraction/availability); and
4   providing a structured process by which to identify explicitly the key uncertainties and associated gaps in information and research.

A catchment scale, multiple stressor ecological risk assessment underway for the Magela Creek catchment in the Alligator Rivers Region (ARR) of northern Australia (Finlayson & Bayliss 2005) provides an example of the application of risk assessment to multiple pressures on wetlands. The assessment is focusing on the relative and cumulative ecological risks of uranium mining, invasive weeds, feral animals and salt water intrusion, the latter threat being one of the major consequences for the region of projected sea-level rise due to climate change. Initial analyses have assessed the probability of adverse change occurring as a consequence of individual pressures and provide a basis for comparing the relative probability of adverse affects. The comparative analyses also provide a basis for reassessing the results and the veracity of the information that was used, particularly if the results were unexpected. Furthermore, it is possible to link ecological models to the risk assessment models.

For the Magela analyses, it is intended to incorporate habitat suitability models for key weeds such as Paragrass *Urochloa mutica* and Mimosa *Mimosa pigra* and conceptual models for the feeding ecology of waterbird populations to assess the relative risks from various pressures including climate change projections. This provides an example of the usefulness of risk assessment in addressing multiple pressures, but it should be emphasized that the success of such assessments will only be realized through the accumulation of essential information. In addition to providing information on the relative risks, the risk assessment model provides a structured way to identify information gaps. In terms of the ongoing assessment of the consequences of climate change for wetlands and waterbirds, the various projections given above could potentially be supported

through application of ecological risk assessment, particularly where multiple pressures may be involved and where probabilistic analyses could be used to identify individual responses and overcome information gaps. This is well known scientifically, but there is insufficient evidence that such approaches are being effectively incorporated into management and monitoring regimes for wetlands and waterbirds.

## IDENTIFIED INFORMATION NEEDS AND GAPS

As noted above, it is widely accepted that human activities are adversely affecting ecosystems and their ability to provide ecosystem services that support humans and life on earth more generally. As climate change and other environmental pressures are inter-linked, we need to assess the effects of these multiple pressures if we are to develop programmes and actions that support sustainable development and human well-being. This assessment includes:

1   obtaining knowledge of the extent of many wetland types, their condition and their hydrology (Finlayson *et al.* 1999);
2   improved understanding of the response of wetlands and wetland species to changes in climatic factors and other pressures (van Dam *et al.* 2002);
3   development of data and models for the geographical distribution of species and their response to climate change at regional level (van Dam *et al.* 2002, IPCC 2002);
4   development of models that include patterns of human land use and water use to provide a realistic projection of the future state of wetlands; and
5   indicators to measure the effect of adaptation and mitigation options for climate change.

Increased desertification resulting from changing climate on its Asian breeding areas is one of the possible causes of the severe decline of the Sociable Plover *Vanellus gregarius*. Photo: Sergey Dereliev.

Increasingly, decision support systems of various complexity are being developed to assist managers make decisions about complex management scenarios, such as that presented by the pressures generated by climate change. Various technical experts have recently promoted ecological risk assessment as a means to support decision making for wetland management (Finlayson *et al.* 2004, Hart 2004). As it is unclear what the interactions are between climate change and the many other pressures affecting wetlands, it is recommended that quantitative wetland risk assessments be undertaken as a means of addressing the uncertainty that currently characterizes many management or adaptation options for sustainable use of wetlands.

## REFERENCES

**AS/NZS.** 1999. Risk Management. Australian Standards, New Zealand Standards, No. 4360. Standards Australia, Canberra, Australia.

**Baker, R.R.** 1978. The Evolutionary Ecology of Animal Migration. Hodder & Stoughton, London, UK.

**Begg, G.W., van Dam, R.A., Lowry, J.B., Finlayson, C.M. & Walden, D.J.** 2001. Inventory and Risk Assessment of Water Dependent Ecosystems in the Daly Basin, Northern Territory, Australia. Supervising Scientist Report 162. Supervising Scientist, Darwin, Australia.

**Berthold, P.** 1988. Evolutionary aspects of migratory behaviour in European warblers. Journal of Evolutionary Biology 1: 195-209.

**Berthold, P.** 1993. Bird Migration. A General Survey. Oxford Ornithology Series. Oxford University Press, U.K.

**Berthold, P. & Terrill, S.B.** 1988. Migratory behaviour and population growth of blackcaps wintering in Britain and Ireland: some hypotheses. Ringing & Migration 9: 153-9.

**Beukema, J.J.** 2002. Expected changes in the benthic fauna of Wadden Sea tidal flats as a result of sea-level rise or bottom subsidence. Netherlands Journal of Sea Research 47: 25-39.

**Burgman, M.A.** 2004. Risks and Decisions for Conservation and Environmental Management. Cambridge University Press, Cambridge, U.K.

**Butler, P.J. & Woakes, A.J.** 1990. The physiology of bird flight. In: E. Gwinner (ed) Bird migration: the physiology and ecophysiology. Springer-Verlag, Berlin: 300-318.

**Crick, H.Q.P. & Sparks, T.H.** 1999. Climate change related to egg-laying trends. Nature 399: 423-424.

**Dann, P.** 1999. Feeding periods and supratidal feeding of Red-necked Stint and Curlew Sandpipers in Western Port, Victoria. Emu 99: 218-222.

**Decker, R. & Beukema, J.J.** 1999. Relations of summer and winter temperatures with dynamics and growth of two bivalves, *Tellina tenuis* and *Abra tenuis*, on the northern edge of their intertidal distribution. Netherlands Journal of Sea Research 42: 207-220.

**Finlayson, C.M. & Bayliss, P.** 2005: Landscape-scale and multiple pressure analyses of services provided by tropical floodplains, in the Alligator Rivers Region, northern Australia. Millennium Ecosystem Assessment, Volume 4, Sub-global program.

**Finlayson, C.M. & D'Cruz, R.** 2005. Inland Water Systems. In: Millennium Ecosystem Assessment, Volume 1,

Conditions and Trends, Millennium Ecosystem Assessment: Strengthening Capacity to Manage Ecosystem Sustainably for Human Well-being. World Resources Institute, Washington D.C.

**Finlayson, C.M., Davidson, N.C., Spiers, A.G. & Stevenson, N.J.** 1999. Global wetland inventory – Status and priorities. Marine and Freshwater Research 50: 717–727.

**Finlayson, C.M., van Dam, R.A., Benzaken, D. & Ingliss, R.** 2004. Towards the development of a decision support system to select wetlands for strategic intervention. Report of a technical workshop held in Townsville, 8-9 December 2003. Australian Government Department of the Environment and Heritage, Canberra, Australia. (http://www.deh.gov.au/coasts/information/pubs/ workshop.pdf)

**Galbraith, H., Jones, R., Park, R., Clough, J., Herrod-Julius, S., Harrington, B. & Page, G.** 2002. Global climate change and sea level rise: potential losses of intertidal habitat for shorebirds. Waterbirds 25: 173-183.

**Gitay, H., Suarez, A., Watson, R.T. & Dokken, D.** (eds). 2002. IPCC Technical Paper V. Intergovernmental Panel on Climate Change, Geneva, Switzerland.

**Gitay, H.** 2006. Methodologies for assessing the vulnerability of wetlands to change in their ecological character. Ramsar Technical Report. Ramsar Convention Secretariat, Gland Switzerland.

**Hart, B.T.** 2004. Environmental risks associated with new irrigation schemes in Northern Australia. Ecological Management and Restoration 5: 107-111.

**Hart, B.T., Lake, P.S., Webb, J.A. & Grace, M.R.** 2003. Ecological risk to aquatic ecosystems from salinity increases. Australian Journal of Botany 51: 689-702.

**Honkoop, P.J.C. & Beukema, J.J.** 1997. Loss of body mass in winter in three intertidal bivalve species: an experimental and observational study of the interacting effects of water temperature, feeding time and feeding behaviour. Journal of Experimental Marine Biology and Ecology 212: 277-297.

**IPCC** 2001. Climate Change 2001: Synthesis Report. A Contribution of Working Groups I, II, and III to the Third Assessment Report of the Intergovernmental Panel on Climate Change. R.T. Watson and Core Writing Team. Cambridge University Press, Cambridge, U.K. and New York, USA.

**IPCC** 2002. Climate Change and Biodiversity. In: H. Gitay, A. Suarez, R.T. Watson & D. Dokken (eds) IPCC Technical Paper V. Intergovernmental Panel on Climate Change, Geneva, Switzerland.

**IPCC & Coastal Zone Management Subgroup.** 1991. Common Methodology for Assessing Vulnerability to Sea Level Rise. Ministry of Transport and Public Works, The Hague, The Netherlands.

**Kingsford, R.T.** 2000. Ecological impacts of dams, water diversions and river management on floodplain wetlands in Australia. Austral Ecology 25: 109-127.

**Kingsford, R.T. & Johnson, W.** 1998. Impact of water diversions on colonially-nesting waterbirds in the Macquarie Marshes of arid Australia. Colonial Waterbirds 21: 159-170.

**Kingsford, R. T. & Norman, F.I.** 2002. Australian Waterbirds – products of the continent's ecology. Emu 102: 47-69.

**Leslie, D.** 2001. Effect of river management on colonially-nesting waterbirds in the Barmah-Millewa forest, south-eastern Australia. Regulated Rivers: Research and Management 17: 2136.

**McDonald, M., Arragutainaq, L. & Novalinga, Z.** 1997. Voices from the Bay. Canadian Arctic Resources Committee and Environmental Committee of the Municipality of Sanikiluaq, Ottawa, Canada. (Also at http://www.isuma.net/).

**Mönkkönen, M.** 1992. Life history traits of Palearctic and Nearctic migrant passerines. Ornis Fennica 69: 161-172.

**Neilson, P.R. & Drapek, R.J.** 1998. Potentially complex biosphere responses to transient global warming. Global Change Biology 4: 505-521.

**Newton, I.** 1998. Population Limitation in Birds. Academic Press, London, U.K.

**Norris, K. & Atkinson, P.W.** 2000. Declining populations of coastal birds in Britain: victims of sea-level rise and climate change? Environmental Reviews 8: 303-323.

**Parmesan, C. & Yohe, G.** 2003. A globally coherent fingerprint of climate change impacts across natural systems. Nature 421: 37-42.

**Peach, W., Baillie, S. & Underhill, L.** 1991. Survival of British sedge warblers *Acrocephalus schoenobaenus* in relation to West African rainfall. Ibis 133: 300-305.

**Pettifor, R.A., Caldow, R.W.G., Rowcliffe, J.M, Goss-Custard, J.D., Black, J.M., Hodder, K.H., Houston, A.I., Lang, A. & Webb, J.** 2000. Spatially explicit, individual-based, behavioural models of the annual cycle of two migratory goose populations. Journal of Applied Ecology 37: 103-135.

**Piersma, T. & Jukema, J.** 1990. Budgeting the flight of a long-distance migrant: changes in nutrient reserve levels of Bar-tailed Godwits at successive staging sites. Ardea 78: 315-337.

**Pollino, C.A., Woodberry, O., Nicholson, A. & Korb, K.** 2005. Parameterising Bayesian Networks: A case study in ecological risk assessment. In: V. Kachitvichyanukul, U. Purintrapiban & P. Utayopas (eds) Proceedings of the 2005 International Conference on Simulation and Modeling.

**Schüz, E, Berthold, P., Gwinner, E. & Oelke, H.** 1971. Grundriß der Vogelzugskunde. Parey, Berlin-Hamburg, Germany.

**Seebohm, H.** 1901. Birds of Siberia. Murray, London.

**Serveiss, V.B.** 2001. Applying ecological risk principles to watershed assessment and management. Environmental Management 29: 145-154.

**Smart, J. & Gill, J.** 2003. Climate change and the potential impact on breeding waders in the U.K. Wader Study Group Bulletin 100: 80-85.

**US EPA (U.S. Environmental Protection Agency).** 1998. Guidelines for Ecological Risk Assessment. EPA/630/R-95/002F. Risk Assessment Forum, Washington, DC, USA.

**US EPA (U.S. Environmental Protection Agency).** 2003. Framework for Cumulative Risk Assessment. EPA/630/P-02/001F. Risk Assessment Forum, Washington, DC, USA.

**van Dam, R.A., Finlayson, C.M. & Humphrey, C.L.** 1999. Wetland risk assessment: a framework and methods for predicting and assessing change in ecological character. In: C.M. Finlayson & A.G. Spiers (eds) Techniques for Enhanced Wetland Inventory, Assessment and Monitoring. Supervising Scientist Report 147. Supervising Scientist, Canberra, Australia: 83-118.

**van Dam, R., Gitay, H., Finlayson, M., Davidson, N.C. & Orlando, B.** 2002. Climate Change and Wetlands: Impacts, Adaptation and Mitigation. Background document (DOC.SC26/COP8-4) prepared for the 26th Meeting of the Standing Committee of the Convention on Wetlands (Ramsar Convention) held in Gland, Switzerland, 3-7 December 2002.

**Waterman, P.** 1996. Australia's coastal vulnerability report. DEST, Canberra, ACT.

**Winkler, D.W., Dunn, P.O. & McCulloch, C.E.** 2002. Predicting the effects of climate change on avian life-history traits. Proceedings of the National Academy of Sciences of the United States of America 99: 13595-13599

**Zöckler, C. & Lysenko, I.** 2000. Waterbirds on the edge. WCMC Biodiversity Series No. 11. UNEP-World Conservation Monitoring Centre, Cambridge, U.K.

**Zwarts, L., Blomert, A.M. & Hupkes, R.** 1990. Increase in feeding time in waders preparing for spring migration from the Banc D'Arguin, Mauritania. Ardea 78: 237-256.

The reduction in the extent of inter-tidal mudflats as a consequence of rising sea-levels will have major implications for waders and other coastal waterbirds. Mudflats in Essex, UK. Photo: Peter Wakely, NCC.

# Sustainable harvest of waterbirds: a global review

*Niels Kanstrup*

*CIC Migratory Bird Commission, Director of Wildlife Management, Danish Hunters' Association, Molsvej 34, DK-8410 Rønde, Denmark. (email: nk@jaegerne.dk)*

Kanstrup, N. 2006. Sustainable harvest of waterbirds: a global review. *Waterbirds around the world.* Eds. G.C. Boere, C.A. Galbraith & D.A. Stroud. The Stationery Office, Edinburgh, UK. pp. 98-106.

## ABSTRACT

Waterbirds have a long tradition of being harvested in various ways. In many countries, the harvest takes place as a primary food source, but recreational hunting is also very popular. Various methods are used. Subsistence hunting of waterbirds has a history that dates back to the dawn of modern mankind. In many remote regions, waterbirds are still an important food resource. At the same time, sustainable utilization at all levels is regarded as a cornerstone in the conservation of nature. Sustainability is considered from the perspectives of two main fields: ecology and socio-economic (political) issues. Aspects of ecological sustainability include the harvest and other direct impacts on bird populations, here regarded as the hunting pressure. Socio-economic aspects include the active participation in nature conservation by local communities, motivated by the access to natural resources and the degree of stability in local communities obtained through nature conservation. In many countries there is a long tradition of detailed wildlife harvest management including programmes for bag surveys and monitoring of harvest levels. In most countries, however, the management of waterbird harvests is poor or completely lacking, and very little information is available on the annual harvest and its impact on populations. In addition, international and flyway based co-ordination is lacking in many regions, and systems need to be developed in order to obtain reliable data on harvest rates in relation to population levels and trends. Models for analysing and achieving sustainability and examples of local and integrated management of waterbird harvest are presented.

## INTRODUCTION

Most people equate sustainability with the definition first introduced in the Brundtland Report "Our Common Future": "The ability of humanity to ensure that it meets the needs of the present without compromising the ability of future generations to meet their own needs" (World Commission for Environment and Development 1987). This fundamental, but not very operational, definition will be the basis for this review. It can be rewritten as "ensuring a high quality of life for everyone, now and for generations to come". This goal will – in this review – be related to the value of the world's waterbirds *per se* and to the value of the human utilization of waterbird resources through sustainable harvest.

Some aspects of the harvest of waterbirds are poorly documented and understood compared to similar aspects for mammals and other wildlife taxa. Due to the high commercial value of meat and trophies, detailed management programmes, including research and monitoring programmes, have been set up for a large number of ungulates and other mammals in all continents. Likewise, it has been shown to be commercially beneficial to establish management programmes for fish

resources, resulting very often in highly sophisticated models for sustainable fishery regimes based on scientific analysis. In contrast, the national and, even more so, international management of wild birds are in a much poorer state, as research and flyway-based harvest programmes still have to be developed in most regions. However, in North America and a number of European countries, there is an elaborate system of monitoring and regulation of waterbird hunting. After many years, a general overview of the impact of bird hunting on populations and sustainability of the harvest is now available for these regions.

Of the 868 species of waterbirds recognized world-wide (Wetlands International 2002), a large proportion are known to be migratory and regularly cross national borders during the course of their migrations. The conservation and sustainable utilization of migratory birds constitute huge challenges in terms of international co-operation, which is very often made difficult by great differences in political regimes, language and culture over relatively short distances. The challenges differ widely from continent to continent. In the Palearctic region in particular, the migratory routes of waterbirds cross a very large number of political borders or limits between political regions where there were until recently (and in some instances, still are) historical and other politically created barriers that impede or prevent the integrated management of bird life. Even though the process of democratization has progressed quite far in many of the world's nations, and even though the last decade has witnessed radically improved means of communication, many countries and regions are lacking the resources and capacity for an elaborate programme of integrated waterbird management that also includes an assessment of harvest.

The terminology of international bird management and harvest assessment is imprecise and far from consistent. In this review, the term "harvest" is used to cover all kinds of active taking of wild bird resources, including any part or product of a bird, whatever the catching method used. Harvest in this sense does not cover the unintentional taking or killing of birds, and thus excludes the by-catch of waterbirds by fishing, and birds killed by oil disasters, traffic, pollution, etc. English terms for activities under this definition of harvest include collecting, gathering, hunting, shooting, wildfowling, trapping and netting.

## ELEMENTS AND TERMS OF SUSTAINABILITY

A widely accepted analysis divides sustainability into three equally important dimensions: ecological, economic and social. This review will focus on the dilemmas between ecological components on the one hand, and social and economic components on the other, and deal less with the significance of the economic resource itself (measured in monetary and meat values) and social dimensions. In the following discussion, social and economic components are treated together under the term "political components".

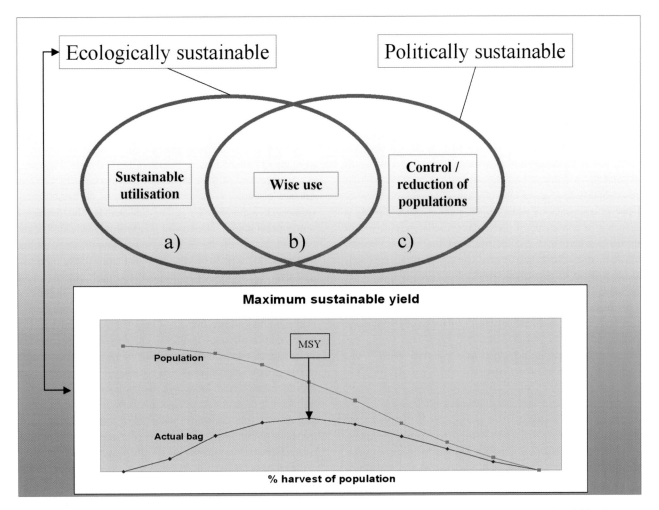

Fig. 1. Terms of sustainability. Fields of activities: a) ecologically, but not politically, sustainable harvest; b) politically acceptable activities that cause reduction or local extinction (regulation) of populations according to clearly set goals; c) ecologically and politically sustainable activities ("wise use"). See text for examples. The maximum sustainable yield (MSY) is defined as the percentage utilization that implies the largest yield and is obtained at intermediate harvest levels. Upper curve (pink): the size of the population; lower curve (blue): the size of the yield in absolute numbers; horizontal axis: the level of utilization of the population in percent.

The simplest component is the ecological one. This comprises the concept of the "harvest principle" which concerns population turnover and population dynamics. Basically, it is about production and mortality and the balance between these two. If production is greater than mortality, the population is growing; if production is smaller than mortality, the population is decreasing. In this context, it is important to consider the concepts of compensatory and additive mortality. The harvest principle is based on the fact that the causes of mortality may to some extent compensate for one another. If one mortality factor is reduced, another one increases, and the overall mortality remains constant. The same goes for mortality as a result of hunting. This effect appears to act within certain limits; it is most pronounced for r-strategists and least for K-strategists. If hunting mortality exceeds a certain limit, compensation mechanisms will no longer be sufficient to ensure that the other mortality factors are correspondingly reduced. Mortality has become additive, and hunting will, over time, cause a reduction in the population (see Fig. 1).

A fundamental concept in this context is maximum sustainable yield (MSY). This is defined on the basis of a given impact of utilization on the population in respect of density dependent productivity. Fig. 1 shows a classic relationship between utiliza-

tion, or harvest, of a population and the response of the population. The maximum sustainable yield is defined as the percentage utilization that implies the largest yield. It may be viewed as an element in the perception of ecological sustainability.

Ecological sustainability is a quantitative concept and requires only that a given harvest causes neither the extinction of the population nor a long-term decline. The term "long-term decline" is an open concept that until recently has not been formally defined in international bird management. At its third Meeting of Parties however, the African-Eurasian Migratory Waterbird Agreement (AEWA 2004) decided that: "A population in 'significant long-term decline' is one where the best available data, information or assessments indicate that it has declined by at least 25% in numbers or range over a period of 25 years or 7.5 generations." When, where and how the harvest takes place is of secondary importance in relation to ecological sustainability. A quantitative optimization of the annual yield may require that the harvest occurs in the period after reproduction and, at least in the case of waterbirds, in a system where the hunting areas and hunting methods are planned in such a way that disturbance is minimized and birds are not prevented from utilizing a given area. To ensure wider ecological sustainability of a given harvest, it is essential that the system is selective in relation to species or species groups, so that the harvest does not unintentionally influence the populations of other species in an unsustainable way through incidental catch or extensive disturbance.

Far more complex is the concept of political sustainability. This will be determined by what is "allowable" within a political region, typically a country, and will vary from region to region. Traditions, culture, ethics and a series of other societal elements will characteristically play a role in political sustainability.

It seems fundamental that a harvest must be ecologically sustainable in order to be politically sustainable, i.e. political sustainability is a subset of ecological sustainability. There is, however, an exception when management is aimed directly at reducing or eliminating a given species in a given area. The means to achieve such an objective maybe seen as ecologically unsustainable utilization – or what one may more appropriately call regulation or population control. Even though – or indeed because – the activity is ecologically unsustainable, it is politically sustainable. Hence, there is an extension of the politically sustainable field that falls outside the ecologically sustainable field (see Fig. 1).

In other words, in this model there are three fields within sustainability as a broad concept:

a) A field that expresses sustainable harvest ecologically, but not politically. Hence, there exists a series of species and species groups which, from a strictly ecological viewpoint, could be hunted, yet in most countries this does not occur because culture, tradition and other socially created conditions do not allow it;

b) A field that describes activities regarded as politically acceptable, in as much as they cause reduction or local extinction (regulation) of populations through management guided by clearly set goals. An example is the control measures taken against populations of waterbirds that damage agricultural crops. Even though there may not be a reduction in the overall population (meta-population), the objective of control is to reduce, or at best eradicate, a local population in a specific area; and

c) A field that describes the overlap between what is ecologically and politically sustainable. This field may be categorized within "wise use", a well-known concept that figures in a number of the international conventions on nature conservation.

On the whole, ecological sustainability may be viewed as a well-founded concept that refers to a mathematical assessment of MSY based on monitoring of populations as well as harvest, while political sustainability varies a great deal between countries and cultures, just as individual persons, on the basis of purely subjective judgement, may have widely differing perceptions of what may be accepted as sustainable utilization of natural resources.

## HARVEST – WHAT AND WHY?

As mentioned above, the term "harvest" is not unambiguous. In this review, the concept covers the "active taking of wild birds and products thereof". This makes a distinction between the gathering of products (collecting), trapping (where the prey is utilized for consumption or in some instances kept or traded alive), and

hunting. Methods differ widely from country to country and from one continent to another. The harvesting of waterbirds has been a very important activity for mankind since the Stone Age, and has been practised particularly by trapping in nets and snares and the collection of products from birds, notably their eggs. Only in recent times has the use of firearms become widespread. Collection of products is still very widespread in many parts of the world. One example is the collection of down of the Common Eider *Somateria mollissima* in Iceland. Here, 400 collectors annually gather 17 gm of down from each of 180 000 nests, amounting to a total harvest of three tonnes (S.B. Hauksson pers. comm.). Another example is the collection of eggs of the Northern Lapwing *Vanellus vanellus* in The Netherlands. This remains a very popular activity. No detailed information is available on the extent of the harvest, but in 2003 the European Court of Justice recognized the activity as legal under the terms of the EC Birds Directive, Article 9, which states that such activities must only account for "small quantities" (European Community 1979).

The capture of waterbirds is still common the world over. Methods differ widely from poisoning to passive trapping with snares, nets or fish traps, and active trapping systems that involve the release of nets by the hunter or the bird itself. The driving of birds, e.g. moulting geese, into nets is also a common activity. Nets are employed on land, in areas of shallow water. e.g. where birds are moulting, and in deeper water where birds are caught during their dives. As one example of waterbird catching on a large scale, more than one million waterbirds may be caught in a single year at Lake Chilwa in Malawi (Malawi Government 2000).

Hunting with weapons began with the use of throwing and thrusting tools such as stones, lances and spears. Over 20 000 years ago, hunting was revolutionized by the development of the bow and arrow. Only much later – less than one thousand years ago – have real firearms come into play. Today, these weapons are crucial for hunting, particularly in Europe and North America, and in many countries, no other method of harvesting is permitted. The rifle is used in some types of hunting, but the shotgun is by far the most important weapon in the hunting of waterbirds.

One example is the hunting of ducks and geese in North America (Table 1). This hunting takes place in autumn during the migration of the birds from their breeding areas to their wintering areas, and also in the wintering areas. Another example is the spring hunting of geese in Siberia. It has been estimated that about 300 000 geese of several species, but particularly the Greylag Goose *Anser anser*, are killed during a single season (E.E. Syroechkovski, Jr. pers. comm.).

Why harvest? Throughout the millennia, the primary motivation for harvest has been to ensure a supply of food and other useful natural products. This is still a very important motivation,

**Table 1. Harvest of Anseriformes in the USA in 1998. After Rothe (1999).**

| Flyway | Ducks | Geese |
|---|---|---|
| Atlantic | 2 371 000 | 498 000 |
| Mississippi | 9 384 000 | 1 424 000 |
| Central | 3 743 000 | 1 187 000 |
| Pacific | 3 643 000 | 396 000 |
| Total | 19 141 000 | 3 505 000 |

not only in developing countries, but also in Arctic regions where access to food resources other than those produced by nature is limited. An element of this "consumptive" motivation is that the harvest may be converted into other values, including monetary value. In much of the developed world, however, the primary motivation for harvest is relaxation, leisure and a passion for the hunt. This may be referred to as "recreational" motivation.

A third motivation for harvest is "management". Here, harvesting activities are carried out as part of the regulation or management of nature. Such activities include the control of wildlife to reduce damage to croplands, fisheries and the like. Usually, a harvest is driven by two of these motivations – or possibly by all three of them.

A typical example of hunting driven by both the need for food and the desire for recreation is the duck hunting in Western Europe, for example in Denmark. Here, the principal motivation is overtly the pleasure and excitement of hunting, but the reward in the shape of fresh, tasty meat is to many an equally strong factor. In Denmark, as in many other countries, one may encounter the whole three-fold motivation, for example in connection with goose hunting, where the hunt, in addition to providing recreation and the prospect of nice meat, may also be driven by a local need for management of the goose populations.

## HOW MUCH IS HARVESTED? – IMPACT AND MONITORING

An obvious question that most people might ask in relation to the harvest of waterbirds is "how much is actually harvested?" In order to assess the ecological sustainability of the harvest, it seems essential to be able to answer this question. Yet there are no surveys or censuses that give anything like a reliable estimate of the global extent of harvest of waterbirds. In North America and a number of Western European countries, quite detailed assessments of the harvest exist. In North America, it is even possible in the case of some species to compare measures of harvest with estimates of population size and thereby obtain an impression of the mortality imposed by hunting on the populations. The Mallard *Anas platyrhynchos* is considered to be the most heavily hunted species in North America. Judging from estimates of population size and harvest, the annual hunting mortality for Mallard is estimated to be below ten percent of the total population in autumn. Other species of waterfowl are pursued less intensively, and it is considered that the hunting mortality for these is in the order of a few percent.

Programmes for the monitoring of hunting harvests exist in a number of countries. In some cases, the reporting of harvests is voluntarily, while in others, it is mandatory. Denmark is one of the countries with the best reporting systems. The official Danish harvest statistics are derived from a mandatory reporting system for all Danish hunters, and have existed since 1942. They indicate that in Denmark about one million waterbirds are brought down annually. Of these, about one-third are thought to be Mallard that have been reared and released for hunting. However, the reporting is not carried out at the species level, but primarily refers to groups of species. For instance, six species of dabbling ducks, Northern Pintail *Anas acuta*, Eurasian Wigeon *A. penelope*, Common Teal *A. crecca*, Gadwall *A. strepera*, Garganey *A. querquedula* and Northern Shoveler *A. clypeata*, are grouped under the heading "other dabbling ducks". Hence,

no direct comparison of harvest and population size can be made at the species level. Therefore the Danish harvest statistics do not constitute a tool that can be used on its own for detailed management of species, either nationally or at the flyway level. First and foremost, the statistics provide basic information that can be used in a broader research context, e.g. interview surveys among hunters. For the last 20 years, the Danish harvest (bag) statistics have been supplemented by the collection of wings of bagged waterbirds and other migratory species. This is a voluntary system and provides valuable insight into the composition of the harvest with respect to species, age and sex. Moreover, it gives a picture of the geographical distribution of the harvest throughout the hunting season, as hunters report on the hunting ground. The number of collected wings has varied over the years, averaging about 11 000 per year (Clausager 2004).

Similar programmes for the collection of bag statistics are found in other countries, while at international level, there are various strategies, with that of Wetlands International's Waterbird Harvest Specialist Group (WHSG) being the most relevant with regard to the integrated monitoring of waterbird harvests.

Statistics on hunting bags are based on reports by the hunters. In this regard, the following analysis is important. Two concepts of yield are employed: the real yield (B) which is unknown, and the reported yield (Br). The real yield (B) may be viewed as a product of the population size (N) of a given species or species group multiplied by the hunting mortality (mh):

$$B = N \times m_h$$

If it is assumed that the hunting mortality is constant, trends in the yield will reflect trends in the population size. If the hunting mortality is known, which is only rarely the case in waterbirds, the yield may be recalculated into an actual population size.

The reported yield (Br) is a product of the real yield and a factor (f h) that expresses the willingness and ability of the hunters to report. Hence,

$$B_r = B \times f_h$$

This factor varies according to a series of circumstances, which include legislation for and promotion of the reporting system, the efficiency of the system, and the scepticism of the hunters towards the use of the data.

Given the above relationship, it must be recognized that the possibility for using reported bags as a reflection of the real bag and population size relies on a series of assumptions, and that sound management requires analysis of the various factors in play. Data, not least data at the flyway level, are considered to be vitiated by such uncertainty that for a broad range of species it is not possible to develop a reliable system that can serve as a stand-alone monitoring tool in international bird management. Assessments of yield are viewed first and foremost as a valuable supplement to internationally co-ordinated population counts, for instance, when special yield surveys are launched in relation to "hot species", e.g. huntable species that according to international standards have an unfavourable conservation status. It is, however, important to note that in many countries game yield statistics constitute a very valuable scientific basis for bird management. The systems that have been developed and the efforts which, for example, Wetlands International's Waterbird Harvest Specialist Group is carrying out at flyway level should therefore be promoted and supported.

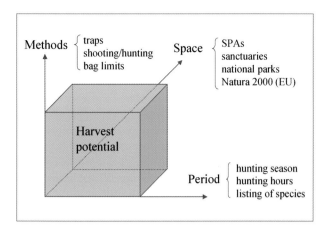

**Fig. 2.** Harvest management tools are the parameters that define the legal potential for harvest, here illustrated as a cube defined by three categories of management tools – period, methods and space – that specify 1) time periods, 2) harvest methodology, and 3) geographical areas, respectively.

## HARVEST MANAGEMENT TOOLS

The world over, there is a large number of different management tools regarding the harvest of waterbirds. In a few regions and countries, there are complete bans on harvest, but in by far the most countries, there is management that allows for harvest within certain limitations. The framework within which harvest can occur may be internationally established. At a global level, for example, the Ramsar Convention on Wetlands (Ramsar, 1971) sets certain guidelines for harvesting by referring generally to the principle of wise use, although it makes no specific demands regarding harvest.

In order to make the management tools operative, it may be useful to divide them into the following categories: (1) tools that specify time periods; (2) tools that specify harvest methodology; and (3) tools that specify geographical areas (Fig. 2).

The classic tool for management of harvest is the establishment of hunting seasons and hunting timetables. In many European countries, the first regulations based on hunting periods were established long ago in the nineteenth century. As mentioned above, the framework for hunting periods is determined in some regions by an international forum, e.g. within the European Union (EU). Hunting seasons are determined at national or sub-national level, and the fundamental principle is that there is no hunting either during spring migration of during the birds' breeding season, but rather immediately after reproduction when populations are at their largest and the biological potential for harvest is at its maximum. In many areas, however, hunting is also carried out before and during the breeding season. Such practice is not necessarily sustainable. In many countries, regulations are made concerning the time of day at which hunting is allowed. Thus, hunting at night is frequently regulated. In some countries, the hunting of geese, for example, is allowed only in the morning hours.

Another management tool which is frequently applied is based on regulation of the harvest in specific geographical management areas. There are a large number of definitions and concepts for such areas world-wide. The World Conservation Union – IUCN has established a series of categories, but the variation is great – from "strict nature reserves" to national parks, wildlife management areas and sanctuaries. Many of these management areas relate to an international classification, while others relate to national legislation. A well-known global network of areas some of which are especially designated for waterbirds are Ramsar sites, designated under the Convention on Wetlands. The Natura 2000 network is a network of sites established under the Birds and Habitats Directives of the EU. Even though the Ramsar Convention and the EU Directives do not specify particular rules for harvest in their respective designated sites, but merely call for general sustainability and a limitation of extensive disturbance, specific limitations on harvest have been established in both Ramsar sites and Natura 2000 sites in a number of countries. These limitations may constitute a complete ban on harvest, but more commonplace is the establishment of core areas with a very restrictive management regime, e.g. with prohibition of harvest, surrounded by a zone in which harvest may be regulated both in time and in the harvest methods that may be employed.

The third category of management tools is based on the methods of hunting and capture. As mentioned earlier, the methods of harvest of waterbirds vary widely throughout the world. Harvest methods are products of culture, tradition and technological development through the millennia. No quantification of the distribution of use of the various methods has ever been made. However, in the vast majority of western countries, the harvesting of waterbirds is carried out almost exclusively with firearms. Several international texts establish particular rules for harvest methods. The AEWA prescribes in its Action Plan (2.1.2 b) that the modes of taking are to be regulated. The EC Birds Directive (European Community 1979) prohibits the methods listed in its Annex IV, *inter alia*, snares, hooks, nets, traps, poisoned or anaesthetic bait, and semi-automatic or automatic weapons with a magazine capable of holding more than two rounds of ammunition. The Directive permits Member States to depart from these rules under certain conditions (Article 9). In many developing countries, firearms are used only to a limited extent in the harvesting of waterbirds. Here, nets, traps and snares are far more widespread.

A frequently used method of regulation is the establishment of bag limits. This is found in many regions of the Americas where the annual harvest is regulated by a special scoring system that sets limits on the number of waterbirds that a hunter may bag in a day. Bag limits are less widespread in Europe, where other means of regulation are more traditional. For certain species, the AEWA Action Plan (2.1.2 c) requires that its Parties to "establish limits on taking, where appropriate, and provide adequate controls to ensure that these limits are observed". Bag limits provide an option for regulating the total size of the harvest. However, the drawback to daily bag limits is that this system contributes to increasing the number of hunting days, and hence potentially increasing the temporal extent of hunting disturbance to waterbirds.

This model, in which management tools are divided into three dimensions (time periods, spatial tools and methods), provides a basis for analysing harvest management and comparing systems from different regions and countries. If the legal potential for harvest (the volume of the blue cube in Fig. 2) is perceived as a level for a sustainable harvest of a given population of waterbirds, it is up to the appropriate authorities in co-operation with stakeholders to organize each one of the dimensions of the cube in such a way that they comply best with

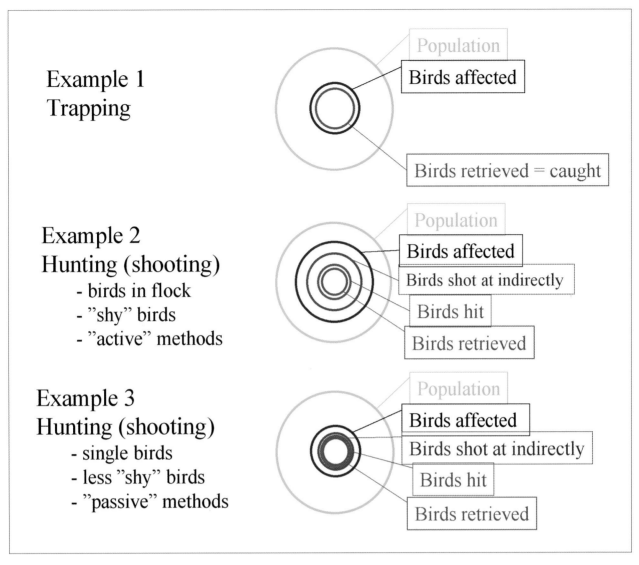

**Fig. 3.** Three examples of the impact of hunting / harvest. Example 1: passive capture, where the indirect effect of the harvest is limited relative to the yield. Example 2: active methods, where the effects are particularly strong, since the birds appear in flocks. Example 3: a situation is imagined where the hunting method is less aggressive and where the birds appear singly. The circles in Example 2 illustrate the gradient from all birds in the population (outer circle) to the birds that are bagged (innermost circle). In between lie the birds that are affected by the disturbance caused by the harvesting activity (circle 2), birds that are shot at indirectly or directly (circle 3), and birds that are hit (circle 4).

local traditions. This may produce an input to flyway-based management of migratory birds, with the Range States within the flyway first and foremost discussing and reaching agreement on levels of harvest, while the actual management takes place nationally or sub-nationally, and thereby in full compliance with the users and considering both ecological and social sustainability.

**IMPACT ON POPULATIONS**

An assessment of the ecological sustainability of a harvest should contain both an assessment of the actual yield and an assessment of the disturbance that a given harvest method inflicts on the population. Yield and disturbance both depend on the choice of harvesting methods. The use of firearms usually gives high selectivity in the yield itself, but has the potential to cause disturbance that has an impact on more species than just the target. The use of methods of passive capture, such as nets, traps and snares, gives low species selectivity, but also has a limited disturbance effect.

Fig. 3 shows a model that describes a gradient from the total number of individuals in a population to the number that are bagged. In between lie the number of birds that are affected by the disturbance caused by the harvesting activity, the birds that are shot at indirectly or directly, and the birds that are hit. It is customary for people involved in the administration of waterbird management to focus on the innermost and outermost quantities, i.e. the yield relative to the population, without giving serious consideration to the quantities lying in between. In effective management, however, it is important to assess sustainability with more refinement, so that it is emphasized in the choice of management that the populations are affected as little as possible relative to the purpose of the harvest. In this context, it is important to keep making a point of both the ecological and the political sustainability of the harvest.

One concrete example from Danish studies is shown in Fig. 4. This shows how the numbers of Eurasian Wigeon resting at Nibe Bredning are affected by the intensity of shooting from two types of shooting punts, i.e. small, flat-bottomed boats used

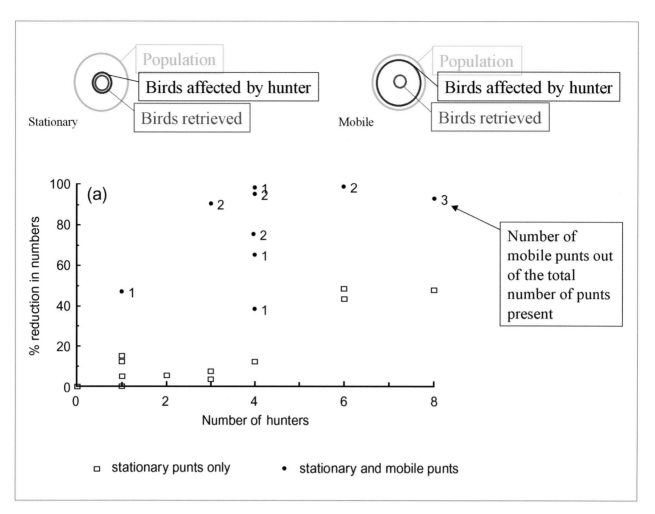

**Fig. 4.** The numbers of Eurasian Wigeon *Anas penelope* resting at Nibe Bredning, Denmark, in relation to 1) the numbers of punts, and 2) the type of hunting practice (stationary/mobile). After Madsen (1998).

for concealment during hunting (Madsen 1998). This analysis could open up a discussion of the selection of hunting methods. As trapping seems to cause less indirect impact on populations than other hunting methods, it might seem obvious to select this method instead of methods with a larger indirect impact. However, in most countries trapping is not seen as being selective (ecological aspects), and is therefore in direct conflict with national and international standards for the harvesting of waterbirds. Furthermore, in many countries, trapping of waterbirds does not meet ethical standards and does not comply with the general motivation for hunting. On the basis of the Danish studies, it could also be questioned why the use of mobile punts is allowed in Denmark. The answer is that mobile hunting can be managed in a sustainable way, even in areas with dense populations, as long as birds are provided with secure refuges (spatial tools). Furthermore, "stalking" birds with mobile punts is seen as a huge challenge, and complies very well with the "joy of hunting" motivation.

One more example to illustrate the model in Fig. 3 relates to circle 4, which describes the number of birds that are hit by shots. From a series of research programmes, it is known that only a subset of these are bagged. The difference between the two sets is calculated as the "non-retrieved harvest" which again may be subdivided into two groups: birds that die, and birds that survive. Birds that die without being retrieved should, from a management viewpoint, be added to the yield in as much as they

are lost to the population. In the USA, the "non-retrieved harvest" must be reported together with the rest of the yield. Birds that survive after being hit are defined as "wounded". This group has been the focus of attention in a number of countries, and the debate has been particularly directed towards the political (ethical) sustainability of the harvest. Experience in Denmark, for example, has shown that it has been possible to reduce the numbers of wounded Pink-footed Goose *Anser brachyrhynchus* by 75% simply by means of a campaign directed at hunters, and without legal interference.

**CO-MANAGEMENT**

In order to ensure political sustainability – in particular, the socio-economic aspects – programmes have been developed in many parts of the world to involve the local population in the management of natural resources, including the harvesting of waterbirds. An overall term for these efforts is "co-management". Co-management may be described in terms of co-operation between international, national and local stakeholders, and between stakeholders at the same level, e.g. various local user interests. Co-management is necessary, partly because many communities around the world are dependent on the utilization of natural resources including wild birds, and partly because no ecosystem is now "beyond the reach" of humans.

An example that illustrates the need for co-management is hunting in Greenland – a vast area with huge natural resources

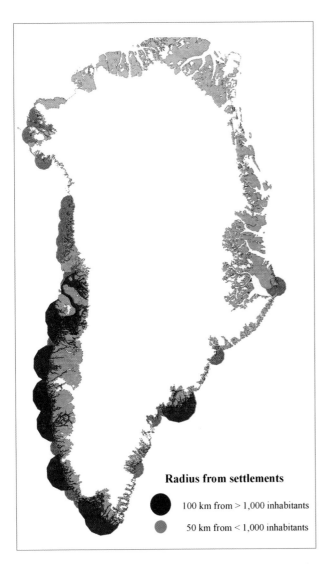

**Radius from settlements**

● 100 km from > 1,000 inhabitants

● 50 km from < 1,000 inhabitants

**Fig. 5.** The regions of Greenland's vast coastal areas that can be reached by motorboat, shown by circles with a radius of 100 km from communities of more than 1 000 inhabitants (blue), and 50 km from settlements of less than 1 000 inhabitants (orange). Communities around the world are dependent on the utilisation of natural resources including wild birds, and no ecosystem is "out of reach" of humans. Source: Due & Ingerslev (2000).

and a very small human population. However, there are indications that waterbird management in Greenland is not sustainable in every respect (Hansen 2001). Greenland has developed from being a vast natural environment which, by virtue of its size, could not be overexploited, into an area that because of modern means of transportation and capture has become vulnerable to human exploitation. Fig. 5 indicates those coastal areas of Greenland within a 100 km radius of communities of more than 1 000 inhabitants and those within a 50 km radius of settlements of less than 1 000 inhabitants. The figure demonstrates that very substantial parts of the west coast of Greenland may be reached in a short time from both small and large villages by modern means of transportation such as fast motor boats.

Another example is found at Lake Chilwa in the southern region of Malawi. This wetland, which has been designated as a Ramsar site (Ramsar Convention 1996), comprises mainly open water, *Typha* swamps, marshes and floodplain grasslands. Every year, Lake Chilwa supports about 153 resident species of waterbirds and 30 species of Palearctic migrants. The Lake Chilwa

catchment has a population density of 162 persons/sq. km, one of the highest in Malawi. Most of these people are subsistence farmers and/or fishermen. The waterbird populations are heavily utilized. There are at least 461 bird trappers using traditional traps and snares. Catching of birds takes place every year with a peak period in the rainy season. Birds are harvested for local consumption and for trade.

Management plans were developed at Lake Chilwa in 2001. The objectives were to enable the local communities to manage the natural resources in a sustainable manner for their own benefit. Bird hunting committees and a bird hunters' association were formed. A project was initiated in 2004 to build capacity in the local community, to encourage the participation of local NGOs in advising communities on sustainable bird management, and to encourage international NGOs to participate in research and monitoring.

## CONCLUSION

Waterbird harvest is widespread and is an important activity in local communities around the world. It is diverse and includes a huge variety of management systems. Although there are some examples of harvest practices being non-sustainable, there seems to be no reason to believe that harvesting/hunting is a general contradiction to the conservation of bird life. On the contrary, the right to use natural resources can motivate local people – especially hunters – to get involved in conservation. Training is a vital element. To build capacity at all levels, more knowledge is needed in terms of (a) the direct impact of harvest (bag, products) and indirect impact (disturbance); (b) population status and trends at flyway, migration route and population level; (c) mankind and nature, *vis-a-vis* development and conservation systems. To secure the conservation of flyways across borders and across continents world-wide, co-operation is needed at all levels – including that of the hunters.

## ACKNOWLEDGEMENTS

Colleagues and friends who supported the preparation of this paper are warmly acknowledged; in particular, Karsten Thomsen, who assisted with the technical aspects and final editing.

## REFERENCES

**AEWA** 2004. Agreement on the Conservation of African-Eurasian Migratory Waterbirds. Available at: http://www.cms.int/species/aewa/aew_text.htm.

**Clausager, I.** 2004. Wing survey from the 2003/04 hunting season in Denmark. Technical Report 504, Danish National Environmental Research Institute.

**Due, R. & Ingerslev, T.** (eds). 2000. Naturbeskyttelse i Grønland [Nature protection in Greenland]. Pinngortitaleriffik, Greenland Nature Institute. Technical Report No. 29. Available at: http://www.natur.gl/filer/Foelsomme_omraeder.pdf.

**European Community** 1979. Council Directive of 2 April 1979 on the conservation of wild birds (79/409/EEC as ammended). Available at: http://europa.eu.int/eur-lex/en/consleg/pdf/1979/en_1979 L0409_do_001.pdf.

**Hansen, K.** 2001. Farvel til Grønlands Natur [Farewell to Greenland's nature]. Gads Forlag.

**Madsen, J.** 1998. Experimental refuges for migratory waterfowl in Danish wetlands. I. Baseline assessment of the disturbance effects of recreational activities. Journal of Applied Ecology 35(3): 386-397.

**Malawi Government** 2000. Lake Chilwa Wetland State of the Environment. Environmental Affairs Department, Ministry of Natural Resources and Environmental Affairs. Report, June 2000.

**Ramsar Convention** 1996. Ramsar Convention Directory of Wetlands of International Importance, Lake Chilwa, Malawi. Wetlands International Site No. 1MW001. Available at: http://www.wetlands.org/reports/index.cfm.

**Rothe, T.C.** 1999. Compilation of data from the USA. U.S. Fish and Wildlife Service, Division of Migratory Bird Management.

**Wetlands International** 2002. Waterbird Population Estimates. Third Edition. Wetlands International Global Series No. 12, Wageningen, The Netherlands.

**World Commission for Environment and Development** 1987. Our Common Future. Oxford University Press, New York.

The Mallard *Anas platyrhynchos* is one of the most widely hunted waterbirds in the world. Photo: Niels Søndergaard.

# Cross-cutting research on a flyway scale - beyond monitoring

*David B. Lank & Silke Nebel[1]*

*Centre for Wildlife Ecology, Department of Biological Sciences, Simon Fraser University, 8888 University Dr., Burnaby, British Columbia, V5A 1S6, Canada. (email: dlank@sfu.ca)*
*[1]Present address: School of Biological, Earth & Environmental Sciences, University of New South Wales, Kensington, Sydney NSW 2052, Australia.*

Lank, D.B. & Nebel, S. 2006. Cross-cutting research on a flyway scale – beyond monitoring. *Waterbirds around the world.* Eds. G.C. Boere, C.A. Galbraith & D.A. Stroud. The Stationery Office, Edinburgh, UK. pp. 107-112.

## ABSTRACT

Research on the population ecology of migratory birds is facilitated by a holistic or "cross-cutting" approach that synthesizes information gathered across the entire flyway, throughout the annual cycle and utilizing different research disciplines. Radio-tracking Western Sandpipers *Calidris mauri* from non-breeding to breeding grounds documented migration timing and usage of stopover sites. Data collected throughout the non-breeding range showed that females migrated farther south than males, and that juveniles were over-represented towards the extremes. Collaboration documented a latitudinal "life-history divide": northerly juveniles migrate and attempt to breed, while southerly juveniles oversummer at non-breeding sites. As predicted by life history theory, southerly birds appear to have higher annual survival rates than migrants. Comparing daily survival rates during breeding, non-breeding and annual periods permits the calculation of survival rates during migratory periods. Integrated studies of behavioral ecology, demography and physiology allowed interpretation of an apparent local population decline in migrating Western Sandpipers. Dramatically decreased usage of a small stopover site occurred despite abundant food resources, and appeared to be caused by a behavioral change in response to increasing falcon populations, rather than a decrease in numbers of migrants. The combination of approaches allowed testing alternative hypotheses as likely causes for the change in site usage.

## INTRODUCTION

Understanding population regulation is a key issue in the study of migratory birds, but it acquires special urgency in species that suffer from decreasing population numbers. In shorebirds (family Scolopacidae), population declines are widespread: more than half of all shorebird populations world-wide are thought to be declining (International Wader Study Group 2003, Stroud *et al.* 2004, 2006), and within North America, this estimate is as high as 80% (Morrison *et al.* 2001).

A long-term research program organized by the Centre for Wildlife Ecology (CWE) at Simon Fraser University, Canada, is using a cross-seasonal and cross-disciplinary approach to study population ecology and, ultimately, population regulation of a migratory shorebird (Nebel & Lank 2003). This holistic approach is based on the synergy gained from synthesizing information sampled across the entire flyway, throughout the annual cycle, and utilizing different research disciplines, creating opportunities for conservation work (Harrington *et al.* 2002).

The Western Sandpiper *Calidris mauri* was chosen as a model species, being the most abundant shorebird on the American Pacific coast. Western Sandpipers breed in western Alaska and eastern Siberia, and overwinter along the American Pacific coast between southern Canada and Peru, and, in smaller numbers, along the Atlantic coast and in the Caribbean (Wilson 1994, Nebel *et al.* 2002). Over 90% of captured birds may be confidently assigned a sex based on bill lengths (Page & Fearis 1971).

The CWE fostered research on diverse aspects of the species' biology by organizing a loose association of researchers working throughout the species' range to collaborate and exchange information (see Acknowledgements). Members consulted with government wildlife managers and non-governmental agency scientists, recruited academics in complimentary fields to work with the species, steered post-doctorate, graduate and undergraduate students towards particular projects, and provided seed funding for researchers elsewhere, particularly in Latin America. The group created a sense of common purpose during annual workshops, which attracted additional participants to the network, and through an electronic list-server.

## CUTTING ACROSS THE FLYWAY

A series of radio-tracking studies of migrant Western Sandpipers conducted over five seasons between 1995 and 2004 during northward migrations from Mexico and California to Alaska capitalized on this network. Collaborators produced detailed information on the movements and stopovers of individual shorebirds with respect to age, sex, time of year, weather conditions, staging site, and year (Iverson *et al.* 1996, Butler *et al.* 1997, Bishop & Warnock 1998, Warnock & Bishop 1998, Butler *et al.* 2002). These studies strengthened the evidence that 80-90% of the Western Sandpiper population use the Copper River Delta, Alaska, towards the end of their northward migration. The length of stay estimated for that site from radio-tracking data was integrated with census data to improve estimates of the species' total population size (Bishop *et al.* 2000). Further analysis of the wealth of data generated by this work will help test individually-based models of migratory strategy, which may be used to predict the population consequences of migratory habitat change.

As a second example, we improved the resolution of a pattern of sexual segregation of Western Sandpipers during the non-breeding season by combining information from 13 different sites, and discovered a novel pattern with respect to age (Nebel *et al.* 2002). Females migrate farther south than males, creating a latitudinal cline between sex ratio and Great Circle distance from the breeding grounds (Fig. 1). The local proportions of juveniles fit a significant U-shape with respect to migration distance (Fig. 2), which interacts with the sexual segregation such that juvenile males are substantially over-represented in samples from the northern end of the distribu-

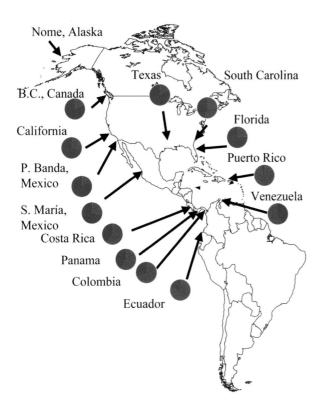

Fig. 1. The proportion of female (red) and male (blue) Western Sandpipers *Calidris mauri* on the non-breeding grounds.

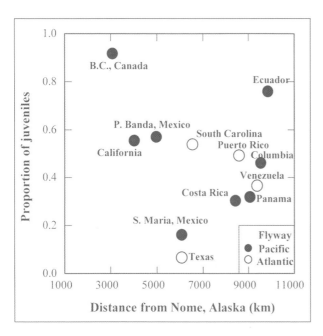

Fig. 2. Age ratios of Western Sandpipers *Calidris mauri* captured at 12 non-breeding locations. The local proportions of juveniles caught at each site vs. migration distance described a U-shaped pattern ($F_{1,22}=5.08$, $P<0.005$; after Nebel *et al.* 2002, reproduced with permission from The Auk).

tion, and juvenile females over-represented in samples from the southern end.

The distributions of sex and age classes also interact with a latitudinal difference in life history strategy (Fernández *et al.* 2004, O'Hara *et al.* 2005). Juveniles at non-breeding sites in Mexico predominantly migrate north and attempt to breed as

one-year-olds, while juveniles in Panama do not migrate, and instead "oversummer" on the non-breeding grounds. We infer that juveniles adopt one of two life history strategies, with shorter-distance migrants opting to attempt migration and breeding at a younger age, and longer-distance migrants maximizing first year survival at the expense of an earlier potential breeding opportunity.

This difference in strategies could map onto biological population differentiation, but none is currently recognized, and disproportionate representation of the sexes at different non-breeding areas makes this seem an unlikely situation. Alternatively, we may have documented two tactics of a conditional strategy (*sensu* Gross 1996), in which case the choice of tactics depends on an environmental cue, such as hatch date, and/or on developmental characteristics, such as body size. In this situation, migration distance itself might follow from a life-history decision based on condition made in Alaska prior to migration, or the opposite might occur, namely that the life history difference might follow from factors determining migration distance (O'Hara *et al.* 2002, O'Hara *et al.* 2005).

If lifetime reproductive success of individuals migrating south to different latitudes is similar, annual survival rates should be higher among oversummering juveniles than among juveniles migrating north in their first year, in order to offset the earlier age of first reproduction of migrants. Western Sandpiper researchers throughout the range and annual cycle have used mark-recapture studies to estimate $\phi$, the rate of local survival, which provides a minimum estimate of true annual survival rate (Table 1), and return rates, which will approach $\phi$ if detection rates are high. Estimates of survival rates obtained at breeding and non-breeding grounds show some general agreement, assuming similar levels of permanent emigration. As predicted, local annual survival is lower in Mexico than Panama. As mark-recapture studies proliferate, comparisons among local survival rates derived from different situations and/or populations may refine our views of local habitat suitability and other aspects of population structure.

## CUTTING ACROSS THE ANNUAL CYCLE

Population managers recognize that partitioning the timing of annual mortality across seasons and locations improves their ability to target conservation action. Studies based on band recovery data can rarely address this question directly. The development and widespread availability of capture-recapture analysis tools (Lebreton *et al.* 1992, White & Burnham 1999) enabled researchers at different sites and seasons to collaborate to obtain the necessary information. The best examples are studies of individually marked geese, which carry conspicuous markers that facilitate re-sightings. For some populations, lower daily survival rates occurred during migration than in winter or summer (Owen & Black 1991, Clausen *et al.* 2001), perhaps due to hunting (Ward *et al.* 1997). Other studies found lower survival rates during breeding seasons (including migratory flights) (Madsen *et al.* 2002), concluded that breeding, wintering and even migration seasons had similar rates of natural mortality (Gauthier *et al.* 2001), or that seasonal patterns differed by sex (Schmutz & Ely 1999). Each study suggests specific management actions, and the ecological reasons for the diversity of situations contribute towards our general understanding of population regulation.

The use of mark-recapture information was taken a step further by combining information derived from different

**Table 1. Annual local survival rates for Western Sandpipers *Calidris mauri* studied at breeding (B) and non-breeding sites (N).**

| Location | Season | Estimates of $\phi$ or return rates (rr) | Source |
|---|---|---|---|
| Nome, Alaska | B | 0.62, 0.57 males* | Sandercock *et al.* 2000 |
| | | 0.59, 0.55 females* | |
| Yukon-Kuskokwim Delta, Alaska | B | rr = 0.58 males | Holmes 1971, Oring & Lank 1984 |
| | | rr = 0.49 females | Ruthrauff & McCaffery, pers. comm. |
| | | 0.67 males** | |
| | | 0.40 females** | |
| Cabo Rojo, Puerto Rico | N | 0.56 adults | Rice 1995 |
| | | 0.61 juveniles | |
| Chitré, Panama | N | 0.54 males | O'Hara *et al.* 2002 |
| | | 0.62 females | |
| Punta Banda, Mexico | N | 0.49 adult males | Fernández *et al.* 2003 |
| | | 0.45 juvenile males | |

\* estimates from two years, samples of nearly all adults
\*\* data from 1998-2002

populations of marked individuals. Sillett & Holmes (2002) obtained estimates of seasonal and annual survival rates from separate local populations of Black-throated Blue Warblers *Dendroica caerulescens* on the breeding grounds in New Hampshire, USA, and on the wintering grounds in Jamaica. Under the assumption that the individuals studied were representative of summer and winter populations, they combined their seasonal estimates with estimates of annual survival rates, and calculated survival rates during the migratory periods, which could not be studied directly. They concluded that the daily mortality rate during migration was 15 times higher than during the two residency seasons. Multiple mark-recapture data sets are becoming available for many non-game species, and comparisons among them may permit additional analyses along these lines. With Western Sandpipers, for example, we hope to develop techniques for combining information from the mark-recapture studies shown in Table 1 to address questions about seasonal survival rates and relative habitat quality.

## CUTTING ACROSS DISCIPLINES

Wildlife managers are often called upon to act in response to changes in local population size. Over the past decade, the cumulative number of Western Sandpipers counted during southward migration at the Sidney Island lagoon, a small stopover site in British Columbia, Canada, declined drastically from c. 16 000 to 4 000 (Ydenberg *et al.* 2004), creating a strong incentive to understand the factors causing this change. Members of the Western Sandpiper research group have collaborated, integrating behavioral, ecological, demographic and physiological studies to address this question.

The Sidney Island lagoon includes c. 100 ha of mudflat, surrounded on three sides by a forest and beach. Across the Strait of Georgia, 40 km east of Sidney Island, is the Fraser River estuary, the major stopover site in British Columbia, with over 5 000 ha of open mudflats that are used by up to a million shorebirds every autumn and spring. We do not know whether population changes have also occurred at the Fraser estuary because the size of the site makes it difficult to census. However, comparisons of attributes of both areas, and of birds captured at them, have

been useful in our analysis of this situation (Lissimore *et al.* 1999, Ydenberg *et al.* 2002, Ydenberg *et al.* 2004).

At Sidney Island, migrating Western Sandpipers were captured, measured, individually marked, and re-sighted daily during the years of population decline; birds were also captured and measured at the Fraser estuary. At Sidney Island, the body mass of captured birds decreased by c. 10% during this period, while no change was observed at the Fraser estuary. Mark-recapture analysis showed a decline in the length of stay of southbound Western Sandpipers using Sidney Island, falling from about eight days in 1992 to about three days in 2001. These changes suggested that deteriorating food conditions at Sidney Island might cause changes in sandpiper numbers.

Western Sandpipers feed on soft-bodied macro-faunal and meio-faunal invertebrates (Sutherland *et al.* 2000, Wolf 2001), making it difficult and time-consuming to measure food abundance directly. However, recent advances in physiological methods offer novel ways to obtain indicator values for the quality of the resources at a site. Blood plasma triglyceride levels in Western Sandpipers correlate with fattening rates as well as with direct measures of food abundance (Williams *et al.* 1999, Guglielmo *et al.* 2005, Seaman 2003). Triglyceride levels of Western Sandpipers caught at Sidney Island in 1996 were twice as high as at the Fraser estuary (Ydenberg *et al.* 2002), casting doubt on lower food availability as an explanation for decreased usage of Sidney Island. Why, then, did Western Sandpipers leave Sidney Island before reaching a body mass comparable to birds at the nearby Fraser Estuary?

The past two decades have seen a steady increase in populations of the Peregrine Falcon *Falco peregrinus* in western North America (Hoffman & Smith 2003), following severe declines caused by the extensive use of DDT after the Second World War. Daily Peregrine sightings during southward migratory periods in the Strait of Georgia increased steeply since at least 1985 (Ydenberg *et al.* 2004). Western Sandpipers are preyed upon by Peregrines, and their escape performance decreases with increasing body mass (Burns & Ydenberg 2002). Individuals accumulating fat for onward migration are therefore especially vulnerable to predators. Peregrines are most successful when

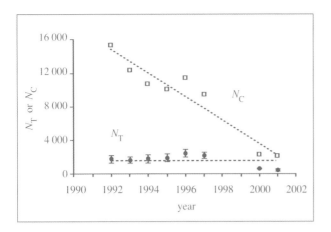

Fig. 3. Comparison of annual cumulative daily counts (NC) of Western Sandpipers *Calidris mauri* stopping over at Sidney Island with estimates of the true number (NT), which take into account the estimate of length of stay. The values for NC indicate a significantly declining trend of c. 18% per year. In contrast, estimates of NT indicate no significant (*P* = 0.24) decline (after Ydenberg *et al.* 2004; reproduced with permission from The Royal Society of London).

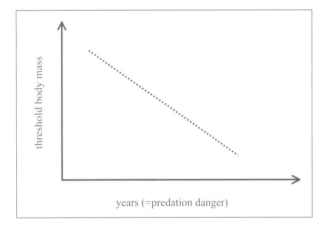

Fig. 4. A bird should switch from a more dangerous but more profitable site to a safer but less profitable site as a function of body mass, which determines its relative escape performance. With increasing predation danger over time, the threshold body mass for changing habitats decreases.

attacking by surprise, which is facilitated by cover, such as high vegetation. The Fraser estuary is large and open, and therefore a relatively safe place for a foraging sandpiper, while Sidney Island is small, enclosed, and inherently more dangerous (Ydenberg *et al.* 2002).

Within this context, Ydenberg *et al.* (2004) developed a hypothesis to explain the change in census numbers at Sidney Island: site choice is driven by a mass-dependent trade-off between local predation danger and foraging profitability. An individual is predicted to switch from a profitable, but dangerous site, to a less profitable, but safer site, contingent on relative marginal fitness values which may be represented as a threshold mass (Fig. 4). With increasing falcon abundance, this trade-off is thought to have led to the following dynamics at Sidney Island: increased danger ⇒ lower mass departure threshold ⇒ shorter length of stay ⇒ fewer birds counted.

Estimates of the true population size of migrants based on census data are particularly sensitive to length of stay. Ydenberg *et al.* (2004) used the mark-recapture data to estimate the actual annual number of birds moving through Sidney Island, incorpo-

rating information on length of stay. There was no evidence that fewer individuals passed through the site in later years (Fig. 3); instead, the steep census decline was accounted for almost entirely by the shortened length of stay. Thus, a change in behaviour, rather than a decrease in local population size, was responsible for the apparent decline.

Recoveries in raptor populations are taking place on continental scales in both the eastern and western hemispheres (Cade *et al.* 1988, Kjellén & Roos 2000, Hoffman & Smith 2003), and must have direct effects on mortality rates of their prey. More important, however, may be indirect effects, such as the changes in habitat usage as illustrated here, in response to changes in environmental danger (*sensu* Lank & Ydenberg 2003). The evidence for declining shorebird populations in North America comes primarily from counts made during migration (Morrison *et al.* 2001). Changes in length of stay alter the cumulative number of birds censused and peak counts, both of which are commonly used as indices in analyses of trends in population size. If changes in the use of smaller stopover sites, which are more easily monitored with precision, are taking place elsewhere, behavioral changes could account for part of the perceived population declines (Ydenberg *et al.* 2004). Other behavioral variables that could affect census data include changes in the timing or route of migration, which also may be influenced by predation danger (Lank *et al.* 2003). The potential effects of habitat or other behavioral changes should be taken into account when designing monitoring programs and interpreting data from them.

## CONCLUSION

The potential benefits of "cross-cutting" approaches to studies of the population ecology of migratory species may seem obvious, but what are the additional costs associated with this approach? These include generating and adopting common protocols for gathering data, steering students towards projects suitable for thesis topics, and spending far more time in the production of multi-authored reports than might be the case for more independent research. Enticing researchers who work in related fields to address questions of interest is potentially a highly cost-effective approach, as these researchers may subsequently bring more resources to the table as their interests grow, but it has the disadvantage that progress with a project will be limited by the schedules of multiple collaborators, each of whom can slow things down. We have invested considerable time in organizing meetings; this time paid off not only with exchange of information, but also in fostering a sense of common purpose and identity that kept participants engaged with the work. But fundamentally, we have found that collaborations are most likely to prosper if they take advantage of pre-existing interests in the populations or topics being addressed. Much of the success of our network came simply by identifying persons already enthusiastic about a question, supporting their individual efforts, and fostering communication and collaboration among them and with ourselves.

## ACKNOWLEDGEMENTS

We thank the Western Sandpiper Research Network, including the persons listed below, each of whom has made a substantial original contribution, knowingly or not. Fred Cooke and Rob Butler (Canadian Wildlife Service) initiated the CWE's focus on this species. For work covered in this review: Nils Warnock, Mary

Anne Bishop and John Takekawa organized northward radio-tracking; Patrick O'Hara worked with Franciso Delgado and others in Panama; Guillermo Fernández worked with Horacio de la Cueva and others in Mexico; Tony Williams and his students Chris Guglielmo and Dana Seaman pursued physiological approaches; and Ron Ydenberg promoted interest in the potential effects of predators on everything. Additional researchers working on the breeding grounds include: Bart Kempenares, Rick Lanctot, Brian McCaffery, Julie Neville, Dan Ruthrauff, Brett Sandercock, and Doug Schamel and family; on migration: Pat Baird, James Burns, Colin Clark, Oliver Egeler, Bob Elner, D.L. Jackson, Gary Kaiser, Barbara Kus, Moira Lemon, Darren Lissimore, James Lyons, Kim Mathot, Edmund Martinez, Amanda Niehaus, Katie O'Reilly, Lew Oring, Brent Ortego, Andrea Pomeroy, Pippa Sheppard, Mary Sewell, Will Stein, Barry Smith, Terri Sutherland, Nick Wolf, Peggy Yen, and Janet Yu; and on the wintering grounds: Felipe Becerril, Alejandra Buenorostro, Roberto Carmona, Jaimie Collazo, Daniel Estrada, Ben Haase, Brian Harrington, Francine Mercier, Susan Rice, Yolanda Sandoval, and Brian Watts.

Barbara Ganter pointed us towards studies of seasonal survival rates in geese, and Ron Ydenberg provided feedback on drafts of the manuscript.

Participants in the Western Sandpiper Research Network have received support from: the Centre for Wildlife Ecology and other programs at Simon Fraser University, The Canadian Wildlife Service and its Latin America Program, Environment Canada, the National Research and Engineering Council of Canada, the Department of Northern and Indian Affairs, Queen's University (Canada), and the Killiam Postdoctoral Program at the University of British Columbia; the US Geological Survey, US Fish and Wildlife Service, National Parks Service, Forest Service, National Science Foundation, Department of Defence, and Environmental Protection Agency; the Smithsonian Tropical Research Station; the Marine Ecosystem Health Program; the National Fish and Wildlife Foundation; Centro de Investigación Científica y de Educación Superior de Ensenada (CICISE); the Consejo Nacional de Ciencia y Tecnología (CONACYT, Mexico); the Patolandia Hunting Club; the European Science Agency; the Konrad Lorenz Institute for Comparative Ethology; the Belgium Fund for Scientific Research; the Point Reyes Bird Observatory; the American Wildlife Research Foundation, Inc.; Chase Wildlife Foundation; Ducks Unlimited; the Lincoln Park Zoo; Sigma Xi; and the John Cooper, Frank M. Chapman, and Jennifer Robinson Memorial Funds.

The authors thank the organizers of the Waterbirds around the world Conference for the invitation to present this work, and Wetlands International for financial support that facilitated Silke Nebel's participation at the meeting.

## REFERENCES

Bishop, M.A. & Warnock, N. 1998. Migration of Western Sandpipers: links between their Alaskan stopover areas and breeding grounds. Wilson Bulletin 110: 457-462.

Bishop, M.A., Meyers, P.M. & McNeley, P.F. 2000. A method to estimate migrant shorebird numbers on the Copper River Delta, Alaska. Journal of Field Ornithology 71: 627-637.

Burns, J.G. & Ydenberg, R.C. 2002. The effects of wing loading and gender on the escape flights of least sandpipers (*Calidris minutilla*) and western sandpipers

(*Calidris mauri*). Behavioral Ecology and Sociobiology 52: 128-136.

Butler, R.W., Williams, T.D., Warnock, N. & Bishop, M.A. 1997. Wind assistance: a requirement for migration of shorebirds? Auk 114: 456-466.

Butler, R.W., Shepherd, P.C.F. & Lemon, M.J.F. 2002. Site fidelity and local movements of migrating western sandpipers on the Fraser River estuary. Wilson Bulletin 114: 485-490.

Cade, T.J., Enderson, J.E., Thelander, C.G. & White, C.M. 1988. Peregrine falcon populations, their management, and recovery. The Peregrine Fund, Inc., Boise, ID.

Clausen, P., Frederiksen, M., Percival, S.M., Anderson, G.Q.A. & Denny, M.J.H. 2001. Seasonal and annual survival of East-Atlantic Pale-bellied Brent Geese *Branta hrota* assessed by capture-recapture analysis. Ardea 89: 101-111.

Fernández, G., de la Cueva, H., Warnock, N. & Lank, D.B. 2003. Apparent survival rates of Western Sandpiper wintering in northwest Baja California, Mexico. Auk 120: 55-61.

Fernández, G., O'Hara, P.D. & Lank, D.B. 2004. Tropical and subtropical Western Sandpipers (*Calidris mauri*) differ in life history strategies. Ornitología Neotropical 15 (S): 385-394.

Gauthier, G., Pradel, R., Menu, S. & Lebreton, J.D. 2001. Seasonal survival of Greater Snow Geese and effect of hunting under dependence in sighting probability. Ecology 82: 3105-3119.

Gross, M.R. 1996. Alternative reproductive strategies and tactics: diversity within sexes. TREE 11: 92-98.

Guglielmo, C.G., Cerasale, D.J. & Eldermire, C. 2005. A field validation of plasma metabolites profiling to assess refueling performance of migratory birds. Physiological and Biochemical Zoology 76: 116-125.

Harrington, B.A., Brown, S.C., Corven, J. & Bart, J. 2002. Collaborative approaches to the evolution of migration and the development of science-based conservation in shorebirds. Auk 119: 914-921.

Hoffman, S.W. & Smith, J.P. 2003. Population trends of migratory raptors in western North America, 1977-2001. Condor 105: 397-419.

Holmes, R.T. 1971. Density, habitat, and the mating system of the Western Sandpiper (*Calidris mauri*). Oecologia 7: 191-208.

International Wader Study Group 2003. Are waders worldwide in decline? Reviewing the evidence. Wader Study Group Bulletin 101/102: 8-12.

Iverson, G.C., Warnock, S.E., Butler, R.W., Bishop, M.A. & Warnock, N. 1996. Spring migration of Western Sandpipers along the Pacific coast of North America: a telemetry study. Condor 98: 10-21.

Kjellén, N. & Roos, G. 2000. Population trends in Swedish raptors demonstrated by migration counts at Falsterbo, Sweden 1942-97. Bird Study 47: 195-211.

Lank, D.B. & Ydenberg, R.C. 2003. Death and danger at migratory stopovers: problems with "predation risk". Journal of Avian Biology 34: 225-228.

Lank, D.B., Butler, R.W., Ireland, J. & Ydenberg, R.C. 2003. Effects of predation danger on migration strategies of sandpipers. Oikos 103: 303-319.

Lebreton, J.-D., Burnham, K.P., Clobert, J. & Anderson, D.R. 1992. Modeling survival and testing biological hypotheses using marked animals: a unified approach with case studies. Ecological Monographs 62: 67-118.

Lissimore, D., Lemon, M., Lank, D.B., Butler, R.W. & Ydenberg, R.C. 1999. Large and consistent body mass differences of migrant *Calidris* sandpipers at adjacent stopover sites: phenomenon and possible explanations. Wader Study Group Bulletin 88: 55-58.

Madsen, J., Frederiksen, M. & Ganter, B. 2002. Trends in annual and seasonal survival of Pink-footed Geese *Anser brachyrhynchus*. Ibis 144: 218-226.

Morrison, R.I.G., Aubry, Y., Butler, R.W., Beyersbergen, G.W., Donaldson, G.M., Gratto-Trevor, C.L., Hicklin, P.W., Johnston, V.H. & Ross, R.K. 2001. Declines in North American shorebird populations. Wader Study Group Bulletin 94: 34-38.

Nebel, S. & Lank, D.B. 2003. Cross-seasonal and cross-disciplinary studies of migratory shorebirds. Wader Study Group Bulletin 100: 118-121.

Nebel, S., Lank, D.B., O'Hara, P.D., Fernández, G., Haase, B., Delgado, F., Estela, F.A., Evans Ogden, L.J., Harrington, B., Kus, B.E., Lyons, J.E., Mercier, F., Ortego, B., Takekawa, J.Y., Warnock, N. & Warnock, S.E. 2002. Western Sandpipers during the nonbreeding season: spatial segregation on a hemispheric scale. Auk 119: 922-928.

O'Hara, P.D., Lank, D.B. & Delgado, F.S. 2002. Is the timing of moult altered by migration? Evidence from a comparison of age and residency classes of Western Sandpipers *Calidris mauri* in Panama. Ardea 90: 61-70.

O'Hara, P.D., Fernández, G., Becerril, F., de la Cueva, H. & Lank, D.B. 2005. Life history varies with migratory distance in Western Sandpipers (*Calidris mauri*). Journal of Avian Biology 36: 191-202.

Oring, L.W. & Lank, D.B. 1984. Breeding area fidelity, natal philopatry, and the social systems of sandpipers. In: J. Burger & B.L. Olla (eds) Shorebirds: Breeding Behavior and Populations. Plenum Publishing Corporation, New York: 125-147.

Owen, M. & Black, J.M. 1991. The importance of migration mortality in non-passerine birds. In: C.M. Perrins, J.-D. Lebreton & G.J.M. Hirons (eds) Bird Population Studies: Relevance to Conservation and Management. Oxford University Press, Oxford: 360-372.

Page, G.W. & Fearis, B. 1971. Sexing Western Sandpipers by bill length. Bird Banding 42: 297-298.

Rice, S.M. 1995. Residency rates, annual return rates and population estimates of Semipalmated and Western Sandpipers at the Cabo Rojo Salt Flats, Puerto Rico. MSc thesis, University of Puerto Rico, Puerto Rico.

Sandercock, B.K., Lank, D.B., Lanctot, R.B., Kempenaers, B. & Cooke, F. 2000. Ecological correlates of mate fidelity in two Arctic-breeding sandpipers. Canadian Journal of Zoology 78: 1948-1958.

Schmutz, J.A. & Ely, C.R.E. 1999. Survival of Greater White-fronted Geese: Effects of year, season, sex, and body condition. Journal of Wildlife Management 63: 1239-1249.

Seaman, D.A. 2003. Landscape physiology: plasma metabolites, fattening rates and habitat quality in migratory Western Sandpipers. MSc thesis, Simon Fraser University, Burnaby.

Sillett, T.S. & Holmes, R.T. 2002. Variation in survivorship of a migratory songbird throughout its annual cycle. Journal of Animal Ecology 71: 296-308.

Stroud, D.A., Davidson, N.C., West, R., Scott, D.A., Haanstra, L., Thorup, O., Ganter, B. & Delany, S. (compilers, on behalf of the International Wader Study Group) 2004. Status of migratory wader populations in Africa and Western Eurasia in the 1990s. International Wader Studies 15: 1-259.

Stroud, D.A., Baker, A., Blanco, D.E., Davidson, N.C., Delany, S., Ganter, B., Gill, R., González, P., Haanstra, L., Morrison, R.I.G., Piersma, T., Scott, D.A., Thorup, O., West, R., Wilson, J. & Zöckler, C. (on behalf of the International Wader Study Group). 2006. The conservation and population status of the world's waders at the turn of the millennium. Waterbirds around the world. G.C. Boere, C.A. Galbraith & D.A. Stroud (Eds.), The Stationery Office, Edinburgh, UK. 643-648.

Sutherland, T.F., Shepherd, P.C.F. & Elner, R.W. 2000. Predation on meiofaunal and macrofaunal invertebrates by western sandpipers (*Calidris mauri*): evidence for dual foraging modes. Marine Biology 137: 983-993.

Ward, D.H., Rexstad, E.A., Sedinger, J.S., Lindberg, M.S. & Dawe, N.K. 1997. Seasonal and annual survival of adult Pacific Brant. Journal of Wildlife Management 61: 773-781.

Warnock, N. & Bishop, M.A. 1998. Spring stopover ecology of migrant Western Sandpipers. Condor 100: 456-467.

White, G.C. & Burnham, K.P. 1999. Program MARK: Survival estimation from populations of marked animals. Bird Study 46 S: 120-138.

Williams, T.D., Guglielmo, C.G., Egeler, O. & Martyniuk, C.J. 1999. Plasma lipid metabolites provide information on mass change over several days in captive Western Sandpipers. Auk 116: 994-1000.

Wilson, W.H. 1994. Western Sandpiper (*Calidris mauri*). In: A. Poole & F. Gill (eds) The Birds of North America. Academy of Natural Sciences, Philadelphia, Pennsylvania; American Ornithologists' Union, Washington, D.C.

Wolf, N. 2001. Foraging ecology and stopover site selection of migrating Western Sandpipers (*Calidris mauri*). MSc thesis, Simon Fraser University, Burnaby.

Ydenberg, R.C., Butler, R.W., Lank, D.B., Guglielmo, C.G., Lemon, M. & Wolf, N. 2002. Trade-offs, condition dependence and stopover site selection by migrating sandpipers. Journal of Avian Biology 33: 47-55.

Ydenberg, R.C., Butler, R.W., Lank, D.B., Smith, B.D. & Ireland, J. 2004. Western sandpipers have altered migration tactics as peregrine populations have recovered. Proceedings of The Royal Society of London B 271: 1263 - 1269.

# Conservation of albatrosses and petrels of the Southern Ocean

*John Cooper*

*Avian Demography Unit, Department of Statistical Sciences, University of Cape Town, Rondebosch 7701, South Africa.*
*(email: jcooper@adu.uct.ac.za)*

Cooper, J. 2006. Conservation of albatrosses and petrels of the Southern Ocean. *Waterbirds around the world.* Eds. G.C. Boere, C.A. Galbraith & D.A. Stroud. The Stationery Office, Edinburgh, UK. pp. 113-119.

## ABSTRACT

Albatrosses and petrels are among the world's most threatened birds, and among the most migratory, undertaking vast movements at sea, including when breeding. Their single-most important threat is from commercial fisheries, especially longlining and demersal trawling. On land, introduced predators constitute the most serious threat, especially to the smaller burrowing species, but human disturbance, habitat degradation and pollution all play a role. A number of initiatives has been undertaken to address these threats. The International Plan of Action for Reducing Incidental Catch of Seabirds in Longline Fisheries, adopted by the Food and Agriculture Organization of the United Nations in 1999, sets out detailed guidelines for nations to follow in adopting their own National Plans of Action (NPOA-Seabirds). Covering a broader suite of threats, the international Agreement on the Conservation of Albatrosses and Petrels (ACAP), which came into force in February 2004, aims to improve the conservation status of albatrosses and the larger petrels, both on land and at sea. At the non-governmental level, the Global Seabird Programme of BirdLife International encourages action by governments and commercial fisheries alike, as do a number of other international and national NGOs. The level of international co-operation achieved between international bodies, national governments and non-governmental organizations to further the conservation of southern albatrosses and petrels can be regarded as an exemplar for the conservation of pelagic seabirds in other oceans.

## INTRODUCTION

Albatrosses and petrels are among the world's most threatened birds (Robertson & Gales 1998, Brooke 2004). According to the latest international listing (BirdLife International 2004a), 60 (47%) of the 129 living species of the order Procellariiformes (tubenoses) have been accorded a global category-of-threat status, ranging from Critically Endangered (extremely high risk of extinction in the wild; 15 species), through Endangered (very high risk of extinction in the wild; 17 species) to Vulnerable (high risk of extinction in the wild; 28 species). A further 14 species are considered to be Near Threatened (Table 1). Within the family Diomedeidae (albatrosses), all but two of the 21 species recognized are considered to be globally threatened. This is a relatively recent phenomenon: the 1979 version of the Red Data Book listed just 12 procellariiforms as globally threatened, of

A 27-year old Wandering Albatross *Diomedea exulans* guards its downy chick on South Africa's Marion Island. Photo: J. Cooper.

**Table 1. Numbers of species and conservation status of procellariiform seabirds (after BirdLife International 2004a).**

| Family | Critical | Endangered | Vulnerable | Near Threatened | Total | % threatened |
|---|---|---|---|---|---|---|
| Albatrosses, Diomedeidae | 2 | 7 | 10 | 2 | 21 | 90.5 |
| Petrels, Procellariidae | 11 | 8 | 17 | 11 | 82 | 43.9 |
| Storm petrels, Hydrobatidae | 2 | 1 | 1 | 1 | 22 | 18.2 |
| Diving petrels, Pelecanoididae | 0 | 1 | 0 | 0 | 4 | 25.0 |
| **Totals** | **15** | **17** | **28** | **14** | **129** | **46.5** |

which only one was an albatross, the Short-tailed Albatross *Phoebastria albatrus*; this was listed as Endangered (King 1979). What has caused this calamitous change in fortunes?

It might be considered that the occurrence of albatrosses and petrels far away from the world's centres of human habitation and activity has lent them a good measure of safety. This might have been so once, but it is assuredly no longer the case. There is some cause for optimism, however, since the threats now facing these charismatic species are being addressed on many fronts. In this paper, I first review the current threats facing albatrosses and petrels, concentrating on those species that frequent the Southern Ocean and its oceanic islands. I then consider the actions underway to enhance their conservation status, and what actions are still required. I end by attempting to show by way of examples of specific initiatives that the level of international co-operation that has been achieved in the Southern Ocean to date may yet allow southern pelagic seabirds to survive this century. At the same time, I suggest that this co-operation stands as an exemplar for the conservation of pelagic seabirds of the other oceans of the world.

## ALBATROSSES AND PETRELS AS MIGRATORY SPECIES

Albatrosses and petrels are arguably the world's most pelagic seabirds, breeding on remote oceanic islands, and ranging over seas far away from continental shores (e.g. BirdLife International 2004b). In so doing, most species migrate over vast distances, especially when not breeding. Several species, notably the albatrosses, can undertake movements that encircle the Southern Ocean, either as non-breeding adults or as juveniles, whereas others may range from Antarctic to subtropical waters (e.g. Weimerskirch *et al.* 1999, BirdLife International 2004b, Croxall *et al.* 2005, P.G. Ryan *in litt.*). Even when breeding and so partially tied to land, albatrosses and petrels may travel hundreds and sometimes a thousand or more kilometres during a single foraging trip (e.g. Nel *et al.* 2000, 2002a). These movements take them out of territorial waters and Exclusive Economic Zones (EEZ) and onto the High Seas. During such movements, they may enter the territorial and EEZ waters of nations other than those of their breeding grounds (Nichols *et al.* 2000, BirdLife International 2004b), making them truly international animals, and thus their conservation a matter of international concern and shared responsibility.

## CURRENT THREATS FACING SOUTHERN ALBATROSSES AND PETRELS

All seabirds, including albatrosses and petrels, are creatures of land, air and sea. The threats they face may be conveniently divided into those that occur on land, and those at sea. These are discussed separately below.

### Land-based threats to southern albatrosses and petrels

The subantarctic and cool-temperate islands of the Southern Ocean were, in the main, discovered around the end of the eighteenth century. Very rapidly, they were visited by sailing vessels that exploited their populations of fur seals *Arctocephalus* spp. and Southern Elephant Seal *Mirounga leonina* to near extinction (e.g. Headland 1990, Richards 1992). At this time, sealers stayed ashore for extended periods, living partially, and at times wholly, off the land. Their diet included seabirds and their eggs, and albatrosses and petrels were not spared. This level of exploitation was very high at times, especially when sealers were marooned or shipwrecked (e.g. Busch 1980). However, a more serious and longer-lasting threat has come from the various alien species that the sealers brought with them. These inadvertent or deliberate introductions have included biota of every description, but the most serious in respect to seabirds have been mammalian predators that have preyed directly on especially the smaller petrels, and herbivores that have altered their habitats. A prime example of the former is the feral domestic cat *Felis catus* which has devastated burrowing petrels on a number of southern islands, most probably causing several local extinctions (Cooper *et al.* 1995, Dingwall 1995, Bester *et al.* 2002). An example of the latter is the European Rabbit *Oryctolagus cuniculus* that has severely affected the megaherb fields of Australia's Macquarie Island (Copson & Whinam 1998). Accounts of other alien species on southern islands that have affected, and in some cases continue to affect, seabirds may be found in papers within Dingwall (1995). In the main, the larger albatrosses (Diomedeidae) have been less seriously affected by introduced species, when compared to the smaller, burrowing petrels (families Procellariidae, Hydrobatidae [Oceanitidae] and Pelecanoididae). Two notable exceptions to this observation are the continuing deleterious effects of the omnivorous domestic pig *Sus scrofa* on New Zealand's Auckland Island (which both disturbs the ground by rooting and can kill and eat albatross chicks; Dingwall 1995) and the House Mouse *Mus musculus*, which, surprisingly, is able to kill large chicks of the Endangered and near-endemic Tristan Albatross *Diomedea dabbenena*, as well as chicks of burrowing petrels, on Gough Island by literally eating them alive (Cuthbert & Hilton 2004, Angel & Cooper 2006, R.M. Wanless pers. comm.).

Anther current land-based threat comes from human disturbance, including by commercial tourists (e.g. de Villiers *et al.* 2005). Scientific research and tourism take place at a number of southern islands, and if not properly managed, have the capacity to reduce breeding success, introduce new disease-bearing agents (Weimerskirch 2004), and ultimately reduce population sizes of albatrosses and petrels. Habitat degradation also plays a role at some breeding localities. This may be caused, for

A group of Endangered Atlantic Yellow-nosed Albatrosses *Thalassarche chlororhynchos* incubating on their pedestal nests among *Phylica* trees on Gough Island, a United Kingdom World Heritage site in the South Atlantic. Photo: J. Cooper.

example, by fires or grazing by introduced herbivores, such as several species of domestic animals on New Zealand's southern islands and on the inhabited main island of Tristan da Cunha (Dingwall 1995).

### Sea-based threats to southern albatrosses and petrels

Southern albatrosses and petrels face their greatest risks at sea. Paramount among these is the mortality caused by fisheries. Attention was first drawn to the large numbers of albatrosses killed by the southern longline fishery for tuna *Thunnus* spp. in the early 1990s (Brothers 1991). Species ranging from the great albatrosses *Diomedea* spp., to the smaller mollymawk albatrosses *Thalassarche* spp., the two species of giant petrels *Macronectes* spp. and burrowing petrels of the genera *Procellaria* and *Puffinus* (shearwaters) are all at serious risk from longlining (see the species accounts in BirdLife International 2004a and references therein). As well as the pelagic tuna fisheries, many southern seabirds are killed by demersal longlining for Patagonian Toothfish *Dissostichus eleginoides* in the Southern Ocean, including by "Illegal, Unreported and Unregulated" (IUU) fishing vessels (Brothers *et al.* 1999). The highest levels of mortality are now thought to take place around the French subantarctic Kerguelen Islands, most especially of White-chinned Petrels *Procellaria aequinoctialis* (Delord *et al.* 2004), although until recently, many birds were killed by both illegal and legal toothfish fisheries elsewhere in the Southern Ocean (e.g. around the South African Prince Edward Islands; Nel *et al.* 2002b).

More recently, it has been shown that demersal trawling in the Southern Hemisphere has the capacity to kill large numbers of albatrosses and petrels, which collide with trawl cables while attempting to feed on offal and discards from factory ships (B. Sullivan *in litt.*, S.L. Petersen pers. comm.). Collisions can result in broken wings and entangled birds being dragged below the surface and drowning.

Albatrosses and petrels face other threats at sea. Ingestion of plastic particles and fish hooks both take their toll (Ryan 1987, Nel & Nel 1999). Entanglement with fishing gear is also a problem (Nel & Nel 1999). Direct persecution of southern albatrosses and petrels at sea now seems to be rare (in the past some species were deliberately caught for human consumption, or shot from sailing vessels for sport or scientific specimens; Robertson & Gales 1998), but isolated cases of birds with their legs apparently tied together deliberately have been reported in recent years (R.M. Wanless pers. comm.). Lastly, changes due to over-fishing and global warming are likely to be affecting the food supplies of albatrosses and petrels adversely in some regions, although offal dumped from fishing vessels can be to the birds' advantage (e.g. Ryan & Moloney 1988).

### ENHANCING THE CONSERVATION STATUS OF SOUTHERN ALBATROSSES AND PETRELS

A number of initiatives has been undertaken to address the threats of pelagic seabirds, including albatrosses and petrels, at the international, national and non-governmental levels. Three of the most significant (although there are many other examples that could have been chosen) are described below.

## The International Plan of Action for Reducing Incidental Catch of Seabirds in Longline Fisheries

The International Plan of Action for Reducing Incidental Catch of Seabirds in Longline Fisheries, adopted by the Food and Agriculture Organization of the United Nations (FAO) in 1999, sets out detailed guidelines for nations to follow in adopting their own National Plans of Action (NPOA-Seabirds; FAO 1999, Cooper *et al.* 2001). Perhaps because it is a voluntary measure, forming part of the FAO Code of Conduct for Responsible Fisheries, few countries have as yet adopted their plans. Formally adopted NPOA-Seabirds exist for Brazil, the Falkland Islands, New Zealand and the USA. Other fishing countries have plans in varying stages of preparation or formalization: these include Australia, Canada, Chile, Japan, Namibia, South Africa and Taiwan.

Existing National Plans of Action vary in their scope and detail, but all list a suite of mitigation measures aimed to reduce seabird mortality to levels defined in terms of the number of individual birds killed or by setting a number of birds killed per thousand hooks. Mitigation measures that are commonly adopted into national regulations include night-setting, use of a bird-scaring "Tori" line, avoiding the dumping of offal and discards during line setting, and adding weights to the line to increase sink rates.

## Agreement on the Conservation of Albatrosses and Petrels

In 1997 and 1999, primarily occasioned by knowledge of the effects of longline mortality, all species of albatrosses and of *Macronectes* and *Procellaria* petrels were listed in the Appendices of the Bonn Convention on the Conservation of Migratory Species of Wild Animals (CMS). Following these listings, Australia took the lead in proposing an Agreement under the CMS to increase the protection of albatrosses and the larger petrels. Successful negotiation meetings were held in Australia and South Africa during 1999 to 2001, and the Agreement on the Conservation of Albatrosses and Petrels (ACAP) came into force with its required five Parties (Australia, Ecuador, New Zealand, South Africa and Spain) in February 2004. By July 2006, four more countries, Chile, France, Peru and the United Kingdom, had become Parties (Cooper & Ryan 2001, www.acap.aq). It is expected that Argentina and Brazil, both signatories to the Agreement, will ratify and become Parties soon. When these two ratifications are achieved, practically all of the breeding range states for ACAP-listed species will be Parties (Fig. 1, Table 2),

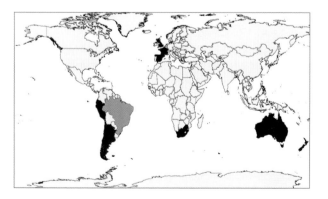

**Fig. 1.** Parties (dark blue) and Signatories (light blue) to the Agreement on the Conservation of Albatrosses and Petrels (as at November 2006).

**Table 2. Albatrosses and petrels listed within the Agreement on the Conservation of Albatrosses and Petrels and their global conservation status.**

| Species | Conservation status (BirdLife International (2004a) |
|---|---|
| Wandering Albatross *Diomedea exulans* | Vulnerable |
| Tristan Albatross *D. dabbenena* | Endangered |
| Antipodean Albatross *D. antipodensis* | Vulnerable |
| Amsterdam Albatross *D. amsterdamensis* | Critical |
| Southern Royal Albatross *D. epomophora* | Vulnerable |
| Northern Royal Albatross *D. sanfordi* | Endangered |
| Waved Albatross *Phoebastria irrorata* | Vulnerable |
| Shy Albatross *Thalassarche cauta* | Near Threatened |
| Salvin's Albatross *T. salvini* | Vulnerable |
| Chatham Albatross *T. eremita* | Critical |
| Buller's Albatross *T. bulleri* | Vulnerable |
| Black-browed Albatross *T. melanophrys* | Endangered |
| Campbell Albatross *T. impavida* | Vulnerable |
| Grey-headed Albatross *T. chrysostoma* | Vulnerable |
| Indian Yellow-nosed Albatross *T. carteri* | Endangered |
| Atlantic Yellow-nosed Albatross *T. chlororhynchos* | Endangered |
| Sooty Albatross *Phoebetria fusca* | Endangered |
| Light-mantled Sooty Albatross *P. palpebrata* | Near Threatened |
| Southern Giant Petrel *Macronectes giganteus* | Vulnerable |
| Northern Giant Petrel. *M. halli* | Near Threatened |
| White-chinned Petrel *Procellaria aequinoctialis* | Vulnerable |
| Spectacled Petrel *P. conspicillata* | Critical |
| Black Petrel *P. parkinsoni* | Vulnerable |
| Westland Petrel *P. westlandica* | Vulnerable |
| Grey Petrel *P. cinerea* | Near Threatened |

Note: The taxonomy followed here is that of BirdLife International (2004a); ACAP has yet to decide on the exact specific taxonomy it will follow.

leading, it is hoped, to a strong Agreement. It is notable that all but four of the species currently listed within ACAP's Annex have a global category of threat ranging from Critically Endangered to Vulnerable (Table 2). The remaining four species are currently considered to be Near Threatened, but this is not grounds for complacency since such species are regarded as being close to qualifying for or likely to qualify for a global threatened category in the near future (IUCN 2001).

The Agreement describes a number of conservation measures to be implemented by Parties, summarized in its Action Plan. These call for a reduction in fishery-induced mortality, eradication of introduced predators at breeding sites, reduction of human disturbance and habitat loss, and measures to reduce marine pollution. The First Session of the Meeting of Parties was held in Hobart, Australia, in November 2004, immediately after an informal Scientific Meeting, when an Advisory Committee was established and rules of procedure discussed and adopted. The first formal meeting of the Advisory Committee was held in July 2005, again in Australia. At this meeting, several initiatives were progressed or commenced. These included formally constituting three working groups to consider taxonomic status, to gather data on population status and trends, and to review the protection and management of breeding sites (www.acap.aq).

The Advisory Committee confirmed a work programme for the inter-sessional period, with the three working groups requested to report back on their findings and recommendations at the next meeting of the Advisory Committee, held in June 2006. An important decision made at the First Advisory Committee was to commence engagements with a number of Regional Fishery Management Organizations (RFMOs) which manage high-seas fisheries that interact with southern seabirds. These include the Convention for the Conservation of Southern Bluefin Tuna (CCSBT), the Indian Ocean Tuna Commission (IOTC) and the Commission for the Conservation of Antarctic Marine Living Resources (CCAMLR). The last has already begun to attend ACAP meetings, and has extended an invitation to ACAP to attend its own meetings. As a first step to collaborative efforts, it was agreed that observer status should be sought by ACAP at meetings of these selected RFMOs, as well as at the biennial meetings of FAO's Committee on Fisheries, where nations' progress with their NPOA-Seabirds is reviewed. An important early decision taken by ACAP is that working documents and information papers submitted to its meetings will be made available publicly on its web-site at www.acap.aq.

## BirdLife International Seabird Conservation Programme

BirdLife International is the world's largest international NGO that advocates the enhanced conservation of birds. In 1997, it initiated a Global Seabird Programme, initially based in South Africa but now managed from the United Kingdom (Cooper 1999, www.birdlife.org). The programme took as its major emphasis longline fishery mortality, but this has now been expanded to consider seabird mortality from trawl fisheries as well. The programme raises awareness through BirdLife's national partners, and is currently active in sponsoring training schemes for fishery observers, undertaking research into mitigation measures and attending and contributing to international meetings, including those of ACAP, the CMS, FAO's Committee on Fisheries and the World Conservation Union (IUCN). It has also recently sponsored reviews and workshops that address aspects of seabird conservation relevant to the protection of albatrosses and petrels of the Southern Ocean (e.g. BirdLife International 2004b, Small 2004).

## Other international initiatives

Other international initiatives include actions taken by RFMOs to reduce longline mortality of seabirds. The leading RFMO in this regard is CCAMLR which has had regulations in place for toothfish vessels in the Southern Ocean to reduce seabird mortality for some time (Small 2004, www.ccamlr.org). However, most RFMOs, significantly including the several that manage tuna fisheries in the Southern Hemisphere, are yet to take such action (Small 2004).

The FAO's Committee on Fisheries has produced guidelines to deter IUU fishing (FAO 2001), but to date few countries appear to have adopted national plans: Chile is a notable exception. Such plans would be an effective way of reducing seabird mortality by longline fisheries, since it is believed that IUU "pirate" fishers are most unlikely to adopt mitigation measures.

Another initiative is the certification of fisheries by the Marine Stewardship Council, *inter alia*, as being "seabird friendly". To date, only one longline fishery has been so certi-

Light-mantled Sooty Albatross *Phoebetria palpebrata*. Photo: Chris Wilson.

fied, that for Patagonian Toothfish around the island of South Georgia (www.msc.org). This fishery now kills very few seabirds, and stands as an example to others in the Southern Ocean.

## A WAY FORWARD

To date, ACAP is essentially a southern agreement, with only species breeding in the Southern Hemisphere being listed in its Annex (Table 2). However, the Agreement text does not make any geographical restrictions, allowing for expansion to the Northern Hemisphere if thought desirable by the relatively simple expedient of adding new species of procellariiform seabirds to those already listed within it. If, for example, the two threatened species of albatross of the North Pacific, the Short-tailed Albatross (Vulnerable) and the Black-footed Albatross *Phoebastria nigripes* (Endangered) (BirdLife International 2004a), are one day included within the Agreement, then many of the fishing nations encircling that region will become range states and might thus be more willing to become Parties to ACAP. Since many of these nations (e.g. China, Japan, South Korea, Taiwan and the USA) are distant-water fishing nations that interact with pelagic seabirds on the High Seas in the Southern Hemisphere, their membership of ACAP should enhance the conservation of southern albatrosses and petrels as well as of their northern counterparts. It is considered that this is a worthy goal for international bodies, national governments and non-governmental organizations alike to work towards over the next decade. At its First Meeting of Parties, ACAP decided to consider which new species might be added to its Annex in the future, and requested that South Africa and Spain take the lead in the matter, by first considering criteria for inclusion and preparing a discussion paper for presentation to and discussion at the third meeting of the Advisory Committee, likely to be held in 2007.

A high level of co-operation has developed between international bodies, national governments and non-governmental organizations to further the conservation of southern albatrosses and petrels. For example, both BirdLife International and the Scientific Committee on Antarctic Research (SCAR), represented by its Group of Experts on Birds, serve on ACAP's Advisory Committee, where they are able to contribute expertise and advise Parties to the Agreement, by way of submitting information papers and contributing to discussions (see examples of submitted papers by both bodies at www.acap.aq). I suggest that this level of co-operation could be extended with effect to improve the conservation of pelagic seabirds in other oceans of the world, in ways that ACAP hopes to achieve in the Southern Ocean. Examples of where such international co-operation might well be advantageous include in both Arctic and Mediterranean waters (Cooper *et al.* 2000, Cooper *et al.* 2003).

## ACKNOWLEDGEMENTS

I thank the organizers of the Waterbirds around the world Conference for funding my attendance and for inviting me to deliver the closing plenary lecture in front of a distinguished audience. I particularly thank Gerard Boere for his editorial patience and Colin Galbraith for enabling me to realize a long-standing ambition to visit Bass Rock.

## REFERENCES

Angel, A. & Cooper, J. 2006. A review of the impacts of introduced rodents on the island of Triston and Gough. RSPB Research Report No. 17. Royal Society for the Protection of Birds, Sandy, UK.

Bester, M.N., Bloomer, J.P., van Aarde, R.J., Erasmus, B.H., van Rensburg, P.J.J., Skinner, J.D., Howell, P.G. & Naude, T.W. 2002. A review of the successful eradication of feral cats from sub-Antarctic Marion Island, southern Indian Ocean. South African Journal of Wildlife Research 32: 65-73.

BirdLife International 2004a. Threatened birds of the World 2004. CD-ROM. BirdLife International, Cambridge, UK.

BirdLife International 2004b. Tracking ocean wanderers. The global distribution of albatrosses and petrels. Results from the Global Procellariiform Tracking Workshop, 1-5 September 2003, Gordon's Bay, South Africa. BirdLife International, Cambridge, UK.

Brooke, M. de L. 2004. Albatrosses and petrels across the World. Oxford University Press, Oxford.

Brothers, N.P. 1991. Albatross mortality and associated bait loss in the Japanese longline fishery in the Southern Ocean. Biological Conservation 55: 255-268.

Brothers, N.P., Cooper, J. & Løkkeborg, S. 1999. The incidental catch of seabirds by longline fisheries: worldwide review and technical guidelines for mitigation. FAO Fisheries Circular No. 937: 1-100.

Busch, B.C. (ed.) 1980. Master of Desolation. The reminiscences of Capt. Joseph J. Fuller. Mystic Seaport Museum, Mystic.

Cooper, J. 1999. BirdLife International Seabird Conservation Programme. World Birdwatch 21(1): 6-7.

Cooper, J. & Ryan, P.G. 2001. The Agreement on the Conservation of Albatrosses and Petrels: implications for research and monitoring at the Prince Edward Islands. South African Journal of Science 97: 78-79.

Cooper, J., Marais, A.v.N., Bloomer, J.P. & Bester, M.N. 1995. A success story: breeding of burrowing petrels (Procellariidae) before and after eradication of feral cats *Felis catus* at subantarctic Marion Island. Marine Ornithology 23: 33-37.

Cooper, J., Dunn, E., Kulka, D.W., Morgan, K.H. & Rivera, K.S. 2000. Addressing the problem: seabird mortality from longline fisheries in the waters of Arctic countries. In: J.W. Chardine, J.M Porter & K.D. Wohl (eds) Workshop on Seabird Incidental Catch in the Waters of

Arctic Countries 26-28 April 2000. Report and Recommendations. Conservation of Arctic Flora and Fauna Technical Report No. 7: 9, 33-42, 61-65.

Cooper, J., Croxall, J.P. & Rivera, K.S. 2001. Off the hook? Initiatives to reduce seabird bycatch in longline fisheries. In: E.F. Melvin & J.K. Parrish (eds) Seabird bycatch: trends, roadblocks and solutions. Sea Grant College Program, Fairbanks: 9-32.

Cooper, J., Baccetti, N., Belda, E.J., Borg, J.J., Oro, D., Papaconstantinou, C. & Sánchez, A. 2003. Seabird mortality from longline fishing in the Mediterranean Sea and Macronesian Waters: a review and a way forward. In: E. Mínguez, D. Oro, E. de Juana & A. Martínez-Abraín (eds) Mediterranean seabirds and their conservation. Scientia Marina 67 (Supplement 2): 57-64.

Copson, G.R. & Whinam, J. 1998. Response of vegetation on subantarctic Macquarie Island to reduced rabbit grazing. Australian Journal of Botany 46: 15-24.

Croxall, J.P., Silk, J.R.D., Phillips, R.A., Afanaseyev, V. & Briggs, D.R. 2005. Global circumnavigations: tracking year-round ranges of nonbreeding albatrosses. Science 307: 249-250.

Cuthbert, R. & Hilton, G. 2004. Introduced House Mice *Mus musculus*: a significant predator of endangered and endemic birds on Gough Island, South Atlantic Ocean? Biological Conservation 117: 483-489.

Delord, K., Gasco, N. & Weimerskirch, H. 2004. Étude de la mortalité accidentale des oiseaux dans la pêcherie a la palangre dans les zones économiques de Crozet et Kerguelen en 2001-2003. Rapport Annuel sur l'État de l'Environnement dans les TAAF, 2002-2004: 39-47.

De Villiers, M.S., Cooper, J. & Ryan, P.G. 2005. Individual variability of behavioural responses by Wandering Albatrosses (*Diomedea exulans*) to human disturbance. Polar Biology 28: 255-260.

Dingwall, P.R. (ed). 1995. Progress in the conservation of subantarctic islands. Proceedings of the SCAR/IUCN Workshop on Protection, Research and Management of Subantarctic Islands, Paimpont, France, 27-29 April, 1992. World Conservation Union, Gland, Switzerland.

FAO 1999. International Plan of Action for Reducing Incidental Catch of Seabirds in Longline Fisheries. International Plan of Action for the Conservation and Management of Sharks. International Plan of Action for the Management of Fishing Capacity. Food and Agriculture Organization of the United Nations, Rome.

FAO 2001. International Plan of Action to Prevent, Deter and Eliminate Illegal, Unreported and Unregulated Fishing. Food and Agriculture Organization of the United Nations, Rome.

Headland, R.K. 1990. Chronological list of Antarctic expeditions and related historical events. Cambridge University Press, Cambridge, UK.

IUCN 2001. IUCN Red List Categories and Criteria: Version 3.1. IUCN Species Survival Commission, Gland, Switzerland, & Cambridge, UK.

King, W.B. 1979. Red Data Book Volume 2: Aves. Second, Revised Edition, Part One. International Union for Conservation of Nature and Natural Resources, Morges, Switzerland.

**Nel, D.C. & Nel, J.L.** 1999. Marine debris and fishing gear associated with seabirds at sub-Antarctic Marion Island, 1996/97 and 1997/98: in relation to longline fishing activity. CCAMLR Science 6: 85-96.

**Nel, D.C., Nel, J.L., Ryan, P.G., Klages, N.T.W., Wilson, R.P. & Robertson, G.** 2000. Foraging ecology of Grey-headed Mollymawks at Marion Island, southern Indian Ocean, in relation to longline fishing activity. Biological Conservation 96: 219-231.

**Nel, D.C., Ryan, P.G., Nel, J.L., Klages, N.T.W., Wilson, R.P., Robertson, G. & Tuck, G.N.** 2002a. Foraging interactions between Wandering Albatrosses *Diomedea exulans* breeding on Marion Island and long-line fisheries in the southern Indian Ocean. Ibis E141-E154.

**Nel, D.C., Ryan, P.G. & Watkins, B.P.** 2002b. Seabird mortality in the Patagonian Toothfish fishery around the Prince Edward Islands, 1996-2000. Antarctic Science 14: 151-161.

**Nicholls, D.G., Murray, M.D., Butcher, E.C. & Moors, P.J.** 2000. Time spent in Southern Ocean Exclusive Zones by non-breeding Wandering Albatrosses (*Diomedea* spp.): implications for national responsibilities for conservation. Emu 100: 318-323.

**Richards, R.** 1992. The commercial exploitation of sea mammals at Iles Crozet and Prince Edward Islands before 1850. Polar Monographs 1: 1-19. Scott Polar Research Institute, Cambridge, UK.

**Robertson, G. & Gales, R.** (eds). 1998. Albatross biology and conservation. Surrey Beatty & Sons, Chipping Norton, Australia.

**Ryan, P.G.** 1987. The incidence and characteristics of plastic particles ingested by seabirds. Marine Environmental Research 23: 175-206.

**Ryan, P.G. & Moloney, C.** 1998. Effect of trawling on bird and seal distributions in the southern Benguela Region. Marine Ecology Progress Series 45: 1-11.

**Small, C.** 2004. Regional Fisheries Management Organizations. Their duties and performance in reducing bycatch of albatrosses and other species. BirdLife International, Cambridge, UK.

**Weimerskirch, H.** 2004. Diseases threatened Southern Ocean albatrosses. Polar Biology 27: 374-379.

**Weimerskirch, H., Catard, A., Prince, P.A., Cherel, Y. & Croxall, J.P.** 1999. Foraging White-chinned Petrels *Procellaria aequinoctialis* at risk from the Tropics to Antarctica. Biological Conservation 87: 273-275.

Southern Giant Petrel *Macronectes giganteus*. Photo: Chris Wilson.

# The Arctic – origin of flyways

*Kenton D. Wohl*

*U.S. Fish and Wildlife Service, Anchorage, Alaska 99503, USA. (email: Kent_Wohl@fws.gov)*

Wohl, K.D. 2006. The Arctic – origin of flyways. *Waterbirds around the world.* Eds. G.C. Boere, C.A. Galbraith & D.A. Stroud. The Stationery Office, Edinburgh, UK. pp. 120-123.

## ABSTRACT

The Arctic and its waterbird resources are unique in at least two respects. In a circumpolar perspective, the eight Arctic nations have common species, shared populations and many similar conservation issues. Such waterbird attributes clearly link the Arctic in a circumpolar manner. The Arctic region is also unique in that it contributes many species of waterbirds to all the major international flyways, linking the Arctic to offshore international waters and to many other countries in both the Northern and Southern Hemispheres. Although Alaska (the U.S. "Arctic") is used to illustrate the international importance of the Arctic, the other seven Arctic countries share a very similar story. In Alaska, about 88% of the regular breeding waterbird species migrate beyond the jurisdiction of the USA, and use as many as eight of the 10 or 11 international flyways. Over 80% of these waterbirds either move to offshore international waters in the North Pacific Ocean or use the four "Americas" flyways en route to Mexico, the Caribbean and South America. The others use the four international flyways to the south and west of Alaska en route to Oceania (Central Pacific), East Asia/Australasia, Central Asia/South Asia, and West Asia/East Africa. These circumpolar and hemispheric linkages imply that countries share a joint responsibility for the conservation of migratory waterbirds. It also suggests that there is a need to improve international collaboration to manage shared populations most effectively.

## INTRODUCTION

I present a brief overview of international waterbird conservation in the Arctic and the Arctic's linkages with flyways and non-breeding areas. The flyway concept and range-wide approach to migratory waterbird management is promoted. The "Birds of Arctic Conservation Concern" project of the Arctic Council's Conservation of Arctic Flora and Fauna program, which highlights waterbird connections within the Arctic and flyways, is summarized.

## ARCTIC WATERBIRD CONSERVATION ISSUES

The key waterbird conservation issues in the circumpolar Arctic are listed below. They are common to all eight Arctic countries (Canada, Finland, Greenland, Iceland, Norway, Russia, Sweden, and the U.S. [Alaska]) and, as such, clearly demonstrate the need to share management, political, legal, and outreach experiences,

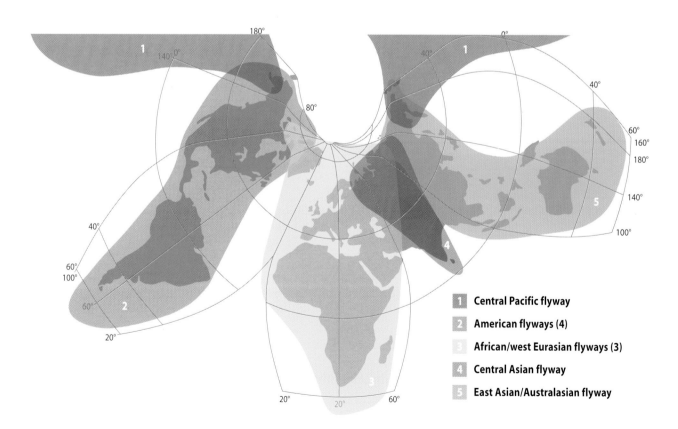

1 Central Pacific flyway

2 American flyways (4)

3 African/west Eurasian flyways (3)

4 Central Asian flyway

5 East Asian/Australasian flyway

**Fig. 1.** International migratory bird flyways originating in the arctic.

approaches, and information with each other, and jointly develop resolutions.

- Harvest (sport, subsistence and unregulated)
- Invasive species
- Habitat alteration
- Oil pollution
- Plastics pollution
- Bycatch in commercial fisheries
- Contaminants
- Diseases
- Human disturbance
- Declining populations
- Climate change

Climate change is an issue receiving increased attention recently and is predicted to produce changes that will not only exacerbate some of the conservation issues above, but will create many new and very visible management conflicts for waterbirds in the near future. These are listed below and have been well-documented by several authors in the Arctic Council's Arctic Climate Impact Assessment Project (Hassol 2004, AMAP 2004):

- Changes in species composition and populations
- Extinction of species
- Changes in phenology/migration/foraging patterns
- Introduction of invasive species and diseases
- Inundation of coastal wetlands
- Drying of interior wetlands
- Changes in terrestrial habitats
- Changes in the values and functions of protected areas

Many of these issues are also shared in a flyway context, with some issues being a higher priority than others, depending on the flyway and the country.

### NEED TO COLLABORATE

It is well known that waterbirds are an important national heritage in the eight Arctic nations, and that the Arctic is the exclusive breeding grounds for many species of waterbirds that are important to Arctic populations of humans. It is not unusual that most work on waterbirds has focused on breeding ecology and population status and trends on the Arctic's breeding grounds. As such, Arctic birders are quite "Arctic-centric".

It is also recognized that most of the Arctic's breeding waterbirds move to offshore regions or migrate to more southerly non-breeding areas via flyways (Fig. 1). For example, in Alaska 89% of the regular breeding seabirds, all of the shorebirds, 73% of the waterfowl, and 92% of the remaining waterbird species migrate beyond the USA when they leave Alaska. When waterbirds leave their Arctic breeding grounds, Arctic birders not only expect them to return the following spring, but also assume or expect that the countries in the non-breeding regions will care for the conservation and protection of these migrants with a similar passion and enthusiasm. However, there are often different legal responsibilities and conservation and protection priorities within a flyway and for particular species or species groups. This necessitates approaching waterbird issues in a range-wide manner and having the international instruments available to promote and execute the communication,

Murre *Uria lomvia.* Photo: U.S. Fish and Wildlife Service.

coordination, and collaboration between countries within a flyway or total range of a given species.

### OPPORTUNITIES FOR INTERNATIONAL COLLABORATION

In the context of common species, shared populations, and similar conservation issues, it is obvious that circumpolar Arctic and flyway approaches are essential to resolve management and conservation issues most effectively. To initiate these approaches requires international frameworks. Such coordination mechanisms are, for example, formal and informal species, habitat, and flyway agreements, and bilateral and multilateral treaties. There are many good examples of flyway and range-wide instruments that provide the necessary mechanisms to create or enhance coordination between countries. In the circumpolar Arctic, the Arctic Council's Conservation of Arctic Flora and Fauna (CAFF) program and its Circumpolar Seabird Expert Group is a recent example of a very successful mechanism aimed at improving coordination of waterbird management issues and monitoring programs throughout the Arctic. The Convention on Migratory Species of Wild Animals (CMS) and its several flyway and species agreements, the Ramsar Convention on Wetlands, the Convention on International Trade in Endangered Species (CITES), and many other regional agreements represent successes in improving the flyway and range-wide approaches to waterbird conservation.

Two interesting movements have occurred in the recent past concerning institutional mechanisms for international cooperation in the conservation of migratory birds. Informal agreements are much more popular today than formal ones because they are much less expensive to implement, operate on a simpler institutional structure and decision-making process, and have the ability to take action on issues in a timelier manner. In addition, flyway or range-wide instruments have been favored over more geographically-limited or regional instruments. Examples are: the bilateral treaties between the USA, Canada, and Mexico, reinvented into a "trilateral" approach; bilateral treaties among the USA, Japan, Russia, China, Australia, and India, some of which are being regrouped into a CMS Central Asian Flyway Agreement; and the many bilateral agreements in the East Asian-Australasian Flyway which are being coordinated by the Asia-Pacific Migratory Waterbird Conservation Committee. Of course, the CMS's African-Eurasian Migratory Waterbirds Agreement (AEWA) is another good example of the flyway approach. Hopefully, there will soon be flyway agreements for the "Americas" flyways and for the Central Pacific Flyway that will unite the two hemispheres into range-wide approaches for waterbirds.

In 1993, the CAFF program gave recognition to the Arctic's important migratory waterbird resources, the commonality of conservation issues, and the need to improve communication in the Arctic when it created the Circumpolar Seabird Expert Group (CSEG), formerly known as the Circumpolar Seabird Working Group. Since the CSEG's first meeting in 1994, it has collaboratively addressed common issues such as seabird bycatch (Chardine *et al.* 2000, Bakken & Falk 1998), seabird harvest (Denlinger & Wohl 2001), and seabird disturbance guidelines (Chardine & Mendenhall 1998). The CSEG has also addressed circumpolar murre and seabird monitoring plans and common species initiatives such as the International Murre and Eider Conservation Strategies (CSWG 1996, CSWG 1997). The CSEG has addressed regional issues such as the North Atlantic murre banding (Petersen & Bakken 2004) and band/ring recovery projects. Another recent project demonstrating circumpolar collaboration is the murre climate change project (Irons *et al.* unpublished). It is an example of birders having a forum; i.e. CSEG, to discuss a common issue, share data and build a common database to develop a circumpolar story about the response of murre populations to climate change. The success of this project will certainly be the prelude for many more circumpolar data-sharing initiatives.

## BIRDS OF ARCTIC CONSERVATION CONCERN

It has often been recognized that Arctic birds are dependent on non-breeding habitats outside the Arctic. In 1996, CAFF commissioned a report that discussed Arctic linkages with other countries for bird species migrating beyond the Arctic (Scott 1998). As a result of that report, CAFF and Wetlands International conducted a workshop to review and prioritize recommendations of the Scott report (Scott 2001). Recognizing the need for improving the cooperation and collaboration for migratory waterbirds beyond the Arctic and value in prioritizing species and conservation issues in both a circumpolar and flyway context, CAFF instructed the CSEG to develop the report "Birds of Arctic Conservation Concern." It is a project that is anticipated to be completed in 2005, and will discuss for each of the eight Arctic countries their migratory bird resources, national and international conservation status, migration routes, non-breeding areas, applicable domestic and international coordination instruments, population status and trends, and list of active international projects and programs. The report will also develop a list of high priority birds called "Birds of Arctic

Conservation Concern". This project will be presented with country, Arctic and flyway perspectives. The report will be the template for documenting each country's priority migratory bird species, international migratory bird programs, and means for international collaboration within the Arctic and the flyways. The document will serve as the template for the Arctic countries to enhance their international migratory bird programs.

## RECOMMENDATIONS

In summary, the eight Arctic nations and their birders have greatly improved their coordination and collaboration as a result of new international coordination mechanisms such as CAFF and its Circumpolar Seabird Expert Group. Arctic waterbird conservation is also greatly benefiting from recent flyway agreements and initiatives and the increasing recognition by Arctic countries of the need to focus on the range-wide and flyway concepts for the most effective approach to waterbird conservation. Effective resolutions to complex Arctic issues such as climate change will necessitate countries uniting for collaborative endeavors to protect shared populations whether on a circumpolar or flyway scale.

The highest priority needs to effect or improve waterbird conservation in the Arctic and the flyways are: 1) to initiate coordinated flyway or range-wide monitoring programs; 2) to create common flyway and circumpolar Arctic databases; and 3) to fill the species and geographic gaps in international coordination frameworks and instruments.

Steller's Eider *Polysticta stelleri*. Photo: Glen Smart, U.S. Fish and Wildlife Sevice.

## REFERENCES

**AMAP - Arctic Monitoring and Assessment Program** 2004. The ACIA international scientific symposium on climate change in the Arctic: extended abstracts. Reykjavik, Iceland, 9-12 November 2004. AMAP Report 2004: 4. Oslo, Norway.

**Bakken, V. & Falk, K.** (eds). 1998. Incidental take of seabirds in commercial fisheries in the Arctic countries. CAFF Technical Report No. 1. Circumpolar Seabird Working Group, Akureyri, Iceland.

**Chardine, J. & Mendenhall, V.** 1998. Human disturbance at Arctic seabird colonies. CAFF Technical Report No. 2. Circumpolar Seabird Working Group, Akureyri, Iceland.

**Chardine, J., Porter, J.M. & Wohl, K.** 2000. Workshop on seabird incidental catch in the waters of Arctic countries. CAFF Technical Report No. 7. Circumpolar Seabird Working Group, Akureyri, Iceland.

**CSWG - Circumpolar Seabird Working Group** 1996. International murre conservation strategy and action plan. CAFF, Akureyri, Iceland.

**CSWG - Circumpolar Seabird Working Group** 1997. Circumpolar eider conservation strategy and action plan. CAFF, Akureyri, Iceland.

**Denlinger, L. & Wohl, K.** 2001. Seabird harvest regimes in the circumpolar nations. CAFF Technical Report No. 9. Circumpolar Seabird Working Group, Akureyri, Iceland.

**Hassol, S.J.** 2004. Impacts of a warming Arctic. Cambridge University Press, Cambridge, UK.

**Irons, D., Anker-Nilssen, J.T., Gaston, A.J., Byrd, G.V., Falk, K., Gilchrist, G., Hario, M., Hjernquist, M., Krasnov, Y., Mosbech, A., Olsen, B., Petersen, A., Reid, J.B., Robertson, G.J., Strom, H. & Wohl, K.D.** unpublished. Fluctuation in circumpolar seabird populations linked to extreme climate shifts.

**Petersen, A. & Bakken, V.** 2004. Distribution of murres outside the breeding season. Circumpolar murre banding program, North Atlantic Region. CAFF Technical Report No. 13. Circumpolar Seabird Expert Group, Akureyri, Iceland.

**Scott, D.A.** 1998. Global overview of the conservation of migratory Arctic breeding birds outside the Arctic. Wetlands International Publication No. 45, CAFF Technical Report No. 4. CAFF, Akureyri, Iceland.

**Scott, D.A.** (ed). 2001. Conservation of migratory Arctic birds, summary report. CAFF & Wetlands International workshop, Songli, Norway, 10-11 November 2000. CAFF Technical Report No. 8. CAFF, Akureyri, Iceland.

Ice near Svartenhuk Halvø, north-west Greenland: an important breeding and moulting area for several waterbird species including the Greenland White-fronted Goose *Anser albifrons flavirostris*. Photo: David Stroud.

# Part 3.

## Geographical regions

## Sections

# 3.1 The Arctic: source of flyways. Workshop Introduction

*Gudmundur A. Gudmundsson*
*Icelandic Institute of Natural History, PO Box 5320, IS-125 Reykjavik, Iceland.*

Gudmundsson, G.A. 2006. The Arctic: source of flyways. Workshop Introduction. *Waterbirds around the world.* Eds. G.C. Boere, C.A. Galbraith & D.A. Stroud. The Stationery Office, Edinburgh, UK. p. 126.

The immense tundra wetlands in the delta of the Lena river, northern Yakutia are the breeding grounds for millions of waterbirds. Whilst human densities are low, these areas are predicted to be widely impacted by changing global climates. Photo: Gerard Boere.

The arctic is the breeding ground for millions of waterbird connected to all global flyways. Environmental and climatic conditions in the arctic are critical for long term flyway conservation and management. The workshop reviewed recent developments in the arctic in relation to local and global changes, legislation and conservation issues, highlighting their importance for the long-term maintenance of the favourable status of migratory waterbirds.

Recent years have seen the active development of much organisational and institutional activity in the arctic, together with the progressive development of a range of multinational agreements and other international treaties (for example the Conservation of Arctic Flora & Fauna – CAFF – a working group of the Arctic Council). These all indicate greatly increased interest in the region.

Ornithological research in various regions of the arctic have focussed on studies of the factors influencing waterbird breeding success, as productivity can strongly vary between years. Soloviev *et al.* report on the development of an international programme to collate information on such between-year changes of productivity. Such fluctuations can also be measured on migration if trapping methods are carried out in a consistent manner as reported by Harebottle using the example of wader productivity as assessed in South Africa – the far migratory terminus of the species' concerned.

Engelmoer *et al.* summarise the long-term and differential population trends of arctic breeding waders as monitored in temperate wintering areas (the Dutch Wadden Sea). The need to standardise much of the monitoring of arctic breeding waders has lead to the establishment of a Committee for Holarctic Shorebird Monitoring (CHASM). Lanctot, on behalf of the Committee, summarises the issues that led to its development and plans for the implementation and development of this important initiative.

In recent years, much more attention, both on the breeding and wintering areas, has been given to endangered arctic waders such as the Spoon-billed Sandpiper *Eurynorhynchus pygmeus*. The reasons for the decline of this species are still unknown. A range of new techniques such as stable isotope analysis have been invaluable in determining the breeding and wintering areas of such rare and threatened species, as reported by Zöckler *et al.*

With climate change predicted to impact more rapidly on the arctic more than on other regions (see the section on the implications of climate change for waterbirds elsewhere in this volume), the need for increased research and conservation effort is strongly stressed.

# Monitoring Arctic-nesting shorebirds: an international vision for the future

*Richard B. Lanctot*

*(on behalf of the Committee for Holarctic Shorebird Monitoring: CHASM)*

*U.S. Fish and Wildlife Service, 1011 East Tudor Road, MS 201, Anchorage, AK 99503, Alaska. (email: richard_lanctot@fws.gov)*

Lanctot, R.B. (on behalf of the Committee for Holarctic Shorebird Monitoring). 2006. Monitoring Arctic-nesting shorebirds: an international vision for the future. *Waterbirds around the world*. Eds. G.C. Boere, C.A. Galbraith & D.A. Stroud. The Stationery Office, Edinburgh, UK. pp. 127-130.

## ABSTRACT

The Pan-Arctic Shorebird/Wader Monitoring and Research Workshop brought together 30 specialists to discuss monitoring and research of Arctic-nesting shorebirds. The meeting was held in Karrebäksminde, Denmark, from 3-6 December 2003. Participants from seven Arctic nations, as well as five nations visited by Arctic migrants during the non-breeding season, convened with two primary objectives: 1) to summarize existing shorebird monitoring protocols and to explore opportunities for integrating them more effectively at a global level; and 2) to discuss the effects of climate change on those populations which have been monitored and studied to date.

This document presents the collective vision of the participants in regard to objective one, and as such, the document outlines the goals, an initial objective, and preliminary recommendations for globally integrated monitoring of Arctic-nesting shorebirds. Participants acknowledged the need to establish an informal working group, which would take the lead on moving the workshop's vision forward. Specifically, this Committee for Holarctic Shorebird Monitoring (CHASM) was formed as the essential first step for guiding the implementation of an effective circumpolar program for monitoring Arctic-nesting shorebirds.

CHASM is a "project" within the International Wader Study Group and is one of seven networks within the Circumpolar Flora and Fauna's Circumpolar Biodiversity Monitoring Program. A circumpolar monitoring program will help ensure that existing monitoring programs continue to be well coordinated and supported, while simultaneously integrating them into a Holarctic program. Participants suggested a number of essential items needed to develop a comprehensive circumpolar Arctic shorebird monitoring plan, and provided more specific recommendations for monitoring shorebirds in breeding and non-breeding areas.

## BACKGROUND

Arctic-nesting shorebirds (or waders) are among the most evocative creatures on our planet. Their tenacity while breeding in harsh northern environments, their spectacular concentrations, prodigious long-distance migrations, and the athletic grace of their aerial acrobatics inspire awe and appreciation. These wonders, however, are in jeopardy. There is a growing agreement among shorebird biologists from around the world that many shorebird populations are declining, some precipitously. A handful of species may soon tumble into the chasm of extinction.

Such declines give cause for concern. The loss of shorebird populations or entire species would be directly counter to the stated desire of world leaders to significantly reduce the rate of loss of biological diversity. Arctic-breeding shorebirds are impor-

tant members of wetland communities. Such habitats are under intense threat from human development and yet support some of the most diverse animal communities on earth. The potential ecological impact on the health and integrity of wetlands caused by the disappearance of shorebirds is unknown. The reduction or loss of shorebird populations may be a symptom of habitat degradation, but it may also be a cause of further degradation as well. Because shorebirds are critically dependent upon distinct staging sites spread across many nations and vast latitudinal distances, they effectively integrate, and thus their status reflects, environmental conditions over much of the globe. The essential reproductive activities of Arctic-nesting shorebirds occur in those northern regions of the planet most likely to experience the earliest and most severe effects of global warming. Sea-level rise induced by climate change also poses a threat to the inter-tidal areas favoured by these birds outside the breeding season. As long-distance migrants from these threatened habitats, shorebirds may serve as important messengers of global climate change.

Our ability to learn lessons from Arctic-nesting shorebirds is currently limited by a lack of sufficiently detailed, scientifically rigorous, and spatially comprehensive population information. Improved and more coordinated monitoring would allow suspected population trends to be confirmed and provide better estimates of the rates of change. This information, in turn, would be used to form many important management decisions, including 1) detecting species at risk, 2) identifying causes of population changes, 3) evaluating conservation and restoration programs, 4) setting priorities for conservation of species and habitats, 5) acting as indicators of anthropogenic impacts in the Arctic and elsewhere, and 6) implementing multilateral environmental agreements. Given this wealth of potential benefits, there is clearly an urgent need for more effective and extensive monitoring of shorebird populations.

### The Pan-Arctic Shorebird/Wader monitoring and research workshop

In response to this need, 30 specialists gathered in Denmark from 3-6 December 2003 to discuss monitoring and research of Arctic-nesting shorebirds. Participants from seven Arctic nations, as well as five nations visited by Arctic migrants during the non-breeding season, convened with two primary objectives: 1) to summarize existing shorebird monitoring protocols and to explore opportunities for integrating them more effectively at a global level; and 2) to discuss the effects of climate change on those populations which have been monitored and studied to date.

For both objectives, there was a concerted effort to expand the discussion beyond a simple presentation of results to date. Instead, workshop participants worked together to explore new and creative avenues for collaboration and coordination. For example, several new analyses were initiated at the workshop, including a synthesis of efforts to estimate shorebird productivity on an annual basis across multiple flyways, as well as a compilation and pan-arctic analysis of short-term climate-related effects on shorebird breeding performance. Perhaps the most important outcome of the workshop, however, was the participants' shared vision concerning the need for an improved approach to monitoring shorebird population sizes and demographics. This document presents the collective vision of the Pan-Arctic Shorebird/Wader Monitoring and Research Workshop, and outlines goals, an initial objective, and preliminary recommendations for globally integrated monitoring of Arctic-nesting shorebirds.

## Vision

To coordinate and integrate monitoring of Arctic-nesting shorebirds at a global scale by collecting and synthesizing information on the population status and trends of all populations of Arctic-nesting shorebirds at all stages of their life cycles, and to make that information available in a timely manner to policy-makers, managers, the scientific community, educators, and the general public.

## Rationale

Monitoring programs allow biologists to assess the status and trends of animals, and to detect and assess the effects of human activities on these same animals. The Arctic region, while generally poor in species diversity, is home to a disproportionately large number of shorebirds. Indeed, roughly 20% of the world's shorebird species and some 30 million of the roughly 100 million individual shorebirds in the world breed in the Arctic. Population estimates have been derived recently for the 100 biogeographical populations of the 37 most typical Arctic-nesting shorebird species. Numerical trends were identified in 52 of these, 12% of which are thought to be increasing, 42% stable, 44% decreasing and 2% probably extinct. All of these Arctic-nesting species migrate to temperate and tropical regions of the globe, and through these migrations, Arctic-nesting shorebirds link every continent except Antarctica and visit nearly every country on earth.

## Goals

1) **Enhance the collection of scientifically rigorous monitoring data, and the coordination and support of existing and new monitoring programs for Arctic-nesting shorebirds**. This goal will be achieved by a) supporting new and continued funding of monitoring programs, b) providing a framework within which shorebird data are collected, analyzed, and integrated across large spatial and temporal scales, and c) preparing regional and global reports on a regular basis.

2) **Integrate these monitoring efforts with the Circumpolar Biodiversity Monitoring Program**. At the 2002 World Summit on Sustainable Development, world leaders expressed their desire to achieve "a significant reduction in the current rate of loss of biological diversity". To achieve this goal, the Conservation of Arctic Flora and Fauna (CAFF) group identified monitoring as a key objective for the conservation of Arctic biodiversity. Accordingly, CAFF initiated the Circumpolar Biodiversity Monitoring Program (CBMP) to "build on national and international work to implement a program to monitor biodiversity at the circumpolar level that will allow for regional assessments, integration with other environmental monitoring programs, and comparison of the Arctic with other regions of the globe". Arctic-nesting shorebirds were among seven monitoring networks chosen by CAFF to provide adequate monitoring of circumpolar biodiversity as initial components of the CBMP. Workshop participants see their interests and concerns dovetailing markedly with those of the CBMP.

3) **Establish formal co-ordination with other international and regional programs**. A variety of existing conservation groups and programs share an interest in shorebirds, other wetlands species, and/or the habitats used by Arctic-nesting shorebirds throughout the year. Examples include the International Wader Study Group (IWSG), the Asia-Pacific Migratory Waterbird Conservation Strategy, the Agreement on the Conservation of African-Eurasian Migratory Waterbirds (AEWA), and the North American Migratory Bird Treaty Act. Concerted efforts should be made to integrate Arctic-nesting shorebird monitoring into the activities of these diverse programs.

## Initial Objective

To sustain the enthusiasm and impetus of the workshop, participants acknowledged the need to establish a formal working group, which would take the lead on moving the workshop's vision forward. Specifically, this Committee for Holarctic Shorebird Monitoring (CHASM) was formed as the essential first step for guiding the implementation of an effective circumpolar program for monitoring Arctic-nesting shorebirds. Such a program should ensure that existing monitoring programs continue to be well coordinated and supported, while simultaneously being integrated into a Holarctic program. As such, the group fulfils the need for a shorebird-monitoring network within the Circumpolar Biodiversity Monitoring Program. In addition, CHASM will also be a project within the IWSG. CHASM's members represent different regions of the circumpolar Arctic as well as temperate areas where Arctic-nesting shorebirds occur during the non-breeding season. Dr Richard Lanctot and Dr Mikhail Soloviev will serve as the first co-chairs of CHASM.

## GENERAL RECOMMENDATIONS

The principle recommendation of the workshop participants is to fully develop and implement a circumpolar Arctic-nesting shorebird monitoring program. Such a program requires the preparation of a plan that will include and build upon the existing Arctic Birds Breeding Conditions Survey and the Program for Regional and International Shorebird Monitoring (and the latter's predecessors such as the International and Maritimes National Shorebird Surveys). It will also be essential to recognize and take advantage of the contribution of existing waterbird population databases compiled by Wetlands International, the results of bird ringing compiled by the British Trust for Ornithology, and smaller monitoring schemes and programs currently underway within and outside the Arctic. The following features should be included in the final plan, although individual components should be completed as time permits with an overall goal of having the entire plan completed by 2006:–

- Description of the existing monitoring programs providing information on Arctic-nesting shorebirds, and the identification of gaps in which species and subspecies are monitored and where additional monitoring is needed in and outside of the Arctic.

- Identification, definition, and encouragement of the collection of a core set of biological variables, including population (e.g. size and structure, seasonal distribution) and demographic (e.g. recruitment and survival) parameters of Arctic-nesting shorebirds.

- Expansion of existing monitoring programs to include the additional shorebird biological parameters identified above, as well as environmental factors important for interpreting the trajectories of population trends, including physical and biological parameters, such as climate, habitat, predator, and alternative prey variables.

- Identification of priority Arctic-nesting shorebirds based on a set of criteria, such as distribution across the circumpolar Arctic, international obligations, current monitoring activities, degree of endangerment, and available information. Such a prioritization will assist managers in determining how and where to allocate limited funds, and determine the potential to form international collaborations.

- Identification of the best locations at which to survey individual shorebird species and subspecies so as to maximize logistical and financial efficiency.

- Sharing and collaborative analyses of regional and global databases, by paying special attention to the design, creation, collection and entry of data. The creation of meta-databases will facilitate the exchange of data for joint analyses and assessments at the regional or global level, and allow comparisons between Arctic and non-Arctic regions. For instance, data exchange and analyses may be enhanced through the use of GIS and web-based tools.

- Improvement of existing status and trend assessments of Arctic-nesting shorebirds by conducting detailed species-by-species syntheses of existing data and knowledge at local and regional levels.

- Integration of short-term biological studies into the long-term monitoring program so as to address immediate management concerns.

## SPECIFIC RECOMMENDATIONS FOR MONITORING IN THE BREEDING AREAS

1  Acknowledging that Moscow University, with the support of Wetlands International and the IWSG, has successfully conducted the "Arctic Birds Breeding Conditions Survey" for more than 10 years, in which Arctic-nesting shorebirds constitute a major part, and that national and bilateral programs exist in several parts of the Arctic, the workshop participants recommend that these programs receive sufficient long-term funding, and that international cooperation and coordination be further developed.

2  Workshop participants further recommend that a number of quantitative elements (e.g. breeding performance, prey and predator abundances) be added to the existing Arctic Birds Breeding Conditions Survey, as deemed necessary and appropriate given the program's overall goals.

3  Immediate funding should be sought to monitor and conduct research on Arctic-nesting shorebirds currently thought to be under severe decline and under threat of becoming endan-

gered or extinct. Potential candidates for study include the Slender billed Curlew *Numenius tenuirostris*, Bristle-thighed Curlew *N. tahitiensis*, Far Eastern Curlew *N. madagascariensis*, Spoon-billed Sandpiper *Eurynorhynchus pygmeus* and Buff-breasted Sandpiper *Tryngites subruficollis*, which are globally threatened according to current IUCN Red List Criteria.

## SPECIFIC RECOMMENDATIONS FOR MONITORING IN THE NON-BREEDING AREAS

1  Acknowledging that monitoring shorebirds on the Arctic breeding grounds will never be geographically extensive enough to provide fully representative data on population trends and demography for the entire Arctic-nesting shorebird community;

And that Wetlands International (through the International Waterbird Census) and others have successfully monitored Arctic-nesting shorebirds and other bird populations along their migration routes for many years in many parts of the world, allowing long-term population indices to be developed for several species, subspecies, and biogeographical populations;

And realizing that tens of thousands of shorebirds are banded every year by volunteer and professional ornithologists alike, enabling changes in discrete populations to be detected on breeding as well as staging and wintering areas;

The workshop participants encourage increased monitoring of Arctic-nesting shorebirds, especially in their wintering areas in the Neotropics (Caribbean, Central and South America), Africa, Australasia, Asia, Europe and Oceania. Such monitoring efforts should include delineation of wintering ranges at the species, subspecies and population levels, establishment of monitoring networks and survey protocols, collection of data by local observers, and sharing of data after they are collected. The International Waterbird Census provides a framework within which internationally coordinated counts can take place.

2  Workshop participants further recommend that monitoring on staging and wintering sites be strengthened by collating, analyzing and publishing results on shorebird recruitment collected from visual observations and banding operations. Biologists studying several populations of swans, geese and ducks have already undertaken similar efforts. Results from such collaborations should be explicitly linked to thresholds (e.g. specific population sizes and/or trends) that will trigger specific types of directed research and management tasks.

## IWSG Workshop on Monitoring Waders In and Outside the Arctic

As a first step in implementing the objectives of this document, a two-day workshop was held during the IWSG meeting in Papenburg, Germany, on the 4 and 5 November 2004. The first day of the workshop focused on improving and coordinating existing programs that monitor shorebirds in their arctic habitats, including measuring population and demographic parameters of shorebirds, habitat use, prey and predator abundances, and environmental factors. The morning session included a number of speakers who described the geographical and logistical constraints faced by Arctic shorebird biologists around the world, and methods for conducting intensive demographic/ecological studies and less intensive checklist/density studies. The remainder of the day was spent on developing protocols and standardizing parameters to be recorded in Arctic field situations. These protocols are scheduled for publication in an upcoming issue of the Wader Study Group Bulletin. The second day of the workshop focused on methods for monitoring recruitment and survival of waders outside the breeding season. Additional goals of this workshop included identifying constraints of the various methods, assessing whether it is possible to obtain population-wide parameters for recruitment and survival, and producing guidelines for undertaking demographic monitoring. The morning session featured a number of speakers who discussed monitoring recruitment at stopovers and flyway termini. These presentations were followed by a discussion that emphasized (1) the need to monitor a population throughout its range for accurate assessment of the absolute level of recruitment rather than just an index of relative recruitment from a few sites, and (2) the importance of considering the effect of changes in the local environment when assessing long-term trends in recruitment. The afternoon session began with a number of speakers discussing survival and population monitoring. Participants addressed the merits and requirements of using individual colour marks and retrapping of individuals during ringing operations to monitor survival. Protocols for monitoring recruitment and survival at staging and non-breeding sites have recently been published (Robinson *et al.* 2005).

## REFERENCES

Robinson, R.A., Clark, N.A., Lanctot, R., Nebel, S., Harrington, B., Clark, J.A., Gill, J.A., Meltofte, H., Rogers, D.I., Rogers, K.G., Ens, B.J., Reynolds, C.M., Ward, R.M., Piersma, T. & Atkinson, P.W. 2005. Long term demographic monitoring of wader populations in non-breeding areas. Wader Study Group Bulletin 106: 17-29.

This paper was first published in the Wader Study Group Bulletin 103: 1-4; 2004.

Participants from the Russian Federation, UK, Germany, Netherlands and WWF in the First International Lena Delta Expedition 1992 at the far outer edge of the delta facing the Arctic Ocean. The extensive landscapes of the arctic provide major logistical challenges to for the survey of shorebirds. Photo: Gerard Boere.

# Breeding performance of tundra waders in response to rodent abundance and weather from Taimyr to Chukotka, Siberia

*Mikhail Y. Soloviev[1], Clive D.T. Minton[2] & Pavel S. Tomkovich[3]*

*[1]Department of Vertebrate Zoology, Biological Faculty, Moscow Lomonosov State University, Moscow, 119992, Russia. (email: soloviev@soil.msu.ru)*

*[2]165 Dalgetty Road, Beaumaris, VIC 3193, Australia. (email: mintons@ozemail.com.au)*

*[3]Zoological Museum, Moscow Lomonosov State University, Boshaya Nikitskaya Street, 6, Moscow, 125009, Russia. (email: pst@zmmu.msu.ru)*

Soloviev, M.Y., Minton, C.D.T. & Tomkovich, P.S. 2006. Breeding performance of tundra waders in response to rodent abundance and weather from Taimyr to Chukotka, Siberia. *Waterbirds around the world.* Eds. G.C. Boere, C.A. Galbraith & D.A. Stroud. The Stationery Office, Edinburgh, UK. pp. 131-137.

## ABSTRACT

Nesting success, rodent abundance and summer temperatures across the breeding ranges of four Arctic waders in eastern Siberia were analysed in conjunction with data on the proportions of juveniles on the non-breeding grounds in south-eastern Australia in 1979-2003 with a view to revealing the response of wader populations to varying environmental conditions during the breeding season. The effect of temperature on the proportion of juveniles was found to increase in the Sharp-tailed Sandpiper *Calidris acuminata*, Curlew Sandpiper *C. ferruginea*, Red-necked Stint *C. ruficollis* and Ruddy Turnstone *Arenaria interpres*, which to some extent corresponds to the increasing severity of their breeding environment. The proportion of juveniles on the non-breeding grounds increased with an increase in rodent abundance across the breeding range in the Sharp-tailed Sandpiper and Red-necked Stint, but not in the Ruddy Turnstone and Curlew Sandpiper. Nesting success measured within the breeding range depended on July temperatures only in the Ruddy Turnstone, and did not depend significantly on rodent abundance in any of the species under investigation. Thus, although the breeding performance of Arctic waders at the level of flyway populations depends on air temperature and rodent abundance during summer, the relative role of these environmental factors differs between species. Mean July temperatures were increasing from 1979 to 2003 across the breeding range of the Red-necked Stint. During this period, the proportion of juveniles was increasing both in this species and the Sharp-tailed Sandpiper.

## INTRODUCTION

Recent research has demonstrated that many populations of waders are declining (International Wader Study Group 2003, Stroud *et al.* 2006). The reasons for these declines are rarely known with certainty, but global climate change is considered to be an important, or even the principal, factor in the declines in Arctic-breeding birds (e.g. Zöckler & Lysenko 2000, Rehfisch & Crick 2003, Zöckler *et al.* 2003).

Arctic-breeding waders are known for the pronounced variation in their breeding success caused by variation in breeding conditions. Given that waders are generally long-lived birds with low adult mortality, variations in breeding success can make a critical contribution to population change. Thus, an understanding of the processes that are occurring on the breeding grounds and their effects on recruitment in wader populations is instrumental for the development of adequate conservation measures in the flyways.

Prey-switching by predators has been suggested as an important factor determining the breeding success of tundra birds, first by Roselaar (1979) and then in a number of other studies. Summers & Underhill (1987) were the first authors to relate presumed predation pressure on the Taimyr Peninsula, Siberia, with the proportion of juveniles in wader populations in their non-breeding areas. However, this relationship has never been analysed over a wide geographical area. Climatic variables may also affect the breeding performance of Arctic waders at scales from local to global (the latter was shown for 1992 by Ganter & Boyd 2000), but their role has rarely been assessed from a long-term perspective (Boyd 1992, Boyd & Piersma 2001) and apparently never in conjunction with the impact of predation pressure.

Thus, existing knowledge of the responses of wader populations to environmental factors on the breeding grounds has been limited in time and space, and has highlighted the role of a single factor. To a large extent, this has been due to a deficiency of large-scale and long-term data from the breeding grounds that would allow formal quantitative processing. Monitoring conducted over a period of 16 years from 1988 to 2003 within the framework of the Arctic Birds Breeding Conditions Survey (a project of the International Wader Study Group) has been able to fill this gap, and has provided data on nesting success and certain environmental factors, such as rodent abundance, within the breeding range of many waders. We have analysed these data in conjunction with the available weather data and data on the proportions of juvenile birds on the non-breeding grounds in south-eastern Australia. This study focuses on processes developing in the East Asian-Australasian Flyway, which until now has received much less attention from researchers than the intensively studied East Atlantic Flyway.

The following specific questions were addressed:

1. How conditions on the breeding grounds relate to nesting success and productivity measured in the non-breeding areas?
2. How the above relations (if any) differ between species?
3. If there are any long-term trends in productivity, and how they relate to possible trends in environmental factors on the breeding grounds?

## METHODS

### Data on nesting success and rodent abundance

Data on the nesting success of waders and rodent abundance on the breeding grounds were gathered during the course of the

Arctic Birds Breeding Conditions Survey (ABBCS), and included estimates from various localities in eastern Siberia (all original data are available at http://www.arcticbirds.ru). The data, which in most cases were not quantitative, were brought to ordinal scale with ranks from 1-3, corresponding to low, average and high estimates of nesting success and rodent abundance. The considerable variation in the precision of the estimates between localities was addressed by ranking the quality of the estimates of nesting success and rodent abundance on a scale of 1-5. These rankings were used for weighting in statistical analyses. Criteria for assigning ranks to estimates of parameters and their quality are explained in Table 1. When quantitative information was lacking, the ranking was based on the mutual agreement of two experts (MYS and PST), who evaluated descriptive information available in the breeding conditions reports. These reports rarely discriminated between species when providing information on nesting success, and the estimates from some localities represented an evaluation of nesting success for the wader community as a whole. Nesting success in this survey was considered strictly as survival of nests, and did not take into account later components of breeding performance, such as the survival of chicks or juveniles.

Relating the information on nesting success and rodent abundance with particular wader species was achieved by interpolating estimates from localities across the ranges of the wader populations under investigation, and averaging the interpolated values. A multiquadratic function with no smoothing (Buhmann 2003) was used for interpolation on a grid with a cell size of 50 km. Averaging the interpolated values resulted in estimates which were no longer ordinal, but still in the same range as the original estimates from point localities (ranks 1-3).

Four species of waders which migrate to south-eastern Australia for the northern winter, and for which good quality data were available for most years, both from the breeding grounds and from the wintering areas, were selected as study species: Ruddy Turnstone *Arenaria interpres*, Sharp-tailed Sandpiper *Calidris acuminata*, Curlew Sandpiper *C. ferruginea* and Red-necked Stint *C. ruficollis*. Delineation of the breeding ranges of the populations of Ruddy Turnstone and Curlew Sandpiper migrating to Australia involved an analysis of long-distance recoveries and flag-sightings, and information from the ABBCS database, Arctic Bird Library at the UNEP World Conservation Monitoring Centre, and Atlas of Breeding Waders of the Russian Arctic (Lappo *et al.* in prep.). The limits of the flyway population of Ruddy Turnstones in the Arctic were set at a point just west of the Lena River delta (120° E) and the Bering Strait (170° W); for the Curlew Sandpiper, the limits were set at Taimyr Lake (100° E) and northern Chukotka (177° E). The flyway populations of the Sharp-tailed Sandpiper and Red-necked Stint encompass the entire ranges of the species.

### Weather data

Weather data were obtained from the web-site of the World Meteorological Organization (National Climatic Data Center, USA). In this study, analyses of weather variables were restricted to mean air temperatures in June and July, although other parameters (e.g. precipitation, timing of snowmelt) could also have been of major importance. However, temperatures were the only variables for which it was possible to obtain consistent, long-term data for an area of interest extending for over 3 500 km from west to east in eastern Siberia.

**Table 1. Criteria for assigning ranks to estimates of nesting success and rodent abundance, and for assigning ranks to the quality of these estimates.**

| Ranks | Nesting success | Rodent abundance |
|---|---|---|
| Criteria for estimates of the parameter | | |
| 1 | <33.3%, if estimated directly as a proportion of hatched nests or using the Mayfield (1975) method; low when based on expert evaluation. | 0-3 specimens per 100 trap-days; low when based on expert evaluation. |
| 2 | 33.3-66.7%, if estimated directly; average when based on expert evaluation. | 4-10 rodents per 100 trap-days; average when based on expert evaluation. |
| 3 | >66.7%, if estimated directly; high when based on expert evaluation. | 11-30 animals per 100 trap-days; high when based on expert evaluation. |
| Criteria for estimates of parameter quality | | |
| 1 | Unsupported evaluation by respondent. | Visual evaluation during a period of less than one month, or interview data, or unknown source. |
| 2 | Evaluation based on abundance of wader broods. | Visual evaluation during a period of less than one month and interview data. |
| 3 | Direct estimates of nesting success with sample of 5-30 nests, or observations of larger numbers of nests terminated before hatching. | Direct counts for a period of less than one month, or visual evaluation for a period exceeding one month, or counts of nests under snow. |
| 4 | Combination of two conditions of rank 3, or combination of any condition of rank 3 with condition of rank 2. | Combination of two conditions of rank 3, or combination of any condition of rank 3 with any condition of rank 1. |
| 5 | Direct estimates of nesting success with sample exceeding 30 nests. | Direct counts for a period exceeding one month. |

We obtained the mean monthly temperatures for June and July for each weather station located to the north of 50° N for the period 1978-2003 (i.e. from the start of cannon-netting for waders in Australia), and then estimated the deviations of these means from the monthly averages over the period 1994-2003. The last 10 years were chosen as a reference period because the available weather data were the most consistent during this period. Deviation values obtained from the weather stations were then interpolated across the whole of the Arctic for each year from 1978 to 2003, and the interpolated values averaged across the flyway population ranges of the four wader species under investigation. The interpolation technique was the same as that used for nesting success and rodent abundance. These average values indicated whether conditions in the respective months across the species' ranges were warmer or colder than the average for the 10-year period 1994-2003.

## Data on proportion of juveniles

The Victorian Wader Study Group has been collecting data on the proportion of juvenile waders in cannon-net catches in south-eastern Australia since 1978. Data on the percentages of juveniles were gathered in 1978-2003 for the Red-necked Stint, in 1979-2003 for the Curlew Sandpiper and Sharp-tailed Sandpiper, and in 1989-2003 for the Ruddy Turnstone. In-depth analyses of the data sampling procedures, possible biases and considerations required during interpretation of data have been published elsewhere (Minton *et al.* 2000). Analyses of the proportions of juveniles in the catches have been made by Minton *et al.* (2001, 2002a, 2002b, 2003a, 2003b, 2004). All catches were made between mid-November and the end of February, except for a few catches of Red-necked Stint and Ruddy Turnstone which were made up to mid-March in some years.

The annual samples of Red-necked Stint and Curlew Sandpiper ranged from several hundred to several thousand birds, while the average annual samples of Sharp-tailed Sandpiper and Ruddy Turnstone were only 180 and 122 birds, respectively. We accounted for the presence of small sample sizes in the latter two species by assigning quality ranks based on the number of birds in the total catches: 1 = <50 birds a year; 2 = 50-99 birds; 3 = 100 or more birds. This scale was chosen to provide the closest match to the previous analyses of juvenile percentage data from the Australian non-breeding grounds, which defined samples below 30 birds as inadequate, and distinguished "small" and "large" catches based on the threshold of 50 birds (e.g. Minton *et al.* 2004).

## Processing and analyses of data

The statistical processing of data was based on fitting regression models, and incorporated weighting of observations with data quality ranks. Outliers were identified using studentized residuals, and excluded from samples when they represented apparently unrealistic values (e.g. 66.7% juveniles in a sample of 66 Sharp-tailed Sandpiper in 1989).

The most general form of dependence of wader productivity on environmental factors was studied by extracting the principal components from two groups of variables: (1) four variables (one per species) corresponding to proportions of juveniles on the wintering grounds; and (2) eight variables corresponding to July temperatures and rodent abundance within the breeding ranges of the four wader species. This analysis was restricted to the period 1989-2003 for which all data were available for all four species.

Spatial analyses were made using Mapinfo GIS (MapInfo Corp. 1996), while statistical processing employed Systat 7.01 (SPSS Inc. 1997).

## RESULTS

### Effects of temperature and rodent abundance on the breeding performance of waders

The principal results of the statistical testing are summarized in Table 2, while Fig. 1 shows the dependence of juvenile proportions on July temperatures and rodent abundance.

An increase in summer air temperatures within the breeding range resulted in an increase in the proportion of juveniles in the non-breeding grounds in each of the four wader species under consideration. The estimated effect of this increase in temperature, expressed as percentage increase in the proportion of juveniles per one degree of increase in the average June and July temperatures across the range of the species, varied from 3.2 in the Sharp-tailed Sandpiper to 14.0 in the Ruddy Turnstone. The effect was most pronounced for mean July temperatures in all species except Sharp-tailed Sandpiper, in which the effect of July temperature, in isolation, was not significant at $P<0.05$. However, when the average June and July temperatures were combined for this species, the effect was significant.

Summer air temperatures had a significant effect on nesting success across the breeding range only in the Ruddy Turnstone, although the marginally significant effect of July temperatures in the Sharp-tailed Sandpiper is noteworthy.

The proportion of juveniles on the non-breeding grounds in south-eastern Australia increased significantly ($P<0.05$) with an increase in rodent abundance in the Sharp-tailed Sandpiper, but not in other species, although an examination of the graphs revealed that a good regression in the case of the Red-necked Stint was adversely affected by a single apparent outlier – the low proportion of juveniles in 2000 (Fig. 1). The relationship between nesting success and rodent abundance was, at best, marginally significant in the Ruddy Turnstone.

Summer temperatures across the breeding ranges of the four species of waders were significantly correlated with each other ($P<0.05$, Spearman correlation of ranks=$S_r$ below), as were the values for rodent abundance ($P<0.05$). However, juvenile proportions in Australia were significantly correlated with each other ($P<0.05$) only in a single pair of species, namely Ruddy Turnstone and Curlew Sandpiper, the only two high Arctic species under consideration.

Extracting the Principal Components[1] from the proportions of juveniles of the four species for the period 1989-2003 aimed at revealing common patterns of variation in the productivity of the different species using a data reduction approach. PC1 explained 54.5% of the total variance of the four variables, and was mostly related to variation in the proportions of juvenile Curlew Sandpiper, Ruddy Turnstone and Red-necked Stint (loadings ranging from 0.68 to 0.94), while correlation with the proportions of juvenile Sharp-tailed Sandpiper was much

---

[1] A Principal Component Analysis is used to simplify a data set; more formally, it is a linear transformation that chooses a new co-ordinate system for the data set such that the greatest variance by any projection of the data set comes to lie on the first axis (then called the first principal component, PC1), the second greatest variance on the second axis (PC2), and so on.

**Table 2.** Estimates of the effects of environmental parameters on the breeding productivity of waders (response variables), and evaluation of trends. The effects are expressed as percentage change in dependent variable per unit change in independent variable; e.g. in the Sharp-tailed Sandpiper, the proportion of juveniles increases by 7.35% when rodent abundance increases by one unit (from "low" to "average", or from "average" to "high"). P-values for the corresponding effects are given in brackets, and estimates of effects significant at P<0.05 are shown in bold.

| Parameter | Species | | | |
|---|---|---|---|---|
| | Red-necked Stint | Curlew Sandpiper | Sharp-tailed Sandpiper | Ruddy Turnstone |
| *Response variable: juvenile proportion* | | | | |
| June temperature | 2.21 | 1.72 | 2.10 | 6.78 |
| | (0.198) | (0.117) | (0.14) | (0.40) |
| July temperature | **6.36** | **6.30** | 1.95 | **11.71** |
| | (0.003) | (0.001) | (0.066) | (0.018) |
| Average of June & July temperatures | **4.65** | **3.50** | **3.16** | **14.01** |
| | (0.027) | (0.024) | (0.032) | (0.045) |
| Rodent abundance | 10.68* | 9.52 | **7.35** | 16.52 |
| | (0.110) | (0.168) | (0.016) | (0.170) |
| *Response variable: nesting success* | | | | |
| June temperature | 0.23 | 0.14 | 0.08 | 0.44 |
| | (0.220) | (0.194) | (0.534) | (0.182) |
| July temperature | 0.25 | 0.18 | 0.17 | **0.28** |
| | (0.125) | (0.155) | (0.086) | (0.038) |
| Average of June & July temperatures | 0.29 | 0.22 | 0.24 | **0.41** |
| | (0.130) | (0.099) | (0.099) | (0.041) |
| Rodent abundance | 0.39 | 0.40 | 0.33 | 0.62 |
| | (0.256) | (0.211) | (0.369) | (0.073) |
| *Linear trends with year* | | | | |
| Juvenile proportion | **0.51** | 0.32 | **0.58** | -0.77 |
| | (0.024) | (0.088) | (0.019) | (0.562) |
| Nesting success | 0.01 | 0.02 | 0.03 | 0.004 |
| | (0.667) | (0.500) | (0.503) | (0.916) |
| Rodent abundance | 0.02 | 0.01 | 0.04 | 0.04 |
| | (0.322) | (0.650) | (0.195) | (0.092) |
| June temperature (1950–2003) | **0.02** | 0.003 | 0.001 | 0.01 |
| | (0.015) | (0.778) | (0.939) | (0.120) |
| July temperature (1950–2003) | **0.02** | 0.01 | **0.03** | **0.03** |
| | (0.026) | (0.183) | (0.020) | (0.001) |

\* The effect of rodent abundance on proportion of juveniles increased to 24.3 (P<0.003) after removal of a single apparent outlier in 2000 from the data set.

smaller (–0.34). Variation in the proportions of juveniles in the latter species was accounted for by PC2 which explained 26.6% of the total variance (loading 0.84 for the Sharp-tailed Sandpiper, and loadings in the range –0.40 to +0.39 for the other three species).

PC1 extracted from the eight environmental variables explained 62.8% of their total variance (loadings in the range 72.1 to 83.6). PC2 explained 24.4% of the total variance, and separated temperature variables (loadings >0.25) from variables of rodent abundance (loadings <–0.45). There is a fairly good linear relationship between PC1 extracted from data on juvenile proportions and corresponding to wader breeding performance, and PC1 extracted from environmental variables on the breeding grounds (Fig. 2), and this is also statistically significant (P<0.05, Sr=0.621).

### Trends in environmental factors in Siberia and the proportions of juveniles in south-eastern Australia

Mean July temperatures increased significantly during the period 1950-2003 at a rate of 0.017-0.029°C per year across the breeding ranges of all species except Curlew Sandpiper, while mean June temperatures increased significantly only in the range of the Red-necked Stint (Table 2). To allow comparison with the trends in breeding performance, we analyzed trends in July temperatures during the periods for which data on juvenile proportions were available for each of the four species. This analysis yielded a highly significant (P<0.003) increasing trend (at a rate of 0.053°C per year) across the breeding range of the Red-necked Stint, and a marginally significant (P=0.057) increasing trend (at a rate of 0.1°C per year) across the breeding range of the Ruddy Turnstone.

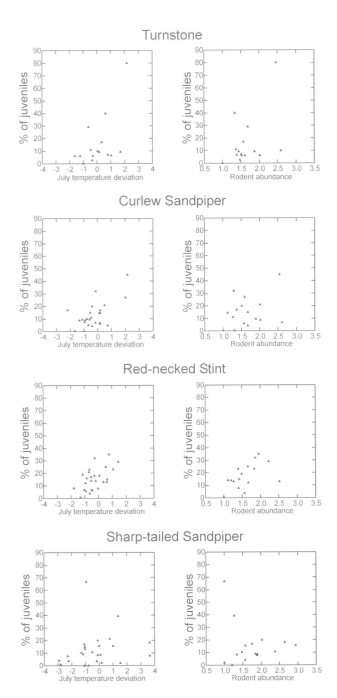

Fig. 1. Percentage of juveniles in four species of waders in south-eastern Australia in relation to deviations in July temperature and rodent abundance on the breeding grounds in eastern Siberia.

In south-eastern Australia, the proportion of juvenile Red-necked Stints and Sharp-tailed Sandpipers increased significantly (*P*<0.03) at an average rate of 0.51% and 0.58% per year, respectively. However, no significant trend was found in the period 1988-2003 either for rodent abundance or wader nesting success across the ranges of the four species, although in the case of the Ruddy Turnstone, the marginally significant value for the effect of year on rodent abundance suggested some tendency for increase. This was probably not confirmed because of the short time series and extremely high variation of the variable.

## DISCUSSION
In this study, we have revealed the relationships between the breeding performance of four Arctic-breeding waders and

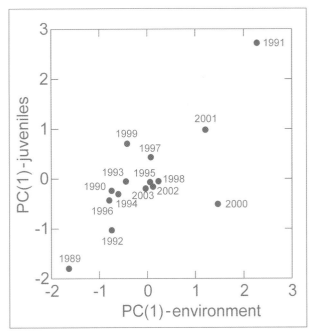

Fig. 2. Environmental factors within the breeding ranges of four species of waders in eastern Siberia (PC(1)-environment) and the percentage of juveniles on the wintering grounds in south-eastern Australia (PC(1)-juveniles).

some environmental variables within their breeding ranges. The magnitude of the effect of June and July temperatures on breeding performance increased with an increase in the severity of environmental conditions. Thus, the Sharp-tailed Sandpiper (which shows an increase of only 3.2% in the proportion of juveniles per degree Centigrade rise in temperature) inhabits southern and typical tundra sub-zones (as defined by Chernov 1985), mires and floodplain habitats with abundant sedge vegetation. This corresponds to the least severe environment compared with that of the other three species. The effects of summer temperatures on the proportions of juvenile Red-necked Stint and Curlew Sandpiper were similar to one another (increasing by 6.4% and 6.3% per degree, respectively). The former species primarily inhabits upper slopes and watersheds in southern and typical tundra, while the latter inhabits slopes and watersheds in typical and Arctic tundra. The severity of the environment in the breeding habitat of these two species is probably, therefore, comparable. Finally, the Ruddy Turnstone inhabits typical and Arctic tundra, but in typical tundra, its breeding range is mostly restricted to the sea coast, where the possibility of adverse weather is considerably higher than in inland areas.

The proportions of juvenile Red-necked Stint, Curlew Sandpiper and Ruddy Turnstone were more strongly correlated with July temperatures than June temperatures, while in the Sharp-tailed Sandpiper, the percentage of juveniles was correlated with June and July temperatures combined. A stronger effect of early summer (June) temperatures seems natural in a species with a southerly distribution. Given that chicks of Arctic waders hatch primarily in July, the greater influence of July temperatures on juvenile production in most species is probably explained by the higher sensitivity of the chicks to adverse weather conditions, especially recently hatched chicks, compared with clutches of eggs. The hypothesis that the primary impact of summer temperatures on breeding performance is via mortality of chicks is also supported by the virtual absence of any relationship between nesting success (up to hatching) and summer temperatures (the Ruddy Turnstone, which inhabits the most severe environment, being the only exception in this study).

The absence of a significant relationship between wader nesting success across the breeding ranges and rodent abundance contradicts the predictions of the Roselaar-Summers prey-switching hypothesis. Our small sample size (16 seasons) and the low quality of data in many years, in particular the data on nesting success, could be a reason for this failure to demonstrate a statistical relationship between these two parameters. The relationship between proportions of juveniles and rodent abundance found in the Sharp-tailed Sandpiper and Red-necked Stint indicates that prey-switching is likely to affect productivity in at least some of the species under consideration, but the reasons why only these species showed a significant relationship are not as yet clear.

The effects of rodent abundance on the nesting success of waders and production of juveniles are less pronounced than the effects of weather. We hypothesize that this is due to the abundance of alternative prey during the incubation period, while temperatures have most effect at the later stage of chick-rearing and thus have a more direct influence on the proportions of juveniles in the population.

The correlation of environmental factors (temperatures and rodent abundance) within the ranges of different species of waders with each other is not surprising given the considerable overlap in the waders' ranges. The absence of a strong correlation in juvenile proportions among most species of waders indicates that the response of waders to similar environmental factors on their breeding grounds differs between species. In particular, the response of the Sharp-tailed Sandpiper to environmental factors differs from that of other species. This may be due to the smaller extent of the Sharp-tailed Sandpiper's breeding range and its more southerly distribution.

Although there are differences between wader species in their response to the Arctic environment, there are also certain similarities. There were years (e.g. 1989 and 1992) in which the combined effects of low summer temperatures and low rodent abundance resulted in very poor breeding performance of all, or nearly all, species, while in other seasons (e.g. 1991) superb environmental conditions resulted in very high reproductive success in all species (Fig. 2). Deviations from this relationship require special consideration. Good environmental conditions in 2000 failed to ensure high breeding performance by waders (Fig. 2). This apparent anomaly was probably the result of an unusual pattern of July air temperatures in eastern Siberia in this year. The very high July temperatures responsible for the relatively high averages across eastern Siberia occurred mostly in eastern Yakutia and western Chukotka – an area which is not inhabited at high density by any of the species under consideration. Conversely, July was cold in western Yakutia, Taimyr and eastern Chukotka, and this probably resulted in the low breeding performance recorded in Australia. Thus, accounting for heterogeneity within the breeding range can greatly aid in the interpretation of results, but the required data have yet to be collated.

In the four species under investigation, the most pronounced long-term increasing trend in juvenile proportions was in the Red-necked Stint, and this corresponds to the most pronounced increasing trend in July temperatures, which occurred within the breeding range of this species. This tallies well with an increase in numbers of Red-necked Stints on the non-breeding grounds, as revealed by monitoring counts in Australia (Minton 2003), and gives persuading evidence of the long-term impact of processes developing on the breeding grounds on recruitment and numbers in wader populations.

While all the evidence points to the positive effects of increasing summer temperatures on wader breeding performance, certain issues remain unclear and require further research to assess the possible impacts of changes in the environment on population productivity and numbers. The following research topics require further investigation:

1  Increasing summer temperatures might, at some point, reach a threshold after which their effect on wader breeding performance will no longer remain beneficial. For example, high summer temperatures could lead to increased dryness of habitats and an associated decrease in the availability of the soil invertebrates on which the waders feed. The consequences for populations of reaching this upper temperature threshold are not known, but could easily be dramatic.

2  Trends in the breeding performance of the Curlew Sandpiper require thorough investigation. The Australian non-breeding population of this species has shown a major decline in numbers, with counts in some areas down to 25% of former levels (Minton 2003). Most of the decline has occurred since 1994 (Minton *et al.* 2002a). However, no evidence was discovered of any deterioration in environmental factors across the breeding range of the species during the present study, implying that stable values of the factors under investigation are not sufficient to support stable populations. It is likely, therefore, that other factors are responsible for the decline in the Curlew Sandpiper population, but what these factors are remains unknown.

3  While summer temperatures affect productivity of all four species of waders to varying degrees, some species also respond to changes in rodent abundance. The reasons for the differences between species in their response to rodent abundance are unknown, as also are the effects of interactions of rodent abundance with temperature. It is also possible that the indirect effect of the lemming cycle on wader productivity differs in various parts of the Arctic, and may, for example, be especially pronounced on the Taimyr Peninsula (e.g. Underhill 1987, Underhill *et al.* 1989). This issue needs verification.

4  The contribution of impacts away from the breeding grounds to changes in juvenile proportions are unknown. Staging sites of migrants in the East Asian-Australasian Flyway are subject to various threats due to intensive development in coastal areas. Studies of population processes in northern Siberia and Australia will hopefully help to interpret correctly those impacts to which birds are exposed on their migration routes.

## ACKNOWLEDGEMENTS

From 1988 to 1996, collection of data on the breeding grounds and data processing were carried out by the Working Group on Waders (Commonwealth of Independent States), while activities in 1997-2004 were conducted within the framework of the ABBCS and with support from the International Wader Study Group, Working Group on Waders (CIS), the Government of The Netherlands, and Wetlands International. We would like to give our special thanks to the large number of people who contributed their data to the ABBCS over a period of 16 years, and all those who participated in the wader-catching activities of the Victorian Wader Study Group over a period of 26 years. Derek Scott provided valuable comments on the manuscript.

## REFERENCES

**Boyd, H.** 1992. Arctic summer conditions and British Knot numbers: an exploratory analysis. Wader Study Group Bulletin 64 (Suppl.): 144-152.

**Boyd, H. & Piersma, T.** 2001. Changing balance between survival and recruitment explains population trends in Red Knot *Calidris canutus islandica* wintering in Britain, 1969-1995. Ardea 89 (2): 301-317.

**Buhmann, M.D.** 2003. Radial Basis Functions. Cambridge University Press, Cambridge.

**Chernov, Y.I.** 1985. The Living Tundra. Cambridge University Press, Cambridge.

**Ganter, B. & Boyd, H.** 2000. A tropical volcano, high predation pressure, and the breeding biology of Arctic Waterbirds: a circumpolar review of breeding failure in the summer of 1992. Arctic 53: 289-305.

**International Wader Study Group** 2003. Waders are declining worldwide. Conclusions from the 2003 International Wader Study Group Conference, Cadiz, Spain. Wader Study Group Bulletin 101/102: 8-12.

**Lappo, E.G., Tomkovich, P.S. & Syroechkovski, E.E., Jr.** In prep. The Atlas of the Breeding Waders of the Russian Arctic.

**MapInfo Corp.** 1996. MapInfo Professional 4.12. (Computer software). Troy, New York.

**Mayfield, H.F.** 1975. Suggestions for calculating nest success. Wilson Bulletin 87: 456-466.

**Minton, C.** 2003. The importance of long-term monitoring of reproduction rates in waders. Wader Study Group Bulletin 100: 178-182.

**Minton, C., Jessop, R. & Hassell, C.** 2000. 1999 Arctic breeding success from an Australian perspective. Arctic Birds: an international breeding conditions survey newsletter 2: 19-20.

**Minton, C., Jessop, R., Collins, P. & Hassell, C.** 2001. Indications of year 2000 Arctic breeding success based on the percentage of first year birds in Australia in the 2000/01 austral summer. Arctic Birds: Newsletter of International Breeding Conditions Survey 3: 31-32.

**Minton, C., Jessop, R. & Collins, P.** 2002a. Variations in apparent annual breeding success of Red-necked Stints and Curlew Sandpipers between 1991 and 2001. Arctic Birds: Newsletter of International Breeding Conditions Survey 4: 43-45.

**Minton, C., Jessop, R., Collins, P. & Hassell, C.** 2002b. Year 2001 Arctic breeding success, as measured by the percentage of first year birds in wader populations in Australia in the 2001/02 austral summer. Arctic Birds: Newsletter of International Breeding Conditions Survey 4: 39-42.

**Minton, C., Jessop, R. & Collins, P.** 2003a. Sanderling and Ruddy Turnstone breeding success between 1989 and 2002 based on data from SE Australia. Arctic Birds: Newsletter of International Breeding Conditions Survey 5: 48-50.

**Minton, C., Jessop, R., Collins, P. & Hassell, C.** 2003b. Arctic breeding success in 2002, based on the percentage of first year birds in wader populations in Australia in the 2002/03 austral summer. Arctic Birds: Newsletter of International Breeding Conditions Survey 5: 45-47.

**Minton, C., Jessop, R., Collins, P., Sitters, H. & Hassell, C.** 2004. Arctic breeding success in 2003, based on juvenile ratios in waders in Australia in the 2003/2004 austral summer. Arctic Birds: Newsletter of the International Breeding Conditions Survey 6: 39-42.

**Rehfisch, M.M. & Crick, H.Q.P.** 2003. Predicting the impact of climatic change on Arctic-breeding waders. Wader Study Group Bulletin 100: 86-95.

**Roselaar, C.S.** 1979. Fluctuaties in aantallen krombekstrandlopers *Calidris ferruginea*. Watervogels 4: 202-210.

**SPSS Inc.** 1997. SYSTAT 7.01 for Windows. (Computer software). Chicago, IL.

**Summers, R.W. & Underhill, L.G.** 1987. Factors related to breeding production of Brent Geese *Branta b. bernicla* and waders (Charadrii) on the Taimyr Peninsular. Bird Study 34: 161-171.

**Stroud, D.A., Baker, A., Blanco, D.E., Davidson, N.C., Delany, S., Ganter, B., Gill, R., González, P., Haanstra, L., Morrison, R.I.G., Piersma, T., Scott, D.A., Thorup, O., West, R., Wilson, J. & Zöckler, C. (on behalf of the International Wader Study Group).** 2006. The conservation and population status of the world's waders at the turn of the millennium. Waterbirds around the world. G.C. Boere, C.A. Galbraith & D.A. Stroud (Eds.), The Stationery Office, Edinburgh, UK. 643-648.

**Underhill, L.G.** 1987. Changes in the age structure of Curlew Sandpiper populations at Langebaan Lagoon, South Africa, in relation to lemming cycles in Siberia. Transactions of The Royal Society of South Africa 46(3): 209-214.

**Underhill, L.G., Waltner, M. & Summers, R.W.** 1989. Three-year cycles in breeding productivity of Knots *Calidris canutus* wintering in southern Africa suggest Taimyr Peninsula provenance. Bird Study 36: 83-87.

**Zöckler, C. & Lysenko, I.** 2000. Water Birds on the edge: First circumpolar assessment of Climate Change impact on Arctic water birds. WCMC Biodiversity Series No. 11. http://www.unepwcmc.org/climate/waterbirds/ WaterBirds_part1.pdf.

**Zöckler, C., Delany, S. & Hagemeijer, W.** 2003. Wader populations are declining – how will we elucidate the reasons? Wader Study Group Bulletin 100: 202-211.

## WEB-SITES

**ABBCS database:** http://arctic.ss.msu.ru/birdspec/.

**Arctic Bird Library:** UNEP World Conservation Monitoring Centre: http://www.unepwcmc.org/arctic/birds/ArcticBird Library.htm.

**World Meteorological Organization:** National Climatic Data Center, USA: http://www.ncdc.noaa.gov/ol/climate/climatere sources.html.

# The Arctic connection: monitoring coastal waders in South Africa - a case study

*Doug M. Harebottle & Les G. Underhill*

*Avian Demography Unit, University of Cape Town, Rondebosch, 7701, South Africa. (email: doug@adu.uct.ac.za)*

Harebottle, D.M. & Underhill, L.G. 2006. The Arctic connection: monitoring coastal waders in South Africa - a case study. *Waterbirds around the world*. Eds. G.C. Boere, C.A. Galbraith & D.A. Stroud. The Stationery Office, Edinburgh, UK. pp. 138-139.

This paper discusses population processes of Arctic-breeding waders in light of global climate change and the birds' occurrence and abundance at non-breeding sites at the southern limits of their migratory range. Curlew Sandpiper *Calidris ferruginea* trends from Langebaan Lagoon, South Africa were selected as a case study to demonstrate the strength of assessing change in Arctic-breeding wader populations through monitoring populations at selected non-breeding sites. Preferred and peripheral sites are described to ensure that monitoring is measurable and valuable. Recommendations are provided to guide future global migratory wader research and conservation.

Arctic-breeding waders constitute an important component of wetland communities, and the ecological impact on the health and integrity of wetland systems is unknown should they disappear (Committee for Holarctic Shorebird Monitoring 2004). There is growing international concern that many wader populations are declining (Wader Study Group 2003, Stroud *et al* 2006) and global warming is likely to impact all habitats used in the annual cycle. Breeding grounds will change due to loss of tundra habitat, while inter-tidal wetlands, both in non-breeding sites and along the migration route, will be impacted as sea-levels rise. The dependence of Arctic waders on critical staging sites will thus reflect environmental conditions across the globe.

It has been suggested that population processes of waders breeding in the Arctic tundra can be monitored at the end of the migratory range, e.g. lemming cycles in Siberia can be observed at the foot of Table Mountain (Underhill 2003). South Africa is host to birds from many of the East Atlantic and West Asia/East Africa Flyway migratory wader populations and the opportunity exists to monitor population trends and processes in these non-breeding areas. Currently, three appropriate sites in South Africa have monitoring programmes for arctic waders: (1) Langebaan Lagoon (Harebottle *et al.* 2006, Underhill 1987), (2) Robben Island (Underhill *et al.* 2001) and (3) Dyer Island (Venter *et al.* 2002). Langebaan Lagoon supports the southern-most large concentration of waders on the East Atlantic Flyway and has the longest running monitoring programme of its kind in the southern hemisphere, operating since 1975.

For our case study, we selected Curlew Sandpiper and examined count data from Langebaan Lagoon over the past 28 years. Long-term trends and breeding productivity are presented in Figs. 1 & 2. Data from mid-summer (January/February) was used to establish overall population trends, while southern winter (July/August) counts were used to measure breeding productivity, as most first-year birds do not migrate (Summers *et al.* 1995). Both numbers of birds and numbers of juveniles at the lagoon have been decreasing over the past 28 years.

The Curlew Sandpiper results from this study have demonstrated that population monitoring at non-breeding sites can be a useful measure of population processes at the breeding grounds.

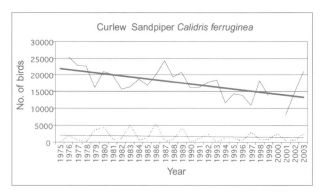

Fig. 1. Summer (solid line) and winter (broken line) counts for Curlew Sandpiper *Calidris ferruginea* at Langebaan Lagoon, South Africa from 1975-2003. Trend lines (dark blue) are shown for each count series.

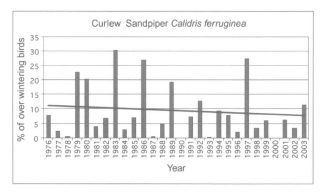

Fig. 2. Breeding productivity of Curlew Sandpiper measured at Langebaan Lagoon, 1976-2003. Figures based on the percentage of winter count of first-year birds versus the previous summer count. Trend line shown in black.

However, it is important that the correct sites are selected for monitoring to be effective. Generally, monitoring sites should be unlikely to undergo any long-term development changes. As such, there is a need to identify preferred and peripheral sites. Preferred sites are those that have roughly the same number of birds each year (e.g. Langebaan Lagoon), while peripheral sites are those that are not occupied every year, or have large annual fluctuations of birds (e.g. Robben Island and Dyer Island).

Based on this case study, the following recommendations are provided for future migratory wader research: (a) the need for improved, coordinated circumpolar monitoring of arctic wader populations to asses their status and population trends, (b) the establishment of networks of preferred and peripheral sites throughout the species' migratory range and (c) the provision of adequate funding to establish monitoring programmes at selected sites, particularly in poorer countries.

We acknowledge financial support from the National Research Foundation.

## REFERENCES

**Committee for Holarctic Shorebird Monitoring** 2004. Monitoring Arctic-nesting Shorebirds: An international vision for the future. Conclusions from the Pan-Arctic Shorebird/Wader Monitoring and Research Workshop, Denmark, 3-6 December 2003. CHASM Publication No. 1

**Harebottle, D.M., Navarro, R.A., Underhill, L.G. & Waltner, M.** 2006. Trends in numbers of migrant waders (Charadrii) at Langebaan Lagoon, South Africa, 1975-2003. Waterbirds around the world. G.C. Boere, C.A. Galbraith & D.A. Stroud (Eds.), The Stationery Office, Edinburgh, UK. 643-648.

**Stroud, D.A., Baker, A., Blanco, D.E., Davidson, N.C., Delany, S., Ganter, B., Gill, R., González, P., Haanstra, L., Morrison, R.I.G., Piersma, T., Scott, D.A., Thorup, O., West, R., Wilson, J. & Zöckler, C.** 2006. The conservation and population status of the world's waders at the turn of the millennium. Waterbirds around the world. G.C. Boere, C.A. Galbraith & D.A. Stroud (Eds.), The Stationery Office, Edinburgh, UK. 643-648.

**Summers, R.W., Underhill, L.G. & Prys-Jones, R.P.** 1995. Does delayed return migration of young waders to their breeding grounds indicate the risk of migration? Ardea 83: 351-357

**Underhill, L.G, Whittington, P.A. & Calf, K.A.** 2001. Shoreline birds of Robben Island, Western Cape, South Africa. Wader Study Group Bulletin 96: 37-39.

**Underhill, L.G.** 2003. Monitoring the Arctic at the foot of Table Mountain. Arctic Bulletin 4/02: 15.

**Venter, A.D., Underhill, L.G., Whittington, P.A. & Dyer, B.M.** 2002. Waders (Charadrii) and other waterbirds at Dyer Island, Western Cape, South Africa. Wader Study Group Bulletin 98: 20-24

**Wader Study Group** 2003. Are waders world-wide in decline? Reviewing the conclusions from the 2003 International Wader Study Group Conference, Cadiz, Spain. Wader Study Group Bulletin 101/102: 8 - 12

Saltmarsh and the southern end of the tidal channel at Langebaan Lagoon.  Photo: Doug Harebottle.

# Thirty years of Arctic wader monitoring in the Dutch part of the Wadden Sea

*Meinte Engelmoer[1], Gerard C. Boere[2] & Ebel Nieboer[3]*

[1] *Senior Consultant Nature Affairs, Province of Frysian, Bentismaheerd 39, Groningen 9736 EC, The Netherlands.*
*(email: m.engelmoer@planet.nl)*
[2] *Dorrewold 22, 7213 TG Gorssel, The Netherlands. (email: gcboere@planet.nl)*
[3] *Park Ondeland 170, 3443 AK Woerden, The Netherlands.*

Engelmoer, M., Boere, G.C. & Nieboer, E. 2006. Thirty years of Arctic wader monitoring in the Dutch part of the Wadden Sea. *Waterbirds around the world.* Eds. G.C. Boere, C.A. Galbraith & D.A. Stroud. The Stationery Office, Edinburgh, UK. pp. 140-146.

## ABSTRACT

Regular wader counting and trapping activities were initiated in the Dutch Wadden Sea about 30 years ago by a group of pioneering ornithologists/ecologists including Jan Rooth, Arie Spaans, Gerard Boere, Ebel Nieboer and Piet Zegers. Since the first count in 1963, there have been over 100 simultaneous counts throughout the Dutch part of the Wadden Sea. Most trapping activities began around 1970, and since then, over 32 000 waders have been trapped. The major aim of the counts and trapping has been to monitor changes in the populations of the wader species occurring in the Wadden Sea, and to obtain insight into changes in the composition of these populations. This paper focuses on the numerical trends and changes in population composition of seven Arctic-breeding waders that occur regularly in the Wadden Sea. Special attention is given to the composition and breeding origins of the populations of Grey Plover *Pluvialis squatarola*, Red Knot *Calidris canutus*, Dunlin *C. alpina* and Bar-tailed Godwit *Limosa lapponica*, as determined by morphometric analysis of wing and culmen lengths.

## INTRODUCTION

When the Arctic breeding season comes to an end, the wader populations from north-eastern Canada in the west to central Siberia in the east begin their migrations to the wintering grounds along the eastern shores of the Atlantic Ocean (e.g. Boere 1977, Smit & Wolff 1981, Smit & Piersma 1989, Meltofte *et al.* 1994, Van de Kam *et al.* 1999, Reneerkens *et al.* 2005). The first step to western Europe is a maximum of about 5 000 km. Nearly all waders in this migration system stay for a shorter or longer period in the international Wadden Sea. Here, western and eastern breeding populations mix. Many birds stay

only for a few weeks, this being long enough for them to refuel for another non-stop flight of 3 000-5 000 km to wintering areas along the coast of West Africa. Those birds that moult in the area stay for a period of between two and four months. Once the moult has been completed, some of the birds migrate to distant wintering grounds in Africa, whilst others depart to winter in coastal regions of south-western Europe and the British Isles. Relatively few waders remain throughout the winter in the Wadden Sea, especially during harsh winters when the area may become devoid of waders. Reverse movements take place in March, April and May, when migrating waders again gather in the Wadden Sea prior to their departure to the breeding grounds. Once again, the area is filled with massive numbers of Arctic-breeding waders.

In order to understand the migrations of these Arctic waders, regular counting and trapping activities were initiated in the Dutch Wadden Sea (Fig. 1) about 30 years ago by a group of ornithologists/ecologists including Jan Rooth, Arie Spaans, Gerard Boere, Ebel Nieboer and Piet Zegers. These pioneers laid the foundations for the organization of regular counting and trapping activities (Fig. 2). The first count was organized by Jan Rooth in 1963, and since then there have been over 100 simultaneous counts throughout the Dutch part of the Wadden Sea. Gerard Boere and Ebel Nieboer started most trapping activities around 1970, after they had been inspired by the trapping activities of Clive Minton and Hugh Boyd on the island of Vlieland in the Dutch Wadden Sea. Since then, over 32 000 waders have been trapped and analysed, resulting in a string of publications, e.g. Nieboer (1972), Boere *et al.* (1973), Boere (1977), Smit & Wolff (1981), Boere *et al.* (1984) and Van der Have *et al.* (1984). Nearly all the younger Dutch ornithologists and ecologists

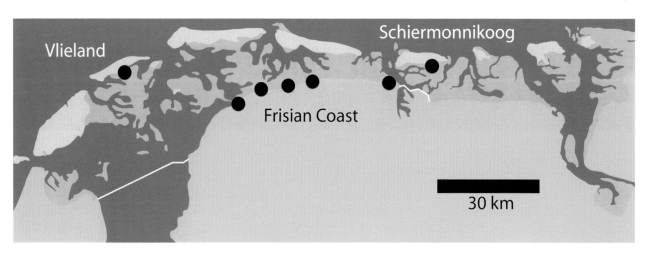

Fig. 1. Wader trapping locations in the Dutch part of the Wadden Sea. The trapping sites are marked with closed circles.

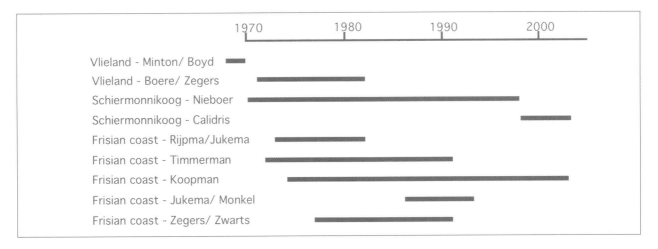

**Fig. 2.** Chronology of wader trapping activities in the Dutch part of the Wadden Sea.

working in the Wadden Sea today became inspired while being involved in these counting or trapping activities in the area. Many of them have since exported their experience to other parts of the world.

Throughout the years, the major aim of organizing counts and trapping activities has been: (1) to monitor changes in the populations of the wader species occurring in the Wadden Sea, and (2) to obtain insight into changes in the composition of these populations. This aim was, and still is, of utmost importance for an understanding of how best to protect the area as a whole. This paper focuses on numerical trends and changes in population composition of seven Arctic-breeding waders that are regularly present in the Dutch Wadden Sea during the non-breeding season. These are: Common Ringed Plover *Charadrius hiaticula*, Grey Plover *Pluvialis squatarola*, Red Knot *Calidris canutus*, Sanderling *C. alba*, Dunlin *C. alpina*, Bar-tailed Godwit *Limosa lapponica* and Ruddy Turnstone *Arenaria interpres*. Some of these species have populations which breed in low Arctic or temperate zones and are regularly present in the Wadden Sea. These populations have also been included in the analyses. Another Arctic species, the Curlew Sandpiper *Calidris ferruginea*, has been excluded because of its restricted occurrence in the Wadden Sea.

Morphometric studies make it possible to produce quantitative estimates of the population composition of mixed wader populations. These estimates are produced with the aid of multivariate data analysis, which includes a comparison of the measurements of birds in the mixed Wadden Sea population with measurements of birds in the breeding populations. Migrant waders in the international Wadden Sea have a mixed breeding origin, but the degree of mixing differs for each species. Measurements of migrants in the Wadden Sea were used to test these new multivariate methods in order to estimate the proportional occurrence of the various breeding populations in the Wadden Sea during the migration seasons and in winter.

## RESULTS

In total, over 32 000 waders have been trapped since the early 1970s. The number of birds trapped annually has fluctuated between 500 and 3 500. In addition, the whole of the Dutch part of the Wadden Sea has been counted three to five times each winter since the early 1970s. P. Zegers and G.C. Boere co-ordinated these counts until 1975 (Boere & Zegers 1974, 1975 & 1977). Zegers continued with the co-ordination until 1992

(Zegers 1985, Zegers & Kwint 1992), and since 1993, SOVON, the Dutch organization for bird monitoring and research, has been responsible for co-ordination (Koffijberg *et al.* 1999, De Boer *et al.* 2001, Kleefstra *et al.* 2002, Van Roomen *et al.* 2002, 2003, 2004, 2005).

### Trends

Most of the Arctic wader species present in the Dutch part of the Wadden Sea show an increasing trend in numbers (Fig. 3). The Red Knot and Ruddy Turnstone have suffered serious declines in the area, but the Ringed Plover, Grey Plover, Sanderling, Dunlin and Bar-tailed Godwit have been increasing in numbers. The early 1980s were characterized by relatively low numbers of Ringed Plover, Sanderling, Dunlin and Bar-tailed Godwit. In the second half of the 1980s, numbers started to recover, with the recovery in Dunlin starting somewhat earlier than in Ringed Plover, Sanderling and Bar-tailed Godwit. The numbers of Red Knot peaked in the first half of the 1990s and have declined since then. Ruddy Turnstone numbers were in continuous decline until the winter of 1999/2000. Since then, numbers have been recovering slowly. Once the trends of mixed populations have been established, it is necessary to unravel them: which populations are on the increase and which are not?

### Population composition in the Wadden Sea

Increases or decreases may be triggered on the breeding grounds, somewhere along the migration routes, on the wintering grounds, or even during the migratory flights. A better understanding is therefore required of population composition throughout the non-breeding season with reference to variability in time and space. When birds are counted, absolute numbers are obtained, resulting in estimates throughout the non-breeding season and a series of index values (Table 1). Conversely, estimates of the composition of populations result in proportional estimates, and can only be obtained when measurements of individual birds are available. Since juveniles and first-winter birds are not fully grown when they arrive in the Wadden Sea, they cannot be compared with samples of adult specimens from the breeding grounds. Thus, in the accounts for Grey Plover, Red Knot, Dunlin and Bar-tailed Godwit that follow, attention is focused on the adult populations.

By comparing the wing and culmen lengths of breeding populations with each other and with those of birds in the mixed

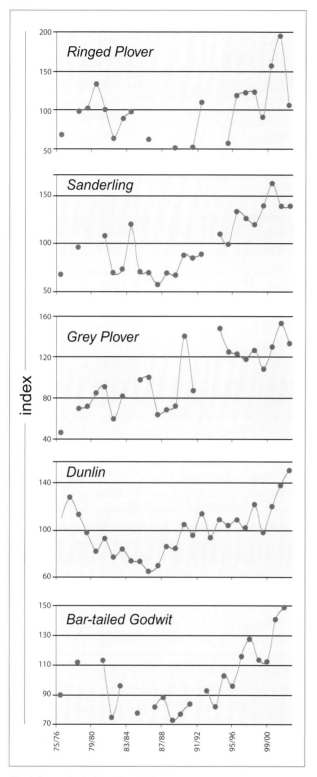

**Fig. 3.** Increasing index values of five Arctic wader species in the Dutch part of the Wadden Sea: 1975/76 - 2001/02. 100 = average over all years.

populations in the Wadden Sea, it is possible to produce estimates of the composition of the wader populations in the Wadden Sea. The methods of comparison are described in Engelmoer (1995), Engelmoer & Roselaar (1998) and Engelmoer (in prep.). Here we focus on the results.

### Grey Plover

Morphometric studies have resulted in the recognition of three different breeding populations of potential relevance to the Wadden

**Table 1.** Indices of wader numbers in the Dutch Wadden Sea: 1975/76 - 2001/02. 100 = average over all years. Data from Sovon Vogelonderzoek Nederland.

| Scientific name | English name | 75/76 | 76/77 | 77/78 | 78/79 | 79/80 | 80/81 | 81/82 | 82/83 | 83/84 | 84/85 | 85/86 | 86/87 | 87/88 | 88/89 | 89/90 | 90/91 | 91/92 | 92/93 | 93/94 | 94/95 | 95/96 | 96/97 | 97/98 | 98/99 | 99/00 | 00/01 | 01/02 |
|---|---|---|---|---|---|---|---|---|---|---|---|---|---|---|---|---|---|---|---|---|---|---|---|---|---|---|---|---|
| *Haematopus ostralegus* | Eurasian Oystercatcher | 78 | 80 | 104 | 107 | 99 | 110 | 105 | 112 | 123 | 118 | 118 | 103 | 123 | 130 | 120 | 109 | 112 | 93 | 95 | 98 | 94 | 73 | 80 | 77 | 82 | 77 | 80 |
| *Recurvirostra avosetta* | Pied Avocet | 94 | 70 | 82 | 92 | 84 | 100 | 97 | 115 | 99 | 125 | 99 | 112 | 109 | 95 | 126 | 146 | 114 | 106 | 87 | 112 | 84 | 88 | 90 | 78 | 87 | 114 | 96 |
| *Charadrius hiaticula* | Common Ringed Plover | 69 | 98 | 103 | 133 | 101 | 64 | 89 | 98 |  |  | 62 |  | 52 | 53 |  |  | 110 |  | 58 |  | 118 | 122 | 123 | 91 | 156 | 194 | 107 |
| *Pluvialis apricaria* | European Golden Plover |  | 90 | 49 | 59 | 61 | 93 | 82 | 48 | 75 | 53 | 70 | 102 | 169 | 69 | 169 | 84 | 82 | 160 | 51 | 104 | 176 | 95 | 135 | 156 | 191 |  |  |
| *Pluvialis squatarola* | Grey Plover | 46 | 70 | 70 | 85 | 88 | 80 | 59 | 82 | 65 | 90 | 90 | 65 | 72 | 72 | 141 | 87 | 120 | 122 | 148 | 126 | 147 | 118 | 127 | 108 | 130 | 153 | 133 |
| *Vanellus vanellus* | Northern Lapwing | 39 | 15 | 51 | 100 | 79 | 119 | 93 | 82 | 53 | 109 | 57 | 66 | 90 | 120 | 51 | 84 | 120 | 204 | 92 | 155 | 59 | 90 | 146 | 122 | 99 | 305 | 190 |
| *Calidris canutus* | Red Knot | 68 | 51 | 70 | 72 | 62 | 108 | 81 | 73 | 103 | 91 | 60 | 65 | 64 | 121 | 85 | 104 | 160 | 181 | 110 | 165 | 92 | 125 | 100 | 146 | 99 | 106 | 72 |
| *Calidris alba* | Sanderling | 68 | 96 | 113 | 70 | 68 | 120 | 69 | 73 | 120 | 70 | 70 | 57 | 69 | 67 | 88 | 85 | 89 | 99 | 110 | 99 | 133 | 127 | 120 | 140 | 163 | 140 | 139 |
| *Calidris alpina* | Dunlin | 110 | 128 | 113 | 112 | 96 | 90 | 82 | 96 | 74 | 78 | 65 | 70 | 86 | 85 | 105 | 96 | 114 | 94 | 109 | 104 | 109 | 102 | 122 | 98 | 120 | 138 | 151 |
| *Limosa lapponica* | Bar-tailed Godwit | 90 |  | 112 | 113 | 95 | 71 | 92 | 76 | 94 | 82 | 94 | 60 | 96 | 101 | 104 | 100 | 144 | 101 | 112 | 132 | 103 | 98 | 106 | 99 | 133 | 145 | 149 |
| *Numenius arquata* | Eurasian Curlew | 93 | 79 | 86 | 70 | 95 | 71 | 92 | 76 | 94 | 82 | 94 | 60 | 96 | 101 | 104 | 100 | 144 | 101 | 112 | 132 | 103 | 98 | 106 | 99 | 133 | 145 |  |
| *Tringa erythropus* | Spotted Redshank | 46 | 79 | 79 | 47 | 87 | 104 | 133 | 107 | 109 | 81 | 34 | 115 | 209 | 109 | 121 | 104 | 128 | 82 | 86 | 143 | 91 | 102 | 89 | 103 | 102 | 84 | 106 |
| *Tringa totanus* | Common Redshank | 120 | 134 |  | 103 |  |  | 94 | 129 | 109 | 76 |  |  | 90 |  | 121 | 104 |  |  |  | 106 | 99 | 82 | 72 | 81 | 109 |  |  |
| *Tringa nebularia* | Common Greenshank | 84 | 96 | 121 |  |  | 95 | 69 | 71 | 77 | 75 | 63 |  | 90 |  | 139 |  |  |  | 82 | 113 | 110 | 42 | 63 | 160 |  | 153 |  |
| *Arenaria interpres* | Ruddy Turnstone | 120 |  | 125 | 103 |  | 116 | 108 | 122 | 139 | 89 |  |  | 99 |  | 139 |  |  |  |  | 74 | 63 | 42 |  |  | 72 |  | 105 |

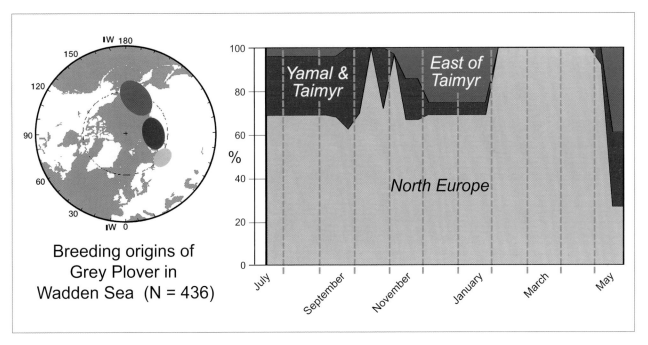

**Fig. 4.** Composition of the non-breeding Grey Plover *Pluvialis squatarola* populations in the Dutch part of the Wadden Sea, based on morphometric analysis of wing and culmen lengths.

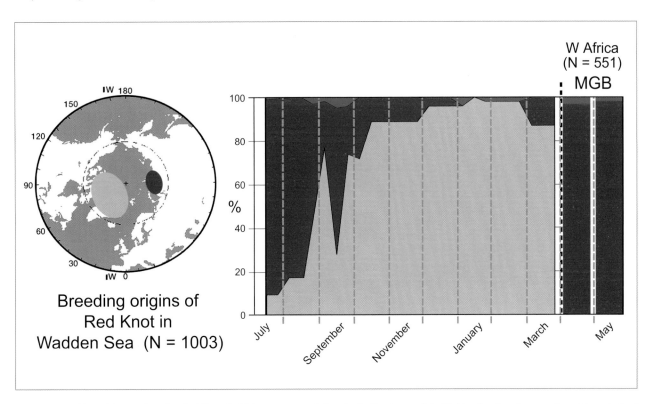

**Fig. 5.** Composition of the non-breeding Red Knot *Calidris canutus* populations in the Dutch part of the Wadden Sea, based on morphometric analysis of wing and culmen lengths. Explanation of patterns: *islandica* (grey); nominate *canutus* (hatched); *piersmai* (black). M = wintering population in Mauritania (WIWO-expeditions, Ens *et al.* 1990); GB = wintering population in Guinea-Bissau (WIWO-expedition, Zwarts 1988).

Sea populations. From west to east, these are: (1) the breeding population in northern Europe; (2) the breeding population in Yamal and Taimyr; and (3) the breeding population east of Taimyr.

The majority of the Grey Plovers in the Wadden Sea apparently belong to the westernmost population breeding in northern Europe (Fig. 4). This breeding population has increased in numbers (Hagemeijer & Blair 1997). The numbers wintering in

western Europe have also increased (e.g. Meltofte *et al.* 1994, Pollitt *et al.* 2003, Van Roomen *et al.* 2004, Engelmoer in prep.), but it is possible that birds from other breeding areas might be involved as well. Grey Plovers from Yamal and Taimyr occur in the Wadden Sea, particularly in July/August and May, and the estimates from the Wadden Sea persistently show the occurrence of a small proportion of Grey Plovers originating from breeding areas east of Taimyr.

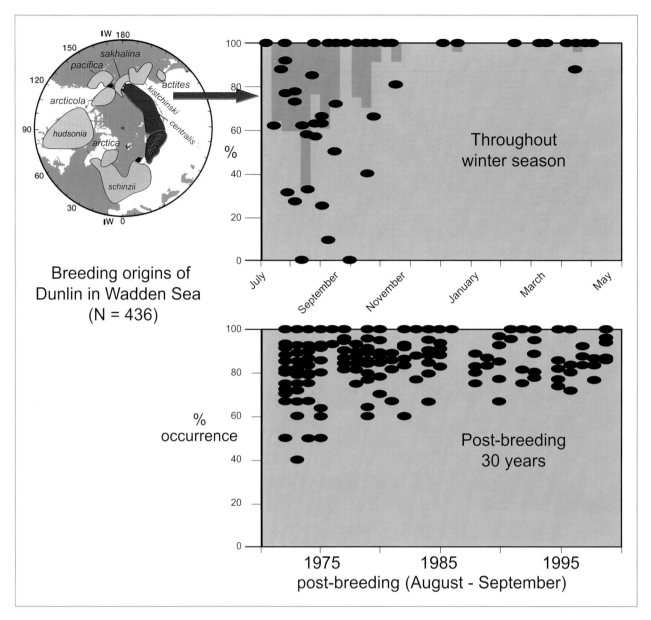

**Fig. 6.** Composition of the non-breeding Dunlin *Calidris alpina* populations in the Dutch part of the Wadden Sea, based on morphometric analysis of wing and culmen lengths. The upper right figure shows the average estimated proportion of the two larger subspecies, *alpina* and *centralis*, in the population by ten-day period throughout the year (dark grey shading). Black dots represent individual samples. The lower right figure shows the change that has occurred over the last 30 years in the proportion of the two larger subspecies in individual samples collected during the post-breeding period.

### Red Knot

Morphometric studies have resulted in the recognition of three breeding populations of potential relevance to the Wadden Sea populations. From west to east, these are: (1) the population of *islandica* breeding in north-eastern Canada; (2) the population of *canutus* breeding in Taimyr; and (3) the population of *piersmai* breeding in the New Siberian Islands.

The majority of Red Knots occurring in the Wadden Sea are the Nearctic subspecies *islandica*, particularly during winter (Fig. 5). Siberian *canutus* are most numerous during July/August and in May, but this subspecies is also regularly present during September/October and March/April. Small numbers of *piersmai* (representing <5%) have been identified in the Wadden Sea in August/September and January/February.

### Dunlin

Four subspecies of Dunlin occur in the Wadden Sea: *arctica* breeding on East Greenland; *schinzii* breeding in north-west

Europe; nominate *alpina* breeding in northern Europe east to Yamal; and *centralis* breeding from Yamal east to 85°E. However, there is overlap in the breeding ranges, as shown by DNA analyses (Wenink 1994), and also overlap in the measurements of the subspecies. The two smallest subspecies, *arctica* and *schinzii*, can easily be separated from the largest subspecies, *centralis*. The measurements of male *alpina* are similar to those of the two smaller subspecies, while female *alpina* are similar in size to *centralis*.

The Dunlin in the Wadden Sea are most often *alpina* or *centralis* (Fig. 6). *Arctica* and *schinzii* occur only during the post-breeding period, with their proportional presence decreasing from July/August to September/October. *Arctica* seems to occur somewhat more regularly than *schinzii*. The late summer occurrence of the two small subspecies, *arctica* and *schinzii*, has decreased markedly since the 1970s in favour of *centralis* and *alpina*. The positive trend in Dunlin numbers since the second half of the 1980s is thus related to larger numbers of *centralis* and *alpina* staging in the Wadden Sea.

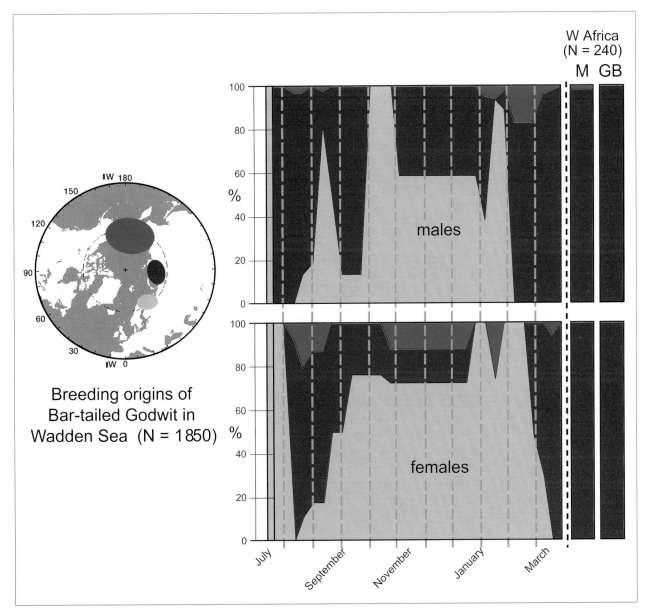

**Fig. 7.** Composition of the non-breeding Bar-tailed Godwit *Limosa lapponica* populations in the Dutch part of the Wadden Sea, based on morphometric analysis of wing and culmen lengths. Explanation of patterns: nominate *lapponica* (grey); *taymyrensis* (hatched); *menzbieri* or further east (black). Ma = wintering population in Mauritania (WIWO-expeditions, Ens *et al*. 1990); GB = wintering population in Guinea-Bissau (WIWO-expedition, Zwarts 1988).

### Bar-tailed Godwit

Morphometric studies have resulted in the recognition of three breeding populations of potential relevance to the Wadden Sea populations. From west to east, these are: (1) nominate *lapponica* breeding in northern Fenno-scandia; (2) *taymyrensis* breeding from Yamal east to the delta of the Anabar River; and (3) *menzbieri* breeding from the Lena Delta east to Chaunsk Bay.

In July and August, immediately after the breeding season, a relatively large proportion of the Bar-tailed Godwits occurring in the Wadden Sea originate from Taimyr, and this is particularly the case amongst the males (Fig. 7). The proportion of *taymyrensis* then decreases during September and October in favour of north European *lapponica*. About 80% of the wintering population of Bar-tailed Godwits in the Wadden Sea are *lapponica* and about 20% *taymyrensis*. Birds from populations breeding east of Taimyr, such as *menzbieri*, occur regularly,

especially females, but always in proportions of less than 10%. *Taymyrensis* is the dominant form again in May, especially amongst the males.

### CONCLUSION

Over the past 30 years, important changes have occurred in the Wadden Sea. Evidence of this has been found from the counting and trapping of Arctic-breeding waders. The combination of counting and trapping has provided quantitative insight into the composition of wader populations with respect to breeding origins, juvenile percentages, and the moulting and refuelling functions of different parts of the area. It has now become clear that the international Wadden Sea should not be considered as a single system for wader migration. Rather, the various areas in the Wadden Sea have different roles and functions for migratory wader populations.

## REFERENCES

**Boere, G.C.** 1977. The significance of the Dutch Wadden Sea in the annual life-cycle of arctic, subarctic and boreal waders. Part 1. The function as a moulting area. Ardea 64: 210-291.

**Boere, G.C. & Zegers, P.M.** 1974. Wadvogeltelling in het Nederlandse Waddengebied in juli 1972. Limosa 47: 23-28.

**Boere, G.C. & Zegers, P.M.** 1975. Wadvogeltellingen in het Nederlandse Waddenzeegebied in april en september 1973. Limosa 48: 74-81.

**Boere, G.C. & Zegers, P.M.** 1977. Wadvogeltellingen in het Nederlandse Waddengebied in 1974 en 1975. Watervogels 2: 161-173.

**Boere, G.C., de Bruijne, J.W.A. & Nieboer, E.** 1973. Onderzoek naar de betekenis van het Nederlandse Waddenzeegebied voor Bonte Strandlopers *Calidris alpina* in nazomer en herfst. Limosa 46: 205-227.

**Boere, G.C., Roselaar, C.S. & Engelmoer, M.** 1984. The breeding origins of Purple Sandpipers *Calidris maritima* present in The Netherlands. Ardea 72: 101-109.

**De Boer, P., Koks, B., van Roomen, M. & van Winden, E.** 2001. Watervogels in de Nederlandse Waddenzee in 1997/98 en 1998/99. SOVON-monitoringrapport 2001/04. SOVON Vogelonderzoek Nederland, Beek-Ubbergen.

**Engelmoer, M.** 1995. The application of discriminant analysis to the morphometrics of waders. In: E.J.M. Hagemeijer & T.J. Verstrael (eds) Bird Numbers 1992. Distribution, monitoring and ecological aspects. Proceedings of 12th International Conference IBCC & EOAC, Noordwijkerhout, The Netherlands: 475-490.

**Engelmoer, M.** (ed). In prep. Morphometrics, weights, moult and migration of the wader populations in the Dutch part of the Wadden Sea.

**Engelmoer, M. & Roselaar, C.S.** 1998. Geographical Variation in Waders. Kluwer Academic Publications, Dordrecht, The Netherlands, and Norwell, U.S.A.

**Ens, B.J., Piersma, T., Wolff, W.J. & Zwarts, L.** (eds). 1990. Homeward bound: problems waders face when migrating from the Banc d'Arguin to their northern breeding grounds in spring. Special volume, Ardea 78.

**Hagemeijer, E.J.M. & Blair, M.J.** (eds). 1997. The EBCC Atlas of European Breeding Birds: Their Distribution and Abundance. T. & A.D. Poyser, London.

**Kleefstra, R., Koks, B., van Roomen, M. & van Winden, E.** 2002. Watervogels in de Nederlandse Waddenzee in 1999/2000. SOVON-monitoringrapport 2002/01. SOVON Vogelonderzoek Nederland, Beek-Ubbergen.

**Koffijberg, K., Koks, B., van Roomen, M. & van Winden, E.** 1999. Watervogels in de Nederlandse Waddenzee in 1996/97, met een samenvattend overzicht van integrale tellingen in 1990/91 - 1995/96. SOVON Monitoringrapport 1999/04, IKC coproductie 23. SOVON Vogelonderzoek Nederland, Beek-Ubbergen.

**Meltofte, H., Blew, J., Frikke, J., Rösner, H.-U. & Smit, C.J.** 1994. Numbers and distribution of waterbirds in the Wadden Sea. IWRB Publication 34, Slimbridge, UK; Wader Study Group Bulletin 74 Special Issue.

**Nieboer, E.** 1972. Preliminary notes on the primary moult in Dunlins *Calidris alpina*. Ardea 60: 112-119.

**Pollitt, M., Hall, C., Holloway, S., Hearn, R., Marshall, P., Musgrove, A., Robinson, J. & Cranswick, P.** 2003. The Wetland Bird Survey 2000-01 Wildfowl and Wader Counts. BTO/ WWT/ RSPB/ JNCC, Slimbridge, UK.

**Reneerkens, J., Piersma, T. & Spaans, B.** 2005. De Waddenzee als kruispunt van vogeltrekwegen. NIOZ-report 2005-4, NIOZ, Texel.

**Smit, C.J. & Piersma, T.** 1989. Numbers, mid-winter distribution and migration of wader populations using the East Atlantic Flyway. In: H. Boyd & J.-Y. Pirot (eds) Flyways and reserve networks for water birds. IWRB Special Publication No. 9. IWRB, Slimbridge, UK: 24-64.

**Smit, C.J. & Wolff, W.J.** (eds). 1981. Birds of the Wadden Sea. Wadden Sea Working Group Report 6, Balkema, Rotterdam.

**Van de Kam, J., Ens, B., Piersma, T. & Zwarts, L.** 1999. Ecologische Atlas van de Nederlandse Wadvogels. Schuyt & Co., Haarlem.

**Van der Have, T.M., Nieboer, E. & Boere, G.C.** 1984. Age-related distribution of Dunlin in the Dutch Wadden Sea. In: P.R. Evans, J.D. Goss-Custard & W.G. Hale (eds) Coastal waders and wildfowl in winter. Cambridge University Press, Cambridge, UK: 160-176.

**Van Roomen, M.W.J., van Winden, E.A.J., Koffijberg, K., Voslamber, B., Kleefstra, R., Ottens, G. & SOVON Ganzen- en Zwanenwerkgroep** 2002. Watervogels in Nederland in 2000/2001. RIZA-rapport BM02.15/ SOVON-monitoringrapport 2002/04. SOVON Vogelonderzoek Nederland, Beek-Ubbergen.

**Van Roomen, M., van Winden, E., Koffijberg, K., Kleefstra, R., Ottens, G., Voslamber, B. & SOVON Ganzen- en Zwanenwerkgroep** 2003. Watervogels in Nederland in 2001/2002. RIZA-rapport BM04.01/ SOVON-monitoringrapport 2004/01. SOVON Vogelonderzoek Nederland, Beek-Ubbergen.

**Van Roomen, M., van Winden, E., Koffijberg, K., Boele, A., Hustings, F., Kleefstra, R., Schoppens, J., van Turnhout, C., SOVON Ganzen- en Zwanenwerkgroep & Soldaat, L.** 2004. Watervogels in Nederland in 2002/2003. RIZA-rapport BM04.09/ SOVON-monitoringrapport 2004/02. SOVON Vogelonderzoek Nederland, Beek-Ubbergen.

**Van Roomen, M., van Turnhout, C., van Winden, E., Koks, B., Goedhart, P., Leopold, M. & Smit, C.** 2005. Trends van benthivore watervogels in de Nederlandse Waddenzee 1975-2002: grote verschillen tussen schelpdiereneters en wormeneters. Limosa 78: 21-38.

**Wenink, P.W.** 2004. Mitochondrial DNA sequence evolution in shorebird populations. Ph.D thesis, University of Wageningen, The Netherlands.

**Zegers, P.M.** 1985. Vogeltellingen in het Nederlandse deel van de Waddenzee 1976-1979. National Forest Service Report 85-10, Utrecht, The Netherlands.

**Zegers, P.M. & Kwint, N.D.** 1992. Vogeltellingen in het Nederlandse deel van het Waddengebied 1979-90. SOVON-report 1992/14. SOVON, Beek-Ubbergen.

**Zwarts, L.** 1988. Numbers and distribution of coastal waders in Guinea-Bissau. Ardea 76: 2-55.

# Stable isotope analysis and threats in the wintering areas of the declining Spoon-billed Sandpiper *Eurynorhynchus pygmeus* in the East Asia-Pacific Flyway

*Christoph Zöckler[1], Evgeny E. Syroechkovskiy, Jr.[2], Elena G. Lappo[3] & Gillian Bunting[1]*

[1] *ArcCona, Ecological Consulting, 30 Eachard Road, Cambridge, CB3 OHY, UK. (email: Christoph.Zockler@unep-wcmc.org)*

[2] *Institute of Ecology and Evolution, Russian Academy of Sciences, Leninski Avenue 3, Moscow 117071, Russia.*

[3] *Institute of Geography, Russian Academy of Sciences, Staromonetny 29, Moscow 109017, Russia.*

Zöckler, C., Syroechkovskiy, E.E., Jr., Lappo, E.G. & Bunting, G. 2006. Stable isotope analysis and threats in the wintering areas of the declining Spoon-billed Sandpiper *Eurynorhynchus pygmeus* in the East Asia-Pacific Flyway. *Waterbirds around the world.* Eds. G.C. Boere, C.A. Galbraith & D.A. Stroud. The Stationery Office, Edinburgh, UK. pp. 147-153.

## ABSTRACT

The Spoon-billed Sandpiper *Eurynorhynchus pygmeus* is a globally threatened species currently classified by IUCN as Endangered. Four expeditions to various parts of the breeding range in Chukotka, eastern Siberia, in 2000-2003 have revealed a sharp decline in numbers. The total population does not exceed 1 000 pairs, and is most likely much lower. The main staging and wintering areas are poorly known, and little information is available on habitat requirements and threats. An analysis of two stable isotopes (deuterium and oxygen-18) in feathers taken from adult birds on the breeding grounds in 2003 indicates wintering areas in the Ganges-Brahmaputra Delta region and South China Sea. Very few of the birds ringed and colour-flagged on the breeding grounds have been re-sighted, and none of the 30 chicks flagged in a core breeding area in 2001 was re-sighted in this area in 2003, suggesting that the main pressures on the species are along the migration route. Various possible reasons for the decline in the species and low return rate of young birds to the breeding areas are discussed. Other migratory waterbirds in the East Asia-Pacific Flyway are undergoing similar declines, and may be affected by the same threats. It is concluded that more effort needs to be given to internationally co-ordinated research and conservation activities if the Spoon-billed Sandpiper is to be safeguarded from extinction.

## INTRODUCTION

The Spoon-billed Sandpiper *Eurynorhynchus pygmeus* is considered to be a globally threatened species and is classified as Endangered (BirdLife International 2004). Four expeditions between 2000 and 2003 to different parts of the breeding range in Chukotka, Russia, revealed a sharp decline. The total population does not exceed 1 000 pairs and is most likely to be much lower (Tomkovich *et al.* 2002, Zöckler 2003, Syroechkovskiy *et al.* in prep.). However, the exact population size and the main wintering sites are not fully known, although there are scattered observations of Spoon-billed Sandpipers in south and south-east Asia. This information and a knowledge of the habitat requirements and threats along the flyway are essential in understanding the recent decline and in implementing the necessary steps towards the protection and safeguarding of a viable population.

The breeding range of the Spoon-billed Sandpiper is confined to the coastal tundra of Chukotka and northern Kamchatka (Figs. 1 and 2). An initial investigation of the three major breeding grounds visited during the surveys did not indicate any specific reasons for the decline in the breeding areas. Although in some of the sites visited, predation of nests and

chicks was very high, in other sites hatching success was very high. There may, however, be other important factors affecting the birds on the breeding grounds, and further research is required to investigate the possible impacts of climate change and other global drivers on conditions in the breeding areas. However, much of the evidence points to threats along the migration route or in the wintering areas.

On migration, the species regularly passes along the coasts of Kamchatka, Sakhalin, Japan and Korea. However, only in Korea are there recent records of the species in substantial numbers, i.e. between 100 and 200 birds annually (Lethaby *et al.* 2000, Jin-Young Park *in litt.*). There have been observations of Spoon-billed Sandpipers in suitable staging and wintering sites in Thailand, Malaysia and Vietnam (Collar *et al.* 2001). Little information is available on staging or wintering areas in Myanmar, Bangladesh and eastern India, and this is often only historical (Howes & Parish 1989, T. Inskipp pers. comm., S. Balachandran pers. comm.). Since 1990, very little information has been received from the wintering grounds, and there have been no observations of groups of more than 20 birds. All this information gives further support to the conclusion that the species is in strong decline.

Unanswered questions on the status of the species still include the exact size of the population and the main wintering areas. The latter is vital in understanding the main reasons for the decline. In view of the paucity of ringing recoveries from potential wintering areas, new technologies are required to reveal the major wintering and stopover sites. In addition to ringing and colour-flagging, the use of stable isotope technology has been demonstrated to be useful in determining the geographical origin of individuals in a population of a species (Hobson & Wassenaar 1997, Marra *et al.* 1998, Webster *et al.* 2002, Atkinson *et al.* in prep.). This technology is now being applied to the Spoon-billed Sandpiper – the first time that a stable isotope analysis has been used on any wader in the Asia-Pacific Flyway. It promises to provide further insight into the location of the pre-breeding moulting areas and the major wintering areas of the Spoon-billed Sandpiper.

## METHODS

### Breeding sites and ringing

Between 2000 and 2003, four expeditions were made to different sites in Chukotka, under the leadership of E.E. Syroechkovskiy, Jr., to investigate the situation of the Spoon-billed Sandpiper on its breeding grounds (see Fig. 2). Breeding densities, hatching and fledging success and various other features of the breeding biology were recorded and compared with the findings of

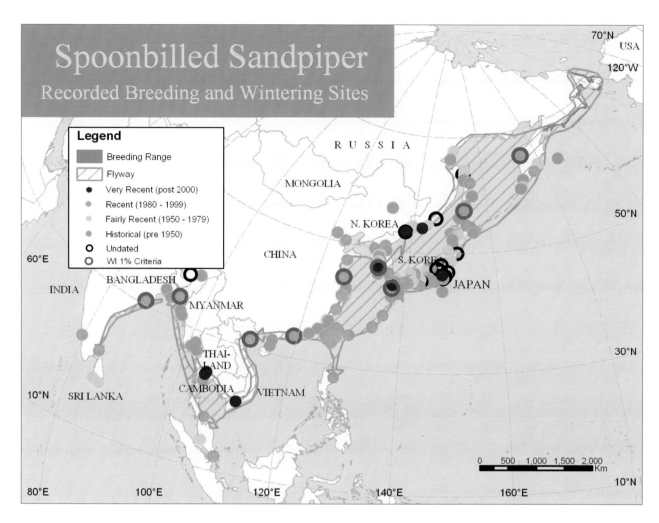

**Spoonbilled Sandpiper**
Recorded Breeding and Wintering Sites

**Legend**
- Breeding Range
- Flyway
- ● Very Recent (post 2000)
- ● Recent (1980 - 1999)
- ● Fairly Recent (1950 - 1979)
- ● Historical (pre 1950)
- ○ Undated
- ◎ WI 1% Criteria

Fig. 1. The distribution of the Spoon-billed Sandpiper *Eurynorhynchus pygmeus*, showing the presumed flyway to south-east Asia.

previous visits. The results of this research will be published elsewhere (Syroechkovskiy *et al.* in prep.). In addition, a number of birds were ringed and colour-flagged. Whenever possible, both members of a breeding pair of Spoon-billed Sandpipers were caught with traps set at or nearby the nest. The adult birds were sexed, and most were ringed and individually colour-flagged. The chicks were also ringed and colour-flagged with light blue flags in North Chukotka and light green flags in South Chukotka.

**Stable isotopes**
In the 2003 season, feather samples were collected for subsequent analyses of stable isotopes. Samples were taken from 28 adult Spoon-billed Sandpipers and one Red-necked Stint *Calidris ruficollis* caught on or near the nest between 13 June and 5 July. Only one or two of the central tail feathers or a couple of scapular feathers were sampled so as not to affect the birds' mobility.

Stable isotopes vary regionally, and the distribution of $\delta^{18}O$ and $\delta^2H$ are promising geographical markers. These isotopes could narrow the location of the species' pre-breeding moulting sites to a smaller geographical region than is currently known. Feather samples from adult breeding birds are assumed to be generated on the wintering grounds, based on a knowledge of closely related species such as other sandpipers (Prater *et al.* 1977), and should therefore bear the signature of the wintering location. At present, the results from the analysis of nine feather

samples are available. Funding for a full analysis of all 29 samples is still lacking.

For the oxygen-18 analysis, 1 mg amounts of feather were weighed into silver capsules. Samples were measured using IAEA-CH-6 (sucrose, $\delta^{18}O = 36.4‰$ vs V-SMOW) as a reference. IAEA-CH-6 and IAEA-C-3 (cellulose, $\delta^{18}O = 32.2‰$ vs V-SMOW) were run as quality control check samples during batch analysis of the samples. IAEA-CH-6 and IAEA-C-3 are inter-comparison materials distributed by the International Atomic Energy Agency, for which the values reported above are generally agreed by the stable isotope analysis community. Both standards and samples were oven-dried at 60°C for more than 72 hours prior to analysis, to remove moisture.

The oxygen isotope analysis was conducted by total conversion at 1080°C in a quartz reactor tube lined with a glassy carbon film, filled to a height of 170 mm with glassy carbon chips and topped with a layer of 50% nickelized carbon (10 mm deep). Carbon monoxide and nitrogen were separated on a GC column packed with molecular sieve 5A at a temperature of 54°C. The isotope ratio mass spectrometer used was a Europa Scientific Geo 20-20 with triple Faraday cup collector array to monitor the masses 28, 29 and 30.

For the deuterium analysis, 1 mg amounts of feather were weighed into silver capsules, and equilibrated with laboratory air moisture for more than 96 hours prior to analysis (Wassenaar & Hobson 2002). Samples were measured using IA-R002 (ISO-Analytical mineral oil, $\delta^2H = -111.2‰$ vs V-SMOW) as a refer-

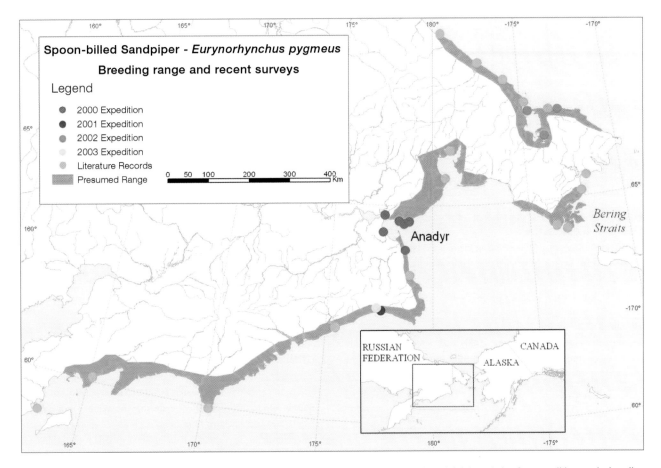

Fig. 2. The breeding distribution of the Spoon-billed Sandpiper *Eurynorhynchus pygmeus* and location of sightings during four expeditions to the breeding grounds in 2000-2003.

ence. IA-R002 and IAEA-CH-7 (polyethylene, $\delta^2H = -100.3\%_0$ vs V-SMOW) were run as quality control check samples during batch analysis of the samples. IAEA-CH-7 is also an inter-comparison material distributed by the International Atomic Energy Agency with an internationally accepted $\delta^2H$ value.

Correction for the exchangeable hydrogen in the feather samples was applied by comparative equilibration of the feathers with BWB-II (whale baleen from the University of Alaska, $\delta^2H = -108\%_0$ vs V-SMOW). The mean measured $\delta^2H$ value for BWB-II was $-101.17\%_0$ vs V-SMOW, providing a comparative equilibration correction factor of 1.0675.

The hydrogen isotope analysis was conducted by total conversion at 1080°C in a quartz reactor lined with a glassy carbon film, filled to a height of 180 mm with glassy carbon chips. Hydrogen was separated from other gaseous products on a GC column packed with molecular sieve 5Å at a temperature of 30°C. The isotope ratio mass spectrometer used was a Europa Scientific Geo 20-20 with a Faraday cup collector array to monitor the masses 2 and 3.

The oxygen-18 and deuterium analyses were carried out by Iso-Analytical Ltd., Cheshire, UK.

## Database of sightings

To support information derived from the stable isotope analyses described above and to provide as much insight as possible into the wintering behaviour of these rare and widely dispersed birds, a database of sightings is being developed. This is directly linked to a GIS system in order to provide a range of map outputs at various scales. These can, in turn, be used for a range of

purposes from giving an overall picture of recent sightings (Fig. 1) to more detailed uses such as planning expeditions and assessing probable threats at the local level.

The database was based on information from Collar *et al.* (2001), but now also includes more recent sightings derived from a range of published and unpublished sources. Two new sites, one in the Gulf of Thailand and one in the Mekong Delta, have recently been included. Additional information from a Wetlands International report (Watkins *et al.* in prep.) has also been added to highlight those sites at which numbers exceeding 1% of the total population have been recorded (blue circles on Fig. 1). Anyone with information on recent sightings, especially of flagged birds, is requested to send it to the authors as well as to the relevant ringing authorities.

Table 1. **Present and past population estimates of the Spoon-billed Sandpiper *Eurynorhynchus pygmeus*.**

| Population estimate (in pairs) | Source | Comments |
|---|---|---|
| 2 000-2 800 | Flint & Kondratiev 1977 | Extrapolation from known breeding grounds. |
| <1 000 | Tomkovich *et al.* 2002 | Based on decline in number of known sites. |
| 560-900 | Syroechkovskiy *et al.* in prep. | If population declined by a factor of 3-5. |
| 400-500 | This study | Based on known numbers and calculated estimates. |

**Table 2. The results of ringing of Spoon-billed Sandpipers** *Eurynorhynchus pygmeus* **during the expeditions to the breeding grounds in 2000-2003.**

| Year | Adults | Chicks | Sightings |
|------|--------|--------|-----------|
| 2000 | 8 | 7 | - |
| 2001 | 1 | 28 | - |
| 2002 | 29 | 30 | 1 juv. |
| 2003 | 55 | 88 | 1 juv. |
| Total | 93 | 153 | 2 |

## RESULTS

### Population estimates

Based on information acquired during the four expeditions in 2000-2003 (see Fig. 2), it is concluded that the total population does not exceed 560-900 pairs, and may be no more than 400-500 pairs (Table 1). For more details, see Syroechkovskiy *et al.* (in prep.).

### Ringing

During the four breeding seasons 2000-2003, a total of 246 birds were ringed and colour-marked with light blue (2002) and light green flags (2000, 2001 and 2003) (Syroechkovskiy *et al.* in prep., Zöckler 2003). Most of these were chicks, but 93 adult birds were also ringed and colour-flagged (Table 2).

### Migration and recoveries

Since the first birds were ringed in 2000, there have been only two re-sightings. A juvenile ringed on 9 July 2002 on Belyaka Spit was sighted in Japan on 25 September 2002, and a juvenile ringed in Meinypil'gyno in 2003 was seen on the mudflats of Saemangeum in South Korea in September 2003, 2.5 months after ringing.

Birds returning to the breeding grounds included two breeding birds re-captured on Belyaka Spit in 2002; these had been ringed in 1988, one as a chick, the other as an adult breeding bird. The site at which the latter individual was breeding was only 200 m away from where it had been ringed 14 years previously (Tomkovich & Soloviev 2000, Tomkovich 2003). This is a remarkable record for two reasons. Firstly, it confirms the high site fidelity of this species on its breeding grounds (Tomkovich 1992, 1995), and secondly, it constitutes the longevity record for the species. Unfortunately, none of the chicks ringed in 2001 was re-sighted in 2003 in Meinypil'gyno.

However, the only adult bird ringed in 2001 was found breeding again in 2003, only a few hundred metres from where it had been ringed.

### Stable isotopes

The stable isotope analysis has so far only been carried out on eight Spoon-billed Sandpipers and one Red-necked Stint. Table 3 shows the results obtained from these nine birds. For comparative purposes, the eight samples from Spoon-billed Sandpipers were compared with that from the Red-necked Stint, a species which is known to follow a different migration route. Hobson & Wassenaar (1997) pointed out that isotope values in feathers differ from those in precipitation. Only about 30% of hydrogen in feathers is derived from drinking water; the remainder (c. 70%) is derived from dietary intake.

Lott *et al.* (2003) have shown that, regardless of species and trophic level, the difference between the values of $\delta^2H$ and $\delta^{18}O$ in precipitation and feathers remains constant at about 18 and 21‰, respectively. According to their research, coastal feeders have a mean value of 36.4‰ (Lott *et al.* 2003). The preferred foraging habitat of the Spoon-billed Sandpiper is coastal lagoons and deltas. This would suggest that there is a high proportion of freshwater or brackish water intake that might reduce the value further towards the freshwater difference. As we do not know enough about the species' diet during the winter months, we have to assume a mix of both deuterium offset values (25‰ and 35‰), resulting in a mean offset of 30‰ of $\delta^2H$ to be added for further approximation. There is no established offset between oxygen-18 in precipitation and feathers. However, taking into account that oxygen-18 in plants is on average 27‰ higher than in precipitation, and in mammals the offset of oxygen-18 is intermediate between that in plants and precipitation, we suggest that oxygen-18 in feathers is very roughly 15-20‰ higher than in precipitation and this needs to be subtracted from the values.

These adjusted values can be compared with the values generated from various research stations as displayed by IAEA (2001) and superimposed with the flyway of the Spoon-billed Sandpiper (see Figs. 3 and 4 for deuterium and oxygen-18, respectively).

If we consider the adjusted $\delta^{18}O$ values of five birds (numbers 2, 3, 4, 24 and 25 in Table 3) and the oxygen-18 distribution within the flyway, we can see that the values coincide well in the Ganges-Brahmaputra Delta region (indicated in

**Table 3. Feather samples from eight Spoon-billed Sandpipers** *Eurynorhynchus pygmeus* **and a Red-necked Stint** *Calidris ruficollis* **obtained during the 2003 expedition to Meinypil'gyno, South Chukotka. All isotope values are expressed in terms of ‰ vs V-SMOW (‰). Adjusted ? values estimate the original precipitation during feather growth.**

| Sample No. | Nest No. | Date | Sex | Ring No. | Ref | $^2H$ | Adjusted $^2H$ | $^{18}O$ | Adjusted $^{18}O$ |
|------------|----------|------|-----|----------|-----|-------|----------------|----------|-------------------|
| 1 | No nest | 13/6 | F | FS11811 | I | -112.70 | -82.70 | 12.00 | -8 to -3 |
| 2 | 31 | 18/6 | F? | | C | -77.83 | -47.83 | 16.25 | -3.75 to 1.25 |
| 3 | 3 | 19/6 | F | | C, I | -90.92 | -60.92 | 16.54 | -3.5 to 1.5 |
| 4 | 1 | 19/6 | M | XT127015 | Zh | -56.29 | -26.29 | 16.36 | -3.6 to 1.4 |
| 5 | 3 | 16/6 | M | FS11812 | C, I | -100.99 | -70.99 | 14.94 | -5.1 to 0 |
| 8 | 14 | 20/6 | M | XT27019 | L | -106.54 | -76.54 | 15.22 | -4.8 to 0 |
| 24 | 56 | 03/7 | F ? | | C, V | -95.15 | -65.15 | 16.27 | -3.8 to 1.2 |
| 25 | 57 | 03/7 | F ? | | L | -87.48 | -57.48 | 16.37 | -3.7 to 1.3 |
| 26 | *C. ruficollis* | 03/7 | F | | C | -48.70 | -18.70 | 19.46 | -0.5 to 4.5 |

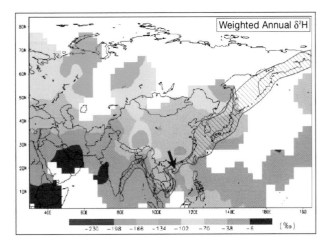

Fig. 3. Distribution of annual mean δ²H, based on IAEA (2001), with overlapping flyway of the Spoon-billed Sandpiper *Eurynorhynchus pygmeus*. The blue arrow points to possible areas of overlapping values and location of the pre-moulting areas

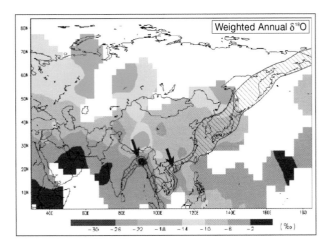

Fig. 4. Distribution of annual mean δ¹⁸O, based on IAEA (2001), with overlapping flyway of the Spoon-billed Sandpiper *Eurynorhynchus pygmeus*. The blue arrows point to possible areas of overlapping values and location of the pre-moulting areas.

red in Fig. 4) and suggest that this is the wintering area of the birds in question. Two birds (numbers 5 and 8 in Table 3) show values in the next lower category (red-brown in Fig. 4) which covers a large area including all the west coast of India, all of Myanmar, Thailand, Malaysia and the area around Hainan in southern China. The value of the first bird sampled (number 1 in Table 3) goes well beyond the values of the others but is still within the range for this second category. Bird 26 in Table 3 shows the only positive value not displayed in the map in Fig. 4. As this sample refers to a different species (Red-necked Stint), the widely differing value of this sample fits quite well with the occurrence of this species in a different flyway.

The values for deuterium vary quite considerably within the nine samples, ranging from −18‰ to below −80‰. Furthermore, the deuterium precipitation map (Fig. 3) does not show as much variation as the δ¹⁸O map (Fig. 4). Only one value coincides with the red-brown range, indicating that the Ganges-Brahmaputra Delta region might be the wintering area of the bird. At the same time, this value could equally refer to the rest of India, Myanmar, Thailand and southern Vietnam. All other

values fall within the next category, which covers an area ranging from central Vietnam north along the Chinese coast as far as North Korea. The only other region of overlap is the area between northern Vietnam and Hainan in southern China, where six of the lower deuterium values in Table 3 overlap with two of the oxygen-18 values (see dark blue arrows in Figs. 3 and 4).

## DISCUSSION
### Stable isotopes
Stable isotopes can be powerful geographical markers. The oxygen-18 values seem to point to the area of the Ganges-Brahmaputra Delta as a wintering area for the Spoon-billed Sandpiper, while overlap in the deuterium and oxygen-18 values of two samples indicates a wintering area in the South China Sea. Both areas are previously known to have held large numbers of Spoon-billed Sandpipers (Collar *et al.* 2001).

However, the results can only been interpreted with caution, as the sample size is very small, the variation within the deuterium values too large, and the scale of the simulated maps very coarse. The results can only be seen as a first approximation, and we hope that funds can be generated to increase the sample size in order to verify these preliminary results.

### Threats during migration
On the basis of our four-year research programme, we can conclude that the Spoon-billed Sandpiper is in serious decline. At the moment, we still do not know what is causing this decline. Compared with all other major flyways, there are particularly serious conditions for waterbirds in the East Asia-Pacific Flyway, with almost all populations declining and many threats recognized (BirdLife International 2003, Syroechkovskiy 2003, Barter 2006, Crosby & Chan 2006). In the Yellow Sea, about 40% of the inter-tidal area has vanished since 1950, and land claim of a further 45% of the remaining area is planned (Barter 2006).

The fact that none of the 30 chicks ringed in 2001 returned to the breeding areas could be interpreted as support for the theory that the main reasons for the decline are to be found on the migration routes or in the wintering areas. However, there are four other possible explanations:

- the birds are still in the wintering areas after two years;
- the returning birds disperse more widely over a larger area and have been overlooked as they spread away from the ringing site;
- the birds did not survive to migrate, which agrees with the very low breeding success observed in Korea (1-2%, Moores 2001); or
- the rings fall off because they were not properly fixed, or the flags harm the birds, increase their vulnerability to predation, or hamper their flight on migration.

In his research on Belyaka Spit in northern Chukotka, Tomkovich (1992, 1994, 1995) found some one- and two-year old birds returning to the vicinity of the ringing site. He noticed that first-time breeders dispersed more widely than older adults, and re-captured two females that had been ringed as chicks 1.5 and 5.5 km from the ringing site, respectively (P.S. Tomkovich *in litt.*). In 2003, we surveyed a 50-60 km stretch of suitable habitat in Meinopil'gyno without finding any ringed birds other than a single breeding bird that had been ringed as an adult and had returned to within a few hundred metres of its ringing site. Although some birds might have been overlooked or moved further away from their natal area, it seems unlikely that all 30 chicks would have been missed, and this again supports the theory that the reasons for the decline are to be found along the flyway or within the breeding area just after hatching.

The possibility that the rings fall off or the flags harm the birds cannot be fully excluded, but most experience with rings and flags in other species of waders has demonstrated that recoveries or re-sightings can be obtained, in some cases, even after 15 years (Tomkovich 2003). There is no research indicating that birds with flags are less well camouflaged or more visible, and thus exposed to a higher risk of predation, than birds without flags. Expeditions to the breeding grounds in 2004 and 2005 should provide further clues, and if young birds are again under-represented among the returning birds, the flagging methods will need to be reviewed.

However, there are some indications that the possible reasons for the decline are to be found in the breeding areas. The most likely is increased predation as a result of changes in the abundance of predators. Climate change and socio-economic changes that have occurred since "perestroika" have led to an increase in the numbers of Arctic Foxes *Alopex lagopus*, and this might have altered the fine balance between lemmings, voles and their predators. No direct research has been carried out yet, and so there is a clear need for further research activities.

It is quite possible that the threats to the Spoon-billed Sandpiper also affect other species within the same flyway. The continuing decline in the population of Dunlin *Calidris alpina* wintering in Japan (M. Kashiwagi *in litt.*) may be relevant here. However, little information is available for other wader populations migrating along the same flyway through south-east Asia. If the widespread declines are a result of the same threats, many wader populations and other migrating species might benefit from conservation efforts for the globally threatened Spoon-billed Sandpiper.

### Future research

We conclude that there is a need for further field expeditions to the breeding areas to monitor the breeding situation and breeding success. However, there is also a need for expeditions to the suspected wintering areas, to investigate wintering numbers, feeding habits and potential threats.

Much more effort needs to be given to internationally co-ordinated research and conservation activities if the species is to be safeguarded from extinction. High priority should therefore be given to the development of a co-ordinated action plan for the species.

### ACKNOWLEDGEMENTS

We are grateful to Steve Brookes and Ian Begley from Iso-Analytical Ltd., Richard Bevan from the University of Newcastle, Phil Atkinson from the British Trust for Ornithology and others for their help and support, and Steve Brookes for comments on the first draft. We would also like to thank Ivan Taldenkov and Vladimir Morozov for providing us with additional feather samples and supporting our surveys, as did Axel Bräunlich, Minoru Kashiwagi, Heikki Karhu, Chris Kelly, James McCallum, Mikhaela Pavlicek, Remo Probst, Chris Schenk, Pavel Tomkovich, Manfred Trobitz and Liu Weiting. We would also like to thank our driver Roman, who brought us to so many remote places, and also many of the other local people who supported our efforts in search of Spoon-billed Sandpipers. The study was supported by the German Ornithological Society (DO-G), the Keidanren Nature Conservation Fund and the Toyota Foundation.

### REFERENCES

**Atkinson, P.W., Baker, A.J., Gonzalez, P.M., Clark, N.A., Robinson, R.A., Peck, M., Cole, K.M. & Bevan, R.M**. In prep. Unravelling the migratory strategies of a long-distance migrant using stable isotopes: Red Knot *Calidris canutus* movements in the Americas.

**Barter, M.A.** 2006. The Yellow Sea – a vitally important staging region for migratory shorebirds. Waterbirds around the world. G.C. Boere, C.A. Galbraith & D.A. Stroud (Eds.), The Stationery Office, Edinburgh, UK. 663-667.

**BirdLife International** 2003. Saving Asia's Threatened Birds: a guide for government and civil society. BirdLife International, Cambridge, UK.

**BirdLife International** 2004. Threatened Birds of the World. Lynx Edicions, Barcelona, & BirdLife International, Cambridge.

**Collar, N., Chen, H. & Crosby, M.** 2001. Threatened Birds of Asia: the BirdLife International Red Data Book. BirdLife International, Cambridge, UK.

**Crosby, M.J. & Chan, S.** 2006. Threatened waterbird species in eastern and southern Asia and actions needed for their conservation. Waterbirds around the world. G.C. Boere, C.A. Galbraith & D.A. Stroud (Eds.), The Stationery Office, Edinburgh, UK. 332-338.

**Flint, V.E. & Kondratiev, A.Ya.** 1977. An experience of evaluating the total number of rare stenotopic species (Spoon-billed Sandpiper *Eurynorhynchus pygmeus* as an example). 7. All-Union Ornithological Conference, Abstracts 2: 250. Naukova Dumka, Kiev. (In Russian).

**Hobson, K.A. & Wassenaar, L.I.** 1997. Linking breeding and wintering grounds of neotropical migrant songbirds using stable hydrogen isotopic analyses of feathers. Oecologica 109: 142-148

**Howes, J. & Parish, D.** 1989. New information on Asian Shorebirds: A preliminary review of the INTERWADER Programme 1983-1989 and priorities for the future. Asian Wetland Bureau Publication 42, Kuala Lumpur.

**IAEA** 2001. GNIP Maps and Animations. International Atomic Energy Agency, Vienna. Accessible at http://isohis. iaea.org.

**Lethaby, N., Moores, N. & Park, Jin-Young.** 2000. Birding in South Korea. Dutch Birding 22: 204-219.

**Lott, C.A., Meehan, T.D. & Heath, J.A.** 2003. Estimating the latitudinal origins of migratory birds using hydrogen and sulphur stable isotopes in feathers: influence of marine prey base. Oecologica 134: 505-510.

**Marra, P.P., Hobson, K.A. & Holmes, R.T.** 1998. Linking winter and summer events in a migratory bird by using stable-carbon isotopes. Science 282: 1884-1886.

**Moores, N. 2001.** Saemankeum: Internationally Significant Wetlands to be 100% Reclaimed. WBK web-site: www.wbkenglish.com.

**Prater, A.J., Marchant, J.H. & Vourinen, J.** 1977. Guide to the Identification and Ageing of Holarctic Waders. BTO Guide 17. British Trust for Ornithology, Thetford, UK.

Syroechkovskiy, E.E. 2003. A review of population decline of waterfowl in East Asia. Proceedings of the International Anatidae Symposium in East Asia & Siberia Region, Seosan, Korea: 48-50.

Syroechkovskiy, E.E., Lappo, E.G., Zöckler, C., Morozov, V.V., Kashiwagi, M. & Taldenkov, I. In prep. The Importance of the Mainopylgyno area, Chukotka, Russia for the breeding of Spoon-billed Sandpiper (*Eurynorhynchus pygmeus*).

Tomkovich, P.S. 1992. Three-year study of breeding Spoon-billed Sandpiper. Asian Wetland News 4(2): 17.

Tomkovich, P.S. 1994. Spatial structure of the Spoon-billed Sandpiper (*Eurynorhynchus pygmeus*) population at the breeding grounds. In: E.N. Kurochkin (ed) Modern Ornithology 1992. Nauka, Moscow: 130-148. (In Russian).

Tomkovich, P.S. 1995. Breeding biology and breeding success of the Spoon-billed Sandpiper *Eurynorhynchus pygmeus*. Russian Journal of Ornithology 4(3/4): 77-91. (In Russian).

Tomkovich, P.S. 2003. Maximum longevity of some waders in Chukotka. In: P.S. Tomkovich & A.O. Shubin (eds) Information materials of the working group on waders, No. 16. Moscow: 55-56. (In Russian with English summary).

Tomkovich, P.S. & Soloviev, M.Y. 2000. Numbers of the Spoon-billed Sandpiper at the north of Kolyuchinskaya Gulf, Chukotka, and count methods for the species on the breeding grounds. Russian Journal of Ornithology, Express Issue 99: 3-10. (In Russian).

Tomkovich, P.S., Syroechkovskiy, E.E., Jr., Lappo, E.G. & Zöckler, C. 2002. Sharp population decline in spoon-billed sandpiper, *Eurynorhynchus pygmeus*, a globally threatened species. Bird Conservation International 12: 1-18.

Wassenaar, L.I. & Hobson, K.A. 2002. Comparative equilibration and online technique for determination of non-exchangeable hydrogen of keratins for use in animal migration studies. Isotopes in Environmental Health Studies 39: 1-7.

Watkins, D. & co-workers. 2004. In prep. Migratory Shorebirds of the East Asian-Australasian Flyway: population estimates and important sites.

Webster, M.S., Marra, P.P., Haig, S.M., Bensch, S. & Holmes R.T. 2002. Links between worlds: unravelling migratory connectivity. Trends in Ecology & Evolution 17: 76-83.

Zöckler, C. 2003. Neues vom Löffelstrandläufer *Eurynorhynchus pygmeus* und seinem alarmierenden Bestandsrückgang. Limicola 17: 188-203.

Breeding habitat of the Spoon-billed Sandpiper *Eurynorhynchus pygmeus* in Chukotka, eastern Russia. Photo: Christoph Zöckler.

# Declines in breeding waterbirds following a redistribution of Arctic Terns *Sterna paradisaea* in West Greenland

*Carsten Egevang[1], Kaj Kampp[1] & David Boertmann[2]*

[1] *Greenland Institute of Natural Resources, PO Box 570, DK-3900 Nuuk, Greenland. (email: egevang@natur.gl)*

[2] *National Environmental Research Institute, Dept. of Arctic Environment, Frederiksborgvej 39, PO Box 358, DK-4000 Roskilde, Denmark.*

Egevang, C., Kampp, K. & Boertmann, D. 2006. Declines in breeding waterbirds following a redistribution of Arctic Terns *Sterna paradisaea* in West Greenland. *Waterbirds around the world.* Eds. G.C. Boere, C.A. Galbraith & D.A. Stroud. The Stationery Office, Edinburgh, UK. p. 154.

The archipelago of Grønne Ejland, consisting of many skerries and four major islands, hosts the largest colony of Arctic Terns *Sterna paradisaea* in Greenland, but the population has undergone some radical changes over the last decades with the decrease in breeding numbers. Arctic Terns inhabited all four major islands twenty years ago but today they are only found on two. The disappearance of the terns from the most easterly island was probably a consequence of Arctic Foxes being present. However, egg harvesting by humans appears to be the main reason why the total tern population has declined. Their disappearance from two islands was followed by a general impoverishment of the islands' birdlife, and the Red Phalarope *Phalaropus fulicarius* disappeared completely after a few years, although numbers remained largely unchanged on the islands still inhabited by terns.

The Red-necked Phalarope *P. lobatus*, on the other hand, still breeds on the islands abandoned by the terns, although some reduction in numbers of pairs has occurred. The response of the Red Phalaropes, and their general co-occurrence with Arctic Terns in West Greenland, suggests that the presence of terns is a necessary condition for Red Phalaropes to breed in this marginal breeding area.

Colonial terns defend their nests and chicks fiercely against avian and mammalian predators, and other birds may benefit from this behaviour by breeding in association with the colonies. Arctic Tern colonies can attract a number of bird species, resulting in both higher species diversity, as well as in higher breeding densities, compared with areas without terns. The Red Phalarope is known to associate with Arctic Tern colonies, but several other species, like ducks and shorebirds, will also occasionally do so. The Red Phalarope is a scarce breeder in West Greenland and all confirmed breeding sites here have been associated with colonies of Arctic Tern.

Six years of data on breeding birds on the four major islands of Grønne Ejland (numbered 1, most westerly, to 4, most easterly, in Tables 1 and 2) from 1980 to 2003 provides estimates of breeding Arctic Tern numbers for 1996, 2002 and 2003 based on line transect analysis, and a rough estimate for 1980 based on extrapolation of breeding densities.

Red Phalaropes were recorded at potential breeding sites; both breeders and migrants feed at the ponds of Grønne Ejland, but breeders were identified by their attachment to a certain area, by their alarm calls, or by direct observation of broods. Breeding Red-necked Phalaropes and other waterbirds were recorded from inspection of the many small ponds of the islands.

Arctic Terns have now abandoned the two easternmost islands (islands 3 & 4, Table 1). For Island 4 this seems to have

**Table 1. Distribution and numbers (breeding pairs) of Arctic Terns *Sterna paradisaea* on the four islands of Grønne Ejland (+ = present, ? = no information).**

| Island | 1980 | 1990 | 1996 | 2002 | 2003 |
|---|---|---|---|---|---|
| 1 | + | ? | 900 | 3300 | 900 |
| 2 | + | ? | 2.800 | 12.300 | 19.300 |
| 3 | + | + | 1100 | 0 | 0 |
| 4 | 10.000 | 0 | 0 | 0 | 0 |
| Total | c. 25.000 | - | 4.800* | 15.600 | 20.200 |

\* The actual number is probably higher but was difficult to estimate due to heavy egg harvesting

**Table 2. Distribution and numbers (pairs) of Red Phalaropes *Phalaropus fulicarius* on Grønne Ejland (? = unknown status).**

| Island | 1979 | 1980 | 1990 | 1996 | 2002 | 2003 |
|---|---|---|---|---|---|---|
| 1 | ? | ? | ? | 0 | 1 | 1 |
| 2 | ca. 10 | ? | ? | 12 | 8 | 7-8 |
| 3 | 2-3 | 0 | ? | 1 | 0 | 0 |
| 4 | 10-20 | 10-11 | 1-2 | 2 | 0 | 0 |

happened between 1982 and 1989. The neighbouring Island 3 was not abandoned until after 1996.

Numbers and distribution of Red Phalaropes on Grønne Ejland have also changed over the last few decades (Table 2), and the species has disappeared from its former stronghold of Island 4. It has also abandoned Island 3, where it was never very numerous. However, on Island 2 the population has been stable or, at most, experienced a moderate decrease. Even the Red-necked Phalarope appears to have decreased on Island 3 and 4, although the earlier counts of this species are less accurate than for Red Phalaropes.

Mallard *Anas platyrhynchos* and Red-breasted Merganser *Mergus serrator*, bred on all the islands, but Long-tailed Duck *Clangula hyemalis* only bred on one island in the central parts of the tern colony.

Our data show that the disappearance of the Arctic Tern from the easternmost islands (Islands 4 and 3) was followed by a gradual but relatively swift disappearance of the Red Phalarope, and supports the view that the Red Phalarope in West Greenland is strongly dependant on breeding Arctic Terns at their breeding site.

# Long-term study of Bewick's Swans *Cygnus columbianus bewickii* nesting in the Nenetskiy State Nature Reserve, Russia: preliminary results and perspectives

*Eileen C. Rees[1] & Anna V. Belousova[2]*

[1]*The Wildfowl & Wetlands Trust, Martin Mere, Burscough, Ormskirk, Lancashire, L40 OTA, UK. (email: Eileen.Rees@wwt.org.uk)*

[2]*All-Russian Research Institute for Nature Protection (ARRINP), Znamenskoye-Sadki, Moscow 117628, Russia. (email: anbelous@online.ru)*

Rees, E.C. & Belousova, A.V. 2006. Long-term study of Bewick's Swans *Cygnus columbianus bewickii* nesting in the Nenetskiy State Nature Reserve, Russia: preliminary results and perspectives. *Waterbirds around the world*. Eds. G.C. Boere, C.A. Galbraith & D.A. Stroud. The Stationery Office, Edinburgh, UK. pp. 155-156.

## INTRODUCTION AND METHODS

A long-term collaborative study of Bewick's Swans *Cygnus columbianus bewickii* breeding on the Russki Zavorot peninsula in the Nenetskiy State Nature Reserve was undertaken by WWT (UK) and ARRINP (Russia) over an eleven year period, from 1991-2000 inclusive and in 2003. Observations were made within a 25 km² study area at Khabuicka, on the east coast of the Russki Zavorot peninsula (68°32'N 53°54'N). The main aim was to determine the extent to which environmental factors (weather, habitat on the breeding territories and predator levels), and also factors relating to individual birds (breeding experience and duration of the pair bond), explain annual variation in breeding attempts, breeding success, and thus recruitment to the population as a whole. Individual swans were identified by the variation in their black-and-yellow bill markings, and by reading the codes on their leg-rings and neck-collars. Nesting density, occupancy of territories and the turnover of pairs on each territory were recorded each year. The breeding success of each pair was measured by recording clutch size, the number of cygnets hatched and the survival of those cygnets through the first 10 days of life. The behaviour of nesting pairs, and of parents with young in the first few days after hatching, was also observed.

## RESULTS

Observations showed that Bewick's Swan *Cygnus columbianus bewickii* pairs occupy the same breeding territories over several summers (Shchadilov *et al.* 1998). Of 184 pairs where both male and female were identified between 1991 and 1995, two (1.1%) were pairs where both members remained together in all five years, eight (4.3%) were birds paired for a minimum of four years, 22 (12.0%) were together for at least three years and 39 (21.2%) for two years. The remaining 113 pairs were seen on territories that they had not occupied in a previous season, and were thought to be newly-formed pairs. Pairs generally returned to the same territory used in the previous year, unless ousted by an incoming pair.

The onset of laying dates ranged from May 23 in 1995 (an early spring) to June 6 in 1994 and 1997 (late springs). Weather conditions influence the timing of arrival on the breeding territories, breeding density and clutch size. The major influence of the timing of the spring thaw on the swans' breeding programme, by reducing the number of breeding pairs and clutch size in late years, agrees with observations of Bewick's Swans on Vaygach Island, which additionally found that cold weather during incubation following an early spring had a detri-

mental effect on hatching success (Syroechkovskiy *et al.* 2002). Preliminary analyses of the Khabuicka data suggest that the effect of previous breeding experience upon brood size at the end of July (by which time the cygnets are about 3-4 weeks old) is more important in some years than in others. This supports observations made in the wintering range, which also found that the number of years that a pair had been together had a greater influence on breeding success (i.e. the number of cygnets associating in winter) in some years than in others (Rees *et al.* 1996).

## CONSEQUENCES AND FUTURE PERSPECTIVES

The long-term Bewick's Swan research programme, together with other ecological studies undertaken in the region in recent years (e.g. van Eerden 2000) have had the positive effect of raising the awareness of local people to the importance of the wildlife in their area. Most of the Russki Zavorot peninsula and the adjacent Korovinkaiya Gulf was designated as a State Nature Reserve (the Nenetskiy zapovednik) by the Russian Government in December 1997 (Kotkin 2000). Scientific staff of the zapovednik are now monitoring biodiversity at the site, and also promote local interest in waterbird conservation through the media and by facilitating education programmes.

Future collaborative programmes planned within Russia include:

- continuing the monitoring programme within the *zapovednik*, with the benefit of modern technology (e.g. GIS) and analyses;
- involving local amateurs in waterbird monitoring, especially during migration;
- raising the awareness of administrators of joint ventures and local enterprises (mainly gas-oil exploitation), to ensure that waterbird conservation and impact assessment is a priority in their business development strategies; and
- the establishment of a network for monitoring waterbird migration (especially Bewick's Swans) along the European flyway.

Further monitoring data will make it possible to develop an inventory of key sites and habitats used by the swans within Russia, and provide guidelines for establishing a network of protected sites. It will also provide a sound scientific foundation for the development of the Russian Bewick's Swan Action Plan, and make a major contribution to a Flyway Management Plan for the species.

## REFERENCES

**Kotkin, N.A.** 2000. Development of network of protected areas in the Nenets Autonomous Okrug. In: B.S. Ebbinge *et al.* (eds). Heritage of the Russian Arctic: Research, Conservation and International Cooperation: 595-599. Ecopros Publishers, Moscow.

**Rees, E.C., Lievesley, P., Pettifor, R. & Perrins, C.** 1996. Mate fidelity in swans: an inter-specific comparison. In: J.M. Black (ed.) Partnerships in birds: the study of monogamy. Oxford University Press, Oxford.

**Shchadilov, Y.M., Belousova, A.V., Rees, E.C. & Bowler, J.M.** 1998. Long-term study of the nesting success in the Bewick's Swans in the coastal tundra in the Nenetskiy Autonomous Okrug. Casarca 4: 217-228.

**Syroechkovsky, E.V., Litvin, K.E. & Gurtovaya, E.N.** 2002. Nesting ecology of Bewick's Swans on Vaygach Island, Russia. In: E.C. Rees, S.L. Earnst & J. Coulson (eds). Proceedings of the Fourth International Swan Symposium, 2001: 221-226. Waterbirds 25, Special Publication 1.

**van Eerden, M.R. (ed.).** 2000. Pechora Delta. Structure and dynamics of the Pechora Delta ecosystems (1995-1999). RIZA report number 2000.037. RIZA Institute for Inland Water Management, Lelystad, The Netherlands.

Dave Paynter (WWT) weighing Bewick's Swans *Cygnus columbianus bewickii* caught on the Korovinskaiya Gulf, Nenetskiy State Nature Reserve (zapovednik), in 2003. The swans are temporarily wrapped in specially designed swan jackets, to protect their plumage whilst being ringed, weighed and measured. Photo: Eileen Rees.

Khabuicka study site in the Nenetskiy State Nature Reserve (zapovednik), with huts and River Khabuicka in the foreground and Lake Khabuicka in the distance, Russia. Photo: Eileen Rees.

## 3.2   Waterbirds in the Neotropics. Workshop Introduction

*Melanie Steinkamp[1] & Roberto Schlatter[2]*
*[1]Atlantic Coast Joint Venture, 11510 American Holly Drive, Room 206C, Laurel, Maryland 20708, USA.*
*[2]Instituto de Zoologia, Universidad Austral de Chile, Casilla 567, Valdivia, Chile. (email: rschlatt@uach.cl)*

Steinkamp, M. & Schlatter, R. 2006. Waterbirds in the Neotropics. Workshop Introduction. *Waterbirds around the world.* Eds. G.C. Boere, C.A. Galbraith & D.A. Stroud. The Stationery Office, Edinburgh, UK. p. 157.

In some regions of the world there is a long history of survey and monitoring of waterbirds, leading to a well-developed understanding of distribution of waterbirds, their status and trends, and the locations of important sites. Throughout the Neotropics however, knowledge of waterbirds, their habitats and ecology, is much more limited, as a consequence of much less data and information.

Many of the papers presented in this workshop describe essential surveys that describe the distribution and numbers of waterbirds so that appropriate conservation measures can be developed. These include surveys in Costa Rica (Quesada), Panama (Sánchez *et al.*), Colombia (Naranjo *et al.*), Brazil (Kober), and Chile (Aparicio).

Generally, a major issue in the Neotropics is a major lack of funding for basic surveys and population monitoring. However, opportunities for funding surveys and conservation can vary between taxa. Whilst significant attention has been focussed on the needs of long-distance, intercontinental migrants, there has been much less research and conservation activity on waterbirds that migrate solely *within* South America. Many of these intra-continental migrant species, and non-migratory waterbirds have poor conservation status and largely unknown populations trends. This is especially the case for Neotropical migrant and resident waterbirds (especially waders) since international sources of funding are not readily available for monitoring, research and conservation.

The progressive development of the Western Hemisphere Shorebird Reserve Network has been an important initiative to raise awareness of the importance of key sites. The role of such areas, their identification and conservation is described from Mexico by Vega *et al.*, for Colombia by Naranjo *et al.*, with the recent development of a more strategic national approach for waterbird conservation in Argentina outlined by Goldfeder & Blanco. The recently established Hemispheric Steering Group for migratory waterbirds, established following the Western Hemisphere Migratory Bird Conference in Chile in 2004, has considerable potential to drive forward conservation activities.

The Symposium presented an overview of existing actions for waterbird flyways in central and South America, and discussed progress to date. A general point which was stressed was an urgent need to update IUCN Red-listings for South America to better reflect the current situation.

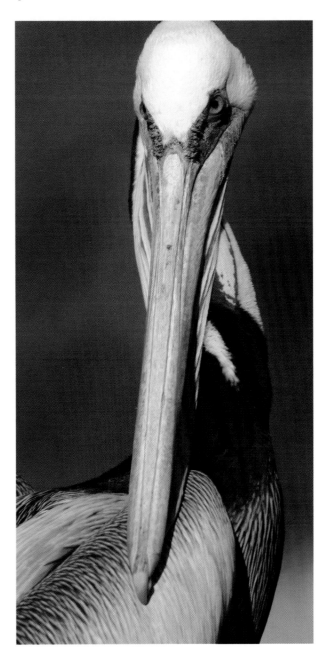

The population of Peruvian Pelican *Pelcanus thagus* is currently increasing and expanding its range. Photo: Chris Wilson.

# Potential new Ramsar sites in northwest Mexico: strategic importance for migratory waterbirds and threats to conservation

*X. Vega[1], M.A. González[2], A. Muñoz del Viejo[3]*

*[1]ITESM-Sinaloa, Boulevard Culiacán 3773, Culiacán 80000, Sinaloa México. (email: xicovega@itesm.mx)*

*[2]Escuela de Biología. Universidad Autónoma de Sinaloa, Ciudad Universitaria, Culiacán, 80000, Sinaloa, G.I.C. México.3.*

*[3]Área de zoología, Facultad de ciencias, Universidad de Extramadura, Auda. de Elvas s/n 06071 Badajoz, Spain. (email: amunoz@unex.es)*

Vega, X., González, M.A. & Muñoz del Viejo, A. 2006. Potential new Ramsar sites in northwest Mexico: strategic importance for migratory waterbirds and threats to conservation. *Waterbirds around the world.* Eds. G.C. Boere, C.A. Galbraith & D.A. Stroud. The Stationery Office, Edinburgh, UK. pp. 158-160.

Northwest Mexico supports a critical series of coastal wetlands that sustain vast numbers of resident and migratory waterbirds using the Pacific Flyway in their annual migrations. These key habitats therefore qualify for possibe designation as Ramsar sites. However, there is a need to further investigate and document these areas in order to protect them. This note presents the locations of potential new Ramsar sites in Northwest Mexico, the species and numbers of birds and the potential threats for their conservation.

Mexico has a coastal shoreline of more than 11 122 km which includes numerous habitats critical for various types of flora and fauna (Riviera-Arriaga & Villalobos, 2001). Northwest Mexico is formed by four States: Baja California Sur, Baja California, Sonora and Sinaloa. It has a shoreline of approximately 5 140 km representing more than 46% of the total coastline of Mexico. Its existence and location along the Pacific Flyway make this region one of the most important and critical areas in the Americas for migratory and neotropical birds (Engilis *et al.* 1998). The coast supports a rich diversity of habitats and high numbers of water-birds that use the area as a stop over, resting or wintering site during migrations. Additionally, there are non-literal shorelines of lagoons and wetlands that are important parts of these biological corridors but are currently under represented because of a lack of systematic studies and evaluation or documentation to warrant their Ramsar nomination (Pérez-Arteaga & Gaston 2004).

According to CONABIO (1997) there are 32 priority wetlands in Mexico, eleven located in Northwest Mexico (Engilis *et al.* 1998). However, Pérez-Artega *et al.* (2002) indi-cated that there are 34 wetlands in Mexico that qualify under Ramsar site-selection Criteria 5 and 6. These wetlands are: Ensenada de Pabellones; Bahía de Santa María; Bahía de Topolobampo; Bahía de Agiabampo; Bahía Santa Barbara; Isla Tobarí; Estero de Lobos; Laguna San Quintín; Laguna Ojo de Liebre and Bahía de San Ignacio. Recently the Mexican Government designated 34 new Ramsar sites, three of which are in the Pacific Northwest Region. There are additional wetlands that may qualify as Ramsar sites, but either there is not yet suffi-cient scientific information or the Federal Government is not aware of their potential importance (Table 1 over).

The Northwest Pacific Coast represents key habitats for several resident and migratory waterbirds, but economic develop-ment with pressure to develop new urban centers is a serious threat. Some of the pressures leading to a loss in bio-productivity follow.

## Aquaculture industry (shrimp farms)

The national production of farmed shrimp reached 16 000 tons in 2000. Of that production, 95% was from the states of Sinaloa and Sonora (Investigación y Desarrollo 1999). The approximate total surface area for shrimp farming was 35 000 ha. Unfortunately most shrimp farms are under-regulated environ-mentally and several have been constructed in fragile ecological ecosystems such as mangroves, intertidal areas, and marsh areas. Effluent contaminated with organic matter and chemical runoff has been pouring directly into adjacent bays as well as altering the natural drainage.

## Agriculture and livestock

Several areas near to the coast have been opened up for agricul-tural or cattle ranching, developments utilizing large applica-tions of agrochemicals with runoff draining directly into adjacent bays. Livestock have been known to cause nesting failure in waterbird colonies (Muñoz & Vega 2002).

## Tourism

Recreational and vocational activities along coasts are major factors of nesting failure and disturbance among waterbirds. Boats, ATVs and pets use these areas without any regulation. A mega-project is proposed by an agency of the Federal Government (Escalera Naútica) for the Northwest region, and several yacht marinas are planned in some of the most important waterbird areas.

## Fishing

The constant influx of new inhabitants into the coastal areas and the development of more "cooperativas" (associations of fish-ermen) have been the principal cause of overexploitation of the bays and coastal areas.

## OTHER ISSUES

In Northwest Mexico, resident and migratory birds are also affected by egg consumption by local people, killing of chicks for bait for crab fishing, building developments and feral animals around breeding colonies and colony disturbance by tourists and fishermen.

## CONCLUSIONS

Although the Federal Government recently designated 34 new Ramsar sites in Mexico, there are other potential sites important for resident and migratory waterbird species. There is a need to establish permanent and systematic monitoring programs in these areas to include wintering and reproductive studies and conservation programs.

Unfortunately, there is a lack of technical and economic resources to undertake such activities. Mexico has partial finan-cial support from the North American Wetland Conservation Act

## Table 1. Sites qualifying as potential Ramsar sites in northwest Mexico.

| Map number | Site | Species | Population | Source |
|---|---|---|---|---|
| 1 | Delta del Río Colorado | Shorebirds | 100 000 | Harrington 1994 |
| 2 | Laguna Ojo de Liebre | *Phalaropus lobatus* | 60 000 | Carmona pers. comm. |
| | | *Podiceps nigricolis* | 60 000 | Carmona pers. comm. |
| | | *Calidris mauri* | 70 000 | Garcia pers. comm. |
| | | *Limosa fedoa* | 120 000 | Vega (own data) |
| | | *Branta bernicla* | 25 000 | Garcia pers. comm. |
| 3 | Laguna San Ignacio | Whale reproduction | | |
| 4 | Parque Nacional Loreto | High biodiversity and endemism | | |
| 5 | Bahía de Santa María | *Calidris mauri* | 550 000 | Vega (own data) |
| | | *Fregata magnificens* | 35 000 | |
| | | *Limnodromus* sp. | 24 000 | |
| | | *Phalaropus tricolor* | 60 000 | |
| | | *Phalacrocorax penicillatus* | 85 000 | |
| 6 | Verde Camacho | Sea turtle nesting site | | |
| 7 | Bahía de San Quintín | Branta bernicla | 60 000 | Garcia pers. comm. |
| 8 | Estero Lobos | Shorebirds | 31 000 | Harrington 1994 |
| 9 | Isla Tobarí | Shorebirds | 55 000 | Harrington 1994 |
| 10 | Bahía de Santa Barbara | Shorebirds | 60 000 | Harrington 1994 |
| 11 | Bahía de Topolombapo | Shorebirds | 47 000 | Harrington 1994 |
| 12 | Ensenada de Pabellones | *Calidris mauri* | 350 000 | Guevara pers. comm. |
| | | *Calidris minutilla* | 150 000 | |
| | | *Recurvirostra americana* | 42 500 | |
| | | *Limnodromus* sp. | 37 000 | |
| 13 | Bahía de Caimanero | Shorebirds | 110 000 | Vega (own data) |
| | | *Recurvirostra americana* | 25 000 | |
| | | *Calidris mauri* | 35 000 | |
| 14 | Bahía de La Paz | *Calidris mauri* | 25 000 | Carmona pers. comm. |
| 15 | Bahía de Magdalena | *Pelecanus occidentalis* | 46 700 | Palacios unpubl. data |
| | | *Fregata magnificens* | 33 500 | |
| | | *Limosa fedoa* | 21 146 | |
| | | *Larus occidentalis* | 9 467 | |
| | | *Larus delawerensis* | 4 950 | |
| 16 | Puerto Peñascos | Shorebirds | 30 000 | Harrington 1994 |
| 17 | Bahía de Kino | Shorebirds | 22 000 | Harrington 1994 |
| 18 | Bahía de Guaymas | Shorebirds | 24 000 | Harrington 1994 |
| 19 | Agiabampo | *Branta bernicla* | 50 944 | Pérez-Arteaga *et al.* 2002 |
| 20 | Isla del Farallon | *Sula nebouxii* | 14 000 | González pers. comm. |
| | | *Sula leucogaster* | 10 000 | |
| | | *Larus hermanii* | 6 000 | |
| 21 | Bahía de Navachiste | *Fregata magnificens* | 25 000 | Gonzáles pers. comm. |
| | | *Sterna maxima* | 10 000 | |
| | | *Branta bernicla* | 5 000 | |
| 22 | Bahía Guadalupana | Shorebirds | 55 000 | Harrington 1994 |
| 23 | Bahía de Ceuta | *Calidris mauri* | 20 000 | Vega (own data) |
| | | *Phalaropus tricolor* | 15 000 | |
| | | *Recurvirostra americana* | 15 000 | |
| | | *Charadrius alexandrinus* | 650 | |
| | | *Sterna maxima* | 2 500 | |

(NAWCA) by the Government of the United States of America for non-governmental organizations and institutions to work on wetland conservation projects. However, the funds are inadequate to support much needed additional scientific research.

The potential Ramsar sites included in this presentation represent the efforts of ornithologists monitoring a diverse array of conservation activities in the Pacific Northwest but whose information has unfortunately not been published or used by the Mexican Government for conservation purposes. There is need to plan, conserve and manage the coastal areas that can help to protect important and crucial waterbird areas; otherwise, the coastal wetlands and waterbirds are going to be further imperiled.

## REFERENCES

**CONABIO** 1997. Provincias biogeográficas de Mexico. Escala 1:4,000,000. CONABIO, Mexico City.

**Engilis, A., Oring, L. W., Carrera, E., Nelson, J.W. & López, A.M**. 1998. Shorebird surveys in Ensenada Pabellones and Bahia Santa María, Sinaloa, Mexico: critical winter habitats for Pacific Flyway shorebirds. Wilson Bulletin 110: 332-341.

**Harrington, B**. 1994. A coastal, shorebird survey in Sonora, Sinaloa and Nayarit Mexico, January 1994. Report for Manomet Bird Observatory. Manomet, Massachusetts.

**Investigación y Desarrollo** 1999. El impacto ecológico de las granjas de camarón. (http://www.invdes.com.mx/anteriores/Abril1999/htm/camaron71.html)

**Pérez-Arteaga, A. & Gaston, K.J.** 2004. Wildfowl population trends in Mexico, 1961-2000: a basis for conservation planning. Biological Conservation 115: 343-355.

**Pérez-Arteaga, A., Gaston, K.J. & Kershaw, M.** 2002. Undesignated sites in Mexico as wetlands of international importance. Biological Conservation 107: 47-57.

**Rivera-Arriaga, E. & Villalobos, G.** 2001. The coast of Mexico: approaches for its management. Ocean and Coastal Management 44: 729-759.

Internationally important numbers of Marbled Godwit *Limosa fedoa* occur at the Bahía de Magdalena, Mexico. Photo: Rob Robinson.

# The importance of Costa Rica for resident and migratory waterbirds

*Ghisselle M. Alvarado Quesada*

*National Museum of Costa Rica, Natural History Department, PO Box 749-1000, San José, Costa Rica. (email: museohn@racsa.co.cr)*

Alvarado Quesada, G.M. 2006. The importance of Costa Rica for resident and migratory waterbirds. *Waterbirds around the world.* Eds. G.C. Boere, C.A. Galbraith & D.A. Stroud. The Stationery Office, Edinburgh, UK. pp. 161-165.

This paper presents a compilation of the available information on Costa Rica's waterbirds: their diversity, distribution, important breeding and wintering areas, nationally and regionally threatened species, and threats to wetland habitats. Costa Rica's waterbird fauna is composed of 167 species in 26 families, and represents 19 percent of the country's total avifauna. Fifty-nine percent of waterbird species are purely migratory, 34% are resident, and 7% have both resident and migratory populations. Costa Rica has over 350 wetlands. The most significant of these for waterbirds (as stopover sites, breeding areas and wintering areas) are Tortuguero, Palo Verde, Cocos Island and Caño Negro, all of which are Ramsar sites. In general, waterbirds use wetlands in the lowlands of the Pacific and Atlantic coasts, and on the north slope, although some waterbirds use small wetlands in the interior of the country, such as the small lakes in the Central Valley. Several islands along the Pacific coast host breeding colonies of colonial waterbirds. Six species of waterbirds are at risk of extinction in Costa Rica, and 12 are considered to be of "High Concern" in the North American Waterbird Conservation Plan.

## INTRODUCTION

Costa Rica is located in the heart of Central America and hosts an abundance of waterbirds, both resident species and migrants that use the many wetlands as stopover points and wintering areas. Most waterbirds occur in the lowlands of the Pacific, Atlantic and North slopes, although some species, including the Snowy Egret *Egretta thula* and Fasciated Tiger-Heron *Tigrisoma fasciatum*, can be found at elevations of up to 2 000 m above sea level (Stiles & Skutch 1989).

Costa Rican waterbirds include seabirds, shorebirds and other freshwater species. Most of the seabirds breed far away from Costa Rica, in places such as New Zealand, Antarctica and Siberia. The migratory waterfowl (Anatidae) and other freshwater species breed in North America, while migratory shorebirds breed mainly in Siberia, Alaska, and north and central Canada (Stiles & Skutch 1989).

Costa Rica has over 350 wetlands, situated both in the lowlands and the highlands; ten of these have been designated as Ramsar sites (Wetlands of International Importance). The Ramsar sites of Palo Verde National Park, Caño Negro, Tortuguero and Cocos Island are the most important for waterbirds. Thousands of cormorants, boobies, herons and egrets, storks, ducks, shorebirds, gulls and terns use these sites for wintering or reproduction.

This paper is a compilation of available information on the waterbirds of Costa Rica: their diversity, distribution, and important breeding and wintering areas; their conservation status at national and regional level; and the threats to their wetland habitats.

## METHODS

The results presented here are based on a review of published literature, as well as bird lists produced by regional experts and unpublished field data held at the National Museum of Costa Rica. For well-studied areas such as the National Parks, comprehensive bird lists are available (e.g. Stiles & Lewis 1980). However, for some areas, information sources had to be combined in order to include all or at least most of the waterbirds occurring there. Maps were created with Arc View 8.2.

## RESULTS AND DISCUSSION

### Waterbird biodiversity

Costa Rica's waterbird fauna is composed of 169 species, representing 19% of the country's total avifauna. These species belong to 26 families, with most species belonging to the Scolopacidae (29), Laridae (27), Ardeidae (18), Anatidae (15) and Rallidae (15). Of all waterbird species, 59% are migratory (passage migrants, winter residents and year-round migrants, with no breeding populations), 34% are resident throughout the year, and 7% have both resident and migratory populations (Table 1).

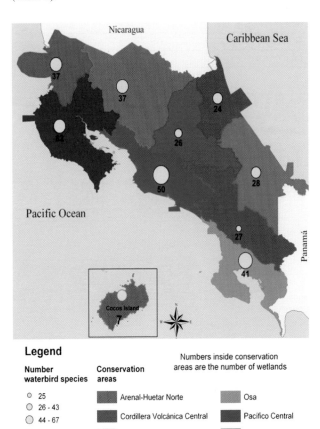

Fig. 1. The distribution of wetlands and waterbirds in Costa Rica by Conservation Area.

**Table 1. The migratory status of waterbirds in Costa Rica, by family.**

| Family | Number of species | Migratory species | Resident species | Resident and migratory |
|---|---|---|---|---|
| Podicipedidae | 2 | 0 | 2 | 0 |
| Procellariidae | 8 | 8 | 0 | 0 |
| Hydrobatidae | 8 | 8 | 0 | 0 |
| Phaethontidae | 1 | 0 | 1 | 0 |
| Sulidae | 4 | 2 | 2 | 0 |
| Pelecanidae | 2 | 1 | 1 | 0 |
| Anhingidae | 1 | 0 | 1 | 0 |
| Fregatidae | 2 | 0 | 2 | 0 |
| Ardeidae | 18 | 3 | 8 | 7 |
| Threskionithidae | 4 | 0 | 4 | 0 |
| Ciconiidae | 2 | 0 | 2 | 0 |
| Anatidae | 15 | 11 | 4 | 0 |
| Charadriidae | 8 | 6 | 0 | 2 |
| Rallidae | 15 | 0 | 13 | 2 |
| Heliornithidae | 1 | 0 | 1 | 0 |
| Eurypygidae | 1 | 0 | 1 | 0 |
| Haematopodidae | 1 | 0 | 0 | 1 |
| Recurvirostridae | 2 | 1 | 1 | 0 |
| Jacanidae | 2 | 0 | 2 | 0 |
| Scolopacidae | 29 | 29 | 0 | 0 |
| Phalaropodidae | 3 | 3 | 0 | 0 |
| Stercorariidae | 4 | 4 | 0 | 0 |
| Laridae | 27 | 23 | 4 | 0 |
| Rhynchopidae | 1 | 1 | 0 | 0 |
| Alcedinidae | 6 | 1 | 5 | 0 |
| **Total** | **167** | **101** | **54** | **12** |

**Table 2. The migratory status of waterbirds in each Conservation Area in Costa Rica.**

| Conservation Area | Number of species | Resident | Migratory | Resident and migratory |
|---|---|---|---|---|
| Cocos Islands | 51 | 6 (12%) | 38 (74%) | 7 (14%) |
| Guanacaste | 72 | 25 (35%) | 35 (49%) | 12 (16%) |
| Arenal and Huetar Norte | 75 | 39 (52%) | 24 (32%) | 12 (16%) |
| Tempisque | 72 | 32 (44%) | 31 (43%) | 9 (13%) |
| Tortuguero | 62 | 24 (39%) | 27 (43%) | 11 (18%) |
| Coordillera Volcánica Central | 43 | 19 (44%) | 17 (40%) | 7 (16%) |
| Central Pacífico | 110 | 37 (34%) | 60 (54%) | 13 (12%) |
| Amistad Caribe | 65 | 25 (39%) | 30 (46%) | 10 (15%) |
| Amistad Pacífico | 25 | 15 (60%) | 6 (24%) | 4 (16%) |
| Osa | 82 | 27 (33%) | 45 (55%) | 10 (12%) |

## Waterbird distribution

Most waterbirds occur in wetlands in the lowlands of the Pacific and Atlantic coasts, and on the north slope. The Pacific coast is more topographically irregular than that of the Atlantic and is characterized by many different habitats, such as beaches, mangrove forests and swamps, which provide excellent foraging areas for waterbirds (Stiles & Skutch 1989). Some herons, ducks, rails, sandpipers and gulls also occur at elevations below 1 800-2 000 m in the Central Valley.

Costa Rica is divided into ten Conservation Areas (including Cocos Island). Fig. 1 shows the numbers of wetlands and waterbird species in Costa Rica by Conservation Area. The Pacifico Central Conservation Area has the greatest species richness, followed by Osa Conservation Area. A higher proportion of waterbirds in the Pacifico Central Conservation Area is migratory than in other parts of the country, with the exception of Cocos Island and Osa (Table 2).

## Ramsar sites important for waterbirds

Costa Rica has 10 Ramsar sites (Wetlands of International Importance). Four of these are extremely important wintering, stopover and breeding areas for waterbirds: Palo Verde National Park, Caño Negro National Park, Tortuguero National Park and Cocos Island (Fig. 2, Table 3). Cocos Island is especially important for seabirds, such as species of Procellariidae and Hydrobatidae, and most of the waterbird fauna here is migratory. These four Ramsar sites are important for waterbirds due to their wetland characteristics (providing opportunities for feeding, breeding and wintering) and because they are located near or along migratory flyways.

## Important breeding sites

Our knowledge of the breeding colonies of waterbirds in Costa Rica is still incomplete. However, some important breeding sites have been identified for species such as the Brown Pelican *Pelecanus occidentalis*, Brown Booby *Sula leucogaster*, Anhinga *Anhinga anhinga*, Magnificent Frigatebird *Fregata magnificens*, Great Egret *Egretta alba*, Cattle Egret *Bubulcus ibis*, Black-crowned Night-Heron *Nycticorax nycticorax*, Boat-billed Heron *Cochlearius cochlearia*, Wood Stork *Mycteria americana*, American White Ibis *Eudocimus albus*, and Bridled Tern *Sterna anaethetus* (Fig. 3). For example, Isla de

Pájaros, located in the lower basin of the Tempisque River, is the most important island for breeding waterbirds in Central America. It is just 2.4 ha in area, and is used as a breeding site by at least eight species of waterbirds: Neotropic (Olivaceous) Cormorant *Phalacrocorax brasilianus*, Anhinga, Great Egret, Cattle Egret, Black-crowned Night-Heron, Boat-billed Heron, Wood Stork, and Roseate Spoonbill *Platalea ajaja*. Cocos Island is used by several breeding seabirds such as Red-footed Booby *Sula sula*, Great Frigatebird *Fregata minor*, Brown

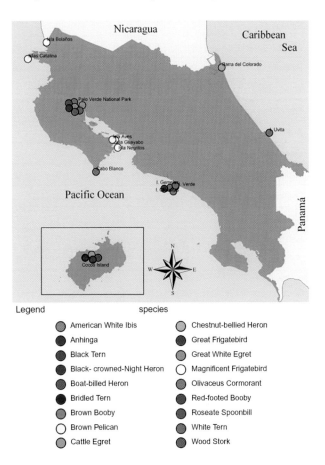

Legend      species

- American White Ibis
- Anhinga
- Black Tern
- Black-crowned-Night Heron
- Boat-billed Heron
- Bridled Tern
- Brown Booby
- Brown Pelican
- Cattle Egret
- Chestnut-bellied Heron
- Great Frigatebird
- Great White Egret
- Magnificent Frigatebird
- Olivaceus Cormorant
- Red-footed Booby
- Roseate Spoonbill
- White Tern
- Wood Stork

Fig. 3. Important sites for breeding colonies of waterbirds in Costa Rica.

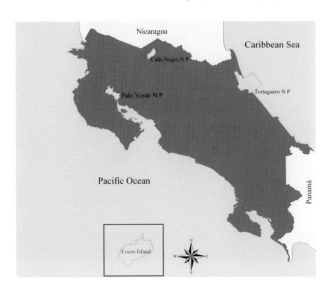

Fig. 2. Ramsar sites important for waterbirds in Costa Rica.

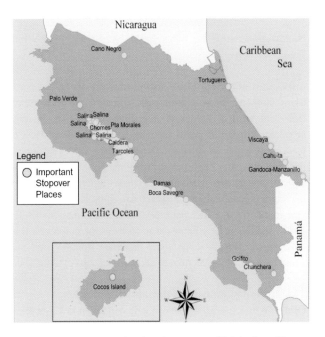

Fig. 4. Important stopover sites for migratory waterbirds in Costa Rica.

**Table 3.** Waterbird biodiversity in the most important Ramsar sites in Costa Rica: Cocos Island, Palo Verde, Tortuguero and Caño Negro.

| Family | Cocos Island | | | Palo Verde | | | Tortuguero | | | Caño Negro | | |
|---|---|---|---|---|---|---|---|---|---|---|---|---|
| | R | M | R-M | R | M | R-M | R | M | R-M | R | M | R-M |
| Podicipedidae | 1 | 0 | 0 | 2 | 0 | 0 | 1 | 0 | 0 | 2 | 0 | 0 |
| Procellariidae | 0 | 3 | 0 | 0 | 0 | 0 | 0 | 0 | 0 | 0 | 0 | 0 |
| Hydrobatidae | 0 | 6 | 0 | 0 | 0 | 0 | 0 | 0 | 0 | 0 | 0 | 0 |
| Sulidae | 2 | 1 | 0 | 0 | 0 | 0 | 2 | 0 | 0 | 0 | 0 | 0 |
| Phalacrocoracidae | 0 | 0 | 0 | 1 | 0 | 0 | 1 | 0 | 0 | 0 | 0 | 0 |
| Pelecanidae | 0 | 0 | 0 | 0 | 0 | 0 | 1 | 0 | 0 | 0 | 1 | 0 |
| Anhingidae | 0 | 0 | 0 | 1 | 0 | 0 | 1 | 0 | 0 | 1 | 0 | 0 |
| Fregatidae | 2 | 0 | 0 | 1 | 0 | 0 | 1 | 0 | 0 | 0 | 0 | 0 |
| Ardeidae | 0 | 1 | 6 | 5 | 1 | 7 | 6 | 1 | 6 | 7 | 1 | 9 |
| Ciconiidae | 0 | 0 | 0 | 2 | 0 | 0 | 0 | 0 | 0 | 2 | 0 | 0 |
| Threskiornithidae | 0 | 0 | 0 | 3 | 0 | 0 | 1 | 0 | 0 | 5 | 0 | 0 |
| Anatidae | 0 | 0 | 0 | 5 | 7 | 0 | 1 | 4 | 0 | 3 | 3 | 0 |
| Aramidae | 0 | 0 | 0 | 1 | 0 | 0 | 0 | 0 | 0 | 0 | 0 | 0 |
| Rallidae | 0 | 0 | 0 | 5 | 1 | 0 | 4 | 0 | 1 | 8 | 1 | 1 |
| Recurvirostridae | 0 | 0 | 0 | 0 | 0 | 1 | 0 | 0 | 1 | 0 | 0 | 1 |
| Jacanidae | 0 | 0 | 0 | 1 | 0 | 0 | 0 | 0 | 0 | 1 | 0 | 0 |
| Heliornithidae | 0 | 0 | 0 | 0 | 0 | 0 | 0 | 0 | 0 | 1 | 0 | 0 |
| Charadriidae | 0 | 3 | 1 | 0 | 1 | 2 | 0 | 2 | 2 | 3 | 1 | 1 |
| Haematopodidae | 0 | 0 | 0 | 0 | 0 | 0 | 0 | 0 | 1 | 0 | 0 | 0 |
| Scolopacidae | 0 | 14 | 0 | 0 | 13 | 0 | 0 | 12 | 0 | 0 | 16 | 0 |
| Stercorariidae | 0 | 2 | 0 | 0 | 0 | 0 | 0 | 0 | 0 | 0 | 0 | 0 |
| Phalaropodidae | 0 | 0 | 0 | 0 | 1 | 0 | 0 | 0 | 0 | 0 | 0 | 0 |
| Laridae | 1 | 7 | 0 | 0 | 5 | 0 | 0 | 7 | 0 | 0 | 0 | 0 |
| Rhynchopidae | 0 | 0 | 0 | 0 | 1 | 0 | 0 | 0 | 0 | 0 | 1 | 0 |
| Alcedinidae | 0 | 1 | 0 | 4 | 1 | 0 | 5 | 1 | 0 | 5 | 1 | 0 |

R = resident; M = migratory; R-M = resident and migratory.

Noddy *Anous stolidus*, Black Noddy *A. minutus* and White Tern *Gygis alba*.

### Important stopover sites and wintering areas
Many thousands of waterbirds pass through Costa Rica during their southward or northward migrations, using river mouths, beaches, swamps, salt ponds and lakes as stopover sites. Most of these move along the Atlantic coast during the southward migration, and along the Pacific coast during the northward migration, with a large number wintering at wetlands in Costa Rica. Many immature herons and egrets, shorebirds, gulls and terns remain year round in Costa Rica until they reach sexual maturity (Stiles 1983), and this is very important in terms of the conservation of these species. Fig. 4 shows some important stopover sites and wintering areas along the Atlantic and Pacific coasts of Costa Rica.

### Threatened species and threats to wetlands
Of the 16 bird species threatened with extinction in Costa Rica, six are waterbirds: Jabiru *Jabiru mycteria*, Roseate Spoonbill,

Red-billed Tropicbird *Phaethon aethereus*. Photo: Albert Chipps.

Sunbittern *Erypyga helias*, Sungrebe *Heliornis fulica*, Fulvous Whistling-Duck *Dendrocygna bicolor* and White-faced Whistling-Duck *D. viduata* (Reglamento a Ley de Conservación de la Vida Silvestre 1997). All of these are resident species. The Costa Rican population of the Jabiru is under 90 individuals, while that of the Roseate Spoonbill is estimated at 300 pairs.

The North American Waterbird Conservation Plan (Kushlan *et al.* 2002) provides a status assessment for 166 colonial waterbirds occurring in the Plan area (from the Arctic to Panama, including the Caribbean Islands and islands of the Pacific). Of the species ranked as "High Concern" (populations are known or thought to be declining, and have some other known or potential threat), 12 occur in Costa Rica: Red-billed Tropicbird *Phaethon aethereus*, Brown Booby, Magnificent Frigatebird, Tricolored Heron *Egretta tricolor*, Little Blue Heron *Egretta caerulea*, Snowy Egret, Bare-throated Tiger-Heron *Tigrisoma mexicanum*, Wood Stork, Jabiru, Gull-billed Tern *Sterna nilotica*, Bridled Tern and Black Skimmer *Rynchops niger*.

Several wetlands in Costa Rica are threatened, the primary threats being human disturbance, industrial and agricultural contamination, sedimentation, drainage and habitat destruction.

## CONCLUSION

Costa Rica is very important for waterbirds, both resident and migratory species. Additional study and careful management of the country's Ramsar sites, conservation areas, migratory flyways, and threatened species are necessary for the health of waterbirds in Costa Rica and throughout the Americas. This compilation is intended to provide a foundation for these actions, which are best carried out within the context of an international initiative, such as Waterbird Conservation for the Americas (www.waterbirdconservation.org).

## ACNOWLEDGEMENTS

I wish to thank Jennifer Wheeler who assisted with the English translation and provided helpful comments on this manuscript, Joaquín Sánchez who made the maps, the National Museum of Costa Rica and in particular Cecilia Pineda for giving me the time to do this work, the Waterbird Council for their letter of support, and the Joint Nature Conservation Committee and organizers of the Waterbirds around the world Conference for financial support to participate in the Conference.

## REFERENCES

Kushlan, J.A., Steinkamp, M., Parsons, K., Capp, J., Acosta, M., Coulter, M., Davidson, I., Dickson, L., Edelson, N., Elliot, R., Edwin, M., Hatch, S., Kress, S., Milko, R., Miller, S., Phillips, R., Mills, K., Saliva, J., Sydeman, B., Trapp, J., Wheeler, J. & Wohl, K. 2002. Waterbird Conservation for the Americas: The North American Waterbird Conservation Plan, Version 1. Waterbird Conservation for the Americas, Washington, D.C.

Reglamento a Ley de Conservación de la Vida Silvestre 1997. La Gaceta No. 233. Diario Oficial (San José, Costa Rica), 3 de diciembre de 1997 (AÑO CXIX).

Stiles, F.G. 1983. Birds. In: D.H. Janzen (ed) Costa Rican Natural History. The Chicago University Press, Chicago.

Stiles, F.G. & Lewis, J. 1980. Lista de Pájaros de Costa Rica, según localidades. Mimeograph.

Stiles, F.G. & Skutch, A.F. 1989. A guide to the Birds of Costa Rica. Ithaca, Comstock Publishing Associates, New York.

Costa Rica's wetlands support an enormous diversity of wildlife and dependent human communities. Manglares de Sierpe – Térraba Reserva Forestal, Costa Rica. Photo: David Stroud.

# Shorebird monitoring in the Upper Bay of Panama

*Loyda E. Sánchez[1], Deborah M. Buehler[1,2] & Alberto I. Castillo[1,2]*

[1]*Panama Audubon Society, PO Box 0843-03076, Panama City, Republic of Panama. (email: lesanch@cwpanama.net)*
[2]*Smithsonian Tropical Research Institute, UNIT 0948, APO AA 34002-0948.*

Sánchez, L.E., Buehler, D.M. & Castillo, A.I. 2006. Shorebird monitoring in the Upper Bay of Panama. *Waterbirds around the world.* Eds. G.C. Boere, C.A. Galbraith & D.A. Stroud. The Stationery Office, Edinburgh, UK. pp. 166-171.

## ABSTRACT

The Republic of Panama occupies an important geographical position connecting North and South America; it hosts an extremely high number of migratory shorebirds in a very restricted area. Within Panama, the Upper Bay of Panama supports enormous numbers of shorebirds during migration. The area qualifies as a globally Important Bird Area; it has been declared a Wetland of International Importance under the Ramsar Convention, and qualifies as a Hemispheric Reserve under the Western Hemisphere Shorebird Reserve Network (WHSRN). This study, conducted by the Panama Audubon Society with support from the Canadian Wildlife Service, collected data on shorebird abundance in the Upper Bay of Panama through aerial and ground surveys during the autumn migration in 2003. The conclusions of the study were as follows: (1) for meaningful comparisons between surveys taken in different years, extended surveys covering the entire migration period are needed; (2) tidal flats within a 30 km stretch to the east of Panama City are extremely important for small shorebirds; (3) studies of productivity, nutrient input and other factors in the inter-tidal zone need to be undertaken to determine why the mudflats between Panama City and the Pacora River are so attractive to shorebirds.

## INTRODUCTION

Shorebirds are among the most migratory of all birds, and spend most of their annual cycle on wintering grounds and migratory staging areas. The viability of their populations thus depends not only on the availability of suitable breeding grounds, but also on the availability and health of highly productive non-breeding areas (Watts 1998). Recent studies indicate that many species concentrate in a small number of essential sites both during migration and in wintering areas. Many shorebird species depend on a network of migration stop-over sites and habitats during their non-breeding season to complete their annual cycles. For conservation to be successful, entire networks, crossing political borders, need to be preserved. Shorebird conservation thus represents an international challenge (Myers 1983, Myers *et al.* 1987, Morrison & Myers 1989), the importance of which is emphasized by recent declines in North American shorebird populations (Morrison *et al.* 2001).

The Republic of Panama occupies an important geographical position connecting North and South America. Due to its position, it hosts an extremely high number of migratory birds in a very restricted area. Aerial surveys by the Canadian Wildlife Service have documented the importance of Panama as a wintering and staging area for shorebirds (Morrison *et al.* 1998). In January 1993, Panama supported a population of 255 000 Nearctic shorebirds; 80% of these birds were within the Upper Bay of Panama. These numbers, concentrated in a very small area, highlight the

crucial importance of Panama for shorebirds. During southward migration in October 1991, counts were even higher, and Morrison *et al.* (1998) counted over 369 000 shorebirds in the Upper Bay alone. Aerial and ground surveys conducted by Watts (1998) during the autumn migration in 1997 found 370 000 shorebirds in a single day. These numbers exceed 100 000 birds annually, and thus qualify the area as a site of international significance under the Western Hemisphere Shorebird Reserve Network (Morrison *et al.* 1995). Based on turnover, Watts estimated that nearly 1.1 million Western Sandpipers *Calidris mauri* alone passed through the area. These estimates of turnover during autumn migration far exceed the WHSRN criterion of 500 000 birds annually, and qualify the Upper Bay of Panama as a site with the highest status under WHSRN (Morrison *et al.* 1995).

Since 1998, as part of the Important Bird Area (IBA) program, the Panama Audubon Society (PAS) has worked to protect this area. Based on a proposal and other information provided by the PAS, ANAM, Panama's National Authority for the Environment, decided to designate part of the area as a Wetland of International Importance under the Ramsar Convention. The site was officially declared a Ramsar site (no. 1 319) on 20 October 2003. It would be beneficial to have this site recognized as a WHSRN Hemispheric Reserve – status that would afford the area further international recognition as a hemispherically important link in a network of important shorebird areas.

The purpose of this study was to conduct additional aerial surveys of the Upper Bay of Panama during the autumn migration of 2003, to build upon the data on abundance, distribution and phenology previously collected by Morrison *et al.* (1998) and Watts (1998), and to conduct extensive ground surveys at five sites (two of which were not previously surveyed).

## STUDY AREA

This study was conducted along the northern shore of the Upper Bay of Panama from Panama Viejo at the eastern edge of Panama City to the Maestra River Estuary, a total distance of 80 km. The study area encompasses the new Ramsar site, which protects all remaining mangroves between Tapia River and the Maestra River Estuary. The area was surveyed by dividing the shoreline into eight 10 km sectors (Fig. 1) which correspond approximately to the sectors used by Watts (1998) and sectors 61 and 62 as designated by Morrison *et al.* (1998). The area consists of mangroves and spectacular inter-tidal mudflats, primarily composed of fine silt and organic compounds, bordering a narrow coastal plain.

Based on criteria established by BirdLife International, the Upper Bay of Panama was determined to be an IBA of global importance (Angehr 2003) and includes 17 000 ha of mangroves and 22 000 ha of mudflats. The mudflats, exposed to seven metre tides, extend out several kilometres from the shore at low

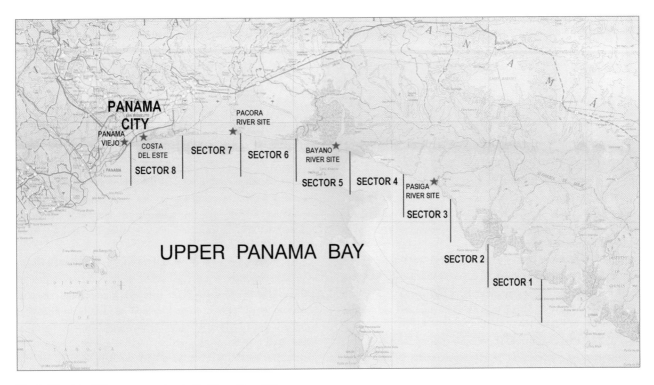

Fig. 1. The eight 10 km survey sectors in the Upper Bay of Panama.

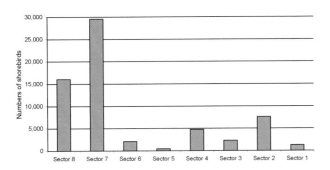

Fig. 2. Spatial distribution of all shorebirds along aerial transects in the Upper Bay of Panama. Sectors are numbered from east to west

tide. The mangroves lie east of the mudflats most heavily used by shorebirds. The prevailing long-shore current flows from east to west, suggesting that mangroves may provide much of the nutrients found in these mudflats (Watts 1998). The western end of the Upper Bay of Panama IBA, a 30 km stretch between the eastern edge of Panama City and the mouth of the Bayano River, harbours the highest density of birds.

## METHODS

The groups of species included in ground and aerial counts were: ducks (Anatidae); raptors, including Ospreys (Pandionidae), hawks (Accipitridae), and falcons and caracaras (Falconidae); long-legged wading birds, including herons and egrets (Ardeidae), ibises and spoonbills (Threskiornithidae), and storks (Ciconiidae); coastal seabirds, including pelicans (Pelecanidae), cormorants (Phalacrocoracidae), frigatebirds (Fregatidae), gulls (Laridae), terns (Sternidae), and skimmers (Rhynchopidae); shorebirds, including jacanas (Jacanidae), oystercatchers (Haematopodidae), stilts (Recurvirostridae), plovers and lapwings, (Charadriidae); sandpipers and relatives (Scolopacidae); and kingfishers (Alcedinidae).

## Ground surveys

Ground surveys were conducted at five sites between 8-27 September 2003. Sites were visited on a rotating basis; however, because of difficult access, the Pasiga River site was visited only once and the Bayano River site only twice. At each site, surveys were carried out with binoculars and telescopes when the tide was 70% to 100% full. The same stretch of shoreline was surveyed each time.

The Panama Viejo site (9°00' 21"N, 79°29" 14"W) is located on the eastern edge of Panama City and was easily accessed on a paved road. The site comprises a broad mudflat with soft black mud, flanked to the east by a tourist centre and to the west by a rocky outcrop. An elevated highway, the Southern Corridor, runs offshore over the outer mudflats, and may have changed tidal circulation patterns since its construction in the late 1990s. The survey was conducted within a 1 km strip of the inter-tidal mudflat and adjacent rocks.

The Costa del Este site (9°00'40"N, 79°27'31"W), at the eastern end of Panama City, is located 3 km east of the Panama Viejo site and was easily accessed on a paved road. It comprises broad mudflats, flanked to the west by the Matías Hernández River and to the east by mangroves. The landward side of the mudflats is flanked by a concrete seawall built to protect a new housing development. This survey included a 3 km stretch of inter-tidal mudflat plus an occasionally flooded 700 m x 300 m area of grassland.

The Pacora River site (9°01'24"N, 79°18'09"W) is 25 km east along the shore from Costa del Este. The area was accessed by four-wheel drive vehicle on a dirt road through privately-owned rice fields to within 500 m of the coast, and then on foot. The site comprises broad mudflats of soft black mud, flanked inland successively by savannah-like grassland with scattered trees and extensive rice fields. The survey included a 2 km stretch of the inter-tidal mudflat, plus some irrigated rice fields surveyed from the road.

The Bayano River site (8°59'54"N, 79°06'18"W), at the

**Table 1.** Summary of information on aerial surveys in Panama in 2003.

| Date | Aircraft | Survey time | Estimated time of high tide | Estimated height of tide (in feet) | Weather |
|------|----------|-------------|------------------------------|-------------------------------------|---------|
| 7 Sept. | Cessna 152 | 11:58-13:03 | 13:14 | 14.7 | Light haze, light wind, 30°C |
| 18 Sept. | Cessna 152 | 07:16-07:50 | 08:17 | 13.3 | Overcast, light wind, 22°C |
| 26 Sept. | Cessna 152 | 15:00-15:33 | 16:39 | 17.4 | Clear, light wind, 32°C |

mouth of the Bayano River, is located 25 km east of the Pacora River site, is accessed by boat from the Bayano River, and comprises a sandy beach. A 2 km stretch of the beach was surveyed on foot, and a 15 km stretch of mangrove forest was surveyed by boat en route to the site.

The Pasiga River site (8°55'16"N, 78°55'14"W) is located 25 km east of the Bayano River site and can only be accessed via the Bayano River and a four hour boat trip by sea. The site comprises a 1 km undisturbed inter-tidal gravel, sand and silt flat at the mouth of Pasiga River.

All five sites are subject to up-welling during the dry season, when westerly winds blow warm surface water offshore and draw cooler, nutrient-rich bottom water to the surface near the coast. Up-welling increases invertebrate activity and reproduction, and makes inter-tidal areas particularly rich in invertebrates which are used as food by shorebirds (Morrison *et al.* 1998).

Counts derived from ground surveys were used to ground-truth the counts obtained during aerial surveys. Since some species were difficult to distinguish from the air, they were counted according to size class (small, medium and large) during the aerial surveys. The number of each species was then estimated by extrapolating from its proportion in flocks based on ground surveys, since the latter provided a more accurate determination of the species composition of large flocks. However, even on ground surveys, some very similar species, such as Semipalmated Sandpiper *Calidris pusilla* and Western Sandpiper, were difficult to distinguish, so they were treated as a single category "peeps". Small shorebirds included peeps (Western and Semipalmated Sandpipers), Least Sandpiper *Calidris minutilla*, Semipalmated Plover *Charadrius semipalmatus* and Wilson's Plover *C. wilsonia*; medium shorebirds included Short-billed Dowitcher *Limnodromus griseus* (the Long-billed Dowitcher *L. scolopaceus* is rare in Panama and has not been recorded in inter-tidal habitats), Red Knot *Calidris canutus,* Black-bellied Plover *Pluvialis squatarola* and Ruddy Turnstone *Arenaria interpres*; large shorebirds included Whimbrel *Numenius phaeopus*, Marbled Godwit *Limosa fedoa* and the two yellowlegs, Greater Yellowlegs *Tringa melanoleuca* and Lesser Yellowlegs *T. flavipes*. Based on habitat similarities, the proportions observed on ground surveys from Pasiga River were used to extrapolate counts for sectors 1-3, the proportions from Bayano River for Sectors 4-6, the proportions from Pacora River for Sector 7, and the proportions from Costa del Este for Sector 8.

**Aerial surveys**

Low-altitude aerial surveys were conducted to determine the abundance of shorebirds during September 2003 (Table 1). Flight dates were selected to try to represent bird numbers at the beginning, middle and end of the survey period. Although it would have been ideal to separate surveys by an equal number

of days, weather conditions and the timing of tides prevented this. Flight times were chosen so that surveys took place when the tide was 70% to 90% full, a time when shorebirds are highly concentrated in a narrow band along the shoreline and are easily surveyed (Watts 1998).

All surveys began at the mouth of Matías Hernández River, at the western edge of the Costa del Este housing development, and ended at the Maestra River Estuary. Methods described in Morrison *et al.* (1998) were followed as closely as possible, using a Cessna 152 (HP1241AS) high-winged aircraft, flying at about 20-30 m above ground level and at a speed of approximately 180 km/hr, depending on bird numbers, habitat, and the directness of the flight path. The flight path was about 25 m offshore from the water's edge, with one observer (DMB) looking inland from the seat behind the pilot, and one observer (AIC) looking forward and seaward from the co-pilots seat. For each sector, DMB also recorded qualitative habitat descriptions which were later used to judge habitat changes since the surveys of Morrison *et al.* (1998) and Watts (1998). All observations were recorded directly into a tape recorder for transcription after the flight.

**RESULTS**

**Habitats**

Major changes in habitat since the surveys of Morrison *et al.* (1998) in 1988, 1991 and 1993 and of Watts (1998) in 1997 have occurred primarily in Sectors 7 and 8 (see Table 2 over). The most obvious change has been the replacement of the Costa del Este marshlands with a housing complex. Additional changes include the loss of most of the sandy beach in Sector 7 due to sand extraction for use in construction, and the construction of the Southern Corridor highway, which now runs across the seaward side of the Panama Viejo mudflat. In addition, the area inland from the Juan Díaz and Tocumen mangroves has become increasingly urbanized, resulting in increasing pressure on these coastal ecosystems, even though development has not yet reached the coast itself. In the Bayano Estuary, a fisherman reported recent cutting in the mangroves for the expansion of a cattle farm, and this was confirmed on the next aerial survey. Since all mangroves are protected in Panama, this cutting is illegal, although the regulations are difficult to enforce in remote areas.

**Abundance**

The 12 ground surveys at five sites resulted in a cumulative total of 307 803 bird observations. Within this cumulative total, shorebirds accounted for 97.0% of all birds, with small shorebirds by far the most numerous (93.6% of total shorebirds). Medium shorebirds accounted for 3.8% of all shorebirds and large shorebirds for 2.6%. Within small shorebirds, peeps, at 90.8%, were by far the most abundant. Watts (1998) calculated

**Table 2.** Major habitats occurring in survey sectors in the Upper Bay of Panama. Breaks in habitat are indicated with diagonal strokes with the first section describing the inter-tidal habitat, the second section describing habitat immediately behind the inter-tidal zone heading inland, and, if necessary, a third section describing habitats further inland. Sectors are numbered from east to west.

| Sector | Habitat Description |
| --- | --- |
| 8 | Broad mudflat with soft black mud / concrete seawall and housing project on western edge and mangroves to the east / housing projects, industrial buildings and Tocumen Airport. |
| 7 | Broad mudflat with soft black mud / savannah scrub forest and grassland with scattered small houses / agricultural land (mainly rice fields) Note: Almost all sandy beaches have been removed by sand trucks. Only a small sandbar at the mouth of Río Pacora remains undisturbed. |
| 6 | Broad mudflats with firmer mud, sand beach / cattle pasture with scattered trees. |
| 5 | Sand and mudflats with some sand beach at the west end of the sector, mangroves up to the water at the mouth of Río Bayano, sand beach at the east end of the sector / some cattle pasture with savannah scrub forest and grassland at the east end of the sector. |
| 4 | Sand beach, flooded mangroves / mostly mangroves, some cattle pasture with savannah scrub forest and grassland at the west end of the sector. |
| 3 | Sand beach, flooded mangroves / mostly mangroves, some cattle pasture with savannah scrub forest and grassland at the west end of the sector. |
| 2 | Muddy flats, sand beach, flooded mangroves / mangroves and some low forest. |
| 1 | Muddy flats, sand beach, flooded mangroves / mangroves and some low forest. |

through mist-netting that Western Sandpipers accounted for 86.9% of peeps. When applied to this study, this proportion would indicate that Western Sandpipers make up 78.9% of small shorebirds and 73.8% of all shorebirds counted.

Non-shorebird species were dominated by gulls and terns, which accounted for 43.7% of the total. Also very abundant were Neotropic Cormorants *Phalacrocorax brasilianus* (23.3%), Brown Pelicans *Pelecanus occidentalis* (17.4%), and long-legged wading birds (11.2%). Magnificent Frigatebirds *Fregata magnificens*, ducks and raptors were rarer at 2.1%, 1.9% and 0.4% of the total respectively.

The three aerial surveys resulted in a cumulative total of 645 791 bird observations, and shorebirds accounted for 97.7% of this total. Shorebird observations were dominated by small shorebirds, which accounted for 91.2% of the shorebird total, while large shorebirds made up 6.1% and medium shorebirds 2.7% of the total. Non-shorebird species were dominated by Neotropic Cormorants (37.3%), Brown Pelicans (29.5%), and gulls and terns (22.4%). Less abundant were long-legged wading birds (8.4%), Magnificent Frigatebirds (1.8%), Black-bellied Whistling-Ducks *Dendrocygna autumnalis* (0.4%) and raptors (0.2%).

### Distribution

Shorebird concentrations were by far the greatest at Costa del Este and Río Pacora, which together had 98% of the shorebird total (45.6% and 52.4%, respectively). All shorebird size classes were concentrated in these two sites, although the concentration of small shorebirds was most pronounced. For small shorebirds, 99% were found in these two sites, whereas medium and large shorebirds were slightly more dispersed, with 85.3% of the medium shorebirds and 84.5% of the large shorebirds being found at Costa del Este and Pacora River. Buff-breasted Sandpipers *Tryngites subruficollis*, Pectoral Sandpipers *Calidris*

*melanotos*, Upland Sandpipers *Bartramia longicauda* and Southern Lapwings *Vanellus chilensis* were only seen in the flooded grassland of Costa del Este.

Non-shorebird species were also concentrated in Costa del Este and Río Pacora, but to a lesser degree, with 40% of the total in Costa del Este, 30% in Río Pacora, 20% in Panama Viejo and 5% in both Río Bayano and Río Pasiga. Again, the habitats present in each site were important for species composition. Cinnamon Teals *Anas cyanoptera* and Savannah Hawks *Buteogallus meridionalis* were only seen in the flooded grassland of Costa del Este. Wattled Jacanas *Jacana jacana*, Rufescent Tiger-Herons *Tigrisoma lineatum*, Muscovy Ducks *Cairina moschata* and Pearl Kites *Gampsonyx swainsonii* were seen only in the rice fields of Río Pacora. Both the flooded grassland of Costa del Este and the rice fields of Río Pacora were important for Wood Storks *Mycteria americana* and White-tailed Kites *Elanus leucurus*. Finally, Black-bellied Whistling-Ducks were seen in large numbers in the flooded pastures along the Bayano River, and in smaller numbers in the Costa del Este flooded grassland.

### Phenology

Collectively, shorebird numbers increased with each successive flight, and also during the course of the ground surveys at Costa del Este and Río Pacora (the two centres of concentration). This was also true for small, medium, and large shorebirds considered separately. For all sizes, peak counts were on the latest survey date. This is similar to the results of Watts (1998), who found that in 1997 counts of medium and large shorebirds peaked in late September and the numbers of small shorebirds were still increasing at the beginning of November. All previous counts in the area indicate that numbers of small shorebirds peak in early to mid-November in Panama. The counts of non-shorebird species remained fairly stable across flights and ground surveys.

## DISCUSSION

### Habitats

The six years between the autumn migration of 1997, when Watts (1998) conducted his surveys, and that of 2003 have seen large changes in shorebird habitat on the eastern edge of Panama City, as urbanization has sprawled eastward, bringing housing complexes, roads and factories. Changes have included the filling-in and paving-over of the Costa del Este marshes for housing, the building of the Southern Corridor highway across the seaward side of the Panama Viejo mudflats, and construction of new factories on the rivers which feed the Upper Bay. The effects of this urbanization are not fully known, and shorebird counts, although very important for monitoring shorebird numbers, are not sufficient to examine fully the effects of urbanization. Further studies on the specific effects of urbanization are needed. For example, chemical studies of sediments are needed to assess whether the paving-over of marshes changes the chemical make-up of the adjacent mudflats, and whether the nutrients that support the food resources used by shorebirds come not only from mangroves and marshes but also from Panama City's untreated sewage. Radio-tracking studies would be helpful in discovering the locations (if they exist) of new high-tide roost sites when (as in Costa del Este) previous sites are paved over. Furthermore, chemical studies on the waste products of factories located on rivers which feed into the Upper Bay are needed to investigate possible reasons for fish kills reported by local people in the area.

### Abundance and phenology

Our aerial counts correspond well with those of Watts (1998). In terms of species composition, our figures are nearly identical, with shorebirds making up well over 90% of total birds, and within shorebirds, small species making up over 90% of the total, large shorebirds around 6%, and medium shorebirds around 2%. Our total counts also matched well. Watts (1998) counted 183 840 shorebirds on 5 September, 216 431 on 20 September, and 254 318 on 27 September, while we counted 141 938 shorebirds on 6 September, 198 730 on 18 September, and 290 536 on 26 September. As a whole, the Upper Bay supported approximately the same number of shorebirds in September 2003 as it did in September 1997. However, the migration of 2003 apparently started somewhat more slowly than in 1997, and there was a large increase in numbers between 18 and 26 September.

Our peak count for small shorebirds was much lower than that of Watts (1998) owing to the fact that we were unable to continue surveys into the peak of Western Sandpiper migration in November. Our peak counts for medium and large shorebirds were also slightly lower than those of Watts (1998), although our survey covered peak dates for all medium and large species except the Willet *Catoptrophorus semipalmatus* (which peaked on 4 October in 1997).

Because Morrison *et al.* (1998) performed aerial surveys at different times in the migration cycle (in late February 1988, late October 1991 and mid-January 1993), we cannot make a direct comparison with their peak counts. However, our peak count of 290 536 on 26 September falls between the January wintering count of Morrison *et al.* (1998) of 209 703 and their autumn migration peak count of 332 838, indicating that our survey covered a period of active migration and included birds that would stay in Panama for the winter, as well as migrants heading further south.

### Distribution

Our data on shorebird distribution also correspond well with those of Watts (1998). Both studies unequivocally indicate the importance of the 30 km stretch of shoreline immediately east of Panama City, especially for small shorebirds. High counts of these birds appear to be linked to the mudflats, composed of soft black mud, that extend from the city's eastern edge to the mouth of the Río Pacora. East of the Río Pacora, the mud becomes firmer and shorebird numbers drop dramatically.

Such high numbers of birds are almost certainly linked to high food productivity due to high nutrient input into these mudflats. The source of this input is not definitely known. Sources may include sediments from rivers, adjacent mangrove forests and dry-season up-welling (Butler *et al.* 1997, Morrison *et al.* 1998). Studies to determine the organic and chemical content of these mudflats and their productivity are necessary to determine exactly why they are attractive to shorebirds.

Ground surveys highlighted fine-scale differences in species distribution between habitats in the Upper Bay of Panama, emphasizing the need to protect a variety of habitats in order to maintain species diversity. The mudflats at all ground sites except for Panama Viejo are protected within the Ramsar site, and although Panama Viejo may not be as important for overall abundance as Costa del Este or Pacora River, it is in some way attractive to medium shorebirds. This is exemplified by the Red Knot. A flock of approximately 100-200 Red Knots was consistently found during surveys at the Panama Viejo site from January to mid-April 2002 (Buehler 2002) and appeared as expected in November 2003. This species was not seen consistently in such numbers at any other ground site.

The Upper Bay of Panama is an extremely important area for shorebirds and other coastal species, and the sheer number of birds that the area supports gives it international importance. The region is diverse and beautiful. To the west, urbanization is encroaching, but to the east, it remains one of few relatively undisturbed habitats in Panama. The bay is important not only biologically, but also socio-economically, providing, among other things, fish and shrimp that are used not only directly by humans as food, but also as feed for the country's chicken industry. Continued monitoring as well as further studies on the effects of urbanization will be needed to understand and protect the Upper Bay of Panama for future generations of shorebirds and humans alike.

## SUMMARY OF CONCLUSIONS AND RECOMMENDATIONS

1) For meaningful comparisons between surveys, long-term surveys which cover the entire migration period are preferred. We recommend that aerial surveys cover all of the autumn migration (August to the end of November) and, if possible, the spring migration (January to the end of April) in order to draw solid conclusions about inter-annual variability between counts. The timing of migration, and thus peak numbers, varies from year to year. Future surveys, which cover the entire migration period and ensure that peak numbers for all categories and species are recorded, will provide a better means for monitoring shorebird abundance in the Upper Bay of Panama.

2) The tidal flats within the 30 km stretch to the east of Panama City are extremely important for small shorebirds. Areas not

included in the Ramsar site (the mudflats of Costa del Este, the Panama Viejo area and the Juan Díaz mangroves) should be protected. Furthermore, protection in areas such as the mangroves of Bayano must be enforced.

3) Studies should be undertaken to determine the factors, especially nutrient flows, which make the mudflats between Panama City and Río Pacora so attractive to shorebirds.

## ACKNOWLEDGEMENTS

This study was funded by a grant from the Canadian Wildlife Service to the Panama Audubon Society. Research would not have been possible without the assistance of many people. Rosabel Miró, current President of PAS, gave the opportunity to work on this project and provided essential logistical and financial assistance. Dr. George Angehr of the Smithsonian Tropical Research Institute provided much needed maps, advice and editing. Carlos Díaz of the Albrook Flight School was a skilled and fearless pilot who kept the project team airborne during low-altitude survey flights. Juan Ramon provided logistical support in obtaining flight permits. Finally the people of Boca de Pacora, Chepo, Puerto Coquira, and Pasiga opened their property and their hearts to the team and provided valuable local information.

## REFERENCES

Angehr, G.R. 2003. Directory of Important Bird Areas in Panama. Panama Audubon Society, Panama City.

Buehler, D.M. 2002. Shorebird counts in Panama during 2002 emphasize the need to monitor and protect the Upper Panama Bay. Wader Study Group Bulletin 99: 41-44.

Butler, R.W., Morrison, R.I.G., Delgado, F.S., Ross, R.K. & Smith, G.E.J. 1997. Habitat associations of coastal birds in Panama. Colonial Waterbirds 20: 518-524.

Morrison, R.I.G. & Myers, J.P. 1989. Shorebird flyways in the New World. In: H. Boyd & J.Y. Pirot (eds) Flyways and reserve networks for water birds. IWRB Special Publication No. 9. IWRB, Slimbridge, UK: 85-96.

Morrison, R.I.G., Butler, R.W., Beyersbergen, G.W., Dickson, H.L., Bourget, A., Hicklen, P.W., Goossen, J.P., Ross, R.K. & Gratto-Trevor, C.L. 1995. Potential Western Hemisphere Shorebird Reserve Network sites for migrant shorebirds in Canada: Second Edition 1995. Canadian Wildlife Service, Ottawa.

Morrison, R.I.G., Butler, R.W., Delgado, F.S. & Ross, R.K. 1998. Atlas of Nearctic shorebirds and other waterbirds on the coast of Panama. Canadian Wildlife Service, Ottawa.

Morrison, R.I.G., Aubry, Y., Butler, R.W., Beyersbergen, G.W., Donaldson, G.M., Gratto-Trevor, C.L., Hicklen, P.W., Johnston, V.H. & Ross, R.K. 2001. Declines in North American Shorebird Populations. Wader Study Group Bulletin 94: 34-38.

Myers, J.P. 1983. Conservation of migrating shorebirds: staging areas, geographic bottlenecks, and regional movements. American Birds 37: 23-25.

Myers, J.P., Morrison, R.I.G., Antas, P.Z., Harrington, B.A., Lovejoy, T.E., Sallaberry, M., Senner, S.E. & Tarak, A. 1987. Conservation strategy for migratory species. American Scientist 75: 18-26.

Watts, B.D. 1998. An Investigation of Waterbirds within the Panama Canal Zone and the Upper Bay of Panama. Center for Conservation Biology, College of William and Mary, Williamsburg, Virginia.

Semipalmated Sandpiper *Calidris pusilla*. Photo: Rob Robinson.

# Rice culture in Cuba as an important wintering site for migrant waterbirds from North America

*Lourdes Mugica[1], Martín Acosta[1], Dennis Denis[1], Ariam Jiménez[1], Antonio Rodríguez[1] & Xavier Ruiz[2]*

[1] *Universidad de la Habana, Facultad de Biología, 25 e J e I Vedado, Ciudad Habana, Cuba. (email: lmugica@fbio.uh.cu)*

[2] *Universitat de Barcelona, Dept. de Biologia Animal. Av. Diagonal 645, 08028-Barcelona, Spain.*

Mugica, L., Acosta, M., Denis, D., Jiménez, A., Rodríguez, A. & Ruiz, X. 2006. Rice culture in Cuba as an important wintering site for migrant waterbirds from North America. *Waterbirds around the world.* Eds. G.C. Boere, C.A. Galbraith & D.A. Stroud. The Stationery Office, Edinburgh, UK. pp. 172-176.

## ABSTRACT

Rice is the second most important crop in Cuba. The main plantations are along the south coast, near natural wetlands. Because rice fields are seasonal and temporary wetlands, they may have an important role as substitute habitat for waterbirds. We studied the bird community associated with rice culture in several plantations in Cuba, and found that 70 bird species were using the paddies mainly as feeding areas, and consuming about 46 different food items. Migrant birds (mainly ducks and shorebirds) comprised 74% of the birds reported; 37% were winter migrants and 37% were species with resident and migratory populations. Most waterbirds utilize both paddies and coastal wetlands as wintering sites. Habitat use during the rice cycle was determined for each of the main guilds in the bird community. The daily consumption of the bird community was determined throughout the year and the rice cycle. In winter, because of the influence of the migrant duck population, daily consumption was five times greater than in summer. We concluded that rice-farming areas in Cuba are playing a key role in the conservation of migratory waterbirds in winter. Cooperative efforts are necessary to understand the complex ecological interactions that are taking place in the paddies and to enhance this important waterbird habitat.

## INTRODUCTION

Rice paddies are among the most productive and dependable agricultural systems devised by humans (Odum 1993), and may be important ecological areas acting as alternative habitat for wetland wildlife (Fasola & Ruíz 1997). Alternating periods of flooding and drying during the rice-growing cycle create a structurally complex habitat which retains many features typical of natural ecosystems. Because waterbirds, with their specific habitat requirements, may be most likely to use those newly created habitats which are most similar to their natural habitat (Cody 1981), the unusually high degree of structural complexity of the rice agro-ecosystem should promote high avian diversity, especially in areas with low usage of pesticides.

After sugar cane, rice is the crop occupying the second highest acreage in Cuba, where it is grown in five provinces. Because of the shape of the island, most of the rice-growing areas are near the south coast. In most places, the coastal belt between the rice fields and the sea is natural wetland, and so the coastal wetlands and paddies may act as a conservation unit for waterbirds. Furthermore, there has been a drastic reduction in the use of chemicals by Cuban farmers in recent years because of the economic crisis, with a consequent increase in the availability of food for waterbirds in the rice-growing areas.

The importance of these areas for wintering waterbirds is enhanced by the fact that Cuba is in the middle of two important

bird migration corridors, the Atlantic and the Mississippi flyways. Thus, Cuba is not only an important wintering area for migrants from North America, but also a very important staging area for birds that are migrating further south. The rice-growing areas may play a key role in the conservation of these species (Mikuska *et al.* 1998).

Although the cultivation of rice is an ancient agricultural practice and rice is now considered the second most important crop in the world (Hoffman 1993), relatively little attention has been given to the complex interactions between the bird community and the rice crop. Some recent studies include those by Fasola & Ruíz (1996), Day & Collwell (1998), Elphick & Oring (1998), Elphick (2000) and Tourenq *et al.* (2001).

Using all of the information collected during a decade (1992-2003) of field studies by the Bird Ecology Group of the University of Havana, our main aims in this paper are: firstly, to summarize data on the diversity, abundance and habitat use of migratory waterbirds using rice fields in Cuba; and secondly, to draw attention to the need for an integrated approach to rice farming that will take into consideration its importance in the conservation of migratory waterbirds.

## STUDY AREAS

The rice-growing regions are huge (c. 20 000 ha), flat areas, usually divided into fields of one hectare. Along the south coast, there is usually a 1 to 5 km wide belt of natural coastal wetlands between the paddies and the sea. During the rice cycle, the development of the rice plant changes with the water regime, and eight different field types have been identified on the basis of water level and vegetation cover (Mugica *et al.* 2003). Samples of the birds using each of these eight field types were taken separately. As the sowing period is spread over several months, many different field types are available at any one time.

## METHODS

We compiled published and unpublished information on the importance of rice fields for migrant birds in Cuba. Most data were collected between 1992 and 2000 during a study of the bird community in the Sur del Jíbaro rice fields in Sancti Spiritus, Cuba (21°35'-21°45'N, 79°5'-79°25'W). Additional data were gathered by sampling the coastal wetlands associated with the rice-growing areas and two other rice-growing areas: Los Palacios, Pinar del Río, in western Cuba, and Amarillas Rice Culture, Matanzas, in central Cuba.

In order to estimate densities of waterbirds and habitat use, the counts were conducted during the first four hours after sunrise (the period of maximum bird activity and relatively low air temperatures) by walking along two transects in each field using a stratified sampling method (each of the eight stages of

**Table 1.** Birds observed during transect counts in rice fields in Cuba, showing annual mean density in birds/ha (MD) with ±95% confidence limits (CL), frequency of occurrence (FO), and months in which the birds were present. Asterisks indicate those species with enough feeding data to be included in the feeding analysis (from Mugica *et al.* 2001).

| Species | MD | CL − | CL + | FO | J | F | M | J | J | A | O | N | D |
|---|---|---|---|---|---|---|---|---|---|---|---|---|---|
| **Resident and migrant populations** | | | | | | | | | | | | | |
| *Podilymbus podiceps* | 0.001 | 0,00 | 0,00 | 11.1 | | | | | | █ | | | |
| *Phalacrocorax brasilianus* | 0.069 | 0,00 | 0,14 | 44.4 | | █ | █ | | | █ | | █ | |
| *Ixobrychus exilis* * | 0.031 | 0,00 | 0,06 | 66.7 | | █ | █ | | | █ | | █ | |
| *Ardea herodias* * | 0.008 | 0,00 | 0,02 | 22.2 | | █ | | | | | | █ | |
| *Ardea (Egretta) alba* * | 0.712 | 0,19 | 1,24 | 100.0 | █ | █ | █ | █ | █ | █ | █ | █ | █ |
| *Egretta thula* * | 2.981 | 0,36 | 5,61 | 100.0 | █ | █ | █ | █ | █ | █ | █ | █ | █ |
| *Egretta caerulea* * | 1.418 | 0,73 | 2,11 | 100.0 | █ | █ | █ | █ | █ | █ | █ | █ | █ |
| *Egretta tricolor* * | 0.027 | 0,00 | 0,05 | 66.7 | █ | █ | █ | | | █ | █ | █ | |
| *Bubulcus ibis* * | 4.716 | 2,89 | 6,55 | 100.0 | █ | █ | █ | █ | █ | █ | █ | █ | █ |
| *Butorides virescens* * | 0.033 | 0,01 | 0,05 | 88.9 | █ | █ | █ | █ | █ | █ | █ | █ | |
| *Nycticorax nycticorax* * | 0.177 | 0,00 | 0,35 | 66.7 | █ | █ | █ | | | █ | | █ | |
| *Nyctanassa violacea* | 0.001 | 0,00 | 0,00 | 11.1 | | █ | | | █ | | | | |
| *Plegadis falcinellus* * | 9.249 | 0,00 | 22,41 | 100.0 | █ | █ | █ | █ | █ | █ | █ | █ | █ |
| *Phoenicopterus ruber* | 0.001 | 0,00 | 0,00 | 11.1 | | | | | █ | | | | |
| *Dendrocygna bicolor* * | 14.963 | 0,00 | 33,10 | 100.0 | █ | █ | █ | █ | █ | █ | █ | █ | █ |
| *Oxyura jamaicensis* | 0.004 | 0,00 | 0,01 | 22.2 | | | | | █ | | | | |
| *Falco sparverius* | 0.001 | 0,00 | 0,00 | 11.1 | | | | █ | | | | | |
| *Rallus elegans* | 0.045 | 0,00 | 0,09 | 55.6 | █ | █ | █ | | | █ | | █ | |
| *Porphyrula martinica* * | 0.086 | 0,01 | 0,16 | 55.6 | █ | █ | █ | █ | █ | █ | █ | █ | █ |
| *Gallinula chloropus* * | 0.353 | 0,10 | 0,61 | 77.8 | █ | █ | █ | █ | █ | █ | █ | █ | █ |
| *Fulica americana* * | 0.147 | 0,00 | 0,29 | 77.8 | █ | █ | █ | █ | █ | █ | █ | █ | █ |
| *Pluvialis squatarola* | 1.190 | 0,00 | 2,50 | 66.7 | █ | █ | █ | █ | █ | █ | █ | █ | |
| *Charadrius vociferus* | 0.507 | 0,00 | 1,19 | 88.9 | █ | █ | █ | █ | █ | █ | █ | █ | █ |
| *Himantopus mexicanus* | 6.448 | 1,18 | 11,71 | 77.8 | █ | █ | █ | █ | █ | █ | █ | █ | █ |
| *Larus atricilla* | 0.084 | 0,00 | 0,18 | 66.7 | █ | █ | █ | █ | █ | █ | █ | █ | |
| *Sterna maxima* | 0.012 | 0,00 | 0,03 | 22.2 | | | | | | | █ | | |
| *Zenaida macroura* | 0.540 | 0,00 | 1,47 | 44.4 | | █ | | | █ | █ | | █ | |
| *Ceryle alcyon* | 0.001 | 0,00 | 0,00 | 22.2 | █ | | | | | | | | █ |
| **Strictly migrant populations** | | | | | | | | | | | | | |
| *Anas acuta* * | 0.008 | 0,00 | 0,02 | 33.3 | █ | | | | | | █ | █ | |
| *Anas discors* * | 23.762 | 1,40 | 46,12 | 66.7 | █ | █ | █ | | | █ | █ | █ | █ |
| *Anas clypeata* * | 0.670 | 0,00 | 1,36 | 55.6 | █ | █ | █ | | | | █ | █ | █ |
| *Aythya collaris* | 0.001 | 0,00 | 0,00 | 22.2 | | | | | | | | █ | █ |
| *Porzana carolina* * | 0.003 | 0,00 | 0,01 | 22.2 | | | | █ | █ | | | | |
| *Laterallus jamaicensis* | 0.001 | 0,00 | 0,00 | 22.2 | | | | | █ | | | | |
| *Charadrius wilsonia* | 0.0,29 | 0,01 | 0,05 | 55.6 | █ | █ | █ | | | █ | █ | | |
| *Charadrius semipalmatus* | 0.051 | 0,00 | 0,14 | 33.3 | █ | █ | | | | | █ | | |
| *Recurvirostra americana* | 0.212 | 0,00 | 0,63 | 22.2 | | | | █ | █ | | | | |
| *Tringa flavipes* | 0.675 | 0,04 | 1,31 | 66.7 | █ | █ | █ | | | █ | █ | █ | █ |
| *Tringa melanoleuca* | 0.437 | 0,00 | 1,01 | 77.8 | █ | █ | █ | █ | █ | █ | █ | █ | █ |
| *Arenaria interpres* | 0.066 | 0,00 | 0,18 | 55.6 | █ | █ | █ | | | █ | █ | █ | |
| *Calidris mauri* | 0.177 | 0,00 | 0,45 | 44.4 | █ | █ | █ | | | | █ | █ | |
| *Calidris minutilla* | 3.614 | 0,00 | 9,10 | 44.4 | █ | █ | █ | | | | █ | █ | |
| *Calidris pusilla* | 0.149 | 0,00 | 0,38 | 33.3 | █ | █ | | | | █ | █ | | |
| *Calidris himantopus* | 0.001 | 0,00 | 0,00 | 22.2 | | █ | █ | | | | | | |
| *Limnodromus griseus* | 0.268 | 0,00 | 0,55 | 44.4 | █ | █ | █ | | | | █ | █ | |
| *Limnodromus scolopaceus* | 0.015 | 0,00 | 0,04 | 33.3 | █ | █ | | | █ | | | | |
| *Gallinago gallinago* | 0.021 | 0,00 | 0,05 | 44.4 | █ | | | | | | █ | █ | █ |
| *Larus argentatus* | 0.003 | 0,00 | 0,01 | 22.2 | | █ | █ | | | | | | |
| *Sterna nilotica* | 0.056 | 0,00 | 0,11 | 44.4 | █ | █ | | | █ | █ | █ | | |
| *Chlidonias niger* | 0.005 | 0,00 | 0,01 | 22.2 | | | | | █ | █ | | | |
| *Sterna antillarum* | 0.000 | 0,00 | 0,00 | 22.2 | | █ | | | | | | | |

the rice cycle was counted independently). Separate tallies of the energetic requirements and 95% confidence intervals were estimated using the allometric equations established by Nagy (1987) for birds (see Mugica 2000 for details of the methodology). The daily consumption of the waterbird community was estimated, taking into account the birds' breeding and non-breeding seasons and the estimated densities of birds in the fields in each month and stage of the rice-growing cycle.

## RESULTS

To date, 97 bird species have been reported using the rice fields and surrounding areas, with the heaviest use of the paddies occurring in winter. Of the 97 species reported, 70 were recorded during transect counts, including 26 species that are migrants and 26 species that have both migrant and resident populations in Cuba (Mugica *et al.* 2001). Thus, 74% of the species recorded in the rice fields are totally or partially migratory, with the migratory populations coming from North America (Table 1). We found that all of the systematic orders of waterbirds reported in Cuba are well represented in the rice fields (Podicipediformes – one species, Pelecaniformes – two spp., Ciconiiformes – 14 spp., Anseriformes – 12 spp., Gruiformes – seven spp., and Charadriiformes – 26 spp.).

The density of waterbirds in the rice fields increased dramatically in winter (Fig. 1) because of the arrival of huge flocks of migrant ducks and shorebirds in October and November. For example, Blue-winged Teal *Anas discors* and Fulvous Whistling-Duck *Dendrocygna bicolor* made up 63% of the birds present in October, whereas in November, the same two species contributed 86% to the total.

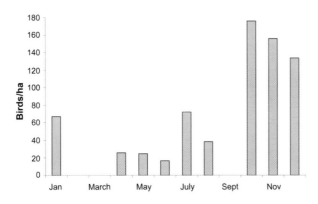

Fig. 1. Monthly variation in bird densities in the Sur del Jibaro rice fields, Sancti Spiritus, Cuba (from Mugica *et al.* 2001.

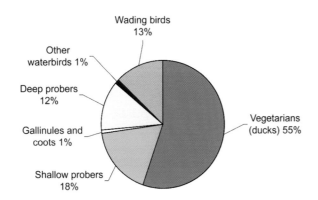

Fig. 2. Composition, by guild, of the waterbird community in the Sur del Jibaro rice fields, Sancti Spiritus, Cuba, based on annual mean densities (from Acosta *et al.* 2002).

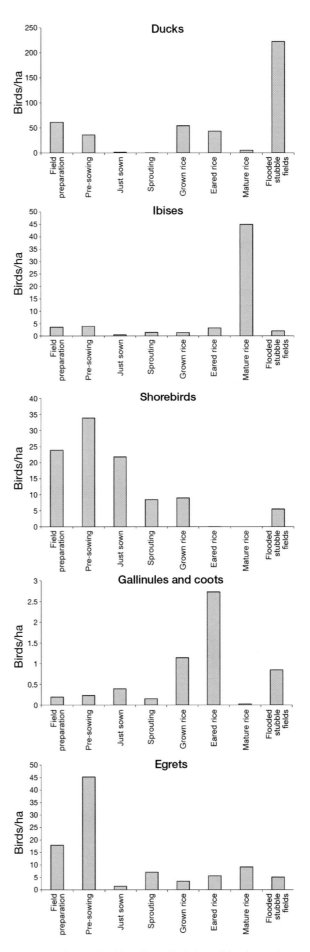

Fig. 3. Annual mean densities of waterbirds, by guild, using each stage of the rice-growing cycle in the Sur del Jibaro rice fields, Sancti Spiritus, Cuba (from Mugica *et al.* 2003).

## GUILD ANALYSIS

The annual mean density was calculated for each guild of water-birds occurring in the rice fields (Fig. 2). Migrant ducks included in the vegetarian guild accounted for more than half of the annual density. The guild of shallow probers, which contains all of the shorebirds, was the second-most important guild, comprising 18% of the annual density. Those guilds containing species with both resident and migratory populations, such as wading birds (herons and egrets) and deep probers (ibises), were next in importance. The differences in density between the guilds were highly significant (Kruskal-Wallis: H = 50.2; p<0.001).

There was marked segregation between the guilds in relation to habitat use (Fig. 3). Ducks preferred those fields flooded after the rice crop had been harvested, as there were many seeds available in the water because of loss during mechanical harvesting. Ibises were most abundant in mature rice after the fields had been drained in preparation for harvesting, particularly in winter, when Glossy Ibises *Plegadis falcinellus* feed mainly on rice seeds (Acosta *et al.* 1996). Shorebirds frequented the first stages of the growing cycle. In these fields, the water level is very low and there is an abundance of small invertebrates, simulating the natural mudflats that these birds usually use for feeding. Gallinules and coots took advantage of the middle stages of the rice cultivation cycle; in these stages, the birds found protection in the vegetation, and frequently used these habitats for resting, nesting and feeding. Wading birds were very opportunistic, and made heavy use of the rice fields when machinery was preparing the soil for sowing and large amounts of food were unearthed by their wheels, making it available for the birds.

### Food intake from the rice culture

The waterbird community uses the rice fields for resting, nesting and feeding. Of these activities, feeding is the most important, because many birds only use the paddies for the time required to meet their daily nutritional needs. Our results have demonstrated that the waterbird community uses at least 46 different food items (Acosta *et al.* 1988, 1990, 1994, 1996, Acosta 1998, Denis *et al.* 2000, Mugica 2000). Most of these food items are plants (58%), with rice playing the key role, followed by about 22 seed-producing species and an aquatic plant *Elodea*. Animal prey includes invertebrates (30%; mainly mollusks, insects and crustaceans) and vertebrates (12%; mainly fishes, frogs and rodents).

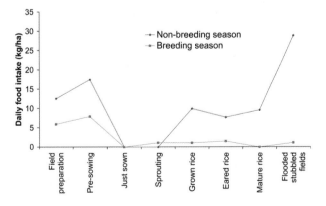

**Fig. 4.** Daily food intake (kg/ha) by the waterbird community in the Sur del Jíbaro rice fields, Sancti Spíritus, Cuba, during the rice-growing cycle in the breeding and non-breeding seasons.

A comparison of the different daily intake rates (in kg/ha) during the various stages of the rice cycle in the breeding and non-breeding periods revealed that the main output of matter and energy through the food was during the winter period (Fig. 4). The most important fields for obtaining food were those at the extremes of the rice cultivation cycle, when the fields were being prepared for sowing and when they had been flooded after the harvest. During the winter months (September to March), the intake of the waterbird community (the total daily consumption throughout the non-breeding period) was 1 606 tons, whereas in the summer months (May to August), the intake was 290 tons. Thus, during the winter months, when migratory waterbirds are present, the daily intake of the waterbird community is five times greater than during the breeding season, when only resident birds are using the paddies (Mugica 2000).

## DISCUSSION

Water level, food supply, season of the year, geographical location of the rice-farming areas, and methods of sowing are important factors determining the usage of rice fields by waterbirds in Cuba. The total number of aquatic birds found in the rice fields was similar to, or higher than, the number reported in several natural wetlands in Cuba (Acosta *et al.* 1992), Florida (Breininger & Smith 1990), Italy (Fasola & Ruiz 1996, 1997) and France (Tourenq *et al.* 2001). The reduction in the use of pesticides and herbicides in Cuba is presumably a major factor in the dramatic increase in the populations of species such as Glossy Ibis and Black-necked Stilt *Himantopus mexicanus*, and may be having an important effect on the entire waterbird community. The number of species recorded from Cuban rice fields is greater than the 46 species reported in rice-growing areas in California (Elphick & Oring 1998). Migratory birds are clearly an important component of the community, and no doubt these play a key role in the energy flow and nutrient cycle in the Cuban rice agro-ecosystem. The proximity of Cuban rice cultivation to roosting, resting and refuge areas in the coastal wetlands is also an important factor. That proximity allows the birds to use both ecosystems, natural and man-made, to provide their daily needs with relatively low energetic cost.

With the increasing problems of loss and degradation of natural wetland habitats, waterbirds will depend more and more on rice fields as an alternative habitat. In this case, the bird community is selecting an anthropogenic ecosystem, based on cues that have been historically associated with reproductive success in similar natural environments. We should keep in mind, however, that negative human interference through farming practices has the potential for drastically affecting wildlife associated with this habitat. For this reason, awareness of the issues surrounding waterbirds and the importance of rice culture to them was promoted among farmers and communities near the paddies through a recent environmental education campaign that involved about 8 000 people from two towns in rural areas. Cooperative efforts are necessary to understand the complex ecological interactions that are taking place in the paddies and to enhance this important waterbird habitat.

## ACKNOWLEDGEMENTS

We thank the organizations that financed our field research and environmental education program, including the American Museum of Natural History, Wilson Ornithological Society,

Wildlife Trust, Whitley Laing Foundation, Wetlands International, the Dutch Ministry of External Affairs, and The West Indian Whistling-Duck Working Group. We would also like to thank Jim Wiley for his revision of the manuscript.

## REFERENCES

**Acosta, M.** 1998. Segregación del nicho en la comunidad de aves del agroecosistema arrocero en Cuba. PhD thesis, University of Havana, Cuba.

**Acosta, M., Torres, O. & Mugica, L.** 1988. Subnicho trófico de *Dendrocygna bicolor* (Vieillot) Aves: Anatidae, en dos arroceras de Cuba. Ciencias Biológicas 19: 41-50.

**Acosta, M., Mugica, L. & Martinez, P.** 1990. Segregación del subnicho trófico en seis especies de Ciconiiformes cubanas. Ciencias Biológicas 23: 68-81.

**Acosta, M., Morales, J., Gonzalez, M. & Mugica, L.** 1992. Dinámica de la comunidad de aves de la Playa La Tinaja, Ciego de Avila, Cuba. Ciencias Biológicas 24: 44-58.

**Acosta, M., Mugica, L. & Valdés, S.** 1994. Estructura trófica de una comunidad de aves acuáticas. Ciencias Biológicas 27: 24-44.

**Acosta, M., Mugica, L., Mancina, C. & Ruiz, X.** 1996. Resource partitioning between Glossy Ibis and American White Ibis in a rice field system in south-central Cuba. Colonial Waterbirds 19(1): 65-72.

**Breininger, D. & Smith, R.** 1990. Waterbird use of coastal impoundments and management implications in east-central Florida. Wetlands 10(2): 223-241.

**Cody, M.L.** 1981. Habitat selection in birds: the roles of vegetation structure, competitors, and productivity. Bioscience 31: 107-111.

**Day, J.H. & Collwell, M.A.** 1998. Waterbird communities in rice fields subjected to different post harvest treatments. Colonial Waterbirds 21 (2): 185-197.

**Denis, D., Mugica, L., Acosta, M. & Jiménez, A.** 2000. Morfometría y alimentación del Aguaitacaimán (*Butorides virescens*) (Aves: Ardeidae) en 2 arroceras cubanas. Biología 14 (2): 133-140.

**Elphick, C.S.** 2000. Functional equivalency between rice fields and the semi-natural wetland habitat. Conservation Biology 14: 181-191.

**Elphick, C.S. & Oring, L.W.** 1998. Winter management of Californian rice fields for waterbirds. Journal of Applied Ecology 35: 95-108.

**Fasola, M. & Ruíz, X.** 1996. The value of rice fields as substitutes for natural wetlands for waterbirds in the Mediterranean region. Colonial Waterbirds 19 (1): 122-128.

**Fasola, M. & Ruiz, X.** 1997. Rice farming and waterbirds: integrated management in an artificial landscape. In: D.J. Pain & M.W. Pienkowski (eds) Farming and birds in Europe. Academic Press Ltd., London: 210-235.

**Hoffman, M.S.** (ed). 1993. The World Almanac. Pharos Books, New York.

**Mikuska, T., Kushlan, J.A. & Hartley, S.** 1998. Key areas of wintering North American Herons. Colonial Waterbirds 21 (2): 125-134.

**Mugica, L.** 2000. Estructura espacio temporal y relaciones energéticas en la comunidad de aves de la arrocera Sur del Jíbaro, Sancti Spiritus, Cuba. PhD thesis, University of Havana, Cuba.

**Mugica, L., Acosta, M. & Denis, D.** 2001. Dinámica temporal de la comunidad de aves asociada a la arrocera Sur del Jíbaro. Biología 15 (2): 86-97.

**Mugica, L., Acosta, M. & Denis, D.** 2003. Variaciones Espacio temporales y uso del hábitat por la comunidad de aves de la arrocera Sur del Jíbaro, Sancti Spiritus, Cuba. Biología 17(2): 105-113.

**Nagy, K.A.** 1987. Field Metabolic Rate and food requirement scaling in mammals and birds. Ecological Monographs 57: 111-128.

**Odum, E.P.** 1993. Ecology and our endangered life-support systems. Sinauer, Sunderland.

**Tourenq, C., Bennetts, R.E., Kowalski, H., Vialet, E., Lucchesi, J.L., Kayser, Y. & Isenmann, P.** 2001. Are rice fields a good alternative to natural marshes for waterbird communities in the Camargue, southern France? Biological Conservation 100: 335-343.

Short-billed Dowitcher *Limnodromus griseus*. Photo: Rob Robinson.

# Waterbird monitoring and conservation in protected areas of the Colombian Pacific

*Luis Germán Naranjo[1,2], Luis Fernando Castillo[1], Richard Johnston-González[1], Carlos Hernández[1], Carlos Ruiz[1] & Felipe Estela[1]*

[1] *Asociación para el estudio y conservación de las aves acuáticas de Colombia – Calidris, Cra 24F Oeete 3-25,*
*Barrio Tejares de San Fernand, Cali, Valle del Cauca 57, Colombia. (email: calidris@telesat.com.co)*
[2] *World Wildlife Fund, Colombia Office, Carrera 35 # 4A- 25 San Fernando, Cali, Colombia. (email: lgnaranjo@wwf.org.co)*

Naranjo, L.G., Castillo, L.F., Johnston-González, R., Hernández, C., Ruiz, C. & Estela, F. 2006. Waterbird monitoring and conservation in protected areas of the Colombian Pacific. *Waterbirds around the world.* Eds. G.C. Boere, C.A. Galbraith & D.A. Stroud. The Stationery Office, Edinburgh, UK. pp. 177-180.

## ABSTRACT

Three Colombian protected areas, the Malpelo Sanctuary and the Gorgona and Sanquianga National Parks, hold the largest known concentrations of Pelecaniformes and shorebirds in the country. The Waterbird Monitoring Program in Protected Areas of the Colombian Pacific was launched in order to establish baseline information on the population sizes of waterbirds and the conservation status of their habitats in these protected areas. Monthly estimates of the various species present at each of the three sites and observations of their reproductive activity allowed the identification of major breeding colonies, breeding cycles and factors influencing their local distribution. Sanquianga is the most important stopover site for shorebirds in the Colombian Pacific, with 20 000-30 000 individuals counted in September and October 2003. An estimated 18 000-23 000 Pelecaniformes have been recorded in this area, demonstrating its importance as a foraging and roosting site for both seabirds and shorebirds. The numbers of seabirds in Gorgona during 2003 fluctuated between 1 200 and 19 000, with the largest number occurring in July. Counts of the Nazca Booby *Sula granti* in the Malpelo Sanctuary confirmed that at least a quarter of the global population of this species nests in this virtually undisturbed area.

## INTRODUCTION

Fifty-seven percent of the species of waterbirds occurring in South America have resident populations in Colombia, and 98% of the migratory waterbirds from the Nearctic occur in the country (Naranjo 1997). Thirteen of these species are threatened to some degree: three at global level and ten at national level (Renjifo *et al.* 2002). Even though there is little information available on the population status of most species at local level, in some parts of the country, as many as 10% of the resident waterbird species are threatened to some extent (Restrepo & Naranjo 1987).

The Colombian Pacific coast is one of the most important areas for waterbirds in Colombia. Sixty percent of the species of waterbirds recorded to date in the country are found in this area (Salaman *et al.* 2001), including 71% of the shorebird species found in Colombia (Naranjo *et al.* 1998). The largest concentrations (both of species and individuals) have been recorded in three protected areas in the southern portion of the Colombian Pacific (Pitman *et al.* 1995, Naranjo *et al.* 1998, Johnston 2000, Castillo & Puyana 2005) where several species of Pelecaniformes nest on a regular basis (Johnston 2000, Cadena 2004, Ospina-Álvarez 2004, Cifuentes 2005). Unfortunately, the available information on population sizes and dynamics is

limited, and this has prevented the development of conservation and management plans for the protected areas that take into account the needs of these species.

In order to fill these gaps, in 2003/04 we initiated a waterbird monitoring program in three protected areas along the southern Pacific coast of Colombia. In each protected area, we estimated the population sizes of all seabirds and shorebirds present, and identified the major breeding colonies, roosting sites and foraging sites in each of the different habitats. In this paper, we present some preliminary results of this program and underline future waterbird research and conservation priorities for the Colombian Pacific.

## STUDY AREA

The Colombian Pacific coast is part of the Choco-Darien Eco-region Complex (Dinerstein *et al.* 1995), and stretches for about 1 300 km between 7°27'N and 1°27'N (Reyna & Solano 1996) (Fig. 1). Three National Protected Areas in the southern portion of this vast area cover all wetland types described for the region: sandy and rocky beaches, mudflats, mangroves and estuaries (Naranjo *et al.* 1998).

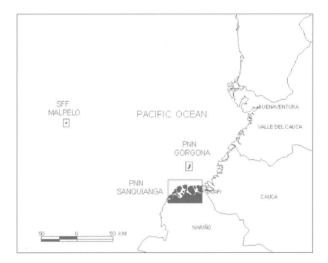

Fig. 1. Location of the three protected areas included in the study: Gorgona and Sanquianga National Parks (PNN) and Malpelo Flora and Fauna Sanctuary (SFF).

The different biophysical characteristics of these three sites, as well as their differing distances from the main harbors, suitability for infrastructure development and management regulations, have given rise to marked differences in resource use and conservation potential for waterbirds. Malpelo is a small

(3.5 km²) volcanic island, 500 km off the coast (Prahl 1990); it is permanently inhabited by five marines (Pitman *et al.* 1995). Gorgona is a small archipelago (617 km²), about 30 km off the coast (Díaz *et al.* 2001); its largest island (13.3 km²) is covered by dense rainforest. Much of the coastline of the main island and a number of small islets have cliffs and tall trees suitable for nesting seabirds. A prison was in operation for several decades on Gorgona Island, but this has been closed down and the archipelago has been declared a National Park; it is currently occupied by less than 20 people on a permanent basis. Sanquianga National Park covers 8 900 km² along a 60-km coastal strip, and is largely covered by dense mangroves. Several estuaries open to the sea within the limits of the park, and large mudflats as well as flooded forests are part of this complex mosaic of habitats. More than 10 000 people inhabit the area (Castaño-Uribe & Sguerra 1998).

## METHODS

We plotted the locations of the largest concentrations of waterbirds on 1:25 000 maps of the three protected areas, based on the published literature (Naranjo *et al.* 1998, Johnston 2000, Johnston *et al.* 2000), field surveys and information from local people. During the initial field trips, we carried out a topographical survey of each site using a GPS, and mapped the major habitats at a scale of 1:5 000.

In Sanquianga National Park, we made monthly censuses at one of the sites (Mulatos-Vigía) where we found the largest numbers of shorebirds, and counted birds at low tide in three different habitats (sandy beaches, mudflats and meadows) to determine the habitat preferences of each species.

Between July 2003 and April 2004, we carried out 51 banding sessions, for a total of 1 133 net/hours. We identified each captured bird to species level and, when possible, we also determined its sex, age, and stage of moult using various field guides (Prater *et al.* 1977, Hayman *et al.* 1986, Canevari *et al.* 2001). All birds were banded using US Fish & Wildlife Service metal rings and an individual combination of colour-bands that would allow us to determine the duration of stay of individual birds at selected sites.

We carried out a number of censuses of waterbirds and seabirds at several roosts and colonies located in the three protected areas. We visited Malpelo twice, on board a Colombian Navy research vessel, and made bird counts from all cliffs accessible on foot (Estela 2003). In Gorgona, we carried out censuses every two weeks from a boat cruising around the nesting colonies (Cadena 2004). In Sanquianga, we made monthly censuses at five roosts/colonies, both in the early morning and before sunset. We also made detailed observations on factors limiting habitat availability for certain nesting seabirds, namely Brown Booby *Sula leucogaster* in Gorgona (Ospina-Álvarez 2004) and in Sanquianga, Neotropic Cormorant *Phalacrocorax brasilianus* (Cifuentes 2005) and Gull-billed Tern *Sterna nilotica*.

## RESULTS

During the 2003/04 winter season, we found 28 species of shorebirds in Sanquianga. As a whole, this area (including the large mudflats located around the northern end of the buffer zone) harbored 20 000-30 000 shorebirds in September/October 2003. Shorebirds were distributed throughout suitable habitats, but were concentrated in two localities: the beaches of Mulatos-Vigía and a sandbar locally known as La Cunita. In these areas, we located three roosts used by Spotted Sandpiper *Actitis macularia* (c. 2 000-5 000), Western Sandpiper *Calidris mauri* (2 000-4 000), Whimbrel *Numenius phaeopus* (>1 000) and smaller numbers of other species.

Mudflats were used by most species, and supported the largest concentrations of shorebirds throughout the field season. Shorebird diversity increased in September and October, when some species made more intensive use of sandy beaches and meadows (Ruiz 2004). We recorded the largest numbers of shorebirds in February 2004, and the highest species diversity in September.

The combined total of Pelecaniformes in the three protected areas in 2003 was in the range 56 455-63 705 (Table 1). The Blue-footed Booby *Sula nebouxii* was much the most abundant species of Pelecaniformes in Gorgona and Sanquianga. The Brown Pelican *Pelecanus occidentalis* also occurred in large numbers at both these sites, while the numbers of Brown Booby were the largest known from any sites on the Pacific coast of Colombia. Gorgona and Sanquianga are only 30 km apart. The main flight directions of the birds and the similar seasonal variation in numbers at both sites suggest that these areas share the same populations, at least in part.

**Table 1. Estimated numbers of Pelecaniformes at three protected areas of the Colombian Pacific in 2003. Data were collected in July at Gorgona and Sanquianga and in October at Malpelo.**

| Species | Sanquianga* | Gorgona† | Malpelo‡ |
| --- | --- | --- | --- |
| Brown Pelican *Pelecanus occidentalis* | 2 000-4 000 | 4 800-5 200 | |
| Neotropic Cormorant *Phalacrocorax brasilianus* | 5 200-5 900 | | |
| Magnificent Frigatebird *Fregata magnificens* | c. 1 000 | 2 400-3 300 | |
| Blue-footed Booby *Sula nebouxii* | 10 000-12 000 | 10 800-11 900 | |
| Brown Booby *Sula leucogaster* | 100-200 | 130-180 | |
| Nazca Booby *Sula granti* | | | c. 20 000 |
| Red-footed Booby *Sula sula* | | | 25 |
| Total | 18 300-23 100 | 18 130-20 580 | c. 20 025 |

* Johnston *et al.* (unpubl. data); †Cadena (2004); ‡ Estela (2003).

## DISCUSSION

Our results confirm the importance of the protected areas along the southern part of the Colombian Pacific coast for shorebirds and Pelecaniformes, previously noted by Naranjo *et al.* (1998). Our counts of Nazca Booby *Sula granti* in Malpelo (c. 20 000) support the estimate by Renjifo *et al.* (2002) indicating that a quarter of the world's population nests in this protected area. Even though the numbers of nesting Pelecaniformes in Gorgona and Sanquianga are not particularly large at a global scale, these two areas are still important at regional level, according to the criteria of the Ramsar Wetlands Convention.

As expected from previous work, the largest concentrations of shorebirds were found on extensive mudflats (e.g. Franke 1987, Blanco *et al.* 2000), particularly in and around Sanquianga National Park (Morrison & Ross 1989). However, our data suggest that the local availability of natural meadows and artificial pastures may be important for some shorebird species, at least during exceptionally high tides or just after heavy rains when the number and size of ponds increase (Johnston *et al.* 2000). Both the spatial and temporal diversity of habitats seem to be greater in Sanquianga than in other areas of the Colombian Pacific, explaining the higher diversity and abundance of shorebirds in the National Park than elsewhere.

Our finding of large shorebird roosts in Sanquianga is noteworthy. As Naranjo & Mauna (1996) noted, the location of important shorebird roosts is patchy, and the availability of suitable habitat for roosting may be a factor influencing the population size of wintering shorebirds, even for species that, to our knowledge, have not been recorded roosting in large numbers, e.g. Spotted Sandpiper and Whimbrel.

Judging from previous information, our preliminary results indicate that the populations of migratory shorebirds and resident Pelecaniformes in these three protected areas are stable. However, a number of factors may pose important threats in some areas, and the combined effects of mangrove fragmentation and conversion, marine pollution, urban sprawl, uncontrolled tourism (Naranjo *et al.* 1998) and hunting (Johnston 2000, Cifuentes 2005) need to be evaluated, if we wish to ensure the continued survival of these important populations of seabirds and shorebirds.

Baseline information obtained during our project points in this direction, and can be used to strengthen local capacity to foresee and solve environmental problems. The three protected areas all meet several of the criteria necessary for their designation as Important Bird Areas (IBAs), and we have used our results to promote the adoption of this conservation category. At the same time, it is necessary to initiate the process leading to the inclusion of Sanquianga and the Cunita area within the Western Hemisphere Shorebird Reserve Network. Our data indicate that this area is a regionally important stopover for the largest number of shorebird species in Colombia. Several barrier islands and mudflats at the Guapi-Iscuandé river mouths close to Sanquianga National Park are important roosting and breeding sites both for Pelecaniformes and shorebirds. These areas are not protected and call for urgent attention.

## ACKNOWLEDGEMENTS

We thank local officers of the Colombian National Parks Unit in Malpelo, Sanquianga and Gorgona, local residents at Mulatos, La Vigía and Amarales, and the Colombian Navy for their logistic support and their hospitality. Help from several volunteers was vital to the success of the field trips. This project is supported by the Colombian National Parks Unit and the Colombian Environmental Action Fund. R. Johnston-González's participation in the Waterbirds Around the World Conference was made possible thanks to financial support from the organizers, the government of Belgium and the Colombian Environmental Action Fund.

## REFERENCES

**Blanco, J.F., Morales, G., Reyes, M. & de Ayala, R.M.** 2000. Dinámica temporal de la distribución y selección de hábitat de aves playeras en Punta Soldado, Pacífico Colombiano. Informe final. Fundación para la promoción de la Investigación y la Tecnología, Banco de la República, Proyecto 853A. Asociación Calidris, Santiago de Cali, Colombia.

**Cadena, G.** 2004. Distribución, abundancia y reproducción de las aves marinas (Pelecaniformes) en el PNN Gorgona durante el año 2003. BSc thesis, Universidad del Valle, Colombia.

**Canevari, P., Castro, G., Sallaberry, M. & Naranjo, L.G.** 2001. Guía de los chorlos y playeros de la región neotropical. American Bird Conservancy, WWF-US, Humedales para las Américas y Manomet Conservation Science, Asociación Calidris, Santiago de Cali, Colombia.

**Castaño-Uribe, C. & Sguerra, S.Y.** 1998. Plan operativo general, Manejo integral de los Parques Nacionales Naturales en el Chocó Biogeográfico. UAESPNN – Ministerio del Medio Ambiente. Santa Fé de Bogotá, Colombia.

**Castillo, L.F. & Puyana, J.** 2005. Colombia: Informe anual 2004. In: B. López-Lanús & D.E. Blanco (eds) El Censo Neotropical de Aves acuáticas 2004. Wetlands International Global Series No. 17. Buenos Aires, Argentina: 57-63.

**Cifuentes, Y.S.** 2005. Éxito reproductivo de *Phalacrocorax brasilianus* (Aves:Pelecaniformes) y su relación con la tala de Árboles en el Parque Nacional Natural Sanquianga, Nariño, Colombia. BSc thesis, Pontificia Universidad Javeriana, Bogotá, Colombia.

**Díaz, J.M., Pinzón, J.H., Perdomo, A.M., Barrios, L.M. & López-Victoria, M.** 2001. Generalidades. In: L.M.S. Barrios & M. López-Victoria (eds) Gorgona Marina: Contribución al conocimiento de una isla única. INVEMAR, serie publicaciones especiales No. 7. Santa Marta, Colombia: 21-25.

**Dinerstein, E., Olson, D.M., Graham, D.J., Webster, A.L., Primm, S.A., Booknider, M.P. & Ledec, G.** 1995. A conservation assessment of the terrestrial ecoregions of Latin America and the Caribbean. The World Bank, Washington, D.C.

**Estela, F.A.** 2003. Línea 5. Aves Marinas Comunidades. In: B.S.L. Beltrán (ed) Informe de actividades Crucero de Investigación Científica 0310 Isla Malpelo. Ministerio del Medio Ambiente, Vivienda y desarrollo territorial, UAESPNN, Santiago de Cali, Colombia: 21-25.

**Franke, R.** 1987. Uso habitacional de los chorlos (Aves: Scolopacidae y Charadriidae) en la Bahía de Buenaventura. Memorias del III Congreso de Ornitología Neotropical, Santiago de Cali, Colombia: 47-51.

**Hayman, P., Marchant, J. & Prater, T.** 1986. Shorebirds: an identification guide to the waders of the world. Houghton Mifflin Company, Boston, USA.

**Johnston, R.G.** 2000. Tamaño poblacional, hábitat y conservación del cormorán neotropical (*Phalacrocorax brasilianus*) en el Parque Nacional Natural Sanquianga (Nariño, Colombia). BSc thesis, Universidad del Valle, Colombia.

**Johnston, R., Angarita, I., Arbeláez, D. & Estela, F.A.** 2000. Expedición Calidris - Sanquianga 2000. UAESPNN – MA, Asociación Calidris, Santiago de Cali, Colombia.

**Morrison, R.I.G. & Ross, R.K.** 1989. Atlas of Nearctic shorebirds on the coast of South America. 2 vols. Canadian Wildlife Service Special Publication. Environment Canada, Ottawa, Ontario.

**Naranjo, L.G.** 1997. Avifauna acuática residente y migratoria en Colombia. In: Corpes Orinoquia (ed) Sabanas, vegas y palmares: Reflexiones sobre el uso sostenible del agua en la Orinoquia. Villavicencio, Colombia: 85-95.

**Naranjo, L.G. & Mauna, J.E.** 1996. Segregation of roosting habitat in migratory shorebirds on the Pacific Coast of Colombia. International Wader Studies 8: 52-54.

**Naranjo, L.G., Aparicio, A. & Falk, P.** 1998. Evaluación de áreas importantes para aves marinas y playeras en el litoral Pacífico colombiano. Informe final de la investigación presentado al Fondo FEN. Asociación Calidris, Santiago de Cali, Colombia.

**Ospina-Álvarez, A.** 2004. Ecología reproductiva y colonialidad del Piquero café *Sula leucogaster* (Aves: Sulidae), en el PNN Gorgona, Pacífico colombiano. BSc thesis, Universidad del Valle, Colombia.

**Pitman, R.L., Spear, L.B. & Force, M.P.** 1995. The marine birds of Malpelo Island, Colombia. Colonial Waterbirds 18 (1): 113-119.

**Prahl, V.H.** 1990. Malpelo, la roca viviente. El Fondo para la Protección del Medio Ambiente, FEN Colombia, Bogotá, Colombia.

**Prater, A.J., Marchant, J.H. & Vourinen, J.** 1977. Guide to identification and ageing of holarctic waders. British Trust for Ornithology 17.

**Rengifo, L.M., Franco-Maya, A.M., Amaya-Espinel, J.D., Kattan, G.H. & López-Lanús, B.** (eds). 2002. Libro rojo de aves de Colombia. Instituto de Investigaciones Biológicos Alexander von Humboldt y Ministerio del Medio Ambiente, Bogotá, Colombia.

**Restrepo, C. & Naranjo, L.G.** 1987. Recuento histórico de la disminución de humedales y la desaparición de aves acuáticas en el Valle geográfico del río Cauca. Memorias del III Congreso de Ornitología Neotropical. Santiago de Cali, Colombia: 43-45.

**Reyna, J.A. & Solano, J.E.** 1996. Informe Final Censo de Áreas de Bajamar Fase I (Nariño). Armada Nacional, DIMAR, Centro de Control de Contaminación del Pacífico, San Andrés de Tumaco, Colombia.

**Ruiz, C.J.** 2004. Distribución espacio-temporal y comportamiento de aves playeras en el Parque Nacional Natural Sanquianga (Nariño, Colombia). BSc thesis, Universidad del Atlántico, Barranquilla, Colombia.

**Salaman, P., Cuadros, T., Jaramillo, J.G. & Weber, W.H.** 2001. Checklist of the birds of Colombia. Sociedad Antioqueña de Ornitología, Medellín, Colombia.

Peruvian Brown Pelicans *Pelecanus thagus* and Peruvian Boobies *Sula variegata*. Photo: Paul Marshall.

# Important areas for waterbirds on the Pacific coast of Colombia

*Luis Germán Naranjo[1,2], Alexandra Aparicio[1,3] & Patricia Falk[1]*

[1] *Asociación Calidris, Carrera 24 F Oeste # 3-25, Tejares de San Fernando, Cali, Colombia.*

[2] *WWF-Programa Colombia, Carrera 35 # 4A- 25 San Fernando, Cali, Colombia. (email: lgnaranjo@wwf.org.co)*

[3] *Organization for Tropical Studies, Apdo. 676-2050, San Pedro, Costa Rica.*

Naranjo, L.G., Aparicio, A. & Falk, P. 2006. Important areas for waterbirds on the Pacific coast of Colombia. *Waterbirds around the world*. Eds. G.C. Boere, C.A. Galbraith & D.A. Stroud. The Stationery Office, Edinburgh, UK. pp. 181-182.

From late 1996 to early 1998, an assessment of waterbird populations on the Pacific coast of Colombia was carried out in order to identify important breeding areas for resident species, foraging and roosting sites for migratory shorebirds, and potential threats to the habitats used by waterbirds along the coast. The most abundant resident species were Brown Pelican *Pelecanus occidentalis*, Neotropical Cormorant *Phalacrocorax brasilianus*, Magnificent Frigatebird *Fregata magnificens* and Brown Booby *Sula leucogaster*, while Semipalmated Plover *Charadrius semipalmatus*, Wilsons' Plover *C. wilsonius*, Whimbrel *Numenius phaeopus*, Spotted Sandpiper *Actitis macularia*, Western Sandpiper *Calidris mauri*, Ruddy Turnstone *Arenaria interpres*, Laughing Gull *Larus atricilla* and Royal Tern *Sterna maxima* were the most abundant migratory species. Major threats identified included habitat conversion, pollution, and disturbance from human activities.

Colombia has a high diversity of bird species, including many wetland dependent species. Of South American waterbirds 57% have resident populations in the country and 98% of migratory North American waterbirds use Colombian wetlands.

Previous studies have shown the regional importance of the Colombian Pacific coast for the conservation of coastal birds. Of shorebirds wintering in Colombia, 75% use the Pacific coast, and 83-92% of species are concentrated in the mangroves south of this coast (Morrison & Ross 1989). It has been suggested that this area is of hemispherical importance at least for Spotted Sandpiper (Hernández 1996). The biggest breeding colony of Brown Pelican *murphyi* in Colombia is on Gorgona Island off the southern coast. One of the biggest breeding colonies of Masked Booby *Sula dactylatra* is on Malpelo Island together with populations of Red-footed Booby *S. sula*, Brown Noddy *Anous stolidus*, Black Noddy *A. minutus* and Swallow-tailed Gull *Creasurus furcatus*. However, much of the available evidence is anecdotal, old, or without a rigorous system of data collection.

This study reviewed 24 sites (10 marine and 14 estuarine wetlands) along the Colombian Pacific coast between late 1996 and early 1998. Wetlands were characterized and counts made along the coast during the austral and boreal winters. Human pressures on the wetlands were identified from interviews with local communities, and classified according to the categories listed in Ramsar Convention protocols.

Eighty species of 16 families were recorded. Most waterbird species recorded were non-breeding residents with only 11% of these species nesting in the region. Proportionately, 26% of species came from the interior of North America, 23% from the Arctic, and only 3% from the North American Atlantic seaboard. Eight key breeding areas for seabirds were identified as were four foraging areas for shorebirds. Three major types of potential

Red-footed Booby *Sula sula*. Photo: Allan Drewitt.

Masked Booby *Sula dactylatra*. Photo: Allan Drewitt.

threats to waterbirds were recognised:

- human activities that change the landscape, e.g. infrastructure construction and mangrove deforestation. The sites most severely disturbed were Buenaventura Bay and Tumaco, both key foraging areas and roosts for shorebirds;
- pollution, e.g. oil spills, insecticides used in malaria eradication programs, heavy metals from gold and silver mines and organic discharges, with Buenaventura and Tumaco bays and the complex Naya estuary-Timbiquí most severely affected; and
- disturbance by human activities that directly and immediately affect waterbird populations, e.g. boat movements, fisheries, hunting and unregulated tourism.

Winter residents included almost all shorebird species from Alaska and the Canadian Arctic, the interior of the United States and Canada, and from the Atlantic coast of North America. Most tern species recorded have breeding populations in other Pacific regions as well as in Central America and the Caribbean area. The presence of species from the Atlantic on the Colombian Pacific coast indicate that the Gulf of Mexico flyway is linked with the Pacific flyway through birds moving across the Panama isthmus.

Climatic variations such as the El Niño - Southern Oscillation event (ENSO) affect the distribution and reproductive success and cause mortality in some species. The presence of species such as Guanay Cormorant *Phalacrocorax bouganvilli*, Peruvian Booby *Sula variegata* and Inca Tern *Larosterna inca* in some years, the massive mortality of Blue-footed Booby *Sula nebouxii* and the almost total absence of shorebirds in some localities in 1997, can be attributed to ENSO effects. Although ENSO is a natural cyclic phenomenon, it can be a severe threat to waterbirds when its effects are combined with the other pressures described above.

Further research to fill information gaps, particularly monitoring specific populations over time are recommended to:

- determine the status of residence of oceanic species;
- determine the factors that affect the reproductive success of resident waterbirds;
- evaluate the populations' responses to environmental stress; and
- monitor the phenology and population numbers of migratory species threatened on a global or regional scale.

The results of this study show the importance for collaboration in the region to understand migratory patterns of species using the Pacific Flyway.

## REFERENCES

**Hernández, C.E.** 1996. Aspectos de la invernada del playerito moteado (*Actitis macularia*) en Punta Soldado, Pacífico colombiano. Tesis de grado en Biología, Universidad del Valle, Colombia.

**Morrison, R.I.G. & Ross, R.K.**. 1989. Atlas of Nearctic shorebirds on the coast of South America. Volume 1-2. Canadian Wildlife Service Special Publication, Ottawa.

Ruddy Turnstone *Arenaria interpres* are abundant on the Pacific coast of Columbia. Photo: Rob Robinson.

# Status of the Black-necked Swan *Cygnus melancorypha* and Coscoroba Swan *Coscoroba coscoroba* in the south of Brazil

*Joao Oldair Menegheti[1] & Joao Carlos Dotto[2]*

*[1]National University of the Rio Grande do Sul, Brazil. (email: meneghet@ufrgs.br)*

*[2]State Foundation of Environmental Protection of the Rio Grande do Sul, Brazil. (email: dottojc@terra.com.br)*

Menegheti, J.O. & Dotto, J.C. 2006. Status of the Black-necked Swan *Cygnus melancorypha* and Coscoroba Swan *Coscoroba coscoroba* in the south of Brazil. *Waterbirds around the world.* Eds. G.C. Boere, C.A. Galbraith & D.A. Stroud. The Stationery Office, Edinburgh, UK. pp. 183-184.

Rio Grande do Sul is the southernmost state of Brazil, situated between 27°03' to 33°45'S and 49°42' to 57°40' W. It has a transitional tropical and subtropical climate, and borders Argentina and Uruguay. Often, in the austral winter, incursions of polar air abruptly change the temperature, rainfall and relative humidity. There is no dry season and rainfall is distributed throughout the year.

This study provides an overview of the current status of the Black-necked Swan *Cygnus melancorypha* and Coscoroba Swans *Coscoroba coscoroba* in the south of Brazil. The Black-necked Swan occurs from Chile and Argentina up to Rio Grande do Sul state, Brazil, occasionally reaching the south of Sao Paulo state and Rio de Janeiro state; the Coscoroba Swan occurs from Patagonia and Chile to Paraguay and Brazil (Nascimento *et al.* 2001).

Annual transect surveys, each lasting about 16 hours, were conducted by helicopter throughout the Coastal Plain of southern Brazil, in late September and early October from 1995 to 2003. Both artificial and natural water bodies were fully surveyed and each was treated as a counting point. The mean annual length of transect was 1 201.56 km, with a 3.15% variation in length between years. The mean annual surface area of water body counting points was 72.72 km$^2$, with a 6.62% variation between years. For big flocks of swans, the number of individuals was estimated, with photographs taken for later verification.

Cox-Stuart tests were used to assess trends, but probabilities associated with the tests indicated an insufficient number of pairs of annual counts (p=0.625) with only four early-later total counts per species being derived. However, a semi-quantitative approach suggests an increasing trend in numbers of both Black-necked and Coscoroba Swans in southern Brazil, since three times as many count pairs showed an increase as showed a decrease. It appears that neither species is decreasing in Rio Grande do Sul. This is consistent with the biogeographic population status assessments made by Schlatter and Canevari in Wetlands International (2002).

In the Rio Grande do Sul Coastal Plain, Black-necked Swans were more abundant than Coscoroba Swans in six of the nine years between 1995 and 2003 (Table 1). Both species are considerably more abundant in the Coastal Plain than other regions of Rio Grande do Sul, but both also occur in the western and southwestern parts of the state (Table 1). However, there were more Black-necked Swans in the southwestern region than in the western region, where it was recorded in only one year (1996), it probably reaches the southwestern region via the Jaguarão river from the coastal plain. The Coscoroba Swan was common in all three regions, but in the western region largely occurred on a single large water reservoir, Sanchuri, where 149 birds were counted in September 2003. This species is known to colonize new water bodies, and the completion of the Rio Negro dam in Uruguay soon attracted Coscoroba Swans (Sick 1972). It is unclear why the Black-necked Swan has not colonized Sanchuri reservoir, since evidence from Chile indicates that the species is also an opportunistic colonizer, e.g. following an earthquake in 1960 a new wetland (Rio Cruces Sanctuary) formed which was soon colonized by Black-necked Swans which had previously been absent from the region (Schlatter *et al.* 2002).

Elsewhere in their range, relative abundance varies but Black-necked Swans are mostly more abundant than Coscoroba Swans. In Uruguay Black-necked Swans were far more abundant

**Table 1.** Total aerial counts of the Black-necked Swan *Cygnus melancorypha* and Coscoroba Swan *Coscoroba coscoroba* in the Coastal Plain, Western and Southwestern regions of the Rio Grande do Sul state, Brazil in austral spring (late September/early October) from 1995 to 2003.

| Year | Coastal Plain Black-necked Swan | Coastal Plain Coscoroba Swan | Western Region Black-necked Swan | Western Region Coscoroba Swan | Southwestern Region Black-necked Swan | Southwestern Region Coscoroba Swan |
|---|---|---|---|---|---|---|
| 1995 | 2 446 | 879 | 0 | 112 | 0 | 10 |
| 1996 | 4 050 | 1 758 | 1 | 396 | 77 | 29 |
| 1997 | 2 348 | 439 | 0 | 211 | 0 | 17 |
| 1998 | 106 | 292 | 0 | 26 | 0 | 4 |
| 1999 | 4 617 | 1 327 | 0 | 55 | 4 | 48 |
| 2000 | 4 372 | 1 902 | 0 | 59 | 187 | 253 |
| 2001 | 1 606 | 768 | 0 | 2 | 19 | 60 |
| 2002 | 323 | 7 420 | 0 | 19 | 4 | 26 |
| 2003 | 3 366 | 4 356 | 0 | 149 | 50 | 141 |

**Table 2. Austral winter and austral summer total counts of the Black-necked Swan *Cygnus melancorypha* and Coscoroba Swan *Coscoroba coscoroba* in Chile from 1990-1999. Data are from the Neotropical Waterbird Census.**

| Year | Austral winter | | Austral summer | |
| | Black-necked Swan | Coscoroba Swan | Black-necked Swan | Coscoroba Swan |
|---|---|---|---|---|
| 1990 | 5 075 | 77 | - | - |
| 1991 | 2 043 | 0 | - | - |
| 1992 | 14 471 | 1 491 | - | - |
| 1993 | 8 792 | 1 154 | 22 | 0 |
| 1994 | 3 351 | 13 | 1 683 | 16 |
| 1995 | 7 458 | 39 | 1 121 | 27 |
| 1996 | 16 535 | 1 963 | 12 969 | 155 |
| 1997 | 2 080 | 55 | 18 265 | 187 |
| 1998 | 6 774 | 0 | 4 121 | 94 |
| 1999 | 1 827 | 0 | 4 535 | 21 |

**Table 3. Austral winter and austral summer total counts of the Black-necked Swan *Cygnus melancorypha* and Coscoroba Swan *Coscoroba coscoroba* in Argentina from 1990-1999. Data are from the Neotropical Waterbird Census.**

| Year | Austral winter | | Austral summer | |
| | Black-necked Swan | Coscoroba Swan | Black-necked Swan | Coscoroba Swan |
|---|---|---|---|---|
| 1990 | 8 055 | 12 195 | - | - |
| 1991 | 908 | 1 096 | - | - |
| 1992 | 10 400 | 17 159 | 31 095 | 7 713 |
| 1993 | 551 | 4 317 | 3 921 | 3 502 |
| 1994 | 1 587 | 2 502 | 16 379 | 8 971 |
| 1995 | 850 | 2 730 | 20 336 | 20 071 |
| 1996 | 291 | 3 504 | 1 589 | 1 787 |
| 1997 | 495 | 852 | 1 036 | 2 259 |
| 1998 | 1 224 | 6 564 | 1 537 | 11 915 |
| 1999 | 289 | 4 074 | 2 904 | 11 866 |

in October 1987 (8 900 birds compared to only 319 Coscoroba Swans, counted by plane – Gambarotta unpublished); and most of the estimated total of 4 000 swans counted on the Laguna de Rocha were Black-necked (Morrison & Ross 1989). Similarly, in Chile Black-necked Swans were consistently the more abundant species in both the austral winter and summer in the 1990s (Table 2), although coverage in some parts of the range of the Coscoroba Swan (Araya & Millie, 1996) was poor. However, in Argentina whilst Black-necked Swans were often the more abundant species in summer, in winter Coscoroba Swans were considerably more abundant in all years from 1990-1999 (Table 3).

## REFERENCES

**Araya, B. & Holman, G.M.** 1996. Guía de Campo de las Aves de Chile. Editorial Universitaria, Santiago, Chile. 400 p.

**Gambarotta, J.C.** Unpublished. Un censo de coscoroba *Coscoroba coscoroba*, cisne de cuello negro *Cygnus melancoryphus* y flamenco *Phoenicopterus chilensis* en Uruguay. Technical Report. 12 pp.

**Menegheti J.O., Rilla, F. & Burger, M.I.** 1990. Waterfowl in South America: their status, trends and distribution. Proceedings of an IWRB Symposium, Astrakhan, USSR, 2-5 October 1989. IWRB Special Publication No. 12: 97-103. Slimbridge, U.K

**Morrison, R.I.G. & Ross, R.K.** 1989. Atlas of Nearctic shorebirds on the coast of South America. Uruguay. C.WS. Special Publication, Ottawa. Vol. 2: 213-217.

**Schlatter, R.P., Navarro, R.A. & Corti, P.** 2002. Effects of El Niño Southern Oscillation on numbers of Black-necked swans at Río Cruces Sanctuary, Chile. Waterbirds 25 (Special Publication 1): 114-122.

**Sick, H.** 1972. A ameaça da avifauna brasileira. Pp. 99-153. In: Academia Brasileira de Ciências (ed.). Espécies da Fauna Brasileira Ameaçadas de extinção, Rio de Janeiro, Brazil. 174 pp.

**Wetlands International** 2002. Waterbird Population Estimates. Third edition. Wetlands International Global Series No. 12. Wageningen, The Netherlands.

# Opportunism required – migratory shorebirds at variable tidal flats in the northeast of Brazil

*Kerstin Kober*

*Center for Marine Tropical Ecology, Fahrenheitstr. 6, 28359 Bremen, Germany. (email: kkober@gmx.de)*

Kober, K. 2006. Opportunism required – migratory shorebirds at variable tidal flats in the northeast of Brazil. *Waterbirds around the world.* Eds. G.C. Boere, C.A. Galbraith & D.A. Stroud. The Stationery Office, Edinburgh, UK. p. 185.

In contrast to the widespread assumption that tropical tidal flats provide a stable food stock for wintering shorebirds (Wolff 1991), recent investigations demonstrate that the abundance of prey in the tropics may show considerable variability (de Goeij *et al.* 2003). Nevertheless, birds which prepare for migration rely on sufficiently abundant and regularly available food stocks. How do they cope with such tropical variability?

This study describes investigations of shorebird ecology on the tropical tidal flats of the Bragantinian peninsula on the northern coast of Brazil between January and June in 2001/2002. Methods of this PhD study are described in Kober (2004). The studied section of the coast is regarded as part of one of the most important wintering areas in South America and shorebirds use this area in spring to accumulate reserves prior to a transoceanic flight to North America (Morrison & Ross 1989).

The tidal flats of the Bragantinian peninsula are characterized by strong variability. Powerful tidal currents with a heavy sediment load generate a small scale mosaic of fluctuating sediment conditions. The pore water salinity of the sediments is altered significantly through the input of fresh water during the rainy season. Presumably as a result of these fluctuations and disturbances, total densities and biomasses of the benthic organisms are low in comparison with other tropical areas. Moreover, a large fraction of the benthic biomass is provided by large molluscs and crustaceans which are too large to be eaten by most shorebirds. Consequently, the food stock available to the birds is extremely low. In addition, the abundance of individual benthic taxa showed high temporal and spatial variability, such that most benthic taxa were frequently unavailable to the birds.

Bird abundance varied seasonally since the majority of the birds were North American migrants, present only during the northern winter. Although their spatial distribution was associated with specific locations, there was noticeable variation which was only weakly related to abiotic factors and prey abundances. Shorebirds showed preferences for certain prey groups, but diets were generally broad. It is assumed that birds in such a poor and variable environment have to forage opportunistically on a large variety of prey items in order to avoid food shortages and the risk of starvation.

## REFERENCES

de Goeij, P., Lavanleye, M., Pearson, G.B. & Piersma, T. 2003. Seasonal changes in the macro-zoobenthos of a tropical mudflat. NIOZ-Report 2003-4. Royal Netherlands Institute for Sea Research (NIOZ) and W.A. Department of Conservation and Land Management. Texel.

Kober, K. 2004. Foraging ecology and habitat use of wading birds and shorebirds in the mangrove ecosystem of the Caeté Bay, Northeast Pará, Brazil. PhD Thesis, Centre of Marine Tropical Ecology, University of Bremen. Bremen.

Morrison, R.I.G. & Ross, R.K. 1989. Atlas of Nearctic shorebirds on the coast of South America. Canadian Wildlife Service, Ottawa.

Wolff, W.J. 1991. The interaction of benthic macrofauna and birds in tidal flat estuaries: a comparison of the Banc d'Arguin, Mauritania, and some estuaries in the Netherlands, p. 299-306. In: Elliot, M. & Ducrotoy, J.-P. [eds.], Estuaries and coasts: Spatial and temporal inter-comparisons. Ohlson & Ohlson, Fredensborg.

As in north-east Brazil, the tidal flats of Suriname are important wintering areas for waders breeding in North America. Photo: Gerard Boere.

# Biodiversity and conservation in the Bañados del Este, southeastern Uruguay

*Adrian B. Azpiroz [1] & Francisco Rilla [2]*

[1]*Department of Biology, R 223, University of Missouri-St. Louis, One University Blvd., St. Louis, MO 63121, USA.*
[2]*CMS/UNEP, Hermann-Ehlers Str. 10, 53113 Bonn, Germany. (email: frilla@cms.int)*

Azpiroz, A.B. & Rilla, F. 2006. Biodiversity and conservation in the Bañados del Este, southeastern Uruguay. *Waterbirds around the world*. Eds. G.C. Boere, C.A. Galbraith & D.A. Stroud. The Stationery Office, Edinburhg, UK. pp. 186-187.

Uruguay, in south-eastern South America, lies within a biogeographical crossroad (*sensu* Spector 2002), where several typical South American biomes meet: the Pampas, the Chaco and the Paranaense forests. The south-eastern part of the country, known as Bañados del Este (BDE), is characterized by extensive freshwater and coastal ecosystems of very significant regional importance. Aquatic habitats include a long strip of Atlantic seashore, coastal sand dunes, coastal lagoons (both freshwater and brackish), mudflats, numerous rivers and streams, inland marshes, and palm swamps. Additionally, the landscape supports extensive areas of grasslands and forests, the latter developing along fast flowing water courses (gallery forests) and on hilly sierras ("bosque serrano"). These form a complex mosaic providing a large variety of habitats for both resident and migratory species, supporting approximately 75% of the country's bird species (Azpiroz 2001).

Although BDE harbours a diverse array of migratory animals, including cetaceans, birds, turtles, fish, and crustaceans (PROBIDES 1999), birds are by far the best studied group, with at least 170 taxa identified. Migratory birds include: 1) Austral migrants breeding in Patagonia and Southern Atlantic islands during the austral summer, moving northwards for the winter. These include several Patagonian passerines and many marine birds (e.g. penguins, albatrosses, petrels) that make extensive use of wet grasslands, and costal waters. 2) Nearctic species, most of which breed in northern North America during the boreal summer and migrate to South America during the austral summer. Most are shorebirds using mudflats surrounding coastal brackish lagoons, seashores and grasslands as feeding grounds. Some species stay in BDE for the whole wintering season, others also use higher latitude destinations. 3) Neotropical migrants

The Band-tailed or Olrog's Gull *Larus atlanticus*, a globally threatened species, is one of many austral migrants that use the Bañados del Este coastal habitats during the austral winter. Photo: Adrian Azpiroz.

breeding in this region during the austral summer and flying northwards for the winter. Most species are insectivorous passerines using diverse terrestrial habitats (Azpiroz 2001). In addition to these "latitudinal" migrants, several other species of waterfowl (e.g. swans and ducks) make regular "horizontal" movements between the large wetland habitats of South America's southern cone (Argentina, Brazil, Chile and Uruguay) (Belton 1984, Arballo & Cravino 1999). The brackish lagoons located along the coast are South America's most important coastal site for American Golden Plover *Pluvialis dominica* (Morrison & Ross 1989). Upland and wet grasslands provide breeding habitat for several threatened capuchino seedeaters *Sporophila palustris, S. cinnamomea, S. zelichi* (Stattersfield *et al.* 1998, Azpiroz 2003). The large water bodies, scattered throughout the region, offer feeding, resting and breeding habitat for many regional migratory waterfowl, such as Coscoroba Swan *Coscoroba coscoroba* and Black-necked Swan *Cygnus melanocoryphus* (Vaz-Ferreira & Rilla 1991).

The importance of the region has been nationally and internationally recognized. It has a Biosphere Reserve (UNESCO), a Wetland of International Importance (Ramsar Convention) and is being considered for addition to the Western Hemisphere Shorebird Reserve Network (WHSRN), which would recognize BDE as a crucial link within the set of key sites of continental importance for migratory shorebirds (Rilla 1993, Blanco & Carbonell 2001).

Although relatively large expanses of pristine habitats still remain, the region is threatened by human activities that have already caused considerable habitat loss and fragmentation. Wetlands have been drained for large-scale development of rice

The White-rumped Sandpiper *Calidris fuscicollis* is probably the most common Nearctic shorebird species in the Bañados del Este. Photo: Adrian Azpiroz.

The Marsh Seedeater *Sporophila palustris* is one of the many globally threatened species that inhabit the region. This species breeds in the Bañados del Este during the austral summer and moves to lower latitudes afterwards. Photo: Adrian Azpiroz.

fields, and cattle ranching has resulted in the replacement of tall grass by short grass species (Bucher & Nores 1988). Agricultural activities and their associated infrastructures (irrigation channels, mini-dams, road networks, etc.) have altered the hydrology (PROBIDES 1999). Forestry activity has increased substantially in recent years, mostly for pulp production, and problems at the coast include tourism encroachment and urban development (Canevari *et al.* 2001) resulting in many illegal settlements. Marine life, in particular sea turtles, is threatened by artisanal and recreational fisheries (López-Mendilaharsu *et al.* 2003).

Although most of Uruguay's effectively protected areas are located within BDE, these are still too few and too small to adequately protect the region's biodiversity. Moreover, the possibility of expanding the current protected area network is particularly limited as most of the land (c. 95%) is privately owned. Thus, the development of conservation activities targeting land-use changes must necessarily involve the active participation of landowners and the private sector.

Substantial additional research is necessary to characterize the processes that maintain the biodiversity values of BDE, and long-term studies are required to establish trends in population sizes and to understand the ecological processes behind species' declines. Finally, the lack of a clear environmental regulatory framework has resulted in contradictory government land-use

policies and limited law enforcement. The implementation of effective conservation measures will largely depend on the ability to address these political issues.

## REFERENCES

**Arballo, E. & Cravino, J.** 1999. Aves del Uruguay. Manual Ornitológico. Editorial Hemisferio Sur, Montevideo, Uruguay.

**Azpiroz, A.B.** 2001. Aves del Uruguay. Lista e introducción a su biología y conservación. Aves Uruguay-Gupeca, Montevideo, Uruguay.

**Azpiroz, A.B.** 2003. Primeros registros del Capuchino de Collar (*Sporophila zelichi*) en Uruguay. Ornitología Neotropical 14: 117-119.

**Belton, W.** 1984. Birds of Rio Grande do Sul, Brazil. Part I. Rheidae through Furnariidae. Bulletin of the American Museum of Natural History 178(4): 369-636.

**Blanco, D.E. & Carbonell, M.** (eds.). 2001. The Neotropical Waterbird Census. The first 10 years: 1990-1999. Wetlands International, Buenos Aires, Argentina & Ducks Unlimited, Inc. Memphis.

**Bucher, E.H. & Nores, M.** 1988. Present status of birds in steppes and savannas of northern and central Argentina. In: P.D. Goriup (ed.). Ecology and Conservation of Grassland Birds. ICBP Technical Publication No. 7. International Council for Bird Preservation, Cambridge, UK: 71-79.

**Canevari, P., Davidson I., Blanco D.E., Castro G. & Bucher, E.H.** 2001. Los humedales de America del Sur: una agenda para la conservación de la biodiversidad y las políticas de desarrollo. Wetlands International, Wageningen, The Netherlands.

**López-Mendilaharsu, M., Bauzá, A., Laporta, M., Caraccio, M.N., Lezama, C., Calvo, V., Hernández, M., Estrades, A., Aisenberg, A. & Fallabrino, A.** 2003. Review and Conservation of Sea Turtles in Uruguay: Foraging habitats, distribution, causes of mortality, education and regional integration. Final Report: British Petroleum Conservation Programme.

**Morrison, R.I.G. & Ross, R.K.** 1989. Atlas of Nearctic shorebirds on the coast of South America. Two volumes. Canadian Wildlife Service, Ottawa, Canada.

**PROBIDES** 1999. Plan Director Reserva de Biosfera Bañados del Este. Rocha, Uruguay.

**Rilla, F.** 1993. Humedales del sureste del Uruguay: situación actual y perspectivas. ICONA, Madrid, Spain.

**Spector, S.** 2002. Biogeographic crossroads as priority areas for biodiversity conservation. Conservation Biology 16(6): 1480-1487.

**Stattersfield, A.J., Crosby, M.J., Long, A.J. & Wege, D.C.** 1998. Endemic Bird Areas of the World. Priorities for biodiversity conservation. BirdLife Conservation Series No.7. BirdLife International, Cambridge, UK.

**Vaz-Ferreira, R. & Rilla, F.** 1991. Black-necked Swans (*Cygnus melancoryphus*) and Coscoroba Swan (*Coscoroba coscoroba*) in a wetland in Uruguay. Wildfowl, Supplement 1: 272-277.

# Abundance, distribution and migration chronology of shorebirds on exposed sandy beaches of south central Chile

*Alexandra Aparicio*[1,2]

[1] *Instituto de Zoología, Universidad Austral de Chile, Casilla 567, Valdivia, Chile.*

[2] *Present address: Organization for Tropical Studies, Apdo. 676-2050, San Pedro, Costa Rica.*

Aparicio, A. 2006. Abundance, distribution and migration chronology of shorebirds on exposed sandy beaches of south central Chile. *Waterbirds around the world*. Eds. G.C. Boere, C.A. Galbraith & D.A. Stroud. The Stationery Office, Edinburgh, UK. p. 188.

The south-central Chilean coast (c. 38°-42°S) is characterized by sandy beaches alternating with inter-tidal flats and rocky shores (Jaramillo 2000). This diversity of habitats, combined with the abundance of potential prey for shorebirds, suggests that the region can support boreal migratory species during their migration to wintering areas in the south, and austral species in their migration to warmer zones of South America. However, basic aspects of the migration of some of these species, such as how many and which sites are used as stopover areas or distances migrated, are still unknown. It has not been clear whether or not this zone is included in migratory routes. Apart from work by Morrison & Ross (1989) on the hemispheric importance of some areas in central and south Chile, the sandy beaches located on the route between the wintering and breeding areas of some migratory species have scarcely been studied. This study evaluates the use of sandy beaches in south-central Chile as stopover areas for shorebirds. A total of 11 shorebird species were recorded, of which five were boreal migrants. Although the number of boreal species was lower than austral species, boreal species were the greater component of this shorebird assemblage, with significantly more individuals.

The study was carried out on five exposed sandy beaches in the south-central Chilean littoral zone near Valdivia (c. 39°S; Curiñanco, Calfuco, La Misión, San Ignacio and Chaihuín) from October 2000 to December 2001, and February 2002. Fortnightly censuses were conducted on each of the beaches during days with spring tides, four times per day on each beach, from high tide to low tide.

Three groups of species were identified: i) "boreal migrants" (Hayes 1995): Whimbrel *Numenius phaeopus*, Sanderling *Calidris alba*, Baird's Sandpiper *C. bairdii*, Surfbird *Aphriza virgata* and Turnstone *Arenaria interpres;* ii) "austral migrants" (Hayes 1995): Rufous-chested Dotterel *Charadrius modestus*, Collared Plover *C. collaris*, Two-banded Plover *C. falklandicus*, Blackish Oystercatcher *Haematopus ater* and Magellanic Oystercatcher *H. leucopodus;* and iii) residents: American Oystercatcher *H. palliatus*. Although the number of boreal species was lower than austral species, there were significantly more boreal individuals counted ($t_{129}$ = 4.74, p < 0.005).

The abundance of boreal migrants was highest in late October 2000 and late February 2001. Austral migrants arrived between March and August, with their abundance relatively constant during the migratory season.

Shorebird assemblages were variable due to a) species arriving from the Northern Hemisphere during the austral spring and summer and b) species from the south arriving during the austral autumn and winter. This explains the greater species richness found in austral winter, when austral species were joined with boreal species that remained in the area. The first abundance peak, October, corresponded to birds arriving from breeding areas in the Northern Hemisphere during the southward migration. The second peak, February, coincides with the return trip of these species to the north of the continent in the northward migration.

Baird's Sandpiper and Surfbirds are examples of species using different migratory routes. The presence of Baird's Sandpiper only during the southward migration suggests this species uses one route during its trip south and another during its return northward migration. In contrast, Surfbirds did not stop in the study area during southward migration but during northward migration in February it used this zone for a short stop. Based on the findings of Vilina & López-Callejas (1996), Tabilo *et al.* (1996) and this work, it appears that the migratory population of Rufous-chested Dotterel disperses and winters on an extensive sector of the Chilean coast, and the number of wintering individuals diminishes towards the north. While there is little information about Collared Plover populations, seasonally fluctuating numbers suggest that the individuals recorded in the study area are part of a migratory population.

In general, the greatest number of birds was recorded at the larger beaches close to other habitats, with no significant concentrations of shorebirds on sandy beaches. However, the results suggest the importance of the zone for migratory shorebirds as the region's system of rivers, inter-tidal beaches and flats offer a diversity of habitats in a relatively small area.

Funding was provided by DID (DID -2001-02), Escuela de Graduados de la Facultad de Ciencias and Instituto de Zoología de la Universidad Austral de Chile, and DAAD (A-98-11018) Doctoral Fellowship. Final analyses and writing were supported with funding from the Barva Transect TEAM Project.

## REFERENCES

Hayes, F.E. 1995. Definitions for migrant birds: what is a neotropical migrant? Auk 112: 521-523.

Jaramillo, E. 2000. The sand beach ecosystem of Chile. In: U. Seeliger, L. Drude de Lacerda & B. Kjerfve (eds.) Coastal Marine Ecosystems of Latin America. Springer-Verlag, Germany.

Morrison, R.I.G. & Ross, R.K. 1989. Atlas of Nearctic shorebirds on the coast of South America. Volume 1-2. Canadian Wildlife Service Special Publication, Ottawa.

Tabilo, E., Jorge, R., Riquelme, R., Moncada, A., Labra, C., Campusano, J., Tabilo, M., Varela, M., Tapia, A. & Sallaberry, M. 1996. Management and conservation of the habitats used by migratory shorebirds at Coquimbo, Chile. International Wader Studies 8: 79-84.

Vilina, Y.A. & López Callejas, M.V. 1996. The Neotropical plovers of Estero El Yali in central Chile. International Wader Studies 8: 85-92.

# The conservation status of migratory waterbirds in Argentina: towards a national strategy

*Sergio D. Goldfeder[1] & Daniel E. Blanco[2]*

*[1]Secretaría de Ambiente y Desarrollo Sustentable, San Martín 459 (1004) Buenos Aires, Argentina. (email: sgoldfeder@medioambiente.gov.ar)*

*[2]Wetlands International, 25 de Mayo 758 10° I, Buenos Aires 1002, Argentina. (email: deblanco@wamani.apc.org)*

*We would like to dedicate this paper to the memory of Pablo Canevari, in recognition of his valuable contribution to the conservation of migratory species in Argentina and the Americas.*

Goldfeder, S.D. & Blanco, D.E. 2006. The conservation status of migratory waterbirds in Argentina: towards a national strategy. *Waterbirds around the world.* Eds. G.C. Boere, C.A. Galbraith & D.A. Stroud. The Stationery Office, Edinburgh, UK. pp. 189-194.

## ABSTRACT

We present a preliminary assessment of the conservation status of migratory species in Argentina, with a focus on waterbirds. This paper will be used as a basis for the organization of the First National Workshop on Migratory Species in 2006. Guidelines for the development of a national conservation strategy will be produced. The present study included a questionnaire survey of experts and an intensive search of the literature. The available information has been compiled and summarized, and the main gaps in knowledge have been identified. A general overview of the results is presented in terms of species distribution, the main flyways, population status (estimates and trends), threats and conservation priorities. We also present some case studies of potential "flagship" species. The experience gained during this first assessment will be used as a basis for the second stage: the National Workshop and its related outputs. The Waterbirds around the world Conference has proved to be an excellent forum for receiving additional input from experts.

## INTRODUCTION

Located in southern South America, Argentina has a wide diversity and abundance of wetlands (e.g. seashores, estuaries, large rivers and associated floodplains, lagoons and marshes, salt lakes, and peatlands) which provide habitat for many waterbird species. Of the 245 species of waterbirds recorded in the country (Mazar Barnett & Pearman 2001), 100 are migrants (41%), and these include many ducks (18 species), flamingos (three species) and shorebirds (29 species).

Nearctic shorebirds that have their main non-breeding areas in Argentina (Canevari *et al.* 2001, Hayman *et al.* 1986) include coastal species (e.g. Hudsonian Godwit *Limosa haemastica*, Red Knot *Calidris canutus* and White-rumped Sandpiper *Calidris fuscicollis*) and grassland species that concentrate in the grasslands of the Pampas (e.g. American Golden Plover *Pluvialis dominica* and Buff-breasted Sandpiper *Tryngites subruficollis*). Moreover, many species migrate within South America, including various Patagonian migrants that have their main breeding areas in Patagonia and main non-breeding sites at lower latitudes (e.g. Magellanic Penguin *Spheniscus magellanicus*, Ruddy-headed Goose *Chloephaga rubidiceps* and Olrog's Gull *Larus atlanticus*) (Yorio *et al.* 1998 & 1999, Madsen *et al.* 2003).

In view of the increase in threats to migratory species in recent years, it has become apparent that there is a need for a national conservation strategy for the conservation of migratory birds. Some efforts have already been made to address biodiversity conservation (SAyDS 2003), and action plans have been prepared for individual species such as the Ruddy-headed Goose (De la Balze & Blanco 2002) and the Andean flamingos (Caziani *et al.* 2001). However, conservation of migratory species has not yet been addressed comprehensively.

The aim of this paper is to make a preliminary assessment of the conservation status of migratory waterbirds in Argentina as a first step towards the development of a comprehensive strategy for their conservation. Basic information is being gathered for broader consultation and the development of a National Workshop.

## METHODS

In this first assessment, we included the waterbirds and seabirds occurring in Argentina, and took the following steps:

1) an intensive literature search to compile background information;
2) selection of species;
3) identification of experts on particular species;
4) questionnaire surveys and telephone interviews; and
5) compilation and analysis of data, including identification of the main gaps in information.

Sources of background information that were consulted included the general literature on Argentinean birds (Canevari *et al.* 1991, De la Peña & Rumboll 1998, Mazar Barnett & Pearman 2001, Narosky & Yzurieta 2003) and international publications (Wetlands International 2002, Hayman *et al.* 1986). Scientific articles and the 'grey literature' were also reviewed. Species were selected on the basis of the following criteria: a) the species should represent different migration types and taxonomic groups; b) they should have a threatened status; c) they should represent different habitat types and conditions, portraying different conservation problems; d) they should be appealing enough to become "flagship" species; and e) there should be sufficient information available.

Questionnaires on selected species were produced and sent to a number of experts. About 93% of the questionnaires were answered effectively, and these responses were followed by telephone interviews. The main points covered in this consultation were:

1) taxonomic information;
2) conservation status;
3) seasonal and spatial distribution, and migration routes;
4) population estimates and trends;
5) the available literature;
6) banding initiatives;

7) threats and the main conservation actions required; and

8) the major requirements for a national conservation strategy.

Background information obtained from the literature and data on selected species provided by experts formed the basis for the present analysis. The taxonomy and systematic order follow Mazar Barnett & Pearman (2001). Information on the conservation status of waterbirds in Argentina was taken from García Fernández *et al.* (1997). Unless otherwise stated, information on population size was taken from Wetlands International (2002).

## RESULTS
### Migratory status
About 100 of the species of waterbirds and seabirds occurring in Argentina are migrants. Taxonomic groups including the highest proportion of migratory species are Phoenicopteriformes (100%, n = 3), Charadriiformes (61%, n = 79), Anseriformes (45%, n = 39) and Procellariiformes (36%, n = 39) (Fig. 1). Species were grouped in the following categories according to their migration patterns:

1) Nearctic migrants: species that breed in the North American tundra and migrate to the Southern Hemisphere during the non-breeding season, reaching Argentina in the austral spring and summer (e.g. Common Tern *Sterna hirundo*, Hudsonian Godwit, Red Knot and White-rumped Sandpiper);

2) Mid-latitudinal migrants: species that breed in Argentina and migrate to central and northern South America during the non-breeding season (e.g. American Wood Stork *Mycteria americana* and Spotted Rail *Pardirallus maculatus*); and

3) Patagonian migrants: species that breed in Patagonia and migrate to northern Argentina, reaching lower latitudes during the non-breeding season (e.g. Ruddy-headed Goose and Rufous-chested Dotterel *Charadrius modestus*).

Two other categories have also been considered:

4) Altitudinal migrants: species that breed in mountainous areas (including the "Puna" region and high plateaux in north-western Argentina) and make seasonal altitudinal migrations, moving to warmer, lower valleys during winter (e.g. the Andean flamingos);

5) Opportunistic migrants: nomadic species that make short- to long-distance movements with no regular pattern in search of favourable habitat conditions providing food and suitable nesting sites (e.g. several grebes, ducks and coots). In many cases, the conditions of the habitat are more important than climatic factors and time of year and, given favourable conditions, these species can breed all year round (Canevari *et al.* 1991).

The dominant migratory type varied between the taxonomic groups that were assessed. The Charadriiformes are dominated by Nearctic migrants, while Patagonian migrants dominate in all other taxa except for the Phoenicopteriformes, which include altitudinal and opportunistic migrants (Fig. 1).

### Case studies
Sixteen species were selected to give as comprehensive an overview as possible (Table 1). In some cases, the information

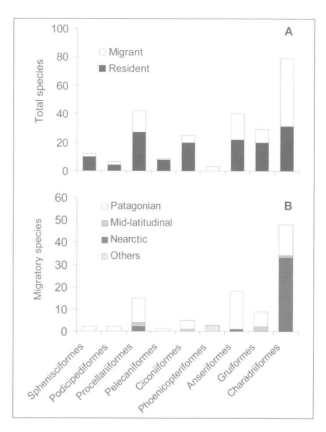

Fig. 1. The numbers of migratory waterbird species in Argentina by Order: (A) in relation to resident species, and (B) in each migrant category.

drawn from literature was revised on the basis of interviews with experts. Eight of the species listed in Table 1 are discussed in greater detail below to illustrate the results of the study. The major gaps in information for these eight species are listed in Table 2.

**Magellanic Penguin *Spheniscus magellanicus*:** This is a Patagonian migrant, breeding along the Patagonian coast from September to March. For the rest of the year (April to August), it is pelagic. The non-breeding range may include southern Brazil (P. Yorio *in litt.*), but no information is available on the migration routes.

**Black-browed Albatross *Thalassarche (Diomedea) melanophris*:** This seabird is another Patagonian migrant, breeding from October to March in the Falklands/Malvinas, South Georgia, the South Sandwich Islands and South Orkney/Orcadas Islands. No specific information is available on its non-breeding areas (April to September), although it is known to reach all southern oceans (F. Rabuffetti *in litt.*). Individual birds are highly faithful to their breeding sites.

**Andean Flamingo *Phoenicopterus andinus*:** This is an altitudinal and opportunistic migrant. During the breeding season (October to April), it occurs in the "Puna" region of the high Andes in north-western Argentina, as well as in Chile, Bolivia and Perú. It migrates to lower areas during the non-breeding season, reaching as far as the central plains of Argentina and southern Perú (S. Caziani *in litt.*).

**Ruddy-headed Goose *Chloephaga rubidiceps*:** The mainland and Tierra del Fuego population of this Patagonian migrant has a very restricted distribution. Breeding pairs concentrate in the surroundings of Punta Arenas and in the northern portion of Tierra del Fuego (Madsen *et al.* 2003). During winter, the birds occur in a small area in southern Buenos Aires province (Blanco *et al.* 2003).

**Table 1.** Selected species of migratory waterbirds in Argentina, indicating migratory and conservation status, listing in Appendices to the Convention on the Conservation of Migratory Species of Wild Animals (CMS), and experts consulted.

| Family | Species | Migratory status | Conservation Status | | CMS | Expert consulted |
|---|---|---|---|---|---|---|
| | | | International | National | | |
| Spheniscidae | *Spheniscus magellanicus\** | PAT | NGT | NLT | No | Pablo Yorio |
| Podicipedidae | *Podiceps gallardoi* | PAT / OPP | NGT | VU | No | Mauricio Rumboll |
| Diomedeidae | *Thalassarche melanophris\** | PAT ? | EN | NLT | II | Fabián Rabufetti |
| Phalacrocoracidae | *Phalacrocorax atriceps* | PAT ? | NGT | NLT | No | Esteban Frere |
| Phoenicopteridae | *Phoenicopterus andinus\** | ALT /OPP | VU | VU | I-II | Sandra Caziani |
| Anatidae | *Chloephaga rubidiceps\** | PAT | NGT | EN | I-II | Daniel Blanco |
| Anatidae | *Anas specularis* | OPP / PAT ? | NGT | NLT ? | II | Mariano Gelain |
| Anatidae | *Tachyeres patachonicus* | PAT | NGT | NLT | II | Pablo García Borboroglu |
| Anatidae | *Netta peposaca* | OPP | NGT | NLT | II | María Elena Zaccagnini |
| Rallidae | *Rallus antarcticus\** | PAT ? | VU | CR | No | Juan Mazar Barnet & Santiago Imberti |
| Rallidae | *Porzana spiloptera* | PAT ? | VU | VU | No | Mark Pearman |
| Pluvianellidae | *Pluvianellus socialis* | PAT | NGT | NLT | II | Silvia Ferrari & Carlos Albrieu |
| Charadriidae | *Oreopholus ruficollis* | PAT | NT | NLT | II | Juan Pablo Isacch |
| Scolopacidae | *Calidris canutus\** | NEA | NT | NLT | II | Patricia González |
| Scolopacidae | *Tryngites subruficollis\** | NEA | NT | NLT | I-II | Daniel Blanco |
| Laridae | *Larus atlanticus\** | PAT | VU | NLT | I | Pablo Petracci |

Migratory status: PAT – Patagonian; NEA – Nearctic; OPP – opportunistic; ALT – altitudinal. Conservation Status: CR – Critically Endangered; EN – Endangered; VU – Vulnerable; NT – Near Threatened; NGT – not globally threatened; NLT – not locally threatened. The eight species selected as case studies are indicated with an asterisk.

**Austral Rail *Rallus antarcticus*:** This small rail is an opportunistic as well as a Patagonian migrant, but little is known about its distribution and movements. There are records from Santa Cruz province in Argentina and Region XII in Chile, but breeding has only been reported from Torres del Paine in November and December (J. Mazar Barnett & S. Imberti *in litt.*).

**Red Knot *Calidris canutus*:** This is a Nearctic migrant shorebird. Most individuals of the subspecies *rufa* migrate annually between breeding sites in the Canadian Arctic and their main non-breeding areas in Tierra del Fuego, in Argentina and Chile (Harrington 2001, P. González *in litt.*).

**Buff-breasted Sandpiper *Tryngites subruficollis*:** This Nearctic migrant has its main non-breeding areas in the Río de la Plata grasslands in Argentina, Uruguay and Brazil, where it is present from September to February (Lanctot *et al.* 2002).

**Olrog's Gull *Larus atlanticus*:** This Patagonian migrant is endemic to southern South America, and the breeding colonies are restricted to the Atlantic coast of Argentina (Buenos Aires and Chubut provinces). No information is available on migration routes (P. Petracci *in litt.*).

## Threats and conservation actions

The threats to the conservation of the selected species were identified. In decreasing order of importance they are:

1) habitat change (either human-induced or natural) and habitat loss;
2) pollution (ranging from oil spills to pesticides);
3) urban development and tourism; and
4) other threats. The latter category includes mining activities,

water management, collection of eggs and guano, overgrazing, pets and feral animals, and biological causes such as low reproductive success and specialized diet during the breeding season.

Further information is given in Table 3 for the eight case studies. Taking into account these threats and the gaps in information that had been identified, a number of conservation actions were suggested by the experts. In decreasing order of importance they were:

1) implementation of protected areas;
2) habitat and species management (including eradication of alien species);
3) education and public awareness;
4) law enforcement;
5) long-term monitoring; and
6) others.

The main conservation actions required for the eight case stuies are listed in Table 3.

A major issue identified by the experts was the need for more research (banding studies, determination of flyways) as a necessary input for better implementation of these conservation actions.

## DISCUSSION

This preliminary analysis provides a basis for the development of a national strategy for the conservation of migratory species in Argentina. The process involved the participation of many

**Table 2.** Population size and trend, revised national conservation status (from Table 1) and main gaps in information for eight species of migratory waterbirds in Argentina. Population estimates follow Wetlands International (2002) except for the two marine species and *Chloephaga rubidiceps*, for which the sources of information are specified.

| Species | Population size | Population trend | National conservation status (revised) | Gaps in information |
|---|---|---|---|---|
| *Spheniscus magellanicus* | 964 000 breeding pairs [1] | No information available | NLT | - Wintering distribution<br>- Migration routes |
| *Thalassarche melanophris* | 1 000 000 – 2 500 000 ind. [2] | Decreasing | VU ? | - Distribution and abundance<br>- Dispersion patterns<br>- Interactions with fisheries |
| *Phoenicopterus andinus* | 34 000 ind. | Decreasing | VU | - Habitat selection<br>- Behaviour<br>- Fluctuations in population size<br>- Breeding biology |
| *Chloephaga rubidiceps* | 900 – 1 178 ind. [3] | Decreasing | EN | - Migration routes and stopover sites<br>- Reproductive success<br>- Local movements in winter |
| *Rallus antarcticus* | 2 500 – 10 000 ind. | No information available | EN ? | - Seasonal movements and distribution<br>- Breeding biology<br>- General ecology (habitat use, behaviour)<br>- Threats |
| *Calidris canutus* | 60 000 ind. | Decreasing | EN | - Size of non-breeding population and demographic parameters in northern South America<br>- Migration routes |
| *Tryngites subruficollis* | 15 000 ind. | Decreasing | NLT | - Migration routes and stopover sites<br>- Population size<br>- Habitat use<br>- Local movements during wintering |
| *Larus atlanticus* | 4 600 ind. | Decreasing | VU | - Migration phenology and flyways<br>- Winter quarters in Argentina, Uruguay and Brazil<br>- Winter quarters in Argentina, Uruguay and Brazil |

[1] Yorio *et al.* (1999), [2] BirdLife International (2000), [3] Blanco *et al.* (this volume)

experts from all around the country who provided updated information on the current status of migratory waterbirds, including natural history, distribution and migration, threats, conservation needs, gaps in information, and so on.

An analysis of the information provided by the experts identified many gaps in information and the need to revise the migratory and conservation status of several waterbird species. There should, in fact, be further discussion regarding the classification of migrants, as several species do not fit into any of the "traditional" categories. In some cases, there is an overlapping of features from different categories. Some species, such as the Black-browed Albatross and Austral Rail, show both Patagonian and opportunistic features, while the Andean Flamingo shows altitudinal and opportunistic characteristics. For many species, basic information on migration patterns is still lacking.

On the other hand, some species are known to be declining, e.g. the Black-browed Albatross. In this case, the available information suggests a decreasing trend for the Falklands/Malvinas colonies, which contain 80% of known breeding pairs (BirdLife

International 2003). The Black-browed Albatross was the main species found in the by-catch on long-line fishing vessels between 1999 and 2001, out of a total of 10 000 albatrosses and petrels counted (M. Favero pers. comm.)

As regards long-distance migrants, many shorebirds are decreasing in South America, including some species that have their main non-breeding areas in Argentina. A particular case is the *rufa* population of the Red Knot, which has been declining significantly for the last two decades, particularly in Tierra del Fuego, where numbers have fallen from 51 000 to 27 000 in 2000-2002, threatening the viability of the subspecies (Baker *et al.* 2004). Another example is the Buff-breasted Sandpiper, which continues to show a declining trend (Lanctot *et al.* 2002).

Patagonian migrants also include some species with an unfavourable conservation status. The mainland and Tierra del Fuego populations of the Ruddy-headed Goose have been in serious decline since the 1950s. This species is now considered to be in danger of extinction both in Argentina and in Chile, with the total population in both countries now estimated at

**Table 3. Main threats and conservation actions identified for eight species of migratory waterbirds in Argentina.**

| Species | Threats | Conservation actions |
|---|---|---|
| *Spheniscus magellanicus* | Oil exploration<br>Interaction with fisheries<br>Disturbance from tourism | Further research?<br>International co-operation? |
| *Thalassarche melanophris* | Interaction with fisheries (including by-catch in long-line fishing, trawling and jigging vessels)<br>Predation by alien species<br>Pollution<br>Disturbance from tourism | By-catch mitigation measures<br>Monitoring breeding colonies<br>Assessment of off-shore distribution and abundance<br>Banding studies |
| *Phoenicopterus andinus* | Habitat changes due to irrigation works<br>Human disturbance in breeding colonies (including egg-collecting and tourism)<br>Mining and poaching<br>Agro-chemicals | Long-term programmes to monitor populations<br>Basin management; regulations on water use and law enforcement |
| *Chloephaga rubidiceps* | Predation by Patagonian Grey Fox Dusicyon griseus<br>Sport hunting and "pest" control<br>Agro-chemicals<br>Habitat changes | Protection of breeding and non-breeding areas<br>Hunting regulations and law enforcement<br>Education and public awareness campaigns<br>Habitat management |
| *Rallus antarcticus* | Overgrazing<br>Irrigation works<br>Alien species? | Management plans for cattle-raising in Patagonian wetlands<br>Water management planning |
| *Calidris canutus* | Tourism and unplanned development<br>Potentially also industrial pollution, oil exploration, sea-farming projects | Management planning<br>Law enforcement<br>Education and public awareness campaigns<br>Monitoring activities |
| *Tryngites subruficollis* | Habitat loss and changes due to agricultural development in former cattle-raising areas<br>Pollution from pesticides in rice fields | Management of grasslands and cattle<br>Regulations on pesticide use<br>Public awareness campaigns<br>Banding initiatives |
| *Larus atlanticus* | Egg-collecting<br>Pollution (heavy metals)<br>Draining works in crab habitats | Improvement of management plans<br>Law enforcement in protected areas<br>Identification of main non-breeding areas and migration routes<br>Protection of the breeding colony at Isla del Puerto |

only about 1 000 birds (Madsen *et al.* 2003, Blanco *et al.* in press). However, the Falklands/Malvinas population of this species has a favourable conservation status (Wetlands International 2002).

In some cases, a revision of the National Conservation Status is needed, as in the case of the Black-browed Albatross, which should be amended to Vulnerable (F. Rabufetti *in litt.*), and the Austral Rail, which should be moved from Critically Endangered to Endangered (J. Mazar Barnett & S. Imberti *in litt.*). In addition, some species such as the Magellanic Penguin and Austral Rail are not included in the CMS Appendices, and thus lack the protection of this international conservation tool.

Moreover, gaps in information have proved to be critical. In some cases, even basic information is lacking (e.g. abundance and distribution, migration routes, wintering areas, habitat use), making the conservation of the species more difficult to accomplish. A lack of knowledge of the distribution and movements of the Austral Rail, for example, prevents the implementation of conservation measures for this species. In the case of the Red Knot, although there is valuable information on the migration of the species (Baker *et al.* 2004), important gaps in knowledge still remain: demographic parameters for the northern South America

and Tierra del Fuego populations, recruitment rates in the breeding areas, late migration and connectivity factors (P. González *in litt.*)

## CONCLUSION

This preliminary assessment has enabled us to collect very valuable information on the migratory waterbirds in Argentina. We have identified many information gaps, the main threats and the main conservation actions required. Furthermore, we have confirmed that a wide consultation amongst waterbird specialists is needed as a next step towards the development of a comprehensive national strategy. With this in mind, a first National Workshop on Migratory Species is planned for 2006.

## ACKNOWLEDGEMENTS

We would like to thank the Secretaría de Ambiente y Desarrollo Sustentable (Argentina), Wetlands International, the Convention on the Conservation of Migratory Species of Wild Animals (CMS), and Colin Galbraith (Chairman) and the Organizing Committee of the Waterbirds around the world Conference.

Our special recognition goes to all those who responded to our questionnaires and provided very valuable information: Carlos Albrieu, Juan Mazar Barnett, Sandra Caziani, Silvia

Ferrari, Esteban Frere, Pablo García Borboroglu, Mariano Gelain, Patricia González, Santiago Imberti, Juan Pablo Isacchs, Mark Pearman, Pablo Petracci, Fabián Rabuffetti, Mauricio Rumboll and Pablo Yorio. We apologize for any omissions.

## REFERENCES

**Baker, A.J., González, P.M., Piersma, T., Niles, L.J., do Nascimento, I.L.S., Atkinson, P.W., Clark, N.A., Minton, C.D.T., Peck, M. & Aarts, G.** 2004. Rapid population decline in Red Knots: fitness consequences of decreased refuelling rates and late arrival in Delaware Bay. Proceedings of the Royal Society of London B. 271: 875–882.

**BirdLife International** 2000. Threatened Birds of the World. Lynx Editions & BirdLife International, Barcelona, Spain, & Cambridge, U.K.

**BirdLife International** 2003. BirdLife's online World Bird Database: the site for conservation. Version 2.0. BirdLife International. Cambridge, U.K. (http://www.birdlife.org).

**Blanco, D.E., Zalba, S.M., Belenguer, C.J., Pugnali, G. & Rodríguez Goñi, H.** 2003. Status and conservation of the ruddy-headed goose *Chloephaga rubidiceps* Sclater (Aves, Anatidae) in its wintering grounds (Province of Buenos Aires, Argentina). Revista Chilena de Historia Natural 76(1): 47-55.

**Blanco, D.E., Matus, R., Blank, O.M., de la Balze, V.M. & Zalba, S.M.** 2006. The Ruddy-headed Goose *Chloephaga rubidiceps* mainland population: a flyway perspective. Waterbirds around the world. G.C. Boere, C.A. Galbraith & D.A. Stroud (Eds.), The Stationery Office, Edinburgh, UK. 195-196.

**Canevari, M., Canevari, P., Carrizo, G.R., Harris, G., Rodríguez Mata, J. & Straneck, R.** 1991. Nueva guía de las aves argentinas. Fundación Acindar, Santiago, Chile.

**Canevari, P., Castro, G., Sallaberry, M. & Naranjo, L.G.** 2001. Guía de los Chorlos y Playeros de la Región Neotropical. American Bird Conservancy, WWF-US, Humedales para las Américas, Manomet Center for Conservation Sciences & Asociación Calidris. Cali, Colombia.

**Caziani, S.M. & Grupo para la Conservación de los Flamencos Altoandinos** 2001. Acciones prioritarias para la conservación de los flamencos altoandinos. Informe final. CMS, GCFA y Fundación Pachamama.

**De la Balze, V.M. & Blanco, D.E.** 2002. El cauquén colorado (*Chloephaga rubidiceps*): una especie amenazada por la caza de avutardas. In: D.E. Blanco, J. Beltrán. & V.M. de la Balze (eds) Primer Taller sobre la Caza de Aves Acuáticas: hacia una estrategia para el uso sustentable de los recursos de los humedales. Wetlands International, Buenos Aires Argentia: 119-122.

**De la Peña, M. & Rumboll, M.** 1998. Birds of southern South America and Antarctica. Collins Illustrated Checklist. Princeton University Press, USA.

**García Fernández, J.J., Ojeda, R.A., Fraga, R.M., Díaz, G.B. & Baigún, R.J.** (compilers). 1997. Libro rojo de mamíferos y aves amenazados de la Argentina. FUCEMA-SAREM-AOP-APN. Avellanada, Argentina.

**Harrington, B.A.** 2001. Red knot (*Calidris canutus*). In: A. Poole & F. Gill (eds) The birds of North America No. 563. Philadelphia, PA. U.S.A.

**Hayman, P., Marchant, J. & Prater, T.** 1986. Shorebirds. Christopher Helm, London. U.K.

**Lanctot, R.B., Blanco, D.E., Dias, R.A., Isacch, J.P., Gill, V.A., Almeida, J.B., Delhey, K., Petracci, P.F., Bencke, G.A. & Balbueno, R.** 2002. Conservation status of the Buff-breasted Sandpiper: historic and contemporary distribution and abundance in South America. Wilson Bulletin 114(1): 44-72.

**Madsen, J., Matus, R., Blank, O., Benegas, L., Mateazzi, G. & Blanco, D.E.** 2003. Population status of the Ruddy-headed Goose (*Chloephaga rubidiceps*) in Tierra del Fuego and mainland Patagonia (Chile and Argentina). Ornitología Neotropical 14(1): 15-28.

**Mazar-Barnett, J. & Pearman, M.** 2001. Annotated checklist of the birds of Argentina. Lynx Edicions, Barcelona. Spain.

**Narosky, T. & Yzurieta, D.** 2003. Guía para la identificación de las aves de Argentina y Uruguay. Ed. Vázquez Mazzini. 15a edición. Buenos Aires.

**SAyDS** 2003. Estrategia Nacional sobre Diversidad Biológica. Secretaría de Ambiente y Desarrollo Sustentable. Resolución 91/03. Buenos Aires, Argentina.

**Wetlands International** 2002. Waterbird Population Estimates – Third edition. Wetlands International Global Series No.12, Wageningen, The Netherlands.

**Yorio, P., Frere, E., Gandini, P. & Harris, G.** (eds). 1998. Atlas de la distribución reproductiva de aves marinas en el litoral patagónico argentino. PMIZCP-FPN-WCS. Buenos Aires, Argentina.

**Yorio, P., Frere, E., Gandini, P. & Conway, W.** 1999. Status and conservation of seabirds breeding in Argentina. Bird Conservation International 9: 299-314.

Paolo Canevari - widely respected for his pioneering contribution to waterbird and wetland conservation in Argentina and the Americas. Photo: Theunis Piersma.

# The Ruddy-headed Goose *Chloephaga rubidiceps* mainland population: a flyway perspective

*Daniel E. Blanco¹, Ricardo Matus², Olivia Blank², Victoria M. de la Balze¹ & Sergio M. Zalba³*

¹ *Wetlands International, 25 de Mayo 758 10° I, Buenos Aires 1002, Argentina. (email: deblanco@wamani.apc.org)*

² *José Robert 0289, Punta Arenas, Chile.*

³ *GEKKO, Universidad Nacional del Sur, San Juan 670 (8000) Bahía Blanca, Argentina.*

Blanco, D.E., Matus, R., Blank, O., de la Balze, V.M. & Zalba, S.M. 2006. The Ruddy-headed Goose *Chloephaga rubidiceps* mainland population: a flyway perspective. *Waterbirds around the world.* Eds. G.C. Boere, C.A. Galbraith & D.A. Stroud. The Stationery Office, Edinburgh, UK. pp. 195-196.

## ABSTRACT

The mainland population of the Ruddy-headed Goose *Chloephaga rubidiceps* is currently estimated at around 1 000 individuals and breeds in southern Patagonia, Chile and Argentina, and winters in southern Buenos Aires province, Argentina. Numbers have seriously declined since the 1950s (Canevari 1996), and at present is considered in danger of extinction in both Argentina and Chile (Glade 1993, García Fernández *et al.* 1997). This study provides an overview of the species' ecology and conservation from research carried out by Wetlands International during the last seven years.

The Ruddy-headed Goose exists in two well-defined populations: a sedentary one restricted to the Malvinas/Falkland Islands and a migratory one that breeds in southern Patagonia, Chile and Argentina and during the winter migrates northwards to the southern Pampas in Buenos Aires Province, Argentina. The latter is the "mainland and Tierra del Fuego" population, currently in serious danger of extinction. Throughout this paper it is referred to as the mainland population.

The Ruddy-headed Goose mainland population is migratory, has a small population size and very restricted distribution (Canevari 1996, Blanco *et al.* 2003a.). Breeding areas are located in mainland Chile along the Straits of Magellan from San Juan to Pali Aike, and in the northern portion of Tierra del Fuego Island (Madsen *et al.* 2003). Brood-rearing sites, such as San Gregorio and San Juan, are characterized by swamps and/or open water offering retreat in case of predation attempts by foxes (Madsen *et al.* 2003).

After the breeding season the Ruddy-headed Goose migrates north to Buenos Aires Province, Argentina. The migration route is still unknown, but twice a year geese fly across Patagonia, which separates the breeding and wintering quarters, covering around 1 500 km. Three uncertain records suggest the use of an inland corridor close to the coast (Wetlands International unpubl. data).

During the non-breeding season the species concentrates in San Cayetano and Tres Arroyos districts, in southern Buenos Aires province (Blanco *et al.* 2003a). This region, where they share the habitat with other *Chloephaga* geese (*Ch. picta* Upland Goose and *Ch. poliocephala* Ashy-headed Goose), is predominantly agricultural with a mosaic of crops, mainly wheat and planted pastures.

Recent studies estimated the mainland population size as 900-1 178 individuals from breeding and wintering areas respectively ((Madsen *et al.* 2003, Blanco *et al.* 2003), (Table 1). Due to its critical status, the species is listed in Appendices I and II of the Bonn Convention (CMS) and was included in CMS Resolutions 4.2 and 5.1 for "Concerted Actions".

The main cause of the population decline appears to be an increase in nest depredation resulting from the introduction in 1951 of the Patagonian Fox *Pseudalopex griseus* to the island of

**Table 1. Ruddy-headed Goose status (Wetlands International 2002)**

| Population | Migration status | Estimate | Trend |
|---|---|---|---|
| Mainland and Tierra del Fuego | Migratory | 900-1 178 [1] | Decreasing |
| Malvinas / Falkland Islands | Sedentary | 42 000-81 000 | Stable |

[1] Confidence interval 95%: 491-1865 (Blanco *et al.* 2003b).

Tierra del Fuego (Madsen *et al.* 2003). A further threat is the location of this population's wintering distribution in the main wheat cropping areas of Argentina, where *Chloephaga* (sheldgeese) have been traditionally persecuted by local farmers who do not distinguish the Ruddy-headed Goose from the other two species (Blanco *et al.* 2001, De la Balze & Blanco 2002). To a lesser degree, sport hunting, habitat modification and agrochemical poisoning are additional threats to the species.

After seven years of studies, Wetlands International and its partners have achieved the following:

* a database with updated information on Ruddy-headed Goose mainland population distribution and numbers;
* a manual and "Action Plan" for the conservation of the species (Blanco *et al.* 2001),
* the creation of the San Juan Reserve, located in the mouth of the San Juan River, 60 km south of Punta Arenas (XII Region, Chile), where Ruddy-headed Goose nests were recently discovered;
* the development of a "Water Management Plan" for the San Gregorio area;
* an intensive public awareness campaign - brochures, magazines articles, posters, etc.; and
* an internet Forum to help track the species during migration.

The critical status of the Ruddy-headed Goose mainland population points to the need for re-categorisation of its status at a global scale. Although more research is needed, there is a possibility that the two populations (mainland and the Malvinas/Falklands) could be different subspecies.

The work was supported by the Convention on Migratory Species of Wild Animals (CMS-UNEP). We thank researchers from Argentina, Chile and Denmark, and especially: Carolina Belenguer, Luis Benegas, Jorge Gibbons, Astrid Knell, Nora Loekemeyer, Jesper Madsen, Gustavo Mateazzi, Flavio Moschione, Pablo Petracci, Germán Pugnali, Silvina Ramírez, Hernán Rodríguez Goñi, Luis Scorolli and Lucas Verniere.

## REFERENCES

**Blanco, D.E., Matus, R., Blank, O.M., Benegas, L., Goldfeder, S., Moschione, F. & Zalba, S.** 2001. Manual para la Conservación del Cauquén (Canquén) Colorado en Argentina y Chile. Wetlands International. Buenos Aires.

**Blanco, D.E., Zalba, S.M., Belenguer, C.J., Pugnali, G. & Rodríguez Goñi, H.** 2003a. Status and conservation of the ruddy-headed goose *Chloephaga rubidiceps* Sclater (Aves, Anatidae) in its wintering grounds (Province of Buenos Aires, Argentina). Revista Chilena de Historia Natural 76(1): 47-55.

**Blanco, D.E., Zalba, S.M., de la Balze, V.M., Petracci, P.F. & Scorolli, A.** 2003b. Distribution and population status of the Ruddy-headed Goose: Preliminary results 2003. Workshop Measuring Waterbird Abundance. 27th Annual Meeting of the Waterbird Society. 24-27 September 2003. Cuiabá, Mato Grosso, Brazil.

**Canevari, P.** 1996. The austral geese (*Chloephaga* spp.) of Southern Argentina and Chile: a review of its current status. Gibier Faune Sauvage, Game & Wildlife. 13: 355-366.

**De la Balze, V.M. & Blanco, D.E.** 2002. El cauquén colorado (*Chloephaga rubidiceps*): una especie amenazada por la caza de avutardas. In: D.E. Blanco, J. Beltrán & V.M. de la Balze (eds.) Primer Taller sobre la Caza de Aves Acuáticas: Hacia una estrategia para el uso sustentable de los recursos de los humedales. Wetlands International, Buenos Aires: 119-122.

**García Fernández, J.J., Ojeda, R.A., Fraga, R.M., Díaz, G.B. & Baigún, R.J.** (compilers). 1997. Libro rojo de mamíferos y aves amenazados de la Argentina. FUCEMA-SAREM-AOP-APN.

**Glade, A.** (ed.). 1993. Libro rojo de los vertebrados terrestres de Chile. Corporación Nacional Forestal, Santiago, Chile.

**Madsen, J., Matus, R., Blank, O.M., Benegas, L., Mateazzi, G. & Blanco, D.E.** 2003. Population status of the Ruddy-headed Goose (*Chloephaga rubidiceps*) in Tierra del Fuego and mainland Patagonia (Chile and Argentina). Ornitología Neotropical 14(1): 15-28.

**Wetlands International** 2002. Waterbird Population Estimates - Third edition. Wetlands International Global Series No. 12. Wageningen, The Netherlands.

Ruddy-headed Geese *Chloephaga rubidiceps*. Photo: Andrew Douse.

# 3.3 Flyway conservation in North America. Workshop Introduction

*Paul R. Schmidt*

*U.S. Fish and Wildlife Service, Migratory Birds and State Programs, 1849 C St. NW, Room 3250, Washington, D.C. 20240, USA.*

Schmidt, P.R. 2006. Flyway conservation in North America. Workshop Introduction. *Waterbirds around the world.* Eds. G.C. Boere, C.A. Galbraith & D.A. Stroud. The Stationery Office, Edinburgh, UK. pp. 197-198.

Delaware Bay on the east coast of North America is a critical staging area for huge numbers of arctic breeding shorebirds that use the site each spring, 'refuelling' especially on abundant Horseshoe Crab *Limulus polyphemus* eggs. Sustaining populations of Horseshoe Crabs is central to the long-term conservation of dependant shorebirds. Photo: Rob Robinson.

## INTEGRATED WATERBIRD HARVEST MANAGEMENT IN NORTH AMERICA

Blohm *et al.* describe the integrated cooperative monitoring efforts to set waterfowl harvest regulations and make management/conservation decisions in North America. Treaties have been developed to define the hunting season and the conditions necessary to implement a hunt.

The Migratory Birds Treaty Act authorized the Secretary of Interior to determine when and how to allow hunting, and to adopt regulations to govern it. Harvest must be compatible with the ability to sustain populations – for both under and overabundant species. In the case of subsistence hunting (traditional use) – treaties have been amended to provide for legal subsistence of migratory birds during the closed season, except during peak of nesting season.

Programs monitoring population, productivity and habitat parameters have been developed to collect data needed to set harvest regulations. Breeding wintering and migration surveys are conducted each year. Spring breeding surveys are done by aircraft using transect lines with ground counts at samples along the same transect lines to correct for detectability of birds from air. Approximately 80 000 miles of survey lines are flown each year. Production surveys are conducted in the summer using the same transects but using a smaller sample. Habitat data is collected during these surveys.

Mid-winter surveys are conducted each year and help to determine continental populations. These surveys provide general information for most waterfowl species, including relative abundance and distribution on the wintering grounds. In Mexico, surveys are conducted cooperatively every three years, with some surveys conducted annually.

Data on productivity is accomplished through large banding programs. Each year, over 200 000 ducks and 150 000 geese/swans are banded. This allows the U.S. Department of Interior to estimate harvest and survival rates. The quality of the data is dependent on band return rates.

Harvest surveys are conducted in the U.S. and Canada where a sample of hunters are asked to provide information particular to their hunt each year. Species specific harvest estimates are conducted and wing surveys provide species age and sex data.

Understanding migration patterns of migratory waterfowl has been the cornerstone of their management. Since 1948, waterfowl species have been managed through four flyways.

Each flyway has a Council with representatives from each province and state in the flyway who develop recommendations about species management. Biologists from the flyways meet a few times annually to review data from surveys and to produce recommendations, which are then presented to for approval. In the U.S., the Assistant Secretary of the Department of Interior gives final approval after review by the U.S. Fish and Wildlife Service. Guidelines or limits on season date, season length, daily bag limits, and shooting hours are set and provided to Sates who then determine their own hunting regulations within these boundaries.

In the U.S, a process called adaptive harvest management is being used to develop waterfowl hunting regulations. Adaptive harvest management is an iterative process of monitoring, assessment, and decision making designed to reduce the uncertainty associated with waterfowl population estimates.

The most pressing issues and challenges in waterfowl management in North America are:–

- Snow Geese *Anser (Chen) caerulescens* and resident Canada Geese *Branta canadensis* – populations are growing at 14% per year in the Atlantic Flyway and rapidly in other flyways as well. This growth has resulted in overabundant populations. New methods of take have been developed and take is allowed during the "closed" migratory bird hunting season.
- Declining species include Scaup *Aythya marila* and Northern Pintail *Anas acuta*. Bag limits have been reduced in response to declining populations throughout the U.S.

## HABITAT CONSERVATION PARTNERSHIPS AND CONTINENTAL PLANNING

Habitat conservation for waterfowl populations in North America has a 75 year history, the success of which has been characterized by the development of partnerships between national governments, regional governments, and the private sector. The first and most important initiative was the North American Waterfowl Management Plan, which, as described by Wheeler, was adopted in the early 1980s as US government policy and later by Canada and Mexico. The implementation strategy involves prioritization of habitat conservation based on habitat goals derived from population goals. A fund was established to provide matching grants for habitat conservation. Inspired by the approach taken in waterfowl, plans were developed for other groups of birds including land birds (Partners in Flight), shorebirds (US Shorebird Conservation Plan) and waterbirds (Waterbird Conservation for the Americas). This activity provided the impetus to develop a cooperative approach, including common approaches to setting goals and common landscape divisions, called Bird Conservation Regions that cover North America. This approach became the North American Bird Conservation Initiative, incorporating not only the taxon based initiative but also Canada and Mexico. The delivery of habitat conservation through the North American Waterfowl Conservation Act was affected through the development of Joint Ventures, which are landscape specific stakeholder partnerships, and which have recently been expanded to include all wetland depended bird species. These partnerships include the Federal government, state governments, and private organizations and interests, which leverage federal funds. Over six million hectares have been protected, restored or enhanced through the North American Waterfowl activities between 1991 and 2004.

Issues and Challenges Facing Migratory Bird Conservation Programmes in North America, involve a wide range of natural and new anthropogenic challenges. There are four principal components: science, legislative policy, habitat, and international. Birds fall into different conservation categories (such as endangered, hunted, and overabundant), which have different challenges. Science issues are critical, including incomplete knowledge, monitoring failures, and communications requiring the right mix of resources and skills to understand the complexities of bird conservation. Legislation includes migratory bird laws and treaties, endangered species laws and environmental protection and assessment laws and policies. Habitat change is a consistent and often the most important threat to species. Habitat conservation needs include habitat loss, contaminants, and climate change. Lessons learned and future strategies in North America, include coordination of monitoring programs, legal consistency, and developing a cohesive Western Hemisphere strategy.

## AN INTEGRAL APPROACH TO WATERBIRD CONSERVATION, MEXICAN PERSPECTIVE

An integral approach includes population, habitat, and socio-economic issues. About 300 species are shared between Mexico and the US but 16% of Mexican species are endemic. The specific legal framework for conservation involve treaties (such as the Ramsar Convention), international funding programs (such as the US North American Waterfowl Conservation Act), and, importantly, the General Law of Wildlife enacted in 2000. This law increased the ownership stake of the local landowner. Implementation and enforcement is still being developed. Important Bird Areas form the network for bird conservation in Mexico. Important Bird Areas include important sites for waterbirds and these sites include some that hold a large proportion of certain waterfowl. The important NGO partners include Ducks Unlimited Mexico and PRONATURA. There is a need for improved international cooperation through international alliances, long term monitoring programs and assessment, and the North American Species Assessment Model.

## SEARCHING FOR EQUILIBRIUM POINTS

Migratory bird conservation must change to meet the goals of keeping common birds common and helping populations in trouble to improve. However it is clear that many species are in trouble, and therefore the goal is not being met. We must search for a balance between historic programming and modern conservation, between targeted conservation action and research and monitoring, and between historic partnerships and new strategic alliances. Historic programs were based on game birds, but there is a growing emphasis on an all bird, multi-species, habitat based approach, while retaining important attention to hunted species. There is a need to design new programs to meet all-bird needs, not just tweak existing programs. We must articulate conservation goals in terms that make broad sense, and must participate in water conservation issues. There is a need be action oriented and also to have a solid understanding of ecological processes. Both are required. The science must be rigorous, reliable, relevant, and resource efficient and have scientifically valid measurable results and monitoring, and continually test key assumptions, such as the relationship between habitat conservation and populations effects. Approaches to bird conservation, such as those for migratory birds and species at risk, need to be brought together. Management decisions are increasingly vulnerable to scientific challenge. Historic alliances, which have achieved good results, are facing new partners and include those from the resource sector. Traditional partnerships must not be neglected and cohesion within the bird community must be strengthened and non-competitive. We need to strive for "working landscapes," in which land must also be used for people, which requires additional linkages to agriculture, fisheries, forestry, and other resource sectors. Continuing to go on the same track will get the same result, and the results are not now sufficient, so change is needed.

# Integrated waterfowl management in North America

*Robert J. Blohm[1], David E. Sharp[2], Paul I. Padding[3], Ronald W. Kokel[1] & Kenneth D. Richkus[3]*

[1]*U.S. Fish and Wildlife Service, 4401 N. Fairfax Drive, Arlington, Virginia 22203, USA. (email: Robert_Blohm@fws.gov)*
[2]*U.S. Fish and Wildlife Service, PO Box 25486 DFC-DMBM, Denver, Colorado 80225, USA.*
[3]*U.S. Fish and Wildlife Service, 10815 Loblolly Pine Drive, Laurel, Maryland 20708, USA.*

Blohm, R.J., Sharp, D.E., Padding, P.I., Kokel, R.W. & Richkus, K.D. 2006. Integrated waterfowl management in North America. *Waterbirds around the world.* Eds. G.C. Boere, C.A. Galbraith & D.A. Stroud. The Stationery Office, Edinburgh, UK. pp. 199-203.

## ABSTRACT

Waterfowl management in North America has its legal foundation in treaties among the continent's three countries that established guidelines for the cooperative management of migratory birds. Within those guidelines, each country determines its own waterfowl hunting regulations each year, based upon the results of cooperative annual programs that monitor the status of waterfowl populations, habitat conditions, migratory movements, and harvest on a continental scale. In the United States, the process for setting regulations involves a cooperative effort by the U.S. Fish and Wildlife Service, representing the Federal government, and Flyway Councils that represent the State governments. This effort culminates with the annual publication of rule-making documents that provide the legal foundation for the establishment of hunting seasons. The United States has recently implemented an adaptive approach for setting annual duck-hunting regulations. This process, called Adaptive Harvest Management, uses model-driven assessments of the results of monitoring programs to set hunting regulations, whereupon the impacts of those regulations are measured in subsequent monitoring efforts, and the cycle is repeated.

## INTRODUCTION

In North America, migratory birds are an important natural resource, with a rich tradition of economic and recreational use and an aesthetic value shared across international boundaries. However, the transitory nature of migratory birds contributes to a unique set of management challenges, due principally to the large number of species and individuals, their widespread distribution, seasonal migration, habitat requirements, and variation in population attributes. The biological complexity is compounded by the fact that these birds migrate to, and through, many different political jurisdictions throughout the continent each year. Furthermore, there are numerous and sometimes competing interests, both within and among jurisdictions, with regard to the management of these species. Thus, managing recreational use, namely the regulation of harvests on the continent, is probably one of the most complicated examples of allocating a renewable resource.

This paper is an overview of the approaches that have been taken in North America to resolve some of the issues that are inherent to managing waterfowl, i.e. migratory ducks, geese, and swans. We describe the legal foundation for cooperation among the nations that share this natural resource, and we provide an overview of cooperative monitoring efforts that establish the biological basis for making sound conservation decisions. Additionally, we describe the administrative processes that are involved in setting annual waterfowl hunting regulations in the United States, including a brief discussion of the Adaptive

Harvest Management protocol that has been adopted for the management of duck harvests in the past decade. Finally, we discuss some of the current issues and challenges that are facing North American waterfowl managers today.

## LEGAL FOUNDATION

Waterfowl, like most migratory birds, are a shared multinational resource. In North America, the importance each country holds for all or portions of the annual cycle of migratory birds is underscored in the respective treaties between those countries. Guidelines for the cooperative protection and management of waterfowl and other migratory bird species were agreed upon and established through treaties (Bean 1983). The first such treaty was the 1916 Convention for the Protection of Migratory Birds between the United States and Great Britain (on behalf of Canada). In 1936, the United States signed a treaty with Mexico at the Mexico Convention for the Protection of Migratory Birds and Game Mammals. This treaty was amended in 1972. Canada and Mexico cooperate under a separate agreement. The United States later entered similar treaties with Japan in 1972 (amended in 1974) and Russia (then the Soviet Union) in 1976. As a result of these treaties, all of the countries involved are jointly responsible for ensuring that healthy migratory bird populations will be available to future generations for all to enjoy.

The treaties define when seasons for hunting are allowed, the species that may be hunted, and the conditions under which hunting seasons may be considered. Within these general guidelines, each nation may implement its own hunting seasons. Each year, representatives of Canada, the United States, and Mexico meet to discuss a wide spectrum of migratory bird topics in order to fulfill their respective mandates for this shared resource.

In the United States, the Migratory Bird Treaty Act of 1918 is the domestic legislation that implements these migratory bird treaties (Bean 1983). Under this Act, the Secretary of the Interior is authorized to determine when and how hunting of migratory game birds can take place, and to adopt regulations for this purpose. Those regulations are written based on the distribution, abundance, economic value, and breeding and migration habits of migratory game birds, and they are updated annually. The Department of the Interior has delegated the federal authority for managing and conserving migratory birds to one of its agencies, the U.S. Fish and Wildlife Service.

The purpose of hunting regulations is to provide opportunities for hunters to take migratory game birds, while ensuring the welfare and long-term sustainability of populations of hunted birds (U.S. Fish and Wildlife Service 1988). This is the common thread that links regulated hunting activities in all three countries on the North American continent. In the United States, our objectives in setting annual hunting regulations are to provide equitable hunting opportunities for all who wish to hunt migratory birds, including sport hunters, subsistence hunters, and those who hunt on Indian reservations. However, we must also ensure that the total annual harvest is compatible with the overall goal of maintaining sustainable populations. In some cases, this means using harvest as a tool to help manage over-abundant species.

Hunting with firearms and falconry are the two legal methods of sport hunting for waterfowl in the United States. As established by treaty, sport hunting of waterfowl may only occur from 1 September to 10 March (open period). The Migratory Bird Treaty Act allows State governments to make and enforce laws or regulations about migratory bird hunting, provided that they do not extend beyond the frameworks that are approved by the Secretary of the Interior (U.S. Fish and Wildlife Service 1988). In other words, States always have the latitude to establish more conservative hunting regulations, but never more liberal regulations. Thus, a key feature of the regulations-setting process for hunting migratory birds in the United States is cooperation with the States.

Although the 1916 treaty between the United States and Canada prohibited the taking of migratory birds from 11 March to 31 August (closed period), native residents of northern Canada and Alaska traditionally harvested migratory birds for nutritional purposes during the spring and summer months (Klein 1966). In recognition of this long-standing, traditional use of migratory birds, the governments of Canada, Mexico, and the United States amended their treaties and agreements in 1997. The amendments provide for the legal subsistence harvest of migratory birds and their eggs in Alaska and Canada during the closed period. However, no take is allowed for a 30-day period during the peak of the nesting season for each species or population.

Beginning with the 1985 hunting season, we have employed separate guidelines and administrative processes for migratory game bird hunting regulations on Indian reservations and ceded lands in the United States (U.S. Fish and Wildlife Service 1988). We developed these parallel guidelines in response to tribal requests for our recognition of their reserved hunting rights, and for some tribes, recognition of their authority to regulate hunting throughout their reservations and ceded lands. In all cases, tribal regulations established under the guidelines must be consistent with the provisions of the international migratory bird treaties, including the outside dates for hunting seasons.

## MONITORING EFFORTS

There are five categories of migratory bird monitoring efforts that are conducted annually in North America: population surveys, productivity surveys, habitat surveys, banding and marking studies, and harvest surveys (Smith *et al.* 1989).

Each year, waterfowl population surveys are conducted on breeding, migration, and wintering areas. The May waterfowl breeding population and habitat survey represents one of the most extensive and respected wildlife surveys in the world. This annual aerial survey has been conducted systematically since 1955, and it is a cooperative effort of the U.S. Fish and Wildlife Service, the Canadian Wildlife Service, and numerous state, provincial, and tribal agencies. The area covered by the survey represents more than 5 400 000 square km of the key waterfowl breeding grounds on the continent. In this survey, pilot-biologists survey the number of breeding waterfowl from aircraft by counting breeding birds seen along established transect lines

(Canadian Wildlife Service & U.S. Fish and Wildlife Service 1977, Reynolds 1987). Biologists on the ground also count birds and assess breeding habitats on a sample of the same transect lines during the same period of time. This provides the basis for correcting the aerial counts to account for the fact that not all birds present along the transect lines can be seen from the air. The corrected counts are expanded to provide species-specific estimates of breeding populations for the entire survey area.

The May breeding population and habitat survey is followed by a July production survey later in the summer, during which broods are counted from the air. The July production survey is conducted on a smaller sample of the same transect lines that are flown during the May breeding population survey. In both surveys, habitat information is an important component of data-gathering efforts. The number and types of ponds are of particular importance as predictors of productivity, and are an important component of the population models that are used to help set hunting regulations. Overall, pilot-biologists fly a total of roughly 128 000 km during the breeding population and production surveys.

The mid-winter survey is another survey of continental waterfowl populations. Conducted annually since 1935, this monitoring program is a census of waterfowl on major wintering areas throughout the United States, and is typically carried out during early January. The mid-winter survey yields general information for most waterfowl species, including relative abundance and distribution on wintering habitats. However, the survey does provide the best population data available for some species, including Tundra Swans *Cygnus columbianus*, Black Brant *Branta bernicla nigricans*, and Snow Geese *Chen (Anser) caerulescens*.

The Mexico waterfowl survey is another aerial survey that is conducted cooperatively by biologists from Canada, Mexico, and the United States. This survey began in 1936, and it augments the mid-winter survey in the United States. The survey covers the major waterfowl wintering grounds of Mexico, including the east coast, the west coast, and the interior highlands. Parts of the survey are conducted annually, but the entire survey is carried out at three-year intervals.

Banding is also an important tool of waterfowl management. To date, biologists in North America have banded more than 63 000 000 birds in total, and have accumulated more than 3 500 000 recoveries. In any one year, biologists will band more than 200 000 ducks and nearly 150 000 geese and swans. In addition to delineating migration routes and chronology, biologists can estimate harvest rates and survival rates for some waterfowl species from band recovery data. These harvest and survival rates are critical pieces of information that are used in efforts to model the population dynamics for particular species or populations (e.g. Anderson & Burnham 1976, Burnham *et al.* 1984). Estimating harvest rates from band recoveries requires accurate estimates of band reporting rates, which reflect the willingness of people who recover bands to report this information to the Bird Banding Laboratory. Band reporting rates were studied extensively in the late 1980s (Nichols *et al.* 1991, Nichols *et al.* 1995), but in recent years, use of a toll-free telephone number imprinted on bands has raised reporting rates significantly from the levels reported earlier. In 2002, biologists began a continent-wide investigation to determine current reporting rates and whether they vary by region and species.

Surveys of sport hunters are conducted annually in both Canada and the United States to assess their level of participation and success during the hunting season. These surveys consist of asking a sample of waterfowl hunters to report the number of ducks and geese they harvested during the hunting season (Martin & Carney 1977, Cooch *et al.* 1978). Both countries also conduct annual wing surveys that provide data on species, age, and sex composition. Additionally, a survey of subsistence hunters is conducted in Alaska each year that provides species-specific estimates of subsistence harvest. These survey systems have been in place since 1961 in the United States, since 1967 in Canada, and for subsistence harvest, since 1980 in Alaska. Harvest surveys provide species-specific estimates of harvest, estimates of hunter effort, and age and sex ratio estimates that are used in population modeling efforts.

## ADMINISTRATIVE PROCESSES

Understanding the migration habits of birds is a primary requisite for all nations participating in the management of our shared waterfowl resource. Long-standing analyses of numerous band recovery records show that waterfowl appear to follow distinct, traditional migration corridors or flyways in their annual travels between breeding and wintering areas (Lincoln 1935, Bellrose 1980). Since 1948, we have managed waterfowl by four administrative Flyways that are based on those migration paths: the Atlantic, Mississippi, Central, and Pacific Flyways (Fig. 1). Some of the important waterfowl hunting regulations that are set each year, including season length and daily bag limits, are specific to these individual Flyways.

Fig. 1. The waterfowl flyways of North America.

Each Flyway has a Flyway Council, which is a formal organization that is composed of one member from each State and Province in that Flyway. Recently, Mexico has also provided representation at Pacific and Central Flyway meetings and discussions. The Flyway Councils are involved in many aspects of migratory game bird management, including development of

recommendations for hunting regulations and assisting in research and habitat management activities.

In the United States, the process of establishing annual hunting regulations is a complex merging of biological, administrative, and legal considerations (U.S. Fish and Wildlife Service 1988). Waterfowl biologists within each Flyway meet several times annually to review the biological data from monitoring programs. Following these reviews, they prepare a series of recommendations for the upcoming hunting season that are presented to their respective Flyway Councils. The recommendations that are adopted by the Flyway Councils are then presented to the U.S. Fish and Wildlife Service's Regulations Committee for consideration. The Regulations Committee evaluates each Flyway's proposals and then submits its findings and recommendations to the Director of the U.S. Fish and Wildlife Service. Final approval is given by the Assistant Secretary of the Department of the Interior, representing the Secretary, whereupon the annual hunting regulations are formally adopted after public review and comment. Throughout this process, the general public are provided with ample opportunity to comment on the recommendations and decisions.

Waterfowl hunting seasons must be established by late August for a few species and areas, and by late September for all of the other species and areas. However, most of the biological data are not available until July. Thus, much of the regulations-setting process in the United States occurs during a very compressed time frame. As one would expect, the processes for developing annual regulations in Canada and Mexico differ from this in terms of both procedures and timing (see Boyd 1979).

The U.S. Fish and Wildlife Service develops waterfowl hunting regulations by establishing the frameworks, or outside limits, for season opening and closing dates, season lengths, bag limits, and shooting hours (U.S. Fish and Wildlife Service 1988). States then select their seasons within these frameworks, considering factors such as distribution, abundance, and timing of migration to and/or from their State, as well as other factors important to their hunting communities. Again, States may always be more restrictive than the federal regulations, but never more liberal.

To help improve the overall regulations-setting process in the United States, the U.S. Fish and Wildlife Service and the States worked together in the early 1990s to develop an Adaptive Harvest Management approach for regulating duck harvest (Johnson *et al.* 1993). Adaptive Harvest Management serves as a way for all interested groups to work cooperatively to review

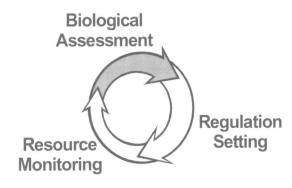

Fig. 2. The monitoring, assessment and decision-making cycle employed annually by the Adaptive Harvest Management process that is used to set annual duck hunting regulations in the United States.

the available biological information and develop as much consensus as possible with regard to setting duck hunting regulations each year. The explicit goal of Adaptive Harvest Management is to optimize long-term hunter opportunity while ensuring healthy waterfowl populations.

Adaptive Harvest Management is an iterative process that each year uses the results of monitoring to inform a series of biological assessments that help establish particular hunting regulations in a given year. The impacts of those regulations are then measured by subsequent monitoring activities, and the cycle is repeated (Fig. 2). The biological assessments are based on statistical models that all parties have agreed to use, which helps promote objective decision-making despite acknowledging an incomplete understanding of the role that harvest plays in duck population dynamics (Williams *et al.* 1996). Annual regulatory decisions about season length and daily bag limits are limited to a fixed set of clear alternatives, and the alternative selected in any given year is based upon the results of the models. The heart of the process is its adaptive nature; when new information is obtained, it is continually incorporated into the process, thereby reducing our uncertainty about the relationship between harvest and duck numbers. This underscores the value of our monitoring programs, and our need to maintain their accuracy and reliability.

The U.S. Fish and Wildlife Service and the States adopted Adaptive Harvest Management in 1995 for regulating duck harvest. Currently, this approach is only used in the United States for the development of duck hunting regulations, particularly for the Mallard *Anas platyrhynchos*. The regulatory alternative that is selected for the Atlantic Flyway is based upon the results of the population models for eastern Mallards, whereas the population models for mid-continental Mallards determine which regulatory alternative is selected for the other three Flyways. Work is ongoing to expand the Adaptive Harvest Management approach to the western Mallard population, recognizing further that stocks vary in their potential to support sport harvest. Additionally, Canada is currently working with the United States to develop an adaptive approach for the harvest of other species or populations of waterfowl besides Mallards, namely, the shared American Black Duck *Anas rubripes* population and the Atlantic population of Canada Geese *Branta canadensis*.

## CURRENT ISSUES

Waterfowl populations typically fluctuate as a function of habitat and environmental conditions; thus periodic increases and decreases are expected. However, the long-term trend information provided by our monitoring efforts indicates that we have cause to be concerned about the status of some species in North America. Results of the waterfowl breeding population survey indicate that Greater Scaup *Aythya marila* and Lesser Scaup *A. affinis* have experienced a long-term decline, particularly since the early 1980s (Afton & Anderson 2001). In response to this decline, the U.S. Fish and Wildlife Service and the Flyway Councils have reduced bag limits for these two species throughout the United States. Contaminants, lower female survival, and reduced recruitment due to changes in the availability of food resources or essential habitats have been suggested as possible reasons for the decline.

The Northern Pintail *Anas acuta* is another species whose numbers have declined significantly. Unlike other prairie ducks, Northern Pintails have not rebounded during the past decade of

generally improved wetland conditions in the prairies of North America. This is probably due to increased vulnerability during the nesting season as a result of modern farming practices, particularly in the grassland areas of the north-central United States and southern Canada (Miller & Duncan 1999). As with Greater and Lesser Scaup, the U.S. Fish and Wildlife Service and the Flyway Councils have reduced the daily bag limit on Northern Pintails to decrease harvest. When low population numbers warrant, they have also reduced the number of days during which hunters may take these birds.

North America is also currently experiencing problems caused by over-abundance of some species. Several populations of Snow Geese and Ross's Geese *Chen (Anser) rossii* have increased dramatically and are causing extensive habitat damage to breeding, migration, and wintering areas (Ankney 1996). To help alleviate this problem, unusual measures have been taken recently to reduce those populations, under the authority of a Conservation Order (U.S. Fish and Wildlife Service 2001). These measures consist mainly of allowing methods of take that previously have been prohibited (e.g. electronic calling) during the period that has traditionally been closed to all migratory bird hunting (i.e. after 10 March). The goals of these efforts are to reduce the Greater Snow Goose *C. c. atlantica* population in the East from 860 000 to 500 000 birds, and to reduce Lesser Snow Goose *C. c. caerulescens* and Ross's Goose populations in the mid-continental region by 50%. These birds number 3 000 000 in mid-winter counts, but estimates from the breeding ground are as high as 5 600 000 birds.

Resident populations of Canada Geese have also experienced high growth rates. These birds reside year-round in much of the United States and parts of southern Canada. Numbers of resident Canada Geese are growing at a rate of 14% per year in the Atlantic Flyway and 6% per year in the Mississippi Flyway, and these geese are increasing rapidly in the Central and Pacific Flyways as well. An over-abundance of these birds has resulted in habitat degradation, crop depredation, and an increasing incidence of conflicts with human activities in urban and suburban areas (Conover & Chasko 1985). Consequently, the U.S. Fish and Wildlife Service is currently considering several alternative management strategies to reduce and control resident Canada Goose populations (U.S. Fish and Wildlife Service 2002).

The results of annual waterfowl monitoring and management efforts in North America are available in a variety of publications and formats, including population status reports, administrative reports, technical reports and scientific papers, proceedings of various conferences and other meetings, and videotapes and DVDs. Reports and other information, including the annual migratory bird hunting regulations, are available on the web sites of the U.S. Fish and Wildlife Service and the Canadian Wildlife Service.

## REFERENCES

**Afton, A.D. & Anderson, M.G.** 2001. Declining scaup populations: A retrospective analysis of long-term population and harvest survey data. Journal of Wildlife Management 65: 781-796.

**Anderson, D.R. & Burnham, K.P.** 1976. Population ecology of the mallard V: Temporal and geographic estimates of survival, recovery and harvest rates. U.S. Fish and Wildlife Service Resource Publication 125, Washington, D.C.

**Ankney, C.D.** 1996. An embarrassment of riches: Too many geese. Journal of Wildlife Management 60: 217-223.

**Bean, M.J.** 1983. The evolution of wildlife law. Prager Publishers, New York, NY.

**Bellrose, F.C.** 1980. Ducks, geese, and swans of North America. Stackpole Books, Harrisburg, PA.

**Boyd, H.** 1979. Federal roles in wildlife management in Canada. Transactions of the North American Wildlife & Natural Resources Conference 44: 90-96.

**Burnham, K.P, White, G.C. & Anderson, D.R.** 1984. Estimating the effect of hunting on annual survival rates of adult mallards. Journal of Wildlife Management 48: 350-361.

**Canadian Wildlife Service & U.S. Fish and Wildlife Service** 1977. Standard operating procedures for aerial water-fowl breeding ground population and habitat surveys in North America. Unpublished report.

**Conover, M.R. & Chasko, G.G.** 1985. Nuisance Canada goose problems in the eastern United States. Wildlife Society Bulletin 13: 228-233.

**Cooch, F.G., Wendt, S., Smith, G.E.J. & Butler, G.** 1978. The Canada migratory game bird hunting permit and associated surveys. In: H. Boyd & G.H. Finney (eds) Migratory game bird hunters and hunting in Canada. Canadian Wildlife Service Report Series No. 43: 8-39.

**Johnson, F.A., Williams, B.K., Nichols, J.D., Hines, J.E., Kendall, W.L., Smith, G.W. & Caithamer, D.F.** 1993. Developing an adaptive management strategy for harvesting waterfowl in North America. Transactions of the North American Wildlife & Natural Resources Conference 58: 565-583.

**Klein, D.R.** 1966. Waterfowl in the economy of the Eskimos of the Yukon-Kuskokwim Delta, Alaska. Arctic 19(4): 319-336.

**Lincoln, F.C.** 1935. The waterfowl flyways of North America. U.S. Department of Agriculture, Circular No. 342, Washington, D.C.

**Martin, E.M. & Carney, S.M.** 1977. Population ecology of the mallard IV: A review of duck hunting regulations, activity, and success, with special reference to the mallard. U.S. Fish and Wildlife Service Resource Publication 130, Washington, D.C.

**Miller, M.R. & Duncan, D.C. 1999.** The northern pintail in North America: Status and conservation needs of a struggling population. Wildlife Society Bulletin 27: 788-800.

**Nichols, J.D, Blohm, R.J., Reynolds, R.E., Trost, R.E., Hines, J.E. & Bladen, J.P.** 1991. Band reporting rates for mallards with reward bands of different dollar values. Journal of Wildlife Management 55: 119-126.

**Nichols, J.D, Reynolds, R.E., Blohm, R.J., Trost, R.E., Hines, J.E. & Bladen, J.P.** 1995. Geographic variation in band reporting rates for mallards based on reward banding. Journal of Wildlife Management 59: 697-708.

**Reynolds, R.E.** 1987. Breeding duck population, production and habitat surveys, 1979-85. Transactions of the North American Wildlife & Natural Resources Conference 52: 186-205.

**Smith, R.I., Blohm, R.J., Kelly, S.T., Reynolds, R.E. & Caswell, F.D.** 1989. Review of data bases for managing duck harvests. Transactions of the North American Wildlife & Natural Resources Conference 54: 537-544.

**U.S. Fish and Wildlife Service** 1988. Issuance of annual regulations permitting the sport hunting of migratory birds. U.S. Department of the Interior, Washington, D.C.

**U.S. Fish and Wildlife Service** 2001. Draft Environmental Impact Statement: Light goose management. U.S. Department of the Interior, Washington, D.C.

**U.S. Fish and Wildlife Service** 2002. Draft Environmental Impact Statement: Resident Canada Goose management. U.S. Department of the Interior, Washington, D.C.

**Williams, B.K., Johnson, F.A. & Wilkins, K.A.** 1996. Uncertainty and the adaptive management of waterfowl harvests. Journal of Wildlife Management 60: 223-232.

Canada Geese *Branta canadensis* have been the subject of a very long term study with results influencing Adaptive Harvest Management policies. Photo: J. Jave.

# Summary of the Workplans for 2005 of the Waterbird Conservation Council's committees

*Jennifer Wheeler*

*U.S. Fish and Wildlife Service, Division of Migratory Bird Management,*
*4401 N. Fairfax Drive, Suite MBSP, Arlington, VA 22203, USA. (email: jennifer_a_wheeler@fws.gov)*

Wheeler, J. 2006. Summary of the Workplans for 2005 of the Waterbird Conservation Council's committees. *Waterbirds around the world*. Eds. G.C. Boere, C.A. Galbraith & D.A. Stroud. The Stationery Office, Edinburgh, UK. pp. 204-205.

The Waterbird Conservation Council (Council) is the keeper of the North American Waterbird Conservation Plan (NAWCP) and has responsibility for coordinating, supporting, communicating implementation of NAWCP and other waterbird plans, updating the plans, and facilitating actions for waterbird conservation throughout the Plan area. The Council is structured to accomplish its work through seven working committees that report to an Executive Committee. The role and workplan for 2005 for each Council committee is summarized in this document.

## EXECUTIVE COMMITTEE

Role: Composed of representatives of the major geographic units of the NAWCP area and committee chairs, this committee oversees and facilitates the work of the Council, and in 2005 has oversight over two ad hoc committees, which will:

- Address the commitments associated with NAWCP "Version 2" as discrete tasks by working committees:
  - Continental-scale treatment of marshbirds as a 2005 task for the Technical Services Committee;
  - Fuller treatment of Latin America and the Caribbean: Underway under "Advancing Range-Wide Waterbird Conservation Throughout the Western Hemisphere;" Regional Committee to facilitate creation of relevant regional plans;
  - Revision of status assessments: Technical Services to develop a strategy to account for hemispheric expansion;
  - Increased conservation actions – Regional Committee to facilitate regional-scale implementation of planned conservation activities; Resources Committee to assess funding opportunities; Conservation Action Committee to continue addressing urgent conservation issues; and
  - Printed Communications Piece: Development led by Communications Committee.
- Develop a strategy of "integration" - identifying opportunities and proposing actions for engaging with existing international organizations and programs to advance waterbird conservation; also promoting integration of waterbird conservation needs with other initiatives at regional levels.
- Outline a plan of action with regard to identifying geographic priorities at multiple levels.

## TECHNICAL SERVICES COMMITTEE

Role: To provide leadership and guidance on a number of technical topics of interest to the Waterbird Conservation for the Americas initiative. The Committee will focus on the most pressing needs identified in the NAWCP, but will also provide input on other technical issues as they emerge

- Secure increased participation from the ranks of scientists
- Priority tasks for 2005:
  - Form a task force and complete the continental-scale marshbirds assessment (i.e. status assessment, and documentation of threats, needs, and partners);
  - Complete the monitoring needs framework currently underway by the committee; and
  - Examine and update the method for status assessment reflecting the Council's decision to include the entire Western Hemisphere in its scope.
- The task of developing guidance for setting resource (population and habitat) objectives is expected to arise from analyses and discussion of bird conservation regions (BCR) and among regional planners.

## REGIONAL PLANNING AND IMPLEMENTATION COMMITTEE

Role: To ensure effective regional waterbird conservation planning and implementation.

- Expand its membership and adjust operations to formally include representatives from each of the planning regions.
- Expand its scope, previously focused on Canada and U.S., to all regions in the NAWCP area, now including South America.
- Priority tasks for 2005:
  - Facilitate completion and endorsement of regional waterbird conservation plans;
  - Facilitate initiation of working group for Mexico to advance a technical assessment of waterbird needs in Mexico; and
  - Assist Central American partners in creating a regional plan from the country reports generated under the Council's project "Advancing Range-Wide Waterbird Conservation Throughout the Western Hemisphere."

## RESOURCES COMMITTEE

Role: To acquire resources to fund the work of the Council and support the implementation of the North American Waterbird Conservation Plan.

- Priority Tasks for 2005 are:
  - Fund the operational budget of the Council for 2005; and
  - Analyze funding opportunities for the waterbird initiative (beginning with the Neotropical Migratory Bird Conservation Act (NMBCA) and the North American Wetlands Conservation Act (NAWCA)).

## COMMUNICATIONS COMMITTEE

Role: To provide communication-related services to support the work of the Council, drawing on its expertise and networks to develop the tools and means of reaching out to target groups with selected messages.

Priority tasks for 2005:
- Expand and improve communications within the committee, the Council, and immediate partners;
- Take responsibility for a new "Executive Summary-like" communications piece on the work and progress of the initiative;
- Assist and guide expansion, revision, and maintenance of the Initiative web site; and
- Oversee an ad hoc committee on "Birds and Rice," which will address A) research needs, B) best practices, C) promotion of "bird-friendly" rice cultivation.

## INTERNATIONAL COMMITTEE

Role: To foster the advancement of the Plan in the widest manner and especially to engage regions in Latin America and the Caribbean.

Priority Tasks for 2005:
- Shift focus from exclusive Latin America/Caribbean areas of initiative to range-wide and cross-boundary issues and make appropriate membership changes;
- Take the lead in approaching South American partners to make links between Council; and
- Continue to oversee the "Advancing Range-Wide Waterbird Conservation Throughout the Western Hemisphere," which funds foundational work for areas south of Mexico, but transition the tasks of producing regional plans (regional=Mexico, Caribbean, Central American and South America) to the Regional Committee.

## CONSERVATION ACTION COMMITTEE

Role: To foster awareness and actions to assure the conservation of waterbird species. Emphasis will be given to those species listed as Highly Imperiled or of High Concern.

Pressing conservation issues will be addressed in a pro-active manner.

Highest priority tasks for 2005
- Continue to promote the importance of the waterbird conservation plan and its implementation and work to obtain increased funding to foster waterbird conservation as outlined in the NAWCP through such measures as Congressional appropriations through the NMBCA, NAWCA, and other sources and co-ordinate actions with the Resources Committee;
- Ensure that conservation strategies facilitate the involvement of international partners across the entire NAWCP area;
- Work to support efforts to prioritize islands in the Americas for eradication of introduced species causing problems for seabirds breeding on these islands; and
- Identify significant threats to 11 imperiled seabird species within the NAWCP plan area, obtain professional peer review of these threats, and foster plans for solutions.

## MEMBERSHIP COMMITTEE

Role: To ensure the on-going vigor of the Council, by identifying and recruiting new members to Council to provide broad and appropriate representation of the many conservation interests (geographical, taxonomic, thematic) of the Waterbird Conservation for the Americas Initiative. In addition, facilitate active participation of members and promote the benefits accruing to members from Council membership.

Resolve issues of Mexican federal-agency representation on Council, as well as the Council's relationship to the North American Bird Conservation Initiative Mexico.

Priority Tasks for 2005 are:
- Revise and release operating guidelines (primarily principles of membership document and Terms of Reference);
- Develop and implement a strategy for populating council based on principles; and
- Promote benefits of membership to existing and prospective members.

Snow Geese *Chen (Anser) caerulescens.* Photo: Michael D. Samuel.

# Canada's Waterbird Conservation Plan – building on 30 years experience on the North American Great Lakes

*Donna L. Stewart[1], D.V. Chip Weseloh[1], Brigitte Collins[2], Steve Timmermans[3] & Jon McCracken[3]*

[1]*Canadian Wildlife Service - Ontario Region, Environment Canada, 4905 Dufferin St., Downsview ON M3H 5T4, Canada. (email: donna.stewart@ec.gc.ca)*

[2]*Canadian Wildlife Service - Ontario Region, Environment Canada, 49 Camelot Dr., Nepean ON K1A 0H3, Canada.*

[3]*Bird Studies Canada, PO Box 160, Port Rowan ON N0E 1M0, Canada.*

Stewart, D.L, Weseloh, D.V.C., Collins, B., Timmermans, S. & McCracken, J. 2006. Canada's Waterbird Conservation Plan – building on 30 years experience on the North American Great Lakes. *Waterbirds around the world.* Eds. G.C. Boere, C.A. Galbraith & D.A. Stroud. The Stationery Office, Edinburgh, UK. p. 206.

Bird conservation in Canada is increasingly being planned and implemented with international cooperation, using integrated approaches under the North American Bird Conservation Initiative (NABCI). Bird species are grouped under the four pillars of NABCI: waterfowl, shorebirds, waterbirds, and landbirds. The vision of waterbird conservation planning in North America is that the distribution, diversity and abundance of populations and the habitats of breeding, migratory, and non-breeding waterbirds are sustained or restored throughout the lands of North America, Central America, and the Caribbean.

To date, this has produced a Canadian Plan (Wings Over Water – WOW) (Milko *et al.* 2003), a North American Plan (Waterbird Conservation for the Americas) (Kushlan *et al.* 2002), and several smaller plans based on multi-jurisdictional regions, provinces or states, and Bird Conservation Regions (BCRs); many more are in preparation.

For the lower Great Lakes, a resource shared between Canada and the United States (U.S.), the Upper Mississippi Valley and Great Lakes Waterbird Conservation Plan will describe the current knowledge, biology, and conservation efforts for the 48 waterbird species which occur in that region. Data compiled in this plan will help fill knowledge gaps, identify information needs and key conservation issues, and promote habitat and site-based conservation actions throughout the region.

In WOW, waterbird species are assessed according to six factor scores: one to two - their North American breeding and non-breeding distributions; three to four - their population size and trend; and five to six - the threats to breeding and non-breeding populations. Canada's "responsibility" for each species is also assessed by the percent of their North American and global populations in Canada. Species are then assigned to Priority Tiers: 1 (high), 2 (medium) and 3 (low). Tier 1 species in Canada are as follows: Common Loon *Gavia immer*, Western Grebe *Aechmophorus occidentalis*, Black-footed Albatross *Diomedea nigripes*, Pink-footed Shearwater *Puffinus creatopus*, Leach's Storm-Petrel *Oceanodroma leucorhoa*, American White Pelican *Pelecanus erythrorhynchos*, American Bittern *Botaurus lentiginosus*, Whooping Crane *Grus americana*, Yellow Rail *Coturnicops noveboracensis*, Heermann's Gull *Larus heermanni*, Bonaparte's Gull *L. philadelphia*, Thayer's Gull *L. thayeri*, Ivory Gull *Pagophila eburnea*, Forster's Tern *Sterna forsteri*, Black Tern *Childonias niger*, Marbled Murrelet *Brachyramphus marmoratus*, Ancient Murrelet *Synthliboramphus antiquus* and Cassin's Auklet *Ptychoramphus aleuticus*.

All colonial waterbird populations in the Canadian and U.S. Great Lakes have been censused three times since the late 1970s,

on a roughly 10-year rotation. Protocols and methods have been standardized between the two countries. Biologists visit all islands in the Great Lakes over a three year period. Nests and eggs of the major species are easily identified and all nests at each site are counted. For example, a large colony of Ring-billed Gulls *Larus delawarensis*, over 50 000 nests, will take a crew of six biologists up to three days to count (Blokpoel & Tessier 1996). Results show, for example, that Double-crested Cormorants *Phalacrocorax auritus* have increased tremendously while Herring Gulls *L. argentatus* have fluctuated. The methods developed on the Great Lakes are being considered for nation-wide surveys.

A volunteer-based Binational Marsh Monitoring Program (MMP) was implemented in 1995. The MMP surveys both birds and calling amphibians; we only provide information for birds here. Volunteers make two evening surveys during the last three hours of daylight between 25 May and 5 July along a route of three to eight previously identified marsh locations. Using passive listening and taped call-backs of selected species, they record all birds seen and heard on field sheets. Some of those results, indicate for example increasing numbers of Common Yellowthroat *Geothlypis trichas* but declining numbers of Black Terns *Chlidonias niger*. Originally, the MMP was implemented in Ontario but recently it has expanded into the Atlantic Provinces and Quebec. Future plans may include Canada-wide implementation.

## REFERENCES

Blokpoel, H. & Tessier, T. 1996. Atlas of colonial waterbirds nesting on the Canadian Great Lakes, 1989-1991. Part 3. Cormorants, gulls and island-nesting terns on the lower Great Lakes system in 1990. Technical Report Series No. 225, Environment Canada, Canadian Wildlife Service-Ontario Region, 74 pp.

Kushlan, J.A., Steinkamp, M.J., Parsons, K.C., Capp, J., Acosta Cruz, M., Coulter, M., Davidson, I., Dickson, L., Edelson, N., Elliot, R., Erwin, R.M., Hatch, S., Kress, S., Milko, R., Miller, S., Mills, K., Paul, R., Phillips, R., Saliva, J.E., Sydeman, B., Trapp, J., Wheeler, J., & Wohl. K. 2002. Waterbird Conservation for the Americas: The North American Waterbird Conservation Plan, Version 1. Waterbird Conservation for the Americas, Washington, DC, U.S.A., 78 pp.

Milko, R.J., Dickson, L., Elliot, R. & Donaldson, G. 2003. Wings Over Water: Canada's Waterbird Conservation Plan. Environment Canada, Canadian Wildlife Service, 56 pp.

# Population declines in North American shorebirds: ecology, life-history and sexual selection

*Gavin H. Thomas[1], Richard B. Lanctot[2] & Tamás Székely[1]*

*[1]Dept. of Biology and Biochemistry, University of Bath, Claverton Down, Bath, BA2 7AY, UK. (email: g.thomas@imperial.ac.uk)*
*[2]U.S. Fish and Wildlife Service, Migratory Bird Management, 1011 East Tudor Road, MS 201, Anchorage, AK 99503, USA.*

Thomas, G.H., Lanctot, R.B., & Székely, T. 2006. Population declines in North American shorebirds: ecology, life-history and sexual selection. *Waterbirds around the world.* Eds. G.C. Boere, C.A. Galbraith & D.A. Stroud. The Stationery Office, Edinburgh, UK. pp. 207-208.

Shorebird populations worldwide are in a perilous state, with 48% of the 200 populations with known trends in decline (International Wader Study Group 2003). Only 16% of the world's shorebird populations with known trends are increasing. These declines are troubling because shorebirds are likely to be important indicators of wetland health on a global scale.

Of North America's 51 breeding species of shorebirds, 22 are in population decline and only three are increasing. To address why these declines are occurring, this study investigated the biological factors (migratory behaviour, biogeography, life-history, sexual selection) that may make some shorebirds more prone to decline than others. Preliminary examination suggests that both the migratory route of a species and their mating system relate to population trends. These initial findings require corroboration using formal statistical analyses to account for the phylogenetic relationships amongst shorebirds.

Typically, extrinsic threats such as habitat loss, predation, climate change, and hunting are cited as the major probable causes of population decline or elevated extinction risk across many taxa. Recent studies indicate that this is only part of the story, and the intrinsic biology of a species influences whether a population is predisposed to decline and extinction (Fisher & Owens 2004). Shorebirds exhibit an unusual diversity in various ecological and behavioural traits among birds, so they are an excellent group to investigate biological correlates of population trends (Székely & Reynolds 1995, Thomas 2004). The focus of this study was to investigate the factors that predispose certain shorebird species to decline, using North American shorebirds as a model group.

Data on population trends of 51 North American breeding shorebirds were taken from the United States, Canadian, and Alaskan shorebird conservation plans (Brown *et al.* 2001, Donaldson *et al.* 2000, Alaska Shorebird Group 2004). In addition, data was collated from the literature on a suite of characters, including: migratory behaviour (distance and route), biogeography (population size, breeding and non-breeding range), life-history (body size, clutch size, adult mortality), and sexual selection (social mating system, testis size).

There are more species with declining populations than stable, or increasing, populations amongst socially polygamous shorebirds, but the reverse is true of socially monogamous shorebirds (Fig. 1a). In addition, shorebirds that migrate across continental North America tend to be declining, rather than stable or increasing, whereas the majority of coastal and oceanic migrants have stable populations (Fig. 1b).

This preliminary examination indicates important biological traits that may predispose some shorebird taxa to decline more than others. However, since closely related species tend to share similar life-histories, ecology, and behaviours (Harvey & Pagel 1991), statistical analyses that incorporate shorebird phylogeny would need to be conducted to separate the effects of common ancestry from biological predisposition (Fisher & Owens 2004).

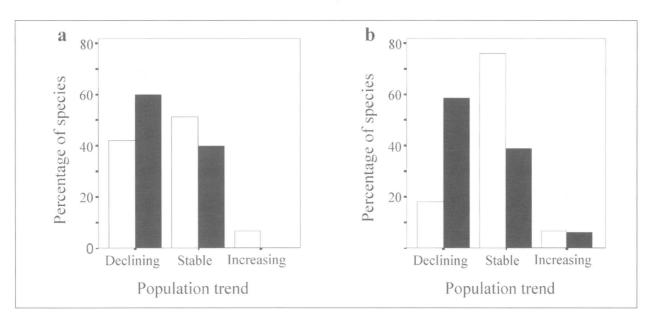

Fig. 1. Population trends of North American shorebirds depending on: a) social mating system (open bars indicate social monogamy, filled bars indicate social polygamy); and b) migration route (open bars indicate coastal or oceanic migration route, filled bars indicate continental migration route).

Furthermore, there is an urgent need to examine the interactions between intrinsic biological traits and extrinsic threats in driving population trends (Fisher & Owens 2004). For instance, Eskimo Curlew *Numenius borealis*, a continental migrant highly dependent on upland grasslands (Gill *et al.* 1998), has declined to near extinction, partially due to the conversion of upland areas into agriculture. Thus, the species dependence on uplands and the concurrent demise of their upland natural habitat interacted to drive the species decline. Since many migratory shorebirds are reliant on small, ephemeral wetlands that are rarely protected adequately (Brown *et al.* 2001), the links between migration routes and habitat change appears to be particularly important in shorebird conservation.

Effective conservation management to halt and reverse recent population declines therefore requires detailed studies of both intrinsic and extrinsic factors that predispose some species to decline more than others on both a regional and global scale.

## REFERENCES

**Alaska Shorebird Group.** 2004. A Conservation Plan for Alaska Shorebirds. Unpublished report, Alaska Shorebird Group, U.S. Fish and Wildlife Service, Migratory Bird Management, Anchorage, Alaska.

**Brown, S., Hickey, C., Harrington, B. & Gill, R.** 2001. The United States shorebird conservation plan, 2nd edn. Manomet, MA: Manomet Center for Conservation Studies.

**Donaldson, G., Hyslop, C., Morrison, R.I.G., Dickson, H.L. & Davidson, I.** 2000. Canadian shorebird conservation plan. Ottawa: Canadian Wildlife Service.

**Fisher, D.O. & Owens, I.P.F.** 2004. The comparative method in conservation biology. Trends in Ecology and Evolution 19: 391-398.

**Gill, R.E., Jr., Canevari, P. & Iverson, E.H.** 1998. Eskimo Curlew (*Numenius borealis*). In *The Birds of North America, No. 347* (eds. A. Poole & F. Gill). The Birds of North America, Inc., Philadelphia, PA.

**Harvey, P.H. & Pagel, M.D.** 1991. The Comparative Method in Evolutionary Biology. New York: Oxford University Press.

**International Wader Study Group.** 2003. Waders are declining worldwide. Conclusions from the 2003 International Wader Study Group Conference, Cádiz, Spain. Wader Study Group Bulletin 101/102: 8-12.

**Székely, T. & Reynolds, J.D.** 1995. Evolutionary transitions in parental care in shorebirds. Proceedings of the Royal. Society of London, Series B 262: 57-64.

**Thomas, G.H.** 2004. Sexual conflict, ecology and breeding systems of shorebirds: phylogenetic analyses. PhD thesis, University of Bath, United Kingdom.

The *rufa* population of Red Knot *Calidris canutus* is in rapid decline, and is being intensively studied to determine reasons. Use of leg flags and colour-marking allows detailed demographic information to be collected on individual birds. Photo: Rob Robinson.

# Coordinated waterbird monitoring in the Pacific flyway of the western U.S.: the Idaho Bird Inventory and Survey (IBIS)

*Rex Sallabanks & Colleen E. Moulton*

*Non-game and Endangered Wildlife Program, Idaho Department of Fish and Game,*
*600 S. Walnut, PO Box 25, Boise, Idaho 83707, USA. (email: rsallaba@IDFG.STATE.ID.US)*

Sallabanks, R. & Moulton, C.E. 2006. Coordinated waterbird monitoring in the Pacific flyway of the western U.S.: the Idaho Bird Inventory and Survey (IBIS). *Waterbirds around the world.* Eds. G.C. Boere, C.A. Galbraith & D.A. Stroud. The Stationery Office, Edinburgh, UK. pp. 209-210.

With the exception of waterfowl surveys for setting harvest limits, waterbird monitoring in the Pacific flyway has generally lacked regional coordination and agreement on standardized protocols. To remedy this situation in Idaho, we launched an all-bird monitoring program called the Idaho Bird Inventory and Survey.

Phase I of the Idaho Bird Inventory and Survey (IBIS) launched in 2004 emphasizes aquatic species and habitats, and focuses on determining the distribution and abundance of waterbirds at Idaho's wetland Important Bird Areas (IBAs) and Idaho Department of Fish and Game Wildlife Management Areas (WMAs). Ultimately, IBIS will generate much-needed inventories of WMAs, initiate permanent surveys at globally-recognized IBAs, yield baseline data for statewide population trend monitoring, and address high priority management issues using short-term species assessments. IBIS is designed to fit within the framework of larger-scale national and international Coordinated Bird Monitoring programs and can easily be adapted for use in other states, especially those within the Pacific flyway of the western U.S.

IBIS is a plan to monitor all birds in Idaho that most wildlife and land-management agencies would contribute to and benefit from. Importantly, IBIS is designed to be part of a relatively new program called "Coordinated Bird Monitoring" (CBM) that is currently being developed at the national level. CBM is a joint effort by managers and bird monitoring specialists to improve the success of bird monitoring programs, and make the information available to all partners. This all-bird coordination effort is modeled after a long-standing program,

implemented by the Flyway Councils, of continent-wide tracking of waterfowl to set management and harvest strategies for game species. As with the waterfowl model, coordinated all-bird monitoring is intended as a feedback system that can provide a scientific basis for management and conservation planning for birds of management concern. This paper focuses on Phase I of IBIS and addresses only waterbirds (terrestrial species are added in Phase II).

Waterbird monitoring will take place at all aquatic IBAs in Idaho, Idaho Department of Fish and Game (IDFG) WMAs and other significant wetlands. Under the framework of CBM, these sites either fall within the Idaho portion of the Northern Rockies Bird Conservation Region (BCR) or the Idaho portion of the Great Basin BCR; these regions correspond to Bird Monitoring Region 50 (BMR-50) in northern Idaho and BMR-51 in southern Idaho, respectively (Fig. 1).

Wetlands in Idaho are used regularly by 119 bird species, 68 of which are considered focal species and potentially of management concern. Providing migration stop-over habitat is probably the most important function of Great Basin wetlands (i.e. those in BMR-51; Fig. 1) for many species of waterfowl, waterbirds and shorebirds. Lake Lowell of Deer Flat National Wildlife Refuge (NWR), for example, is a site of regional importance for shorebirds. American Falls Reservoir is a major stop-over site for most aquatic species, and especially for shorebirds. Major breeding colonies of Western Grebes *Aechmophorus occidentalis* and Franklin's Gulls *Larus pipixcan* also depend on these

Fig. 1. Bird monitoring regions in Idaho (shaded state) in which the Idaho Bird Inventory and Survey (IBIS) statewide coordinated all-bird monitoring plan is being implemented. Bird Monitoring Region 50 (BMR-50) corresponds to the Idaho portion of the Northern Rockies Bird Conservation Region (BCR) and BMR-51 corresponds to the Idaho portion of the Great Basin BCR.

American Avocets *Recurvirostra americana* at Bear River Migratory Bird Refuge. Photo: US Fish & Wildlife Service.

habitats, and Grays Lake NWR supports the largest breeding concentration of Sandhill Cranes *Grus canadensis* in the world. Many permanent wetlands serve as wintering habitat for waterfowl, such as Harriman State Park and Bear River NWR for Trumpeter Swans *Cygnus buccinator*.

Abundance of waterbirds is usually determined using area searches by foot, boat, or plane across all of a site or in a series of randomly selected plots. Because vegetation may change between years, which could result in substantial changes in numbers recorded even if the number of birds present does not change, careful attention must be paid to estimating detection rates where birds are obscured by vegetation. Site descriptions, including survey protocols, are provided for all major aquatic sites in Idaho in the full IBIS plan.

As IBIS is a new program, monitoring data have yet to be generated. Results are therefore pending the collection of data in the initial 2004–2006 period. Management issues to be addressed with these data include: (1) identifying species at risk and causes of declines; (2) inventory of WMAs for birds in all seasons; (3) effects of wetland loss and degradation; and (4) conflicts between piscivorous birds and fish populations. Additional issues will be addressed in v2.0 of IBIS when terrestrial habitats and species are added to the monitoring plan.

## ACKNOWLEDGMENTS

Financial support for the initial development and implementation of IBIS (v1.0) was provided by the U.S. Geological Survey – Snake River Field Station (USGS), the Nongame and Endangered Wildlife Program of IDFG, the Bureau of Land Management, and through a State Wildlife Grant administered by the U.S. Fish and Wildlife Service. We are especially grateful to Elisabeth Ammon (Great Basin Bird Observatory) and Jonathan Bart (USGS) for technical assistance with writing v1.0; Rita Dixon, Steve Rust, Jeff Gould, John Augsburger, and Greg Kaltenecker also helped with developing management issues and/or describing monitoring strategies.

Franklin's Gull *Larus pipixcan* in Chile. These migratory gulls breed in central North America including Idaho, and spend the non-breeding season on the Pacific coasts of South America. Photo: Chris Wilson.

# Individual behaviour, population genetics, and phylogeography of North American mergansers

*John M. Pearce[1,2]*

[1]*Alaska Science Center, U.S. Geological Survey, 1011 E. Tudor Road, Anchorage, Alaska, 99503, USA.*
[2]*Institute of Arctic Biology and Department of Biology and Wildlife, University of Alaska, Fairbanks, Alaska, 99775, USA.*
*(email: John_Pearce@usgs.gov)*

Pearce J.M. 2006. Individual behaviour, population genetics, and phylogeography of North American mergansers. *Waterbirds around the world*. Eds. G.C. Boere, C.A. Galbraith & D.A. Stroud. The Stationery Office, Edinburgh, UK. pp. 211-212.

Our understanding of population status and trends of the three species of merganser that inhabit North America is limited. This project is investigating factors involved in population dynamics of common and red-breasted mergansers using mark-recapture and DNA data collected from across North America.

As with eider and scoter populations 10 years ago, little is known about the habits and ecology of the three species of merganser that inhabit North America: the Common *Mergus merganser*, Red-breasted *M. serrator* and Hooded Merganser *Lophodytes cucullatus*. While trend data suggest that in North America all species are stable, if not increasing, our under-standing of population status and trends of these species is limited (Dugger *et al.* 1994, Titman 1999, Mallory & Metz 1999). Aerial surveys flown throughout North America are not designed to sample large sections of river and coastal areas commonly used by mergansers. When encountered, mergansers are not differentiated to species, but lumped into a single "merganser" category. As a result, surveys detect variable numbers of birds each year, poorly describe the distribution of mergansers, and leave large portions of the distribution of these species unsurveyed (e.g., Hodges *et al.* 1996). All mergansers occupy portions of the boreal forest in Alaska and Canada and this ecozone is experiencing rapid conversion to agriculture in Canada, declining by as much as 0.89% per year since 1974 (Hobson *et al.* 2002). The lack of basic biological information for mergansers has prompted the North American Sea Duck Joint Venture (SDJV) Management Board (2001) to list "Population Dynamics" as the highest priority and most urgent information need for the management of Common and Red-breasted Mergansers, and "Population Delineation" as the highest priority for Hooded Mergansers.

The distributions of all three species of merganser differ markedly across North America, and populations may differ demographically and genetically (Hewitt 2000). This project therefore proposes to investigate factors involved in population dynamics of common and red-breasted mergansers, such as nesting ecology and annual fidelity to breeding areas. Since field-based estimates of fidelity may not be representative of larger regions, DNA samples will be collected from across North America. This linkage of multiple markers such as banding and genetic data is important because both historical and contempo-rary factors influence the distribution and genetic differentiation of populations (Pearce & Talbot 2006). The combination of these different markers should allow more confident conclusions about the location of population mixing and a possible mechanism for genetic similarity across the arctic. Since many arctic dwelling species have only recently colonized deglaciated areas, genetic similarity could mean that fidelity takes place, but is not mani-fested in genetic data. Therefore, direct estimates from banding

and telemetry data are crucial to fully understand population movements in relation to genetic patterns (Pearce & Talbot 2005).

On field sites in south central Alaska, I am using standard mark-recapture techniques (leg bands and radio transmitters) for marking individuals. Pre-nesting females and brood-rearing females will be marked with radio transmitters to find nests and to quantify brood survival respectively. Sub-adult birds will also be implanted with 2-year radio transmitters prior to fledging to provide information on general movements and dispersal. Mark-recapture data will be analyzed using Program MARK (White & Burnham 1999) as has been done recently with historic data on Common Mergansers (Pearce *et al.* 2005a).

Standard genetic methods discussed elsewhere (Pearce *et al.* 2005b) will be used to amplify nuclear and mitochondrial (mt) DNA and assess population patterns at variable loci. Samples are being acquired throughout Alaska, across North America and in Europe and Russia. Ultimately, our goal is to combine inferences from demographic and genetic data for a better understanding of population patterns at both local and continental scales.

Initial analysis of historical banding data for Common Mergansers suggests that coastal and interior breeding areas may differ in their migratory tendency and survival rates (Pearce *et al.* 2005a). Similar patterns are also being investigated using historical banding data for Hooded Mergansers (Pearce *et al.*, unpublished data). In a preliminary analysis of 437 base pairs of mtDNA control region (domain I), I observed little differentia-tion between Pacific and Atlantic migratory flyways. Nucleotide and haplotypic diversities of these two flyways suggest a colonization event from the east or contemporary female-mediated gene flow between continental populations.

Further work is needed to adequately quantify levels of contemporary movement and gene flow among populations of all mergansers species. Additional quantification of population patterns using markers with both historic (genetic) and more contemporary (banding, stable isotopes) perspectives are being pursued and will allow more robust inferences regarding levels of gene flow and population dynamics of these species.

## Request for assistance

I am seeking additional DNA samples from both breeding and wintering birds of all merganser species. DNA can come from blood, tissue, developing eggs, or nest feathers and egg shell membranes (Pearce *et al.* 1997). Please contact John Pearce at the address above for details.

## ACKNOWLEDGEMENTS

Thanks to D. Derksen, P. Flint, M. Lindberg, K. McCracken, J. Morton, M. Olson, J. Reed, J. Schamber, K. Winker. P. Padding assisted with DNA sampling of Hooded Mergansers. Funding was provided by the North American Sea Duck Joint Venture and the Alaska Science Center, U.S. Geological Survey.

## REFERENCES

Dugger, B.D., Dugger, K.M. & Fredrickson, L.H. 1994. Hooded Merganser *Lophodytes cucullatus*. In: A. Poole & F. Gill (ed) The Birds of North America, No. 98. The Birds of North America, Inc., Philadelphia, PA.

Hewitt, G. 2000. The genetic legacy of the Quaternary ice ages. Nature 405: 907-913.

Hobson, K.A., Bayne, E.M. & van Wilgenburg, S.L. 2002. Large-scale conversion of forest to agriculture in the boreal plains of Saskatchewan. Conservation Biology 16: 1530-1541.

Hodges, J.J., King, J.G., Conant, B. & Hanson, H.A. 1996. Aerial surveys of waterbirds in Alaska 1957-94: population trends and observer variability. National Biological Service Information and Technology Report 4. 24 pp.

Mallory, M. & Metz, K. 1999. Common Merganser *Mergus merganser*. In: A. Poole & F. Gill (ed) The Birds of North America, No. 442. The Birds of North America, Inc., Philadelphia, PA.

Pearce, J.M., Fields, R.L. & Scribner, K.T. 1997. Nest materials as a source of genetic data for avian ecological studies. Journal of Field Ornithology 68: 471-481.

Pearce, J.M., J. A. Reed, J.A. & Flint, P.L. 2005a. Geographic variation in survival and migratory tendency among North American Common Mergansers. Journal of Field Ornithology 76: 109-118.

Pearce, J.M, Talbot, S.L., Petersen, M.R. & Rearick, J.R. 2005b. Gene flow and population structure in the threatened Steller's Eider. Conservation Genetics, 6: 743-757

Pearce, J.M. & Talbot, S.L. 2005. Demography, genetics, and the value of mixed messages. Condor, 108: 474-479

Sea Duck Joint Venture Management Board. 2001. Sea Duck Joint Venture Strategic Plan: 2001-2006. SDJV Continental Technical Team. Unpubl. Report.

Titman, R.D. 1999. Red-breasted Merganser *Mergus serrator*. In: A. Poole & F. Gill (ed) The Birds of North America, No. 443. The Birds of North America, Inc., Philadelphia, PA.

White, G.C. & Burnham, K.P. 1999. Program MARK: survival estimation from populations of marked animals. Bird Study 46: 120138.

Pair of Red-breasted Mergansers *Mergus serrator* in Alaska. Photo: Margaret Petersen, U.S. Geological Survey.

# Using national plans in North America to conserve shorebirds at an international scale

*Garry Donaldson[1], Brad Andres[2], Aurea Estrada[3] & Stephen Brown[4]*
[1]*Canadian Wildlife Service, 351 St. Joseph Blvd., Gatineau, Quebec, K1A 0H3, Canada.*
[2]*U.S. Fish and Wildlife Service, 4401 North Fairfax Drive, Arlington, Virginia, 22203, USA.*
[3]*Ducks Unlimited de México, Fracc. Bosques de Aragón, EdoMex, Mexico.*
[4]*Manomet Center for Conservation Sciences, Manomet, Massachusetts, USA.*

Donaldson, G., Andres, B., Estrada, A. & Brown, S. 2006. Using national plans in North America to conserve shorebirds at an international scale. *Waterbirds around the world.* Eds. G.C. Boere, C.A. Galbraith & D.A. Stroud. The Stationery Office, Edinburgh, UK. p. 213.

A recent report on the status of shorebirds breeding in Canada and the United States indicated that there were 35 species with enough information to determine population trends and 18 species with insufficient information (Morrison *et al.* 2001a). Of those species with trend indicators, 28 showed negative trends (19 were statistically significant) and seven showed positive trends (one was statistically significant). This information illustrates the need for immediate management action to reverse the large number of negative population trends. However, effective conservation efforts will be challenging given a dearth of information on some of the most basic biological parameters for shorebirds in North America. The most recent report on shorebird population numbers indicated the following accuracy ratings: high (accurate and precise), two species; good (estimates on which confidence limits can be placed), five species; moderate (within 50% of true number) 13 species; low (estimate within correct order of magnitude) 21 species; and poor (based on educated guess) 12 species (Morrison *et al.* 2001b).

Recognizing that implementing conservation actions is best done using national or regional instruments, in Canada and the United States it was decided that planning for shorebird conservation at the national level was most appropriate. The Canadian (Donaldson *et al.* 2000) and US (Brown *et al.* 2001) shorebird conservation plans were developed in parallel and contain the framework necessary for regional implementation while recognizing the importance of international collaboration. Given the mobility of shorebirds among nations, it was also noted that a high level of communication was needed to ensure that the two plans were compatible and would support a high level of collaboration. Subsequently, when Mexico began development of their national shorebird conservation plan, the two established plans were used as tools and it is expected that the final version of the Mexican plan will also describe a framework for regional implementation and international collaboration.

Just as the national plans allow for stepping down to regional actions or up to international efforts, shorebird-specific implementation of habitat monitoring and research occurs at the various levels through three different programs. The Western Hemisphere Shorebird Reserve Network (WHSRN) was established in 1985 and is working in a growing number of countries in the Americas to address shorebird habitat issues. The Program for Regional and International Shorebird Monitoring (PRISM) is designed to tackle monitoring for shorebird species during breeding, migration and non-breeding periods of the year using a variety of methods in a coordinated manner at all scales. The Shorebird Research Group of the Americas (SRGA) facilitates communication among researchers by promoting the establishment of species specialist working groups that tackle information gaps for species and those that relate to determination of conservation needs and direction for conservation actions. It is important to note that all of these initiatives have been designed to be inclusive of shorebird conservation needs in all parts of the Americas, so while they may have had their initiation in the north, all aim to be inclusive of all countries of the Western Hemisphere. All recognize that incorporation of additional conservation needs may be warranted as more countries become involved.

## REFERENCES

**Brown, S., Hickey, C., Harrington, B. & Gill R.** (eds.). 2001. United States Shorebird Conservation Plan, 2nd Ed. Manomet Center for Conservation Sciences, Manomet, Massachusetts. http://www.fws.gov/shorebirdplan/USShorebird.htm

**Donaldson, G.M., Hyslop, C., Morrison, R.I.G., Dickson, H.L. & Davidson, I.** 2000. Canadian Shorebird Conservation Plan. Canadian Wildlife Service, Environment Canada, Ottawa. http://www.cws-scf.ec.gc.ca/publications/spec/cscp/index_e.cfm

**Morrison, R.I.G., Aubry, Y., Butler, R.W., Beyersbergen, G.W., Donaldson, G.M., Gratto-Trevor, C.L., Hicklin, P.W., Johnston, V.H. & Ross R.K.** 2001a. Declines in North American Shorebird Populations. Wader Study Group Bulletin 94: 34-38.

**Morrison, R.I.G., Gill, R.E. Jr., Harrington, B.A. , Skagen, S., Page, G.W., Gratto-Trevor, C.L. & Haig, S.M.** 2001b. Estimates of shorebird populations in North America. Canadian Wildlife Service Occasional Paper No. 104, Canadian Wildlife Service, Ottawa.

Waders over Mispillion, Delaware Bay. Photo: Rob Robinson.

# Issues and challenges facing migratory bird conservation programs in North America

*Steve Wendt[1], Paul Schmidt[2] & Garry Donaldson[1]*

[1] *Canadian Wildlife Service, 351 St. Joseph Blvd., Gatineau, Quebec K1A 0H3, Canada. (email: Garry.Donaldson@ea.gc.ca)*

[2] *U.S. Fish and Wildlife Service, 4401 North Fairfax Drive, Arlington, Virginia 22203, USA.*

Wendt, S., Schmidt, P. & Donaldson, G. 2006. Issues and challenges facing migratory bird conservation programs in North America. *Waterbirds around the world.* Eds. G.C. Boere, C.A. Galbraith & D.A. Stroud. The Stationery Office, Edinburgh, UK. pp. 214-216.

## ABSTRACT

Many species of North American birds continue to experience population declines of a magnitude and duration that warrant concern. Although relatively few species are in immediate danger of being lost from the most northern areas, a large number require conservation efforts to ensure sustainability and reverse declines before expensive recovery actions are needed. The purpose of this paper is to examine, in general terms, the major conservation issues facing these bird species, and challenges that complicate the delivery of solutions. National wildlife agencies in Canada and the United States have recently developed national strategies for the conservation of migratory birds. These planning efforts help us to propose the general framework for a national bird conservation program that incorporates the following components: science (knowing the status of birds, what is affecting their populations, and how to mitigate adverse effects), legislation and policy (government tools for promoting and compelling protective actions for birds and their habitats), habitat (ensuring natural spaces are available where birds can carry out their lives), and international considerations (coordinate conservation efforts so that population sustainability is not threatened by failure in non-participating nations).

## INTRODUCTION

The purpose of this paper is to examine the major issues facing migratory bird conservation programs in North America and the challenges that complicate the delivery of conservation solutions. For definition purposes, North America includes Mexico, the United States and Canada only because these countries have recently developed mechanisms for cooperation on bird conservation; we recognize that the North American continent includes many other nations of importance to migratory birds whose bird conservation perspectives are not reported here.

Migratory bird programs have many important characteristics among nature programs that tend to keep them at the forefront of conservation:–

- Bird conservation is reflected in national or higher level legislation and jurisdiction. This is partly because birds are highly migratory, and so cannot be dealt with effectively by more local levels of government.
- Many international conservation fora have been established for birds because cooperation among the nations that share species through the annual migratory cycle is needed.
- Biological information on birds is relatively good. This fact owes much to the flying ability of birds which gives them some freedom from attack by mammals (such as people). As a consequence, birds can afford to advertise their presence through attractive plumages and vocalizations that not only provide for ease of study but also create fondness for the species by people.
- Birds attract strong public interest for their beauty and cultural value, and also for their ecology and as food.

Birds have high vagility, and therefore high value as ecological indicators – in effect, birds reflect the current state of habitats better than most other organisms because they have freedom of movement.

Bird conservation faces powerful challenges. Before the sixteenth century, natural forces, combined with sometimes very significant land-use factors wielded by the indigenous people of North America, had operated on birds with positive and negative population effects that resulted in a particular distribution of birds across the continent. This situation is tempting to consider as a target for conservation because modern anthropogenic factors were absent.

Although birds face many new population pressures, it is not always easy to determine which are significant. Birds occur in every North American ecological region, and so they can be affected by almost every kind of economic activity. As favoured species for conservation, birds can be used in arguments against many societal undertakings, sometimes with little regard for evidence of effects on bird populations. Scientific studies of birds along with solid monitoring programs are needed to determine which factors must most urgently be addressed by bird conservation programs. However, what should conservation programs do in the absence of scientific certainty?

Factors that could be used to model population change in birds include natural processes, land use, water use, climate change, invasive species, environmental contaminants, and harvest (from Mac *et al.* 1998). An effective science-based program should attempt to quantify such factors in the context of their impact on birds. Without complete information, progress can still be made by assessing the potential scale of impact and developing habitat oriented approaches that have promise in softening anthropogenic effects for incompletely predicted benefit of birds and other natural resources. If very general habitat approaches are not at the outset sufficiently tied to research on birds, or, as is more often the case, if some scientific understanding is in place but it develops more slowly than habitat project work, bird conservation managers should be looking for improved scientific validation of work underway on an ongoing basis: the underlying philosophy of adaptive management.

North Americans are developing a framework for bird conservation, the North American Bird Conservation Initiative. More recently, both the U.S. Fish and Wildlife Service (2004) and the Canadian Wildlife Service (in prep.) have drafted strategic plans for migratory birds. These planning efforts help us to propose the general framework for a national bird conservation program that incorporates the following: science (knowing the status of birds, what is affecting their populations, and how to mitigate adverse effects), legislation and policy (government tools for promoting and compelling protective actions for birds and their habitats), habitat (ensuring natural spaces are available where birds can carry out their lives), and international considerations (coordinate conservation efforts so that population sustainability is not threatened by failure in non-participating nations).

## SCIENCE ISSUES

To understand the issues that arise in science, it is useful to begin with a simple version of a bird conservation program designed to make appropriate use of science. Assuming a system that begins with the designation of conservation categories for species, there should be bird population monitoring sufficient to assign all species to the correct conservation categories, and make sure that category changes are detected within a reasonable timeframe. Research should be sufficient for understanding the requirements of priority species, and to allow development of conservation actions oriented to those species and their habitats. Although this is simply put, the research supporting conservation actions may require significant socio-economic components. Science is also required for evaluation, development of new models, structured learning, and revision of plans.

It is difficult to predict all the issues that will arise in bird conservation science. This is partly because of the wide range of scientific disciplines that may be applied to problems about birds, and partly because the natural environment poses such a wide range of questions. Nevertheless, a number can be described.

Population monitoring provides a basis for bird conservation. We know that there are currently monitoring failures, and this is an issue that reduces the quality of program delivery. For example, we have poor knowledge of the status of rails (Rallidae) and other, similar marsh species. The issue becomes the need to establish adequate monitoring systems. Nocturnal species, boreal species, and some tundra-nesting shorebirds are also outside the coverage of current bird monitoring programs.

Many issues arise in knowing what factors are reducing populations, and in getting knowledge to drive conservation. For example, what is limiting populations of the Loggerhead Shrike *Lanius ludovicianus* in Canada, and what can be done about it? What has been the population effect of West Nile virus on North American birds? What design factors are important to reduce bird collisions with buildings, wind turbines, and stationary towers? Are there important sub-lethal effects from a wide range of contaminants present in the environment of birds?

Among the science issues, it is important to know that there is currently a general lack of habitat monitoring in North America, and often only rudimentary knowledge of how habitat variables that we can measure relate to bird populations.

There is growing recognition of ongoing failures in communication of results and loss of scientific knowledge. Working against this are advances in technology and use of the Internet for sharing information. Sometimes it is possible to recover long-lost data from archives and bring them back into use, as the Arctic Goose Joint Venture intends to do with a number of century-old surveys of waterfowl that U.S. scientists carried out in Mexico.

As important as any other science issue is the need to use science to evaluate and improve conservation programs. This lies at the heart of adaptive management. A current example is the planned biological evaluation of the conservation initiatives through the North American Waterfowl Management Plan.

## LEGISLATIVE AND POLICY ISSUES

When migratory bird legislation was introduced in North American countries, the immediate conservation issues were excessive hunting, especially market hunting, and collection of birds, feathers, nests, or eggs for personal use. Such practices had already led to the extinction of some species. Therefore, although habitat requirements for birds were recognized, the main thrust of regulatory tools dealt with hunting and prohibitions against possession of birds. The migratory bird treaties date from the first half of the twentieth century, but their overall intention, the preservation of migratory birds, remains valid.

Things have changed since the original treaties were developed. Additional legislative tools are available such as those that deal with endangered species and requirements for environmental assessments of new development and activities on the landscape. Governments are also increasingly committing themselves to conservation approaches through various international agreements for wildlife and habitat. An example of the latter is the Ramsar Convention on Wetlands. Unfortunately, human impacts on birds have accelerated, so that the indirect take of birds, as described below, now numbers in the many millions and is becoming an issue of high priority for North American governments.

Among the legislative issues facing us, we feel that three should be highlighted from the current perspective: forestry management systems need to support sustained populations of forest birds; agricultural programs need to encourage preservation of threatened bird habitats such as wetlands and native grasslands; and governments need effective tools to manage the incidental take of birds caused by economic or industrial activity. Examples of the latter include the occurrence of birds oiled at sea and the damage to bird populations as a result of fishing and forestry practices.

## HABITAT AND CONSERVATION ISSUES

When assessing conservation from a risk or assessment point of view, it is almost impossible to remove the role of habitat. Among the conservation issues affecting birds, there is such a wealth of possible risks, combined with a lack of information about how the risks could affect the sustainability of bird populations, that it is not possible to provide rankings. Wetlands continue to disappear, old growth forests and native prairies are shrinking. Habitat quality is under threat from overuse, pollution, and disturbance by exotic species. Increased contaminants including airborne global pollutants are finding their way into even those ecosystems quite recently thought to be pristine. At the risk of being unspecific, we note the following list of issues that are active concerns because of their potential impact on birds:

- Habitat loss and nest destruction
    - Expansion of farms, urban development; transportation and other linear development
    - Wetland drainage and modification
    - Unplanned consequences of fire management, livestock management, shrimp farming, tourism development, salt extraction, energy development, mining, aquaculture and many other human activities

- Contaminants
  - Oil at sea and oil tailings and production spills
  - Pesticides
  - Lead from fishing and hunting
  - Hazardous industrial wastes
- Introduced predators, competitors or diseases
- Environmentally triggered diseases (botulism)
- Physical threats - entanglement in fishing gear, collisions
- Hunting taking place outside conservation frameworks

Wetlands in all parts of the continent are of importance to a variety of species. Because the diversity of activities that occur near wetlands and wetland types are richer in Mexico, we have chosen to summarize the wetland issues in that country as an example of the diverse challenges for conservation in these habitats. The following issues were extracted from Inventory of Mexican Wetlands (Carrera & de la Fuente 2003): stream flow reduction by reservoirs, sedimentation, salt extraction industries, shrimp farming, tourism development, agricultural expansion, contamination, extraction of water for other uses, and drainage for reclamation.

One of the more quantitative recent works on conservation issues for birds was the review of the extent that birds may be affected by collisions and electrocutions associated with man-made objects in the United States (Manville 2005). Estimates were reported for vehicles strikes ($10^7$ birds), building and window collisions ($10^7$ - $10^8$ birds), smoke stack casualties ($10^4$ - $10^5$ birds), power line electrocutions ($10^4$ - $10^5$ birds), power line impacts ($10^5$ - $10^7$ birds), communication tower accidents ($10^6$ - $10^7$ birds), and wind turbine impacts ($10^5$ birds). This would amount to a total mortality of $10^8$ to $10^9$ birds annually. This information was adapted from the U.S. report; however, we state the results rounded to powers of 10, in recognition of the difficulty in coming up with precise estimates of these problems. The take-home message is that the cumulative impact of collisions is probably very significant.

The impact of climate change on birds is mostly predicted by models, rather than having much evidence from direct results. That is why we can hypothesize major impacts on the distribution and abundance of birds from climate model predictions, while, at a species level, climate change is not often identified as a current threat. Gross predictions of changes in moisture distribution can be applied to landscapes and the birds that occur there. That is not to say that the authors do not recognize the future threat of climate change on bird habitats, but that there is generally a lack of sufficient information to characterize it for particular bird species.

## INTERNATIONAL COORDINATION ISSUES

The creation of national boundaries across landscapes used by wildlife can impose considerable challenges to wildlife that may encounter widely ranging differences in land use depending on the country they are in. Economic status, government structures and priorities, and differing cultural practices and values among other factors will vary among countries and influence the availability and quality of habitats for wildlife. Considerations for North American migratory birds include the countries of the Western Hemisphere as well as countries across the Atlantic and Pacific oceans that birds may access if originating at northern latitudes.

Communication and coordination are key elements of successful international conservation efforts. For example,

effective internationally coordinated monitoring efforts for migratory birds will ensure that all countries in a species' range have access to information on distribution, abundance and trends. In addition, international collaboration on monitoring will allow for discussion on how best to monitor species so that efforts are directed to the best locations and times of year. Other key elements include:

- Consistency among legal protection mechanisms
- Access to international conservation resources for birds
- Meeting the obligations for wetlands, and expansion of international focus beyond wetlands.

Conservation at a national level is often challenging in terms of capacity to coordinate a variety of interests and participants (e.g. government and non-governmental organizations); these challenges are multiplied when efforts move into the international arena. There is a need in the Americas to bring together governments and citizens to develop a framework for the conservation of migratory wildlife among nations. Environment Ministers at the 2001 Summit of the Americas in Quebec City recognized this and called for just such an effort.

## CONCLUDING REMARKS

Considering the challenges presented by issues of science, habitat, legislation and international cooperation, the task at hand is not to be taken lightly. An increasing trend is towards the development of partnerships among governments, non-governmental organizations, academia and industries to come together to work towards common goals. By working together to identify conservation priorities and develop action plans that take advantage of each partner's strengths and capacities, the seemingly complicated task of effecting positive change becomes more tangible. To this end, the North American Bird Conservation Initiative (NABCI) is bringing people and organizations together on local, regional, national and international scales to meet common conservation goals in Mexico, the United States and Canada. NABCI's principles and achievements to date offer an example to other regions of a model that can be adopted or modified in other countries to address conservation using a partner-driven approach.

## REFERENCES

**Canadian Wildlife Service** (in prep.). Migratory Bird Program Plan. Canadian Wildlife Service, Gatineau, Quebec.

**Carrera, E. & de la Fuente, G.** 2003. Inventario y clasificatión de humedales en México. Parte 1. Ducks Unlimited de México, A.C. México.

**Mac, M.J., Opler, P.A., Puckett Heaker, C.E. & Doran, P.D.** 1998. Status and trends of the nation's biological resources. Two volumes. U.S. Department of the Interior, U.S. Geological Survey, Reston, Virginia.

**Manville, A.M., II.** 2005. Bird Strikes And Electrocutions At Power Lines, Communication Towers, And Wind Turbines: State Of The Art And State Of The Science – Next Steps Toward Mitigation. USDA Forest Service General Technical Report PSW-GTR-191.

**U.S. Fish and Wildlife Service** 2004. A Blueprint for the Future of Migratory Birds, Migratory Bird Program Strategic Plan 2004-2014. USFWS, Arlington, Virginia.

# 3.4   Intra-African migration. Workshop Introduction

*Issa Sylla[1] & Tim Dodman[2]*
[1]*Wetlands International, West African Programme, PO Box 8060, Dakar-Yoff, Senegal.*
[2]*Wetlands International, Hundland, Papa Westray, Orkney, KW17 2BU, UK.*

Sylla, I. & Dodman, T. 2006. Intra-African migration. Workshop Introduction. *Waterbirds around the world*. Eds. G.C. Boere, C.A. Galbraith & D.A. Stroud. The Stationery Office, Edinburgh, UK. p. 217.

Great White Pelicans *Pelecanus oncrotalus* roost together at very great densities at the Doudj National Park in Senegal. Photo: Sergey Dereliev.

Many of Africa's migratory and resident waterbirds have poor conservation status and largely unknown population trends. Whilst there has been some research and conservation of migratory birds in Africa, this has focussed largely on African-Eurasian migrants, and the status and needs of most intra-African migrants are much less clear.

The workshop aimed to identify actions that would be important to promote development of research and conservation of intra-African migrants and resident waterbirds, including through the implementation of the African-Eurasian Waterbird Agreement. It reached the following recommendations:

### Identifying actions needed for the conservation of intra-African migratory waterbirds

A key issue that hampers the conservation of African waterbirds is a limited knowledge of their conservation needs, particularly related to their movements, which are often unpredictable. It is also difficult to identify key site networks in some areas, due to the irregular but important role of temporary wetlands. In order to promote development of research and conservation of African waterbirds, the following recommendations are proposed. These are drawn largely from the issues affecting intra-African migration presented in the workshop and subsequent discussions. Dodman & Diagana provide further information about intra-African migration:–

1   Improve our knowledge of the status of African waterbirds and their migratory patterns through:
   - Applied research of weather patterns, site conditions and waterbird seasonality;
   - Extending the African Waterbird Census to other seasons and other areas;

   - Use/analysis of existing African Waterbird Census and other data to identify site linkages and migratory patterns;
   - Increased adoption of satellite telemetry (Childress *et al.* gives an example as to the value of this technology in elucidating sites networks for Lesser Flamingo *Phoenicopterus minor*);
   - Initial conservation focus on a series of 'high profile species';
   - Monitoring, research and conservation of threatened species (Young's description of research on the ecology of Madagascar Teal *Anas bernieri* is a good example of what is needed); and
   - Development of AFRING.

2   Identify key sites and site networks for intra-African migrants, especially threatened species (Mlingwa & Baker highlight the key importance of networks of sites for Lesser Flamingo *Phoenicopterus minor* in the soda lakes of Tanzania).

3   Develop Species Action Plans for African waterbirds.

4   Promote increased focus on intra-African migrants in the implementation of the African-Eurasian Waterbird Agreement.

5   Adopt a precautionary principle; it is often necessary to implement conservation action before knowing the full picture.

6   Enhance awareness of African waterbirds, especially their values and ecological roles.

7   Highlight the plight and lack of knowledge of threatened African waterbirds.

8   Mobilise resources for conservation and monitoring of intra-African migrants, especially through development and subsequent implementation of a Conservation Strategy for African Waterbirds.

# Conservation dilemmas for intra-African migratory waterbirds

*Tim Dodman[1] & Cheikh Hamallah Diagana[2]*

[1] *Wetlands International, Hundland, Papa Westray, Orkney, KW17 2BU, UK. (email: tim@timdodman.co.uk)*

[2] *Wetlands International, West African Programme, PO Box 8060, Dakar-Yoff, Senegal.*

Dodman, T. & Diagana, C.H. 2006. Conservation dilemmas for intra-African migratory waterbirds. *Waterbirds around the world.* Eds. G.C. Boere, C.A. Galbraith & D.A. Stroud. The Stationery Office, Edinburgh, UK. pp. 218-223.

## ABSTRACT

Africa is a vast and diverse continent, rich in coastal and inland wetlands, permanent and temporary, tropical and temperate. Waterbirds in Africa have developed diverse strategies to exploit this wetland diversity. Some species are largely sedentary, especially those in relatively static tropical climates. However, most demonstrate movements in response to changing seasons and environmental conditions. The onset of rain is an important trigger for migration within Africa. Some waterbirds are harbingers of the rainy season, whilst others follow in the wake of rain. However, levels and timing of rain can be unpredictable, and rain may not fall at all in some years. When rain falls in arid and semi-arid areas, productive temporary wetlands can appear overnight, and attract large numbers of waterbirds, many of which display some nomadic tendencies. This unpredictability presents difficult management scenarios. Overall, waterbird movements within Africa are poorly understood, and there are few clearly identifiable "named" flyways. This directly limits our abilities to conserve waterbirds in Africa, and to implement the African-Eurasian Migratory Waterbird Agreement. It will take major resources and many years before we have clear pictures of waterbird movements within Africa. Yet conservation measures are needed now, especially for those species in decline.

## INTRODUCTION

This paper constitutes a desk-study review of the movements of waterbirds within Africa, drawing on published references, analyses of African Waterbird Census (AfWC) data and observations. As these movements are poorly understood, we aim to illustrate some intra-African migratory strategies and behaviours, and use these to draw up recommendations for conservation purposes and, in particular, improved implementation of the African-Eurasian Migratory Waterbird Agreement (AEWA) in Africa.

## METHODS

The methodological process of the review was to identify potential conservation dilemmas for migratory waterbirds in Africa and, as far as possible, to illustrate in the "results" the migratory strategies adopted by waterbirds in relation to these dilemmas and to Africa's geography and climate, whilst the focus of the discussion is on drawing up recommendations. However, the first dilemma concerns definitions, and is best considered under the methodology.

### Dilemma 1: Definition disorders

**Waterbird:** The Convention on Wetlands (Ramsar, 1971) defines "waterfowl" as species of birds that are ecologically dependent upon wetlands, and "waterbird" as being synonymous with "waterfowl" (Wetlands International 2002). Rose & Scott (1994) define "waterfowl" more precisely as all species of 32 families,

essentially comprising the main waterbird groups falling between the Gaviidae (divers) and the Rhynchopidae (skimmers) following the traditional sequence of bird families (Morony *et al.* 1975). This group of families is noted, non-exclusively, by the Convention on Wetlands for application of waterbird criteria, although not all their members are wetland-dependent, such as the Crowned Plover *Vanellus coronatus* and coursers. Conversely, there are wetland-dependent birds in other families, such as the Osprey *Pandion haliaetus*, and some kingfishers, coucals and warblers.

### Migration, nomadism and "wintering":

Using the definition of the Convention on the Conservation of Migratory Species of Wild Animals, "migratory species" refers to "the entire population or any geographically separate part of the population of any species or lower taxon of wild animals, a significant proportion of whose members cyclically and predictably cross one or more national jurisdictional boundaries". In terms of migratory waterbirds, the northwards and southwards movements of birds breeding in the Northern Hemisphere during the northern summer and spending the northern winter further south are arguably the most clearly understood and fit within this definition very well. Intra-African movements are often less clear, as they are sometimes neither cyclical nor predictable. Several species usually referred to as "migrants" in Africa are essentially "nomads" or "dispersers", whilst many often described as "residents" do perform regular migrations within Africa. Waterbirds have developed a range of strategies to survive Africa's changing seasons and to exploit temporary habitats, most usually linked to rainfall.

The term "**migratory species**" can also be misleading, as some species have both discrete migratory and sedentary populations. An example is the Eurasian Spoonbill *Platalea leucorodia*, which has four populations occurring in Africa. Two are migratory populations breeding in Europe and spending the northern winter in Africa, whilst there are also two (largely) resident populations, *balsaci* in coastal Mauritania and *archeri* in the Red Sea and Somalia.

**Intra-African migration** is generally accepted to refer to movements within Africa. In this paper, intra-African migration is considered as "the movement of birds within Africa and around its coastline according to local triggers and continental weather patterns, especially rainfall". Movements between the African continent and its outlying islands are also considered here.

**Nomadism** is displayed by animals that move irregularly; nomads are wanderers, though their movements away from and to particular areas may be predictable, usually relating to climatic conditions.

"**Wintering**" is a term that is widely used to describe birds temporarily residing in areas during winter, usually the northern winter. It is often more widely applied, such that "wintering areas" are taken to be the main places of residence when not breeding. As there are two winters in Africa (north and south of the equator) and no winter at all in the tropics, the term is very misleading in an African context, where most movements of birds bear no relation to winter as such. "Non-breeding" is proposed here as an alternative term for "wintering".

## RESULTS

### Dilemma 2: Complicated arrows (diverse migratory behaviour)

Familiar flyway maps depict migratory routes, mostly in north-south directions and often reasonably well-defined and characterized by bottlenecks, such as the Straits of Gibraltar, coastlines, such as the East Atlantic Flyway, and major rivers, such as the Nile. By comparison, intra-African movements are more complex, with "arrows" in all directions. Some movements occur across a broad front, some are "one-way tickets", some are of greatly varying lengths, whilst some species disperse widely in a wide range of directions. Recoveries of the Red-billed Teal *Anas erythrorhyncha* ringed in southern Zambia, for instance, are from further north in Zambia, west in Namibia, south in South Africa and Botswana, and east in Zimbabwe (Dowsett & Leonard 2001). Complex movements like these present difficult challenges for waterbird conservation, such as the identification of key sites for different stages in the life cycle.

The main causal factor for waterbird movements within Africa is the availability of food and water, which is principally affected by the climate, notably rainfall. Marine productivity also affects food availability for coastal species. Other factors, such as breeding, altitude, moulting and fire, are all important parts of "the migration equation", but mostly relate to the underlying importance of food availability. There are several different "migratory behavioural types":

- **Local movers / short-distance migrants.** Some waterbirds move relatively short distances between a network of key sites. Their migrations are fairly regular and predictable. An example is the sub-population of the Black Crowned Crane *Balearica pavonina* breeding in marshy floodplains of the Casamance of southern Senegal between August and November, then migrating to wetlands of Guinea-Bissau, where numbers peak in January (Diagana *et al.* in prep.).
- **Rains migrants / arid migrants.** This group includes a large number of species for which rainfall or, conversely, dwindling water resources are the principal triggers for movement, as discussed below (Dilemma 3).
- **Nutrition migrants / post-roost dispersers.** Some waterbirds share common night roosts and disperse widely by day in search of food. White Pelicans *Pelecanus onocrotalus* can cover large distances during a single day: in some areas, their roosts may be far from any water source. They are essentially day migrants, flying to distant wetlands daily from secure roosts or breeding colonies. Some large White Pelican roosts or breeding sites, however, are found very close to their main feeding areas, such as those in the lower Senegal Valley, so the need for undisturbed roosts may be the principal factor behind their migratory behaviour.
- **Post-breeding dispersers.** Many birds disperse after breeding and also fall into other "migration categories", such

as rains migrants. Some, however, disperse widely away from breeding sites in different directions, an example being the Grey-headed Gull *Larus cirrocephalus*. Ringing recoveries from birds ringed at colonies in South Africa (on the eastern Witwatersrand) show striking dispersal, with movements to Mozambique, Zimbabwe, Zambia, Botswana, Namibia and Angola, and within South Africa to the southwest and east coasts (Underhill *et al.* 1999). It is hard to determine if these constitute migratory movements, as it is not clear if the same birds are returning to breed in the area or colony where they were themselves born.

- **Nomads.** True nomads are not migrants, as they do not move in a cyclical or predictable manner. However, some nomadic movements are predictable to a certain extent, in that they are usually in response to, often irregular, climatic or environmental conditions, for instance in semi-arid areas with irregular rainfall. In such areas, temporary wetlands may attract large numbers of waterbirds, even when they only appear every few years. The Lesser Flamingo *Phoenicopterus minor* can be considered as a nomad, with birds in eastern Africa moving frequently and unpredictably between a series of known key sites in the Rift Valley, as demonstrated by Childress *et al.* (2006).
- **Altitudinal migrants.** Some waterbirds, particularly in eastern Africa, are at least partial altitudinal migrants. One example is the (Eastern) African Snipe *Gallinago nigripennis aequatorialis*, which breeds in highland bogs up to 4 000 m above sea level, from where altitudinal migration takes place to lower-lying and warmer areas during the non-breeding season (Gichuki *et al.* 2000).
- **Environmental response migrants.** Some waterbirds move opportunistically as a result of, sometimes irregular, environmental conditions and local habitat changes. Apart from rainfall, other environmental conditions such as fire and locust eruptions can precipitate movement. Movements of the Lesser Black-winged Lapwing *Vanellus lugubris*, for instance, may in part be dictated by brush fires in some areas, which cause new grass growth suitable for nesting (Urban *et al.* 1986).

### Dilemma 3: Complex rain patterns

The main trigger for intra-African migration of waterbirds is food availability in relation to rainfall. In Africa, rainfall derives primarily from the Inter-Tropical Convergence Zone (ITCZ), where moist maritime air meets dry continental air, along which rain then falls on a broad front (Jones 1995). The movement of the ITCZ north and south across the equator gives rise to the annual pattern of rainy seasons. In general, the broad rainy season north of the equator, including the Sahel zone, is between May and November, and in southern Africa between November and April, with rain in equatorial regions occurring all year round and with a pattern of variable twin rains in eastern Africa (Fig. 1). However, rainfall is not always regular, nor is it reliable in its duration and amount. Sometimes there is no rain at all in semi-arid and arid areas, such as south-western Africa. Rainfall is the major trigger for migration, and some species are trans-equatorial migrants, such as Abdim's Stork *Ciconia abdimi*, which leaves the Sahel after rains and visits eastern and southern Africa as rains begin.

Direct effects of local rainfall are particularly apparent in semi-arid areas, for instance the filling of ephemeral wetlands in

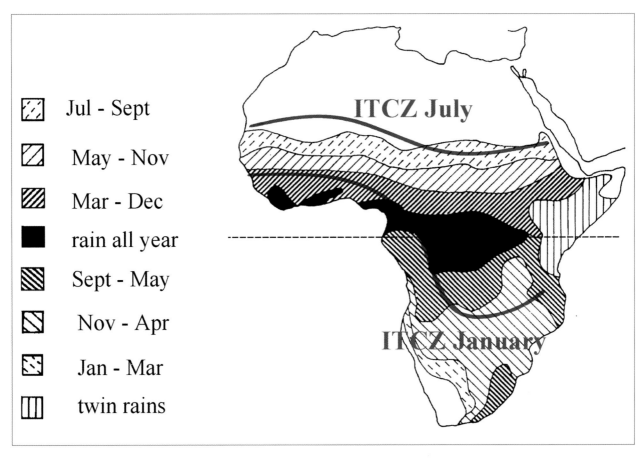

**Fig. 1.** The timing and duration of rainfall in sub-Saharan Africa (Jones 1995). The thick lines show the July (northern midsummer) and January (northern midwinter) positions of the Inter-Tropical Convergence Zone (ITCZ).

semi-arid Namibia and Niger. In Namibia, widespread rains reduce bird numbers at permanent wetlands, when birds disperse widely to newly flooded parts, whilst some breed opportunistically as wetlands fill up. This occurred in 1996/97, when the Common Coot *Fulica atra*, Lesser Moorhen *Gallinula angulata*, Whiskered Tern *Chlidonias hybridus* and Black-necked Grebe *Podiceps nigricollis* bred *en masse* at Nyae Nyae Pan in central north-east Namibia (R. Simmons in Dodman *et al.* 1997). Several species of wetland birds in Namibia directly follow rain fronts, descending onto pans as they fill (Simmons *et al.* 1999). In Niger, isolated temporary wetlands provide an important resource for waterbirds, with the smaller lakes usually having a higher nutrient load and supporting high densities of waterbirds as they gradually dry out (Mullié *et al.* 1999).

Another feature of rainfall that drives the movements of waterbirds is the cycle of flooding and changing water levels of riverine wetlands. This is particularly important in floodplain areas, such as those found on the Niger, Nile and Zambezi rivers. The flooding patterns do not relate so much to local rainfall as rainfall in the headwaters and wider catchments of the rivers. The effect is particularly strong on the middle stretches of the Nile and Niger rivers, where rainfall in the Sahel zone is limited, whilst rainfall in the upper reaches of these rivers is much more significant. This effect of "indirect rain" is important in understanding the movements of birds into and out of extensive wetlands such as the Inner Niger Delta. Here, peak floods occur between November and January (Zwarts & Diallo 2002), several months after the period of peak rainfall from June to August in the upper reaches of the Niger River in Guinea.

**Diverse rain triggers waterbird movements**
Within this dynamic picture of rainfall in Africa, there are different triggers for the movements of waterbirds. These include:

- ***Sudden availability of productive wetlands.*** This is usually caused by direct rainfall, and is particularly apparent in semi-arid areas, with filling of ephemeral wetlands. Many prey items for waterbirds are prolific at the onset of rains, and ephemeral wetlands can support high biomass densities. In Niger, for example, small lakes tend to have the highest fish production and highest densities of waterbirds (Mullié *et al.* 1999).

- ***Rising water levels / flooding.*** Rising water levels are attractive for some floodplain waterbirds, especially those that feed on wetland plants and on prey items in swamps. The inundated wetlands and rice-fields of Guinea-Bissau are attractive for some Palearctic migrants such as the Black-tailed Godwit *Limosa limosa*, but they also support good numbers of intra-African migrants, notably herons, egrets, rails and Black Crowned Cranes (Dodman *et al.* 2004). The Wattled Crane *Grus carunculatus* also favours floodplains; its diet includes the tubers of floodplain plants (Meine & Archibald 1996). Conversely, rising water levels drive some waterbirds out of wetlands, especially shorebirds, which lose the habitat of exposed mud or lake edge. Almost the entire Zambian population of Kittlitz's Plover *Charadrius pecuarius* leaves during high floods (Urban *et al.* 1986), when its preferred semi-arid floodplain habitat becomes inundated.

- **Falling water levels / edge effects.** As dry seasons set in or as floods of major rivers recede, many wetlands start to shrink. This provides rich new food sources for many waterbirds, as previously unobtainable mud-dwelling invertebrates become exposed and as nutrient loads in smaller wetlands increase. As waters gradually recede, feeding conditions are optimal for birds which forage at the water's edge, and wader densities in particular can increase. Predatory species such as the Great Cormorant *Phalacrocorax carbo* and Marabou Stork *Leptoptilos crumeniferus* are attracted to shrinking pools, where concentrations of prey, such as catfish, can become very high. Water levels fall in the Inner Niger Delta mainly between January and April (Zwarts & Diallo 2002), providing optimum feeding conditions for several species of Palearctic-breeding waders. Some intra-African migrants also start to increase in number in the delta from February/March as floods recede, as detailed in van der Kamp & Diallo (1999): Kittlitz's Plover colonizes the dried flats, where it breeds, whilst the Spur-winged Plover *Vanellus spinosus* appears almost as soon as floods start to recede.

- **Lack of rain / increasing aridity.** In semi-arid areas where there are limited permanent water sources such as larger rivers, wetlands are only available for a relatively short period. When these ephemeral wetlands finally dry up, there can be a sudden exodus of waterbirds. In such cases, it is the prevailing arid conditions that act as the trigger for migration, not the onset of rains elsewhere. Some birds exploit the last shrinking wetlands until they dry up completely. There are several ephemeral pools in Botswana's Makgadikgadi System, including Rysana Pan. In January 2001, this pan was dry except for ten remnant pools; some of the last birds to leave here were Kittlitz's Plover, Chestnut-banded Plover *Charadrius pallidus*, Caspian Plover *Charadrius asiaticus* and Little Stint *Calidris minuta*, whilst a pair of South African Shelducks *Tadorna cana* still remained at one dwindling pool (Tyler 2001).

Most of the main rains/water-related triggers for migration, such as flooding, falling water levels and direct rainfall, can thus serve as instigators of arrival or departure. This may be illustrated by comparing the movements of two storks: Abdim's Stork and the African Openbill *Anastomus lamelligerus*. Both are trans-equatorial migrants. Abdim's Stork breeds in the Sahel belt of west-central Africa between May and August and migrates after breeding to eastern and southern Africa, stopping en route in productive feeding areas. Popular migration routes and key non-breeding sites have recently been described by Peterson *et al.* (in press), who tracked storks moving from breeding areas in Niger across to north-west Tanzania and further south, eventually moving back, following the rains north, to the same area to breed. Conversely, the African Openbill breeds mainly in southern and eastern Africa, usually late in the rainy season and into the dry season, with some thence migrating north of the equator, where it is mainly a dry season visitor, arriving after the rains and staying for a good part of the dry season. It also has some irregular mass migrations. The preferred food of Abdim's Stork is grasshoppers, whilst the African Openbill feeds almost exclusively on snails and freshwater mussels. Optimal feeding conditions for Abdim's Stork

are during wet periods, when there is plenty of food available in grasslands and floodplains. It pays for this stork to leave its breeding area as food resources become scarcer during the dry season, and to move into areas just as rains begin. However, for the African Openbill, molluscs are more readily available well into the rainy season and as wetlands start to recede.

One species that is often quick to exploit productive wetlands is the Fulvous Whistling Duck *Dendrocygna bicolor*, which can appear periodically in very large numbers, suggesting that it is highly mobile (Scott & Rose 1996). Whistling-ducks display semi-nomadic tendencies, exploiting diverse wetland habitats such as floodplains, coastal lagoons and ephemeral wetlands, congregating at large wetlands for moulting and feeding. The White-faced Whistling Duck *D. viduata* is also regular within the forest block. The importance of the forest block of Central Africa as a refuge and stopover zone for intra-African migrants is poorly understood.

### Dilemma 4: Divergent coastal movements
#### Madagascar-Africa migration

A handful of birds migrate between continental Africa and Madagascar. Two are of particularly unfavourable conservation status. The Madagascar Squacco Heron *Ardeola idae* leaves Madagascar around April after breeding and heads for southern and central-southern Africa, where it is mainly present during the dry season. It has declined dramatically, possibly due to competition with the Squacco Heron *A. ralloides*, which appears to be spreading in Madagascar and is more adaptable to man-made habitats (Morris & Hawkins 1998). The Madagascar Pratincole *Glareola ocularis* migrates to coastal eastern Africa, where it is mainly present from April to September. It breeds mostly in eastern Madagascar and migrates to Madagascar's west coast, before uplifting for coastal Tanzania, thence moving along the coastal belt of Kenya to southern Somalia. As the only pratincole to occur in Madagascar, its migratory behaviour may have originated in Africa, in pursuit of suitable breeding localities. Whatever the reason, it is a species in decline (Dodman 2002) and in need of conservation action at key non-breeding sites and in breeding areas.

The Madagascar Teal *Anas bernieri*, however, is a short-distance migrant within Madagascar. After breeding in the mangroves of western Madagascar, this globally threatened duck moves to secluded areas for the moult, and then to wetland refugia during the dry season (Young 2004, 2006); conservation measures must take account of the networks of sites essential to the teal during the different stages of this annual cycle.

### Coastal migration

There are divergent movements of waterbirds all around Africa's coastline, with varying patterns in West Africa, the Red Sea, the Mediterranean and the Mozambique Channel; but what are the main triggers for movement? A key factor affecting the distribution of many species is the availability of suitable breeding areas. Movement is mainly governed by marine productivity and the life cycles of pelagic fish, with breeding occurring when feeding conditions are optimal near breeding islands, and with subsequent dispersal afterwards in pursuit of profitable feeding areas. The Royal Tern *Sterna maxima* depends on a range of breeding sites in West Africa, mostly low-lying sandy islands, where it breeds in May. Yet estuarine systems and off-shore sandy archipelagos are fairly dynamic, and some breeding islands may disappear completely in strong seas, as happened recently in Guinea (N. Keita pers. comm.). However, as the terns depend on a network of sites, they can breed elsewhere within a similar area. Indeed, there are regular fluctuations in breeding numbers at several sites monitored in Senegal, The Gambia and Mauritania (Veen *et al.* 2003). After breeding, the terns disperse along the coast. The Caspian Tern *S. caspia* also breeds on similar islands off West Africa, although it differs in having an extended breeding season, enabling birds to be much more flexible in their annual life cycle. Annual variations in timing of breeding of the Roseate Tern *S. dougallii* and Lesser Noddy *Anous tenuirostris* on Aride Island, Seychelles, reflect the unpredictability of food supplies at the start of the breeding season (Ramos & Monticelli in press).

## DISCUSSION

### Conservation management dilemmas

There are a number of difficulties in attempting to manage migratory species and to maintain populations in a healthy conservation status. Such challenges have been widely discussed in the past, and indeed formed the bedrock of international co-operation that led to the creation of the Ramsar Convention on Wetlands. More recently, the AEWA was launched as another vehicle for international co-operation. However conservation of intra-African migrants presents additional difficulties, in particular:

- Many African flyways are diffuse, and not easy to specify.
- Some sites are only important irregularly, e.g. once every few years, especially temporary wetlands.
- Site networks are not always obvious, and may include large numbers of small wetlands or sites that are not used regularly.
- Several species exploit wetlands at different periods and for different reasons, such that sites cannot be maintained in a constant state; rather it is important to permit natural flooding and other cycles.
- Many waterbirds are nomadic and are not faithful to specific routes or annual seasons.
- It is difficult to monitor intra-African migrants: current procedures under the AfWC focused on co-ordinated bi-annual censuses are not effective enough in identifying migratory strategies.
- On a practical level, there are low resources and capacity for conserving intra-African migrants, whilst other issues also influence monitoring, such as inaccessibility and security.

### Recommendations for the conservation of intra-African migrants

The high diversity of "movement strategies" of African waterbirds and the often limited ability to predict movements render their management and conservation quite difficult. The life cycles and movements of most African waterbirds are not precisely known, and the networks of key sites not well determined. In light of this, and taking account the issues summarized above, the following recommendations are proposed:

1 Improve our knowledge of the status of African waterbirds and their migratory patterns through:
   - Applied research of weather patterns, site conditions and waterbird seasonality;

   - Extending the AfWC to other seasons and other areas;
   - Use/analysis of existing AfWC and other data to identify site linkages and migratory patterns;
   - Increased adoption of satellite telemetry;
   - Initial conservation focus on a series of "high profile species";
   - Monitoring, research and conservation of threatened species;
   - Development of AFRING (African bird ringing scheme).
2 Identify key sites and site networks for intra-African migrants, especially threatened species.
3 Develop Species Action Plans for African waterbirds.
4 Promote increased focus on intra-African migrants in the implementation of the AEWA.
5 Adopt a precautionary principle; it is often necessary to implement conservation action before knowing the full picture.
6 Enhance awareness of African waterbirds, especially their values and ecological roles.
7 Highlight the plight and lack of knowledge of threatened African waterbirds.
8 Mobilize resources for conservation and monitoring of intra-African migrants, especially through development and subsequent implementation of a Conservation Strategy for African Waterbirds.

## ACKNOWLEDGEMENTS

We acknowledge the support of Wetlands International and the Government of The Netherlands in enabling us to participate in the Waterbirds Around the World Conference. We thank all participants and supporters of the African Waterbird Census. Special thanks to Dr Peter Jones for permission to reproduce the map. Thanks also to Dr Gerard Boere for accepting our rather late submission and to an anonymous referee for constructive comments.

## REFERENCES

**Childress, B., Hughes, B., Harper, D., Van den Bossche, W., Berthold, P & Querner, U.** 2006. Satellite tracking documents the East African Flyway and key site network of the Lesser Flamingo *Phoenicopterus minor.* Waterbirds around the world. G.C. Boere, C.A. Galbraith & D.A. Stroud (Eds.), The Stationery Office, Edinburgh, UK. 234-238.

**Diagana, C.H., Dodman, T. & Ndiaye, I.** In prep. Conservation Status of Black Crowned Crane at selected wetlands in Sahelian Africa (working title). Wetlands International, Dakar, Senegal.

**Dodman, T.** 2002. Waterbird Population Estimates in Africa. Unpublished consultation draft, Wetlands International.

**Dodman, T., de Vaan, C., Hubert, E. & Nivet, C.** 1997. African Waterfowl Census 1997 / Les Dénombrements Internationaux d'oiseaux d'eau en Afrique, 1997. Wetlands International, Wageningen, The Netherlands.

**Dodman, T., Barlow, C., Sá, J. & Robertson, P.** 2004. Zonas Importantes para as Aves na Guiné-Bissau / Important Bird Areas in Guinea-Bissau. Wetlands International, Dakar; Senegal. Gabinete de Planificação Costeira, ODZH, Bissau.

**Dowsett, R.J. & Leonard, P.M.** 2001. Results from Bird Ringing in Zambia. In: P. Leonard, C. Beel & P. Van

Daele (eds) 1999 Zambia Bird Report. Zambian Ornithological Society, Lusaka, Zambia: 6-46.

**Gichuki, C.M., Gichuki, N.N. & Kairu, E.** 2000. Population biology and breeding ecology of the African Snipe (*Gallinago nigripennis*) in central Kenya. In: H. Kalchreuter (ed) Fifth European Woodcock and Snipe Workshop – Proceedings of an International Symposium of the Wetlands International Woodcock and Snipe Specialist Group, 3-5 May 1998. Wetlands International Global Series No. 4, International Wader Studies 11, Wageningen, The Netherlands: 45-50.

**Jones, P.** 1995. Migration strategies of Palearctic passerines in Africa. Israel Journal of Zoology, Vol. 41: 393-406.

**Meine, C.D. & Archibald, G.W.** (eds). 1996. The Cranes: Status Survey and Conservation Action Plan. IUCN, Gland, Switzerland, and Cambridge, UK.

**Morony, J.J., Jr., Bock, W.J. & Farrand, J.** 1975. Reference List of the Birds of the World. Department of Ornithology, American Museum of Natural History, New York, USA.

**Morris, P. & Hawkins, F.** 1998. Birds of Madagascar: A Photographic Guide. Pica Press, UK.

**Mullié, W.C., Brouwer, J., Codjo, S.F. & Decae, R.** 1999. Small isolated wetlands in the Central Sahel: a resource shared between people and waterbirds. In: A. Beintema & J. van Vessem (eds) Strategies for Conserving Migratory Waterbirds. Proceedings of Workshop 2 of the 2nd International Conference on Wetlands and Development held in Dakar, Senegal, 8-14 November 1998. Wetlands International Publication No. 55, Wageningen, The Netherlands.

**Peterson, B.S., Falk, K., Jensen, F.P. & Christensen, K.D.** In press. Abdim's Stork movements: Where to go year round in search of grasshoppers. In: Proceedings of the Eleventh Pan-African Ornithological Congress, Djerba, Tunisia, 20-25 November 2004. Ostrich Supplement.

**Ramos, J.A. & Monticelli, D.** In press. Long-term studies on productivity of Roseate Terns and Lesser Noddies on Aride Island, Seychelles. In: Proceedings of the Eleventh Pan-African Ornithological Congress, Djerba, Tunisia, 20-25 November 2004. Ostrich Supplement.

**Rose, P.M. & Scott. D.A.** 1994. Waterfowl Population Estimates. IWRB Publication 29, Slimbridge, UK.

**Scott, D.A. & Rose, P.M.** 1996. Atlas of Anatidae Populations in Africa and Western Eurasia. Wetlands International Publication No. 41, Wageningen, The Netherlands.

**Simmons, R.E., Barnard, P.E. & Jamieson, I.G.** 1999. What precipitates influxes of birds to ephemeral wetlands in arid landscapes? Observations from Namibia. Ostrich 70: 145-148.

**Tyler, S.** 2001. A review of waterbird counts in Botswana, 1991-2000. Babbler Special Supplement No. 1.

**Underhill, L.G., Tree, A.J., Oschadleus, H.D. & Parker, V.** 1999. Review of Ring Recoveries of Waterbirds in Southern Africa. Avian Demography Unit, University of Cape Town, Cape Town, South Africa.

**Urban, E.K., Fry, C.H. & Keith, S.** 1986. The Birds of Africa Volume II. Academic Press, London, UK.

**Van der Kamp, J. & Diallo, M.** 1999. Suivi écologique du Delta Intérieur du Niger: Les Oiseaux d'Eau comme bio-indicateurs. Recensements crue 1998-1999. Mali-PIN publication 99-02. Wetlands International, Sévaré, Mali, and Altenburg & Wymenga, Veenwouden, The Netherlands.

**Veen, J., Peeters, J., Leopold, M.F., van Damme, C.J.G. & Veen, T.** 2003. Les Oiseaux piscivores comme indicateurs de la qualité de l'environnement marin: suivi des effets de la pêche littorale en Afrique du Nord-Ouest. Alterra Report 666, Wageningen, The Netherlands.

**Wetlands International** 2002. Waterbird Population Estimates – Third Edition. Wetlands International Global Series No. 12, Wageningen, The Netherlands.

**Young, H.G.** 2004. Madagascar Teal *Anas bernieri*: the ecology and conservation of a short distance migrant. In: Abstracts Book: Waterbirds Around the World: A global review of the conservation, management and research of the world's major flyways, 3-8 April 2004, Edinburgh, UK. Wetlands International, Wageningen, The Netherlands.

**Young, H.G.** 2006. Madagascar Teal *Anas bernieri:* the ecology and conservation of a short distance migrant. Waterbirds around the world. G.C. Boere, C.A. Galbraith & D.A. Stroud (Eds.), The Stationery Office, Edinburgh, UK. 252-254.

**Zwarts, L. & Diallo, M.** 2002. Eco-hydrologie du Delta. In: E. Wymenga, B. Kone, J. van der Kamp & L. Zwarts (eds) Delta Intériur du Niger. Ecologie et gestion durable des resources naturelles. Mali-pin publication 2002-01. Wetlands International, Sévaré, Mali; RIZA, Rijkswaterstaat, Lelystad, The Netherlands; Altenburg & Wymenga conseilleurs écologiques, Veenwouden, The Netherlands.

Both humans and waterbirds depend on healthy wetlands. Sudan. Photo: Niels Gilissen - MIRATIO.

# An investigation into inter-colony movements of African Penguins *Spheniscus demersus*

*Philip A. Whittington[1,2], J. Griffin[1], P. Bartlett[3], R.J.M. Crawford[4], N.T.W. Klages[5], R.M. Randall[6] & A.C. Wolfaardt[1,7]*

[1]*Avian Demography Unit, Department of Statistical Sciences, University of Cape Town, Rondebosch, 7700, South Africa.*

[2]*Present address: Department of Zoology, PO Box 77000, Nelson Mandela Metropolitan University, Port Elizabeth, 6031, South Africa.*

[3]*Ministry of Fisheries and Marine Resources, PO Box 394, Lüderitz, Namibia.*

[4]*Marine and Coastal Management, Private Bag X2, Roggebaai, 8012, South Africa.*

[5]*Institute for Environmental and Coastal Management, PO Box 77000, Nelson Mandela Metropolitan University, Port Elizabeth, 6031, South Africa.*

[6]*South African National Parks, Box 176, Sedgefield, 6573, South Africa.*

[7]*Western Cape Nature Conservation Board, Private Bag X5014, Stellenbosch, 7599, South Africa.*

Whittington, P.A., Griffin, J., Bartlett, P., Crawford, R.J.M., Klages, N.T.W, Randall, R.M. & Wolfaardt, A.C. 2006. An investigation into inter-colony movements of African Penguins *Spheniscus demersus*. *Waterbirds around the world*. Eds. G.C. Boere, C.A. Galbraith & D.A. Stroud. The Stationery Office, Edinburgh, UK. pp. 224-225.

The African Penguin *Spheniscus demersus* is endemic to southern Africa, breeding mainly on offshore islands from the coast of central Namibia to Algoa Bay in the Eastern Cape Province of South Africa. The population of this species declined by 90% during the 20th century and it is considered Vulnerable under the IUCN Red Data List criteria. African Penguins visit breeding colonies other than those at which they are known to breed or at which they were born, and are occasionally recorded outside their breeding range (Randall *et al.* 1987, Randall 1989, Whittington *et al.* 2005a).

Breeding colonies of the African Penguin fall geographically into three main groups: the Algoa Bay islands in the Eastern Cape of South Africa, colonies in the Western Cape of South Africa and those in Namibia. These three groups are each about 600 km apart and were used as the three regions in the analysis. A total of 52 260 African Penguins was flipper-banded between 1970 and June 1999 (Whittington *et al.* 2005a). Searches were made for flipper-banded penguins at breeding colonies and the band numbers were read in the field using binoculars or a tele-scope. Most re-sightings were made between August 1994 and October 1999.

Movements were analysed for birds banded as chicks and for those banded when in adult plumage, attained at 12–22 months of age (Randall 1989). Those banded as chicks were further separated into birds re-sighted when two years old or younger and those re-sighted when over two years of age. A movement was defined as the outward journey away from the breeding or natal colony; most birds later returned to their colony. Movements to the west and/or north were termed as "clockwise" while those to the south and/or east as "anticlockwise". The proportions of birds moving in each direction from each region were calculated, along with the numbers moving between regions.

Between 1970 and 1999, 42 267 re-sightings were made of 10 470 banded birds and a further 1 217 birds were recovered dead. Of the birds banded as chicks that were re-sighted, 35% were recorded away from their natal colony and 9% of adults re-sighted had also visited colonies other than the one at which they were known to breed.

**Table 1.** Directions of movements of chicks re-sighted away from the natal colony when two years old or less and when greater than two years old. Z-values are positive for clockwise movement or negative for anticlockwise movement. Values greater than 1.96, or less than –1.96, shown in bold type, are significant at the 5% level.

| | Clockwise | | Anticlockwise | | Z-value | |
|---|---|---|---|---|---|---|
| | ≤ 2 years | > 2 years | ≤ 2 years | > 2 years | ≤ 2 years | > 2 years |
| Eastern Cape | 102 | 22 | 1 | 18 | **9.95** | 0.63 |
| Western Cape | 96 | 209 | 86 | 155 | 0.74 | **2.83** |
| Namibia | 85 | 118 | 111 | 113 | -1.86 | 0.33 |

**Table 2.** Movements of chicks between breeding regions; re-sightings made when two years old or less and when over two years old.

| | To | | | | | |
|---|---|---|---|---|---|---|
| | Eastern Cape | | Western Cape | | Namibia | |
| | ≤ 2 years | > 2 years | ≤ 2 years | > 2 years | ≤ 2 years | > 2 years |
| Eastern Cape | 11 | 25 | 89 | 13 | 2 | 2 |
| From Western Cape | 2 | 4 | 160 | 328 | 19 | 32 |
| Namibia | 0 | 2 | 12 | 54 | 184 | 175 |

African Penguins banded in the Eastern Cape Province showed a marked clockwise movement around the coast during their first two years of life. This was less pronounced in birds re-sighted when over two years of age, although birds of this age group banded in the Western Cape did show a significant clockwise pattern of movements (Table 1). Birds banded as adults in the Eastern Cape also showed a significant clockwise movement (Z = 4.09, P = < 0.05). Adults banded in the Western Cape and in Namibia exhibited mainly anticlockwise movements but these were not statistically significant.

Most movements were made to other colonies within the natal region (Table 2) or, in the case of adult birds, to other colonies within the region of their breeding colony. However, 87% of the birds banded as chicks within the Eastern Cape and recorded at other colonies when aged two years or younger were recorded at colonies in the Western Cape and two were found in Namibia.

Of 598 birds that were banded as chicks and subsequently recorded breeding, 514 (86%) were breeding at their natal colony (Whittington *et al.* 2005b). Most of the remaining 84 birds settled to breed at non-natal colonies within their natal region. Most emigrants from Namibian colonies were found breeding in the Western Cape.

Nine birds, eight of which were banded in adult plumage, were reliably recorded breeding at more than one locality. The ninth bird, banded as a chick, was first recorded breeding at its natal colony (Robben Island) before apparently emigrating to nearby Dassen Island two years later (Whittington *et al.* 2005b).

This study confirms that in their first two years of life African Penguins disperse away from their natal colonies and may travel considerable distances. Birds from the Eastern Cape moved west towards nutrient rich areas around Agulhas Bank and in the Benguela upwelling system off the West Coast. Pelagic shoaling fish such as Sardine *Sardinops sagax* and Anchovy *Engraulis encrasicolus*, which form the major part of the African Penguin's prey, are abundant in these areas (Randall *et al.* 1987, Randall 1989). Most African Penguin colonies in the Western Cape lie within the Benguela upwelling system or on Agulhas Bank, while those in Namibia are situated within the Benguela upwelling system, giving birds in these regions the possibility of finding adequate food resources in either direction. Adult birds were less likely to be seen at other colonies than young birds, and the distances travelled tended to be shorter. It is likely that most of the journeys made by adults were foraging trips.

Most African Penguins banded as chicks returned to their natal colony to breed, which is the normal pattern for this species (Randall *et al.* 1987). Those that emigrated were thought to have done so in response to a change in distribution and abundance of prey species (Crawford 1998, Whittington *et al.* 2005b). This study provides the first documented evidence of African Penguins breeding at more than one locality. The eight birds banded as adults that did so were all survivors of the *Apollo Sea* oil spill and had been cleaned and subsequently released by the Southern African Foundation for Conservation of Coastal Birds (SANCCOB). Five of them made their first breeding attempt within a year of being cleaned. It is possible that the trauma of oiling, petro-chemical poisoning and stress undergone during the rehabilitation procedure, caused the birds to be disorientated, resulting in them attempting to breed at a colony other than the one at which they finally chose to settle.

Support from British Petroleum, Chicago Zoological Society, the Darwin Initiative, Earthwatch Institute, International Fund for Animal Welfare, Marine Living Resources Fund, National Research Foundation, WWF South Africa and a Jagger scholarship from the University of Cape Town is gratefully acknowledged. Western Cape Nature Conservation Board, South African National Parks, Robben Island Museum, The Department of Correctional Services and Eastern Cape Nature Conservation gave permission and arranged accommodation for work at penguin colonies under their administration. The Marine and Coastal Management section of the Department of Environmental Affairs and Tourism, the South African Defence Force, Robben Island Museum, The Department of Correctional Services, Wilfred Chivell, Port Elizabeth Museum and Portnet provided transport to offshore islands. We thank all those who contributed re-sightings to the penguin database.

## REFERENCES

**Crawford, R.J.M.** 1998. Responses of African Penguins to regime changes of sardine and anchovy in the Benguela system. South African Journal of Marine Science 19: 355–364.

**Randall, R.M.** 1989. Jackass Penguins. In: A.I.L. Payne & R.J.M. Crawford (eds) Oceans of life off southern Africa. Vlaeberg, Cape Town: 244–256.

**Randall, R.M., Randall, B.M., Cooper, J., La Cock, G.D. & Ross, G.J.B.** 1987. Jackass Penguin *Spheniscus demersus* movements, inter-island visits, and settlement. Journal of Field Ornithology 58(4): 445–455.

**Whittington, P.A., Randall, R.M., Randall, B.M., Wolfaardt, A.C., Crawford, R.J.M., Klages, N.T.W., Bartlett, P.A., Chesselet, Y.J. & Jones, R.** 2005a. Patterns of movements of the African Penguin in South Africa and Namibia. African Journal of Marine Science 27(1): 215–229.

**Whittington, P.A., Randall, R.M., Crawford, R.J.M., Wolfaardt, A.C., Klages, N.T.W., Randall, B.M., Bartlett, P.A., Chesselet, Y.J. & Jones, R.** 2005b. Patterns of immigration to and emigration from breeding colonies by African Penguins. African Journal of Marine Science 27(1): 205–213.

Part of the moulting flock of African Penguins *Spheniscus demersus* on Robben Island in December. Penguins come ashore to moult, and do not feed for about a month during the process. Photo: Les Underhill.

# Anatidae numbers and distribution in West Africa in winter

*Bertrand Trolliet & Olivier Girard*

*Office National de la Chasse et de la Faune Sauvage, F-85340 L'Ile d'Olonne, France. (email: bertrand.trolliet@oncfs.gouv.fr)*

Trolliet, B. & Girard, O. 2006. Anatidae numbers and distribution in West Africa in winter. *Waterbirds around the world.* Eds. G.C. Boere, C.A. Galbraith & D.A. Stroud. The Stationery Office, Edinburgh, UK. pp. 226-227.

In West Africa, the largest wetland areas are associated with large hydrographic basins. This paper summarises recent information on wintering Anatidae numbers in three large wetland systems in West Africa, from west to east, the Senegal Delta, the Inner Niger Delta and the Lake Chad Basin.

The Senegal Delta (Senegal and Mauritania), is very artificial with dams, canalisation of the river, and rice field developments; the estimates of Anatidae numbers are based on annual counts made between 1990 and 2001. The Inner Niger Delta (Mali), is a large area seasonally flooded by the overflow of the Niger river; aerial counts were made in this area in January 1999, 2000 and 2001. The Lake Chad basin (Chad, Cameroon, Nigeria, Niger), consists of Lake Chad itself, the Logone floodplain and numerous seasonal wetlands situated close to the Chari river, and Lake Fitri. Aerial counts were made in this area in the winters of 1999-2000 and 2003-2004.

Overall, the numbers of Palearctic ducks counted in these three major wetlands averaged 240 000 for the Senegal Delta, 610 000 for the Inner Niger Delta, and 500 000 for the Lake Chad Basin. During the winter of 1999-2000, the total number of Palearcticducks counted simultaneously in the three areas was 1.7 million birds. Taking into account censuses made elsewhere in West Africa, and those areas not censused, it is estimated the regional Anatidae population numbers are 2 - 2.5 million birds.

In all areas, the Garganey *Anas querquedula* was the most abundant Palearctic duck, forming on average nearly 80% of the total population. The average number counted in the three main areas amounted to a little over one million birds, and the total regional population number is probably over 1.5 million. The Northern Pintail *Anas acuta* represents c. 20% of Palearctic ducks and its regional number is now probably less than 500 000. The Northern Shoveler *Anas clypeata* is abundant only in the Senegal Delta, with 19 000 birds. Among the other Palearctic ducks, Common Teal *Anas crecca*, Eurasian Wigeon *Anas penelope*, Common Pochard *Aythya ferina* and Tufted Duck *Aythya fuligula* and, in rarer cases, Common Shelduck *Tadorna tadorna*, are only present in small numbers. However, the recent counts made in Mali and Chad, found unexpectedly high numbers of Ferruginous Ducks *Aythya nyroca,* with up to 14 000 in Mali and 8 500 in Chad.

The total numbers of Afrotropical Anatidae counted in these three areas amounted to 31 400 for the Senegal Delta, 55 000 for the Inner Niger Delta, and 180 000 for the Lake Chad Basin. During the winter of 1999-2000, a total of 480 000 Afrotropical Anatidae were counted in the region, including other wetlands. On the basis of what is known of the distribution of these birds, and of the areas covered by these counts, it is estimated that the total regional Afrotropical Anatidae population is approximately 700 000 birds.

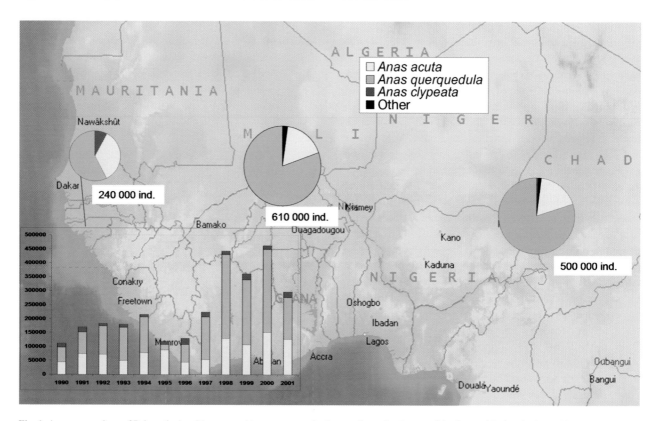

Fig. 1. Average numbers of Palearctic Anatidae counted in recent years in three main wetland areas of the Senegal Delta, the Inner Niger Delta and the Lake Chad Basin.

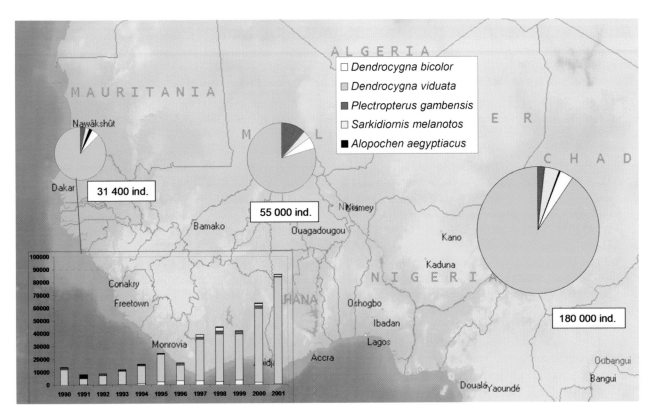

**Fig. 2.** Average numbers of Afrotropical Anatidae counted in recent years in three main wetland areas of the Senegal Delta, the Inner Niger Delta and the Lake Chad Basi

The White-faced Whistling Duck *Dendrocygna viduata* is the most abundant species in all three major areas, representing c. 85% of the total. Other Afrotropical Anatidae present are Fulvous Whistling Duck *Dendrocygna bicolor* (5%), Comb Duck *Sarkidiornis melanotos* (5%), and Spur-winged Goose *Plectropterus gambensis* (4%). The Egyptian Goose *Alopochen aegyptiacus* and African Pygmy-goose *Nettapus auritus* also occur but are uncommon (Fig. 2). Further information on numbers of Anatidae and other waterbirds in West Africa is provided by Dodman & Diagana (2003) and Trolliet *et al.* (2003).

**REFERENCES**

**Dodman, T. & Diagana, C.H.** 2003. African Waterbird Census / Les dénombrements d'oiseaux d'eau en Afrique 1999, 2000 & 2001. Wetlands International Global Series No. 16. Wageningen, The Netherlands.

**Trolliet, B., Girard, O.** & **Fouquet, M.** 2003. Evaluation des populations d'oiseaux d'eau en Afrique de l'Ouest. Rapport scientifique 2002, ONCFS: 51-55.

The Inner Niger Delta holds 2-40% of the West African population of Northern Pintail *Anas acuta*.  Photo: Paul Marshall.

# Anatidae wintering in the Inner Niger Delta, Mali

*Olivier Girard*

*Office National de la Chasse et de la Faune Sauvage, F-85340 L'Ile d'Olonne, France. (email: o.girard@oncfs.gouv.fr)*

Girard, O. 2006. Anatidae wintering in the Inner Niger Delta, Mali. *Waterbirds around the world.* Eds. G.C. Boere, C.A. Galbraith & D.A. Stroud. The Stationery Office, Edinburgh, UK. pp. 228-229.

In January 1999, 2000 and 2001, aerial counts were made in the Inner Niger Delta in Mali. Aerial counts are the only method for surveying such a vast (c. 35 000 km²) and inaccessible area as the Inner Niger Delta in a relatively short time span. The surveys required 40 to 50 flight-hours to count 85% to 90% of the flooded areas containing Anatidae.

Ten species of Anatidae were observed. Six were Afrotropical species: Fulvous Whistling Duck *Dendrocygna bicolor*, White-faced Whistling Duck *Dendrocygna viduata*, Egyptian Goose *Alopochen aegyptiacus*, Spur-winged Goose *Plectropterus gambensis*, Knob-billed Duck *Sarkidiornis melanotos* and African Pygmy-goose *Nettapus auritus*, and four were Palearctic: Garganey *Anas querquedula*, Pintail *Anas acuta*, Northern Shoveler *Anas clypeata* and Ferruginous Duck *Aythya nyroca*. Numbers varied from 10 600 to 77 600 for Afrotropical species and from 258 000 to 922 600 for Palearctic species (Table 1).

The most numerous Afrotropical Anatidae were White-faced Whistling Duck (more than 70 000 in 2001), Fulvous Whistling Duck (almost 8 000 in 2000) and Spur-winged Goose (almost 6 000 in 2000). The most numerous Palearctic species were Garganey (almost 745 000 in 2001) and Pintail (almost 165 000 in 2001).

The majority of the birds were north of latitude 14°30'N, in the largest area of inundation in the Inner Niger Delta; an area with the largest lakes, a very large number of inundated depres-

sions, many backwaters and rivers, and extensive floodplains. Among the 1 380 flocks of ducks that were counted, 605 were single-species flocks. Spur-winged Goose and Garganey were the two species most often encountered in monospecific flocks, whilst Knob-billed Ducks were almost always associated with at least one other species.

Comparison between the numbers counted during the three years of this study and those from counts made at the beginning of the 1970s shows very great fluctuations in population numbers for all species (Table 2). However, with the exception of the Northern Shoveler, a species that seems to be declining considerably in numbers, there is no trend for any of the other species. Between 10% to 50% of wintering Anatidae estimated to be present in West Africa are found in the Inner Niger Delta (Table 3). This region is of major importance for the globally Near Threatened Ferruginous Duck, with 8 000 to 15 000 birds wintering on just a few lakes situated in the northwestern part of the delta.

There was no relationship between the degree of inundation of the Delta and total population numbers (r = -0.10), the numbers of Afrotropical Anatidae (r = -0.02) or Palearctic Anatidae (r = -0.11) (Fig. 1). The best year, 1978, and the worst, 1974, were observed with similarly low water levels. The difference between the maximum and minimum numbers counted between 1999 and 2001, under quite similar flooding conditions, was a factor of four.

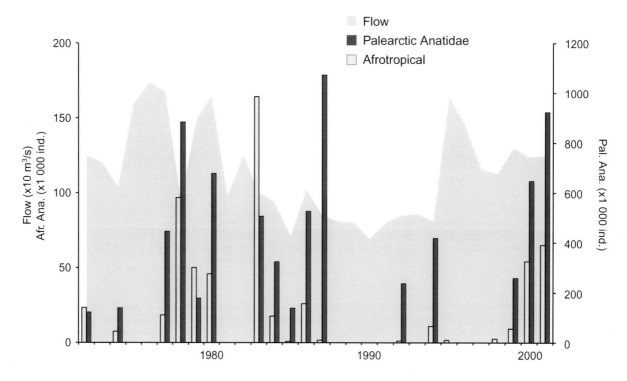

**Fig. 1.** Changes between 1972 and 2001 in the numbers of Palearctic and Afro-tropical Anatidae, and the flow rate of the Niger River downstream of the Inner Niger Delta.

**Table 1. Number of Anatidae counted by plane in the Inner Niger Delta (Mali) in January 1999, 2000 and 2001.**

| Species | Number of Anatidae counted in | | |
|---|---|---|---|
| | 1999 | 2000 | 2001 |
| **Afrotropical** | | | |
| Fulvous Whistling Duck | 88 | 7 733 | 2 795 |
| White-faced Whistling Duck | 7 760 | 47 310 | 70 950 |
| Egyptian Goose | 6 | 87 | 0 |
| Spur-winged Goose | 2 450 | 5 760 | 3 220 |
| Knob-billed Duck | 330 | 4 300 | 610 |
| African Pygmy Goose | 0 | 5 | 12 |
| Subtotal | 10 634 | 65 195 | 77 587 |
| **Palearctic** | | | |
| Pintail | 41 100 | 116 650 | 164 160 |
| Garganey | 209 130 | 515 680 | 744 000 |
| Northern Shoveler | 0 | 200 | 195 |
| Ferruginous Duck | 7 800 | 13 020 | 14 300 |
| Subtotal | 258 030 | 645 550 | 922 655 |
| **Total (rounded numbers)** | **269 000** | **711 000** | **1 000 000** |

**Table. 2. Changes in the numbers of Anatidae, between 1972 and 2001 in the Inner Niger Delta (Mali).**

| Species | Number (1 000 individuals) of Anatidae in years | | | | | | | | | | | | | | | |
|---|---|---|---|---|---|---|---|---|---|---|---|---|---|---|---|---|
| | 1972 | 1974 | 1977 | 1978 | 1979 | 1980 | 1983 | 1984 | 1985 | 1986 | 1987 | 1992 | 1994 | 1999 | 2000 | 2001 |
| Fulvous Whistling Duck | 0.3 | 0.2 | 3 | 23 | 1.1 | 2.1 | 70.6 | 31.4 | ? | 12.3 | ? | ? | 7 | 0.1 | 7.7 | 2.8 |
| White-faced Whistling Duck | 21 | 7.8 | 14 | 70 | 43.5 | 46.6 | 114.3 | 33.8 | ? | ? | ? | 0,3 | 1.9 | 7.8 | 47.3 | 71 |
| Egyptian Goose | 2.6 | 0.2 | 0.7 | 1.9 | 0.3 | ? | 1.7 | 0.9 | 0.4 | 0.3 | ? | ? | 0.1 | 0 | 0.1 | 0 |
| Spur-winged Goose | 1.5 | 0.7 | 2.9 | 1.6 | 5.6 | 0.7 | ? | 5.2 | 0.6 | 18 | 1.3 | ? | 0.1 | 2.5 | 5.8 | 3.2 |
| Knob-billed Duck | 2.5 | 0.2 | 1.4 | 20 | 9.1 | 5.5 | 10.8 | 1,7 | ? | ? | 0.6 | 1 | 4.3 | 0.3 | 4.3 | 0.6 |
| Pintail | 27 | 69 | 100 | 400 | 65 | 204 | 156 | 126 | (?) | 76 | 166 | 140 | 150 | 41 | 117 | 164 |
| Garganey | 94 | 69 | 334 | 480 | 108 | 467 | 350 | 148 | 131 | 450 | 900 | 95,7 | 267 | 209 | 516 | 744 |
| Northern ∂Shoveler | ? | ? | 6.9 | 2.2 | 0.4 | 2.2 | ? | 0.2 | ? | ? | ? | ? | ? | 0 | 0.2 | 0.2 |
| Ferruginous Duck | ? | ? | 4 | 0.9 | 3.9 | 3.4 | 0.3 | 2.9 | 6.4 | ? | 5.6 | ? | ? | 7.8 | 13 | 14.3 |

**Table. 3. Estimated numbers of Anatidae wintering in West Africa and in the Inner Niger Delta (IND) in Mali.**

| Species | Estimated numbers for West Africa | Estimations for the IND | Percentage of IND in West Africa |
|---|---|---|---|
| Fulvous Whistling Duck | 35 000 to 100 000 | 8 000 to 10 000 | 10-30 % |
| White-faced Whistling Duck | ca 600 000 | 50 000 to 70 000 | 10 % |
| Spur-winged Goose | ca 50 000 | 8 000 to 10 000 | 15-20 % |
| Knob-billed Duck | ca 50 000 | 5 000 to 20 000 | 10-40 % |
| Pintail | < 500 000 | 100 000 to 200 000 (sometimes more?) | 20-40 % |
| Garganey | > 1 500 000 | 500 000 to 800 000 | 30-50 % |
| Ferruginous Duck | > 15 000 | 8 000 to 15 000 | 50-100 % |

# Lesser Flamingo *Phoenicopterus minor* counts in Tanzanian soda lakes: implications for conservation

*Charles Mlingwa[1] & Neil Baker[2]*

[1]*Tanzania Wildlife Research Institute, PO Box 661, Arusha, Tanzania. (email: tawiri@habari.co.tz)*
[2]*Tanzania Bird Atlas Project, c/o Tabora Research Station, PO Box 52, Tabora, Tanzania. (email: neilandliz@ntlword.com)*

Mlingwa, C. & Baker, N. 2006. Lesser Flamingo *Phoenicopterus minor* counts in Tanzanian soda lakes: implications for conservation. *Waterbirds around the world.* Eds. G.C. Boere, C.A. Galbraith & D.A. Stroud. The Stationery Office, Edinburgh, UK. pp. 230-233.

## ABSTRACT

Counts of the Lesser Flamingo *Phoenicopterus minor* in Tanzanian soda lakes have been carried out since the 1960s. We present here data on population estimates for this species in Tanzania. Despite the sporadic nature of the counts, the available data indicate the nomadic nature of this species within the soda lakes in northern Tanzania. The lowest number of birds recorded was 68 163 in 1969, and the highest, 2 759 026 in 1995. The total population of the Lesser Flamingo in East Africa may be at least four million birds, if data from Kenya are included. It is evident from the data currently available that a full set of soda lakes, regardless of size, is necessary in order to secure the conservation of the Lesser Flamingo in East Africa.

## INTRODUCTION

The Lesser Flamingo *Phoenicopterus minor* occurs in eastern, southern and western Africa, as well as in Pakistan and north-western India. In East Africa, the Lesser Flamingo is a charac-teristic bird of soda lakes in the Rift Valley where it is highly gregarious and nomadic (Britton 1980, Zimmerman *et al.* 1996). The East African Rift Valley lakes may host about 95 percent of the total world population of this species, which is estimated at

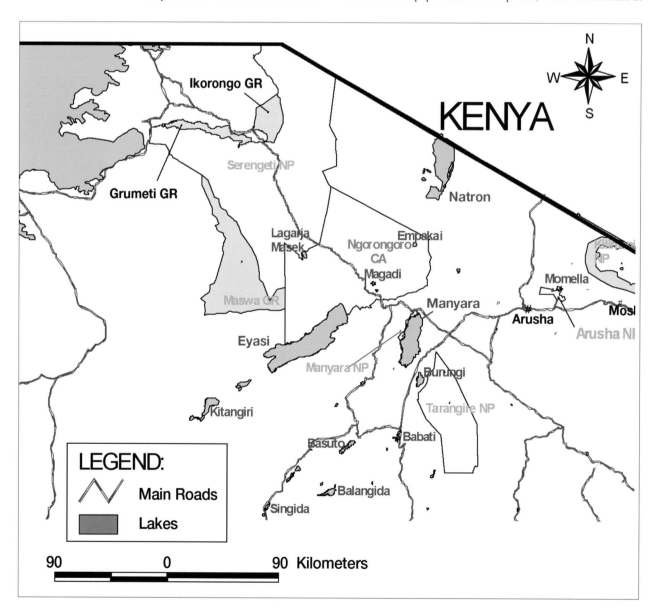

Fig. 1. Soda lakes in northern Tanzania.

**Table 1. Counts of the Lesser Flamingo *Phoenicopterus minor* at soda lakes in Tanzania during the period 1969-2004. The numbers preceding the year indicate the months in which the censuses were carried out.**

| | Year | 3-1969 | 1991 | 1&2-1992 | 7&11-1994 | 1-1995 | 3-2000 | 1-2002 | 1&2-2004 |
|---|---|---|---|---|---|---|---|---|---|
| **LAKES** | Area (km²) | | | | Numbers | | | | |
| Natron | 850.0 | 25 195 | - | 372 670 | 507 117 | >400 000 | - | 102 410 | - |
| Magadi | 14.1 | 5 686 | - | - | 7 765 | - | - | 1 000 | 6 090 |
| Empakai | 8.2 | - | - | - | 400 000 | 4 026 | - | - | 18 011 |
| Lagarja | 6.4 | 4 100 | - | - | 0 | - | - | 1 250 | - |
| Masek | 1.0 | | | | | | | | |
| Manyara | 410.0 | 1 313 | 1 940 000 | - | 78 320 | >1 000 000 | 0 | 8 264 | 382 500 |
| Burungi | 40.0 | - | - | - | 71 030 | 0 | - | 46 | 0 |
| Basuto | 36.2 | - | - | - | - | - | 100 000 | - | - |
| Eyasi | 1 160.0 | 28 288 | - | - | 0 | 800 000 | 12 000 | 502 066 | - |
| Kitangiri | 44.0 | 104 | - | - | - | 500 000 | - | 0 | 25 |
| Singida | 3.2 | - | - | - | - | 55 000 | - | - | 500 |
| Balangidas | 7.3 | 3 452 | - | - | - | 0 | - | 2 000 | 23 120 |
| Momellas | 2.4 | 25 | - | 220 000 | - | 0 | - | 17 404 | 3 746 |
| **TOTAL** | | **68 163** | **1 940 000** | **592 670** | **1 064 232** | **>2 759 026** | **112 000** | **634 440** | **433 992** |

about 3-4 million birds (Baker 1996, Njaga & Githaiga 1999). Lake Natron is the main and only regular breeding site in East Africa for this species, with nesting recorded most frequently during the dry period from August to November (Brown & Root 1971, Brown & Britton 1980). The Lesser Flamingo is considered to be Near Threatened globally because of its restricted distribution and the loss of habitat as a result of siltation in some of the soda lakes (Collar *et al.* 1994). It has been the subject of a number of censuses dating back to the 1960s (Batholomew & Pennycuick 1973), but these censuses have been sporadic, even at individual sites. The aim of this paper is to present an overview of the census data collected in Tanzania during the period from 1969 to the present. We use these data to assess the importance of each of the soda lakes and the implications for the conservation of this species.

## METHODS

Data on the numbers of Lesser Flamingos at various soda lakes (Fig. 1) are derived from aerial censuses carried out in 1969, 1991, 1992, 1994, 1995, 2000 and 2002 using the Aerial Point Survey technique (Northon-Griffiths 1978), and total ground counts (Bibby *et al.* 1998) in 2000 at Basuto lake only, in 2002 at the Momella lakes only, and in 2004 at all lakes counted in this year. Each site was counted in a single day. The census data are scattered in the published literature (e.g. Bartholomew & Pennycuick 1973, Baker 1996, Baker & Baker 2002), as well as in unpublished reports at the Conservation Information and Monitoring Unit of the Tanzania Wildlife Research Institute in Arusha, Tanzania. In all cases, total counts were obtained either by counting birds on the spot during ground surveys, or by counting birds in photographs taken during aerial surveys (Norton-Griffiths 1978). At no time of year, however, did the censuses cover all of the soda lakes indicated in Fig. 1, even in those years when extensive surveys were carried out (1969, 1994, 1995, 2002 and 2004).

## RESULTS

Table 1 lists the 13 soda lakes in northern Tanzania where flamingo counts were carried out during the period 1969-2004. However, in none of the years was there a complete survey of all the lakes. Furthermore, the counts in any one year were not carried out on the same day. Thus it has never been possible to gain a complete picture of the occurrence of Lesser Flamingos at the study lakes at any one time. Despite these limitations, it is evident that high numbers of Lesser Flamingos were present in Tanzania in 1991 and 1995, with populations of nearly two million (at a single lake, Manyara) in 1991 and three million in 1995 (Fig. 2). The lowest numbers were recorded in 1969, although eight lakes were surveyed, and 2000, when only three lakes were surveyed. The occurrence of Lesser Flamingos at each of the 13 soda lakes surveyed during the period 1969 to 2004 is indicated in Fig. 3. Numbers ranged from none at many lakes to nearly two million at a single lake (Lake Manyara). In all five surveys at Lake Natron, Lesser Flamingos were present, albeit in widely varying numbers (Fig. 3). Seven of the 13 soda lakes held 100 000 or more Lesser Flamingos on at least one occasion (Table 1 & Fig. 3). These seven included two of the

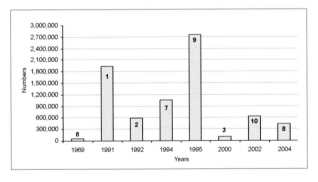

**Fig. 2.** Population estimates of Lesser Flamingo *Phoenicopterus minor* in Tanzania during the period 1969 to 2004. The figure with each bar indicates the total number of soda lakes surveyed.

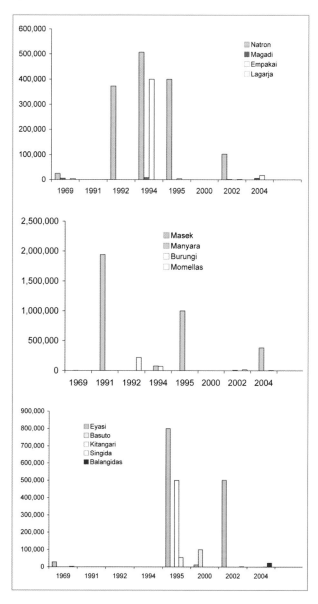

**Fig. 3.** Counts of the Lesser Flamingo *Phoenicopterus minor* at various soda lakes in Tanzania. Only those years in which surveys were conducted are included. Lake Lagarja includes Lake Masek.

smaller lakes, the Momella Lakes and Lake Empakai, which held as many as 220 000 and 500 000 birds, respectively. No similar concentrations were recorded at the other small lakes.

## DISCUSSION

According to the census data currently available, the distribution of the Lesser Flamingo in Tanzania is restricted to soda lakes within the Rift Valley and Volcanic Highlands in the northern part of the country. It is possible, however, that other saline lakes, such as Lake Rukwa in south-western Tanzania, may also hold populations of this species (Baker 1996). Due to their highly nomadic movements, populations of the Lesser Flamingo are hard to estimate within a given region in any one year unless surveys are conducted at all suitable lakes within the space of a few days. Previous rough estimates for Kenya and Tanzania, the stronghold for this species, have been about five million birds (Brown 1959), and more recently, around four million birds (Baker 1996). Assuming that during any given period in January 1995, Tanzania held close to three million birds (see Table 1 & Fig. 2), while there were nearly one million birds in Kenya

(Nasirwa & Bennun 1995), the total population of the Lesser Flamingo in East Africa at that time may have been close to four million birds, particularly if Ethiopia were included. However, the total count of Lesser Flamingos in Kenya and Tanzania on the same day in January 2002 amounted to only about 1.5 million birds (TAWIRI 2002), although no surveys were carried out in Ethiopia at that time. The nomadic behaviour of the Lesser Flamingo is demonstrated by annual fluctuations in the total number of birds counted countrywide, ranging from less than 100 000 birds in March 1969 to nearly three million in January 1995. This situation is further demonstrated by annual changes in numbers at individual lakes. It has been noted that the distribution and abundance of flamingos are related to food supply (Tuite 1981, Burgis & Symoens 1987). Thus, changes in the numbers of flamingos at a particular soda lake during the year and between years may reflect fluctuations in the availability of the food supply. The Lesser Flamingo is specialized for feeding on *Spirulina*, a species of blue-green algae that is found in alkaline water. The abundance of these algae at a particular site may attract large numbers of birds irrespective of the size of the lake, as demonstrated at Momellas and Empakai. Any other factors accounting for the differing abundance of the flamingos among the lakes may be indirect by affecting the food supply. For example, Lagarja and Masek lakes, which are only two kilometres apart, are sometimes diluted to fresh water during years with high rainfall, and become joined together to form a single lake (Baker 1996). Under such conditions, no *Spirulina* can grow and the lakes are avoided by the flamingos.

## Conservation implications

The Lesser Flamingo is a highly nomadic species that is dependent on a range of soda lakes to complete its annual cycle. Changes in the annual counts for the entire country give an indication of the numbers of birds that may be occurring outside Tanzania at certain times. Furthermore, annual changes in flamingo counts at individual sites may indicate changes in the importance of each of the soda lakes both within years and between years. This situation may be caused by changes in the food supply of *Spirulina* at each lake. The soda lakes in Kenya and Tanzania are the most important habitat for the Lesser Flamingo in Africa. However, most of the important lakes in Tanzania are outside the network of highly protected national parks and game reserves. For example, only a portion of Lake Manyara is within the Lake Manyara National Park. Empakai, Lagarja, Masek and the Momella lakes are the only lakes located within highly protected areas. Increased siltation and chemical pollution from agricultural activities pose a major threat to most of the lakes which are not well protected (pers. obs). A similar situation is also found for the soda lakes in Kenya (Nyaga & Githaiga 1999). The two countries should therefore take responsibility for preserving all of the existing soda lakes, regardless of size, in order to ensure the continued survival of this near-threatened species as well as other waterbird species. Any human activities that can be detrimental to the Rift Valley drainage system should be discouraged (Nyaga & Githaiga 1999). No simultaneous counts of Lesser Flamingos have been made in all African countries where soda lakes could be important for this species. Thus estimates of the Lesser Flamingo population for Africa as a whole remain incomplete. We therefore suggest that there be a continent-wide, co-ordinated count of Lesser Flamingos in order to improve our understanding of the temporal and spatial distribution and abundance of these birds, and hence to assist in the planning of effective conservation action for the species.

## ACKNOWLEDGEMENTS

CM would like to thank the Secretariat of the African-Eurasian Waterbird Agreement and the Conference Organizing Committee for sponsoring his attendance at the Waterbirds around the world Conference.

## REFERENCES

Baker, N.E. 1996. Tanzania waterbirds count. Wildlife Conservation Society of Tanzania, Dar es Salaam, Tanzania.

Baker, N.E. & Baker, L.M. 2002. Important Bird Areas in Tanzania: A first inventory. Wildlife Conservation Society of Tanzania, Dar es Salaam, Tanzania.

Bartholomew, G.A. & Pennycuick, C.J. 1973. The flamingo and pelican populations of the Rift Valley Lakes in 1968-69. East African Wildlife Journal 11: 189-198.

Bibby, C., Jones, M. & Marsden, S. 1998. Bird Surveys. Royal Geographical Society, London.

Britton, P.L. (ed). 1980. Birds of East Africa. East Africa Natural History Society, Nairobi.

Brown, L.H. 1959. The mystery of flamingos. Country Life, London.

Brown, L.H. & Britton, P.L. 1980. The Breeding Seasons of East African Birds. East Africa Natural History Society, Nairobi.

Brown, L.H. & Root, A. 1971. The breeding behaviour of the Lesser Flamingo, *Phoeniconaias minor*. Ibis 113: 147-172.

Burgis, M.I. & Symoens, J.T. 1987. African wetlands and shallow water bodies: directory. Institute Francais de Recherche Scientifique pour le Development en Cooperation, Paris.

Collar, N.J., Crosby, M.J. & Stattersfield, A.J. 1994. Birds to Watch 2: The World List of Threatened Birds. Conservation Series No. 4. BirdLife International, Cambridge, UK.

Nasirwa, O.O. & Bennun, L.A. 1995. Monitoring of waterbirds in central Kenya, July 1994 and January 1995. The National Museums of Kenya. Centre for Biodiversity Research Report: Ornithology No. 19.

Nyaga, N. & Githaiga, J. 1999. Ewaso power project kills the flamingo. The East African Newspaper; March 4-11, 1999.

Norton-Griffiths, M. 1978. Counting Animals. Second Edition. African Wildlife Federation, Nairobi, Kenya.

TAWIRI 2002. Aerial Censusing of Flamingos in the Rift Valley Lakes, January 2002. Tanzania Wildlife Research Institute, Arusha, Tanzania.

Tuite, C. 1981. Flamingos in East Africa. SWARA (East Africa Wildlife Society) 4 (4): 36-38.

Zimmerman, D.A., Turner, D.A. & Pearson, D.J. 1996. Birds of Kenya and northern Tanzania. Russel Friedman Books, Halfway House, SA.

An unusually high number of Lesser Flamingos *Phoenicopterus minor* were found dead at Lake Nakuru in 2006. Such, and more serious mortality events, have occurred in the Rift Valley lakes with increasing frequency. The root causes of this mortality remain unknown although it is likely to involve the interaction of environmental factors as well as impacts on the lake ecosystem which combine to influence the susceptibility of flamingos to both toxic and infectious disease. Integrated studies are urgently required better to understand the long-term implications of such die-offs. Photo: Ruth Cromie.

# Satellite tracking documents the East African flyway and key site network of the Lesser Flamingo *Phoenicopterus minor*

*Brooks Childress[1,2,3], Baz Hughes[1], David Harper[2], Wim Van den Bossche[4], Peter Berthold[5] & Ulrich Querner[5]*

[1]*Threatened Species Unit, The Wildfowl & Wetlands Trust, Slimbridge, GL2 7BT, UK. (email: Brooks.Childress@wwt.org.uk)*
[2]*Department of Biology, University of Leicester, Leicester, LE1 7RH, UK.*
[3]*Department of Ornithology, National Museums of Kenya, PO Box 40658, Nairobi, Kenya.*
[4]*BirdLife Belgium, Kardinaal Mercierplein 1, 2800 Mechelen, Belgium.*
[5]*Research Centre for Ornithology, Max Planck Society, Vogelwarte Radolfzell, 78315 Radolfzell, Germany.*

Childress, B., Hughes, B., Harper, D., Van den Bossche, W., Berthold, P. & Querner, U. 2006. Satellite tracking documents the East African flyway and key site network of the Lesser Flamingo *Phoenicopterus minor*. *Waterbirds around the world*. Eds. G.C. Boere, C.A. Galbraith & D.A. Stroud. The Stationery Office, Edinburgh, UK. pp. 234-238.

## ABSTRACT

The itinerant Lesser Flamingo *Phoenicopterus minor* is dependent on a network of specialized sites for its survival. To study the movements of individual birds and define this network in East Africa, four adult male Lesser Flamingos were tagged with satellite transmitters (PTTs) at Lake Bogoria, Kenya, in October 2002. During the first 15 months, there was no significant difference in the length of their inter-lake flights. However, there were significant differences in the number of flights and the number of days spent at each stopover. One bird flew 2 964 km, making 20 visits to eight different lakes (mean stay 21.8 days), while another made 18 visits to six different lakes (mean stay 24.1 days), flying 3 012 km. A third bird moved among lakes 70 times, visiting 11 different lakes (mean stay 6.4 days) and flew 7 870 km. The fourth bird's PTT stopped transmitting after 38 days. There were no flights outside East Africa. The flyway for the Lesser Flamingo in East Africa consisted of a 940 km north-south range between Lake Logipi, Kenya, and Lake Bahi, Tanzania. The network of sites used by the study birds consisted of nine alkaline lakes in Kenya and Tanzania. The conservation status of these nine sites varies from well-protected to completely unprotected.

## INTRODUCTION

The Lesser Flamingo *Phoenicopterus minor* is the smallest and most numerous of the world's six flamingo species, and is estimated to number between 2 220 000 and 4 230 000 individuals (Wetlands International 2002). It occurs in four regional populations in Africa and central Asia, the largest of which (2.0-4.0 million birds) occurs on the alkaline lakes of East Africa (Wetlands International 2002). Hundreds of thousands of birds frequently gather on these lakes in Kenya and Tanzania (Brown 1975, Vareschi 1978, Howard 1994), a spectacle that is vital to eco-tourism in this region.

The species is classified by IUCN as Near Threatened, due to its dependence on a limited number of unprotected breeding sites and a narrow range of required breeding conditions that occur irregularly and infrequently (BirdLife International 2000). The East African population is known to have bred successfully at only one location during the past 40 years, Lake Natron in Tanzania, and this lake, on the border with Kenya, is unprotected. Schemes such as the recently proposed soda-ash extraction business and hydroelectric power generation at Lake Natron could result in rapid population declines (BirdLife International 2000).

The Lesser Flamingo is an itinerant species (Evans 1985), moving frequently and unpredictably from lake to lake within the Rift Valley (Brown 1975, Vareschi 1978, Tuite 1979, Brown *et al.* 1982, Tuite 2000), and between salt pans and other wetlands in southern Africa (Borello *et al.* 1998, McCulloch *et al.* 2003), but returning to the same breeding sites. The frequent inter-lake movements have traditionally been thought to be associated with fluctuation in food abundance (Vareschi 1978, Tuite 1979). However, it is not clear that this alone is responsible. At Lake Bogoria, the Lesser Flamingo population can double or halve during periods as short as two weeks, despite a constant density of *Arthrospira fusiformis*, the Lesser Flamingo's primary food in East Africa (Brown 1975, Vareschi 1978, BC unpubl. data). Other hypotheses have included changes in the availability of fresh water, changes in the conductivity of the lake water, movement to breeding sites, and disturbance by predators (Vareschi 1978). However, with the exception of movement to breeding sites, none of these hypotheses seemed viable to Vareschi (1978).

Historically, it was thought that the three African populations of the Lesser Flamingo were separate and that no regular interchange took place (Brown 1973). However, circumstantial evidence has been assembled to show that East African Lesser Flamingos may fly to Botswana and Namibia to breed during periods when the Etosha and Makgadikgadi salt pans are flooded (Tuite 1979, Borello *et al.* 1998, Simmons 2000, McCulloch & Borello 2000), and that there may be interchange between the West African and other African populations (Trolliet & Fouquet 2001). However, very little is known about the movements of individual Lesser Flamingos. The only previous study to use satellite tracking was by McCulloch *et al.* (2003), who followed three Lesser Flamingos in southern Africa.

The primary aim of the present multi-year study was to use satellite tracking to document the flyway and network of key sites used by this Near Threatened species in East Africa during different periods of the year to support the development of an effective international site conservation plan. Secondary aims were to improve understanding of the movements of individual Lesser Flamingos and document whether there was any regular interchange between the East African population and the smaller populations elsewhere in Africa and India.

## STUDY SITE

This study was based at Lake Bogoria in Kenya (0°11'-0°20'N, 36°06'E), located within the Lake Bogoria National Reserve, a

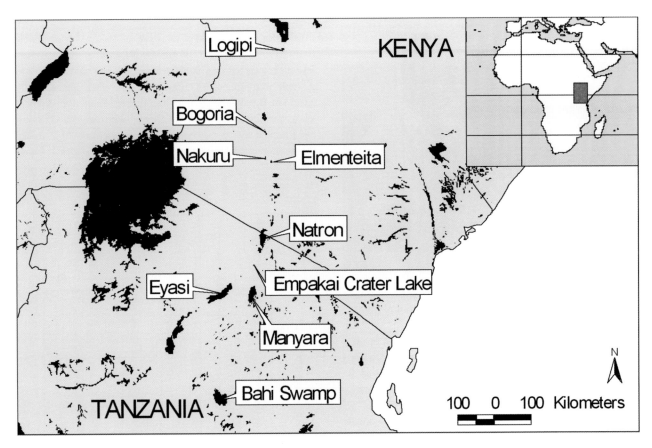

Fig. 1. Key sites for Lesser Flamingos *Phoenicopterus minor* in East Africa: November 2002 – January 2004.

protected area of 10 700 ha (Bennun & Njoroge 1999), 64 km north of Nakuru town in the eastern Rift Valley (Fig. 1). A recently-designated Ramsar site, Lake Bogoria is one of the two main feeding lakes for the Lesser Flamingo in Kenya, and regularly holds several hundred thousand birds. It is a long (16 km), narrow (3 km), shallow (max. depth 10.2 m), alkaline (1 160 ± 14.2 meq l$^{-1}$) lake with a pH of 10.2-10.3, situated at 975 m above sea level (Harper *et al.* 2003, Vareschi 1978).

## METHODS

In October 2002, four adult male Lesser Flamingos were captured and tagged with satellite transmitters (PTTs): two with solar-powered PTTs and two with battery-powered PTTs. The birds were captured using loops of 50 lb test polyethylene fishing line attached to a 120 x 245 cm grid of 3 mm wire mesh squares (7.5 x 7.5 cm) (Childress *et al.* 2004). Approximately 50 loops were tied to the grid. The grid was placed in the water perpendicular to the shoreline in a shallow, flat area where flamingos gathered and walked back and forth. The birds were captured when their feet became entangled in the loops.

Microwave Telemetry, Inc. supplied the two battery-powered PTTs. They were PTT-100 45 g units with estimated transmission lifetimes of 1 200 hours. The pre-set duty cycle specified for both was eight hours on and 60 hours off, which was estimated to result in operational periods of approximately 15 months. These units represented 2.2% and 2.3% of the body mass of the birds to which they were affixed. The two solar-powered PTTs had been reconditioned by their manufacturers, North Star Science and Technology, LLC, and Microwave Telemetry, Inc., respectively. The duty cycle of the North Star PTT (weight 40 g) was pre-set to be on for eight hours and off for 18 hours. As a test, the Microwave Telemetry PTT (weight 35 g) had no pre-set duty cycle. With no pre-set duty cycle, the PTT shuts itself off when its battery power is low, and then restarts automatically every six hours. If its battery has recharged sufficiently, it continues to transmit; if not, it shuts down for another six hours. These PTTs represented 1.6% and 1.9% respectively of the body mass of the birds to which they were affixed, and were expected to have operational lifetimes of three to five years.

We used a "backpack" harness specially designed for multi-year studies of large birds such as storks and flamingos (Van den

Table 1. Summary of number of inter-lake flights, number of different lakes visited, mean number of days spent at each stop, and approximate total distance moved by three satellite-tagged adult male Lesser Flamingos *Phoenicopterus minor* in the Rift Valley, East Africa, November 2002 – January 2004.

| Bird | No. inter-lake flights | No. different wetlands visited | Mean days spent at each stop ± SD (range) | Approx. inter-lake distance flown |
|---|---|---|---|---|
| Safari | 18 | 6 | 24.1 ± 28.4 (1-87) | 3 012 km |
| Bahati | 20 | 8 | 21.8 ± 34.1 (2-137) | 2 964 km |
| Imara | 70 | 11 | 6.4 ±15.1 (0-110)* | 7 870 km |

* 0 = less than one day

Fig. 2. Lesser Flamingo *Phoenicopterus minor* ready for release at Lake Bogoria, Kenya, showing position of PTT. Photo: Richard Webster.

Bossche 2002), consisting of 3 mm braided nylon cord inside a Teflon sleeve (Childress *et al.* 2004). The PTTs were positioned as high as possible on the birds' backs (Fig. 2). We fitted the harness to allow all four fingers of a flat hand to pass easily between the transmitter and the bird.

Argos CLS (Collecte Localisation Satellites) in Ramonville Cedex, France, calculated and reported the locations of the study birds utilizing the National Oceanic and Atmospheric Administration (NOAA) satellite system to receive transmissions from the PTTs. Argos's multi-satellite service was used to enable location calculations from all six satellites that passed over the Rift Valley regularly during the study.

We used locations in Argos's classes 0-3 (0: >1 000 m with no upper limit; 1: 1 000 m; 2: <350 m; 3: <150 m; Taillade 1992), as our purpose was only to identify the lake or wetland being used by the study birds during each transmission period. The length of each stopover visit was determined by subtracting the first date a location calculation was received from that lake (assumed date of arrival) from the first date a location calculation was received from a succeeding lake. We assumed that the date of departure from one lake and date of arrival at a new lake were the same, although this may not have been the case in all instances, as we were unable to tell when a movement was made if it was made when the PTT was in its "off" phase (60 hours out of every 68 hours). In most cases, the distance between the lakes and the quality of the location calculations were sufficient to determine that the bird had indeed moved from one lake to another. However, in some cases, the quality of the location calculations received was too poor to enable us to distinguish between two locations that were fairly close to each other. In these cases, we assumed that the bird had not moved.

Statistical analyses of inter-lake flight distances and lengths of stopovers were conducted with Kruskal-Wallis and Mann-Whitney tests in Minitab Statistical Software, Release 13 (Minitab Inc. 2000), as these data were either counts (length of stopovers) and/or not randomly distributed (both). We named the four birds "Bahati", "Safari", "Imara" and "Bendera" for discussion purposes.

## RESULTS

### Inter-lake movements

Between November 2002 and January 2004, Safari made 18 inter-lake flights, visited six different lakes, spent 24.1 days (SD ±28.4) at each stop (range 1-87 days) and travelled approximately 3 012 km; Bahati made 20 inter-lake flights, visited eight different lakes, spent 21.8 days (SD ± 34.1) at each stop (range 2-137 days), and travelled approximately 2 964 km; Imara made 70 inter-lake flights and visited 11 different lakes and wetlands, spent 6.4 days (SD ±15.1) at each stop (range <1-110 days), and travelled

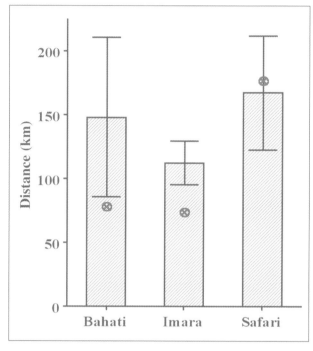

Fig. 3. Mean and median lengths of inter-lake flights by three Lesser Flamingos *Phoenicopterus minor*, with 95% confidence intervals for the means; cross-hair symbols are medians: November 2002 – January 2004.

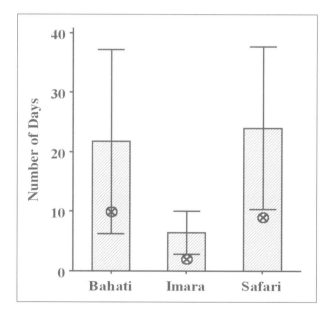

Fig. 4. Mean and median lengths of stopovers by three Lesser Flamingos *Phoenicopterus minor*, with 95% confidence intervals for the means; cross-hair symbols are medians: November 2002 – January 2004.

7 870 km (Table 1). Bendera's PTT stopped transmitting after 38 days at Lake Bogoria. The movement sensor on the PTT indicated no movement throughout the final day of transmission.

There were no significant differences among the three birds in terms of the length of their inter-lake flights (H = 4.76, DF = 2, P > 0.05 adj. for ties, $N_1$ = 18, $N_2$ = 20, $N_3$ = 70; Kruskal-Wallis Test), although there was a significant difference between Imara and Safari on this dimension (W = 1 018.5, P < 0.05 adj. for ties, $N_1$ = 18, $N_2$ = 70; Mann-Whitney Test) (Fig. 3). There were significant differences among the three birds in terms of the number of days spent at each stopover (H = 23.5, DF = 2, P < 0.001 adj. for ties, $N_1$ = 19, $N_2$ = 21, $N_3$ = 71; Kruskal-Wallis Test), and these differences were between Imara and the other two birds (Fig. 4), as there was no significant difference between Bahati and Safari on this dimension (W = 370.5, P > 0.05 adj. for ties, $N_1$ = 19, $N_2$ = 21; Mann-Whitney Test).

### The East Africa flyway and key site network

Ninety-nine percent of all flights by the three study birds were within the Rift Valley along a 940 km range between Lake Logipi in northern Kenya and Lake Bahi in central Tanzania (Fig. 1). There were no flights outside these two countries.

The three birds spent 99.9% of their combined stop over days at nine alkaline lakes in Kenya and Tanzania (Logipi, Bogoria, Nakuru, Elmenteita, Natron, Empakai Crater, Eyasi Manyara and Bahi), and 73.1% on just four lakes (Bogoria, Logipi, Manyara and Nakuru).

## DISCUSSION
### Movements

During the first fifteen months of this multi-year study, the three tagged birds remained within the Rift Valley, travelling north and south along a 940 km range between Lake Logipi in northern Kenya and Lake Bahi in central Tanzania. They spent 99.9% of their combined time on alkaline lakes, Bahati moved between lakes 20 times, Safari moved 18 times, and Imara moved 70 times.

The reasons for these movements are still unclear. The birds moved independently of one another, and it was often the case that one of the tagged birds would depart from a lake within days of another arriving at the same lake, or that another remained on the lake for several days/weeks after the first bird had departed. This phenomenon has become more apparent with the addition of a further four tagged birds to the study in June-July 2003, and indicates that the movements are probably not related to major fluctuations in food availability. There are occasions, such as those reported by Tuite (2000) and Vareschi (1978), where substantial changes in food availability result in large-scale population shifts away from or towards one particular lake. However, these large-scale changes in food availability do not occur overnight (Vareschi 1978), and do not seem to be directly related to the daily arrivals and departures of Lesser Flamingos at a given lake. There may be seasonal patterns in the movements, related either to the rains or the annual breeding season (October-December) at Lake Natron, or both. However, too few data are available to form any conclusions at this stage. Although Lesser Flamingos bred in large numbers at Lake Natron during both the 2002 and 2003 breeding seasons, none of the tagged birds appeared to have made an effort to breed. During October-December 2002, two of the three tagged birds did not visit Lake Natron at all, while the third made seven visits to that lake, all of between one and three days in length.

During October-December 2003, two of the three tagged birds did not visit Lake Natron, while the other visited the lake for 12 days in October and three days in November, but not at all in December. All four tagged birds added to the study in 2003 made one three-day visit to Lake Natron in November, but no visits in October or December. It appears that all of the study birds were non-breeders during these two years.

Although the number and frequency of movements by the three birds differed substantially between Bahati and Safari, and Imara, there was no significant difference in the length of their inter-lake flights. On the other hand, there was a significant difference between Bahati and Safari, and Imara, in the length of their stopovers, even though all three birds spent long periods of time (e.g. 45-137 days) at several different lakes.

The reasons for these differences in movement patterns are as unclear as the reasons for the inter-lake movements themselves. Since Lesser Flamingos rarely fly alone, all of the recorded movements are believed to have been made within flocks of other Lesser Flamingos. This confirms the general view that the Lesser Flamingo is a truly itinerant species. During the 15-month period reported here (and the subsequent period to March 2004), there were no flights outside Kenya and Tanzania, either by the initial three birds tagged or the four tagged birds added to the study in July 2003. Thus the study has provided no direct evidence as yet of any interchange between the East African population and any of the other smaller populations.

Conditions at the Makgadikgadi salt pans in Botswana and at Etosha Pan in Namibia during the 2002-03 breeding season were not conducive to Lesser Flamingo breeding, as it was a drought year and both locations were too dry for nest-building (G. McCulloch & R. Simmons *in litt.*). The 2003-04 breeding season was wetter, and Lesser Flamingo breeding occurred at both locations (G. McCulloch & R. Simmons *in litt.*). However, because there was breeding at Lake Natron during both 2002 and 2003, the finding that the tagged birds showed no interest in breeding at Lake Natron probably indicates that conditions in southern Africa had no effect on the movements of the tagged birds during these periods.

### Key site network: implications for protection and conservation

On a combined basis, the initial three tagged birds spent 99.9% of their time at nine alkaline lakes in Kenya and Tanzania (Logipi, Bogoria, Nakuru, Elmenteita, Natron, Empakai Crater, Eyasi, Manyara and Bahi), and these nine lakes, appear to comprise the key site network for Lesser Flamingos in East Africa. It has been known for many years that these nine alkaline wetlands are important for this species in East Africa (e.g. Bartholomew & Pennycuick 1973). This study documents their relative importance.

The conservation status of the nine lakes varies considerably. In Kenya, Lakes Bogoria and Nakuru are well protected, both being Ramsar sites and Lake Bogoria being entirely within a national reserve, while Lake Nakuru is within a national park. Lake Elmenteita is partly within a private wildlife sanctuary and partly unprotected (Bennun & Njoroge 1999). It is a small lake (1 800 ha) with several tourist facilities around its perimeter. Lake Logipi is completely unprotected and suffers from high levels of insecurity and overgrazing (W. Kimosop pers. comm.).

In Tanzania, the Empakai Crater Lake is well protected, being within the Ngorongoro Conservation Area. However, only the north-western quadrant of Lake Manyara is within the Lake Manyara National Park. The remainder of the lake, where the Lesser Flamingos congregate most frequently, is outside the park and thus unprotected. Incredibly, Lake Natron, the only successful breeding location for the East African population of Lesser Flamingos during the past 40 years, is also unprotected. This lake has been threatened in recent years by proposals for a major dam and hydroelectric power generation project on one of the major inflows from Kenya and a new soda ash extraction scheme (BirdLife International 2000), and there is currently a proposal for a new tourist lodge and facilities along its shore (N. Baker *in litt.*). Lake Eyasi and Lake Bahi are not protected in any way, and their surrounding areas are under heavy pressure from deforestation, overgrazing and agriculture (Baker & Baker 2002, N. Baker *in litt.*).

In view of the critical importance of these nine sites to the survival of the Lesser Flamingo in East Africa, it seems clear that there is an urgent need to protect those sites that remain unprotected. Proposals for such protection will be included in the forthcoming AENA/CMS Flamingo Conservation Action Plan currently being prepared by the Wetlands International/IUCN-SSC Flamingo Specialist Group, and supported by the findings from this study.

## ACKNOWLEDGEMENTS

This study was conducted under the auspices of the Department of Ornithology, National Museums of Kenya, the Baringo and Koibatek County Councils, and William Kimosop, Senior Warden, Lake Bogoria National Reserve. DH thanks the Ministry for Science and Technology for permission to conduct research in Kenya. In addition to their own organizations, the authors thank the following organizations and individuals for their financial and logistical support: International Flamingo Foundation, Darwin Initiative, Earthwatch Institute, Vodafone Group Foundation, Peter Scott Trust for Education and Research in Conservation, Ms Cicely Port, Mr Anthony Van Nice and Mr Errett Van Nice. We also thank the volunteers in Earthwatch Institute's Lakes of the Rift Valley research programme for their assistance with the fieldwork.

## REFERENCES

**Baker, N.E. & Baker, E.M.** 2002. Important bird areas in Tanzania: a first inventory. Wildlife Conservation Society of Tanzania, Dar es Salaam.

**Bartholomew, G.A. & Pennycuick, C.J.** 1973. The flamingo and pelican populations of the Rift Valley lakes in 1968-1969. East African Wildlife Journal 11: 189-198.

**Bennun, L. & Njoroge, P.** 1999. Important bird areas in Kenya. Nature Kenya, The East Africa Natural History Society, Nairobi.

**BirdLife International** 2000. Threatened Birds of the World. Lynx Edicions and BirdLife International, Barcelona and Cambridge.

**Borello, W.D., Mundy, P.J. & Liversedge, T.N.** 1998. Movements of Greater and Lesser Flamingos in southern Africa. In: E. Leshem, E. Lachman & P. Bertold (eds) Migrating Birds Know No Boundaries. Torgos Publication 28: 201-218.

**Brown, L.H.** 1973. The Mystery of the Flamingos. Second edition. East African Publishing House, Nairobi.

**Brown, L.H.** 1975. East Africa. In: J. Kear & N. Duplaix-Hall (eds) Flamingos. T. & A. D. Poyser, Ltd., Berkhamsted, England: 38-48.

**Brown, L.H., Urban, E.K. & Newman, K.** 1982. The Birds of Africa, Volume I. Academic Press, London.

**Childress, B., Harper, D., Van den Bossche, W., Berthold, P. & Querner, U.** 2004. Satellite tracking Lesser Flamingo movements in the Rift Valley, East Africa: pilot study report. Ostrich 75: 57-65.

**Evans, P.R.** 1985. Migration. In: B. Campbell & E. Lack (eds) Dictionary of Birds. T & AD Poyser, Calton, UK: 349.

**Harper, D.M., Childress, R.B., Harper, M.M., Boar, R.R., Hickley, P., Mills, S.C., Otieno, N., Drane, T., Vareschi, E., Nasirwa, O., Mwatha, W.E., Darlington, J.P.E.C. & Escuté-Gasulla, X.** 2003. Aquatic Biodiversity and Saline Lakes: Lake Bogoria, National Reserve, Kenya. Hydrobiologia 500: 259-276.

**Howard, G.** 1994. East African flamingos surveyed. IUCN Wetlands Programme Newsletter No.10.

**McCulloch, G.P. & Borello, W.D.** 2000. The importance of the Makgadikgadi salt pans in Botswana for flamingos in Africa. In: G.A. Baldassarre, F. Arengo & K.L. Bildstein (eds) Conservation biology of flamingos. Waterbirds 23 (Special Publication 1): 64-68.

**McCulloch, G., Aebischer, A. & Irvine, K.** 2003. Satellite tracking of flamingos in southern Africa: the importance of small wetlands for management and conservation. Oryx 37: 480-483.

**Minitab, Inc.** 2000. MINITAB™ Statistical Software, Release 13.0 for Windows® . Minitab, Inc., State College, Pennsylvania, USA.

**Simmons, R.E.** 2000. Declines and movements of Lesser Flamingos in Africa. In: G.A. Baldassarre, F. Arengo & K.L. Bildstein (eds) Conservation biology of flamingos. Waterbirds 23 (Special Publication 1): 40-46.

**Taillade, M.** 1992. Animal tracking by satellite. In: G. Priede & S.M. Swift (eds) Wildlife telemetry; remote monitoring and tracking of animals. Ellis Horwood, Chichester: 149-160.

**Trolliet, B. & Fouquet, M.** 2001. La population ouest-africaine du Flamant nain *Phoeniconaias minor*: effectifs, répartition et isolement. Malimbus 23: 87-92.

**Tuite, C.H.** 1979. Population size, distribution, and biomass density of the Lesser Flamingo in the Eastern Rift Valley, 1974-76. Journal of Applied Ecology 16: 765-775.

**Tuite, C.H.** 2000. The distribution and density of Lesser Flamingos in East Africa in relation to food availability and productivity. In: G.A. Baldassarre, F. Arengo & K.L. Bildstein (eds) Conservation biology of flamingos. Waterbirds 23 (Special Publication 1): 52-63.

**Van den Bossche, W.** 2002. Eastern European White Stork Populations: Migration Studies and Elaboration of Conservation Measures. BfN (German Federal Agency for Nature Conservation), Skripten 66: 197.

**Vareschi, E.** 1978. The ecology of Lake Nakuru (Kenya). I. Abundance and feeding of the Lesser Flamingo. Oecologia 32: 11-35.

**Wetlands International** 2002. Waterbird Population Estimates – Third edition. Wetlands International Global Series No.12, Wageningen, The Netherlands.

# Movements of three Greater Flamingos *Phoenicopterus ruber roseus* fitted with satellite transmitters in Tanzania

*N.E. Baker[1], E.M. Baker[1], W. Van den Bossche[2] & H. Biebach[3]*

[1] *Tanzania Bird Atlas Project, PO Box 1605, Iringa, Tanzania. (email: tzbirdatlas@yahoo.co.uk)*

[2] *Co-chair WI / IUCN SSC Storks, Ibises & Spoonbills Specialist Group, Heindonksesteenweg 277, 2830 Willebroek, Belgium. (email: wimvandenbossche@yahoo.co.uk)*

[3] *Max-Planck-Institut für Ornithologie, Von der Tann Str. 7, 82346 Andechs, Germany. (email: biebach@orn.mpg.de)*

Baker, N.E., Baker, E.M., Van den Bossche, W. & Biebach H. 2006. Movements of three Greater Flamingos *Phoenicopterus ruber roseus* fitted with satellite transmitters in Tanzania. *Waterbirds around the world.* Eds. G.C. Boere, C.A. Galbraith & D.A. Stroud. The Stationery Office, Edinburgh, UK. pp. 239-244.

## ABSTRACT

In April 2002, backpack PTTs were fitted to three Greater Flamingos *Phoenicopterus ruber roseus* at two sites in northern Tanzania. To maximise battery life, the transmitters were programmed to send signals for 12 hours at intervals of 192 hours. All three batteries lasted into 2004, having provided more than 24 months of data. This paper maps the recorded movements of the three birds, comments on each individual and raises issues related to the conservation of the species within Tanzania and Kenya.

## BACKGROUND

Satellite transmitters have revolutionised our understanding of large animal movements at the level of the individual (Meyburg & Lobkov 1994, Hughes *et al.* 1998, Stuwe *et al.* 1998). Advances in technology have enabled lighter transmitters to be fitted to an increasing range of species but weight constraints are still a significant issue. However, the most significant drawback remains that of cost. The transmitters alone are far from cheap and the added download and computer time means the technology still remains beyond everyday use. Movements of a few of the larger wetland birds between the Western Palearctic and the Afrotropics have featured in most studies undertaken to date in Africa (Berthold *et al.* 2001). Movements of waterbirds within the Afrotropical Region are still largely conjectural but advances have been made in recent years with long-term studies of Lesser Flamingo *Phoeniconaias minor* in southern Africa (McCulloch *et al.* 2003) and East Africa (Childress *et al.* in press). More recent studies have focussed on Abdim's Stork *Ciconia abdimii* between the breeding grounds in the northern Tropics and wintering grounds south of the equator, mainly in Tanzania (Flemming Pagh Jensen, pers. comm.).

During discussions about knowledge gaps with colleagues at the Max-Plank-Institut für Ornithologie Vogelwarte Radolfzell the possibility arose of redirecting three transmitters from their White Stork project and fitting these to Greater Flamingos. MPI Radolfzell duly provided the transmitters and the download costs while the Tanzanian Bird Atlas Project provided logistical support and capture of the birds. The birds were tagged with battery powered satellite backpack transmitters. These were PTT-100 platform transmitter terminals (PTTs) from Microwave Telemetry (USA) weighing 45 g. Each unit was programmed to emit a signal for 12 hours duration at intervals of 192 hours. The transmitter was attached to the bird's back as a backpack by a continuous strip of a 3.5 mm nylon rope with the 250 mm antenna angled backwards and free.

The PTTs transmitted with an impulse of 53 seconds, the length of one impulse was about 300 millisecond. Each impulse contained information in code regarding identification number, battery level, temperature and activity. The signals were received 850 km above the earth by NASA-satellites of the TIROS-series and forwarded to the ARGOS ground-station in Toulouse, France. ARGOS then calculated the PTT location using doppler shift analysis and their own algorithms, and the processed data were received at Radolfzel by email.

The Argos computer system assigns a 'location class' (LC) to each data record. Poor weather and low battery conditions can adversely affect signal reception by the satellites and therefore birds can not always be located with the same degree of accuracy. There are seven LCs of which only the four most accurate (from 150 m to 1 km) were used.

## TRAPPING METHODS

Slipknots made from 0.5 mm clear fishing line were attached at intervals of 30 cm to 50 m lengths of nylon rope. These lines were sunk in shallow water in a 'V' formation and held in place by locally occurring stones. The trap lines were under constant surveillance throughout and birds were removed within minutes of being caught. The two females were fitted with metal numbered rings from the East African Ringing Scheme (available rings were not large enough for the male bird) and red plastic rings. Standard measurements including weight were taken from all birds and are given in Table 1.

The transmitter + harness weight of 48 gm represented 1.75%, 2.06% and 2.34% of body weight, well within the recommended limit of 5%.

**Table 1. Biometric data from the three birds.**

| Date | Site | Ring | Species | Age | Sex | Weight (g) | Wing (mm) | Tarsus (mm) | Remarks |
|------|------|------|---------|-----|-----|-----------|-----------|-------------|---------|
| 30/3/02 | Manyara | - | *Phoenicopterus ruber* | AD | M | 2750.0 | 424.0 | 340.0 | 27187 - Leo |
| 7/4/02 | Magadini | W0902 | *Phoenicopterus ruber* | AD | F | 2330.0 | 380.0 | 264.0 | 27188 - Jane |
| 18/4/02 | Magadini | W0903 | *Phoenicopterus ruber* | imm | F | 2050.0 | 397.0 | 275.0 | 27186 - Paola |

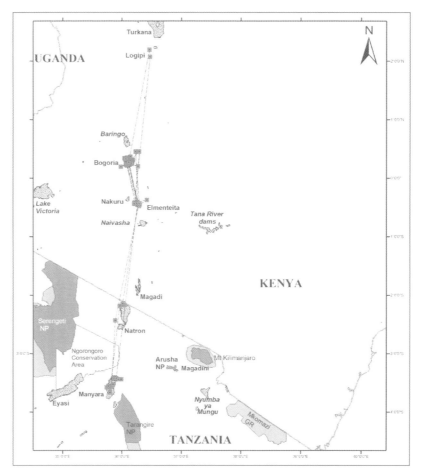

Fig. 1. Satellite tracking of three Greater Flamingos April 2002 to June 2004: Leo.

## LOGISTICS

There was much debate on where to catch the birds. Core areas would perhaps provide more insight into movements for most birds but those in peripheral areas would perhaps move greater distances. In the end, financial and time constraints dictated that birds should be captured in core areas close to the Rift Valley in northern Tanzania.

The first location of choice was Lake Manyara which is well known to hold significant numbers of flamingos. Much of the northern shallows where the flamingos feed occur outside Lake Manyara National Park and are subject to considerable disturbance from fishermen, tourists and bird catchers (Baker & Baker 2002). During the visit in March 2002 the latter were particularly active, trapping Yellow-billed Storks *Mycteria ibis* from the adjacent active breeding colony and even Blacksmith Plovers *Vanellus armatus* and Chestnut-banded Sandplovers *Charadrius pallidus* for the apparently insatiable export market. Levels of disturbance were such that flamingo flocks were severely agitated and it proved difficult to herd them in the direction of the trap lines. During discussions with one of the bird trappers it was established that several Greater Flamingos had been caught in recent weeks and were being held in a house in Mto wa Mbuu, the nearest village. The Park Ecologist from Lake Manyara National Park, who had accompanied us in the field, quickly located the house and we negotiated to purchase (for only $10) the largest and healthiest bird from the dozen or so walking around an empty room in a recently constructed house. It is not appropriate to go into detail here concerning the bird trade, but suffice it to say that the smear lines on the walls clearly

indicated that this particular room had held numbers of birds of varying heights for many days.

The second site of choice was to be Lake Natron, known to be a breeding site for the Greater Flamingo but far more important for Lesser Flamingos. Large numbers of Lesser Flamingo were present at all the surveyed areas of this lake and much time would have been lost attempting to target the fewer Greater Flamingo present in those areas which were accessible.

We chose not to trap birds within protected areas and it was decided to limit our search to those lakes known to regularly harbour smaller numbers of birds. Magadini is a small, seasonal rainfed alkaline lake between Mounts Meru and Kilimanjaro and barely 10 km from the Momella Lakes within Arusha National Park. This lake is known to hold numbers of both flamingo species on a regular basis. It was also only a few kilometres from our home base at the time on the south-west slopes of Mt. Kilimanjaro.

## RESULTS

The movements of the male bird tagged at Lake Manyara are shown in Fig. 1.

It must be emphasised that during the 192 hr interval any of these birds could (and most probably did) move considerable distances. The straight lines on the maps link sequential accurate fixes and do not therefore even pretend to map flight paths. This should be taken into account when interpreting the maps.

As this was the first bird caught and tagged and he had been held in captivity for an undetermined number of days, there were obvious concerns about his well-being. However, within minutes

**Table 2. Movement summary for Leo, the adult male: 100 usable fixes from 30 March 2002 to 21 June 2004 - 813 days.**

| | | Leo 27187 | |
|---|---|---|---|
| date | date | location | Days |
| 30.03.02 | 15.06.02 | Manyara | 78 |
| 22.06.02 | 22.06.02 | Elmenteita | ? |
| 30.06.02 | 31.01.03 | Bogoria | 216 |
| 07.02.03 | 10.03.03 | Elmenteita | 32 |
| 18.03.03 | 18.03.03 | Natron | ? |
| 26.03.03 | 10.05.03 | Manyara | 45 |
| 18.05.03 | 02.06.03 | Natron | 15 |
| 10.06.03 | 10.06.03 | Elmenteita | ? |
| 18.06.03 | 18.06.03 | Bogoria | ? |
| 25.06.03 | 03.08.03 | Elmenteita | 40 |
| 10.08.03 | 12.12.03 | Bogoria | 125 |
| 19.12.03 | 11.01.04 | Elmenteita | 24 |
| 03.02.04 | 20.04.04 | Bogoria | 77 |
| 28.04.04 | 06.05.04 | Logipi | 9 |
| 21.05.04 | 21.06.04 | Elmenteita | 33 |

**Five sites over 814 days**

**Table 3. Movement summary for Paola, an adult female: 69 usable fixes from 18 April 2002 to 9 April 2004 - 721 days.**

| | | Paola 27186 | |
|---|---|---|---|
| date | date | location | days |
| 18.04.02 | 06.06.02 | Magadini | 50 |
| 14.06.02 | 15.09.02 | Arusha NP | 94 |
| 23.09.02 | 23.09.02 | Manyara | ? |
| 01.10.02 | 17.11.02 | Arusha NP | 48 |
| 25.11.02 | 24.05.03 | Manyara | 181 |
| | no further fixes until | | |
| 18.09.03 | 18.09.03 | Manyara | ? |
| 04.10.03 | 04.10.03 | Burungi | ? |
| 12.10.03 | 12.10.03 | Manyara | ? |
| 19.10.03 | 13.12.03 | Burungi | 56 |
| 21.12.03 | 21.12.03 | Empakai | ? |
| 06.01.04 | 06.01.04 | Manyara | ? |
| 14.01.04 | 14.01.04 | Rasini Bay | ? |
| 21.01.04 | 09.04.04 | Natron | 79 |

**Seven sites over 721 days**

**Table 4. Movement summary for Jane, an immature female: 95 usable fixes from 21 April 2002 to 9 June 2004 - 779 days.**

| | | Jane 27188 | |
|---|---|---|---|
| date | date | location | days |
| 07.04.02 | 21.04.02 | Magadini | 15 |
| 29.04.02 | 29.04.02 | Nyumba ya Mungu | ? |
| 06.05.02 | 29.12.02 | Manyara | 238 |
| 03.01.03 | 03.01.03 | Natron | ? |
| 08.01.03 | 04.05.03 | Manyara | 117 |
| 12.05.03 | 20.05.03 | Natron | 9 |
| 28.05.03 | 07.08.03 | Elmenteita | 72 |
| 14.08.03 | 14.08.03 | Mida Creek | ? |
| 22.08.03 | 22.03.04 | Rasini Bay | 211 |
| 08.05.04 | 08.05.04 | ? | ? |
| 24.05.04 | 09.06.04 | Manyara | 17 |

**Seven sites over 793 days**

of being released he appeared to be walking and feeding normally within a small flock of some 80 birds. During subsequent observations he was seen to preen the antenna and did not appear to be disturbed by it, the backpack transmitter or the harness. Worthy of note is that he may have spent some 418 days at Bogoria, was the only bird to visit Logipi in the far north near Lake Turkana, and that he did not visit the coast.

The movements of the adult female bird tagged at Magadini are shown in Fig. 2.

This bird was the only one of the three to visit Lake Burungi and may have stayed on this small lake for nearly two months. She was also the only bird to visit Empakai Crater lake within the Ngorongoro Conservation Area, although this was only a single fix so her visit was a short one. Perhaps the most interesting of her movements was the visit to Rasini Bay in coastal Kenya. This single fix indicates a stay of no more than 15 days and it could have been far less than this. Lake Manyara was obviously important to this bird during the two years with a potential long single stay and many return visits.

The movements of the immature female bird tagged at Magadini are shown in Fig. 3.

The long stay of this bird on Lake Manyara seems at first to be quite remarkable. Fixes were so close together for so many weeks that it was feared she had died and we were seeing simple errors in accuracy. Equally, her long stay on the Kenyan coast was also surprising but due to the long intervals between fixes it is not possible to draw firm conclusions from these two long stays as single sites. There is no significant wetland within several kilometres of the fix on the 8 May 2004 and at a time of 13:12 GMT this would not suggest a bird on a long overland flight. Lake Chala, a small steep sided crater lake (unsuitable for flamingos) is some 15 km to the north-east of this fix and Lake Jipe (which would be suitable as a stopover site) is 20 km to the south-east. The shortest distance between Elmenteita and Mida Creek on the Kenyan coast is 520 km but it cannot be stated from these results that this distance was covered in a single flight.

## Habitat usage on Lake Manyara

Many of the flamingo lakes within the Rift Valley are quite small and little can be inferred from satellite tracking movement of individual birds due to inaccuracies inherent in the methodology and the lack of choice when birds are disturbed for any reason. However, the results mapped here for Lake Manyara show quite remarkable individual choice of habitat selection within the lake.

Fig. 4. details the 81 fixes from all three birds during their visits to Lake Manyara.

Of the 45 fixes for Jane, 40 (88%) were from the southern half of the lake with two clear concentrations in the south-east. Yet only one fix from 16 and one fix from 20 were recorded for Leo and Paola respectively from this part of the lake. The latter is actually well to the southeast of the lake and she may well

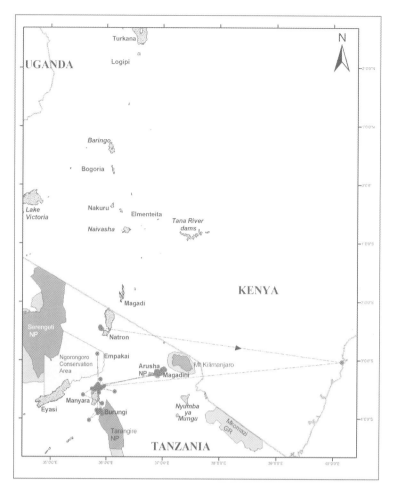

Fig. 2. Satellite tracking of three Greater Flamingos April 2002 to June 2004: Paola.

have been on her way to Lake Burungi. Ten of the 16 fixes for Leo are in the far north-east section of the lake, close to where he was caught and released and although 17 of the 20 fixes for Paola are in the same general area they are clearly well to the south of the habitat preferred by Leo.

Long intervals between fixes make it difficult to be more dogmatic about these results but these three birds clearly showed individual choice in their usage of this lake.

## CONSERVATION IMPLICATIONS

These comments relate only to the lakes visited by these three birds and not to all the lakes in East Africa utilised by the Greater Flamingo.

The importance of **Lake Manyara** to this species cannot be over emphasised. Of special note here is that these birds spend the majority of their time in the eastern and southern portions of the lake that are not included within the National Park. The entire lake area should be protected as suggested in the national Important Bird Areas inventory (Baker & Baker 2002).

Although only one of the three birds utilised **Lake Burungi** this lake is known to be seasonally important to both flamingo species (Baker 1997, Baker & Baker 2002) and it is surely an oversight that this lake has not yet been incorporated into Tarangire National Park lying as it does just outside the current protected area boundary.

That **Lake Natron** is critical for the entire Rift Valley population of Lesser Flamingos is well understood (Mlingwa & Baker 2006) but it is less clear how significant this lake is to the much smaller population of Greater Flamingos although it does appear to be a regular breeding site for this species too. All three tagged birds used the lake to varying degrees and its status as a Ramsar site should prevent undue damage to this unique ecosystem. However, renewed calls to exploit the soda ash and the threat of a tarmac road through the valley certainly give cause for concern.

**Lake Bogoria** is protected as a National Reserve managed by the local county councils and as such is free from undue disturbance (Bennun & Njoroge 1999).

**Lake Elmenteita** is largely protected by private ownership (Bennun & Njoroge 1999) but requires some formal protection, perhaps best served for now by bringing it within the Ramsar Convention.

**Rasini Bay** is used here to denote two small bays along the southern shoreline of Ungwana (Formosa) Bay in coastal Kenya. Rasini is the southern most bay and Fundisa a few kilometers to the north. Within the context of this study and accepting the limitations imposed by the 192 day signal interval, Jane spent 211 consecutive days here between August 2003 and March 2004. In contrast Paola visited this part of the Kenyan coast for less than two weeks giving a single fix on 14 January 2004. Little is known about this site and only the northern shoreline was included in the Kenya Important Bird Areas (Bennun & Njoroge 1999). It would seem worthwhile to include the whole of this area in future waterbird counts and in particular to conduct regular counts of Great Flamingo here to ascertain the importance of this site to this species.

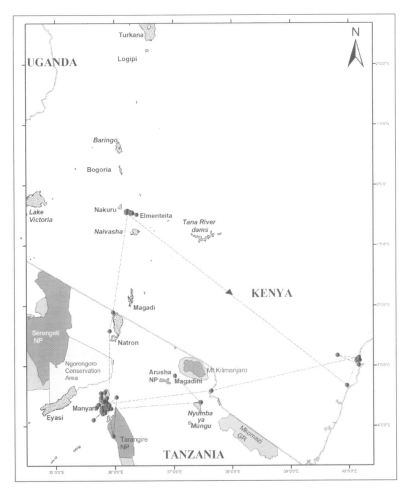

**Fig. 3.** Satellite tracking of three Greater Flamingos April 2002 to June 2004: Jane.

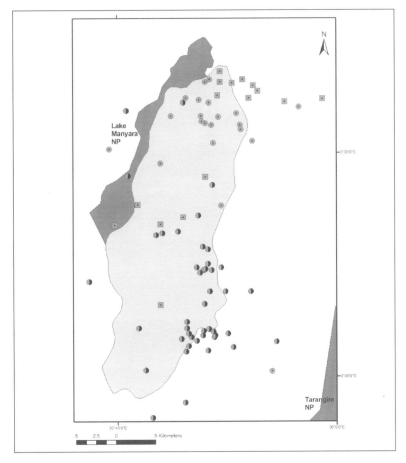

**Fig. 4.** Satellite tracking of three Greater Flamingos during visits to Lake Manyara, from April 2002 to June 2004: ▣ Leo; ◉ Paola; and ◖ Jane.

## ACKNOWLEDGEMENTS

The generosity of Peter Berthold and Ulrich Querner of the Max-Planck-Institut für Ornithologie Radolfzell in providing transmitters, download costs and computer time is fully acknowledged and very much appreciated. NEB acknowledges the research clearance afforded by the Tanzania Commission for Science and Technology. We thank Emilion Kihwele, the Park Ecologist at Lake Manyara National Park for accompanying us in the field while working on the shores of Lake Manyara.

## REFERENCES

Baker, N.E. 1997. Tanzania Waterbird Count: the first co-ordinated count on the major wetlands of Tanzania. Wildlife Conservation Society of Tanzania. Dar es Salam.

Baker, N.E., & Baker, E.M 2002. Important Bird Areas in Tanzania. Wildlife Conservation Society of Tanzania. Dar es Salaam.

Bennun, L. & Njoroge, P. 1999. Important Bird Areas in Kenya. Nature Kenya. Nairobi.

Berthold, P., van den Bossche, W., Fiedler, W., Gorney, E., Kaatz, M., Leshem, Y., Nowak, E. & Querner, U. 2001. Der Zug des Weißstorchs *Ciconia ciconia*: eine besondere Zugform auf Grund neuer Ergebnisse. Journal fur Ornithologie 142: 73-92.

Childress, B., Hughes, B., Harper, D., Van den Bossche, W., Berthold, P. and Querner, U. in press. East African flyway and key site network of the Lesser Flamingo *Phoenicopterus minor* documented through satellite tracking. Proceedings of the Pan African Ornithological Congress XI, 20-25 November 2004; Djerba, Tunisia.

Hughes, G.R., Luschi, P., Mencacci, R. & Papi, F. 1998. The 7000-km oceanic journey of a leatherback turtle tracked by satellite. Journal of Experimental Marine Biology and Ecology 229: 209-217.

McCulloch, G., Aebischer, A. &Irvine, K. 2003. Satellite tracking of flamingos in southern Africa: the importance of small wetlands for management and conservation. Oryx 37(4): 480-483.

Meyburg, B.-U. & Lobkov, E.G. 1994. Satellite tracking of a juvenile Steller's Sea Eagle *Haliaeetus pelagicus*. Ibis 136: 105-106.

Mlingwa, C. & Baker, N. 2006. Lesser Flamingo *Phoenicopterus minor* counts in Tanzanian soda lakes: implications for conservation. Waterbirds around the world. G.C. Boere, C.A. Galbraith & D.A. Stroud (Eds.), The Stationery Office, Edinburgh, UK. 230-233.

Stuwe, M., Abdul, J.B., Mohd, B. & Wemmer, C.B. 1998. Tracking the movements of translocated elephants in Malaysia using satellite telemetry. Oryx 32: 68-74.

Lesser Flamingos *Phoenicopterus minor* feeding at Lake Nakuru, Kenya. Photo: Sergey Dereliev.

# Waterbirds in Tanzania: what we know and what we do not; where are the knowledge gaps?

*N.E. Baker & E.M. Baker*

*Tanzania Bird Atlas Project, PO Box 1605, Iringa, Tanzania. (email: tzbirdatlas@yahoo.co.uk)*

Baker, N.E. & Baker, E.M. 2006. Waterbirds in Tanzania: what we know and what we do not; where are the knowledge gaps? *Waterbirds around the world*. Eds. G.C. Boere, C.A. Galbraith & D.A. Stroud. The Stationery Office, Edinburgh, UK. pp. 245-249.

This paper presents a summary of current knowledge of water-bird numbers in Tanzania. Reports from earlier surveys contained in the literature have been supplemented by recent survey work. Recommendations are made for monitoring.

Prior to 1995 only four sites had been "counted" in Tanzania for the African Waterbird Census (Table 1). Counting waterbirds on some of the larger lakes and swamps is extremely difficult. At 945 000 km$^2$ Tanzania is the size of Germany, The Netherlands and France combined (941 965 km$^2$) (Times Atlas 1985). It is estimated that 5.8% (5 439 000 ha) of Tanzania is covered by lakes and swamps but this does not include the many seasonal wetlands (Hughes & Hughes 1992).

With close to 15 million waterbirds frequenting Tanzania and 42 sites known to hold internationally important numbers (1% of populations) it is clear that coverage remains poor and must be improved upon.

The larger lakes, swamps and dams are listed in Table 2. Many of the swamps have boundaries that are difficult to define and only now are they beginning to be mapped with any degree of accuracy. There are many hundreds of small cattle dams and many thousands of ephemeral ponds, lakes and swamps. The lengths of coastline and shorelines of the larger lakes are also given in Table 2 but again these have yet to be delineated accurately. The major wetlands are shown on Map 1.

The preliminary Atlas map for the African Fish Eagle *Haliaeetus vocifer* gives an indication of how few dry squares there are in Tanzania (Map 2). The pale grey squares on all these maps indicate poor coverage and clearly indicate sites for future fieldwork.

In 1995 the first co-ordinated count of the major wetlands took place with significant assistance from the Royal Society for

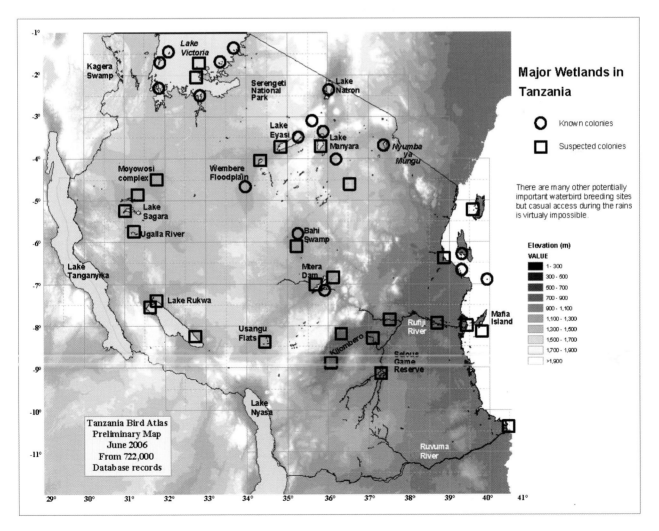

Fig. 1. Major wetlands in Tanzania.

**Table 1. African Waterbird Census results for Tanzania.**

African Waterbird Census: Tanzania - January waterbird counts

| Year | Sites | Species | Numbers | Reference |
|------|-------|---------|---------|-----------|
| 1992 | 1 | 1 | 372 670 | Perennou 1992 |
| 1993 | - | - | - | |
| 1994 | 3 | 56 | 46 377 | Taylor & Rose 1994 |
| 1995 | 107 | 148 | 1 735 963 | Dodman & Taylor 1995; Baker 1997 |
| 1996 | ? | 109 | 57 324 | Dodman & Taylor 1996 |
| 1997 | ? | 54 | 22 891 | Dodman *et al.* 1997 |
| 1998 | ? | 126 | 207 430 | Dodman *et al.* 1998 |
| 1999 | 1 | 27 | 5 192 | Dodman & Diagana 2003 |
| 2000 | 7 | 84 | 22 265 | Dodman & Diagana 2003 |
| 2001 | 16 | ? | 91 518 | Dodman & Diagana 2003 |

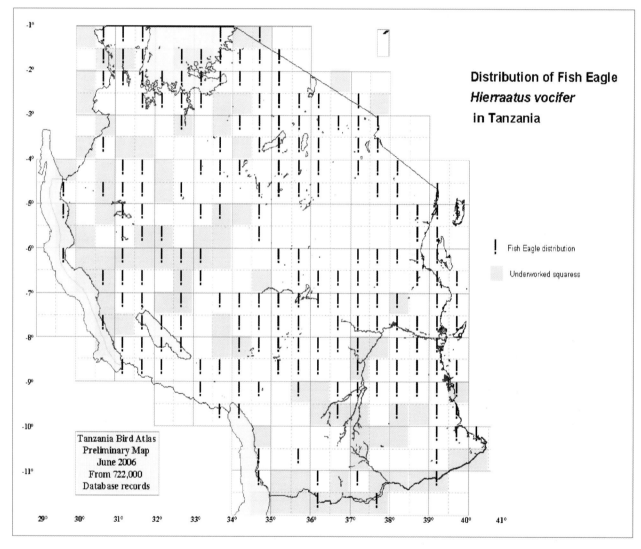

**Fig. 2.** Distribution of the Fish Eagle *Haliaeetus vocifer* in Tanzania.

the Protection of Birds and the Global Environmental Facility. The publication of these results and the first waterbird population estimates for Tanzania provided the raw data to designate shadow Ramsar sites (Baker 1997). These data were also used to designate sites of global importance using IUCN Red List criteria and Ramsar 1% levels. Of the sites holding 1% of a population, 41 are listed in the IBA inventory (Baker & Baker 2002) and more are being added with continuing fieldwork.

The second co-ordinated count took place in January 2005 (N.E. Baker in prep.). The Tanzania Bird Atlas database held 105 000 records in 1996: by May 2006 it held 722 000 records of which 114 600 (15.8%) are for waterbirds. With records being submitted on a regular basis from a growing number of observers it is anticipated that the one million mark will be reached within three years. From this increased knowledge base it is possible to revise the population estimates for many waterbird species utilising Tanzania.

## Table 2. The larger and potentially most important wetlands in Tanzania.

| Name | Size (ha) | Knowledge | 1% Levels | Status | Comments | Reference |
|---|---|---|---|---|---|---|
| Kagera valley lakes | 35 000 | very poor | ? | (Ramsar) | 15 000 ha in Rwanda | Hughes & Hughes 1992 |
| Moyowosi swamps | 320 000 | poor | yes | NO | | Hughes & Hughes 1992 |
| Moyowosi floodplain | 250 000 | poor | ? | Ramsar | in wet years | Hughes & Hughes 1992 |
| Ugalla floodplain | 90 000 | very poor | yes | Ramsar | | Hughes & Hughes 1992 |
| Lake Sagara | 85 000 | poor | yes | Ramsar | in wet years | Hughes & Hughes 1992 |
| Masirori Swamp | 30 000 | unknown | ? | NO | papyrus swamp | Hughes & Hughes 1992 |
| Nyumba ya Mungu | 22 000 | good | yes | NO | impoundment | Baker & Baker 2002 |
| Pangani River | 90 000 | poor | ? | NO | some papyrus | Hughes & Hughes 1992 |
| Wami floodplain | 80 000 | very poor | ? | NO | some papyrus | Hughes & Hughes 1992 |
| Ruvu floodplain | 43 200 | poor | ? | NO | | Hughes & Hughes 1992 |
| Kilombero floodplain | 626 500 | quite good | yes | Ramsar | | Hughes & Hughes 1992 |
| Ihefu Swamp | 4 000 | poor | yes | GR | | Hughes & Hughes 1992 |
| Usangu Flats | 150 000 | poor | yes | NO | in wet years | Hughes & Hughes 1992 |
| Mtera reservoir | 66 000 | quite good | yes | NO | area of open water | Baker & Baker 2002 |
| Lake Rukwa | 600 000 | very poor | yes | NO | some GR | Baker & Baker 2002 |
| Katavi National Park | 67 000 | poor | yes | NP | floodplain | Hughes & Hughes 1992 |
| Katavi National Park | 2 520 | poor | ? | NP | lakes | Hughes & Hughes 1992 |
| Bahi Swamp | 125 000 | poor | yes | NO | worked in 2005 | Hughes & Hughes 1992 |
| Wembere floodplain | 140 000 | poor | yes | NO | in wet years | Hughes & Hughes 1992 |
| Lake Kitangire | 11 500 | poor | yes | NO | are of open water | Hughes & Hughes 1992 |
| Lake Eyasi | 116 000 | poor | yes | NO | in wet years | Hughes & Hughes 1992 |
| Yaida Swamp | 16 200 | poor | yes | NO | seasonal lake / swamp | Baker & Baker 2002 |
| Lake Natron | 85 500 | poor | yes | Ramsar | lake level in wet years | Hughes & Hughes 1992 |
| Lake Natron | 12 000 | poor | yes | Ramsar | swamp | Hughes & Hughes 1992 |
| Lake Manyara | 41 300 | good | yes | NO | west shore only in NP | Hughes & Hughes 1992 |
| Lake Burungi | 4 000 | poor | yes | NO | | Baker & Baker 2002 |
| Shuriro swamp | 36 000 | unknown | ? | NO | in wet years | Hughes & Hughes 1992 |
| Tarangire NP swamps | >60 000 | poor | yes | NP | in wet years | Hughes & Hughes 1992 |
| Lake Buigi | 7 000 | poor | ? | GR | | Hughes & Hughes 1992 |
| Lake Ikamba | 12 500 | unknown | ? | NO | | Hughes & Hughes 1992 |
| Lake Victoria | 3 375 600 | poor | yes | NO | area in Tanzania | Hughes & Hughes 1992 |
| Lake Tanganyika | 1 350 736 | very poor | ? | NO | area in Tanzania | Hughes & Hughes 1992 |
| Lake Nyasa | 2 975 000 | very poor | ? | NO | none in Tanzania ??? | Hughes & Hughes 1992 |
| The Balangidas | 10 000 | poor | yes | NO | | Hughes & Hughes 1992 |
| Latham Island | <3 | good | yes | NO | major seabird colonies | Baker & Baker 2002 |
| Lake Victoria shoreline | 1 420 km | poor | yes | NO | | Hughes & Hughes 1992 |
| Tanganyika shoreline | 650 km | very poor | ? | NO | | Hughes & Hughes 1992 |
| Nyasa shoreline | 305 km | unknown | ? | NO | | Hughes & Hughes 1992 |
| Indian Ocean coast | >1 500 km | variable | yes | NO | Rufiji Delta - Mafia Ramsar | Hughes & Hughes 1992 |
| Zanzibar coastline | ? | good | yes | NO | includes Pemba island | Baker & Baker 2002 |

GR = Game Reserve   NP = National Park   NO = not protected

Currently 201 species from 31 families of waterbirds are known from Tanzania, 28 of these are vagrants and 14 are not actually wetland birds (Table 3). Records of the remaining 159 species have been used to plot known waterbird concentrations at the level of the Atlas square (½ degree x ½ degree, approximately 2 500 km² at the equator) shown on Map 3.

**How many waterbirds?** Table 4 below lists crude population estimates (guesses in some cases) for the total number of waterbirds utilising Tanzania. These figures are currently being refined at the species level but the rough figure of 15 million birds appears to be credible. There are 16 million cows in

Tanzania and one rarely sees cattle without a seemingly similar number of Cattle Egrets!

**Breeding species:** Known and suspected colonies are marked on Map 1. Our knowledge of these major breeding sites the numbers involved threats and their success rates are poorly known. Access during the rainy season is the greatest problem. Aerial surveys and counts are essential if our knowledge of these sites is to be improved.

**The knowledge gaps:** From the above it is clear that far more effort is required to visit more wetlands and to count the birds on them as accurately as possible. All wetlands should be

**Table 3. Families and species of waterbirds\* occurring in Tanzania.**

| Family | Species | Vagrant | Non wetland | Species used |
|---|---|---|---|---|
| Dendrocygnidae | 2 | | | 2 |
| Anatidae | 20 | 5 | | 15 |
| Gruidae | 2 | | | 2 |
| Heliornithidae | 1 | | | 1 |
| Rallidae | 18 | | 2 | 16 |
| Scolopacidae | 27 | 3 | | 24 |
| Rostratulidae | 1 | | | 1 |
| Jacanidae | 2 | | | 2 |
| Burhinidae | 3 | 1 | 1 | 1 |
| Haematopodidae | 1 | | | 1 |
| Recurvirostridae | 2 | | | 2 |
| Charadriidae | 22 | 1 | 4 | 17 |
| Dromadidae | 1 | | | 1 |
| Glareolidae | 8 | 1 | 4 | 3 |
| Lariidae | 28 | 7 | | 21 |
| Accipitridae | 7 | 1 | 2 | 4 |
| Podicipedae | 3 | | | 3 |
| Phaethontidae | 1 | | | 1 |
| Sulidae | 4 | 3 | | 1 |
| Anhingidae | 1 | | | 1 |
| Phalacrocoracidae | 2 | | | 2 |
| Ardeidae | 20 | 2 | | 18 |
| Scopidae | 1 | | | 1 |
| Phoenicopteridae | 2 | | | 2 |
| Threskiornithidae | 5 | | 1 | 4 |
| Pelecanidae | 2 | | | 2 |
| Balaenicipitidae | 1 | | | 1 |
| Ciconiidae | 8 | | | 8 |
| Fregatidae | 2 | | | 2 |
| Diomedeidae | 1 | 1 | | 0 |
| Procellariidae | 3 | 3 | | 0 |
| **Totals from 31 families** | **201** | **28** | **14** | **159** |

order follows Hockey *et al.* 2005

\* waterbirds are defined here as those species counted each year under the AfWC

mapped using current GIS technology. All the known or suspected colonies require monitoring. To achieve this, dedicated teams are required within the two major conservation bodies, National Parks and Wildlife Division and the Tanzania Wildlife Research Institute. Other bodies such as International and National NGOs should be encouraged to support these efforts. WWF, IUCN, African Wildlife Foundation, Frankfurt Zoological Society, the Wildlife Conservation Society and the Wildlife Conservation Society of Tanzania are all active in Tanzania and all are in one way or another involved with wetlands. Tanzania is a signatory to both the Ramsar and the Bonn Convention and has a National Wetlands Working Group in place. Enough resources exist to support regular monitoring of known sites and surveys of new sites - it just requires supporting and organising.

**Table 4. Waterbird population estimates for Tanzania.**

| Family | Estimate | Notes |
|---|---|---|
| Dendrocygnidae | 80 000 | |
| Anatidae | 350 000 | |
| Gruidae | 3 000 | |
| Heliornithidae | 3 000 | |
| Rallidae | 1 000 000 | (guess) |
| Scolopacidae | 1 000 000 | from regular counts |
| Jacanidae | 300 000 | |
| Burhinidae | 50 000 | |
| Recurvirostridae | 60 000 | |
| Charadriidae | 500 000 | from regular counts |
| Dromadidae | 30 000 | |
| Glareolidae | 20 000 | |
| Lariidae | 2 200 000 | 2 million White-winged Terns |
| Accipitridae | 5 000 | |
| Podicipedae | 100 000 | |
| Sulidae | 10 000 | |
| Anhingidae | 10 000 | |
| Phalacrocoracidae | 250 000 | |
| Ardeidae | 5 400 000 | 5 million Cattle Egrets !! |
| Scopidae | 150 000 | |
| Phoenicopteridae | 2 500 000 | 50 000 Greater Flamingos ? |
| Threskiornithidae | 135 000 | |
| Pelecanidae | 50 000 | |
| Ciconiidae | 450 000 | 250 000 Abdim's Storks |
| **Total** | **14 656 000** | |

These figures are being refined at the species level (Baker in prep)

Greater Flamingo *Phoenicopterus roseus*. Photo: Phil Shepherd.

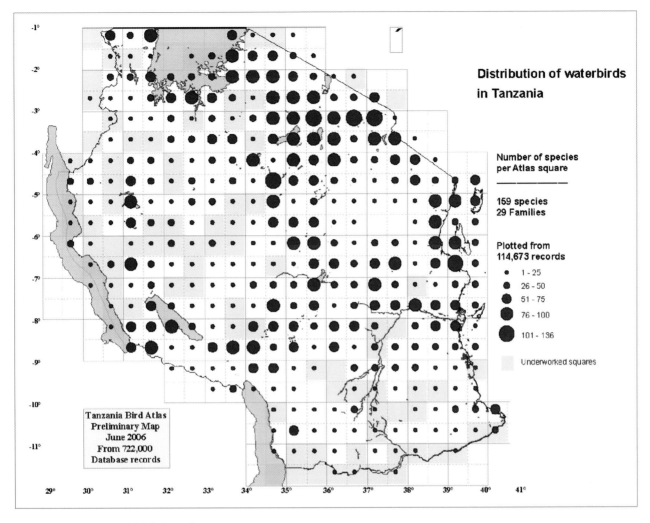

**Distribution of waterbirds in Tanzania**

Number of species per Atlas square

159 species
29 Families

Plotted from
114,673 records

- • 1 - 25
- • 26 - 50
- • 51 - 75
- ● 76 - 100
- ● 101 - 136

Underworked squares

Tanzania Bird Atlas
Preliminary Map
June 2006
From 722,000
Database records

**Fig. 3.** Distribution of waterbirds in Tanzania.

## ACKNOWLEDGEMENTS
The Leverhulme Trust awarded NEB a research grant to allow fieldwork to continue in Tanzania during 2004/2005. Frankfurt Zoological Society provided funds that enabled NEB to attend the Edinburgh Conference. Both organisations are fully acknowledged and thanked for their support. The Commission for Science and Technology are thanked for granting research permits in Tanzania.

## REFERENCES
**Baker, N.E.** 1997. Tanzania Waterbird Count: the first coordinated count on the major wetlands of Tanzania January 1995. Wildlife Conservation Society of Tanzania. Dar es Salaam.

**Baker, N.E. & Baker, E.M.** 2002. Important Bird Areas in Tanzania: A first inventory. Wildlife Conservation Society of Tanzania.

**Baker, N.E.** in prep. Waterbirds and Wetlands in Tanzania: Results from the January 2005 count and current status of species and sites. Wildlife Division Dar-es Salaam Tanzania.

**Dodman, T. & Taylor, V.** 1995. African Waterfowl Census 1995. The International Waterfowl and Wetlands Research Bureau. Slimbridge. UK.

**Dodman, T. & Taylor, V.** 1996. African Waterfowl Census

1995. The International Waterfowl and Wetlands Research Bureau. Slimbridge. UK.

**Dodman, T., de Vaan, C. Hubert, E. & Nivet, C.** 1997. African Waterfowl Census 1997. Wetlands International. Wageningen. The Netherlands.

**Dodman, T., Béibro, H.Y., Hubert, E. & Williams, E.** 1999. African Waterbird Census 1998. Wetlands International. Dakar. Senegal.

**Dodman, T. & Diagana, C.H.** 2003. African Waterbird Census 1999, 2000 & 2001. Wetlands International Global Series No. 16. Wageningen, The Netherlands.

**Hockey, P.A.R., Dean, W.R.J. & Ryan, P.G.** (eds.) 2005. Roberts – Birds of Southern Africa. VIIth ed. The Trustees of the John Voelcker Bird Book Fund. Cape Town.

**Hughes, R.H. & Hughes, J.S.** 1992. A Directory of African Wetlands. IUCN, Gland, Switzerland and Cambridge, UK/UNEP, Nairobi, Kenya / WCMC, Cambridge, UK.

**Perennou, C.** 1992. African Waterfowl Census 1992. The International Waterfowl and Wetlands Research Bureau. Slimbridge. UK

**Taylor, V. & Rose, P.** 1994. African Waterfowl Census 1994. The International Waterfowl and Wetlands Research Bureau. Slimbridge. UK

**The Times Atlas of the World**. 1985. Times Books. London.

# Conservation biology of an endemic waterbird of Madagascar, the Madagascar Plover *Charadrius thoracicus*: distribution, surveys and photographs

*Sama Zefania[1] & Tamás Székely[2]*

[1] *Lot II N 26 KA Analamahitsy Antananarivo Madagascar. (email: samazefania@yahoo.fr)*
[2] *Department of Biology and Biochemistry, University of Bath, Bath, BA2 7AY, UK. (email: T.Szekely@bath.ac.uk)*

Zefania, S. & Székely, T. 2006. Conservation biology of an endemic waterbird of Madagascar, the Madagascar Plover *Charadrius thoracicus*: distribution, surveys and photographs. *Waterbirds around the world.* Eds. G.C. Boere, C.A. Galbraith & D.A. Stroud. The Stationery Office, Edinburgh, UK. pp. 250-251.

The Madagascar Plover *Charadrius thoracicus* is an endemic shorebird classified as Near Threatened by the International Union for the Conservation of Nature (IUCN), but is close to being classified as Vulnerable, with little known of its biology. We present the results of surveys in 2002 and 2003 of the distribution and ecology of the Madagascar Plover.

Major wetlands were surveyed in the west coast of Madagascar both during the wet and dry seasons. The surveys showed that the Madagascar Plover has wider geographic distribution than previously thought, the breeding sites are scattered, and the number of plovers appears to fluctuate at most sites. The Madagascar Plover coexists with two other plover species, Kittlitz's Plover *Charadrius pecuarius* and the White-fronted Plover *Charadrius marginatus*, with which it appears to compete for nest sites. We designated areas for a population study, ringed adults and chicks and took morphological measurements. We anticipate that the surveys and population monitoring will enable us to estimate the total number of individuals of this endemic plover, and we will then be able to project its future population changes.

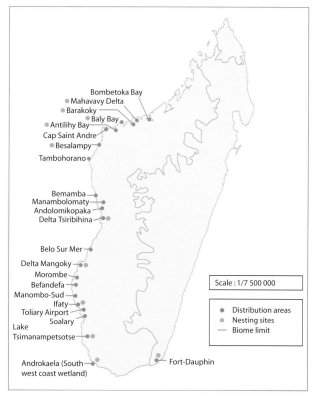

Fig. 1. Wetlands (24) surveyed during dry and wet seasons 2002 and 2004 in the west cost of Madagascar; 11 are nesting areas of Madagascar Plover *Charadrius thoracicus* in which we found nests with eggs, chicks and juveniles.

The status and the distribution of the Madagascar Plover have been changing from year to year. Previous records and the new survey results from the west coast during the dry and wet seasons of 2002, 2003 and 2004 show a wider geographic distribution with a scattered breeding sites (see Fig. 1); the analysis identified some competitor species and an alarmingly small population (see Table 1). The species occupied mainly wetland in the west cost of Madagascar between Mahajanga (north) and Fort Dauphin (south). The size of the population is very low and fluctuates each year - 370 individuals in the dry season of 2003 and 262 in the wet season of 2003-2004. An accurate estimate of population numbers is urgently required.

The competition of this species with the White-fronted Plover and Kittlitz's Plover in both their nesting and feeding areas is more than previously known. The Three-banded Plover *Charadrius tricollaris* is rarely seen with the Madagascar Plover.

Madagascar Plover *Charadrius thoracicus* adult at Mahavavy delta (Andolomikopaka), August 2003.

**Table 1.** Variation in population size of Madagascar Plover *Charadrius thoracicus* according to census season and surveyed sites.

| POPULATION ESTIMATES | Recent surveys | Previous data | | | | | | | | | | |
|---|---|---|---|---|---|---|---|---|---|---|---|---|
| SITES | December 2003 - March 2004 | August - November 2003 | January - July 2003 | 2002 | 2001 | January 2000 | July 2000 | September 2000 | 1999 | 1998 | 1993 | 1990 |
| Mahavavy delta and around | 3 | 3 | | | | | | | 5 | | | |
| Bombetoka bay | 3 | 4 | | | | | | | 3 | | | |
| Marambitsy bay or Barakoky | 44 | 86 | 64 | 32 | | | | | 1 | | | |
| PN Baly bay | 21 | 92 | 7 | 24 | 23 | 2 | 14 | 7 | 19 | | 1 | |
| East of Antilihy bay | 0 | 14 | | | | | | | | | | |
| Antilihy bay | 0 | 8 | | | | | | | | | | |
| Cap Sainte André | 0 | 6 | | | | | | | | | | |
| Tambohorano | 6 | 4 | | | | | | | 2 | 61 | | |
| Besalampy | 0 | 19 | | | | | | | | | | |
| Tsiribihina delta | 15 | 21 | | | | | | | | 47 | 14 | |
| Belo sur mer | 24 | 40 | | | | | | | | | | |
| Morombe | 10 | 20 | | 6 | | | | | | | | |
| South of Mangoky delta | 4 | 6 | | | | | | | 15 | | | |
| Mangoky delta | 17 | 27 | | | | | | 50 | | | | |
| Toliary Airport | 8 | 10 | | 11 | | | | | | | | |
| Mangily / Ifaty | 9 | 9 | | 9 | | | | | | | | |
| Soalary | 0 | 1 | | | | | | | | | | |
| Bemamba | 0 | | | | | | | | | 2 | | |
| Ampatifaty (Manambolomaty) | 0 | | | 1 | 5 | | | | | | | |
| Antsotsa/Besara (Manambolomaty) | 0 | | | 12 | | | | | | | | |
| Bevango (Manambolomaty) | 0 | | | 5 | | | | | | | | |
| PN Tsimanampetsotsa | 63 | | | 14 | | | | 55 | | | | |
| Befandefa | 0 | | | | 11 | | | | | | | |
| Manombo South | 0 | | | | 7 | | | | | | | |
| Andrikaela (ZH South west cost) | 33 | | | | | | | | | 25 | | |
| Fort-Dauphin | 0 | | 11 | | | | | | | | | 16 |
| Andolomikopaka (Manambolo) | 2 | | | | | | | | | | | |
| Total | 262 | 370 | 11 | 32 | 18 | 2 | 14 | 7 | 15 | 25 | 2 | 16 |

A Madagascar Plover adult at Ifaty in its prefered habitat, ringed December 2002 (Yellow on left leg), seen again February 2004.

A nest with two eggs of Madagascar Plover at Lake Tsimanampetsotse, February 2004.

Madagascar Plover juvenile captured at Androkaela, February 2004.

# Madagascar Teal *Anas bernieri*: the ecology and conservation of a short distance migrant

*Hywel Glyn Young*

*The Durrell Wildlife Conservation Trust, Les Augrès Manor, Trinity, Jersey, JE3 5BP, UK.*

Young, H.G. 2006. Madagascar Teal *Anas bernieri*: the ecology and conservation of a short distance migrant. *Waterbirds around the world.* Eds. G.C. Boere, C.A. Galbraith & D.A. Stroud. The Stationery Office, Edinburgh, UK. pp. 252-254.

This paper describes the breeding behaviour and ecology of the Madagascar Teal *Anas bernieri* based on field observations from Madagascar and Durrell Wildlife.

The Madagascar Teal is the western-most representative of the Australo-Asian grey teal (genus *Anas*) and limited data suggest that breeding occurs in Madagascar during the wet-season in seasonally flooded mangrove in tree-holes produced by decay (Young *et al.* 2001, Young 2002). Teal are, however, more widely reported from shallow saline lakes and estuaries during the dry-season, April-December, and flightless birds have been found annually at a moult site (Lake Antsamaky) in May-June (Young 2002). Field study in western Madagascar during the wet-season, December-March, has proven difficult as roads flood and mosquito numbers increase.

To understand Teal ecology, the captive population at Durrell Wildlife (Young 2000) was used to study reproductive behaviour. Results were compared with data on the related (Young *et al.* 1997) Grey Teal *A. gracilis* to predict ecology of the Madagascan endemic and integrated with known distribution and field data, resulting in a comprehensive synthesis of the species' biology interpreted in terms of implications for conservation planning (Young 2002).

Captives were studied 1998-2000 and pairs allowed to nest in conditions mimicking those in the wild (Young 2002). Behaviour (courtship, nest sites, pair-bonds, parental care, duckling development, moults) was compared with published information on Grey Teal, particularly in Queensland, Australia, (Lavery 1970, 1972a,b,c, Prawiradilaga 1985, Marchant & Higgins 1990).

Study showed that both sexes of Madagascar Teal were aggressive to congeners during group encounters and that synchronous displaying, a common feature of most dabbling ducks, was not observed. The display repertoire is smaller than that of Grey Teal, the differences most obvious in male agonistic and post-copulatory displays. Madagascar Teal has no Down-up, a display widely used by dabbling ducks in group displays (Davis 1997), or Chin-lift, another appeasement display in Grey

Teal courtship (see Prawiradilaga 1985) further suggesting that Madagascar Teal rarely indulge is social courtship and most likely live in habitats unsuited to these behaviours (Young 2002).

Madagascar Teal nesting preferences were unknown. However, related species, including Grey Teal, predominantly nest in tree-cavities (Marchant & Higgins 1990, Young *et al.* 2001) and it was predicted that Madagascar Teal would nest similarly. When supplied with boxes etc. that mimic tree-cavities this was confirmed. Nesting pairs showed that females at any stage of the reproductive cycle, particularly when foraging, were rarely unaccompanied. This concurs with observations made during the dry-season in Madagascar (Green *et al.* 1994, pers. obs 1992-1994 and 2004), when birds were principally in pairs, even within small flocks and inter-pair aggression was high (Green *et al.* 1994).

Unlike many dabbling ducks (see Johnson *et al.* 1999), Teal remained paired throughout brood-rearing and males were highly vigilant and protective of their mate and offspring. In common with the Grey Teal, Madagascar Teal exhibited a breeding strategy that involves high male input and pair-bonds that may last through consecutive seasons.

Ducklings fledged in 45-49 days (quicker than Grey Teal) and can, therefore, leave nesting areas within eight weeks of hatching. Adults moult body feathers throughout most of the year and are probably able to avoid high energy costs associated with short intense moults. Both sexes replace their wing feathers following completion of the breeding cycle, even if they have failed to rear young, and this moult and subsequent flightlessness can be delayed if environmental conditions such as rainfall delay nesting: breeding or moulting may not occur in the same month in consecutive years.

Madagascar Teal shun vegetated wetlands during the dry-season preferring open areas: this habitat choice and preferences at other times are not conducive to social encounters, and the species thus has a simplified display repertoire and marked levels of intra-specific aggression.

Madagascar Teal may have been restricted to mangrove for nesting through competition for natural cavities with other

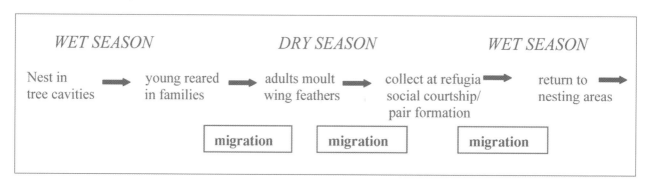

Fig. 1. Predicted annual cycle of Madagascar Teal *Anas bernieri*.

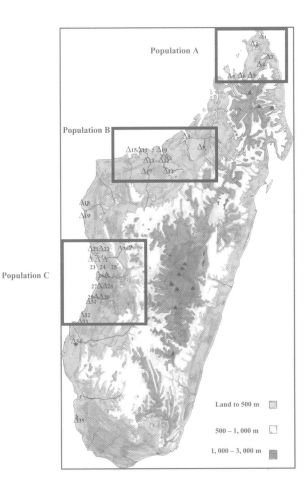

**Fig. 2.** Distribution of Madagascar Teal *Anas bernieri* showing currently known sub-populations (A).

users, notably lemurs (Young 2002, Kear 2003). All natural nests found in Madagascar (Fig. 3) have been in seasonally flooded, not tidal, areas of Black Mangrove *Avicennia marina* on the landside of littoral forest. Nesting birds must leave these sites as they dry and move short distances to nearby shallow wetlands (Figs. 1 & 4); and, as these also dry, they move further inland or to coasts and estuaries. Following brood-rearing, it is unsafe to moult wing feathers in the drying nesting-areas, and Teal move to safe sites such as Antsamaky where flightless adults have been caught and ringed annually in May-June since 1997. It is possible that in other areas, particularly in the wetter northwest, adults may moult within breeding areas before leaving for dry-season sites such as the Betsiboka Delta (Thorstrom & Rabarisoa 1997) or Ankazomborona (Razafindrajao *et al.* 2001).

Migrations between nesting, moulting and dry-season sites may include the whole Teal population in that area moving possibly only a few kilometres (Fig. 1).

Teal are threatened by subsistence hunting when nesting, clearance of mangrove for shrimp farming, trapping when in moult and the conversion of shallow coastal wetlands for rice-cultivation. Distribution of known sites (Fig. 2) suggests that three isolated sub-populations have developed as habitat conversion makes areas unsuitable. A further threat may be the potential loss of genetic diversity resulting from isolation as the species' naturally limited dispersal reduces mixing. Small numbers of Teal occur within only one protected area, at Kirindy Mitea, and future conservation strategies for this species must include adequate protection of nesting, moulting and dry-season sites from each sub-population.

**Fig. 3.** Mangroves, with Madagascar Teal *Anas bernieri* tree-hole nest site, Lake Andio, Kirindy Mitea National Park, Madagascar, 8 October 2004.

**Fig. 4.** Dry season site for Madagascar Teal *Anas bernieri*, Lake Ambondro, Kirindy Mitea National Park, Madagascar, 10 October 2004.

## REFERENCES

**Davis, E.S**. 1997. The Down-Up display of the mallard: one display, two orientations. Animal Behaviour 53: 1025-1034.

**Green, A.J., Young, H.G., Rabarisoa, R.G.M., Ravonjiarisoa, P. & Andrianarimisa, A.** 1994. The dry season diurnal behaviour of the Madagascar Teal *Anas bernieri* at Lake Bemamba. Wildfowl 45: 124-133.

**Johnson, K.P., McKinney, F. & Sorenson, M.D.** 1999. Phylogenetic constraint on male parental care in the dabbling ducks. Proceedings of the Royal Society of London 266: 759-763.

**Kear, J**. 2003. Cavity-nesting ducks: why woodpeckers matter. British Birds 96: 217-233.

**Lavery, H.J.** 1970. Studies of waterfowl (Anatidae) in north Queensland. 4. Movements. Queensland Journal of Agricultural and Animal Sciences 27: 411-424.

**Lavery, H.J.** 1972a. The Grey Teal at saline drought-refuges in north Queensland. Wildfowl 23: 56-63.

**Lavery, H.J.** 1972b. Studies of waterfowl (Anatidae) in north Queensland. 8. Moults of the Grey Teal (*Anas gibberifrons gracilis* Buller). Queensland Journal of Agricultural and Animal Sciences 29: 209-222.

**Lavery, H.J.** 1972c. Studies of waterfowl (Anatidae) in north Queensland. 9. Grey Teal (*Anas gibberifrons gracilis* Buller) at saltwater habitat. Queensland Journal of Agricultural and Animal Sciences 29: 223-235.

**Marchant, S. & Higgins, P.J.** 1990. Handbook of Australian, New Zealand and Antarctic Birds, Vol. 1. Oxford University Press, Oxford.

**Prawiradilaga, D.M**. 1985. A comparative study of the courtship behaviour of the Grey Teal (*Anas gibberifrons*) and Chestnut Teal (*Anas castanea*). MSc thesis, University of New England, Armidale, Australia.

**Razafindrajao, F., Lewis, R., Nichols, R. & Woolaver, L.** 2001. Discovery of a new breeding population of Madagascar Teal *Anas bernieri* in north-west Madagascar. Dodo 37: 60-69.

**Thorstrom, R. & Rabarisoa, R.G.M**. 1997. An observation of Madagascar Teal *Anas bernieri* in northwestern Madagascar. Wildfowl 47: 212-215.

**Young, H.G**. 2000. The Madagascar Teal at the Jersey Zoo: an *ex situ* breeding programme. Threatened Waterbird Specialist Group Newsletter 12: 57-62.

**Young, H.G**. 2002. Predicting the ecology of Madagascar's endemic dabbling ducks using captive populations and related taxa: implications for conservation. PhD thesis, University of Kent, Canterbury, UK.

**Young, H.G., Lewis, R.E. & Razafindrajao, F**. 2001. A description of the nest and eggs of the Madagascar Teal *Anas bernieri*. Bulletin of the British Ornithologists' Club 121: 64-67.

**Young, H.G., Sorenson, M.D. & Johnson, K.P**. 1997. A description of the Madagascar Teal *Anas bernieri* and an examination of its relationships with the Grey Teal *A. gracilis*. Wildfowl 48: 174-180.

# Subsistence use of waterbirds at Lake Chilwa, Malawi

*Roy Bhima*

*Department of National Parks and Wildlife, PO Box 30131, Lilongwe, Malawi.*

Bhima, R. 2006. Subsistence use of waterbirds at Lake Chilwa, Malawi. *Waterbirds around the world.* Eds. G.C. Boere, C.A. Galbraith & D.A. Stroud. The Stationery Office, Edinburgh, UK. pp. 255-256.

## ABSTRACT

Lake Chilwa in southern Malawi is an important habitat for waterbirds. About 160 species have been recorded, including many migrants. Around 1.5 million birds occur in the wetland, including 12 species in numbers exceeding 1% of their flyway populations. The Lake Chilwa catchment area has a human density of 162 person/km$^2$, one of the highest in Malawi. Most of the people are subsistence farmers and fishermen, but they also harvest waterbirds for local consumption and trade. At least 460 trappers use traditional traps and snares to catch waterbirds, and bird-catching takes place every year with a peak period in the rainy season. A Lake Chilwa Management Plan was developed in 2000 with the objective of enabling local communities to manage the natural resources on a sustainable basis for their own benefit. Bird Hunting Committees and a Bird Hunters Association were formed, but have not been legally established. The Danish Hunters Association began a project in 2003 to improve the Bird Hunters Association, and works with various government agencies and NGOs to regulate hunting, advise communities on sustainable management of waterbirds, and carry out research and monitoring.

## INTRODUCTION

Lake Chilwa in southern Malawi is an important wetland for waterbirds, providing breeding, resting and feeding areas for large numbers of birds in the West Asian-East African Flyway. About 160 species have been recorded at the lake, including 41 migratory species. Based on counts in 2000, it was estimated that the wetland supports around 1.5 million resident and migratory waterbirds. The numbers of 12 species exceed 1% of their flyway populations, including Glossy Ibis *Plegadis falcinellus*, Fulvous Whistling-Duck *Dendrocygna bicolor*, Black Crake *Amaurornis flavirostris*, Allen's Gallinule *Porphyrio alleni*, Lesser Moorhen *Gallinula angulata* and Grey-headed Gull *Larus cirrocephalus*.

The Lake Chilwa catchment area has a human density of about 162 persons/km$^2$. This is one of the highest densities in the country, which has an average of 104 persons/km$^2$. The population of the catchment is largely in rural areas and is directly dependent on natural resources such as land, water, trees, birds, fish, rodents and others for survival. Waterbirds are a major source of protein and are hunted in very large numbers at Lake Chilwa. This paper reviews information on the utilization of waterbirds at Lake Chilwa and discusses the management efforts that are being undertaken.

## STUDY AREA

Lake Chilwa is a tropical lake in southern Malawi. It is located to the north of Phalombe plain between the Zomba and Mulanje mountains at latitude 15°00'-15°30'S and longitude 35°30'-36°10'E. The water level of the lake is at an altitude of 627 m

above sea level. The lake has no outlet, and varies considerably is size depending on precipitation in the catchment, with a small increase in water level resulting in a tremendous increase in surface area. The entire wetland area is roughly 40 km across from east to east and 60 km from north to south, and has a total area of about 2 400 km$^2$. In "normal" years, open water can cover about 1 500 km$^2$; one-third of this is swamp and marshes, and one-third is floodplain. The entire catchment area is 8 349 km$^2$, of which 5 669 km$^2$ are in Malawi and the rest in Mozambique. The lake and its surrounding swamps, marshes and floodplain contain water most of the time, but during the last 100 years, several recessions have occurred including three incidents of complete drying out. The maximum depth of the lake is less than 5 m, and due to this shallowness, wind action keeps the water column completely mixed throughout the year. Plant biomass production of as much as 20-30 tonnes per hectare per year has been recorded from the predominant lake habitat of *Typha* and *Phragmites* reeds.

## METHODS

Information has been obtained from various reports that were compiled in preparation for the listing of Lake Chilwa as a Ramsar site (e.g. Wilson & van Zegeren 1998). While most of the reports on the birds of the Lake Chilwa area are concerned mainly with ecology, scattered information is available on the subsistence use of waterbirds, and this information has been brought together in the present study. A management plan (Environmental Affairs Department 2000) gives detailed information on various natural resources of the wetland, and the project documents of the Danish Hunters Association (DHA) in Malawi give information on methods of bird hunting and sustainable utilization in the area.

## RESULTS AND DISCUSSION

### Subsistence use of waterbirds

Most of the people in the Lake Chilwa catchment are smallholder subsistence farmers and fishermen. They grow maize, rice, groundnuts, cassava and tobacco. Productivity is totally dependent on adequate rainfall to recharge the lake annually and to maintain the water balance in the wetlands. The fishery is the most important natural resource in and around the lake, and yields about 25 000 tonnes per year. This is dependent on the water level in previous years. When the lake re-floods after drying out, the fishery recovers within two to three years.

Many species of birds breed during the months of January to July at various sites around the lake (Wilson 1999). Most birds favour the river mouths for breeding, as these areas are largely inaccessible to the local people and offer protection to the breeding birds because of the dense marsh vegetation.

The local people rely heavily on waterbirds as a source of protein, and usually go bird hunting when fish catches are low,

particularly during periods of drought. Bird hunting at Lake Chilwa typically involves the use of traditional methods such as birdlime, snares or string, tangling nets, fish traps and drop-nets baited with millet or rice. These are very cheap methods of catching birds, and do not require high investment.

There are at least 460 bird trappers in the Lake Chilwa catchment (Wilson 1999). An estimated 1.2 million birds are trapped every year, with an economic value of US$ 215 000. Species trapped in large numbers include Common Moorhen *Gallinula chloropus*, Lesser Moorhen, Allen's Gallinule, Blake Crake, Fulvous Whistling-Duck, White-faced Whistling-Duck *Dendrocygna viduata* and Hottentot Teal *Anas hottentota* (Wilson & van Zegeren 1998, Wilson 1999). There are also a number of licensed hunters. Trapping and shooting of birds take place every year with a peak period in the rainy season. In unusual years when the water level in the lake is low, bird catching increases by 300-500%.

Birds are harvested for local consumption and trade. During the months of December, January and February, many households experience food shortages, and birds are a major source of protein during this period. Many roasted birds can be found on sale in recreation areas such as bars in nearby towns.

### Management of Lake Chilwa

There is no formal management of the wetland and its waterbirds. The Department of National Parks and Wildlife, which is responsible for management of wildlife in the country, has had little presence in the area as it concentrates most of its activities in national parks and wildlife reserves. However, Lake Chilwa was listed as a Ramsar site under the Ramsar Convention on Wetlands on 1 November 1997. Surveys have shown that the wetland fulfils several of the Ramsar criteria for the designation of wetlands of international importance: it regularly supports 20 000 waterbirds; it regularly supports substantial numbers of individuals from particular groups of waterbirds indicative of wetland values, productivity and diversity; and it regularly supports at least 1% of the individuals in a population of one species or subspecies of waterbirds.

The wetland was listed as a Ramsar site to ensure that there would be wise and sustainable use of all natural resources. Despite the limited presence of the Department of National Parks and Wildlife, the Ramsar listing attracted international attention to the wetland. The Danish Development Agency (DANIDA), for example, supported the development of the Lake Chilwa Wetland and Catchment Project.

A Lake Chilwa Management Plan was developed in 2001. Based on enabling policies such as the Wildlife Policy of 2000, Community Based Natural Resource Management (CBNRM) programmes were developed. The Lake Chilwa Bird Hunters Association (BHA), known locally as the "Mwayi wa Mbalame", was formed in September 2001 by eighteen bird hunters' clubs in and around the Lake Chilwa basin to promote CBNRM activities for birds and thereby promote sustainable utilization. Twenty-nine bird sanctuaries, where trapping and shooting of birds are not allowed, have been established to provide secure breeding areas and roosting sites for birds (Wilson 2001). However, the Bird Hunters Association has yet to be legally established.

The Danish Hunters Association (DHA) has recently begun to work with the bird hunters' clubs in the Lake Chilwa area. The DHA proposes to use its experience from working at similar sites in Denmark to develop restricted use in some of the 29 bird sanctuaries and to introduce a more sustainable management of the waterbird harvest (DHA & Malawi CBNRM NGOs 2003). A DHA project entitled "Capacity Development of Bird Hunters Association of the Lake Chilwa" was initiated in 2003, and is being carried out in collaboration with various government agencies and NGOs to regulate hunting, advise communities on sustainable management of waterbirds, and carry out research and monitoring. The immediate objective of the project is "to build the capacity of the Lake Chilwa Bird Hunters Association to better organize themselves to sustainably manage the long term utilization of sedentary and migratory birds" (DHA & WESM 2003). With the listing of Lake Chilwa as a Ramsar site and the presence of the Danish Hunters Association at the lake, it is now hoped that sustainable hunting and management of waterbirds can be achieved.

### REFERENCES

**Danish Hunters Association & Malawi CBNRM NGOs** 2003. Capacity Development of NGO CBNRM Network. DANIDA, Malawi.

**Danish Hunters Association & Wildlife and Environmental Society of Malawi** 2003. Capacity Development of Bird Hunters Association. DANIDA, Malawi.

**Environmental Affairs Department** 2000. Lake Chilwa Wetland state of the environment. Ministry of Natural Resources and Environmental Affairs, Lilongwe, Malawi.

**Wilson, J.G.M.** 1999. The waterfowl of Lake Chilwa and their utilization by local communities and conservation measures as required by the Ramsar Convention. State of the Environment Study No. 20, Lake Chilwa Wetland Project, Zomba, Malawi.

**Wilson, J.G.M.** 2001. The development of community management of waterfowl on Lake Chilwa Wetland. Lake Chilwa Wetland and Catchment Management Project. Ministry of Natural Resources and Environmental Affairs, Lilongwe, Malawi.

**Wilson, J.G.M. & van Zegeren, K.** 1998. The Birds of Lake Chilwa. In: K. van Zegeren & M.P. Munyenyembe (eds) The Lake Chilwa Environment – A Report of the 1996 Ramsar site study. Department of Biology, Chancellor College, Zomba, Malawi.

# Waterbird ringing in Africa

*H. Dieter Oschadleus*

*Avian Demography Unit, Department of Statistical Sciences, University of Cape Town, Rondebosch, 7701, South Africa.*
*(email: dieter@adu.uct.ac.za)*

Oschadleus, H.D. 2006. Waterbird ringing in Africa. *Waterbirds around the world.* Eds. G.C. Boere, C.A. Galbraith & D.A. Stroud. The Stationery Office, Edinburgh, UK. pp. 257-262.

## ABSTRACT

An overview of bird ringing in Africa is presented, specifically relating to waterbirds. Summaries for West Africa and East Africa are based mainly on annual ringing reports. SAFRING's database is used for the analysis of ringing in southern Africa, the region where most waterbird ringing has occurred. Bird ringing started in southern Africa in 1948, and nearly 600 000 waterbirds have been ringed since then. There have been 15 000 recoveries of these birds (2.5%), and at least one recovery for 101 species. In addition, there have been 52 000 recaptures and re-sightings of marked birds (8.7%). There have been 1 900 recoveries and recaptures of waterbirds ringed in Europe. The annual ringing totals and recovery rates in different groups of waterbirds are investigated. More Pelecaniformes have been ringed than any other group, largely because of the large-scale ringing of Cape Gannets *Morus capensis* in southern Africa, but the highest recovery rate is found in the Gruiformes. Waterbird ringing has decreased in the last two decades, but efforts are being made to revitalize this. SAFRING is computerizing ringing data, as these provide large amounts of as yet unutilized data for analysis. Efforts are being made to expand waterbird ringing in Africa through training programmes and species projects with funding from UNEP/AEWA.

## INTRODUCTION

In 1909, the London Times announced the recovery of a European-ringed White Stork *Ciconia ciconia* found dead in South Africa. This was the first recovery of a bird migrating across the equator. The stork had been ringed in Hungary on 10 July 1908 and recovered in Himeville, KwaZulu-Natal, South Africa, in January 1909 (ring number 209). While bird ringing started in Europe in 1899, it only began in Africa some 50 years later. To date, at least 600 000 waterbirds have been ringed in Africa, and although the recovery rate is low, valuable data on migration and other movements have been collected. Ringing schemes in Africa have not operated consistently, except for two schemes, one in southern Africa and one in eastern Africa. This paper provides a general overview of waterbird ringing activities in Africa, and gives more details for waterbird ringing in southern Africa, where the vast majority of waterbirds have been ringed. Finally, the paper looks at the AFRING concept in the past, present and future.

## METHODS

To investigate the extent of waterbird ringing in Africa, the literature was searched for annual ringing reports. For southern Africa, statistics relating to waterbird ringing were extracted from the SAFRING database. As most of the waterbird ringing in Africa has been in southern Africa, more extensive analyses are presented for this region than for other parts of the continent. The literature was searched to investigate the history of the AFRING concept, while a summary of potential future waterbird ringing projects in Africa was drawn from Underhill *et al.* (1999).

## RESULTS

### Waterbird ringing in Africa outside southern Africa

General bird ringing has been sporadic throughout most of Africa. The first ringing scheme was started in 1948 in southern Africa; this is now known as SAFRING. Annual ringing reports have been published in the journals Ostrich and Safring News (now Afring News) (see Appendix I). Reports of recoveries have been published separately from ringing reports since 1993. The former are not listed in Appendix I, but are easy to trace as they always directly follow the ringing reports. More details of waterbird ringing in southern Africa are given below.

Ringing started in Zambia in the early 1960s, and initially used South African rings (address: Zoo Pretoria). Zambian rings (address: Livingstone Museum) were introduced in 1969, but by the early 1980s, it had become obvious that an independent scheme was not justified, and so Kenyan rings (address: Nairobi) and SAFRING rings (address: SAFRING UCT) replaced Zambian rings (Dowsett & Leonard 2001). Low numbers of waterbirds were ringed during the period 1985-1999; ringing totals of over 500 are listed for African Openbill *Anastomus lamelligerus* (667), Red-billed Teal *Anas erythrorhyncha* (2 121), Hottentot Teal *A. hottentota* (525), Collared Pratincole *Glareola pratincola* (518), Blacksmith Plover *Vanellus armatus* (719) and Wood Sandpiper *Tringa glareola* (852). Ringing totals for the years up to 1999 have been published by Dowsett & Leonard 2001. A total of 212 waders were ringed in Zambia between 1997 and 2003, mostly using Zambian rings but also some SAFRING rings.

### East Africa

The East African Ringing Scheme (address: Nairobi) started in 1950, and concentrated on passerine migrants at Ngulia (from 1969 to the present), resident passerines in Nairobi, and Palearctic waders on the Kenya coast (mostly at Mwamba Bird Observatory, Watamu). The area covered by this ringing scheme includes Kenya, Tanzania, Uganda and Sudan, with small numbers of "Nairobi" rings also being used in Djibouti, Ethiopia, Rwanda, Somalia and Zambia (Backhurst 1988). Rings from other schemes have also been used in Kenya, e.g. 8 000 Lesser Flamingos *Phoenicopterus minor* were ringed with British Trust for Ornithology rings. A total of 44 927 waterbirds were ringed in East Africa between 1960 and 1987, including over 3 000 waders at Lake Magadi in the Rift Valley and Mida Creek on the coast (Backhurst 1988). Annual ringing reports were published by Backhurst and covered the years 1966-1987 (see Appendix I); in addition many reports (published or only cyclostyled) are available for bird ringing activities at Ngulia.

Liz and Neil Baker compiled separate annual ringing summaries for Tanzania. Their totals are included in the East African totals, as Nairobi rings were used. There was also a ringing scheme in operation in Ethiopia from 1969 to 1980 (Ash 1981). Annual ringing reports for this period were published by Ash; recovery reports were produced for at least two years (see Appendix I).

## West Africa

From 1958 to 1983, R. Sharland published a series of annual bird ringing reports for Nigeria in the journals Nigerian Field, Bulletin of the Nigerian Ornithological Society and Malimbus. Ringing in Ghana was included in these reports for the years 1960-1963. A full list of reports is provided in Appendix I; some of these were duplicated in different journals.

A ringing scheme was started again in Ghana in 1991, and there was some ringing in Senegal in 1991-1993 (Djoudj ringing project), but these schemes have not been consistent. There have been various expeditions from Europe to West Africa to ring passerine migrants, and the Dutch Working Group for International Wader and Waterfowl Research (WIWO) has undertaken expeditions to West Africa to ring migrant waders. Waders were also ringed in Mauritania by W. Dick. Brussels rings have been used in Senegal, and Jan Veen ringed gulls and terns with SAFRING rings.

## Waterbird ringing in southern Africa

Waterbird ringing began in southern Africa in 1948 with the ringing of five ducks, 15 plovers, 19 migrant sandpipers and one Caspian Tern *Sterna caspia*. Over the next 55 years, almost 600 000 waterbirds were ringed. The waterbird species reported here are the species listed in the African-Eurasian Waterbird Agreement (AEWA), as well as some seabirds and some non-AEWA waterbirds (e.g. Long-tailed Cormorant *Phalacrocorax africanus*). The annual totals of waterbirds ringed and recovered have been extracted from the SAFRING database. Many recoveries are from the Palearctic region (Fig. 1).

To understand how ringing effort has changed in southern Africa, it is practical to divide the first five decades of ringing into two periods, each of about 25 years, here referred to as the first (1948-1974) and second (1974-1999) periods. The total number of birds ringed by July 1999 was 1.8 million, of which 45% were ringed in the first period (Oschadleus & Underhill 1999). A list of the top 10 species ringed over the 50-year period includes various non-waterbird species, two seabirds (Cape Gannet *Morus capensis* and African Penguin *Spheniscus demersus*) and two waterbirds (Yellow-billed Duck *Anas undulata* and Cattle Egret *Bubulcus ibis*).

It is striking that in the period up to 1974, the emphasis was on waterbird ringing. Thus 97% of all Cattle Egrets were ringed in this first period. Similarly 74% of the Yellow-billed Ducks were ringed in the same period. This reflects the efforts of ringers working at Barberspan, North-west Province, and Rondevlei, Western Cape, ringing egret chicks and trapping adult waterfowl in walk-in traps. Unfortunately, most of the people who were ringing during this period have either retired or passed away, and there is an acute lack of skills in using these techniques. A large amount of dam construction has taken place in southern Africa since 1974, and it is likely that the patterns of movements of waterbirds have changed since then. Some waterbirds are migratory within Africa, e.g. Comb Duck *Sarkidiornis melanotos*, while others show dispersal as far as central Africa, e.g. Cattle Egret (Underhill *et al.* 1999). These would make interesting subjects for co-operative research projects between African countries.

During the second period, the overwhelming majority of ringers focused on mist-netting. Terns, gulls and waders began to appear in the top twenty most frequently ringed species (see Oschadleus & Underhill 1999). While not many Common Terns *Sterna hirundo* have been ringed in South Africa, large numbers have been recovered in this country. This species could be studied along Africa's coastline to obtain more information on its migration, e.g. the locations of stopover sites, and the timing and rate of migration.

## Ringing and recovery totals by waterbird groups

A breakdown of waterbird ringing in southern Africa is given in Table 1. The most frequently ringed group is the Pelecaniformes due to the large number of Cape Gannet chicks that are ringed. This is followed by the Anseriformes. The highest recovery rate is for the cranes (Gruiformes), possibly because these are large birds and thus easily seen. The next highest recovery rate is for species of Anseriformes, probably because many of these are hunted and then reported, or recovered at the site of ringing. Other groups with high recovery rates include the storks (Ciconiiformes) and flamingos (Phoenicopteriformes). Very few

**Table 1. Numbers of waterbirds ringed and recovered in southern Africa.**

| Order | Group | Ringed by 2000* | Recovered by Sept 2003 | Percent recovered | Re-sighted or recaptured | Percent re-sighted or recaptured | Foreign recoveries |
|---|---|---|---|---|---|---|---|
| Sphenisciformes | Penguins | 75 382 | 2 511 | 3.3 | 27 250 | 36.1 | 0 |
| Podicipediformes | Grebes | 135 | 0 | 0.0 | 0 | | 0 |
| Pelecaniformes | Pelicans etc. | 162 331 | 3 955 | 2.4 | 21 816 | 13.4 | 0 |
| Ciconiiformes | Storks etc. | 69 766 | 1 027 | 1.5 | 88 | 0.1 | 809 |
| Phoenicopteriformes | Flamingos | 1 754 | 10 | 0.6 | 6 | 0.3 | 0 |
| Anseriformes | Ducks | 106 637 | 3 793 | 3.6 | 66 | 0.1 | 15 |
| Gruiformes | Cranes | 28 559 | 1 304 | 4.6 | 188 | 0.7 | 0 |
| Charadriiformes, Charadrii | Waders | 92 718 | 645 | 0.7 | 930 | 1.0 | 45 |
| Charadriiformes, Laridae | Gulls & terns | 60 617 | 1 780 | 2.9 | 1 959 | 3.2 | 1 036 |
| Totals | | 597 899 | 15 025 | 2.5 | 52 303 | 8.7 | 1 905 |

* Only the ringing totals up to 2000 were available at the time of writing.

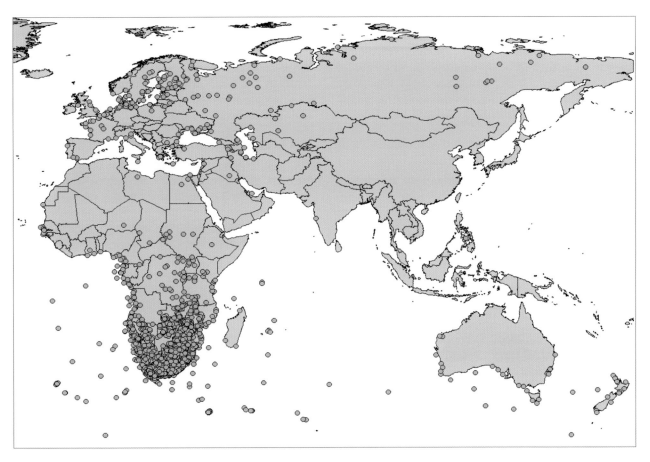

**Fig. 1.** Recoveries of seabirds and waterbirds ringed in southern Africa (from the SAFRING database).

grebes (Podicipediformes) have been ringed and none has been recovered. The larger birds tend to have higher recovery rates, partly because the corpses of dead birds are more visible. These rates are well over 1%, and thus mass ringing of large birds should be encouraged. Waders (Charadriiformes, Charadrii) have a lower recovery rate, and yet ringing of this group has produced spectacular information on migration routes. The highest recapture rate is in the African Penguin (36%), which has been the subject of an intensive recapture effort because of its endangered status. The next highest recapture rate is for the Great White Pelican *Pelecanus onocrotalus* (re-sightings), followed by the Cape Gannet (recaptures of birds on nests). Gulls and terns (Charadriiformes, Laridae) also have high recapture rates, while waders have a higher recapture rate than recovery rate. The highest numbers of foreign recoveries and recaptures are for the White Stork and Common Tern.

Marking projects – colour rings and satellite transmitters

Colour rings and flags have been used on a wide variety of seabirds, waders and other waterbirds in southern Africa, usually to identify cohorts rather than individual birds. Engraved rings are becoming popular as they can be used for re-sightings of individual birds. These are being used on African Black Oystercatchers *Haematopus moquini*, Hartlaub's Gulls *Larus hartlaubii* and other seabirds, and will be used in projects currently being planned for the Sacred Ibis *Threskiornis aethiopicus*.

Satellite tags are still little-used in southern Africa, partly because of the high costs involved. Satellite transmitters were fitted to three African Penguins after the oil spill in June 2000

from the tanker Treasure (Crawford *et al.* 2000), before the cleaned birds were released. These three birds, Peter, Percy and Pamela, went on to make world news headlines, e.g. on the front cover of Time magazine. White Storks migrate from Europe to spend the non-breeding season in South Africa, and do not normally breed there. For the last 60 years, however, a few pairs have bred regularly in the Western Cape, and many of their chicks have been fitted with satellite transmitters. Satellite transmitters have also been used by the Crane Working Group on Blue Cranes *Grus paradisea*.

## AFRING – extending waterbird ringing throughout Africa

The concept of AFRING was first proposed in 1969, at a meeting of bird ringers during the Third Pan-African Ornithological Congress in Kruger National Park (Anon. 1971). The meeting recognized the need to establish close co-operation between ringing schemes in Africa, and between African and European schemes, and concluded that to achieve this, it was necessary to develop a code for recoveries, and to compose a numbered checklist for African species. It was agreed that another meeting should be organized within six months to develop the code for recoveries. Accordingly, an AFRING meeting was held at the 15th International Ornithological Congress in The Hague, The Netherlands, in 1970. Countries represented at this meeting included Angola, Congo, Ethiopia, Kenya, Nigeria, Senegal, South Africa, Tanzania, Uganda and Zambia. Two aims were established, namely to standardize recovery data, and to put all African recovery records on standard forms (Anon. 1970).

Ornithologists from South Africa played a leading role, but due to the political climate, these ornithologists could no longer easily be involved in African meetings. The concept of AFRING was thus not realized for nearly three more decades, although Prof. Les Underhill (at the Avian Demography Unit in the University of Cape Town) at various times applied for funding for AFRING, and made the following suggestions:

- Model AFRING on EURING;
- Standardize codes and methods;
- Facilitate bird ringing through training, the provision of rings and the establishment of a database;
- Provide leadership in all aspects of bird-marking in Africa;
- Promote collaborative projects (country/continent/flyway);
- Provide a secure backup for data;
- Curate primary data of defunct schemes; and
- Analyse data, especially with respect to conservation and management issues.

The Second International Conference on Wetlands and Development, held in Dakar, Senegal, in November 1998, recommended that the development of an intra-African ringing co-ordination scheme (AFRING) be accorded a very high priority. This opened the way for Wetlands International to apply for funding and establish the co-ordination of waterbird ringing schemes in Africa. The Avian Demography Unit received the tender for this project in January 2004. Doug Harebottle (Avian Demography Unit) was appointed to co-ordinate the project. A stakeholders' meeting was held at the Waterbirds around the world Conference in Edinburgh in April 2004, and a follow-up meeting was planned for the Eleventh Pan-African Ornithological Congress in Tunisia in November 2004.

During their review of recoveries of waterbirds in southern Africa, Underhill *et al.* (1999) identified a number of specific waterbird ringing projects in Africa, and these were presented in Israel (Oschadleus 2002). From this list of projects, a short list of species was chosen for immediate consideration: Great White Pelican, Sacred Ibis, Greater Flamingo *Phoenicopterus ruber*, Lesser Flamingo, Comb Duck, Wood Sandpiper, Sandwich Tern *Sterna sandvicensis*, Royal Tern *S. maxima* and Great Crested (Swift) Tern *S. bergii*.

An important requirement for ringing schemes is to computerize historical ringing data. These data can be used to provide information on past ringing activities and on the timing of arrival and departure of migrants (e.g. Wood Sandpiper, Oschadleus & Underhill 2002), and are required for the analysis of survival rates, moult patterns and biometrics. They can also be used to study changes in historical distribution.

## ACKNOWLEDGEMENTS
The main sponsors of SAFRING are the University of Cape Town, the South African Department of Environmental Affairs and Tourism, BirdLife South Africa and the Namibian Ministry of the Environment and Tourism. Helpful comments were provided by Marienne de Villiers and Doug Harebottle.

## REFERENCES
**Anon.** 1970. S.A.O.S. ringing report. Bokmakierie 22: 93.

**Anon.** 1971. Third Pan-African Ornithological Congress Ringing Meeting. Ostrich Supplement 8: 529-530.

**Ash, J.S.** 1981. Bird-ringing results and ringed bird recoveries in Ethiopia. Scopus 5: 85-101.

**Backhurst, G.C.** 1988. Eastern African Ringing Report 1981-87. Scopus 12 (1/2): 1-52.

**Crawford, R.J.M., Davis, S.A., Harding, R.T., Jackson, L.F., Leshoro, T.M., Meyer, M.A., Randall, R.M., Underhill, L.G., Upfold, L., van Dalsen, A.P., van der Merwe, E., Whittington, P.A., Williams, A.J. & Wolfaardt, A.C.** 2000. Initial impact of the *Treasure* oil spill on seabirds off western South Africa. South African Journal of Marine Science 22: 157-176.

**Dowsett, R.J. & Leonard, P.M.** 2001. Results from bird ringing in Zambia. Zambia Bird Report 1999: 16-46.

**Oschadleus, H.D.** 2002. Bird-ringing projects in Southern Africa. Wings over Africa: 125-132.

**Oschadleus, H.D. & Underhill, L.G.** 1999. SAFRING ringing totals over 50 years. Safring News 28: 11-13.

**Oschadleus, D. & Underhill, L.** 2002. Twenty five years of Wood Sandpiper ringing from southern Africa. Wader Study Group Bulletin 99: 19-20.

**Underhill, L.G., Tree, A.J., Oschadleus, H.D. & Parker, V.** 1999. Review of Ring Recoveries of Waterbirds in Southern Africa. Cape Town: Avian Demography Unit, University of Cape Town, South Africa.

## APPENDIX I. SELECTED PUBLISHED REPORTS ON BIRD RINGING IN AFRICA.

### West Africa
Annual ringing reports

Sharland, R.E. 1969. Ringing in Nigeria, 1968. Eleventh Annual Report. Bulletin of the Nigerian Ornithological Society 6(21): 26-29.

Sharland, R.E. 1970. Ringing in Nigeria, 1969. Twelfth Annual Report. Bulletin of the Nigerian Ornithological Society 7(28): 94-99.

Sharland, R.E. 1972. Ringing in Nigeria, 1970. 13th Annual Report. Bulletin of the Nigerian Ornithological Society 9: 1-6.

Sharland, R.E. 1972. Ringing in Nigeria 1971. 14th Annual Report. Bulletin of the Nigerian Ornithological Society 9: 13-16.

Sharland, R.E. 1974. Ringing in Nigeria 1972 & 1973. 15th and 16th Annual Reports. Bulletin of the Nigerian Ornithological Society 10: 69-73.

Sharland, R.E. 1975. Ringing in Nigeria 1974. 17th Annual Report. Bulletin of the Nigerian Ornithological Society 11(40): 50-52.

Sharland, R.E. 1976. Ringing in Nigeria 1975. 18th Annual Report. Bulletin of the Nigerian Ornithological Society 12(41): 38-40.

Sharland, R.E. 1977. Ringing in Nigeria. 19th Annual Report. Bulletin of the Nigerian Ornithological Society 13(43): 64-65.

Sharland, R.E. 1978. Ringing in Nigeria 1977. 20th Annual Report. Bulletin of the Nigerian Ornithological Society 14(45): 24-26.

Sharland, R.E. 1979. Ringing in Nigeria 1978. 21st Annual Report. Malimbus 1(1): 43-46.

Sharland, R.E. 1980. Ringing in Nigeria 1979. 22nd Annual Report. Malimbus 2(1): 71-72.

Sharland, R.E. 1981. Ringing in Nigeria in 1980. 23rd Annual Report. Malimbus 3(2): 39-40.

Sharland, R.E. 1982. Ringing in Nigeria in 1981. 24th Annual Report. Malimbus 4(2): 105-106.

Sharland, R.E. 1983. Ringing in Nigeria in 1982. 25th Annual Report. Malimbus 5(2): 78-78.

Sharland, R.E. 1984. Ringing in Nigeria in 1983. 26th Annual Report. Malimbus 6(1, 2): 90-91.

Sharland, R.E. 1985. Ringing in Nigeria 1984. Malimbus 7: 140-140.

Sharland, R.E. 1986. Ringing in Nigeria 1985. Malimbus 8(1): 44-45.

Some other relevant reports

Yates, J.M.St.J. 1937. Ringed birds recovered on the West Coast, 1935-36. Nigerian Field 6(2): 70.

Matthews, J.W. 1955. Correspondence: Ringed Gannets. Nigerian Field 20(2): 91-93.

Young, C.G. 1955. Correspondence: Ringed Gannets. Nigerian Field 20(4): 185.

Sharland, R.E. 1997. Ringing recoveries between Nigeria and eastern Europe. Malimbus 19(2): 103-103.

**East Africa**

Annual ringing reports for Ethiopia

Ash, J.S. 1970. Birds ringed in Ethiopia, October 1969 - 31 December 1970. Cyclostyled report.

Ash, J.S. 1971. Bird ringing in Ethiopia, 1969-1971. Cyclostyled report.

Ash, J.S. 1972. Bird ringing in Ethiopia, 1969-1972. Cyclostyled report.

Ash, J.S. 1973. Bird ringing in Ethiopia, 1969-1973. Cyclostyled report.

Ash, J.S. 1974. Bird ringing in Ethiopia, 1969-1974. Cyclostyled report.

Ash, J.S. 1975. Bird ringing in Ethiopia, 1969-1974. Safring News 4/1: 22.

Ash, J.S. 1976. Bird-ringing in Ethiopia. Report No.5, 1969-1975. USNAMRU No.5 Technical Report 1: 1-17.

Ash, J.S. 1976. Bird ringing in Ethiopia. Report No.6, 1969-1976. Cyclostyled report.

Ash, J.S. 1977. Bird ringing in Ethiopia. Report No.7, 1969-1977. Cyclostyled report.

Ash, J.S. 1978. Bird ringing in Ethiopia. Report No.8, 1969-1978. Cyclostyled report.

Ash, J.S. 1981. Bird-ringing results and ringed bird recoveries in Ethiopia. Scopus 5: 85-101.

Ash, J.S. 1994. Bird-ringing recoveries from Ethiopia and Eritrea II. Scopus 17(2): 113-118.

Annual ringing reports for Kenya

Reynolds, F.L. 1960. Bird Ringing in East Africa. Journal of East African Natural History Society 23: 198-199.

Backhurst, G.C. 1968. East Africa ringing report: 1966-67. Journal of East African Natural History Society & National Museum 27(116): 61-65.

Backhurst, G.C. 1969. East Africa ringing report: 1967-68. Journal of East African Natural History Society & National Museum 27(118): 217-225.

Backhurst, G.C. 1970. Bird ringing report: 1968-1969. Journal of East African Natural History Society & National Museum 28(119): 16-26.

Backhurst, G.C. 1971. East Africa ringing report: 1969-70. Journal of East African Natural History Society & National Museum 28(123): 1-14.

Backhurst, G.C. 1972. East Africa ringing report: 1970-71. Journal of East African Natural History Society & National Museum 136: 1-16.

Backhurst, G.C. 1973. East Africa ringing report: 1971-72. Journal of East African Natural History Society & National Museum 144: 1-15.

Backhurst, G.C. 1975. East Africa ringing report: 1972-74. Journal of East African Natural History Society & National Museum 146: 1-9.

Backhurst, G.C. 1978. East Africa ringing report: 1974-77. Journal of East African Natural History Society & National Museum 163: 1-10.

Backhurst, G.C. 1981. Eastern Africa ringing report: 1977-81. Journal of East African Natural History Society & National Museum 174: 1-19.

Backhurst, G.C. 1988. Eastern African Ringing Report: 1981-87. Scopus 12 (1/2): 1-52.

Annual ringing reports for Tanzania

Best, C. (compiler). 1993. Bird ringing in Tanzania. Safring News 22: 31.

**Southern Africa**

Annual ringing reports

Ashton, E.H. 1950. Progress Report: Bird Ringing. Ostrich 21: 106-112.

Ashton, E.H. 1952. Second Progress Report: Bird Ringing 1950-1951. Ostrich 23: 56-61.

Ashton, E.H. 1954. Third Progress Report: Bird Ringing 1951-1952. Ostrich 25: 2-12.

Ashton, E.H. 1954. Fourth Progress Report: Bird Ringing 1952-1953. Ostrich 25: 130-138.

Ashton, E. 1956. Fifth Progress and Ringing Report (Part I). Ostrich 27: 5-13.

Ashton, E. 1957. Sixth Ringing Report. Ostrich 28: 98-115.

McLachlan, G.R. 1961. Seventh Ringing Report. Ostrich 32: 36-47.

McLachlan, G.R. 1962. Eighth Ringing Report. Ostrich 33 (3): 29-37.

McLachlan, G.R. 1963. Ninth Ringing Report. Ostrich 34: 102-109.

McLachlan, G.R. 1964. Tenth Ringing Report. Ostrich 35: 101-110.

McLachlan, G.R. 1965. Eleventh Ringing Report. Ostrich 36: 214-223.

McLachlan, G.R. 1967. Twelfth Ringing Report. Ostrich 38: 17-26.

McLachlan, G.R. 1969. Thirteenth Ringing Report. Ostrich 40: 37-50.

Elliott, C.C.H. & Jarvis, M.J.F. 1970. Fourteenth Ringing Report. Ostrich 41: 1-118.

Elliott, C.C.H. & Jarvis, M.J.F. 1972. Fifteenth Ringing Report. Ostrich 43: 236-295.

Elliott, C.C.H. & Jarvis, M.J.F. 1973. Fifteenth Ringing Report (cont.). Ostrich 44: 34-78.

Elliott, C.C.H. 1974. Sixteenth ringing report for southern Africa. Ostrich 45: 161-166.

Vernon, C.J. 1975. Seventeenth ringing report for southern Africa. Ostrich 46: 125-128.

Vernon, C.J. 1976. Eighteenth ringing report for southern Africa. Ostrich 47: 89-94.

Vernon, C.J. 1977. Nineteenth ringing report for southern Africa. Ostrich 48: 106-109.

Morant, P.D. 1979. Twentieth ringing report for southern Africa. Ostrich 50: 83-87.

Morant, P.D. 1980. Twenty-first ringing report for southern Africa. Ostrich 51: 204-214.

Morant, P.D. 1981. Twenty-second ringing report for southern Africa. Ostrich 52: 44-53.

Oatley, T.B. 1982. Some local bird ringing statistics for 1979-1981. Safring News 11: 9-15.

Oatley, T.B. 1983. Twenty-third ringing report for southern Africa. Ostrich 54: 141-149.

Oatley, T.B. 1984. Local bird ringing statistics for the 1982/1983 ringing year. Safring News 13: 18-24.

Newton, I.P. 1985. Local bird ringing statistics for the 1983/1984 ringing year. Safring News 14: 36-41.

Oatley, T.B. 1986. SAFRING statistics for the 1984-1985 ringing year. Safring News 15: 29-36.

Oatley, T.B. 1988. SAFRING statistics for the 1985-1986 and 1986-1987 ringing years. Safring News 17: 15-21.

Oatley, T.B. 1989. SAFRING statistics for the 1987-1988 ringing year. Safring News 18: 49-55.

Oatley, T.B. 1990. SAFRING statistics for the 1988-1989 ringing year. Safring News 19: 27-35.

Oatley, T.B. 1992. Report on the 1990-1991 ringing year. Safring News 21: 22-31.

Oatley, T.B. 1992. Annual report on the 1991-1992 ringing year. Safring News 21: 61-70.

Oatley, T.B. 1993. Annual report for the 1992-1993 ringing year. Safring News 22: 57-65.

Oatley, T.B. 1994. Annual report for the 1993-1994 ringing year. Safring News 23: 83-87.

Oatley, T.B. 1995. Report on the ringing year: 1994-1995. Safring News 24: 63-67.

Oatley, T.B & Best, C.C. 1996. Report on the 1995-1996 ringing year. Safring News 25: 55-59.

Oatley, T.B. & Best, C.C. 1997. Report on the 1996-1997 ringing year. Safring News 26: 67-71.

Oschadleus, D. 1998. Report on the 1997-98 ringing year. Safring News 27: 21-25.

Oschadleus, H.D. 1999. Report on the 1998-1999 ringing year. Safring News 28: 31-34.

Oschadleus, H.D. 2000. Report on the 1999-2000 ringing year. Safring News 29: 90-92.

Oschadleus, H.D. 2001. Report on the 2000-2001 ringing year. Afring News 30: 71-73.

Oschadleus, H.D. 2003. Report on the 2001-2002 ringing year. Afring News 32: 16-18.

**Some other relevant reports**

McLachlan, G.R. 1966. The first ten years of ringing in South Africa. Ostrich Supplement 6: 255-263.

Skead, D.M. 1979. A brief report of ringing at Barberspan including the 1978/79 report. Safring News 8: 51-56.

Oschadleus, H.D. & Underhill, L.G. 1999. SAFRING ringing totals over 50 years. Safring News 28: 11-13.

Immature Crab Plover *Dromas ardeola*. Photo: Dieter Oschadleus.

# 3.5 Flyway conservation in the Central Asian Flyway. Workshop Introduction

*Taej Mundkur*

*Wetlands International - South Asia, A-25, 2nd Floor, Defence Colony, New Delhi - 110 024, India.*

Mundkur, T. 2006. Flyway conservation in the Central Asian Flyway. Workshop Introduction. *Waterbirds around the world.* Eds. G.C. Boere, C.A. Galbraith & D.A. Stroud. The Stationery Office, Edinburgh, UK. p. 263.

The permanent wetlands of the Karakum desert in Turkmenistan are of great importance for waterbird populations migrating through this region. Photo: Sergey Dereliev.

The Central Asian Flyway covers a large continental area of Eurasia between the arctic and Indian Oceans. This flyway comprises several important and overlapping migration routes for different species of waterbirds, most of which extend from Siberia to south and southwest Asia. The limited existing information that is available on waterbird populations needs to be strengthened, but existing data appears to show that many species are declining. The semi-arid condition of the Central Asian region and the effects of climatic changes observed on wetlands there have considerable impacts on the distribution and status of waterbirds, as described by Kreuzberg-Mukhina.

Most of the countries along this flyway have developing economies or economies in transition, and the focus of governments is to improve the living standards and conditions of their peoples. Accordingly, there is an inadequate allocation of resources for research and conservation, and for the involvement of local stakeholders in the sustainable management of wetlands. In addition, changes in political systems and instabilities in some countries, language and other barriers, have hindered co-operation to be developed between the agencies of the countries within the flyway. Thus there has been more limited co-operation in information sharing, research and conservation activities compared to other flyway systems or geographical regions.

The symposium made the following recommendations:

- An international framework for the development of conservation initiatives for migratory waterbirds and wetlands in the Central Asian Flyway is urgently required to promote co-operative action.
- An Action Plan for wetland and migratory waterbird conservation for the Central Asian Flyway identifying regional priorities should be finalised and endorsed by the governments of the region, in co-operation with other major stakeholders (e.g. multi-lateral environmental conventions, non-governmental organisations and others). Implementation of the plan will require active participation and resources from agencies within and outside the flyway.
- A network of internationally important sites in the Central Asian Flyway should be established to raise awareness and promote the conservation of migratory waterbirds and wetlands in the context of sustainable development.
- Trans-boundary wetland and waterbird projects should be developed with international support, involving local agencies and organisations in each participating country.
- Strong networks of people in each country within the flyway should be established for undertaking surveys and monitoring waterbirds and their habitats.
- Key threatened species which need immediate attention should be short-listed and conservation efforts for them initiated.

# Waterbirds in the valleys of the Ob river tributaries (Western Siberia) and their conservation

*Tatiana K. Blinova[1], I.V. Gromyshev[1] & M.M. Samsonova (Mukhacheva)[2]*

[1] *Tomsk State University, 14 Kirov ave, of. 32, Tomsk, 634034, Russia. (email: btk@green.tsu.ru)*

[2] *Tomsk State University, Institute of Biology, 36 Lenin ave, Tomsk, 634050, Russia. (email: maria_samsonova@mail.ru)*

Blinova, T.K., Gromyshev, I.V. & Samsonova (Mukhacheva), M.M. 2006. Waterbirds in the valleys of the Ob river tributaries (Western Siberia) and their conservation. *Waterbirds around the world.* Eds. G.C. Boere, C.A. Galbraith & D.A. Stroud. The Stationery Office, Edinburgh, UK. p. 264.

Previous studies of the avifauna of the swamps and taiga forests in the Chulym and Vasugan river areas (Western Siberian plain) are scarce. This study describes waterbird species of the taiga zone: numbers, distribution and species assemblages of the different landscapes in the region.

Surveys were made in the eastern part of the Western Siberian plain in the Chulym-river area (Ob river right tributary) in May – July from 1996 – 2002 and in the Vasugan-river area (left tributary) in 2003 (Blinova & Samsonova 2004). Birds were counted from cutters, motorboats and hovercraft in different types of lakes and water areas of medium and small rivers. In total the surveys covered about 2 000 kilometers.

A total of 27 species of waterfowl were found during the surveys, including; Black-throated Diver *Gavia arctica*, Black-necked Grebe *Podiceps nigricollis*, Mute Swan *Cygnus olor*, Whooper Swan *Cygnus cygnus*, Bewick's Swan *Cygnus bewickii*, some species of river and diving ducks, terns and gulls and 23 other wetland associated species, including birds of prey; White-tailed Eagle *Haliaeetus albicilla*, Osprey *Pandion haliaetus*, Black Kite *Milvus migrans*, Grey Heron *Ardea cinerea*, Black Stork *Ciconia nigra*, Bittern *Botaurus stellaris*, sandpiper species, Sedge Warbler *Acrocephalus schoenobaenus*, Grey Wagtail *Motacilla cinerea*, and Sand Martin *Riparia riparia*; in total about 30 % of the region's avifauna.

Among these, 11 species (one-fifth of the total) are listed as rare (Red Data Book of the Tomsk region 2002): Great Crested Grebe *Podiceps cristatus*, Grey Heron, Black Stork, Greater Flamingo *Phoenicopterus roseus*, Whooper and Bewick's Swans, White-tailed Eagle, Osprey, Common Crane *Grus grus*, Oystercatcher *Haematopus ostralegus* and Kingfisher *Alcedo atthis*.

Other species vulnerable to the effects of human activity are those at the limits of their distribution: Bittern, Common Pochard *Aythya ferina*, Coot *Fulica atra*, Little Tern *Sterna albifrons*, Black Tern *Chlidonias niger*, White-winged Black Tern *Chlidonias leucopterus*, Great Crested Grebe and Water Rail *Rallus aquaticus*, species rare on the flyway; Ruff *Philomachus pugnax*, Greater Scaup *Aythya marila*, and passage species Herring Gull *Larus argentatus* and Mute Swan.

Species living near reservoirs and watercourses are influenced by anthropogenic factors (hunting, felling of riverside trees, spring fires, grass cutting). The most damage is from poaching, including the hunting of rare species. Spring fires affect early-nesting birds near river banks, and also destroy dead wood, which White-tailed Eagles and Ospreys use for nesting. Tree-felling also destroys White-tailed Eagle, Osprey, and Black Stork nesting sites.

In recognition of its ornithological importance, four Important Bird Areas (IBAs) of federal importance have been identified in the Chylum river basin:

- The Middle Chulym river basin IBA includes the river section between Tomsk and Krasnoyarsk oblasts and its surrounding landscapes. White-tailed and Golden Eagles *Aquila chrysaetos* nest there, and regular records of Black Stork and Osprey suggest that they also probably breed there (Blinova, et al., 2001). Corncrakes *Crex crex* are common on the flooded meadows. In winter, Gyrfalcon *Falco rusticolis* and Snowy Owl *Nyctea scandiaca* occur;

- The Bolshie Chertany Lake IBA is of great importance as a migratory bird staging area. Birds include Whooper, Bewick's and Mute Swans, Black-throated Diver, Greater Scaup, Goosander *Mergus merganser*, Osprey, Greater Spotted Eagle *Aquila marila* also use the lake, and Aquatic Warblers *Acroephalus paludicola* occur in the riparian scrub on the banks;

- The Dikoye Lake IBA is situated between the Ob and Chulym rivers, with nesting species including White-tailed Eagle, Osprey and Whooper Swan; and

- The Lower Chulym IBA occupies a 50 km length of river from its mouth and the neighboring biotopes. Osprey and White-tailed Eagle nest here. Oystercatchers occur on the sandbanks of the Chulym, with Eagle Owl *Bubo bubo* in the forests and Horned Grebe *Podiceps auritus*, Tufted Duck *Aythya fuligula*, Whooper Swan and Little Tern in the wetlands. Black Stork also occurs as does Gyrfalcon in winter.

Measures to secure the conservation of waterbirds in the region include identification of further IBAs, the strengthening of species conservation in Nature Reserves, the prevention of accidental spills during extraction and transportation of petroleum, communication with hunters and local communities to prevent direct persecution by hunting and poaching, and placing notices near nests.

## REFERENCES

**Blinova, T. & Samsonova, M. (Mukhacheva).** 2004. Birds of the Tomsk Prichulymie. Northampton: STT; Tomsk: STT. 344 pp.

**Blinova, T., Mukhacheva, M. & Kudryavtsev, A.** 2001. The southern taiga region of the Chylum river basin (W. Siberia) as an International Important Bird Area. Bird Census News. 14(1): 14 – 15.

**Red Data Book of Tomsk region.** 2002. Tomsk State University Press, Tomsk. 402 pp.

# Study and conservation of the Lesser White-fronted Goose *Anser erythropus* on the Putorana plateau, southern Taimyr: results and perspectives

*Alexey A. Romanov*

*State Nature Reserve "Putoransky", Norilsk, Russia.*
*Present address: Izmailovsky proyezd, 20-1-15, 105037 Moscow, Russia. (email: ring@bird.msk.ru)*

Romanov A.A. 2006. Study and conservation of the Lesser White-fronted Goose *Anser erythropus* on the Putorana plateau, southern Taimyr: results and perspectives. *Waterbirds around the world.* Eds. G.C. Boere, C.A. Galbraith & D.A. Stroud. The Stationery Office, Edinburgh, UK. p. 265.

On the Taimyr Peninsula in Siberia the main Lesser White-fronted Geese *Anser erythropus* breeding areas are concentrated in the Dudypta and Kheta River basins. The Putorana plateau is the southernmost stronghold of the species range in Taimyr. Until recently, knowledge of Lesser White-fronted Geese breeding areas on the Putorana plateau was based only on surveys made before 1990. At that time breeding of these rare geese was only confirmed at two lakes: Keta and Kutaramakan, and thus, the Putorana plateau was thought to be at the edge of the species' breeding range with only solitary pairs breeding there.

During this time the general status of the Lesser White-fronted Goose population was recognised as seriously deteriorating. This prompted the Goose, Swan and Duck Study Group (GSDSG) of Northern Eurasia and the mining and smelting enterprise "Norilsk Nikel" to initiate a joint project in 1999 to study Lesser White fronted Geese on the Putorana plateau.

From 1999 to 2003 eight tectonic mountain lakes with depressions from 45 to 130 km long were surveyed, confirming for the first time that the Putorana plateau is a key area for Lesser White-fronted Geese breeding within the Taimyr part of the species range.

In the 30 000 sq. km area of the western part of this mountainous country, 200 Lesser White-fronted Goose pairs breed annually, comprising 10-15% of the Taimyr population. Their breeding range includes the whole western Putorana, stretching south up to 66°58'N. Therefore, the southernmost boundary of the range is situated 250 km further south than previously recognised.

From 1999 to 2003 Lesser White-fronted Geese continued to occur at many large water bodies on the plateau and successfully breed at some of them. Stable and relatively large breeding populations were found around the following lakes: Kutaramakan (30-40 breeding pairs); Dyupkun (100); Agata Nizhnyaya (30-40); and Severnoye (10-15). Dyupkun Lake probably hosts the largest breeding concentration on the Putorana plateau and certainly one of the largest on the Taimyr Peninsula.

The main landscape feature around all Putorana lakes is a flat, wide shoreline stretching for tens of kilometres, richly overgrown with willows, sedges and meadow herbs. These habitats provide Lesser White-fronted Geese with readily available and rich food, as well as safe shelters in case of danger. At many sites, flat shorelines are adjacent to vast near-shore shallows, which gradually dry out with an annual water level decline in the summer, resulting in late summer vegetation growth which provides the birds with food for longer periods.

Low levels of human disturbance and low predator pressure on broods are among the critical factors for the survival of breeding populations. The valleys of the Muksun River and the Glubokoye, Sobachye, and Nakomyaken lakes are probably still important as breeding areas. although for only a small portion of the population, but other lakes (Lama and Keta) suffer considerable human disturbance.

On the Putorana plateau, Lesser White-fronted Geese are breeding in both forest tundra and taiga areas when favourable habitats are available. Mean breeding density in the most favourable habitats is one pair per 5 km of the shore line. Mean brood size (n=18) was 4.2 goslings. The largest joint broods consist of 10 adults and 23 young.

The conservation perspectives for the unique Putorana plateau breeding populations are fairly good since the plateau is almost uninhabited due to extremely hard access. Furthermore, Kutaramakan and Dyupkun lakes are situated within the State Nature Reserve "Putoransky". However, this project had recognised that constant efforts in environmental education and raising awareness of the need for protection of the species are important for their conservation, for example, through publications in the federal and local media, and through the distribution of booklets and posters calling for the endangered species' protection. Future actions within the framework of the project include searching for new breeding sites on the Putorana plateau with the help of satellite imagery, migration studies using satellite telemetry, and establishing protected areas.

# Waterbird surveys in the Tobolo-Irtyshskaja forest-steppe and steppe of Western Siberia

*Sergei A. Soloviev*

*Omsk State Pedagogical University, Russia. (email: solov_sa@mail.ru)*

Soloviev, S.A. 2006. Waterbird surveys in the Tobolo-Irtyshskaja forest-steppe and steppe of Western Siberia. *Waterbirds around the world.* Eds. G.C. Boere, C.A. Galbraith & D.A. Stroud. The Stationery Office, Edinburgh, UK. p. 266.

The south-west of the West Siberian plain, Omsk oblast, is a region of Tobolo-Irtyshskaja forest-steppe and steppe. Waterbird populations using both African-Eurasian and Asian-Australasian flyways occur in this area of the Central Palearctic. Finsh (1877) reported in the 19th century that there were plentiful waterbirds in this area, with many ducks and swans being observed on all rivers and lakes. In the steppe areas of the study area (an area rich in herbs, sod-grass and gramineous steppe) there are also a number of large lakes. There are very few trees, except for some areas of birch. Records of waterbird species, which include globally-threatened species such as Dalmatian Pelican *Pelecanus crispus* and Black-winged Pratincole *Glareola nordmanni*, in some of the most important wetland areas from recent surveys are summarized below.

The 75 000 ha Steppe State Zakaznik (54°28'N; 75°35'E) has Whooper Swan *Cygnus cygnus*, Greylag Goose *Anser anser* and Common Crane *Grus grus* nesting on reservoirs. Up to 100 000 Greylag Goose and up to 5 000 Common Crane concentrate here on migration. White-tailed Eagle *Haliaeetus albicilla*, Red-breasted Goose *Branta ruficollis*, Lesser White-fronted Goose *Anser erythropus*, Avocet *Recurvirostra avosetta*, Black-winged Stilt *Himantopus himantopus*, and Common Curlew *Numenius arquata* have also been recorded. There was a large colony of Common Gull *Larus canus* and 12 pairs of Avocets on an island in Lake Chebakly, and flocks of 15-30 Ruff *Philomachus pugnax*, 20-50 White-fronted Goose *Anser albifrons* and two Demoiselle Cranes *Anthropoides virgo* were present around the lake. On Lake Terenkul there was a colony of Little Gulls *Larus minutus* and a pair of Mute Swan *Cygnus olor*, with Common Pochard *Aythya ferina*, Tufted Duck *A. fuligula*, Common Coot *Fulica atra*, White-winged Black Tern *Chlidonias leucopterus*, Red-necked Grebe *Podiceps griseigena*, and Marsh Harrier *Circus aeruginosus* present. Near Lake Ataechje the steppe form of Merlin *Falco columbarius* was observed. On Lake Zholtyrkol there were two Whooper Swans and one Black-winged Pratincole.

On the wet meadows of the Irtysh oxbow near Zarechje settlement in the "Novovorshavskiy site of Irtysh steppe bottomland" nesting Oystercatcher *Haematopus ostralegus*, and White-winged Black Tern and three Great White Egret *Egretta alba* were recorded in June 2003.

The 2 300 ha Lake Alabota (53°59'N, 74°01'E), more than 1 000 White-fronted Geese were observed on 16 May 2002 and 59 Mute Swans were seen at the end of the summer. A colony of 15 pairs of Black-winged Pratincoles was found on 15 June, and up to 340 Greylag Geese breed here. Other waterbirds included Black-winged Stilt (26 birds), Demoiselle Crane (52 birds), Red-necked Grebe, Common Pochard, Garganey *Anas querquedula*, Shoveler *A. clypeata*, Ruff *Philomachus pugnax*, Avocet, Black-headed Gull *Larus ridibundus*, Little Ringed Plover

*Charadrius dubius*, Gadwall *A. strepera*, Northern Lapwing *V. vanellus*, Yellow-legged Gull *Larus cachinnans*, Marsh Harrier, Common Crane (20 birds), and Whooper and Mute Swan.

A chain of 22 saline lakes occur along the western bank of the river Irtysh from (54°57'N; 72°19'E) up to the Kazakhstan border. On Lake Piketnoe there was a pair of Mute Swans and Avocet (1), Black-winged Stilt (5), Common Curlew and a significant number of Common Pochard. A flock of about 10 Turnstones *Arenaria interpres* was seen on the slightly saline lake Krivoe on 5 June 2003, near the settlement of Severnoe in the area of Isilkulskogo. Here there was also a colony of 34 Avocet nests with clutch sizes of five (one nest), four (14 nests), three (six nests), two (two nests) and one (one nest). One nest (four eggs) of Black-winged Stilt was found on the same date, and chicks were seen on 12 June.

At Lake Bolshe-Murla (55°56'N, 74°32'E), in a valley of the Irtysh river, a White-tailed Eagle was seen on 20 June 2004.

At Mangutskii lake (55°49'N, 70°56'E), there were up to 80 Whooper Swans, 800 White-fronted Geese, various species of ducks including Goldeneye *Bucephala clangula*, White-winged Black Tern, two nesting pairs and 10 individual Black-tailed Godwits, and three White-tailed Eagles.

The 57 000 ha Bairovskii Republican Zakaznik (56°N, 73°E) has 68 lakes, with nesting Whooper Swan, Greylag Goose, Common Crane and Common Curlew. On the lake system "Saltaim-Tenis" (56°07'N 71°45'E), at Lake Tenis (36 000 ha) and Lake Saltaim (40 000 ha) there are the most northern colonies in the world of Dalmatian Pelican (200 individuals) and Common Cormorant *Phalacrocorax carbo*, along with breeding Grey Heron *Ardea cinerea* and Yellow-legged Gull.

On Lake Achikul (56°18'N, 71°50'E), there were Dalmatian Pelican (2-10 birds), Common Cormorant (eight birds), nesting Whooper Swan (25 birds), Grey Heron (four birds), Garganey (10 birds), Greylag Goose (30 birds), Hen Harrier *Circus cyaneus*, Marsh Harrier, Common Buzzard *Buteo buteo*, Spotted Eagle *Aquila clanga*, Hobby *Falco subbuteo*, Common Kestrel *F. tinnunculus*, Corncrake *Crex crex*, Northern Lapwing, Common Curlew (four birds), Common Tern *Sterna hirundo*, Common Gull and Yellow-legged Gull.

On the Verhneoshskiy river (56°10'N, 72°30'E) there were 46 Grey Herons, 42 Greylag Geese, 30 Whooper Swans, 292 Garganey and also Black-necked Grebe *Podiceps nigricollis*, Teal *Anas crecca*, Gadwall, Shoveler, Common Pochard, Tufted Duck, White-tailed Eagle, Black Kite *Milvus migrans*, Marsh Harrier, Pallid Harrier *C. macrourus*, Black-winged Stilt, Oystercatcher and Black-winged Pratincole.

## REFERENCE

Finsh, O. 1877. Ornithological letters from the Bremen Expedition to Western Siberia. Ibis 1: 48-65.

# Waterbird populations in the Barabinsk Lowland, Russia, 1976-2003

*Alexander P. Yanovsky*
*Institute of Animal Systematics and Ecology of the Siberian Division of the Russian Academy of the Sciences, Novosibirsk, Russia.*

Yanovsky, A.P. 2006. Waterbird populations in the Barabinsk Lowland, Russia, 1976-2003. *Waterbirds around the world*. Eds. G.C. Boere, C.A. Galbraith & D.A. Stroud. The Stationery Office, Edinburgh, UK. pp. 267-268.

The Barabinsk Lowland is both a waterfowl nesting site and situated on a major flyway. Data on the population dynamics of waterfowl are important for developing policies for nature protection and sustainable hunting. This area around Novosibirsk contains forest-steppe, woods, and wetland habitats. There are 12 600 ha of freshwater lakes and 8 800 ha of brackish and saline lakes, including Lakes Malye Chany (freshwater) and Bolshye Chany (brackish). Data is available for the period from 1976 to 2003, and was compiled from surveys of reservoirs, migration observations, monitoring of nesting sites, and hunting bag surveys. In total there were 2 556 hours of observations of migrating birds, 1 203 nests monitored, and 3 678 birds from hunting bags examined. Fourteen species of waterfowl were nesting in the area on a regular basis.

Mute Swan *Cygnus olor* are mainly found to the south of Lake Malye Chany. In the 1970s and 1980s Mute Swans progressively settled on an increasing number of lakes, although they are now less abundant than Whooper Swans *Cygnus cygnus*. Almost every year in the survey pairs of Mute Swan have been seen in the vicinity of Lake Malye Chany during the breeding season.

Whooper Swans are amongst the most common large waterbirds on the lakes of northern forest-steppe. To the north of the Trans-Siberian railway numbers gradually increased in the 1980s and early 1990s. In June 1994 nesting pairs were observed on one of three freshwater lakes, with a density of six adults, mainly nesting, per 1 000 ha of freshwater lakes.

Greylag Geese *Anser anser* usually nest in areas to the south of Lake Bolshye Chany, on the Bagan reservoir and the Karasuk lake systems. Nests have been found amongst reeds in the shallows of wetlands near to the islands and peninsulas of Lake Chany. Numbers increased in the late 1990s, especially in areas where grain fields are close to wetlands. Since then numbers have decreased, due to droughts from 1998 to 2000 during which the surface area of lakes was reduced, and due also to the impacts of spring hunting.

Shelduck *Tadorna tadorna* occur to the north of Tatarsk, Barabinsk and Novosibirsk and often to the south and southwest of Lake Chany on saline lakes. Around Bagansk, Shelduck were observed in June 1994 at a density of about four adult individuals per 1 000 ha of saline lakes. However, breeding success was low, with only 2-12% of pairs having chicks. This appears to be due to the lack of suitable nesting places, and also the periodic drying of lakes.

Mallard *Anas platyrhynchos* were widespread, occurring on most reservoirs, including those in settlements. They have stable, high numbers where hunting is closed. In the 1970s, nesting on lakes and islands averaged about two males ha[-1], and one to four males ha[-1] in boggy woods.

Teal *Anas crecca* nest to the north of Lake Chany and in a valley of the Ob river, sometimes close to reservoirs in thickets or woods. Numbers have remained relatively stable over past decades, owing to the stability of conditions in wooded areas.

Gadwall *Anas strepera* nest in the central Barabinsk lowland. Numbers have decreased less than those of other ducks, probably owing to their later arrival and their tendency to nest in more protected areas such as the islands of Lake Chany with its colonies of waterbirds, and lakeside scrub and birch woods. On the island of Uzkoredky in the northern part of Lake Chany numbers of males decreased from 67 in 1987 to only 16 in 2000, but numbers increased again to 43 in 2001, and 110 in 2003.

Wigeon *Anas penelope* nest mainly to the north of the Trans-Siberian highway in birch woods and southern taiga, and also in a valley of the Ob river. In some years, small numbers have also been observed in southern forest-steppe, nesting on lakes with larger islands.

Common Terns *Sterna hirundo* colonies provide protection for other breeding waterbirds. Photo: Sergey Dereliev.

Pintail *Anas acuta* prefer to nest in open habitats. However, these areas have frequently been converted to agricultural use, resulting in c. 80% of nests being destroyed and a large (30-fold) decrease in numbers since the 1970s and 1980s, with high levels of spring hunting also likely to have contributed to the population decrease.

During the 1970s, especially between 1976-1979, Garganey *Anas querquedula* was amongst the most abundant nesting ducks in the Barabinsk lowland and the wetlands of the upper Ob river. Since then numbers have decreased 20-fold, due to low nesting success in its preferred open habitats which are no longer available.

Shoveler *Anas clypeata* were numerous in the mid 1970s, but numbers are now reduced and variable, dependent on weather conditions, and now forming about 5% of numbers of *Anas* spp. present.

Pochard *Aythya ferina* mostly nests in typical lake forest-steppe and the upper Ob river. Numbers were stable in the 1970s, averaging 0.5-0.8 males ha$^{-1}$ in areas with small islands. Between the 1990s and 2000s numbers first slowly decreased and then, for no clear reason, have decreased rapidly, especially to the north of Lake Malye Chany.

Tufted Duck *Aythya fuligula* form nesting aggregations on lakes in woods and forest-steppe where there are colonies of gulls, usually Black-headed Gull *Larus ridibundus*, or Common Tern *Sterna hirundo*. Although nesting density is variable, depending on spring water levels, numbers have generally decreased. In 1978 average density was 140 males ha$^{-1}$ on small islands on Lake Menzelinskoe, with an overall density on lakes of 0.05 males ha$^{-1}$.

Goldeneye *Bucephala clangula* nest in hollow trees along the wooded shores of lakes and small rivers. Over the last decades hollow trees suitable for nesting have disappeared as a result of tree felling and the species now depends on artificial nest boxes along the wooded shores of reservoirs. From experimental studies the optimal number of nest boxes is 2-3 per km$^2$, more than is recommended for northern and western Europe.

In addition to these regularly breeding 14 species, Red-crested Pochard *Netta rufina*, Ruddy Shelduck *Tadrona ferruginea*, and White-headed Duck *Oxyura leucocephala* nest occasionally on a small number of lakes in the southwest Barabinsk lowland. Bean Goose *Anser fabalis* and White-fronted Goose *Anser albifrons* occur annually on spring and autumn passage. Three species of *Mergus*, Smew *M. albellus*, Red-breasted Merganser *M. serrator* and Goosander *M. merganser*, occur on autumn migration, as occasionally do Long-tailed Duck *Clangula hyemalis* and Scaup *Aythya marila*. Velvet Scoter *Melanitta fusca*, Bewick's Swan *Cygnus bewickii*, Red-breasted Goose *Branta ruficollis*, Lesser White-fronted Goose *Anser erythropus* and Ferruginous Duck *Aythya nyroca* occur very rarely.

Tufted Ducks *Aythya fuligula* form nesting aggregations on lakes in woods and forest-steppe especially close to gull colonies. Photo: Paul Marshall.

# Past and current status of Anatidae populations in Kazakhstan

*Sergey N. Yerokhov*

*Institute of Zoology of the Ministry of Education and Science, Academgorodok, Al-Farabi Street 93, Almaty, 480060, Kazakhstan.
(email: Syerokhov@nursat.kz)*

Yerokhov, S.N. 2006. Past and current status of Anatidae populations in Kazakhstan. *Waterbirds around the world.* Eds. G.C. Boere, C.A. Galbraith & D.A. Stroud. The Stationery Office, Edinburgh, UK. pp. 269-274.

## ABSTRACT

Thirty-nine species of Anatidae are known to occur in Kazakhstan, including several globally threatened species. Twenty-two species are present throughout the year; five occur only during the breeding, moulting and migration seasons; five only during the migration seasons; and seven only as rare visitors. The total number of Anatidae recorded annually in Kazakhstan has decreased from about 30 million in the first half of the twentieth century to 13 million in 1999-2003. There has been a steady degradation of wetland habitats in recent years, and this has been the main factor affecting the number and distribution of Anatidae. Economic hardship has led to increased levels of illegal hunting, and this has resulted in a decline in some species. Human disturbance, caused primarily by intensive fishing, also poses a serious threat to waterfowl populations. The high level of water consumption for industry and agriculture is another important factor, while inefficient technologies are leading to water pollution in many wetlands. Since the period of economic transition, government agencies and Non-Governmental Organisations (NGOs) concerned with the conservation of Anatidae and their habitats have been more active, and in 2003, the Government initiated a national Program for the Conservation, Reproduction, Sustainable Utilization and Study of Waterfowl.

## INTRODUCTION

The wetlands of Kazakhstan are the largest and most important in Central Asia for Anatidae (ducks, geese and swans). About 40 species of Anatidae occur in the wetlands of Kazakhstan, including many common species that may be hunted and several globally threatened and near threatened species, such as the Lesser White-fronted Goose *Anser erythropus*, Red-breasted Goose *Branta ruficollis,* White-headed Duck *Oxyura leucocephala* and Ferruginous Duck *Aythya nyroca*.

This paper presents the results of an analysis of the current status of some Anatidae populations, the trends in their numbers and the changes in their distribution within the most significant habitats. The main natural and human-related disturbance factors and threats are discussed, and recent measures that have been taken for the conservation and management of Anatidae in Kazakhstan are reviewed.

## METHODS

The data from 25 years of study of Anatidae in Kazakhstan were analysed, as were archive material at the National Institute of Zoology and the existing literature. In addition, an analysis was made of counts and estimates of quarry species provided by the Fauna Protection Inspectorates and Hunting Societies, and obtained by interview. The author studied state and governmental documents relating to the protection and utilization of waterfowl and their habitat, the laws of Kazakhstan on biodiversity, and specially protected natural territories. The current evaluation of the numbers of Anatidae was made possible as a result of the implementation of the long-term program "Monitoring of Waterfowl in the Main Habitats of Kazakhstan" (1999-2003). In parallel, the author took part in a number of international projects including "Monitoring and Assessment of Lesser White-fronted Goose in the Autumn Migration Period in North Kazakhstan" and "The Current Status of White-headed Duck in Central Asia". Information obtained in these projects has been used in this report.

## RESULTS

### Species of Anatidae in Kazakhstan

Thirty-nine species of Anatidae in 17 genera occur in Kazakhstan (Table 1). Changes in species diversity during the last 100 years relate only to the occurrence of rare species. At the end of the nineteenth and during the first half of the twentieth century, 40 species of Anatidae occurred in Kazakhstan (Dolgushin 1960). Subsequent research has failed to confirm the continuing existence of two species, the Harlequin Duck *Histrionicus histrionicus* and King Eider *Somateria spectabilis*. However, the Barnacle Goose *Branta leucopsis* was first recorded in Kazakhstan during the spring migration of 1999. Thus, the current list of Anatidae in Kazakhstan (Table 1) includes 39 species (Yerokhov 2003).

The distance of Kazakhstan from the sea determines the distribution of Anatidae within the country. Most of the breeding species are dabbling ducks and diving ducks, although the Greylag Goose *Anser anser*, Ruddy Shelduck *Tadorna ferruginea* and Common Shelduck *T. tadorna* also breed. During the migration seasons, and especially in autumn, large numbers of waterfowl that breed in coastal areas of the Arctic Ocean regularly stop over in the northern regions of Kazakhstan. These include the Greater White-fronted Goose *Anser albifrons*, Lesser White-fronted Goose, Red-breasted Goose, Goosander *Mergus merganser* and Smew *Mergellus albellus*.

### Status and distribution

Most of the Anatidae species occurring in Kazakhstan are present during all stages in their annual biological cycle: 22 species breed, undertake their moult, occur on migration and can also be found in winter. Five species breed, moult and occur on migration, and another five species are found only as non-breeders in summer and during their seasonal migrations. The remaining seven species are rare visitors, and are recorded only occasionally and in small numbers.

Anatidae are very common throughout most of Kazakhstan's territory, and can be found in all landscapes including high mountainous areas, e.g. the Bar-headed Goose *Anser indicus* and Ruddy Shelduck. The important breeding and moulting areas are located mainly in the northern part of Kazakhstan. The most important

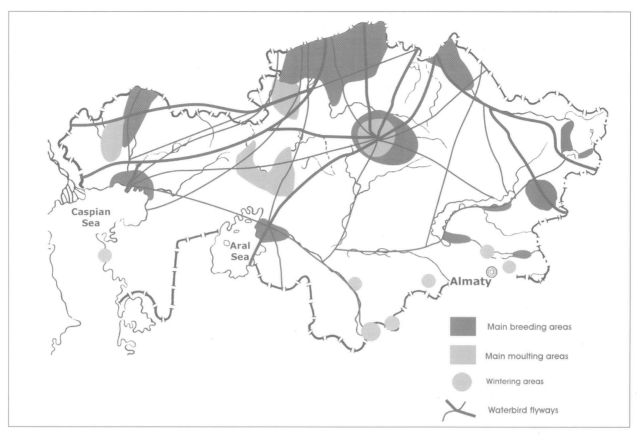

Fig. 1. The principal habitats and flyways of Anatidae in Kazakhstan.

### Table 1. The number of species of Anatidae occurring in Kazakhstan.

| Group | No. of species |
| --- | --- |
| Swans | 3 |
| Geese | 10 |
| Shelducks | 2 |
| Dabbling ducks | 10 |
| Diving ducks | 8 |
| Scoters | 3 |
| Mergansers | 3 |
| Total | 39 |

stopover sites for migrating populations are in the southern part of the country, while the main wintering areas are in the south and south-east. Two major waterbird flyways, the Siberian-Black Sea-East African Flyway and the Central Asian-South Asian Flyway, pass through Kazakhstan. The former passes mainly through the northern, west-central, north-western and western regions of the country. The latter passes through the north-eastern, eastern, east-central, south-eastern and southern regions. However, no clear-cut geographical boundary can be drawn between these two flyways as there is considerable overlap (Fig. 1).

### Population levels in the last century and at present

No information is available on the total numbers of Anatidae in Kazakhstan during the first half of the twentieth century. However, it has been estimated that the total number of geese during that period was about 8-10 million (Solomatin 1971). Assuming that the ratio of geese to ducks in Kazakhstan at that

time was close to the current ratio (1:2), we might suppose that the number of ducks was about 20 million, giving a total of 30 million for all Anatidae. However, even in the first half of the twentieth century, waterfowl specialists were reporting a considerable decrease in the number of many species, especially Greylag Goose and dabbling ducks (Gavrin 1969). Approximately 40 years later, in 1991-1994, the total number of Anatidae was estimated at about 17 million (Krivenko 1996). Since then, the pressure on Kazakhstan's natural resources has increased considerably, due to the transition to a market economy. The annual estimation of Anatidae populations has gained special relevance because of the importance of waterfowl hunting, and the recording of numbers of waterfowl has become more regular. Based on records from 1999-2003, the annual total of Anatidae in Kazakhstan was 13 million birds (Table 2). The main limiting factor during this period was a series of severe droughts in 1998-2001 resulting in serious degradation of wetland conditions in the northern and central parts of Kazakhstan. This, in turn, resulted in a considerable reduction in the numbers of birds.

### DISCUSSION
#### Population trends

An analysis of information on the abundance of Anatidae in Kazakhstan reveals that the total numbers have decreased from perhaps as many as 30 million in the first half of the twentieth century to about 13 million in recent years. The current status of the 39 species of Anatidae occurring in Kazakhstan, based on observations in 1999-2003, is summarized in Table 3. In some species, the numbers have fluctuated widely from year to year, while in others, the numbers have remained relatively stable.

**Table 2. The current numbers of Anatidae in Kazakhstan, based on counts in 1999-2003 (in thousands).**

| Region | Swans | Geese | Shelducks | Dabbling ducks | Diving ducks | Sea-ducks | Total |
|---|---|---|---|---|---|---|---|
| Ural-Caspian | 10.0 | 560.0 | 15.0 | 1 800.0 | 750.0 | 3.0 | **3 138.0** |
| Northern Kazakhstan | 2.0 | 1 500.0 | 25.0 | 2 500.0 | 1 000.0 | 4.0 | **5 031.0** |
| Central Kazakhstan | 3.0 | 800.0 | 270.0 | 1 700.0 | 1 300.0 | 4.0 | **4 077.0** |
| Eastern Kazakhstan | 0.5 | 75.0 | 50.0 | 65.0 | 35.0 | 2.0 | **227.5** |
| South-eastern Kazakhstan | 0.5 | 40.0 | 70.0 | 250.0 | 200.0 | 7.0 | **567.5** |
| **Total** | **16.0** | **2 75.0** | **430.0** | **6 315.0** | **3 285.0** | **20.0** | **13 041.0** |

**Table 3. The current status of Anatidae populations in Kazakhstan.**

| Category | Group | Population size | Variation in numbers |
|---|---|---|---|
| Abundant, relatively stable | *Tadorna tadorna*<br>*Tadorna ferruginea*<br>*Anas platyrhynchos*<br>*Anas strepera*<br>*Anas penelope*<br>*Anas crecca*<br>*Anas querquedula*<br>*Netta rufina*<br>*Aythya fuligula*<br>*Aythya ferina* | Over 50 000 | Relatively stable distribution and numbers |
| Abundant, variable | *Anser anser*<br>*Anser albifrons*<br>*Branta ruficollis* *<br>*Cygnus olor*<br>*Anas acuta*<br>*Anas clypeata*<br>*Bucephala clangula* | Over 50 000 | Considerable variation in distribution and numbers |
| Scarce, relatively stable | *Anser fabalis*<br>*Anser erythropus* *<br>*Cygnus columbianus bewickii* *<br>*Aythya marila*<br>*Aythya nyroca* *<br>*Mergus merganser*<br>*Mergus serrator* | Under 10 000 | Relatively stable distribution and numbers |
| Scarce, variable | *Cygnus cygnus* *<br>*Branta bernicla*<br>*Melanitta fusca* *<br>*Melanitta deglandi* *<br>*Clangula hyemalis*<br>*Oxyura leucocephala* *<br>*Mergellus albellus* | Under 10 000 | Considerable variation in distribution<br>*and numbers; mainly declining* |
| Rare, irregular | *Chen caerulescens*<br>*Anser indicus* *<br>*Branta leucopsis*<br>*Anas falcata*<br>*Anas formosa*<br>*Melanitta nigra* * | Single birds or<br>small groups | N/A |
| Undefined | *Anser cygnoides* *<br>*Marmaronetta angustirostris* * | Very few<br>observations<br>of single birds | N/A |

* specially protected species.

## Natural threats

Anatidae populations in Kazakhstan are affected by the unstable hydrological regime of wetlands, and this is especially important in northern and central Kazakhstan. The lakes in this region are typically inland drainage systems that become much reduced in size during dry periods, and refill only during years of high snowfall and rainfall. This normally occurs on a cycle of 8-12 years. Three to five years after re-flooding, habitat conditions in these lakes are favourable for Anatidae. Some years later, as the area of the lakes becomes reduced and the salinity increases, conditions for Anatidae deteriorate considerably. By the end of the dry period, many of the lakes are less suitable for waterfowl, and the number of Anatidae in northern and central Kazakhstan decreases by 3-5 times compared to the normal period.

## Threats caused by humans

### Transformation of habitats

Recent decades have been characterized by a steady degradation of wetland habitats for most species of waterbirds in Kazakhstan (Yerokhov & Stuge 1997), and this has been the main factor affecting the number and distribution of Anatidae. Typical habitats include freshwater, brackish and moderately saline lakes. The hydrological regime is maintained primarily by river flow or flood waters.

Over-regulation of the flow of most rivers, irretrievable consumption of water supplies and the redistribution of water cause unnatural fluctuations in water level. At the same time, there is considerable pollution from industrial, agricultural and domestic waste. About 40% of the annual inflow of rivers in Kazakhstan is irretrievably utilized or rendered unusable by pollution (Anon. 2004).

### Unstable hydrological regime

Changes in water level in wetlands are seasonal and depend on the amount of water utilized for the generation of hydroelectric power and irrigation of arable land. About half of the sites where mass concentrations of waterfowl occur are artificial water-storage reservoirs. It is normal for there to be a considerable rise or fall in water level in such reservoirs during the waterfowl breeding season, and this has a negative effect on egg-laying and the survival of broods.

### Fishing

Fishing activities have negative effects on the status and numbers of Anatidae at many of the most important wetlands in Kazakhstan. Economic challenges have encouraged a large number of people to take up fishing, the intensity of which has now reached an unprecedented scale. As a result, Anatidae are under double pressure. Hundreds of ducks, mostly young birds, perish in fishing nets, while the disturbance caused by fishing activities is an even more serious problem for the birds because of the human presence, noise of motor boats, etc. As a result, birds are forced to leave wetlands where fishing is intensive. For example, at Alakol and Sasykkol lakes in eastern Kazakhstan, the number of nesting Greylag Geese has fallen by 30-40 times within the last decade, and the number of nesting Gadwall *Anas strepera* and Red-crested Pochard *Netta rufina*, by 15-20 times (N. Berezovikov pers.comm.). A similar situation has been observed at other lakes in eastern Kazakhstan.

### Illegal hunting

Illegal hunting is quite common in some parts of Kazakhstan, and includes hunting with fire-arms or other means, the collection of eggs from nests, and the capture of ducks and geese during the moulting period.

### Uncontrolled visits and tourism

Uncontrolled access to lake shores and open-water areas for tourists and other visitors can be almost as serious as illegal hunting in terms of its negative impacts on waterfowl. Bird-watching activities are becoming more common, especially in central and south-eastern Kazakhstan. These activities often occur in areas where there is insufficient infrastructure to cater for the bird-watchers. At some sites around Alakol Lake, at the lakes along the Ile River and in the Tengis-Kurgaljin lakes, the problem of unregulated tourism has become more and more serious, and very few steps have been taken to address this.

## Conservation measures

At national level, the main political approaches to the conservation of biodiversity (including Anatidae) are determined by the Law on Protection, Rehabilitation and Use of Fauna (1993). In accordance with this law, the Government of Kazakhstan has adopted a List of Rare and Endangered Animal Species which contains 11 species of Anatidae (see Table 3). In 2002, a proposal from waterfowl specialists led to the inclusion of the globally threatened Lesser White-fronted Goose in this list. A special clause in the above-mentioned Law contains the provision for a Red Book of Kazakhstan. Another significant legal instrument is the Law on Specially Protected Natural Territories (SPNT), which lists the most significant waterfowl habitats in a special SPNT category: internationally significant wetlands. To date, the highest level of reserve status has been assigned to only three wetlands of global significance: Tengis-Kurgaljin lakes, Naursum Lake and Alakol Lake. The Tengis-Kurgaljin lakes have been designated as a Ramsar site under the Ramsar Convention on Wetlands (1975), as have the Irgiz-Turgai lakes. By a decision of the Government of Kazakhstan in 2003, a special Fishery Committee has been established which will implement a more efficient regulation of fishing activities and reduce their negative effects on waterfowl. In 1999, the Government of Kazakhstan developed and adopted a National Strategy and Action Plan for Conservation and Balanced Utilization of Biological Diversity. Other priority measures foresee the establishment in Kazakhstan of a network of specially protected wetlands as habitats of migratory birds. In addition, in recent years more emphasis is being placed on the efficient management of waterfowl resources that are open to hunting. One practical step is the Government's Program of Conservation, Reproduction, Sustainable Utilization and Study of Waterfowl, affected in 2003.

A joint project of the Government of Kazakhstan and Global Environment Facility entitled "Integrated Conservation of Priority Globally Significant Wetlands as Habitats of Migratory Birds - Demonstration in three Sites" is focused on the demonstration of comprehensive approaches to the conservation of waterfowl populations and their habitats. Three globally significant wetlands, Tengis-Kurgaljin lakes, the delta of the Ural River, and the Alakol lakes system, located on the most important migration routes of waterfowl in Kazakhstan, have been selected as demonstration sites. The project, which is envisioned to have a seven-year term, commenced in 2004 within the UN Sustainable Development Program in Kazakhstan.

In 2002, the Program of Mandatory Environmental Education was adopted at national level with a view to providing training in basic environmental knowledge, primarily through an introduction to biodiversity and the problems of biodiversity conservation for students and high school children as well as specialists in various fields of activity.

At local level, the main efforts for the conservation of Anatidae are largely focused on the efficient management of hunting resources. Temporary difficulties resulting from the economic reform have forced some groups of people, especially rural populations, to exploit natural resources, particularly fish and waterfowl, and this had led to violations of the law. Since 2003, regional authorities concerned with the management of hunting have been obliged to perform annual monitoring in waterfowl reserves, and this will be used as a basis for the establishment of hunting quotas.

Considerably more attention is now being given to strengthening the existing protected areas and establishing new protected areas at local level in the most significant habitats for Anatidae. In 2000, all such territories were subject to state registration. Specific users responsible for their management and conservation have been appointed. At present, there are 14 locally protected wetlands (zakazniks) and over 100 "rest zones", including the lakes where waterfowl hunting is fully prohibited or restricted, in Kazakhstan.

Kazakhstan has recently become involved in international co-operation in the conservation and study of Anatidae species in Central Asia. The legal framework for such co-operation is determined by a special international agreement concluded in

1995 by the Ministries of Environment of Kazakhstan, Kyrgyzstan, Uzbekistan and Tajikistan. The priority objectives of regional co-operation include efficient management of transboundary water resources, resolution of the consequences of shrinkage of the Aral Sea, and conservation of biodiversity in the region. Kazakhstani experts are playing an active role in developing the initiative proposed by Wetlands International for joint actions along the Central Asian Flyway. In particular, in recent years they have taken part in such projects as: 'The Present-day Status of White-headed Duck (*Oxyura leucocephala*) in Central Asia'; 'Assessment of the Present Conditions of the World Population of Ferruginous Duck (*Aythya nyroca*)'; and 'The Record of Wintering Waterfowl in Central Asia'. Since 2003, Kazakhstan and other regional partners (Russia, China and Islamic Republic of Iran) have started to implement the GEF/UNEP project 'Conservation of the Network of Effectively Protected Territories on the Migration Flyways of the Western Population of Siberian Crane *Grus leucogeranus* and Other Globally Endangered Waterfowl Species' - a project envisaged to continue for six years.

Kazakhstan was one of the first countries to accede to the Convention on Biological Diversity (1994), and is at the final stages of approving the necessary documents to accede to the Ramsar Convention on Wetlands (1975). Approval has also been given for Kazakhstan to accede to the Convention on the Conservation of Species of Migratory Wild Animals (1979). For many years, Kazakhstan has been co-operating with other countries in the region within the framework of international memoranda on the conservation of endangered species such as the Siberian Crane, Slender-billed Curlew *Numenius tenuirostris* and Sociable Lapwing *Vanellus gregarius*.

Kazakhstan is co-operating in a range on international conservation collaborations including the Convention on Migratory Species' Memorandum of Understanding on the Siberian Crane *Grus leucogeranus*. Participants of the 5th Meeting of the Range States, Moscow, April 2004. Photo: Crawford Prentice.

## PROJECTIONS FOR THE FUTURE

As a result of global warming, the southern limits of the breeding ranges of species that breed only in northern and northeastern Kazakhstan, i.e. Eurasian Wigeon *Anas penelope*, Northern Pintail *A. acuta*, Tufted Duck *Aythya fuligula*, scoters *Melanitta* spp. and Goosander, will move to the north or northeast and beyond the boundaries of Kazakhstan. However, species with a more southerly or westerly range in Kazakhstan, such as the Ruddy Shelduck, Red-crested Pochard, White-headed Duck and possibly Marbled Teal *Marmaronetta angustirostris*, will increase in number during the breeding season.

Industrial and agricultural development will lead to increased water consumption, and there will be an increase in the number of polluted water bodies. However, economic growth will enable the Government to allocate sufficient finance for in-depth scientific studies of Anatidae species. The scientific knowledge obtained from these studies will be used to develop practical measures for the efficient management and conservation of Anatidae. Solving environmental and protection problems will be given higher priority. In addition to economic development, further development and improvements will be made in the legal and legislative systems in relation to natural resources, particularly as they relate to waterfowl and their habitats.

Slowly but steadily, the overall level of environmental knowledge will increase among the population of Kazakhstan. Attitudes towards the exploitation of the nation's natural heritage will change with increasing understanding of the fragility and vulnerability of the environment and the full dependence of biodiversity upon human activities. Existing voluntary public associations (NGOs) and the development of new NGOs in Kazakhstan will make a larger contribution to the conservation of waterfowl and their habitats. Anatidae in Kazakhstan have a promising future.

## ACKNOWLEDGEMENTS

The author gives credit to his colleagues, Kazakh ornithologists, who have taken an active part in the study of Anatidae (Eduard Gavrilov, Nikolai Berezovikov, Anatoly Gistsov, Vladimir Vilkov, Nikolai Andrusenko, Vasily Zhulyi and others). Recent surveys in northern Kazakhstan were made possible with the support and co-operation of the Regional Environmental Agency in Hame, Finland, and especially Dr. Erkki Kellomiaki. For many years, the Goose, Swan and Duck Study Group of Northern Eurasia and the Duck Specialist Group of Wetlands International have helped in the development and funding of surveys. With their support, the author has been able to report on the results of surveys at annual meetings. In recent years, fruitful co-operation has been developed with government agencies in Kazakhstan, the Forestry and Hunting Committee, hunting inspectorates and hunting societies, individual hunters and naturalists. The author wishes to thank all those who have contributed in the development of this report, and looks forward to co-operating with them in the future.

## REFERENCES

**Anon.** 2004. Water Resources of Kazakhstan in the New Millennium: Outlook. Publications of the United Nations Development Program in Kazakhstan. UNDP 07, Almaty: 30-33.

**Dolgushin, I.A.** 1960. Birds of Kazakhstan. Vol. 1. Anseriformes. Almaty: 238-411.

**Gavrin, V.F.** 1969. Kostanay Wetlands. Hunting and Hunting Management 9: 12-13.

**Krivenko, V.G.** 1996. Anatidae in the former USSR. Game and Wildlife 13 (2): 303-319.

**Solomatin, A.O.** 1971. Dynamics of the Number of Geese and Brants in Northern Kazakhstan. Bulletin of the Moscow Nature Surveyors Society, Biology Section. LXXVI: 89-98.

**Yerokhov, S.N.** 2003. Current status and trends of Anatinae population numbers in Kazakhstan. In: Proceedings of International Symposium on Management and Conservation of Waterfowl Populations in Northern Eurasia, Petrozavodsk: 53-54.

**Yerokhov, S.N. & Stuge, T.S.** 1997. Conditions of Mass Moulting Sites of Dabbling and Diving Ducks in Kurgaljin Lakes. Natural Reserve Fund of Kazakhstan, Scientific Technical Collection, Almaty: 41-44.

Greylag Geese *Anser anser* are amongst the more abundant wildfowl in Kazakhstan. Photo: Paul Marshall.

# Creating protected areas on Lake Balkhash and Ile River Delta in the Kazakhstan Republic

*Altay Zhumakan-Uly Zhatkanbayev*

*Institute of Zoology of the Ministry of Education and Science, Akademgorodok, Almaty, 480060, Kazakhstan.*

Zhatkanbayev, A.Z-U. 2006. Creating protected areas on Lake Balkhash and Ile River Delta in the Kazakhstan Republic. *Waterbirds around the world.* Eds. G.C. Boere, C.A. Galbraith & D.A. Stroud. The Stationery Office, Edinburgh, UK. pp. 275-276.

The Republic of Kazakhstan is a new, independent state created after the disintegration of the Soviet Union. Occupying an area of 2 717 300 km², it is the ninth largest country in the world. Due to its large expanses of arid and largely uninhabitable territory, Kazakhstan is an unevenly and sparsely populated country of c.15 million people. The climate in most areas is predominantly arid, although nearly all types of climate occur, with the exception of tropical and subtropical.

Flat lands occupy up to 90% of the Republic, of which, 63% fall within semi-arid and fully arid zones. A Government Nature Reserve (zapovednik) is the highest form of protection for natural areas, protecting typical landscapes and also particularly valuable or vulnerable areas. These reserves are one example of the Soviet (now considered Russian) system of protecting natural territories, and have been preserved in the majority of the other newly independent post-Soviet states, with the exception of the three Baltic States, Estonia, Latvia and Lithuania, which have changed their systems of protected territories. In the 1980s and 1990s, during the Soviet and post-Soviet periods of development, the North American system of National Parks for protected areas became popular, there are already six in Kazakhstan under the control of central government. Additionally, in Kazakhstan and neighboring Kyrgyzstan, the German Union for Nature Protection (NABU) is attempting to introduce Biosphere Reserves. However, no Biosphere Reserves have yet been created in Kazakhstan.

Currently there are ten Nature Reserves (zapovedniks) in Kazakhstan with a combined area of 950 000 hectares, about 0.35% of the Republic's territory. Many people working in conservation would like to increase this amount of protected land to match those of other countries. Unfortunately, in the typical Soviet desire to pursue high figures, the quality of such protected areas has been forgotten. Quality, nonetheless, should always prevail over quantity. Kazakhstan currently lacks the ecological, social and economic prerequisites to increase the number of Nature Reserves or the amount of protected land. In today's conditions, even the most basic attributes are lacking, and have been for some time. In many of the existing reserves, the protected status of the land is not observed in any sense and there are inadequate numbers of staff to carry out preservation work or conduct a full state programme of scientific work. In some reserves there are no scientific staff at all, and the necessary funding and equipment is lacking. In practically all zapovedniks there is opposition to the protected status of the land by those who favor traditional, historical uses of the biological and other natural resources by local communities. Additionally, in almost all local nature reserves, some type of economic activity or use of natural resources is permitted in violation of existing nature protection legislation. This situation has arisen as a result of the top-down management of the

reserves during the long Soviet period of their existence, and it reflects the need to improve, or transform, the existing system. It is urgent for this to take place in the near future in order to ensure the necessary economic, social and environmental conditions for development in Kazakhstan.

Of the ten zapovedniks, five are situated in the Tyan Shan mountains, in the southern and southeastern part of the Republic, and the Altai mountains, in the eastern part. Five are located in zones of varying aridity: Usturt, Barsa-Kelmes, Nauryzym, Korghalzhin and Alakol. Seven of the ten were established during the Soviet period, and all of them, including the most recently established, were created according to the principle of protecting typical, representative landscapes. The preservation and rehabilitation of threatened animal species and plants was a secondary issue.

The region around Lake Balkhash is the most attractive area for creating new reserves. During the Soviet years the Kazak National Academy of Sciences developed a long-term plan for the development of a network of protected natural territories, and provided scientific grounds for creating a flat-land reserve of 210 000 hectares formed from three areas, including both desert and wetland areas, in this region of the Southern Balkhash.

These new zapovednik would preserve not only representative landscapes but also a wide assortment of Kazak desert animals, including those listed in the 1996 Red Data Book of Kazakhstan, such as Bobrinski's Bat *Eptesicus bobrinskii*, Persian Gazelle *Gazella subgutturosa*, Asiatic Wild Ass *Equus hemionus*, Marbled *Vormela peregusna*, Short-toed Snake-Eagle *Circaetus gallicus*, Steppe Eagle *Aquila rapax*, Imperial Eagle *Aquila heliaca*, Houbara Bustard *Chlamydotis undulata*, Black-bellied Sandgrouse *Pterocles orientalis*, Pin-tailed Sandgrouse *Pterocles alchata*, Pallas's Sandgrouse *Syrrhaptes paradoxus*, Eagle Owl *Bubo bubo* but also high endemic species that are the typical inhabitants of desert territories: Thick-tailed Pygmy Jerboa *Salpingotus pallidus* and Ile's Pander's Ground-Jay *Podoces panderi ilensis*. The need for specially protected areas for small vertebrates, however, is not as important as for large hoofed animals and especially many waterbird species, which are often hunted by poachers.

The Ile River drains the northern Tyan-Shan mountains and enters Lake Balkhash, creating a delta of c. 817 000 hectares, which consists of an extensive network of river channels, bordered by dense riparian scrub, lakes of standing and running water, reed beds and desert areas. The typical wetland area of c. 168 000 hectares is the largest in Kazakhstan.

Currently, this almost completely natural area hosts breeding sites of such globally threatened and near-threatened bird species as Dalmatian Pelican *Pelecanus crispus*, White-Headed Duck *Oxyura leucocephala*, Ferruginous Duck *Aythya nyroca*,

White-tailed Eagle *Haliaeetus albicilla*, Pallid Harrier *Circus macrourus*, Black-winged Pratincole *Glareola nordmanni*, White-winged Woodpecker *Dendrocopus leucopterus* and Pale-backed Pigeon *Columba eversmanni*.

Ten native fish species *Schizothorax argentatus argentatus, Diptychus dybowskii, Diptychus maculatus, Phoxinus phoxinus phoxinus, Perca schrenki, Noemacheilus strauchi strauchi, Noemacheilus labiatus, Noemacheilus dorsalis, Noemacheilus stoliczkai stoliczkai* and *Noemacheilus sewerzowi* occur amongst the total of 28 species which inhabit the Ile-Balkhash basin since18 species have been artificially introduced here. Two of the native fish species, (*S. a. argentatus* and *P. schrenki*) are globally threatened, and *S. a. argentatus* is almost extinct.

In 1996, the commercial fishery on Lake Balkhash and Ile River Delta, consisted respectively (in tons): *Abramis brama* (3424 and 29), *Stizostedion lucioperca* (535 and 3), *Silurus glanis* (298 and 80), *Cyprinus carpio* (127 and 10) and *Aspius aspius* (93 and 13). The fishery on Lake Balkhash is better developed than in the delta and is increasing now that it has opened up to the newly evolving private sector with the economic changes brought about following the break-up of the USSR.

The major factor affecting waterfowl, other birds and general wildlife in the delta is the increasing annual burning of reeds and riparian scrub by local hunters, fishermen and farmers to provide fresh areas for fishing, grazing, harvesting of reeds and open areas for hunting Muskrats *Ondatra zibetica*. Burning and illegal hunting are uncontrolled and occur throughout the delta, even in the wetter parts. An integrated approach to land and water-use management in this largest wetland in Kazakhstan is needed, particularly the regulation of water flow through the Kapshaghay dam, so as to reintroduce natural flow regimes. Fires and poaching are a major threat for wildlife, but much of this can be overcome if local people can be encouraged to avoid burning and hunting, especially during the breeding season for wildlife. There is a need for raising awareness, promoting educational programmes and encouraging environmental tourism, which could bring real benefits to the wetland and the local communities. Finally, as result of conservation efforts, the designation of protected areas as national natural parks or nature reserves (zapovednik) is important in these largest and highest priority wetlands in Kazakhstan, such as Lake Balkhash and Ile River Delta.

The globally threatened Ferruginous Duck *Aythya nyroca* breeds at Lake Balkhash in Kazakhstan. Photo: Nikolai Petkov.

# The effect of habitat change on the distribution of waterbirds in Uzbekistan and the possible implications of climate change

*Elena A. Kreuzberg-Mukhina*

*Institute of Zoology of Uzbekistan Academy of Science, Niyasov str.-1, Tashkent, 700095, Uzbekistan.*
*(email: iucn_uz@mail.ru)*

Kreuzberg-Mukhina, E.A. 2006. The effect of habitat change on the distribution of waterbirds in Uzbekistan and the possible implications of climate change. *Waterbirds around the world.* Eds. G.C. Boere, C.A. Galbraith & D.A. Stroud. The Stationery Office, Edinburgh, UK. pp. 277-282.

## ABSTRACT

In recent decades, a significant change has been observed in the climate in Central Asia. To some extent, this has been caused by the large-scale development of irrigated agriculture in the region leading to redistribution of water resources and transformation of ecosystems. Degradation of the Aral Sea and creation of new water-storage reservoirs in the desert regions have affected the climate at both local and regional level. At the same time, significant warming has been observed in the global climate. An analysis of data on the current status of waterbirds wintering in Uzbekistan has shown that waterbirds are sensitive indicators of the climate change that has occurred in the region. Historically, two wintering zones (warm and cold) have been recognized in Uzbekistan, divided by the 0°C isotherm in January. Most of the waterbirds that overwinter in Uzbekistan occur in the warm wintering zone, which was formerly confined to southern regions of the country. Waterbirds occur in the cold wintering zone mostly in autumn, before the appearance of ice cover on the reservoirs. As a result of the warming in climate, the northern limit of the warm wintering zone is shifting permanently to the north. This paper discusses the response of waterbirds to the creation of new wintering habitat and warming in climate in Uzbekistan during the last two decades.

## INTRODUCTION

The region of Central Asia covers about four million km$^2$ and has a human population of about 45 million. In recent decades, it has become evident that a significant change is occurring in the region's climate. On the one hand, this is a reflection of global climate warming processes. On the other hand, large-scale development and irrigation projects in Central Asia have led to climate change in the region through their influence on desertification and salinization processes and transformation of ecosystems. New artificial water-storage reservoirs have been constructed in arid agricultural regions, and these have partially compensated for the loss of extensive wetland habitats in the basin of the Aral Sea. The degradation of the Aral Sea and the creation of new reservoirs within its basin have both had an influence on the climate at local and regional level.

Historically, the wetlands in the Aral Sea deltas served as stopover sites for large numbers of waterbirds migrating between breeding grounds in Western Siberia and Kazakhstan and wintering areas in south-west Asia, Africa and the Indian subcontinent (Isakov 1975, Gavrilov 1979, Dolnik 1982). As a result of the desiccation of the Aral Sea and degradation of wetlands in the Amu-Darya and Syr-Darya deltas, the richest biological resources in this region were destroyed. At the same time, the

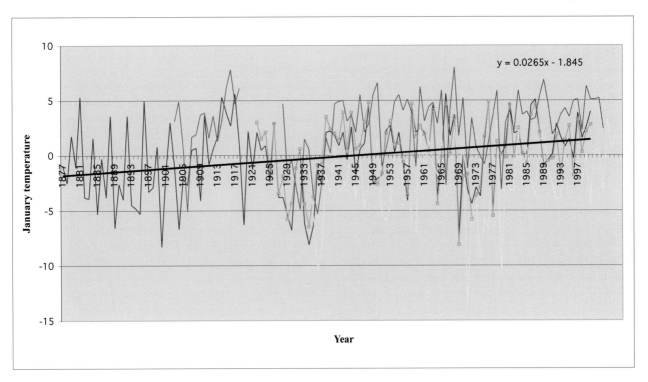

**Fig. 1.** Average January air temperatures at four locations in Uzbekistan since 1877. Tashkent – blue and linear regression, Bukhara – green, Tamdy – yellow, Termez – red.

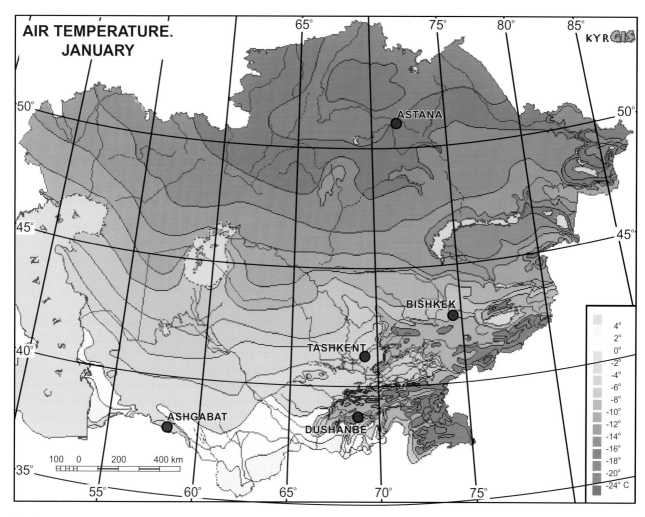

**Fig. 2.** Average January air temperatures in Central Asia.

appearance of new artificial wetlands in the south of the region, which had historically been very dry, resulted in a redistribution of waterbirds during the migration seasons and in winter.

It is evident that there has been a warming of the climate in Uzbekistan in recent decades (Fig. 1) and as a result of this warming, new wintering sites have become available for many species of waterbirds. Mid-winter waterbird counts conducted in the late 1980s and during the last few years (2000-2004) have shown that the limit of the warm wintering zone has shifted northwards by 300-500 km since the 1980s. In contrast, meteor-ological records suggest that during the preceding 100 years, the January isotherm shifted northwards by only about 200 km (data from National Institute of Hydro-meteorological Research).

An analysis of data on the current status of waterbirds wintering in Uzbekistan has shown that waterbirds are sensitive indicators of the climate change that is taking place throughout the region. The redistribution of wintering waterbirds is not only of scientific interest, but also has an influence on the develop-ment of local economies and is of considerable practical value. However, the development of appropriate conservation measures for waterbirds has been hampered by the current lack of national and regional strategies and wetland management plans, a lack of knowledge, a lack of training, education and awareness programmes, and an absence of dialogue with stakeholders concerning wetland resources. It is essential, both for the conser-vation of threatened waterbird species and for the sustainable

use of waterbirds as a game resource, that a long-term programme for the monitoring and management of wetlands and waterbirds in Uzbekistan be initiated on the basis of proper scientific assessment.

**METHODS**

A special investigation of the status and distribution of water-birds in Uzbekistan was conducted in 1986-1988 as part of a national programme for the compilation of information on game species (Shernazarov 1996, Atajanov *et al.* 1999, Nazarov & Mukhina 2002). This investigation involved aerial censuses in the Zeravshan, Syr Darya and Amu Darya basins, and covered 39 water-storage reservoirs during the autumn migration season and 23 water-storage reservoirs during the winter months. In 2000, aerial censuses of wintering waterbirds were carried out at a total of 25 water-storage reservoirs mostly in the south of Uzbekistan, although some sites in the north of the country were also counted (Atajanov *et al.* 2000). In addition, in 2000-2004, ground counts of wintering waterbirds were conducted at 30 water bodies in Uzbekistan (Lanovenko & Kreuzberg 2002). In general, the same important wintering sites were covered each year, although coverage in 1986-1988 was somewhat more extensive than in 2000-2004. During the course of these mid-winter surveys, data were gathered on the numbers and distribu-tion of 50 species of waterbirds. The present analysis is based on the published results of these surveys.

## RESULTS

### Changes in the numbers of waterbirds wintering in Uzbekistan

Historically, a warm wintering zone and a cold wintering zone have been recognized in Uzbekistan, divided by the 0°C isotherm in January (Kashkarov 1994, 1999). The dividing line between the two zones runs to the north of the lower course of the Zeravshan River (Fig. 2). About 80% of all waterbirds wintering in Uzbekistan are found in the southern regions of the country. The northern regions, which support the remaining 20%, are characterized by unstable conditions and significant fluctuations in waterbird numbers (Atajanov *et al.* 1999). The mid-winter waterbird surveys in the 1980s revealed that during this period the total number of wintering waterbirds was between 200 000 and 300 000 (Kashkarov 1999, Nazarov & Mukhina 2002). The aerial survey in 2000 revealed that there had been a significant increase in the total number of wintering waterbirds to about 978 000 (Atajanov *et al.* 2000). Of these, 327 300 (33.5%) were in the cold wintering zone, and 651 200 (66.5%) in the warm wintering zone (Lanovenko *et al.* 2001). The increasing trend in the numbers of waterbirds wintering in Uzbekistan continued in 2002-2004. Taking into account the relatively poor coverage of ground surveys at large reservoirs, the numbers of wintering waterbirds recorded in 2002-2004 were significant. In 2002, when only the 14 largest reservoirs were counted, 374 600 waterbirds (72.7% of the total) were recorded on reservoirs in the southern regions of Bukhara and Surkhandarya (warm wintering zone), while 102 400 (27.3%) were recorded in the Aydar-Arnasay wetland system in the north (cold wintering zone). Thus, it appears from these surveys that the total number of waterbirds wintering in Uzbekistan has been increasing over the past two decades, and that the birds are becoming more evenly distributed between the warm and cold wintering zones.

A comparison of the results of the aerial surveys in the 1980s with those of the similarly comprehensive aerial survey in 2000 reveals that there have been some changes in the relative abundance of the most abundant wintering species in Uzbekistan (Table 1). Data on 44 species of waterbirds were gathered during the mid-winter surveys in 1986-1988 (Nazarov & Mukhina 2002). Among game species, the Common Coot *Fulica atra* was the most numerous, accounting for 40% of all waterbirds counted. The Mallard *Anas platyrhynchos* and Common Teal *A. crecca*

were also numerous, and represented about 30% and 10% of all birds counted, respectively. Other species of Anatidae, such as Red-crested Pochard *Netta rufina*, Common Pochard *Aythya ferina*, Tufted Duck *A. fuligula*, Smew *Mergellus albellus* and Goosander *Mergus merganser*, together comprised about 10% of the total (Kashkarov 1999). In 2000, data were collected on 38 species of waterbirds (Atajanov *et al.* 2000). Among these, the Common Coot made up 43.0% of all birds counted, the Mallard 11.7%, and the Common Teal 3.8%. Other common species in 2000 included the Greylag Goose *Anser anser* (3.3% of all birds counted), Common Pochard (3.3%), Red-crested Pochard (1.6%), Great Cormorant *Phalacrocorax carbo* (1.6%), and pelicans *Pelecanus* spp. (0.5%). In the 1980s, the six most abundant species accounted for almost 81% of the total waterbirds wintering in Uzbekistan, while in 2000, the nine most abundant species accounted for only about 70% of the total. This demonstrates greater diversity in the wintering concentrations of waterbirds in 2000 than in the 1980s.

Although aerial surveys permit coverage of most of the water-storage reservoirs in Uzbekistan, including areas that are inaccessible from the ground, it is necessary to note some shortcomings of these surveys. For example, it is difficult to identify and count some species, such as divers (Gaviidae) and grebes (Podicipedidae), which do not take off from the water during the surveys. Ground surveys conducted in January 2000 at reservoirs in the Djizak, Samarqand and Bukhara regions (mostly in the warm wintering zone) enabled data to be gathered on 49 species of waterbirds. These included a total of 1 822 grebes belonging to five species, as compared with only 72 individuals counted during the aerial survey (Atajanov *et al.* 2000). Concentrations of grebes were observed on many reservoirs in Uzbekistan during the ground surveys in 2001-2004 (Kreuzberg-Mukhina & Snegur 2002).

The numbers of waterbirds on the reservoirs of Uzbekistan can show wide fluctuations during the winter months depending on fluctuations in temperature. The largest concentrations of waterbirds are observed after unexpected and sharp falls in temperature. For example, at the beginning of December 2001, following sharp frosts in northern regions of the country, huge flocks of ducks appeared on reservoirs in the south. At this time, a concentration of over 36 000 Red-crested Pochards was recorded on Karakyr Lake in the Bukhara region, and migrating flocks of 831 Goosanders and 225 Red-breasted Mergansers

**Table 1. The most abundant species of waterbirds wintering in Uzbekistan in the 1980s and in 2000.**
**Status: B – breeding bird; M – passage migrant; W – winter visitor.**

| Species | Status in Uzbekistan | Proportion in 1980s (%) | Proportion in 2000 (%) |
|---|---|---|---|
| Pelican species *Pelecanus* spp. | B, M, W | * | 0.5 |
| Great Cormorant *Phalacrocorax carbo* | B, M, W | * | 1.6 |
| Great Egret *Egretta alba* | B, M, W | * | 0.9 |
| Greylag Goose *Anser anser* | B, M, W | 1.0 | 3.3 |
| Mallard *Anas platyrhynchos* | B, M, W | 27.6 | 11.7 |
| Common Teal *Anas crecca* | M, W | 9.7 | 3.8 |
| Red-crested Pochard *Netta rufina* | B, M, W | 0.9 | 1.6 |
| Common Pochard *Aythya ferina* | B, M, W | 1.5 | 3.3 |
| Common Coot *Fulica atra* | B, M, W | 40.0 | 43.0 |
| Other waterbirds | - | 19.3 | 30.3 |

*: Present in very small numbers and included in "Other waterbirds".

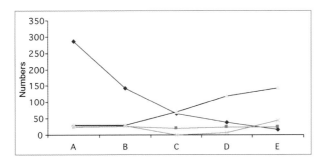

Fig. 3. Numbers of wintering waterbirds (in thousands) on several lakes in the Bukhara region, Uzbekistan. Counts were conducted in: A – January 2000; B – February 2000; C – January 2002; D – January 2003; E – January 2004. Blue – Dengizkul Lake; Green – Zekry Lake; Pink – Tudakul Lake; Yellow – Kuyumazar Reservoir.

*Mergus serrator* were observed on reservoirs in the Khoresm region. By January 2002, these birds were more widely dispersed within the various wetlands of the Bukhara region. In relatively warm winters with stable temperatures, the waterbirds are more evenly distributed throughout the wetlands of Uzbekistan and do not form such large concentrations.

Furthermore, the number of birds at a particular reservoir can remain stable or fluctuate from year to year depending on local ecological conditions. For example, at four wetlands in the Bukhara region (Dengizkul Lake, Zekry Lake, Tudakul Lake and Kuyumazar Reservoir), the number of wintering birds changed both within a winter (2000) and also from year to year (Fig. 3). At Dengizkul Lake, the first wetland to be designated as a Ramsar site in Uzbekistan, the number of birds fell from 287 000 in January 2000 to only 16 000 in January 2004 as a result of the unstable water regime in the lake. At the small Zekry Lake, where the number of wintering birds depends on the inflow of irrigation water from agricultural land, numbers fluctuated widely from 27 000 in 2000 to 8 000 in 2003 and 44 000 in 2004. At Tudakul Lake, which has a stable water regime, the number of wintering birds was relatively stable in 2000-2004, with numbers fluctuating between 21 000 and 25 000. At Kuyumasar Reservoir, also with a stable water regime, the wintering population of Mallard increased from about 30 000 in 2000 to about 140 000 in 2004. Thus is appears that the waterbirds wintering in Uzbekistan are responding quickly both to changes in the climate and to ecological changes at the wetlands.

## The shift in wintering zones and response of waterbirds to climate change

The ground and aerial surveys of wetlands in Uzbekistan in 2000-2004 revealed that new wintering areas were being established in areas that had not previously supported large numbers of waterbirds. The surveys also led to the discovery of species which had not previously over-wintered in Uzbekistan or had been recorded only in very small numbers, such as the Common Crane *Grus grus*, Black Stork *Ciconia nigra*, Ruddy Shelduck *Tadorna ferruginea* and White-headed Duck *Oxyura leucocephala*. Until recently, even regular over-wintering by species of grebes was unknown in Uzbekistan. The increase in numbers of wintering birds has been most pronounced in geese, swans, pelicans, cormorants, herons, White-tailed Eagle *Haliaeetus albicilla* and White Stork *Ciconia ciconia* – species which formerly wintered in Uzbekistan in very small numbers.

An analysis of the data has revealed that major changes have occurred in the winter distribution of a number of waterbird species in Uzbekistan. Five such species are discussed below.

The total wintering population of the Greylag Goose in Uzbekistan was formerly estimated at between 2 000 and 5 000 individuals (Nazarov & Mukhina 2002). However, current assessments of the wintering population range from 50 000 to 100 000 individuals (Atajanov *et al.* 2000). Most of these geese spend the winter in the reed-beds of Karakyr Lake where, according to the hunting inspectorate, over 100 000 individuals have been recorded during the winter season. About 28 000 Greylag Geese were counted at this lake during the mid-winter survey in 2000 (Atajanov *et al.* 2000). Between 12 000 and 17 000 geese were recorded annually from 2001 to 2003 in the border zone between Uzbekistan and Afghanistan (Kreuzberg-Mukhina & Lanovenko 2003), and over 20 000 geese were recorded flying out to feed in fields of cereals in the Kashkadarya region in January 2004. Significant numbers of wintering geese also congregate on wild cereals in the Kyzylkum desert between Aydar Lake and the Nuratau range. It is evident, therefore, that the number of Greylag Geese wintering in Uzbekistan has increased by at least 10-15 times in recent decades. Irrigated cereals and wild cereals, which now continue to grow throughout the winter months, provide suitable feeding conditions for the geese, and the proximity of wetlands to the feeding areas encourages the birds to remain in these areas.

In the past, the Ruddy Shelduck was recorded in Uzbekistan only in very small numbers in southern regions of the country (Kashkarov 1987). Its numbers never exceeded several hundred individuals. In recent years, this duck has been extending its range in winter to water-storage reservoirs in the vicinity of agricultural land (Kreuzberg-Mukhina & Lanovenko 2001, Lanovenko *et al.* in press). Estimates from the various provinces of Uzbekistan indicate a wintering population in recent years of between 1 000 and 15 000 individuals. However, this is likely to be an underestimate, as this species, which spends much of its time on agricultural land, is easily overlooked during the counts.

The White-headed Duck was formerly an extremely rare species in Uzbekistan, recorded in very small number only at the beginning of the twentieth century (Kashkarov 1987). The unexpected rediscovery of the White-headed Duck at Sudochie wetland in autumn 1999 was followed by a series of records of this globally threatened species in Uzbekistan (Kreuzberg-Mukhina & Lanovenko 2000). The species was first recorded at Dengizkul Lake during the winter of 2000 (Lanovenko *et al.* 2000, Kreuzberg-Mukhina 2003). The number of wintering birds increased rapidly, and an almost unbelievable total of 5 135 White-headed Ducks was recorded at this lake in January 2003. The birds were more widely dispersed in January 2004, when a total of 1 194 were recorded at Karakyr, Tudakul, Khadicha, Zekry and Dengizkul lakes. The optimum conditions for White-headed Ducks wintering in Uzbekistan have yet to be determined, but it is clear that this is another species that is spreading from the south and taking advantage of water-storage reservoirs to extend its wintering range.

In February 2001, about 5 500 Common Cranes were recorded on abandoned agricultural land and wheat fields near the Amu Darya River in the border zone between Uzbekistan and Afghanistan (Lanovenko & Kreuzberg-Mukhina 2002). This was the first observation of Common Cranes wintering in Central Asia. Previously, the nearest wintering areas of Common Cranes were in India (Flint 1987). Surveys along the Amu Darya River in the winters of 2002 and 2003 recorded totals of 15 500 and 15 600 Common Cranes, respectively. In 2004, however, the cranes were found over 500 km to the north of Surkhandarya region – in Bukhara, Kashkadarya, Samarkand and Djizak regions. In that year, there were about 2 500 cranes in Kashkadarya region alone.

The Northern Lapwing *Vanellus vanellus* was formerly recorded as a wintering species only in southern regions of Uzbekistan. In recent years, this species has been observed in suitable habitat throughout southern and central regions of Uzbekistan, and is slowly extending its range northwards. Thus, while in 2001 Northern Lapwings were observed only in Surkhandarya region in the south of country, in 2003 and 2004, they were recorded near lakes Aydar and Achinskoe in Djizak and Kashkadarya regions.

Similar changes have been observed in the wintering distribution of the Great Crested Grebe *Podiceps cristatus*, Black-necked Grebe *P. nigricollis*, Great Cormorant, Pygmy Cormorant *Phalacrocorax pygmeus*, Dalmatian Pelican *Pelecanus crispus*, Grey Heron *Ardea cinerea*, White Stork, Black Stork, Mute Swan *Cygnus olor* and some other species. In general, these species have shown a tendency to spend the winter at recently constructed water-storage reservoirs.

## DISCUSSION

### Climate change and the possible consequences for waterbirds

It has been predicted that as a result of the warming in climate, by the year 2030 the boundary between the dry tropical and temperate climatic zones will have shifted northwards by a further 150-200 km, while altitudinal climatic zones will have moved upwards by 150-200 m (Spektorman 2002). By the same time, the duration of the frost-free period will have increased by 8-15 days. An increase of 1.5-2.0°C in air temperatures in the central Kyzylkum desert will result in a change from the existing cold winter regime to a regime of relatively mild winters throughout which plant growth is possible. It is already apparent that such changes are creating suitable conditions for over-wintering by many species of waterbirds in parts of the cold deserts of Central Asia that were formerly frozen in winter. At the same time, the construction of large water-storage reservoirs and other artificial wetlands in these arid regions has created appropriate ecological conditions for wintering waterbirds. One might therefore expect there to be an extension in the wintering zone of waterbirds in Central Asia, an increase in the numbers and diversity of waterbirds wintering in the region, and the establishment of permanent over-wintering sites for some species and groups of species. The tendency for birds to return to the same areas in successive winters has been observed in the Dalmatian Pelican, Great Egret, Grey Heron, Mute Swan, Greylag Goose, Mallard and some other species. In contrast, the grebes and many species of ducks change their wintering areas both within winters and from year to year.

A similar change in the climate has been observed at other seasons, but the existing ornithological data are insufficient for any analysis to determine if there have been comparable changes in species distribution and numbers during the migration and breeding seasons.

Large-scale abstraction of water from the Amu Darya and Syr Darya rivers for irrigation purposes led to the Aral Sea crisis. This has been discussed elsewhere (Anon. 1999, Gorelkin *et al.* 2002, Agaltsova & Borovikova 2002, Tuchin *et al.* 2003), but it is worth adding here that the expected climate change will have further negative consequences for wetland ecosystems in the region, such as increasing evaporation rates, increasing salt migration, exhaustion of underground water resources, decreasing soil fertility, increasing mineralization of stagnant lakes, and an acceleration in the eutrophication processes in water-storage reservoirs. Furthermore, there are no climate change scenarios that show an increase in the flow of the Amu Darya and Syr Darya rivers. On the contrary, it is expected that there will be a decrease in flow during the growing season, and this might be expected to worsen the crisis in the Aral basin. As a result of global warming, there will be an increase in the occurrence of extreme climatic events such as periods of drought and high summer temperatures, further affecting the water regime and with additional negative consequences for natural ecosystems and people (CAREC 2003).

## CONCLUSION

During the last two decades, there has been a significant increase in the extent of agricultural land in Uzbekistan, while at the same time, a rise in winter temperatures has enabled the growth of desert plants to continue throughout the winter. It is clear that both of these factors have had an influence on the wintering status of many waterbird species. It seems that waterbirds are sensitive indicators of the changes that are occurring in the structure of ecosystems as a result of climate change. In view of the high value of many waterbird species in local economies in Uzbekistan, there is an urgent need to implement special measures for the proper management and wise use of waterbirds in the region.

The changes in climate that are occurring in Central Asia are aggravating the ecological problems in the Aral Sea basin and require appropriate response measures. If socio-economic development is to be sustainable, it is necessary to co-ordinate development activities with a comprehensive water policy that includes reconstruction of agriculture, the use of water-saving technologies, and the management and conservation of water resources.

## ACKNOWLEDGEMENTS

First of all, the author wishes to express her gratitude to the international organizations that have sponsored surveys of wintering waterbird in Uzbekistan: the Agricultural Department of the Royal Netherlands Embassy in Moscow (2001-2003), the Ramsar Small Grants Programme (1998-2000), and Wetlands International (2003-2004). The idea for this analysis of information on wintering waterbirds in relation to climate change came from Dr D.Yu. Kashkarov (1937-2003). The collection of data on wintering waterbirds in Uzbekistan was undertaken by many specialists from the Institute of Zoology, National University and hunting inspectorates of Bukhara, Tashkent, Djizak, Samarkand, Navoi, Kashkadarya and Surkhandarya provinces of Uzbekistan. Special thanks should be given to colleagues from the Institute of Zoology who participated in the mid-winter waterbird counts in 2001-2004: Dr E. Shernazarov, Dr E. Lanovenko, A. Filatov, S. Zagrebin, A. Ten and D. Snegur. Special thanks should also be given to Dr N.Ye. Gorelkin from the National Institute of Hydro-meteorological Research for kindly providing information on climate change and the current status of water-storage reservoirs in Uzbekistan and elsewhere in Central Asia.

## REFERENCES

**Agaltsova, N.A. & Borovikova, L.N.** 2002. Complex approaches in the assessment of water-resources vulnerability in conditions of climate change. In: Proceedings Book, Bulletin No. 5: Assessment of climate change in the territory of the Republic of Uzbekistan: development of methodological guidelines for the evaluation of natural environment fragility. Tashkent: 26-36. (In Russian).

**Anon.** 1999. First national report of the Uzbekistan Republic to the UN Convention on Climate Change. Tashkent.

**Atajanov, A., Filatov, A., Lanovenko, Y., Zagrebin, S., Chernogaev, E. & Khodjaev, J.** 1999. Summary of existing data on past waterfowl surveys in Uzbekistan. Project of the Ramsar Small Grants Programme. Protection of Uzbekistan's Wetlands and their Waterfowl. Report on Phase 2. Tashkent.

**Atajanov, A., Filatov, A., Lanovenko, Y., Zagrebin, S., Chernogaev, E. & Khodjaev, J.** 2000. Aerial survey of wetlands in Uzbekistan. Project of the Ramsar Small Grants Programme. Protection of Uzbekistan's Wetlands and their Waterfowl. Report on Phase 3. Tashkent.

**CAREC** 2003. The aims of Central Asia in sustainable development. Environment, Water and Safety in Central Asia. CAREC - Regional Ecological Centre of Central Asia.

**Dolnik, V.R.** 1982. The problems of bird migration through arid and mountain territories of Central Asia. Ornithology, Moscow 17: 13-17.

**Flint, V.E.** 1987. Family Gruidae. In: Birds of USSR. Nauka, Leningrad: 266-334.

**Gavrilov, E.I.** 1979. Seasonal bird migrations in the territory of Kazakhstan. Alma-Ata.

**Gorelkin, N.Ye., Goroshkov, N.I., Nurbaev, D.D. & Talskykh, V.N.** 2002. Assessment of the state of collectors and lakes of the right bank of the Amu Darya River. In: The problems of desert development. No. 2: 49-57. (In Russian).

**Isakov, Yu.A.** 1975. Scientific and organizational aspects of migratory bird conservation. In: Materials of the All-Union Conference on Bird Migration. Part 1. Moscow: 39-43.

**Kashkarov, D.Yu.** 1987. Order Anseriformes. In: Birds of Uzbekistan. Vol. 1, FAN, Tashkent: 57-122. (In Russian).

**Kashkarov, D.Yu.** 1994. On principles for the compilation of the prognoses of waterfowl numbers in the conditions of Central Asia. In: Rare and insufficiently known birds of Uzbekistan and neighbouring countries. Tashkent: 26-28. (In Russian).

**Kashkarov, D.Yu.** 1999. Problems of bird diversity conservation and their rational use in Uzbekistan. DSc thesis, University of Tashkent, Uzbekistan.

**Kreuzberg-Mukhina, E.A.** 2003. Review of the current status of the eastern populations of the White-headed Duck.

Casarca - Bulletin of the Working Group on Anseriformes of Northern Eurasia No .8: 277-294. Moscow. (In Russian).

**Kreuzberg-Mukhina, E. & Lanovenko, E.** 2000. White-headed Duck at the Sudochie Wetlands, Uzbekistan. TWSG News 12: 15-16.

**Kreuzberg-Mukhina, E.A. & Lanovenko, E.N.** 2001. On Ruddy Shelduck wintering in Uzbekistan. Casarca - Bulletin of the Goose, Swan and Duck Study Group of Northern Eurasia 7: 208- 210. Moscow. (In Russian).

**Kreuzberg-Mukhina, E. & Lanovenko, E.** 2003. New goose wintering site at the Uzbekistan-Afghanistan state border. In: Management and conservation of waterfowl populations in Northern Eurasia (with special focus on the White Sea - Baltic Flyway). Abstracts Book. Petrozavodsk: 204-205.

**Kreuzberg-Mukhina, E. & Snegur, D.** 2002. Grebes and some trends in the change of their current status in Uzbekistan. In: The current problems of ornithology in Siberia and Central Asia. II International Ornithology Conference. Part 2. Ulan-Ude: 55-58.

**Lanovenko, E.N. & Kreuzberg E.A.** 2002. On the Common Crane status in Uzbekistan. In: Cranes of Eurasia (Distribution, numbers, biology). Moscow: 178-182.

**Lanovenko, E., Filatov, A. & Zagrebin, S.** 2000. White-headed Duck at the Dengizkul lake, Uzbekistan. TWSG News 12: 16.

**Lanovenko, E.N., Filatov, A.K. & Zagrebin, S.V.** 2001. Value of the water storage reservoirs of Uzbekistan for the conservation of biodiversity of wintering birds. In: Actual problems of the study and conservation of birds of Eastern Europe and Northern Asia. Proceedings of the International Conference, Kazan: 358-359.

**Lanovenko, E.N., Zagrebin, S.V., Kreuzberg, E.A., Filatov, A.K. & Shernazarov E.** In press. On the importance of the Aydar-Arnasay lake system for the sustainable use of avifaunal resources.

**Nazarov, O. & Mukhina, E.** 2002. Status overview of waterbirds and wetlands in Uzbekistan. In: Birds of Wetlands and Grasslands: Proceedings of the Salim Ali Centenary Seminar, Bombay: 73-80.

**Shernazarov, E.Sh.** 1996. Anthropogenic transformation of the fauna, populations and ecology of waterbirds and shorebirds in Uzbekistan. DSc thesis, University of Tashkent, Uzbekistan.

**Spektorman, T.Yu.** 2002. Methods of constructing climate scenarios in the territory of Uzbekistan on the basis of the concept of the "best forecast". Information on the fulfilment by Uzbekistan of its commitments to the UNFCCC. Bulletin 5: 83-88. Tashkent.

**Tuchin, A.I., Gromyko, K.V. & Ruziev, I.B.** 2003. Ecological problems of the Southern and Northern Aral Sea regions and suggestions on their rehabilitation and stabilization. In: Ecological Sustainability and Advanced Methods for the Management of Water Resources in the Aral Sea Basin. NIC, MKVK, Almaty & Tashkent: 341-351. (In Russian).

# The Aral Sea basin: changes in migratory and breeding waterbird populations due to major human-induced changes to the region's hydrology

*Elena A. Kreuzberg-Mukhina*

*Institute of Zoology of Uzbekistan Academy of Science, Niyasov str.-1, Tashkent, 700095, Uzbekistan.*
*(email: iucn_uz@mail.ru)*

Kreuzberg-Mukhina, E.A. 2006. The Aral Sea basin: changes in migratory and breeding waterbird populations due to major human-induced changes to the region's hydrology. *Waterbirds around the world.* Eds. G.C. Boere, C.A. Galbraith & D.A. Stroud. The Stationery Office, Edinburgh, UK. pp. 283-284.

Most of Central Asia is located in an arid zone within the inland drainage area of the Aral Sea basin. In the mountain systems of Tien-Shan and Pamir-Alai the seasonal thaw of snow and glaciers, combined with rain, feeds the two biggest rivers, the Amu Darya and Syr Darya. Between 1960 and 1980 the wide-spread development of dams and irrigation systems began to divert substantial amounts of water from the Amu Darya and Syr Darya rivers for agricultural irrigation, mainly for cotton production, and this has had major ecological impacts of an unparalleled scale on the Aral Sea and its catchments, including on waterbirds.

The water level of the Aral Sea itself has fallen by 16 m, with major increases in salinity and drying out much of the former lake bed and the deltas of the Amu Darya and Syr Darya rivers. These ecologically rich deltas, originally wetland habitats rich in biodiversity, are threatened by desertification and significant

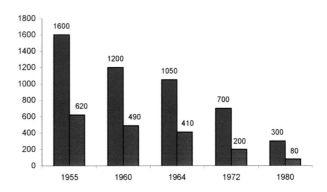

Fig. 1. Decreases in the waterflow into the Amu Darya river into the Aral Sea 1955-1980. Blue - water flow into the delta (m³ sec⁻¹); red: - total total area of lakes in delta (km²)

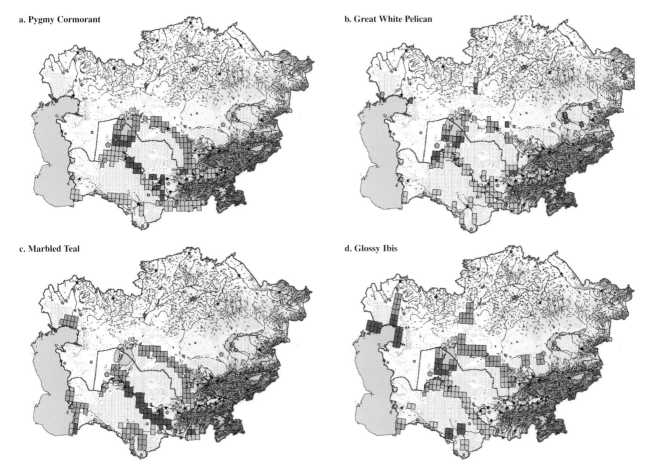

**Fig. 2.** Changes in the breeding and non-breeding distribution of four globally-threatened waterbirds (Pygmy Cormorant *Phalacrocorax pygmaeus*, Great White Pelican *Pelecanus onocrotalus*, Marbled Teal *Marmaronetta angustirostris*, and Glossy Ibis *Plegadis falcinellus*). Legend: Green cells are the past breeding area of species distribution; brown cells are the current breeding area, yellow cells are the non-breeding areas. Bright green cells are protected areas.

loss of waterbird species. These Aral Sea basin wetlands were very important for breeding colonial waterbirds such as pelicans, cormorants, herons, egrets, swans and ducks. In the early 1960s there were approximately 2 600 lakes in the Amu Darya delta but this had fallen to only 400 by 1985. Decreases in river flows and delta lake area are shown in Fig. 1. These changes have had major impacts on the climatic, ecological, economic and social conditions of the Aral Sea region.

Recognition of these impacts has led to some wetland restoration efforts (e.g. in the Sudochie wetland). In addition, many new artificial water-bodies have been created associated with water management for the 7 million ha of irrigated land. These include 94 reservoirs and 24 000 km of channels (Gorelkin 1988, Gorelkin *et al.* 2002). These new water bodies have to some extent replaced the functions of the original lake systems as migratory sites for waterbirds using migratory flyways from Western Siberia and Kazakhstan to Caspian and African wintering areas, and are also used as recreational areas for fishing and hunting by local communities.

However, the loss of wetlands has led to major changes to the species composition, numbers and distribution of waterbirds. At the beginning of the 20th century the Aral Sea and its neigh-bouring territories supported 319 bird species, 179 of which were nesting (Zarudny 1916, Gladkov 1936, Kostin 1956). By the early 1970s the number of species had dropped to 168 and only 32 species were nesting in the coastal strip of the Syr Darya delta (Gubin 1999). Between 1999 and 2002, during ecological monitoring of the Sudochie wetland, 230 bird species were recorded in the Amu Darya deltya. These included 101 waterbird species, but only 68 species (41 of which were waterbirds) were recorded nesting (Kreuzberg-Mukhina & Lanovenko 2003).

The wetland systems surrounding the new human-made waterbodies, such as Aydar-Arnasay lake system, Kairakum, Chardara, Tudakul, Karakir, Dengizkul, Khadicha reservoirs, have provided refuges for many migratory waterbirds. Although some species have attempted breeding in these new wetlands, breeding success has been relatively poor and waterbird diversity in these new wetlands during summer is generally low. However, some species have expanded their breeding ranges southwards along the Amu Darya and Syr Darya river valleys.

Recent surveys of the Aral Sea basin have found waterbirds gathering in unexpected places, and include the discovery of new major breeding, moulting and wintering areas for globally threatened species including White-headed Duck *Oxyura leuco-cephala*, Dalmatian Pelican *Pelecanus crispus* and Pygmy Cormorant *Phalacrocorax pygmaeus*. Major wintering areas for Eurasian Crane *Grus grus*, Greylag Goose *Anser anser* and Lesser White-fronted Goose *Anser erythropus* now occur in the upper parts of Amu-Darya river on the border between Uzbekistan and Afghanistan, within newly-irrigated areas.

Despite this, overall there has been a major decline in the distribution of a number of globally and regionally threatened waterbirds (Fig. 2).

## ACKNOWLEGEMENTS

Water-bird species data gathering in the Aral Sea basin was conducted with financial support of many international organiza-tions including NABU (German Union of the Nature Protection) (1995-1998), the Chicago Zoological Society (1995-1997), the Global Environmental Facility (1999-2002), the Agricultural

Lesser White-fronted Geese *Anser erythropus* now occur in the upper parts of the Amu-Darya river on the border between Uzbekistan and Afghanistan. Photo: Paul Marshall.

Department of the Royal Netherlands Embassy in Moscow (2001-2003), Wetlands International (2003-2004), and INTAS (2000-2003). Thanks are due to the many specialists, and partic-ularly to Eugenia Lanovenko and Elmurat (ornithological surveys in Uzbekistan). Elena Bykova, Stiven Ling and Larisa Stogova secured the compiling of Central Asian database and preparation of GIS maps for threatened species. Special thanks go to Dr. E.J. Milner-Gulland who coordinated the INTAS project.

## REFERENCES

**Gladkov, N.A.** 1936. Ecological peculiarities of the Amu Darya flood lands in relation to inhabiting it ornithological fauna. In: Questions of ecology and biocenology. Leningrad. 3: 253-265. (In Russian).

**Gorelkin, N.Ye.** 1988. Changes in the structure of lakes in the plain territory of Central Asia under influence of water-economy constructions. In: Proceedings of the Uzbek geographical society. Tashkent, "FAN". V. 14: 25-31. (In Russian).

**Gorelkin, N.Ye., Goroshkov, N.I., Nurbaev, D.D. & Talskykh, V.N.** 2002. Assessment of the state of collectors and lakes of the right banks of the Amu Darya River. In: The problems of the deserts development. 2: 49-57. (In Russian).

**Gubin, B.M.** 1999. The present state of the North Aral Sea avifauna and its conservation problem. In: Sustainable use of Natural Resources of Central Asia. Almaty: 112-119. (In Russian).

**Kostin, V.P.** 1956. Notes on the ornithological fauna of the lower parts of Amu Darya and Ustyurt. In: Proceedings of the Institute of Zoology and Parasitology of the Uzbek Academy of Science. Tashkent. 8: 78-129. (In Russian).

**Kreuzberg-Mukhina, E. & Lanovenko, E.** 2003. New goose wintering site at the Uzbekistan – Afghanistan state border. In: Management and conservation of waterfowls populations in Northern Eurasia (with special focus on White Sea – Baltic Flyway). Book of abstracts, Petrozavodsk: 204-205.

**Zarudny, N.A.** 1916. Birds of Aral Sea. In: News of the Turkestan Department of the Russian Geographical Society. V. 12. P.1. Tashkent: 1-229. (In Russian).

# The importance of Uzbekistan's wetlands for wintering waterfowl of the Central Asian Flyway

*Yevgeniya Lanovenko*

*Institute of Zoology, Uzbek Academy of Sciences, A.Niyazov str., 1, 700011, Tashkent, Uzbekistan. (email: filatov@comuz.uz)*

Lanovenko,Y. 2006. The importance of Uzbekistan's wetlands for wintering waterfowl of the Central Asian Flyway. *Waterbirds around the world*. Eds. G.C. Boere, C.A. Galbraith & D.A. Stroud. The Stationery Office, Edinburgh, UK. pp. 285-286.

The current ecological situation in Central Asia is very different from the early part of the last century, especially regarding waterbird habitats. The Aral Sea region has experienced both major habitat loss and re-creation as a result of human activities. This paper shows that both natural and artificial wetlands are attractive for wintering waterbirds which spend the winter in central and southern regions of Uzbekistan, within the migration flyway from North-Western Asia to Iran-Caspian and Indian-Pakistani wintering grounds.

In the second half of the 20th century anthropogenic transformations of arid ecosystems took place throughout Central Asia. This especially affected the flat lands of Uzbekistan, which were developed for agriculture. Development of an irrigation and drainage network in arid areas has resulted in changes in levels of groundwater and the creation of a large number of filtration and waster-water lakes. The degradation of the Aral Sea and the deltas of the Amudarya and Syrdarya rivers has resulted in major loss of habitats for nesting and migrating birds in Central Asia. Consequently, the importance of existing and newly created lakes increased. Over 200 000 waterbirds over-winter on the inland wetlands of Uzbekistan (Kashkarov 1994).

Uzbekistan is situated in the middle and south-eastern part of the Turanian plain. Research was undertaken in the south-eastern part part i.e. central and southern regions of Uzbekistan. This region has comparatively mild climatic conditions for wintering waterbirds, and 10 to 33% of the total number of waterbirds in the Central Asian-Caspian region overwinter there (Kashkarov 1994). Wetlands in the southern regions of Central Asia and southern Uzbekistan are situated in the zone of warm Central Asian wintering grounds, whereas wetlands in northern Uzbekistan are in the zone of cold Central Asian wintering grounds and are frequently frozen which results in high fluctuations in numbers of wintering birds over different years.

Wetlands studied included large and small lakes, water reservoirs and two stretches of the Syrdarya river: a stretch in Uzbekistan between the Tajikistan and Kazakhstan boundaries (approximately 80 km long), and a stretch on the border with Afghanistan (approximately 20 km long).

**Table 1. Distribution of wintering waterbirds in Uzbekistan wetlands in January.**

| Region | Wetland | No. of waterbirds counted | | |
| --- | --- | --- | --- | --- |
| | | 2000 | 2003 | 2004 |
| **Region of cold wintering grounds** | | **412 346** | **241 171** | **331 373** |
| Mid-stream of the Syrdarya River | Syr Darya river | 19 456 | 128 028 | 97 578 |
| | Aydar-Arnasay lakes system | 284 539 | 96 643 | 60 708 |
| | Tuyabuguz water reservoir | - | 16 500 | 28 914 |
| Bukhara region | Ayakagitma | 23 281 | - | - |
| | Karakir lakes system | 85 070 | - | 144 173 |
| **Region of warm wintering grounds** | | **559 419** | **317 092** | **442 146** |
| Bukhara Region | Kuyumazar and Tudakul water reservoirs | 55 345 | 143 392 | 168 533 |
| | Shorkul | 13 864 | - | - |
| | Solyonoye and Zamonbobo lakes | 16 379 | - | - |
| | Khadicha Lake | 8 395 | - | 1 620 |
| | Deukhona Lake | 5 813 | 6 018 | 3 262 |
| | Zekry Lake | 26 663 | 8 377 | 43 745 |
| | Dengizkul | 286 634 | 39 345 | 18 503 |
| Kashkadarya region | Talimarjan water reservoir | 66 698 | - | 53 128 |
| | Sichankullake | 7 637 | - | - |
| | Chimkurgan water reservoir | 19 254 | - | - |
| | Achinskoye Lake | 52 737 | | 28 637 |
| Surhandarya Region | Amudarya river | - | 52 427 | 62 632 |
| | Uchkyzyl water reservoir | - | 9 915 | 8 638 |
| | Aktepe water reservoir | - | 21 267 | 26 331 |
| | Kumkurgan water reservoir | - | 36 351 | 27 117 |
| **Total** | | **971 765** | **558 263** | **773 519** |

Aerial surveys were carried out in 2000 on 32 Uzbekistani wetlands in both cold and warm wintering ground zones, with over 900 000 wintering waterbirds counted (Lanovenko *et al.* 2001). Mixed surveys (by foot and motorboat) counted 558 263 waterbirds wintering on 13 wetlands in 2003, and 773 519 waterbirds on 15 wetlands in 2004. All censuses were carried out in January (Table 1).

More than 50 waterbird species were recorded, nine of which are globally threatened: Dalmatian Pelican *Pelecanus crispus*, Lesser White-fronted Goose *Anser erythropus*, White-headed Duck *Oxyura leucocephala*, Ferruginous Duck *Aythya nyroca*, White-tailed Eagle *Haliaeetus albicilla,* Red-breasted Goose *Branta ruficollis*, Marbled Teal *Marmaronetta angustirostris*, Pallas's Sea Eagle *Haliaeetus leucoryphus* and Pygmy Cormorant *Phalacrocorax pygmaeus*. The creation of the new waterbodies has modified the territorial distribution of waterbirds in the Central Asian region and are especially important for White-headed Duck and White-tailed Eagle.

In Table 1, comparison with the 1990s population estimates (Perennou *et al.* 1994), indicates that 17% of Red-crested Pochard from the Western-Central-Asian/South-Western Asia population, 33.8% of Mallard from Western Siberia/Southern-Western Asia population, 42.8% of Ruddy Shelduck *Tadorna ferruginea* from Western-Asian/Caspian/Iranian-Iraq population, and up to 30% of White-headed Duck from Southern-Eastern Europe/Turkish/Southern-Western Asia are wintering in Uzbekistan.

In cold weather conditions, as in 2000 and 2003, waterbirds concentrated on the larger wetlands and deeper rivers. In relatively warm weather, as in 2004, waterbirds distributed over a larger number of shallow small lakes and fields near the deep rivers and big lakes.

In 2004, a very warm winter with good water levels in lakes and water reservoirs, the distribution of some species changed. White-headed Duck, for example, had previously concentrated

only on Dengizkul Lake, but in 2004 it was recorded also on the many small, shallow lakes in Bukhara region and at the Aydar Arnasay lakes system in the Syrdarya river basin.

These surveys illustrated the importance of Uzbekistani wetlands for wintering waterbirds on the Central Asian flyway with the identification of nine wetlands as having international importance for the support of wintering waterbirds. Three of these have Special Protected Area status, which corresponds to IUCN protected areas category IV. Only one of these, Dengizkul Lake, has Ramsar status as a Wetland of International Importance.

The surveys were made possible by a Ramsar Small Grant Fund in 2000, and in 2003 and 2004 through support from the Dutch government in the framework of the Central Asian Flyway Project (Wetlands International, WWF Russia). The enthusiasm of the members of the Working Group on Uzbekistan's Wetlands contributed greatly to the success of these surveys.

## REFERENCES

**Kashkarov, D.Yu.** 1994. On Principles of making prognoses of waterfowl numbers under conditions of Middle Asia. Rare and little-studied birds of Uzbekistan and adjacent territories. Proceedings of IV National Ornithological Conference. Uzbekistan,Tashkent.

**Lanovenko, Ye.N., Zagrebin, S.V. & Filatov, A.K**. 2001. Importance of Uzbekistan's wetlands for conservation biodiversity of wintering birds. Actual problems of surveys and conservation birds of Eastern Europe and Nothern Asia. International conference. Russia, Kazan: 358-359.

**Perennou, C., Mundkur, T. & Scott, D.A.** 1994. The Asian Waterfowl Census 1987-91: distribution and status of Asian waterfowl. AWB Publication No. 86. IWRB Publication No. 24.

The Northern Lapwing *Vanellus vanellus* has recently expanded its wintering range northwards and now occurs throughout central and southern Uzbekistan. Photo: Paul Marshall.

# A review of the wetlands of Afghanistan

*Ahmad Khan*

*University of Wisconsin at Madison/The International Crane Foundation, 11376 Shady Lane Road, Baraboo, Wisconsin 53913, USA.*
*Present address: Mohallah Ibrahim Khel, Village Udigram, District Swat, Pakistan. (email: snowleop@psh.paknet.com.pk)*

Khan, A. 2006. A review of the wetlands of Afghanistan. *Waterbirds around the world.* Eds. G.C. Boere, C.A. Galbraith & D.A. Stroud. The Stationery Office, Edinburgh, UK. pp. 287-291.

## ABSTRACT

Afghanistan is a landlocked arid country with a rich biodiversity represented in various life forms and their habitats. The existence of water in arid climates such as that of Afghanistan plays a significant role not only in maintaining human livelihoods but also in creating pristine ecosystems that provide essential services to the local communities. Such wetland habitats in an arid country are important resting, feeding and staging areas for a number of migratory bird species. This paper reviews the wetlands of Afghanistan from the perspective of current status, conservation issues and recommendations for initiatives in the future.

## INTRODUCTION

Afghanistan is a landlocked country of about 65.2 million ha in Central Asia. The country's natural resources include forests (2.2 million ha), arable land (7.9 million ha) and rangelands (5.0-14.7 million ha). Altitudes range from 400 m above sea level in the Seistan basin to over 6000 m in the Zebak. The country lies at the confluence of the Palearctic and Indo-Malayan biogeographical realms, and is endowed with rich biodiversity. The climate is characterized by arid and semi-arid conditions with hot summers and cold winters (ICIMOD 1997). Afghanistan's diverse habitats host 119 species of mammals, 400 species of birds, two species of amphibians and 4 000 species of vascular plants. The country is divided into three distinct regions, the Hindu Kush highlands, the Northern Plains and the Southern Plains (Smith *et al.* 1973), and this has given rise to the ethno-cultural division of the country into Pukhtoon, Hazara, Uzbek and Tajik.

Soviet troops invaded Afghanistan in 1979, hampering any development activity and resulting in decades of war. The war in Afghanistan not only brought suffering to communities already living at subsistence level, but devastated structures and institutions. The management and conservation of the country's natural resources, including wetlands and their associated biodiversity, were not spared.

The wetland habitats of Afghanistan consist of three major types: rivers, lakes and marshes, and man-made reservoirs. Since most of Afghanistan is very dry, the few wetlands that exist are of considerable ecological and social importance. Most of the watercourses are liable to great seasonal variation in water level, and they are subject to intensive human use. Many of Afghanistan's rivers drain into depressions where they have no outlet, resulting in the formation of large shallow saline lakes and marshes. Many thousands of birds use the internationally significant wetlands of Ab-i-Estada, Dasht-i-Nawar, Band-i-Amir and Kol-e-Hashmat Khan (ICIMOD 1997).

## METHODS

This review of the wetlands of Afghanistan is based primarily upon my thesis research on assessment of the post-war status of Lake Ab-i-Estada. I used a combination of approaches including literature review, field surveys, formal and informal interviews, and personal observations to collect information about the lake. The literature review was carried out in various libraries including those of the University of Kabul (Afghanistan), University of Wisconsin (USA), University of Peshawar (Pakistan) and United Nations branch in Islamabad (Pakistan). Interviews with local communities were carried out during field surveys at Lake Ab-i-Estada. In addition, I visited the wetlands of Dasht-i-Nawar, Band-i-Amir and Kol-e-Hashmat Khan. Information on protected areas, including key wetland habitats in central Afghanistan, was derived from interviews and personal observation.

## DISCUSSION

### Important wetlands of Afghanistan

The drainage systems in Afghanistan mostly end in endorreic (closed) basins (UNEP 2003). The Amu Darya, Helmand, Arghandab, Gardez, Ghazni, Mahara and other rivers receive their input from rainfall, snowmelt and glaciers, and create lakes and marshes which are important wetland ecosystems. The rivers are a source of water for irrigation, while the lakes raise the humidity in the surrounding areas and reduce the need for irrigation of crops – a much needed saving in arid climatic conditions. The small number of wetlands formed by these rivers support a wide variety of wetland-dependent birds, particularly migratory waterbirds. Most of the wetlands are used by migratory birds for feeding and resting, while some are used for breeding (UNEP 2003, Sauey 1985). In addition to their importance for birds, these wetlands have great importance for the human communities living around them.

### Band-i-Amir

Band-i-Amir consists of a chain of six lakes formed by travertine dams in the Hazarajat Mountains of the western Hindu Kush, in Bamyan Province (IUCN 1991). These lakes, named Ghulaman, Qambar, Haibat, Panir, Pudina and Zulfiqar, are noted for their distinctive scenic beauty and are also home to a variety of waterbirds. Qambar Lake has been drained and converted to marshland, providing suitable habitat for rails, coots and birds dependent on reed-beds. Ghulaman Lake has thick reed vegetation and provides habitat for waterbirds such as rails and coots. The four other lakes are deeper, and are frequented by diving ducks and grebes. The area is one of the most beautiful landscapes in Afghanistan, and has been a popular tourist attraction since the 1950s, with day tours visiting the site from Bamyan (IUCN 1991). In response to a request from the Afghan Tourist Organization (ATO), the site was declared a National Park in 1973. The National Park covered an area of 41 000 ha, but could not be notified in the official gazette. There has been little impact on the physical condition of this National Park since the 1970s, and the lakes remain in good shape (UNEP 2003). However, lack of awareness of the importance of the site, unorganized tourism, the influence of warlords in the area, illicit fishing through dynamiting and netting, and the extreme poverty of the local communities are some of the key conservation issues here.

### Dasht-i-Nawar Lake

This lake lies in a vast depression at high altitude in the Koh-e-Baba range, an offshoot of the Hindu Kush (Fig. 1). It was formerly a perennial lake with a huge area of mudflats and numerous islands. The lake provided breeding grounds for the Greater Flamingo *Phoenicopterus (ruber) roseus* and a staging area for thousands of migratory waterbirds of various species. The Government of Afghanistan declared the lake a Waterfowl and Flamingo Sanctuary in 1974. In 1999, however, the lake dried up completely due to a severe drought. A study of the lake in 2002 revealed that there were several small ponds fed by spring waters which provided some habitat for waterbirds during drought years. Several species of ducks, including Mallard *Anas platyrhynchos*, Common Teal *A. crecca* and Common Pochard *Aythya ferina*, were present on the ponds in early September 2002 (UNEP 2003). In comparison with other wetlands in Afghanistan, the problems at Dasht-i-Nawar are of relatively low intensity, and the wetland has high resistance to extreme conditions because of the presence of springs as a permanent source of water. However, a lack of awareness and lack of recognition of the important values of the wetland are key issues.

### Kol-e-Hashmat Khan

Kol-e-Hashmat Khan, in the south-eastern outskirts of Kabul, is situated at an elevation of 1 973 m and has an area of 191 ha. This lake, which is surrounded by dense reed-beds, was one of the most important and well-protected wetlands until the onset of war in 1979. The lake was formerly a royal hunting ground and was declared a Waterfowl Reserve by King Zahir Shah in the 1930s. Over 150 species of migratory birds have been recorded in the area, and the lake has supported as many as 30 000-35 000 waterbirds. From 1973 until the war, the protection of Kol-e-Hashmat Khan was the responsibility of the Guard-i-Jamhuriat (military). The lake dried out in 1999 due to the severe drought in the region. Prior to the war, it received water from a branch of the Logar River, but this was dammed in various places and became silted up. In addition, water from the Logar River was diverted for irrigation. The local community has encroached on the lake, and settlements have extended all around it. Recent reports suggest that the government has decided to drain the wetland to accommodate the ever-increasing human population of Kabul.

### Ab-i-Estada

The Gardez, Ghazni and Mahara rivers and a few unclassified streams drain into a large depression in the Koh-e-Baba and Koh-e-Pughman foothills of the Hindu Khush, and form the large saline lake of Ab-i-Estada (literally "standing water"; Fig. 2). Located between 32°30'N and 67°50'E and at an altitude of 2 070 m, this lake was a Waterfowl and Flamingo Sanctuary prior to the war in 1979. The wetland covers 27 000 ha, including 13 000 ha of surface water and 14 000 ha of mudflats. The width of the mudflats surrounding the lake varies from 0.5 km on the western shore to 7 km in the east. The lake has two small islands near its south-eastern shore. The tiny island of

Kuchney ghundai (500 m²) is 0.3 km from the shore, while the island of Loya ghundai (2 500 m²) is 2.2 km from the shore (Shank & Rodenburg 1977, Khan 2000). In the central basin of the watershed (over 19 400 km²), there are dams on the Gardez River (Band-i-Sardeh) and Ghazni River (Band-i-Sultan).

Bird counts at Ab-i-Estada and in the surrounding area have included 122 species of 84 genera, 45 families and 17 orders (Paludan 1959, Shank & Rodenburg 1977; local information and pers. obs). The importance of the lake for migratory birds is due to its location on an important flyway between breeding grounds in Siberia and Kazakhstan and wintering grounds in Pakistan and India – a flyway characterized by the paucity of stopover sites providing water and wetland habitats. The lake was formerly a very important stopover site for the critically endangered Siberian Crane *Grus leucogeranus* (Khan 2001). Wader species such as the Pied Avocet *Recurvirostra avosetta*, Black-winged Stilt *Himantopus himantopus*, Kentish Plover *Charadrius alexandrinus* and Greater Sandplover *C. leschenaultii* have bred at the lake (Niethammer 1970). The two small islands have provided breeding habitat for Greater Flamingos as well as for Slender-billed Gulls *Larus genei* and Gull-billed Terns *Gelochelidon nilotica*.

### Past history of wetland management in Afghanistan

The wetlands of Afghanistan attracted international attention in the late 1960s, and the significance of Ab-i-Estada and Dasht-i-Nawar was recognized at the International Conference on the Conservation of Wetlands and Waterfowl (Ramsar, Iran, 1971) at which the final text of the Ramsar Convention on Wetlands was adopted. Following this conference, the Government of Afghanistan and custodian Department of Wildlife and National Parks declared Band-i-Amir as a National Park in 1973, and Ab-i-Estada and Dasht-i-Nawar as Waterfowl and Flamingo Sanctuaries in 1974 (Shank & Rodenburg 1977). The proposal to declare Ab-i-Estada as a National Park in 1993 (IUCN 1993) did not materialize because of political unrest in the country.

The boundaries of the reserves were delineated and clearly defined. At Ab-i-Estada, the reserve boundaries were drawn by R.G. Petocz to maintain, wherever possible, a 2 km zone around the lake, while including all mudflats and excluding all cultivated areas. Consequently, the boundaries extended some 7 km from the lake in the east where there are extensive mudflats, whereas in the west, where farming is most intensively practiced, the boundary approached to within 0.5 km of the lakeshore in some places (Shank & Rodenburg 1977).

A ban on hunting was strictly enforced to protect the fauna of the protected areas in Afghanistan, and protection staff were recruited for the purpose. The government at the time appointed 10 guards for protection purposes at Ab-i-Estada, six from the army or republican guard (Jandrama) and four from the local community. Four wildlife guards were appointed for the protection of Kol-e-Hashmat Khan Waterfowl Reserve. Similarly, guards were posted for the protection of wildlife at Band-i-Amir National Park and Dasht-i-Nawar Waterfowl and Flamingo Sanctuary. These guards were responsible for patrolling the protected areas to control hunting and report any illegal hunting. There was a fine of 500 Afghanis for illegal hunting. The untrained guards (wildlife protection officers) at Ab-i-Estada were later supplemented with professional wildlife guards trained in Iran (Shank & Rodenburg 1977).

A system of water regulation was introduced at Ab-i-Estada and Kol-e-Hashmat Khan to maintain the water surface during the dry summer months. Water was allocated to Ab-i-Estada from the upstream Band-i-Sardeh during the summer months, and no diversion of water upstream of the lake was allowed for any purpose. Similarly, water was allocated to Kol-e-Hashmat Khan from the Kabul and Gardez rivers during the dry months of the year (Khan 2000).

## War and the management of wetlands in Afghanistan

Prior to the war, the interest of the Government of Afghanistan in the conservation of its natural resources had been increasing and by 1970 had attracted international attention. However, all its efforts were hampered by the invasion of troops from the former Soviet Union in 1979. Since then, the conservation status of the country's natural resources has been drastically weakened due to various reasons which can be summarized as follows:

- massive emigration from the country resulting in a critical loss of trained professionals;
- restricted access to former protected areas and high security risks;
- dissolution of the country into small kingdoms under different warring factions;
- increased availability and accessibility of arms (rifles, machine guns, automatic rifles, rocket launchers and missiles) and ammunition;
- destruction of infrastructure such as roads, bridges and water supply systems;
- destruction and loss of existing records and a halt to research and all other information gathering;
- uncontrolled exploitation of natural resources due to disputed ownership; and
- lack of alternative resources.

The problem of uncontrolled shooting of wildlife was further increased due to the great flow of arms and ammunition into the country, making them widely available and accessible. During the war, individuals and groups of fighters reportedly used birds and mammals for target practice. Forests were burned to expose enemies or cut to provide funds for the purchase of weapons.

## Effects of war (1979-2001) on the wetlands

Little is known about the status of wetlands in Afghanistan between 1979 and the present. Most of the information available has been provided by verbal accounts from local communities. During the period of fighting, most people left the affected areas and took refuge elsewhere within Afghanistan, while some fled the country. Information from the local community at Ab-i-Estada indicates that about 60% of the community became refugees, while between 23% (UNIDATA 1992) and 33% (UNHCR 1990) of the local community at Dasht-i-Nawar were refugees in Pakistan. Very few people, mostly the old and children, were left behind. About 2.2% of the local people around Dasht-i-Nawar were killed and another 3.2% were disabled (UNIDATA 1992). Government troops were deployed in the area around Ab-i-Estada and are reported to have hunted freely at the lake. Soviet troops in helicopters are reported to have fired several times on waterbirds at this lake, mostly in the flamingo colonies.

The wetlands lost their protection when they lost the guards that had been posted there. Six of the guards at Ab-i-Estada reportedly left the area, and the four guards from the local villages were old and have since died. A tower built at Ab-i-Estada for the effective protection of the lake was completely destroyed. Two of the guards at Kol-e-Hashmat Khan died during the war, while the other two were restored to their duties by the Taliban Government in 1998. Local communities were able to hunt waterbirds and collect eggs with no controls. As a likely result of these activities, there was an alarming decline in the central population of the Siberian Crane at this time. The population of 100 in 1967-68 (Sauey 1985) had declined to 57 by 1976 and to only 23 by 1989 (New York Times 1989). All tourism organized by the Afghanistan Tourism Organization ceased during the war. The wetlands also lost their traditional water allocation systems, and local communities began to encroach on the land (pers. obs). The community upstream of Ab-i-Estada began diverting water from the Gardez and Ghazni rivers for irrigation, and this might have contributed to the drying up of the lake. The local community around Kol-e-Hashmat Khan occupied land at the margins of the lake, thus reducing its area.

## Current status of wetlands in Afghanistan

### Land ownership

The local communities at Ab-i-Estada, Kol-e-Hashmat Khan, Dasht-i-Nawar and Band-i-Amir have no claims to ownership of the land, and admit government ownership (according to personal discussions with the local communities in 1999, 2000 and 2002). However, a number of nomadic groups (Kochis) who migrate into these areas with their livestock claim that they have traditional grazing rights which are recognized as legal by the government (Khan 2004). This grazing, along with grazing by livestock belonging to the local communities, could result in a change in vegetation structure around the wetlands. The local community at Dasht-i-Nawar came into conflict with the Kochis on the use of this area in 1999.

### Legal protection and management

At present, there are no protection staff at any of the wetlands. The local communities at Ab-i-Estada and Kol-e-Hashmat Khan regularly hunt waterbirds for fresh meat. At Ab-i-Estada, almost every man in the local community is a part-time hunter, and at least 10% are full-time hunters (Khan 2000, 2004). Falcon trapping was introduced into the Ab-i-Estada area by falcon trappers from Pakistan, and is becoming a common activity. In 2002, there were numerous falcon-trapping camps operated by people from the surrounding villages (Khan 2000, UNEP 2003). At Band-i-Amir, unorganized local tourism creates problems of water pollution and disturbance to migratory birds. On the other hand, informants state that the previous rules regarding wildlife protection have been put back in place and will be implemented when the government has sufficient funds to do this (Khan 2000, 2004, UNEP 2003).

### Grazing and collection of fuel wood

At present, grazing and the collection of fuel wood in the vicinity of Ab-i-Estada are open to anyone. Nomads exercise their grazing rights during the summer months, and local people take year round benefit of the wetland's status as "no man's land". The uncontrolled grazing activity is likely to have brought

Over-grazing by domestic stock, and deforestation are major issues throughout much of Central Asia. These hillsides have been heavily grazed by goats and sheep leading to soil erosion; note the high concentration of livestock on the right. A short distance up the valley, in the Chatkal State Nature Reserve, Uzbekistan, the hillsides are fully wooded (see p. 885). Photo: David Stroud.

about changes in vegetation cover and species composition of the plant communities. Some effects of the overgrazing and collection of fuel wood on the vegetation have already been reported (Goudie 1986).

### River flows and traditional water management

The Ghazni and Gardez rivers are the main sources of water for Ab-i-Estada. The Band-i-Sardeh (dam) on the Gardez River was constructed by the Soviets under the Sardeh Irrigation Project (1967-76) to irrigate 18 752 ha of land. This dam can potentially provide water to irrigate about 80 000 ha in Khawaja Omri, Deh Yak and Ghazni districts; however, at present only 40% of this area is under cultivation because of the poor state of the irrigation canals. The reservoir of the Band-i-Sardeh covers an area of about 9 600 ha when full; however, at present only half of the capacity is being used (UNIDATA 1992). A second dam, the Band-i-Sultan, restricts the flow of the Ghazni River and diverts water for irrigation. Both these dams have decreased the flow of water in the rivers that reach the lake. The full effects of the change in the lake's hydrology caused by these marked reductions in water flow have not yet been studied.

Downstream from the two dams, the local communities of Dilla and other villages have constructed small dams on the Ghazni and Gardez rivers to divert water for the irrigation of agricultural land. This additional diversion of water increases the adverse impacts on the hydrology of the lake, particularly in dry years when no water may reach the lake, especially from the Ghazni River. In the past, a few days of water flow were reserved

for the lake during the dry summer months, but this practice is no longer in operation.

### CONCLUSIONS AND RECOMMENDATIONS

There are very few wetlands in Afghanistan's arid landscape that provide habitat for large numbers of waterbirds in addition to functioning as a source of water for drinking, irrigation and other human needs. Band-i-Amir, Dasht-i-Nawar, Kol-e-Hashmat Khan and Ab-i-Estada are the most important wetland habitats in Afghanistan for migratory waterbirds and must be protected. There were good rains and heavy snowfalls in the watersheds of these wetlands in 2002 and 2003, and as a result, Kol-e-Hashmat Khan and Dasht-i-Nawar have been restored. Ab-i-Estada has received some water and here the wetland habitats have recovered to a considerable extent (officials of the Save the Environment-Afghanistan pers. comm.). The Government of Afghanistan must now consider re-designation of these wetlands as protected areas with appropriate legal status.

There is a need to develop comprehensive management plans for these wetlands based on a preliminary management plan for Ab-i-Estada and Dasht-i-Nawar prepared in 1977 (Shank & Rodenburg 1977) and guidelines developed by the University of Wisconsin at Madison (Khan 2004). The management plans should emphasize the following objectives:

- Strengthening institutional structures for a "watch and ward" system for the wetlands, with provision for the participation of local communities;

- Protecting migratory birds visiting the wetlands for breeding, feeding, resting and staging;
- Maintaining the essential hydrological inputs and hydro-dynamics of the lakes;
- Encouraging, facilitating and supporting research on various aspects of the wetlands and rural life in surrounding areas;
- Creating awareness amongst the local communities through various approaches;
- Integrating development issues with conservation of the wetlands and their resources;
- Developing cross-boundary co-operation and networks for the conservation of wetlands important for migratory water-birds.

## ACKNOWLEDGEMENTS

I was able to accomplish this work with support from the International Crane Foundation (George Archibald, Claire Mirande and Jim Harris), University of Wisconsin (Prof. Tim Moermond and Prof. Stan Temple), Save the Environment-Afghanistan (Abdul Wali Mudaqiq, Ghulam Muhammad and Naseer Ahmad Ahmadi), WWF-Pakistan (Chairman of Scientific Committee and Chief Technical Advisor Ashiq Ahmad Khan, and Director General Ali Hassan Habib), the NWFP Wildlife Department (Dr Muhammad Mumtaz Malik), and other friends and colleagues. I am grateful to Gerard Boere for the invitation to attend the Waterbirds around the world Conference and for sponsoring my participation.

## REFERENCES

**Goudie, A.** 1986. The Human Impact on the Natural Environment. The MIT Press, Cambridge, UK.

**ICIMOD** 1997. Regional consultation on Bio-diversity Assessment in the HKH eco-region. Country Report of Afghanistan, ICIMOD.

**IUCN** 1991. Opportunities for Improved Environmental Management in Afghanistan. UNOCA.

**Khan, A.** 2000. Research Feasibility Study at Lake Ab-i-Estada in Afghanistan in preparation for MS degree course in Conservation Biology and Sustainable Development from the University of Wisconsin at Madison (USA). Web-site of the Afghanistan Living Natural Resources Group.

**Khan, A.** 2001. Status Survey of Ab-i-Estada in Afghanistan to Develop a Draft Management Program Using Siberian Cranes (*Grus leucogeranus*) as a Flagship Species. University of Wisconsin & ICF. Unpublished report.

**Khan, A.** 2004. Habitat status and hunting pressure on migra-tory cranes in Pakistan and Assessment of Lake Ab-i-Estada in Afghanistan with proposed conservation plans for selected wetlands. MS (CBSD) thesis, University of Wisconsin at Madison, USA.

**Neithammer, V.G.** 1970. Vogelleben am Ab-i-Estada, Ghazni Province, Afghanistan: 221-227.

**New York Times** 1989. Afghan war threatens flock of rare cranes. New York Times, 18 May 1989.

**Paludan, K.** 1959. On the birds of Afghanistan. Videnskabelige Meddelelser fra Dansk Naturhistorisk Forening 122: 1-332.

**Sauey, R.** 1985. The Range, Status, and Winter Ecology of the Siberian Crane (*Grus leucogeranus*). PhD dissertation, Cornell University, Ithaca, New York, USA.

**Shank, C. & Rodenburg, W.F.** 1977. Management Plan for Ab-i-Estada and Dasht-i-Nawar Flamingo and Waterfowl Sanctuaries. UNDP/FAV/DFRMA.

**Smith, H.H., Bernier, D.W., Bunge, F.M., Rints, F.C., Shinn, R.S. & Tolki.** 1973. Area Handbook for Afghanistan. US Government Printing Office, Washington, D.C.

**UNEP** 2003. Afghanistan, Post Conflict Environmental Assessment. United Nations Environment Program, Post Conflict Assessment Unit, Geneva. (http://postconflict.unep.ch/afghanistan/report/afghanistanpcajan-uary2003.pdf)

**UNHCR** 1990. Background Report, Ghazni Province. Data Collection for Afghan Repatriation Project.

**UNIDATA** 1992. Afghanistan, Ghazni Province, a Socio-Economic Profile. A project of UNDP/OPS & UNOCA.

Pair of Siberian Cranes *Grus leucogeranus* at Fereydoon Kenar, Iran. Abi-i-Estada in Afghanistan was formerly an important staging area for this species. Photo: Crawford Prentice.

# Strategic role of Pakistan wetland resources: prospects for an effective migratory waterbird conservation network

*Kashif M. Sheikh & Naseem Kashif*

*Canadian Circumpolar Institute, University of Alberta, Suite 308, 8625-112 St., Edmonton T6G 0H1, Alberta, Canada. (email: kashif.sheikh@ualberta.ca)*

Sheikh, K.M. & Kashif, N. 2006. Strategic role of Pakistan wetland resources: prospects for an effective migratory waterbird conservation network. *Waterbirds around the world.* Eds. G.C. Boere, C.A. Galbraith & D.A. Stroud. The Stationery Office, Edinburgh, UK. pp. 292-293.

## ABSTRACT

Pakistan, situated in the north-west of Southern Asia, provides staging grounds for large numbers of migratory birds from Siberia, Central Asia and Europe. Common and threatened species overwinter in wetlands throughout the country. There have been few studies to monitor the migratory bird populations and their use of wetlands, primarily due to the absence of an effective network that could successfully generate accurate ecological data and information. Current flyway management systems rely on information from local hunters, erratic wildlife surveys and raw estimates. Information gaps exists for key wetland sites including Mangla Lake, Rawal Lake, Zangi Nawar Lake, the high mountain wetlands in northern Pakistan including the Naltar wetland complex, wetlands of Deosai plains and many others. There have been several reports of Black Storks *Ciconia nigra* and cranes; with flocks of Marbled Teal *Marmaronetta angustirostris* reported from drought-hit areas where wetlands have recently revived due to heavy rains. Linkages and partnerships with neighboring countries are also weak. The establishment of an information system through the creation of banding/research stations is recommended. These could then serve as potential nature-based tourism localities to raise public awareness and further sustainable and wise use of wetlands. However, strong support from international wetland organisations would be necessary to build capacity in Pakistan wetland communities. The network would also help in creating much needed knowledge exchange systems, improving public awareness and environmental education for wetlands and waterbirds.

## INTRODUCTION

Pakistan lies in the northwestern part of southern Asia bordering with Afghanistan, Iran, China, India and in the south, the Arabian Sea. Wetland habitats, both natural and man-made, cover approximately 7 800 km$^2$ (9.7% of the total area of Pakistan). The Indus river system and its flood plains form the main inland wetland areas. From the northern mountains to the southern coast, wetland areas provide refuge for large numbers of wintering migratory birds. Ducks, geese and swans pass through the high mountains to reach lowlands rich with lakes and man-made wetlands. Bar-headed Geese *Anser indicus* fly over high altitude passes as high as 6 000 m and above in a single flight. The most breathtaking experience for bird-watchers is in the Indus Delta and its coastal mangrove forests where the entire area is a magnet for terns, gulls, fish-eagles and Osprey *Pandion haliaetus,* although in some remote areas these birds are still traditionally hunted by local indigenous communities.

Waterbird migration patterns and distribution have not been well studied in Pakistan. There have had been sporadic efforts to research and count birds, but no consistent or reliable data is available to assist in the development of conservation policy. Lack of ringing facilities and basic field data is also a major problem. Wetlands International's Asian Waterbird Census (Li & Mundkar 2004) covered 94 wetlands in Pakistan between 1997 and 2001, with wider coverage in some past years such as 1993 when 269 sites were covered; and with the help of various experts and contacts, provides valuable data on waterbird populations and their distribution and status, but its coverage is still incomplete. WWF have reported that Pakistan's wetlands and their rich biological resources are threatened by over-exploitation, habitat destruction and polluted environments. The main causes for wetland degradation are ineffective management, poor stakeholder participation and lack of coordination for management strategies.

## METHODS

Between 1991 and 2001 various wetland studies were undertaken to collect detailed information on habitat ecology, species diversity, limnology, feeding habits of various migratory species, conservation measures, hunting activities and a census of migratory birds. The studies included field projects, indirect and direct consultations with relevant government departments; professional field biologists and site managers, as well as a literature review. The wetland sites and areas studied during this period included Zangi Nawar lake, Lulukdan wetlands, Zhob river, Haleji lake, Indus Delta, Indus river, Taunsa Barrage, Chashma barrage, Rangla wetland complex, Kharal lake, Gamaghar lake, Ucchali complex, Namal lake, Mangla reservoir, Tarbela reservoir, Borith lake, Naltar wetland complex, Gilgit river, Hunza river and many others.

## RESULTS

Pakistan has more than 670 species of birds, of which one third are waterbirds, with most of these being migratory species, including geese, ducks, swans, waders and other waterbirds. Species that require urgent attention include Siberian Crane *Grus leucogeranus*, Sarus Crane *Grus antigone*, Dalmatian Pelican *Pelicanus crispus*, Sociable Plover *Vanellus gregarius*, Lesser White-fronted Goose *Anser erythropus* and Pallas's Fish Eagle *Heliaeetus leucoryphus.*

The convergence of three high mountain ranges gives rise to a great variety of landscapes and wetland habitats (glacial lakes, running streams, nullahs or dry watercourses). The unique canal system and combination of man-made and natural wetlands attract millions of birds in unique patterns and congregations at numerous sites throughout Pakistan. Some of the important wetland sites are: Ucchali Lake situated in the Salt range, important for globally threatened White-headed Duck *Oxyura leucocephala*; Zangi Nawar lake in the deserts of southern Pakistan in Balochistan province which is important for the globally threatened Marbled Teal *Marmaronetta angustirostris;* and mountain wetlands important for the globally threatened Ferrguinous Duck *Aythya nyroca.* Many wetlands in the western and southern parts of the country, such as the Indus river delta, Zhob river (for Siberian Crane*)* and Haleji Lake, are important for millions of waterbirds either wintering or using them as staging grounds.

There is a lack of consistency in the data for many important sites, and most sites lack regular monitoring of migratory species. Although there have been efforts to survey wetlands sites and their resources, there is a real lack of an effective network of specialists who could successfully generate accurate data and information for developing conservation policies for flyways. Most information has been derived from local hunters, sporadic wildlife surveys and wild estimates. Local efforts to determine the routes of migratory species, their role in ecosystem functioning and demands for conservation action have been erratic. Some waterbird species such as White-headed Duck and Marbled Teal received attention and projects have been launched for their protection and recovery but migratory behavior and flyway routes of many species have not been studied due to the absence of an efficient network that could have linked the information.

There have been several reports of Black Storks *Ciconia nigra* in the northern areas as well as sightings of flocks of Cranes *Grus* spp. in the southern parts of the North-West frontier, Punjab and Balochistan. Some flocks of Marbled Teal have been reported from the southern parts of the country where wetlands had dried up due to long periods of drought but now after many years some wetlands have revived due to recent heavy rains. However, many wetland sites have not been visited for a long time and need urgent attention. One example is Kharal Lake, which formerly supported White-headed Ducks but is now drying out due to human activities causing wetland habitat deterioration and a consequent decline in its biodiversity.

There are major information gaps for important wetland sites such as Mangla Reservoir, Rawal Lake, Zangi Nawar Lake and the high mountain wetlands in northern areas e.g. Naltar lakes and many wetlands of Sindh and Punjab province. IUCN and other conservation organizations, especially WWF and the Ornithological Society of Pakistan (OSP), along with scientists and conservationists have been actively working to provide the necessary backing for the protection of sites and efforts are underway to develop a national wetland conservation strategy along with an enabling policy framework.

## DISCUSSION

It has long been felt that migratory birds require a specific system and an association of active field scientists who would work on a regular basis to document migratory species records. Such a *'Bird Conservation Network'* would require support from various international wetland agencies to help establish an effective information and monitoring system to inform decisions and assist in developing an effective policy framework. The network would enable comprehensive and coordinated species surveys and monitoring which could lead to species recovery plans and further conservation actions as well as supporting the wise use of wetlands. To establish such a network, it is recommended that:

- a team of dedicated amateur and professional researchers, university students, hunters and managers from all parts of Pakistan establish a network for recording up to date information on the distribution and movements of migratory birds. Representation from all regions covering all habitats would be necessary to ensure equal progress in developing and delivering effective conservation action.
- two bird ringing and recording stations are established: one in the northern mountains (Karamabar valley or Chitral Valley) and another in the freshwater or coastal and marine parts of the country (Sindh or Balochistan areas falling within the central Asian flyway or along the Zhob river in Balochistan).
- a regional research project is developed including Pakistan, Iran, India and Afghanistan with scientists, volunteers and researchers to share information and develop useful conservation strategies.

## ACKNOWLEDGEMENTS

We thank the many local communities, local authorities, conservation organisations and hunters for their support in the surveys, providing valuable information and help in visiting their areas.

## REFERENCE
**Li, Z.W.D. & Mundkur, T.** 2004. Numbers and distribution of waterbirds and wetlands in the Asia-Pacific region. Results of the Asian Waterbird Census: 1997-2001. Wetlands International, Kuala Lumpur, Malaysia.

Ferruginous Duck *Nyroca ferruginea.* Photo: Nikolai Petkov.

# Decreases in size of lakes and numbers of birds in selected wetlands in Pakistan

*Zulfiqar Ali[1] & Muhammad Akhtar[2]*
*[1]Department of Wildlife and Ecosystem, University of Veterinary and Animal Sciences, Lahore, Pakistan.*
*(email: zulfiqarali68@yahoo.com)*
*[2]Zoology Department, University of the Punjab, Lahore, Pakistan.*

Ali, Z. & Akhtar, M. 2006. Decreases in size of lakes and numbers of birds in selected wetlands in Pakistan. *Waterbirds around the world.* Eds. G.C. Boere, C.A. Galbraith & D.A. Stroud. The Stationery Office, Edinburgh, UK. pp. 294-295.

Pakistan has an estimated 780 000 ha of wetlands and over 225 important wetland resources have been documented. These freshwater and marine wetlands, which include 19 Ramsar sites, support unique assemblages of biodiversity including globally important habitats, species and genomes. However, in general, these wetlands are degrading under a broad spectrum of anthropogenic threats, most of which are a direct consequence of poverty, but many of which are also exacerbated by human ignorance and mismanagement.

Pakistan lies at the crossroads of Asia's major Palaearctic bird migration routes. At different times in the annual cycle there are substantial concentrations of passage migrants,influxes of winter visitors from northern breeding grounds and summer breeding migrants from the Indus Plains or northern alpine regions.

The Indus Flyway is one of the world's major migration routes, running from Siberia to various destinations in Pakistan over the Karakorum, Hindu Kush and Suleiman mountain ranges, along the Indus River and down to the delta. It is important for its diverse species and large numbers of birds that use this flyway, including globally threatened species such as White-headed Duck *Oxyura leucocephala*, Houbara Bustard *Chlamydotis undulata* and Siberian Crane *Grus leucogeranus*. Based on regular counts at different Pakistani wetlands, it is estimated, that between 700 000 and 1 200 000 birds arrive in Pakistan via the Indus Flyway every year.

This study, conducted from 1993 to 2003, collected data on avian diversity at selected wetlands in Pakistan, and made an overall assessment of ecosystem health. Censuses were made by the point counts method (Haldin & Ulfvens 1987). Depending on the size of each lake one to five count points per lake were selected from which the whole area could be observed with the aid of a telescope. Using GPS coordinates, elevation was recorded and the morphometry of lakes assessed.

Nine sites were selected from Punjab Pakistan, including the Uchalli Wetlands Complex (Jahlar, Khabbaki and Uchalli Lakes) which is a Ramsar Site. It was estimated that overall surface area of these nine lakes was reduced by 46% between 1993 and 2003. The total number of birds recorded in 1993 was 177 671, but by 2003 this had reduced to 89 010 (Table 1). Significant losses were observed at the Salt Range Wetlands Complex where the morphometry was reduced by 56%, and there was a reduction in bird numbers from 35 090 in 1993 to only 5 275 by 2003.

These lakes are not only shrinking in surface area but are also experiencing deterioration of water quality. This poses a serious health hazard to wildlife in general, and birds in particular. Due to a number of ecological changes mainly induced by human pressure, the health and very life of these lakes is threatened.

Think of a world without birds; singing, humming, flying, fluttering, flocking, diving, hopping, dipping, gliding, playing around, and spreading colour in the sky, on the ground and on water, making each day interesting and beautiful - the fascination never ends. Bird migration superbly demonstrates the complexity and the wonder of the web of life. The evolution of individual migratory strategies of many different bird species over the past tens of thousands of years represents the delicate balance of nature, which is very sensitive to the impacts of human activity.

**Table 1.** **Maximum bird counts and changes in extent of nine Punjab (Pakistan) lakes from 1993 to 2003.**

| Name of Site | | Maximum bird count 1993 | Maximum bird count 2003 | Size reduction |
|---|---|---|---|---|
| Rawal Lake | | 7 652 | 3 089 | 30% |
| Kallar Kahar Lake | | 6 793 | 1 246 | 30% |
| Jahlar Lake | Salt Range Wetlands Complex | 721 | 370 | 40% |
| Khabakki Lake | | 9 624 | 342 | 100% |
| Uchalli Lake | | 13 291 | 1 591 | 60% |
| Nammal Lake | | 4 661 | 1 726 | 50% |
| Rangpur Marsh | | 8 752 | 9 256 | 0% |
| Chasma Reservoir | | 122 950 | 71 008 | 0% |
| Kharar Lake | | 3 227 | 382 | 100% |
| **Total** | | **177 671** | **89 010** | **46%** |

Wetlands are of vital importance not only for birds, but also for Pakistan, as their importance to human populations in arid zones is huge. The microclimate around wetlands creates favourable conditions for the settlement of communities which depend on the wetlands for their livelihood. They exploit the wetlands directly for products such as water, food and fuel, they benefit indirectly from wetland services such as groundwater recharge, storm protection, flow regulation, flood alleviation, sediment and nutrient retention, not forgetting the less tangible attributes of wetlands, such as biodiversity and aesthetic beauty. It is the use of all these various services that gives wetlands their high economic value and supports the local people directly, as well as providing goods and services to the world outside the wetland. Wetlands protect our environment, our property, our safety and the economy.

To ensure a better future for these important wetlands, the following recommendations are made:

- wildlife monitoring programmes should be conducted on a regular basis to determine population trends;
- raising awareness, environmental education and capacity building should be promoted to enable people to manage their natural wetland resources sustainably;
- eco-tourism should be developed for international recognition of the area's beauty and biodiversity;
- effective measures should be taken to prevent water pollution, especially due to land-based sources;
- effective solid waste management programmes should be initiated; and
- strategies to manage and protect wetlands from degradation and to safeguard migratory birds should be implemented.

## REFERENCES

**Haldin, M. & Ulfvens, J.** 1987. On the efficiency of censusing waterbirds by boat. Ornis Fennica 64: 74-75.

One of eight individually marked young Siberian Cranes *Grus leucogeranus* caught in Kytalyk, Yakutia. The Indus Flyway is important for this species. Photo: Crawford Prentice.

# The decline in wader populations along the east coast of India with special reference to Point Calimere, south-east India

*S. Balachandran*

*Bombay Natural History Society, Hornbill House, S.B. Singh Road, Mumbai, 400 023, India.*
*(email: balachand@hotmail.com & bnhs@bom4.vsnl.net.in)*

Balachandran, S. 2006. The decline in wader populations along the east coast of India with special reference to Point Calimere, south-east India. *Waterbirds around the world.* Eds. G.C. Boere, C.A. Galbraith & D.A. Stroud. The Stationery Office, Edinburgh, UK. pp. 296-301.

## ABSTRACT

The main wintering grounds for waders (shorebirds) in the Central Asian/South Asian Flyway are located in India, especially along the east coast. Until the 1990s, Point Calimere was the most important site for waders on the east coast, supporting hundreds of thousands of birds throughout the migration season. Point Calimere is now degraded as a result of human interference, and a decline of over 70% has been noted in the wader populations. This decline has become apparent by comparing trapping data and transect counts from the early 1980s and early 1990s with those from 1998-2002. The decline has been reflected in wader numbers at other important habitats on the east coast, particularly Pulicat Lake and the Gulf of Mannar, which ringing recoveries have shown are used by the same wader populations. The decline has been highest in the two commonest sandpipers, Curlew Sandpiper *Calidris ferruginea* and Little Stint *C. minuta*. These species are now becoming uncommon at many sites where they formerly occurred in many thousands. Several thousand Pied Avocets *Recurvirostra avosetta* and Black-winged Stilts *Himantopus himantopus* wintered at Point Calimere in the 1980s, but these have now become scarce. Two species, the Crab Plover *Dromas ardeola* and Eurasian Oystercatcher *Haematopus ostralegus*, have not been sighted since 1992. The major causes of the decline are discussed, and some recommendations are made for further research and restoration of the important wetlands at Point Calimere.

## INTRODUCTION

The Central Asian/South Asian Flyway lies entirely within the Northern Hemisphere and is the shortest flyway in the world. It is also the most poorly known flyway, and for a high proportion of its wader populations, nothing is known of population size or trends. India is the major wintering area for waders in this flyway, but information on wader populations is patchy and mostly over a decade old. Thus, contemporary knowledge of waders is almost absent. Between 1970 and 1990, the Bombay Natural History Society (BNHS) carried out bird ringing on a large scale in various parts of the country, and highlighted the importance of a number of wetlands and the status of migratory birds dependent on those wetlands. This work accumulated a vast amount of data on migration patterns and flyways, seasonal movements, biometrics, moult, longevity, weight changes etc. The study helped to obtain comprehensive information on breeding areas, staging areas (both within India and abroad) and wintering areas that are globally important for the protection of migratory birds.

Recoveries of ringed birds have shown that most of the migratory waders occurring in India are from northern and central Siberia, although some populations from north-eastern and eastern Siberia also winter in India. Birds ringed in India have been recovered in the former USSR during spring passage

at over 60°N and over 117°E, and during autumn passage at lower latitudes between 60°E and 80°E. The recoveries have generated good data for some species, especially two *Calidris* sandpipers (Curlew Sandpiper *C. ferruginea* and Little Stint *C. minuta*) and the Ruff *Philomachus pugnax*. However, the available data are still insufficient to arrive at a meaningful conclusion with regard to the migration patterns of many species. The BNHS study was not able to document the total population of waterbirds in the wetlands under investigation. These and other gaps in knowledge can be filled only with the active collaboration of all countries within the Central Asian/South Asian Flyway.

## Migration patterns of waders in India and overlap in flyways

Among waders, the Arctic-breeding species such as Little Stint and Curlew Sandpiper undertake a loop migration within India before departing in spring. Most waders migrate to India during early autumn, mainly through the north and north-west. From here, some birds continue on south-west to wintering areas in Africa (as confirmed in the Ruff), while others move south-east to the east coast of India, as demonstrated by a Curlew Sandpiper that was ringed at Bharatpur (north-west India) and recovered in the same winter at Point Calimere (south-east India). A similar migratory divide between birds wintering in India and those wintering in south-west Asia and Africa may also occur in Kazakhstan, as most of the recoveries during autumn passage of birds ringed in India have been from Kazakhstan. The spring passage of waders along the east coast of India is relatively well known (Ali 1981, Balachandran 1998, Hussain 1991).

Although the bulk of the waders wintering in India follow the Central Asian/South Asian Flyway, some ringing recoveries provide evidence of overlap with the East Asian/Australasian and West Asian/East African Flyways in eastern and western India, respectively. The recovery of a birds ringed at Point Calimere, in Australia and birds ringed at Bharatpur, in Africa are examples of this overlap. Thus, it is possible that there are migratory divides in both eastern and western India, with some birds moving on to their respective wintering grounds in the Southern Hemisphere.

## Recent migration and related ecological studies in India

Systematic studies of bird migration in India through bird ringing came to an end when the bird migration projects sponsored by the US Fish and Wildlife Service were concluded in 1992. There was no ringing of waterbirds in India between 1993 and 1997, but in 1998, ringing was resumed on a small scale through a project sponsored by the US Fish and Wildlife Service to train volunteers in bird ringing and related studies. Under this

Fig. 1. Major habitats for waders in India.

programme, nearly 4 800 waterbirds were ringed in various parts of the country between 1998 and 2002. The bulk of the catch (68%) was at Point Calimere in the south-east.

In the last two years, a few locally sponsored ringing programmes have been organized at Basai Wetland near Delhi, and two 10-day programmes have been organized at Point Calimere through the BNHS Conservation Fund (Daniel & Balachandran 2003). The Himachal Pradesh State Government has recently sponsored a 20-day training programme on bird ringing at Pong Dam, a Ramsar site. Through these programmes, over 1 000 waterbirds have been ringed and data generated on the current status of waterbirds at these wetlands.

Regular bird ringing has been carried out at Chilika Lake for the last two years as part of a three-year project on waterbird populations sponsored by the Chilika Development Authority, Government of Orissa. Over 5 000 birds have been ringed, most of them waders. A bird atlas of Chilika Lake is now being prepared, based on the distribution of waterbirds (including waders) in different zones of the lake. Various conservation measures have been suggested for the creation of additional habitat for migratory waterbirds as well as the breeding birds, and these are being followed up and implemented by the government.

## MATERIALS AND METHODS

The numbers of waders ringed and recorded at four wetlands on the east coast of India (Point Calimere, Gulf of Mannar, Pulicat Lake and Chilika Lake) under the Bird Migration Project of the BNHS between 1980 and 1992 were taken as the baseline data to assess the size of the wader populations during the 1980s and 1990s. The ringing and census data obtained at Point Calimere and Pulicat Lake under the Bird Banders' Training Programme of the BNHS between 1998 and 2003 and the bird counts carried out in Chilika Lake by the BNHS between 2001 and 2003 were compared with the earlier data to assess the decline in wader populations. The numbers of each species ringed and the capture rate per day were also used for comparison.

## MAJOR WADER HABITATS ON THE EAST COAST MONITORED FOR BIRD MIGRATION
### Point Calimere Wildlife Sanctuary and the adjoining Great Vedaranyam Swamp

The Point Calimere Wildlife Sanctuary (10°18'N, 79°51'E) is situated on a low promontory on the Coromandel Coast (southern Deccan Plateau) in the Bay of Bengal (Fig. 1). The adjoining Great Vedaranyam Swamp stretches parallel to the Palk Strait for about 48 km, and is separated from it by a sandbank. Its north-south dimensions vary from about 10 km at its broadest in the east, to about 8 km in the central part and about 6 km in its western portion. Five freshwater channels connected to the Cauvery River empty into the swamp. There is a gradual slope from north to south. The total area is about 349 sq. km.

In about two-thirds of the swamp, the habitat varies seasonally. During the monsoon and periods of south-westerly winds, there is a continuous expanse of fresh, brackish or saline water extending to the northern tip of the swamp. At other times, the area of open water gradually dries up from north to south. During the drying stage, there are exposed flats and shallow pools. The extreme eastern promontory of the swamp, comprising Kodikkarai and Kodikkadu Reserve Forest, has been declared a wildlife sanctuary. This sanctuary, the Point Calimere Wildlife Sanctuary, supports both littoral and terrestrial life zones (Ali 1980, Manakadan 1992). It comprises 26 sq. km of tropical dry evergreen forest intermingled with scrub jungle and mangrove vegetation, and intersected by numerous tidal inlets and creeks.

Exploitation of the Great Vedaranyam Swamp for salt extraction and other marine-based industries is fast growing. Two private chemical firms have been operating in the leased swamp areas adjoining the wildlife sanctuary. The manufacture of salt involves three stages. Sea water is pumped into reservoirs and then condensed before it is finally allowed to flow into salt-pans, where the salt crystallizes. The reservoirs alter the ecosystem to some extent since they are, in the absence of tidal fluctuation, more or less stagnant. The composition of the littoral communities and microfauna is drastically altered under such conditions. The condensers have a relatively high salinity and temperature which create an ecological barrier for most marine organisms from April to October. Only the monsoon makes this environment temporarily habitable for marine organisms.

Point Calimere and Great Vedaranyam Swamp are an important wintering and staging area for over 1 000 000 waders and other waterbirds, and are the only site that has been intermittently monitored by bird ringing studies for the last three decades. The swamp is of great importance as a staging area for migrants on their way to and from Sri Lanka and other wintering grounds.

### Chilika Lake

Chilika Lake, a designated Ramsar site, is the world's second largest brackish-water lagoon, situated between 19°28'N and 19°54'N and between 85°05'E and 85°38'E (Fig. 1). The water surface of the lake varies from a maximum of 1 165 sq. km during the monsoon to a minimum of 906 sq. km during the summer. The various habitats include marshes, mudflats, freshwater pools and areas of open water with varying depths and salinity.

**Table 1. Declines in the catches of waders at Point Calimere, India.**

| Species | No. ringed in one season and maximum catch in a single day | | | Average catch/day | | |
|---|---|---|---|---|---|---|
| | 1980-82 | 1990-92 | 2000-02 | 1980-82 | 1990-92 | 1999-03 |
| *Charadrius mongolus* | 1 063　(45) | 658　(48) | 705　(34) | 7 | 8 | 7 |
| *Calidris minuta* | 9 876 (376) | 1 137 (170) | 513　(40) | 56 | 20 | 5 |
| *Calidris ferruginea* | 3 569 (180) | 1 330 (110) | 599　(35) | 20 | 14 | 6 |
| *Philomachus pugnax* | 564　(80) | 184　(47) | 74　(17) | 3 | 2 | 1 |

During the dry season (December to May), a large island is exposed (Nalabana Island), and this has extensive mudflats which attract over 300 000 waterbirds. This island was declared as a Bird Sanctuary in 1987. The island supports the largest concentrations of waders in the lake, and is also utilized by several ground-nesting birds for breeding.

Despite its large size, the lake has no areas of shallow water and mudflats until Nalabana Island emerges in December. Hence, small and medium-sized waders are scarce until December. The numbers of most wader species begin to increase from late December and reach a peak in late January. For the smaller waders, the lake serves mainly as a staging area during the northward migration in spring. However, the large and long-legged Black-tailed Godwit *Limosa limosa* has been seen in good numbers from November to March, indicating that this species utilizes the lake during the winter.

### Gulf of Mannar Biosphere Reserve

The 21 islands in the Gulf of Mannar extend from Rameshwaram Island in the north to Tuticorin in the south, and comprise an island ecosystem that is unique on the east coast of India (Fig. 1). These islands, along with their marine environment between latitudes 8° 47' and 9°15'N and longitudes 78°12' and 79°14'E, have been notified as India's first Marine Biosphere Reserve. Most of the islands support a luxuriant growth of mangroves, while the sandy shores offer excellent nesting grounds for sea turtles. The sea bed around the inshore islands is carpeted with sea-grass beds which not only serve as feeding grounds for Sea Cows *Dugong dugong*, but also harbour a diverse animal community including birds. The highly productive fringing and patchy coral reefs that surround the islands are a treasure house of colourful marine fishes. Extensive inshore areas exposed during low tide at Manali and Hare islands are frequented by coastal waders, especially those species that prefer sand-flats such as the Crab Plover *Dromas ardeola*, Eurasian Oystercatcher *Haematopus ostralegus*, Grey Plover *Pluvialis squatarola*, Lesser Sandplover *Charadrius mongolus*, Greater Sandplover *C. leschenaultii*, Bar-tailed Godwit *Limosa lapponica*, Eurasian Curlew *Numenius arquata*, Ruddy Turnstone *Arenaria interpres*, Great Knot *Calidris tenuirostris*, Red Knot *C. canutus* and Sanderling *C. alba*. Other areas with major concentrations of waterbirds are Dhanuskodi Lagoon on Rameswaram Island and Pillaimadam Lagoon on the mainland near Mandapam. These lagoons are frequented by thousands of small waders, mainly Lesser Sandplover, Little Stint and Curlew Sandpiper, as well as Greater Flamingos *Phoenicopterus (ruber) roseus*. During the 1980s, the Gulf of Mannar as a whole supported about 50 000 waterbirds (Balachandran 1990 & 1995).

### Pulicat Bird Sanctuary

Pulicat Lake is situated on the south coast of Andhra Pradesh (13°25'-13°55'N, 80°03'- 80°19'E), on the eastern seaboard of India (Fig. 1). It covers an area of about 450 sq. km, and is the second largest brackish-water lagoon in India after Chilika Lake in Orissa. The lake was declared as a bird sanctuary by the Andhra Pradesh Forest Department in 1976. The entire area is a vast, brackish to saline lagoon with extensive mud- and sand-flats. The sanctuary is bounded on its eastern side by the spindle-shaped Sriharikota Island, 185 km in length. This island was probably formed by recession of the sea, and is mostly flat with a few sand dunes ranging from 4.5 to 6 m in height. Over 200 000 waterbirds were recorded at Pulicat Lake in 1988 and 1989, including over 30 000 Greater Flamingos. The most abundant waders were Lesser Sandplover, Black-tailed Godwit, Little Stint, Curlew Sandpiper and Ruff.

## POPULATION DECLINES IN WATERBIRDS
### Point Calimere

The decline in waterbird populations at Point Calimere is very conspicuous not only to ornithologists, but also to laymen in the area. Any local villager, especially anyone over 40 years of age, can recall the drastic changes that have occurred in the numbers of waders and other waterbirds in the Great Vedaranyam Swamp. The disappearance of the fabulous clouds of waterbirds (waders, ducks, terns, flamingos, egrets) that passed through the villages on their way between feeding and roosting sites up until the late 1980s is a visible indicator of the decline. The appearance of large mounds of salt on the mudflats, which were once thronged by thousands of waders, ducks and flamingos, is an indication of the habitat loss and degradation.

As no simultaneous counts were made throughout the swamp, it is difficult to quantify the decline. The data generated from the small areas sampled for bird counts during the 1980s and personal observations of the waterbird populations in the past and present have helped to provide qualitative estimates for some of the common species. Furthermore, the bird ringing data collected between 1980 and 1991 and the recent skeletal ringing data collected between 1998 and 2003 have helped in estimating the scale of the decline.

The ringing and census data from Point Calimere indicate that there has been a decline of over 70% in certain species of waders since the 1980s. This decline in wader populations is apparent from changes in the numbers of birds caught per day, in the total numbers of birds caught per season, and in the numbers of birds counted in areas that were monitored in the 1980s and 1990s. The number of birds caught per day has decreased for several species of wader, despite a doubling of

## Table 2. Population estimates for common waders at Point Calimere, India.

| Species | 1980s | 1990s | 2000-03 |
|---|---|---|---|
| *Himantopus himantopus* | >15 000 | 3 000 | >1 000 |
| *Recurvirostra avosetta* | >7 000 | >500 | <100 |
| *Charadrius mongolus* | >10 000 | >75 000 | <40 000 |
| *Limosa limosa* | >50 000 | >40 000 | >15 000 |
| *Calidris minuta* | >200 000 | >100 000 | <20 000 |
| *Calidris ferruginea* | >150 000 | >80 000 | <25 000 |
| *Philomachus pugnax* | >100 000 | 30 000 | <10 000 |

effort per day in recent years (Table 1). The population estimates for the common waders from the 1980s, 1990s and 2000-2003 indicate that although there was a decline in all species between the 1980s and 1990s, this has become much more pronounced in recent years (Table 2). Certain species that prefer the inter-tidal zone have either disappeared or declined drastically (e.g. Crab Plover, Eurasian Oystercatcher and Sanderling), as also have some inland waders (e.g. Spotted Redshank *Tringa erythropus*, Ruff and Black-winged Stilt *Himantopus himantopus*).

The most affected species are the two Arctic-breeding *Calidris* sandpipers, Little Stint and Curlew Sandpiper, which were formerly the most abundant winter visitors at Point Calimere. The reservoirs, inter-tidal zone and other brackish areas at Point Calimere provided enormous feeding areas for these species, with numbers of Little Stint in the 1980s exceeding 200 000 and those of Curlew Sandpiper, 150 000. During the last four years, however, neither of these species has been recorded in numbers exceeding 25 000. It appears that these two species formerly benefited from the shallow water levels in the reservoirs which carried many littoral organisms (crustaceans, polychaetes) into the environment. The plentiful rains also helped to increase the productivity of these habitats during the wet season. The extension of salt-based industries, the diminishing rainfall and disturbances caused by fishermen have now altered these habitats.

## Causes for the decline in wader populations at Point Calimere

### Poaching

There is intensive illegal hunting of Little Stints and Curlew Sandpipers by professional bird-trappers who depend on birds for their livelihood. These bird-trappers operate outside the sanctuary limits, and employ three traditional methods of trapping: clap-traps, mesh-nets (similar to gill-nets and operated at night) and nooses. The gregarious Little Stint and Curlew Sandpiper are particularly vulnerable to clap-traps, as they forage on mudflats with shallow water, i.e. in areas that are ideal for the use of this type of trap. It is interesting to note that in a single day in 1980, one clap-trap yielded 376 Little Stints for ringing. Similarly, 180 Curlew Sandpipers have been caught by this method in a single day.

The scale of the poaching was formerly huge. In the 1980s and 1990s, over 100 trappers were operating these highly effective traps throughout the migration season from August to March in the Muthupet and Adirampatinam areas outside the wildlife sanctuary. In recent times, however, the number of trappers involved in poaching has fallen, as trapping is no longer as productive as it was due to the fall in numbers of waders.

### Depletion of groundwater and saltwater intrusion

The extraction of groundwater has increased manifold in recent years to cater to the needs of the floating population of fisherfolk who are on the increase. Groundwater recharge is inadequate because of the consistently diminishing rainfall in the area over the last two decades.

The flushing and dilution of the highly saline water stored in the reservoirs, condensers and salt-pans have been hampered by embankments constructed in the swamp by chemical companies and other salt-works. Formerly, the incursion of seawater into large areas of the swamp caused by the strong summer winds not only made the swamp habitable for waterbirds during the summer months, but also helped to prevent the mudflats from drying out completely.

The saline incursion has made the area unsuitable for raising traditional crops such as paddy, while water in the freshwater wells is no longer potable. The hyper-saline conditions have not only altered the texture of the mudflats in the reservoirs, but have also affected the adjacent habitats for birds.

### Cessation of monitoring activities by the BNHS

The presence of a BNHS monitoring station at Point Calimere from 1979 to 1992 maintained a check on the activities of the salt-based chemical companies operating in the area. However, since the cessation of research activities by the BNHS at the end of 1992 due to a lack of funds, there has been little to restrain the chemical companies in their alteration of the habitat for commercial goals.

Ringing and bird censusing activities were resumed at Point Calimere in 1999, and since then, researchers have been present for 20-30 days each season. This has helped to monitor habitat changes in the area. During the migration season of 2003/04, following a relatively good monsoon, the chemical companies drained the water from the reservoirs to strengthen the earthen embankments. The continuing habitat changes have resulted in extensive compaction of the soft muddy substrate, making it less productive for the smaller organisms which form the bulk of the food resources for waders in the area. It is imperative, therefore, that in deciding the future of Great Vedaranyam Swamp, the greatest care be exercised in striking a balance between the commercial demands of the salt industry and the requirements of the migratory birds.

### Wader populations at other sites.

Large declines have also been observed in the numbers of many species of waders wintering at Pulicat Lake and in the Gulf of Mannar since the 1980s (Tables 3 & 4). The declines were most apparent in coastal waders, and those species preferring inland and brackish habitats, such as the Black-tailed Godwit and Ruff, were less affected (Table 3). In contrast, the numbers of waders at Chilika Lake have remained high (Table 5), and here there was an increasing trend during the three migration seasons between 2001 and 2004. The possible increase at Chilika may be due to a movement of birds away from Point Calimere and other sites in the south. However, the numbers of Little Stint, the most abundant wader on the east coast of India, have never exceeded 100 000 in recent years. This indicates that there has been a decline in the South Asian wintering population of this species, possibly because of the degradation of its key wintering site at Point Calimere.

## Table 3. Population estimates for common waders at Pulicat Lake, India.

| Species | 1988-89 | 1998-99 |
|---|---|---|
| *Himantopus himantopus* | >5 000 | 3 000 |
| *Recurvirostra avosetta* | >1 000 | >400 |
| *Charadrius mongolus* | >25 000 | >15 000 |
| *Limosa limosa* | >20 000 | >18 000 |
| *Calidris minuta* | >60 000 | >35 000 |
| *Calidris ferruginea* | >35 000 | >20 000 |
| *Philomachus pugnax* | >40 000 | 30 000 |

## Table 4. Population estimates for common waders in the Gulf of Mannar, India.

| Species | 1985-88 | 1993 | 2001 |
|---|---|---|---|
| *Dromas ardeola* | 900 | 150 | 65 |
| *Pluvialis squatarola* | 970 | 230 | 180 |
| *Charadrius mongolus* | >13 000 | >8 000 | >4 000 |
| *Numenius arquata* | 450 | 120 | 67 |
| *Tringa nebularia* | 250 | >3 500 | 180 |
| *Calidris tenuirostris* | 350 | 140 | 450 |
| *Calidris canutus* | 300 | 85 | 90 |
| *Calidris minuta* | >8 000 | >3 000 | >2 000 |
| *Calidris ferruginea* | >10 000 | >8 000 | >5 000 |

## Table 5. Peak counts of common waders at Chilika Lake, India (2001-2004).

| Species | Peak count |
|---|---|
| *Himantopus himantopus* | 5 000 |
| *Recurvirostra avosetta* | >500 |
| *Charadrius mongolus* | 56 000 |
| *Limosa limosa* | 55 000 |
| *Calidris minuta* | 24 000 |
| *Calidris ferruginea* | 54 000 |
| *Philomachus pugnax* | 10 000 |

## DISCUSSION

It is well known that many long-distance migrant waders are highly dependent on a series of key staging areas – essential "stepping stones" – between their wintering areas and more northerly breeding areas (see, for example, Stroud, and Baker, this volume). Up until the late 1980s, Point Calimere served both as a major wintering site for waders and as a key staging area for waders wintering elsewhere in India. This area now appears to be inhospitable for the bulk of the migratory wader populations because of anthropogenic pressures. The transit populations of waders en route to other wintering areas in autumn and their breeding areas in spring have disappeared. This is mainly due to the prevalence of dry and highly saline conditions during both autumn and spring as a result of intense industrial activities. Thus, the degradation of this crucial "stepping stone" for migrant waders has had a great impact on the biogeographical populations of the species dependent on it.

This is especially apparent in the drastic decline of the Curlew Sandpiper and Little Stint on the east coast of India. These species were never observed at any of the coastal wetlands of India in such huge concentrations as those observed at Point Calimere. The linkage between this coastal wetland and other major wader habitats both within India and abroad has been well established through ringing recoveries. Recoveries outside India involve not only other countries in the Central Asian/South Asian Flyway, but also countries in neighbouring flyways. Hence, the role of this wetland in maintaining the global populations of some wader species is unquestionable.

The occurrence of globally threatened waders, such as the Spoon-billed Sandpiper *Eurynorhynchus pygmeus*, Spotted Greenshank *Tringa guttifer* and Asian Dowitcher *Limnodromus semipalmatus*, at Point Calimere also emphasizes its global importance. Hence, there is an urgent need for more and better population monitoring. In the first instance, and as a minimum requirement, an adequately funded national monitoring programme needs to be established, to develop an internationally co-ordinated research initiative to discover more about the causes of the declines.

## RECOMMENDATIONS

1) A permanent bird migration study centre should be established in India to impart training on bird migration and related studies, and to strengthen collaboration with other countries in the Central Asian/South Asian Flyway and neighbouring flyways in the dissemination of knowledge on bird migration.

2) The monitoring of flyway populations in collaboration with other countries in the Central Asian/South Asian Flyway should be improved by strengthening and streamlining the mid-winter waterbird counts and through joint expeditions.

3) Species study groups should be formed for the species identified for further research under the Indo-Russian Protocol.

4) Further analyses of the status of waders in the Central Asian/South Asian Flyway should be carried out, using existing data and information, to highlight common patterns and processes in the declining populations.

### Recommendations relevant to Point Calimere

1) Dialogue should be initiated between the Wildlife Department, local communities, environmentalists and corporate bodies operating in the area, as a confidence building measure.

2) Areas of common concern and mutual benefit for industrial ventures, conservationists and other stakeholders should be identified, to reduce loss and modification of habitat as a result of commercial activities.

3) Detrimental practices, especially with regard to the salt/chemical industry, should be highlighted and appropriate mitigation measures elaborated after mutual consultation with such industries in the Great Vedaranyam Swamp.

4) A Joint Working Group comprising the stakeholders (Wildlife Department, local communities, corporate bodies and NGOs) and specialists should be set up to monitor modification of the habitat in the Great Vedaranyam Swamp. The

Joint Working Group would suggest and implement measures for the restoration of the swamp.

5) Restoration measures should be implemented in the known traditional wintering and passage sites for waders with the involvement of local communities and NGOs.

## ACKNOWLEDGEMENTS

I am grateful to Wetlands International for sponsoring my trip to Scotland to present this paper at the Waterbirds Around the World Conference. I would like to thank my colleagues, namely Mr V. Kannan, Mr P. Sthiyaselvam, Ms Vibhuti Dedhia, Dr Ranjit Manakadan, Mr Gopi Naidu and Ms Divya Fernandus, for assisting in the preparation of this paper.

## REFERENCES

**Ali, S.** 1980. Ecological Reconnaissance of Vedaranyam Swamp, Thanjavur District, Tamil Nadu. Report for the Bombay Natural History Society, Bombay.

**Ali, S.** 1981. Population Structure and Movement of Indian Avifauna. Annual Report I (1980-81). Bombay Natural History Society, Bombay.

**Balachandran, S.** 1990. Studies on coastal birds of Mandapam and neighbouring islands, Peninsular India. PhD thesis, Annamalai University, Annamalai Nagar, India.

**Balachandran, S.** 1995. Shorebirds of the Gulf of Mannar Marine National Park, Tamil Nadu. Journal of the Bombay Natural History Society 92(3): 303-313.

**Balachandran, S.** 1998. Bird Migration Studies in India. Final Report (1980-1992). Phase I: Population Structure and Movement of Indian Avifauna (1980-1986). Final Report. Phase II: Bird Migration (1987-1992). Final Report. Bombay Natural History Society, Mumbai.

**Daniel, J.C. & Balachandran, S.** 2003. Bird Banders' Training Programme. Final Report (1998-2002). Bombay Natural History Society, Mumbai.

**Hussain, S.A.** 1991. Population Structure and Movement of Indian Avifauna. Bird Migration. Annual Report I (1990-91). Bombay Natural History Society, Bombay.

**Manakadan, R.** 1992. Ecology of waterbirds of Point Calimere Wildlife Sanctuary with special reference to impact of saltworks. Unpublished thesis, University of Bombay, India.

Ruddy Turnstone *Arenaria interpres*. Photo: Rob Robinson.

# Important Bird Areas in western India

*Aeshita Mukherjee[1] & Burkhard Wilske[2]*
[1] *AINP on Applied Ornithology, Gujarat Agricultural University, Anand, India. (email: aeshitam@rediffmail.com)*
[2] *Max Planck Institute of Chemistry, Mainz, Germany.*

Mukherjee, A. & Wilske, B. 2006. Important Bird Areas in western India. *Waterbirds around the world.* Eds. G.C. Boere, C.A. Galbraith & D.A. Stroud. The Stationery Office, Edinburgh, UK. p. 302.

This paper briefly discusses recent population estimates of some wetland bird species in some potential Important Bird Areas (IBA) in the state of Gujerat in western India.

The Important Bird Areas Programme (IBA) of Bird Life International identifies sites of international significance for bird conservation. They are part of a wider, integrated approach to conservation that embraces site, species and habitat protection and will be used to reinforce and existing protected areas network. The IBA Programme aims to gather and disseminate information on key bird species and sites through the active participation in conservation of communities living in and around IBAs.

Over 1 200 bird species across the world are currently under threat of extinction, which is about 12% of the world's bird species. In India, 78 bird species are globally threatened, and to address this, the Indian IBA Programme was launched by the Bombay Natural History Society in March 1999. One of the major aims is to identify and protect IBAs throughout the country using a set of standard global criteria.

Work has been carried out in western India in the state of Gujarat, which has an arid to semiarid climate. There, canal-linked reservoirs play an important role in sustaining both human and bird life, including a large number of migrant waterfowl. These are adapted to wetlands, but they occupy the ecosystems that are highly productive and dynamic with abundant resources available. These migratory movements may be non-stop or may include some stopover point between the wintering and breeding areas, depending on the habitat conditions and the flyways being followed. The Saurashtra Region of Gujarat is a paradise for the wintering cranes, particularly the Demoiselle Crane *Grus virgo* and the Common Crane *Grus grus*. The present study started by focusing on the estimation of the size of crane populations and identification of internationally important sites. Both site specific and broad based strategies were then suggested for future management, including designation as Ramsar sites.

We recorded about 65 000 Demoiselle Cranes, with the largest concentration being 39 080 at Ghee Dam, Jamnagar. Shian Dam, 20 km from Ghee Dam, supported more than 10 000 Demoiselle Cranes and 3 500 Common Cranes (Mukherjee & Parasharya 1999). At the Charakla Salt Farm, Jamnagar, we recorded more than 200 Black-necked Grebes *Podiceps nigricollis*. This species is an uncommon winter visitor and this record was the largest number ever recorded in India (Parasharya & Mukherjee 1998).

At Porbander, a coastal town of Gujarat, we recorded White-cheeked Terns *Sterna repressa* (35), White-winged Black Terns, *Chlidonias leucopterus* (3) and Little Terns, *Sterna albifrons* (2). These three species are uncommon to this area. Additional records of the Slender-billed Gull *Larus genei* from the Gujarat coast also add to the importance of the area (Parasharya *et al.* 2000, Parasharya & Mukherjee 2001).

## REFERENCES

**Mukherjee, A. & Parasharya, B.M.** 1999. Concentration of wintering cranes in Saurashtra. Pavo 37: 81-84.

**Parasharya, B.M., Mathew, K.L. & Mukherjee A.** 2000. Additional site record of Slender-billed Gull *Larus genei* from Gujarat coast. Journal of the Bombay Natural History Society 97: 279-280.

**Parasharya, B.M. & Mukherjee, A.** 1998. A record number of Black-necked Grebe *Podiceps nigricollis* from Gujarat. Journal of the Bombay Natural History Society 95: 335-336.

**Parasharya, B.M. & Mukherjee, A.** 2001. Sighting of White-winged Black Tern *Chlidonias leucopterus* and Black-shafted Tern *Sterna saundersi* at Porbander coast, Gujarat. Journal of the Bombay Natural History Society 98: 113-114.

Sites supporting Demoiselle Cranes *Grus virgo* in the Saurashtra region of Gujarat qualify as Ramsar sites. Photo: Sergey Dereliev.

# Importance of wetlands for conservation of bird life in the dry lands of western India

*Aeshita Mukherjee[1] & Burkhard Wilske[2]*

[1] *AINP on Applied Ornithology, Gujarat Agricultural University, Anand, India. (email: aeshitam@rediffmail.com)*
[2] *Max Planck Institute of Chemistry, Mainz, Germany.*

Mukherjee, A. & Wilske, B. 2006. Importance of wetlands for conservation of bird life in the dry lands of western India. *Waterbirds around the world.* Eds. G.C. Boere, C.A. Galbraith & D.A. Stroud. The Stationery Office, Edinburgh, UK. pp. 303-304.

This study discusses the habitat requirement of the waterfowl population in canal-linked reservoirs of Kheda District, Gujarat, India. We also attempted to identify factors that contribute to the attraction of waterfowl to these reservoirs and to suggest management and planning strategies for maintaining waterfowl in environments supporting high human population densities.

The need for maintaining and enhancing urban and suburban populations of wildlife has greatly increased in recent decades (Washington 1978), but planning for wildlife in urban areas is often stifled by inadequate support from resource agencies and lack of awareness and expertise in wildlife matters by urban planners (Davey 1967, Geis 1980). The solution to this dilemma is either to encourage greater collaboration between wildlife regulatory agencies and municipal planners or, as discussed in this paper, to familiarize the planners with the wildlife resources through literature relevant to both the disciplines (Greer 1983).

Canal-linked reservoirs play an important role in sustaining both human and bird life in the dry lands of India. The population of waterfowl at artificial wetlands, mainly reservoirs and canals, was studied in Gujarat, western India, from 1988 to 2000. Observations were made in January each year from 1998 to 2000 at three reservoir study sites when the migratory waterfowl population was greatest: 112 waterbird species were observed. Habitat size and complexity were important factors influencing the species diversity, while factors contributing to waterbird presence included abundant food supply and safe roosting sites. In addition to reservoirs, flooded set-aside farmlands were of immense importance to more than 30 000 waterbirds of 66 species, suggesting that fallow inundated fields serve as a key supplementary habitat for the waterbirds, especially during the dry period. Both site specific and broad based strategies are suggested for future management.

Narda Reservoir is a 57 ha storage reservoir designed for irrigation purposes with a discharge which averages 65 cfs. The water quality is good and is used for fisheries. In summer, the reservoir becomes shallow and overgrown with aquatic vegetation. The surrounding area is agricultural landscape and the main crop grown is paddy rice *Oryza sativa.*

Pariej Reservoir is a 445 ha perennial water storage reservoir for the district, fulfilling the drinking water requirement of the surrounding 52 villages. The surrounding area is mostly saline and as a result no crops are grown. Due to water seepage from the reservoir, the whole area is waterlogged and behaves as a permanent marsh with a heavy growth of the reed *Typha angustata* and other aquatic vegetation. Commercial fishing is practiced in this reservoir.

Kanewal Reservoir, with an area of 625 ha, is the largest reservoir in the district. The land surrounding the reservoir is salt affected and remains dry during summer. During the monsoon, the whole area is inundated and migratory waterfowl enjoy a temporary wetland. The reservoir provides drinking water to 57 villages, and there is occasional fishing.

Waterfowl counts were made in alternate weeks in January from 1988 to 2000. Plant composition and vegetation cover for the entire study area was also recorded using the quadrat (1 m x m) method.

Paddy rice and wheat are the principal cultivated crops in the district. Undisturbed vegetation was found mostly on the banks of reservoirs. A total of 19 plant species were found around Narda Reservoir, predominantly *Echinocloa colonum. Cyperus rotundus* was dominant around Pariej Reservoir. *Typha angustata* was the next most abundant and provided breeding grounds for three species of bittern. At Kanewal Reservoir, *Najas gramina* was most abundant, followed by *Typha angustata.*

Observations at the three sites showed that the waterfowl initiated their activity in early morning about 30 min before sunrise. Most of the activities (foraging, preening, swimming and feeding) ceased within 15 min after initiation. The movements of the birds were a function of their feeding preference. Morning counts were best because they included all birds utilizing the reservoir, and there was little human disturbance.

At Narda Reservoir, the waterfowl were attracted due to shallow aquatic vegetation, specially *Cyperus* species. Migratory waterfowl arrived by October and diversity increased significantly to between 12-36 species over the winter months. The density of ducks ranged between 0.2–15.4 per ha, and for other waterbird species was 1.7–78.2 per ha. Coots *Fulica atra* were the most abundant species. Ducks were mostly found feeding in the adjacent paddy fields because these provided secure food supplies and a relatively fixed water depth (less than 1 m).

Pariej Reservoir had a comparatively higher diversity than Kanewal and Narda, with between 36 and 85 species. The Dalmatian Pelican *Pelecanus crispus* was attracted to this reservoir due to its abundant fish supply. However, coots were dominant all year. Gadwall *Anas strepera*, Northern Shoveler *Anas clypeata*, Northern Pintail *Anas acuta*, Eurasian Wigeon *Anas penelope* were also common and regularly observed; the density of ducks ranged from 0.3–9.0 individuals per ha and other waterbirds between 9.6–59.1 per ha. The reservoir is a potential breeding site for Great-crested Grebe *Podiceps cristatus.*

Kanewal Reservoir, having short grass and emergent vegetation, attracted many migratory waterfowl, with densities of 1.0–9.0 individuals per ha. Ducks congregated mostly to feed on tubers of *Najas minor.* The number of species varied from 26 to 95 because this is the only water body in the area, and is shallow with abundant food. The density of other waterbirds was 20.0–64.0 individuals per ha. Dalmatian Pelicans, Red-crested

Pochards *Netta ruffina* and Demoiselle Cranes *Grus virgo* were regularly attracted to the reservoir.

Each site differed with respect to size and habitat complexity. These interrelationships suggest that for feeding, several distinct locations with different habitat qualities are needed. The study also suggested that these reservoirs are not totally dependent on each other but acted as independent micro-habitats in the sustenance of migratory waterfowl.

In conclusion, the following action is required:

- Familiarize land managers and planners with wildlife resources in the biologically managed environment.
- Elucidate the habitat requirements of waterfowl populations using reservoirs and adjacent areas.

- Attempt to focus the factors influencing waterfowl attraction to these reservoirs and possible ways to manage them.

## REFERENCES

Davey, S.P. 1967. The role of wildlife in an urban environment. Transactions of North American Wildlife Natural Resources Conference 32: 50-60.

Geis, A.D. 1980. Elements of urban wildlife program. The Wildlifer 180.

Greer, D.M. 1983. Urban waterfowl population. Ecological evaluation of management and planning. Environmental Management 6: 217-229.

Washington, T. 1978. Wildlife and urban connection. Colorado Outdoors 27: 38-42.

Significant numbers of Red-crested Pochards *Netta ruffina* are regularly attracted to Kanewal Reservoir. Photo: N. Zbinden.

# Status of migratory shorebirds at Bhitarkanika and Chilika wetlands on the east coast of India

*Anup Kumar Nayak*

*Wildlife Warden, Bhitarkanika; 1865/1866, Nuasahi Nayapalli (near Post Office), Bhubaneswar-751012, Orissa, India.*
*(email: bravo_123@sancharnet.in)*

Nayak, A.K. 2006. Status of migratory shorebirds at Bhitarkanika and Chilika wetlands on the east coast of India. *Waterbirds around the world*. Eds. G.C. Boere, C.A. Galbraith & D.A. Stroud. The Stationery Office, Edinburgh, UK. pp. 305-307.

This paper describes the status of migratory shorebirds at Bhitarkanika wetland based on counts conducted in July 2002-2003 and Chilika wetlands based on counts made in January 2001, 2002 and 2003.

Bhitarkanika wetland extends to over 672 sq km in the north eastern part of Orissa State on the east coast of India and is the second most viable mangrove eco system in India after Sundarban. Bhitarkanika was declared a Wildlife Sanctuary in 1975 and a Ramsar site in 2002, but has been little studied. The Sanctuary area is divided into seven areas: Raipatia, Jaudia, Satabhaya, Barunei mouth and chataka, Udabali Island, Babubali Island and sand bars, mudflats along Bhitarkanika and Maipura rivers and Dangmal and Bhitarkanika meadows.

Visits were made twice a month during July 2002 to July 2003 by observers in boats or vehicles, and all shore birds sighted were listed. A total of 37 species of shorebirds and seven other important species were identified during the 13 months of observation.

A small number of over-summering shore birds were observed up to June 2003. Golden Plover *Pluvialis fulva* and Terek Sandpiper *Xenus cinereus* were present all year except for June and July. Whimbrel *Numenius phaeopus* were sighted most of the year, and may be breeding somewhere within Bhitarkanika. Early migrants included Great Knots *Calidris tenuirostris* which were seen in flocks of about 500 during

August to December, and Ruff *Philomachus pugnax* were found in large numbers as early as October 2002, indicating they were heading south.

Chilika is the largest brackish water lagoon in India, and is situated along the east coast of Orissa. Surveys were carried out on 12th and 13th of January 2001, 2002 and 2003 by boat. Results are given in the Table 2.

The presence of rare shorebird species like the Spoon-billed Sandpiper *Eurynorhynchus pygmeus*, Asian Dowitcher *Limnodromus semipalmatus* and Broad-billed Sandpiper *Limicola falcinellus* in Chilika wetland emphasizes the importance of this wetland along the east coast of India. The Bombay Natural History Society (BNHS) has recommended that the Bhusandpur and Tinimuhan areas of about 60 sq km be declared as a new bird sanctuary in addition to the existing sanctuary at Nalaban island. Large numbers of Fulvous Whistling Duck *Dendrocygna bicolor*, Lesser Whistling Duck *Dendrocygna javanica* and Cotton Teal *Nettapus coromandelianus* and other migratory birds support such an action.

The threats faced by the Chilika lagoon are due to siltation, shrinkage of the area, choking of the inlet channel, proliferation of invasive fresh water species like Water Hyacinth *Eichornia crassipes*, increased aquaculture activities, eutrophication and nest trampling by buffaloes.

Common Sandpiper *Actitis hypoleucos* occur frequently at Chilika Lake. Photo: Paul Marshall.

**Table 1. Shorebirds sighted at Bhitarkanika July 2002-July 2003.**

| name | | Max. number counted at a site on a trip | Habitat |
|---|---|---|---|
| Oystercatcher | *Haematopus ostralegus* | 10 | Udabali |
| Avocet | *Recurvirostra avosetta* | 80 | Satabhaya |
| Black-winged Stilt | *Himantopus himantopus* | 58 | Satabhaya |
| Collared Pratincole | *Glareola pratincola* | 500 | Jaudia |
| Red-wattled Lapwing | *Vanellus indicus* | 53 | Jaudia |
| Yellow-wattled Lapwing | *V. malabaricus* | 10 | Jaudia |
| Grey-headed Lapwing | *V. cinereus* | 38 | Satabhaya |
| Great Knot | *Calidris tenuirostris* | 500 | Gupti |
| Grey Plover | *Pluvialis squatarola* | 5 | Mudflat |
| Long-billed Plover | *Charadrius placidus* | 10 | Raipatia |
| Little Ringed Plover | *C. dubius* | 8 | Raipatia |
| Pacific Golden Plover | *Pluvialis fulva* | 200 | Jaudia |
| Kentish Plover | *C. alexandrinus* | | Raipatia |
| Lesser Sand Plover | *C. mongolus* | 2 000 | Goja island |
| Indian Skimmer | *Rynchops albicollis* | 70 | Barunei mouth |
| Black-tailed Godwit | *Limosa limosa* | 5 000 | Raipatia |
| Whimbrel | *Numenius phaeopus* | 50 | Mudflat |
| Eurasian Curlew | *N. arquata* | 20 | Babubali island |
| Spotted Redshank | *Tringa erythropus* | 4 | Satabhaya |
| Common Redshank | *T. totanus* | 50 | Raipatia |
| Common Greenshank | *T. nebularia* | 10 | Satabhaya |
| Spotted Greenshank | *T. guttifer* | 2 | Stabhaya |
| Marsh Sandpiper | *T. stagnatilis* | 10 | Raipatia |
| Green Sandpiper | *T. ochropus* | 5 | Raipatia |
| Wood Sandpiper | *T. glareola* | 10 | Raipatia |
| Common Sandpiper | *Actitis hypoleucos* | 10 | Mudflat |
| Terek Sandpiper | *Xenus cinereus* | 22 | Mudflat |
| Ruddy Turnstone | *Arenaria interpres* | 5 | Chataka |
| Pintail Snipe | *Gallinago stenura* | 2 | Dangmal |
| Jack Snipe | *Lymnocryptes minimus* | 2 | Dangmal |
| Little Stint | *Calidris minuta* | 2 000 | Raipatia |
| Temminck's Stint | *C. temminckii* | 10 | Raipatia |
| Long-toed Stint | *C. subminuta* | 5 | Raipatia |
| Dunlin | *C. alpina* | 10 | Raipatia |
| Curlew Sandpiper | *C. ferruginia* | 200 | Raipatia |
| Ruff | *Philomachus pugnax* | 50 | Raipatia |
| Greater Painted Snipe | *Rostratula benghalensis* | 2 | Dangmal |
| Common Snipe | *Gallinago gallinago* | 5 | Dangmal |
| Lesser-crested Tern | *Sterna bengalensis* | 50 | Chataka |
| Great-crested Tern | *Sterna bergii* | 5 | Chataka |
| Eurasian Spoonbill | *Platalea leucorodia* | 10 | Goja island |
| Black-necked Stork | *Ephippiorhynchus asiaticus* | 1 | Dangmal |
| Lesser Adjutant | *Leptoptilos javanicus* | 10 | Mahisamada |
| Gray Pelican | *Pelecanus philippensis* | 13 | Dangmal |

**Table 2. Survey data for birds in Chilika lake.**

| Name | | 2001 | 2002 | 2003 |
|---|---|---|---|---|
| Greater Painted Snipe | *Rostratula benghalensis* | - | 26 | 2 |
| Avocet | *Recurvirostra avosetta* | 6 | 218 | - |
| Black-winged Stilt | *Himantopus himantopus* | 2 924 | 2 957 | 2 131 |
| Little Pranticole | *Glareola lactea* | 1 556 | 704 | |
| Red-wattled Lapwing | *Vanellus indicus* | 114 | 75 | 53 |
| Yellow-wattled Lapwing | *V. malabaricus* | 4 | 40 | 4 |
| Grey-headed Lapwing | *V. cinereus* | - | - | 257 |
| Grey Plover | *Plurialis squatarola* | 23 | 516 | 11 |
| Long-billed Plover | *Charadrius placidus* | 25 | 42 | - |
| Little Ringed Plover | *C. dubius* | 325 | 260 | 569 |
| Pacific Golden Plover | *Pluvialis fulva* | 1 886 | 1 536 | 427 |
| European Golden Plover | *Pluvialis apricaria* | 6 | 50 | 53 |
| Kentish Plover | *C. alexandrinus* | 1 273 | 1 577 | 73 |
| Lesser Sand Plover | *C. mongolus* | 13 306 | 15 330 | 5 760 |
| Greater Sand Plover | *C. leschenaultii* | 25 | 20 | 19 |
| Black-tailed Godwit | *Limosa limosa* | 14 071 | 57 963 | 9 279 |
| Bar-tailed Godwit | *L. lapponica* | 225 | 54 | 41 |
| Whimbrel | *Numenius phaeopus* | 1 301 | 22 | 22 |
| Eurasian Curlew | *N. arquata* | 516 | 2052 | 40 |
| Spotted Redshank | *Tringa erythropus* | 65 | 80 | 12 |
| Common Redshank | *T. totanus* | 2 082 | 1 119 | 333 |
| Common Greenshank | *T. nebularia* | 82 | 73 | 60 |
| Spotted Greenshank | *T. guttifer* | - | 12 | - |
| Marsh sandpiper | *T. stagnatilis* | 8 168 | 4 047 | 1 870 |
| Green Sandpiper | *T. ochropus* | 80 | 21 | 23 |
| Wood Sandpiper | *T. glareola* | 2 538 | 1 459 | 3 427 |
| Common Sandpiper | *Actitis hypoleucos* | 4 582 | 1 677 | 588 |
| Terek Sandpiper | *Xenus cinereus* | 46 | - | - |
| Ruddy Turnstone | *Arenaria interpres* | - | 130 | 1 |
| Common Snipe | *Gallinago gallinago* | 257 | 266 | 329 |
| Pintail Snipe | *Gallinago stenura* | - | 7 | - |
| Jack Snipe | *Lymnocryptes minimus* | 15 | 49 | 14 |
| Sanderling | *Calidris alba* | 4 | - | — |
| Little Stint | *C. minuta* | 8 952 | 9 140 | 5 366 |
| Temminck's Stint | *C. temminckii* | 510 | 34 | 82 |
| Long-toed Stint | *C. subminuta* | 4 | 3 | 16 |
| Dunlin | *C. alpina* | 266 | 292 | 473 |
| Curlew Sandpiper | *C. ferruginea* | 1 366 | 9 928 | 2 676 |
| Spoonbilled Sandpiper | *Eurynorhynchus pygmeus* | 2 | 1 | 6 |
| Ruff | *Philomachus pugnax* | 1 | 1 536 | 659 |
| Asian Dowitcher | *Limmodromus semipalmatus* | 2 | 4 | - |
| Broadbilled Sandpiper | *Limicola falcinellus* | 2 | 4 | 2 |
| Red Knot | *Calidris canutus* | - | - | 6 |
| Great Knot | *Calidris tenuirostris* | - | - | 6 |
| **Total species** | | **38** | **39** | **34** |

# Residential, population and conservation status of Indian wetland birds

*Arun Kumar, P.C. Tak & J.P. Sati*
*Zoological Survey of India, Dehra Dun- 248 195 (Uttaranchal), India.*

Kumar, A., Tak, P.C. & Sati, J.P. 2006. Residential, population and conservation status of Indian wetland birds. *Waterbirds around the world.* Eds. G.C. Boere, C.A. Galbraith & D.A. Stroud. The Stationery Office, Edinburgh, UK. p. 308.

Wetland birds play a significant cultural and social role in local communities as well as being an important component of wetland ecosystem. Increasing attention to the conservation of wetlands in India has resulted in extensive research; this paper assesses the current status of 310 Indian wetland birds (Kumar *et al.* in press) with the emphasis on threatened species.

Out of 310 Indian wetland species 130 (c. 42%) are migrant, 173 resident, however the status is unknown for seven species. Of the migrants, 107 are winter migrants, six have some passage population(s), 13 are summer migrants, and the remaining four are purely passage migrants. Of the 173 resident species, 53 are completely resident, 38 are part resident and part winter migrant, and 50 undertake local movements chiefly depending on water conditions. In terms of abundance, Indian wetland birds can be categorized as Very Common (four species), Common (26), Locally Common (115), Un-Common (45), Rare (67), Very Rare (five), Vagrant (47) and Probably Extinct (one).

Wetland drainage and conversion is the major threat for Asian waterbirds, including the infilling (or 'reclamation') of intertidal coastal wetlands, principally for agriculture and aquaculture. The most recently published checklist was the "Threatened Birds of Asia: the BirdLife International Red Data Book (2001)", followed by "Saving Asia's Threatened Birds: A Guide for Government and Civil Society (2003)".

The Waterbird Population Estimates Third edition by Wetlands International (2002) lists 2 271 biogeographical populations of 868 species. The largest number of waterbird populations (697) is found in Asia, followed by Africa (611) and the Neotropics (540). Out of 310 Indian wetland birds, seven species are endemic, three fall in to the Restricted Range Species category and one comes under data deficient category; 11 are Biome-Restricted Species of which five species are from Eurasian High Mountain (Biome 05), three from Sino-Himalayan Subtropical Forest (Biome 08), one from Indo-Chinese Tropical Moist Forest (Biome 09), and two from Indo-Malayan Tropical Dry Zone (Biome 11) (Jhunjhunwala *et al.* 2001).

Regarding distribution and status, 51 species occur in wetlands, six in forests, five in grasslands, and one is a seabird. Of the 51 wetland species, five are found in wetlands of Tibetan Plateau (W09), 15 in North Indian Wetlands (W12), five in South Indian and Sri Lankan Wetlands (W13), 16 in Assam and Sylhet Plains (W14), and 10 in Bay of Bengal Coast (W15); of six forest dwelling species, one occur in Sino-Himalayan Mountain Forests (F04), two in Indian Peninsula and Sri Lankan Forests (F05), and three in Indo-Burmese Forests. Of the five grassland species, four are found in Indo-Gangetic Grassland (G02) and one in South Asian Arid Habitats (G03). Only one species is a seabird (S01).

Altogether 23 species are listed under the Convention on International Trade in Endangered Species of Wild Fauna and Flora (CITES 2002). A total of 51 species come under the Convention on Migratory Species (CMS); 21 are listed under Schedule-I and 231 under Schedule-IV of the Wildlife (Protection) Act, 1972 (WL(P) Act).

Approximately 12% of Asian birds are globally threatened with extinction. Many species are edging close to extinction through disturbance or habitat loss as well as intensive hunting pressure. An analysis of threatened wetland birds indicates that of a total of 242 species, 82 species are in Asia and 39 in India. Of the 310 wetland bird species in India, 51 (ca. 16%) are Threatened of which 34 are Globally Threatened (four Critical, seven Endangered, 23 Vulnerable); 16 Near Threatened (NT) and one Data Deficient (DD). Of the 51 Threatened species, 39 show a declining population trend, while three are increasing, five are stable, and the trends of three species are indeterminate. The remaining one species, Pink-headed Duck *Rhodonessa caryophyllacea* globally threatened, has probably disappeared from India.

Of the 34 globally threatened species, only 16 are listed under CITES (11 in Appendix I and five in Appendix II), while the others are not listed in CITES Appendices, thus imposing no restriction on their trade. Eight of the 34 species are listed under Schedule-I of the WL (P) Act, while 22 are relegated to Schedule-IV; two species, Masked Finfoot, *Heliornis fulica* and Indian Skimmer, *Rynchops albicollis* (with an estimated total population for the South Asian region of 5 000 birds each), are not included under the WL (P) Act at all. Similarly, two of the most highly threatened Indian Waterbirds, Sarus Crane *Grus antigone* and Black-necked Stork *Ephippiorhynchus asiaticus*, are again listed under Schedule-IV with threshold populations of 90 and four respectively.

A broad range of national policies on forestry, agriculture, wetlands and fisheries can have significant impacts on biodiversity conservation. By ensuring that policies and laws at local, provincial and national levels also take into account the principle of conservation, threats to species can be minimized.

## REFERENCES

**BirdLife International** 2001. Threatened Birds of Asia. The BirdLife International Red Data Book. Cambridge, UK: BirdLife International. 3 026 pp.

**BirdLife International** 2003. Saving Asia's threatened birds: a guide for government and civil society. Cambridge, U.K.: BirdLife International. 246 pp.

**Jhunjhunwala, S., Rahmani, A.R., Ishtiaq, F. & Islam, Z.** 2001. The Important Bird Areas Programme in India. Buceros 6(2): 1-50.

**Kumar, A. Sati, J.P., Tak, P.C. & Alfred, J.R.B.** in press. Handbook on Indian Wetland Birds and their conservation. Rec. Zool. Surv. India, (Published - Director, Zoological Survey of India, Kolkata 700 020).

**Wetlands International** 2002. Waterbird Population Estimates-Third edition, Wetlands International Global Series No. 12. Wageningen, The Netherlands.

# Protection of habitat of Sarus Crane *Grus antigone* in the Bhoj wetland, India

*Pradip Kumar Nandi*

*Lake Conservation Authority of Madhya Pradesh, Paryavaran Parisar, E-5, Arera Colony, Bhopal - 452016, India.*
*(email: nandipk56@rediffmail.com)*

Nandi, P.K. 2006. Protection of habitat of Sarus Crane *Grus antigone* in Bhoj wetland, India. *Waterbirds around the world.* Eds. G.C. Boere, C.A. Galbraith & D.A. Stroud. The Stationery Office, Edinburgh, UK. pp. 309-310.

The Bhoj wetland is comprised of upper and lower lakes, and was declared as a Ramsar site in 2002. The southern part is the preferred site for all birds including the Sarus Crane. More than 160 Sarus Cranes (>1% of the reported total population in India) have been counted here, and the wetland has been identified as an IBA. The current population status of the Sarus Crane is described in this note.

In Asia, out of 2 700 bird species, 323 are reportedly threatened due to habitat degradation; in India alone, 130 species are of conservation concern. About 20% of those species are reportedly threatened due to degradation of wetland habitat. The Sarus Crane *Grus antigone,* the world's tallest flying bird (Archibald *et al.* 2003), is the only resident breeding Crane in India and Southeast Asia, has suffered a rapid population decline within a few decades (Choudhury *et al.* 1999). The current range of the Indian Sarus Crane includes the plains of northern, north-western, and western India and the western half of Nepal's Tarai lowlands. Gole (1989) estimated <13 000 Sarus Cranes in its entire distribution range in India. Degradation of wetland habitats, poaching, nest destruction, changes in agricultural practices and conflict with farmers in the catchment of the wetlands have been the main factors behind this decline, which seems likely to continue unless appropriate protection measures are taken (Gole 1989, Meine & Archibald 1996, Kaur & Choudhury 2003).

The Upper lake in Bhopal is the oldest large man-made lake in India and is now an part of an important wetland. It has a submergence area of about 36 sq km at full tank level and a catchment area of 361 sq km spread over two districts, Bhopal and Sehore. Sixty percent of the catchment area of the lake is predominantly agricultural. The lake has been subjected to pollution due to discharge of untreated sewage and runoff carrying silt and agricultural chemicals. Various preventive and curative measures including fringe area plantation over about 1 000 ha land were undertaken under an integrated conservation and management plan.

No systematic study of the avian fauna was conducted until March 2000-September 2001; one of the objectives was to record the population and spatial distribution of Sarus Cranes within different areas of the Upper lake.

The study area was divided into three zones based on the topography, pattern of land use and levels of anthropogenic interventions. The eastern and northeastern zones have water up to 9 m; the area is highly disturbed and is used extensively for water related recreational activities. A 5 ha forest cushions the southeastern zone with a protected zone: encompassing about 5 km of the total 56 km periphery of the lake, this area sports the richest biodiversity. Since there is little impact from human habitation, most nesting birds including the Sarus Crane were observed here.

The third section comprises of the western and southwestern zones of the lake. This zone is studded sporadically by rural

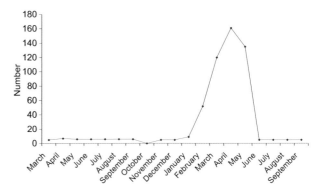

Fig. 1. Monthly variation in the population of Sarus Cranes in the southwestern zone of Upper lake during 2000-01.

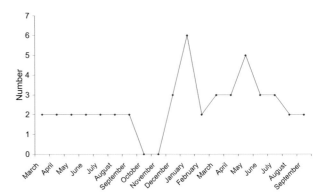

Fig. 2. Monthly variation in population of Sarus Cranes in the southeastern zone of Upper lake during 2000-01.

settlements, a number of which are located within 2-3 km of the full tank level of the lake, with extensive fallow land and recent patches of buffer zone plantation created by the Capital Project (Forest Division) Bhopal during 1989-2004 under the conservation and management plan. The key feature of this zone is its low depth of water, low direct human disturbance and less pollutant influx due to restricted urbanization.

Direct total counts were done from widely spread out fixed vantage points. Since the Sarus Crane is a huge bird and visible from a distance, we presume our counts are accurate as only a very small proportion of the lake periphery (<10%) within the selected zones (South East, South West and West) was unapproachable. Bi-hourly counts from 0600-1800 hrs four times a month, during the four-month period of significant population change, and once in a month for other period of the study, were conducted. The highest of these counts were finally termed as the minimum monthly populations of the species.

In 2000, the Sarus Crane population in the southwest to western zone was found to be fewer than 10. However, during February to May of 2001, it showed a dramatic increase, with a peak of 161 in the month of April (Fig. 1). No such change was observed in the south–eastern zone, where the observed population was fewer than 10 during the entire period of the study (Fig. 2).

One breeding pair of Sarus Cranes was observed and monitored in the south western region where they had made a nest on a mound created while work for deepening and widening of the spill channel was undertaken. This nest was seen first in November 2000, and the family of three monitored to the end of the study in September 2001.

During the study period, mechanized removal of silt from the southern part of the lake was in progress, but the noise and dust did not appear to deter Sarus Cranes from foraging within 50 m of the machines.

Sarus Cranes are mostly non-migratory in India, but often make short seasonal movements between dry and wet season habitats. Indian Sarus Cranes have adapted to the dense human population, and interact closely with people in areas where traditions of tolerance prevail. Their optimal habitat includes a combination of small seasonal marshes, floodplains, high altitude wetlands, human-altered ponds, fallow and cultivated lands, and rice paddy. Often they focus their foraging on underground tubers of native wetland vegetation such as *Eleocharis* spp. Breeding pairs nest in a wide variety of natural wetlands, along canals and irrigation ditches, beside village ponds and in rice paddies. More than other Crane species, Sarus Cranes also utilize wetlands in open forests as well as open grasslands. Where possible, nests are located in shallow water where short emergent vegetation is dominant, and the use of human-dominated wetlands is common in India. In this case, the fringe area plantation may have been a positive factor in the Sarus Crane favouring the Upper lake.

Absence of the Sarus Crane in the north and north east zones of the Upper lake indicates a dislike of the high level of human disturbance and the lack of contiguity of usable habitat. A dramatic increase in population of Sarus Cranes in summer of 2001 could be attributed to the shrinkage of wetland habitat in and around Bhopal due to a poor rains in consecutive years. This phenomenon may assume greater importance and calls for appropriate protection measures for the habitat around the Upper lake.

The future of the Indian Sarus Crane is closely tied to the quality of small wetlands in India that experience heavy human use and suffer from high rates of sewage inflow, extensive agricultural runoff, high levels of pesticide residues, and intensification of agricultural systems. The magnitude of the decline in Sarus Crane population is such that it has been categorized as a threatened species, and there are proposals to move the species from the schedule IV to schedule I of the Wildlife Protection Act (1972, amended in 1991) and take some special measures for its

Sarus Crane *Grus antigone.* Photo: P.K. Nandi.

conservation. In the case of the Upper lake, the following initiatives may be taken:

- Declaration of the entire buffer zone plantation area around Upper lake and the shallow part of the lake as a conservation area.
- Public Awareness Programmes: Citizens of Bhopal and the adjoining villages need to be encouraged to take part in the conservation programme.
- Creation of Sarus Watch groups: under the guidance of wild life experts, students may be encouraged to form voluntary groups who will monitor the Sarus Crane population through out the year and help villagers understand the need to protect this bird.
- Encourage commercial companies to help protect vulnerable species and their habitat as part of their social responsibility: Infrastructure development due to the lake conservation plan implementation has encouraged tourism, and the Capital Project (Forest Division) is also encouraging eco-tourism.

## REFERENCES

Archibald G.W., Sunder, K.S.G. & Barzen, J. 2003. A review of three species of Sarus Crane *Grus antigone*. Journal of Ecological Society. 16: 5-15.

Choudhury, B.C., Kaur, J. & Sunder, K.S.G. 1999. Sarus Crane count, Wildlife Institute of India.

Gole, P. 1989. The Status and Ecological Requirements of Sarus Crane. Phase I. Ecological Society, Pune, India. 45 pp.

Kaur, J. & Choudhury, B.C. 2003. Stealing of Sarus Crane eggs. Current Science, 85(11): 1515-16.

Meine, C.D. & Archibald, G.W. (eds) 1996. The Cranes:- Status Survey and Conservation Action Plan. IUCN, Gland, Switzerland and Cambridge, UK. 249 pp.

# Nesting sites and breeding success of Black-necked Crane *Grus nigricollis* in Ladakh, India

*Pankaj Chandan[1], Parikshit Gautam & Archana Chatterjee*

[1]*Senior Project Officer, WWF-India, Field Office, Hemis Complex, Zangsti Road, Leh - 194101, Ladakh, India.*
*(email: pchandan@wwfindia.net)*

Chandan, P., Gautam, P. & Chatterjee, A. 2006. Nesting sites and breeding success of Black-necked Crane *Grus nigricollis* in Ladakh, India. *Waterbirds around the world.* Eds. G.C. Boere, C.A. Galbraith & D.A. Stroud. The Stationery Office, Edinburgh, UK. pp. 311-314.

Ladakh contains some of the world's most unique and spectacular wetlands and is the only known breeding ground of Black-necked Crane *Grus nigricollis* in India. The study area was situated in the Changthang region of eastern Ladakh, part of the Trans-Himalayas of the Tibetan Plateau. (Fig. 1). This harsh environment, at an altitude of 4 000 m and above, is a cold, sparsely vegetated desert, with a short summer season, home to only highly adapted flora and fauna. Strong and unpredictable winds make the area highly inhospitable, with summer temperatures from 0°C to 30°C and winter from -10°C to -40°C (Mishra & Humbert-Droz 1998). The region has numerous brackish and freshwater wetlands, which apart from their hydrological importance, are home to a wide variety of flora and fauna. Most of these wetlands are of glacial origin and remain frozen from December to March. A unique nomadic tent dwelling tribe, the Changpas, roam the wetlands of Ladakh in search of pasturelands.

To identify appropriate wetlands to survey, a thorough literature review was carried out and based on this information, 22 wetlands were identified for an intensive survey. Surveys were undertaken from 2000 to 2003: a limited survey of a few wetlands in 2000 and 2001 and a survey of all wetlands in 2002 and 2003. All known and probable nesting and feeding sites were visited from April to November during each year. Data was collected on the number of nests, eggs laid, hatching success and survival of fledglings. Rapid surveys were made in March and April, and October to November to establish arrival and departure dates. The day a Black-necked Crane was first sighted was treated as arrival date (Oring & Lank 1982), and the last day when the species was sighted was considered as its departure date (Bhupathy *et al.* 1998).

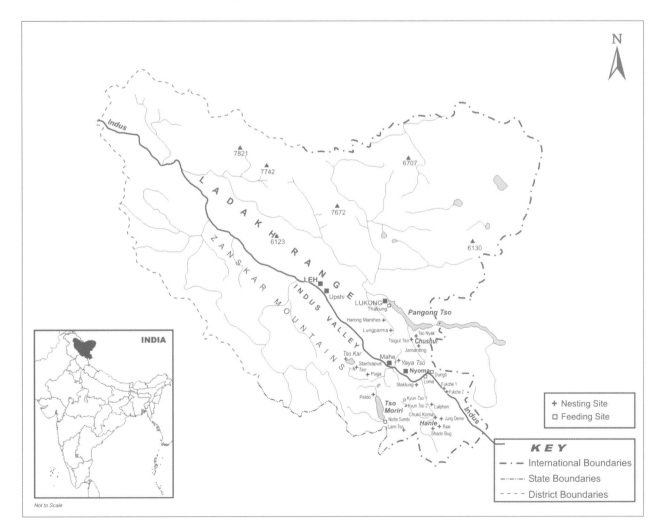

**Fig. 1.** Map of feeding and nesting sites of Black-necked Cranes *Grus nigricollis* in Ladakh.

**Table 1.** Surveys and breeding records of Black-necked Crane *Grus nigricollis* in Ladakh.

| Month / Year | No. of wetlands covered | No. of Black-necked Cranes | | No. of chicks fledged | Reference |
| --- | --- | --- | --- | --- | --- |
| | | Total sightings | Breeding pairs | | |
| June 1919 | 2 | 3 | 1 | - | Ludlow (1920) |
| June 1924 | 7 | 11 | 4 | - | Osmaston (1925) |
| May-June 1926 | 8 | 10 | 5 | - | Meinertzhagen (1927) |
| June 1976 | 4 | 5 | 2 | - | Hussain (1976) |
| July 1978 | 10 | 12 | 1 | - | Gole (1981) |
| May-June 1980 | 10 | 14 | 3 | - | Gole (1983) |
| June 1982 | 9 | 13 | 3 | - | Nurbu (1983) |
| June 1983 | 6 | 7 | 2 | - | Hussain 1985 |
| August-October 1986 | 8 | 16 | 2 | - | Narayan *et al.* (1987) |
| July-November 1987 | 5 | 9 | 1 | - | Akhtar (1989) |
| Sep-October 1992 | 14 | 17 | 4 | - | Chacko (1992) |
| May-Sep 1995 | 18 | 22 | 5 | 6 | Chacko (1995) |
| May-August 1996 | 18 | 25 | 12 | 9 | Chacko (1996) |
| June-September 1997 | 18 | 38 | 12 | 9 | Pfister (1998) |
| April– December 2002 | 22 | 59 | 15 | 10 | This study |
| April- November 2003 | 22 | 60 | 16 | 10 | This study |

Data for estimating breeding productivity was collected from 15 pairs of birds in 2002 and 16 pairs in 2003. The reproductive output of each nest was followed through the various stages of the life cycle, from the clutch laid, through hatching/fledging and recruitment into the breeding population. As there were few sub-adults present, these were included in the adult category. Productivity was calculated as the number of young reared per successful female in the population in a year. The Mayfield (1961) method (successful nests / all nests) was used to determine nesting success.

Black-necked Cranes arrived in the wetlands of Changthang, their only known nesting area in India, in the last week of March or first week of April and leave in the last week of October or first week of November, along with their chicks. Other waterbirds also bred in these wetlands: Bar-headed Goose *Anser indicus*, Brown-headed Gull *Larus brunicephalus*, Great-crested Grebe *Podiceps cristatus*, Ruddy Shelduck *Tadorna ferruginea* and Lesser Sand Plover *Charadrius mongolus*.

Table 1 summarises numbers and breeding records from previous surveys and this survey. In 2002 and 2003, totals (adults and chicks) of 59 and 60 birds respectively were recorded; the highest number ever recorded in Ladakh. Six new breeding sites were found (Table 2). A total of 15 nests were found in 2002, and 16 in 2003. Nesting success was 33.3% in 2002 and 31.5% in 2003, less than recorded in previous years: 60% in 1995, 43% in 1996, 37.5% in 1997. In each year 10 chicks were reared – a productivity of 0.66 in 2002 and 0.62 in 2003, lower than in previous studies of Black-necked Cranes in Ladakh between 1992 and 1997 - 0.75 – 1.2 young per pair (Chacko 1995, 1996, Pfister 1998), but within the range of productivity reported for other crane species of 0.23-1.39 young per pair (Pomeroy 1980, Walkinshaw 1981, Neumann 1987; Tarboten *et al.* 1987, Mafabi 1991, Prange & Mewes 1991, Winter 1991).

The 2002 April to December survey of 22 wetlands found Black-necked Cranes nesting in all wetlands except for Tsomoriri and Kyun Tso 1, Kyun Tso 11 and Pangong Tso. Three new nesting sites (Yaya Tso, Chukil Koma and Staklung)

were recorded, the Yaya Tso site (altitude 4 720 m) was the highest recorded breeding location in India. Of the 15 breeding pairs, 14 laid two eggs each and one pair laid only one egg. At many nests, eggs were eaten by feral dogs. Of the 12 chicks that hatched two were lost: the chick at Jung Demo was eaten by a feral dog, but the cause of the loss a chick at Lungparma could not be ascertained. In October, 10 healthy chicks and 49 adults were recorded in different wetlands. A Crane tagged at Hanle, Ladakh in 1995 was recorded in 2002 in a breeding pair, but the nest was abandoned after the egg was eaten by a dog.

Although the 2000 and 2001 surveys covered only four wetlands (Tsomoriri, Tsokar, Startsapuk Tso & Puga), nesting at the northern end of Tsomoriri in 2000 was the first record for the area. This nest was washed out by a major water level rise. No nesting was recorded at Puga or Tsokar in 2000, but in 2001, one nest was found at each wetland; again first nesting records for these sites. The Tsokar nest was unusual as it was built within an area of mounds near Thukjay village, rather than the more usual sites with open visibility. All four eggs at the Tsokar and Puga sites were eaten by dogs. However, the nest at Startsapuk Tso successfully produced two chicks during 2000 and 2001.

In January 2003, a pair of Cranes was recorded overwintering at Lam Tso Chumur wetland which was completely frozen, their survival due to nomads in that area feeding them. This is the first recorded case of a pair of Black-necked Cranes staying during the harsh Ladakh winter.

Although our more extensive surveys found a larger breeding population than previously recorded its overall breeding productivity appears to be declining. This seems to be due to increased human activities such as unplanned development and grazing. However, our frequent observations of dogs taking eggs during incubation suggest that this is the major threat to the breeding population of cranes in Ladakh.

**ACKNOWLEDGEMENTS**
The success of this study in such a hostile environment with its challenging terrain and severe climate is entirely due to the whole hearted support of numerous individuals and organizations.

Table 2. Wetlands in which Black-necked Cranes *Grus nigricollis* have been recorded nesting in Ladakh. * indicates sites covered during present study. Sites with geographic coordinates and altitude provided are those where nesting was recorded in 2002.

| Name of Site | First year nesting recorded | Location | Altitude (m) | Reference |
|---|---|---|---|---|
| Tsigul Tso, Chuchul * | 1978 | 33°34' 43.4"N 78°37' 27.6"E | 4 445 | Gole (1983) |
| Shado Bug, Hanle * | 1980 | 32°44' 42.3"N 78°58' 25.3"E | 4 298 | Gole (1983) |
| Lam Tso Chumur * | 1980 | 32°42' 38.0"N 78°33' 22.2"E | 4 405 | Gole (1983) |
| Mankhang/Lalphari * | 1994 | 32°57' 18.8"N 78°54' 15.8"E | 4 215 | Chacko (1995) |
| Tso Nyak, Chuchul * | 1995 | 33°37' 43.8"N 78°40' 36.6"E | 4 348 | Chacko (1995) |
| Sato (Horong Marshes) * | 1996 | | | Chacko (1996) |
| Lungparma * | 1996 | 33°46' 29.5"N 78°22' 50.5"E | 4 558 | Chacko (1996) |
| Jamarding, Chuchul * | 1996 | 33°35' 29.0"N 78°41' 01.6"E | 4 394 | Chacko (1996) |
| Fukche 1 * | 1995 | 32°57' 21.4"N 79°11' 56.3"E | 4 180 | Chacko (1996) |
| Fukche 11 * | 1997 | 32°57' 51.4"N 79°11' 56.3"E | 4 178 | Pfister (1998) |
| Raar, Hanle * | 1996 | 32°46' 47.3"N 78°57' 02.0"E | 4 326 | Chacko (1996) |
| Jung Demo, Hanle * | 1996 | 32°48' 07.6"N 78°57' 41.6"E | 4 305 | Chacko (1996) |
| Startsapuk Tso * | 1996 | | | Chacko (1996) |
| Peldo, Tsomoriri | 2000 | | | This study |
| Puga | 2001 | | | This study |
| Tsokar | 2001 | 33°19' 45.6"N 78°02' 07.7"E | 4 582 | This study |
| Staklung | 2002 | 33°05' 20.7"N 78°42' 25.9"E | 4 173 | This study |
| Chukil, Hanle | 2002 | 32°46' 53.9"N 78°59' 20.9"E | 4 276 | This study |
| Yaya Tso | 2002 | 33°18' 59.2"N 78°29' 08.8"E | 4 720 | This study |

We are greatly indebted to Ladakh Autonomus Hill Development Council, Department of Wildlife Protection Jammu and Kashmir, Indian Army and Indo Tibetan Border Police for their cooperation and support during various stages of the study. Our warm thanks go to Dr. George Archibald, Dr. S. A. Hussain, Col. R. T. Chacko, Otto Pfister, K. S. Gopi Sundar, Ashfaq Ahmed and Li Fengshan for providing the crucial and relevant literature which facilitated the study. We are also thankful to Dr. Biksham Gujja, WWF International and Leen de Jong, WWF-Netherlands, for their support.

## REFERENCES

**Akhtar, S.A.** 1989. Some Observations on the Breeding Behaviour of the Black-necked Crane *Grus nigricollis* in Ladakh. Asia Crane Congress, Rajkot, India. 17 pp.

**Bhupathy, S., Vijayan, V.S. & Mathur, R.** 1998. Population Ecology of Migratory Waterfowl in Keoladeo National Park. Bharatpur. Journal of the Bombay Natural History Society 95: 287-294.

**Chacko, R.T.** 1992. A Summer Study of the Black-necked Cranes Breeding in Some Remote High Altitude Areas of Ladakh, India. Unpublished Report.

**Chacko, R.T.** 1995. A Summer 95 Study of the Black-necked Cranes Breeding in Some Remote High Altitude Areas of Ladakh, India. Unpublished Report.

**Chacko, R.T.** 1996. A Summer 96 Study of the Black-necked Cranes Breeding in Some Remote High Altitude Areas of Ladakh, India. Unpublished Report.

**Gole, P.** 1981. Black-necked Cranes in Ladakh. Crane Research Around the World: Proceedings of The International Crane Symposium at Sapporo, Japan in 1980.

**Gole, P.** 1983. Future of Black-necked Cranes in Indian Sub-continent. In G.W. Archibald & R.F. Pasquier (eds). Proceedings International Crane Workshop 1983, Bharatpur, India: 51-54.

**Hussain, S.A.** 1976. Preliminary report. Bombay Natural History Society/World Wildlife Fund – India. Ladakh Expedition.

**Hussain, S.A.** 1985. Status of Black-necked Crane in Ladakh – 1983, Problems and Prospects. Journal of the Bombay Natatural History Society 82: 449-458.

**Ludlow, F.** 1920. Notes on the Nidification of Certain Birds in Ladak. Journal of the Bombay Natatural History Society, 27: 141-146.

**Mayfield, H.** 1961. Nesting Success Calculated from Exposure. Wilson Bulletin 73 : 255-61.

**Mafabi, P.G.** 1991. The Ecology and Conservation Status of the Grey Crowned Crane in Uganda. In: J. Harris (ed), Proceedings 1987 International Crane Workshop. International Crane Foundation, Baraboo, Wisconsin, USA: 363-367.

**Meinertzhagen, R.** 1927. Systematic Results of Birds Collected at High altitudes in Ladakh and Sikkim, Part 11. Ibis 69: 624.

**Mishra, C. & Humbert-Droz, B.** 1998. Avifaunal Survey of Tsomoriri Lake and Adjoining Nuro Sumdo Wetland in Ladakh, Indian Trans-Himalaya. Forktail 14: 865-867.

**Narayan, G., Akhtar, A., Lima, R. & D'Cunha, E.** 1987. Black-necked Crane *Grus nigricollis* in Ladakh 1986. Journal of the Bombay Natatural History Society, 83 (Supplement): 180-195.

**Neumann, T.** 1987. Breeding Status of the Common Crane in the Federal Republic of Germany. In G.W. Archibald & R.F. Pasquier, (eds.), Proceedings of the 1983 International Crane Workshop. International Crane Foundation, Baraboo, Wisconsin, USA: 243-245.

**Nurbu, C.** 1983. Notes on the Black-necked Crane in Ladakh. In G.W. Archibald & R.F. Pasquier, eds., Proceedings of the 1983 International Crane Workshop, Bharatpur India. International Crane Foundation, Baraboo, Wisconsin, USA: 55-56.

**Osmaston, B.B.** 1925. On the Birds of Ladakh. Ibis 12: 662.

**Oring, L.W., & Lank, D. W.** 1982. Sexual Selection, Arrival Times, Philopatry and Site Fidelity in the Polyandrous Spotted Sandpiper. Behavioural Ecology Sociobiology 10: 185-191.

**Pfister, O.** 1998. The Breeding Ecology and Conservation of the Black-necked Crane *Grus nigricollis* in Ladakh India. Unpublished Thesis. University of Hull, UK.

**Pomeroy, D.E.** 1980. Aspects of the Ecology of Crowned Cranes *Balearica regulorum* in Uganda. Scopus 4:29-35.

**Prange, H. & Mewes, W.** 1991. The Common Crane in the German Democratic Republic. In J. Harris, (ed.), Proceedings of the 1987 International Crane Workshop. International Crane Foundation, Baraboo, Wisconsin, USA: 263-269.

**Tarboton, W.R., Barnes, P. R. & Johnson, D.N.** 1987. The Wattled Crane in South Africa during 1978-1982. In G.W. Archibald & R.F. Pasquier, (eds.), Proceedings of the 1983 International Crane Workshop. International Crane Foundation, Baraboo, Wisconsin, USA: 353-361.

**Walkinshaw, L.H.** 1981. The Sandhill Cranes. In J.C. Lewis & H. Masatomi, (eds.), Proceedings of the International Crane Symposium, Sapporo, Japan, 1980. International Crane Foundation USA: 151-162.

**Winter, S. W.** 1991. The Demoiselle Crane in the Agricultural Landscape of the Ukrainian Steppe Zone. In J. Harris, (ed.), Proceedings of the 1987 International Crane Workshop. International Crane Foundation, Baraboo, Wisconsin, USA: 285-295.

Russian experts taking biometrics of juvenile Siberian Crane *Grus leucogeranus* in Kytalyk, Yakutia. Photo: Crawford Prentice.

# 3.6 East Asia-Pacific Flyway. Workshop Introduction

*Taej Mundkur*

*Wetlands International - South Asia, A-25, 2nd Floor, Defence Colony, New Delhi - 110 024, India.*

Mundkur, T. 2006. East Asia-Pacific Flyway. Workshop Introduction. *Waterbirds around the world.* Eds. G.C. Boere, C.A. Galbraith & D.A. Stroud. The Stationery Office, Edinburgh, UK. p. 315.

Oyster farm in Luoyuan Bay, Fujian Province, China. The inter-tidal mudflats of the Chinese coast, as elsewhere in East Asia, are subject to a very high intensity of use by populations of dependent humans as well as waterbirds. Photo: Mark Barter.

The waterbirds of Asian-Australasian flyways are the most poorly known of the world's waterbird migration systems, and the greatest number of globally threatened waterbirds occurs here. This flyway extends across the most densely populated part of the world, where there are extreme pressures not only on unprotected wetlands but also on protected sites (many of which also either contain or provide the livelihoods of very large numbers of people). Effective protection of wetlands of major importance is a critical need, as in other regions of the world. There are huge, and crucial, challenges in ensuring effective wise-use of key sites, as well as ensuring that consumptive uses of waterbirds are sustainable.

The symposium reviewed existing policies, case studies and problems within the East Asian flyway, and discussed the effectiveness of the different approaches.

The following recommendations were made:–

- Networks of internationally important sites provide a sound foundation for flyway conservation initiatives. Chan presented the example of the North-east Asian Crane Network as a model. Voluntary conservation initiatives can provide a successful model for migratory waterbirds and wetland conservation. Significant voluntary effort has been expended in recent years to better understand wader conservation needs. Recent work was outlined by Straw *et al.* and Huettmann *et al.*

- Conservation of migratory waterbirds must be achieved increasingly through delivery of sustainable development.

- Conservation of migratory waterbirds must address the needs of local communities and national governments if they are to be successful in the longer term.

- Developing networks of wetland education centres should be promoted to create greater local awareness and support, and provide the foundation for conservation of migratory waterbirds through strong and functional flyway site networks. Young summarised the role of Asian wetland centres in the conservation of wetlands and migratory waterbirds.

- Management of migratory waterbirds requires sound monitoring information covering their annual life cycles. Development and strengthening of such monitoring programmes requires long-term investments across flyways. Li *et al.* describe a range of recent initiatives.

# Shorebird migration studies in Kamchatka

*Yuri N. Gerasimov*

*Kamchatka Branch, Pacific Institute of Geography, Russian Academy of Science Rybakov 19a, Petropavlovsk-Kamchatsky, 683024, Russia.*

Gerasimov, Y.N. 2006. Shorebird migration studies in Kamchatka. *Waterbirds around the world.* Eds. G.C. Boere, C.A. Galbraith & D.A. Stroud. The Stationery Office, Edinburgh, UK. pp. 316-318.

Kamchatka, a large (1 200 km long) peninsula in far eastern Russia, is of great importance as a staging and breeding area for many species of shorebirds on the East Asian flyway, with a total of fifty species of Charadriidae being recorded there. Research on shorebird migration in Kamchatka began in the mid 1970s, becoming more intensive from 1989 onwards when special counts of shorebirds during northward spring migration were started (Gerasimov 1980, 1988, Lobkov 1980, 2003), for further information and additional references see Gerasimov (2005). From 1990 to 2003 nine counts were made at eight different locations on the peninsula. Each count was carried out over a 15–30 day period during late April to early June, with additional daily counts being made on mudflats in Korf Bay. In addition, for southwards (northern autumn) migration, a large study was undertaken at the Penzhina Estuary in 2002 (12 July–10 August) and 2003 (11 August–10 September), at the northern end of the peninsula, as part of the implementation of the Action Plan for the Conservation of Migratory Shorebirds in the East Asian-Australasian Flyway: 2001–2005 (Shorebird Working Group of Wetlands International 2001). Five to six hour counts on mudflats were undertaken along a fixed 10 km shoreline length. Additionally, shorebirds were counted flying past the study area, and at night estimates were made based on the calls of birds flying past. The only previous autumn survey was of the Moroshechnaya Estuary between 2-18 August 1989. Survey locations and periods are shown in Fig. 1, and counts from selected years in Table 1.

Additional information on shorebird migration on Kamchatka was obtained from banded and flagged shorebirds, and satellite tracking of Eastern Curlew *Numenius madagascariensis* (Ueta *et al.* 2002). In the 1990s Dunlin *Calidris alpina* were also banded with plastic colour-rings. A series of papers on different shorebird species have been published from this research (Gerasimov & Gerasimov 2000b, 2001, 2002).

Observations of northward migration on west Kamchatka show that this coast is very important for shorebirds. Species including Dunlin, Red-necked Stint *Calidris ruficollis*, Great Knot *Calidris tenuirostris*, Bar-tailed Godwit *Limosa lapponica*, and Whimbrel *Numenius phaeopus* arrive either at the southwest and western coasts and migrate northwest, or arrive on in the southeast and migrate along the northeast coast. The largest shorebird concentrations were observed in 1990 at the mouth of the Moroshechnaya River on the mid-west coast of the peninsula, although full counts for all species (except for Great Knot) could not be made, and it is probable that total numbers of Dunlin, Red-necked Stint and Bar-tailed Godwit were much higher than counted.

Thousands of Wood Sandpipers *Tringa glareola*, Black-tailed Godwits *Limosa limosa* and Common Greenshanks *Tringa nebularia* were counted in 1999 at Karchinskoe Lake in central Kamchatka, but significant migration of these species

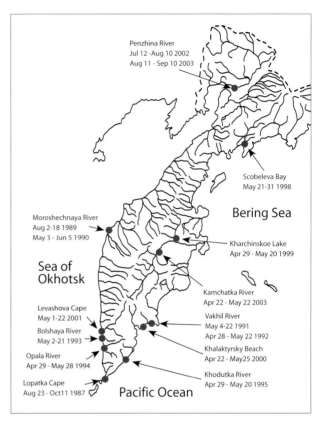

Fig. 1. Main locations where shorebird migration studies have been carried out on Kamchatka. Observations at Lopatka Cape were conducted by Lobkov (2003); all other observations were carried out by the author).

was not seen on west coast of the peninsula. So these species may be arriving at Kamchatka at high altitude and flying into the central part of the peninsula only after crossing its eastern mountain range, before dispersing to breed throughout the peninsula. Thousands of Common Snipe *Gallinago gallinago* and Long-toed Stints *Calidris subminuta* pass by Kharchinskoe Lake during the second half of May, but accurate counts could not be made as these species were migrating mainly at night. In contrast to the west coast, surveys in 1991, 1992, 1995 and 2000 found only small number of shorebirds using different parts of the south-east coast of the peninsula (Gerasimov 2001).

The various surveys permit a minimum estimation of the total numbers of different shorebirds using the peninsula during northward migration (Table 2).

There is much less information available for southward (autumn) migration. However, both areas surveyed – the mouth of Penzhina River in north-east Kamchatka and the Moroshechnaya Estuary on its mid-east coast – are important as staging places for shorebirds (Gerasimov & Gerasimov 1997, 1999, Huettmann & Gerasimov 2002, Gerasimov 2003, 2004). However, observations showed that shorebirds generally remain

**Table 1. Numbers of shorebirds counted in different parts of Kamchatka.**

| Species | Northward migration (spring) | | | | | Southward migration (autumn) |
|---|---|---|---|---|---|---|
| | 1990 | 1991 | 1993 | 1994 | 1999 | 2002 & 2003 |
| | Moroshechnaya Estuary | Vakhil River mouth | Bolshaya River mouth | Opala River mouth | Karchin-skoe Lake | Penzhina River mouth |
| | E coast | SE coast | SW coast | SW coast | central | NE coast |
| Pacific Golden Plover | 156 | 43 | 3 | 1 | 122 | 475 |
| Grey Plover | 129 | 5 | – | – | – | 85 |
| Common Ringed Plover | – | – | – | – | 1 | 55 |
| Lesser Sand Plover | 393 | 279 | 71 | 43 | 683 | 48 |
| Eurasian Oystercatcher | 440 | – | 1 | – | – | 1 |
| Red-necked Phalarope | – | – | – | – | – | 10 776 |
| Grey Phalarope | – | – | – | – | – | 2 |
| Ruddy Turnstone | 353 | 49 | 86 | 8 | 4 | 2 |
| Dunlin | 39 509 | 1 347 | 54 993 | 33 821 | 7 290 | 370 136 |
| Long-toed Stint | – | 33 | – | – | 130 | 18 |
| Temminck's Stint | – | – | – | – | 8 | 109 |
| Red-necked Stint | 19 489 | 60 | 1 583 | 894 | 1 101 | 62 774 |
| Sharp-tailed Sandpiper | – | – | – | – | – | 5 |
| Sanderling | 2 | – | – | – | – | 30 |
| Red Knot | 188 | 77 | – | 90 | – | 51 |
| Great Knot | 35 985 | 364 | – | 343 | 46 | 12 |
| Spoon-billed Sandpiper | 107 | 1 | – | – | – | 1 |
| Ruff | – | – | – | – | 6 | 22 |
| Wood Sandpiper | 87 | 75 | 1 | 2 | 3 600 | 1 260 |
| Spotted Redshank | 2 | 4 | – | 1 | 13 | 321 |
| Common Greenshank | 13 | 55 | 22 | 6 | 1 652 | 48 |
| Grey-tailed Tattler | – | – | – | – | 24 | 195 |
| Wandering Tattler | – | – | – | – | – | 1 |
| Common Sandpiper | 5 | 2 | 4 | – | 10 | 76 |
| Terek Sandpiper | 162 | – | – | – | 18 | 383 |
| Long-billed Dowitcher | – | – | – | – | – | 210 |
| Black-tailed Godwit | 54 | 40 | 16 | 14 | 3 722 | – |
| Bar-tailed Godwit | 1 813 | 726 | 284 | 2 747 | 60 | 145 |
| Eastern Curlew | 80 | 434 | 173 | 552 | 56 | 19 |
| Whimbrel | 1 959 | 2 542 | 137 | 5 341 | 1 | 125 |
| Common Snipe | 3 | 3 | 5 | 1 | * | 53 |
| **TOTAL** | **100 929** | **6 119** | **57 379** | **43 865** | **18 547** | **447 438** |

**Table 2.** Estimates of minimum numbers of the main shorebird species using Kamchatka during northwards (spring) migration.

| Species | West coast | Central peninsula | East coast | Total |
|---|---|---|---|---|
| Grey Plover | 1 000 | – | 1 000 | 2 000 |
| Pacific Golden Plover | 1 000 | 500 | 500 | 2 000 |
| Lesser Sand Plover | 2 000 | 1 000 | 2 000 | 5 000 |
| Ruddy Turnstone | 1 000 | – | 2 000 | 3 000 |
| Eurasian Oystercatcher | 500 | – | – | 500 |
| Wood Sandpiper | 10 000 | 10 000 | 5 000 | 25 000 |
| Common Greenshank | 5 000 | 5 000 | 2 000 | 12 000 |
| Red-necked Stint | 100 000 | 10 000 | 10 000 | 120 000 |
| Dunlin | 200 000 | 20 000 | 30 000 | 250 000 |
| Great Knot | 40 000 | 500 | 2 000 | 42 500 |
| Red Knot | 3 000 | – | – | 3 000 |
| Eastern Curlew | 1 000 | 200 | 300 | 1 500 |
| Whimbrel | 10 000 | – | 5 000 | 15 000 |
| Black-tailed Godwit | 1 000 | 5 000 | 1 000 | 6 000 |
| Bar-tailed Godwit | 10 000 | – | 1 000 | 11 000 |
| **TOTAL** | **385 500** | **52 200** | **61 800** | **498 500** |

at the Penzhina River mouth in north-east Kamchatka for only one day, as there are no suitable roosting places for species such as Dunlin and Red-necked Stint during high tide. In addition, large numbers of shorebirds overfly the mudflats and so are not included in the mudflat counts.

During recent years shorebird migration studies on Kamchatka have been supported by the Australian Department of Environment and Heritage (DEH). We also sincerely thank all those people who have helped us with data gathering on migration of shorebirds on Kamchatka over the years.

## REFERENCES

**Gerasimov, N.N.** 1980. Spring migration of Great Knot and Red Knot on west coast of Kamchatka. New in studies of biology and distributions of waders. Moscow: 96-98.

**Gerasimov, N.N.** 1988. Whimbrel on Kamchatka. Waders in the USSR: distribution, biology and conservation. Moscow: 26–31.

**Gerasimov, N.N. & Gerasimov, Yu.N.** 1997. Shorebird Use of the Moroshechnaya Estuary. Shorebird Conservation in the Asia-Pacific Region. Melbourne, 138–140.

**Gerasimov, N.N. & Gerasimov, Yu.N.** 1999. The estuary of the Moroshechnaya River as a place of wader concentration. The biology and conservation of the birds of Kamchatka 1: 47–52. Moscow.

**Gerasimov, Yu.N.** 2001. Observation on spring migration of waterbirds along southeast coast of Kamchatka. The biology and conservation of the birds of Kamchatka 3: 86–95. Moscow.

**Gerasimov, Yu.N.** 2003. Shorebird studies in North Kamchatka from July 5 – August 12 2002. The Stilt 44: 19–28.

**Gerasimov, Yu.N.** 2004. Southward migration in 2003 of shorebirds at the Penzhina River mouth, Kamchatka, Russia. The Stilt 45: 33–38.

**Gerasimov, Yu.** 2005. The Penzhina River Estuary, Kamchatka, Russia – a very important shorebird site during southward migration. In: P. Straw (ed.), Status and Conservation of Shorebirds in the East Asian-Australasian Flyway; Proceedings of the Australasian Shorebirds Conference 13-15 December 2003, Canberra, Australia. Wetlands International Global Series 18/International Wader Studies 17: 161-167.

**Gerasimov, Yu.N. & Gerasimov, N.N.** 2000b. Information on the northward migration of Great Knot *Calidris tenuirostris* in Kamchatka, Russia. The Stilt 36: 35–38.

**Gerasimov, Yu.N. & Gerasimov, N.N.** 2001. Records of northward migration of Dunlin *Calidris alpina* through Kamchatka, Russia. The Stilt 39: 37–40.

**Gerasimov, Yu.N. & Gerasimov N.N.** 2002. Whimbrel *Numenius phaeopus* on Kamchatka, Russia. The Stilt 41: 48–54.

**Huettmann, F. & Gerasimov, Yu**. 2002. Using sampling to obtain density estimates for Whimbrels (*Numenius phaeopus*) and other birds in the coastal tundra of the Moroshechnaya River Spit, Sea of Okhotsk, during fall migration. Avian Ecology and Behaviour 8: 49–69.

**Lobkov, E.G.** 1980. Migration and hunting of Whimbrel on Eastern Kamchatka. New studies of the biology and distribution of waders. Moscow: 111–112.

**Lobkov, E.G.** 2003. Autumn migration of waterbirds and seabirds on Lopatka Cape. The biology and conservation of the birds of Kamchatka. 5: 27–54, Moscow.

**Shorebird Working Group of Wetlands International**. 2001. Action Plan for the Conservation of Migratory Shorebirds in Asia Pacific: 2001–2005. Environment Australia, Canberra.

**Ueta, M., Antonov, A., Artukhin, Yu. & Parilov, M.** 2002. Migration routes of Eastern Curlews tracked from Far East Russia. Emu 102: 345–348.

A Red-necked Stint *Calidris ruficollis* colour marked in Australia. Many thousands of stints pass through Kamchatka on spring and autumn migration, and colour-marking has assisted in understanding the migration ecology of this species on the East Asian – Australasian Flyway. Photo: Chris Wilson.

# Conserving migrating shorebirds in the Yellow Sea region

*C. Kelin & X. Qiang*

*Wetlands International, Room 501, Grand Forest Hotel, No. 3A, Bei Sanhuan Zhonglu Road, Beijing 100029, China.*
*(email: ckl@wetwonder.org or xq@wetwonder.org)*

Kelin, C. & Qiang, X. 2006. Conserving migrating shorebirds in the Yellow Sea region. *Waterbirds around the world.* Eds. G.C. Boere, C.A. Galbraith & D.A. Stroud. The Stationery Office, Edinburgh, UK. p. 319.

The Yellow Sea Region lies between North and South Korea to the east and China to the west, and covers an area of 458 000 sq km. Biodiversity in the inter-tidal zone of the Yellow Sea Region is high: excellent feeding and roosting areas accommodate many different species of waterbirds, and preliminary records indicate that the coastal zone of the Yellow Sea eco-region supports about 200 breeding, staging and wintering waterbird and seabird species.

The Yellow Sea eco-region is a very important component of the East Asian-Australasian Flyway. It serves as an essential staging site for shorebird migration between the south and north: its position is crucial for shorebird migration as it acts as an energy station due to its large coastal inter-tidal flats. Shorebirds breeding in the Russian Far East, northeast China and northern China can either migrate along the coastline and winter in the middle and lower Chang Jiang and South China, or continue to fly southward to winter in Southeast Asia, Australia or New Zealand. The northern coast of the Yellow Sea is probably the final staging site for many shorebird species flying to their breeding sites.

In order to assess the shorebird resources in the Yellow Sea and to accurately understand the utilization of the region by shorebirds during their northward and southward migration, Wetlands International-China has for the past nine years organized experts to conduct regular field surveys along the most of the coasts of the Yellow Sea.

A total of 54 shorebird species have so far been found in the Yellow Sea during southward or northward migration, of which 34 species occurred in internationally important numbers (more than 1% of its estimated biogeographic population) at one or more sites. This number represents 60% of the migratory shorebird species in the East Asian – Australasian Flyway. It is estimated that at least 2 million shorebirds, approximately 40% of all migratory shorebirds population in the Flyway, use the Yellow Sea Region during northward migration. Large numbers of shorebirds, perhaps exceeding 1 million, also pass through this region during southward migration. A total of 14 sites have been identified in the Yellow Sea-China coast where at least one shorebird species has been recorded in internationally important numbers.

The majority of one globally threatened species, the Spotted Greenshank *Tringa guttifer*, uses the Yellow Sea for both northward and southward migrations, and nine sites have been identified as internationally important for this species. Almost the entire migratory population of five shorebird species uses the Yellow Sea: Curlew Sandpiper *Calidris ferruginea*, Bar-tailed Godwit *Limosa lapponica*, Eurasian Curlew *Numenius arquata*, Great Knot *Calidris tenuirostris* and Kentish Plover *Charadrius alexandrinus*. Approximately 80% of the estimated population of Eastern Curlew *Numenius madagascariensis* and 40% of Asian Dowitcher *Limnodromus semipalmatus* were represented in the Yellow Sea during northward migration.

Seven species occur in internationally important concentrations in the southern part of the Yellow Sea during the non-breeding season, i.e. the Eurasian Curlew *Numenius arquata*, Spotted Redshank *Tringa erythropus*, Common Greenshank *Tringa nebularia*, Sanderling *Calidris alba*, Eurasian Oystercatcher *Haematopus ostralegus*, Pied Avocet *Recurvirostra avosetta* and Kentish Plover *Charadrius alexandrinus*. The Oriental Pratincole *Glareola maldivarum* breeds in the Yellow Sea in internationally important numbers.

Based on the analysis of the survey results, it is clear that shorebird use of the Yellow Sea Region is very varied. Some species occur at high densities within limited wetland sites, while some species are distributed in many sites but at lower density.

Approximately 600 million people from China, South Korea and North Korea live in the Yellow Sea Region. The rapid growth of the population and economy of China and South Korea has resulted in degradation and a serious loss of wetland habitat along the Yellow Sea and regionally due to environmental pollution, reduced river flows and human disturbance.

Successful shorebird conservation will depend on positive national policies and plans and wise and sustainable development and use of inter-tidal mudflat and coastal resources. Coordination and cooperation between related agencies will be important as a basis for the successful realization of these national policies and plans. In addition to traditional approaches, further efforts should be made to facilitate regional environment improvement and shorebird conservation. These may include:

- regular surveys, assessment and monitoring of wetland and shorebirds in the Yellow Sea;
- initiation of a long-term general and overall protection plan for the Yellow Sea Eco-region;
- define a set of key fields and priorities for conservation in the Yellow Sea Region;
- increase public awareness activities; and
- establish a wetland and shorebird conservation network for the Yellow Sea eco-region.

# The North East Asian Crane Site Network

*Simba Chan*

*Flyway Officer of the North East Asian Crane Site Network, Wild Bird Society of Japan, WING 2-35-2 Minamidaira, Hino, Tokyo 191-0041, Japan. (email: simba@birdlife-asia.org)*

Chan, S. 2006. The North East Asian Crane Site Network. *Waterbirds around the world.* Eds. G.C. Boere, C.A. Galbraith & D.A. Stroud. The Stationery Office, Edinburgh, UK. pp. 320-323.

## ABSTRACT

The North East Asian Crane Site Network was launched in 1997. The main goal of the Network is to conserve crane species and their habitats in north-east Asia. As of October 2003, there are 26 sites important for cranes and storks in the six north-east Asian countries that have joined the Crane Network. Since its launch in 1997, the Crane Network has organized a number of workshops, symposia and training courses with a view to improving site management and promoting public awareness of the need for site conservation. At the workshops and training courses, the Crane Network has provided opportunities for reserve staff, researchers and conservation organizations from the six countries in north-east Asia to share their experiences and to establish closer bonds both within these countries and with countries outside the region.

## BACKGROUND

Cranes have long been regarded as symbols of longevity and happiness in north-east Asia, and there has been a long history of crane protection in the region. In recent decades, cranes have been amongst the first species to be given legal protection and to benefit from the designation of special sanctuaries. Cranes are therefore important flagship species for the conservation of wetland habitats in north-east Asia.

Of the fifteen species of cranes in the world, seven are found in north-east Asia (Mongolia, China, North Korea, South Korea, Japan and the eastern part of Russia). Four of these species are largely or wholly confined to the region and are globally threatened: Siberian Crane *Grus leucogeranus*[1], Red-crowned Crane *G. japonensis*, White-naped Crane *G. vipio*, and Hooded Crane *G. monacha*. North-east Asia is thus the most important region for crane conservation in the world. As cranes are birds of very high cultural significance, they are also ideal flagship species for wetland conservation in the region.

## HISTORY

In 1990, the Wild Bird Society of Japan (WBSJ), together with the Yamashina Institute for Ornithology and other researchers in the region, began using satellite-tracking to study the migration of cranes in Asia. This work resulted in the identification of many important migration routes and stopover sites for cranes. In 1993, WBSJ organized an international workshop "The Future of Cranes and Wetlands" in Tokyo and Sapporo, Japan, to discuss the next steps in the conservation of cranes in the region. The concept of building a network of important sites was raised at this workshop.

In December 1994, representatives from 16 East Asian and Australasian countries attended a workshop on the conservation of migratory waterbirds in Kushiro, Japan. The meeting was organized under the auspices of the Environment Agency of Japan[2] and the Australian Nature Conservation Agency[3], with assistance from the Asian Wetland Bureau[4] and the International Waterfowl and Wetlands Research Bureau - Japan Committee[5]. WBSJ was a strong supporter of the workshop. The workshop produced a summary statement known as the "Kushiro Initiative" which called for the following:

- preparation of a conservation strategy for migratory water-birds in the region;
- development of Action Plans for species groups; and
- development of networks of internationally important sites for species groups.

In 1997, the North East Asian Crane Site Network (hereafter referred to as the Crane Network) was launched at an international conference on wetlands and waterbirds held at Beidaihe, China. The Crane Network is one of three networks that have been established for particular groups of waterbirds under the Asia-Pacific Migratory Waterbird Conservation Strategy, the others being for Anatidae (ducks, geese and swans) and shorebirds. The Working Group of the Crane Network was established in 1997 to give guidance to the activities of the Crane Network. It consists of national representatives from all six countries in the region, researchers and international crane experts. The Crane Flyway Officer implements the activities as discussed and decided upon by the Crane Working Group. Since 2000, the Crane Network has also covered activities relating to the conservation of stork species in north-east Asia, particularly the globally endangered Oriental White Stork *Ciconia boyciana*.

By April 2004, 26 sites of importance for cranes and storks had joined the Crane Network. They include sites from all six north-east Asian countries and some of the most important wetlands in north-east Asia. Twelve of the sites have already been listed as Ramsar sites under the Ramsar Convention on Wetlands, and all 26 sites have been identified as Important Bird Areas under the BirdLife International global programme. A list of the Crane Network Sites is given in Table 1 (see also Fig. 1).

## ACTIVITIES

Since 1997, the Crane Network has organized a number of workshops on research and management, symposia to promote public

---

[1] There is a very small population of this species in central and western Asia, but more than 99% of the global population occurs in north-east Asia.

[2] Now known as the Ministry of the Environment, Japan.

[3] Now known as the Department of the Environment and Heritage, Australia.

[4] Now part of Wetlands International.

[5] Now known as Wetlands International Japan.

**Table 1. List of sites in the North East Asian Crane Site Network.**

| Country and sites | Geographical co-ordinates |
|---|---|
| **Russian Federation** | |
| Kytalyk Resource Reserve | 70°46'- 72°20'N, 143°35'- 152°30'E |
| Khingansky Nature Reserve and Ganukan Game Reserve | 49°30'N, 130°15'E |
| Lake Khanka Nature Reserve | 44°53'N, 132°26'E |
| Daursky Nature Reserve | 50°05'N, 115°45'E |
| **Mongolia** | |
| Mongol Daguur Strictly Protected Area | 49°42'N, 115°06'E |
| Khurkh-Khuiten Valley, Mongolia | 48°19'N, 110° 22'E; 48°16'N, 110°45'E |
| Ugtam Nature Reserve, Mongolia | 49°14'- 49°25'N, 113°34'- 113°57'E |
| **People's Republic of China** | |
| Zhalong National Nature Reserve | 46°52'- 47°32'N, 123°47'- 124°37'E |
| Sanjiang National Nature Reserve | 47°26'- 48°28'N, 133°41'- 135°05'E |
| Xingkai Lake National Nature Reserve | 45°10'N, 132°21'E |
| Xianghai National Nature Reserve | 44°50'- 45°19'N, 122°05'- 122°35'E |
| Shuangtai Hekou National Nature Reserve | 40°45'- 41°10'N, 121°30'- 122°00'E |
| Yellow River Delta National Nature Reserve | 37°50'N, 118°10'E |
| Yancheng National Nature Reserve | 33°40'N, 120°30'E |
| Shengjin Hu National Nature Reserve | 30°15'- 30°30'N, 116°55'- 117°15'E |
| Poyang Lake National Nature Reserve | 29°15'N, 116°00'E |
| Cao Hai National Nature Reserve | 26°48'N, 104°10'E |
| **Democratic People's Republic of Korea** | |
| Kumya Wetland Reserve | 39°25'N, 127°20'E |
| Mundok Wetland Reserve | 39°30'N, 125°20'E |
| **Republic of Korea** | |
| Han River Estuary | 37°45'N, 126°40'E |
| Cholwon Basin | 38°15'N, 127°13'E |
| **Japan** | |
| Kiritappu Marsh | 43°05'N, 145°05'E |
| Akkeshi Lake and Bekanbeushi Marsh | 43°03'N, 144°54'E |
| Kushiro Marsh | 43°09'N, 144°26'E |
| Yashiro | 34°01'N, 131°54'E |
| Izumi-Takaono Wildlife Protection Area | 32°05'N, 130°20'E |

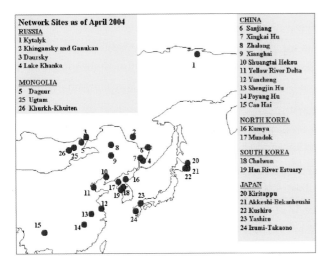

Fig. 1. North East Asian Crane Site Network: Network Sites as at April 2004.

Siberian Crane *Grus leucogeranus* breeding grounds at Kytalyk Resource Reserve, Yakutia – one of the sites in the North East Asian Crane Site Network. Photo: Crawford Prentice.

awareness of conservation issues, and training courses for local stakeholders. The Crane Network has published manuals on research and management techniques, as well as newsletters for the dissemination of information.

The meetings of the Crane Network not only serve their academic, training and management purposes, but perhaps more importantly, provide opportunities for reserve workers,

**Table 2. Main activities of the North East Asian Crane Site Network.**

| Main activities of the North East Asian Crane Site Network | |
| --- | --- |
| **1997** - July | Establishment of the Crane Network Working Group |
| **1998** - March | First issue of the Crane Network Newsletter published |
| - September | Research workshop at Muraviovka Park, Russia. First Meeting of the Working Group |
| **1999** - February | Preparatory meeting for the symposium and forum on conservation of cranes at Sunchoen, South Korea, in February 2000 |
| - May | Atlas of Key Sites for Cranes in the North East Asian Flyway published |
| - December | Research Handbook (outputs of the Muraviovka workshop) published |
| **2000** - February | Symposium and forum on conservation of cranes in Suncheon, South Korea<br>Children's art exhibition held in Suncheon, South Korea<br>Second Meeting of the Working Group. Discussion of the Action Plan |
| - September | Training course for nature reserves on the breeding grounds of cranes, held at Khingansky Nature Reserve, Russia |
| - October | Children's art exhibition held in Naha, Okinawa<br>Third Meeting of the Working Group and adoption of the Action Plan<br>Children's art exhibition held in Mongolia |
| - December | Second issue of the Crane Network Newsletter published |
| **2001** - January | Launch of the Action Plan 2001-2005 |
| - March | Crane Dispersal Meeting held in Beijing, China<br>Education and Eco-tourism Workshop (I) held at Yellow River Delta Nature Reserve, China<br>Fourth Meeting of the Working Group<br>Children's art exhibition held in China |
| **2002** - February | Fifth Meeting of the Working Group held in Kushiro, Japan |
| - February/March | Education and Eco-tourism Workshop (II) held in Kushiro, Japan |
| - March | Symposium on crane conservation held in Kushiro, Japan<br>Children's art exhibition held in Kushiro, Japan<br>Discussion on Crane dispersal held in Incheon, South Korea |
| - June | Designation of six new Network Sites in China |
| - August | Presentation of certificates for the six new Chinese Crane Network Sites at the International Crane Workshop, Beijing, on 8 August 2002<br>National workshop of Chinese Crane Site Network managers at the International Crane Workshop |
| **2003** - March | Meeting with the Korean Crane Network in Gumi, South Korea<br>Discussion of the possibility of maintaining suitable crane wintering grounds in Gumi, Korea |
| - July | Designation of two new Network Sites in Mongolia |
| - August | Sixth Meeting of the Working Group held in Ulaan Baatar, Mongolia<br>Symposium on crane and wetland conservation held in Ulaan Baatar, Mongolia<br>Presentation of certificates for the two new Mongolian Crane Network Sites at the symposium in Ulaan Baatar, Mongolia<br>Training course on education and visitor management, held in Daguur, Mongolia |
| - November | Workshop and symposium on crane conservation in Japan, held in Kushiro, Japan |
| - December | Third issue of the Crane Network Newsletter published |

researchers and conservation organizations from the six countries in north-east Asia to share their experiences and to establish closer ties between these countries and with countries outside the region. For example, in 2001, 2002 and 2003, the Crane Network organized workshops and training courses on education and visitor management in China, Japan and Mongolia. At each meeting, there were over 50 participants from various countries. Translation has always been a challenge, but it is a very good sign that people from countries throughout the region are now interested to know what their foreign counterparts are doing. Good communication within the region has started.

The main focus of the Crane Network is to empower reserve managers in north-east Asia, and to provide opportunities for multinational co-operation in conservation. The 15 principal activities in the Crane Network Action Plan for the period 2001-2005 cover the following major areas: development of the Crane Network, improvement of management skills of site managers, promotion of education programmes at the sites, research and monitoring of crane populations, and exchange of information within the region. A chronological list of the main activities of the Crane Network up to March 2004 is given in Table 2. The Working Group of the North East Asian Crane Site Network is currently preparing a new action plan for the period 2006-2010.

## THE FUTURE

There seems to have been some recovery in the numbers of cranes in north-east Asia in recent years as a result of effective protection. There are now at least 10 000 Hooded Cranes, 6 000 White-naped Cranes, 2 000 Red-crowned Cranes and 3 000 Siberian Cranes in the wild. However, the continuing increase in the human population and higher expectations in living standards resulting from rapid economic growth in north-east Asia will no doubt place higher demands on the already limited land resources in this region. More land will be claimed for agriculture, industry and housing, and agriculture in existing farmlands will become more intensive. This is certainly not good news for wildlife, particularly species such as cranes which are adapted to semi-agricultural habitats in their wintering areas.

Cranes are now becoming increasingly concentrated at a few wintering sites. The situation is very serious in Japan and South Korea, and a similar trend has also been noted in China. If we do not save enough sites now, within one or two decades the cranes in north-east Asia will end up having to survive at only a handful of sites. Unlike the situation in the late nineteenth century, the biggest threat to cranes now is not human persecution, but habitat destruction, as it is to most other threatened wildlife. For this reason, we should not think that the cranes are "saved" just because there has been an increase in numbers. In fact, cranes are facing a very serious threat from habitat loss in north-east Asia.

One of the major research topics in the Crane Network Action Plan for 2001-2005 is to study the feasibility of dispersing over-concentrated crane populations, particularly the populations of Hooded Cranes and White-naped Cranes wintering at Izumi in Japan. This is a very difficult task, not only because suitable alternative wintering sites have to be identified, but also because the support and co-operation of local communities is essential. While on the one hand, it is important to disperse the over-concentrated cranes at some sites, on the other, it is important to prevent over-concentration of cranes in other countries, particularly in China.

This is why site conservation and proper management are very important. The Crane Network can play a role in empowering local stakeholders and strengthening co-operation between different sites and different countries. In the coming five years, and certainly in the long term, the Crane Network will work with researchers, conservationists and stakeholders to improve the management of sites important for cranes in north-east Asia, and bring these people together in closer co-operation.

## ACKNOWLEDGEMENTS

The Ministry of the Environment of Japan has been supporting the Crane Network from the outset. Since its launch, the Crane Network has also received support from the State Committee for Environmental Protection of the Russian Federation, the Ministry of Nature and the Environment of Mongolia, the State Forestry Administration of the People's Republic of China, the Nature Conservation Center of the Democratic People's Republic of Korea, and the Forestry Administration and Ministry of Environment of the Republic of Korea. Their support and guidance are essential for the success of crane conservation in north-east Asia.

The International Crane Foundation and other national crane research groups and experts have provided advice and assistance in the formation of the Crane Network. We are particularly grateful to the Amur Chapter of the Socio-ecological Union (Russian Federation), the Muraviovka Park for Sustainable Land Use (Russian Federation), the National Institute of Environmental Research (Republic of Korea), the City Government of Dongying (China), Wetlands International Japan, the City Government of Kushiro (Japan), the Mongolian Academy of Sciences, and the UNDP Eastern Steppe Biodiversity Project (Mongolia) for assistance at meetings, training courses and symposia. Ligue pour la Protection des Oiseaux assisted in raising funds to organize education workshops. Activities of the Crane Network have been generously funded by the Japan Fund For Global Environment, Japan Trust for Global Environment, Keidanren Nature Conservation Fund (Japan), Ministry of Environment (Republic of Korea), City Government of Suncheon (Republic of Korea), Société des Eaux Minérales d'Evian of the Danone Corporate Group (France), French Global Environment Facility, and UNEP/GEF Siberian Crane Wetlands Project.

Education and awareness raising are critical aspects of crane conservation. Dr Evgeny Bragin explaining use of radio telemetry equipment to monitor Siberian Cranes *Grus leucogeranus* in Yakutia as part of the UNEP/GEF Siberian Crane Wetlands project.     Photo: Crawford Prentice.

# The role of Asian wetland centres in the conservation of wetlands and migratory waterbirds

*Lew Young*

*Mai Po Nature Reserve, WWF Hong Kong, Mai Po, San Tin, Yuen Long, Hong Kong. (email: lyoung@wwf.org.hk)*

Young, L. 2006. The role of Asian wetland centres in the conservation of wetlands and migratory waterbirds. *Waterbirds around the world*. Eds. G.C. Boere, C.A. Galbraith & D.A. Stroud. The Stationery Office, Edinburgh, UK. pp. 324-327.

## ABSTRACT

The establishment of visitor centres to raise awareness of the importance of wetlands and migratory waterbirds probably began in the UK in the 1940s. Since then, a network of similar wetland centres has been developed around the world, and wetland education has become one of the key tools in the conservation of wetlands and their wildlife. These centres are often associated with important wetlands, and may play a significant role in the study and conservation of these sites. Since the early 1980s, interest in the development of wetland centres in Asia has gained considerable momentum. This paper provides a brief history of a few of the wetland centres in Asia and the efforts that have been made to conserve migratory shorebirds through education programmes and management of the wetland habitats associated with the centres. Special attention is given to the work of the education centres associated with the Mai Po Inner Deep Bay Ramsar site in Hong Kong, P.R. China.

## INTRODUCTION

The concept of establishing education centres to raise awareness of the importance of wetlands and their wildlife probably began with the opening of the centre at Slimbridge (UK) in 1946 by Sir Peter Scott. Since then, a network of similar centres has been built around the world, and wetland education has become one of the key tools in the conservation of wetlands and their wildlife.

However, these centres do not just focus on wetland education and public awareness. They are often carefully located on the edge of an important wetland so that the centre may also play an important role in the management of the wetland, conducting monitoring and research, working with local communities and lobbying government to ensure the "wise use" of the wetland and its long-term protection.

Over the past decade, wetland centres around the world have been working together more closely through the Wetland Link International (WLI) initiative in order to share resources and ideas for programmes, and to carry out co-operative projects. This has been particularly true in Asia, where a number of established wetland centres have played important roles in providing support for the establishment of new protected wetland sites and associated centres in other countries. These centres have recently decided to form an Asian Chapter of WLI to help promote greater co-operation between Asian wetland centres.

## THE ROLE OF WETLAND CENTRES AND WETLAND NATURE RESERVES

### Education and awareness

One of the advantages of having an education centre built adjacent to a wetland is that the wetland can be used as an educational tool where students and other visitors can be guided and shown first-hand the variety of wildlife that wetlands support and the ecological stories that they can reveal.

To facilitate the visitors' appreciation and understanding of the wetland, facilities such as an exhibition room, nature trails, notice boards, bird-watching hides and boardwalks are often available. Educational material such as books and leaflets are usually produced to explain the various aspects of the ecology of the wetland and its wildlife. A range of special (e.g. guided) education and public awareness programmes are also often offered, targeting the general public (including the disabled), students, decision makers and others. There may also be programmes for volunteers to help with the daily management of the reserve and centre.

### Conserving and managing habitats for wetland wildlife, including waterbirds

Wetland centres may, or may not, also be responsible for the management of the adjacent wetland. If so, then the work will involve maintaining the ecological value of the site. This may include providing habitat for the various species of wildlife for which the wetland is important, and balancing the need to conserve the site with maximizing opportunities for visitors to enter and learn about the site, and value its importance.

### Monitoring and research

In order to manage a wetland in a manner that can maximize its ecological value, regular baseline ecological monitoring needs to be conducted. This will ensure that any adverse changes are detected quickly, and allow action to be taken immediately to resolve the problem. Such monitoring may include the quality of water in the wetland and changes in the diversity and abundance of waterbirds for which the site is important.

Research projects may be carried out by staff of the wetland centre or, alternatively, co-operative links may be established with local colleges or universities and projects conducted by students or academic staff. Examples of such projects may include investigating the optimum means of managing certain habitats in the reserve in order to maximize its value for key wildlife species. It is important that the data and reports from such monitoring and research projects are published and made available to the reserve staff who can then take appropriate management action.

### Training

Wetland centres can often provide training for overseas site managers and decision makers on topics such as habitat management, waterbird identification and survey techniques, waterbird catching and banding, and environmental education techniques. This training can be achieved by inviting participants to the centre, by staff from the centre visiting overseas sites, remotely via e-mail (such as the Shorebird Sister Schools Programme), or by twinning sites.

Mai Po Wildlife Education Centre, Hong Kong. Photo: Lew Young.

## WETLAND CENTRES IN ASIA

The development of wetland centres in Asia originally lagged behind that in "western" countries, but since the early 1980s, interest in providing such centres has gained momentum. This is especially so in those Asian countries whose economies have been growing rapidly in recent decades. The following section provides a brief history of a few of these centres in Asia, their importance for shorebirds, and the work that has been carried out to conserve these birds through education programmes and management of the wetland habitats associated with the centres.

### Wetland Centres around Deep Bay, P.R. China

#### Mai Po Marshes Wildlife Education Centre and Nature Reserve, Hong Kong

The Mai Po Marshes form part of the complex of wetlands around Deep Bay in the north-western corner of Hong Kong, and have been well known as a site for wetland wildlife since the end of the 1800s. At present, some 54 000 waterbirds winter in these wetlands, and an additional 20 000-30 000 shorebirds pass through the area during the spring and autumn migration. At least 177 species of waterbirds have been recorded in Deep Bay. Forty of these (almost 23%) are of special importance either because they are threatened species, or because they occur in numbers that exceed 1% of the flyway population (Carey & Young 1999).

Due primarily to the importance of the area for migratory waterbirds, in 1995 the Hong Kong government designated an area of 1 500 ha of wetlands around Deep Bay as a Wetland of International Importance under the Ramsar Convention on Wetlands. This Ramsar site includes the Deep Bay mudflats, the Mai Po Marshes Nature Reserve, and an area of commercial fishponds on the land-ward edge of the site.

In 1984, WWF Hong Kong took over the management of the 380 ha Mai Po Marshes Wildlife Education Centre and Nature Reserve (MPNR) with a view to promoting education and conservation in collaboration with the Hong Kong government. The MPNR is made up of 24 traditionally operated shrimp ponds (locally known as "*gei wai*"), each of about 10 ha in size and supporting a mixture of mangroves, reed-beds and areas of open water. Shorebirds feed on the inter-tidal mudflats in Deep Bay, but at high tide, they fly into the reserve and roost in a number of specially managed "*gei wai*" that provide areas of shallow water during spring or autumn passage and throughout the winter period. In summer, however, the water level in these ponds is kept high to prevent the encroachment of reeds from the edges of the pond into the areas of open water. The height of the vegetation around the roost sites is also kept low so as not to obstruct the flight lines of the shorebirds; this also allows the shorebirds to see the approach of aerial predators (Lawler 1995).

MPNR staff also carry out some management of the shorebirds' feeding areas on the adjacent mudflat. This is necessary because the mangroves that fringe the mudflat are slowly advancing out over the mud. Each autumn, the mangrove seedlings in an area of approximately 30 ha in front of the bird-watching hides on the edge of the mudflat are removed manu-ally. This not only keeps the view from the hides unobstructed, but also maintains an open area of mudflat for feeding shore-birds and other waterbirds.

Through a programme of specially guided visits to the reserve, students and the general public can get a first-hand understanding of the importance of wetlands and waterbirds, and the need for their conservation. However, due to the small size of the reserve, visitor numbers have to be controlled so as to minimize disturbance to the wildlife. As a result, only around

40 000 people visit MPNR each year. These include about 400 groups of primary and secondary school students on specially guided programmes sponsored by the government's Education Department. Teams of volunteers also help with reserve management at various times of the year.

## Wetland Park, Hong Kong

In 1987, reclamation work began on an area of 300 ha of fish-ponds in the south-western corner of the Deep Bay wetlands for the construction of a new town (Tin Shui Wai) that would eventually house some 135 000 people. However, with increasing awareness of the importance of wetlands, the government proposed in 1995 to set aside an area of 64 ha at the development site as mitigation for the loss of wetlands caused by the construction of the new town. This area would also act as a buffer between the new town and the Mai Po Inner Deep Bay Ramsar site.

After further discussions, the government decided in 1999 to expand the ecological mitigation area into a Wetland Park for both local residents and overseas visitors. This was partly in response to the increasing demand from people wishing to visit Deep Bay and obtain a greater understanding of the wetlands, but unable to do so because of a lack of space on the guided tours at MPNR. The facility will have a modern wetland education centre as well as a range of demonstration wetland habitats, including a high-tide roosting site for shorebirds and other waterbirds. Work began on the Tin Shui Wai Wetland Park in 2000, and the park was finally opened in May 2006. The Wetland Park is managed by the Agriculture, Fisheries and Conservation Department of the Hong Kong SAR government.

Being less ecologically sensitive than MPNR, this new wetland centre will have a capacity of up to 400 000 visitors per year. It will therefore be able to bring the message of the importance of the Deep Bay wetlands and waterbirds to a much larger and wider audience.

## Futian National Nature Reserve, Shenzhen

A range of wetlands, such as mudflats, mangroves, shrimp ponds and fishponds, is also found along the northern, Mainland China side of Deep Bay. Some protection was afforded to these wetlands in 1984, and in 1988, the area was upgraded to a National Nature Reserve (NNR). The boundaries of the Futian National Nature Reserve were confirmed in 1998, and enclose an area of 368 ha; the reserve is managed by the Department of Agriculture and Forestry, Shenzhen SEZ.

Many of the shorebirds that use Deep Bay feed on the mudflats on both the Hong Kong and Shenzhen sides of the bay. However, at high tide, the majority of these birds fly to MPNR to roost on the shallow ponds there, because of the lack of suitable high-tide roosts at Futian NNR.

In the late 1990s, the reserve began to develop a range of visitor facilities, such as a floating boardwalk and a tower hide for bird-watching that overlooks the mudflats. In December 2003, the reserve launched its education programme with the opening of a wetland education centre which works with local school teachers to promote environmental education in Shenzhen's schools. This provides a good opportunity to spread the message of the importance of the Deep Bay wetlands to the community on the Shenzhen side of the bay and, hopefully, will lead to co-ordinated conservation management of the whole Deep Bay catchment.

Photo: David Stroud.

## Guandu Nature Park, Taipei

The coastal wetlands at Guandu in northern Taiwan have always been an important site for bird-watching, and so in 1986 the Taipei government agreed to establish the Guandu Nature Park. A committee was formed to investigate the ecology of the site and plan its management. In 1988, the committee published its report, and the government began acquiring land for management. Finally in 1993, the government announced that an area would be set aside for the Guandu Nature Park. By 1996, an area of 57 ha had been taken over, and this was granted to the Wild Bird Society of Taipei (WBST) for management.

Some 23 species of shorebirds have been recorded on the coastal mudflats, with the commonest being Pacific Golden Plover *Pluvialis fulva*, Common Greenshank *Tringa nebularia*, Wood Sandpiper *T. glareola* and Common Snipe *Gallinago gallinago*. A further three species of shorebirds have been recorded within the Nature Park, namely Greater Painted-Snipe *Rostratula benghalensis*, Black-winged Stilt *Himantopus himantopus* and Little Ringed Plover *Charadrius dubius*.

At present, the peak numbers of shorebirds are about 500, but prior to 1997, there were over 2 000 Kentish Plover *Charadrius alexandrinus* and Dunlin *Calidris alpina* alone. The decline in shorebird numbers is thought to have been due to a decline in the area of mudflat adjacent to the Nature Park as a result of encroachment by mangroves. However, the WBST has recently created a high-tide roost site within the Nature Park, and a group of 60 Dunlin was recorded there in November 2003.

The Nature Park has an active wetland education programme attended by some 120 000 visitors annually. This programme includes many types of activities:

- Teachers organize special activities for school students on themes selected by the teachers themselves. These activities are mainly for primary school students;
- During weekends and holidays, a variety of activities are offered for the public and for family groups. Depending on the season, these activities may include courses on wetland ecology, such as studying the local birds, aquatic plants and frogs. Other educational activities which further increase wetland awareness include creating models of waterbirds and dragonflies from folded paper, and pressing flowers. Other topics may also be offered, such as watching the stars at night;

- Teachers also help to lead volunteers into the Nature Park to carry out various types of work that not only promote greater appreciation amongst the volunteers of how to maintain the ecological value of wetlands, but also help to improve the environment of the Nature Park; and

- Special annual events are organized, such as an annual International Bird Fair in November.

### Sungei Buloh Wetland Reserve, Singapore

This coastal wetland dominated by mangroves is located on the northern shore of Singapore. Historically, local fishermen had impounded the area for shrimp farming using inter-tidal ponds, but in 1989 an area of 87 ha was designated as a Nature Park, and this was opened to the public in 1993. In 2001, its status was upgraded to Nature Reserve and it was listed as a Shorebird Network Site. The size was expanded to 130 ha in 2003.

Some 35 species of shorebirds have been recorded at Sungei Buloh, with peak numbers of between 1 500 and 2 500 birds being recorded at any one time. These shorebirds feed mainly on the nearby mudflat but roost inside the reserve. There is an active shorebird banding programme, with some 500 shorebirds being banded each year and recoveries coming from as far afield as Russian Yakutia. A colour-flagging programme was initiated in 2003.

One of the problems that the reserve faces is from mangrove encroachment both over the mudflat and around the shorebird roosting sites within the reserve. Whilst mangrove seedlings are removed from the mudflat on an annual basis, a programme to control mangroves inside the reserve has yet to begin.

The Sungei Buloh Wetland Reserve has an active programme of wetland education for the 100 000 local and over-seas visitors that it receives annually. With assistance from Hong Kong and Shanghai Banking Corporation (HSBC), a Sungei Buloh Education Fund was established in 1997 to support a series of nature outreach programmes at the reserve. These programmes range from self-guided walks to specialized thematic trails such as "Heron Watch" and "Prawn Watch". For walk-in visitors, volunteer guides are available on Saturdays at specific times to explain the ecology of the reserve. For organized groups, a series of "Nature Hunts" has been developed to allow these visitors to explore and learn more about the reserve. In 1999, the reserve began a programme with local schools whereby a school can adopt a particular part of the reserve and be responsible for its maintenance.

### DISCUSSION

From the early 1980s, there has been a growing awareness in Asia of the importance of wetland conservation and the need to communicate this message to the public through the establish-ment of wetland education centres. These wetland centres now play a very important role in promoting wetland education and public awareness, and in many cases, their staff are also involved in the active management and conservation of the wetland of which they are a part.

With the growing economic affluence in many Asian coun-tries, more and more education centres are being built, many of which are the first centres of their kind in the countries concerned. As a result, the message of wetland conservation will continue to spread across the continent. This is now especially the case, as many of the wetland centres are beginning to network amongst themselves to share resources and experience so as to make their work more effective.

### ACKNOWLEDGEMENTS

The following persons generously provided information and comments on this paper: Ruby Fang (Guandu Nature Park, Taipei), James Gan (Sungei Buloh, Singapore) and Christine Prietto (The Wetland Centre, Australia).

### REFERENCES

**Carey, G.J. & Young, L.** 1999. The importance to waterfowl of the Mai Po Marshes and Inner Deep Bay Ramsar Site. Hong Kong Bird Report 1997: 141-149.

**Lawler, W.** 1995. Wader roost construction in Moreton Bay. Queensland Wader Study Group, Australia.

Boardwalks through the mangroves at Mai Po allow visitors to have close contact with wetland flora and fauna. Photo: David Stroud.

# Shorebird research in the East Asian-Australasian Flyway: looking to the future

*Phil J. Straw[1], Ken B. Gosbell[2] & Clive D.T. Minton[3]*

*[1]Avifauna Research & Services, PO Box 2006, Rockdale Delivery Centre, Rockdale 2216, Australia.*
*(email: philstraw@avifaunaresearch.com)*
*[2]17 Banksia Court, Heathmont, 3135 Australia. (email: ken@gosbell.id.au)*
*[3]165 Dalgetty Road, Beaumaris, 3193 Australia. (email: mintons@ozemail.com.au)*

Straw, P.J., Gosbell, K.B. & Minton, C.D.T. 2006. Shorebird research in the East Asian-Australasian Flyway: looking to the future. *Waterbirds around the world.* Eds. G.C. Boere, C.A. Galbraith & D.A. Stroud. The Stationery Office, Edinburgh, UK. pp. 328-331.

## ABSTRACT

Large-scale wader studies, revolving around ringing and wader counts, started in the early 1980s and have progressed to co-operative studies over much of Australia, New Zealand and the Asia-Pacific region. Despite extensive ringing and colour-flagging programmes and counting programmes over an increasing area of the East Asian-Australasian Flyway, research is hardly keeping pace with the loss of wader habitats and declines in many of the wader populations of this flyway. Plans to extend a network of researchers and volunteers across the three flyways of the Asia-Pacific region are underway with collaborative studies and the establishment of a multi-lingual wader studies newsletter.

## INTRODUCTION

This paper seeks to highlight some of the achievements towards our understanding of migratory waterbirds in the Asia-Pacific region, and some of the issues that need to be addressed in the future, if we are to effectively protect migratory and non-migratory waterbirds and their habitats. The views are from an Australian perspective and focus on waders, but essentially cover significant events in the move towards conservation of migratory waterbirds in the Asia-Pacific region.

The Asia-Pacific region is made up of three recognized wader flyways, the Central Asian-South Asian Flyway, the East Asian-Australasian Flyway and the Western (or Central) Pacific Flyway (Fig. 1). The best known is undoubtedly the East Asian-Australasian Flyway due to the extensive research carried out there in recent years. The East Asian-Australasian Flyway alone is home to at least five million migratory waders and an untold number of non-migratory waders. Migratory species fly along the three identified flyways crossing 57 countries and territories in the region. During their migration, these birds depend on strategically located staging areas where birds stop to rest and "refuel", by building up fat deposits, before continuing their migration. Many of these birds pass through heavily populated regions that encompass more than 45% of the world human population who compete for resources and space with the waders.

Over the past twenty-five years, a number of wader studies have been carried out in the East Asian-Australasian Flyway. These studies have identified the range, migration routes, staging areas and breeding grounds of many species. A result of these studies has also clearly illustrated the worrying decline in available habitat, critical for the long-term survival of many species.

At a recent International Wader Study Group Conference in Cadiz, Spain, wader experts found that the majority of wader populations are in decline. However, the Asia-Pacific region is of special concern as it has the largest number of populations under

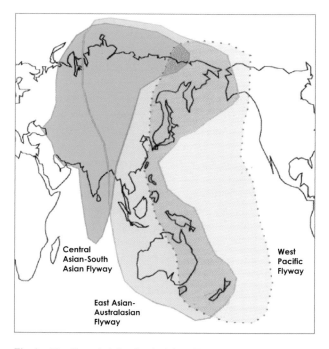

**Fig. 1.** The Central Asian-South Asian, East Asian-Australasian and Western Pacific Flyways (Wetlands International image).

threat or least understood. These concerns are not restricted to waders; other waterbirds such as cranes and Anatidae are also under threat or in decline. For migratory species to survive, they must have secure breeding, staging and non-breeding areas where there are sufficient food resources and minimal disturbance. At this stage, it is not known to what extent the loss of inter-tidal habitat in the Yellow Sea (the most important staging area for a large proportion of migratory waders in the East Asian-Australasian Flyway) has had an effect on migratory waders, an area of research obviously needing further investigation.

## RESEARCH

Research on migratory species in the Asia-Pacific region has slowly gained momentum over the past twenty-five years. Prior to this, large-scale research had been carried out only in New Zealand where shorebird researchers have been active since the 1960s.

Serious research on populations and migration in Australia was not initiated until 1981 after the formation of the Australasian Wader Study Group (AWSG), a Special Interest Group of the Royal Australasian Ornithologists' Union (Curry 1981). Prior to this, little was known about the wader populations over much of the Australian continent and even less about those of the rest of the Asia-Pacific flyways.

In 1981, the AWSG conducted its first national wader counts at known key non-breeding (overwintering) sites in an effort to understand changes in numbers of various migratory species, as well as providing information on wader movements (Martindale 1981). During these early surveys, 303 volunteers surveyed accessible sites over a single weekend, counting a total of about 400 000 waders. Some of the more remote areas of Australia, such as the Gulf of Carpentaria and the north-west coastline, were surveyed during the same season from the air using small, fixed-winged aircraft. These surveys revealed large concentrations of waders and highlighted the need to explore these areas in more detail.

The first major ground expedition to the north-west of Australia was carried out in 1981 with financial and logistic support from the Western Australia Government. This, and subsequent surveys, revealed internationally significant numbers of about 20 species of migratory waders, including most of the world's population of Great Knot *Calidris tenuirostris*. Even now, new discoveries are being made about wader populations in these sparsely populated areas of Australia. It was not until the 1990s that the Northern Territory coastline was investigated. Counts in this region were due to the efforts of a single individual who deviated from standard aerial fauna surveys to discover over two million waders of 40 species along this coastline. An example of an even more recent discovery is the occurrence of an estimated 2.9 million Oriental Pratincoles *Glareola maldivarum* along 80 Mile Beach in northern Western Australia in February 2004. Prior to this, the previous population estimate for this species in Australia was 60 000 (Sitters *et al.* 2004).

Despite the amount of work carried out so far in Australia, there is no long-standing tradition of focussed wader research in Australian universities or other research institutes, as there is, for example, in Europe. Most wader research in Australia has been carried out by volunteers. A great deal has been learned through their efforts, but volunteers working in their own time are not well placed to carry out ecological studies that require long periods of continuous fieldwork, prolonged analysis, or expensive field equipment. Such studies, for example of foraging ecology or precise roosting requirements, are often needed for science-based management of wader sites. The need for professional studies in Australia, and the Asia-Pacific region as a whole, is likely to increase as human development encroaches further into wader sites.

### Bird ringing as a research tool

Although wader ringing has been carried out in New Zealand, and to some extent in Australia, since the 1960s, large-scale ringing did not start until the late 1970s with the introduction of cannon-netting by ringers from the UK. Since then, over 320 000 migratory waders have been ringed in Australia by various wader study groups, though mainly in the north-west and south-east of the country. Ringing recoveries have played a major role in plotting migration routes and identifying major staging areas throughout the East Asian-Australasian Flyway. Recoveries come from retrapped birds, hunters, or rings returned by members of the public from birds found dead. By far the most numerous recoveries have been from hunters and, to some extent, ringing recoveries were a measure of the density of hunters and hunting activity, rather than large concentrations of birds as may have previously been thought. Nevertheless, ringing provided useful information locating important wader sites and these have been

**Fig. 2.** Great Knot *Calidris tenuirostris* with alpha-numeric colour flag visible in the field. Photo: Adrian Boyle.

supported by ground surveys. The situation was vastly improved with the introduction of colour-flagging in Australia in 1990 (Minton 2005). Colour flags are basically coloured plastic (darvic) rings that are shaped so that a tab extends from the ring providing a much larger viewable surface area than conventional colour rings. The results of introducing flagging have been impressive. Many bird-watchers, armed with binoculars or a spotting scope, are now able to see the various combinations of colour flags which identify the locality where the birds were marked. The reporting rate from flags has far outstripped the recovery rate from conventional ringing (Minton 2005). Flag sightings are now regularly reported from Arctic Russia and Alaska, either of birds observed at the nest or, in the case of Bar-tailed Godwits *Limosa lapponica* in Alaska, of birds congregating before departing on their southward migration.

There are now 20 different locations throughout the East Asian-Australasian Flyway where colour flagging in taking place. With new ringing sites being established in the flyway, new discoveries are made each season, such as a Dunlin *Calidris alpina* caught while overwintering in the Yangtze River estuary, China, and then observed nesting on Barrow Island, Alaska. This is the first known connection of this species between China and the USA. Some individuals of species such as the Great Knot have been observed in successive years on their nesting grounds in Siberia and at their non-breeding grounds in north-western Australia. Even when only small numbers of birds are colour-flagged at their breeding grounds, as in the case of the endangered Spoon-billed Sandpiper *Eurynorhynchus pygmeus*, very useful "recoveries" have been made along their migration routes and in the non-breeding grounds, providing invaluable information for their long-term conservation.

It has been possible, for some time, to identify individual birds in the field by placing a combination of colour bands on their legs. However, this relies on accurate observations to determine the position of a number of bands, and wrongly reported combinations can be a problem, especially as some colours tend to fade over time. In 2004, a trial using alpha-numeric engraved colour flags was undertaken in Australia with a high degree of success. This system is now used increasingly throughout the East Asian-Australasian Flyway with very rewarding results, especially with the advent of digital cameras and "digiscoping" enabling photographs to be taken of flagged birds through a telescope (see Fig. 2).

Recent moves to train people in ringing and survey techniques have resulted on some large-scale ringing and flagging in mainland China with some spectacular results. Birds ringed in Asia that migrate to Australia and New Zealand have a high probability of being observed by bird-watchers and interested members of the public; they are also observed in other regions with high numbers of bird-watchers, such as Japan and parts of China (Taiwan and Hong Kong), Russia (study sites on the breeding grounds) and Alaska.

Bird ringing and colour-flagging have provided a lot of information on movements of birds between breeding and non-breeding areas and on longevity, while the data collected at the time of capture (morphometrics, weights, etc.) have provided invaluable information on the timing of moult and weight gains, which in turn provide an indication of distance travelled between one site and another. In an attempt to understand recruitment and mortality rates, recent emphasis has been on the determination of the proportion of first-year birds (identified by plumage differences) at a range of sites in south-eastern Australia, particularly Victoria and South Australia. These are correlated with observations made of breeding conditions in the Arctic (Minton *et al.* 2005).

### Radio and satellite tracking

Radio and satellite tracking have been carried out by a number of researchers in Australia to determine the movements of shorebirds locally or globally. The advantage of radio tracking is the small nature of the transmitters involved enabling them to be used on the smallest waders without causing significant inconvenience to the birds. The downside of radio transmitters is the short range of operation. Despite this, useful information has been gained using this equipment tracking birds between foraging habitats and roost sites, especially at night when visual observations are virtually impossible. Such studies have played important roles in providing information for wildlife and land managers, including local and state government agencies. Examples include Rohweder (2000) and Todd (2000) whose studies located previously unknown nocturnal roost sites and foraging habitat.

Satellite tracking holds no geographic bounds and is providing invaluable data about the precise migration routes taken by migrating shorebirds and the time spent at staging areas and time taken to fly between sites. The first successful attempt to track migratory shorebirds in this flyway was worked carried out by the Queensland Wader Study Group, in association with the Wild Bird Society of Japan, between 1997 and 1999 when Far Eastern Curlews *Numenius madagascariensis* were fitted with transmitters using custom-made harnesses to attach the transmitter. Although the project tracked a number of birds between their non-breeding grounds in Australia and breeding grounds in Russia and northern China, the majority of birds abandoned their migration and returned to the sites at which they were trapped. It would appear that the weight and/or wind drag of the transmitters were too great. More recently, work carried out in Alaska on Bar-tailed Godwits that migrate between Alaska and eastern Australia and New Zealand has demonstrated that this species is able to carry satellite transmitters during this apparent 11 000 km non-stop flight (Gill 2006). In this study, new technology was available, enabling relatively small transmitters to be surgically implanted in the abdominal cavity of the bird. Although the transmitters failed to function, the birds, marked with individually

numbered leg flags, were observed after their arrival in Australia and New Zealand. Without doubt it is only a matter of time before such flights will be tracked accurately, providing much needed data for shorebird management in the Asia-Pacific region.

### Population monitoring

An ongoing population monitoring programme (PMP) of Australian waders has been carried out since a pilot study in 1981. The purpose of the programme is to monitor year to year changes in populations of migratory and non-migratory waders at selected sites across the continent. Counts are made twice each year: in February, when migratory species have finished any southward movement, enabling counts to be carried out at many sites without fear of double counting; and again in late June to early July, when all migratory species that breed in the Northern Hemisphere are on their breeding grounds, leaving only non-breeding (largely immature birds) behind. Twenty-three key sites were among those counted in 1981, and additional important sites have been added since as a result of increased knowledge of site use by key species. Regular monitoring has shown alarming declines in some wader populations, such as the Curlew Sandpiper *Calidris ferruginea*. More subtle or slow changes in Australian wader populations cannot be detected easily with the existing array of count sites, and it has been stressed that the PMP needs to be expanded (Wilson 2001). In 2004, the AWSG, in conjunction with the Australian Government (Department of Environment and Heritage), commenced a programme in Australia aimed at monitoring waders that utilize the Yellow Sea as a stopover en route to/from Australia, to determine any short-term trends in the populations of species likely to be impacted by the significant inter-tidal land claim in this region, particularly at Saemangeum in South Korea. This programme also has an objective of testing methodological approaches that could improve the sensitivity of population monitoring on the non-breeding grounds.

Fluctuations in population sizes detected in Australia are thought to be as a result of the influence of some impact along the flyway rather than in Australia. There do not seem to be major impacts in the way of habitat loss or disturbance of waders, other than at some local sites, in Australia, or obvious changes in the Arctic breeding grounds. Concerns about the impacts of habitat loss on migratory species have led to a programme of surveys in East Asia, especially the Yellow Sea area (Barter 2002). Surveys conducted since 1996 in China and Korea show that the extensive inter-tidal areas and near-coastal wetlands of the Yellow Sea support very large numbers of migratory waders during both northward and southward migrations.

In the Asia-Pacific region, the Asian Waterbird Census (AWC) was initiated in 1987 as in integral part of the International Waterbird Census co-ordinated by Wetlands International. The AWC provides the most comprehensive waterbird count programme in the region. The census is undertaken in January each year, and is carried out primarily by a volunteer-based network to monitor the populations and distribution of waterbirds and the status of wetland habitats, while at the same time enhancing public awareness about waterbird and wetland conservation. Since the establishment of the AWC, more than 5 700 sites across 25 countries have been counted at least once by thousands of volunteers. This project is linked to the shorebird monitoring programme in Australia, Anatidae and shorebird censuses in Japan and waterbird counts in Hong Kong.

## LOOKING TO THE FUTURE

We are very fortunate in having several long-term counting programmes in Australia, New Zealand and parts of Asia (through the AWC), as well as long-term ringing programmes in northern Western Australia, south-eastern Australia, New Zealand and Japan. We also have long-term productivity data from measurements of the percentage of juvenile birds in catches each year. Studies in New Zealand have provided some of the essential foundations for conservation actions as a result of long-term research programmes, providing knowledge of populations and changes to populations over time. Such studies should continue and be extended into other countries in the region.

As a result of the efforts put in by many people over the past 25 years, we are now able to identify some of the major issues that need to be addressed if we are to ensure the conservation of waterbird populations and their habitats in the Asia-Pacific region. A network of important sites for migratory waders has been identified and supported by the governments of many of the countries in the East Asian-Australasian Flyway through the efforts of Wetlands International, with support from the Australian, Dutch, Japanese and U.S. Governments.

Future counts of waterbird populations, including migratory waders, and wetland surveys will need to include a network of a large number of people on the ground, more than the membership/staff of any single group. This will take the collaborative efforts of international, national and local bird groups and conservationists, as well as the establishment of an effective communication network in a region with a high diversity of languages.

It has recently been proposed that an Asia-Pacific wader specialist group, or network, be formed, working in close association with other international groups, such as Wetlands International, WWF, BirdLife International and special interest groups (e.g. International Wader Study Group), regional groups, such as the AWSG, and national and local bird and conservation groups in all of the countries within the Asia-Pacific region.

A major challenge for this new group will be to establish a network of university researchers in the Asia-Pacific region. To some extent, this has started to happen through co-operative work co-ordinated by Wetlands International with major input from members of the AWSG and New Zealand Wader Study Group. Researchers from Fudan University and the East China Normal University in Shanghai, Beijing Normal University in Beijing, and Tunghai University in Taiwan, have been involved in collaborative ringing and flagging projects and wader surveys along the east coast of China and the Yellow Sea for the past ten years, as well as conducting research projects in shorebird ecology. While it is likely that research is being carried out at universities in other countries in the Asia-Pacific region, communication has been difficult. To a large extent, this is being addressed by the translation of a newsletter for the East Asian-Australasian Flyway (The Tattler) into Chinese and Indonesian and an increased circulation now covering countries in all of the flyways in the Asia-Pacific region.

International concerns publicized during recent wetland reclamation projects have helped to focus attention on the tragic loss of essential wetland habitats in Japan, China and Korea. However, it is essential to have rigorous scientific data to back up arguments for protection against future losses, rather than solely depending on the emotional side of wildlife conservation. Hopefully the lessons learned from the losses in Japan and the impending loss of more than 40 sq. km of inter-tidal habitat at Saemangeum in South Korea will help to prevent similar disasters in the future. An international research project is planned, starting in 2006, to monitor the effects of the loss of wader feeding habitat at Saemangeum on waders in the Yellow Sea as well as in Australia and New Zealand.

Planning for the future would include improved monitoring of waders over a wide range of wetlands, increasing the networking of researchers and conservationists, and extending training programmes to provide expertise in bird identification, ecology and survey techniques as well as the effective management of wetlands.

## ACKNOWLEDGEMENTS

The authors would like to acknowledge constructive comments on early drafts by Phil Battley, Mark Barter and Doug Watkins.

## REFERENCES

**Barter, M.A.** 2002. Shorebirds of the Yellow Sea: Importance, threats and conservation status. Wetlands International Global Series 9, International Wader Studies 12. Canberra, Australia.

**Curry, P.** (ed). 1981. Australian Wader Study Group; its history and progress to date. The Stilt 1: 1.

**Gill, B.** 2006. Good News, Band News, and Great News: Satellite tagged Bar-tailed Godwits. Tattler; Newsletter for the Asia Pacific Flyways, January 2006: 4.

**Martindale, J.** 1981. AWSG Wader Counts in Australia. The Stilt 1: 1.

**Minton, C.D.T.** 2005. What have we learned from banding and flagging waders in Australia? In: P. Straw (ed) Status and Conservation of Shorebirds in the East Asian-Australasian Flyway. Proceedings of the Australasian Shorebirds Conference, 13-15 December 2003, Canberra, Australia. Wetlands International Global Series 18, International Wader Studies 17. Sydney, Australia.

**Minton, C.D.T., Jessop, R., Collins, P. & Gosbell, K.** 2005. Monitoring shorebird breeding productivity by the percentage of first year birds in populations in S.E. Australian non-breeding areas. In: P. Straw (ed) Status and Conservation of Shorebirds in the East Asian-Australasian Flyway. Proceedings of the Australasian Shorebirds Conference, 13-15 December 2003, Canberra, Australia. Wetlands International Global Series 18, International Wader Studies 17. Sydney, Australia.

**Rohweder, D.A.** 2000. Day-night use by five species of migratory shorebird in the Richmond River Estuary, Northern New South Wales, Australia. PhD thesis, Southern Cross University, Australia.

**Sitters, H., Minton, C., Collins, P., Etheridge, B., Hassell, C. & O'Connor, F.** 2004. Extraordinary numbers of Oriental Pratincoles in NW Australia. The Stilt 45: 43-49.

**Todd, M.K.** 2000. Feeding ecology of Latham's Snipe *Gallinago hardwickii* in the lower Hunter Valley (New South Wales). Emu 100: 133-138.

**Wilson, J.R.** 2001. The Australasian Wader Studies Group population monitoring project: where to now? Perspectives from the Chair. The Stilt 39, July 2001.

# Threatened waterbird species in eastern and southern Asia and actions needed for their conservation

*Michael J. Crosby[1] & Simba Chan[2]*

[1]*BirdLife International, Wellbrook Court, Girton Road, Cambridge, CB3 0NA, UK. (email: mike.crosby@birdlife.org.uk)*
[2]*Birdlife Asia Division, Toyo-Shinjuku Building, 2nd floor, 1-12-15 Shinjuku, Shinjuku-Ku, Tokyo 160-0022, Japan.*

Crosby, M.J. & Chan, S. 2006. Threatened waterbird species in eastern and southern Asia and actions needed for their conservation. *Waterbirds around the world.* Eds. G.C. Boere, C.A. Galbraith & D.A. Stroud. The Stationery Office, Edinburgh, UK. pp. 332-338.

## ABSTRACT

This paper outlines three priority-setting projects conducted by the BirdLife International Asia Partnership which are relevant to threatened waterbirds in the East Asia-Pacific Flyway, all of which are designed to collect the best available information on these birds, their habitats and key sites, and to use this to define the most appropriate actions for their conservation. Many projects are already underway to implement the recommendations resulting from these priority-setting analyses. The development of a network for the conservation of the endangered Black-faced Spoonbill *Platalea minor* is given as an example of an approach that could be used more widely in the region.

## INTRODUCTION

Asia is immensely rich in waterbirds, but these birds and their wetland habitats are under great pressure, linked to a combination of rapid economic development and increasing human population. As a consequence, many Asian waterbird species are globally threatened. This paper presents an overview of three projects of the BirdLife Asia Partnership[1], conducted in collaboration with Wetlands International and other organizations, which are relevant to the conservation of threatened waterbirds in eastern and southern Asia.

### The Asia Red Data Book

BirdLife International (formerly ICBP) has been identifying and documenting globally threatened bird species since the 1960s. In addition to global checklists of threatened birds (e.g. Collar *et al.* 1994, BirdLife International 2000), regional bird Red Data Books have been published for Africa (Collar & Stuart 1985), the Americas (Collar *et al.* 1992) and, most recently, a large part of Asia (BirdLife International 2001). The publication of *Threatened birds of Asia: the BirdLife International Red Data Book* in 2001 was the culmination of a six-year project involving well over 1 000 compilers and data contributors. This book covers the whole of eastern and southern Asia from the Pacific west as far as the valley of the Yenisey in the north and Pakistan in the south (hereafter referred to as "the Asia region"). It documents in great detail the 323 globally threatened bird species that regularly occur in this region, in two volumes totalling over 3 000 pages of text and maps. The Red Data Book has been produced on CD-ROM, and the species accounts can be viewed and downloaded on the Internet (www.rdb.or.id). There is a facility on the web-site to add new data on threatened birds to the species accounts, which will make it possible to keep these accounts up to date. Thousands of copies of the book, CD-ROM and species accounts have been distributed and are being widely used within the Asia region.

### Saving Asia's threatened birds

Although the Asian Red Data Book is a valuable resource for many in the conservation community, it is not suitable for some target audiences, for example government officials with responsibility for land-use planning but without any specialist knowledge of birds. A follow-up to the Red Data Book was therefore produced, *Saving Asia's threatened birds: a guide for government and civil society* (BirdLife International 2003). This was designed as an advocacy document to present the main conclusions of the Red Data Book to decision-makers in a clear and highly visual format. It is based upon a synthesis of the detailed information from the Red Data Book, with a particular focus on recommendations for the conservation of birds and their key sites and habitats. In addition to its technical content, *Saving Asia's threatened birds* includes approximately 200 photographs of birds, habitats and conservation issues designed to illustrate that Asia's threatened birds and their habitats are a beautiful and spectacular part of Asia's heritage that must be saved. Over 1 000 copies of the book have been distributed to government and civil society in the Asia region.

### Important Bird Areas in Asia

BirdLife's Important Bird Area (IBA) Programme is a worldwide initiative aimed at identifying, documenting and working towards the conservation and sustainable management of a network of critical sites for the world's birds. These sites are selected through the application of standard, internationally recognized criteria, based upon the most up-to-date information available on bird distributions and populations. The IBA approach is particularly appropriate for waterbird conservation because many species have a tendency to congregate at particular wetland sites. This means that many of their conservation needs can be addressed by actions focussed on certain key sites. Two of the four standard global selection categories used to identify IBAs are relevant to waterbirds. One of these is used to select sites that support significant numbers of one or more globally threatened species, while the other is used to select sites because they support internationally important congregations of one or more waterbird species. The Asian IBA Programme was launched in 1996, and has so far resulted in the publication of *Important Bird Areas in Asia: key sites for conservation* (BirdLife International 2004) and directories of IBAs in Cambodia (Seng Kim Hout *et al.* 2003), India (Islam & Rahmani 2004), several regions of Indonesia (Rombang & Rudyanto 1999, Holmes & Rombang 2001, Holmes *et al.* 2001, Rombang *et al.* 2002), Laos (Ounekham & Inthapatha 2003), the Philippines (Mallari *et al.* 2001), Taiwan (Wild Bird Federation

---

[1] BirdLife International is a world-wide partnership of organizations working to conserve all bird species and their habitats. In Asia, BirdLife has Partner and Affiliate organizations or Country Programmes in 17 countries and territories, and works with research contacts in all of the other countries and territories in the region.

**Table 1.** Globally threatened waterbird species in eastern and southern Asia. The table includes the threatened categories allocated to waterbird species in Collar *et al.* (1994), BirdLife International (2001) and BirdLife International (2004). If the 1994 or 2001 columns are blank, the threatened category is the same as that given in the 2004 column.

| Scientific name | English name | 1994 | 2001 | 2004 |
|---|---|---|---|---|
| *Pelecanus crispus* | Dalmatian Pelican | | LR/cd | VU |
| *Pelecanus philippensis* | Spot-billed Pelican | | | VU |
| *Egretta eulophotes* | Chinese Egret | EN | | VU |
| *Ardea insignis* | White-bellied Heron | | | EN |
| *Gorsachius magnificus* | White-eared Night-Heron | CR | | EN |
| *Gorsachius goisagi* | Japanese Night-Heron | VU | | EN |
| *Mycteria cinerea* | Milky Stork | | | VU |
| *Ciconia stormi* | Storm's Stork | | | EN |
| *Ciconia boyciana* | Oriental Stork | | | EN |
| *Leptoptilos javanicus* | Lesser Adjutant | | | VU |
| *Leptoptilos dubius* | Greater Adjutant | | | EN |
| *Pseudibis davisoni* | White-shouldered Ibis | EN | | CR |
| *Thaumatibis gigantea* | Giant Ibis | | | CR |
| *Nipponia nippon* | Crested Ibis | CR | | EN |
| *Platalea minor* | Black-faced Spoonbill | CR | | EN |
| *Oxyura leucocephala* | White-headed Duck | VU | | EN |
| *Anser cygnoides* | Swan Goose | VU | | EN |
| *Anser erythropus* | Lesser White-fronted Goose | | | VU |
| *Branta ruficollis* | Red-breasted Goose | | | VU |
| *Tadorna cristata* | Crested Shelduck | | | CR |
| *Cairina scutulata* | White-winged Duck | | | EN |
| *Anas luzonica* | Philippine Duck | LR/nt | | VU |
| *Anas formosa* | Baikal Teal | | | VU |
| *Marmaronetta angustirostris* | Marbled Teal | | | VU |
| *Rhodonessa caryophyllacea* | Pink-headed Duck | | | CR |
| *Aythya baeri* | Baer's Pochard | | | VU |
| *Mergus squamatus* | Scaly-sided Merganser | VU | VU | EN |
| *Grus leucogeranus* | Siberian Crane | EN | | CR |
| *Grus antigone* | Sarus Crane | LR/nt | | VU |
| *Grus vipio* | White-naped Crane | | | VU |
| *Grus monacha* | Hooded Crane | LR/cd | | VU |
| *Grus nigricollis* | Black-necked Crane | | | VU |
| *Grus japonensis* | Red-crowned Crane | VU | | EN |
| *Coturnicops exquisitus* | Swinhoe's Rail | | | VU |
| *Gallirallus okinawae* | Okinawa Rail | | | EN |
| *Aramidopsis plateni* | Snoring Rail | | | VU |
| *Gymnocrex rosenbergii* | Blue-faced Rail | | | VU |
| *Gymnocrex talaudensis* | Talaud Rail | NE | | EN |
| *Habroptila wallacii* | Invisible Rail | | | VU |
| *Heliopais personata* | Masked Finfoot | | | VU |
| *Rhinoptilus bitorquatus* | Jerdon's Courser | EN | | CR |
| *Vanellus macropterus* | Javanese Lapwing | EX | | CR |
| *Vanellus gregarius* | Sociable Lapwing | VU | VU | CR |
| *Scolopax mira* | Ryukyu Woodcock | | | VU |
| *Scolopax rochussenii* | Moluccan Woodcock | VU | | EN |
| *Gallinago nemoricola* | Wood Snipe | | | VU |
| *Numenius tahitiensis* | Bristle-thighed Curlew | | | VU |
| *Tringa guttifer* | Spotted Greenshank | | | EN |
| *Eurynorhynchus pygmeus* | Spoon-billed Sandpiper | VU | VU | EN |
| *Larus saundersi* | Saunders's Gull | EN | | VU |
| *Larus relictus* | Relict Gull | LR/nt | | VU |
| *Rissa brevirostris* | Red-legged Kittiwake | | | VU |
| *Sterna bernsteini* | Chinese Crested Tern | | | CR |
| *Rynchops albicollis* | Indian Skimmer | | | VU |

Key: EX = Extinct; CR = Critical; EN = Endangered; VU = Vulnerable; LR/cd = Lower Risk (Conservation Dependent); LR/nt = Lower Risk (Near Threatened); NE = Not Evaluated.

Taiwan 2001), Thailand (Bird Conservation Society of Thailand 2004) and Vietnam (Tordoff 2002). Several other national directories are in preparation.

The Asian IBA Programme has five long-term objectives: (i) to provide a basis for the development of national conservation strategies and protected areas programmes; (ii) to highlight areas that should be safeguarded through wise land-use planning, national policies and regulations, and the grant-giving and lending programmes of international banks and development agencies; (iii) to provide a focus for the conservation efforts of civil society, including national and regional NGO networks; (iv) to highlight sites that are threatened or inadequately protected, so that urgent remedial measures can be taken; and (v) to guide the implementation of global conservation conventions and migratory bird agreements.

## RESULTS

BirdLife International (2001) documented a total of 323 globally threatened bird species that regularly occur in the Asia region. These include 54 waterbird species (of which six also range into Europe), a higher total than for any other region of the world (Table 1, Fig. 1). This high total reflects both the richness of Asia in waterbird species, and the great pressures on the region's wetlands and their birds.

Many of the threatened waterbird species in Australasia, Africa and the Americas are island endemics or continental species with restricted ranges. When these restricted-range species are excluded from the regional totals, a more dramatic picture is apparent (Fig. 2). Eastern and southern Asia have a much higher total of widespread threatened waterbirds than any other region of the world. These include northern migrants such as Swan Goose *Anser cygnoides*, Siberian Crane *Grus leucogeranus* and Spoon-billed Sandpiper *Eurynorhynchus pygmeus*, some of which disperse very widely outside the breeding season. They also include tropical waterbirds such as Spot-billed Pelican *Pelecanus philippensis*, Lesser Adjutant *Leptoptilos javanicus* and Indian Skimmer *Rynchops albicollis*, which were formerly found throughout much of south and south-east Asia. The protection of these widespread threatened waterbirds is a particularly difficult conservation challenge, because they are often shared between several countries and occur at many sites.

BirdLife International (2001) illustrated the major declines and localized extinctions suffered by many of Asia's threatened waterbirds. For example, the Indian Skimmer has virtually disappeared from south-east Asia, and the species is now largely restricted to the northern Indian subcontinent (Fig. 3).

Many of the 323 threatened species in the Asia region overlap in range and habitat requirements, and a single conservation action can often benefit several species. In BirdLife International (2003), these threatened species were subdivided into groups according to their distributions and the habitats that they occupy. This analysis identified nine major forest regions, three grassland regions and twenty wetlands regions. The twenty wetland regions (Fig. 4) together cover all significant breeding, passage and wintering habitats for threatened waterbirds in the Asia region. Fifteen of these wetland regions lie within the East Asia-Pacific Flyway. BirdLife International (2003) included a standard account for all of the forest, grassland and wetland regions. This documented the threatened species that occur in the region and the key habitats and IBAs for their conservation, with an analysis

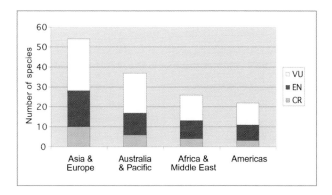

Fig. 1. Numbers of globally threatened waterbirds by region of the world.

Key: VU = Vulnerable; EN = Endangered; CR = Critically Endangered. Columns represent Regions of the world: 1 = Asia and Europe; 2 = Australasia and the Pacific; 3 = Africa and the Middle East; 4 = The Americas.

The totals for "Asia and Europe" (column 1) include the Critically Endangered Slender-billed Curlew *Numenius tenuirostris*, which occurs in Europe and western Asia outside the region covered in BirdLife International (2001) and is therefore not listed in Table 1. The Sarus Crane *Grus antigone* and Red-legged Kittiwake *Rissa brevirostris* occur outside the Asia region, in Australasia and the Americas, respectively, but are included in the total for "Asia and Europe" (column 1) because substantial proportions of their ranges lie within Asia. Six species, Dalmatian Pelican *Pelecanus crispus*, Lesser White-fronted Goose *Anser erythropus*, Marbled Teal *Marmaronetta angustirostris*, White-headed Duck *Oxyura leucocephala*, Sociable Lapwing *Vanellus gregarius* and Slender-billed Curlew, have most of their ranges in Europe and Asia and are therefore included in the totals for "Asia and Europe" (column 1), but they also range into the Middle East and/or Africa. The Bristle-thighed Curlew *Numenius tahitiensis* occurs in the Asia region and was documented in BirdLife International (2001), but most of its range is in the Pacific and North America, and it is included in the totals for "Australasia and the Pacific" (column 2). Note that the Socotra Cormorant *Phalacrocorax nigrogularis* and Northern Bald Ibis *Geronticus eremita*, which are included in the totals for "Africa and the Middle East" (column 3), range into south-west Asia.

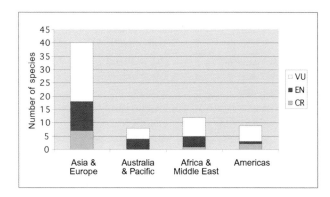

Fig. 2. Numbers of "widespread" globally threatened waterbirds by region of the world.

Key: VU = Vulnerable; EN = Endangered; CR = Critically Endangered. Regions of the world: 1 = Asia and Europe; 2 = Australasia and the Pacific; 3 = Africa and the Middle East; 4 = The Americas.

of the threats to birds and their habitats, and the conservation measures required to address these threats. The main conservation issues (and proposed conservation measures) in each region

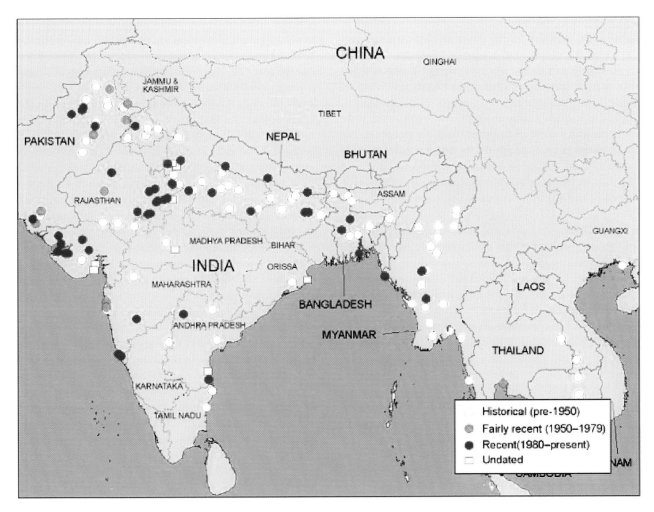

Fig. 3. The decline in the range of Indian Skimmer *Rynchops albicollis*.

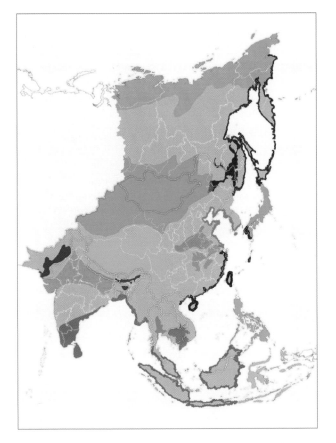

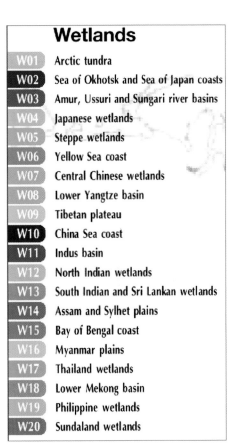

## Wetlands

| | |
|---|---|
| W01 | Arctic tundra |
| W02 | Sea of Okhotsk and Sea of Japan coasts |
| W03 | Amur, Ussuri and Sungari river basins |
| W04 | Japanese wetlands |
| W05 | Steppe wetlands |
| W06 | Yellow Sea coast |
| W07 | Central Chinese wetlands |
| W08 | Lower Yangtze basin |
| W09 | Tibetan plateau |
| W10 | China Sea coast |
| W11 | Indus basin |
| W12 | North Indian wetlands |
| W13 | South Indian and Sri Lankan wetlands |
| W14 | Assam and Sylhet plains |
| W15 | Bay of Bengal coast |
| W16 | Myanmar plains |
| W17 | Thailand wetlands |
| W18 | Lower Mekong basin |
| W19 | Philippine wetlands |
| W20 | Sundaland wetlands |

Fig. 4. Key wetland regions for threatened birds in the Asia region.

are grouped under four main headings: (i) habitat loss and degradation; (ii) protected areas coverage and management; (iii) exploitation of birds; and (iv) gaps in knowledge.

BirdLife International (2004) documented a total of 2 293 IBAs in the 28 countries and territories in the Asia region (Fig. 5). These sites cover a total area of 2 331 560 sq.km, equivalent to 7.6% of the region's land area. Eighty-two percent of the IBAs were identified because of their significance for globally threatened bird species, including the 54 threatened waterbird species that occur in the Asia region. Forty-one percent of the IBAs were identified because they hold globally significant congregations of waterbirds, seabirds and/or migratory raptors or cranes.

## DISCUSSION

The projects outlined above have compiled comprehensive, up-to-date information on threatened waterbirds in eastern and southern Asia. They have identified the wetland regions where these threatened waterbirds are concentrated and the Important Bird Areas that are critical for their long-term survival. A large number of measures have been proposed for the conservation of these waterbirds, and their habitats and key sites. These projects therefore provide a sound basis for waterbird and wetland conservation in eastern and southern Asia. However, there are still many gaps in knowledge of Asia's waterbirds, and our perceptions of the priority actions required for their conservation are likely to change in the light of new information and as new threats affect Asia's birds and their habitats.

The main threats to Asia's waterbirds include conversion of wetlands to agricultural land and for development, and unsustainable levels of exploitation. Conservation NGOs can carry out some of the measures recommended in BirdLife International (2001, 2003) to help address these threats; for example, through projects to improve the protection and management of key IBAs, by raising awareness of waterbirds and the threats that they face, and through surveys and monitoring. However, there are many actions that can only be taken by governments or the corporate sector. For example, the governments of China, North Korea and South Korea have plans to reclaim almost half of the remaining inter-tidal wetlands around the Yellow Sea, which would have a devastating impact on coastal ecosystems and east Asian endemic shorebirds such as Spotted Greenshank *Tringa guttifer*. The conservation community needs to persuade governments to review and revise potentially damaging plans of this type, and should seek to be involved in the processes to assess the environmental impact of new projects. Large numbers of copies of *Threatened Birds of Asia, Saving Asia's threatened birds* and *Important Bird Areas in Asia* have been distributed to government and civil society with the aim of raising awareness and motivation for the conservation of threatened birds throughout the Asia region.

The BirdLife Partnership is currently developing two mechanisms for the protection and management of IBAs, the "Site Support Group" (SSG) concept and IBA monitoring. SSG is a generic term used to describe groups of local stakeholders who share a common commitment to the conservation of an IBA. SSG activities vary according to local circumstances and priorities, but often include monitoring of biodiversity and threats, implementing education and awareness programmes, and developing eco-tourism or other income-generating activities with benefits for local livelihoods and biodiversity. At formally

protected IBAs, SSGs can complement the work of protected area management staff; where appropriate, this relationship can be formalized to allow the SSG to participate in protected area management. At IBAs that are not designated as formal protected areas, SSGs can support local authorities, local people and/or private land owners to conserve biodiversity, or even take responsibility for site management themselves. In addition to supporting site management, SSGs are frequently well positioned to campaign against immediate threats to biodiversity or to lobby for change in policies that undermine IBA conservation.

A prerequisite for effective conservation action for the IBA network is accurate, up-to-date information on the nature and severity of threats to biodiversity, the status of bird populations and habitats, and the type and effectiveness of conservation action at IBAs. To this end, a region-wide monitoring system needs to be established, comprising site-based monitoring at individual IBAs linked to national and regional mechanisms to manage data on the IBA network as a whole. Such a system could generate information to guide policy development at the national and regional levels, as well as supporting site safeguard policies, by providing early warnings about threats to biodiversity at sites. Furthermore, an IBA monitoring system could facilitate adaptive management of individual IBAs, by identifying priority conservation actions and evaluating their effectiveness. Given the scale of the IBA network and the finite resources available for its conservation, the monitoring system needs to be cost effective and engage as broad a spectrum of stakeholders as possible.

There is a much higher number of widespread threatened waterbird species in the Asia region than in any other region of the world, and many of these require conservation action in several of their range states. An international network established for the endangered Black-faced Spoonbill *Platalea minor* provides a good example of a mechanism to stimulate and co-ordinate conservation actions for a widespread threatened waterbird. The Black-faced Spoonbill is a rare waterbird which breeds on islets in the Yellow Sea off the coasts of Korea and China, and winters in several east Asian countries. Kennerley (1990) published a review that showed that the known population of the species at that time was only 288 individuals, leading to increased concern for its conservation. In 1995, an international workshop was held for the species in Taipei, and this led to the production of a Black-faced Spoonbill Action Plan (Severinghaus *et al.* 1995). Follow-up workshops, also involving experts from all range states, were held in Beijing in 1996 and Tokyo in 1997, and a regional network for the conservation of the species has been developed.

Many of the recommendations from the Black-faced Spoonbill Action Plan and from the workshops have been implemented, including the production of education leaflets and posters on the conservation of the species in the national languages of all range states, and co-operation on satellite tracking to study its migration. An international census of Black-faced Spoonbills has been carried out every January since 1997. This census has recorded increasing numbers of birds since it began in 1997, but it is unclear whether this is the result of a real increase in numbers or can be entirely accounted for by improved coverage of the species' wintering sites. The increased interest in the species has led to effective conservation action in many parts of its range, including improved protection of

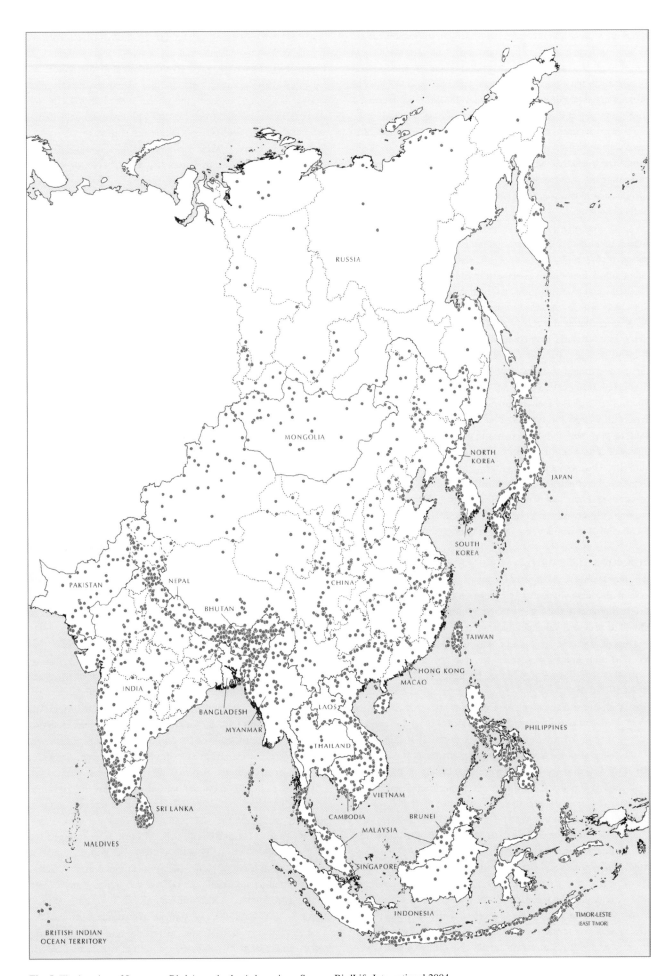

**Fig. 5.** The location of Important Bird Areas in the Asia region. Source: BirdLife International 2004.

wintering sites in several range states through the establishment of new protected areas and designation of new Ramsar sites. For example, the most important wintering site for Black-faced Spoonbills in the world is on the west coast of Taiwan. This site is under considerable pressure from development, but increased concern for the conservation of the spoonbill has resulted in the site being designated as a new protected area. Several spoonbills were shot in this area in the early 1990s, apparently by local people frustrated that the presence of this threatened species was preventing the reclamation of the mudflats for development, but a round-the-clock watch by local bird clubs prevented any further shooting.

Other networks are being developed for the benefit of threatened waterbirds in eastern and southern Asia under the co-ordination of Wetlands International. Three networks of sites of international importance have been established under the Asia-Pacific Migratory Waterbird Conservation Strategy: the Anatidae Site Network in the East Asian Flyway; the East Asian-Australasian Shorebird Site Network; and the North East Asian Crane Site Network. Numerous activities have been undertaken at network sites, including public awareness and education, surveys and training courses in wetland management, while international and national meetings have been held to share information and skills relevant to wetland management. The annual Asian Waterbird Census involves large numbers of people in counting waterbirds at thousands of wetlands in the region, and the project therefore plays an important role in monitoring waterbird numbers. However, there is potential for the Asian Waterbird Census to be broadened to monitor the sites themselves and the pressures that they face. There is also potential for participants in the three flyway networks and the Asian Waterbird Census to become involved in IBA Site Support Groups.

## ACKNOWLEDGEMENTS

We are grateful for the input of the many people who contributed to, and are acknowledged in, *Threatened Birds of Asia, Saving Asia's threatened birds* and *Important Bird Areas in Asia*. Taej Mundkur provided valuable guidance during the preparation of this paper, and the manuscript was improved by comments received from an anonymous reviewer.

## REFERENCES

**Bird Conservation Society of Thailand** 2004. Directory of Important Bird Areas in Thailand: key sites for conservation. Bird Conservation Society of Thailand and BirdLife International, Bangkok, Thailand.

**BirdLife International** 2000. Threatened birds of the world. Lynx Edicions/BirdLife International. Barcelona, Spain, and Cambridge, UK.

**BirdLife International** 2001. Threatened Birds of Asia: the BirdLife International Red Data Book. BirdLife International, Cambridge, UK.

**BirdLife International** 2003. Saving Asia's threatened birds: a guide for government and civil society. BirdLife International, Cambridge, UK.

**BirdLife International** 2004. Important bird areas in Asia: key sites for conservation. BirdLife Conservation Series No. 13. BirdLife International, Cambridge, UK.

**Collar, N.J. & Stuart, S.N.** 1985. Threatened birds of Africa and related islands: the ICBP/IUCN Red Data Book. (Third edition, Part 1). International Council for Bird Preservation and International Union for Conservation of Nature and Natural Resources, Cambridge, UK.

**Collar, N.J., Gonzaga, L.P., Krabbe, N., Madroño Nieto, A., Naranjo, L.G., Parker, T.A. & Wege, D.C.** 1992. Threatened birds of the Americas: the ICBP/IUCN Red Data Book (Third edition, Part 2). International Council for Bird Preservation, Cambridge, UK.

**Collar, N.J., Crosby, M.J. & Stattersfield, A.J.** 1994. Birds to Watch 2. BirdLife Conservation Series No. 4. BirdLife International, Cambridge, UK.

**Holmes, D. & Rombang, W.M.** 2001. Daerah Penting bagi Burung: Sumatera. PKA/BirdLife International Indonesia Programme, Bogor, Indonesia. (In Indonesian).

**Holmes, D., Rombang, W.M. & Octaviani, D.** 2001. Daerah Penting bagi Burung di Kalimantan. PKA/BirdLife International Indonesia Programme, Bogor, Indonesia. (In Indonesian).

**Islam, M.Z. & Rahmani, A.R.** 2004. Important Bird Areas in India: priority sites for conservation. Indian Bird Conservation Network, Bombay Natural History Society, Bombay, India, and BirdLife International, Cambridge, UK.

**Kennerley, P.R.** 1990. A review of the status and distribution of the Black-faced Spoonbill. Hong Kong Bird Report 1989: 116-125.

**Mallari, N.A.D., Tabaranza, B.R. & Crosby, M.J.** 2001. Key conservation sites in the Philippines: a Haribon Foundation and BirdLife International directory of Important Bird Areas. Bookmark Inc., Manila.

**Ounekham, K. & Inthapatha, S.** 2003. Directory of Important Bird Areas in Lao P.D.R. Forest Inventory and Planning Division, the Division of Forest Resource Conservation, BirdLife International in Indochina and the Wildlife Conservation Society Lao Program, Vientiane.

**Rombang, W.M. & Rudyanto** 1999. Daerah Penting bagi Burung di Jawa dan Bali. PKA/BirdLife International Indonesia Programme, Bogor, Indonesia. (In Indonesian).

**Rombang, W.M., Trainor, C. & Lesmana, D.** 2002. Daerah Penting bagi Burung: Nusa Tenggara. PKA/BirdLife Indonesia, Bogor, Indonesia. (In Indonesian).

**Seng Kim Hout, Pech Bunnat, Poole, C.M., Tordoff, A.W., Davidson, P. & Delattre, E.** 2003. Directory of Important Bird Areas in Cambodia: key sites for conservation. Department of Forestry and Wildlife, Department of Nature Conservation and Protection, BirdLife International in Indochina and the Wildlife Conservation Society Cambodia Programme, Phnom Penh.

**Severinghaus, L.L., Brouwer, K., Chan, S., Chong, J.R., Coulter, M.C., Poorter, E.P.R. & Wang, Y.** 1995. Action plan for the Black-faced Spoonbill *Platalea minor*. Bird Conservation Research Series No. 10. Wild Bird Society of Taiwan, Taipei.

**Tordoff, A.W.** (ed) 2002. Directory of Important Bird Areas in Vietnam: key sites for conservation. BirdLife International in Indochina and the Institute of Ecology and Biological Resources, Hanoi.

**Wild Bird Federation Taiwan** 2001. Important Bird Areas in Taiwan. Wild Bird Federation Taiwan, Taipei.

# Monitoring waterbirds in the Asia-Pacific region

*David Li Zuo Wei & Taej Mundkur*

*Wetlands International, 3A39, Block A, Lobby C, Kelana Centre Point, Jalan SS7/19, Petaling Jaya, Selangor, 47301, Malaysia.*
*(email: david@wiap.nasionet.net)*

Li, Z.W.D. & Mundkur, T. 2006. Monitoring waterbirds in the Asia-Pacific region. *Waterbirds around the world.* Eds. G.C. Boere, C.A. Galbraith & D.A. Stroud. The Stationery Office, Edinburgh, UK. pp. 339-342.

## ABSTRACT

The Asian Waterbird Census (AWC) provides the most comprehensive monitoring programme for waterbirds in the Asia-Pacific region. It was initiated in 1987 as an integral part of the International Waterbird Census, and is co-ordinated by Wetlands International. Since the establishment of the AWC, more than 5 700 sites across 26 countries have been counted at least once, and this has involved the active participation of thousands of volunteers. This regional census has close links with a number of comprehensive national schemes that are undertaken in January and at other times of the year. These include the long-running shorebird monitoring programme in Australia, the censuses of Anatidae and shorebirds in Japan, and waterbird counts in Hong Kong. The AWC also has close links with the international monitoring programme for the Black-faced Spoonbill *Platalea minor*. Countries within the Asia-Pacific region have occasionally organized censuses of waterbirds at site level, and the Arctic breeding grounds of many migratory waterbirds are being monitored through an extensive annual International Breeding Conditions Survey. This paper provides an overview of the ongoing monitoring schemes; it identifies present weaknesses, and recommends various measures that should be taken to improve the monitoring of waterbirds throughout the region.

## INTRODUCTION

Migratory waterbirds are one of the most remarkable components of global biodiversity. Their long migrations and tendency to concentrate in large numbers on particular wetlands make them both visible and charismatic. They are important indicators of the ecological condition and productivity of wetland ecosystems, and their presence is widely valued by numerous stakeholders including local human populations, tourists, associated enterprises and research biologists throughout the world. They also offer many opportunities for using wetlands on a sustainable basis, particularly through eco-tourism.

Many species of waterbirds are relatively easy to count because at certain times of the year they occur in conspicuous concentrations. No other group of birds has been so comprehensively and frequently surveyed. There is a strong tradition in Europe and North America, and a growing tradition in other parts of the world, of using long-term waterbird census data as a basis for estimating the sizes and trends of waterbird populations.

This paper provides a brief overview of waterbird monitoring programmes in the Asia-Pacific region. It identifies gaps in coverage of the existing programmes, and recommends a number of way in which these programmes could be improved to achieve more effective monitoring of migratory waterbirds throughout the Asia-Pacific flyways.

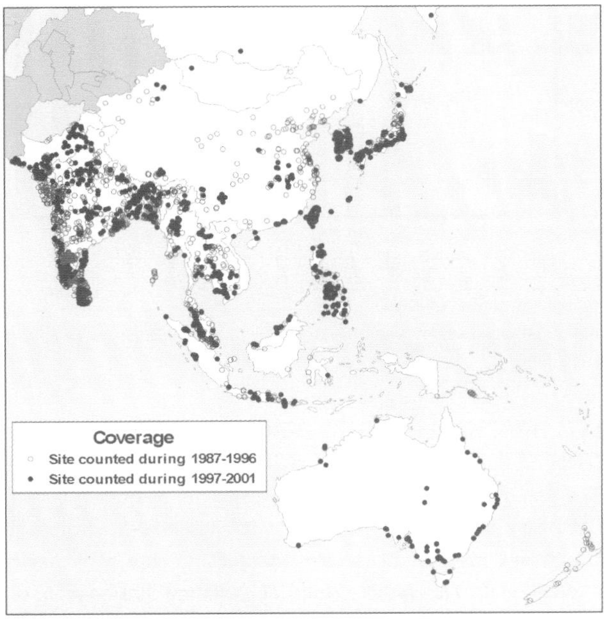

## ASIAN WATERBIRD CENSUS

### Introduction

The Asian Waterbird Census (AWC) was initiated in 1987 and runs in parallel with other waterbird censuses carried out in Africa, Europe, central and western Asia, and Latin America under the umbrella of the International Waterbird Census (IWC), which is co-ordinated by Wetlands International. The IWC is the largest and longest-running international monitoring programme of animals in the world (although some national programmes are older).

The IWC (and thus the AWC) aims to contribute to the conservation of waterbirds and their habitats by:

- providing the basis for estimates of waterbird populations;
- monitoring changes in waterbird numbers and distribution by regular, standardized counts at representative wetlands;
- improving knowledge of little-known waterbird species and wetland sites;
- identifying and monitoring networks of sites that are important for waterbirds and, in particular, identifying and monitoring sites that qualify as Wetlands of International Importance under the Ramsar Convention on Wetlands;
- providing information on the conservation status of waterbird species for use by international agreements; and
- increasing awareness of the importance of waterbirds and their wetland habitats at local, national and international levels.

The AWC also aims to build and strengthen national networks of enthusiastic volunteers and facilitate their training. It takes place once a year, during the second and third weeks of January. The census was initiated in 1987 on the Indian subcontinent, and has grown rapidly to cover most countries in southern and eastern Asia,

Fig. 1. Regional coverage of the Asian Waterbird Census (AWC).

**Coverage**
- Site counted during 1987-1996
- Site counted during 1997-2001

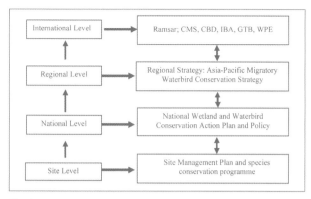

**Fig. 2.** The contribution of the Asian Waterbird Census to national and international conservation frameworks.

Key: Ramsar – Convention on Wetlands; CMS – Convention on Migratory Species; CBD – Convention on Biological Diversity; IBA – BirdLife International's *Important Bird Areas* programme; GTB – IUCN/BirdLife International's *Globally Threatened Birds Update* programme; WPE – Wetlands International's *Waterbird Population Estimates* programme.

as well as Australasia (Fig. 1). A total of 5 700 sites in 26 countries have been counted at least once since 1987. The data collected by the AWC have been used in various reports and contribute to a range of conservation activities from local to global level (Fig. 2).

### Results of AWC: 1997-2001

The results of the AWC from 1997 to 2001 have been summarized by Li & Mundkur (2004) as follows:

* A total of 1 392 sites in 22 countries were covered at least once, including a total of 61 internationally important wetlands listed under the Ramsar Convention, 32 Migratory Waterbird Network Sites in the East Asian–Australasian Flyway, and 43 Important Bird Areas (IBAs) in Cambodia, Lao PDR, the Philippines, Taiwan and Vietnam (as at 31 December 2003). The highest count was in 2001, when 4 571 522 birds were recorded at a total of 770 sites;

* Eighty-two sites in 10 countries (about 6% of the total number of sites counted) were reported to support more than 20 000 birds;

* In total, 291 species of waterbirds and 15 species of wetland-dependent raptors (birds of prey) were recorded. Thirty-seven of these species are listed as globally threatened by BirdLife International (2004). They include three Critically Endangered, 12 Endangered and 23 Vulnerable species. Thirty-one of the globally threatened species are restricted to the region covered by the AWC. In addition, 16 Near Threatened species were recorded; and

* One hundred and forty-five species recorded during the census are listed in the Appendices to the Convention on Migratory Species; 26 species are listed by the Convention on International Trade in Endangered Species of Wild Fauna and Flora (CITES).

Li & Mundkur (2004) found, however, that it was still difficult to determine population sizes and trends for most species of waterbirds in the Asia-Pacific region on the basis of data available from the AWC, because of inconsistent coverage of sites in some countries.

### Future development of the AWC: a strategy for 2004-2006

In order to improve the AWC to meet the needs of waterbird and wetland conservation, a strategy has been developed to guide the development of the AWC during the period 2004-2006 (Wetlands International 2003). The objectives of the strategy include the following:

* enhance geographic and site coverage of the AWC;
* improve the quality of AWC data to achieve the aim of monitoring of waterbird populations;
* enhance communication amongst AWC co-ordinators and the networks of counters;
* develop training, communication and public awareness programmes for the AWC;
* develop a fundraising strategy for the AWC, and to seek funding opportunities to support its development;
* support improved decision making and policy development on waterbird and wetland conservation at international and national levels through enhanced use of AWC data; and
* develop a co-ordination mechanism for the AWC.

### INTERNATIONAL BLACK-FACED SPOONBILL CENSUS

In 1993, Tom Dahmer initiated an international census of the Black-faced Spoonbill *Platalea minor*, a globally threatened species confined to eastern Asia and listed as Endangered by BirdLife International (2004). This is the only single-species monitoring programme for a waterbird in the Asia-Pacific region. The Hong Kong Bird Watching Society has taken over responsibility for the International Black-faced Spoonbill Census since 2003. The results of the census show an apparent increase in numbers from only 294 birds during a preliminary survey in January 1989 to at least 1 206 birds in January 2004 (Yu 2004; see Fig. 3).

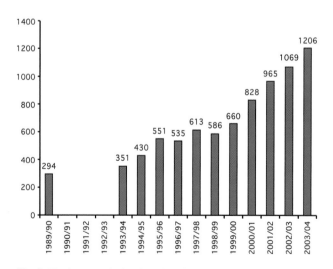

**Fig. 3.** Total counts of wintering Black-faced Spoonbills *Platalea minor*, 1989-2004.

### INTERNATIONAL ARCTIC BIRDS BREEDING CONDITIONS SURVEY (ABBCS)

The International Arctic Birds Breeding Conditions Survey (ABBCS) is a joint project of the International Wader Study Group and the Goose and Swan Specialist Groups of Wetlands International. The project aims at collating information on environmental conditions on the breeding grounds of birds nesting in the Arctic. Data on bird numbers and breeding performance during the Arctic summer are analyzed in relation to climatic factors and predation levels. Information is available online on waterbird breeding success, rodent abundance and certain weather characteristics in the Arctic for the summers of 1992 to 2003 inclusive. Information is available for 83 sites in the summer of 2002 (Soloviev & Tomkovich 2003).

## NATIONAL AND SUB-NATIONAL MONITORING PROGRAMMES

### Shorebird monitoring programme in Australia

In 1981, the Australasian Wader Studies Group began regular counts of shorebirds (waders) at a selection of 23 sites in February and June (Gosbell 2003). The results of the counts have been used in estimating population trends in shorebirds. Cannon-netting is providing data from re-traps and information on the proportion of juveniles in the populations to supplement the counting programme. Additional information is being obtained from the re-sighting of birds marked with flags.

### Waterbird counts in Hong Kong

Regular waterbird censuses in Hong Kong include monthly waterbird counts, heron and egret counts, and shorebird counts. The synchronized monthly waterbird counts are undertaken throughout the year by voluntary waterbird counters at assigned sites; the January count coincides with the AWC. Counts of herons and egrets are carried out every year at the breeding colonies, where the numbers of nests are also counted. Shorebird counts are carried out throughout the year by professional counters, the main aim of this programme being to monitor the usage of the Mai Po Ramsar site by shorebirds.

### Anatidae and shorebird censuses in Japan

An Anatidae monitoring programme was initiated in Japan in 1971. A nation-wide census is undertaken in mid-January every year, and covers all species of Anatidae. The counts are co-ordinated by Prefecture governments, and the annual national reports are compiled by the Ministry of Environment. Since 1989, the data have been digitized and stored in the Japan Integrated Biodiversity Information System (J-IBIS).

The shorebird monitoring programme started in 2000. Three surveys are conducted each year: during the northward migration, during the southward migration, and in winter. The censuses are undertaken by WWF-Japan with financial support from the Ministry of Environment. The results of the shorebird censuses have been published in a range of survey reports.

## OTHER WATERBIRD SURVEYS

Other waterbird surveys in the Asia-Pacific region have included the following:

- surveys undertaken by governments at national and local level;
- surveys conducted at regional, national and local level as part of various on-going wetland and waterbird projects;
- surveys conducted by specialist groups in the implementation of the three Actions Plans for the conservation of Anatidae, cranes and shorebirds, respectively, in the East Asian-Australasian Flyway; and

- surveys conducted by groups or individuals with an interest in a particular species or group of species.

## DISCUSSION

The monitoring of waterbirds in the Asia-Pacific region continues to suffer from a number of deficiencies:

- the AWC is unable to fulfil its role in monitoring the population sizes and trends of waterbirds during the non-breeding season for several reasons. Site coverage is poor and inconsistent in some countries, and the data received from some counters are of poor quality. Important sites that are not popular for counters, or are difficult to access, are often omitted, while some of the commoner waterbird species, as well as some little-known species, are often not well monitored. Furthermore, there is often a lack of financial support for activities at national level;
- comprehensive national waterbird monitoring programmes are not being undertaken by developing countries due to funding constraints and limited capacity;
- the ABBCS programme covers only a limited part of the breeding grounds of migratory waterbirds, and information on the breeding populations of waterbirds breeding outside the Arctic is not being collected in a comprehensive and co-ordinated manner;
- there are no regular ongoing monitoring programmes at most of the important staging areas, and comprehensive information on these sites is lacking; and
- surveys at national and site level are conducted irregularly. The results of many surveys are not readily accessible as the data are often published only in the local language, or are not published at all and remain widely dispersed.

## RECOMMENDATIONS

The following measures should be taken to improve the effectiveness of monitoring programmes for waterbirds in the Asia-Pacific region:

1  promote the application of the Asian Waterbird Census as a flagship programme for monitoring waterbird populations and trends;
2  implement the AWC Strategy 2004-2006 to enhance coverage of the census, build local capacity and improve data quality;
3  extend the AWC to cover the island nations of the Pacific;
4  promote the Black-faced Spoonbill Census as one tool to enhance coverage of the AWC in countries throughout the range of this species;
5  complement the coverage of the ABBCS to monitor populations of migratory waterbirds in all breeding areas in the region;
6  encourage the establishment of comprehensive monitoring programmes for migratory waterbirds at important staging areas in the flyway;
7  identify sites of international and national importance (Important Bird Areas, Ramsar sites, network sites, national parks, etc.) that should be given high priority in monitoring programmes;
8  strengthen co-operation between institutions and organizations to promote greater sharing of information on water-

birds and wetlands, and establish appropriate co-ordination mechanisms to facilitate comprehensive monitoring of waterbirds throughout the region;

9 improve current monitoring programmes to assess the status of wetlands and waterbirds at different times of the year;

10 produce and regularly update flyway atlases for waterbird groups to promote awareness of the importance of sites for conservation;

11 increase the resources available for local, national and regional waterbird monitoring networks to improve the collection and collation of information and effective dissemination and use of outputs; and

12 ensure that land-use and management decisions are being based on the best information available.

## REFERENCES

**BirdLife International** 2004. Threatened Birds of the World 2004. BirdLife International, Cambridge, UK. CD-ROM.

**Gosbell, K.** 2003. Shorebird Monitoring in Australia. Report to the first Meeting of Asian Waterbird Census Co-ordinators, 9-10 October 2003. Unpublished report.

**Li, Z. W. D. & Mundkur, T.** 2004. Numbers and distribution of waterbirds and wetlands in the Asia-Pacific region. Results of the Asian Waterbird Census: 1997-2001. Wetlands International, Kuala Lumpur, Malaysia.

**Soloviev, M. & Tomkovich, P.** (compilers). 2003. Arctic Birds 5 (2003). Newsletter of International Breeding Conditions Survey.

**Wetlands International** 2003. Strategy for Development of the Asian Waterbird Census: 2004-2006. Wetlands International, Kuala Lumpur, Malaysia. Unpublished report.

**Yu, Y.T.** 2004. International Black-faced Spoonbill Census: 16-18 January 2004. The Hong Kong Bird Watching Society, Hong Kong.

## USEFUL WEB-SITES

**Asian Waterbird Census (AWC):**
www.wetlands.org/IWC/awc/awcmain.html.
**Australian shorebird monitoring programme:**
www.tasweb.com.au/awsg/index.htm.
**Black-faced Spoonbill Census:**
www.hkbws.org.hk/waterbird/bfs.html.
**Hong Kong waterbird counts:**
www.hkbws.org.hk/waterbird/index.html.
**International Arctic Birds Breeding Conditions Survey (ABBCS):** www.arcticbirds.ru.
**Japan Integrated Biodiversity Information System (J-IBIS):** ww.biodic.go.jp.

Counting shorebirds from a high vantage point at Yalu Jiang National Nature Reserve in the Yellow Sea, Liaoning Province, China. Photo: Mark Barter.

# Shorebird abundance and diversity in Sungei Buloh Wetland Reserve, Singapore

*James T.W.M. Gan & R.K. Ramakrishnan*

*National Parks Board, Sungei Buloh Wetland Reserve, 301 Neo Tiew Crescent, Singapore 71892.*
*(email: James_Gan@NParks.gov.sg)*

Gan, J.T.W.M. & Ramakrishnan, R.K. 2006. Shorebird abundance and diversity in Sungei Buloh Wetland Reserve, Singapore. *Waterbirds around the world.* Eds. G.C. Boere, C.A. Galbraith & D.A. Stroud. The Stationery Office, Edinburgh, UK. pp. 343-344.

The Sungei Buloh Wetland Reserve of Singapore hosts appreciable numbers of migratory shorebirds during the northern winter. Shorebirds have been counted regularly at the wetland since 1990 providing information on the abundance, species composition and population trends. The information indicates those shorebird species and numbers that might be expected in similar wetland sites in the vicinity and on scores of, as yet, ornithologically unsurveyed islands south of Singapore.

Sungei Buloh Wetland Reserve (SBWR) is a gazetted nature reserve and wetland of 131 hectares comprising habitats such as mangrove forest, coastal mudflats and brackish water ponds (National Parks Board 2003). Counts have been done at various sites in Singapore since the 1980s, notably by the former organisation INTERWADER and the Asian Waterfowl Census. However, regular weekly long-term shorebird counting programmes have only been done in SBWR.

The census area was within SBWR and counts were made at least once a month using binoculars and telescopes during daylight hours, at both high and low tide, along a prescribed route, although counts prior to 1993 sought to capture a snapshot of the numbers of shorebirds in the area and did not necessarily adhere to this route. The maximum shorebird count for a session in each month is shown in Table 1. The daily peak counts highlight some clear patterns. The southward migration period, September to December, consistently tends to see larger numbers

of shorebirds (c. 2 000 birds), compared to the northward migration, February to May (c. 1 000 birds). Numbers typically start to build up from July reaching a peak in September with a second peak in November before declining in December. Numbers then start to increase again, with evidence of spring peaks with lesser peaks between February and April before declining very rapidly in May. Very small numbers of shorebirds remain in the wetland between May to July these being largely Common Redshank *Tringa totanus* and Whimbrel *Numenius phaeopus*.

In terms of species diversity and abundance, seven species of shorebirds dominate. Their maximum and minimum numbers recorded from 2001 to 2003 for each month are provided in Table 2. The most numerous species at the wetland is the Pacific Golden Plover *Pluvialis fulva* whose numbers tend to peak in November with a mean monthly maximum of 1 086. A limitation of the data in Table 2 is that a substantial influx of passage shorebirds may be missed since count sessions are from one to almost four weeks apart. Closer spaced counts would help refine and clarify the magnitude and timing of passage peaks. However, these data do give an overall picture of the seasonal abundance of shorebirds at SBWR.

## REFERENCES

**National Parks Board** 2003. Sungei Buloh Wetland Reserve: A Decade of Wetland Conservation, Singapore.

**Table 1.** **Sungei Buloh shorebird census data 1990-2003, peak counts in each month ("NC" indicates no count).**

| | Shorebird census data 1990-2003 - Day peak counts in each month | | | | | | | | | | | |
|---|---|---|---|---|---|---|---|---|---|---|---|---|
| | Month | | | | | | | | | | | |
| Year | Jan | Feb | Mar | Apr | May | Jun | Jul | Aug | Sep | Oct | Nov | Dec |
| 1990 | | | | | | | | | 955 | 488 | 405 | 1212 |
| 1991 | 539 | 417 | 215 | NC | NC | NC | NC | 543 | 1262 | 2430 | 667 | 1613 |
| 1992 | 245 | 864 | 1097 | NC | NC | NC | NC | NC | NC | NC | 1412 | 880 |
| 1993 | 791 | 476 | 440 | 42 | NC | NC | NC | 1233 | 2572 | 2213 | 4332 | 2018 |
| 1994 | 1065 | 840 | 1276 | 439 | 52 | 0 | 5 | 532 | 976 | 2443 | 5091 | 3572 |
| 1995 | 1570 | 2049 | 1586 | 178 | 42 | 25 | 51 | 185 | 4495 | 5262 | 3841 | 1504 |
| 1996 | 1002 | 180 | 977 | 321 | 83 | 35 | 48 | 619 | 1263 | 1269 | 2088 | NC |
| 1997 | NC | NC | NC | NC | NC | NC | NC | 724 | 2172 | 2119 | 2306 | 2045 |
| 1998 | 1160 | 876 | 702 | 984 | NC | NC | 2 | 728 | 1825 | 2281 | 2711 | 2586 |
| 1999 | 1472 | 1862 | 1013 | 1056 | NC | NC | NC | NC | 188 | 2517 | 2275 | 2066 |
| 2000 | 1998 | 1772 | 1079 | 367 | NC | NC | 21 | 478 | 1607 | 1448 | 1605 | 2078 |
| 2001 | 1738 | 1391 | 755 | 1622 | 45 | 20 | 32 | 407 | 1787 | 1968 | 2213 | 2470 |
| 2002 | 1018 | 1539 | 1126 | 355 | 16 | 17 | 38 | 230 | 1431 | 1525 | 2071 | 1057 |
| 2003 | 923 | 1211 | 747 | 484 | 88 | 0 | 5 | 169 | 683 | 1718 | 2643 | 1283 |

**Table 2.** **Maximum and minimum monthly counts of selected species recorded at Sungei Buloh from 2001 - 2003.  (Values are rounded to the nearest whole number).**

| Monthly counts of selected species recorded at Sungei Buloh from 2001-2003 | | | | | | | | | | | | | |
|---|---|---|---|---|---|---|---|---|---|---|---|---|---|
| | | Months | | | | | | | | | | | |
| | | Jan | Feb | Mar | Apr | May | Jun | Jul | Aug | Sep | Oct | Nov | Dec |
| Common Greenshank | Max | 191 | 134 | 119 | 135 | 11 | 0 | 1 | 24 | 56 | 106 | 191 | 189 |
| | Min | 73 | 77 | 33 | 7 | 0 | 0 | 0 | 2 | 21 | 32 | 101 | 78 |
| Common Redshank | Max | 104 | 156 | 44 | 66 | 15 | 2 | 17 | 140 | 336 | 199 | 223 | 175 |
| | Min | 54 | 49 | 10 | 13 | 1 | 0 | 4 | 24 | 140 | 63 | 116 | 52 |
| Curlew Sandpiper | Max | 27 | 0 | 0 | 0 | 0 | 0 | 0 | 39 | 53 | 121 | 233 | 123 |
| | Min | 0 | 0 | 0 | 0 | 0 | 0 | 0 | 4 | 4 | 35 | 137 | 68 |
| Marsh Sandpiper | Max | 329 | 371 | 296 | 184 | 1 | 0 | 0 | 2 | 62 | 277 | 237 | 327 |
| | Min | 107 | 223 | 108 | 1 | 0 | 0 | 0 | 0 | 5 | 63 | 150 | 131 |
| Lesser Sandplover | Max | 270 | 191 | 35 | 37 | 3 | 0 | 1 | 79 | 317 | 228 | 198 | 203 |
| | Min | 148 | 71 | 35 | 4 | 0 | 0 | 0 | 1 | 141 | 177 | 119 | 152 |
| Pacific Golden Plover | Max | 283 | 373 | 320 | 389 | 0 | 0 | 0 | 92 | 449 | 915 | 1086 | 676 |
| | Min | 145 | 172 | 133 | 1 | 0 | 0 | 0 | 4 | 115 | 358 | 505 | 469 |
| Whimbrel | Max | 210 | 193 | 166 | 165 | 24 | 10 | 19 | 21 | 107 | 184 | 300 | 188 |
| | Min | 58 | 88 | 52 | 20 | 5 | 3 | 0 | 0 | 44 | 60 | 114 | 61 |

The Sungei Buloh Wetland Reserve, Singapore holds significant numbers of waterbirds over the northern winter.  Photo: Alistair Crowle.

# Using predictive modelling to investigate large-scale shorebird migration in the Russian Far East for Great Knot *Calidris tenuirostris*, Red Knot *Calidris canutus* and Bar-tailed Godwit *Limosa lapponica*

*Kyle Kusch[1] & Falk Huettmann[2]*

[1]*University of Calgary, Geography Dept, Calgary T2N 1N4 Canada.*
[2]*University of Alaska-Fairbanks -EWHALE lab- Institute of Arctic Biology, Biology and Wildlife Department, Fairbanks, Alaska, 99775-7000 USA. (email: fffh@uaf.edu)*

Kusch, K. & Huettmann, F. 2006. Using predictive modelling to investigate large-scale shorebird migration in the Russian Far East for Great Knot *Calidris tenuirostris*, Red Knot *Calidris canutus* and Bar-tailed Godwit *Limosa lapponica*. *Waterbirds around the world*. Eds. G.C. Boere, C.A. Galbraith & D.A. Stroud. The Stationery Office, Edinburgh, UK. p. 345.

Predictive modelling allows the presentation of relative probabilities of occurrence for species of interest. This approach is particularly useful for large areas which have only been poorly studied. The Sea of Okhotsk in the Russian Far East is such an area with a huge coastline along the East Asian-Australasian (EAA) Flyway. It comprises large mudflats, estuaries and wetlands; some of them never inventoried. Detailed shorebird survey data are missing or only locally known for this region. We used "presence only" and "confirmed absence" information from an extensive review of Russian literature (Huettmann 2003) as the basis for predicting the occurrence of shorebirds in this large region. In addition, the predictive model used six years of data from an international field research project that investigated shorebird migration in spring and autumn based on identified, representative mudflats and estuaries in eastern and southern Kamchatka, Magadan region, Sakhalin Island and southern Kurile Islands (Antonov & Huettmann 2004). These compiled sources in a GIS (ArcView) format represent the best available digital data set on shorebirds in the region. For data transparency reasons they are described with FGDC NBII metadata in XML format, available for public review, quality review and further extension.

A progressive modelling approach was used (Manly *et al.*, 2002, Scott *et al.* 2002) using GIS, modified S-PLUS code (Huettmann and Linke 2003) and statistical linear and non-linear modelling algorithms (Huettmann & Diamond 2001, Yen *et al.* 2004) in order to predict where Great Knot *Calidris tenuirostris*, Red Knot *Calidris canutus* and Bar-tailed Godwit *Limosa lapponica* occur during autumn and spring migration on the shores of the Sea of Okhotsk. Significant model predictors such as tidal range, river type and size, substrate type and mudflat size were derived from Remote Sensing layers, software tools, hardcopy maps and others.

From the compiled locations with known shorebird occurrences, it appeared that the three species prefer tidal saltwater locations with organic matter and freshwater inflow. The model showed a difference between spring and autumn migration, suggesting different migration strategies.

The models indicated a good agreement with known shorebird migration "hotspots". This is important for obtaining population estimates and quantifying turn-over rates. However, more field work is needed to further improve these quantitative prediction accuracies and to learn more about the migration strategies. This predictive shorebird GIS model is the first of its kind, and can contribute greatly to conservation decisions and advanced field research. Together with other it can support development and implementation of conservation strategies for shorebird species along the EAA Flyway. Eventually, it could be used in a spatial Population Viability Analysis (PVA) framework and for environmental impact studies. These modelling applications should become further recognized and improved, and eventually be used to support international conservation management policy decisions such as through the Ramsar and Bonn Conventions.

## REFERENCES

**Antonov, A. & Huettmann, F.** 2004. On the southward migration of Great Knot in the western Sea of Okhotsk: results and conclusions from coordinated surveys on northern Sakhalin Island and in Schastia Bay-Mainland Russian Far East, 2002. Stilt 41: 14-20.

**Huettmann, F.** 2003. Literature Review: Shorebird migration in the Sea of Okhotsk region, Russian Far East, along the East Asian Australasian flyway for selected species (Great Knot *Calidris tenuirostris*, Red Knot *Calidris canutus*, Bar-tailed Godwit *Limosa lapponica*). Report for Environment Australia, Wetlands International, Canberra.

**Huettmann, F. & Diamond, A.W.** 2001. Seabird colony locations and environmental determination of seabird distribution: A spatially explicit seabird breeding model in the Northwest Atlantic. Ecological Modelling 141: 261-298.

**Huettmann, F. & Linke, J.** 2003. An automated method to derive habitat preferences of wildlife in GIS and telemetry studies: A flexible software tool and examples of its application. European Journal of Wildlife Research 49: 219-232.

**Manly, B. J., McDonald, L. L., Thomas, D.L., McDonald, T. L. & Erickson, W.P.** 2002. Resource Selection by Animals. Kluwer Academic Publishers, Dordrecht.

**Scott, J.M., Heglund, P.J. & Morrison, M.L.** 2002. Predicting Species Occurrences: Issues of Accuracy and Scale. Island Press, Washington, D.C.

**Yen, P., Huettmann, F. & Cooke, F.** 2004. Modelling abundance and distribution of Marbled Murrelets (*Brachyramphus marmoratus*) using GIS, marine data and advanced multivariate statistics. Ecological Modelling 171: 395-413.

# Status and conservation of the Little Curlew *Numenius minutus* on its over-wintering grounds in Australia

*M.G. Bellio[1], P. Bayliss[1], S. Morton [2] & R. Chatto[3]*

[1] *Environmental Research Institute of the Supervising Scientist, GPO Box 461, Darwin NT 0801, Australia.*

[2] *CSIRO Environment & Natural Resources, GPO Box 2697, Canberra ACT 2601, Australia.*

[3] *Parks and Wildlife Commission of the Northern Territory, PO Box 496, Palmerston NT 0831, Australia.*

Bellio, M.G., Bayliss, P., Morton, S. & Chatto R. 2006. Status and conservation of the Little Curlew *Numenius minutus* on its over-wintering grounds in Australia. *Waterbirds around the world*. Eds. G.C. Boere, C.A. Galbraith & D.A. Stroud. The Stationery Office, Edinburgh, UK. pp. 346-348.

## ABSTRACT

The Little Curlew *Numenius minutus*, the smallest member of the genus *Numenius,* is strongly migratory with a restricted breeding range in eastern Siberia and wintering grounds in Australia and elsewhere in the South Pacific region (Marchant & Higgins 1996, van Gils & Wiersma 1996). Since Gould's discovery of the Little Curlew in Australia in 1840 and the collection of the first specimens from their breeding area in northern Siberia, further studies, both on their breeding and wintering grounds, have added to our knowledge of this bird (Labutin *et al.* 1982, Marchant & Higgins 1996, Watkins 1993, van Gils & Wiersma 1996).

Nevertheless, the species has received little attention in terms of detailed studies of its distribution and biology and it is probably one of the least known waders that migrate from Siberia to Australia.

This paper reviews the literature on this species, in particular that available on its wintering-grounds in Australia, and highlights further research which could assist the species' conservation.

## WINTERING DISTRIBUTION IN AUSTRALIA

Movements of Little Curlew *Numenius minutus* in Australia are poorly understood and information is highly biased toward months when wetlands are most accessible. Little Curlews are nomadic and very mobile across Australia and while their occurrence can be predictable at certain sites, at other locations their distribution is highly unpredictable and variable between years. Some sites are used only for short periods, or not at all in some years. The triggers that drive movements are likely to be a combination of availability and accessibility to suitable roosting and feeding habitat (Collins & Jessop 2001). No quantitative studies have been attempted to investigate the cause/effect of these movements. Each year individuals stage in large numbers across the Top End of Northern Australia, including Darwin, from their arrival from their breeding grounds till the onset of the wet season (Crawford 1972, 1978; Garnett & Minton 1985; Mc Kean *et al.* 1986, Lane 1987, Bamford 1988, 1990, Jaensch 1994, Collins & Jessop 2001, Barter 2002, Bellio 2004). By the end of February, they disappear from the sub-coastal floodplains of northern Australia and disperse inland. The role of ephemeral wetlands, such as the systems of intermittent lakes (e.g. Lake Woods, Sylvester, Corella) of inland Australia need to be investigated in more detail, and the patterns of northward migration are still subject to debate.

Northern Australia wetlands, such as those of the Alligator Rivers Region, seem unsuitable during northward migration periods, with large areas still inundated. Nevertheless, there are occasional records (usually in small numbers) of Little Curlews in April for Darwin and the Alligator Rivers Region (Morton *et al.* 1991, Niven McCrie & David Donato pers comm.). These observations coincide with El Niño years or with exceptional cyclone events in the Gulf of Carpentaria in Queensland. In the context of climate change scenarios, climatic events at a local (rainfall patterns) and large scale (cyclones, El Niño/La Niña events) need to be investigated. Investigating movements with radio-telemetry and using remote sensing techniques to map habitat availability at varying scales could be used to relate movements to habitats and climatic conditions.

## DIET AND HABITAT USAGE

In Australia, Little Curlews are closely associated with grasslands, including dry floodplains such as those of Kakadu National Park (Northern Territory) and the black-soil plains of the northern interior (Bamford 1988, 1990). They are one of the few migratory birds to utilise urban grassed areas, such as lawns, ovals and airstrips (Collins & Jessop 2001). Little Curlews are omnivorous, feeding on a wide range of plant and animal material, and seem to respond opportunistically to peaks of one type or other food resource. During a pilot study at Darwin airport, between October 2003 and January 2004, the stomach contents of six Little Curlews were analysed. Termites (*alatae*) represented 90% of stomach items, the remaining 10% comprised stones and plant parts (of genera *Scleria* and *Eleocharis*). The stomach content of one individual collected in Kakadu National Park comprised entirely seeds of wild rice (*Oryza* sp.) (Bellio 2004).

Few quantitative studies have been carried out on diet, foraging behaviour, and on physical structure of habitats (vegetation and water depth) and how this influences suitability. The ecological conditions posed by the highly variable environment of Australia and the relative suite of behavioural and physiological adaptations of the species remain largely unknown. Some of the questions that remain to be answered include:

- how they harvest their food resources?
- their foraging niche in relation to other species?
- conspecific relationships with respect to habitat, time of the year and kind of resources available?

Understanding mechanisms of habitat selection is central to addressing how vulnerable this long-distance migrant may be to rapidly changing conditions.

## POPULATION ESTIMATES AND BANDING STUDIES

The minimum population estimate for Little Curlew in the East-Asian-Australasian Flyway is 200 000 individuals (Barter 2002).

Several studies have been published on the distribution, abundance, and areas of significance on Australian wintering grounds (Garnett & Minton 1985, McKean *et al.* 1986, Lane 1987, Bamford 1988, 1990, Morton *et al.* 1991, Jaensch 1994). Banding studies have been carried out in the Northern Territory (Kakadu National Park), and Western Australia (Anna Plains) by the Australian Wader Study Group (AWSG), but only a few have been caught. Biometrics suggest the existence of possible distinct populations, but this hypothesis has not been tested (Bamford 1988, 1990, Barter 1992c). The AWSG has collected much data on Little Curlew moulting strategies, with results soon to be published. Nevertheless, more banding studies are required in order to estimate survival between years, and to provide information on population dynamics and trends. Further banding studies will also increase our knowledge on movements in Australia and elsewhere along the East-Asian-Australasian Flyway. Targeted surveys aimed at reassessing population estimates should also be planned, as the population estimates for their wintering ground are based on surveys more than 20 years old (Morton *et al.* 1991, Barter 2002).

## THREATS TO HABITAT

As for many other migratory shorebirds, the Little Curlew faces threats due to habitat loss and/or habitat modification. The extent of these threats are difficult to evaluate, due to a lack of long term monitoring data, but they are likely to include the species' breeding sites, stop-over sites along flyway, and wintering grounds. As an example, the Alligator Rivers Region in Northern Australia, and Kakadu National Park in particular, have been long recognised as important for Little Curlew during southward migration (Morton *et al.* 1991, Bamford 1988,1990, Barter 2002). The wetlands of Alligator Rivers Region are considered pristine in comparison to those elsewhere in Australia.

Nevertheless, over the past two decades many pressures have been identified that are or will adversely affect the ecological condition of these wetlands (Storrs & Finlayson 1997, Finalyson *et al.* 1988), including: loss of extent and diversity of habitat due to weeds such as *Mimosa pigra* (Walden & Bayliss 2003, Walden *et al.* 2004), and introduced grasses such as Olive Hymenachne *Hymenachne amplexicaulis* and Para Grass *Brachiaria mutica* (Finlayson *et al.* 1997), consequences of rising sea levels including saltwater intrusion (Bayliss *et al.* 1997; Eliot *et al.* 1999; Waterman *et al.* 2000) and damage to micro and macro-scale habitat caused by feral animals such as pigs and buffalos (Skeat *et al.* 1996, East 1996). Without quantitative studies on species-habitat relationships, sound predictions on the consequences of these pressures on Little Curlew habitat are difficult.

## CHALLENGES FOR THE FUTURE

The Little Curlew differs from its relatives within the genus *Numenius* both in terms of morphological and behavioural characters and it seems to be a close relative of the almost extinct Eskimo Curlew *Numenius borealis* (Labutin *et al.* 1982). Habitat loss and hunting have been recognised as the major factors responsible for the disappearance of the Eskimo Curlew. In order to save its Asian-Australian counterpart, the following key data and information is needed:

- ecological studies;
- quantitative studies on species-habitat relationships;

- population dynamics and trends in population established by banding studies (proportional survival of juveniles and adults);
- cause/effect mechanisms of movements in relation to climatic events at local and broad scales;
- mapping of habitat suitability at landscape-scale using GIS and remote sensing;
- patterns of movements using radiotelemetry; and
- identification of areas of importance and significance, across its breeding grounds, along the flyway and on its wintering areas.

## ACKNOWLEDGMENTS

The information summarised here would not have been possible to collate without much valuable data and comments provided by Australian scientists, bird-watchers and public who have undertaken research and made field observations for many years and were happy to share their knowledge for the benefit of the species. As such we would like to thank and acknowledge the following people/organisations: Alan Anderson (CSIRO – Darwin), Birds Australia, Jared Archibald (NT Museum), Walter Boles (Australian Museum, Sydney), Pete Collins (AWSG), Ian Cowie (NT Herbarium), David Donato (NT Field Naturalist Group), Peter Dostine (DIPE, NT), Lunar Eclipse (Darwin Airport), Roger Jaensch (WI), Wayne Longmore (Museum Victoria), Niven McCrie (NT Field Naturalist Group), Clive Minton (AWSG), Robert Palmer (ANWC CSIRO), Danny Roger (AWSG), Pavel Tomkovich (Zoological Museum Moscow) and Doug Watkins (WI).

## REFERENCES

**Bamford, M.J.** 1988. Kakadu National Park: a Preliminary survey of migratory waders October/November 1987. RAOU Report No. 41.

**Bamford, M.J.** 1990. RAOU Survey of Migratory Waders in Kakadu National Park: Phase III. Report to the Australian National Parks and Wildlife Service. RAOU Report No. 70.

**Barter, M.** 1992. Morphometric and moult of the Little curlew *Numenius minutus* in north western Australia. The Stilt 21: 20-21.

**Barter, M.** 2002. Shorebirds of the Yellow Sea. Importance, threats and conservation status. Wetland International Global Series 9: 19.

**Bayliss, B.L., Brennan, K.G., Eliot, I., Finlayson, C.M., Hall, R.N., House, T., Pidgeon, R.W.J., Walden, D. & Waterman, P.** 1997. Vulnerability assessment of the possible effects of predicted climate change and sea level rise in the Alligator Rivers Region, Northern Territory, Australia. Supervising Scientist Report 123, Supervising Scientist, Canberra. 134 pp.

**Bellio, M.G.** 2004. Results on the analysis of stomach contents of six individuals of the Little Curlew (*Numenius minutus*) at Darwin Airport, Northern Territory, Australia Unpublished Report to Parks and Wildlife Commission of the Northern Territory- July, Darwin.

**Collins, P. & Jessop, R.** 2001. Arrival and departure dates and habitat of Little Curlew *Numenius minutus* at Broome, North-Western Australia. The Stilt 39: 10-12.

**Crawford, D.N.** 1972. Birds of the Darwin area. Emu 72: 131-174.

**Crawford, D.N.** 1978 . Notes on the Little Curlew on the sub-coastal plains, Northern Territory. Australian Bird Watcher 7: 270-272.

**Eliot, I., Finlayson, C.M. & Waterman, P**. 1999. Predicted climate change, sea-level rise and wetland management in the Australian wet-dry tropics. Wetlands Ecology and Management 7: 63-81.

**East, T.J.** 1996. Landform evolution. In: C.M. Finlayson & I. von Oertzen (eds.), Landscape and Vegetation Ecology of the Kakadu Region, Northern Australia. Kluwer Academic Publishers, The Netherlands: 37-55.

**Finlayson, C.M., Bailey, B.J., Freeland, W.J. & Fleming, M.** 1988. Wetlands of the Northern Territory. In: A.J. McComb & P.S. Lake (eds.) The Conservation of Australian Wetlands: 103-106. Surrey Beatty & Sons, Sydney.

**Finlayson, C.M., Storrs, M.J. & Lindner, G.** 1997. Degradation and rehabilitation of wetlands in the Alligator Rivers Region of northern Australia. Wetlands Ecology and Management 5: 19-36.

**Garnett, S. & Minton, C.** 1985. Notes on the Movements and Distribution of Little Curlew *Numenius minutus* in Northern Australia. Australian Bird Watcher 11: 69-73.

**Jaensch, R.** 1994. Lake Finniss: an internationally significant site for the Little Curlew. The Stilt 25: 21.

**Labutin, Y.V., Leonovitch, V.V. & Verprinstev, B.N.** 1982. The Little Curlew *Numenius minutus* in Siberia. Ibis 124: 302-319.

**Lane, B.A.** 1987. Shorebirds in Australia. Nelson, Melbourne.

**McKean, J.L., Shurcliff, K.S. & Thompson, H.A.F.** 1986. Notes on the status of Little Curlew *Numenius minutus* in the Darwin area, Northern Territory. Australian Bird Watcher 11 :259-260.

**Marchant, S. & Higgins, P.** 1996. Handbook of Australian, New Zealand & Antarctic Birds. Volume 3: Snipes to Pigeons. Oxford University Press, Melbourne Australia: 95-102.

**Morton, S.R., Brennan, K.G. & Armstrong, M.D.** 1991. Distribution and abundance of waterbirds in the Alligator Rivers Region, Northern Territory. Supervising Scientist for the Alligator Rivers Region, Open File Record, 86: 1-460.

**Skeat, A.J., East, T.J. & Corbett, L.K.** 1996. Impact of feral water buffalo. In: Landscape and Vegetation Ecology of the Kakadu Region, Northern Australia. C.M. Finlayson & I. von Oertzen (eds.). Kluwer Academic Publishers, The Netherlands: 157-179.

**Storrs, M.J. & Finlayson, C.M.** 1997. Overview of the conservation status of wetlands of the Northern Territory. Supervising Scientist Report 116, Supervising Scientist, Canberra.

**van Gills, J. & Wiersma, P.** 1996. Family Scolopacidae (Sandpipers, Snipes and Phalaropes). In: J. del Hoyo, A. Elliott & J. Sargatal (eds). Handbook of the Birds of the World. Vol. 3. Lynx Edicions, Barcelona, Spain. 502 pp.

**Walden, D. & Bayliss, P.** 2003. An ecological risk assessment of the major weeds on the Magela Creek floodplain, Kakadu National Park, preliminary report. Internal Report 439, Supervising Scientist, Darwin. Unpublished paper.

**Walden, D., van Dam, R., Finlayson, C.M., Storrs, M., Lowry, J. & Kriticos, D.** 2004. A risk assessment of the tropical wetland weed *Mimosa pigra* in northern Australia. Supervising Scientist Report 177, Supervising Scientist, Darwin NT.

**Waterman, P., Finlayson, C.M. & Eliot, I.** 2000. Assessment and monitoring of coastal change in the Alligator Rivers Region, northern Australia: a review of initial activities. In: I. Eliot, M. Saynor, M. Eliot & C.M. Finlayson (eds.), Assessment and monitoring of coastal change in the Alligator Rivers Region, northern Australia. Supervising Scientist Report 157, Darwin: 149-161.

**Watkins, D.** 1993. A national Plan for Shorebird Conservation in Australia. RAOU Report No 90.

Little Curlew *Numenius minutus*. Photo: Nick Davidson.

# 3.7 Sustainable use of natural resources in the African-Eurasian Flyway. Workshop Introduction

*Bert Lenten*

*Executive Secretary of AEWA, UN Campus, Hermann Ehlers-Str. 10, Bonn 53113, Germany. (email: blenten@unep.de)*

Lenten, B. 2006. Sustainable use of natural resources in the African-Eurasian Flyway. Workshop Introduction. *Waterbirds around the world*. Eds. G.C. Boere, C.A. Galbraith & D.A. Stroud. The Stationery Office, Edinburgh, UK. p. 349.

The widespread Mallard *Anas platyrhynchos* is one of the commonest duck species in many countries and makes up a large proportion of the annual harvest of waterbirds across Eurasia. Photo: Paul Marshall.

Conservation of migratory waterbirds can only be achieved by connecting the protection of migratory waterbird populations and the conservation of their habitats to the sustainable use of their populations themselves and the natural resources they depend upon.

However, in African-(West) Eurasian Flyways, the generally good knowledge of waterbirds is not being effectively transferred into necessary national and local actions. Nor have conservation efforts led to maintaining or restoring the health of many waterbird populations, including globally threatened species (see Davidson & Stroud, this volume).

There are urgent needs to integrate waterbird conservation as part of sustainable development, to the greater benefit of local communities and other stakeholders dependent on wetlands as well as benefiting biodiversity. The African-Eurasian Waterbird Agreement (UNEP/AEWA) provides a good basis to achieve this.

Traditional knowledge in the use of these resources by local human communities is more and more in danger of being lost and should be safe-guarded: it should be taken into account when developing action and management plans. The impact of intensive and/or detrimental use of natural resources, be it intensive marine fisheries or hunting, has to be reduced and controlled in order not to interfere with traditional sustainable use. However, there are some highly-unsustainable practises that need to be stopped (such as the use of lead gunshot in wetlands).

The Agreement on the Conservation of African-Eurasian migratory waterbirds entered into force in 1999. Since then, 57 out of 119 potential Range States have ratified the Agreement to become Contracting Parties. The Preamble to the Agreement stresses that any taking of waterbirds must be undertaken sustainably, taking account of the conservation status of the specie concerned. A number of projects in the Agreement's International Implementation Priorities have addressed the sustainable use of natural resources. Accordingly, the Agreement provides a valuable framework within which to consider these issues.

A major African-Eurasian-Flyway GEF Project was approved in November 2003 and will start to be implemented in mid 2006. This project, which will be executed by Wetlands International in close cooperation with BirdLife International, will especially focusing on: capacity building, cooperative research and monitoring and communication activities.

# The Agreement on the Conservation of African-Eurasian Migratory Waterbirds

*Bert Lenten*

*Executive Secretary of AEWA, UN Campus, Hermann-Ehlers Str. 10, Bonn 53113, Germany. (email: blenten@unep.de)*

Lenten, B. 2006. The Agreement on the Conservation of African-Eurasian Migratory Waterbirds. *Waterbirds around the world*. Eds. G.C. Boere, C.A. Galbraith & D.A. Stroud. The Stationery Office, Edinburgh, UK. pp. 350-353.

## ABSTRACT

The Agreement on the Conservation of African-Eurasian Migratory Waterbirds (AEWA) – an agreement developed under the aegis of the Convention on the Conservation of Migratory Species of Wild Animals – was concluded in The Netherlands in June 1995 and entered into force in November 1999. The geographical coverage of the Agreement extends from north-eastern Canada and Arctic Siberia to the southernmost tip of Africa, and includes 119 countries. The Agreement adopts a flyway approach, and provides for co-ordinated conservation action to be taken by the Range States throughout the migration systems of the 235 species of waterbirds to which it applies. By the end of 2006, 58 countries had joined the Agreement. This paper gives a brief history of the Agreement and reviews the progress that has been made in its implementation. Recent activities relating to sustainable hunting, the African waterbird ringing scheme, climate change and avian influenza are discussed. The paper concludes by looking at some of the future challenges for the AEWA and emphasizing the need to strengthen co-operation with other multinational environmental agreements and organizations.

## INTRODUCTION

The Agreement on the Conservation of African-Eurasian Migratory Waterbirds (AEWA) is the largest of its kind hitherto developed under the Convention on the Conservation of Migratory Species of Wild Animals (CMS). It was concluded on 16 June 1995 in The Hague, The Netherlands, and entered into force on 1 November 1999 after the required number of at least fourteen Range States, comprising seven from Africa and seven

**Table 1. Contracting parties to the Agreement on the conservation of African-Eurasian Migratory Waterbirds as at the end of 2006.**

| Contracting Party | Date of entry into force | Contracting Party | Date of entry into force |
|---|---|---|---|
| **Eurasia** | | Sweden | 01-11-1999 |
| Albania | 01-09-2001 | Switzerland | 01-11-1999 |
| Belgium | 01-06-2006 | Syria | 01-08-2003 |
| Bulgaria | 01-02-2000 | Ukraine | 01-01-2003 |
| Croatia | 01-09-2000 | United Kingdom | 01-11-1999 |
| Czech Republic | 01-09-2006 | Uzbekistan | 01-04-2004 |
| Denmark | 01-01-2000 | **Africa** | |
| European Community | 01-10-2005 | Algeria | 01-10-2006 |
| Finland | 01-01-2000 | Benin | 01-01-2000 |
| France | 01-12-2003 | Congo (Brazzaville) | 01-11-1999 |
| Georgia | 01-08-2001 | Djibouti | 01-05-2004 |
| Germany | 01-11-1999 | Egypt | 01-11-1999 |
| Greece | 14-05-1998* | Equatorial Guinea | 01-12-1999 |
| Hungary | 01-03-2003 | Gambia | 01-11-1999 |
| Ireland | 01-08-2003 | Ghana | 01-10-2005 |
| Israel | 01-11-2002 | Guinea | 01-11-1999 |
| Italy | 01-02-2006 | Guinea-Bissau | 01-11-2006 |
| Jordan | 01-11-1999 | Kenya | 01-06-2001 |
| Latvia | 01-01-2006 | Libyan Arab Jamahirya | 01-06-2005 |
| Lebanon | 01-12-2002 | Mali | 01-01-2000 |
| Lithuania | 01-11-2004 | Mauritius | 01-01-2001 |
| Luxembourg | 01-12-2003 | Morocco | 19-11-1997* |
| Macedonia FYR | 01-02-2000 | Niger | 01-11-1999 |
| Moldova | 01-04-2001 | Nigeria | 01-07-2004 |
| Monaco | 01-11-1999 | Senegal | 01-11-1999 |
| Netherlands | 01-11-1999 | South Africa | 01-01-2000 |
| Portugal | 01-03-2004 | Sudan | 01-11-1999 |
| Romania | 01-10-1999 | Tanzania | 01-11-1999 |
| Slovakia | 01-07-2001 | Togo | 01-11-1999 |
| Slovenia | 01-10-2003 | Tunisia | 01-10-2005 |
| Spain | 01-11-1999 | Uganda | 01-12-2000 |

* Date of signing; ratification is still pending

Fig. 1. Area of the Agreement on the Conservation of African-Eurasian Migratory Waterbirds (AEWA).

from Eurasia, had ratified. Since then, the Agreement has been an independent international treaty.

The AEWA covers 235 species of birds ecologically dependent on wetlands for at least part of their annual cycle, including many species of divers, grebes, pelicans, cormorants, herons, storks, rails, ibises, spoonbills, flamingos, ducks, swans,

Fig. 3. Tenth anniversary celebration and opening ceremony of the AEWA exhibition "Impressions of travelling birds" by the Federal Minister for the Environment, Nature Conservation and Nuclear Safety, Mr. Jürgen Trittin, at the Museum Alexander Koenig in Bonn, Germany, on 4 July 2005. Photo: Sergey Dereliev.

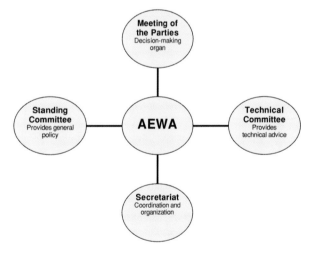

Fig. 2. Subsidiary bodies of the African-Eurasian Migratory Waterbird Agreement (AEWA).

geese, cranes, waders, gulls, terns and even the African Penguin *Spheniscus demersus*.

The Agreement covers 119 countries in Europe, parts of Asia and Canada, the Middle East and Africa. In fact, the geographical area of AEWA stretches from the northern reaches of Canada and the Russian Federation to the southernmost tip of Africa. The Agreement provides for co-ordinated and concerted action to be taken by the Range States throughout the migration system of the waterbirds to which it applies. Of the 119 Range States, 58 coun-

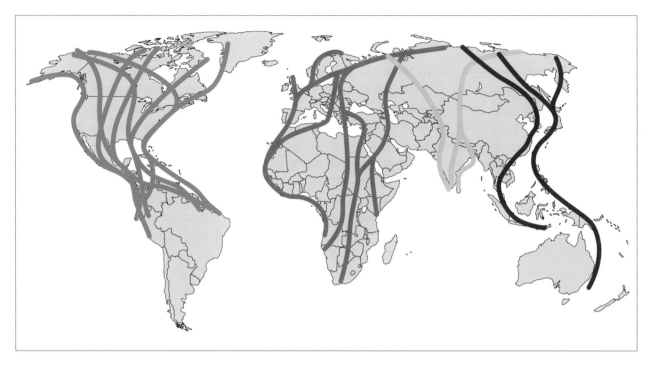

**Fig. 4.** The principal flyways of migratory waterbirds breeding in the Northern Hemisphere. (Note that many waterbirds migrate in directions other than those indicated here (Boere & Stroud, this volume, p. 40)).

tries have joined the AEWA, Guinea-Bissau being the latest Contracting Party as of 1 November 2006 (see Fig. 1 and Table 1).

Parties to the Agreement are called upon to engage in a wide range of conservation actions which are described in a comprehensive Action Plan (2006-2008). This detailed plan addresses such key issues as: species and habitat conservation, management of human activities, research and monitoring, education and information, and implementation.

After the conclusion of the Agreement on 16 June 1995, an Interim Secretariat was established. The first Meeting of the Parties (Cape Town, South Africa, November 1999) decided to establish a permanent Secretariat integrated in the United Nations Environment Programme (UNEP) and co-located with the Secretariat of the CMS in Bonn, Germany. This materialized in mid-2000.

To support and oversee the implementation of the Agreement, two subsidiary bodies have been established, namely the Technical Committee and, after the Second Meeting of the Parties (Bonn, Germany, September 2002), also a Standing Committee (Fig. 2). The latter took over all matters relating to policy, governance, administration and finance.

In 2005, AEWA celebrated its 10th Anniversary (Fig. 3). Although the Agreement is still relatively young, it has already proven to be quite successful. Thanks to support given by the European Union, Denmark, France, Germany, Switzerland, the Netherlands, Sweden and the United Kingdom, good progress has been made with the implementation of the Agreement. Much more could, of course, be done, but as always, lack of resources is the main bottleneck in this respect.

A welcome development will be the implementation of the African-Eurasian Flyways GEF (Global Environment Facility) project, which began in late 2006. This project has been designed by Wetlands International in close co-operation with BirdLife International and in consultation with the Ramsar Bureau and the AEWA Secretariat, and will be implemented by

Wetlands International and BirdLife International within the next five years. The main focus of the project will be on capacity building, co-operative research and monitoring, and communication activities.

## FLYWAY APPROACH

In the mid-1980s, the Ministry of Agriculture, Nature Management and Fisheries (LNV) in The Netherlands decided to take the lead in drafting the Agreement on the Conservation of African-Eurasian Migratory Waterbirds. Being a Contracting Party to the CMS, The Netherlands felt that it was one of their obligations to support the CMS in developing such a regional agreement for migratory waterbirds. Waterbirds are of extreme interest for The Netherlands which, being located more or less in the middle of the East Atlantic Flyway, provide breeding grounds for several species of waders that overwinter in West Africa, as well as wintering areas for geese that breed in the high Arctic. Furthermore, LNV was convinced that conservation of migratory species is only possible through international co-operation and therefore strongly promoted the "flyway approach".

As noted above, implementation of the AEWA is well underway. One of the success stories is that the "flyway approach" (Fig. 4) has been widely accepted not only by experts, but also by decision makers and policy makers. It is clear that for the conservation of migratory birds, international co-operation is needed. Without co-operation, all efforts made to conserve a species in country A could be in vain if, for example, unsustainable taking is accepted in country B. The flyway approach means that all the threats that a particular species encounters during its migrations between its breeding grounds and its wintering areas are identified and tackled, or at least mitigated, through international co-operation of the countries along the flyway. This concept is easy to understand even for non-experts, which is the reason why the AEWA Secretariat has been able to raise more awareness and to convince many countries to join the Agreement.

The AEWA is the first multilateral environmental agreement dealing with the conservation of migratory waterbirds. It is seen as a model that could be replicated within the CMS framework in other regions of the world.

## AEWA ACTIVITIES SINCE THE EDINBURGH CONFERENCE

Since the Waterbirds around the world conference, the AEWA has been active on a range of issues addressed in Edinburgh. The Third Meeting of the Parties took place in October 2005 in Dakar, Senegal, and adopted 20 Resolutions – thus paving the way for further development of the Agreement. The Parties strongly endorsed the concluding statement of the Waterbirds around the world conference, and committed themselves to the implementation of the Edinburgh Declaration (this volume).

### Sustainable hunting

In order to raise awareness among hunters and the relevant authorities on the issue of lead poisoning, the AEWA Secretariat planned several workshops on this subject, one of which took place in Senegal in October 2004. This workshop was organized in close co-operation with ONCFS, Wetlands International, CIC, OMPO, FNC and the Government of Senegal, and adopted 11 recommendations dealing with topics such as improving waterbird surveys and the setting of quotas for the number of birds that may be harvested. Two more workshops are planned for 2006 and 2007. These will be jointly organized with BirdLife International and will take place in Lebanon and Tunisia.

### African Waterbird Ringing Scheme

Ringing studies in Europe have contributed greatly to our current understanding of waterbird migration and ecology. In order to develop an African Ringing Scheme (AFRING) which, it is hoped, will provide long-term international co-ordination between the various ringing schemes in Africa, the AEWA Secretariat supported the first AFRING waterbird ringing course, which was held in September 2004 in East Africa (Kenya). The next course is planned for Ghana in 2006.

### Waterbirds and climate change

The impacts of climate change on migratory waterbirds are an important and complex issue that the AEWA will have to deal with in future in order to develop policies that adapt waterbird conservation to changes in climate. A desk study was suggested at the Third Meeting of the Parties; this will summarize understanding of the current and future responses of migratory waterbirds to actual and predicted climate change, and practical means of adaptation.

### Avian influenza

The Third Meeting of the Parties also responded to the recent spread of the Asian lineage of highly pathogenic avian influenza (HPAI) subtype H5N1, and emphasized the need for national surveillance and monitoring mechanisms, especially in African countries, as well as for international co-operation in order to identify and eliminate HPAI H5N1. The Parties stressed the key role of the AEWA as a member of the International Scientific Taskforce on Avian Influenza, which has been set up under the auspices of the CMS, in disseminating information and scientific assessments related to the developing situation.

Launch of World Migratory Birds Day at Laikipia, Kenya, 9 April 2006. Photo: David Stroud.

## FUTURE OF THE AEWA

According to the United Nations, there are 191 sovereign states world-wide. Taking into account that 119 Range States are located in the AEWA region, it is clear that we have to deal with a very complex situation. Nowhere else on the globe do birds have to cross so many political borders. These borders make no sense for the birds, but could have an impact on their chances of survival. One of the challenges for the Secretariat is to convince more Range States to join the Agreement in the near future. The number of Contracting Parties is 58 (as of November 2006), and several more Range States are in the process of joining. However, this means that approximately 60 Range States still have to be convinced of the benefits of joining the Agreement.

Another issue is the question of whether the scope of the Agreement should be broadened in the sense of geographical and species coverage. Both options have been in discussion in the subsidiary bodies of the Agreement for several years, and will be a major issue for the next decade.

Last but not least, a challenge will be to increase the implementation of the Agreement. A great deal has already been achieved, but much more remains to be done. The recent Third Meeting of the Parties has shown that a major challenge for the AEWA is to strengthen co-operation with other multilateral environmental agreements and organizations. Current incidents such as the spread of highly pathogenic avian influenza H5N1 require prompt reaction. This implies close co-operation with other organizations, particularly non-governmental organizations which have the means and mechanisms to implement short-term projects. Moreover, the discussions on the impacts of climate change have made it clear that waterbird conservation needs to be dealt with as one aspect of nature conservation in general, rather than in isolation, and that adaptive policies have to be developed in close co-operation with other agreements and key partners. The AEWA is ready to contribute to the 2010 target as set by the World Summit on Sustainable Development (Johannesburg, South Africa, 2002) to reduce the current rate of loss of biodiversity by 2010. This can, of course, only be achieved by putting all our efforts together.

# Conservation problems of migratory waterfowl and shorebirds and their habitats in the Kaliningrad region of Russia

*Dimitri Grishanov*

*Kaliningrad State University, Universitetskaya str., 2, Kaliningrad 236040, Russia. (email: grishanov@email.albertina.ru)*

Grishanov, D. 2006. Conservation problems of migratory waterfowl and shorebirds and their habitats in the Kaliningrad region of Russia. *Waterbirds around the world.* Eds. G.C. Boere, C.A. Galbraith & D.A. Stroud. The Stationery Office, Edinburgh, UK. p. 354.

The Kalingrad region is an important area for migrating water-fowl, but is threatened by changes in agricultural practice and oil pollution. Current and potential threats to wildfowl and habitat in the area are described as well as their present status.

The Kaliningrad region of Russia is situated on the south-east coast of the Baltic Sea, and is part of the Belomoro-Baltiyskiy migratory flyway; it provides many sites for short- and long-term stop-over by large numbers of migratory water-fowl and shorebirds. Particularly numerous migrants are the White-fronted Goose *Anser albifrons*, Bean Goose *A. fabalis*, Greylag Goose *A. anser*, Mallard *Anas platyrhynchos*, Wigeon *A. penelope*, Pintail *A. acuta*, Tufted Duck *Aythya fuligula*, Long-tailed Duck *Clangula hyemalis*, Goosander *Mergus merganser*, Coot *Fulica atra*, Ringed Plover *Charadrius hiaticula*, Lapwing *Vanellus vanellus*, Ruff *Philomachus pugnax*, Dunlin *Calidris alpina*, Common Snipe *Gallinago gallinago* and many others. Some rare and threatened species (e.g. Bewick's Swan *Cygnus columbarius bewickii*, Lesser White-fronted Goose *Anser erythropus*, Ferruginous Duck *Aythya nyroca* and others) have also been recorded in the region.

The main migratory stop-over sites in the Kaliningrad region are the coastal waters of the Baltic Sea, shores of the Curonian and Vistula lagoons and reservoirs, peat-bogs, marshes and river valleys. The current state of the main long-term migratory stop-over sites for waterfowl and shorebirds is relatively favourable. However, there are many negative factors affecting habitat quality, the most important in the Kaliningrad region being the following.

*Petroleum pollution of the coastal waters of the Baltic Sea.* Sources of land-based petroleum pollution land are badly equipped petroleum terminals, numerous storehouses of mineral oil, industrial, agricultural and transport agencies, boilers, poor drainage from industrial enterprises and municipal services, and storm drains of cities and vehicles. From official data, pollution by mineral oil and sewage is estimated to be from 50 to 90 tons per year. Potential threats of petroleum pollution are oil recovery operations on land and sea, and oil pipelines and large oil storage depots. However, the basic sources of shoreline pollution by mineral oil in the Kaliningrad region are from the sea – prob-ably from large petroleum terminals abroad. In the last decade, pollution of mineral oil in coastal areas was estimated (for example in 1996) at hundreds kilograms up to more than 100 tons. Sources of pollution in all cases were outside the territorial waters of Russia. Cases of mass destruction of a waterfowl population from petroleum pollution on the Kaliningrad coast are rare, but each year high mortality of Long-tailed Ducks is very noticeable.

*Drainage.* As a result of land drainage for use by agriculture and extraction of peat, many ecosystems including wetlands are being destroyed. Drainage of swamps, flooded meadows and raised bogs round the borders of lagoons and in the valleys of the larger rivers results not only fewer sites being available to migra-tory birds, but also in the reduction of the value of the habitat for use during migration. It is noticeable that in such cases the migration of many waterbirds has become transitory.

*Overgrowing of the low-grass meadows by shrubs and tall grass.* The change in use of meadows from mowing and moderate grazing has resulted in low-grass meadows becoming high-grass meadows, frequently overgrown by shrubs and reeds. This type of habitat change dominated the Kaliningrad region at the end of the twentieth century, and as a result, the quality of coastal meadow habitats of birds has declined, with many sites becoming unsuitable as migratory stop-over sites for geese and shorebirds.

*Peat-extraction.* Recently, five raised bogs where many migra-tory species of geese, ducks and shorebirds stopped, have been destroyed in full or in part. Modern legislation and the strategy of nature management in the region do not provide adequate protection of marsh habitats. As a result, only three large raised bogs remain in a condition thought to be suitable for migratory waterfowl and shorebirds to utilize as stop-over sites.

*Burning and mowing of reeds on the shores of the lagoons and in the mouths of rivers.* In winter and early spring a large quan-tities of reeds are mowed, contrary to recommended practice, with the result that total area of mowed sites is increasing. From the middle of March, reeds in many places are set on fire. Sites of partly mowed and partly burned reeds become unattractive for birds and lose their value as migratory stop-over sites.

*Spring and illegal hunting.* Legal hunting for waterfowl opens in April (in 2004, for example, from April 3 to April 22), causing stress to the birds and compelling them to leave traditional migratory stop-over sites prematurely. In addition to a high level of legal hunting there is also a very high level of poaching, even in protected areas.

In conclusion, the basic problems of protection are the following:

- many valuable stop-over sites for migratory birds are not protected, and there are no areas protected under the Ramsar Convention;
- in those reserves that are protected, habitat conservation for of birds is lacking or ineffective; and
- management plans for the major migratory stop-over sites are not yet developed in any detail.

# The state and conservation problems of key stop-over sites of migratory Common Snipe *Gallinago gallinago* in the Kaliningrad region of Russia

*Julia Yarovikova*

*Kaliningrad State University, Universitetskaya str., 2, Kaliningrad 236040, Russia.*
*(email: grishanov@email.albertina.ru)*

Yarovikova, J. 2006. The state and conservation problems of key stop-over sites of migratory Common Snipe *Gallinago gallinago* in the Kaliningrad region of Russia. *Waterbirds around the world.* Eds. G.C. Boere, C.A. Galbraith & D.A. Stroud. The Stationery Office, Edinburgh, UK. p. 355.

In the Kaliningrad region, Common Snipe *Gallinago gallinago* migrate in large numbers during both spring and autumn. Their migration route covers all areas of the region, but mostly they move along the large rivers Neman and Pregolia, and along the coasts of the Curonian and Vistula lagoons.

Abundance and availability of food resources are the major factors determining their distribution. Results of field research show that the optimal conditions for foraging migratory Common Snipe are soil humidity being wet to very wet, vegetation height being from 10 to 25 cm, and vegetation cover from 40 to 60%.

The key stopover sites in this region are seasonally flooded meadows and swamp meadows, located in the Neman River delta, and the eastern and southern coasts of the Curonian lagoon. In some years, favorable conditions in some meadows leads to densities of more than 500 resting and feeding Common Snipe per 10 ha. However, the location and suitability of these habitats changes each year according to water levels during a migration season, and from the levels and types of agricultural use.

The hydrological regime of these areas fluctuates as a result of water management works and to a large extent the weather conditions of the season. During the last decade management works have been irregular and at a local scale. At some sites, especially if there was no agricultural usage, meadows were flooded, and have become boggy and overgrown by shrubs. Currently, within the framework of the Federal target program in the Kaliningrad region, major work on the restoration of water management systems is being undertaken. This has led to increased drainage of floodplains and the loss of suitable staging habitats for migratory Common Snipe.

The location, intensity and type of agricultural use, such as haymaking and grazing, determine the structure of vegetative cover and thus the abundance of food resources. Late mowing and moderate grazing (80-90 cows on 100 ha) promotes favorable vegetative characteristics for Common Snipe foraging. However, excessive grazing results in the degradation of vegetation cover, which in turn negatively influences the abundance of food resources. In the Kaliningrad region agricultural use depends upon the economic situation of individual farms. For the last decade, grazing and hay making in the region has become erratic owing to the sharp reduction in numbers of livestock, from 468 000 in 1990 to 240 000 in 2000. As a result, some meadows are now completely trodden down due to high levels of grazing, while others are overgrown with high grass and shrubs due to no agricultural usage. In both situations these habitats thus have become unsuitable for migratory Common Snipe. Due to lack of haymaking, vegetation is burnt on some sites. Early spring fires in some areas improve the state of stopover sites during spring migration.

The stopover sites of migratory Common Snipe situated in the Important Bird Area of the Neman river Delta and Curonian Lagoon coast, also includes three state nature zoological reserves, Diunniy, Gromovskiy and Zapovedny with a total area of 57 000 ha. These reserves are managed by the Kaliningrad Regional Hunting Department, but there is no special conservation strategy for migratory Common Snipe and their key stopover sites.

Common Snipe *Gallingao gallinago* feed in seasonally flooded wetlands during migratory stop-overs in Kaliningrad. Photo: Simon Stirrup.

# The Neman River Delta: a potential Ramsar site in Kaliningrad, Russia

*Gennady Grishanov [1] & Dimitri Grishanov[2]*

[1] *Chair of Ecology and Zoology, Kaliningrad State University, Universitetskaya str., 2, Kaliningrad 236040, Russia.*
[2] *Kaliningrad State University, Universitetskaya str., 2, Kaliningrad 236040, Russia.*
*(email: grishanov@email.albertina.ru)*

Grishanov, G. & Grishanov, D. 2006. The Neman River Delta: a potential Ramsar site in Kaliningrad, Russia. *Waterbirds around the world*. Eds. G.C. Boere, C.A. Galbraith & D.A. Stroud. The Stationery Office, Edinburgh, UK. p. 356.

The delta of the Neman River and the adjacent eastern coast of the Curonian Lagoon is the main stop-over site of migratory waterbirds in the Kaliningrad region. It is a complex mosaic of wetland and forest habitats, with rivers, canals, marshes, meadows and forests. These unique, pristine wetlands are the largest such area in the south Baltic region and play a key role in maintaining the biodiversity of the region.

The northern part of the Neman River delta is located in Lithuania and was designated as a Ramsar site in December 1993. The southern part of the delta is Russian territory and despite its huge significance for migratory birds still does not have Ramsar status although it meets the Ramsar criteria for identifying wetlands of international importance in the following respects:

- the site is a representative and unique example of a coastal wetland complex, characteristic of the Eastern Baltic Region (Criterion 1);
- the site is very important for the conservation of biological diversity and for the natural hydrological regime of the region (Criterion 3);
- the site supports significant numbers of rare, vulnerable or endangered species of birds, mammals and plants. Among these are numerous species of fauna and flora of European conservation concern (Criterion 2);
- the site regularly supports more than 20 000 waterbirds (Criterion 5).

There are 16 priority habitat types in the delta which are included on Annex 1 of the EU Habitats Directive. Approximately 250 bird species occur in the delta, including 156 breeding species and up to 50 species with special conservation status. The wetlands are important as a stop-over site for migratory waterbirds such as Greylag Goose *Anser anser*, White-fronted Goose *A. albifrons*, Bean Goose *A. fabalis*, Tufted Duck *Aythya fuligula*, Pochard *A. ferina*, Wigeon *Anas penelope*, Pintail *A. acuta* and Mallard *A. platyrhynchos* which form large concentrations of more than 20 000 individuals in the autumn.

Thirteen species of birds have been recorded breeding in the Neman River delta which are listed in The Red Data Book for the Russian Federation: Spotted Eagle *Aquila clanga*, Lesser Spotted Eagle *A. pomarina*, White-tailed Eagle *Haliaeetus albicilla*, Osprey *Pandion haliaetus*, Eagle Owl *Bubo bubo*, Little Tern *Sterna albifrons*, Curlew *Numenius arquata*, Oystercatcher *Haematopus ostralegus*, Avocet *Recurvirostra avosetta*, Great Grey Shrike *Lanius excubitor*, Middle Spotted Woodpecker *Dendrocopos medius*, Black Stork *Ciconia nigra* and Golden Plover *Pluvialis apricaria*. The following Russian Red Data Book listed species are regularly recorded on migration in the delta: Black-throated Diver *Gavia arctica*, Red Kite *Milvus milvus*, Golden Eagle *Aquila chrysaetos*, Peregrine *Falco peregrinus*, Dunlin *Calidris alpina*, Caspian Tern *Sterna caspia*; and the globally threatened Lesser White-fronted Goose *Anser erythropus*, Ferruginous Duck *Aythya nyroca*, Spotted Eagle, Corncrake *Crex crex*, Great Snipe *Gallinago media*, Aquatic Warbler *Acrocephalus paludicola*. The delta also hosts the largest density of breeding Bittern *Botaurus stellaris*, Montagu's Harrier *Circus pygargus*, White-tailed Eagle, Spotted Crake *Porzana porzana*, Corncrake, Crane *Grus grus*, Little Tern and Black Tern *Chlidonias niger* in the region.

Two State Zoological Nature Reserves, Diunny and Zapovedny are located in the wetlands. However, they provide insufficient protection to maintain ecological and biological diversity or the hydrological regime of the area. Economic development projects are a threat to conservation of the key habitats. Urgent measures are required to regulate certain kinds of human economic activities such as the proposed works for deepening part of the Neman river and the coastal part of the Curonian lagoon which are of particular concern for this region.

Increasing human disturbance, such as the unregulated development of water-based tourism, threaten this unique natural complex. Frequent spring fires in large areas of reed thickets, peat bogs and woods, regular fires on the embankments of dams and increased poaching are also cause for concern.

The long term plan for nature conservation in the Kaliningrad region includes the establishment of a State Nature Complex (landscape) Reserve with zonation plans for differing uses and levels of protection. Designating the wetlands of the Neman River delta as a Ramsar site would be an important step towards conserving these valuable habitats for waterbirds. Their unique landscape and biodiversity value is significant for the whole Baltic region and should provide the basis for further protection and conservation status, such as working with Lithuania to establish a possible transfrontier protected area of European significance. Such transfrontier sites are especially encouraged by the Ramsar Convention.

# The migration routes of waterfowl and their protection in Baikal Siberia

*Yuri I. Mel'nikov*

*State Nature Reserve 'Baikalo-Lenskiy', Irkutsk, 291 B Baikalskaja St. a/b 3580, 664050, Russia. (email: zapoved@irk.ru)*

Mel'nikov, Yu.I. 2006. The migration routes of waterfowl and their protection in Baikal Siberia. *Waterbirds around the world*. Eds. G.C. Boere, C.A. Galbraith & D.A. Stroud. The Stationery Office, Edinburgh, UK. pp. 357-362.

## ABSTRACT

Long-term studies have been used to determine features of the migration of waterfowl (ducks, geese and swans) in Baikal Siberia. For the first time, the major and minor migratory routes have been identified, and the way in which these have developed in relation to the mountainous areas and plains of the region has been revealed. Important staging areas, supporting at least 20 000 individuals during the migration seasons, are identified. It is estimated that at least 10-12 million waterfowl pass through Baikal Siberia in autumn. However, there is a poor level of protection for waterfowl in the region. The existing specially protected areas, primarily hunting reserves, do not provide adequate protection for waterbirds, and a decrease in the numbers has been observed in recent years. There is now an urgent need for the creation of a special system of protected areas for the protection and rational use of waterfowl in the region.

## INTRODUCTION

The waterfowl and shorebirds of Baikal Siberia migrate along the East Asian-Australasian Flyway. An analysis of the recoveries from about 170 000 ringed birds (Pizhjanov 1998) has shown that the western limits of the wintering range of waterbirds from Baikal Siberia are in central and eastern India (Mel'nikov 1999), while the majority of birds winter in Japan, China, South-east Asia, the Philippines, New Guinea and Australia (Skryabin *et al.* 1978, 1981, Pizhjanov 1998, Mel'nikov 1999). The migration routes of waterfowl in the East Asian-Australasian Flyway are poorly known. In Baikal Siberia, investigations have been carried out only at the most important staging areas and along the main migration routes. Little information is available on the numbers of waterfowl present, and details of the migration routes through the highlands of this region are practically unknown.

## STUDY AREA, MATERIALS AND METHODS

The extensive territory in the south of eastern Siberia, located around Lake Baikal, is referred to as Baikal Siberia (Peshkova 1972). It lies at the centre of the Asian continent on the boundary between the steppe and forest zones, and is an important ecological barrier in the distribution of many species of animals and plants. The Sajan-Baikal plateau, with its uplifted and strongly shattered ranges (2 500-3 500 m), divides the south of the region into two parts: Prebaikalia and Transbaikalia. Land to the north and south of the plateau has low- and mid-mountainous relief (800-1 800 m), with numerous depressions in the south (Florensov & Oljunin 1965). The Angara valley in the central Sajan-Baikal plateau is open to a southerly air-stream from the valley of the Selenga River to the south, and this warm air supports steppe and forest-steppe zones along the Angara River and lower portions of its tributaries, on Olkhon Island and in Priolkhonje (Peshkova 1972).

Baikal Siberia is characterized by continental climatic conditions. This is especially marked in inter-montane depressions (Zhukov 1965). There is relatively little precipitation, and there are few large lake systems. Coniferous taiga forest dominates everywhere, and there are only small areas of forest-steppe and steppe in the relatively warm, inter-montane basins. Permafrost is widely distributed almost throughout the territory.

This paper is based on the results of 40 years of personal research, and makes use of the published literature and interviews with the local population, waterfowl hunters and forestry experts. Over 15 000 km were covered on foot or by boat during the course of the research, and about 2 000 hours were spent making observations from fixed observation posts. Fieldwork was carried out in most of the large wetland systems in the region. The migration of waterfowl was studied in detail at fixed observation posts at the mouth of the Irkut River, in the Selenga River delta, and in the basins of rivers in East Sajan (Oka, Goloustnaja, Uda, Zima, Malyi Tagul and Toisik). The results of some of these studies have already been published (Mel'nikov 2000a, 2000b, 2001). On the basis of the published material and personal research, migration routes of waterfowl in the region have been mapped.

## RESULTS

### Spring migration

Two major migration routes (flyways) pass through southern Transbaikalia: the Selenga and the Khingan. They are formed in Mongolia and China (Mel'nikov 1999, 2000b). In early spring, the Selenga flyway reaches the delta of this river, and then divides into several smaller flyways. The Khingan flyway divides into two in the region of Dalay-nor Lake, with one branch following the Argun River (Khingan-Argun) and the other proceeding to the Torej lakes (Khingan-Torej). The first of these soon leaves the limits of Baikal Siberia in the basin of the Aldan River (Gavrin & Rakov 1960). The second divides into three smaller flyways: the Torej-Olekma, Torej-Kirenga-Tunguska and Torej-Baikal-Angara.

Migrating waterfowl first appear in southern Transbaikalia (in the region of Kyakhta and the Torej basin) in the second half of March (Molleson 1897, Gavrin & Rakov 1959). In years with an early spring, small groups of Ruddy Shelduck *Tadorna ferruginea*, and sometimes Mallard *Anas platyrhynchos*, have already appeared in the Selenga River delta and at Verchnee Priangarie (Irkutsk and Ust-Orda) by the end of March. The first large wave of migrating waterfowl appears in southern Transbaikalia as soon as the average daily air temperature exceeds 0°C (Gavrin & Rakov 1959, Shinkarenko 1988). This usually occurs with a significant intrusion of warm air from Mongolia and China at the beginning of April. Waterfowl arriving at this time include early-breeding dabbling ducks, such as Mallard, Common Teal *Anas crecca*, Northern Pintail *A. acuta*

Female Mallard *Anas platyrhynchos* and young. Photo: Paul Marshall.

and Eurasian Wigeon *A. penelope*, and Common Goldeneye *Bucephala clangula*. The north-south orientation of the basins in Transbaikalia promotes rapid penetration of warm air to the north, and the wave of migrants quickly reaches the northern-most areas of forest-steppe, although the numbers are much lower in the north.

The movement of birds far to the north in the first stages of the spring migration is facilitated by a gap in the mountain ranges in the area of the Selenga River delta and a tributary of the Angara River, and also the large areas of steppe on the Irkutsk-Cheremchovo plain and on the edge of the Prebaikalia lowlands. There is already, in the early stages of spring migra-tion in southern Baikal, a well-defined flyway (Baikal-Angara-Yenisei) that leaves in a north-westerly direction to the Yenisei via the extensive Irkutsk-Cheremchovo plain and southern edge of the Leno-Angara plateau.

From this major flyway, smaller flyways diverge to the north and north-east, passing through Verkholeniy (Kachug settlement) and Ust-Kut in the Lena valley, where there are small areas of steppe and agricultural land. Around Irkutsk, the Baikal-Angara-Yenisei flyway divides into two branches. The main branch continues on in a north-westerly direction, while the other (the Baikal-Angara-Tunguska flyway) turns north and follows the valley of the Nizyhnjaja Tunguska River to Erbogachen plain, where it joins up with the Torej-Kirenga-Tunguska flyway. Birds reaching the basin of the Lena River follow this valley in a north-easterly direction. Other flyways formed in the Selenga River delta are insignificant in size, and are used by birds moving to breeding areas within Baikal Siberia.

In this first period of the spring migration, the birds migrate exclusively along river valleys, as the land between the valleys

remains under snow and presents a serious barrier to the birds. Both north-easterly and south-westerly movements of birds have been observed along the eastern edge of Lake Baikal at this time of year (Skryabin 1975), and it has not been possible to identify separate migration routes in this area. Groups of ducks that breed locally are already arriving on their breeding grounds in southern Prebaikalia in the middle of April, often before the first major wave of spring migrants (Mel'nikov 1998).

The appearance of the first migrants in early spring always occurs during short warm spells, which are usually followed by cold periods (of three to four days), with air temperatures of –5 to –7°C. The mass migration of waterfowl begins when the average daily air temperatures rises above 0°C throughout much of the territory (Shinkarenko 1988). This usually occurs at the end of April or the beginning of May, although there may still be short cold spells. However, snow cover in the low mountain ranges between the rivers disappears and conditions for migra-tion improve considerably. Migration occurs on a much broader front, with birds beginning to appear on the southern slopes of high mountainous areas. At this time, birds begin to fly through some of the lower passes in the mountain ranges of East Sajan to reach the Uda river valley, which they follow in a northerly or north-westerly direction. However, the main Yenisei flyway, which includes birds from the East Tuva staging area (Emeljanov & Savchenko 2000), is rather poorly represented in Baikal Siberia.

In other mountain ranges in East Sajan, there are minor flyways of birds from the Khangaiy flyway which originates in Mongolia. These minor flyways, having passed around the high, snow-covered mountain ranges, enter large river valleys with favourable conditions for further migration. However, the number of birds involved is small. Also during this period, a rather small flyway (Vitim-Paton) is formed in the large lake system in the Vitim Mountains (Ivano-Arahley, Eravna and Baunt lakes), and this has several minor branches in the high-lands of the Vitim, Severo-Baikal and Patom plateaux (Mel'nikov 2000a).

In the second half of May, waterfowl migration in southern Baikal Siberia comes to an end, while in northern areas, the mass migration begins. At this time of year, migration occurs every-where on a broad front, and large concentrations of birds can be found at staging areas at large lake systems. The location of these staging areas determines the directions of the minor flyways. Concentrations of birds elsewhere along the flyways are observed only at certain strategically important locations and, in high mountains, in certain mountain passes. At present, there is a well-defined flyway through the Baikal Mountains leading to the Nizhnjaja Tunguska river valley.

## Moult migration

A return migration of the drakes of some waterfowl species is observed at moulting areas even before the end of the spring migration. The timing of the moult migration is closely linked to the breeding phenology of the birds. Even within southern Baikal Siberia, there is a two-week difference in dates of first egg-laying between the earliest breeders in southern areas and those in northern areas. Differences in the main egg-laying period are more indicative in this respect. The difference between breeders in northern Baikal Siberia (Nizhnjaja Tunguska river valley) and those in the south (Selenga River delta) is three weeks. In years with an early spring, drake Mallard and Northern Pintail begin to pursue females in the first few days of May. Some 10-15 days after disintegration of the pair bond, the drakes form small flocks (Mel'nikov 1998), and start to undertake local movements to good feeding areas. The number of drakes involved in these movements rapidly builds up, and by early June, drakes greatly outnumber nesting birds at the important moulting sites. By the beginning of July, the moulting drakes have been joined by many females (sometimes 30-35%), presumably birds that have had an unsuccessful breeding season.

The first species to begin their moult migration are those that nest earliest, e.g. Mallard, Common Teal, Garganey *Anas querquedula* and Northern Pintail. Moult migrations occur on a broad front and under very favourable conditions, with moulting flocks of drakes occurring on practically all wetlands in Baikal Siberia. The direction of the moult migrations basically coincides with the spring and autumn flyways (Mel'nikov 2000b). The long duration of the moult migrations (ranging from 2.0 to 3.5-4.0 months according to species) is a result of the length of the breeding season. Even in mid-July, some ducks remain paired and are still breeding. This late nesting is due to the laying of one or even two replacement clutches, being most common in Gadwall *Anas strepera*, Tufted Duck *Aythya fuligula*, Common Pochard *A. ferina*, Common Goldeneye and Smew *Mergellus albellus*. The moult migration of these late breeders may be delayed until the end of August. Furthermore, birds from northern breeding areas migrate to southern areas to moult, and having nested later than southern breeders, also undertake their moult later. This further extends the duration of the moulting period.

In Baikal Siberia, mass moulting of waterfowl occurs only in the south of the region, in the Selenga River delta and Torej lakes. Depending on water levels, there are between several hundred and up to 30 000-50 000 moulting drakes in these areas. However, throughout Baikal Siberia, some of the drakes moult in their breeding areas, and do not undertake long-distance moult migrations. Usually these are late breeders which gather in groups of five to ten individuals in secure areas with optimum feeding conditions. Only on those lakes with the best conditions are there moulting concentrations of up to some hundreds (but no more than 1 000) individuals. The scarcity of important moulting areas in Baikal Siberia, particularly for diving ducks and dabbling ducks that feed on invertebrates, such as the Northern Shoveler *Anas clypeata*, is thought to be due to the small number of reservoirs in the region, and their low productivity. Even in the northern limits of the forest-steppe zone, conditions are still very poor for moulting birds, although there are some fairly large concentrations of moulting drakes in this area.

### Autumn migration

The autumn migration begins under favourable conditions in the middle or at the end of August. Large concentrations of birds that have bred locally gather on the largest lake systems in the region, and the first dabbling ducks begin to depart. Formerly there were appreciable movements of Baikal Teal *Anas formosa* at this time, but this is now an extremely rare species in Baikal Siberia. The last birds to depart are the diving ducks, sawbills, geese and swans.

The main directions of the movements in spring and autumn almost exactly coincide. Migration occurs on a broad front, with some funnelling along flyways in certain areas. The minor flyways are used by only small numbers of birds, mostly on their way to the main staging areas where they congregate in larger flocks. The number of birds migrating through high mountainous areas, even in favourable conditions, is insignificant, although almost all species migrate in small numbers along flyways at low and middle elevations in the mountains.

Migration through mountain passes is far from uniform. During some seasons, it can occur on a large scale. It is clearly related to weather conditions, with birds not flying through some passes if there is a deterioration in the local weather. In periods of very severe weather, when most or all of the passes are closed, the bird congregate on lakes in the river valleys where they remain until the weather improves.

Three or four waves of migration are observed during autumn, each producing a big increase in the numbers of birds at the main staging areas. The species composition of each wave differs, but Mallard, Common Teal, Northern Pintail, Eurasian Wigeon, Tufted Duck and Common Goldeneye dominate in all waves. The first consists mainly of dabbling ducks, and the last, mainly diving ducks, geese and swans. The total number of birds seen migrating along the main flyways varies considerably from year to year (by as much as eight fold), and obviously depends on conditions along the migration route. Observations made from the ground take into account only those birds flying at low level, while non-stop migration at high altitude (true migration) goes unrecorded.

With the onset of heavy snowfall in the high mountains in the first half of September, migration through these areas almost stops, although there are occasional flocks of geese and Whooper Swans *Cygnus cygnus*. Discrete flyways begin to appear in the valleys, and these are well pronounced by late autumn, when the shallow lakes become covered in ice. In Prebaikalia, the last of the migrants gather on the reservoirs of Ust-Ilym, Bratsk and Irkutsk, and the large lakes of Irkutsk-Cheremhovo plain and Prebaikala plain (Ochaul, Berikul, Kondakov and others). The last wave of the autumn migration appears in the second ten days of November, and passes through the Verkhnee Priangaryei, Primorskyi ridge, Selenga River delta and Torej lakes on the way to Mongolia and China.

### Staging areas

The most important staging areas during the spring, moult and autumn migrations are the large lake systems along the major flyways. The largest of these are located on the border of the forest-steppe and steppe zones, the most significant being the Torej lakes and Selenga River delta. Staging areas in the Baikal basin (Barguzin river valley, Arangatujy lakes, Verkhnjaja Angara and Kichera river mouths, and Verkhneangarsk expansion) are less important. The chain of Angarsk reservoirs is an important staging area, as also are the Irkutsk, Bratsk and Ust-Ilym reservoirs. One of the most important staging areas in northern Baikal Siberia is Erbogachen plain, in the Nizhnjaja Tunguska valley. Many other smaller sites support up to about 20 000 waterfowl during the migration seasons. The location of these staging areas determines the direction of many of the minor flyways, as bird move from one staging area to another.

The total number of a waterfowl using the staging areas in Baikal Siberia is considerable. Unfortunately, it is very difficult to provide a reliable estimate of numbers on the basis of the available data. However, counts of the large concentrations of waterfowl during autumn migration at the two most important staging areas in Baikal Siberia (Selenga River delta and Torej lakes) allow us to make a tentative estimate of total numbers. It should be noted that there are few areas of mass concentration of waterfowl near the southern borders of Baikal Siberia, and most of these are much less important than the Selenga River delta and Torej lakes. An exception is the Argun River along which migrate at least half of the waterfowl entering Russian territory via the Khingan flyway. However, waterfowl following the Khingan-Argun flyway soon leave Baikal Siberia via the Aldan valley. There has been no accurate estimation of numbers in this flyway for many years, and as the flyway lies largely outside Baikal Siberia, it has not been considered here.

At the end of twentieth century, some research was carried out on the migration of waterfowl in the Selenga River delta and Torej lakes, and this included an estimation of numbers. This work has shown that, depending on the year, between two million and five million waterfowl stop off in the Selenga River delta during the autumn migration (Skryabin 1995), while between three million and five million waterfowl stop off in the Torej lakes (Goroshko 1998). It has been estimated that a further two million birds occur at the many other, less important sites, including sites that hold less than 20 000 individuals. Hence, the total number of waterfowl occurring at staging areas in Baikal Siberia during the autumn migration is estimated at 10-12 million individuals. This is a minimum estimate for the number

Rare waterbirds to Baikal Siberia such as the Bewick's Swan *Cygnus columbianus bewickii* sometimes occur at important staging areas in the north of the region. Photo: Paul Marshall.

Moulting flocks of drake Mallards *Anas platyrhynchos* as well as other ducks occur in autumn on practically all wetlands in Baikal Siberia. Photo: Crawford Prentice.

of waterfowl passing through Baikal Siberia, as an unknown proportion passes through southern Baikal Siberia without stopping to rest. Significant annual fluctuations in the numbers of waterfowl recorded at staging areas are related to the condition of the wetlands. In years with high water levels, the numbers of birds increase sharply, while in years with low water levels, numbers are greatly reduced.

### Protection of waterfowl

Sites of importance for the protection of waterfowl are poorly represented in the current network of specially protected natural territories (SPNT), which includes various categories of protected area. Indeed, most of the internationally important wetlands are unprotected. Furthermore, the fact that a site of high importance as a breeding or staging area for waterfowl has been designated as a SPNT at local level (territorial hunting reserve) does not mean that it is well protected. Infringement of the regulations concerning the exploitation of wildlife resources in territorial hunting reserves is now the usual situation. Only twelve of the 30 most important areas for waterfowl are formally protected; in two reserves (Dauria and Olekma), two national parks (Prebaikalian and Transbaikalian) and eight hunting reserves. All of these are sites of international importance.

With a few exceptions, important staging areas for waterfowl on the main flyways in Baikal Siberia are not specially protected, and this is the main deficiency in waterfowl protection in the region. Many of these staging areas are unique wetlands and support a high diversity of waterfowl. The southern lake systems are especially interesting in this respect, as they often support a number of specially protected species such as Greylag Goose *Anser anser*, Swan Goose *A. cygnoides*, Baer's Pochard *Aythya baeri* and Baikal Teal. Important staging areas in the north of the region support rare species such as Bewick's Swan *Cygnus columbianus bewickii*, Middendorff's Bean Goose *Anser fabalis middendorffi*, Lesser White-fronted Goose *A. erythropus*, Harlequin Duck *Histrionicus histrionicus* and White-winged Scoter *Melanitta (fusca) deglandi*, and also require more protection.

The extreme importance of the Selenga River delta for waterfowl was recognized in the 1980s, and yet this site remains unprotected. The establishment of a protected area in the delta is a high priority, as also is the establishment of an ornithological reserve to protect the Inarigda lake complex in the Nizhnjaja Tunguska valley (Nizhnetungusskiy). All other important sites require, if not full protection, then at least regulations concerning the economic exploitation of waterfowl resources. In the creation of the SPNT network, no consideration was given to the special protection of waterfowl, although this group of birds includes many species that require special attention. Special approaches are required in the planning of a system of protection and management for waterfowl, as well as for various other groups of birds.

### DISCUSSION

Hitherto, the waterfowl flyways of Baikal Siberia have been poorly investigated. The information collected by us and the general information available in the literature have enabled us to present the first overview of the main directions and character of movements of waterfowl within the limits of this extensive territory. The main flyways along which birds reach Baikal Siberia during the spring migration converge on the important staging areas in the Selenga River delta and Torej basin, and then divide into a series of smaller flyways. A significant proportion of the birds finish their migration in Baikal Siberia, and settle down to breed here and in adjoining regions. During the autumn migration, birds use a wide network of minor flyways to reach the main staging areas in Baikal Siberia, whence they continue along the major flyways to their wintering areas.

The large and well-defined flyways reflect the main directions of the migrations of long-distance migrants: north-west in spring and south-east in autumn. In spring, these flyways appear much earlier in southern Baikal Siberia than flyways in other directions, and in autumn, continue until the middle of November, when migration on other flyways has ceased. Many of the birds in these major flyways breed in central and eastern Taymyr, where there are very high breeding densities of many species of waterfowl.

The formation of well-pronounced flyways in Baikal Siberia is principally caused by the natural features and climatic conditions of the region. The Sajan-Baikal plateau is relatively low in elevation, and has gaps through which southerly air streams can penetrate in early spring, bringing warm air to the Selenga and Angara valleys. This is reflected in the presence of large areas of steppe vegetation. Other, less well-pronounced flyways are formed later in the spring, and are connected with the movement of birds through high mountain ranges (2 500-3 000 m). It has been demonstrated that orographic features and the latitudinal distribution of vegetation zones have a big influence on the direction and intensity of the migration routes of waterfowl.

Despite the scarcity of large lake systems in Baikal Siberia, very large concentrations of waterfowl occur at staging areas during the spring and autumn migration seasons. There would appear to be abundant food resources for the migrating birds, as the quality of the wetlands in Baikal Siberia has essentially not changed in recent decades. However, the numbers of migrating waterfowl are now much lower than they were in the middle of twentieth century.

The wetlands of southern Baikal Siberia are of great importance for migratory waterfowl, providing staging areas where the birds can build up their fat reserves before continuing their migration. However, the present system of state protected territories is obviously insufficient to provide adequate protection for waterfowl and maintain species diversity. The main reason for this is that, until now, the creation of a system of protected areas has focused exclusively on the preservation of fur-bearing animals because of their high economic value. The development of a special system of protected territories is therefore required for the protection of breeding and migrating waterfowl.

### REFERENCES

**Emeljanov, V.I. & Savchenko, A.P.** 2000. Specific structure, ratio and spatial structure of goose flyways in southern Priynicei Siberia. In: Ts.Z. Dorzhiev (ed) Modern problems of ornithology of Siberia and Central Asia. Buryat State University Press, Ulan-Ude: 107-112. (In Russian).

**Florensov, N.A. & Oljunin, V.N.** 1965. Relief and geological structure. In: I.P. Gerasimov (ed) Prebaikalia and Transbaikalia. Science Press, Moscow: 23-90. (In Russian).

**Gavrin, V.F. & Rakov, N.V.** 1959. Materials from studying the spring flight of waterfowl in the headwaters of the Argun river. The message I. In: V.S. Pokrovskii (ed) Migratory animals, 1. USSR Academy Press, Moscow: 59-66. (In Russian).

**Gavrin, V.F. & Rakov, N.V.** 1960. Materials from studying the spring flight of waterfowl in the headwaters of the Argun river. The message II. Features of flight of different species. In: V.S. Pokrovskii (ed) Migratory animals, 2. USSR Academy Press, Moscow: 146-174. (In Russian).

**Goroshko, O.A.** 1998. Some results of a study of birds of a Torej hollow (Russia and Mongolia) and prospects for their preservation. Boundaries of especially protected natural territories of Northern Eurasia: the theory and practice. The Scientific – Practical Bulletin 1. IUCN-WCPA Press, Moscow: 23-26. (In Russian).

**Mel'nikov, Yu.I.** 1998. Dynamics of sexual structure and migration of waterfowl on the average current Oka river (Leno-Angarsk plateau). In: V.V. Popov (ed) Proceedings of the Baikalo-Lenskyi State Reserve 1. Inkombook Press, Moscow: 78-84. (In Russian).

**Mel'nikov, Yu.I.** 1999. Migration routes and territorial connections of shorebirds and waterfowl in Prebaikalia. In: S.A. Bukreev & V.A. Zubakin (eds) Inventory, monitoring and protection of key ornithological territories in Russia. Russian Union of Protection of Birds, Moscow: 143-147. (In Russian).

**Mel'nikov, Yu.I.** 2000a. Observations of migrating shorebirds and waterfowl through the mountain ranges of Eastern Siberia. In: Ts.Z. Dorzhiev (ed) Questions for the study of biodiversity and monitoring of condition of terrestrial ecosystems of the Baikal region. Russian Academy of Science Press, Ulan-Ude: 125-130. (In Russian).

**Mel'nikov, Yu.I.** 2000b. The Waterfowl of the Central Palearctic Flyway Region: Migrations, Use, Protection. In: T. Hughson & C. Ruckstuhl (eds) ISCORD 2000: Proceedings of the Sixth International Symposium on Cold Region Development, Hobart, Tasmania, Australia, 31 January - 4 February 2000. Melbourne: 323-326.

**Mel'nikov, Yu.I**. 2001. Number, distribution and migrations of the Bean Goose in the south of Eastern Siberia. In: Yu.I. Mel'nikov (ed) Proceedings of the Baikalo-Lenskyi State Reserve, 2. Listok Press, Irkutsk: 82-100. (In Russian).

**Molleson, V.S.** 1897. Observation of the spring flight of birds on the Chikoyi river in 1896. Report Troizkosavsko-Kjahta Branch, Priamur Branch RGO 4: 3-28.

**Peshkova, G.A.** 1972. Steppe flora of Baikal Siberia. Science Press, Novosibirsk.

**Pizhjanov, S.V.** 1998. Baikal as an avifaunal unit. In: V.I. Evsikov (ed) Problems in the preservation of biodiversity. Science Press, Novosibirsk: 81-85. (In Russian).

**Shinkarenko, A.V.** 1988. The dynamics of flight of waterfowl and meteorological conditions. In: N.G. Skryabin (ed) Ecology of the terrestrial vertebrates of Eastern Siberia. Irkutsk State University Press, Irkutsk: 6-17. (In Russian).

**Skryabin, N.G.** 1975. Waterfowl of Baikal. The East-Siberian Book Publishing House, Irkutsk. (In Russian).

**Skryabin, N.G.** 1995. Selenga river delta - the largest staging area for waterfowl on Baikal. In: A.I. Diemin (ed) The eco-geographical characteristics of Prebaikalia. State Pedagogical Institute Press, Irkutsk: 101-108. (In Russian).

**Skryabin, N.G., Sadkov, V.S. & Pizhjanov, S.V.** 1978. Role of Baikal in the migration of shorebirds. In: E.V. Gvozdev (ed) The Second All-Union Conference on Migrations of Birds 1. Science Press, Alma-Ata: 162-164. (In Russian).

**Skryabin, N.G., Sadkov, V.S., Pizhjanov, S.V., Gilevich, A.L., Safronov, N.N., Popov, V.D. & Mel'nikov, Yu.I.** 1981. Results of ringing gulls and terns on Baikal. In: I.M. Ganja (ed) Ecology and protection of birds. Shtiinza Press, Kishinev: 209. (In Russian).

**Zhukov, V.M.** 1965. Climate. In: I.P. Gerasimov (ed) Prebaikalia and Transbaikalia. Science Press, Moscow: 91-126. (In Russian).

Occasional flocks of Whooper Swans *Cygnus cygnus* migrate through Baikal Siberia in autumn.  Photo: Paul Marshall.

# Enigmas about Whimbrel *Numenius phaeopus* in the East Atlantic Flyway

*Bertrand Trolliet*

*Office National de la Chasse et de la Faune Sauvage, Chanteloup-85340, Ile d'Olonne, France.*
*(email: bertrand.trolliet@oncfs.gouv.fr)*

Trolliet, B. 2006. Enigmas about Whimbrel *Numenius phaeopus* in the East Atlantic Flyway. *Waterbirds around the world.*
Eds. G.C. Boere, C.A. Galbraith & D.A. Stroud. The Stationery Office, Edinburgh, UK. p. 363.

Current estimates of the number of Whimbrel *Numenius phaeopus* breeding in Europe are between 322 200 to 369 000 pairs, of which 250 000 are in Iceland (Thorup 2006). However, surveys in (northern) summer in Guinea and the Banc d'Arguin have shown that around 50% of the numbers in winter do not migrate north in spring. Thus, taking into account that a proportion of birds do not return to breeding grounds but oversummer in their wintering areas, the number of breeding pairs should be multiplied by four to estimate the wintering numbers, which would thus amount to 1.3 to 1.5 million individuals.

These birds are thought to winter along the West African coast, with small numbers wintering in Europe, which is confirmed by ring recoveries. The total number of wintering birds, counted or estimated, in Europe and West Africa (from Morocco to Gabon), is approximately 111 000 individuals (Trolliet & Fouquet 2004), i.e. 7.5 to 8.5% of the estimated breeding population. This implies that more than one million individuals could be wintering in areas that have not been surveyed, possibly mangrove areas. These figures also would imply that Whimbrel is the most abundant coastal wader in Africa. There is no data showing that European-breeding Whimbrel winter further south in Africa (where, anyway, known numbers are small).

Between Africa and the breeding grounds in Iceland and north continental Europe, only a few areas are known where Whimbrel stopover during their spring migration. The total peak numbers (which occur almost simultaneously) on these known stopover places does not exceed 70 000 individuals.

One of these stopover sites is Chanteloup, Vendée, in western France. Counts made at this roosting site, biometric analysis of more than 2 100 Whimbrels captured there in spring, and estimates of energy requirements, indicate that the birds staging on these known stopover places represent at most 1.1 million days x individuals, corresponding to less than 220 000 individuals. Birds must stage for an average of more than five days to deposit enough energy reserves to reach their breeding areas. This would mean that well in excess of 424 000 Whimbrels stopover in known staging areas in spring.

This implies that either these birds:

- stopover elsewhere, although it seems unlikely that such large numbers have been missed; or,
- they fly directly from Africa to their breeding areas.

To fly direct, birds breeding in continental Europe would need to cover at least 6 000 km. However, studies in Mauritania are not compatible with the departure from there of hundreds of thousands of Whimbrel going direct to their breeding areas. This suggests that the great majority of Icelandic Whimbrel would have to depart from more southerly areas, situated at least 5 800 km from Iceland. Estimates of energy expenditures

suggest that such long nonstop flights are probably impossible. However, metabolism rates and the energy costs of flight under the actual conditions of migratory flights over long distances are insufficiently known and may differ considerably from predictions of theoretical models.

Thus we have to conclude that breeding numbers are over-estimated, particularly in Iceland. However, this over estimation is probably not so excessive, and enigmas remain about populations sizes, winter distribution and migrations of European Whimbrels.

To answer these questions, it is suggested that studies begin, or continue, on:

- numbers breeding in Iceland;
- numbers wintering in West Africa's mangroves, notably in Nigeria;
- the birds' movements, ecology and physiology in West Africa in April, and
- surveys to locate other spring migratory stopover places in Europe.

## REFERENCES

**Thorup O.** (compiler) 2006. Breeding waders in Europe 2000. International Wader Studies 14.

**Trolliet, B. & Fouquet, M.** 2004. Wintering waders in Coastal Guinea. Wader Study Group Bulletin 103: 56-62.

Whimbrels *Numenius phaeopus* on a Seychelles beach. Photo: Ian Francis.

# The European Non-Estuarine Coastal Waterbird Survey

*Steve J. Holloway, Niall H.K. Burton & Mark M. Rehfisch*
*British Trust for Ornithology, The Nunnery, Thetford, Norfolk, IP24 2PU, UK. (email: niall.burton@bto.org)*

Holloway, S.J., Burton, N.H.K. & Rehfisch, M.M. 2006. The European Non-Estuarine Coastal Waterbird Survey. *Waterbirds around the world.* Eds. G.C. Boere, C.A. Galbraith & D.A. Stroud. The Stationery Office, Edinburgh, UK. pp. 364-365.

This paper provides a brief overview of the background and results of the European Non-Estuarine Coastal Waterbird Survey (NEWS), which reported on the wader populations wintering on the non-estuarine coasts of 12 European countries.

NEWS was the first co-ordinated survey of waders wintering on the continent's non-estuarine coasts. The survey aimed to provide population estimates for waterbirds using the non-estuarine habitats in different participant countries, which would complement information from better-monitored estuarine sites.

In total 12 different countries participated in the survey, covering non-estuarine shores from Sweden to Croatia (Table 1). Most counts took place in the winter of 1997/98, with some in 1999/2000.

The survey's results will be published in an International Wader Studies volume (Burton *et al.* in prep.). For each country, papers report on the numbers of waders recorded during the survey and provide population estimates for their non-estuarine coasts. Numbers of other waterbirds recorded are also summarised.

In total, 25 wader species were recorded during the survey. Most widespread were Oystercatcher *Haematopus ostralegus*, Grey Plover *Pluvialis squatarola*, Sanderling *Calidris alba*, Purple Sandpiper *C. maritima*, Dunlin *C. alpina*, Redshank *Tringa totanus* and Turnstone *Arenaria interpres* (Table 1).

The United Kingdom held most non-estuarine waders, with a total estimated population of 380 100 birds (Rehfisch *et al.* 2003). The non-estuarine coasts of the countries surveyed support large proportions (>20%) of the biogeographic populations of Ringed Plover *Charadrius hiaticula*, Sanderling, Purple Sandpiper, Curlew *Numenius arquata*, Redshank and Turnstone.

## ACKNOWLEDGEMENTS

Thanks are due to all those who participated in the survey and particularly the national organisers and authors: K. Devos (Belgium), D. Radović, V. Sćetarić Legan, J. Kralj, D. Blažina (Croatia), O. Thorup, H. Ehrup, N. Burton (Denmark), B. Deceuninck, R. Mahéo, F. Gabillard, (France), J. Blew, K. Günther, J.-J. Kieckbusch, H.-W. Nehls (Germany), J. Cortes (Gibraltar), K. Colhoun, G. Austin, S. Newton (Ireland), C. Soldatini, A. De Berardinis, N. Baccetti (Italy), L. Mendes, M. Dias, R. Rufino (Portugal), F. Hortas, A. Pérez-Hurtado, F. Robledano, C. Álvarez Laó, R. Salvadores (Spain), L. Nilsson (Sweden), M. van Roomen, G. Keijl, B. Koks, K. Mostert (The Netherlands), S. Holloway, M. Rehfisch, G. Austin and the Wetland Bird Survey (UK and Isle of Man). We would also like to thank the International Wader Study Group, and the UK's Joint Nature Conservation Committee and Northumbrian Water Ltd who helped to finance the publication of the survey's results.

## REFERENCES

**Burton, N.H.K.** *et al.* in prep. The European Non-Estuarine Coastal Waterbird Survey. International Wader Studies 18.

**Rehfisch, M.M., Holloway, S.J. & Austin, G.E.** 2003. Population estimates of waders on the United Kingdom's and the Isle of Man's non-estuarine coasts in 1997-98. Bird Study 50: 22-32.

The non-estuarine shores of the United Kingdom hold internationally important numbers of waterbirds, especially waders. Much of the coast of the island of Tiree has been designated as a Ramsar site to protect the large numbers of waders which over-winter there. Photo: David Stroud.

**Table 1. Participant countries in the European Non-Estuarine Coastal Waterbird Survey and wader species recorded.**

| Species | Belgium | Croatia | Denmark | France | Germany | Gibraltar | Ireland | Italy | Portugal | Spain | Sweden | Netherlands | UK |
|---|---|---|---|---|---|---|---|---|---|---|---|---|---|
| Oystercatcher *Haematopus ostralegus* | X | X | X | X | X | | X | | X | X | X | X | X |
| Avocet *Recurvirostra avosetta* | X | | | X | | | | | | | | X | |
| Ringed Plover *Charadrius hiaticula* | X | | X | X | | | X | | X | X | | X | X |
| Kentish Plover *Charadrius alexandrinus* | | X | | X | | | | X | X | X | | | X |
| Golden Plover *Pluvialis apricaria* | | | | X | X | | X | | | X | | X | X |
| Grey Plover *Pluvialis squatarola* | X | X | X | X | X | | X | X | X | X | X | X | X |
| Lapwing *Vanellus vanellus* | | X | | X | X | | X | | | X | X | X | X |
| Knot *Calidris canutus* | X | | | X | X | | | | | | X | X | X |
| Sanderling *Calidris alba* | X | X | X | X | X | | X | X | X | X | X | X | X |
| Little Stint *Calidris minuta* | | | | X | | | | X | | X | | | |
| Purple Sandpiper *Calidris maritima* | X | X | | X | X | | X | | X | X | X | X | X |
| Dunlin *Calidris alpina* | X | X | X | X | X | | X | X | | X | X | X | X |
| Ruff *Philomachus pugnax* | | | | | | | | | | X | | | |
| Jack Snipe *Lymnocryptes minimus* | | X | | | | | | | | | | | X |
| Common Snipe *Gallinago gallinago* | | X | | | X | | X | | | | | | X |
| Black-tailed Godwit *Limosa limosa* | X | | | X | | | | | | | | | X |
| Bar-tailed Godwit *Limosa lapponica* | X | X | | X | X | | X | | | X | X | X | X |
| Whimbrel *Numenius phaeopus* | | | | | | X | | | X | X | | | |
| Curlew *Numenius arquata* | X | X | | X | X | | X | | | X | X | X | X |
| Spotted Redshank *Tringa erythropus* | X | | | X | | | | | | | | | X |
| Redshank *Tringa totanus* | X | X | X | X | X | | X | | | | X | X | X |
| Greenshank *Tringa nebularia* | | X | | X | | | X | | | | | | X |
| Green Sandpiper *Tringa ochropus* | | | | X | | | | | | | | | |
| Common Sandpiper *Actitis hypoleucos* | | X | | X | | | | X | X | X | | | X |
| Turnstone *Arenaria interpres* | X | X | X | X | X | | X | X | X | X | | X | X |

# The evaluation of some key wetlands for waterfowl in Central Anatolia, Turkey

*Utku Perktaş, Atil Bariş Albayrak & Zafer Ayaş*
*Hacettepe University, Faculty of Science, Department of Biology (Zoology Section), Beytepe, Ankara, Turkey.*
*(email: perktas@hacettepe.edu.tr)*

Perktaş, U., Albayrak, A.B. & Ayaş, Z. 2006. The evaluation of some key wetlands for waterfowl in Central Anatolia, Turkey. *Waterbirds around the world.* Eds. G.C. Boere, C.A. Galbraith & D.A. Stroud. The Stationery Office, Edinburgh, UK. pp. 366-367.

This paper presents the results of waterfowl population surveys carried out in five areas in the Central Anatolia region of Turkey between 1998 and 2001.

Turkey contains a significant number of wetlands important on a continental scale within Europe. Although these wetlands are known to be important for breeding and wintering waterfowl populations, little quantitative information is known about the population status of the bird species that use them (Tucker & Heath 1994, Scott & Rose 1996, Tucker & Evans 1997). However, because of the loss or degradation of wetlands across Turkey, wetland dependent species are at high risk, and we therefore examined the number of breeding and wintering waterfowl and looked at the importance of the selected wetlands for some protected waterfowl species.

Our study was conducted from 1998 to 2001 across five different wetlands in the Central Anatolia region of Turkey (Fig. 1): Nallihan Bird Paradise (900 ha); Balikdami on the Sakarya River; Seyfe Lake (max. 9 350 ha); Palas Lake (saline, 2 330 ha); and Sultansazliği in the Develi closed basin. The wetland includes a series of salt, brackish and freshwater lakes, and extensive marshes. *Salicornia* steppe encloses the salt-lakes environs, and southern marshes include large *Phragmites* reedbeds.

Between 1998 and 1999, we worked in the Seyfe Lake, Palas Lake and Sultansazliği areas, and in 2000 and 2001 in Nallihan Bird Paradise and Balikdami. We used the survey methodology suggested by Bibby *et al.* (1992) to determine the individual numbers of wintering and breeding waterfowl. European Threat Status (ETS) suggested by Tucker & Heath (1994) was also used to evaluate waterfowl conservation status.

A total of 41 waterfowl species were recorded in the five study sites between 1998 and 2001 (Table 1), and many waterfowl species were recorded in both wintering and breeding seasons. A total of 17 species were of unfavourable conservation status. Twelve of these species were recorded in Sultansazliği. Turkey has rich and diverse bird habitats that are vulnerable to the habitat destruction that has been continuing for about 30 years (Özesmi 1989).

In conclusion, the status of bird populations in Turkey appears to be different from that of the rest of Europe. However further population work will be necessary to clarify the changes in species numbers over time and their relationship to habitat change.

## ACKNOWLEDGEMENTS

We are especially grateful to Hacettepe University Research Foundation, ENCON Com. Ltd., Assoc. Prof. Dr. Levent Turan, Çağatay Tavşanoğlu, and Kadir Yiğit US for their great support.

## REFERENCES

**Bibby, C.J., Burgess, N.D. & Hill, D.A.** 1992. Bird Census Techniques. Academic Press, London.

**Özesmi, U.** 1989. Protection of Sultan Marshes, Turkey. Sandgrouse 11: 73-75.

**Scott, D.A. & Rose, P.M.** 1996. Atlas of Anatidae Populations in Africa and Western Eurasia. Wetlands International Publication No. 41, Wetlands International, Wageningen, The Netherlands.

**Tucker, G.M. & Evans, M.I.** 1997. Habitats for birds in Europe: a conservation strategy for the wider environment. BirdLife International (BirdLife Conservation Series No. 6), Cambridge.

**Tucker, G.M. & Heath, M.F.** 1994. Birds in Europe: their conservation status. BirdLife International (BirdLife Conservation Series No. 3), Cambridge.

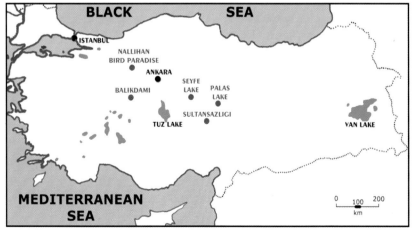

Fig. 1. Study areas in Turkey.

**Table 1.  Recorded maximum number of birds in all study areas. B = breeding season; W = wintering season.**

| SPECIES | COMMON NAMES | EUROPEAN THREAT STATUS | NALLIHAN BIRD PARADISE | | BALIKDAMI | | SEYFE LAKE | | PALAS LAKE | | SULTANSAZLIGI | |
|---|---|---|---|---|---|---|---|---|---|---|---|---|
| | | | Season | Population Max. | Season | Population Max. | Season | Population Max. | Season | Population Max. | Season | Population Max. |
| Tachybaptus ruficollis | Little Grebe | secure | W | 431 | B | 11 | - | - | - | - | B | 18 |
| Podiceps cristatus | Great Crested Grebe | secure | W | 31 | - | - | - | - | - | - | B | 4 |
| Phalacrocorax carbo | Cormorant | secure | w | 662 | - | - | - | - | - | - | - | - |
| Phalacrocorax pygmeus | Pygmy Cormorant | vulnerable | - | - | - | - | - | - | - | - | B | 350 |
| Nycticorax nycticorax | Night Heron | declining | B | 76 | B | 77 | - | - | - | - | - | - |
| Ardeola ralloides | Squacco Heron | vulnerable | B | 16 | B | 38 | - | - | - | - | B | 19 |
| Egretta garzetta | Little Egret | secure | B | 168 | B | 83 | - | - | - | - | B | 89 |
| Egretta alba | Great White Egret | secure | W | 237 | W | 8 | - | - | - | - | W | 11 |
| Ardea cinerea | Grey Heron | secure | B | 262 | - | - | - | - | - | - | B | >500 |
| Ardea purpurea | Purple Heron | vulnerable | - | - | B | 8 | - | - | - | - | B | 4 |
| Ciconia nigra | Black Stork | rare | B | 62 | - | - | - | - | - | - | - | - |
| Ciconia ciconia | White Stork | vulnerable | B | 159 | B | 252 | B | 30 | B | 340 | B | >100 |
| Phoenicopterus ruber | Greater Flamingo | localized | - | - | - | - | B | 1 573 | B | 684 | B | >20 000 |
| Anser albifrons | White-fronted Goose | secure | - | - | - | - | W | 20 000 | - | - | - | - |
| Anser anser | Greylag Goose | secure | - | - | - | - | W | 48 | - | - | - | - |
| Tadorna ferruginea | Ruddy Shelduck | vulnerable | B / W | 223 / 598 | B | 108 | B | 250 | B | 171 | B | 198 |
| Tadorna tadorna | Shelduck | secure | - | - | - | - | B | 48 | W | 186 | B | 110 |
| Anas penelope | Wigeon | secure | W | 15 | W | 500 | - | - | - | - | B | 90 |
| Anas strepera | Gadwall | vulnerable | - | - | - | - | W | 90 | - | - | W | >100 |
| Anas crecca | Teal | secure | W | 24 | W | 1 137 | - | - | - | - | B | >500 |
| Anas platyrhynchos | Mallard | secure | W | 676 | - | - | B | 70 | - | - | B | 1 000 |
| Anas acuta | Pintail | vulnerable | - | - | W | 144 | B | 12 | - | - | B | 90 |
| Anas querquedula | Garganey | vulnerable | W | 84 | - | - | B | 100 | - | - | B | 90 |
| Anas clypeata | Shoveler | secure | W | 374 | W | 500 | B | 38 | - | - | B | 100 |
| Netta rufina | Red-crested Pochard | declining | - | - | - | - | W | 5 | - | - | B | 100 |
| Aythya ferina | Pochard | secure | W | 220 | - | - | W | 90 | - | - | W | >500 |
| Aythya nyroca | Ferruginous Duck | vulnerable | - | - | - | - | - | - | - | - | B | 90 |
| Mergus albellus | Smew | vulnerable | - | - | - | - | - | - | W | 101 | - | - |
| Gallinula chloropus | Moorhen | secure | - | - | - | - | - | - | W | 101 | B | 16 |
| Fulica atra | Coot | secure | W | 602 | W / B | 796 / 338 | W | >1 000 | - | - | W / B | 801 / >1 000 |
| Himantopus himantopus | Black-winged Stilt | secure | - | - | - | - | B | 42 | B | 150 | B | 20 |
| Recurvirostra avosetta | Avocet | localized | - | - | - | - | B | 12 | B | 150 | W | >500 |
| Charadrius alexandrinus | Kentish Plover | declining | - | - | - | - | B | 12 | B | 90 | B | 100 |
| Vanellus spinosus | Spur-winged Plover | (endangered) | - | - | - | - | B | 6 | - | - | - | - |
| Vanellus vanellus | Lapwing | (secure) | - | - | B | 118 | B | 9 | B | 90 | B | 150 |
| Calidris minuta | Little Stint | (secure) | - | - | B | 32 | - | - | - | - | - | - |
| Philomachus pugnax | Ruff | (secure) | - | - | - | - | W | >10 000 | - | - | - | - |
| Tringa totanus | Redshank | declining | - | - | W | 85 | - | - | - | - | W | 160 |
| Tringa nebularia | Greenshank | secure | - | - | - | - | W | 38 | - | - | - | - |
| Larus ridibundus | Black-headed Gull | secure | B / W | 2 149 / 1 169 | - | - | B | 10 000 | - | - | B | 93 |
| Larus genei | Slender-billed Gull | (secure) | - | - | - | - | W | 950 | - | - | - | - |

# Changes in abundance and diversity of waders and wintering waterfowl on the southern coast of the Caspian Sea

*Ahmad Barati[1] & Olia Gholi Khalilipoor[2]*

*[1]Department of Environmental Sciences, Bu-Ali Sina University of Hamedan, Iran. (email: abarati@basu.ac.ir)*

*[2] Department of Environmental Sciences, University of Khorramshahr, Iran.*

Barati, A. & Khalilipoor, O.G. 2006. Changes in abundance and diversity of waders and wintering waterfowl on the southern coast of the Caspian Sea. *Waterbirds around the world*. Eds. G.C. Boere, C.A. Galbraith & D.A. Stroud. The Stationery Office, Edinburgh, UK. pp. 368-369.

Changes in the abundance and diversity of waterbirds on the southern coast of the Caspian Sea were studied using mid-winter census data collected by Department of Environment of Iran during 1999-2003. We investigated changes in the size and diversity of waterbird populations in the southern coastal zones of the Caspian Sea. In this paper, population trends and species distribution of waders and wintering waterfowl in different years and regions are presented.

Iran has about 105 important wetland bird habitats hosting about 502 species (Firouz 1974). Due to their geographic and ecological situation, Iranian wetlands are used as wintering sites by many wader and waterfowl populations (Rabiee 2002). A census has been conducted since 1982 by the Department of Environment of Iran in the main wetlands from Makhtum Gholi bay to Astarain. These wetlands lie in the three northern provinces of Iran, Golestan, Mazandaran and Gila, from where we have utilised data from 15, 17 and 25 water bodies/wintering sites respectively. The census carried out total counts every year in early January till February. Population trends in each region were assessed and summarized for the period 1999-2003.

The waterfowl population in the southern coastal zones of Caspian Sea reached a maximum of 2 835 800 birds in 2003 and a minimum in 1999. The largest and smallest populations waders in 2003 and 2002 was about 166 990 and 16 600 birds respectively.

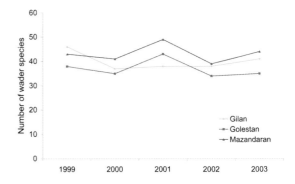

Fig. 2. Changes in wader diversity in southern coastal zones of the Caspian Sea.

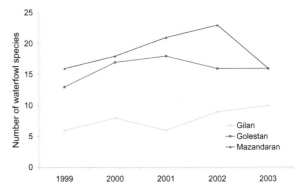

Fig. 3. Changes in the number of waterfowl species in southern coastal zones of the Caspian Sea.

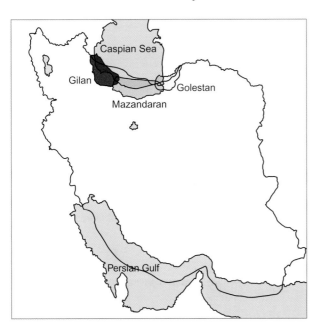

Fig. 1. Location of Gilan, Mazandaran and Golestan in Iran.

The number of all wintering species varied from 87 in 2001 and 2003 to 80 in 2000, with waders varying from 61 in 2003 to 53 in 2000, and waterfowl from 27 in 2001 to 22 in 1999 (Figs. 2-4, Table 1). In all regions the highest number of species belonged to the Anatidae family and the lowest to the Threskiornithidae, Dromadidae, Gruidae, Phoenicopteridae, Haematopodidae, and Burhinidae.

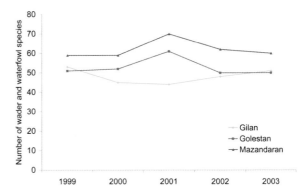

Fig. 4. Changes in waders and waterfowl species on southern Caspian Sea coasts.

## Table 1. Check list of southern Caspian Sea waterbirds.

| | |
|---|---|
| Aythya marila | Greater Scaup |
| Bucephala clangula | Common Goldeneye |
| Mergus albellus | Smew |
| Mergus serrator | Red-breasted Merganser |
| Mergus merganser | Goosander |
| Oxyura leucocephala | White-headed Duck |
| Grus leucogeranus | Siberian Crane |
| Rallus aquaticus | Water Rail |
| Porzana parva | Little Crake |
| Porzana porzana | Spotted Crake |
| Porphyrio porphyrio | Purple Swamphen |
| Gallinula chloropus | Common Moorhen |
| Fulica atra | Eurasian Coot |
| Haematopus ostralegus | Eurasian Oystercatcher |
| Himantopus himantopus | Black-winged Stilt |
| Recurvirostra avosetta | Eurasian Avocet |
| Glareola pratincola | Collared Pratincole |
| Glareola nordmanni | Black-winged Pratincole |
| Vanellus vanellus | Northern Lapwing |
| Pluvialis apricaria | Eurasian Golden Plover |
| Pluvialis squatarola | Grey Plover |
| Charadrius hiaticula | Ringed Plover |
| Charadrius dubius | Little Ringed Plover |
| Charadrius alexandrinus | Kentish Plover |
| Charadrius leschenaultii | Greater Sand Plover |
| Scolopax rusticola | Common Woodcock |
| Lymnocryptes minimus | Jack Snipe |
| Gallinago solitaria | Solitary Snipe |
| Gallinago media | Great Snipe |
| Gallinago gallinago | Common Snipe |
| Limosa limosa | Black-tailed Godwit |
| Limosa lapponica | Bar-tailed Godwit |
| Numenius phaeopus | Whimbrel |
| Numenius arquata | Common Curlew |
| Tringa erythropus | Wood Sandpiper |
| Tringa totanus | Redshank |
| Tringa stagnatilis | Marsh Sandpiper |
| Tringa nebularia | Greenshank |
| Tringa glareola | Spotted Redshank |
| Xenus cinereus | Terek Sandpiper |
| Actitis hypoleucos | Common Sandpiper |
| Arenaria interpres | Ruddy Turnstone |
| Calidris alba | Sanderling |
| Calidris minuta | Little Stint |
| Calidris ferruginea | Curlew Sandpiper |
| Calidris alpina | Dunlin |
| Limicola falcinellus | Broad-billed Sandpiper |
| Philomachus pugnax | Ruff |
| Phalaropus lobatus | Red-necked Phalarope |
| Stercorarius parasiticus | Arctic Skua |
| Stercorarius pomarinus | Pomarine Skua |
| Larus canus | Common Gull |
| Larus argentatus | Herring Gull |
| Larus fuscus | Lesser Black-backed Gull |
| Larus ichthyaetus | Great Black-headed Gull |
| Larus ridibundus | Black-headed Gull |
| Larus genei | Slender-billed Gull |
| Larus minutus | Little Gull |
| Sterna caspia | Caspian Tern |
| Sterna sandvicensis | Sandwich Tern |
| Sterna hirundo | Common Tern |
| Sterna albifrons | Little Tern |
| Chlidonias hybridus | Whiskered Tern |
| Chlidonias leucopterus | White-winged Tern |

Population estimates of waterfowl, waders and waterbirds in the three provinces are presented in Figs. 5-7 below.

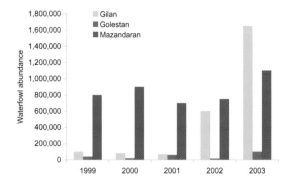

Fig. 5. Waterfowl populations in southern coastal zones of Caspian Sea.

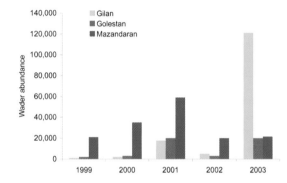

Fig. 6. Waders population in southern coastal zones of Caspian Sea.

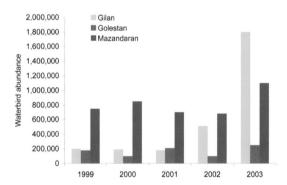

Fig. 7. Waterbirds population in southern coastal zones of Caspian Sea.

Within the last five years some significant changes in populations and diversity have taken place. There was a rapid increase of waterbirds and waders in Gilan while in other regions we did not find spectacular fluctuations. In total, the mean size of waterbird populations was greater in Mazandaran than in other regions.

In general, there has been an increasing trend in the size of waterbird populations in the southern coastal zones of Caspian Sea. Mazandaran was the most abundant and diverse region in northern Iran as Mazandaran wetland seems to have food resources and large-scale water bodies.

## REFERENCES

**Firouz, E.** 1974. Environment Iran. Natural Society for the Conservation of Natural Resources and Human Environment.Tehran. 51 pp.

**Rabiee, K.** 2002. Waterbird mid-winter census report. Local office of Department of Environment, Mazandaran, Iran.

# Results of eight years of monitoring wintering and nesting waterbirds in Azerbaijan

*Elchin Sultanov*

*Azerbaijan National Academy of Sciences, Azerbaijan Ornithological Society Mukhtarov str. 13, ap.16, 370001, Baku, Azerbaijan. (email: sultanov@azdata.net)*

Sultanov, E. 2006. Results of eight years of monitoring wintering and nesting waterbirds in Azerbaijan. *Waterbirds around the world.* Eds. G.C. Boere, C.A. Galbraith & D.A. Stroud. The Stationery Office, Edinburgh, UK. pp. 370-371.

This paper discusses counts of waterbirds in Azerbaijan between 1993-2005. Most counts were conducted in winter and some have already been reported (Paynter *et al.* 1996, Sultanov & Haddow 1997, Sultanov *et al.* 1998, 1999, 2000, Sultanov *et al.* 2004).

Azerbaijan has about 1.25 million wintering waterbirds that use the Caspian-West Siberian-East African Flyway (Sultanov & Mustafayev 1994, Sultanov 1997), and it is estimated that along the shores of Azerbaijan there are no fewer than 250 000 breeding waterbirds of which over 40 000 winter on islands and old oil platforms (Sultanov & Kerimov 1999). We estimate the number of migratory birds to be 8-10 times higher than wintering birds. During winter, the major species are ducks

**Table 1. Main waterbird sites in Azerbaijan.**

| Sites | Months XI-II | III-IV IX-X (for one day counts) | V-VI | Importance |
|---|---|---|---|---|
| Lake Agzybir | Up to 30 000 | Up to 20 000 | Up to 10 000 | II |
| Yashma island | Up to 30 000 | Up to 10 000 | Up to 5 000 | II |
| Mardakan-Buzovna coast | 1 719-3 663 | | | II |
| Pirallahy Island | Up to 35 000 | Up to 5 000 | | I |
| Shakhdili-Tava | Up to 100 000 | Up to10 000 | Up to 10 000 | I |
| Tukan-Hovsan-Zikh | Up to 25 000 | | | II |
| Baku bay | Up to 30 000 | Up to 10 000 | Up to 5 000 | II |
| Lake Gyzylgyol | 575-3 720 | | | |
| Factory "Shelf"- Sahil Settlement | Up to 100 000 | Up to 10 000 | Up to 10 000 | I |
| Sangachal cape | Up to 30 000 | | | I |
| Gobustan Settlement | Up to 20 000 | Up to 15 000 | | I |
| Alat Bay | Up to 60 000 | Up to 5 000 | | II |
| Islands of Baku archipelago (all) | Up to 30 000 | Up to 20 000 | | I |
| Zenbil Island | | | Up to 5 000 | I |
| Gil Island | | | Up to 10 000 | I |
| Garasu Island | | | Up to 10 000 | I |
| Babur-Gutan Island | Up to 20 000 | Up to 5 000 | Up to 5 000 | I |
| Cape Pirsagat | Up to 15 000 | | | II |
| Lake of Shirvan National Park ("Flamingo", "Gushggol", "Shorgol") | 2 717-31 238 | Up to 10 000 | | I |
| Kura River Delta | Up to 75 000 | Up to 30 000 | Up to 10 000 | I |
| Gyzylagach State Reserve | 263 314 - 450 000 up to 1 000 000 | Up to 100 000 | | I |
| Lake Makhmudchala | Up to 40 000 | | | I |
| Lake Hajigabul | Up to 25 000 | Up to 25 000 | | I |
| Lake Sarysu | 75 000-311 000 | | | I |
| Lake Aggyol | 43 000-150 000 | | | I |
| Agrychay water reservoir | 176-2 096 | | | II |
| Lake Ajinohur | Up to 10 000 | | | II |
| Varvara water reservoir | 962-13 694 | 478-1 398 | | II |
| Samukh | Up to 6 500 | | | II |
| Yenikend water reservoir | 1 224-1 462 | | | II |
| Lake Jandar | 2 351-11 957 | 547-964 | | II |
| Araz water reservoir (Nakhchivan) | 2 183 | 1 410 | | II |

(more than 1 000 000), coot (nearly 200 000), geese (40 000), many swans (up to 30 000 in extremely cold winters) and pelicans (up to 3 000). During the breeding period, herons, ibises, terns, gulls, cormorants and moorhens are present, while waders occur during migration.

The sharp increase in Caspian Sea oil production represents an escalation of an already severe risk of oil pollution, and it is therefore essential to conduct regular monitoring. During the period of monitoring, bird populations fluctuated on the sites along the Caspian Sea coast from a low of 70 000 (April 1997, 10-12% of the maximum number in winter) to a high of 1 076 000 in winter 2002-2003 (Sultanov 2004). In inland wetlands where there is less migration, there is a sharp increase in the number of birds in the beginning-middle of December and then a decrease during February.

We can distinguish sites by their importance in terms of the number of birds: the most important have congregations of more then 30 000 waterbirds during at least one season of year, while other sites have fewer then 30 000 birds.

Thirteen threatened species were observed in the survey area, the most important wintering species being White-headed Duck *Oxyura leucocephala*, Lesser White-fronted Goose *Anser erythropus* and Dalmatian Pelican *Pelecanus crispus*, and the most important resident species Pygmy Cormorant *Phalacrocorax pygmeus*.

Lakes Aggyol, Sarysu, Mahmudchala, Agzybir, Hajigabul, Kura river Delta Varvara water reservoir and Gyzylagach State reserve have large mixed colonies of pelicans and storks that can include up to 11 species numbering from two to 60 thousand for Gyzylagach State reserve (Konovalova 1979).

In most important inland wintering areas, diving and surface-feeding ducks are in equal proportion. For example at Aggyol and Makhmudchala lakes and Sarysu (about 90% of all waterbirds are Red-crested Pochard *Netta rufina*, Pochard *Aythya ferina* and Tufted Duck *Aythya fuligula*). Surface–feeding ducks predominate in Lake Hajigabul (Mallard *Anas platyrhynchos* and Shoveler *Anas clypeata*). In total, 108 species of waterbirds have been identified.

## REFERENCES

**Konovalova, N.A.** 1979. The state of colonies of Ciconiiformes and Pelecaniformes birds in Kyzylagach reserves. In: "Natural conditions and birds of coasts of the Caspian Sea and bordering lowlands "Proc. of Kyzylagach State Reserve part1 Baku Azernashr 83-88. (In Russian.)

**Paynter, D., Aarvak, T. & Sultanov, E.** 1996. Winter counts of threatened species in Azerbaijan. TWSG News, Slimbridge, UK 9: 39-42.

**Sultanov, E.H.** 2004. An ornithological study of the Azerbaijan Caspian coast islands and regions of oil production. Sandgrouse 26: 112-126.

**Sultanov, E.H. & Mustafayev, G.T.** 1994. The basic results of the winter aircount of birds in Azerbaijan. A Bird of Caucasus, Stavropol: 38-40. (In Russian.)

**Sultanov, E. & Haddow, C.** 1997. AIOC ornithological survey in Azerbaijan. December 1995 to February 1997. Proceeding of the fourth Baku International Congress on Energy, Ecology and Economy. Baku: 134-141.

**Sultanov, E.H.** 1997. The basic results of the aircount of waterbirds in Azerbaijan in 1996. Scientific inheritance of N.Y. Dinnik and his role in development of modern natural sciences. Stavropol: 123-125. (In Russian.)

**Sultanov, E., Mosley, P., Paynter, D. & Aarvak, T.** 1998. Results of counts of wintering geese and swan in Azerbaijan in 1993 and 1996. Berkut 7(1-2): 30-31.

**Sultanov, E.H. & Kerimov, T.A.** 1999. Places of concentration and annual dynamics of number of birds at the Absheron archipelago. Ecological monitoring of coastal zone Great Baku and Sumgait Baku: 17-22. (In Azeri.)

**Sultanov, E., Gavashelishvili, A., Kerimov, T., Javakhi, Z. & Agayeva, N.** 1999. Saving Humbatova. Ecological monitoring with the public's participation at sites noted for high biodiversity and vulnerability of ecosystems along Baku-Supsa oil pipeline. Baku-Tbilisi. 124 pp. (In Azeri, Georgian, English and Russian.)

**Sultanov, E., Kerimov, T., Aliyev, S., Humbatova, S. & Agayeva, N.** 2000. Potential Ramsar Sites of Azerbaijan. Baku. Wetlands International-AEME Publication. 152 pp. (In Azeri and Russian.)

Extensive reed-beds in Azerbaijan. Photo: Peter Cranswick.

# Evolution of freshwater lagoons in Daghestan and their importance for waterbirds on the west Caspian coast

*E.V. Vilkov*

*Russian Academy of Sciences, Daghestan Scientific Centre, Republican Ecologico-Biological Centre of Pupils, Pr. Gamidova (Kirova), 367003 Makhachkala, Daghestan, Russia. (email: evberkut@mail.ru; eberkut@xtreem.ru)*

Vilkov, E.V. 2006. Evolution of freshwater lagoons in Daghestan and their importance for waterbirds on the west Caspian coast. *Waterbirds around the world.* Eds. G.C. Boere, C.A. Galbraith & D.A. Stroud. The Stationery Office, Edinburgh, UK. p. 372.

The Caspian Sea is important for migrating and wintering water-fowl. In 1979 there was a significant rise in sea level of approximately 3 m which lasted until 1996; during this time, a group of brackish lagoons free from surface vegetation appeared on the west coast. These 52 km - long lagoons are located along the routes of migratory birds flying along the western side of the Caspian. This paper considers the effects these lagoons have had on waterbird populations.

The narrowing of a migration corridor towards the plain of the Caspian coast has created a "bottleneck" effect resulting in a mixture of terrestrial and waterbird populations. Since their initial formation, the lagoons have become naturally desalinated and have developed freshwater wetland flora. This makes them especially attractive for a variety of waterfowl with reeds serving as natural protection, and algal meadows occupied by 13 fish species. What is most surprising is that this adjoins a lifeless semi-desert-steppe landscape.

Lagoons that do not freeze during winters have become increasingly used for over-wintering by coots, ducks, swans, gulls and cormorants that previously used to migrate to more remote areas of the southern Caspian Coast and to southeast Africa. The lagoons have therefore increased the biodiversity of the western Caspian Coast not only during migration periods, but also during winter. During one migration season, >12 million birds flew through this area, with many stopping for rest on the lagoons. Over 40 000 Tufted Duck *Aythya fuligula* have been sighted in four hours during peak migration.

Surveys have identified 283 species of birds, amounting to 79.2% of the total recorded in the Republic of Daghestan. Of those, 46 are listed in the Red Book, including the Pygmy Cormorant *Phalacrocorax pygmeus*, Dalmatian Pelican *Pelecanus crispus*, White Pelican *Pelecanus onocrotalus*, Glossy Ibis *Plegadis falcinellus*, Lesser White-fronted Goose *Anser erythropus*, Marbled Teal *Marmaronetta angustirostris* and White-tailed Eagle *Haliaeetus albicilla*. Some of them, such as the Dalmatian Pelican, Lesser White-fronted Goose, Marbled Teal and Corncrake *Crex crex*, are globally threatened. The lagoons thus directly contribute to the conservation of these and other rare birds. The Turalin and Sulak lagoons are the most important as, unlike others, they are little affected by fluctuations in the level of the Caspian Sea and changes in groundwater levels because of rivers running into them. The ecological importance of the lagoons continues to grow as most birds migrating through this region now stop here regularly to rest and feeding; whilst some nesting birds have since spread along a wider area of the central Daghestan Caspian coast.

The lagoons of Daghestan are unique and have transformed a coast previously deserted and scorched by the sun into a unique wetland filled with life. Now the lagoons are a popular place for zoological excursions, where anyone can become familiar with the biodiversity of the region. The gulfs are unique places for ecological education and training, where not only young ornithologists and ecologists, but also teachers, biologists, students and pupils can learn. This "open-air study" will undoubtedly develop an active environmental and civic responsibility in the new generation, and change society as a whole.

The increased numbers of fish and birds now attract poachers who hunt for anything from the widespread Coot *Fulica atra* or Purple Gallinule *Porphyrio porphyrio* to the ordinary wild duck, endangered Ferruginous Duck *Aythya nyroca*, Red-breasted Geese *Branta ruficollis* and Lesser White-fronted Geese. However, poaching does not cause as much devastation as the remodeling of the beach around the Turalin lagoon, where a four hectare area of sandy bar separating the lagoon from the sea was leveled in the spring of 1999. That September, drainage of the lagoon was begun through a deep channel connected to the sea. The level of water in the lagoon catastrophically decreased by 0.7-0.9 m, causing a reduction in the composition, number and species of waterfowl present.

The fact is that the land occupied by Turalin lagoon represents a perfect place for the construction of country villas, where future owners, potentially ignorant of their own actions may one day replace the lagoon with luxury housing. This means that the Turalin and Sulak lagoons are under active threat of destruction. The unique habitats as well as a number of new bird species will be lost forever unless we undertake urgent measures to preserve them. In this respect there is an urgent necessity to establish Natural Areas of Preferential Protection (NAPP) in the area of the two most important lagoons of Daghestan: Turalin and Sulak. Fortunately, three years ago the author of this paper managed to register these wetlands in the official list of "Key Ornithological Territories of Russia of World Importance." Subsequently, two projects aimed at the establishment of NAPP in areas of Turalin and Sulak lagoons were prepared and passed assessment by the Ministry of Nature of the Republic of Daghestan, the Makhachkala Interregional Committee on Ecology and Nature Management of the Makhachkala Administration with the Center of Preservation of Biodiversity at the State Committee of Ecology of Russia, and the Union of Protection of Birds in Russia.

In 2000, the ornithological association of pupils "Berkut," together with the research club "Ecosphere" (Azerbaijan) successfully implemented a project called "Ecological education of pupils for revealing potential NAPP along the Western Caspian Coast". This bilateral project has received the highest marks of experts in the Initiative for Social Action and Renewal in Eurasia's (ISAR) Caspian Program. This group is currently trying to promote the establishment of ornithological micro-reserves at Turalin and Sulak lagoons through the city administration, and urging the Government of Daghestan to promote the official assignment of NAPP status to these areas.

# An overview of the Office National de la Chasse et de la Faune Sauvage (ONCFS) research programmes on Anatidae

*Vincent Schricke*

*Office National de la Chasse et de la Faune Sauvage, CNERA Avifaune Migratrice, 53 rue Russeil, 44000 Nantes, France.*
*(email: v.schricke@oncfs.gouv.fr)*

Schricke, V. 2006. An overview of the Office National de la Chasse et de la Faune Sauvage (ONCFS) research programmes on Anatidae. *Waterbirds around the world*. Eds. G.C. Boere, C.A. Galbraith & D.A. Stroud. The Stationery Office, Edinburgh, UK. p. 373.

The Office National de la Chasse et de la Faune Sauvage (ONCFS) Anatidae research team have developed programmes on duck and geese population dynamics, studies of monitoring schemes, waterfowl habitats, and hunting bags, and contribute to several actions at European and international scales, such as the EU management plan for species with an unfavourable conservation status (Schricke 2001, 2002), and the African-Eurasian Waterbird Agreement international action plan for the Dark-bellied Brent Goose *Branta b. bernicla*.

The duck population studies concern Teal *Anas crecca*, Pochard *Aythya ferina* and Tufted Duck *Aythya fuligula*. A new research program in 2002 included the launch of a new ringing and marking scheme involving individual nasal marks applied to several hundred birds in 2003, a population dynamics model based on capture-recapture (in contrast to previous models using other parameters and population sizes), and behaviour-based individual models with predictive aspects (Guillemain *et al.* 2003). These studies were made in cooperation with CNRS Montpellier and Chizé, University of Coimbra (Portugal) and Kristiansad (Sweden).

A further research programme, concerning the physiological state of ducks in winter, has been undertaken in cooperation with CNRS Strasbourg; the main objective being to build a model to estimate the body condition of four species, Teal, Pochard, Tufted Duck and Mallard *Anas platyrhynchos* in normal winters or during cold spells.

Studies of geese are focussed on two species: Brent Geese, in co-operation with CNRS Chizé (involved in the EU funded Coast Bird Diversity programme); and Greylag Geese *Anser anser*, studied on the Atlantic coast to determine how geese use saltmarshes in relation to different management actions and disturbances (Fritz *et al.* 2004), and also, on the Mediterranean coast, to determine the impact of Greylags on the increasing use of *Scirpus maritimus* communities in a nature reserve (in co-operation with Tour du Valat, Camargue).

Monitoring schemes at a national scale include: midwinter counts in co-operation with Ligue pour le Protection des Oiseaux (BirdLife France), winter counts during December to February, studies of spring migration and breeding chronology, and at an international scale: waterfowl monitoring in West Africa, particularly since 1989 in the Senegal Basin in co-operation with Wetlands International and the Senegal National Parks Directorate (Diouf *et al.* 2003). Waterfowl habitat studies include the impact of management of a maritime hunting reserve on wintering ducks (Baie du Mont Saint-Michel), the evaluation of trophic potential for ducks, and the management of pond banks for breeding ducks.

## REFERENCES

**Diouf, S., Rigolot, J.B., Peeters, J. & Schricke, V.** 2003. Rapport national pour le Sénégal. In: T. Dodman & C.H Diagana. African Waterfowl Census/Les Dénombrements d'Oiseaux d'eau en Afrique 1999, 2000 & 2001. Wetlands International Global Series No 16: 69-73.

**Fritz, H., Blais, S., Durant, D., Poisbleau, M., Desmonts, D., Joyeux, E & Schricke, V.** 2004. Differential responses to disturbances by Greylag and Brent geese wintering in the baie de l'Aiguillon, western France. 8th Annual Meeting of the Goose Specialist Group of Wetlands International, Odessa, Ukraine, 5-10 March 2004, Abstract Book: 35-37.

**Guillemain, M., Leray, G., Caizergues, A. & Schricke, V.** 2003. Dynamique de population de la Sarcelle d'hiver *Anas crecca*. In: Rapport Scientifique ONCFS 2002: 55-57.

**Schricke, V.** 2001. Elements for a Garganey *Anas querquedula* management plan. Gibier Faune Sauvage, Game and Wildlife, 18(1): 9-41.

**Schricke, V.** 2002. Elements for a Pochard *Aythya ferina* management plan. Gibier Faune Sauvage, Game and Wildlife, 19(2): 143-178.

Greylag Goose *Anser anser*. Photo: Paul Marshall.

# Waterbirds of Baie de Baly, Madagascar

*Rivo Rabarisoa[1], Odon Rakotonomenjanahary[2] & Julien Ramanampamonjy[3]*
[1]*Organisation Takatra, BP 8505 (101) Antananarivo, Madagascar. (email: takatra@wanadoo.mg)*
[2&3]*Asity Association, BP 4096 (101) Antananarivo, Madagascar. (email: asity@yahoo.mg)*

Rabarisoa, R., Rakotonomenjanahary, O. & Ramanampamonjy, J. 2006. Waterbirds of Baie de Baly, Madagascar. *Waterbirds around the world*. Eds. G.C. Boere, C.A. Galbraith & D.A. Stroud. The Stationery Office, Edinburgh, UK. pp. 374-375.

The Baie de Baly, Mahajanga province, is located c. 450 km northeast of Antananarivo, the capital of Madagascar. It is in the centre of the 57 418 ha National Park of Baie de Baly, created in December 1997, and was identified as an Important Bird Area in 1999. The establishment in 1999 of a commercial shrimp farm inside the mangrove habitat, necessitated the development of a strategy to maintain the stability of the wetland ecosystem. Since 2000, the Malagasy League for Bird Conservation in Madagascar (Asity) in collaboration with the shrimp farm society "Aquaculture des Macareigne" have made regular visits to record waterbirds as a tool for monitoring changes to the wetland ecosystem.

The survey site (15°57' - 16°08'S, 45°17' - 45°27'E) includes 7 200 ha of mangrove, 700 ha of marshes, approximately 35–40 km of rivers and coast, and the 300 ha Sarika lake. The mangrove vegetation is dominated by *Avicennia* spp. and *Rhizophora* spp. with 220 ha of the mangrove area converted into a shrimp farm (Autrant & Rafomanana 1998). Sarika is an open permanent lake (3 200 m long) in a savannah palm area, with dry deciduous forest at its south eastern end. The lake shore is partly covered by aquatic reeds, mostly *Phragmites* spp., used as bird roosts. The marshes are the flood plain of the Ambolobozo river which joins the eastern part of the mangrove, and is used by the local community for growing rice.

Since 2000, waterbird counts have been conducted in January, July and September. Surveys were carried out by boat, using African Waterbird Census techniques (Perennou 1991).

During the 12 counts undertaken from 2000 to 2003, 54 species of waterbirds were recorded (Table 1). The most diverse families were Ardeidae (11 species), Charadriidae (nine species) and Scolopacidae (seven species). Seven were endemic Malagasy sub-species (Young *et al.* 1993). Nine other species are also endemic to Madagasacar, of which five are globally threatened: the Madagascar Heron *Ardea humbloti,* Black-banded Plover *Charadrius thoracicus*, Madagascar Fish-eagle *Haliaeetus vociferoides,* Madagascar Sacred Ibis *Threskiornis bernieri* and Madagascar Little Grebe *Tachybaptus pelzelnii.* In addition, two individuals of Madagascar Squacco Heron *Ardeola idea* were recorded in one count. This species breeds only in Madagascar from October to March and leaves from May to October to spend the austral winter in east and central Africa, visiting coastal and inland waters (Stevenson & Fanshawe 2002). Both Lesser Flamingo *Phoenicopterus minor* and Greater Flamingo *Phoenicopterus ruber roseus* were recorded during July and September visits, but rarely seen in January.

Six species, including Little Grebe *Tachybaptus ruficollis*, Madagascar Little Grebe, African Pygmy Goose *Nettapus auritus* and Hottentot Teal *Anas hottentota* were particularly dependent on freshwater lake ecosystems. However, the most important waterbird concentrations, mainly waders and herons, foraged on mudflats near mangroves and in the coastal zone.

During high tide, herons and egrets rested on mangrove trees, and waders and flamingos moved to the back of the mangroves. Two important nesting sites were noted at Sarika lake: a nesting and roosting site for the Yellow-billed Stork *Mycteria ibis* and Madagascar Sacred Ibis and a nesting area for Darter *Anhinga rufa*, Cattle Egret *Bubulcus ibis*, Dimorphic Egret *Egretta dimorpha,* Great Egret *Egretta alba*, and Madagascar Sacred Ibis in a group of mangrove trees in the eastern part of the study area, which is also used by roosting bats *Pteropus rufus.*

Five tern species frequent the Bay de Baly, the most important being the migratory Lesser Crested Tern *Sterna bengalensis* (now known also to breed in north-west Madagascar, Le Corre & Bemanaja 2004) and the Common Tern *Sterna hirundo*. Two species breed in Madagascar, Greater Crested Tern *Sterna bergii* and Caspian Tern *S. caspia* (Goodmand & Benstead 2004), whilst the others are migratory. These species usually frequent the bay and were abundant during January, but were infrequent or absent in July and September. Lesser Crested, Greater Crested and Caspian Terns were attracted by the shrimp farm and sometimes followed fishing boats all along the coast. The fifth species, Saunder's Tern *Sterna saundersi* was always seen inside the bay near the mangrove estuary. Changes in physico-chemical parameters inside the shrimp farm force shrimps to the surface which attracts terns and other bird species like the Dimorphic Egret *Egretta dimorpha* and Black Kite *Milvus migrans.*

Out of the 19 migratory species recorded, 16 were Palaearctic waders, but numbers were very low compared with those visiting mainland African wetlands. Only one species, the Crab Plover *Dromas ardeola,* occurred in numbers over their 1% population threshold. The Pacific Golden Plover *Pluvialis fulva* is considered as a vagrant species in Madagascar (Goodman & Benstead 2004) but was seen regularly in low numbers, two to six individuals, in the coastal area of Baie de Baly, usually associated with other waders such as the Greater Sand Plover *Charadrius leschenaultii* and the Common Greenshank *Tringa nebularia*. Numbers of migratory waders are low in July and September, but much higher in January.

Despite four years of regular monitoring, it is likely that not all waterbirds using the area have been recorded. For example, the Madagascar Teal *Anas bernieri,* a globally threatened and endemic species to Madagascar, was recorded in the mangroves in 1999 (Safford 1993), but has not been seen during monitoring counts.

From the waterbird monitoring, the Baie de Baly has been identified as qualifying as a wetland of international importance since it supports more than 1% of the populations of 12 waterbird species (Wetlands International 2002). Of these, five species exceeded 1% thresholds in at least half the counts: Dimorphic Egret, Madagascar Heron, Madagascar Sacred Ibis, Madagascar Openbill *Anastomus lamelligerus madagascariensis* and White-fronted Plover *Charadrius marginatus*. In addition, three pairs (6% of the world population) of the Madagascar Fish-eagle were

**Table I. Maximum numbers of each waterbird species inside the Baie de Baly wetland from 2000 to 2003.**

| Species | Status | Maximum number |
|---|---|---|
| *Tachybaptus ruficollis* | B | 4 |
| *Tachybaptus pelzelnii* | VU, E | 2 |
| *Phalacrocorax africanus pictillis* | SE | 11 |
| *Anhinga rufa vulsini* | SE | 27 |
| *Nycticorax nycticorax* | B | 16 |
| *Ardeola ralloides* | B | 15 |
| *Ardeola idae* | EN, M, B | 2 |
| *Bubulcus ibis* | B | 855 |
| *Butorides striatus rutenbergi* | SE | 32 |
| *Egretta ardesiaca* | B | 93 |
| *Egretta dimorpha* | E | 554 |
| *Egretta alba* | B | 165 |
| *Ardea purpurea* | B | 6 |
| *Ardea cinerea firasa* | SE | 21 |
| *Ardea humbloti* | EN, E | 28 |
| *Mycteria ibis* | B | 51 |
| *Threskiornis bernieri* | EN | 93 |
| *Anastomus lamelligerus madagascariensis* | SE | 71 |
| *Plegadis falcinellus* | B | 30 |
| *Platalea alba* | B | 200 |
| *Phoenicopterus ruber* | M | 1 940 |
| *Phonicopterus minor* | NT, M | 1 249 |
| *Dendrocygna viduata* | B | 308 |
| *Dendrocygna bicolor* | B | 15 |
| *Sarkidiornis melanotos* | B | 58 |
| *Nettapus auritus* | B | 4 |
| *Anas hottentota* | B | 2 |
| *Haliaeetus vociferoides* | CR, E | 5 |
| *Dromas ardeola* | M | 1 411 |
| *Dryolimnas cuvieri* | E | 15 |
| *Gallinula chloropus pyrrhorrhoa* | SE | 18 |
| *Himantopus himantopus* | B | 10 |
| *Charadrius marginatus* | B | 234 |
| *Charadrius thoracicus* | VU, E | 18 |
| *Charadrius pecuarius* | B | 155 |
| *Charadrius tricollaris bifrontatus* | SE | 18 |
| *Charadrius leschenaultii* | M | 82 |
| *Charadrius mongolus* | M | 71 |
| *Charadrius hiaticula* | M | 33 |
| *Pluvialis fulva* | V | 9 |
| *Pluvialis squatorala* | M | 13 |
| *Numenius phaeopus* | M | 345 |
| *Tringa nebularia* | M | 95 |
| *Xenus cinereus* | M | 121 |
| *Actitis hypoleucos* | M | 90 |
| *Arenaria interpres* | M | 241 |
| *Calidris ferruginea* | M | 2 159 |
| *Calidris alba* | M | 130 |
| *Sterna caspia* | B | 15 |
| *Sterna bergii* | B | 262 |
| *Sterna bengalensis* | M | 2 500 |
| *Sterna saundersi* | M | 98 |
| *Sterna hirundo* | M | 1 500 |
| *Alcedo vintsioides* | E | 20 |

Status is E: endemic species; SE: endemic sub-species; VU: Vulnerable; CR: Critically Endangered; EN: Endangered; NT: Near Threatened; M: migratory; B: breeding. BirdLife International 2004, Goodman & Benstead 2003.

regularly recorded at Baie de Baly (Rabarisoa *et al.* 1997).

Using waterbirds as a tool to monitor changes in the wetland ecosystem has led to recommendations that both the National Park and Shrimp Farm management take measures to avoid biodiversity loss. The presence of a shrimp farm in the National Park requires not only good collaboration between these two institutions but also the involvement of local authorities. Shrimp aquaculture attracts many people for employment which in the long term can threaten biodiversity without any adequate prevention. Recommendations have been made for an effective public awareness campaign concerning the importance of wetland biodiversity and the sustainable use of natural resources, since commercial shrimp farming can induce changes in natural resource use and livelihoods resulting in environmental deterioration through the acceleration of mangrove habitat destruction, water pollution, land encroachment, and social disruption (Barraclough & Finger-Stich 1996). Continued waterbird monitoring is recommended to provide early warning of any changes in the Baie de Baly wetlands.

## ACKNOWLEDGEMENTS

We would like to thank all counters for their active participation and the following institutions for their support: the Aquaculture des Mascareigne (Aquamas), The "Eaux & Forêts" representative at Soalala, the Commune of Soalala, the "Association National pour la Gestion des Aires Protégées" (ANGAP), Wetlands International, and the Ministère de l'Environnement à Madagascar.

## REFERENCES

**Autrant, M. & Rafomanana, G.** 1998. Etude de Schema d'Amenagement de l'aquaculture de crevette à Madagascar. Consortium OSIMO, FTM, PHO & ORSTOM.

**Barraclough, S. & Finger-Stich, A.** 1996. Some ecological and social implications of commercial shrimp farming. United Nations Research Institute for Social Development. UNRISD, Palais des Nations, 1211 Geneva, Switzerland.

**BirdLife International.** 2004. Threatened birds of the world 2004. Species factsheet for globally threatened birds. BirdLife International, Cambridge.

**Goodman, S. & Benstead, J.** 2003. The Natural History of Madagascar. The University of Chicago Press. Chicago and London.

**Le Corre & Bemanaja.** 2004. Status and conservation of seabirds at Madagascar. Unpublished poster.

**Perennou, C.** 1991. African Waterfowl Census: counting waterbirds. IWRB, Slimbridge, UK.

**Rabarisoa, R., Watson, R.T., Thorstom, R. & Berkelman, J.** 1997. Status of the Madagascar Fish Eagle *Haliaeetus vociferoides* in 1995. Ostrich 68(1):12

**Safford, R. J.** 1993. The Madagascar Teal *Anas bernieri*: a preliminary survey from Antsalova to Morondava. Dodo 29: 95-102.

**Stevenson, T. & Fanshawe, J.** 2002. Field guide to the birds of Africa, Eastern Africa: Kenya, Tanzania, Uganda, Rwanda & Burundi. T. & A.D. Poyser Ltd, London.

**Wetlands International.** 2002. Waterbird Population Estimates – Third edition. Wetlands International Global series No. 12, Wageningen, The Netherlands.

**Young, H.G., Safford, R., Green, A., Ravonjiarisoa, P. & Rabarisoa, R.** 1993. Survey and capture of the Madagascar Teal *Anas bernieri* at lac Bemamba Madagascar July – August 1993. Dodo 29: 77-94.

# Trends in numbers of migrant waders (Charadrii) at Langebaan Lagoon, South Africa, 1975-2003

*Doug M. Harebottle[1], Rene A. Navarro[1], Les G. Underhill[1] & Manfred Waltner[2]*

[1] *Avian Demography Unit, University of Cape Town, Rondebosch, 7701, South Africa. (email: doug@adu.uct.ac.za)*
[2] *Western Cape Wader Study Group, 5 Montagu Way, Pinelands, 7405, South Africa. (email: mwalt@mweb.co.za)*

Harebottle, D.M., Navarro, R.A., Underhill, L.G. & Waltner, M. 2006. Trends in numbers of migrant waders (Charadrii) at Langebaan Lagoon, South Africa, 1975-2003. *Waterbirds around the world.* Eds. G.C. Boere, C.A. Galbraith & D.A. Stroud. The Stationery Office, Edinburgh, UK. pp. 376-378.

Population trends of seven Palearctic wader species were investigated at Langebaan Lagoon, South Africa. Over 28 years, summer (January/February) counts indicated there were major declines for Curlew Sandpiper *Calidris ferruginea*, Red Knot *C. canutus* and Sanderling *C. alba*, and smaller declines for Grey Plover *Pluvialis squatarola* and Ruddy Turnstone *Areneria interpres*. In contrast, data for Whimbrel *Numenius phaeopus* and Bar-tailed Godwit *Limosa lapponica* suggest that populations may be increasing. Winter counts (July/August) were used to assess breeding productivity based on over-wintering juveniles and suggested declining productivity for Grey Plover, Curlew Sandpiper, Ruddy Turnstone, Red Knot and Bar-tailed Godwit. The results are discussed in light of monitoring population changes for Arctic waders at the end point of their migratory range.

(a)

(b)

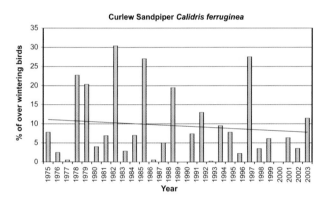

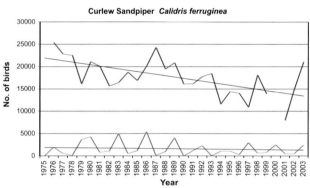

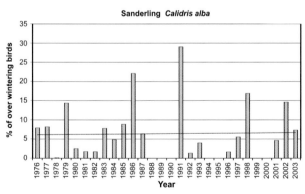

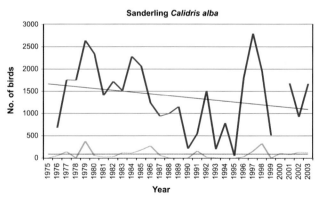

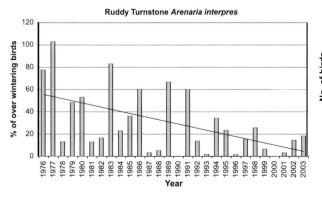

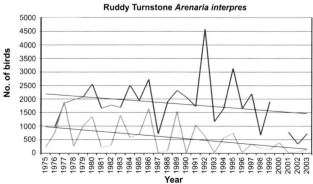

(a)  (b)

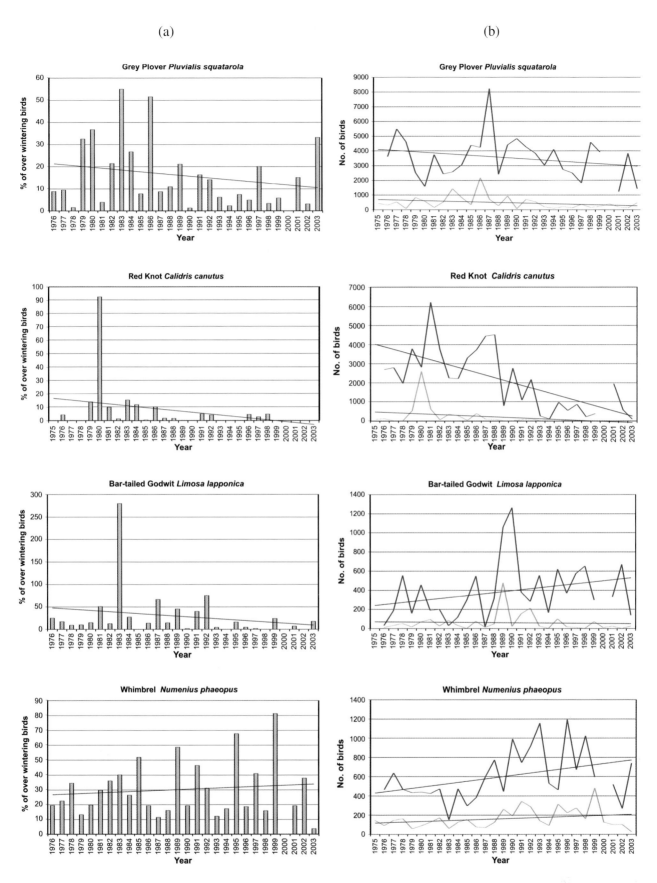

A large number of Palearctic waders occur annually during the austral summer at Langebaan Langoon which is the southernmost major wetland on the East Atlantic and West Asia/East Africa Flyways (Underhill 1987). Counts of migrant waders at this locality started in 1975 and an earlier analysis of this dataset revealed no clear trends for migrant wader species (Underhill

1987). This paper updates (for 1975-2003) trends for seven of the most common migrant wader species occurring at the lagoon.

Langebaan Lagoon is a large (5 600 ha), sheltered arm of Saldanha Bay situated on the west coast of South Africa. It is located within the West Coast National Park, which is also a designated Important Bird Area (Barnes 1998). The lagoon was designated as a Ramsar site in 1988 and includes 1 650 ha of intertidal sand- and mudflats and over 600 ha of saltmarshes, the latter representing about 32% of the total saltmarsh habitat in South Africa. Most Palearctic waders are found in these salt-marshes.

Bi-annual counts of non-breeding Palearctic waders and other waterbirds have been conducted at Langebaan Lagoon since July 1975. Data from 28 mid-summer (January/February) counts were used to determine long-term trends using linear regression while data from the 28 mid-winter (July/August) counts were used to assess breeding productivity based on the proportion of over-wintering juveniles (see Summers *et al.* 1995).

Population trends (summer) and breeding productivity (winter) are shown for Grey Plover, Ruddy Turnstone, Curlew Sandpiper, Sanderling, Red Knot, Bar-tailed Godwit and Whimbrel in Fig. 1.

Declines are evident for Curlew Sandpiper, Grey Plover, Red Knot, Sanderling and Knot, but are most noticeable for Curlew Sandpiper, Red Knot and Sanderling. In contrast, an increasing trend in numbers is evident for Whimbrel and Bar-tailed Godwit.

In terms of breeding success, trends suggest declining productivity for Curlew Sandpiper, Ruddy Turnstone, Red Knot, Bar-tailed Godwit and Grey Plover.

This analysis has demonstrated that population trends of arctic waders can be monitored at the end point of their migratory range, which may be significant in light of these wetlands being sensitive to global climate change and changes in overall population sizes. Future monitoring at the lagoon should focus on more frequent (i.e. monthly) monitoring in order to reduce the variability of the six-monthly counts.

We thank the Western Cape Wader Study Group and numerous other observers for helping with the counts; South African National Parks are thanked for permission to conduct

The southern shoreline of Langebaan Lagoon. Photo: Doug Harebottle.

counts in the West Coast National Park; The National Research Foundation provided financial assistance.

## REFERENCES

**Barnes, K.N.** (ed) 1998. Important Bird Areas in southern Africa. BirdLife South Africa, Johannesburg.

**Summers, R.W., Underhill, L.G. & Prys-Jones, R.P.** 1995. Does delayed return migration of young waders to their breeding grounds indicate the risk of migration? Ardea 83: 351-357.

**Underhill, L.G.** 1987. Waders (Charadrii) and other waterbirds at Langebaan Lagoon, South Africa, 1975-1986. Ostrich 58: 145-155.

There has been a long-term decline in numbers of Grey Plovers *Pluvialis squatarola* at Langebaan Lagoon. Significant numbers have been ringed in South Africa yielding important information on movements. Photo: Dieter Oschadleus.

# The breeding sites and distribution of Red-crested Pochard *Netta rufina* in Hungary

*Attila Bankovics*

*Hungarian Natural History Museum, H-1088 Budapest, Baross u. 13. Hungary.*

Bankovics, A. 2006. The breeding sites and distribution of Red-crested Pochard *Netta rufina* in Hungary. *Waterbirds around the world*. Eds. G.C. Boere, C.A. Galbraith & D.A. Stroud. The Stationery Office, Edinburgh, UK. p. 379.

The Red-crested Pochard *Netta rufina* is one of the least studied European duck species (Keller 2000). Overall breeding distribution in the western part of Europe in the first half of the 20th century is well reported (Cramp *et al.* 1977), but its occurrence and current status in the Carpathian basin is less well known. Hagemeijer and Blair (1997) mentioned it, but even recently published field identification books on European birds do not show Hungary as a breeding area for Red-crested Pochard. This paper summarises the current status of this species since its status has changed in Hungary during the last three decades.

Sporadic records published in different Hungarian ornithological periodicals and this author's, so far unpublished, observations were compiled, covering records from the period between 1960 and 2003.

Until 1960 Red-crested Pochard was one of the rarest duck species in Hungary. Keve (1960) mentioned only 16 earlier records. Between 1960 and 1975 observations increased slowly with a total of 23 records by 1975, i.e. seven new observations were made in this 15 year period (Keve 1976, 1984, Schmidt 1973). The first four of which came from Transdanubia.

There were three observations in the eastern half of Hungary in the spring of 1967 at Petőfiszállás, on Lake Péteri, with three males and one female observed on 12 and 15 March and one male and one female on 3 April (Bankovics 1968).

Since 1975 the number of records has grown more rapidly. There were 33 new reports between 1975 and 1983, most from the Lake Fertő area in Transdanubia (Kárpáti 2000). During that period the species was regarded as a rare, but regular, passage migrant in Hungary.

The first breeding of Red-crested Pochard was proved in 1986 at two breeding sites: the Kis-Balaton (in the newly established water-reservoir) and Lake Fertő (Futó 1990, Kárpáti 1987). Since then it has became a regular breeding bird in both sites and has begun to spread as a breeding bird, initially into the area of Transdanubia in the western half of the country.

From the mid-1990s Red-crested Pochard have started to occupy new breeding sites east from the Danube, in the area between the Danube and the Tisza rivers. It has bred at Lake Riha on Mohács Island in the Danube in the Duna-Dráva National Park (Kárpáti 2000). In 2003 it was first confirmed as breeding in Dzsidva Fishponds at Szakmár (Tamás, Ádám pers. comm.). The breeding population has also continued to spread in the Transdanubian region, in 2001 there was a new breeding site in the Fertő-Hanság National Park, in the Hanság region at Bősárkány (Bankovics *et al.* 2002).

The most important recent breeding sites and the estimated numbers of breeding pairs (in parenthesis) are: 1. Lake Fertő (30),
2. Hanság (2), 3. Kis-Balaton (20), 4. Fonyód (5), 5. Balatonlelle (5), 6. Dinnyés (15), 7. Mocsa (3), 8. Rétszilas (3), 9. Soponya (3), 10. Riha-tó (Mohácsi-sziget) (3), and 11. Szakmár (1).

Comparing numbers of Red-crested Pochard in Hungary between the 1960s and the 1990s indicates major changes: it was a rare vagrant until the mid-1960s, became a regular visitor locally after 1975, and a regular passage migrant in the 1990s. It has bred in Hungary since 1986, with a current estimated breeding population of approximately 90 pairs.

I am grateful to Erika Bankovics and Orsolya Mile for their help in elaborating the data, Péter Batáry for helping with the English translation and all the field-workers for providing the records.

## REFERENCES

Bankovics, A. 1968. Red-crested Pochards on the pond of Péteri. Aquila 75: 296.

Bankovics, A., Fülöp, T., Hadarics, T., Mogyorósi, S. & Pellinger, A. 2002. The Birds of Fertő-Hanság National Park and their Importance in Nature Conservation Aspect. In: Mahunka S. (ed.) The fauna of the Fertő-Hanság National Park: 745-785.

Cramp, S. (ed.) 1978. Handbook of the Birds of Europe, the Middle East and North Africa: the Birds of the Western Palearctic. Vol. I. Oxford University Press, Oxford.

Futó, E. 1990. Recent nesting bird species at the Kis-Balaton Water Reservoir, Section 1. Aquila 96-97: 154.

Hagemeijer, E. J. & Blair, M. J. (eds.) 1997. The EBCC Atlas of European Breeding Birds: their distribution and abundance. T. & A.D. Poyser, London.

Kárpáti, L. 1987. Üstökös réce (*Netta rufina*) fészkelése a Fertő hazai oldalán. Madártani Tájékoztató 1987. január-június: 29-31.

Kárpáti, L. 2000. Üstökös réce, *Netta rufina*. – in Haraszthy L. (szerk.): Magyarország madarai. Pp. 59-60. Mezőgazda, Budapest.

Keller, V. 2000. Winter distribution and population change of Red-crested Pochard *Netta rufina* in southwestern and central Europe. Bird Study 47: 176-185.

Keve, A. 1960. Nomenclator Avium Hungariae. Pp. 1-90. Budapest.

Keve, A. 1976. Adatok a Kis-Balaton madárvilágához. Aquila 82: 49-79.

Keve, A. 1984. Nomenclator Avium Hungariae. Pp. 1-100. Akadémiai Kiadó, Budapest.

Schmidt, E. 1973. Faunisztikai jegyzetek 1. Aquila 76-77: 183-186.

# The Lesser White-fronted Goose *Anser erythropus* at the verge of the millennium

*Vladimir V. Morozov*

*Russian Research Institute of Nature Protection, Znamenskoye-Sadki, Moscow, 113628, Russia.*

Morozov, V.V. 2006. The Lesser White-fronted Goose *Anser erythropus* at the verge of the millennium. *Waterbirds around the world.* Eds. G.C. Boere, C.A. Galbraith & D.A. Stroud. The Stationery Office, Edinburgh, UK. pp. 380-381.

This paper analyses the current state of the Lesser White-fronted Goose *Anser erythropus* in Russia, discusses present threats and proposes conservation measures.

Members of a specially formed Lesser White-fronted Goose group undertook a number of field trips to ring and mark Lesser White-fronted Geese in breeding areas in Western Siberia, Taimyr, and Yakutia and the Bolshezemelskaya tundra.

One of the main goals of the field studies was to obtain information on the current migration stopover sites of the Lesser White-fronted Goose and on the location of their wintering grounds. Previously, we had postulated the existence of several geographical populations of the Lesser White-fronted Geese which differed greatly in numbers and habitats (Morozov 1995). New data did not confirm this supposition: on the contrary, the results of satellite tracking of birds marked in Fennoscandia and ringed on the Polar Urals favoured the concept of a single population inhabiting the territories from the north of the Scandinavian peninsula to the east of Taimyr. Nevertheless, the structure of mtDNA of the Fennoscandian Lesser White-fronted Geese differs considerably from that of the birds from other areas of the species' breeding range (Ruokonen & Lumme 1999), indicating a great degree of isolation and allowing us to consider them as a separate geographical population.

Lesser White-fronted Geese inhabiting the tundras of European Russia, like some Fennoscandian ones, cross the Ural mountains in autumn heading to the Turgaiskaya depression. Migration routes of Lesser Whitefronts with satellite transmitters demonstrate that geese from breeding grounds located in the European part of the Russian tundras cross the Ural and migrate along the Ob River valley to the stopover sites in Northern Kazakhstan (Morozov & Aarvak in press).

The migration stopovers in Northern Kazakhstan gather Lesser White-fronted Geese not only from Taimyr, Gydan and Yamal but also from the Bolshezemelskaya tundra and even Fennoscandia, as demonstrated by the structure of mtDNA of the birds hunted in Kazakhstan (Ruokonen & Lumme 1999). Unfortunately, no data on migrations of the Lesser White-fronted Geese nesting east of Taimyr confirmed by ringing or marking results are available. The structure of mtDNA of the geese shot in China indicates a considerable genetic isolation of these birds (Ruokonen & Lumme 1999). However, we know nothing about the distribution of these individuals within the breeding grounds because no samples have been collected there. Thus, we can only assert that the eastern part of the breeding range of this species is occupied by at least one geographic population, though the existence of more than one is also possible.

The total estimate presented in the previous review was 30 000–50 000 individuals at the end of the breeding season (Morozov 1995). The number of 50 000 birds was rather an assumption, because we had no data on the Lesser White-fronted

Developing awareness of the conservation needs of waterbirds, including the requirement to limit hunting, is key in Russia and neighbouring countries. Awareness mural, Dunaiskie Plavni Nature Reserve, Danube Delta, Ukraine. Photo: David Stroud.

Goose numbers on Taimyr, which was supposed to be inhabited by one of the largest territorial groups of these geese. The first special studies carried out on Taimyr have yielded quite different results: numbers of Lesser White-fronted Geese appear to be much lower than expected (Syroechkovski Jr. 1996), and the total number inhabiting Taimyr and the areas west of it was re-estimated at 8 500–17 000 birds (Lorentsen *et al.* 1999).

Analysis of the current estimates made on the migration stopovers in Kazakhstan suggest that the present numbers of the species may be estimated by the end of the breeding season as follows: Western Siberia and Taimyr, including the Putorana Plateau - 8 000 to 11 000; Kanin Peninsula and Taimyr - 9 000 to 12 000. Winter censuses conducted in China over the last years are fairly reliable, and we agree with the mid-winter estimate of 12 000–17 000 inhabiting Yakutia and the Far East. The total world population of the Lesser White-fronted Geese in the post-breeding period may thus be 20 000 to 25 000 individuals in different years, although the estimate of our colleagues from Western Europe is 24 000–30 000 individuals (Lorentsen *et al.* 1999, Markkola 2001).

Increased mortality of birds due to the hunting pressure along the migration routes and on the wintering grounds is considered now the main and virtually the only cause of the decline in numbers. The losses of the marked birds during migration vividly demonstrate a very high mortality rate in this population after the breeding season (Lorentsen *et al.* 1998, 1999, Øien *et al.* 1999). However, other populations also suffer from both legal and illegal hunting. For example, in autumn 2000, eight people using poisoned grain baits killed 667 Lesser White-fronted Geese at Lake Dongting (Lei 2001): 5 to 10% of the total number of this species wintering in China. Population losses on the wintering grounds will be considerably higher, taking into account the difficulties in distinguishing the Lesser White-fronted Geese from the White-fronted Geese in flight, the low level of the public hunting standards, and the fact that the hunting legislation is very often violated in Russia and in a number of neighboring countries (Ukraine, Kazakhstan and Azerbaijan).

Hunting pressure, especially in spring, is a crucial factor in the dramatic decline of the Lesser White-fronted Goose, which is the rarest goose species in Eurasia. The following measures seem realistic and constructive:

- wider advocacy of Lesser White-fronted Goose protection by hunters' societies and the Department of Game Management at the federal and regional levels;
- strict regulation and banning of hunting on all goose species in spring and autumn along the migration routes, on the breeding grounds and in the stopover sites; and
- support for professional and qualified amateur ornithologists in Lesser White-fronted Goose studies.

## REFERENCES

Aarvak, T., Arkiomaa, A., Tolvanen, P., Øien, I.J. & Timonen, S. 2004. Inventories and catching attempts of Lesser White-fronted Geese *Anser erythropus* at Lake Kulykol, Kazakstan, in 2002 and 2003. Fennoscandian Lesser White-fronted Goose conservation project. Report 2001–2003 (eds. T. Aarvak, & S. Timonen,). WWF Finland Report No. 20 & NOF Rapportserie Report No.1-2004. Helsinki–Klæbu: 36–40.

Lei, G. 2001. Conservation of Lesser White-fronted Goose at East Dongting lake, China in 2000. Fennoscandian Lesser White-fronted Goose conservation project. Annual report 2000 (eds. P. Tolvanen, I.J. Øien, & K. Ruokolainen.). WWF Finland Report No. 13 & NOF Rapportserie Report No.1-2001. Helsinki–Klæbu: 48.

Lorentsen, S.H., Øien, I.J. & Aarvak, T. 1998. Migration of Fennoscandian Lesser White-fronted Geese *Anser erythropus* mapped by satellite telemetry. Biological Conservation 84: 47–52.

Lorentsen, S.H., Øien, I.J., Aarvak, T., Markkola, J., von Essen, L., Farago, S., Morozov, V., Syroechkovsky, E. Jr. & Tolvanen P. 1999. Lesser White-fronted Goose *Anser erythropus*. Goose populations of the Western Palearctic. A review of status and distribution (eds. J. Madsen, G. Cracknell, & T. Fox.). Wetlands International Publication No. 48. Wetlands International, Wageningen, The Netherlands. Pp. 144–161.

Markkola, J. 2001. The Finnish Lesser White-fronted Goose EU Life/Nature project 1997–2000. Fennoscandian Lesser White-fronted Goose conservation project. Annual report 2000 (eds. P. Tolvanen, I.J. Øien, & K. Ruokolainen). WWF Finland Report No. 13 & NOF Rapportserie Report No.1-2001. Helsinki–Klæbu: 40–44.

Morozov, V.V. 1995. The status, distribution and trends of the Lesser White-fronted Goose *Anser erythropus* population in Russia. Bulletin of Goose Study Group of Eastern Europe and Northern Asia 1: 131–144.

Ruokonen, M. & Lumme, J. 1999. Phylogeography and population genetic structure of the Lesser White-fronted Goose. Fennoscandian Lesser White-fronted Goose conservation project. Annual report 1998 (eds. P. Tolvanen, I.J. Øien, & K. Ruokolainen). WWF Finland Report No. 10 & NOF Rapportserie Report No. 1-1999: 51–52.

Syroechkovski, Jr. E.E. 1996. Present status of the Lesser White-fronted Goose populations *Anser erythropus* in Taimyr and some peculiarities of the system of species migration in the Western Palearctic. Casarca 2: 71–112.

Tolvanen, P., Karvonen, R., Pynnönen, P. & Leito, A. 2000. Monitoring of Lesser White-fronted Geese in western Estonia in 1999. Fennoscandian Lesser White-fronted Goose conservation project. Annual report 1999 (eds. P. Tolvanen, I.J. Øien, & K. Ruokolainen). WWF Finland Report No. 12 & NOF Rapportserie Report No. 1-2000. Helsinki–Klæbu. 18–21.

Øien, I.J., Tolvanen, P., Aarvak, T., Litvin, K.E. & Markkola, J. 1999. Survey and catching of Lesser White-fronted Geese at Taimyr Peninsula 1998 – preliminary results on autumn migration routes mapped by satellite telemetry. Fennoscandian Lesser White-fronted Goose conservation project. Annual report 1998 (eds. P. Tolvanen, I.J. Øien, & K. Ruokolainen) WWF Finland Report No. 10 & NOF Rapportserie Report No. 1-1999. 37–41.

# Part 4.

# Cross-cutting issues

## Sections

# 4.1 The implications of climate change for waterbirds. Workshop Introduction

*Mark O'Connell*

*The Wildfowl & Wetlands Trust, Slimbridge, Gloucestershire, GL2 7BT, UK.*

O'Connell, M. 2006. The implications of climate change for waterbirds. Workshop Introduction. *Waterbirds around the world*. Eds. G.C. Boere, C.A. Galbraith & D.A. Stroud. The Stationery Office, Edinburgh, UK. p. 384.

The widespread and long-term retreat of glaciers in Greenland is a signal of the changes currently occurring in the arctic environment. Modelling has shown that climate change will profoundly affect the extent and ecological character of arctic waterbird habitats. Photo: David Stroud.

Climate determines the distribution and movements of waterbirds and the wetland habitats they use. Global climates, however, are changing, and as a result of human activities are doing so faster than historic levels. Importantly, species within communities will respond differently to climate change, and will alter their distribution at different speeds, thereby creating the potential to form new assemblages. Some waterbird populations will be able to track changes in resource/habitat distribution (Rehfisch & Austin give examples of changing distributions of wintering waterbirds in the UK), although some will not be able to adapt in this fashion. In relation to climate changes and waterbirds the research community has four key conservation challenges, outlined below,

## 1. To describe what will happen

To be able to tease out effects of climate change from long-term fluctuation and effects of a range of human activities, there will be a need for relevant information and data at the flyway level. A further need will be to understand impacts of climate change on wetland processes and functions, as well as some of the 'hidden' effects of climate change on waterbird populations, such as some of the subtle differential effects of return rates of seabirds to their breeding colonies (as described by Favero & Becker). It will also be important to understand the capacity of waterbirds to react to extreme weather events, and to understand and agree what constitutes a 'significant' population change.

## 2. To identify where it will happen

The generic challenges will be to identify potential changes in the distribution of flyway resources (both abiotic and biotic), and to predict how waterbirds will spatially track these changes.

## 3. To develop or enhance research methods

There will be a need to ensure research access to relevant data and information as well as the supporting development of appropriate methods for determining what will happen and where it will happen (above).

## 4. To support the action agenda

It will be particularly important to facilitate the flow of relevant information and data to support the action agenda, for example as part of action plans within flyway Agreements and other multilateral instruments. It is therefore of high priority to ensure that the results of climate change studies are disseminated appropriately and that stakeholders are engaged fully at all stages of future research.

As well as undertaking new work to fill gaps in current knowledge, scientists must also consider how to utilise the considerable amount of information that is already available for analysis. There is also a universal need to support financially the continuance of long-term, wide-scale monitoring of species and habitats. These data are the foundation on which our response and adaptation to climate change will be based.

The consequences of climate change for waterbirds will be multiple and greatly exacerbate ongoing negative impacts such as habitat loss and degradation. Landscape scale planning will be required to reduce or mitigate the impacts of climate change on waterbird populations and their habitats. Research that explores a range of potential future scenarios will therefore be required to underpin this landscape scale planning, and will need data from long-term monitoring and surveillance (as described by O'Connell *et al.* in the specific case of north-west European goose populations).

# Developing an integrated approach to understanding the effects of climate change and other environmental alterations at a flyway level

*M.J. O'Connell[1], A.H.L. Huiskes[2], M.L. Loonen[3], J. Madsen[4], M. Klaassen[5] & M. Rounsevell[6]*

[1] *The Wildfowl & Wetlands Trust, Slimbridge, Gloucestershire, GL2 7BT, UK.*
[2] *Netherlands Institute of Ecology, Yerseke, The Netherlands.*
[3] *University of Groningen, Groningen, The Netherlands.*
[4] *National Environmental Research Institute, Dept. of Arctic Environment, Frederiksberg 39, PO Box 358, DK-4000 Roskilde, Denmark.*
[5] *Netherlands Institute of Ecology, Maarssen, The Netherlands.*
[6] *Université Catholique de Louvain, Louvain-la-Neuve, Belgium.*

O'Connell, M.J., Huiskes, A.H.L., Loonen, M.L., Madsen, J., Klaassen, M. & Rounsevell, M. 2006. Developing an integrated approach to understanding the effects of climate change and other environmental alterations at a flyway level. *Waterbirds around the world*. Eds. G.C. Boere, C.A. Galbraith & D.A. Stroud. The Stationery Office, Edinburgh, UK. pp. 385-397.

## ABSTRACT

The environmental consequences of global climate change are predicted to have their greatest effect at high latitudes and have great potential to impact fragile tundra ecosystems. The Arctic tundra is a vast biodiversity resource and provides breeding areas for many migratory geese. Importantly, tundra ecosystems also currently act as a global carbon "sink", buffering carbon emissions from human activities. In January 2003, a new three-year project was implemented to understand and model the interrelationships between goose population dynamics, conservation, European land use/agriculture and climate change. A range of potential future climate and land-use scenarios will be applied to the models and combined with information from field experiments on grazing and climate change in the Arctic. This paper describes the content of the research programme as well as issues in relation to engaging stakeholders with the project.

## INTRODUCTION

### Changes to European landscapes

Socio-economic, agricultural and demographic changes have imposed modifications on the European landscape to such a degree that habitats over most of the region have been altered in some way, degraded, or removed entirely. Although many of these changes have resulted in negative impacts for European fauna and flora, some species have benefited, and indeed increased their distribution and abundance to a point where they come into "conflict" with human interests (Patterson 1991, Cope *et al.* 2003). In addition to the direct impacts of change on different elements of the European landscape, human activities involving the burning of fossil fuels during the last two hundred years have now altered climate and weather patterns beyond pre-industrial "background" levels (Jones *et al.* 1998, Huang *et al.* 2000, IPCC 2001, Jones & Mann 2004). Many of these environmental alterations have not been in the form of large "step" changes, but have often been slow, insidious, ongoing, patchy, and spread over wide spatial extents. These characteristics complicate efforts to detect and measure the changes as they happen, and to predict future patterns of change. They also make it difficult for appropriate authorities to develop strategies to halt and reverse the impacts of such change (O'Connell & Yallop 2002, Caro *et al.* 2004).

### Changes to European migratory goose populations

The relatively large size and aggregative behaviour of geese, coupled with a large number of skilled volunteer observers across Europe, have made it possible to measure general changes in goose populations, i.e. overall abundance, distribution, and use of key sites (for a review, see Madsen *et al.* 1999). Long-term and large-scale capture-recapture efforts (e.g. ringing) have also produced data that can be used to model the trajectory of goose populations by analysing the demographic factors of survival, fecundity, dispersal and recruitment (e.g. Alisaiskas 2002, Cope *et al.* 2003, Frederiksen *et al.* 2004). However, quantifying general changes in goose abundance and knowing their population trajectory does not necessarily provide an understanding of the causes of the changes in measured demographic parameters, or facilitate the development of holistic approaches to conservation strategies (i.e. those encompassing the widest possible range of biotic, abiotic and human factors that operate at an ecosystem or landscape level).

### Holistic research: the "ecosystem approach"

The term "ecosystem" came to prominence in the 1930s, but had been in use as a general concept since the 1860s (Botkin 1990). The view of populations connected through interactions with their proximate biotic and abiotic environment developed into a paradigm where ecological groupings were viewed within reasonably closed and self-regulating systems. Ecologists later expanded these ideas within a framework of "systems analysis" which provided a methodology to understand very complex systems and feedback loops (Odum 1953). However, the "ecosystem approach" (Hartig *et al.* 1998, Wang 2004) has a number of conceptual problems. O'Neill (2001) highlighted three key issues: (1) the selection of elements to be included within a named ecosystem is often subjective and based on *a priori* knowledge; (2) ecosystem research foci are often selected subjectively and based on favoured or "easy target" ecosystem elements; and (3) human activities are invariably seen merely as "external" disturbances to ecosystems.

In relation to ecosystem management, a further critical assessment was made by O'Connell (2003) who identified five assumptions underlying actions to protect ecosystems and manage them on a sustainable basis:

a) There is adequate inventory and monitoring to provide appropriate information for action;

b) That change in the ecosystem can first be detected and then measured;

c) That it is possible to identify the underlying causes of change;

d) There is the ability to predict the likely consequences of change in all parts of a system; and

e) There is knowledge of remedial action to halt or reverse the detected and measured change.

In most cases, these assumptions will not be met, and there is a great deal of fundamental research needed to address this situation.

### The "flyway" concept

Migratory birds also raise additional difficulties for the ecosystem approach. Migration results in species moving between and within a variety of "systems", and this presents problems when trying to understand the full range of their environmental interactions and population drivers. To address some of these problems, the idea of avian "flyways" was developed. Conceptually, a flyway can be thought of as possessing ecosystem-like qualities (i.e. many interacting biotic and abiotic elements interacting within a relatively closed and self-sustaining system). But for practical applications, a flyway can also be defined simply as the network of sites (and routes) required to fulfil the annual life cycle of individuals within a migratory population. As well as providing a useful research framework for migratory species, the flyway concept also facilitates transboundary conservation measures and monitoring (Boere 2003).

### Integrated flyway studies

An increasing number of migratory bird studies are being been made at the conceptual level of flyways, i.e. they consider life-history events at the breeding, non-breeding and migration sites (Francis *et al.* 1992, Hoffman *et al.* 2002, Hötker *et al.* 1998,

Malcolm & ReVelle 2002, Otis 2004). However, although covering appropriate spatial scales, many of these studies still focus on only one or a small number of life history factors occurring at this scale, e.g. survival, habitat requirements, hunting levels, phenology, etc. Data limitations and research costs mean that few studies have been able to take a more holistic "whole system" approach integrating the large number of different biotic and abiotic elements impacting both species and landscapes within a flyway. The potential benefit of an integrated approach is to go beyond quantitative description, and to generate an understanding of the relative importance of different processes within a flyway system and how these interact at different spatial and temporal scales. In turn, this provides a means to forecast the likely impacts of change on individual system elements, and explore system responses under a combination of different environmental change scenarios. The central components of a framework for flyway level research is shown in Fig. 1.

## COMPONENTS OF ARCTIC BREEDING GOOSE FLYWAYS

Eight species of geese breed on Arctic tundra habitats in the European Arctic (mostly beyond 65˚N) and migrate to wintering grounds in climatically temperate zones (generally between 40˚N and 60˚N). The study described in this paper refers to a Northern Hemisphere flyway where two goose populations utilize tundra systems on the Svalbard archipelago for breeding and then migrate (via a number of stopover sites) to wintering areas on estuarine and agricultural habitats in north-western Europe. The two goose populations (described in detail below) have very different breeding site requirements and feeding ecology, and have spatially separated wintering areas.

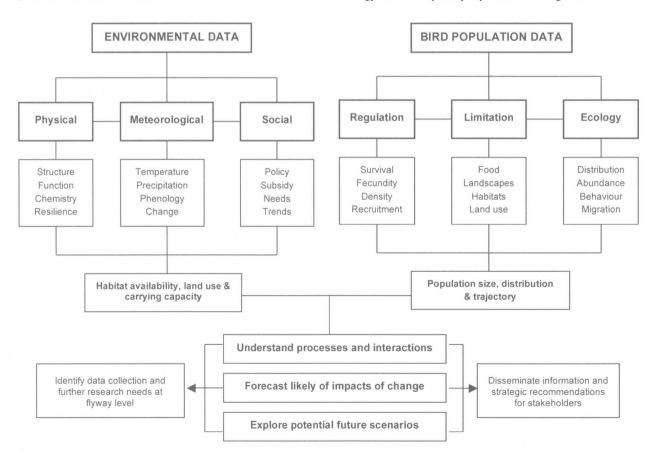

Fig. 1. Information needs and analytical outcomes of a flyway-level, integrated research approach.

## Structural and functional characteristics of tundra

Globally, tundra habitats cover approximately 9% of the world's surface (Clausen 1996), with Arctic tundra occupying a circumpolar area of nearly six million sq. km. Tundra is characterized by low biotic diversity, short and simple vegetation structure, and shallow root systems. Many of the 1 700 species of plants recorded in the Arctic region can photosynthesize at low temperatures and light intensities, and most are wind-adapted and robust to soil perturbation (Epstein *et al.* 2004). Tundra soils are generally thin, generated slowly, seasonally thawed, and lie on a layer of permanently frozen subsoil (permafrost) consisting mostly of gravel and finer material. This vertical profile results in poor drainage, and where water saturates the upper surface, bogs and ponds are often present. Rainfall varies considerably within the Arctic region, but average yearly precipitation (including melting snow) is often less than 25 cm.

This combination of physical, chemical and climatic factors results in environmental conditions where atmospheric carbon dioxide is sequestered by tundra habitats, which have been estimated to contain up to 30% of the world's soil carbon stocks (Gilmanov & Oechel 1995, Waelbroeck *et al.* 1997, McGuire *et al.* 2002). This makes tundra systems particularly important in terms of global carbon balance. Tundra plant communities which are grazed by geese are often dominated by graminoids and bryophytes. However, elevated temperatures and over-grazing by geese cause a shift towards increased graminoid and decreased bryophyte dominance, and result in warming and drying of the soil, faster nutrient cycling, and increased carbon efflux. Another key characteristic of tundra ecosystems is their low nutrient status, particularly in relation to nitrogen. Increases in the rate of nutrient cycling may result from both soil warming and grazing. This is known to alter species composition and increase productivity of both terrestrial and aquatic tundra communities. In addition, increased nitrogen availability decreases the carbon : nitrogen ratio of plant tissue, thus increasing the rate at which it will decompose and hence the carbon efflux from the system (Fahnstock *et al.* 1999, Brooks *et al.* 2005). The responses of habitats to elevated temperatures can be characterized by their sensitivity, adaptability and vulnerability. "Sensitivity" defines the thresholds of climate change that result in altered composition, structure and functioning of an ecosystem. "Adaptability" is the degree to which systems can adjust in response to altered environmental conditions. "Vulnerability" defines the extent to which climate change may damage or harm a system, i.e. is related to both sensitivity and adaptability. Empirical evidence suggests that tundra habitats show high sensitivity, low adaptability and high vulnerability (Forbes *et al.* 2001, Chapin *et al.* 2004).

## Svalbard tundra

The Svalbard archipelago (78˚30'N, 18˚00'E) consists of nine main islands with an area of just over 62 000 sq. km. The islands are mountainous (up to 1 700 m), with glaciers and snowfields covering more than 60% of the land surface in high summer and 100% in winter. The relatively milder western areas comprise a large number of steep-sided fjords with tundra habitats in the lower drainage basins and river beds.

## Arctic climates and climate change

The Arctic experiences both polar maritime (i.e. influenced by oceanic factors) and continental (i.e. influenced by terrestrial land masses) climates. Weather patterns are characterized by high spatial variability, and although the region receives a large amount of solar energy in summer, the high reflectivity (albedo) of snow and ice surfaces keeps absorption of solar energy low. Heat gained during long summer days can therefore be relatively small. Maritime climate conditions prevail in coastal Alaska, Iceland, northern Norway and adjoining parts of Russia. Winters are often cold and stormy; summers are cloudy but mild with a mean temperature of about 10˚C. Annual precipitation is generally between 60 cm and 125 cm, and there are normally at least six months of snow cover. At lower latitudes, "continental" climates result in much more severe winters, although precipitation is lower. Permanently frozen ground (permafrost) is widespread and, in summer, only the top one to two metres of ground thaws. This results in a poorly drained "active layer" that often remains waterlogged and on which tundra habitats can develop.

Since the end of the nineteenth century, the average temperature of the earth's surface has risen by 0.6˚C, and sea levels have risen by between 10 cm and 20 cm. By 2100, temperatures are predicted to increase further by between 1.4 and 5.8 degrees, with an additional sea level rise of 9 to 88 cm. The 1990s were the warmest decade of the last millennium, and 1998 the warmest year. Mean air temperatures in the Arctic have increased by about 5˚C over the last 100 years, and the extent of sea ice has decreased by 14% since the 1970s. These increases in temperature represent larger changes than any century-long trend in the last ten thousand years (Weaver & Green 1998). By the year 2100, winter temperatures in many parts of the Arctic are predicted to rise by 40% more than the global average change.

## Arctic migratory geese

The Arctic region provides vast areas of relatively disturbance-free wilderness in which animals can breed. There are plentiful food resources (although relatively limited in variety) and, at higher latitudes, up to 24 hours of daylight in which to feed offspring. Approximately 430 bird species breed in the Arctic (Zöckler 1998), of which 130 are migratory waterbirds (Wetlands International 2002). There are 15 species of "true" geese within the genera *Anser* and *Branta*, and 12 of these breed both in the Arctic and elsewhere, with eight breeding exclusively in the Arctic region. Thirty-four subspecies are represented in the region (with 24 exclusive to the Arctic), comprising 67 populations of which 50 breed in the Arctic. The latter group has been estimated to total more than eight million individuals, representing 67% of the total world population of the genera *Anser* and *Branta* (Madsen *et al.* 1996).

All Arctic breeding populations of geese migrate to lower latitudes during the non-breeding season. Many species migrate on a narrow geographical front, with fixed routes and a small number of stopover sites at which the birds rest, socialize and replenish body fat reserves (Choudhury *et al.* 1996, Madsen *et al.* 2002, Prop *et al.* 2003). Traditionally, wintering birds made use of coastal and estuarine habitats, particularly coastal marshes. In these areas, large numbers of birds have been hunted by humans, and by the middle of the twentieth century the population of many species had been reduced to levels that were a fraction of their previous "natural" state (Madsen 1991, Pettifor *et al.* 2000). During the latter half of the century, changes in agricultural practices resulted in new, plentiful and seasonally reliable food sources for wintering geese (van Eerden *et al.* 1996,

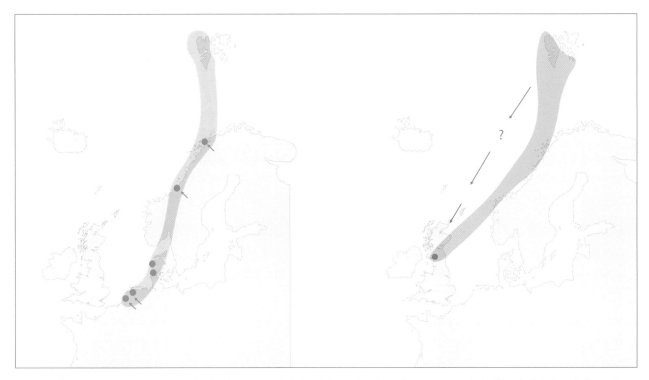

**Fig. 2.** Principal breeding, migration and wintering areas of Svalbard Barnacle Geese *Branta leucopsis* (red) and Pink-footed Geese *Anser brachyrhynchus* (blue).

Therkildsen & Madsen 2000). This, coupled with improved legislative protection and positive site management regimes (e.g. refuge areas and cold-weather hunting bans), resulted in a change in the fortunes of many goose populations, many of which are increasing or stable (Wetlands International 2002).

### Svalbard geese

Geese breeding on the Svalbard archipelago are recognized as distinct "populations", i.e. are groups that do not experience significant immigration or emigration (Wetlands International 2002). The Svalbard Barnacle Geese *Branta leucopsis* breed colonially, mainly in the west of the archipelago. They often (but not exclusively) utilize steep rocky areas, and many colonies are on islands (Mitchell *et al.* 1998). Most of the population over-winters on the Scottish side of the Solway Firth in the UK (Fig. 2), although changes have been occurring in the timing and spatial extent of the population's wintering distribution. It is likely that the population constituted as few as 300 individuals in 1948, and came close to extinction (Pettifor *et al.* 1998). As a result of conservation measures in the mid-1950s and a switch to feeding on agricultural habitats, there was a gradual increase in the population during the last half of the twentieth century. The population is currently estimated to be nearly 28 000 birds. Although density dependence in productivity and survival has been found on the breeding grounds, it does not appear to regulate the population as a whole. At present the population is growing (Fig. 3a), presumably because birds are still colonizing new breeding habitat (Black 1998, Trinder *et al.* 2005). There is no evidence that the population has reached the carrying capacity of either the summer or winter ranges. If breeding is being regulated by population density, then further increases in population size may be small. Aggregation into relatively confined breeding and wintering areas makes this population vulnerable to stochastic events, such as adverse conditions on

the breeding grounds, disease or adverse conditions during migration. The most sensitive demographic factor is adult survival (Tombre *et al.* 1998, Schmutz *et al.* 1997), and Trinder *et al.* (2005) suggest that the loss of as few as 350 individuals annually produces a median equilibrium population at its current size of nearly 28 000, with the likelihood of long-term population decline increasing markedly if additional annual losses exceeded 1 000.

While Barnacle Geese are restricted to nesting on cliffs or islands that offer protection from Arctic Foxes *Alopex lagopus*, Svalbard Pink-footed Geese *Anser brachyrhynchus* nest more widely in loose colonies on the open tundra, being capable of defending the nest from fox attacks. The species breeds in the western part of Svalbard, whereas in the eastern part, the summer season is too short to execute both nesting and brood-rearing. The population migrates via stopover sites in Norway to wintering grounds in Denmark, The Netherlands and Belgium (Fig. 2). The population increased from 12 000-20 000 in the mid-1960s to 40 000-50 000 by 2003 (Fig. 3b). The rapid increase in the 1970s was probably due to improved survival caused by relaxation of winter shooting pressure (Ebbinge *et al.* 1984), but changes in winter food supplies towards agricultural crops may also have played a role in the more recent increase (Fox *et al.* 2005). Today, the species is still subject to hunting in Svalbard, Norway and Denmark, but hunting mortality does not seem to be a factor controlling population size (Madsen *et al.* 2002).

Although not included in the present study, Brent Geese *Branta bernicla* also breed on Svalbard. The Brent Goose has a circumpolar breeding distribution with a range extending from Greenland to Svalbard and northern Russia, continuing through Alaska to the Canadian Arctic Archipelago. There are three subspecies. One of these, the Light-bellied Brent Goose *B. b. hrota*, occurs generally in the western Arctic (Canada to Svalbard and Franz Joseph Land), and has three distinct popula-

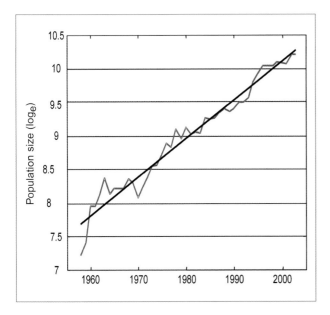

Fig. 3a. Svalbard Barnacle Goose *Branta leucopsis* ($\log_e$) population size: 1957 to 2004.

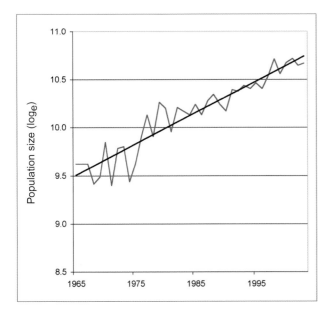

Fig. 3b. Svalbard Pink-footed Goose *Anser brachyrhynchus* ($\log_e$) population size: 1965 to 2003.

tions breeding in Canada, Greenland and Svalbard. The population on Svalbard currently numbers only about 5 000 individuals. It is probable that the population was previously around 50 000 individuals during the early twentieth century, but had declined to 2 000 individuals by the 1970s (Scott & Rose 1996), with a more recent recovery to about 6 600 (Denny *et al.* 2004). This decline, in common with other Brent Goose populations, has been attributed to a disease-related die-off in their favoured food resource (eel grass *zostera*), combined with shooting and disturbance. Despite currently being protected throughout its range, the Svalbard Light-bellied Brent Goose population remains depressed and is one of the most vulnerable goose populations in the world. Suggested explanations for this slow recovery include competition with the expanding Barnacle Goose population on Svalbard, and predation there by Polar Bears *Ursus maritimus* and Arctic Foxes (Madsen *et al.* 1989, 1992).

## Herbivory by geese

Grazing by geese and other herbivores can have a large effect on tundra systems (Cooch *et al.* 1991, Jano *et al.* 1998). The selective removal of biomass can alter vegetation composition and the amount and quality of litter produced. Goose grazing can also alter the nitrogen cycle (when goose droppings function as a source of nitrogen), and hence increase the productivity of their forage. It is clear that increases in the populations of geese grazing on tundra will have implications for the carbon and nitrogen balance of the system. Geese have also direct and indirect effects on Arctic freshwater ecosystems, by altering nitrogen and phosphorous regimes in lakes and ponds. For very nutrient-poor sites, faecal droppings provide a valuable input for the systems, while coastal ponds may be severely eutrophied by increased loading of nutrients. Nitrogen and phosphorous are key determinants of productivity, biodiversity, ecosystem processes and food-web dynamics in these freshwater systems (Antoniades *et al.* 2003, Graneli *et al.* 2004).

## Goose migration sites

Barnacle Geese spend approximately one month on their traditional spring staging areas in Helgeland in mid-Norway (Gullestad *et al.* 1984, Black *et al.* 1991, Prop & Black 1998). In recent years, the outer islands in Helgeland have been depopulated, and Barnacle Geese have spread into new areas in the north and east (Black *et al.* 1991, Prop *et al.* 1998, Shimmings 1998). In these areas, they feed on sown pastures and heavily managed and fertilized swards (Black *et al.* 1991). Today, the geese therefore stage in either traditional maritime habitats (e.g. outer islands), or newly-exploited agricultural habitats on inland islands. In recent years, Barnacle Geese also stage in Vesterålen in northern Norway (Shimmings 2003, Tombre *et al.* 2004). Here they overlap with Svalbard Pink-footed Geese, feeding mainly on farmland close to the coast. Most of the farmland is cultivated grassland used for sheep and cattle grazing and hay. Along the coastline, some areas of salt-marsh and seashore vegetation remain, although most are overgrown through the lack of summer grazing by livestock.

The Svalbard population of Pink-footed Geese has spring staging areas in mid-Norway and Vesterålen in northern Norway. Here the population aggregates during April and May, foraging on a combination of pastures and spring-sown cereals (mid-Norway only). In recent years, conflicts between farming interests and Pink-footed Geese have given rise to organized scaring of geese from pastures in Vesterålen, which has resulted in geese departing earlier to the breeding grounds without accumulating essential nutrient stores (Madsen & Klaassen 2006) which are a prerequisite for successful breeding as well as survival (Fox *et al* 2005, J. Madsen & M. Klaassen, unpubl. data). A spring migration dynamic model predicts that an abrupt intensification of the scaring campaign, which is currently being considered in both staging areas in Norway, will have dramatic impacts on the population due to the scale of the campaign and the limited possibilities that the geese will have to gain sufficient experience and, hence, adapt to the scaring regime (Klaassen *et al.* 2006).

## Goose wintering grounds, land use and climate

Up to the 1960s, Europe was a net importer of many food items, and most agricultural production was achieved by low intensity, high labour methods. As agriculture mechanized and intensified during the immediate post-war period and the European

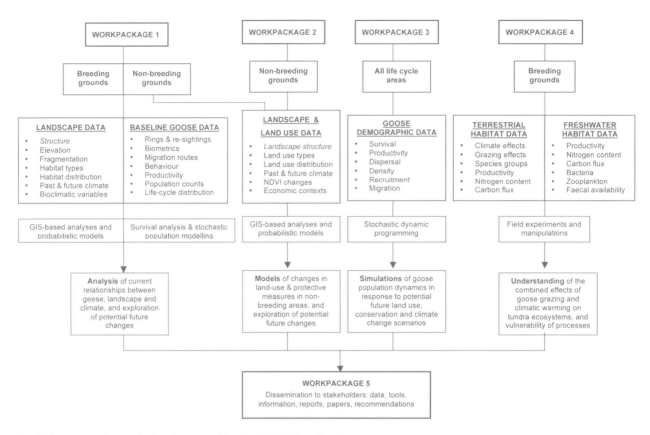

Fig. 4. Flyway area, data, methods and outputs of the five FRAGILE work packages.

economy became more service-oriented, the proportion of the labour force working on the land dropped from more than 20% in the 1950s to 5% today. However, more than ten million Europeans still work in the agricultural sector and more than 40% of the land area is dedicated to food production. Agricultural intensification in the European Union has been facilitated by the development of the Common Agricultural Policy (CAP) in the 1960s, which had the effect of favourably regulating internal and external agricultural markets. During the 1980s, the prohibitive costs associated with maintaining the CAP and a number of trade disputes with other countries prompted the EU to adopt a series of policy reforms in 1992. The "MacSharry reforms" led to reductions in domestic intervention prices, the introduction of compensatory payments, and the implementation of compulsory land "set aside" provisions (Patterson 1997, Matthews 1996, Dauberg 2003). These reforms were further developed and extended through Agenda 2000. The EU has recently expanded its area to include ten central and eastern European countries. Further CAP reforms are, therefore, necessary and are currently being developed and implemented.

These important changes in agricultural policy have been accompanied by the additional drivers of rapidly shifting consumer food preferences, and changes in crop phenology resulting from new "cold hardy" plant varieties that can be sown in winter (Commission of the European Communities 2003). This dynamic and often radically changing system has meant huge changes in what is grown, where it is grown, how it is grown, and when it is grown. In the past, Svalbard geese have spent the winter months on a mixture of naturally occurring salt-marsh (merse) and other coastal and estuarine habitats. Most Svalbard Barnacle Geese spend the winter on the Scottish side of the Solway Firth, whilst Pink-footed Geese winter principally

in Denmark, The Netherlands and Belgium. Both populations now spend a considerable proportion of the winter feeding on agricultural fields, pastures and polders (Pink-footed Geese: Fox *et al.* 2005). This alteration in habitat preference has been a result of the geese exploiting new opportunities presented by changes in agricultural production methods and timing, as well as declines in the quality and extent of "natural" habitats.

Several studies have now attempted to analyse future changes in land use and agriculture through the use of scenario development techniques (for a review see Alcamo *et al.* in press). How human societies, technology and the climate will evolve in the future is simply unknown, and prediction of changes in these drivers is simply not possible. In the face of such large uncertainties, scenario development is an important research and decision support tool that can assist in the exploration of alternative futures. Scenarios of changes in the agriculture sector have now explored the role of socio-economic, policy, technology and climate change on future land use and agricultural production strategies (e.g. Alcamo *et al.* in press, Abildtrup *et al.* 2006, Ewert *et al.* in press, Rounsevell *et al.* in press). Whilst each scenario has its own particular assumptions and interpretations, a general trend from many scenarios is of declining agricultural land-use areas. Some scenarios also suggest an increase in extensive land management practices either in combination with declining areas, or as an adaptation to the pressures that cause the area changes. Whilst such trends do not constitute a prediction, they suggest very strongly that future agricultural landscapes will be very different from the present. One of the major areas of concern for goose population dynamics is that grassland areas may decline significantly in some regions of Europe. This will result from continued technological development and the reduced demand for livestock products, but also depends entirely on the ways in which policy makers will or will not respond to such developments. Currently, large areas of agricultural grassland in Europe are protected through measures such as the Less Favoured Areas scheme (LFAs). Thus, the future of goose over-wintering sites may depend as much on future European rural development policy as on, for example, the direct effects of climate change. Most authors seem to agree that climate change will, in practice, have a much less important effect on agriculture in north-west Europe than socio-economic, technological and policy change (Rounsevell *et al.* 2006). There is still an open question, however, about what will happen to the areas of land that are no longer used for agriculture. Further development in the cultivation of bioenergy crops (such as biofuels, short-rotation coppice or *Myscanthus*) seems plausible, but the "abandonment" of agricultural land in some areas seems likely. These types of land-use changes will have important implications for goose overwintering areas.

## DEVELOPING AN "INTEGRATED" APPROACH
### European framework research
Every four years, the European Commission sets out a "framework" of the priorities for research, technological development and demonstration activities to be commissioned during a particular time period. Framework 5 (1998 to 2002) included an area of work on "Global Change, Climate and Biodiversity", with a sub-action on "Ecosystem vulnerability". The aim was to "develop the scientific, technological and socio-economic basis and tools necessary for the study and understanding of changes in the environment". In 2002, a partnership of twelve organizations and universities across Europe put together a successful bid for funding under Framework 5. The research team combined the requisite skills, experience, knowledge and long-term data needed to attempt a holistic flyway level study. The study was called: "FRagility of Arctic Goose habitats: Impacts of conservation, Land use and climate changE" (FRAGILE).

### Project drivers
The development of the project was precipitated by five observations:

* The effects of global climate change will be most acute at high latitudes;
* The distribution and abundance of many tundra breeding geese have been increasing for 40 years;
* Arctic tundra ecosystems can be functionally damaged if over-grazed by geese;
* Severe alterations to tundra result in system switches, i.e. from carbon sink to source; and
* Interactions between geese and agricultural interests in north-west Europe have increased as geese have exploited new agricultural areas during the wintering period.

These observations and the potential impacts arising from them have been recognized (and studied) within individual fields of expertise for some time. But scientists, conservationists, competent agencies, and stakeholder groups recognized a large gap in our knowledge in terms of the interactions and combined effects of these factors at large spatial extents (flyway level). Developing strategies, legal instruments and management regimes to address potential impacts requires outputs that: (a) quantify the current ecosystem/flyway state, and then (b) allow

a range of potential future states to be explored on the basis of different socio-economic and climate scenarios. The FRAGILE project was therefore designed to integrate the five driver elements (above) and answer questions within four main areas:

* *Goose populations*: what have been the primary demographic parameters driving population changes?
* *Tundra landscapes*: how are tundra habitats distributed in relation to landscape and climatic factors, and how are geese spatio-temporally distributed within and between available habitats?
* *European land use*: how is European land use influenced by landscape, policy, socio-economic factors and climate?
* *Tundra ecosystems*: how do climate and grazing by geese influence tundra ecosystem function?

These areas form the main themes of the FRAGILE project. In their own right, each will generate a range of extremely useful data, information and analyses. However, the central rationale of the project is to integrate the four elements to provide:

* An understanding of the environmental and climatic drivers of observed changes in goose population parameters. This will allow an exploration of how the distribution and abundance of goose populations might change given a range of future socio-economic, land use and climate scenarios; and
* An understanding of which tundra ecosystem processes are most vulnerable to the combined effects of goose grazing pressure and climatic warming, and an ability to determine thresholds for ecosystem degradation.

Using the above framework, the overall project aim is therefore to provide a mechanistic and explorative basis for understanding the relationships between goose populations, habitats and land use. The three major contexts to this research framework are climate change, European socio-economic and agricultural policies, and international conservation instruments.

### Stakeholder engagement
The project will produce a range of outputs in the form of data, information, models, analyses, exploration tools, reports, scientific papers, etc. An explicit element of the FRAGILE approach has been to engage stakeholders and potential end-users of these outputs. A stakeholder group was established at the start of the project, and a workshop held. This served to inform the group of proposed methods and outputs, and provided an opportunity to discuss and incorporate stakeholder perspectives. A post-project stakeholder workshop will also be convened.

### Methods, data sources and integration
The project is divided into a series of discrete "work packages", representing different skill, knowledge and data groupings within the FRAGILE research team. Fig. 4 shows the data requirements, generic methods and analytical outputs of the five work packages. The vast amount of data and information used within the work packages was accessed from five generic sources:

* *Monitoring data*: counts of birds and productivity assessments at key sites, largely provided through volunteer-based moni-

toring schemes and records from individual fieldworkers;

- *Ringing and re-sighting data*: records of individually marked birds, again largely sustained by volunteer-based activities and records from key fieldworkers;
- *Remote sensing data*: Landscape and climate data in the form of satellite images, and data from satellite tracking devices attached to migrating geese;
- *Publicly accessible data*: Climate, land use and many other types of data available on the internet or on request from specific institutions; and
- *Empirical field data*: behavioural observations, experimental plots and habitat ground-truthing.

Fig. 5 schematically represents the integration of outputs from the different work elements.

### How can outputs from flyway studies be utilized?
Outputs from integrated research of this nature have a variety of direct and indirect uses. Through pro-active dissemination to appropriate agencies, FRAGILE data, information, models, simulation tools and recommendations will be used to support policy and legislative instruments within the Svalbard-North-west Europe flyway (and possibly beyond). The major relevant instruments are shown in Table 1. Most of these instruments were created in such a way as to respond directly to what was, at the time, perceived to be the main environmental problem, i.e. habitat loss. Whilst habitat loss and degradation remain major environmental issues, climate change may speed up these processes, render them irreversible in many areas, or create a new suite of issues not adequately addressed by the obligations and actions of established legislative instruments (Boere 2003). For example, UNEP/CMS (2002) identified that climate change will impact migratory species by (1) changing physiological responses, (2) altering the timing of life-cycle events, (3) changing the physical location, extent and condition of breeding,

staging and wintering areas, and (4) altering atmospheric and oceanic circulation thus impacting elements such as food resources. Whilst it would be impossible to alter current international conventions in the light of these new factors, it is vital that information on all impacts of climate change are made available to competent agencies involved in their implementation. This is a major role of integrated projects such as FRAGILE and the exploratory tools they can produce. The ability to explore potential population and behavioural outcomes in response to a range of future scenarios also provides an invaluable tool in formulating and improving local, national and flyway level goose management policies (Kruse *et al.* 2004).

In addition to outputs such as data, models, simulation tools, etc., projects that attempt to analyse and integrate such a wide gamut of data also provide other indirect strategic benefits. For example, the FRAGILE project has highlighted the importance of financial support for volunteer-based monitoring activities (often seen as a poor cousin to "hard science"). Long-term, repeated measure, large-scale monitoring and ringing data are central pillars to flyway research, although our analyses have also identified a number of shortcomings in these data where improvements and modifications could be made. These will be fed back to relevant organizations and individuals and reported in later papers. The project has also provided useful lessons in relation to the actual process of attempting such a large integrated flyway research programme (considered in more detail below), and in identifying future research needs.

### DISCUSSION
At the time of writing, the FRAGILE project still has a year left to run, and our results, data, models and other outputs will be published elsewhere. The aim of this paper is to provide a working example of: (1) how an integrated and flyway level project can be constructed; (2) the types of data required; (3) the types of outputs that can be produced; and (4) how the outputs

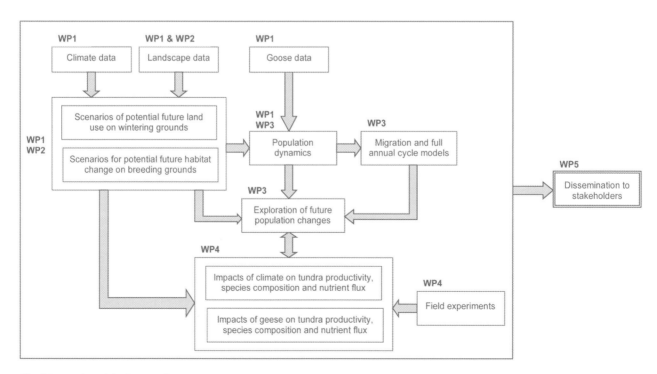

**Fig. 5.** Integration of the five FRAGILE work packages (WP1-5).

**Table 1. Key legislative instruments where FRAGILE outputs can be used.**

| Legislative instrument | Relevant articles | Relevant actions |
|---|---|---|
| Council Directive on the conservation of wild birds | Articles 2, 3.1, 3.2, 4.1b, 4.1c, 4.1d, 4.2, 4.3, 4.4, 7.4, 10.1, 10.2, 12. | Deterioration of habitats within and outside SPAs; protection of habitats for migratory species; information needed to ensure sustainable use of quarry species; encouraging research on bird population dynamics; national reporting. |
| Council Directive on the conservation of natural habitats and of wild fauna and flora | Articles 2.1, 2.2, 2.3, 3, 4, 6.1, 6.2, 10, 11, 12.1d, 17, 18.1, 18.2. | Protection of goose wintering areas; research needs for protecting habitats; inventory of important sites; development of management plans; prevention of deterioration of breeding habitats; national reporting. |
| Framework Convention on Climate Change | Articles 5a-b, 6, 9, 12 Decision 5/CP.1 Recommendation 9/CP.3 Kyoto Protocol. | Methodologies and tools to evaluate climate change impacts and adaptation; transference of scientific knowledge; quantification of C and N fluxes; assessment of ecosystems as carbon sources/sinks. |
| Ramsar Convention on Wetlands | Articles 3.2, 4.4. Operational objectives 2.5, 2.7, 3.1, 3.2, 5, 6. | Prevention of ecological change of wetlands; encourage research and data exchange; environmental impact assessment; management including local people; develop education and public awareness of wetland habitats and issues. |
| Convention on Biological Diversity | Articles 7a-d, 12a-c, 13a-b, 17.1, 17.2, 25. | Identification of processes and categories of human activities likely to have adverse effects on habitats and species; encourage research and training; raise public awareness; exchange of scientific and technological information; national reporting. |
| Convention on the Conservation of Migratory Species of Wild Animals | Articles 2.3a, 3.4a, 5.5b-f. | Promotion of research into migratory species; conservation of habitats for migratory species; develop management plans; research ecology and population dynamics of migratory species; exchange information; maintain networks of suitable sites; AEWA Action Plan. |
| Convention on the Conservation of European Wildlife and Natural Habitats | Articles 2, 4.3, 4.4, 5, 10.1, 11b, 14. SC recommendation 3/84. | Maintenance of tundra habitats and species; establishment of peatland inventories. Norway has agreed to include Svalbard under this convention (except with reference to the Arctic Fox *Alopex lagopus*). |
| European Landscape Convention | Articles 5, 6a-c, 7, 8, 9. | Promotion of landscape protection; information on landscapes and transformation threats; raising public awareness; trans-frontier co-operation. |
| Pan-European Biological and Landscape Diversity Strategy | Action themes 1.1, 1.4, 3.1, 3.2, 4.1, 7.1, 7.2, 7.5. | European ecological network sites in goose wintering areas; Action 7.5 focuses on regions with emphasis on tundra in northern Europe. |
| Council Directive on reporting | Transfer of information from Member States to European Commission. | Results will be submitted for national reporting under Birds & Habitats Directives, FCCC, CBD, CMS, Berne, Ramsar. |

can be used for conservation and sustainable resource management. We also hope that lessons can be learnt from some of the problems encountered during the implementation of the research.

The varied nature and sheer volume of the data required are two major problems with undertaking a research programme at ecosystem level. Many of the data are in "raw" format (from field observations) and need to be collated, managed, manipulated and interrogated. This raises a range of issues in terms of quality assessment and control, and where "sampling" data are used, information about sampling effort is required. Where long-term species data are employed, there can be significant changes in the number and quality of observers within the temporal extent of the data, as well as changes in the spatial extent of the data. The analytical methods for analysing presence/absence data and changes in species/habitat distributions also need careful consideration and methodological development in relation to the types of data available to the study (Fielding & Bell 1997, Brito *et al.* 1999, Thuiller *et al.* 2003, Wisz 2004). Even the range and spatial scale of information from satellites have changed radically in the last ten years. At the opposite end of the scale, where field-based data are newly acquired, three years of

research funding may not be an adequate time-scale for observation. It is also true that for research into some ecosystems, data at any spatial or temporal scale simply will not be available.

Using an enormous amount of varied environmental data from a range of sources also requires a broad array of appropriate data management and analytical skills within the collaborating research groups. This and other factors inevitably make the costs of research at this scale a significant aspect of attempts to fund such work. It will therefore be important to learn and disseminate lessons from the FRAGILE project, as well as to develop rapid assessment techniques in parallel with more detailed research programmes (Boere 2003). One of the other major lessons is that true integration of outputs needs to be carefully considered. It is very easy to implement a study where different elements are being researched independently and are merely under the same project title, but quite a different matter to ensure that outputs and results (not just data) from one group are actually being utilized within the conceptual framework of the research in another collaborating group.

One of the most important features of the FRAGILE project has been the avoidance of references to making "predictions".

A prediction implies a single discernible trajectory or end point for the processes being studied. For many elements of the project, this would have been at best irrelevant, and at worst enormously misleading. Instead, the project is seeking to present species, habitat and system responses under a range of potential future scenarios of climatic, environmental and socio-economic change. Whilst in some quarters this tool-based and explorative approach might be perceived as not producing "concrete" results, it is in fact of far greater application to the intended stakeholder groups.

An explorative approach also recognizes that potential changes in habitat-species associations under new scenarios of climate change will present a number of difficult issues in relation to developing appropriate conservation and management strategies. At the present time, most strategies, conventions, action plans and management policies are fundamentally centred on "current" and narrowly defined ecosystem assemblages. However, differential species' responses to climate change will almost certainly lead to structural and phenological realignment between species comprising an ecosystem, thus making it likely that some current definitions (e.g. those within the current EC Habitats Directive) will cease to exist (Visser *et al.* 1998, Carpenter & Turner 2000). This is also another reason why integrating field experimentation (e.g. the FRAGILE manipulations on Svalbard) is so important in evaluating the combined impacts of climate change on the structure and function of systems, and empirically testing causal links suggested by analyses of numbers from monitoring, etc. Far more research of this nature (i.e. exploring re-combination and structuring at an ecosystem level) is urgently needed.

## ACKNOWLEDGEMENTS

The FRAGILE project was funded by the EC under Framework 5, and is a collaboration between 13 organizations and universities across Europe. We would like to take this opportunity to acknowledge the work of all members of the team.

## REFERENCES

**Abildtrup, J., Audsley, E., Fekete-Farkas, M., Giupponi, C., Gylling, M., Rosato, P. & Rounsevell, M.** 2006. Socio-economic scenario development for assessment of climate change impacts on agricultural land use. Environmental Science and Policy 9 (2): 101-115.

**Alcamo, J., Kok, K., Busch, G., Priess, J., Eickhout, B., Rounsevell, M., Rothman, D. & Heistermann M.** In press. Searching for the future of land: scenarios from the local to global scale. Chapter 8. In: H. Geist & E. Lambin (eds) The LUCC Synthesis book, Springer-Verlag.

**Alisauskas, R.T.** 2002. Arctic climate, spring nutrition, and recruitment in midcontinent lesser snow geese. Journal of Wildlife Management 66 (1): 181-193.

**Antoniades, D., Douglas, M.S.V. & Smol, J.P.** 2003. Comparative physical and chemical limnology of two Canadian high arctic regions: Alert (Ellesmere Island, NU) and Mould Bay (Prince Patrick Island, NWT). Archiv fur Hydrobiologie 158 (4): 485-516.

**Black, J.M.** 1998. Movement of barnacle geese between colonies in Svalbard and the colonisation process. In: F. Mehlum, J.M. Black & J. Madsen (eds) Research on

Arctic Geese. Proceedings of the Svalbard Goose Symposium, Oslo, Norway, 23-26 September 1997. Norsk Polarinstitutt Skrifter 200: 115-128.

**Black, J.M., Deerenberg, C. & Owen, M.** 1991. Foraging behaviour and site selection of barnacle geese *Branta leucopsis* in a traditional and newly colonised spring staging habitat. Ardea 79: 349-358.

**Boere, G.C.** 2003. Global activities on the conservation, management and sustainable use of migratory water-birds: an integrated flyway/ecosystem approach. Wader Study Group Bulletin 100: 96-101.

**Botkin, D.** 1990. Discordant harmonies. Oxford University Press, New York, USA.

**Brito, J.C., Crespo, E.G. & Paulo, O.S.** 1999. Modelling wildlife distributions: logistic multiple regression vs overlap analysis. Ecography 22: 251-260.

**Brooks, P.D., McKnight, D. & Elder, K.** 2005. Carbon limitation of soil respiration under winter snowpacks: potential feedbacks between growing season and winter carbon fluxes. Global Change Biology 11 (2): 231-238.

**Caro, T., Engilis, A., Fitzherbert, E. & Gardner, T.** 2004. Preliminary assessment of the flagship species concept at a small scale. Animal Conservation 7 (1): 63-70.

**Carpenter, S.R. & Turner, M.G.** 2000. Hares and tortoises: Interactions of fast and slow variables in ecosystems. Ecosystems 3 (6): 495-497.

**Chapin, F.S., Peterson, G., Berkes, F., Callaghan, T.V., Angelstam, P., Apps, M., Beier, C., Bergeron, Y., Crepin, A.S., Danell, K., Elmqvist, T., Folke, C., Forbes, B., Fresco, N., Juday, G., Niemela, J., Shvidenko, A. & Whiteman, G.** 2004. Resilience and vulnerability of northern regions to social and environmental change. Ambio 33 (6): 344-349.

**Choudhury, S., Black, J.M. & Owen, M.** 1996. Body size, fitness and compatibility in barnacle geese *Branta leucopsis*. Ibis 138 (4): 700-709.

**Clausen, M.** 1996. Variability of global biome patterns as a function of initial and boundary conditions in a climate model. Climate Dynamics 12: 371-379.

**Commission of the European Communities** 2003. The agricultural situation in the European Union: 2002 Report. Report in conjunction with the General Report on the Activities of the European Union, 2002. Brussels and Luxembourg.

**Cooch, E.G., Lank, D.B., Rockwell, R.F. & Cooke, F.** 1991. Long-term decline in body size in a snow goose population - evidence of environmental degradation. Journal of Animal Ecology 60 (2): 483-496.

**Cope, D.R., Pettifor, R.A., Griffin, L.R. & Rowcliffe, J.M.** 2003. Integrating farming and wildlife conservation: the Barnacle Goose Management Scheme. Biological Conservation 110 (1): 113-122.

**Daugbjerg, C.** 2003. Policy feedback and paradigm shift in EU agricultural policy: the effects of the MacSharry reform on future reform. Journal of European Public Policy 10 (3): 421-437.

**Denny, M.J.H., Clausen, P., Percival, S.M., Anderson, G.Q.A., Koffijberg, K. & Robinson, J.A.** 2004. 2004 Light-bellied Brent Goose *Branta bernicla hrota* (East Atlantic population) in Svalbard, Greenland, Franz Josef

Land, Norway, Denmark, the Netherlands and Britain 1960/61 - 2000/01. Waterbird Review Series, The Wildfowl & Wetlands Trust/Joint Nature Conservation Committee, Slimbridge, UK.

Ebbinge, B.S., Meulen, H. van der & Smit, J.J. 1984. Changes in winter distribution and population size of the pink-footed geese in Svalbard. Norsk Polarinstitutt Skrifter 181: 11-17.

Epstein, H.E., Beringer, J., Gould, W.A., Lloyd, A.H., Thompson, C.D., Chapin, F.S., Michaelson, G.J., Ping, C.L., Rupp, T.S. & Walker, D.A. 2004. The nature of spatial transitions in the Arctic. Journal of Biogeography 31 (12): 1917-1933.

Ewert, F., Rounsevell, M.D.A., Reginster, I., Metzger, M. & Leemans, R. In press. Future scenarios of European agricultural land use. I: Estimating changes in crop productivity. Agriculture, Ecosystems and Environment.

Fahnestock, J.T., Jones, M.H. & Welker, J.M. 1999. Wintertime $CO_2$ efflux from arctic soils: Implications for annual carbon budgets. Global Biogeochemical Cycles 13 (3): 775-779.

Fielding, A.H. & Bell, J.F. 1997. A review of methods for the assessment of prediction errors in conservation presence/absence models. Environmental Conservation 24: 38-49.

Forbes, B.C., Ebersole, J.J. & Strandberg, B. 2001. Anthropogenic disturbance and patch dynamics in circumpolar arctic ecosystems. Conservation Biology 15 (4): 954-969.

Fox, A.D., Madsen, J., Boyd, H., Kuijken, E., Norriss, D.W., Tombre, I.M. & Stroud, D.A. 2005. Effects of agricultural change on abundance, fitness components and distribution of two arctic-nesting goose populations. Global Change Biology 11 (6): 881-893.

Francis, C.M., Richards, M.H., Cooke, F. & Rockwell, R.F. 1992. Long-term changes in survival rates of lesser snow geese. Ecology 73 (4): 1346-1362.

Frederiksen, M., Hearn, R.D., Mitchell, C., Sigfusson, A., Swann, R.L. & Fox, A.D. 2004. The dynamics of hunted Icelandic goose populations: a reassessment of the evidence. Journal of Applied Ecology 41 (2): 315-334.

Gilmanov, T.G. & Oechel, W.C. 1995. New estimates of organic matter reserves and net primary productivity of the North American tundra ecosystems. Journal of Biogeography 22 (4-5): 723-741.

Graneli, W., Bertilsson, S. & Philibert, A. 2004. Phosphorus limitation of bacterial growth in high Arctic lakes and ponds. Aquatic Sciences 66 (4): 430-439.

Gullestad, N., Owen, M. & Nugent, M.J. 1984. Numbers and distribution of Barnacle Geese *Branta leucopsis* on Norwegian staging islands and the importance of the staging area to the Svalbard population. Norsk Polarinstitutt Skrifter 181: 57-65.

Hartig, J.H., Zarull, M.A. & Law, N.L. 1998. An ecosystem approach to Great Lakes management: Practical steps. Journal of Great Lakes Research 24 (3): 739-750.

Hoffman, S.W., Smith, J.P. & Meehan, T.D. 2002. Breeding grounds, winter ranges, and migratory routes of raptors in the Mountain West. Journal of Raptor Research 36 (2): 97-110.

Hötker, H., Lebedeva, E., Tomkovich, P.S., Gromadzka, J., Davidson, N.C., Evans, J., Stroud, D.A., West, R.B. (eds).1998. Migration and international conservation of waders: Research and conservation on north Asian, African and European flyways. International Wader Studies 10. 500pp.

Huang, S., Pollack, H.N. & Shen, P.Y. 2000. Temperature trends over the past five centuries reconstructed from borehole temperatures. Nature 403: 756-758.

IPCC 2001. IPCC Third Assessment Report: Climate Change 2001. International Panel on Climate Change, Geneva, Switzerland.

Jano, A.P., Jefferies, R.L. & Rockwell, R.F. 1998. The detection of vegetational change by multitemporal analysis of LANDSAT data: the effects of goose foraging. Journal of Ecology 86 (1): 93-99.

Jones, P.D. & Mann, M.E. 2004. Climate over the past millennia. Reviews of Geophysics 42: RG2002, doi:10.1029/2003RG000143.

Jones, P.D., Briffa, K.R., Barnett, T.P. & Tett, S.F.B. 1998. High-resolution paleoclimatic records for the last millennium: interpretation, integration and comparison with General Circulation Model control-run temperatures. The Holocene 8: 455-471.

Klaassen, M., Madsen, J., Bauer, S. & Tombre, I. 2006. Modelling behavioural and fitness consequences of disturbance for geese along their spring flyway. Journal of Applied Ecology 43 (1): 92-100.

Kruse, J.A., White, R.G., Epstein, H.E., Archie, B., Berman, M., Braund, S.R., Chapin, F.S., Charlie, J., Daniel, C.J., Eamer, J., Flanders, N., Griffith, B., Haley, S., Huskey, L., Joseph, B., Klein, D.R., Kofinas, G.P., Martin, S.M., Murphy, S.M., Nebesky, W., Nicolson, C., Russell, D.E., Tetlichi, J., Tussing, A., Walker, M.D. & Young, O.R. 2004. Modelling sustainability of arctic communities: An interdisciplinary collaboration of researchers and local knowledge holders. Ecosystems 7 (8): 815-828.

Madsen, J. 1991. Status and trends of goose populations in the Western Palearctic in the 1980s. Ardea 79 (2): 113-122.

Madsen, J. 1995. Impacts of disturbance on migratory waterfowl. Ibis 137: S67 – S74

Madsen, J. & Klaassen, M. 2006. Assessing body condition and energy budget components by scoring abdominal profiles in free-ranging pink-footed geese *Anser brachyrhynchus*. Journal of Avian biology 37 (3): 283.

Madsen, J., Bregnballe, T. & Mehlum, F. 1989. Study of the Breeding Ecology and Behaviour of the Svalbard Population of Light-Bellied Brent Goose (*Branta bernicla hrota*). Polar Research 7: 1-21.

Madsen, J., Bregnballe, T. & Hastrup, A. 1992. Impact of the Arctic Fox *Alopex lagopus* on nesting success of geese in southeast Svalbard, 1989. Polar Research 11 (2): 35-39.

Madsen, J., Reed, A. & Andreev, A. 1996. Status and trends of geese (*Anser* sp., *Branta* sp.) in the world: Review, updating and evaluation. Gibier Faune Sauvage, Game and Wildlife 13: 337-353.

**Madsen, J., Cracknell, G. & Fox, A.D.** 1999. Goose Populations of the Western Palearctic. A review of status and distribution. Wetlands International Publication No. 48, Wetlands International, Wageningen, The Netherlands; National Environmental Research Institute, Rønde, Denmark.

**Madsen, J., Frederiksen, M. & Ganter, B.** 2002. Trends in annual and seasonal survival of Pink-footed Geese *Anser brachyrhynchus*. Ibis 144 (2): 218-226.

**Malcolm, S.A. & ReVelle, C.** 2002. Rebuilding migratory flyways using directed conditional covering. Environmental Modelling and Assessment 7 (2): 129-138.

**Matthews, A.** 1996. The disappearing budget constraint on EU agricultural policy. Food Policy 21 (6): 497-508.

**McGuire, A.D., Wirth, C., Apps, M., Beringer, J., Clein, J., Epstein, H., Kicklighter, D.W., Bhatti, J., Chapin, F.S., de Groot, B., Efremov, D., Eugster, W., Fukuda, M., Gower, T., Hinzman, L., Huntley, B., Jia, G.J., Kasischke, E., Melillo, J., Romanovsky, V., Shvidenko, A., Vaganov, E. & Walker, D.** 2002. Environmental variation, vegetation distribution, carbon dynamics and water/energy exchange at high latitudes. Journal of Vegetation Science 13 (3): 301-314.

**Mitchell, C., Black, J.M. & Evans, M.** 1998. Breeding success of cliff-nesting and island-nesting barnacle geese in Svalbard. In: F. Mehlum, J.M. Black & J. Madsen (eds) Research on Arctic Geese. Proceedings of the Svalbard Goose Symposium, Oslo, Norway, 23-26 September 1997. Norsk Polarinstitutt Skrifter 200: 141-146.

**O'Connell, M.J.** 2003. Detecting, measuring and reversing changes to wetlands. Wetland Ecology and Management 11 (6): 397-401.

**O'Connell, M.J. & Yallop, M.L.** 2002. Research needs in relation to the conservation of biodiversity in the UK. Biological Conservation 103: 115-123.

**Odum, E.P.** 1953. Fundamentals of ecology. W.B. Saunders, Philadelphia, Pennsylvania, USA.

**O'Neill, R.V.** 2001. Is it time to bury the ecosystem concept? (with full military honors, of course!) Ecology 82 (12) 3275–3284.

**Otis, D.L.** 2004. Mallard harvest distributions in the Atlantic and Mississippi flyways during periods of restrictive and liberal hunting regulations. Journal of Wildlife Management 68 (2): 351-359.

**Patterson, I.J.** 1991. Conflict between geese and agriculture - does goose grazing cause damage to crops? Ardea 79 (2): 178-186.

**Patterson, L.A.** 1997. Agricultural policy reform in the European community: A three-level game analysis. International Organization 51 (1): 135-165.

**Pettifor, R.A., Black, J.M., Owen, M., Rowcliffe, J.M. & Patterson, D.** 1998. Growth of the Svalbard barnacle goose *Branta leucopsis* winter population 1958-1996: An initial review of temporal demographic changes. In: F. Mehlum, J.M. Black & J. Madsen (eds) Research on Arctic Geese. Proceedings of the Svalbard Goose Symposium, Oslo, Norway, 23-26 September 1997. Norsk Polarinstitutt Skrifter 200: 147-164.

**Pettifor, R.A., Caldow, R.W.G., Rowcliffe, J.M., Goss-Custard, J.D., Black, J.M., Hodder, K.H., Houston, A.I., Lang, A. & Webb, J.** 2000. Spatially explicit, indi-vidual-based, behavioural models of the annual cycle of two migratory goose populations. Journal of Applied Ecology 37: 103-135.

**Prop, J. & Black, J.M.** 1998. Food intake, body reserves and reproductive success of barnacle geese *Branta leucopsis* staging in different habitats. Norsk Polarinstitutt Skrifter 200: 175-193.

**Prop, J., Black, J.M., Shimmings, P. & Owen, M.** 1998. Expansion of the spring staging area of Barnacle Geese in relation to food limitation. Biological Conservation 86: 339-346.

**Prop, J., Black, J.M. & Shimmings, P.** 2003. Travel schedules to the high arctic: barnacle geese trade-off the timing of migration with accumulation of fat deposits. Oikos 103 (2): 403-414.

**Rounsevell, M.D.A., Ewert, F., Reginster, I., Leemans, R. & Carter, T.R.** In press. Future scenarios of European agricultural land use. II: Projecting changes in cropland and grassland. Agriculture, Ecosystems and Environment.

**Rounsevell, M.D.A, Reginster, I., Araújo, M.B., Carter, T.R., Dendoncker, N., Ewert, F., House, J.I., Kankaanpää, S., Leemans, R., Metzger, M.J., Schmit, C., Smith, P. & Tuck, G.** 2006. A coherent set of future land use change scenarios for Europe. Agriculture, Ecosystems and Environment 114: 57-68.

**Schmutz, J.A., Rockwell, R.F. & Petersen, M.R.** 1997. Relative effects of survival and reproduction on the population dynamics of emperor geese. Journal of Wildlife Management 61: 191-201.

**Scott, D.A. & Rose, P.M.** 1996. Atlas of Anatidae Populations in Africa and Western Eurasia. Wetlands International Publication No. 41, Wageningen, The Netherlands.

**Shimmings, P.** 1998. Hvitkinngås ved rasteplasser langs norskekysten - forandringer i områdebruk medfører konflikt med jordbruksinteresser. Vår Fuglefauna 21: 11-15. (In Norwegian).

**Shimmings, P.** 2003. Spring staging by Barnacle Geese *Branta leucopsis*, and the effects of a management plan in the Herøy district in Nordland, Norway. Report to Directorate for Nature Management.

**Therkildsen, O.R. & Madsen, J.** 2000. Energetics of feeding on winter wheat versus pasture grasses: a window of oppor-tunity for winter range expansion in the pink-footed goose *Anser brachyrhynchus*. Wildlife Biology 6 (2): 65-74.

**Thuiller, W., Araujo, M.B. & Lavorel, S.** 2003. Generalised models versus classification tree analysis: predicting spatial distributions of plant species at different scales. Journal of Vegetation Science 14: 669-680.

**Tombre, I.M., Black, J.M. & Loonen, M.J.J.E.** 1998. Critical components in the dynamics of a barnacle goose colony: a sensitivity analysis. Norsk Polarinstitutt Skrifter 200: 81-89.

**Tombre, I.M., Madsen, J., Tømmervik, H. & Eythórsson, E.** 2004. Vårrastende kortnebbgjess i Vesterålen. Konflikter med landbruket, årsaker og konsekvenser. NINA Report: NINA Fagrapport 77. Norsk institutt for naturforskning. (In Norwegian).

**Trinder, M., Rowcliffe, M., Pettifor, R., Rees, E. & Griffin, L.** 2005. Status and population viability of Svalbard barnacle geese. Information paper.

**UNEP/CMS** 2002. Biodiversity in Motion. Migratory Species and their Value to Sustainable Development. A CMS/Secretariat contribution to the World Summit on Sustainable Development, 26 August – 4 September 2002, South Africa. http://www.wcmc.org.uk/cms/cop7/list_of_docs/WSSDmotion.html.

**van Eerden, M.R., Zijlstra, M., van Roomen, M. & Timmerman, A.** 1996. The response of Anatidae to changes in agricultural practice: long-term shifts in the carrying capacity of wintering waterfowl. Gibier Faune Sauvage, Game and Wildlife 13: 681-706.

**Visser, M.E., van Noordwijk, A.J., Tinbergen, J.M. & Lessells, C.M.** 1998. Warmer springs lead to mistimed reproduction in great tits (*Parus major*). Proceedings of the Royal Society of London, Series B 265: 1867-1870.

**Waelbroeck, C., Monfray, P., Oechel, W.C., Hastings, S. & Vourlitis, G.** 1997. The impact of permafrost thawing on the carbon dynamics of tundra. Geophysical Research Letters 24 (3): 229-232.

**Wang, H.L.** 2004. Ecosystem management and its application to large marine ecosystems: Science, law, and politics. Ocean Development And International Law 35 (1): 41-74.

**Weaver, A.J. & Green, C.** 1998. Global climate change: Lessons from the past - policy for the future. Ocean and Coastal Management 39 (1-2): 73-86.

**Wetlands International** 2002. Waterbird Population Estimates – Third Edition. Wetlands International Global Series No. 12, Wageningen, The Netherlands.

**Wisz, M.S.** 2004. Modelling Potential Distributions of Sub-Saharan Birds: Techniques and Applications for Conservation and Macroecology. Unpublished PhD thesis, University of Cambridge, UK.

**Zöckler, C.** 1998. Patterns in Biodiversity in Arctic Birds. World Conservation Monitoring Centre Bulletin 3.

Integrated population monitoring, such as that which has been undertaken for the population of Greenland White-fronted Geese *Anser albifrons flavirostris* over 20 years, provides the best chance of understanding the nature and consequences of climate change impacts on waterbirds. Photo: Alyn Walsh.

# Climate change and coastal waterbirds: the United Kingdom experience reviewed

*Mark M. Rehfisch & Graham E. Austin*

*British Trust for Ornithology, The Nunnery, Thetford, IP24 2PU, UK.  (email: Mark.Rehfisch@bto.org)*

Rehfisch, M.M. & Austin, G.E. 2006. Climate change and coastal waterbirds: the United Kingdom experience reviewed. *Waterbirds around the world*.  Eds. G.C. Boere, C.A. Galbraith & D.A. Stroud.  The Stationery Office, Edinburgh, UK.  pp. 398-404.

## ABSTRACT

Climate change is occurring world-wide, and its effects are already visible in species and their habitats. The internationally important populations of waterbirds in the UK, and waders in particular, are already affected by climate change. So far, changes in distribution, timing of arrival to winter and to breed, and laying dates have been linked to it. Changes in the distributions of certain wintering waders, linked to changing winter temperatures, have affected the proportions of their flyway populations on sites designated as being of conservation importance for the species. This has major implications for conservation policy. Waders are declining in the UK and world-wide, and it is possible that climate change is in part responsible, both directly by affecting their energy balance, and indirectly by affecting the availability, quantity and quality of their habitats. Waders appear to be good indicators of climate change, and the development of reliable scenarios of waterbird distributions occurring under future, changed climate scenarios would help with nature conservation planning, raise public awareness and, perhaps, lead to constructive political action to curb greenhouse gas emissions. However, before such scenarios can be developed, much work is necessary to help define appropriate parameters for such models.

## INTRODUCTION

Globally, the ten hottest years on record occurred between 1991 and 2004; during the last century temperatures have risen by 0.6ºC, and global sea level has risen by 20 cm (Houghton *et al.* 2001). Ice caps are disappearing from mountain peaks, and Arctic sea ice has thinned by 40% (Wadhams 1997). Thus, climate change is occurring and the causal link to increased greenhouse emissions is established (Houghton *et al.* 2001). The Chief Scientific Adviser to the British Government has suggested that climate change is the most severe problem being faced today (King 2004). In 2003, in France and the United Kingdom (UK), 20 000 people died as a consequence of an unprecedented heat wave that the French Ministry of the Environment expects to occur henceforth every three to four years. By 2080, extreme tidal events that are now expected in the UK once every 100 years could be occurring every three years, and 3.5 million people could be at "high" risk of flooding, with hundreds of millions at risk world-wide (King 2004). The distribution and phenology of a wide range of biota have been affected by changing weather over recent decades world-wide (Parmesan & Yohe 2003, Root *et al.* 2003).

The UK, with its extensive coastline and low-lying land, is internationally important for its wintering waterbird populations. This paper concentrates on the Sub-order Charadrii or waders (shorebirds), of which the UK holds over 20% of the flyway populations of 10 species (Rehfisch *et al.* 2003a). World-wide, 103 out of 207 wader populations with known trends are prob-

ably extinct or in decline for reasons that are unclear (International Wader Study Group 2003, Stroud *et al.* 2006). In Great Britain, the numbers of eight out of 14 common species of wintering wader are in decline (Rehfisch *et al.* 2003a), with particularly large declines being apparent on non-estuarine coasts (Rehfisch *et al.* 2003b). Waders include the world's longest-distance migrants, with some breeding in the circumpolar tundra and wintering in the Southern Hemisphere. These "integrators" of change could be particularly prone to the effects of factors, such as climate change, that occur on vast spatial scales (Piersma & Lindström 2004). In the UK, it has been suggested that declines may be due to a combination of factors that include habitat changes resulting from land-claim, dredging, loss of salt-marsh and urbanization (Goss-Custard *et al.* 1995, Dolman & Sutherland 1995), shell-fisheries (Atkinson *et al.* 2003), human disturbance (Liley 2000, Burton *et al.* 2002), and water abstraction. Furthermore, recent legislation that is limiting the amount of organic nutrients entering coastal waters could be lowering the biomass of the invertebrate prey of waders (Burton *et al.* 2003).

Principally using the example of the present and predicted future situation in the UK, this paper briefly reviews climate change itself, and considers its effects on sea level and coastal geomorphology, on the plant and invertebrate food resources and habitats of waterbirds, and on the waterbirds themselves. The possible mitigation of any adverse effects within present legal frameworks is considered, and research priorities that could help make it possible to develop scenarios of the likely effect of climate change on waterbirds are identified.

## REVIEW

### Climate change

In the UK, summer and winter isotherms increase from north to south, and east to west, respectively. During the twentieth century, temperatures in central England rose by almost 1˚C, and the decade of the 1990s was the warmest since records began in the 1660s. Average sea level is rising by about 1 mm per year, and winters across the UK have been getting wetter, with a larger proportion of the precipitation falling on days of heavy rainfall (Hulme *et al.* 2002a). Average minimum temperatures increased by about 1.5˚C between 1984/85 and 1997/98 (Austin & Rehfisch 2005).

Some degree of further climate change is inevitable over the next 30-40 years as a consequence of past and present emissions of greenhouse gases and the inertia of the climate system. However, the greenhouse gases emitted over the next few decades will influence the climate of the second half of the twenty-first century and beyond. Based on future global emissions of greenhouse gases, Hulme *et al.* (2002a, 2002b) detail four scenarios (low emissions, medium-low emissions, medium-high emissions and high emissions) of how climate change will affect the UK climate by 2020, 2050 and 2080. By 2080, under the medium-high emissions scenario, the UK climate will become warmer by 2.3-3.2°C. Warming will be greatest in the south and east and in the summer and autumn. Temperatures in coastal waters will increase, and very cold winters will become increasingly rare. Winters will become wetter and summers drier. By 2080, summer soil moisture may be reduced by over 40% over large parts of England, while snowfall will decrease on average by 60-90% in Scotland. Heavy winter precipitation will become more frequent. The relative sea-level rise around the UK will vary according to local isostatic forces, and will range from -2 to 86 cm above the current level in Britain. Under the medium-high emissions scenario, extremely high sea levels could occur 10-20 times more frequently by the 2080s than at present.

## Coastal geomorphology

The present coastal configuration of the UK reflects unregulated pre-twentieth century development. In England alone, over 860 km of soft cliffs are protected from erosion (23% of the coastline), and in excess of 1 259 km of sea-defences provide flood protection for 2 347 square km of embanked lowlands where over two million people live and half of the highest-grade agricultural land is found (Crooks 2004). The remaining coastal natural resources, including coastal birds, are suffering from a sustained net decline largely related to coastal squeeze of inter-tidal habitat (Carpenter & Pye 1996). Large-scale coastal land-forms are currently adjusting to two major perturbations: rising sea level and the loss of flood plains with their hydraulic functions (Crooks 2004). Because of the land-ward migration of coastal landforms, coastal "roll-over" and the redistribution of sediments, maintaining the coast in its present state is not possible. The existence and quality of certain landforms, such as dune-fields and shingle ridges, are dependent upon allowing natural migration. Management intervention to prevent migration will result in degradation of the natural form of these systems and their associated biodiversity values. Maintaining fixed flood defences will, with rising sea level, result in the loss of many of the inter-tidal foraging grounds of the UK's waders unless a policy of land ward coastal realignment is enacted. Such a policy, however, would conflict with the maintenance of fresh-water lowland habitats (Lee 2001) and the interests of a human population with assets entrenched behind flood defences.

## Plant and invertebrate resources

Salt-marshes are areas of high primary productivity subject to tidal inundation. Their greatest significance for coastal birds is probably as the base of estuarine food webs, for salt-marshes export considerable amounts of organic carbon to adjacent habitats, particularly to the invertebrates of mudflats; in addition, they provide sites for feeding, nesting and roosting (Hughes 2004). Climate change can affect salt-marshes in a number of ways, including through sea-level rise. When the sea level rises, the marsh vegetation moves upward and inland, but sea-walls that prevent this lead to coastal squeeze and loss of marsh area. However, evidence from south-east England indicates that sea-level rise does not necessarily lead to loss of marsh area, for marshes accrete vertically and maintain their elevation with respect to sea level, where the supply of sediment is sufficient. Lower down the shore, the abundance and productivity of brown algae is likely to decrease as the climate warms and the

increasing size of waves and frequency of storms increase exposure (Kendall *et al.* 2004). This would represent a loss of feeding grounds for species such as Ruddy Turnstone *Arenaria interpres* that feed on invertebrates associated with the seaweed. Furthermore, algal debris exported to sediments boosts the production of bacteria at the base of the food web.

In the British Isles, some coastal invertebrates live close to the geographical limits of their distribution. With climate change, some of these southerly species might be expected to extend their range as climatic restraints are relaxed (Kendall *et al.* 2004). In most cases, the effects on the distribution of water-birds are likely to be small; for example, the replacement of the northern limpet *Patella vulgata* by the southern *Patella depressa* is unlikely to have an adverse effect on predators such as Eurasian Oystercatchers *Haematopus ostralegus*. An increase in sea level will only have a major impact on the extent of invertebrate communities on rocky shores, where shore topography prevents the upward migration of the biota. Where a seawall limits shores, for example, biological production will be curtailed as the area available for colonization decreases. However, environmental cues control or synchronize the reproductive cycle of many marine invertebrates, and climate change will modify the relationship between temperature and photoperiod (Lawrence & Soame 2004). It is uncertain whether such invertebrates, the major prey of overwintering coastal birds, will be able to adapt sufficiently rapidly to changing conditions to avoid major population change and local extirpations.

## Waterbird phenology

Meta-analyses confirm the changing phenology of bird populations (Parmesan & Yohe 2003, Root *et al.* 2003). The timing of arrival and breeding of migrant waders in the UK can be responsive to ambient temperatures and, where long-term trends exist, they can often be explained by trends in climate. Records of the first arrival of Common Sandpipers *Actitis hypoleucos* at four bird observatories around the British Isles show no trend over time or relationship with spring temperatures (Loxton & Sparks 1999). Similar results are obtained for the Common Sandpiper, Eurasian Oystercatcher, Northern Lapwing *Vanellus vanellus* and Common Redshank *Tringa totanus* in north-east Scotland over the period 1974-1999, although the arrival date of the Eurasian Curlew *Numenius arquata* became 25 days earlier (Jenkins & Watson 2000). Between 1950 and 1998, the first arrival dates of Little Ringed Plovers *Charadrius dubius* and Whimbrels *Numenius phaeopus* in south-east England became earlier by six and 22 days per decade, and three and six days per °C in relation to mean January to March temperatures, respectively (Sparks & Mason 2001). In a study that included seven species of waterbirds wintering in Britain, the duration of stay did not change, but the first arrival date of Tundra Swan *Cygnus columbianus* advanced by seven days per decade, while that of Jack Snipe *Lymnocryptes minimus* regressed by six days per decade, between 1966-67 and 2000-01 (Sparks & Mason 2004).

In the UK, the Common Ringed Plover *Charadrius hiaticula* exhibits no overall trend in laying date between 1944 and 1995. However, its laying date has become earlier in relation to mean monthly temperatures at a rate of 1.1 days per °C, the temperatures in the relevant months showing little trend over time (Crick & Sparks 1999). Although the Eurasian Oystercatcher demonstrates a curvilinear trend in average laying date between 1962 and 1995 (peaking in the mid-1970s), this is not related to temperature, but partially to precipitation in May, becoming earlier at the rate of 0.06 day per mm.

## Waterbird distributional shifts

The breeding distributions of some British birds have extended northwards with climate change (Thomas & Lennon 1999). Eurasian Golden Plover *Pluvialis apricaria* and Common Sandpiper populations in the Pennine Mountains of England fluctuate in relation to changes in the North Atlantic Oscillation (NAO), a meteorological feature that determines the weather affecting north-west Europe (Forchhammer *et al.* 1998). Eurasian Golden Plover numbers increase two years after warm and moist winters, presumably as a result of improved juvenile survival. Common Sandpiper numbers increase after cool, dry winters, perhaps due to changes in food supplies or habitat on their African wintering grounds.

The distribution of wintering waders in Britain has changed since the 1970s (Austin *et al.* 2000). Since the mid-1980s, with an increase of 1.5°C in the mean winter temperature in the UK, the estuarine distributions of seven out of nine common wader species have moved in an eastwards direction across the winter isotherms (Fig. 1), with the smaller species showing the greatest shifts, as is expected if mediated by temperature (Austin & Rehfisch 2005). Between the 1984-85 and 1997-98 winter surveys of Britain's non-estuarine coasts, the distributions of eight wader species moved in an eastwards and/or northwards direction with increasingly mild winter temperatures and changes in mean rainfall, wind speed and wind-chill (Rehfisch *et al.* 2004). In both instances, the waders appear to be wintering closer to their breeding grounds, which are predominantly to the north and east of Britain, as milder winter weather has diminished the risk of cold-induced mortality in the colder east. The recent decline in eight of the 14 species of common coastal waders in Britain (Rehfisch *et al.* 2003a, 2003b) could be due to the waders now wintering even further to the north and east, on the European mainland (Rehfisch & Crick 2003).

national thresholds, respectively (Baker & Stroud 2006). As wader distributions in Britain change with climate change, the numbers of some species at some British SPAs are dropping below the thresholds upon which the designations are based. For example, the number of Dunlin *Calidris alpina* wintering on the Severn Estuary has dropped from an average count of over 40 000 in the mid-1970s to below the international threshold of 14 000 in recent winters up to and including the winter of 2000-01 (Austin & Rehfisch 2005). This is not an isolated example. Many species of wader are declining more rapidly in the west of Britain than in the east, as illustrated by the Common Ringed Plover (Fig. 2: Austin *et al.* 2004).

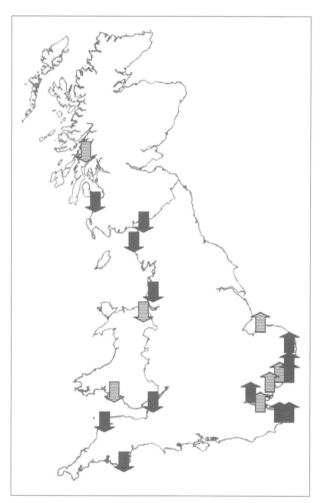

Fig. 2. Change in Common Ringed Plover *Charadrius hiaticula* numbers on Britain's SPAs designated for the species (Austin *et al.* 2004). Upward- and downward-pointing arrows indicate SPAs where numbers increased and decreased between 1994-95 and 1999-2000, respectively; filled and hatched arrows indicate changes of 50% and 25% in smoothed numbers during that period, respectively.

## Conservation implications for waterbirds

Waders are designated features of Special Protection Areas (SPAs) that regularly hold one percent or more of their flyway population or British wintering population, the international and

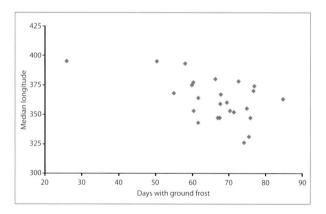

Fig. 1. Relationship between the median longitude of Common Ringed Plover *Charadrius hiaticula* distribution in Britain and the average number of days with ground frost recorded across 39 British weather stations (Rehfisch & Austin 1999).

## Scenarios of future change

Hughes (2000) suggests that the challenge for ecologists, physiologists and land managers is to predict the effects of human-induced climate and atmospheric change on species and on communities. Such predictions should include effects on physiology, distribution, phenology and individual adaptation. Whereas it is impossible to predict accurately future responses of biota to climate change, it has become acceptable to suggest a range of scenarios of possible change (Lawton 1996, Danell *et*

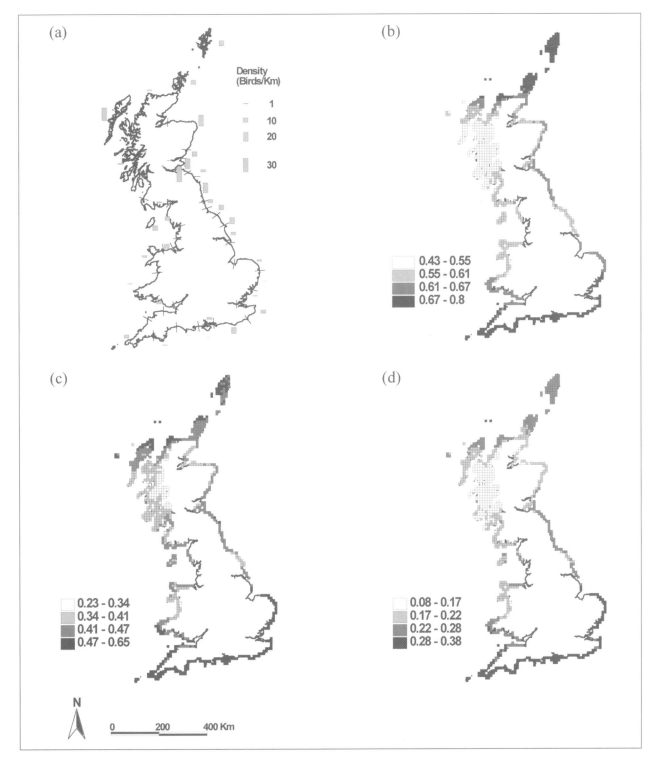

**Fig. 3.** (a) Ruddy Turnstone *Arenaria interpres* densities on the non-estuarine coast of each of Great Britain's counties during the winter of 1984-85; and (b) to (d) predicted relative change in their numbers at a scale of 10-km square under various UKCIP climate change scenarios: (b) 2020 medium-low versus 1961-1990 baseline; (c) 2080 medium-low versus 1961-1990 baseline; (d) 2080 high versus 1961-1990 baseline. 1 = no change, <1 = decrease, > 1 = increase (Rehfisch *et al.* 2004). All changes in (b) to (d) are <1, thus indicating declines.

*al.* 1999). However, modelling the future status of waterbirds or any other biota under climatic conditions that are out of the range of human knowledge is a major challenge. To develop realistic models of the likely effect of climate change on water-birds that can migrate annually over huge distances, the factors and interactions that influence their demographics must be much better understood than at present (Rehfisch & Crick 2003, Piersma & Lindström 2004). For example, the single issue of

time-lag leading to phenological disjunction is of considerable conservation importance (Sutherland 2004), since climate change is expected to occur very rapidly (Houghton *et al.* 2001), and yet there is much uncertainty as to whether biota have the capacity to respond sufficiently quickly and whether habitat responses will take years or centuries. Examples of biota finding it difficult to remain in step with their environment already exist. Although Great Tits *Parus major* can lay earlier in response to early, warm spring weather, often in parallel to the emergence of the caterpillars of winter moths on which they feed their young (Perrins 1991), they cannot significantly decrease their incubation period. However, the caterpillars can halve their development time in sufficiently warm weather, leading to an early shortage of food for young Great Tits (Buse *et al.* 1999). There is also some evidence that long-distance migrants have not responded as rapidly to climate change as short-distance migrants (Jenkins & Watson 2000, Penuelas *et al.* 2002).

Scenarios of how biota may change with climate change already exist, but their value is dependent on critical assumptions being met. Three examples are discussed. First, Austin and Rehfisch (2003) use habitat association models to suggest that in 2020 and 2050, sufficient estuarine habitat will be available to sustain the present numbers of waterbirds wintering in the UK under four UK Climate Impacts Programme (UKCIP) scenarios of sea-level rise. For these predictions to be correct, the present associations between estuarine morphology and habitat must remain true in the warmer future, and habitats must continue to hold at least the present quantity of the resources of waterbirds. Rehfisch *et al.* (2004) tentatively suggest that the numbers of some wader species wintering on the UK's non-estuarine coasts may decline considerably under the 2080 UKCIP scenarios (Fig. 3). However, for these scenarios of decline to be correct, at the very least the observed relationships between weather and wader distributions must continue to hold true outside of the present range of weather, and flyway wader populations must be large enough to provide sufficient numbers of potentially over-wintering individuals. Finally, to help guide UK conservation policy, the MONARCH project (Monitoring Natural Resource Responses to Climate Change) was established to attempt to predict how biodiversity will change with climate change. The first set of MONARCH predictions, based on a bioclimatic approach, took no account of plant and animal dispersal capabilities, geographical impediments to movement, and changing socio-economic conditions with a warming climate (Harrison *et al.* 2001). Subsequent regional predictions have addressed some of these factors, but the dispersal capacity of the organisms and phenological disjunction that may occur between interdependent species remain to be considered. Thomas *et al.* (2004) may also be underestimating the scale of future extinction of species, as their work also suffers these limitations. At best, without major information gathering to increase the reliability of model parameters, such scenarios of change can only be broadly indicative of what could happen, and must be treated with caution.

## DISCUSSION AND CONCLUSIONS

Climate is changing now (Houghton *et al.* 2001, Hulme *et al.* 2002a, 2002b), and its effect on biota is apparent world-wide (Parmesan & Yohe 2003, Root *et al.* 2003). Waterbirds are, and will continue to be, increasingly affected by rising temperatures and rising sea levels that change their habitat (Crooks 2004) and the communities of plants and animals on which they depend (Hughes 2004, Kendall *et al.* 2004, Lawrence & Soame 2004). These changes are reflected in existing changes in waterbird phenology (Cricks & Sparks 1999, Rehfisch & Crick 2003, Crick 2004, Sparks & Mason 2004) and distributional shifts (Austin *et al.* 2000, Rehfisch *et al.* 2004, Austin & Rehfisch 2005). However, much of the basic information necessary to describe the existing effects of climate change on waterbirds, quite apart from allowing the development of realistic predictions to be

made, is missing. Existing analyses have been patchy. For example, distributional changes with changing weather have been described for wintering waders, but not for other wintering waterbirds such as swans, geese and ducks. Only recently have wider scale analyses started to determine whether there is evidence that similar winter distributional shifts are occurring outside the boundaries of the UK and into Continental Europe. There has been no attempt to detect large-scale distributional changes in breeding waterbirds with changing weather. A few changes in the arrival and departure dates of migrant waterbirds have been described, but no systematic attempt has been made to analyse the main data sets of counts of breeding or wintering birds to determine whether there is evidence that changes in phenology are detectable at a national level or in the sequential usage of sites. Critically, no attempt has been made to determine whether the observed changes in wader distributions are causally related to the changes in the weather itself (temperature, Austin & Rehfisch 2005; temperature, precipitation and wind, Rehfisch *et al.* 2004), or whether the weather is having an indirect effect on the waders by affecting their habitat and resources. Increasing temperature has a direct effect on waders by lessening their energy losses and thus their energy requirements (Wiersma & Piersma 1994) and, as such, could allow birds living near the limit of their metabolic requirements (Piersma 1994) to winter in areas previously too energetically expensive. Changing weather can also have indirect effects on waterbirds. For example, increasing temperatures lead to rising sea levels and thus habitat change, as well as changing distributions (Kendall *et al.* 2004) and availability (Pienkowski 1983) of wader invertebrate prey. Determining the causal drivers of change would make it possible to generate more realistic scenarios of changing waterbird numbers with climate change.

## Planning for the future

Realistic scenarios of change allow statutory agencies to plan for the future. Understanding how wildlife will react to climate change makes it easier for them to attempt to fulfil their legal obligations towards wildlife on designated sites and to help species at risk of major decline. Already some of the legal tools necessary to protect waterbirds in a changing environment exist (Boere & Taylor 2004), and there is an increasing understanding of how suitable waterbird habitat can be created (Atkinson *et al.* 2004, Zedler 2004). The latter is useful, for example, if bird distributions are changing rapidly at a time when rapid sea-level rise is leading to major habitat loss.

Scenarios of change can (i) allow generally scarce conservation resources to be effectively targeted at priority species, (ii) concentrate the public's attention on the effects of human-induced climate change on wildlife (e.g. Thomas *et al.* 2004) and by extension themselves, and (iii) following raised public awareness, make it easier for politicians to take action that may be unpopular with voters.

However, much work is necessary before scenario models inspiring confidence can be generated. If the future weather scenarios of the Intergovernmental Panel on Climate Change (IPCC) are correct, the predictions will have to be made for climatic conditions not yet encountered, making it particularly difficult to predict accurately the likely scale of changes to waterbirds and other biota. The development of scenarios will be particularly complex for waterbirds, as the scenarios will have to allow for events occurring on often spatially extensive flyways.

## Opportunities

Assuming that the IPCC future weather scenarios are broadly correct, the Earth is about to change radically with possibly largely disastrous consequences for humans and the first human-induced massive extinction of biota (Thomas *et al.* 2004). Even with a complete and immediate switch to renewable energy, the Earth would continue to warm and sea level to rise for decades due to the time lags within atmospheric systems. Solutions to the effects of climate change on waterbirds and other fauna require changes in human behaviour. A useful first step would be to radically change the discounting philosophy that gives a very low value to long-term benefits and makes politicians reluctant to affect present economic growth for even major long-term benefits (Henderson & Sutherland 1996).

A change in the direction of the economy presents great opportunities for technological development in almost all fields of human endeavour, including renewable energy, energy conservation and thus car, house and industrial design, and agriculture. This would provide a major stimulus for growth, and the fact that countries are largely rejecting this opportunity is disappointing. The excuse that reducing carbon emissions makes humans poorer is apparently false: between 1990 and 2000, Great Britain's economy grew by 30%, employment increased by 4.8% and yet the intensity of greenhouse gas emissions fell by 30% and overall emissions fell by 12% (King 2004).

## ACKNOWLEDGEMENTS

The waterbird research cited here would have been impossible without the combined efforts of the counters who supply the data to the Wetland Bird Survey, a partnership of the BTO, WWT, RSPB and JNCC (on behalf of EN, SNH, CCW & EHS (NI)), the British Atmospheric Data Centre that allowed access to their weather data, and the UKCIP that allowed access to their baseline data and predictions. Thanks are due to Mark O'Connell for organizing the session at the Waterbirds Around the World Conference, to an anonymous referee for improving the manuscript, to the British Ornithologists' Union for providing the opportunity to produce the volume on the effects of climate change on waterbirds that much of this paper is based on (available free online http://www.bou.org.uk/pubibis.html), and to Sarah Jackson for producing Figure 2.

## REFERENCES

Atkinson, P.W., Clark, N.A., Clark, J.A., Bell, M.C., Dare, P.J. & Ireland, P.L. 2003. Changes in commercially fished shellfish stocks and shorebird populations in the Wash, England. Biological Conservation 114: 127-141.

Atkinson, P.W., Crooks, S., Drewitt, A., Grant, A., Rehfisch, M.M., Sharpe, J. & Tyas, C. 2004. Managed realignment in the UK – the first five years of colonization by birds. Ibis 146 (Suppl. 1): S101-S110.

Austin, G. & Rehfisch, M.M. 2003. The likely impact of sea level rise on waders (Charadrii) wintering on estuaries. Journal for Nature Conservation 11: 43-58.

Austin, G. & Rehfisch, M.M. 2005. Shifting non-breeding distributions of migratory fauna in relation to climatic change. Global Change Biology 11: 31-38.

Austin, G.E., Peachel, I. & Rehfisch, M.M. 2000. Regional trends in coastal wintering waders in Britain. Bird Study 47: 352-371.

Austin, G.E., Jackson, S.F. & Mellan, H.J. 2004. WeBS Alerts 2000/2001: Changes in numbers of wintering waterbirds in the United Kingdom, its Constituent Countries, Special Protection Areas (SPAs) and Sites of Special Scientific Interest (SSSIs). BTO Research Report No. 349 to the Wetland Bird Survey Partnership. British Trust for Ornithology, Thetford, UK.

Baker, H & Stroud, D.A. 2006. Establishment of a UK network of Special Protection Areas for waterbirds: the SPA review and future directions. Waterbirds around the world: 675-679.

Boere, G.C. & Taylor, D. 2004. Global and regional governmental policy and treaties as tools towards the mitigation of the effects of climate change on waterbirds. Ibis 146 (Suppl. 1): S111-S119.

Burton, N.H.K., Armitage, M.J.S., Musgrove, A.J. & Rehfisch, M.M. 2002. Impacts of man-made landscape features on the numbers of estuarine waterbirds at low tide. Environmental Management 30: 857-864.

Burton, N.H.K., Jones, T.E., Austin, G.E., Watt, G.A., Rehfisch, M.M. & Hutchings, C.J. 2003. Effects of reductions in organic and nutrient loading on bird populations in estuaries and coastal waters of England and Wales. Phase 2 Report. EN Research Report, Peterborough.

Buse, A., Dury, S.J., Woodburn, R.J.W., Perrins, C.M. & Good, J.E.G. 1999. Effects of elevated temperature on multi-species interactions: the case of Pedunculate Oak, Winter Moth and Tits. Functional Ecology 13 (Suppl. 1): 74-82.

Carpenter, K. & Pye, K. 1996. Saltmarsh changes in England and Wales – its history and causes. Environment Agency R&D Technical Report W12. H.R. Wallingford Ltd & Foundation for Water Resources, Marlow.

Crick, H.Q.P. 2004. The impacts of climate change on birds. Ibis 146 (Suppl. 1): S48-S56.

Crick, H.Q.P. & Sparks, T.H. 1999. Climate related to egg-laying trends. Nature 399: 423.

Crooks, S. 2004. The effect of sea-level rise on coastal geomorphology. Ibis 146 (Suppl. 1): S18-S20.

Danell, K., Hofgaard, A., Callaghan, T.V & Ball, J.P. 1999. Scenarios for animal responses to global change in Europe's cold regions: an introduction. Ecological Bulletins 47: 8-15.

Dolman, P.M. & Sutherland, W.J. 1995. The response of bird populations to habitat loss. Ibis 137: S38-S46.

Forchhammer, M.C., Post, E. & Stenseth, N.C. 1998. Breeding phenology and climate. Nature 391: 2930.

Goss-Custard, J.D., Clarke, R.T., Caldow, R.W.G., Durell, S.E.A. le V. dit & Ens, B.J. 1995. Population consequences of winter habitat loss in a migratory shorebird. II. Model predictions. Journal of Applied Ecology 32: 337-351.

Harrison, P.A., Berry, P.M. & Dawson, T.P. 2001. Climate Change and Nature Conservation in Britain and Ireland – modelling natural resource responses to climate change (the MONARCH project). UKCIP Technical Report, Oxford.

Henderson, N. & Sutherland, W.J. 1996. Two truths about discounting and their environmental consequences. Trends in Ecology & Evolution 11: 527-528.

Houghton, J.T., Ding, Y., Griggs, D.J., Noguer, M., van der Linden, P.J., Dai, X., Maskell, K. & Johnson, C.A. 2001. Climate Change 2001: The scientific basis. Cambridge University Press, Cambridge, UK, and New York, USA.

Hughes, L. 2000. Biological consequences of global warming: is the signal already apparent? Trends in Ecology & Evolution 15: 56-61.

Hughes, R.G. 2004. Climate change and loss of saltmarshes: consequences for birds. Ibis 146 (Suppl. 1): S21-S28.

Hulme, M., Jenkins, G.J., Lu, X., Turnpenny, J.R. Mitchell, T.D., Jones, R.G., Lowe, J., Murphy, J.M., Hassell, D., Boorman, P., McDonald, R. & Hill, S. 2002a. Climate Change scenarios for the United Kingdom: the UKCIP02 scientific report. Tyndall Centre for Climate Change Research, Norwich, UK.

Hulme, M., Turnpenny, J. & Jenkins, G. 2002b. Climate Change scenarios for the United Kingdom: the UKCIP02 briefing report. Tyndall Centre for Climate Change Research, Norwich, UK.

International Wader Study Group 2003. Are waders world-wide in decline? Reviewing the evidence. Wader Study Group Bulletin 101/102: 8-12.

Jenkins, D. & Watson, A. 2000. Dates of first arrival and song of birds during 1974-99 in mid-Deeside, Scotland. Bird Study 47: 249-251.

Kendall, M.A., Burrows, M.T., Southward, A.J. & Hawkins, S.J. 2004. Predicting the effects of marine climate change on the invertebrate prey of the birds of rocky shores. Ibis 146 (Suppl. 1): S40-S47.

King, D.A. 2004. Climate change science: adapt, mitigate, or ignore? Science 303: 176-177.

Lawrence, A.J. & Soame, J.M. 2004. Effects of climate change on the reproduction of coastal invertebrates. Ibis 146 (Suppl. 1): S29-S39.

Lawton, J.H. 1996. Population abundances, geographic ranges and conservation: 1994 Witherby Lecture. Bird Study 43: 3-19.

Lee, M. 2001. Coastal defence and the Habitats Directive: prediction of change in England and Wales. Geographical Journal 167: 39-56.

Liley, D. 2000. Predicting the consequences of human disturbance, predation and sea level rise for Ringed Plover populations. PhD thesis, University of East Anglia, UK.

Loxton, R.G. & Sparks, T.H. 1999. Arrival of spring migrants at Portland, Skokholm, Bardsey and Calf of Man. Bardsey Observatory Report 42: 105-143.

Parmesan, C. & Yohe, G. 2003. A globally coherent fingerprint of climate change impacts across natural systems. Nature 421: 37-42.

Penuelas, J., Filella, I. & Comas, P. 2002. Changed plant and animal life cycles from 1952 to 2000 in the Mediterranean region. Global Change Biology 8: 531-544.

Perrins, C.M. 1991. Tits and their caterpillar food supply. Ibis 133: S49-S54.

Pienkowski, M.W. 1983. The effect of environmental conditions on feeding rates and prey selection of shore plovers. Ornis Scandinavica 14: 227-238.

Piersma, T. 1994. Close to the edge: energetic bottlenecks and the evolution of migratory pathways in knots. PhD thesis, Rijksuniversiteit Groningen, Groningen.

Piersma, T. & Lindström, Å. 2004. Migrating shorebirds as integrators of global environmental information. Ibis 146 (Suppl.1): S61-S69.

Rehfisch, M.M. & Austin, G. 1999. Ringed Plovers go east. BTO News 223: 14-15.

Rehfisch, M.M. & Crick, H.Q.P. 2003. Predicting the impact of climatic change on Arctic-breeding waders. Wader Study Group Bulletin 100: 86-95.

Rehfisch, M.M., Austin, G.E., Armitage, M.J.S., Atkinson, P.W., Holloway, S.J., Musgrove, A.J. & Pollitt, M.S. 2003a. Numbers of wintering waterbirds in Great Britain and the Isle of Man (1994/95-1998/99): II. Coastal waders (Charadrii). Biological Conservation 112: 329-341.

Rehfisch, M.M., Holloway, S.J. & Austin, G.E. 2003b. Population estimates of waders on the non-estuarine coasts of the United Kingdom and the Isle of Man during the winter of 1997-98. Bird Study 50: 22-32.

Rehfisch, M.M., Austin, G.E., Freeman, S.N., Armitage, M.J.S. & Burton, N.H.K. 2004. The possible impact of climate change on the future distributions and numbers of waders on Britain's non-estuarine coast. Ibis 146 (Suppl. 1): S70-S81.

Root, T.L., Price, J.T., Hall, K.R., Schneider, S.H., Rosenzweig, C. & Pounds, J.A. 2003. Fingerprints of global warming on wild animals and plants. Nature 421: 57-60.

Sparks, T.H. & Mason C.F. 2001. Dates of arrivals and departures of spring migrants taken from the Essex Bird Reports 1950-1998. Essex Bird Report 1999: 154-164.

Sparks, T.H. & Mason, C.F. 2004. Changes in phenology of winter migrant birds in Essex. Ibis 146 (Suppl. 1): S57-S60.

Stroud, D.A., Baker, A., Blanco, D.E., Davidson, N.C., Delany, S., Ganter, B., Gill, R., González, P., Haanstra, L., Morrison, R.I.G., Piersma, T., Scott, D.A., Thorup, O., West, R., Wilson, J. & Zöckler, C. (on behalf of the International Wader Study Group). 2006. The conservation and population status of the world's waders at the turn of the millennium. Waterbirds around the world: 643-648.

Sutherland, W.J. 2004. Climate change and coastal birds: research questions and policy responses. Ibis 146 (Suppl. 1): S120-S124.

Thomas, C.D. & Lennon, J.L. 1999. Birds extend their ranges northwards. Nature 399: 213.

Thomas, C.D., Cameron, A., Green, R.E., Bakkenes, M., Beaumont, L.J., Collingham, Y.C., Erasmus, B.F.N., De Siqueira, M.F., Grainger, A., Hannah, L., Hughes, L., Huntley, B., Van Jaarsveld, A.S., Midgley, G.F., Miles, L., Ortega-Huerta, M.A., Peterson, A.T., Phillips, O.L. & Williams, S.E. 2004. Extinction risk from climate change. Nature 427: 145–148.

Wadhams, P. 1997. Ice in the ocean. Gordon & Breach, London.

Wiersma, P. & Piersma, T. 1994. Effects of microhabitat, flocking, climate and migratory goal on energy expenditure in the annual cycle of red knots. The Condor 96: 257-279.

Zedler, J.B. 2004. Compensatory mitigation for damages to wetlands: can net losses be reduced? Ibis 146 (Suppl. 1): S92-S100.

# Effects of the North Atlantic Oscillation and El Niño-Southern Oscillation on return rates, body mass and timing of migration of Common Terns *Sterna hirundo* breeding in Germany

*Marco Favero[1] & Peter H. Becker[2]*

[1] *Biology Department, University of Mar del Plata – CONICET, Funes 3250 (B7602AYJ), Mar del Plata, Argentina.*

[2] *Institut für Vogelforschung "Vogelwarte Helgoland", An der Vogelwarte 21, D-26386, Germany.*

Favero, M. & Becker, P.H. 2006. Effects of the North Atlantic Oscillation and El Niño-Southern Oscillation on return rates, body mass and timing of migration of Common Terns *Sterna hirundo* breeding in Germany. *Waterbirds around the world.* Eds. G.C. Boere, C.A. Galbraith & D.A. Stroud. The Stationery Office, Edinburgh, UK. pp. 405-409.

## ABSTRACT

Environmental variability at breeding and wintering areas may have complex effects on populations of migratory seabirds. Here, we report on the correlation of climate variability in the winter quarters and at migration stopover sites with return rates, individual condition and migration strategy of Common Terns *Sterna hirundo* breeding in northern Germany. Climate variability was defined by the North Atlantic Oscillation Index (NAOI) and Southern Oscillation Index (SOI, a measure of the El Niño-Southern Oscillation). Data on Common Terns were obtained over the last ten years at a breeding colony in the Banter See (northern Germany) by systematically marking adults and fledged chicks with transponders. The return rate of breeders was negatively correlated with the NAOI in the previous year, but for two-year-old sub-adults was positively correlated with the lagged SOI, indicating possible dependence for survival on food availability at migration stopover sites and in the wintering areas, respectively. Sub-adults also arrived later at the breeding colony after years of high NAO, suggesting that conditions at the wintering sites and during spring migration strongly influence the survival and behaviour of prospecting terns. The sub-adults appear to be more dependent on climatic conditions at wintering and migration stopover sites than adults, possibly as a result of different migratory behaviour, or foraging experience and the breeding requirements of adults. Studies on the wintering and migration strategies of the species are required to confirm the mechanisms linking migration and climate variability.

## INTRODUCTION

There is much evidence of biological responses to climate variability in marine and terrestrial ecosystems (Holmgren *et al.* 2001, Beaugrand & Reid 2003). Studies on bird species have demonstrated impacts of climate change and oscillations in climate on many aspects of their life history, including survival, recruitment, reproductive output, population dynamics and timing of migration. Many species of migratory birds now arrive considerably earlier in spring than just a few decades ago, and several studies have shown that fluctuations observed in populations are regulated by climate change (Sillett *et al.* 2000, Moss *et al.* 2001, Møller 2002, Both *et al.* 2004, Hüppop & Hüppop 2002, Saino *et al.* 2004). For seabirds, the impact of climate change and oscillations has been observed predominantly at breeding colonies (e.g. Thompson & Ollason 2001, Croxall *et al.* 2002, Simeone *et al.* 2002). Therefore, an understanding of the dynamic consequences of climate oscillations and environmental conditions operating in the winter quarters and along migration routes is required for these marine predators.

The Common Tern *Sterna hirundo* is one of the most cosmopolitan tern species, breeding mostly in the Northern Hemisphere and wintering in the tropics and temperate regions of the Southern Hemisphere (Nisbet 2002, Becker & Ludwigs 2004). Common Terns breeding in Europe spend the winter along the coast of Africa, from north-west Africa to Cape Town, and migrate along the East Atlantic coast. The Common Terns from breeding colonies in the Banter See in northern Germany winter predominantly in West Africa between the equator and 20°N (Becker & Ludwigs 2004). Most of the 47 recaptures of birds ringed in the Banter Sea have been in West Africa, although some birds have been recovered as far south as 10°S (P.H. Becker unpubl. data). In general, sub-adult Common Terns remain in their winter quarters throughout their first two years, returning to the breeding colonies as prospectors when they are two years old. The age of first breeding ranges from two to five, but is most commonly three (Becker *et al.* 2001, Ludwigs & Becker 2002, Dittmann & Becker 2003).

A major source of inter-annual variability in the atmospheric circulation of the Northern Hemisphere is the North Atlantic Oscillation (NAO), which is associated with changes in the surface westerly winds across the North Atlantic into Europe. Whereas warm, wet and stormy winters in the north-east Atlantic and northern Europe are associated with a high North Atlantic Oscillation Index (NAOI), these conditions are associated with a low NAOI in southern Europe (Hurrell 1995). However, unlike the tropical Pacific, seasonal climate variability in the tropical Atlantic is not dominated by any single process (Sutton *et al.* 2000). This region is subject to multiple competing forces among which El Niño-Southern Oscillation (ENSO) teleconnections have been linked to important environmental processes such as enhanced upwelling phenomena in equatorial West Africa (Roy & Reason 2001). These large-scale climatic factors may affect ecological patterns and processes in both marine and terrestrial systems, changing the relative amount of resources and habitats available in the breeding grounds, and consequently affecting the life history, demography and population dynamics of the species (Alerstam & Hedenström 1998, Stenseth *et al.* 2002). Hemispheric systems, such as the NAO or ENSO, may potentially influence migrants beyond their breeding ranges – during migration as well as in the wintering areas. Variability in arrival mass and date of arrival for individual migration strategies could be an expression of phenotypic plasticity (Saino *et al.* 2004), and ecological conditions during winter may affect the energetic balance, individual condition and moult of birds, and therefore the timing of departure and migration strategy (Marra *et al.* 1998), with significant consequences for life history.

**Table 1.** Multiple regression and partial correlation analyses of arrival date, return rate and arrival mass of Common Terns *Sterna hirundo* breeding in Germany, with North Atlantic Oscillation (NAOI) and Southern Oscillation (SOI) indices as independent variables.

| | Breeders | | | Prospectors | | |
| --- | --- | --- | --- | --- | --- | --- |
| | Date of arrival | Arrival mass | Return rate | Date of arrival | Arrival mass | Return rate |
| Multiple R | 0.554 | 0.284 | 0.689 | 0.798 | 0.306 | 0.833 |
| Multiple $R^2$ | 0.307 | 0.081 | 0.475 | 0.638 | 0.094 | 0.694 |
| $F^{2,7}$ | 1.553 | 0.307 | 3.171 | 6.175 | 0.361 | 7.938 |
| (p) | (0.277) | (0.745) | (0.105) | (0.028) | (0.709) | (0.016) |
| Partial correlations | | | | | | |
| Lag NAOI β | 0.173 | 0.267 | -0.684 | 0.658 | -0.302 | -0.489 |
| (p) | (0.599) | (0.486) | (0.041) | (0.023) | (0.429) | (0.049) |
| Lag SOI β | -0.537 | -0.114 | -0.053 | -0.496 | 0.069 | 0.699 |
| (p) | (0.132) | (0.763) | (0.852) | (0.066) | (0.855) | (0.012) |

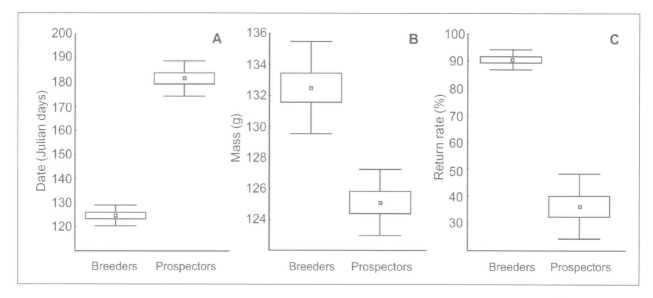

**Fig. 1.** Date of arrival (A), arrival mass (B), and return rate (C) of breeding and prospecting Common Terns *Sterna hirundo* throughout the study period. Means – dots; standard errors – boxes; standard deviations – error bars.

This study aimed to analyse the long-term variability observed in migration schedule, body mass at arrival and return rate of prospecting and breeding Common Terns in relation to oscillations in climate operating across the species' distribution, hypothesising a significant effect of climate on body mass, timing of migration and return rates.

## METHODS

Common Tern data were collected at a breeding colony located at Banter See, Wilhelmshaven, Northern Germany. Between 1992 and 2001, complete cohorts of fledged Common Terns (n = 2 081) and 101 adults were implanted with transponders. The migration schedule (date of arrival), individual arrival mass and return rates of breeders (individuals older than four years) and prospectors (two-year-old sub-adults; 91% of the sub-adults return at the age of two years; Dittmann & Becker 2003) were automatically recorded every season over a 10 year study period (1994 to 2003), using antennas and electronic balances located at resting sites throughout the breeding colony (for details, see Wendeln & Becker 1996, Becker & Wendeln 1997, Becker *et al.* 2001).

Environmental variability was defined in this study by the North Atlantic Oscillation Index (NAOI) and El-Niño-Southern Oscillation (ENSO; indicated by the Southern Oscillation Index, SOI). High positive values of SOI indicate La Niña conditions, and low, negative values indicate El Niño conditions. For all analyses, we used annual mean monthly values of the standardized NAOI and SOI for each calendar year. The NAOI data set was obtained from the Climate Prediction Centre website, and the SOI data set from the Commonwealth Bureau of Meteorology website. Temporal auto-correlation in the NAOI and SOI during the study period was found to be non-significant ($F_{1,9}$= 0.01, $r^2$= 0.001, P= 0.939, and $F_{1,9}$= 0.48, $r^2$= 0.056, P= 0.510, respectively).

We measured the effects of the NAO and ENSO on the return rates, timing of migration and individual condition of prospecting and breeding Common Terns. Mean index values from the year before were correlated to parameter values collected for Common Terns (i.e. average indices of the year *i* paired with parameters from the breeding season for the year *i*+1). The annual schedule of Common Terns from the study site was assumed as follows: breeding season from May to late

August, autumn migration from September to November, winter season from December to March, and spring migration from late February to May. For each breeding season of the ten-year study period, average arrival mass, date of arrival and return rate were calculated. The arrival mass was the mean body mass during the first three days after arriving at the colony. The return rate for breeders was the percentage of birds breeding in the previous year that were recorded, and for prospectors was the percentage of successful fledglings from two years previously. The ranges of annual sample sizes were as follows: date of arrival of adults, 56-388 (total N = 1 785); date of arrival of prospectors, 14-228 (total N = 808); return rate of adults, 53-273 (total N = 1 466); return rate of prospectors, 103-502 (total N = 2 078); arrival mass of adults, 40-160 (total N = 947), arrival mass of prospectors, 9-113 (total N = 406). Multiple regression and partial correlation analyses of all three parameters were performed with NAOI and SOI as independent variables.

## RESULTS

Significant differences were found between breeders and prospectors in the three parameters under consideration. Breeders arrived at the colony significantly earlier than sub-adults ($T_{18}$= 21.41, P< 0.0001, Fig. 1a). Breeders were about 5% heavier than sub-adults when they arrived at the colony ($T_{18}$= 6.53, P< 0.0001, Fig. 1b), and the proportion of breeders returning to the colony was almost three times higher than the proportion of sub-adults returning after two years ($T_{18}$= 13.68, P< 0.0001, Fig. 1c).

The return rate in breeders was negatively correlated with the lagged NAOI, while in prospectors it was positively correlated with the lagged SOI (Table 1, Fig. 2a). Prospectors arrived later following high NAO years, and both prospectors and breeders showed similar but non-significant trends following low SOI years (Fig. 2b). All significant correlations explained nearly 40% of the variability in the parameters under consideration. The arrival masses of breeders and prospectors were not correlated with the NAOI or SOI.

Multiple regression models with both lagged NAOI and SOI as independent variables explained significant proportions of the variability in the prospectors' date of arrival (64%) and return rate (69%) (Table 1). Post-hoc partial correlations indicated that the NAOI explained nearly 66% of the variability in the prospectors' date of arrival, 50% in the prospectors' return rate and 68% in the breeders' return rate; the SOI explained 70% of the variability in the prospectors' return rate (Table 1).

## DISCUSSION

Higher adult survival and earlier arrival of prospectors following low NAO years were most likely attributable to favourable foraging conditions during the spring migration. Higher abundance of marine fish, including Herring *Clupea harengus* (a key prey for Common Terns in Europe; Greenstreet *et al.* 1999) in estuarine areas (Attrill & Power 2002), as well as higher copepod abundance in the North Atlantic (Heath 1999) have been observed following winters characterized by low NAOI values. Consequently low NAOI values should indicate better feeding conditions in breeding areas and along the migration routes between north-west Africa and Europe.

While the return rates in adults were not correlated with the SOI (an index of ENSO conditions), the return rates of prospecting terns were significantly explained by variability in the SOI, being higher after cold La Niña events (i.e. high SOI). The impact of La Niña on local climate and the intensification of Atlantic trade winds cause concomitant upwellings in coastal West Africa (Roy

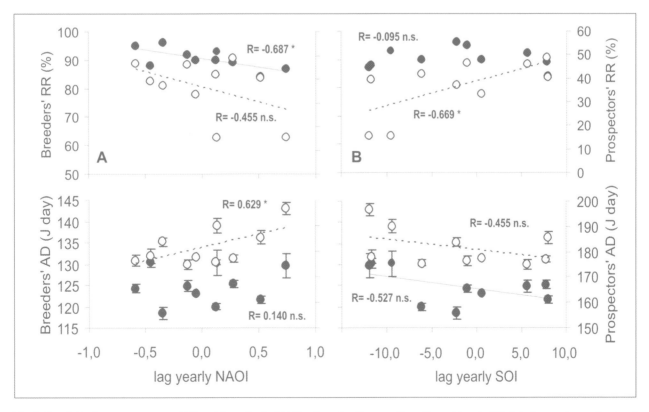

**Fig. 2.** Correlation between return rate (RR) and date of arrival (AD) of breeding Common Terns *Sterna hirundo* (filled circles, continuous lines) and prospectors (open circles, dashed lines), and one year lagged (A) North Atlantic Oscillation (NAOI) and (B) Southern Oscillation (SOI) indices for 1994-2003 (n = 10 years). * = P< 0.05; n.s. = non-significant correlation.

& Reason 2001), which are likely followed by increases in food availability. Subsequent increases in rainfall (Nicholson & Selato 2000, Holmgren *et al.* 2001) might increase river runoff in the vicinity of wintering areas, enhancing local productivity and food availability for Common Terns, as has been observed in the winter quarters off southern South America (Favero *et al.* 2001, Acha *et al.* 2004). Individuals departing in better physical condition from the wintering areas should therefore arrive earlier at the breeding grounds than those departing in poor condition (Forchhammer *et al.* 2002), as observed for prospecting sub-adults (Fig. 2b).

Prospectors showed higher variability in all three parameters than did adult terns, and their parameters followed more closely fluctuations observed in the NAO and ENSO. This may be because adults have to return to the breeding colonies earlier than prospecting sub-adults in order to breed, irrespective of climatic conditions. Multiple regression models explained more than 80% of the variability in timing of migration and return rate of prospectors, showing the differential responses of age classes to climate and environmental variability (Alerstam & Hedenström 1998). The absence of an effect of large-scale climate variability on body mass at arrival could be related to the fact that local food availability (affected by short-term processes) may immediately influence body mass in small seabirds, such as terns, that possess low energetic reserves (Greenstreet *et al.* 1999). The lower variability observed in adult terns could be related to the fact that more experienced individuals might be able to cope better with fluctuations in environmental conditions, as the increase in body mass with age shows (Dittmann & Becker 2003, Limmer & Becker unpubl. data). The stronger effects of variability in the ENSO on the survival of sub-adults (expressed as the observed return rates over a two-year period) could also be related to the fact that the birds spend their first two winter seasons in West Africa (Becker & Ludwigs 2004), where ENSO teleconnections have a strong influence.

Higher adult return rates and earlier arrival of prospectors were observed after low NAO years, while higher return rates of prospectors corresponded with cold ENSO events. For the moment, the reasons for these parallel trends between climate variability and return rates, body mass and timing of migration in the Common Tern are rather speculative. Further analyses and experimental studies examining local weather and environmental manifestations of climate (e.g. sea surface temperature, productivity) at wintering, staging and breeding areas are required for a better understanding of the effects of climate on variability in the migration and survival of Common Terns.

## ACKNOWLEDGEMENTS

This study was supported by the DFG (Be 916/5) and German Academic Exchange Service (DAAD Grant A/02/19132), and was a collaboration between the Institute for Avian Research "Vogelwarte Helgoland" and the National University of Mar del Plata (15E/238). We give special thanks to Stephen Oswald for his helpful comments on this paper.

## REFERENCES

Acha, E.M., Mianzan, H.W., Guerrero, R.A., Favero, M. & Bava, J. 2004. Coastal marine fronts at the southern cone of South America. Physical and ecological processes. Journal of Marine Systems 44: 83-105.

Alerstam, T. & Hedenström, A. 1998. The development of bird migration theory. Journal of Avian Biology 29: 343-369.

Attrill, M.J. & Power, M. 2002. Climatic influence on a marine fish assemblage. Nature 417: 275-278.

Beaugrand, G. & Reid, P.C. 2003. Long-term changes in phytoplankton, zooplankton and salmon related to climate. Global Change Biology 9: 1-7.

Becker, P.H. & Ludwigs, J.D. 2004. *Sterna hirundo* Common Tern. In: D. Parkin (ed) Birds of the Western Palearctic Update Vol. 6, Nos. 1-2, Oxford University Press, Oxford: 91-137.

Becker, P.H. & Wendeln, H. 1997. A new application for transponders in population ecology of the Common Tern. Condor 99: 534-538.

Becker, P.H., Wendeln, H. & González-Solís, J. 2001. Population dynamics, recruitment, individual quality and reproductive strategies in common terns *Sterna hirundo* marked with transponders. Ardea 89: 241-252.

Both, C., Artemyev, A.V., Blaauw, B., Cowie, R.J., Dekhuijzen, A.J., Eeva, T., Enemar, A., Gustafsson, L., Ivankina, E.V., Järvinen, A., Metcalfe, N.B., Nyholm, N.E.I., Potti, J., Ravussin, P.A., Sanz, J.J., Silverin, B., Slater, F.M., Sokolov, L.V., Török, J., Winkel, W., Wright, J., Zang, H. & Visser, M.E. 2004. Large-scale geographical variation confirms that climate change causes birds to lay earlier. Proceedings of the Royal Society of London B, 271: 1657-1662.

Croxall, J.P., Trathan, P.N. & Murphy, E.J. 2002. Environmental change and Antarctic seabird populations. Science 297: 1510-1514.

Dittmann, T. & Becker, P.H. 2003. Sex, age, experience and condition as factors affecting arrival date in prospecting Common Terns, *Sterna hirundo*. Animal Behaviour 65: 981-986.

Favero, M., Bachmann, S., Copello, S., Mariano-Jelicich, R., Silva, M.P., Ghys, M., Khatchikian, C. & Mauco, L. 2001. Aves Marinas del Sudeste Bonaerense. In: O. Iribarne (ed) Reserva de Biósfera Mar Chiquita: Características Físicas, Biológicas y Ecológicas. Ed. Martin – UNESCO, Argentina: 251-267.

Forchhammer, M.C., Post, E. & Stenseth, N.R. 2002. North Atlantic Oscillation timing of long- and short-distance migration. Journal of Animal Ecology 71: 1002-1014.

Greenstreet, S.P.R., Becker, P.H., Barrett, R.T., Fossum, P. & Leopold, M.F. 1999. Consumption of pre-recruit fish by seabirds and the possible use of this as an indicator of fish stock recruitment. ICES Cooperative Research Report 232: 6-17.

Heath, M.R. 1999. Climate fluctuations and the spring invasion of the North Sea by *Calanus finmarchicus*. Fisheries Oceanography 8 (Supplement 1): 163-176.

Holmgren, M., Scheffer, M., Ezcurra, E., Gutierrez, J.R. & Morhen, M.J. 2001. El Niño effects on the dynamics of terrestrial ecosystems. Trends in Ecology and Evolution 16: 89-94.

Hüppop, O. & Hüppop, K. 2002. North Atlantic Oscillation and timing of spring migration in birds. Proceedings of the Royal Society of London B, 270: 233-140.

Hurrell, J.W. 1995. Decadal trends in the North Atlantic Oscillation: regional temperatures and precipitation. Science 269: 676-679.

Ludwigs, J.D. & Becker, P.H. 2002. The hurdle of recruitment: Influences of arrival date, colony experience and sex in the Common Tern *Sterna hirundo*. In: C. Both & T. Piersma (eds) The avian calendar: exploring biological hurdles in the annual cycle. Proceedings of the Third Conference of the European Ornithologists' Union. Ardea 90: 389-399.

Marra, P.P., Hobson, K.A. & Holmes, R.T. 1998. Linking winter and summer events in a migratory bird by using stable-carbon isotopes. Science 282: 1884-1886.

Møller, A.P. 2002. North Atlantic Oscillation (NAO) effects of climate on the relative importance of first and second clutches in a migratory passerine bird. Journal of Animal Ecology 71: 201-210.

Moss, R., Oswald, J. & Baines, D. 2001. Climate change and breeding success: decline in capercaillie in Scotland. Journal of Animal Ecology 70: 47-61.

Nicholson, S.E. & Selato, J.S. 2000. The influence of La Niña on African rainfall. International Journal of Climatology 20: 1761-1776.

Nisbet, I.C.T. 2002. Common Tern *Sterna hirundo*. In: A. Poole & F. Gill (eds) The Birds of North America, No. 618. Cornell Laboratory of Ornithology and The Academy of Natural Sciences.

Roy, C. & Reason, C. 2001. ENSO related modulation of coastal upwelling in the eastern Atlantic. Progress in Oceanography 49: 245-255.

Saino, N., Szep, T., Romano, M., Rubolini, D., Spina, F. & Møller, A.P. 2004. Ecological conditions during winter predict arrival date at the breeding quarters in a trans-Saharan migratory bird. Ecology Letters 7: 21–25.

Sillet, T.S., Holmes, R.T. & Sherry, T.W. 2000. Impacts of a global climate cycle on population dynamics of a migratory songbird. Science 288: 2040-2042.

Simeone, A., Araya, B., Bernal, M., Diebold, E.N., Grzybowski, K., Michaels, M., Teare, J.A., Wallace, R.S. & Willis, M.J. 2002. Oceanographic and climatic factors influencing breeding and colony attendance patterns of Humboldt penguins *Spheniscus humboldti* in central Chile. Marine Ecology Progress Series 227: 43-50.

Stenseth, N.C., Mysterud, A.T., Ottersen, G., Hurrell, J.W., Chan, K.S. & Lima, M. 2002. Ecological Effects of Climate Fluctuations. Science 297: 1292-1296.

Sutton, R.T., Jewson, S.P. & Rowell, D.P. 2000. The elements of climate variability in the tropical Atlantic region. Journal of Climate 13: 3261-3284.

Thompson, P.M. & Ollason, J.C. 2001. Lagged effects of ocean climate change on fulmar population dynamics. Nature 413: 417-420.

Wendeln, H. & Becker, P.H. 1996. Body mass change in breeding Common Terns (*Sterna hirundo*). Bird Study 43: 85-95.

Common Terns *Sterna hirundo* at the southern terminus of their migration, at Dyer Island, South Africa. Photo: Dieter Oschadleus.

## 4.2   Disease emergence and impacts in migratory waterbirds. Workshop Introduction

*Tonie Rocke*

*National Wildlife Health Center, 6006 Schroeder Rd., Madison, WI 53711, USA.*

Rocke, T. 2006. Disease emergence and impacts in migratory waterbirds. Workshop Introduction. *Waterbirds around the world.* Eds. G.C. Boere, C.A. Galbraith & D.A. Stroud. The Stationery Office, Edinburgh, UK. pp. 410-411.

The increasing frequency of several waterbird diseases, many of which are zoonotic, has highlighted the important need for more systematic disease surveillance at national and international scales. Current concerns regarding avian influenza have focussed attention on how best to undertake the scientific support functions. Photo: Paul Marshall.

The frequency and magnitude of disease losses amongst waterbirds (from emerging or re-emerging disease agents) have increased to the extent that they demand attention. These diseases not only affect waterbirds, but have impacts on the economic, health and cultural values of humans. Solutions require the integration of numerous scientific disciplines in an ecological approach.

The symposium reviewed existing diseases frequently carried and transported by migratory waterbirds, including botulism (Rocke), avian influenza (Shortridge & Melville) and avian cholera (Samuel).

A number of common themes and conclusions emerged from the presentations:

- Disease (both newly emerging and previously established agents) has increased in prominence as a cause of mortality in wild waterbirds and significantly impacts certain water-

bird populations, as reported by Friend, Rocke and Kuiken *et al..* Novel etiologies now cause recurring waterbird mortalities as reported by Cole & Franson.

- Some waterbird diseases also have human and domestic animal implications and vice versa. Communication, collaboration and co-ordination between ornithologists, conservation biologists, wildlife health experts, veterinarians, and public health officials are critical to improve knowledge of these diseases and facilitate their mitigation.

- Underlying factors for emergence of diseases are related to increases in human populations, human consumption patterns, the redistribution of species and/or further aggregation of gregarious species in a manner that facilitates disease transmission.

- Improvements in disease surveillance, diagnosis and prevention are critically needed to address and manage disease problems in waterbirds.

- Integration and understanding of underlying concepts and impacts of disease are critical for global waterbird conservation.
- Education of the public, government officials and the media on the role of wild birds in disease transmission should be mandatory to prevent common misperceptions. Proactive approaches to engage with the media are necessary.

The following four recommendations were made:

1. There is a need to increase awareness, and to educate others, that disease in waterbird populations should be viewed in an ecological context, responsive to environmental changes and perturbations.
2. A global wildlife health policy should be instituted that provides standardized methods for investigation, diagnosis and reporting of mortality events in waterbirds and other wildlife (similar to those put in place for domestic animals and humans, by, for example, the World Health Organisation and the World Organisation for Animal Health - OIE).
3. Discourse and interaction between conservation biologists, animal welfare proponents and the food animal industry should be strongly encouraged so that animal welfare considerations do not jeopardise wildlife conservation (*i.e.* proximity of open range animal production to wetlands).
4. Active steps should be undertaken to curtail the excessive movement of wild animals through the exotic pet trade so as to reduce the risk of disease transmission and to enhance the conservation of wild species.

The workshop called, in particular, for urgent action to mitigate disease emergence and losses in waterbirds by integrating fundamental disease concepts into global strategies for waterbird conservation.

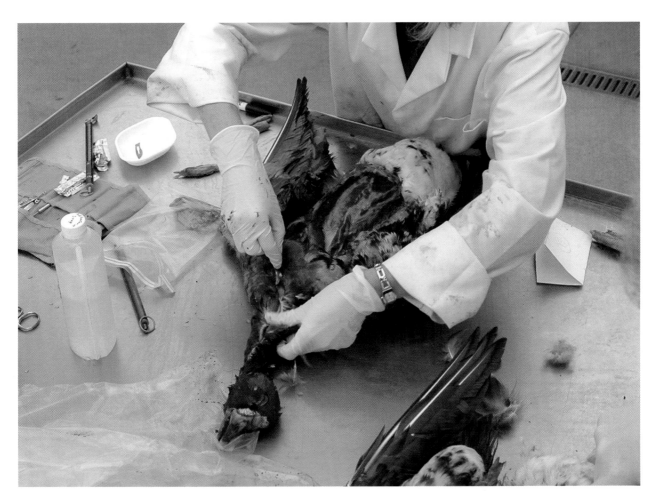

There is an urgent need to better integrate animal health surveillance into programmes of waterbird monitoring so as to better understand the consequences of disease for both individual birds and for populations. The UK Wildfowl & Wetlands Trust have embarked on long-term health screening of Greenland White-fronted Geese *Anser albifrons flavirostris* as an adjunct to the internationally co-operative research and monitoring of this population. Photo: Alyn Walsh.

# Evolving changes in diseases of waterbirds

*Milton Friend*

*National Wildlife Health Center, 6006 Schroeder Rd., Madison, Wisconsin 53711, USA. (email: milton_friend@usgs.gov)*

Friend, M. 2006. Evolving changes in diseases of waterbirds. *Waterbirds around the world.* Eds. G.C. Boere, C.A. Galbraith & D.A. Stroud. The Stationery Office, Edinburgh, UK. pp. 412-417.

## ABSTRACT

The emergence of infectious diseases is a hallmark of the twentieth century, along with the resurgence of diseases thought to have been "conquered". This continuing problem is global in scope, involves humans (e.g. AIDS, hantavirus pulmonary syndrome, and tuberculosis), domestic animals (e.g. bovine spongiform ecephalopathy "mad cow disease", Nipah virus infections, and foot-and-mouth disease), and wildlife (e.g. mobillivirus infections, chronic wasting disease, and inclusion body disease of cranes). The emergence of diseases in wildlife involves virtually all classes of vertebrates and is occurring in all types of habitats. The number of diseases involved and the magnitude of losses are such that disease emergence and resurgence are posing an unprecedented challenge for the conservation of wildlife, including some waterbird populations.

## INTRODUCTION

Changes over time in the occurrence of diseases in waterbirds are reflective of broader disease increases worldwide. This presentation focuses on the occurrence of disease in North American waterbirds, primarily waterfowl. The scientific literature, disease databases maintained by the U.S. Geological Survey's National Wildlife Health Center (NWHC) and personal experiences gained during more than 40 years as a wildlife disease practitioner are the foundation for this evaluation. The great amount of North American literature involving waterfowl and diagnostic findings of their causes of mortality provide a reasonable basis for retrospective evaluations of the occurrence of major disease events and when various diseases reached sufficient notoriety to be reported. Changes that have occurred include the types of disease agents involved (noninfectious vs. infectious), geographic occurrence for specific diseases, and the magnitude of losses.

## HISTORICAL PERSPECTIVE

The foundation for investigations of waterbird diseases in the USA is the Bear River Wildlife Disease Station established early in the 1900s by the Bureau of Biological Survey. The station leader was Alexander Wetmore, who later became the most distinguished American ornithologist of the nineteen thirties and forties (Ripley & Steed 1987). Dr. Wetmore's classical studies on what we now know to be type C avian botulism (Wetmore 1918) and his investigations of lead poisoning (Wetmore 1919) are the first in-depth studies of disease in wild waterbirds.

Avian botulism (type C *Clostridium botulinum*) emerged as a problem during the late 1800s (Jensen & Price 1987), and was the most common of the few diseases receiving attention by waterfowl biologists prior to the 1960s. Avian cholera (*Pasteurella mutocidia*) first appeared in North American waterbirds in 1944 (Quortup *et al.* 1946), but for several decades had only a limited geographic distribution (Friend 1981). Leucocytozoonosis (*Leucocytozoon simondi*) became a concern during the 1920s and 1930s. By the 1950s, this disease was a focus for investigation in Canada and some of the northern areas of the USA (Fallis & Trainer 1964, Wobeser 1981). Early in the 1950s, the gizzard worm *Amidostomum* spp. was incriminated as a factor in Canada Goose *Branta canadensis* mortality in localized areas of the Atlantic seaboard of the USA (Herman & Wehr 1954). Lead poisoning was recognized as a problem for waterfowl as early as 1874 in the USA (Friend 1999a). There also was an awareness of aspergillosis as an occasional cause of bird deaths (O'Meara & Witter 1971).

## INCREASED PROMINENCE OF INFECTIOUS DISEASE

The number of infectious diseases of concern in waterbirds has increased, as has the frequency of disease events they cause. Avian cholera, currently the greatest global cause of waterbird

---

**Table 1.** **Examples of avian cholera epizootics in marine environments.**

| Geographic area | Primary species | Populations affected | |
| --- | --- | --- | --- |
| | | Breeding colony | Other |
| **North America** | | | |
| Canada | Waterfowl | • | |
| USA | Waterfowl | • | • |
| **South America** | | | |
| Chile | Waterfowl | | • |
| **Europe** | | | |
| The Netherlands | Waterfowl, gulls | • | • |
| Denmark | Waterfowl, gulls, others | • | • |
| **Africa** | | | |
| South Africa | Gulls, cormorants | • | • |
| **Antarctica** | Brown Skua *Catharacta antarctica* | | • |
| **New Zealand** | Rockhopper Penguin *Eudyptes chrysocome* | • | |

mortality by an infectious disease, first appeared as a disease of wild waterbirds in Africa in 1940 and in the USA in 1944 (Rosen 1971). It is noteworthy that in their extensive review of water-fowl disease, Phillips & Lincoln (1930) state, "We do not have a single well-authenticated case of its occurrence [avian cholera] among wild North American waterfowl." Because of concern about this disease, they urged that it be watched for. Since 1944, avian cholera has gradually expanded its North American range and is now enzootic in several major waterfowl areas across the USA and in Canada (Friend 1999b). Globally, avian cholera has caused epizootics among marine birds from the Antarctic to the coast of Africa and in other areas (Table 1), but most commonly occurs in freshwater environments. Avian cholera has also become a "disease for all seasons", with outbreaks occurring on summer breeding grounds, in wintering areas, and along spring and autumn staging and migration areas.

A wide variety of other infectious diseases have appeared in captive and wild bird populations within the USA (Friend *et al.* 2001). Duck plague (duck virus enteritis - DVE) entered the USA in 1967 (Leibovitz & Hwang 1968), and has since become enzootic (Converse & Kidd 2001, Friend 1999c). The 1996 occurrence of the trematode *Leyogonimus polyoon* has resulted in enzootic establishment, with repeated outbreaks in Wisconsin (Cole & Friend 1999). American White Pelicans *Pelecanus erythrorhynchos* are among the many avian and other species being impacted by West Nile fever (WNF) since its appearance in North America in 1999 (NWHC unpubl. data).

Avian pox was first reported in wild waterfowl on the USA mainland in 1978 (Morton & Dieterich 1979), and pox in Bald Eagles *Haliaeetus leucocephalus* quickly followed (Hansen 1999). Personal investigation of a major epizootic of avian pox in Laysan Albatrosses *Diomedea immutabilis* and Black-footed Albatrosses *D. nigripes* on Midway Atoll within that same time-frame also involved the appearance of a new disease in a waterbird population. Many years of banding albatrosses on Midway by others had not disclosed the presence of this highly visible disease (pers. unpubl. data), except for an isolated case

report of pox in a Red-tailed Tropicbird *Phaethon rubicauda* (Locke *et al.* 1965).

Newcastle disease (ND) is another example of increased prominence by an infectious disease. Lethal strains of ND were eliminated from the poultry industries of Canada and the USA during the early 1970s. However, ND has periodically been killing large numbers of Double-crested Cormorants *Phalacrocorax auritus* since 1990 in Canada and since 1992 in the USA (Docherty & Friend 1999). These and other diseases that have appeared (Table 2) illustrate the increasing challenge that infectious disease poses for the conservation of wild birds (Friend *et al.* 2001).

## GEOGRAPHIC EXPANSION OF DISEASE

Expansion of the historic geographic distribution for many diseases is another outcome from disease emergence and resur-gence, and involves both non-infectious diseases such as avian botulism and established infectious diseases such as avian cholera. Originally, type C avian botulism was considered to be a disease of western North America, but since the 1930s it has occurred throughout most of the USA, including Hawaii (Rocke & Friend 1999) and on all continents with the exception of Antarctica. During the winter of 2002/2003, Taiwan experienced avian botu-lism for the first time in wild waterbirds (Rocke, this volume).

The first reported avian cholera epizootic in waterbirds occurred in Kenya during 1940 (Rosen 1971). The global occur-rence of this disease is attested to by Table 1. Continued global expansion is evident from the 2003 epizootic that killed more than 13 000 Baikal Teal *Anas formosa* wintering in Cheonseo Bay. This was the first occurrence of avian cholera in Korea (Kwon & Kang 2003). The geographic spread of avian cholera as a disease of North American waterbirds began during the 1960s after nearly two decades of localized occurrences in California and Texas. During the 1970s and 1980s, epizootics occurred across the USA and accompanied waterbirds from their breeding grounds in northern Canada to wintering areas in the southern USA and Mexico (Brand 1984, Friend 1999b).

**Table 2. Examples of novel disease occurrences in North American waterbirds since 1960.**

| Disease | Type | Year | Primary Taxa | Comments |
|---|---|---|---|---|
| Duck Plague | Virus | 1967 | Anatidae | Now enzootic |
| Erysiphelothrix | Bacteria | 1975 | Podicipedidae | Later die-off of Brown Pelicans *Pelecanus occidentalis* |
| Streptococcosis | Bacteria | 1977 | Podicipedidae | First record in any wild bird |
| Avian pox | Virus | 1978 | Anatidae | Pox in Bald Eagles *Haliaeetus leucocephalus* followed |
| Inclusion body disease of cranes | Virus | 1978 | Gruidae | Captive breeding colony |
| Newcastle disease | Virus | 1990 | Phalacrocoracidae | Recurring epizootics of highly virulent disease |
| Avian botulism | Bacterial toxin | Mid-1980s | Pelecanidae | First type C epizootics in fish-eating birds |
| Avian tuberculosis | Bacteria | 1980s | Gruidae | Major causes of demise of "satellite" flock of Whooping Cranes *Grus americana* |
| Mycotoxicosis | Fungal toxin | 1982 | Gruidae | Associated with peanut farming |
| Unknown | Unknown | 1992 | Podicipedidae | Persistent problem recognizable by clinical signs |
| Avian vascular mylenopathy | Unknown | 1994 | Rallidae, Anatidae, Accipitridae | Persistent and expanding problem first seen in Bald Eagles |
| Trematodiasis | Metazoan parasite | 1996 | Rallidae | Now enzootic |
| West Nile fever | Virus | 2002 | Pelecanidae | First occurrence in 1999 in Corvidae |

**Table 3. North American examples (excluding type C avian botulism) of disease emergence and geographic expansion causing 5 000 or more waterbird deaths since 1970.**

| Location | Disease | Year | Estimated loss | Primary species |
|---|---|---|---|---|
| Chesapeake bay, Maryland | Avian Cholera | 1970 | 80 000 | Scoters *Melanitta* spp., Long-tailed Duck *Clangula hyemalis* |
| Lake Andes, South Dakota | Duck Plague | 1973 | 40 000 | Mallard *Anas platyrhynchos* |
| Great Salt lake, Utah | Erysipelas | 1975 | 5 000 | Eared Grebe *Podiceps nigricollis* |
| Great Salt Lake, Utah | Streprococcosis | 1977 | 7 500 | Waterfowl, shorebirds |
| Hudson Bay, Canada | Avian cholera | 1979 | 5 000+ | Snow Goose *Chen caerulescens* |
| Rainwater Basin, Nebraska | Avian cholera | 1980 | 80 000 | Waterfowl |
| Texas Panhandle | Mycotocicosis | 1985 | 5 000 | Sandhill Crane *Grus canadensis* |
| Saskatchewan, Canada | Avian cholera | 1988 | 5 000+ | Redhead *Aythya americana* |
| Salton Sea, California | Salmonellosis | 1989 | 5 000 | Cattle Egret *Ardea ibis* |
| Lower Therien, Canada | Newcastle disease | 1992 | 20 000 | Double-crested Cormorant *Phalacrocorax auritus* |
| Salton Sea, California | Unidentified | 1992 | 155 000 | Eared Grebe |
| Banks Island, Northwest Territories | Avian cholera | 1995 | 30 000 | Snow Goose |
| Shawano Lake, Wisconsin | Trematodiasis | 1986 | 12 700 | American Coot *Fulica americana* |
| Salton Sea, California | Newcastle disease | 1998 | 6 000 | Double-crested Cormorant |
| Great Salt Lake, Utah | Avian cholera | 1998 | 50 000 | Eared Grebe |
| Tensas, Louisiana | Aflatoxicosis | 1999 | 10 500 | Snow Goose |
| Mid-and Western USA | West Nile fever | 2003 | 5 000+ | American White Pelican *Pelecanus erythrorhynchos* |

The rapid geographic spread within North America by some newly emerged avian diseases such as WNF and house finch conjunctivitis has been without precedence. It took less than four years for WNF to appear in all of the contiguous 48 states within the USA following its appearance in New York City in 1999 (NWHC unpubl. data). In less than three years following the 1994 index case of conjunctivitis in a House Finch *Carpodacus mexicanus* at a bird feeder in the Washington D.C. area, this disease spread across the entire geographic range of the eastern populations of this species (Fischer *et al.* 1997). Further geographic spread to the western House Finch population followed. Spread to Canada and Mexico has also occurred for WNF and conjunctivitis. The rate of spread for duck plague across the USA and into Canada (Friend 1999c) has been less aggressive than the infectious diseases just noted. Isolated and sporadic epizootic with limited geographic spread has been characteristic of still other avian diseases (Friend & Franson 1999). However, further spread of these diseases may still occur.

**MAGNITUDE OF LOSSES**

The greatest loss of waterbirds from a single disease event may have been the 1910 avian botulism outbreak that occurred on the Bear River marshes in Utah. That year also likely marked the greatest single-year loss from one disease. The millions of waterbirds that died from botulism that summer on the Bear River marshes and in California stimulated the beginning of real concern about the effects of this disease on waterfowl populations within the USA (Jensen & Williams 1964). There are no reports of disease events in wild birds of similar magnitude prior to that time. Also, although epizootics due to parasites, fungi, or bacteria may have occurred, Phillips & Lincoln (1930) stated that they "...have no knowledge that disease – which in modern times [1920s] has so decimated the [waterfowl] flocks – was an important factor..."

With the exception of the early avian botulism events, individual disease events involving waterbirds rarely exceeded losses of 5 000 until the occurrence of avian cholera. Past eval-

uations of North American waterfowl losses from disease resulted in a total estimated loss during 1930-1964 of nearly 1.9 million birds and a yearly average of approximately 55 000 birds (Stout & Cornwell 1976). Since the 1970s, single events during many years have killed more than 50 000 birds (NWHC unpubl. data). In another evaluation, Bellrose (1976) estimated that during the period of 1955-1973, non-hunting mortality (disease, predation, and accidents) resulted in the loss of 20 million game ducks each year and noted that "Disease directly or indirectly accounts for the largest proportion of non-hunting deaths". Much of this mortality (two to three percent of the waterfowl population) was due to lead poisoning (1.6 to 2.4 million game ducks).

Since the 1970s, both the frequency of reported disease events in waterbirds and the number of large-scale losses due to individual events have increased greatly over the previous half-century (Table 3). The characteristics of these disease events also differ from previous times. A greater number of diseases are involved, disease is occurring over a greater geographic area, and these events are occurring throughout the year rather than being seasonal.

**POPULATION IMPACTS**

In 1948, Ira Gabrielson, then Director of the Fish and Wildlife Service, referred to botulism and other disease as minor factors in the decline of North American waterfowl populations (Gabrielson 1948). Gabrielson's perspectives towards disease were consistent with long-reigning beliefs by many within the wildlife conservation community. Those beliefs minimized the toll of avian botulism within the western USA despite reports that "...the disease outbreaks in the West are particularly disastrous and it is conceivable that because of them it might be necessary to shorten shooting seasons or bag limits..." (Phillips & Lincoln 1930).

As noted by Toft (1991) and others (e.g. Haldane 1949, May 1988), the long-standing failure of many within the wildlife conservation community to accept the importance of disease has deep roots that have their origin in the teachings and writings of eminent ecologists and biologists. In the past, "…ecologists and evolutionary biologists virtually ignored parasites [including microbes]…, even as a source of mortality for host species [wildlife] of primary interest" (Toft 1991). However, within recent years, a shifting in perspective towards the impacts of disease on avian populations has emerged within some components of the wildlife conservation community. In 1980, Price noted that "…parasites [includes microbes] affect the life and death of practically every other living organism" and a decade later (1991) stated "…parasites are likely to play a role in practically every aspect of the evolutionary biology of birds, and probably vertebrates in general. Such a view has been a long-time in gestation, probably because in a fetal condition it was roundly thwarted by two eminent ecologists".

Those ecologists were Charles Elton and David Lack. Their conclusions may have been appropriate for the time period and species for their study. However, the conditions of today are different and present an array of increased challenges for avian populations world-wide (Friend *et al.* 2001, Friend & Franson 1999). Admittedly, "the ability to determine and evaluate the effect of disease on the population dynamics of free-ranging avifauna is fraught with difficulties and confounded by a host of factors that complicate the determination of cause-and-effect relationships" (Friend *et al.* 2001). Regardless, examples of waterbird populations being threatened by disease are currently not difficult to find.

Although the cause has yet to be determined, disease is suspected to be a major factor in the decline of Common Eiders *Somateria mollissima* in the Gulf of Finland (Hollmén *et al.* 1999, 2000). That population is declining at an annual rate of 6-10% (Hario 1998). In the late 1980s, duckling survival dropped to 1-5% in some areas, and mortality events have killed large numbers of young and some adult Eiders (Hollmén *et al.* 1999, 2000). Also, the 2004 avian cholera outbreak on Dyer Island, South Africa, killed fledgling as well as adult Cape Cormorants *Phalacrocorax capensis* and Crowned Cormorants *P. coronatus*, two species whose populations are in decline and classified as near-threatened. This is the third consecutive year for outbreaks of avian cholera on this Cape Nature Conservation reserve (Pro Med 2004). Avian cholera is also a major mortality factor for the Ruddy Duck *Oxyura jamaicensis* at California's Salton Sea. Substantial numbers of Eared Grebes (Black-necked Grebes) *Podiceps nigricollis* have also been killed by avian cholera at the Salton Sea and the Great Salt Lake (Friend 2002).

In general, disease evaluations primarily involve fledged birds. Far less is known about disease as a factor in effecting recruitment, even though mortality occurs on a large scale. Newcastle disease, avian cholera, salmonellosis, and eustrongyides are diseases causing mass mortality in breeding colonies of waterbirds (Friend & Franson 1999). For example, Newcastle disease killed most of the production of Double-crested Cormorants at the Salton Sea during 1997 and again during 1998 (Friend 2002). The emergence of diseases that impact embryo survival and other aspects of reproduction are potentially of even greater importance. Therefore, the high prevalence of antibodies to infectious bursal disease virus (IBDV) in Common Eiders nesting in the Gulf of Finland (Hollmén *et al.* 2000) and antibodies to IBDV in wild Emperor Penguins *Aptenedytes fosteri* and Adelie Penguins *Pygoscelis*

*adalaiae* in the Antarctic (Gardner *et al.* 1997a, 1997b) is of special concern.

## DISCUSSION

Disease emergence is real, global in scope, and affecting wildlife as well as domesticated species and humans. Infectious disease has increased in prominence as a cause of mortality for wild birds, and is aided by environmental conditions that redistribute and further aggregate gregarious species in a manner that facilitates disease transmission. Aquatic environments are an important habitat for disease emergence in humans and should be viewed with similar concern for wild waterbirds. A recent evaluation cited 17 different pathogenic microbes and infectious human diseases recognized since 1972 for which water may play a role (Koopmans 2001). Examples of disease in waterbirds within this presentation clearly demonstrate that aquatic environments are also important for disease emergence in birds. It is important to recognize that examples have been provided, rather than a holistic overview of the increasing array of diseases taking a toll of waterbirds.

Losses from disease are much greater today than they have been for nearly a century. These losses have increased consequences because direct and indirect effects of habitat loss have reduced the resilience of wildlife populations to compensate for the cumulative impacts from disease. Further habitat degradation and loss are assured for the foreseeable future (Ayensu *et al.* 1999). Thus, past approaches to disease in wildlife need to be improved upon. Reactive response to epizootics is an inadequate approach and should not be our primary defense against disease in waterbirds. The conservation of these species requires a more proactive approach involving disease prevention and control as a mainstream activity if we are truly serious about global waterbird conservation.

## REFERENCES

**Ayensu, E., Claasen, D. van R., Collins, M., Dearing, A., Fresco, L., Gadgil, M. & Gitau, H.** 1999. International ecosystem assessment. Science 286: 685-686.

**Bellrose, F.C.** 1976. Ducks, Geese and Swans of North America. Stackpole Books, Harrisburg, Pennsylvania.

**Brand, C.J.** 1984. Avian cholera in the Central and Mississippi Flyways during 1979-1980. Journal of Wildlife Management 48: 299-406.

**Cole, R.A. & Friend, M.** 1999. Miscellaneous parasitic diseases. In: M. Friend & J.C. Franson (eds) Field Manual of Wildlife Diseases: General Field Procedures and Disease of Birds. U.S. Geological Survey, Biological Resources Division Information and Technology Report 1999-2001: 249-258.

**Converse, K.A. & Kidd, G.A.** 2001. Duck plague epizootics in the United States, 1967-1995. Journal of Wildlife Disease 37: 347-357.

**Docherty, D.E. & Friend, M.** 1999. Newcastle Disease. In: M. Friend & J.C. Franson (eds) Field Manual of Wildlife Diseases: General Field Procedures and Disease of Birds. U.S. Geological Survey, Biological Resources Division Information and Technology Report 1999-2001: 175-179.

**Fallis, A.M. & Trainer, D.O., Jr.** 1964. Blood parasites. In: J.P. Linduska & A.L. Nelson (eds) Waterfowl Tomorrow. U.S. Department of the Interior, Washington, D.C.: 343-348.

**Fisher, J.R., Stallknecht, D.E., Luttrell, M.P., Dhondt, A.A. & Converse, K.A.** 1997. Mycoplasma conjunctivitis in wild song birds: The spread of a new contagious disease in a mobile host population. Emerging Infectious Diseases 3: 69-72.

**Friend, M.** 1981. Waterfowl diseases – changing perspectives for the future. Fourth International Waterfowl Symposium, New Orleans, Louisiana: 189-196.

**Friend, M.** 1999a. Lead poisoning. In: M. Friend & J.C. Franson (eds) Field Manual of Wildlife Diseases: General Field Procedures and Disease of Birds. U.S. Geological Survey, Biological Resources Division Information and Technology Report 1999-2001: 317-334.

**Friend, M.** 1999b. Avian cholera. In: M. Friend & J.C. Franson (eds) Field Manual of Wildlife Diseases: General Field Procedures and Disease of Birds. U.S. Geological Survey, Biological Resources Division Information and Technology Report 1999-2001: 75-92.

**Friend, M.** 1999c. Duck plague. In: M. Friend & J.C. Franson (eds) Field Manual of Wildlife Diseases: General Field Procedures and Disease of Birds. U.S. Geological Survey, Biological Resources Division Information and Technology Report 1999-2001: 141-151.

**Friend, M.** 2002. Avian disease at the Salton Sea. Hydrobiologia 473: 293-306.

**Friend, M. & Franson, J.C.** (eds). 1999. Field Manual of Wildlife Diseases: General Field Procedures and Disease of Birds, U.S. Geological Survey, Biological Resources Division Information and Technology Report 1999-2001, Reston, Virginia. http://www/nwhc.usgs.gov/pub_metadata/index.html

**Friend, M., McLean, R.G. & Dein, F.J.** 2001. Disease emergence in birds: challenges for the twenty-first century. The Auk 118: 290-303.

**Gabrielson, I.N.** 1948. Wildlife Conservation. The Macmillan Company, New York.

**Gardner, H., Brouwner, S., Gleeson, L., Kerry, K. & Riddle, M.** 1997a. Poultry virus infection found in Antarctic penguins. Penguin Conservation 10: 8-21.

**Gardner, H., Knowles, K., Riddle, M. Brouwner, S. & Gleeson, L.** 1997b. Poultry virus infection in Antarctic penguins. Nature 387: 245.

**Haldane, J.B.S.** 1949. Disease and evolution. La Ricerca Science Supplement 19: 68-76.

**Hansen, W.** 1999. Avian pox. In: M. Friend & J.C. Franson (eds) Field Manual of Wildlife Diseases: General Field Procedures and Disease of Birds. U.S. Geological Survey, Biological Resources Division Information and Technology Report 1999-2001: 163-169.

**Hario, M.** 1998. Recent trends and research results for four archipelago bird species – common eider, velvet scoter, herring gull and lesser black-backed gull. In: T. Solonen & E. Lammi (eds) The Yearbook of the Linnut Magazine. Bird Life Finland, Kuopio, Finland: 12-24.

**Herman, C.M. & Wehr, E.E.** 1954. The occurrence of gizzard worms in Canada geese. Journal of Wildlife Management 18: 509-513.

**Hollmén, T., Leighton, J.T., Sankari, S., Soveri, T. & Hario, M.** 1999. An experimental study on the effects of polymorphisms in common eider ducklings. Journal of Wildlife Diseases 35: 466-473.

**Hollmén, T., Franson, J.C., Docherty, D.E., Kilpi, M., Hario, M., Creekmore, L.H. & Petersen, M.R.** 2000. Infectious bursal disease virus antibodies in eider ducks and herring gulls. Condor 102: 688-691.

**Jensen, W.I. & Price, J.I.** 1987. The global importance of type C botulism in wild birds. In: M.W. Eklund & V.R. Dowell, Jr. (eds) Avian Botulism: An International Perspective. Charles C. Thomas, Springfield, Illinois: 33-54.

**Jensen, W.I. & Williams, C.S.** 1964. Botulism and fowl cholera. In: J.P. Linduska & A.L. Nelson (eds) Waterfowl Tomorrow. U.S. Department of the Interior, Washington, D.C.: 333-341.

**Koopmans, M.P.G.** 2001. Emerging issues: new risks. Microbial Pathogens and Disinfection by-products in Drinking Water: 181-190.

**Kwon, Y.K. & Kang, M.I.** 2003. Outbreak of fowl cholera in Baikal teals in Korea. Avian Disease 47: 1491-1495.

**Leibovitz, L. & Hwang, J.** 1968. Duck plague on the American continent. Avian Diseases 12: 361-378.

**Locke, L.N., Writz, W.O. & Brown, E.E.** 1965. Pox infection in a red-tailed tropic bird (*Phaeton rubricauda*). Bulletin of the Wildlife Disease Association 1: 60-61.

**May, R.M.** 1988. Conservation and disease. Conservation Biology 2: 28-30.

**Morton, J.K. & Dieterich, R.A.** 1979. Avian pox infection in an American green-winged teal (*Anas crecca carolinensis*) in Alaska. Journal of Wildlife Diseases 15: 451-453.

**O'Meara, D.C. & Witter, J.F.** 1971. Aspergillosis. In: J.W. Davis, R.C. Anderson, L. Karstad & D.O. Trainer (eds) Infectious and Parasitic Diseases of Wild Birds. Iowa State University Press, Ames, Iowa: 153-162.

**Phillips, J.C. & Lincoln, F.C.** 1930. American Waterfowl: Their Present Situation and the Outlook For Their Future. Houghton Mifflin Co., Boston, Massachusetts.

**Price, P.W.** 1980. Evolutionary Biology of Parasites. Princeton University Press, Princeton, New Jersey.

**Price, P.W.** 1991. Forward. In: J.E. Loye & M. Zuk (eds) Bird-Parasite Interactions-Ecology, Evolution and Behavior. Oxford University Press, Oxford: v-vii.

**Pro Med** 2004. Avian cholera, cormorants – South Africa. 6 January 2004, Capetown Times. http://www.capetimes.co.za/index.php?fArticleId=318667

**Quortrup, E.R., Queen, F.B. & Merovka, L.J.** 1946. An outbreak of pasterellosis in wild ducks. Journal of the American Veterinary Medical Association 108: 94-103.

**Ripley, S.D. & Steed, J.A.** 1987. Alexander Wetmore. Biological Memoirs 56: 597-626.

**Rocke, T.E. & Friend, M.** 1999. Avian botulism. In: M. Friend & J.C. Franson (eds) Field Manual of Wildlife Diseases: General Field Procedures and Disease of Birds. U.S. Geological Survey, Biological Resources Division Information and Technology Report 1999-2001: 271-281.

**Rosen, M.N.** 1971. Avian cholera. In: J.W. Davis, R.C. Anderson, L. Karstad & D.O. Trainer (eds) Infectious and Parasitic Diseases of Wild Birds. Iowa State university Press, Ames, Iowa: 59-74.

**Stout, I.J. & Cornwell, G.W.** 1976. Nonhunting mortality of fledged North American waterfowl. Journal of Wildlife Management 40: 681-693.

**Toft, C.A.** 1991. Current theory of host-parasitic interactions. In: J.E. Loye & M. Zuk (eds) Bird-Parasite Interactions – Ecology, Evolution and Behavior. Oxford University Press, Oxford: 3-15.

**Wetmore, A.** 1918. The Duck Sickness in Utah. U.S. Department of Agriculture Bulletin No. 672, Washington, D.C.

**Wetmore, A.** 1919. Lead Poisoning in Waterfowl. U.S. Department of Agriculture Bulletin No. 793, Washington, D.C.

**Wobeser, G.A.** 1981. Disease of Wild Waterfowl. Plenum Press, New York.

The appearance of new diseases in susceptible waterbird populations often results in catastrophic losses, such as this occurrence of duck plague that killed approximately 40 000 Mallards *Anas platyrhynchos* at a National Wildlife Refuge in the USA. Photo: Milton Friend courtesy of the U.S. Geological Survey.

Carcasses being incinerated as part of cleanup activities associated with a major outbreak of avian botulism at a National Wildlife Refuge in the USA. Photo: Milton Friend, courtesy of the U.S. Geological Survey.

# Emerging viral diseases in waterbirds

*Thijs Kuiken, Ron A.M. Fouchier, Guus F. Rimmelzwaan & Albert D.M.E. Osterhaus*
*Department of Virology, Erasmus Medical Centre, Dr. Molewaterplein 50, 3015 GE Rotterdam, The Netherlands.*

Kuiken, T., Fouchier, R.A.M., Rimmelzwaan, G.F. & Osterhaus A.D.M.E. 2006. *Emerging viral diseases in waterbirds. Waterbirds around the world.* Eds. G.C. Boere, C.A. Galbraith & D.A. Stroud. The Stationery Office, Edinburgh, UK. pp. 418-421.

Emerging viral diseases in waterbirds include Newcastle disease, West Nile fever and avian influenza. These are important not only because of their impact on the species themselves, but also because they may be transmitted to domestic animals, humans, or both, with economic consequences and consequences for human health. Pathogenic Newcastle disease virus emerged in Double-crested Cormorants *Phalacrocorax auritus* in south-central Canada in 1990, and spread widely across North America in subsequent years. It affects mainly juvenile cormorants, with up to 90% mortality in affected colonies. Newcastle disease is economically important because it is a reportable disease infectious for poultry. Its emergence may have been associated with rapid population growth of cormorant populations, largely due to anthropogenic factors. West Nile virus first appeared in New York in 1999, and has spread rapidly across North and Central America. Mortality of infected wild birds, particularly crows (Corvidae) but also waterbirds, has been unexpectedly high. The virus is occasionally transmitted to humans, horses and other mammals. In 2003, over 9 000 human cases were reported in the USA, of which nearly 300 were fatal. Wild birds, mainly waterbirds, are thought to be the reservoir for influenza A viruses in nature. In 2003, highly pathogenic avian influenza A (H7N7) virus probably evolved from low pathogenic viruses in free-living Mallard *Anas platyrhynchos* and caused high mortality in poultry in The Netherlands. The virus was also transmitted to humans, resulting in conjunctivitis, influenza-like illness and one fatal case of pneumonia. The emergence of H7N7 virus may be related to the rapid growth of free-range chicken farms in The Netherlands. Overall, the underlying factors for the emergence of infectious diseases in recent years are anthropogenic social and environmental changes. We need to recognize and address these factors in order to decrease the rate of emergence and to make the transition to a more sustainable society.

## INTRODUCTION

Since the 1980s, the emergence and re-emergence of infectious diseases in humans, domestic animals and wildlife have been reported with increasing frequency (Daszak *et al.* 2000, Kuiken *et al.* 2003). Waterbird species around the world have also been affected by emerging infections, including viruses, bacteria and protozoa (Table 1). Here we concentrate on three outbreaks, Newcastle disease, West Nile fever and avian influenza, and discuss possible underlying factors and future measures.

## NEWCASTLE DISEASE

Newcastle disease in Double-crested Cormorants *Phalacrocorax auritus* (reviewed in Kuiken 1999) emerged in North America in 1990, when extensive mortality was observed in breeding colonies at several lakes in the central provinces of Canada. This was considered extraordinary because the causative agent, a pathogenic strain of Newcastle disease virus, was exotic to North America, and because it was the first time that this disease had caused high mortality in wild birds.

The clinical signs of Newcastle disease in Double-crested Cormorants include lameness of one or both wings or legs, loss of balance, uncoordinated movements, exudation from the eyes, and abnormal posture. The nervous signs correspond to a characteristic non-suppurative inflammation of the brain and spinal cord (encephalomyelitis) and the presence of Newcastle disease virus antigen in neurons, glial and endothelial cells, as shown by immunohistochemistry. Although the above clinical signs and pathologic changes are suggestive, the definitive diagnosis of Newcastle disease depends on identification of the virus by isolation or reverse transcriptase-polymerase chain reaction, and determination of its pathogenicity.

Since its emergence in 1990, Newcastle disease in Double-crested Cormorants has become more widespread, appearing in western Canada, the Great Lakes area and the north-central states

**Table 1. Selected emerging infectious diseases in wild birds in the past two decades (data from Daszak *et al.* 2000 and Kuiken *et al.* 2003).**

| Disease | Pathogen | Hosts | Geography of emergence |
|---|---|---|---|
| Highly pathogenic avian influenza | Influenza A virus (H5N1) | Humans, waterfowl, waders, poultry | Asia |
| Highly pathogenic avian influenza | Influenza A virus (H7N7) | Humans, waterfowl, poultry | The Netherlands |
| West Nile fever | West Nile virus | Humans, horses, other mammals, birds, mosquitoes | North and Central America |
| Newcastle disease | Newcastle disease virus | Double-crested Cormorant, pelicans, gulls, poultry | Canada, USA |
| Mycoplasmal conjunctivitis | *Mycoplasma gallisepticum* | House Finch* and other garden birds | Canada, USA |
| Salmonellosis | *Salmonella typhimurium* DT40 | Wild finches | UK |
| Avian malaria | *Plasmodium* spp. | Wide range of native birds | Hawaii |

* *Carpodacus mexicanus*

of the USA in 1992, and extending to the west coast of the USA in 1997. These outbreaks have affected mainly Double-crested Cormorants, and are limited to young of the year, with up to 90% mortality in affected colonies. In other bird species present at these outbreaks, Newcastle disease has been diagnosed only in an American White Pelican *Pelecanus erythrorhynchos*, a Ring-billed Gull *Larus delawarensis*, a Black-crowned Night-Heron *Nycticorax nycticorax*, and a Caspian Tern *Sterna caspia*. No evidence of Newcastle disease was found in 22 species of birds occurring at a breeding colony of Double-crested Cormorants where an outbreak of Newcastle disease was followed closely.

Newcastle disease is important for the poultry industry because of the devastating epidemics it causes, and because of its far-reaching effects on trade in poultry products. There is one recorded instance of transmission of Newcastle disease from Double-crested Cormorants to poultry. This was in 1992 at Devils Lake, North Dakota, where Newcastle disease was diagnosed in a flock of domestic free-range turkeys located less than 7 km from an affected cormorant colony (Meteyer *et al.* 1997).

A possible underlying factor for the emergence of Newcastle disease in Double-crested Cormorants is the dramatic increase in the size of its population since the late 1970s, resulting in a greater risk of transmission of the Newcastle disease virus and increased severity of the outbreaks. This is especially true for the population in the Canadian and US interior, which increased from about 6 000 in 1969 to 220 000 in 1992 (Hatch 1995). There appear to be five factors that have contributed to this population explosion (Wires *et al.* 2001):

- the ban on DDT in 1972;
- increased protection for the Double-crested Cormorant in 1972, under the Migratory Bird Treaty Act;
- human-induced changes (e.g. the introduction of exotic fish species and over-fishing of predatory fish) in lakes in the breeding range, resulting in an increased food supply;
- the development of aquaculture (e.g. catfish farms) in the wintering range, resulting in an increased food supply; and
- the creation of additional breeding and foraging habitat (e.g. reservoirs and artificial islands).

## WEST NILE VIRUS

The emergence of West Nile virus infection in North America is impressive because of its dramatic impact on the health of humans, domestic animals and wild birds. It spread from its original range in Africa, the Middle East and Europe to New York in 1999, where it was first described as a fatal neurological disease of unknown cause in humans. When mortality and nervous signs were also observed in a variety of exotic and native birds, especially crows (Corvidae), the investigators realized that they were dealing with a new disease in North America, West Nile fever (Lanciotti *et al.* 1999).

West Nile virus infection is mosquito-borne, and is amplified and maintained in birds. It is occasionally transmitted, usually by mosquito bites, to humans, horses and other mammals, but these are incidental hosts that do not play an important role in the life cycle of the virus. The nervous signs observed in West Nile fever are related to virus infection and subsequent inflammation of the central nervous system, with expression of virus antigen in neurons and glial cells of affected tissue (Campbell *et al.* 2002, Steele *et al.* 2000).

Wild birds are important for the epidemiology of West Nile virus. Modelling indicates that infected birds spread the virus over long distances along their migratory routes, while mosquitoes are important for local dissemination (Peterson *et al.* 2003). As a result, the West Nile virus has spread rapidly across North America, from New York in 1999 as far west as California and as far south as Mexico and the Caribbean by 2003, and is likely to spread further south into Central and South America (Kuiken *et al.* 2003). According to reports to the Centers for Disease Control and Prevention (2004a), mortality from West Nile virus infection has been recorded in over 100 wild bird species in the USA, including several species of waterbirds. This is surprising, because mortality in birds is low in the historic range of West Nile virus (McLean *et al.* 2002). Two possible reasons for the high mortality in wild birds in North America are that North American birds have not co-evolved with West Nile virus and are therefore more susceptible to disease, and/or that the strain of West Nile virus in North America is particularly pathogenic. Information on the impact of West Nile virus on wild birds at the population level remains scant. Yaremych *et al.* (2003) found an annual survival rate of 17.9% in American Crows *Corvus brachyrhynchos* in an area where West Nile virus occurred, compared with an average annual survival rate of 89.6% for breeding-age American Crows not affected by West Nile virus infection. In another study, West Nile virus infection was diagnosed as the cause of death in American White Pelicans at nine sites in the USA where more than ten pelicans died in 2002 and 2003 (Rocke *et al.* in press).

West Nile virus also has a large impact on the health of humans and horses in North America. As expected in a human population that had not previously been exposed to West Nile virus infection, there has been a relatively high proportion of potentially fatal neurological cases. A total of 9 862 human cases were reported in the USA in 2003 alone, and 264 of these were fatal (Centers for Disease Control and Prevention 2004b). In horses, a total of 5 181 cases were reported in the USA in 2003 (USDA 2004), with substantial morbidity and mortality from West Nile virus encephalitis (Kleiboeker *et al.* 2004).

The underlying factors for the emergence of West Nile virus in North America are poorly understood. There was an increase in the number of cases of West Nile meningoencephalitis in the original range of the West Nile virus between 1994 and 2000 (Campbell *et al.* 2002), and by phylogenetic analysis, the 1999 New York isolate most closely resembled that of an isolate from Israel in 1997, suggesting that it originated from the Middle East (Lanciotti *et al.* 2002). How this occurred is not known; possible mechanisms include migratory birds, legal or illegal importation of birds, persons travelling at the incubation stage of West Nile virus infection, and transport of infected mosquitoes by aeroplane.

## AVIAN INFLUENZA A VIRUS

Avian influenza A virus has recently received widespread attention because of large-scale outbreaks in poultry and virus transmission from poultry to humans, in some cases with fatal consequences (Fouchier *et al.* 2004, Tran *et al.* 2004). Wild birds, mainly waterbirds, are involved with these outbreaks because they are thought to be the reservoir for influenza A viruses in nature. For this reason, the Department of Virology at the Erasmus Medical Centre in The Netherlands is engaged in a long-term surveillance study to screen migratory birds for the presence of influenza A virus (Fouchier *et al.* 2003). To date, influenza A viruses representing 15 haemagglutinin subtypes and nine neuraminidase subtypes have been described in birds. Of these, the subtypes H5 and H7 may become highly pathogenic in poultry and result in so-called fowl plagues (Fouchier *et al.* 2004). The recent H5N1 virus outbreaks are described elsewhere in these Proceedings (Melville & Shortridge 2006). Here we will concentrate on the H7N7 virus outbreak in The Netherlands in 2003 (Fouchier *et al.* 2004, Koopmans *et al.* 2004).

In February 2003, an infectious disease with high lethality for poultry emerged in The Netherlands and subsequently spread to poultry in Germany and Belgium. In total, around 30 million chickens, representing about 28% of the total chicken population in The Netherlands, died or were pre-emptively culled. The causative agent of this outbreak was identified as highly pathogenic avian influenza A (H7N7) virus. By sequencing and phylogenetic analysis of the genome of this virus, it was found to be most closely related to low pathogenic virus isolates obtained from Dutch Mallard *Anas platyrhynchos* during the course of the above-mentioned surveillance study. Evolution from a low pathogenic to a high pathogenic pathotype presumably occurred after the virus had been introduced into poultry farms, as has been shown on several other occasions (Ito *et al.* 2001).

Responses to health questionnaires revealed that 453 people involved in the control of the avian influenza outbreak had health complaints, consisting of conjunctivitis (349 cases), influenza-like illness (90 cases) and other complaints (67 cases). Influenza A (H7) virus was isolated from 89 of these cases, most of which had conjunctivitis. One veterinarian died from pneumonia followed by acute respiratory distress syndrome caused by H7N7 virus, two weeks after visiting an affected poultry farm.

Over 100 carcasses of free-living wild birds were collected around affected poultry farms to determine whether H7N7 virus was transmitted from poultry to wild birds ("spill-back"). However, none of these carcasses tested positive for influenza A virus, and there was therefore no evidence for a role of wild birds in spreading the H7N7 virus from affected poultry farms to other areas.

Underlying factors for the emergence of H7N7 virus in The Netherlands are unclear. It is possible, however, that it is associated with the rapid increase in the number of free-range chickens in The Netherlands, from none in 1991 to 305 000 in 2001. This fits with the association between outbreaks of highly pathogenic avian influenza outbreaks and the presence of free-range poultry farms or "wet" markets in other parts of the world (Kuiken *et al.* 2003).

## DISCUSSION

The above examples illustrate our lack of knowledge of the factors underlying the emergence of infectious diseases in individual cases. However, when reviewed together, emerging infectious diseases in humans, domestic animals and wildlife show a common set of underlying factors (Table 2). These result from the combined weight of human numbers and their consumption patterns that are overloading the planet's biophysical and ecological capacity (Daszak *et al.* 2000, Daszak *et al.* 2001, McMichael 2001).

Early detection of emerging infectious diseases will be facilitated by improved disease surveillance in humans, domestic animals and wildlife. Furthermore, we have the technological capability to respond rapidly to such events in terms of identifying the causative agent and developing diagnostic techniques,

**Table 2. Factors underlying the emergence of infectious diseases (from Daszak *et al.* 2000).**

- International travel and commerce (introduction of species)
- Demographic changes
- Agricultural changes
- El Niño Southern Oscillation
- Global climate change
- Technological change
- Microbial adaptation
- Breakdown in health or international traffic infrastructure
- Increased interaction with vectors/wildlife/humans/domestic animals
- Immuno-suppression/heightened susceptibility
- Increased surveillance

and, to a lesser degree, developing vaccines and therapeutic agents (Kuiken *et al.* 2003). However, these measures do not deal with the source of the problem. The emergence and re-emergence of infectious diseases will only increase in the future, unless we address the increase in human population and consumption patterns, and make the transition to a more sustainable society.

## REFERENCES

Campbell, G.L., Marfin, A.A., Lanciotti, R.S. & Gubler, D.J. 2002. West Nile virus. Lancet Infectious Diseases 2: 519-529.

Centers for Disease Control and Prevention 2004a. Web-site: http://www.cdc.gov/ncidod/dvbid/westnile/bird-species.htm, accessed 12 February 2004.

Centers for Disease Control and Prevention 2004b. Web-site: http://www.cdc.gov/ncidod/dvbid/westnile/surv&control CaseCount03_detailed.htm, accessed 18 June 2004.

Daszak, P., Cunningham, A.A. & Hyatt, A.D. 2000. Emerging infectious diseases of wildlife – threats to biodiversity and human health. Science 287: 443-449.

Daszak, P., Cunningham, A.A. & Hyatt, A.D. 2001. Anthropogenic environmental change and the emergence of infectious diseases in wildlife. Acta Tropica 78: 103-116.

Fouchier, R.A., Olsen, B., Bestebroer, T.M., Herfst, S., van der, K.L., Rimmelzwaan, G.F. & Osterhaus, A.D. 2003. Influenza A virus surveillance in wild birds in Northern Europe in 1999 and 2000. Avian Diseases 47: 857-860.

Fouchier, R.A., Schneeberger, P.M., Rozendaal, F.W., Broekman, J.M., Kemink, S.A., Munster, V., Kuiken, T., Rimmelzwaan, G.F., Schutten, M., Van Doornum, G.J., Koch, G., Bosman, A., Koopmans, M. & Osterhaus, A.D. 2004. Avian influenza A virus (H7N7) associated with human conjunctivitis and a fatal case of acute respiratory distress syndrome. Proceedings of the National Academy of Sciences of the U.S.A. 101: 1356-1361.

Hatch, J.J. 1995. Changing populations of Double-crested Cormorants. Colonial Waterbirds 18 (Special Publication 1): 8-24.

Ito, T., Goto, H., Yamamoto, E., Tanaka, H., Takeuchi, M., Kuwayama, M., Kawaoka, Y. & Otsuki, K. 2001. Generation of a highly pathogenic avian influenza A virus from an avirulent field isolate by passaging in chickens. Journal of Virology 75: 4439-4443.

Kleiboeker, S.B., Loiacono, C.M., Rottinghaus, A., Pue, H.L. & Johnson, G.C. 2004. Diagnosis of West Nile virus infection in horses. Journal of Veterinary Diagnostic Investigation 16: 2-10.

Koopmans, M., Wilbrink, B., Conyn, M., Natrop, G., van der, N.H., Vennema, H., Meijer, A., van Steenbergen, J., Fouchier, R., Osterhaus, A. & Bosman, A. 2004. Transmission of H7N7 avian influenza A virus to human beings during a large outbreak in commercial poultry farms in the Netherlands. Lancet 363: 587-593.

Kuiken, T. 1999. Review of Newcastle disease in cormorants. Waterbirds 22: 333-347.

Kuiken, T., Fouchier, R.A., Rimmelzwaan, G.F. & Osterhaus, A. 2003. Emerging viral infections in a rapidly changing world. Current Opinion in Biotechnology 14: 641-646.

Lanciotti, R.S., Roehrig, J.T., Deubel, V., Smith, J., Parker, M., Steele, K., Crise, B., Volpe, K.E., Crabtree, M.B., Scherret, J.H., Hall, R.A., MacKenzie, J.S., Cropp, C.B., Panigrahy, B., Ostlund, E., Schmitt, B., Malkinson, M., Banet, C., Weissman, J., Komar, N., Savage, H.M., Stone, W., McNamara, T. & Gubler, D.J. 1999. Origin of the West Nile virus responsible for an outbreak of encephalitis in the northeastern United States. Science 286: 2333-2337.

Lanciotti, R.S., Ebel, G.D., Deubel, V., Kerst, A.J., Murri, S., Meyer, R., Bowen, M., McKinney, N., Morrill, W.E., Crabtree, M.B., Kramer, L.D. & Roehrig, J.T. 2002. Complete genome sequences and phylogenetic analysis of West Nile virus strains isolated from the United States, Europe, and the Middle East. Virology 298: 96-105.

McLean, R.G., Ubico, S.R., Bourne, D. & Komar, N. 2002. West Nile virus in livestock and wildlife. Current Topics in Microbiology and Immunology 267: 271-308.

McMichael, A.J. 2001. Human frontiers, environments and disease: past patterns, uncertain futures. Cambridge University Press, Cambridge, UK.

Melville, D.S. & Shortridge, K.F. 2006. Migratory waterbirds and avian influenza in the East Asian-Australasian Flyway with particular reference to the 2003-2004 H5N1 outbreak. Waterbirds around the world. G.C. Boere, C.A. Galbraith & D.A. Stroud (Eds.), The Stationery Office, Edinburgh, UK. 432-438.

Meteyer, C.U., Docherty, D.E., Glaser, L.C., Franson, J.C., Senne, D.A. & Duncan, R. 1997. Diagnostic findings in the 1992 epornitic of neurotropic velogenic Newcastle disease in double-crested cormorants from the upper midwestern United States. Avian Diseases 41: 171-180.

Peterson, A.T., Vieglais, D.A. & Andreasen, J.K. 2003. Migratory birds modeled as critical transport agents for West Nile virus in North America. Vector Borne Zoonotic Diseases 3: 27-37.

Rocke, T., Converse, K., Meteyer, C. & McLean, B. In press. The impact of disease in American White Pelicans in North America. Waterbirds.

Steele, K.E., Linn, M.J., Schoepp, R.J., Komar, N., Geisert, T.W., Manduca, R.M., Calle, P.P., Raphael, B.L.,

Pathogenic Newcastle disease virus emerged in Double-crested Cormorants *Phalacrocorax auritus* in south-central Canada in 1990, and spread widely across North America in subsequent years. Photo: Rob Robinson.

Clippinger, T.L., Larsen, T., Smith, J., Lanciotti, R.S., Panella, N.A. & McNamara, T.S. 2000. Pathology of fatal West Nile virus infections in native and exotic birds during the 1999 outbreak in New York City, New York. Veterinary Pathology 37: 208-224.

Tran, T.H., Nguyen, T.L., Nguyen, T.D., Luong, T.S., Pham, P.M., Nguyen, V.C., Pham, T.S., Vo, C.D., Le, T.Q., Ngo, T.T., Dao, B.K., Le, P.P., Nguyen, T.T., Hoang, T.L., Cao, V.T., Le, T.G., Nguyen, D.T., Le, H.N., Nguyen, K.T., Le, H.S., Le, V.T., Christiane, D., Tran, T.T., Menno, D.J., Schultsz, C., Cheng, P., Lim, W., Horby, P. & Farrar, J. 2004. Avian influenza A (H5N1) in 10 patients in Vietnam. New England Journal of Medicine 350: 1179-1188.

USDA 2004. Web-site: http://www.aphis.usda.gov/vs/nahps/equine/wnv/map2003.html, accessed 18 June 2004.

Wires, L.R, Cuthbert, F.J., Trexel, D.R. & Joshi, A.R. 2001. Status of the double-crested cormorant (*Phalacrocorax auritus*) in North America. Final report to U.S. Fish and Wildlife Service.

Yaremych, S.A., Warner, R.E., Van de Wyngaerde, M.T., Ringia, A.M., Lampman, R. & Novak, R.J. 2003. West Nile virus detection in American crows. Emerging Infectious Diseases 9: 1319-1321.

# The global importance of avian botulism

*Tonie E. Rocke*

*National Wildlife Health Center, 6006 Schroeder Rd., Madison, Wisconsin 53711, USA. (email: tonie_rocke@usgs.gov)*

Rocke, T. E. 2006. The global importance of avian botulism. *Waterbirds around the world.* Eds. G.C. Boere, C.A. Galbraith & D.A. Stroud. The Stationery Office, Edinburgh, UK. pp. 422-426.

## ABSTRACT

On a world-wide basis, avian botulism is the most significant disease of waterbirds. Type C botulism has been reported in waterbirds from every continent except Antarctica, and outbreaks with one million or more waterbird deaths have been reported by the USA, Canada, and Russia. Unfortunately, population impacts of avian botulism have not been well studied. Species that are numerous, geographically widespread, and have a high reproductive potential (e.g. Mallard *Anas platyrhynchos*) may be able to withstand sporadic high losses, while populations of other, less common or endangered species whose populations are disproportionately exposed to botulism, may not be as resilient (e.g. Northern Pintail *Anas acuta*, Black-faced Spoonbill *Platalea minor*). The effect of botulism on local or regional waterbird populations is also significant. The 1996 botulism outbreak at the Salton Sea, California, killed nearly 15% of the western population of American White Pelicans *Pelecanus erythrorhynchos*. Because the occurrence of avian botulism is largely controlled by environmental factors and not dependent on waterbird density, this disease has the potential to cause significant population declines in some species, seriously impeding conservation efforts.

## INTRODUCTION

During the last century, avian botulism killed many millions of birds, especially waterfowl and shorebirds, and was the most significant disease of waterbirds in total mortality. Large outbreaks of "duck sickness", later recognized to be type C botulism, were first documented in the western USA and Canada in the early 1900s (Hobmaier 1932). Millions of waterfowl died in three widely separated regions of North America – the deltas of the Great Salt Lake, Utah, the southern San Joaquin Valley,

California, and the Elfros region of Saskatchewan, Canada. Outside North America, the first outbreaks of botulism in wild birds were recorded in Australia in 1934 (Pullar 1934), in Russia (formerly USSR) in 1957 (Kuznetzov 1992), and in Europe in 1963 (Jensen & Price 1987), first in Sweden and shortly after in Denmark (1965), Great Britain (1969), and The Netherlands (1970). Botulism was also confirmed in South Africa (1965), New Zealand (1971), Japan (1973), Argentina (1979) and Brazil (1981). To date, type C botulism has been diagnosed in wild waterbirds in at least 28 countries and on every continent with the exception of Antarctica. More than a million deaths from type C avian botulism have been reported during single outbreaks in some wetlands in North America and Russia (Table 1), and outbreaks with losses exceeding 50 000 birds have been relatively common. Even though most of the large outbreaks of avian botulism occurred in North America, the global importance of the disease and its potential to cause massive and even catastrophic losses of birds are evident.

## ETIOLOGY AND HOST RANGE OF THE DISEASE

The agent which causes avian botulism is a neurotoxin produced by the bacterium *Clostridium botulinum*, a strict anaerobe that forms dormant spores in adverse conditions. Botulinum toxin is produced only after the spores germinate during vegetative growth of the bacteria. Birds primarily acquire the disease by ingesting toxin-laden food items; thus, the disease is usually a food poisoning and not an infection. It can also be caused by "toxico-infections", when botulinum toxin-producing bacteria colonize the intestinal tract of an individual or secondarily infect a wound. Seven different neurotoxins are produced by strains of *C. botulinum*, designated types A to G (Smith & Sugiyama 1988). Most botulism outbreaks in birds are caused by type C toxin, but sporadic die-offs among fish-eating birds, primarily in the Great Lakes of North America, have been caused by type E toxin.

Botulinum toxin causes a flaccid paralysis in birds, with loss of motor control, flight and ambulation. A common sign of botulism in birds is paralysis of the nictitating membrane. In the final stages of the disease, birds are unable to lift their heads; thus, the disease has also been called "limberneck". Death usually results from respiratory failure or drowning. All birds are probably susceptible to botulinum toxin, with the exception of vultures and possibly other scavenging birds, which may have an innate resistance to the disease. Upon review of the literature and over 2 000 diagnostic records at the USGS National Wildlife Health Center (NWHC), confirmed reports of type C botulism were found for 264 species of birds representing 39 families; most of these (22) were waterbird families. Foraging behavior appears to be the most significant risk factor for avian botulism (Rocke & Friend 1999). Filter feeding and dabbling waterfowl, such as Mallard *Anas platyrhynchos*, Green-winged Teal *A. crecca*, and Northern Shoveler *A.*

**Table 1. Type C avian botulism outbreaks with losses of over 50 000 birds.**

| Location | Year | Estimated losses |
|---|---|---|
| Utah and California, USA | 1910 | Millions |
| Lake Malheur, Oregon, USA | 1925 | 100 000 |
| Great Salt Lake, Utah, USA | 1929 | 100 000-300 000 |
| Tulare Basin, California, USA | 1941 | 250 000 |
| Tule Lake, California, USA | 1948 | 65 000-150 000 |
| California, USA | 1969 | 140 000 |
| Montana, USA | 1970 | 100 000 |
| Great Salt Lake, Utah, USA | 1980 | 110 000 |
| Caspian Sea, former USSR | 1982 | 1 000 000 |
| Lake Pakowki, Alberta, Canada | 1995 | 100 000 |
| Whitewater Lake, Manitoba, Canada | 1996 | 117 000 |
| Old Wives Lake, Saskatchewan, Canada | 1997 | 1 000 000 |
| Great Salt Lake, Utah, USA | 1997 | 514 000 |

*clypeata*, are among the species at greatest risk for contracting type C botulism, as well as probing shorebirds such as sandpipers (Scolopacidae), and avocets and stilts (Recurvirostridae).

## EPIZOOTIOLOGY

Much of the collective knowledge about the epizootiology of avian botulism derives from observations of the massive outbreaks in waterfowl in wetlands in western North America. However, the epizootiology of botulism in birds is more complex than previously believed and also quite diverse, being dependent on local environmental conditions as well as the foraging behavior of the birds involved. Several distinct patterns in the occurrence of type C botulism in waterbirds are evident and will be discussed here.

### Botulism in freshwater wetlands

Avian botulism in freshwater wetlands typically occurs during the warmer months of summer or autumn, but outbreaks are unpredictable, sometimes occurring annually in certain wetlands but not in adjacent ones with similar habitat and patterns of bird use. Also, losses from botulism vary greatly from year to year and from species to species. Only a few hundred birds may die from botulism in a wetland one year, whereas tens of thousands or more may die the following year at the same location.

Botulinum spores are highly resistant to heating and drying, can remain viable for years, and are widely distributed in wetland habitats (Smith *et al.* 1978). Spores can also be found in the tissues of most wetland inhabitants, including aquatic insects, mollusks and crustacea, and many vertebrates, including birds and fish (Reed & Rocke 1992). Wetlands where botulism outbreaks have occurred multiple times are heavily contaminated with spores and have a higher probability of subsequent outbreaks than wetlands with no known history of the disease (Wobeser *et al.* 1987). However, spores can be carried in the tissues of birds and distributed to new environments in their feces (Matveev & Konstantinova 1974), and outbreaks have occurred in recent years in wetlands with no known history of the disease (NWHC unpubl. data). In a 40 sq km multi-wetland complex where numerous botulism outbreaks have occurred in the past, Sandler *et al.* (1993) found no association between the density of spores in an individual wetland and the occurrence of outbreaks. Once botulinum spores are established in a wetland, their density is probably not a limiting factor for the occurrence of the disease.

Wetland conditions seem to be a more important determinant in the occurrence of botulism. A recent study of 32 wetlands with botulism outbreaks and paired control wetlands in nine states in the USA (Rocke & Samuel 1999) demonstrated that the risk of botulism outbreaks was associated with several measurable wetland characteristics. These relationships could be modeled, but they were complex, involving both non-linear and multivariate associations. The most important factor was water pH, but its effect was strongly influenced by water temperature and redox potential. In general, the risk of botulism outbreaks increased when pH was between 7.5-9.0, redox potential was negative, and water temperature was over 20°C. Risk declined in wetlands with a pH under 7.5 or over 9.0, when redox potential was positive (over +100 mv), and water temperature was lower (10-15°C). Although these variables have been shown to influence spore germination and bacterial replication in the laboratory, the

underlying mechanism for their association with the risk of botulism outbreaks in natural wetlands is unknown. Also, the investigators emphasized that even when wetland conditions were indicative of high risk, other, more proximate factors, such as invertebrate density, bird abundance and other sediment and water characteristics, probably interact to determine whether botulism actually occurs in a specific wetland and may also influence its severity. For example, in a multi-wetland refuge complex in northern California, botulism outbreaks in high-risk wetlands occurred in direct relation to increasing invertebrate abundance and increasing temperature (Rocke *et al.* 1999).

Presumably, wetland conditions enable bacterial growth and toxin production, resulting in a high-risk situation, but an outbreak will only occur if toxic food items are encountered and ingested by birds. In some cases, decaying organic matter that contains toxin may be directly ingested by birds. Toxin has been produced readily in high protein organic matter and decaying invertebrate tissues both in the field and in the laboratory (Hobmaier 1932, Kalmbach & Gunderson 1934, Bell *et al.* 1955, Rocke unpubl. data). Birds that sift through the mud to feed, such as Mallard and other dabbling ducks, and filter feeders, such as Northern Shoveler, are likely to ingest a wide variety of decaying organic matter or dead invertebrates that may contain sufficient levels of toxin to cause botulism. Waterbirds may also be poisoned upon consumption of zooplankton or wetland invertebrates that have consumed toxic material. The carcass-maggot cycle, described in more detail below, is a classic example of secondary poisoning through consumption of toxin-laden invertebrates, but other aquatic animals may serve in this role as well. Wetlands are home to numerous invertebrates and zooplankton that consume organic debris, particularly in the benthos, and type C botulinum toxin has been demonstrated in free-living aquatic invertebrates (Kalmbach & Gunderson 1934, Rocke unpubl. data), crustacea (Rocke unpubl. data), and zooplankton (Neubauer *et al.* 1988). Unfortunately, direct evidence that clarifies the role of invertebrates in the initiation of botulism outbreaks is lacking. Instead, most research has focused on the role of sarcophagous larvae on carcasses and the carcass-maggot cycle of botulism.

### Carcass-maggot cycle of avian botulism

It is well known that decomposing tissues containing botulinum spores can support high levels of toxin production (Bell *et al.* 1955, Reed & Rocke 1992). Fly larvae and other invertebrates are unaffected by the toxin and, as they feed on decaying matter, they effectively act to concentrate the toxin. Toxin levels in maggots as high as 400 000 mouse lethal doses (MLD)/g have been found on waterfowl carcasses (Duncan & Jensen 1976). With a 50% lethal dose for type C botulinum toxin in waterfowl estimated at 36 000-43 000 MLD/kg of body weight (Rocke *et al.* 2000), ingestion of only a single toxic maggot could be lethal. Although most waterfowl will not directly consume a vertebrate carcass, many would ingest maggots that fall off. In this way, botulism outbreaks in waterfowl often become self-perpetuating. This has become known as the carcass-maggot cycle of botulism, and it is thought that toxic maggots have the greatest potential to cause massive die-offs of birds (Wobeser 1997).

Waterbirds that have ingested botulinum spores and die from any cause are as likely to initiate outbreaks through the carcass-maggot cycle as birds that ingested pre-formed toxin and died from the disease (Reed & Rocke 1992). Thus the presence of decaying carcasses from other mortality events can lead to a botulism outbreak. Bird collisions with power transmission lines have initiated botulism outbreaks in Montana, USA (Malcolm 1982) and elsewhere (NWHC unpubl. data). Other sources of mortality, e.g. hailstorms and algal poisoning, and even other disease agents may precipitate botulism outbreaks through the carcass-maggot cycle.

Many factors influence the carcass-maggot cycle, including fly density and environmental conditions such as temperature and wind speed that facilitate fly egg-laying, maggot development and maggot dispersal from carcasses (Reed & Rocke 1992, Wobeser *et al.* 1997). However, the most critical factor is the density of carcasses that are toxigenic, i.e. contain botulinum spores that germinate and produce toxin (Reed & Rocke 1992). Some investigators (Duncan & Jensen 1976) found that 85-90% of maggot-infested carcasses contained toxic maggots, while in another study (Reed & Rocke 1992), the rate varied from 29% to 69%. Although not every carcass will become maggot-infested or produce toxic maggots, factors that reduce the availability of toxic carcasses in wetlands, such as the presence of scavenging predators and carcass pick-up, may lower the risk of waterbird exposure to botulinum toxin.

### Winter outbreaks of avian botulism

Most outbreaks of botulism occur in the summer and autumn months when wetland temperatures rise and are more favorable for bacterial growth and toxin production. However, on occasion, outbreaks of type C botulism in waterbirds have been documented in late winter or early spring (Haagsma 1973, Graham *et al.* 1978, Wobeser *et al.* 1983, Hubalek & Halouzka 1991). Outbreaks of botulism have occurred in winter in California, USA, Saskatchewan, Canada, and also in the Norfolk Broads, UK. Typically, these outbreaks are preceded by a botulism die-off in the same location the previous autumn and often involve diving ducks. The spring outbreaks may be the result of toxin-bearing maggots that fell to the bottom of the wetland the previous autumn and are accessible in the spring only to diving ducks (Wobeser *et al.* 1983).

### Type C botulism in fish-eating waterbirds

In 1996, over 15 000 pelicans, herons, and other fish-eating birds became sick or died from type C botulism at the Salton Sea in southern California, a 97 000 ha (375 sq. miles) inland sea that provides critical wintering habitat for numerous birds. Nearly half the birds that died at the Salton Sea were either American White Pelicans *Pelecanus erythrorhynchos* or Brown Pelicans *P. occidentalis*. This was the largest die-off ever reported for pelicans anywhere in the world from any agent. Prior to this event, type C botulism in fish-eating birds was considered infrequent and incidental to larger outbreaks in waterfowl, and most previous reported botulism outbreaks that involved large numbers of fish-eating birds (mostly divers, Gaviidae, and gulls, Laridae), were caused by type E botulinum toxin (Rocke & Friend 1999). The largest reported loss of pelicans from botulism before 1996 was 223 birds at Long Lake, North Dakota, in 1988 (Rocke *et al.* in press). Although type C botulism recurred in fish-eating birds at the Salton Sea from 1997 to 2001, the total loss over this period (approximately 1 000-3 000 birds) was lower than in 1996.

The primary source of toxin for birds at the Salton Sea was

thought to be Tilapia *Oreochromis mossambicus*, an introduced fish that dominated the Sea at that time. Toxin was found in nearly 50% of sick and dead Tilapia and also in undigested fish remains regurgitated by sick pelicans (Rocke *et al.* 2004). Systematic research at the Salton Sea demonstrated that live Tilapia (both sick and healthy) harbored botulinum cells in their gastrointestinal tracts (Nol *et al.* 2004), and the prevalence of the bacteria varied from year to year as did mortality in pelicans. The investigators hypothesized that the high summer water temperatures (often over 37°C) and other environmental stresses, combined with the Tilapia's reduced foraging efforts in the summer months, created an altered, possibly static gut environment that was conducive to spore germination (Nol *et al.* 2004). The epizootiology of the disease at the Salton Sea appears to be very unusual.

### Avian botulism associated with landfills

Several outbreaks of type C botulism in gulls have been associated with landfills and refuse tips in Britain (Lloyd *et al.* 1976), Scotland (MacDonald & Standring 1978), Ireland (Quinn & Crinion 1984), the Virgin Islands (Norton 1986), and most recently Israel (Gophen *et al.* 1991). The refuse itself is not thought to be the source of the bacteria; rather, botulinum spores are probably transferred by birds attracted to the sites. The presence of the spores, coupled with rotting organic matter and the concomitant rise in environmental temperatures, promote bacterial replication and toxigenesis, and ultimately result in botulism in birds scavenging at the sites. In the case of the die-off in Israel, waste products from a chicken slaughterhouse were found to be improperly buried and probably contributed to the die-off (Gophen *et al.* 1991).

### DISCUSSION

Although avian botulism is arguably the most significant disease for waterbirds, its effect on populations is poorly understood. Unfortunately, the information required to measure its impact on populations, such as annual and spatial variation in botulism occurrence and estimates of populations at risk, is difficult to obtain for most waterbird species. Generally, mortality estimates during die-offs are based on the retrieval of carcasses. However, it has been demonstrated that the retrieval of carcasses underestimates mortality by between three times (Cliplef & Wobeser 1993) and as much as 10 times (Stutzenbaker *et al.* 1986). Also, numerous outbreaks probably go undetected as scavenging animals can consume large numbers of carcasses (Stutzenbaker *et al.* 1986).

Botulism outbreaks often involve several species of waterbirds. Some species may be able to withstand high losses, while others may not be as resilient. The Mallard, which is numerous and geographically widespread and has a high reproductive potential, can probably withstand sporadic heavy losses from botulism. Other, less common species whose populations are disproportionately exposed to botulism may be more severely impacted. From 1994 to 1997, outbreaks of avian botulism killed over four million waterfowl in Canada and the USA, and the Northern Pintail *Anas acuta* accounted for a large proportion (15-20%) of the recorded mortality (NWHC unpubl. data). At the same time, surveys showed that Northern Pintail populations in North America remained low, while populations of other dabbling ducks increased in response to improving water conditions in the prairie pothole regions (US Fish and Wildlife Service 1998). Although the reasons for this trend are unknown, it is thought that botulism may be one of several factors contributing to low pintail numbers. The effects of botulism on local or regional populations can also be important. During the 1996 outbreak at the Salton Sea, an estimated 15% of the western sub-population of the American White Pelican died (Rocke *et al.* 2004).

Endangered species are especially vulnerable to a disease like botulism that is not density dependent. Threatened or endangered waterbirds in the USA that have contracted botulism include the Brown Pelican and four Hawaiian species, the Hawaiian Goose (Nene) *Branta sandvicensis*, Hawaiian Duck *Anas wyvilliana*, Hawaiian Coot *Fulica alai*, and Hawaiian Stilt *Himantopus mexicanus knudseni*. Waterbird species with a limited distribution or that winter or breed in only a few wetlands are most at risk. During the winter of 2002/2003, avian botulism killed 73 Black-faced Spoonbills *Platalea minor* out of about 500 individuals at the Tseng-Wen Estuary in Tainan, Taiwan, a critical wintering area for the species; this loss represented approximately 7% of the total global population of this species (BirdLife International 2004). If the disease recurs at the Tseng-Wen Estuary, it could have serious implications for the conservation of the Black-faced Spoonbill.

In the past, numerous management actions were recommended to prevent botulism outbreaks in wetlands, such as removing rotting vegetation, agitating stagnant water, stabilizing water levels, creating shorelines with steep banks, removing vertebrate carcasses that served to perpetuate outbreaks through the carcass-maggot cycle of botulism, and even killing invertebrates with pesticides. Of these recommendations, only the removal of carcasses has been effective in reducing botulism losses (Reed & Rocke 1992), but unfortunately, carcass monitoring and removal activities are costly, labor intensive and not an efficient prevention strategy, especially in very large wetlands. Additional research is needed to understand the various environmental factors that promote outbreaks in different situations. The development of predictive or risk-assessment models based on demonstrated associations between wetland and other conditions and the occurrence of botulism outbreaks could be used in an adaptive management approach to identify wetlands at high risk for waterbirds, to develop and evaluate alternative strategies for reducing the risk to waterbirds, and to evaluate how current wetland and waterbird management practices influence the risk of botulism outbreaks.

## ACKNOWLEGEMENTS

The author's work on this manuscript was supported by the U.S. Geological Survey, Biological Resources Division. Many thanks to J. C. Franson and K. Converse for helpful editorial comments and to the organizers of the Waterbirds around the world Conference.

## REFERENCES

Bell, J.F., Sciple, G.W. & Hubert, A.A. 1955. A microenvironment concept of the epizoology of avian botulism. Journal of Wildlife Management 19: 352-357.

BirdLife International 2004. State of the world's birds 2004: indicators for our changing world. BirdLife International, Cambridge, UK.

Cliplef, D.J. & Wobeser, G. 1993. Observations on waterfowl carcasses during a botulism epizootic. Journal of Wildlife Diseases 29: 8-14.

Duncan, R.M. & Jensen, W.I. 1976. A relationship between avian carcasses and living invertebrates in the epizootiology of avian botulism. Journal of Wildlife Diseases 12: 116-126.

Gophen, M., Cohen, A., Grinberg, K., Pokamunski, S., Nili, E., Wynne, D., Yawetz, A., Dotan, A., Zook-Rimon, A., Ben-Shlomo, M. & Ortenberg, Z. 1991. Implications of botulism outbreaks in gulls (*Larus ridibundus*) on the watershed management of Lake Kinneret (Israel). Environmental Toxicology and Water Quality 6: 77-84.

Graham, J.M., Smith, G.R., Borland, E.D. & MacDonald, J.W. 1978. Botulism in winter and spring and the stability of *Clostridium botulinum* type C toxin. Veterinary Record 102: 40-41.

Haagsma, J. 1973. Etiology and epidemiology of botulism in waterfowl in the Netherlands. BronderOffset B.V., Rotterdam.

Hobmaier, M. 1932. Conditions and control of botulism (duck disease) in waterfowl. California Fish and Game 18: 5-21.

Hubalek, Z. & Halouzka, J. 1991. Persistence of *Clostridium botulinum* type C toxin in blow fly (Calliphoridae) larvae as a possible cause of avian botulism in spring. Journal of Wildlife Diseases 27: 81-85.

Jensen, W.I. & Price, J.I. 1987. The global importance of type C botulism in wild birds. In: M.W. Eklund & V.R. Dowell, Jr. (eds) Avian botulism: an international perspective. Charles C Thomas, Springfield, Illinois: 33-54.

Kalmbach, E.R. & Gunderson, M.F. 1934. Western duck sickness: a form of botulism. U.S. Department of Agriculture Technical Bulletin 411.

Kuznetzov, E.A. 1992. Botulism in wild waterfowl in the USSR. In: Diseases and Parasites of Wild Animals. Ministry of Ecology and Natural Resources of Russia, Moscow: 112-122. (In Russian).

Lloyd, C.S., Thomas, G.J., MacDonald, J.W., Borland, E.D., Standring, K. & Smith, J.L. 1976 Wild bird mortality caused by botulism in Britain 1975. Biological Conservation 10: 119-129.

MacDonald, J.W. & Standring, K.T. 1978. An outbreak of botulism in gulls on the Firth of Forth, Scotland. Biological Conservation 14: 149-155.

Malcolm, J.M. 1982. Bird collisions with a power transmission line and their relation to botulism at a Montana wetland. Wildlife Society Bulletin 10: 297-304.

Matveev, K.I. & Konstantinova, M.D. 1974. The role played by migrating birds in the distribution of the botulism agent. Hygiene and Sanitation 12: 91-92.

Neubauer, M., Hudec, K. & Pellantova, J. 1988. The occurrence of *Clostridium botulinum* type C bacterium and botulotoxin in an aquatic environment in southern Moravia. Folia Zoologica 37: 255-262.

Nol, P., Rocke, T.E., Gross, K. & Yuill, T.M. 2004. Prevalence of neurotoxic *Clostridium botulinum* type C in the gastrointestinal tracts of tilapia (*Oreochromis mossambicus*) in the Salton sea. Journal of Wildlife Diseases 40: 414-419.

**Norton, R.L.** 1986. Case of botulism in laughing gulls at a land-fill in the Virgin Islands, Greater Antilles. Florida Field Naturalist 14: 97-98.

**Pullar, E.M.** 1934. Enzootic botulism amongst wild birds. Australian Veterinary Journal 10: 128-135.

**Quinn, P.J. & Crinion, R.A.P.** 1984. A two year study of botulism in gulls in the vicinity of Dublin Bay. Irish Veterinary Journal 38: 214-219.

**Reed, T.M. & Rocke, T.E.** 1992. The role of avian carcasses in botulism epizootics. Wildlife Society Bulletin 20: 175-182.

**Rocke, T.E. & Friend, M.** 1999. Avian Botulism. In: M. Friend & J. C. Franson (eds) Field Manual of Wildlife Diseases: General Field Procedures and Diseases of Birds. Biological Resources Division Information and Technology Report 1999-2001: 271-281.

**Rocke, T.E. & Samuel, M.D.** 1999. Water and sediment characteristics associated with avian botulism outbreaks in wetlands. Journal of Wildlife Management 63: 1249-1260.

**Rocke, T.E., Euliss, N. & Samuel, M.D.** 1999. Environmental characteristics associated with the occurrence of avian botulism in wetlands on a northern California wetland. Journal of Wildlife Management 63: 358-368.

**Rocke, T.E., Samuel, M.D., Swift, P.K. & Yarris, G.S.** 2000. Efficacy of a type C botulism vaccine in green-winged teal. Journal of Wildlife Diseases 36: 489-493.

**Rocke, T.E., Nol, P., Pelizza, C. & Sturm, K.** 2004. Type C botulism in pelicans and other fish-eating birds at the Salton Sea. Studies in Avian Biology 27: 136-140.

**Rocke, T.E., Converse, K., Meteyer, C. & McLean, R.** In press. The impact of disease in American White Pelicans in North America. Waterbirds.

**Sandler, R.J., Rocke, T.E., Samuel, M.D. & Yuill, T.M.** 1993. Seasonal prevalence of *Clostridium botulinum* type C in sediments of a northern California wetland. Journal of Wildlife Diseases 29: 533-539.

**Smith, G.R., Milligan, R.A. & Moryson, C.J.** 1978. *Clostridium botulinum* in aquatic environments in Great Britain and Ireland. Journal of Hygiene 80: 431-438.

**Smith, L.D.S. & Sugiyama, H.** 1988. Botulism: the organism, its toxins, the disease. Second edition. Charles C Thomas, Springfield, Illinois.

**Stutzenbaker, C.D., Brown, K. & Lobpries, D.** 1986. Special report: an assessment of the accuracy of documenting waterfowl die-offs in a Texas coastal marsh. In: J.S. Feierabend & A.B. Russell (eds) Lead Poisoning in Wild Waterfowl, a workshop. National Wildlife Federation, Washington, D.C., USA: 88-95.

**U.S. Fish and Wildlife Service** 1998. Waterfowl population status. U.S. Fish and Wildlife Service, Washington, D.C., USA.

**Wobeser, G.A.** 1997. Avian botulism – another perspective. Journal of Wildlife Diseases 33: 181-186.

**Wobeser, G.A., Rainnie, D.J., Smith-Windsor, T.B. & Bogdan, G.** 1983. Avian botulism during late autumn and early spring in Saskatchewan. Journal of Wildlife Diseases 19: 90-94.

**Wobeser, G.A., Marsden, S. & MacFarlane, R.J.** 1987. Occurrence of toxigenic *Clostridium botulinum* type C in the soil of wetlands in Saskatchewan. Journal of Wildlife Diseases 23: 67-76.

**Wobeser, G., Baptiste, K., Clark, E.G. & Deyo, A.W.** 1997. Type C botulism in cattle in association with a botulism die-off in waterfowl in Saskatchewan. Canadian Veterinary Journal 38: 782.

Mallards *Anas platyrhynchos* are amongst those dabbling and filter-feeding ducks most likely to contract type C botulism. Photo: Sergey Dereliev.

# Domestic poultry and migratory birds in the interspecies transmission of avian influenza viruses: a view from Hong Kong

*Kennedy F. Shortridge[1] & David S. Melville[2]*

[1]*Emeritus Professor, The University of Hong Kong, Hong Kong SAR, China; and Honorary Professor, Department of Molecular Medicine and Pathology, The University of Auckland, Auckland, New Zealand. (email: kennedyfs@xtra.co.nz)*

[2]*Dovedale, R.D. 2 Wakefield, Nelson, New Zealand. (email: david.melville@xtra.co.nz)*

Shortridge, K.F. & Melville, D.S. 2006. Domestic poultry and migratory birds in the interspecies transmission of avian influenza viruses: a view from Hong Kong. *Waterbirds around the world*. Eds. G.C. Boere, C.A. Galbraith & D.A. Stroud. The Stationery Office, Edinburgh, UK. pp. 427-431.

## ABSTRACT

Agricultural practices in southern China provide an abundance of avian influenza viruses in the environment through the medium of the domestic duck. This is the backdrop to a series of remarkable genetic changes by the recently recognized Asian lineage of highly pathogenic H5N1 virus involving multiple poultry hosts, particularly the chicken, and in the case of the 2003/2004 outbreak in east and south-east Asia, the domestic duck as well as the chicken. While there is little evidence to support the role of migratory birds in the spread of this outbreak, the widening range of hosts suggests that they could in the future. The implications arising from the spread of the H5N1 virus for humans, poultry and wildlife in the Asian region and beyond are great. Ornithologists have much to contribute in dealing with these issues.

## INTRODUCTION

The recognition of an antigenic relationship between the surface haemagglutinin glycoproteins (HA) of the pandemic H3N2 influenza A virus that emerged through Hong Kong from neighbouring Guangdong Province, China, in 1968, and a virus previously isolated from a duck in the Ukraine, engendered a zoonotic perspective of pandemic influenza (Webster & Laver 1975). It led the World Health Organization (WHO) to foster studies on the ecology of influenza viruses (1) to determine the range of influenza viruses in nature, (2) to see if it is possible to recognize a virus before it appears in pandemic form in humans, and (3) to see whether this would facilitate quick and effective vaccine production. In other words, it was the goal to try to get ahead of the next pandemic influenza virus – a first-ever step toward significant influenza pandemic preparedness (Stuart-Harris 1970).

Financial and other support through the National Institutes of Health, Bethesda, USA, were instrumental in getting this goal off the ground in the early 1970s. More structured ecological studies have been pursued by influenza virologists since then, but with little input from ornithologists. The apparent lack of interest by ornithologists may have its roots in the fact that there have been no observable signs of avian influenza recorded for wild birds (Hansen 1999), there being only one case of large-scale mortality in Common Terns *Sterna hirundo* apparently caused by an H5N3 virus (Rowan 1962, Becker 1966).

Given the historical association of Asia and especially China as the source of a number of pandemics over the last 1 000 years (Potter 1998), narrowing to southern China in the last century, ecological studies of influenza viruses have been conducted in Hong Kong since 1975 on local and imported domestic poultry and animals, notably the pig, as well as migratory birds, with a view to getting ahead of the next pandemic. In this sense, Hong Kong has functioned as an influenza sentinel post for southern China and the wider region for almost 30 years.

In 1997, a highly pathogenic avian influenza (HPAI) virus, H5N1/97, was detected in chickens in the sentinel post itself, leading to human deaths and sparking fears of the next pandemic (Claas *et al.* 1998). A pandemic was probably averted by the slaughter of poultry across the Hong Kong SAR (Shortridge *et al.* 2000). A second H5N1 pandemic alarm occurred in late 2003 and early 2004. This time, an H5N1 virus manifested in chickens and ducks en masse in a number of countries in east and south-east Asia, resulting in human fatalities in two of them, and raising the question of whether wild birds played a role in the spread of the virus (see Melville & Shortridge 2004 & this volume). This report notes factors, past and present, contingent upon the dynamics of avian influenza virus (AIV) in the region.

## SOUTHERN CHINA

Waterfowl (Anatidae), and to a lesser extent shorebirds and gulls (Charadriiformes), are the primary reservoirs of AIV. The virus occurs asymptomatically in the birds, multiplying mainly in the intestine and being spread by faecally contaminated water (Markwell & Shortridge 1982, Webster *et al.* 1992). The domestication of the duck in eastern China, notably in the south around 2500 BC (Needham 1986), brought AIV into the "influenza farmyard" where these birds were mainly raised along river banks (Fig.1). The system changed around the start of the Ching Dynasty (1644 AD), when the ducks were raised as an adjunct to rice farming, initially as a means of controlling rice pests, in a beautifully balanced ecosystem conserving precious grain needed for humans (Fig. 2). This practice of duck raising reached its zenith in southern China and spread to varying extents throughout south-east Asia. (The goose was probably domesticated in China at about the same time as the duck.)

This practice meant that AIV could occur year-round in domestic ducks in southern China, a situation confirmed through virus surveillance studies. The overall isolation rates from the cloaca and trachea of aquatic ducks, partially aquatic geese and terrestrial chickens in a study conducted in Hong Kong from 1975-1980 on poultry from southern China were 6.5%, 1.11% and 0.41%, respectively (Shortridge 1992). The isolation rate of AIV from migratory ducks and shorebirds sampled over a number of years at a Hong Kong wetland was about the same as that from chickens (Chin, Shortridge, Liu, Suen & Melville unpubl. data).

The isolation of H3N2 viruses resembling the 1968 pandemic and contemporary human variants in virus surveillance studies of pigs in 1976 indicated that this domestic animal

Fig. 1. A photograph taken in 1980 in the Pearl River Delta, Guangdong Province, China, showing the traditional method of raising ducks along river banks. The "duck herder" can be seen amongst the ducks. This method of duck raising would be rare today.

Fig. 2. Ducks on a flooded rice field in Guangdong Province, China. The ducks feed on insects, crabs, etc. and are removed from the field when the rice blossoms, held on waterways and ponds, and introduced onto the dry field to fatten on unharvested, fallen grain. There are five crops of ducks a year, the two main ones in conjunction with the summer and autumn rice crops (Shortridge 1992 & 1997).

had a role to play in the "influenza farmyard" of southern China (Shortridge *et al.* 1977), possibly as a "mixing vessel" for the two-way exchange of avian and human influenza viruses (Scholtissek *et al.* 1985).

The newly recognized influenza ecology outlined above, the close association of the large human population with domestic animals in the region providing increased opportunity for interspecies transmission of avian influenza viruses, and the historical link of China (particularly southern China) with influenza

pandemics, led to southern China being designated as a hypothetical epicentre for the emergence of pandemic influenza viruses (Shortridge & Stuart-Harris 1982). This was the anchor for pandemic preparedness. Humans are considered as part of a matrix of interconnected AIV ecology (Fig. 3), with recognition of untoward respiratory disease or virus activity at any point in the matrix offering the prospect of preparedness and action. The key to this would lie in virus surveillance at all levels.

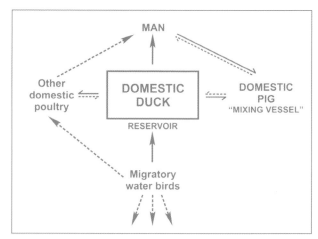

Fig. 3. Diagram showing the likely ecological relationship among the influenza A viruses of birds, pigs and humans in southern China, with the domestic duck as the central reservoir. The solid line indicates a more certain relationship, which in the case of ducks, humans and pigs has a genetic basis. The broken line indicates a less certain relationship (Shortridge 1988 & 1992).

### THE H5N1/97 VIRUS AND CONSEQUENCE

In 1997, Hong Kong found itself in the midst of an incipient pandemic situation; the first time that it had been possible to recognize one. The chicken in retail, live poultry markets was the principal source of H5N1/97 virus for humans (Shortridge 1999, Shortridge *et al.* 2000). Ancestry of this incident can be traced back to a precursor H5N1 virus that caused an outbreak of disease in domestic geese with 40% mortality in Guangdong Province in 1996 (Tang *et al.* 1998, Xu *et al.* 1999). It is worth noting that H5 viruses had been isolated from domestic ducks and a goose in the 1975-1980 surveillance studies (Shortridge 1992). Perhaps the most striking aspect of the generation of the triple reassortant H5N1/97 virus was the apparent role of the quail *Coturnix* sp., a minor poultry (Guan *et al.* 2000, Li *et al.* 2003), as the facilitator or avian "mixing vessel" for this (Fig. 4). More recent studies on H9 viruses have indicated that the quail can act as an intermediate host facilitating interspecies transmission from ducks to chickens (Perez *et al.* 2003).

The importance of domestic poultry, i.e. chickens rather than migratory birds, as the principal H5N1/97 virus source lies in the fact that in east Asia, and particularly in southern China, they are raised in close proximity to humans on small holdings and farms, making them a potential source of virus for humans. This situation has been exacerbated in the last 20 years or so because of the intensification of chicken production in southern China (and elsewhere around the world) increasing the opportunity for interspecies transmission, virus amplification and disease. The fact that precursor H5N1, H9N2 and H6N1 viruses continued to exist after 1997 (Guan *et al.* 2002a, Chin *et al.* 2002, Webster

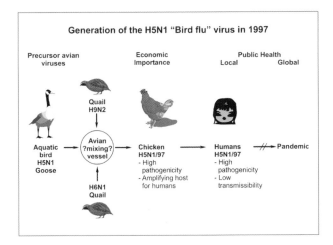

Fig. 4. Results of intensive virus surveillance post-1997, showing the most likely chain of events in the generation of the H5N1/97 virus, a triple reassortant highly pathogenic for chickens and humans. A goose H5N1 virus provided the gene encoding the H5 HA surface glycoprotein, a quail H9N2 virus provided the six genes encoding the internal proteins, and a quail H6N1 virus provided the gene encoding the second surface glycoprotein, the N1 neuraminidase, with the quail probably acting as a "mixing vessel" for these events (Guan *et al.* 1999, Hoffmann *et al.* 2000).

*et al.* 2002) suggested that an H5N1/97-like virus could be regenerated or that each of the precursors could be of pandemic potential in this changing AIV milieu (Shortridge *et al.* 2001).

## H5N1 VIRUS REAPPEARS

The HPAI H5N1/97 virus has not been isolated in the Hong Kong sentinel post since 1997. Instead, the precursor H5N1 virus was detected in geese in 1999 (Cauthen *et al.* 2000), changing hosts to ducks and undergoing re-assortment with unknown, aquatic AIV in 2000 (Webster *et al.* 2002, Guan *et al.* 2002b). It moved to chickens in 2001 and 2002 in changing ranges of genotypes (Guan *et al.* 2002a, Sturm-Ramirez *et al.* 2004), with one genotype, "Z", predominating and, in some cases, a closely related genotype "Z+" being detected. These genotypes, particularly the "Z+" genotype, were isolated from fatal infections in wild and captive waterfowl in Hong Kong in 2002 (Sturm-Ramirez *et al.* 2004, Guan *et al.* 2004), the first time a lethal influenza virus had been isolated from wild aquatic birds since 1961 (Becker 1966). The "Z+" genotype was also isolated from two Hong Kong residents following a visit to Fujian Province, to the north of Guangdong Province, in early 2003 (Guan *et al.* 2004). An H5N1 virus was isolated from a dead Peregrine Falcon *Falco peregrinus* in Hong Kong in early 2004 (Li *et al.* 2004).

The "Z" genotype that predominated in chickens by 2002 also predominated in chickens and ducks in the disastrous H5N1 virus outbreak in east and south-east Asia in late 2003 and early 2004 (Li *et al.* 2004). Although the "Z+" genotype was isolated from dead wild birds in Hong Kong, there was no convincing evidence that wild birds played a role in the spread of H5N1 virus in the region. Indeed, intensive virus surveillance around this time at a Hong Kong wetland did not yield H5N1 virus (Y. Guan pers. comm.). Poor hygiene and biosecurity probably played the major role in the spread of the virus (Melville & Shortridge 2004 & this volume).

## RINGING IN CHANGES

Given the lack of transparency in acknowledging a virus disease that was undoubtedly spreading in the region from an epicentre in south-eastern China over at least two years, there is every prospect that the H5N1 virus, in particular the "Z" genotype, will become endemic in avian hosts (Melville & Shortridge 2004, Li *et al.* 2004). The H5N1 situation is another phase in the influenza story (Fig. 5), the virus having established itself as a threat to the world. The fact that the chicken "Z" genotype has transferred to ducks (Li *et al.* 2004) not only affects the evolutionary dynamics of H5N1, but also makes the virus more available for spread by migratory birds. Better understanding of the elements of the Asian-Australasian Flyway, including systematic

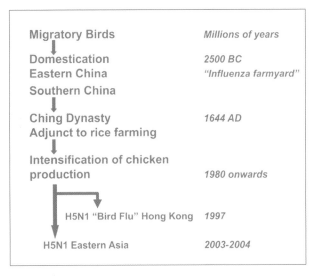

Fig. 5. A chronology of notable events in relation to current H5N1 problems.

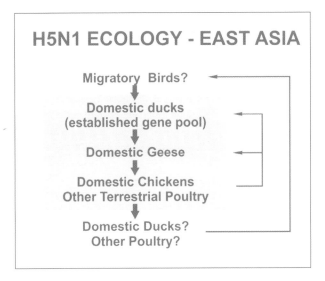

Fig. 6. A schematic approach for exploring a possible link between migratory birds and domestic poultry against the background of the 2003/2004 H5N1 incident in east Asia. The shaded area indicates a more certain relationship and the outer area a less certain relationship.

Note. Since this article was written in mid 2004, H5N1 virus has been isolated from Migratory birds in eastern and western China and has become endemic in domestic poultry, notably ducks and geese in southern China and probably in parts of southeast Asia (Chen *et al.* 2006).

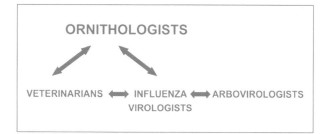

Fig. 7. The need for greater interaction in dealing with avian influenza problems. Ornithologists can make important contributions to understanding, disease control and prevention.

AIV surveillance and exploration of the domestic poultry/migratory bird niches that facilitate AIV exchange, are of paramount importance (Fig. 6). Ornithologists have an important role to play in this scenario, interacting with veterinarians and influenza virologists who can learn much in virus ecology from their arbovirus colleagues (Fig. 7). The spreading of West Nile virus exemplifies this (Rappole & Hubalek 2003). Such interaction serves to enhance our understanding of infectious zoonotic diseases.

The Migratory Animals Pathological Survey (1963-1971) laid the groundwork for bird migration studies in Asia (McClure 1974). There has been considerable progress in bird ringing in a number of countries over the past three decades, but no attempt has been made to synthesize the results across the region, and many data remain unpublished and inaccessible. As a priority, ringing schemes should co-operate in a regional review of ringing data for waterbirds, as this would facilitate a greater understanding of the relationships between species and between flyways which may be important in considering the natural spread of novel AIV forms. Consideration should be given to the establishment of long-term AIV intelligence at ringing stations in east Asia, as is currently undertaken at some sites in Europe (De Marco *et al.* 2003), and wildlife managers should be encouraged to submit dead birds for post-mortem examination. There remain many unknowns regarding the ecology of AIV in wild birds, and there is scope for extensive work on topics such as the effects of changes in gut morphology and physiology before/during/after migration (Piersma & Gill 1988) on the survival of viruses, and hence their possible spread. "Only when we are at peace with Nature will disease begin to melt away" (Shortridge 2003).

## REFERENCES

Becker, W.B. 1966. The isolation and classification of Tern virus: Influenza Virus A/Tern/South Africa/1961. Journal of Hygiene (Cambridge) 64: 309-320.

Cauthen, A.N., Swayne, D.E., Schultz-Cherry, S., Perdue, M.L. & Suarez, D.L. 2000. Continued circulation in China of highly pathogenic avian influenza viruses encoding the hemagglutinin gene associated with the 1997 H5N1 outbreak in poultry and humans. Journal of Virology 74: 6592-6599.

Chen, H., Smith, G.J.S., Li, K.S., Wang, J., Fan, Y.H., Rayner, J.M., Vijaykrishna, D., Zhang, J.X., Zhang, L.J., Guo, C.T., Cheung, C.L., Xu, K.M., Duan, L., Huang, K., Qin, K., Ceung, Y.H.C., Wu, W.L., Lu, H.R., Chen, Y., Xia, N.S., Naipospos, T.S.P., Yuen, K.Y., Hassan, S.S., Bahri, S., Nguyen, T.D., Webster, R.G., Peiris, J.S.M. & Guan, Y. 2006. Establshment of multiple sublineages of H5N1 influenza virus in Asia: implications for pandemic control. Proceedings of the National Academy of Sciences of the U.S.A. 103: 2845-2850.

Chin, P.S., Hoffmann, E., Webby, R., Webster, R.G., Guan, Y., Peiris, M. & Shortridge, K.F. 2002. Molecular evolution of H6 influenza viruses from poultry in Southeastern China: prevalence of H6N1 influenza viruses possessing seven A/Hong Kong/156/97(H5N1)-like genes in poultry. Journal of Virology 76: 507-516.

Claas, E.C.J., Osterhaus, A.D.M.E., Van Beck, R., de Jong, J.C., Rimmelzwaan, G.F., Senne, D.A., Krauss, S., Shortridge, K.F. & Webster, R.G. 1998. Human influenza A (H5N1) virus related to a highly pathogenic avian influenza virus. Lancet 351: 472-473.

De Marco, M.A., Foni, E., Campitelli, L., Raffini, E., Delogu, M. & Donatelli, I. 2003. Long-term monitoring for avian influenza viruses in wild bird species in Italy. Veterinary Research Communications 27 (Supplement) 1: 107-114.

Guan, Y., Shortridge, K.F., Krauss, S. & Webster, R.G. 1999. Molecular characterization of H9N2 influenza viruses: were they the donors of the "internal" genes of H5N1 viruses in Hong Kong? Proceedings of the National Academy of Sciences of the USA 96: 9363-9367.

Guan, Y., Shortridge, K.F., Krauss, S., Chin, P.S., Dyrting, K.C., Ellis, T.M., Webster, R.G. & Peiris, M. 2000. H9N2 influenza viruses possessing H5N1-like internal genomes continue to circulate in poultry in Southeastern China. Journal of Virology 74: 9372-9380.

Guan, Y., Peiris, J.S., Lipatov, A.S., Ellis, T.M., Dyrting, K.C., Krauss, S., Zhang, L.J., Webster, R.G. & Shortridge, K.F. 2002a. Emergence of multiple genotypes of H5N1 avian influenza viruses in Hong Kong SAR. Proceedings of the National Academy of Sciences of the USA 99: 8950-8955.

Guan, Y., Peiris, M., Fong, K.F., Dyrting, K.C., Ellis, T.M., Sit, T., Zhang, L.J. & Shortridge, K.F. 2002b. H5N1 viruses isolated from geese in southeastern China: evidence for genetic reassortment and interspecies transmission to ducks. Virology 292: 16-23.

Guan, Y., Poon, L.L.M., Cheung, C.Y., Ellis, T.M., Lim, W., Lipatov, A.S., Chan, K.H., Sturm-Ramirez, K.M., Cheung, C.L., Leung, Y.H.C., Yuen, K.Y., Webster, R.G. & Peiris, J.S.M. 2004. H5N1 influenza: a protean pandemic threat. Proceedings of the National Academy of Sciences of the USA 101: 8156-8161.

Hansen, W. 1999. Avian influenza. In: K.M. Friend & J.C. Franson (eds) Field Manual of Wildlife Diseases. U.S. Geological Survey, Washington. http://www.nwhc.usgs.gov/pub_metadata/field_metadata/field_manual.html

Hoffmann, E., Stetch, J., China, M.P.S., Leneva, I., Krauss, S., Scholtissek, C., Peiris, J.S.M., Shortridge, K.F. & Webster, R.G. 2000. Characterization of the influenza A virus gene pool in avian species in southern China: was H6N1 a derivative or a precursor of H5N1? Journal of Virology 74: 6309-6315.

Li, K.S., Xu, K.M., Peiris, J.S.M., Poon L.L.M., Yu, K.Z., Yuen, K.Y., Shortridge, K.F., Webster, R.G. & Guan, Y. 2003. Characterization of H9 subtype influenza viruses from the ducks of southern China: a candidate for the next influenza pandemic in humans? Journal of Virology 77: 6988-6994.

Li, K.S., Guan, Y., Wang, J., Smith, G.J.D., Xu, K.M., Rahardjo, A.P., Puthavathana, P., Buranthai, C., Dung, N.T., Estoepangestie, A.T.S., Chaisingh, A., Auewarakul, P., Long, H.T., Hahn, N.T.H., Lim, W., Webby, R.J., Poon, L.L.M., Chen, H., Shortridge, K.F., Yuen, K.Y., Webster, R.G. & Peiris, J.S.M. 2004. Genesis of a dominant highly pathogenic, potentially pandemic H5N1 influenza virus in Eastern Asia. Nature 430: 209-213.

Markwell, D.D. & Shortridge, K.F. 1982. Possible waterborne transmission and maintenance of influenza viruses in domestic ducks. Applied and Environmental Microbiology 43: 110-116.

McClure, H.E. 1974. Migration and survival of the birds of Asia. US Army Medical Component, SEATO Medical Project, Bangkok.

Melville, D.S. & Shortridge, K.F. 2004. Influenza: time to come to grips with the avian dimension. Lancet Infectious Diseases 4: 261-262.

Melville, D.S. & Shortridge, KF. 2006. Migratory waterbirds and avian influenza in the East Asian-Australasian Flyway with particular reference to the 2003-2004 H5N1 outbreak. Waterbirds around the world. G.C. Boere, C.A. Galbraith & D.A. Stroud (Eds.), The Stationery Office, Edinburgh, UK. 432-438.

Needham, J. 1986. Biology and biological technology. Part 1. In: J. Needham (ed) Biological Pest Control, Science and Civilization in China. Vol. 6. Cambridge University Press, Cambridge: 550-553.

Perez, D.R., Lim, W., Seiler, J.P., Guan, Y., Peiris, M., Shortridge, K.F. & Webster, R.G. 2003. Role of quail in the interspecies transmission of H9 influenza A viruses: molecular changes on HA that correspond to adaptation from ducks to chickens. Journal of Virology 77: 3148-3156.

Piersma, T. & Gill, R.E. 1998. Guts don't fly: small digestive organs in obese Bar-tailed Godwits. Auk 115: 196-203.

Potter, C.W. 1998. Chronicle of influenza pandemics. In: K.G. Nicholson, R.G. Webster & A.J. Hay (eds) Textbook of Influenza. Blackwell Science, Oxford: 3-18.

Rappole, J.H. & Hubalek, Z. 2003. Migratory birds and West Nile virus. Journal of Applied Microbiology 94 (Supplement): 47-58.

Rowan, M.K. 1962. Mass mortality among Common Terns in South Africa in April - May 1961. British Birds 55: 103-114.

Scholtissek, C., Burger, H., Kistner, O. & Shortridge, K.F. 1985. The nucleoprotein as a possible major factor in determining host specificity of influenza H3N2 viruses. Virology 147: 278-294.

Shortridge, K.F. 1988. Pandemic influenza: a blueprint for control at source. Chinese Journal of Clinical and Experimental Virology 2: 82-90.

Shortridge, K.F. 1992. Pandemic influenza: a zoonosis? Seminars in Respiratory Infections 7: 11-25.

Shortridge, K.F. 1997. Is China an influenza epicentre? Chinese Medical Journal 110: 637-641.

Shortridge, K.F. 1999. Poultry and the H5N1 outbreak in Hong Kong, 1997: abridged chronology and virus isolation. Vaccine 17 Supplement 1: S26-29.

Shortridge, K.F. 2003. Severe acute respiratory syndrome and influenza virus incursions from southern China. American Journal of Respiratory and Critical Care Medicine 168: 1416-1420.

Shortridge, K.F. & Stuart-Harris, C.H. 1982. An influenza epicentre? Lancet ii: 812-813.

Shortridge, K.F., Webster, R.G., Butterfield, W.K. & Campbell, C.H. 1977. Persistence of Hong Kong influenza virus variants in pigs. Science 196: 1454-1455.

Shortridge, K.F., Gao, P., Guan, Y., Ito, T., Kawaoka, Y., Markwell, D., Takada, A. & Webster, R.G. 2000. Interspecies transmission of influenza viruses: H5N1 virus and a Hong Kong SAR perspective. Veterinary Microbiology 74: 141-147.

Shortridge, K.F., Peiris, M., Guan, Y., Dyrting, K., Ellis, T. & Sims, L. 2001. H5N1 virus: beaten but is it vanquished? In: B. Dodet & M. Vicari (eds) Emergence and Control of Zoonotic Ortho- and Paramyxovirus Diseases. John Libbey Eurotext, Paris: 91-97.

Stuart-Harris, C.H. 1970. Pandemic influenza: an unresolved problem in prevention. Journal of Infectious Diseases 122: 108-115.

Sturm-Ramirez, K.M., Ellis, T., Bousfield, B., Bissett, L., Dyrting, K., Rehg, J.E., Poon, L., Guan, Y., Peiris, M. & Webster, R.G. 2004. Reemerging H5N1 influenza viruses in Hong Kong in 2002 are highly pathogenic to ducks. Journal of Virology 78: 4892-4901.

Tang, X., Tian, G., Zhao, J. & Zhou, K.Y. 1998. Isolation and characterization of prevalent strains of avian influenza viruses in China. Chinese Journal of Animal and Poultry Infectious Diseases 20: 1-5. (In Chinese).

Webster, R.G. & Laver, W.G. 1975. Antigenic variation of influenza viruses. In: E.D. Kilbourne (ed) The Influenza Viruses and Influenza. Academic Press, New York: 269-314.

Webster, R.G., Bean, W.J., Gorman, O.T., Chambers, T.M. & Kawaoka, Y. 1992. Evolution and ecology of influenza viruses. Microbiological Reviews 56: 152-179.

Webster, R.G., Guan, Y., Peiris, M., Walker, D., Krauss, S., Zhou, N.N., Govorkova, E.A., Ellis, T.M., Dyrting, K.C., Sit, T., Perez, D. & Shortridge, K.F. 2002. Characterization of H5N1 influenza viruses that continue to circulate in geese in southeastern China. Journal of Virology 76: 118-126.

Xu, X., Subbarao, K., Cox, N.J. & Guo, Y. 1999. Genetic characterization of the pathogenic influenza A/Goose/Guangdong/1/96 (H5N1) virus: similarity of its hemagglutinin gene to those of H5N1 viruses from the 1997 outbreaks in Hong Kong. Virology 261: 15-19.

# Migratory waterbirds and avian influenza in the East Asian-Australasian Flyway with particular reference to the 2003-2004 H5N1 outbreak

*David S. Melville[1] & Kennedy F. Shortridge[2]*

*[1] Dovedale, R.D. 2 Wakefield, Nelson, New Zealand. (email: david.melville@xtra.co.nz)*

*[2] Emeritus Professor, The University of Hong Kong, Hong Kong SAR, China; and Honorary Professor, Department of Molecular Medicine and Pathology, The University of Auckland, New Zealand. (email: kennedyfs@xtra.co.nz)*

Melville, D.S. & Shortridge, K.F. 2006. Migratory waterbirds and avian influenza in the East Asian-Australasian Flyway with particular reference to the 2003-2004 H5N1 outbreak. *Waterbirds around the world*. Eds. G.C. Boere, C.A. Galbraith & D.A. Stroud. The Stationery Office, Edinburgh, UK. pp. 432-438.

## ABSTRACT

Wild birds, especially waterfowl, can act as reservoirs for avian influenza A viruses and migrant wild birds may potentially transport viruses over long distances. Concern was expressed regarding the possible role of wild birds in the 2003-2004 outbreak of H5N1 avian influenza in East/Southeast Asia, but it seems unlikely that they directly contributed to the spread of the disease. There is an urgent need for increased virus surveillance work together with studies to increase understanding of bird migration in the region.

## INTRODUCTION

The outbreak of H5N1 highly pathogenic avian influenza (HPAI) in East and Southeast Asia in late 2003-early 2004 was unprecedented in both scale and severity. Over 100 million domestic poultry (mostly chickens) died or were slaughtered and there were 34 human cases, of which 23 were fatal (WHO 2004b, FAO 2004a). Media speculation suggested that wild birds had spread the virus (e.g. Kim 2004) and concern has been expressed regarding the potential pandemic threat posed by H5N1 (Guan *et al.* 2004). This paper outlines the ecology of avian influenza, considers the possible role of wild birds in the 2003-2004 outbreak and highlights the urgent need for multidisciplinary studies.

## ECOLOGY OF AVIAN INFLUENZA

There are 16 haemagglutinin and 9 neuramidase subtypes of avian influenza A virus (AIV), all of which have been isolated from wild birds (Alexander 2000, Fouchier *et al.* 2005). Poultry are not the normal host for AIV but some strains, particularly H5 and H7, can be highly pathogenic resulting in high mortality. AIV infection in wild birds is usually asymptomatic (Webster *et al.* 1992).

AIV in birds replicates mainly in the intestinal tract, being shed in the faeces (Webster *et al.* 1978). Infected wild ducks may shed virus for two to four weeks (Delogu 2003) and transmission is considered to be principally via the faecal-oral route (Webster *et al.* 1992). However contemporary H9 viruses show an increased ability to replicate in the respiratory tract (Webster *et al.* 2002, Perez *et al.* 2003), and Sturm-Ramirez *et al.* (2004) considered that aerosol transmission and oral-oral contamination via drinking water could be important avenues for transmission of the late 2002 early 2003 H5N1 virus. It has been suggested that this may have happened at a wildlife rescue centre in Cambodia in 2004 (FAO 2004d).

The method(s) of transmission between wild and domestic birds remain largely speculative. Some outbreaks have provided strong circumstantial evidence suggesting that virus was intro-

duced from wild birds (Campitelli *et al.* 2004), for example by contaminating drinking water (Karunakaran *et al.* 1983), whereas in some other studies it was possible that wild birds might have become infected from domestic birds (Nestorowicz *et al.* 1987).

Birds that occur in dense aggregations and which inhabit wetlands and/or aquatic environments are prime candidates for infection and this is reflected in relative infection rates. Waterbirds generally, and waterfowl (Anatidae) in particular, having higher infection rates (~15%) than terrestrial species (~2%) (Alexander 2000, Stallknecht & Shane 1988). Although Hansen (1999) reported 'frequent' occurrence of infection in waders, terns and gulls (Charadriiformes), it appears that waders generally are seldom infected (Melville unpublished).

Avian influenza, based on virus isolates and/or serological evidence, has been recorded from 47 species of wild birds in East Asia (Table 1), and from a further 70 species that occur in East Asia, but in which infection was recorded elsewhere (Table 2).

## THE 2003-2004 H5N1 OUTBREAK

The 2003-2004 outbreak of H5N1 occurred in poultry almost simultaneously throughout much of the East/Southeast Asian region with the first cases being reported in Cambodia on 15 December 2003 and in South Korea on 17 December. Outbreaks were confirmed in early January from Vietnam (8th), Japan (12th), Thailand (23rd), China and Laos (27th), and finally Indonesia on 2 February (FAO 2004d, WHO 2004a). Interestingly there was no outbreak in poultry in Hong Kong although H5N1 was isolated from a Peregrine Falcon[1] found dead on 19 January 2004.

These were the first ever outbreaks of HPAI in South Korea, Vietnam, Thailand, and Indonesia, and the first case in Japan since 1925. Subsequently no further countries reported incidents of H5N1. By March the outbreak appeared to have largely subsided, however outbreaks reappeared in Vietnam, Thailand and China in mid 2004 (FAO 2004e).

Populations of migratory waterbirds in East Asia include over 10 million ducks and geese, six million egrets and herons, seven million shorebirds, 20 million seabirds and substantial but un-estimated numbers of rails (Delaney & Scott 2002, Kondratyev *et al.* 2000).

The majority of seabirds remain at sea during the winter and most would be unlikely to come in to contact with domestic poultry, gulls in Asia notably being far less associated with human agricultural activities than in Europe or North America, although a case of H5N1 in a Black-headed Gull in Hong Kong in January 2003 (AFCD 2003) should not be overlooked.

[1] Scientific names are given in Tables 1 & 2

**Table 1. Species of wild bird in which avian influenza has been recorded in East/Southeast Asia\***

| Species | | Locality |
|---|---|---|
| Little Grebe | *Tachybaptus ruficollis* | Thailand |
| Great Cormorant | *Phalacrocorax carbo* | China |
| Little Egret | *Egretta garzetta* | Hong Kong |
| Grey Heron | *Ardea cinerea* | Hong Kong |
| Chinese Pond Heron | *Ardeola bacchus* | Hong Kong |
| Black-crowned Night Heron | *Nycticorax nycticorax* | China |
| Asian Openbill | *Anastomus oscitans* | Thailand |
| Mute Swan | *Cygnus olor* | Japan |
| Tundra Swan | *Cygnus columbianus* | Japan |
| Whooper Swan | *Cygnus cygnus* | China, Mongolia |
| Bar-headed Goose | *Anser indicus* | China, Mongolia |
| Ruddy Shelduck | *Tadorna ferruginea* | China |
| Eurasian Wigeon | *Anas penelope* | Japan |
| Falcated Duck | *Anas falcata* | Russian Far East |
| Baikal Teal | *Anas formosa* | Russian Far East |
| Common Teal | *Anas crecca* | Japan, Russian Far East |
| Mallard | *Anas platyrhynchos* | Japan, Russian Far East |
| Spot-billed Duck | *Anas poecilorhyncha* | Japan |
| Northern Pintail | *Anas acuta* | Japan, Russian Far East |
| Tufted Duck | *Aythya fuligula* | Japan |
| Peregrine Falcon | *Falco peregrinus* | Hong Kong |
| Brown Crake | *Amaurornis akool* | China |
| Bar-tailed Godwit | *Limosa lapponica* | China |
| Whimbrel | *Numenius phaeopus* | China |
| Common Snipe | *Gallinago gallinago* | Russian Far East |
| Curlew Sandpiper | *Calidris ferruginea* | Hong Kong |
| Dunlin | *Calidris alpina* | Japan |
| Black-tailed Gull | *Larus crassirostris* | Japan, Russian Far East |
| Black-headed Gull | *Larus ridibundus* | Hong Kong |
| Relict Gull | *Larus relictus* | China |
| Brown-headed Gull | *Larus brunnicephalus* | China |
| Great Black-headed Gull | *Larus ichthaetus* | China |
| Guillemot | *Uria aalge* | Russian Far East |
| Black/Spectacled Guillemot | *Cepphus grylle/carbo* | Russian Far East |
| Red Turtle Dove | *Streptopelia tranquebarica* | Thailand |
| Little Cuckoo Dove | *Macropygia ruficeps* | Thailand |
| Yellow-vented Bulbul | *Pycnonotus goiaver* | Malaysia |
| Oriental Magpie Robin | *Copsychus saularis* | Hong Kong |
| Japanese White-eye | *Zosterops japonica* | Hong Kong |
| White-rumped Munia | *Lonchura striata* | Hong Kong |
| Scaly-breasted Munia | *Lonchura punctulata* | Hong Kong |
| Eurasian Tree Sparrow | *Passer montanus* | China, Hong Kong |
| Crested Mynah | *Acridotheres tristis* | Hong Kong |
| Black Drongo | *Dicrurus macrocercus* | Thailand |
| Common Magpie | *Pica pica* | South Korea, Hong Kong, China |
| House Crow | *Corvus splendens* | Hong Kong, Thailand |
| Large-billed Crow | *Corvus macrorhynchus* | Japan, Cambodia, Hong Kong |

\* after Stallknecht & Shane (1988) and Olsen *et al.* (2006) with additions.

**Table 2. Species of wild bird which occur in East/Southeast Asia and in which avian influenza has been recorded elsewhere***

| | | | |
|---|---|---|---|
| Red-throated Diver | *Gavia stellata* | Black-throated Diver | *Gavia arctica* |
| Great Crested Grebe | *Podiceps cristatus* | Wedge-tailed Shearwater | *Puffinus pacificus* |
| Little Cormorant | *Phalacrocorax niger* | Glossy Ibis | *Plegadis falcinellus* |
| Eurasian Spoonbill | *Platalea leucorodia* | Greater White-fronted Goose | *Anser albifrons* |
| Greylag Goose | *Anser anser* | Brent Goose | *Branta bernicla* |
| Common Shelduck | *Tadorna tadorna* | American Wigeon | *Anas americana* |
| Gadwall | *Anas strepera* | Garganey | *Anas querquedula* |
| Northern Shoveler | *Anas clypeata* | Red-crested Pochard | *Netta rufina* |
| Common Pochard | *Aythya ferina* | Greater Scaup | *Aythya marila* |
| Tufted Duck | *Aythya fuligula* | Long-tailed Duck | *Clangula hyemalis* |
| Velvet Scoter | *Melanitta fusca* | Common Scoter | *Melanitta nigra* |
| Goosander | *Mergus merganser* | Red-breasted Merganser | *Mergus serrator* |
| Smew | *Mergus albellus* | Saker Falcon | *Falco cherrug* |
| Northern Goshawk | *Accipiter gentilis* | Common Buzzard | *Buteo buteo* |
| Ring-necked Pheasant | *Phasianus colchicus* | Purple Swamphen | *Porphyrio porphyrio* |
| Common Moorhen | *Gallinula chloropus* | Common Coot | *Fulica atra* |
| Pied Avocet | *Recurvirostra avosetta* | Black-winged Stilt | *Himantopus himantopus* |
| Eurasian Oystercatcher | *Haematopus ostralegus* | River Lapwing | *Vanellus dauvcelii* |
| Eurasian Curlew | *Numenius arquata* | Eurasian Woodcock | *Scolopax rusticola* |
| Common Redshank | *Tringa totanus* | Spotted Redshank | *Tringa erythropus* |
| Green Sandpiper | *Tringa ochropus* | Ruddy Turnstone | *Arenaria interpres* |
| Sharp-tailed Sandpiper | *Calidris acuminata* | Red-necked Stint | *Calidris ruficollis* |
| Red Knot | *Calidris canutus* | Sanderling | *Calidris alba* |
| Temminck's Stint | *Calidris temmincki* | Ruff | *Philomachus pugnax* |
| Pomarine Skua | *Stercorarius pomarinus* | South Polar Skua | *Catharacta maccormicki* |
| Slender-billed Gull | *Larus genei* | Herring Gull | *Larus argentatus* |
| Black-legged Kittiwake | *Rissa tridactyla* | Common Tern | *Sterna hirundo* |
| Arctic Tern | *Sterna paradisaea* | Little Tern | *Sterna albifrons* |
| Sooty Tern | *Sterna fuscata* | White-winged Tern | *Chlidonias leucopterus* |
| Black Tern | *Chlidonias niger* | Collared Dove | *Streptopelia decaocto* |
| Great Spotted Woodpecker | *Dendrocopus major* | Barn Swallow | *Hirundo rustica* |
| Yellow Wagtail | *Motacilla flava* | White Wagtail | *Motacilla alba* |
| Common Whitethroat | *Sylvia communis* | Yellow-breasted Bunting | *Emberiza aureola* |
| Black-faced Bunting | *Emberiza spodocephala* | House Sparrow | *Passer domesticus* |
| Common Starling | *Sturnus vulgaris* | Carrion Crow | *Corvus corone* |

* after Stallknecht & Shane (1988) and Olsen *et al.* (2006) with additions

The large areas of rice paddy throughout much of the region (74 million ha, of which some 38% is in China; IRRI 2004) provide artificial, freshwater wetland habitats which may be used by a wide variety of waterbirds including ducks, geese, waders, storks, ardeids and rallids. All of these birds potentially could come into contact with the large numbers of domestic ducks (Shortridge & Melville 2005) which are widely used for pest control and scavenge in paddis during and immediately after harvest - there being some 19 million in the Mekong delta alone (Bui *et al.* 1998). However most poultry affected by H5N1 were chickens, not ducks, suggesting that direct transfer of virus was unlikely. Furthermore, the outbreak occurred in mid-winter, at a time when most waterfowl populations are thought to be fairly sedentary, although there is evidence of mobility in some ducks populations (Pradel *et al.* 1997), and mid-winter movements of presumed waterfowl have been recorded by radar in Hong Kong (Melville 1980). There were no particularly unusual weather events reported in East Asia which might have resulted in mass movements of waterfowl in the region.

The highest concentrations of migratory Anatidae occur in Japan, South Korea and eastern and central China, south of the 0°C January isotherm (Li & Mundkur 2004). Relatively few migratory ducks occur in Indochina and Thailand, and even less in Indonesia, which suggests that they were unlikely to be carriers of virus in these areas. Ringing data show that at least some ducks migrate from Japan through Taiwan to the Philippines (Yamashina Institute for Ornithology records) yet Taiwan alone was affected by a mildly pathogenic form of H5N2, rather than H5N1, and no avian influenza outbreaks were reported from the Philippines – a situation hard to reconcile with the suggestion that wild birds were the main means of virus transport.

It is unclear whether the 'first reported' dates really reflect the situation on the ground, especially since Vietnam had potential human cases as early as October 2003 (WHO 2004a). Thus it is possible that virus was present for some time before being reported, in which case wild birds might have assisted its spread. For example, large numbers of rails migrate from mainland Asia to Indonesia where they are trapped for food, being sold in markets together with domestic poultry (M. Silvius pers. comm.) and this could have allowed for transmission of virus in the autumn of 2003. Little is known of AIV infection rates in rallids: Delogu (2003) reported 1.2% infection in Eurasian Coots in Italy. However, if waterbirds were responsible for introducing the virus to Indonesia it might be expected that at least some of the birds would also have passed through Malaysia and/or The Philippines, yet there were no reports of H5N1 from either country.

Transmission of virus by terrestrial bird species which occur around fish and duck farms, such as, in Southern China, Rufous Turtle Dove *Streptopelia orientalis*, Barn Swallow, Red-billed Starling *Sturnus sericeus* and Eurasian Tree Sparrow is a possibility (virus isolations are known from the swallow and sparrow, and from congeners of the dove and starling), and all four are to a greater or lesser extent migratory, but the timing and extent of the outbreak does not fit known movement patterns.

Most reported cases affected chickens, but domestic ducks and geese were also affected in some areas. Information on mortality in wild birds remains sketchy with a number of unconfirmed reports. The provenance of the Peregrine Falcon found dead in Hong Kong is uncertain (P.J. Leader *in litt.*) and it may have been held in captivity. Large-billed Crows and Common Magpies were reported dead in association with poultry farms in Japan and South Korea, respectively, but presence of H5N1 has not been confirmed. In Thailand several hundred Asian Openbills were reported dead and H5N1 was isolated from at least one individual (The Influenza Sequence Database 2004), while in Cambodia several birds at a wildlife rehabilitation centre were reportedly positive, including free-flying wild Large-billed Crows (FAO 2004d, D.W. Geale *in litt.* 2004). It is noteworthy that no wild waterfowl were recovered anywhere, and extensive surveillance in Hong Kong failed to find any H5N1 virus in wild waterfowl faeces (L. Young *in litt.* 2004).

There are no known wild bird reservoirs of HPAI (Swayne and Suarez 2000). Although there are some instances of HPAI virus isolation from wild birds associated with outbreaks in poultry (as apparently in 2003-2004), the fact that such birds have been found dead suggests that HPAI causes mortality in at least some wild birds, in which case they are unlikely to be effective carriers of infection (Capua *et al.* 2000).

It is noteworthy that despite fears that migratory birds might carry H5N1 northwards in the spring of 2004, there is no evidence that this occurred – although it was suggested that migratory birds and wild waterfowl could have transmitted the disease to a poultry farm near Chau Hu, Anhui, China (OIE 2004), the timing of the outbreak in early July makes this unlikely and the lake apparently supports relatively few waterfowl even in winter (M. Barter, in litt.). A reported die-off of wild birds in Mongolia in mid-March (FAO 2004c) was apparently the result of another cause.

It remains unclear why the 2003-2004 outbreak occurred in such an explosive manner. It seems likely that human activity resulted in at least some of the spread, as in the case of an outbreak in Lhasa, Tibet which appears to have resulted from the introduction of chickens from Lanzhou, Gansu – some 1 500 km away (FAO 2004b). The trade in wild song birds, for example, laughingthrushes *Garrulax* spp. from China to Indonesia (Melville & Lau 1993), also might have provided an avenue for dissemination of virus, while the Buddhist practise of 'merit release' of caged birds might have resulted in local transmission as birds joined local wild populations. It seems more likely

however, that the virus had been 'smouldering' for some time, possibly partly masked due to vaccination programmes in some countries (MacKenzie 2004) and that most of the spread was human mediated, aided by poor hygiene standards and biosecurity protocols (Melville and Shortridge 2004).

The 2003-2004 outbreak has highlighted how little we know of both birds and avian influenza in East Asia.

## INTER-FLYWAY CONNECTIONS

Whilst migrant waterfowl may not have played a significant role in the spread of H5N1 in 2003-2004, their potential role in the spread of viruses should not be overlooked. Not only is there potential for North-South spread along the East Asian-Australasian Flyway but also for East-West spread. Although the differing Eurasian and North American influenza A virus lineages are thought to have arisen as a result of the general lack of interchange between birds in these land masses there is mixing of some populations. Wrangel Island, for example, is used as a post-breeding moulting ground by Brent Geese from both Siberian and Alaskan breeding areas (Ward *et al.* 1993), and ~2% of recoveries of Pintail ringed wintering in Japan have been in North America (Yamashina Institute for Ornithology records). Dunlin winter in large numbers along the coast of eastern China and inland, and DNA analysis indicates that at least some of these birds are from the Alaskan breeding population (Wenink & Baker 1996), and thus may mix with those that winter along the west coast of the USA south to California (Warnock & Gill 1996).

Webby *et al.* (2002) postulated that an outbreak of H6N2 influenza in California which had genetic similarities to viruses from chickens in Eurasia might indicate convergent evolution in which common mutations arose as viruses adapted to the chicken host, but there remains the possibility of importation of Eurasian genes via migratory waterfowl.

Our knowledge of the East and Central Asian Flyways is limited, but they appear to overlap extensively in western China, Mongolia and central Siberia allowing for interchange between them. Thus Bar-headed Geese *Anser indicus* migrate from the Tibetan plateau to winter in India or southwest China ( Zhang & Yang 1997) and Great Cormorants from the same area also winter in India (Kumar 2003). In view of the fact that the Thai breeding population of Asian Openbills migrates to Bangladesh (McClure 1974), isolation of H5N1 from at least one of these birds highlights the potential for spread of this virus to the Indian subcontinent. Such movements potentially could provide a route for the westward spread of novel virus forms from South China, the hypothetical epicentre for the emergence of pandemic influenza viruses (Shortridge & Stuart-Harris 1982).

## THE FUTURE

Avian influenza is asymptomatic in wild birds, and the only record of significant mortality was of 1 300 Common Terns in South Africa (Becker 1966). This pales to insignificance in comparison with some other pathogens such as fowl cholera which killed over ten thousand Baikal Teal in Korea in 2000 (Kwon & Kang 2002), and botulism which resulted in the death of four to five million wild waterfowl in the western USA in 1952 (Locke & Friend 1987). This may help explain the scant attention that avian influenza has received from most ornithologists to date – it did not even feature in a review of avian related zoonoses (Cooper 1990). With the potential for a new pandemic there is an urgent need for ornithologists to work with influenza virologists to implement widespread surveillance in wild birds, as well as promoting migration studies, to help elucidate the role of wild birds in the ecology of avian influenza.

## ACKNOWLEDGEMENTS

We are grateful to M. Barter, D.W. Geale, P.J. Leader, M. Silvius and L. Young for providing information.

## REFERENCES

**Agriculture, Fisheries & Conservation Department** 2002. Pathogenic H5N1 avian influenza in waterfowl and wild birds, final report, Hong Kong, China. www.afcd.gov.hk/quarantine/text/vetnews/download/oiebirds.pdf

**Alexander, D.J.** 2000. A review of avian influenza in different bird species. Veterinary Microbiology 74: 3-13.

**Becker, W.B.** 1966. The isolation and classification of a Tern virus: Influenza Virus A/Tern/South Africa/1961. Journal of Hygiene, Cambridge 64: 309-320.

**Bui, X.M., Ogle, B. & Preston, T.R.** 1998. Studies on duck production in the Mekong Delta, Vietnam. In: E.L. Foo & T.D. Senta (eds.). Integrated bio-systems in zero emissions applications. Proceedings of the Internet Conference on Integrated Bio-systems. http://www.ias.unu.edu/proceedings/icibs

**Campitelli, L., Mogavero, E., De Marco, M.A., Delogu, M., Puzelli, S., Frezza, F., Facchini, M., Chiapponi, C., Foni, E., Cordioli, P., Webby, R., Barigazzi, G., Webster, R.G. & Donatelli, I.** 2004. Interspecies transmission of an H7N3 influenza virus from wild birds to intensively reared domestic poultry in Italy. Virology 323: 24-36.

**Capua, I., Grossele, B., Bertoli, E., & Cordioli, P.** 2000. Monitoring for highly pathogenic avian influenza in wild birds in Italy. Veterinary Record 147: 640.

**Cheng, M.C., Lee, M.S., Wang C.H., & Kida, H.** 2002. Influenza virological surveillance in migratory waterfowl in Taiwan from 1998 to 2002. Options for the Control of Influenza V. Okinawa. Conference Abstract WO9P-06: 123.

**Cooper, J.E.** 1990. Birds and zoonoses. Ibis 132: 181-191.

**Delaney, S. & Scott, D.A.** 2002. Waterbird population estimates. 3rd. ed. Wetlands International Global series no. 12. Wetlands International, Wageningen.

**Delogu, M.** 2003. Avian influenza: ecology and risk factors for humans and poultry production. CEVA Scientific Seminar, Budapest, 7 November 2003.

**FAO** 2004a. Bird flu in Asia: control campaigns need to continue. http://www.fao.org/newsroom/en/news/2004/37727/index/html

**FAO Avian Influenza Technical Task Force.** 2004b. FAO AIDE news. 6. Summary of situation as of 23/02/2004. http://www.fao.org/ag/againfo/subjects/en/health/diseases-cards/avian_update.html

**FAO Avian Influenza Technical Task Force.** 2004c. FAO AIDE news. 12. Summary of situation as of 16/04/2004. http://www.fao.org/ag/againfo/subjects/en/health/diseases-cards/AVIbull012.pdfl

**FAO Avian Influenza Technical Task Force.** 2004d. FAO AIDE news. 16. Summary of situation as of 14/07/2004.

http://www.fao.org/ag/againfo/subjects/en/health/diseases-cards/AVIbull016.pdf

**FAO Avian Influenza Technical Task Force.** 2004e. FAO AIDE news. 18. Summary of situation as of 29/06/2004. http://www.fao.org/ag/againfo/subjects/en/health/diseases-cards/AVIbull018.pdfl

**Fouchier, R.A.M, Munster, V., Wallensten, A., Bestebroer, T.M., Herfst,S., Smith, D., Rimmelzwaan, G.F., Olsen, B. & Osterhaus, A.D.M.E.** 2005. Characterization of a novel influenza A virus hemagglutinin subtype (H16) obtained from Black-headed Gulls. Journal of Virology 79: 2814-2822.

**Guan, Y., Poon, L.L.M., Cheung, C.Y., Ellis, T.M., Lim, W., Lipatov, A.S., Chan, K.H., Sturm-Ramirez, K.M., Cheung, C.L., Leung, Y.H.C., Webster, R.G. & Peiris, J.S.M.** 2004. H5N1 influenza: a protean pandemic threat. Proceedings of the National Academy of Sciences of the USA 1001: 8156-8161.

**Hansen, W.** 1999. Avian influenza. In: M.Friend & J.C. Franson (eds.). Field manual of wildlife diseases. US Geological Survey, Washington. http://www.nwhc.usgs.gov/pub_metadata/field_manual/field_manual.html

**International Rice Research Institute.** 2004. Table 2. Rough rice area (000 ha), by country and geographical region, 1961-2002. http://www.irri.org/science/ricestat/pdfs/Table%2002.pdf

**Karunakaran, D., Hinshaw, V., Poss, P., Newman, J. & Halvorson, D.** 1983. Influenza A outbreaks in Minnesota turkeys due to subtype H10N7 and possible transmission by waterfowl. Avian Diseases 27: 357-366.

**Kim, B.H.** 2004. Bird flu carried by migrant birds. Joongang Ilbo 3 February 2004: 8. In Korean – English translation at www.wbkenglish.com/avflu.asp

**Kondratyev, A. Ya., Litvinenko, N.M. & Kaiser, G.W.** (eds.). Seabirds of the Russian Far East. Environment Canada, Ottawa.

**Kumar, R.S.** 2003. Ring recovery from Great Cormorants *Phalacrocorax carbo* in India. Journal of the Bombay Natural History Society 100: 621-624.

**Kwon, Y.K. & Kang, M.I.** 2002. Outbreak of fowl cholera in Baikal Teal in Korea. Avian Diseases 47: 1491-1495.

**Li, D.Z.W. & Mundkur, T.** 2004. Numbers and distribution of waterbirds and wetlands in the Asia-Pacific Region. Results of the Asian Waterbird Census: 1997-2001. Wetlands International, Kuala Lumpur.

**Li, K.S., Guan, Y., Wang, J., Smith, G.J.D., Xu, K.M., Duan, L., Rahardjo, A.P., Puthavathana, P., Buranathai, C., Nguyen, T.D., Estoepangestie, A.T.S., Chaisingh, A., Auewarakul, P., Long, H.T., Hahn, N.T.H., Webby, R.J., Poon, L.L.M., Chen, H., Shortridge, K.F., Yuen, K.Y., Webster, R.G. & Peiris, J.S.M.** 2004. Genesis of a highly pathogenic and potentially pandemic H5N1 influenza virus in eastern Asia. Nature 430: 209-213.

**Locke, L.N. & Friend, M.**1987. Avian botulism. In: M. Friend & C.J. Laitman (eds.) Field guide to wildlife diseases. Vol. 1. General field procedures and diseases of migratory birds. Resource Publication 167. US Department of the Interior, Fish and Wildlife Service, Washington, DC.

**MacKenzie, D.** 2004. Bird flu outbreak started a year ago. New Scientist 181 (2432): 10-11.

McClure, H.E. 1974. Migration and survival of the birds of Asia. US Army Medical Component, SEATO Medical Project, Bangkok.

Melville, D. 1980. Bird migration through Hong Kong observed by radar and its implications for birdstrike control. Agriculture and Fisheries Department, Hong Kong. pp. 23.

Melville, D.S. & Lau, A. 1993. Hong Kong (with special reference to China). In: Nash, S. Sold for a song: trade in Southeast Asian non-CITES bids. TRAFFIC, Cambridge: 53-62.

Melville, D.S. & Shortridge, K.F. 2004. Influenza: time to come to grips with the avian dimension. Lancet Infectious Diseases 4: 261-262.

Nestorowicz, A., Kawaoka, Y., Bean, W.J. & Webster, R.G. 1987. Molecular analysis of the haemagglutinin genes of Australian H7N7 influenza viruses: role of passerine birds in maintenance or transmission? Virology 1670:411-418.

OIE. 2004. Highly Pathogenic Avian Influenza in China (People's Rep. of~). OIE Disease Information 9 July 2004. 17 (28). http://www.oie.int/eng/info/hebdo/aIS_37.htm#/Sec1

Olsen, B., Munster, V.J., Wallensten, A., Waldenstrom, J., Osterhaus, A.D.M.E. & Fouchier, R.A.M. 2006. Supporting online material for Global patterns of influenza A virus in wild birds. http://www.sciencemag.org/cgi/content/full/312/5772/384/DCI

Perez, D.R., Lim, W., Seiler, J.P., Guan, Y., Peiris, M., Shortridge, K.F. & Webster, R.G. 2002. Role of quail in the interspecies transmission of H9 influenza viruses: molecular changes on HA that correspond to adaptation from ducks to chickens. Journal of Virology 77: 3148-3156.

Pradel, R., Rioux, N., Tamisier, A. & Lebreton, J-D. 1997. Individual turnover among wintering Teal in Camargue: a mark-recapture study. Journal of Wildlife Management 61: 816-821.

Shortridge, K.F. & Melville, D.S. 2005. Domestic poultry and migratory birds in the interspecies transmission of avian influenza viruses: a view from Hong Kong. Waterbirds around the world: 427-431.

Shortridge, K.F. & Stuart-Harris, C.H. 1982. An influenza epicentre? Lancet 2: 212-213.

Stallknecht, D.E. & Shane, M.E. 1988. Host range of influenza virus in free-living birds. Veterinary Research Communications 12: 125-141.

Sturm-Ramirez, K.M., Ellis, T., Bousfield, B., Bissett, L., Dyrting, K., Rehg, J.E., Poon, L., Guan, Y., Peiris, M. & Webster, R.G. 2004. Reemerging H5N1 influenza viruses in Hong Kong in 2002 are highly pathogenic to ducks. Journal of Virology 78: 4892-4901.

Swayne, D.E. & Suarez, D.L. 2000. Highly pathogenic avian influenza. OIE Scientific and Technical Review 19: 463-482.

The Influenza Sequence Database. 2004. http://flutest.lanl.gov/search/index. (database accessed 21 June 2004)

Ward, D.H., Derksen, D.V., Kharitonov, S.P., Stishov, M. &

Baranyuk, V.V. 1993. Status of Pacific Black Brant *Branta bernicla nigricans* on Wrangel Island, Russian Federation. Wildfowl 44: 39-48.

Warnock, N.D. & Gill, R.E. 1996. Dunlin (*Calidris alpina*). In: A. Poole & F. Gill (eds.). The birds of North America. No. 203. The Academy of Natural Sciences, Philadelphia, and The American Ornithologists' Union, Washington, D.C.

Webby, R.J., Woolcock, P.R., Krauss, S.L. & Webster, R.G. 2002. Reassortment and interspecies transmission of North American H6N2 influenza viruses. Virology 295: 44-53.

Webster, R.G., Yakhno, M., Hinshaw, V.S., Bean, W.J. & Morti, K.G. 1978. Intestinal influenza: replication and characterization of influenza viruses in ducks. Virology 84: 268-278.

Webster, R.G., Bean, W.J., Gorman, O.T., Chambers, T.M. & Kawaoka, Y. 1992. Evolution and ecology of influenza A viruses. Microbiological Reviews 56: 152-179.

Webster, R.G., Guan, Y., Peiris, M., Walker, D., Krauss, S., Zhou, N.N., Govoroka, E.A., Ellis, T.M., Dyrting, K.C., Sit, T., Perez, D. & Shortridge, K.F. 2002. Characterization of H5N1 influenza viruses that continue to circulate in geese in southeastern China. Journal of Virology 76: 118-126.

Wenink, P.W. & Baker, A.J. 1996. Mitochondrial DNA lineages in composite flocks of migratory and wintering Dunlins (*Calidris alpina*). Auk 113: 744-756.

WHO 2004a. H5N1 avian influenza: a chronology of key events. 12 February 2004. http://www.who.int/csr/disease/avian_influenza/chronology/en/print.html

WHO 2004b. Confirmed human cases of avian influenza A (H5N1). http://www.who.int/csr/disease/avian_influenza/country/cases_table_2004_03_24/en/

Yamashina Institute for Ornithology. 1979-1997. Reports of the Bird Migration Research Center. Yamashina Institute for Ornithology, Chiba/Tokyo. In Japanese

Zhang, F.Y. & Yong, R.L. 1997. Bird migration research in China. China Forestry Publishing House. In Chinese pp. 364.

## Update June 2006

Avian influenza is now endemic in poultry in Southeast Asia and, as of 20 June 2006, there have been 228 human cases with 130 deaths (WHO 2006). Whilst there is currently little evidence of human-to-human transfer of virus (Williamson 2006), there remains concern that a readily transmissible form may emerge and start a pandemic (WHO 2005).

In April/May 2005 some 6,000 waterfowl were reported dead at Qinghai Hu, China, including Great Cormorant, Bar-headed Goose, Ruddy Shelduck, Great Black-headed Gull and Brown-headed Gull. H5N1 virus taken from these birds was closely related to viruses circulating in poultry and wild birds in southern China (Chen *et al*. 2005, Liu *et al*. 2005). In early August H5N1 was recovered from a Bar-headed Goose and three Whooper Swans found dead in Mongolia (OIE 2005), and H5N1 was reported from poultry and wildfowl in Russia and Kazakhstan in August.

Throughout late 2005 and early 2006, H5N1 apparently spread westwards across parts of Central Asia and Europe, reaching

Africa in February 2006, infecting both domestic poultry and a variety of wild birds - Mute Swans in particular appeared to suffer high mortality in Europe. A virus from birds in Western Siberia and Europe is very similar to that from Qinghai (Brown *et al.* 2006.), however, the role of wild birds in spreading the virus remains uncertain and trade in live poultry and products has been implicated in some cases (Melville & Shortridge 2006). Highly pathogenic H5N1 virus has been isolated from apparently healthy ducks and Eurasian Tree Sparrows in China (Chen *et al.* 2006, Kou *et al.* 2005) and H5N1 virus seems to be moving between domestic and wild birds and back again (Chen *et al.* 2006). In April/May 2006 there were further outbreaks in wild waterfowl in both China and Mongolia (FAO 2006), but the situation in Bar-headed Geese has become further complicated with the discovery that these are being artificially reared in Qinghai (Butler 2006).

## REFERENCES

Brown, I.H., Londt, B.Z., Shell, W., Manvell, R.J., Banks, J., Gardner, R., Outtrim, L., Essen, S.C., Sabirovic, M., Slomka, M. & Alexander, D.J. 2006. Incursion of H5N1 'Asian lineage virus' into Europe: source of introduction? http://www.fao.org/ag/againfo/subjects/en/health/diseases-cards/conference/documents/I.Brown.pdf

Butler, D. 2006. Blogger reveals China's migratory goose farms nears site of flu outbreak. Nature 441: 263.

Chen,H., Smith, G.J.D., Zhang, S.Y., Qin, K., Wang, J., Li, K.S., Webster, R.G., Peiris, J.S.M. and Guan, Y. 2005. H5N1 virus outbreak in migratory waterfowl. Nature 436 (7048): 191-192.

Chen, H., Smith, G.J.D., Li, K.S., Wang, J., Fan, X.F., Rayner, J.M., Vijaykrishna, D., Zhang, J.X., Zhang, L.J., Guo, C.T., Cheung, C.L., Xu, K.M., Duan, L., Huang, K., Qin, K., Leung, Y.H.C., Wu, W.L., Lu, H.R., Chen, Y., Xia, N.S., Naipospos, T.S.P., Yuen, K.Y., Hassan, S.S., Bahri, S., Nguyen, T.D., Webster, R.G., Peiris, J.S.M. & Guan, Y. 2006. Establishment of multiple sublineages of H5N1 influenza virus in Asia: implications for pandemic control. Proceedings of the National Academy of Sciences 103: 2845-2850.

FAOAvian Influenza Technical Task Force. 2006. FAOIDEnews. 40. Update of the Avian Influenza situation (as of 19/06/2006). http://www.fao.org/docs/eims/upload//209858/AVIbull040.pdf

Kuo, Z., Lei, F.M., Yu, J., Fan, Z.J., Yin, Z.H., Jia, C.X., Xiong, K.J., Sun, Y.H., Zhang, X.W., Wu, X.M., Gao, X.B., & Li, T.X. 2005. New genotype of avian influenza H5N1 virus isolated from Tree Sparrows in China. Journal of Virology 79: 15460-15466.

Liu, J.H., Xiao, H.X., Lei, F.M., Zhu, Q.Y., Qin, k., Zhang, X.W., Zhang, X.G., Zhao, D.M., Wang, G.H., Feng, Y.J., Ma, J.C., Liu, W.J., Wang, J. and Gao, G.F. 2005. Highly pathogenic H5N1 influenza virus infection in migratory birds. Science 309 (5738): 1206.

Melville, D.S. & Shortridge, K.F. 2006. Spread of H5N1 avian influenza virus: an ecological conundrum. Letters in Applied Microbiology 42: 435-437.

OIE. 2005. Highly Pathogenic Avian Influenza in Mongolia in migratory birds (follow-up report No. 2). http://www.oie.int/eng/info/hebdo/aIS_55.htm#Sec0

WHO 2005. Geographical spread of H5N1 avian influenza in birds - update 28 Situation assessment and implications for human health. http://www.who.int/csr/don/2005_08_18/en/index.html

WHO 2006. Cumulative Number of Confirmed Human Cases of Avian Influenza A/(H5N1) Reported to WHO 20 June 2006. http://www.who.int/csr/disease/avian_influenza/country/cases_table_2006_06_20/en/index.html

Williamson, L. 2006. Family vector for Sumatra bird flu. http://news.bbc.co.uk/1/hi/world/asia-pacific/5110084.stm

Bar-headed Geese *Anser indicus,* Brown-headed Gulls *Larus brunnicephalus* and a Great Black-headed Gull *Larus ichthyaetus* at Qinghai Hu, China, about a week before the outbreak of HPAI H5N1 there in May 2005. The close mixing of these species indicates the potential for viral transmission between species. Photo: Jemi & John Holmes.

# Recurring waterbird mortalities of unusual etiologies

*Rebecca A. Cole & J. Christian Franson*

*United States Geological Survey, National Wildlife Health Center, 6006 Schroeder Road, Madison, Wisconsin 53711, USA.*
*(email: Rebecca_Cole@usgs.gov)*

Cole, R.A. & Franson, J.C. 2006. Recurring waterbird mortalities of unusual etiologies. *Waterbirds around the world*. Eds. G.C. Boere, C.A. Galbraith & D.A. Stroud. The Stationery Office, Edinburgh, UK. pp. 439-440.

## ABSTRACT

Over the last decade, the National Wildlife Health Center of the United States Geological Survey has documented various large-scale mortalities of birds caused by infectious and non-infectious disease agents. Some of these mortality events have unusual or unidentified etiologies and have been recurring. While some of the causes of mortalities have been elucidated, others remain in various stages of investigation and identification. Two examples are discussed: 1) *Leyogonimus polyoon* (Class: Trematoda), not found in the New World until 1999, causes severe enteritis and has killed over 15 000 American Coot *Fulica americana* in the upper mid-western United States. The geographic range of this parasite within North America is predicted to be limited to the Great Lakes Basin. 2) In the early 1990s, estimates of up to 6% of the North American population of the Eared Grebe *Podiceps nigricollis* died at Salton Sea, California, with smaller mortalities occurring throughout the 1990s. Birds were observed to have unusual preening behaviour, and to congregate at freshwater drains and move onto land. Suggested etiologies included interactions of contaminants, immuno-suppression, an unusual form of a bacterial disease, and an unknown biotoxin. During studies carried out from 2000 to 2003, Eared Grebe mortality did not approach the level seen in the early 1990s and, although bacteria were identified as minor factors, the principal cause of mortality remains undetermined. The potential population impact of these emerging and novel disease agents is currently unknown.

## INTRODUCTION

Causes of avian mortality events are often difficult to identify. As birds are highly mobile and can travel great distances during their migrations, the identification of disease agents, often in concert with temporal or seasonal factors, can be elusive. The two events discussed herein were recurring, which facilitated multi-year investigations and research. The disease agents in these events have never previously been identified in North America and/or were agents that caused signs of disease which were unusual or unconventional for that disease agent.

### *Leyogonimus polyoon* (Class: Trematoda) infection of American Coot *Fulica americana* in Shawano Lake, Wisconsin

Shawano Lake is the headwater drainage lake for the Wolf River and has a surface area of 6 063 acres (2 452 ha) with an average depth of 6 ft (1.83 m) and maximum depth of 42 ft (12.8 m). The lake is covered in ice for approximately six months of the year. In 1997, a large mortality event involving primarily American Coot and some waterfowl, mostly Lesser Scaup *Aythya affinis*, occurred. By the end of the 1997 mortality event, over 11 000 American Coot and 800 Lesser Scaup had been

American Coot *Fulica americana*. Photo: Gary Kramer, USFWS.

collected. In subsequent years, mortality events have waned, with the last documented mortality event occurring in 2002. Post mortem examinations of American Coots in 1997 revealed that a trematode *Leyogonimus polyoon*, previously only found in the Eurasian Coot *Fulica atra* and Common Moorhen *Gallinula chloropus* in Europe and Russia, was the cause of mortality in the American Coot. Ten American Coots, six males, one female and three of unknown sex, were submitted for necropsy. Body condition of birds was as follows: five poor, three moderate, one good and one not recorded. Those birds in poor flesh had no subcutaneous fat and a very prominent keel. The duodenum and jejunum had multi-focal areas approximately 1-1.5 cm in length which were distended and firm upon palpation. The intestines contained fibrinous to caseous cores of necrotic debris which occluded the lumen. All other organs were unremarkable. Cultures for *Salmonella* spp. and fungi were negative. Microscopic examination of intestinal sections from the coots revealed a general enteritis characterized by mucosal sloughing in areas where cores of necrotic debris were found with trematodes embedded into the tunica muscularis with occasional mult-inucleated giant cells surrounding the parasites. In one bird, over 40 000 trematodes were removed from the intestine. This is a conservative count, given that many worms were embedded in the intestinal tissue and not available for enumeration.

The life cycle of this trematode was not documented in the literature; neither was it reported to cause mortality in birds. We found that the snail *Bithynia tentaculata* was infected with *L. polyoon* cercariae (first larval stage). This snail was introduced into the United States in the 1870s (Mills *et al.* 1993). Various insect larvae from Shawano Lake were infected with the metacercariae (second larval stage, infectious for birds) of the parasite. Laboratory reared American Coots that were fed insects infected with metacercariae passed parasite eggs in their feces approximately 10-13 days after feeding, and were found to have adult worms in the small intestine upon necropsy.

Two other pathogenic trematodes, *Sphaeridiotrema globulus* and *Cyathocotyle bushiensis*, which also use *B. tentaculata* as an intermediate host, were found in Lesser Scaup and some American Coot in the latter stages of the mortality event. These parasites were first recorded in North America in the early 1900s, and have been reported as causes of mortality in Lesser Scaup and other waterfowl in Canada and the United States. *C. bushiensis* and *S. globulus* are also reported to infect waterbirds in Europe, but do not cause mortality events.

Ongoing research has indicated that *B. tentaculata* has moved west into the Mississippi River and has carried *S. globulus* and *C. bushiensis* into that waterway (National Wildlife Health Center, unpubl. results). At this point, control activities would most likely be focused on the snail, with the intention of decreasing the number of snails in certain water bodies where snails gather to overwinter. Various molluscicides are being tested for their effectiveness in killing snails in the early spring months.

## Eared Grebe (Black-necked Grebe) *Podiceps nigricollis* mortality at the Salton Sea, California

The Salton Sea in southern California is the state's largest lake, at approximately 375 square miles (97 000 ha) in surface area. The Sea is below sea level and its salinity is greater than that of the Pacific Ocean. From January to March, during staging for spring migration, more than one million Eared Grebes may congregate at the Salton Sea (Jehl & McKernan 2002). In late 1991 and early 1992, an undiagnosed disease event at the Sea killed an estimated 150 000 Eared Grebes, representing about 6% of the North American population (Meteyer *et al.* 2004). During the die-off, feathers of affected grebes often appeared disheveled or wet, and the birds exhibited unusual preening behaviour, congregated at freshwater drains where they were observed to gulp fresh water, moved onto the shore, and allowed people to approach and capture them (Meteyer *et al.* 2004). Trace elements, organochlorine contaminants, salt toxicosis, and botulism were ruled out, and, although avian cholera was diagnosed in some grebes collected along the north and west shorelines of the Sea, it was not found in grebes that died on the south shore and was not determined to be the major cause of mortality. Potential causes for the 1991-1992 die-off were suggested to include interactions of contaminants, immuno-suppression, an unknown biotoxin or pathogen present at the Sea, or a unique form of avian cholera (Meteyer *et al.* 2004). Previous Eared Grebe die-offs have been noted at the Salton Sea, and one in 1989, in particular, was of large magnitude (Jehl 1996).

Eared Grebe mortality continued to occur through the 1990s, but none of the die-offs approached the magnitude of the 1992 event. From early 2000 to early 2003, the Salton Sea Authority Wildlife Disease Surveillance Program reported that the number of Eared Grebe carcasses picked up ranged from a low of 37 in 2002 to 2 973 in 2003, with a total of 5 094 during the four-year period. As in previous years, most of the Eared Grebe mortality occurred from January to May. Of the carcasses picked up from 2000 to 2003, 214 were recovered that were in suitable post mortem condition for full or partial diagnostic evaluation at the National Wildlife Health Center. About 28% of the carcasses were described as having wet plumage, compared with 19% in the 1992 die-off (Meteyer *et al.* 2004). The weights of Eared Grebes found sick or dead in 2000-2003 were similar to the weights reported by Meteyer *et al.* (2004) for grebes that were emaciated or in poor to fair condition in the 1992 die-off. Carcass weights did not differ between grebes found sick or dead, but weights of dead grebes decreased as the spring season progressed. This finding suggests a chronic process and may indicate that grebes can tolerate a greater loss of body mass as the temperature increases. In other words, it could be expected that grebes should be able to thermoregulate with a lower body mass in warm weather than in cold weather. *Pasteurella multocida* (the bacterial agent of avian cholera) was a minor factor in the Eared Grebe mortality that occurred at the Salton Sea in 2000 and 2001, but none of the grebes tested in 2002 and 2003, when mortality was highest, was positive for *P. multocida*. Most of the *P. multocida* isolates were from grebes collected on the north and north-west shorelines of the Sea. Similarly, in the 1992 mortality event, most of the avian cholera cases were found in Eared Grebes collected on the north and west shorelines of the Sea (Meteyer *et al.* 2004).

*Salmonella* sp. was also associated to a relatively low degree with Eared Grebe mortalities in 2000 to 2002, but none of the grebes tested in 2003 was positive for *Salmonella* sp. and no isolates were found in the 1992 mortality event (Meteyer *et al.* 2004). No viruses were isolated from Eared Grebes from 2000 to 2003. Enveloped RNA viruses were isolated from two Eared Grebes in the 1992 die-off, but they were not lethal to embryos and were not characterized further (Meteyer *et al.* 2004). Botulism toxins were not detected in any of the Eared Grebes that were tested during 2000-2003, and there was no evidence to attribute Eared Grebe mortality at the Salton Sea during this period to avian botulism. In summary, despite investigative efforts over the years, no single responsible etiology has been identified as the cause of the Eared Grebe mortality events occurring at the Salton Sea between the early 1990s and 2003.

## REFERENCES

Jehl, J.R., Jr. 1996. Mass mortality of eared grebes in North America. Journal of Field Ornithology 76: 471-476.

Jehl, J.R., Jr. & McKernan, R.L. 2002. Biology and migration of eared grebes at the Salton Sea. Hydrobiologia 473: 245-253.

Meteyer, C.U., Audet, D.J., Rocke, T.E., Radke, W., Creekmore, L.H. & Duncan, R. 2004. Investigation of a large-scale eared grebe (*Podiceps nigricollis*) die-off at the Salton Sea, California, in 1992. Studies in Avian Biology 27: 141-151.

Mills, E.L., Leach, J.H., Carlton, J.T. & Secor, C. 1993. Exotic Species in the Great Lakes: A History of Biotic Crises and Anthropogenic Introductions. Journal of Great Lakes Research 19: 1-54.

# Consequences of an unforeseen event: effects of foot-and-mouth disease on the Barnacle Goose *Branta leucopsis* population wintering on the Solway Firth

*Larry Griffin[1], Mark O'Brien[2] & Eileen C Rees[3]*

[1]*The Wildfowl & Wetlands Trust, Eastpark Farm, Caerlaverock, Dumfries, Dumfriesshire, DG1 4RS, UK.*

[2]*The Royal Society for the Protection of Birds, Dunedin House, 25 Ravelston Terrace, Edinburgh, EH4 3TP, UK.*

[3]*The Wildfowl & Wetlands Trust, Martin Mere, Burscough, Ormskirk, Lancashire, L40 0TA, UK.*

Griffin, L., O'Brien, M. & Rees, E.C. 2006. Consequences of an unforeseen event: effects of foot-and-mouth disease on the Barnacle Goose *Branta leucopsis* population wintering on the Solway Firth. *Waterbirds around the world*. Eds. G.C. Boere, C.A. Galbraith & D.A. Stroud. The Stationery Office, Edinburgh, UK. pp. 441-442.

The outbreak of foot-and-mouth disease (FMD) in Britain in February 2001 had a major impact on farming activity around the Solway Firth the following summer, with many farmers losing their cattle and sheep. The changes in farming practices associated with FMD were considered likely to have consequences for the Svalbard Barnacle Goose *Branta leucopsis* population (which winters almost exclusively on the Solway Firth), because the geese generally feed on short, well fertilised pastures which have been grazed by sheep and cattle, and/or cut for hay or silage. They also spend time feeding on grazed merse (Owen *et al.* 1987). Longer or unfertilised swards, fields being put to arable crops, or an increase in set-aside in some parts of their wintering range could have caused shifts in goose feeding distribution in winter 2001/02. Moreover, variation in feeding opportunities could have led to a detrimental effect on body condition in winter 2001/02, which in turn might have influenced breeding success in summer 2002 and survival to the 2002/03 season.

Goose distribution before and after FMD was analysed to determine whether the reduction in livestock grazing rendered traditional feeding sites less attractive to the birds. Sward characteristics were measured to describe variation in food quality and quantity, and thus explain any changes in distribution. Demographic parameters recorded since the 1970s were used to determine whether a post-FMD change in food supply had longer-term effects on the population, by influencing survival and breeding success. This short note presents a summary of the results of the study. They are presented in full in Griffin *et al.* (2004).

To quantify the effects of FMD on farming activity, farmers were asked to complete questionnaires describing, for both 2000 and 2001, the main crop in each field, the number and timing of cuts for hay/silage, type of livestock and duration of grazing, fertiliser application, the year in which the field was last reseeded (if <10 years ago), and whether the farmer lost sheep, cattle, or both types of livestock due to FMD. In 2001-2002, more detailed monthly habitat assessments were also undertaken, to provide data to investigate causal links between farming activity and goose feeding site selection. Mean sward length was recorded for 177 fields, and sward biomass and protein content for a stratified sample of 64 fields (Griffin *et al.* 2004).

Changes in goose distribution across the Solway was monitored by: (i) weekly counts of numbers present in each field along a fixed route on the north side of the estuary, and (ii) coordinated weekly total population censuses covering all the main areas used by the geese. Fixed route counts recorded in 2001/02

were compared with similar route counts made each winter since 1993/94 so as to determine any local changes in feeding site selection. The latest total population counts were compared with population counts undertaken at least once a winter since 1993/94, and monthly since winter 1999/2000 (Phillips *et al.* 2000, Griffin & Coath 2001), to determine whether there was a more major shift in distribution across the Solway.

The potential of longer-term effects of FMD to affect goose survival and breeding success was assessed by comparing abdominal profile (body condition) scores for the geese in 2001/02 with those recorded in previous winters, using the method described by Owen (1981). Breeding success in summer 2002 (post-FMD) was assessed subjectively by considering the proportion of juveniles recorded in winter 2002/03 with observations made in the previous nine winters. Resightings of Barnacle Geese marked with plastic leg-rings were analysed using the MARK programme (White & Burnham 1999), to determine whether post-FMD survival (i.e., from winter 2001/02 to winter 2002/03) differed from annual survival rates recorded since the colour-ringing programme commenced in 1973.

The questionnaire interviews with farmers revealed that those affected by FMD reduced their fertiliser application in summer 2001, and switched grassland management from grazing to mowing. There was no significant change in the proportion of land that was tilled and cropped, rather than left as grass, in comparison with earlier years. Sward height on 'FMD affected farms' (those that lost both cattle and sheep) was taller than on 'unaffected farms' (those that lost sheep but not cattle) in October, but not from December onwards. At the Wildfowl and Wetlands Trust (WWT) Caerlaverock Reserve (FMD affected) the sward was taller in autumn 2001 than any previous autumn for which data had been collected (1997 to 2000 inclusive; Fig. 1). Otherwise, there was little variation in the sward variables (i.e., live biomass, forage quality and protein content) between FMD affected and unaffected sites in winter 2001/02.

The total population censuses found no evidence for a major shift in goose distribution between the southern (English) and northern (Scottish) sides of the Solway Firth in the winter immediately following FMD, in comparison with earlier and subsequent years, nor for a major movement to feeding sites outside the traditional wintering area. Individual flock sizes were smaller in 2001/02, and the geese used a greater number of fields in comparison with previous winters and with 2002/03, suggesting that the birds were more widely dispersed across their traditional feeding areas in 2001/02.

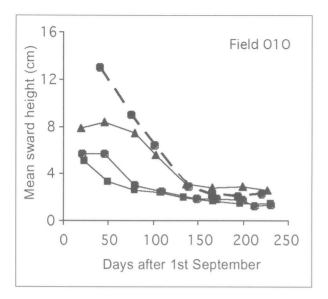

**Fig. 1.** Variation in winter sward height in a typical pasture field at WWT Caerlaverock, for three winters before FMD (solid lines) and one winter after FMD (dashed line).

**Table 1.** The ability of the model to predict the frequency of occurrence of Barnacle Geese on a field-by-field basis in 2000/01 compared with 2001/02. The Chi-squared values given are the goodness of fit of the model.

|  | 2000/01 winter | 2001/02 winter |
|---|---|---|
| October | 4.78* | 57.53*** |
| November | 41.24*** | 64.67*** |
| December | 102.61*** | 42.17*** |
| January | 67.10*** | 94.77*** |
| February | 71.15*** | 96.22*** |
| March |  | 59.89*** |
| April |  | 29.31*** |

* $P<0.05$; *** $P<0.001$

Changes in field management between 2000 and 2001 had some effect on goose distribution in the early part of winter 2001/02: fewer geese were recorded in fields in October 2001 where cattle grazing was lower during summer 2001 than the previous year, and fewer geese were recorded in November 2001 where a post-FMD reduction in sheep grazing had occurred. This supports earlier studies indicating that livestock grazing regimes can prepare the optimal sward for geese in autumn (Owen *et al.* 1987). However, there was little evidence that changes in field management influenced goose usage of fields from December onwards, or that the sward parameters measured influenced goose distribution in a substantial manner. Moreover, it seemed that the geese would feed on longer swards than had previously been considered optimal.

Modelled factors that affected goose distribution prior to FMD (for winters 1997/98 1999/2000 inclusive) were that, the disturbance regime for each field (fields having been classified as reserve, feeding, buffer and scaring zones each year, as part of the Solway Goose Management Scheme) was more closely associated with distribution than other variables. This is likely to have been due to the scheme reflecting feeding site fidelity in previous years, since previous use of a field by the geese is taken into account on determining the zone to which a field is assigned. Crop type was also significantly associated with goose distribution, with young pasture more frequently used by the geese than old pasture in early winter, while merse was used more frequently from February to April inclusive (Griffin *et al.* 2004).

A model of goose distribution in winters 1997/98 to 1999/2000 appeared better able to predict distribution in the winter immediately after FMD (2001/02) than in the previous 'control' year (2000/01) (Table 1). This confirmed the analyses of changes in goose distribution, which indicated that there was no major shift in feeding site selection in the winter following FMD

Low goose body condition in 2001/02 reflected a long-term decline, associated with poorer condition on arrival in October. Thus, there was no evidence for FMD-related changes in food

supply affecting the birds' condition in 2001/02. Similarly, low survival to winter 2002/03 reflected an ongoing trend, which may be related to other factors, such as density-dependent effects on the breeding grounds. Breeding success in 2002, recorded during winter 2002/03, was better than in the previous two years, and approached the ten-year mean of 10.8%.

Overall, the study found no evidence for FMD having a major effect on the Svalbard Barnacle Goose population. This may perhaps reflect the lack of variation in sward quantity and quality between FMD affected and unaffected sites, which in turn may be due to the farmers switching from grazing to mowing, and to the short time period involved. Further experimental work is needed to confirm whether sward condition and large-scale goose distribution are affected if changes in grazing and fertiliser regimes are maintained.

## REFERENCES

**Griffin, L.R. & Coath, D.C.** 2001. WWT Svalbard Barnacle Goose Project Report 2000- 2001. WWT Internal Report, Slimbridge.

**Griffin, L., O'Brien, M. & Rees, E.C.** 2004. Effects of foot-and-mouth disease on farming activity within the Solway Goose Management Scheme and consequences for the Svalbard Barnacle Goose population wintering on the Solway Firth. WWT and RSPB report to the Scottish Executive Environmental and Rural Affairs Department. 109 pp.

**Owen, M.** 1981. Abdominal profile - a condition index for wild geese in the field. Journal of Wildlife Management 45: 227-230.

**Owen, M., Black, J.M., Agger, M.C. & Campbell, C.R.G.** 1987. The use of the Solway Firth by an increasing population of Barnacle Geese in relation to changes in refuge management. Biological Conservation 39: 63-81.

**Phillips, R.A., Davis, S.E., Garner, M.G., Mackley, E.K. & Robinson, A.P.** 2000. WWT Svalbard Barnacle Goose Project Report 1999-2000. WWT Internal Report, Slimbridge.

**White, G. C. & Burnham, K.P.** 1999. Program MARK: survival estimates from populations of marked animals. Bird Study 46: 120-138.

# Snow Goose *Chen caerulescens caerulescens* overabundance increases avian cholera mortality in other species

*Michael D. Samuel*

*USGS-National Wildlife Health Center, 6006 Schroeder Road, Madison, WI 53711, USA.*
*Present address: USGS-Wisconsin Cooperative Wildlife Research Unit, Department of Wildlife Ecology, 204 Russell Labs,*
*University of Wisconsin, Madison, WI 53706, USA. (email: mdsamuel@wisc.edu)*

Samuel, M.D. 2006. Snow Goose *Chen caerulescens caerulescens* overabundance increases avian cholera mortality in other species.
*Waterbirds around the world.* Eds. G.C. Boere, C.A. Galbraith & D.A. Stroud. The Stationery Office, Edinburgh, UK. pp. 443-445.

## ABSTRACT

Avian cholera is a highly infectious disease caused by the bacterium *Pasteurella multocida* that affects >100 species of waterbirds worldwide. Current information on avian cholera indicates Lesser Snow Goose *Chen caerulescens caerulescens* to be a likely reservoir of the disease, though more birds survive outbreaks than was previously believed, and many of the birds that survive infection could be carriers of the disease agent. North American snow geese have increased dramatically, they are frequently involved in larger avian cholera outbreaks, they associate in dense winter aggregations that can enhance disease transmission, and these birds nest in colonies that facilitate continuation of the disease cycle during the summer. In the Rainwater Basin, an internationally recognized migration area for waterbirds, increasing populations of snow geese are associated with increasing avian cholera mortality, especially in other waterfowl species using the area each spring. High avian cholera in snow geese increases the risk of disease transmission and the magnitude of disease outbreaks in the community of waterfowl hosts using this area.

## INTRODUCTION

Avian cholera is a highly infectious disease caused by the bacterium *Pasteurella multocida* and is the most important infectious disease affecting waterfowl in North America (Wobeser 1997). The bacteria are primarily transmitted by ingesting or inhaling contaminated water from wetlands where birds die from the disease and from bird-to-bird contact. Wetlands with high densities of waterfowl can increase the risk of disease transmission and potentially the magnitude of disease outbreaks. Because the bacterium affects >100 species of waterbirds (Botzler 1991) factors such as bird density, disease transmission, and species mortality rates may depend on the community of waterfowl hosts using an area. Although much remains unknown about the ecology of avian cholera, recent evidence indicates that Lesser Snow Geese *Chen caerulescens caerulescens*, and possibly other waterbirds, are probable carriers of this disease agent (Samuel *et al.* 2005). Although avian cholera has killed >100 000 birds during single outbreaks the disease also appears to cause ongoing, low-level mortality within waterfowl populations (Botzler 1991, Wobeser 1992, Samuel *et al.* 1999*b*). Current management strategies to control avian cholera losses in waterfowl have been reactive, consisting primarily of collecting and disposing of carcasses when outbreaks occur (Wobeser 1992).

The Rainwater Basin (RWB) in Central Nebraska is internationally recognized as a key focal point in the spring migration of millions of ducks, geese, shorebirds, and cranes. However, large scale habitat changes in the RWB have produced at least two notable effects on migratory waterfowl. First, the dramatic reduction in habitat has produced extremely high concentrations (>500 000) of birds on many of the remaining wetlands. These crowded conditions can enhance transmission and spread of infectious diseases (Friend 1992). Since the 1970s avian cholera has been a recurrent disease problem in the RWB (Windingstad *et al.* 1984, 1988) where mortality occurs annually and in some years (e.g. 1998) estimated losses exceeded 100 000 birds. Risk and severity of diseases like avian cholera may have been further exacerbated by concurrent reductions in wetland quality (Friend 1981). Secondly, over the past decade, the skyrocketing population of mid-continent Lesser Snow Geese has shifted its principal spring migration corridor from eastern to central Nebraska. These birds have apparently been attracted to the abundance of nutrient and energy subsidy provided to waterfowl feeding on waste agricultural crops in the RWB.

## METHODS

The RWB encompasses >10 000 km$^2$ in south-central Nebraska with <10% of the pre-settlement wetland basins remaining (Smith & Higgins 1990). Because the vast majority of wetlands have been destroyed, the remaining basins exist in an intensive agricultural environment. The RWB is also recognized as the focal passageway for 7-9 million ducks and 5-7 million geese migrating from their wintering grounds in the southern United States and Mexico to their breeding grounds in Canada and the Arctic (Gersib *et al.* 1992). Avian cholera was first reported in the RWB in 1975 when an estimated 25 000 birds died (Zinkl *et al.* 1977). Since that time, avian cholera has occurred almost annually with most losses during spring migration, but fall outbreaks have occasionally occurred. Estimated losses have varied each year with peak mortality reported in 1980 (Brand 1984) and again in 1998.

We used data on carcasses collected by U.S. Fish and Wildlife Service and Nebraska Game and Parks Commission staff during spring avian cholera mortality events in the RWB from 1984-1999 to evaluate species composition of mortality and the relation between Lesser Snow Goose mortality and mortality in four of the predominate species of waterfowl: White-fronted Geese *Anser albifrons*, Canada Geese *Branta canadensis*, Mallard *Anas platyrhynchos*, and Northern Pintail *Anas acuta*. Carcass collection for remaining waterfowl species were considered as "other waterfowl" mortality. We used regression methods to evaluate the relation between the number of Snow Goose carcasses collected during outbreaks and those of other species collected during the same outbreaks. A separate regression analysis was conducted to compare Snow Geese to each of the waterfowl species collected.

**Table 1.** Carcasses collected during spring (February-April) avian cholera outbreaks in the Rainwater Basin, Nebraska, 1984-99 and reported to the National Wildlife Health Center. No avian cholera losses were reported during spring 1993 and 1994.

| Year | Lesser Snow Geese *Chen c. caerulescens* | White-fronted Geese *Anser albifrons* | Canada Geese *Branta canadensis* | Northern Pintail *Anas acuta* | Mallard *Anas platyrhynchos* | Other |
|------|------|------|------|------|------|------|
| 1984 | 38 | 92 | 107 | 75 | 85 | 68 |
| 1985 | 69 | 82 | 127 | 67 | 59 | 56 |
| 1986 | 266 | 173 | 123 | 170 | 42 | 79 |
| 1987 | 544 | 271 | 155 | 124 | 47 | 240 |
| 1988 | 440 | 635 | 551 | 118 | 95 | 110 |
| 1989 | 862 | 232 | 35 | 84 | 21 | 57 |
| 1990 | 274 | 147 | 116 | 55 | 37 | 67 |
| 1991 | 2 708 | 623 | 134 | 384 | 82 | 126 |
| 1992 | 3 610 | 670 | 154 | 147 | 107 | 40 |
| 1995 | 1 306 | 78 | 21 | 79 | 37 | 21 |
| 1996 | 5 223 | 505 | 92 | 1 013 | 321 | 454 |
| 1997 | 2 771 | 257 | 104 | 92 | 60 | 143 |
| 1998 | 20 290 | 962 | 239 | 2 575 | 1 267 | 892 |
| 1999 | 1 153 | 81 | 14 | 60 | 69 | 83 |
| **Total** | **39 554** | **4 808** | **1 972** | **5 043** | **2 329** | **2 436** |

## RESULTS

The severity of avian cholera losses among waterfowl populations has varied annually from endemic to epizootic wherever this disease has become established (Windingstad *et al.* 1998). Mortality levels may be influenced by a number of factors including species susceptibility, waterfowl density, age/sex of birds, stress, and weather (Rosen 1969, McLandress 1983, Botzler 1991, Samuel *et al.* 1999b, Windingstad *et al.* 1998). From 1984 to 1999, >56 000 carcasses of known species composition were collected during spring avian cholera outbreaks in Nebraska's RWB (Table 1). Lesser Snow Geese comprised the majority of carcasses (70.5%), followed in frequency by Northern Pintail (9.0%), White-fronted Geese (8.6%), other waterfowl species (4.3%), Mallard (4.1%), and Canada Geese (3.5%). The number of carcasses collected in the RWB varied annually, generally reflecting severity of avian cholera losses. However, the number of carcasses collected typically was much smaller than estimated mortality during the outbreak. For example, in 1998 <25 000 carcasses were collected and identified to species compared with an estimated total mortality >100 000 birds. The number of Snow Goose carcasses collected was positively related to the number of White-fronted Geese (slope = 0.040, $t_{12}$ = 3.80, $P$ = 0.003), Northern Pintail (slope = 0.127, $t_{13}$ = 17.1, $P$ < 0.0001), Mallard (slope = 0.060, $t_{13}$ = 20.9, $P$ < 0.0001), and other waterfowl species (slope = 0.046, $t_{13}$ = 9.83, $P$ < 0.0001) collected. However, there was no relationship between Snow Goose carcasses and the number of Canada Geese collected (slope = 0.004, $t_{12}$ = 0.56, P = 0.58).

## DISCUSSSION

The RWB appears to provide nearly ideal conditions for regular outbreaks of avian cholera (Wobeser 1992: 678), increasing Lesser Snow Geese, and crowding on a markedly reduced wetland base further contribute to the increased risk of avian cholera (Friend 1992). Current information indicates that Snow Geese are a likely reservoir of the disease (Samuel *et al.* 2005)

and may be particularly important in the ecology of avian cholera because populations have increased dramatically, they are frequently involved in larger avian cholera outbreaks, they associate in dense winter aggregations that can enhance disease transmission, and they nest in colonies which facilitate continuation of the disease cycle during the summer (Samuel *et al.* 1999a). In the RWB, Snow Geese are associated with increasing avian cholera mortality in other waterfowl species using the area each spring. Thus, there appears to be considerable potential for overabundant Snow Goose populations to adversely impact other species of birds by increasing the risk of disease transmission and outbreaks. Clearly a better understanding of the ecology of avian cholera is needed, including factors that promote and terminate outbreaks; the frequency of carrier birds and their role in the disease cycle; and how bird density, species composition, carcass density, and wetland conditions affect transmission of the disease. In the RWB and other areas with endemic avian cholera mortality it appears that management actions that reduce bird density, increase habitat available to waterfowl, reduce stress on birds, and provide habitat that encourages separation of ducks and geese would be beneficial.

## REFERENCES

Botzler, R.G. 1991. Epizootiology of avian cholera in wildfowl. Journal of Wildlife Diseases 27: 367-395.

Brand, C.J. 1984. Avian cholera in the Central and Mississippi Flyways during 1979-80. Journal of Wildlife Management 48: 399-406.

Friend, M. 1981. Waterfowl management and waterfowl disease: Independent or cause and effect relationships? Transactions of the North American and Natural Resources Conference 46: 94-103.

Friend, M. 1992. Environmental influences on major waterfowl diseases. Transactions of the North American Wildlife and Natural Resources Conference 57: 517-525.

Gersib, R.A., Dinan, K.F., Kauffeld, J.D., Gabig, P.J., Cornely, J.E., Jasmer, G.E., Hyland, J.M., & Strom, K.J. 1992. Rainwater Basin Joint Venture implementation plan. Nebraska Game and Parks Commission, Lincoln, Nebraska. 56 pp.

McLandress, R.M. 1983. Sex, age, and species differences in disease mortality of Ross' and lesser snow geese in California: implications for avian cholera research. California Fish and Game 69: 196-206.

Rosen, M.N. 1969. Species susceptibility to avian cholera. Bulletin of the Wildlife Disease Association 5: 195-200.

Samuel, M.D., Shadduck, D.J., Goldberg, D.R., Baranyuk, V., Sileo, L. & Price, J.I. 1999a. Antibodies against *Pasteurella multocida* in snow geese in the western arctic. Journal of Wildlife Diseases 35: 440-449.

Samuel, M.D., Takekawa, J.Y., G. Samelius, G. & Goldberg, D.R. 1999b. Avian cholera in lesser snow geese nesting on Banks Island, Northwest Territories. Wildlife Society Bulletin 27: 780-787.

Samuel, M.D., Shadduck, D.J., Goldberg, D.R. & Johnson, W.P. 2005. The role of lesser snow and Ross's geese as carriers of avian cholera in the Playa Lakes Region. Journal of Wildlife Diseases. 41: 48-57.

Smith, B.J. & Higgins, K.F. 1990. Avian cholera and temporal changes in wetland numbers and densities in Nebraska's Rainwater Basin Area. Wetlands 10: 1-5.

Windingstad, R.M., Hurt, J.J., Trout, A.K. & Cary, J. 1984. Avian cholera in Nebraska's rainwater basins. Transactions of the North American Wildlife and Natural Resources Conference 49: 577-583.

Windingstad, R.M., Kerr, S.M., Duncan, R.M. & Brand, C.J. 1988. Characterization of an avian cholera epizootic in wild birds in western Nebraska. Avian Diseases 32: 124-131.

Windingstad, R.M., Samuel, M.D., Thornburg, D.D. & Glaser, L.C. 1998. Avian cholera mortality in Mississippi Flyway Canada geese. In: D.H. Rusch, M.D. Samuel, D.D. Humburg & B.D. Sullivan (eds.) Biology and management of Canada geese. Proceedings of the international Canada goose symposium, Milwaukee, Wisconsin: 283-289.

Wobeser, G. 1992. Avian cholera and waterfowl biology. Journal of Wildlife Diseases 28: 674-682.

Wobeser, G. 1997. Disease of wild waterfowl. Second edition. Plenum Press, New York, New York. 324 pp.

Zinkl, J. G., Dey, N., Hyland, J.M., Hurt, J.J. & Heddleston, K.L. 1977. An epornitic of avian cholera in waterfowl and common crows in Phelps County, Nebraska, in the spring, 1975. Journal of Wildlife Disease 13: 194-198.

Snow Geese *Chen caerulescens caerulescens* are a likely reservoir of avian cholera. Photo: Michael D. Samuel.

# Ukraine as an ecological corridor for the transcontinental migration of birds in the Afro–Eurasian region and questions of epidemiological safety

*I. Rusev[1] & A. Korzuykov[2]*

[1]*Ukrainian I.I. Mechnikov Antiplague Research Institute, Laboratory of Ecomonitoring, 1A Ap., 42 Home Pastera str., Odessa, 65026, Ukraine. (email: wildlife@paco.net)*

[2]*Odessa I.I. Mechnikov National University, Biological Department, 2, Shampansky str., Zoological Department, Odessa, Ukraine. (email: olegk@te.net.ua)*

Rusev, I. & Korzuykov, A. 2006. Ukraine as an ecological corridor for the transcontinental migration of birds in the Afro-Eurasian region and questions of epidemiological safety. *Waterbirds around the world.* Eds. G.C. Boere, C.A. Galbraith & D.A. Stroud. The Stationery Office, Edinburgh, UK. p. 446.

Ukraine acts as an ecological corridor for the transcontinental migration of birds in the Afro-Eurasian region. This paper suggests that migrating birds may carry potentially dangerous viruses from Africa to Europe via the Ukraine.

A total of 416 species of birds reside in Ukraine for at least some part of the year (Fesenko & Bokotej 2002); of these, 19 are listed on the IUCN Red List and 67 in the Red Book of Ukraine. These include a number of important migratory birds. Over 100 of the 170 birds listed in the African-Eurasian Migratory Waterbird Agreement either nest in Ukraine or stop during migration: the Azov-Black sea coastal area is therefore a very important migration ecological corridor for many species of birds from Europe, Asia and Africa. Snake Island in the Black Sea is a key point for migrating non-passerine birds (Korzuykov *et al.* 1998).

The wetlands in the coastal areas of the Azov- Black Sea, particularly in the deltas of the Danube and Dniester, and along the Azov-Black Sea corridor provide habitat or resting sites for over then 200 species of waterfowl many of which migrate to Africa and some to Asia (Shegolev & Rusev 1993; Rusev & Barker 1995). For example, the well-known Night Heron *Nycticorax nycticorax* nesting population which in the Dniester delta consists of only 2 500 pairs, migrates to Mali, Chad and Niger (Rusev 1999). Some birds have also been found in Russia to the east, and to the west in France, Germany, Spain and Italy (Fig. 1).

It is known that Africa has many natural foci of arboviruses – West Nile Fever, Sindbis fever and others (Lvov & Ilichev 1979), and this natural migration root could be a possible transmission route for viruses and infection of people. Our previous serological and virology investigations of ticks, mosquitoes and birds in the Azov-Black Sea region during 1986-2002 showed that they are significant factors in the potential spread of infection to human populations, and a practical system of monitoring and managing the epidemiological situation is needed (Rusev & Boshenko 1977; Rusev *et al.*1998). This is particularly relevant given the need to monitor avian influenza in Europe and elsewhere.

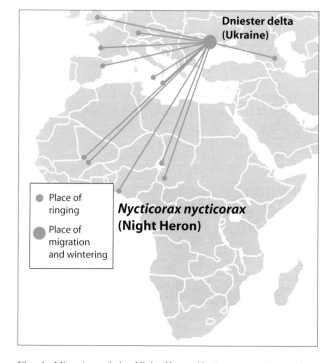

Fig. 1. Migration of the Night Heron *Nycticorax nycticorax* from Dniester delta population.

## REFERENCES

Fesenko, G. & Bokotej, A. 2002. The bird fauna of Ukraine. The Ukrainian Society for the Protection of Birds. Kiev. 411 pp.

Korzuykov, A., Rusev, I. & Gerjik, I. 1998. Coast of the NW Black Sea as migration root of birds Europe and Asia. Proceedings of the 1996 EUCC international symposium: Management and conservation of the Northern-Western Black sea coast. Odessa: 83.

Lvov, D. & Ilichev, V. 1979. Migration of birds and transmission of infections. Nauka, Moscow 270 pp.

Rusev, I.T. 1999. Migration and wintering of *Nycticorax nycticorax* from the Dnestr delta population. The Ring: ringing-migration-monitoring 21(1): 12.

Rusev, I. & Barker, N. 1995. The wetlands of the Dnestr delta: present situation and management. In M.G. Healy & J.P. Doody 1995. Directions in European coastal management: 519-524.

Rusev, I. & Boshenko, Yu. 1977. System of monitoring of natural foci ecosystems. In: Sanitary protection of territory of Ukraine and prophylactic of especially dangerous infections. Odessa: 180-183.

Rusev, I., Boshenko, Yu. & Dubina, D. 1998. Transcontinental migration of birds as factor of forming of foci arboviruses in coastal zone of NW of the Black Sea. In: Proceedings of the 1998 EUCC international symposium: Management and conservation of the Northern-Western Black sea coast, Odessa: 54.

Schegolev, I. & Rusev, I. 1995. The coastal wetlands of the Ukrainian Black Sea: present situation and conservation proposals. In: Proceedings of the 4th EUCC conference (1993), Coastal Management and Habitat Conservation 1: 385-394.

## 4.3 Flyway monitoring – rising to the challenge. Workshop Introduction

*Ward Hagemeijer[1] & Leon Bennun[2]*
*[1]Wetlands International, PO Box 471, 6700 AL Wageningen, The Netherlands.*
*[2]BirdLife International, Wellbrook Court, Girton Road, Cambridge, CB3 0NA, UK.*

Hagemeijer, W. & Bennun, L. 2006. Flyway monitoring – rising to the challenge. Workshop Introduction. *Waterbirds around the world.* Eds. G.C. Boere, C.A. Galbraith & D.A. Stroud. The Stationery Office, Edinburgh, UK. p. 447.

Monitoring waterbirds in Sudan. Photo: Niels Gilissen - MIRATIO.

Counts of migratory waterbirds in their breeding, staging and non-breeding areas have taken place for many decades. For non-breeding birds, the International Waterbird Census (IWC) organised by Wetlands International, has developed into a systematic global programme since its introduction in the 1960s. Summaries of national monitoring programmes were presented for a number of countries, including for North America (Blohm *et al.*), Sweden (Nilsson), the Netherlands (van Roomen *et al.*), the Czech Republic (Musilova *et al.*), and Slovakia (Ridzon). Long-term monitoring of breeding birds is also well-established at particular sites (such at the Bulgarian Bourgas wetlands reported by Profirov *et al.*) as well as for single species. However, it is clear that many gaps remain and there are many challenges in obtaining and using the data needed for more effective flyway management.

At a flyway scale, the symposium aimed to provide an overview of present monitoring approaches and programmes, identifying important gaps, and discussing ways to improve coverage and effectiveness. It suggested ways to link monitoring and results more closely to waterbird conservation and management.

It concluded that monitoring under the IWC is a strong contribution to the current knowledge of the status and trends of waterbird flyway populations; and also that there are many challenges ahead to improve monitoring so as to effectively address data needs in relation to flyway management.

The following five recommendations were made:-

1. The expansion of spatial and temporal coverage of the IWC, and improvement in the quality of data obtained, through capacity building and the training of observers in data deficient regions, as well as the monitoring of sites during migration and breeding seasons.
2. Strengthening the monitoring of demographic parameters. An integrated approach to the monitoring of waterbirds gives cost-effective identification of the reasons for waterbird population changes. There are good examples of the collection of demographic information and its integration with census data. Further such national and especially international schemes should be strongly encouraged and funded.
3. Incorporating data obtained by various methods including hunting bag statistics, ringing and other marking methods.
4. Development of monitoring site characteristics and threats to sites using methods including remote sensing.
5. Improvement in co-operation between Wetlands International, BirdLife International and other organisations so as to ensure optimum efficiency.

# Monitoring North America's waterfowl resource

*Robert J. Blohm[1], David E. Sharp[2], Paul I. Padding[3] & Kenneth D. Richkus[3]*

[1]*U.S. Fish and Wildlife Service, 4401 N. Fairfax Drive, Arlington, Virginia 22203, USA. (email: Robert.Blohm@fws.gov)*

[2]*U.S. Fish and Wildlife Service, PO Box 25486 DFC-DMBM, Denver, Colorado 80225, USA.*

[3]*U.S. Fish and Wildlife Service, 10815 Loblolly Pine Drive, Laurel, Maryland 20708, USA.*

Blohm, R.J., Sharp, D.E., Padding P.I. & Richkus, K.D. 2006. Monitoring North America's waterfowl resource. *Waterbirds around the world*. Eds. G.C. Boere, C.A. Galbraith & D.A. Stroud. The Stationery Office, Edinburgh, UK. pp. 448-452.

## ABSTRACT

Monitoring programs are an essential component of successful waterfowl management in North America. Five major categories of waterfowl monitoring efforts are conducted annually: population surveys; production surveys; habitat surveys; banding and marking programs; and harvest surveys. These surveys and programs are cooperative in nature, and rely on integrated partnerships between federal, state, and provincial agencies, as well as private organizations throughout the continent. Results from these surveys provide estimates of waterfowl population size, recruitment, survival rates, and harvest, as well as a means of evaluating habitat quality. Quantitative assessments of these key parameters provide the foundation for understanding waterfowl population dynamics and making and evaluating harvest management decisions.

## INTRODUCTION

One of the primary goals of waterfowl harvest management is to provide equitable hunting opportunity while ensuring the long-term sustainability of the hunted populations. Monitoring bird populations is an essential element in facilitating this task, and is the common basis for regulating hunting activities in all three countries in North America. The signatories of the various migratory bird treaties (United States, Canada, Mexico, Russia, and Japan) share responsibility for conducting the monitoring efforts that are needed to ensure sustainability.

In this paper, we provide an overview of the monitoring programs in North America, which are critical components of successful waterfowl management. There are five major categories of waterfowl monitoring efforts that are conducted annually: population surveys, production surveys, habitat surveys, banding and marking programs, and harvest surveys. These surveys and programs are cooperative in nature, involving biologists and other personnel from federal, state, and provincial agencies, as well as some non-governmental organizations. Information collected in these surveys results in estimates of waterfowl population size, recruitment, survival rates, and harvest, and also provides a means of appraising habitat quality. Together, these estimates provide the foundation for understanding waterfowl population dynamics and making and evaluating harvest management decisions.

## POPULATION SURVEYS

Each year, waterfowl population surveys are conducted on breeding and wintering grounds, and during migration. Most of these surveys are broad-scale in nature, wherein pilot-biologists count many species simultaneously, but some are designed to be species- or population-specific. These are primarily aerial surveys, and the data they provide are used independently or in conjunction with other information to derive annual estimates or indices of abundance for most species of ducks and populations of geese.

### Breeding Ground Surveys

The May breeding population and habitat survey is the most extensive and most important of North America's waterfowl population surveys. This survey was initiated on an experimental basis in 1947, became fully operational in 1955 (Martin *et al.* 1979), and has since been conducted annually. This survey is a cooperative effort of the United States Fish and Wildlife Service (USFWS), the Canadian Wildlife Service (CWS), and state, provincial, and tribal agencies. From 1955 to 1995, the May breeding population and habitat survey annually sampled more than 3.6 million square km of waterfowl breeding habitat throughout central Canada, north-central United States, and Alaska (Smith 1995). In 1996, the survey area was expanded to include an additional 1.8 million square km in the north-eastern United States and eastern Canada. In its entirety, this area represents a large portion of the primary duck nesting areas in North America.

The methodology for the May breeding population and habitat survey is described in detail in manuals of standard operating procedures (CWS & USFWS 1977, 1987) and elsewhere (e.g. Reynolds 1987); therefore we will only outline it briefly here. To sample the North American waterfowl breeding habitat efficiently, the area is divided up into 65 strata or areas of similar waterfowl habitat and waterfowl densities. Within each stratum are transect lines that were established to sample the stratum from the air (Fig. 1). Different strata are sampled at different intensities depending on waterfowl densities within the strata. Each transect is further divided into a series of 28.8 km segments (25.6 km in Alaska). In total, over 85 000 km of transects are flown each year using 13 fixed-wing aircraft.

Air crews, each of which consists of a pilot-biologist and an observer, fly along each transect line at an altitude of 30-45 m and a speed of 145-170 km per hour. The pilot-biologist identifies and counts all ducks and geese within 200 m of the transect line on the left side of the aircraft, while the observer is responsible for identifying and counting waterfowl within 200 m on the right side. Observed birds are identified as singles, pairs, flocks, or groups (CWS & USFWS 1977, 1987). Until recently, pilot-biologists and observers recorded their observations on tape recorders, and later transcribed and summarized the data onto paper forms or into a computer. Today, observations are recorded directly in a computer, and each observation is geo-referenced with point locations from the aircraft's Global Positioning System (GPS, see Hodges & Thorpe 2002).

When the survey was first established, population estimates derived from the aerial counts were not adjusted for birds that

**Fig. 1.** Strata and transect lines of the May waterfowl breeding population and habitat survey that is flown annually in North America.

could not be seen from the air. To correct for this bias, a sub-sample of segments was chosen for more intensive scrutiny by biologists on the ground. Ground crews consisting of two to four people coordinate with the air crews and conduct their waterfowl counts on sample segments within three days after the air crew has flown the segment. The ground crew uses GPSs, aerial maps, and past experience to check every wetland and count and identify each duck or goose observed on the sample segments. The use of these "air-ground comparison segments" was first tested in 1959, and the system became fully operational in 1961 in Canada and in 1974 in the United States. Currently, in the United States and Canadian prairies there are 163 air-ground comparison segments. The ground counts provide the basis for developing visibility correction factors to account for the fact that not all birds within 200 m of the transect can be seen from the air. In some northern and eastern strata, where ground access is problematic due to lack of roads, helicopters are used instead of ground crews (e.g. Malecki *et al.* 1981). In these areas, transects are flown by the fixed-wing aircraft and then followed up by a helicopter crew using procedures similar to those used by the ground crews in the prairie areas.

Species-specific estimates of breeding populations are derived by taking the counts obtained from fixed-wing aircraft, adjusting them based on the visibility correction factors, and expanding them over the survey area in each stratum. Martin *et al.* (1979) provided a detailed explanation of the statistical analyses used to derive population estimates and the associated variances.

Although the May breeding population and habitat survey covers a large portion of North America's primary waterfowl breeding areas, it is not all-encompassing. Many populations of geese nest in the arctic or sub-arctic regions of Alaska and Canada, and the remoteness and extensive distribution of their habitats make it difficult to acquire population estimates at this season. Therefore, biologists must rely on other surveys to obtain indices of abundance for many populations of geese, including Snow Geese *Chen (Anser) caerulescens*, Ross's Geese *C. (A.) rossii*, Greater White-fronted Geese *Anser albifrons*, and Canada Geese *Branta canadensis*. One such survey is the arctic-nesting goose survey, where biologists from federal, state, and provincial agencies, and universities, count geese at various locations on the nesting grounds. These surveys are usually conducted from helicopters over historical goose nesting areas (e.g. Reed & Changon 1987), and they are used in conjunction with other population surveys conducted during autumn and winter to provide annual goose population estimates.

### Wintering Ground Surveys

The mid-winter survey is another survey of continental waterfowl populations that includes most species of ducks and geese. Conducted annually since 1935, this survey provides estimates of waterfowl on major wintering areas throughout the United States. It is a cooperative effort between federal and state personnel that is usually conducted in January. Unlike the transect-based May survey, the mid-winter survey is primarily a cruise survey during which pilot-biologists and their observers attempt to census birds in the areas they survey. Unfortunately, survey methodology has varied among states, and coverage has varied over years. This lack of standardization, coupled with the cost of conducting the survey, has been the origin of some criticism (e.g. Eggeman & Johnson 1989). However, although the mid-winter survey only yields general information for most waterfowl species, such as relative abundance and distribution on wintering habitats, it does provide the best population data available for some species, including Tundra Swan *Cygnus columbianus*, Black Brant *Branta bernicla nigricans*, and some other goose populations (Trost *et al.* 1990).

The Mexican waterfowl survey is another winter aerial survey that is conducted cooperatively by biologists from Canada, Mexico, and the United States. Starting in the mid-1930s, this cruise survey covers the major waterfowl wintering grounds of Mexico, including the east coast from Laguna Madre to Tampico, the west coast including the Baja Peninsula, and the interior highlands (Saunders 1952). Parts of the survey are conducted annually, but the entire survey is now carried out at three-year intervals. The Mexican waterfowl survey is not part of the mid-winter survey; however, it augments the winter surveys conducted in the United States by providing additional coverage of waterfowl species that winter extensively in Mexico. For example, species such as Mallard *Anas platyrhynchos* are well covered by the mid-winter survey, but a large proportion of some species such as Blue-winged Teal *A. discors*, Northern Pintail *A. acuta* and Redhead *Aythya americana* winter far into Mexico.

### Migration Surveys

In addition to surveys on the breeding and wintering grounds, some population surveys are also conducted during the spring and autumn migrations. An example of a migration survey is the mid-continent Sandhill Crane *Grus canadensis* survey, which is conducted in late March. Nearly the entire population gathers in Nebraska's Platte River Valley at that time, during the northward spring migration. The survey consists of a pilot-biologist and his observer counting birds along established transect lines. It also uses aerial photography of a sub-sample of crane flocks to quantify errors made by the pilot-biologist and observer in the estimation of flock sizes, thereby enabling the development of correction factors to obtain a more accurate estimate of the population size (Benning & Johnson 1987). Another example is the September survey of mid-continent Greater White-fronted Geese that is conducted in the Canadian prairie, where the population gathers during the southward autumn migration.

## PRODUCTIVITY SURVEYS

The July duck production survey is very similar to the May breeding population and habitat survey, but instead of counting breeding pairs, pilot-biologists count duck broods, and, whenever possible, identify the broods by age class. They also count pairs and lone males to obtain an index of the late nesting effort, an important component of overall productivity for some species (Reynolds 1987). The survey area is a subset of the May survey area, and fewer transects are sampled. Ducklings cannot be identified to species from the air, and brood counts are not corrected for pilot/observer visibility because broods are difficult to count from the ground. As a result, this survey provides an index of annual production for all ducks in the survey area, but not species-specific estimates.

The wintering grounds are another place for biologists to estimate productivity, especially for Tundra Swans and some species of geese. Adult Tundra Swans and their young of the year are easily distinguishable from the air, because the adults are white and the young birds have dull gray plumage. The winter productivity counts are generally conducted with the mid-winter surveys, and consist of both transect and cruise surveys.

## HABITAT SURVEYS

Knowledge of habitat conditions is an important component in any attempt to predict changes in the size of duck populations. The two major operational surveys used for this purpose are the May breeding population and habitat survey and the July duck production survey. In addition to counting ducks and geese during these surveys, pilot-biologists and their observers also count ponds and assess habitat conditions over the key breeding areas in North America. Pond counts and the changes in pond numbers between May and July have been critical components of the process that predicts annual duck production in the Prairie Pothole Region of the United States and Canada. Furthermore, annual pond counts obtained during the May survey serve as major inputs into the models used to determine annual hunting seasons and regulations (Johnson *et al.* 1997).

Satellite imagery and remote sensing are also two techniques currently being used and/or evaluated to monitor and estimate habitat conditions. For example, biologists can access LANDSAT satellite imagery to determine the amount and distribution of upland and wetland habitat available for breeding waterfowl (Koeln *et al.* 1988). Such imagery is important for targeting where habitat management projects should be undertaken. In addition, Advanced Very High Resolution Radiometry (AVHRR) has recently been used to monitor the timing of snow melt in some of the arctic habitats used by nesting geese (Strong & Trost 1994). In the arctic and sub-arctic regions, the phenology of snow melt and timing of the spring break-up are important variables used for predicting the timing of nest initiation by geese, and ultimately annual goose productivity. Production is usually poor if nesting is delayed much beyond 15 June. These approaches to quantifying and qualifying habitat not only hold promise for improving our estimates of available habitat, but will allow pilot-biologists and observers to concentrate their efforts on counting ducks (Smith *et al.* 1989).

## BANDING AND MARKING PROGRAMS

Banding is another important source of information for waterfowl managers. The first large-scale North American banding program was established in 1922 (USFWS & CWS 1989), but it was not until 1946 that an international banding effort was organized to address specific management objectives for ducks (Smith *et al.* 1989).

One of the first uses of banding and recovery location data was to help biologists determine migration routes (Lincoln 1935). Determining the four major migratory pathways, or flyways, in North America led to the establishment of the Flyway System in 1948; Flyways are still the administrative units by which we manage waterfowl today. Understanding migration routes for various species gives biologists insight into the distribution and derivation of the harvest, which allows us to better manage individual populations.

Biologists can also estimate both annual harvest rates and annual survival rates for some waterfowl species from band recovery data. The annual variation in harvest and survival rates has helped biologists understand how breeding habitat conditions and harvest regulations affect survival (e.g. Burnham *et al.* 1984).

Thus, these harvest and survival rates are critical pieces of information that are used to help determine appropriate hunting regulations each year, i.e. the regulations that will result in sustainable harvest levels (Williams *et al.* 1996). Estimating harvest rates from band recoveries requires a thorough understanding of band reporting rates. Reporting rates reflect the willingness of people who recover bands to report this information to the Bird Banding Laboratory. In recent years, use of a toll-free telephone number imprinted on bands has raised reporting rates significantly from the levels that Nichols *et al.* (1995) estimated for the late 1980s. We are currently conducting a comprehensive multi-year investigation to determine what the reporting rates are now, and whether they vary by region, species, and sex.

Currently, biologists band more than 200 000 ducks and nearly 150 000 geese and swans in North America each year. To date, we have concentrated most of our duck banding efforts on Mallards. The Mallard is the most commonly harvested duck in the United States and Canada (USFWS 2003), and much of what we know regarding waterfowl population dynamics and harvest management is due to the continued success of the banding effort devoted to this species.

## HARVEST SURVEYS

National surveys of sport hunters have been conducted annually since 1952 in the United States and since 1967 in Canada. Although they have undergone significant changes since their inception, these surveys are still conducted by mail, and consist of asking samples of waterfowl hunters to report the number of ducks and geese they harvest during the hunting season (Martin & Carney 1977, Cooch *et al.* 1978). The surveys provide annual information that allows biologists to evaluate long-term trends in harvest, hunter numbers, hunting pressure, and waterfowl population demographics (Trost *et al.* 1987). This information, coupled with data from other surveys, allows biologists to generate population models that are used to help determine harvest management prescriptions for several species, such as Mallard, Northern Pintail, and Canvasback *Aythya valisineria*.

Both countries currently require all hunters of migratory birds to provide their name and address, either through a migratory bird hunter registration system (United States) or a special migratory bird hunting permit (Canada). This yields sample universes from which the USFWS and CWS select samples of hunters for their "harvest diary" surveys. Each sampled hunter is asked to report the date, location, and the number of ducks and geese taken for each day of waterfowl hunting. Hunters' responses are used to estimate the mean number of ducks and geese harvested per hunter for each state or province. The total number of ducks and geese harvested in each state or province is then estimated by expanding these means by the number of hunters in each state or province.

Both countries also select another sample of hunters annually, and ask them to participate in "parts collection" surveys. Hunters who agree to participate are mailed postage-paid wing envelopes and are asked to send back a wing from every duck and the tail feathers of every goose that they shoot throughout the hunting season. Biologists identify the species, age, and sex of each duck wing in the sample and the species and age of each goose tail. Thus, these surveys yield estimates of the species, sex, and age composition of the harvest. Results of the parts collection surveys are combined with the results of hunting diary surveys to provide species-specific harvest estimates (Martin & Carney 1977, Cooch *et al.* 1978).

Additionally, a survey of the annual harvest of subsistence hunters has been conducted in Alaska since 1985. For this survey, a sample of households is selected in the parts of Alaska where subsistence harvesting of birds and eggs is legal. Survey forms that show pictures of the various species of birds are hand-delivered to the sample households, and participants are asked to record how many birds and eggs of each species they take over the entire subsistence harvest period (April-October). Harvest estimates are derived in a similar fashion as sport harvest in the United States and Canada, except that species-specific estimates are derived directly from the household reports rather than from a wing survey.

## CONCLUSION

Monitoring programs are integral components of migratory bird management in North America. Together, results from these surveys and programs comprise the largest data set on any wildlife species group in the world. Results from these surveys serve as crucial inputs for many waterfowl population models, and are used to help guide biologists in setting and evaluating harvest management and habitat management programs. Furthermore, the success of North America's monitoring efforts is entirely dependent upon cooperation at all levels among the agencies and organizations that are charged with managing this important wildlife resource.

## REFERENCES

**Benning, D.S & Johnson, D.H.** 1987. Recent improvements to sandhill crane surveys in Nebraska's central Platte River Valley. Proceedings of the North American Crane Workshop 7: 165-172.

**Burnham, K.P., White, G.C. & Anderson, D.R.** 1984. Estimating the effect of hunting on annual survival rates of adult mallards. Journal of Wildlife Management 48: 350-361.

**Canadian Wildlife Service & U.S. Fish and Wildlife Service** 1977. Standard operating procedures for aerial waterfowl breeding ground population and habitat surveys in North America. Unpublished report.

**Canadian Wildlife Service & U.S. Fish and Wildlife Service** 1987. Standard operating procedures for aerial waterfowl breeding ground population and habitat surveys in North America; revised. Unpublished report.

**Cooch, F.G., Wendt, S., Smith, G.E.J. & Butler, G.** 1978. The Canada migratory game bird hunting permit and associated surveys. In: H. Boyd & G.H. Finney (eds) Migratory game bird hunters and hunting in Canada. Canadian Wildlife Service Report Series No. 43: 8-39.

**Eggeman, D.R. & Johnson, F.A.** 1989. Variation in effort and methodology for the Midwinter Waterfowl Inventory in the Atlantic Flyway. Wildlife Society Bulletin 17: 227-233.

**Hodges, J. & Thorpe, P.P.** 2002. Voice/GPS survey program manual for the breeding population and production surveys. Unpublished report.

**Johnson, F.A., Moore, C.T., Kendall, W.L., Dubovsky, J.A., Caithamer, D.F., Kelley, Jr., J.R. & Williams, B.K.** 1997. Uncertainty and the management of mallard harvests. Journal of Wildlife Management 61: 202-216.

**Koeln, G.T., Jacobson, J.E., Wesley, D.E. & Rempel, R.S.** 1988. Wetland inventories derived from LANDSAT data for waterfowl management planning. Transactions of the North American Wildlife and Natural Resource Conference 53: 303-310.

**Lincoln, F.C.** 1935. The waterfowl flyways of North America. U.S. Department of Agriculture, Circular No. 342, Washington, D.C.

**Malecki, R.A., Caswell, F.D., Bishop, R.A., Babcock, K.M. & Gillespie, M.M.** 1981. A breeding ground survey of EPP Canada geese in northern Manitoba. Journal of Wildlife Management 45: 46-53.

**Martin, E.M. & Carney, S.M.** 1977. Population ecology of the mallard, IV: A review of duck hunting regulations, activity, and success, with special reference to the mallard. U.S. Fish and Wildlife Service Resource Publication 130, Washington, D.C.

**Martin, F.W., Pospahala, R.S. & Nichols, J.D.** 1979. Assessment and population management of North American migratory birds. In: J. Carins, Jr., G.P. Patil & W.E. Waters (eds) Environmental biomonitoring, assessment, prediction and management – certain case studies and related quantitative issues. International Co-operative Publication House, Burtonsville, Maryland: 187-239.

**Nichols, J.D, Reynolds, R.E., Blohm, R.J., Trost, R.E., Hines, J.E. & Bladen, J.P.** 1995. Geographic variation in band reporting rates for mallards based on reward banding. Journal of Wildlife Management 59: 697-708.

**Reed, A. & Changon, P.** 1987. Greater snow geese on Bylot Island, Northwest Territories, 1983. Journal of Wildlife Management 51: 128-131.

**Reynolds, R.E.** 1987. Breeding duck population, production, and habitat surveys, 1979-85. Transactions of the North American Wildlife and Natural Resource Conference 52: 187-205.

**Saunders, G.B.** 1952. Waterfowl wintering grounds of Mexico. Transactions of the North American Wildlife and Natural Resource Conference 17: 89-100.

**Smith, G.W.** 1995. A critical review of the aerial and ground surveys of breeding waterfowl in North America. Biological Science Report 5. U.S. Department of the Interior, Washington, D.C.

**Smith, R.I., Blohm, R.J., Kelly, S.T., Reynolds, R.E. & Caswell, F.D.** 1989. Review of the data bases for managing duck harvests. Transactions of the North American Wildlife and Natural Resource Conference 54: 537-544.

**Strong, L.L. & Trost, R.E.** 1994. Forecasting production of arctic nesting geese by monitoring snow cover with advanced very high resolution radiometer (AVHRR) data. Proceedings of the Pecora Symposium 12: 425-430.

**Trost, R.E., Sharp, D.E., Kelly, S.T. & Caswell, F.D.** 1987. Duck harvests and proximate factors influencing hunting activity and success during the period of stabilized regulations. Transactions of the North American Wildlife and Natural Resource Conference 52: 216-232.

**Trost, R.E., Gamble, K.E. & Nieman, D.J.** 1990. Goose surveys in North America: Current procedures and suggested improvements. Transactions of the North American Wildlife and Natural Resource Conference 55: 338-349.

**U.S. Fish and Wildlife Service** 2003. Harvest Information Program: Preliminary estimates of waterfowl hunter activity and harvest during the 2001 and 2002 hunting seasons. Administrative Report. Laurel, Maryland.

**U.S. Fish and Wildlife Service & Canadian Wildlife Service** 1989. The North American banding program - a revised approach. Unpublished report.

**Williams, B.K., Johnson, F.A. & Wilkins, K.A.** 1996. Uncertainty and the adaptive management of waterfowl harvests. Journal of Wildlife Management 60: 223-232.

American White Pelicans *Pelecanus erythrorhynchos*.  Photo: U.S. Fish and Wildlife Service.

# The African Waterbird Census (1991-2004): fourteen years of waterbird surveys in Africa

*Cheikh Hamallah Diagana[1], Tim Dodman[2] & Seydina Issa Sylla[1]*

[1]*Wetlands International, BP 8060 Dakar-Yoff, Senegal. (email: diaganawet@sentoo.sn)*

[2]*Hundland, Papa Westray, Orkney, KW17 2BU, UK.*

Diagana, C.H., Dodman, T. & Sylla, S.I. 2006. The African Waterbird Census (1991-2004): fourteen years of waterbird surveys in Africa. *Waterbirds around the world.* Eds. G.C. Boere, C.A. Galbraith & D.A. Stroud. The Stationery Office, Edinburgh, UK. pp. 453-456.

## ABSTRACT

The African Waterbird Census (AfWC) is one of several co-ordinated international waterbird censuses carried out under the umbrella of the International Waterbird Census (IWC). The census was initiated in 1991, and since 1998 has been managed from the Wetlands International office in Dakar, Senegal. To date, over 900 sites in 36 countries have been counted at least once during the census, and thousands of volunteers and professionals have participated in the counts. Over 9.2 million waterbirds were counted in the census of January 2000. This paper provides a brief history of the AfWC, and reviews some of the problems and challenges that it faces. A strategy for the development of the AfWC during the period 2004-2006 is discussed, and a number of priorities are identified.

## INTRODUCTION

The African Waterbird Census (AfWC) runs parallel to other international waterbird censuses in Asia, the Western Palearctic and the Neotropics under the umbrella of the International Waterbird Census (IWC). The AfWC, which concerns sub-Saharan Africa, was initiated in 1991, when 15 countries participated. Gradually, the AfWC has extended its coverage to reach most parts of the continent and Africa's outlying islands, particularly in the Indian Ocean, such as Madagascar. The main objectives of the AfWC are to:

- establish a monitoring programme for African wetlands;
- determine distribution and migratory strategies of waterbirds in Africa;
- develop estimates of the populations of waterbirds in Africa;
- create a network grouping persons involved in the survey, management and use of waterbirds and wetlands; and
- promote education and public awareness concerning wetlands and waterbirds.

During its implementation, Wetlands International has benefited from the financial support of several partners for the AfWC, including the Government of The Netherlands, the Swiss Agency for Environment and Forests, the Ramsar Convention Bureau, and the Secretariat of the African-Eurasian Migratory Waterbird Agreement (AEWA), whilst other partners have contributed to the programme directly through parallel initiatives, including the Office National de la Chasse et de la Faune Sauvage (ONCFS) in West Africa and the Wildfowl and Wetlands Trust (WWT) in Eastern Africa.

## Participation, coverage and national co-ordination

After the opening of Wetlands International's Africa Programme Office in Dakar, Senegal, in 1998, the database was transferred to Dakar and is managed there, whilst regular contact is maintained with the IWC database at the headquarters of Wetlands International in The Netherlands. To date, the database holds data from more than 900 sites in 36 countries, and thousands of volunteers and professionals have participated in the waterbird census in one way or another.

There is an on-going effort to strengthen national co-ordination of the AfWC, especially through the nomination of National Co-ordinators; so far 38 have been nominated. There are also voluntary Regional Co-ordinators for the five identified sub-regions of West Africa, Central Africa, Eastern Africa, Southern Africa, and Madagascar and the Indian Ocean islands.

## Network development

In 1997, *A Preliminary Waterbird Monitoring Strategy for Africa* (Dodman 1997) was published. This used the results of an international workshop, questionnaires and other sources to propose a strategy for applied programmes of waterbird monitoring in Africa. An African Waterbird Census Steering Committee was formed on the recommendation of the AfWC network, and this met for the first time in November 1998, when a number of action points were developed. Just before the 10th Pan-African Ornithological Congress in Kampala Uganda, in 2000, Wetlands International organized an AfWC development workshop. The main theme "from census to conservation" translates the desire to link the AfWC closely to the conservation of waterbirds and wetlands in Africa. About fifty resource persons attended the workshop including many AfWC National Co-ordinators. This provided a good basis for the development of the AfWC in the coming years. Regional recommendations were formulated, lending a new dynamism to this pioneering conservation network.

## Some results from the AfWC programme

The results of the census from 1991 to 2001 demonstrate that tremendous efforts have been made by the network to cover a wide range of sites. The total counts have varied considerably from year to year (Fig. 1), often reflecting the coverage more than actual decreases or increases in birds at individual sites. The high count in 2000 can be explained by the coverage of some sites of high productivity where birds concentrate, such as the Banc d'Arguin (Mauritania), Lake Bogoria (Kenya), and some large breeding colonies such as Bird Island (Seychelles). Indeed, these sites alone accounted for more than 50% of the numbers of birds counted in January 2000.

The number of participating countries has generally increased since the initiation of the census, with around 30 countries now regularly participating in the programme (Fig. 2). However, there are often difficulties in maintaining the census in certain countries,

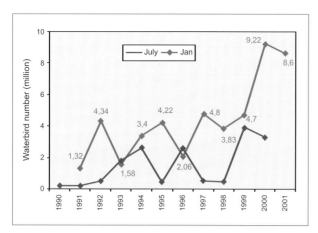

**Fig. 1.** Number of waterbirds counted under the African Waterbird Census: 1991-2001.

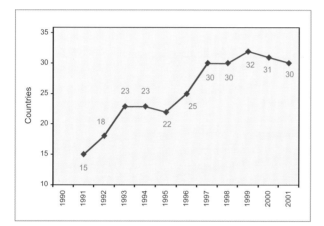

**Fig. 2.** Number of countries counted under the African Waterbird Census: 1991-2001.

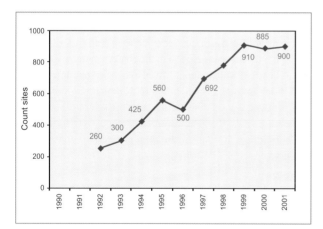

**Fig. 3.** Number of sites participating in the African Waterbird Census: 1992-2001.

due to insecurity, lack of financial resources, lack of commitment, changes in national co-ordination and other reasons. The availability of a small grants programme for the AfWC managed by Wetlands International has assisted greatly in assuring the participation of a number of countries, and extending the census to new countries. In addition, the inclusion of AfWC surveys within some regional projects has significantly helped to strengthen networks, especially in West and Eastern Africa.

The number of sites covered by the programme increased significantly from 1991 to 1999, a period which saw many new

countries joining the AfWC network, but this has tailed off since then (Fig. 3). This is to be expected, and a key challenge for the AfWC, if it is to function as a monitoring programme, is to maintain the regular coverage of key sites.

The outputs of the AfWC are multiple. Of particular significance, the AfWC has provided an excellent platform for capacity building of national networks, through training, exchanges, provision of equipment and by simply enabling people to get involved in fieldwork on a regular basis. The census also benefits from participation of a wide range of partners at all levels. This has helped strengthen partnerships between organizations.

## Use of AfWC information

The main data collected under the AfWC are the numbers of birds counted at different wetlands. However, additional information is requested through the compilation of census forms, which include sections for site condition, weather and other variables. Site forms are also requested to be completed for each site, where standard information may be recorded and a site map provided. However, the quality of these additional data are often poor, and the level of data inadequate. Another challenge for the census is to improve the site data and the regular monitoring of site conditions, including threats. These may help, in the long run, to improve analysis and thereby usefulness of the data.

Some of the main current uses of the AfWC data are:–

- Increasing knowledge of waterbird populations, their migratory strategies and conservation status. Data have been used extensively in the development of Waterbird Population Estimates (Rose & Scott 1994, Rose & Scott 1997, Wetlands International 2002) and waterbird atlases (Scott & Rose 1996, Delany *et al.* in prep.), and in developing strategic analyses of waterbirds (e.g. Perennou 1991, Scott 1999, Dodman 2002). Data have been used for the identification of Important Bird Areas (IBAs) in Africa (Fishpool & Evans 2001). Data are also used for assessments of the status of particular species, such as the Cape Teal *Anas capensis* (Baker 2005).
- Development of Species Action Plans. AfWC data were used in particular for developing a conservation action plan for the Black Crowned Crane *Balearica pavonina* (Williams *et al.* 2002).

Long-toed Lapwing *Vanellus crassirostris*, Lake Naivasha, Kenya. Photo: Ian Francis

- Monitoring the ecological character and productivity of wetlands. Regular repeated surveys can contribute to quantifying changes in wetland character and measuring the impacts of developments. This is achieved through measuring basic site characteristics as well as through recording waterbirds numbers and distribution.
- Provide baseline data that may be referred to if a wetland is threatened by land use developments, such as draining or conversion to irrigation. Data may thus be used in contributing to Environmental Impact Assessments (EIAs) and in highlighting important and/or sensitive areas.
- Support development and implementation of the Convention on Wetlands (Ramsar, Iran 1971) and the AEWA in Africa. Data have been in used in particular for the identification of new and potential Sites of International Importance under the Ramsar Convention (Ramsar sites) and of key site networks under the AEWA.

## Constraints for the development of the AfWC

There are many and diverse challenges facing the AfWC at different levels. Some of the common constraints are given below:

### Weak financial and organizational support for the AfWC.

Surveys cost money, and many African organizations lack the financial means to execute surveys on a regular basis. Wetlands International does provide small grants and sometimes more substantial funds for surveys and related activities, but such funds are generally limited, whilst provision of external funds on a regular basis cannot be seen as a sustainable means of support. Countries are encouraged to build the AfWC into more regular conservation or monitoring programmes, but this is often difficult to achieve, and most nature management organizations in Africa depend to a large extent on external funds for specific short-term projects. National Co-ordinators themselves are often not in a position to dedicate much time to the AfWC, and the material means at their disposal are derisory for achieving good results on a regular basis.

### Inadequate communication and commitment.

Good communication is an essential component of an effective functioning network. Whilst recent technological developments have facilitated communication in Africa, there is still limited communication between most members of the network. This is partly due to the fact that the network is rather dynamic, outputs are irregular and there have been no means of late to permit National Co-ordinators to meet together at a regional or continental level. Poor communication generally leads to lowered commitment to the census, especially if feedback is not provided often enough.

### Limited expertise and data quality control.

At the national level, there is generally only limited expertise in the AfWC, from planning surveys to identification of waders to collection and input of data. There is also a limited ability to check data carefully and thoroughly, for instance, before submission to Wetlands International. This situation can result in errors in the database, published reports and resulting analyses.

Goliath Heron *Ardea goliath* at Lake Baringo, Kenya. Photo: Colin Galbraith.

## Priorities for the future

Although the AfWC remains one of the few regional monitoring schemes in Africa and enjoys a wide participation of countries and network members, constant attention needs to be paid to its execution and development. Five key practical requirements for the coming years are as follows:

### Enhance communication within the AfWC network.

National Co-ordinators in particular need time and resources (availability of computers, e-mail etc.) for effective communication within the network. Organization of regular workshops, creation and regular updating of an AfWC web-site and production of a biannual newsletter would also be useful. These and other actions could be included in an AfWC communication strategy.

### Institutional strengthening of the AfWC network.

To help build the census into national planning schemes, National and Regional Co-ordinators need organizational support to enable them to carry out census activities, and in particular, for national co-ordination and data collation. They and managers of key sites also need field equipment to enable their national networks to carry out wetland surveys, including binoculars, telescopes, identification guides, GPS, digital cameras etc.

### Develop a fundraising strategy for operation and development of the AfWC.

There are requirements to meet the core running costs of the AfWC, such as network support, data entry, regular reporting and database management. Additional funds are needed so that action can be taken on the basis of the results of the AfWC, for instance conservation of species that are (or appear to be) in decline.

Improve the data quality of the AfWC.

The quality of the data needs to be improved at site, national and international levels. There is scope for involving the Wetlands International Specialist Group network in checking data and reports.

Develop a training and public awareness programme.

The AfWC network is large and dynamic, with many new recruits each year. Training is needed widely at different levels, whilst awareness needs to be raised, especially concerning the value and application of the AfWC, linked to the importance of conservation of wetlands.

## REFERENCES

**Baker, N.** 2003. A reassessment of the northern population of the Cape Teal *Anas capensis*. Scopus 23: 29-43.

**Delany, S.N., Scott, D.A. & Dodman, T.** In prep. Atlas of Wader Populations in Africa and Western Eurasia. International Wader Study Group and Wetlands International.

**Dodman, T.** 1997. A Preliminary Waterbird Monitoring Strategy for Africa. Wetlands International, Wageningen, The Netherlands.

**Dodman, T.** In review 2002. Waterbird Population Estimates in Africa. Unpublished report to Wetlands International, Wageningen, The Netherlands.

**Fishpool, L.D.C. & Evans, M.I.** (eds). 2001. Important Bird Areas in Africa and associated islands: Priority sites for conservation. Pisces Publications and BirdLife International (BirdLife Conservation Series No. 11), Newbury and Cambridge, UK.

**Perennou, C.** 1991. Les recensements internationaux d'oiseaux d'eau en Afrique Tropicale. IWRB Special Publication No. 15. Slimbridge, UK.

**Rose, P.M. & Scott, D.A.** 1994. Waterfowl Population Estimates. IWRB Publication 29. Slimbridge, UK.

**Rose, P.M. & Scott, D.A.** 1997. Waterfowl Population Estimates 2. Wetlands International, Wageningen, The Netherlands.

**Scott, D.A.** 1999. Report on the Conservation Status of Migratory Waterbirds in the Agreement Area. Report to the Interim Secretariat of the African-Eurasian Migratory Waterbird Agreement. AEWA, Bonn.

**Scott, D.A. & Rose, P.M.** 1996. Atlas of Anatidae populations in Africa and Western Eurasia. Wetlands International Publication No. 41. Wetlands International, Wageningen, The Netherlands.

**Wetlands International** 2002. Waterbird Population Estimates – Third Edition. Wetlands International Global Series No. 12, Wageningen, The Netherlands.

**Williams, E.T.C., Beilfuss, R. & Dodman, T.** 2002. Status Survey and Conservation Action of the Black Crowned Crane *Balearica pavonina*. Wetlands International, Dakar, Senegal, & International Crane Foundation, Baraboo, Wisconsin, USA.

Waterbird counters in Sudan. Photo: Tim Dodman.

# Ten years of continuous waterbird monitoring at Lutembe Bay, Lake Victoria, Uganda

*Achilles Byaruhanga & Dianah Nalwanga*

*Nature Uganda, East Africa Natural History Society, PO Box 2703, 4 Kampala, Uganda.*
*(email: achilles.byaruhanga@natureuganda.org)*

Byaruhanga, A. & Nalwanga, D. 2006. Ten years of continuous waterbird monitoring at Lutembe Bay, Lake Victoria, Uganda. *Waterbirds around the world* (Eds. G.C. Boere, C.A. Galbraith & D.A. Stroud). The Stationery Office, UK. pp. 457-458.

Lutembe Bay lies on the northern shores of Lake Victoria at the mouth of Murchison Bay between Entebbe and Kampala, at an altitude of 1 130 m, covering an area of 500 ha. It is shallow, papyrus-fringed, and almost completely cut off from the main body of Lake Victoria by two papyrus islands. The dominant vegetation is a mosaic of papyrus on the main open waterside of the lake, with *Miscanthus* and *Vossia* species towards dry land (Langdale-Brown *et al.* 1964). The bay extends into a *Miscanthus* swamp and merges with forest remnants to the north and horticultural farms to the northwest on the landward side, with shallow waters and scattered islets of mud in the open area of the bay.

*Nature Uganda* has carried out waterbird counts at least twice a year since 1994, and monthly since 1998. Total counts were made of all birds seen or heard from a slow moving canoe. In addition, birds such as crakes, coucals or fish eagles *Haliaeetus vocifer* heard calling from fringing habitats were recorded. Species abundance was calculated as encounter rates (number of individual birds per field hour).

Lutembe Bay is one of 30 Important Bird Areas (IBAs) in Uganda due to its globally, regionally, nationally and locally important biodiversity (Byaruhanga *et al.* 2001, Birdlife International 2001). The bay regularly supports 20 000 – 50 000 roosting and feeding waterbirds and seven globally threatened species occur: Papyrus Yellow Warbler *Chloropeta gracilirostris*, Papyrus Gonolek *Laniarius mufumbiri*, Shoebill *Balaeniceps rex*, African Skimmer *Rhynchops flavirostris*, Pallid Harrier *Circus macrouros*, Great Snipe *Gallinago media* and Madagascar Squacco Heron *Ardeola idea*. There are 24 species of regional concern. As well as supporting a large diversity of African species it is an important non-breeding area for huge congregations of Palearctic migrants. It regularly holds over 70% of the global population of White-winged Black Terns *Chlidonias leucopterus* (Byaruhanga *et al.* 2002, Byaruhanga 2003), and there are often large numbers of Grey-headed Gulls *Larus cirrocepharus*, Black-headed Gulls *Larus ridibundus* and Gull-billed Terns *Sterna nilotica*.

A total of 207 species were recorded during 63 counts between January 1994 and July 2003 (Dodman & Taylor 1993, 1994, 1995, 1997, Scott *et al.* 1994, Omoding *et al.* 1996, Wetlands International 2002). Of these, 76 were waterbirds, with the others being associated with fringing wetland habitats or remnant forests, bushes and gardens. The largest number of species (82) was recorded December 2000, and the smallest number (13) in May 1998. Species diversity varied seasonally, with more species present during the boreal winter when Palearctic migrant species are present: monthly averages were 34.5-51.7 species between September and March, and 22.5-36.0 species between April and August.

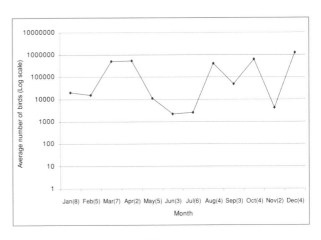

Fig. 1. Monthly average counts of birds in Lutembe Bay, Uganda between 1994-2003. Numbers in parentheses are the number of counts in each month.

Similarly, the numbers of birds counted were lowest in June and July (average 2 449 birds; n=9 counts), and variable but often much higher between August and April, with the highest monthly average being in December (1 237 769 birds; n=4 counts) (Fig. 1). The highest count was 2 639 567 birds in December 1999, with counts exceeding 1 million birds on five other occasions (March and August 2000, April and October 2002, and March 2003).

The great variations in the number of birds counted was largely a consequence of the frequent but not consistent presence of very large numbers of White-winged Black Terns. Averaged over the 63 counts, this species formed >95% of all birds present. The largest numbers were present in December 1999 (2 567 540 birds), with other high counts being 2 056 000 (March 2000), 1 238 723 (October 2002) and 1 041 700 (March 2003).

Only three other species (all Palearctic migrants) occurred in large numbers: Whiskered Tern *Chlidonias hybridus*, with its largest number (102 800 birds) in March 2000; Gull-billed Tern (largest count 12 640 birds in February 1997); and Black-headed Gull (largest count 16 460 birds in January 2002. Black-headed Gull numbers appear to have increased considerably since 2000. The site also hosts hundreds of Palearctic ducks, notably Garganey *Anas querquedula* (Byaruhanga & Arinaitwe 1996). Gulls and terns roost on muddy islets when the water level is low, especially between September to March. The exceptionally low count (308 birds) in January 1998 was probably due to "El Nino" rains which raised water levels that flooded most of the islets in the bay on which many birds breed or roost.

Among Afro-tropical migrants, the Open-billed Stork *Anastomus lamelligerus* was the most abundant (encounter rate five birds per hour). The most common resident waterbirds were

Long-toed Plover *Vanellus crasirostris* (encounter rate 94 birds per hour), Long-tailed Cormorant *Phalacrocorax africanus*, Yellow-billed Duck *Anas undulata* and African Jacana *Actophilornis africanus*.

Of globally threatened species, the Madagascar Squacco Heron was recorded twice (one in July 1994 and two in January 2002); Shoebill was recorded four times (March 1995, July 1997, August 2000 and January 2002); and a pair of African Skimmer was seen in January 2001. The near-threatened Papyrus Gonolek was regularly recorded calling. Other notable species included the Black Heron *Egretta ardesiaca*, recorded in 18 counts, with a maximum of 15 birds in December 2000.

Whilst Lutembe Bay is of major importance for waterbirds, including globally and regionally threatened species (Arinaitwe 1997), it is also very important in supporting local community livelihoods as a source of raw materials for building, local crafts, water for domestic use and, probably more importantly, fish as food and income. Since it is also close to Uganda's capital, Kampala, it also has high potential for income-generation through eco-tourism. However, Lutembe Bay faces degradation in its ecological character: agro-chemicals used by five flower farms close to the Bay have been detected in its waters. Monitoring needs to be put in place to assess the potentially adverse impacts from these and other developments such as sand mining and stone quarrying.

## REFERENCES

**Arinaitwe, J.** 1997. Some aspects of the distribution of water-bird communities along the north western shores of Lake Victoria. PhD Thesis. Makerere University, Kampala.

**BirdLife International.** 2001. Important Bird Areas in Africa. BirdLife International, Cambridge.

**Byaruhanga, A., Arinaitwe, J. & Williams, C.** 2002. Large congregations of White-winged Black Terns *Chlidonias leucopterus* at Lutembe Bay, Lake Victoria. Bulletin of the African Bird Club 9(1): 25-26

**Byaruhanga, A. & Arinaitwe, J.** 1996. The status and distribution of Anatids (Anatidae) in Uganda: A review. Gibier Faune Sauvage, Game and Wildlife. 13: 251-260.

**Byaruhanga, A.** 2003. Lutembe bay – An important bird area on the brink of destruction. The Naturalist: A newsletter of Nature Uganda. The East Africa Natural History Society 7(1): 5.

**Byaruhanga, A., Kasoma, P. & Pomeroy, D.** 2001. Important Bird Areas in Uganda. East Africa Natural History Society, Kampala.

**Dodman, T. & Taylor, V.** 1993, 1994, 1995, 1997. African Waterfowl Census. IWRB, Slimbridge, UK.

**Langdale-Brown, I., Osmaston, H.A. & Wilson, G.** 1964. The Vegetation of Uganda and its bearing on Land uses. Uganda Government Printers, Entebbe.

**Omoding, J., Otim, T., Etiang, P. & Mutekanga, N.** 1996. Inventory of wetland biodiversity in Uganda. Activities, methodologies and results. National Wetlands Programme, Kampala.

**Scott, D., Byaruhanga, A., Kagoda, M., & Mbeiza Mutekanga, N.** 1994. Wetland Biodiversity Inventory for Uganda. UNO/RAF/006/GEF Project Field document 2.

**Wetlands International** 2002. African Waterbird Census 1999, 2000, 2001. Wetlands International Global Series 16.

Weaverbirds nesting on an island of papyrus *Cyperus papyrus*, Lake Mburo National Park, Uganda. Photo: David Stroud.

# Priority needs for co-ordinated research at flyway level to improve monitoring and management of waterbird populations, as identified by the French National Observatory of Wildlife

*Michel Vallance & Yves Ferrand*

*ONCFS Base administrative St Benoist, 78610 AUFFARGIS, France. (email: m.vallance@oncfs.gouv.fr)*

Vallance, M. & Ferrand, Y. 2006. Priority needs for co-ordinated research at flyway level to improve monitoring and management of waterbird populations, as identified by the French National Observatory of Wildlife. *Waterbirds around the world*. Eds. G.C. Boere, C.A. Galbraith & D.A. Stroud. The Stationery Office, Edinburgh, UK. pp. 459-462.

## ABSTRACT

The National Observatory of Wildlife was created by the French Government in 2003 to provide high scientific standards to underpin for the implementation of regulations and government decisions relating to game management, with special reference to enforcement of the European Union (EU) Birds Directive. The main priority is to set up integrated monitoring schemes for waterbird populations at flyway level, starting with the more vulnerable species. One illustration of the methods to be developed is the monitoring scheme for Eurasian Woodcock *Scolopax rusticola* run for the last 20 years by the Office National de la Chasse et de la Faune Sauvage (ONCFS). This comprises intensive ringing programmes, monitoring of breeding areas, and analysis of hunting bags. The priorities for research have now been identified more clearly, and have highlighted the need for co-operative research programmes at flyway level. Two such programmes include stable isotope analysis to infer population origins, and improved interpretation of data through modelling.

## INTRODUCTION

In ensuring that we make the right decisions in migratory bird management, integrated population monitoring is an appropriate and useful management tool. However, initial studies have highlighted that some key data are missing for a good understanding of the status of migratory bird populations. The situation can be improved through the application of new research techniques and better international co-operation. This leads us from a national point of view towards an international flyway approach.

## THE NATIONAL OBSERVATORY OF WILDLIFE (FRANCE)

The National Observatory of Wildlife was created by the French Government in February 2003 to provide high scientific standards for the implementation of statutory regulations and government decisions relating to game management, especially the national implementation of the European Union (EU) Directive on the conservation of wild birds. It comprises a scientific council of 11 experts whose expertise must be based on the best information and scientific data available. Material for the meetings of the council is prepared by the national wildlife agency, the Office National de la Chasse et de la Faune Sauvage (ONCFS).

The Government has asked the question: are we making good rules? Neither the hunters nor the conservation associations think that this is the case. Obviously, not all questions have a clear answer. Serious problems can arise in the interpretation of data and scientific discussion. For example:

a) Different sub-populations of the same species can confuse the situation (long-distance migrants, short-distance migrants, residents, birds that migrate east, birds that migrate west, etc.). They may be exposed to different habitat conditions and may differ in conservation status, requiring different management decisions;

b) Huge variations in the raw data sets – from one year to another, and from one site to another – are also confusing. It is necessary to separate out environmental variation and census errors (statistical variation) from demographic variation as far as possible;

c) Turnover among wintering birds can cause problems. The birds that we count on 15 December are not always the same as those that we count on 15 January. At some large sites, it would be informative to have an estimate of turnover, e.g. by determining the mean duration of stay; and

d) Finally, difficulties can arise as a result of different sampling bases (breeding or wintering populations). These two sampling bases do not overlap, causing discrepancies and uncertainties.

Not all these problems can be resolved at the present time.

## INTEGRATED MONITORING

In the best cases, all of the existing knowledge and data sets can be organized in a management tool known as "integrated monitoring". This requires the following:

a) Intensive data collection over long time periods;

b) Data analysis to provide estimates of key demographic and other parameters; and

c) Modelling to give an understanding of the real situation, to facilitate adaptive management, and to forecast the results.

As an example of an integrated monitoring scheme, we give a short account of the monitoring scheme for Eurasian Woodcock *Scolopax rusticola* in France. One important factor is the statistical quality of the sampling (geographical coverage). At present, statistical methods give indices of relative abundance, and not estimates of absolute population numbers. Ringing has been an important aspect of the work on Woodcock, and has been carried out continuously and intensively since the 1980s in close co-operation with hunting associations, which has ensured good recovery rates of rings (Fig. 1). Wing examination (for ageing) and national hunting bag statistics have been used in the analyses of hunting bags.

This fieldwork has given us a very long time-series of data to analyse. The long-term trend in Woodcock populations wintering in France has been stable (Ferrand *et al.* 2003), but shows some important annual fluctuations (Fig. 2). It is impor-

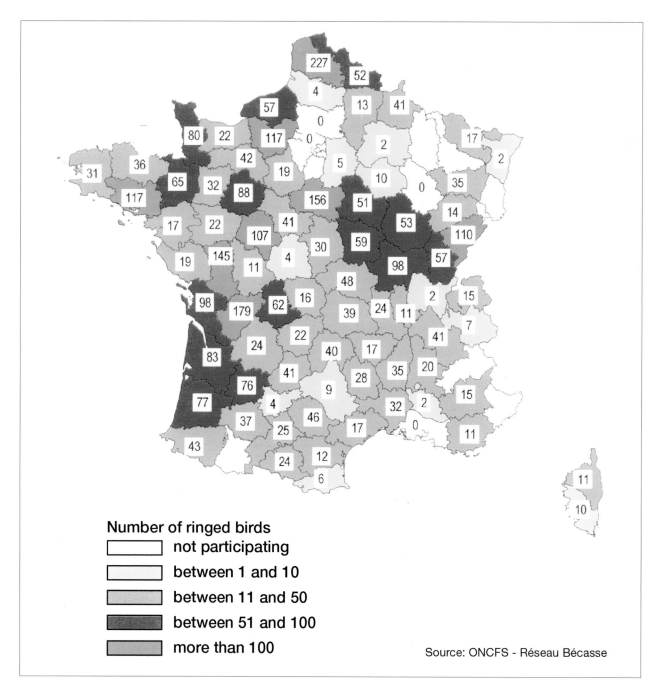

**Fig. 1.** Numbers of Eurasian Woodcocks *Scolopax rusticola* ringed in France during the winter of 2002/03, by department. A total of 3 417 Woodcocks were ringed. Colours indicate the numbers ringed in each district.

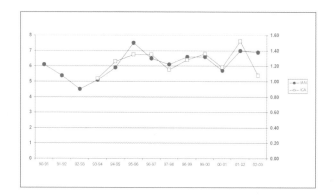

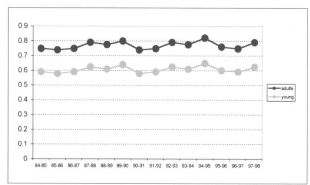

**Fig. 2.** Population trends in Eurasian Woodcocks *Scolopax rusticola* wintering in France. ICA = hunting abundance index; IAN = contact index during night ringing sessions. All figures are national averages.

**Fig. 3.** Survival rates of Eurasian Woodcocks *Scolopax rusticola* wintering in France (Tavecchia *et al.* 2002).

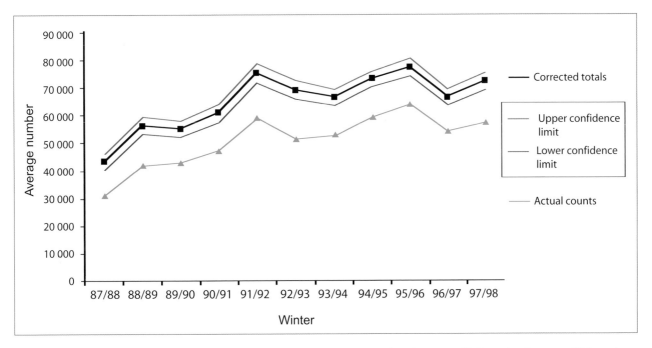

**Fig. 4.** Demographic trends of wintering Common Teal *Anas crecca* in France (average of numbers counted in December, January and February).

tant to bear in mind, however, that these variations are also linked to the precision of the estimates. With respect to survival rates (Fig. 3), we see that the curve has good precision because of the large number of ringing recoveries (over 4 000 Woodcocks have been ringed every winter for ten years). When we consider our attempts to obtain an indirect estimation of breeding success, we see the importance of a flyway approach: our French data on age ratios (from wing examinations) are combined with Danish data, which are collected earlier in the year along the migration route.

As a management tool, this monitoring scheme is already rather ueful (Ferrand & Gossman 2001). It will become fully effective when we can integrate more data from Russia (breeding area, breeding density, reproduction rate). Ultimately, we will be able to construct a demographic model to inform hunting management decisions and adapt measures and rules in response to demographic trends in woodcock populations.

In many cases, however, we need more sophisticated research to make progress in our understanding of populations of migratory birds. Possible ways to achieve this are illustrated by two international research programmes making use of new scientific methods in a global flyway approach: stable isotope tracking to infer population origins, and improved interpretation of data through modelling.

## STABLE ISOTOPE TRACKING TO INFER POPULATION ORIGINS

The wintering population of a migratory bird species often comprises a mixture of individuals from several sub-populations which cannot be separated on the basis of phenotypic differences. The idea behind stable isotope tracking is to track birds by means of the isotope signatures of their feathers. This technique is being used by ONCFS in co-operation with the Canadian Wildlife Service. We first verified that there was a correlation between Deuterium isotope ratios in feathers and in rainwater samples (Hobson *et al.* 2004). This correlation had already been used in North America, but had not yet been veri-

fied and used in Europe. A map showing the geographical variation in stable isotope ratios gives a clear geographic pattern that can be used to determine whether birds have originated from northern Europe, central Europe or southern Europe. Important progress can now be made in the identification of birds' origins, and this will allow more information to be derived from the analyses of European hunting bags and ringing data sets.

## DATA INTERPRETATION: THE HELP OF MODELS

The direct and simplistic interpretation of raw data may be misleading, as highlighted by Common Teal *Anas crecca* (Fig. 4). The conservation status of this species in France is a priority issue for policy makers, since only 70 000-90 000 birds are counted in midwinter, while over 330 000 are harvested by hunters. In addition to the analysis of existing ringing data, a new ringing and marking programme has been launched at six sites scattered around France. As well as being ringed, some birds are fitted with nasal saddles, allowing long-distance recognition of individuals. This marking activity is being co-ordinated with scientists in Portugal and Sweden, and has already resulted in a number of international re-sightings (Fig. 5). To date, 1 356 Common Teal have been ringed, of which 708 have also been fitted with nasal saddles. There have

**Table 1. Preliminary results of Common Teal *Anas crecca* ringing and marking programme (ONCFS, France; Kristianstad University, Sweden; Coimbra University, Portugal).**

|  | Metal ring only | Metal ring & nasal saddle |
|---|---|---|
| Marked | 648 | 708 |
| Recoveries (dead birds) | 28 | 33 |
| Recaptures & re-sightings | 207 | 1 455 |
| At least one report (% of birds) | 19.8% | 49.9% |

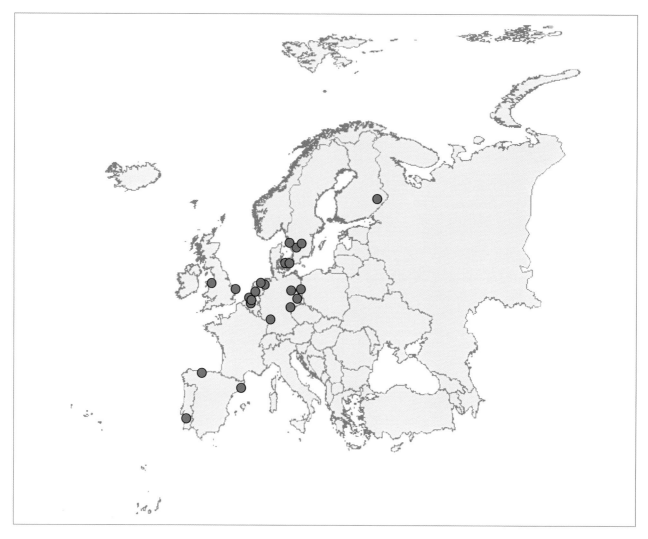

Fig. 5. Each dot represents a wetland at which one or more birds have been observed. In total, there were 87 observations of 26 different birds outside France between November 2002 and June 2004.

been 1 195 observations of birds with nasal saddles, involving 298 different individuals. In all, 42% of marked individuals have been recaptured or re-sighted at least once during the first two years of the programme (Table 1). Nasal saddles have therefore proved to be much more efficient than metal rings in building up a large data set quickly. The results are also more rewarding, since in addition to providing useful information on residence times at sites, survival rates, etc., the use of individually marked birds provides a scientific basis for the determination of parameters for a behaviour-based model of population dynamics.

Modelling at a flyway scale will hopefully give us, in the near future, a better understanding of fluctuations in populations and turnover of individuals, and allow us to predict the potential outcome of human activities on population trends, thus helping us to make the right decisions for policy-making. This type of model has already been developed and successfully validated for Eurasian Wigeon *Anas penelope* (Guillemain *et al.* 2002).

## ACKNOWLEDGEMENTS
We would like to give our special thanks to the hunters' federations, the French Woodcock clubs and the field staff of ONCFS, as well as the Station Biologique de la Tour du Valat, for their participation in the collection of field data and valuable help in the acquisition of this scientific knowledge.

## REFERENCES

Ferrand, Y. & Gossmann, F. 2001. Elements for a Woodcock (*Scolopax rusticola*) management plan. Gibier Faune Sauvage, Game and Wildlife 18(1): 115-139.

Ferrand, Y., Gossmann, F., Bastat, C. & Guénézan, M. 2003. What census method for migrating and wintering woodcock populations? Proceedings of the Sixth Woodcock & Snipe Workshop, 24-28 November 2003, Nantes, France.

Guillemain, M., Caldow, R.W.G., Stillman, R.A. & Goss-Custard, J.D. 2002. Towards behaviour-based models of dabbling duck population dynamics. European Journal of Wildlife Research 48, Supplement: 1-6.

Hobson, K.A., Bowen, B.J., Wassenaar, L.I., Ferrand, Y. & Lormée, H. 2004. Using stable hydrogen and oxygen isotope measurements of feathers to infer geographical origins of migrating European birds. Oecologia 141: 477- 488.

Tavecchia, G., Pradel, R., Gossmann, F., Bastat, C., Ferrand, Y. & Lebreton, J.D. 2002. Temporal variation in annual survival probability of the Eurasian woodcock *Scolopax rusticola* wintering in France. Wildlife Biology 8(1): 21-30.

# Long-term waterbird monitoring in The Netherlands: a tool for policy and management

*Marc van Roomen[1], Kees Koffijberg[1], Ruurd Noordhuis[2] & Leo Soldaat[3]*

[1] *SOVON Dutch Centre for Field Ornithology, Rijksstraatweg 178, 6573 DG, Beek-Ubbergen, The Netherlands. (email: marc.vanroomen@sovon.nl; kees.koffijberg@sovon.nl)*

[2] *RIZA, PO Box 17, 8200 AA Lelystad, The Netherlands. (email: R.Noordhuis@riza.rws.minvenw.nl)*

[3] *Statistics Netherlands, PO Box 4000, 2270 JM, Voorburg, The Netherlands. (email: LSLT@CBS.nl)*

Roomen, M. van, Koffijberg, K., Noordhuis, R. & Soldaat, L. 2006. Long-term waterbird monitoring in The Netherlands: a tool for policy and management. *Waterbirds around the world.* Eds. G.C. Boere, C.A. Galbraith & D.A. Stroud. The Stationery Office, Edinburgh, UK. pp. 463-470.

## ABSTRACT

The monitoring of waterbirds in The Netherlands has a long tradition. It has evolved from various regional, seasonal and species-specific projects into an integrated monitoring scheme which aims to assess waterbird trends at site and national level, and operates within the framework of a governmental network of ecological monitoring. It is also incorporated in international monitoring programmes such as the International Waterbird Census (IWC) and the Wadden Sea Trilateral Monitoring and Assessment Programme (TMAP). The backbone of the scheme comprises monthly counts at all sites supporting large numbers of non-breeding waterbirds. This paper provides an overview of the monitoring scheme, starting with its aims and targets. It describes the census scheme, and discusses the sites that are covered and the methods used to calculate indices and trends. It also shows how data are used for policy and management issues, taking the EU Birds Directive as an example. Data from the waterbird monitoring project have been used extensively to designate Special Protection Areas in The Netherlands. Population trends in individual species are used to assess conservation status which is then translated into the aims of future management plans. Monitoring will gain importance by assessing the numbers and trends against targets and a system of alerts. As waterbirds are highly dependent on their food supplies and often respond quickly to changes in food availability, they are cost-effective indicators of changes in the broader ecological quality of their habitats.

## INTRODUCTION

The Netherlands are of outstanding importance for many waterbirds. The country's position along the East Atlantic Flyway, the large amount of wetland habitat and the prevailing mild winters attract internationally important numbers of waterbirds during all stages of their life cycle. The monitoring of waterbirds in The Netherlands has a long tradition. As early as the 1950s and 1960s, waterbird counts were being carried out regularly. The start of the International Waterbird Census (IWC) in the late 1960s further improved the network and stimulated many volunteer and professional bird-watchers to participate. In addition to the international midwinter counts, several regional (often monthly) censuses were established in important wetlands, e.g. in the Wadden Sea, along the River Rhine and its tributaries, at Lake ijsselmeer, and in the Delta area in the south-west of the country. Counts of geese and swans had already started in the 1960s, both in wetlands and in agricultural areas. In response to the growing need for comprehensive national monitoring data, all these surveys have recently been combined in a national waterbird monitoring scheme (Koffijberg *et al.* 2000). This scheme is part of the so-called Network Ecological Monitoring, a governmental instrument to collect monitoring data for various groups of species including, for example, plants, dragonflies and mammals (van Strien 2005). Through this scheme, data required for international treaties and conventions, such as the European Union (EU) Birds and Habitats Directives, Ramsar Convention on Wetlands, and African-Eurasian Migratory Waterbird Agreement (AEWA) of the Bonn Convention, also become available.

Waterbird monitoring in The Netherlands is currently a joint scheme of the Ministry of Agriculture, Nature and Food Quality, the Ministry of Transport, Public Works and Water Management, BirdLife The Netherlands and Statistics Netherlands, and is co-ordinated by the SOVON Dutch Centre for Field Ornithology. At present about 1 500 observers, of whom a large proportion are dedicated volunteers, participate in the scheme each year. This paper provides an overview of the monitoring programme, and gives examples of results and their role in the development of environmental policies and management plans.

## WHY WATERBIRDS?

Statistics on the status and trends in numbers of waterbirds are required for the conservation of bird populations and biodiversity, as well as for the conservation of their (wetland) habitats. This acknowledges the role of waterbirds as indicator species. Waterbird numbers can be assessed rather accurately by counts, and since they often respond quickly to changes in their environment, their status can be a powerful indicator of changes in other organisms in the ecosystem, which are often more difficult to measure or for which only recent data are available. At Lake Veluwemeer, for instance, a close relationship was found between the numbers of some waterbird species and the amount of submerged macrophytes (Fig. 1). In the 1970s and 1980s, submerged vegetation was very limited because of eutrophication. As a consequence, the numbers of waterbirds were low. However, an improvement in water quality led to an increase in aquatic vegetation, which was followed by an increase in waterbird numbers. By using this relationship, it was possible to reconstruct the ups and downs in the abundance of submerged vegetation and other aspects of the ecosystem before the 1970s, when only bird numbers were being surveyed. In this way, qualitative descriptions of the lake could be underpinned with (modelled) data. Several additional relationships exist between waterbird numbers, food supply, water quality parameters, and policy and management issues in which waterbirds might act as effective indicators of underlying processes at lower trophic levels (Noordhuis & Koffijberg 2004).

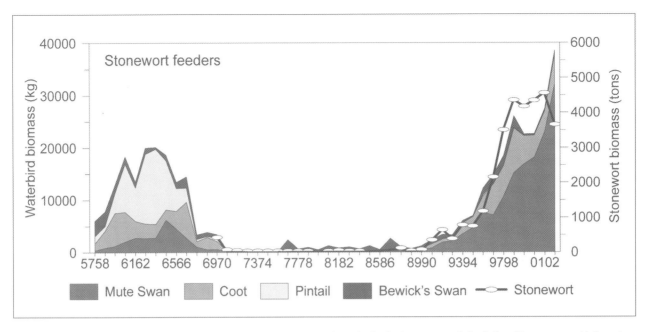

Fig. 1. Trends in biomass of herbivores and stonewort in Lake Veluwemeer, The Netherlands. A strong correlation is found between waterbird numbers (expressed in biomass to account for consumption by species of different size) and stonewort biomass (r = 0.96, df = 29).

## AIMS OF THE MONITORING PROGRAMME

A clear definition of the aims and targets of a monitoring scheme will help to direct efforts to improve the programme and provide the information that is required. This includes selection of the target species which are to be covered and a definition of the geographical scale for which data are required. Fortunately, waterbirds are relatively easy to count, and it is often the case that numbers of all species can be assessed when visiting a site. All species of divers, grebes, cormorants, herons and allies, swans, geese, ducks, rails, coots, waders, gulls and terns occurring in The Netherlands are included in the counts. Non-native species which have been introduced or escaped are also covered. In addition, a few species of raptors and passerines, which are specific to wetlands and easy to cover while counting other waterbirds, are included. For analyses and trend calculations (see below), priority is given to species which are important in

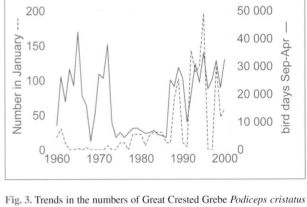

Fig. 3. Trends in the numbers of Great Crested Grebe *Podiceps cristatus* at Lake Veluwemeer, The Netherlands, based on numbers from January counts (dashed line) and on bird-days calculated from monthly counts in September-April (solid line).

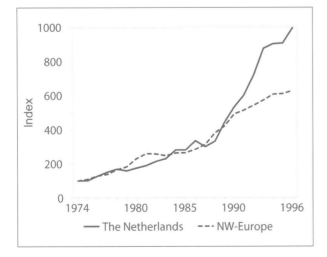

Fig. 2. Trends in the numbers of Gadwall *Anas strepera* in The Netherlands and in North-west Europe. The trend in North-west Europe is taken from Delany *et al.* (1999). Numbers in The Netherlands have grown faster than those in North-west Europe (t = -12.4; df = 12, p < 0.001, based on a non-linear regression analysis).

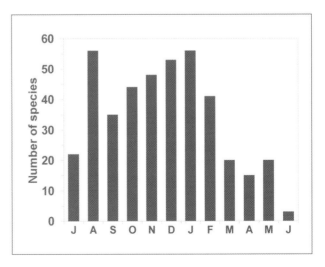

Fig. 4. Phenology of the number of target species of waterbirds (Annex I of the EU Birds Directive and indicator species in national freshwater bodies) occurring in The Netherlands. Species are only included for a given month if their numbers in that month are equal to at least 80% of the peak count during the 12-month period.

relation to the EU Birds Directive. This aims to safeguard bird species and their habitats within the EU, and obliges member states to carry our regular monitoring at important sites (Special Protection Areas, SPAs).

At present, indices and trends are calculated for 53 species (van Roomen *et al.* 2004). These are calculated at three different geographical scales: individual sites, regions and the country as a whole (national trends). Priorities for trend analyses at site level are SPAs designated under the EU Birds Directive (in most cases these sites have also been designated as Ramsar sites under

the Ramsar Convention on Wetlands), national freshwater bodies (water bodies managed by the government and overlapping to a large extent with SPAs), and agricultural sites important for geese and swans (these often lack any protection status).

In addition to these national aims, the counts also contribute to international monitoring programmes, including the International Waterbird Census (IWC) co-ordinated by Wetlands International and the Trilateral Monitoring and Assessment Programme (TMAP) for the international Wadden Sea. The latter is a trilateral co-operation between The Netherlands,

**Fig. 5.** Monitoring sites in The Netherlands used for the calculation of national trends in populations of waterbirds (except for swans, geese and seaducks).

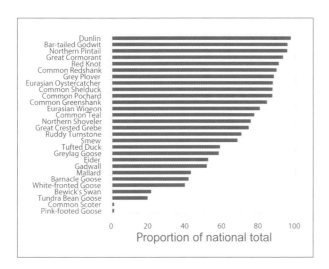

Fig. 6. The proportions of the national January totals of 28 species of waterbirds that occur within the monitoring sites shown in Fig. 5.

Germany and Denmark for monitoring and management policies in the Wadden Sea. International population estimates and trends are important references for national monitoring. They are necessary for separating trends at national or site level from trends at flyway level (Fig. 2).

## OUTLINE OF THE MONITORING PROGRAMME
### Several counts a year

A single count in January is the best strategy for an international monitoring scheme, since the distribution of waterbirds at this time of year is rather stable, and in many countries a large survey effort can only be achieved once a year. However, for monitoring at national level and at the level of individual sites, more counts are required per year, since a single count in January covers only a tiny part of the annual cycle of waterbirds. For example, species occurring on migration in spring and autumn and those occurring in moulting concentrations in late summer are not covered at all in January, but might be the most important species at many sites. Moreover, as phenology patterns or wintering strategies might change in time (e.g. a switch in distribution as a result of global warming), national monitoring of waterbirds benefits from counts which are carried out at all times of the year. Thus, trends in January may give a very misleading picture of the overall abundance of a species, as shown in Fig. 3 for the Great Crested Grebe *Podiceps cristatus* at Lake Veluwemeer. When only the January counts are considered, it appears that Great Crested Grebes were very scarce in the 1960s and 1970s, and increased after the mid-1980s. However, it is known that the species did occur in substantial numbers in the 1960s and 1970s, but mainly in spring and autumn, with only a few birds remaining in January. This only becomes apparent when one takes into account all monthly counts between September and April. It then becomes clear that the current use of the site is rather similar to that in the 1960s and 1970s. The recent increase in January is simply the result of an increase in the numbers of wintering birds (i.e. a prolonged stay of birds in autumn).

Since most countries will have a mixture of resident species, passage migrants and winter visitors, waterbird counts should ideally cover all months of the year. In The Netherlands, each month of the year appears to be of some importance as regards the number of target species occurring in important numbers

(Fig. 4). The main reason for this is the large variation in phenology of the species involved. In freshwater lakes and other inland sites, the period September-April has the highest abundance of waterbirds. Some large lakes are also used in other months, e.g. when moulting concentrations occur in late summer. In estuaries, however, all months of the year are important. Based on these patterns, it was decided to use monthly counts between September and April to cover inland sites and monthly counts throughout the year to cover coastal estuaries (e.g. the Wadden Sea and Delta area) and some large freshwater lakes (e.g. Lake IJsselmeer). In the Wadden Sea, monthly counts are achieved through a combination of monthly counts at a sample of sites and five total counts throughout the year. This area is so large that monthly total counts would be beyond the capability of the volunteer counters.

### Selection of sites for monitoring

Because of the large amount of wetland habitat in The Netherlands and large part of the year in which important numbers of waterbirds are present, it would be a considerable task to include all water bodies in the monitoring scheme. Therefore, a selection of sites has been identified which covers all important waterbird concentrations (Fig. 5). This selection includes all SPAs and national freshwater bodies, and thus all priorities for site monitoring. For most waterbird species except geese, swans and seaducks, these sites together support a high proportion of the national populations (Fig. 6). The core areas for geese and swans are in agricultural areas, and additional counts are carried out for these species in these areas (Fig. 7). Seaducks occur in large numbers only in the coastal zone of the North Sea and open waters of the Wadden Sea. Both of these areas are not covered by monthly land-based counts, but are counted once a year (in January) by an aerial survey. Additional waterbird counts are made in January at less important sites as part of the International Waterbird Census.

### Missing counts and trend analysis

Due to the different history of the various census projects, not all sites have similar and comparable series of data. Some sites have monthly counts dating back to 1975, while others have counts starting in the 1980s or lack counts in important months. Even though coverage has increased over the decades (Fig. 8), some counts are still missed because of poor weather conditions (e.g. fog), absence of the observer or other reasons. Thus, when compiling uniform data sets for trend analyses, consideration has to be given to the missing counts. Standardized methods have been developed to estimate numbers at the sites not counted (imputing). In The Netherlands, we have adopted the method used in the Wetland Bird Survey in the British Isles (for background, see Underhill & Prys-Jones 1994). Species-specific models are used to account for site, month and year factors. This imputing is performed by using the U-index package (Bell 1995). Missing counts are imputed on the basis of the smallest count units, and count units are stratified according to their seasonal and annual patterns (Soldaat *et al.* 2004).

Trend analyses are based on annual estimates of occurrence per species for a certain geographical area (either site, regional or national level). This annual estimate of occurrence is defined as the seasonal sum of the counted and estimated (imputed) numbers throughout the year (or in September-April, depending

**Fig. 7.** Staging sites of swans and geese in The Netherlands used for the calculation of national trends.

on the site; see above). Trends are calculated by using a linear regression of the log-transformed seasonal sums, and are assessed for different periods (e.g. since the start of monitoring or over the last 10 years). The output is classified according to certain definitions, including definitions of stable and fluctuating trends. In the near future, trend calculations will be extended by incorporating flexible trends (Visser 2004) which are better able to deal with strong fluctuations.

## USE OF WATERBIRD DATA IN RELATION TO THE EU BIRDS DIRECTIVE

The EU Birds Directive has become increasingly important for nature conservation policy and management in The Netherlands (and other EU countries). Together with the EU Habitats Directive, a network of sites, the so-called Natura 2000 sites, has been set up within the EU for the conservation of biodiversity. Special Protection Areas (SPAs) are a part of this Natura 2000

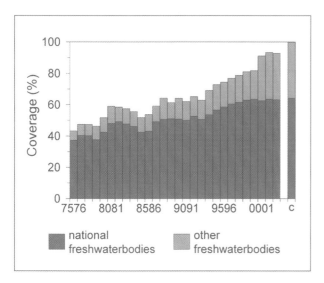

**Fig. 8.** The availability of count data for freshwater monitoring sites in The Netherlands since 1975/76. Coverage is expressed as a percentage of all possible main count unit/month combinations. Column C indicates complete coverage of all sites.

network. As a first step, national waterbird counts (and breeding bird surveys) were used to identify SPAs on the basis of the list of target species (species listed in Annex I of the Birds Directive) and 1% threshold values of the Ramsar Convention (van Roomen *et al.* 2000). To date, 79 sites have been designated as SPAs in The Netherlands. These include all important wetland sites but do not cover many agricultural sites important for populations of geese and swans.

Designation of important sites is only a first step towards better protection of the species involved. The conservation status of the species needs to be assessed regularly, both at national and site level, and monitoring plays an important role in evaluating trends in abundance. A methodology for assessing the conservation status of species against the formulated targets is currently being developed. Overviews of the trends in waterbird species listed in the EU Birds Directive are already available at site level (Fig. 9). However, judgements on the favourable or unfavourable conservation status of a species (and thus the direction of the observed trends) are not always easy to make. EU environmental policies not only cover biodiversity, but also deal, for example, with improved environmental conditions in water bodies. The Water Framework Directive (WFD), for instance, aims to tackle the problem of eutrophication. A decline in the nutrients in water bodies, however, might change the food web and thus have a (negative) effect on the abundance of some waterbirds. An example of this paradox is the relationship between the numbers of Tufted Ducks *Aythya fuligula* and stocks of the Zebra Mussel *Dreissena polymorpha* at Late Markermeer. As the levels of eutrophication were reduced, mussel stocks declined and the water became more turbid. The numbers of Tufted Ducks responded negatively and declined (Fig. 10). From the viewpoint of the Water Framework Directive, the lower eutrophication levels can be regarded as a success, but according to the EU Birds Directive, site management should undertake action to halt the decline in Tufted Ducks. Therefore, definitions of favourable conservation status should not simply refer to bird numbers, but should also take into account the ecological potential of a site.

## DISCUSSION
### The monitoring programme

The monitoring of waterbirds in The Netherlands is only possible at the present time because of the high interest and co-operation of many volunteer bird-watchers. The participation and commitment of many site managers and institutions are also essential. We are very fortunate that as early as the 1970s monthly censuses had started in several important wetland systems. These censuses provided a firm basis for the current monitoring scheme. Although we now have a smooth-running and well-used scheme, a number of compromises had to be made while re-designing the programme.

Firstly, because of the limitations to observer effort, we work with a selection of monitoring sites, e.g. SPAs, national fresh-water bodies and internationally important goose and swan staging areas (Figs. 5 & 7). One could argue that these sites only represent optimal sites and do not take into account dynamics in site use. As is known from studies of individual species (e.g. of Dark-bellied Brent Goose *Branta bernicla bernicla*, Ebbinge 1992), optimal sites are often the first to become saturated when a population increases, and less optimal sites are abandoned as soon as a population experiences a downward trend. The impact of such processes is thought to be very small in our monitoring scheme. For many species, 50% or more of the national population is included within the selection of sites. For some goose species, nearly the entire national (or even international) population is covered by the current selection of monitoring sites. Thus, the dynamics in site use are well taken into account, as a large number of sub-optimal sites are already part of the network of monitoring sites. The January census, which covers many more sites, might eventually indicate sites that are becoming increasingly important, at least in winter.

Secondly, underestimation of bird abundance might occur, since the monthly counts will not always cover all the migration peaks of a species, especially when these occur during a period of only a few days or always between the mid-monthly counts. Therefore, monitoring in the Wadden Sea within the framework of the Trilateral Monitoring and Assessment Programme was initially set up with twice-monthly counts in sample census areas (Rösner 1994, Günther 2003). However, in the Dutch Wadden Sea, no representative sample of sites could be established. Hence, the errors in estimates of bird abundance caused by the non-representative sample of sites were larger than in the less accurate numbers derived from monthly counts in the entire area (van Roomen *et al.* 2002). Monthly counts represent reliable estimates of the abundance of birds, especially for the purposes of long-term trend analysis. Only in the case of very small sites, or to derive numbers for qualification purposes (e.g. when designating SPAs), are additional counts needed to arrive at a more reliable estimate of numbers or to assess peak counts.

Thirdly, we use imputing techniques to arrive at estimates for sites not covered by the counts. In recent years, this has involved only a few sites, but when using the older data, the amount of imputed data increases and this might result in erroneous trend estimates. Moreover, the calculation of standard errors is theoretically questionable because we are not dealing with a sample of sites but with more or less complete counts. The results from a recent experiment with "artificial" gaps in a complete data set have shown that trend estimates might be fairly reliable even with a high proportion of imputed data

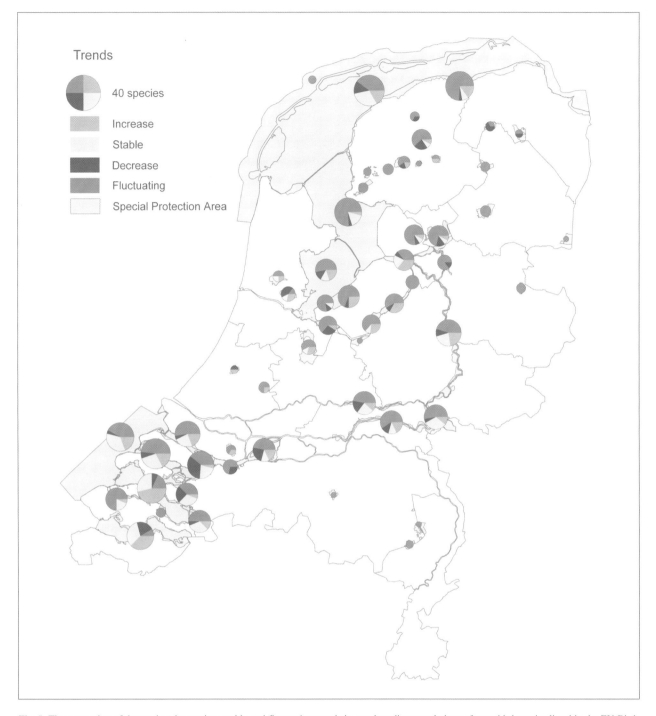

**Fig. 9.** The proportion of decreasing, increasing, stable and fluctuating trends in non-breeding populations of waterbird species listed in the EU Birds Directive, for each of the relevant Special Protection Areas in The Netherlands (SPAs that only support terrestrial species are not taken into account). The size of the circles represents the number of species per site.

(Soldaat *et al.* 2004). The results of this study are now being used to fine-tune the imputing technique.

## Data for policy and management

The need for monitoring data has increased substantially in the last decade. While the first waterbird counts focussed on estimates of total population size and identification of key sites, the monitoring of individual key sites has become increasingly important and is an obligation in the implementation of the EU Birds and Habitats Directives. As a consequence, periodical assessment of the conservation status of species is required, and management plans have to be written to formulate conservation objectives.

Developing alert limits will be an essential tool to judge the observed trends and to point at detrimental or negative impacts at the designated sites (de Nobel *et al.* 2002, Austin *et al.* 2003).

Furthermore, in the case of negative trends it will be important to separate between local (site) trends, national trends and international (flyway) trends. Comparing site trends with international trends will help policy makers and site managers to make the right decisions regarding the underlying causes. If the trends at a particular site seem to be caused by local factors, the relationship between the waterbirds and their food supply needs to be investigated. The numbers of waterbirds are often regulated by their food supply or their possibilities to exploit this

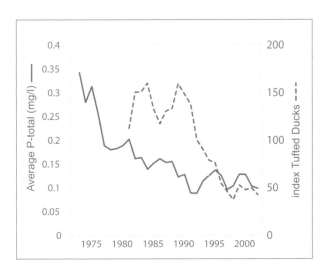

Fig. 10. Trends in the numbers of Tufted Duck *Aythya fuligula* and levels of eutrophication (expressed as mg/l of phosphorus) at Lake Markermeer, The Netherlands.

supply (carrying capacity theory). As waterbirds can be readily divided into guilds according to their food preferences (herbivores, fish-eating birds, etc.), and as long time-series of count data exist, re-constructions of the development in numbers (monitoring) will be of great help in unravelling the causes of any unfavourable development. The same relationships will help to formulate effective measures to restore a favourable conservation status.

## ACKNOWLEDGEMENTS

First of all, we would like to thank all observers participating in the waterbird monitoring project in The Netherlands. The waterbird monitoring scheme is financially supported by the Ministry of Agriculture, Nature and Food Quality, the Ministry of Transport, Public Works and Water Management, and BirdLife The Netherlands (Vogelbescherming Nederland). Jeroen Nienhuis and Erik van Winden (SOVON) transformed the first drafts of the figures into more presentable versions.

## REFERENCES

Austin, G.E., Armitage, M.J.S., Atkinson, P.W., Burton, N.H.K., Leech, D.I., Marshall, A.R., Mellan, H.J., Musgrove, A.J., Pollit, M. & Rehfisch, M.M. 2003. WeBS Alerts 1999/2000: Changes in numbers of wintering birds in the United Kingdom, its constituent countries, Special Protection Areas (SPAs) and Sites of Special Scientific Interest (SSSIs). BTO Research Report No. 306. British Trust for Ornithology, Thetford, UK.

Bell, M.C. 1995. UINDEX4. A computer programme for estimating population index numbers by the Underhill method. The Wildfowl & Wetlands Trust, Slimbridge, UK.

Delany, S., Reyes, C., Hubert, E., Pihl, S., Rees, E., Haanstra, L. & van Strien, A. 1999. Results from the International Waterbird Census in the Western Palearctic and Southwest Asia, 1995 and 1996. Wetlands International Publication No. 54, Wageningen, The Netherlands.

de Nobel, P., van Turnhout, C., van der Winden, J. & Foppen, R. 2002. An alert system for bird population changes on a national level and for EU Bird Directive monitoring: a Dutch approach. SOVON Research Report 2002/04. SOVON Dutch Centre for Field Ornithology, Beek-Ubbergen, The Netherlands.

Ebbinge, B.S. 1992. Regulation of numbers of Dark-bellied Brent Geese on spring staging areas. Ardea 80: 203-228.

Günther, K. 2003. Rastvogel Monitoring im Schleswig-Holsteinischen Wattenmeer 2001-2002. WWF, Husum, Germany.

Koffijberg, K., van Roomen, M., Berrevoets, C. & Noordhuis, R. 2000. Tellen van watervogels in Nederland: verdere ontwikkelingen en integratie vanaf 2000. SOVON-Onderzoeksrapport 2000/05. SOVON Vogelonderzoek Nederland, Beek-Ubbergen, The Netherlands.

Noordhuis, R. & Koffijberg, K. 2004. Watervogels als indicatoren: presentatie van trends in relatie tot beleidsdoelstellingen. RIZA-rapport 2004.003/SOVON-onderzoeksrapport 2004/01. RIZA, Lelystad, The Netherlands.

Rösner, H.-U. 1994. Population indices for migratory birds in the Schleswig-Holstein Wadden Sea from 1987 to 1993. Ophelia, Supplement 6: 171-186.

Soldaat, L., van Winden, E., van Turnhout, C., Berrevoets, C., van Roomen, M. & van Strien, A. 2004. De berekening van indexen en trends bij het watervogelmeetnet. SOVON-onderzoeksrapport 2004/02. Centraal bureau voor de Statistiek, Voorburg/Heerlen, The Netherlands.

Underhill, L.G. & Prys-Jones, R.P. 1994. Index numbers for waterbird populations. (I) Review and methodology. Journal of Applied Ecology 31: 463-480.

van Roomen, M., Boele, A., van der Weide, M.J.M., van Winden, E.A.J. & Zoetebier, D. 2000. Belangrijke vogelgebieden in Nederland, 1993-97. Actueel overzicht van Europese vogelwaarden in aangewezen en aan te wijzen speciale beschermingszones en andere belangrijke gebieden. SOVON-informatierapport 2000/01. SOVON Vogelonderzoek Nederland, Beek-Ubbergen, The Netherlands.

van Roomen, M., van Turnhout, C., Nienhuis, J., Willems, F. & van Winden, E. 2002. Monitoring van watervogels als niet-broedvogel in de Nederlandse Waddenzee: evaluatie huidige opzet en voorstellen voor de toekomst. SOVON-onderzoeksrapport 2002/01. SOVON Vogelonderzoek Nederland, Beek-Ubbergen, The Netherlands.

van Roomen, M., van Winden, E., Koffijberg, K., Boele, A., Hustings, F., Kleefstra, R., Schoppers, J., van Turnhout, C., SOVON Ganzen- en zwanenwerkgroep & Soldaat, L. 2004. Watervogels in Nederland in 2002/2003. SOVON-monitoringrapport 2004/02, RIZA-rapport BM04/09, SOVON Vogelonderzoek Nederland, Beek-Ubbergen, The Netherlands.

van Strien, A. 2005. Landelijke natuurmeetnetten van het NEM in 2004. Centraal Bureau voor de Statistiek, Voorburg/Heerlen, The Netherlands.

Visser, H. 2004. Estimation and detection of flexible trends. Atmospheric Environment 38: 4135-4145.

# Monitoring geese in the Vinogradovo floodplain - the core stop-over site in Moscow region

*Alexander L. Mischenko, Olga V. Sukhanova & Sergej P. Kharitonov*
*Russian Bird Conservation Union, Shosse Entuziastov, 60, bld.1, Moscow 111123, Russia. (email: almos@redro.msk.ru)*

Mischenko, A.L., Sukhanova, O.V. & Kharitonov, S.P. 2006. Monitoring geese in the Vinogradovo floodplain - the core stop-over site in Moscow region. *Waterbirds around the world.* Eds. G.C. Boere, C.A. Galbraith & D.A. Stroud. The Stationery Office, Edinburgh, UK. pp. 471-472.

The Vinogradovo floodplain is particularly valuable as a spring stop over station for large geese flocks: this paper presents the results of monitoring migrating goose numbers there from 1979 to 2003.

The Vinogradovo floodplain of the Moskva River (c. 50 sq km) is included in the Ramsar Shadow List of the Russian Federation, and is important as a spring stopover for large flocks of geese. It is an "island ecosystem", wedged in a ring of settlements of cottages and fields on terraces. The floodplain is characterized by a mosaic of habitats, including meadows (c. 30 sq km), small lakes, fens, abandoned pastures and small forage fields, drainage ditches and bushes, and is one of the few well-preserved floodplain sites in the densely populated Moscow Region. In 1986 a regional state nature reserve (Zakaznik) was established in the most important part of this area (c. 20 sq km). Monitoring of migrating goose numbers has been conducted there since the late 1970s.

In the Vinogradovo floodplain counts of geese were conducted using two methods: observation of feeding geese from raised viewpoints using a telescope, and observation of geese flying to the floodplain (morning) or to surrounding fields for feeding (evening) using binoculars. The maximum numbers of staging geese during the period of monitoring are shown in the Table 1, from which it can be seen that there is no obvious dependence of geese numbers upon a level of spring flood.

The White-fronted Goose *Anser albifrons* formed the majority of migrating geese in Vinogradovo in all years except

**Table 1.** **Dynamics of geese numbers on spring stop-over in Vinogradovo.**

| Years | Maximum quantity of staging geese | Level of spring flood |
|---|---|---|
| 1979-1983 | 12 000 - 15 000 | |
| 1984-1990 | 13 000 -16 000 | |
| 1995 | 5 000-6 000 | Low |
| 1997 | 10 000 | Low |
| 2000 | 8 000-10 000 | High |
| 2002 | 12 000 | Very low |
| 2003 | 7 000 | Medium |

See Zubakin *et al.* 1988, Kontorschikov *et al.* 1991, and Zubakin 2000 for more detailed information on these geese.

for 2002, when peak numbers (just over 3 000 birds) were much lower than in other years. In 2003 the maximum number of staging White-fronted Geese (c. 7 000) was also considerably lower than in 1980-1990. The maximum numbers of staging Bean Goose *Anser fabalis* were no more than 350 geese in the early and mid-1980s, 870-1 000 in 1997 and 2000, and about 120 individuals in 2003. In 2002 there was a very early, dry spring and very low spring flood, and very high numbers of migrating Bean Geese were recorded: at the peak of migration (4 April 2002) - the number of Bean Geese exceeded 8 700 individuals – about 80% of all goose numbers in that year.

The Vinogradovo floodplain is an important spring staging area for nominate race of White-fronted Goose *Anser albifrons*. Photo: Paul Marshall.

The maximum number of the migrating Greylag Goose *Anser anser* did not exceed 50 birds annually, while no more than four Lesser White-fronted Goose *Anser erythropus* were observed at one time in any year. In springs with low floods (e.g. 2002) resting goose flocks concentrated in swamps and flooded areas in the southern and north-eastern sectors of the floodplain, while in springs with normal floods (2003) geese dispersed throughout the floodplain.

Migrating geese fed on plants of meadow grass on the floodplain and fields beyond the river valley. Usually White-fronted Geese passed over to forage in fields far further away, but in 2002 foraging Bean Geese concentrated in the corn fields and perennial crops on the terrace of Moskva River, close to the floodplain and 4-5 km from the main resting sites. In early May 2002 Geese also used the floodplain for roosting: before dawn, they left the floodplain for the fields and returned after 9:00; between 17:30 and 21:00, they flew out to forage and returned to roost in complete darkness.

It is impossible to estimate the total number of geese migrating across the Vinogradovo floodplain without large-scale colour marking, but on the basis of a comparison between changes in the number and species composition in different migration waves, no fewer than 22 000 geese stopped over in the area, and the actual number could approach 30 000. Large flocks of resting Bean Geese can be observed in the Vinogradovo floodplain only in years with extremely early springs, as most Bean Geese normally fly through the floodplain without stopping.

Within last decade recreation pressures in the floodplain have sharply increased, resulting in illegal shooting and disturbance to geese, while the areas of corn fields and perennial crops used by geese for feeding near the floodplain have greatly decreased. For all of those reasons, the general numbers of White-fronted Geese in Vinogradovo floodplain has been decreasing.

Development of a management plan for the Vinogradovo floodplain has started. and will include guidelines on more efficient protection, agricultural management, expansion of the reserved area and establishment of the protected zone with spring hunting banned.

### ACKNOWLEDGEMENTS:
We express sincere gratitude to the Administration of Voskresensk District (Moscow Region) for financial support of our research in 2002-2003. Also we thank Dr. Victor Zubakin and Dr. Sergej Volkov for assistance with goose counts in 2002 and 2003.

### REFERENCES
**Zubakin, V.A., Morozov, V.V., Kharitonov, S.P., Leonovich, V.V. & Mischenko, A.L.** 1988. The birds of the Moscow-river meadowland near Vinogradovo, Moscow Region. In: O.L. Rossolimo (ed.) Birds of reclaiming territories. Moscow University Press, Moscow: 126-167. (In Russian).

**Kontorschikov, V.V., Zubakin, V.A., Pegova, A.N., Rubtsov, A.S., Semernin, I.V. & Yakhontov, E.L.** 1991. The places of geese concentrations in Moscow Region. In: V.D. Ilyichev (ed.) Proceedings of 10th All-Russian Ornithological Conference. Part 2, vol. 1. Navuka i tekhnika, Minsk: 299-300. (In Russian).

**Zubakin, V.A.** 2000. Faustovo floodplain of the river Moskva. In: T.V. Sviridova & V.A. Zubakin (eds) Important Bird Areas of Russia. Vol. 1. Russian Bird Conservation Union, Moscow: 238-239. (In Russian).

Fewer than 50 Greylag Geese *Anser anser* occur annually on the Vinogradova flood plain.  Photo: Paul Marshall.

# Estuarine waterbirds at low tide: the WeBS low tide counts 1992-93 to 1998-99

*Andy Musgrove*

*British Trust for Ornithology, The Nunnery, Thetford, Norfolk, IP24 2PU, UK. (email: webs@bto.org)*

Musgrove, A. 2006. Estuarine waterbirds at low tide: the WeBS low tide counts 1992-93 to 1998-99. *Waterbirds around the world.* Eds. G.C. Boere, C.A. Galbraith & D.A. Stroud. The Stationery Office, Edinburgh, UK. p. 473.

UK estuaries are of key international importance for non-breeding waterbirds. Whilst the numbers of birds frequenting these estuaries have been well monitored by a large team of experienced volunteers for many years, notably through the Wetland Bird Survey (WeBS), the UK has shown a further commitment to the conservation of estuarine waterbirds by undertaking a national "Low Tide Counts" scheme from the winter of 1992-93 onwards. The WeBS Low Tide Counts Scheme aims to investigate the within-site distribution of estuarine waterbirds at low tide, in order to improve understanding of site usage and thus to focus conservation efforts to greater effect. The data arising from the first seven winters have now been summarised for a book, *Estuarine Waterbirds at Low Tide* (Musgrove *et al.* 2003). The introduction to the book includes background information about estuarine habitats, estuarine wildlife, human influences on estuaries and the monitoring of estuarine waterbirds. There then follows a detailed account and discussion of the methods used during the WeBS Low Tide Counts, both for the survey itself and for subsequent data processing and presentation. The coverage achieved by the scheme during the seven winters 1992-93 to 1998-99 is detailed, with 62 UK estuaries being included during that period.

The main bulk of the book is a set of 62 site accounts. For each of these, background information about the site is given, along with the coverage of the site achieved by the scheme, including a discussion of the degree of overlap with the boundaries of designated Special Protection Areas and Ramsar Sites.

The waterbird distribution at the site is then discussed in a broad sense, and the distribution of all key waterbirds at each site is also mapped. Following the site accounts, the data are discussed by species, with fuller accounts for 29 key species, reduced accounts for 32 species and brief notes on a further 47 species. The book is completed by a discussion of the use of Low Tide Counts for the purposes of nature conservation casework, along with a broad discussion of the findings of the survey and aims for the future.

The Wetland Bird Survey is a partnership between the British Trust for Ornithology, The Wildfowl & Wetlands Trust (WWT), Royal Society for the Protection of Birds (RSPB) and the Joint Nature Conservation Committee (JNCC, on behalf of English Nature, Scottish Natural Heritage, the Countryside Council for Wales and the Environment and Heritage Service in Northern Ireland). However, although *Estuarine Waterbirds at Low Tide* was a joint production between these partners, it could not have been produced without the hard work of hundreds of dedicated volunteer fieldworkers who contributed data to the scheme. The International Wader Study Group (WSG) is also thanked for its hard work in the final production of the book.

## REFERENCES

Musgrove, A.J., Langston, R.H.W., Baker, H. & Ward, R.M. (eds). 2003. *Estuarine Waterbirds at Low Tide: the WeBS Low Tide Counts 1992/93 to 1998/99.* WSG / BTO / WWT / RSPB / JNCC, Thetford. 310 pp

UK Environment Minister Elliot Morley MP, who is himself a keen waterbird counter, receiving the first copy of the WeBS Low Tide Count Atlas on his counting site at the Humber estuary, eastern England. Photo: Gareth Hartford.

# Waterfowl marking in Portugal: main results and future perspectives

*David Rodrigues[1], M. Ester Figueiredo[2], António Fabião[2] & Paulo Tenreiro[3]*

[1] *Departamento Florestal – Escola Superior Agrária de Coimbra, Bencanta 3040-316 Coimbra, Portugal.*
*(email: drodrigues@mail.esac.pt)*

[2] *Departamento de Engenharia Florestal – Instituto Superior de Agronomia, Tapada da Ajuda, 1349-017 Lisboa, Portugal.*

[3] *Coordenação de Coimbra – Instituto da Conservação da Natureza, Mata Nacional do Choupal, 3000 Coimbra, Portugal.*

Rodrigues, D.J.C., Figueiredo, M.E., Fabião, A. & Tenreiro, P. 2006. Waterfowl marking in Portugal: main results and future perspectives. *Waterbirds around the world.* Eds. G.C. Boere, C.A. Galbraith & D.A. Stroud. The Stationery Office, Edinburgh, UK. pp. 474-475.

The recent integrated monitoring of some Portuguese waterfowl populations has allowed several studies of their ecology, biology and management (Figueiredo 2003, Rodrigues 2001, Rodrigues & Fabião 1997, Rodrigues & Tenreiro 1996, Rodrigues *et al.* in press). This paper reports and discusses some results related to capture and marking processes used with waterfowl in Portugal.

We started the regular capture of waterfowl in Portugal in June 1993, and by the end of March 2004 we had marked 7 519 ducks and 1 047 rails. We also nasal-saddled ducks and obtained more than 21 000 resightings. The use of nasal saddles on ducks improved the results obtained (e.g. information on Mallard international movements increased 225%) and allowed new data analyses.

Ducks and Rails were captured on baited swim-in and walk-in traps, and marked with metal rings. Ducks were also nasal marked with flexible PVC, rubber (Rodrigues *et al.* 2001) or Polyurethane saddles (D. Rodrigues, unpubl. data). Nasal saddling started in 1993 with *Anas platyrhynchos* and continued with Wigeon *Anas penelope*, Gadwall *A. strepera*, Pintail *A. acuta* and Shoueler *A. clypeata* (from 1998), Teal *A. crecca* and Garganey *A. querquedula* (from 1999), and Tufted Duck *Aythya fuligula* (from 2003). Different colours and alphanumerical codes on the nasal saddles allowed individual identification. Capture took place from July 1993 to the end of March 2004.

Capture totals, recoveries and resightings are summarised in Table 1. Most captured duck species have higher International resighting rates than recovery rates. Teal and Wigeon moulting primaries were captured between September and early December.

Nasal marks proved to be an efficient tool in the study of duck movements and migration. They increased the amount of information obtained from marked birds, allowed the estimate of survival rates (Rodrigues 2001), and will allow the assessment of returning rates of migratory ducks. The study has become less dependent on hunter reports, which gave a recovery rate of only 2.6%.

According to Rodrigues *et al.* (2000), Mallard populations from Central and Northern Portugal (from Mondego River basin to the north) are more related to Galicia and North Atlantic populations (Atlantic flyway) than to the Southern Portuguese populations (from Tagus basin to south). The latter should be more related to the southern Spanish and Mediterranean populations. This separation should probably also be applied to migratory species since ducks wintering in central and north Portugal prefer to use the Atlantic flyway, and birds wintering in south

**Table 1.** Total birds ringed and nasal marked within the study, recovered and resighted in Portugal, and recovered and resighted abroad.

| Species | N (N marked) | Recoveries in Portugal | Resightings in Portugal | International recoveries | International resightings (N birds) |
|---|---|---|---|---|---|
| *Anas acuta* | 8 (2) | 0 | 0 | 1 (12.5%) | 0 |
| *Anas clypeata* | 44 (33) | 0 | >80 | 2 (4.7%) | 8 (4-12.1%) |
| *Anas crecca* | 1 502 (847) | 1 (0.1%) | >1000 | 61* (4.1%) | 26 (14-1.7%) |
| *Anas carolinensis* | 2 (=) | 0 | >25 | 0 | 0 |
| *Anas penelope* | 157 (138) | 1 (0.6%) | >210 | 4 (2.5%) | 10 (5-3.6%) |
| *Anas platyrhynchos* | 5 739 (5 689) | 216 (3.8%) | >20 000 | 20 (0.4%) | 80 (54-0.9%) |
| *Anas querquedula* | 3 (2) | 0 | 11 | 0 | 0 |
| *Anas strepera* | 21 (18) | 0 | >35 | 1 (4.8%) | 0 |
| Hybrid of *Anas* | 1 (=) | 0 | 7 | 0 | 0 |
| *Aythya collaris* | 1 (=) | 0 | >20 | 0 | 0 |
| *Aythya ferina* | 5 (0) | 0 | 0 | 1 (20%) | 0 |
| *Aythya fuligula* | 36 (10) | 1 (2.8%) | >55 | 1* (2.8%) | 3 (1-10.0%) |
| *Fulica atra* | 104 (-) | 4 (3.9%) | - | 0 | - |
| *Gallinula chloropus* | 846 (-) | 5 (0.6%) | - | 0 | - |
| *Porphyrio porphyrio* | 2 (-) | 0 | - | 0 | - |
| *Porzana porzana* | 1 (-) | 0 | - | 0 | - |
| *Rallus aquaticus* | 94 (-) | 0 | - | 0 | - |
| Total | 8 566 (6 739) | 228 (2.6%) | >21 000 | 91 (1.2%) | 127 (78-1.2%) |

* includes one recapture

Portugal have a higher component of the Central European and Mediterranean flyway, but this must be confirmed with more captures in the south.

The capture of Teal and Wigeon moulting primaries reinforced the importance of the Iberian wetlands as both wintering areas and as moulting grounds for those species that do not nest in Portugal (Rufino 1989)

## ACKNOWLEDGEMENTS

The research work was funded within projects STRD/AGR/0038 (JNICT, Lisbon), PAMAF 4031 (INIA, Lisbon), POCTI/PNAT/AGR/15032/1999 (FCT, Lisbon) and Centro de Estudos Florestais, Lisbon. David Rodrigues was funded through a doctoral scholarship (Programs CIENCIA and PRAXIS XXI).

## REFERENCES

**Figueiredo, M.** 2003. Ecology and Management of Teal *Anas crecca* L. on Central Portugal. Master Thesis. Faculty of Science and Technology, University of Coimbra, Portugal. (In Portuguese with English abstract)

**Rodrigues, D.J.C.** 2001. Ecology and Management of Mallard *Anas platyrhynchos* L. Populations on Portuguese Wetlands. PhD Thesis, Agronomics High Institute, Technical University of Lisbon, Portugal. (Introduction and Discussion in Portuguese, Chapters and Abstract in English)

**Rodrigues, D.J.C. & Tenreiro, P.J.Q.** 1996. Importance of refuge areas on Rail population game management: the example of the Madriz Marsh for the Moorhen population of the River Arunca valley. Revista Florestal 9: 319-327. (In Portuguese with English summmary).

**Rodrigues, D. & Fabião, A.** 1997. Loss and change of habitat and possible effects on mallard populations of Mondego and Vouga river basins. In: J. D. Goss-Custard, R. Rufino & A. Luis (eds.). Effect of Habitat Loss and Change on Waterbirds. The Stationery Office, London: Pp.127-130.

**Rodrigues, D.J.C., Fabião, A.M.D., Figueiredo, M.E.M.A. & Tenreiro, P.J.Q.** 2000. Migratory status and movements of the Portuguese Mallard *Anas platyrhynchos.* Vogelwarte 40: 292-297.

**Rodrigues, D.J.C., Fabião, A.M.D. & Figueiredo, M.E.M.A.** 2001. The use of nasal markers for monitoring Mallard populations. *In* R. Field, R.J. Waren, H. Okarma & P.R. Sievet (eds.) Wildlife, land, and people: priorities for the 21st century. Proceedings of the Second international Wildlife management Congress. The Wildlife Society, Bethesda, Maryland, USA. Pp. 316-318.

**Rodrigues, D.C., Figueiredo, M.E. & Fabião, A.** In press. A preliminary model for a Portuguese Mallard population in Central Portugal. Folia Zoologica.

**Rufino, R.** 1989. Atlas das Aves que nidificam em Portugal Continental. SNPRCN. Lisbon, Portugal.

Mallard *Anas platyrhynchos* are one of several duck species to have been individually marked in Portugal. Photo: Paul Marshall.

# Britain's first Winter River Bird Survey: a new approach to surveying waterbirds on linear waterways

*James A. Robinson, Melanie Kershaw, Jenny Worden & Peter Cranswick*

*The Wildfowl & Wetlands Trust, Slimbridge, Gloucestershire, GL2 7BT, UK. (email: jenny.worden@wwt.org.uk)*

Robinson, J.A., Kershaw, M., Worden, J. & Cranswick, P.A. 2006. Britain's first Winter River Bird Survey: a new approach to surveying waterbirds on linear waterways. *Waterbirds around the world.* Eds. G.C. Boere, C.A. Galbraith & D.A. Stroud. The Stationery Office, Edinburgh, UK. pp. 476-477.

Rivers are essential to large numbers of wetland birds that visit the UK during the winter. The distribution and numbers of waterbirds using rivers need to be monitored so that correct and effective conservation action can be triggered if numbers decline. Currently, linear waterways such as rivers and canals are poorly covered by existing surveys compared with other wetland habitats. The aim of a national Winter River Bird Survey would

be to increase the coverage of linear waterways to improve the accuracy of national population estimates for relevant species and to evaluate the extent to which current surveys underestimate these populations.

A pilot survey was undertaken in January and February 2000 and 2001 to investigate methods for a full national survey (Robinson *et al.* 2003). Since a full survey could not hope to

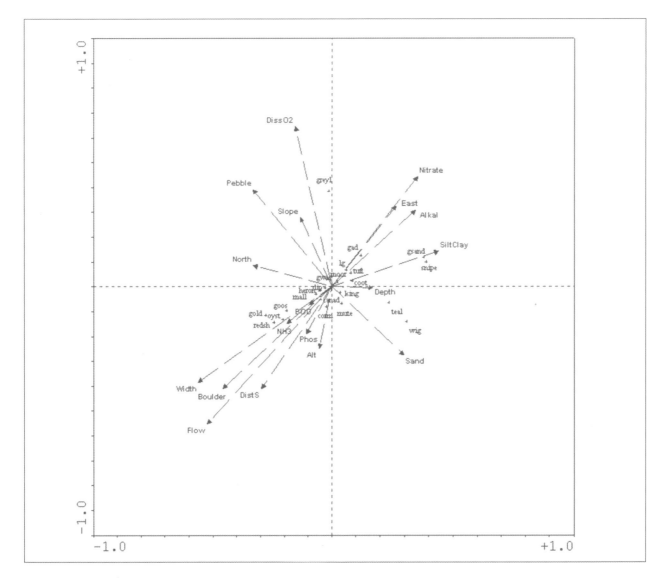

Fig. 1. A plot of the scores of the first and second axes of the CCA ordination of the environmental variables and bird scores (Abbreviations used: canad = Canada Goose *Branta canadensis*, corm = Cormorant *Phalacrocorax carbo*, dip = Dipper *Cinclus cinclus*, gad = Gadwall *Anas strepera*, gold = Goldeneye *Bucephala clangula*, goos = Goosander *Mergus mergus*, gsand = Green Sandpiper *Tringa ochropus*, gwag = Grey Wagtail *Moticilla cinerea*, heron = Grey Heron *Ardea cinerea*, king = Kingfisher *Alcedo atthis*, lg = Little Grebe *Tachybaptus ruficollis*, mall = Mallard *Anas playtyrhynchos*, moor = Moorhen *Gallinula chloropus*, mute = Mute Swan *Cygnus olor*, oyst = Oystercatcher *Haematopus ostralegus*, redsh = Redshank *Tringa totanus*, tuft = Tufted Duck *Aythya fuligula*, wig = Wigeon *Anas penelope*; Alakl = Alkalinity, Alt = Altitude, DissO2 = Dissolved O2, DistS = Distance from source, Phos = Phosphate).

cover all river lengths in the UK, a randomised sampling approach would be used to derive population estimates. Stratified random sampling gives more accurate results than unstratified sampling, since bird density is predicted to vary according to factors such as region, river width, flow rate etc. The pilot survey identified the most suitable strata for a national survey, allowed selection of the most appropriate length of river to use as a count unit, and assessed the level of coverage required to generate estimates with a given confidence interval.

During the pilot, 30 rivers and canals were surveyed, representing a wide range of geographical, physical and environmental waterway types. Each river and canal was divided into 500 m sections and each stretch was visited once to record the numbers of each species present. Over 27 400 birds were counted, and data analysed for 22 species. The following environmental variables had been measured by the Environment Agency for each stretch in England and Wales and were used in statistical analyses: width; depth; alkalinity; % silt or clay; % sand; % pebbles or gravel; % boulders or cobbles; altitude; distance from source; slope; mean phosphate; mean nitrate; BOD; dissolved oxygen; ammonia; easting; northing; flow category; and General Quality Assessment biology grade.

Count data were used to identify suitable strata for the national survey, based on bird densities in river channels, so as to minimise the within-stratum variance in bird density. Multivariate analyses were used to identify major patterns of distribution for different species and the relationships between density, and the various environmental variables were quantified using Canonical Correspondence Analysis (CCA), a form of direct gradient analysis which attempts to explain species distribution patterns.

An indirect gradient analysis technique was used to test whether the measured environmental variables were adequate to explain the major variation in species composition. Unlike CCA, this technique does not attempt to constrain the species

responses to any environmental variables. It therefore represents major patterns in the species data without making any assumptions about the factors associated with these gradients.

A biplot of the first and second axes of the CCA ordination of the river and bird scores is shown in Fig. 1. The first axis is primarily a width/flow axis separating stretches that are wide with high flow rates from narrower stretches with lower flows. Having run the CCA analysis with all variables included, forward selection was then used to rank environmental variables in terms of their importance for determining the species data. Automatic selection was used to sequentially select the best five variables on the basis of maximum extra fit. The five environmental variables most important in explaining the species data were: water flow, northing, easting, dissolved oxygen and % silt or clay.

A nine-level stratification was identified based on region and flow combinations. The full survey will aim to cover 8 000 x 500 m stretches of river across nine strata, based on low and high flows and regions within England and Wales, to produce population estimates with +/-10% precision for a variety of species. Means for stratifying coverage in Scotland are being pursued.

## ACKNOWLEDGEMENTS
We thank Ron Thomas, Graeme Storey and Emily Orr for providing large amounts of environmental data from the Environment Agency's databases. This work was funded by a partnership between the British Trust for Ornithology, The Wildfowl & Wetlands Trust, the Royal Society for the Protection of Birds and the Joint Nature Conservation Committee.

## REFERENCES
**Robinson, J.A., Kershaw, M., Thomas, R. & Storey, G.** 2003. WeBS Pilot Riverine Survey 2000-2001: Data analysis and recommendations for national survey design. WWT Research Report, Slimbridge.

The River Nene in Northamptonshire, England, filling its floodplain after heavy rains. Photo: David Stroud.

# Fluctuations and trends in Swedish waterfowl populations during the last four decades

*Leif Nilsson*

*Department of Animal Ecology, University of Lund, Ecology Building S-223 62 Lund, Sweden. (email: leif.nilsson@zooekol.lu.se)*

Nilsson, L. 2006. Fluctuations and trends in Swedish waterfowl populations during the last four decades. *Waterbirds around the world.* Eds. G.C. Boere, C.A. Galbraith & D.A. Stroud. The Stationery Office, Edinburgh, UK. pp. 478-479.

Regular waterfowl counts have been undertaken in Sweden since 1959/60, and Sweden has participated in the international midwinter counts of the International Waterbird Census since their start in January 1967. The counts aimed at the fullest

possible coverage during the years 1969-78, after which a standardized net of sites were counted each year for the calculation of annual indices. In addition, country-wide surveys of south Sweden were undertaken in 1971-73, 1987-89 (partial - no aerial

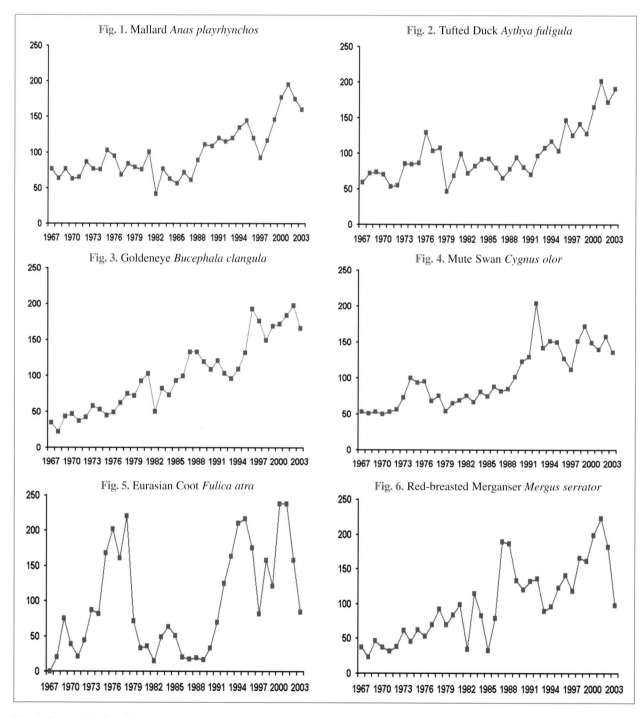

**Figs. 1–6.** Annual indices for some common species based on pair-wise comparisons of counts on sites for two consecutive years. The values so obtained have been recalculated so that the mean for the series =100 (January data for the period 1987–2003).

**Table. 1. Totals for some species from country-wide surveys in Sweden 1971- 73 and 2004. All inshore coastal areas and the majority of inland sites were covered.**

| Species | 1971-73 | 2004 |
|---|---|---|
| *Anas platyrhynchos* | 86 000 | 11 0000 |
| *Anas penelope* | 40 | 5 000 |
| *Aythya fuligula* | 65 000 | 201 000 |
| *Bucephala clangula* | 24 000 | 69 000 |
| *Somateria mollissima* | 9 000 | 43 000 |
| *Mergus serrator* | 3 400 | 4 400 |
| *Mergus merganser* | 11 000 | 17 000 |
| *Cygnus olor* | 10 000 | 30 000 |
| *Fulica atra* | 15 000 | 17 500 |
| *Phalacrocorax carbo* | 1 900 | 8 100 |

surveys in Baltic archipelagos) and 2004. Areas further north are normally ice-covered in January and thus not important for waterfowl numbers. Midwinter indices are presented here for six species out of ten which were analysed (Figs. 1-6). Significantly increasing trends were found for seven species, whereas there were no long-term trends in the indices for the other three species. The index for the Eider, being representative only for

the southern part of the winter area on the Swedish west coast, showed a peak in the 1970s, then very low numbers followed by an increase in the 1990s. In the Coot *Fulica atra* there was a marked peak in the late 1970s after the previous mild winters, and then the population crashed after the cold 1979 winter, remaining at a low level until it once again increased during the 1990s. In most cases the increasing trends in the Swedish International Waterfowl Census (IWC) indices reflect changes in the winter distribution of the different species in relation to the milder winters in recent years. In some cases the increase can be a combination of distribution changes and a real population change. These questions can only be answered by the coming international analysis of the IWC data gathered in several countries in the flyway. Almost complete aerial surveys were undertaken in the Baltic archipelagos and the west coast in 1971-73 and 2004, with complete land-based coverage along the open coasts and on all important inland sites. Preliminary totals for 2004 are compared with country-wide surveys in 1971-73 in Table 1, and trends for individual species are shown in Fig. 1–6. Updates of the results from the Swedish mid-winter counts are found on the homepage of the project: www.biol.lu.se/zooekologi/ waterfowl/index.htm. A major analysis of the data from the Swedish midwinter counts has started and will be finished in late 2005.

Numbers of Swedish Mute Swans *Cygnus olor* have stabilised in the last decade after an earlier period of increase. Photo: Chris Wilson.

# Conflicting trends in Ruddy Shelduck *Tadorna ferruginea* populations: a myth or reality?

*Anastasia B. Popovkina*

*Goose, Swan and Duck Study Group of Northern Eurasia*

*Dept. Vertebrate Zoology, Biol. Faculty, Moscow State University, Moscow 119992, Russia. (email: nastya@soil.msu.ru)*

Popovkina, A.B. 2006. Conflicting trends in Ruddy Shelduck *Tadorna ferruginea* populations: a myth or reality? *Waterbirds around the world.* Eds. G.C. Boere, C.A. Galbraith & D.A. Stroud. The Stationery Office, Edinburgh, UK. pp. 480-481.

This paper discusses changes in the numbers of different populations of the Ruddy Shelduck *Tadorna ferruginea* in Europe and Asia, changes which are not well understood, and describes a new initiative to assist in collecting and analysing population data.

Six populations (Ethiopian, Northwest African, Black Sea–East Mediterranean, Southwest and Central Asian, Central–Southern–Southeast Asian, and East Asian) of the Ruddy Shelduck are presently recognised (Penennou *et al.* 1994, Scott & Rose 1996). Noticeable fluctuations in numbers and certain shifts of the range of the species have been observed over the last three centuries. Mid-winter counts have indicated a dramatic decline in the western populations between the 1980s and mid-1990s, while at the same time the population numbers of Ruddy Shelducks in the Asian part of the range have undergone no noticeable changes over the past century and, moreover, seem to increase there. The recent influx of the Ruddy Shelducks in Western Europe cannot be explained by the dispersal of the escapes from captivity and still puzzles the experts. These facts have led some experts to assume that the species is being gradually driven out of the western parts of its range and that the range is shifting eastwards.

Ruddy Shelduck is listed as a species of European Conservation Concern (SPEC3: unfavorable – Europe). Its threat status in Europe is Vulnerable. The species is listed in the EU Wild Birds Directive (Annex I), Bern Convention (Appendix II), and Bonn Convention (Appendix II).

Different experts suggest the following reasons for the decline of the Ruddy Shelduck populations:

- habitat changes due to agricultural development (drainage of shallow marshland, subterranean water extraction for irrigation, over-grazing, etc.);
- coastal housing development;
- dramatic decline of marmot populations in steppe habitats;
- excessive shooting, particularly at the wintering grounds;
- nest-site disturbance; and
- natural causes (global and local climate changes, degradation of habitats, etc.).

The future of the species in Europe seems greatly dependent on the implementation of conservation measures, particularly prevention of shooting at its wintering grounds. However, increases of Ruddy Shelduck populations have been reported in the last decades for Bulgaria and European Russia. An increase in numbers from the early 1970s to the late 1980s has been reported for Kazakhstan and the Caspian region. Along with a noticeable (about 96%) decline in Pakistan, the population wintering in Iran has increased dramatically in the last 20 years,

the mid-winter counts suggesting that a five- or six-fold increase has occurred (Penennou *et al.* 1994).

In some experts' opinion, the recent increase in Ruddy Shelduck numbers in particular areas was caused by:

- direct conservation measures (Red Listings, banning of hunting, etc.);
- expansion of favourable habitats (dispersal and increase in numbers of marmots due to conservation measures; construction of dams and water reservoirs; depression in agriculture due to stagnation of economic development, etc.);
- reintroduction; and
- natural causes (global and local climate changes; improvement of habitats).

We have reviewed whether re-distribution of birds between the western and eastern populations has occured, or are we witnessing the extinction of certain populations and the increase of others? The question could be answered if the existence of isolated populations is confirmed and if boundaries between populations (if any) are determined. Ringing recovery data would be of great help although very few Ruddy Shelducks have been ringed so far. For population studies, DNA-analysis would also help. Global censuses (primarily those conducted by Wetlands International) provide data on the species numbers on wintering grounds, while those for the breeding areas are of great value.

With a view to understanding population trends and providing valuable information for international conservation efforts, a few years ago the Goose, Swan, and Duck Study Group of Northern Eurasia launched a Project to study recent changes in numbers and

Ruddy Shelducks *Tadorna ferruginea*. Photo: Anastasia Popovkina.

range. Questionnaires containing questions on the numbers and local distribution of Ruddy Shelducks and status of their populations in particular areas were compiled and distributed primarily in the regions inhabited by the species, and information from many European and Asian regions of Russia and other countries was obtained. Data provided by numerous respondents have been entered into a database and regularly updated. Analysis of published data provides an understanding of the long-term population trends.

Data on recent Ruddy Shelduck numbers were reported by more than 130 respondents from 49 countries.

We encourage people to support this project by filling in the questionnaire available from the Project Coordinator at nastya@soil.msu.ru. Joint international efforts could facilitate

both better understanding of the Ruddy Shelduck population dynamics at a global level and implementation of the necessary conservation measures.

## REFERENCES

Penennou, C., Mundkur, T., Scott, D. A., Follestad, A. & Kvenild, L. 1994. The Asian Waterfowl census 1987–91: Distribution and Status of Asian Waterfowl. AWB Publication No. 86. IWRB Publication No 24. AWB, Kuala Lumpur, Malaysia and IWRB, Slimbridge, UK: 1–372.

Scott, D. A. & Rose, P. M. 1996. Atlas of Anatidae Populations in Africa and Western Eurasia. Wetlands International Publication, 41: 1–336.

Ruddy Shelducks *Tadorna ferruginea*. Photo: Anastasia Popovkina.

# The Swan Goose *Anser cygnoides* research and conservation programme in Russia

*Nikolay D. Poyarkov*

*Lomonosov Moscow State University; Goose, Swan and Duck Study Group of Northern Palearctic, Russia.*
*(email: Poyarkov@soil.msu.ru)*

Poyarkov, N.D. 2006. The Swan Goose *Anser cygnoides* research and conservation programme in Russia. *Waterbirds around the world.* Eds. G.C. Boere, C.A. Galbraith & D.A. Stroud. The Stationery Office, Edinburgh, UK. pp. 482-483.

Up to the middle of the 20th century, Swan Geese *Anser cygnoides* were quite common in Russia, from Predbaikalie to the Lower Amur (Nizhneye Priamurie), Priamorie region, and northern Sakhalin. Since the 1950s, the range of this species has been progressively shrinking and its numbers declining under increasing anthropogenic impacts.

The Swan Goose is the most vulnerable goose species in East Asia, due to its nesting in densely populated and easily accessible flood plains, and intensive and uncontrolled hunting at its wintering grounds.

In 2000, a Russian-Japanese joint program of Swan Goose research and conservation was initiated with financial support from the Keidanren Science Foundation (Japan), with the goal of developing conservation measures at national and international levels. The main objectives were to: census Swan Geese in

known nesting sites and to study the peculiarities of their biology; mark geese of different populations; establish the need for specially protected areas; raise awareness in local communities about the need for protecting Swan Geese; adjust hunting regulations to avoid accidental shooting of Swan Geese; and develop procedures for restoration of the species within its range.

During the pilot phase (2000-2003) achievements included:

* the establishment, in 2002, of an International Task Force for Swan Geese with the participation of China, Japan, Korea, Mongolia and Russia;
* the publication of all available original and published data on numbers and biology of Swan Geese (Poyarkov, 2001, 2003);
* the survey of all known and potential nesting sites of Swan Geese in the Russian Far East, with the discovery of some

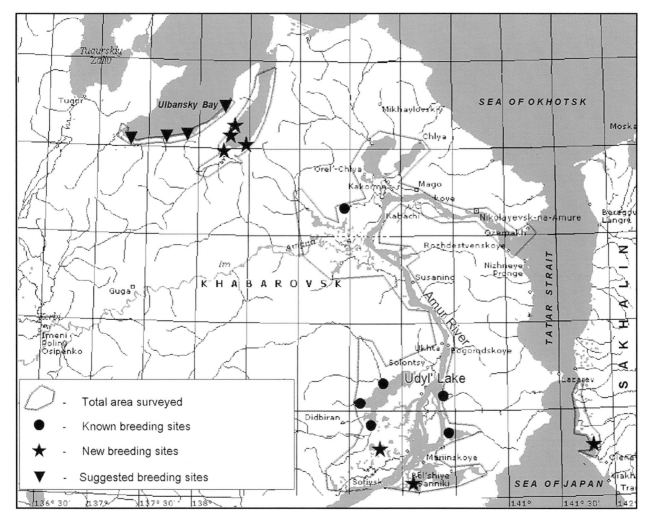

Fig. 1. Total area surveyed and the breeding sites of Swan Geese *Anser cygnoides* in the Priamurie, the Far East.

previously unknown nesting sites (Fig. 1) as well as obviously vacant and poorly occupied sites;

- recognising an increase in goose numbers in Udyl' Zakaznik (refuge), identified through the monitoring of Swan Geese population on Udyl' lake (Russian Far East), as a result of raising public awareness and education;
- coordination of an Swan Geese research program in the transboundary region of Transbaikalia with Dr. Oleg Goroshko (Daurskiy State Nature Reserve), who undertook research and compiled all available published data and original materials on the status and biology of Swan Geese in the region (Goroshko 2001, 2003a, Goroshko & Liu Sangtao 2003);
- the discovery of some characteristics of the species, including; nesting in different types of habitats, the mobility of populations and brood amalgamations, the relationship between population condition in Dauria and long-term climatic cycles, and the extremely high proportion of non-breeding birds during a drought period (Goroshko 2003b);
- marking of Swan Geese with neck collars at Udyl' (139°48'E, 52°10'N) and Torey (115°41'E, 50°00'N) lakes;
- indications that a Korean stopover area is very important for Far Eastern Swan Geese breeding populations from recoveries made at Han River estuary (126°41'E, 37°48'N);
- the establishment of the Zakaznik "Kholan" for the protection of the nesting Swan Geese in the Russian Far East, in 2001;
- implementation of large-scale public awareness and education campaigns targeting local communities with hundreds of stickers, posters, and booklets printed and distributed, radio clips recorded and played as advertisement on radio, and lectures for students;
- the confiscation of nine young Swan Geese from local people, which were taken to Moscow Zoo to be used as basic stock for a captive breeding program of Swan Geese populations; and
- the collection of sample feathers for population structure studies by molecular genetic methods.

Unfortunately, proposals for changing some hunting regulations in the Far East were not supported by the Khabarovsk Department of Game Management.

Besides activities in Russia, the Task Force members have started work in other regions with a review of general information on the status of Swan Geese in Mongolia (Gombobaatar *et al.,* 2003), and China (Liu, 2004), the monitoring of Swan Geese, marking with neck collars and obtaining new data on Swan Geese feeding ecology at its Korean stopover site (Lee, 2004). Based on this data, it appears that the Swan Geese breeding range is divided into two parts: Far Eastern and Daurian. Questions regarding their degree of separation should be the focus of future studies.

Further work on Swan Geese research and protection is planned under the framework of the Task Force:

- monitoring of Swan Geese populations, research into the "bottlenecks" in species ecology and GIS-analysis of the areas inhabited by Swan Geese to reveal and examine potential nesting sites;
- banding of geese and fitting radio and satellite transmitters;
- molecular-genetic analyses of different populations to understand the population structure;
- supporting existing special protected areas and establishing new ones to enhance Swan Goose conservation;
- developing further public awareness and education programmes;
- developing and implementing a restoration program for a Swan Goose population in its former range to guarantee the survival of the species in the winter period; and
- developing a monitoring system of the Russian populations at the wintering grounds in China.

## REFERENCES

Gombobaatar, S., Tseveenmyadag, N. & Nyambayar, B. 2003. Current status of research and future trends of Swan Goose *Anser cygnoides* and Baikal Teal *Anas formosa* in Mongolia. 2003 International Anatidae Symposium in East Asia & Siberia Region. Seosan, Korea: 79-82.

Goroshko, O. A. 2001. Swan Goose in the eastern Transbaikalia and Mongolia. Casarca 7: 68-98. (In Russian with English summary).

Goroshko, O. A. 2003a. Swan Geese on Torey Lakes, Transbaikalia, in 2002. Casarca 9, Moscow: 96-99. (In Russian with English summary).

Goroshko, O. A. 2003b. 2003–extremely unfavourable year for Swan Geese in Dauria transboundary region (Russia and Mongolia). 2003 International Anatidae Symposium in East Asia & Siberia Region. Seosan, Korea: 83-92.

Goroshko, J., A. & Liu Sangtao. 2003. Numbers and habitats of Swan Geese and Ruddy Shelducks in Dalai Lake Nature Reserve, North-Eastern China. Casarca 9: 372-376. (In Russian with English summary).

Lee, K. 2004. Swan Geese on Han River estuary. Presentation at Anatidae Working Group, Seosan, Korea, Oct. 2004.

Liu, D. 2004. Survey and Distribution of Anatidae in China. Presentation at Anatidae Working Group, Seosan, Korea, Oct. 2004.

Poyarkov, N. D. 2001. The Swan-Goose: its origin, number dynamics, biology, and conservation. Casarca 7: 51-67. (In Russian with English summary).

Poyarkov, N. D., 2003. The first results of Russian-Japanese joint programme of the Swan-Goose conservation in Russia. Casarca 9: 87-95.

# Current status of the International Waterbird Census in the Czech Republic

*Zuzana Musilová & Petr Musil*

*Deptartment of Zoology, Faculty of Science, Charles University, Vinicna 7, CZ-128 44 Praha 2, Czech Republic.*
*(email: iwccz@post.cz)*

Musilová, Z. & Musil, P. 2006. Current status of the International Waterbird Census in the Czech Republic. *Waterbirds around the world*. Eds. G.C. Boere, C.A. Galbraith & D.A. Stroud. The Stationery Office, Edinburgh, UK. pp. 484-486.

Monitoring of wintering waterbirds has a long tradition in the Czech Republic. The International Waterbird Census (IWC) was established (in former Czechoslovakia) in the winter of 1965/66 and has been carried out annually ever since, with results regularly published in national journals and bulletins (Pellantová 1995, 1996, 1997, 1998). Up to 2003, monitoring and counts were undertaken on 35 to 199 wetlands located in various parts of Bohemia and Moravia. However, this initial IWC monitoring scheme was designed in the 1970s, and no longer corresponds to the current distribution of wintering waterfowl in the Czech Republic.

In order to optimize coverage of the IWC, the "*Complete Wintering Waterbird Census*" project was undertaken from 2004 - 2006 to assess the current distribution and numbers of wintering waterbirds. The results of this project will be analysed to update the IWC in the Czech Republic, with the aim of

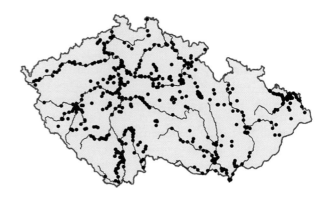

Fig. 1. Distribution of wetland sites covered in the "*Complete Wintering Waterbird Census*" in January 2004.

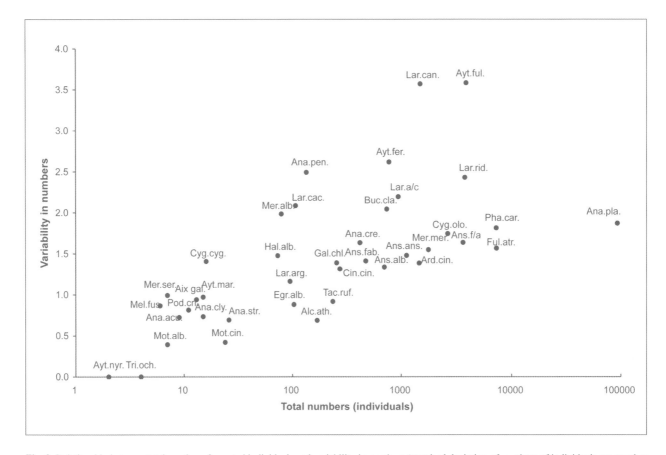

Fig. 2. Relationship between total number of counted individuals and variability in numbers (standard deviation of numbers of individuals per number of occupied sites). Species which show non-equal pattern of distribution, i.e. those which were counted in only a few places in high numbers are located in upper part of figure. For species abbreviations see Table 1.

**Table 1.** List of species recorded by mid-January International Waterbird Census on 478 wetland sites in the Czech Republic in January 2004. The abbreviations of species names listed in the second column are those used in Fig. 2.

| Species | Abbreviated name for Fig. 2 | no of sites | Number of birds counted | | | | | | | |
|---|---|---|---|---|---|---|---|---|---|---|
| | | | TOTAL | West Bohemia | North Bohemia | Central Bohemia | South Bohemia | East Bohemia | South Moravia | North Moravia |
| Number of sites | | | 478 | 51 | 38 | 114 | 73 | 78 | 56 | 68 |
| *Gavia stellata* | Gav.ste. | 5 | 13 | 4 | | | 2 | | 7 | |
| *Tachybaptus ruficollis* | Tac.ruf. | 69 | 236 | 10 | 38 | 92 | 5 | 9 | 38 | 44 |
| *Podiceps cristatus* | Pod.cri. | 5 | 11 | 1 | 1 | 9 | | | | |
| *Phalacrocorax carbo* | Pha.car. | 154 | 7 248 | 391 | 1 531 | 2 415 | 227 | 348 | 1 160 | 1 176 |
| *Phlacrocorax pygmeus* | Pha.pyg. | 1 | 1 | | | 1 | | | | |
| *Botaurus stellaris* | Bot.ste. | 1 | 1 | | | | | | 1 | |
| *Egretta alba* | Egr.alb. | 37 | 103 | 3 | 1 | 2 | 12 | 1 | 62 | 22 |
| *Ardea cinerea* | Ard.cin. | 268 | 1 456 | 138 | 132 | 320 | 214 | 154 | 250 | 248 |
| *Cygnus olor* | Cyg.olo. | 150 | 2 640 | 132 | 408 | 597 | 637 | 297 | 401 | 168 |
| *Cygnus cygnus* | Cyg.cyg. | 3 | 16 | 14 | 1 | | | | 1 | |
| *Anser fabalis* | Ans.fab. | 10 | 471 | 6 | 4 | 222 | | 87 | 122 | 30 |
| *Anser albifrons* | Ans.alb. | 2 | 701 | | | | | | 701 | |
| *Anser anser* | Ans.ans. | 11 | 1 119 | | 1 | | 1 | | 1 112 | 5 |
| *Anser* spp. | Ans.f/a | 6 | 3 625 | | 350 | | | 12 | 3 263 | |
| *Branta leucopsis* | Bra.leu. | 2 | 2 | 2 | | | | | | |
| *Cairina moschata* | Cai.mos. | 1 | 1 | | | | | | | 1 |
| *Aix galericulata* | Aix gal. | 6 | 13 | | | 2 | 1 | 6 | 1 | 3 |
| *Aix sponsa* | Aix spo. | 1 | 1 | | | | | 1 | | |
| *Anas penelope* | Ana.pen. | 8 | 134 | 4 | 2 | 2 | 1 | | 124 | 1 |
| *Anas strepera* | Ana.str. | 8 | 26 | 2 | 8 | 4 | | 1 | 11 | |
| *Anas crecca* | Ana.cre. | 31 | 418 | 14 | 16 | 49 | 1 | 54 | 266 | 18 |
| *Anas platyrhynchos* | Ana.pla. | 365 | 93 102 | 9 020 | 9 791 | 20 581 | 21 281 | 9 074 | 15 439 | 7 916 |
| *Anas acuta* | Ana.acu. | 5 | 9 | 1 | 6 | | 2 | | | |
| *Anas clypeata* | Ana.cly. | 4 | 15 | 1 | | 2 | | | 7 | 5 |
| *Aythya ferina* | Ayt.fer. | 41 | 775 | 4 | 126 | 578 | 3 | 16 | 41 | 7 |
| *Aythya nyroca* | Ayt.nyr. | 2 | 2 | | | 2 | | | | |
| *Aythya fuligula* | Ayt.ful. | 67 | 3 874 | 23 | 2 017 | 1 689 | 14 | 74 | 24 | 33 |
| *Aythya marila* | Ayt.mar. | 5 | 15 | | 3 | 12 | | | | |
| *Mellanitta fusca* | Mel.fus. | 3 | 6 | | | 4 | | | 1 | 1 |
| *Bucephala clangula* | Buc.cla. | 36 | 740 | 33 | 328 | 111 | 7 | 38 | 216 | 7 |
| *Mergus albellus* | Mer.alb. | 16 | 79 | 1 | 10 | 19 | | 1 | 46 | 2 |
| *Mergus serrator* | Mer.ser. | 3 | 7 | | 5 | 2 | | | | |
| *Mergus merganser* | Mer.mer. | 92 | 1 770 | 202 | 591 | 496 | 24 | 158 | 190 | 109 |
| *Anatinae* spp. | Anas | 13 | 43 | 3 | 1 | 6 | 1 | 1 | 31 | |
| *Haliaeetus albicilla* | Hal.alb. | 29 | 73 | 1 | 3 | 11 | 20 | | 35 | 3 |
| *Gallinula chloropus* | Gal.chl. | 54 | 256 | 7 | 25 | 202 | 1 | 10 | 9 | 2 |
| *Fulica atra* | Ful.atr. | 123 | 7 284 | 97 | 2 209 | 3 875 | 33 | 394 | 362 | 314 |
| *Gallinago gallinago* | Gal.gal. | 1 | 1 | | | | | 1 | | |
| *Tringa ochropus* | Tri.och. | 4 | 4 | | | 2 | | | 1 | 1 |
| *Larus ridibundus* | Lar.rid. | 49 | 3 782 | 8 | 198 | 3 097 | 4 | 19 | 42 | 414 |
| *Larus canus* | Lar.can. | 20 | 1 489 | 8 | 7 | 78 | 2 | | 1 33 | 1 261 |
| *Larus argentatus* | Lar.arg. | 9 | 95 | 2 | 58 | 1 | | | 34 | |
| *Larus cachinnans* | Lar.cac. | 7 | 107 | | | 2 | | | 100 | 5 |
| *Larus cachinans/argentatus* | Lar.a/c | 7 | 940 | | 800 | 126 | | | | 14 |
| *Alcedo atthis* | Alc.ath. | 91 | 169 | 48 | 17 | 34 | 7 | 28 | 14 | 21 |
| *Motacilla cinerea* | Mot.cin. | 16 | 24 | 3 | 4 | 8 | 4 | | 2 | 3 |
| *Motacilla alba* | Mot.alb. | 5 | 7 | 2 | 1 | 2 | | | | 2 |
| *Cinclus cinclus* | Cin.cin. | 61 | 275 | 12 | 8 | 23 | 10 | 132 | 13 | 77 |
| *Emberiza schoeniclus* | Emb.sch. | 1 | 4 | | | | | 4 | | |
| **Number of individuals** | | | 133 183 | 10 197 | 18 703 | 34 676 | 22 514 | 10 920 | 24 260 | 11 913 |
| **Number of species** | | | 49 | 32 | 35 | 36 | 25 | 25 | 36 | 31 |

achieving almost complete coverage of suitable wetlands (Musilová *et al.* 2003, Musilová & Musil 2004).

In January 2004, 300 volunteers recorded 133 183 individuals of 50 waterbird species on 478 wetland sites. Sites included small rivers, sections of larger rivers, reservoirs, the most important fishpond areas, gravel and sand pit lakes, industrial wetlands and also flooded riverine habitats in south Moravia (Fig. 1). A web site www.iwccz.wz.cz was established to assist volunteers involved in this monitoring programme.

Mallard *Anas platyrhynchos* was by far the most abundant bird species, followed by Great Cormorant *Phalacrocorax carbo*, Coot *Fulica atra*, Tufted Duck *Aythya fuligula* and Black-headed Gull *Larus ridibundus*. Mallard was also the most frequent waterbird species recorded, followed by Grey Heron *Ardea cinerea*, Great Cormorant *Phalacrocorax carbo*, Mute Swan *Cygnus olor* and Coot *Fulica atra* (see Table 1, Fig. 2).

White-fronted Goose *Anser albifrons* and Greylag Goose *Anser anser* occurred mainly in South Moravia, and Bean Goose *Anser fabalis* in Central Bohemia and South Moravia. Little Grebe *Tachybaptus ruficollis*, Pochard *Aythya ferina*, Tufted Duck *Aythya fuligula*, Goosander *Mergus merganser* and Coot *Fulica atra* were most abundant in North and Central Bohemia, but Black-headed Gull *Larus ridibundus* and Moorhen *Gallinula chloropus* were the most abundant in Central Bohemia and Goldeneye *Bucephala clangula* occurred mainly in Central Bohemia and South Moravia. Teal *Anas crecca*, Great White Egret *Egretta alba*, Smew *Mergus albellus* and White-tailed Eagle *Haliaetus albicilla* were recorded mainly in South Moravia. Large numbers of Common Gulls *Larus canus* were recorded in North Moravia. Yellow-legged Gull *Larus cachinnans* and Herring Gull *Larus argentatus* were most abundant in North and Central Bohemia and in South Moravia. High numbers of Dippers *Cinclus cinclus* occurred mostly in the highland regions of East Bohemia and North Moravia. Grey Heron *Ardea cinerea*, Mute Swan *Cygnus olor* and Kingfisher *Alcedo atthis* were distributed widely across the whole country (Table 1, Fig. 2).

The following species which are endangered and/or rare in the Czech Republic were recorded: Pygmy Cormorant *Phalacrocorax pygmeus*, Bittern *Botaurus stellaris*, Whooper Swan *Cygnus cygnus*, Barnacle Goose *Branta leucopsis*, Pintail *Anas acuta*, Shoveler *Anas clypeata*, Ferruginous Ducks *Aythya nyroca*, Scaup *Aythya marila* and Velvet Scoter *Melanitta fusca*.

## REFERENCES

**Musilová, Z. & Musil, P.** 2004. The International Waterbird Census in the Czech Republic in 2004. CSO News 59: 33-37. [In Czech with English summary].

**Musilová, Z., Musil, P. & Pellantová, J.** 2003. The International Waterbird Census in the Czech Republic in 1998 - 2003. CSO News 57: 17-23. [In Czech with English summary].

**Pellantová, J.** 1995. The International Waterbird Census in the Czech Republic in winter season 1993/1994. CSO News 40: 3-7. [In Czech with English summary].

**Pellantová, J.** 1996. The International Waterbird Census in the Czech Republic in winter season 1994/1995. CSO News 42: 3-7. [In Czech with English summary].

**Pellantová, J.** 1997. The International Waterbird Census in the Czech Republic in winter season 1995/1996. CSO News 44: 3-8. [In Czech with English summary].

**Pellantová, J.** 1998. The International Waterbird Census in the Czech Republic in winter season 1996/1997. CSO News 46: 2-6. [In Czech with English summary].

Mute Swans *Cygnus olor* in the Czech Republic often over-winter on urban wetlands.  Photo: Katerina Svadova.

# Waterbird censuses in Slovakia

*Jozef Ridzoň*

*Spoloã nos pre ochranu vtáctva na Slovensku, Mlynské nivy 41, 82109 Bratislava, Slovakia. (email: ridzon@sovs.sk)*

Ridzoň, J. 2006. Waterbird census in Slovakia. *Waterbirds around the world.* Eds. G.C. Boere, C.A. Galbraith & D.A. Stroud. The Stationery Office, Edinburgh, UK. p. 487.

The first International Waterbird Census in Slovakia took place in 1967. Initially only the most important sites, such as the Danube River, the Southslovak lowland and some water reservoirs, were counted. These sites were divided into 20 - 40 sections, e.g. such that the length of one section of the Danube River being approximately 8 km.

In 1993 a winter waterbird census was inaugurated in the mountainous region of Orava North Slovakia. From 1994 to 2003, regular waterbird counts were conducted at rivers and brooks covering a total length of 373 km. The streams were divided into between 33 and 59 counting sections (Karaska 1998, 1999, 2000). Nearly all sites with a possible occurrence of waterbirds were counted – even those where only one White-throated Dipper *Cinclus cinclus* wintered. This census in the Orava region provided precise and valuable information about the wintering of rare and dispersed species, such as Jack Snipe *Lymnocryptes minimus*, Common Snipe *Gallinago gallinago,* White-throated Dipper, Green Sandpiper *Tringa ochropus*, and Water Rail *Rallus aquaticus.* The only way to obtain data on such species in Slovakia is to achieve a complete count of streams and lakes.

In 1999 only two regions in Slovakia were counted thoroughly, the Danube River near Bratislava, the most important region for the occurrence of waterbirds and Orava, one of the least important regions for wintering waterbirds. Only a small amount of data concerning the occurrence of waterbirds was available from the other regions in Slovakia. Therefore, in 2000 counts according to the model used in Orava began in all regions of Slovakia where there were enough willing ornithologists and birdwatchers to make counts. In November, December, February and March monthly counts were added, as most sites in Slovakia are frozen in January and at that time of year it is impossible to determine their importance for the migration of waterbirds. The number of counted sites rose from 90 in January 1999, to 377 in January 2003.

The increased extent of the census significantly influenced total numbers counted. In January 1999, a total of 69 220 individuals of 42 species, was counted. In January 2003, after the introduction of the wider census, 101 070 individuals of 51 species were counted. In the other months of the 2002/2003 winter season, only half of the count sections in Slovakia were covered, and consequently the numbers of waterbirds were lower: 57 989 individuals of 51 species in November 2002; 121 257 individuals of 49 species in December 2002; 64 785 individuals of 45 species in February 2003; and 53 698 individuals of 52 species in March 2003.

The most numerous species in all the winter months of 2002/2003 was Mallard *Anas platyrhynchos.* In January, it reached its highest dominance, 46%, although a large number of census sites were rivers, where Mallard is a monodominant species. The second most numerous species for all months was Tufted Duck *Aythya fuligula,* with its dominance fluctuating between 11% and 23%. The third most numerous species from November until January was Pochard *Aythya ferina* with dominance from 8% to 13%, but in February the third most dominant was Goldeneye *Bucephala clangula* (8% dominance), and in March Lapwing *Vanellus vanellus* (14% dominance).

In January 2003, due to the more detailed coverage compared with January 1999, significantly higher numbers of wintering individuals representing more species were recorded, representing an estimated 86% of all waterbirds wintering in Slovakia. The increase in recorded numbers of different species was (number of individuals in January 1999/number in January 2003): Cormorant *Phalacrocorax carbo* 989/5 934; Great Egret *Ardea alba* 35/205, Grey Heron *Ardea cinerea* 158/689, Mute Swan *Cygnus olor* 445 /1 755, Teal *Anas crecca* 273 /727, Mallard *A. platyrhynchos* 22 780 /47 732 , Goosander *Mergus merganser* 99 /439, Green Sandpiper *Tringa ochropus* 7 /16, Kingfisher *Alcedo atthis* 10 /84, Dipper *Cinclus cinclus* 317 /453 .

The most important site for wintering waterbirds in Slovakia was in Hrušovská· zdrž. In December 2002, 74 395 birds were counted there. In January 2003, the most numerous species at this site was the Tufted Duck *Aythya fuligula*, representing 86% of its Slovak population.

The increased number of count sites has provided much improved information about the importance of sites. Along the Váh river, 16 136 wintering waterbirds were recorded, which makes it the second most important river for waterbirds after the Danube river. The Malý Dunaj river was counted along all its entire length for the first time from 2000 – 2003, and in January 2003 a total of 6 064 waterbirds wintered there, representing 6% of the Slovak population of wintering birds.

The counts undertaken from 2000 to 2003 were a near complete census of the most important Slovak rivers, numerous tributaries and the biggest water reservoirs. Such a census has considerably improved the information on the distribution of waterbirds in different winters.

## REFERENCES

Karaska, D. 1998. Zimné sčítavanie vodného vtáctva na Orave v rokoch 1993 – 1998. Zborník Oravského múzea, 15: 175 – 182.

Karaska, D. 1999. Zimné sčítanie vodného vtáctva na Orave v roku 1999. Zborník Oravského múzea, 16: 221 – 224.

Karaska, D. 2000. Zimné sčítanie vodného vtáctva na Orave v roku 2000. Zborník Oravského múzea, 17: 265 – 269.

# Measuring wader recruitment

*Jacquie A. Clark, Robert A. Robinson, Nigel A. Clark & Philip W. Atkinson*
*British Trust for Ornithology, The Nunnery, Thetford, Norfolk, IP24 2PU, UK. (email: Jacquie.Clark@bto.org)*

Clark, J.A., Robinson, R.A., Clark, N.A. & Atkinson, P.W. 2006.  Measuring wader recruitment.  *Waterbirds around the world.* Eds. G.C. Boere, C.A. Galbraith & D.A. Stroud.  The Stationery Office, Edinburgh, UK.  pp. 488-489.

This paper describes methods of measuring wader recruitment from catches of waders in winter. We show how best to analyse the data by using generalized linear models that allow us to account for the nature of the data. We produce national indices for two species and show that breeding populations may differ in their patterns of recruitment.

Counts of waders in the non-breeding season allow us to measure population change, but any changes are driven by variation in recruitment, survival and dispersal. Survival and dispersal can be measured using ringing recoveries and recruitment is normally measured as productivity (chicks/pair) on the breeding grounds. However, the productivity of well-dispersed breeding waders in remote areas is difficult to measure and information for each year is generally only available from a few breeding sites. As waders are easier to study on the non-breeding grounds, an alternative approach is to measure juvenile recruitment there using the proportion of juveniles in catches. For this work, age ratio data from all cannon net catches of waders in winter (November to March) in Britain between 1992 - 1993 and 2002 - 2003 were examined to determine the best way to calculate an index.

Two alternative methods of calculating an index of recruitment were investigated. For the 'Catch' index the proportion of juveniles in each catch is calculated and a mean of the proportions is worked out. However, the 'Catch' index is strongly affected by small catches, which tend to contain a high proportion of juveniles (Boyd & Piersma 2001). This problem can be overcome to some extent by weighting the importance of catches by catch size. However, this is an arbitrary solution. A catch index for all Dunlin *Calidris alpina* and for those in catches of more than 10 and more than 20 birds was calculated.

To avoid the problem of small catches making a disproportionate contribution to the index, an 'Individual' index was calculated. For the 'Individual' index each bird was treated as an individual sample. A linear model with a logit link, binomial error distribution and an overdispersion factor was used. Using this linear model removes the effect of small catches, accounts for aggregation, produces confidence limits and also allows the inclusion of site and other factors (e.g. region). 'Individual' indexes for all Dunlin and all Oystercatchers *Haematopus ostralegus* were calculated. The Oystercatcher data was also split into eastern Britain (where most wintering Oystercatchers are from the breeding population in Norway) and western Britain (where most wintering Oystercatchers are from the breeding population in Iceland).

The 'Catch' index for Dunlin is shown in Fig. 1 and demonstrates how the proportion of juveniles calculated from the catches reduces when small catches are excluded. Fig. 2 shows the 'Individual' index for Dunlin with 95% confidence limits. Figs. 3-5 show the 'Individual' index for Oystercatcher for the whole of Britain. 'Individual' indexes are also show for eastern

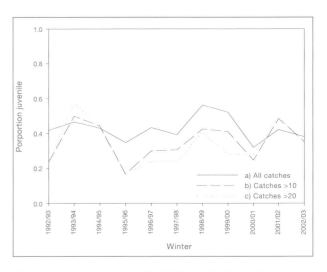

Fig. 1. 'Catch' index for Dunlin *Calidris alba* from all cannon net catches of waders in winter (November to March) in Britain between 1992/93 and 2002/03. All catches, catches with more than 10 birds, and catches with more than 20 birds are shown.

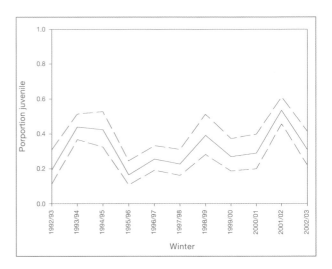

Fig. 2. 'Individual' index for Dunlin *Calidris alba* from all cannon net catches of waders in winter (November to March) in Britain between 1992/93 and 2002/03 with 95% confidence limits.

(largely Norwegian breeders) and western Britain (largely Icelandic breeders). The different patterns of recruitment between regions may reflect differing conditions on the breeding grounds.

This investigation of the calculation of wader recruitment has suggested that an 'Individual' index using linear modelling should be used. This approach allows statistical testing to take place and factors which might affect a catch to be taken into account. It also avoids the over-representation of small catches that tend to contain a higher proportion of juveniles than larger catches.

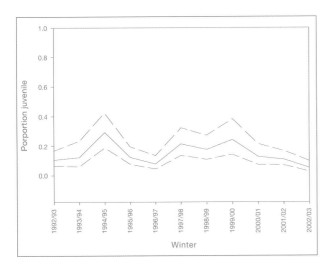

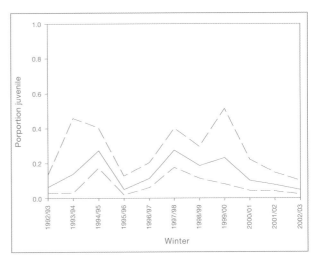

**Fig. 3.** 'Individual' index for Oystercatcher *Haematopus ostralegus* from all cannon net catches of waders in winter (November to March) in Britain between 1992/93 and 2002/03 with 95% confidence limits.

**Fig. 5.** 'Individual' index for Oystercatcher *Haematopus ostralegus* from cannon net catches of waders in winter (November to March) in eastern Britain between 1992/93 and 2002/03 with 95% confidence limits.

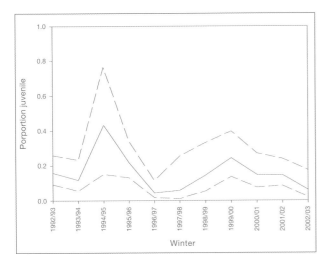

**Fig. 4.** 'Individual' index for Oystercatcher *Haematopus ostralegus* from cannon net catches of waders in winter (November to March) in western Britain between 1992/93 and 2002/03 with 95% confidence limits.

It is relatively easy to obtain data on the proportion juvenile of waders present on the non-breeding grounds in order to monitor recruitment, but these data may not be a straightforward representation of productivity. Further work comparing results from the breeding and non-breeding areas needs to be carried out to validate this technique. In addition, aspects of the birds' biology need to be considered in interpreting the data. For example, birds wintering in one area may be from more than one breeding population. Also adults and juveniles may not be randomly distributed geographically (on a variety of scales).

## ACKNOWLEDGEMENTS

Thanks to all the ringers who worked hard to collect the data on which this paper is based. The British Trust for Ornithology (BTO) Ringing Scheme is funded by a partnership of the BTO, the Joint Nature Conservation Committee (on behalf of English Nature, Scottish Natural Heritage and the Countryside Council for Wales, and also on behalf of the Environment and Heritage Service in Northern Ireland), National Parks and Wildlife (Ireland) and the ringers themselves. This work was funded under the Joint Nature Conservation Committee Advice Contract. Thanks to Steve Freeman, Graham Austin, David Stroud and Hans Meltofte for discussions and comments and to Mark Collier, who input the data.

## REFERENCES

**Boyd, H. & Piersma, T**. 2001. Changing balance between survival and recruitment explains population trends in Red Knots *Calidris canutus islandica* wintering in Britain, 1965-1995. Ardea 89: 301-317.

Gathering and recording biometric and other information from a Dunlin *Calidris alpina*. Photo: Rob Robinson.

# Dynamics of breeding duck populations over the last two decades in key wetlands of the Moscow region

*Olga V. Sukhanova & Alexander L. Mischenko*

*Russian Bird Conservation Union, Shosse Entuziastov, 60, bld.1, Moscow 111123, Russia. (email: almos@redro.msk.ru)*

Sukhanova, O.V. & Mischenko, A.L. 2006. Dynamics of breeding duck populations over the last two decades in key wetlands of the Moscow region. *Waterbirds around the world.* Eds. G.C. Boere, C.A. Galbraith & D.A. Stroud. The Stationery Office, Edinburgh, UK. p. 490.

The Moscow region is one of the most populated and economically developed regions in Russia. The Vinogradovo floodplain and the small number of lakes in the region have remained important for breeding ducks, and different types of artificial wetlands (fishponds, storage reservoirs etc.) have also been created. In the 1980s large numbers of breeding diving ducks used the artificial wetlands and the Vinogradovo floodplain. In the first half of the 1980s, Tufted Duck *Aythya fuligula* broods accounted for more than 50% of all recorded broods of ducks in fishponds with Pochard *Aythya ferina* accounting for approximately 30%. On the Vinogradovo floodplain Tufted Duck broods accounted for 10-13%, Pochard 15-17%; and Pintail *Anas acuta* 8-10%. Broods of Gadwall *Anas strepera* were sporadic.

By the beginning of the 1990s, numbers of breeding ducks in the region had sharply declined and colonies of Black-headed Gull *Larus ridibundus* had almost disappeared from most wetlands. This was primarily due to an increase in recreational activities and the intensity of spring hunting everywhere in the region. On some ponds, paid sport fishing has been introduced. On some systems of fish ponds, employees undertake unregulated hunting in the autumn season. Property development has also increased and many ponds are now surrounded by large groups of dachas and cottages. In the Vinogradovo floodplain cover by emergent water plants has spread widely. All of these factors have negatively affected the regional populations of waterbirds.

From the mid-1980s to the end of the 1990s, the total number of ducks on two pilot fishponds were reduced 1.6 and 2.1-fold and the number for the same period on the Vinogradovo floodplain decreased four-fold. By the end of the 1990s there was a catastrophic decrease in the number of Tufted Duck and Pochard. In 2001-2002 broods of these species were observed in only one fishpond and there were none in the Vinogradovo floodplain. Pintail has completely ceased to breed in the floodplain or in any artificial wetland in the region. However, there was an appreciable growth of the Gadwall population in the Vinogradovo floodplain; forming approximately 15% of all broods in 2001.

Taking into account the very restricted funds of fishpond owners, associations of hunters and local authorities for nature protection, the best way forward for the wise management of fish ponds is an implementation of simple changes or additions to the usual management procedures. These should focus on the creation of islets, the maintenance of the meadow stage of succession and maintenance of emergent vegetation fringing islands. This type of habitat management is cheap; does not require the involvement of many additional people nor any substantial increase in costs for fishpond management.

A management plan for the maintenance of breeding ducks' populations in the Vinogradovo floodplain is under development. It will include guidelines on the expansion of the reserve area, more efficient management of recreation, "waterbird-friendly" agricultural management and cleaning spreading emergent water plants from lakes.

Floodplain wetlands in western Siberia hold important populations of breeding waterbirds as well as providing people with a wide range of ecosystem services, especially fisheries. Photo: Gerard Boere.

# Spotted Crakes *Porzana porzana* breeding in the UK - a history and evaluation of current status

*Ian Francis[1] & David A. Stroud[2]*

*[1]Royal Society for the Protection of Birds, 10 Albyn Terrace, Aberdeen, AB10 1YP, UK. (email: Ian.Francis@rspb.org.uk)*

*[2]Joint Nature Conservation Committee, Monkstone House, City Road, Peterborough, PE1 1JY, UK. (email: David.Stroud@jncc.gov.uk)*

Francis, I. & Stroud, D.A. 2006. Spotted Crakes *Porzana porzana* breeding in the UK - a history and evaluation of current status. *Waterbirds around the world.* Eds. G.C. Boere, C.A. Galbraith & D.A. Stroud. The Stationery Office, Edinburgh, UK. pp. 491-492.

The Spotted Crake *Porzana porzana* is a rare breeding bird in the UK, with around 30-70 pairs nesting annually. It may have increased in recent decades. However, recording standards are poor and an intensive search of new information showed that in most years more than twice as many pairs were breeding than the official record suggested. Totals also reflected observer effort. A failure of observers to submit records is hampering the protection of sites of importance for Spotted Crakes, and the process of rectifying this is time-consuming. Better information flows are urgently needed.

Spotted Crakes are rare breeding birds favouring a small number of sites where suitable wetlands exist. Most records are of singing birds. Some of these records are passed to local bird recorders and then to the UK Rare Breeding Birds Panel, which includes both of the current authors. The panel's reports estimated a UK population of around 30 pairs. A more intensive national survey in 1999 recorded 73 singing males. This study shows that previous annual figures are also underestimates in most years.

Unpublished and published data sources were searched, mainly local bird reports, and many extra records of Spotted

Male Spotted Crake (right) caught in 2000 at Insh Marshes, Scotland and fitted with radio tag, leading to discovery of a nest and chicks (above). Photos: C. Donald, I. Mackenzie.

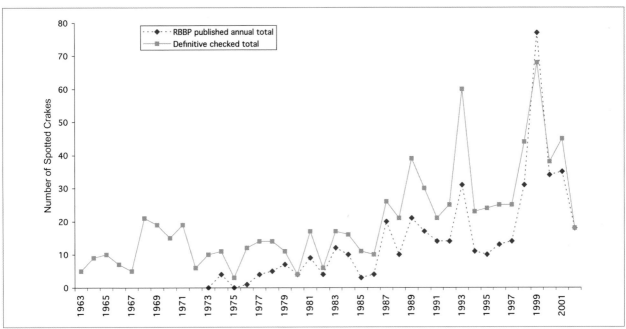

Fig. 1. Graph shows comparison of UK totals (Sharrock 1976, Gibbons *et al.* 1993, Gilbert 2002)

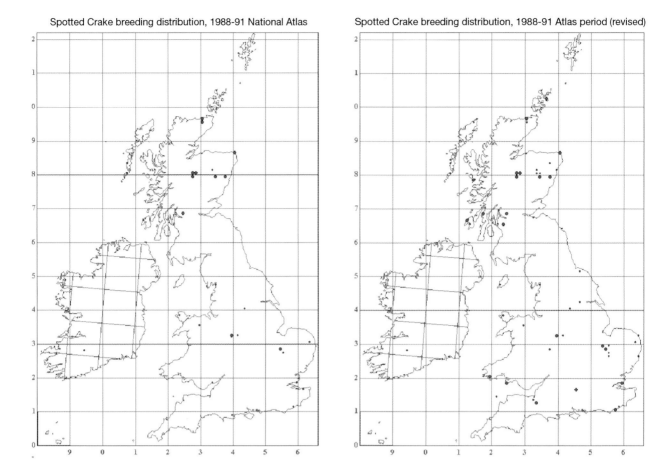

Spotted Crake breeding distribution, 1988-91 National Atlas

Spotted Crake breeding distribution, 1988-91 Atlas period (revised)

**Fig. 2.** Comparison of published UK Atlas map (1988-91) (left) with revised map for same period (right).

Crakes each year were found. Many of these had been poorly recorded and normal reporting processes had not been effective. UK totals were adjusted to take account of the new information and the population trend since the early 1800s was reassessed together with current status and distribution.

Evidence from the 19th Century indicates that Spotted Crakes were once significantly more abundant. During the early 20th Century records were few, but this probably implies very little recording. Since the 1960s, numbers have apparently increased, but periods of more intensive survey, such as national breeding bird atlases and the 1999 survey, produced more records (Fig. 1). However, in all years except 1999, the known totals were significant underestimates and even published atlas maps provide an incomplete picture (Fig. 2).

To protect important sites for rare breeding birds such as Spotted Crakes, good information flows are required, at both local and national levels. This study has highlighted deficiencies in UK data collation processes, and shown that they can be rectified. But this is time-consuming, and an improved system for capture of site-based conservation data is urgently needed.

## ACKNOWLEDGEMENTS

We are grateful to all local observers and county recorders for submitting records to RBBP and to JNCC, the Statutory Country Agencies, RSPB and BTO for provision of information.

Spotted Crake *Porzana porzana* nesting location in Scotland. Photo: Ian Francis

## REFERENCES

**Sharrock, J.T.R.** 1976. The Atlas of Breeding Birds in Britain and Ireland. T. & A.D. Poyser, Calton.

**Gibbons, D.W., Reid, J.B. & Chapman, R.A.** 1993. The New Atlas of Breeding Birds in Britain and Ireland 1988-1991. T. & A.D. Poyser, London.

**Gilbert, G.** 2002. The status and habitat of Spotted Crakes *Porzana porzana* in Britain in 1999. Bird Study 49: 79-86.

# The sixth International White Stork Census: 2004-2005

*Kai-Michael Thomsen & Hermann Hötker*

*Michael-Otto-Institut im NABU, Goosstroot 1, 24861 Bergenhusen, Germany (email: NABU-Inst.Thomsen@t-online.de)*

Thomsen, K. & Hötker, H. 2006. The sixth International White Stork Census: 2004-2005. *Waterbirds around the world*. Eds. G.C. Boere, C.A. Galbraith & D.A. Stroud. The Stationery Office, Edinburgh, UK. pp. 493-495.

The decline of the White Stork *Ciconia ciconia* population early in the 20th century has often been used to highlight problems in the environment, notably the loss of wetlands and the changes in agriculture. This paper presents population trends since 1994/95 and first results of the sixth International White Stork Census.

White Storks have been intensively studied in the past: since 1934 there have been five international censuses (1934, 1958, 1974, 1984, 1994/95). The next international census in 2004-05 is to be co-ordinated again by the German Society for Nature Conservation (NABU, the BirdLife Partner in Germany) and the

Michael-Otto-Institute. The Sixth International White Stork Census is a project of BirdLife International, and it is supported by the Royal Society for the Protection of Birds (RSPB) (BirdLife Partner in Great Britain). Altogether, 40 countries in Europe, Northern Africa, the Middle East and Central Asia will take part in the project. The White Stork will be used as a flagship species for public awareness campaigns by several national BirdLife partner organisations.

The International White Stork Census is taking place in 2004 and 2005. In each country a national coordinator or organ-

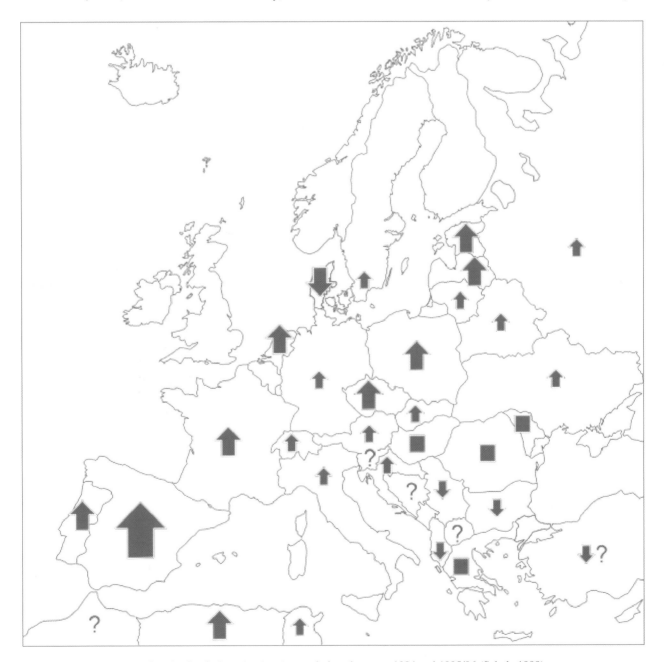

Fig. 1. Population trends of White Stork *Ciconia ciconia* populations between 1984 and 1995/96 (Schulz 1999).

**Table 1. Population trends since 1995/96 in some regions (names of White Stork subpopulations after Schulz 1999).**

| Country | Coverage | Year | Population size | Source | Population change (%) |
|---|---|---|---|---|---|
| **Eastern core population** | | | | | |
| Austria | Total country | 2002 | 366 | BirdLife Austria (in litt.) | +4,6 |
| Czech Republic | Total country | 2003 | 811 | Rejmann 2004 | -4,9 |
| Slovakia | Total country | 2003 | 1 250 | Fulin 2003 | +10,9 |
| Latvia | Estimate | 1999 | | Janaus 2001 | Increase |
| Poland | Obra Valley, Western Poland | 2000 | 43 | Tryjanowski & Kuzniak 2002 | -27,1 |
| Hungary | Total country | 1999 | 5 500 | Lovaszi 2001 | +13,4 |
| Romania | Projection | 1999 | 4 400 | Kósa 2001 | -12,0 |
| Belarus | Projection | 1999 | 11 500 | Samusenko 2000 | -2,5 |
| Ukraine | Estimate | 2003 | 25 000-30 000 | Grishchenko 2004 | ≥42,9 |
| **North western peripheral population** | | | | | |
| Denmark | Total country | 2003 | 1 | Skov in litt. | -83,3 |
| Germany | Total country | 2003 | 4 162 | NABU-BAG Weißstorchschutz 2004 | +2,4 |
| The Netherlands | Total country | 1998 | 326 | van der Have (in litt.) | +22,6 |
| Switzerland | Total country | 2003 | 191 | Storch Schweiz 2004 | +14,4 |
| **South eastern peripheral population** | | | | | |
| Serbia and Montenegro | Vojvodina | 1999 | 998 | Gergelij *et al.,* 2000 | +23,2 |
| **South western core population** | | | | | |
| France | Charente-Maritime | 1998 | 70 | Sériot *et al.,* 1998 | +62,8 |
| **Maghreb population** | | | | | |
| Tunisia | Total country | 1999 | 405 | Azafzaf 2002 | +15,7 |
| Algeria | Total country | 2001 | 5 147 | Moali (in litt). | +92,1 |

**Table 2. Preliminary results of the Sixth International White Stork Census from some participating countries.**

| Country | 1994/95 | 2004 | National co-ordinator |
|---|---|---|---|
| **Western Core Population** | | | |
| Portugal | 3 302 | 7 630 | SPEA, G. Rosa, V. Encarnacao, M. Candelária |
| France | 315 | 941 | Groupe Cigogne France, Aprecial, G. Wey |
| **North western peripheral population** | | | |
| Belgium | ? | 50 | BirdLife Belgium, W. van den Bosche |
| Denmark | 6 | 3 | DOF, H. Skov |
| Germany | 4 063 | 4 710 | NABU, C. Kaatz |
| Sweden | 11 | 29 | O. Olson |
| Switzerland | 167 | 198 | Storch Schweiz, M.& P. Enggist |
| The Netherlands | 266 | 528 | Vogelbescherming Nederland, R. Rietfeld |
| **Eastern core population** | | | |
| Austria | 350 | 392 | BirdLife Austria, E. Karner-Ranner |
| Slovakia | 1 127 | 1 330 | SOVS, M. Fulin |
| Slovenia | ? | 236 | DOPPS, D. Denac |
| Hungary | 4 850 | 5 300 | MME, P. Lovászi |
| **South eastern peripheral population** | | | |
| Greece | 1 500 | 2 139 | T. Kominos |

isation (national BirdLife partners) is responsible for the collection and analysis of data. Where possible the census will cover the total area of the country.

Twenty-four countries participated in the fourth International White Stork Census. This census documented the all time low of the population and revealed a world population size of no more than 135 000 breeding pairs (Rheinwald 1989,

Schulz 1999). Over ten years since the previous census the decline in the western population (20%) was much greater than in the eastern population (10%) (Rheinwald 1989).

Ten years later the fifth International Census documented a population increase of 23%, and the new population estimate was 166 000 pairs (Schulz 1999). White Stork populations had increased in nearly all countries and regions, except Denmark,

Serbia, Bulgaria, Albania and perhaps Turkey (Fig. 1). The western population has increased by about 75% since 1984 whereas the eastern population has increased by only 15%.

There are different reasons for the population increase between 1984 and 1994/95. The strong increase of the western population is attributed to better climatic conditions in the wintering areas in the western Sahel and the development of a wintering population in southern Spain (Tortosa *et al.* 1995). On the Iberian peninsula the increase in the number of irrigated fields and the attractiveness of large garbage dumps for storks may have improved feeding conditions for breeding storks (Schulz 1999).

The reasons for the smaller increase in the eastern population are not clear. The economic difficulties in central and eastern Europe after 1990 and their influence on the intensity of farming possibly had a positive effect on the reproductive success of White Storks.

Since the last (fifth) international census White Stork populations have changed in different ways. In south-western Europe and in the Maghreb region numbers of Storks have increased rapidly. In western central Europe there has been an increase until 2000 and a slight decrease thereafter (Table 1). In most countries the numbers of White Stork are nowadays higher than in 1994/95.

We have received preliminary results of the Sixth International Census from eleven countries (Table 2). In most of them populations of White Storks have increased since the previous census. The largest increases in population size were recorded in those regions inhabited by storks migrating on the western flyway. Here the numbers went up by more than 100%. Populations also increased, however, in the regions hosting storks that migrate on the eastern flyway.

## REFERENCES

**Rheinwald G.** 1989. Versuch einer Bilanz. In: G. Rheinwald, J. Ogden & H. Schulz (eds.) Weißstorch - White Stork. Proceedings of the First International Stork Conservation Symposium. Schriftenreihe des DDA 10: 221-227.

**Schulz H.** (ed.) 1999. Weißstorch im Aufwind? White Storks on the up? Proceedings of an International Symposium on the White Stork, Hamburg 1996. NABU (Naturschutzbund Deutschland e.V.), Bonn: 351-365.

**Tortosa F.S., Mannez M. & Barcell M.** 1995. Wintering white storks (*Ciconia ciconia*) in south west Spain in the years 1991 and 1992. Vogelwarte 38: 41–45.

White Storks *Ciconia ciconia* in the Turkish region of Uluabat Lake. These birds have always had a long association with houses and other man-man structures. Photo: Kai-Michael Thomsen.

# Monitoring of waterbirds at Bourgas wetlands, Bulgaria

*Lyubomir Profirov[1], Milko Dimitrov[1], Tanyo Michev[2] & Konstantin Nyagolov[1]*

[1] *Bourgas Wetlands Project, 8000 Bourgas, PO Box 189, Bulgaria. (email: lovebird@techno-link.com)*
[2] *Laboratory for General Ecology, 2 Gagarin Str., Central, 1113 Sofia, Bulgaria.*

Profirov, L., Dimitrov, M., Michev, T. & Nyagolov, K. 2006. Monitoring of waterbirds at Bourgas wetlands, Bulgaria. *Waterbirds around the world.* Eds. G.C. Boere, C.A. Galbraith & D.A. Stroud. The Stationery Office, Edinburgh, UK. pp. 496-497.

The Bourgas wetlands are the most important ornithological complex in Bulgaria and play a significant role in the conservation of biodiversity in the country. In 1984 Atanasovsko Lake was declared a Ramsar site. Since February 2003, three further sites have gained Ramsar status: Pomoriysko Lake – 814 ha, Vaya Lake – 2 900 ha and Poda Lagoon, including Foros Bay – 307 ha. These sites have been important for many international and Bulgarian ornithologists since the second half of the 19th century (Reiser 1894, Jordans 1940, Patev 1950, Mountfort & Fergusson-Lees 1961, Prostov 1964, Nankinov & Darakchiev 1977, Michev & Profirov 2003, Michev *et al.* 2004).

This paper presents the results of the monthly ornithological monitoring of the Bourgas wetlands from 1996 to 2002. The monitoring covered all natural and some selected artificial wetlands in the Bourgas wetland region, with a total area of c. 9 500 ha. All data were collated to form a single "average" year. This hypothetical year starts with spring migration (March, April and May), followed by the breeding season (June and July), autumn migration (August, September, October and November) and winter (December, January and February). Aerial surveys were conducted by plane and helicopter to count birds breeding in colonies in the reed beds of lakes and to obtain the exact positions of all breeding localities.

Of the 153 species of waterbirds found in the region six are residents, 48 are breeding summer visitors, 34 non-breeding summer visitors, 105 migrants, 92 winter visitors and 17 vagrants. These results indicate that the Bourgas wetlands have the highest diversity of waterbird species during migration time. Highest numbers are observed in the winter period, with large concentrations of geese, ducks, diving ducks, waders etc. During the breeding season, species diversity is relatively poor. The highest number of waterbird species in a single monitoring scheme was in September 1999, with 71 species recorded and

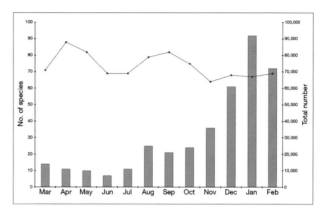

**Fig. 1.** Average total numbers and average species number of waterbirds in all Bourgas lakes.

the highest total number of waterbirds recorded was in December 2000, with 186 236 individuals. The seasonal dynamic of average total numbers of waterbirds and average species numbers are presented in Fig. 1, with the average monthly numbers of all waterbirds at the different lakes of the Bourgas wetlands presented in Fig. 2.

The biggest concentrations of waterbirds were recorded during the winter months from December to February in the freshwater basins of Vaya and Mandra lakes. The ten most numerous waterbird species in the Bourgas wetlands are presented in Table 1.

The results obtained indicate that the Bourgas wetlands are of international importance for many waterbird species. Among them are several globally threatened species with the maximum numbers recorded as follows: Pygmy Cormorant *Phalacrocorax pygmeus* 10 600 in December 1999; Dalmatian Pelican *Pelecanus crispus* 647 wintering in January 1999, Red-breasted

**Table 1. Bourgas wetland monthly average numbers of the ten most numerous waterbird species in descending order of their highest average monthly numbers.**

| Species Month | Mar | Apr | May | Jun | Jul | Aug | Sep | Oct | Nov | Dec | Jan | Feb |
|---|---|---|---|---|---|---|---|---|---|---|---|---|
| *Anser albifrons* | 666 | 8 | 1 | 2 | 0 | 0 | 0 | 75 | 2 | 3 927 | 45 545 | 40 456 |
| *Aythya ferina* | 1 598 | 432 | 156 | 81 | 419 | 907 | 1 549 | 6 372 | 11 448 | 14 387 | 9 566 | 7 879 |
| *Fulica atra* | 1 703 | 194 | 26 | 36 | 103 | 1 180 | 1 946 | 3 793 | 5 843 | 10 859 | 12 000 | 7 065 |
| *Anas platyrhynchos* | 1 002 | 222 | 108 | 518 | 247 | 798 | 2 032 | 2 334 | 2 663 | 9 232 | 6 298 | 4 009 |
| *Aythya fuligula* | 729 | 137 | 2 | 1 | 14 | 10 | 7 | 835 | 627 | 2 946 | 5 602 | 7 176 |
| *Larus ridibundus* | 231 | 592 | 302 | 350 | 3 299 | 5 962 | 3 118 | 1 505 | 1 304 | 2 184 | 1 438 | 1 102 |
| *Phacrocorax carbo* | 769 | 609 | 628 | 837 | 742 | 1 395 | 1 520 | 2 203 | 2 178 | 4 138 | 3 969 | 2 654 |
| *Branta ruficollis* | 1 | 0 | 0 | 0 | 0 | 0 | 0 | 0 | 0 | 15 | 3 981 | 676 |
| *Phalacrocorax pygmeus* | 1 071 | 433 | 33 | 5 | 7 | 67 | 134 | 260 | 787 | 3 626 | 2 710 | 513 |
| *Anas crecca* | 364 | 104 | 5 | 2 | 1 | 24 | 314 | 1 099 | 2 025 | 3 153 | 976 | 872 |

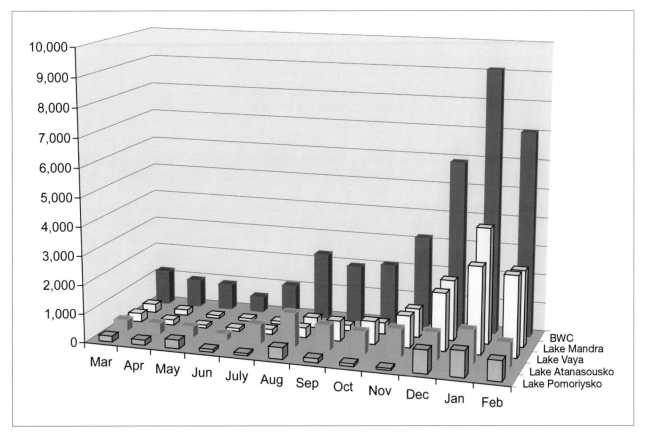

**Fig. 2.** Average monthly numbers of all waterbirds seen at the different Bourgas Lakes.

Goose *Branta ruficollis* 23 738 in January 1996, White-headed Duck *Oxyura leucocephala* 2 260 in March 1999, Ferruginous Duck *Aythya nyroca* 111 in September 1999.

With so many Ramsar sites in one ecological complex the perspective of our future activities is very clear; to develop the project "Bourgas Wetlands" to establish a National Wetland Center and increase international cooperation.

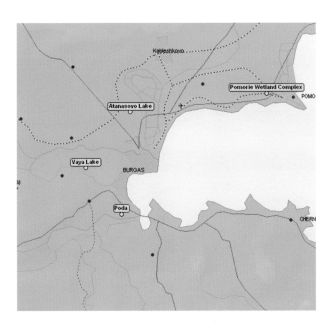

**Fig. 3.** Bourgas Ramsar sites map. Source: Ramsar Sites Information Service (RSIS); © Wetlands International.

## REFERENCES

**Dimitrov, M., Michev, T., Profirov, L. & Nyagolov, K.** In press. Waterbirds of Bourgas Wetlands: results and evaluation of the monthly waterbird monitoring 1996-2002. Bulgarian Biodiversity Foundation & Publishing House Pensoft, Sofia.

**Jordans, A.V.** 1940. Ein Beitrag zur Kenntnis der Vögelwelt Bulgariens. Mitt. Naturw. Inst., Sofia 13: 49-152.

**Michev, T. & Profirov, L.** 2003. Midwinter Numbers of Waterbirds in Bulgaria (1977-2001). Results from 25 years of mid-winter counts carried out at the most important Bulgarian Wetlands. Publishing House Pensoft, Sofia. 160 pp.

**Michev, T., Profirov, L., Dimitrov, M. & Nyagolov, K.** 2004. The Birds of Lake Atanasovsko: Status and Check List. Second Edition. Bourgas Wetlands Publication Series 5. Bulgarian Biodiversity Foundation, Project "Bourgas Wetlands", Bourgas. 44 pp.

**Mountfort, G.J. & Fergusson-Lees, J.** 1961. Observation on the Birds of Bulgaria. Ibis 103a: 443-471.

**Patev, P.** 1950. The Birds of Bulgaria. Sofia: Bulgarian Academy of Sciences: 364 pp. [In Bulgarian with English summary].

**Prostov, A.** 1964. Contribution on the Ornithofauna of Bourgas Region. Bull. de l'Institut de zoologie et musée, Sofia 15: 5-68. [In Bulgarian with Russian and German summary].

**Reiser, O.** 1894. Materialien zu einer Ornis balcanica. II. Bulgarien. In: Commission bei Carl Gerold's Sohn, Wien. 204 pp.

# Monitoring overlapping populations: the Greylag Goose *Anser anser* in the Iceland-Britain flyway

*Richard Hearn[1] & Morten Frederiksen[2,3]*

[1] *The Wildfowl & Wetlands Trust, Slimbridge, Gloucestershire, GL2 7BT, UK. (email: Richard.Hearn@wwt.org.uk)*

[2] *Icelandic Institute of Natural History, PO Box 5320, IS-125 Reykjavik, Iceland.*

[3] *Present address: Centre for Ecology & Hydrology, Hill of Brathens, Banchory, Aberdeenshire, AB31 4BW, UK.*

Hearn, R. & Frederiksen, M. 2006. Monitoring overlapping populations: the Greylag Goose *Anser anser* in the Iceland-Britain flyway. *Waterbirds around the world.* Eds. G.C. Boere, C.A. Galbraith & D.A. Stroud. The Stationery Edinburgh, Office, UK. pp. 498-499.

Greylag Geese *Anser anser* in Britain are comprised of three populations. This paper discusses the difficulties of monitoring these populations and reports on changes in survey procedures designed to overcome these difficulties.

Three populations of Greylag Goose are currently recognised in the UK: the Iceland Greylag Goose – a migratory population present between October and April, and two sedentary populations - the NW Scotland Greylag Goose and the re-established Greylag Goose. NW Scotland Greylag Geese are the remnant of a population that was once more widespread in Britain, and predominantly occur in western Scotland with others in mainland northern Scotland. The re-established Greylag Goose was reintroduced into this former range, predominantly by hunters, between the 1930s and 1960s, and in most cases stock derived directly from the NW Scotland population. Whilst the two sedentary populations have increased in abundance and distribution in recent years, best available data indicate that the Iceland Greylag Geese declined by approximately 20% during the 1990s.

Monitoring population parameters for most UK goose populations is achieved through The Wildfowl & Wetlands Trust's (WWT) Goose Monitoring Programme (GMP): a suite of integrated surveys that provide estimates of abundance and distribution, reproductive success, movements and survival. Estimates of abundance of Iceland Greylag Geese have been made annually since 1960 through the Icelandic-breeding Goose Census (IGC): counts of the two sedentary populations are conducted at least annually in most key areas, and are supported by more comprehensive surveys on a nine-yearly basis. All are currently site-based look-see surveys, with no attempt to locate birds away from sites known to support them.

In recent decades, changes in abundance and distribution mean that these populations now overlap in many areas where they were formerly discrete. This has provided complications for monitoring protocols, and thus the assessment of conservation status. Recent modelling (see Frederiksen *et al.* 2004) found that the IGC and estimates of harvest rate in Iceland were incompatible for Iceland Greylag Goose; using each of these data sources

The Loch of Strathbeg in Aberdeenshire is of international importance as a roost for the Icelandic population of Greylag Geese *Anser anser*, holding over 3% of the total population, with peak use in the mid-winter period. Photo: David Stroud.

in population models provided widely differing estimates of abundance. In other words, either the Icelandic hunting bag was over-estimated or the IGC missed a proportion of the population (or both to a lesser degree).

Examination of the way in which hunting bag data in Iceland are reported found no evidence of widespread identification problems, or that double-reporting was an important bias. This suggested that underestimation of the autumn population size was a problem, either through undercounting in the UK or due to a large part of the population wintering outside the UK. A workshop that reviewed the results of Frederiksen *et al.* (2004) lead to the production of a series of recommendations for future monitoring effort (Frederiksen 2001) that are now providing the basis for initiatives under development as part of the GMP.

Progress has already begun with a number of these. Closer collaboration with other countries supporting wintering Iceland Greylag Geese has been developed, so that counts from there are now included as part of the IGC. This includes Norway, where recent re-encounters of marked birds have highlighted the presence of a regular flock, previously believed to be over wintering birds from the Northwest Europe population. Surveys have yet to establish whether other flocks of Iceland Greylag Geese occur regularly. Recommendations on methodological changes to the current IGC that would establish whether large numbers of Iceland Greylag Geese in the UK are currently undetected have been made, and moves to implement these are underway. This includes the development of a September count and a stratified sample survey. Finally, material is being collected for stable isotope analysis to test whether this is an effective way of estimating the proportion of migratory and sedentary Greylag Geese in different parts of the UK, and thus address the identification problems posed by the presence of other populations.

The current difficulties with monitoring Greylag Geese in the UK pose a number of problems for conservationists wishing to secure a favourable conservation status for these populations and achieve effective allocation of conservation resources. They also highlight issues for all surveys dealing with overlapping populations: changes in biological patterns may require methodological changes to be made to surveillance tools, and it is vital that methods are reviewed as part of any monitoring programme in order to ensure continued effectiveness. Questions are also raised about the future likelihood of continuing to monitor three separate Greylag Goose populations in the Iceland-Britain flyway and the consequences of this for biodiversity conservation.

## ACKNOWLEDGEMENTS

The contribution to this work by a number of colleagues, notably Carl Mitchell, Arnór Sigfússon and Bob Swann is gratefully acknowledged. A partnership between the Wildfowl & Wetlands Trust and the Joint Nature Conservation Committee has provided funding for much of the count surveys to date. The Peter Scott Trust for Education and Research in Conservation also provided invaluable support for the continuation of other fieldwork, notably ringing. Finally, the GMP would not exist without the support of a network of dedicated volunteer fieldworkers that collect data and ring birds – their continued support is very much appreciated.

## REFERENCES

**Frederiksen, M**. 2001. Icelandic-British workshop on grey geese, Hvanneyri, Iceland, 28-30 September 2001: Proceedings and recommendations. Náttúrufræðistofnun Íslands, Reykjavík.

**Frederiksen, M., Hearn, R.D., Mitchell, C., Sigfússon, A. Swann, R.L. & Fox, A.D.** 2004. The size and dynamics of Icelandic-breeding goose populations: a reassessment of the evidence. Journal of Applied Ecology 41: 315-334.

Greylag Goose *Anser anser*. Photo: Paul Marshall.

# Monitoring and mapping of waders breeding in northernmost Sweden

*Åke Lindström*

*Department of Animal Ecology, Lund University, Ecology Building, S - 223 62 Lund, Sweden. (email: ake@lindstrom@zooekol.lu.se)*

Lindström, Å. 2006. Monitoring and mapping of waders breeding in northernmost Sweden. *Waterbirds around the world*. Eds. G.C. Boere, C.A. Galbraith & D.A. Stroud. The Stationery Office, Edinburgh, UK. p. 500.

Wader species of the northern taiga and tundra regions are difficult to map and monitor on their breeding grounds. Many of them, for example the *Tringa* sandpipers and snipes, are difficult to follow also during winter due to their wide wintering areas and lack of large concentrations. Good monitoring data are scarce for most of these species.

The northern half of Sweden, approximately 61-69° N, consists mainly of taiga, rich in small water bodies suitable for waders, with areas of mountainous tundra farthest to the west and north. Systematic data on distribution and population trends have so far been lacking for the 25 waders species breeding in the area. The Swedish Breeding Bird Atlas (Svensson *et al.* 1999) recorded the presence or absence of birds in 5 km x 5 km squares in the 1970s and 1980s, but only 18% of the area was well covered and data were only available for one year for each square.

A scheme with 724 fixed routes systematically distributed over the whole of Sweden was launched in 1996 as a part of the Swedish Bird Survey (Fig. 1). The aim is to complement the system of point count routes running since 1975 that mainly covers southern Sweden. Routes are positioned on fixed coordinates on the Swedish Grid, and there are 25 km between the routes in W-E and N-S direction. The systematic distribution of routes should result in a representative coverage of the most widespread habitats.

A fixed route consists of an 8 km line transect, formed as a 2 x 2 km square with a 5 minute point count every full km. The route is walked clockwise, starting 04:00. All birds seen or heard are recorded. The person counting may deviate 200 m from the transect, but outside this distance counting stops. It is resumed when the line ± 200 m can be reached again. Census date varies between late May and early July depending on latitude. Although the scheme best covers passerines, many waders are also recorded.

About 400 of the fixed routes are situated in the northern taiga and tundra regions. Some of them are located in inaccessible areas involving one or two days of walking to reach the route, but a network of roads (due to forestry activities) make most routes readily accessible by car. The aim is to count each route annually, but in practice, many routes will only be visited every 2-5 years. About 200 routes were counted in northern Sweden in 2003, the best year so far. About half of these were carried out by volunteers and the other half by paid people. The scheme has been adopted by several Regional Administrative Boards as their regional monitoring tool, and the economic and logistic support from this cooperation greatly helps covering the routes.

As an example, relative densities of the Wood Sandpiper *Tringa glareola* increase from about 1.2 birds per 8 km line transect in the southern part of its range to 5.6 birds per 8 km line transect in the far north (Fig. 1). There is no significant population trend in 1996-2003 (Fig. 2).

For the first time there is the potential to monitor population trends and relative densities of species like Golden Plover *Pluvialis apricaria* (369 birds recorded on 50 different northern

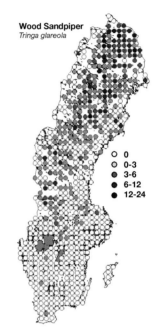

Fig. 1. The average number of Wood Sandpipers *Tringa glareola* recorded per year on the 8 km line transects (1-8 years per route). Each dot represents a fixed route. Empty spaces indicate routes no yet censused.

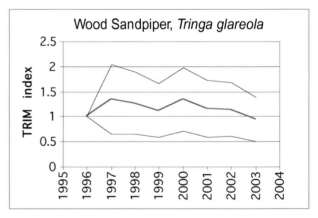

Fig. 2. Yearly indices (in red) with 95% CI for each year in relation to the starting year. Calculated using TRIM (Pannekoek & van Strien 2001).

routes in 2003), Whimbrel *Numenius phaeopus* (124/46), Wood Sandpiper (423/110), Greenshank *Tringa nebularia* (217/77) and Spotted Redshank *Tringa erythropus* (32/18), on their remote breeding grounds.

## REFERENCES

**Pannekoek, J. & van Strien, A. 2001.** TRIM 3 Manual (TRends and Indices for Monitoring data). Statistics Nederlands, Voorburg.

**Svensson, S., Svensson, M. & Tjernberg, M. 1999.** Svensk Fågelatlas. Vår Fågelvärld, supplement 31, Stockholm.

# The development of a database for the Spoon-billed Sandpiper *Eurynorhynchus pygmeus*

*Gillian Bunting & Christoph Zöckler*

*World Conservation Monitoring Center, 219 Huntington Road, Cambridge, CB3 ODL, UK. (email: Christoph.Zockler@wcmc.org.uk)*

Bunting, G. & Zöckler, C. 2006. The development of a database for the Spoon-billed Sandpiper *Eurynorhynchus pygmeus*. *Waterbirds around the world*. Eds. G.C. Boere, C.A. Galbraith & D.A. Stroud. The Stationery Office, Edinburgh, UK. pp. 501-502.

Recent research on the breeding areas of the Spoon-billed Sandpiper *Eurynorhynchus pygmeus* indicated a sharp decline in the population (Tomkovich *et al.* 2002, Zöckler *et al.* 2006, Syroechkovski *et al.* in press). The species has been upgraded in the Red List and is now considered as Endangered (BirdLife 2004). At the seventh Conference of the Parties to the Convention on the Conservation of Migratory Species of Wild Animals (CMS) in Bonn, 2002, it was agreed to promote and support the development of a species Action Plan. Furthermore, the globally threatened status and lack of knowledge about the Spoon-billed Sandpiper led to the formation of a Recovery Team, which had its first meeting at the conference giving rise to these proceedings.

The Action Plan requires accurate, comprehensive and up to date data on species distribution and abundance, in the form of a species database. Although this information is largely available for breeding areas (Lappo *et al.* in press), data on migration or wintering grounds are missing and have not been captured in a central database.

The ultimate aim of the database is to allow easy analysis of the data both over time, to formulate population trends, and spatially, to assess distribution and migration patterns. However, for cost effectiveness and flexibility, the database structure has been kept as simple as possible. A relational database in MS Access has been constructed, with two linked tables. One contains the information specific to a particular location, while the other details individual sightings.

The Locations table is based on information published by Birdlife (2001). Information on the location of sites is available for each species from the Birdlife web site at www.birdlife.org As well as a site name and coordinates, to link to GIS, this table contains all available information on habitats. However, information is currently limited and there is scope for further development.

The Observations table is also based on information by Birdlife (2001), textual information from the species account has been converted to tabular form. Key fields include the date of observation, number of birds, observers name or published reference and the site name. Where available, data on age, sex and ring recoveries are also added. Many historical records, which did not contain full date or site information, could not be

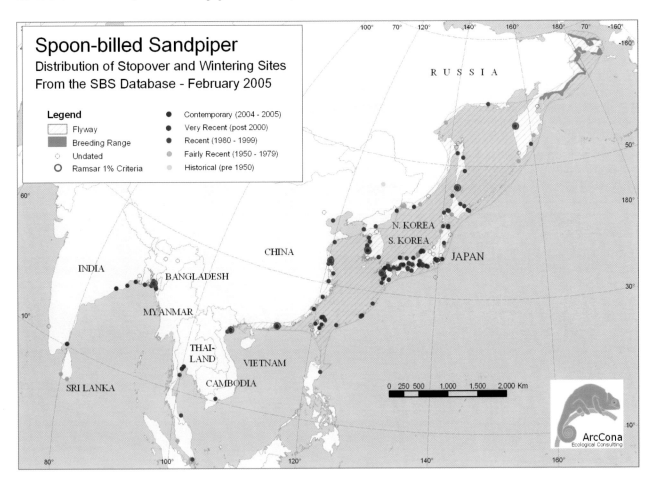

**Fig. 1.** Distribution of stopover and wintering sites for the Spoon-billed Sandpiper *Eurynorhynchus pygmeus*.

included in this structure. Work is currently progressing to bring the information content of the database up do date, and records published on the internet from 2001 to the present are captured as well as many unpublished observations. At present, the database contains 250 site location records and 300 discrete observations. The authors are aware of many more observations, which are not yet included, and anyone with observations is kindly requested to send it to the authors.

Four new locations have been added to the 'Locations' table. These include the Indian Sunderbans, the Mekong Delta, a new area of the Inner Gulf of Thailand and Yuboo Island in South Korea, all of which are highly significant.

In the Indian Sundarbans delta, Sharma (2003) describes observations from eight different locations made in November and December 2001, with up to 14 sightings recorded. Although these observations were not substantiated in 2005 (Zöckler *et al.* in press) large flocks in neighbouring Bangladesh point to potentially crucial wintering sites in this region. The largest flock ever recorded outside a breeding area was in the outer sandbanks of the Ganges Delta in Bangladesh (Howes & Parish 1989). This evidence, combined with early results from stable isotope analysis (Zöckler *et al.*, this volume) suggest that the Ganges delta may be a core area of the wintering range.

In the Mekong Delta, an observation made in southern Vietnam is significant, as it was the first from that region. Its location, at the southern tip of Indochina, supports the suggestion that at least some birds migrate along the coastline instead of taking an overland route.

The Inner Gulf of Thailand is one of the most closely watched areas within the wintering range, due to its proximity to the city of Bangkok. It is not unexpected, therefore, that Spoon-billed Sandpiper were observed for the first time at Pak Thale in Thailand. However, it is of some concern that this site, and other parts of the Gulf, are apparently under threat from a major infrastructure development project.

Finally, Yuboo Island is the location of one of the very few recoveries of a leg-flagged Spoon-billed Sandpiper. A juvenile bird was seen there in late September 2004, which was ringed in July 2004 in Meinopylgino, Chukotka, Russia.

Continuation of data collection and recording is essential for both species conservation and the development of the Action Plan. The development of the database and the Action Plan are closely linked and should be developed jointly, in close collaboration with BirdLife International and Wetlands International. The analysis of data feed directly into the Action Plan, which will prioritise future research and conservation efforts.

## ACKNOWLEDGEMENTS

Without the vision and experience of E.E. Syroechkovski the present fragile status of the species would not have been recognised. We thank the organiser of the Russian Arctic expeditions and the many co-workers. We also thank Mike Crosby from BirdLife International for his continuing support.

## REFERENCES

**Birdlife International** 2001. Threatened Birds of Asia, Birdlife International, Cambridge, UK.

**BirdLife International** 2004. Threatened Birds of the World. Lynx & BirdLife International, Barcelona, Cambridge. CD –Rom

**Howes, J., & Parish, D.** 1989. Shorebirds in Asia: Progress on studies and priorities for future activities. Presented at the ICBP/East Asian Bird Protection Conference. 17th-20th April 1989, Bangkok, Thailand.

**Sharma, A.** 2003. First records of Spoon-billed Sandpiper *Calidris pygmaeus* in the Indian Sundabarns delta, West Bengal. Forktail 19: 136-137.

**Syroechkovski, E.E., Lappo, E.G., Zöckler, C., Morozov, V.V., Kashiwagi, M. & Taldenkov, I**. in press. The Importance of the Mainopylgyno area, Chukotka, Russia for the breeding of Spoon-billed Sandpiper (*Eurhynorhynchus pygmeus*)

**Tomkovich, P.S., Syroechkovski Jr. E.E., Lappo, E.G. & Zöckler, C.** 2002. Sharp population decline in spoon-billed sandpiper, *Eurynorhynchus pygmeus*, the globally threatened species. Bird Conservation International 12: 1-18.

**Zöckler, C., Syroechkovski, E. E., Lappo, E. G. & Bunting, G. C.** 2006. Stable Isotope analysis to determine the wintering sites of the declining Spoon-billed Sandpiper (*Eurynorhynchus pygmeus*) in the Asian Pacific Flyway. Waterbirds around the world. G.C. Boere, C.A. Galbraith & D.A. Stroud (Eds.), The Stationery Office, Edinburgh, UK. 147-153.

Southern Chukotka, breeding habitat of Spoon-billed Sandpiper *Eurynorhynchus pygmeus*. Photo: Christoph Zöckler.

# Population size and trend of the Red-crested Pochard *Netta rufina* in southwest/central Europe: an update

*Verena Keller*

*Schweizerische Vogelwarte/Swiss Ornithological Institute, CH-6204 Sempach, Switzerland. (email: verena.keller@vogelwarte.ch)*

Keller, V. 2006. Population size and trend of the Red-crested Pochard *Netta rufina* in southwest/central Europe: an update. *Waterbirds around the world*. Eds. G.C. Boere, C.A. Galbraith & D.A. Stroud. The Stationery Office, Edinburgh, UK. pp. 503-504.

The southwest/central European flyway population of the Red-crested Pochard *Netta rufina* is assumed to be a distinct population separate from the eastern European and Asian ones (Scott & Rose 1996, Defos du Rau 2002). An analysis of the results of the International Waterbird Census (IWC) up to 1994 indicated that the overall population size of the southwest/central European flyway population had not increased but that birds had shifted their winter distribution (Keller 2000a, 2000b). This was most likely the consequence of a drought period in Spain and improved wintering conditions in central Europe. This paper updates the situation to 2001, based on the data from the mid-winter counts of the IWC.

Since 1994, wintering numbers of the Red-crested Pochard in central Europe have continued to increase, but numbers in the western Mediterranean have been fluctuating (Fig. 1). Trends and Indicators for Monitoring Data (TRIM) analyses (Pannekoek & van Strien 1998) indicate a significant increase of the total flyway population for the period 1990 to 2001 (overall index trend: $1.0698 \pm 0.0115$). However, high overdispersion and strong fluctuations of numbers at individual sites result in a poor statistical fit of the model. Thus the long-term trend is difficult to interpret, also because coverage by the IWC of sites

used by Red-crested Pochard prior to 1990 was limited (Keller 2000a).

Since the 1990s, Red-crested Pochards have overwintered mainly in Spain and Switzerland/Germany (Fig. 2). They are concentrated on a small number of sites. The six most important sites - Albufera de Valencia and Delta del Ebro in Spain, Bodensee (Switzerland, Germany and Austria), Lac de Neuchâtel and Vierwaldstättersee in Switzerland and Camargue in France hold, on average, about 75% of the total flyway population.

Red-crested Pochards can shift between sites in large numbers within short periods. If censuses are not well co-ordinated the risk of double-counting, or of missing large flocks, is high. Shifts and the high concentrations on a few sites may result in high proportions of the population being missed or double-counted. In 1999, the year with a peak count of 40 000 individuals, the waterbird census on the three main lakes in Switzerland/Germany took place on the same date (17 January). Censuses in Spain were also carried out in mid-January, but exact counting dates are not available.

In the second edition of Waterbird Population Estimates (Rose & Scott 1997) the size of the southwest/central European flyway population was estimated at 25 000 individuals. In the

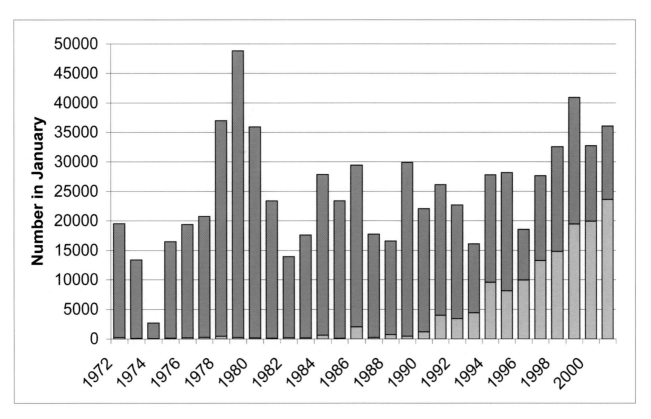

Fig. 1. Mid-winter numbers of Red-crested Pochards *Netta rufina* in the western Mediterranean (mainly Spain, Portugal and France; dark) and in central Europe (mainly Switzerland and Germany; light) 1972—2001. Data from the International Waterbird Census (IWC).

**Fig. 2.** Main wintering sites of Red-crested Pochards *Netta rufina* in south-west and central Europe in the 1990s.

third edition (Wetlands International 2002) the estimate was increased to 50 000, a revision based largely on the 40 000 individuals counted in January 1999. Although this 1999 census result appears to be realistic, even though double counts cannot be excluded, the total population estimate of 50 000 seems to be rather high. The main sites used by Red-crested Pochards have been well covered from 1996 onwards, making it unlikely that 10 000 individuals were missed in these years.

## ACKNOWLEDGEMENTS

Thanks go to all the waterbird counters collaborating in the IWC and to the national coordinators for permission to use their data. Special thanks go to B. Deceuninck and J. Wahl who provided additional data for France and Germany and to R. Martí, B. Molina and J.C. del Moral who answered many questions on the Spanish data.

## REFERENCES

**Defos du Rau, P.** 2002. Elements for a red-crested pochard (*Netta rufina*) management plan. Gibier Faune Sauvage, Game and Wildlife 19: 89-141.

**Keller, V.** 2000a. Winter distribution and population change of Red-crested Pochard *Netta rufina* in southwestern and central Europe. Bird Study 47: 176-185.

**Keller, V.** 2000b. Winterbestand und Verbreitung der Kolbenente *Netta rufina* in der Schweiz und im angrenzenden Ausland. Ornithol. Beobachter. 97: 175-190.

**Pannekoek, J. & van Strien, A.** 1998. TRIM 2.0 for Windows (Trends & Indices for Monitoring data). Research paper No. 9807. Statistics Netherlands, Voorburg.

**Rose, P.M. & Scott, D.A.** 1997. Waterfowl Population Estimates - Second Edition. Wetlands International Publication 44. Wetlands International, Wageningen.

**Scott, D.A. & Rose, P.M.** 1996. Atlas of Anatidae Populations in Africa and Western Eurasia. Wetlands International Publication No. 41. Wetlands International, Wageningen.

**Wetlands International** 2002. Waterbird Population Estimates - Third Edition. Wetlands International Global Series No. 12. Wageningen.

Red-crested Pochards *Netta rufina* in Lucerne, Switzerland. Photo: N. Zbinden.

# 4.4 Migration ecology. Workshop Introduction

*Theunis Piersma[1] & Nils Warnock[2]*

[1]*Department of Marine Ecology & Evolution, Royal Netherlands Institute for Sea Research (NIOZ), PO Box 59,*
*1790 AB Den Burg, Texel, The Netherlands; and: Animal Ecology Group, Centre for Ecological and Evolutionary Studies,*
*University of Groningen, PO Box 14, 9750 AA Haren, The Netherlands.*
[2]*PRBO Conservation Science, 4990 Shoreline Hwy, Stinson Beach, CA 94970, USA.*

Piersma, T. & Warnock, N. 2006. Migration ecology. Workshop Introduction. *Waterbirds around the world.* Eds. G.C. Boere, C.A. Galbraith & D.A. Stroud. The Stationery Office, Edinburgh, UK. p. 505.

Greenland White-fronted Geese *Anser albifrons flavirostris* flying to staging areas in western Iceland. Recent research, including the use of satellite telemetry, has given a clearer understanding of the energetic implications of the lengthy two-stage migration undertaken by these geese. Photo: Chris Wilson.

Over the last decade many research projects have been undertaken to investigate the ways by which migratory birds handle their energetic needs in relation to flight ranges (including individual decisions of birds regarding these routes), the selection of stopover or staging areas, and the use of available food resources.

The aim of the workshop was to identify the conservation consequences of the many different ecological and life-history strategies that waterbird species use during their annual cycle; to identify and discuss the value of modern research techniques (stable isotopes, geo-locators, satellite tracking); and to formulate priorities for further research.

The advent of satellite tracking has revolutionised understanding of the migration systems of waterbirds, providing near real-time information to be gathered on the location of individual birds. Recent studies of the movements of East Canadian High Arctic Light-bellied Brent Geese *Branta bernicla hrota* are summarised by Robinson *et al.* This technology will probably always be relatively expensive and thus applicable only to small numbers of individuals. In contrast, new techniques such as genetic analysis (as presented by Svazas for Common Snipe *Gallinago gallinago*) and the use of stable isotopes (as summarised by Atkinson *et al.* for determining population structures of Nearctic Red Knot *Calidris canutus rufa*) have significant potential to help elucidate flyways, and thus assist conservation managers. Although not a waterbird, using the example of the Redwing *Turdus iliacus,* Coiffait *et al.* show how that combined use of stable isotope and DNS analysis can be an effective tool in clarifying population identity – with potential implications for population studies of waterbirds.

The extent of migration can be very considerable. Gill *et al.* present evidence of one of the most extreme: an 11 000 km non-stop flight by Bar-tailed Godwits *Limosa lapponica* from Alaska to New Zealand and eastern Australia. Understanding the eco-physiological constraints of such flights, focuses attention on the critical importance of adequate feeding (re-fuelling) possibilities at the termini of such flights (and on intermediate staging areas where these are used).

# Elucidating the movements of migratory birds through the combined use of stable isotope 'signatures' and DNA markers

*Lisette Coiffait[1], Richard Bevan[1], Chris Redfern[2], Jason Newton[3] & Kirsten Wolff[1]*

[1]*School of Biology, University of Newcastle, Newcastle upon Tyne NE1 7RU, UK. (email: lisette.coiffait@ncl.ac.uk)*
[2]*Northern Institute for Cancer Research, Paul O'Gorman Building, University of Newcastle, Newcastle upon Tyne, NE2 4HH, UK.*
[3]*NERC Life Sciences Mass Spectrometry Facility, Scottish Universities Environmental Research Centre, East Kilbride, Glasgow, G75 0QF, UK.*

Coiffait, L., Bevan, R., Redfern, C., Newton, J. & Wolff, K. 2006. Elucidating the movements of migratory birds through the combined use of stable isotope 'signatures' and DNA markers. *Waterbirds around the world*. Eds. G.C. Boere, C.A. Galbraith & D.A. Stroud. The Stationery Office, Edinburgh, UK. pp. 506-507.

This paper presents the preliminary results of a study using a combination of stable isotope 'signatures' and DNA markers to establish the migratory patterns of Redwing *Turdus iliacus* passing through Wales and England. The approach is of application to waterbirds and is of significance in the light of the increasing use of these techniques to elucidate the breeding or wintering areas of waterbird species, especially those which are highly threatened.

For many birds, migration is a fundamental aspect of their life history, and knowledge of the links between breeding, wintering and intermediate stopover sites is crucial for determining at which points in the annual cycle avian populations are most vulnerable. Whilst there is a considerable amount of information available concerning migration at the species level, far less is known at the population and intra-population level (Bairlein 2001). Groups of birds may be spatially distinct at some stages of the annual cycle, but the extent to which individuals from the same breeding area migrate to the same wintering area and vice versa is largely unresolved.

The conventional technique of ringing birds has limited potential for population level studies because it relies on recapturing individuals, and the probability of this is extremely low. A novel approach combining the use of stable isotope ratios of carbon, nitrogen and hydrogen with multiple DNA markers has therefore been used to examine the migratory movements of the Redwing *Turdus iliacus* and the European Blackbird *T. merula*. The Redwing has a breeding range that covers a vast area from Iceland to eastern Siberia, while a second race *T. i. coburni* nests in Iceland and the Faeroes and differs markedly from nominate *T. i. iliacus* in several aspects of its migration (Milwright 2002). Blackbirds are partial migrants, with a highly complex pattern of movements; their breeding range spans most of Europe (Chamberlain & Main 2002). In this preliminary study, body feathers were sampled from populations of *T. i iliacus* and *T. i. coburni* (Table 1).

Feathers were washed in 0.25M NaOH followed by deionised water, and dried at 50° C. Carbon, nitrogen and hydrogen isotope ratios were analysed via continuous-flow stable isotope mass spectrometry (CF-IRMS) capable of measuring $\delta^{15}N$, $\delta^{13}C$ and $\delta D$ to $\pm$ 0.2 ‰, 0.1 ‰ and $\pm$ 2 ‰ respectively. A Multivariate Analysis of Variance (MANOVA) was used to investigate whether mean stable isotope ratios of $\delta 15N$, $\delta 13C$ and $\delta D$ differed between birds of different origins. Posthoc testing (Tukey's) was carried out to determine where statistical differences occurred.

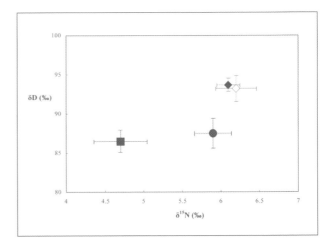

Fig. 1. Mean feather, $\delta^{15}N$ and $\delta D$ values of adult and first-year Redwings *T. iliacus* collected from three different populations overwintering in the UK, and a single Icelandic breeding population. Values are reported in parts per thousand (‰). Each point represents the mean ($\pm$ SE) of all birds sampled at that location. Bardsey birds are represented by a diamond (◆ autumn; ◇ spring), Farne Island birds by a circle (●) and Icelandic birds by a square (■).

The two Bardsey populations did not differ significantly for any of the three isotope ratios ($\delta^{13}C$, $\delta^{15}N$; Fig. 1) ($F_{1,130} = 1.041$; P = 0.377), and are therefore discussed as a single population hereafter. There was a highly significant difference in both $\delta D$ and $\delta^{15}N$ between birds of Icelandic origin and the Bardsey birds

**Table 1. Sampling location and size of four populations of Redwing used to investigate the relationship between feather $\delta^{13}C$, $\delta^{15}N$ and $\delta D$ values and breeding origin.**

| Species | Sample site | Breeding origin | n | Collection date |
|---|---|---|---|---|
| *T. i. iliacus* | Bardsey, North Wales, UK | Unknown; presumed Continental | 111 | Oct 1995 |
| *T. i. iliacus* | Bardsey, North Wales, UK | Unknown; presumed Continental | 21 | Mar 1998 |
| *T. i. iliacus* | Farne Islands, Northumberland§, UK | Unknown; presumed Continental | 10 | Nov 2004 |
| *T. i. coburni* | Iceland | Iceland | 20 | Sep 2004 |

($F_{1,150} > 9.09$; $P \leq 0.003$). $^{13}$C did not differ significantly between these two populations. Isotope ratios ($\delta^{13}$C, $\delta^{15}$N and $\delta$D) from the Farne Island birds were not significantly different from either the Icelandic or the Bardsey populations, perhaps due to a lack of statistical power.

The highly significant differences in $\delta$D and $\delta$15N between the Bardsey Redwings and the Icelandic birds indicate that this method offers real potential for discriminating between redwings of different breeding origin. The lack of significant difference between the autumn- and spring-sampled Bardsey birds may be expected since, in both cases, the feather isotopic ratios reflect those of the breeding origins. The breeding range of Redwing is known to extend from Iceland to eastern Siberia (Milwright 2002) and the wide range of $\delta$D values birds indicates that they have originated from numerous sites within its range. However, during the course of migration, these birds have subsequently converged into a relatively small area, and whilst the destination of the autumn birds and origin of the spring birds cannot be established, one can speculate that the former were heading for southwest Britain/Ireland, while the latter had overwintered there (Milwright 2002).

A recent study by Hobson *et al.* (2004) indicates that hydrogen isotope ratios in Europe vary with latitude, generally decreasing (i.e. becoming more negative) on a south to north geographical gradient, but that there is little discrimination between the east and west. The next stage of the project is to sample Redwings at representative breeding sites (of different latitudes), to determine whether isotopic ratios of feathers from known breeding sites can be correlated with those collected at overwintering sites. Combining several genetic markers with the stable isotope 'signatures' and biometric data (e.g. Clegg *et al.* 2003, Wennerberg 2001) may reveal population- or regionally-specific groupings and migratory movements as has recently been done with Wilson's Warbler *Wilsonia pusilla* (Clegg *et al.* 2003).

## ACKNOWLEDGEMENTS

We thank Tómas Gunnarsson, The Natural History Society of Northumbria and the National Trust Farne Islands' wardens for their assistance with collecting samples for this project. We thank NERC for providing funding for the project.

## REFERENCES

**Bairlein, F.** 2001. Results of bird ringing in the study of migration routes. Ardea 89: 7-19.

**Chamberlain, D. & Main, I**. 2002. Common blackbird Turdus merula. In: The Migration Atlas: movements of the birds of Britain and Ireland. C.V. Wernham, M.P. Toms, J.H. Marchant, J.A. Clark, G.M. Siriwardena & S.R. Baillie (eds). T. & A.D. Poyser, London: 521-526.

**Clegg, S.M., Kelly, J.F., Kimura, M. & Smith, T.B**. 2003. Combining genetic markers and stable isotopes to reveal population connectivity and migration patterns in a Neotropical migrant, Wilson's warbler (*Wilsonia pusilla*). Molecular Ecology 12: 819-830.

**Hobson, K.A., Bowen, G.J., Wassenaar, L.I., Ferrand, Y. & Lormee, H**. 2004. Using stable hydrogen and oxygen isotope measurements of feathers to infer geographical origins of migrating European birds. Oecologia 141: 477–488.

**Milwright, D.** 2002. Redwings *Turdus iliacus*. In: The Migration Atlas: movements of the birds of Britain and Ireland. Eds. C.V. Wernham, M.P. Toms, J.H. Marchant, J.A. Clark, G.M. Siriwardena & S.R. Baillie (eds). T. & A.D. Poyser, London: 534-537.

**Wennerberg, L.** 2001. Breeding origin and migration pattern of dunlin (*Calidris alpina*) revealed by mitochondrial DNA analysis. Molecular Ecology 10: 1111-1120.

Icelandic Redwing *Turdus iliacus coburni*. Photo: Alistair Crowle.

# Long-term trends in numbers and distribution of wintering geese in the Oostkustpolders, Flanders (Belgium)

*Eckhart Kuijken[1,2], Christine Verscheure[1], Wouter Courtens[1] & Patrick Meire[3]*

[1] *Institute of Nature Conservation, Kliniekstraat 25, B-1070 Brussels, Belgium. (email: eckhart.kuijken@inbo.bt)*

[2] *University of Ghent, Biology Department, K.L. Ledeganckstraat 35, B-9000 Ghent, Belgium.*

[3] *University of Antwerp, Ecosystem Management Department, Universiteitsplein 1, 2610 Wilrijk, Belgium.*

Kuijken, E., Verscheure, C., Courtens, W. & Meire, P. 2006. Long-term trends in numbers and distribution of wintering geese in the Oostkustpolders, Flanders (Belgium). *Waterbirds around the world.* Eds. G.C. Boere, C.A. Galbraith & D.A. Stroud. The Stationery Office, Edinburgh, UK. pp. 508-511.

Long-term goose counts in Flanders, especially in the Oostkustpolders, started in 1959 and still continue on a fortnightly basis. The two main wintering species are White-fronted Geese *Anser albifrons* and Pink-footed Geese *A. brachyrhynchus*. This paper summarise changes in their numbers, distribution, phenology and habitat selection.

Five wintering areas are important: (1) Oostkustpolders, (2) NO-Vlaanderen (Kreken area), (3) Beneden Schelde (lower Scheldt river), (4) IJzervallei and (5) Maasvallei (Border Meuse) (Fig. 1). Pinkfeet occur almost exclusively in (1); Whitefronts also started mainly in (1), but have developed increasing winter populations in the other areas, notably (2) and (4); (5) has been frequented more recently. Other goose species are less important except for Greylag Geese *Anser anser,* which have increased up to 6 000, especially in (1), (3) and (4), partly as a result of increased breeding. Bean Geese *Anser fabalis* mostly appear in small numbers in (2) and (3). Barnacle Geese *Branta leucopsis* rarely reach above 1 000 and prefer the coastal areas in (1), but this species is developing fast-growing feral breeding populations. Dark-bellied Brent Geese *Branta b. bernicla* pass through on migration and only some flocks stop along the coast, mainly in (1).

Pinkfeet in Flanders are increasing faster than the Svalbard population, while Oostkustpolders has become the regular southernmost mid-winter haunt during the last decade, with up to 90% of this population. The actual average maximum is about 35-38 000. White-fronted Geese have not increased as fast as the Baltic-North Sea population, with an average maximum of 25-35 000, representing 2-4% of the estimated total population.

The increase in wintering geese numbers has been affected by the harsh winter of 1978/79, when almost entire populations of Pinkfeet and Whitefronts moved from the north to Belgium and France. Many birds 'discovered' new sites, especially the coastal polders, and with another three hard winters in the 1980s, the birds returned in increasing numbers. A national goose shooting ban was instituted in 1981 and this is still in force, resulting in a further build up of wintering numbers (Fig. 2).

The steady increase of geese in the Oostkustpolders since 1959 has had several consequences on their regional distribution patterns. In the first decade, most birds stayed at Damme (near Bruges), where goose hunting was stopped locally on a voluntary basis. During and after 1978/79 a shift to the west occurred in the coastal areas up to the Oostende region. Whitefronts later

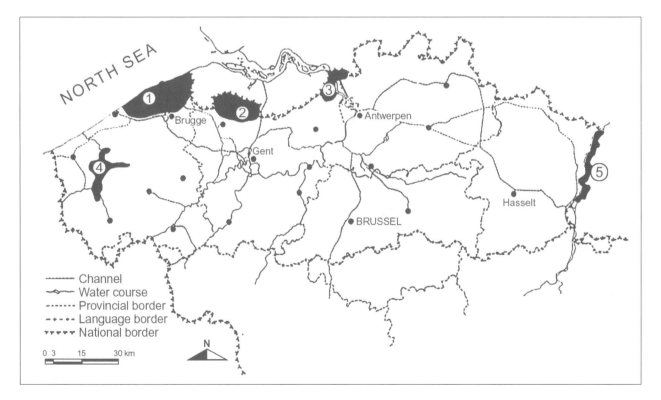

**Fig. 1.** Wintering areas of geese in Flanders (Belgium):
(1) Oostkustpolders, (2) NO-Vlaanderen (Kreken area), (3) Beneden Schelde (lower Scheldt river), (4) IJzervallei and (5) Maasvallei (Border Meuse).

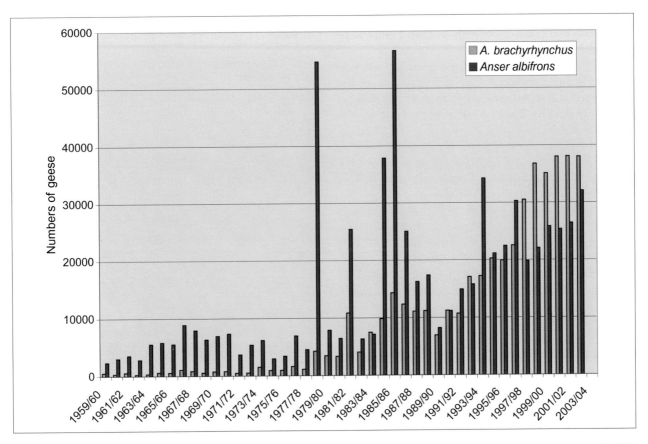

**Fig. 2.** Winter maxima of White-fronted *Anser albifrons* and Pink-footed Geese *A. brachyrhynchus* in the Oostkustpolders, (Flanders, Belgium) 1959-2003.

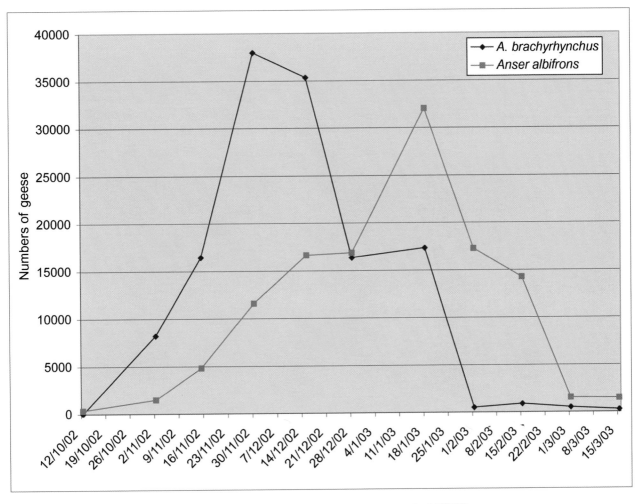

**Fig. 3.** Phenology of wintering geese in the Oostkustpolders based on fortnightly counts; example of 2002/03.

'discovered' the IJzervallei (site 2 in Fig. 1): this species is much more mobile than Pinkfeet, which show a high fidelity to the Oostkustpolders site.

The distribution dynamics of the geese changed when the carrying capacity of traditional wintering grounds was reached and an overflow to secondary haunts started in the mid seventies (Kuijken 1969, 1975). This then led to shifting processes with cyclic use of feeding grounds (Meire *et al.* 1988, Meire & Kuijken 1991). In recent times most of the suitable wintering areas in the Oostkustpolders (ca 30 000 ha) are visited from the beginning of the season, and the intensive exchanges between sites no longer have a clear cyclic character.

In Fig. 3, the counts for winter 2002/03 show an average phenology for both species, with the peak number dates differing by almost one month. Also the distribution tends to show inter-specific avoidance the more numbers increase (Fig. 4).

Research is continued on feeding ecology, influence of disturbance and changes of agriculture, especially in the coastal polders (Kuijken *et al.* 2001). There has been an important loss of the preferred habitat, "permanent semi-natural wet grasslands with micro-relief". Both goose species started using arable land more frequently. Integrated protection of traditional polder grasslands is a real need for wintering geese, breeding meadow birds and botanical diversity as important conservation values are threatened by the intensification of agriculture.

The goose shooting ban resulted in less disturbance and enabled a spontaneous goose distribution to the most suitable

Pink-footed Geese *Anser brachyrhynchus*. Photo: Paul Marshall.

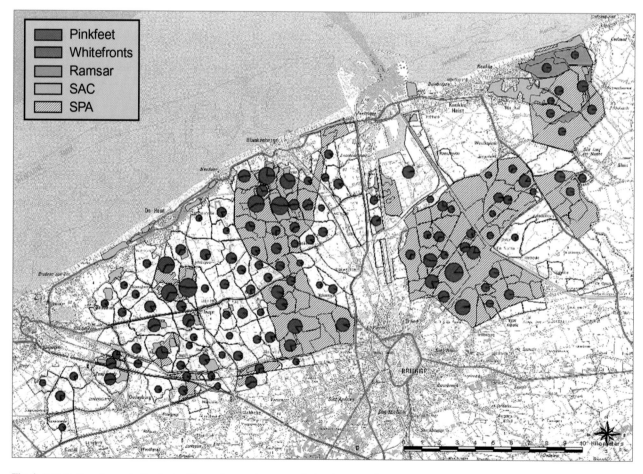

**Fig. 4.** Distribution of geese in Oostkustpolders and protection status of wintering grounds; most core areas (large circles) are classified under European Union's nature Directives as either Special Protection Areas and/or as Special Areas of Conservation (Natura 2000); note some segregation of Pink-footed and White-fronted Geese.

sites without overall agricultural damage, as the total wintering area increased more than the goose numbers themselves. On average the grazing pressure is c. 200 goosedays/ha, with a maximum duration of stay of 4.5 months, and with peak numbers above 10 000 during only 10 weeks. As most geese stay on permanent grasslands (on average 85-95%), the amount of damage to agricultural crops is very limited.

In most winters 90% of the geese have left the Oostkustpolders when spring regrowth of vegetations starts - Pinkfeet especially can leave as early as mid-January, although normally mid- February. Only exceptionally do birds return (pers. obs. 1996).

The effects of the shooting ban caused a change in distribution of wintering geese preferring grassland complexes, the core areas of which have been protected as shown in Fig. 4. A proposal to designate parts of the Oostkustpolders as a new Ramsar site was not finalised. The IJzervalley floodplain is designated as both a Ramsar site and as a Natura 2000 site. For both sites the presence of geese was one of the main criteria.

The Flemish Ecological Network also includes goose areas, and specific projects aim to restore old permanent grasslands, hopefully helping to unify former extensive complexes as optimal habitats for wintering waterbirds and thus avoid conflicts with agriculture. Finally, some core polders are partly managed as nature reserves (Damme, Uitkerke, Blankaart & IJzervalley etc.) and contribute to the public interest for wild geese.

## REFERENCES

**Kuijken, E**. 1969. Grazing of Wild Geese on Grasslands at Belgium. Wildfowl 20 : 4754.

**Kuijken, E.** 1975. Oecologie van overwinterende ganzen te Damme (W.-Vl.) in Westeuropees verband. PhD. Thesis Univ. Gent. (In Dutch). 280 pp.

**Kuijken E., Courtens W., Teunissen W., Vantieghem S., Verscheure C. & P. Meire**. 2001. Numbers and distribution dynamics of wintering geese in Flanders (Belgium): Data application in conservation policy; unpubl. Report VLINA-project 00/03. (In Dutch).

**Meire, P., Kuijken E. & Devos K.** 1988. Numbers and distribution of White-fronted and Pink-footed Geese in Flanders (Belgium) 1981-87 in a North West European context. Wildfowl 39:71-81.

**Meire P. & Kuijken E.** 1991. Factors affecting the number and distribution of wintering geese in Flanders, Belgium, and some implications for their conservation. Ardea 79: 143-158.

Pink-footed Geese *Anser brachyrhynchus*. Photo: Paul Marshall.

# East-Atlantic flyway populations of seaducks in the Barents Sea region

*Yuri Krasnov[1], Maria Gavrilo[2], Natalie Nikolaeva[3], Yuri Goryaev[1] & Hallvard Strøm[4]*

[1] *Murmansk Marine Biological Institute, 14 Vladimirskaya st., Murmansk, Russia. (email: maria@yai.usr.pu.ru)*

[2] *Arctic & Antarctic Research Institute, 38 Bering st., Saint-Petersburg, 199397, Russia. (email: mashuka@aari.nw.ru)*

[3] *WWF Russia, building 3, 19 Nikoloyamskaya st., Moscow, 109240, Russia.*

[4] *Norsk Polarinstitutt, Polar Center, NO 9296, Tromsø, Norway.*

Krasnov, Yu., Gavrilo, M., Nikolaeva, N., Goryaev, Yu. & Strøm, H. 2006. East-Atlantic flyway populations of seaducks in the Barents Sea region. *Waterbirds around the world*. Eds. G.C. Boere, C.A. Galbraith & D.A. Stroud. The Stationery Office, Edinburgh, UK. pp. 512-513.

This study provides information on the distribution of nine species of seaducks in Kandalaksha and Onega Bays, in the southern part of the Barents Sea, and the northern part of the White Sea and identifies the principal marine areas important for seaducks (Table 1). The most extensive observations were carried out in varying seasons from 1993-2003. Data were collected using various methods including static observations, land-based line and spot counts, aerial surveys by helicopter and fix-winged aeroplane in both coastal and open waters. The major wintering grounds of seaducks were in open coastal areas of the ice-covered north-west portion of the White Sea and the unfrozen Murman coast of the Barents Sea.

In early April 2003, a 500 km transect of the coastline was surveyed, identifying c. 19 500 Barents Sea Common Eider *Somateria mollissima*, 7 000 Atlantic Steller's Eider *Polysticta stelleri* and 4 500 King Eider *Somateria spectabilis* (Krasnov *et al*. 2004). Long-tailed Ducks *Clangula hyemalis* winter mostly along the western Murman coast (Nygård *et al*., 1995). The distribution of wintering seaducks appeared to be determined by climatic conditions, particularly the extent of ice (Krasnov *et al*. 2004).

During spring migration most seaducks pass through the area, but during autumn migration the southern Barents Sea and northern White Sea provide important staging opportunities, with principal stopover sites in the eastern Pechora Sea shallows. The Black Scoter *Melanitta nigra* is the most abundant species, with flocks of up to 15 000 birds recorded. Steller's Eider and King Eider were observed during migration from Novaya Zemlya and the Kara Sea to the eastern Pechora Sea. Major

Male Common Eider *Somateria mollissima*. Photo: Colin Galbraith.

moulting concentrations of King Eider (c. 40 000 birds) and Black Scoter were found in shallow areas of the south-eastern Barents Sea, while moulting Common and Steller's Eider were found mostly in the north-western White Sea along the shores of the Kola Peninsula (Isaksen *et al*. 2000, Krasnov *et al*. 2002, Strom *et al*. 2004). The Terskiy and Murman coasts of the Kola Peninsula support high numbers of three species of eiders and Long-tailed Ducks during their moulting and wintering seasons while the south-east Barents Sea supports migrating scoters and moulting King Eiders. Both areas meet the conditions for recognition as marine Important Bird Areas (IBAs).

The rapidly increasing off-shore oil industry in the Russian part of the southern Barents Sea and the White Sea is considered

**Table 1. Status of seaducks as observed in coastal regions of the study area.**

| Species | White Sea | | Barents Sea | | |
| | Kandalaksha Bay | Terskiy Coast | East Murman | Kola Bay | Pechora Sea |
|---|---|---|---|---|---|
| *Clangula hyemalis* | M W | MO W B | MO M W B | W | B MO M W |
| *Somateria mollissima* | B MO W | B MO W | B MO M W | MO W B | B MO W |
| *Somateria spectabilis* | M OW | M MO W | M W | W | B M MO W |
| *Polysticta stelleri* | M W | M MO W | M MO W | W | RB M MO |
| *Melanitta fusca* | B M | MO M W | M W | S | B M |
| *Melanitta nigra* | RB M | MO | M | W | B M MO |
| *Mergus serrator* | B MO | B MO | B MO | W | B MO M |
| *Mergus merganser* | MO | MO M | MO W | W | MO M |
| *Bucephala clangula* | B MO M | MO | - | MO W | MO |

B – breeding (only species breeding along the seashore and on maritime islands are included); RB – rare breeding; MO – moulting; M – migrating through the area; W – overwintering; OW – occasionally/rare overwintering a major hazard to seaduck populations. The current system of wildlife conservation in the region is based mainly on a network of special protection areas (SPAs) which cannot guarantee sufficient protection for seaducks and their marine habitats against oil-related hazards in shelf areas. It is essential to identify population connections and the demographic structure of Common Eider sub-populations in different areas of the study region, and to obtain numeric data on eiders wintering in Onega Bay and moulting along southern Novaya Zemlya to support enhancing the conservation of seaduck populations in the region.

## REFERENCES

Isaksen, K., Strøm, H., Gavrilo, M. & Krasnov, Yu. 2000. Distribution of seabirds and waterfowl in the Pechora Sea, with emphasis on post-breeding marine ducks. In: H. Strøm, K. Isaksen & A.N. Golovkin (eds) Seabirds and wildfowl surveys in the Pechora Sea during August 1998. Norwegian Ornithological Society. Report 2-2000: 7–44.

Krasnov, Yu.V., Goryaev, Yu.I., Shavykin, A.A., Nikolaeva, N.G., Gavrilo, M.V. & Chernook, V.I. 2002. Atlas of the Pechora Sea birds: distribution, abundance, dynamics, problems of protection. Apatity: Kola Sci. Center RAS. (In Russian with English summary)

Krasnov, Yu.V., Strøm, H., Gavrilo, M.V. & Shavykin, A.A. 2004 (in press) Seabirds wintering in polynyas along Terskiy coast of the White Sea. Ornitologiya, Moscow, Vol. 30. (In Russian with English summary)

Nygård, T., Jordhoy, P., Kondakov, A. & Krasnov, Yu. 1995. A survey of waterfowl and seal on the coast of the southern Barents Sea in March 1994. NINA Oppdragsmelding 361: 1–24.

Strøm, H., Krasnov, Yu., Gavrilo, M. & Shavykin, A. 2004 (in prep.) Seaduck survey in the southern Barents Sea region in 2003. Norwegian Polar Institute Report Series, Norwegian Polar Institute, Tromsø.

Female Common Eider *Somateria mollissima* with young. Photo: Colin Galbraith.

# Changes in migration patterns and wintering areas of south Swedish Greylag Geese *Anser anser*

*Leif Nilsson*

*Department of Animal Ecology, University of Lund, Ecology Building, S-223 62  Lund, Sweden.*
*(email: leif.nilsson@zooekol.lu.se)*

Nilsson, L. 2006. Changes in migration patterns and wintering areas of south Swedish Greylag Geese *Anser anser*. *Waterbirds around the world*. Eds. G.C. Boere, C.A. Galbraith & D.A. Stroud. The Stationery Office, Edinburgh, UK. pp. 514-516.

## ABSTRACT

Neck-banding of Greylag Geese *Anser anser* started in south-western Scania, southern Sweden, in 1984, as a part of a Nordic programme to carry out a detailed study of the migration routes of Greylag Geese from different regions of the Nordic countries. By 2002, 2 347 Greylag Geese had been neck-banded in Scania, and these had resulted in about 14 000 readings of neck-bands from abroad. During the course of the study, there was a northward shift in the main winter quarters from a majority of the geese wintering in south-western Spain to a majority wintering in The Netherlands. During the same period, the timing of the autumn and spring migrations also changed. In 2002, the median arrival date of geese staging in The Netherlands in autumn was about 40 days later than in 1986, while in spring, the geese returned to their breeding areas in Scania about 20 days earlier. The implications of these changes for the population dynamics of the species are discussed.

## INTRODUCTION

The population of Greylag Geese *Anser anser* in Sweden, as in most other countries in north-west Europe, has increased markedly during recent decades (Nilsson *et. al.* 1999). Thus the September totals in Sweden are now close to ten times higher than they were when the counts started in 1984 (L. Nilsson unpubl. data). The increasing Greylag Goose populations during the late 1970s and early 1980s led to the establishment of many new concentrations of geese in a number of agricultural areas in the Nordic countries, and this gave rise to conflicts with agricultural interests. In response to this, the Nordic Council for Wildlife Research (NKV) started a neck-banding programme in the Nordic countries in 1984. The main aim of this programme was to study the migration patterns and local movements of Greylag Geese in the four Nordic countries (Andersson *et al.* 2001). The presence of a large number of neck-banded Greylag Geese in the population was used to study various aspects of the ecology of the geese, especially in south-western Scania, in southern Sweden (see, for example, Nilsson *et al.* 2001, Nilsson & Persson 1993, 1994, 1996, Nilsson *et al.* 1997).

When the neck-banding programme started in 1984, the majority of the marked geese migrated from the Nordic countries to staging areas in The Netherlands and then continued on to the traditional wintering areas in the Marismas of Quadalquivir in southern Spain (Andersson *et al.* 2001, Paludan 1973, Lund 1971). Some geese remained throughout the winter in The Netherlands in the first year of the study, but this proportion increased during the period of the study. There were also differences in the migration patterns and wintering areas between the various Nordic study populations. The Nordic project was terminated in the early 1990s (Andersson *et al.* 2001), but neck-banding programmes continued in Norway and south-western Scania, southern Sweden.

This paper provides an updated review of the migration patterns of Greylag Geese from south-west Scania since the joint Nordic analysis (Andersson *et al.* 2001) and, more specifically, attempts to elucidate the changes that have occurred in the migration patterns and wintering areas of the Greylag Geese from Scania, and to analyse these changes in relation to different aspects of the population ecology of the species.

## METHODS

Families of flightless Greylag Geese were captured by driving them into nets at four different breeding lakes in a study area in southern Scania in southernmost Sweden. The study area and methods of capture have been described in other reports from the study (Andersson *et al.* 2001, Nilsson & Persson 1994). During the period 1984-2002, a total of 2 321 Greylag Geese were neck-banded in the study area, comprising 588 adults and 1 733 yearlings.

Intensive observations were undertaken in the study area to establish the presence and return rate of the marked geese on an annual basis and to establish their breeding success. In some years, intensive checks were also undertaken as a part of other local studies. Observations were made in the staging and wintering areas by a network of more than a thousand voluntary observers who regularly checked their local areas. National marking programmes in the various countries along the migration route also co-operated in the study. Furthermore, during several years of the present study, Hakon Persson was undertaking a special study of the geese in Spain.

## RESULTS

Of the 2 321 geese which were marked, 98% of the adults and 86% of those marked as young birds were seen after marking. A total of 467 adults (81% of all those marked and seen after marking) and 1 086 birds marked as yearlings (73%) were encountered abroad, providing information on migration patterns and wintering areas. The largest numbers of observations of marked birds were in The Netherlands, followed by Spain (Fig. 1).

Small numbers of Greylag Geese from Scania were recorded in The Netherlands during the summer, especially during the first years of the study, when Oostvaardersplassen in Flevoland was still the major moulting site for Greylag Geese from Scania (Nilsson *et al.* 2001). During the first two periods of the study (1984-1990 and 1990-1996), the main migration into The Netherlands occurred in October, but in the period 1996-2002, the main arrival occurred in November (Fig. 2). Peak numbers were recorded in October in the first study period, and in November and December in the second and third periods, respectively. Throughout the study, there has been a significant trend in the later arrival of Scanian Greylag Geese in The

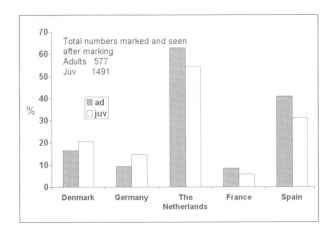

Fig. 1. Percentages of neck-banded Greylag Geese *Anser anser* from south-west Scania, southern Sweden, that were seen abroad (as a percentage of those seen after marking).

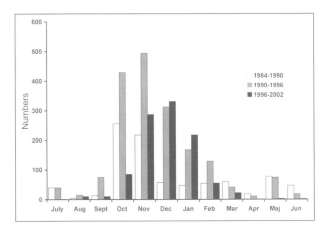

Fig. 2. Monthly distribution of observations of neck-banded Greylag Geese *Anser anser* from south-west Scania, southern Sweden, seen in The Netherlands during three time periods. Each individual is included only once per month and year.

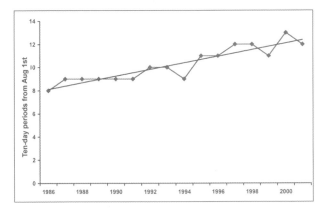

Fig. 3. Median arrival time (in ten-day periods from 1 August) in The Netherlands of neck-banded Greylag Geese *Anser anser* from south-west Scania, southern Sweden (R= 0.92, P<0.001).

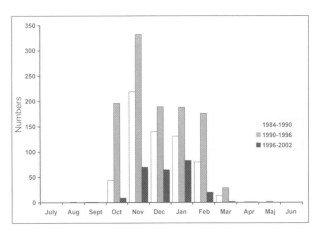

Fig. 4. Monthly distribution of observations of neck-banded Greylag Geese *Anser anser* from south-west Scania, southern Sweden, seen in Spain during three time periods. Each individual is included only once per month and year.

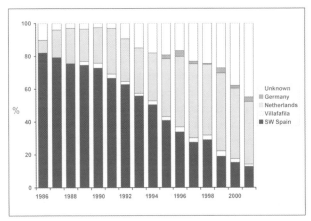

Fig. 5. Percentage distribution of Greylag Geese *Anser anser* from south-west Scania, southern Sweden, in their wintering areas in 1986-2001.

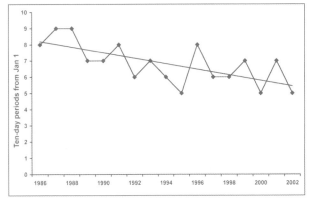

Fig. 6. Median arrival time (in ten-day periods from 1 January) of neck-banded Greylag Geese *Anser anser* in the breeding/marking areas in south-west Scania, southern Sweden (R= 0.67, P<0.001).

Netherlands, the median arrival date now being about 40 days later than it was at the start of the study (Fig. 3).

During the first part of the study, Scanian Greylag Geese had already arrived in their wintering areas in southern Spain in October, after a short stay in The Netherlands (Andersson *et al.* 2001), but the main arrival occurred later in later years (Fig. 4).

However, it is more difficult to establish the true peak in the occurrence of marked geese in south-west Spain, as the birds often move into areas in the Marismas where the reading of neck-bands is very difficult.

Over the years, there has been a gradual shift in the winter distribution of Scanian Greylag Geese. A higher proportion of the geese remain throughout the winter in the Dutch Delta area, and fewer birds migrate to Spain (Fig. 5). Some geese now spend the winter on the German North Sea coast, and a wintering tradition has even been established in Sweden, where there has been a wintering population of about 5 000 birds in January in the last few years (L. Nilsson unpubl. data).

The spring migration has also changed. The median date of arrival at the breeding areas is now about one month earlier than it was in the earliest period of the study (Fig. 6).

## DISCUSSION

The changes in the migration pattern of the Scanian Greylag Goose population are not unique. Within the Nordic Greylag Goose Project, a similar change has been noted in the Norwegian population, with the geese now arriving at the staging areas in The Netherlands later than was formerly the case (A. Follestad & L. Nilsson unpubl. data). Similarly, in Sweden, there has been a marked northward shift in the distribution of autumn staging Taiga Bean Geese *Anser fabalis fabalis* in recent years (Nilsson 2000).

The changes seen in the migration pattern of the Greylag Goose, as in other species, can most probably be related to the recent trend in milder winters and earlier springs. In Sweden, the last really cold winter was in 1987; winters since then have been mild or with only short cold periods, at least in southernmost Sweden (Swedish Meteorological Institute Monthly reports). In the province of Scania, mean February and March temperatures show an increasing trend since the goose project started in 1986, but the situation is better described as a marked change in winter temperatures after the cold winter of 1987, with much milder temperatures since then.

Even if milder winters and earlier springs are important factors behind the change in migration patterns, changes in agriculture may also be of importance (Nilsson & Persson 2000). In Sweden, there has been an increase in the acreage of autumn-sown cereals in recent years, offering the geese good feeding conditions after the ploughing of stubble fields and root crops.

It is interesting to speculate what effects these changes in winter distribution and migration pattern can have on the Greylag Goose populations. Nilsson & Persson (1996) found a significantly higher survival rate for Greylag Geese wintering in The Netherlands than for those wintering in Spain. This difference was most probably related to differences in hunting pressure, but it was also found that drought conditions in the Marismas led to higher mortality rates in some years. The difference in the length of the migration is probably of minor importance.

The geese wintering in The Netherlands showed a higher breeding success than the geese wintering in Spain (Nilsson & Persson 1996). The recruitment rate of young geese into the breeding population was, among other factors, also found to be related to the choice of winter quarters by the parents (Nilsson *et al.* 1997). Nilsson & Persson (1994) found a significant relationship between early arrival and high breeding success, and this could be related to the location of the winter quarters, as geese wintering in The Netherlands are in a better position to return early to the breeding areas in Scania than geese wintering in Spain.

To conclude, the results demonstrate the importance of continuing the neck-banding programmes in Europe, in order to monitor and analyse ongoing and future changes in the migration patterns and wintering distributions of European geese in relation to a variety of underlying factors.

## ACKNOWLEDGEMENTS

The Nordic marking programme was started by the Nordic Council for Wildlife Research (NKV), which also funded the programme during the early years. Further support was obtained from the Swedish Environmental Protection Agency, the Carl Trygger Foundation for Scientific Research and the Öresunds Bro Consortium. The catching and marking of the geese was undertaken by Hakon Persson. The study would not have been possible without the participation of over a thousand voluntary observers in many countries who reported their neck-band readings.

## REFERENCES

**Andersson, Å., Follestad, A., Nilsson, L. & Persson, H.** 2001. Migration patterns of Nordic Greylag Geese *Anser anser*. Ornis Svecica 11: 19-58.

**Lund, H. M-K.** 1971. Ringmerking av Grågjess i Norge. Sterna 10: 247-250.

**Nilsson, L.** 2000. Changes in numbers and distribution of staging and wintering goose populations in Sweden, 1977/78 – 1998/99. Ornis Svecica 10: 33-49.

**Nilsson, L. & Persson, H.** 1993. Variation in survival in an increasing population of the Greylag Goose *Anser anser* in Scania, southern Sweden. Ornis Svecica 3: 137-146.

**Nilsson, L. & Persson, H.** 1994. Factors affecting the breeding performance of a marked Greylag Goose *Anser anser* population in south Sweden. Wildfowl 45: 33-48.

**Nilsson, L. & Persson, H.** 1996. The influence of the choice of winter quarters on the survival and breeding performance of Greylag Geese (*Anser anser*). In: M. Birkan, J. van Vessem, P. Havet, J. Madsen, B. Trolliet & M. Moser (eds) Proceedings of the Anatidae 2000 Conference, Strasbourg, France, 5-9 December 1994. Gibier Faune Sauvage, Game and Wildlife 13: 557.

**Nilsson, L. & Persson, H.** 2000. Changes in field choice among staging and wintering geese in southwestern Scania, south Sweden. Ornis Svecica 10: 33-49.

**Nilsson, L., Persson, H. & Voslamber, B.** 1997. Factors affecting survival of young Greylag Geese and their recruitment into the breeding population. Wildfowl 48: 72-87.

**Nilsson, L., Follestad, A., Koffijberg, K., Kuijken, E., Madsen, J., Mooij, J., Mouronval, J.B., Persson, H., Schrcke, V. & Voslamber, B.** 1999. Greylag Goose *Anser anser*: Northwest Europe. In: J. Madsen, G. Cracknell & A.D. Fox (eds) Goose populations of the Western Palearctic. A review of status and distribution. Wetlands International Publication No.48, Wetlands International, Wageningen, The Netherlands, & National Environmental Research Institute, Rönde, Denmark: 182-201.

**Nilsson, L., Kahlert, J. & Persson, H.** 2001. Moult and moult migration of Greylag Geese *Anser anser* from a population in Scania, south Sweden. Bird Study 48: 129-138.

**Nilsson, L., Green, M. & Persson, H.** 2002. Field choice in spring and breeding performance of Greylag Geese *Anser anser* in southern Sweden. Wildfowl 53: 7-25.

**Paludan, K.** 1973. Migration and survival of *Anser anser* ringed in Denmark. Videnskabelige Meddelser fra Dansk Naturhistorisk Forening 138: 217-232.

# Identifying and characterising the feeding areas of Dark-bellied Brent Geese *Branta bernicla bernicla* in and around Special Protection Areas in the UK

*Helen E. Rowell & James A. Robinson[1]*

*The Wildfowl & Wetlands Trust, Slimbridge, Gloucestershire, GL2 7BT, UK. (email: helen.rowell@wwt.org.uk)*
*[1]Present address: RSPB Northern Ireland, Belvoir Park Forest, Belfast, BT8 4QT, UK.*

Rowell, H.E. & Robinson, J.A. 2005. Identifying and characterising the feeding areas of Dark-bellied Brent Geese *Branta bernicla bernicla* in and around Special Protection Areas in the UK. *Waterbirds around the world*. Eds. G.C. Boere, C.A. Galbraith & D.A. Stroud. The Stationery Office, Edinburgh, UK. pp. 517-518.

In 2003, The Wildfowl & Wetlands Trust (WWT) undertook a survey to identify and characterise the inland feeding areas of Dark-bellied Brent Geese *Branta bernicla bernicla* around the 19 Special Protection Areas (SPAs) in the UK for which it is a qualifying species. The Dark-bellied Brent Goose is a winter visitor to the UK from its breeding grounds in Siberia. Most winter on estuaries with extensive intertidal areas in southern and eastern England. A flyway population increase from 22 000 in 1960/61 to around 300 000 in the late 1990s resulted in a rapid seasonal depletion of natural foods such as eel-grass *Zostera* spp., green algae *Enteromorpha* spp. and saltmarsh plants. This has led to an increase in the use of cropped habitats such as coastal grasslands and cultivated cereal crops.

Nineteen SPAs were selected for the study of Dark-bellied Brent Geese in the UK. These generally included only intertidal areas and those immediately adjacent to them. However, Dark-bellied Brent Geese are known to rely on inland agricultural habitats for feeding. In general, sites having a low degree of 'naturalness', such as a large proportion of improved agricultural land, have not been selected for SPA classification in the UK, but these areas could be considered the 'most suitable areas' for species such as the Dark-bellied Brent Goose. The regularity of use, and the types of cropped habitats used, by this species around existing SPA boundaries were investigated to inform any subsequent process for site identification and the inclusion of cropped land within existing SPAs.

A questionnaire was sent out to local experts for each SPA requesting information on whether or not Dark-bellied Brent Geese had used coastal/estuarine feeding areas within/around the SPA during the previous five winters (1998/99-2002/03), and which estuaries were visited by birds recorded within the SPA. It also asked for inland feeding areas within/around the SPA to be marked on 1:25 000 maps of the sites. Experts were also asked to estimate the percentage of the total numbers on the site using different inland habitats in autumn, winter and spring, to mark on the map the land use type of each field used by birds, and to indicate the average number of birds within individual fields over the previous five winters.

There were marked differences in the amount and types of information provided for the survey, and general patterns in habitat use across the SPA suite shown by the results should therefore be treated with caution. However, inland feeding was recorded at all sites for which information was provided. The results showed a general pattern of birds feeding on their traditional estuarine habitats after they arrived in autumn, moving inland to feed as the winter progressed and back to estuarine areas in the spring. The site maps showed that, for each SPA, inland feeding areas were generally located just outside the SPA boundary see Fig. 1 for one example. Overall, feeding on permanent pasture was recorded at 38% of sites, on fertilised pasture (63%), on winter cereals (88%), on oilseed rape (38%), on golf courses (19%), on amenity/recreational land (25%), and on other grassed habitats (19%). There were no records of birds feeding on spring cereals.

The proportion of time spent feeding on improved permanent pasture, winter cereals and oilseed rape peaked in winter (Fig. 2). The use of permanent pasture increased through to spring. Birds only used golf courses and amenity/recreational land after November.

A large number of Dark-bellied Brent Geese associated with many SPAs feed on cropped habitats outside the SPA boundary. Consideration should thus be given to the inclusion of these areas within the SPA as part of a functional site for the birds, in

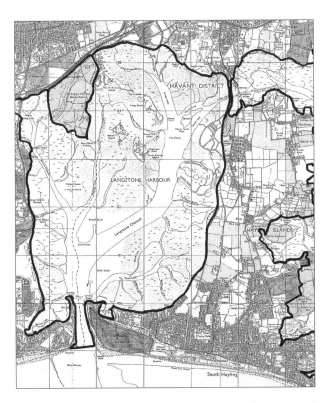

**Fig. 1.** Feeding areas for Dark-bellied Brent Geese in and around Langstone Harbour SPA (boundary indicated by black line) (key to habitats: Yellow-arable, Green-pasture, Red-amenity, Purple-unknown). Reproduced from 1:25 000 Pathfinder & Outdoor Leisure maps with permission of The Controller of Her Majesty's Stationery Office, © Crown Copyright.

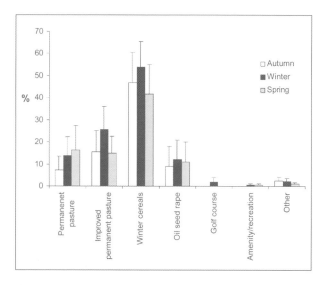

**Fig. 2.** Mean percentage use of different inland feeding habitats by Dark-bellied Brent Geese in and around SPAs in the UK (bars represent 1 standard error)

keeping with the principle of the 'most suitable territories'. The study also demonstrated that although there is a large amount of information gathered on habitat use by this species, detail varies markedly between sites and information is generally not collected using any standard methodology. To improve monitoring of habitat use for this and other large herbivorous waterbirds, there is a need to develop standardised methods to inform the future conservation and management of site networks.

## ACKNOWLEDGEMENTS

This study was funded by the WWT/JNCC Partnership. Information was kindly supplied by Richard Caldow, Bob Chapman, Steve Groves, Chris Lewis, Alan Parker, Anne de Potier, Michael Rooney, Jim Scott, Rod Smith, Rick Vonk, John Walker, Eddie Wiseman and Derek Wood.

Dark-bellied Brent Geese *Branta bernicla bernicla* occur on many of the estuaries of the south and east coasts of England, and sometimes regularly forage on surrounding areas of arable farmland and wet grassland. Photo: Peter Wakely, English Nature.

# Flyways of the East Canadian High Arctic Light-bellied Brent Goose *Branta bernicla hrota:* results of a satellite telemetry study

*James A. Robinson[1], G.A. Gudmundsson & P. Clausen*
*[1]Present address: RSPB Northern Ireland, Belvoir Park Forest, Belfast, BT8 4QT, UK.*

Robinson, J.A., Gudmundsson, G.A. & Clausen, P. 2006. Flyways of the East Canadian High Arctic Light-bellied Brent Goose *Branta bernicla hrota*: results of a satellite telemetry study. *Waterbirds around the world.* Eds. G.C. Boere, C.A. Galbraith & D.A. Stroud. The Stationery Office, Edinburgh, UK. p. 519.

In 2002, six East Canadian High Arctic Light-bellied Brent Geese *Branta bernicla hrota* were tracked by satellite telemetry from staging grounds in Iceland, via Greenland, to breeding grounds in Canada, and back to wintering grounds in Ireland. This was the first time that this migration route had been tracked. The study confirmed the importance of the west coast of Iceland as a staging area in the spring and autumn and identified areas used briefly by birds on the east and west coasts of Greenland and northeast Canada. The distribution of these geese during the summer was also assessed, identifying the probable locations of breeding and moulting sites. The study also identified some of the threats faced by these geese during migration. One of the geese died from natural causes in Iceland, probably raptor predation, whilst at least one other goose was shot in Canada. The results of the study made media headlines across the world and a web site 'Brent Goose 2002', hosted by the Wildfowl & Wetlands Trust, was designed to enable others to follow the journeys made by these geese. Additional satellite telemetry work is planned for 2004 and 2005 to improve our understanding of the migratory routes of this population of geese.

Light-bellied Brent Goose *Branta bernicla hrota* wearing satellite telemetric transmitter. Photo: Chris Wilson.

Decoys are an effective means of encouraging Light-bellied Brent Geese *Branta bernicla hrota* into cannon-net range. Photo: Chris Wilson.

# A review of the effects of intensive fish production on waterbird breeding populations

*Petr Musil[1]*

[1] *Dept. Zoology, Faculty of Science, Charles University, Vinicna 7, CZ-128 44 Praha 2, Czech Republic. (email: p.musil@post.cz)*

Musil, P. 2006. A review of the effects of intensive fish production on waterbird breeding populations. *Waterbirds around the world.* Eds. G.C. Boere, C.A. Galbraith & D.A. Stroud. The Stationery Office, Edinburgh, UK. pp. 520-521.

The breeding populations of most water bird species in the Czech Republic increased until the 1970s and then dropped. Fishpond management has been shown to be an important factor, and this paper summarizes current knowledge about effect of fishpond management on waterbird breeding populations.

In the Czech Republic, breeding populations of many resident water bird species (e.g. Black-necked Grebe *Podiceps nigricollis*, Gadwall *Anas strepera*, Pochard *Netta rufina*, Marsh Harrier *Circus aeruginosus*, Black-headed Gull *Larus ichthyaetus* have increased during the past 100 years, whilst species such as Mute Swan *Cygnus olor*, Tufted Duck *Aythya fuligula*, Red-crested Pochard *Netta rufina* and Goldeneye *Bucephala clangula* have started to breed, frequently in new areas (Hudec & Černý 1977, Hudec 1994). However, since the early 1980s numbers of grebes, ducks, coots and Black-headed Gulls started to decline. By the mid 1980s, the population of several duck species had declined by 30%. Moreover, the gradual decline in the size of the breeding population of other species (e.g. Teal *Anas crecca*, Garganey *Anas querquedula*, Shoveler *Anas clypeata*, Common Snipe *Gallinago gallinago*) continued as the result of changes in landscape use, especially the draining of wetlands (Šťastný *et al.* 1987, Musil & Fuchs 1994, Šťastný *et al.* 1997, Musil *et al.* 2001).

One cause of this decrease may have been the direct effect of fishpond management, especially the negative effect of increasing fish stocks (Musil & Šálek 1994, Musil *et al.* 2001). Fishponds represent the most common wetland type in the Czech Republic, with about 20 000 fishponds covering 50 000 ha. These fishponds are the result of landscape modifications by several generations that have led to the development of shallow, eutrophic water bodies, often over-grown with littoral macrophytes, and thus suitable for breeding, resting or migrating waterfowl. Fish production (mostly Carp *Cyprinus carpio*) was about 50 kg/ha until the end of the 19th century, increasing to more than 1 000 kg/ha from 1950 to 1980.

More recently, the important grazing effect of fish (especially Carp) has been recognised as a factor affecting benthic and plankton communities, the extent of littoral vegetation, and consequently water transparency and chemistry. As a result, there is an overgrowth of phytoplankton, water turbidity increases, and the light cannot penetrate to the deeper water layers where anaerobiosis may occur.

Negative effects of fish stock density on the July density of diving ducks were found by Pykal & Janda (1994) in fishponds in South Bohemia. A similar relationship was also found in Mallard, Gadwall, Pochard, Tufted Duck and Coot in fishponds near Ismaning – an important moulting site for waterfowl in the whole Central European Region (Krosick & Köhler 2000). The numbers and reproductive output of waterfowl in non-fishpond wetlands have also been negatively affected by fish stock density

(Eriksson 1978, Giles 1994). The response of individual waterbird species to competition for food with fish depends on many factors, but the most vulnerable are specialised species requiring certain groups or a certain size of benthic animals (Draulans 1982, Giles 1994; Winfield & Winfield 1994). The survival rate of the flightless young may be affected by the availability of food close to nesting sites (Cox *et al.* 1998, Sjöberg *et al.* 2000).

A preference for fishponds with younger fish stock and higher water transparency was found in diving duck broods (Musil *et al.* 1997, 2002) and in Little Grebe (Cepák *et al.* 1999) in fishponds of the Třeboň Biosphere Reserve, and in several duck and grebe species (Pavelka & Košťál 2000) in fishponds of the Poodfií Landscape Protected Area in North Moravia. Comparisons of habitat selection in adults and broods of Pochard and Tufted Duck (Musil *et al.* 2002, Musil *et al.* in litt.) show that fishponds with younger fish stock and higher water transparency were preferred especially by broods and adults in July (i.e. in the moulting period). On the other hand, larger, isolated fishponds with well developed littoral stands are more preferred in March and April (Musil *et al.* in litt.).

Fishponds currently represent the most important habitat for waterfowl breeding in the Czech Republic (Musil *et al.* 2001). Although any management recommendations have to respect the original purpose of fishponds, fish stock density could be lowered in some selected fishponds, such as those in SPAs or Nature Reserves. The development of natural food supplies (large zooplankton, benthos, littoral fauna) should be supported and the physical characteristics of fishponds improved, especially water transparency.

Fishponds with conditions suitable for breeding waterbird species are those having a fish stock density less than 400 kg/ha and water transparency more than 50 cm. Generally, a typical fish stock composed of Carp should be replaced by a mixed fish stock of Tench and Pike or Perch. The biomass of fish in mixed stock has to be lower in the first year of a two-year cycle (c. 100-150 kg/ha). Fishpond systems should include ponds with fry (i.e. fish hatched in the current year) which may be very important for waterfowl broods moving to habitats with low fish-competition and high invertebrate food availability (Pykal 1995, Musil *et al.* 2001).

## REFERENCES

Cepák, J., Musil, P. & Voldánová, G. 1999. Trends in breeding populations of grebes in the Czech Republic: indicators of environmental changes. Vogelwelt 120: 283-288.

Cox, R.R. Jr., Hanson, M.A., Roy, C.C., Euliss, N.H., Johnson, D.H. & Butler, M.G. 1998. Mallard duckling growth and survival in relation to aquatic invertebrates. Journal of Wildlife Management 62: 124-133.

**Draulans, D.** 1982. Foraging and size selection of mussels by the Tufted Duck *Aythya fuligula*. Journal of Animal Ecology 51: 943-956.

**Eriksson, M.O.G.** 1978: Lake selection by Goldeneye ducklings in relation to the abundance of food. Wildfowl 29: 81-85.

**Giles, N.** 1994. Tufted Duck (*Aythya fuligula*) habitat use and brood survival increases after fish removal from gravel pit lakes. Hydrobiologia 279/280: 587-592.

**Hudec, K.** (ed.) 1994. Fauna of the Czech and Slovak Republics, Birds 1. Academia Praha. [In Czech with German summary].

**Hudec, K. & Černý, W.** (eds) 1977. Fauna of the CSSR, Birds 2. Academia, Praha. [In Czech with German summary].

**Krosick von, E. & Köhler, P.** 2000. The long-term changes in numbers and distribution of moulting waterbirds according to changes in trophic level, fish stock and water level in Ramsar site "Ismaninger Speichersee mit Fischteichen". Orn. Anz. 39: 135-158. [In German with English summary].

**Musil, P., Albrecht, T., Cepák, J., Fialová, Š. a kol**. 2002. Population dynamics and habitat preferences of Pochard (*Aythya ferina*) and Tufted Ducks *(Aythya fuligula)*. Abstracts of national conference "Zoologické dny – Brno 2002": 102. [In Czech].

**Musil, P. Cepák, J., Hudec, K. & Zárybnický, J**. 2001. The long- term trends in the breeding waterfowl populations in the Czech Republic. OMPO & Institute of Applied Ecology, Kostelec nad Černými lesy. 120 pp.

**Musil, P. & Fuchs, R.** 1994. Changes in abundance of water birds species in southern Bohemia (Czech Republic) in the last 10 years. Development in Hydrobiology. In: J.J. Kerekes. (ed.) Aquatic birds in trophic web of lakes. Hydrobiologia 279/280: 511-519.

**Musil, P., Pichlová, R., Veselý, P. & Cepák, J**. 1997. Habitat selection by waterfowl broods on intensively managed fishponds in South Bohemia (Czech Republic). Wetlands International Publication 43: 169-176.

**Musil, P. & Šálek, M.** 1994. Changes in abundance of water and wetland birds in South Bohemia during the last decade: summary review. In: G. Aubrecht, G. Dick, & C. Prentice (eds.) Monitoring of Ecological Change in Wetlands of Middle Europe. Proceedings of International Workshop, Linz, Austria, 1993. Stapfia 31, Linz, Austria, and IWRB Publication No. 30, Slimbridge, UK: 55-60.

**Pavelka, K. & Košťál, J.** 2000. Water and wetland birds on fishponds with different carp fishstocks in the Poodfií floodplain, 1993-98. *Sylvia* 36(supplement): 17.

**Pykal, J. & Janda, J.** 1994. Numbers of waterbirds on south Bohemian fishponds in relation to fishpond management. *Sylvia* 30: 3-11. [In Czech with English summary].

**Pykal, J.** 1996. Recommendation for pro management of Important Bird Areas on fishponds. Proc. IBA in the Czech Republic, Kostelec nad âernˇmi Lesy 1995: 80-84. [In Czech with English summary].

**Sjöberg, K., Pöysä, H., Elmberg, J. & Nummi, P.** 2000. Response of Mallard ducklings to variation in habitat quality: an experiment of food limitation. Ecology 81(2): 329-335.

**Šťastný, K., Bejček, V. & Hudec, K.** 1997. Atlas breeding birds in the Czech Republic in 1985-1989. H & H, Jinoãany. [In Czech with English summary].

**Šťastný, K., Randík, A. & Hudec, K**. 1987. Atlas breeding birds in Czechoslovakia hnízdního rozšíření ptáků v ČSSR 1973/77. Academia Praha. [In Czech with English summary].

**Winfield, D.K. & Winfield, I.J.** 1994. Possible competitive interactions between overwintering Tufted Duck *Aythya fuligula* and fish population of Lough Neagh, Northern Ireland: evidence from diet studies. Hydrobiologia 279/280: 377-386.

Low intensity fish ponds managed at low intensity are of great importance for waterbirds in central Europe. Orsoya fishpond, Bulgaria. Photo: Nikolai Petkov.

# Identification of Common Snipe *Gallinago gallinago* flyways in the Western Palearctic by analysis of ringing recoveries and genetic studies

*Saulius Svazas[1] & Algimantas Paulauskas[2]*

[1]*Institute of Ecology of Vilnius University, Akademijos 2, LT-2600 Vilnius, Lithuania. (email: svazas@ekoi.lt)*

[2] *Vytautas Magnus University, Vileikos 8, LT-3035 Kaunas, Lithuania.*

Svazas, S. & Paulauskas, A. 2006. Identification of Common Snipe *Gallinago gallinago* flyways in the Western Palearctic by analysis of ringing recoveries and genetic studies. *Waterbirds around the world.* Eds. G.C. Boere, C.A. Galbraith & D.A. Stroud. The Stationery Office, Edinburgh, UK. pp. 522-523.

The Common Snipe *Gallinago gallinago* is a common and widely distributed species in the Western Palearctic. It is mostly migratory in Europe, although those breeding in Ireland, UK and maritime countries of Western Europe are only partially migratory or sedentary (Cramp & Simmons 1983). There are major gaps in our knowledge about the flyways of the Common Snipe in the Western Palearctic, notably how breeding and wintering grounds are linked.

As a secretive and widely dispersed bird, the Common Snipe is one of the most difficult species to count within the framework of the International Waterbird Census (IWC). The maximum regional IWC count total of about 20 000 birds is much smaller than 1% of the total European population of the Common Snipe (Gillissen *et al.* 2002). The great majority of ring recoveries are from Western Europe and these are of mainly passage migrants of unknown origin. The main flyways outside Western Europe are poorly known.

A new ringing scheme for the Common Snipe was recently developed by the international association "Migratory Birds of the Western Palearctic" ("OMPO") in Lithuania, NW Russia, Belarus and Poland. In 1998-2003 about 3 500 Common Snipe were ringed and measured, including 486 birds from breeding populations of Lithuania, NW Russia and Belarus (juveniles or adults mist-netted in the nesting territory). A total of 38 ringing recoveries have been reported.

Analysis of recoveries of Common Snipe of Lithuanian origin indicates a tendency of these birds to concentrate in the autumn-winter period along the North Sea coast of France. More than 80% of all recoveries were from northern France (Svazas *et al.* 2002). A similar pattern of recoveries has been reported for Common Snipe ringed in NW Russia (Kharitonov 1998). The great majority of migrating Common Snipe ringed at the Baltic coast of Poland were also recovered in northern France, with some recoveries also from Ireland and Britain (Meissner 2000).

There is a different pattern of recoveries of Common Snipe ringed in Belarus (Mongin 2002): only a few from northern Belarus were from northern France, and southern Belarus breeding birds migrate towards the West Mediterranean region. Ringing data indicate that Belarus is located on a dividing line between two different flyways.

Analysis of the genetic structure of the Common Snipe population was performed to determine possible genetic divergence within different sub-populations of this species. A total of 164 samples were collected for genetic analysis from breeding populations in Lithuania, Belarus and NW Russia, and from migratory/wintering populations in France, Britain and Morocco. The random amplified polymorphic DNA (RAPD) method was applied. Ten primers were used for amplification. Three primers, each consisting of ten base pairs, were effectively used for amplification by means of the RAPD method. All three

primers formed a certain number of fragments of the genomic DNA. The fragments of a different size corresponded to various analyzed sampling units. The value of genetic similarity between different populations was defined calculating the number of common fragments and total number of fragments.

The results of this analysis have revealed that the breeding population in the Eastern Baltic region is very similar, with a high coefficient of genetic similarity (0.888) to the genetic structure of wintering birds collected in northern France (Paulauskas & Svazas 2002). Genetically similar birds were collected in southern France and in breeding sites located in southern Belarus (coefficient of genetic similarity 0.727). Common Snipe sampled in central and eastern France represented a genetically transitional population structure, intermediate between the NW Europe and Central Europe/West Mediterranean populations. The genotype of sub-species *Gallinago gallinago faroeensis,* collected in the Hebridean islands, was significantly different from all other investigated populations.

Combined ring recoveries data and the results of these genetic studies suggest that there are four flyways of the Common Snipe in the Western Palearctic (Fig. 1). The Northeast Atlantic flyway includes breeders from Iceland, the Faeroe Islands and northern Scottish islands, wintering mostly in Ireland and Britain. The NW

Fig. 1. Designated flyways of the Common Snipe in the Western Palearctic: Northeast Atlantic flyway (1), North-West Europe flyway (2), Continental Europe flyway (3), and South-East Europe flyway (4).

Europe flyway includes breeders from northern Russia, Fennoscandia, Baltic States, northern Belarus, northern Poland and maritime countries of Western Europe, wintering in northern France, Britain, Ireland and in NW Africa. Results of this study indicate the existence of a distinct Continental Europe flyway, including breeders of central Russia, southern Belarus, western Ukraine and Central Europe, migrating largely towards the West Mediterranean region. According to available direct recoveries, Common Snipe wintering in Central and Western Africa can be ascribed to the Continental Europe flyway (Kharitonov 1998, Rouxel 2000). Kharitonov (1998) has defined the SE Europe flyway, linking breeding grounds of Common Snipe in southern Russia and eastern Ukraine with their wintering sites located in the Black Sea/East Mediterranean region, Eastern Africa and the Middle East.

The designated population limits are very similar to those suggested by Hemery & Nicolau-Guillaumet (1979), from analysis of more than 1 500 recoveries of the Common Snipe in France. The suggested NW Europe flyway of the Common Snipe is identical to population limits defined by means of analysis of ring recoveries of Fennoscandian birds (Kålås 1980). Kharitonov (1998) has suggested the existence of two major migratory routes of the Common Snipe in the Western Palearctic: European-West African and Southern Russia and Central/East African/Middle East. These were defined from analysis of nearly 200 ring recoveries available in the former USSR. The data from our study indicate that the European-West African migratory route, suggested by Kharitonov (1998), includes two different NW Europe and Continental Europe flyways.

The defined limits of different flyways of Common Snipe in the Western Palearctic are essential for conservation and wise management of this species. A continuous chain of available key habitats stretching throughout the whole flyway is an obligatory condition for the survival of the Common Snipe population (Devort *et al.* 1997, Rouxel 2000).

## ACKNOWLEDGEMENTS

This study would not have been possible without the support of OMPO who funded field surveys and the genetic study of the Common Snipe in Eastern Europe, and provided samples of Common Snipe for genetic analysis from Western Europe and Africa.

## REFERENCES

**Cramp, S. & Simmons, K.F.L. (eds).** 1983. The birds of the Western Palearctic. Vol. 3., Oxford University Press, Oxford.

**Devort, M., Chevallier, F., Lethier, H., Olivier, G.-N. & Veiga, J.** 1997. The Common Snipe. Elements of an action plan. Editions Confluences & OMPO, Bordeaux.

**Gillissen, N., Haanstra, L., Delany, S., Boere, G. & Hagemeijer, W.** 2002. Numbers and distribution of wintering waterbirds in the Western Palearctic and South West Asia in 1997, 1998 and 1999. Results from the International Waterbird Census. Wetlands International Global Series No. 11, Wageningen.

**Hemery, G. & Nicolau-Guillaumet, P.** 1979. Geographical routes of Common Snipes migrating and wintering in France. Bulletin ONC 79: 43-69. (In French).

**Kålås, J.A.** 1980. Migration of Common Snipes ringed in Fennoscandia. Fauna Norvegica 3: 84-88.

**Kharitonov, S.** 1998. Migration and some population parameters for Common Snipe in Eastern Europe and North Asia. In: C. Zykov (ed) Study of the status and trends of migratory bird populations in Russia. OMPO & Severtzov Institute of Ecology and Evolution, Moscow: 136-155.

**Meissner, W.** 2000. Long-term ringing data of snipes in the coastal region of Poland. OMPO Newsletter 21: 63-73.

**Mongin, E.** 2002. Snipes in Belarus. In: S. Svazas (ed) Snipes of the Eastern Baltic region and Belarus. OMPO Vilnius, Vilnius: 15-36.

**Paulauskas, A. & Svazas, S**. 2002. Genetic study of Western Palearctic populations of the Common Snipe. In: S. Svazas (ed) Snipes of the Eastern Baltic region and Belarus. OMPO Vilnius, Vilnius: 82-95.

**Rouxel, R.** 2000. Snipes of the Western Palearctic. OMPO & Eveil Nature, Paris.

**Svazas, S., Raudonikis, L., Jusys, V. & Zydelis, R**. 2002. Snipes in Lithuania. In: S. Svazas (ed) Snipes of the Eastern Baltic region and Belarus. OMPO Vilnius, Vilnius: 63-82.

Common Snipe *Gallinago gallinago.* Photo: Simon Stirrup.

# Crossing the ultimate ecological barrier: evidence for an 11 000 km long non-stop flight from Alaska to New Zealand and eastern Australia by Bar-tailed Godwits *Limosa lapponica*

*Robert E. Gill, Jr.[1], Theunis Piersma[2], Gary Hufford[3], Rene Servranckx[4] & Adrian Riegen[5]*

[1]*Alaska Science Center, U.S. Geological Survey, 1011 E. Tudor Road, Anchorage, Alaska 99503, USA. (email: robert_gill@usgs.gov)*

[2]*Animal Ecology Group, Center for Ecological and Evolutionary Studies, University of Groningen, PO Box 14, 9750 AA Haren, The Netherlands, and Department of Marine Ecology and Evolution, Royal Netherlands Institute for Sea Research (NIOZ), PO Box 59, 1790 AB Den Burg, Texel, The Netherlands.*

[3]*National Weather Service, National Oceanic and Atmospheric Administration, Alaska Region, 222 W. 7th Ave. No. 23, Anchorage, Alaska 99513, USA.*

[4]*Canadian Meteorological Service, 2121 N. Service Road, Trans Canada Highway, Dorval, Quebec, H9P 1J3, Canada.*

[5]*231 Forest Hill Road, Waiatarua, Auckland 8, New Zealand.*

Gill, R.E., Jr., Piersma, T., Hufford, G., Servranckx, R. & Riegen, A. 2006. Crossing the ultimate ecological barrier: evidence for an 11 000 km long non-stop flight from Alaska to New Zealand and eastern Australia by Bar-tailed Godwits *Limosa lapponica*. *Waterbirds around the world*. Eds. G.C. Boere, C.A. Galbraith & D.A. Stroud. The Stationery Office, Edinburgh, UK. pp. 524-534.

## ABSTRACT

Populations of the Bar-tailed Godwit *Limosa lapponica* embark on some of the longest migrations known among birds. The *baueri* race breeds in western Alaska and spends the non-breeding season a hemisphere away in New Zealand and eastern Australia; the *menzbieri* race breeds in Siberia and migrates to western and northern Australia. Although the Siberian birds are known to follow the coast of Asia during both migrations, the southern pathway followed by the Alaska breeders has remained unknown. Two questions have particular ecological importance: (1) do Alaska godwits migrate directly across the Pacific, a distance of 11 000 km; and (2) are they capable of doing this in a single flight without stopping to rest or refuel? We explored six lines of evidence to answer these questions. The distribution of resightings of marked birds of the *baueri* and *menzbieri* races was significantly different between northward and southward flights, with virtually no marked *baueri* resighted along the Asian mainland during southward migration. The timing of southward migration of the two races further indicates the absence of a coastal Asia route by *baueri*, with peak passage of godwits in general occurring there a month prior to the departure of most birds from Alaska. The use of a direct route across the Pacific is also supported by significantly more records of godwits reported from within a direct migration corridor than elsewhere in Oceania, and during the September to November period than at other times of the year. The annual but rare occurrence of Hudsonian Godwits *Limosa haemastica* in New Zealand and the absence of records of this species along the Asian mainland also support a direct flight, and are best explained by Hudsonian Godwits accompanying Bar-tailed Godwits from known communal staging areas in Alaska. Flight simulation models, extreme fat loads, and the apparent evolution of a wind-selected migration from Alaska further support a direct, non-stop flight.

Note: This paper is an abbreviated version of the original that appeared in the February 2005 issue of The Condor.

## INTRODUCTION

The timing of human settlement of the Earth's biomes appears to be related not only to the physical extent of ecological barriers encountered but also to their inhospitable nature. In this sense, the Pacific Ocean arguably represents the most formidable ecological barrier, with human expansion into the far reaches of Oceania occurring only within the past 3 000-4 000 years (Hurles *et al.* 2003). But does the Pacific Ocean present a similar ecological barrier to birds? Obviously not to those forms adapted for existence on and from the sea. And surprisingly it appears not to for many land-birds, as more of these species have migrations crossing portions of the Pacific than across any other ocean (Williams & Williams 1999). For example, several species of shorebirds migrating from Alaska must cross a minimum of 3 500 km of open ocean before reaching Hawaii, and even large portions of these populations overfly the Hawaiian Archipelago en route to the next available land 3 000 km farther south (Thompson 1973, Williams & Williams 1988, 1990, 1999, Marks & Redmond 1994, Johnson 2003). The limits of such non-stop flights are pushed even further by Red Knots *Calidris canutus* and Bar-tailed Godwits *Limosa lapponica* that migrate northward from southeastern Australia and New Zealand to staging sites along the coast of the Yellow Sea, a distance of over 8 000 km (Battley 1997, Battley & Piersma 2005, J. Wilson and C. Minton unpubl. data).

Two subspecies of the Bar-tailed Godwit occur in the central Pacific basin (Higgins & Davies 1996, Engelmoer & Roselaar 1998, McCaffery & Gill 2001). The *L. l. menzbieri* population breeds in central northern Siberia and spends the non-breeding season in western and northern Australia. Members of the *L. l. baueri* population nest in Alaska and spend the non-breeding season in New Zealand and eastern Australia. In the Anadyr Basin area of Chukotka, there is a third, much smaller breeding population of unresolved taxonomic affinity (Engelmoer & Roselaar 1998, see Discussion). The *menzbieri* population, numbering about 170 000 birds, appears to migrate both north and south in a two-stage flight with the leg from western Australia to the Yellow Sea and Korean Peninsula entailing a 6 000 km-long non-stop effort (Barter & Wang 1990, Wilson & Barter 1998, J. Wilson and C. Minton unpubl. data), and the southward leg an 8 000 km-long flight from the Sea of Okhotsk (M. Barter pers. comm.). The *baueri* population is slightly smaller (Gill & McCaffery 1999, McCaffery & Gill 2001, Minton in press), and during northward migration birds are thought to undertake a single flight of between 5 000 and 8 000 km (Riegen 1999, J. Wilson and C. Minton unpubl. data). The advent of intensive marking programs initiated in New Zealand and Australia in the late 1970s (Riegen 1999, J. Wilson and C. Minton unpubl. data) has shown that birds marked within the non-breeding range of *baueri* do not occur along the Asian coast during southward migration. This led Barter (1989) and others (Barter & Wang 1990, Riegen 1999, J. Wilson and C. Minton unpubl. data) to speculate that the southward flight is instead direct across the Pacific, a minimum distance of about 9 700 km to north-eastern Australia and 10 800 km to New Zealand.

Māori folklore lends support to godwits crossing this large ecological barrier. When living on a small Pacific island north of New Zealand, they noticed that the kūaka (Bar-tailed Godwit) migrated every year in a southerly direction. From this evidence, they deduced that land was to be found to the south, and canoes were outfitted for a voyage that eventually led to the discovery of Aotearoa (New Zealand), their new home (Gudgeon 1903, Te Paa 1912, Phillipps 1966, Riley 2001).

Building upon these millennia-old observations, our objective here is to answer two fundamental and oft-pondered questions concerning the southward migration of the *baueri* race of the Bar-tailed Godwit: (1) do birds migrate across the Pacific Ocean between Alaska and New Zealand, a distance of 11 000 km, and (2) are they capable of doing this in a single flight without stopping to rest or refuel? We address these questions by exploring six lines of evidence: (1) distributional records and chronology of occurrence of godwits during migration periods; (2) differential resighting rates of leg-flagged birds seen during northward and southward migrations; (3) comparisons between departure and arrival events recorded at migration termini; (4) annual occurrence of a congener, the Hudsonian Godwit *L. haemastica*, in Oceania; (5) analyses of maximum flight ranges; and (6) synoptic weather and wind-field analyses across the Pacific and atmospheric trajectory models at the time of known departures from Alaska.

## METHODS
### Distributional records and chronology throughout Oceania

If godwits undertake a direct trans-Pacific flight from Alaska to New Zealand and eastern Australia, they would be expected to occur in central Oceania either as occasional fall-outs from migrating flocks or at regularly used stopover sites. To assess this, we turned to three principal sources (see Gill *et al.* 2005 for details). Combined, they represent over 300 field assessments (with 568 monthly records) collected since the early 1920s (see Gill *et al.* 2005 for assumptions).

We also assessed seasonal occurrence from census data obtained at sites where counts have been conducted throughout the annual cycle (Gill *et al.* 2005).

### Band recoveries and sightings of leg-flagged birds

We used band recovery and resighting data to assess seasonal migration routes of godwits. The banding databases for godwits contain a combined total of about 14 000 records, including about 10 000 since the early 1980s representing birds on which various colors of leg flags, specific to individual countries or regions, were applied. Much of the information for godwits has previously been summarized by Riegen (1999), Minton *et al.* (2002), and J. Wilson and C. Minton (unpubl. data). Almost annually since the mid-1990s, there have been efforts dedicated to observing marked godwits, both on the migration staging

grounds in Alaska (Gill & McCaffery 1999) and at migration stopover sites in Japan, Korea, and China (J. Wilson and C. Minton unpubl. data).

### Timing of arrival and departure

To assess levels of concordance between periods of departure and arrival, we relied on available seasonal census data from breeding, non-breeding, and migratory stopover sites of both the *baueri* and *menzbieri* subspecies. Most of these studies were conducted independently of each other and focused on site-specific issues and not broad geographic regions or range-wide assessments. Nevertheless, they are of sufficient number and scope that comparisons can be made, especially within the past decade, when we made concerted efforts to document departures from Alaska and arrivals in New Zealand.

### Maximum flight range predictions

For an energy-based evaluation of the proposed 11 000 km-long trans-Pacific flight by godwits, we computed maximum flight ranges (i.e. the distance flown in still-air conditions until the fuel store is depleted) and changes in other variables using an advanced program that encompasses the family of flight-mechanic models presented in Pennycuick (1989). These were later modified to account for use of protein stores during long-distance flights (Pennycuick 1998). The variables used in program FLIGHT and assumptions we make for several of these variables are presented in Table 1 of Gill *et al.* (2005).

### Environmental data

In the previous predictions, we assumed that flight speed was unaffected by winds, but a number of waterbird species staging in south-western Alaska have been shown to have wind-aided southward migrations (see Discussion). To learn if departures of godwits from Alaska were correlated with weather, we looked at synoptic weather and wind-field data from the September-November migration period. From this, we wanted to learn not only what weather characteristics were associated with known departure events, but also the frequency, intensity, and track of storms that occurred throughout the North Pacific during the staging period. This investigation also lead us to look at en route winds, both those associated with departures and those across the central and southern Pacific Ocean. To learn the extent of favorable winds provided by storms during departure, we used a Lagrangian atmospheric trajectory model (CMC 2001).

To assess winds over the Pacific Ocean once birds had departed on migration, we used two sources. For the observed departure in 1987, we obtained data (2.5° latitude x 2.5° longitude grid) from the NOAA-CRIES Climate Diagnostic Center (CDC 2004); for all other departures, we used data (presented by 0.9° x 0.9° grid) from the CMC Global Data Assimilation and Forecast System (CMC 2004). (For this effort, both have been converted to a 10° x 10° grid). Even though it is unlikely that birds migrate at a constant altitude, we simplified our analysis by selecting winds at the 850 mb (c. 1 500 m) level, a general height at which shorebirds in other studies have been shown to migrate (citations in Green 2003). See Gill *et al.* (2005) for additional details.

### Statistical analyses

Reported values are means ± SD. For assumptions associated with various statistical tests, see Gill *et al.* (2005).

**Table 1.** Variables used in the simulation of flight ranges (distance to depletion of fuel store) for male Bar-tailed Godwits *Limosa lapponica* departing Alaska on an 11 000 km-long flight[a] to New Zealand and eastern Australia (Program Flight, version 1.15).

| Variables (SI-units) | Values |
|---|---|
| **General assumptions[b]** | |
| Basal metabolic rate equation[c] | for non-passerines |
| Induced power factor | 1.2 |
| Profile power ratio | 0.903 |
| Acceleration due to gravity (m sec$^{-1}$) | 9.81 |
| Fat energy density (J kg$^{-1}$) | $3.90 * 10^7$ |
| Dry protein density (J kg$^{-1}$) | $1.83 * 10^7$ |
| Protein hydration ratio[d] | 2.2 |
| Conservation efficiency | 0.23 |
| Circulation and respiration factor | 1.1 |
| Density of muscle (kg m$^{-3}$) | 1 060 |
| Mitochondria inverse power density (m$^3$ W$^{-1}$) | $1.2 * 10^{-6}$ |
| Power density of mitochondria | constant |
| **Specific assumptions[e]** | |
| Altitude of flight (m) | 0 or 1 500 |
| Air density (kg m$^{-3}$) | 1.23 |
| Starting ratio V:V$_{mp}$ | 1.2 |
| Flight speed during trip[f] | constant |
| Specific work | constant |
| Minimum energy from protein (%) | 5 |
| Body drag coefficient | 0.1 or 0.05 |
| **Bird-related measurements** | |
| Wing span (m)[g] | 0.73 |
| Aspect ratio[h] | 9.3 |
| Wing area (m2)[i] | 0.0573 |
| Body mass at start (g)[j] | 455, 485, or 515 |
| Fresh mass of pectoral muscle at start (g)[j] | 67, 72, or 76 |
| Fat mass at start (g)[j] | always 200 |
| Airframe mass at start (g)[j] | 188, 213, 239 |

[a] The great circle distance between the most northerly Alaska staging site (Yukon Delta) and the northern tip of New Zealand is 10 700 km; that between the most southerly staging site (Nelson Lagoon) and northern Queensland, Australia, is 9 700 km. We assume godwits follow a great circle route (orthodrome), although a constant compass course (loxodrome route) would likely add little additional distance since the departure and arrival sites occur along a north-south axis.

[b] Based on standard settings in the program Flight and as verified by Pennycuick & Battley (2003).

[c] Changing it to the passerine equation in view of high BMR in many shorebirds (Kersten & Piersma 1987) has remarkably little effect on the model outcomes (see program FLIGHT).

[d] This is the ratio of water released and lost through respiration as dry protein is combusted, assuming that water makes up 69% of wet protein.

[e] Specific to southward migrating *baueri* godwits, with the body drag coefficient and altitude being varied.

[f] Flight speed (i.e. true air speed; see program FLIGHT) is a function of the starting body mass.

[g] Based on a sample of 26 male *baueri* godwits from non-breeding grounds in New Zealand (Battley & Piersma 2005).

[h] Based on a sample of wing tracings of three *baueri* godwits from Alaska (C. J. Pennycuick pers. comm.).

[i] Computed from wing span and aspect ratio.

[j] Based on a variety of body mass and body composition values.

## RESULTS

### Seasonal occurrence, distribution, and numbers of birds in Oceania

We found records of godwits in Oceania during every month of the year (Fig. 1A), but most frequently during the southward migration period (September-November) when 49% of all monthly records ($n = 254$) are attributed. No other month accounted for more than 8% of the total. We found a similar temporal pattern at Suva Point, Fiji, the only site in Oceania at which systematic counts of godwits have been conducted for extended periods (Fig. 1B).

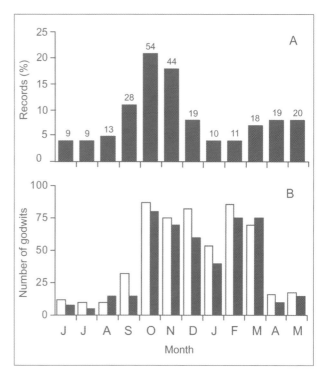

Fig. 1. (A) Percentage of total records of occurrence ($n = 254$) of Bar-tailed Godwits *Limosa lapponica* throughout Oceania each month. Numbers above bars show number of records. (B) Number of godwit records during monthly censuses at Suva Point, Fiji; solid bars from Skinner (1983) and open bars from D. Watling (unpubl. data).

The geographic occurrence of godwits in Oceania was widespread, with birds noted from most (77%) of the 30 major archipelagoes and from over 350 different atolls and islands within. Only from central and eastern Polynesia (e.g. Southern Cook, Marquises, Austral, Gambier, Line, most of the Tuamotu, and Pitcairn islands) have birds not been recorded.

We also found a significant difference between the southward migration period and the rest of the year ($21 = 32.4$, $P < 0.001$) when we looked at geographic distribution of records in Oceania by season. Most sites where godwits were recorded during the September-November period occurred throughout a corridor linking Alaska and the non-breeding grounds in eastern Australia and New Zealand (Fig. 2). The same pattern was found when total maximum counts per site were compared inside and outside the migration corridor. When adjusted for sites with multi-year records, 93% ($n = 868$) of all godwits noted during the southward migration period came from sites within the likely migration corridor. The proportion increased to 97% when records just outside but east of the corridor (Hawaiian and Cook

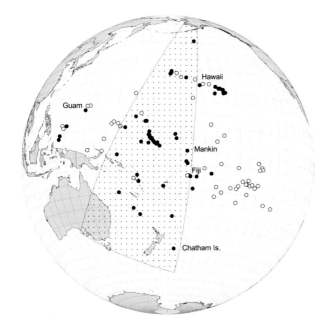

**Fig. 2.** Distribution of records of Bar-tailed Godwits *Limosa lapponica* throughout Oceania during the southward migration period (September-November). Filled circles = sites reporting godwits; unfilled circles = sites at which no godwits were noted during the period. Map projection = Orthographic (central meridian = 180; reference latitude = –10). Lateral bounds of stippled region = plotted great circle routes.

islands) were also considered (Fig. 2). Most (87%) of the 868 birds were recorded from four sites in the southern half of the migration corridor: Mankin Atoll (120 birds) in the Tungaru Islands, Rewa River (200 birds) and Suva Point (121 birds) in Fiji, and Chatham Island (314 birds) east of New Zealand (Fig. 2). When these four sites are not considered, the average maximum number of godwits recorded at sites elsewhere in Oceania during southward migration was similar both outside (4.6 ± 7.1, range 1–21) and inside (2.8 ± 3.9, range 1–20) the corridor (Mann-Whitney $U$-test: $z = 0.9$, $n = 13, 37$, $P = 0.19$).

### Resightings of marked birds
The proportions of color-flagged godwits of the two subspecies that were resighted along the coast of Asia during northward

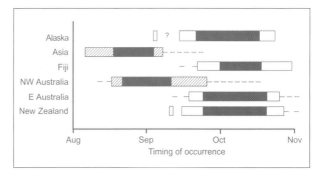

**Fig. 3.** Timing of southern passage of Bar-tailed Godwit *Limosa lapponica* races *baueri* (unfilled bars) and *menzbieri* (cross-hatched bars) at different locations along their migration route. Filled portions of bars indicate periods of peak passage; dashed lines indicate periods of movement. See Gill *et al.* (2005) for sources.

and southward migrations differed markedly (Table 2; $\chi_1^2 = 36.8$, $P < 0.001$). On northward migration, both *baueri* and *menzbieri* regularly used intermediate stopover sites; during southward migration, however, *menzbieri* were still commonly sighted along the coast of Asia whereas *baueri*, with but three exceptions, have gone unreported. Sightings of marked *baueri* ($n = 136$; R. Gill and B. McCaffery unpubl. data), but not of marked *menzbieri*, on the Alaska staging grounds from late August through September (1999-2004) further indicate the extent of separation of the two subspecies during southward migration.

### Timing of departure and arrival
The average peak departure of godwits from Alaska and peak arrival in Fiji, New Zealand, and south-eastern Australia occur within a two- to three-week period from late September to mid-October (Fig. 3). Both departure from Alaska and arrival in New Zealand can be earlier, however, as recorded in 2003, when birds were seen leaving during the first week of September (Table 3) and the first arrivals were noted in New Zealand 6-10 days later (A. Riegen and P. Battley unpubl. data). In contrast, the southward passage of *menzbieri* godwits along the coast of Asia and arrival in Western Australia is a month earlier and essentially over before *baueri* godwits depart Alaska (Fig. 3).

**Table 2.** Seasonal distribution of resightings and recoveries of the *baueri* and *menzbieri* subspecies of the Bar-tailed Godwit *Limosa lapponica* along the coast of East Asia during the northward and southward migration. All putative *baueri* were marked on the non-breeding grounds in New Zealand and eastern Australia; *menzbieri* were marked in western Australia (but see footnotes for the few exceptions). See Gill *et al.* (2005) for sources of data.

| | Northward | | Southward | |
|---|---|---|---|---|
| Sighted in | *baueri* | *menzbieri* | *baueri* | *menzbieri* |
| Russia | 2 | 3 | 2 | 5 |
| Japan | 84[a] | 1 | | 2 |
| North Yellow Sea | 18 | 38 | 1 | 2 |
| Republic of Korea | 62 | 54 | | 35 |
| Hong Kong, Taiwan, SE China[b] | 2 | 52 | | 1 |
| **Total** | **168** | **148** | **3** | **45** |

[a] Includes one bird flagged in Japan in August and seen in New South Wales, Australia, in the subsequent February.

[b] Includes 40 birds (one *baueri* and 39 *menzbieri*) shot by hunters; the remainder are resightings of flagged birds including one juvenile flagged in Hong Kong and recovered in north-western Australia.

**Table 3.** **Conditions during departures of Bar-tailed Godwits** *Limosa lapponica* **on southward migration from sites on the Alaska Peninsula.**

| Departure period[a] | No. birds (no. flocks)[b] | Storm characteristics | | | Departure site winds | | Tail-wind component[d] | | |
| | | Low center position | Pressure (mb) | Distance & direction[c] from departure point | Speed (m sec⁻¹) | Direction | Speed (m sec⁻¹) | Direction | Fetch (km)[e] |
|---|---|---|---|---|---|---|---|---|---|
| 20 Oct 1987 (09:30) | >9 (?) | 47°N, 174°W | 976 | 1 100 km; 225° | 10 | N | 10–21 | NNW-NW | 1 200 |
| 24 Sep 1996 (03:00–07:00) | 492 (1) | 43°N, 175°W | 974 | 1 650 km; 237° | 4–8 | NNE | 8–23 | N-NW | 1 300 |
| 10–11 Oct 2000 (04:00–20:00) | >4 000 (?) | 55°N, 160°W | 986 | 650 km; 184° | 5–10 | NNE | 13–23 | N-NW | 900 |
| 3–5 Sep 2003 (09:00–10:00) | 5 090 (15) | 47°N, 162°W | 998 | 900 km; 183° | 0–5 | N | 8–15 | N-NNW | 1 100 |

[a] 1987 departure point: Cold Bay (55°20'N, 162°50'W); 1996 and 2000: Nelson Lagoon (56°00'N, 161°00'W); 2003: Egegik Bay (58°10'N, 157°30'W). All times Coordinated Universal Time (add 10 hr for local, Alaska Daylight Time).

[b] For details of 1987 departure see Piersma & Gill (1998); 1996 observation by R. Gill and M. Owens; 2000 observation by R. Gill; 2003 observation by R. Gill and D. Ruthrauff.

[c] Direction relative to true north from departure site.

[d] Winds along likely initial migration route from departure site.

[e] Fetch = longest distance with sustained winds from tail or quartering tail direction.

**Table 4.** **Predicted performance (according to program Flight) of male Bar-tailed Godwits** *Limosa lapponica* **initiating flight with given fuel stores and flight parameters (see Table 1) and flying until fat stores are depleted. Program FLIGHT assumes that a small part of the energy used comes from burning protein, primarily from pectoral muscle but also from other components of lean mass as well (see Methods for specifics).**

| Body drag coefficient | At start of flight | | | | At fat depletion | | Distance covered (km)[a] | Days in the air | Air speed (m sec⁻¹) |
| | Body mass (g) | Lean mass (g) | Fat mass (g) | Pectoral muscle mass(g) | Body mass (g) | Pectoral muscle mass (g) | | | |
|---|---|---|---|---|---|---|---|---|---|
| 0.10 | 455 | 255 | 200 | 67 | 183 | 28 | 9 303 | 7.0 | 15.3 |
| 0.10 | 485 | 285 | 200 | 72 | 213 | 32 | 8 154 | 6.0 | 15.6 |
| 0.10 | 515 | 315 | 200 | 76 | 243 | 36 | 7 240 | 5.3 | 15.9 |
| 0.05 | 455 | 255 | 200 | 67 | 188 | 30 | 12 883 | 8.2 | 18.2 |
| 0.05 | 485 | 285 | 200 | 72 | 214 | 33 | 11 308 | 7.0 | 18.6 |
| 0.05 | 515 | 315 | 200 | 76 | 244 | 37 | 10 049 | 6.1 | 19.0 |
| 0.05 | 485 | 285 | 200 | 54 | 213 | 24 | 11 308 | 7.0 | 18.6 |
| 0.05 | 515 | 285 | 230 | 76 | 202 | 29 | 12 928 | 7.9 | 19.0 |

[a] Distances covered based on flight at sea level.

## Maximum flight range predictions

With a starting body mass of 485 g, a fat mass of 200 g (= 41% body fat), and pectoral muscles adjusted to body mass, male Bar-tailed Godwits would be able to cover 11 000 km under still air conditions only if their body drag coefficient would be as low as 0.05 (Table 4, Fig. 4). Under either assumption for body drag, arrival body mass (213–214 g, or 75% of the lean mass at start) would be reasonable. (Note that Battley *et al.* 2000 found lean mass of Great Knots *Calidris tenuirostris* that arrived after a 5 400 km long flight to be c. 80% of lean mass at departure). Pectoral muscle masses of godwits at arrival (21-33 g) were small, but not unrealistically so (Landys-Ciannelli *et al.* 2003). A body drag coefficient of 0.05 appears to be realistic for godwits, since it produces a more consistent prediction of air speed (18.6 m sec⁻¹, or 67 km hr⁻¹), i.e. a value that is much closer to empirical values obtained by radar for godwits of the *L. l. taymyrensis* subspecies

during northward migration (18.4 m sec⁻¹; M. Green and T. Piersma unpubl. data), than for air speeds (15.6 m sec⁻¹) obtained with a body drag coefficient of 0.1 (Table 1).

Reducing body mass by 30 g and leaving fat mass at 200 g (44% fat) enhanced the predicted maximum flight range (Fig. 4), but led to inappropriately low arrival masses and very small pectoral muscle masses (Table 4). Increasing body mass by 30 g lean tissue (39% fat) led to lower maximum flight ranges but also to reasonable values for remaining body and pectoral muscle masses at the point of fat depletion (Table 4). When we decreased pectoral muscle mass at departure to 54 g based on the fraction of body mass measured in the sample of *baueri* from New Zealand (0.111; Battley & Piersma 2005), final body mass was of the right order but pectoral muscle mass (24 g) remaining after the flight was certainly too low (Table 4). When we gave birds with a lean mass of 285 g an extra 30 g of fat (thus

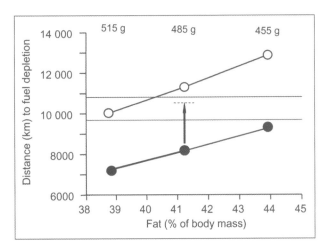

**Fig. 4.** Predicted maximum flight range (the distance to fuel depletion) in male Bar-tailed Godwits *Limosa lapponica*. Plot is a function of body mass (515, 485, or 455 g), variation in the percent fat of body mass at the start of the flight from Alaska (39-44%; with correlated variation in body mass, fat-free mass, and pectoral muscle mass, but with a constant fat load of 200 g), and two values for body drag coefficient (BDC). Solid circles indicate simulations using a BDC value of 0.1; unfilled circles indicate simulations using a value of 0.05. The solid horizontal lines represent great circle distances transited by godwits: the upper line at 10 800 km is the distance between the northernmost staging site in Alaska (Yukon Delta) and the northern tip of North Island, New Zealand; the lower line at 9 700 km is the distance between the southernmost staging site in Alaska (Nelson Lagoon) and Townsville, Queensland, Australia, the suspected northern portion of the non-breeding range of *baueri* in Australia. For a bird with a starting body mass of 485 g, a BDC of 0.1, an average constant flight speed of 15.4 m sec$^{-1}$, but with an average tail wind of 4.5 m sec$^{-1}$ for the entire distance, the flight range would be increased by 2 000 km, as indicated by the arrow and broken horizontal line. A similar proportional increase in flight range would occur in birds having a BDC of 0.05 (unfilled circles).

increasing pectoral muscle mass from 72 g to 76 g), they increased their maximum flight range, but reduced final body mass and pectoral muscle mass to quite low values.

### Departures in relation to weather

Actual departures of birds on southward migration from Alaska were observed on four occasions between 1987 and 2003 (Table 3; Gill *et al.* 2005). Observed departures spanned almost a seven-week period between early September and mid-October (Table 3). All four events occurred in association with moderate troughs with imbedded storms having central pressures between 976 and 998 mb (average 984 mb) and centered between 650 and 1 400 km south of the departure sites (Table 3, Fig. 5). Such storms are propagated in the Aleutian low pressure system along a track that, beginning in September, passes south along the Aleutian Islands and then northward into the Gulf of Alaska. During the period 1976-2000, storms with central pressure of between 975 and 1 000 mb occurred annually along this track on average twice in September, between two and three times in October, and just over three times in November. Local winds during the departure events varied in both direction and intensity, ranging between 0 and 10 m sec$^{-1}$ from north to north-east. The positions of the storm centers at the time of departure (Fig. 5) suggest that birds would have to have flown on a slight

west-south-west heading (200-240°) before obtaining maximum benefit from tail winds, but once positioned within the "upstream" side of the systems, birds flying in a southerly direction would have encountered strong direct to quartering tail winds averaging 15 m sec$^{-1}$ (mid-point of ranges, Table 3). Winds of this approximate speed and direction would have been maintained on average over a distance of about 1 000 km, with conditions associated with the 1996 departure, for example, extending almost 1 500 km south (Table 3, Fig. 6).

Winds during the mid-portion (latitudes 20° N to 20° S) of each of the four suspected flights (Fig. 5) were very similar and characterized by light (2-8 m sec$^{-1}$) crosswinds or quartering tail to head winds. Once into the southern realm of the south-east trades and austral westerlies at about days five and six of the flight, godwits again experienced strong direct tail or quartering tail winds over the last 1 000 km of the flight, especially if New Zealand was the destination. Any birds attempting to go to eastern Australia during the 2003 event would have experienced moderate to strong head winds from central Queensland south to Victoria, but mostly calm winds if landfall were in northern Queensland (Fig. 5).

### DISCUSSION

The evidence we present supporting a direct non-stop flight by *baueri* godwits between Alaska and New Zealand is straightforward and compelling: (1) *baueri* godwits are extremely rare along the central East Asian mainland on southward migration; (2) peak southward departure from Alaska and peak arrival in New Zealand occur within the same relatively short period, and both are a month later than for godwits (*L. l. menzbieri*) that do follow a continental Asia route; (3) too few godwits have been noted in Oceania to suggest any regularly used intermediate stopover site(s), but the birds that are recorded there peak in occurrence and number in October and within a direct corridor linking Alaska and New Zealand/eastern Australia when fallout of transients would be expected; (4) the annual occurrence of Hudsonian Godwits in New Zealand and eastern Australia (but their absence from mainland Asia) can best be explained by their accompanying Bar-tailed Godwits on a trans-Pacific flight; (5) birds appear energetically and mechanically capable of such a flight based on current knowledge of aerodynamics and measured fuel sources; and (6) known departures from Alaska coincide with favorable winds for a southward flight but are in opposition to a more south-westerly continental route. Aspects of several of these lines of evidence warrant additional discussion.

### Factors constraining flight range

The simulations with program Flight suggest that even under still air conditions Bar-tailed Godwits leaving staging sites in Alaska with realistic body and fat mass values should be able to reach New Zealand in a non-stop flight of between 9 800 and 10 700 km. If the godwits are able to use tail winds routinely en route (see below), we can relax the assumption of a body drag coefficient of 0.05 (but see Elliott *et al.* 2004) and accept a value closer to the more often used 0.1 (Kvist *et al.* 2001, Pennycuick & Battley 2003). In addition to fat as fuel, protein availability and water (dehydration) can limit flight range (Klaassen 1995, Jenni & Jenni-Eiermann 1999). For the *L. l. taymyrensis* subspecies during a 4 300 km-long northward flight from western Africa to Europe, Landys *et al.* (2000) concluded that

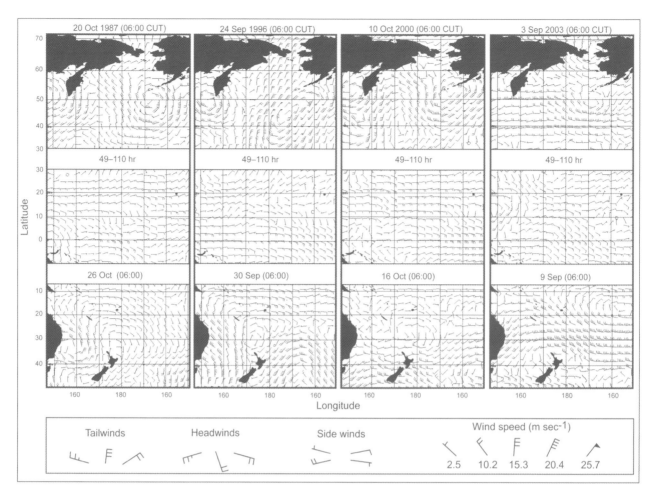

Fig. 5. En route winds (850 mb altitude) associated with the four recorded departures of Bar-tailed Godwits *Limosa lapponica* from Alaska. See Table 3 for location of departure sites. The upper panels represent winds at time of departure (± 3 hr, CUT = Coordinated Universal Time), middle panels show typical conditions between the 49th and 110th hr of the flight, and lower panels the conditions at the end (but are also representative of the preceding 24-36 hr). The long, unflagged portion of the axis of each wind bar points towards the direction the wind is blowing; the number and type of short flags perpendicular to the long axis of each wind bar indicate wind speed. The original wind vectors are depicted in knots and converted here to m sec⁻¹. The legend indicates the range of directions that would be tail winds, head winds, or side winds along the proposed trans-Pacific migratory corridor between Alaska and eastern Australia and New Zealand.

flights ranging in altitude from sea level to 3 000 m would avoid dehydration, and in fact found no evidence for dehydration in arriving godwits. Interestingly, Landys *et al.* (2000) also had to assume a body drag coefficient as low as 0.05 for the virtual godwits to complete their flight.

Our simulations have made clear that the necessary minimum protein use during non-stop flights does limit maximum flight range. Birds leaving Alaska with a lean mass lower than 275 g are predicted to have exhausted their fat when their lean mass is as low as 200 g and their pectoral muscles have become tiny (Table 4). The small-sized juvenile Bar-tailed Godwits with a lean mass of only 166 g and a fat store of 200 g that died during a collision probably just after take-off on a southward flight (Piersma & Gill 1998) are predicted (using the assumptions listed in Table 1) to be able to cover more than 11 000 km non-stop. Not surprisingly, they are also predicted to arrive with perhaps unrealistically low lean and pectoral muscle masses (for a body drag coefficient of 0.05, lean mass after 11 000 km of flight under still air conditions would be 170 g and pectoral muscle mass 25 g; with a coefficient of 0.1, the predicted final mass values are 130 g and 20 g, respectively). Given such values upon arrival in New Zealand, it seems unwar-

ranted to expect these birds to have been capable of reaching the South Pole, an additional distance of 6 000 km, as predicted by Pennycuick & Battley (2003) who accommodated unrealistic lean mass values. Lowering the minimum energy obtained from protein to 2% does not resolve the problem. In view of the absence of hard data on body composition for adult godwits, and the problematic departure condition of the juveniles from 1987, detailed studies on body condition at departure in relation to performance during the ensuing flight and pin-pointing the exact arrival time in New Zealand are clearly needed.

### A direct route or one with stopovers?
#### A direct flight by a congener
Hudsonian Godwits breed in subarctic and temperate North America and migrate to southern South America (Elphick & Klima 2002), yet are rare annual visitors to New Zealand (Higgins & Davies 1996, Elphick & Klima 2002) and occasionally elsewhere in Oceania (Watling 2001), with up to nine different individuals seen in a single year. What might explain the regular appearance of this species a hemisphere removed from its normal non-breeding range? It is highly unlikely that the Hudsonian Godwit, although also a long-distance migrant

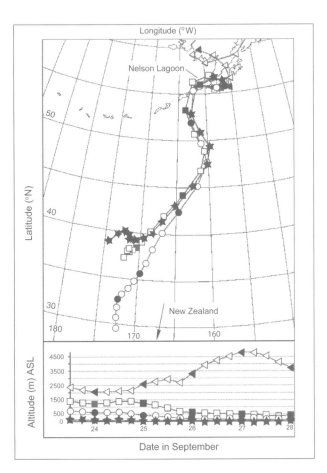

**Fig. 6.** Air flow over a five-day period for objects entering the air column at Nelson Lagoon, Alaska, at the time of the observed departure of Bar-tailed Godwits *Limosa lapponica* on 23 September 1996. The objects, entered into the air column at various altitudes, are then tracked at successive six-hour intervals; filled star = surface, unfilled circle = 750 m, unfilled square = 1 500 m, and unfilled triangle = 2 500 m elevation above sea level (ASL). Their respective filled symbols denote 24-hour periods. During the initial 60 hours of the model run between Nelson Lagoon and about 40° N latitude, winds at 750 m and 500 m altitude varied between 10 and 15 m sec⁻¹. The arrow to New Zealand approximates the direction but not necessarily the route taken.

(McCaffery & Harwood 2000), reaches southern Oceania by following a continental route via the east Asian mainland, a distance of over 16 000 km. Indeed, we could find only a single record of the species from Asia, and that from Chukotka, almost 150 years ago (in Kessel & Gibson 1978). It is also highly unlikely that birds reach New Zealand via a 9 000 km-long flight across the Southern Ocean after an initial flight of 8 000 to 11 000 km from eastern Canada to southern South America. The most logical explanation for their occurrence in New Zealand is that they accompany Bar-tailed Godwits on the godwits' southward flight across the Pacific (see also Kessel & Gibson 1978). Recent observations of small numbers of Hudsonian Godwits (all juveniles to date) support this idea.

## Stopovers

As it is energetically more favorable to cover a certain migration distance in many small steps than in one long hop (Piersma 1987), the assembled evidence that some 150 000 Bar-tailed Godwits annually make an 11 000 km-long non-stop flight from Alaska to New Zealand/eastern Australia begs the question of

why do they not make stopovers, either along the east Asian mainland, if such a route is followed, or during a trans-Pacific crossing. First, the evidence we have assembled fails to support use of a continental route, with or without use of stopover sites. Given the paucity of records of *baueri* along the east Asian mainland during southward migration, if they were migrating along the Asian coast, this would entail a non-stop flight of almost 16 000 km, i.e. 40% longer than a flight directly across the Pacific. Such a long flight is improbable, given the fuel loads of departing godwits and predicted arrival mass upon fuel depletion (contra Pennycuick & Battley 2003). In addition, during the recorded departures, birds would have initially encountered moderate to strong head winds and then a long fetch of strong southerly winds if they had followed a more south-westerly route along the Asian mainland. Such a flight would have forced birds either to fly into opposing winds or to detour around the systems, both of which would have added substantially to energetic costs.

We likewise found no evidence suggesting use of intermediate stopover sites if birds followed a direct route across the Pacific. Arguably, the Pacific Ocean is vast and it could harbor yet undiscovered stopover site(s), but the region has received considerable attention from ornithologists, and its indigenous peoples are intimately in tune with their natural resources. We find it beyond reason to expect the annual use by 150 000 godwits at stopover site(s) in Oceania to have gone undetected by either group of people. Indeed, the 80-year span of records that we searched accounted for a total of only about 4 000 godwits having been recorded throughout all of Oceania – this from a projected total of some 12 million godwits that could have stopped somewhere en route during this period. Although we cannot rule out that birds alight on open ocean waters during transit, it is likely that this would be for relatively short periods and then related to adverse conditions (Piersma *et al.* 2002) and not for rest.

Thus, a single flight over the Pacific is not only likely but in several ways advantageous as it may be safer (there are rarely aerial predators in central Oceania; cf. Ydenberg *et al.* 2002), healthier (as encounters with pathogens will be avoided; Piersma 1997), and faster and more direct (as the time required to settle at new stopover areas is avoided; Alerstam & Lindström 1990). It could also indicate the high quality of the western Alaskan staging sites relative to potential staging/stopover areas along the east Asian coastline or throughout Oceania (Gill & Handel 1990, Gudmundsson *et al.* 1991). Indeed, soft substrate intertidal habitat, the preferred feeding substrate for non-breeding godwits, is extremely limited throughout Oceania, occurring mostly on Fiji, the one site in Oceania that regularly hosts godwits (Watling 2001). See Gill *et al.* (2005) for a more detailed discussion of this topic.

### The role of wind systems over the Pacific

The *baueri* subspecies of the Bar-tailed Godwit can be added to a growing list of birds that have evolved wind-sensitive migration strategies, especially southward migrations, within the subpolar marine low pressure belt that circles the Northern Hemisphere (Richardson 1979, Åkesson & Hedenström 2000, Green 2003, M. Green and T. Piersma unpubl. data). This phenomenon is especially evident in the North Pacific, where the Aleutian low pressure system shapes and dominates weather and wind patterns throughout the year (Christoforou & Hameed 1997, Overland *et al.* 1997). In particular, two taxa of large-bodied, medium-distance migrant geese, the Brent Goose *Branta bernicla* and Cackling Canada Goose *B. canadensis minima*, annually initiate trans-oceanic flights from the Alaska Peninsula to the Pacific coast of North America in conjunction with the passage of moderate to strong low pressure systems (Dau 1992, Gill *et al.* 1997). Not surprisingly, even small-bodied birds, such as the Dunlin *Calidris alpina*, with similar non-breeding ranges often depart on the same weather systems as those used by geese (Warnock & Gill 1996, R. Gill unpubl. data). The emerging pattern is that godwits, geese, and Dunlin can use the same storms, only varying their departures in accordance with the position of the storm center and the birds' final destination.

Evolving a migration system in conjunction with winds at the departure site is one thing, but in the case of godwits which are crossing the entire Pacific, they must pass through at least five other latitudinal zones of defined winds and pressure. It is beyond the scope of this paper to present a thorough analysis of wind conditions along the entire projected flight path (cf. Piersma & Jukema 1990, Piersma & van de Sant 1992, Åkesson & Hedenström 2000). However, what emerges from the four cases we studied suggests that winds were generally favorable throughout the migration corridor during the calculated six-day transit time, and certainly in no instance was there strong opposing wind for any appreciable distance. The most obvious question relating to this is to what extent local departure cues are related to favorable "downstream" winds. Is weather across the Pacific structured (teleconnected) such that certain departure cues at northern latitudes translate to assure relatively favorable conditions along most of the route (McCaffery & Gill 2001)? The Aleutian low pressure center is a large-scale dominating feature of the North Pacific (Christoforou & Hameed 1997, Overland *et al.* 1997) that has obviously shaped the evolution of equally large-scale geographical migration patterns similar to systems described elsewhere in the Northern Hemisphere (citations in Green 2003). However, the godwits' migration strategy, involving flights that span hemispheres, is unlikely to have been selected for solely on the basis of factors occurring over just a portion of the range and independently of those elsewhere along the migration corridor.

This raises obvious questions about global climate change and its affects on wind regimes and thus on wind-selected avian migrants. The ecological effects of climate fluctuations are many, and are projected to be most profound in regions with large-scale patterns of climate variability such as the North Atlantic and North Pacific (Stenseth *et al.* 2002). Models of global climate change suggest an intensification of propagating weather systems moving across the North Pacific. Such would result in a shift of the Aleutian Low center eastward that would in turn increase the number and intensity of storms and bring stronger northerly winds over a longer fetch on the backside of individual low pressure centers. Godwits may, however, be able to adapt to this as the Aleutian Low and adjacent Hawaiian High have been found to shift position and intensity (seesaw pattern) on a decadal scale during most of the twentieth century (Christoforou & Mameed 1997, Overland 1999). The phenomenon, however, also needs to be assessed in the Southern Hemisphere as well in terms of the teleconnection patterns between the two hemispheres.

Development of suitable remote-sensing satellite technology would greatly enhance our understanding of the complexity of the godwits' migration system and flight behaviour of long-distance trans-oceanic migrants in general. With such technology, answers would be forthcoming to questions about (1) mechanisms of orientation, (2) how birds select winds (vertical and lateral) at all stages of the flight, (3) whether they adjust air speed for wind drift, (4) whether they adjust air speed during the course of the flight, and (5) the extent to which they can assess and react to changes in downstream flight conditions.

## ACKNOWLEDGMENTS

This work benefited from numerous discussions with colleagues throughout the Pacific basin, including M. Barter, D. Rogers, and C. Minton in Australia; P. Battley in New Zealand; G. McCormack in the Cook Islands; P. Tomkovich and Y. Gerasimov in Russia; and C. Dau, C. Handel, B. McCaffery, and D. Ruthrauff in Alaska. Unpublished information on the occurrence of godwits throughout Oceania was provided by P. Bruner, P. Donaldson, W. Johnson, J. Marks, G. McCormack, R. Pyle, F. Ward, and D. Watling. A cadre of New Zealanders helped assess the arrival of godwits following observed departures in Alaska, especially P. Battley, H. and Z. Clifford, T. Habraken, D. Lawrie, D. Melville, R. Schuckard, and B. and B. Woolley. M. Whalen helped prepare our graphics. Earlier versions of the manuscript benefited by comments and suggestions from P. Battley, M. Barter, D. Dobkin, R. Drent, C. Handel, M. Klaassen, C. Minton, L. Tibbitts, and two anonymous reviewers.

## REFERENCES

**Åkesson, S. & Hedenström, A.** 2000. Wind selectivity of migratory flight departures in birds. Behavioural Ecology and Sociobiology 47: 140-144.

**Alerstam, T. & Lindström, Å.** 1990. Optimal bird migration: the relative importance of time, energy, and safety. In: E. Gwinner (ed) Bird Migration: physiology and ecophysiology. Springer, Berlin: 331-359.

**Barter, M.** 1989. Bar-tailed Godwit *Limosa lapponica* in Australia. Part 1: races, breeding areas and migration routes. Stilt 14: 43-48.

**Barter, M. & Wang, T.H.** 1990. Can waders fly non-stop from Australia to China? Stilt 17: 36-39.

**Battley, P.F. 1997.** The northward migration of Arctic waders in New Zealand: departure behaviour, timing and possible migration routes of Red Knots and Bar-tailed Godwits from Farewell Spit, North-West Nelson. Emu 97: 108-120.

**Battley, P.F. & Piersma, T.** 2005. Body composition and flight ranges of Bar-tailed Godwits (*Limosa lapponica baueri*) from New Zealand. The Auk. 122(3): 922-937

**Battley, P.F., Piersma, T., Dietz, M.W., Tang, S., Dekinga, A. & Hulsman, K.** 2000. Empirical evidence for differential organ reductions during trans-oceanic bird flight. Proceedings of the Royal Society of London B 267: 191-195.

**Christoforou, P. & Hameed, S.** 1997. Solar cycles and the Pacific 'centers of action.' Geophysical Research Letters 24: 293-296.

**CDC (Canadian Diagnostic Centre)** 2004 (online). NCEP/NCAR reanalysis data. Retrieved from the

NOAA-CRIES Climate Diagnostic Center World Wide Web. http://www/cdc/noaa.gov/cdc/data.ncep.reanalysis. html; 28 January 2004.

CMC (Canadian Meteorological Centre) 2001 (online). Atmospheric transport models for environmental emergencies. http://gfx.weatheroffice.ec.gc.ca/cmc_library /data/; 15 January 2004.

CMC (Canadian Meteorological Centre) 2004 (online). Global Forecast System. Retrieved from the Canadian Meteorological Centre World Wide Web Library. http://www/smc-msc.ec.gc.ca/cmc/op_systems/global_ forecasr_e.html; 28 January 2004.

Dau, C.P. 1992. The fall migration of Pacific Flyway Brent *Branta bernicla* in relation to climatic conditions. Wildfowl 43: 80-95.

Elliott, K.H., Hewtt, M., Kaiser, G. & Blake, R.W. 2004. Flight energetics of the Marbled Murrelet, *Brachyramphus marmoratus*. Canadian Journal of Zoology 82: 644-652.

Elphick, C.S. & Klima, J. 2002. Hudsonian Godwit (*Limosa fedoa*). In: A. Poole & F. Gill (eds). The Birds of North America, No. 629. The Birds of North America, Inc., Philadelphia, PA.

Engelmoer, M. & Roselaar, C. 1998. Geographical variation in waders. Kluwer Academic Publications, Dordrecht, The Netherlands.

Gill, R.E., Jr. & Handel, C.M. 1990. The importance of subarctic intertidal habitats to shorebirds: a study of the central Yukon-Kuskokwim Delta, Alaska. The Condor 92: 702-725.

Gill, R.E., Jr. & McCaffery, B.J. 1999. Bar-tailed Godwits *Limosa lapponica* in Alaska: a population estimate from the staging grounds. Wader Study Group Bulletin 88: 49-54.

Gill, R.E., Jr., Babcock, C.A., Handel, C.M., Butler, W.R., Jr. & Raveling, D.G. 1997. Migration, fidelity, and use of autumn staging grounds in Alaska by Cackling Canada Geese *Branta canadensis minima*. Wildfowl 47: 42-61.

Gill, R.E., Piersma, T., Hufford, G., Servranckx, R. & Riegen, A. 2005. Crossing the ultimate ecological barrier: evidence for an 11 000-km-long nonstop flight from Alaska to New Zealand and eastern Australia by Bar-tailed Godwits. The Condor 107: 1-20.

Green, M. 2003. Flight strategies in migrating birds: when and how to fly. PhD thesis, Department of Ecology, Lund University, Sweden.

Gudgeon, W.E. 1903. The whence of the Mäori, Part 3. Journal of the Polynesian Society, Vol. 12.

Gudmundsson, G.A., Lindström, Å. & Alerstam, T. 1991. Optimal fat loads and long-distance flights by migrating Knots *Calidris canutus*, Sanderlings *C. alba* and Turnstones *Arenaria interpres*. Ibis 133: 140-152.

Higgins, P.J. & Davies, S.J.J.F. (eds). 1996. Handbook of Australian, New Zealand and Antarctic Birds. Volume 3: Snipe to Pigeons. Oxford University Press, Melbourne.

Hurles, M.E., Matisoo-Smith, E., Gray, R.D. & Penny, D. 2003. Untangling Oceanic settlement: the edge of the knowable. Trends in Ecology and Evolution 18: 531-540.

Jenni, L. & Jenni-Eiermann, S. 1999. Fat and protein utilisation during migratory flight. International Ornithological Congress 22: 1437-1449.

Johnson, O.W. 2003. Pacific and American Golden-Plovers: reflections on conservation needs. Wader Study Group Bulletin 100: 10-13.

Kersten, M. & Piersma, T. 1987. High levels of energy expenditure in shorebirds: metabolic adaptations to an energetically expensive way of life. Ardea 75: 175-187.

Kessel, B. & Gibson, D. 1978. Status and distribution of Alaska birds. Studies in Avian Biology 1.

Klaassen, M. 1995. Water and energy limitations on flight range. Auk 112: 260-262.

Kvist, A., Lindström, Å., Green, M., Piersma, T. & Visser, G.H. 2001. Carrying large fuel loads during sustained bird flight is cheaper than expected. Nature 413: 730-732.

Landys, M.M., Piersma, T., Visser, G.H., Jukema, J. & Wijker, A. 2000. Water balance during real and simulated long-distance migratory flight in the Bar-tailed Godwit. The Condor 102: 645-652.

Landys-Ciannelli, M.M., Piersma, T. & Jukema, J. 2003. Strategic size changes of internal organs and muscle tissue in the Bar-tailed Godwit during fat storage on a spring stopover site. Functional Ecology 17: 151-159.

Marks, J.S. & Redmond, R.L. 1994. Migration of Bristle-thighed Curlews on Laysan Island: timing, behavior and estimated flight range. The Condor 96: 316-330.

McCaffery, B.J. & Gill, R.E., Jr. 2001. Bar-tailed Godwit (*Limosa lapponica*). In: A. Poole & F. Gill (eds). The Birds of North America, No. 581. The Birds of North America, Inc., Philadelphia, PA.

McCaffery, B.J. & Harwood, C.M. 2000. Status of Hudsonian Godwits on the Yukon-Kuskokwim Delta, Alaska. Western Birds 31: 165-177.

Minton, C., Jessop, R., Collins, P., Deleyev, J. & Beasley, L. 2002. Sightings of waders leg-flagged in Victoria: report number 9. Stilt 42: 56-72.

Overland, J.E., Adams, J.M. & Bond, N.A. 1997. Decadal variability in the Aleutian low and its relation to high latitude circulation. Journal of Climate 12: 1542-1548.

Pennycuick, C.J. 1989. Bird flight performance: a practical calculation manual. Oxford University Press, Oxford.

Pennycuick, C.J. 1998. Computer simulation of fat and muscle burn in long-distance bird migration. Journal of Theoretical Biology 191: 47-61.

Pennycuick, C.J. & Battley, P.F. 2003. Burning the engine: a time-marching computation of fat and protein consumption in a 5420-km non-stop flight by Great Knots *Calidris tenuirostris*. Oikos 103: 323-332.

Phillipps, W.J. 1966. Maori life and custom. A.H. & A.W. Reed, Wellington, New Zealand.

Piersma, T. 1987. Hop, skip or jump? Constraints on migration of arctic waders by feeding, fattening, and flight speed. Limosa 60: 185-194.

Piersma, T. 1997. Do global patterns of habitat use and migration strategies co-evolve with relative investments in immunocompetence due to spatial variation in parasite pressure? Oikos 80: 623-631.

Piersma, T. & Gill, R.E., Jr. 1998. Guts don't fly: small digestive organs in obese Bar-tailed Godwits. Auk 115: 196-203.

Piersma, T. &. Jukema, J. 1990. Budgeting the flight of a long-distance migrant: changes in nutrient reserve levels of

Bar-tailed Godwits at successive staging sites. Ardea 78: 315-337.

**Piersma, T. & van de Sant, S.** 1992. Pattern and predictability of potential wind assistance for waders and geese migrating from West Africa and the Wadden Sea to Siberia. Ornis Svecica 2: 55-66.

**Piersma, T., Spaans, B. & Dekinga, A.** 2002. Are shorebirds sometimes forced to roost on water in thick fog? Wader Study Group Bulletin 97: 42-44.

**Richardson, W.J.** 1979. South-eastward shorebird migration over Nova Scotia and New Brunswick in autumn: a radar study. Canadian Journal of Zoology 57: 107-124.

**Riegen, A.C.** 1999. Movements of banded Arctic waders to and from New Zealand. Notornis 46: 123-142.

**Riley, M.** 2001. Maori bird lore. Viking Seven Seas NZ, Ltd., Paraparaumu, New Zealand.

**Stenseth, N., Mysterud, A., Ottersen, G., Hurrell, J., Chan, K.-S. & Lima, M.** 2002. Ecological effects of climate fluctuations. Science 297: 1292-1296.

**Te Paa, W.** 1912. The story of the Kuaka's flight. Journal of the Polynesian Society 21.

**Thompson, M.** 1973. Migratory patterns of Ruddy Turnstones in the central Pacific region. Living Bird 12: 5-23.

**Warnock, N. & Gill, R.E., Jr.** 1996. Dunlin (*Calidris alpina*). In: A. Poole & F. Gill (eds). The Birds of North America, No. 203. The Academy of Natural Sciences, Philadelphia, and The American Ornithologists' Union, Washington, D.C.

**Watling, D.** 2001. A guide to the birds of Fiji and western Polynesia including American Samoa, Niue, Samoa, Tokelau, Tonga, Tuvalu and Wallis and Futuna. Environmental Consultants (Fiji) Ltd., Fiji.

**Williams, T.C. & Williams, J.M.** 1988. Radar and visual observations of autumnal (southward) shorebird migration on Guam. Auk 105: 460-466.

**Williams, T.C. & Williams, J.M.** 1990. The orientation of transoceanic migrants. In: E. Gwinner (ed) Bird Migration: physiology and ecophysiology. Springer, Berlin: 9-21.

**Williams, T.C. & Williams, J.M.** 1999. The migration of land birds over the Pacific Ocean. International Ornithological Congress 22: 1948-1957.

**Wilson, J.R. & Barter, M.A.** 1998. Identification of potentially important staging areas for "long jump" migrant waders in the East Asian – Australasian Flyway during northward migration. Stilt 32: 16-27.

**Ydenberg, R.C., Butler, R.W., Lank, D.B., Guglielmo, C.G., Lemon, M. & Wolf, N.** 2002. Trade-offs, condition dependence and stopover site selection by migrating sandpipers. Journal of Avian Biology 33: 47-55.

**Program Flight** (Windows version 1.13, July 2003) can be downloaded at: http://detritus.inhs.uiuc.edu/wes/pennycuick.html.

Bar-tailed Godwit *Limosa lapponica* – one of the world's extreme long-distance migrants.  Photo: Paul Marshall.

# Using stable isotope ratios to unravel shorebird migration and population mixing: a case study with Red Knot *Calidris canutus*

*Philip W. Atkinson[1], Allan J. Baker[2], Karen A Bennett[3], Nigel. A. Clark[1], Jacquie A. Clark[1], Kimberly B. Cole[4], Amanda Dey[5], Andre G. Duiven[6], Simon Gillings[1], Patricia M. González[7], Brian A. Harrington[8], Kevin Kalasz[3], Clive D.T. Minton[9], Jason Newton[10], Lawrence J. Niles[5], Robert A. Robinson[1], Ines de Lima Serrano[11] & Humphrey P. Sitters[12]*

[1] *British Trust for Ornithology, The Nunnery, Thetford, Norfolk, IP24 2PU, UK. (email: phil.atkinson@bto.org)*

[2] *Centre for Biodiversity and Conservation Biology, Royal Ontario Museum, 100 Queen's Park, Toronto, Ontario M5S 1C6, Canada, and Department of Zoology, University of Toronto, Queen's Park, Ontario, Canada.*

[3] *Delaware Division of Fish and Wildlife, DNREC, 4876 Hay Point Landing Road, Smyrna, DE 19977, USA.*

[4] *Delaware Coastal Programs, Division of Soil and Water Conservation, DNREC, 89 Kings Highway, Dover, DE 19901, USA.*

[5] *Endangered and Nongame Species Program, New Jersey Division of Fish and Wildlife, PO Box 400, Trenton, NJ 08625, USA.*

[6] *Peter Sellershof 176, 1325 GZ Almere, The Netherlands.*

[7] *Fundación Inalafquen, Pedro Morón 385 (8520) San Antonio Oeste, Río Negro, Argentina.*

[8] *Manomet Center for Conservation Sciences, 81 Stage Road, PO Box 1770, Manomet, MA 02345, USA.*

[9] *165 Dalgetty Road, Beaumaris, Victoria, Australia.*

[10] *NERC Life Sciences Mass Spectrometry Facility, Scottish Universities Environmental Research Centre, Rankine Avenue, Scottish Enterprise Technology Park, East Kilbride, G75 0QF, UK.*

[11] *Centro de Pesquisas para Conservação das Aves Silvestres (CEMAVE-IBAMA), C. Postal 102, João Pessoa PB, CEP 58.440-970, Brazil.*

[12] *Limosa, Old Ebford Lane, Ebford, Exeter, EX3 0QR, UK.*

Atkinson, P.W., Baker, A.J., Bennett, K.A., Clark, N.A., Clark, J.A., Cole, K.B., Dey, A., Duiven, A.G., Gillings, S., González, P.M., Harrington, B.A., Kalasz, K., Minton, C.D.T., Newton, J., Niles, L.J., Robinson, R.A., de Lima Serrano, I. & Sitters, H.P. 2006. Using stable isotope ratios to unravel shorebird migration and population mixing: a case study with Red Knot *Calidris canutus*. *Waterbirds around the world*. Eds. G.C. Boere, C.A. Galbraith & D.A. Stroud. The Stationery Office, Edinburgh, UK. pp. 535-540.

## ABSTRACT

Identifying demographic mechanisms is fundamental to understanding the causes of population change in waterbirds. This may be relatively easy for static breeding and wintering populations, but populations of mixed breeding or wintering origin often occur in stopover sites in spring and autumn, and thus estimates of survival and recruitment from these areas are inevitably representative of all the birds marked, rather than individual populations. We used stable isotope analysis of flight feathers to identify the different wintering populations of Red Knot *Calidris canutus rufa* that passed through Delaware Bay, north-eastern USA, in the springs of 2004 and 2005. Here, they feed and fatten on an abundance of Horseshoe Crab *Limulus polyphemus* eggs before flying to their Arctic breeding areas. $\delta^{13}N$ values separated birds from wintering areas in southern South America ("southern" birds) and Brazil/south-eastern USA ("northern" birds). Northern birds were further separated using $\delta^{13}C$ values. Approximately 55% of the birds caught within Delaware Bay were from the southern population, 22.5% from Brazil, and 12.5% from the south-eastern USA, while 10% were of unknown (although most likely "northern") origin. At a site on the Atlantic coast of Delaware Bay, where only Mussel *Mytilus* spp. spat were available, the proportion of short-distance migrants from the south-eastern USA was much higher, and is most likely related to their shorter-hop migration strategy that allows them to take advantage of this hard-shelled prey resource.

## INTRODUCTION

The migration of shorebirds is one of the most inspiring and impressive spectacles in the natural world. The Red Knot *Calidris canutus* is a flagship species among long-distance shorebird migrants. In the Americas, populations winter in the south-eastern USA, in northern Brazil and the Caribbean, and at sites in Tierra del Fuego and Patagonia. In order to reach breeding grounds in the Canadian Arctic, some individuals make an annual round-trip of 30 000 km. For these birds, Delaware Bay is the last major northward staging site where they join hundreds of thousands of other shorebirds to feed on the eggs of Horseshoe Crabs *Limulus polyphemus*. During a 10-14 day stopover, Red Knots increase their body mass by over 70%, gaining the fuel for their final non-stop flight to the breeding grounds.

Over the past five to ten years there has been a dramatic reduction in the numbers of Red Knot passing through Delaware Bay (Baker *et al.* 2004), with similar declines noted in the South American wintering areas (Morrison *et al.* 2004) but apparently not in the relatively poorly known population wintering in the south-eastern USA (Niles *et al.* in prep.). For a species that makes such long distance migrations to tight deadlines (Piersma *et al.* 2005), there are many potential pressure points in the annual cycle.

One of the major aims of a study, initiated in 1997, is to determine the causes of the change in the Red Knot populations of the West Atlantic Flyway by marking individuals and using survival and recruitment models (White & Burnham 1999) to estimate demographic rates. However, one of the problems of studying birds on passage sites is that individuals from several different populations may mix. Ideally, demographic rates would be estimated for each population separately, thereby enabling better understanding of the issues under study. This requires a means of assigning individuals to different populations, which in the case of shorebirds is often difficult owing to no single clear distinguishing feature. Morphometrics and genetic markers can sometimes partly or wholly distinguish different subspecies of shorebirds (Wenink *et al.* 1994, Baker 2002) but not individual birds. One technique, used successfully in other species, is measurement of light element stable isotope ratios in feathers (Chamberlain *et al.* 1997, Hobson 1999, Webster *et al.* 2002, Bearhop *et al.* 2005).

Using carbon and nitrogen stable isotopes in flight feathers from a pilot sample of 100 individual Red Knots sampled in Delaware Bay in spring 2003, Atkinson *et al.* (2005) showed that birds from at least four different wintering populations passed through Delaware Bay in spring 2003. The basic technique involves measuring isotope ratios in feathers moulted in known wintering areas, then deriving comparable figures from individuals caught in Delaware Bay so that they can be assigned with confidence to one of the wintering areas. This paper develops and applies this method to 1 220 and 947 individual Red Knots caught during spring staging in Delaware Bay in 2004 and 2005, respectively. We determine the proportion of birds originating from the major wintering areas, and seek to give guidance on the use of stable isotopes in migration studies.

## METHODS

### FEATHER SAMPLING AND ISOTOPE ANALYSIS

To determine the wintering area of birds caught in Delaware Bay, we took a sample of the sixth primary covert, measured ascendantly, from each bird caught. This feather was used because it is moulted at the time of the birds main primary moult and is likely to be indicative of the main wintering area (for full details see Atkinson *et al.* 2005). Each feather was washed in a solution of 0.25M sodium hydroxide to remove dirt and grease, rinsed thoroughly in distilled water, then dried overnight in an oven at 75°C. Each sample was finely chopped using surgical scissors into pieces no longer than 2 mm in length, and between 0.5 and 1 mg of each feather was accurately weighed into tin capsules and loaded into an automatic sampler. Stable isotope ratio measurements of carbon and nitrogen were made using CF-IRMS (Continuous Flow Isotope Ratio Mass Spectrometry). All stable isotope values are reported in permil (‰) using the delta ($\delta$) notation:

$$\delta \text{ isotope} = \left[ \left( \frac{R_{sample}}{R_{sample}} \right) - 1 \right] \times 1000$$

where $\delta$ isotope is the sample isotope ratio ($^{13}$C or $^{15}$N) relative to a standard (traceable to a primary international standard), and R is the ratio of heavy to light isotopes ($^{13}$C/$^{12}$C or $^{15}$N/$^{14}$N) in the sample or standard. $\delta^{13}$C and $\delta^{15}$N are reported relative to their primary international standards, namely Peedee Belemite (V-PDB) and atmospheric nitrogen (V-AIR), respectively. Routine measurements were precise to within 0.1‰ for $\delta^{13}$C and 0.3‰ for $\delta^{15}$N.

### STATISTICAL ANALYSIS

First, a small number of sub-adult birds were identified by having a carbon isotope signature ($\delta^{13}$C <-19.5‰) typical of the freshwater systems where their feathers were grown. These birds were therefore hatched in the previous summer and were approximately 10-11 months old. A two-stage process was then used to estimate the origins of adult birds caught in Delaware Bay in 2004 and 2005: first, birds were divided into northern or southern winterers; second, northern winterers were divided into those of USA or Brazilian/Caribbean origin.

Atkinson *et al.* (2005) showed that there was a clear division in the values of $\delta^{15}$N between birds wintering in Patagonia and

**Table 1.** $\delta^{13}$C values of primary coverts of adult Red Knot *Calidris canutus* known to belong to the two northern wintering populations based either on birds caught or individually-marked birds observed in the wintering areas. Winter refers to the boreal winter in which the coverts were grown.

| Winter | Brazil | n | Florida/Georgia | n |
|---|---|---|---|---|
| 2003/2004 | -16.06 ± 1.06 | 8 | -17.31 ± 0.8 | 18 |
| 2004/2005 | -15.3 ± 1.03 | 33 | -16.58 ± 0.41 | 19 |

Tierra del Fuego ($\delta^{15}$N >13.5‰, termed "southern" birds) and elsewhere ($\delta^{15}$N <13.5‰, termed "northern" birds). Northern birds comprise two geographically distinct populations, in the southern-eastern USA and Brazil, but the isotope signatures of birds from each overlap. We therefore calculated the mean and SD of the $\delta^{13}$C values of birds known to winter in each area from birds either caught there (33 birds caught in Maranhaõ State, Brazil, in November 2004 and February 2005) or observations of known individuals which had been sampled the previous spring in Delaware Bay (Table 1). To estimate the proportion of individuals originating from each wintering area, we assumed that the distribution of $\delta^{13}$C values of northern birds caught in Delaware Bay was a composite of two overlapping normal distributions, one of $\delta^{13}$C values from Brazilian birds and the other of $\delta^{13}$C values from birds from the south-eastern USA. We used a least squares method to fit two normal curves (based on the means and SDs of $\delta^{13}$C values of birds from known wintering areas) to the observed frequency distribution of the $\delta^{13}$C values from birds in Delaware Bay. $\delta^{15}$N values were not used, as there was little difference between the two means. We excluded any outlying "northern" type birds that had $\delta^{13}$C or $\delta^{15}$N values more than 2 SD from either of the two known reference sample means, and classed these birds as unknown. The proportion of birds from each wintering area was adjusted until the overall sum of squares of the observed minus estimated numbers for each $\delta^{13}$C category was minimized. As isotope values may differ annually, year-specific values of $\delta^{13}$C were used. This method gave a means of estimating the relative proportion of birds from Brazil versus the south-eastern USA, but did not permit individual northern birds to be allocated to one of these populations, although it was, of course, possible to assign the probability of belonging to each population based on the $\delta^{13}$C values.

### RESULTS AND DISCUSSION

#### Origin of the birds passing through Delaware Bay in 2004 and 2005

In both 2004 and 2005, stable isotope ratios of individual Red Knots separated well (Fig. 1) according to the divisions used by Atkinson *et al.* (2005). Sub-adult birds (i.e. birds < 1 year old) made up a small proportion of the total birds caught in Delaware Bay, with 28 individuals in 2004 and 31 in 2005. Averaged across the two years, 51.8% of the adult birds were from the southern population (Tierra del Fuego/Patagonia) and 48.2% were from the northern population (south-eastern USA/Brazil and other as yet unknown areas). Approximately 20% of northern adults deviated by >2 SD from the $\delta^{13}$C and $\delta^{15}$N means of birds from known wintering areas (Fig 1, box) and

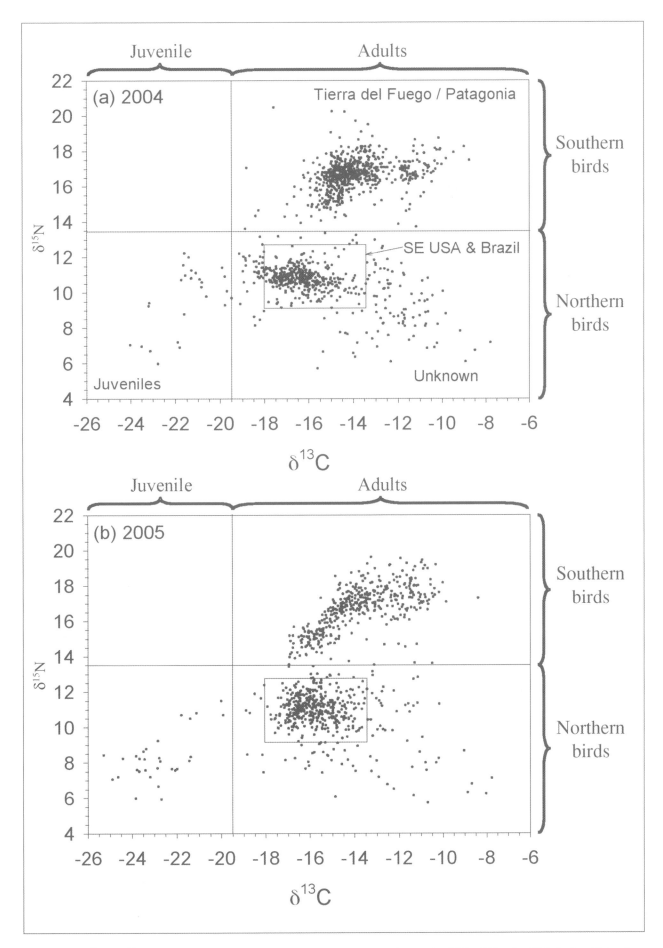

**Fig 1.** Plots of $\delta^{13}C$ and $\delta^{15}N$ values of Red Knot *Calidris canutus* caught in Delaware Bay in (a) spring 2004 and (b) spring 2005. Southern birds refer to the population wintering in Patagonia and Tierra del Fuego; northern, to those wintering in north-western Brazil, the Caribbean and the south-eastern USA.

**Table 2.** Wintering origin (numbers and percentage) of adult and sub-adult Red Knot *Calidris canutus* caught on passage in Delaware Bay in spring 2004 and 2005. Unknown refers to northern wintering birds whose δ¹³C values were outside the range of the Brazilian and south-eastern USA wintering population. (Sub-adults are birds less than one year old and still with juvenile primary coverts grown soon after hatching).

| Year | Number of individuals | | Southern adults | Northern adults | | |
|------|-------|-----------|------------------|---------|---------|---------|
| | *Adults* | *Sub-adults* | | *SE USA* | *Brazil* | *Unknown* |
| 2004 | 1 192 | 28 | 669 (56.1%) | 150 (12.6%) | 262 (22.0%) | 111 (9.3%) |
| 2005 | 916 | 31 | 434 (47.4%) | 206 (22.5%) | 185 (20.2%) | 91 (9.9%) |

were labelled as of unknown origin. Decomposition of the frequency distribution of δ¹³C values of the remaining northern birds then divided into approximately 45:55 south-eastern USA to Brazil (Fig. 2). These translate into proportions of the Delaware passage population as 21.1% from Brazil, 17.6% from the south-eastern USA and 9.6% unknown, with mostly small differences between years (Fig. 1, Table 2). There was one major difference in the composition of the catches between years. More birds with a south-eastern USA origin were caught in 2005 than in 2004, due to a change in catching locations. In 2004, all individuals were caught within the confines of the bay

itself, whereas in 2005, catches were also made on the beaches and marshes on the Atlantic coast of Delaware Bay. These latter catches contained a much higher proportion of the shorter-distance migrants from the south-eastern USA.

Prior to this study, it was originally thought that the majority of the birds passing through Delaware Bay were from the populations wintering in Tierra del Fuego and Patagonia. However, the stable isotope data indicate that in 2004 and 2005 only approximately half of the individuals were from there.

### Use of stable isotopes in studies of birds on passage sites

These results show that the use of stable isotopes can be an extremely useful tool for assigning individual birds to distinct populations in cases where these populations have distinct stable isotope signatures. In this case, birds from very different geographical areas (northern and southern groups) were distinguishable. As a tool for population biologists, this is extremely useful because it may help to explain the basis of heterogeneity in survival and re-sighting rates, and opens the door to calculating population-level demographic parameters from mixes of populations. For instance, in coming years it will be possible to evaluate survival, recruitment, passage times and staging behaviour for specific Red Knot wintering populations, thus helping to elucidate the causes of declines and best management for recovery.

To use stable isotopes successfully in this way, it is necessary to collect reference material from known wintering areas, and this is labour-intensive if the species in question migrates to many different areas. Fortunately in this case, Red Knot are only known to winter in a small number of well-known and well-studied sites, although even for this species, around 10% of the passage birds in Delaware Bay were classed as unknown. This is not to say that they are necessarily from different wintering locations, but these unknowns could be birds adopting a different diet or moulting at a different time of year. Indeed they might be two year old birds. Isotope ratios vary temporally in response to, for example, changing seasons, and Red Knot in their first year of life do not return to the breeding grounds the following summer. Instead, they remain on or near the wintering areas and tend to undergo a full primary moult several months earlier than the adults returning from the breeding areas. Although poorly understood at present, this is likely to be the explanation for the "unknown" northern signatures and will be the subject of further study.

As well as discriminating between locations separated by large geographical distances, isotope ratios may change over a relatively small scale. Isotope signatures from Red Knot known to winter in Bahia Lomas in Chile and Rio Grande in Argentina,

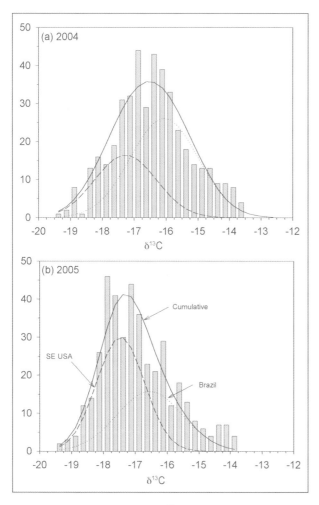

**Fig 2.** Frequency distribution of δ¹³C values from adult Red Knot *Calidris canutus* of the "northern" wintering population captured in Delaware Bay during spring passage in a) 2004 and b) 2005. Bars show the actual frequency distribution; lines show the individual fitted normal curves from reference samples, and cumulative fitted curve for south-eastern USA and Brazilian birds.

Red Knot *Calidris canutus rufa* at Delaware Bay, May 2006.  Photo: Rob Robinson.

approximately 160 km apart, are found to be very different (Atkinson *et al.* 2005). This is most likely due to the fact that the city of Rio Grande is at the head of the estuary and discharges from the city are likely to alter $\delta C^{13}$ and $\delta N^{15}$ values in the sediments surrounding the estuary. In this case, such differences are useful. This also prompts caution in applying broad-scale isotopic gradients to large areas without knowledge of the processes operating on the ground.

This method relies on birds growing feathers or other tissues in areas with predictably different isotope ratios. For species that are more widespread in winter, or use similar habitats in different locations, such clear-cut results may not be achieved. For example, in a study of the American Golden Plover *Pluvialis dominica* and Pacific Golden Plover *P. fulva*, feathers grown in the wintering grounds showed no differences in $\delta D$, $\delta^{13}C$ and $\delta^{15}N$ values between species, despite wintering on different continents (Rocque 2003).

These results also show that some isotope ratios are prone to annual fluctuations, probably related to climate. Thus, although the threshold $\delta^{15}N$ and $\delta^{13}C$ values used to distinguish northern and southern birds, and adults and sub-adults (still with juvenile primaries), appear to be robust from year to year, there were more marked annual differences in the south-eastern USA/Brazil distinction. This suggests that samples should be collected over several years to help evaluate natural variation in isotope signatures and limit its impact on misclassification of individuals. Analysis of additional isotopes may also help classification, but may be prohibitively expensive.

### Linking breeding and wintering locations

In certain circumstances, stable isotopes allow researchers to draw links throughout the flyway of individual species. Provided the necessary reference samples have already been discriminated, samples from adults on the breeding grounds may enable direct linkages to be drawn between breeding and wintering

locations. However, for high Arctic breeders such as the Red Knot, sampling feathers from juveniles on the wintering grounds to identify breeding grounds is less productive. This is because there appear to be few consistent and predictable geographic patterns in isotope ratios in the largely terrestrial/freshwater tundra habitats. For lower latitude breeders, differences may be more apparent where large-scale differences in geology or primary production exist. For instance, the strontium signature found in bones of the Common Redshank *Tringa totanus* can be used to distinguish birds from Iceland, with a relatively young geology, from those breeding in Scotland, where rocks are much older (Evans 2004).

In conclusion, stable isotopes coupled with colour-marking birds as individuals can offer a useful way of distinguishing mixed populations of shorebirds on passage sites. In situations similar to Delaware Bay, their usage offers the opportunity of calculating parameters such as survival, recruitment, mass gain, stopover time etc. for populations that winter many thousands of kilometres apart.

### ACKNOWLEDGEMENTS
We would like to thank all the volunteers who helped out with the shorebird banding programmes in Argentina, Chile and Delaware Bay. We are grateful to the U.S. Fish and Wildlife Service and National Environment Research Council (NERC) for funding the isotope analyses, and would like to acknowledge Greg Breese for his help and support of the project. The fieldwork was funded, in part, through a grant from the Delaware Division of Fish and Wildlife with funding from the Division of Federal Aid, U.S. Fish and Wildlife Service, under State Wildlife Grants appropriation 05020201-2330. Stable isotope analyses were carried out at the NERC Life Sciences Mass Spectrometry Facility under a grant from NERC, by Dr Alina Marca at the Stable Isotope Laboratory at the University of East Anglia and by Dr Tom Maddox at the University of Georgia.

## REFERENCES

**Atkinson, P.W., Baker, A.J., Bevan, R.M., Clark, N.A., Cole, K.B., Gonzalez, P.M., Newton, J., Niles, L.J. & Robinson, R.A.** 2005. Unravelling the migration and moult strategies of a long-distance migrant using stable isotopes: Red Knot *Calidris canutus* movements in the Americas. Ibis 147: 738-749.

**Baker, A.J.** 2002. The deep roots of bird migration: inferences from the historical record preserved in DNA. In: C. Both & T. Piersma, T. (eds) The avian calendar: exploring biological hurdles in the annual cycle. Proceedings of 3rd Conference of the European Ornithologists' Union, Groningen, August 2001. Ardea 90: 503-513.

**Baker, A.J., González, P.M., Piersma, T., Niles, L.J., de Lima Serrano do Nascimento, I., Atkinson, P.W., Clark, N.A., Minton, C.D.T., Peck, M. & Aarts, G.** 2004. Rapid population decline in red knots: fitness consequences of decreased refuelling rates and late arrival in Delaware Bay. Proceedings of the Royal Society B: 271: 875-882.

**Bearhop, S., Fiedler, W., Furness, R.W., Votier, S.C., Waldron, S., Newton, J., Bowen, G.J., Berthold, P. & Farnsworth, K.** 2005. Assortative mating as a mechanism for rapid evolution of a migratory divide. Science 310: 502-504.

**Chamberlain, C.P., Blum, J.D., Holmes, R.T., Feng, X., Sherry, T.W. & Graves, G.R.** 1997. The use of isotope tracers for identifying populations of migratory birds. Oecologia 109: 132-141.

**Evans, J.** 2004. You are what you eat: isotopes and migration studies. Transactions of the Leicester Literary & Philosophical Society 98: 14-15.

**Hobson, K.A.** 1999. Tracing origins and migration of wildlife using stable isotopes: a review. Oecologia 120: 314-326.

**Morrison, R.I.G., Ross, R.K. & Niles, L.J.** 2004. Declines in wintering populations of Red Knots in southern South America. Condor 106: 60-70.

**Niles, L.J., Sitters, H.P., Dey, A.D., Baker, A.J., Morrison, R.I.G, Hernandez, D.E., Clark, K., Harrington, B.A., Peck, M.K., Gonzalez, P.M., Atkinson, P.W., Clark, N.A. & Minton, C.D.T.** (in prep.). Status of the Red Knot (*Calidris canutus rufa*) in the Western Hemisphere. New Jersey Department of Environmental Protection. Trenton, New Jersey.

**Piersma, T., Rogers, D.I., González, P.M., Zwarts, L., Niles, L.J., de Lima do Nascimento, I., Minton, C.D.T. & Baker, A.J.** 2005. Fuel storage rates before northward flights in red knots worldwide: facing the severest constraint in tropical intertidal environments? In: R. Greenberg & P.P. Marra (eds) Birds of Two Worlds. Smithsonian Institution Press, Washington D.C.: 262-273.

**Rocque, D.A.** 2003. Intrinsic markers in avian populations: explorations in stable isotopes, contaminants and genetics. PhD thesis, University of Alaska, Fairbanks.

**Webster, M.S., Marra, P.P., Haig, S.M., Bensch, S. & Holmes, R.T.** 2002. Links between worlds: Unravelling migratory connectivity. Trends in Ecology and Evolution 17: 76-82.

**Wenink, P.W., Baker, A.J. & Tilanus, M.G.J.** 1994. Mitochondrial control-region sequences in two shorebird species, the turnstone and the dunlin, and their utility in population genetic studies. Molecular Biology and Evolution 11: 22-31.

**White, G.C. & Burnham, K.P.** 1999. Program MARK: Survival estimation from populations of marked animals. Bird Study 46 (Supplement): 120-138.

Ringing and measuring Dunlin *Calidris alpina* caught at Delaware Bay. Photo: Rob Robinson.

# Geographical segregation in wintering Dunlin *Calidris alpina* populations along the East Atlantic Flyway: evidence from mitochondrial DNA analysis

*Ricardo J. Lopes[1] & Liv Wennerberg[2]*

[1] *CIBIO - Centro de Investigação em Biodiversidade e Recursos Genéticos, Campus Agrário de Vairão, 4485-661 Vairão, Portugal. (email: ricardolopes@mail.icav.up.pt)*

[2] *National History Museum, University of Oslo, PO Box 1172 Blindern, N-0318 Oslo, Norway. (email: Liv.Wennerberg@nhm.uio.no)*

Lopes, R.J. & Wennerberg, L. 2006. Geographical segregation in wintering Dunlin *Calidris alpina* populations along the East Atlantic Flyway: evidence from mitochondrial DNA analysis. *Waterbirds around the world*. Eds. G.C. Boere, C.A. Galbraith & D.A. Stroud. The Stationery Office, Edinburgh, UK. pp. 541-544.

## ABSTRACT

The Dunlin *Calidris alpina* is the most abundant species of shorebird using the East Atlantic Flyway. This flyway links breeding areas in Greenland, Iceland, northern Europe and northern Russia with wintering areas in western Europe and Africa. Differences in migration pattern and segregation between Dunlin populations on their wintering grounds have already been indicated by analyses of morphometric data and ringing recoveries. Here, we use genetic markers (mitochondrial DNA) to analyse the extent of such segregation along the flyway, comparing birds from different stopover sites and wintering areas. We sampled birds from different wintering areas (Sweden, Portugal, Morocco, Guinea-Bissau) and compared their mtDNA haplotype frequencies. All birds from wintering areas in north-west Africa had the western (European) haplotype, while the eastern (Siberian) haplotype was present in all samples from wintering areas in Europe, with the highest frequencies occurring furthest north (in Sweden). Comparison with the haplotype frequencies in breeding populations revealed that birds from Greenland, Iceland and northern Europe were predominant in wintering areas in West Africa, while populations wintering in western Europe (the Iberian Peninsula and Sweden) originated from more eastern breeding grounds in Russia.

## INTRODUCTION

A comparison of the migration ecology of waders reveals a large variation in migration patterns between species (Pienkowski & Evans 1984, del Hoyo *et al.* 1996, Wernham *et al.* 2002). In some species, this variability also occurs between populations, sex or age classes that may be segregated, fully or partially, on their wintering grounds (Nebel *et al.* 2002). This seems to be the case for populations of the Dunlin *Calidris alpina* that use the East Atlantic Flyway, the main migration flyway connecting breeding areas from Canada to Siberia with wintering areas in western Europe and Africa (Smit & Piersma 1989). At least three subspecies of Dunlin, *C. a. arctica*, *C. a. schinzii* and *C. a. alpina*, migrate along the East Atlantic Flyway to reach wintering areas extending from southern Scandinavia to West Africa (del Hoyo *et al.* 1996).

It is known that breeding populations from northern Scandinavia, European Russia and Siberia winter mainly in the northern parts of the wintering range, while populations from Greenland, Iceland and north-west Europe winter mainly in West Africa (Pienkowski & Evans 1984). These conclusions were based mainly on analyses of morphometric data and ringing recoveries (Pienkowski & Dick 1975, Wymenga *et al.* 1990). However, both of these methods have their limitations.

Morphological measurements differ between subspecies, but as there is also some sexual dimorphism, substantial overlap exists between the subspecies (Greenwood 1986) and this complicates determination of breeding origin based on morphometric data from unsexed birds. The potential of ringing recoveries to reveal the breeding origin of wintering birds has been limited by the scarcity of ringing recoveries from Arctic breeding areas as well as from wintering grounds in West Africa (e.g. Greenwood 1984, Wymenga *et al.* 1990, Gromadzka & Ryabitsev 1998).

Genetic methods have been used to identify breeding populations of the Dunlin on a global scale (Wenink & Baker 1996, Wennerberg 2001). Within the breeding areas of Dunlin using the East Atlantic Flyway, sequencing of mitochondrial DNA (mtDNA) has revealed the presence of two mtDNA lineages: a European haplotype and a Siberian haplotype. The frequency of the European haplotype decreases with longitude of the breeding area, while the frequency of the Siberian haplotype increases (Wennerberg 2001). By comparing the haplotype composition in a flock of non-breeding Dunlin with that of various breeding populations, the breeding origin of the flock can be estimated. This methodology has been applied mainly to migrating flocks (Wenink & Baker 1996, Tiedemann 1999, Wennerberg 2001, Wennerberg *et al.* 2001), and there have been few attempts to analyse wintering populations, probably because of the difficulty of obtaining DNA samples from some of the wintering areas. We here update current knowledge of the wintering distribution of Dunlin along the East Atlantic Flyway using these genetic markers to investigate the presence of geographical segregation.

## MATERIAL AND METHODS

Dunlin were sampled at wintering sites along the East Atlantic Flyway (Sweden, Portugal, Morocco and Guinea Bissau) during the winters of 1995 to 2001. Blood samples were taken from all birds and DNA was extracted according to standard procedures. The mtDNA was amplified by Polymerase Chain Reaction (PCR), and PCR products were digested with the restriction enzyme *Alu* I (for details, see Lopes 2004). *Alu* I was chosen because it cuts the mtDNA at positions that separate the two mtDNA lineages: the European and Siberian haplotypes (Wenink *et al.* 1996). Published data on the haplotypes of wintering flocks in Spain and Sweden (from Wennerberg 2001) have also been included in the analysis. Information on breeding populations has been obtained from the published results of mtDNA analyses of 280 breeding birds from 22 breeding populations (Wenink *et al.* 1993, 1996, Wennerberg *et al.* 1999, Wennerberg 2001) and some additional unpublished data (Wennerberg unpubl. data).

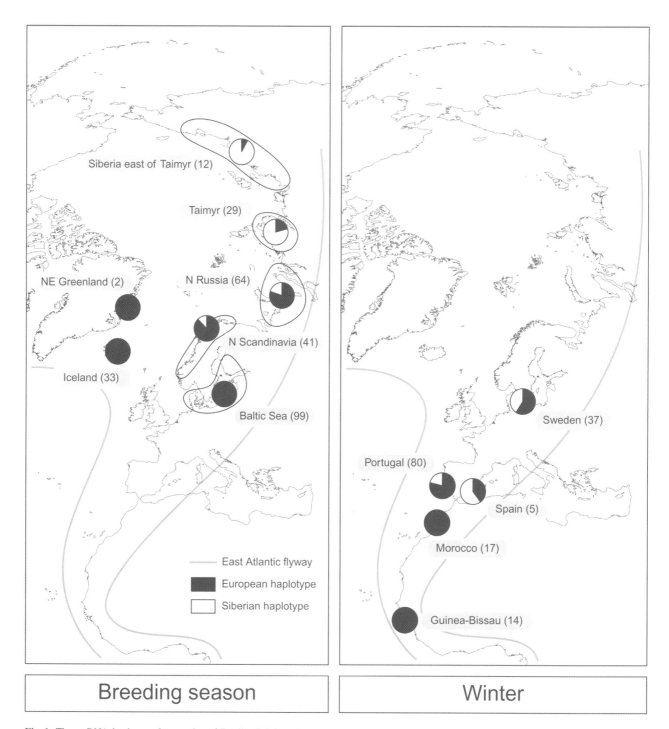

**Breeding season**

**Winter**

Fig. 1. The mtDNA haplotype frequencies of Dunlin *Calidris alpina* sampled during winter along the East Atlantic Flyway. For comparison, the European haplotype frequencies of Dunlin sampled in the breeding regions are also shown. Sample sizes are shown in brackets.

## RESULTS AND DISCUSSION

### Population segregation in the wintering areas

Our data confirm the results obtained from analyses of morphometric data and ringing recoveries, and show that there is partial segregation of Dunlin populations during winter. The mtDNA haplotype frequencies of wintering Dunlin populations differed between locations along the East Atlantic Flyway (Fig. 1). A clear distinction was observed between West Africa, where only the European haplotype was present in wintering flocks, and western Europe, where both the European and Siberian haplotypes were present. A major shift occurred between Morocco and the Iberian Peninsula. Within Iberia, Dunlin from the east coast (Tarragona, Spain) tended to include more birds

with the Siberian haplotype than birds from the west coast (Tagus estuary, Portugal), but the sample size from Spain was too small for any firm conclusions to be drawn (Fig. 1). Birds wintering in southern Sweden, which comprise one of the northernmost wintering populations in the flyway, had a higher frequency of the Siberian haplotype than any wintering population further south (Fig. 1).

### Assignment of breeding origin

Wintering flocks could be assigned to their respective breeding areas by comparing their haplotype frequencies with those from breeding populations (Fig. 1). The frequency of haplotypes from the West African winter assemblages corresponded to frequencies found on breeding areas in the western part of the breeding range (Greenland, Iceland, Baltic Sea). The Portuguese winter assemblage was similar to the northern Scandinavian and northern Russian breeding populations (Fig. 1). Although the sample from Spain was very small, it was possible to identify a northern Scandinavian or Russian breeding origin for these birds as well, based on the occurrence of Siberian haplotypes in the sample. The mtDNA haplotype frequencies from birds wintering in Sweden corresponded to breeding populations in northern Russia and the Taimyr Peninsula (Fig. 1).

These would be the obvious conclusions if there was no mixing of birds from different breeding populations in the wintering areas. However, in some parts of the wintering range, there is evidence of considerable mixing of breeding populations (Pienkowski & Dick 1975, Batty 1993). For example, evidence from ringing has shown that *C. a. schinzii* breeding in the Baltic region (and lacking the Siberian haplotype) may winter in several different areas, including France, Iberia and Morocco (Jönsson 1986). Recoveries of birds from the British breeding population of *C. a. schinzii* suggest that these birds winter mainly in West Africa, although a few may also winter in the Iberian Peninsula (Wernham *et al.* 2002). Thus, it is possible that the haplotype frequencies reported in Iberia might include some birds from breeding populations in which the frequency of the European haplotype is 100%. If this is the case, the other birds that contribute to the Iberian wintering flocks must originate from breeding populations with a high proportion of the Siberian haplotype, as in the eastern part of the breeding range, mainly in Russia.

In addition to confirming the presence of segregation on the wintering grounds, the results of the present study give more information on the composition of the winter assemblages in terms of their breeding origins, especially in Morocco and Iberia (see below). Analyses of morphometric data and ringing recoveries show that it is unlikely that there is a large influence of the nominate subspecies in Guinea-Bissau and Mauritania (Wymenga *et al.* 1990, Wintermans 1998). The results of the present study point to the occurrence of birds from northern Russia and Siberia in northern Europe in winter, as also indicated by the small number of ringing recoveries that link breeding grounds in northern Russia and western Siberia with wintering areas in northern Europe (Hardy & Minton 1980, Petterson *et al.* 1986, Greenwood 1984, Gromadzka 1989, Wernham *et al.* 2002). Our results also provide evidence that birds from these northeastern breeding populations occur as far south as Iberia.

### Morocco

Morphometric data indicate the presence of a considerable proportion of the nominate subspecies in Morocco during winter; minimum estimates of 20-25% *C. a. alpina* have been suggested (Pienkowski & Dick 1975, Greenwood 1984, Kersten *et al.* 1983). There have also been recoveries in Morocco of birds ringed on passage in Scandinavia and believed to have originated from breeding grounds further to the east (Pienkowski & Dick 1975, Greenwood 1984, Kersten *et al.* 1983). However, our study did not record any birds with the Siberian haplotype in Morocco, as would have been expected if birds from the eastern breeding populations were present. Further work with larger samples and over a number of years is required to clarify this question and determine the importance of Morocco as a wintering area for the nominate subspecies.

### Iberian Peninsula

The Iberian Peninsula has been considered to be one of the wintering areas of the nominate subspecies and also a wintering area for *C. a. schinzii*. Batty (1993) analysed bill lengths of birds wintering at Ria Formosa (southern Portugal), and concluded that most of the Dunlin were *C. a. schinzii*. In contrast to these results, an analysis of all ringing recoveries in Portugal (Lopes 2004) showed that most of the birds found in Portugal during winter (December and January) were recorded in the eastern part of Great Britain, the Wadden Sea, the Baltic region and northern Scandinavia, indicating eastern migration routes. The results of our genetic analysis clearly support the occurrence of wintering assemblages with a high proportion of the nominate subspecies in Iberia.

### Future applications and integration of methods

The analysis of ringing recoveries requires the compilation of data throughout an extended sampling period, in most cases decades, before any clear picture emerges. However, there is an urgent need to develop research tools that can be used to study the relatively quick responses in the population dynamics of migratory birds to environmental factors, such as habitat alteration and climate change, so that actions can be implemented in time. Furthermore, there are still some major gaps in our knowledge of the migration patterns and winter distribution of the Dunlin (e.g. occurrence of segregation between age classes or the sexes). Morphometric studies can play a major role in this regard. By using genetic sexing methods for smaller samples, we will be able to analyse the differences between populations much more accurately, from local to flyway scale (e.g. Lopes 2004).

Genetic population markers, such as the ones used in this study, have also a big potential for monitoring wintering populations. Other genetic techniques (e.g. micro-satellites, nuclear DNA sequencing, and amplified fragment polymorphisms – AFLP) and bio-geochemical approaches (e.g. ratios of stable isotopes) may prove to be useful in discerning between populations (e.g. Clegg *et al.* 2003). Techniques such as AFLP provide an efficient way of screening the nuclear genome for population markers. Genetic markers with higher mutation rates, such as micro-satellites, are potentially useful for distinguishing populations on a smaller geographical scale.

### CONCLUSIONS

Although the genetic markers which have been used to date lack enough resolution to pinpoint the breeding origin of each bird individually, their use has narrowed the range of possible breeding origins and made it possible to reject other regions with a high degree of confidence. This has allowed us to review and confirm our current understanding of the segregation of Dunlin populations, as revealed by morphometric data and ringing recoveries. The use of the methodology based on genetic markers can help to improve the conservation of the Dunlin as well as other long-distance migrants, and can be integrated with other methods for monitoring and management purposes.

### ACKNOWLEDGEMENTS

We would like to thank all those who have helped with the sampling of birds, especially Theunis Piersma (Guinea-Bissau), José L. Arroyo (Morocco) and Christer Persson (Sweden).

This research was funded by Fundação para a Ciência e a Tecnologia (FCT) through the grant PRAXIS XXI/BD/16250/98 and by the National Centre for Biosystematics, National History Museum, University of Oslo.

## REFERENCES

Batty, L. 1993. Computer analysis of wader morphometric data. Wader Study Group Bulletin 70: 23-27.

Clegg, S.M., Kelly, J.F., Kimura, M. & Smith, T.B. 2003. Combining genetic markers and stable isotopes to reveal population connectivity and migration patterns in a Neotropical migrant, Wilson's warbler (*Wilsonia pusilla*). Molecular Ecology 12: 819-830.

del Hoyo, J., Elliott, A. & Sagatal, J. 1996. Handbook of the Birds of the World. Vol. 3: Hoatzins to Auks. Lynx Edicions, Barcelona.

Greenwood, J.G. 1984. Migration of Dunlin *Calidris alpina*: a world-wide overview. Ringing and Migration 5: 35-39.

Greenwood, J.G. 1986. Geographical variation and taxonomy of the Dunlin *Calidris alpina* (L.). Bulletin of the British Ornithologists' Club 106: 43-56.

Gromadzka, J. 1989. Breeding and wintering areas of Dunlin migrating through southern Baltic. Ornis Scandinavica 20: 132-144.

Gromadzka, J. & Ryabitsev, V.K. 1998. Siberian Dunlins *Calidris alpina* migrate to Europe: first evidence from ringing. In: H. Hötker, E. Lebedeva, P.S. Tomkovich, J. Gromadzka, N.C. Davidson, D.A. Stroud & R.B. West (eds) Migration and international conservation of waders. Research and conservation on north Asian, African and European flyways. International Wader Studies 10: 88-90.

Hardy, A.R. & Minton, C.D.T. 1980. Dunlin migration in Britain and Ireland. Bird Study 27: 8192.

Jönsson, P.E. 1986. The migration and wintering of Baltic Dunlins *Calidris alpina schinzii*. Vår Fågelvärld Supplement 11: 7178.

Kersten, M., Piersma, T., Smit, C. & Zegers, P. 1983. Wader migration along the Atlantic coast of Morocco, March 1981. RIN report 83/20, Research Institute for Nature Management, Texel, The Netherlands.

Lopes, R.J. 2004. Migration and winter dynamics of the Dunlin *Calidris alpina* in Portugal. PhD thesis, University of Coimbra, Portugal.

Nebel, S., Lank, D.B., O'Hara, P.D., Fernandez, G., Haase, B., Delgado, F., Estela, F.A., Ogden, L.J.E., Harrington, B., Kus, B.E., Lyons, J.E., Mercier, F., Ortego, B., Takekawa, J.Y., Warnock, N. & Warnock, S.E. 2002. Western sandpipers (*Calidris mauri*) during the nonbreeding season: Spatial segregation on a hemispheric scale. Auk 119 (4): 922928.

Pettersson, J., Sandström, A. & Johansson, K. 1986. Wintering areas of migrants trapped at Ottenby Bird Observatory. Special report from Ottenby Bird Observatory, No.6. Ottenby, Sweden.

Pienkowski, M.W. & Dick, W.J.A. 1975. The migration and wintering of Dunlin *Calidris alpina* in north-west Africa. Ornis Scandinavica 6: 151-167.

Pienkowski, M.W. & Evans, P.R. 1984. Migratory behavior of shorebirds in the western Palearctic. In: J. Burger & B.L. Olla (eds) Behavior of Marine Animals. Vol.6. Shorebirds. Migration and Foraging Behavior. Plenum Press, New York: 73123.

Smit, C.J. & Piersma, T. 1989. Numbers, midwinter distribution and migration of wader populations using the East Atlantic flyway. In: H. Boyd & J.Y. Pirot (eds) Flyways and reserve networks for water birds. IWRB Special Publication No. 9, Slimbridge, UK: 24-63.

Tiedemann, R. 1999. Seasonal changes in the breeding origin of migrating Dunlins (*Calidris alpina*) as revealed by mitochondrial DNA sequencing. Journal für Onithologie 140: 319323.

Wenink, P.W. & Baker, A.J. 1996. Mitochondrial DNA lineages in composite flocks of migratory and wintering dunlins (*Calidris alpina*). The Auk 113 (4): 744-756.

Wenink, P.W., Baker, A.J. & Tilanus, M.G.F. 1993. Hypervariable control region sequences reveal global population structuring in a long-distance migrating shorebird, the dunlin (*Calidris alpina*). Proceedings of the National Academy of Sciences of the United States of America 90: 9498.

Wenink, P.W., Baker, A.J., Rösner, H.U. & Tilanus, M.G.F. 1996. Global mitochondrial DNA phylogeography of Holarctic breeding Dunlins (*Calidris alpina*). Evolution 50: 318330.

Wennerberg, L. 2001. Breeding origin and migration pattern of dunlin (*Calidris alpina*) revealed by mitochondrial DNA analysis. Molecular Ecology 10: 1111-1120.

Wennerberg, L., Holmgren, N.M.A., Jönsson, P.E. & von Schantz, T. 1999. Genetic and morphological variation in breeding dunlin *Calidris alpina* in the Palearctic tundra. Ibis 141: 391-398.

Wennerberg, L., Pettersson, J. & Holmgren, N.M.A. 2001. The timing of autumn migration and moult in two mtDNA haplotypes of Dunlin *Calidris alpina* at a stopover site in the Baltic Sea. In: L. Wennerberg, Genetic variation and migration of waders. PhD thesis, Lund University, Sweden: 115-127.

Wernham, C.V., Toms M.P., Marchant, J.H., Clark, J.A., Siriwardena, G.M. & Baillie, S.R. (eds). 2002. The Migration Atlas: movements of the birds of Britain and Ireland. T. & A.D. Poyser, London.

Wintermans, G. 1998. Geographical breeding origin, plumage and weight of waders wintering in the Arquipelago dos Bijagos. In: W.J. Wolf (ed) The end of the east-atlantic flyway – Waders in Guinea Bissau. WIWO Report 39, Zeist: 9-38.

Wymenga, E., Engelmoer, M., Smit, C.J. & van Spanje, T.M. 1990. Geographical breeding origin and migration of waders wintering in West Africa. Ardea 78: 83-112.

# Spring migration patterns in Western Sandpipers *Calidris mauri*

*Mary Anne Bishop[1,2], Nils Warnock[3,4] & John Y. Takekawa[5]*

[1]*Copper River Delta Institute, USDA Forest Service, PO Box 1460, Cordova, AK 99574 & Department of Fisheries, University of Washington, Seattle, WA 98195, USA.*

[2]*Present address: Prince William Sound Science Center, PO Box 705, Cordova, AK 99574, USA.*
*(email: mbishop@pwssc.gen.ak.us)*

[3]*Environmental Resource Sciences, University of Nevada, Reno, NV 89512, USA & Department of Biological Sciences, Simon Fraser University, Burnaby, BC V5A 1S6, Canada.*

[4]*Present address: PRBO Conservation Science, 3820 Cypress Drive, 11, Petaluma, CA 94954, USA.*

[5]*U.S. Geological Survey, Western Ecological Research Center, San Francisco Bay Estuary Field Station, 505 Azuar Drive, Vallejo, CA 94592, USA.*

Bishop, M.A., Warnock, N. & Takekawa, J.Y. 2006. Spring migration patterns in Western Sandpipers *Calidris mauri*. *Waterbirds around the world*. Eds. G.C. Boere, C.A. Galbraith & D.A. Stroud. The Stationery Office, Edinburgh, UK. pp. 545-550.

## ABSTRACT

One hundred and thirty-two Western Sandpipers *Calidris mauri* were radio-marked at two sites on the Pacific coast of North America (San Francisco Bay, California, and Grays Harbor, Washington) and at an interior wetland in the western Great Basin (Honey Lake, California). The northward migration of these birds was monitored at a network of 12 major stopover sites and four breeding areas. Eighty-eight percent of the birds were relocated at 10 stopover sites and two breeding areas between San Francisco Bay and the Yukon-Kuskokwim Delta, Alaska (c. 4 200 km). On average, birds were relocated at fewer than two sites, with the Copper River Delta in Alaska being the single most important stopover site. Migrant birds radio-marked at the interior site shifted to the coast between Oregon and Washington, and then continued their migration along the Pacific coast. Individual birds used a wide variety of migration strategies, from stopping at sites 200-300 km apart to flying as far as 2 100 km in under 48 hours. At the population level, we observed heterogeneity in phenology and site use, a strategy well adapted to the changing landscape that Western Sandpipers must navigate during migration, especially in interior regions.

## INTRODUCTION

Large-scale marking studies have been successful in providing information on bird migration routes and stopover areas (Lincoln 1959, Butler *et al.* 1996). Determining how individual, small (<35 g) birds such as Calidrid sandpipers migrate over large distances has been challenging because of technological, logistical, and financial constraints. Systematic data on sites used or not used by individual shorebirds along major segments of their migration flyways did not exist until Iverson *et al.* (1996) first documented the coastal migration routes of individual Western Sandpipers *Calidris mauri* between San Francisco Bay, California, and Cook Inlet, Alaska, during spring 1992.

The Western Sandpiper, a mid- to long-distance migrant (Johnson & Herter 1990), is the most numerous shorebird along the Pacific Flyway. In some years, its population can number over four million individuals (Bishop *et al.* 2000). This Nearctic shorebird breeds principally in western Alaska, with smaller numbers in north-eastern Russia and northern and central Alaska (Kessel 1989, Wilson 1994, Bishop & Warnock 1998). The wintering areas extend from California to Peru, and from the southern

Atlantic coast of the USA and the Gulf of Mexico to northern South America (Wilson 1994).

Along the Pacific Flyway, five coastal migratory stopover sites have been documented which support over 500 000 migrant Western Sandpipers in spring: San Francisco Bay (Stenzel & Page 1988), Grays Harbor, Washington (Wilson 1993), Fraser River Delta, British Columbia (Butler *et al.* 1987, Butler 1994), Stikine River Delta, Alaska (G. Iverson unpubl. data) and Copper River Delta, Alaska (Isleib 1979, Bishop *et al.* 2000). Areas in the Central Valley of California and the western Great Basin of the United States also host large numbers of migrating Western Sandpipers (Harrington & Perry 1997, Oring & Reed 1997), but the use of these interior areas by Western Sandpipers and other shorebirds remains poorly understood.

Our previous work has shown that Western Sandpipers migrate northward from San Francisco Bay along the Pacific coast using a rapid, short-flight migration strategy (Iverson *et al.* 1996) which includes short (1-3 days) stays at large estuarine habitats (Warnock & Bishop 1998). Males precede females, and between the sexes there are differences in the likelihood of a stopover being used (Bishop *et al.* 2004). Our research also provided evidence that the Yukon-Kuskokwim Delta in Alaska is the final breeding destination for many of the birds migrating through San Francisco Bay and other areas on the Pacific coast (Bishop & Warnock 1998).

Here, we examine spring migration by individual Western Sandpipers radio-marked in 1995 and 1996 in North America at two sites on the Pacific coast and an interior site in the Great Basin. We describe and analyze the effects of year and banding location on phenology and use of stopovers during the northward migration to the breeding grounds, a distance of more than 4 000 km. We also describe a previously unknown migration route of Western Sandpipers through the western Great Basin.

## METHODS

We captured Western Sandpipers from 17 to 30 April 1995 and 17 April to 3 May 1996 at two sites on the Pacific coast, San Francisco Bay (hereafter referred to as San Francisco; 37°46'N, 122°26'W) and Grays Harbor (46°57'N, 124°03'W), and at an interior wetland in the Great Basin, Honey Lake, California (40°14'N, 120°21W; Fig. 1). Generally, capture dates corresponded with the peak migration at the trapping sites. Birds were trapped in mist-nets placed in salt ponds, mudflats, and

**Fig. 1.** Banding and monitoring sites for Western Sandpiper *Calidris mauri* telemetry study, spring 1995 and 1996. Combined monitoring sites include: Grays Harbor and Willapa Bay, Washington; Fraser River Delta and Tofino Beach, British Columbia; eastern and western Cook Inlet, and Bristol Bay, Alaska (combines two stopover and two breeding areas).

freshwater ponds during daylight hours. Each bird was weighed to the nearest 0.5 g, and the exposed culmen, flattened wing chord, and tarsus were measured (in mm). Sex was determined by length of exposed culmen (males <24.2 mm; females >24.8 mm; unknown 24.2-24.8 mm; Page & Fearis 1971); birds were not aged.

Radio-transmitters weighing 0.9 g (Model BD-2; Holohil Systems Ltd., Woodlawn, Ontario, Canada) were glued to the lower backs of 132 Western Sandpipers (1995, $n = 61$; 1996, $n = 71$), following methods described in Warnock & Warnock (1993). Retention time was previously found to be more than seven weeks in this species (Warnock & Takekawa 1996). The transmitter averaged about 3% of a bird's body mass, and

the expected battery life was more than four weeks. The battery life of test transmitters averaged $39.0 \pm 2.5$ days ($n = 5$).

We searched for radio-marked Western Sandpipers from the ground and fixed-wing aircraft at 15 sites in 1995 and 19 sites in 1996 (Fig. 1, Table 1; see Bishop & Warnock 1998 and Warnock & Bishop 1998 for dates and locations). Monitoring began north of the banding sites as soon as radio-marked birds were suspected of departing and continued until either all radio-marked birds had departed, or when minimal migratory activity was observed. The number and timing of flights varied by area and year. In 1996, daily flights occurred at Grays Harbor, in the Fraser River Delta, and in the Stikine River Delta, Yakutat Forelands, Copper River Delta and Kachemak Bay in Alaska (Fig. 1). During peak migration in 1996, two flights were flown per day at the Fraser River Delta ($n = 2$ days) and Copper River Delta ($n = 6$ days).

For our analyses, we combined monitoring sites into 11 sites (Fig. 1). Each site beyond the banding location where an individual bird's radio signal was detected was counted as one relocation, with a maximum of one detection per monitoring site, regardless of how many times the bird was detected at that site. We assumed that all radio-marked birds present at a banding or monitoring site were detected regardless of the monitoring method. High winds prevented monitoring at the Copper River Delta on 6 May 1995; we assumed that birds detected on 7 May had arrived on 6 May ($n = 7$). Of the 71 radio-marked birds in 1996, four radio frequencies were identical to transmitters on Caribou *Rangifer rangifer* at Bristol Bay in western Alaska, and were only monitored at more southerly sites. Where appropriate, these four birds and one bird that died or lost its radio at Stikine River Delta were excluded in some analyses.

Statistical analyses were performed using STATA (Computing Resource Center, Santa Monica, California 1992). Data were examined for departures from normality and homogeneity by preliminary graphing and testing of data. For analyses, yearly dates were converted into Julian dates (JD). When reporting results, we adjusted all 1996 dates to 1995 (1996 date + 1 day), since 1996 was a leap year. For all tests, significance was determined if $P \leq 0.05$. Means are reported $\pm$ one standard deviation (SD).

## RESULTS
### Relocations
In 1995, we relocated 51 of the 61 Western Sandpipers (84%) a total of 85 times at eight of the nine monitoring sites. In 1996, 64 of 69 Western Sandpipers (93%) were relocated a total of 140 times at 10 of the 11 monitoring sites (Table 2, Fig. 2). For all monitoring sites, the number of birds relocated between years was not significantly different ($\chi^2_1 = 2.65$, $P = 0.10$). We failed to relocate 15 birds after departure from their banding site (six males and nine females), both years combined. The number of birds not found was not significantly different among banding sites ($\chi^2_2 = 0.91$, $P > 0.60$).

In 1995, birds banded at San Francisco stopped at an average of $1.6 \pm 0.6$ sites (max. 3); birds banded at Honey Lake at $1.6 \pm 0.8$ sites (max. 3); and birds banded at Grays Harbor at $1.7 \pm 0.5$ sites (max. 2). In 1996, with more extensive aerial monitoring efforts at five sites (Humboldt Bay, Grays Harbor, Yakutat Forelands, Copper River Delta, and Bristol Bay), San Francisco radio-marked birds were relocated at an average of $2.6 \pm 1.1$ sites (max. 5), Honey Lake birds at $1.6 \pm 0.7$ sites

**Table 1.  Distance (km) between banding sites of radio-marked Western Sandpipers *Calidris mauri* and more northerly monitoring sites.**

| Monitoring site | Banding site | | |
|---|---|---|---|
| | San Francisco CA | Honey Lake CA | Grays Harbor WA |
| Humboldt Bay CA | 410 | | |
| Grays Harbor WA | 1 110 | 790 | |
| Fraser River Delta BC | 1 350 | 1 030 | 240 |
| Stikine River Delta AK | 2 410 | 2 090 | 1 300 |
| Yakutat Forelands AK | 2 940 | 2 620 | 1 830 |
| Copper River Delta AK | 3 250 | 2 930 | 2 140 |
| Cook Inlet AK | 3 590 | 3 270 | 2 480 |
| Mulchatna River AK | 3 880 | 3 560 | 2 770 |
| Bristol Bay AK | 4 000 | 3 680 | 2 890 |
| Yukon-Kuskokwim Delta AK | 4 200 | 3 880 | 3 090 |

CA = California, USA; WA = Washington, USA; BC = British Columbia, Canada; AK = Alaska, USA.

**Table 2. Numbers of Western Sandpipers *Calidris mauri* radio-marked and percent relocated at least once to the north. Spring 1995 and 1996.**

| Banding location | | 1995 Banded | % Relocated | 1996 Banded | % Relocated |
|---|---|---|---|---|---|
| San Francisco, CA | Male | 16 | 94 | 15 | 100[1] |
| | Female | 13 | 69 | 15 | 87 |
| Honey Lake, CA | Male | 12 | 83 | 7 | 71 |
| | Female | 6 | 67 | 5 | 100 |
| | Unknown | 0 | 0 | 1 | 0[2] |
| Grays Harbor, WA | Male | 7 | 100 | 21 | 95 |
| | Female | 7 | 86 | 6 | 100 |
| | Unknown | 0 | 0 | 1 | 100 |

[1] One bird not included due to overlap with Caribou frequency at northern site.

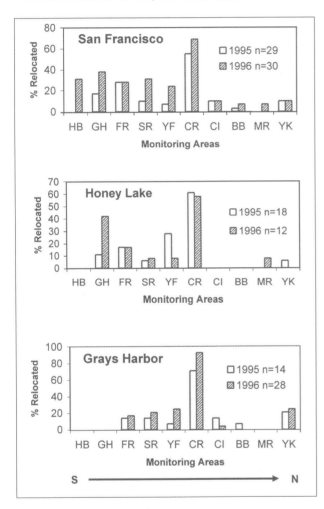

Fig. 2. Relocations (%) of radio-marked Western Sandpipers *Calidris mauri* at areas north of banding sites in spring 1995 and 1996. Stopover areas, beginning at the southernmost monitoring site: HB = Humboldt Bay, California; GH = Grays Harbor and Willapa Bay, Washington; FR = Fraser River Delta and Tofino Beach, British Columbia; SR = Stikine River Delta, Alaska; YF = Yakutat Forelands, Alaska; CR = Copper River Delta, Alaska; CI = Cook Inlet, Alaska; BB = Bristol Bay, Alaska (a stopover and breeding area). Breeding areas: MR = Mulchatna River, Alaska; YK = Yukon-Kuskokwim Delta, Alaska. There were no relocations at Malheur Lake, Oregon.

(max. 3), and Grays Harbor birds at 1.6 ± 0.6 sites (max. 3). In 1996, we relocated three San Francisco birds (two males, one female) at five stopover sites.

The Copper River Delta was the stopover site with the highest number of relocations, with 61% of marked birds stopping there in 1995 and 80% in 1996. Significantly more radio-marked birds were relocated at the Copper River Delta in 1996 than in 1995 ($\chi^2_1 = 4.97$, $P = 0.03$). San Francisco birds had the fewest relocations (55%, 1995), while Grays Harbor birds had the most relocations (93%, 1996; Fig. 2). In 1996, we conducted twice-daily flights on the Copper River Delta during six days and relocated 40 different radio-marked birds. Four birds (10%) were detected on one flight only, indicating that these birds migrated through the Copper River Delta in less than 12 hours.

We also relocated radio-marked Western Sandpipers at Humboldt Bay, Willapa Bay, Yakutat Forelands, Bristol Bay (a stopover and breeding area), and two other breeding areas in Alaska (Fig. 1). Although Willapa Bay is only 35-90 km (depending on location) south of Grays Harbor, no sandpipers relocated at Willapa Bay were detected within Grays Harbor. However, one Willapa bird was detected at the mouth of Grays Harbor on the outer beach. At the Yakutat Forelands, sandpipers were located along a 100 km stretch from Yakutat Bay southeast to the East Alsek River, with the majority of relocations occurring between Ocean Cape and the Seal Creek-Ahrnklin River estuary. On the breeding grounds, birds were relocated on Alaska's Yukon-Kuskokwim Delta in both years and near the confluence of the Nushagak and Mulchatna Rivers in 1996, the only year that this site was monitored.

Despite extensive coverage in both years, no radio-marked birds were relocated north of Redoubt Bay (north-western Cook Inlet) or along the Alaska Peninsula between Naknek and Unimak Island. Nor were radio-marked birds relocated during our one year of monitoring efforts at Malheur Lake in eastern Oregon (Fig. 1) and at Cape Peirce, Alaska (west of Bristol Bay). In 1995, no birds were detected at Humboldt Bay in northern California, although they were detected in 1996 when we increased our effort.

### Phenology

The mean departure dates of radio-marked Western Sandpipers from the three banding sites ranged from 26 April to 3 May in 1995 and from 27 April to 8 May in 1996 (Table 3). The average arrival dates at sites monitored ranged from 29 April at Humboldt Bay to 20 May at the Yukon-Kuskokwim Delta (Fig. 3). For radio-marked birds departing from San Francisco, this indicates a 25 day migration period over the final c. 4 000 km of their migration route. Depending on the year, for monitoring sites up to and

**Table 3.** Banding and mean departure dates from banding sites of radio-marked Western Sandpipers *Calidris mauri* captured at three locations. Dates adjusted so that the 1996 leap year dates equal 1995 (1996 date + one day).

| Banding location | Year | Banding dates | Mean departure date | Range | N |
|---|---|---|---|---|---|
| San Francisco CA | 1995 | 17-19, 21-23 Apr | 28 Apr | 20 Apr - 5 May | 29 |
| | 1996[1] | 18-23 Apr | 28 Apr | 22 Apr - 9 May | 30 |
| Honey Lake CA | 1995 | 27, 28, 30 Apr | 1 May | 27 Apr - 8 May | 18 |
| | 1996[1] | 26 Apr | 27 Apr | 27 Apr - 30 Apr | 13 |
| Grays Harbor WA | 1995 | 24, 25, 28 Apr | 3 May | 24 Apr - 9 May | 14 |
| | 1996 | 28-30 Apr, 1,3,4 May | 8 May | 3 May - 13 May | 28 |

[1] 1996 includes two birds dropped from other analyses (one from San Francisco and one from Honey Lake).

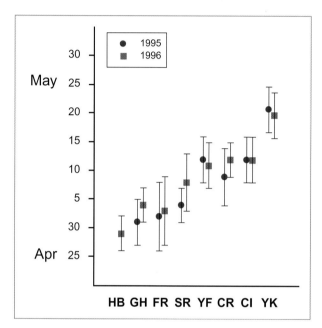

**Fig. 3.** Mean arrival dates (± SD; dates adjusted for leap year) for radio-marked Western Sandpipers *Calidris mauri* at stopover and breeding sites where four or more relocations were recorded; spring 1995 and 1996. Stopover areas: HB = Humboldt Bay, California; GH = Grays Harbor and Willapa Bay, Washington; FR = Fraser River Delta and Tofino Beach, British Columbia; SR = Stikine River Delta, Alaska; YF = Yakutat Forelands, Alaska; CR = Copper River Delta, Alaska; CI = Cook Inlet, Alaska. Breeding area: YK = Yukon-Kuskokwim Delta, Alaska.

including the Copper River Delta, the migration window for radio-marked birds (number of days between the first arrival of a radio-marked bird and last departure of a radio-marked bird) was shortest (10 days) for Humboldt Bay, Grays Harbor and Stikine River Delta, and longest for the Fraser River Delta and Copper River Delta (20 days each). At the Copper River Delta, the mean arrival dates for Western Sandpipers banded at San Francisco were 7 May 1995 ± 4 days (*n* = 16) and 10 May 1996 ± 4 days (*n* = 20); Honey Lake, 14 May 1995 ± 3 days (*n* = 11) and 13 May 1996 ± 2 days (*n* = 7); and Grays Harbor, 8 May 1995 ± 5 days (*n* = 10) and 14 May 1996 ± 2 days (*n* = 26).

## DISCUSSION

### Stopover use
Overall, individual radio-marked Western Sandpipers showed a wide variety of migration strategies, from stopping at sites 200-300 km apart to flying as far as 2 100 km in less than 48 hours.

On average, individual radio-marked Western Sandpipers were relocated at fewer than two of the 10 monitoring sites (including stopover and breeding sites). We may have missed some birds at our monitoring sites (i.e. birds passing through a site in less than 24 hours), but from our twice-daily flights at the Fraser and Copper River Deltas, the number of birds missed does not appear to be over 10%. It seems likely that birds were stopping at smaller, unmonitored sites, since travel times between known stopover areas were too long for uninterrupted flight (Bishop *et al.* 2004).

Iverson *et al.* (1996) concluded that Western Sandpipers from San Francisco were more likely to be detected at stopover sites with increasing latitude. This study fails to support that contention. At Humboldt Bay, c. 400 km north of San Francisco, we relocated 30% of birds radio-marked at San Francisco in 1996 when we increased ground coverage and added aerial coverage. Relocations at Grays Harbor were slightly higher than the more northerly sites of Stikine River Delta and Yakutat Forelands during both years of this study, even though fewer aerial surveys were conducted at Grays Harbor. We suggest that the low stopover use at Grays Harbor (3.4% of 58 birds) found by Iverson *et al.* (1996) was probably a result of insufficient coverage. Their monitoring at Grays Harbor in 1992 only included Bowerman Basin (approximately 10% of the exposed mudflats within Grays Harbor; Wilson 1993), and monitoring was from the ground, rather than from the air. More perplexing are the differences in stopover use at the Fraser River Delta, where monitoring coverage was comparable between the two studies. Whereas Iverson *et al.* (1996) recorded only 8.6% of San Francisco radio-marked birds stopping at the Fraser River Delta in 1992, we relocated 27-28% in both 1995 and 1996.

At the population level, all of the sites that were regularly monitored north of San Francisco up to and including the Copper River Delta were used by at least 20% of the radio-marked Western Sandpipers during one of the two years of this study. If we assume that the radio-marked birds are representative of the Western Sandpiper's Pacific Flyway population, then each of these stopover sites qualifies, at a minimum, as an "international shorebird site" under the criteria used by the Western Hemisphere Shorebird Reserve Network (WHSRN), i.e. a site used by at least 10% of the flyway population of a species. As of January 2005, Humboldt Bay, Grays Harbor, the Fraser River Delta and the Copper River Delta are official WHSRN sites. However, Controller Bay, an area of high shorebird use (M.A. Bishop unpubl. data) located just east of the Copper River Delta, is not part of the Copper River Delta WHSRN hemispheric site designation. Alaska's Stikine River Delta and Yakutat Forelands also lack WHSRN designation.

Similar to previous studies (Iverson *et al.* 1996, Bishop *et al.* 2000, Bishop *et al.* 2004), our relocations revealed the importance of the Copper River Delta in south-central Alaska for Western Sandpipers. It has been asserted that virtually all of the world's population of Western Sandpipers stops at the Copper River Delta during their northward migration (Wilson 1994). Even accounting for birds that pass through too quickly to be relocated, it appears that in some years, some western Great Basin and San Francisco birds may not be stopping at the Copper River Delta. For birds radio-marked at Grays Harbor however, the high numbers of relocations recorded in both years (>71%) indicate that the Copper River Delta is of great importance for birds migrating through this site. In contrast, the Fraser River Delta (240 km to the north of Grays Harbor) in British Columbia had lower use (<15%) by Grays Harbor birds, and relocations at Stikine River Delta and Yakutat Forelands were only slightly higher.

Our study has also revealed the importance of Yakutat Forelands for the Pacific Flyway population of Western Sandpipers. Radio-marked birds from all three banding sites used Yakutat Forelands in both years, in particular the area between the town of Yakutat and the Ahrnklin River. Subsequent ground surveys at the Seal Creek-Ahrnklin River estuary confirmed that Western Sandpipers are the most abundant shorebird in spring in this area (Andres & Browne 1998).

## Migration routes

The western Great Basin is one of the least studied areas in North America for shorebirds (Neel & Henry 1997). For the first time, we established a northward migration route for Western Sandpipers passing through the western Great Basin. Western Great Basin birds, represented by birds marked at Honey Lake, were relocated at coastal sites from Grays Harbor to the Copper River Delta. However, no Honey Lake birds were detected at Humboldt Bay in either year, nor were Honey Lake birds detected inland at Malheur National Wildlife Refuge, Oregon, in spring 1996 during four monitoring days that included one aerial survey. Many sites used by Western Sandpipers in the western Great Basin are dry in some years (Robinson & Warnock 1997). The springs of 1995 and 1996 were wet (N. Warnock unpubl. data) and habitat was abundant. In wet years, these birds may be moving more slowly through the Great Basin than in dry years, before shifting to the coast.

Western Sandpipers can be abundant in the Willamette Valley of Oregon during spring (Paulson 1993). A possible migration route for these interior migrating birds is to travel up the western side of the Great Basin through the Klamath Basin in northern California, into the Willamette Valley of Oregon to the Columbia River, and then shift westward onto the Washington coast. Greater White-fronted Geese *Anser albifrons* migrating through the Central Valley of California, just west and parallel to the western Great Basin, follow a similar route to their breeding grounds (Ely & Takekawa 1996) which overlap with those of the Western Sandpiper

## Effects of radio-marking on phenology

Several studies have shown that shorebirds lose body mass during and immediately after capture (Pienkowski *et al.* 1979, Davidson 1984, Lindström 1995, Warnock *et al.* 1997). Our previous work suggests that radio-marked birds may require additional days to regain weight and adjust to the radio (Warnock & Bishop 1998, Warnock *et al.* 2004). In this study, we radio-marked birds just prior to and during peak migration at San Francisco (about 20-25 April; Storer 1951, Stenzel & Page 1988) and at Grays Harbor (late April to early May, N. Warnock unpubl. data). Nevertheless, the average departure from both sites occurred a few days later than peak migration in both years. This pattern was repeated at other stopover sites. We cannot rule out an effect of capture or the radio-transmitter on the migration timing of the marked birds; however, it appears to be a short-term effect, as evidenced by our very high relocation rate at sites to the north, including the breeding grounds. For some birds, there was no apparent capture effect. For instance, two Grays Harbor birds left the day they were captured and were seen at Fraser River one day later.

## CONCLUSIONS

At the individual level, data on inter-annual differences and flight strategies used by shorebirds during migration are still lacking. This would involve trapping and tracking the same individual in consecutive years, an improbable event in the case of Western Sandpipers, or use of a long-lived transmitter and attachment. At the population level, however, this study suggests that the migration strategies of Western Sandpipers vary, as they do in other shorebirds (Myers *et al.* 1990, Davidson & Wilson 1992, Skagen & Knopf 1994, Warnock *et al.* 2004). There appears to be heterogeneity in phenology and site use during migration, a strategy that is well adapted to the changing landscape that Western Sandpipers must navigate during migration, especially in interior regions.

In future studies, it would be valuable to examine the migration strategies of Western Sandpipers during early and late spring migration and during autumn migration, periods not covered by this study. Our study reveals the importance of maintaining a network of stopover sites along the coast and interior of the Pacific Flyway. At the same time, our study demonstrates the singular importance of the Copper River Delta for migrant Western Sandpipers in spring. The conservation of Western Sandpipers clearly hinges on this network of stopover areas.

## ACKNOWLEDGEMENTS

Funding was provided by: Canadian Wildlife Service/NSERC Wildlife Ecology Research Program; Chase Wildlife Foundation; Lake Clark National Park; National Fish and Wildlife Foundation's Neotropical Migratory Bird Conservation Initiative; Simon Fraser University; Skaggs Foundation; U.S. Fish and Wildlife Service, Ecological Services, San Francisco Bay Program; U.S. Fish and Wildlife Service, Region 7, Coastal Marine Bird Program; U.S. Fish and Wildlife Service, Region 1, Refuges and Wildlife; and USDA Forest Service, Region 10, Alaska. We wish to thank the following people for assistance with banding and radio-tracking birds: J. Hanson, E. Burns, D. Orthmeyer, S. Warnock, K. Foerster, P. Schmidt, J. Smith, R. Mathis, J. Solzberg, K. Kovacs, P. Schmidt, L. Oring, and L. Powers in California; G. Ivey in Oregon; R. Schuver, W. Schuver, D. Williamson, L. Vicencio, J.E. Takekawa, R. Van Deman, G. Reardon, S. MacKay, and S. Marston in Washington; M. Lemon and P. Shepard in Canada; and P. Walsh, S. Posner, P. Robertson, B. Andres, B. Browne, R. Capitan, V. Harke, D. Walter (deceased), E. Lance, L. Lobe, J. Carnes, G. West, J. Hupp, K. Bollinger, R. Gill, A. Bennett, L. Bennett,

L. Alsworth, R. Kleinleder, L. Slater, D. Dewhurst, H. Moore, B. Smoke, N. Varner, G. Ruhl, A. Aderman, C. Dau, R. King, M. Wege, D. Cox, and G. Walters in Alaska. We thank the following individuals and their agencies for loaning equipment: J. Bodkin, D. Esler, J. Hupp and D. Munson, D. Irons, D. Orthmeyer, and S. Ranney. Special thanks are extended to Holohil Systems, R. Butler, F. Cooke, A. Dalsimer, S. Haig, M. Kolar, D. Lank, R. Morat, L. Oring, P. Stangel, K. Wohl, and T. Zimmerman. We thank our reviewers for their comments. Support during the writing of this paper was provided to MAB through a grant from the Prince William Sound Oil Spill Recovery Institute.

## REFERENCES

Andres, B.A. & Browne, B.T. 1998. Spring migration of shorebirds on the Yakutat Forelands, Alaska. Wilson Bulletin 110: 326-331.

Bishop, M.A. & Warnock, N. 1998. Migration of Western Sandpipers: links between their Alaskan stopover area and breeding grounds. Wilson Bulletin 110: 457-462.

Bishop, M., Meyers, P.M. & McNeley, P.F. 2000. A method to estimate migrant shorebird numbers on the Copper River Delta, Alaska. Journal of Field Ornithology 71: 627-637.

Bishop, M.A., Warnock, N. & Takekawa, J.Y. 2004. Differential spring migration by male and female Western Sandpipers at interior and coastal sites. Ardea 92: 185-196.

Butler, R.W. 1994. Distribution and abundance of Western Sandpipers, Dunlins and Black-bellied Plovers in the Fraser River estuary. In: R.W. Butler & K. Vermeer (eds). Abundance and distribution of birds in estuaries in the Strait of Georgia. Canadian Wildlife Service Occasional Paper No. 83, Ottawa: 13-23.

Butler, R.W., Kaiser, G.W. & Smith, G.E.J. 1987. Migration, chronology, length of stay, sex ratio, and weight of Western Sandpipers (*Calidris mauri*) on the south coast of British Columbia. Journal of Field Ornithology 58: 103-111.

Butler, R.W., Delgado, F.S., De La Cueva, H., Pulido, V. & Sandercock, B.K. 1996. Migration routes of the Western Sandpiper. Wilson Bulletin 108: 662-672.

Davidson, N.C. 1984. Changes in the conditions of Dunlin and Knots during short-term captivity. Canadian Journal of Zoology 62: 1724-1731.

Davidson, N.C. & Wilson, J.R. 1992. The migration system of the European-wintering Knot, *Calidris canutus islandica*. Wader Study Group Bulletin 64, Supplement: 39-51.

Ely, C.R. & Takekawa, J.Y. 1996. Geographic variation in migratory behavior of Greater White-fronted Geese (*Anser albifrons*). Auk 113: 889-901.

Harrington, B.A. & E. Perry. 1997. Important shorebird staging sites meeting Western Hemisphere Shorebird Reserve Network criteria in the United States. U.S. Fish & Wildlife Service, Washington, D.C.

Isleib, M.E. 1979. Migratory shorebird populations on the Copper River Delta and eastern Prince William Sound, Alaska. Studies in Avian Biology 2: 125-129.

Iverson, G.C., Warnock, S.E., Butler, R.W., Bishop, M.A. & Warnock, N. 1996. Spring migration of Western Sandpipers (*Calidris mauri*) along the Pacific coast of North America: a telemetry study. Condor 98: 10-21.

Johnson, S.R. & Herter, D.R. 1990. Bird migration in the Arctic: a review. In: E. Gwinner (ed). Bird migration, physiology and ecophysiology. Springer-Verlag, Berlin: 22-43.

Kessel, B. 1989. Birds of the Seward Peninsula, Alaska. University of Alaska Press.

Lincoln, F.C. 1952. Migration of birds. Doubleday, Doran & Company, Garden City, New York.

Lindström, A. 1995. Stopover ecology of migrating birds: some unsolved questions. Israel Journal of Zoology 41: 407-416.

Myers, J.P., Sallaberry, M., Ortiz, A.E., Castro, G., Gordon, L.M., Maron, J.L., Schick, C.T., Tabilo, E., Antas, P. & Below, T. 1990. Migration routes of new world Sanderlings (*Calidris alba*). Auk 107: 172-180.

Neel, L.A. & Henry, W.G. 1997. Shorebirds of the Lahontan Valley, Nevada, USA: a case history of western Great Basin shorebirds. International Wader Studies 9: 15-19.

Oring, L.W. & Reed, J.M. 1997. Shorebirds of the western Great Basin of North America: overview and importance to continental populations. International Wader Studies 9: 6-12.

Page, G.W. & Fearis, B. 1971. Sexing Western Sandpipers by bill length. Bird-Banding 42: 297-298.

Paulson, D. 1993. Shorebirds of the Pacific Northwest. University of Washington Press, Seattle.

Pienkowski, M.W., Lloyd, C.S. & Minton, C.D.T. 1979. Seasonal and migrational weight changes in Dunlins. Bird Study 26: 134-148.

Robinson, J.A. & Warnock, S.E. 1997. The staging paradigm and wetland conservation in arid environments: shorebirds and wetlands of the North American Great Basin. International Wader Studies 9: 37-44.

Skagen, S.K. & Knopf, F.L. 1994. Residency patterns of migrating sandpipers at a midcontinental stopover. Condor 96: 949-958.

Stenzel, L.E. & Page, G.W. 1988. Results of the first comprehensive shorebird census of San Francisco and San Pablo bays. Wader Study Group Bulletin 54: 43-48.

Storer, R.W. 1951. The seasonal occurrence of shorebirds on Bay Farm Island, Alameda County, California. Condor 53: 186-193.

Warnock, N. & Bishop, M.A. 1998. Spring stopover ecology of migrant Western Sandpipers. Condor 100: 456-467.

Warnock, N. & Warnock, S.E. 1993. Attachment of radio-transmitters to sandpipers: review and methods. Wader Study Group Bulletin 70: 28-30.

Warnock, N., Page, G.W. & Sandercock, B.K. 1997. Local survival of Dunlin wintering in California. Condor 99: 906-915.

Warnock, N., Takekawa, J.Y. & Bishop, M.A. 2004. Migration and stopover strategies of individual Dunlin along the Pacific Coast of North America. Canadian Journal of Zoology 82: 1687-1697.

Warnock, S.E. & Takekawa, J.Y. 1996. Wintering site fidelity and movement patterns of Western Sandpipers *Calidris mauri* in the San Francisco Bay estuary. Ibis 138: 160-167.

Wilson, W.H. 1993. Conservation of stop-over areas for migratory waders: Grays Harbor, Washington. Wader Study Group Bulletin 67: 37-40.

Wilson, W.H. 1994. Western Sandpiper (*Calidris mauri*). In: The birds of North America, No. 90. The Academy of Natural Sciences, Philadelphia, and The American Ornithologists' Union, Washington, D.C.

# Indicators of body condition, energy demand and breeding success in the Ruddy Turnstone *Arenaria interpres*, a species of concern

*Deborah E. Perkins & Rebecca L. Holberton*

*Department of Biological Sciences, University of Maine, Orono, ME 04469-5751, USA. (email: pourmeariver@gci.net)*

Perkins, D.E. & Holberton, R.L. 2006. Indicators of body condition, energy demand and breeding success in the Ruddy Turnstone *Arenaria interpres*, a species of concern. *Waterbirds around the world.* Eds. G.C. Boere, C.A. Galbraith & D.A. Stroud. The Stationery Office, Edinburgh, UK. pp. 551-552.

Although the Ruddy Turnstone *Arenaria interpres* is a species of high concern in Canada (Donaldson *et al.* 2000) and the United States (Brown *et al.* 2001), its breeding ecology is poorly understood (Nettleship 2000). Reproductive physiological and energetics studies are critical to understanding how environmental conditions affect breeding success and population viability. The breeding ecology and behavioral endocrinology of Ruddy Turnstones were studied at East Bay, Southampton Island, Nunavut, Canada in 2003. Hormonal patterns associated with energy regulation and sex-specific parental efforts were investigated to understand better how high latitude breeders meet energy demands. Normally, plasma corticosterone (CORT; the major energy-regulating hormone) is low, but can rise rapidly to help an individual through periods of potential stress (the adrenocortical response; Wingfield 1994, Harvey *et al.* 1984). While acute high CORT levels redirect behavior to life saving activities, chronic levels can compromise reproduction (Wingfield 1994). Previous studies have shown some Arctic-breeding birds reduce this response during critical breeding stages (Wilson & Holberton 2004, Reneerkens *et al.* 2002, Holberton & Wingfield 2003, O'Reilly & Wingfield 2001), possibly increasing the threshold for life-saving responses that may otherwise compromise breeding success, e.g. desertion.

The study used the Mayfield method to estimate nest success (Bart & Robson 1982). Incubation period was assumed to be 23 days (Nettleship 2000). Body condition was assessed by size-corrected body mass, with the body mass divided by the flattened wing length cubed (Winker *et al.* 1992, Summers 1988, Davidson 1983). Relative incubation effort was assessed during twelve 24-hour behavioural watches: six at mid-incubation (eight to fifteen days after onset of incubation) and six at late incubation (sixteen to twenty-three days after onset of incubation). To measure the adrenocortical response at different parental stages, blood samples for CORT were taken within four minutes (baseline) and at 10 and 30 minutes after capture during mid-incubation and early brooding, which includes the stage from when the first chick is hatched to when all chicks were hatched and found in the immediate vicinity of the nest. A direct radioimmunoassay procedure was used to determine CORT concentrations (Wingfield *et al.* 1992).

Nest success was 0.33 (95% CI 0.19-0.55; 321 exposure days); 42% of nests were lost to predators.

Overall, incubating females were significantly leaner than incubating males (stages pooled; t = 2.254, *P* = 0.032). There was some indication that body condition varied by stage, and this difference approached significance (main effect of stage: $F_{2,51}$ = 3.067, *P* = 0.055). However, there were no differences in body condition between the sexes within each stage (stage * sex

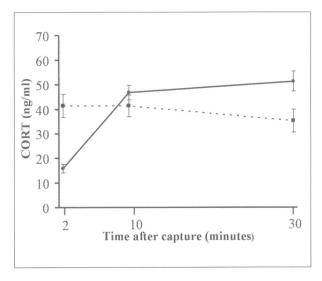

Fig. 1. The adrenocortical response of Ruddy Turnstones *Arenaria interpres* at East Bay, Southampton Island, Nunavut, Canada, during mid-incubation (day 8-15) and early brooding (with 1-2 day old chicks). Sexes pooled. Solid line = mid-incubation (n = 21); dashed line = brooding (n = 15).

interaction: $F_{2,51}$ = 0.070, *P* = 0.932). Females were somewhat leaner than males within the mid-incubation stage, and this difference approached significance (t = 2.01, *P* = 0.059).

Regarding parental effort and CORT secretion, breeding pairs shared incubation duties equally (total contribution by either sex did not differ significantly from 50% at either mid- or late-incubation; t = 1.1, *P* = 0.321, t = 0.79, *P* = 0.467, respectively), and this was reflected in their similar patterns of CORT secretion. Specifically, males and females showed extremely similar adrenocortical responses during mid-incubation (main effect of sex: $F_{1,18}$= 0.344, *P* = 0.565; sex * time interaction: $F_{2,36}$ = 0.797, *P* = 0.458, two factor repeated-measures ANOVA, *P* > 0.05 for all Tukey post hoc comparisons of each sampling interval). As during the mid-incubation stage, males and females showed extremely similar CORT profiles during the early brooding stage (main effect of sex: $F_{1,13}$= 0.478, *P* = 0.501; sex * time interaction: $F_{2,26}$ = 0.530, *P* = 0.595, two factor repeated-measures ANOVA, *P* > 0.05 for all Tukey post hoc comparisons of each sampling interval).

In contrast to the mid-incubation period, brooding birds did not express an adrenocortical response: CORT concentrations did not increase significantly in response to capture and handling during early brooding (repeated measures ANOVA, within subjects: $F_{2,26}$ = 1.326, *P* = 0.283). CORT concentrations were not significantly different between the sexes at any time during sampling (*post hoc* for repeated measures time 0, *P* = 1.00; time

10, $P = 0.725$; time 30, $P = 0.447$).

However, both males and females (sexes pooled) showed dramatic changes in adrenocortical secretion patterns between mid-incubation and brooding (main effect of stage: $F_{1,33} = 0.116$, $P = 0.736$; stage * time interaction: $F_{2,66} = 29.18$, $P < 0.001$, two factor repeated-measures ANOVA; Fig. 1). Baseline CORT was significantly higher during the brooding stage (Tukey, $P < 0.001$; Fig. 1). While ten minute values did not differ, CORT concentrations at the 30 minute sampling period were significantly lower during the brooding stage as compared to the mid-incubation stage (Tukey: $P = 0.015$; Fig. 1).

Nest success of Ruddy Turnstones at East Bay was relatively low in 2003 compared to other years (1.00 in 2000, 0.83 in 2001; P. Smith, pers. comm.), and the predation rate (42%) was higher than estimates from other areas within their North American breeding range (18-27%; Nettleship 1967, Parmelee & MacDonald 1960).

In this study, incubating females were significantly leaner than incubating males, possibly owing to their greater initial reproductive investment via egg production. Due to the severe environment in which they breed, females breeding at high latitudes may not be able to regain energy reserves until brood desertion is a viable option for them during the early to mid-fledging period. Poor condition upon arrival may subsequently affect parental effort and breeding success in both sexes, as effects may be cumulative throughout the breeding season. If a female begins the season in poor condition, a male's ability to compensate for her early desertion would depend on his own energy reserves. Further research is needed during spring migration and throughout the annual cycle to identify factors limiting arrival condition, and, thus, breeding success of both sexes in high latitude breeders.

Previous studies of Arctic-breeding shorebirds have not compared parental effort, as reflected by the adrenocortical response, during the brood care and incubation phases. Caring for precocial young can be demanding (Hegyi & Sasvari 1998), especially for high latitude breeders facing time and energy constraints (Ashkenazie & Safriel 1979, Byrkjedal 1989). An increase in baseline CORT during brooding may be the proximate mechanism that helps parents meet the demands of parental care at high latitudes by facilitating the additional foraging and feeding required to meet their own energy needs while caring for offspring. The reduced expression of the adrenocortical response during brooding may be a mechanism to increase the threshold for abandonment during this period of greater parental effort, especially when faced with few or no re-nesting opportunities.

## ACKNOWLEDGEMENTS

Canadian Wildlife Service and American Museum of National History for funding.

## REFERENCES

Ashkenazie, S., & Safriel, U.N. 1979. Time energy budget of the Semipalmated Sandpiper *Calidris pusilla* at Barrow Alaska. Ecology 60: 783-799.

Bart, J., & Robson, D.S. 1982. Estimating survivorship when the subjects are visited periodically. Ecology 63: 1078-1090.

Brown, S., Hickey, C., Harrington, B. & Gill, R. 2001. The U.S. Shorebird Conservation Plan. Manomet, MA, Manomet Center for Conservation Sciences.

Byrkjedal, I. 1989. Time constraints and vigilance breeding season diet of the Dotterel *Charadrius morinellus*. Journal Für Ornithologie 130: 293-302.

Donaldson, G.M., Hyslop, C., Morrison, R.I.G., Dickson, H.L. & Davidson, I. 2000. Canadian Shorebird Conservation Plan, Authority of the Minister of Environment, Canadian Wildlife Service.

Harvey, S., Phillips, J.G., Rees, A. & Hall, T.R. 1984. Stress and adrenal function. Journal of Experimental Zoology 232: 633-645.

Hegyi, Z., & Sasvari, L. 1998. Parental condition and breeding effort in waders. Journal of Animal Ecology 67: 41-53.

Holberton, R.L., & Wingfield, J.C.. 2003. Modulating the corticosterone stress response: A mechanism for balancing individual risk and reproductive success in Arctic-breeding sparrows? Auk 120: 1140-1150.

Nettleship, D.N. 1967. Breeding biology of Ruddy Turnstones and Knots at Hazen Camp, Ellesmere Island, N. W. T. M. Sc. thesis, University of Saskatchewan, Saskatoon.

Nettleship, D.N. 2000. Ruddy Turnstone: *Arenaria interpres*. In: A. Poole & F. Gill (eds.) The Birds of North America, No. 537. Philadelphia, PA, The Birds of North America.

O'Reilly, K.M., & Wingfield, J.C. 2001. Ecological factors underlying the adrenocortical response to capture stress in Arctic-breeding shorebirds. General & Comparative Endocrinology 124: 1-11.

Parmelee, D.F., & MacDonald, S.D. 1960. The birds of west-central Ellesmere Island and adjacent areas. National Museum of Canada Bulletin No. 169 (Biological Series No. 78): 1-229.

Reneerkens, J., Morrison, R.I.G., Ramenofsky, M., Piersma, T. & Wingfield, J.C. 2002. Baseline and stress-induced levels of corticosterone during different life cycle substages in a shorebird on the high Arctic breeding grounds. Physiological & Biochemical Zoology 75: 200-208.

Summers, R.W. 1988. The use of linear measurements when comparing masses. Bird Study 36: 77-79.

Wilson, C.M., & Holberton, R. 2004. Personal risk versus immediate reproductive success: a basis for latitudinal differences in the adrenocortical response to stress in Yellow Warblers, *Dendroicha petechia*. Auk 121: 1238-1249.

Wingfield, J.C. 1994. Modulation of the adrenocortical response in birds, In: K.G. Davey, R.E. Peter, and S.S. Tobe (eds). Perspectives in Comparative Endocrinology, National Research Council of Canada: 520-528

Wingfield, J.C., Vleck, C.M. & Moore, M.C. 1992. Seasonal changes of the adrenocortical response to stress in birds of the Sonoran Desert. Journal of Experimental Zoology 264: 419-428.

Winker, K., Warner, D.W. & Weisbrod, A.R. 1992. Daily mass gains among woodland migrants at an inland stopover site. Auk 109: 853-862.

# Migration of Pontic Gulls *Larus cachinnans* form *'ponticus'* ringed in the south of Ukraine: a review of recoveries from 1929 to 2003

*Antonina G. Rudenko*

*The Black Sea Biosphere Reserve, Lermontov Street 1, Golaya Pristan 75600, Kherson Region, Ukraine.*
*(email: arudenko@gopri.hs.ukrtel.net)*

Rudenko, A.G. 2006. Migration of Pontic Gulls *Larus cachinnans* form *'ponticus'* ringed in the south of Ukraine: a review of recoveries from 1929 to 2003. *Waterbirds around the world.* Eds. G.C. Boere, C.A. Galbraith & D.A. Stroud. The Stationery Office, Edinburgh, UK. pp. 553-559.

## ABSTRACT

The Pontic Gull *Larus cachinnans* form *'ponticus'* breeds on islands and lagoons along the coast of the Black Sea and Sea of Azov. Censuses in 1998 revealed a total of population of 28 226 pairs. Pontic Gulls have been ringed at breeding colonies in the south of Ukraine since the late 1920s, and by 2003 there had been 1 169 recoveries of birds ringed in the Black Sea Biosphere Reserve, Swan Islands and Sivash. A total of 817 gull chicks were colour-ringed in the Black Sea Biosphere Reserve between 1999 and 2002, and 20 of these have subsequently been recovered or re-sighted. This paper reviews the recoveries of Pontic Gulls ringed in Ukraine, and compares the movements of young birds with those of adults. The great majority of adults remain within the Azov-Black Sea region throughout the year. Most young birds also remain in the region, but a small number of birds undertake lengthy migrations in their first calendar year, mostly in a south-westerly direction (Romania, Bulgaria, Turkey, Cyprus, Greece and Egypt) or north-westerly direction (Poland, Germany, Denmark and The Netherlands). Some of these birds continue their nomadic movements in their second year.

## INTRODUCTION

Large white-headed gulls of the *Larus argentatus/cachinnans* complex breed in the south of Ukraine (Stepanyan 1990). Some authors assign the birds breeding in the Black Sea, Caspian Sea and eastern Kazakhstan to a distinct species, the Caspian Gull L. cachinnans (Olsen & Larsson 2002), while those birds breeding in the northern Black Sea and Sea of Azov have been assigned to the form "ponticus" – Pontic Gull. In Ukraine, the breeding area of the Pontic Gull lies between latitudes 45° and 47°N and longitudes 29° and 39°E, and includes islands and lagoons along the coast of the Black Sea and Sea of Azov. The westernmost colonies are situated in the Danube Delta, and the easternmost,

on Krivaya Spit in the Sea of Azov. The northern limit of the breeding range is probably in the region of the Kiev water storage basin, and the southern limit is on the coast of the Crimean Peninsula (Kistyakovsky 1957, Klestov & Fesenko 1990, Siokhin & Grinchenko 1988; Fig. 1).

### Size of the breeding population in the Azov-Black Sea region

The main breeding colonies of the Pontic Gull are located in Yagorlitsky Bay (Konsky and Krugly Islands) and Tendra Bay (Orlov and New Islands) in the Black Sea Biosphere Reserve, on islands in Jarylgachsky Bay, in the Sivash (e.g. Kitaj, Martinaychy and Chongarsky Islands), on the Swan Islands (Lebayzhie) in Karkinitsky Bay (Kistaykovsky 1957, Klimenko 1951, Sabinevsky 1958, Kostin 1983), and on Molochny Lagoon, Obitochnaya Spit and Krivaya Spit. In the mid-1990s, there were large colonies at Kuyanlitsky and Alibay Lagoons in the Odessa region (Siokhin & Grinchenko 1988, Siokhin 2000a).

#### Jarylgachsky Bay

In 1929, Jarylgach Island was included in the Black Sea Reserve. Here there were about 100 breeding pairs of Pontic Gulls (kistaykovsky 1957). In the last 70 years, the number of pairs breeding on islands in Jarylgachsky Bay has remained relatively stable. Some increase was observed in the 1980s and 1990s, when the population reached 3 500-3 900 pairs (Ardamatskaya 2000), and at the beginning of this century, there were about 4 500 pairs in this area (Ardamatskaya *et al.* 2000).

#### Black Sea Biosphere Reserve

When Jarylgach Island was excluded from the Black Sea Biosphere Reserve (in 1951), the Pontic Gulls moved onto islands in Tendra Bay, where the numbers increased to 3 100 pairs (Sabinevsky 1958). At the beginning of the 1950s, the main colonies were located on Babin Island. In 1956-1958, Pontic Gulls were eradicated from islands in Tendra Bay, as they posed an appreciable threat to other bird species nesting on the islands (Sabinevsky 1958).

Since the end of the 1950s, the main breeding colonies in the Black Sea Biosphere Reserve have been located on Konsky and Krugly Islands in Yagorlitsky Bay. In 1984-1986, the number of pairs on Konsky Island varied between 2 000 and 3 500 (Trubka 1986, Rudenko 1992). On Krugly Island, there were between 200 and 500 pairs. During the 1990s, the number of Pontic Gulls in the Black Sea Biosphere Reserve increased to 5 000 pairs. The numbers breeding on islands in Tendra Bay have increased from 50-60 pairs in 1990 to 1 500 pairs in recent years. Other colonies are located on Orlov Island and New Island

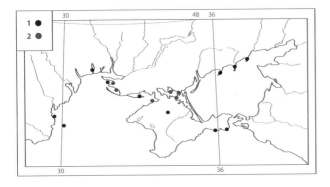

**Fig. 1.** Breeding areas of the Pontic Gull *Larus cachinnans* and ringing sites in the south of Ukraine. 1 – breeding areas; 2 – ringing sites.

(Yaremchenko pers comm.). The total number of breeding pairs in the reserve in the early 2000s was about 4 000.

### Swan Islands (Lebayzhie)

The largest colonies of Pontic Gulls have always been on the Swan Islands. Here the numbers increased from 1 750 pairs in the 1950s (Kistyakovsky 1957) to 9 417 pairs in the early 1980s (Kostin 1983). During the 1980s, the population remained relatively stable at 10 000 pairs, but by the end of the 1990s, numbers had fallen by almost half to 5 000-7 000 pairs (Tarina *et al.* 2000).

### Sivash

There are large breeding colonies of Pontic Gulls in the Sivash. In the 1970s and 1980s, up to 2 000 pairs bred on Kitaj Island, up to 300 pairs on Martinaychy (Kostin 1983), 2 030 pairs on the Chongarsky Islands, and 5 500 pairs in eastern Sivash. There were also 2 500 pairs at Molochny Lagoon and 785 pairs on Krivaya Spit (Siokhin & Grinchenko 1988). In the 1990s, the total number of breeding pairs in the Sivash was over 14 000 (Siokhin 2000a).

According to the results of censuses in 1998, the total number of Pontic Gulls in the Azov-Black Sea region was 28 226 pairs (Siokhin 2000b). The relative stability in the total numbers of Pontic Gulls in Sivash and Karkinitsky, Jarylgachsky, Tendra and Yagorlitsky Bays in the Black Sea, despite considerable fluctuations in numbers at each of these sites, the synchronization of breeding, and the movements of individuals between colonies, have led to the conclusion that these colonies form part of a single Azov-Black Sea population (Sabinevsky 1958, 1966). This conclusion is supported by the fact that many of the breeding birds remain throughout the year in the Azov-Black Sea region, and there are no essential differences in the nomadic movements of birds from the various ringing sites. After breeding, birds from the various colonies are widely distributed along the coasts of the Sea of Azov and Black Sea, and also in the Danube, Don and Kuban regions.

## RESULTS AND DISCUSSION

### A brief history of Pontic Gull ringing in the south of Ukraine

The ringing of Pontic Gulls with metal rings began in the south of Ukraine, and in particular in the Black Sea Biosphere Reserve, at the end of the 1920s. In the reserve archives, there are recoveries of birds ringed on islands in Tendra and Yagorlitsky Bays in the Black Sea Biosphere Reserve, on the Swan Islands in Karkinitsky Bay, and on Kitaj, Martinaychy and Kuyuk-Tuk Islands in Sivash (Table 1). The presence of all this material is a legacy of the many ornithologists who have worked in the region, especially A.B. Kistaykovsky (1920s), M.I. Klimenko (1950s), B.V. Sabinevsky (1950s-1960s) and T.B. Ardamatskaya (1950s-1970s) in the Black Sea Biosphere Reserve and Sivash, and Yu.V. Kostin and N.A. Tarina on the Swan Islands.

An analysis of the results of gull ringing in the Black Sea Biosphere Reserve during the period 1944-1950 was undertaken by Klimenko (1950, 1951, 1953), and later by Sabinevsky (1958, 1966), while Ardamatskaya (1977) produced a report on the migration of gulls including the Pontic Gull.

The author has been involved in the ringing of Pontic Gulls in the south of Ukraine since 1984. Since 1993, a colour-ringing

programme has been in operation under the co-ordination of Norman van Swelm (Ornithological Station Voorne, The Netherlands). About 2 000 nestlings have been colour-ringed since this programme began. An independent study of the migration of the Pontic Gull using ringing has also been carried out by the Melitopol Pedagogical University (Koshelev 2000).

The following analysis of the results obtained from the ringing of Pontic Gull chicks includes the results from both metal- and colour-ringing, and uses published material as well as recent unpublished material. In total, 1 169 Pontic Gulls ringed with metal rings have been recovered. Gull chicks were ringed in spring and summer, primarily in May and June. Seventy-six adult birds were ringed in April and May in 1984 and 1985, and eight adults were ringed in 1990. Colour-ringing of Pontic Gulls was carried out on Konsky and Krugly Islands in Yagorlitsky Bay and at Potievsky in Tendra Bay in the Black Sea Biosphere Reserve. In this paper, only the results obtained from colour-ringing during the five-year period 1999-2003 are discussed.

### Results from ringing with metal rings

Most recoveries, irrespective of age, were recorded as "killed by a hunter" (Table 2). A large proportion of the recoveries were recorded as "circumstances unknown", but the majority of these were probably birds killed by man. Over two-thirds of the recoveries (67.1%) were of birds recovered in their first calendar year. Somewhat fewer (19.2%) were of birds in their second and third year of life, and only 9.5% were of birds aged 4-6 years old (Table 3). The maximum age recorded was 21 years and seven months; this was a bird ringed as a chick in the Black Sea Biosphere Reserve in May 1954 and recovered in the Crimea in January 1976. The annual survival rate of Pontic Gulls increases after the birds have achieved an age of two years. However, the low recovery rates of older birds can also be explained by the loss of metal rings, which disintegrate with age (Ardamatskaya 1977).

### Post-fledging roosts and autumn migration

Most eggs hatch at the beginning of May, and the first young birds fledge in the first ten days of June. In the Black Sea Biosphere Reserve, the first young were seen on the wing on 6-8 June in 1984-1989 and on 28 May in 1990. The nesting sites are abandoned by the young gulls in the last ten days of August (25-31 August in 1984-1990s), and only a few young birds from late broods remain on the islands in autumn. There are only

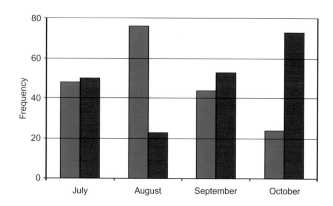

Fig. 2. Numbers of immature (blue) and adult (red) Pontic Gulls *Larus cachinnans* at roosts of non-breeding birds on Tendra Island, south Ukraine, in July to October.

**Table 1. Numbers of Pontic Gulls *Larus cachinnans* ringed at three localities in the south of Ukraine: 1929-2003.**

| Place of ringing | Years and months of ringing | Numbers of birds ringed | | Recoveries of birds ringed as chicks | | Ringers |
|---|---|---|---|---|---|---|
| | | chicks | adults | Total | % | |
| Black Sea Biosphere Reserve (BSBR) | 1929-1955 May-June | 9 231 | - | 308 | 3.3 | Kistaykovsky, Sabinevsky, Klimenko & Ardamatskaya (with BSBR funding) |
| | 1984-1986, 1990 May-June | 391 770 | 68 8 | - 1 | - 0.1 | Rudenko (with BSBR funding) |
| | 1999-2003 June-July | 813 | - | 20 | 2.5 | van Swelm & Rudenko |
| Swan Islands | 1949-1957, 1983-1987 May-June | 6 307 2 643 | - - | 408 5 | 6.5 0.2 | Sabinevsky (with BSBR funding); Kostin & Tarina |
| Sivash | 1934-1960 May-June | No data | No data | 455 | - | Sabinevsky (with BSBR funding) |
| Total | 1929-2003 | 20 155 | 76 | 1 197 | 3.7* | |

\* Excluding Sivash.

**Table 2. Details of recoveries of Pontic Gulls *Larus cachinnans* ringed in the south of Ukraine.**

| | Place of ringing | | | | | |
|---|---|---|---|---|---|---|
| | Black Sea Biosphere Reserve | | Swan Islands (Lebyazhie) | | Sivash | |
| Details of recovery | Total recoveries | % | Total recoveries | % | Total recoveries | % |
| Killed by hunter | 236 | 77.2 | 256 | 62.7 | 264 | 58.0 |
| Found dead | 18 | 5.8 | 35 | 8.6 | 29 | 6.4 |
| Found sick or wounded and dying | 13 | 4.2 | 23 | 5.6 | 16 | 3.5 |
| Remains of bird found | 3 | 0.9 | - | - | 3 | 0.7 |
| Found wounded or killed by man | 1 | 0.2 | 1 | 0.2 | 2 | 0.4 |
| Caught alive and released | 6 | 1.9 | 25 | 6.1 | 35 | 7.7 |
| Caught alive, but details unknown | 2 | 0.7 | - | - | - | - |
| Finding circumstances unknown | 25 | 8.2 | 61 | 15.0 | 105 | 23.1 |
| Caught alive and taken to zoo | 1 | 0.3 | - | - | - | - |
| Ring found | 1 | 0.3 | 2 | 0.5 | 1 | 0.2 |
| Ring number read in field | - | - | 1 | 0.2 | - | - |
| Caught alive and released with a new ring or without a ring | - | - | 4 | 1.0 | - | - |

**Table 3. Year of recovery of Pontic Gulls *Larus cachinnans* ringed at three localities in the south of Ukraine.**

| Pace of ringing | Number & % | First calendar year | Years after ringing | | | | | | | | | | | Age unknown | Total |
|---|---|---|---|---|---|---|---|---|---|---|---|---|---|---|---|
| | | | 1 | 2 | 3 | 4 | 5 | 6 | 7 | 8 | 11 | 17 | 21 | | |
| Black Sea Biosphere Reserve | Number | 163 | 26 | 51 | 18 | 21 | 4 | 4 | 3 | 2 | | 1 | 1 | 12 | 306 |
| | % | 53.3 | 8.5 | 16.7 | 5.9 | 6.9 | 1.3 | 1.3 | 1.0 | 0.7 | | 0.3 | 0.3 | 3.9 | |
| Swan Islands | Number | 276 | 21 | 62 | 17 | 13 | 4 | 3 | 4 | 2 | | | | 6 | 408 |
| | % | 67.6 | 5.1 | 15.2 | 4.2 | 3.2 | 1.0 | 0.7 | 1.0 | 0.5 | | | | 1.5 | |
| Sivash | Number | 345 | 25 | 39 | 17 | 12 | 6 | 7 | 3 | | 1 | | | | 455 |
| | % | 75.8 | 5.5 | 8.6 | 3.7 | 2.6 | 1.3 | 1.5 | 0.7 | | 0.2 | | | | |
| Total | Number | 784 | 72 | 152 | 52 | 46 | 14 | 14 | 10 | 4 | 1 | 1 | 1 | 18 | 1 169 |
| | % | 67.1 | 6.2 | 13.0 | 4.4 | 3.9 | 1.2 | 1.2 | 0.8 | 0.3 | 0.1 | 0.1 | 0.1 | 1.5 | |

minor differences in the basic phenology of the breeding season between the Swan Islands and Sivash (Kostin 1983, Siokhin & Grinchenko 1988).

Having abandoned the islands, the great majority of young birds from the Black Sea Biosphere Reserve spend the first two to three weeks within 3-5 km of their birthplace, forming large roosts on bay shores, alongside roads and in fields. By the beginning of August, and less often by the end of July, the young birds reach Tendra Island, where they disperse along the coast. Here the young birds congregate with adults in large post-breeding roosts (Rudenko & Ardamatskaya 1993; Fig. 2).

Young birds from the Swan Islands and Sivash, having abandoned their colonies, appear along the coasts of Karkinitsky Bay

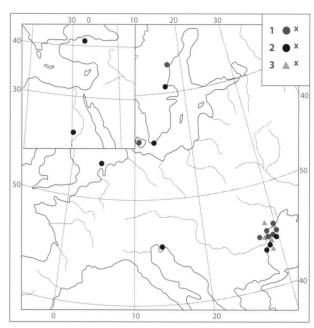

**Fig. 4.** Distribution of foreign recoveries of Pontic Gulls *Larus cachinnans* ringed as chicks or adults in the Black Sea Biosphere Reserve (1x), Swan Islands (2x), and Sivash (3x). Month of recovery: 6-12 (June to December).

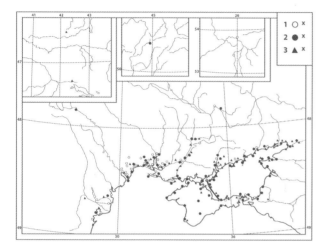

**Fig. 3.** Distribution of autumn recoveries of Pontic Gulls *Larus cachinnans* ringed as chicks in the Black Sea Biosphere Reserve (1x), Swan Islands (2x), and Sivash (3x). Month of recovery: 6-10 (June to October). The Black Sea Biosphere Reserve (1x), Swan Islands (2x), and Sivash (3x). Month of recovery: 6-10 (June to October).

and the Sea of Azov. Some weeks after ringing, some individuals migrate along the northern and eastern coasts of the Sea of Azov, and have been recovered 300-500 km from the place of ringing. A young bird ringed on the Swan Islands on 27 June was recovered a few days later on Krivaya Spit in the Sea of Azov, about 300 km away. Many birds ringed as chicks in May and June have been recovered in June and July between 50 and 500 km from the place or ringing, or even more (Fig. 3); of the 72 recoveries of birds in this period, only 11 (15.3%) were from within 50 km of the place of ringing. Some of the young birds undertake a long-distance migration in a north-westerly direction. For example, four gulls were observed one month after ringing on the River Neman in Byelorussia (825 km), and two birds, ringed on 23 May on the Swan Islands and 27 May in the Black Sea Biosphere Reserve respectively, were recovered in Sweden (Fig. 4). The bird ringed on 27 May was recovered in Sweden as early as June. Some young birds move south-west, reaching the Danube Delta and coasts of Romania and Bulgaria (one recovery) in June and July, while others migrate in an easterly direction, e.g. a young gull reached Cimlyansky water storage basin (850 km from the place of ringing) by 26 July.

The majority of recoveries of birds in their first calendar year have been in the month of August, and this is also the peak month for recoveries of adults (Fig. 5). The distribution of recoveries of

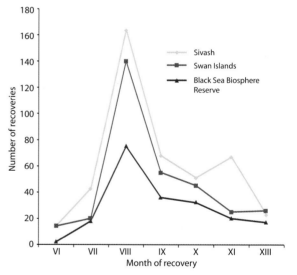

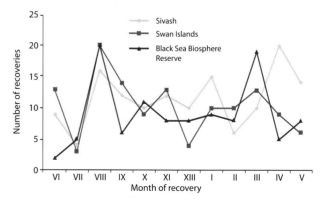

**Fig. 5.** Recoveries by month of Pontic Gulls *Larus cachinnans* ringed in the Black Sea Biosphere Reserve (1), Swan Islands (2), and Sivash (3). A: immature birds in their first calendar year; B: adults. Month of recovery: I-XII (January to December).

young birds in August is similar to the distribution of recoveries in June and July (Fig. 3). The birds are widely dispersed along the northern coasts of the Black Sea and Sea of Azov from the Danube to the Don and Kuban in the Crimea. In the south-west, some birds reach the coast of Romania (260 km from the place of ringing). It appears that young birds reaching the Romanian and Bulgarian coasts in their first year of life prolong their nomadic wanderings in subsequent years, as there have been 12 recoveries of immature gulls from Romania and three from Bulgaria in various seasons in later years. There is also one recovery of an immature bird in August in the Chernovtsy region, indicating that a part of the population continues to migrate in a north-westerly direction towards the Baltic coast. Immature birds in their second year of life have been found in the port of Copenhagen in Denmark, over 1 700 km from the place of ringing. Other young birds follow the Don and Manich river valleys to Lake Manich (675-680 km from the place of ringing), and there has been one recovery further north-east in the Penza region, about 1 160 km from the ringing site.

The recoveries of young birds in September and October indicate that the great majority of birds remain along the shores of the Black Sea and Sea of Azov. Some birds continue to move in a north-westerly direction, reaching the coast of Denmark (Zealand) and Germany (Heligoland), while others move east as far as the coast of the Caspian Sea (two recoveries in the Astrachansky region, 1 160-1 170 km from the place of ringing). There have also been recoveries of young birds in September and October from Greece (1 250 km) and from Lake Brollos in lower Egypt (c. 2 500 km).

The recoveries of adults after the end of the breeding season and in autumn indicate that these birds disperse along the coasts of the Black Sea and Sea of Azov (Fig. 6). Field observations have revealed that adults and young birds migrate in mixed flocks.

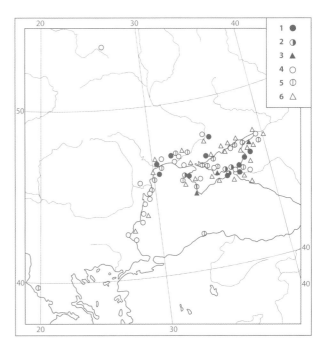

**Fig. 7.** Distribution of winter recoveries of Pontic Gulls *Larus cachinnans* ringed as chicks in the Black Sea Biosphere Reserve (1 and 4), Swan Islands (2 and 5), and Sivash (3 and 6). 1-3 = first-year birds; 4-6 = immature and adult birds.

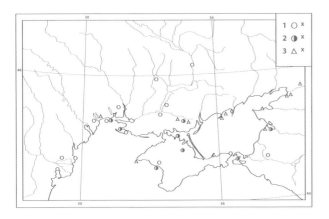

**Fig. 6.** Distribution of recoveries of adult Pontic Gulls *Larus cachinnans* ringed as chicks in the Black Sea Biosphere Reserve (1x), Swan Islands (2x), and Sivash (3x). Month of recovery: 1-12 (January to December).

### Wintering period

During the wintering period (from the end of November to the end of February), most Pontic Gulls in all age groups remain within the Azov-Black Sea region in Odessa, Nikolaev, Kherson, Zaporozhye, Crimea, Donetsk and Rostov territories in Ukraine and Krasnodar Territory in Russia (89.0% of all winter recoveries; n = 163). This region can be considered to be the centre of

the wintering range of the Azov-Black Sea population of the Pontic Gull (Fig. 7). The recoveries suggest that most of the adult birds remain throughout the winter in this region. However, some immature birds winter on the coast of Romania, Bulgaria, Greece and Turkey (10.4% of recoveries), and one bird has been recovered in winter in Byelorussia.

### Spring migration period

The date of return of Pontic Gulls to their breeding grounds varies somewhat from year to year. In the Black Sea Biosphere Reserve, the main arrival of adults at the colonies usually occurs between 20 February and 10 March, but in severe winters with late springs, the arrival may be delayed until the second ten days in April. The adults arrive on the breeding islands in small flocks of between three and eight individuals. Egg-laying usually commences at the end of March or beginning of April. Immature birds remain dispersed along the coasts of the Sea of Azov and Black Sea south to Romania (Fig. 8). Thus, the distribution of immature Pontic Gulls in spring scarcely differs from that in autumn. The main concentrations (88.8% of recoveries) are in the Odessa, Kherson, Crimea, Zaporozhye and Rostov regions in Ukraine, and on the coast of Krasnodar Territory in Russia. However, some birds remain in the Baltic Sea, and there has been one recovery of an immature on the River Narva in Estonia in May.

Pontic Gulls ringed on islands in the Black Sea Biosphere Reserve have been recovered in May in the Rostov region, and birds ringed on the Swan Islands have been recovered at the height of the breeding season on islands in the Black Sea Biosphere Reserve. These recoveries indicate that there is some interchange of individuals between breeding colonies.

### Results from colour-ringing

In the period 1999 to 2002, 817 Pontic Gull chicks were ringed with red colour-rings. Reports of 20 of these birds have been

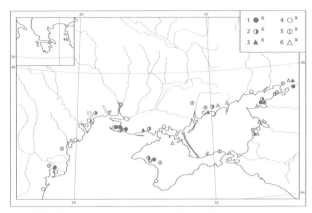

Fig. 8. Distribution of spring recoveries of Pontic Gulls *Larus cachinnans* ringed as chicks or adults in the Black Sea Biosphere Reserve (1x and 4x), Swan Islands (2x and 5x), and Sivash (3x and 6x). 1x -3x = adult birds; 4x-6x = immature birds. Month of recovery: 3-5 (March to May).

**Table 4. Recoveries and re-sightings of Pontic Gulls *Larus cachinnans* colour-ringed as chicks at Yagorlitsky Bay, Konsky Islands, in the south of Ukraine in 1999-2002.**

| Date of ringing | Number of chicks ringed | Recoveries/re-sightings | |
|---|---|---|---|
| | | Total | % |
| 29.06.1999 | 430 | 15 | 3.5 |
| 13.07.2000 | 275 | 3 | 1.1 |
| 14.07.2001 | 100 | 1 | 1.0 |
| 28.07.2002 | 12 | 1 | 8.3 |
| Total | 817 | 20 | 2.4 |

received from the Kiev and Moscow Ringing Centres and Norman van Swelm (Table 4). Nine birds were reported in the year of ringing, seven in the following calendar year, two in the third year, and two in the fifth year. Sixteen of the birds were seen alive, and the number on the colour ring was read in the field; four birds were found dead. Three of these were found dead in the calendar year after ringing, although they were less than one year old (7-10 months). One bird was found dead four months after ringing. Most of the live birds were re-sighted in winter (seven) and summer (six).

Four of the birds were reported in Ukraine, and the remainder (17 re-sightings of 16 birds) were found in seven countries further west in Europe: Poland (6), Germany (3), Romania (3), Cyprus (2), Denmark (1), The Netherlands (1) and Bulgaria (1) (Table 5). Most of these birds were seen in natural habitats (on sea coasts, along rivers and at lakes), but two birds were found at rubbish tips in Poland, two birds were seen at Nicosia airport in Cyprus, and one bird was seen in the city of Berlin in Germany (Rudenko & Rudenko 2004).

## CONCLUSIONS

On the basis of evidence from the recovery of ringed birds, it can be concluded that there are no essential differences between the migration routes of Pontic Gulls nesting on islands in the Black Sea Biosphere Reserve and those nesting in the Sivash or on the Swan Islands (Lebyazhie). There appears to be regular inter-

**Table 5. Distribution of recoveries and re-sightings, by country and month, of Pontic Gulls *Larus cachinnans* ringed in the Black Sea Biosphere Reserve in the south of Ukraine in 1999-2002.**

| Country | Number of recoveries/ re-sightings | % of total recoveries/ re-sightings | Month of recovery/ re-sighting |
|---|---|---|---|
| Bulgaria | 1 | 4.8 | I |
| Cyprus | 2 | 9.5 | I, I |
| Denmark | 1 | 4.8 | XII |
| Germany | 3 | 14.3 | X, XII, XII |
| Netherlands | 1 | 4.8 | XII |
| Poland | 6 | 28.6 | VIII, X, XI, XI, XI, XII |
| Romania | 3 | 14.3 | VIII, VIII, VIII |
| Ukraine | 4 | 19.0 | IV, IV, IV, X |
| Total | 21 | | |

change between these breeding populations, confirming the earlier conclusion of Sabinevsky (1966) concerning the uniform nature of the Azov-Black Sea population of the Pontic Gull. The bulk of the population is resident within the region, and this tendency to remain in the area appears to increase with age. Only young birds undertake long-distance migrations, migrating in two main directions: in a south-westerly direction to Romania, Turkey, Bulgaria and Cyprus, and in a north-westerly direction towards Poland, Germany, Denmark and The Netherlands. The movements of adult birds in autumn, winter and spring are largely confined to the limits of the Azov-Black Sea region.

## ACKNOWLEDGEMENTS
I would like to thank all the generations of ornithologists in the Black Sea Biosphere Reserve who have taken part in ringing of Pontic Gulls on islands in the Azov-Black Sea region. Special thanks go to Dr Tatiana Ardamatskaya for giving me the opportunity to analyse the recoveries resulting from her field work and that of Dr Boris Sabinevsky. I would also like to thank Norman van Swelm for enabling me to participate in the Pontic Gull colour-ringing programme, and Gerard Boere for encouraging me to prepare this paper.

## REFERENCES
**Adamatskaya, T.B.** 1977. Seasonal distribution and migrations of larids nesting in the Black Sea Reserve. Information of the Baltic Commission on learning about the migration of birds. Tartu, 1977, No. 2: 87-113. (In Russian).

**Ardamatskaya, T.B.** 2000. Ornithofauna and ornithocomplexes. In: T.I. Kotenko & Yu. R. Shelyag-Sosonko (eds). Biodiversity of the Jarylgach: modern state and ways for conservation. Vestnik Zoologii Supplement, Special Issue, Kiev: 74-82. (In Russian).

**Ardamatskaya, T.B., Siokhin, V.D. & Poluda, A.M.** 2000. Jarilgachsky Bay. In: V.D. Siokhin (ed). Number and distribution of breeding waterbirds in the wetlands of Azov-Black Sea Region of Ukraine. Branta, Melitopol-Kiev: 145-167. (In Russian).

**Kistyakovsky, A.B.** 1957. Fauna of Ukraine. A: Birds. Naukova Dumka Publication, Kiev. (In Russian).

**Klestov, N.L. & Fesenko, G.V.** 1990. Laridae in the water storage basin of Dneprovsky. Publication 90.3, Institute of Zoology, Academy of Sciences, Ukraine SSR, Kiev. (In Russian).

**Klimenko, A.I.** 1950. Seasonal migrations of Laridae on the northern Black Sea coast. Transactions of the Black Sea Reserve, Kiev, Vol. 1: 3-52. (In Russian).

**Klimenko, A.I.** 1951. On the seasonal migrations of Laridae in the south of Ukraine. Abstracts of the Ornithological Conference, Riga, p. 11. (In Russian).

**Klimenko, A.I.** 1953. On the migration of Laridae of the south Ukrainian SSR. In: Migration of birds in the European part of the USSR, Riga: 117-125. (In Russian).

**Koshelev, A.I.** 2000. Migratory movements of the North Azov Pontic Gull (*Larus cachinnans*). In: I. Rusev, A. Korzyukov & V. Stoilovsky (eds). Birds of the Azov-Black Sea region on the border of the Millennium. Astroprint Publications, Odessa: 25-26. (In Russian).

**Kostin, Yu.V.** 1983. Birds of Crimea. Nauka Publications, Moscow.

**Olsen, K.M. & Larsson, H.** 2002. Gulls of Europe, Asia and North America. C. Helm and Princeton University Press.

**Rudenko, A.G.** 1992. The modern status of the Pontic gull (*Larus cachinnans*) populations in the Black Sea Reserve. In: Ornithological Investigations in Reserves. Nauka Publications, Moscow: 113-128. (In Russian).

**Rudenko, A.G. & Ardamatskaya, T.B.** 1993. Roosts of gulls on Tendra Island Seashore in the Black Sea Biosphere Reserve. Bulletin of the Moscow Society of Natural Investment, Department of Biology, 98,(4) 3-16. (In Russian).

**Rudenko, A.G. & Rudenko, V.P.** 2004. Results of colour ringing of the Pontic Gull (*Larus cachinnans*) in the Black Sea Biosphere Reserve in 1999-2003. In: V.V. Serebryakov (ed). Modern problems in zoological science. Kiev University Publication: 148-150. (In Ukrainian).

**Sabinevsky, B.V.** 1958. Economic value of the Pontic gull in requirements of the Black Sea Reserve. Transactions of the Black Sea Reserve, Golaya Pristan, 2: 65-81. (In Russian).

**Sabinevsky, B.V.** 1966. A problem of the Azov-Black Sea population of the Pontic gull in terms of items of information about its seasonal placement and new economic problems. In: Proceedings of the IV Inter-University Zoogeographic Conference, Odessa: 234-236. (In Russian).

**Siokhin, V.D.** 2000a. Sivash. In: V.D. Siokhin (ed) Number and distribution of breeding waterbirds in the wetlands of the Azov-Black Sea Region of Ukraine. Branta, Melitopol-Kiev: 190-200. (In Russian).

**Siokhin, V.D.** 2000b. Characteristics of the distribution and numbers of breeding birds in the wetlands of the Azov-Black Sea costs. In: V.D. Siokhin (ed). Number and distribution of breeding waterbirds in the wetlands of the Azov-Black Sea Region of Ukraine. Branta, Melitopol-Kiev: 412-444. (In Russian).

**Siokhin, V.D. & Grinchenko, A.B.** 1988. The Herring Gull. In: Colonial hydrophilic birds of the south of Ukraine. Naukova Dumka Publications, Kiev: 24-33. (In Russian).

**Stepanyan, L.S.** 1990. In: V.E. Sokolov (ed). Conspectus of the ornithological fauna of the USSR. Science Publication, Moscow: 217-228. (In Russian).

**Tarina, N.A., Kostin, C.Yu. & Bagricova, N.A.** 2000. Karkinitsky Bay. In: V.D. Siokhin (ed). Number and distribution of breeding waterbirds in the wetlands of the Azov-Black Sea Region of Ukraine. Branta, Melitopol-Kiev: 168-189.

**Trubka, A.G.** 1986. An estimation of some methods of the registration of the Pontic Gull on Konsky Islands in Yagorlitsky Bay. In: All-Union Conference on the problem of a cadastre and registration of fauna, Abstracts, Vol. 1, Moscow: 203-205. (In Russian).

Gulls nest on the strandline of the Ukrainian part of the Danube Delta, the westernmost limit of the breeding distribution of Pontic Gull *Larus cachinnans*. Photo: David Stroud.

# Modelling survival and movement probability of Little Tern *Sterna albifrons* at a post-breeding moulting site: the effect of the colony of origin

*Giacomo Tavecchia[1], Nicola Baccetti[2] & Lorenzo Serra[2]*

[1]*IMEDEA – UIB/CSIC, 21, c. M. Marques,07190, Esporles, Spain.*
[2]*Istituto Nazionale per la Fauna Selvatica, 40064 Ozzano Emilia BO, Italy.*

Tavecchia, G., Baccetti, N. & Serra, L. 2006. Modelling survival and movement probability of Little Tern *Sterna albifrons* at a post-breeding moulting site: the effect of the colony of origin. *Waterbirds around the world.* Eds. G.C. Boere, C.A. Galbraith & D.A. Stroud. The Stationery Office, Edinburgh, UK. pp. 560-561.

Safeguarding the main stopover or moulting sites for migratory birds along each flyway has long been long recognised and is a high priority in general strategies for bird conservation. These sites act as 'spatial funnels', attracting individuals dispersed over vast areas giving a unique opportunity to obtain a snapshot of the population at a larger scale. Moulting areas are usually sites with low predation pressure and abundant food resources that meet the high energy demands of feather replacement. The location of moulting areas and the extent to which they attract individuals from different breeding areas are often unknown, but have important consequences for population dynamics and conservation strategies.

In 1990, a large post-breeding roost of Little Terns *Sterna albifrons* was discovered at Venice Lagoon, Italy. This species is in decline throughout its European range and is threatened by human activities (del Hoyo *et al.* 1996). Recaptures of ringed birds suggested that the moulting area at Venice Lagoon attracts adults and juveniles from an area encompassing the entire east Adriatic coast (Cherubini *et al.* 1996). A large number of breeding colonies are within this range, hosting a total of about 6 000 pairs, the highest of any European country for this species (Fasola *et al.* 1989, Muselet 1997).

The extent to which the breeding colony of a bird's birth influenced the probability of it reaching the moulting site was investigated by combining information collected from multiple breeding colonies with that obtained at the moulting site. Moreover, the capture-recapture data provided the opportunity to estimate Little Tern post-fledging and annual adult survival probabilities for the first time.

The capture-recapture information collected between 1990 and 1997 came from two main sources, a) birds ringed as chicks on the main Adriatic breeding colonies and b) juveniles and adults captured after the breeding season on a roosting site in the Venice Lagoon near the moulting area. Survival probability was estimated by maximum likelihood procedure from individual encounter histories (Lebreton *et al.* 1993). The local survival parameter is the product between the local survival probability and a movement probability, called here "survival/movement" as a residual of these two components. A total of 12 185 capture-recapture histories were analysed.

The best model describing these data assumed a negative relationship between the survival/movement parameter and the distance of the colony of birth for juveniles. However, this relationship disappeared in adults, whose survival was considered constant. The average annual adult survival/movement probability was 0.899 (95% confidence interval: 0.963-0.836). Juvenile survival between June and September was 0.601 (95% confidence interval: 0.287-0.850), calculated assuming that all juveniles born near the roosting site would actually visit it in their first winter. First-year survival was estimated to be 0.578 (95% confidence interval: 0.737-0.418).

The results suggest that the moulting area could act as a 'population funnel' within a system of moult migration that involves birds breeding up to 500 km away. However, other unknown moulting sites must exist within the Southern Adriatic Sea, given that a large proportion of Southern birds did not use the Venice Lagoon moulting site, that could be important for the conservation of the species.

The survival/movement parameter in juveniles varied according to birth location, being negatively related to the distance from the moulting site. The effect of the distance on survival cannot be disentangled from the probability of reaching the site. However, the most likely explanation is that distance affected the movement probability. In contrast, the average value of yearly local survival/movement was constant and very similar to the survival estimate found for other species of terns (Spendelow *et al.* 1995; del Hoyo *et al.* 1997). This suggests that individuals that have visited the moulting site at least once tend to visit it again, with a similarly high probability, regardless to their location of birth. Fixation upon the moulting site would probably be achieved the first time they visit it as juveniles, consistent with the general mechanism of site fixation (Ketterson & Nolan 1990).

The northern Adriatic Sea is a particularly productive area due to the large fresh-water input from the Po and other rivers, combined with the mixing effect caused by strong winds and tidal movements. Nearly 5% of birds born at the range limits of the site's breeding catchment are estimated to moult in the Venice lagoon. This further emphasises the importance of moulting sites but also suggests that other similar sites are likely to attract the majority of birds originating from southern areas of the Adriatic Sea, but their catchment ranges are not known. Patches of rich waters coupled with coastal lagoons have been found along the south-eastern coasts of the Adriatic Sea, but whether any of these sites are used as moulting areas by Little Terns, especially by individuals coming from Italian colonies is, currently, unknown (Tavecchia *et al.* 2005).

## REFERENCES

**Cherubini, G., Serra, L. & Baccetti, N.** 1996. Primary moult, body mass and moult migration of Little Tern *Sterna albifrons* in NE Italy. Ardea 84: 99-114.

**Fasola, M., Saino, N., Canova, L. & Bogliani, G.** 1989. Breeding and summering populations of gulls and terns in coastal wetlands on the Adriatic Sea. Le Gerfaut 79: 177-184.

**del Hoyo, J., Elliott, A. & Sargatal, J.** 1996 Handbook of the Birds of the World. Vol 3. Hoatzin to Auks Lynx Edicions, Barcelona.

**Ketterson, E.D. & Nolan, V. Jr.** 1990. Site attachment and site fidelity in migratory birds: experimental evidence from the field and analogies from neurobiology. In: E. Gwinner, (ed.) Bird Migration, Springer Verlag, Berlin: 117-129.

**Lebreton, J.-D. Pradel, R., & Clobert, J.** 1993. The statistical analysis of survival in animal populations. TREE 8: 91-95.

**Muselet, D.** 1985. Les quartiers d'hivernage des sternes naines européennes *Sterna albifrons*. L'Oiseau et la Revue Francaise d'Ornithologie 55: 183-193.

**Spendelow, J.A., Nichols, J.D., Nisbet, I.C.T., Hays, H., Cormons, G.D., Burger, J., Safina, C., Hines, J.E. & Gochfeld, M.** (1995) Estimating annual survival and movement rates of adults within a metapopulation of Roseate Terns. Ecology 76: 2415-2428.

**Tavecchia, G., Baccetti, N. & Serra, L.** 2005. Colony specific variation in the use of a moulting site in a migratory seabird. Journal of Avian Biology 36: 501-509.

Little Tern *Sterna albifrons* feeding chick. Photo: Brian McKean.

# Greater Flamingo *Phoenicopterus ruber* ringing at Lake Uromiyeh, I.R. Iran

*Sadegh Sadeghi Zadegan*

*Department of Environment, Pardisan Eco-park, Wildlife Bureau, Tehran, I.R. Iran. (email: sadeghizadegan@abtdi.net)*

Zadegan, S.S. 2006. Greater Flamingo *Phoenicopterus ruber* ringing at Lake Uromiyeh, I.R. Iran. *Waterbirds around the world.* Eds. G.C. Boere, C.A. Galbraith & D.A. Stroud. The Stationery Office, Edinburgh, UK. pp. 562-563.

Uromiyeh Lake (483 000 ha) is a large, shallow, hypersaline lake with numerous islands and extensive fringing brackish to saline marshes, in a large internal drainage basin in the uplands of northwestern Iran. The lake is of great importance as a breeding area for many species of waterfowl, notably Greater Flamingo *Phoenicopterus ruber* and is protected as a National Park and Ramsar site. This note describes the results of the ringing programme started in 1970.

Large breeding colonies of the Greater Flamingo were first located in 1965 and 1966 (Fig. 1). Crude estimates place the total flamingo population on Lake Uromiyeh at 10 000-12 000 in 1965 and 1966, while aerial censuses of the breeding colonies in 1971-72 put the population at 15 000-20 000 breeding pairs, with an additional 5 000-10 000 non-breeders present (Scott 1973). Numbers appear to be increasing slightly, with perhaps as many as 25 000 breeding pairs in the last decade. In Iran as whole, wintering flamingo populations are estimated at 85 000-160 000 individuals.

The Flamingo Ringing Project at Lake Uromiyeh started in 1970, and has continued annually from early July to late August in most years. In 1970, 2 250 flamingo pulli (chicks) were neck-banded with blue collars and 242 adults were ringed with metal leg-rings. Since 1970 only metal leg- rings have been used, and by the end of the 1999 breeding season, a total of 30 002 birds had been marked (leg rings and collars). A colour ringing program was initiated in 1999, starting with 295 pulli. Data are summarised in Table 1.

By the end of December 2002, 216 recoveries (0.72 %) had been reported from 28 countries, including Morocco, Sudan, Ethiopia, Somalia, Azerbaijan, Kazakhstan, India, Sri Lanka and Iran (Table 2). This demonstrates a very wide post-juvenile dispersal of flamingos that had not hitherto been suspected. The adult birds from the Lake Uromiyeh colony, however, seem to winter almost entirely in central Fars and along the coast of Persian Gulf and Oman Sea.

The rate of recovery increased until 1974 (1.23%), but from 1975 this has steadily decreased to 0.72% in 1999. This indicates that metal ringing is not a suitable method for marking flamingos, and we should explore more effective methods such as satellite tracking and colour ringing. From 689 adult ringed birds only 7 have been recovered (three from Iran, two from Kazakhstan, one from Egypt and one from the UAE), and those between 10 months and 15 years after ringing. It seems that ringed adults survive better than ringed chicks. Only two colour rings have been recovered, both in Khue Dubai in 2002 and 2005.

**Table 1.** Greater Flamingo *Phoenicopterus ruber* ringing and recovery statistics.

| Year | Total birds ringed | No. of sdults | No. of chicks | No. of recoveries (all) | % Rcvd. year of ringing | % Rcvd./total | Cumulative ringed birds* | Cumulative recovery | Cumulative % success* |
|------|------|------|------|------|------|------|------|------|------|
| 1970 | 2 492 | 242 | 2 250 | 8(5+3) | 0.32 | 3.70 | 2 492 | 8 | 0.321 |
| 1971 | 1 000 | 0 | 1 000 | 18 | 1.80 | 8.33 | 3 492 | 26 | 0.744 |
| 1972 | 1 495 | 0 | 1 495 | 31 | 2.07 | 14.35 | 4 987 | 57 | 1.143 |
| 1973 | 1 499 | 0 | 1 499 | 20 | 1.33 | 9.26 | 6 486 | 77 | 1.187 |
| 1974 | 1 450 | 0 | 1 450 | 20 | 1.38 | 9.26 | 7 936 | 97 | 1.222 |
| 1975 | 977 | 103 | 874 | 1 | 0.10 | 0.46 | 8 913 | 98 | 1.099 |
| 1976 | 1 762 | 257 | 1 505 | 11(7+4) | 0.62 | 5.09 | 10 675 | 109 | 1.021 |
| 1977 | 2 037 | 16 | 2 021 | 22 | 1.06 | 10.18 | 12 712 | 131 | 1.030 |
| 1978 | 2 326 | 0 | 2 326 | 22 | 0.94 | 10.18 | 15 038 | 153 | 1.017 |
| 1980 | 904 | 4 | 900 | 4 | 0.44 | 1.85 | 15 942 | 157 | 0.984 |
| 1981 | 1 408 | 8 | 1 400 | 9 | 0.64 | 4.17 | 17 350 | 166 | 0.957 |
| 1982 | 1 054 | 4 | 1 050 | 9 | 0.85 | 4.17 | 18 404 | 175 | 0.951 |
| 1983 | 1 802 | 55 | 1 747 | 15 | 0.83 | 6.94 | 20 206 | 190 | 0.940 |
| 1985 | 850 | 0 | 850 | 5 | 0.59 | 2.31 | 21 056 | 195 | 0.926 |
| 1986 | 496 | 0 | 496 | 2 | 0.40 | 0.92 | 21 552 | 197 | 0.914 |
| 1987 | 800 | 0 | 800 | 1 | 0.12 | 0.46 | 22 352 | 198 | 0.886 |
| 1988 | 1 100 | 0 | 1 100 | 2 | 0.18 | 0.92 | 23 452 | 200 | 0.853 |
| 1989 | 1 500 | 0 | 1 500 | 3 | 0.20 | 1.39 | 24 952 | 203 | 0.813 |
| 1994 | 1 500 | 0 | 1 500 | 5 | 0.33 | 2.31 | 26 452 | 208 | 0.786 |
| 1995 | 1 500 | 0 | 1 500 | 4 | 0.27 | 1.85 | 27 952 | 212 | 0.758 |
| 1997 | 650 | 0 | 650 | 1 | 0.15 | 0.46 | 28 602 | 213 | 0.745 |
| 1998 | 650 | 0 | 650 | 1 | 0.15 | 0.46 | 29 252 | 214 | 0.731 |
| 1999 | 750 | 0 | 750 | 2 | 0.27 | 0.92 | 30 002 | 216 | 0.720 |
| Total: | 30 002 | 689 | 29 313 | 216 | 0.720 | 100 | 30 002 | 216 | 0.720 |

*Waterbirds around the world*

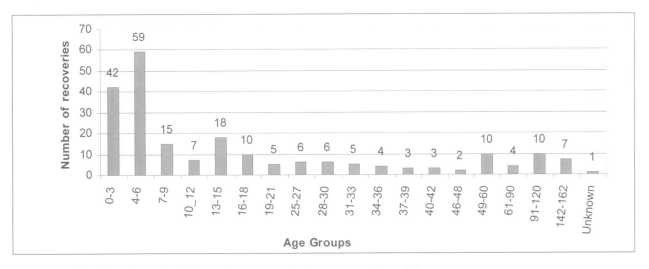

Fig. 2. Recoveries of ringed Greater Flamingos *Phoenicopterus ruber* by age groups (in months).

Fig. 2 shows recovery periods varying from 1-162 months. A total of 99 recoveries (46.3%) occurred 1-6 months after ringing, and 113 recoveries (52.8%) 1-9 months after ringing, showing a high mortality during the juvenile period, caused perhaps by the following:

- until five months, chicks do not have enough strength to fly, and therefore cannot escape enemies;
- chicks are not familiar with threats and are easily injured;

- differences in migration routes - adults are thought to winter mainly in Iran and juveniles outside Iran; and
- recovery data show that although flamingos are a protected species, they are widely hunted, and most recoveries come from shot birds.

**REFERENCES**

Scott, D.A. 1973. The Greater Flamingo *Phoenicopterus ruber* in Iran, Ornithology Unit, Department of Environment, Tehran, Iran.

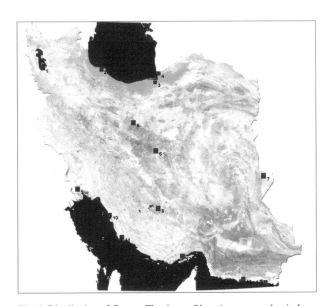

Fig. 1. Distribution of Greater Flamingos *Phoenicopterus ruber* in Iran.
1- Lake Uromiyeh (National Park, Ramsar Site and Biosphere Reserve)
2- Sefid Rud Delta (Protected Area and Ramsar site)
3- Miankaleh (Ramsar Site and Wildlife Refuge)
4- Gomishan (No Hunting Area)
5- Qom Salt Lake (included in Kavir National Park and Kavir Biosphere Reserve)
6- Gav Khoni (Ramsar site)
7- Hamun Lakes (Ramsar Site and Protected Area)
8- Tashk and Bakhtegan Lakes (National Park and Ramsar site)
9- Shadegan Marsh (Ramsar Site and Wildlife Refuge)
10- Helleh (Protected Area)
11- Mond (Protected Area)
12- Hara (Protected Area, Ramsar Site and Biosphere Reserve)
13- Gagin and Gabrik
14- Chabahar Bay

**Table 2. Recoveries in different countries.**

| Rank | Recovery Countries | No. of Recoveries | % Recovery/ Total |
|---|---|---|---|
| 1 | I. R. Iran | 49 | 22.68 |
| 2 | India | 21 | 9.72 |
| 2 | Pakistan | 21 | 9.72 |
| 3 | Iraq | 19 | 8.80 |
| 4 | Turkey | 19 | 8.80 |
| 5 | Libya | 13 | 6.02 |
| 6 | Egypt | 10 | 4.63 |
| 7 | Kazakhstan | 8 | 3.70 |
| 8 | UAE | 7 | 3.24 |
| 9 | Oman | 5 | 2.31 |
| 10 | Bahrain | 4 | 1.85 |
| 10 | Ethiopia | 4 | 1.85 |
| 10 | Syria | 4 | 1.85 |
| 10 | Qatar | 4 | 1.85 |
| 10 | Tunisia | 4 | 1.85 |
| 11 | Saudi Arabia | 3 | 1.39 |
| 11 | Somalia | 3 | 1.39 |
| 11 | Sudan | 3 | 1.39 |
| 12 | Azerbaijan | 2 | 0.93 |
| 12 | Cyprus | 2 | 0.93 |
| 12 | Greece | 2 | 0.93 |
| 12 | Israel | 2 | 0.93 |
| 12 | Morocco | 2 | 0.93 |
| 13 | Djibouti | 1 | 0.46 |
| 13 | Italy | 1 | 0.46 |
| 13 | Kuwait | 1 | 0.46 |
| 13 | Sri Lanka | 1 | 0.46 |
| 13 | Turkmenistan | 1 | 0.46 |

# The Sivash Bay as a migratory stopover site for Curlew Sandpiper *Calidris ferruginea*

*Sergei V. Khomenko*

*Schmalhausen Institute of Zoology, National Academy of Sciences of Ukraine, Vul. B. Khmelnitskogo, 15, Kyiv-30, MPS, UA-01601, Ukraine. (email: khomenko@izan.kiev.ua)*

Khomenko, S.V. 2006. The Sivash Bay as a migratory stopover site for Curlew Sandpiper *Calidris ferruginea*. *Waterbirds around the world*. Eds. G.C. Boere, C.A. Galbraith & D.A. Stroud. The Stationery Office, Edinburgh, UK. pp. 564-567.

## ABSTRACT

During migration periods the Sivash Bay of the Azov Sea supports up to 1.5% of the world population of Curlew Sandpiper *Calidris ferruginea* (c. 66 000 – 120 000 birds). In spring most birds pass through in the first ten days of May. They stopover for four to five days during which they accumulate as much as 41% of extra body mass. Curlew Sandpipers' main prey during this time is Brine Shrimp *Artemia salina*, whose distribution is restricted to the hypersaline waters of the Sivash. Feeding upon Brine Shrimps is highly profitable: spending 79% of foraging time, with pecking rates of 90 per minute, birds are able to gain 4.3 g of reserve tissue daily. The flight range of birds departing from the Sivash in spring is estimated at 2 – 2 500 km. In autumn, Curlew Sandpipers leave for wintering grounds located all over the African continent with sufficient fat reserves to travel 4 – 4 500 km. Ringing recoveries link this stopover site with staging areas in the Mediterranean, Baltic and East-Atlantic. Birds breed in the Taimyr Peninsula, although morphometric data suggests that some birds may come from areas further east.

## INTRODUCTION

Compared with the East-Atlantic flyway, stopover sites of waders in wetlands around the Mediterranean, Black and Caspian Seas, the Afro-Eurasian continental flyway corridor, remains rather poorly studied. Curlew Sandpipers show a clear preference for this continental flyway corridor in both spring and autumn (Eliot *et al.* 1976, Wilson *et al.* 1980). This paper summarizes results of several studies on Curlew Sandpiper in the Sivash Bay (Khomenko *et al.* 1999, Dyadicheva *et al.* 1999).

## METHODS

Counts and mist-netting of Curlew Sandpipers were carried out during regular expeditions of the Azov-Black Sea Ornithological Station to the the Sivash Bay (S Ukraine, SE Europe) between 1992-1998. By 1998, a total of 6 400 Curlew Sandpipers were ringed and 79 long-distance recoveries (0.6%) obtained in the Southern Ukraine (including the Sivash). Spatial coverage of counts varied between years, the most complete censuses being carried out in May 1993, 1996 and August 1998. Since the periods of catching and ringing varied between years, all data from 1992 to 1998 was pooled by five day periods (Bertold's pentads) to analyze the seasonality of morphometrics, body mass dynamics and moult (19 pentads, $275 \pm 424$ birds per pentad analyzed). Only samples $\geq 20$ adult birds were included in the analyses providing totals of 3 313 birds in spring and 1 414 birds in autumn. Birds were measured, weighed and aged according to standard methodologies (Prater 1977; pre-print by H. Schekkerman 1990). Plumage characteristics were described according to Chernichko (1988). The average wing to bill ratio was calculated for each sample to identify sex ratios (Khomenko & Dyadicheva 1999).

Time budgets were determined by activity scanning (184 hours of observations, six activities distinguished; for details see Khomenko *et al.* (1999). The average daily body mass gain was calculated by comparing the expenditure (BMR + activity costs + moult) and income (consumption of food per unit of time * energy equivalent * assimilation coefficient of the prey) of the energy budgets according to a standard evaluation procedure (Dolnik 1982). The production of 1 g of reserve tissue was considered to cost 34.2 kJ (Verkuil *et al.* 1993). The maximum flight distance (MFD, km) was calculated as the formula: MFD=95.447 *

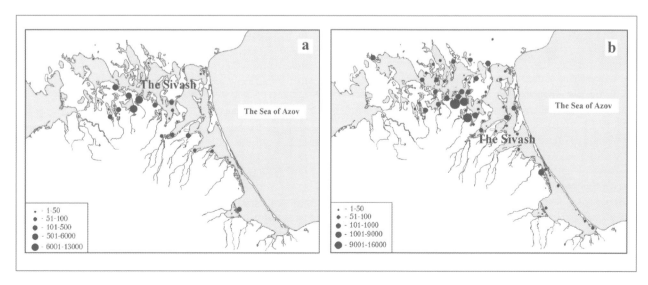

**Fig. 1.** Distribution of Curlew Sandpiper *Calidris ferruginea* gatherings in the Sivash according to absolute counts carried out in 1990-1998. Only maximum figures for each counting locality are presented. a – spring, b – autumn.

$V(T^{0.302}-M^{0.302})$; where V – flight speed (km/h), T – initial body mass (g), M – arrival body mass (g) (Gavrilov 1992).

## RESULTS

### Numbers, distribution and migration pattern

The largest gatherings of Curlew Sandpipers were found in the southern part of the country, where birds occur in most coastal wetlands. In the Sivash area, c. 33 000 and c. 72 000 birds were counted here simultaneously at the peak of spring and autumn migration respectively. Smaller numbers, totaling up to c. 10 000, were counted in autumn in the estuaries of the Azov-Black Sea coast (Dyadicheva *et al.* 1999). The largest concentrations in both spring and autumn were in Central Sivash (Fig. 1).

Seasonal trends in the wing/bill ratio (Fig. 2) indicate that males migrate earlier than females in both spring and autumn (Cramp & Simmons 1983). In spring migration, two waves can be distinguished; the first, around 10 May with a maximum c. 33 000 birds counted simultaneously and a second, five times smaller, around 22 May. The migration pattern suggests that most birds stay in the area for five to six days. Autumn migration, which begins with the arrival of males in mid-July, is more prolonged. Most males leave the area by 8 August. A pronounced peak in numbers is recorded around 20 August, when females replace males in the staging area. In autumn, males and females are estimated to stay for two to four weeks, with females tending to have shorter stopover periods than males.

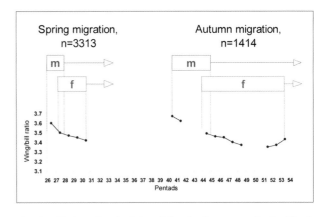

Fig. 2. Timing of male (m) and female (f) stopover in the Sivash according to the wing/bill ratio dynamics.

## FEEDING ECOLOGY, PRE-MIGRATORY FATTENING AND FLIGHT RANGE

The habitat choice of Curlew Sandpipers in the Sivash (Fig. 2) clearly shows that birds prefer Brine Shrimps to other (mainly freshwater) prey species that are available (Khomenko *et al.* 1999). Contrary to many other waders (e.g. Zwarts *et al.* 1990) Curlew Sandpipers in both the Central and Eastern Sivash feed only during the daytime. Maximum feeding activity occurs in the morning (Fig. 3), during periods of maximum availability of Brine Shrimps. In the Central Sivash, Curlew Sandpipers foraged significantly longer (79.4 ± 22.3%) than in the Eastern

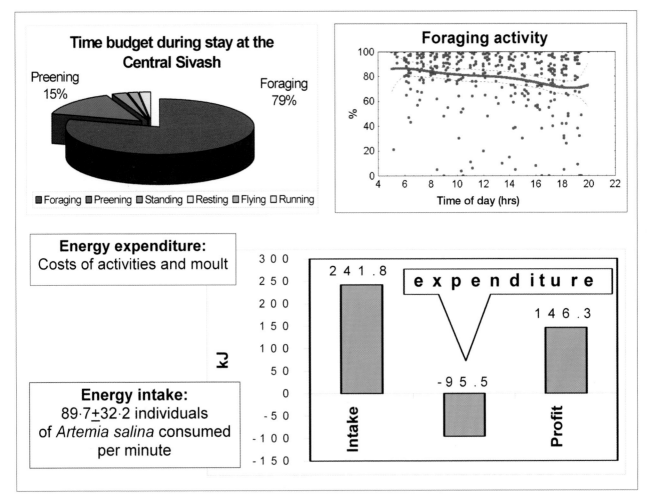

Fig. 3. Time and energy budgets of Curlew Sandpipers *Calidris ferruginea* foraging on Brine Shrimps *Artemia salina*.

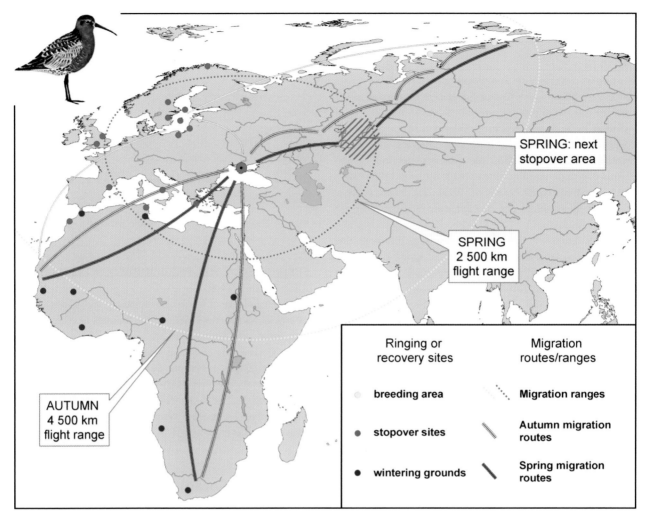

**Fig. 4.** Recoveries of Curlew Sandpipers *Calidris ferruginea* ringed or recovered in the S Ukraine by seasons (wintering, migration and breeding) and scheme of migration routes and estimated flight ranges.

(74.5 ± 23.8%), mainly due to a decreasing time for resting from 6.7 ± 12.0 to 0.2 ± 0.5% (Mann-Whitney test, p<0.01).

Pecking rates of Curlew Sandpipers in the Central Sivash were measured (n=517) to estimate the consumption of this prey per unit of time. It averaged 89.7 ± 32.2 specimens per minute, which was significantly higher than in Dunlin (Mann-Whitney test, p<0.01). Energy intake was estimated on the basis of daily food consumption (Fig. 3). Dependent on the time spent foraging it varied from 180.8 to 273.8 kJ/day (average = 241.8 ± 32.5 kJ/day). This fully compensated estimated daily energy expenditures leaving an average of 146.3 ± 38.4 kJ/day (72.1-185.5 kJ/day) available for building up fat reserves. With this amount of energy Curlew Sandpipers were estimated to gain body mass at a rate of 2.1-5.4 g/day (on average 4.3 ± 1.1 g/day). During the spring staging period, which is estimated to be no longer than five to six days (Khomenko *et al.* 1999), birds can gain as much as 33 – 41% of extra body mass. Their flight range should then be around 2 000 – 2 500 km, which is clearly not enough to go directly to the breeding grounds (Fig. 4). In autumn, average body mass is generally in the range of 70 to 78 g. The estimated flight range to the wintering grounds is approximately 4 000 – 4 500 km.

## DISCUSSION

Given the assessment of Curlew Sandpiper numbers in the Sivash it seems that the area is probably one of the most important stopover sites for this species in the world. If the turnover rate is taken into account, according to our estimates up to 9% (c. 66 000 birds) of the African wintering population pass the area in spring and around 21% (c. 160 000 birds) – during autumn migration. These figures correspond to 0.5 and 1.5% of the world population of Curlew Sandpiper (Rose & Scott 1994). Nowhere else have such large concentrations of Curlew Sandpiper been recorded.

There is no doubt that large numbers of birds are attracted to the area by high densities of Brine Shrimps. Research has shown that Curlew Sandpipers using this food during pre-migratory fattening can gain body mass at a daily rate close to the maximum ever recorded (5.5 g/day, sedimentation fields in Bahrain, Hirschfeld *et al.* 1990). Therefore, fat reserves sufficient for flying some 2 – 2 500 km can be accumulated in an extremely short period of time (four to five days). It is important to stress the fact that most birds depart from the Sivash with 33 - 41% of extra body mass as early as mid-May, which is approximately one month before their arrival at the breeding grounds. They have one more stopover area on route to the breeding grounds, which is most likely to be located somewhere in the south of Western Siberia (Fig. 4).

The particular preference of Curlew Sandpiper for hypersaline environments has also been recorded in Hungary, where up to 61% of birds occurred in salt pans (Sterbetz 1993). This raises the question as to whether the species may be dependent on the food resources of galinic water bodies during migrations via continental Eurasia. The exclusively diurnal feeding and high efficiency of foraging upon Brine Shrimps recorded in the Sivash clearly distinguish Curlew Sandpiper from other sandpiper species, and Dunlin in particular (Khomenko *et al.* 1999). These peculiarities of its feeding ecology suggest that birds do not just feed on Brine Shrimps by chance, but to a certain extent, specialize on such food. Moreover, it is known that saline water bodies (e.g. Manych-Gudilo, the Caspian coast, salt lakes of the south of Western Siberia) predominate in the areas Curlew Sandpipers pass through during migration to the breeding grounds and back.

Breeding grounds of Curlew Sandpipers ringed or recovered in S Ukraine are located in NW and N Taimyr (n=2), although analysis of morphometrics suggest (Khomenko *et al.* 1999) that a faction of smaller-billed birds may come from the areas to the east (up to the Lena River mouth). Wintering areas are apparently rather large and include N, W, S and Central Africa. Many recoveries (n=25) link S Ukraine and NW Europe (mostly Scandinavia and Baltic). Frequent re-trapping of birds between these two areas indicate that some Curlew Sandpipers using the East-Atlantic Flyway in autumn may move from NW Europe to S Ukraine via the Dnipro River valley just like Dunlins (Chernichko 1982). Another frequently used route links S Ukraine and the Mediterranean area (n=37). Two direct recoveries (in Spain and Italy) indicate a south-western movement in autumn. The seasonal distribution of recoveries suggests that birds use the Mediterranean flyway both during spring and fall migrations. The distribution of ringing recoveries suggests a wide wintering range of birds passing the Sivash (Fig. 4). Also the pattern of connections between the area and other stopover sites along the East-Atlantic flyway (as well as wintering and breeding grounds) seems to be more complicated than originally thought (Eliot *et al.* 1976, Wilson *et al.* 1980). The most likely migration routes taken by Curlew Sandpipers staging over in the Sivash are shown in Fig. 4. The scheme proposed by Eliot *et al.* (1976) and Wilson *at al.* (1980) can be accomplished by combining the Baltic – Black Sea route (which is apparently used by birds during autumn passage to the southern African wintering grounds) and the supposed Black Sea – south of Western Siberia route (which brings birds to the next stopover area on route to the breeding grounds).

Although both the Central and Eastern Sivash have already been designated as Ramsar sites, the future development of agricultural irrigation poses a serious threat to Curlew Sandpipers. A large-scale discharge of irrigation and drainage waters would freshen the saline lagoons and reduce availability of halophytic Brine Shrimps. Therefore, efforts should be made to safeguard this unique stopover site from the threat of possible desalination which would help to protect migratory populations of Curlew Sandpiper at a global scale.

## REFERNCES

Chernichko, I.I. 1988. A manual for study of population peculiarities of Dunlin migrations (catching and data collection). Information of the Working Group on Waders: 244-245. Vladivostok. [In Russian]

Chernichko, I.I., Yurchuk R.N. & Zmienko, A.B. 1992. Migrations of waders on the Southwestern coast of Ukraine. In: Seasonal migrations of birds in Ukraine: 164-182. Kiev: Naukova dumka. [In Russian]

Cramp, S. & Simmons, K.E.L. 1983. The birds of the Western Palearctic. Vol. 3. Oxford: Oxford University Press.

Dolnik, V.R. 1982. Time and energy budgets in free-living birds. Leningrad: Zoological Institute of the Academy of Sciences of USSR. Vol. 6: 3-37. [In Russian]

Dyadicheva, E.A., Khomenko, S.V., Zhmud, M.E., Chernichko, I.I., Garmash, B.A., Kinda, V.V. 1999. Numbers and migration patterns of Curlew Sandpipers in Ukraine Branta: Transactions of the Azov-Black Sea Ornithological Station. Issue 2. Melitopol: Branta: 91-112. [In Russian with English resume, tables and figures]

Elliott, C.C.H., Waltner, M., Underhill, L.G., Pringle, J.S. & Dick, W.J.A. 1976. The migration system of the Curlew Sandpiper *Calidris ferruginea* in Africa. Ostrich 47: 191-213.

Gavrilov, V.V. 1992. Methodological recommendations on the estimation of flight energy and maximum flight ranges of waders. Information of the Working Group on Waders: 24-27. Ekaterinburg: Nauka. [In Russian]

Gavrilov, V.V. 1998. Morphometric characteristics in waders breeding at North-East Yakutia. Ornithologia 28: 200-207. [In Russian]

Hirschfeld, E., Mohamed, S.A. & Stwarczyk. 1992. Bahrain wader study. WIWO report 42, WIWO, Zeist.

Khomenko, S.V. & Dyadicheva, E.A. 1999. Biometrics, moult and geographical relations of Curlew Sandpipers migrating via southern Ukraine. Branta: Transactions of the Azov-Black Sea Ornithological Station. Issue 2. Melitopol: Branta: 113-134. [In Russian with English resume, tables and figures]

Khomenko, S.V., Garmash, B.A., Metzner, J., Nikel, , M. 1999. Feeding ecology and time budgets of Curlew Sandpiper and Dunlin during spring stopover in the Sivash, Ukraine. Branta: Transactions of the Azov-Black Sea Ornithological Station. Issue 2. Melitopol: Branta: 77-90.

Prater, A.J., Marchant, J.H. & Vuorinen, J. 1977. Guide to the identification and ageing of Holarctic Waders. BTO Guide 17. Tring: British Trust for Ornithology.

Rose, P.M. & Scott, D.A. 1994. Waterfowl Population Estimates. IWRB Publ. 29, Slimbridge, IWRB.

Verkuil, Y., van de Sant, S., Stikvoort, E., van der Winden, J., Zwinselman, B. 1993. Breeding ecology of waders in the Sivash. In: T.M. van der Have & S. van de Sant (eds.) Waterbirds in the Sivash, Ukraine, spring 1992: 39-64. WIWO-report 36, Zeist: WIWO.

Wilson, J.R., Czajkowski, M.A. & Pienkowski, M.W. 1980. The migration through Europe and wintering in West Africa of Curlew Sandpipers. Wildfowl 31: 107-122.

Zwarts, L., Ens, B.J., Kersten, M. & Piersma, T. 1990. Moult, mass and flight range of waders ready to take off for long-distance migrations. Ardea 78(1/2): 83-112.

# 4.5   Migration and flyway atlases. Workshop Introduction

*Jacquie Clark*
*British Trust for Ornithology, The Nunnery, Thetford, Norfolk, IP24 2PU, UK.*

Clark, J. 2006. Migration and flyway atlases. Workshop Introduction. *Waterbirds around the world.* Eds. G.C. Boere, C.A. Galbraith & D.A. Stroud. The Stationery Office, Edinburgh, UK. p. 568.

Over one hundred years of bird ringing have provided a wealth of ringing recoveries. Much of this information has only incidentally been used in studies of single species or in depth population studies. Recently a few countries have produced bird migration atlases in which the results of bird ringing play a major rôle.

This workshop provided an overview of the present atlases; the various methods used to present the available ringing data integrated with information from other sources to give international overviews of the distribution and movements of waterbirds.

## INTERNATIONAL COLLABORATION

Whilst a number of migration atlases have been published, most only cover a subset of bird species, and almost all produced to date are based on ringing and recovery data from single countries (as for example, described by Dobrynina & Kharitonov for Russian waterbirds). There is a strong need for atlases using data from all countries, within a continent or sub-continent (for example, as noted by Oschadleus for southern Africa), in a flyway, or best of all, based on the biology of the birds.

Spina & Clark of EURING demonstrate how ringing schemes from different countries can collaborate productively, but there is still a long way to go.

## BROADENING THE TECHNOLOGICAL BASE OF INFORMATION

Most analyses for the atlases published so far are based on recoveries of metal rings. We need better integration with such data, of other data from colour-ringing and similar individual marking, telemetry, stable isotope analyses and genetic markers.

## COMBINING RINGING AND COUNT DATA

Systematic analyses for atlases confirm the value of ringing studies in assessing the conservation status of breeding, wintering and stop-over sites within the context of whole flyways.

Systematic analysis of data on waterbird ringing recoveries should continue to be a priority so as to give a better assessment of distributional limits of biogeographical populations. This work should be encouraged on a co-operative, international basis, and integrated with reviews of waterbird survey and census information. Such integration of count data with ringing data will allow the assessment of the conservation status of such sites even more clearly, and to better understand how each species uses the parts of its entire range.

## FLYWAY SCALE ATLASES

The mapped depiction of the geographic limits of the different biogeographical populations of waterbirds has long been seen as a conservation priority. Indeed, IWRB organised a whole international symposium in 1976 on the subject of mapping waterbird distributions, at which was discussed a proposal for an atlas of wetlands and waterfowl so as to map flyways and key sites for ducks, geese and swans. As discussed by Delany & Scott, this

George Atkinson-Willes pioneered IWRB's initial mapping of European waterbird distributions. Modern technology has vastly enhanced the capability to organise spatial information and modern bird atlases are using increasing sophisticated analytical methods. Photo: Wildfowl & Wetlands Trust.

project was eventually realised fifteen years later by Scott & Rose with their 1996 *Atlas of the distribution of African and West Eurasian Anatidae* — a land-mark publication by Wetlands International summarising existing knowledge. However, since then there has been slow progress in developing population atlases for other waterbird taxa, although a major publication on waders is currently in preparation.

## DEVELOPING ANALYTICAL TECHNIQUES

Systematic analyses of ringing data are needed for five reasons:-

1. Describe the distributional patterns of birds in space, how these vary seasonally, and long-term changes in distribution and movements.
2. Reliably distinguish the patterns of different populations, ages and sexes.
3. When ringing data are computerised, modern computing technology provides immense analytical power. Techniques such as geographical information systems expand this beyond the more obviously statistical methods.
4. Various analytical methods have been developed for ringing data and there is active progress in developing further methods; this must continue.
5. The major need is to overcome biases associated with geographical variation in reporting rates and with method of recovery. We need to overcome the impacts of these biases on the apparent differences in migration of different populations, ages and sexes.

# EURING: its role in migration and flyway atlases

*Fernando Spina[1] & Jacquie Clark[2]*

[1] *Istituto Nazionale per la Fauna Selvatica, Via Ca' Fornacetta 9, I-40064 Ozzano Emilia BO, Italy. (email: fernando.spina@infs.it)*

[2] *British Trust for Ornithology, The Nunnery, Thetford, Norfolk, IP24 2PU, UK. (email: jacquie.clark@bto.org)*

Spina, F. & Clark, J. 2006. EURING: its role in migration and flyway atlases. *Waterbirds around the world*. Eds. G.C. Boere, C.A. Galbraith & D.A. Stroud. The Stationery Office, Edinburgh, UK. pp. 569-573.

## ABSTRACT

Knowledge of the complex biological systems represented by migration routes is best obtained through the study of individually marked birds. The oldest and most widespread technique to follow the movements of birds is ringing. In Europe, EURING (The European Union for Bird Ringing) has ensured that ringing and recovery data are collected and stored in a standardized manner in its EURING Data Bank (EDB). These data can be used to perform large-scale analyses of the geographical distribution of flyways, seasonality of movements and ecological requirements of waterbirds migrating within the Palearctic and between Europe and Africa. This paper gives a brief review of the ringing and recovery data available for waterbirds in the EDB, and suggests some ways in which these data might be used, particularly in the compilation of migration atlases. EURING continues to improve the EDB, and offers its long-term expertise to assist in the analysis of recoveries of ringed birds on a flyway scale.

## INTRODUCTION

Migratory birds freely cross political boundaries and represent a natural heritage belonging to the international community. Sound conservation and management policies need to be based on a large-scale approach, involving many countries and also different continents. For species which are hunted, this implies the need for shared international legal instruments to ensure common actions and prescriptions in terms of habitat management and harvesting. Important examples are offered by the EU Wild Birds Directive 79/409 and the African-Eurasian Migratory Waterbirds Agreement (AEWA) under the Convention on Migratory Species of Wild Animals (CMS).

Knowledge of the complex biological systems represented by migration routes (including breeding, moulting, migration stopover and wintering areas) is best obtained through the study of individually marked birds. The oldest and most widespread technique to follow the movements of birds is ringing (also known as banding).

The original aim of bird ringing was to describe the routes used by birds during their migrations. A century after the first ringing activities were carried out, scientific bird ringing remains a highly versatile and extremely efficient research and monitoring technique. As well as identifying the movements of birds and the location of their breeding and wintering grounds in all continents, ringing has allowed the investigation of many aspects of bird biology, behaviour and demography which can only be analysed if individuals can be identified.

In Europe, EURING (The European Union for Bird Ringing, www.euring.org), a network of 38 national ringing schemes, has ensured that data are collected and stored in a standardized manner. EURING maintains the EURING Data Bank (EDB),

which constitutes an invaluable asset for analysts by bringing together reports of ringed birds that were either ringed or subsequently reported (recovered, recaptured or re-sighted) anywhere in Europe. These data can be used to perform large-scale analyses of the geographical distribution of flyways, seasonality of movements and ecological requirements of waterbirds migrating within the Palearctic and between Europe and Africa. This information can assist in objective decision making, to ensure that appropriate site protection and sustainable hunting guarantee the favourable conservation status of the various species.

## MIGRATION ATLASES AND THE ANALYSIS OF RINGING DATA

A series of recently produced national migration atlases and a geographical index of the contents of the EDB provide practical examples of the potential for analysis of ringing recoveries to serve as a tool for the management of migratory birds. The analytical approaches which were adopted in these atlases and the strategy adopted by EURING to stimulate further large-scale applied analyses of ringing data were the subject of a session devoted to migration and flyway atlases at the Waterbirds around the world Conference.

The migration atlas for Britain and Ireland (Wernham *et al.* 2002) is based on an impressive sample of recoveries that have been accumulated over almost a century, and offers interesting examples of novel analyses. Frequency distributions of the distances moved by ringed birds allow the migratory tendency of a species and the differential migration of sub-populations of that species to be investigated and quantified. The historical coverage of data also offers a unique opportunity to describe temporal changes in migration routes as a possible consequence of global climate change.

The influence of global change on bird migration patterns is also shown by some of the analyses performed on another huge sample of recoveries, held at the Bird Ringing Centre of Russia and illustrated by Sergei Kharitonov, based on analyses carried out with the late Inna Dobrynina (Dobrynina & Kharitonov, this volume). The importance of having continuous coverage of ringing activities over many years, and hence long-term sets of recoveries, is illustrated by species such as the Red-breasted Goose *Branta ruficollis*. Until the 1970s, the main winter quarters of this species were located in the south-west corner of the Caspian Sea, but in the early 1970s, the entire population moved to the north-west corner of the Black Sea, and since the late 1990s, some birds have begun to spend the winter along the north coast of the Black Sea and around the Sea of Azov (Dereliev, this volume). Such complex patterns of movements also emphasize the need for international legislation to take account of the geographical distribution of birds and to respond to any changes. Without adequate monitoring, significant changes in the network of important areas for a particular species (a crucial component of sound international conservation policies) may be missed.

This is especially true when huge geographical areas are involved, as shown by the data on recoveries held at the SAFRING Ringing Centre at the Avian Demography Unit, University of Cape Town, South Africa, and published in a series of atlases (e.g. Underhill *et al.* 1999). During the boreal winter, the southernmost latitudes of the African continent are home to a number of species that breed thousands of kilometres away to the north, in the highest latitudes of the Palearctic. The problems affecting birds which spend parts of their annual cycle in areas so far apart and pass across a large number of countries, often with very diverse legislation, during their migrations are a great challenge for bird conservation, and can only be evaluated through methods that involve marking birds individually, such as ringing.

As many waterbirds congregate in a relatively small number of sites outside the breeding season, they are also regularly monitored by direct counts. The International Waterbird Census (IWC), coordinated by Wetlands International, covers a huge geographical area and a large number of species. This long-term project has provided numerical estimates of populations not only at the species level, but also at the level of biogeographical populations, and has contributed to the publication of a series of atlases (Delany & Scott, this volume), the first of which was the Atlas of Anatidae Populations in Africa and Western Eurasia (Scott & Rose 1996). These very important atlases show the geographical boundaries of the flyways followed by each of the different populations of a species. It is clear that in the integrated management and sustainable harvesting of migratory waterbirds, consideration has to be given both to the number of individuals of a given species and to the different populations funnelling along their respective flyways.

**Table 1.** **Recovery data available for analysis in the EURING Data Bank for some AEWA species.**

| EURING code | Scientific name | Live recoveries | Dead recoveries | Total recoveries |
|---|---|---|---|---|
| 05820 | *Larus ridibundus* | 105 707 | 82 087 | 187 794 |
| 01520 | *Cygnus olor* | 80 439 | 28 349 | 108 788 |
| 05920 | *Larus argentatus* | 24 926 | 65 590 | 90 516 |
| 01860 | *Anas platyrhynchos* | 7 692 | 61 394 | 69 086 |
| 01340 | *Ciconia ciconia* | 39 327 | 17 059 | 56 386 |
| 01610 | *Anser anser* | 36 333 | 7 021 | 43 354 |
| 01840 | *Anas crecca* | 1 526 | 40 386 | 41 912 |
| 01440 | *Platalea leucorodia* | 39 143 | 695 | 39 838 |
| 05900 | *Larus canus* | 7 367 | 24 719 | 32 086 |
| 04500 | *Haematopus ostralegus* | 12 935 | 18 092 | 31 027 |
| 02060 | *Somateria mollissima* | 8 353 | 16 745 | 25 098 |
| 01590 | *Anser albifrons* | 19 854 | 4 797 | 24 651 |
| 00720 | *Phalacrocorax carbo* | 1 790 | 19 580 | 21 370 |
| 01660 | *Branta canadensis* | 11 831 | 8 387 | 20 218 |

## THE ROLE OF EURING

An ideal development in the compilation of migration atlases would be represented by an atlas integrating data on the distribution of waterbirds based on counts with data from the recoveries of individually marked birds. In order to provide better access to the contents of its unique data bank (EDB) and to stimulate such integrated analyses, EURING has produced a geographical index of the 2.7 million coded and computerized recoveries available for 426 species of birds. The EDB contains large data sets for many of the waterbird species covered by the AEWA (Table 1), and

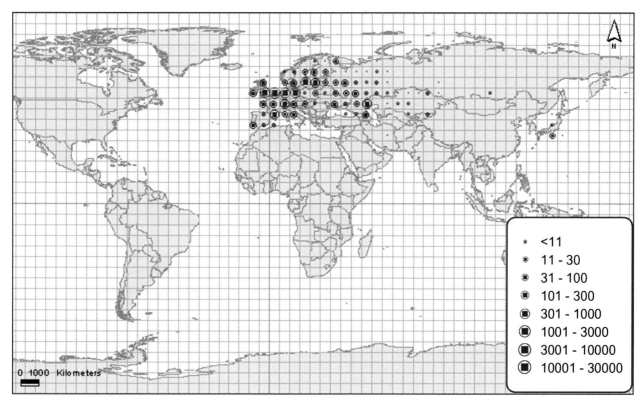

Legend:
- · <11
- 11 - 30
- 31 - 100
- 101 - 300
- 301 - 1000
- 1001 - 3000
- 3001 - 10000
- 10001 - 30000

**Fig. 1.** Ringing data available for the Mallard *Anas platyrhynchos* in the EURING Data Bank, by 5° grid square.

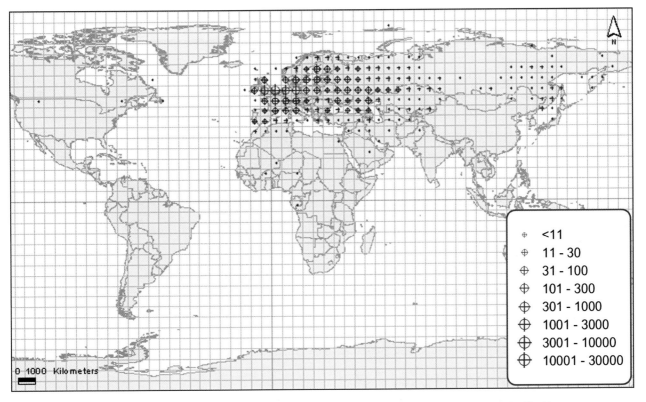

| | |
|---|---|
| ⊕ | <11 |
| ⊕ | 11 - 30 |
| ⊕ | 31 - 100 |
| ⊕ | 101 - 300 |
| ⊕ | 301 - 1000 |
| ⊕ | 1001 - 3000 |
| ⊕ | 3001 - 10000 |
| ⊕ | 10001 - 30000 |

0 1000 Kilometers

Fig. 2. Recovery data (dead recoveries only) available for the Mallard *Anas platyrhynchos* in the EURING Data Bank, by 5° grid square.

**Table 2. Number of recoveries of the Mallard *Anas platyrhynchos* in the EURING Data Bank per decade. A distinction is made between birds recovered dead and those recaptured alive or re-sighted.**

| Time period | Records of dead recoveries | Records of live recaptures/re-sightings |
|---|---|---|
| Pre 1940 | 373 | 1 |
| 1940-1949 | 1 839 | 14 |
| 1950-1959 | 12 820 | 1 333 |
| 1960-1969 | 20 430 | 1 315 |
| 1970-1979 | 13 943 | 1 372 |
| 1980-1989 | 9 762 | 1 368 |
| 1990-1999 | 1 979 | 1 784 |
| Post 1999 | 245 | 505 |

these are available for analysis. The EURINDEX project has been accomplished with the involvement of the NIOO in Heteren, The Netherlands, the INFS in Bologna, Italy, and the BTO in Thetford, UK; the results were published in July 2004 on EURING's web site (http://www.euring.org/edb/index.htm). The index is structured on a grid of 5° longitude x 5° latitude, and shows the amount of data available for each of the grid cells. Two maps showing the number of birds ringed and the number of dead recoveries, respectively, are presented for a total of 173 species with over 500 lines of data available (see examples for the Mallard *Anas platyrhynchos* in Figs. 1 & 2), while for another group of 160 species, a further two maps show the geographical distribution of ringing and live recaptures/re-sightings, respectively.

Summary tables also give the amount of data available per decade, starting from before the 1940s, and make a distinction between dead recoveries and live recaptures/re-sightings (Table 2);

this is important when planning analyses of long time-series, as the composition of the samples may change over time through changes in human/bird interactions (e.g. through changes in the finding circumstances). The contribution of data by each ringing scheme with over 500 recoveries is also reported (Table 3).

Although the AEWA covers a huge range of countries, it is apparent from the distribution of ringing/recovery data points in the EURINDEX maps that the geographical boundaries of the Agreement do not necessarily match those of the populations involved in migratory movements within the AEWA region. For example, the distribution of the recoveries of Eurasian Wigeon *Anas penelope* (Fig. 3) and Northern Pintail *A. acuta* (Fig. 4) includes the whole of Eurasia east to the Pacific coast. This suggests that further analyses are required for a better understanding of the complex flyways involving AEWA species and the Agreement area. As regards Africa, the geographical distribution of recoveries of the Sandwich Tern *Sterna sandvicensis* (Fig. 5) confirms that the boundaries of the Agreement area should extend to the southernmost latitudes of this continent.

Ringing recoveries are the best available source of information for the analysis of survival rates. This is especially important when considering the complex issues relating to the sustainable harvest of waterbirds, for which survival rates need to be taken into account. EURING can also make an important contribution in this respect. Through its analytical meetings, where statisticians and ornithologists work together for the better use of CMR (capture/mark/recapture) data, new models have been developed and are now available for the derivation of reliable survival estimates.

## CONCLUSION

EURING continues to maintain and improve its data bank, the EDB, and offers its long-term expertise to assist in the analysis

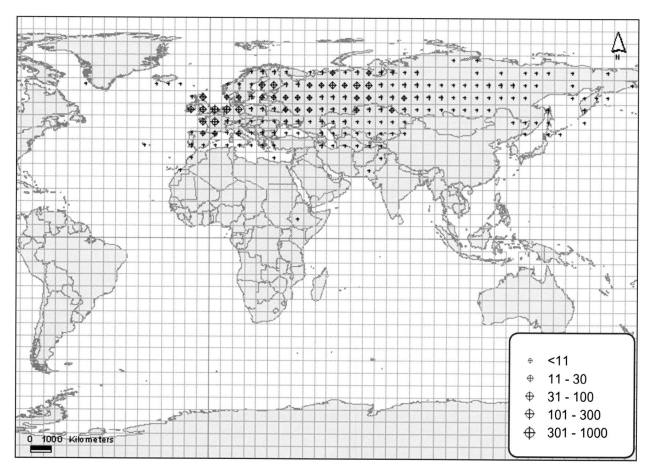

| | |
|---|---|
| ⊕ | <11 |
| ⊕ | 11 - 30 |
| ⊕ | 31 - 100 |
| ⊕ | 101 - 300 |
| ⊕ | 301 - 1000 |

**Fig. 3.** Recoveries of the Eurasian Wigeon *Anas penelope* in the EURING Data Bank, by 5° grid square.

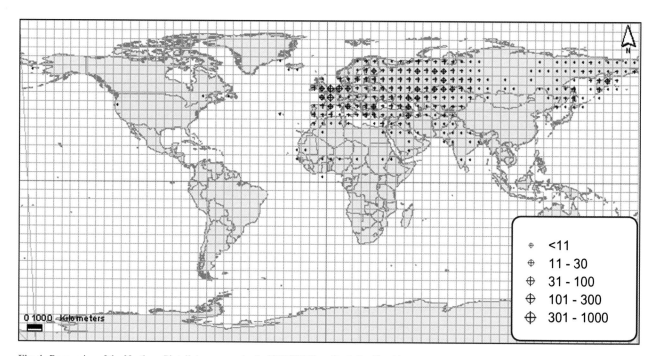

| | |
|---|---|
| ⊕ | <11 |
| ⊕ | 11 - 30 |
| ⊕ | 31 - 100 |
| ⊕ | 101 - 300 |
| ⊕ | 301 - 1000 |

**Fig. 4.** Recoveries of the Northern Pintail *Anas acuta* in the EURING Data Bank, by 5° grid square.

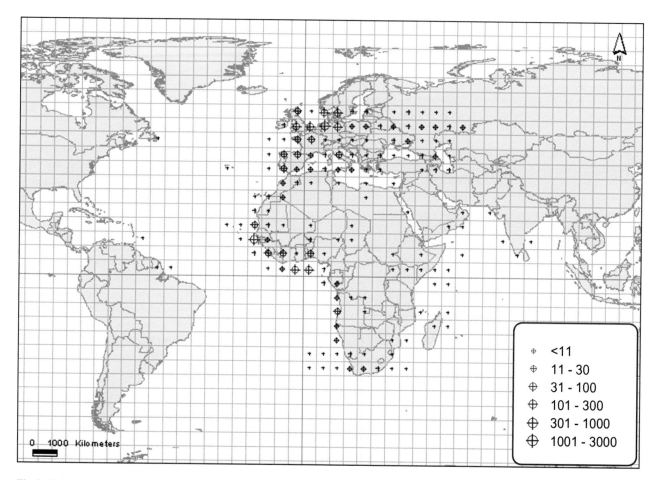

**Fig. 5.** Recoveries of the Sandwich Tern *Sterna sandvicensis* in the EURING Data Bank, by 5° grid square.

**Table 3. Number of recoveries of the Mallard *Anas platyrhynchos* in the EURING Data Bank from each ringing scheme with over 500 recoveries. The average time between ringing and recovery (duration) is given in years.**

| Scheme | Country | Scheme name | No. of dead recoveries | Duration | No. of live recoveries | Duration |
|---|---|---|---|---|---|---|
| BLB | Belgium | Bruxelles | 4 061 | 1.38 | - | - |
| DEH | Germany | Hiddensee (DEH) | 1 061 | 1.90 | 2 193 | 1.87 |
| DER | Germany | Radolfzell | 932 | 1.43 | - | - |
| DFH | Germany | Wilhelmshaven (Helgoland) | 2 112 | 1.56 | - | - |
| DFR | Germany | Radolfzell/Rossiten | 504 | 1.29 | - | - |
| DKC | Denmark | Copenhagen | 4 401 | 1.98 | 2 047 | 2.52 |
| FRP | France | Paris | 1 698 | 1.73 | - | - |
| GBT | UK & Ireland | London (British Museum/Tring/Thetford) | 23 784 | 1.59 | - | - |
| HES | Switzerland | Sempach | 1 019 | 2.13 | - | - |
| IAB | Italy | Bologna Ozzano (BO) | 590 | 1.44 | 634 | 0.70 |
| NLA | Netherlands | Arnhem | 6 661 | 1.69 | - | - |
| SFH | Finland | Helsinki Museum | 1 512 | 1.23 | - | - |
| SUM | USSR | Moskwa | 5 560 | 1.34 | - | - |
| SVS | Sweden | Stockholm Museum | 4 156 | 1.86 | - | - |

of recoveries of ringed birds on a flyway scale. The EURING information should aid decision makers (e.g. the AEWA Secretariat, European Commission and national governments) in establishing appropriate controls on factors such as the timing of hunting seasons, to ensure the sustainable use of waterbird resources for the benefit of biodiversity conservation and all sectors of society.

## REFERENCES

**Scott, D.A. & Rose, P.M.** 1996. Atlas of Anatidae Populations in Africa and Western Eurasia. Wetlands International Publication No. 41, Wageningen, The Netherlands.

**Underhill, L.G., Tree, A.J., Oschadleus, H.D. & Parker, V.** 1999. Review of Ring Recoveries of Waterbirds in Southern Africa. Avian Demography Unit, University of Cape Town, Cape Town.

**Wernham, C.V., Toms, M.P., Marchant, J.H., Clark, J.A., Siriwardena, G.M. & Baillie, S.R.** (eds). 2002. The Migration Atlas: movements of the birds of Britain and Ireland. T. & A.D. Poyser, London.

# Wetlands International's Flyway Atlas series: establishing the geographical limits of waterbird populations

*Simon N. Delany[1] & Derek A. Scott[2]*

[1] *Wetlands International, PO Box 471, 6700 AL Wageningen, The Netherlands. (email: simon.delany@wetlands.org)*

[2] *c/o Castletownbere Post Office, Castletownbere, 6. Cork, Ireland. (email: derekscott@eircom.net)*

Delany, S.N. & Scott, D.A. 2006. Wetlands International's Flyway Atlas series: establishing the geographical limits of waterbird populations. *Waterbirds around the world*. Eds. G.C. Boere, C.A. Galbraith & D.A. Stroud. The Stationery Office, Edinburgh, UK. pp. 574-581.

## ABSTRACT

Waterbird conservation takes place increasingly at the level of flyways of individual biogeographical populations. Wetlands International provides triennial updates of waterbird population estimates at global level on behalf of the Ramsar Convention on Wetlands. Practitioners using these estimates as the basis of waterbird conservation policies and plans need to know which estimates to apply in which geographical areas, and Wetlands International has produced a series of Flyway Atlases to facilitate this process. The *Atlas of Anatidae Populations in Africa and Western Eurasia* was produced in 1996 on behalf of the Secretariat of the African-Eurasian Migratory Waterbird Agreement (AEWA). This was followed by atlases of Anatidae and cranes in East Asia, which form the basis of the Asia-Pacific Migratory Waterbird Conservation Strategy site networks for Anatidae and cranes. *Goose Populations of the Western Palearctic* followed in 1999, and work on an *Atlas of Wader Populations in Africa and Western Eurasia* is currently underway. Plans for future atlases include volumes covering all the other waterbird populations included in AEWA, and interactive presentation on the AEWA web-site will be established. Modern developments in electronic media have opened up new possibilities for presentation which are being explored during production of the Wader Atlas.

## INTRODUCTION

Waterbird conservation takes place increasingly at the level of flyways of individual biogeographical populations. The concept of a flyway as the geographical area used by the migratory population of a species during every stage of its life cycle is well-established. Flyways were first described in Eurasia for a number of duck species by Isakov (1967), who developed the concept to embrace more generalised "flyways" which are used by a number of species with similar geographical ranges and migration habits.

When attempting the conservation of any species, it is essential to have as much information as possible about the numbers of individuals that exist, where they are found, and whether their numbers are decreasing, stable or increasing. Since 1994, Wetlands International has provided this information at global level for about 870 species recognised as "waterbirds", which are divided for the purposes of conservation into about 2 200 "populations". The first edition of the Wetlands International publication *Waterbird Population Estimates* was published in 1994 (Rose & Scott 1994), the second in 1997 (Rose & Scott 1997) and the third in 2002 (Wetlands International 2002). A fourth edition is in press at the time of writing (Wetlands International in press). An important policy instrument supported by this publication is the Ramsar Convention on Wetlands. Wetlands of International Importance (so called "Ramsar sites") are recognised under this international agree-

ment using nine criteria. Criterion 6 states that any site regularly holding 1% of a waterbird population qualifies as a Wetland of International Importance.

In order to know which sites hold 1% of a population, it is necessary to have an estimate for the total size of the population (which is provided by *Waterbird Population Estimates*), and also to know the geographical limits of each population. The geographical information provided about each species in *Waterbird Population Estimates* comprises a map of global distribution at species level together with verbal descriptions, which are necessarily brief, of the geographical range of each population during the breeding and non-breeding seasons. Practitioners using these estimates as the basis of waterbird policies and plans need to know precisely which estimates to apply in which geographical area. The information in *Waterbird Population Estimates* is not sufficient to enable detailed understanding of the population boundaries of each species. For this purpose, detailed maps showing the population boundaries of each species are required. In response to this need, Wetlands International is producing a series of Flyway Atlases which are the subject of this paper.

## WETLANDS INTERNATIONAL'S ATLASES OF WATERBIRD POPULATIONS

Wetlands International has produced three atlases of waterbird populations. The first to be published was the *Atlas of Anatidae Populations in Africa and Western Eurasia* (Scott & Rose 1996). This identified "biogeographical populations" for all 61 species of Anatidae which occur regularly in Africa and Western Eurasia, and shows the limits of these populations in a series of maps. This atlas was followed by a similar *Atlas of Key Sites for Anatidae in the East Asian Flyway* (Miyabayashi & Mundkur 1999) and an *Atlas of Key Sites for Cranes in the North East Asian Flyway* (Chan 1999). A related publication, *Goose populations of the Western Palearctic: A review of status and distribution* (Madsen *et al.* 1999) provided much greater detail for the 23 populations of nine species of geese (*Anser* spp. and *Branta* spp.) occurring in Europe and western Asia. Wetlands International is now working on the largest and most ambitious atlas to date – an *Atlas of Wader Populations in Africa and Western Eurasia* (Delany *et al.* in prep.).

Scott & Rose (1996) and Delany *et al.* (in prep.) cover the region of the African-Eurasian Migratory Waterbird Agreement (AEWA), and provide crucial technical information needed for conservation of waterbird populations under this agreement. Miyabayashi & Mundkur (1999) and Chan (1999) do the same for the Asia-Pacific Migratory Waterbird Conservation Strategy (APMWCS), forming the basis of site networks under the strategies for Anatidae and cranes, respectively.

For each species, the maps in these publications show the breeding range, the boundaries of each biogeographical population (the total geographical range within which each 1% threshold applies) and key sites (i.e. sites that regularly hold >1% of the population). Also presented is a list of key sites for each species with details of counts, and this information is summarized in a site gazetteer, by country, combining information from all species. The species texts provide interpretation of the maps and tables and relevant background information about each population. An important concept running through all these atlases is that of sites forming a network.

## METHODS

The data and information used in the compilation of atlases of waterbird populations come from a number of sources. The most important single source is the International Waterbird Census (IWC), initiated in Europe in 1967 and now involving more than 15 000 waterbird counters (most of whom are voluntary birdwatchers) in over 100 countries in all parts of the world except North America. Each year in January, this network undertakes detailed, standardised counts of between 30 and 40 million waterbirds, details of which are sent to Wetlands International and stored on the IWC database.

These count data provide the information needed to estimate the numbers of many populations, to identify the geographical ranges at species level, and to identify the key sites used by the populations. Important information on the movements of birds in these populations comes largely from the results of bird ringing and other migration studies.

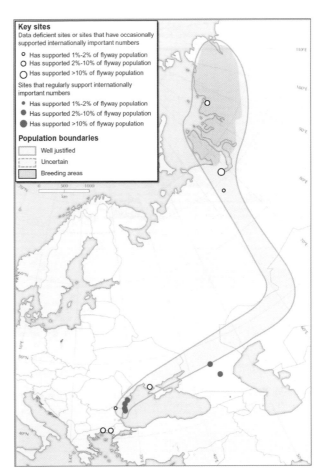

Fig. 2. Population boundaries of the Red-breasted Goose *Branta ruficollis* (from Scott & Rose 1996).

Millions of birds have been ringed in the past 100 years, and published information is available about the movements of most waterbird species (e.g. Spina & Clark, this volume). These published data provide a sound basis for the separation of many waterbird populations, but they usually relate only to birds ringed and/or recovered in a single country (e.g. Underhill *et al.* 1999, Fransson & Pettersson 2001, Bakken *et al.* 2003). One of the aims of EURING is to facilitate international-level analyses of data relating to birds ringed in Europe, but all except the most generalised data are inaccessible to third parties. It is therefore still difficult to conduct large-scale analyses which include data collected by both counting and ringing activities at international level.

## TYPES OF BIOGEOGRAPHICAL POPULATION

Various types of "biogeographical populations" have been recognized in *Waterbird Population Estimates* and the flyway atlases, and these are best demonstrated and explained by using examples from Wetlands International's publications.

Isakov (1967) first presented biogeographical population boundaries for Anatidae in Western Eurasia (Fig. 1). In 1974, at an international conference at Heiligenhafen, Isakov offered his "Thoughts on an Atlas of distribution of waterfowl and wetlands". These biogeographical populations are still recognised today, and form the basis of many of the populations in the Anatidae Atlas of Scott & Rose (1996). The approach fits well with the Convention on Biodiversity's "Ecosystem Approach" because the flyway of each population encompasses the entire ecosystem that it uses. Isakov's populations were supported by

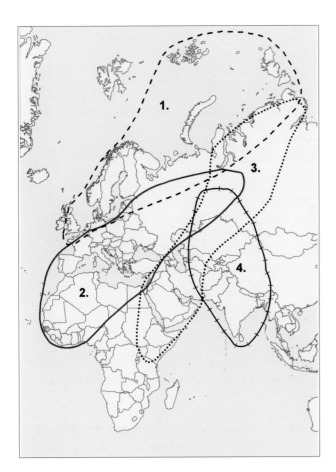

Fig. 1. The four main geographical populations of Anatidae in Western Eurasia as identified by Isakov (1967).

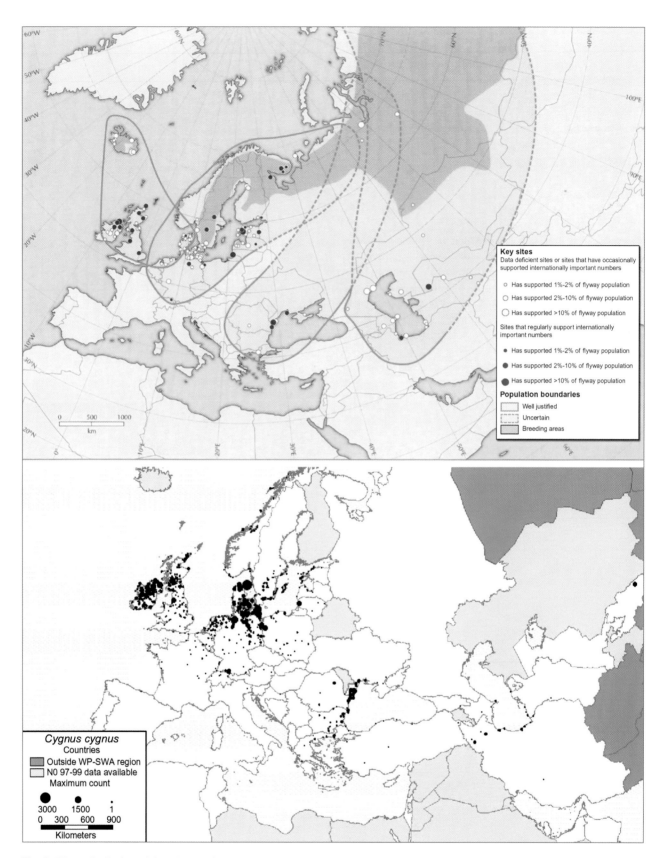

**Fig. 3.** Winter distribution of the Whooper Swan *Cygnus cygnus* in Europe, 1997-1999, as revealed by IWC counts (Gilissen *et al.* 2002), and population boundaries established by Scott & Rose (1996).

Shevareva (1970) who analysed 10 600 recoveries of ducks ringed in the former USSR and confirmed the basic geographical populations for the Mallard *Anas platyrhynchos*, Common Teal *A. crecca*, Northern Pintail *A. acuta*, Eurasian Wigeon *A. penelope* and Garganey *A. querquedula*.

The simplest type of waterbird population is illustrated in Fig. 2. The Red-breasted Goose *Branta ruficollis* is a monotypic species with a relatively small population. The migration routes and key sites are quite well known (although information is still lacking on key spring staging areas). There is only a single

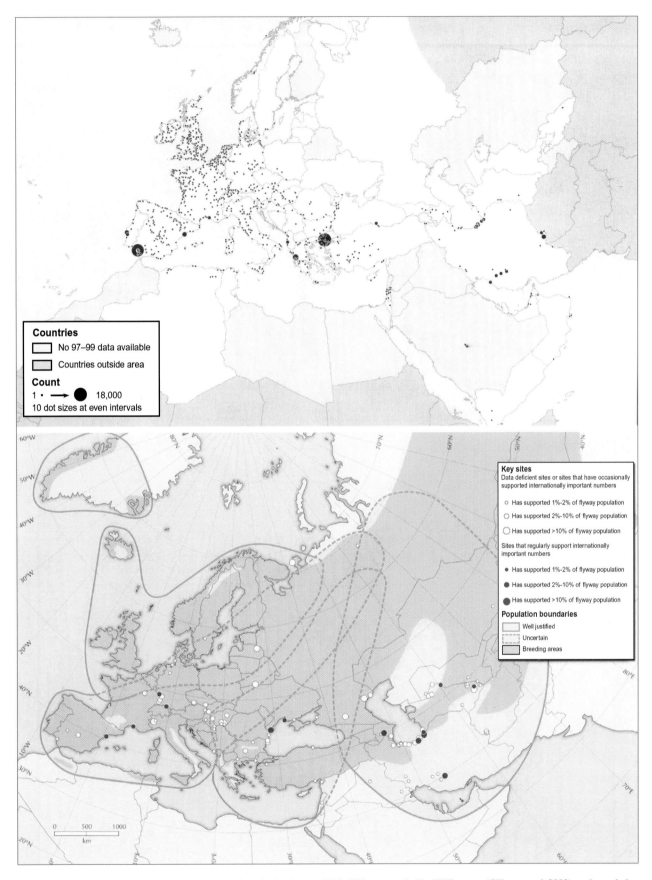

**Fig. 4.** Winter distribution of the Mallard *Anas platyrhynchos* in Europe, 1997-1999, as revealed by IWC counts (Gilissen *et al.* 2002), and population boundaries established by Scott & Rose (1996).

population, the geographical limits of which comprise the entire range of the species.

A similar approach can be used for many polytypic species,

where each subspecies occupies a different flyway. This type of population division is used for the Red Knot *Calidris canutus* which has six subspecies, each of which occupies largely sepa-

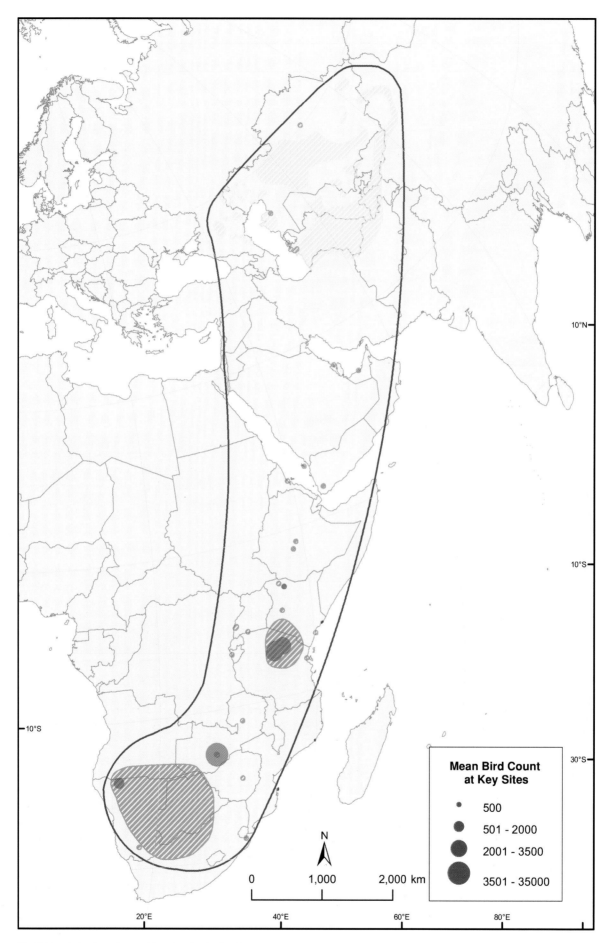

**Fig. 5.** Population boundary and key sites for the Caspian Plover *Charadrius asiaticus* (from Delany *et al.* in prep). Key sites: Lake Turkana, Kenya; Oponono Lake, Namibia; Lake Manyara, Ngorongoro Conservation Area, Serengeti National Park and Singida Lake, Tanzania; Kafue Flats, Zambia.

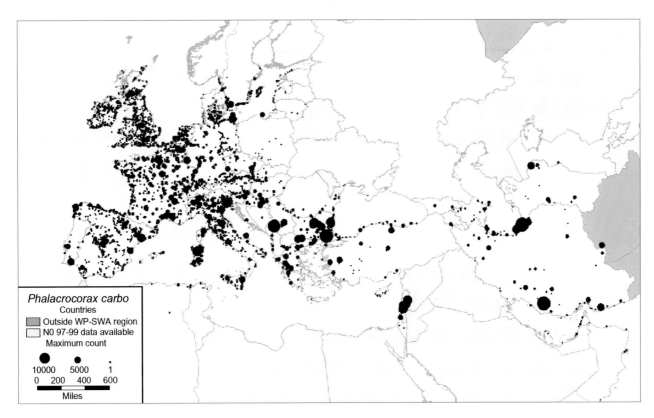

Fig. 6. Winter distribution of the Great Cormorant *Phalacrocorax carbo* in Europe, 1997-1999, as revealed by IWC counts (Gilissen *et al.* 2002).

rate breeding and non-breeding ranges, although in some cases, two subspecies use the same sites during migration.

Fig. 3 shows another type of population division. The Whooper Swan *Cygnus cygnus* is a monotypic species divided into five populations on the basis of geographically separate wintering ranges. Fig. 3 shows four of these populations; a fifth occurs in East Asia and appears in Miyabayishi & Mundkur (1999). The lower map in Fig. 3 shows the distribution of Whooper Swans in Europe and western Asia in the three winters 1997-1999, plotted directly from IWC count data. The justification for the population divisions is clear, and is supported by published ringing data which show that birds wintering in Ireland and the UK breed in Iceland and comprise a discrete population, while the other three populations, identified on the basis of their geographically separated wintering areas, mix to a considerable extent on their breeding grounds in northern Russia.

The distribution and movements of many waterbird species are more continuous and complex, and do not allow ready division into populations on purely biological grounds. The most extreme example in the AEWA region is the Mallard. The range of this species in Europe, as plotted from IWC data collected in the three winters 1997-99, is shown in Fig. 4 above the population boundaries identified by Scott & Rose (1996). The range is nearly continuous, and movements are complex, with resident birds in western and central Europe being joined by migrants from the east in winter.

For the Mallard, Scott & Rose (1996) based the population boundaries on those proposed by Isakov (1967) and supported by Shevareva (1970), but they identified one additional population by splitting the Mediterranean population into western and eastern portions. Apart from the separate and distinct population breeding in Greenland, these "population boundaries" are not biologically very meaningful, and even with this division, very

few key sites are recognised for this species, which rarely forms very large concentrations. The Mallard is an extreme case, and division into populations using this "practical approach" based on "wintering regions" has been successfully undertaken for many species which cannot be reliably divided using a purely biological approach. Furthermore, it has often been found that the same "wintering regions" are appropriate for a number of species of waterbirds with similar habitat requirements and migration strategies, e.g. the North-west Europe, Black Sea/Mediterranean and South-west Asia regions for various dabbling ducks and diving ducks in Western Eurasia.

It is accepted that in most widespread and numerous species there is a considerable amount of overlap between adjacent "wintering populations" during the migration seasons and on the breeding grounds. However, under the "practical approach", the individuals wintering in a particular region are treated as a single population regardless of their distribution at other times of year. This approach was refined by Atkinson-Willes (1976, 1978) in the 1970s, then by Rüger *et al.* (1986), Monval & Pirot (1989) and others in the 1980s, before being used by Scott & Rose for the Anatidae Atlas in 1996. The approach is supported by ringing evidence, e.g. Perdeck & Clason 1980.

For many migratory species of waterbirds, particularly those that are widely dispersed outside the breeding season, far more is known about the breeding populations at northern latitudes than about the non-breeding populations at southern latitudes, where the birds may mix with sedentary populations of the same species and be indistinguishable to counters (e.g. some herons and egrets breeding in Western Eurasia and wintering in Africa). In such cases, population units have often been identified on the basis of the breeding populations within relatively well-defined geographical areas. As with populations identified on the basis of their wintering regions, such populations may mix with other popula-

**Table 1. Definitions of "biogeographical population".**

**Biological approach**

- The entire population of a monotypic species (e.g. Red-breasted Goose *Branta ruficollis*).
- The entire population of a recognized subspecies (e.g. the six subspecies of Red Knot *Calidris canutus*).
- A discrete population of a migratory species or subspecies that rarely if ever mixes with any other population of that species or subspecies at any time of the year (e.g. the population of Whooper Swans *Cygnus cygnus* breeding in Iceland).
- A regional group of sedentary, nomadic or dispersive birds with an apparently rather continuous distribution and no major gaps between breeding units sufficient to prohibit interchange of individuals during their normal nomadic wanderings and/or post-breeding dispersal (e.g. the Madagascar population of Hottentot Teal *Anas hottentota*).

**Practical approach**

- The individuals of a migratory species or subspecies which spend the non-breeding-season ("winter") in a particular, discrete geographical region (e.g. the populations of Mallard *Anas platyrhynchos* in Western Eurasia). There may, however, be a considerable amount of overlap between two adjacent populations during the migration seasons and on the breeding grounds. The "wintering" regions used by these population units should:
  a) be large and varied enough for the "populations" to stay within their boundaries for the whole winter;
  b) be bounded by unsuitable habitats, or by zones in which birds are absent; and
  c) include the migration routes leading to them.
- The individuals of a migratory species or subspecies which spend the breeding season in a particular, discrete geographical region (e.g. the European breeding population of Eurasian Woodcock *Scolopax rusticola*). There may, however, be a considerable amount of overlap between two adjacent populations during the migration seasons and on the non-breeding ("wintering") grounds.

Flyway populations of Sanderlings *Calidris alba* will be mapped in the forthcoming Wader Atlas to be published in 2007. Photo: Paul Marshall.

population units on the basis of degree of isolation from other populations of the same species in relation to the known extent of the dispersive and/or nomadic movements of the species. They defined such populations as "a regional group of sedentary, nomadic or dispersive birds with an apparently rather continuous distribution and no major gaps between breeding units sufficient to prohibit interchange of individuals during their normal nomadic wanderings and/or post-breeding dispersal".

The various types of "biogeographical population" that have been adopted in *Waterbird Population Estimates* and Wetlands International's flyway atlases are summarized in Table 1.

**Wader Atlas**

The latest in the series of Wetlands International's atlases of waterbird populations is the *Atlas of Wader Populations in Africa and Western Eurasia* (Delany *et al.* in prep.), which is being produced jointly by the International Wader Study Group and Wetlands International. Work started on this atlas as long ago as 1998. It has weathered a number of organisational and financial crises and is likely to be finished in 2007.

The wader atlas includes all the information provided in earlier flyway atlases, but is based on a wider selection of data sources. Its maps have also been produced and presented using more modern, GIS software. BirdLife International have made data available from their IBA database to help identify key sites in periods not covered by the IWC (principally, spring and autumn migration). An example of a map from the Wader Atlas is provided in Fig. 5.

**DISCUSSION**

Atlases of waterbird populations produced by Wetlands International to date have covered those groups of species for which most data of high quality are available. In the late 1980s, the number of species included in the IWC was expanded from just "wildfowl and waders" to include all waterbirds. Now that these additional species have been counted for 15 years, enough data have accumulated to make it possible to prepare similar atlases for most other waterbird species in Africa and Western

tions of the same species at other times of the year. For a number of species with extensive breeding ranges in Western Eurasia, two populations have been identified – a European breeding population and a West Asian breeding population, separated by the Ural Mountains. In many species, this practical approach appears to have some biological validity as evidence from ringing suggests that the bulk of the individuals breeding western of the Urals migrate south-west to spend the non-breeding season in western and southern Europe and West Africa, while birds breeding east of the Urals spend the non-breeding season mainly in the Middle East and eastern and southern Africa.

While much of the emphasis in the flyway atlases has been given to identifying "flyways" for migratory populations of waterbirds, an attempt has also been made to identify "populations" of sedentary or nomadic species which would be appropriate for conservation management purposes. Scott & Rose (1996) gave some consideration to this matter, and identified

Eurasia. The existence of the AEWA as a legally binding instrument, with 53 Contracting Parties in January 2006, has created a strong demand for high-quality published information about migratory waterbird populations which gives great impetus to this work in the AEWA region.

Fig. 6 shows the distribution of the Great Cormorant *Phalacrocorax carbo* in Europe in the three winters 1997-1999, as revealed by the IWC counts. The IWC data are now in place for this and many additional species, and a review of literature concerning ringing recoveries, combined with these data, will provide the basis for population atlases for these additional species in years to come.

Future analyses for migration atlases would benefit greatly from an ability to use data from bird ringing in direct combination with the waterbird count data in the IWC database. It is to be hoped that developments at EURING will make this possible in the not too distant future.

Modern approaches to the presentation of spatial data will broaden the scope and improve the accessibility of future atlases. It will be possible to present maps in hardcopy for ease of use, but at the same time to make them available electronically on CD ROM and web-sites. Electronic formats will allow users to go deeper into the data by selecting map layers which could include, for example, count data for selected species in selected geographical regions, and related environmental data sets such as those relating to climate and land use. Zöckler *et al.* (2003) presented ideas for future presentation of waterbird data using an interactive, web-based interface which would allow data and information from a number of different web-based sources to be integrated and queried in a so-called "web portal". These methods will offer considerable scope for future work which will provide insight into factors beyond the current need to know the geographical limits of populations.

## ACKNOWLEDGEMENTS

The basis of Wetlands International's work on waterbird numbers and distribution is the network of over 15 000, mostly voluntary, waterbird counters in more than 100 countries. We salute their skill and dedication. Thanks also to Jacquie Clark, Fernando Spina and Carl Mitchell for helpful discussions.

## REFERENCES

**Atkinson-Willes, G.L.** 1976. The Numerical Distribution of Ducks, Swans and Coots as a Guide in Assessing the Importance of Wetlands in Midwinter. In: M. Smart (ed) Proceedings of the International Conference on Conservation of Wetlands and Waterfowl, Heiligenhafen, Federal Republic of Germany, December 1974. IWRB, Slimbridge, UK: 199-254.

**Atkinson-Willes, G.L.** 1978. The numbers and distribution of sea ducks in northwest Europe, January 1967-73. In: A. Andersson & S. Fredga (eds) Proceedings of the Symposium on Sea Ducks, 16-17 June 1975, Stockholm, Sweden. National Swedish Environment Protection Board, Stockholm, and IWRB, Slimbridge, UK: 28-67.

**Bakken, V., Runde, O. & Tjorve, E.** 2003. Norwegian Bird Ringing Atlas. Volume 1. Divers – Auks. Stavanger Museum, Stavanger.

**Chan, S.** 1999. Atlas of Key Sites for Cranes in the North East Asian Flyway. Wetlands International – Japan, Tokyo.

**Delany, S.N., Scott, D.A. & Dodman, T.** In prep. Atlas of Wader Populations in Africa and Western Eurasia. International Wader Study Group and Wetlands International.

**Fransson, T. & Pettersson, J.** 2001. Swedish Bird Ringing Atlas. Volume 1. Divers – Raptors. Stockholm.

**Isakov, Y.A.** 1967. MAR Project and Conservation of Waterfowl breeding in the USSR. In: Z. Salverda (ed) Proceedings of the Second European Meeting on Wildfowl Conservation, Noorrdwijk aan Zee, The Netherlands. Ministry of Cultural Affairs, Recreation and Social Welfare, The Netherlands: 125-138.

**Madsen, J., Cracknell, G. & Fox, A.D.** (eds). 1999. Goose populations of the Western Palearctic: A review of status and distribution. Wetlands International Publication No. 48. Wetlands International, Wageningen, The Netherlands; National Environmental Research Institute, Rønde, Denmark.

**Miyabayashi, Y. & Mundkur, T.** 1999. Atlas of Key Sites for Anatidae in the East Asian Flyway. Wetlands International – Japan, Tokyo, and Wetlands International – Asia Pacific, Kuala Lumpur.

**Monval, J.-Y. & Pirot, J.-Y.** 1989. Results of the IWRB International Waterfowl Census 1967-1986. IWRB Special Publication No. 8. Slimbridge, UK.

**Perdeck, A.C. & Clason, C.** 1980. Some Results of Waterfowl Ringing in Europe. IWRB Special Publication No. 1. Slimbridge, UK.

**Rose, P.M. & Scott, D.A.** 1994. Waterfowl Population Estimates. IWRB Publication No. 29. Slimbridge, UK.

**Rose, P.M. & Scott, D.A.** 1997. Waterfowl Population Estimates – Second Edition. Wetlands International Publication No. 44, Wageningen, The Netherlands.

**Rüger, A., Prentice, C. & Owen, M.** 1986. Results of the IWRB International Waterfowl Census 1967-1983. IWRB Special Publication No. 6. Slimbridge, UK.

**Scott, D.A. & Rose, P.M.** 1996. Atlas of Anatidae Populations in Africa and Western Eurasia. Wetlands International Publication No. 41. Wetlands International, Wageningen, The Netherlands.

**Shevareva, T.** 1970. Geographical Distribution of the Main Dabbling Duck Populations in the USSR, and the Main Directions of their Migrations. In: Y.A. Isakov (ed) Proceedings of the International Regional Meeting on Conservation of Wildfowl Resources, Leningrad, USSR, 25-30 September 1968. Moscow: 46-55.

**Spina, F. & Clark, J.** 2006. EURING: its role in migration and flyway atlases, Waterbirds around the world, G.C. Boere, C.A. Galbraith & D.A. Stroud (Eds). The Stationery Office, Edinburgh, UK. pp. 569-573.

**Underhill, L.G., Tree, A.J., Oschadleus, H.D. & Parker, V.** 1999. Review of Ring Recoveries of Waterbirds in Southern Africa. Avian Demography Unit, University of Cape Town, Cape Town.

**Wetlands International** 2002. Waterbird Population Estimates – Third Edition. Wetlands International Global Series No. 12, Wageningen, The Netherlands.

**Wetlands International** In press. Waterbird Population Estimates – Fourth Edition. Wetlands International Global Series, Wageningen, The Netherlands.

# The Russian waterbird migration atlas: temporal variation in migration routes

*Inna N. Dobrynina & Sergei P. Kharitonov[1]*

[1]*Bird Ringing Centre of Russia, Leninskiy prospect, 86-310, 119313, Moscow, Russia. (email: ring@bird.msk.ru)*

Dobrynina, I.N. & Kharitonov, S.P. 2006. The Russian waterbird migration atlas: temporal variation in migration routes. *Waterbirds around the world.* Eds. G.C. Boere, C.A. Galbraith & D.A. Stroud. The Stationery Office, Edinburgh, UK. pp. 582-589.

## ABSTRACT

Ringing recovery data from the database of the Bird Ringing Centre of Russia were used for this analysis, which examines variation in the mean distance of ringing recoveries for various waterbirds over ten-year periods. Many species of waterbirds which inhabit inland wetlands show a consistent trend of increasing migration distance throughout the last century. Several species of ducks demonstrate a more complicated pattern, with the mean distance of recoveries first decreasing and then increasing, although the overall trend is for the migration distance to increase over the past century. In seaducks, the migration distance has remained relatively constant throughout the period under review. A comparable analysis for some passerines reveals that in some groups (e.g. thrushes) there has been a progressive increase in the length of the migration, while in others (e.g. finches), the mean distance of ringing recoveries has decreased. Some waterbirds undertake "non-migratory" movements in autumn, continuing to move in the direction of their spring migration after breeding or moulting. We propose that bird migration atlases should reflect the changes that have occurred in migration routes throughout the entire study period of bird migration. Non-migratory movements of birds in autumn can be regular, and should also be reflected in migration atlases.

## INTRODUCTION

By March of 2004, the Bird Ringing Centre of Russia held details of almost 200 000 recoveries of ringed birds, of which 78 000 (for 380 species and subspecies) were computerized. For 67 species (including 54 waterbirds), the full set of recoveries was already in the computer database. The majority of recoveries are of birds found since 1926. These recoveries cover a huge territory incorporating the breeding areas and long, and sometimes quite sophisticated, migration routes (Fig. 1). In bird migration atlases, it is usual to present the recoveries of ringed birds in a geographical way (Brewer *et al.* 2000, Wernham *et al.* 2002, Bakken *et al.* 2003). Here, we would like to stress that in such atlases it is useful to consider not only geographical areas, but also different time periods, which should be presented separately. The main aim of this paper is to demonstrate the importance of this statement.

### Materials and methods

This paper was written on the basis of ringing recovery data taken from the database of the Bird Ringing Centre of Russia. The main parameter of the recoveries under analysis was the mean distance between the ringing location and recovery location. All available recoveries were used to calculate the average length of movement during a particular time period, and no distinction was made between birds ringed in Russia and recovered abroad and those ringed abroad and recovered in Russia.

We examined changes in the mean recovery distance for various waterbirds since 1926. In most cases, we used ten-year periods (decades) as the standard time period for sampling. In the following account, we discuss species on the basis of the fluctuations in the mean distance of their migration during the study period, rather than in systematic order.

For plotting the recoveries, we used the MapInfo-5.5 programme with an additional tool written by Sergei Kharitonov in Map Basic language and installed into the body of the MapInfo

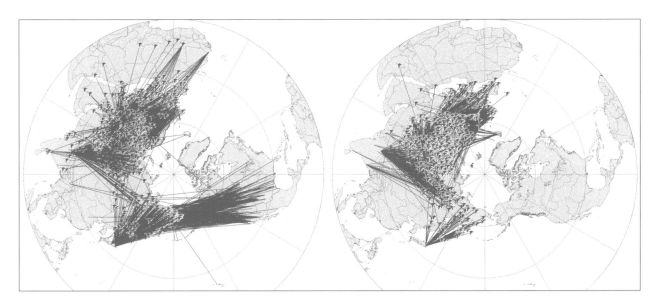

Fig. 1. Ringing recoveries of Northern Pintail *Anas acuta* (left map; 6 775 recoveries) and Eurasian Wigeon *Anas penelope* (right map; 2 829 recoveries) in the database of the Bird Ringing Centre of Russia. Duck symbols indicate the recovery locations.

**Table 1.** Migration distances of the Eurasian Woodcock *Scolopax rusticola* in the four decades from 1951 to 1990.

| Decade | Mean distance of recoveries (km) | Number of recoveries | Significance of change between decades | Significance of change since 1951-1960 |
|---|---|---|---|---|
| 1951-1960 | 1 519.5 | 23 | | |
| 1961-1970 | 1 553.9 | 18 | P=0.93 | P=0.93 |
| 1971-1980 | 1 927.8 | 42 | P=0.08 | P=0.046 |
| 1981-1990 | 2 300.9 | 67 | P=0.008 | P<0.0001 |

**Table 2.** Mean distance of ringing recoveries of the Eurasian Woodcock *Scolopax rusticola* according to direction of flight.

| | Mean distance of recovery for north-south flights (bearing 315°-45° and 135°-225°) | | | Mean distance of recovery for east-west flights (bearing 45°-135° and 225°-315°) | | |
|---|---|---|---|---|---|---|
| Decade | Distance (km) | Number of recoveries | Significance of change from 1951-1960 | Distance (km) | Number of recoveries | Significance of change from 1951-1960 |
| 1951-1960 | 1 458.9 | 12 | | 1 585.5 | 11 | |
| 1961-1970 | 1 392.3 | 4 | P=0.59 | 1 600.0 | 14 | P=0.84 |
| 1971-1980 | 1 742.9 | 13 | P=0.37 | 2 040.9 | 29 | P=0.15 |
| 1981-1990 | 2 301.3 | 7 | P=0.013 | 2 300.8 | 60 | P=0.0015 |

programme. This tool allows lines to be drawn on a map between ringing locations and recovery locations. As a test for statistical differences, we used the Mann-Whitney test (Fowler & Cohen 1995).

## RESULTS

### Variations in the recovery distances of waterbirds

The "classic" example of a species of waterbird making a major change in its migration route in recent decades is the Red-breasted Goose *Branta ruficollis*. Up until the late 1970s, this species wintered in the south-western corner of the Caspian Sea. The birds then suddenly changed their wintering grounds to the north-eastern corner of the Black Sea, mostly around Shabla and Durankulak lakes in Bulgaria (see review in Syroechkovski 1995). In the late 1980s, flocks of wintering Red-breasted Geese re-appeared in the Caspian region (Syroechkovski 1995).

Analysis of the average recovery distances in different groups of waterbirds during the eight decades from 1920 to 2000 has

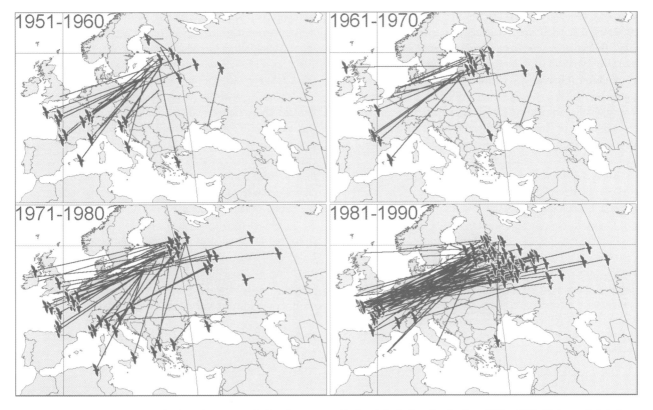

**Fig. 2.** Recoveries of Eurasian Woodcock *Scolopax rusticola* ringed or recovered in Russia in the four decades from 1951 to 1990. Wader symbols indicate the recovery locations.

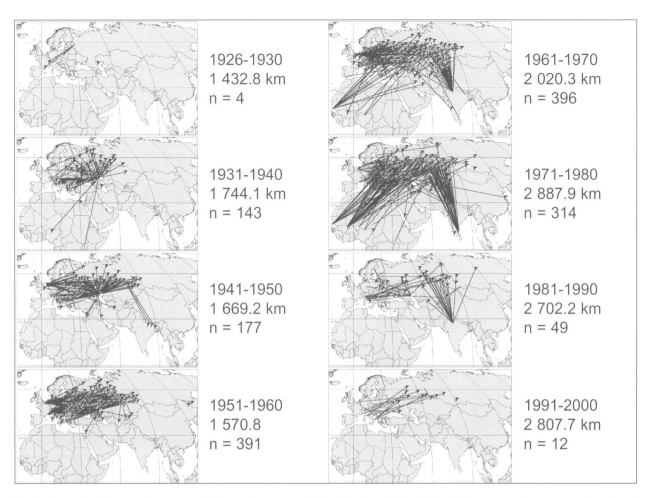

**Fig. 3.** Recoveries of Garganey *Anas querquedula* ringed or recovered in Russia by decade since 1926, with the average distance and total number of recoveries in each decade. Duck symbols indicate the recovery locations.

revealed interesting patterns of variation in the length of the migration. Several species that inhabit freshwater wetlands (Common Teal *Anas crecca*, Garganey *A. querquedula*, Common Snipe *Gallinago gallinago* and Common Coot *Fulica atra*), wet meadows (Northern Lapwing *Vanellus vanellus*) and moist places in the forest (Eurasian Woodcock *Scolopax rusticola*) show a consistent increase in the length of their migration route throughout the last century. This steady increase in the length of the migration is especially well pronounced in the Eurasian Woodcock (Fig. 2, Table 1). In this species, the increase is apparent both in terms of latitude and longitude (Table 2).

Another good example of an increase in length of migration is shown by the ringing recoveries of Garganey (Fig. 3). This increase is apparent even if we compare only those decades when most of the recoveries were in Europe (e.g. 1951-60 and 1991-2000; P=0.002). A third example is provided by the Common Coot (Fig. 4). It can be seen from Fig. 4 that there has been a considerable increase in the recovery distances of birds ringed in India, with the recoveries shifting farther and farther north in each successive decade as the birds perform longer and longer journeys (differences are significant: between 1961-1970 and 1971-1980, P=0.0013; between 1971-1980 and 1981-1990, P=0.0002).

Several species of dabbling ducks (Northern Pintail *Anas acuta*, Mallard *A. platyrhynchos* and Northern Shoveler *A. clypeata*) and diving ducks (Common Pochard *Aythya ferina* and Tufted Duck *A. fuligula*) demonstrate a more complicated

pattern. The mean recovery distance first decreases, and then increases (Fig. 5). In the case of the Northern Pintail (Fig. 6), the mean recovery distance of birds ringed in the vast moulting area in the Volga Delta (Astrakhan Nature Reserve) decreased from 1 652.5 km in 1927-1940 (N=156) to 1 372.4 km in 1941-1980 (N=1 215; P=0.0015).

A similar pattern of change has been observed in Black-throated Diver *Gavia arctica*. Eurasian Wigeon *Anas penelope* shows an almost constant mean recovery distance until the 1970s, then an increase; the Gadwall *A. strepera* and Caspian Tern *Sterna caspia* show a more or less constant distance until the 1950s, and then a sharp increase, while Common Goldeneye *Bucephala clangula* (a lake duck) shows a steady increase throughout.

In two seaducks, Common Eider *Somateria mollissima* and Steller's Eider *Polysticta stelleri*, the mean recovery distance has fluctuated in recent decades, although in the case of Steller's Eider, there has probably been some increase in the length of the migration in recent years (Table 3). Unlike most ducks, the Greylag Goose *Anser anser* shows a more or less constant mean recovery distance throughout the twentieth century.

**Variations in the recovery distances of land-birds**

For comparison, we carried out similar analyses for several species of passerines that are not associated with wetlands (Fig. 7). Song Thrush *Turdus philomelos* has shown almost no increase in mean recovery distance since the 1950s (1 899.3 km in 1951-1960, N=117; 2 028 km in 1991-2000, N=66; P=0.66).

**Table 3.** Migration distances of the Common Eider *Somateria mollissima* and Steller's Eider *Polysticta stelleri* in the five decades from 1951 to 2000.

| Decade | Common Eider | | | Steller's Eider | | |
|---|---|---|---|---|---|---|
| | Mean distance of recoveries (km) | Number of recoveries | Significance of change from 1951-1960 | Mean distance of recoveries (km) | Number of recoveries | Significance of change from 1961-1970 |
| 1951-1960 | 780.9 | 6 | | | | |
| 1961-1970 | 498.1 | 19 | P=0.36 | 2 516.7 | 43 | |
| 1971-1980 | 419.9 | 27 | P=0.08 | 3 078.4 | 84 | P=0.001 |
| 1981-1990 | 629.7 | 4 | P=0.46 | 2 718.7 | 17 | P=0.5 |
| 1991-2000 | | | | 3 335.6 | 308 | P<0.0001 |

In Redwing *T. iliacus* and Fieldfare *T. pilaris*, there has been a significant increase in the mean recovery distance since the 1950s: in the Redwing, from 1 899.3 km in 1951-1960 (N=61) to 2 886.3 km in 1991-2000 (N=38, P=0.0084); and in the Fieldfare, from 1 946.9 km in 1951-1960 (N=103) to 2 860.2 km in 1991-2000 (N=26, P=0.007). In the Brambling *Fringilla montifringilla*, the recovery distance showed a decreasing trend from the 1950s until the 1980s (1 771.4 km in 1951-1960, N=110; 1 305.4 km in 1981-1990, N=48; P=0.0005), and then a probable increase in the 1990s (1 305.4 km in 1981-1990, N=48; 1 501.8 km in 1991-2000, N=25; P=0.37). The Chaffinch *F. coelebs* shows a similar pattern, but with the decrease continuing in the 1990s (1 578.4 km in 1951-1960, N=360; 1 016.6 km in 1991-2000, N=101; P<0.0001).

## "Non-migratory" movements

Some waterbirds undertake lengthy movements in addition to their normal spring and autumn migrations. These movements usually take place after the breeding season and during the protracted autumn migration season. After the breeding season has ended, or in the event of breeding failure, some waterbirds use the time before the onset of the autumn migration to move elsewhere. In some species, the pattern of these post-breeding movements can be quite regular. These "non-migratory" movements have an interesting peculiarity in that the birds follow the spring migration routes. While the normal direction of the autumn migration in eastern Europe and Western Siberia is to the south, south-west or west, the non-migratory movements in autumn are to the north, north-east or east.

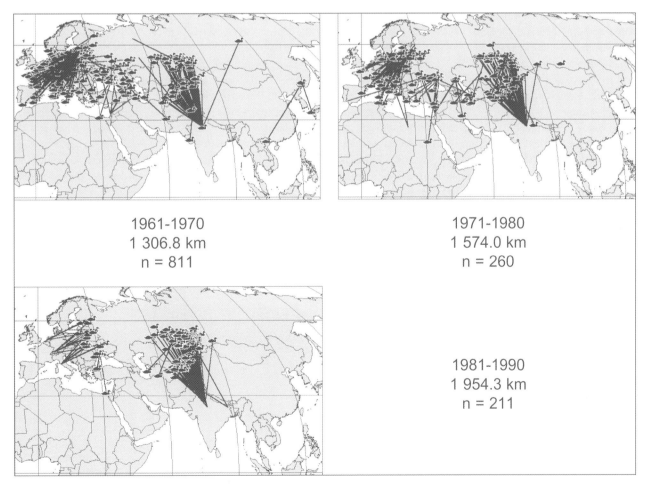

1961-1970
1 306.8 km
n = 811

1971-1980
1 574.0 km
n = 260

1981-1990
1 954.3 km
n = 211

**Fig. 4.** Recoveries of Common Coot *Fulica atra* ringed or recovered in Russia in the three decades from 1961 to 1990, with the average distance and total number of recoveries in each decade. Duck symbols indicate the recovery locations.

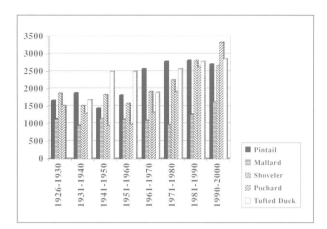

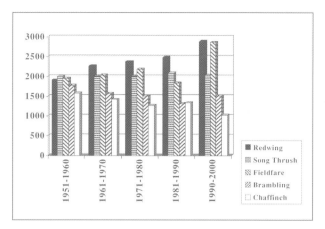

**Fig. 5.** Mean distances of ringing recoveries for three dabbling ducks (Northern Pintail *Anas acuta*, Mallard *A. platyrhynchos* and Northern Shoveler *A. clypeata*) and two diving ducks (Common Pochard *Aythya ferina* and Tufted Duck *A. fuligula*) ringed or recovered in Russia by decade since 1926. The Y-axis gives the mean distance of recovery in km.

**Fig. 7.** Mean distances of ringing recoveries of three thrushes (Redwing *Turdus iliacus*, Song Thrush *T. philomelos* and Fieldfare *T. pilaris*) and two finches (Brambling *Fringilla montifringilla* and Chaffinch *F. coelebs*) ringed or recovered in Russia by decade since 1950. The Y-axis gives the mean distance of recovery in km.

The movements of Black-headed Gulls *Larus ridibundus* in a non-migratory direction are well known as a result of studies by Jānis Vīksne in the Baltic States (Vīksne 1968). Black-headed Gulls ringed in the Baltic States have been recovered up to 506 km away in a non-migratory direction. Such movements also take place in central Russia, where movements of up to 370 km have been recorded (Fig. 8). Similar movements have been found in Gadwall which, after finishing the moult, may move as far as 300 km in a non-migratory direction.

The database of the Bird Ringing Centre of Russia contains three recoveries of Common Snipe which made non-migratory movements, travelling 984, 986 and 2 445 km, respectively (Fig. 9). In addition to these direct recoveries, a comparison of ringing and recovery dates in different parts of Europe indicates that, during the autumn migration, Common Snipe from eastern and middle Europe initially move far to the east or north-east (Kharitonov 1998). Later in the year, these birds turn back and migrate in the "normal" autumn direction, i.e. to the west and south-west. It seems that a considerable part of the European population of Common Snipe first moves in a north-easterly direction in autumn (Kharitonov 1998). Further support for these findings is provided by additional data from Paulauskas & Svazas (2002).

## DISCUSSION

In this study, we have found several interesting changes in the migration routes of waterbirds. However, studies based on the recoveries of ringed birds are always open to the question: to what extent do the ringing recovery data reflect the real movements of birds, and to what extent are they biased by regional and temporal differences in the reporting rate by humans. In order to prove our findings, we must take into account a variety of factors that could bias the results.

The most common objection to ringing recovery data is that the pattern of recoveries reflects the distribution of hunters, rather than the distribution of the birds. One way to test this is to compare the distribution of the recoveries of two closely related species in the same area. The database of the Bird Ringing Centre of Russia provides a good possibility for such a comparison because we can perform the comparison in the very sparsely populated areas of central and eastern Siberia. If we plot the recoveries of Northern Pintail on a map, we can see an obvious gap between the Japanese and North American population and the European, African, Central Asian and Indian populations (Fig. 1). It could be argued that this gap is not real, and is caused by the low numbers of hunters in central Siberia. However, if we plot all recoveries of Eurasian Wigeon, we can see many recov-

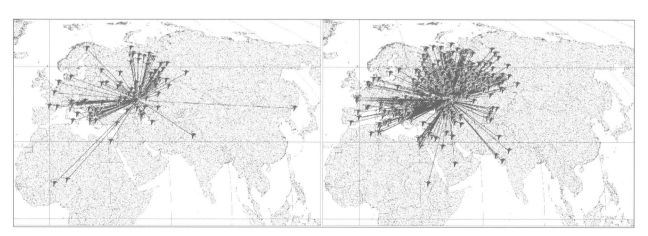

**Fig. 6.** Recoveries of Northern Pintail *Anas acuta* ringed in the moulting area in the Volga Delta in 1927-1940 (left map) and 1941-1980 (right map). Duck symbols indicate the recovery locations.

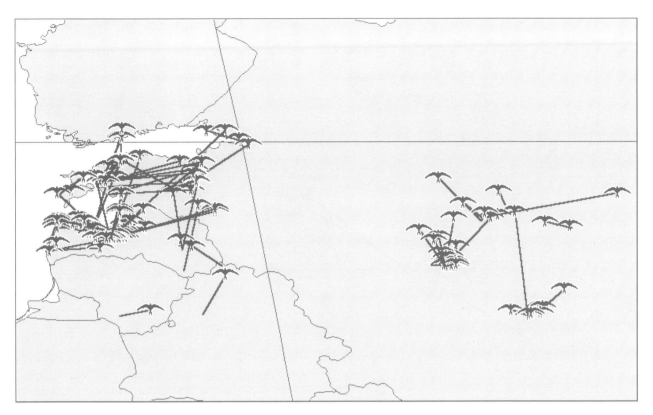

Fig. 8. Autumn movements of Black-headed Gulls *Larus ridibundus* in a northerly or easterly direction in the Baltic States and central Russia. Gull symbols indicate the recovery locations.

eries exactly from this "gap". Therefore, the gap for Northern Pintail is real, and not biased by the distribution of hunters. Similarly, the recoveries of Eurasian Wigeon show a gap between the birds wintering in Japan and all other wintering populations. This gap is also real, because there are many recoveries of Northern Pintail within it (Fig. 1).

The second common objection to ringing recovery data is that the distribution of hunters might change through time. To investigate this possibility, we looked more closely at the well pronounced and highly significant increase in the length of the migration route of the Eurasian Woodcock from 1971-1980 to 1981-1990. To check for a possible change in the distribution of hunters, we analysed the distances over which letters containing bird rings had been posted to reach the Ringing Centre, i.e. we analysed the distance from Moscow to the recovery location for all species of birds in 1971-1980 (10 587 letters from the former USSR) and 1981-1990 (13 444 letters from the former USSR). The average distance for letters in these two decades decreased significantly from 2 080.5 km in 1971-1980 to 1 743 km in 1981-1990 (P<0.0001). This situation is quite understandable, given that the economic situation was deteriorating in the 1980s, postage costs were increasing, and people were sending fewer letters from remote areas. However, in spite of the decline in numbers of letters from remote areas, the mean recovery distance of the Eurasian Woodcock clearly increased. We therefore conclude that the increase in length of the migration route is real, and is not caused by a change in the distribution of hunters or their reporting habits.

A third possible problem might arise as a result of the establishment of new bird ringing locations in successive decades. Such a problem might affect the recoveries of Garganey (Fig. 3), since many new ringing locations appeared in Africa during the study period. However, for this species, we made a special comparison restricted to recoveries within Europe and only during the two decades 1951-60 and 1991-2000, when the European ringing locations were about the same (see above).

As regards specific ringing locations, we should stress that the trend in length of migration route observed at a particular ringing location might be the opposite of that observed in the population as a whole. A good example of this is provided by the Northern Pintail. Although the average recovery distance of Northern Pintail from the important ringing site in the Volga Delta decreased significantly between 1927-1940 and 1941-1980 (see above), the overall trend in this species was one of increase, with the mean recovery distance increasing from 1 834.9 km in 1926-1940 (N=263) to 2 197.7 km in 1941-1980 (N=5 702; P<0.0001).

On the basis of these analyses, we conclude that there was a real increase in the length of the migration routes of many waterbirds of freshwater habitats throughout the last century. A probable reason for this tendency for migration routes to increase in length in each successive decade is the progressive shrinkage of wetlands and other moist areas in Europe and northern Asia. It seems that many areas are getting drier. Almost no changes were found in the migrations of seaducks, probably because these birds use marine habitats rather than inland water-bodies, and are therefore unaffected by the loss of wetland habitat.

It is not clear why, in several duck species, the length of the migration route first decreased and then increased. However, the overall trend in these species is increasing, because the initial decrease in the length of the migration route was less than the subsequent increase.

Global warming might be affecting land-birds such as the Chaffinch and Brambling. In these two species, the trend is the opposite of that for many waterbirds, with the length of the migration route decreasing during the last century. These

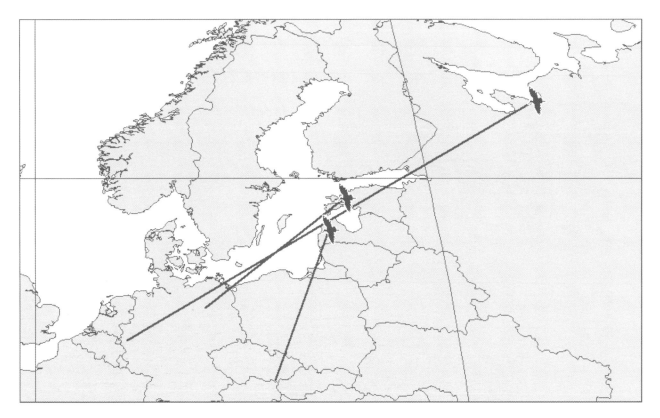

Fig. 9. Autumn movements of Common Snipe *Gallinago gallinago* in a northerly or easterly direction. Wader symbols indicate the recovery locations.

species, and probably many other passerines, are evidently spending the winter closer to their breeding grounds.

This analysis has revealed that the migration patterns of birds can change significantly even during the relatively short period when bird ringing activities have been carried out. The causes of these changes are poorly understood, but could include climate change and related factors.

In some species, it appears that the breeding and/or moulting areas are not really the terminal points of the birds' spring migration. In autumn, some birds continue their "spring migration" after breeding or moulting. There is evidence that some Gadwall, before migrating to their wintering grounds, first visit their previous breeding sites (Kharitonov 2002).

## CONCLUSIONS

In waterbirds that inhabit freshwater wetlands, lakes or other inland water-bodies, the length of the migration routes has been progressively increasing during the last century. Birds which live in more stable water conditions (e.g. seaducks) do not demonstrate this gradual increase in their migration routes.

As a result of this analysis, we recommend that efforts be made to identify periods in which significant changes in the length of migration routes have occurred. The dynamics of migration routes should then be reflected in bird migration atlases in order to define the places where species should be protected. It would also be worthwhile in migration atlases to indicate the non-migratory movements of waterbirds in late summer and autumn, especially when this pattern of migration is characteristic of a population. This type of movement might be particularly important for rare and vulnerable species. As regards the widespread increase in lengths of migration routes during the twentieth century, here we simply try to draw atten-

tion to this interesting phenomenon. Further and more detailed studies are clearly required.

## ACKNOWLEDGEMENTS
We would like to thank all staff members of the Bird Ringing Centre of Russia who computerize the ringing recovery data. The work was performed with the support of a grant from the Russian Fund of Fundamental Investigations (Grant No. 01-04-48382).

## REFERENCES

**Bakken, V., Runde, O. & Tjørve, E.** 2003. Norsk ringmerkingsatlas. Vol. 1. Stavanger Museum, Stavanger.

**Brewer, D., Diamond, A., Woodsworth, E.J., Collins, B.T. & Dunn, E.H.** 2000. Canadian Atlas of Bird Banding. Vol.1: Doves, Cuckoos, and Hummingbirds through Passerines, 1921-1995. Canadian Wildlife Service Special Publication: 1-396.

**Fowler, J. & Cohen, L.** 1995. Statistics for Ornithologists. Second edition. BTO Guide 22. British Trust for Ornithology, Thetford.

**Kharitonov, S.P.** 1998. Migration and some population parameters for Common Snipes (*Gallinago gallinago*) in Eastern Europe and North Asia. In: Proceedings of the Programme: Study of the Status and Trends of Migratory Bird Populations in Russia. Second issue. Moscow: 136-155.

**Kharitonov, S.P.** 2002. Migration and some population parameters of the Gadwall *Anas strepera* in Europe and North Asia. In: Proceedings of the Programme: Study of the Status and Trends of Migratory Bird Populations in Russia. Fourth issue. World & Family Publishing House, Sankt-Petersburg: 123-142.

**Paulauskas, A. & Svazas, S.** 2002. Genetic study of Western Palearctic populations of the Common Snipe *Gallinago gallinago*. Snipes of the Eastern Baltic region and Belarus. OMPO Special Publication, OMPO Vilnius, Vilnius: 82-95.

**Syroechkovski, E.E., Jr.** 1995. Changes in distribution and numbers of Red-breasted Goose in 1980-90s. Bulletin of Geese Study Group of Eastern Europe and Northern Asia No. 1: 89-102. Moscow.

**Vīksne, J.A.** 1968. The role of the post-nesting dispersal of the Black-headed Gull (*Larus ridibundus*) for its breeding dispersion (on the east Baltic population data). Ecology of waterfowl of Latvia. Ornithological Study 5: 167-206. Riga.

**Wernham, C., Toms, M., Marchant, J., Clark, J., Siriwardena, G. & Ballie, S.** (eds). 2002. The Migration Atlas: movements of the birds of Britain and Ireland. T. & A.D. Poyser, London.

Ringing recoveries show that movements of Eurasian Coots *Fulica atra* ringed in India have been increasing in length. Birds are now migrating further north into Russia and the central Asian Republics, compared to the 1950s. Photo: Paul Marshall.

Recoveries of Russian ringed Black-headed Gulls *Larus ridibundus* show a non-directional pattern of movements rather than directional migration. Photo: Paul Marshall.

# Logistics of a migration atlas project for a small ringing scheme: the waterbird migration atlas of southern Africa

*H. Dieter Oschadleus*

*Avian Demography Unit, Department of Statistical Sciences, University of Cape Town, Rondebosch, 7701, South Africa. (email: dieter@adu.uct.ac.za)*

Oschadleus, H.D. 2006. Logistics of a migration atlas project for a small ringing scheme: the waterbird migration atlas of southern Africa. *Waterbirds around the world.* Eds. G.C. Boere, C.A. Galbraith & D.A. Stroud. The Stationery Office, Edinburgh, UK. pp. 590-594.

## ABSTRACT

By 1999, there were 11 656 recoveries of waterbirds recorded in the database of the South African Bird Ringing Unit (SAFRING). Producing a review atlas of ringing recoveries within a relatively small ringing scheme entailed several challenges. One of these was a time constraint: less than a year was available for completion of the atlas in order to meet the publication deadline of two international meetings. The biggest challenge related to data systems and a range of data integrity issues. In the previous year, SAFRING had converted all recovery data from mainframe multi-files to a consistent database, but was still fine-tuning the new database system. Other problems that were overcome included limited numbers of staff (volunteers were recruited to help with data checking), finances and the analysis and writing of the species texts.

## INTRODUCTION

There is a need to summarize and review the recoveries obtained from bird ringing to make the information widely available, especially information on survival rates and migration routes. Several ringing schemes around the world have begun to produce "migration atlases" which typically analyse bird ringing data by species, e.g. the BTO migration atlas for Britain and Ireland (Wernham *et al.* 2002), the Norwegian atlas (Bakken *et al.* 2003) and the Swedish atlas (Fransson & Pettersson 2001). The South African Bird Ringing Unit (SAFRING) produced its first review of ringing recoveries for raptors and owls (Oatley *et al.* 1998). This was followed by a similar review for waterbirds (Underhill *et al.* 1999), which covered about seven times as many recoveries as the review for raptors and owls, and presented much new information. Producing this review atlas within a relatively small ringing scheme posed several challenges. These challenges and how they were overcome are discussed in this paper.

## METHODS

By 1999, there were details of 11 656 recoveries of 101 species of waterbirds in the SAFRING database. These data were analysed and published for the first time in "A Review of Ring Recoveries of Waterbirds in Southern Africa" (Underhill *et al.* 1999). This review is limited to species of waterbirds occurring in southern Africa. Only species in the families listed as waterbirds by Rose & Scott (1997) were considered. These include pelicans, cormorants, herons, storks, ibises, flamingos, ducks, cranes, waders, gulls and terns. The review considered only those species for which there was at least one ringing recovery available in the SAFRING database. For each species, the atlas provides text, tables with details of the most significant and interesting recoveries, and maps and other graphics. As an

example, the information provided for the Sanderling *Calidris alba* is reproduced in Figs. 1, 2 and 3.

## RESULTS

### Challenge 1: Funds

The cost of running the project was covered by SAFRING. Each recovery was printed on one page, but to save costs, this paper was later re-used on the second side, and then recycled. Six paid student volunteers were trained to check these pages against the original ringing schedules and recovery letters. The analyses and the writing of species texts were undertaken by four authors on an unpaid basis. The publication costs were sponsored.

### Challenge 2: Data system and data integrity

Recovery data had previously been entered onto a mainframe computer. At one point in time, a substantial number of correct records had been deleted and the incorrect records intended for deletion had survived. A structured database (Paradox™) was designed for a PC computer. The mainframe data were collated, checked for integrity, and added to the database. Additional problems with the early ringing data, i.e. for the period 1948-1975, were as follows:-

(a) different numerical age codes were used at different stages by different ringers. The original SAFRING age codes were modified, with currently-used codes officially adopted on 1 October 1974 (Elliott 1974). It is, however, unclear whether all ringers made the change to the new age codes exactly on that date. The lesson to be learned is that if codes are changed, the new codes should be distinguishable from the old ones;

(b) data were submitted on hand-written cards, not on standardized forms, and as a result, some data (e.g. age) were sometimes omitted;

(c) no identification numbers were allocated to ringers;

(d) some records were lost when the scheme was moved to a new location; and

(e) the nearest town was entered as the ringing site, rather than the geographical co-ordinates of the site.

The data are also affected by scheme issues (as described in Oatley *et al.* 1998):-

(a) the return address on rings was changed;

(b) recoveries of foreign birds are not all received by SAFRING; and

(c) a large body of recapture and resighting data is held by ringers.

### Challenge 3: Analysis and species texts

For each species, standard maps and tables of all the recovery records were produced to aid write-ups by species experts.

**Table 64.** *Recoveries of Sanderling.*

| No. | Ring | Ring date | Age | | Ringing place | Finding date | | Finding place | Elapsed | Dist | Code |
|---|---|---|---|---|---|---|---|---|---|---|---|
| 1 | 241005 | 23.09.71 | Ad | 3346 2540 | Coega, EC | 03.01.77 | 2244 1431 | Swakopmund, Na | 5y 3m | 2028 | 751 |
| 2 | 246091 | 22.04.72 | Ad | 3305 1802 | Langebaan Lagoon, WC | 13.06.72 | 7325N 8038 | Krasnojarsk, Ru | 1m 22d | 12715 | 210 |
| 3 | 282579 | 03.05.75 | Ad | 3305 1802 | Langebaan Lagoon | 31.05.77 | 4253N 4738 | Dagestan, Az | 2y 1m | 8964 | 210 |
| 4 | 282592 | 04.10.75 | Ad | 3305 1802 | Langebaan Lagoon | 29.06.79 | 7329N 8046 | Dikson, Ru | 3y 9m | 12722 | 104 |
| 5 | 286530 | 01.03.78 | Ad | 3408 1819 | Kommetjie, WC | 24.02.84 | 4712N 3829 | Natalyvks, Ru | 6y 0m | 9261 | 210 |
| 6 | 292623 | 22.03.75 | 1Y | 3311 1805 | Langebaan Lagoon | 25.07.77 | 5450N 1038 | Ristinge, Dk | 2y 4m | 9808 | 100 |
| 7 | 868713 | 26.05.97 | Ad | 6403N 2242W | Sangerdi, Is | 19.03.99 | 2259 1427 | Walvis Bay, Na | 1y 10m | 10194 | 761 |
| 8 | B00195 | 13.09.91 | Ad | 0456N 0221W | Esiama, Gh | 01.05.92 | 2226 1428 | Wlotzkasbaken, Na | 7m 18d | 3549 | 390 |
| 9 | BB10731 | 22.03.75 | Ad | 3305 1802 | Langebaan Lagoon | 11.08.79 | 4705N 3810 | Donetsk, Ua | 4y 4m | 9134 | 104 |
| 10 | BB11070 | 28.11.75 | U | 3142 1811 | Olifants R, WC | 03.01.77 | 2239 1439 | Swakopmund, Na | 1y 1m | 1065 | 761 |
| 11 | BB12755 | 08.02.75 | U | 3142 1811 | Olifants R | 22.05.75 | 3553N 1434 | Malta, Mt | 3m 12d | 7521 | 210 |
| 12 | BB12884 | 09.02.75 | U | 3142 1811 | Olifants R | 14.05.77 | 4343N 1029 | Pisa, It | 2y 3m | 8419 | 759 |
| 13 | BB21821 | 16.04.78 | Ad | 3306 1802 | Langebaan Lagoon | 15.12.79 | 3507N 2612 | Crete, Gr | 1y 8m | 7629 | 210 |
| 14 | BB44099 | 17.05.69 | Ad | 5235N 0028 | The Wash, Uk | 13.02.77 | 3305 1802 | Langebaan Lagoon | 7y 9m | 9705 | 759 |
| 15 | BB77266 | 11.03.88 | Ad | 3408 1819 | Kommetjie | 02.07.90 | 7605N 9838 | L Taimyra, Ru | 2y 4m | 13420 | 211 |
| 16 | SA462968 | 12.05.73 | U | 3652N 1018 | Rades, Tn | 03.05.75 | 3305 1802 | Langebaan Lagoon | 2y 0m | 7812 | 759 |

**Table 65.** *Recoveries of Ruff.*

| No. | Ring | Ring date | Age | | Ringing place | Finding date | | Finding place | Elapsed | Dist | Code |
|---|---|---|---|---|---|---|---|---|---|---|---|
| 1 | 424399 | 22.09.73 | 2Y F | 2610 2822 | Benoni, GP | 08.12.73 | 3355 1828 | Cape Town, WC | 2m 16d | 1283 | 751 |
| 2 | 427857 | 29.11.75 | Ad F | 2617 2812 | Germiston, GP | 24.08.83 | 1625 3509 | Blantyre, Mw | 7y 9m | 1311 | 643 |
| 3 | 448610 | 16.02.83 | Ad F | 3355 1828 | Cape Town | 20.05.85 | 5057N 6924 | Atbasar, Kz | 2y3m | 10665 | 261 |
| 4 | 454890 | 22.12.84 | Ad F | 3333 2654 | Port Alfred, EC | 20.08.90 | 1758 3039 | Norton, Zw | 5y 8m | 1772 | 108 |
| 5 | 518202 | 07.02.71 | Ad M | 2618 2813 | Germiston | 15 04.71 | 3700N 4528 | Naghadeh, Ir | 2m 6d | 7263 | 210 |
| 6 | 522186 | 18.09.73 | Ad M | 2633 2536 | Barberspan NR, NW | 02.06.74 | 7035N 14821 | Chokudakh, Ru | 8m 14d | 13962 | 210 |
| 7 | 64305856 | 07.09.72 | Ad | 2633 2536 | Barberspan NR | 24.04.73 | 0149N 3119 | Butiaba, Ug | 7m 16d | 3212 | 751 |
| 8 | 64307524 | 22.08.70 | Ad | 2942 3105 | Umhlanga, KZ | 17.02.72 | 3342 1858 | Paarl, WC | 1y 6m | 1228 | 199 |
| 9 | 64308081 | 08.12.68 | 1Y F | 3336 2653 | Port Alfred, EC | 31.05.71 | 6651N 16400 | Magadan, Ru | 2y 6m | 15392 | 210 |
| 10 | 7013108 | 28.08.69 | Ad F | 5236N 1253 | Potsdam, De | 10.02.70 | 3150 1828 | Doringbaai, WC | 5m 14d | 9400 | 199 |
| 11 | B43746 | 27.09.83 | 1Y F | 2715N 7730 | Bharatpur, In | 02.01.84 | 3333 2654 | Port Alfred | 3m 4d | 8612 | 759 |
| 12 | D08080 | 09.09.93 | 1Y M | 1808 3007 | Chegutu, Zw | 18.05.94 | 6210N 13045 | Tyungyulyu, Ru | 8m 8d | 12328 | 255 |

**Table 66.** *Recoveries of African Snipe.*

| No. | Ring | Ring date | Age | | Ringing place | Finding date | | Finding place | Elapsed | Dist | Code |
|---|---|---|---|---|---|---|---|---|---|---|---|
| 1 | 523027 | 29.10.72 | Ad | 1746 3053 | Harare, Zw | 15.12.72 | 1740 3050 | Harare | 1m 17d | 12 | 210 |
| 2 | 59308717 | 15.12.63 | Ad | 1750 3120 | Harare | 22.01.68 | 1738 3102 | Harare | 4y 1m | 39 | 210 |
| 3 | 59308728 | 21.12.63 | Ad | 1750 3120 | Harare | 27.08.64 | 1757 3054 | Harare | 8m 7d | 48 | 210 |
| 4 | D01479 | 22.10.90 | Ad | 1752 3031 | Norton, Zw | 01.07.94 | 1745 3010 | Chegutu, Zw | 3y 8m | 39 | 274 |

**Table 67.** *Recoveries of Pied Avocet.*

| No. | Ring | Ring date | Age | | Ringing place | Finding date | | Finding place | Elapsed | Dist | Code |
|---|---|---|---|---|---|---|---|---|---|---|---|
| 1 | 525652 | 10.04.83 | Ad | 3312 1807 | Langebaan Lagoon, WC | 07.11.85 | 3117 2011 | Calvinia, NC | 2y 7m | 288 | 269 |
| 2 | 525658 | 19.01.85 | Ad | 3312 1807 | Langebaan Lagoon | 21.09.86 | 2930 2009 | Pofadder, NC | 11y 8m | 454 | 299 |
| 3 | 531111 | 18.10.75 | Ad | 2617 2812 | Germiston, GP | 04.11.79 | 2641 2755 | Vereeniging, GP | 4y 1m | 53 | 199 |
| 4 | 63408221 | 14.11.87 | Ad | 2004 2834 | Bulawayo, Zw | 04.12.87 | 2004 2836 | Bulawayo, Zw | 20d | 4 | 644 |
| 5 | 637050 | 12.03.99 | Ad | 2259 1427 | Walvis Bay, Na | 01.05.99 | 2300 1431 | Walvis Bay | 1m 20d | 7 | 653 |
| 6 | A06355 | 22.02.58 | U | 3404 1830 | Rondevlei NR, WC | 13.11.59 | 3235 2508 | Pearston, EC | 1y 9m | 638 | 199 |

**Table 68.** *Recoveries of Spotted Dikkop.*

| No. | Ring | Ring date | Age | | Ringing place | Finding date | | Finding place | Elapsed | Dist | Code |
|---|---|---|---|---|---|---|---|---|---|---|---|
| 1 | 520815 | 04.04.72 | Imm | 3357 2535 | Port Elizabeth, EC | 06.02.89 | 3400 2533 | Port Elizabeth | 16y 10m | 6 | 399 |
| 2 | 523963 | 02.12.72 | Ad | 3317 2631 | Grahamstown, EC | 23.06.83 | 3317 2631 | Grahamstown | 10y 7m | 0 | 644 |
| 3 | 612653 | 08.07.77 | Ad | 2559 2751 | Randburg, GP | 20.02.78 | 2609 2610 | Lichtenburg, NW | 7m 14d | 169 | 100 |
| 4 | 64506717 | 30.01.73 | Ad | 3358 1828 | Cape Town, WC | 06.02.84 | 3358 1828 | Cape Town | 11y 0m | 0 | 261 |
| 5 | 64506718 | 30.01.73 | Ad | 3358 1828 | Cape Town | 10.07.84 | 3357 1829 | Cape Town | 11y 5m | 2 | 199 |
| 6 | 64506736 | 25.02.73 | Ad | 3400 2534 | Port Elizabeth | 24.10.94 | 3358 2535 | Port Elizabeth | 21y 8m | 4 | 686 |
| 7 | 64506762 | 24.05.73 | Ad | 3318 2632 | Grahamstown | 08.06.84 | 3317 2631 | Grahamstown | 11y 0m | 2 | 261 |
| 8 | 665422 | 19.05.91 | U | 2539 2818 | Pretoria, GP | 25.07.91 | 2540 2755 | Hartbeespoort, NW | 2m 6d | 38 | 252 |

**Fig. 1.** Extracts from the *Review of Ring Recoveries of Waterbirds in Southern Africa* (Underhill *et al.* 1999), showing the table of interesting recoveries for the Sanderling *Calidris alba*.

Fig. 49. Ringing and recovery sites of Sanderling.

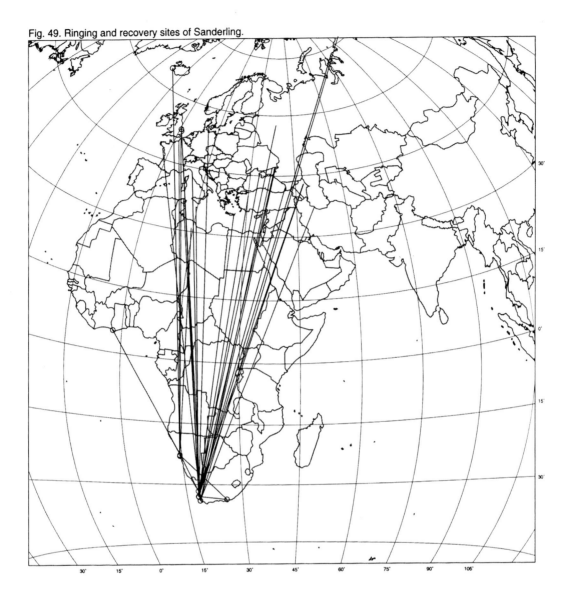

# 281 Sanderling

*Calidris alba*

The Sanderling has a fragmented breeding distribution in the northernmost zone of the tundra; it breeds most extensively in northeastern Canada and Greenland with a series of isolated populations from the Taimyr Peninsula eastwards to Yakutia, Russia. It migrates to most of the world's coastlines between *c.* 60° N and the southern limits of South America, Africa and Australia. In southern Africa it is almost exclusively coastal. The timing of scattered inland records, which peak in September to November (Penry 1994 for Botswana; Tree 1999b for Zimbabwe), suggests that these are mainly young birds on their first southward migration. Throughout its nonbreeding range, it occurs at sandy beaches, wave-cut platforms, and sheltered bays and inlets with a sandy or muddy substrate. The highest densities in southern Africa are found on the west coast, especially in central Namibia, the Northern Cape and the Western

Cape. The population visiting southern Africa has been estimated to be 78 000 in Namibia and South Africa, and at least 5000 in southern Mozambique (Summers *et al.* 1987b; HBW3 520; ASAB1 422–423; Parker 1999).

The provenance of birds reaching southern Africa is currently considered to be Siberia and all recoveries have been interpreted to fit this hypothesis, although it had long been suggested that Sanderlings breeding in Greenland also occur (e.g. Summers 1976; Summers *et al.* 1987a; Hockey & Douie 1995; ASAB1 422–423). Arrival starts in September and departure is in April and early May, with the eastern and southern coasts having been vacated by March. Considerable numbers of young nonbreeders remain through the southern winter .

2916 Sanderlings ringed have generated 32 recoveries of which 22 were made in Eurasia (Table 64, Fig. 49). In addition there are five recoveries on the southern African west coast of birds ringed in Iceland (7), Great Britain (two, e.g. 14), Tunisia (16) and Ghana (8). We interpret the pattern of the recoveries as follows. Eight birds reported between 6 August and 15

**Fig. 2.** Extracts from the *Review of Ring Recoveries of Waterbirds in Southern Africa* (Underhill *et al.* 1999), showing the Sanderling *Calidris alba* map.

October (median date 6 September) from the Black and Caspian Sea region were adults on southward migration from Siberia. Four recoveries in England, Denmark (6) and France (two) between 25 July and 9 August (median date 3 August) and the control in Namibia of a Sanderling ringed in Ghana on 15 September (8) were on southward migration from Greenland. In support of this interpretation, we point out that there have been no recoveries from the intervening Mediterranean basin area during southward migration and that the median date of passage in the west was 28 days earlier than in the east. Breeding in Greenland is completed earlier than breeding in Siberia.

During northward migration, nine recoveries can be assigned to three areas. (A) Four recoveries between 15 and 28 May in France, England (two) and Iceland. We believe that these birds were migrating to Greenland. (B) Four birds in the central Mediterranean basin between 1 and 22 May (Tunisia (16), Malta (two, e.g. 11) and Italy (12)). These are likely to have migrated along the west coast of Africa to the Gulf of Guinea and then crossed the Sahara Desert, and belong to the Siberian population. (C) One recovery from the Caspian Sea on 31 May (3). This bird is likely to have been returning to Siberia via the east coast of Africa. There are three recoveries close to or on the Siberian breeding grounds on dates between 13 June and 2 July: two birds were recovered near Dikson, western Taimyr, and one in northern Taimyr (2, 4 & 15).

If the above interpretation of the migration routes of Sanderlings is correct, it suggests that many Siberian birds undertake a loop migration southwards along the east coast of Africa and northwards along the west coast. There are controls of ringed birds and several other strands of evidence to support this. Three controls show 'westward' movement within southern Africa, but are not within the same year: two birds caught on the same night, 22–23 September 1971, near Port Elizabeth, were controlled in the Western Cape on 30 December 1973 and on the central Namibian coast on 3 January 1977 (1), respectively, and a bird ringed in the Western Cape on 28 November 1975 was controlled in the same 3 January 1997 catch in Namibia. High reporting rates for Sanderling occur from September to January in southern Mozambique (Parker 1999); numbers at two sites in Algoa Bay, Eastern Cape, were highest from December to February (Martin & Baird 1987; Spearpoint *et al.* 1989), and reporting rates along the coastline of the Northern Cape and Namibia were highest in March, and densities along the Skeleton Coast, Namibia, were high in March (Tarr & Tarr 1987; ASAB1 422–423). These observations also support the notion of loop migration.

Recoveries of Sanderlings ringed in the Western Cape, dated 15 December 1979 in Crete (13) and 24 February 1984 in the Black Sea (5), are far more likely to represent reporting dates (and not dates of death) than to be examples of birds that have changed their nonbreeding areas. They have been excluded from the argument above, but their dates suggest that they were delayed reports of recoveries made on southward migration a few months earlier.

The longest elapsed time between ringing and recovery was of a bird ringed as an adult in England on 17 May 1969 and controlled 7 y 8 m later in the Western Cape (14). One of the shortest elapsed times was of an adult ringed at Langebaan Lagoon on 22 April 1972, close to departure date, and recovered 52 days later, within the breeding range in Siberia, 12 715 km distant (2). The date of recovery, 13 June, is four days later than the mean arrival date in their arctic tundra breeding areas (Syroechkovski & Lappo 1994).

# 284 Ruff

## *Philomachus pugnax*

The Ruff has a large breeding range in Eurasia, from the Netherlands eastwards to Chukotka. It breeds from temperate latitudes to north of the Arctic Circle, with high breeding densities in forest tundra and in the shrub tundras subzone of Siberia. The entire population migrates in a southwesterly direction; the vast majority are in sub-Saharan Africa during the nonbreeding season. It occurs widely in the interior of southern Africa, with concentrations in the Okavango basin of Botswana, the central watershed of Mashonaland in Zimbabwe and the panveld region of the Free State, Gauteng and North West provinces of South Africa. Relatively few Ruff occur in coastal habitats. The provenance of Ruff visiting southern Africa appears to be eastern Asia (Tree 1985; HBW3 530–531; ASAB1 424–425).

The Ruff occurs in marshy, short-grassed habitat but also feeds in pastures and stubble. It favours mesotrophic and eutrophic wetland conditions. Arrival in southern Africa commences in early August and continues to November. It is highly nomadic, moving in response to rainfall events which create or drown suitable habitat. Males depart mainly during February; females depart from late March to early May. Winter records

Fig. 3. Extracts from the *Review of Ring Recoveries of Waterbirds in Southern Africa* (Underhill *et al.* 1999), showing the text for the Sanderling *Calidris alba*.

Les Underhill and Vincent Parker wrote the texts for the orders Pelecaniformes, Ciconiiformes, Phoenicopteriformes, Anseriformes and Gruiformes. Tony Tree wrote the texts for most of the Charadriiformes, and Les Underhill wrote the remainder.

About 10 recoveries per species were illustrated in the publication. The selection aimed to provide a representative set of interesting recoveries, showing distances moved and elapsed times between ringing and recovery. The authors attempted to choose both birds with the longest elapsed times between recoveries, and those that showed rapid movement over relatively long distances.

Where there was sufficient information to show movement, the recoveries for a species were illustrated on a map at the appropriate scale for the species. The authors were unable to provide uniform summary statistics of distances moved and elapsed times between ringing and recovery, although this had been one of their objectives. The reasons are described in detail in Underhill *et al.* (1999). For example, for species such as the White Stork and the Palearctic terns, the SAFRING database consists mainly of records of birds ringed on the breeding grounds and recovered in southern Africa; statistics based on distances and elapsed times are then based on a fraction of the total database for these species, and are not useful. The discussions of distances and elapsed times therefore tended to be qualitative, rather than quantitative.

The first paragraph of each species text provided a brief description of distribution, habitat and the current understanding of movements. Species for which there was little previously published information on movements and migrations had longer texts, as did species for which new insights into patterns of movement were presented.

### Challenge 4: Time constraint
The review was completed in less than a year, from the development of the concept to the dates of two important meetings in South Africa where the review was to be presented. These two meetings were the Sixth Conference of the Parties to the Convention on the Conservation of Migratory Species of Wild Animals, and the First Meeting of the Parties to the African-Eurasian Migratory Waterbird Agreement.

### DISCUSSION
A large body of data on bird movements exists at SAFRING, but until recently, these data have not been readily accessible. The upgraded computer system made it possible to analyse results for any species, and this led to a review of the results obtained from the ringing of raptors and owls (Oatley *et al.* 1998), followed by a similar review for waterbirds (Underhill *et al.* 1999). It was the intention of SAFRING to produce such reviews annually to cover other species groups, but this has not yet happened.

For some waterbird species, the accumulated information is meagre. For other species, the body of data now available is sufficient for more detailed analysis than was possible in the review by Underhill *et al.* (1999). For many species, the information presented had never previously been summarized and made available; for most species, additional information has accumulated since the last review of that species' movements was published. For a few species, notably Ruddy Turnstone *Arenaria interpres* and Sanderling, additional information obtained while the review was being undertaken has led to a radical reassessment of their migration systems.

From a statistical perspective, the production of this review was a substantial exercise in data mining (Adriaans & Zantinge 1996). A major component of data mining is data verification. Oatley *et al.* (1998) described some of the problems associated with the checking of old SAFRING records; these apply equally to the atlas analysis. As far as the limitations of the preserved records allowed, recoveries were individually checked against the original ringing and recovery information. There were tight time constraints on the production of the 1999 review, and it was inevitable that, in spite of the authors' best efforts, some errors remained. However, the quality of the SAFRING database of waterbird recoveries has been enormously improved through the production of this review; ongoing maintenance will occur as SAFRING becomes aware of errors. Underhill *et al.* (1999) regarded the database to be adequately clean so that researchers can use the data for individual species for further analyses.

### ACKNOWLEDGEMENTS
The main sponsors of SAFRING are the University of Cape Town, BirdLife South Africa and the Namibian Ministry of the Environment and Tourism. The National Zoological Gardens of South Africa, Pretoria, and especially Dr Ferdi Schoeman, act as a clearing house, and efficiently send the recovery information to SAFRING. Les Underhill and Marienne de Villiers provided helpful comments on an earlier draft. An anonymous reviewer helped produce a more concise paper.

Acknowledgements for the production of Underhill *et al.* (1999) are as follows. The publication costs were sponsored by the Department of the Royal Netherlands Embassy, Pretoria, and the South African Post Office. Giselle Murison, Simone Maharaj, Kevin McDonald, Tafadzwa Mhlanga, Lizzie Turner and Gill van Zijl assisted with the task of data cleaning. Rob Crawford (cormorants and terns), James Harrison, Phil Hockey (African Black Oystercatcher) and Terry Oatley commented on species accounts, and Sue Kuyper and Jane Underhill proof-read the text.

### REFERENCES
**Adriaans, P. & Zantinge, D.** 1996. Data mining. Addison-Wesley, Harlow.

**Bakken, V., Runde, O. & Tjorve, E.** 2003. Norwegian Bird Ringing Atlas. Volume 1. Divers – Auks. Stavanger Museum, Stavanger.

**Elliott, C.C.H.** 1974. NUBRA 1974. Safring News 3 (3): 13-15.

**Fransson, T. & Pettersson, J.** 2001. Swedish Bird Ringing Atlas. Volume 1. Divers – Raptors. Stockholm.

**Oatley, T.B., Oschadleus, H.D., Navarro, R.A. & Underhill, L.G.** 1998. Review of Ring Recoveries of Birds of Prey in Southern Africa: 1948-1998. Endangered Wildlife Trust, Johannesburg.

**Rose, P.M. & Scott, D.A.** 1997. Waterfowl Population Estimates – Second Edition. Wetlands International Publication 44. Wageningen, The Netherlands.

**Underhill, L.G., Tree, A.J., Oschadleus, H.D. & Parker, V.** 1999. Review of Ring Recoveries of Waterbirds in Southern Africa. Avian Demography Unit, University of Cape Town, Cape Town.

**Wernham, C.V., Toms, M.P., Marchant, J.H., Clark, J.A., Siriwardena, G.M. & Baillie, S.R.** (eds). 2002. The Migration Atlas: movements of the birds of Britain and Ireland. T. & A.D. Poyser, London.

# Progress on the 'The Atlas of the breeding waders of the Russian Arctic'

*E.G. Lappo[1], P.S. Tomkovich[2] & E.E. Syroechkovski Jr.[3]*

*[1]Institute of Ecology Geography, Russian Academy of Science, Staromonetny Pereulok, 29, 109017, Moscow, Russia.*
*[2]Zoological Museum of Moscow State University, Bolshaya Nikitskaya Street, 6, 125009, Moscow, Russia.*
*[3]Institute of Ecology and Evolution, Russian Academy of Science, Leninski Prospect, 33, 119071, Moscow, Russia.*

Lappo E.G., Tomkovich P.S. & Syroechkovski E.E. Jr. 2006. Progress on the 'The Atlas of the breeding waders of the Russian Arctic'. *Waterbirds around the world.* Eds. G.C. Boere, C.A. Galbraith & D.A. Stroud. The Stationery Office, Edinburgh, UK. pp. 595-596.

In total, 75 wader species have been recorded in the Russian part of the Arctic. This paper describes progress to date on a new atlas of breeding waders of the Russian Arctic.

The authors are currently working with colleagues on 'The Atlas of the breeding waders of the Russian Arctic', which will present a series of maps illustrating the distribution of breeding wader species, abundance and breeding range. The last set of detailed maps of breeding wader distribution in the former USSR was published over 40 years ago (Kozlova 1961, 1962), and the new Atlas is planned to be the first publication to present detailed information on waders in the Arctic or treeless northern areas of Russia as well as on other species that have recently expanded into the Arctic.

For the purposes of the Atlas, we consider the Russian Arctic as a super region north of the Arctic Circle (European Russia, West Siberia, Taimyr, northern Yakutia, Chukotka) as well as other adjacent tundra-like northern treeless areas (islands and the coastal White Sea, extensive north-boreal bogs of West Siberia, Magadan Region, Kamchatka, northern Sakhalin Island). Our team has been involved in collecting original data in the Russian Arctic since 1988: of 56 wader species that breed in the Russian Arctic, 51 were chosen for detailed analysis of their ranges.

Data entered into the Access database include the species, study sites with geographical coordinates, information on timing of observations, weather data, rodent/predator information, data on status of each species, breeding density in certain habitats, and a list of publications and data sources.

Data entry and editing are possible from within a single form, and there is a set of standardized queries and reports. Data have been entered from over 1 375 sources of information from 1 504 localities (Fig. 1), but data for nearly 22% of the sources, including those from museum collections, are not yet published. All data are currently being analysed.

The database is linked to ArcView software with the help of AccessLink, and this allows the production of maps of species distribution. All localities within the database can be reflected on the map, and in this way up to three breeding distribution maps for any wader species in the Russian Arctic can be produced. These maps can show breeding records (point coverage), breeding abundance (point coverage) and an extrapolated breeding range (polygon coverage). We are utilising a method of species breeding range extrapolation based on landscape and vegetation maps that has previously been used in Russia (Uspenski 1969, Brunov 1982, Lappo 1996, Tomkovich 1997), and is known as the method of "landscape extrapolation". This method is suited to the analysis of irregular and incomplete records of breeding and habitats. Preferences for breeding habitats are determined for each species, and the presence of birds in habitats within these landscapes is extrapolated to a group of

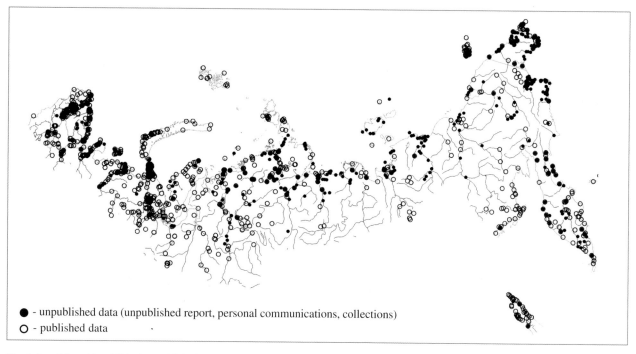

● - unpublished data (unpublished report, personal communications, collections)
○ - published data

**Fig. 1.** Localities with published, unpublished sources and data from collections on waders breeding records in the Russian Arctic.

similar landscapes. Margins of the breeding range are digitized according to a landscape network with some extra limits added in accordance with the currently known breeding distribution. GIS (Geographic Information Systems) provide the possibility of using the method of landscape extrapolation by providing landscapes, topography, rivers and lakes, soils, and natural zonation as different layers on available maps in various combinations.

Maps of the breeding distribution of each species will be accompanied in the Atlas by a detailed account describing general species distribution, population structure, migration links and some key characteristics of the species biology. An extended English summary will be provided.

The available preliminary data show that ranges and numbers of majority of the Arctic waders were apparently stable during the 20th century. Surprisingly few wader species had negative trends in at least some of their populations. The number of species with changes in range is larger than those with changes in number, probably due to the almost complete absence of monitoring of these processes in the Russian Arctic. The prevalence of positive over negative trends in wader distribution can be partly explained by subjective factors: it is much easier to record range extension than range shrinkage. The majority (n=13) of the species actively spreading north, especially to western European Russia, West Siberia and the Far East, are of southern origin.

## ACKNOWLEDGEMENTS

The Ministry of Agriculture, Nature Management and Fisheries of The Netherlands and the Royal Netherlands Embassy in Moscow are supporting the project financially. We are pleased to acknowledge many people including those who assisted in obtaining original data in the field, and especially those who kindly provided us with unpublished information - Dr. Yuri Gerasimov, Petr Glazov, Viktor Golovnyuk, Vladimir Morozov and Grigory Tertitski. Dr. Mikhail Stishov created the database and ArcView links. Dr. Christoph Zöckler and Dr. Symon Blyth of the World Conservation Monitoring Centre (Cambridge, UK) have kindly provided the background digitised maps.

## REFERENCES

**Brunov, V.V.** 1982 Methods of quick compilation of maps for bird ranges. Bulletin. of Moscow Society of Naturalists, Biology Section. 87(6): 66-73. In Russian.

**Kozlova, E.V.** 1961 & 1962. Charadriiformes. Suborder Limicolae. In: Fauna of the USSR. Birds. Vol.2, issue 1, parts 2 & 3. Moscow & Leningrad, USSR Academy of Sciences Publ., 503 & 433 pp. In Russian.

**Lappo, E.G.** 1996. Comparisons of breeding range structure for Dunlin *Calidris alpina* and Curlew Sandpiper *Calidris ferruginea*: conservative and nomadic tundra waders. Wader Study Group Bulletin. 80: 41-46.

**Tomkovich, P.S.** 1997. Breeding distribution, migrations and conservation status of the Great Knot *Calidris tenuirostris* in Russia. Emu 97(4): 265-282.

**Uspenski, S.M.** 1969. Die Strandläufer Eurasiens (Gattung *Calidris*). Die Neue Brehm-Bücherei 420. Wittenberg Lutherstadt, Ziemsen Verlag. 78 pp.

The extensive tundra of Taimyr Peninsula, northern Siberia, July 1993. These wetlands are the breeding grounds of several million waterbirds which migrate via a number of flyways to Europe, Africa, various parts of Asia and Australia. The region is an important study area for international teams, working closely with their Russian colleagues, researching waterbird ecology and migration. Photo: Gerard Boere.

Many indigenous peoples live throughout the Russian arctic for whom waterbirds are an important seasonal source of food.  Photo: Gerard Boere.

Patterned high-arctic tundra in the Lena Delta, Russia – the breeding habitat of huge numbers of migratory waterbirds.  Photo: Gerard Boere.

# Part 5.

## Integrated approaches to waterbird conservation

## Sections

# 5.1 Flyway management for species of conservation concern. Workshop Introduction

*Baz Hughes*
*The Wildfowl & Wetlands Trust, Slimbridge, Gloucestershire, GL2 7BT, UK.*

Hughes, B. 2006. Flyway management for species of conservation concern. Workshop Introduction. *Waterbirds around the world.* Eds. G.C. Boere, C.A. Galbraith & D.A. Stroud. The Stationery Office, Edinburgh, UK. pp. 600-601.

The Black-winged Pratincole *Glareola nordmanii* is globally threatened and the population is in rapid decline. An international species action plan has been developed under the auspices of the African-Eurasian Waterbirds Agreement. Photo: Sergey Dereliev.

For migratory species of conservation concern, common or complementary approaches to conservation at an international scale are necessary to ensure their survival throughout their annual cycle. The last decade has seen a number of initiatives to seek co-operation for single species of threatened migratory waterbirds at international or flyway scales. As summarised by the following papers; some of these initiatives have been more successful than others.

The workshop reviewed flyway management planning initiatives with the aim of deriving 'best practice', in particular those features of procedure or policy that lead to effective implementation and conservation delivery, and reached the following recommendations:

- **Plan Production**. Production of species action plans needs to involve all stakeholders, ideally through holding focused participatory workshops using an established structure.
- **Plan Structure**. Action plans need to be produced to an established format with clear, specific, measurable, attainable, and prioritised targets backed up by thorough annual work programmes and realistic funding plans. They should facilitate the monitoring and evaluation of subsequent implementation, linking threats, actions and measurable objectives.

- **Plan Endorsement/Affiliation**. Endorsement by relevant international institutions, conventions, agreements, conservation organisations and national governments is highly desirable, although this in itself does not determine success or failure.
- **Plan Implementation**. Action plan implementation needs to based on the twin premises of sound science and collaboration. International plans need to be transcribed into national action plans so as to ensure government commitment and support. Ideally, national action plans should be enshrined in national legislation (e.g. to implement national biodiversity action plans). In many cases, local community involvement is critical for successful implementation, and specific recommendations on this issue should be included in action plans. Greater priority needs to be afforded to communication, education and public awareness activities. Where relevant, building network capacity to enable sound implementation should be an integral factor in the action planning process. The success of long-term implementation may be enhanced if there is measurable short-term progress, demonstrating the success of plans to key stakeholders and funders at an early stage.
- **Plan Review & Update.** Plans need to include a predetermined process for monitoring and regular update in order to

learn from past successes and failures, i.e. an appropriate feedback mechanism. Most importantly, plans should be viewed as "living" rather than "static" documents incorporating an iterative monitoring and re-evaluation process to refresh priorities in order to react to inabilities to achieve the ideal agreed objectives. If the other issues identified in this series of recommendations can be addressed, the only (but totally defeating) reason for failure may be the lack of flexibility in an action plan to deal with evolving constraints.

- **Species Recovery Team.** The existence and enthusiasm of a highly motivated, multi-disciplinary Species Recovery Team, comprising key individuals and bodies that will be involved in plan implementation, is critical to successful implementation. A dynamic coordinator with the long-term commitment and organisational backing to drive the implementation process is essential. Recovery Team spirit needs to be maintained through regular communication between members, for example through team meetings and list servers. All Recovery Team members should be in agreement over the goal and priorities outlined in the action plan thus engendering a strong sense of plan ownership. Recovery Team members should be sensitive to cultural differences between Range States and of the effects of human and logistical capacity limitations on the timescale for plan implementation.

- **Plan Funding.** Existence of national or international funding instruments (e.g. EU-LIFE funding) increase the chance of successful implementation. However, Species Recovery Teams need to incorporate fund-raising expertise in order to make the most of these opportunities. Species Recovery Teams also need to exploit all possible 'marketing' opportunities.

- **NGO Involvement.** The wholehearted, and ideally financial, backing of national or international non-governmental organisations is probably the most crucial factor in determining the success or failure of Species Action Plans.

Communication, education and public awareness are all crucial elements to any species recovery programme. Awareness materials have been provided for use at crane breeding sites in Yakutia (Russia) as part of international crane conservation initiatives. Photo: Crawford Prentice.

# Saving Europe's most endangered birds: lessons to be learned from implementing European Species Action Plans

*Szabolcs Nagy[1] & Ian Burfield[2]*

*[1]Wetlands International, Droevendaalsesteeg 3, Wageningen 6700 AC, The Netherlands. (email: Szabolcs.Nagy@wetlands.org)*
*[2]BirdLife International, Droevendaalsesteeg 3, Wageningen 6700 AC, The Netherlands. (email: ian.burfield@birdlife-europe.nl)*

Nagy, S. & Burfield, I. 2006. Saving Europe's most endangered birds: lessons to be learned from implementing European Species Action Plans. *Waterbirds around the world*. Eds. G.C. Boere, C.A. Galbraith & D.A. Stroud. The Stationery Office, Edinburgh, UK. pp. 602-607.

## ABSTRACT

In 1993, BirdLife International started the development of European species action plans in collaboration with Wetlands International. These action plans were endorsed in 1996 by the Ornis Committee of the European Union's Directive on the conservation of wild birds and by the Standing Committee of the Bern Convention. In 2003, the European Commission commissioned BirdLife International to review the implementation of the plans in the 25 Member States of the European Union. This paper summarizes the results with special reference to waterbirds.

## INTRODUCTION

The concept of international species action plans was developed in the 1970s to protect threatened populations of certain North American waterbird species with special economic and social importance. The format for these plans was developed under the framework of the North American Waterfowl Management Plan (Heredia *et al.* 1996). The preparation of species action plans was also triggered by the U.S. Endangered Species Act. These plans were used as a basis for recovery efforts in the UK, Australia, New Zealand and several other countries. The requirement of the Convention on Biological Diversity to prepare biodiversity action plans provided further impetus for the preparation of species action plans.

In 1993, BirdLife International and Wetlands International drew up action plans for 23 species then considered to be globally threatened or near-threatened (Collar *et al.* 1994), with support from the European Commission and the Royal Society for the Protection of Birds (RSPB, BirdLife Partner in the UK). For each species, a workshop of experts and interested parties from range states was held to ensure that the latest scientific and practical information was available. Each workshop also provided an opportunity to discuss the merits of different conservation strategies and to develop recommendations based on the outcome of the discussion. In order to secure high-level stakeholder commitment, several drafts were circulated to experts and government agencies under the auspices of international conservation bodies.

In 1996, the first set of 23 plans was endorsed by the Ornis Committee of the European Union's Directive on the conservation of wild birds, and by the Standing Committee of the Bern Convention. The plans were published in 1996 (Heredia *et al.* 1996). Almost one third of the species covered by action plans in this book were waterbirds, namely the Pygmy Cormorant *Phalacrocorax pygmeus*, Dalmatian Pelican *Pelecanus crispus*, Lesser White-fronted Goose *Anser erythropus*, Red-breasted Goose *Branta ruficollis*, Marbled Teal *Marmaronetta angustirostris*, White-headed Duck *Oxyura leucocephala* and Slender-billed Curlew *Numenius tenuirostris*.

Since then, many more action plans have been produced under the auspices of the Ornis Committee, the Bern Convention, and the relevant Memoranda of Understanding of the Convention on Migratory Species of Wild Animals as well as the African-Eurasian Waterbird Agreement (see Table 1).

In October 2003, the European Commission commissioned BirdLife International to review the implementation of the first 23 action plans in the 25 countries that are now Member States of the EU. In 2000, BirdLife International carried out a pan-European assessment of progress in the implementation of these action plans, based solely on the information provided by its Partner organizations (Gallo-Orsi 2001). This earlier report therefore provided some basis for comparison with the more recent EU-level assessment.

## MATERIALS AND METHODS

### Data collection

The latest review of the implementation of species action plans broadly followed the methodology already used in *Saving Europe's most threatened birds* (Gallo-Orsi 2001), in order to obtain indices which could be aggregated across the EU. The review took place in three stages. First, available information was collected for provision to national contacts (usually national BirdLife Partners). The main data sources at this stage were:

- BirdLife International's *Birds in Europe 2* database, which provided information on the current population size and trend of each species over the period of 1990–2000;
- BirdLife International's World Bird Database, which provided information on Important Bird Areas (IBAs) of global importance already identified for the species;
- the European Commission's Natura 2000 database, which provided information on Special Protection Areas (SPAs); and
- the EU LIFE Project Database, which provided information on LIFE projects.

In the second stage, the available information was sent to the national contacts, together with a questionnaire for each species relevant to their country. These questionnaires were based on the recommendations in the relevant action plans. The actions in each plan were converted into target statements, to enable measurement of progress in implementation. The correspondents were asked to:

- review and if necessary correct the available information (i.e. information on population size, population in IBAs and protected areas, existence of management plans, LIFE and other Community funding);
- report on measures taken in relation to each action;
- evaluate distance to target by assigning an implementation score;

## Table 1. Species with international species action plans.

| Species | Year of action plan approval | EU25 Threat Status | European Threat Status | Global IUCN Red List Category | 1990-2000 EU25 breeding population trend | 1990-2000 EU25 winter population trend | Which targets are achieved? | Revision / new plan in preparation |
|---|---|---|---|---|---|---|---|---|
| *Pterodroma madeira* | 1995 | Critically Endangered | (CR) | CR | Stable | - | Long | |
| *Pterodroma feae* | 1995 | Vulnerable | VU | NT | Stable | - | Short | |
| *Phalacrocorax pygmeus* | 1995 | Rare | S | NT | Moderate increase | Stable | Long | |
| *Pelecanus crispus* | 1995 | Rare | R | VU | Moderate increase | - | Long | |
| *Anser erythropus* | 1995 | Critically Endangered | EN | VU | Large decline | Stable | None | AEWA, Ornis |
| *Branta ruficollis* | 1995 | Localized | VU | VU | - | Stable | Medium | |
| *Marmaronetta angustirostris* | 1995 | Endangered | (VU) | VU | Stable | Large increase | None[1] | |
| *Oxyura leucocephala* | 1995 | Vulnerable | VU | EN | Large increase | Large increase | Medium | Ornis, AEWA, Bonn |
| *Aegypius monachus* | 1995 | Rare | R | NT | Large increase | - | Long | |
| *Aquila heliaca* | 1995 | Rare | R | VU | Large increase | - | Long | |
| *Aquila adalberti* | 1995 | Endangered | (EN) | EN | Stable | - | Medium | |
| *Falco naumanni* | 1995 | Depleted | H | VU | Stable | - | Short | |
| *Crex crex* | 1995 | Depleted | H | NT | Large increase | - | Medium | Ornis, AEWA, Bonn |
| *Chlamydotis undulata fuerteventura* | 1995 | Vulnerable | (VU) | VU | Unknown | - | Unknown | |
| *Otis tarda* | 1995 | Vulnerable | VU | VU | Stable | - | None | |
| *Numenius tenuirostris* | 1995 | - | NE | CR | - | - | None | |
| *Larus audouinii* | 1995 | Localized | L | NT | Large increase | - | Long | |
| *Columba trocaz* | 1995 | Rare | (R) | NT | Stable | - | Medium | |
| *Columba bollii* | 1995 | Rare | (R) | NT | Stable | - | Short | |
| *Columba junoniae* | 1995 | Endangered | EN | EN | Unknown | - | Unknown | |
| *Acrocephalus paludicola* | 1995 | Vulnerable | (VU) | VU | Large decline | - | None | |
| *Fringilla teydea* | 1995 | Rare | R | NT | Stable | - | Short | |
| *Pyrrhula murina* | 1995 | Endangered | (EN) | EN | Stable | - | None | |
| *Botaurus stellaris* | 1999 | Depleted | H | | Stable | - | | |
| *Aythya nyroca* | 1999 | Vulnerable | (VU) | NT | Moderate decline | Stable | | AEWA |
| *Polysticta stelleri* | 1999 | Localized | L | | - | Stable | | |
| *Gypaetus barbatus* | 1999 | Vulnerable | (VU) | | Large increase | - | | |
| *Aquila pomarina* | 1999 | Declining | (D) | | Moderate decline | - | | |
| *Aquila clanga* | 1999 | Endangered | EN | VU | Stable | - | | |
| *Hieraaetus fasciatus* | 1999 | Endangered | EN | | Large decline | - | | |
| *Tetrax tetrax* | 1999 | Vulnerable | VU | NT | Large decline | - | | |
| *Puffinus mauretanicus* | 2000 | Critically Endangered | CR | CR | Large decline | - | | |
| *Phalacrocorax aristotelis desmarestii* | 2000 | Not evaluated[2] | | | | | | |
| *Accipiter gentilis arrigonii* | 2000 | Not evaluated | | | | | | |
| *Accipiter nisus granti* | 2000 | Not evaluated | | | | | | |
| *Falco eleonorae* | 2000 | Declining | D | | Moderate decline | - | | |
| *Falco biarmicus* | 2000 | Vulnerable | VU | | Moderate decline | - | | |
| *Falco rusticolus* | 2000 | Rare | (R) | | Stable | - | | |
| *Alectoris graeca whitakeri* | 2000 | Not evaluated | | | | | | |
| *Perdix perdix italica* | 2000 | Not evaluated | | | | | | |
| *Porphyrio porphyrio* | 2000 | Localized | L | | Large increase | - | | |
| *Fulica cristata* | 2000 | Critically Endangered | CR | | Moderate decline | Moderate decline | | |
| *Cursorius cursor* | 2000 | Endangered | (EN) | | Unknown | - | | |
| *Sterna dougallii* | 2000 | Rare | R | | Stable | - | | |
| *Dendrocopos major canariensis & thanneri* | 2000 | Not evaluated | | | | | | |
| *Loxia scotica* | 2000 | Data Deficient | DD | DD | Unknown | | | |

[1] Based on range contraction reported from Spain.

[2] Subspecies were not evaluated separately by BirdLife International.

- estimate the size of the population affected by the measure; and
- estimate the response of the population.

Implementation scores ranged from 0-4 according to the level of progress towards the target:

0   Action not needed/not relevant;

1   Little or no work (0-10%) carried out (only piecemeal actions, without being part of a strategic approach);

2   Some work started (11-50%), but no significant progress yet;

3   Significant progress (51-75%), but target still not reached; and

4   Action fully implemented; no further work required except continuation of ongoing work (e.g. monitoring).

In the third stage, the information returned by these national correspondents was sent to the respective members of the Ornis Committee's Scientific Working Group for checking (copies were also sent to the national representative on the Ornis Committee).

The final responses were then returned to BirdLife for checking and analysis. Some scores were corrected if there were inconsistencies between the answer and the score, or if the action was not relevant for the particular country. When in doubt, replies were checked by consulting the compilers individually.

## EVALUATION

The evaluation of the action plans was based on two questions:

- To what extent have the recommendations of the action plan been implemented?
- Have the short-, medium- or long-term biological aims of the action plan been achieved?

### Implementation

Implementation was evaluated from the Implementation Scores assigned in the previous process. As explained above, these scores measure the distance to target. The overall level of implementation at national level was characterized by the National Implementation Score (NIS), which combines for each country the priority of the actions with the level of implementation. The NIS ranges between 1 and 4, where 1 represents little or no progress while 4 represents full implementation.

The overall implementation of the action plan was evaluated by calculating an Average Implementation Score (AIS) from the National Implementation Scores. In order to obtain a rough idea of the overall level of implementation of the action plans in a given country, an Average of National Implementation Scores (ANIS) was calculated for each Member State, based on the NIS of all the species occurring in the country.

### Effectiveness

The outcome of the implementation of the action plans was measured in relation to the short-, medium- and long-term aims set in the action plan (Table 2). On this basis, the following categories were distinguished:

- None of the aims was achieved;
- Short-term aims achieved;
- Medium-term aims achieved;

- Long-term aims achieved; and
- Status unknown.

## RESULTS

### Implementation

The level of implementation of the action plans varied markedly between Member States, with NIS ranging between 0 (for endemic species) and 2.69 (for White-headed Duck).

The highest efforts were directed towards Critically Endangered species such as Zino's Petrel *Pterodroma madeira* and Slender-billed Curlew, but no clear tendency was observed in other Red List categories (Table 3). The AIS for Vulnerable species was slightly higher than that for Near Threatened species. Interestingly, the AIS for the Endangered species was somewhat lower than for other Red List categories. Furthermore, a tendency towards higher level of implementation for waterbirds can be observed compared to other species.

The UK achieved the highest level of implementation, indicating the benefits of the UK Biodiversity Action Plan process. It was followed by some other countries where species are the subject of targeted actions, such as The Netherlands, Hungary, Portugal, Austria, France and Sweden. Although some regions of Spain also carry out excellent species conservation work, this is not reflected in the ANIS of Spain because the country's overall score was often reduced due to more limited actions in other regions.

The level of implementation in the ten new Member States was generally lower than in the existing fifteen Member States. This was probably due to the lack of EU funding instruments, such as LIFE-Nature, Interreg and agri-environmental programmes, during the decade preceding their accession to the EU. It also shows that much more assistance is needed in eastern European and African countries if a higher level of implementation of the action plans is to be achieved there.

An analysis of the distribution of LIFE-Nature funding revealed that this funding played a major role in the implementation of the action plans, especially in the Mediterranean Member States. Regarding waterbirds, LIFE-Nature funding played an especially important role in Greece (Pygmy Cormorant, Dalmatian Pelican, Lesser White-fronted Goose, White-headed Duck and Slender-billed Curlew) and Spain (White-headed Duck and Marbled Teal).

The European Union also played an important role in the implementation of the action plans through its conservation Directives. Article 5 of the Birds Directive provides a strong legal framework and guidelines for the Member States to give adequate legal protection to the action plan species, all of which are listed on Annex I of the Directive. However, it was reported in several cases (especially for raptors and waterbirds) that the enforcement of legal protection is still insufficient (e.g. Pygmy Cormorant and Dalmatian Pelican in Greece, and raptors in Portugal, Spain and Greece).

The obligations arising from Article 4 of the Birds Directive have also played an important role in the conservation of the action plan species. For most species, most or all of the IBAs are covered to some extent by SPAs, and the accession process has also accelerated the protection of key sites in the new Member States (Z. Waliczky *in litt.*). However, the results of this analysis also showed that the extent of SPAs and nationally protected areas tend to be much smaller than that of IBAs.

**Table 2. Recovery targets set in the international species action plans.**

| Species Name | Aim of Action Plan |
|---|---|
| Zino's Petrel<br>*Pterodroma madeira* | To increase the breeding population to at least 40 pairs by the year 2000. |
| Slender-billed Curlew<br>*Numenius tenuirostris* | S: to prevent the extinction of the Slender-billed Curlew.<br>M: to prevent any further decrease in the Slender-billed Curlew population.<br>L: to secure a significant increase in the number of Slender-billed Curlews. |
| White-headed Duck<br>*Oxyura leucocephala* | S: to maintain the current population and area of occupancy of the White-headed Duck throughout its range.<br>M: to promote population increase within its current range.<br>L: to promote expansion of the breeding population to other suitable areas.<br>To prevent hybridization of the White-headed Duck by eradicating the introduced North American Ruddy Duck *Oxyura jamaicensis* in the Western Palearctic. |
| Spanish Imperial Eagle<br>*Aquila adalberti* | To increase the numbers and distribution of the Spanish Imperial Eagle to a degree that will allow its reclassification as a species of least concern. |
| White-tailed Laurel Pigeon<br>*Columba junoniae* | S: to conserve the population at no less than its 1985 level.<br>M-L: to promote the expansion of its range. |
| Azores Bullfinch<br>*Pyrrhula murina* | To increase the Azores Bullfinch population to 150-200 pairs by 2010.<br>To extend the area of the laurel forest by 80 ha, reversing its continuing large-scale deterioration through the invasion of exotic flora. |
| Dalmatian Pelican<br>*Pelecanus crispus* | S: to prevent any further declines below 1994 levels in the population size and distribution of the Dalmatian Pelican.<br>M-L: to increase the population size of the Dalmatian Pelican to a level at which it no longer qualifies as a globally threatened species. |
| Lesser White-fronted Goose<br>*Anser erythropus* | S: to maintain the current population in known areas throughout its range.<br>M-L: to ensure an increase in the Lesser White-fronted Goose population. |
| Red-breasted Goose<br>*Branta ruficollis* | S: to maintain Red-breasted Goose numbers at no less than 70 000 birds. |
| Marbled Teal<br>*Marmaronetta angustirostris* | S: to maintain the current population and area of occupancy of the Marbled Teal throughout its range (based on 1985-94 figures).<br>M: to promote population increase of the species within its current range.<br>L: to promote expansion of the breeding population to other suitable areas. |
| Imperial Eagle<br>*Aquila heliaca* | S: to maintain the numbers of Imperial Eagle throughout its present range.<br>M-L: to ensure range expansion. |
| Lesser Kestrel<br>*Falco naumanni* | S: to maintain all known breeding colonies at 1994 levels or larger.<br>M-L: to increase the population size so that it no longer qualifies as a globally threatened species. |
| Great Bustard<br>*Otis tarda* | S: to maintain the populations of the Great Bustard throughout its range.<br>M-L: to enable population growth and range expansion. |
| Aquatic Warbler<br>*Acrocephalus paludicola* | S: to maintain the current population throughout its range.<br>M-L: to promote expansion of the breeding population to other suitable areas. |
| Fea's Petrel<br>*Pterodroma feae* | S: to protect and maintain the breeding population of Fea's Petrel.<br>M: to promote its expansion to all available habitat on the island of Bugio.<br>L: to promote its expansion to all available habitat on Deserta Grande. |
| Pygmy Cormorant<br>*Phalacrocorax pygmeus* | S: to prevent declines below 1994 levels of population size and distribution.<br>M-L: to increase the population size to a level at which it no longer qualifies as near threatened. |
| Cinereous Vulture<br>*Aegypius monachus* | S: to maintain and enhance the existing populations in Europe.<br>L: to encourage the re-colonization of the former range. |
| Corncrake<br>*Crex crex* | S: to prevent declines below 1994 levels in the population size and distribution of the Corncrake to enable it to be removed from the list of globally threatened birds.<br>M: to ensure recovery of small breeding populations at risk of extinction. |
| Houbara Bustard<br>*Chlamydotis undulata* | S: to maintain the range and population of the Canary Islands' Houbara Bustard at no less than the 1994 levels.<br>M-L: to promote an increase in the population and range expansion. |
| Audouin's Gull<br>*Larus audouinii* | S: to maintain the current population throughout its range.<br>M-L: to ensure expansion of the species' range and numbers particularly in smaller colonies. |
| Dark-tailed Laurel Pigeon<br>*Columba bollii* | S: to conserve the population at no less than its 1993 level.<br>M: to promote the expansion of its range. |
| Madeira Laurel Pigeon<br>*Columba trocaz* | S: to maintain the population at no fewer than 3 500 individuals.<br>M: to ensure its continued increase towards occupying all suitable habitats.<br>L: to enable re-colonization of areas of its former range through habitat restoration. |
| Blue Chaffinch<br>*Fringilla teydea* | S: to conserve the range and populations at no less than the present level.<br>M-L: to increase the Gran Canaria population to a level at which it is no longer classified as a near threatened species. |

**Table 3. Implementation of the international species action plans in decreasing order of Average Implementation Scores (AIS).**

| Species name | AIS |
|---|---|
| Zino's Petrel *Pterodroma madeira* | 3.31 |
| Slender-billed Curlew *Numenius tenuirostris* | 3.21 |
| Dalmatian Pelican *Pelecanus crispus* | 3.05 |
| Madeira Laurel Pigeon *Columba trocaz* | 2.94 |
| Lesser White-fronted Goose *Anser erythropus* | 2.81 |
| Cinereous Vulture *Aegypius monachus* | 2.80 |
| Marbled Teal *Marmaronetta angustirostris* | 2.75 |
| Great Bustard *Otis tarda* | 2.55 |
| Blue Chaffinch *Fringilla teydea* | 2.51 |
| Red-breasted Goose *Branta ruficollis* | 2.47 |
| Pygmy Cormorant *Phalacrocorax pygmeus* | 2.44 |
| Imperial Eagle *Aquila heliaca* | 2.39 |
| Aquatic Warbler *Acrocephalus paludicola* | 2.39 |
| White-tailed Laurel Pigeon *Columba junoniae* | 2.38 |
| Dark-tailed Laurel Pigeon *Columba bollii* | 2.38 |
| Fea's Petrel *Pterodroma feae* | 2.27 |
| Spanish Imperial Eagle *Aquila adalberti* | 2.19 |
| Corncrake *Crex crex* | 2.14 |
| Houbara Bustard *Chlamydotis undulata* | 2.04 |
| Audouin's Gull *Larus audounii* | 2.01 |
| Azores Bullfinch *Pyrrhula murina* | 2.00 |
| White-headed Duck *Oxyura leucocephala* | 1.87 |
| Lesser Kestrel *Falco naumanni* | 1.84 |

In most cases, there was not a large difference between the population recorded within IBAs and that within SPAs, although the data in the Natura 2000 database and the World Bird Database are not readily comparable. Some major gaps in the coverage of IBAs by SPAs were identified for some species, especially farmland birds, whereas the coverage for globally threatened waterbirds was found to be almost complete for the breeding populations. Coverage of the key stopover sites would require further investigation.

Although significant progress has been made in designating the key sites for globally threatened waterbirds as SPAs, much less progress has been made in preparing and implementing management plans. On the basis of the available information, only a small fraction of the sites was covered by management plans.

**Effectiveness**

Assessing the population size, distribution and trends (BirdLife International 2004a) in relation to the short- (1-3 years), medium- (1-5 years) and long-term (1-10 years) aims set out in the action plans suggested that the status of the action plan species has generally improved since the drafting of the plans. For 15 species, at least the short-term targets have been achieved. For 11 of these, the medium-term targets have also been met, and in six cases even the long-term targets have been reached. It is also encouraging that a separate analysis found that Annex I species with species action plans did better than Annex I species without an action plan, based on their population trends (BirdLife International 2004b).

The group of species where the long-term targets were achieved includes two waterbirds with fairly concentrated populations: Pygmy Cormorant and Dalmatian Pelican. On the other hand, the group where even the short-term objectives of the action plan were not achieved also includes three waterbirds: Slender-billed Curlew, Lesser White-fronted Goose and Marbled Teal. The first two of these species are long-distance migrants, and the development of their populations is likely to be heavily influenced by factors operating on their breeding or wintering grounds outside the European Union.

Despite these results, it was not possible to detect any association between the AIS and the level of recovery. This is partly because AIS scoring was a qualitative measure that focused at the level of implementation of all actions relevant in a given country, and did not take into account the size of the population in that country. An example is White-headed Duck, where the AIS is fairly low because of poor measures in many potential White-headed Duck range states, even though effective measures in certain regions of Spain have contributed significantly to the increase of the population. In the case of Great Bustard *Otis tarda*, however, the positive effects of many ongoing conservation measures were reduced by the ongoing range contraction. Another factor contributing to the lack of association relates to differences in the species' biology and their reaction to changes induced by political and economic changes. For example, Corncrake *Crex crex* has responded positively to the reduced intensity of farming in the new Member States, despite the fact that little progress has been made towards targeted agri-environmental measures for it.

International action plans were drawn up to build consensus amongst the individuals and organizations involved in the conservation of the species. Therefore, an analysis was made to show whether species with a "champion" did better than those without. Of the 23 species, 16 had an organization leading on the species' conservation (e.g. species specialist groups, conservation teams or dedicated NGOs, such as the Black Vulture Conservation Foundation). In general, species with a "champion" reached a higher level of recovery target than species without one, although this difference was not significant.

**CONCLUSIONS AND RECOMMENDATIONS**

This evaluation shows that the species action plans have played a positive role in improving the conservation status of Europe's most threatened birds, because Annex I species with action plans did better than Annex I species without action plans (BirdLife International 2004b).

In almost two-thirds of the action plan species (15 species), further population decline or range contraction in the EU has been stopped. In the case of 11 species, medium-term targets were also reached, and in six cases even the long-term recovery target was met.

The recovery of action plan species can be explained partly by the generally higher level of site protection, but also by their priority status for LIFE-Nature funding. LIFE-Nature was a major instrument in promoting the implementation of the action plans. Unfortunately, LIFE-Nature provided only project funding, and activities often ceased after the funding ended.

Apart from LIFE-Nature funding, species 'champions' have played a major role in promoting the implementation of the action plans. Their activities were supported partly by LIFE-Nature funds, but substantial amounts of private and corporate funding were also mobilized through NGOs. However, the lack of a significant difference in the performance of species with and without "champions" suggests that government commitment to regulations, law enforcement, site designation and management is essential.

Research and monitoring to fill gaps in knowledge and to provide feedback about the effectiveness of measures also require stable funding. Collaborative arrangements at national level, involving different stakeholders, based on national action plans and supported by adequate funding, are necessary for effective species recovery. At international level, the European Union has played a major role, but for migratory species it is essential to expand the scope of the plans to cover the entire range of the species.

## ACKNOWLEDGEMENTS

We thank Wetlands International and in particular Baz Hughes (WWT) for inviting us to present the preliminary results of our study in Edinburgh, and Gerard Boere for his encouragement and patience during the process of preparing the manuscript.

Micheál O'Briain (DG Environment) played an instrumental role in initiating this study and promoting the action planning process in the European Union. Our BirdLife colleagues Umberto Gallo-Orsi, Nicola Crockford, Canan Orhun, Marianne de Rijk, Stuart Butchart and Frans van Bommel all provided invaluable help in collecting and analysing the data.

## REFERENCES

**BirdLife International** 2004a. Birds in Europe: population estimates, trends and conservation status. BirdLife International, Cambridge, UK.

**BirdLife International** 2004b. Birds in the European Union: a status assessment. BirdLife International, Wageningen, The Netherlands.

**Collar, N., Crosby, M. & Stattersfield, A.** 1994. Birds to Watch 2. BirdLife International, Cambridge, UK.

**Gallo-Orsi, U.** 2001. Saving Europe's most threatened birds. BirdLife International, Wageningen, The Netherlands.

**Heredia, B., Rose, L. & Painter, M.** 1996. Globally threatened birds in Europe. Council of Europe, Strasbourg.

Considerable effort has been expended to locate the breeding grounds in Russia of the Critically Threatened Slender-billed Curlew *Numenius tenuirostris*. Dr Sasha Yurlov, Novosibirsk, discussing with local farmers the difference between the three curlew species. Photo: Gerard Boere.

# Conservation action plans for the Black Crowned Crane *Balearica pavonina* and Black Stork *Ciconia nigra* in Africa

*Cheikh Hamallah Diagana[1], Tim Dodman[2] & Seydina Issa Sylla[1]*

[1] *Wetlands International, West African Programme, PO Box 8060, Dakar-Yoff, Senegal. (email: diaganawet@sentoo.sn)*

[2] *Wetlands International, Hundland, Papa Westray, Orkney, KW17 2BU, UK. (email: tim@timdodman.co.uk)*

Diagana, C.H., Dodman, T. & Sylla, S.I. 2006. Conservation action plans for the Black Crowned Crane *Balearica pavonina* and Black Stork *Ciconia nigra* in Africa. *Waterbirds around the world*. Eds. G.C. Boere, C.A. Galbraith & D.A. Stroud. The Stationery Office, Edinburgh, UK. pp. 608-612.

## ABSTRACT

Conservation action plans have been drawn up for the Black Crowned Crane *Balearica pavonina* and Black Stork *Ciconia nigra* in Africa. The action plans present overviews of the species and their different populations, with a particular emphasis on status and threats. Key components of the plans are recommended actions for implementation. The conservation action plan for the Black Crowned Crane has already led to follow-on actions that contribute to implementation of the plan. Participation is essential in the action planning process.

## INTRODUCTION

The Black Crowned Crane *Balearica pavonina* is a resident of the Sahel and Sudan Savannah regions of Africa, ranging from the Senegal basin and Guinea-Bissau drainage in West Africa to the western Ethiopian Highlands and south-west Rift Valley in East Africa. The West African Crowned Crane *B. p. pavonina* occupies the western part of this range, from Senegal to Chad. The Sudan Crowned Crane *B. p. ceciliae* occurs in eastern Africa, with its largest concentration in Sudan (Walkinshaw 1964, 1973, Johnsgaard 1983). It is classified as Near Threatened (BirdLife International 2005). Current population estimates are 15 000 for *B. p. pavonina* (Dodman 2002) and 43 000-55 000 for *B. p. ceciliae* (Beilfuss *et al.* in press). Due to the rapid decrease of populations in certain areas and a lack of knowledge about status in other areas, the International Crane Foundation (ICF) and Wetlands International launched the Black Crowned Crane Programme in 1999 in order to determine the species' conservation status and to prepare an action plan for its conservation.

The Black Stork *Ciconia nigra* is a fairly widespread but generally scarce bird in Africa, where it occurs in three separate populations (Rose & Scott 1994). The estimate of the population breeding in south-west Europe and spending the northern winter in West Africa is the lowest of these, at 1 300-1 370 individuals (Wetlands International 2002). Whilst various projects and conservation programmes are underway for this population in south-west Europe, its conservation status is much less clear in West Africa, where awareness of the stork is also rather low. Results from recent initiatives, including some pioneering satellite-tracking programmes, have helped identify preferred migration routes and important sites in West Africa (Jadoul *et al.* 2003). The much larger population that breeds in central and eastern Europe and spends the northern winter in south-west Asia and sub-Saharan Africa north of the equator numbers around 19 500-28 000 individuals (Wetlands International 2002). Birds from this population cross into Africa at both the Straits of Gibraltar and the Sinai. Of 10 birds fitted with trans-

mitters in the Czech Republic between 1995 and 1999, six followed the south-west migratory route and four followed the south-east flyway into Africa (Bobek *et al.* 2001). There is also a resident population of Black Storks in southern Africa with an estimated population of 1 560-4 050 individuals, key countries being Zimbabwe, Zambia and South Africa (Dodman 2002). With the support of the Ramsar Convention Secretariat, Wetlands International has developed a preliminary conservation action plan for the Black Stork in Africa, focusing largely on West Africa.

## METHODS

### Black Crowned Crane

Using resources from diverse sources, Wetlands International and ICF supported a range of activities aimed at ascertaining the status of the Black Crowned Crane across its range, and employed a full-time Black Crowned Crane Programme Co-ordinator in December 1999, based at the Wetlands International office in Dakar, Senegal. Preliminary activities included an analysis of gaps in information and a detailed questionnaire survey, whilst a wide range of field surveys were supported in twenty countries across the range. Over a two-year period, a total of 187 of 226 target sites were covered by field surveys or questionnaires, or both (Williams *et al.* 2003). Target sites included all sites known or suspected to harbour cranes, as identified from the African Waterbird Census database, previous reports and publications, and personal communication with survey participants.

The questionnaire surveys aimed to supplement and expand on the fields surveys, and the questionnaires were widely distributed. Questions were asked on distribution, population size, status and movements, diet, breeding activity, threats, local attitudes, and legal protection concerning the Black Crowned Crane. Field and questionnaire survey data were analysed to develop population estimates for discrete "sub-populations" or "Crane Areas". The survey results were also used as the basis for developing the Conservation Action Plan, which was reviewed during a Round Table Discussion at the 10th Pan African Ornithological Congress in Uganda in 2000 (Williams *et al.* 2001). The action plan was published in 2003, whilst a technical poster and an awareness-raising poster (labelling the crane as the "Jewel of the Sahel") were also produced.

### BLACK STORK

The aim of the "Conservation Action for Black Storks in Africa" project was to determine the status of, and threats to, Black Storks in (West) Africa, initiate actions for their conservation, and build awareness of this charismatic migratory species in Africa. The

**Table 1.** Estimates by country of the Black Crowned Crane *Balearica pavonina* from 1985 (Urban 1987), 1994 (Urban 1996) and 2004 (after Beilfuss *et al.* in press).

| | 1985 | 1994 | 2004 |
|---|---|---|---|
| *B. p. pavonina* | | | |
| Benin | 50? | 50? | 50 |
| Burkina Faso | 100? | 100? | 50 |
| Cameroon | 2 000 | 2 000-3 500 | 3 000 |
| Central African Republic | Several 100s | Several 100s | 500 |
| Chad | Few 1 000s | 3 500-5 000 | 5 500 |
| Congo | 600-700 | 0? | 0 |
| Côte d'Ivoire | - | Vagrant? | <30 |
| The Gambia | ? | 100 | 100 |
| Ghana | 50 | 50 | <50 |
| Guinea | - | - | 200 |
| Guinea-Bissau | 0? | ? | 1 500 |
| Mali | 7 000–8 000 | 3 000-3 500 | 100 |
| Mauritania | 200 | 200 | 500 |
| Niger | Several 100s | <1 000 | 1 300 |
| Nigeria | Few 100s | <100 | 20 |
| Senegal | 1 000 | 1 000-2 000 | 1 900 |
| Togo | 50 | 50 | 50 |
| **Subspecies total** | 15 000-20 000 | 11 500-17 500 | 15 000 |
| | | | |
| *B. p. ceciliae* | | | |
| Democratic Republic of Congo | - | - | occasional visitor |
| Egypt | - | Vagrant? | 0 |
| Ethiopia | Few 1 000s | Few 1 000s | 2 500 |
| Kenya | Few 100s | 100s | 250 |
| Sudan | 50 000 | 50 000 | 25 000-52 000 |
| Uganda | 500 | 500 | 50 |
| **Subspecies total** | 50 000-70 000 | 55 000-60 000 | 28 000-55 000 |
| **Species total** | 65 000-90 000 | 66 500-77 500 | 43 000-70 000 |

main objectives were: to determine the conservation status of the Black Stork in (West) Africa; to identify key sites for, and threats to, the species in (West) Africa; to develop a conservation strategy (action plan) for (West) Africa; and to increase awareness of the Black Stork and importance of wetlands in West Africa.

As in the Black Crowned Crane programme, questionnaires were also used for developing the preliminary action plan, although no specific surveys were organized. Field data were mainly drawn from existing data held in the African Waterbird Census database, whilst information on migration and other aspects was obtained via parallel projects (e.g. Bobek *et al.* 2001, Jadoul *et al.* 2003). The preliminary study was carried out in 2002, priority actions were identified in 2003, and a preliminary action plan (consultation review) was produced in 2005. A poster was produced and presented at the Waterbirds around the world Conference in Edinburgh, UK, in 2004. A technical poster was also produced, and both posters are being distributed in Africa.

## RESULTS
### Black Crowned Crane

New population estimates were produced based on the surveys of 2000-2001, with 14 500 *B. p. pavonina* and >27 500 *B. p. ceciliae* yielding a global species estimate of >42 000 individuals (Williams *et al.* 2003). Population estimates have subsequently been revised and now stand at 15 000 *B. p. pavonina*

and 28 000-55 000 *B. p. ceciliae* (Table 1; Beilfuss *et al.* in press, Wetlands International in press). These figures are significantly lower than previous estimates of Urban (1987), Urban (1996) and Meine & Archibald (1996), mainly due to a substantial revision in the estimated population of the Sudan Crowned Crane (Table 1). Both populations were found to be in decline, with significant declines noted in Nigeria and Mali, whilst a hitherto largely undetected sub-population was discovered in Guinea-Bissau. A distribution map was drawn up, in which the discrete Crane Areas were identified. The action plan also detailed information on crane breeding ecology, habitat, feeding ecology, protection status, threats and local attitudes, and used this information to develop a set of recommended conservation actions, as detailed below.

### Recommended conservation actions for the Black Crowned Crane (from Williams *et al.* 2003)

1 Launch public awareness programmes for the Black Crowned Crane as a flagship species for wetland conservation.

2 Initiate case studies to find solutions to key threats facing the Black Crowned Crane.

3 Develop integrated management programmes for critical wetlands and catchments that support Black Crowned Cranes.

4   Advocate the designation of Black Crowned Crane sites as Wetlands of International Importance and the implementation of the Ramsar Convention on Wetlands.

5   Transfer the Black Crowned Crane from CITES Appendix II to Appendix I.

6   Strengthen the Black Crowned Crane network and working group to promote further research, monitoring and exchange of information.

7   Convene international and range-wide workshops to plan future conservation measures for the Black Crowned Crane.

Further specific actions were developed for each subspecies (Williams *et al.* 2003). Since the action plan was developed (in 2001, printed in 2003), Wetlands International and ICF have continued to work together to address the main recommendations of the plan. In particular, a number of specific case studies have been achieved and/or are still underway. These include:

*   investigating the status of cranes and factors behind the live crane trade in Mali;
*   investigating factors affecting breeding and movements of cranes in an area where wetlands have been converted to agricultural land in Senegal;
*   surveys and conservation of cranes in the rice-growing zone of coastal West Africa from the Casamance of Senegal to Guinea, with a special focus on Guinea-Bissau;
*   a survey and Participatory Rural Appraisal in selected communities in the crane's range in Nigeria.

**Black Stork**

Key sites for Black Storks in West Africa were identified, including potential Wetlands of International Importance (sites that meet the Ramsar Convention's 1% criterion for the Black Stork), as well as other key (non-wetland) stopover sites. The main threats to Black Storks in Africa were also identified, and their conservation requirements determined. Awareness of the Black Stork was built into the African Waterbird Census network and other networks in Africa.

The Black Stork Conservation Action Plan is currently under technical review prior to publication. It presents information on the status of the three populations, their distribution and migration strategies, count data from the African Waterbird Census, habitat and ecology, breeding, threats and current conservation measures and legislation. In Africa, the main threats identified are the loss and degradation of habitat, hunting, and factors relating to inadequate legislation. Habitat degradation in West Africa is due to desertification, changing landscapes with agricultural intensification, and related factors such as pollution caused by the concentration of pesticides and other chemicals in wetlands. In eastern Mauritania, an important staging area for Black Storks, natural wetlands have been lost due to the building of dams and clearing land for agriculture, a trend that is likely to continue given current national policies directed towards food security (Shine 2003).

The main aim of the preliminary action plan is to prevent, in the short term, further degradation of wintering sites in West Africa through local community-based conservation initiatives, and in the long term, to augment the populations wintering in

Black Crowned Cranes *Balearica pavonina* displaying at the Plaine de Monchon in Guinea, January 2006.  Photo: Menno Hornman.

Poster raising awareness of Black Storks *Ciconia nigra*.
Photo: Tim Dodman.

West Africa through site restoration and the conservation of the stork's main habitats. The specific objectives of the plan are given below.

## Specific objectives of the preliminary Black Stork Conservation Action Plan

1 Promote the restoration and conservation of suitable wintering habitat for Black Storks in West Africa.
2 Encourage the application of national and international legislation in favour of the protection of the Black Stork and its habitat, notably its wintering habitat in Sahelian Africa.
3 Regularly monitor the populations of Black Storks in Africa.
4 Initiate case studies to define threats to Black Storks in their winter quarters in Sahelian Africa and identify solutions to minimize threats.
5 Develop and launch a public awareness and education programme on storks in general and the need to protect their fragile habitats in Africa.
6 Strengthen co-operation between breeding and non-breeding zones (staging and wintering zones) of the Black Stork, especially through a network of managers of key sites for storks across their flyways.
7 Strengthen communication of the network.

The action plan further provides management options and measurable indicators for each objective and a series of "sub-objectives", and describes mechanisms for putting the plan into practice. The plan details specific recommendations for each of the main wintering zones in West Africa, namely the western zone (Mauritania, Senegal and western Mali), the central zone (Mali), and the eastern zone (Burkina Faso, Niger, Benin, Nigeria, Togo and Ghana), as well as a buffer zone for staging areas in Mauritania.

## DISCUSSION

There have been significant outputs from the follow-on projects launched since the development of the Black Crowned Crane Conservation Action Plan. These have included community awareness and training activities and related outputs; conservation awareness materials produced and locally distributed; site guardians appointed; site conservation agreements developed with local communities; and local training materials produced in Creole and other languages. Training has mainly focused on informing local communities about the importance and values of wetlands and about cranes and other waterbirds. The plan thus remains as a useful living conservation tool that is still under implementation. It has certainly acted as a stimulus for focusing and prioritizing further conservation action and for raising funds for these actions.

By contrast, the Black Stork Conservation Action Plan has not yet been completed, due to a prolonged review process, and no new specific follow-up actions have been developed. There is also a need to integrate further information and conservation priorities for the discrete population in southern Africa, for which further communications are also required. Nevertheless, the plan promises to be a useful document for prioritizing future conservation actions for this species, and for potentially expanding some components to embrace other storks in the region. Significant research is conducted on Black Storks in Europe, where this is widely regarded as a high priority species for conservation. There is much to be gained through a strengthened network for Black Stork conservation and exchange between partners in Europe and Sahelian countries of Africa. The series of international conferences on the Black Stork and the Stork, Ibis and Spoonbill Specialist Group of Wetlands International are positive vehicles for achieving this.

Conservation action plans are useful planning tools for focusing and prioritizing attention on species, in particular threatened species, for which concerted and co-ordinated action is often needed for their successful conservation. It may arguably be easier to raise funds and enthusiasm for the implementation of plans for charismatic or well-known species than for less-known or drab species. However, whatever the success in raising funds, clear and prioritized recommended actions are extremely useful, and will be widely respected if appropriate networks have been involved in drawing them up. The African-Eurasian Migratory Waterbird Agreement (AEWA) advocates the development of Species Action Plans, and has produced a number of plans under its technical series, e.g. UNEP/AEWA (2004). There are also specific national action plans in some countries, such as the Botswana Wattled Crane Action Plan (Motsumi *et al.* 2003). The BirdLife African Species Working Group and the Royal Society for the Protection of Birds (RSPB) have established a project to enhance the conservation of key bird species in Africa through the development and implementation of Species Action Plans. A key step in the BirdLife Species Action Plan approach is the organization of participative species action planning workshops (BirdLife International, no date). Participation is certainly a key element in the success of developing and implementing action plans, and in their monitoring and evaluation.

## ACKNOWLEDGEMENTS

We would like to acknowledge the input of Emmanuel Williams and Rich Beilfuss, both co-authors of the "Status Survey and Conservation Action Plan for the Black Crowned Crane *Balearica pavonina*", upon which parts of this paper are based. Other key collaborators in implementation of the Black Crowned Crane Conservation Action Plan are Bakary Kone, Idrissa Ndiaye and Joãzinho Sá. We particularly acknowledge the financial support of the Disney Wildlife Conservation Fund, the North of England Zoological Society, the Programme of International Nature Management of the Ministries of Agriculture, Nature Management and Fisheries (LNV) and Foreign Affairs (NEDA) in The Netherlands, and the Ramsar Convention Secretariat.

## REFERENCES

**Beilfuss, R.D., Dodman, T. & Urban, E.K.** In press. Status of Cranes in Africa 2005. In: Craig, A. (ed) Proceedings of the 11th Pan African Ornithological Congress. Ostrich.

**BirdLife International** 2005. Species factsheet: *Balearica pavonina*. Downloaded from http://www.birdlife.org on 8 March 2006.

**BirdLife International** No date. Planning for the future: Species Action Plans for threatened birds in Africa. BirdLife International / RSPB / Nature Uganda, Kampala, Uganda.

**Bobek, M., Simek, J., Pojer, F. & Peske, L.** 2001. Ecology of Black Storks from the same breeding ground wintering in different parts of Africa: a telemetry project. Ostrich Supplement 15: 88.

**Dodman, T.** 2002. Waterbird Population Estimates in Africa. Unpublished consultation draft. Wetlands International.

**Jadoul, G., Hourlay, F. & Toussaint, A.-C.** 2003. Suivi de la migration automnale de la Cigogne noire (*Ciconia nigra*) par télémétrie satellitaire. Aves 40(1-4): 155-164.

**Johnsgaard, P.A.** 1983. Cranes of the World. Indiana University Press, Bloomington, Indiana.

**Meine, C.D. & Archibald, G.W.** 1996. The cranes: status survey and conservation action plan. IUCN, Gland, Switzerland.

**Motsumi, S., Hancock, P., Borello, W., Tyler, S. & Evans, S.W.** (eds). 2003. Botswana Wattled Crane (*Bugeranus carunculatus*) Action Plan. Final Workshop Report. BirdLife Botswana and BirdLife South Africa, Johannesburg, South Africa.

**Rose, P.M. & Scott, D.A.** 1994. Waterfowl Population Estimates. IWRB Publication 29. IWRB, Slimbridge, UK.

**Shine, T.** 2003. The Conservation Status of Eastern Mauritania's ephemeral wetlands and their role in the Migration and Wintering of Black Storks (*Ciconia nigra*). Aves 40(1-4): 228-240.

**UNEP/AEWA** 2004. International Single Species Action Plan for the Conservation of the Sociable Lapwing *Vanellus gregarius*. AEWA Technical Series No. 2, Bonn.

T-shirts are among the means of raising awareness of the need to conserve Black Storks *Ciconia nigra*. Photo: Sergey Dereliev.

**Urban, E.K.** 1987. The cranes of Africa – an overview. In: G.W. Archibald & R.F. Pasquier (eds) Proceedings of the 1983 International Crane Workshop. International Crane Foundation, Baraboo, Wisconsin: 307-315.

**Urban, E.K.** 1996. Status of cranes in Africa, 1994. In: R.D. Beilfuss, W.R. Tarboton & N.N. Gichuki (eds) Proceedings African crane and wetland training workshop. International Crane Foundation, Baraboo, Wisconsin: 53-59.

**Walkinshaw, L.H.** 1964. The African crowned cranes. Wilson Bulletin 76(4): 355-77.

**Walkinshaw, L.H.** 1973. Cranes of the World. Winchester Press, New York.

**Wetlands International** 2002. Waterbird Population Estimates – Third Edition. Wetlands International Global Series No. 12, Wageningen, The Netherlands.

**Wetlands International** In press. Waterbird Population Estimates – Fourth Edition. Wageningen, The Netherlands.

**Williams, E.T.C., Dodman, T. & Beilfuss, R.** 2001. Reviewing a status survey and conservation action plan for the Black Crowned Crane *Balearica pavonina*. Ostrich Supplement 15: 238.

**Williams, E.T.C., Beilfuss, R.D. & Dodman, T.** 2003. Status survey and conservation action plan for the Black Crowned Crane *Balearica pavonina*. Wetlands International, Dakar, Senegal, and International Crane Foundation, Baraboo, Wisconsin, USA.

# Approaches to freshwater bird species conservation – Wattled Cranes *Bugeranus carunculatus* and Shoebill Storks *Balaeniceps rex* in Zambia

*Hewitt Chizyuka*

*WWF Southern Africa Regional Program Office, No 10 Lanark Road, Belgravia, PO Box Cy 1409, Causeway, Harare, Zimbabwe.*
*(e-mail: Hchizyuka@wwf.org.zw)*

Chizyuka, H. 2006. Approaches to freshwater bird species conservation – Wattled Cranes *Bugeranus carunculatus* and Shoebill Storks *Balaeniceps rex* in Zambia. *Waterbirds around the world.* Eds. G.C. Boere, C.A. Galbraith & D.A. Stroud. The Stationery Office, Edinburgh, UK. p. 613.

At first sight, there may not be many compelling reasons why freshwater bird species in their own right merit particular conservation efforts. However, many large conservation issues, such as habitat protection, management of certain important landscapes, water and wetland management issues and promotion of improved local livelihoods and tourism, can benefit from bird species conservation initiatives.

The World Wide Fund for Nature (WWF) has recently embarked on large-scale freshwater conservation initiatives in Southern Africa. A strategic decision has been made to implement freshwater management interventions that address conservation at river basin level and prominently factor in livelihood issues in order to promote the positive socio-economic progress of local communities while reducing the pressures that lead to ecological damage of these ecosystems.

Work is currently underway in the Kafue flats wetlands of Zambia to promote wise use of wetland resources, and special attention is being paid to the protection of habitats for the Wattled Cranes *Bugeranus carunculatus,* an endangered bird species in the area whose low numbers remain a matter of grave concern. According to the International Crane Foundation the future of Wattled Cranes in Africa depends on Zambia, which supports more than half of the global population in the country's major wetlands and flood plains, such as the Bangweulu Swamps and the Kafue Flats.

Recent surveys in countries previously thought to be strongholds for the crane – Botswana, Mozambique, Tanzania and especially Zambia – have indicated that populations of Wattled Cranes may now only be half previous estimates. Zambia's crane population was recently estimated at around 4 000 to 4 500 compared to 1985 estimates of around 11 000 and 1994 estimates of around 7 000 to 8 000. Loss and degradation of wetland habitat is the most significant threat to the Wattled Crane, and human encroachment into the habitat, dry season fires on the grassland plains and even harvesting of crane eggs for food have all been detrimental.

Breeding and feeding cycles of Wattled Cranes are linked to the natural flood cycles of rivers. Pairs begin nesting as flood waters start to recede following peak flooding since nesting in shallow waters protects the nests from predators and wildfires, but unfortunately not from man as the intensification of artisinal fishing activities in relatively shallow waters has resulted in increased disturbance and the loss of eggs. In the Kafue Flats, river regulation has had a very adverse impact on the cranes. Since the construction of the Itezhi Tezhi dam on the Kafue river, Wattled Cranes have experienced significant constraints to their breeding and feeding sites. The ICF estimates that during a year of normal flooding conditions, about 40% of Wattled Crane pairs

attempt to breed but when floods fail only about 3% of all pairs breed. The absence of floods also decreases tuber productivity, an important food source for cranes. Wattled Cranes are not the only victims: farmers and fishermen who depend on natural hydrological variations in river-floodplains for their livelihoods are also affected by river regulations which give rise to artificial flooding and drying. Throughout Southern Africa large dams have brought hardship for subsistence farmers and fishermen whose livelihoods depend upon the natural flow regimes of rivers. Altered flooding patterns have impacted on water supply, fuelwood, grasses for livestock grazing and fish stocks.

WWF is also working in the Bangweulu basin, also in Zambia, where they are seeking solutions to arrest the decline of the very rare Shoebill Stork *Balaeniceps rex*. This is one of the most rare and elusive birds in Africa and has lured many visitors to the swamps in hope of a sighting in one of their last remaining habitats. The biggest threat to this bird species has been loss of nesting sites due to human encroachment, flooding and occasional fires.

In both cases the conservation of these rare bird species is not only critical for biodiversity in the Kafue Flats and the Bangweulu basin but also for enhancing the livelihoods of local communities through eco-tourism.

A globally threatened Shoebill *Balaeniceps rex* at Mabamba Bay Wetland System, Uganda, recently designated in September 2006 as a Ramsar site. Photo: Dwight Peck.

# Co-ordinating conservation action across the Atlantic: development of a Flyway Management Plan for the East Canadian High Arctic Light-bellied Brent Goose *Branta bernicla hrota*

*James A. Robinson*

*The Wildfowl & Wetlands Trust, Slimbridge, Gloucestershire, GL2 7BT, UK.*

*Present address: RSPB Northern Ireland, Belvoir Park Forest, Belfast, BT8 4QT, UK. (email: james.robinson@rspb.org.uk)*

Robinson, J.A. 2006. Co-ordinating conservation action across the Atlantic: development of a Flyway Management Plan for the East Canadian High Arctic Light-bellied Brent Goose *Branta bernicla hrota*. *Waterbirds around the world*. Eds. G.C. Boere, C.A. Galbraith & D.A. Stroud. The Stationery Office, Edinburgh, UK. pp. 614-618.

## ABSTRACT

The East Canadian High Arctic (ECHA) Light-bellied Brent Goose *Branta bernicla hrota* breeds in Canada's eastern Queen Elizabeth Islands and winters mainly on the coast of the island of Ireland. The key threats to the population are habitat loss/degradation, natural disasters, changes in the dynamics of native food species, and pollution. In light of the small number of countries involved, it has been deemed appropriate by the Range States to take an international approach to the conservation of the population, with the production of an International Single Species Action Plan (SSAP) within the framework of the Agreement on the Conservation of African-Eurasian Migratory Waterbirds (AEWA). The broad aim of this SSAP will be to restore the ECHA Light-bellied Brent Goose to a favourable conservation status. The SSAP is being developed using internationally agreed standards for identifying actions, and has been prepared specifically to facilitate the monitoring and evaluation of subsequent implementation, linking threats, actions and measurable objectives. The ECHA Light-bellied Brent Goose Working Group will oversee the implementation of the SSAP, and will comprise representatives of the five countries involved (Canada, Greenland, Iceland, Ireland and the UK), relevant international interest groups and several technical advisors.

**Fig. 1.** Global distribution of the East Canadian High Arctic Light-bellied Brent Goose *Branta bernicla hrota* (breeding areas – dark blue; non-breeding areas – grey; delimitation of flyway – hatched line).

## INTRODUCTION

Single species action plans are prepared and reviewed regularly for many species/populations of birds with an unfavourable conservation status. These plans address the status of the species/population, identify recovery options, and recommend management activities (Bell & Merton 2002). Targeted conservation activity for species and populations is essential to ensure that effective use is made of limited resources.

The East Canadian High Arctic (ECHA) population of the Light-bellied Brent Goose *Branta bernicla hrota* breeds in Canada's eastern Queen Elizabeth Islands; the great majority winter on the coastline of the island of Ireland, with smaller numbers in the Channel Islands and northern France (Fig. 1). The population comprises around 20 000 individuals in winter (Wetlands International 2002), and is listed under Category A (2) of the Agreement on the Conservation of African-Eurasian Migratory Waterbirds (AEWA) (see AEWA web-site). The AEWA has been developed under the Convention of Migratory Species of Wild Animals (CMS) and encompasses Europe, Central Asia, the Middle East and Africa. The Agreement covers 235 species of birds ecologically dependent on wetlands for at least a part of their annual cycle. Populations listed in Category A (2) are deemed to deserve the production of national action plans with a view to improving their overall conservation status.

In light of the small number of countries within the range of the ECHA Light-bellied Brent Goose, and given the history of co-operative international conservation and research initiatives, it has been deemed appropriate by the Range States to take an international approach to the conservation of this population, with the production of an AEWA International Single Species Action Plan (SSAP) which can also be used to frame conservation action in countries that are not Contracting Parties to the Agreement. The broad aim of the SSAP will be to restore the ECHA Light-bellied Brent Goose population to a favourable conservation status.

This paper describes the development of the SSAP for the ECHA Light-bellied Brent Goose, from the convening of an international workshop in autumn 2003 to the drafting of the plan itself in 2004, using the format for AEWA SSAPs developed by BirdLife International (BirdLife International 2002). The future success of the plan and its implementation are also discussed.

## PLAN DEVELOPMENT
### International workshop

The first international workshop for the ECHA Light-bellied Brent Goose was convened at the Wildfowl & Wetlands Trust (WWT) visitor centre at Castle Espie (on the shores of Strangford Lough in Northern Ireland) in autumn 2003. This workshop followed discussions between various stakeholders across the flyway who were eager to see more targeted and secured conservation action for the population in the future. Much of the impetus came from the Irish Brent Goose Research Group, a small group of Brent Goose enthusiasts from Ireland and the UK including individuals from government departments, non-governmental organizations and research institutions, as well as amateurs. Without this group of keen individuals, it is unlikely that such rapid progress in the production of the plan would have been possible.

The workshop was designed to promote co-operation and exchange of knowledge between researchers and conservationists involved with the Brent Goose population. Experts attended from throughout the range of the population and, on the first day, gave various presentations on the biology of the species and its conservation requirements. On the second day, "wall-storming" sessions and discussions within small groups enabled the participants to identify the threats facing the population and the actions required to improve its conservation status. Workshop activities were designed to elicit contributions from all of the delegates present, to promote a sense of "ownership" of the SSAP at a very early stage in the process.

Bert Lenten attended the workshop on behalf of the UNEP/AEWA Secretariat, presenting a synthesis of the aims and objectives of the AEWA Secretariat and its ability to support the production and implementation of SSAPs. The workshop resulted in formal support for the production of an AEWA SSAP for this population of Brent Geese. The WWT (an international non-governmental organization based in the UK) agreed to undertake the work necessary to produce the plan, supported by funds from the Environment & Heritage Service (Northern Ireland) and the National Parks and Wildlife Service (Ireland).

## Threats analysis

The threats facing this population of Brent Geese were identified at the international workshop and derived using the interactive "wall storming" approach detailed in Robinson & Callaghan (2003). To ensure consistency between this and other AEWA SSAPs, all threats were identified according to categories listed in the IUCN Species Survival Commission's Threats Authority files (see IUCN Species Survival Commission web-site).

The results of this analysis and additional research (e.g. Robinson *et al.* 2004) indicated that the ECHA Light-bellied Brent Goose faces various threats throughout its range. In order to prioritize conservation action to address these threats, the following scoring system was adopted:

- Critical - a factor causing or likely to cause very rapid declines (>30% over 10 years);
- High - a factor causing or likely to cause rapid declines (20-30% over 10 years);
- Medium - a factor causing or likely to cause relatively slow, but significant, declines (10-20% over 10 years);
- Low - a factor causing or likely to cause fluctuations;
- Local - a factor causing or likely to cause negligible declines; and
- Unknown - a factor that is likely to affect the population, but it is not known to what extent.

The main threats to the ECHA Light-bellied Brent Goose are listed in Table 1.

## Structure of the plan

After the international workshop, the WWT took the lead in producing the first draft of the SSAP. The first major section of the SSAP provides a summary of the best scientific information available on the population, its ecology, threats and conservation status (both for the population and its habitats in each of the Range States). Much of this information is provided in more detail in a recent review of the population (Robinson *et al.* 2004). The second major section, entitled "Framework for Activity", identifies and defines the Goal, Purpose and Results of the SSAP, and sets targets and means of verification for its implementation.

The Goal is the higher level of objective to which the SSAP will contribute. Overall, the Goal of the SSAP will be to secure the favourable conservation status of the ECHA Light-bellied Brent Goose. The Purpose is the objective or effect of the plan. The five Purposes listed for the SSAP are to:

- end illegal and accidental shooting by 2014;
- ensure that permitted harvest levels continue to remain sustainable;
- provide protection and management of sufficient habitat across the range to support 25 000 birds (as measured in winter) by 2014;
- understand population dynamics fully by 2014; and
- understand fully the effects and impacts of currently unquantified threats by 2014.

The Results are the changes that will need to have been brought about by the plan if the Purpose is to be realized. Objectively Verifiable Indicators (OVIs) specify the meaning of the Results. They are designed to measure the impact of an activity, rather than the process undertaken to achieve it, and are measured by Means of Verification, which are time-bound. The Goal, Purpose, Results and Activities of the plan have been designed to be specific, measurable, agreed, realistic and time-bound. An example of the relationship between Purpose, Result, Objectively Verifiable Indicator and Means of Verification is shown in Table 2. Limited space here does not allow the listing of all the Results and Activities identified in the second draft of the SSAP.

The section of the SSAP entitled "Activities by Range State" identifies a series of activities for each country. The activities needed to achieve each Result are listed with their priority and urgency. Many of the required activities were identified at the international workshop and are linked directly to specific threats. The lists of activities are relatively short for each Range State and require achievable conservation action.

## A FRAMEWORK FOR IMPLEMENTATION
### Creation of an International Species Working Group

The ECHA Light-bellied Brent Goose Working Group will act as the International Species Working Group (ISWG) for implementation of the SSAP, working under the auspices of the AEWA Technical Committee. This group will comprise representatives of each of the five Range States, representatives of relevant international interest groups including each of the relevant treaties (e.g. AEWA Technical Committee), and several technical advisors.

AEWA Range States will have a responsibility to monitor their national populations of the species and its habitat, to

**Table 1.** Relative importance of threats to the East Canadian High Arctic Light-bellied Brent Goose *Branta bernicla hrota* during the breeding and non-breeding seasons.

| Threat category | Breeding | Non-breeding |
|---|---|---|
| 1. Habitat loss/degradation (human induced) | | |
|    1.1. Agriculture | | |
|       1.1.6. Marine aquaculture | - | LOCAL |
|    1.4. Infrastructure development | | |
|       1.4.1. Industry | - | HIGH |
|       1.4.2. Human settlement | - | HIGH |
|       1.4.3. Tourism/recreation | - | HIGH |
|       1.4.6. Dams (barrages etc.) | - | HIGH |
|    1.5. Invasive alien species (directly impacting habitat) | - | MEDIUM |
| 2. Invasive alien species (directly affecting the species) | | |
|    2.1. Competitors | - | LOCAL |
| 4. Accidental mortality | | |
|    4.2. Collision | | |
|       4.2.1. Pylons and buildings | - | LOCAL |
| 5. Persecution | | |
|    5.1. Pest control | - | LOCAL |
| 6. Pollution (affecting the habitat and/or species) | | |
|    6.1. Atmospheric pollution | | |
|       6.1.1. Global warming/oceanic warming | CRITICAL? | CRITICAL? |
|    6.3. Water pollution | | |
|       6.3.1. Agricultural | - | LOW |
|       6.3.2. Domestic | - | LOW |
|       6.3.3. Commercial/industrial | LOW | HIGH |
|       6.3.6. Oil slicks | LOW | HIGH |
| 7. Natural disasters | | |
|    7.1. Drought | HIGH | HIGH |
|    7.2. Storms/flooding | HIGH | HIGH |
| 8. Changes in native (food) species dynamics | | |
|    8.5. Pathogens/parasites | LOW | CRITICAL |
| 9. Intrinsic factors | | |
|    9.2. Poor recruitment/reproduction/regeneration | MEDIUM | - |
|    9.9. Restricted range | MEDIUM | HIGH |
| 10. Human disturbance | | |
|    10.1. Recreation/tourism | - | MEDIUM |
|    10.4. Transport | - | MEDIUM |
|    10.6. Other (agricultural) | - | MEDIUM |
|    10.6. Other (industrial) | LOCAL | MEDIUM |

**Table 2.** An example of the relationship between Purpose, Result, Objectively Verifiable Indicator and Means of Verification.

| Purpose | Result | Objectively Verifiable Indicator | Means of Verification |
|---|---|---|---|
| To end illegal and accidental shooting by 2014 | Strict enforcement of species protection legislation across the range by 2008 | By 2008, a measurable increase in the number of penalties issued to those infringing national and international legislation regarding the species and its habitat | Within three years:<br>• All known incidences of illegal shootings investigated<br>• Guilty parties penalized according to national legislative requirements<br><br>Within six years:<br>• Financial penalties for contravening national legislation<br>• Annual assessment of illegal shootings |

monitor the actions taken, including their impact on the species and its habitat, and to report on successes and problems. This should be undertaken by the National Species Working Groups (NSWG), as recommended by the AEWA Conservation Guidelines No. 1 (National Single Species Action Plans). To ensure that lessons are learnt and shared internationally, this information will be communicated to the ECHA Light-bellied Brent Goose Working Group and thus to other Range States, including via the relevant international treaties.

To improve action for the species, the ECHA Light-bellied Brent Goose Working Group will aim to catalyse and co-ordinate the collection of further information relevant to the conservation of the species, including details of size and distribution of the breeding population, migration habits, wintering range and ecology (e.g. habitat use and diet).

Thus, the work of the ECHA Light-bellied Brent Goose Working Group will include the following:

- Developing guidelines for population censusing and monitoring.
- Organizing a co-operative ringing programme.
- Developing guidelines for habitat management practices.
- Facilitating the development of a population model where this will be helpful to focus conservation effort (for example through identifying parameters for which improved data are most needed).
- Assisting in and co-ordinating the preparation of National Action Plans.
- Co-ordinating and facilitating exchange of information between Range States (NSWGs) and between the AEWA and the Range States.
- Collecting country data and annual reports on the implementation of the SSAP from the NSWGs.
- Monitoring implementation of the SSAP through the preparation of an annual international report by the ISWG.
- Organizing intermediate meetings with groups of Range States (training, emergency measures, etc.).
- Preparing and organizing the triennial review meeting between Range States.
- Preparing and submitting a review of the SSAP to the triennial meeting of the Range States and to the triennial Meeting of the Parties to the AEWA.

Detailed "Terms of Reference" based on the above description of activities will be prepared by the AEWA Technical Committee, and hopefully endorsed by the Range States to assist the ECHA Light-bellied Brent Goose Working Group with its work.

## Country actions

To assist in the implementation of the SSAP, it is hoped that each Range State will, as a minimum, commit itself to:

- Endorse the Terms of Reference of the ECHA Light-bellied Brent Goose Working Group.
- Endorse the SSAP.
- Establish a National Species Working Group.
- Report to the ECHA Light-bellied Brent Goose Working Group (through the AEWA Secretariat) on relevant issues in the country, at least by contributing information for the preparation of the annual report by the ISWG.

- Prepare a National Action Plan within one year, in co-operation with the NSWG and based on the International SSAP (see AEWA Conservation Guidelines No. 1).
- Implement the National Action Plan.
- Prepare a review of the National Action Plan every three to five years.
- Maintain and further develop adequately funded research and monitoring programmes to deliver key data.

A timetable for monitoring, evaluation and communication has also been developed and is an integral component of the SSAP.

## NEXT STEPS

In February 2004, the first draft of the SSAP was circulated among the participants of the international workshop and other experts and key stakeholders who were unable to attend. Comments received during the consultation period were used to improve the first draft, and a new draft was finalized in May 2004. This was submitted to the AEWA Secretariat which, in turn, has now circulated it among the key contacts identified by each of the relevant government departments in the Range States. The SSAP was formally adopted at the Third Meeting of Parties to the AEWA in October 2005. It is hoped that it will also be adopted by those countries within the range of the population that are not as yet parties to the AEWA (Greenland and Iceland). Beyond that, it will be the responsibility of the International Species Working Group to oversee and monitor implementation.

The process of developing the plan has been effective so far. The interactive nature of the international workshop and the use of an action plan format that a) uses agreed standards in the definition of threats and identification of required actions, b) is easily understood and used by the target audience, and c) follows a common format adopted by other international treaties, have promoted involvement from stakeholders. It remains to be seen how effective the SSAP will be, but the structure of the plan facilitates monitoring and evaluation of the implementation through indicators of "means" (e.g. production of reports) and "ends" (e.g. increases in goose numbers).

## ACKNOWLEDGEMENTS

This work would not have been possible without contributions from Ken Abraham, Dave Allen, Stuart Bearhop, Hugh Boyd, Sean Boyd, Bob Brown, Kendrew Colhoun, Kathy Dickson, Bart Ebbinge, Ian Enlander, Gudmundur Gudmundsson, Jim Hines, Richard Inger, John McCullough, Graham McElwaine, Kerry Mackie, Paddy Mackie, Mark Mallory, Oscar Merne, Ian Montgomery, James Orr, Alex Portig, Austin Reed, Tony Richardson, David Thompson, Matthew Tickner, Lynne Tinkler and Hugh Thurgate. Thanks also go to Bert Lenten and Yuki Itakura (both of the UNEP/AEWA Secretariat) and Lorraine Robinson who provided support during the preparation of the International Single Species Action Plan. Much of the text has been derived from BirdLife International (2002).

## REFERENCES

**Bell, B.D. & Merton, D.M.** 2002. Management of critically endangered populations. In: K. Norris & D.J. Pain (eds) Conserving Bird Biodiversity: General Principles and their Application. Cambridge University Press, Cambridge: 105-138.

**BirdLife International** 2002. Format for the AEWA International Single Species Action Plan. Report prepared for the Secretariat of the African-Eurasian Waterbird Agreement.

**Robinson, J.A. & Callaghan, D.** 2003. The Ferruginous Duck as a Near Threatened Species: Problems, Causes and Solutions. In: N. Petkov, B. Hughes & U. Gallo-Orsi (eds) Ferruginous Duck: From Research to Conservation. BirdLife International Conservation Series No. 6, BSPB-TWSG, Sofia: 138-143.

**Robinson, J.A., Colhoun, K., Gudmundsson, G.A., Boertmann, D., Merne, O., Ó Bríain, M., Portig, A., Mackie, K. & Boyd, H.** 2004. Light-belled Brent Goose *Branta bernicla hrota* (East Canadian High Arctic population) in Canada, Ireland, Iceland, France, Greenland, Scotland, Wales, England, the Channel Islands and Spain 1960/61-1999/2000. Waterbird Review Series, The Wildfowl & Wetlands Trust/Joint Nature Conservation Committee, Slimbridge, UK.

**Wetlands International** 2002. Waterbird Population Estimates – Third Edition. Wetlands International Global Series No. 12, Wageningen, The Netherlands.

**Web-sites**
**AEWA:**http://www.unepaewa.org/documents/agreement_text/eng/agree/ag_t1.htm.
**IUCN Species Survival Commission:**
http://www.iucn.org/themes/ssc/sis/authority.htm.

The east Canadian population of Light-belled Brent Goose *Branta bernicla hrota* over-winters mainly in the estuaries of Ireland. Photo: Chris Wilson.

# The Red-breasted Goose *Branta ruficollis* in the new millennium: a thriving species or a species on the brink of extinction?

*Sergey G. Dereliev*

*Bulgarian Society for the Protection of Birds / BirdLife Bulgaria, PO Box 50, 1111 Sofia, Bulgaria. (email: dereliev@gmail.com)*
*Present address: AEWA Secretariat, Hermann-Ehlers-str. 10, D-53113 Bonn, Germany. (email: sdereliev@unep.de)*

Dereliev, S.G. 2006. The Red-breasted Goose *Branta ruficollis* in the new millennium: a thriving species or a species on the brink of extinction? *Waterbirds around the world.* Eds. G.C. Boere, C.A. Galbraith & D.A. Stroud. The Stationery Office, Edinburgh, UK. pp. 619-623.

## ABSTRACT

The Red-breasted Goose *Branta ruficollis* is a globally threatened species breeding in the Russian arctic, migrating through Kazakhstan and Russia, and wintering in Ukraine, Romania and Bulgaria. In the 1960s, the single population of the species shifted its wintering range from the south-west Caspian Sea to the north-west Black Sea. Coinciding with this shift, the numbers were thought to have declined by about 50%, from 60 000 birds in the 1960s to 30 000 in the 1970s. A recovery in numbers was recorded as early as the beginning of the 1990s, and during the next decade the population increased to 88 000. Numbers then plummeted to only 23 000 in 2002, since when there has been a moderate recovery. Because of these rapid declines, the species' IUCN Red List category could be upgraded from Vulnerable to Endangered. Past and present conservation, research and monitoring activities throughout the flyway have achieved some results, but full implementation of activities has been hampered by constraints such as lack of human, logistic and financial capacity in the Range States. To improve the situation, it is necessary to review and update the International Species Action Plan for the Red-breasted Goose, and to launch a major project for the species throughout the flyway.

## INTRODUCTION

This paper focuses attention on the globally threatened Red-breasted Goose *Branta ruficollis*, its population history and particularly its current status, the extent of our knowledge, and the past and ongoing conservation, research and monitoring programmes. The main purpose of the paper is to review the present situation and outline the constraints and priorities for future work.

## METHODS

This paper is based mainly on information from published studies and reports, reviews, unpublished reports and theses, and the personal comments of a number of contributors.

## RESULTS AND DISCUSSION

### Range and flyway

The Red-breasted Goose is a monotypic species occurring in central and western Eurasia (Fig. 1). Its breeding range is confined to the Russian arctic, where it occurs on three peninsulas in west-central Siberia: the Taimyr (c. 70% of the population), Yamal and Gydan (Madsen *et al.* 1999). The northern and southern limits of the breeding grounds are at about 73°N and 68°N, respectively. The eastern limit is generally considered to be in the Taimyr at 108-110°E. However, in the late 1990s,

Red-breasted Geese were discovered breeding in Yakutia, which extends the species' range to 114°E (Syroechkovskiy, Jr. 1999).

The first section of the migration route of the Red-breasted Goose is oriented in a south-westerly direction down the eastern side of the Ural Mountains towards Kazakhstan, along a "corridor" only 100-150 km wide (Hunter & Black 1996). In this section, there are several staging areas in the Ob River floodplains, the first of which is still north of the Arctic Circle. Further south, there are staging areas in the middle Ob near Khanty-Mansisk and in the region between Surgut and the River Vakh. On reaching Kazakhstan, the geese stage at several sites in the north-western part of the country (Kustanay region): in the Tobol-Ishim forest-steppe, and in the watersheds of the Ubagan, Ulkayak and Irgizin rivers in the Kazakh uplands. From there, the orientation of the flyway turns westwards, and the next known staging sites are at the Manych-Gudilo Lakes and Velvskoye Reservoir in Russia, to the west of the northern end of the Caspian Sea (Scott & Rose 1996).

From these last known staging areas, the geese enter their wintering range. Most of the recent literature on the Red-breasted Goose gives the contemporary wintering range of the entire population as the west coast of the Black Sea. However, in the last few years it has been shown that under certain conditions some geese may spend the winter along the north coast of the Black Sea and even around the Sea of Azov. The most important wintering sites are the Shabla and Durankulak lakes in Bulgaria, the Razelm-Sinoie complex and Danube Delta in Romania, Sivash Lagoon and the deltas of the Danube, Dnester and Dnepr

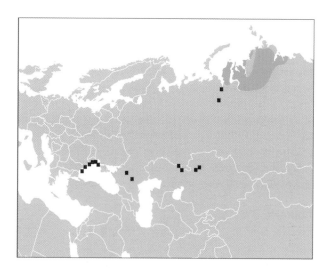

**Fig. 1.** The range of the Red-breasted Goose *Branta ruficollis* (green polygon – breeding range; red dots – staging or wintering areas) (after Cramp & Simmons 1977, Syroechkovskiy, Jr. 1995, 1999).

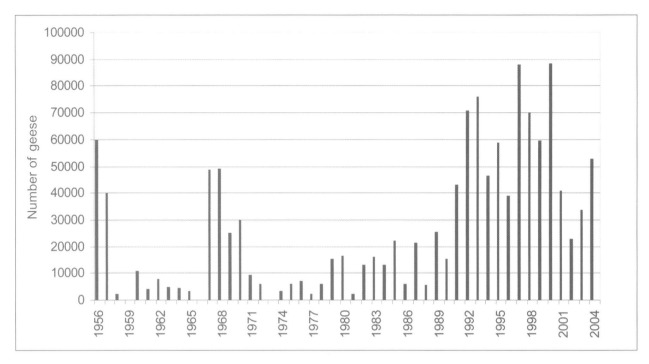

**Fig. 2.** Maximum counts or estimates (where count data are not available) of Red-breasted Geese *Branta ruficollis* in their wintering areas or staging areas (Kazakhstan) for the period 1956-2004. (The winter of 1955/56 is listed as 1956, the winter of 1956/57 as 1957, and so on). (Sources: Uspenskiy & Kishko 1976, Hunter & Black 1996, Dereliev 1998, Tolvanen & Pynnonen 1998, Madsen *et al.* 1999, Dereliev 2000a, Dereliev *et al.* 2000, Hulea 2002, B. Ivanov *in litt.*, S. Yerokhov *in litt.*).

rivers and adjacent "limans" in Ukraine (Dereliev 2000a, 2000b, Dereliev *et al.* 2000, Hulea 2002, Rusev *et al.* 1998, 1999) and, in warm winters, even the Kuma-Manych Depression in Russia (E.E. Syroechkovskiy, Jr. pers. comm.). Recent observations have shown that the Red-breasted Goose, although showing much higher fidelity to coastal areas than other wintering geese such as the Greater White-fronted Goose *Anser albifrons*, can be found over 100 km inland.

The wintering range of the Red-breasted Goose has not always been as it is today. In the twentieth century, there occurred a significant westward shift in the winter quarters by about 1 800 km. Up until the 1960s, the entire population spent the winter on the south-west coast of the Caspian Sea, particularly in the Kizil-Agach area in Azerbaijan. In that decade, the entire population abandoned the Caspian coast and moved to winter on the Black Sea coast. The last observations of large flocks (25 000 birds) in Azerbaijan were in 1970. Already in the late 1960s, similar numbers of Red-breasted Geese were being recorded on the west coast of the Black Sea in Romania. Large flocks of Red-breasted Geese (15 000 birds) were first recorded in Bulgaria in the late 1970s. This major shift in wintering range has been attributed to reduced food availability in the south-west Caspian because of a change from cereals and rice crops to cotton and vineyards, habitat loss, excessive hunting pressure, and possibly some other unknown factors (Isakov 1979).

## Population history

Records prior to 1954 are scarce, but it is thought that the numbers of Red-breasted Geese were similar to, or larger than, those of today. The first reliable estimation of numbers comes from 1956, when 60 000 Red-breasted Geese were reported to winter in the Caspian region (Fig. 2). Between 1956 and 1967, the population was thought to vary between 50 000 and 60 000

individuals (Uspenskiy & Kishko 1976). Coverage in 1967 and 1968 was the best that had been achieved up to that time, and produced a total of 49 000 birds, equally divided between the Caspian Sea and Black Sea regions. From 1969 to 1990, however, the maximum numbers recorded in the non-breeding areas did not exceed 30 000 (Hunter & Black 1996). There are suggestions that the population might have crashed as a consequence of the birds being forced to leave their traditional, but degraded, winter quarters in the Caspian region, and/or because of the effects of DDT on populations of the Peregrine Falcon *Falco peregrinus*, which is known to protect nesting geese from Arctic Foxes *Alopex lagopus* (Vinokurov 1990, Syroechkovskiy, Jr. 1995). However, it has been suggested that this decline was less dramatic than has been supposed, and that the big difference in numbers was due to a lack of adequate monitoring in the newly established wintering areas (Syroechkovskiy, Jr. 1995, Hulea 2002).

In 1991, a total of 43 180 birds were counted – the first time that over 30 000 had been recorded since the end of the 1960s. This was followed by a count of 75 881 in 1993 – the highest population size ever recorded for the species. In the following few years, fluctuating numbers were recorded, but the overall trend was one of increase. Peak numbers of 88 000 were recorded in 1996 in the staging areas in Kazakhstan, and again in 2000 in the wintering areas (Tolvanen & Pynnonen 1998, Hulea 2002, S. Yerokhov *in litt.*). However, within a period of only two years, numbers in the wintering areas crashed by more than 70% to only 23 000 birds in 2002. Several hypotheses have been put forward to explain this rapid decrease: (1) a new shift in the wintering range; (2) insufficient coverage of monitoring in recent years; and (3) a genuine population decline. The first of these hypotheses has been the subject of much discussion, but there have been no signs of a return of birds to Azerbaijan

(Sultanov pers. comm.) or establishment of new wintering areas elsewhere. Although there was some reduction in monitoring efforts in Romania in 2001-2002, the International Waterbird Census (a mid-January count) was carried out in all the countries in the wintering range, and covered the major roost sites.

The hypothesis that there was a genuine decline in the population between 2000 and 2002 has received the greatest support. S. Yerokhov (pers. comm.) reported a rapid decline in the numbers of staging Red-breasted Geese in Kazakhstan over the same period, and this was confirmed by Tolvanen *et al.* (2001). In Bulgaria at least, food was very scarce in the winters of 2000/01 and 2001/02 because of the limited amount of winter cereals in these years. The Red-breasted Geese were forced to concentrate along roads to feed on spilled grain – an unprecedented situation. Starvation and the harsh winters most probably led to high mortality. These events coincided with poor breeding conditions in the tundra. Reports of the breeding seasons of 2000 and 2001 in the annual bulletin of the International Arctic Birds Breeding Conditions Survey (Soloviev & Tomkovich 2001, 2002) from most of the monitored localities on the Yamal, Gydan and Taimyr peninsulas indicated an absence or low numbers of lemmings and voles, numerous predators (Arctic Foxes), low density of breeding birds of prey (Peregrine Falcon and Rough-legged Buzzard *Buteo lagopus*), and unstable, dry and unfavourable weather conditions: all prerequisites for low breeding success of the Red-breasted Goose population. Other "traditional" adverse factors at staging and wintering areas, such as excessive hunting pressure and disturbance, could also have contributed to the population decline.

Counts of geese in the next two winters (2002/03 and 2003/04) indicate that there has been a gradual recovery in the population to about 52 800 birds. This might have been a consequence of improved breeding conditions due to higher numbers of lemmings and lower predation levels in 2002 (Soloviev & Tomkovich 2003), and improved conditions in winter due to better food availability.

The geometric mean of the number of birds recorded in the last four winters (2000/01 to 2003/04) is only 35 900. This compares with a geometric mean of 75 500 in the previous four winters (1996/97 to 1999/2000), and represents a decline of 52%.

The future of the Red-breasted Goose seems uncertain. All the available information indicates that this species is highly susceptible to rapid fluctuations in population size due to slight changes in environmental conditions. Recoveries from population crashes might not always be quick and successful. Some critical sites in the wintering range are under increased threat from infrastructure development due to growing investments in Bulgaria and Romania. Global climate change poses an even greater threat. Based on modelling of climate change, it has been predicted that between 67% (scenario with moderate temperature rise of 1.7°C) and 85% (scenario with extreme temperature rise of 5°C) of the breeding tundra habitat will be lost by 2070-2099 because of changes in the vegetation (Zöckler & Lysenko 2000).

## Conservation status

The Red-breasted Goose is a globally threatened species currently classified as Vulnerable according to B2a + b(iii) of the IUCN Red List criteria (BirdLife International 2004a). It was also listed in the category Vulnerable in the 1994 and 2000 editions of the IUCN Red List, and was listed in the category Threatened in the 1988 edition.

The recently recorded decline ranges between >70% (from the highest count in 2000 to the lowest count in 2002) and 52% (from the mean numbers in 1996-2000 to the mean numbers in 2001-2004). Since this decline was observed over a very short period of time (less than 10 years), it meets IUCN Red List criterion A1a (≥70% population decline) or A2 (≥50% population decline), and the status of the species could therefore be upgraded to Endangered.

At European level, the Red-breasted Goose is classified as SPEC 1 (Species of European Conservation Concern, Category 1) due to its globally threatened status (BirdLife International 2004b).

## Conservation activities, research and monitoring

World-wide conservation activities for the Red-breasted Goose are co-ordinated through an International Species Action Plan, which was elaborated by the Wildfowl & Wetlands Trust on behalf of BirdLife International and published with the support of the European Commission, DG Environment (Hunter & Black 1996). This Action Plan was endorsed by the European Union through the Ornis Committee as well as by the Bern Convention. Some of the Range States have developed their own National Species Action Plans.

In the autumn of 1996, an International Red-breasted Goose Working Group was established within the framework of the Wetlands International Goose Specialist Group. The Working Group consists mainly of experts from the species' range states, and has been chaired by the Bulgarian Society for the Protection of Birds (BSPB)/BirdLife Bulgaria.

Most of the conservation activities throughout the range of the Red-breasted Goose are in some way related to the protection of roosting sites. Many wetlands where Red-breasted Geese congregate during the non-breeding season are managed in accordance with management plans officially endorsed by the state, or are the subject of management plans currently under development. In addition, some existing protected areas are being extended.

Since the geese are dependent on winter cereals as a food supply during the winter months, purchase schemes have been implemented by NGOs in Bulgaria and Romania. The general idea is to create buffer zones of protected agricultural land around the wetlands or to establish secure feeding areas inland. These schemes are in direct competition with investors whose plans are to establish tourist infrastructure and facilities near and around the coastal lakes. Since the investors are able to afford much higher prices than the NGOs, these schemes are only partially successful and the threat of habitat destruction at the key sites remains very high.

Despite the efforts of state authorities and NGOs to control hunting, shooting is still a major problem in some countries. Although a protected species throughout its range, the Red-breasted Goose is still being shot because it forms mixed flocks with the huntable Greater White-fronted Goose. Some key roosting sites, although protected, are often in winter practically under siege by hunters, who approach critically close to the wetlands and sometimes even to the shoreline. This hunting not only results in some direct mortality of Red-breasted Geese, but also has an indirect negative impact on the population as a whole because of the strong disturbance factor. Shooting causes distur-bance not only at the roosting sites, but also in the feeding areas, which are unprotected. Hunting is also a problem in the staging areas, but the severity of this is often unknown.

In the last decade, there have been very few studies that have focused on the Red-breasted Goose and its habitat. In the second half of the 1990s, Dr. John Quinn carried out a detailed scientific study of the behavioural ecology of the Red-breasted Goose in arctic Russia as part of his PhD study at the University of Oxford (Quinn 2000). This research deals, among other issues, with the habitat choice of breeding geese and nesting associations of geese and birds of prey. The winter feeding ecology of the Red-breasted Geese in Romania was studied by Dr. Dan Hulea during his PhD study at the University of East Anglia (Hulea 2002). In addition to habitat selection, food availability and feeding pref-erences, foraging dynamics and crop damage, this study covers the numbers and regional movements of the geese. Research by the author (for the Bulgarian-Swiss Biodiversity Conservation Programme, BSPB/BirdLife Bulgaria and Sofia University) in Bulgaria in the second half of the 1990s focused on phenology and dynamics of numbers, distribution at roosting and feeding sites, age ratio and body condition, diet and crop damage (Dereliev 2000a, 2000b).

The wintering range is currently the best monitored part of the species' flyway. Already by the end of the 1960s, with the start of the International Waterbird Census, most of the key sites were being covered with the aid of sporadic expeditions by western ornithologists. The first monitoring schemes to cover the entire wintering period commenced as early as the beginning of the 1990s. In Bulgaria, B. Ivanov (*in litt.*) attempted monthly counts at Shabla and Durankulak lakes for a period of three years in the early 1990s, and BSPB/BirdLife Bulgaria has been running a monitoring scheme of fortnightly counts since the winter of 1995/96. In this winter and the next, simultaneous monthly counts were carried out with Romania, and these were also attempted, with varying degrees of success, from 1998/99 to 2000/01.

The BirdLife Partnership launched a promising new initia-tive in the winter of 2003/04 as part of the activities of the International Red-breasted Goose Working Group. This initia-tive is known as the Red-breasted Goose Common Monitoring and Research Programme (RBGCMRP). Its general goal is to provide up-to-date information on the status of the species and its habitats, movements, ecology and conservation needs to facilitate the drawing up and implementation of adequate conservation activities. The initiative is co-ordinated by BSPB/BirdLife Bulgaria, and currently operates only within the wintering range (in Romania by SOR/BirdLife Romania and in Ukraine by UTOP/BirdLife Ukraine). In the first stage of the programme, it is planned to extend the scope of the simultaneous counts in the coastal wetlands in the three countries and to strengthen the programme. Later, it is planned to expand the programme to cover the entire range of the species. The programme receives financial support from RSPB/BirdLife UK in Romania and Ukraine, and from WWT in Bulgaria.

No special monitoring of the Red-breasted Goose has been carried out in the staging and breeding areas in recent years. However, there have been regular expeditions to Kazakhstan mainly by Finnish and Norwegian ornithologists supported by local experts. The main focus of these expeditions has been staging Lesser White-fronted Geese *Anser erythropus*, but they have contributed invaluable data on the Red-breasted Geese there. The second notable monitoring scheme is the Annual International Arctic Birds Breeding Conditions Survey, which has been carried out since 1998 and provides important data from the breeding grounds.

## Constraints and priorities for the future

Whether the Red-breasted Goose will be a thriving species in the new millennium or a species on the brink of extinction largely depends on adequate conservation measures. The formulation and implementation of such measures should be backed by rigorous research and monitoring programmes. All of these activities suffer from the same constraints of lack of sufficient human, logistic and financial capacity. Even in the wintering range, where conservation, research and monitoring activities have been most concentrated in the last decade, such problems hinder effective implementation. The situation is most serious in Ukraine, where the geese occupy vast coastal areas but human capacity is not adequately developed. Similar constraints exist in Romania as well, and to a much lesser extent also in Bulgaria. The ongoing activities rely on small grants, which do not allow institutional development and the necessary increase in capacity. In the staging and breeding areas, we are facing an even more complicated situation. In some parts of the flyway ("white spots"), no information has been available for a number of years because of a total absence of projects and expert coverage.

Largely for the above-mentioned reasons, the International Red-breasted Goose Working Group has not yet been able to provide co-ordination of activities outside the wintering range. It is an unfortunate fact that the species' flyway stretches across five countries, all of which are either developing or in transition (OECD 2003). Thus, the governments are encountering difficul-ties in providing financial and other support for implementation of necessary activities as described in the International and National Species Action Plans. NGOs in these countries are not well developed institutionally and are financially unstable, depending almost entirely on external funding. In addition, the framework of the International Species Action Plan is not suffi-ciently operational to provide good guidance to implementers.

Short- and medium-term actions should be undertaken in order to overcome these handicaps. In the first place, the International Species Action Plan should be reviewed, updated and rewritten in the shorter AEWA format, with a view to improving its usefulness at the operational level. A major part of the further implementation of the Action Plan should be carried out within the framework of a large-scale flyway project (GEF or similar). While supporting basic scientific research and the strengthening of ongoing monitoring and conservation activities, the project should focus mainly on human and institutional capacity building. Thus, firstly it would improve international co-ordination, and secondly it would have a catalytic effect on the development of networking throughout the flyway.

## ACKNOWLEDGEMENTS

I would like to thank several experts from the Range States – members of the International Red-breasted Goose Working Group – not simply for their contribution to this paper, but for their long-standing commitment to the conservation, research and monitoring of this remarkable species: Elchin Sultanov in

Azerbaijan; Dimitar Georgiev, Ivaylo Ivanov, Nicky Petkov and Viktor Vasilev in Bulgaria; Sergey Yerokhov in Kazakhstan; Dan Hulea, Attila Sandor, Alexandru Dorosencu and Eugen Petrescu in Romania; Evgeny Syroechkovski, Jr., Vladimir Morozov and Konstantin Litvin in Russia; and Ivan Rusev, Anatoly Korzyukov and Mykhailo Zhmud in Ukraine. I would also like to extend this acknowledgement to the donor organizations, RSPB (represented by Norbert Schaffer), WWT (represented by Baz Hughes) and other sponsors, for their invaluable support.

## REFERENCES

**BirdLife International** 2004a. Threatened Birds of the World 2004. CD-ROM. BirdLife International, Cambridge, UK.

**BirdLife International** 2004b. Birds in Europe: population estimates, trends and conservation status. BirdLife Conservation Series No. 12. BirdLife International, Cambridge, UK.

**Cramp, S. & Simmons, K.E.L.** (eds). 1977. The Birds of the Western Palearctic. Vol. 1. Oxford University Press, Oxford.

**Dereliev, S.** 1998. Monitoring of the Red-breasted Geese in Bulgaria in the 1990s. Threatened Waterfowl Specialist Group News: 38-40.

**Dereliev, S.** 2000a. Dynamics of numbers and distribution of the Red-breasted Goose *Branta ruficollis* (Pallas, 1769) in its main wintering area in the region of lakes Shabla and Durankulak. MSc thesis, Faculty of Biology, Sofia University "St. Kliment Ohridski", Bulgaria. (In Bulgarian).

**Dereliev, S.** 2000b. Results from the monitoring of wintering geese in the region of lakes Durankulak and Shabla for the period 1995-2000. BSBCP & BSPB/BirdLife Bulgaria, Sofia. Unpublished report. (In Bulgarian).

**Dereliev, S., Hulea, D., Ivanov, B., Sutherland, W.J. & Summers, R.W.** 2000. The numbers and distribution of Red-breasted Geese *Branta ruficollis* at winter roosts in Romania and Bulgaria. Acta Ornithologica 35: 63-66.

**Hulea, G.D.** 2002. Winter feeding ecology of the Red-breasted Goose (*Branta ruficollis*). PhD thesis, University of East Anglia, UK.

**Hunter, J. & Black, J.M.** 1996. Red-breasted Goose. In: B. Heredia, L. Rose & M. Painter (eds) Globally threatened birds in Europe: action plans. Council of Europe, Strasbourg, France: 79-98.

**Isakov, Yu.A.** 1979. Migration of the Red-breasted Goose. In: D.S. Pavlov (ed) Migration of birds of Eastern Europe and Northern Asia: Anseriformes. Nauka Publication, Moscow. (In Russian).

**Madsen, J., Cracknell, G. & Fox, A.D.** (eds). 1999. Goose populations of the Western Palearctic. A review of status and distribution. Wetlands International Publication No. 48, Wetlands International, Wageningen, The Netherlands; National Environmental Research Institute, Ronde, Denmark.

**OECD** 2003. DAC List of Aid Recipients as at 1 January 2003. Organisation for Co-operation and Development, Paris, France.

**Quinn, J.L.** 2000. Red-breasted Goose behavioural ecology in arctic Russia. PhD thesis. Oxford University, UK.

**Rusev, I.T., Zhmud, M.E., Korziukov, A.I., Gerzhik, I.P., Satzyk, S.F., Potapov, O.V. & Roman, E.G.** 1998. Patterns of bird wintering in north-western Black Sea region in 1998. In: Winter bird counts Ukrainian Azov-Black Sea coast. Proceedings of the XVIII Conference of the Azov-Black Sea Ornithological Working Group, 4-6 February 1998, Alushta-Kiev: 22-47. (In Russian).

**Rusev, I.T., Korziukov, A.I. & Satzyk, S.F.** 1999. Monitoring of wintering birds in north-western Black Sea region in 1999. In: Winter bird counts Ukrainian Azov-Black Sea coast. Proceedings of the XIX Conference of the Azov-Black Sea Ornithological Working Group, 18-21 February 1999, Melitopol-Odessa-Kiev: 46-60. (In Russian).

**Scott, D.A. & Rose, P.M.** 1996. Atlas of Anatidae Populations in Africa and Western Eurasia. Wetlands International Publication No. 41. Wetlands International, Wageningen, The Netherlands.

**Soloviev, M. & Tomkovich, P.** 2001. Arctic Birds: Newsletter of the International Breeding Conditions Survey, No. 3. Moscow.

**Soloviev, M.Y. & Tomkovich, P.S.** 2002. Arctic Birds: Newsletter of the International Breeding Conditions Survey, No. 4. Moscow.

**Soloviev, M. & Tomkovich, P.** 2003. Arctic Birds: Newsletter of the International Breeding Conditions Survey, No. 5. Moscow.

**Syroechkovskiy, E.E. Jr.,** 1995. Changes in distribution and numbers of Red-breasted Goose in 1980-1990s. Casarca 1: 89-102. (In Russian).

**Syroechkovskiy, Jr., E.E.** 1999. Eastward expansion of the Red-breasted Goose breeding range: first nesting records in Yakutia. Casarca 5: 95-100. (In Russian).

**Tolvanen, P. & Pynnonen, P.** 1998. Monitoring the autumn migration of Lesser White-fronted Goose *Anser erythropus* and other geese in NW Kazakhstan in October 1996. In: P. Tolvanen, K. Ruokolainen, J. Markkola & R. Karvonen (eds) Finnish Lesser White-fronted Goose Conservation Project. Annual Report 1997. WWF Finland Report No. 9: 19-20.

**Tolvanen, P., Aarvak, T. & Bragina, T.** 2001. Conservation work for the wetlands and monitoring the autumn staging of Lesser White-fronted Goose in the Kustanay region, north-west Kazakhstan, in 2000. In: P. Tolvanen, I.J. Øien & K. Ruokolainen (eds) Fennoscandian Lesser White-fronted Goose conservation project. Annual report 2000. WWF Finland Report No. 13 & Norwegian Ornithological Society, NOF Rapportserie Report No. 1-2001: 30-33.

**Uspenskiy, S.M. & Kishko, Yu.I.** 1976. Wintering of Red-breasted Geese in Eastern Azerbaidjan. Problems of the North V 2. Moscow: 235-243. (In Russian).

**Vinokurov, A.A.** 1990. *Branta ruficollis* in the USSR. In: G.V.T. Matthews (ed) Managing Waterfowl Populations. IWRB Special Publication No. 12, Slimbridge, UK: 197-198.

**Zöckler, C. & Lysensko, I.** 2000. Water Birds on the Edge: first circumpolar assessment of climate change impact on Arctic breeding water birds. World Conservation Press, Cambridge, UK.

# Conservation of the White-headed Duck *Oxyura leucocephala* in Central and South Asia

*David Li Zuo Wei[1], Taej Mundkur[1,2], Elena A. Kreuzberg-Mukhina[3], Sergey Yerokhov[4], Alexander Solokha[5], Zulfiqar Ali[6] & Abdul Aleem Chaudhry[7]*

[1] *Wetlands International, 3A39, Block A, Kelana Centre Point, Jalan SS7/19, Petaling Jaya, 47301 Selangor, Malaysia. (email: david@wiap.nasionet.net)*

[2] *Swarankit, Plot No 6, Mahatma Housing Society, Kothrud Pune City 411 029, Maharashtra State, India. (email: crabplover@yahoo.co.uk)*

[3] *Institute of Zoology of Uzbekistan Academy of Science, Niyasov str.-1, Tashkent, 700095, Republic of Uzbekistan. (email: iucn_uz@mail.ru)*

[4] *Institute of Zoology, Al-Farabi Str.93, Academgorodok, 480060 Almaty, Kazakhstan. (email: instzoo@nursat.kz)*

[5] *Wetlands International - Russia Office, Nikoloyamskaya Ulitsa, 19, strn.3, Moscow 109240, Russia. (email: asolokha@wwf.ru)*

[6] *University of Veterinary and Animal Sciences, Lahore, Pakistan. (email: zulfiqarali68@yahoo.com and zulfiqaruvas@yahoo.co.in)*

[7] *84 B III Johar Town, Lahore, Pakistan. (email: mhaleemi@yahoo.com)*

Li, Z.W.D., Mundkur, T., Kreuzberg-Mukhina, E.A., Yerokhov, S., Solokha, A., Ali, Z. & Chaudhry, A.A. 2006. Conservation of the White-headed Duck *Oxyura leucocephala* in Central and South Asia. *Waterbirds around the world.* Eds. G.C. Boere, C.A. Galbraith & D.A. Stroud. The Stationery Office, Edinburgh, UK. pp. 624-628.

## ABSTRACT

The White-headed Duck *Oxyura leucocephala* is the only stiff-tail (Oxyurini) indigenous to the Palearctic. The global population, which was probably over 100 000 in the early twentieth century, has decreased to 8 000-13 000 individuals in 2002. In the Central Asian region, the details of the life cycle of the species and its precise migratory habits largely remain an enigma. As the region undergoes an extended periodic drying cycle, there is a challenge of ensuring maintenance of wetlands in their natural condition, and ensuring allocation to these wetlands of regular water supplies, given that human impacts on wetlands increase from domestic, industrial and agricultural uses. The fate of the small population of White-headed Ducks that migrate to Pakistan remains in question. In 2003, Wetlands International undertook a comprehensive survey and collation of information to ascertain the status and conservation needs of the

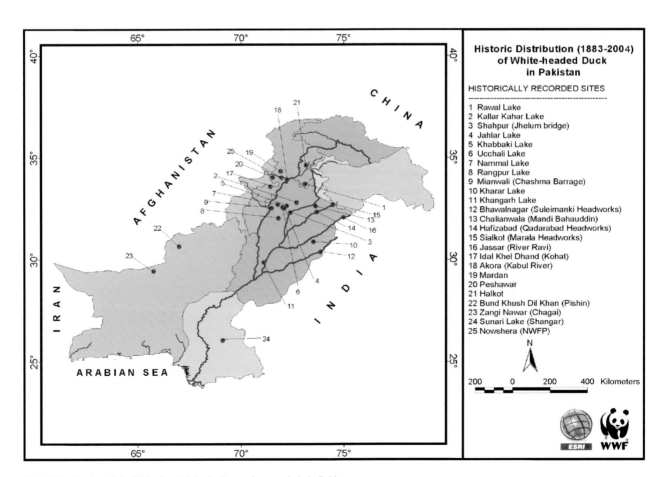

**Fig. 1.** Distribution of the White-headed Duck *Oxyura leucocephala* in Pakistan.

species, the results of which were published in a report. Surveys in Uzbekistan, Kazakhstan and Pakistan in 2003 and 2004 have provided new information on the important sites for the species. This paper provides an update on the status and conservation needs of the species.

## INTRODUCTION

The White-headed Duck *Oxyura leucocephala* is a globally threatened species, currently evaluated as Endangered in the IUCN Red List of Threatened Species (BirdLife International 2004). Its range and population size have decreased drastically since 1900, as a result of habitat destruction and hunting pressure (Green & Hughes 2001). The global population of the White-headed Duck was probably over 100 000 individuals in the early twentieth century, but had fallen to an estimated 19 000 birds in 1991 (Green & Hughes 1996). Since then, numbers have probably declined to as few as 8 000-13 000 individuals (Wetlands International 2002). This has aroused great concern for the conservation of this species.

With funding from the Convention on Conservation of Migratory Species of Wild Animals (CMS), Wetlands International carried out a comprehensive review of the status of the White-headed Duck in 12 Central Asian countries in 2002, and made a series of recommendations for its conservation. This report focused on the status of the White-headed Duck in Afghanistan, China, India, Iran, Kazakhstan, Kyrgyzstan, Mongolia, Pakistan, Russia (east of the Ural Mountains), Tajikistan, Turkmenistan and Uzbekistan. The report was published in February 2003 (Li & Mundkur 2003). A review of the status of the species in the Central Asian countries of the former USSR was published in 2002 (Kreuzberg-Mukhina 2002).

This paper presents the latest information available on the species in Central and South Asia, based on these reports and additional observations in Pakistan, Kazakhstan, Mongolia and Uzbekistan in 2003 and 2004.

## STATUS OF THE WHITE-HEADED DUCK IN PAKISTAN

In Pakistan, the White-headed Duck has been widely recorded at more than 25 sites across four provinces, namely Punjab, Baluchistan, North-West Frontier Province (NWFP) and Sindh (Fig. 1). The numbers of White-headed Duck have dropped from 1 039 in 1968 and 733 in 1987 to only about 10 birds in January 2001. In January-February 2002, Abdul Aleem Chaudhry carried out a field survey in northern Pakistan (Chaudhry 2002); only five birds were observed during the survey in January (at Jahlar Lake), and this number had fallen to three in February. However,

**Table 1. Recent counts of the White-headed Duck *Oxyura leucocephala* and status of its wetland habitats in Pakistan.**

| Site name | Last count of White-headed Duck | Status of wetlands in January-February 2002 | Status of wetlands in January 2004 | Threats to White-headed Ducks in Pakistan |
|---|---|---|---|---|
| Jahlar | 8 individuals on 5 January 2004 | Following light showers, there was some water in the lake. In the previous year, the lake had been completely dry. | The water storage capacity of the lake had been drastically reduced. | |
| Khabekki | 5 individuals in January 2001 | Due to a failure of the rains for the last few years, only about one eighth of the lake area was flooded. Very few waterbirds were seen. | Completely dry. | |
| Ucchali | 19 individuals on 15 February 2004 | Due to a failure of the rains, the water level was very low. Only a few waterbirds were observed on the lake. | The extent of water had decreased to only about 100 ha. | Drought. Habitat loss and modification. Hunting and disturbance. Introduction of fishes, e.g. Grass Carp and Tilapia. |
| Kharal | 14 individuals in January 1990 | The lake had been drained and was completely dry. | | |
| Kallar Kahar | 46 individuals in January 1984 | The lake has been developed into a recreational resort, and because of disturbance, very few waterbirds now visit the lake. | | |
| Nammal | 3 individuals on 15 December 2003 | No appreciable change in character except that the water level had dropped | | |
| Rawal | 7 individuals on 28 January 2003 | A recreational resort was being developed | Increased disturbance from general public, boating etc. | |

higher numbers were recorded in the next two seasons: 33 birds were recorded in January 2003, and 24 birds in January 2004 Abdul Aleem Chaudhry pers. obs., February 2004). Loss of habitat due to development and drought has been the major threat to the White-headed Duck in Pakistan (Table 1).

## POPULATION SIZE AND TRENDS OF NON-BREEDING/WINTERING BIRDS

The following summary of the population status of the White-headed Duck in South and Central Asia is based on Li & Mundkur (2003), but incorporates the latest information available from Pakistan and Uzbekistan (Table 2 and Fig. 2).

### South Asian population

As noted above, the wintering (non-breeding) population in Pakistan decreased rapidly from 1 039 birds in 1968 to only about 10 birds in 2001 and 2002, 33 birds in January 2003, and 25 birds in January 2004. The species is rarely recorded in India, and the last record is of a single individual in January 1997 in Uttar Pradesh.

### East Mediterranean & South-west Asia population

The numbers of birds recorded in Iran and Turkmenistan in January vary widely from year to year, with the total for the two countries reaching a peak of 1 300-1 500 birds.

In Uzbekistan, large numbers of White-headed Ducks were recorded for the first time in January 2000, when 1 137 birds were counted. Only 14 birds were counted in January 2002, but this low number should be treated with caution, as the count at Dengizkul Lake, where most of the White-headed Ducks were recorded in 2000, was incomplete because of poor access due to flooding. In January 2003, there was a very high count of 5 146 birds in Uzbekistan, mostly at Dengizkul Lake which in this year was being affected by natural drought and abstraction of water for agriculture. In January 2004, a total of 1 192 birds were recorded at several wetlands in Bukhara Province in Uzbekistan. It should be noted that in 2004 a significant amount of water that had been used for agricultural purposes was discharged into Dengizkul Lake. This changed the ecological conditions of the lake and led to a decrease in the numbers of wintering waterbirds including White-headed Ducks (Elena A. Kreuzberg-Mukhina pers. obs., March 2004). Observations have shown that there are no regular wintering sites for the White-headed Duck in Uzbekistan. Rather, it seems that the birds move from site to site depending on where conditions are favourable. Records of climatic conditions indicate that there has been a northward shift in the 0°C isotherm in January, and this is enabling birds to spend the non-breeding period further north than in previous years.

The numbers of White-headed Ducks in Turkey and Azerbaijan have fallen consistently over the past ten years. In

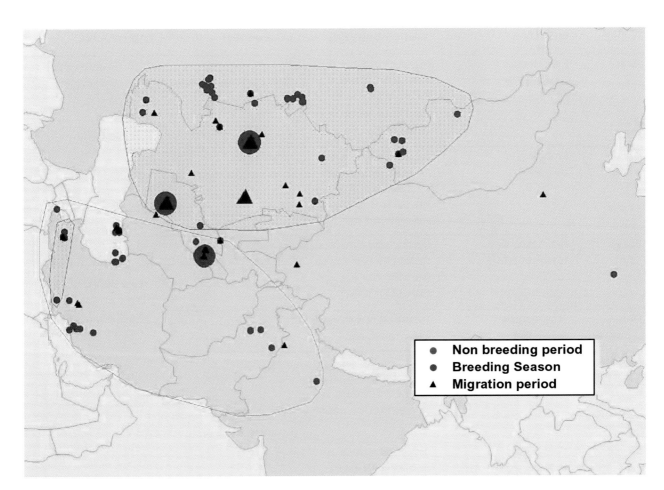

**Fig. 2.** Distribution of the White-headed Duck *Oxyura leucocephala* in Central and South Asia in 1990-2004.
**Notes:** Blue circles indicate breeding areas; red circles indicate wintering (non-breeding) areas; black triangles indicate staging areas during the migration periods. The large symbols indicate sites at which there have been counts of over 1 000 White-headed Ducks during the last five years.

**Table 2. Mid-winter counts of the White-headed Duck *Oxyura leucocephala*: 1990-2004.**

| Country | 1990 | 1991 | 1992 | 1993 | 1994 | 1995 | 1996 | 1997 | 1998 | 1999 | 2000 | 2001 | 2002 | 2003 | 2004 |
|---|---|---|---|---|---|---|---|---|---|---|---|---|---|---|---|
| **South Asian population** | | | | | | | | | | | | | | | |
| India | - | - | - | - | - | - | - | 1 | 0 | 0 | 0 | 0 | 0 | 0 | 0 |
| Pakistan | 76 | 64 | 146 | 145 | 148 | 51 | 32 | 52 | 56 | 36 | 23 | 10 | 10 | 33 | 24 |
| **East Mediterranean & South-west Asia population** | | | | | | | | | | | | | | | |
| Afghanistan | - | - | - | - | - | - | - | - | - | - | - | - | - | - | - |
| Iran | 0 | 19 | 20 | 82 | 482 | 1 485 | 13 | 356 | - | 26 | - | 4 | 591 | - | - |
| Turkmenistan | 0 | 223 | - | 3 | - | - | - | - | 820 | 7 | 287 | 476 | 723 | - | - |
| Uzbekistan | - | - | - | - | - | - | - | - | - | - | 1 137 | - | 14 | 5 146 | 1 192 |
| Albania | - | - | - | - | - | 4 | - | 0 | 0 | 0 | 0 | 0 | - | - | - |
| Azerbaijan | - | 3 520 | - | - | - | 1 | 136 | 210 | 1 100 | - | 334 | - | - | - | - |
| Bulgaria | - | 8 | 81 | 186 | 34 | - | 76 | 0 | 175 | 634 | - | 1970 | 554 | - | - |
| Greece | 423 | 170 | 54 | 5+ | 349 | 900 | 632 | 2213 | 689 | 261 | 1 472 | - | - | - | - |
| Georgia | - | - | - | - | - | - | - | - | 2 | - | - | - | - | - | - |
| Israel | 410 | 191 | 256 | 140 | 19 | 75 | 1 | 127 | 72 | 62 | 102 | 274 | - | - | - |
| Romania | 18 | 5 | 3 | 4 | 75 | 17 | 9 | 12 | 284 | 350 | 520 | - | - | - | - |
| Syria | - | - | - | 30 | 35 | 140 | - | - | - | - | - | - | - | - | - |
| Turkey | 7 526 | 10 927 | 4 478 | 3 576 | 3 428 | 2 970 | 1 300 | - | 1 002 | 2 575 | 1 000 | 989 | 1 378 | - | - |
| Yugoslavia | - | - | - | 6 | - | 6 | - | 0 | 0 | 0 | - | - | - | - | - |

Published sources of information are listed in Li & Mundkur 2003. Additional information provided by: Abdul Aleem Chaudhry (Pakistan), Alex Filatov (Uzbekistan), Andy Green (overall range), Bahtiyar Kurt (Turkey), Baz Hughes (overall range), Behrouz Behrouzi-Rad (Iran), Elena Kreuzberg-Mukhina (Uzbekistan), Evgeniya Lanovenko (Uzbekistan), Gradimir Gradev (Bulgaria), Hamid Amini (Iran), Hichem Azafzaf (Tunisia), José Torres (Spain), M. Zafar-ul Islam (India), Myrrhy Gauser (Turkmenistan), Paul Isenmann (Tunisia and Algeria), Rahat Jabeen (Pakistan), Sadegh Sadeghi Zadegan (Iran), Vladislav Vasilyev (Turkmenistan), Yavar Shahbazi (Iran), and Zulfiqar Ali (Pakistan).

Note: Most counts were undertaken in January. In some countries where coverage has been poor, data from November and December of the previous year and February have been included.

Turkey, numbers have fallen from 10 927 birds in January 1991 to about 1 000 birds in January 2000, 2001 and 2002, and in Azerbaijan, from 3 520 birds in January 1991 to 334 in January 2000. However, in the eastern Mediterranean, White-headed Duck numbers have apparently increased: 2 213 and 1 472 birds were recorded in Greece in January 1997 and 2000, respectively; 1 970 birds were recorded in Bulgaria in January 2001; and 520 birds were recorded in Romania in January 2001. This could suggest that the main wintering grounds of the White-headed Duck are shifting westwards.

During the period 1998 to 2002, the total number of White-headed Ducks recorded in January in the East Mediterranean & South-west Asia region was between 3 260 and 4 852. However, these data may give an incomplete picture of the wintering population in this region, as there was a lack of information from some countries in some years. In the 2003 review, Li & Mundkur (2003) therefore used the highest count of 4 852 birds (in January 2000) as the minimum estimate for the East Mediterranean & South-west Asia population, and gave the population estimate as around 5 000-10 000 birds. This estimate now needs to be revised in light of the new data from Uzbekistan, where 5 146 birds were recorded in January 2003.

**UPDATE FROM MONGOLIA AND KAZAKHSTAN ON MIGRATION AND BREEDING POPULATIONS**

According to Li & Mundkur (2003), the White-headed Duck breeds mainly in Kazakhstan, southern Russia, Uzbekistan and western Mongolia. Their report suggests that the Mongolian breeding population could be around 250 pairs and that in Kazakhstan, at least 300-500 pairs. Recent observations in Mongolia and Kazakhstan have provided further information on the size the breeding populations in these two countries. In Mongolia, 400 White-headed Ducks were observed in Khar Us Lake in July 2004 (Simba Chan pers. comm., September 2004). Belyalov & Kovshar (2004) provide information on the White-headed Duck in Kazakhstan in 2003. Highlights of their report include: a total of 1 021 adult birds with (uncounted) juveniles and chicks in the Tengiz-Korgalzhyn Lakes region in late August; 2 000 birds at Kyzylkol Lake, southern Kazakhstan, in September; and 162 birds at Sorbulak Lake in early April. Observations of birds at new sites include: a pair in Ustkamenogrsk region, eastern Kazakhstan, in June; 17 birds in Karaganda region, central Kazakhstan, in September; up to five birds at south Balchasch Lake (Lepsy River and Topar Lake) during May and June; and three to four birds at Sasykkol Lake, south-eastern Kazakhstan, from May to August.

## THREATS TO THE WHITE-HEADED DUCK
### Drought
The drought in Central Asia in 2000-2002 has greatly reduced the amount of wetland habitat for White-headed Ducks and other waterbirds. Many important sites for the White-headed Duck have dried out completely, or have had a much lower water level and greatly reduced water surface in some years. The long-term effects of drought on the viability of the White-headed Duck population are unknown but potentially serious.

### Habitat loss
The natural drought conditions have caused significant loss of habitat for the White-headed Duck. In addition, the unsustainable use of water resources for irrigation and the pollution of wetlands have further reduced the extent of suitable habitat. Water levels in the remaining wetlands of importance for the White-headed Duck have also been reduced.

### Hunting and disturbance
Although hunting of the White-headed Duck is banned in most countries, illegal hunting still occurs. Additionally, fishing, overgrazing and agricultural activities in and around lakes have both direct and indirect effects on the White-headed Duck.

## RECOMMENDATIONS
Li & Mundkur (2003) made six main recommendations for the conservation of the White-headed Duck in Central Asia, and these remain a priority.

- All countries need to undertake a review of their national policy and legislation to ensure adequate legal protection for the White-headed Duck and its enforcement. (National government agencies in the Range States).
- Sustainable management of water resources is needed to ensure adequate allocation of water to maintain the viability of wetland habitats used by the White-headed Duck. (National government agencies in the Range States).
- Site conservation measures, such as the establishment of an international network of sites of importance for migratory waterbirds including the White-headed Duck, need to be pursued. (Convention on Migratory Species and national government agencies in the Range States).
- A flyway-wide project should be developed for the conservation of the White-headed Duck and its wetland habitats through building and strengthening links between wetland managers and organizations involved in the conservation of the White-headed Duck across the region. (Convention on Migratory Species, national government agencies in the Range States, Wetlands International).
- A comprehensive population-monitoring programme should be developed to monitor the distribution and status of the White-headed Duck in the Central Asian region during the wintering, migratory and breeding seasons. (National government agencies in the Range States, site management authorities, NGOs).
- Research is urgently required to define the migration routes of the White-headed Duck and identify the population boundaries. Population surveys at all historical sites and all potential sites for the species are an immediate concern. (Research institutes, universities, NGOs).

## ACKNOWLEDGEMENTS
We thank a number of experts who have kindly contributed valuable information to this study. They include: A.K. Yurlov, Alex Filatov, Alexander Yakovlev, Anatoli Ostachenko, Andrie Gavrilov, Andrew Grieve, Andy J. Green, Axel Braunlich, Bahtiyar Kurt, Batdelger Dashnamjilyn, Baz Hughes, Behrouz Behrouzirad, D. Salmakeyev, Derek Scott, Elchin H. Sultanov, Eldar A. Rustamov, Evgeniya Lanovenko, Goetz Eichhorn, Nadejda S. Gordienko, Gradimir Gradev, Hamid Amini, He Fenqi, Hichem Azafaf, Holger Schielzeth, Islom Abdusalamov, Joerg Ratayczak, Joost van der Ven, Juma Saparmuradov, Lars Lachmann, Lei Gang, M. Zafar-ul Islam, Ma Ming, Maria Panayotopoulou, Myrrhy Gauser, N. Tseveenmyadag, Niels Gilissen, Nyambayar Batbayar, Paul Isenmann, Rahat Jabeen, S. Gombobaatar, Sadegh Sadeghi Zadegan, Serey Bukreev, Sergey Sklyarenko, Thomas Heinicke, Torres Esquivias, Vladislav Vasilyev, Will Cresswell, Yavar Shahbazi, Yehoshua Shkedy and Zulfiqar Ali. We would also like to thank Simba Chan and Oleg Belyalov who have contributed up-to-date information for Mongolia and Kazakhstan.

We also thank the Convention on Migratory Species (CMS) for providing financial support for compilation and dissemination of the 2003 status overview report.

## REFERENCES
**Belyalov, O.V. & Kovshar, V.A.** (compilers). 2004. Kazakhstan Ornithologist Bulletin 2003. Almaty. (In Russian).

**BirdLife International** 2004. Threatened Birds of the World 2004. CD-ROM, BirdLife International, Cambridge, UK.

**Chaudhry, A.A.** 2002. White-headed Duck Survey in Pakistan: 2002. Wetlands International, Kuala Lumpur, Malaysia. Unpublished report.

**Green, A.J. & Hughes, B.** 1996. Action plan for the White-headed Duck *Oxyura leucocephala*. In: B. Heredia, L. Rose & M. Painter (eds) Globally threatened birds in Europe. Council of Europe Publishing, Strasbourg: 119-146.

**Green, A.J. & Hughes, B.** 2001. White-headed Duck *Oxyura leucocephala*. In: D.B. Parkin (ed) BWP Update: the Journal of Birds of the Western Palearctic 3(2): 79-90. Oxford University Press, Oxford.

**Kreuzberg-Mukhina, E.A.** 2002. Review of the current status of the eastern populations of the White-headed Duck. Casarca 8: 277-294.

**Li, Z.W.D. & Mundkur, T.** 2003. Status Overview and Recommendations for Conservation of the White-headed Duck *Oxyura leucocephala* in Central Asia. Wetlands International Global Series No. 15. Wetlands International, Kuala Lumpur, Malaysia.

**Wetlands International** 2002. Waterbird Population Estimates – Third Edition. Wetlands International Global Series No.12. Wetlands International, Wageningen, The Netherlands.

# The Lesser White-fronted Goose *Anser erythropus* in the south-east Caspian region of Turkmenistan

*Vladislav V. Vasiliev[1], Mirra E. Gauzer[1], Eldar A. Rustamov[1] & Anna V. Belousova[2]*

[1] *Program IBA/RSPB in Turkmenistan, 19, Bakhry-Khazar street, Turkmenbashi, 745000, Turkmenistan.*
*(email: elldaru@mail.ru)*

[2] *All-Russian Research Institute for Nature Protection, Znamenskoye-Sadki, Moscow 117628, Russia. (email: anbelous@online.ru)*

Vasiliev, V.V., Gauzer, M.E., Rustamov, E.A. & Belousova, A.V. 2006. The Lesser White-fronted Goose *Anser erythropus* in the south-east Caspian region of Turkmenistan. *Waterbirds around the world*. Eds. G.C. Boere, C.A. Galbraith & D.A. Stroud. The Stationery Office, Edinburgh, UK. pp. 629-632.

## ABSTRACT

The south-east Caspian region of Turkmenistan is an important staging and wintering area for the globally threatened Lesser White-fronted Goose *Anser erythropus*. During the period 1975-2003, surveys carried out in late autumn and mid-winter recorded Lesser White-fronted Geese at a total of 14 sites. The numbers of geese fluctuated widely from a maximum of 1 850 individuals in November 1999 to none in several years. The most important sites were the Turkmenbashi, Balkan, Mihkailovskiy and Severo-Cheleken Bays in the central part of the Caspian coast of Turkmenistan, and the delta of the Atrek River in the southern part. Changes in the distribution and numbers of geese have occurred as a result of habitat degradation or alteration and other anthropogenic pressures, especially hunting. Various measures are proposed for the protection and management of the Lesser White-fronted Goose in Turkmenistan, and it is suggested that these measures could be used in the development of an international action plan for the conservation of the species in the Caspian region as a whole.

## INTRODUCTION

The basin of Caspian Sea is an important wintering area for the globally threatened Lesser White-fronted Goose *Anser erythropus*. However, the recent status and distribution of the species in the region, particularly in the south-east Caspian, have not been described in the literature. Information concerning the wintering populations of Lesser White-fronted Geese in the Caspian Sea basin has been lacking for a number of years (Morozov & Syroechkovskiy 2002). Furthermore, no attempts have been made to develop special measures for the conservation and management of the species in the Caspian region, in spite of the fact that the species is included in the national Red Data Books of the Caspian states. This paper provides a summary of recent information on the distribution and numerical abundance of the Lesser White-fronted Goose in the south-east Caspian region of Turkmenistan, and suggests a number of measures that should be taken for the protection and management of the population.

## METHODS

This paper is based on surveys carried out by V.I. Vasiliev in the south-eastern part of the Caspian Sea between 1980 and 2003, and also on data gathered by A.A. Karavaev in the lower basin of the Atrek River between 1975 and 1991 (Karavaev 1991). The surveys were undertaken by car, on foot, or in some years from a motor-launch, between October and March, usually twice a year – in the last ten days of November and first ten days of December, and in

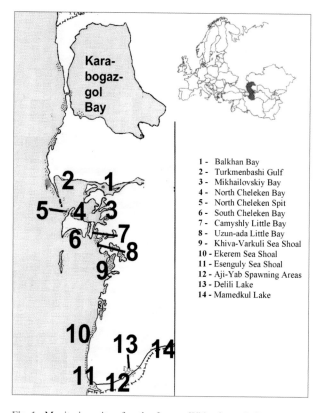

1 - Balkhan Bay
2 - Turkmenbashi Gulf
3 - Mikhailovskiy Bay
4 - North Cheleken Bay
5 - North Cheleken Spit
6 - South Cheleken Bay
7 - Camyshly Little Bay
8 - Uzun-ada Little Bay
9 - Khiva-Varkuli Sea Shoal
10 - Ekerem Sea Shoal
11 - Esenguly Sea Shoal
12 - Aji-Yab Spawning Areas
13 - Delili Lake
14 - Mamedkul Lake

Fig. 1. Monitoring sites for the Lesser White-fronted Goose *Anser erythropus* in the south-east Caspian region of Turkmenistan.

the first ten days of January. These time periods coincided with the end of the autumn migration / start of the wintering period, and middle of the wintering period. Forty-six surveys were carried out on the Caspian seashore, and 54 surveys in the delta of the Atrek River. Waterfowl were recorded at a total of 36 wetlands, and Lesser White-fronted Geese were observed at 14 of these sites (Fig. 1). In total, 6 241 Lesser White-fronted Geese were recorded. Only 5 774 individuals have been included in the present analysis, as the remainder were birds counted during general avifaunal surveys and may not have been correctly identified.

## RESULTS

The Lesser White-fronted Goose did not occur annually at any of the sites under investigation. During the 29 years under review (1975-2003), the maximum number of birds counted was 1 850 individuals in November 1999; the minimum number (in years when at least some geese were located) was only two individuals in November 1982. There were no observations of the species in the years 1976-1978, 1986-1987 and 1992-1996.

**Table 1. Counts of the Lesser White-fronted Goose *Anser erythropus* at monitoring sites in the south-east Caspian region of Turkmenistan. Monitoring sites are numbered as in Fig. 1.**

| Date | Monitoring sites | | | | | | | | | | | | | |
|---|---|---|---|---|---|---|---|---|---|---|---|---|---|---|
| | 1 | 2 | 3 | 4 | 5 | 6 | 7 | 8 | 9 | 10 | 11 | 12 | 13 | 14 |
| 15-25.01.1979 | | | | | | | | | | | | 31 | | |
| 27.11-02.12.1980 | | | | | | | | | | | 139 | | | |
| 10-20.01.1981 | | | | | | | | | | | | 39 | | |
| 20-30.11.1981 | | | | | | | | | | | | 10 | | |
| 20-30.12.1981 | | | | | | | | | | | | 10 | | |
| 20-30.11.1982 | | | | | | | | | | | | 2 | | |
| 01-10.02.1983 | | | | | | | | | | | | 53 | | |
| 05.12.1984 | 87 | | | | | | | | | | | | | |
| 28.01.1985 | | | | | | | | | | | | | 95 | |
| 26.11-03.12.1985 | | 79 | | | | | | | | 14 | | 4 | | |
| 15-23.01.1988 | | | | | | | | | | | | 78 | | |
| 20-30.12.1988 | | | | | | | | | | | | 6 | | |
| 22.01.1989 | | | | | | | | | | | | | 759 | |
| 20-30.11.1990 | | | | | | | | | | | | 3 | | |
| 19.01.1991 | | | | | | | | | | | 135 | | | |
| 30.11-06.12.1997 | 41 | | | | | | | | | | | | | |
| 26.11-02.12.1998 | 153 | | | | | | | | | | | | | |
| 17-24.11.1999 | 147 | | 464 | | 486 | 490 | 93 | | | | | 174 | | |
| 11-19.11.2000 | | | | | | | | | | | | 144 | | 18 |
| 14-21.01.2001 | | | | | | | | | | | | 96 | | |
| 21-30.11.2001 | 430 | | 36 | | | | | | | | | 650 | 17 | |
| 08-19.01.2002 | | 149 | | 75 | | | | | | | | 176 | | |
| 27.11.2002 | 194 | | | | | | | | | | | | | |
| 06-23.01.2003 | 4 | | | | | | 42 | 5 | 54 | | 73 | 12 | 7 | |

However, the possibility that Lesser White-fronted Geese occurred at other wetlands along the south-east Caspian shore in these years cannot be excluded, as most of the wetlands possess habitat that is potentially suitable for the species during the migration seasons or wintering period.

The two most important factors influencing the distribution and population dynamics of the geese in Turkmenistan are changes in the hydrological regime of the wetlands and hunting pressure. The largest concentrations of Lesser White-fronted Geese were found in protected areas in Turkmenbashi (formerly Krasnovodskiy), Balkan, Mihkailovskiy and Severo-Cheleken Bays in the central part of the Caspian shore at the limit of the State Khazarskiy (formerly Krasnovodskiy) Strictly Protected Area (zapovednik) (Fig 1). Over the period under review, an average of 40% of all Lesser White-fronted Geese recorded in autumn in the south-east Caspian region were found in these areas, and an average of 53% of all those recorded in winter.

The Aji-Yab wetlands (Aji-Yab spawning areas) in the lower basin of the Atrek River were formerly almost as important as the wetlands on the central Turkmenistan coast, with the numbers of geese ranging from 16% to 38% of the total population. Unfortunately, these sites have recently lost their value for Lesser White-Fronted Geese and other waterfowl as a result of drainage.

Table 1 gives details of the numbers of Lesser White-fronted Geese recorded in late autumn and winter at the 14 monitoring sites in the south-east Caspian region. The fluctuations in numbers at wetlands in the central part of the Turkmenistan coast showed slightly different tendencies from those in the southern part (Atrek Delta). The numbers of geese were more or less stable in the central part (470-600 individuals) and the southern part (maximum 667) during the autumn migration and early winter in 1999-2002. During the mid-winter period, the total number of geese usually falls: in 2002 the number in the central part decreased to 224 individuals, and in the southern part, to 176 individuals. The distribution of the species differed in some years. In January 1989 (in the middle of the wintering period), there were 759 Lesser White-fronted Geese in the lower Atrek Delta, and no birds in the central part. Similarly, in January 1991, there were 135 geese in the lower Atrek Delta and none in the central part. It should be noted that during the period 1975-1991, 84.4% of all Lesser White-fronted Goose observations in the Atrek Delta came from the period 1975-1983, and only 15.6% from the period 1984-1991 (Karavaev 1991).

The seasonal migrations of the Lesser White-fronted Goose in the south-east Caspian region produce two peaks: in autumn, in the first part of November, and in spring, in February, although the spring migration usually continues until March. The earliest date that Lesser White-fronted Geese have been observed in the lower part of the Atrek River is 25 October 1982, and the latest, 21 March 1983 (Karavaev 1991).

## DISCUSSION

The distribution and population dynamics of Lesser White-fronted Geese in the south-east Caspian region are characterized by fluctuations which are determined by habitat degradation or alteration and other anthropogenic pressures, chiefly hunting. A similar situation occurs on the breeding grounds where the goose populations face similar pressures (Morozov & Syroechkovskiy 2002).

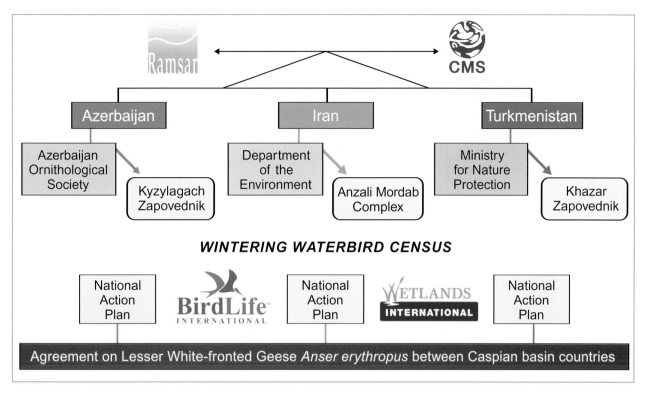

**Fig. 2.** Proposed model for integrated management of the Lesser White-fronted Goose *Anser erythropus* in the south Caspian region.

No strategy or action plan has yet been elaborated for the conservation of the species at regional level. In view of the present poor status of the Lesser White-fronted Goose in the region (e.g. erratic distribution, frequent movements between sites, low numbers and large fluctuations), we propose that the following measures be undertaken in Turkmenistan. These measures could be used in the future development of a strategy and action plan for the conservation of the species in the Caspian Sea region as a whole.

### Improvement of national legislation, particularly hunting regulations

- Application of international instruments relevant to the conservation of wetlands and waterbirds, including the Ramsar Convention on Wetlands (Ramsar, 1971) and Framework Convention on the Protection of the Caspian Sea Marine Environment (Tehran, November 2003). Turkmenistan should ratify the Ramsar Convention and designate as its first Wetland of International Importance (Ramsar site) the wetlands in the State Khazarskiy Strictly Protected Area, which constitute one of the most important staging and wintering areas for the Lesser White-fronted Goose. These international instruments could be used for the protection of Lesser White-fronted Goose habitat.
- Revision of the National Hunting Regulations. The Lesser White-fronted Goose is included in the Turkmenistan Red Data Book (1995-1999), and hunting of the species is prohibited throughout Turkmenistan. However the species could easily be shot during the autumn-winter hunting season together with other grey geese (*Anser* spp.) because of the difficulties in identification and low level of hunters' awareness. The hunting of geese should be carefully controlled or prohibited in certain areas where the Lesser White-fronted Goose occurs in high numbers. Greater effort

should be made to control illegal hunting, and the penalties for hunting Lesser White-fronted Geese should be increased several fold.

### Monitoring and conservation

- Continuation and expansion of the monitoring of Lesser White-fronted Geese during the migration and wintering periods in the south-east Caspian region, especially in Turkmenbashi, Balkhan, Miklhailovskiy and Severo-Cheleken Bays, and in the Atrek Delta. The monitoring should include censuses of the population, mapping of habitat, and ringing.
- Preparation of a wetland inventory to document sites of known importance for the Lesser White-fronted Goose and to identify sites of potential importance.
- Establishment of a network of Important Bird Areas in the Caspian region, with the co-operation of BirdLife International. This network should aim to provide the optimal system of protected areas for the Lesser White-fronted Goose, and could help to raise the awareness of local communities.
- Elaboration of a National Action Plan for the conservation of the Lesser White-fronted Goose in Turkmenistan.

### Education and awareness

- Raising awareness of the species' vulnerability. The Turkmenistan Society for Nature Protection should provide a programme of education in all settlements along the Caspian coast to raise awareness amongst local people, especially in Essenguly, Khazar, Turkmenbashi and Karabogaz.
- Providing education for hunters and raising their awareness through the Turkmenistan Society for Hunters and Fishermen, taking into account the recommendations of the Turkmenistan Ministry for Nature Protection.

- Drawing the attention of the central and local environmental organizations (government departments, NGOs and local societies) to the activities for raising awareness that are being undertaken within the framework of the UNDP-GEF Project on the sustainable use of the ecosystem in the State Khazarskiy Strictly Protected Area.
- Developing an action plan for the management of the principal habitats of the Lesser White-fronted Goose in the Turkmenistan sector of the Caspian Sea coast, to provide optimal management of protected areas as well as unprotected areas and hunting reserves.

We should like to stress that we are eager to co-operate in future investigations on the Lesser White-fronted Goose, not only in Turkmenistan, but also in Iran and Azerbaijan, with a view to the elaboration of an integrated action plan for the international management of the migration routes, stopover sites and wintering areas of the Lesser White-fronted Goose in the south Caspian region. The main steps in the elaboration of such an action plan are shown in Fig. 2.

## REFERENCES

Karavaev, A.A. 1991. Number and distribution of waterfowl at South-eastern Caspian Sea shore (Grebes, Pelicans, Ciconiiformes, Anseriformes). In: Natural Environment and Fauna of South-eastern Part of Caspian Sea Shore. Trudy Krasnovodskogo Gos. Zapovednika 2. Moscow: 37-143.

Morozov, V.V. & Syroechkovskiy, E.E., Jr. 2002. Lesser White-Fronted Goose on the Verge of the Millennium. Casarca 8: 233-276.

Lesser White-fronted Goose *Anser erythropus*. Photo: Rob Robinson.

# Reintroduction of the Lesser White-fronted Goose *Anser erythropus* in Fennoscandia with the help of microlight aircraft

*Johan Mooij[1], Axel Paulsch[2] & Wolfgang Scholze[3]*

[1]*Johan H. Mooij, Biologische Station im Kreis Wesel, Freybergweg 9, D -46483 Wesel, Germany. (email: johan.mooij@bskw.de).*

[2]*Axel Paulsch, Ibn (Institute of Biodiversity– Network e.V.), Johann-Maier-Stresse 4, D-93049 Regensburg, Germany. (email: Paulsch@biodiv.de)*

[3]*Wolfgang Scholze, DAeC- e.V., Hermann-Blenk-Straße 28, 38108 Braunschweig, Germany. (email: w.scholze@daec.de)*

Mooij, J., Paulsch, A. & Scholze, W. 2006. Reintroduction of the Lesser White-fronted Goose *Anser erythropus* in Fennoscandia with the help of microlight aircraft. *Waterbirds around the world.* Eds. G.C. Boere, C.A. Galbraith & D.A. Stroud. The Stationery Office, Edinburgh, UK. pp. 633-634.

The Lesser White-fronted Goose *Anser erythropus* is a monotypic species that formerly had a continuous distribution in the southern tundra between Lapland and Chukotka. Since the first population estimates of the 1950s, a drastic decrease in numbers was recorded from more than 100 000 to fewer than 27 000 birds in the 1990s. During the 1930s flocks of c. 50 000 Lesser Whitefronts were regularly recorded in the Western Palaearctic. During the 1950s the Western Palaearctic population was still estimated at more than 50 000 birds, but in the 1990s numbers recorded in this region during midwinter counts never exceeded 10 000 – 13 000.

Population numbers have decreased about 5% annually since the 1980's on most regularly monitored sites, and at present the wild Fennoscandian subpopulation is close to extinction. The reasons for this decline are changing conditions in stop-over and wintering sites, as well as hunting along migration routes in spite of the fact that hunting of the species is not permitted in most countries. The Lesser White-fronted Goose is included in Appendix 1 of the Bonn Convention, in Appendix II of the Bern Convention and in Annex I of the EC Directive on the Conservation of Wild birds. However, hunting of the quite similar looking Greater White-fronted Goose *Anser albifrons* causes high mortality of Lesser White-fronted Geese. Complete abandonment of hunting would be the best protection measure, but for at present this is not feasible.

The late Dr. Lambart von Essen started a re-introduction programme in Sweden in 1981. He avoided the main threats by creating a new safe migration route to safe wintering grounds using semi-domestic Barnacle Geese *Branta leucopsis* as foster parents for Lesser White-fronted goslings, which in this way learned to migrate to safe wintering grounds in Western Europe. With this programme von Essen showed that geese are imprinted on the area where they learned to fly and that young geese must be guided by their parents to the winter quarters. The Swedish re-introduction project founded the only expanding Lesser White-fronted Goose population worldwide. Today it consists of about 100-150 birds, all migrating to the Netherlands to winter. Although this project has been very successful, there are some genetic problems. Since 1991, a number of hybrids between Barnacle and Lesser-White fronted Geese were recorded in the range of the Swedish introduction scheme (Anderson & Larsson 2006).

The method of using microlight aircraft as foster parents was developed about a decade ago by Bill Lishman. Today it is an approved method used in Northern America, Europe and Asia, and already adopted for several endangered bird species, e.g. Whooping Crane *Grus americana,* Trumpeter Swan *Cygnus buccinator,* Bald Ibis *Geronticus eremita* and Siberian Crane *Grus leucogeranus.*

Aktion Zwerggans and its Swedish and Finnish partners intend to re-introduce Lesser White-fronted Geese in Fennoscandia by means of the microlight method. Within a period of four years, it is planned to guide a total of about 400 genetically 'clean' Lesser White-fronted Geese from the former breeding areas in Fennoscandia along a western migratory route from Finnish Lapland via Sweden and Denmark to western Germany. In the selected wintering site wild Lesser White-fronts are observed wintering every year. Along the planned migratory route hunting of Greater White-fronted Geese is forbidden. A test flight in 1999 showed that the microlight method has high survival rates comparable to the Swedish Barnacle Goose method. Changing traditional migratory routes and wintering areas is not uncommon in wild goose species (for example Greater White-fronted Goose and Red-breasted Goose *Branta ruficollis* (Dereliev 2006) in the second half of the 20th century).

The microlight method seems to be very promising and, together with the Barnacle Geese foster parent method already used by the Swedish re-introduction project, will hopefully save the Fennoscandian Lesser White-fronted Geese from extinction. In addition, the re-introduction of young Lesser White-fronted Geese by microlight aircraft would exclude the risk of hybridisation with Barnacle Geese. Several conclusions may be drawn from this:

- In spite of all past measures, the local Fennoscandian subpopulation is decreasing by about 5% annually and will be halved in about 10 years. According to modern population genetics the critical size for small isolated populations is likely to be a few hundred individuals (Baker 2006). At present the population size is clearly below this level and the population has little chance to recover again without a strong input of new genetic material.

- Re-enforcement of the Fennoscandian subpopulation by 'genetic upgrading' through the re-introduction of Lesser White-fronted Geese from other breeding lines could help restore the viability of the population.

- The re-introduction of artificially bred Lesser White-fronted Geese of non-hybrid origin may be helpful in saving the Fennoscandian subpopulation from extinction.

- Re-introduced Lesser White-fronted Geese should be forced to adopt alternative migratory routes in a part of the range with low hunting pressure to reduce mortality rates.

• The Swedish method of re-introducing Lesser White-fronted Geese with the help of Barnacle Geese as foster parents is successful but carries a high risk of hybridisation between the two species. The re-introduction of young Lesser White-fronted Geese with the help of microlight aircraft has proved to be as successful as the Swedish method but excludes the risk of hybridisation.

## REFERENCES

**Anderson, A. & Larsson, T.** 2006. Reintroduction of Lesser White-fronted Goose *Anser erythropus* in Swedish Lapland. Waterbirds around the world. G.C. Boere, C.A. Galbraith & D.A. Stroud (Eds.), The Stationery Office, Edinburgh, UK. 635-636.

**Baker, A.J.** 2006. Population declines and the risk of extinction in waders: genetic and ecological consequences of small population size. Waterbirds around the world. G.C. Boere, C.A. Galbraith & D.A. Stroud (Eds.), The Stationery Office, Edinburgh, UK. 668-671.

**Dereliev, S.G.** 2006. The Red-breasted Goose *Branta ruficollis* in the new millenium: a thriving species or a species on the verge of extinction? Waterbirds around the world. G.C. Boere, C.A. Galbraith & D.A. Stroud (Eds.), The Stationery Office, Edinburgh, UK. 619-623.

Lesser White-fronted Geese *Anser erythropus* flying alongside a microlight (inset). Photos: Christian Moullec.

# Reintroduction of Lesser White-fronted Goose *Anser erythropus* in Swedish Lapland

*Åke Andersson[1] & Torsten Larsson[2]*

[1] *Swedish Lesser White-fronted Goose Project, Ringgatan 39 C, SE-752 17 Uppsala, Sweden. (email: ake_a@swipnet.se)*
[2] *Swedish Environmental Protection Agency, SE-106 48 Stockholm, Sweden.*

Andersson, Å. & Larsson, T. 2006. Reintroduction of Lesser White-fronted Goose *Anser erythropus* in Swedish Lapland. *Waterbirds around the world.* Eds. G.C. Boere, C.A. Galbraith & D.A. Stroud. The Stationery Office, Edinburgh, UK. pp. 635-636.

The Lesser White-fronted Goose *Anser erythropus* used to be a common breeding bird in the mountainous area of Swedish Lapland but by the late 1970s the Swedish, as well as the whole Fennoscandian, population had declined severely (Norderhaug & Norderhaug 1984, Lorentsen *et al.* 1999). Today, probably less than 5% of the original population remains in the region. The last known and fully verified breeding record of the original breeding population in Sweden is from 1989 (von Essen 1999), and in Finland breeding ceased during the 1990s, but a small population of about 30-45 pairs still breeds in Norway (Øien & Aarvak 2002). The main reasons for the decline are thought to have been hunting pressure and environmental changes in the southeastern wintering areas. In 1981 the Swedish Association for Hunting and Wildlife Management started to reintroduce the Lesser White-fronted Goose to a former breeding area in Swedish Lapland. The aim of this programme was to establish a new population which would migrate to safer and better wintering areas.

A captive stock of Lesser White-fronted Goose has been kept at Öster Malma Wildlife Management School in central Sweden where, just before fledging, young birds are reared and released in Swedish Lapland with Barnacle Geese *Branta leucopsis* as foster parents (von Essen 1996). The goslings are imprinted on the release area and are guided by their foster parents to winter quarters in The Netherlands. In spring, the immature Lesser White-fronted Geese accompany the Barnacle Geese to central Sweden and then continue alone to the area in Lapland where they were released. All released goslings are individually ringed with leg rings and an observation network has been organized to study migration routes, return rate and breeding success.

During 1981 – 1999, a total of 301 goslings and 47 one-to-two year old geese were released in a well-known former breeding area in the mountainous area of Swedish Lapland. More than 47 breeding attempts have resulted in fledged young (Fig. 1). During the last five years at least 29 broods with a total of 83 immature birds have been recorded in early autumn. The size of the reintroduced population was estimated to be about 100 birds in autumn 2003.

The introduced Lesser White-fronted Geese use the area around Hudiksvall in central Sweden as a stopover site during both spring and autumn, with some geese also moulting there. The Hjälstaviken Ramsar site, in central Sweden, is used by some geese especially during autumn, but few families show up there. There is no other known regularly used autumn stopover site between Hudiksvall and the North Sea coast of Germany and the Netherlands, indicating that at least some geese make this journey as a non-stop flight. The established geese stay in coastal areas in The Netherlands during winter, where in recent years 60-80 birds have been regularly reported.

Genetic investigations on Lesser White-fronted Geese have confirmed that some of the birds in the Öster Malma stock were contaminated with genes from White-fronted Goose *Anser albifrons* (Tegelström *et al.* 2001). Pending the outcome of genetic studies, the release of birds in Lapland has been temporarily stopped and captive birds found to carry genes from White-fronted Goose have been destroyed. Efforts are now being made to recreate a breeding stock in captivity founded on wild birds.

The project is run by the Swedish Association for Hunting and Wildlife Management in cooperation with the Swedish Environmental Protection Agency, WWF-Sweden and Sveriges Vildnad. It is also supported by The Swedish Wetland Fund, Alvin Fund and Göran Gustafsson Foundation.

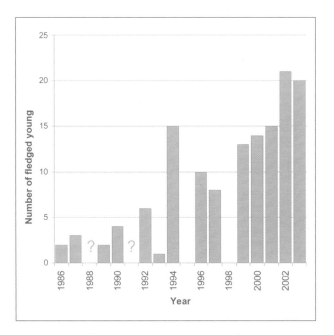

**Fig. 1.** Number of fledglings recorded from introduced geese or their descendants. In 1995, no breeding took place because of cold weather and in 1998 the ice broke up very late, causing high nest predation.

## REFERENCES

**von Essen, L.** 1996. Reintroduction of Lesser White-fronted Geese *Anser erythropus* in Swedish Lapland (1981-1991). In: M. Birkan, J. van Vessem, P. Havet, J. Madsen, B. Trolliet, & M. Moser, (eds). Proceedings of the Anatideae 2000 Conference, Strasbourg, France, 5-9 December 1994. Gibier Faune Sauvage, Game and Wildlife 13: 1169-1180.

**von Essen, L.** 1999. The Swedish reintroduction project on Lesser White-fronted Geese. In: P. Tolvanen, I.J. Øien,

& K. Ruokolainen (eds). Fennoscandian Lesser White-fronted Goose conservation project. Annual report 1998. WWF Finland Report 10 & Norwegian Ornithological Society, NOF Rapportserie no. 1-2000: 22-23.

**Lorentsen, S.-H., Øijen, I.J., Aarvak, T., Markkola, J., von Essen, L., Farago, S., Morozov, V., Syroechkovsky, Jr., & Tolvanen, P.** 1999. Lesser White-fronted Goose *Anser erythropus*. Pp. 144-161. In: J. Madsen, G. Cracknell, & A.D. Fox, (eds) Goose populations of the Western Palearctic. A review of status and distribution. Wetlands International Publ. No. 48. Wetlands International, Wageningen, The Netherlands National Environmental Reseach Institute, Rønde, Denmark.

**Norderhaug, A. & Norderhaug, M.** 1984. Status of the Lesser White-fronted Goose, *Anser erythropus*, in Fennoscandia. Swedish Wildlife Research 13: 171-185.

**Øien, I.J. & Aarvak, T.** 2002. Fortsatt håp for den syngende gåsa Vår Fuglefauna 25(3): 117-122.

**Tegelström, H., Ruokonen, M. & Löfgren, S.** 2001. The genetic status of the captive Lesser White-fronted Geese used for breeding and reintroduction in Sweden and Finland. In: P. Tolvanen, I.J. Øien, & K. Ruokolainen (eds). Fennoscandian Lesser White-fronted Goose conservation project. Annual Report 2000. WWF Finland Report 13 & Norwegian Ornithological Society, NOF Rapportserie no. 1-2001: 22-23.

A pair of Lesser White-fronted Geese *Anser erythropus* at Valdak Marshes, Northern Norway. Photo: Ingar Jostein Øien.

# Twenty-five years of population monitoring – the rise and fall of the Greenland White-fronted Goose *Anser albifrons flavirostris*

*A.D. Fox[1], A.J. Walsh[2], D.W. Norriss[3], H.J. Wilson[3], David A. Stroud[4] & Ian Francis[5]*

[1]*Department of Wildlife Ecology and Biodiversity, National Environmental Research Institute, Kalø, Grenåvej 12, DK-8410 Rønde, Denmark. (email: tfo@dmu.dk)*

[2]*Department of the Environment, Heritage and Local Government, Wexford Wildfowl Reserve, North Slob, Wexford, Ireland.*

[3]*Department of the Environment, Heritage and Local Government, 7 Ely Place, Ely Square, Dublin 2, Ireland.*

[4]*Joint Nature Conservation Committee, Monkstone House, City Road, Peterborough, PE1 1JY, UK.*
*(email: david.stroud@jncc.gov.uk; anseralbifronsflavirostris@hotmail.com)*

[5]*Royal Society for the Protection of Birds, 10 Albyn Terrace, Aberdeen, AB10 1YP, UK.*

Fox, A.D., Walsh, A.J., Norriss, D.W., Wilson, H.J., Stroud, D.A. & Francis, I.S. 2006. Twenty-five years of population monitoring – the rise and fall of the Greenland White-fronted Goose *Anser albifrons flavirostris*. *Waterbirds around the world*. Eds. G.C. Boere, C.A. Galbraith & D.A. Stroud. The Stationery Office, Edinburgh, UK. pp. 637-639.

This paper describes changes in the populations of the White-fronted Goose during the past 25 years, discusses possible reasons for these and suggests courses of action required now.

The Greenland White-fronted Goose *Anser albifrons flavirostris* breeds in west Greenland and migrates through Iceland to winter exclusively in Britain and Ireland. It is the most morphologically and geographically distinct sub-species of the circumpolar White-fronted Goose *Anser albifrons* (Ely *et al.* 2005). The global population declined from 17 500-23 000 in the 1950s to 14 300-16 600 in the late 1970s (Ruttledge & Ogilvie 1979), when it was protected from hunting and many of the sites supporting internationally important concentrations were given statutory protection (Stroud 1992, 1993). Subsequently the population recovered, and at the major Irish wintering site at least, the expansion in numbers fitted that modelled on the assumption of completely additive mortality during the previous period of hunting (Fox 2003).

Under protection measures, and helped by a series of good breeding seasons, the Greenland White-fronted Goose increased from 17 000 in 1982/3 to 35 500 in 1998/9. However, in the subsequent years, numbers have fallen dramatically to less than 27 000 in 2001/2, a 25% decline in three years

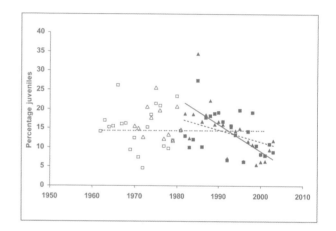

Fig. 2. Trends in reproductive output amongst Greenland White-fronted Geese at Wexford (triangles) and Islay (squares) based on sampled age ratios of juvenile geese. Data are presented for the period prior to (open symbols) and post-protection from hunting on the wintering grounds (filled symbols). Broken horizontal line shows the long term overall average. The declines since protection are statistically significant at Wexford (solid regression model line), but not on Islay (dotted line).

(Fig. 1). Because the population is closed and the annual population census covers all known wintering resorts, the change cannot be the result of changes in immigration or emigration, and must result from changes in birth or death rates. Evidence from survival estimates based on resightings of collared individuals suggest no major changes since protection in 1982/3, a conclusion supported by the results of population modelling based on counts at the two major resorts, Islay (Inner Hebrides, Scotland) and Wexford (southeast Ireland, see Fox 2003). However, the proportion of young returning to winter at Islay and Wexford shows declining trends since protection (Fig. 2). Evidence from detailed observations of collared birds at Wexford shows that known aged birds have shown an increased delay in the age of first breeding, and that an increasingly small proportion (<5%) of all goslings surviving their first winter survive to ever breed at all (Fox 2003). The recent decline in numbers is due to the failure to replace annual losses that have not changed substantially over a period of decades, and may be explained by a sustained decline in reproductive output rather than a small increase in mortality, although the causes for this long-term decline remain unknown.

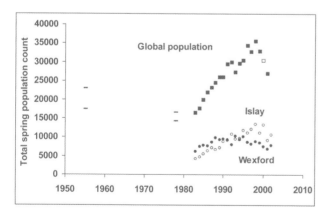

Fig. 1. Total population estimates for the Greenland White-fronted Goose based on literature sources in the 1950s and late 1970s (upper and lower levels shown as lines), and based on total spring counts of all known haunts since winter 1982/1983 (filled squares). Note the value for 2001 is estimated because of the Foot and Mouth epidemic that year. Annual spring counts are shown for the two most important wintering resorts, Wexford Slobs (filled circles, southeast Ireland) and Islay (open circles, Inner Hebrides, Scotland).

Declines in breeding success are ultimately due to extrinsic factors such as changes in nest predation rate or intrinsic factors to do with female body condition. There is no evidence for any change in nest predation rate in west Greenland, and it seems unlikely that such a change would occur synchronously throughout such an extended latitudinal range. Factors affecting the ability of females to attain breeding condition could potentially act on geese during their period on the wintering grounds, spring staging or breeding areas. Several potential factors could act at each point in the life cycle: (i) increases in local density, (ii) climate change and (iii) habitat change.

On the wintering grounds, analysis shows no consistent evidence for density dependent decreases in reproduction at the site level and no general evidence of effects of climate change. There is evidence that flocks wintering on intensively managed farmland have higher breeding success than those using bogland and semi-natural habitats, suggesting shifts from traditional habitats in the last 30 years have been associated with increased, not decreased, reproductive success (Fox *et al.* 2005).

On the spring staging areas and breeding areas, there is little evidence for climate or habitat change affecting breeding success (A.D. Fox *et al.* unpublished data). There are no obvious consistent effects of density dependence in breeding success detectable at the population level amongst Greenland White-fronted Geese (A.D. Fox *et al.* unpublished data). It therefore seems likely that some other factor, perhaps operating directly on the breeding grounds, may be responsible for the long-term decline in breeding success.

The population of Canada Geese *Branta canadensis interior* that breeds in northern Quebec and winters in the eastern United States has colonised west Greenland in the last 20 years, an expansion confirmed by satellite telemetry, ringing recoveries, resightings and DNA analysis (Fox *et al.* 1996, Kristiansen *et al.* 1999, Scribner *et al.* 2003). Studies of interactions between Canada Geese and Greenland White-fronted Geese on the summer areas show the behavioural dominance of Canada Geese, at least during the flightless moult, which results in local displacement of White-fronted Geese (Kristiansen & Jarrett 2002). Extensive aerial survey of the west Greenland breeding grounds showed that in spite of favouring the same geographical region, the two species were less likely to occur together than expected by chance, suggesting some segregation at large spatial scales (Malecki *et al.* 1999). However, more detailed studies and extensive surveys are required to determine whether this is the major factor involved in depressing breeding success in Greenland White-fronted Geese, and repeat aerial surveys of the breeding grounds will be carried out during the summer of 2005 to confirm changes in the local abundance and summer distribution of both species over the last six years.

In conclusion, while there are several explanations for the recent decline in Greenland White-fronted Goose productivity, the most likely would seem to be the interactions on the breeding areas with the increasing numbers of Canada Geese that are appearing in west Greenland from North America (Fox *et al.* 2006). However, we really require some detailed studies of the breeding biology of the two species in sympatry and allopatry before we can conclude cause and effect.

The Greenland White-fronted Goose has adapted to novel feeding opportunities presented by rapid changes in grassland management and modern agriculture in Iceland and on the wintering areas, apparently enabling the population to adjust to the massive changes in the extent and quality of its natural peatland and wetland habitats that have occurred since 1940 (Fox *et al.* 2005). In addition, protection from hunting permitted its increase during the 1980s and 1990s. It is therefore somewhat ironic that changes in another hemisphere (agricultural improvement during the last century and hunting regulation since the 1990s in North America) have encouraged the expansion in numbers of another similar sized goose, *B. c. interior*, to the point where that population has colonised West Greenland. This extension of range may have now affected the reproductive success, and hence the population size, of another goose species wintering on the western fringe of Europe (Fox *et al.* 2006).

Canada Geese have become legal quarry in Greenland since spring 2004. Whilst there is no doubt that such exploitation may reduce their numbers locally, this will not solve the problem of declining reproductive success amongst Greenland White-fronted Geese. Care must also be taken to avoid increasing the kill of Whitefronts in West Greenland. The Greenland White-fronted Goose remains a quarry species in Greenland (where only a few hundred are thought killed each year because of their inaccessibility) and in Iceland, where the bag has shown a significant increase from 2 947 in 1996 to 3 685 in 2001 (data from the Icelandic Wildlife Management Institute). This increase, coincident with the decline in global population size, means that the Iceland hunting kill has risen from 8% to 12%, and now contributes a significant, and increasing, element of overall annual mortality. Whilst it is clear that the autumn hunt in Greenland and Iceland was sustainable during the period of population expansion of the 1980s and 1990s, the present level of kill cannot assist in returning the population to favourable conservation status. Furthermore, while the cessation of the autumn hunt cannot halt the current decline in the overall population, it is one tangible conservation action that will contribute to the slowing of the rate of decrease in numbers. In June 2006, the Icelandic government announced protection of Greenland White-fronted Geese, effective from autumn 2006. This is a most valuable contribution to the conservation of the population.

It is important that the management plan (Stroud 1992, 1993), drafted and agreed for this population in Wexford, Ireland in 1992 but never formally signed by the Range States (Ireland, United Kingdom, Iceland and Greenland), be reconvened and updated to establish research and monitoring priorities for action (Fox *et al.* 2006). Failing this, bilateral agreements between range states should be concluded. Actions must be targeted to secure the population for the future to ensure that the international investment in the protection of the population that occurred in the 1980s and 1990s was not in vain.

## REFERENCES

Ely, C.R., Fox, A.D., Alisauskas, R.T., Andreev, A., Bromley, R.G., Degtyaryev, A.G., Ebbinge, B., Gurtovaya, E.N., Kerbes, R., Kondratyev, A., Kostin, I., Krechmar, A.V., Litvin, K., Miyabayashi, Y., Mooij, J.H., Oates, R.M., Orthmeyer, D.L., Sabano, Y., Simpson, S.G., Solovieva, D.V., Spindler, M.A., Syrochkovskii, Y.V., Takekawa, J.Y. & Walsh, A.J. 2005. Circumpolar variation in morphological characteristics of Greater White-fronted Geese *Anser albifrons.* Bird Study 52(2): 104-119.

Fox, A.D. 2003. The Greenland White-fronted Goose *Anser albifrons flavirostris* - the annual cycle of a migratory herbivore on the European continental fringe. D. Sc. thesis, University of Copenhagen. Available at: http://www2.dmu.dk/1_viden/2_Publikationer/3_Ovrig e/rapporter/tony1.asp

Fox, A.D., Glahder, C., Mitchell, C., Stroud, D.A., Boyd, H. & Frikke, J. 1996. North American Canada Geese *Branta canadensis* in west Greenland. Auk 113: 231-233.

Fox, A.D., Stroud, D.A., Walsh, A., Wilson, H.J., Norriss, D.W. & Francis, I.S. 2006. Recent changes in abundance of the Greenland White-fronted Goose. British Birds 99:242-261.

Fox, A.D., Madsen, J., Boyd, H., Kuijken, E., Norriss, D.W., Tombre, I.M. & Stroud, D.A. 2005. Effects of agricultural change on abundance, fitness components and distribution of two arctic-nesting goose populations. Global Change Biology 11: 881-893.

Kristiansen, J.N., Fox, A.D. & Jarrett, N.S. 1999. Resightings and recoveries of Canada geese *Branta canadensis* ringed in West Greenland. Wildfowl 50: 199–203.

Kristiansen, J.N. & Jarrett, N.S. 2002. Inter-specific competition between Greenland white-fronted geese *Anser albifrons flavirostris* and Canada geese *Branta canadensis* interior moulting in West Greenland: mechanisms and consequences. Ardea 90: 1-13.

Malecki, R.A., Fox, A.D. & Batt, B.D.J. 2000. An aerial survey of nesting White-fronted and Canada Geese in West Greenland. Wildfowl 51: 49-58.

Ruttledge, R.F. & Ogilvie, M.A. 1979. The past and current status of the Greenland White-fronted Goose in Ireland and Britain. Irish Birds 3: 293–363.

Scribner, K.T., Malecki, R.A., Batt, B.D.J., Inman, R.L., Libants, S. & Prince, H.H. 2003. Identification of source population for Greenland Canada geese: genetic assessment of a recent colonization. Condor 105: 771–782.

Stroud, D.A. 1992. Greenland White-fronted Goose International Conservation Plan. Draft working document: Full plan (184 pp.) and Executive summary (21 pp.). Prepared for National Parks and Wildlife Service/International Waterfowl and Wetlands Research Bureau. Available from: Peterborough, United Kingdom: Joint Nature Conservation Committee, Monkstone House, City Road, Peterborough PEI IUA, United Kingdom.

Stroud, D.A. 1993. The development of an international conservation plan for *Anser albifrons flavirostris*, the Greenland White-fronted Goose: In: M. Moser, R.C. Prentice, and J. van Vessem, eds. Waterfowl and wetland conservation in the 1990s: A global perspective. Proceedings of the IWRB Symposium, St. Petersburg Beach, Florida, U.S.A. IWRB Special Publication No. 26. Slimbridge, U.K: 142-148.

Greenland White-fronted Geese *Anser albifrons flavirostris* on their staging grounds, Hvanneyri, west Iceland during September 2005. Photo: Chris Wilson.

# Experimental disturbance of moulting Greenland White-fronted Geese *Anser albifrons flavirostris*

*Christian M. Glahder[1] & Alyn J. Walsh[2]*

[1]*National Environmental Research Institute, Department of Arctic Environment, Denmark. (email: cmg@dmu.dk)*

[2]*Department of the Environment, Heritage and Local Government, National Parks & Wildlife, Wexford Wildfowl Reserve, Ireland.*

Glahder, C.M. & Walsh, A.J. 2006. Experimental disturbance of moulting Greenland White-fronted Geese *Anser albifrons flavirostris*. *Waterbirds around the world.* Eds. G.C. Boere, C.A. Galbraith & D.A. Stroud. The Stationery Office, Edinburgh, UK. p. 640.

Undisturbed wetlands are vital to waterfowl during their wing moult. In many Arctic goose populations, immature and non-breeding birds migrate to remote areas that contain both refuge lakes, safe from predators, and adequate food supplies for the moulting period. In West Greenland, even the most remote areas are today affected by many different human activities during summer. Moulting areas can be disturbed by mineral exploration (2.5-14.6% of ice-free land covered by licences in the 1990s), by hunters, their numbers increased 70% from 1994 to 2002, who now have the ability to reach most coastal areas in their motor-boats (20-fold increase since 1939), and by tourists (e.g. cruise liners have doubled over the last decade). In order to advise Greenland authorities, the aim of this study was to assess the behavioural and spatial response of moulting geese flocks to human intrusion.

Human disturbance was deliberately made to Greenland White-fronted Geese *Anser albifrons flavirostris* moulting on the Naternaq plain in central West Greenland. This Ramsar site holds about 10% of the total population of the Greenland White-fronted Goose (25-30 000). The study was carried out in July 1999 and 2000 in a 75 km² lowland tundra area dotted with lakes (68°18'N, 55°55'W). The hypothesis was that moulting geese would react to an intruding person in a similar way to their reaction to an attacking Arctic Fox *Alopex lagopus*: the geese would flee to a refuge lake and stay there until the intruder had disappeared, then normal behaviour would be resumed after a relatively short period. Prior to experimental disturbance, behaviour and distribution patterns of goose flocks were observed during one third of the moulting period (total c. 25 days). Goose flocks used lake systems of on average 4.4 lakes (SD=2.3, n=23) where distances between lakes were on average 52.9 m (SD=58.8, n=107). According to goose dropping counts, a strip no more than c. 20 m from lake shores was used for feeding and resting. There was a linear relationship between available feeding habitat and the number of moulting geese present at a lake (y = 5.96x – 3.56, df = 147, R² = 0.74, P< 0.001). This suggests that the food resource determines the number of moulting geese. The minimum feeding habitat that held geese was c. 2.3 ha. Furthermore, the distance from the nearest lake affected the presence of goose flocks: the shorter the distance the higher the likelihood of goose presence. A logistic regression model including feeding habitat and distance to nearest lake as variables, gave a highly significant description of the probability of a moulting goose flock to use a lake (Likelihood ratio G² = 37.89, df = 2, P<0.0001). From these analyses, it appears that the study area supports 70-75% of optimal goose numbers, indicating that few potential sites were vacant.

When a person disturbed the geese by walking straight towards a flock, it became alert at an average distance of 653 m

(SD=263, n=14) and fled at a significantly shorter distance of 448 m (SD=155, n=14). Fleeing flocks continued running and swimming for on average 26 minutes (SD=15, n=16) and traversed 1.1 km (SD=0.6, n=16). Moulting habitats from where geese were disturbed were either reoccupied (average period without moulting geese 3.2 days (SD=1.0, n=9)) or not reoccupied during the moulting period (average period 6.3 days (SD=3.4, n=7)). On average, the vacant period lasted for 4.6 days (SD=2.7, n=16) or about 20% of the moulting period. The observed disturbance reactions can impact the geese by (i) reducing their feeding ability because undisturbed habitats are likely to be occupied or not suitable, (ii) causing energy loss of a minimum of 5% of daily energy intake (one incident) due to prolonged running and swimming, and (iii) exposing them to Arctic Fox attacks during fleeing, returning and within inadequate habitats.

Simulations of a person traversing 10 randomly chosen transect lines (width 1 km) through the study area were made. On average 10.4% (SD=10) of all lakes in the study area holding geese were disturbed.

The disturbance effect of one intruding person was much more profound than hypothesised, since the period where geese were affected was measured in days and not in minutes or hours. About half of the moulting habitats stayed vacant for 10-15% of the moulting period, while remaining habitats where flocks were disturbed were unoccupied for the rest of the moulting period. Fleeing geese were not likely to find other adequate moulting habitats because a high proportion were already occupied.

The wetlands of Naternaq Ramsar site hold about 10% of the world population of Greenland White-fronted Goose *Anser albifrons flavirostris*. Photo: David Stroud.

# 5.2 Declining waterbirds: problems, processes and sites. Workshop Introduction

*David A. Stroud*

*Joint Nature Conservation Committee, Monkstone House, City Road, Peterborough, PE1 1JY, UK. (email: DavidStroud@jncc.gov.uk)*

Stroud, D.A. 2006. Declining waterbirds: problems, processes and sites. Workshop Introduction. *Waterbirds around the world.* Eds. G.C. Boere, C.A. Galbraith & D.A. Stroud. The Stationery Office, Edinburgh, UK. pp. 641-642.

The globally threatened Spoon-billed Sandpiper *Eurynorhynchus pygmeus* is in rapid decline for reasons that are not understood. The destruction and degradation of key sites on its East Asian flyway, especially in the Yellow Sea, will further impact on the species. Photo: Christoph Zöckler.

The status of many waterbird populations is poor, with major declines reported for many taxa, in many parts of the world as reported by many studies throughout this volume. Habitat loss and degradation remains the principle driver for these declines, although many other factors are significant, including the impact of over-exploitation as noted for geese by Syroechkovskiy in East Asia. For long-distant migrants, the ecological quality of major staging areas appears to be of key importance in sustaining populations. This has been noted especially for long-distance migrant waders (e.g. Barter, Syroechkovskiy and Stroud *et al.*).

The workshop reviewed the status of waterbirds and explored the processes underlying current observed declines. In particular, it considered issues at a number of 'mega-sites' which have been implicated as causes of declines of migrant waterbirds in those areas.

Whilst much conservation attention has been focused on the needs of migratory species — the subject of several international legal instruments concerning their conservation — a high proportion of globally or near threatened waterbird species are sedentary. Some of these species are much more poorly known and have a significantly worse conservation status than migrants. Evaluation of their current status suggests these species should receive urgent priority conservation attention, especially in light of the absence of international structures (such as, for example, the Convention on Migratory Species) to promote their conservation.

Of particular conservation concern is the declining environmental status of several key staging areas (such as inter-tidal wetlands of the Yellow Sea described by Barter), which provide energetic spring-boards for long-distance migrants. The degradation of these areas compromises the status of many migrant waders and other waterbirds. The rapid collapse of populations, forced below threshold levels, has been predicted theoretically, and now appears to be occurring in a number of rapidly declining populations. Baker describes the genetic and ecological consequences of small population sizes in waders – issues of significance to other waterbird taxa also.

Conservation responses must urgently address causes of wetland loss and degradation, as well as enhancing monitoring and research so as better to inform appropriate conservation policies. National and international strategies and conservation instruments have scope to help, but need to be much more strategic in their implementation so as to address root causes.

The completion of the 33 km seawall at Saemangeum in South Korea will destroy 40 100 ha of tidal-flat and shallows - an estuarine system which on present knowledge is the most important wader site in the whole of the Yellow Sea, supporting internationally important numbers of at least 17 species of waders (including several globally threatened species). Photo: Mark Barter.

A range of actions are desirable:

- There is urgent need for more and better population monitoring. As a minimum, adequately funded national monitoring programmes are required. The International Waterbird Census co-ordinated by Wetlands International offers an effective framework within which such monitoring can be organised.
- Internationally co-ordinated programmes should be developed to assess waterbird productivity and survival. This information would aid in the development of more focussed and cost-effective conservation responses. Interpretation of

multiple information sources and especially spatial data is greatly helped by Geographic Information Systems.

- The application of IUCN Red-list criteria at sub-species/population level should be encouraged to highlight the conservation status of individual biogeographic populations. This information is especially valuable in the context of listings under various international treaties.
- Further comparative analyses, using existing data and information, of waterbird status in different regions and flyways should be undertaken.
- The status of waterbirds worldwide should continue to be reviewed with the aim of continuing to provide technical advice to international conventions and other organisations as to those populations which should receive major attention with respect to their conservation, monitoring and research.

World leaders at the World Summit on Sustainable Development, Johannesburg, in 2002, established a target of "*a significant reduction in the current rate of loss of biological diversity*" by 2010. The declines reported in from all over the world suggest that, for many groups of waterbirds, it will be extremely challenging to achieve these targets without major changes to economic processes and the attitudes of society.

World leaders noted that to achieve this target "*will require the provision of new and additional financial and technical resources to developing countries*". It was noted also that at a minimum, significantly greater investment is urgently needed not only in developing countries, but also in developed nations. This is required to establish and maintain national monitoring schemes, as well as to understand the causes of population declines so that appropriate, targeted conservation responses may be made.

The rapid collapse of waterbird populations has been predicted theoretically and now appears to be occurring in a number of rapidly declining populations, including that of the Nearctic Red Knot *Calidris canutus rufa*. Photo: Rob Robinson.

# The conservation and population status of the world's waders at the turn of the millennium

*David A. Stroud, A. Baker, D.E. Blanco, N.C. Davidson, S. Delany, B. Ganter, R. Gill, P. González, L. Haanstra, R.I.G. Morrison, T. Piersma, D.A. Scott, O. Thorup, R. West, J. Wilson & C. Zöckler (on behalf of the International Wader Study Group)[1]*

*[1] Correspondence: David Stroud, Joint Nature Conservation Committee, Monkstone House, City Road, Peterborough, PE1 1JY, UK. (email: David.Stroud@jncc.gov.uk)*

Stroud, D.A., Baker, A., Blanco, D.E., Davidson, N.C., Delany, S., Ganter, B., Gill, R., González, P., Haanstra, L., Morrison, R.I.G., Piersma, T., Scott, D.A., Thorup, O., West, R., Wilson, J. & Zöckler, C. (on behalf of the International Wader Study Group). 2006. The conservation and population status of the world's waders at the turn of the millennium. *Waterbirds around the world.* Eds. G.C. Boere, C.A. Galbraith & D.A. Stroud. The Stationery Office, Edinburgh, UK. pp. 643-648.

## ABSTRACT

Using information from many sources, but especially data collated for the third edition of Wetlands International's *Waterbird Population Estimates*, we review the status of the world's waders in the late 1990s. There are widespread declines in most regions and biotopes caused principally by loss and degradation of wetland (and other) habitats. On different flyways, between 33% and 68% of populations are in decline, compared with only 0% to 29% increasing. Non-migratory, island species have especially poor status, with about half of all island waders being globally threatened with extinction. Of particular conservation concern is the declining environmental status of several key staging areas, which provide energetic 'spring-boards' for long-distance migrants. The degradation of these areas compromises the status of many migrant waders. The rapid collapse of populations, forced below threshold levels, has been predicted theoretically, and now appears to be occurring in a number of rapidly declining populations. Conservation responses must urgently address causes of wetland loss and degradation, as well as enhancing monitoring and research so as better to inform appropriate conservation policies. National and international strategies and conservation instruments have scope to help, but need to be much more strategic in their implementation so as to address root causes.

## INTRODUCTION

Other than in Antarctica, waders (or shorebirds) occur on nearly every shoreline of the world, as well as in many other biotopes. They are attractive birds, of economic and ecological importance, and accordingly in some parts of the world are well-studied. For some migratory waders, very large numbers occur at low densities over extensive breeding areas, but gather at much higher densities in the non-breeding season at a few localities, enabling their population status to be regularly assessed. They are thus amongst the better known groups of birds, and with their range of specialized feeding and migration ecologies, they are sensitive environmental indicators. Information on their international population status can accordingly be used to indicate the wider health of their environments: indeed, the task of ensuring the favourable conservation status of waders is inseparable from that of ensuring the conservation and wise use of their wetland and other habitats. Regrettably however, the loss and degradation of wetlands and other habitats continue apace all around the world (Millenium Ecosystem Assessment 2005), and are the underlying cause of the poor conservation status of so many species. Habitat changes have complex ecological, demographic and genetic consequences for waders.

In 2003, a conference of the International Wader Study Group (WSG) in Cádiz, Spain, brought together 132 specialists from 20 countries to review the population and conservation status of waders around the world. The global status of waders was assessed using the best available data, drawing on several major programmes that have compiled recent data, e.g. Dodman (in review 2002) and Thorup (2002), and summaries by Wetlands International (2002) and Zöckler *et al.* (2003). In particular, a major WSG review of the status of waders in Africa and Western Eurasia collated extensive new data (Stroud *et al.* 2004).

## RESULTS AND DISCUSSION

Following the taxonomy adopted by Wetlands International (2002), the scope of this review covers 511 populations of 214 species of waders in eleven families (Rostratulidae, Dromadidae, Haematopodidae, Ibidorhynchidae, Recurvirostridae, Burhinidae, Glareolidae, Charadriidae, Scolopacidae, Pedionomidae and Thinocoridae). Three of these species (and populations) are extinct; of the other 508 populations, trends are available for only 210.

Around the world, most populations of waders of known population trend are declining (Table 1) – a matter of international conservation concern. On different flyways, between 33% and 68% are in decline (overall 48%), compared with only 0-29% increasing (overall 16%): thus three times as many populations are in decline as are increasing. The reasons for these declines are diverse, although they are generally caused by habitat loss or degradation (Zöckler *et al.* 2003).

### Flyways in Western Eurasia and Africa

Comparisons between the three main wader flyway systems in Western Eurasia and Africa show that knowledge is better for populations using the largely coastal East Atlantic Flyway than for the other two: it has been possible to assess trends for 44 (93%) of East Atlantic Flyway populations, but for only 25 (76%) of the Black Sea/Mediterranean populations and for just 18 (35%) of West Asian/East African wader populations (Table 1; Stroud *et al.* 2004). Overall, the East Atlantic Flyway appears in the healthiest state: only a little over one-third (37%) of populations are decreasing. This is in contrast to the Black Sea/Mediterranean Flyway where, of populations with known trends, 65% are declining, and the West Asian/East African Flyway which has 53% of known populations in decline. Island populations – specifically those on the Canary and Cape Verde Islands, St. Helena and Madagascar – have a particularly poor conservation status and include most of the region's globally threatened species.

**Table 1. Status of the world's waders at the turn of the millennium. Data summarized from Wetlands International (2002). Figures include both migratory and sedentary species and populations.**

| Totals by Ramsar region[1] | Total no. wader species | Total no. wader popns. | No. popns. definitely or possibly extinct | No. Globally Threatened wader species[2] | No. Near Threatened wader species | No. popns. definitely or probably declining | No. popns. with definitely or probably stable nos. | No. popns. definitely or probably increasing | No. popns. with unknown trends |
|---|---|---|---|---|---|---|---|---|---|
| Africa | 81 | 202 | 1 | 5 | 4 | 40 | 36 | 14 | 111 |
| Europe | 39 | 98 | 0 | 2 | 1 | 30 | 28 | 12 | 28 |
| Asia | 65 | 198 | 1 | 10 | 7 | 31 | 16 | 7 | 143 |
| Oceania | 41 | 79 | 4 | 11 | 6 | 11 | 7 | 7 | 50 |
| Neotropics | 56 | 109 | 1 | 1[3] | 5 | 25 | 22 | 4 | 57 |
| North America | 42 | 86 | 1 | 4 | 2 | 31 | 20 | 6 | 28 |
| GLOBAL TOTALS | 214 | 511 | 7 | 23 | 19 | 96 | 72 | 32 | 304 |

**Other regions and specific flyways[4,5]**

| | | | | | | | | | |
|---|---|---|---|---|---|---|---|---|---|
| East Atlantic Flyway | 29 | 47 | 0 | 0 | 0 | 16 | 19 | 9 | 3 |
| Black Sea/Mediterranean | 31 | 33 | 0 | 1 | 1 | 17 | 5 | 3 | 8 |
| West Asia/East Africa | 44 | 51 | 0 | 2 | 1 | 9 | 9 | 0 | 33 |
| Sub-Saharan Africa | 7 | 10 | 0 | 0 | 0 | 1 | 0 | 2 | 7 |
| Central/South Asia | 59 | 71 | 0 | 6 | 1 | 7 | 3 | 4 | 57 |
| East Asia/Australasia[6] | 67 | 79 | 1 | 5 | 7 | 9 | 1 | 1 | 67 |
| Australasian endemics[7] | 24 | 35 | 2 | 7 | 2 | 6 | 4 | 6 | 17 |
| Central Pacific[8] | 9 | 9 | 2 | 4 | 0 | 2 | 3 | 0 | 2 |
| North America/inter-continental | 46 | 71 | 1 | 3 | 2 | 25 | 20 | 3 | 22 |
| South America | 26 | 42 | 0 | 0 | 4 | 6 | 7 | 2 | 27 |

[1]  Some species or populations may occur in more than one Ramsar region.
[2]  Including extinct species.
[3]  There is an urgent need to update formal IUCN Red-listings for Neotropical waders as a number of species are clearly of this status but are not currently categorised as such.
[4]  Totals also included in Ramsar Regions; some populations occur on more than one of the flyways.
[5]  Comparable information is not yet available for the following flyways: Pacific North America, Central North America, Mississippi, Atlantic North America – given the apparently major overlaps south of the breeding areas, data for these flyways are combined in the "North America/inter-continental" flyway category.
[6]  Excludes Australian, New Zealand and associated island endemic populations.
[7]  Australian, New Zealand and associated island endemic populations.
[8]  Excludes New Zealand and associated island endemic populations.

Comparison with the status of 66 populations in the 1980s (Smit & Piersma 1989) indicates that more populations are in long-term decline (13) than are either stable (eight), or in long-term increase (four). Some populations are severely threatened and in decline, and extremely rapid population declines (>50% since the mid-1980s) have been recorded for four populations: the two populations of Sociable Lapwing *Vanellus gregarius*, the single population of Black-winged Pratincole *Glareola nordmanni*, and the western European breeding population of Black-tailed Godwit *Limosa limosa limosa*. None of Africa's globally threatened waders are increasing their small population sizes.

### Central and South Asian Flyway

This is shortest of the world's wader flyways, lying entirely in the Northern Hemisphere. It is also one of the most poorly known, with a high proportion of its wader populations being unknown in either size or population trend (80% of populations; Davidson 2003a). Furthermore, nearly all existing estimates are over ten years old, meaning that contemporary knowledge of the waders in this part of the world is almost unknown. Nonetheless, the best available information indicates that about twice as many wader populations are declining as are increasing. There is an urgent need both to assess recent data for this flyway and to improve processes of basic data gathering and analysis.

There are five globally threatened waders in the flyway; the populations of four are in active decline, whilst the current status of the remaining species is unknown. A further six small populations have unknown status, and at least one of the species concerned, the Long-billed Plover *Charadrius placidus*, clearly qualifies for IUCN Red-listing. The proposed establishment of a Central Asian Flyway Agreement under the Convention on the Conservation of Migratory Species of Wild Animals (CMS) is a welcome step forward towards better understanding and conservation of waders on this flyway, but the scale and range of issues indicate that it will need to be highly strategic in its operation to have positive impacts.

### East Asian and Australasian Flyway

There are enormous human population pressures in this region which contains over a third of the world's human population as well as some of the world's fastest growing economies (Wilson 2003). This has major direct consequences for waders: over 80% of wetlands in east and south-east Asia are classified as threatened, with over half under serious threat. Of inter-tidal wetlands in South Korea, 43% have been destroyed by land-claim (with more underway), as also have 37% of inter-tidal wetlands on China's coastline (e.g. Barter 2002).

The East Asian/Australasian Flyway is the flyway with the highest number of wader populations and also the highest proportion of populations for which information on numbers and trends is lacking (85% of populations – see Table 1). For populations of known trend on this flyway, 82% are declining and only 9% increasing. The status of Australasian[1] endemic populations is better known (49% with unknown trend), and equal numbers (38%) are declining and increasing.

[1]  Australia, New Zealand and its associated islands

Asia and Oceania between them hold 29 globally threatened and near threatened species – 69% of all such waders globally. Of the 12 globally threatened species on the East Asian/ Australasian Flyway, one is possibly extinct, six are actively declining (including the Spoon-billed Sandpiper *Eurynorhynchus pygmeus*, which appears to be undergoing rapid population collapse; Tomkovich *et al.* 2002), and the status of the remaining five is unknown. None is recovering its status. The development of non-binding international mechanisms (APMWCS 2001) for conservation and monitoring is a welcome step forward, although there are huge challenges to secure the conservation of wetlands of global significance to waders so as to reverse current negative trends. This is especially so, given the intense socio-economic pressures within the region.

## Central Pacific Flyway

The region contains relatively few waders, but these are mostly small populations with poor conservation status (Gill *et al.* 2003), and there are more Critically Threatened and Endangered waders here than in any other part of the world. Excluding species endemic to New Zealand and its associated islands (which for the purposes of this paper are included in the East Asian/Australasian Flyway), 40% of populations are declining and none is increasing.

Whilst conservation actions have been taken for a few endemic species, the status of many other endemic and migratory species and populations is poorly known throughout this flyway. For endemic species, knowledge is better for species occurring in New Zealand and Australia than in the central and south Pacific (e.g. for species such as the Tuamotu Sandpiper *Prosobonia cancellata*).

Given the small population sizes and declines, there is an urgent need for greater conservation attention for endemic and especially migrant waders in the central Pacific. Limited conservation "capacity" of many Pacific island states and other nations' overseas territories in the region is currently a significant constraint on reversing the unfavourable conservation status of many Pacific waders.

## North America (including inter-continental migrants)

Migrant waders use four main flyway systems in North America (Pacific, Central, Mississippi and Atlantic: Morrison 2003), with most migrants overwintering in Central and South America. There are six globally threatened and near threatened species: one of these, the Eskimo Curlew *Numenius borealis*, is probably extinct, and four of the five remaining tiny populations may still be in decline.

Population trend analyses have indicated extensive declines in wader populations in many parts of North America, especially in Atlantic areas of the USA and Canada (Morrison *et al.* 2001). Overall, 52% of populations using the North American flyways are in decline, and only 6% are increasing. These widespread declines, which include alarming examples such as the recent extremely rapid decline of the Red Knot *Calidris canutus rufa*, indicate that conservation concerns and actions around the world must be extended to include species that are not currently listed as "at risk". Completion of Shorebird Conservation Plans in Canada (Donaldson *et al.* 2000) and the USA (Brown *et al.* 2001) are welcome national initiatives which have the potential to address the major issues, but it remains to be seen if they will be

adequately funded by governments. As yet, their implementation seems not to have led to improved population status of waders.

## South America (residents and intra-continental migrants)

None of the resident waders or intra-continental migrants in South America is currently recognized as globally threatened, and there are only four near threatened species. There is, however, an urgent need to update the IUCN Red List for South America to better reflect the current situation (González & Blanco 2003). South America also supports a significant number of endemic species and one endemic family of waders, the seedsnipes (Thinocoridae).

There is very poor knowledge of the population sizes and trends of South American waders, with this information lacking for 64% of all populations occurring only within South America (compared with only 31% of North American migrants). Of populations with known trend, 40% are declining and only 13% are increasing.

There is a major lack of funding for basic survey and population monitoring. This is especially the case for Neotropical migrant and resident waders, since international sources of funding are not readily available for monitoring, research and conservation.

## CONCLUSIONS

### The importance of staging sites for long-distance migrants

Long-distance migrant waders are highly dependent on the continued existence, in favourable conservation status, of a few key staging areas – the essential "stepping stones" to more northerly breeding areas. The importance of maintaining the ecological character of these vital places has been repeatedly stressed: what happens on staging areas such as the Wadden Sea in Europe, Delaware Bay in North America, the Yellow Sea in Asia and the Banc d'Arguin in Africa, seems to control much of the rest of the annual cycle – and survival – of these waders (e.g. Ens *et al.* 1990, Piersma 1994, van de Kam *et al.* 2004).

Declining food resources and reduced suitability of staging sites have major implications for the survival and reproduction of these migrants (Davidson 2003b). "Virtual habitat loss" can occur in these areas as a consequence of poor management arising from unsustainable exploitation of natural resources, disturbance and other local perturbations. This leads to damage to the ecological character of these wetlands with major consequences for their ability to continue to support waders.

### Loss of key staging areas

Major conservation issues currently face three internationally important coastal wetlands of critical importance to migratory waders:

- The completion of the 33 km seawall at Saemangeum in South Korea will destroy 40 100 ha of tidal-flat and shallows – an estuarine system which, on present knowledge, is the most important site for waders in the whole of the Yellow Sea, supporting internationally important numbers of at least 17 species of waders, including several globally threatened species. The Yellow Sea is itself by far the most important staging area on the East Asian/Australasian Flyway, hosting

**Table 2. Conservation status of wader populations occurring on islands compared to continental land masses. Species status from BirdLife International (2000).**

| | Total no. of wader populations | Total no. of wader populations not Red Listed | Total no. of wader populations Red Listed | IUCN Red List Status | | | | | |
| --- | --- | --- | --- | --- | --- | --- | --- | --- | --- |
| | | | | Extinct | Critical | Endangered | Vulnerable | Near Threatened | Data Deficient |
| Island | 53 | 27 | 26 | 3 | 2 | 4 | 6 | 11 | 0 |
| populations | | 51% | 49% | 6% | 4% | 8% | 11% | 21% | 0.0% |
| Continental | 458 | 425 | 33 | 0 | 3 | 2 | 9 | 18 | 1 |
| populations | | 92.8% | 7.2% | 0.0% | 0.7% | 0.4% | 2.0% | 3.9% | 0.2% |

at least two million waders of 36 species during northward migration (Barter 2002). At least 25 000 people also depend econ-omically on this wetland system, for fishing and shell-fishing.

- Delaware Bay is a critically important spring staging area in eastern North America. Over-exploitation by humans of food resources used by waders may now be affecting the ability of waders using this site to reach their Arctic breeding areas and to breed there successfully. This appears to be leading to drastic and rapid population declines in some species, especially the Red Knot *Calidris canutus rufa*.

- In the Dutch part of the international Wadden Sea, there is now compelling scientific evidence to indicate that unsustainable levels of industrial shell-fishing have led to redistribution of birds from the high quality feeding areas (e.g. Piersma & Koolhaas 1997, Piersma *et al.* 2001, van de Kam *et al.* 2004). Declines of the biogeographical populations of long-distance migrant waders most heavily dependent on the Wadden Sea have occurred and are continuing (Davidson 2003b). However, recent decisions in the European Court over the legality of the shell-fishery in relation to the nature conservation directives of the European Union mean that this over-exploitation has now ceased.

- The Banc d'Arguin National Park in Mauritania is a major wintering area for waders on the East Atlantic Flyway, yet fishing on an industrial scale by international fleets in the waters just outside the park is depleting fish resources and possibly impacting on the wider ecosystem.

### Agricultural intensification
Intensification of agriculture is a major driver of change to wetlands (Millenium Ecosystem Assessment 2005) and remains a major adverse factor affecting the status of waders not only in western Europe, with its long-established agricultural landscapes, but also in other regions such as eastern Europe and central Asia, where natural steppe landscapes have now been replaced by arable cultivation and other forms of agriculture. In North and South America, loss of natural habitats to agriculture is also of significant concern.

### Climate change
The ecological consequences of changing climate will be complex, but effects such as altered distributions already appear to be occurring (Rehfisch *et al.* 2004). Changed climate patterns, such as increased desertification of continental steppe regions, will exacerbate habitat loss and degradation.

### Status of short-distance, intra-continental migrants
Short-distance, intra-continental migrants have generally been afforded less attention than inter-continental migrants. In South America, Asia and Africa especially, there is a severe lack of information on intra-continental migrant waders (González & Blanco 2003, Stroud *et al.* 2004). For migrant waders which move long distances between rich and poor countries, there are several international mechanisms that fund research and conservation initiatives. However, for those species which move solely between southern, developing countries, there are few such international funding opportunities. This constrains essential monitoring and conservation activity.

### Status of non-migratory waders
Whilst much conservation attention has, correctly, been focused on the needs of migratory species – the subject of several international legal instruments concerning their conservation – about two-thirds (60%) of globally or near threatened wader species are sedentary. Some of these species are much more poorly known and have a significantly worse conservation status than migrants. Evaluation of their current status suggests that these species should receive urgent attention, especially in light of the absence of international structures to promote their conservation.

Many of the world's rarest and most threatened waders occur on islands (Table 2). About half of all island waders are globally threatened (compared to just 7% of populations occurring in continental areas), and these comprise a significant proportion of all globally threatened waders (Table 2). The conservation challenges faced by independent island nations and self-governing overseas territories of other nations are many, and there is often limited human capacity to address these. International organizations and conventions should assist these islands to develop appropriate conservation programmes as a matter of priority.

### Monitoring and research
There is urgent need for more and better population monitoring. As a minimum, adequately funded national monitoring programmes are required. The International Waterbird Census co-ordinated by Wetlands International offers an effective framework within which such monitoring can be organized. Monitoring might be most effectively undertaken through targeted enhancements focused on particular populations, especially those associated with certain geographic regions or habitats.

Characteristics of the population dynamics of waders, especially the larger species, are such that under certain circumstances, very rapid population "collapses" occur. Examples include the probably extinct Eskimo Curlew, the *rufa* population of Red Knot, and the globally threatened Slender-billed Curlew *Numenius tenuirostris*, Sociable Lapwing and Spoon-billed Sandpiper. For this reason, and on a precautionary basis, it is desirable that population monitoring systems at national and international levels are as responsive as possible. Formal alerting systems should accordingly be developed to warn of significant declines (e.g. Atkinson *et al.* 2006). Integrating population monitoring with demographic information should be developed to provide further "early-warning" systems.

In view of the extensive declines noted for many species of migratory waders, there is an urgent need to develop internationally co-ordinated research initiatives to uncover reasons for the declines, and also to understand why some populations are able to increase on flyways which have many populations in decline. Funding for such programmes should be a global priority.

### Genetic consequences for small populations

Genetic studies indicate not only that small populations are especially vulnerable to the accumulation of harmful genetic mutation (genetic drift), but also that "effective population sizes" are significantly smaller than "census population sizes" (Baker 2003, 2006). That is, not all individuals in a population contribute to the gene pool. Owing to the low genetic variability (homozygosity) of waders, there is particular concern as to the long-term genetic consequences of populations falling below 15 000 individuals (Baker 2006). A total of 140 wader populations, comprising 28% of the global total, are estimated to be smaller than this threshold. Special attention is needed for declining populations which are getting close to this threshold, since they may still have the capacity to recover.

### Further analyses to guide conservation actions

A range of actions are desirable:

- Internationally co-ordinated programmes should be developed to assess wader productivity and survival. This information would aid in the development of more focussed and cost-effective conservation responses to information from count programmes. Interpretation of multiple information sources and especially spatial data is greatly helped by Geographic Information Systems.
- The application of IUCN Red List criteria at subspecies/population level should be encouraged to highlight the conservation status of individual biogeographical populations. This information is especially valuable in the context of listings under various international treaties.
- Further comparative analyses, using existing data and information, of the status of waders in different regions and flyways should be undertaken.
- The status of waders world-wide should continue to be reviewed, with the aim of continuing to provide technical advice to international conventions and other organizations as to those populations which should receive major attention with respect to their conservation, monitoring and research.

World leaders at the World Summit on Sustainable Development, Johannesburg, in 2002 established a target of "a significant reduction in the current rate of loss of biological diversity" by 2010. Before that, in 2001, European Union Heads of State at Göteborg adopted the more challenging target "that biodiversity decline should be halted with the aim of reaching this objective by 2010." The declines reported in this paper from all over the world suggest that, for waders at least, it will be extremely challenging to achieve these targets.

World leaders noted that to achieve this target "will require the provision of new and additional financial and technical resources to developing countries". We agree, and also note that at a minimum, significantly greater investment is urgently needed not only in developing countries, but also in developed nations. This is required to establish and maintain national monitoring schemes, as well as to understand the causes of population declines so that appropriate, targeted conservation responses can be made.

### ACKNOWLEDGEMENTS

Many individuals actively participated in the International Wader Study Group's workshop on declining waders in Cádiz in September 2003, upon which this summary paper is based, and contributed to the preparation of the WSG's analysis of the status of migratory wader populations in Africa and Western Eurasia. We thank them all.

### REFERENCES

**APMWCS - Asia-Pacific Migratory Waterbird Conservation Committee** 2001. Asia Pacific Migratory Waterbird Conservation Strategy. Wetlands International - Asia Pacific. Kuala Lumpur, Malaysia.

**Atkinson, P.W., Austin, G.E., Rehfisch, M.M., Baker, H., Cranswick, P., Kershaw, M., Robinson, J., Langston, R., Stroud, D.A., van Turnhout, C. & Maclean, I.M.D.** 2006. Identifying declines in waterbirds: the effects of missing data, population variability and count period on the interpretation of long-term survey data. Biological Conservation 130: 549-559

**Baker, A.J.** 2003. Genetic and ecological consequences of near extinctions (population bottlenecks) of waders. Wader Study Group Bulletin 101/102: 17.

**Baker, A.J.** 2006. Population declines and the risk of extinction in waders: genetic and ecological consequences of small population size. Waterbirds around the world. G.C. Boere, C.A. Galbraith & D.A. Stroud (Eds.), The Stationery Office, Edinburgh, UK. 668-671.

**Barter, M.** 2002. Shorebirds of the Yellow Sea. Importance, threats and conservation status. International Wader Studies 12.

**BirdLife International** 2000. Threatened birds of the world. Lynx Edicions and BirdLife International, Barcelona, Spain, and Cambridge, UK.

**Brown S., Hickey, C., Harrington, B. & Gill, R.** (eds). 2001. The U.S. Shorebird Conservation Plan. Second edition. Manomet Center for Conservation Sciences, Manomet, Massachusetts, USA.

**Davidson, N.C.** 2003a. Status of wader populations on the Central/South Asian flyway. Wader Study Group Bulletin 101/102: 14-15.

**Davidson, N.C.** 2003b. Declines in East Atlantic wader populations: is the Wadden Sea the problem? Wader Study Group Bulletin 101/102: 19-20.

**Dodman, T.** In review 2002. Waterbird Population Estimates in Africa. Unpublished report. Wetlands International, Dakar, Senegal.

**Donaldson, G.M., Hyslop, C., Morrison, R.I.G., Dickson, H.L. & Davidson, I.** 2000. Canadian Shorebird Conservation Plan. CWS, Ottawa.

**Ens, B.J., Piersma, T., Wolff, W.J. & Zwarts, L.** (eds). 1990. Homeward bound: problems waders face when migrating from the Banc D'Arguin, Mauritania, to their northern breeding grounds in spring. Ardea 78 (1/2).

**Gill, R., Jr., Pierce, R., Riegen, A., Tibbitts, L. & Johnson, O.** 2003. The status of shorebird populations in Oceania. Wader Study Group Bulletin 101/102: 15.

**González, P.M. & Blanco, D.E.** 2003. Are shorebirds in decline in the Neotropical region? Wader Study Group Bulletin 101/102: 16.

**Millenium Ecosystem Assessment.** 2005. Ecosystems and human well-being: wetlands & water synthesis. World resources Institute, Washington, D.C. 68 pp.

**Morrison, R.I.G.** 2003. Shorebird populations in North America: numbers and trends. Wader Study Group Bulletin 101/102: 16.

**Morrison, R.I.G., Aubry, Y., Butler, R., Beyersbergen, G.W., Donaldson, G.M., Gratto-Trevor, C.L., Hicklin, P.W., Johnston, V.H. & Ross, R.K.** 2001. Declines in North American shorebird populations. Wader Study Group Bulletin 94: 34-38.

**Piersma, T.** 1994. Close to the edge: energetic bottlenecks and the evolution of migratory pathways. Hen Open Boek, Den Burg, The Netherlands.

**Piersma, T. & Koolhaas, A.** 1997. Shorebirds, shellfish(eries) and sediments around Griend, Western Wadden Sea, 1988-1996. Single large-scale exploitative events lead to long-term changes in the intertidal birds-benthos community. NIOZ-Rapport 1997-7. Netherlands Instituut voor Onderzoek der Zee, The Netherlands.

**Piersma, T., Koolhaas, A., Dekinga, A., Beukema, J.J., Dekker, R. & Essink, K.** 2001. Long-term indirect effects of mechanical cockle-dredging on intertidal bivalve stocks in the Wadden Sea. Journal of Applied Ecology 38: 976-990.

**Rehfisch, M.M., Austin, G.E., Freeman, S.N., Armitage, M.J.S. & Burton, N.H.K.** 2004. The possible impact of climate change on the future distributions and numbers of waders on Britain's non-estuarine coast. Ibis 146 (Supplement 1): 70-81.

**Smit, C. & Piersma, T.** 1989. Numbers, midwinter distribution, and migration of wader populations using the East Atlantic Flyway. In: H. Boyd & J.-Y. Pirot (eds) Flyways and reserve networks for waterbirds. IWRB Special Publication No. 9: 24-63.

**Stroud, D.A., Davidson, N.C., West, R., Scott, D.A., Haanstra, L., Thorup, O., Ganter, B. & Delany, S.** (compilers on behalf of the International Wader Study Group). 2004. Status of migratory wader populations in Africa and Western Eurasia in the 1990s. International Wader Studies 15: 1-259. (www.waderstudygroup.org).

**Thorup, O.** (ed). 2002. Consultation draft for Breeding Waders in Europe 2000 [as at June 2002]. International Wader Studies 14.

**Tomkovich, P.S., Syroechkovski, E.E., Jr., Lappo, E.G. & Zöckler, C.** 2002. First indications of a sharp population decline in the globally threatened Spoon-billed Sandpiper *Eurynorhynchus pygmeus*. Bird Conservation International 12: 1-18.

**Van de Kam, J., Ens, B., Piersma, T. & Zwarts, L.** 2004. Shorebirds. An illustrated behavioural ecology. KNNV Publishers, Utrecht, The Netherlands.

**Wetlands International** 2002. Waterbird Population Estimates – Third Edition. Wetlands International Global Series No. 12. Wageningen, The Netherlands.

**Wilson, J.** 2003. The East Asian-Australasian Flyway. Wader Study Group Bulletin 101/102: 15.

**Zöckler, C., Delany, S. & Hagemeijer, W.** 2003. Wader populations are declining – how will we elucidate the reasons? Wader Study Group Bulletin 100: 202-211.

Over a third of the world's human population occurs in East Asia and Australasia. The region's wetlands support dense human populations and are subject to a wide range of pressures and threats which have major implications for the many waterbirds that share these areas. Shellfishing in Fujian Province, China (Yellow Sea). Photo: Mark Barter.

# Long-term declines in Arctic goose populations in eastern Asia

*Evgeny E. Syroechkovskiy, Jr.*

*Institute of Ecology and Evolution, RAS, Goose, Swan and Duck Study Group of Northern Eurasia, Leninskiy prospect 33, Moscow, 119071, Russia.  (email: ees@gcnet.ru)*

Syroechkovskiy, Jr., E.E.  2006.  Long-term declines in Arctic goose populations in eastern Asia.  *Waterbirds around the world.* Eds. G.C. Boere, C.A. Galbraith & D.A. Stroud.  The Stationery Office, Edinburgh, UK.  pp. 649-662.

## ABSTRACT

Originally, the wetlands of eastern Asia were probably comparable in size to those of the Western Palearctic and North America, and it is likely that as recently as 200-300 years ago, the size of the goose populations was similar. However, it is estimated that there are now only about half a million geese in eastern Asia, as compared with 4.5 million in the Western Palearctic and 17 million in North America. In recent decades, most goose populations in eastern Asia have undergone very rapid declines and several are now at critically low levels. Two notable exceptions are the populations of Greater White-fronted Goose *Anser albifrons* wintering in Japan and Korea, where successful conservation measures and improvements in feeding conditions for geese have led to recent increases. Available information indicates that the main threat to east Asian geese is the loss of habitat in the staging and wintering areas, especially in China, although hunting is also a problem in many areas. We summarize field surveys on the breeding grounds in northern Russia in 1991-2005, and focus on the declines in population and changes in distribution of four species: Greater White-fronted Goose, Bean Goose *A. fabalis*, Lesser White-fronted Goose *A. erythropus* and Brent Goose *Branta bernicla*. It is hoped that the results of these studies will help us to find better solutions for the conservation of the threatened goose populations of eastern Asia.

## INTRODUCTION

The poor status of the goose populations in eastern Asia has been mentioned by many local research workers as well as authors of wide-scale reviews (e.g. Andreev, 1997, Madsen *et al.* 1996, Mooij & Zöckler 2000, Syroechkovskiy 1997a, 2001, 2003). In this paper, we try to analyse population trends and major range changes in the geese of north-eastern Russia, which comprise the great majority of east Asian geese. Our analysis is focused on Arctic geese, which make up the majority of geese in Asia. It does not concern three species with a more southerly distribution: Greylag Goose *Anser anser*, Swan Goose *A. cygnoides* and Bar-headed Goose *A. indicus*. However, many authors who have looked at these species have reported similar trends to those in Arctic geese (e.g. Dugintsov 1996, Babenko & Poyarkov 1998, Poyarkov 2001, Kear 2005, Cao *et al.* 2006a, 2006b).

## MATERIALS AND METHODS

We have studied the dynamics of goose populations in the eastern regions of the Russian Arctic for 15 years. In this paper, the term "eastern Asia" is not used in a strict geographical sense, but is simply used to describe that part of eastern Asia inhabited by populations of "true geese" (the genera *Anser* and *Branta*). The region stretches across Russia east of the Yenisey River basin, and includes China, Japan and Korea. The boundary between Western and Eastern Palearctic populations of geese

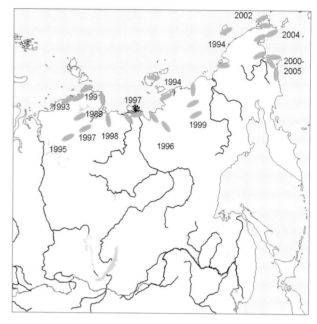

Fig. 1.  Goose population monitoring areas surveyed by the author and his team in the eastern Russian Arctic in 1991-2005. The years in which the areas were monitored are indicated.

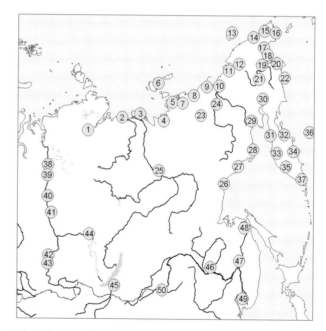

Fig. 2.  Key breeding areas and stopover sites for East Asian goose populations in Russia. The numbering of the sites follows Table 1.

varies between species. However, in this study, we have considered the Taimyr Peninsula as the western boundary of our study area. Here, the westernmost population of east Asian Bean Geese *Anser fabalis* reaches the western limits of its breeding

**Table 1. Territories of key importance for goose populations in the Russian part of East Asia, 1. The sources used for compilation of the table are listed in References.**

| | Area | Status of birds (breeding, moulting, migrating, wintering) | Protection status of the area | Key species of the Asian goose populations most numerous within the area 2, 3 | Recent rate of importance of the area for Asian goose populations | Monitoring scope since 1995 | Prevailing trends of goose species since 1995 |
|---|---|---|---|---|---|---|---|
| 1. | Plains of the southern and eastern Taimyr | breeding, moulting | partly protected | Bean Goose | low | poor | increase [5] |
| 2. | Plain north of the Pronchischeva mountain range between the Anabar and Oleniok rivers | breeding, moulting | unprotected | White-fronted Goose | medium | poor | increase [5] |
| 3. | The Lena River Delta | breeding, moulting | protected | Bean Goose, White-fronted Goose, Black Brant, Lesser White-fronted Goose | high | extensive | stable |
| 4. | Lower reaches of the Yana and Chondon rivers | breeding, moulting, migrating | unprotected | Bean Goose, White-fronted Goose, Black Brant | medium | intermediate | unknown |
| 5. | Lake plains adjacent to Lake Bustakh | breeding, moulting, migrating | partly protected | Bean Goose, White-fronted Goose | unknown | poor | unknown |
| 6. | Novosibirskie Islands (Novaya Sibir', Faddeevskiy, and the northern part of Bolshoy Liakhovskiy Island) | breeding, moulting | protected | Bean Goose, White-fronted Goose, Black Brant [3] | lost | no monitoring | unknown |
| 7. | Lower reaches of the Khroma River | breeding, moulting, migrating | unprotected | White-fronted Goose, Bean Goose | unknown | no monitoring | unknown |
| 8. | Lower reaches of the Indigirka River | breeding, moulting, migrating | partly protected | White-fronted Goose, Bean Goose, Black Brant | low | intermediate | decline |
| 9. | Alazeya tundras, including the Kuropatochia River basin | breeding, moulting, migrating | partly protected | Bean Goose, White-fronted Goose, Lesser White-fronted Goose | low | no monitoring | unknown |
| 10. | Kolyma tundras, including the Chukochii rivers basin | breeding, moulting, migrating | partly protected | Bean Goose, White-fronted Goose, Lesser White-fronted Goose | medium | poor | decline |
| 11. | Kyttyk-Ajon tundras | moulting, breeding, migrating | unprotected | Lesser White-fronted Goose, White-fronted Goose | medium | poor | unknown |
| 12. | Chaunskaya tundra | breeding, moulting, migrating | partly protected | White-fronted Goose | low | poor | decline |
| 13. | Wrangel Island | breeding, moulting, migrating | protected | Black Brant [3] | lost | extensive | - |
| 14. | Vankaremskaya lowland | breeding, moulting, migrating | unprotected | Emperor Goose, Black Brant[3], White-fronted Goose | high | poor | unknown |

**Table 1 (cont). Territories of key importance for goose populations in the Russian part of East Asia, 2. The sources used for compilation of the table are listed in References.**

| | Territory | | | Species | | Monitoring | Trend |
|---|---|---|---|---|---|---|---|
| 15. | Koliuchinskie tundras | breeding, moulting, migrating | unprotected | Emperor Goose, Black Brant[3] | medium | extensive | stable |
| 16. | Mechigmenskie tundras | migrating, breeding | partly protected | Emperor Goose, Black Brant[3], White-fronted Goose | low | intermediate | stable |
| 17. | Konerginskaya tundra | breeding, moulting, migrating | unprotected | White-fronted Goose, Emperor Goose[3] | high | no monitoring | unknown |
| 18. | Uelkalskie tundras | breeding, moulting, migrating | unprotected | White-fronted Goose | high | no monitoring | unknown |
| 19. | Taniurer-Kanchalanskie tundras | breeding, moulting, migrating | unprotected | White-fronted Goose | medium | no monitoring | unknown |
| 20. | Nizhneanadyrskaya (Low Anadyr) tundra | breeding, moulting, migrating | partly protected | White-fronted Goose, Emperor Goose[3], Bean Goose | high | intermediate | increase |
| 21. | Sredne-Anadyrskaya (Middle Anadyr) plain | breeding, migrating | partly protected | White-fronted Goose | lost | no monitoring | unknown |
| 22. | Lagoons of the northern Koryakia (Meinypilgyno, Khatyrka, etc.) | breeding, moulting, migrating | unprotected | White-fronted Goose, Bean Goose, Emperor Goose[3] | high | extensive | increase |
| 23. | Abyiskaya lowland | migrating, breeding, moulting | unprotected | Lesser White-fronted Goose | high | intermediate | fluctuating |
| 24. | Sredne-Koleimskaya lowland | migrating | unprotected | White-fronted Goose, Bean Goose | medium | no monitoring | unknown |
| 25. | Forty islands (the middle reaches of the Lena River north of the Viliuy River mouth) | migrating | partly protected | Bean Goose, White-fronted Goose | high | poor | fluctuating |
| 26. | Okhotsko-Kukhtuiskaya plain | migrating | unprotected | White-fronted Goose, Bean Goose | unknown | poor | unknown |
| 27. | Kava-Tauiskaya plain | migrating, breeding | protected | White-fronted Goose, Bean Goose | medium | extensive | stable |
| 28. | Malakchanskaya tundra | migrating | partly protected | White-fronted Goose, Bean Goose | high | poor | fluctuating |
| 29. | Gizhiginskaya plain | migrating | unprotected | Bean Goose, White-fronted Goose | unknown | no monitoring | unknown |
| 30. | Manilskie lakes (the lower reaches of the Penzhina River) | migrating | unprotected | Bean Goose, White-fronted Goose, Lesser White-fronted Goose | high | poor | slight increase following mass decline |
| 31. | Parapolskiy Dol lowland | breeding, migrating | protected[4] | White-fronted Goose, Bean Goose, Lesser White-fronted Goose | medium | poor | unknown |

**Table 1 (cont). Territories of key importance for goose populations in the Russian part of East Asia, 3. The sources used for compilation of the table are listed in References.**

| No. | Site | Use | Protection | Species | Importance | Monitoring | Trend |
|---|---|---|---|---|---|---|---|
| 32. | Malamvayam Lagoon (eastern Kamchatka) | migrating | protected | Black Brant [3] | high | no monitoring | unknown |
| 33. | Interfluve of the Utkholok and Kvachina rivers (western Kamchatka) | moulting, breeding, migrating | protected[4] | Bean Goose | high | poor | stable |
| 34. | Lake Kharchinskoe | migrating | protected | White-fronted Goose, Lesser White-fronted Goose | high | extensive | increase |
| 35. | Lower reaches of the Moroshechnaya River (western Kamchatka) | breeding, moulting, migrating | protected[4] | Bean Goose | high | extensive | increase for breeding geese |
| 36. | Commander Islands and the Kronotsk coast of Kamchatka | wintering | protected | Emperor Goose[3] | low | | unknown |
| 37. | Interfluve of the Opala and Galygina rivers (south-western Kamchatka) | breeding, moulting, migrating | protected | Bean Goose | high | intermediate | decline following the growth in the 1990s |
| 38. | Bolshoe Konoshelie Island and its vicinities (the lower reaches of the Enisey River) | migrating | unprotected | Bean Goose | unknown | no monitoring | unknown |
| 39. | The Nizhniaya baikha River (the middle reaches of the Enisey River) | migrating, breeding | unprotected | Bean Goose | lost | poor | increase[5] |
| 40. | Eloguy-Artiuginskaya floodplain (the middle reaches of the Enisey River) | migrating | unprotected | Bean Goose | unknown | no monitoring | unknown |
| 41. | Vorogovskoye mnogoostrovie [area with numerous islands] (the middle reaches of the Enisey River) | migrating | unprotected | Bean Goose | unknown | no monitoring | unknown |
| 42. | Lake Kosogol and the Serezh River floodplain (the south of the Krasnoyarsk Kray) | migrating | partly protected | Bean Goose | high | poor | decline |
| 43. | Altayskiy district of Khakassia | migrating | partly protected | Bean Goose | high | extensive | decline |
| 44. | Kezhemskoe mnogoostrovie [area with numerous islands] at the Angara River | migrating | partly protected | Lesser White-fronted Goose | high | intermediate | decline |
| 45. | The Selenga River Delta | migrating | protected | Bean Goose | lost | extensive | - |

Table 1 (cont). Territories of key importance for goose populations in the Russian part of East Asia, 4. The sources used for compilation of the table are listed in References.

| No. | Territory | | | Species | | Importance | Trend |
|---|---|---|---|---|---|---|---|
| 46. | Zeysko-Bureinskaya plain (between the Zeya and Bureya rivers) | migrating | partly protected[4] | Bean Goose, White-fronted Goose, Lesser White-fronted Goose | high | intermediate | decline |
| 47. | Lake Bolon | migrating | protected[4] | White-fronted Goose, Bean Goose | high | intermediate | decline |
| 48. | Lower reaches of the Amur River (Evoron-Chukchagir, Udyl-Kizi, and Amur-Amgun lowlands) | migrating | partly protected (Lake Udyl[4]) | White-fronted Goose, Bean Goose | medium | intermediate | decline |
| 49. | Lake Khanka | migrating | protected[4] | White-fronted Goose, Bean Goose | high | extensive | decline |
| 50. | Torey Lakes | migrating | partly protected | Bean Goose | low | intermediate | decline |

1 The territories important for the Asian goose populations wintering in North America are also included.

2 Snow Goose is excluded, since virtually all geese of this species occurring on the named areas belong to the American populations.

3 Black Brant and Emperor Goose numerous within the area are included. Most of the geese of these species belong to the American populations, though some birds may winter in Asia and belong to the threatened populations with extremely low numbers. All the areas important for the both species are included in the list of Important Goose Areas of Asia unless and until the precise pattern of distribution of the Asian populations of these species is determined.

4 Area is included in the Ramsar List.

5 Increase due to immigration of birds from the Western Palearctic goose populations.

range. This species penetrates farther west than any other east Asian goose (Kistchinskiy 1979). Our studies of east Asian goose populations were carried out between 1991 and 2005 in the region from Taimyr to Chukotka (Fig. 1).

For our analyses of population trends, we conducted a literature review, mostly of Russian sources including so-called "grey literature", largely unavailable to English-speaking readers, and field studies to determine the present status of goose population and make comparisons with data from previous years. We used standard techniques in our field studies, as described in our earlier publications (e.g. Syroechkovskiy 1997a, 1999, Artyukhov & Syroechkovskiy 1999).

Our estimates of goose populations were based on data compiled by Wetlands International (Wetlands International 2002), local estimates from the Russian literature, and unpublished data received from our Russian, Japanese and Korean colleagues. The population estimates given here mostly correspond to our knowledge up to 2003, and have not been adjusted on the basis of data acquired in 2004-2006. As only rough estimates are given in publications from the beginning and middle of the twentieth century (and also in some later publications), and as counts were conducted using a variety of methods, we have often had to use qualitative methods of estimating goose numbers to determine population trends.

## RESULTS AND DISCUSSION
### Key areas for Arctic geese in eastern Russia
Recent knowledge of the main breeding grounds and migration routes of Anseriformes in Russia allows us to identify key breeding and staging areas for the goose populations. The great majority of these areas are either already included in lists of Important Bird Areas (IBAs) and wetlands of international importance, or will be in the near future (Krivenko 2000, unpublished data of RBCU, etc.).

The most important areas for east Asian geese are shown in Fig. 2. The list of sites (Table 1) includes the areas which are still important, as well as a number of sites that have lost some of their importance because of the drastic decline in goose populations in eastern Asia in recent decades (see below). Most of the latter areas are, however, still suitable for geese, and it is possible that they may regain their former importance if goose populations begin to increase again, as is now occurring in some regions of Kamchatka and Chukotka.

### Populations and trends of east Asian geese
The population estimates and trends for each of the populations of the six goose species considered are summarized in Table 2. The population differentiation of east Asian geese remains poorly studied. Based on current knowledge, we recognize 14 migratory populations of geese breeding in north-eastern Russia. Three of these (both populations of the Snow Goose *Anser (Chen) caerulescens* and the largest population of the Brent Goose *Branta bernicla*) winter exclusively in North America. Much the largest part of the wintering range of the Emperor Goose *Anser canagicus* is in Alaska. However, there are some data which suggest the existence of a separate "Asian" Emperor Goose population (Syroechkovskiy, in prep.). Recent studies have revealed a spring and autumn migration route running from the breeding and moulting grounds in southern Chukotka along the Korayk Mountains to the Kamchatka coast. There is also increasing evidence of the possible wintering of Emperor Geese

**Table 2.** Estimated numbers and trends of east Asian Arctic goose populations. Based on Andreev (1997), Gerasimov (1996), Kerbes *et al.* (1999), Li & Mundkur (2004), Lopez & Mundkur (1997), Madsen (1991), Madsen *et al.* (1999), Mooij *et al.* (1996), Perennou *et al.* (1994), Scott & Rose (1996), Tetsuro (1996), Wetlands International (2002), Yemelyanov (2000), unpublished data of JAWGP, GSDSG NE, V.V. Baraniuk and Yu.N. Gerasimov (pers. comm.).

| Species | Subspecies/population | Numbers in mid-1980s | Numbers in 2000-2002 | Population trends |
|---|---|---|---|---|
| *Anser fabalis* | *A. f. middendorffii*[1] | c. 140 000[2] | 70 000 | Decreasing |
| | *A. f. serrirostris* (south Kamchatka – Japan) | 6 000 | 6 000-7 000 | Approximately stable, fluctuating |
| | *A. f. serrirostris* (excluding Kamchatka population) | c. 240 000[2] | c. 60 000 | Decreasing |
| | *A. f. rossicus* (Yenisey – China) | ? | <10 000 | Decreasing |
| *Anser albifrons* | Wintering in China | 250 000[2] | 30 000-50 000 | Decreasing |
| | Wintering in Korea | 5 000-30 000 | 60 000- 110 000 | Increasing |
| | Chukotka – Japan | 20 000 | 75 000 | Increasing |
| *Anser erythropus* | Eastern Russia – China[3] | c. 40 000 | 220 000 | Decreasing |
| *A. caerulescens* | Two populations on Wrangel Island | 80 000 | 105 000 | First decreasing, now increasing slowly |
| *A. canagicus* | Total (summer estimates in Russia) | 165 000 (5 000-10 000) | 85 000 (25 000) | First decreasing, now increasing slowly |
| *Branta bernicla* | *B. b. nigricans* wintering in North America (summer estimates in Russia) | 185 000 (?) | 130 000 (40 000) | Decreasing then increasing |
| | *B. b. nigricans* wintering in China[3] | 3 000-4 000 | 4 000-5 000 | First decreasing, now stable |
| | *B. b. nigricans* wintering in Japan | 700 | 1 000 | First decreasing, now stable |
| **TOTAL** | **14+ populations** | **c. 925 000** | **490 000** | |

[1] Current knowledge allows us to recognize at least three migratory populations of Taiga Bean Goose (subspecies *middendorffii*) in eastern Asia: an Okhotsk/Kamchatka-Japan population; a Yakutian-China population; and a Sayany-China population. There is likely more differentiation but further studies are needed. The Taiga Bean Goose is recorded in the Arctic but the main breeding areas are further south, and so this form has not been considered in detail here.

[2] Estimates based on a combination of data from direct counts and extrapolations and estimates based on a study of trends in various parts of the range.

[3] This most likely comprises several migratory populations.

along the Kronotsk coast (Yu.N. Gerasimov pers. comm.). The level of isolation of this population from the North American population has still to be determined. It is also possible that in the case of the Greater White-fronted Goose *Anser albifrons*, Lesser White-fronted Goose *A. erythropus* and Bean Goose, more detailed studies will allow further subdivision of populations, especially between birds wintering in China and those wintering in Korea. As can be seen from Table 2, the great majority of populations which are "pure Asian" have either declined dramatically and are still declining, or have stabilized at very low numbers, critical for their existence.

## Comparison with in goose populations in Western Eurasia and North America

To determine if such a decline in goose numbers was the general trend in Eurasia, we analysed data from Wetlands International on numbers and population trends of geese in Western Eurasia. In Fig. 3, the increases and decreases in goose populations in Western Eurasia since the mid-1980s are compared with those in Eastern Eurasia. It is obvious that negative population trends totally dominate in eastern Asia, while positive trends dominate in the goose populations wintering in Europe. Since the mid-1980s, the proportion of "European" geese in the total goose population in Russia has increased from 57% to 82% due to the increase in

most goose populations in Europe and simultaneous decrease in Asian populations (Syroechkovskiy 2001, 2003). In Fig. 4, we compare the total numbers of all goose species in three large regions of the Northern Hemisphere: Western Palearctic, Eastern Palearctic and North America. These three regions are very similar in size and have similar habitats suitable for migratory goose populations. It seems likely that long ago, and perhaps only 200-300 years ago, the total numbers of geese inhabiting these three regions were approximately similar. The current situation is alarming: the goose population of the Eastern Palearctic, numbering only about half a million birds, comprises little over 2% of the total goose numbers in the Northern Hemisphere. We suggest that this situation reflects the attitudes of the states in these three regions to the conservation of migratory birds and their habitats and the support they give to nature conservation. Most of the populations of even "common" geese in eastern Asia are now at such low numbers that they would immediately be given threatened status if they inhabited Europe or North America.

## Local population trends of geese in eastern Russia

We analysed data on local changes in goose numbers to assess regional variations in trends in goose populations in eastern Asia. This analysis was based on data from long-term population monitoring and the results of current studies, and was conducted

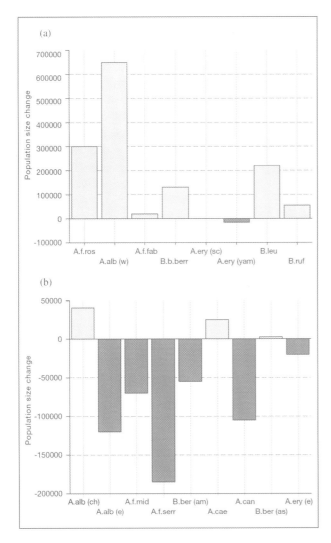

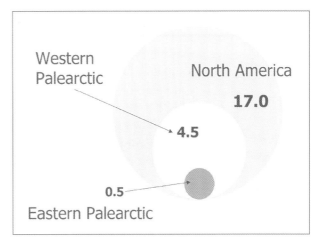

**Fig. 4.** Comparison of the size of the goose populations in the Eastern Palearctic, Western Palearctic and North America (Nearctic).

for the two most abundant species with vast ranges in eastern Asia: the Greater White-fronted Goose (Fig. 5) and eastern Tundra Bean Goose *A. f. serrirostris* (Fig. 6). Publications by research workers in the early and mid-twentieth century rarely contain detailed count data, but still give a good enough idea of the relative abundance of geese in certain study areas. When it was not possible to compare quantitative data, we used qualitative comparisons of relative abundance.

It is possible to evaluate whether the estimates of trends shown in Figs 5 & 6 are representative by comparing them to Fig. 2, which depicts key IBAs, the most important sites for

**Fig. 3.** Changes in numbers in the goose populations in a) western Russia, and b) eastern Russia in the last 20 years. Numbers in the mid-1980s are given as the "zero level". The size of the columns show by how much the populations have increased or decreased since the mid-1980s. The names of the populations are represented by the first letters of the scientific names of the species/subspecies. Sources as in Table 2.

A group of 300 moulting Brent Geese *Branta bernicla*, caught in the delta of the Nishnyaya Taimyra river, Eastern Taimyr, July 1990, on the first Dutch-Russian-German-UK Siberian expedition. This expedition was the start of a long term research programme on the ecology and migration of Brent Geese and arctic waders between the Russian Federation and the Netherlands. Annually since 1990, Russian-Dutch expeditions to Taimyr have taken place with a changing number of participants from other countries. Photo: Gerard Boere.

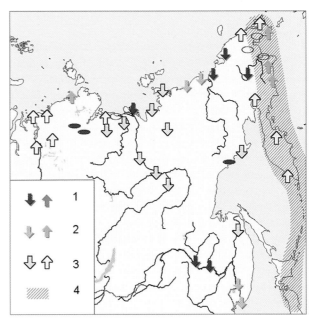

**Fig. 5.** Local population trends of the Greater White-fronted Goose *Anser albifrons* as monitored in eastern Russia during the last 40 years. Trends: upward pointing arrow – increasing trend; downward pointing arrow – declining trend; oval – relatively stable numbers. Methods of estimating trends: 1 – comparison of counts; 2 – results of counts combined with estimates from experts; 3 – combination of data from various sources, including qualitative and numerical data and information from local residents. The shaded area (4) shows the range of the increasing Russian-Japanese population. Sources as listed in References, with additional information from N.D. Poyarkov and Yu.V. Shibaev (pers. comm.).

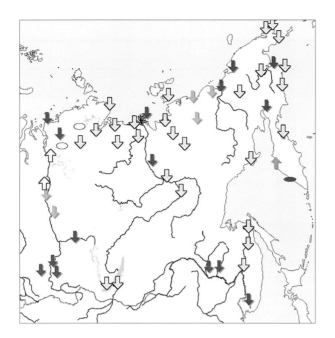

**Fig. 6.** Local population trends of the Tundra Bean Goose *Anser fabalis serrirostris* and *A. f. rossicus* monitored in eastern Russia during the last 40 years. Legend as in Fig. 5. Sources as listed in References, with additional information from N.D. Poyarkov and Yu.V. Shibaev (pers. comm.).

geese in eastern Asia. It is clear that population trends have been estimated mainly in the most important areas for geese, and so in general we can conclude that the data are quite representative for the entire flyways.

## Population differentiation and trends in Asian geese

### Greater White-fronted Goose

In this study, we have not considered subspecific differentiation, which has been discussed by Mooij & Zöckler (2000). Here we consider only the differentiation of Asian populations of the Greater White-fronted Goose, which are poorly known. There is an assumption that considerable mixing between populations ("pan-mixia") can occur in Asia, as it does in the Western Palearctic populations of this species (Mooij *et al.* 1996). It is possible that mixing occurs to some extent between the populations wintering in China and Korea , as their migration routes partly overlap. However, data from satellite transmitters (M. Kurechi pers. comm.) and a colour-marking programme in Chukotka in 2001-2005 have revealed the existence of a quite separate Chukotka-Japan population of White-fronted Geese. Of 120 birds marked by our team in southern Chukotka in the last five years, 25% were recorded on wintering grounds in Japan or on the way there. No birds were recorded in Korea, where more and more attention has been given to geese in recent years, nor were any birds recorded in other parts of the species' range.

Over a considerable part of Russian east Asia, the trends in White-fronted Goose populations have been negative throughout recent decades (Figs. 5, 7 & 8). A comparative analysis of the changes in numbers on the wintering grounds in China and Korea is of interest. In China, where the Greater White-fronted Goose was abundant in the past and possibly the most numerous of the geese, the population has been steadily declining and now probably comprises no more than 30 000 birds concentrated in the Yangtze valley (Cao *et al.* 2006a, 2006b). At the same time, in Korea the numbers of this species have been increasing. Counts

in the late 1980s (Perennou *et al.* 1994) revealed less than 5 000 birds in Korea. It is likely that this was a considerable underestimate, but the total wintering population of the species in Korea was clearly small. The official mid-winter (January) counts in Korea in 1997-2001 gave estimates of 10 000-61 000 birds (Li & Mundkur 2004). However, according to Korean goose researchers (Lee Ki-Sub pers. comm.), the true number of this species in Korea since 2000 has exceeded 100 000 birds; e.g. 108 000 were counted in early winter concentrations in South Korea in November 2002 (Han *et al.* 2003). It was presumed that most of these birds would have been missed by the January counts because they disperse widely over agricultural land when the water bodies in the demilitarized zone freeze over.

In any event, there has been considerable growth in the Greater White-fronted Goose population in the Korean wintering grounds during the last decade. This is undoubtedly related to the favourable conditions that have existed for geese in Korea in recent years. The hunting of geese has been totally banned since the 1980s, and many areas of inter-tidal mudflat and salt marsh on the west coast have been turned into rice fields and have become ideal wintering grounds for geese (Lee Honsoo pers. comm.). These changes have not only favoured geese but also some ducks and, in particular, have contributed to the large increase in numbers of Baikal Teal *Anas formosa*. The big increase in the wintering population of Greater White-fronted Geese in Korea might be partly due to natural population growth, and partly to immigration from the wintering areas in China, where numbers have been declining in recent decades. This can only be clarified by undertaking co-ordinated international counts and large-scale colour-marking of geese in the region.

The warmer winters, as a result of global climate change, may be contributing to the establishment of a more stable over-wintering population of geese in Korea, which is located at the northern climatic limit of potential goose wintering range in eastern Asia.

Analysis of local trends in north-eastern Russia (Fig. 5) reveals that in the greater part of this region (in Yakutia), a steady decrease in the numbers of Greater White-fronted Geese has been recorded almost everywhere. This is consistent with the negative trends in the wintering areas in China which have been linked with the breeding areas in Yakutia by ringing recoveries (data from Bird Ringing Centre of Russia). The situation is different in Kamchatka and Chukotka. Here, the observations of a research group supervised by N.N. Gerasimov and Yu.N. Gerasimov and our expeditions since 2000 have revealed considerable growth in the goose populations, especially in areas adjacent to the Pacific coast. This is obviously a reflection of the increase in numbers of geese on the wintering grounds in Japan in the 1980s and 1990s (Kurechi 2005, M. Kurechi pers. comm.), and later also in Korea. An analysis of the population dynamics of Greater White-fronted Geese in the region of the Anadyr Estuary has revealed that during the period from the early 1990s until 2003, there was a gradual replacement of birds wintering mainly in China (Kondratyev 1993) by birds wintering in Japan (E.E. Syroechkovskiy and A.I. Artyukhov, unpubl. data). We also observed an increase in numbers and range expansion in the Greater White-fronted Goose populations in southern and eastern Chukotka Peninsula in 2000-2004 (Fig. 5), compared with the situation in the 1960s, 1970s and 1980s

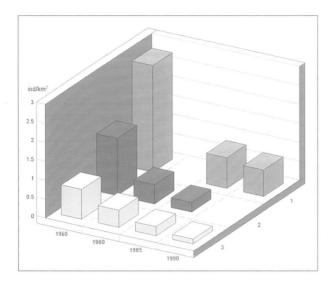

**Fig. 7.** Decrease in numbers of geese (individuals km$^{-2}$) counted during aerial surveys on the breeding grounds in northern Yakutia between 1960 and 1990. Locations (from west to east): 1 – Lena Delta; 2 – Yana-Indigirka Lowland; 3 – Kolyma-Alazeya Lowland. Based on Yegorov (1965), Degtyarev (1994) and A.V. Andreev (unpublished data).

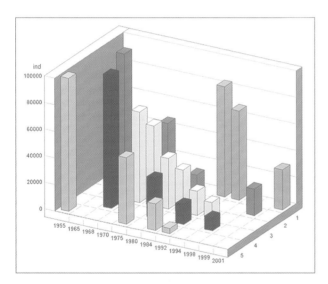

**Fig. 8.** Population (number of individuals) decline on migration stopovers of Bean and White-fronted Geese at southern Siberia and Russian Far-East from 1950s onwards.

Based on (Dymin, 1986; Gerassimov, 1988; Dugintsov, 1996; Andreev, 1997; Antonov, 2000; Yemeliyanov, 2000; Rozenfield, Smirenskiy, 2001)

1 Zeya Lowland (middle Amur, south-west of city of Blagovestchensk) numbers of both Bean and White-fronted Geese

2 Khakassiya (Southern Central Siberia) – Bean Goose numbers

3 Zeya Lowland – Bean Goose numbers only

4 Apkhara Lowland (central Amur, east of Bureya River mouth); Khinganskiy Zapovednik -Bean and White-fronted Geese

5 Penzhina (north western Kamchatka peninsula) – mainly Bean Goose including some White-fronted Geese

(e.g. Portenko 1972, Tomkovich & Sorokin 1983). These observations are confirmed by local people in the settlements of Novoye Chaplino, Sireniki, Yanrakynnot, Lorino and Lavrentiya, and reindeer herders visiting the basins of the Yoniveem, Igelveem, Chegitun, Kurupka, Erguveem and Seutakan rivers and the Konnerginskaya tundra. In the last decade, Greater White-

fronted Geese have become much commoner in these areas than they were in the 1980s. We suggest that this increase is related to the occurrence in these areas of geese from the favourable wintering grounds in Japan and Korea. These birds are probably now partly replacing birds from the Chinese wintering population which were formerly common here.

From the results of our aerial survey in 2002, we conclude that the present breeding range of the Greater White-fronted Geese wintering in Korea and Japan includes the Koryak Mountains, Anadyr Bay coasts, Kanchalakskaya, Uelkalskaya and Konnerginskaya tundras, Amguema River basin, north and west coasts of the Tenkyrgynpilkhen Estuary (up to Smidt Cape), and most of the Chukotka Peninsula except perhaps for the north coast of Koluchin Bay and Neshkanskaya tundra. The exact distribution of birds from different populations in the Chukotka area has still to be determined.

The current status of the Greater White-fronted Goose in the middle reaches of the Anadyr River also has to be clarified. The Chinese wintering population of Greater White-fronted Geese inhabited this area about 30 years ago and then almost completely disappeared (Krechmar 1986, Krechmar *et al.* 1991, A.V. Krechmar pers. comm.). It is possible that the area is now inhabited by birds from the Japanese and Korean wintering populations.

The supposition that there is exchange between the Chukotkan and Alaskan populations of Greater White-fronted Goose seems to us poorly justified and based on a misinterpretation of observations of goose migration in the vicinity of Arakamchechen Island. Our observations in 2004 and an analysis of information derived from questioning local people in Providenskiy District of Chukotka do not confirm this supposition.

The local people living in the lower reaches of the Anabar River in extreme north-western Yakutia reported an increase in the Greater White-fronted Goose population at the end of the twentieth century. According to them, since the early 1990s most Greater White-fronted Geese arriving on the lower reaches of Anabar River in spring arrive from the west, from the direction of Taimyr, while the traditional arrival from the south has almost ceased. At Ystankh-Khocho village in the summer of 1997, we observed Greater White-fronted Geese migrating from the west towards the Lena River delta, on their way to the moulting sites. It is possible, therefore, that a considerable proportion of the Greater White-fronted Geese from the western Yakutian tundra, and particularly those from the moulting sites north of the Pronchishcheva Mountains, belong to the Western Palearctic populations.

The observations discussed above suggest that a process of territorial re-distribution is occurring between migratory populations of Greater White-fronted Geese in eastern Asia. Vast areas of tundra in Yakutia and Chukotka, where the numbers of geese have drastically declined due to the shrinkage of the wintering grounds in China, are gradually being occupied by birds penetrating into the area from other, more successful populations in Taimyr and Koraykia. Thus, large shifts in goose populations are occurring in eastern Asia as a result of anthropogenic factors.

### Bean Goose

It is commonly accepted that only one subspecies of Tundra Bean Goose *A. f. serrirostris* inhabits eastern Asia (Alphéraky 1905, Stepanyan 2003, Delacour 1954, Mooij & Zöckler 1999, and others). Whether or not the subspecies *A. f. rossicus* can be subdivided into separate migratory populations remains unclear. Most global reviews, including the most recent (Kear 2005), indicate that *A. f. rossicus* migrates only to Europe, and consider it as belonging wholly to the Western Palearctic. However, most Russian research workers (e.g. Ptushenko 1952, Kistchinskiy 1979, Mel'nikov 2001), including those who have made a thorough study of the morphology and taxonomy of the species (Yemelyanov 2000), have shown that most Bean Geese from Taimyr, although belonging to the subspecies *rossicus*, migrate southwards along the Yenisey River valley and its tributaries at least as far as Lake Baikal. China is the only region where birds passing through this area might spend the winter. This suggests that both *serrirostris* and *rossicus* share wintering grounds in China. We are not aware of any thorough taxonomic study of Bean Goose subspecies wintering in China, but such a study could solve the puzzle as to whether or not there are separate migratory populations of *rossicus*.

Population differentiation in east Asian Bean Geese is not clearly understood. Our present knowledge allows us to identify at least four migratory populations (Table 2), although in reality there are probably more. In recent decades, Asian Tundra Bean Geese have experienced huge anthropogenic pressures. In the mid-twentieth century, they were among the most abundant and widespread geese in eastern Asia. In the past, the east Asian populations of Bean Geese extended across the whole of Taimyr, for almost a thousand kilometres from east to west, whereas the westernmost of the east Asian populations of Greater White-fronted Geese probably penetrated only as far west as eastern Taimyr. Bean Geese also differ from Greater White-fronted Geese in having a migration route along the Yenisey. Birds follow this route in spring from the wintering grounds in China to central Siberia as far as the edges of the West Siberian Plain and Gydan Peninsula (Syroechkovskiy 1965, Kistchinskiy 1979, Rogacheva 1992).

In the mid-twentieth century, Bean Geese were abundant everywhere in the tundra areas of Taimyr, Yakutia, Chukotka and Kamchatka (Ptushenko 1952, Vorobyev 1963, Uspenskiy *et al.* 1962, Yegorov 1965, Portenko 1972, Rogacheva 1992). At that time, according to our estimates, Asian Bean Goose populations exceeded one million birds. However, many researchers recorded a steady decline in Bean Goose populations in the 1960s, 1970s and 1980s: in the breeding areas in Taimyr, the lower Lena River and eastern tundra in Yakutia (Kokorev 1989, Rogacheva 1992, V.I. Pozdnyakov pers. comm.), and along the migration routes in the middle reaches of the Amur River, Kamchatka and other regions in the Russian Far East, as well as along the Yenisey migration route (Rogacheva 1992, Yemelyanov 2000, Savchenko *et al.* 2003) (Figs. 6 & 8). Our studies conducted at key wetlands in northern Yakutia and Chukotka in 1994-2004 revealed a further decline in numbers. The breeding range has now become highly fragmented. Formerly a common species, the species now inhabits only small patches of suitable habitat, often situated tens or even hundreds of kilometres apart (Syroechkovskiy 1997). In our annual three-month surveys of geese in the lower reaches of the Anabar, Olenek Yana and Indigirka rivers in 1996-1999, we were able to find a total of fewer than ten nests of this species and only a few moulting sites, with fewer than 1 000 birds.

Despite the relatively favourable conditions on the wintering grounds in Japan in recent years, there has been no sustained growth in the southern Kamchatka-Japan Bean Goose population, as there has in the Greater White-fronted Goose population. This Bean Goose population began to increase in 1980, but never became abundant and is now probably declining again (Yu.N. Gerasimov pers. comm.). The number of Bean Geese wintering in Korea is low, and if the rate of decline is the same as that in China, the population will be close to extinction within the next decade.

The only area where positive trends have been recorded in an Asian population of Bean Goose in recent years is in the extreme west, in the vast bogs and flood-lands in the upper and middle reaches of the Nizhnyaya Baikha River, in the middle reaches of the Enisey River. According to staff of Turukhansk Hunting Inspectorate, the Taiga Bean Goose had become rare in this area after a long-term decline in the numbers of migrating and breeding birds, but in the early 1990s, this trend was reversed as a result of a considerable increase in the numbers of geese arriving from the south-west. In the late 1990s, staff of the Hunting Inspectorate in Ust-Eniseysk District of Taimyr Autonomous Region also recorded an increase in the numbers of Bean Geese arriving in spring from the direction of the West Siberian Plain. Thus, it would seem that the process of population replacement in Asia, as described for Greater White-fronted Geese, has only just begun for Bean Geese.

The overall status of Bean Geese in eastern Asia is depressing. We suggest that the remaining populations of the Tundra Bean Goose represent only about 10-15% of the total numbers in eastern Asia about a century ago. It is obvious that the hunting of all subspecies of Bean Geese should be banned immediately throughout their ranges in eastern Russia, and the strictest measures should be taken to protect the species' staging and wintering sites.

## Lesser White-fronted Goose

Information on population trends in Lesser White-fronted Geese, which is easily mistaken for Greater White-fronted Geese, is even scarcer than for the other species of geese in eastern Asia. A review of the population decline and range fragmentation in this species has recently been published elsewhere (Morozov & Syroechkovskiy 2002). Little is known about population differentiation in this species, although it most likely exists. It is difficult to believe that the birds following a migration route along the Angara River in central Siberia belong to the same migratory population as those passing through Kamchatka. Scattered observations of this species on passage (Portenko 1972, Rogacheva 1992, Dugintsov 1996, Yu.N. Gerasimov pers. comm., pers. obs) suggest the existence of at least three migration routes: Central Siberian (Angarian), Amur-Yakutian and Far Eastern. The latter may have two branches: Kamchatka-Chukotian and Okhotsk-Kolymian. There is an urgent need for studies with the help of satellite transmitters to resolve this. It is possible that there have been some shifts in the wintering populations similar to those that are now occurring in the Greater White-fronted Goose, as the only known wintering area for the Asian populations of the Lesser White-fronted Goose is at Dongting Lake in China. The Asian populations of this species are in a critical state, with total numbers now less than 20 000 birds (Cao *et al.* 2006a, 2006b). Population trends have been found to be negative wherever they have been investigated during the last 20 years (Morozov & Syroechkovskiy 2002).

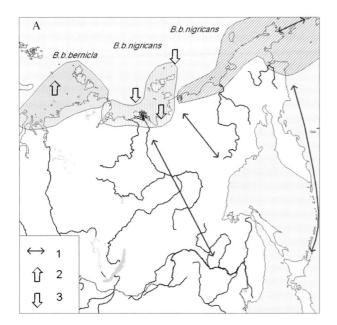

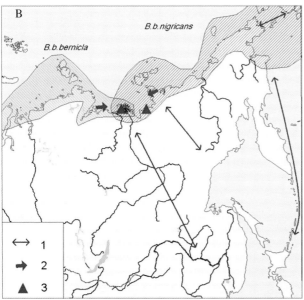

Fig 9. Re-distribution of three populations of Black Brant in Yakutian tundra in the second half of 20th century.

A) Middle 20th century,

1 – migration routes

2 – records of increasing trends in the breeding grounds

3 – records of decreasing trends in the breeding grounds

B) End of 20th century.

1 – migration routes

2 – directions of expansion of populations replacing decreasing Asian population of Black Brant

3 – possible areas of remaining breeding of Asian population of Black Brant

## Brent Goose

The population dynamics and changes in range of the Asian populations of the Brent Goose (subspecies *nigricans*, often known as Black Brant) in Russia have been studied in some detail (Syroechkovskiy 1995, 1997b, 1999, Syroechkovskiy *et al.* 1998, etc.). Declines in the populations of Brent Geese throughout the

Russian Arctic in the second half of the twentieth century resulted in fragmentation of the breeding range. Only scattered colonies of this species have survived. In the 1960s and 1970s, the total number of Brent Geese in the Russian Arctic was in the region of 20 000-30 000 birds. Since the 1970s, the North American population of *nigricans* and the population of the nominate subspecies in Western Eurasia have been increasing, but this has not happened in the Asian populations of *nigricans*. As a result of the drastic population decline (Fig. 9), the areas formerly inhabited by the Asian populations of *nigricans* have been gradually occupied by birds of the nominate subspecies invading from the west and North American birds coming in from the direction of Chukotka. These conclusions have been confirmed by ringing recoveries and direct observations.

The Asian populations of *nigricans* are very small, poorly studied and close to extinction. The wintering sites in China are poorly known, and the breeding areas, which are thought to be on the lower Lena and Yana rivers, have not been surveyed. In view of the high anthropogenic pressures and speed of development in the Chinese coastal areas where Brent Geese winter (Barter 2002), we surmise that these populations will soon be extinct unless urgent measures are taken to safeguard them. To some extent, the breeding populations might be maintained by immigration of birds from the North American population. Ringing recoveries from Japan suggest that this may already be occurring (T. Ikeuchi pers. comm., V.I. Pozdnyakov pers. comm., data of the Bird Ringing Centre of Russia). The migration system of Brent Geese wintering in Japan and observed on migration along coastal Kamchatka still remains unclear. It is probable that there is a loop migration, with birds crossing the Asian mainland in spring (Pozdnyakov & Germogenov 1988, Syroechkovskiy 1999) and returning via the Pacific coast in autumn, with a major stopover at the Malamvayam Estuary in Kamchatka (Gerasimov & Gerasimov 1999, Syroechkovskiy 1999). However, these suppositions need thorough verification, preferably with the help of satellite transmitters.

## CONCLUSIONS

Various authors have described the poor conditions for goose populations, large-scale poaching and loss of suitable wetland habitat in China (Degtyarev 1995, Goroshko 2000, Barter 2002, Cao *et al.* 2006a), but no special studies of these problems are known to us. Although some positive steps have been taken to mitigate the impacts of development on wetlands and waterbirds (Anonymous 2002), much remains to be done to improve the situation for east Asian geese. A detailed analysis of the situation should be the subject of a separate study and publication.

Our main conclusions regarding the trends in east Asian goose populations are as follows:

- The majority of east Asian goose populations are in long-term decline, in contrast to most populations of geese in the Western Palearctic and North America.
- There are only about half a million geese left in the whole of eastern Asia. This huge area is inhabited by less than 2.5% of the geese in the Northern Hemisphere.
- Although all countries in eastern Asia with populations of geese have contributed to their decline in numbers due to habitat change and excessive hunting, the critical bottlenecks for the goose populations are the staging and

wintering areas in China. Further studies and awareness campaigns are urgently required there.

- Some east Asian goose populations have reached critically low levels below 20 000 birds (Lesser White-fronted Goose, the two Asian Brent Goose populations); most of the other, formerly abundant populations have recently fallen below 100 000 birds and are in urgent need of conservation measures throughout their flyways.

- Both the Greater White-fronted Goose and the Bean Goose are still hunted in the Asian part of Russia, despite their declining trends and low numbers. The Russian Far East should impose a temporary (but long-term) ban on goose hunting, most importantly in spring, but in many areas also in autumn. Special rights could be given to indigenous minorities, and the hunting law should be strictly enforced throughout eastern Russia.

- Shifts in breeding range have been reported in the eastern and western parts of our study area. Fragmented breeding areas abandoned by the declining Asian populations of Greater White-fronted Goose and Bean Goose are being occupied by birds from the increasing populations in neighbouring flyways, which have more secure wintering areas in Western Europe, Japan and North America.

- Thirty years of conservation efforts for the Greater White-fronted Goose and Bean Goose in Japan have had positive results, resulting in the stabilization and increase in numbers of several populations, and setting an excellent example recognized by the international conservation community. The experience gained in Japan in the conservation of geese and especially habitat restoration could be widely used in other parts of Asia, especially in China.

- The rapid increase in the Greater White-fronted Goose population in Japan, which followed rather simple habitat conservation and restoration efforts, shows the high adaptive potential of geese. It has demonstrated the potential for future reestablishment of goose populations in Asia, even in highly industrialized developed countries, especially in association with "goose friendly" rice-production technologies which result in very low levels of conflict with farming interests and increasing numbers of geese.

- The increase in numbers of geese wintering in South Korea should be subject to further study and documentation. South Korea could be the second "growing point" for goose populations in eastern Asian after Japan.

## ACKNOWLEDGEMENTS

Firstly, I would like to thank the Japanese Association for Wild Geese Protection, and especially President Masyuki Kurechi and Yoshihiko Miyabayashi, for their constant help, both by assisting us financially and by providing information and advice at all stages in our work, through the implementation of the Asia-Pacific Migratory Waterbird Conservation Strategy. I also thank the Administrations at all levels in Chukotka and Yakutia for supporting our surveys, and the friendly people of the Arctic villages who helped us enormously in our field work. Our work received financial support from many sources, especially the Russian Academy of Sciences, Toyota Foundation, Kei Dan Ren Science Foundation, Santory Whisky Foundation, CIC Migratory Bird Commission, Arctic Ecology and Anthropology Research Centre (Moscow), U.S. Fish & Wildlife Service, Foundation for Support of Domestic Science (Russia) and Dr Werner Trense. Volunteers from eight countries have contributed greatly to our field surveys: C. Schenk, P. Palmer, J. O'Sullivan, M. Trobits, M. Boegehausen, T. Kuppel, G. Eihorn, J. Lugert, R. Probst, M. Pavlichev, A. Braunlich, H. Karhu, J. MacCalum, C. Kelly, T. Jakkonen, T. Noach, V. Nilssen, M. Lieser, M. Stensmyr and A. Tree. Field data were collected with the help of many colleagues, and I would especially like to mention E.G. Lappo, C. Zöckler, P.S. Tomkovich, S.V. Volkov and A.I. Artiukhov for their major contributions to the surveys of Arctic waterfowl during our expeditions. Comments from Yu.N. Gerasimov, K. Livin, N. Poyarkov, A. Kondratyev, E. Lappo and anonymous reviewers have improved the text.

## REFERENCES

**Alphéraky, S.N.** 1905. Geese of Russia. Kutschnerew & Co., Moscow. [In Russian].

**Andreev, A.V.** 1997. Monitoring of geese in Northern Asia. In: Andreev A.V. (ed) Species diversity and population status of waterbirds in North-East Asia Magadan: 5-36.

**Anonymous** 2002. China National Wetland Conservation Action Plan (English version). China Forestry Publishing House, Beijing, China.

**Antonov, A.I.** 2000. Terms of seasonal geese migrations and changes of geese numbers in Arkhara Lowland, Amur Region, Russia, for the last thirty years. Casarca 6: 320-322. [In Russian].

**Artyukhov, A.I. & Syroechkovskiy, Jr., E.E.** 1999. New data on distribution of Lesser White-fronted Goose in the Abyi Lowland (Eastern Yakutia). Casarca 5: 136-143. [In Russian].

**Babenko, V.G. & Poyarkov, N.D.** 1998. Geese and swans in low Amur area. Casarca 4: 297-312. [In Russian].

**Barter, M.A.** 2002. Shorebirds of the Yellow Sea – Importance, threats and conservation status. Wetlands International Global Series 9, International Wader Studies 12, Canberra, Australia.

**Cao, L., Barter, M., Lei, G. & Yang, Q.** 2006a. Anatidae in the Yangtze floodplain in winter 2004 and 2005. Casarca 11. (In press).

**Cao, L., Wang, X., Wang, Q. & Barter, M.** 2006b. Wintering Anatidae in China – a preliminary analysis. Casarca 11. (In press).

**Degtyarev, A.G.** 1994. Location and conservation of places of moulting concentrations of geese in northern Yakutia. In: G.A. Voronov (ed) Nature protected areas: Problems of recognition, research and system organisation. Volume 2. Perm University Publications, Perm: 43-44. [In Russian].

**Delacour, J.** 1954. The Waterfowl of the World. Volume 1. Country Life, London.

**Dugintsov, V.A.** 1996. Importance of south part of Zeya-Bureya Lowland in the period of spring migration. In: N.M. Litvinenko (ed) Birds of the wetlands of the southern Russian Far East and their protection. Nauka Publications, Vladivostok: 144-156. [In Russian].

**Dymin, V.A.** 1986. Estimates of Bean Goose numbers at the south of Zeya-Bureya Lowland based on spring counts. Studies, conservation and wise use of birds in the USSR. Nauka Publications, Leningrad: 212-213. [In Russian].

Gerasimov, N.N. 1996. The wild geese of Kamchatka Peninsula. Russian Ornithological Journal 5(3/4): 77–80. [In Russian].

Gerasimov, Yu.N. & Gerasimov, N.N. 1999. A register of important waterfowl wetlands in Kamchatka. Biology and conservation of birds of Kamchatka. Issue 1. Dialog-MGU Publications, Moscow: 37-46. [In Russian].

Goroshko, O.A. 2000. Wintering waterfowl on Poyang Lake in China. Casarca 6: 323-328. [In Russian].

Han, S.-W., Yoo, S.-H., Lee, H., Lee, K., Paek, W.-K. & Song, M. 2003. A study on the wintering population of geese in Cheolwon, Korea. In: Proceedings of the 2003 International Anatidae Symposium in East Asia and Siberia region. Hanseo University, Seosan, Korea: 95-101.

Kear, J.K. (ed). 2005. Ducks, Geese and Swans. Oxford University Press, Oxford.

Kerbes, R.H., Baranyuk, V.V., Hines, J.E. 1999. Estimated size of the Western Canadian Arctic and Wrangel Island Lesser Snow Goose populations on their breeding and wintering grounds. In: Kerbes, R.H. *et al.* (ed) Distribution, survival and numbers of Lesser Snow Geese of the Western Canadian Arctic and Wrangel Island, Russia. Canadian Wildlife Service Occasional paper 98: 25-38.

Kistchinskiy, Ä.Ä. (ed). 1979. Migration of birds of Eastern Europe and North Asia. Anseriformes. Nauka Publications, Moscow. [In Russian].

Kokorev, Y.I. 1989. The dynamics of populations of waterfowl of the Pura river basin. In: A.I. Solomakha (ed) Mammals and birds of North of Central Siberia, Novosibirsk: 137-150. [In Russian].

Kondratyev, A.V. 1993. Breeding biology, habitat distribution and numbers of four species of geese at south-western coast of Anadyr Liman. The Russian Journal of Ornithology 2(3): 287-302. [In Russian].

Kretchmar, A.V. 1986. White-fronted Goose in the middle reaches of Anadyr river. Zoological Journal 65 (6): 889-900. [In Russian].

Kretchmar, A.V., Andreev, A.V. & Kondratyev, A.Y. 1991. Birds of Northern Plains. Nauka Publications, Leningrad. [In Russian].

Krivenko, V.G. (ed). 2000. Wetlands in Russia. Volume 3: Wetlands on the Ramsar shadow list. Wetlands International Global Series 3, Moscow.

Kurechi, M. 2005. Restoration of networks of goose and other waterfowl habitats by using winter flooding rice fields in Japan. In: Abstracts of the Third International Symposium on Waterfowl of Northern Eurasia, CD version: 69

Li, Z.W.D. & Mundkur, T. 2004. Numbers and distribution of waterbirds and wetlands in the Asia-Pacific region. Results of the Asian Waterbird Census: 1997-2001. Wetlands International, Kuala Lumpur, Malaysia.

Lopez, A. & Mundkur, T. (eds). 1997. The Asian Waterfowl census 1994-1996. Results of the coordinated waterbird census and an overview of the status of wetlands in Asia. Wetlands International, Kuala Lumpur, Malaysia.

Madsen, J. 1991. Status and trends of goose populations in the Western Palearctic in the 1980s. Ardea 79(2): 113-122.

Madsen, J., Reed, A. & Andreev, A. 1996. Status and trends of geese (Anser sp., Branta sp.) in the world: a review, updating and evaluation. In: M. Birkan, J. van Vessem, P. Havet, J. Madsen, B. Trolliet & M. Moser (eds) Proceedings of the Anatidae 2000 Conference, Strasbourg, France, 5-9 December 1994. Gibier Faune Sauvage (Game and Wildlife) 13: 337-353.

Madsen, J., Cracknell, G. & Fox, A.D. (eds). 1999. Goose populations of the Western Palearctic: A review of status and distribution. Wetlands International Publication No. 48, Wetlands International, Wageningen, The Netherlands, and National Environmental Research Institute, Rønde, Denmark.

Mel'nikov, Yu.I. 2001. Numbers, distribution and migration of Bean Goose in the south of Eastern Siberia. In: Proceeding of State Nature Reserve "Baikalo-Lenskiy". Issue 2, Irkutsk: 82-98. [In Russian].

Mooij, J.H. & Zöckler, C. 2000. Reflections on the systematics, distribution and status of Anser albifrons. Casarca 6: 91-107.

Mooij, J., Ebbinge, B.S., Kostin, I.O., Burgers, J. & Spaans, B. 1996. Panmixia in White-fronted Geese of the Western Palearctic. In: J. Mooij (ed) Ecology of geese wintering at the Lower Rhine area (Germany). Biologishe Station im Kreis Wesel.

Morozov, V.V. & Syroechkovski, Jr., E.E. 2002. Lesser White-fronted Goose on the verge of the Millenium. Casarca 8: 233-276. [In Russian].

Perennou, C., Mundkur, T., Scott, D.A., Follestad, A. & Kvelnid, L. 1994. The Asian Waterfowl Census 1987-91: Distribution and Status of Asian Waterfowl. AWB Publication No. 86; IWRB Publication No. 24. AWB, Kuala Lumpur, Malaysia, and IWRB, Slimbridge, UK.

Portenko, L.A. 1972. Birds of Chukotski Peninsula and Wrangel Island. Vol. I. Nauka Publications, Leningrad. [In Russian].

Poyarkov, N.D. 2001. The Swan Goose: its origin, number dynamics, biology and conservation. Casarca 7: 51-67. [In Russian].

Pozdynakov, V.I. & Germogenov, N.I. 1988. Migration and numbers of Brent Goose in Yakutia . In: Y.G. Shevetsov (ed) Rare vertebrate animals of Siberia. Nauka Publications, Siberian Branch, Novosibirsk: 164-169. [In Russian].

Ptushenko, Y.S. 1952. Order Anseriformes. In: Birds of the Soviet Union. Vol. 4. Academy of Sciences Publications, Moscow. [In Russian].

Rogacheva, H.V. 1992. Birds of the Central Siberia. Husum-Druck & Verlagsgesellschaft, Husum, Germany.

Rozenfeld, S.B. & Smirenskiy, S.M. 2001. Survey of spring stopovers of geese and recommendations for their conservation in the Amur oblast'. Casarca 7: 413-420. [In Russian].

Savchenko, A.P., Yemelyanov, V.I., Karpova, N.V., Yangulova, A.V. & Savchenko, I.A. 2003. The resources of hunting birds of Krasnoyarsk Territory. Krasnoyarsk State University (edited by V.V. Lutskiy). [In Russian].

Scott, D.A. & Rose, P.M. 1996. Atlas of Anatidae Populations in Africa and Western Eurasia. Wetlands International

Publication No. 41. Wetlands International, Wageningen, The Netherlands.

**Stepanyan, L.S.** 2003. Conspectus of the ornithological fauna of Russia and adjacent territories (within the borders of the USSR as a historic region). Academkniga, Moscow. [In Russian].

**Syroechkovskiy, E.E.** 1965. Central Siberian Flyway and waterfowl resources of Krasnoyarskiy Region. Geography of waterfowl resources in USSR, Moscow. Issue 2: 59-61. [In Russian].

**Syroechkovskiy, Jr., E.E.** 1995. Current status of Asian population of Brant *Branta bernicla nigricans*. Bulletin of the Goose Working Group of Eastern Europe and North Asia No. 1: 57-67. [In Russian].

**Syroechkovskiy, Jr., E.E.** 1997a. Species, status and population distribution of Russian Arctic Geese. Gibier Faune Sauvage (Game and Wildlife) 13: 381-396.

**Syroechkovskiy, Jr., E.E.** 1997b. Mixed colonies of two subspecies of Brant in Olenyok Bay. Casarca 3: 72-76. [In Russian].

**Syroechkovskiy, Jr., E.E.** 1999. Brent Goose (*Branta bernicla* L.) in Russia: ecology, distribution, problems of conservation and sustainable use of resources. PhD thesis, IPEE RAS, Moscow.

**Syroechkovskiy, Jr., E.E.** 2001. Geese of the Russian Arctic: dynamics of ranges, population trends and problems of wise use and conservation – Studies and conservation of waterfowl in Eastern Europe and North Asia. In: Abstracts of the First Symposium of the Goose Study Group of Eastern Europe and North Asia, Moscow: 117-118.

**Syroechkovski, Jr., E.E.** 2003. The problems of conservation of the Anseriformes in the Russian Arctic. Management and conservation of waterfowl populations in Northern Eurasia (with special focus on the White Sea – Baltic Flyway). In: V.B. Zimin, A.B. Popovkina & E.E. Syroechkovskiy, Jr. (eds) Abstracts of International Symposium, Petrazavodsk: 234-236. [In Russian].

**Syroechkovski, Jr., E.E., Zöckler, C. & Lappo, E.** 1998. Status of Brent Goose (*Branta bernicla*) in northwest Yakutia, East Siberia. British Birds 91 (12): 565-572.

**Tetsuro, S.** 1996. Thick-billed and Middendorff's Bean geese: ecological difference between the subspecies. Japanese Society for Bird Protection Monthly Journal Nature 417: 18-21. [In Japanese with English summary].

**Tomkovich, P.S. & Sorokin, A.G.** 1983. Bird fauna of Eastern Chukotka. Distribution and systematics of birds (Studies of Fauna of the USSR). Moscow Zoological Museum of Moscow State University MGU Publication 21: 77-159. [In Russian].

**Uspenskiy, S.M., Beome, R.L., Priklonski, S.G. & Vekhov, V.N.** 1962. Birds of northeast of Yakutia. Ornithologia 4: 39-45, & 5: 49-66. [In Russian].

**Vorobyev, K.A.** 1963. Birds of Yakutia. USSR Academy of Sciences Publications, Moscow. [In Russian].

**Wetlands International** 2002. Waterbird Population Estimates. Third Edition. Wetlands Global Series No. 12, Wageningen, The Netherlands.

**Yegorov, O.V.** 1965. Numbers of waterfowl and some other birds in Lena delta and Yana-Indigirka tundra based on results of aerial surveys. In: Nature of Yakutia and its conservation. Yakutsk: 124-127. [In Russian].

**Yemelyanov, V.I.** 2000. Morphometric analysis of the Bean Goose (*Anser fabalis* Lath.) as a basis for protection and rational use of the geese in Priyenisejskaya Siberia. Krasnoyarks State University. [In Russian].

Swan Geese *Anser cygnoides*, Tundra Swans *Cygnus columbianus jankowskii* and Ruddy Shelducks *Tadorna ferruginea* at Poyang Lake National Nature Reserve, Jiangxi Province, China. Photo: Mark Barter.

# The Yellow Sea – a vitally important staging region for migratory shorebirds

*Mark A. Barter*

*21 Chivalry Avenue, Glen Waverley, VIC 3150, Australia. (email: markbarter@optusnet.com.au)*

Barter, M.A. 2006. The Yellow Sea – a vitally important staging region for migratory shorebirds. *Waterbirds around the world.* Eds. G.C. Boere, C.A. Galbraith & D.A. Stroud. The Stationery Office, Edinburgh, UK. pp. 663-667.

## ABSTRACT

Surveys conducted during the last 11 years show that the extensive inter-tidal areas and near-coastal wetlands of the Yellow Sea are the most important staging region for migratory shorebirds in the East Asian-Australasian Flyway. Thirty-six species have so far been found to occur in internationally important numbers at one or more sites in the Yellow Sea; two of the species are classified as globally-threatened, whilst another two are near-threatened. Twenty-seven sites have been identified as supporting at least one species in internationally important numbers. The rapid growth of the human populations and economies of China and South Korea is causing serious loss and degradation of coastal habitats. Achieving effective conservation of migratory shorebirds and their wetland habitats around the Yellow Sea coastline will be particularly challenging due to the high dependence of the local communities on inter-tidal resources. The exceptional importance of the Yellow Sea biodiversity, both on a global scale and as a shared resource for the three littoral countries, makes it highly desirable that conservation activity be implemented at eco-region level.

## INTRODUCTION

The East Asian-Australasian Flyway, one of eight shorebird flyways around the world, stretches from Siberia and Alaska southwards through east and south-east Asia to Australia and New Zealand, and supports over seven million shorebirds of which some five million are migratory (Bamford *et al.* 2005).

The shorebirds of the East Asian-Australasian Flyway face the challenge of sharing it with more than one-third of the world's human population, many of whom live in countries that have some of the fastest developing economies in the world. The resulting economic and social pressures are posing major threats to wetlands, with more than 80% of the significant wetlands in east and south-east Asia being classified as threatened in some way; 51% of these are under serious threat (Scott & Poole 1989).

Much has been learnt about the breeding and non-breeding portions of shorebirds' lives within the flyway. However, relatively little is known of the migration strategies of the individual species – a deficiency which is particularly serious, given that the key wetlands used during migration in east and south-east Asia are the most threatened in the flyway (Melville 1997). This need for greatly improved information on important shorebird staging sites has led to extensive survey and counting activity over the last 20 years, particularly along the coastline of the Yellow Sea.

## THE YELLOW SEA AND SHOREBIRD STUDIES

The Yellow Sea is a semi-enclosed shallow sea, with extensive inter-tidal areas, located between the Korean Peninsula in the east and China to the west (Fig. 1). The Chinese coastline consists of extensive stretches of tidal flats separated by the

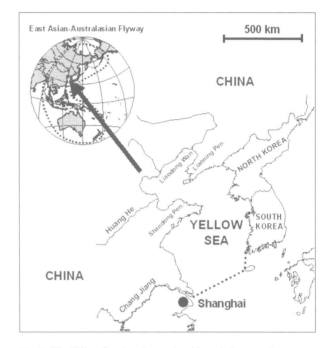

**Fig. 1.** The Yellow Sea: location, national boundaries, constituent parts and major rivers.

rocky regions of the Shandong and Liaoning Peninsulas and north-west Liaodong Wan, whilst the west coast of South Korea consists of large tidal flats which are contained in broad estuaries in the north and surround islands in the south-west. The total area of inter-tidal flats in the Yellow Sea, including the south coast of South Korea, is about 20 000 sq. km. The tidal ranges of the central west coast of the Korean Peninsula are amongst the highest in the world.

Since 1996, Wetlands International – China has been carrying out surveys during the northward migration period for shorebirds around the Yellow Sea coastline of China. In South Korea, staff of the Avian Laboratory, Ministry of Environment, have been conducting intensive counts of important sites in the Yellow Sea on both northward and southward migration since 1993. Non-governmental organizations in South Korea have also made a major contribution in recent years. Unfortunately, very little information is available from North Korea. The data collected up to 2000 have been analysed and published in the monograph *Shorebirds of the Yellow Sea – importance, threats and conservation status* (Barter 2002) and form the basis for this paper.

## SURVEY RESULTS

### Species present in internationally important concentrations

A total of 36 shorebird species has so far been found to occur in internationally important numbers at one or more sites in the

**Table 1. Species ranked according to the number of sites at which they occur in internationally important numbers.**

| Species | Number of sites of international importance | | | | |
| --- | --- | --- | --- | --- | --- |
| | Total | Northward migration | Southward migration | Non-breeding season | Breeding season |
| Kentish Plover *Charadrius alexandrinus* | 21 | 11 | 16 | 4 | 2 |
| Eurasian Curlew *Numenius arquata* | 15 | 7 | 11 | 6 | - |
| Terek Sandpiper *Xenus cinereus* | 14 | 9 | 13 | - | - |
| Far Eastern Curlew *Numenius madagascariensis* | 13 | 12 | 7 | - | - |
| Grey Plover *Pluvialis squatarola* | 13 | 12 | 7 | - | - |
| Great Knot *Calidris tenuirostris* | 12 | 11 | 3 | - | - |
| Black-tailed Godwit *Limosa limosa* | 12 | 7 | 6 | - | |
| Dunlin *Calidris alpina* | 11 | 10 | 5 | - | - |
| Lesser Sandplover *Charadrius mongolus* | 11 | 10 | 7 | - | - |
| Common Greenshank *Tringa nebularia* | 11 | 4 | 8 | 1 | - |
| Whimbrel *Numenius phaeopus* | 9 | 9 | - | - | - |
| Spotted Greenshank *Tringa guttifer* | 9 | 4 | 6 | - | - |
| Bar-tailed Godwit *Limosa lapponica* | 8 | 8 | 1 | - | - |
| Eurasian Oystercatcher *Haematopus ostralegus* | 7 | 3 | 4 | 2 | 2 |
| Red-necked Stint *Calidris ruficollis* | 5 | 5 | 2 | - | - |
| Black-winged Stilt *Himantopus himantopus* | 5 | 4 | 3 | - | 2 |
| Marsh Sandpiper *Tringa stagnatilis* | 5 | 3 | 4 | - | - |
| Red Knot *Calidris canutus* | 5 | 3 | 2 | - | - |
| Broad-billed Sandpiper *Limicola falcinellus* | 5 | 2 | 4 | - | - |
| Asian Dowitcher *Limnodromus semipalmatus* | 4 | 4 | 3 | - | - |
| Spotted Redshank *Tringa erythropus* | 4 | 4 | 2 | 1 | - |
| Little Ringed Plover *Charadrius dubius* | 4 | 4 | 2 | - | - |
| Ruddy Turnstone *Arenaria interpres* | 3 | 3 | 1 | - | - |
| Sanderling *Calidris alba* | 3 | 1 | 3 | 1 | - |
| Common Redshank *Tringa totanus* | 2 | 2 | 1 | - | 2 |
| Sharp-tailed Sandpiper *Calidris acuminata* | 2 | 2 | 1 | - | - |
| Curlew Sandpiper *Calidris ferruginea* | 2 | 2 | - | - | - |
| Northern Lapwing *Vanellus vanellus* | 2 | 1 | 2 | - | - |
| Grey-tailed Tattler *Heteroscelus brevipes* | 2 | 1 | 1 | - | - |
| Pied Avocet *Recurvirostra avosetta* | 2 | 1 | - | 1 | - |
| Spoon-billed Sandpiper *Eurynorhynchus pygmeus* | 2 | - | 2 | - | - |
| Grey-headed Lapwing *Vanellus cinereus* | 2 | - | 2 | - | - |
| Little Curlew *Numenius minutus* | 1 | 1 | - | - | - |
| Oriental Plover *Charadrius veredus* | 1 | 1 | - | - | - |
| Red-necked Phalarope *Phalaropus lobatus* | 1 | - | 1 | - | - |
| Oriental Pratincole *Glareola maldivarum* | 1 | - | - | - | 1 |

Yellow Sea (Table 1). This number represents 60% of the migratory shorebird species in the East Asian-Australasian Flyway.

Table 2 provides a summary of the estimated numbers of birds using the Chinese and South Korean portions of the Yellow Sea during northward migration for those species for which sufficient count data are available (see Barter 2002 for an explanation of how these estimates were made). An estimate is also given of the proportion of the flyway breeding populations being supported at this time of the year. The use of proportions of breeding populations is the most appropriate way to measure of the Yellow Sea's importance, as this does not include the often significant numbers of non-migrating immature birds remaining on the non-breeding grounds further south.

The great importance of the Yellow Sea for shorebirds during northward migration is demonstrated by the fact that it supports 30% or more of the flyway breeding populations of 18 species; for six of these species, the region supports almost the entire flyway breeding population.

The Yellow Sea is particularly important for four species of special conservation concern: the Endangered Spotted Greenshank *Tringa guttifer* and Vulnerable Spoon-billed Sandpiper *Eurynorhynchus pygmeus*, and the Near-Threatened Far Eastern Curlew *Numenius madagascariensis* and Asian Dowitcher *Limnodromus semipalmatus*. All four of these are endemic to the East Asian-Australasian Flyway. It is highly likely that the great majority of the Spotted Greenshank and Spoon-billed Sandpiper populations use the Yellow Sea during both northward and southward migrations. More than 90% of the estimated breeding population of the Far Eastern Curlew migrate through the Yellow Sea on northward migration, and 50% of the Asian Dowitchers.

In total, it is estimated that a minimum of 2 000 000 shorebirds use the wetlands around the Yellow Sea during northward migration, i.e. approximately 40% of the estimated flyway popu-

**Table 2. Proportion of the breeding populations of shorebirds supported by the Yellow Sea during northward migration.**

| Species | Population estimate | % breeding of population |
|---|---|---|
| Great Knot | 290 000 | >90 |
| Bar-tailed Godwit | 230 000 | >90 |
| Grey Plover | 110 000 | >90 |
| Kentish Plover | 90 000 | >90 |
| Far Eastern Curlew | 32 000 | >90 |
| Eurasian Curlew | 32 000 | >90 |
| Dunlin | 660 000 | 70 |
| Whimbrel | 33 000 | 70 |
| Lesser Sandplover | 32 000 | 65 |
| Spotted Redshank | 20 000 | 60 |
| Asian Dowitcher | 9 300 | 50 |
| Red Knot | 67 000 | 40 |
| Marsh Sandpiper | 39 000 | 40 |
| Red-necked Stint | 87 000 | 35 |
| Common Greenshank | 15 000 | 35 |
| Terek Sandpiper | 14 000 | 35 |
| Broad-billed Sandpiper | 5 100 | 35 |
| Black-tailed Godwit | 48 000 | 30 |
| Ruddy Turnstone | 4 500 | 20 |
| Little Curlew | >>17 000 | >10 |
| Sharp-tailed Sandpiper | 17 000 | 10 |
| Curlew Sandpiper | 18 000 | <10 |

**Fig. 2.** Locations of sites in the Yellow Sea at which internationally important numbers of at least one species of shorebird have been recorded. South Korean sites: 1 Ganghwa Do; 2 Yong Jeong Do; 3 Daebu Do; 4 Namyang Man; 5 Hongwon Ri; 6 Asan Man; 7 Seosan Reclaimed Area; 8 Geum Gang Hagu; 9 Mangyeung Gang Hagu; 10 Dongjin Gang Hagu; 11 Paeksu Tidal Flat; 12 Hampyeong Man; 13 Meian Gun Tidal Flat; 14 Aphae Do; 15 Suncheon Man; 16 Nakdong Gang Hagu.

lation of migratory shorebirds. Perhaps 1 000 000 shorebirds pass through the region on southward migration.

### Internationally important sites

Twenty-seven internationally important sites have been identified around the Yellow Sea coastline (Fig. 2). Ten of these sites are located in China, one in North Korea and 16 in South Korea. Six of the ten Chinese sites, the North Korean site and a small part of one of the 16 South Korean sites are within protected areas. A summary of information on the numbers of internationally important species and highest seasonal counts at each site is presented in Table 3.

The sites exhibit a great diversity in the number of species of shorebirds that they support in internationally important numbers. Half of the sites carry at least five species in internationally numbers, whilst six support 15 or more species. At five sites, the highest counts of shorebirds have exceeded 100 000 on northward migration, whilst one site supports almost 250 000 shorebirds on southward migration. Some sites support a high proportion of the flyway population of one or more species; those sites holding >5%, >10% and >20% of the estimated flyway populations are listed in Table 4. These sites have very important conservation significance.

Six extremely important regions within the Yellow Sea have been identified:

- central and northern Jiangsu coast (Yancheng NNR and Dongsha);
- Bohai Wan (Huang He NNR, Tianjin Municipality and Shi Jiu Tuo);
- northern Liaodong Wan (Shuangtaizihekou NNR and Linghekou);
- Yalu Jiang NNR;
- Namyang and Asan Mans;
- the Mangyeung and Dongjin estuaries.

Each of these regions supports peak numbers well in excess of 100 000 shorebirds on northward migration, whilst the Jiangsu coast holds more than 250 000 on southward migration and is also the most important area within the Yellow Sea during the non-breeding season.

### Threats

The rapid growth of the human populations and economies of China and South Korea is causing serious loss and degradation of coastal habitats. Approximately 37% of the inter-tidal areas existing in the Chinese portion of the Yellow Sea in 1950 and 43% of those in the South Korean part in 1917 have been reclaimed to date. China has plans to reclaim a further 45% of its current mudflats and South Korea an additional 34%. The two largest rivers flowing into the Yellow Sea, the Huang He (Yellow River) and Chang Jiang (Yangtze River), are undergoing significant changes that will greatly reduce the input of sediments, and it is predicted that future loss of inter-tidal areas will occur at an increasing rate due to the combined effects of reclamation and reduced accretion. The declining river flows and high levels of pollution are leading to reduced benthic productivity and thus a decline in food supplies for shorebirds. Human disturbance, by affecting feeding and roosting birds, and competition, through unsustainable harvesting of benthic fauna, may also have a serious impact on shorebirds.

**Table 3. Sites in the Yellow Sea ranked according to the number of species of shorebirds occurring in internationally important numbers and the highest seasonal counts (see Fig. 2 for site locations).**

| Site | No. of species occurring in internationally important numbers | Highest count | | |
|---|---|---|---|---|
| | | Northward migration | Southward migration | Non-breeding season |
| Yancheng NNR | 23 | 111 285 | 82 530 | 27 181 |
| Huang He NNR | 17 | 130 122 | 70 748 | - |
| Tianjin Municipality | 17 | 73 553 | - | - |
| Dongjin Gang Hagu | 16 | 126 145 | 36 181 | - |
| Mangyeung Gang Hagu | 16 | 115 054 | 53 178 | - |
| Shi Jiu Tuo | 15 | - | - | - |
| Shuangtaizihekou NNR | 14 | 63 641 | 25 780 | - |
| Dong Sha | 13 | 72 584 | 244 176 | 44 737 |
| Namyang Man | 12 | 53 359 | 26 470 | 2 303 |
| Asan Man | 11 | 70 507 | 10 362 | 635 |
| Yalu Jiang NNR | 10 | 151 708 | - | - |
| Geum Gang Hagu | 10 | 34 198 | 12 212 | 4 084 |
| Yeong Jong Do | 10 | 22 886 | 21 038 | 240 |
| Ganghwa Do | 9 | 28 715 | 15 317 | 1 183 |
| Jiu Duan Sha | 7 | 5 780 | 843 | 4 190 |
| Chongming Dao PNR | 6 | 24 770 | 2 889 | 4 871 |
| Nakdong Gang Hagu | 4 | 14 198 | 2 857 | - |
| Suncheon Man | 4 | 14 170 | 3 443 | 3 770 |
| Aphae Do | 4 | 12 862 | 9 162 | 606 |
| Seosan Reclaimed Area | 3 | 10 696 | 408 | - |
| Meian Gun Tidal Flat | 3 | 2 180 | 6 466 | 585 |
| Linghekou | 2 | 34 445 | - | - |
| Hampyeong Man | 2 | 5 728 | 6 549 | 964 |
| Daebu Do | 1 | - | 3 668 | - |
| Paeksu Tidal Flat | 1 | 1 511 | 2 060 | - |
| Hongwon Ri | 1 | - | - | - |
| Mundok MBWR | 1 | - | - | - |

Key: NNR = National Nature Reserve; PNR = Provincial Nature Reserve; MBWR = Migratory Bird Wetland Reserve.

The adverse effects of the various threats being encountered by shorebirds in the Yellow Sea are most significant during northward migration, when shorebirds are not only preparing for their final long flight into the breeding grounds, but also gaining additional reserves to sustain them during the period immediately after arrival, when feeding conditions may be poor but territories have to fought for and eggs laid.

Of particular concern is the ongoing reclamation of the Mangyeung and Dongjin estuaries as part of the 401 sq. km Saemangeum Reclamation Project. These estuaries are the most important sites in South Korea during both northward and southward migration, in terms of both maximum counts and numbers of species occurring in internationally important concentrations. During the northward migration period, the two estuaries jointly carry 30% of the Great Knot *Calidris tenuirostris* breeding population. The estuaries also support the most significant concentrations within the Yellow Sea of the endangered Spotted Greenshank and vulnerable Spoon-billed Sandpiper during southward migration. Between them, the two estuaries support the highest recorded concentrations in the Yellow Sea during northward migration of three species, and during southward migration of seven.

## CONSERVATION STATUS OF SHOREBIRDS IN THE YELLOW SEA

The widespread and ongoing reclamation of inter-tidal areas, excessive pollution levels and high levels of human disturbance indicate very clearly that migratory shorebirds are already encountering serious problems in the Yellow Sea. These difficulties can be expected to increase. Thus, the conservation status of shorebirds is poor and is likely to decline further. Effective conservation of migratory shorebirds and their wetland habitats is a challenging task at any time, but it is particularly difficult around the Yellow Sea coastline, where development activities are generally undertaken with little regard for environmental consequences.

The traditional approach to nature conservation, i.e. the creation of a network of protected areas with severe limitations being placed on human activities, is inappropriate in the Yellow Sea due to the very extensive nature of the inter-tidal areas in the region and the high dependence of the local communities on the inter-tidal resources. Even nature reserves in China have large human populations, e.g. 90 000 people live within the Yancheng National Nature Reserve.

**Table 4.** Sites supporting >20%, >10% and >5% of an estimated shorebird flyway population during northward migration, southward migration or the non-breeding season.

| Sites | >20% | >10% | >5% |
|---|---|---|---|
| Chongming Dao PNR | | | Kentish Plover (NM) |
| Dong Sha | | | Asian Dowitcher (SM) |
| Yancheng NNR | | Spotted Redshank (SM) | Spotted Redshank (NM) |
| | | Marsh Sandpiper (NM) | Marsh Sandpiper (SM) |
| | | Sanderling (NM) | Sanderling (NB) |
| | | Little Ringed Plover (SM) | Dunlin (NM) |
| | | | Kentish Plover (SM) |
| Huang He NNR | Eurasian Curlew (NM) | Grey Plover (NM) | |
| | Kentish Plover (NM) | Little Curlew (NM) | |
| Tianjin Municipality | | Black-winged Stilt (NM) | Eurasian Curlew (NM, SM, NB) |
| | | | Red Knot (NM) |
| | | | Curlew Sandpiper (NM) |
| | | | Grey Plover (NM) |
| Shi Jiu Tuo | Eurasian Curlew (SM) | | Eurasian Curlew (NM) |
| | | | Black-winged Stilt (SM) |
| | | | Grey-headed Lapwing (SM) |
| | | | Northern Lapwing (SM) |
| | | | Kentish Plover (SM) |
| Shuangtaizihekou NNR | | | Great Knot (NM) |
| Yalu Jiang NNR | | Great Knot (NM) | Far Eastern Curlew (NM) |
| | | Bar-tailed Godwit (NM) | Grey Plover (NM) |
| Ganghwa Do | | | Far Eastern Curlew (NM) |
| Namyang Man | | | Eurasian Curlew (NM, SM) |
| | | | Spotted Greenshank (NM) |
| | | | Great Knot (NM) |
| Asan Man | | Black-tailed Godwit (NM) | Great Knot (NM) |
| Geum Gang Hagu | Eurasian Oystercatcher (NB) | Eurasian Oystercatcher (NB) | Eurasian Curlew (SM) |
| Mangyeung Gang Hagu | | Great Knot (NM) | Black-tailed Godwit (SM) |
| | | Kentish Plover (SM) | Spotted Greenshank (SM) |
| | | | Dunlin (NM) |
| | | | Lesser Sandplover (NM, SM) |
| Dongjin Gang Hagu | | Great Knot (NM) | Spotted Greenshank (SM) |
| | | | Kentish Plover (SM) |
| | | | Lesser Sandplover (NM, SM) |

NM = northward migration; SM = southward migration; NB = non-breeding season.

Successful conservation activity will depend on the adoption of suitable national policies and plans for the appropriate use of inter-tidal and sub-coastal areas. These will need to be harmonized across the three littoral countries. Local community support will be an essential factor in creating the necessary political environment for the development and successful implementation of these policies and plans.

## REFERENCES

**Bamford, M.J., Watkins, D.G., Bancroft, W. & Tischler, G.** 2005. Population Estimates and Importance of Sites for Shorebirds in the East Asian-Australasian Flyway. In: P. Straw (ed) Status and Conservation of Shorebirds in the East Asian-Australasian Flyway. Proceedings of the Australasian Shorebirds Conference 13-15 December 2003, Canberra, Australia. Wetlands International Global Series 18, International Wader Studies 17. Sydney, Australia.

**Barter, M.A.** 2002. Shorebirds of the Yellow Sea – Importance, threats and conservation status. Wetlands International Global Series 9, International Wader Studies 12, Canberra, Australia.

**Melville, D.S.** 1997. Threats to waders along the East Asian-Australasian Flyway. In: P. Straw (ed) Shorebird Conservation in the Asia-Pacific Region. Australasian Wader Studies Group of Birds Australia, Melbourne.

**Scott, D.A. & Poole, C.M.** 1989. A Status Overview of Asian Wetlands. Publication No. 53. Asian Wetland Bureau, Kuala Lumpur.

# Population declines and the risk of extinction in waders: genetic and ecological consequences of small population size

*Allan J. Baker*

*Department of Natural History, Royal Ontario Museum, and Department of Zoology, University of Toronto, Toronto, Ontario, Canada.*

Baker, A.J. 2006. Population declines and the risk of extinction in waders: genetic and ecological consequences of small population size. *Waterbirds around the world.* Eds. G.C. Boere, C.A. Galbraith & D.A. Stroud. The Stationery Office, Edinburgh, UK. pp. 668-671.

## ABSTRACT

World-wide population declines in waders are of great concern because many species have not yet recovered from loss of genetic variation caused by population bottlenecks in the late Pleistocene. Therefore genetically effective population sizes are much smaller than census population sizes. Genetic drift can be more important than selection in determining the fate of new mutations in small populations, in which case populations are expected to accumulate deleterious mutations. The fixation of such deleterious alleles is expected to reduce reproductive success of a species and lead to extinction unless new beneficial mutations are fixed by selection and help restore part of the lost fitness. Critical effective size could be as small as a few hundred individuals, above which a population will persist without extinction due to genetic load. However, this requires an approximately 10-fold higher census population size because of the variance in breeding success and fluctuations in numbers in different generations. In populations such as the Red Knot *Calidris canutus rufa* which is currently undergoing a drastic decline in numbers due to bad ecological conditions, the risk of extinction is exacerbated. This paper reviews genetic and ecological evidence of why the population is declining, and argues that an increasing number of species may be in the same risk category.

## INTRODUCTION

Wader species and their constitutive populations are of international conservation concern, following a recent review of population trends around the world (International Wader Study Group 2003, Stroud *et al.* 2006). For those species in which population trends were reported, three times as many are in decline as are expanding. Forty-two of 214 species (19.6%) listed by the International Wader Study Group were assessed as either Globally Threatened or Near Threatened. Although this number includes some species that are already thought to be extinct, it is a strong indication that the loss of biodiversity in this charismatic group of birds is accelerating. The causes of this increasing risk of extinction in waders are poorly understood, and raise important issues in conservation management generally, as well as specific questions about how to halt global declines and engage in population restoration.

While the loss of wetlands and destruction of associated food supplies is likely implicated in most population declines, it is often not appreciated fully that the risk of extinction involves both genetic and ecological consequences of small population size. The purpose of this paper is to bring to the attention of wader biologists some recent theoretical work on the genetic risks of extinction of small populations (Whitlock 2000), and to emphasize that ecological and genetic risks operate in different time frames. However, both need to be considered in the restoration of small populations if we are to try to give them a future in other millennia.

## LOW GENETIC VARIATION IN WADERS

Assays of genetic variation in waders have uncovered the rather surprising fact that many species and populations are genetically impoverished, relative to other groups of birds such as passerines. This was first reported by Baker & Strauch (1988) using protein electrophoresis (see Table 1). Low genetic variability is evident not only in small populations of threatened endemics such as the African Black Oystercatcher *Haematopus moquini* and Mountain Plover *Charadrius montanus*, but also in migratory species with much larger population sizes (e.g. Purple Sandpiper *Calidris maritima* and Willet *Catoptrophorus semipalmatus*). The latter implies that at some time in their recent past, Purple Sandpipers and Willets were reduced to small ancestral populations, thereby losing genetic variation, and have expanded subsequently to larger populations. Not enough time has elapsed since the populations expanded for many mutations to accumulate in the genomes of these species and restore the genetic variation expected in equilibrium populations.

## HISTORICAL DEMOGRAPHY AND GENETIC BOTTLENECKS

One source of loss of genetic variation in wader populations dates back to previous episodes of population declines in the last glacial maximum (LGM) about 22 000 years ago in the Northern

**Table 1. Estimates of genetic variability at 30 loci of some wader species based on protein electrophoresis.**

| Species | N | No. alleles/locus | % Polymorphic loci | Average heterozygosity |
|---|---|---|---|---|
| African Black Oystercatcher *Haematopus moquini* | 13 | 1.1 | 8.3 | 0.019 |
| Grey Plover *Pluvialis squatarola* | 13 | 1.1 | 7.5 | 0.011 |
| Mountain Plover *Charadrius montanus* | 10 | 1.0 | 0.0 | 0.000 |
| Red Knot *Calidris canutus* | 25 | 1.3 | 17.9 | 0.020 |
| Purple Sandpiper *Calidris maritima* | 35 | 1.1 | 6.9 | 0.006 |
| Dunlin *Calidris alpina* | 25 | 1.1 | 13.8 | 0.009 |
| Willet *Catoptrophorus semipalmatus* | 23 | 1.1 | 5.0 | 0.002 |
| Passerine average | | | | 0.053 |

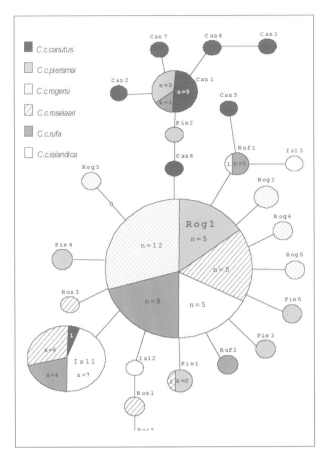

**Fig. 1.** Minimum spanning network connecting 91 haplotypes found in 657 bp of the mitochondrial DNA control region in globally distributed populations of the Red Knot *Calidris canutus*. The star-like pattern is created because most haplotypes differ by one mutation from the common haplotypes. From Buehler & Baker (2005).

Hemisphere, or possibly earlier glacial maxima in the Pleistocene. Especially for migratory waders breeding in the high Arctic tundra, such as the Red Knot *Calidris canutus*, the genetic footprint of a small population that survived the LGM is readily apparent in the very limited variation in mitochondrial DNA sequences of the six subspecies (Baker *et al.* 1994). Only 25 haplotypes were found in 675 bp sequences of the control region, the fastest evolving part of the mtDNA molecule. Furthermore, the 91 individuals that were sequenced were sampled over the global range of the species (Buehler & Baker 2005). The minimum spanning network has the pattern expected under a demographic contraction and population bottleneck in the LGM: a few ancestral common haplotypes that survived the bottleneck, and most of the remainder arising by mutations of one or a few bases subsequently as the population expanded (Fig. 1).

Such a star-like phylogeny is typical of small populations of recently bottlenecked species. Although such a pattern can also be generated by selection acting on linked genes in the nucleus, this is unlikely in Red Knots because (1) the same star-like pattern has been found in other species of waders suggesting a general demographic contraction in response to harsh Pleistocene environmental conditions, and (2) a similarly low level has been found in nuclear loci (Table 1) and in genomic scans of Red Knots using amplified fragment length polymorphisms (AFLP, Table 2). The scans also show that waders such as the Red Knot and Dunlin *Calidris alpina* have less genetic variation at hundreds of nuclear loci than a range of other bird species. The lowest value was recorded in the Red Knot (all subspecies included), even though a larger number of loci (836) were scanned than in passerine taxa.

## POPULATION PERSISTENCE AND THE GENETIC RISK OF EXTINCTION IN SMALL POPULATIONS

In a seminal paper, Whitlock (2000) assessed the genetic risk of extinction in small populations in which he not only considered the fixation of deleterious alleles that thereby affect the fitness of all individuals, but also factored in the fixation of beneficial mutations that can reduce this genetic load. Beneficial alleles are more likely to be lost and deleterious alleles are more likely to be fixed in small populations because random genetic drift is more important relative to selection. Thus small populations have a high probability of extinction because of the inexorable decline in fitness.

However, Whitlock showed that there is a critical threshold size (*Ne, crit*) above which populations are expected to persist indefinitely because the loss of fitness from the fixation of deleterious alleles is countered by the fixation of beneficial alleles. This critical effective size in populations varies according to a number of factors. First, if the rate of beneficial mutation is large relative to the rate of deleterious mutation, the loss of fitness will be restored in smaller populations than would be the case if the rates were reversed. Second, when the mean effects of mutation are high, the importance of genetic drift of nearly neutral alleles is decreased, and thus critical effective size is lower. Third, if beneficial mutations are likely to be more frequent or have a larger effect in compensating for a previous decline in fitness, then *Ne, crit* will be lower. Fourth, a high ratio of effective population size (and hence the number of breeding adults) to census population size will decrease the critical threshold size for population persistence. Finally, sexual selection could also lower this threshold by removing deleterious alleles, as alleles that decrease productivity are also likely to reduce mating success (Whitlock 2000).

Due to uncertainty and lack of empirical estimates of these parameters, the critical effective size can only be approximated, but is thought to be in the range of hundreds of individuals. However, the ratio of effective population size to census population size in waders (Buehler & Baker 2005) is typically about 0.1, as it is in other wildlife (Frankham 1995). Therefore, as Whitlock (2000) pointed out, census population size for population persistence in the longer term needs to be at least 10 times larger than the critical effective size, typically in the thousands.

## POPULATION PERSISTENCE AND THE ECOLOGICAL RISK OF EXTINCTION IN SMALL POPULATIONS

Ecological and demographic factors such as breeding failure and low recruitment rates, low adult annual survival and worsening environmental conditions present much more immediate risks of extinction than genetic factors (Lande 1998). This is because ecological pressures can operate on a much shorter time frame of a few generations in long-lived organisms such as waders, whereas genetic problems accumulate slowly through time. In the *rufa* population of Red Knots, for example, the immediate threats are more likely to be ecological. Late arrival at Delaware Bay in spring and inadequate refuelling at this last stopover before migrating to the Arctic breeding grounds have resulted in

**Table 2. Genomic diversity in bird taxa estimated with amplified fragment polymorphisms (AFLP).**

| Species | No. amplified loci | No. polymorphic loci | % polymorphic loci |
|---|---|---|---|
| House Finch *Carpodacus mexicanus* | 363 | 223 | 61.4 |
| Chiffchaff *Phylloscopus collybita* | 251 | 141 | 56.2 |
| Bluethroat *Luscinia svecica* | 232 | 81 | 34.9 |
| Willow Flycatcher *Empidonax trailli* | 708 | 197 | 27.8 |
| Dunlin *Calidris alpina* | 900 | 203 | 22.6 |
| Red Knot *Calidris canutus* | 836 | 129 | 15.4 |
| Average | 585.4 | 150.2 | 31.4 |

decreased annual survival of adults and low recruitment rates in the period 2000-2001 (Baker *et al.* 2004). The further loss of 13 000 birds from the over-wintering population in Tierra del Fuego, as recorded by an aerial census in February 2005, considerably increases the risk of extinction of this population. In the short period of five years, the population has declined from about 53 532 to 17 653.

The large-scale losses of birds could, in part, be a lag effect of inadequate refuelling at stopover sites, increased risk of breeding in unpredictable climatic conditions in the Arctic due to global climate change, and increased susceptibility to pathogens and parasites. In small populations, the latter can be associated with the loss of adaptive variation and the accumulation and fixation of deleterious mutations which reduce fitness. We therefore expect such populations to be more prone to large mortalities in unfavourable ecological circumstances such as annual food failures, increased incidence of pathogens, and pollution. The joint effects of environmental stochasticity and genetic processes could increase the risk of extinction even further, as appears to be the case in the Red Knot. Not only have refuelling problems and late arrival at stopover sites been implicated in the severe decline in the Tierra del Fuego population, but also spring migrants passing through Lagoa do Piexe in southern Brazil in 1997 were observed dying in small flocks after foraging on ocean beaches. The cause of this mortality could not be determined, but was possibly due to a viral pathogen.

The interaction of genetic and ecological risk factors was the basis for the "parasite" hypothesis of wader migration which predicted that long-distance migrants such as the Red Knot have to winter in low-parasite marine environments (Piersma 1997), because they trade-off increased energy expenditure for immune system suppression. This in turn was also predicated on the observation that many species of waders are genetically impoverished as a result of population bottlenecks in the late Pleistocene (Baker & Strauch 1988, Baker *et al.* 1994), and thus have reduced levels of adaptive variation. The salient point about species that have survived a prolonged bottleneck (as in the millennial duration of glacial maxima) is that a population must exist at a much larger size for a very long time to recover from the negative effects on fitness suffered when the population was small (Whitlock 2000).

Migratory waders are vulnerable not only because of their life history characteristics and specialized ecologies, but also because of the genetic erosion of adaptive genetic variation from small population size in the past (Piersma & Baker 1999). We should thus not be surprised that so many migrant waders are declining world-wide and many species will be in the same risk

Dunlin *Calidris alpina* surface-tension feeding. Dunlins have lower genetic diversity than many other bird species. Photo: Rob Robinson.

category, and must be cognizant that restoration of their populations probably depends on managing for larger census population sizes than implied in the old 50 : 500 rule of thumb. This rule suggests that an effective population size of 50 breeding adults may be adequate in avoiding inbreeding depression, whereas an effective size of about 500 is required to prevent the loss of genetic variation in quantitative traits with high heritability (Harris *et al.* 1987, Simberloff 1988). This rule implies a census population size of about 5 000 adults for minimum viable population size, but if the ratio of beneficial to deleterious mutations is low, then it is wise to manage for at least double this population size to increase the chances of long-term persistence.

Although critical threshold size for population persistence has large uncertainties associated with it, larger census populations are good insurance in mitigating ecological and genetic risk factors. Finally, it is better to act earlier in declaring species or populations threatened or endangered. Rather than waiting until numbers have dwindled to hundreds or a few thousands, population restoration has to be attempted much sooner when the population is correspondingly bigger. Not only will this decrease adverse genetic effects, but it will also increase the prospects for a demographic expansion and reduce the risk of extinction.

## REFERENCES

**Baker, A.J. & Strauch, J.G.** 1988. Genetic variation and differentiation in shorebirds. Proceedings of XIX International Ornithology Congress, Ottawa, June 1986. Symposium 27: 1639-1645.

**Baker, A.J., Piersma, T. & Rosenmeier, L.** 1994. Unraveling the intraspecific phylogeography of knots (*Calidris* *canutus*) - A progress report on the search for genetic markers. Journal für Ornithologie 135: 599-608.

**Baker, A.J., Gonzalez, P.M., Piersma, T., Niles, L.J., do Nascimento, I.L.S., Atkinson, P.W., Clark, N.A., Minton, C.D.T., Peck, M.K. & Aarts, G.** 2004. Rapid population decline in red knot: fitness consequences of decreased refuelling rates and late arrival in Delaware Bay. Proceedings of the Royal Society of London 271: 875-882.

**Buehler, D.M. & Baker, A.J.** 2005. Population divergence times and historical demography in red knots and dunlins. Condor 107: 497-513.

**Frankham, R.** 1995. Effective population size/adult population size ratios in wildlife: a review. Genetical Research 65: 95-107.

**Harris, R.B., Maguire, L.A. & Shaffer, M.L.** 1987. Sample sizes for minimum viable population estimation. Conservation Biology 1: 72-76.

**International Wader Study Group** 2003. Are waders world-wide in decline? Reviewing the evidence. Wader Study Group Bulletin 101/102: 8-12.

**Lande, R.** 1998. Risk of population extinction from fixation of deleterious and reverse mutations. Genetica 102/103: 21-27.

**Piersma, T.** 1997. Do global patterns of habitat use and migration strategies co-evolve with relative investments in immunocompetence due to spatial variation in parasite pressure? Oikos 80: 623-631.

**Piersma, T. & Baker, A.J.** 1999. Life history characteristics and the conservation of migratory shorebirds. In: L.M. Gosling & W.J. Sutherland (eds) Behaviour and Conservation. Cambridge University Press: 105-123.

**Simberloff, D.** 1988. The contribution of population and community biology to conservation science. Annual Reviews of Ecology and Systematics 19: 473-511.

**Stroud, D.A., Baker, A., Blanco, D.E., Davidson, N.C., Delany, S., Ganter, B., Gill, R., González, P., Haanstra, L., Morrison, R.I.G., Piersma, T., Scott, D.A., Thorup, O., West, R., Wilson, J. & Zöckler, C. (on behalf of the International Wader Study Group).** 2006. The conservation and population status of the world's waders at the turn of the millennium. Waterbirds around the world. G.C. Boere, C.A. Galbraith & D.A. Stroud (Eds.), The Stationery Office, Edinburgh, UK. 643-648.

**Whitlock, M.C.** 2000. Fixation of new alleles and the extinction of small populations: drift load, beneficial alleles, and sexual selection. Evolution 54: 1855-1861.

As with a number of other wader species, although now abundant, the Willet *Catoptrophorus semipalmatus* has very low genetic variability implying that they have been through a recent population bottleneck. Photo: Rob Robinson.

## 5.3 Building effective ecological networks. Workshop Introduction

*Leon Bennun[1] & Ward Hagemeijer[2]*
[1]*BirdLife International, Wellbrook Court, Girton Road, Cambridge, CB3 0NA, UK.*
[2]*Wetlands International, PO Box 471, 6700 AL Wageningen, The Netherlands.*

Bennun, L. & Hagemeijer, W. 2006. Building effective ecological networks. Workshop Introduction. *Waterbirds around the world.*
Eds. G.C. Boere, C.A. Galbraith & D.A. Stroud. The Stationery Office, Edinburgh, UK. p. 672.

Lake Durankulak on the Bulgarian Black Sea coast is one of the major wintering areas for Red-breasted Geese *Branta ruficollis*. The species is has only ever been recorded from 115 sites worldwide and of these 70% qualify for Ramsar designation. The long-term viability of this species will depend on the conservation of these ecologically linked sites. Photo: Sergey Dereliev.

Flyway-level conservation requires attention to site networks, not just individual sites. Such wide-scale consideration (sometimes at continental scales) provides a practical challenge to planners and managers. Among other problems and constraints are limited resources, patchy data, restricted opportunities for new designations of protected sites, and the wide distributions of migratory species in space and time. Especially in response to the latter, with the advent of climate-mediated distributional shifts, approaches to the creation of site-networks are required that have a dynamic quality: with processes that allow regular assessment of effectiveness – and adaptation to 'fine-tune' effectiveness.

The symposium reviewed and discussed different approaches to: identifying key sites; building a coherent ecological network; linking site networks with the Convention on Biological Diversity's 'ecosystem approach'; recognition and practical conservation of site networks. Examples of national (or wider) networks were reviewed from the UK (Baker & Stroud), the Western Hemisphere Shorebird Reserve Network (Duncan), as well as in the context of the specific needs of individual species such as for Lesser White-fronted *Anser erythropus* and Red-breasted Geese *Branta ruficollis* (Dereliev), Greater Flamingo *Phoenicopterus ruber* (Bechet *et al.*), as well as for Siberian Crane *Grus leucogeranus* (Prentice *et al.*).

Pritchard stressed that the objectives of a site network must foster a synergy of the functions and values of its parts. The objectives (and strategies) of key site networks should have a sound scientific basis, so that it can be a credible statutory objective and a yardstick for measuring success. Pritchard challenged the workshop to be more specific about the ecological meaning that underpins our network concepts, including as related to site network coherence within existing legal frameworks.

# Towards coherence in site networks

*Dave E. Pritchard*

*BirdLife International/RSPB, The Lodge, Sandy, Bedfordshire, SG19 2DL, UK. (email: dave.pritchard@rspb.org.uk)*

Pritchard, D.E. 2006. Towards coherence in site networks. *Waterbirds around the world.* Eds. G.C. Boere, C.A. Galbraith & D.A. Stroud. The Stationery Office, Edinburgh, UK. pp. 673-674.

## ABSTRACT

When does a collection of sites become a network? And when does a network become coherent? Network administrators are often vague in defining the purposes and targets for individual networks. As a result, "coherence" often means little more than "a network that includes all my sites". Objectives of a site network must foster a synergy of the functions and values of its parts. The objectives (and strategies) of key site networks are explored to give the concept a more scientific basis, so that it can be a credible statutory objective and a yardstick for measuring success. Issues include: cost-effectiveness (geographical concentration); risk reduction (geographical spread); "capture"; "completion"; representativity; and viability. These objectives have implications for the way statutory site frameworks are operated, and the policy choices to be made. This paper challenges us to be more specific about the ecological meaning that underpins our network concepts, and also briefly comments on site network coherence within existing legal frameworks.

## INTRODUCTION

When we talk about site networks, we need to be clear about the objectives we have in mind. Those objectives also need to be ecologically meaningful at the network scale. Historically, much emphasis has been put on criteria for choosing sites. This generates a list of sites, but it does not necessarily follow that the list will have functions at the level of a network. In recent years, more emphasis has been put on management and on objectives for individual sites. This might help to secure the integrity of the individual sites, but again it does not necessarily contribute to coherence of the network. So what is this "coherence"? When does a collection of sites become a network? And when does a network become coherent?

## DISCUSSION

### Network-level objectives

To make a list of sites into a network, probably the minimum element required is a defined common purpose to which all the sites contribute. Network administrators face the question of whether their collection of sites is designed to provide scientific reference points, to serve as flagship cases to rally the conservation cause, to be used as demonstration sites for management techniques, to preserve the values that made each site qualify for designation, to restore more "natural" conditions, or something else. These questions get one as far as being able to say why any particular sites belong to a common collection. It is very important to relate sites to some context like this, but that in itself will not produce network coherence.

So perhaps coherence is an issue to do with the relationships between sites, and the properties of the "glue" which holds them together in some kind of unity. That is unlikely, because these things relate merely to the mechanism producing coherence.

The coherence itself resides instead in the resulting state of what the dictionary definition calls "being well held together". It is an expression of what the totality represents.

One can be slightly more strategic by adding a thought such as "if we wish to add more sites to the network, what scheme of priorities are we working to?" But even doing this does not necessarily involve defining an end-objective or target state for the network as a whole. Rather, what is really required is to define an objective which is concerned with the network in total having more functions and values than simply the sum of its parts. This, moreover, will be different in each case: it is not something which is possessed in a general way, automatically, by any plurality of sites.

If the common purpose is, for example, "sites holding examples of a rare species" or "the best quality examples of an ecosystem", then even if the strategy which has been adopted is a reactive site-by-site one, it is implicit that there is a job being done by the system, as well as the job being done by any one site within it. So in the first example referred to, this would be the function of making a specified contribution to the fate of the species, or in the second example, the function of representing within the network a sample of a value-set which extends outside the network. Alternatively, the system might be aiming at objectives such as making a contribution to sustaining an economic resource, or increasing overall capacity to support a particular species or habitat.

Once this has been resolved and an objective for the system has been defined, coherence also involves a second somewhat harder question. Threshold issues need to be addressed which assist in deciding when there are enough of the right kind of sites in the system to accomplish the end objective. Some examples of the objectives of site networks are examined below.

### Risk reduction/cost-effectiveness objectives

One goal for a site network may be to provide a sustainable representation of the range of distribution of the species or habitats at stake, as an expression of ecological character, biological diversity or population dynamics. Two potentially competing objectives towards achieving this goal are risk reduction and cost-effectiveness.

In order to minimize vulnerability and risk, a strategy of selecting sites so that the variety of values at stake is spread throughout the largest possible number of sites (geographical spread) may be appropriate. A strategy such as this is an insurance against the total loss of a resource being caused by localized impacts such as fire, flooding, disease or inappropriate land-use decisions. This kind of strategy also helps the chances of recovery from such events by offering a spread of gene-pools for potential re-colonization. In addition, site networks might need to include some "spare" resources for emergencies, such as sheltered refuges for birds in unusually severe weather. Spreading sites across several geopolitical jurisdictions may also help, to guard against the effects of political support for conservation fluctuating from time to time and from place to place.

If an objective of minimizing the cost per unit benefit is adopted, the opposite kind of strategy (geographical concentration) might be produced, because this would suggest that the maximum variety and abundance of values should be concentrated in the smallest possible number of sites. This could also maximize complementarity, i.e. each site being as different from the others as possible.

A social question which potentially affects the number and distribution of sites within a network is whether to have an objective of maximizing accessibility of sites to people. This might be important if the aims of the system include considerations such as human enjoyment of natural areas for bird-watching, or provision of amenity "greenspace".

### "Capture" and "completion" objectives

These spreading or concentrating approaches do not necessarily say anything in themselves about the composition of the sites that make up the network. To address this, one would require an approach to site selection based upon an objective something to the effect of maximizing the diversity of what is covered by the network. This is what could be thought of as a "capture objective", defining what the system aims to capture and hold within it. However, objectives to "maximize" something do not help to quantify the target end-state, unless it is genuinely intended that the system will cover 100% of whatever is of interest. Hence, while they could be called capture objectives, they could not normally be thought of as "completion objectives".

Completion objectives go further, by addressing the issue of how to know when to stop, i.e. when the network is coherent in the sense of containing enough sites of the right type. If this can be defined, then one can also search for sites to fill gaps in coverage. Two main strategies for completion objectives are representativity and viability. These are probably the main areas of benefit involved in moving from a single site to a site network.

### Representativity strategy

Representativity is a strategy for including enough sites or types of site within the network to demonstrate the range of functions, values and attributes at stake, and to enable a contribution to be made to the conservation of each of these. This is not just a matter of presenting samples: it has the crucial additional element of sufficiency.

Examples of "representation" objectives might be those targeting:

- the "best manifestations" of whatever is valued;
- the typical or reference type examples of whatever is valued;
- examples which demonstrate a particular aspect of knowledge or understanding;
- the cases least affected by human influence;
- sufficient cases to represent the full range of variety;

- a "basic minimum" of the heritage to pass on to future generations; and
- examples from each spatial subdivision of the geographical scope of the network.

### Viability strategy

Viability is a strategy for including in the network a sustainable minimum of something, such as a self-sustaining population, so that it can be conserved within the sites, perhaps on a basis of assuming a scenario where the aspect of value is lost from everywhere outside the network. Network concepts as such, as distinct from the question of simply having a large total area, come into their own especially in respect of the multiple site requirements of migratory or otherwise mobile taxa. This is a question of designing a network to include all the different geographical, climatic and other factors which play different roles at different times, and combine together to support the population.

Some networks may have an objective of including sites which play a "critical" role in relation to viability. This may include seasonal, climatic or biophysical "bottlenecks" of some kind in the life cycle or population cycle of a species.

### Site network coherence within existing legal frameworks

The coherence of site networks already features in one or two legal regimes. The Strategic Framework for Ramsar sites under the Convention on Wetlands contains a reference to network coherence, in that case at national level.

Under the European Union's Habitats Directive, if a project which is likely to damage a designated site nevertheless meets various public interest tests and has to be approved, there is a requirement for habitat compensation which has to serve an aim of protecting the overall coherence of the designated site network. It can be seen that this could translate into an idea of using maintenance of network coherence as one criterion for judging the adequacy of mitigation and compensation measures, more generally.

One assumption being made here is that overall network coherence can be preserved even if there are changes in the individual constituent sites. The concept therefore admits some interchangeability among the ingredients which go to make it up. The corollary, though, is that an impact on any one part of the system has to be considered in terms of its implications for the whole system.

### CONCLUSION

In conclusion, it seems clear that a coherent network cannot simply be thought of as "a network that includes all the sites I want it to include"! This paper has explored a few ways of giving the concept a more scientific and functional basis. This is an area that should be developed further in future, so that coherence can be a credible statutory objective and a yardstick for measuring success.

# Establishment of a UK network of Special Protection Areas for waterbirds: the SPA review and future directions

*Helen Baker & David A. Stroud*

*Joint Nature Conservation Committee, Monkstone House, City Road, Peterborough, PE1 1JY, UK.*
*(email: Helen.Baker@jncc.gov.uk)*

Baker, H. & Stroud, D.A. 2006. Establishment of a UK network of Special Protection Areas for waterbirds: the SPA review and future directions. *Waterbirds around the world*. Eds. G.C. Boere, C.A. Galbraith & D.A. Stroud. The Stationery Office, Edinburgh, UK. pp. 675-679.

## ABSTRACT

Special Protection Areas (SPAs) are sites designated under the European Union Directive on the Conservation of Wild Birds (79/409/EEC). The first analyses of the SPA network in the UK were published in the early 1990s. These reviews approached network creation on the individual merits of each site. Another network review was published in 2001, following agreement of formal UK SPA selection guidelines. The 2001 review was significantly different in its species-based approach; protection requirements of each species were assessed and a *suite* of SPAs selected accordingly. The national *network* comprises the aggregated SPA suites for 103 species or biogeographical populations, with 242 sites designated. The UK is of international importance for its waterbird populations and high proportions of many populations occur within the SPA network. Sites of importance for assemblages of over 20 000 non-breeding waterbirds are also included. The 2001 review highlighted gaps in the network, especially in the marine environment, which are now being addressed. National standards in monitoring SPA condition have been implemented, with each site assessed every six years. This will aid management of individual SPAs, and will allow regular assessment of the effectiveness of the national network in contributing to species conservation.

## INTRODUCTION

Special Protection Areas (SPAs) are strictly protected sites designated in accordance with the European Union (EU) Directive on the Conservation of Wild Birds (79/409/EEC; the "Birds Directive"). SPAs are designated for rare and vulnerable species within the EU (listed in Annex I of the Directive), and also for other regularly occurring migratory species. SPAs, together with Sites of Community Importance (SCI; identified under the EU Directive on the Conservation of Natural Habitats and of Wild Fauna and Flora - 92/43/EEC; "the Habitats Directive"), form the Natura 2000 network, which is intended to be a coherent ecological network. Designation of an area as a Natura 2000 site provides a high level of habitat protection, with explicit procedures and strict tests to be followed in relation to proposed developments affecting the site. SPA management is focused on the requirements of the species for which the site has been selected ("qualifying species"); potential impacts of activities that might negatively affect the site are assessed against effects on these birds.

Despite the intention that SPAs will contribute to a coherent European ecological network of protected sites, there are no detailed guidelines or criteria agreed at the EU level for selecting SPAs. The Directive provides broad guidance stating that the most suitable territories in number and size shall be classified and that these should ensure survival and reproduction within the species' area of distribution. In addition, for migratory species, SPA provision should take into account breeding, moulting and wintering areas and staging posts along the migration route, paying particular attention to protection of internationally important wetlands. The specific mention of internationally important wetlands is an implicit reference to the Convention on Wetlands (Ramsar, 1971) and an indication that the Ramsar site selection criteria should guide selection of SPAs for migratory waterbirds (Temple-Lang 1982).

Since the Birds Directive came into force, legal cases have influenced development of SPA selection approaches. Of greatest significance was Case C-3/96 *Commission v Netherlands* [1998] ECR I-3031, which established that in the absence of a scientific evaluation published by a government, the European Court of Justice could assess Member State SPA provision against BirdLife International's Important Bird Area (IBA) network (Grimmett & Jones 1989). The IBA identification process uses specific criteria for selecting sites, but there has been no formal adoption of these criteria as a common standard for selecting SPAs at either UK or European Union scales. The IBA process makes no reference to network coherence, and no IBA suites for species are identified, although its stated aim is to provide a network of sites that are of importance for the long-term viability of those populations amenable to site-based conservation across their biogeographical range. BirdLife International considers the IBA network to be the minimum essential to ensure the survival of these species (Heath & Evans 2000).

The means of achieving the SPA components of a coherent ecological network of Natura 2000 sites are therefore not clear. The Habitats Directive states that the designation of habitats, either alone or in order to support species, should be proportional to their occurrence. However, the Directive provides no guidance on what proportions would be adequate to contribute to a coherent ecological network. During moderation of national SCI lists, arbitrary levels of biogeographical representation were used to prioritize further network development (EU Habitats Committee 1997). When the proposed SCIs within a region supported more than 60% of a habitat or species, the consideration of more sites was of low priority. This level was chosen as it is likely to ensure that in most cases the objectives of the Habitats Directive would be met. However, the selection of SCIs is guided by more specific criteria than the Birds Directive provides for SPAs, and no similar target has been established for assessing the European SPA network.

In this paper, we describe the approach in the UK to establishing a network of SPAs, and the UK SPA selection guidelines. We also explore what the network provides specifically for

Britain was carried out and published in 1990, with site details published in 1992 (Stroud *et al.* 1990, Pritchard *et al.* 1992). SPAs in Northern Ireland were evaluated, adopting an approach similar to that used in Great Britain, on an All-Ireland basis in the early 1990s (Way *et al.* 1993). These reviews approached the task of defining a network of sites from an assessment of "best" sites on their own individual merits, rather than an assessment of the national, or international, needs of the species for which the network was being established. This type of approach was based on that for IBAs and the identification of potential Ramsar sites through its series of directories of wetlands of international importance (e.g. Carp 1980). The UK had designated 33 SPAs at the time of completion of the 1990 review, but critically the review identified a further 190 areas that should be considered for designation. A further list identified other areas where more data were required before further assessment of status could be made.

In 1994, the UK government requested that the Joint Nature Conservation Committee (JNCC) co-ordinate another review of the network and provide guidance on site selection. This resulted in the publication of formal UK SPA selection guidelines (JNCC 1999; Box 1) and a full review of terrestrial SPAs (Stroud *et al.* 2001).

The 2001 review was significantly different from previous reviews in that it approached site selection from a species perspective; site protection needs of both Annex I species occurring in the UK and other regularly occurring migratory species were assessed. Integral was the application of the UK SPA selection guidelines through a clearly defined decision-making process (Stroud *et al.* 2001). SPAs were not selected for Annex I or migratory species that are widely dispersed (and therefore deemed unsuitable for site-based conservation measures), but at least one SPA was selected for each of 103 species or biogeographical populations. The review assessed the protection requirements of each species or population in detail, and for each of these, derived a *suite* of SPAs accordingly. The overall UK *network* of SPAs is derived from the combination of all 103 suites for species or populations.

## THE UK SPA SELECTION GUIDELINES

The formal UK SPA selection guidelines (JNCC 1999) rely very much on the international precedence set by both the contemporary Ramsar Criteria and IBA Criteria, whilst taking into consideration the requirements of the Birds Directive and the desire for a more species-led approach. The UK SPA selection guidelines are not criteria – the application process is a two stage process, and it allows a degree of ecological assessment to inform the selection of the "most suitable" sites (see Box 1). Hence, the SPA suite for a particular species may not necessarily comprise all nationally or internationally important areas for that species, but may contain sites with fewer birds that have been added, for example, to improve coverage of a species' distribution.

## THE UK SPA NETWORK

The UK SPA network currently comprises 242 designated SPAs, and extends to more than 1 470 300 ha – about 6% of the UK's land surface. It includes suites of SPAs for 103 species or biogeographical populations, and incorporates 115 Ramsar sites.

The UK is of major international importance for several groups of birds. These include: breeding seabirds; wintering and

---

## Box 1. The UK Special Protection Area Selection Guidelines (JNCC 1999).

Application of the guidelines involves two stages. Stage 1 is intended to identify areas that are likely to qualify for SPA status. These areas are then considered further, using one or more of the judgements in Stage 2 to select the most suitable areas in number and size for SPA classification.

### Stage 1

1. An area is used regularly by 1% or more of the Great Britain (or in Northern Ireland, the all-Ireland) population of a species listed in Annex I of the Birds Directive (79/409/EEC as amended) in any season.
2. An area is used regularly by 1% or more of the biogeographical population of a regularly occurring migratory species (other than those listed in Annex I) in any season.
3. An area is used regularly by over 20 000 waterfowl (waterfowl as defined by the Ramsar Convention) or 20 000 seabirds in any season.
4. An area which meets the requirements of one or more of the Stage 2 guidelines in any season, where the application of Stage 1 guidelines 1, 2 or 3 for a species does not identify an adequate suite of most suitable sites for the conservation of that species.

### Stage 2

1. *Population size and density*
   Areas holding or supporting more birds than others and/or holding or supporting birds at higher concentrations are favoured for selection.
2. *Species range*
   Areas selected for a given species provide as wide a geographic coverage across the species' range as possible.
3. *Breeding success*
   Areas of higher breeding success than others are favoured for selection.
4. *History of occupancy*
   Areas known to have a longer history of occupation or use by the relevant species are favoured for selection.
5. *Multi-species areas*
   Areas holding or supporting the larger number of qualifying species under Article 4 of the Directive are favoured for selection.
6. *Naturalness*
   Areas comprising natural or semi-natural habitats are favoured for selection over those which do not.
7. *Severe weather refuges*
   Areas used at least once a decade by significant proportions of the biogeographical population of a species in periods of severe weather in any season, and which are vital to the survival of a viable population, are favoured for selection.

---

waterbirds. Finally, we provide a brief overview of monitoring and the future development of the UK SPA network.

## DEVELOPMENT OF THE UK SPA NETWORK

The UK began its programme of SPA designation in 1982. In order to assess progress, a full analysis of the SPA network in

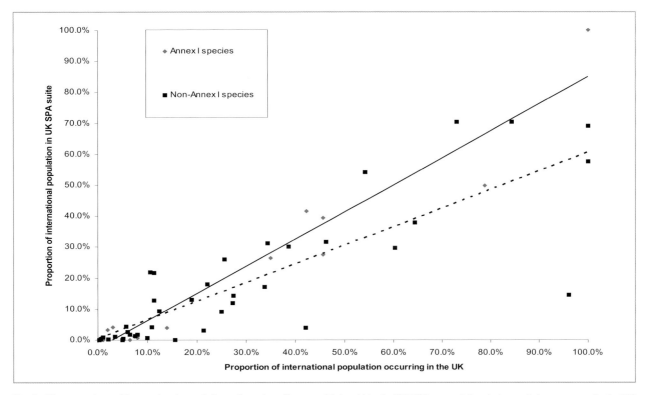

Fig. 1. The proportions of international populations of non-breeding waterbirds within the UK SPA network in relation to their occurrence in the UK (from Stroud *et al.* 2001). Solid line: linear relationship for Annex I species; y = 0.8743x – 0.0261; R² = 0.9353. Broken line: linear relationship for non-Annex I migratory species; y = 0.6018x + 0.0044; R² = 0.7029.

passage waterbirds; birds of Britain's distinctive uplands; and birds of Caledonian pinewoods. A high proportion (in some cases all) of the national and international populations of such species are contained within the UK SPA network. The habitat protection provided for these birds is a major contribution to their international conservation. Those species of greatest conservation concern in the context of the Birds Directive tend to have the highest proportions of their populations within the UK SPA network, as do those that have the smallest geographical ranges, and those where the UK holds a high proportion of international numbers (Fig. 1). Such figures allow an assessment of whether a network of sites is achieving its conservation aims in terms of providing a sufficient extent and geographical range of habitats for any given species.

The UK is of outstanding international importance for its waterbird populations, a consequence of its mild winter climate and strategic location on migratory flyways. In the mid-1990s, the SPA network supported an average of over 2 186 000 non-breeding waterbirds, approximately 40% of all waterbirds present in the UK in mid-winter. Fifty-seven sites of importance for assemblages of over 20 000 non-breeding waterbirds have been selected. In addition, a further 62 SPAs support internationally and/or nationally important numbers of waterbirds.

The performance of the UK SPA network for non-breeding waterbirds has been assessed and shown to be good (Jackson *et al.* 2004), but can be demonstrated more generally by a brief review of a few examples. Many species have high representation in the UK SPA network, with sites meeting most of the species' needs. For example, the network supports over 60% of the British breeding population of Black-throated Divers *Gavia arctica*, with sites providing nesting, roosting and feeding requirements during the breeding period. A number of waders

are well represented in the non-breeding season, such as the Bar-tailed Godwit *Limosa lapponica*, Dunlin *Calidris alpina alpina*, Red Knot *Calidris canutus* and Grey Plover *Pluvialis squatarola* for which the UK SPA network supports 70-90% of the British populations. In the case of the Annex I listed Bar-tailed Godwit, the network supports around 40% of the *lapponica* subspecies. For these species, SPAs include both feeding and roosting habitats, and so meet the birds' ecological needs during migration and in winter.

SPA provision in the UK for the Icelandic population of the Pink-footed Goose *Anser brachyrhynchus* is a good example of how a network of protected sites can make a significant contribution to the conservation of a species' population. This non-Annex I migratory population winters almost exclusively in the UK and is highly aggregated: 24 SPAs have been selected for it, supporting approximately 80% of UK numbers and 70% of the biogeographical population. Birds have been shown to use these SPAs as a true network, taking advantage of the different sites within the suite as they make seasonal movements to alternative feeding areas (Mitchell & Hearn 2004). The level of representation of the species in the UK network can be considered to be adequate, and the need for additional sites, given the current quality of habitats in the network and behaviour of the population, to be unnecessary. Hence, in this respect the network meets the requirements of Article 4 of the Birds Directive. However, these figures could be considered to be misleading in the sense that the focus of site protection for the species is primarily to provide safe roosting areas; the suite contains very little foraging habitat, which for this species is primarily intensively managed farmland. The designation of SPAs to include such habitat may not be appropriate, given that the species has been highly adaptable to changes in agriculture over the last 40 years and has derived significant benefit from this (Mitchell & Hearn 2004, Fox *et al.* 2005). To achieve a coherent ecological network for this species, a complementary approach to SPA designation of some form of wider landscape management that would ensure the perpetuation of suitable foraging areas, and access to them, may be more effective. Defining disturbance-free feeding zones around the sites within the network, and possibly also corridors (in the form of daytime resting places), could be beneficial in such a landscape approach. However, there is no defined mechanism for this kind of approach within the Birds Directive, although Article 3 could be interpreted as seeking the establishment of protected areas with a less strict level of protection than Natura 2000 sites. Other mechanisms may also be available to ensure that feeding areas have some degree of protection, such as agri-environmental provisions. For such species, including many other Anatidae, it may be that agri-environmental policies should aim to define a certain overall *extent* of feeding habitat within a defined distance of major roosts without being overly concerned about specific feeding locations. However, further assessment of the protection requirements of foraging habitats for those species using arable crops is required.

Not all species are as well represented within the UK SPA network, for a number of reasons. For example, less than 5% of British Mallards *Anas platyrhynchos* occur within the SPA network (representing less than 1% of the biogeographical population) due to the species being more widely dispersed during the non-breeding period. The contribution that protected sites can make to the conservation of dispersed species will be small, and wider countryside measures become of primary, but complementary, importance. The concept of a coherent ecological network for the conservation of such species must be developed at landscape-scale.

Overall, the terrestrial component of the UK SPA network is considered by the UK government to be substantially complete and the representation of each species within the network to be, in the majority of cases, at a sufficient level to meet the objectives of Article 4 of the Birds Directive. However, as no quantitative targets are set by the Birds Directive and few studies of conservation strategies for birds have been made that define optimal levels of site protection, there is no contemporary guidance on acceptable levels of population representation in the network. There have been previous attempts to define target ranges for species representation in a network of protected sites (e.g. Stroud *et al.* 1990, based on Bezzel 1980), but the final ranges produced remain arbitrary. Nevertheless, this kind of approach, which uses variables such as range occupancy, abundance, trends and international responsibility to highlight levels of high, moderate and low provision, seems intuitively useful. Furthermore, setting levels of population representation to assist in selecting networks of protected sites has been shown to be an effective approach (Jackson *et al.* 2004). Further refinement of a target-setting approach for population representation, based on testing of outcomes, would perhaps provide a simple and meaningful way to guide the definition of national and international networks.

Utilizing the standard Natura 2000 data submitted by Member States to the European Commission (available from the European Topic Centre on Biological Diversity), it is possible to begin to develop an understanding of how the overall European SPA network contributes to the conservation of populations. For example, there have been at least 235 SPAs designated for Bewick's Swan *Cygnus columbianus bewickii* throughout the EU15. Numbers peak in eastern European sites in autumn and spring, as birds migrate through the Baltic countries, and in western European sites, in winter. The UK has designated 15 SPAs for this population, and these support over 95% of British numbers and around 30% of the biogeographical population. However, it is difficult to assess the degree to which the EU15 SPA network provides support for this population from the standard data alone. The development of meaningful evaluation techniques, at population level, of the Natura 2000 network is essential, but to ensure that this network meets its objectives, the component national networks need to be of a sufficient standard. However, national action must be placed within the context of the full range of the species, especially for migratory species. Clearer approaches to target setting for national networks and guidance on achieving a coherent European ecological network is essential if SPA provision is to be a truly effective conservation tool at pan-European level. The long-term performance of the network will ultimately be assessed by the conservation status of the populations concerned.

## THE FUTURE DEVELOPMENT AND MONITORING OF THE UK SPA NETWORK

The 2001 UK SPA review highlighted cases where current data are inadequate to allow the selection of SPAs for certain species or at certain times of the year. These include sites for gulls and raptors in winter, and for mixed populations of passage waders. In addition, the review had a terrestrial focus, and a separate review process has been initiated for birds in the marine environment.

The UK government established a post-review scientific consultative group in 2001 (UK SPA and Ramsar Scientific Working Group – see http://www.jncc.gov.uk/page-1770 for more information) to advise it on the development of the SPA network, its monitoring and management. This group includes representatives from the government, non-governmental conservation organizations, and land and marine industrial sectors. One of the group's work areas is to review the importance of cropped habitats as feeding areas (for species such as the Pink-footed Goose) and evaluate possible approaches to the conservation and management of these areas in the context of the Birds Directive. Another area of work is to develop further a target-setting approach for population representation that may aid in further assessment and development of the SPA network.

The establishment of a network of SPAs must be accompanied by effective monitoring and management. EU Member States are obligated to avoid both the deterioration of habitats within SPAs and significant disturbance to the birds using these sites.

Monitoring protocols for SPAs, termed "Common Standards Monitoring", have been developed in the UK: all qualifying species will be monitored on each SPA at least once every six years (JNCC 2004). The aim is to provide an "alerts" type system which warns of unfavourable changes in the condition of the qualifying bird features, the causes of which can then be further explored and site management modified if appropriate (see Austin *et al.* 2006). Standardized monitoring of birds is already in place for many sites, with national schemes, such as the BTO/WWT/RSPB/JNCC Wetland Bird Survey for waterbirds, providing regular counts of birds, and in some cases trends, in many SPAs. Such schemes are heavily reliant on the considerable efforts of volunteer bird-watchers, and both major non-governmental conservation organizations and the government have aided the development of such monitoring capacity. However, some sites are infrequently monitored, especially those in remote areas, and for these, the Common Standards Monitoring approach (JNCC 2004) will provide a valuable opportunity to enhance the collection of information and use this to better focus the conservation management of individual SPAs. It will also allow periodic assessment, at national network scale, of the continuing effectiveness of SPAs in contributing to the conservation of certain bird populations.

## CONCLUSIONS

The UK Special Protection Area network comprises 242 designated sites, with suites of sites for each of 103 bird species or populations, and extends to about 6% of the UK's land area (Stroud *et al.* 2001). A species-based approach to building the network has allowed the selection of sites that not only support large numbers of birds, but are also sufficient to maintain species' ranges within the UK. Although substantially complete in the terrestrial environment, the network remains in development and SPA provision for birds in the marine environment is the current priority for such development. The key challenge remains understanding when the network is sufficient to meet the conservation needs of a species in the context of the species' ecology and other complementary measures. We believe that a species-based approach is intuitively the best way to build a coherent network, but recognize that setting targets is conceptually and scientifically difficult to do and that sufficiency is likely always to be measured in terms of scientific judgement; this should not detract from striving to create effective protected site networks.

## REFERENCES

**Austin, G.E., Maclean, I.M.D., Atkinson, P.W. & Rehfisch, M.M**. 2006. The UK Waterbirds Alerts System. Waterbirds around the world. G.C. Boere, C.A. Galbraith & D.A. Stroud (Eds.), The Stationery Office, Edinburgh, UK. 705-710.

**Bezzel, E.** 1980. An assessment of the endangered status of Europe's breeding birds and the importance of their biotopes as a basis for protective measures. Report (DOC.ENV/22/80) to European Commission.

**Carp, E.** 1980. Directory of Wetlands of International Importance in the Western Palearctic. UNEP/IUCN, Gland, Switzerland.

**EU Habitats Committee** 1997. Criteria for assessing national lists of pSCI at biogeographical level (Hab. 97/2 rev. 4).

**Fox, A.D., Madsen, J., Boyd, H., Kuijken, E., Norriss, Tombre, I.M. & Stroud, D.A.** 2005. Effects of agricultural change on abundance, fitness components and distribution of two arctic-nesting goose populations. Global Change Biology 11: 881-893.

**Grimmett, R.F.A. & Jones, T.A.** 1989. Important bird areas in Europe. ICBP Technical Publication No. 9, Cambridge, UK.

**Heath, M.F. & Evans, M.I.** (eds.). 2000. Important Bird Areas in Europe: priority sites for conservation. Two volumes. BirdLife Conservation Series No. 8. BirdLife International, Cambridge, UK.

Loch Badanloch, part of the peatlands of Caithness and Sutherland (the Flow Country), selected as part of the UK SPA network on the basis of its internationally important populations of breeding waterbirds including Golden Plover *Pluvialis apricaria*, Dunlin *Calidris alpina* and Greenshank *Tringa nebularia*. Photo: SNH.

**Jackson, S.F., Kershaw, M. & Gaston, K.J.** 2004. The performance of procedures for selecting conservation areas: waterbirds in the UK. Biological Conservation 118: 261-270.

**JNCC** 1999. The Birds Directive: selection guidelines for Special Protection Areas. Joint Nature Conservation Committee, Peterborough, UK.

**JNCC** 2004. Common Standards Monitoring. Joint Nature Conservation Committee, Peterborough, UK. (Available only online http://www.jncc.gov.uk/csm/default.htm).

**Mitchell, C.R. & Hearn, R.D.** 2004. Pink-footed goose *Anser brachyrhynchus* (Greenland/Iceland population) in Britain 1960/61 – 1999/2000. Waterbird Review Series, The Wildfowl & Wetlands Trust/Joint Nature Conservation Committee, Slimbridge, UK.

**Pritchard, D.E., Housden, S.D., Mudge, G.P., Galbraith, C.A. & Pienkowski, M.W.** 1992. Important Bird Areas in the United Kingdom including the Channel Islands and the Isle of Man. RSPB/JNCC, Sandy, UK.

**Stroud, D.A., Mudge, G.P. & Pienkowski, M.W.** 1990. Protecting internationally important bird sites: a review of the EEC Special Protection Area network in Great Britain. Nature Conservancy Council, Peterborough, UK. 230 pp.

**Stroud, D.A., Chambers, D., Cook, S., Buxton, N., Fraser, B., Clement, P., Lewis, P., McLean, I., Baker H. & Whitehead, S.** 2001. The UK SPA network: its scope and content. Three vols. Joint Nature Conservation Committee, Peterborough, UK. Available at http://www.jncc.gov.uk/UKSPA/default.htm.

**Temple-Lang, J.** 1982. The European Community Directive on bird conservation. Biological Conservation 22: 11-25.

**Way, L.S., Grice, P., MacKay, A., Galbraith, C.A., Stroud, D.A. & Pienkowski, M.W.** 1993. Ireland's internationally important bird sites: a review of sites for the EC Special Protection Area network. Joint Nature Conservation Committee, Peterborough, UK. Report to the National Parks and Wildlife Service of the Office of Public Works, Dublin and the Department of the Environment (Northern Ireland), Belfast. 231 pp.

# Waterbird Review Series: site inventories for swan and goose populations in Britain and Ireland

*Peter Cranswick[1], Matthew Denny[2], Richard Hearn[1], Carl Mitchell[1], James Robinson[1], Helen Rowell[1], Robin Ward[1] & Jenny Worden[1]*

[1] *The Wildfowl & Wetlands Trust, Slimbridge, Gloucestershire, GL2 7BT, UK. (e-mail: peter.cranswick@wwt.org.uk)*

[2] *Vine Cottage, Middletown, Hailey, Witney, Oxon, OX29 9UB, UK.*

Cranswick, P.A., Denny, M.J.H., Hearn, R.D., Mitchell, C.R., Robinson, J.A., Rowell, H.E., Ward, R.M. & Worden, J. 2006. Waterbird Review Series: site inventories for swan and goose populations in Britain and Ireland. *Waterbirds around the world.* Eds. G.C. Boere, C.A. Galbraith & D.A. Stroud. The Stationery Office, Edinburgh, UK. pp. 680-681.

Great Britain is of major importance for many populations of swans and geese, supporting during winter five entire or near-entire biogeographical populations, and a significant proportion of a further six (Table 1). A long-history of wildfowl (Anatidae) monitoring in Britain, particularly by The Wildfowl & Wetlands Trust (WWT) and supported by the Joint Nature Conservation Committee (JNCC) and its predecessor organisations, has developed into a programme of targeted surveys for these populations. Detailed information on the numbers and trends of these species at their key haunts is vital to the conservation and management of these populations at site, national and international levels. The need for national inventories is widely recognised by international conservation agreements and single species management plans; for example, the UK implementation plan for the African-Eurasian Waterbird Agreement specifically identifies the need for waterbird inventories to underpin habitat conservation. The Waterbird Review Series provides a comprehensive tool for conservation practitioners and decision makers, whether working at international level or as site managers.

The Waterbird Review Series brings together up to four decades of data and knowledge from the long-term monitoring programmes of swan and migratory goose populations that winter in Britain and Ireland. In each review, introductory sections describe abundance, distribution and ecology, particularly in Britain and Ireland but also throughout the population's range. Central to each review is a detailed inventory of impor-

tant sites. Population numbers and trends are presented (e.g. Fig. 1) along with a summary of site protection status, habitats and site usage by the population. Information is provided for all sites of international and national importance in the late 1990s, but also for sites of former importance where numbers have since declined. An overview of historical importance is provided at a regional level. The reviews demonstrate the value of long-term monitoring programmes, particularly in being able to highlight the dynamic distributions of many of these species, their expansion into new areas, their declines in others and, in some cases, apparent switching between favoured roost sites at a local scale.

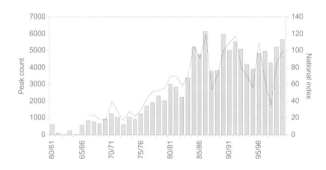

Fig. 1. Bewick's Swans at the Ouse Washes: peak counts (bars) and British index (line) 1960/61-1999/2000

**Table 1.** Native swan and goose populations occurring in Britain: 'Estimate' is the number of birds in Britain except for East Canadian High Arctic Light-bellied Brent Geese, where the estimate is for birds in Ireland.

| Species/sub-species | Population/race | Estimate | % of flyway population |
|---|---|---|---|
| Mute Swan *Cygnus olor* | Britain | 37 500 | 100 |
| Whooper Swan *Cygnus cygnus* | Iceland | 5 720 | 27 |
| Bewick's Swan Cygnus *columbarius bewickii* | NE Europe | 8 070 | 28 |
| Taiga Bean Goose *Anser f. fabalis* | *fabalis* | 400 | <1 |
| Tundra Bean Goose *Anser fabalis rossicus* | *rossicus* | 100 | <1 |
| Pink-footed Goose *Anser brachyrhynchus* | Greenland/ Iceland | 241 000 | 100 |
| Greenland White-fronted Goose *Anser albifrons flavirostris* | *flavirostris* | 20 900 | 77 |
| European White-fronted Goose *Anser a. albifrons* | Baltic/North Sea | 5 790 | <1 |
| Greylag Goose *Anser anser* | Iceland | 81 900 | 100 |
| Barnacle Goose *Branta leucopsis* | E Greenland | 45 000 | 83 |
| Barnacle Goose *Branta leucopsis* | Svalbard | 22 000 | 100 |
| Dark-bellied Brent Goose *Branta b. bernicla* | W Siberia | 98 100 | 46 |
| Light-bellied Brent Goose *Branta bernicla hrota* | Svalbard/N Greenland | 2 900 | 58 |
| Light-bellied Brent Goose *Branta bernicla hrota* | East Canadian High Arctic | 20 000 | 100 |

These reviews have highlighted the need for continued and enhanced monitoring, particularly of demographic variables such as productivity and survival, in order to track changes more closely, particularly at a site level, and to understand the processes driving changes at a population level. Although the reviews focus upon wetland sites, many swan and goose species also use semi-natural and agricultural habitats, but systematic information on the use of these areas is lacking for most sites. This remains a priority area for future surveys in order to relate feeding areas to roost sites, to understand the changing distributions of these species, and to enable effective conservation and management. The Waterbird Review Series is available on WWT's web site: http://www.wwt.org.uk/monitoring/waterbirdreviews/.

## ACKNOWLEDGEMENTS

The largest thank you is to the many thousands of counters, mostly volunteers, who have contributed the vast amount of data upon which these reviews are based. Without such skilled and dedicated people, these reviews would not have been possible.

Many people, too numerous to mention here, contributed towards the production of the Waterbird Review Series, but special thanks go to Helen Baker, David Boertmann, Hugh Boyd, Allan & Lyndesay Brown, Preben Clausen, Kendrew Colhoun, Gudmundur A Gudmundsson, Paul Marshall, Graham McElwaine, Oscar Merne, Eileen Rees, Chris Spray and David Stroud. The Waterbird Review Series was funded under the WWT/JNCC Partnership.

In winter, the UK supports the entire Svalbard population of Barnacle Goose *Branta leucopsis* and over 80% of the east Greenland population. The conservation and appropriate management of their key sites is critical to the long-term viability of these populations. Photo: Paul Marshall.

# The Western Hemisphere Shorebird Reserve Network (WHSRN)

*Charles D. Duncan*

*Manomet Center for Conservation Sciences, 76 Emery Street, Portland, Maine 04102, USA. (email: cduncan@manomet.org)*

Duncan, C.D. 2006. The Western Hemisphere Shorebird Reserve Network (WHSRN). *Waterbirds around the world.* Eds. G.C. Boere, C.A. Galbraith & D.A. Stroud. The Stationery Office, Edinburgh, UK. pp. 682-686.

## ABSTRACT

The Western Hemisphere Shorebird Reserve Network (WHSRN) is a voluntary coalition of people and communities linked through association with sites that host biologically important numbers of shorebirds. WHSRN's mission is to protect shorebird species through a network of key sites in the Americas. The focus is on site-based actions, particularly actions that can best be accomplished through a network of partners acting in concert. The Network was started in 1985 and now includes 60 sites in eight countries, with some 250 partner organizations, representing approximately eight million ha. Sites qualify at one of three levels: "hemispheric" (used by over 500 000 shorebirds per year, or at least 30% of a flyway population), "international" (over 100 000 per year, or at least 10%) or "regional" (over 20 000 per year, or at least 5%). In all cases, a site's landowners must agree to its inclusion in the Network before it can be accepted. Recent data indicating rapid declines in the populations of many shorebird species suggest that many additional sites need to be protected and included within the Network. Targeted conservation actions for species undergoing steep declines, having small populations, or otherwise at risk, are urgently needed. WHSRN has recently completed a thorough review of its mission, conservation vision, and strategy, including goals and objectives, for 2004-2008. With these has come a new organizational structure of nested geographic councils. The Network's Office continues to be a program of the Manomet Center for Conservation Sciences. Tasks ahead for the Network and a summary of lessons learned since the Network's founding are presented.

## HISTORY

The Western Hemisphere Shorebird Reserve Network (WHSRN) is one of the oldest flyway-scale conservation organizations. It traces its origin to a proposal by Guy Morrison of the Canadian Wildlife Service (CWS) for an international "series of protected areas linking key sites" for shorebirds throughout their range, made in 1982 at an International Waterfowl and Wetlands Research Bureau (IWRB) symposium (Morrison *et al.* 1995). The original concept, for totally protected "sister parks," was intimately connected with the CWS atlas work being carried out by Morrison and Ken Ross to quantify the use of the South American "wintering" grounds by shorebirds breeding in Canada, as well as with work of the International Shorebird Surveys operated out of Manomet Observatory (now Manomet Center for Conservation Sciences, and hereafter simply "Manomet"). The idea was developed with Morrison and other researchers by J.P. Myers, first at the Philadelphia Academy of Natural Sciences and then at the National Audubon Society.

Myers and Pete McLain (of the New Jersey Department of Fish, Game and Wildlife, USA) presented the idea to the International Association of Fish and Wildlife Agencies (IAFWA) in 1985. IAFWA adopted the plan and pledged to collaborate with the World Wildlife Fund-US (WWF) in advancing the network, by then formally named WHSRN (Myers *et al.* 1987). This was a key step because it brought the concept to the attention of a wide variety of wildlife managers across North America and served as justification for work on shorebirds (Morrison *in litt.* 2004). Other organizations, including Audubon, CWS, and Manomet, soon joined with IAFWA and WWF.

WHSRN was the first hemispheric system of linked reserves to protect important shorebird habitats. Fittingly for a Network concerned about protection of stopover and staging areas, hemispherically important Delaware Bay, USA, was the first site accepted into the Network. The site was nominated by the governors of the states of New Jersey and Delaware; it was declared in November 1985, and dedicated at a ceremony on 21 May 1986.

From the first, WHSRN's governance has consistently been through a voluntary, representative Council. The first Council meeting included representatives from the U.S. Fish and Wildlife Service (USFWS), CWS, the Suriname Forest Service, Manomet, the University of Córdoba, Argentina, and IAFWA. Many of these have been key institutional partners and leaders throughout WHSRN's history. Many other organizations have also made important contributions, especially at the regional level, both in recruiting and supporting site nominations and in expanded shorebird conservation actions. WHSRN's Office, under a variety of names, has been variously housed over the years at the following organizations and locations: Wildlife Habitat Canada (Ottawa); Buenos Aires, Argentina; National Audubon Society (New York City, USA); and Manomet (Massachusetts, USA).

### Site criteria

Sites qualify for inclusion in WHSRN in one of the following three categories:

- Regional significance: at least 20 000 shorebirds per year, or at least 5% of a flyway population for a species;
- International significance: over 100 000 shorebirds per year, or at least 10% of a flyway population; or
- Hemispheric significance: over 500 000 shorebirds per year, or at least 30% of a flyway population.

To qualify, sites must also have the explicit agreement of the landowner(s) and their commitment to:

- make shorebird conservation a priority at the site;
- protect and manage habitat for shorebirds; and
- update the Network at least annually of any changes in the site's status or contact information.

While many sites represent discrete sections of beach or coastline, others, such as Delaware Bay, comprise much larger landscapes. The only requirement concerning the scale of a site is that the number of landowners be such that the Network can communicate with them all and that all have agreed to be enrolled. A complete listing of current sites is available at Manomet's web-site.

Despite the Network's activities to date, the populations of many shorebird species continue to decline. The United States Shorebird Conservation Plan (USSCP) has shown that 22 of North America's shorebird taxa are in significant decline (Brown *et al.* 2001), and the International Wader Study Group has concluded that 48% of the world's shorebirds with known population trends are declining, while only 16% are increasing (International Wader Study Group 2003, Stroud *et al.* 2006). Analysis of migration data from eastern North America shows that nine species are declining and none is increasing. Most severely among these, the American Golden Plover *Pluvialis dominica* was found to be declining at a rate of 7.2% annually (Bart *et al.* 2004).

## THE NEW STRATEGY

As a result of these and other realities, a thorough re-examination of the Network's purpose and structure was initiated in May 2003. This strategic planning process sought to ensure that the Network adapted to changes since its creation, and to craft a strategy for the ensuing five years aimed at halting and even reversing the negative population trends. The review began as a series of discussions among many individuals who have been close to WHSRN and to shorebird conservation over a number of years. A day-long session, held at the VIIth Neotropical Ornithological Congress in Puyehue, Chile, in October 2003 and attended by 43 participants from 14 nations, was of inestimable value in creating the draft plan. The draft was then made available for review on the Internet. Comments received were considered before the preparation of the final version by WHSRN staff. The final document, available in English and Spanish at Manomet's web-site, outlines WHSRN's mission, vision, goals, and operating strategy in the context of the current state of shorebird conservation, including that for individual species, as well as conservation programs that may have overlapping goals. The Strategic Plan for 2004-2008 was adopted by the WHSRN Council in April 2004.

### Mission and guiding principles

WHSRN's mission, as refined during the creation of the Strategic Plan, is the conservation of shorebird species and their habitats across the Americas through a network of key sites. Two critical words in this mission statement are "network" and "sites." WHSRN seeks to accomplish shorebird conservation by engaging in actions collaboratively, actions that no one site could undertake on its own, but where a collection of sites – a network – can achieve results. Similarly, WHSRN emphasizes activities that are site-based rather than trying to be involved in all aspects of shorebird conservation.

WHSRN has five guiding principles:

- Site designation and conservation action are based on the best available scientific and other information.
- Site-based conservation is the centerpiece for accomplishing WHSRN's mission within the larger ecological context of each site.
- Traditional and local ecological knowledge and cultural practices are recognized, valued and respected.

- Integration and collaboration at local, national and international scales both within the Network and with other conservation groups and programs enhance WHSRN's capacity to achieve its vision.
- Communication and voluntary partnerships are key to an effective network and achieving common conservation goals.

### Strategy

Many species of shorebirds are highly migratory and often highly concentrated at a small number of places. Their vast breeding grounds and the remote areas where they spend their non-breeding season both face severe threats. The underpinning of WHSRN's conservation strategy is two-fold. First, shorebird conservation requires site-based action at a grand, indeed, hemispheric, scale. Second, the power of WHSRN is the power of co-operation: to accomplish goals as an alliance of partners which could not be achieved by the sum of the separate efforts of these people and organizations. Thus, the goals and objectives developed in the Strategic Plan were selected for being site-based and best accomplished through a network of partners acting in concert.

These two criteria also define what WHSRN is not. WHSRN's role is not to be the be-all and end-all of shorebird conservation. It is not, for instance, a designer of monitoring schemes, nor primarily a group lobbying for increased funding or legislative changes. Instead, WHSRN seeks opportunities where its own efforts can support other groups that do such work, including the several national shorebird conservation plan councils. Similarly, there are many times when the goals of these groups and councils can best be accomplished through WHSRN's network of sites. Thus, collaboration and communication among all members of the conservation community is a requisite for all of WHSRN's efforts.

### Goals and objectives

WHSRN's new Strategic Plan established four major goals for 2004-2008, as follows:

A. Conservation Planning: Ensure that the Network's conservation actions are the effective and appropriate application of the best available information.
B. Conservation Action: Implement shorebird conservation action at Network sites throughout the Americas.
C. Shorebird Conservation Communities: Create and maintain informed, involved, empowered and interconnected human communities at Network sites.
D. Strengthening the Network: Become the strongest network of sites possible to meet the challenges and threats to shorebirds.

Within each goal, specific objectives with measurable outcomes have been defined. These objectives form the basis of the Network's activities over the coming five years. The activities will be the responsibility of the several governing bodies and implementing groups, described below.

### Related programs

WHSRN, of course, is not the only conservation program that focuses its attention on sites. The 1971 Ramsar Convention on Wetlands predates WHSRN significantly and has a global reach.

Several "Important Bird Area" (IBA) programs have also been created to identify sites and lend support for conservation, with that of BirdLife International having the greatest geographic coverage. The East Asian-Australasian Shorebird Site Network, started in 1996, applies WHSRN's approach to its own geographic area. While these programs have their own sets of criteria, they are, broadly speaking, entirely compatible with WHSRN's approach. In fact, it will be the rare exception when a WHSRN site would not also qualify as a Ramsar site or as an IBA. (One unlikely case might be where a WHSRN site supports large numbers of shorebirds of several species, but where no one species reaches the IBA criterion). In recognition of the complementarity of missions and approaches, senior staff members from these programs have been invited to serve on the WHSRN Hemispheric Council. Within the Western Hemisphere, Ramsar, BirdLife, and WHSRN have begun to cooperate more closely in the identification, designation, and conservation-planning of new sites.

## Organizational structure

While the sites are the backbone of WHSRN, three groups are critical for the implementation of the five-year strategy, as well as longer-term plans. These are: Site Partners, the people on the ground at each WHSRN site; Network Partners, the organizations that support the Site Partners and the Network overall; and the Advisory Committees. In this last category is the Scientific Advisory Committee, providing scientific support to both Members and Partners.

Leadership of WHSRN is implemented at several scales. The WHSRN Hemispheric Council is the body responsible for the strategic direction of the Network and matters affecting the WHSRN program as a whole. The Hemispheric Council works closely with Manomet, the anchoring institution. National Councils design and implement pertinent activities that contribute to the achievement of the Network's mission. Communication among the several components and levels of WHSRN's structure is a shared responsibility of all participants. The new Network structure, schematized in Fig. 1, is designed specifically to serve the conservation needs of the Site Partners and to de-centralize other activities, such as identification and enrollment of new sites.

The WHSRN Office provides executive staff and services to the Network's Members, Partners, governing Councils, and the Scientific Advisory Committee, for the implementation of the Strategic Plan and work programs. The staff is employed by Manomet, and supervised with input from the Hemispheric Council.

## Funding

Funding for specific projects continues to be obtained from grants and contracts with a variety of funding bodies including Manomet, as it has since WHSRN's creation. The new strategy, however, contemplates that members of the Hemispheric Council will also have responsibility for ensuring that funds are available for WHSRN activities.

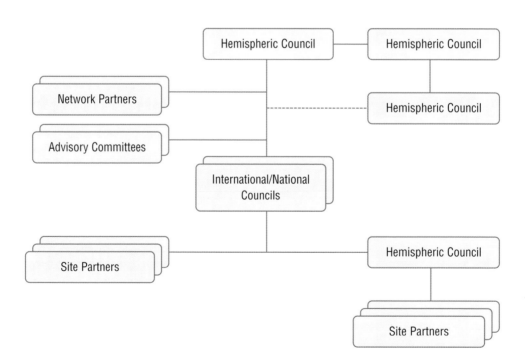

**Fig. 1.** The structure adopted by WHSRN to implement its 2004-2008 Strategic Plan.

**Notes:**

1. International and National Councils are involved when the Site Partners and/or Network Partners within a nation or group of nations choose to create them.

2. Some Site Partners may work directly with an International Council (lower left branch), others with their respective National Councils (lower right).

3. National Councils for large and active nations may work directly with the Hemispheric Council. They may also choose to be affiliated with an International Council.

4. The WHSRN Office is a program of, and supervised by, Manomet, with input from the Hemispheric Council. It serves to support all elements of the Network.

# THE FUTURE

## Tasks ahead

The Western Hemisphere Shorebird Reserve Network has grown in an organic way with sites added where there has been a convergence of shorebird usage, willing owners, and an awareness of the Network's existence. The resulting distribution of sites has been heavily biased toward North America, with only nine of the 60 current sites in South America and only one in Central America. The present goal is to add sites based on their importance to shorebirds, rather than on geopolitical or cultural convenience.

The declines observed in some species are severe, and action is urgently required. The American Golden Plover *Pluvialis dominica,* for instance, is declining at 7.2% annually in eastern North America (Bart *et al.* 2004). WHSRN will emphasize protecting key sites as well as catalyzing site-based conservation action for species such as the American Golden Plover with small, declining, or threatened populations.

The Network's Office, working with the Hemispheric Council and the newly forming national councils, will take a pro-active approach to recruiting sites, particularly those that qualify as being of "international" or "hemispheric" importance. For many species, especially poorly known resident species and austral migrants, identifying these will involve the creation of working groups to establish species priorities and refine knowledge of their distribution throughout the annual cycle.

Management of WHSRN sites for shorebirds can benefit from application of a uniform analysis of the key threats and the sources of the threats that each site faces, followed by the design of conservation strategies to abate the threats. Evaluation measures permitting monitoring of progress toward threat reduction and achieving population goals must be determined *a priori*. Particularly important is the identification of multi-site and multi-scale threats that the Network may be able to address more efficiently than can managers of individual sites.

For those species already known to be of highest conservation concern based on prioritization schemes such as that of the USSCP (Brown *et al.* 2001) or BirdLife International (see website), WHSRN is working urgently with site partners. Examples include a tri-national project for the New World race of Red Knot *Calidris canutus rufa* in the USA, Argentina and Chile, and another to protect and manage wintering habitat for the Buff-breasted Sandpiper *Tryngites subruficollis* in Brazil, Uruguay and Argentina. Where species-specific working groups already exist, WHSRN will collaborate and seek to ensure that the geographic scope of their work covers the entirety of the species' range. Where such groups are lacking, WHSRN will seek to catalyze their formation and their functioning with the goal of rapid identification of an initial set of priority sites for conservation action and inclusion in WHSRN.

Many communities involved with WHSRN sites have expressed the need for educational and outreach material, and the Network has responded wherever feasible. WHSRN will continue to provide these information products, and indeed, seeks to refine them through analysis of the needs of target audiences, be they school groups, local or regional governments, park guards or people engaged in the eco-tourism industry.

## Lessons learned

Over the course of WHSRN's almost 20 years of existence, it has become evident that strong networks for flyway-scale conservation have a variety of requisites. First among these, perhaps self-evidently, is the need for strong partnerships. An immediate corollary is a high degree of trust, and this must be consciously and actively built and maintained. International networks, by definition, involve people with distinct cultural, historical and, frequently, linguistic backgrounds. Every effort must be made to acknowledge these differences so that they do not impede progress toward the shared goals of the several partners. Typically this will mean that correspondence and other network documents, including web pages, should be translated into the appropriate languages.

Because flyway-scale conservation is inherently complex, and because the relationships of trust just described are not quickly built, it is imperative that rapid turn-over of staff be avoided. Generally this requires, at minimum, a stable base of core funding. Donors frequently like to give to "projects" where their contributions are felt to have immediate conservation impact. It is equally important to guarantee that stable structures and staffing be in place throughout the system to achieve the changes they seek to effect.

Building local capacity to protect and manage habitat at network sites is another crucial element. The designation of a site by an international network carries weight beyond what may be given to local efforts. Nonetheless, building lasting support in the host communities, adapting to changing conditions, and monitoring the effectiveness of conservation action is best done by people intimately familiar with the local situation. Progress toward the network's goals at the site will be greatly advanced if there is a mechanism to provide the training and other resources needed to people based there.

Accomplishing results at the level of biogeographical populations for highly migratory species such as shorebirds turns an old dictum on its head. To succeed globally, we need to think - and act - locally. If our goal is protecting global populations and even reversing declines, we must craft strategies that work at local levels. Frequently, well-designed measures of success that are applicable at the local level for monitoring progress toward the larger goal have been lacking. One reads proposals all too often that include "number of posters printed," or "number of meetings with local officials" among the standards by which it is proposed that the project can be evaluated. A needed conceptual advance is a way for locally applied projects to measure their progress and their contribution to population-level targets.

A collaborative network is only as effective as its communication tools. In this regard, current networks have tools that were inconceivable when WHSRN was started in 1985. Electronic mail and the now ubiquitous web-sites have facilitated communication on an unprecedented scale, and at a virtually instantaneous pace. Digital photography and spatially explicit tools such as geographic information systems affect the content of communications. The ways that ideas are presented affect how the ideas are conceptualized. There is no reason to imagine that such technological change in communication is ending, or even slowing down. Conservation networks need to plan, and budget, for rapid adoption of appropriate new communications technologies if they are to keep pace with the acceleration of threats to the species they hope to protect.

A crucial advance for shorebird conservation in the Western Hemisphere was the creation of national shorebird conservation plans in the USA (Brown *et al.* 2001) and Canada (Donaldson *et al.* 2000). Prior to the creation of these plans, information on the sizes and trends of shorebird populations was fragmented and disorganized. The compilation of the best available knowledge in the plans allowed species to be ranked according to the degree of conservation concern, clearly indicating those that need the most immediate action by WHSRN and its partners. These compilations and syntheses need to be maintained and updated where already begun, and need to be expanded geographically to the entirety of the Western Hemisphere. WHSRN places a high priority on supporting and expanding the continuation of these scientific collaborations, as indicated under its "best available information" goal. Indeed, transparent, shared access to scientif-ically-sound conservation planning information is essential to the effective use of scarce conservation dollars.

## ACKNOWLEDGMENTS

This manuscript has benefited from the comments of Stephen Brown, Linda Leddy, and an anonymous reviewer. It is a pleasure to thank them for their helpful reviews.

## REFERENCES

**Bart, J., Brown, S., Harrington, B. & Morrison, G.** 2004. Population Trends of North American Shorebirds. In review.

**Brown S., Hickey, C., Harrington, B. & Gill, R.** (eds.). 2001. The U.S. Shorebird Conservation Plan. Second edition. Manomet Center for Conservation Sciences, Manomet, Massachusetts, USA.

**Donaldson, G.M., Hyslop, C., Morrison, R.I.G., Dickson, H.L. & Davidson, I.** (eds.). 2000. Canadian Shorebird Conservation Plan. Canadian Wildlife Service Special Publication, Ottawa, Ontario, Canada.

**International Wader Study Group** 2003. Waders are declining worldwide. Conclusions from the 2003 International Wader Study Group Conference, Cádiz, Spain. Wader Study Group Bulletin 101/102: 8-12.

**Morrison, R.I.G., Butler, R.W., Beyersbergen, G.W., Dickson, H.L., Bourget, A., Hicklin, P.W., Goossen, J.P., Ross, R.K. & Gratto-Trevor, C.L.** 1995. Potential Western Hemisphere Shorebird Reserve Network Sites for Shorebirds in Canada. Second Edition. Canadian Wildlife Service Technical Report Series No. 227. Canadian Wildlife Service, Ottawa.

**Myers, J.P., Morrison, R.I.G., Antas, P.Z., Harrington, B.A., Lovejoy, T.E., Salaberry, M., Senner, S.E. & Tarak, A.** 1987. Conservation Strategy for Migratory Species. American Scientist 75: 19-26.

**Stroud, D.A., Baker, A., Blanco, D.E., Davidson, N.C., Delany, S., Ganter, B., Gill, R., González, P., Haanstra, L., Morrison, R.I.G., Piersma, T., Scott, D.A., Thorup, O., West, R., Wilson, J. & Zöckler, C. (on behalf of the International Wader Study Group).** 2006. The conservation and population status of the world's waders at the turn of the millennium. Waterbirds around the world. G.C. Boere, C.A. Galbraith & D.A. Stroud (Eds.), The Stationery Office, Edinburgh, UK. 643-648.

### Web-sites

http://www.manomet.org/WHSRN/sites.php for a complete listing of current WHSRN sites.

http://www.manomet.org/WHSRN/strategic_plan.htm for English version of WHSRN's Strategic Plan for 2004-2008.

http://www.manomet.org/WHSRN/RHRAP/plan_estrategico.htm for Spanish version of WHSRN's Strategic Plan for 2004-2008.

http://www.birdlife.net/datazone/species.html for BirdLife International's work on species of conservation concern.

Anahuac National Wildlife Refuge, Texas, was named a WHSRN site because of the high numbers of Whimbrels *Numenius phaeopus* that use it each April and May (> 2 200). These are presumed to be mostly or entirely of the *hudsonicus* subspecies and therefore >10% of the estimated biogeographic population of 18,000 for that subspecies. Photo: Paul Marshall.

# Conservation of waterbirds and wintering areas through Important Bird Areas in India

*M. Zafar-ul Islam*

*Bombay Natural History Society, Hornbill House, Shaheed Bhagat Singh Road, Mumbai – 400 023, India.*
*(email: zafar_bnhs@rediffmail.com  or zafarul@gmail.com)*

Islam, M.Z. 2006. Conservation of waterbirds and wintering areas through Important Bird Areas in India. *Waterbirds around the world.* Eds. G.C. Boere, C.A. Galbraith & D.A. Stroud. The Stationery Office, Edinburgh, UK. p. 687.

India is among the top ten nations of the world for high levels of biodiversity. Its immense biological diversity represents about 7% of the world's flora and 6.5% of its fauna. It embraces 10 biogeographical zones and 26 biotic provinces (Rodgers *et al.* 2000). There are 614 amphibians and reptiles, 1 300 birds and 350 species of mammals in India. Among the larger animals, 173 mammals, 78 birds (BirdLife International 2001), and 15 reptile species are considered endangered. This large range of species inhabit the country's various habitats, from its crowded and colourful corals reefs to icy, alpine grasslands. However, there is very little information on the biology of the vast majority of these, many of which have not yet been named. Their value as sources of genes, food, medicine, or as essential parts of ecological systems, has been little assessed.

Wetlands in India include marshes, swamps, flood-plains, bogs, peatlands, shallow ponds, littoral zones of larger water bodies, tidal marshes etc., and are hugely diverse. But whether they are ponds, marshes, coral reefs, peatlands, lakes or mangroves, they all share one fundamental feature: the complex interaction of their basic components - soil, water, animals and plants. This feature fulfils many functions and provides many products that have sustained humans over the centuries. In India, wetlands are distributed in all the biogeographic regions and exhibit significant ecological diversity, primarily because of the variability of climate conditions and the changing topography. They provide a multitude of ecosystem services - including water purification; regulation of flow; fisheries; habitats for plants, animals and micro-organisms; opportunities for recreation and tourism; and so forth. Their hydrological processes buffer against such extremes as droughts and flooding. Many wetlands have been converted for agriculture, industry and settlements, some have been affected by industrial effluents, sewage, household waste and sedimentation due to degradation of catchments.

Indian wetlands support spectacular concentrations of wetland-dependent wildlife, such as the million or more shorebirds visiting Point Calimere Wildlife Sanctuary (Tamil Nadu), Chilika Lake (Orissa), Pitti Islands (Lakshadweep), and the islands of Gujarat.

BirdLife International, its UK partner, the Royal Society for the Protection of Birds (RSPB) and the designated partner in India, the Bombay Natural History Society (BNHS), have come together to establish the Indian Bird Conservation Network (IBCN), which includes NGOs and individuals wishing to contribute towards bird conservation in India. One of the aims of the Network is to identify and protect Important Bird Areas (IBA) throughout the country, and an IBA Programme was officially launched in March 1999. For identified sites, the IBA programme collects information including bird populations, conservation issues, management problems and threats. Through this programme BNHS has been working on wetland conservation since 1999, and has been involved with activities such as waterbird counts, education and public awareness work, and lobbying with the government, at both Union and State level. There is now a fully-fledged, sustained conservation programme focusing on wetlands which has evolved from these initial activities.

Analysis of the 466 IBAs shows that 425 sites have globally threatened species, 205 sites hold restricted range species, and 99 sites qualify as biome restricted assemblages, and 136 sites fit in the congregatory criteria. Many sites fit more than one criterion, and some sites such as Keoladeo National Park and Chilka Lake qualify for all four criteria (Islam & Rahmani 2004).

Around 90% of IBAs in India are important for one or more of the 78 globally threatened species in India, and 47% for the 74 restricted range species found in India. Almost all IBAs fall under at least one biome and hold some of the 374 bird species that fall in the biome criterion. The IBAs are also important for congregatory terrestrial birds, wintering and passage waterbirds and breeding seabirds, and almost 17% of IBAs have been identified for these.

However, identification of these important areas is alone not sufficient to conserve India's biodiversity. Even many protected areas face serious conservation problems, despite their status. Also, very few of India's protected areas were chosen to specifically conserve birds. The IBA approach is one of the ways to conserve bird species through the protection or conservation of important sites.

Most of the Red Data Book species are distributed across the Indian sub-continent, with 17 migratory species and 57 others that seasonally migrate within India. Migratory species face severe threats from hunting and loss of habitat. To protect those that cross one or more border, where conservation deficiencies in one country will affect the measures undertaken by other countries, the Indian IBA program, together with the Convention on the Conservation of Migratory Species of Wild Animals (Bonn Convention) will try to facilitate international agreements between countries to protect and manage migratory species with an unfavorable conservation status.

## REFERENCES

**BirdLife International** 2001. Threatened Birds of Asia: the BirdLife International Red Data Book. Cambridge, U.K.: BirdLife International.

**Islam, M.Z. & Rahmani A.R.** 2004. Important Bird Areas in India: Priority sites for conservation. Indian Bird Conservation Network, Bombay Natural History Society and BirdLife International (UK). 1,200 pp.

**Rodgers, W.A., Panwar, H.S. & Mathur, V.B.** 2000. Wildlife Protected Area Network in India: A Review, Executive Summary. Wildlife Institute of India, Dehradun.

# Metapopulation networks as tools for research and conservation: the Greater Flamingo *Phoenicopterus roseus* in the Mediterranean and West Africa

*Arnaud Béchet[1], Christophe Germain[1], Juan A. Amat[2], Charina Cañas[2], Manuel Rendon Martos[3], Araceli Garrido[3], Nicola Baccetti[4], Paolo Dall'Antonia[4], Özge Balkız[1,5], Yelli Diawara[6], Francesc Vidal i Esquerré[7] & Alan Johnson[1]*

[1] *Station Biologique de la Tour du Valat,Le Sambuc, 13200 Arles, France. (email: bechet@tourduvalat.org)*

[2] *Estación Biológica de Doñana, Apdo. 1053, 41080 Sevilla, Spain.*

[3] *Reserva Natural Laguna de Fuente de Piedra, Apdo. Correos N° 1, 29520 Fuente de Piedra, Malaga, Spain.*

[4] *Istituto Nazionale per la Fauna Selvatica, Via Ca Fornacetta, 9, 40064 Ozzano BO, Italy.*

[5] *Erciyes Üniversitesi Çevre Müh. Böl. 38039 Kayseri, Turkey.*

[6] *Parc National du Banc d'Arguin, B.P. 5355, Nouakchott, République Islamique de Mauritanie.*

[7] *Parc Natural del Delta de l'Ebre, Av. de Catalunya, 46, 43580 Deltebre, Spain.*

Béchet,A., Germain, C., Amat, J.A., Cañas, C., Martos, M.R., Garrido, A., Baccetti, N., Dall'Antonia, P., Balkız, Ö., Diawara, Y., Esquerré, F.V. & Johnson, A. 2006. Metapopulation networks as tools for research and conservation: the Greater Flamingo *Phoenicopterus roseus* in the Mediterranean and West Africa. *Waterbirds around the world.* Eds. G.C. Boere, C.A. Galbraith & D.A. Stroud. The Stationery Office, Edinburgh, UK. p. 688.

Observations in the 1990s of Greater Flamingos *Phoenicopterus roseus* banded as chicks in France and breeding in Spain and Italy, suggested that the French population was not closed. Rather, flamingos breeding at different colonies of the western Mediterranean were part of a metapopulation, i.e. important exchanges of breeding waterbirds occur among colonies. To enhance understanding of the population dynamics of this species and to propose sound conservation planning, a network was developed of partners working on flamingos at their main breeding sites.

The Greater Flamingo network was initiated in 2002 through a workshop uniting French, Italian, Spanish and Turkish partners, with Mauritania joining the network in 2003. The broad objective of the network is to study environmental and individual factors influencing juvenile and adult dispersal in order to provide sound conservation planning at an appropriate scale. The network core is a database of 400 000 resightings of more than 30 000 flamingos banded in four countries (France, Spain, Italy, Turkey) and eight colonies. The database is in four languages (French, Spanish, Italian, English) with life histories in five languages (including Turkish). Resighting efforts are coordinated over critical time-periods according to a standardized seasonal sampling scheme.

The Greater Flamingo network surveys a total of 19 breeding sites in five countries (France, Spain, Italy, Turkey and Mauritania). Of these sites, 36% are in active salinas and their existence relies on continued salt production together with appropriate island and water management. The main threat for other sites is water shortage, due to conflicts between agricultural and environmental requirements.

In the western Mediterranean, the number of Flamingo colonies has increased in the last decade, as well as an overall increase of the breeding population and numbers of chicks fledged. This increase probably resulted from the dispersal of juveniles and adults born at the large colonies of Salins de Giraud (Camargue, France) and Fuente de Piedra (Andalucia, Spain) where breeding has occurred every year for 25 and eight years respectively.

We made the hypothesis that the distribution of breeding flamingos among colonies of the western Mediterranean was despotic, following an age-related behavioural dominance where old experienced birds breed at large and long-established colonies (Salin de Giraud, France and Fuente de Piedra, Spain) and younger birds breed at small and recently-established colonies (Rendon *et al.* 2001).

We tested the prediction that flamingos hatched at the major breeding sites of Salin de Giraud and Fuente de Piedra would breed younger at the smaller colonies i.e. Saline di Comacchio, Italy (<1 000 pairs), Salinas de la Trinitat, Spain (<2 000) and Molentargius, Sardinia (<7 000)) than at Salin de Giraud and Fuente de Piedra.

The breeding status of banded flamingos was assessed from a hide. The following categories of birds were considered as breeders (i) flamingos incubating an egg, (ii) flamingos incubating more than 48 hr on a nest, (iii) flamingos with a chick on a nest or (iv) flamingos feeding a chick.

Flamingos hatched at Fuente de Piedra and then breeding at Salinas de la Trinitat were the same age as those breeding at Salins de Giraud (G-test, G = 3.8, df = 2, P = 0.14).

Flamingos hatched at Salin de Giraud and breeding at Salinas de la Trinitat tended to grow older with time (G = 16.5, df = 9, P = 0.056) which could be a consequence of an ageing pool of breeders. Contrary to predictions, these flamingos were no younger than those breeding at Fuente de Piedra (all paired G-tests non significant). At Molentargius, no temporal trend could be detected and French flamingos were no younger than those breeding at Fuente de Piedra (all paired $\chi^2$ tests non significant). Finally, at Saline di Comacchio, French flamingos observed breeding in 2002 were younger than those at Fuente de Piedra (G = 74.7, df = 3, P < 0.001). In 2003, only nine French flamingos were observed breeding at Comacchio, yet the trend was the same as that observed in 2002 (G = 30.9, df = 3, P < 0.001).

Our results suggest that the smallest colonies, such as Saline di Comacchio, could allow early recruitment of Greater Flamingos into the overall breeding population. This implies that small breeding sites could play a critical role in the metapopulation dynamics of the Greater Flamingos and should thus be included in conservation planning.

## REFERENCES

Rendon, M.A., Garrido, A. , Ramirez, J.M. , Rendon-Martos, M. & Amat, J.A. 2001. Despotic establishment of breeding colonies of Greater Flamingos, *Phoenicopterus ruber*, in southern Spain. Behavioural Ecology and Sociobiology 50: 55-60.

# The globally threatened Lesser White-fronted Goose *Anser erythropus* and Red-breasted Goose *Branta ruficollis*: current status and future priorities for the Ramsar site network in Europe and Asia

*Sergey G. Dereliev*

*Bulgarian Society for the Protection of Birds/BirdLife Bulgaria, PO Box 50, 1111 Sofia, Bulgaria. (email: dereliev@gmail.com)*
*Present address: AEWA Secretariat, Hermann-Ehlers-Str. 10, D-53113 Bonn, Germany. (email: sdereliev@unep.de)*

Dereliev, S.G. 2006. The globally threatened Lesser White-fronted Goose *Anser erythropus* and Red-breasted Goose *Branta ruficollis*: current status and future priorities for the Ramsar site network in Europe and Asia. *Waterbirds around the world*. Eds. G.C. Boere, C.A. Galbraith & D.A. Stroud. The Stationery Office, Edinburgh, UK. p. 689.

The Lesser White-fronted Goose *Anser erythropus* and the Red-breasted Goose *Branta ruficollis* are both globally threatened species, both categorized as Vulnerable (VU) (BirdLife International 2004). The global population of the Lesser White-fronted Goose (LWfG) is currently estimated at some 25 000–30 000 individuals, with three biogeographical populations recognised – European, Siberian-Caspian and East Asian. The single population of the Red-breasted Goose (RbG) has declined between 2000 and 2003 by more than 70% from 88 000 birds, although in the last season observed there were >52 000 birds counted within the winter range, suggesting a slight recovery. Both species are strongly dependent upon wetlands for their flyways. This analysis assesses the extent to which the sites important for conservation of these two species are covered by the Ramsar Convention's network of Wetlands of International Importance ("Ramsar sites").

A literature review of 47 publications was used to identify important locations for these geese, which was then compared with Ramsar Sites information (www.ramsar.org). Only data from the last two decades (1982–2002) were used. Information was summarized by species and by country with: name of site, area (ha), Ramsar designation status (yes/no, ha), statutory protection status (yes/no, overlap), goose numbers (max, year), % of biogeographical population, and numbers of other goose species observed (max, year). This preliminary information was circulated to national experts to verify and add to or correct the list of sites and other data. Only Ramsar site designation Criterion 2 (threatened species) and 6 (>1% of biogeographical population) were used to assess sites' potential qualification for Ramsar site designation.

A total of 115 sites worldwide were identified where the RbG has been known to occur and 215 sites where LWfG have been known to occur. The largest number of sites was in Europe and the smallest number in E Asia. Of these sites, 65% (LWfG) and 70% (RbG) qualify for Ramsar designation either under Criterion 2 (predominantly for LWfG) or Criteria 2 and 6 (predominantly for RbG). However, for quite a large proportion of the sites, information is deficient.

Less than one third of all sites which appear to meet the Ramsar criteria for either of the two species have been desig-nated as Ramsar sites so far. Of the sites which are lacking Ramsar designation, more than half for each species qualify under Criterion 2 only, i.e. are sites where no significant congre-gations (>1% of the biogeographical population) have been observed. However, even for those sites with Ramsar designa-tion, about 50% have only part of the relevant area for geese designated: site extensions should be considered in these sites. Only a few sites have full protection (10% for RbG and 20% for LWfG), while around one third (LWfG) and more than half (RbG) are lacking any statutory designation.

Many of the sites as important for the LWfG or the RbG, are also significant for other species of geese: around 40% of the LWfG sites and 60% of the RbG sites qualifying for designation under Criterion 2 and/or Criterion 6.

A few sites are of outstanding importance for the survival and conservation of LWfG or RbG populations, in that they support >10% of the biogeographical populations. For LWfG there is one site in Russia for the European population; four sites in three countries (Kazakhstan, Russia and Iran) for the Siberian-Caspian population; and seven sites in two countries (China and Russia) for the E Asian population. For RbG there are 14 outstanding sites in five countries (Bulgaria, Romania, Ukraine, Kazakhstan and Russia) with particular concentrations along the W-NW Black Sea coast and in NW Kazakhstan.

Future priorities for the conservation of these globally threatened species should be:

- the accession of Kazakhstan, Turkmenistan and Iraq to the Ramsar Convention and designation of Ramsar sites for these goose species;
- full designation of all wetlands qualifying as Ramsar sites (70% of RbG and 75% of LWfG sites);
- extension of the partially designated Ramsar sites (55% of RbG and 45% of LWfG sites);
- full statutory protection of all sites (79% of RbG and 60% of LWfG sites currently lack partial or complete protection);
- focusing on securing the future conservation of the outstanding sites (supporting >10% of a population) as a matter of urgency and priority; and
- updating information on goose populations for all sites.

# Flyway site network development in Asia: wetland conservation using the Siberian Crane *Grus leucogeranus* as a flagship species

*Crawford Prentice[1], Claire Mirande[1], Elena Ilyashenko[2] & James Harris[1]*

[1]*International Crane Foundation, PO Box 447, Baraboo, Wisconsin 53913-0447, USA. (email: crawford@savingcranes.org)*
[2]*Siberian Crane Flyway Co-ordination Centre, Moscow Zoo, Moscow, Russian Federation.*

Prentice, C., Mirande, C., Ilyashenko, E. & Harris, J. 2006. Flyway site network development in Asia: wetland conservation using the Siberian Crane *Grus leucogeranus* as a flagship species. *Waterbirds around the world.* Eds. G.C. Boere, C.A. Galbraith & D.A. Stroud. The Stationery Office, Edinburgh, UK. pp. 690-696.

## ABSTRACT

The Siberian Crane *Grus leucogeranus* is a critically endangered species dependent upon shallow wetland habitats along its migration routes. Three routes are currently known: a West Asian flyway that leads from breeding grounds in Western Siberia to the Caspian lowlands of northern Iran; a Central Asian flyway connecting Western Siberian breeding grounds to the wintering site in northern India; and an East Asian flyway leading from Yakutia to the central Yangtze floodplain lakes in China. A UNEP/GEF project involving four countries (People's Republic of China, Islamic Republic of Iran, Republic of Kazakhstan and the Russian Federation) is being implemented under the co-ordination of the International Crane Foundation, and aims to conserve key wetlands along the West and East Asian flyways. The Siberian Crane is a large, attractive bird of great cultural significance to many of the peoples along these flyways, and is being used to generate public awareness and support for wetland conservation. The project addresses threats at 16 internationally important wetlands along the flyways, and seeks to secure their ecological integrity for the benefit of the wide range of flora and fauna that they support. The project has a major international component, improving co-ordination and strengthening capacity for flyway conservation efforts, and supporting international flyway conservation efforts within the framework of existing strategies and agreements. The project facilitates the development of networks of wetland sites in Asia, and provides resources and training for the conservation of selected sites within these networks.

## INTRODUCTION

Over the past 25 years, the International Crane Foundation (ICF) has been working with a network of experts in a number of Asian countries to discover basic information about the Siberian Crane *Grus leucogeranus*, including the location of its breeding grounds, the migration routes that it uses, and the range of threats that it encounters. This research has resulted in a good understanding of the life history of the species, which is briefly summarized here (for further information, see Sauey 1985 and Meine & Archibald 1996). More recent work giving the results of satellite-tracking studies for the eastern population has been published by Kanai *et al.* (2002).

The Siberian Crane is the most specialized of the cranes, utilizing shallow wetland habitats at all stages of its migration cycle. It is Critically Endangered (BirdLife International, 2001), with a world population of less than 3 000 individuals, the vast majority of which belong to the eastern population. While recent winter counts (January 2001 – December 2006) at Poyang Lake Basin have exceeded this number, the accuracy of these counts

requires validation. The western population held between nine and 14 birds until the late 1990s, but has declined since then, with only two wild individuals being reported in winter 2005/6. The central population declined dramatically from perhaps 80 birds at the wintering site in the 1960s to a single pair in 2001. In the summer of 2002, a pair, presumably the same as that recorded in 2001, was observed for the last time on the breeding grounds in Russia. There have been unconfirmed reports, however, of several (four to seven) cranes in other areas within the breeding range of this population, and of a single crane along the migration route in Uzbekistan and Pakistan, and on the wintering grounds in India. The migration routes for the three populations are shown in Fig. 1.

Efforts for the conservation and recovery of this critically endangered species gained momentum in recent years through the Memorandum of Understanding concerning Conservation Measures for the Siberian Crane concluded under the Convention on the Conservation of Migratory Species of Wild Animals in 1993 (UNEP/CMS 2005). These measures have included substantial investment in captive-breeding programmes that support efforts to undertake re-introductions where population levels have declined to non-viable levels, in combination with habitat conservation and other measures.

## THREATS TO SIBERIAN CRANES AND THEIR WETLAND HABITATS

Due to the destruction and disturbance of key wetlands throughout Asia, numerous migratory waterbirds are in serious decline (APMWCC 2001, BirdLife International 2001). The deterioration in the integrity of wetland ecosystems and decline in waterbird populations are primarily due to the impact of human activities, including the killing and disturbance of waterbirds. The situation is extremely precarious for the Siberian Crane, necessitating urgent conservation measures: the bird itself, although protected throughout its range, relies on a series of shallow wetlands along its flyways that are under serious pressure from a range of human activities. Attrition of wetland habitat is a major phenomenon throughout Asia (for example, see Scott & Poole 1989). Threats at the local level include: over-utilization and disturbance from hunting, fishing, trapping, logging and grazing; reclamation for agriculture; overuse or diversion of water resources; development of oil and gas fields; construction of dams and other forms of river regulation; and degradation of watersheds. It should be noted that the types and levels of threat are highly site-specific, and that the risks posed by hunting also affect the birds outside their key sites.

The Siberian Cranes' wintering sites are used for prolonged periods and are most severely threatened due to high human popu-

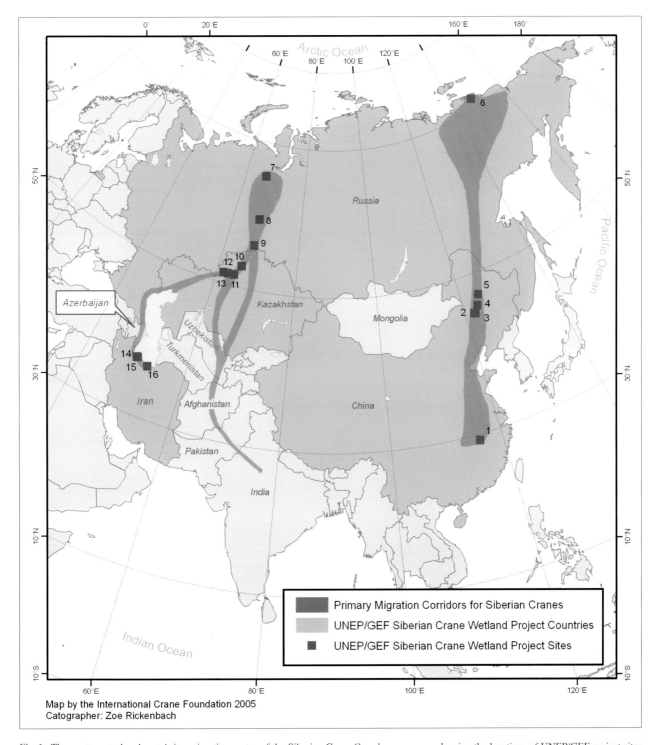

**Fig. 1.** The west, central and east Asian migration routes of the Siberian Crane *Grus leucogeranus*, showing the locations of UNEP/GEF project sites along the west and east Asian routes.

lation density, habitat loss and disturbance. While the cranes can be concentrated into relatively small areas, changing hydrological conditions at Poyang Lake Basin in China often require the flocks to move to different locations during the winter or between different years. Wintering Siberian Cranes are territorial at Fereydoon Kenar in Iran and defend scarce resources; thus this small site can support only a few families. Alternate wintering sites in the Caspian lowlands must be identified and protected. The cranes' energetic balance on departure for spring migration can have an impact on breeding success, a factor largely determined by the quality of over-wintering habitats (Chavez-Ramirez 1996). In some Arctic-breeding goose species, there is evidence

that spring feeding conditions on the over-wintering grounds and migration staging areas affect breeding performance (for instance, in Barnacle Geese *Branta leucopsis* and Brent Geese *B. bernicla*). While multiple factors such as wind conditions during northward migration and predation by Arctic Foxes affect reproductive success in Brent Geese, heavier female birds in spring are more likely to return to the wintering grounds in autumn with offspring (Ebbinge 1989, Ebbinge & Spaans 1995, Prop & Black 1998). Maintaining the feeding quality of habitats used during the over-wintering and spring migration periods should therefore be carefully considered in site management for migratory waterbirds such as the Siberian Crane.

**Table 1.** Protection status and international significance of wetlands selected as UNEP/GEF project sites.

| Country | Site name (numbers refer to points in Fig. 1) | International recognition & designations | National protection status | IUCN protected area category | Globally threatened and near threatened bird species recorded at sites. (see Table 2 for scientific names). |
|---|---|---|---|---|---|
| China | 1. Poyang Lake Basin (Jiangxi) | Ramsar (part), NEACSN, Global 200 Ecoregion, AWI, IBA | NNR (part), MAB network site | IV (part) | Dalmatian Pelican, Oriental White Stork, Black-faced Spoonbill, Lesser White-fronted Goose, Swan Goose, Baikal Teal, Mandarin Duck, Baer's Pochard, Scaly-sided Merganser, Greater Spotted Eagle, Imperial Eagle, Siberian Crane, Hooded Crane, White-naped Crane, Swinhoe's Rail, Great Bustard, Grey-headed Lapwing, Saunders's Gull, Japanese Marsh Warbler. |
| China | 5. Zhalong Nature Reserve (Heilongjiang) | Ramsar, AWI, NEACSN, IBA | NNR | IV | Oriental White Stork, Black-headed Ibis, Swan Goose, Lesser White-fronted Goose, Baikal Teal, Baer's Pochard, Greater Spotted Eagle, Siberian Crane, Hooded Crane, Red-crowned Crane, White-naped Crane, Swinhoe's Rail, Great Bustard, Grey-headed Lapwing, Far Eastern Curlew, Asian Dowitcher, Japanese Marsh Warbler. |
| China | 3. Xianghai Nature Reserve (Jilin) | Ramsar, AWI, NEACSN, IBA | NNR, MAB network site | IV | Oriental White Stork, Swan Goose, Lesser White-fronted Goose, Baikal Teal, Baer's Pochard, Steller's Sea Eagle, Greater Spotted Eagle, Lesser Kestrel, Siberian Crane, Hooded Crane, Red-crowned Crane, White-naped Crane, Great Bustard, Grey-headed Lapwing, Far Eastern Curlew, Asian Dowitcher, Jankowski's Bunting. |
| China | 4. Momoge Nature Reserve (Jilin) | AWI, IBA | NNR | IV | Oriental White Stork, Swan Goose, Baer's Pochard, Siberian Crane, Hooded Crane, Red-crowned Crane, White-naped Crane, Great Bustard, Grey-headed Lapwing, Far Eastern Curlew, Asian Dowitcher. |
| China | 2. Keerqin Nature Reserve (Inner Mongolia) | AWI, IBA | NNR, MAB network site | IV | Oriental White Stork, Swan Goose, Baer's Pochard, Greater Spotted Eagle, Siberian Crane, Hooded Crane, Red-crowned Crane, White-naped Crane, Great Bustard, Grey-headed Lapwing, Far Eastern Curlew, Asian Dowitcher. |
| Iran | 16. Fereydoon Kenar, Ezbaran & Sorkhe Rud Damgahs | Ramsar, IBA, MIWE | Non-shooting Area | IV (part) | Dalmatian Pelican, Pygmy Cormorant, Lesser White-fronted Goose, Red-breasted Goose, Ferruginous Duck, White-tailed Eagle, Imperial Eagle, Greater Spotted Eagle, Siberian Crane, Great Snipe. |
| Iran | 15. Amirkelayeh & Rud Posht | Ramsar, IBA, MEWI | Wildlife Refuge (part) | 1a (part) | Pygmy Cormorant, Marbled Teal, Ferruginous Duck, White-tailed Eagle. |
| Iran | 14. Bujagh / Sefid Rud Delta | Ramsar, IBA, MEWI | National Park | IV | Dalmatian Pelican, Pygmy Cormorant, Lesser White-fronted Goose, Red-breasted Goose, White-headed Duck, White-tailed Eagle, Imperial Eagle. |
| Kazakhstan | 11. Naurzum Lake System (including Sarykopa Lake System and Lake Kulagol) | Nominated Ramsar Site; nominated World Heritage Site | Strict Nature Reserve (Zapovednik) | 1a | Dalmatian Pelican, Lesser White-fronted Goose, Red-breasted Goose, Ferruginous Duck, White-headed Duck, White-tailed Eagle, Imperial Eagle, Siberian Crane, Little Bustard. |
| Kazakhstan | 13. Kulykol Lake | | Local NHA | IV | Lesser White-fronted Goose, Red-breasted Goose, White-headed Duck, Siberian Crane, Little Bustard, Sociable Lapwing. |
| Kazakhstan | 12. Zharsor and Urkash Lakes | | None | - | Lesser White-fronted Goose, Red-breasted Goose, Ferruginous Duck, White-tailed Eagle, Imperial Eagle, Siberian Crane, Little Bustard, Sociable Lapwing. |
| Kazakhstan | 10. Tantegir Hollow – Zhanshura Lake | | None | - | Lesser White-fronted Goose, Red-breasted Goose, Siberian Crane, Little Bustard. |
| Russia | 6. Kytalyk Resource Reserve | NEACSN; proposed World Heritage Site, IBA | Resource Reservation, incl. two Nature Reserves (zakazniks) | VI, IV (part) | Lesser White-fronted Goose, Baikal Teal, Spectacled Eider, Steller's Eider, White-tailed Eagle, Siberian Crane. |

**Table 1 (cont). Protection status and international significance of wetlands selected as UNEP/GEF project sites.**

| Country | Site name (numbers refer to points in Fig. 1) | International recognition & designations | National protection status | IUCN protected area category | Globally threatened and near threatened bird species recorded at sites. (see Table 2 for scientific names). |
|---|---|---|---|---|---|
| Russia | 7. Kunovat River Basin Wetlands | Ramsar | Three Nature Reserves (zakazniks) | VI, IV | Lesser White-fronted Goose, Red-breasted Goose, Siberian Crane. |
| Russia | 8. Konda and Alymka Rivers Basin (Uvat Region) | | Two Nature Reserves (zakazniks) | VI, IV | Lesser White-fronted Goose, Red-breasted Goose, White-tailed Eagle, Imperial Eagle, Siberian Crane, Great Snipe, Slender-billed Curlew, Aquatic Warbler. |
| Russia | 9. Trans-boundary Wetlands in Tyumen and Kurgan Regions | Ramsar | Five Nature Reserves (zakazniks), one Nature Monument, temp. Wildlife Refuges | IV, III (part) | Dalmatian Pelican, Lesser White-fronted Goose, Red-breasted Goose, White-headed Duck, Siberian Crane, Corncrake, Sociable Lapwing. |

Key:

**AWI** - Asian Wetlands Inventory (Scott 1989);

**IBA** - Important Bird Area (Evans 1994, BirdLife International 2004);

**MEWI** - Middle East Wetlands Inventory (Scott 1995);

**NEACSN** - NE Asia Crane Site Network (Chan 1999); Ramsar - Ramsar site;

**NHA** - Non-hunting Area;

**NNR** - National Nature Reserve;

**MAB** - Man & Biosphere Reserve.

Siberian Cranes require migratory stopover sites to rest and replenish depleted energy reserves to complete migration and to breed successfully. Population pressure and conflicts with water and wetland use threaten the important sites on Songnen Plain in north-eastern China in particular. Summering areas for sub-adult Siberian Cranes (age 1-5 years) are largely unknown for all populations and must be identified, assessed and protected. Siberian Cranes are highly sensitive to disturbance on their breeding grounds and pairs require large territories. The main threats at these far northern sites are disturbance from human activities such as oil exploration, timber extraction and collection of natural produce.

## CAUSE OF THREATS

The causes of many of the threats include: increasing human pressure on natural resources; unsustainable exploitation of wetlands by rural communities; lack of co-ordination among sectoral agencies; lack of capacity and financial resources for protected area management and species protection; poor levels of environmental awareness and understanding; weak legislation or enforcement related to nature protection; and a lack of integration of conservation concerns into development planning and water management. Also related to human impacts are the long-term implications of climate change on wetlands in the region. At the international level, existing international co-operation and capacity for international co-ordination of conservation efforts are limited, and limited information is available about migration routes and sites for many waterbird species. This problem includes a lack of systematically collected information on the status of wetland resources and threats to wetlands in Asia.

## GLOBAL ENVIRONMENT FACILITY (GEF) PROJECT

Following on from the CMS Memorandum of Understanding, the next stage in the long-term conservation programme for the Siberian Crane was the development of an international project funded by the GEF and other donors and with the United Nations Environment Programme (UNEP) serving as the Implementing Agency (UNEP 2002). This project focuses specifically on the conservation of the international network of wetlands upon which the Siberian Crane depends, together with other migratory waterbirds and a wide range of other wetland fauna and flora. It aims to facilitate the development and expansion of a network of protected wetland sites and wider application of the approaches that have been developed in each participating country.

The Siberian Crane is being used as "flagship species" for the conservation of large open wetlands, in the same way that other charismatic species have been used to attract public attention for conservation issues. The project area covers two of the three migration routes used by populations of the Siberian Crane in Asia, targeting key wetland sites located in China, Iran, Kazakhstan and Russia (Table 1, Fig. 1). It does not cover the Central Asian migration route of the Siberian Crane outside Russia and Kazakhstan, as this is being addressed by parallel conservation activities under the CMS Memorandum of Understanding.

The project's intervention strategy reflects the life history of the Siberian Crane in that the selection of project sites covers the main known breeding, wintering and staging areas for both western and eastern populations. Those sites that are of greatest importance for the species are given priority in the first three-year phase of the project. These include the eastern population's main breeding grounds (in Kytalyk) and main wintering site (at Lake Poyang), and sites under most immediate threat (staging areas at Zhalong and Xianghai in China). Similarly, protection measures at the western population's main wintering site at Fereydoon Kenar in Iran are being addressed. Targeted research designed to fill gaps in our knowledge of migration routes and to identify further critical sites is also given priority. Less urgent sites and activities will be addressed in a second three-year phase. Sites covered by other major projects have generally been omitted in order to avoid duplication of effort. Close co-ordination and exchange of information will be maintained to ensure that the requirements of the cranes will be incorporated into other programmes.

## IMPORTANCE OF SIBERIAN CRANE SITES FOR OTHER GLOBALLY THREATENED WATERBIRDS

The wetlands that have been identified as sites for project intervention all meet the criteria of the Ramsar Convention on Wetlands for identifying Wetlands of International Importance, and many have existing international designations (see Table 1). The flyways used by the Siberian Cranes are shared with many other species of migratory waterbirds, including at least 32 globally threatened or near threatened waterbird species (see Table 2), and thus have significance far beyond conservation of the Siberian Crane alone. For example, Zhalong Nature Reserve, one of China's project sites, supports at least 12 other globally threatened and near threatened bird species, including the largest breeding population of Red-crowned Cranes *Grus japonensis* in the world; Poyang Lake, another Chinese project site, supports at least 14 species of globally threatened and near threatened birds, including half the world population of White-naped Cranes *G. vipio* throughout the winter. These flyway site networks sustain millions of migratory waterbirds along their migration routes, which span the Asian continent between northern breeding grounds and southern wintering areas (see APMWCC 2001 for further information). These wetlands are also of considerable socio-economic and cultural importance, supporting the livelihoods of local communities, as well as contributing to regional and national economic development in many cases. (See Annex 9E in GEF Project Document for details).

## AIMS AND ACTIVITIES OF THE GEF PROJECT

The project aims to secure the ecological integrity of a network of globally important wetlands that are of critical importance for migratory waterbirds and other wetland biodiversity, using the globally threatened Siberian Crane as a flagship species. To address threats and underlying causes, the project will undertake actions principally at three levels, as described below.

### Site level

The project aims to address threats to key wetlands of international importance that are of critical importance for the conservation of the Siberian Crane and other migratory waterbirds (see Table 1). A range of measures will be undertaken at each site in relation to specific threats, in order to ensure its future ecological integrity. These measures involve a high degree of stakeholder participation, and will contribute to local community development through pilot sustainable livelihood projects where these are a priority. Site activities include strengthening legal protection and enforcement, developing and implementing site management plans, capacity building for site management, environmental education and public awareness programmes, and alternative livelihood projects. (See Annex 9B1 of Project Document for details). The timeframe for these activities is designed to allow adequate time for capacity building, education and community participation approaches to yield the targeted conservation results.

### National level

The project will undertake specific actions to strengthen the national legislative, policy and planning framework for wetland and waterbird conservation, strengthen capacity for international co-operation, and undertake national activities that support site conservation, such as monitoring, training, education and public awareness programmes. These activities are being co-ordinated with UNDP/GEF national wetlands projects in China, Iran and Kazakhstan as well as other projects. They also aim to strengthen mechanisms for integrated wetland management through improved inter-sectoral collaboration. In China, improvements in the co-ordination of waterbird monitoring within the country will be a priority.

### International level

The project will focus on building capacity for the co-ordination of flyway networks of wetlands along the West/Central and East Asian flyways for migratory waterbirds, led by sites of importance for the Siberian Crane as a flagship species. These networks are being carefully co-ordinated with other flyway or regional conservation initiatives, such as the Asia-Pacific Migratory Waterbird Conservation Strategy 2001-2005 (APMWCS), Central Asian Flyway (CAF) project, Agreement on the Conservation of African-Eurasian Migratory Waterbirds (AEWA), Crane Working Group of Eurasia, and UNEP/GEF Econet project in Central Asia, in order to form an integrated programme, and will contribute significantly towards the implementation of international conventions. The networks will also contribute to the delivery of activities under the Conservation Plans of the CMS Memorandum of Understanding concerning Conservation Measures for the Siberian Crane. This component will be accompanied by applied field research (such as satellite telemetry studies) in support of flyway conservation.

A regional co-ordination centre has been established in Moscow, which links with the above-mentioned initiatives. A centralized database and GIS have been designed, which will facilitate exchange of information on waterbird species and the project sites and undertaking of regional assessments. The project is also strengthening capacity for co-ordination of the North East Asia Crane Site Network's activities in China and Yakutia; it supports the operation of a Task Force on the Siberian Crane under the Crane Working Group (part of the APMWCS co-ordination structure), and facilitates an enhanced level of flyway conservation activities in line with existing plans and institutional frameworks.

The project is working with other partners (CMS, Wetlands International and national governments) to develop a Western/Central Asia Site Network for Siberian Cranes (and Other Waterbirds) within the wider frameworks of the Central Asian Flyway project and the CMS Memorandum of Understanding. This effort will transfer experience gained by the North East Asia Crane Site Network and help towards the establishment of a wider network of waterbird sites for the Central Asian flyway.

Activities supporting the flyway site networks include the production and distribution of public education materials to support Crane Festivals (conducted at 28 sites in 2004), training in data management (workshop in Kazakhstan in September 2004), staff exchanges between sites, satellite telemetry research on Siberian Crane migration routes, and improved access to information through the regional database, English and Russian language web-sites, a newsletter and an email migration-tracking communication system.

## CHALLENGES FOR SITE NETWORKS

This project covers a selection of key sites for the Siberian Crane, and some other key sites are covered by other projects.

**Table 2. Globally threatened and near threatened species of migratory waterbirds using wetlands selected as UNEP/GEF project sites.** *(Adapted from Asia Pacific Migratory Waterbird Conservation Committee, 2001).*

| Species[1] | English Name | Category of Threat[2,3] | Global (G) / Regional (R) Population Estimate[3] | Regional Population[3] |
|---|---|---|---|---|
| *Pelecanus crispus* | Dalmatian Pelican | VU | 9 800-12 400 R | SW, S Asia |
| *Phalacrocorax pygmeus* | Pygmy Cormorant | LR/Nt | 25 000 - 100 000 R | SW Asia |
| *Ciconia boyciana* | Oriental Stork | EN | 3 000 G | |
| *Threskiornis melanocephalus* | Black-headed Ibis | LR/Nt | <100 R | E Asia |
| *Platalea minor* | Black-faced Spoonbill | EN | 970 G | |
| *Anser cygnoides* | Swan Goose | EN | 50 000-60 000 G | |
| *Anser erythropus* | Lesser White-fronted Goose | VU | 14 000 R1 | E China |
| *Anser erythropus* | Lesser White-fronted Goose | VU | 8 000-13 000 R2 | N Europe, W Siberia |
| *Branta ruficollis* | Red-breasted Goose | VU | 88 000 G | |
| *Aix galericulata* | Mandarin Duck | LR/Nt | 70 000 G | |
| *Anas formosa* | Baikal Teal | VU | 300 000 G | |
| *Marmaronetta angustirostris* | Marbled Teal | VU | 5 000-15 000 R | SW Asia |
| *Aythya baeri* | Baer's Pochard | VU | 10 000-20 000 (G) | |
| *Aythya nyroca* | Ferruginous Duck | LR/Nt | 25 000-100 000 R1 | SW Asia |
| *Aythya nyroca* | Ferruginous Duck | LR/Nt | 25 000 - 1 000 000 R2 | S,E & SE Asia |
| *Polysticta stellerii* | Steller's Eider | LR/Lc | 220 000 G | |
| *Somateria fischeri* | Spectacled Eider | LR/Lc | 330 000-390 000 G | |
| *Mergus squamatus* | Scaly-sided Merganser | VU | 3 600-4 500 (G) | |
| *Oxyura leucocephala* | White-headed Duck | EN | 10 R1 | South Asia |
| *Oxyura leucocephala* | White-headed Duck | EN | 5 000-10 000 R2 | E Med, SW Asia |
| *Grus monacha* | Hooded Crane | VU | 8 500 G | |
| *Grus japonensis* | Red-crowned Crane | EN | 2 400 G | |
| *Grus vipio* | White-naped Crane | VU | 7 200 G | |
| *Grus leucogeranus* | Siberian Crane | CR | 3 000 G | |
| *Coturnicops exquisitus* | Swinhoe's Rail | VU | <10 000 G | |
| *Crex crex* | Corncrake | VU | >1 000 000 G R? | Asian population unknown |
| *Glareola nordmanni* | Black-winged Pratincole | DD | 29 000-45 000 G | |
| *Vanellus gregarius* | Sociable Lapwing | VU | 400-1 200 G | |
| *Vanellus cinereus* | Grey-headed Lapwing | LR/Nt | 25 000-100 000 G | |
| *Charadrius placidus* | Long-billed Plover | LR/Nt | <10 000 G | |
| *Numenius tenuirostris* | Slender-billed Curlew | CR | <50 G | |
| *Numenius madagascariensis* | Far Eastern Curlew | LR/Nt | 38 000 G | |
| *Gallinago media* | Great Snipe | LR/Nt | 100 000-1 000 000 R | W Siberia, NE Europe |
| *Limnodromus semipalmatus* | Asian Dowitcher | LR/Nt | 23 000 G | |
| *Larus saundersi* | Saunder's Gull | VU | 7 100-9 600 G | |

REFERENCES: 1: Collar *et al.* (1994) 2: BirdLife International (2001) 3: Wetlands International (2002).

NOTES: **CR**=Critically Endangered **EN**=Endangered **VU**=Vulnerable **DD**=Data Deficient **LR**=Lower Risk **Lc**=Least Concern **Nt**=Near threatened

The birds, however, use additional sites that need to be identified through satellite tracking studies and surveys, and protected as appropriate.

The management capacity at the known key sites needs to be strengthened – a key aim of the present GEF project. Ecological research is focusing on habitat requirements of the eastern population on their critical wintering grounds at Poyang Lake.

Although hunting of Siberian Cranes is illegal in all four GEF countries, hunting still poses a significant threat to this species and other migratory waterbirds. The education of hunters throughout the flyways and improved legislation and enforcement are needed in order to allay this threat. High-profile projects in Asia similar to that undertaken by Operation Migration in the USA for the Whooping Crane *Grus americana* (migration of released birds led by hang-glider) would be a dramatic way of raising awareness, with education activities at stopovers along the route.

Finally, the only way to verify whether this multi-level conservation effort is being successful is through improved monitoring of waterbird populations throughout the flyways concerned. At present, coverage (for example, by the Asian Waterbird Census) is very limited in key regions such as China; the quality of data available has to be improved, and this is being addressed under the project.

## ADDED VALUE OF THE FLYWAY APPROACH

The flyway approach increases the complexity of project co-ordination and management, and increases the level of risk for projects working at this level. This approach adds to the costs of conservation when combined with activities at national and site levels. Such an approach, however, is essential for enabling the comprehensive and effective management of migratory species throughout their life cycles. It also facilitates the improved representation of wetland habitats in protected area systems along an entire flyway, supporting both wetland and waterbird conservation. Co-operation among a range of conservation initiatives at flyway, national and site levels should improve the efficiency of efforts by focusing attention on priorities and improving access to information on sites and species, and applying lessons learned to other sites.

## ACKNOWLEDGEMENTS

The authors gratefully acknowledge assistance from their colleagues at ICF, including George Archibald, Li Fengshan, Patricia Gleason, Dorn Moore, Elena Smirenski, Zoe Rickenbach and Luan Haiyan. This project would not have been possible without the support of UNEP Task Managers Mark Zimsky and Max Zieren. We are grateful to the national project teams and wish to acknowledge the valuable leadership of Wang Wei, Zhang Dehui and Qian Fawen (China); Anoushiravan Najafi, Mohammed Ayatollahi and Sadegh Sadeghi-Zadeghan (Iran); Sergey Yerokhov, Evgeny Bragin, Tatiana Bragina, Anatoly Kovshar and staff of the Forest and Hunting Committee, Ministry of Agriculture (Kazakhstan); and Alexander Sorokin, Anastassia Shilina, Victor Vlasenko, Alexander Ermakov, Tatiana Belyakova and Nikolai Germogenov (Russian Federation). Project design benefited greatly from the advice and assistance of organizations including CMS, UNDP, Wetlands International, Ramsar Convention Bureau, Cracid Breeding and Conservation Center, and the World Bank. Many other individuals and organizations assisted in the preparation of this project and we acknowledge them here.

## REFERENCES

**APMWCC - Asia-Pacific Migratory Waterbird Conservation Committee** 2001. Asia-Pacific migratory waterbird conservation strategy: 2001-2005. Wetlands International – Asia Pacific, Kuala Lumpur. http://www.wetlands.org/IWC/publications.aspx

**BirdLife International** 2001. Threatened birds of Asia: the BirdLife International Red Data Book. BirdLife International, Cambridge, UK. http://www.rdb.or.id/

**BirdLife International** 2004. Important Bird Areas in Asia: key sites for conservation. BirdLife Conservation Series No. 13. BirdLife International, Cambridge, UK.

**Chan, S.** 1999. Atlas of key sites for cranes in the North East Asian Flyway. Wetlands International Japan, Tokyo, Japan. http://www.wing-wbsj.or.jp/english_hp/

**Chavez-Ramirez, F.** 1996. Food availability, foraging ecology, and energetics of Whooping Cranes wintering in Texas. PhD thesis, Texas A&M University, College Station, Texas.

**CMS - Convention on the Conservation of Migratory Species of Wild Animals** 1999. Conservation measures for the Siberian Crane. CMS Technical Series Publication 1. UNEP/CMS Secretariat, Bonn, Germany.

**Collar, N.J., Crosby, M.J. & Stattersfield, A.J.** 1994. Birds to watch 2, the world list of threatened birds: the official source for birds on the IUCN red list. BirdLife Conservation Series No. 4. BirdLife International, Cambridge, UK.

**Ebbinge, B.S.** 1989. A multifactorial explanation for variation in breeding performance of Brent Geese *Branta bernicla*. Ibis 131: 196-204.

**Ebbinge, B.S. & Spaans, B.** 1995. The importance of body reserves accumulated in spring staging areas in the temperate zone for breeding in Dark-bellied Brent Geese *Branta b. bernicla* in the high Arctic. Journal of Avian Biology 26: 105-113.

**Evans, M.I.** 1994. Important Bird Areas in the Middle East. BirdLife International, Cambridge, UK.

**Kanai, Y., Ueta, M., Germogenov, N., Nagendran, M., Mita, N. & Higuchi, H.** 2002. Migration routes and important resting areas of Siberian Cranes (*Grus leucogeranus*) that migrate between northeastern Siberia and China as revealed by satellite tracking. Biological Conservation 106: 339-346.

**Meine, C.D. & Archibald, G.W.** 1996. The cranes: status survey and conservation action plan. IUCN, Gland, Switzerland.

**Prop, J. & Black, J.M.** 1998. Food intake, body reserves and reproductive success of Barnacle Geese *Branta leucopsis* staging in different habitats. In: F. Mehlum, J.M. Black & J. Madsen (eds) Research on Arctic Geese. Proceedings of the Svalbard Goose Symposium, Oslo, Norway, 23-27 September 1997. Norsk Polarinstitutt Skrifter 200: 175-193.

**Sauey, R.T.** 1985. The range, status and winter ecology of the Siberian Crane (*Grus leucogeranus*). PhD thesis, Cornell University.

**Scott, D.A.** 1989. A Directory of Asian Wetlands. IUCN - The World Conservation Union, Gland, Switzerland.

**Scott, D.A.** (ed). 1995. A Directory of Wetlands in the Middle East. IUCN, Gland, Switzerland, and International Waterfowl and Wetlands Research Bureau, Slimbridge, UK.

**Scott, D.A. & Poole, C.M.** 1989. A status overview of Asian wetlands. Asian Wetland Bureau, Kuala Lumpur, Malaysia.

**UNEP - United Nations Environment Programme** 2002. Regional: China, Iran, Kazakhstan and Russian Federation – Development of a Wetland Site and Flyway Network for Conservation of the Siberian Crane and Other Migratory Waterbirds in Asia. GEF Project Brief. Unpublished document. Can be downloaded from: http://www.scwp.info/documents/ProDocICF15Jan2003.doc/

**UNEP/CMS ed. 2005.** Conservation measures for the Siberian Crane, Third Edition. CMS Technical Series Publication No. 10. UNEP/CMS Secretariat, Bonn, Germany. 242 pp.

**Wetlands International** 2002. Waterbird Population Estimates – Third Edition. Wetlands International Global Series No. 12, Wageningen, The Netherlands.

**Web-sites**
**UNEP/GEF P Siberian Crane Wetland Project**
http://www.scwp.info/

# Site networks for the conservation of waterbirds

*Ward Hagemeijer*

*Wetlands International, PO Box 471, 6700 AL Wageningen, The Netherlands. (email: ward.hagemeijer@wetlands.org)*

Hagemeijer, W. 2006. Site networks for the conservation of waterbirds. *Waterbirds around the world.* Eds. G.C. Boere, C.A. Galbraith & D.A. Stroud. The Stationery Office, Edinburgh, UK. pp. 697-699.

## ABSTRACT

In a flyway approach to the conservation of waterbird populations, the sites used throughout the year provide us with one of the tangible conservation tools with which we can work. Sound management of these sites can safeguard waterbird populations as they move from breeding grounds to staging sites and on to wintering sites. All these sites have a role to play in the birds' annual cycle. The network of critical sites (or critical network of sites) is the minimum network that needs to be maintained to support waterbird populations indefinitely. The functions of the sites and the functional links between sites are important attributes of this critical site network, which is more than just a list of important sites. A lot of information exists on the numbers of birds using sites at various times of the year, particularly in midwinter (January), but knowledge about the function of sites for waterbirds and their role in the annual cycle is rather poor, and needs to be improved. One of the aims of the UNEP-GEF African Eurasian Flyways Project is to bring together these various strands of information to compile a network of critical sites for waterbirds in African and Western Eurasia.

## INTRODUCTION: FLYWAY CONSERVATION

Migratory waterbirds can range over thousands of kilometres in their movements between breeding and non-breeding areas, relying on the availability of suitable habitat throughout their range. Most species are highly migratory, covering large distances and concentrating in large numbers at often a small number of places, making them vulnerable to external influences but at the same time attractive for bird-watching and ecological tourism. They are often an important resource for traditional sustainable use (Kanstrup 2006).

The definition of a flyway is generally understood to mean the entire range of a migratory waterbird species (or group of species, or distinct population of a single species) from the breeding grounds to the wintering areas, including the intermediate resting and feeding areas and the often relatively narrow corridor within which the birds migrate (see, for example, Scott & Rose 1996). The concept was first developed in North America, and is now widely used when attempting to define the overall problems that a migratory waterbird encounters in its life cycle and determine which countries should co-operate to protect and manage the populations on a sustainable basis.

The term "flyway" is to some extent a theoretical concept. It is not the same as a "migration route", which may be defined as the travel lanes of individual birds on their way from any particular breeding area to their winter quarters. Flyways, on the other hand, may well be conceived as those broader areas in which related migration routes are associated or blended in a definite geographic region. In addition, they have also become to have an administrative meaning (http://www.birdnature.com/flyways.html).

The term flyway can be used at various taxonomic, geographic and political "scales", as described in Boere & Stroud 2006, this volume.

The conservation of migratory waterbirds along a flyway poses a great challenge to international environmental co-operation. This is because of the vast distances covered by many species of waterbirds in the completion of their annual cycles and the large number of range states involved. Inadequate or inappropriate management measures by just one range state can jeopardize the conservation status of one or many species throughout the flyway. Thus, a high degree of international co-operation is essential throughout the areas used by the populations of the species involved: this is called the "flyway approach". Such co-operation requires international co-ordination at the levels of research, planning and monitoring, common standards for legislation, protected area designation and management, sustainable use, sharing of information and transfer of know-how. In this regard, the role of international conventions and agreements, such as the Convention on Biological Diversity (CBD), the Ramsar Convention on Wetlands, the Convention on Migratory Species (CMS) and the Agreement on the Conservation of African-Eurasian Migratory Waterbirds (AEWA) under the CMS, is essential.

Besides functioning at international, regional and national levels, an effective conservation programme for migratory waterbirds needs to focus right down to the site level, covering all scales in time (when are the sites used and by what) and space, and should provide tools to help the implementation of conservation actions at all appropriate levels.

At the species level, a flyway is in fact the entire ecosystem needed for a migratory waterbird in order to survive, including all the habitat types needed to accommodate breeding, resting and wintering during the whole annual cycle. As such, the concept fully supports the ecosystem approach required under the CBD.

Flyway conservation is the holistic approach to conservation of waterbirds and the systems they use – with their specific habitats – for the benefit of people and biodiversity. It evolves along four main axes: species, sites, habitats and people. A site network is one of the tools that bring together all four axes, and as such is a very important component of flyway conservation.

The flyway concept, by definition, requires close co-operation between all the Range States involved. It can strongly stimulate co-operation between states to build up networks of scientists, conservationists and reserve managers, and stimulate a wealth of small-scale initiatives in all fields of biodiversity and habitat conservation. Migratory waterbirds are a biodiversity resource shared by all countries of the world; conserving migratory waterbirds and using them on a sustainable basis helps to protect the biodiversity of many countries at the same time.

Migratory species really force Range States to work together because of the shared interest in conserving each other's biodiversity and ensuring that the use of a species in one country is co-ordinated with that in other countries to avoid, for instance, unsustainable use of populations.

For many of these species, wetlands are the most important habitat type[1]. These habitats are usually rather discrete and separated from each other by vast areas of non-wetland habitat, causing waterbirds to concentrate at these sites. Wetlands are highly productive habitats and can therefore support large concentrations of waterbirds, despite their sometimes limited size. One of the ways to indicate the importance of individual sites is by the numbers of birds which habitually use them, year after year (see Scott & Rose 1996).

To complete their annual cycles, migratory waterbirds are dependent on a network of important sites throughout their range. Each site in the network plays a vital role, enabling the individuals that use it to reach the next (or another) site. Loss of one such site in the network could result in the distance between sites becoming too long, or in the location for a certain process (e.g. moult) no longer being available. This would "disconnect" the sites before and after it, and be equivalent to losing a link in a chain.

Wetlands are among the most threatened habitats in the world, having suffered losses exceeding 50% of the original area in many countries during recent decades (Millennium Ecosystem Assessment 2005). Large wetland complexes have been reduced in size, and some isolated wetlands have completely disappeared (Finlayson & Moser 1991). If, as a consequence of these losses, a site disappears from the network, the birds need to be able to find an alternative. The flexibility to be able to do this is determined by a complex of many factors. It is obvious that the network, if thinned beyond the species' flexibility, can no longer support the population, leading to a decrease in numbers and eventually a crash. Waterbirds require the network of sites as stepping stones along their migration routes. This means that there is an absolute minimum size and configuration of this network that needs to be maintained to support waterbird populations indefinitely. This is what is meant by the network of critical wetland areas, or critical network of wetland areas[2]. This network may be considered as a minimum essential to ensure the survival of these species across their ranges should remaining habitat elsewhere be lost. Because all sites are, or may increasingly become, refuges, if any one of them is lost the consequences may be disproportionately large. Any comprehensive conservation initiative for migratory waterbirds should therefore take the safeguarding of this network of sites into account: without these sites, the species will not survive. As such, the network of critical sites is one of the pillars of the flyway approach to the conservation of waterbirds

Waterbirds are not the only users of these wetland sites. In many cases, local communities depend on the goods and services provided by these wetlands. Changes in human activities caused, for example, by increasing population densities are resulting in more and more unsustainable use and in clashes of interest between human activities and waterbird requirements. However, in cases of sustainable use or through targeted intervention aimed at restoration, good conditions for wetland biodiversity, including waterbirds, can be maintained and population levels can stay or become healthy. Site-based conservation should strive at these "win-win" situations.

## NETWORK OF CRITICAL SITES AS A TOOL FOR CONSERVATION

From the above, it is clear that the network of critical sites is a powerful tool in an effective conservation programme for the benefit of populations of migratory waterbirds, the habitats on which they depend and the people sharing these habitats. It is a mechanism for incorporating internationally co-ordinated measures for site conservation, species monitoring and conservation, including sustainable use and regulation of any forms of harvest. Defining the network of critical sites sets the geographic priorities for the implementation of these conservation actions. Knowledge of this network is therefore a basic need for the implementation of policy tools such as the Ramsar Convention at the global scale and regional initiatives such as AEWA, Western Hemisphere Shorebird Reserve Network and East Asian-Australasian Flyway Site Network.

Although a list of sites covering a certain area is often referred to as a network, a network in the true sense of the word is more than this. In a network, the functions of sites and the functional links between sites are important attributes. Sites can serve various functions to birds, e.g. as breeding grounds, stopover sites (either for roosting, feeding, moulting or other ecologically important components of the life cycle such as pair bonding), wintering sites, and refuges in severe weather. It is well documented that birds are often quite traditional in their use of sites, not only on the breeding grounds and in the wintering areas, but also at staging areas along the migration routes. These functions of, and links between, sites will differ between and within species and may even change over the years, for example as a result of changing weather conditions. Although most waterbirds seem to be quite flexible in their response to changing environmental conditions, those with more traditional migration strategies and high site fidelity, such as the Lesser White-fronted Goose *Anser erythropus* and certain species of waders, are particular vulnerable. Little is known about these aspects of a site network except in a few cases where in-depth research has been undertaken, e.g. in the case of the Greenland White-fronted Goose *Anser albifrons flavirostris* (Fox *et al.* 1994, Fox & Stroud 2002). For most species, more work is needed before it is possible to identify the critical sites and assess their roles in the annual cycle. In most cases, therefore, it would be too ambitious at the present time to aim at building site networks by relying heavily on knowledge of the functional aspects site linkages.

A temporary solution might be found at an intermediate stage, by subdividing the annual cycle into three main life-cycle components (breeding, passage and over-wintering) and analysing the network on this basis. Traditionally, waterbirds have mostly been counted in the month of January within the framework of the International Waterbird Census (IWC) co-ordinated by Wetlands International. Thus, for many sites information is lacking on their role in the migration seasons. In many cold regions, where most if not all sites are completely frozen over in winter (January), relatively little is known about the importance of sites for waterbirds. The Important Bird Areas (IBA) project and database of BirdLife International have, to some extent, mobilized information about numbers of waterbirds in periods other than mid-winter, and it is therefore important to combine this information with information from the IWC.

---

[1] It is important to note that some migratory waterbirds may also depend on non-wetland sites for part of their annual cycle.

[2] Both forms of wording contribute to an understanding of the concept: the network aspect as well as the site aspect are critical for the survival of the species

One specific role that sites can play in a site network is that of providing flexibility in case of shifting distributions. Against the background of climate change, this would appear to be an increasingly important characteristic of a site network (Boere & Taylor 2004).

The word "critical" in the strict sense implies that the removal of any one of the sites from the network would have a serious impact on the population of waterbirds that the network as a whole supports. This concept of a minimum configuration of sites is straightforward in itself, but difficult to apply in practice, because it cannot be underpinned by scientific data, and cannot be tested. To date, initiatives to establish conservation approaches based on site selection have therefore taken a pragmatic approach and expressed selection criteria in numerical terms, the most famous being the 1% criterion[3] as used, for example, in compiling lists of important sites under the Ramsar Convention and within the framework of the Important Bird Areas project.

The Ramsar Convention has adopted the following definition of the term "critical site", as given in the *Strategic framework for the List of Wetlands of International Importance* published by the Ramsar Bureau: "Critical sites for mobile or migratory species are those which contain particularly high proportions of populations gathered in relatively small areas at particular stages of life cycles. This may be at particular times of the year or, in semi-arid or arid areas, during years with a particular rainfall pattern. For example, many waterbirds use relatively small areas as key staging points (to eat and rest) on their long-distance migrations between breeding and non-breeding areas. For Anatidae species, moulting sites are also critical. Sites in semi-arid or arid areas may hold very important concentrations of waterbirds and other mobile wetland species and be crucial to the survival of populations, yet may vary greatly in apparent importance from year-to-year as a consequence of considerable variability in rainfall patterns."

Although these criteria for the identification of sites for inclusion in specific lists have been the subject of extensive discussion in the past, they do not consider "complementarity" between sites, or different "roles" of sites in the flyway. It is therefore worth looking at these criteria again, to evaluate whether there is scope for better incorporation of the functionality of sites in a network into the selection criteria.

It should be said that the creation and implementation of new criteria should only be promoted if there is clear indication that this will significantly improve the functioning of the resulting network. In other cases, it is preferable to adhere to existing criteria, to avoid loading additional burden on the shoulders of countries that will have to work with the criteria and to avoid losing the conservation value and credit build up with the existing sites. Instead of replacing existing criteria, it may therefore be necessary to define additional criteria to accommodate the functional component of the network.

There is also a need to look at the efficiency or effectiveness of the selected network. Evaluation of the effectiveness of a proposed network should be undertaken on a species (or species group) basis, and involves bringing together data from various existing data sets to check to what extent the network covers the distribution of the species (or species group) and fulfils the various roles in the annual life cycle.

## UNEP-GEF AFRICAN EURASIAN FLYWAYS PROJECT

For the effective conservation of migratory waterbirds, it is important to be able to make the step from lists of key sites to networks of critical sites. Inadequate knowledge and understanding of waterbirds and the way they use sites have, until now, hampered this step forward. UNEP-GEF and several major co-funders, including the German Government and the AEWA Secretariat, have therefore decided to support a flyways project for the African-Eurasian region. This project, entitled "Enhancing conservation of the critical network of sites required by Migratory Waterbirds on the African/Eurasian Flyways" (or UNEP-GEF African Eurasian Flyways Project in short) is being developed by Wetlands International and will run for the period 2006-2011. The project will address the issues mentioned above, and will develop a network of critical sites for the African-Eurasian region. The need for the development of such a network of sites of critical importance to migratory waterbirds is well established and supported by both the Ramsar Convention and AEWA.

## REFERENCES

**Boere, G.C. & Taylor, D.** 2004. Global and regional governmental policy and treaties as tools towards the mitigation of the effect of climate change on waterbirds. Ibis 146 (Supplement 1): 111-119. http://www.blackwell-synergy.com/doi/full/10.1111/j.1474-919X.2004.00335.x

**Finlayson, M. & Moser, M.** (eds.). 1991. Wetlands. International Waterfowl and Wetlands Research Bureau (IWRB), Facts on File, Oxford, New York.

**Fox, A.D., Norriss, D.W., Stroud, D.A. & Wilson, H.J.** 1994. Greenland White-fronted Geese in Ireland and Britain 1982/83-1993/94 - the first twelve years of international conservation monitoring. Greenland White-fronted Goose Study Research Report No. 8. GWGS, Aberystwyth & National Parks and Wildlife Service, Dublin. 55 pp. http://www.greenlandwhitefront.homestead.com/report1.html

**Fox, A.D. & Stroud, D.A.** 2002. The Greenland White-fronted Goose *Anser albifrons flavirostris*. BWP Update 4(2): 65-88.

**Kanstrup, N.** 2006. Sustainable harvest of waterbirds: a global review. Waterbirds around the world. G.C. Boere, C.A. Galbraith & D.A. Stroud (Eds.), The Stationery Office, Edinburgh, UK. 98-106.

**Millennium Ecosystem Assessment** 2005. Ecosystems and human well-being: wetlands and water synthesis. World Resources Institute, Washington DC. 68 pp.

**Scott, D.A & Rose, P.M.** 1996. Atlas of Anatidae Populations in Africa and Western Eurasia. Wetlands International publication No. 41. Wetlands International, Wageningen, The Netherlands.

---

[3] Ramsar Criterion 6: A wetland should be considered internationally important if it regularly supports 1% of the individuals in a population of one species or subspecies of waterbird. http://ramsar.org/key_guide_list2006_e.htm

## 5.4 Integrating waterbird conservation: populations, habitats and landscapes. Workshop Introduction

*Jim Kushlan*

*Smithsonian Environmental Research Centre, PO Box 1930, Edgewater, MD 21037-1930 USA. (email: jkushlan@earthlink.net)*

Kushlan, J. 2006. Integrating waterbird conservation: populations, habitats and landscapes. Workshop Introduction. *Waterbirds around the world*. Eds. G.C. Boere, C.A. Galbraith & D.A. Stroud. The Stationery Office, Edinburgh, UK. p. 700.

Orsoya fishpond, Bulgaria. The conservation of such traditional fishponds - which are subject to a low intensity of management - is important to maintain associated waterbirds included the globally threatened Ferruginous Duck *Aythya nyroca*. Photo: Nikolai Petkov.

The long-term conservation of waterbirds requires conservation activities to be undertaken at a wide range of scales and in respect to the different periods of annual life cycles.

Development of strategies and policies for effective conservation and/or management will vary greatly according to the ecology and distribution of different waterbird species. Species which are highly aggregating will occur at high densities at a few sites. The identification, protection and management of these key sites will be an effective means of conserving significant proportions of populations — especially where groups of such sites are managed as networks (as explored by the papers in the preceding section: Building effective ecological networks).

For species that aggregate less densely, wider measures may be necessary to secure their favourable status, especially where these species occur at low densities across wetland or other landscapes. For many species a mix of site-related and wider-countryside measures are needed. This will include species such as some geese and swans which roost at high densities on sites which can be protected as refuges or through similar site-related measures, but during the day then range more widely, at lower densities, to feed on farmland or other habitats. Integrated conservation approaches are needed in such circumstances.

Landscape-scale measures can be of either formal or informal nature. Formal measures include government-led agri-environment policies that seek to deliver environmental benefits through subsidies provided to farmers and other land-managers.

The development of wider policies for waterbird conservation is aided by clarity as to objectives and targets, and in this respect, Johnson *et al.* summarise the US experience in planning for bird conservation at landscape scales.

As with all conservation management, there is a need to monitor the effectiveness of wider conservation measures so that these policies may be adapted or modified in the light of changing circumstances. Such monitoring needs necessarily to be wide-scale, and Bart presents the development of the North American Program for Regional and International Shorebird Monitoring (PRISM) which aims to collect a range of population parameters on shorebirds at continental scales. Austin *et al.* summarise the development by the UK Wetland Bird Survey of a waterbird 'alerts' system. This provides annual feedback to conservation managers and others on the status of sites and species using objective analysis of trends and the application of pre-defined criteria to assess significant declines. The system has already been effective in guiding priority setting by conservationists in the UK.

Wider policies are valuable not just in the context of cropped habitats. Petkov highlights the value of traditional fishponds, managed at low-intensity in some eastern European countries, for the conservation of the threatened Ferruginous Duck *Aythya nyroca*. In this example, policies which might result in either the abandonment of current fish-farming practises on the one hand, or its intensification on the other, might be extremely damaging to the status of Ferruginous Duck.

Straw & Saintilan highlight the importance of tropical open shores for inter-tidal waders and highlight the implications of the loss of this habitat following invasion by mangrove species. This suggests that the development of proposals to afforest shores with mangroves should be approached with caution and always following an environmental impact assessment that considers wider implications such as this.

# The Program for Regional and International Shorebird Monitoring (PRISM) in North America

*Jonathan Bart*

*Forest and Rangeland Ecosystem Science Center, US Geological Survey, 970 Lusk Street, Boise, Idaho 83706, USA.*
*(email: jopn_bart@usgs.gov)*

Bart, J. 2006. The Program for Regional and International Shorebird Monitoring (PRISM) in North America. *Waterbirds around the world*. Eds. G.C. Boere, C.A. Galbraith & D.A. Stroud. The Stationery Office, Edinburgh, UK. pp. 701-704.

The Program for Regional and International Monitoring (PRISM) provides guidance on how to monitor shorebirds that regularly nest in Canada and the United States. PRISM has five goals, but work so far has focused on one of the goals, namely estimating trends in population size. An accuracy target has been adopted and a substantial amount of work has been completed to design surveys in the arctic, boreal, and temperate regions of Canada and the United States. Less work has been done on surveys to be conducted in winter.

## INTRODUCTION

National shorebird conservation plans in Canada (Donaldson 2001) and the United States (Brown *et al.* 2001), completed in the past few years, both recommended a comprehensive approach to monitoring shorebird populations in North America. These calls to action led to the formation of PRISM, the Program for Regional and International Shorebird Monitoring (Skagen *et al.* 2004, Bart *et al.* 2005a). The national plans identified 74 shorebird taxa, including 49 species, with populations in Canada and the United States large enough to warrant monitoring. PRISM has five goals:

- Estimate the size of breeding populations of shorebirds in Canada and the United States.
- Describe the distribution, abundance, and habitat relationships of shorebirds.
- Monitor trends in the size of shorebird populations.
- Monitor shorebird numbers at stopover locations.
- Assist local managers in meeting their shorebird conservation goals.

Estimating trends in population size was thought to be the most difficult goal to achieve, and so initial work has focused on this goal. PRISM has adopted the following accuracy target for trend estimation:

*80% power to detect a 50% decline in population size, occurring during no more than 20 years, using a two-tailed test with a 0.15 significance level, and acknowledging effects of potential bias.*

A three-part approach for trend estimation has been developed to achieve this goal:

- Surveys on the breeding grounds.
- Surveys on migration.
- Surveys on the wintering grounds.

Progress in the development of each of these surveys is described below.

## SURVEYS ON THE BREEDING GROUNDS

Separate programs are being conducted in arctic, boreal, and temperate regions. During surveys, all shorebirds encountered are recorded, but in each region, programs are designed to survey only those species for which one-third or more of the population occurs in the region. For example, surveys in both the arctic and boreal regions are designed to survey Red-necked Phalaropes *Phalarope lobatus*, because more than one-third of their population is thought to occur in each region, but surveys in the Arctic are not designed specifically to monitor Semipalmated Plovers *Charadrius semipalmatus*, although they do occur in the Arctic, because more than two-thirds of their population are believed to breed in the boreal region.

### Arctic regions

A great deal of work has been carried out in the arctic portions of Canada and Alaska during the past five years. Methods for surveying shorebirds were developed at a research station on the delta of the Colville River, using support from the US Fish and Wildlife Service and the US Geological Survey. The approach uses double sampling. A large sample of plots is selected, using formal probability methods, and surveyed a single time. A sub-sample of these plots is surveyed intensively to determine the number of shorebirds actually present. The number of birds "present" on a plot is defined as the number of territorial males whose first nest of the season, or territory centroid for non-nesters, is within the plot. This number is then doubled to obtain the estimate of population size. Other methods of estimation are needed if a substantial number of the males are non-territorial, but this is a situation that we have not yet encountered. The ratio of number recorded on rapid surveys of the intensive plots to number actually present is used as a correction factor to adjust results from the rapid plots and obtain an unbiased estimate of numbers actually present. Geographic information systems (GIS) methods are used to stratify the study area, and habitat-based models are used to extrapolate findings from the sample to the entire region. Two- or three-stage sampling is used to select survey plots depending on sampling intensity within the region. The field methods are described in Bart & Earnst (2002, 2005); the sampling plan and derivation of the estimators are described in Bart *et al.* (2005b).

Once the basic method was developed, tests were made to evaluate and refine it for use throughout the Arctic in Alaska and Canada. Trials were carried out in 15 sites, widely distributed across the Arctic (Fig. 1). A manuscript summarizing results and presenting a proposed plan for conducting the surveys during the next 10-20 years has been prepared and is undergoing peer review by a panel of experts. Following peer review, the plan will be revised as needed, submitted for publication in a scientific journal, and then implemented in the coming years.

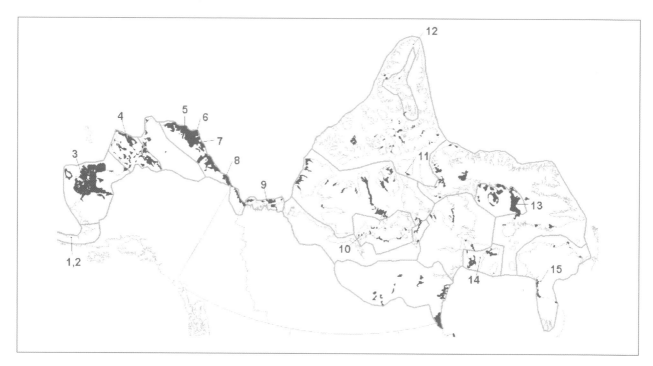

Fig. 1. North American Arctic (i.e. Alaska and northern Canada), showing location of field sites at which the methods for the long-term survey were developed (numbers 1-15) and the regions (thick gray lines) which form the starting point for the sampling plan. Black areas are wetlands, as indicated by the Circumpolar Arctic Vegetation Map (CAVM Team 2003).

The next step in developing the PRISM arctic surveys is to broaden coverage, where appropriate, to include other birds and perhaps to collect data on other organisms and environmental parameters. A decision was made in 2003 that surveys in Canada would record all species, because many of the areas being surveyed have rarely if ever been visited by biologists on the ground. A commitment has also been made to contact other Arctic researchers to determine the importance of collecting other kinds of information.

## Boreal regions

The Boreal PRISM committee carried out an assessment of methods for surveying shorebirds in the boreal region (Aubry *et al.* 2004). They identified nine priority species, of 19 species that breed regularly in boreal regions, and considered how best to survey each one in each boreal Bird Conservation Region (BCR). A primary conclusion was that methods currently used to survey species other than shorebirds should be used rather than developing methods solely for shorebirds. The assessment discusses methods used for land-birds (North American Breeding Bird Survey, off-road point counts), waterfowl (helicopter aerial surveys of wetlands, roadside waterfowl surveys), marsh birds (Marsh Bird Monitoring), and migrant shorebirds (aerial and ground-based stopover site surveys). Their conclusions (Aubry *et al.* 2004, p. 33) were:

Because of differences among boreal species in geographic distribution and habitat use, no one survey type can be used to monitor all boreal shorebirds. For some species, such as the high alpine breeders Surfbird *Aphriza virgata* and Wandering Tattler *Heteroscelus incanus*, adequate population monitoring

on the breeding grounds may not be feasible in the near future, and surveys during migration and wintering should be further investigated. For species with very limited breeding ranges, such as Hudsonian Godwit *Limosa haemastica* and Short-billed Dowitcher *Limnodromus griseus*, species-specific surveys may be required within small geographic areas. For some species, expanding coverage of the Breeding Bird Survey, which is well established and relatively inexpensive to conduct, to encompass the many roads within the boreal region that are not currently surveyed, may prove adequate for population monitoring. Roadside surveys which target wetlands, such as roadside waterfowl surveys and marsh bird surveys, may also be valuable, cost-effective tools for monitoring some boreal shorebirds.

Their report includes numerous recommendations on work needed to determine how the existing survey protocols and programs can best be used to survey each of their high priority species.

In Canada, bird monitoring in the boreal forest has recently gained prominence through programs initiated by both government (e.g. Canadian Wildlife Service) and non-government (e.g. Ducks Unlimited) agencies. Boreal PRISM is viewed as one part of a broader boreal bird monitoring effort. The PRISM program will collaborate closely with boreal monitoring by other bird groups to ensure maximum program efficiency. We anticipate proceeding with testing the adequacy of existing methods for monitoring boreal shorebirds in the spring of 2005.

## Temperate regions

Seventeen shorebird species nest in temperate regions in sufficient abundance to be focal species for this region. The PRISM accuracy target appears to be met for Piping Plovers *Charadrius melodus* and American Woodcock *Scolopax minor*, and may be met for five other species that are frequently recorded on the Breeding Bird Survey, although more work is needed to assess potential bias. A detailed survey has been made for American Oystercatchers *Haematopus palliatus* that nest within the United

States (Brown *et al.* 2005). In 2004, a three-year study was initiated to study Long-billed Curlews *Numenius americanus*. The results will achieve the PRISM trend monitoring target as well as providing information on habitat relationships and conservation priorities for this species. A comprehensive plan is needed for monitoring the other eight species. Comprehensive programs recently initiated in several States may be helpful, but work focused on these shorebird species will also be needed.

## SURVEYS ON MIGRATION

Most shorebird species can be monitored during migration, and much work has been carried out to develop rigorous surveys for this period. The International Shorebird Survey (Howe *et al.* 1989, Brown *et al.* 2001) and the Maritimes Shorebird Survey (Morrison *et al.* 1994, 2001) have collected information on migrating shorebirds since the mid-1970s, but without a well-defined sampling frame or written, site-specific protocols. PRISM investigators have developed approaches for defining the sampling frame and preparing survey protocols. Canada and the United States have been divided into bird monitoring regions, created by intersecting a Province and State map with a map of Bird Conservation Regions (BCRs) which were delineated by the North American Bird Conservation Initiative (NABCI 2000). This approach permits stepping up results either to the Province and State level or to the BCR level. Each bird monitoring region is partitioned into two or more strata. One stratum consists of "designated sites", i.e. sites with a sufficient number of birds, and people to survey them, for them to be non-randomly selected for inclusion in the shorebird survey. The rest of the region is referred to as the matrix, and may be sub-divided into two or

Long-billed Curlew *Numenius americanus*. Photo: Gary Kramer.

more matrix strata depending on shorebird distribution and appropriate survey methods. For example, reservoirs might be common in one part of a region and might be surveyed by boat; another part of the region might contain extensive marshes where ground surveys would be needed, and the rest of the region might have too few shorebirds to be worth surveying.

---

**Table 1. Information recorded about each designated site in the PRISM migrating shorebird monitoring program.**

1. **Boundaries and ownership** – A brief description of who owns the land. If special permission or permits are needed to access the site, note this. Include local contact names and phone numbers, if appropriate. Briefly describe habitat at the site.

2. **Focal species using the site and timing of use** – Describe shorebird use of the site including species, numbers, and timing.

3. **Location of Type 1 and 2 habitat within the site** – Delineate the areas used most intensively by birds (Type 1 habitat) and areas used less frequently but often enough to warrant occasional surveys (Type 2 habitat). Try to define these areas so that >75% of the bird-days are in Type 1 habitat and >20% of the bird days are in Type 2 habitat.

4. **Access to Type 1 and 2 habitat and the visibility of the birds** – Describe access to the site, including observation points, boat access and permission requirements. Identify any areas that are inaccessible. Describe problems with seeing all birds during a survey, if any. If visibility is different for different species note this (e.g. "large waders are easily detected, but distances are too great to accurately identify smaller waders").

5. **Past and current surveys** – Briefly describe past or current surveys at the site. Summarize any available survey data briefly.

6a. **Potential survey methods: description** – Identify and describe the best methods for surveying the site. Consider access, visibility and past survey results. Consider differences in survey methods among seasons, if appropriate. Consider when during the day surveys should be conducted. In general, all surveys in a site should be made during a single period. Timing of surveys is especially important at tidal sites but may be important at other sites due to the sun or other factors. Note that if the number of birds present varies rapidly, as is often the case with tidal areas, then the survey period should be brief. Otherwise, surveyors may gradually learn when surveys will yield the highest counts and may be tempted to visit at these times.

6b. **Potential survey methods: selection bias** – If some areas are not accessible, then discuss whether density in surveyable portions of the site may differ from the site-wide density and, if so, whether long-term trends might occur in the ratio: (density in the surveyable area)/(overall density). Any such trend will cause bias in the trend estimate. Consider whether occasional surveys might be conducted (e.g. from the air) of the entire site.

6c. **Potential survey methods: measurement error and bias** – Missing birds cause measurement error; a trend in the proportion of birds that are missed causes measurement bias. Discuss the potential for measurement bias and ways to minimize it (e.g. by intensive surveys on a sub-sample of plots).

7. **Needed Pilot Studies** – Identify any information needed to complete the sampling plan.

---

In such a case, three matrix strata might be distinguished. Sampling frames, following this approach, have been developed for the east coast of the United States (see http://www.shorebird-world.org/fromthefield/PRISM/PRISM1.htm) and several western States and areas (e.g. see http://www.gbbo.org/abc_maps.htm), and work in several other States is proceeding. A comprehensive list of designated sites and matrix strata is in the final stages of preparation for the continental United States.

Detailed guidelines have also been prepared for developing site-specific survey methods (Table 1). The guidelines include a description of the site (boundaries, habitat, ownership, access), species likely to be encountered, and survey methods. Particular attention is given, in the survey methods section, to the potential for selection bias (because some portions of the site are inaccessible), measurement error (because some birds in surveyed areas are not detectable), and measurement bias (because a long-term trend exists in the proportion of the birds detected). A final section identifies any pilot studies needed before the surveys can be fully designed. Examples of site descriptions are provided in Bart *et al.* (2005c) and at the internet sites above.

## SURVEYS ON THE WINTERING GROUNDS

Extensive surveys of wintering shorebirds have been carried out by Morrison *et al.* (1998) and Morrison & Ross (1989), and some species-specific surveys have been conducted. Most of this work preceded the formation of PRISM, or has been carried out independently of it. An exception is the detailed survey, mentioned above, of American Oystercatchers, carried out as part of PRISM by the Manomet Center for Conservation and colleagues (Brown *et al.* 2005). A comprehensive strategy for surveying shorebirds on their wintering grounds is still needed, and will need to be developed cooperatively with countries that would host these surveys. Collaboration between those who have developed PRISM and organizers of the Wetlands International mid-winter waterbird counts would be especially valuable. Such discussions should include the possibility of expanding those counts into the USA and Canada.

## ACKNOWLEDGMENTS

PRISM has been developed by dozens of shorebird experts and hundreds of dedicated technicians during the past five years. Reviews by S. Skagen and V. Johnston helped improve the manuscript. My work on PRISM has been supported by the US Geological Survey, the US Fish and Wildlife Service, and the Canadian Wildlife Service.

## REFERENCES

Aubry, Y., Bart, J., Johnston, V., Ross, K., Sinclair, P., Smith, P. & Tibbits, L. 2004. Boreal shorebirds: An assessment of conservation status and potential for population monitoring. Unpublished report by the Canadian Wildlife Service available from Pam.Sinclair@ec.gc.ca

Bart, J. & Earnst, S.L. 2002. Double sampling to estimate bird density and population trends. Auk: 119: 36-45.

Bart, J. & Earnst, S.L. 2005. Methods for shorebird surveys in the arctic. In: C.J. Ralph & T.R. Rich (eds.) Proceedings of the third international Partners in Flight International Symposium. US Forest Service, General Technical Report, Arcata, California, USA.

Bart, J., Andres, B., Brown, S., Donaldson, G., Harrington, B.,

Johnston, V., Jones, S., Morrison, R.I.G. & Skagen, S. 2005a. The Program for Regional and International Shorebird Monitoring (PRISM). In: C.J. Ralph & T. R. Rich (eds.) Proceedings of the third international Partners in Flight International Symposium. US Forest Service, General Technical Report, Arcata, California, USA.

Bart, J., Andres, B., Brown, S., Donaldson, G.M., Johnston, V., McCaffrey, B., Morrison, R.I.G., Smith, P.A. & Wightman, C. 2005b. Design of long-term surveys for shorebirds in the arctic. Unpublished manuscript available from jon_bart@usgs.gov.

Bart, J., Manning, A., Thomas, S. & Wightman, C. 2005c. Preparation of Regional Shorebird Monitoring Plans. In: C.J. Ralph & T.R. Rich (eds.) Proceedings of the third international Partners in Flight International Symposium. US Forest Service, General Technical Report, Arcata, California, USA.

Brown, S., Hickey, C., Harrington, B. & Gill, R. (eds.). 2001. United States Shorebird Conservation Plan, second edition. Manomet Center for Conservation Sciences, Manomet, Massachusetts, USA.

Brown, S.C., Schulte, S., Harrington, B., Winn, B., Bart, J. & Howe, M. 2005. Population size and winter distribution of eastern North American oystercatchers. Journal of Wildlife Management. 69(4): 1538-1545.

CAVM Team 2003. Circumpolar Arctic Vegetation Map. Scale 1:7 500 000. Conservation of Arctic Flora and Fauna (CAFF) Map No. 1. U.S. Fish and Wildlife Service, Anchorage, Alaska.

Donaldson, G.M., Hyslop, C., Morrison, R.I.G., Dickson, H.L. & Davidson, I. (eds.). 2001. Canadian Shorebird Conservation Plan. Canadian Wildlife Service, Ottawa, Canada.

Howe, M.A., Geissler, P.A. & Harrington, B.A. 1989. Population trends of North American shorebirds based on the International Shorebird Survey. Biological Conservation 49: 185-199.

Morrison, R.I.G. & Ross, R.K. 1989. Atlas of Nearctic shorebirds on the coast of South America. Two volumes. Canadian Wildlife Service, Ontario, Canada.

Morrison, R.I.G., Downes, C. & Collins, B. 1994. Population trends of shorebirds on fall migration in eastern Canada 1974-1991. Wilson Bulletin 106: 431-447.

Morrison, R.I.G., Butler, R.W., Delgado, F.S. & Ross, R.K. 1998. Atlas of Nearctic shorebirds and other waterbirds on the coast of Panama. Canadian Wildlife Service, Special Publication, Ottawa, Ontario, Canada.

Morrison, R.I.G., Aubry, Y. , Butler, R.W., Beyersbergen, G.W., Donaldson, G.M., Gratto-Trevor, C.L., Hicklin, P.W., Johnston, V.H. & Ross, R.K. 2001. Declines in North American shorebird populations. Wader Study Group Bulletin 94: 34-38.

NABCI 2000. North American Bird Conservation Initiative: Bringing it all together. U.S. Fish and Wildlife Service, Arlington, Virginia, USA.

Skagen, S.K., Bart, J., Andres, B., Brown, S., Donaldson, G., Harrington, B., Johnston, V., Jones, S.L. & Morrison, R.I.G. 2004. Monitoring the shorebirds of North America: towards a unified approach. Wader Study Group Bulletin 100: 102-104.

# The UK Waterbirds Alerts System

*Graham E. Austin, Ilya M.D. Maclean, Philip W. Atkinson & Mark M. Rehfisch*
*British Trust for Ornithology, The Nunnery, Thetford, IP24 2PU, UK.  (email: Graham.Austin@bto.org)*

Austin, G.E., Maclean, I.M.D., Atkinson, P.W. & Rehfisch, M.M.  2006.  The UK Waterbirds Alerts System. *Waterbirds around the world*.  Eds. G.C. Boere, C.A. Galbraith & D.A. Stroud.  The Stationery Office, Edinburgh, UK.  pp. 705-710.

## ABSTRACT

The UK hosts internationally important numbers of waterbirds, and to conserve and manage these populations effective monitoring protocols are needed. The Alerts System, by adopting a standardized method for identifying the direction and magnitude of changes in waterbird numbers at a range of spatial and temporal scales, provides an effective means of doing so. The system makes use of generalized additive models (GAMs) to produce smoothed indices of abundance, and is applied to assess trends at several spatial and temporal scales. To flag population changes, High and Medium Alerts are issued if population declines exceed 50% and 25%, respectively. Several of the key findings from the most recent Alerts analysis are presented.

## INTRODUCTION

Waterbirds, perhaps more than any other taxonomic group, have been used to select areas for conservation. Their sensitivity to environmental change, the relative ease with which they can be counted and their tendency to congregate at key locations make them effective proxies for aspects of wider biodiversity (Stroud *et al.* 2001). The UK holds internationally important numbers of non-breeding waterbirds (Stroud *et al.* 2001). Whilst some of these individuals breed within the UK, many originate from breeding areas in the Arctic and are attracted in such large numbers by the combination of relatively mild winters and extensive areas of inter-tidal mudflats (Davidson *et al.* 1991). Protecting these species is a high conservation priority, and the UK Government has agreed to international obligations to do so (Stroud *et al.* 2001). For example, the European Union's Directive on the conservation of wild birds (EC/79/409) requires Member States to take a range of actions to sustain bird populations, and includes establishing and maintaining a national network of sites, known as Special Protection Areas (SPAs) (Stroud *et al.* 2001). Numerous wetland sites have been designated on the basis of the number of waterbirds they contain, and there are legal obligations to ensure that their favourable status is maintained (Stroud *et al.* 2001).

The monitoring of wildlife populations is essential if they, and the sites on which they depend, are to be managed and conserved effectively (Greenwood *et al.* 1995). However, conservation resources are finite and effective means of identifying priorities are needed. One way in which this can be achieved is to monitor population changes at a variety of spatial and temporal scales. Through this process, resources can be targeted towards protecting the most threatened species and areas. In Britain, numbers of wintering waterbirds have been recorded as part of a national scheme called the Wetland Birds Survey (WeBS). This scheme has been in place since the winter of 1947/48, and coverage similar to that seen today has been maintained for over 35 years, providing one of the largest and most detailed, long-running biological data sets available.

The Alerts System was developed to provide a standardized method of identifying the direction and magnitude of changes in numbers at a variety of spatial and temporal scales for a range of waterbird species for which sufficient WeBS data are available. Species that have undergone major changes in numbers can then be flagged by issuing an Alert. Alerts are intended to be advisory and, subject to interpretation, should be used as a basis on which to direct research and subsequent conservation efforts if required.

## DATA COLLECTION METHODS

Waterbird data used in the calculation of Alerts are collected by a network of counters as part of the WeBS scheme (Pollit *et al.* 2003). This scheme is an amalgamation of two previous long-term monitoring schemes, the Birds of Estuaries Enquiry (BoEE) and the National Wildfowl Count Scheme (NWC), and aims to identify important sites and monitor changes in numbers and distribution of divers, grebes, cormorants, herons, wildfowl, rails, waders, gulls, terns and kingfishers in the UK, contributing data also to the International Waterbird Census. Whilst WeBS data are collected using several counting schemes, only data from counts termed "Core Counts" are currently used to calculate Alerts. Core Counts are made at approximately 2 000 wetland sites in both coastal and inland locations around the UK. Typically, these are conducted monthly on a synchronized date, and coastal sites are usually counted at high-tide. Whilst a wide variety of wetland habitats are included in the Core Count scheme, a large proportion of the total area covered consists of estuaries and large still waters of which over 70% are covered nationally. Many of the sites included in the scheme are, or have been proposed as, Ramsar sites, SPAs, or Sites or Areas of Special Scientific Interest (SSSIs/ASSIs).

## SPECIES AND SITE COVERAGE

The WeBS Alerts System is concerned solely with highlighting changes in the abundance of waterbirds outside the breeding season. The type of habitat in which many of these species breed is not covered by the WeBS scheme, and WeBS data from the breeding season are therefore generally not suitable for determining changes in the numbers of breeding waterbirds. Wildfowl (Anatidae) data have been collected from the majority of English, Scottish and Welsh sites since the winter of 1966/67, with wader (shorebird) data available from 1969/70. Earlier, less nationally complete counts date back to the winter of 1947/48, although these data have not been computerized. The survey was extended to include the Common Coot *Fulica atra* and Great Crested Grebe *Podiceps cristatus* from 1983/84, the Little Grebe *Tachybaptus ruficollis* from 1985/86 and the Great Cormorant *Phalacrocorax carbo* from 1986/87. Wader numbers have been recorded from sites in Northern Ireland since 1970/71, with numbers of other waterbirds recorded since

**Table 1. List of species currently included in WeBS Alerts analysis.**

| |
|---|
| Little Grebe *Tachybaptus ruficollis* |
| Great Crested Grebe *Podiceps cristatus* |
| Great Cormorant *Phalacrocorax carbo* |
| Little Egret *Egretta garzetta* |
| Bewick's Swan *Cygnus columbianus bewickii* |
| Whooper Swan *Cygnus cygnus* |
| European White-fronted Goose *Anser albifrons albifrons* |
| Dark-bellied Brent Goose *Branta bernicla bernicla* |
| Light-bellied Brent Goose (Canada/Greenland population) *Branta bernicla hrota* |
| Light-bellied Brent Goose (Svalbard population) *Branta bernicla hrota* |
| Common Shelduck *Tadorna tadorna* |
| Eurasian Wigeon *Anas penelope* |
| Gadwall *Anas strepera* |
| Common Teal *Anas crecca* |
| Mallard *Anas platyrhynchos* |
| Northern Pintail *Anas acuta* |
| Northern Shoveler *Anas clypeata* |
| Common Pochard *Aythya ferina* |
| Tufted Duck *Aythya fuligula* |
| Greater Scaup *Aythya marila* |
| Common Eider *Somateria mollissima* |
| Common Scoter *Melanitta nigra* |
| Velvet Scoter *Melanitta fusca* |
| Common Goldeneye *Bucephala clangula* |
| Red-breasted Merganser *Mergus serrator* |
| Goosander *Mergus merganser* |
| Common Coot *Fulica atra* |
| Eurasian Oystercatcher *Haematopus ostralegus* |
| Pied Avocet *Recurvirostra avosetta* |
| Common Ringed Plover *Charadrius hiaticula* |
| Eurasian Golden Plover *Pluvialis apricaria* |
| Grey Plover *Pluvialis squatarola* |
| Northern Lapwing *Vanellus vanellus* |
| Black-tailed Godwit *Limosa limosa* |
| Bar-tailed Godwit *Limosa lapponica* |
| Eurasian Curlew *Numenius arquata* |
| Common Redshank *Tringa totanus* |
| Ruddy Turnstone *Arenaria interpres* |
| Red Knot *Calidris canutus* |
| Sanderling *Calidris alba* |
| Dunlin *Calidris alpina* |
| Ruff *Philomachus pugnax* |

1986/87. Of the species recorded during WeBS "Core Counts", 40 (plus two additional populations of the Brent Goose *Branta bernicla*) are encountered frequently enough for inclusion in the Alerts System when considering national alerts. These are given in Table 1.

The numbers of some species of geese are not well monitored by monthly WeBS core counts and thus are not included.

Other waterbird species, including the Slavonian Grebe *Podiceps auritus*, Great Bittern *Botaurus stellaris* and Long-tailed Duck *Clangula hyemalis*, which, although recorded by WeBS, are either encountered too infrequently or in numbers too small from which to derive trends.

In addition to analysis of national trends, if possible, SPAs and SSSIs of importance for over-wintering waterbirds are assessed annually. Currently, sufficient data are available to assess trends on 68 SPAs and 26 SSSIs. A number of SPAs and many SSSIs cannot be assessed because count data for all cited species were unavailable or largely incomplete. Additionally, a few SPAs and many SSSIs cannot be assessed until ongoing work on establishing coincidence between WeBS count-sector boundaries and designated site boundaries has been completed. The areas surveyed during WeBS "Core Counts" at WeBS sites are matched as accurately as possible to designated site boundaries. Where WeBS count-sectors and SPA boundaries do not coincide, the optimum match is assessed. In many cases, there may be practical reasons for discrepancy. For example, most WeBS counts of estuaries are made at high tide because birds can be more reliably counted as they arrive or when they settle at roost, whereas some statutory site boundaries only encompass the inter-tidal habitat and exclude the adjoining areas where such roosts form. When birds are distributed across large expanses of inter-tidal flats, it can be extremely difficult to assess numbers accurately.

For each site, the species considered are those for which the site is important and thus for which decreases in numbers give cause for particular concern to conservationists. The suite of species was derived from Stroud *et al.* (2001), ignoring those cited as qualifying in a SPA due to important passage or breeding numbers. This selection process applies principally to SPAs. In the case of SSSIs, sites have often been designated for their "general waterbird interest" without specific information regarding the species composition being readily available. Consequently, species for SSSI assessment were selected on the basis that they were either listed specifically within the valid citation, or are likely to be a component of an undefined assemblage, such as "wintering waterfowl" listed in the citation.

## DATA ANALYSES
### Calculating annual indices
The index value for a particular winter is the number of birds present in that winter (summed monthly counts) expressed relative to the number of birds present in the most recent winter used in data analysis. Annual indices are calculated using count data collected between September and March, and within this period, the months for which the numbers of a given species are at their most stable are those used. This period differs between species, and further details can be found in Maclean *et al.* (2005). The same period is adopted for the assessment of Alert status.

Since it is often the case that sites do not contain complete time-series of count data, the Underhill indexing method (Underhill & Prŷs-Jones 1994) is used to estimate missing counts. The Underhill indexing method essentially imputes missing observations using other completed counts, but taking account of trends occurring elsewhere. These values are incorporated into the index, and serve as a complete data matrix for input into the General Additive Models used to generate smoothed trends.

## Calculating smoothed trends

Natural temporary fluctuations in numbers can differ in size and/or direction from longer-term trends, hindering their interpretation. Extreme values may trigger false Alerts due to misinterpretation of temporary, short-term declines as longer-term trends. Alternatively, long-term trends that may have led to Alerts being flagged could be obscured by short-term fluctuations. In order to avoid such misinterpretations and misidentifications when calculating Alerts, the Alerts System uses general additive models (GAMs) (Hastie & Tibshirani 1990) to fit a smoothed trend curve to the annual indices. The degree of smoothing depends on the number of degrees of freedom available to the GAMs. As the number of degrees of freedom is decreased from ($n$ -1), which would be identical to the Underhill index provided data are complete, the trend become increasingly smooth until ultimately with one degree of freedom the smoothed curve becomes a linear fit. The WeBS Alert System adopts a standard $n/3$ degrees of freedom (rounded up to the nearest integer) to produce a level of smoothing that, while removing temporary fluctuations not likely to be representative of long-term trends, captures those aspects of the trends that may be considered to be important (Atkinson *et al.* 2006).

Changes in numbers calculated using values from a smoothed GAM trend are less likely to be due to the effects of temporary fluctuations in numbers, or to counting errors, than results produced were annual index values to be used. Thus, the use of GAMs reduces the probability that a decline from a short-lived unsustainable peak in numbers would be responsible for triggering an Alert. A decline from a period of sustained high numbers, however, would trigger an Alert using GAMs, and clearly would be worthy of investigation. It should be noted that, because a standard degree of smoothing has been applied across all species and spatial scales, the arithmetic derivation could trigger alerts for species showing large year-to-year fluctuations in numbers. In these cases, knowledge of their ecology and population dynamics is essential for correct interpretation. This is addressed partially by the WeBS Alerts Biological Filter, the purpose of which is to fine tune the general rule for triggering an Alert in a species-specific manner.

## Biological filters

The smoothing used to produce the fitted trends goes some way towards preventing alerts being triggered when apparent decreases are due to natural fluctuations in numbers between winters. However, because the degree of smoothing has been standardized across all species, spatial scales and locations, it can be expected to achieve better results for some species than others. Rather than sustain the considerable extra processing costs that would be necessary to assess individually the optimal degree of smoothing for each species / spatial scale / location combination (itself is a process with a degree of subjectivity attached to it), a "biological filter" has been applied to reduce the chance of triggering false Alerts.

The aim of the biological filter is to attach a cautionary note to alerts being triggered when the observed decline for a given period is not uncharacteristic of that which might occur occurring due to inherent fluctuations exhibited by some species. The biological filter takes into account a number of aspects of the population dynamics and behaviour of each species that can be expected to affect the observed level of fluctuation. Several sources of information are used to assess this. Full details are given in Maclean *et al.* (2005), but a brief summary is given here.

To address the issue of varying population stability amongst species, the mean absolute percentage change between subsequent winters has been calculated. Species have been assigned a *Fluctuation Score*, based on this value, such that those which show higher annual fluctuations scored low and stable species scored high. To address the issue of expected links between longevity and the degree of annual fluctuation, species have been assigned a *Longevity Score* by using ringing recovery data. Those which are longer-lived have been scored high, whereas shorter-lived species have been score low. To address the issue of site-faithfulness between winters, ringing data have been used to assign a *Between Winter Movement Score*, based on the median distance of movements between winters. Site-faithful species have been scored highly, whereas highly mobile species are assigned a low score. To address the issue of site faithfulness within winters, ringing data have again been used to assign a *Within Winter Movement Score*. This was based on the median distance of within winter movements, such that site-faithful species scored high, whereas highly mobile species scored low. In all instances, only data from the UK are used. The overall *Biological Filter Score* (BFS) is calculated by summing the four contributing scores. In instances where contributing scores cannot be calculated, the maximum value (2) was used, thus adopting a conservative approach ensuring that no species is down-graded due to lack of information. Thus each species was assigned a BFS of between 0 and 8, with short-lived and/or fluctuating and/or highly mobile species being assigned the lowest score.

## Calculating Alerts

Proportional changes in the smoothed GAM trend in numbers over short-term (5-year), medium-term (10-year), long-term (25-year) and since site designation (variable) time-frames are calculated by subtracting the smoothed GAM trend value at the start of the time-frame from the smoothed GAM trend value in the penultimate winter. The final winter is not used, as GAMs have a tendency to exhibit disproportional upward or downward inflections at either end of the time-series used. Where data are not available for a 25-year period, the longest possible period (second to penultimate winter) is used instead. Calculated change values are expressed as a percentage of the index at the start of the period. Larger values therefore indicate larger proportional changes in numbers, with positive values equating to relative increases in the numbers, and negative values equating to relative decreases over the specified time period. These values are then categorized according to their magnitude and direction. Declines of between 25% and 50% inclusive are flagged as Medium Alerts and declines of greater than 50% as High Alerts. In order to facilitate comparison of decreases and increases in numbers, increases of between 33% and 100% are described as Medium increases, whilst increases of greater than 100% are described as High increases. This accommodates the fact that proportionally greater increases are required to return numbers to their former level following a given decrease.

The Biological Filter Score is then applied to provide a cautionary flag where required. For those species with a BFS of eight, cautionary flags are not applied. For those species with a

BFS of six or seven, cautionary flags are applied to short-term Medium Alerts. For those species with a BSF of four or five, cautionary flags are applied to short-term Alerts. For those species with a BSF of less than four, cautionary flags are applied except when medium and long-term High Alerts are issued.

After Biological Filter Scores have been applied, Alerts are considered at various spatial scales. All species currently included in the WeBS Alerts scheme are considered for Great Britain and Northern Ireland. Country-wide trends for each of Wales, England and Scotland are also considered for each species. The suite of species for which site trends are evaluated is restricted to those for which a designated site is considered important during the winter and for which there were sufficient data for evaluation. Regional trends are also calculated to enable comparison with site trends. To aid such comparisons, the proportions of both the regional and national populations hosted by each site are also calculated. This process goes some way to enabling downward trends driven by large-scale population or regional population shifts to be distinguished from those driven by adverse conditions on site.

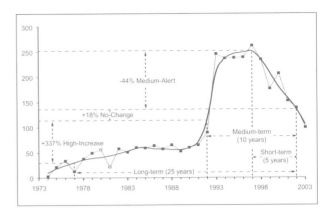

**Fig. 1.** Example of a plot generated by the WeBS Alerts analysis (Grey Plover *Pluvialis squatarola* on the Firth of Forth). The smoothed GAM trend shows a long-term high increase, a short-term decline triggering a Medium Alert, and no change in the medium term. The site was designated as an SPA in 2001, so insufficient time has elapsed to establish any meaningful change in the population trend over this period.

## WHAT HAS WEBS ALERTS SHOWN US?
### National population changes

The most recent Alerts analyses (Maclean *et al.* 2005) has revealed that High Alerts have been triggered for three species and Medium Alerts for a further three species. In the long term,

the smoothed trend reveals that the Bewick's Swan *Cygnus columbianus bewickii*, European White-fronted Geese *Anser albifrons albifrons* and Ruff *Philomachus pugnax* have all undergone declines of more than 50% and thus High Alerts have been triggered. The Mallard *Anas platyrhynchos* has undergone a

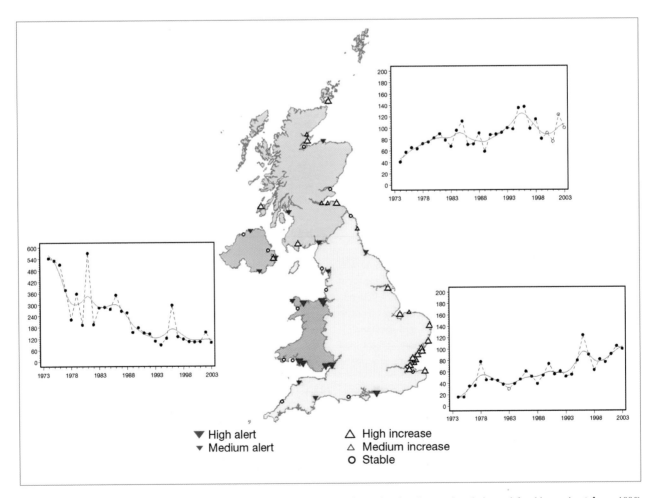

▼ High alert
▼ Medium alert

△ High increase
△ Medium increase
O Stable

**Fig. 2.** Long-term trends in the number of Common Ringed Plover *Charadrius hiaticula* wintering on sites designated for this species (△ - >100% increase; △ - 50-100% increase; O - no change; ▼ - 25-50% decrease; ▼ - >50% decrease). Regional trends are also shown. In the long term, numbers have decreased in Wales and the south of England, and increased in Scotland and the east of England. The apparent shift in the population has been attributed to climate change.

decline of greater than 25%, triggering a Medium Alert. The Whooper Swan *Cygnus cygnus*, Eurasian Wigeon *Anas penelope*, Common Teal *A. crecca*, Common Eider *Somateria mollissima*, Common Goldeneye *Bucephala clangula*, Goosander *Mergus merganser* and Eurasian Coot have undergone moderate increases, and the Light-bellied Brent Goose *B. b. hrota* (Svalbard population), Gadwall *Anas strepera*, Greater Scaup *Aythya marila*, Pied Avocet *Recurvirostra avosetta*, Northern Lapwing *Vanellus vanellus*, Eurasian Golden Plover *Pluvialis apricaria*, Grey Plover *P. squatarola* and Black-tailed Godwit *Limosa limosa* have all undergone large increases. In the medium term, High Alerts have been triggered for Bewick's Swan and European White-fronted Goose, and Medium Alerts for Dark-bellied Brent Goose *B. b. bernicla* and Common Shelduck *Tadorna tadorna*. The Little Grebe, Gadwall, Eurasian Golden Plover and Black-tailed Godwit have undergone moderate increases, and the Light-bellied Brent Goose (Svalbard population) and Pied Avocet have undergone large increases. In the short term, High Alerts have been triggered for the Bewick's Swan and European White-fronted Goose, and a Medium Alert has been triggered for the Goosander. The Pied Avocet has undergone moderate increases and the Little Egret *Egretta garzetta* has undergone large increases. Some species, such as Little Egret (which has undoubtedly increased in the long term), have not been monitored by WeBS for sufficiently long to examine population trends over all time periods. It is noteworthy that several species, such as the Grey Plover (Fig. 1), have undergone short-term declines or increases against a background of long-term directional changes in the opposite direction. Such examples serve to illustrate the need to determine trends over a range of time periods.

## Large-scale population shifts

The Alerts System has also been instrumental in highlighting several species which have undergone marked re-distributions in their populations. For example, a number of wader species have undergone declines in the west of the UK, but are increasing in the east (Fig. 2). Such patterns, revealed through Alerts analyses at the site level but examined at larger spatial scales, have sometimes been the catalyst for further research. For example, it is now well established that population shifts first revealed through the Alerts process have occurred in response to climate change (Rehfisch *et al.* 2004, Austin & Rehfisch 2005, Rehfisch & Austin 2006). On average, estuaries on the south and east coasts of Britain have muddier sediments than those on the west coast, and thus support a higher biomass of invertebrate prey for waders. With the warming of winter temperatures by 1.5°C since the mid-1980s, the risk of weather-induced mortality on the colder east coast estuaries has diminished, and consequently populations have shifted in the expected easterly direction (Austin & Rehfisch 2005, Rehfisch & Austin 2006).

## Site-level changes

One of the primary aims of the Alerts System and subsequent reporting has been to establish important changes in waterbird numbers occurring on the UK's network of wetland and coastal SPAs. Numerous alerts have been triggered at the site level, but not all of these are indicative of unfavourable conditions at the site (Maclean *et al.* 2005). However, similar trends occurring within groups of species with closely related resource require-

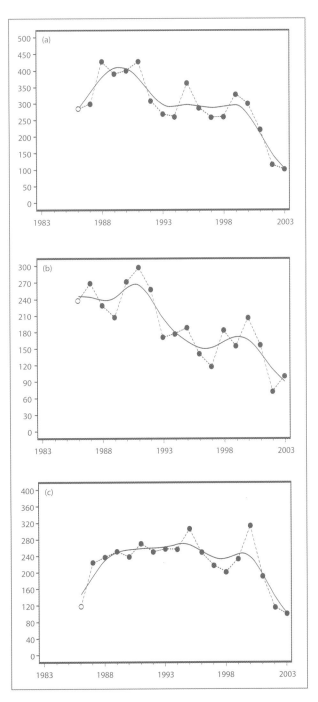

**Fig. 3.** Trends in the numbers of Common Pochard *Aythya ferina* (a), Tufted Duck *A. fuligula* (b), and Common Goldeneye *Bucephala clangula* (c) over-wintering on Lough Neagh and Lough Beg. In the short term particularly, all three species have undergone major declines, with recent analysis suggesting climate-change-related distributional shifts (Allen *et al.* 2004).

ments can be a useful indicator that such sites may be experiencing problems. For example, in the most recent Alerts analyses, one of the most dramatic revelations has been the plight of diving ducks over-wintering on the Lough Neagh and Beg SPA. This site hosts nationally and internationally important numbers of the Common Pochard *Aythya ferina*, Tufted Duck *A. fuligula* and Common Goldeneye. Upwards of 25 000 Common Pochard, over 7.5% of the North-east and North-west European wintering population (Stroud *et al.* 2001) and over 50% of the UK population (Pollitt *et al.* 2003), were regularly recorded at this site during the early 1990s. In a relatively short period of time (as revealed by the triggering of a short-term High Alert), the population has crashed and now numbers less than 7 000. Similar decreases have also been observed in the numbers of Tufted Duck and Common Goldeneye (Fig. 3). Recent detailed analysis triggered by these declines suggest that the declines are probably linked to climate-change related distributional shifts (Allen *et al.* 2004).

## CONCLUSIONS

The monitoring of wildlife populations and the sites on which they depend is an essential component of effective conservation management. The need to conserve and manage waterbird populations is evident, given the number of international treaties which place emphasis on waterbird populations. The Alerts System, by providing a standardized method for identifying the direction and magnitude of changes in waterbird numbers, provides one means of monitoring waterbird populations, and has already been instrumental in highlighting a range of conservation priorities.

## ACKNOWLEDGEMENTS

The monitoring of waterbird populations would not be possible without the combined efforts of the numerous volunteers who supply data. Our thanks also to Helen Baker, Peter Cranswick, Mel Kershaw, James Robinson, Rowena Langstone, David Stroud and Chris van Turnhout, who have all been instrumental in the development of the Alerts protocol. The Wetland Bird Survey is jointly organized by the British Trust for Ornithology, The Wildfowl and Wetlands Trust, the Royal Society for the Protection of Birds and the Joint Nature Conservation Committee (the latter on behalf of English Nature, Scottish Natural Heritage, Countryside Council for Wales, and Environment and Heritage Service in Northern Ireland).

## REFERENCES

Allen, D., Mellon, C., Enlander, I., & Watson, G. 2004. Lough Neagh diving ducks: recent changes in wintering populations. Irish Birds 7: 327-336.

Atkinson, P.W., Austin, G.E., Rehfisch, M.M., Baker, H., Cranswick, P., Kershaw, M., Robinson, J., Langston, R.H.W., Stroud, D.A., van Turnhout, C. & Maclean, I.M.D. 2006. Identifying declines in waterbirds: the effects of missing data, population variability and count period on the interpretation of long-term survey data. Biological Conservation 130: 549-559.

Austin, G.E. & Rehfisch, M.M. 2005. Shifting nonbreeding distributions of migratory fauna in relation to climate change. Global Change Biology 11: 31-38.

Davidson, N.C., Lafoley, D.d'A., Doody, J.P., Way, L.S., Gordon, J., Key, R., Drake, C.M., Pienkowski, M.W., Mitchell, R. & Duff, K.L. 1991. Nature conservation and estuaries in Britain. Nature Conservancy Council, Peterborough, UK.

Greenwood, J.J.D., Baillie, S.R., Gregory, R.D., Peach, W.J. & Fuller, R.J. 1995. Some new approaches to conservation monitoring of British breeding birds. Ibis 137, Supplement 1: S16-S28.

Hastie, T.J. & Tibshirani, R.J. 1990. Generalized additive models. Chapman & Hall, London.

Maclean, I.M.D., Austin, G.E., Mellan, H.J. & Girling, T. 2005. WeBS Alerts 2003/2004: Changes in numbers of wintering waterbirds in the United Kingdom, its Constituent Countries, Special Protected Areas (SPAs) and Sites of Special Scientific Interest (SSSIs). BTO Research Report No. 416 to the WeBS partnership. BTO, Thetford, UK. Available at: http://blx1.bto.org/webs/alerts/index.htm.

Pollitt, M.S., Hall, C., Holloway, S.J., Hearn, R.D., Marshall, P.E., Musgrove, A.J., Robinson, J.A. & Cranswick, P.A. 2003. The Wetland Bird Survey 2000-01: Wildfowl and Wader Counts. BTO/WWT/RSPB/JNCC, Slimbridge, UK.

Rehfisch, M.M. & Austin, G.E. 2006. Climate change and coastal waterbirds: the United Kingdom experience reviewed. Waterbirds around the world. G.C. Boere, C.A. Galbraith & D.A. Stroud (Eds.), The Stationery Office, Edinburgh, UK. 398-404.

Rehfisch, M.M., Austin, G.E., Freeman, S.N., Armitage, M.J.S. & Burton, N.H.K. 2004. The possible impact of climate change on the future distributions of waders on Britain's non-estuarine coast. Ibis 146: S70-81.

Stroud, D.A., Chambers, D., Cook, S., Buxton, N., Fraser, B., Clement, P., Lewis, P., McLean, I., Baker, H. & Whitehead, S. (eds.). 2001. The UK SPA network: its scope and content. Three volumes. JNCC, Peterborough, UK. Available at http://www.jncc.gov.uk/UKSPA/default.htm.

Underhill, L.G. & Prŷs-Jones, R. 1994. Index numbers for waterbird populations. I. Review and methodology. Journal of Applied Ecology 31: 463-480.

Recent analyses of UK waterbird monitoring data has highlighted the shifting distributions of a number of species including Ringed Plovers *Charadrius hiaticula* and which have been attributed to changing climate. Recent decreases in eastern England have coincided with increases further east and north elsewhere in Europe. Photo: Paul Marshall.

# Biological planning for bird conservation at the landscape scale: developing shared conservation strategies in the United States

*Rex R. Johnson, Seth E. Mott & David A. Smith*

*Division of Bird Habitat Conservation, U.S. Fish and Wildlife Service, 4401 N. Fairfax Drive, Arlington, Virginia 22203, USA.*

Johnson, R.R., Mott, S.E. & Smith, D.A. 2006. Biological planning for bird conservation at the landscape scale: developing shared conservation strategies in the United States. *Waterbirds around the world.* Eds. G.C. Boere, C.A. Galbraith & D.A. Stroud. The Stationery Office, Edinburgh, UK. pp. 711-716.

## ABSTRACT

The magnitude of the challenge of conserving the full spectrum of migratory birds and their habitats dwarfs traditional wildlife management resources. To be successful, partnerships of government agencies and non-governmental organizations require explicit estimates of habitat objectives that are adequate to fulfill population conservation mandates, and cost-effective conservation strategies that are based on a systematic application of the best available science, and are therefore credible. In the United States, biological planning partnerships are an increasingly common means of developing shared visions and strategies for the community of conservation implementers. Biological planning is founded on the use of models describing population-habitat relationships, and the application of models to spatial data to reflect consensus-based management decision processes. An example of model-based biological planning is presented that illustrate how its use can: (1) increase management efficiency; (2) yield transparent and defensible conservation strategies; (3) serve as a framework for identifying and prioritizing among management information needs; (4) enable development of coordinated conservation strategies for multiple groups of wildlife; and (5) direct habitat restoration conducted with programs seeking diverse environmental and socio-economic benefits, but for which wildlife benefits are secondary goals, thereby enhancing the impact of these programs on bird populations.

## INTRODUCTION

The mandate to conserve bird populations in perpetuity is vast. Compared to this mandate, legal authorities and funding appropriated for habitat conservation are severely limited. In the United States, natural resource management agencies preside over a slow but inexorable deterioration of environmental function, including the capacity to sustain populations of most species. The challenges we face demand new approaches to the conservation enterprise – approaches based on applied science, coordinated conservation, and the cooperative communication of compelling conservation strategies.

The purpose of this paper is to illustrate (1) the importance of partnerships in affecting conservation at landscape-scales, and (2), more specifically, the role of biological planning in forging these partnerships and insuring that our collective conservation actions are effective and efficient. This paper is not intended to be a comprehensive description of the process of biological planning and evaluation, or of the diverse literature on various aspects of this iterative process.

## CONSERVATION PARTNERSHIPS

In the U.S., political boundaries – among states and various government programs – have contributed to a traditionally frag-mented and piecemeal approach to conservation with needs expressed implicitly rather than explicitly. Our challenge in the conservation of migratory birds is to coalesce the pieces of the conservation puzzle vested in diverse agencies into a comprehensive international, multi-agency strategy for conservation. When a conservation strategy is developed and implemented through partnerships, it reflects a community vision, with each partner committing their programs and influence with external entities to delivering components of the whole.

One challenge in developing a community conservation strategy is that partners' jurisdictional boundaries often do not conform to a common theme. Most are based on states or aggregates of states. This facilitates program management but is not particularly conducive to the strategic management of populations and habitats. In the U.S., the geographic currency of partnerships is joint ventures initially formed under the banner of the North American Waterfowl Management Plan. Aligned along ecological boundaries, thereby transcending political barriers, joint ventures are partnerships of government agencies, non-governmental organizations, and others whose purpose is the efficient conservation of migratory birds.

Joint ventures are only valuable to the extent that they enable conservation that exceeds the sum of the potential actions of the individual agencies and organizations that comprise them. Joint ventures are uniquely structured to capture this added value. An ideal joint venture is comprised of two parts – a management board and a biological planning and evaluation team. The biological planning and evaluation team is charged with developing a science-based community conservation strategy. The role of management board members is to exert influence on the political process, and to shape how government agencies deliver their programs, to support implementation of the community strategy. Through this dual structure, joint ventures position themselves as a nexus for information between the scientific community and the agencies and programs seeking natural resource enhancement benefits through habitat conservation. Neither half of the joint venture can function effectively without the other. To use a different paradigm, a business is comprised of manufacturing and sales. A joint venture's product is a science-based conservation strategy. This product is marketed by the management board.

## BIOLOGICAL PLANNING AND EVALUATION

Most wildlife management agencies are charged with the conservation of populations. Habitat management on public and private lands is an important tool in attaining this goal. As land-use pressures escalate, the question "How much habitat is enough?" is being asked more and more often. To make a compelling case for additional conservation resources and authorities, agencies need to articulate explicit goals and efficient strategies for attaining them.

Translating a population goal into an estimate of how much habitat is enough to attain this goal requires that we consider similarities and differences in the ways different species relate to habitats and respond to management, i.e. our planning must be spatially explicit, and we must design a landscape that maximizes collateral benefits and accounts for management conflicts. The development of spatial analysis techniques that integrate the biological foundation for management with digital spatial data using Geographic Information System (GIS) technology has been instrumental to science-based strategic conservation.

Collectively, a landscape design and habitat objectives predicted to sustain populations at desired levels constitute a conservation strategy (Fig. 1). The reliability of our assumptions about population-habitat relationships, and the degree to which managers are able to conform to the landscape design in delivering conservation, determine the relevance of our habitat objectives.

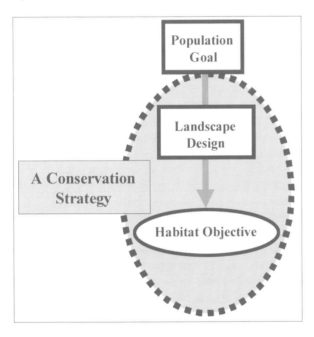

Fig. 1. A comprehensive biologically-based conservation strategy consists of explicitly stated goals and habitat objectives emanating from a landscape design predicted to sustain populations at goal levels.

This type of strategy is not a stack of papers that is bound and sits on a shelf gathering dust. It is a living suite of tools that are continually augmented, updated and refined through the iterative process of evaluation and planning anew. Different components of our strategy speak to different audiences. For example, regional or national habitat objectives mean little to a field-level manager; however, landscape designs that help managers decide where to apply management treatments, e.g. protect grass or wetlands, reforest, etc., are invaluable. The opposite is true for agency administrators that need clear statements of regional and national habitat objectives to gain support for conservation programs from elected officials.

The scientific foundation for a conservation strategy is inevitably imperfect. In practice, this foundation is a set of assumptions about how species are predicted to respond to landscape structure, patch-scale dynamics, and management actions.

Often, these assumptions are founded on very limited information. Yet the process of guiding management actions by articulating clear goals, applying the information that does exist, stating our underlying management assumptions (hypotheses) explicitly, evaluating the validity of our assumptions, and feeding refined assumptions into future management decisions is incredibly powerful. Most will recognize this process as adaptive resource management. Adaptive management of bird populations is founded on biological planning and evaluation for habitat conservation.

## Model-based approaches

Biological models are the vehicles for translating science into conservation strategies. The sole purpose of models is to improve the outcomes of management decisions. A model is simply a set of assumptions expressed in measurable terms. Models are commonly developed for focal species, i.e. priority species that are sensitive to landscape structure, patch-scale characteristics, and management that affects the structure of the plant community. Focal species are presumed to represent the habitat needs of a wider array of other species that are often less sensitive to these factors, although evaluation of this assumption is critical.

A model's value is measured by the extent to which it adds useful information to the management of focal species. Generally speaking, as model complexity goes up, so does the added value for decision making because model predictions move beyond our capacity for intuition. For example, models such as range maps or basic habitat associations offer managers little that they do not already know. In fact, if a species' habitat relationships are adequately described by a basic habitat type (e.g. emergent wetland or deciduous forest), it is probably a poor candidate for a focal species for biological planning, because it captures little of the more refined habitat needs of other species which respond to factors such as landscape configuration or patch size.

Models are applied to digital spatial data to predict the potential population impacts of delivering a particular management treatment at a specific place in the landscape. Typically, the potential of every unit of the landscape is assessed in developing these decision support tools (DSTs) for the management of focal species.

Biological planners commonly use models that fall into two broad categories. Conceptual models, which may or may not include empirically-based parameter estimates, are compiled from a variety of sources including the personal experiences of individuals knowledgeable about the interactions of a species and its habitat. Conceptual models are sometimes called heuristic models, in that they carry a heavy burden to evaluate their inherent assumptions and future improvement in model performance is expected accordingly. Conversely, empirical models are more initially data driven and are typically developed from discrete data sets. Empirical model coefficients also require regular assessment, but if their foundation is long-term, spatially extensive data sets – clearly the preferred source – evaluation and model updating are inherent components of the periodic data collection protocol. Both types of models are data driven in the iterative biological planning and evaluation paradigm.

Lastly, while assessing apparent habitat suitability is often useful, developing a comprehensive conservation strategy that includes priority areas for specific conservation actions and habitat objectives requires that we use models that reliably predict carrying capacity or some other measure of population potential, developed in an awareness of the ecological factors or processes that limit populations.

## QUALITY CONTROL IN PARTNERSHIP-BASED CONSERVATION

Why do partnerships such as joint ventures invest in biological planning and evaluation? (1) It can increase their efficiency – vital, given the magnitude of their mandate relative to the resources available to them; (2) it is a transparent and defensible application of sound science which enhances the partnership's credibility – collectively and individually; (3) it is a framework for identifying critical information gaps for actual management decisions rather than things we would simply like to know more about, which has characterized much of our past statement of research needs; (4) it enables the development of coordinated conservation strategies for multiple groups of wildlife; and (5) it sets the stage for greater influence in the implementation of other State and Federal programs. To return to our business paradigm, biological planning and evaluation represent joint venture quality control.

### Efficiency

The benefits of biological planning are predicated on the idea that every unit of a landscape, and every alternative management action at that location, has a unique potential to affect populations and unique costs to management agencies and society of doing so. Balancing these factors in pursuit of high impact per dollar expended is the essence of efficient conservation. While calculation of management costs may be relatively simple, assessing the probable impacts of applying a particular treatment at a particular location to populations of multiple species requires applications of science in a spatially-explicit environment.

### Transparency and defensibility

Application of science to clearly defined management goals and information needs yields inherently defensible management strategies and decisions. The only question is whether the science is adequate to support a particular action that otherwise would not occur. In the U.S., biological planning serves two fundamental roles:

- targeting existing program resources and activities; and
- assessing the need for additional resources and programs.

When strategies and decisions are based on explicitly described assumptions, founded on the best available science, the decision-making environment is inherently transparent and defensible. Moreover, by acknowledging that our assumptions are based on imperfect knowledge, we isolate the decision process from its outcomes, and we set the stage for a productive dialogue on strengthening the biological foundation.

Finally, the maps and other products of biological planning are powerful tools that enable managers to communicate effectively with elected officials and the public, both to support their proposed actions and to resist actions that may be inefficient or undesirable.

### Building the biological foundation

A model is really just a set of assumptions described in measurable terms. All assumptions are imperfect. As we go through the biological planning process, it is often obvious which assumptions are the most tenuous. Furthermore, refinement of some assumptions will have little impact on the decision we make. Others will have a large impact. Assumptions that are the most tenuous and that have the greatest potential impact on our management decisions are the highest priorities for research. Thus, model-based biological planning is a systematic way of identifying and prioritizing information needs, i.e. identifying missing critical research and monitoring, and distinguishing these needs from things about which we are simply curious. This is a more strategic approach to building the biological foundation for conservation than traditional, more haphazard means of identifying research needs.

### Coordination of conservation for multiple species

When biological planning is conducted in a spatially-explicit context, collateral benefits for multiple species can be assessed and management conflicts can be resolved. Maximizing site-level collateral benefits, within the constraints of program purposes and priorities, and minimizing collateral adverse impacts at landscape or eco-regional scales are essential to efficient conservation. Furthermore, the process of spatially-explicit planning is open-ended, i.e. other environmental and socio-economic functions of habitats can be assessed in the same fashion and integrated with spatial decision support tools developed for wildlife.

### Greater influence

In intensively altered ecosystems, relatively little land is typically in public ownership. A private land conservation solution is required. A variety of Federal land management programs and environmental protection policies exert a profound impact on these landscapes. In the U.S., none is more important than the U.S. Department of Agriculture's "Farm Bill". The Farm Bill supports the apparently conflicting goals of sustaining high agricultural production by subsidizing farming operations, while simultaneously paying land owners to convert farmland into habitat for prevention of soil erosion, enhancing water quality, and providing wildlife habitat. In recent years, Farm Bill expenditures have exceeded by nearly 200 times the combined total of all Federal agencies for bird conservation. Clearly, influencing these farming subsidies and agricultural programs is of paramount importance in conserving birds. As the ultimate responsible entity for migratory bird conservation, the U.S. Fish and Wildlife Service (USFWS) has a special interest in Farm Bill policies and programs; however, in the political process of establishing these policies, the USFWS requires the support of state and non-governmental partners.

As noted, the products of landscape-scale biological planning can be compelling, because of their visual impact and because they are transparently derived and built on sound science. Being compelling, they provide a vehicle for reaching out beyond traditional conservation programs to other programs that affect public and private land-use management. Despite long-standing challenges in working with agriculture, bird conservationists in the U.S. have recently had success is targeting Farm Bill conservation programs, amounting to millions of dollars each year, in regions of the country where the capability for biological planning and evaluation exists.

## A CASE STUDY

We illustrate these concepts in the following case study from an area of five counties in the Prairie Pothole Region of Minnesota. Although the models and maps of species-specific landscape priority areas are real, the population goals and some assumptions, and thus the integrated landscape design and habitat objectives, are hypothetical.

Our case study begins with the identification of an ecological perturbation (grassland habitat loss and fragmentation) and focal species that are sensitive to it. We consider the full suite of priority grassland-dependant birds in light of their response to stand height and density, patch size, and landscape structure. For our example, we chose three focal species. The Marbled Godwit *Limosa fedoa*, an apparently area-sensitive priority breeding shorebird, uses native or disturbed tame grasslands, studded with shallow wetlands, in landscapes with low terrain relief. The Greater Prairie Chicken *Tympanuchus cupido* is similarly sensitive to patch size and landscape structure. It requires short grass for nesting, but uses taller stands for brood rearing and other functions. Lastly, we chose to use the Mallard *Anas platyrhynchos* as a focal species. Mallards are grassland generalists and are relatively insensitive to grassland landscape structure; however, they require the juxtaposition of grasslands and wetlands, and there is great public demand for this species, with correspondingly high population goals.

A diverse conservation partnership is active in this five-county area. For each of our focal species, the partnership established population goals (Table 1). Above minimum viable population sizes, a partnership's population goals are value-based predictions of public demand for wildlife and public willingness to pay the costs of attaining those goals. Ideally, population goals should be established iteratively by setting goals, assessing costs, and revisiting goals and costs until an acceptable level of consensus is achieved.

We assembled models and other assumptions that relate focal species populations to grasslands. An empirical model for Greater Prairie Chickens that included only remotely-sensed variables was published by Niemuth (2003). This logistic regression predicted the probability of a site supporting a Greater Prairie Chicken lek. This model predicted relative habitat suitability, and it was necessary to make additional assumptions about average population size of leks, ratio of males to females in the vicinity

of leks, and size of the females' home range (Fig. 2).

A poisson regression was developed for Mallards from pre-existing field survey data. This regression predicted the capacity (in number of breeding pairs) of individual wetland basins, based on basin size and water regime. These estimates were combined with other data on the maximum travel distance of female Mallard from wetlands to upland nesting sites to estimate the number of ducks that could nest in a tract of grassland based on the number and characteristics of surrounding wetlands (Fig. 2).

Pre-existing survey data were inadequate to construct empirical models for Marbled Godwits. We developed a conceptual model in consultation with biologists with some expertise in habitat use by godwits (Diane Granfors, U.S. Fish and Wildlife Service, unpubl. model) (Fig. 2). As with the model for Greater Prairie Chickens, it was necessary to make additional assumptions to relate godwit populations to potential habitat.

Each of these models required assessment. We used pre-existing data, such as state Heritage Society data, to check model predictions, and, coincident with conservation delivery, collected additional field data to evaluate model assumptions and performance.

Models were applied to spatial data on grasslands and wetlands to:

- assess current eco-regional capacity to sustain populations of focal species;
- establish restoration objectives;
- assess contributions of lands currently in the conservation estate (Table 1); and
- identify priority sites and landscapes to protect and restore habitats in order to conserve populations as effectively as possible at goal levels (Fig. 2).

Establishing restoration objectives implies an awareness of current carrying capacity and assumptions about probable future loss of existing capacity. In most cases, it is unrealistic to try to protect all existing capacity. These losses must be offset by restoration. Furthermore, it is desirable to consider the amount of existing capacity that should be formally protected versus the amount that should remain in private, unprotected status. This proportion will depend on the importance of the landscape to a species' range-wide population and the risk of habitat loss over a finite time-scale. In our case study, we chose a strategy of perpetual protection of the full habitat potential needed to secure our population goals.

**Table 1. Population goals may be crafted into habitat objectives for future conservation by assessing current landscape potential, collateral conservation impacts, and contributions of the existing conservation estate.**

|  | Mallard (pairs/recruits) | Marbled Godwit (pairs) | Greater Prairie Chicken (hens) | Total habitat |
|---|---|---|---|---|
| Partnership's population goal | 26 000/32 000 | 60 | 184 | |
| Contribution of the existing conservation estate | 9 163/9 536 | 32 | 104 | |
| Conserved population deficit | 16 837/22 464 | 28 | 80 | |
| Species-specific habitat objectives (ha) | 106 098 | 10 781 | 37 195 | 154 074 |
| Collateral impacts | | | | |
| Mallard | | 12 | 72 | |
| Marbled Godwit | 1 487/1 863 | | 24 | |
| Greater Prairie Chicken | 4 365/5 675 | 16 | | |
| Integrated habitat objectives (ha) | | | | 115 027 |

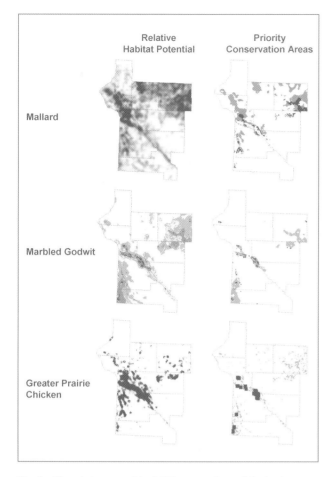

Fig. 2. The relative potential of different portions of the landscape to support populations of focal species, and priority conservation areas for each species based on population goals and relative potential to sustain populations. In the latter, priority protection areas are depicted in dark blue, and priority restoration areas in light blue.

By developing priority sites and landscapes for individual species, it is possible to develop species-specific habitat objectives (Table 1). Summing these species-specific habitat objectives indicates that approximately 154 000 ha of additional grassland must be conserved to attain our population goals.

Driven by program priorities, which are often defined in legislation, different agencies and organizations will play different roles in attaining goals for a particular focal species; however, implementation of one program often has collateral impacts, positive or negative, on other focal species (Table 1). An awareness of these collateral impacts is essential to efficient attainment of population goals. Therefore, we develop an integrated landscape design by combining priority areas for multiple focal species. This integrated landscape design is the foundation for our actual habitat objectives (Fig. 3).

This integration of species-specific priority conservation areas may result in conflicts based on impacts of grassland management on our focal species. For example, Marbled Godwits and Greater Prairie Chickens require native prairie or disturbed tame grasslands, while Mallards select tall, rank idled grasslands for nesting when available. This conflict was resolved in each area that is a priority for Mallards and for Greater Prairie Chickens or Marbled Godwits. We used an *ad hoc* process based on prediction of adverse impact on Mallards of managing grassland patches for prairie chickens/godwits and vice versa, and the relative importance of each conflicted geographic unit to each species in our integrated landscape design. This altered the predicted carrying capacity for each species of our landscape design, and required that the design, and our habitat objectives, be adjusted accordingly. Thus, like all other aspects of biological planning, the development of an integrated landscape design is iterative.

Based on our integrated landscape design, we estimate that approximately 115 000 ha of additional grassland habitat must be conserved, in the context of our integrated landscape design,

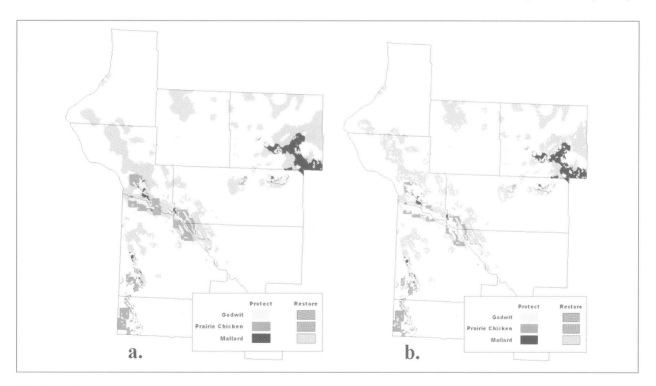

Fig. 3. (a) An integrated landscape design was created by merging species-specific priority conservation areas and reconciling management conflicts, based on differential responses to management of habitat structure. (b) The same integrated landscape design after the existing conservation estate was masked out. This is the foundation for habitat objectives, and for future grassland protection and restoration.

to attain the partnership's population goals (Table 1). Compared to our previous estimate of 154 000 ha, this represents a 25% increase in conservation efficiency. How close this habitat objective is to the amount of habitat we ultimately have to conserve to attain our population goals depends on how closely we are able to conform to our integrated landscape design. In practice, this habitat objective is a minimum estimate because some deviation from an optimal strategy is inevitable.

Despite our increased efficiency, restoring and providing some degree of protection to 115 000 ha of grassland habitat is still a massive challenge which underscores the need to capture the full wildlife conservation potential of the U.S. Farm Bill and other Federal programs.

## PREDICTED SPECIES RICHNESS MAPS

In some cases, the increased availability of remotely-sensed digital land-cover data and GIS technology has led to the use of simple habitat associations (e.g. emergent wetland or deciduous forest) in lieu of more informative models, and to the creation of maps of predicted species richness by overlaying deterministic predictions of apparent habitat suitability for large numbers of species. At best, these maps provide little information for management, and at worst result in a misallocation of program resources, for the following reasons:

*Process deficiencies*
- Overlaying deterministic species-specific predictions about habitat suitability results in high, but seldom estimated, uncertainties in predicted species richness.
- The product fails to provide information on what form conservation should take at a particular location. The implied action is protection of existing habitat, which is only one tool available to managers.
- The process does not acknowledge conflicting species responses to management, and does not accommodate resolution of potential management conflicts.
- The process does not consider populations, and does not result in defensible, population-based habitat objectives.
- Because of the simplicity of models and the failure of models to make explicit predictions of abundance or vital rates, the process does not connect management with research/monitoring.

*Model deficiencies*
- The need to use overly simplistic species-population relationships (models) because of the large number of species being considered.
- A failure to consider limiting factors or larger-scale habitat or landscape factors influencing actual habitat suitability, carrying capacity, or vital rates.
- A failure to consider population viability driven by "patch" and landscape-scale factors.

*Scale deficiencies*
- The scale of assessment is disconnected from the scale of management when species richness is "summed" for larger units such as 7.5 quadrangles of 7.5 x 7.5 geographical minutes, or watersheds, which are almost always larger than the scale at which management is applied on the ground, thus violating the assumption that all of the species accounted for in the species richness estimate will be benefited by a single management action.

In short, single maps of species richness (biodiversity) are typically poor predictors of actual or potential species distributions, are often driven by local or landscape-scale habitat heterogeneity more than importance to populations, often are not useful for management unless they are dissimilated into the elements used to construct them, and as such, have little value for directing conservation actions. Nevertheless, maps of species richness are often compelling, as is the idea of using them to conserve biodiversity. As such, they can inadvertently impede more sophisticated approaches to landscape design, based on higher level critical thinking about trust responsibilities, limiting factors, management compatibility and spatial scales.

## CONCLUSIONS

Biological planning is critical to efficient, transparent, and credible management decisions. Planners and managers are forced to be explicit about their assumptions about population-habitat relationships. Thus, it provides a foundation for strengthening the biological foundation through evaluation which in turn contributes to reliable future conservation strategies. When conducted in a spatially-explicit environment, biological planning provides a means of integrating the conservation needs of migratory birds with other species of wildlife, and other environmental and socio-economic functions of habitat.

The magnitude of our mandate dwarfs traditional conservation resources. Wildlife conservation agencies must use their programs strategically to conserve the habitats that are most critical to their mission, and must develop the capacity to engage other government agencies and the public and more effectively harness their conservation potential. Partnerships for the development of community conservation strategies and for outreach are invaluable to conservation.

This implies that wildlife conservation agencies will rethink their roles and responsibilities. Rather than think of their roles as solely one of active habitat and population management, agencies have to view their role as equally one of nurturing, stewarding, and promoting the biological foundation and strategies for migratory bird conservation, i.e. we must provide leadership and an explicit strategy for the conservation of migratory birds, and coordination of conservation partnerships. The foundation for this leadership will be biological planning at landscape scales.

## REFERENCES

**Niemuth, N.D.** 2003. Identifying landscapes for greater prairie chicken translocation using habitat models and GIS: a case study. Wildlife Society Bulletin 31(1): 145-155.

# Loss of shorebird habitat as a result of mangrove incursion due to sea-level rise and urbanization

*Phil Straw[1] & Neil Saintilan[2]*

[1] *Avifauna Research & Services, PO Box 2006, Rockdale Delivery Centre, NSW 2216, Australia.*
*(email: philstraw@avifaunaresearch.com)*
[2] *Centre for Environmental Restoration and Stewardship, Australian Catholic University, Mackillop Campus. PO Box 968,*
*North Sydney, NSW 2059, Australia. (email: neil.saintilan@environment.nsw.gov.au)*

Straw, P. & Saintilan, N. 2006. Loss of shorebird habitat as a result of mangrove incursion due to sea-level rise and urbanization. *Waterbirds around the world.* Eds. G.C. Boere, C.A. Galbraith & D.A. Stroud. The Stationery Office, Edinburgh, UK. pp. 717-720.

## ABSTRACT

Most migratory shorebird species require areas of open habitat such as tidal flats and salt-marshes where they can forage, rest and moult. The expansion of mangroves into shorebird feeding and roosting habitats due to sea-level rise and increased sedimentation is presenting a significant problem in closed situations such as estuaries in Hong Kong, Taiwan and eastern Australia. Seaward invasion of mangroves onto tidal mudflats as a result of excessive sedimentation caused by poor watershed management is affecting shorebird feeding areas. Landward invasion of mangroves in response to sea-level rise is affecting salt-marsh areas important as shorebird roosting and feeding habitat. Options for management intervention, such as the controlled removal of accreting mangrove seedlings and saplings from key shorebird feeding grounds, as well as the restoration and creation of mudflat and salt-marsh habitat, are discussed.

## SHOREBIRD HABITAT REQUIREMENTS

Most migratory shorebirds prefer to feed on open areas of undisturbed mudflats where they have a clear view of the approach of avian or terrestrial predators. Roosting sites are also selected to provide an open view and easy escape in case a predator approaches. Only under certain circumstances, where they have no alternative, will shorebirds utilize habitats close to tall vegetation or structures that obscure their view.

In a survey of 63 inter-tidal flats in nine New South Wales estuaries on the east coast of Australia, Lawler (1996) determined estuarine features which related to abundance in the feeding habitat of six species. The Bar-tailed Godwit *Limosa lapponica* selected large, low-lying flats for feeding; Whimbrel *Numenius phaeopus* favoured mangrove-lined flats in high-sediment regimes; and Far Eastern Curlew *N. madagascariensis* and Pacific Golden Plover *Pluvialis fulva* favoured large complexes of flats. Common Greenshanks *Tringa nebularia* frequented feeding areas of any size, provided they were wet, nutrient-rich and mangrove-fringed. Grey-tailed Tattlers *Heteroscelus brevipes* were more likely to feed adjacent to mangroves and on flats with some ground cover.

During high tide, when tidal flats are submerged, shorebirds require roosting sites such as beaches, sand spits, salt-marshes, and structures such as infrequently used jetties, barges, rock walls and oyster platforms. A few species, such as the Grey-tailed Tattler and Whimbrel, frequently roost on exposed branches of mangrove trees.

One of the most significant findings of Lawler (1996) was the extent to which most shorebirds avoided trees while roosting.

In a study of 134 sites used by roosting shorebirds in 18 estuaries in New South Wales, Lawler described the roosting habitat of five species with respect to a range of variables. Of the ground roosts, of which there were 93, only two were within 10 m of vegetation over 5 m tall, and 83% were at least 30 m distant from trees 5 m tall. Ninety percent of ground roosting sites were further than 10 m from 2 m high trees and bushes. Beaches accounted for 55% of roost sites, salt-marshes for 15%, mangrove trees for 19%, and artificial structures for 11%.

Studies of the Hunter Estuary in New South Wales have revealed that shorebirds abandon diurnal roost sites on sand spits and river-training walls where terrestrial predators, such as foxes, might be able to approach under the cover of darkness (Clarke & van Gessel 1983, Geering 1995, Straw 2000). The sites chosen at night are flooded back-swamps: usually salt-marsh or shallow lagoons where predators would be reluctant to stalk roosting shorebirds and where they would be more obvious. As there are few studies of nocturnal roost sites, it is unknown how widespread this practice is.

## THE MANGROVE ENVIRONMENT

Mangroves form an important part of the coastal ecology in southern Asia and throughout Australasia, together with sea-grasses and open tidal flats on the seaward side and salt-marsh communities on the landward side of the mangrove belt. The width of mangrove woodland varies from a few metres to several kilometres, depending on the latitude and coastal topography. The most extensive forests tend to exist in the tropics along shallow coastlines where there are many species of mangrove, whereas in temperate regions only one or two species occur.

The widespread loss and degradation of mangrove forests throughout South-east Asia and on the eastern coast of Australia are well documented. Logging and conversion for aquaculture are among the most frequently cited causes in South-east Asia, while the conversion of mangrove forests into waterfront residential and resort accommodation has been one of the main causes in Australia. Over the years, awareness regarding the ecological and economic importance of mangroves has grown. As a result, many authorities are engaged in efforts to restore this valuable resource, and this is reflected in the increasing number of publications and workshops dedicated to the subject (e.g. JAM 1994, Khemnark 1995, Field 1996). In New South Wales, the removal of mangroves without a licence now carries heavy penalties, with fines of AUS$ 55 000 for individuals and AUS$ 100 000 applying for corporations (Diver 2003). Any licences that are granted usually require the planting of at least one mangrove for every one removed in a place where they have a high likelihood of survival.

Unfortunately, many mangrove restoration projects move immediately into planting mangroves without determining why natural recovery has not occurred (Lewis 1998). Mangrove planting efforts have been conducted both in degraded former mangrove areas as well as in areas where mangroves have not previously occurred. Various South-east Asian countries have carried out large-scale planting of mangrove seedlings on inter-tidal mudflats (which cannot be considered "restoration") as part of well-intentioned mangrove restoration programmes. Though limited in success, these efforts have resulted in afforestation of significant tracts of open tidal flats over the past decade, substantially reducing the area of inter-tidal mudflat habitat (Erftemeijer & Lewis 2000). Land-ownership issues appear to play a major role in targeting mudflats for such planting programmes, as mudflats are "easily" accessible (with no-one claiming ownership), while access to abandoned shrimp ponds in former mangrove areas - which should be the real target for restoration - usually involves complicated legal claims over land ownership. Furthermore, such areas are prone to land speculation, especially in coastal areas where there is need for room for expansion of industrial and residential areas.

## LOSS OF HABITAT AS A RESULT OF MANGROVE INVASION

Another less well-known cause of the loss of shorebird habitat is the spread of mangroves through poorly understood processes in both a seaward and landward direction. Recent studies have shown that mangroves have invaded large areas of salt-marsh and open tidal mudflats, two types of habitat utilized by shorebirds. This situation is most pronounced in areas of rapid coastal development where coastal wetlands, including tidal mudflats, have been substantially reduced. The accretion of mangroves onto tidal mudflats is thought to be a result of increased silt loads and nutrient levels due to uncontrolled development and soil erosion in upstream catchment areas. Mangroves follow such fertile areas of mud accretion, and their establishment in such environments may lead to a reduction in the extent of open tidal flat habitat available to shorebirds (Augustinus 1995). Mangrove expansion in a landward direction over the past five decades may be attributed to a rise in sea level, which has exposed upper inter-tidal environments to mangrove colonization. Wilton (2001) demonstrated that while salt-marsh losses in recent decades have been greatest in urbanized estuaries, the component of loss due to mangrove encroachment is relatively constant between estuaries, at a median figure of 30%. The overall sea-level rise in the period 1940-2000 (70 mm at the Fort Dennison datum in Sydney Harbour) represents approximately 30% of the vertical range of the salt-marsh. The consistency of the trend between estuaries, the similarity between the approximate degree of loss and the degree of sea-level rise, and the pattern of encroachment along drainage lines (Saintilan & Williams 1999), all suggest that at least some component of salt-marsh loss is related to sea-level trends.

**Table 1. Mangrove increase/decrease over the past few decades at 31 selected sites in Australia.**

| Location | Mangrove increase (percent) | Period | Source |
|---|---|---|---|
| Johnstone River, Queensland | 14.8 | 1943-1991 | Duke 1995 |
| Hinchinbrook Channel | 5.8 | 1943-1991 | Duke 1995 |
| Coolangatta to Caloundra | -8.4 | 1974-1987 | Hyland & Butler 1988 |
| Oyster Point | 119 | 1944-1983 | McTainsh *et al.* 1988 |
| Morton Bay | 10 | 1944-1983 | Morton 1994 |
| Tweed River | 86 | 1930-1994 | Saintilan 1998 |
| Hunter estuary (overall) | 31 | 1954-1994 | Williams *et al.* 1999 |
| - Kooragang Island | 20 | 1954-1994 | Williams *et al.* 1999 |
| - Tomago/Fullerton/Stockton | 46 | 1954-1994 | Williams *et al.* 1999 |
| - South Bank | 41 | 1954-1994 | Williams *et al.* 1999 |
| - Throsby Creek | -91 | 1954-1994 | Williams *et al.* 1999 |
| Couranga Point, Hawkesbury | 30 | 1954-1994 | Saintilan & Hashimoto 1999 |
| Berowra Creek, Hawkesbury | 30 | 1941-1994 | Williams & Watford 1997 |
| Careel Bay | 551 | 1940-1996 | Wilton 2001 |
| Homebush Bay | 65 | 1930-2000 | Rogers & Saintilan 2001 |
| Port Jackson/Parramatta River | -19 | 1930-1985 | Thorogood 1985 |
| Kurnell Peninsula | 33 | 1956-1996 | Evans & Williams 2001 |
| Towra Point | 36 | 1942-1997 | Mitchell & Adam 1989 |
| Minnamurra Estuary | 69.6 | 1938-1997 | Chafer 1998 |
| Currambene Creek | 32 | 1949-1993 | Saintilan & Williams 2000 |
| Cararma Inlet | 15 | 1949-1993 | Saintilan & Williams 2000 |
| Moruya River | 43.4 | 1949-1999 | Phillips 2001 |
| Merimbula | 122 | 1948-1994 | Meehan 1997 |
| Pambula | 84 | 1948-1994 | Meehan 1997 |
| Kooweerup, Westernport | 60 | 1940-1999 | Rogers & Saintilan 2001 |
| Rhyll, Westernport | 20 | 1939-1999 | Rogers & Saintilan 2001 |
| French Island, Westernport | 2 | 1967-1999 | Rogers & Saintilan 2001 |
| Quaill Island, Westernport | 32 | 1973-1999 | Rogers & Saintilan 2001 |
| North Arm Creek, S.A. | 19.6 | 1979-1993 | Coleman 1998 |
| Swan Alley, S.A. | 189 | 1935-1979 | Burton 1982 |
| River Light, S.A. | 117 | 1949-1979 | Burton 1982 |

Of 31 case studies in south-eastern Australia (Table 1), only four reported a decline in mangrove area. These were associated with construction and development works. Unfortunately, there are few data describing the distribution of estuarine macrophytes prior to the use of aerial photography.

This trend of mangrove proliferation has placed pressure on other estuarine habitat types. In a review of 29 photogrammetric surveys covering over 20 estuaries in Queensland, New South Wales, Victoria and South Australia, Saintilan & Williams (1999, 2000) described an increase in the area of mangroves, and a corresponding decrease in the salt-marsh habitat. In 70% of estuaries surveyed, salt-marsh losses due to mangrove incursion have exceeded 30%, and in some situations losses have approached 100%. These impacts have heightened pressure on salt-marsh already impacted by agricultural and urban developments (Kratochvil *et al.* 1972, Zann 1997, Finlayson & Rea 1999). In a world unaltered by humans, the movement of mangroves into salt-marsh habitat as a result of sea-level rise would be offset by a similar movement in a landward direction by salt-marsh. However, in many situations salt-marsh is being squeezed out of existence between an advancing front of mangroves on one side and landfill and development on the other.

Accurate mapping, and therefore measurement, of the loss of tidal flats due to the spread of mangroves has yet to be completed in Australia. Mapping of mangroves at Mai Po Nature Reserve in Hong Kong has shown that the mangroves are spreading seaward at a rate of 5 m a year, and have expanded from 197 ha in 1987 to 394 ha in 2000 (WWF Hong Kong 2003). A similar situation has occurred at Guandu Nature Park, Taipei (R. Fang pers. comm.).

The prognosis for coastal wetlands in south-eastern Australia in the context of further sea-level rise is continued mangrove expansion landward and on a much wider front in a seaward direction if sedimentation rates remain high (Stolper 2002).

## MANAGING MANGROVES

The loss of shorebird habitat continues throughout the Asia-Pacific region. The most dramatic loss is due to land reclamation by humans through increasingly larger projects, e.g. at Seamangeum in South Korea. The answer to the problem is clear, although at times seemingly impossible: the cessation or even the reversal of land-filling projects. However, the situation relating to mangrove incursion into shorebird habitat needs more study, and the solutions are less clear. At some sites, such as Mai Po Nature Reserve in Hong Kong and parts of the Hunter River estuary, New South Wales, Australia, teams of volunteers periodically remove mangrove seedlings and saplings from relatively small but critically important shorebird feeding habitat and roosting sites. However, such management interventions may not be viable in the long term and at larger scales. To prevent the continual re-colonization by mangroves through seeds from other coastlines, tidal mudflats may have to be restored to levels below that suitable for mangrove colonization.

In areas where space is limited, such as in Sydney, Mai Po and many places in the UK, alternative habitats have been created for shorebirds in the form of shallow ponds or "scrapes". These sites are manipulated to create wet, muddy shores through changing water levels, either through sluice gates from nearby tidal waters or by pumping water in and out of the site. Constructed or modified sites such as these in South-east Asia and Australia have to be managed in such a way as to exclude mangrove seeds from entering the site from nearby mangrove forests. A number of systems are currently being designed to allow tidal flows and fish passage while preventing flotsam, including mangrove seeds and floating pollutants, from entering the site.

## CONCLUSIONS

For a long-term, sustainable solution to the problem of mangrove invasion into feeding and roosting habitats of migratory shorebirds, the underlying causes of sedimentation and sea-level rise should be addressed. Integrated river basin management approaches may help to reduce the problem of excessive sedimentation. Recent advances in ecological engineering have helped in the successful restoration and/or artificial creation of mudflat and salt-marsh habitats (Evans *et al.* 1999, Short *et al.* 2000, Simenstad & Warren 2002). Policies and interventions aimed at reducing the emissions of greenhouse gases may, in the long run, help to slow down the rate of sea-level rise. In the short term, the management of the spread of mangroves through weeding as seedlings appear and the construction of shorebird habitat excluding mangroves (two strategies being carried out in Hong Kong and Australia) are protecting threatened shorebird communities.

## ACKNOWLEDGEMENTS

The authors are grateful for constructive criticism and suggested changes to this paper from P.L.A. Erftemeijer.

## REFERENCES

**Augustinus, P.G.E.F.** 1995. Geomorphology and sedimentology of mangroves. In: G.M.E. Perillo (ed.) Geomorphology and Sedimentology of Estuaries. Chapter 12: Developments in Sedimentology 53: 333-357.

**Burton, T.** 1982. Mangrove changes recorded north of Adelaide. Safic 6: 8-12.

**Chafer, C.J.** 1998. A spatio-temporal analysis of estuarine vegetation change in the Minnamurra River 1938-1997. Minnamurra Estuary Management Committee.

**Clarke, C.J. & van Gessel, F.** 1983. Habitat Evaluation – Birds. In: J. Moss (ed.) An Investigation of Natural Areas Kooragang Island, Hunter River. Department of Environment and Planning, Sydney.

**Coleman, P.S.J.** 1998. Changes in a mangrove/samphire community, North Arm Creek, South Australia. Transactions of the Royal Society of South Australia 122(4): 173-178.

**Diver, L.** 2003. Legislation for the protection and conservation of marine vegetation. In: P. Straw (ed.) Status and Management of Migratory Shorebirds in Sydney. Sydney Olympic Park Authority.

**Duke, N.C.** 1995. Mangrove in the Great Barrier Reef World Heritage Area: current status, long-term trends, management implications and research. In: D. Wachenfeld, J. Oliver & K. Davis (eds.) State of the Great Barrier Reef World Heritage Area Workshop. Proceedings of a Technical Workshop held in Townsville, Queensland, Australia, 27-29 November 1995. Great Barrier Reef Marine Park Authority: 288-299.

**Erftemeijer, P.L.A. & Lewis, R.R. III** 2000. Planting mangroves on intertidal mudflats: Habitat restoration or habitat conversion? In: V. Sumantakul *et al.* (eds) Enhancing Coastal Ecosystem Restoration for the 21st Century. Proceedings of Regional Seminar for East and Southeast Asian Countries: ECOTONE VIII, Ranong & Phuket, 23-28 May 1999: 156-165.

**Evans, M.J. & Williams, R.J.** 2001. Historical distribution of estuarine wetlands at Kurnell Peninsula, Botany Bay. Wetlands (Australia) 19 (2): 61-71.

**Evans, P.R., Ward, R.M., Bone, M. & Leakey, M.** 1999. Creation of temperate-climate intertidal mudflats: factors affecting colonization and use by benthic invertebrates and their bird predators. Marine Pollution Bulletin 37: 535-545.

**Field, C.D.** (ed.). 1996. Restoration of Mangrove Ecosystems. International Society for Mangrove Ecosystems, Okinawa, Japan.

**Finlayson, C.M. & Rea, N.** 1999. Reasons for the loss and degradation of Australian wetlands. Wetlands Ecology and Management 7: 1-11.

**Geering, D.** 1995. Ecology of Migratory Shorebirds in the Hunter River Estuary. Report by Shortland Wetlands Centre Ltd. to Kooragang Wetland Rehabilitation Project.

**Hyland, S.J. & Butler, C.T.** 1988. The distribution and modification of mangroves and saltmarsh-claypans in southern Queensland. Queensland Department of Primary Industries, Information Series QI89004.

**JAM** 1994. Development and Dissemination of Re-afforestation Techniques of Mangrove Forests. Proceedings of the Workshop on ITTO Project, Bangkok, 18-20 April 1994. ITTO Japan Association for Mangroves, NATMANCOM, Bangkok, Thailand.

**Khemnark, C.** (ed.). 1995. Ecology and Management of Mangrove Restoration and Regeneration in East and Southeast Asia. Proceedings of the ECOTONE IV, 18-22 January 1995, Surat Thani, Thailand.

**Kratochvil, M., Hannon, N.J. & Clarke, L.D.** 1972. Mangrove swamp and saltmarsh communities in eastern Australia. Proceedings of the Linnaean Society of New South Wales 97: 262-274.

**Lawler, W.** 1996. Guidelines for Management of Migratory Shorebird Habitat in Southern East Coast Estuaries, Australia. Master of Resource Science thesis, University of New England.

**Lewis, R.R.III** 1998. Restoration of mangrove forests and seagrass meadows: how do we improve training and avoid repeating the same mistakes? Paper presented at the First Joint Meeting of the CEST Panel of the UJNR, Hayama, 17-20 March 1998.

**McTainsh, G., Iles, B. & Saffigna, P.** 1988. Spatial and temporal patterns of mangroves at Oyster Point Bay, Southeast Queensland, 1944-83. Proceedings of the Royal Society of Queensland 99: 83-91.

**Meehan, A.** 1997. Historical changes in seagrass, mangrove and saltmarsh communities in Merimbula Lake and Pambula Lake. BSc Honours thesis, Faculty of Science, University of Wollongong.

**Mitchell, M.L. & Adam, P.** 1989. The decline of saltmarsh in Botany Bay. Wetlands (Australia) 8: 37-46.

**Morton, R.M.** 1994. Fluctuations in wetland extent in southern Moreton Bay. In: J.G. Greenwood & N.J. Hall (eds.) Future marine science in Moreton Bay. School of Marine Science, University of Queensland: 145-150.

**Phillips, R.C.M.** 2001. Assessment of saltmarsh communities in the Moruya River including community structure and long-term change. Bachelor of Environmental Science Honours thesis, University of Wollongong.

**Rogers, K. & Saintilan, N.** 2001. Homebush Bay Mangrove and Saltmarsh Monitoring Program. Produced for the Sydney Olympic Park Authority, Australian Catholic University, August 2001.

**Saintilan, N.** 1998. Photogrammetric Survey of the Tweed River wetlands. Wetlands (Australia) 17: 74-82.

**Saintilan, N. & Hashimoto, T.R.** 1999. Mangrove-saltmarsh dynamics on a bay-head delta in the Hawkesbury River estuary, New South Wales, Australia. Hydrobiologia 413: 95-102.

**Saintilan, N. & Williams, R.** 1999. Mangrove transgression into saltmarsh environments in eastern Australia. Global Ecology and Biogeography 8: 117-124.

**Saintilan, N. & Williams, R.** 2000. Short Note: the decline of saltmarsh in southeast Australia: Results of recent surveys. Wetlands (Australia) 18 (2): 49-54.

**Short, F.T., Burdick, D.M., Short, C.A., Davis, R.C. & Morgan, P.A**. 2000. Developing success criteria for restored eelgrass, salt marsh and mud flat habitats. Ecological Engineering 15: 239-252.

**Simenstad, C.A. & Warren, R.S.** (eds.). 2002. Dike/Levee Breach Restoration of Coastal Marshes. Restoration Ecology 10(3) (Special Issue): 1-602.

**Stolper, D.** 2002. Modelling the evolution of estuaries, their intertidal zones and mangrove habitats. PhD thesis, University of Sydney.

**Straw, P.** 2000. Hunter Estuary Wader Habitat Investigation Stage 2. Report by Avifauna Research & Services to NSW National Parks and Wildlife Service.

**Thorogood, C.A.** 1985. Changes in the distribution of mangroves in the Port Jackson-Parramatta River estuary from 1930 to 1985. Wetlands (Australia) 5: 91-93.

**Williams, R.J. & Watford, F.A.** 1997. Change in the distribution of mangrove and saltmarsh in Berowra and Marramarra Creeks, 1941-92. Report to Hornsby Shire Council by NSW Fisheries.

**Williams, R.J., Watford, F.A. & Balashov, V.** 1999. Kooragang Wetland Rehabilitation Project: Changes in wetland fish habitats of the lower Hunter River. NSW Fisheries Office of Conservation, Fisheries Research Institute, Cronulla.

**Wilton, K.** 2001. Changes in coastal wetland habitats in Careel Bay, Pittwater, N.S.W. from 1940-1996. Wetlands (Australia) 19 (2): 72-86.

**WWF Hong Kong** 2003. HSBC Wetland Management Training Manual. WWF Hong Kong.

**Zann, L.P.** 1997. Our sea, our future. Major findings of the State of the Marine Environment Report for Australia. Department of Environment, Sport and Territories, Canberra.

# Migratory waterbirds in the Bagga riverine wetland of central Sudan: challenges for integrated wetland management

*Ali Kodi Tirba*

*Wildlife Conservation Administration, PO Box 336, Khartoum, Sudan. (email: tirbakh@maktoob.com)*

Tirba, A.K. 2006. Migratory waterbirds in the Bagga riverine wetland of central Sudan: challenges for integrated wetland management. *Waterbirds around the world.* Eds. G.C. Boere, C.A. Galbraith & D.A. Stroud. The Stationery Office, Edinburgh, UK. pp. 721-724.

## ABSTRACT

The River Nile is one of the most important flyways for migratory waterbirds moving between Africa, Europe and western Asia. Sudan has a longer portion of the Nile than any other country in the region and many wetlands that provide suitable conditions for migrant birds. These conditions are to a large extent dictated by the geomorphologic structure of the Nile and the prevailing human activities. One of the most important stopover sites for migratory waterbirds is Bagga riverine wetland in central Sudan, south of Khartoum. This wetland has six main habitat types: shrub-scrub, seasonally flooded grassland, permanently flooded swamps, papyrus swamp, riverbank habitat, and open water. Censuses in 2003 indicated the presence of 170 000 waterbirds of 50 species. About 5 000 people live in the area and utilize the wetland for fishing, cultivation, livestock grazing, papyrus harvesting, water consumption and woodcutting, while visitors from elsewhere engage in sport hunting and other recreation. The impact of some of these activities (over-fishing, over-grazing, illegal hunting) has resulted in a marked deterioration in the wetland. This is an issue that needs to be addressed through the implementation of a variety of management strategies aimed at ensuring sustainable utilization of the wetland resources.

## INTRODUCTION

### Background

Sudan is the largest country in Africa, with an area of approximately 2.5 million sq. km. The country is gently sloping towards the north. It is generally flat with some scattered hills and mountains. There are nine major habitat types (ecological zones): desert; semi-desert; low rainfall woodland savannah; high rainfall woodland savannah; equatorial forest; the Sudd region; montane regions; floodplains; and the Red Sea coast. Wetland habitats make up 20% of the total area of the country. They include the Sudd swamps, the River Nile and its tributaries (a drainage network of 9 000 km), 750 km of coastline along the Red Sea, a number of inland lakes, 2 000 "haffirs", and 10 000 km of canals in the Gezira irrigation scheme. In addition, there are innumerable seasonal swamps.

Wetlands in Sudan are vital to the global conservation of migratory waterbirds, as the country is situated on one of the main migration routes of waterbirds breeding in Europe and western Asia and spending the non-breeding season in Africa. Moreover, the wetlands contribute profoundly to the welfare of the people and wildlife in general.

The River Nile is one of the main flyways of migratory waterbirds moving between Africa, Europe and the Middle East. The Sudanese portion of the River Nile is longer than that in any other country in the region, and provides a considerable amount of suitable habitat for the migrant birds. The condition of the wetlands is, to a large extent, dictated by the geomorphologic structure of the Nile and the prevailing human activities.

The principal uses of wetlands along the River Nile in Sudan vary according to location. South of latitude 12°N, the use of wetlands is largely confined to the direct exploitation of wetland resources, e.g. farming, fisheries, harvesting of minor wetland products, and other non-consumptive uses such as transportation and recreation. However, along the northern portion of the Nile, from latitude 12°N to the Egyptian border, the river runs through exceptionally dry areas characterized by excessively high temperatures, low relative humidity and low precipitation. Human activities in these areas are entirely dependent upon the wetlands. Here, in addition to fishing, human settlement, transportation and recreation, the wetlands are used as a source of water for irrigation, with water being abstracted in very large quantities to irrigate agricultural schemes along the riverbanks. This portion of the river is very densely populated, and wetlands are primarily confined to the river channel. The nearest extensive swampy area to this portion of the River Nile is Bagga riverine wetland to the south.

### Policy and legislative framework

The Wildlife Conservation Act of 1986 governs and regulates practices inside the protected areas in Sudan. Thus declaration of Bagga riverine wetland as a protected area should be the foundation for ensuring the sustainable development of this important area.

Ratification of the Ramsar Convention on Wetlands (Ramsar, 1971) by Sudan in 2005 could now provide international recognition for Bagga wetland, especially as the last bird census in the area indicated the presence of 170 000 waterbirds of 50 species, which fulfils one of the criteria of the Ramsar Convention for the inclusion of sites in the List of Wetlands of International Importance.

Sudan is a Party to the Convention on the Conservation of Migratory Species of Wild Animals (Bonn, 1979), and therefore has obligations to conserve wetlands that harbour migratory waterbirds, such as Bagga wetland.

## BAGGA WETLAND

### General information

#### Location, site definition and boundary

Bagga wetland is an extensive swampy area of about 250 sq. km along the banks of the White Nile south of Khartoum. The wetland is situated between latitudes 10°35'-10°56'N and between longitudes 35°11'- 35°19'E. The principal components of the wetland are the main river channel and a number of small islands and peninsulas. There are nine villages scattered throughout the wetland, namely Tabour, Birka Island, Saafa, Argally Island, Shawal, Amgar Island, Um Shimayla, Gardood Island and

Um Nari Island. The wetland is a staging area for thousands of migratory waterbirds. Waterbird censuses in February and June 2003 indicated the presence of 168 572 birds of 50 species.

Bagga wetland has, for a long time, been subject to various types of human exploitation. The site has been designated by the Wildlife Conservation General Administration as a Bird Concession for sport hunting. Two safari companies, Decy Safaris and Blue-Sky Safaris, manage the sport hunting in the area, and bring tourists from various parts of Europe and Asia to the site, as well as Sudanese residents. The wetland is also used extensively by the local people for various purposes such as fishing, mechanized agriculture, "geref" farming, livestock grazing, transportation, drinking water and recreation.

All these activities have made the site attractive to a diverse range of competing economic activities. These activities need to be harmonized to ensure long-term sustainable utilization of the wetland resources. There is therefore a need for a long-term management plan that takes into account the interests of all the stakeholders in the decision-making process and subsequent management activities.

## Environmental information
### Physical characteristics

(i) Geology

The wetland is situated in a region of Precambrian metamorphic rocks that are dominated by gneisses and schists of the basement complex. Deposits of sedimentary rocks are clearly visible along the riverbanks.

(ii) Topography

The terrain is generally flat with some scattered sandy hills and depressions. There is a very weak drainage network, and the site is gently sloping towards the north. The soils are sandy to loamy.

(iii) Climate

The climate is typical of the low rainfall woodland savannah. The average annual precipitation varies between 300 and 700 mm; the rains begin at the end of May, reach a peak in the middle of August, and end in October. The relative annual humidity is between 55% and 60%. Average annual temperatures range between 30˚ and 35˚C.

(iv) Hydrology

The hydrological regime of Bagga wetland is, to a large extent, linked to the hydrological regime of the White Nile, with the river being much the most important source of water for the wetland. The flooding period is between mid-August and mid-September. The inflow regime consists of discharge from the White Nile, the River Alaen and various small streams, as well as surface runoff, seepage and direct rainfall. The outflow regime consists of return flow into White Nile, evaporation and transpiration.

## Ecological characteristics

Bagga wetland can be broadly classified into six main habitat types: shrub-scrub, seasonally flooded grassland, permanently flooded swamps, papyrus swamp, riverbank habitat, and open water.

(i) Shrub-scrub

The shrub-scrub habitat occurs in peripheral areas of the wetland. It is composed of acacia trees and grasses. The ecological function of this habitat is to provide a shelter belt that protects the wetland from siltation by wind-blown sand and clay transported by surface runoff. This habitat also contributes to soil fertility by producing leaf litter and providing shade for soil micro-organisms. The common tree species associated with this habitat are *Acacia nilotica*, *A. tortilis* sub. *tortilis*, *A. tortilis* sub. *seyal*, *A. nubica*, *A. senegal A. seyal*, *Balanites aegyptiaca* and *Ziziphus spinocristi*. Common bird species include the Yellow-billed Kite *Milvus aegyptius*, pigeons, doves, warblers and crows.

(ii) Seasonally flooded grassland

This habitat type is located in the inner parts of the wetland from the shrub-scrub zone towards the main river channel. It consists of open grassland intermingled with scattered shrubs of *Acacia nilotica*, and provides grazing areas for domestic livestock and thatching material for the local houses. The main grass species are *Hyperrinia* sp. and *Cloris giana*.

(iii) Permanently flooded swamps

These are swampy areas adjacent to the river channel that retain water throughout the year. Various emergent and submerged macrophytes are found in this habitat type, including the Water Hyacinth *Eichhornia crassipes*, Red Water Fern *Azolla filiculoides*, Hippo Grass *Vossia cuspidata*, Reed Mace *Typha capensis* and *T. domingensis*. Common bird species include the Great White Egret *Egretta alba*, Intermediate Egret *E. intermedia*, Little Egret *E. garzetta*, African Openbill *Anastomus lamelligerus*, Woolly-necked Stork *Ciconia episcopus*, Sacred Ibis *Threskiornis aethiopicus*, Glossy Ibis *Plegadis falcinellus*, African Spoonbill *Platalea alba*, Egyptian Goose *Alopochen aegyptiacus* and African Jacana *Actophilornis africana*.

(iv) Papyrus swamp

Pure stands of papyrus occur as scattered patches within the permanently flooded swamps. Various types of fish species are found in this habitat. The main bird species include Maccoa Duck *Oxyura maccoa*, White-backed Duck *Thalassornis leuconotus*, Southern Pochard *Netta erythrophthalma*, African Jacana and Little Tern *Sterna albifrons*.

(v) Riverbank habitat

This habitat is created between the swamps and the river when the flood waters recede. The main bird species found in this area include the Black-winged Stilt *Himantopus himantopus*, Pied Avocet *Recurvirostra avosetta*, Little Stint *Calidris minuta*, Ruff *Philomachus pugnax* and gulls *Larus* spp.

(vi) Open water

This habitat comprises the open waters of the main river channel. The river is normally 4-6 m deep from October to July, and varies between 10 m and 15 m deep during the height of the flood in August and September.

## Land tenure system

The land tenure system in Sudan is governed by the Land Act of 1943, in which all unregistered lands are the property of the State. Bagga wetland is under state ownership, except for areas of the riverbanks that are seasonally flooded and cultivated after the flood recedes. Such areas are in the ownership of certain families who inherited them from their grandfathers a long time ago. The Land Act of 1943 recognizes this land ownership as property under legal ownership. Other forms of land ownership within the wetland, i.e. as found in the small villages, are not recognized by the Land Act of 1943. However, the Department of Land Planning normally tackles such cases and formalizes registration procedures to legalize ownership on the basis of the Land Act. Research needs to be undertaken to determine the percentages of land given over to each of the various main uses. This could be carried out in collaboration with the national remote-sensing authorities.

## Management infrastructure

The area is managed by Bagga Local Council, which is part of the White Nile State managerial structure. Some areas have been allocated as sites for bird shooting concessions under the responsibility of the Wildlife Conservation General Administration. Bagga Local Council is responsible for providing a better livelihood for the local community. It collects government revenue and taxes, and pays for public services such as schools and hospitals. The Wildlife Conservation General Administration has the power to invest in all government owned lands throughout the country in collaboration with the local authorities. The Wildlife Administration generates revenue from sport hunting, and the revenue is divided between the Wildlife Administration and the local councils, with 40% going to the department and 60% to the local councils.

## Cultural characteristics

About 5 000 people live in and around the wetland. These belong mainly to the Hassania tribe, Gaafra, Hawaweer, Hamr and Bederia, but there are also some individuals from western Sudan, mainly the Nuba tribe, Four, Masaleet and Bargoo, while others from northern Sudan include the Shaygia, Gaalia, Mahas and Danagla.

## Wetland benefits

Various direct benefits are drawn from the wetland, e.g. fishing, farming, grazing of livestock, water consumption, harvesting of papyrus, woodcutting, sport hunting and recreation.

## Fishing

Fishing is carried out in the wetland by a variety of methods. The fish catches are either transported fresh for marketing in nearby urban centres such as Kosti and Doeum, or dried using traditional techniques. The dried fish are either canned and sold in urban centres such as Khartoum, or packed in special bags and used to feed labourers in the rain-fed mechanized agricultural schemes in central and eastern parts of the country.

Over-fishing is a problem, and there is an urgent need for research to establish an annual fishing quota. Otherwise, fishing activities will have to be banned to allow the situation to improve.

## Farming

Seasonally flooded areas are used to raise cash crops when the flood waters recede. These areas have very fertile soil that has been deposited by the flood waters from the Nile. Furthermore, this soil retains moisture for a very long time after the floods have receded, thus reducing the need for irrigation using diesel pumps.

## Livestock grazing

The local people own large herds of domestic livestock of various types, but mainly sheep, as these are adapted to the local climate and provide the favourite meat of the Sudanese. The wetland provides grazing areas for livestock especially during poor rainy seasons, when the natural pastures support very little vegetation. The livestock provide large quantities of milk for domestic use and a flourishing cheese industry, and the area is well known for the unique quality of its cheese.

## Water consumption

Water from the wetland is used for various purposes: for domestic use in the nearby villages, for irrigating agricultural crops, and for drinking by livestock. The river is used for boat transportation to carry people and their products from the wetland to the various villages, and to bring products from remote areas to centres with transport facilities to other areas.

## Papyrus harvesting

The patches of papyrus are used by the local community for roofing material and to make various types of handicrafts, such as mats and baskets. The papyrus industry is an important source of revenue for the local community. Loaded trucks move daily to various parts of central Sudan including Khartoum, which is the main market for these products.

## Woodcutting

The shrub-scrub habitat surrounding the wetland is the main source of firewood, charcoal and building materials for the local community. Bagga wetland is located in the semi-desert region of the country, and vegetation is fairly scarce. Thus, the wetland plays a vital role in providing the local community with a source of fuel.

## Sport hunting

Hunting licenses for the sport hunting of waterfowl are issued to tourists by the Wildlife Conservation General Administration. Several professional safari companies are involved in this type of hunting, and bring clients from many parts of the world to shoot waterfowl in the area. The revenue generated from this sport hunting has a perceptible impact on the overall revenue generation of the Wildlife Administration.

## Recreation

Camping sites at various places in the wetland are used for recreation. Some sites are natural, while others are constructed by tour operators. People are brought from the urban centres during their vacations and on public holidays to spend time along the edge of the wetland.

## STRATEGIES FOR THE MANAGEMENT OF BAGGA WETLAND

There is a need for the effective participation of all stakeholders in addressing the problems that face the management of Bagga wetland. The following strategies will therefore be adopted to enhance the participation of all stakeholders in the management of the wetland.

### Partnerships

The involvement of all stakeholders in the decision-making process will help to achieve community empowerment and enhance public trust. To achieve this goal, government officials should be encouraged to accept members of the local community in the decision-making process.

### Ecosystem approach

There is a need to adopt an ecosystem approach to environmental management in Bagga wetland. The implementation of this strategy requires co-ordinating initiatives and data from various sectors.

### Management structure

The implementation of the management strategy needs to operate within a sound overall management structure that supports participation by all stakeholders. There is a need for flexibility in dealing with diverse interests and sectors, and the development of participation regimes that can adapt to changing circumstances is of primary importance.

### Zonation

The management plan should recognize the multiple functions that the wetland can provide in combining biodiversity, wilderness and aesthetic values with compatible forms of sustainable development activities. The concept of Biosphere Reserves, as developed by UNESCO through the MAB Programme, will be used to guide zonation. Three zones will be delineated: a core zone, a buffer zone and a transitional zone.

### Core zone

The core zone should include areas of high sensitivity to exploitation which have to be protected to ensure the conservation of ecological processes and life support systems. Priorities for the core zone include:

- conservation of biodiversity and scenery;
- realization of the maximum potential of the educational and research values;
- realization of the recreational values without jeopardizing higher priorities.

### Buffer zone

The buffer zone provides protection for the core zone. Activities in this zone should be carried out as pilot projects subject to research, and should be regulated so that they do not interfere with the priorities of the core zone. All activities within this zone should be subjected to environmental impact assessment prior to implementation.

### Transitional zone

The transitional zone covers the rest of the wetland. In this zone, multiple uses will be encouraged. All activities should be subjected to environmental impact assessment to ensure compatibility with the priorities in the core and buffer zones.

## CONCLUSION

The area is facing real challenges, and a balance needs to be adopted between the need to cater for the growing demands of the local population and the stringent need for wetland conservation. Proper management and utilization on a sustainable basis are urgently required.

Papyrus *Cyperus papyrus* swamps are important habitats for waterbirds and other wildlife as well as being an valuable economic resource for human populations throughout much of Africa. Lake Mburo National Park, Uganda. Photo: David Stroud.

# Impacts of the restoration of the hydrological cycle on bird populations and socio-economic benefits in and around the Parc National du Diawling in Mauritania

*Yelli Diawara[1] & Cheikh Hamallah Diagana[2]*

[1] *Parc National du Banc d'Arguin Mauritanie, BP 5355, Nouakchott, Mauritania. (email: yelli-pnba@mauritania.mr)*
[2] *Wetlands International, West Africa Programme, PO Box 8060, Dakar-Yoff, Senegal. (email: diaganawet@sentoo.sn)*

Diawara, Y. & Diagana, C.H. 2006. Impacts of the restoration of the hydrological cycle on bird populations and socio-economic benefits in and around the Parc National du Diawling in Mauritania. *Waterbirds around the world.* Eds. G.C. Boere, C.A. Galbraith & D.A. Stroud. The Stationery Office, Edinburgh, UK. pp. 725-728.

## ABSTRACT

Until the 1960s, the hydrology of the lower Senegal delta in Mauritania was basically determined by the natural flooding of the Senegal River and tidal action. Each year, the area experienced periods of drought and flood with water that was alternately fresh, brackish and saline. Thousands of migratory waterbirds of both Palearctic and Afrotropical origin occurred in the area when conditions were favourable. With the construction of the Diama Dam and impoundment of the right bank of the Senegal River, the former floodplain between the island of Mboyo and Keur Macène was deprived of a freshwater supply for approximately 10 years. This resulted in a reduction in the numbers of migratory water-birds to a few dozens or hundreds during the period 1986 to 1993. Water management projects undertaken in the Parc National du Diawling have been aimed at restoring the previous conditions in the lower delta through recreating the normal hydrological cycle and thereby restoring the ecological values (bird, fish and plants) and socio-economic values of the park and its surroundings.

## INTRODUCTION

Wetlands in the lower Senegal delta (situated between 16°10'-16°35'N) were formerly amongst the richest and most extensive in West Africa. This delta system was comprised of a mosaic of floodplains and estuaries, alternately flooded with fresh, brackish and saline during the natural flood cycle of the Senegal River. This variation in salinity favoured the development of a rich diversity of plant species (Diawara *et al.* 1998). The floodplains were important spawning grounds for the fish fauna in the lower delta, and important foraging and nesting areas for a wide variety of waterbirds (Hamerlynck *et al.* 1997). These diverse ecosystems have long sustained a population of hundreds of thousands of people who were closely dependent upon the natural resources of the wetlands.

Since the beginning of the 1970s, the natural ecosystems of the lower Senegal delta have changed considerably, firstly because of deterioration caused by environmental factors (drought and soil degradation), and secondly, because of the construction of the Diama Dam and other water impoundments in the Senegal River valley. The environmental and social impacts of these developments were underestimated, and degradation of the ecosystems increased, especially downstream from the Diama Dam. Since the construction of the dam, the future of the lower delta ecosystem has been the subject of a number of debates at national and sub-regional level. The government of Mauritania eventually resolved in favour of the preservation of a sample of the lower delta ecosystem. Consequently, on 11 January 1991, a decree (Decree 91-005) was enacted, establishing a National Park, the "Parc

National du Diawling", on 16 000 ha of the former floodplains (Fig. 1). The general objectives of the National Park are the conservation and wise use of the resources of a sample of the ecosystem of the lower Senegal delta. In particular, the park seeks to ensure the harmonious and sustainable development of the activities of the indigenous people.

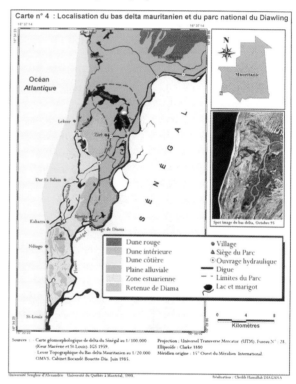

Fig. 1. Location of the lower Senegal delta and Parc National du Diawling in Mauritania.

## HYDROLOGY OF THE PARC NATIONAL DU DIAWLING

Before the construction of the two dams, Manantali and Diama, upstream and downstream on the River Senegal respectively, the hydrology of the lower delta was mainly dependent upon rainfall. It is important to highlight the exceptional nature of rivers in the Sahel zone which are located in an area where, because of the imbalance between rainfall and evaporation, no permanent surface water exists for long periods of time. The natural flood waters (freshwater) reach the delta between mid-August and September. Water movements in the lower delta were formerly complex and could change direction depending on water levels in the coastal zone. In years of low rainfall (a situation which has often occurred since 1970), seawater could penetrate up to 300 km inland from the mouth of the river.

In order to simulate the previous hydrology of the lower delta, the Parc National du Diawling has installed, with the involvement of the local population, six hydraulic structures (two for water supply, and four two-way structures) and dikes of 1.5 to 2.0 m IGN that make it possible to divide the park into three great basins (Diawling, Bell and Gambar).

The Gambar basin is currently an integral part of the Diama reservoir. The management of the dam prevents any incursion of salt water, thus ensuring that water bodies upstream of the dam remain fresh. This basin, which was formerly a fishing, gathering and grazing area for the indigenous population, has now become unavailable because it has become completely overgrown with an invasive plant, *Typha australis* (as a consequence of the freshwater reservoir). This has had a detrimental effect on the biodiversity and productivity of the environment, and has resulted in the disappearance of *Nymphaea lotus*, *Sporobolus robustus* and grazing areas.

The management of the park is currently focused on the hydrological functioning of the other two major basins: Bell and Diawling. The Diawling basin is gradually filled by the Cheyal structure upstream and the Berbar and Lekseir structures downstream. The aim has been to attain a water level of 1.0 m IGN in August and increase this to 1.30 m IGN by the end of the season, i.e. in September and October. The Bell basin is supplied by the Lemer structure upstream and the Bell 1 and Bell 2 structures downstream. The aim has been to attain a water level of 1.05 m IGN two weeks after the opening of the structures, and then to maintain this level for nearly one month, to enable the vegetation to develop. The level is then increased gradually to 1.20-1.30 m IGN. The basin has to be drained quickly starting from November, as directed by the management plan, to reflect the normal receding of water under natural conditions.

## MAXIMUM WATER LEVELS IN THE BASINS

Since the filling of the basins in the national park and its surroundings in 1995, the maximum water levels have fluctuated from one year to the next (Fig.2). A number of factors are involved in these variations in water level; in particular, the opening date of the structures, the head of water, the opening of gates, the high level of water in the lower part of the park, and the management of minor works.

The management of water levels has been better in the Bell basin than in the Diawling basin. In the Bell basin, it has always been possible to reach the planned water level at a given period, whereas in the Diawling basin, it has rarely been possible to exceed a level of 1.20 m IGN because of the size of the basin and its opening to other depressions starting from one metre IGN, such as the Tombos marshes and the Aftout (a depression over 50 km in length). The low water levels in both basins in 1996 (Fig. 2) correspond to low opening of the gates because of maintenance works on the left bank dike, and the high levels in 1999 correspond to an exceptional flood year when it was impossible to control water levels from downstream.

## BIRD FAUNA IN THE PARC NATIONAL DU DIAWLING

The wetlands in the lower Senegal delta are one of the first sites to be reached by migratory waterbirds from the Western Palearctic after crossing the Sahara in autumn. The freshwater and brackish marshes in the delta also support large numbers of Afrotropical waterbirds, and are important nesting sites for several bird species.

In 1995, the Parc National du Diawling began flooding the basins. With this resumption of the hydrological cycle, the park and its surroundings have once again become an internationally important area for waterbirds. The area has held over 1% of the West African population of several species, notably Great White Pelican *Pelecanus onocrotalus*, Great Cormorant *Phalacrocorax carbo*, Greater Flamingo *Phoenicopterus roseus*, Eurasian Spoonbill *Platalea leucorodia*, Black Stork *Ciconia nigra*, and some Palearctic and Afrotropical Anatidae, e.g. Northern Pintail *Anas acuta*, Northern Shoveler *A. clypeata*, Garganey *A. querquedula* and White-faced Whistling-Duck *Dendrocygna viduata*.

The series of waterbird counts conducted in Parc National du Diawling and the surrounding area began well before 1995. The first results of waterbird counts in the lower Senegal delta in Mauritania were provided by the International Waterfowl and Wetlands Research Bureau (IWRB) even before the creation of the national park in 1991. Park personnel then benefited from the support of IWRB during the international census periods until 1996. Since 1997, the census in the lower Senegal delta has benefited from the support of the Office National de la Chasse (ONCSF) in France. From January 1996 to 1999, the international census results revealed a significant increase in the numbers of Palearctic ducks wintering in the delta (Fig. 3). However, since 2000 the numbers of Palearctic and Afrotropical ducks (Northern Pintail, Northern Shoveler and White-faced Whistling-Duck) have been relatively low (Dodman & Diagana 2003). This change in numbers is mainly related to changes in water level in the different basins in the park.

The annual waterbird counts were generally conducted between 14-16 January. At this time of the year, the water level in the basins can often be favourable for ducks, as was the case in the years from 1996 to 1999. At the beginning of the implementation of the Parc National du Diawling management plan, water management was mainly aimed at restoring the ornithological values of the lower Senegal delta. The emphasis was then shifted to other values, such as fish fauna, flora and the activities of the local population on the periphery of the park. When all these other values had been taken into consideration, the water levels in January were no longer suitable for large concentrations of waterbirds in the great lakes, as little foraging habitat was available around the lakes (especially in the Bell basin, where the water level varies between 1.0 m and 1.15 m IGN). Since 2000, large concentrations of ducks have not been

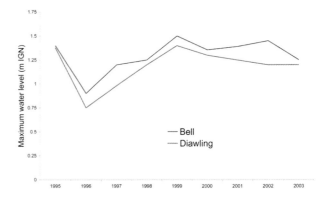

**Fig. 2.** Fluctuations in water level in two basins in the Parc National du Diawling, Mauritania: 1995-2003.

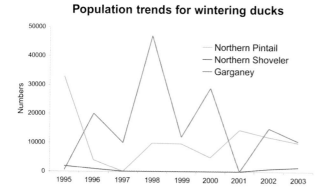

**Population trends for wintering ducks**

— Northern Pintail
— Northern Shoveler
— Garganey

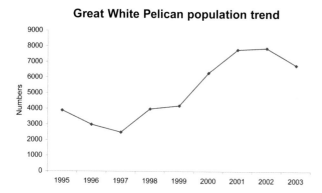

**Greater Flamingo population trend**

**Great White Pelican population trend**

Fig. 3. Numbers of three species of ducks, Greater Flamingos *Phoenicopterus roseus* and Great White Pelicans *Pelecanus onocrotalus* in the Parc National du Diawling, Mauritania: 1995-2003.

observed until February, except in the case of the Northern Pintail which occurs mainly in November and December.

## ORNITHOLOGICAL VALUES AND ECONOMIC BENEFITS

The most important breeding bird colonies in the Mauritanian part of the lower Senegal delta were found in the mangrove forests along the tidal creeks of the delta. Colonies of fish-eating birds were present in the Gueyeloube area, as well as at the Bell-Khurubam confluence. This area was colonized by a mangrove forest (*Avicennia germinans* and *Rhizophora racemosa*) and a plant community in which *Tamarix senegalensis* and *Sesuvium portulacastrum* predominate. As elsewhere in the delta, in the mid-1960s the Diawling area hosted several breeding species, e.g. African Darter *Anhinga rufa* (c. 10 000), Great Egret

*Egretta alba* (10-100) and Sacred Ibis *Threskiornis aethiopicus* (10-15). The breeding success was related to the richness of the environment in nutrients (fish, shellfish, amphibians and insects). The lower delta was not only important for breeding birds, but also for large numbers of wintering Palearctic ducks (e.g. Garganey) and Afrotropical ducks and geese (e.g. White-faced Whistling-Duck, Egyptian Goose *Alopochen aegyptiacus* and Spur-winged Goose *Plectropterus gambensis*).

With the construction of the right bank dike along the Senegal River, the floodplains were cut off from the natural flooding from the river. As a result, there was a gradual deterioration in the natural resources, including waterbird populations which disappeared almost completely (only one or two waterbirds were present in 1991), until artificial management restored the flood cycle to a part of the lower delta. Since the flooding of the basins in 1995, hundreds of thousands of waterbirds have again been observed in the Parc National du Diawling and surrounding areas (205 000 waterbirds were counted in 1996, and 135 000 in 1998).

The local people living around the periphery of the national park have a tradition of fishing in the wetlands throughout the year, and soon became aware of the interest that there was in the bird fauna in the lower delta. It has now become usual for the fishermen from neighbouring villages to organize themselves and establish a series of fishing areas, and this has been of benefit to fish-eating birds in particular.

The ornithological resources of the Parc National du Diawling and its surroundings are today the main attraction for tourists in the area, hence the creation of an important sector, that of eco-tourism. Initially, the national park studied the feasibility of different types of tourism, including mass tourism and beach tourism, but in the light of the park's objectives, eco-tourism seems to be the most relevant. Since 1998, this sector has been receiving nearly one thousand visitors per season through Mauritanian and Senegalese private operators. Currently, there are only a few local operators who take advantage of the benefits that can be derived from eco-tourism, and with the private sector controlling most of the new activities (tourism, market-gardening, handicrafts, needlework, etc.), there has been scarcely any perceptible change in the incomes of the local population.

## CONCLUSION

The hydrological management of the Parc National du Diawling remains complex, considering the varying water requirements for the restoration of the ecosystem and the demands of the local population for socio-economic activities at various times of the year. Currently, the Parc National du Diawling is the only area available for the grazing of hundreds of livestock (cattle, goats and camels) that spend the rainy season on the red dunes of the Trarza. The people living on the periphery of the park are requesting that the basins be flooded in two phases. The first phase coincides with the natural flood period, and the second phase with the dry season. This dry-season flooding would make it possible to sustain livestock during the lean period. However, after more than four months of inundation by natural flood waters, all the depressions become invaded by noxious aquatic plants. There are already several zones of invasive plants (*Typha australis*, *Potamogeton nodosus* and *Utricularia inflexa*) in the Diawling and Bell basins that had, until recently, been spared.

The implementation of dry-season flooding would favour the colonization of the open water areas of the lakes and, consequently, reduce the resting and foraging areas for several species of migratory waterbirds (ducks, waders, etc.) as well as some sedentary species. Furthermore, the conditions would favour invasive plants to the detriment of other plant species such as *Sporobolus robustus*, an herbaceous perennial much sought after by the local people for use in handicrafts. The third basin in the national park (Diama impoundment) exemplifies the systematic reduction in biodiversity caused by the permanent presence of water, which favours colonization by invasive plants.

## REFERENCES

**Diawara, Y., Ba Amadou & Kloff, S.** 1998. Les plantes envahissantes au bas delta du fleuve Sénégal. Actes 2 conférence internationale sur les zones humides et le développement, Dakar, 8-15 novembre 1998.

**Dodman, T. & Diagana, C.H.** 2003. African Waterbird Census / Les Dénombrements des Oiseaux d'Eau en Afrique 1999, 2000 & 2001. Wetlands International Global Series No. 16, Wageningen, The Netherlands.

**Hamerlynck, O. et al.** 1997. Plan Directeur d'Aménagement du Parc National du Diawling. Tome I et II.

The Parc National du Diawling holds internationally important numbers of Great White Pelicans *Pelecanus onocrotalus*. Photo: Sergey Dereliev.

# Population size, population development and habitat use of Avocets *Recurvirostra avosetta* in Western Europe at the end of the 20th century

*Hermann Hötker[1] & Rodney West[2]*

[1]*Michael-Otto-Institut im NABU, Goosstroot 1, 24861 Bergenhusen, Germany. (email: NABU-Inst.Hoetker@t-online.de)*
[2]*Flint Cottage, Stone Common, Blaxhall, Woodbridge, Suffolk, IP12 2DP, UK.*

Hötker, H. & West, R. 2006. Population size, population development and habitat use of Avocets *Recurvirostra avosetta* in Western Europe at the end of the 20th century. *Waterbirds around the world.* Eds. G.C. Boere, C.A. Galbraith & D.A. Stroud. The Stationery Office, Edinburgh, UK. pp. 729-730.

After having been at very low levels at the end of the 19th century, populations of Avocets *Recurvirostra avosetta* breeding in Western Europe have shown a dramatic increase in recent decades (Glutz von Blotzheim *et al.* 1977). In this paper we try to investigate whether this increase is continuing, and whether it has occurred at the same time and with the same speed at all sites. We also try to give an overview of population size, population development and habitat use of Avocets breeding in Western Europe. The paper is based on a workshop "Understanding population dynamics of Avocets" held during the annual conference of the International Wader Study Group in 1999 (see Hötker & West 2005 and other papers in Wader Study Group Bulletin 107).

By the end of the 1990s, the total population of Avocets breeding in Western Europe was 29 658 pairs (Table 1). The most important countries were The Netherlands, Germany, Spain and Denmark; the single most important site was the coast of the Wadden Sea, shared between Denmark, Germany and the Netherlands, where about 12 000 pairs bred. Given that the present population is nearly 30 000 breeding pairs in the East Atlantic Region, we calculate that the total population of western Europe may reach 90 000 individuals.

On the coasts of the North Sea and the Baltic Sea, Avocets mainly breed on saltmarshes, and in some places colonies are asso-

ciated with coastal engineering works. Coastal lagoons and embankments with freshwater or brackish water are also important in certain regions. On the coasts of the Atlantic and the Mediterranean saltpans both used and disused are by far the most important habitats. In the central European hinterland and also in inland Spain, Avocets mainly breed at alkaline lakes and fishponds.

Avocets were very rare at the beginning of the 20th century, but from that time populations began to recover in many countries (Glutz von Blotzheim *et al.* 1977, Fig. 1). From about 1940 onwards, many populations increased exponentially until the late 1980s; exceptions occurred in Portugal, the Mediterranean part of France, and Austria where populations remained stable (although fluctuating annually) for long periods.

In the late 1980s, the population dynamics changed within a very few years but the overall population has remained more or less stable since then. From the peak of population trend, developments in different countries started to diverge. In the core area of the breeding distribution in the Wadden Sea and the delta of the Rivers Rhine, Maas and Schelde, the population declined significantly between 1989 and 1998 (annual rate of loss 265 pairs, t=-3.27, p=0.01), while populations continued to be stable in those areas where Avocet populations had not changed much before, such as Portugal, Mediterranean France and Austria. In other parts of Western Europe, the population is still increasing, although less quickly, for example in Estonia, Lithuania, United Kingdom, France, Spain, and Italy. Moreover, there are breeding attempts in formerly uncolonised countries, for example, Norway (BLI/EBCC 2000) and Poland (Chylarecki pers. comm.)

Although the reasons for the population recovery in the 20th century are not entirely understood, the most likely is better protection of Avocets from hunting and egg collecting. Many reserves with a ban on hunting have been established, at first in the breeding sites but later also in wintering sites, and more than 90% of the western European Avocet population is now breeding in nature reserves. Avocets can thus be regarded as a nature protection success story. Other factors which may have had an effect on the increase of the population throughout the 20th century include the eutrophication of coastal waters, climatic changes and habitat change through coastal engineering. Several authors relate numbers of Avocets in non-breeding sites to the degree of water pollution (van Impe 1985, Prop 1998) which has caused a general increase in density in many estuarine invertebrates (Beukema & Cadee 1986). In particular polychaetes, an important part of the diet of Avocets, have profited from the increase of nutrients in the water (Reise *et al.* 1989).

However, the population is still relatively small compared to many other wader species, and Avocets tend to congregate in

**Table 1. Most recent estimates of Avocets *Recurvirostra avosetta* breeding in Western Europe (BirdLife International & European Bird Census Council 2000).**

| Country | Pairs | Year |
|---|---|---|
| Estonia | 125 | 1998 |
| Lithuania | 10 | 1998 |
| Sweden | 1 068 | 1995 |
| Norway | 3 | 1990 |
| Denmark | 4 613 | 1998 |
| Germany | 5 860 | 1997 |
| The Netherlands | 6 921 | 1998 |
| Belgium | 240 | 1997 |
| UK | 654 | 1997 |
| France (Atlantic) | 1 200 | 1996 |
| France (Mediterranean) | 860 | 1999 |
| Spain | 5 750 | 1998 |
| Portugal | 150 | 1995 |
| Austria | 120 | 1998 |
| Italy | 1 922 | 1998 |
| **Total** | **29 496** | |

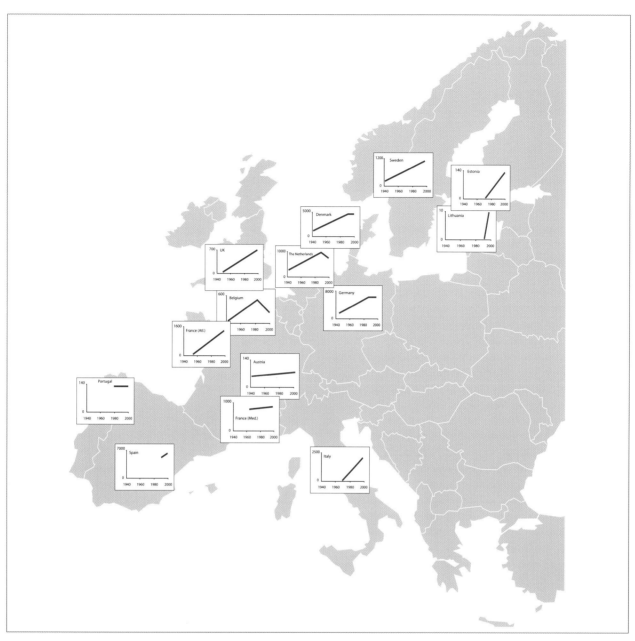

**Fig. 1.** Population developments of Avocets *Recurvirostra avosetta* breeding in western European countries.

relatively few estuaries outside the breeding season where they may be threatened by environmental disasters like oil spills. Many nesting habitats sites require "hands-on" habitat management, and part of the population is therefore conservation dependant. Habitat loss occurs in particular in southern Europe where saltpans are disused or transformed into fishponds without suitable breeding habitats for Avocets. Global temperature increases leading to rising sea levels will probably destroy much of the breeding habitats of the Avocets nesting on salt marshes.

## REFERENCES

Beukema, J.J. & Cadee, G.C. 1986. Zoobenthos responds to eutrophication of the Dutch Wadden Sea. Ophelia 26: 55-64.

BirdLife International and European Bird Census Council (BL/EBCC) 2000. European bird populations: estimates and trends. BirdLife International, Cambridge, BirdLife Conservation Series 10.

Glutz von Blotzheim, U.N., Bauer K.M. & Bezzel, E. 1977. Handbuch der Vögel Mitteleuropas. Band 7. Charadriiformes (2.Teil). Akademische Verlagsgesellschaft, Wiesbaden.

Hötker, H. & West, R. 2005. Population size, population development and habitat use of Avocets in Western Europe at the end of the 20th century. Wader Study Group Bulletin 107: 57-65.

Prop, J. 1998. Effecten van afvalwaterlozingen op trekvogels in de Dollard: een analyse van tellingen uit de periode 1974-1995. In: K. Essink & P. Esselink (eds.). Het Eems-Dollard estuarium: interacties tussen menselijke beïnvloeding en natuurlijke dynamiek. Rapport RIKZ-98.020, Haren.

Reise, K., Herre, E. & Sturm, M. 1994. Historical changes in the benthos of the Wadden Sea around the island of Sylt in the North Sea. Helgoländer Meeresuntersuchungen 43: 417-433.

van Impe, J. 1985. Estuarine pollution as a probable cause of increase of estuarine birds. Marine Pollution Bulletin 16: 271-276.

# Transboundary management of Kura Basin wetlands as an important step towards waterbird conservation in the South Caucasus region

*Karen Jenderedjian*

*Head of Division of Animal Resource Management, Agency of Bioresource Management of the Ministry of Nature Protection, Government Building 3, Republic Square, Yerevan 375010, Armenia. (email: jender@arminco.com)*

Jenderedjian, K. 2006. Transboundary management of Kura Basin wetlands as an important step towards waterbird conservation in the South Caucasus region. *Waterbirds around the world*. Eds. G.C. Boere, C.A. Galbraith & D.A. Stroud. The Stationery Office, Edinburgh, UK. pp. 731-732.

This paper describes current initiatives to establish and co-ordinate multi-lateral planning for landuse and conservation management in the Kura-Arax river basin within the Caucasus Region.

Situated between the Black Sea and Caspian Lake, the Caucasus is among the planet's 25 most diverse and endangered areas. It covers 580 000 km$^2$ including parts of Armenia, Azerbaijan and Georgia, the North Caucasus portion of the Russian Federation, north-eastern Turkey and part of north-western Iran. Landscapes in the Caucasus range from high mountains to semi-deserts and wetlands; vegetation types include snowfields and glaciers, steppe, broadleaf and coniferous forests, alpine and subalpine meadows, and alder and Caucasian wing-nut swamp forests. The 2002 IUCN Red List identifies one species of plant and 50 species of globally threatened animals in the Caucasus. Of 11 species of globally threatened birds, six are waterbirds: Lesser White-fronted Goose *Anser erythropus*, Red-breasted Goose *Branta ruficollis*, Marbled Teal *Marmaronetta angustirostris*, White-headed Duck *Oxyura leucocephala*, Corncrake *Crex crex* and Sociable Plover *Vanellus gregarius*. Large numbers of waterbirds from Eastern Europe and Western Siberia migrate across the Caucasus to the Middle East and East Africa: of those, 115 species are listed in Annex II of the AEWA. One waterbird species, the Armenian Gull *Larus armenicus*, is endemic to the region.

Important wetland ecosystems are found throughout the Caucasus, and wetland vegetation covers large areas along the coastal zones of the Black and Azov seas, Caspian Lake and Terek, Sulak, Kuban, Samur, Rioni and Kura rivers. The catchment of the Kura River is of exceptional international importance, and is shared between five countries - Armenia, Azerbaijan, Georgia, Iran and Turkey (Fig. 1). The Kura River is the largest hydrological watercourse in the South Caucasus, originating on the northeast slopes of Kizil-Giadik (Turkey) and flowing through Georgia and Azerbaijan into the Caspian Lake. The river is 1 515 km in length and the area of the basin is 205 037 km$^2$. Together with its major tributary the River Arax, the entire basin occupies the greater part of the South Caucasus, and supports a population of 6.8 million people. The waters of the river system are used for drinking, hydropower and irrigation, especially in Armenia, Georgia and Azerbaijan. Although wetlands make up only 0.9% of the river system, 21 wetland-dependent Important Bird Areas (IBA) have been identified, of which Lake Arpi (3 139 ha) and Lake Sevan (489 100 ha) in Armenia and Agh-Ghol (500 ha) in Azerbaijan are designated Ramsar sites.

Unfortunately, the waters of the Kura-Arax river system are extensively polluted, with the concentrations of impurities

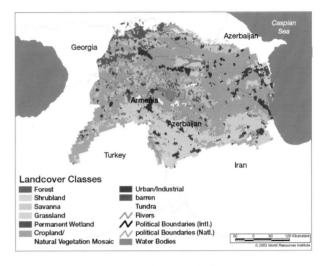

Fig. 1. Landcover classes in the Kura-Arax basin.

exceeding allowable limits by as much as 10 times for phenol, 14 times for phosphate and 20 times for oil. Pollution plus drastic political and economic upheaval, uncontrolled use of water resources and poaching have brought ecological instability and loss of biodiversity in general and of waterbirds in particular. The situation is aggravated because of the absence of a common approach between Armenia, Azerbaijan, Georgia, Iran and Turkey towards integrated management of water and wetland resources. Problems arise due to:

- limited capacity of the institutions responsible;
- underdeveloped environmental legislation at national and regional levels;
- inefficient control and lack of financial mechanisms to prevent pollution;
- weak system of water monitoring and lack of reliable data on pollution; and
- lack of mechanisms for co-operation and co-ordination of action plans.

There are several ongoing programs initiated by the European Commission and the UNDP to improve water management in Kura-Arax basin through the harmonization of legislation, monitoring and regional planning. The "Eco-regional Nature Protection Programme for the South Caucasus Region", part of the Caucasus Initiative launched by the German Ministry of Co-operation and Development aims to promote cooperation on the development of a coherent strategy to ensure biodiversity conservation in the region. A number of wetlands will be given the status of protected areas on the both sites of Armenian-Georgian border, while the following activities will be financed from the recently approved €2 200 000 programme "Establishment of Protected Areas in the Armenian Javakheti Region":

- to establish a National Park in accordance with IUCN guidelines including Lake Arpi and its water catchment areas bordering Georgia and Turkey;
- to investigate the potential for possible establishment of wetland sanctuaries (such as Akhuryan and others);
- to integrate the National Park into the land use of the project area;
- to develop selected support programs to decrease the pressure on the National Park and sanctuaries and to foster acceptance by the population; and
- to promote transboundary cooperation in the biodiversity conservation in the Javakhety Region.

The Critical Ecosystem Partnership Fund (CEPF) is developing a strategy based on the results of stakeholder workshops and background reports coordinated by the WWF Caucasus Programme. The strategy is underpinned by targets against which the success of investments can be measured, namely species (extinctions avoided), sites (areas protected) and landscapes (corridors created). Four strategic directions guide CEPF's approach in the Caucasus:

- support society efforts to promote transboundary cooperation and improve protected area systems;
- strengthen mechanisms to conserve biodiversity of the area with emphasis on species, site and corridor outcomes;
- implement models demonstrating sustainable resource use; and

- increase the awareness and commitment of decision-makers to biodiversity conservation.

The CEPF provides special attention to wetlands and international cooperation, and the Wetland Management Training Course for the Staff of Sevan National Park (Armenia) and Kolkheti National Park (Georgia) has recently been approved for funding. Prospective wetlands for transboundary conservation are Ararat Valley fish-ponds and floodplain marshes on Mount Ararat, shared with Armenia, Turkey and the Nakhichevan enclave of Azerbaijan and Iran.

There is no doubt that cooperation on transboundary conservation of the Caucasus and Kura Basin wetlands will positively influence not only waterbird diversity but will also mitigate the effects of the uneasy political situation in the South Caucasus Region.

## FURTHER INFORMATION

http://earthtrends.wri.org/text/water-resources/map-324.html

http://ruzgar.aznet.org/ruzgar/1-7.htm

http://seu.iatp.ge/Kura-Araks.html

http://www.azeribirds.org/eng/e_ob_xarak.html

http://www.iucn.org/themes/wani/eatlas/html/eu16.html

http://www.kura.iabg.de/inventarisierung_engl.htm

http://www.undp.org.ge/Projects/kura.html

The Ramsar site of Lake Sevan in Armenia is one of the largest waterbodies in the Caucasus and supports several endemic species. Photo: David Stroud.

# The importance of extensive fishponds for Ferruginous Duck *Aythya nyroca* conservation

*Nikolai Petkov*

*BirdLife International Ferruginous Duck Conservation Team, c/o Bulgarian Society for the Protection of Birds/BirdLife Bulgaria.*
*(email: nicky.petkov@bspb.org; www.bspb.org/nyroca)*

Petkov, N. 2006. The importance of extensive fishponds for Ferruginous Duck *Aythya nyroca* conservation. *Waterbirds around the world.* Eds. G.C. Boere, C.A. Galbraith & D.A. Stroud. The Stationery Office, Edinburgh, UK. pp. 733-734.

This paper reviews the importance of the extensive fishponds as a basic wetland habitat for Ferruginous Duck *Aythya nyroca* in Europe. The data for this evaluation are taken from the BirdLife International IBA database and the Ferruginous Duck workshop in Sofia, Bulgaria in October 2002.

The Ferruginous Duck is listed as Near Threatened by BirdLife International (2000). Once one of the commonest breeding duck species in Europe, it is now declining in most of its European breeding grounds. The largest breeding populations known are in Romania (2 000-6 000 pairs) and Croatia (1 000-3 000), although it is declining in both countries. In Asia, the species is scattered and little is know about actual breeding numbers. Currently the European population is estimated at 12 000 – 18 000 pairs (BirdLife International 2004). It is found in shallow and eutrophic wetlands, and in Central and Eastern Europe, where many of the natural wetlands and habitats of the species have been destroyed, it has adapted to using extensive fishponds. It is presumed that the species breeds in 41 countries and the estimates for the trends in 18 countries suggested declines of 20-50% (Robinson 2002). In many parts of its European range it has populated artificial wetlands such as extensively managed fishponds. In 2002 an international workshop was held in Sofia, Bulgaria to re-evaluate the threats and status of the species and develop a Species Action Plan under the AEWA (African-Eurasian Waterbird Agreement). Though it is now considered that over half of the population breeds in Asia, there are no real data on breeding sites with significant breeding populations that can confirm this suggestion. The breeding population in Europe is much better known and the largest breeding populations depend on artificial wetlands especially fishponds.

Extensive fishponds are fishfarms that were created 40-60 years ago for fish farming in Central and Eastern Europe and due to less intensive management have evolved into semi-natural wetlands supporting high biodiversity including important bird populations. They are mostly used to grow Carp *Cyprinus carpio*. To some extent they have replaced the natural marshes which they resemble, and they shelter a high diversity of aquatic macrophytes and emergent vegetation, a far cry from the more intensive fish farming systems of Western Europe.

Croatia, Serbia, Romania, Hungary and Bulgaria account for nearly 63% of the European population of Ferruginous Duck (BirdLife International 2004); the most important breeding habitat is the fishpond with more than half of the breeding sites. A total of 186 IBAs for Ferruginous Duck have been identified in Europe, of which 126 are fishponds (BirdLife International IBA database, 2004). The fishponds are the only wetlands beside large river deltas where moulting and migration concentrations occur (Petkov *et al* 2003).

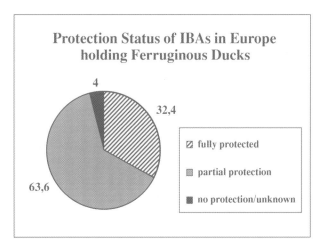

**Fig. 1.** Protection status of sites important for Ferruginous Duck *Aythya nyroca* in Europe

The abandonment and change in management of extensive fish ponds has brought a significant reduction in Ferruginous Duck breeding numbers in some countries and in some specific fishponds. For example, in Poland the breeding population has decreased from 400 pairs in the 1980s to 40 pairs currently, with much of this decline attributable to the drainage and/or intensification of the fishpond management (Wieloch 2003). In Croatia, the Crna Malaka fishpond, where over 4 000 birds concentrated for moulting and migration in the 1990s (Schneider-Jacoby 2003), is one of the most important breeding and moulting sites in Europe. However, as a result of management changes, numbers there have dropped significantly and the species population in Central and Eastern Europe is endangered. In Bulgaria, Mechka Fishpond (IBA BG024), the most important breeding site with over 30 pairs and with moulting and migration concentrations in the 1990s up to 3 000 Ferruginous Ducks, currently holds 10-20 pairs and no more than 80-100 birds on migration. Within the five years from 1997 to 2002, fishponds in Bulgaria lost their key position as the most important wetlands for the breeding of the species with the percentage of the breeding pairs occurring in them dropping from 49% to 42% (Petkov 2004).

The main problems identified for the fishponds are:

- transformation into intensive fishfarms due to low profitability of more extensive management;
- abandonment because of transformation of the ponds for arable cultivation;
- mismanagement and deterioration after privatisation resulting in overgrowing vegetation and consequent reduction in wetland biodiversity;

- lack of state policy to support extensive fishponds, and policy preferences that lead to their abandonment or transformation to other types of agriculture;
- reed cutting and burning during breeding season leading to loss of clutches, low breeding success and high mortality of reed breeding species;
- drying up of basins in key periods during migration; and
- illegal hunting of Ferruginous Ducks in unprotected fishponds, resulting from a desire of fishponds owners to increase income.

Currently the existence of the breeding population in Europe is under severe threat due to neglect or poor management of the fishponds; if these are transformed or intensified this will lead to a significant decrease in the Ferruginous Duck population in Europe, driving it to the brink of extinction in a number of countries in Europe.

There is a need for conservationists, fishpond managers, state nature conservation and aquaculture and fisheries institutions to combine their efforts to formulate best practice guidelines for the management of extensive fishponds which combine fish farming and Ferruginous Duck conservation. Sustainable fish-farming should be included in the priority measures of the national agri-environmental programmes of the new Member States of the EU where much of these habitats are found. For others it should be a priority to develop state funds and policies and systems of incentives and compensation, both financial and nonfinancial.

## REFERENCES

**BirdLife International** 2000. Threatened birds of the world. Lynx Edicions and BirdLife International, Barcelona and Cambridge.

**BirdLife International** 2004. Birds in Europe- population estimates, trends and conservation. Cambridge UK. BirdLife International Conservation Series No 12. 374 pp.

**BirdLife International World Bird Data Base** 2004. Cambridge, UK.

**Petkov, N., Hughes, B. & Gallo-Orsi, U.** (eds.). 2003. Ferruginous Duck: from research to conservation. BSPB Conservation Series No 6. BirdLife International – BSPB – TWSG. 144 pp.

**Petkov, N.V.** 2004. Comparative study on the ecological requirements of the ferruginous Duck *Aythya nyroca* and Pochard *Aythya ferina* during breeding season in Bulgaria. PhD Thesis, Central Laboratory of General Ecology at the Bulgarian Academy of Sciences, Sofia. 220 pp.

**Robinson, J**. 2002. International Species Review *Aythya nyroca*. CMS, AEWA, WWT, BirdLife International.

**Schneired-Jacoby, M**. 2003. Lack of Ferruginous Duck protection in Croatia: a reason for the decline in Central Europe. In: N. Petkov, B. Hughes & U. Gallo-Orsi (eds.). Ferruginous Duck: from research to conservation. BSPB Conservation Series No 6. BirdLife International- BSPB – TWSG:. 44-54.

**Wieloch, M**. 2003. The status of the Ferruginous Duck in Poland. In: N. Petkov, B. Hughes & U. Gallo-Orsi (eds.). Ferruginous Duck: from research to conservation. BSPB Conservation Series No. 6. BirdLife International- BSPB – TWSG: 28-32.

Extensive fishfarms have evolved under less intensive management into semi-natural wetlands supporting high biodiversity including important bird populations. Orsoya fishpond, Bulgaria. Photo: Nikolai Petkov.

# Monitoring needs and landscape level planning for conservation of waterbirds in Abu Dhabi, United Arab Emirates

*Sálim Javed, Shahid Khan, Yasser Othman, John Newby & Frederic Launay*

*Environmental Agency – Abu Dhabi, PO Box 45553, Abu Dhabi, United Arab Emirates. (email: sjaved@erwda.gov.ae)*

Javed, S., Khan, S., Othman, Y., Newby, J. & Launay, F. 2006. Monitoring needs and landscape level planning for conservation of waterbirds in Abu Dhabi, United Arab Emirates. *Waterbirds around the world.* Eds. G.C. Boere, C.A. Galbraith & D.A. Stroud. The Stationery Office, Edinburgh, UK. pp. 735-736.

The mudflats of the southern Gulf support several million water-birds during spring and autumn migration and an estimated 250 000 shorebirds use the vast inter-tidal zone of the United Arab Emirates (UAE) at peak periods (Evans 1994, Butler *et al.* 2001). The Emirate of Abu Dhabi, with nearly 70% of the total land area of the Emirates, a 340 km coastline and nearly 40 big and small islands, supports a rich assemblage of birds, particularly waterbirds and nationally and regionally important breeding colonies of seabirds. Nearly 40% of all bird species recorded in the Emirate are waterbirds.

On several islands in the Emirate breeding colonies of the regionally endemic, and globally threatened, Socotra Cormorant *Phalacrocorax nigrogularis* are of global significance. Breeding colonies of Crab Plover *Dromas ardeola*, restricted to only two islands, are internationally important. Important breeding populations of White-cheeked Tern *Sterna repressa* and four other terns *Sterna* spp, Sooty Gull *Larus hemprichii* and Red-billed Tropicbird *Phaethon aethereus* are also found in the Emirate (Aspinall 1995, Aspinall 1996). Fifteen key islands in the Emirate contain 85% of all the IBAs, 85% of all tern colonies in the UAE, almost the entire breeding populations of five terns (*Sterna* spp.), nearly 80% of the Socotra Cormorant breeding population and all the breeding population and colonies of Crab Plover and Red-billed Tropicbird in the UAE (Javed & Khan 2003). Fifteen globally, and several regionally, threatened species are found in the country (BirdLife International 2005, Hornby & Aspinall 1996).

Rapid urban and industrial infrastructure development in the country, mostly along the coast and islands, has put many breeding colonies under threat (Evans 1994). Between 1995 and 2002 numbers of Socotra Cormorant breeding colonies have declined by more than 50%, from 13 colonies in 1995 to only six by 2002 (Aspinall 1996, Javed & Khan 2004). However, inconsistencies in methods, timings and data gaps do not allow any meaningful comparison of trends in overall breeding seabird numbers.

Conservation of waterbirds in the Emirate has three inherent weaknesses. First, information on waterbird populations is inconsistent and sporadic. Second, the network of protected coastal and island sites is inadequate. Third, the coastline and many islands are under severe developmental pressure and are being altered rapidly due to the absence of any policy or Coastal Zone Management Plan.

Systematic, long-term population monitoring is fundamental to acquire information on important bird populations, both to monitor changes and recommend actions. Abu Dhabi's Environment Agency (EAD) waterbird programme is a step in that direction. Such monitoring programmes, initiated locally,

should also develop into bigger programmes for the entire region. The Middle East is, and will remain, a political hotspot because of strategic oil reserves and increasing global energy demands, and will pose threats to waterbirds from oil spills and conflicts such as the Gulf War (Evans & Keijl 1993, Symens & Suhaibaini 1993). A regional waterbird monitoring programme with networks of individuals and organisations will be important for capacity building, monitoring and rapid response to oil spills and other events.

The long-term future of species and sites cannot be guaranteed without protection. Important islands for waterbirds should be declared as protected immediately (Javed & Khan 2003), to add to the existing protected areas under the Morrawah Marine Protected Area (MMPA) which currently has nine islands with an area of 4 225 km². IBAs or areas listed in the Directory of wetlands in the Middle East (Scott 1995) do not guarantee protection for sites, but they do provide international recognition to sites and it is imperative to further protect them.

Landscape patterns influence bird assemblages, and the understanding of such patterns provides opportunities and challenges (Clark *et al.* 2004). As migratory waterbirds use large geographical areas and move across them, a landscape based approach to monitor and conserve the wintering, staging and breeding waterbirds and their habitat is essential. However, management of areas along the coast is not only very difficult, but also extremely challenging due to such areas often being of high economic value for property development, tourism and industry. A landscape-scale management approach is needed to secure the conservation of waterbirds while enabling the UAE, and the Emirate in particular, to develop sustainably through maintaining natural ecosystem processes and the integrity and well being of coastal and inland ecosystems.

## REFERENCES

**Aspinall, S.** 1995. United Arab Emirates. In: D.A. Scott (ed.) A Directory of the wetlands in the Middle East. IUCN Gland, Switzerland, and IWRB Slimbridge, UK.

**Aspinall, S.** 1996. The breeding birds of the United Arab Emirates. Hobby Publications, UK.

**BirdLife International** 2005. Threatened birds of the World. www.birdlife.org

**Butler, R.W., Davidson, N.C. & Morrison, R.I.G.** 2001. Global-scale shorebird distribution in relation to productivity of near-shore ocean waters. Waterbirds 24: 224-232.

**Clark, R.G. Hobson, K.A., Nichols, J.D. & Bearhop, S.** 2004. Avian dispersal and demography/l scaling up to the landscape and beyond. The Condor 106: 717-719.

**Evans, M.** 1994. Important Bird Areas in the Middle East. BirdLife International, UK.

**Evans, M.I. & Keijl, G.O.** 1993. Impact of Gulf War oil spills on the wader populations of the Saudi Arabian Gulf Coast. Sandgrouse 15: 85-105.

**Hornby, R. & Aspinall, S.** 1996. Red Data List for Birds of the United Arab Emirates. Tribulus 6.2: 13-17.

**Javed, S. & Khan, S.B.** 2004. Status of breeding seabirds in the Abu Dhabi Emirate. Unpublished Report. Environmental Research and Wildlife Development Agency, Abu Dhabi.

**Javed, S. & Khan, S.B.** 2003. Important islands for bird conservation in the Abu Dhabi Emirate. Unpublished Report. Environmental Research and Wildlife Development Agency, Abu Dhabi.

**Scott, D.A** (ed.) 1995. A Directory of the wetlands in the Middle East. Gland, Switzerland, IUCN and IWRB Slimbridge, UK.

**Symens, P. & Suhaibaini, A.** 1993. Impact of Gulf War oil spills on the wintering seabird populations along the northern Arabian Gulf coast of Saudi Arabian, 1991. Sandgrouse 15: 37-43.

The United Arab Emirates hold an important breeding population of Red-billed Tropicbird *Phaethon aerthereus*. Photo: Simon Stirrup.

## 5.5 The marine environment: challenges for conservation implementation. Workshop Introduction

*John Croxall*

*Chair of Global Seabird Programme, BirdLife International, Wellbrook Court, Girton Road, Cambridge, CB3 0NA, UK.*

Croxall, J. 2006. The marine environment: challenges for conservation implementation. Workshop Introduction. *Waterbirds around the world*. Eds. G.C. Boere, C.A. Galbraith & D.A. Stroud. The Stationery Office, Edinburgh, UK. pp. 737-738.

Royal Albatross *Diomedea* sp. in New Zealand. The conservation of pelagic seabirds such as albatrosses and petrels is both a pressing and urgent conservation challenge. Photo: Colin Galbraith.

This workshop, the only one of the conference devoted exclusively to a marine theme, recognised that some of the world's greatest conservation challenges are in the marine environment, both within territorial (Exclusive Economic Zone) waters and on the high seas.

Amongst the biggest challenges for marine conservation are:

a) implementation of precautionary ecosystem-based approaches to sustainable use of resources; and
b) minimization of the environmental consequences of human activities.

Progress on both topics requires the identification of species, sites and areas needing particularly sensitive management, including the context and scope of Marine Protected Areas.

The presentations illustrated some current approaches to these issues, both methodological and practical, mainly focusing on sea ducks and coastal areas in the Northern Hemisphere.

Two presentations illustrated the use of new methods and instrumentation. Mosbech *et al.* describes the use of satellite telemetry to define migration routes and offshore key habitats during winter for King Eiders *Somateria spectabilis* in arctic Greenland by attaching transmitters to birds from three moulting sites in west Greenland and a breeding site in arctic Canada. With increasing potential human impacts from oil activities and fisheries more knowledge on the key habitats outside the breeding areas is needed. Surveys by plane or ship can give snapshots of distribution and provide important data for population estimates. However, offshore surveys whether by plane or ship are costly and are limited by light and bad weather during the Arctic winter, where ice also limit the accessibility for ships. Therefore satellite telemetry provides an important supplementary tool. West Greenland though in the Arctic, provides areas of open water during winter and is an important wintering area for Arctic marine birds.

Garthe & Skov report that the German Baltic Sea was one the first areas in which the Special Protection Areas (SPA) of the

EC Directive on the conservation of wild birds were selected on the basis of offshore concentrations of seabirds. In 2002, a GIS and geostatistical procedure was applied to define concentration areas for seabirds, mainly sea ducks. From this exercise it was concluded that it is possible to describe offshore aggregations of seabird species exhibiting high aggregations by applying geostatistical routines. For species showing widespread distributions this procedure is much more difficult and needs to be further developed. For modelling purposes, co-variates (*e.g.* water depth) should be taken into account in the future. Also, the spatial variation of the boundary lines describing concentrations should be calculated to estimate the reliability of the data as well as the relevance of the areas selected.

Nikolaeva *et al.* reported that although the present system of Russian protected areas has established over 100 strictly protected nature reserves (zapovedniks), these do not currently include marine protected areas. An important goal is to establish 13 strictly protected reserves with offshore areas for protection of seabirds and waterfowl and coastal marine habitats. Recently the combined efforts of experts have resulted in a set of proposed Marine Protected Areas with special reference to seabird and sea duck conservation. Some of the most important proposed protected areas in the Barents and White Sea include: (1) east Murman coast including the archipelagos of the Kandalaksha state strictly protected reserve and the most important seabird colonies; (2) the main moulting, migrating and stopover areas of waterfowl in the Pechora Sea area; (3) the main breeding moulting, migrating and wintering areas in the White Sea area. In the very near future rapid oil and gas development and transportation on the Russian arctic shelf will come into conflict with the existing habitat protection strategy for seabirds and waterfowl. It is evident that development of an appropriately designed network of marine protected areas is urgently needed as an effective way

to mitigate the environmental impact of the above activities and to maintain normal ecosystem functioning.

Overall, the workshop agreed that sufficient data, expertise and relevant methodological approaches now exist to identify key sites for protecting breeding and wintering concentrations of seabirds and sea duck within coastal areas, notably Exclusive Economic Zones (EEZs). The challenge here is primarily to integrate the necessary species and habitat protection into an appropriate overall system for managing all aspects of such habitats in a way that will provide suitable protection against pollution, over-fishing and other ecosystem-destabilizing influences. Even within coastal areas and EEZs, however, much more work is needed to identify important staging areas and to define key habitats for species which are not congregatory.

For high seas areas and pelagic marine systems, however, considerable new work is required to develop approaches for identifying critical habitats and biodiversity hot-spots for marine vertebrates, especially seabirds. This will require combining existing data from at-sea surveys with records from remote-tracking sources and developing new analytical and modeling approaches for visualizing and integrating such data with information from other marine taxa and with data on the physical and biological marine environment. New standards of management and governance of the high seas will also need to be implemented, particularly by Regional Fisheries Management Organizations and others with high seas jurisdictions, closely linked to parallel initiatives and equivalent standards being implemented in adjacent areas within EEZs under coastal state jurisdiction. This will entail large-scale multinational initiatives and will need to involve data holders and stakeholders from both conservation and resource exploitation constituencies, together with relevant government, intergovernmental and non-governmental organizations if open-ocean areas are to be managed and protected in appropriate ways.

With issues to address in both terrestrial and marine environments, birds such as penguins present challenging conservation problems. More than 3 000 Magellanic Penguins *Spheniscus magellanicus* at Harberton, Beagle Channel, Argentina. Photo: Chris Wilson.

# Selection of suitable sites for marine protected areas for seabirds: a case study with Special Protection Areas (SPAs) in the German Baltic Sea

*Stefan Garthe[1] & Henrik Skov[2]*

[1] *Research and Technology Centre (FTZ), University of Kiel, Hafentörn, D-25761 Büsum, Germany. (email: garthe@ftz-west.uni-kiel.de)*

[2] *DHI Water & Environment, Agern Allé 11, DK-2970 Hørsholm, Denmark. (email: hsk@dhi.dk)*

Garthe, S. & Skov, H. 2006. Selection of suitable sites for marine protected areas for seabirds: a case study with Special Protection Areas (SPAs) in the German Baltic Sea. *Waterbirds around the world.* Eds. G.C. Boere, C.A. Galbraith & D.A. Stroud. The Stationery Office, Edinburgh, UK. pp. 739-742.

## ABSTRACT

This paper is an abbreviated and updated version of two publications: Garthe (2003), Verteilungsmuster und Bestände von Seevögeln in der Ausschließlichen Wirtschaftszone (AWZ) der deutschen Nord- und Ostsee und Fachvorschläge für EU-Vogelschutzgebiete, and Garthe (2006), Identification of areas of seabird concentrations in the German North Sea and Baltic Sea using aerial and ship-based surveys. It gives a brief overview of the field methods used to study the distribution of seabirds at sea in the German Baltic Sea. It also shows how the data were analysed, how seabird concentrations may be delineated, and how suggestions for protected areas were derived from the data.

## INTRODUCTION

Marine protected areas (MPAs) for seabirds are currently being established under various international instruments and marine conventions (e.g. OSPAR, HELCOM), and also under the main nature conservation directives of the European Union. When Germany adopted its Federal Nature Conservation Act in April 2002 in order to select Natura 2000 sites including sites within the Economic Exclusion Zone (EEZ), the need arose to obtain an up-to-date overview of the distribution and status of seabirds in German waters of the North and Baltic Seas. This paper briefly describes the field methods used in studying the distribution of seabirds at sea, how the data were analysed, how seabird concentrations may be identified, and how suggestions for protected areas were derived from the data.

## FIELD METHODS

Seabird distribution in the south-western Baltic Sea was studied by transect counts from ships and aircraft. This method basically aims at assessing distribution patterns and numbers of seabirds at sea, but ships and aircraft are differently suited for these purposes (see Camphuysen *et al.* 2004 and Garthe *et al.* 2004 for recent reviews). Aerial surveys are able to cover a much larger area in a much shorter time and at a lower cost per kilometre than surveys from ships. However, they are only feasible under conditions of low wind speed, and there are limitations to species identification from the air (e.g. groups such as grebes, gulls, terns and auks cannot usually be identified to species level). Ship-based surveys enable the collection of additional information on the behaviour of the birds and usually allow for sampling environmental data, such as hydrography, which proves very useful for understanding species distribution patterns.

The methodology for counts from ships was first described by Tasker *et al.* (1984) and has been largely standardized internationally. Due to the presence of high densities of birds that quite often fled from approaching ships, it proved necessary to search regularly or continuously for birds using binoculars and to deploy at least two observers, as suggested by Webb & Durinck (1992) and Garthe *et al.* (2002). Birds were counted from either the top deck or the bridge-wing, usually on 300 m wide transects set to one or both sides of the vessel. Flying birds were counted employing the "snapshot" method (Tasker *et al.* 1984, Garthe *et al.* 2002). The position of the survey vessel was recorded automatically by onboard or portable GPS instruments.

Seabirds were counted from aircraft using a transect methodology recently described by Diederichs *et al.* (2002). Flights were conducted from twin-engine aircraft (e.g. Partenavia P-68) flying over German waters from the coast to the outer limit of the EEZ. Transects were usually set perpendicular to the coast to obtain variation over major habitat features such as water depth, distance to coast, and frontal systems. Transects were 10 km apart in the North Sea (20 km in areas far from the coast) and mostly 8 km apart in the Baltic Sea. Flights were conducted at an altitude of 250 ft (78 m) and a speed of 100 knots (185 km/hour). During the counts, all bird observations were recorded on a portable voice recorder; the data recorded included: time (to the nearest second), species, number, general behaviour (five categories) and also, if possible, age and sex. Geographic position was recorded every five seconds onboard the aircraft.

## SPECIES SELECTION

Gellermann *et al.* (2003) catalogued those species occurring in German waters which must be considered in the selection of SPAs. They distinguished three different levels of importance for species. In the selection of SPAs, only those species that were categorized in their list as of high or medium importance were used. Three groups of bird species comprised this category. The first group comprises the species that are listed in Annex I of the EU Birds Directive (species that shall be the subject of special conservation measures) and that occur regularly in the offshore waters of the German parts of the Baltic Sea. These are Red-throated Diver *Gavia stellata*, Black-throated Diver *G. arctica*, Slavonian Grebe *Podiceps auritus*, and four species of terns. The second group comprises migratory species that regularly occur in offshore areas. The EU Birds Directive does not define "migratory species", and the definition used in practice is the one provided by the Convention on Migratory Species of Wild Animals (Bonn Convention). This Convention defines migratory species as species in which a significant proportion of the population cyclically and predictably crosses one or more national jurisdictional boundaries. In both study areas, this includes all seabird species. For these species, especially those that occur in major concentrations, the most important areas (or a few of the most important areas) were recommended for selection as SPAs.

The identification of SPAs focused on the German EEZ, and preferably on areas that were important for more than one species. The third group comprises rare offshore species and species occurring only along the coast (e.g. diving ducks, geese and swans).

Analysis of the data was equal for the first two groups, i.e. Annex I species and migratory species. However, concentrations of Annex I species were considered to be much more important and were thus more decisive for the designation of SPAs than areas with only migratory bird species. The third group (i.e. species that were rare offshore or confined to the coast) was not relevant to the SPA selection process in the EEZ because of the virtual absence of these species in this area.

## SPECIES DISTRIBUTION

All species distribution maps are based on densities, i.e. the number of individuals per unit area. Some species are distributed over large areas and usually exhibit only short-term aggregations (e.g. gulls), while other species are often densely concentrated and are predictable in their distribution (e.g. seaducks). For all relevant species in the German Baltic Sea, a spatial interpolation procedure based on ordinary kriging (Kitanidis 1997) and used by Skov *et al.* (2000) was adopted and further developed (Garthe 2003, Garthe & Skov in prep.). With this procedure, distributional data were interpolated and smoothed between survey lines on the basis of the species-specific spatial abundance structure (which is measured by the software in use). Fig. 1 gives one example for the Long-tailed Duck *Clangula hyemalis*.

## SPA SELECTION

The boundaries of areas of bird concentration were determined by an analysis investigating the gradient of density change over space. In order to do this, the modelled distributional data were projected into a two-dimensional map. In each case, the modelled isoline of bird density (i.e. the line drawn through the same level of bird density) located just outside the strongest gradient in spatial density was chosen as the boundary of a

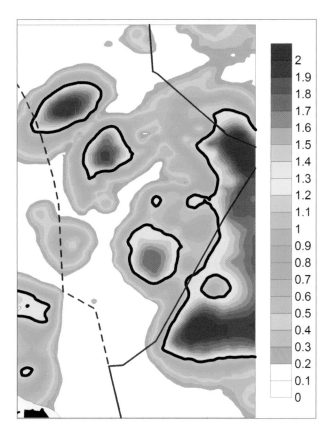

**Fig. 1.** Distribution of the Long-tailed Duck *Clangula hyemalis* in the German Baltic Sea in winter (December-March); 1986-2002. Colours represent different densities (values as logarithmic density; see legend). Black areas were not studied sufficiently. The dashed red line indicates the seaward limit of German territorial waters; the continuous red line indicates the seaward limit of the German EEZ.

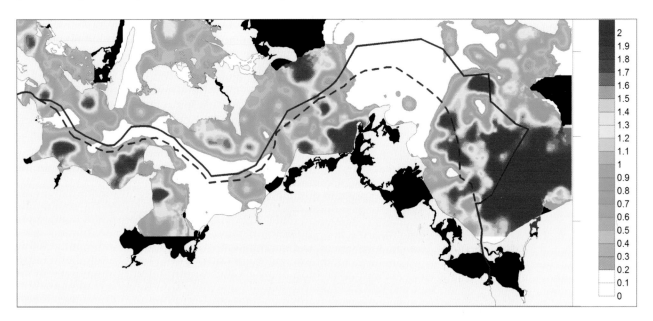

**Fig. 2.** Distribution of the Velvet Scoter *Melanitta fusca* in the Pommeranian Bay in winter (December-March); 1986-2002. Colours represent different densities (values as logarithmic density [log (density + 1)]; see legend). The dashed red line indicates the seaward limit of German territorial waters; the continuous red line indicates the seaward limit of the German EEZ.

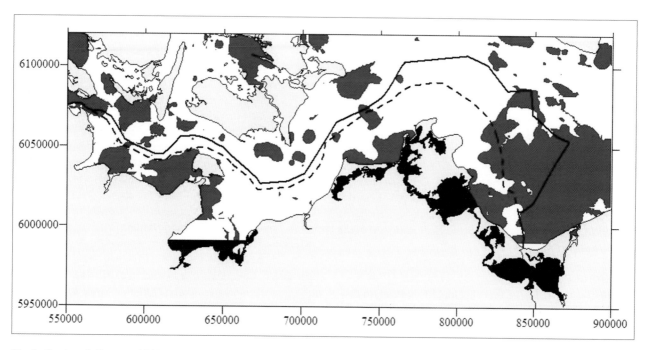

**Fig. 3.** Overlay of all areas exhibiting concentrations of the species of interest in this study in the south-western Baltic Sea (blue colour). Black areas were not studied sufficiently. The dashed line indicates the seaward limit of German territorial waters, the continuous line indicates the seaward limit of the German EEZ.

concentration (see Fig. 2 for one example). In this way, the major part of the concentration is included in the selected area. The density value of the boundary line was noted and used as the species- and season-specific minimum density defining a seabird concentration. This value was then taken for plotting the contour line showing the spatial extent of the respective concentration.

The areas of concentration and contour lines for each of the species of interest derived from the list of Annex I and migratory bird species were then combined so that a set of areas for potential conservation was identified (Fig. 3). From this map, one potential SPA was suggested.

## DISCUSSION

The data collected by ship-based and aerial surveys have been extremely useful for describing the current distribution patterns of all seabird species in the two study areas. Both field methods have their advantages and disadvantages because of their different characteristics. A combination of both methods is ideal for most purposes, including those discussed in this paper. It is important to select these field methods carefully, with respect both to the spatio-temporal scale envisaged for such a study and to the species under consideration.

The robustness of the results has been the focus of considerable attention by various groups in the light of proposals for two large SPAs within the German EEZ in the Baltic and North Seas (Garthe 2003). Most promising was the finding that all surveys carried out after finalization of the SPA proposals (i.e. all surveys in 2003 and 2004) identified the same areas of major concentration as in previous years. This demonstrates that even if the boundaries of the areas of concentration shift slightly, as might be expected in seabirds living in a dynamic environment, the major results are stable and reproducible. However, on a larger time-scale it is possible that the distribution of seabird species could change, especially if environmental conditions change. In the Baltic Sea, this could be the case, for instance, in

relation to winter ice distribution, since nearly all of the data collected for this study were from mild and normal winters only. In the North Sea, recent major changes in food availability (which have led to breeding failures in the north-western North Sea) may influence distribution patterns in the German Bight, at least in those species ranging over wide areas of the North Sea.

The analytical methods outlined in this paper are still at an early stage in being adopted as standard procedures for designating SPAs, since most Member States of the European Union have not yet delineated such protected sites in offshore areas. However, these methods have been very useful for selecting areas of seabird concentration and SPAs. More recent work by British colleagues highlights the way forward (e.g. McSorley *et al.* 2004, Webb *et al.* 2004). For species exhibiting a widely dispersed distribution, the procedure for identifying areas of concentration is much more difficult than for aggregated species. To date, no proposals have been made as to how to deal with sea areas in which the only species present are rather evenly or at least widely distributed. In such cases, vast areas would need to be designated to capture a meaningful percentage of bird numbers. This is often politically impossible and might also be less easy to justify scientifically. This problem needs further consideration. For modelling purposes, e.g. in future site selection, covariates (e.g. water depth) should be included. Also, attention might be given to the reliability of data by calculating (statistically) the spatial variation of the boundary lines describing concentrations. If such boundary lines vary substantially over space (e.g. within a standard deviation), then the baseline data and/or aggregation characteristics of the bird species may be less evident than when the boundaries are more stable over space.

## ACKNOWLEDGEMENTS

This work is based on several projects that have been conducted in recent years. Funding has been received primarily from Bundesamt für Naturschutz, Bundesministerium für Umwelt,

Naturschutz und Reaktorsicherheit, Freunde und Förderer der Inselstation der Vogelwarte Helgoland e.V., Ornithologische Arbeitsgemeinschaft für Schleswig-Holstein & Hamburg e.V. and Forschungs- und Technologiezentrum Westküste (FTZ) der Universität Kiel. Field observations have been carried out by many observers over the years. Many private and governmental institutions permitted work on their boats. Furthermore, many people have contributed to this work by collecting, summarizing and analysing data, by helping to shape the procedures for SPA designation, and by general comments. From these, at least, the following need to be mentioned: C.J. Camphuysen, V. Dierschke, O. Engelhard, N. Guse, O. Hüppop, J. Kotzerka, J. Krause, U. Kubetzki, K. Ludynia, N. Markones, T. Merck, M. Scheidat, P. Schwemmer, H. Skov, N. Sonntag, A. Webb and T. Weichler.

## REFERENCES

**Camphuysen, C.J., Fox, A.D., Leopold, M.F. & Petersen, I.K.** 2004. Towards standardised seabirds at sea techniques in connection with environmental impact assessments for offshore wind farms in the U.K. Final report to COWRIE, COWRIE-BAM-02-2002.

**Diederichs, A., Nehls, G. & Petersen, I.K.** 2002. Flugzeugzählungen zur großflächigen Erfassung von Seevögeln und marinen Säugern als Grundlage für Umweltverträglichkeitsstudien im Offshorebereich. Seevögel 23: 38-46.

**Garthe, S.** 2003. Verteilungsmuster und Bestände von Seevögeln in der Ausschließlichen Wirtschaftszone (AWZ) der deutschen Nord- und Ostsee und Fachvorschläge für EU-Vogelschutzgebiete. Berichte zum Vogelschutz 40: 15-56.

**Garthe, S.** 2006. Identification of areas of seabird concentrations in the German North Sea and Baltic Sea using aerial and ship-based surveys. In: H. von Nordheim, D. Boedeker & J.C. Krause (eds.) Advancing towards effective marine conservation in Europe: Natura 2000 sites in German offshore waters. Springer.

**Garthe, S. & Skov, H.** In prep. Selection of suitable sites for marine protected areas for seabirds: a case study with Special Protection Areas (SPAs) under the EU Birds Directive in the Baltic Sea.

**Garthe, S., Hüppop, O. & Weichler, T.** 2002. Anleitung zur Erfassung von Seevögeln auf See von Schiffen. Seevögel 23: 47-55.

**Garthe, S., Dierschke, V., Weichler, T. & Schwemmer, P.** 2004. Rastvogelvorkommen und Offshore-Windkraftnutzung: Analyse des Konfliktpotenzials für die deutsche Nord- und Ostsee. Unpublished final report of sub-project 5 of the project MINOS to the Federal Environmental Ministry, Berlin.

**Gellermann, M., Melter, J. & Schreiber, M.** 2003. Ableitung fachlicher Kriterien für die Identifizierung und Abgrenzung von marinen Besonderen Schutzgebieten (BSG) nach Art. 4 Abs. 1 und 2 der Vogelschutzrichtlinie bzw. Vorschlagsgebieten gemäß Art. 4 Abs. 1 der FFH-Richtlinie für die deutsche ausschließliche Wirtschaftszone. Unpublished report to the Federal Environmental Ministry, Berlin.

**Kitanidis, P.** 1997. Introduction to geostatistics – Applications in hydrogeology. Cambridge University Press, New York.

**McSorley, C.A., Webb, A., Dean, B.J. & Reid, J.B.** 2004. Inshore marine Special Protection Areas: a methodological evaluation of site selection and boundary determination. JNCC Report 344. Joint Nature Conservation Committee, Peterborough, UK.

**Skov, H., Vaitkus, G., Flensted, K.N., Grishanov, G., Kalamees, A., Kondratyev, A., Leivo, M., Luigojoe, L., Mayr, C., Rasmussen, J.F., Raudonikis, L., Scheller, W., Sidlo, P.O., Stipniece, A., Struwe-Juhl, B. & Welander, B.** 2000. Inventory of coastal and marine important bird areas in the Baltic Sea. BirdLife International, Cambridge, UK.

**Tasker, M.L., Jones, P.H., Dixon, T.J. & Blake, B.F.** 1984. Counting seabirds at sea from ships: a review of methods employed and a suggestion for a standardized approach. Auk 101: 567-577.

**Webb, A. & Durinck, J.** 1992. Counting birds from ships. In: J. Komdeur, J. Bertelsen & G. Cracknell (eds) Manual for aeroplane and ship surveys of waterfowl and seabirds. IWRB Special Publication 19, Slimbridge, UK: 24-37.

**Webb, A., McSorley, C.A., Dean, B.J., Reid, J.B., Cranswick, P.A., Smith, L. & Hall, C.** 2004. An assessment of the numbers and distributions of inshore aggregations of waterbirds using Liverpool Bay during the non-breeding season in support of possible SPA identification. Unpublished JNCC report. Joint Nature Conservation Committee, Peterborough, UK.

# Existing and proposed marine protected areas and their relevance for seabird conservation: a case study in the Barents Sea region

*Natalia G. Nikolaeva[1], Vassily A. Spiridonov[2] & Yury V. Krasnov[3]*

[1]*Russian Bird Conservation Union, 60 bd. 1, Entuziastov shosse, Moscow, 111123 Russia. (email: n_nikolaeva@neehon.com)*
[2]*World Wide Fund for Nature, Russian Programme Office, 19 bd. 3, Nikoloyamskaya st., Moscow, 109240 Russia.*
[3]*Murmansk Marine Biological Institute, 17 Vladimirskaya st., Murmansk, 183010 Russia.*

Nikolaeva, N.G., Spiridonov, V.A. & Krasnov, Y.V. 2006. Existing and proposed marine protected areas and their relevance for seabird conservation: a case study in the Barents Sea region. *Waterbirds around the world.* Eds. G.C. Boere, C.A. Galbraith & D.A. Stroud. The Stationery Office, Edinburgh, UK. pp. 743-749.

## ABSTRACT

The present system of Russian protected areas has resulted in the establishment of 100 strictly protected nature reserves. However, Russia has not yet established any system of marine protected areas. The most important goal of the 12 existing strictly protected reserves that include marine waters is the protection of waterbirds and their coastal habitats. During the last few years, various experts working together have produced a proposal for a series of marine protected areas with special reference to the conservation of seabirds and seaducks. Some of the most important proposed marine protected areas in the Barents Sea region include: 1) the eastern Murman coast, including the archipelagos of Kandalaksha State Strictly Protected Reserve and the most important seabird colonies; 2) the main moulting and staging areas for waterbirds in the Pechora Sea; and 3) the main breeding, moulting, staging and wintering areas in the White Sea. In the near future, rapid oil and gas development and transportation on the Russia Arctic shelf will come into conflict with the existing strategy for the protection of seabirds and waterbirds. The development of an appropriately designed network of marine protected areas is proving to be an effective way to ensure that the normal ecosystem functions are maintained.

## INTRODUCTION

The present system of protected areas in Russia has a history of almost 90 years, and has resulted in the establishment of 100 strictly protected nature reserves (zapovedniks). Some of these are Ramsar sites and a few others are protected under the World Heritage Convention. A characteristic of Russian zapovedniks is the presence of research departments that

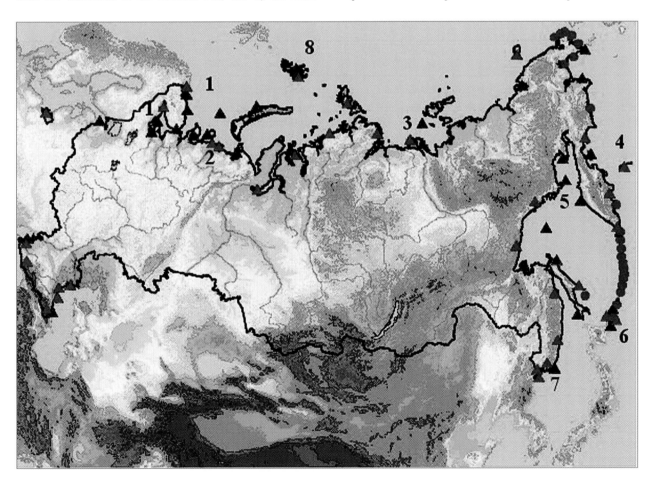

Fig. 1. Russian protected areas with offshore areas: (1) Kandalaksha Reserve in the Barents Sea and White Sea; (2) Nenets Reserve in the Barents Sea; (3) Ust'-Lena Reserve in the Laptev Sea; (4) Commander Islands in the Bering Sea; (5) Magadan Reserve in the Sea of Okhotsk; (6) Kuril Reserve in the Sea of Okhotsk; (7) Far Eastern Marine Reserve in the Sea of Japan; (8) Franz-Josef Land Reserve in the Barents Sea.

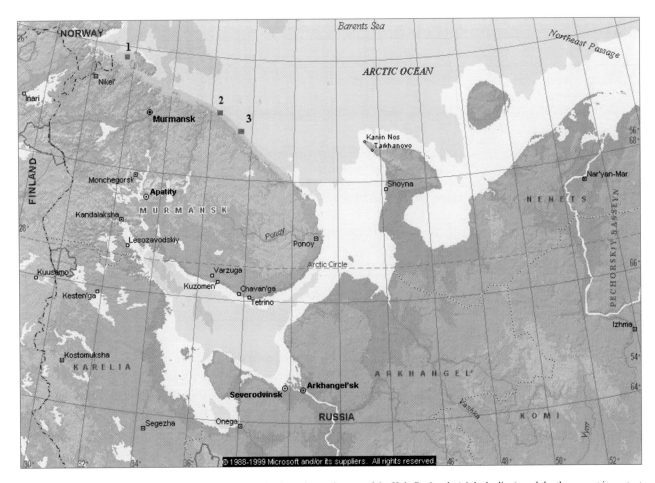

Fig. 2. The most important wintering areas for some seaducks along the north coast of the Kola Peninsula (pink shading), and the three most important breeding areas for the Common Eider *Somateria mollissima*: (1) Ainov Islands; (2) Gavrilovskiye Islands; (3) Seven Islands in Kandalaksha State Strictly Protected Reserve.

conduct a programme of monitoring biological observations (the so-called "Chronicle of Nature"). However, Russia has not yet established any system of marine protected areas.

Existing reserves that are of special importance for the protection and investigation of seabirds and seaducks are the strictly protected reserves of Kandalaksha (White Sea and Barents Sea), Nenets (Barents Sea), Ust'-Lena (Laptev Sea), Commander Islands (Bering Sea), Magadan (Sea of Okhotsk), Kuril (Sea of Okhotsk) and Far Eastern Marine (Sea of Japan), and the Franz-Josef Land Reserve (Barents Sea) (Fig. 1). Amongst other protected areas that either do not have a high protection status or are under regional jurisdiction, the Solovki and Kuzova Islands (White Sea), Beringia Nature Park and several small coastal reserves in the Russian Far East are worthy of mention.

During the last few years, the joint efforts of a number of experts on marine wildlife, including experts on seabirds and waterbirds, have culminated in the mapping of several important and especially sensitive areas. A series of marine protected areas (MPAs) has been proposed on the basis of a gap analysis, with special attention being given to conservation targets for seabirds and seaducks. Of particular importance is the establishment of marine protected areas and introduction of other conservation and management measures along the East Atlantic Flyway in the Barents Sea and White Sea (Krasnov *et al.* this volume). Data on the abundance, population dynamics and distribution of seabirds and seaducks were collected using various methods. These included land-based stationary observations and aerial surveys

by helicopter and special aeroplane in the coastal and open waters of the Barents and White Seas.

According to Russian national legislation, marine waters are under federal jurisdiction, and only those marine areas given federal protection may be considered as marine protected areas in the strict sense. Thirteen of the strictly protected reserves (IUCN category I) in Russia include offshore areas, and four others have marine buffer zones. In addition, there are eight federal reserves which include marine areas, and most of these have been designated as Ramsar sites or are potential Ramsar sites. The most important management goal of most of these reserves is the protection of seabirds and waterbirds and their coastal habitats.

The increasing human activity in the waters surrounding the islands which already have some protection is poorly regulated, resulting in a need for the establishment of other protected areas (especially marine) within the Barents and White Seas to ensure that there is a representative and functional network of marine protected areas. A set of marine protected areas for the conservation of seabirds and seaducks has therefore been proposed for the Barents and White Seas. Some examples of the most important of these proposed protected areas are considered below.

## EASTERN MURMAN COAST FROM THE RIBACHIY PENINSULA TO SVYATOINOS CAPE

The coastal waters off the north coast of the Kola Peninsula (Fig. 2) are an extremely important wintering area for several species of seaducks (Bianki *et al.* 1993). Over 70 000 seaducks,

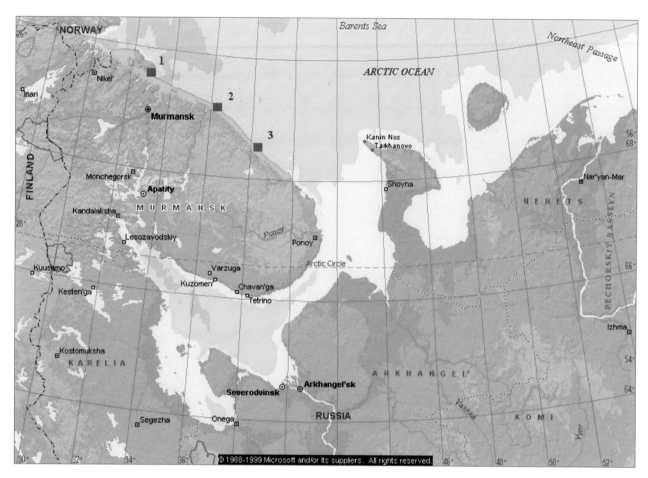

Fig. 3. Proposed marine protected areas along the north coast of the Kola Peninsula: (1) Gorodetskiy seabird colony and surrounding waters off the Rybachiy Peninsula; (2) Yarnishnaya Inlet with Krutik Cape and Dalnezelenetskaya Inlet; (3) Dvorovaya Bay.

including large numbers of Steller's Eider *Polysticta stelleri*, spend the winter in this area (Nygård *et al.* 1995). Two of the most abundant wintering species are the Common Eider *Somateria mollissima* and the King Eider *S. spectabilis*, while the Common Eider also breeds here (Belopol'skii 1957). As many as 6 000-7 000 pairs of Common Eiders have been found nesting (Karpovich 1987). The wintering population of this species is about 50 000 birds, and thus greatly exceeds the number of breeding individuals. However, nothing is known about the origin and breeding areas of the wintering birds as there are no ringing recoveries. At present, the most important threats include illegal egg-collection and disturbance in the breeding areas, but oil spills and chronic oil pollution may pose a serious threat in the future. The most important breeding areas for the Common Eider are situated on the islands of three archipelagos: Ainov, Gavrilovskiye and Seven Islands (Fig. 2) in Kandalaksha State Strictly Protected Reserve in the Barents Sea (Karpovich 1984). Unfortunately, in the last few years a strict protection regime has not been maintained at these islands because of serious management problems in the reserve. Furthermore, the wintering grounds of the Common Eider are unprotected. Thus, the main priority for this area is to re-establish a real protection regime in the islands.

There are three important seabird colonies on the coast of the Kola Peninsula without any protection status. Gorodetskiy seabird colony on the Ribachiy Peninsula (Fig. 3) is the largest colony along the entire Kola coast, with over 50 000 Black-legged Kittiwake *Rissa tridactyla* nests and about 4 000 guillemots *Uria*

spp. This seabird colony and the surrounding waters off the Rybachiy Peninsula deserve federal reserve (zakaznik) status.

Farther east, Krutik Cape supports 4 000 Black-legged Kittiwake nests and Dvorovaya Bay supports 32 000 Kittiwake nests and over 1 000 guillemots. The main limiting factor influencing the dynamics of seabird colonies in recent years has been the state of the food resources, such as Herring *Clupea harengus*, Capelin *Mallotus villosus* and sand eels *Ammodytes* spp. (Krasnov *et al.* 1995, Krasnov & Barrett 1995). The size of the fish stocks is determined not only by environmental factors, but also to a considerable extent by fisheries activities. Because of the low level of the Capelin stock in 2003, Black-legged Kittiwakes failed to breed at the colonies along the Kola Peninsula coast. Thus, the depletion of food resources, oil spills and chronic oil pollution have been identified as the most important threats to seabird colonies in this area.

Another marine area which requires special protection status (e.g. specially protected marine waters) is the Yarnishnaya Inlet together with Krutik Cape and Dalnezelenetskaya Inlet near Dalniye Zelentsi settlement (Fig. 3). This area has been a scientific study area of the Murmansk Marine Biological Institute for many years. A third important area in this region is Dvorovaya Bay (Fig. 3), where federal reserve (zakaznik) status combined with a monitoring programme would be desirable.

## THE PECHORA SEA

The establishment of marine protected areas in the Pechora Sea is a high priority. The area is of great importance for seabirds

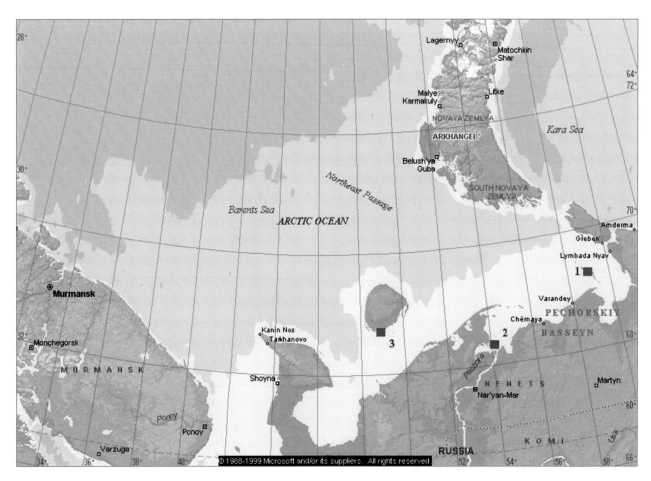

Fig. 4. Proposed marine protected areas in the Pechora Sea: (1) the waters around Dolgiy Island; (2) the Pechora Estuary; (3) the waters off the south coast of Kolguev Island.

and waterbirds because of its extensive breeding grounds, moulting sites and staging areas for birds on migration (Krasnov *et al.* 2002). The problem of the Pechora Sea is that it is a mosaic of local oil fields, which makes it difficult to design effective protected areas. In the proposal for the establishment of protected areas, we will compare the pros and cons of two possible ways of developing a protected area: 1) through nomination of the Nenetskiy Zapovednik for UNESCO Biosphere Reserve status and establishment of a cluster of biosphere polygons in offshore areas; or 2) through the establishment of a network of protected areas with some other status, under the special control of the Russian maritime and environmental authorities. We consider the first option below.

### Dolgiy Island

The waters surrounding Dolgiy Island (Fig. 4) hold the largest concentration of moulting and migrating seaducks in northwestern Russia. King Eider and Common Scoter *Melanitta nigra* are two of the most abundant species. Flocks of over 10 000 seaducks have been observed in the area (Isaksen *et al.* 2000). At the same time, this area borders on the Prirazlomnoye oil field, and the seaducks could therefore be at great risk of exposure to oil spills, chronic oil pollution, human disturbance and degradation of food resources during oil exploration.

### Pechora Estuary

The Pechora Estuary (Fig. 4) is the only marine staging area for swans *Cygnus* spp. along the migration route to their wintering

areas. During autumn, large flocks of Bewick's Swans *Cygnus columbianus bewickii* and Whooper Swans *C. cygnus* numbering several hundred birds pass through the area (Krasnov *et al.* 2002). In addition, some seaducks and dabbling ducks spend the winter in the estuary. Current threats include illegal hunting and human disturbance, while chronic oil pollution from oil exploration could pose a threat in the future. The presence of the Nenetskiy State Zapovednik provides a good opportunity to develop offshore protected areas through raising the status of the zapovednik to Biosphere Reserve and adding some offshore areas as biosphere polygons with a special management regime. Some areas could be directly associated with the Nenetskiy Zapovednik, or at least with the Nenetskiy Zakaznik, particularly an area in the Pechora Estuary and the waters surrounding Dolgiy Island.

### Kolguev Island

The waters off the south coast of Kolguev Island (Fig. 4) are an important moulting area and staging area for migrating seaducks. The King Eider is the most numerous species in these waters, while the Bean Goose *Anser fabalis* and Greater White-fronted Goose *A. albifrons* are present during autumn (Ponomaryeva 1995, Krasnov *et al.* 2002). The main threats are hunting, human disturbance, and the increasing possibility of oil spills and chronic oil pollution. The original model territory of Kolguev Island that combined local, traditional use of natural resources and modern oil exploration led to the establishment of a specially protected ethno-ecological territory. The possible

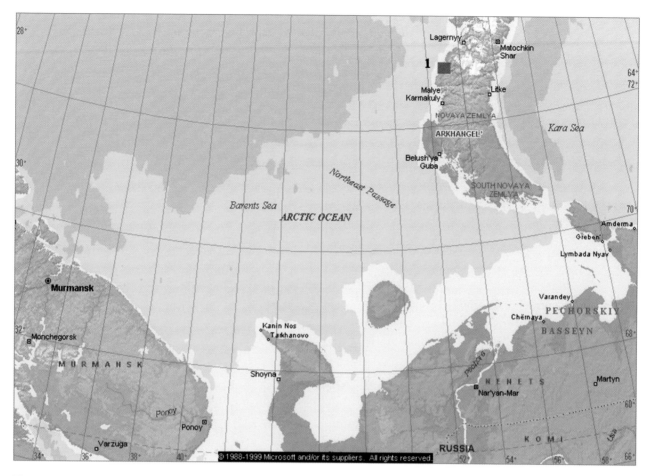

Fig. 5. The proposed marine protected area near Novaya Zemlya, including Bezimyannaya and Gribovaya Bays (1).

addition of a 12-mile marine zone and marine reserve around the island is under discussion.

## NOVAYA ZEMLYA

The largest and most important colonies of Common Eider and seabirds (including c. 1 000 000 Brunnich's Guillemot *Uria lomvia*) in northern European Russia are situated along the south-west coast of the Novaya Zemlya archipelago (Uspenskiy 1956, Uspenskiy & Khakhin 1993). Two bays on the south-west coast of Novaya Zemlya (Bezimyannaya and Gribovaya Bays; Fig. 5) hold the majority of the breeding population of Common Eiders and some seabird species, but these were under strict protection only until 1952. The current number of breeding Common Eiders, their systematic status and their wintering areas are unknown. The main threats in the area are human disturbance on the eider breeding grounds during future development of mineral resources along the coast, depletion of the food resources of seabirds (e.g. over-fishing of Polar Cod *Boreogadus saida*, one of the most important food items of seabirds in the area), and possible pollution of coastal waters from the Shtokmanovskoye gas field. The proposed protection regime for the breeding, moulting and possible wintering areas of seaducks and seabirds includes establishing a network of protected areas of various types in the waters surrounding the most important bird habitats on Novaya Zemlya, and re-establishing the strict protection status of Bezimyannaya Bay.

## THE WHITE SEA

The most abundant species of seaduck in the White Sea is the Common Eider. The isolated population of eiders in this area is estimated to be about 40 000-60 000 birds (Bianki & Karpovich 1983, Bianki 1991).

### The Terskiy coast

The Terskiy coast of the Gorlo in the White Sea (Fig. 6) is one of the most important staging areas for migrating birds in the East Atlantic Flyway and one of the most important moulting and wintering areas for seaducks in the region. In summer, moulting seaducks, mainly Common Eiders (c. 6 000 birds) and Steller's Eiders (c. 4 000 birds), congregate in Terskiy coastal waters (Krasnov *et al.* 2006). The Terskiy coastal zone is the only area in the Russian Arctic that supports a large population of Steller's Eiders throughout the year (Krasnov *et al.* 2006) and, at the same time, is a key moulting area for this species (Kokhanov 1979). The system of polynyas along the Terskiy coast supports huge wintering flocks of Common Eiders (c. 16 000 birds), King Eiders (c. 6 500) and Steller's Eiders (4 000) (Strøm *et al.* in press), and is currently one of the most important wintering areas for the King Eider in northern European Russia. Most of the potential problems in the area are thought to be related to unregulated tourism, oil spills, chronic oil pollution and shipping (during transportation of oil from the Kandalaksha, Onega and Arkhangelsk oil terminals to the Murmansk oil terminal). One possible location for the proposed pipeline from Siberia to Murmansk would pass through the area. An offshore federal reserve (zakaznik) encompassing the moulting and wintering areas of seaducks has been proposed for the Terskiy coast of the White Sea.

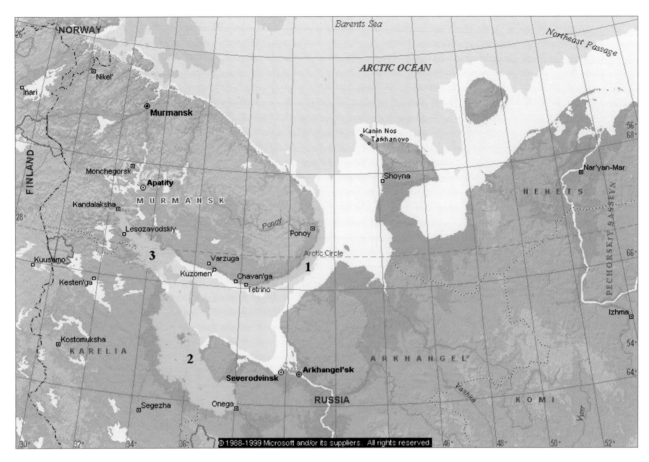

Fig. 6. Proposed marine protected areas in the White Sea: (1) the Terskiy coast of the Gorlo in the White Sea; (2) Onega Bay; (3) Kandalaksha Bay.

## Onega Bay

Almost half of the White Sea Common Eider population breeds on islands in Onega Bay (Fig. 6), and the majority of males moult within this region. In autumn, numerous flocks of seabirds and waterbirds in the East Atlantic Flyway stop over in Onega Bay (Bianki 1991) on passage to their wintering grounds. In winter, polynyas in Onega Bay hold the majority of the White Sea Common Eider wintering population. The most serious potential threats in the area include human disturbance, illegal hunting and egg-collection, and chronic oil pollution during oil transportation from the Onega Bay ports. Detailed proposals will be developed concerning the boundaries and protection regime for offshore marine reserves (zakaznik) in the wintering areas of the Common Eiders and off the Solovetskiy Archipelago.

## Kandalaksha Bay

The archipelagos of small islands in Kandalaksha Bay (Fig. 6) support over half of the breeding population of Common Eiders in the White Sea. Thousands of seaducks spend their moulting period in this area, and during autumn, numerous flocks of migrating seaducks and flocks of Whooper Swans and Bean Geese stage here (Bianki 1991). The main threats to seabirds and waterbirds in the bay are illegal egg-collection, human disturbance, and oil spills and chronic oil pollution during oil transportation from Kandalaksha oil terminal to Murmansk. Since 1975, Kandalaksha Bay has been one of Russia's Ramsar sites. The Kandalaksha State Nature Reserve in Kandalaksha Bay includes four separate archipelagos. However, as in the Barents Sea branch of the Kandalaksha Reserve, a strict protection

regime has not been enforced at some of the protected islands in recent years, because of serious management problems in the reserve. Thus, the main priority for this area is to re-establish an effective protection regime in the islands within the reserve.

## CONCLUSION

The potential contamination of marine habitats by oil pollution could be the most important threat for seabirds and waterbirds along the Russian part of the East Atlantic Flyway. Significant deficiencies in regulatory documents defining an ecological policy for Russian oil and gas companies on the marine shelf were identified in the course of this analysis. There is no doubt that the rapid development of oil and gas resources on the Russia Arctic shelf and the transportation of these products will, in future, come into conflict with the existing protection strategies for seabirds and waterbirds based on establishing and broadening protected natural areas. Nevertheless, it is evident that development of an appropriately designed network of marine protected areas could prove to be an effective way to mitigate the environmental impact of the oil and gas industry and secure a normal functioning ecosystem.

## REFERENCES

**Belopol'skii, L.O.** 1957. Ecology of colonial seabirds of the Barents Sea. Israel Program for Scientific Translations, Jerusalem. (Translated from Russian, 1961).

**Bianki, V.V.** 1991. Birds. Oceanographic conditions and biological productivity of the White Sea. Polar Research Institute of Fisheries and Oceanography Press House, Murmansk: 1-115. (In Russian).

**Bianki, V.V. & Karpovich, V.N.** 1983. The present-day status of the Common Eider on the White Sea and on the Murman coast. Communications of the Baltic Commission for the Study of Bird Migration, Tartu. 16: 55-68. (In Russian).

**Bianki, V.V., Kokhanov, V.V., Koryakin, A.S., Krasnov, Yu.V., Paneva, T.D., Tatarinkova, I.P., Chemyakin, R.G., Shklyarevich, F.N. & Shutova, E.V.** 1993. Birds of Kola - White Sea Region. Russian Ornithological Journal, St. Petersburg 2(4): 491-586. (In Russian).

**Isaksen, K., Strøm, H., Gavrilo, M. & Krasnov, Yu.V.** 2000. Distribution of seabirds and wildfowl in the Pechora Sea during August 1998. Norwegian Ornithological Society, Report No. 2: 7-38.

**Karpovich, V.N.** 1984. Kandalaksha zapovednik. Murmansk Press House, Murmansk. (In Russian).

**Karpovich, V.N.** 1987. On possible cycles in the population dynamics of the Common Eider. Problems of study and protection of Pribelomorye nature. Murmansk Press House, Murmansk: 55-64. (In Russian).

**Kokhanov, V.D.** 1979. Steller's Eider *Polysticta stelleri* (Pall.) at Murman and in the White Sea. Ecology and morphology of eider ducks in the USSR. Nauka Press, Moscow: 208-216. (In Russian).

**Krasnov, Yu.V.** 1995. Seabirds (retrospective analysis of population development). In: The environment and ecosystems of Novaya Zemlya. Archipelago and shelf. Kola Scientific Centre. Russian Academy of Science Press, Apatity: 138147. (In Russian)

**Krasnov, J.V. & Barrett, R.T.** 1995. Large-scale interaction among seabirds, their prey and humans in the southern Barents Sea. In: H.R. Skjoldal, C.C.E. Hopkins, K.E. Erikstad & H.P. Leinaas (eds) Ecology of Fjords and Coastal Waters. Elsevier Science, Amsterdam: 443-456.

**Krasnov, Yu.V., Matishov, G.G., Galaktionov, K.V. & Savinova, T.N.** 1995. The colonial seabirds of Murman. Nauka Press, St. Petersburg. (In Russian).

**Krasnov, Yu.V., Goryaev, Yu.I., Shavikin, A.A., Nikolaeva, N.G., Gavrilo, M.V. & Chernook, V.I.** 2002. Atlas of the birds of the Pechora Sea: distribution, abundance, dynamics, problems of protection. Kola Scientific Centre. Russian Academy of Science Press, Apatity. (In Russian).

**Nygård, T., Jordhøy, P., Kondakov, A. & Krasnov, Y.** 1995. A survey of waterfowl and seals on the coast of the southern Barents Sea in March 1994. NINA Oppdragsmelding 361: 1-24.

**Ponomaryeva, T.S.** 1995. Nesting avifauna of Kolguev island territory. Ornithology. Moscow State University Press, Moscow. 26: 92-96. (In Russian).

**Strøm, H., Krasnov, J., Gavrilo, M. & Shavykin, A.** In press. Survey of wintering seaducks along the Terskiy and Murman coast, April 2003. Norwegian Polar Institute Report Series, Norwegian Polar Institute, Tromsø.

**Uspenskiy, S.M.** 1956. Bird bazaars of Novaya Zemlya. Translated by the Department of Northern Affairs and National Resources, Canada, 1958.

**Uspenskiy, S.M. & Khakhin, G.V.** 1993. Novaya Zemlya today. Hunt and Hunting Management 1: 1-3. (In Russian).

Helicopters are essential to survey waterbirds in the remote and inaccessible areas of northern Eurasia. Photo: Crawford Prentice.

# Revision of Danish EU Bird Directive SPAs in relation to the development of an offshore wind farm: a case study

*Ib Krag Petersen*

*National Environmental Research Institute, Grenåvej 14, DK-8410 Rønde, Denmark. (email: ikp@dmu.dk)*

Petersen, I.K. 2006. Revision of Danish EU Bird Directive SPAs in relation to the development of an offshore wind farm: a case study. *Waterbirds around the world*. Eds. G.C. Boere, C.A. Galbraith & D.A. Stroud. The Stationery Office, Edinburgh, UK. pp. 750-751.

Danish marine inshore waters are major staging and wintering grounds for huge numbers of migratory waterbirds. At least five to seven million individuals of more than 30 species winter in these areas, and much greater numbers exploit them for staging on migration (Laursen *et al.* 1997). In some cases, these concentrations constitute the entire breeding or flyway populations of northwest Palearctic species and are of major international importance (Rose & Scott 1994, 1997, Laursen *et al.* 1997, Delany & Scott 2002). As a consequence, Denmark has obligations under international legislation and as a signatory to international conventions, such as the African – Eurasian Migratory Waterbird Agreement under the Bonn Convention, the Ramsar Convention and the EU Birds Directive. Such treaties require states to protect the habitats and maintain the populations of migratory birds using the territory of those states. The majority of Danish SPAs (Special Protection Areas) under the EU Birds Directive are marine, all of which were classified in 1983.

As part of a programme to develop renewable energy sources, a government action plan launched five offshore demonstration wind farm projects in Danish waters in 1997. The aim of the projects was to provide information about their engineering and economic feasibility as well as assessing their effects on the environment, especially the potential impacts on waterbirds. All projects were obliged to undertake full Environmental Impact Assessments (EIAs) prior to construction, as well as post-construction monitoring. Results from these projects would provide background information to support the development of policy relating to future offshore wind farm developments.

One such wind farm, consisting of 33 wind turbines spread over an area of approximately 20 km², was planned south of the island of Læsø. Bird numbers and distributions were studied within a 5 600 km² survey area. This large study area was chosen because of the intention of extending the windfarm and developing capacity to exploit up to 2 000 MW of wind power in the area. In addition, these shallow waters were considered to constitute a single biogeographical unit for Common Scoter *Melanitta nigra*.

Between 1999 and 2001 a total of 15 aerial surveys were conducted by the National Environmental Research Institute (NERI) using a high winged, twin-engined Partenavia P-68 Observer, designed for general reconnaissance purposes. Survey flight altitude was 76 m and cruising speed approximately 185 km/t (100 knots). The whole study area was covered by a total of 30 north-south parallel transects, flown at 3 km intervals, covering a total linear track of 1 800 km.

The surveys revealed huge concentrations of wintering, as well as moulting, Common Scoter (Figs.1 & 2). Although the existence of these concentrations were already known (Laursen *et al.* 1997) and previous aerial surveys had encountered up to 900 000 Common Scoters in the study area, this was the first survey to

establish their total extent and detailed geographical distribution. Data presented from this study are based on the number of birds encountered from the line transect samples, so the actual number of birds is expected to be at least two or three times higher than the number of individuals encountered (Petersen *et al.* 2003).

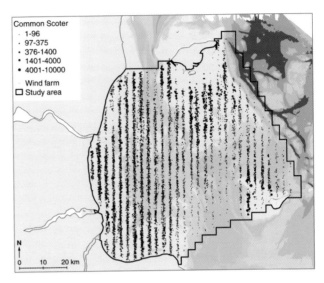

**Fig. 1.** Distribution of wintering Common Scoter *Melanitta nigra* in the survey area (October to April).

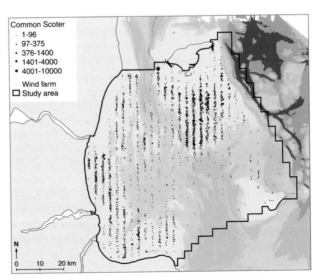

**Fig. 2.** Distribution of Common Scoter *Melanitta nigra* in the survey area during the moulting period (July to September).

During winter, Common Scoters were scattered over shallow areas of the study area, particularly in the vicinity of the proposed wind farm and in the western parts of the area. In the moulting period (July to September) the birds were concentrated in the vicinity of the proposed wind farm, with lower concentrations in the western parts of the study area.

Thus the location of the proposed wind farm was close to concentrations of wintering and moulting Common Scoters, giving some cause for concern for their future favourable conservation status. Based on this new information it was decided to adjust the position of the proposed wind farm by 10 km, in order to avoid conflict with concentrations of Common Scoter. In addition it became clear that less than half of Common Scoters present in the study area were detected within boundaries of existing SPAs. This led to the enlargement of two SPAs and the designation of one new area so as to include 98% of the Common Scoters in the study area.

## REFERENCES

**Delany, S. & Scott, D.A.** 2002. Waterbird population estimates. Third Edition. Wetlands International Global Series 12. Wageningen, The Netherlands. 226 pp.

**Laursen, K., Pihl, S., Durinck, J., Hansen, M., Skov, H., Frikke, J., & Danielsen, F.** 1997. Numbers and distributions of waterbirds in Denmark 1987-1989. Danish Review of Game Biology 15(1): 1-184.

**Petersen, I.K., Fox, A.D. & Clausager, I.** 2003. Distribution and numbers of birds in Kattegat in relation to the proposed offshore wind farm south of Læsø - Ornithological impact assessment. Report commissioned by Elsam Engineering A/S. National Environmental Research Institute. 116 pp.

**Rose, P.M. & Scott, D.A.** 1994. Waterfowl population estimates. IWRB Publication 29. Slimbridge, UK. 102 pp.

**Rose, P.M. & Scott, D.A.** 1997. Waterfowl population estimates. Second Edition. Wetlands International Publication No. 44. Wageningen, The Netherlands. 106 pp.

Although breeding on freshwater wetlands, Common Scoters *Melanitta nigra* overwinter in Danish inshore waters in internationally important numbers. Photo: Daníel Bergmann.

# Extending the boundaries of seabird breeding colony protected areas into the marine environment

*Claire A. McSorley, Ben J. Dean, Andy Webb & James B. Reid*
*Joint Nature Conservation Committee Seabirds and Cetaceans Team, Dunnet House, 7 Thistle Place, Aberdeen, AB10 1UZ, UK.*

McSorley, C.A., Dean, B.J., Webb, A. & Reid J.B. 2006. Extending the boundaries of seabird breeding colony protected areas into the marine environment. *Waterbirds around the world*. Eds. G.C. Boere, C.A. Galbraith & D.A. Stroud. The Stationery Office, Edinburgh, UK. pp. 752-753.

During the breeding season, many seabird species engage in essential maintenance behaviours in the waters immediately adjacent to the colony and, therefore, should be accorded some protection within these marine areas. We investigated distribution patterns of Northern Gannet *Morus bassanus*, Common Guillemot *Uria aalge*, Razorbill *Alca torda* and Atlantic Puffin *Fratercula arctica* engaged in maintenance behaviours adjacent to their breeding colonies. We recommend a 2 km seaward boundary extension to existing Northern Gannet breeding colony Special Protection Areas (SPAs), and a 1 km extension for existing auk SPAs.

SPAs provide for the protection of the habitats of naturally occurring wild birds under the provisions of the EC Birds Directive. UK SPAs are mostly limited to terrestrial, freshwater and estuarine environments (Stroud *et al.* 2001). However, the Directive also applies to the geographical sea area. The Joint Nature Conservation Committee (JNCC) provides advice to government to support the classification of SPAs in the marine environment.

During the seabird breeding season, the inshore waters adjacent to colonies are used by many seabirds for essential preening, bathing and courtship behaviours (maintenance behav-

iours). The distribution patterns of seabirds engaged in maintenance behaviours are assumed to be independent of site characteristics and, therefore, generic to all colonies. In 2001, the JNCC conducted boat-based surveys around six UK seabird colonies. The aim was to determine appropriate generic seaward boundary extensions to existing seabird colony terrestrial SPAs that include the important marine areas used by seabirds engaged in maintenance behaviour.

A survey vessel navigated a series of transects extending up to 5 km from the coast of Skokholm and Skomer, Grassholm, the Farne Islands, the Bass Rock, the Isle of May, and Fowlsheugh. The species, number, location and behaviour of all seabirds observed on the water were recorded in one minute samples. Data analyses were performed separately for Northern Gannets, Common Guillemots, Razorbills and Atlantic Puffins.

Bird density data were interpolated using ordinary kriging, which makes use of the inherent spatial autocorrelation in the recorded densities modelled in a semivariogram. This generates a grid of predicted densities for each species. To investigate a possible generic solution for seabird colony SPA boundary extensions we plotted mean predicted density against distance from the colony shore for all sites.

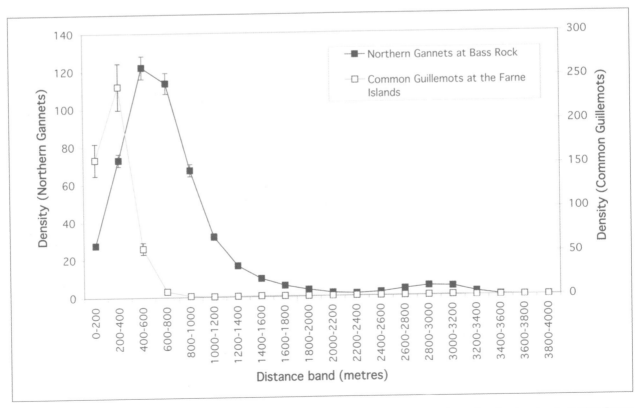

Fig. 1. Distance band analysis showing relationship between mean predicted density (birds km²; standard error bars) and distance from the colony shore for Northern Gannets *Morus bassanus* and Common Guillemots *Uria aalge*.

Predicted density of seabirds engaged in maintenance behaviour decreased with distance from the shore. This relationship was consistent within and between sites, but often at different density scales for each species and for each site. Northern Gannets engaged in maintenance behaviour formed significant aggregations within 2 km of the colony shore, and auks formed similar aggregations within 1 km of the colony shore (Fig. 1).

Based on these findings we recommend extending the boundary of existing terrestrial seabird colony SPAs into the marine environment by 2 km from mean low water mark (mean low water springs in Scotland) for Northern Gannet SPAs, and similarly, by 1 km for auk SPAs (McSorley *et al.* 2003).

## ACKNOWLEDGEMENTS

JNCC is funded by the three country agencies; Scottish Natural Heritage, English Nature and the Countryside Council for Wales. Thanks to all those people who participated in the surveys and provided comments on the work.

## REFERENCES

McSorley, C.A., Dean, B.J., Webb, A. & Reid, J.B. 2003. Seabird use of waters adjacent to colonies: Implications for seaward extensions to existing breeding seabird colony Special Protection Areas. JNCC Report No. 329. http://www.jncc.gov.uk/Publications/JNCC329/default.htm

Stroud, D.A., Chambers, D., Cook, S., Buxton, N., Fraser, B., Clement, P., Lewis, P., McLean, I., Baker, H. & Whitehead, S. (eds.) 2001. The UK SPA network: its scope and content. JNCC, Peterborough. Three volumes. (90 pp.; 438 pp.; 392 pp.) http://www.jncc.gov.uk/UKSPA/default.htm

Britain and Ireland support a large proportion of the world population of Northern Gannet *Morus bassana*. Photo: Ward Hagemeijer.

# Assessing the numbers and distribution of waterbirds in UK inshore marine waters

*Peter Cranswick, Colette Hall & Lucy Smith*

*The Wildfowl & Wetlands Trust, Slimbridge, Gloucestershire, GL2 7BT, UK. (email: peter.cranswick@wwt.org.uk)*

Cranswick, P.A., Hall, C. & Smith, L. 2006. Assessing the numbers and distribution of waterbirds in UK inshore marine waters. *Waterbirds around the world.* Eds. G.C. Boere, C.A. Galbraith & D.A. Stroud. The Stationery Office, Edinburgh, UK. pp. 754-755.

An assessment of waterbird numbers and distribution is essential for determining conservation priorities, for identifying and monitoring important sites, and for assessing the results of targeted conservation action. Long-term monitoring of waterbirds in the UK is well developed, covering a range of species and habitats, but systematic surveys of marine waters have historically been limited to offshore ship-based surveys, missing nearshore areas that are potentially important for divers and seaducks. In 2001/2002, a new aerial survey technique was adopted, enabling coverage of large areas in a short timescale and minimising disturbance to the target species (Common Scoters *Melanitta nigra* and Red-throated Divers *Gavia stellata*).

Distance-sampling methodology was adopted to provide a statistically robust means of determining numbers. The use of a Global Positioning System provided high spatial resolution data. A twin-engined plane followed transects separated at 2 km intervals and running perpendicular to the main environmental gradients. Between 2001/2002 and 2003/2004, surveys were undertaken by The Wildfowl & Wetlands Trust (WWT) in Liverpool Bay, the Thames Estuary, and parts of the Greater Wash, primarily in winter (e.g. WWT Wetlands Advisory Survey 2003, Cranswick *et al.* 2003, Cranswick *et al.* 2004).

Large numbers of Common Scoters were recorded at several sites in the Irish Sea, notably Carmarthen, Cardigan and Liverpool Bays. Distribution regularly extended up to 10 km from shore and, at one site – Shell Flat, a shallow sandbank off the Lancashire coast – up to 20 km from shore (Fig. 1). Most birds were found in waters less than 10 m deep. Distribution was broadly similar within and between winters, although there was some evidence of a gradual movement to deeper water during the course of a winter.

Analysis of survey data from February 2003 showed that 70 000 birds were present in Liverpool Bay alone. More than half of these were at Shell Flat, a site that before aerial surveys was not recognised as supporting any Common Scoter, but which at times is probably the most important site for this species in UK waters. In the early 1990s, fewer than 30 000 Common Scoter were estimated to winter in British waters.

Red-throated Divers were recorded during winter months, and although present at all sites, numbers and distribution were more variable than for scoters. Birds were distributed sparsely, up to 15 km from shore at many sites. Marked concentrations were, however, recorded on occasion in the Thames Estuary and provisional estimates suggest that at least 5 000, and perhaps as many as 10 000, were present in late winter. This compares with a current estimate of 4 850 for British waters as a whole. Distribution within the site, and the aggregation of birds into groups, varied between months, and marked movements were observed during the course of an individual aerial survey.

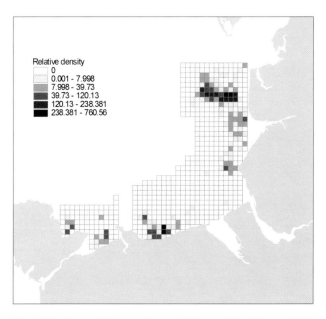

Fig. 1. Distribution of Common Scoter in Liverpool Bay, February 2003 (numbers are corrected for survey effort in 2x2 km cells).

Results from just a few winters' aerial survey have greatly increased the knowledge of numbers and distribution of waterbirds in UK waters: current estimates of wintering numbers are clearly considerable underestimates, and new sites of international importance have been identified, as have the offshore limits of distribution.

A strategy for monitoring waterbirds in UK inshore waters is currently under development. This advocates the use of aerial survey as the principal means of providing information for site monitoring and designation, complemented by boat-based and land-based surveys where conditions allow. Aerial data have already been used to underpin the designation of the UK's first marine Special Protection Area (Carmarthen Bay, SW Wales), for Common Scoter, and the precise spatial data enabled the site boundary to be defined.

Aerial survey will also be used increasingly by the expanding offshore wind industry, providing accurate information on waterbirds to inform Environmental Impact Assessments and to monitor the effects of windfarms. The ability to cover large areas near-synchronously will also enable assessment of the cumulative impacts of these developments. The aerial survey technique provides a robust and repeatable method for meeting these varied requirements for informing waterbird conservation in inshore waters.

WWT gratefully acknowledges funding from the Countryside Council for Wales, English Nature, and wind farm development companies, and the advice and encouragement of Tony Fox and Ib Petersen.

## REFERENCES

**Cranswick, P.A., Hall, C. & Smith, L.** 2003. Aerial surveys of birds in proposed strategic areas for offshore wind-farm development, round 2: preliminary report, winter 2002/03. The Wildfowl & Wetlands Trust, Slimbridge.

**Cranswick, P.A., Hall, C. & Smith, L.** 2004. All Wales Common Scoter survey: report on 2002/03 work programme. WWT Wetlands Advisory Service report to Countryside Council for Wales, CCW Contract Science Report No. 615.

**WWT Wetlands Advisory Service** 2003. All Wales Common Scoter Survey: report on 2001/02 work programme. CCW Contract Science Report No. 568.

The development of new aerial survey techniques has resulted in radical re-assessment of the international importance of the waters around Britain for wintering waterbirds. Photo: Peter Cranswick.

# An effective survey technique for large groups of moulting sea ducks

*G. Randy Milton[1], Paul Illsley[2], & Frances M. MacKinnon[1]*

*[1]Nova Scotia Department of Natural Resources, 136 Exhibition Street, Kentville, Nova Scotia, B4N 4E5, Canada.*
*(email: miltongr@gov.ns.ca)*
*[2]Centre of Geographic Sciences, 50 Elliott Road RR #1, Lawrencetown, Nova Scotia, B0S 1M0, Canada.*

Milton, G.R., Illsley, P. & MacKinnon, F.M. 2006. An effective survey technique for large groups of moulting sea ducks. *Waterbirds around the world.* Eds. G.C. Boere, C.A. Galbraith & D.A. Stroud. The Stationery Office, Edinburgh, UK. pp. 756-757.

## ABSTRACT

We report on a system that can be obtained at a reasonable cost for use in a standardized methodology to survey numbers within aggregations of sea ducks. Results are compared using digital analyses software and manual counts.

Common Eider *Somateria mollissima dresseri* gather in large moulting flocks in the Gulf of St. Lawrence and along the Atlantic coasts of Nova Scotia and Maine from July through August. Numbers of birds are often visually estimated from low flying aircraft, even though analyses of aerial photographs of these flocks have been shown to provide more accurate and repeatable results [see Bajzak & Piatt (1990) and review in Lavigne *et al.* (1977)]. This has been due in-part to costs associated with developing and printing large numbers of images, followed by hours of manual counting.

Low cost high-resolution digital cameras are now available, and advances in digital analyses software can be used to partially automate the counting process. Here we describe a system to record locations and acquire images of flocks of molting birds, and the use of commercially available software for digital image analyses.

## Image acquisition and preparation:

Flown at 300-400 feet (91-122 m), images were acquired (12 August 2002) using a Canon D60 digital camera equipped with a high resolution 2000 X 3000 pixel RGB CMOS image sensor, 1/500 sec shutter speed, and 24 mm wide-angle lens focused to infinity to provide a uniform pixel resolution of 3.1 cm. (at 328 ft/100 m) for vertical images. Aircraft drift can cause oblique images (more than 3 degrees from vertical) with pixel resolution varying across the image.

Waypoints of flocks were recorded on a scanned and geo-

Fig. 2. Objects are classified using eCognition as eider and grouped into memberships of one (red) or two (green) birds. The green area is one object representing two birds. * compare with Fig. 1.

registered 1:50 000 topographic map entered into a moving map software package (Fugawi) linked to a Garmin 12XL GPS unit. The camera's time stamp was synchronized with GPS time as displayed on the moving map software. Overlapping images were required for large flocks.

Enhancement on some images using the 'One Step Photo Enhance' command in Jasc Paint Shop Pro 8 increased contrast between the water and ducks. Count breaklines were identified to avoid double counting of birds in flocks with overlapping images.

## Image analyses using ArcView

Images were imported to ArcView 3.2, and a line shapefile enclosing the count area was created. Individual eiders were recorded using a point shape file (Fig. 1) and the total number of records per point shape file was entered on a spreadsheet (Excel) with the time required for the count.

## Image analyses using eCognition

The eCognition software segments the image into similar objects. The size of the objects is dependent upon the scale parameter used. Objects can then be classified using membership functions, e.g. area of objects, image band values, and relation to other objects.

Images were imported into ArcView 3.2 and a shapefile was created around the entire image to form the image boundary. A second shapefile for the area of the image between the breaklines was created, and the two shapefiles were joined and the ID value for the area of interest set to 1. The image and the thematic shapefile were loaded into eCognition with the Protocol (see

Fig. 1. Eiders are recorded by placing a point on each individual within a point shape file created for each count area using ArcView.

below) and executed. Results (Fig. 2) were edited and identifiable errors in classification corrected. Processing and edit times were entered on the spreadsheet.

### eCognition Protocol

The Protocol is an executable program that separates the area of interest from the rest of the image, and then segments water from non-water. Objects are classified as water for values above a brightness threshold for channel 1, and non-water objects are further divided into ducks and non-ducks using a second brightness threshold value for channel 2. Multiple ducks were often grouped as an object because of minimal separation, and the number of birds in a group was determined using the area membership function. Thresholds can vary between images due to angle and height of acquisition. Once classified and results viewed, threshold values in the membership function can be changed and the image reclassified to improve accuracy. Run time for classification is minimal (c.10 seconds) once the segmentation process is complete.

### RESULTS

The ArcView approach recorded 36 981 Common Eider in 55 flocks (7-5 588 birds) distributed among 32 waypoints. Eleven flocks (each >1 000 birds) accounted for 63.4%, 8 flocks (500-1 000 birds) provide an additional 16.2% with the remaining 36 flocks contributing 20.4% of the total number. The analyses of the 145 images required 11:33:34 hr. Most images (87.6%) had fewer than 500 birds, 9.6% had 500-1 000 birds and 2.8% had more than 1 000 birds.

The true number is however greater than the 36 981 recorded. Several flocks had repeated passes and total counts varied from less than 1% to 4.4% and 6.1%. We speculate this variation is due to partially masked or hidden birds, and birds which may have surfaced or dove between acquisitions. A correction factor of 5% adjusts the estimate to 38 830 Common Eider, of which less than 1.5% are female (unpubl. data).

### Comparison of ArcView and eCognition approaches

A subset of the 145 images was selected for the eCognition approach. The number of eider in the count areas of 35 images (ArcView approach) varied from 13 to 2 556 birds and represents 45.7% of the total recorded. Between approaches, there was no difference in three count areas while an additional 16 varied between one and three birds, with count area totals ranging from 13 to 240 birds. Using a difference threshold of ±4%, 10 count areas differed by 4-69 birds; in five instances the

ArcView approach had higher totals. The four images with the greatest number of birds are included within the ±4% threshold, three had lower totals using eCognition. On the remaining six count areas, eCognition recorded 17 543 birds, an increase of 656 (3.9%) over ArcView, with individual counts varying from 6.8% to 15.0%.

Total time (processing and edit) to analyze an image is more for the eCognition approach, but does not require intervention once the protocol is executed. A more valid comparison is eCognition edit time versus ArcView time. In most cases, edit time is similar or significantly less than for ArcView time, particularly as the number of birds increase. Subjectively, images with separation between birds and less water reflectance required less edit time. The time required for the manual ArcView approach (4:48:53 hr) was approximately twice that of the alternate method (2:26:33 hr) for a 3.9% difference in total birds.

### DISCUSSION

Readily available and used by many natural resource management agencies, utilizing ArcView in this approach can provide accurate results and a permanent record but can also be time consuming and a potential health risk (repetitive motion syndrome). The object based eCognition software can provide the same or comparable accuracy with reduced expenditure of time and health risk.

The use of photography in low altitude aerial censuses of aggregations of animals has been repeatedly shown to provide more accurate numbers than visual estimates, and provide a permanent record. High-resolution digital cameras and moving map software linked to GPS provide increased flexibility and enhanced data acquisition and reporting capabilities. The system reported here can be readily obtained at a reasonable cost and be part of a standardized methodology for surveying aggregations of sea ducks. Ensuring images are vertical as opposed to oblique, a fast shutter speed (>1/500) to reduce blurring, and undertaking surveys in conditions which reduce surface water reflectance glare will reduce the error associated with this approach.

### REFERENCES

**Bajzak, D. & Piatt, J.F.** 1990. Computer-aided procedure for counting waterfowl on aerial photographs. Wildlife Society Bulletin 18: 125-129.

**Lavigne, D.M., Øritsland, N.A. & Falconer, A.** 1977. Remote sensing and ecosystem management. Skrifter No 166. Norsk Polarinstitutt, Oslo. 51 pp.

Flock of Common Eider *Somateria mollissima* on the Ythan Estuary, Aberdeenshire, Scotland. Photo: Colin Galbraith.

# Ramsar site designation, marine sites and seaducks: a Scottish perspective

*Chris M. Waltho*

*73 Stewart Street, Carluke, Lanarkshire, ML8 5BY, UK. (email: Chris.waltho@eider.org.uk)*

Waltho, C.M. 2006. Ramsar site designation, marine sites and seaducks: a Scottish perspective. *Waterbirds around the world.* Eds. G.C. Boere, C.A. Galbraith & D.A. Stroud. The Stationery Office, Edinburgh, UK. pp. 758-759.

The Convention on Wetlands of International Importance especially as Waterfowl Habitat (Ramsar, Iran, 1971) defines wetlands as: "areas of marsh, fen, peatland or water, whether natural or artificial, permanent or temporary, with water that is static or flowing, fresh, brackish or salt, including areas of marine water the depth of which at low tide does not exceed six metres" (Article 1.1 of the Convention). However, concerning the designation of Wetlands of International Importance (Ramsar sites), Article 2.1 provides that wetlands: "*may incorporate riparian and coastal zones adjacent to the wetlands, and islands or bodies of marine water deeper than six metres at low tide lying within the wetlands*". The intent of this provision is to permit flexibility in the boundary delineation of Ramsar sites so as to include connectivity within functional ecological units where appropriate.

This paper examines how well these provisions can be, and are being, applied to cover areas of coastal waters internationally important for seaducks – species which are included within the Convention's definition of waterbirds. In marine waters, there is a continuum offshore in bird species distribution, from inshore waterbirds to pelagic seabirds. Seaducks form part of the inshore waterbirds guild occupying relatively shallow waters, but much of the marine area upon which they depend is deeper that the core six metre depth provision of the Convention.

The Ramsar Convention Manual (Ramsar Convention Secretariat 2003a) suggests that "*The* [6 metre] *figure is thought to come from the maximum depth to which sea ducks can dive whilst feeding*". However, subsequent extensive research on seaducks (see e.g. Cramp & Simmons 1977) has shown that this depth is too shallow to capture many seaduck feeding sites (see also Petersen, this volume). Most seaduck species regularly feed in deeper water, some considerably deeper. As extreme examples, King Eider *Somateria spectabilis* feed over offshore banks in water depths of 23–35 m in West Greenland (Mosbech *et al.* 2002) and Spectacled Eider *Somateria fischeri* feed in 40-70 m depths in the Bering Sea (Lovvorn *et al.* 2003).

Seaduck feeding sites are generally large in area (100s of km²). Coverage within Ramsar sites of the whole of nearshore marine areas important for seaducks could be achieved in two ways: either the inclusion of such large areas seawards of coastal systems such as estuaries, and/or the designation of offshore Ramsar sites where there are shallow offshore banks which are in water less than 6 m deep. However, sea areas such as those used by King Eider and Spectacled Eider in the above examples would still be excluded from this approach.

Using the example of Ramsar sites in Scotland, how effective is the existing Ramsar site network in covering the sea areas important for seaducks?

Most nearshore marine areas important for seaducks in Scotland are large (Table 1, mean 400 km², n=6). Even at this scale, Scottish seaduck sites are well below the average for European Ramsar sites covering seaduck areas (mean 660 km², n=16; source: Ramsar Sites Database). Where designated Ramsar sites in Scotland do include areas important for seaducks, coverage is at best only a small part of these areas: on average 27% of the area used by seaducks (n=6). In addition, four seaduck areas are wholly outside the suite of designated Ramsar sites (Table 1). Only the Solway Firth Ramsar site substantially covers the area important for seaducks (87% coverage), and three other Ramsar sites have less than 10% coverage of the seaduck area.

**Table 1. Scottish seaduck sites and current Ramsar coverage.**

| Seaduck Site (see Fig. 1) | approx area (km²)* | Relevant coastal/marine Ramsar Site(s) | approx area (km²)** | Estimated % Ramsar coverage |
|---|---|---|---|---|
| 1 Solway Firth | 500 | Upper Solway Flats and Marshes | 436.4 | 87.3 |
| 2 Firth of Clyde | 360 | Inner Clyde Estuary | 18.3 | 5.1 |
| 3 Other West Coast | not available | none | | |
| 4 Western Isles | not available | none | | |
| 5 Orkney | not available | none | | |
| 6 Shetland | not available | none | | |
| 7 Moray Firth | 700 | Cromarty Firth/Dornoch Firth; Loch Fleet/Moray & Nairn Coast | 125.9 | 18 |
| 8 Aberdeenshire coast | 45 | Ythan estuary & Meikle Loch | 3.1 | 7 |
| 9/10 Montrose/Angus coast; Tay/St Andrews Bay | 300 | Montrose Basin; Firth of Tay & Eden Estuary | 37.9 | 12.6 |
| 11 Firth of Forth | 500 | Firth of Forth | 31.6 | 6.3 |
| **Mean (n=6)** | **400.8** | | **108.8** | **22.7** |

* Range estimated by author from aerial survey maps in Dean *et al.* (2003, 2004a, 2004b).

** Estimated area of Ramsar site(s) relevant for seaduck distribution.

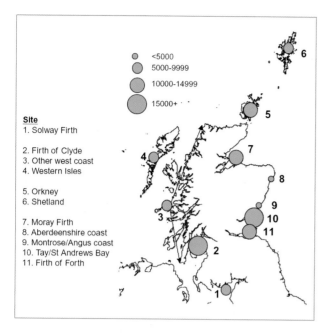

Fig. 1. Scottish seaduck sites.

Scottish seaduck sites and populations are well covered by areas included within Integrated Coastal Zone Management (ICZM) strategies (>70% of all seaduck numbers (n=111 860) and seaduck sites (n=11)). However, the significance of these areas for seaducks is poorly recognised by these ICZM strategies: seaducks are recognised in only two of the five published strategies, although all these strategies recognise designated Ramsar sites.

In the short to medium term, it is highly unlikely that the well-established definition of wetlands and 6 m depth scope of the Ramsar Convention text could be readily amended to widen coverage to deeper marine waters, since this would require amendments of major significance to the Convention text to be adopted and ratified by Contracting Parties. However, there are a number of practical steps which could be taken now to recognise all areas important for seaducks within protected areas networks. These include:

i)   improving the clarity of existing guidance for Ramsar site designation in relation to the acceptability of incorporating marine areas with a water depth of more than 6 m within Ramsar site boundaries, particularly in relation to ensuring improved coverage of areas important for off-shore seaduck concentrations, in a manner similar to the clarification on this matter provided for marine ecosystems such as coral reefs - see Ramsar's *Strategic Framework and guidelines for the future development of the List of Wetlands of International Importance* (Ramsar Convention Secretariat 2003b);

ii.  boundary extensions of existing designations of coastal Ramsar sites to fully cover the adjacent marine areas important for seaduck populations;

ii.  designation as Ramsar sites of marine areas important for seaducks where these include offshore banks in less than 6 m water depth;

iii  better recognition within ICZM strategies of areas important for seaducks, whether or not these areas are included within designated Ramsar sites; and

iv.  the application of other mechanisms, both national (e.g. Marine Protected Areas) and international (e.g. Special Protection Areas under the EU Birds Directive), for the designation of marine (deep sea) protected areas to fully cover the areas important for seaducks.

Implementing a combination of these approaches would enhance, for seaducks, the global and flyway-scale coherent and comprehensive networks of Ramsar sites called for by the Convention's *Strategic Framework* (Ramsar Convention Secretariat 2003b).

## REFERENCES

Cramp, S & Simmons, K.E.L. (eds.) 1977. The birds of the Western Palearctic Vol. 1. Oxford University Press, Oxford.

Dean, B.J., Webb, A., McSorley, C.A. & Reid, J.B. 2003. Aerial surveys of UK inshore areas for wintering seaduck, divers and grebes: 2000/01 and 2001/02. JNCC Report No. 333. ISSN 0963 8091.

Dean, B.J., Webb, McSorley, C.A, Reid, J.B. 2004a. Surveillance of wintering seaduck, divers and grebes in UK inshore areas: aerial surveys 2002/03. JNCC Report No. 345. 60 pp. ISSN 0963 8091.

Dean, B.J., Webb, A., McSorley, C.A. Schofield, R.A. and Reid, J.B. 2004b. Surveillance of wintering seaducks, divers and grebes in UK inshore areas: aerial surveys and shore-based counts 2003/04, November 2004. JNCC Report No. 357. ISSN 0963-8091.

Lovvorn, J.R., Richman, S.E., Grebmeier, J.M., Cooper, L.W. 2003. Diet and body condition of spectacled eiders wintering in pack ice of the Bering Sea. Polar Biology 26: 259–267.

Mosbech, A., Merkel, F. & Boertmann, D. 2002. The king eider (*Somateria spectabilis*) population in Western Greenland during autumn and winter determined by aerial surveys and satellite telemetry. Paper presented at Workshop on Baltic/North Sea common eider populations. Seaduck Specialist Group, Roosta, Estonia, April 2002.

Ramsar Convention Secretariat 2003a. The Ramsar Convention Manual: a guide to the Convention on Wetlands (Ramsar, Iran, 1971). Third edition. Ramsar Convention Secretariat, Gland, Switzerland.

Ramsar Convention Secretariat 2003b. Strategic Framework and guidelines for the future development of the List of Wetlands of International Importance. Ramsar Wise Use Handbook 7, Second edition. Ramsar Convention Secretariat, Gland, Switzerland.

# Potential impacts of marine fisheries on migratory waterbirds of the Afrotropical Region: a study in progress

*John Cooper*

*Avian Demography Unit, Department of Statistical Sciences, University of Cape Town, Rondebosch 7701, South Africa.*
*(email: jcooper@adu.uct.ac.za)*

Cooper, J. 2006. Potential impacts of marine fisheries on migratory waterbirds of the Afrotropical Region: a study in progress. *Waterbirds around the world*. Eds. G.C. Boere, C.A. Galbraith & D.A. Stroud. The Stationery Office, Edinburgh, UK. pp. 760-764.

## ABSTRACT

A study of the potential impacts of marine fisheries on AEWA-listed waterbirds of the Afrotropical Region is described. A total of 43 waterbirds of eight families forage in marine waters in the region. Nearly one-third are gulls and terns, the rest of the assemblage being made up of a penguin, cormorants, a gannet, pelicans, phalaropes and a grebe. Only four of the species are considered to be globally threatened, and three of these are southern African endemics. Nearly half the species considered are breeding residents. Palearctic migrants make up the next largest category. The listed species are affected by a broad range of fisheries, both directly by mortality and indirectly by competition for resources. The fisheries of most concern are longlining, demersal trawling and purse-seining. The species most affected are the African Penguin *Spheniscus demersus*, Cape Gannet *Sula (Morus) capensis*, Cape Cormorant *Phalacrocorax capensis* and Great Crested Tern *Sterna bergii* in southern Africa, and probably Palearctic gulls and terns further north on the Continent. These species are recommended for future study and monitoring.

## INTRODUCTION

The First Session of the Meeting of the Parties to the African-Eurasian Migratory Waterbird Agreement (AEWA), held in Somerset West, South Africa, in November 1999, adopted Resolution 1.4 "International Implementation Priorities for AEWA 2000-2004" that listed a number of projects considered to be of international importance and for which international cooperation was needed (AEWA 1999, 2000). Funding to undertake Project 24 "Study of the potential impacts of marine fisheries on migratory waterbirds" was not attained by the AEWA Secretariat until the end of 2001. For a number of years, there has been significant concern about the potential impacts of commercial marine fisheries on bird populations. Whereas research has been conducted on seabird species (e.g. Tasker *et al.* 2000), there has been no overview on the potential impacts on waterbirds listed within Annex 2 of AEWA, a number of which are known to feed on marine prey. Such a review would identify candidate species and areas for more detailed study or monitoring.

In May 2002, a contract was awarded by the AEWA Secretariat to the Avian Demography Unit, University of Cape Town, to undertake the study. Following discussion, it was agreed that the study would be a "desk study", reviewing published and unpublished ("grey literature") sources, and would be largely restricted to the Afrotropical Region (Africa south of the Sahara). A first consideration of the species then listed within AEWA revealed that 33 species foraged to a greater or lesser extent in marine Afrotropical waters (here defined as commencing below low-water mark, and thus excluding birds that forage in the inter-tidal zone, such as most waders (shore-birds) and the large wading birds (Ciconiiformes).

A CAMP (Conservation Assessment and Management Plan) workshop held jointly by the Avian Demography Unit, University of Cape Town, and the IUCN/SSC Conservation Breeding Specialist Group in Cape Town, South Africa, in February 2002 recommended that 10 species of southern African breeding coastal seabirds should be nominated by South Africa for inclusion within Annex 2 of AEWA (du Toit *et al.* 2003). The workshop report included draft nomination texts which were then submitted by South Africa to the AEWA Secretariat. These nominations were accepted by the Second Session of the AEWA Meeting of the Parties, held in Bonn, Germany, in September 2002 (AEWA 2002), and were added to those birds to be included within the review of marine fisheries impacts, giving a total of 43 species spread over eight families (Table 1).

## METHODS

For each species, a literature review has been conducted and a species account has been drafted under the headings: description and taxonomy, distribution, migration and movements, habitat, breeding, population size and trends, foraging behaviour and diet, potential and actual impacts of marine fisheries, other related conservation concerns, and recommendations. The text of each species account is to be accompanied by a distribution map and a selected bibliography. An example of a species text, that for Great Crested Tern *Sterna bergii*, is given as Appendix 1.

Regional reviews of Afrotropical commercial marine fisheries in relation to potential impacts on waterbirds are to be undertaken separately for three regions: western (Mauritania to Congo), southern (Angola to Mozambique) and eastern (Tanzania to Sudan).

## A PRELIMINARY ANALYSIS

### Taxonomic and threatened status

Most (31; 72%) of the 43 marine-foraging species are gulls and terns. Cormorants (five species) form the next largest grouping. The pelecaniform order is also represented by one gannet and two pelicans. There are single species of grebes and penguins and two phalaropes (Table 1).

Only four of the 43 species have been accorded globally threatened status by the World Conservation Union (BirdLife International 2004). Three are southern African endemic species (African Penguin *Spheniscus demersus*, Vulnerable; Cape Gannet *Sula (Morus) capensis*, Vulnerable; and Bank Cormorant *Phalacrocorax neglectus*, Endangered). The fourth is the Vulnerable Socotra Cormorant *P. nigrogularis*, which is a non-breeding visitor to the Afrotropical Region (Gulf of Aden and southern Red Sea). No species has been categorized as

**Table 1. Waterbird species listed in Annex 2 of the African-Eurasian Migratory Waterbird Agreement that forage within Afrotropical marine waters.**

**SPHENISCIDAE**

African Penguin *Spheniscus demersus**

**PODICIPEDIDAE**

Black-necked Grebe *Podiceps nigricollis*

**PELECANIDAE**

Great White Pelican *Pelecanus onocrotalus*

Dalmatian Pelican *Pelecanus crispus*

**SULIDAE**

Cape Gannet *Sula (Morus) capensis**

**PHALACROCORACIDAE**

Crowned Cormorant *Phalacrocorax coronatus**

Bank Cormorant *Phalacrocorax neglectus**

Great Cormorant *Phalacrocorax carbo**

Socotra Cormorant *Phalacrocorax nigrogularis*

Cape Cormorant *Phalacrocorax capensis**

**SCOLOPACIDAE**

Red-necked Phalarope *Phalaropus lobatus*

Grey Phalarope *Phalaropus fulicaria*

**LARIDAE**

White-eyed Gull *Larus leucophthalmus*

Sooty Gull *Larus hemprichii*

Audouin's Gull *Larus audouinii*

Kelp Gull *Larus dominicanus**

Heuglin's Gull *Larus heuglini*

Armenian Gull *Larus armenicus*

Yellow-legged Gull *Larus cachinnans*

Lesser Black-backed Gull *Larus fuscus*

Great Black-headed Gull *Larus ichthyaetus*

Grey-headed Gull *Larus cirrocephalus**

Hartlaub's Gull *Larus hartlaubii**

Common Black-headed Gull *Larus ridibundus*

Slender-billed Gull *Larus genei*

Mediterranean Gull *Larus melanocephalus*

Little Gull *Larus minutus*

Sabine's Gull *Xema sabini*

Gull-billed Tern *Sterna nilotica*

Caspian Tern *Sterna caspia*

Royal Tern *Sterna maxima*

Lesser Crested Tern *Sterna bengalensis*

Great Crested Tern *Sterna bergii*

Sandwich Tern *Sterna sandvicensis*

Roseate Tern *Sterna dougallii*

Antarctic Tern *Sterna vittata**

Common Tern *Sterna hirundo*

Arctic Tern *Sterna paradisaea*

Little Tern *Sterna albifrons*

Saunders's Tern *Sterna saundersi*

Damara Tern *Sterna balaenarum*

White-cheeked Tern *Sterna repressa*

Black Tern *Chlidonias niger*

*Species added to Annex 2 of AEWA in 2002 following nomination by South Africa.
Note: Taxonomy, nomenclature and sequence after AEWA (2002).

Critically Endangered. Five species have been categorized as Near Threatened, including an additional three southern African endemics: the Crowned Cormorant *P. coronatus*, Cape Cormorant *P. capensis* and Damara Tern *Sterna balaenarum*, and two gulls, White-eyed *Larus leucophthalmus* and Audouin's *L. audouinii*. The White-eyed Gull is endemic to the Red Sea; Audouin's Gull is a non-breeding visitor to the western Afrotropics (Mauritania and Senegal) from the Mediterranean.

When considered on a regional basis, it is noteworthy that six of the nine threatened and near threatened species are endemic to southern Africa. The absence from the Afrotropics of threatened gulls and terns is also noticeable, with only two of the 31 species being considered as near threatened.

## Migratory and regional status

Nearly half (19; 44%) of the 43 AEWA species under consideration are breeding residents of the Afrotropical Region (although some of these may also be regarded as intra-African migrants). Twenty-three (53%) are Palearctic migrants, of which eight species also have breeding populations within the Afrotropical Region. A single species, the Antarctic Tern *S. vittata*, is a non-breeding visitor from the Southern Ocean to southern Africa.

The regional distribution of AEWA marine-foraging Afrotropical species shows some intriguing patterns (Table 2). Not surprisingly, there are more Palearctic visitors to western and eastern Africa than to southern Africa. Perhaps most significant is that southern Africa supports more breeding species than do the other two regions. On a taxonomic basis, southern Africa supports the largest numbers of pelecaniform species (due to the presence of four species of marine cormorants, three of which are

**Table 2. Regional distribution and origins of marine-foraging AEWA-listed species within the Afrotropical Region.**

| Category | Region | | |
|---|---|---|---|
| | Western | Southern | Eastern |
| Breeders | 4 | 14 | 8 |
| Breeders/Palearctic migrants | 5 | 1 | 5 |
| Intra-African migrants | 2 | 2 | 0 |
| Palearctic migrants | 14 | 7 | 12 |
| Southern Ocean migrants | 0 | 1 | 0 |
| **Totals** | **25** | **25** | **25** |

**Table 3. Taxonomic distribution of marine-foraging AEWA-listed species within the Afrotropical Region.**

| Taxon | Region | | |
|---|---|---|---|
| | Western | Southern | Eastern |
| Penguins | 0 | 1 | 0 |
| Grebes | 1 | 1 | 1 |
| Pelicans and allies | 3 | 6 | 4 |
| Phalaropes | 1 | 1 | 1 |
| Gulls | 9 | 4 | 9 |
| Terns | 11 | 12 | 10 |
| **Totals** | **25** | **25** | **25** |

endemic to the region), but supports less than half the number of gulls that occur in the other two regions, since a number of Palearctic migrant gulls do not venture that far south (Table 3).

## Impacts of marine fisheries

Southern African fisheries are mainly by trawl, purse-seine and longline, whereas western African fisheries are more diverse, with a significant artisanal component (as is the case for eastern Africa). Each of these fisheries impacts upon seabirds in negative and in positive ways, as summarized below.

### Longline fisheries

Longline fisheries are well known for their injurious effects on many seabird populations, mainly members of the Procellariiformes (albatrosses and petrels). However, there is little evidence that AEWA species are significantly affected within the Afrotropics. The exception may be the Cape Gannet, which has been recorded caught on longlines off South Africa and Namibia (Cooper & Ryan 2003). Although evidence is lacking, gulls may be at risk in western Africa, since the migrant visitors Audouin's Gull and Yellow-legged Gull *L. cachinnans* are killed by longlines set in the Mediterranean Sea (Cooper *et al.* 2003). Longlining does offer some advantages to seabirds, in the form of discarded offal and non-target species, but this has not been assessed within the Afrotropics.

### Trawling

Demersal trawling off southern Africa is an important source of food (discards and offal) for several AEWA species, most especially the Cape Gannet, and to a lesser extent the Kelp Gull *L. dominicanus* (Abrams 1983, Ryan & Moloney 1988). However, birds may become trapped in trawls, and be killed or injured by collisions with trawl warps (S.L. Petersen pers. com., pers. obs). Published information is lacking from elsewhere within the Afrotropics.

### Purse-seining

This type of fishery acts indirectly by reducing the food supply of several AEWA species. Significant examples are a suite of species that prey upon small shoaling fish in southern African waters (African Penguin, Cape Gannet, Cape Cormorant and Great Crested Tern; see, for example, Crawford & Dyer 1995 and Crawford 2003). Quantitative information from the western Afrotropical Region is largely absent, but several species of terns are known to consume fish prey also taken by purse-seine and beach-seine fisheries (Brenninkmeijer *et al.* 2002, Veen *et al.* 2003).

### Traps

Traps set for Cape Rock Lobster *Jasus lalandii* have been known occasionally to entrap and drown Bank Cormorants in southern African waters, but this is not thought to be a significant cause of mortality (Cooper 1981, 1985). However, over-fishing of rock lobster may be adversely affecting this Endangered and decreasing species indirectly, since the lobster forms an important part of its prey in most of its breeding range (unpubl. data)

### Gill nets

Gill and set nets have occasionally drowned African Penguins in South African waters (pers. obs). However, as these nets are

Great Crested Terns *Sterna bergii* breeding on Robben Island, South Africa. Photo: Dieter Oschadleus.

mainly used within sheltered bays and estuaries, the drownings that they cause are not thought to be a significant cause of mortality to the species.

### Indirect fishery impacts

Discarded gear can lead to entanglements and ingestion, as has been reported for Great Crested Terns in southern Africa (Cooper *et al.* 1990). All of the species under consideration are potentially at risk, but information on species and regional differences is essentially lacking. The catching of birds, such as gannets and terns, by fishers for food nowadays is largely restricted to artisanal fisheries, although hard evidence is generally lacking.

## CANDIDATE SPECIES FOR MONITORING

The following species are suggested for further study and monitoring to assess the effects of marine fisheries on their populations within the Afrotropical Region. Within the southern African region, continued demographic and dietary studies of the African Penguin, Cape Gannet, Cape Cormorant, Bank Cormorant and Great Crested Tern are warranted, following on from the large body of work undertaken over the last 50 years (e.g. Crawford 2003 and references therein). In the western and eastern regions, far less is currently known, and new studies should continue to concentrate on those migrant and resident gulls and terns which are known or are thought to overlap in their prey with commercial fisheries (e.g. Brenninkmeijer *et al.* 2002, Veen *et al.* 2003).

## ACKNOWLEDGEMENTS

The study reported here has been funded by the African-Eurasian Migratory Waterbird Agreement. The author thanks the Organizing Committee of the Waterbirds around the world Conference for funding his attendance. Gerard Boere is acknowledged for his extraordinary editorial patience and perseverance. Samantha Petersen and Genevieve Jones contributed to the species and regional reviews, respectively.

## REFERENCES

**Abrams, R.** 1983. Pelagic seabirds and trawl-fisheries in the southern Benguela Current region. Marine Ecology Progress Series 11: 151-156.

**AEWA** 1999. Proceedings of the First Session of the Meeting of the Parties to the Agreement on the Conservation of

African-Eurasian Migratory Waterbirds. Cape Town, South Africa, 6-9 November 1999. Secretariat of the African-Eurasian Waterbird Agreement, Bonn.

**AEWA** 2000. International implementation priorities for the Agreement on the Conservation of African-Eurasian Migratory Waterbirds 2000-2004. Secretariat of the African-Eurasian Waterbird Agreement, Bonn.

**AEWA** 2002. Proceedings of the Second Session of the Meeting of the Parties to the Agreement on the Conservation of African-Eurasian Migratory Waterbirds. Bonn, Germany, 25-27 September 2002. Secretariat of the African-Eurasian Waterbird Agreement, Bonn.

**BirdLife International** 2004. Threatened birds of the world 2004. CD-ROM. BirdLife International, Cambridge, UK.

**Brenninkmeijer, A., Stienen, E.W.M., Klaassen, M. & Kersten, M**. 2002. Feeding ecology of wintering terns in Guinea-Bissau. Ibis 144: 602-613.

**Cooper, J.** 1981. Biology of the Bank Cormorant. Part 1: distribution, population size, movements and conservation. Ostrich 52: 208-215.

**Cooper, J.** 1985. Biology of the Bank Cormorant. Part 3: foraging behaviour. Ostrich 56: 86-95.

**Cooper, J. & Ryan, P.G.** 2003. South African National Plan of Action for Reducing the Incidental Catch of Seabirds in Longline Fisheries. University of Cape Town, Cape Town.

**Cooper, J., Crawford, R.J.M., Suter, W. & Williams, A.J.** 1990. Distribution, population size and conservation of the Swift Tern *Sterna bergii* in southern Africa. Ostrich 61: 56-65.

**Cooper, J., Baccetti, N., Belda, E.J., Borg, J.J., Oro, D., Papaconstantinou, C. & Sánchez, A.** 2003. Seabird mortality from longline fishing in the Mediterranean Sea and Macronesian waters: a review and a way forward. Scientia Marina (Supplement 2): 57-64.

**Crawford, R.J.M.** 2003. Influence of food on numbers breeding, colony size and fidelity to localities of Swift Terns in South Africa's Western Cape, 1987-2000. Waterbirds 26: 44-53.

**Crawford, R.J.M. & Dyer, B.M.** 1995. Responses by four seabird species to a fluctuating availability of Cape Anchovy *Engraulis capensis* off South Africa. Ibis 137: 329-339.

**Du Toit, M., Boere, G.C., Cooper, J., de Villiers, M.S., Kemper, J., Lenten, B., Petersen, S.L., Simmons, R.E., Underhill, L.G., Whittington, P.A & Byers, O.P.** (eds) 2003. Conservation and Assessment Plan for southern African coastal seabirds. Avian Demography Unit, University of Cape Town, and IUCN/SSC Conservation Breeding Specialist Group, Cape Town and Apple Valley.

**Ryan, P.G. & Moloney, C.L.** 1988. Effect of trawling on bird and seal distributions in the southern Benguela region. Marine Ecology Progress Series 45: 1-11.

**Tasker, M.L., Camphuysen, C.J., Cooper, J., Garthe, S., Montevecchi, W.A. & Blaber, S.J.M.** 2000. The impacts of fishing on marine birds. ICES Journal of Marine Science 57: 531-547.

**Veen, J., Peeters, J., Leopold, M.F., van Damme, C.J.G. & Veen, T.** 2003. Les oiseaux piscivores comme indacateurs de la qualité de l'environnement marin: suivi des effets de la pêche littorale en Afrique du Nord-Ouest. Alterra, Wageningen, The Netherlands.

---

## APPENDIX 1

### GREAT CRESTED TERN *STERNA BERGII*
Family: Laridae
Other names: Swift, Crested, Greater Crested Tern

### Description
The Great Crested Tern is a large, slender marine tern with long, narrow, strongly angled wings, a long deeply forked tail, a yellow bill and black legs and feet. It is grey above and white below with a black cap and a shaggy crest. Breeding adults have a black cap covering the upper forehead, crown and nape. The cap covers the eye and is separated from the bill by a narrow white forehead. Non-breeding adults differ from breeding birds in that the forehead is white, merging into a black-spotted or streaked crown. The hind crown and crest are matt black and may have faint white grizzling. The crest feathers are shorter and more rounded than those of adults in breeding plumage. The juvenile has a brownish black head and the crown is more mottled forming a paler cap. Juvenile upperparts are grey with brown and white mottling and barring.

### Distribution
Five subspecies have been recognized, four of which occur within the Afrotropical Region:

- *S. b. bergii* (smallest and palest subspecies) is endemic to southern Africa, with records extending from Luanda, Angola, in the west to Maputo, Mozambique, in the east. Breeding by *bergii* has been recorded at 27 localities, from Swakopmund, Namibia, to Stag Island, Algoa Bay, Eastern Province, South Africa.
- *S. b. enigma* occurs from the Zambezi Delta, Mozambique, south to Durban, KwaZulu-Natal, South Africa, and is believed to breed on islands off Mozambique and Madagascar.
- *S. b. thalassina* (largest and darkest race) breeds in East Africa and the central Indian Ocean.
- *S. b. velox* breeds in the Red Sea, East Africa, Arabian Sea, Persian Gulf and the northern Indian Ocean.

Note: only the African and south-western Asian populations are included in Appendix II of the Bonn Convention on Migratory Species.

### Movements
The southern African population is mobile. Adults leave breeding sites at the end of the breeding season and most move east to the Indian Ocean coastline of the Eastern Cape and KwaZulu-Natal, South Africa. Many fledglings move east from colonies in Namibia and Western Cape as shown by band recoveries. For example, a nestling banded at Lüderitz, Namibia, was recovered

at Umzumbe, KwaZulu-Natal (2 169 km), and a bird banded at Robben Island, Western Cape, was recovered at Sodwana Bay, KwaZulu-Natal (1 716 km). Other fledglings move substantial distances north, e.g. from Marcus Island, Western Cape, to Swakopmund, Namibia. Areas used by post-breeding adults and immatures overlap. Birds frequently change breeding sites between years, both changing sites of colonies at islands and moving between islands or mainland breeding localities.

The *thalassina* subspecies winters along the east African coast north to Kenya and Somalia and may move as far south as Durban, South Africa. Populations of *velox* breeding from the Persian Gulf eastwards appear to be sedentary or dispersive rather than migratory, but the population breeding in the Red Sea is partly migratory, wintering south along the east African coast to Kenya.

### Habitat

Great Crested Terns breed colonially on offshore islands, lagoons and salt pans. They may roost or loaf on sandy or rocky shores and less often on artificial structures such as boats, pilings and harbour buildings. In Namibia, they favour poles in cultivated oyster beds or raised salt encrustations in lagoons. They occur on their own or in flocks of up to several hundred birds, sometimes with gulls or other species of terns.

The species does not occur far out to sea, being restricted to the continental shelf usually within sight of land. It ventures inland at only a few localities when birds may forage at water bodies up to 3 km from the sea and cross narrow strips of land that separate water bodies, such a between Table and False Bays near Cape Town, South Africa.

### Breeding

Great Crested Terns breed in colonies, often in association with other seabirds. They are monogamous and the pair bond is maintained during the year and sometimes lasts from year to year. Mean colony size is significantly related to the abundance of pelagic fish prey. The nest consists of a shallow scrape in the sand on open flat or occasionally sloping ground. It is often unlined, but sometimes includes stones or the bones of cuttlefish *Sepia* spp. One, occasionally two, eggs are laid and incubated for 25-30 days during the months of January to early July in the Western Cape. Newly hatched chicks are very pale, with sparse black speckling. They are brooded and fed by both parents. Older chicks form crèches or loose groups. Young fledge at 38-40 days. Some fledged young accompany their parents after leaving colonies and most remain dependent until at least four months of age.

### Population size and trends

The species' total population within the Afrotropical Region is unknown. Best estimates follow:

| | | |
|---|---|---|
| Madagascar and Mozambique | *enigma* | 8 000-10 000 individuals |
| Eastern Africa & Seychelles | *thalassina* | 2 550-4 500 individuals |
| Red Sea & north-eastern Africa | *velox* | numbers unknown |
| Southern Africa | *bergii* | 20 000 individuals |

Note: The breeding population of *bergii* was 4 835 pairs in 1984 and 6 336 pairs in 2000 in South Africa, and up to 1 682 pairs have nested in Namibia.

### Food and feeding

In the Western Cape (1977-1986), fish formed 86% of all prey items consumed. The remainder was made up of cephalopods, crustaceans and insects. Prey size ranged from 7-138 mm in length and 0.1-30.0 g in mass. Shoaling pelagic fish, notably Anchovy *Engraulis capensis* and Sardine *Sardinops sagax*, are especially important in the diet. In Namibia, Great Crested Terns feed mainly on Pelagic Goby *Sufflogobius bibarbatus* and hakes *Merluccius* spp. Immature birds are often kleptoparasitized by Kelp Gulls *Larus dominicanus* in Namibia. On Stag/Seal Island in the Eastern Cape, young were mainly fed on *Petalichthys capensis*. Fiddler Crabs *Uca stenodactyla* have been reported as prey in Tanzania.

Great Crested Terns feed mostly at sea by plunge diving or by dipping and food is usually swallowed in mid air. They are restricted to the top one metre of the ocean and birds may forage up to 10 km from land in the breeding season.

### Impacts of marine fisheries

Although this species is not threatened in southern Africa, large fluctuations in numbers of Great Crested Terns breeding in the Western Cape of South Africa are significantly related to fluctuations in the abundance of pelagic fish on which they prey. These are intensively exploited by a purse-seine fishery, which could thus have deleterious indirect effects on prey availability.

Great Crested Terns *Sterna bergii* breeding on Robben Island, South Africa. Photo: Dieter Oschadleus.

# Seabird populations of Britain and Ireland: the last 30 years

*P. Ian Mitchell[1], Steven F. Newton[2], Norman Ratcliffe[3] & Timothy E. Dunn[1]*

[1]*Joint Nature Conservation Committee Seabirds and Cetaceans Team, Dunnet House, 7 Thistle Place, Aberdeen, AB10 1UZ, UK.*
*(email: ian.mitchell@jncc.gov.uk)*
[2]*BirdWatch Ireland, Rockingham House, Newcastle, Co. Wicklow, Republic of Ireland.*
[3]*Royal Society for the Protection of Birds, The Lodge, Sandy, Bedfordshire, SG19 2DL, UK.*

Mitchell, P.I., Newton, S.F., Ratcliffe, N.R. & Dunn, T.E.  2006.  Seabird populations of Britain and Ireland: the last 30 years. *Waterbirds around the world.*  Eds. G.C. Boere, C.A. Galbraith & D.A. Stroud.  The Stationery Office, Edinburgh, UK.  pp. 765-766.

This note summarises the results of *Seabird 2000*, a census of all 25 species of seabird breeding in Britain and Ireland. Comparisons with two previous censuses enable trends over the last 15-30 years to be assessed.

The British Isles are one of the most important areas in the world for breeding seabirds. The coastal population of Britain and Ireland has been censused three times: in 1969-70, 1985-88 and most recently during *Seabird 2000* in 1998-2002. *Seabird 2000* also surveyed inland colonies of terns, gulls and Great Cormorants *Phalacrocorax carbo* and provided the first accurate estimates of shearwater and petrel numbers.

Standardised recording methods were employed by over 1 000 surveyors (Mitchell *et al.* 2004). Population estimates were obtained from complete counts or from sample surveys of large colonies of ground-nesters.

Numbers of seabirds breeding in Britain and Ireland have increased from approximately five million in 1969-70, to over six million in 1985-88, then to almost eight million in 1998-2002. However, since 1985-88, populations of only seven species have increased in size by more than 10%; while five have changed by less than 10% and eight have declined by more than 10% (Table 1).

**Table 1.  Numbers of seabirds breeding in Britain & Ireland 1969-2002.  All counts are of pairs unless otherwise stated.**

| Species | Coastal colonies only[1] | | | | | Inland & coastal |
|---|---|---|---|---|---|---|
| | 1969-70 | 1985-88 | 1998-2002 | % change since 1969-70 | % change since 1985-88 | 1998-2002 |
| Northern Fulmar *Fulmarus glacialis* | 308 960 | 536 577 | 537 991 | 74% | 0% | 537 991 |
| Manx Shearwater *Puffinus puffinus*[2] | | | 332 267 | | | 332 267 |
| European Storm-petrel *Hydrobates pelagicus*[2] | | | 124 775 | | | 124 775 |
| Leach's Storm-petrel *Oceanodroma leucorhoa*[2] | | | 48 357 | | | 48 357 |
| Northern Gannet *Morus bassanus* | 137 661 | 186 508 | 259 311 | 88% | 39% | 259 311 |
| Great Cormorant *Phalacrocorax carbo* | 8 010 | 10 806 | 11 560 | 44% | 7% | 13 681 |
| European Shag *Phalacrocorax aristotelis* | 33 876 | 42 970 | 32 306 | -5% | -25% | 32 306 |
| Arctic Skua *Stercorarius parasiticus* | 1 039 | 3 388 | 2 136 | 106% | -37% | 2 136 |
| Great Skua *Stercorarius skua* | 3 079 | 7 645 | 9 635 | 213% | 26% | 9 635 |
| Mediterranean Gull *Larus melanocephalus* | 0 | 1 | 113 | | | 113 |
| Black-headed Gull *Larus ridibundus* | 74 927 | 77 573 | 79 392 | 6% | 2% | 141 890 |
| Common Gull *Larus canus* | 12 983 | 15 471 | 21 475 | 65% | 39% | 49 780 |
| Lesser Black-backed Gull *Larus fuscus* | 50 035 | 64 417 | 91 323 | 83% | 42% | 116 684 |
| Herring Gull *Larus argentatus* | 343 586 | 177 065 | 147 114 | -57% | -17% | 149 177 |
| Great Black-backed Gull *Larus marinus* | 22 412 | 20 892 | 19 691 | -12% | -6% | 19 713 |
| Black-legged Kittiwake *Rissa tridactyla* | 447 967 | 539 645 | 415 995 | -7% | -23% | 415 995 |
| Sandwich Tern *Sterna sandvicensis* | 12 073 | 16 047 | 14 252 | 18% | -11% | 14 252 |
| Roseate Tern *Sterna dougallii* | 2 384 | 550 | 790 | -67% | 44% | 790 |
| Common Tern *Sterna hirundo* | 14 890 | 14 861 | 14 497 | -3% | -2% | 14 497 |
| Arctic Tern *Sterna paradisaea* | 52 288 | 78 764 | 56 123 | 7% | -29% | 56 123 |
| Little Tern *Sterna albifrons* | 1 917 | 2 857 | 2 153 | 12% | -25% | 2 153 |
| Common Guillemot *Uria aalge*[3] | 652 175 | 1 182 791 | 1 559 484 | 139% | 32% | 1 559 484 |
| Razorbill *Alca torda*[3] | 167 683 | 176 135 | 216 087 | 29% | 23% | 216 087 |
| Black Guillemot *Cepphus grylle*[4] | | | 42 683 | | | 42 683 |
| Atlantic Puffin *Fratercula arctica* | 452 069 | 506 626 | 600 751 | 33% | 19% | 600 751 |

[1]  inland colonies were not surveyed during 1969-70 and 1985-88.
[2]  not surveyed during 1969-70 and 1985-88.
[3]  counts of individuals.
[4]  counts of pre-breeding adults; pre-breeding surveys were not conducted during 1969-70 and were not conducted in the Republic of Ireland during 1985-88.

Over 50% of Britain and Ireland's seabirds are comprised of four species, whose abundance increased considerably between 1960-70 and 1985-88. Subsequently, numbers of Common Guillemot *Uria aalge* and Atlantic Puffin *Fratercula arctica* have continued to increase, but numbers of Northern Fulmars *Fulmarus glacialis* are stable and Black-legged Kittiwakes *Rissa tridactyla* have declined by 23% (Table 1). Herring Gulls *Larus argentatus* are the only species that have decreased in number between all three censuses.

Food supply and habitat availability have been the major factors affecting breeding seabird numbers in Britain and Ireland over the last 30 years. All species that have declined by more than 10% since 1985-88 (Table 1), with the exception of Herring Gull, are reliant on small fish, mainly sandeels *Ammodytes marinus*, to feed themselves and their chicks. Since the late 1980s, colonies of these species in the Northern Isles and along the North Sea coast of Britain have experienced successive years of poor breeding success due to sandeel shortages (Mavor *et al.* 2004). This period coincided with increased sea-surface temperature in the North Sea and consequent changes to the plankton commu-nity (Beaugrand *et al.* 2003) that may have reduced sandeel recruitment (Arnott & Ruxton 2002). If sea-surface temperatures continue to increase, sandeel-dependent seabird populations will decline further. Climate change may also have direct effects on breeding seabirds: rising sea levels may reduce the amount of breeding habitat available for shoreline nesting species such as terns; winter storms can cause large-scale 'wrecks' of seabirds; and summer storms can cause wide scale breeding failure.

Another major source of food — discards and offal produced by commercial fishing — is set to decline in the future following the recent reductions of white fish stocks in the North Sea. This will probably impact on large gulls, skuas and Northern Fulmars that rely on such sources.

Predation by mammals has had a significant impact on the size of seabird populations, particularly on ground-nesters, by limiting availability of safe nesting habitat. For instance, the distribution of Storm-petrels is limited to offshore islands free of rats. American Mink *Mustela vison* can swim to offshore islands and their habit of surplus taking of eggs and killing chicks and adult seabirds has significantly impacted on gulls and terns in NW Scotland and throughout Ireland. Eradication of Rats *Rattus norvegicus* and Mink from some islands has led to recolonisa-tion by breeding seabirds.

*Seabird 2000* was a partnership between JNCC, RSPB, Scottish Natural Heritage, English Nature, Countryside Council for Wales, Environment & Heritage Service Northern Ireland, the Seabird Group, Shetland Oil Terminal Environmental Advisory Group, BirdWatch Ireland and the National Parks & Wildlife Service – Republic of Ireland. Many other organisa-tions and individuals contributed time and funds to the census.

Marwick Head on the west coast of Orkney is classified as a Special Protection Area for its internationally important populations of seabirds. It holds about 75 000 seabirds in the breeding season, including Kittiwakes *Rissa tridactyla* and Guillemots *Uria aalge*. Photo: David Stroud.

## REFERENCES

**Arnott, S.A. & Ruxton, G.D.** 2002. Sandeel recruitment in the North Sea: demographic, climatic and trophic effects. Marine Ecology Progress Series 238: 199-210.

**Beaugrand, G., Brander, K.M., Lindley, A., Souissi, S. & Reid, P.C.** 2003. Plankton effect on cod recruitment in the North Sea. Nature 426: 661-664.

**Mavor, R.A., Parsons, M., Heubeck, M. & Schmitt, S.** 2004. Seabird numbers and breeding success in Britain and Ireland, 2003. Joint Nature Conservation Committee, Peterborough. (UK Nature Conservation No. 28.)

**Mitchell, P.I., Newton, S.F., Ratcliffe, N. & Dunn, T.E.** 2004. Seabird populations of Britain and Ireland. T. & A.D. Poyser; London.

# The UK Seabird Monitoring Programme

*Matthew Parsons, Roderick A. Mavor & P. Ian Mitchell*

*Joint Nature Conservation Committee Seabirds and Cetaceans Team, Dunnet House, 7 Thistle Place, Aberdeen, AB10 1UZ, UK. (email: matt.parsons@jncc.gov.uk)*

Parsons, M., Mavor, R.A. & Mitchell, P.I. 2006. The UK Seabird Monitoring Programme. *Waterbirds around the world.* Eds. G.C. Boere, C.A. Galbraith & D.A. Stroud. The Stationery Office, Edinburgh, UK. pp. 767-768.

The UK Seabird Monitoring Programme (SMP) facilitates the co-ordination of breeding seabird monitoring on a UK-wide basis and is one of the most extensive and detailed of its kind, collecting annual demographic data on 26 species. Population trends of three abundant and widespread species with different feeding strategies are presented, and likely causative factors discussed.

The Joint Nature Conservation Committee's (JNCC) Seabird Monitoring Programme has, since 1986, co-ordinated the monitoring of breeding seabirds on a UK-wide basis (Mavor *et al.* 2004). The aim of the SMP is to ensure sufficient data on seabird numbers and breeding success are collected to enable their conservation status to be assessed. The programme assists JNCC and partner organisations in providing advice relevant to government and others on the conservation needs of breeding seabirds.

Standardised methods of collecting field data on breeding numbers and breeding success were used (Walsh *et al.* 1995) and promoted nationwide to ensure comparability of results. UK-wide breeding numbers are presented as indices, whereby the number of birds counted in a sample of colonies in a particular year is expressed as a percentage of the number present in the same colonies when the SMP was initiated in 1986.

Fig. 1 shows the annual UK breeding population indices of three abundant and widespread seabird species from 1986 to 2003. Black-legged Kittiwakes *Rissa tridactyla* have declined significantly since 1995, at a mean rate of -5.8% per annum

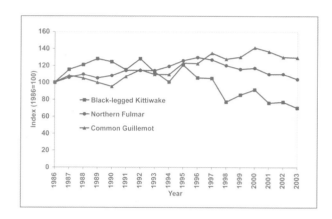

Fig. 1. UK population indices of Black-legged Kittiwake *Rissa tridactyla*, Northern Fulmar *Fulmarus glacialis* and Common Guillemot *Uria aalge*, 1986-2003.

(t=5.04, P<0.001), in contrast to increases in the population of Common Guillemots *Uria aalge* (though the latter has declined since 2000). These trends are thought to be related to the feeding strategies of each species: the former restricted to feeding near the sea surface (mostly taking small sandeels *Ammodytes* spp.) while the latter can dive to reach a wider range of fish. Sandeel recruitment in the North Sea has been negatively affected by sea temperature increases in recent decades (Arnott & Ruxton 2002)

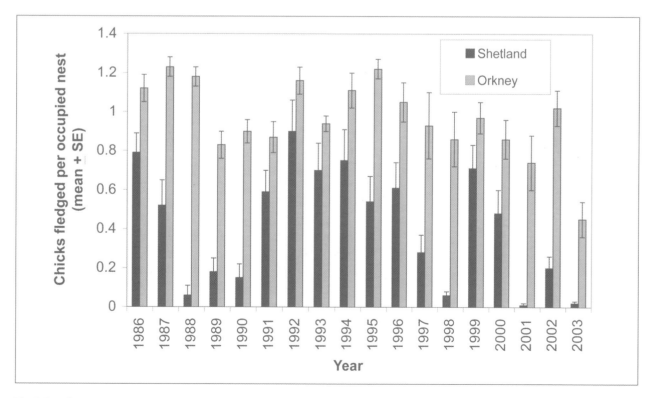

Fig. 2. Breeding success of Black-legged Kittiwake *Rissa tridactyla* on Orkney and Shetland, 1986-2003.

and it is likely that their availability to surface-feeders such as Kittiwakes also declined, at least locally. For example, in Shetland in 1988-90, 1997-98 and 2001-2003, the breeding success of Black-legged Kittiwakes was extremely low (Fig. 2), a phenomenon that has been correlated with low local availability of sandeels in that region (Oro & Furness 2002). In contrast, in adjacent Orkney the species was much more successful in each year and, presumably, sandeels more available.

The Northern Fulmar *Fulmarus glacialis* feeds on fish, zooplankton and discards and offal from fishing boats. The increase in numbers (up to *c*. 1996; Fig. 1.) may be attributed to moderate levels of fishing activity (and associated feeding opportunities); recent declines are perhaps due to decreased fishing effort and to declines in zooplankton and sandeels (Tasker 2004).

JNCC is funded by Scottish Natural Heritage, English Nature and the Countryside Council for Wales. Lead partners in the SMP are RSPB and Shetland Oil Terminal Environmental Advisory Group. Many others have contributed data, including volunteers funded via the Seabird Group.

Common Guillemots *Uria aalge*. Photo: Ian Mitchell.

### REFERENCES

**Arnott, S.A. & Ruxton, G.D.** 2002. Sandeel recruitment in the North Sea: demographic, climatic and trophic effects. Marine Ecology Progress Series 238: 199-210.

**Oro, D. & Furness, R.W.** 2002. Influences of food availability and predation on survival of kittiwakes. Ecology 83(9): 2516-2528.

**Mavor, R.A., Parsons, M., Heubeck, M. & Schmitt, S**. 2004. Seabird numbers and breeding success in Britain and Ireland, 2003. Joint Nature Conservation Committee. Peterborough. (UK Nature Conservation No. 28.)

**Tasker, M.L.** 2004. Fulmar *Fulmarus glacialis*. In: P.I. Mitchell, S.F. Newton, N. Ratcliffe & T.E. Dunn (eds). Seabird populations of Britain and Ireland. T&A.D. Poyser; London: 49-62.

**Walsh, P.M., Halley, D.J., Harris, M.P., del Nevo, A., Sim, I.M.W. & Tasker, M.L.** 1995. Seabird monitoring handbook for Britain and Ireland. JNCC/RSPB/ITE/ Seabird Group, Peterborough.

Standardised methods are used to collect data on breeding seabird productivity in the UK, with a sample of sites assessed each year. Photo: Matt Parsons.

# Use of satellite telemetry to locate key habitats for King Eiders *Somateria spectabilis* in West Greenland

*Anders Mosbech[1], Rikke S. Danø[1], Flemming Merkel[2], Christian Sonne[1], Grant Gilchrist[3] & Annette Flagstad[4]*

[1] *National Environmental Research Institute, Department of Arctic Environment, PO Box 358, Frederiksborgvej 399, DK-4000 Roskilde, Denmark. (email: amo@dmu.dk)*

[2] *Greenland Institute of Natural Resources, PO Box 570, DK-3900 Nuuk, Greenland, Denmark.*

[3] *Canadian Wildlife Service, Raven Road, K1A 0H3, Ottawa, Canada.*

[4] *Copenhagen Royal Veterinary and Agricultural University, Department of Small Animal Science, Dyrlægevej 16, DK-1870 Frederiksberg, Denmark.*

Mosbech, A., Danø, R.S., Merkel, F., Sonne, C., Gilchrist, G. & Flagstad, A. 2006. Use of satellite telemetry to locate key habitats for King Eiders *Somateria spectabilis* in West Greenland. *Waterbirds around the world.* Eds. G.C. Boere, C.A. Galbraith & D.A. Stroud. The Stationery Office, Edinburgh, UK. pp. 769-776.

## ABSTRACT

Satellite transmitters were implanted in King Eiders *Somateria spectabilis* at three moulting sites in West Greenland (26 birds) and a breeding site in Arctic Canada (10 birds). The tracked birds showed a diversity of migration routes and staging areas. However, regardless of the implantation locality, almost half of the tracked birds wintered at the Store Hellefiskebanke and adjacent coast in West Greenland (68°N) at some point in November, December and January. Locations on Store Hellefiskebanke were centred in areas with a water depth of 23-35 m and up to 70 km from the coast. A bird with a depth transducer showed a diurnal diving pattern, preferentially diving during daylight. The maximum depth of dive recorded was 43 m. Satellite telemetry has proven to be an important supplementary tool to locate key habitats for marine birds in remote areas.

## INTRODUCTION

There is increasing human use of marine areas for fishing, recreation and mineral extraction in polar environments. Consequently, it is important to identify key habitats used by wildlife to minimize unforeseen environmental impacts from anthropogenic activities. For example, surveys by plane or ship have provided important data on bird distribution and population estimates of several marine bird species in West Greenland (Mosbech & Johnson 1999, Merkel *et al.* 2002). However, the results generated by surveys are often restricted to short time periods. In the Arctic, offshore surveys whether by plane or ship are costly and are limited by light and bad weather, and during the Arctic winter, also by ice.

Satellite telemetry can provide supplementary data to identify key habitats by showing bird locations daily or several times a week for up to a year. However, to give reliable information, transmitters have to be small and attached to the birds in ways that do not alter their behaviour. Among seaducks, implantable transmitters with protruding external antenna have proven to function well; for example with Spectacled Eiders *Somateria fischeri* (Petersen & Douglas 1995, Petersen *et al.* 1999). Satellite transmitter data also have the potential to provide information on behaviour if the transmitters contain appropriate sensors on board. Depth transducers have often been used in satellite telemetry in marine mammals. Here we test a satellite transmitter prototype with a depth transducer in a seaduck to obtain information on diving behaviour which can elucidate how much and when birds actually forage in a remote staging area.

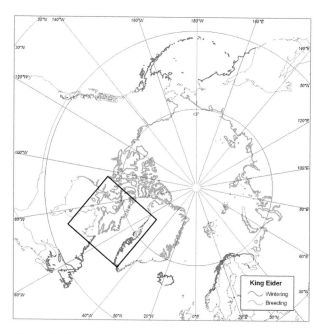

Fig. 1. Distribution of breeding and wintering King Eiders *Somateria spectabilis* with the study area indicated. (Distribution based on Pearce *et al.* 2004, Cramp & Simmons 1977, and this study).

West Greenland is an important moulting, staging and wintering area for the King Eider *Somateria spectabilis* (Salomonsen 1968, Frimer 1995, Lyngs 2003, Mosbech & Boertmann 1999; Fig. 1). Based on surveys covering different parts of West Greenland in different years, about 300 000 King Eiders have been estimated to winter there (Mosbech & Johnson 1999). Most of these breed in the eastern Canadian Arctic and some in north-western Greenland, while King Eiders do not breed in West Greenland. Surveys of moulting areas in West Greenland (Mosbech & Boertmann 1999) and a breeding area in Canada (the Rasmussen Lowlands, Gratto-Trevor *et al.* 1998) indicate a decreasing population size. Because of the large flock sizes of King Eiders (up to 25 000 individuals) and very uneven distribution of flocks in West Greenland, knowledge of habitat use and movements are needed to plan a dedicated survey that can cover the key areas, both on the offshore banks and in the coastal zone.

In this study, we present an initial analysis of location data from King Eiders tracked through the autumn and winter of 2003/04, together with tracking data from the autumn and winter of 1999/2000 (Mosbech *et al.* 2001). King Eiders were tracked from three moulting sites in West Greenland and a breeding site in Arctic Canada to locate key autumn and winter habitats. We also examine diving data from a satellite transmitter with pressure transducer from a King Eider staging in West Greenland.

## STUDY AREA

During winter, Baffin Bay and the western part of the Davis Strait between Canada and Greenland are covered with ice (90-100%), except for a few polynyas (i.e. spaces of open water in the midst of ice in the Arctic seas). However, along the south-west coast of Greenland in the eastern Davis Strait (62-67°N), there are large areas with open water and open drift ice all year round. The area is called the South-west Greenland Open Water Area, and is a very important wintering area for auks (Alcidae) and eiders (Boertmann *et al.* 2004). The south-west Greenland continental shelf is up to 120 km wide north of the open water area, and narrows down to 50 km in the south. The shelf includes several shoals or banks which range in depth from 20 m to 100 m. The largest continuous offshore area with depths less than 50 m in West Greenland is on the northern part of Store Hellefiskebanke (about 5 000 sq. km) in the marginal ice zone north of the Open Water Area. During winter, there are usually drifting ice floes with at-sea ice coverage of 10-80%. Within the West Greenland area, fishing and hunting are intensive, and oil exploration activities are increasing. Consequently, there is a need for careful assessment of potential environmental impacts on eider populations (CAFF 1997).

## METHODS

In 2003, a total of 26 King Eiders were tracked during autumn and winter using intra-abdominally implanted satellite transmitters. In July 2003, 10 King Eiders (seven females and three males) were tracked from a breeding site at East Bay, Southampton Island, Nunavut, in Arctic Canada. In September 2003, 16 King Eiders (six females and 10 males) were tracked from the moulting sites in Mellemfjord and Nordfjord at Disko Island, Greenland. In addition, in August 1999, 10 King Eiders (three females and seven males) were tracked from the moulting site at Umiarfik, in the Upernavik region of West Greenland (Mosbech *et al.* 2001), and these location data are included in the analysis.

At moulting sites, birds were captured in mist nets set between floating platforms (Mosbech *et al.* 2001) or in modified fishing nets. In the fish gillnets, birds were captured one at a time while escape-diving. Specially designed surface-floating fishing nets (Daconetmonofil cod nets 3.3 m deep, 41 m long, equipped with floats and a light lead line, and with a mesh size of 55 mm) were set from fast boats moving in front of a diving bird. The nets had very little weight at the bottom so a bird caught in the net could surface and breathe.

At the breeding site, birds were caught in large mist nets as they flew around an island colony, or in wire funnel traps placed over nests (Gilchrist 2003). After capture, the birds were immediately freed from the net and held in a box of plywood or cardboard lined with puppy nappies prior to and after surgery. Birds were released close to the capture site 2-16 hours after surgery.

The satellite transmitters (PTTs - Platform Transmitter Terminals) were pressure-proof implantable PTT-100 from Microwave Telemetry Inc. weighing about 50 g. The PTTs have expected battery life for 700 transmission hours. To obtain as detailed information as possible, some PTTs were programmed

with fast duty cycles (i.e. four hours transmission and 30 hours off) giving detailed information on local movements, while others were programmed with slow duty cycles (e.g. four hours transmission and 60 hours off). In some cases, the latter provided locations for more than a year. Some of the PTTs were fitted with pressure transducers, which reduced expected battery life to 400-500 transmission hours.

The surgical implantation procedure was performed according to Korschgen *et al.* (1996) with a few modifications (Mosbech *et al.* in prep.).

Location data were received through the Argos Location Service Plus system in DIAG format. Locations are classified according to accuracy by Argos. Location Class (LC) 3, 2 and 1 locations have an estimated accuracy (within one SD) of <150 m, 150-350 m, and 350-1 000 m, respectively, whereas the accuracy of non-standard locations (LC 0, A and B) are >1 000 m or unknown (Argos User's Manual: http://www.cls.fr/manuel). However, most of the LC 0 and A locations are within 9 km of the true location (Britten *et al.* 1999). For the general analysis of staging areas, location class 3, 2, 1 and 0 locations were included in this analysis. For one bird, a more detailed analysis of home range combined with dive behaviour has been performed, including non-standard locations when there was positional redundancy within 5 km (using the PC-SAS ARGOS filter by Douglas 2003). For home range calculations, we used the ArcView GIS extension "Animal Movements" (Hooge *et al.* 1999). We used the fixed-kernel home range estimator (Worton 1989) to estimate the 50% and 95% utilization distribution, and to determine the smoothing parameters, we applied least squares cross-validation (Seaman & Powell 1996, Hooge *et al.* 2004). The information on diving behaviour from the pressure transducer was processed in the PTT in 4-hour time frames, and the compressed data transmitted as number of dives, average dive duration, and time spent at different depth intervals for each 4 hour time frame. The depth intervals used were the intervals 0-1 m (surface), 1-10 m, 10-20 m, 20-30 m, 30-40 m and >40 m.

## RESULTS

This analysis includes location data received until March 2004, at which time there were still 16 active transmitters of the 26 PTTs deployed in 2003 (Table 1).

Table 1. **Number of locations received from King Eiders** *Somateria spectabilis* **tracked from East Bay (Canada) and Disko (Greenland) in 2003-2004, and the relative abundance of the tracked King Eiders at Store Hellefiskebanke. (Based on Argos location classes 3, 2, 1 and 0).**

| Month | Total | | Store Hellefiskebanke | |
|---|---|---|---|---|
| | No. of locations | No. of birds | No. of birds | % birds |
| September | 337 | 26 | 0 | 0 |
| October | 567 | 26 | 5 | 19 |
| November | 519 | 22 | 10 | 45 |
| December | 476 | 22 | 11 | 50 |
| January | 384 | 22 | 10 | 45 |
| February | 203 | 16 | 6 | 38 |

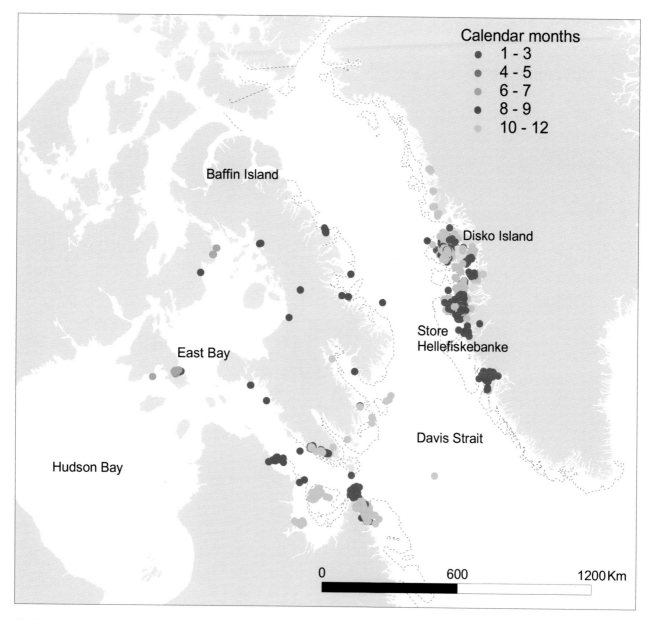

**Fig. 2.** PTT locations received until 29 March 2004 from 10 King Eiders *Somateria spectabilis* tracked from June 2003 from East Bay, and 16 King Eiders tracked from September 2003 from Disko Island (Argos Standard Locations). The location colour code refers to the calendar month.

For the 10 King Eiders with transmitters implanted at the breeding site in East Bay, nine transmitted throughout the autumn (past 15 November), and these nine birds showed a diversity of migration routes and staging areas (Fig. 2). Six of the nine King Eiders migrated to Greenland (four of the six females; two of the three males) and arrived in Greenland between the end of August and the beginning of December. Three birds crossed Baffin Island during the autumn migration. Moulting areas have been identified for six birds based on the fact that during the flightless wing moult period the birds have restricted movements during a period of over three weeks. Three of the six birds performed wing moult in Greenland (one of the two males and two of the four females). The three birds from East Bay which moulted in Greenland moulted at three different sites; two of these are outside the localities where high concentrations of moulting birds have previously been identified (Mosbech & Boertmann 1999).

Satellite tracking of 16 King Eiders from moulting areas in two fjords (Mellemfjord and Nordfjord) at western Disko Island, Greenland, showed that in the period from the start of tracking on 7 September to 10 October 2003 the birds stayed close to their moulting areas with small daily movements. Soon after 10 October, most of the birds initiated their migration southward to Store Hellefiskebanke (an offshore bank) and the nearby coast off the mouth of Nassuttooq fjord (Nordre Strømfjord).

In 1999, the birds were tracked from just before wing moult (the end of July) in a moulting area in southern Upernavik. The birds moulted in the area and stayed in the vicinity of southern Upernavik until October. Six birds were tracked beyond October 1. Five of these birds went to Store Hellefiskebanke about 450 km further south, while one male stayed in southern Upernavik until the end of transmissions in February 2000.

### Store Hellefiskebanke

Store Hellefiskebanke and the adjacent coast off Nassuttooq were a very important winter staging area for birds tracked in 2003/04 (Figs. 2 & 3). In the winter, Store Hellefiskebanke occurs in the marginal drift ice zone just north of the West Greenland Open Water Area. Birds arrived in the area from 13

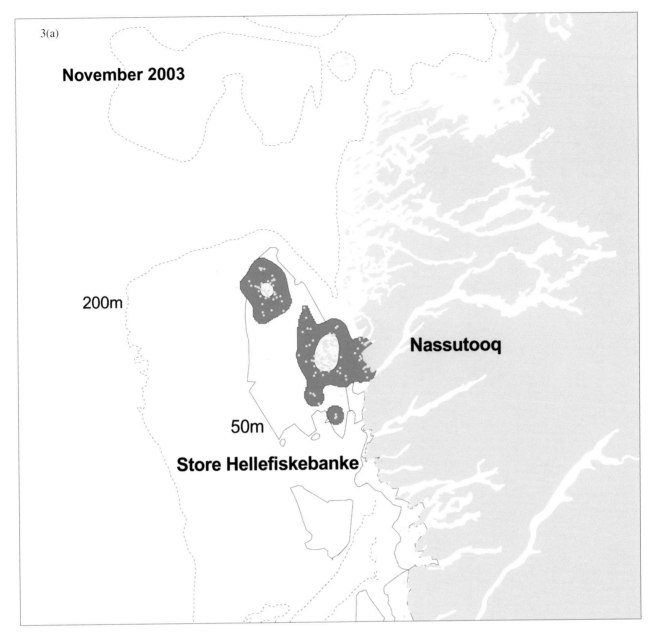

Fig. 3. PTT locations (yellow dots) and kernel home range contours, 50% (green shading) and 95% (light green shading), for tracked King Eiders *Somateria spectabilis* on Store Hellefiskebanke in November 2003 and January 2004. The solid black line is the 50m depth contour; the dotted line is the 200 m depth contour. The thick blue line in 3b is the edge of the drift ice when new ice formation began on the Bank between the drift ice and the coast in January 2004.

October with a median arrival date of 15 November. From October to March, 16 out of a total of 25 birds staged for some period in this area: five of the nine birds tracked from the East Bay breeding site in Canada (five of the six birds which migrated from Canada to Greenland), and 11 of the 16 birds tracked from the Disko moulting areas (Nordfjord and Mellemfjord).

In the period November to March, 31-38% of the total number of PTT locations received each month came from Store Hellefiskebanke, and in the period November to January, about half of the birds with active PTTs staged in this area (Table 1). Four out of seven males stayed for less than a week (range 1-6 days between first and last PTT location in the area), while the remaining three males and nine females spent between 33 days and 164 days (median 78 days between first and last PTT location in the area). In 1999, six birds from the moulting area in Upernavik were tracked during autumn. Five of the six birds

went to Store Hellefiskebanke (median arrival date 30 October), and stayed until the last transmitted locations in January 2000. Combining PTT location data from the two winters 1999/2000 and 2003/04, a total of 21 out of 31 King Eiders tracked during winter staged at Store Hellefiskebanke.

The locations from King Eiders at Store Hellefiskebanke in 1999 were centred on areas with a water depth of 23-35 m, which typically occurred about 50 km from the coast. The daily movements of the birds within Store Hellefiskebanke were relatively small. Ice cover on Store Hellefiskebanke from November 1999 to February 2000 was variable but never exceeded 90% (Danish Meteorological Institute ice charts based on Radarsat and NOAA satellite data), and no clear relationship between the movements of the birds and changes in ice cover could be detected. In November 2003, King Eider locations were centred on the same shallow areas of this offshore bank as in 1999 (Fig. 3), and there

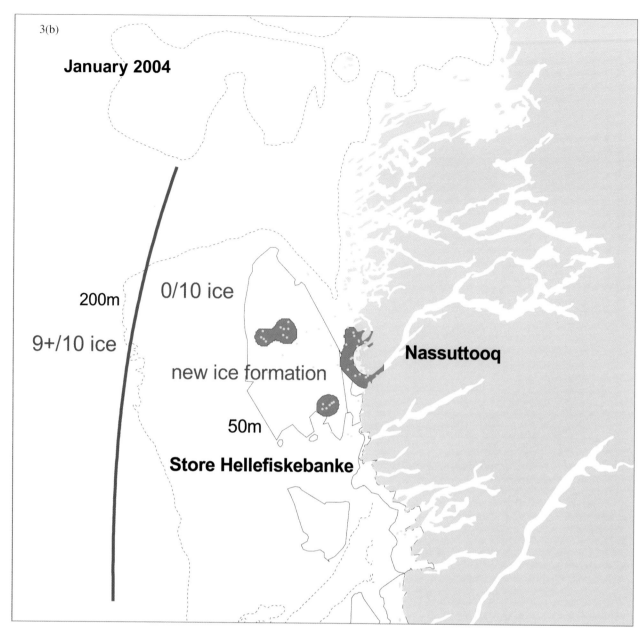

3(b)

**January 2004**

200m

**0/10 ice**

**9+/10 ice**

new ice formation

**Nassuttooq**

50m

**Store Hellefiskebanke**

were ice-free conditions on the bank from November to January. However, by January, the Danish Meteorological Institute ice charts showed formation of new ice on the bank potentially covering the sea surface completely for a period. At this time, we detected a significant movement of the kernel home range towards the coast just north of Nassuttooq (Fig. 3). The area of the more coastal home range in January was only about half the size of the home range in November (95% contour: 986 sq. km and 2 195 sq. km, respectively; 50% contour: 145 sq. km and 277 sq. km, respectively). Along the coast north of Nassuttooq, the tidal amplitude is 4 m, and strong tidal currents typically ensure that there is always some open water. In February and March, the kernel home range moved slowly away from the coast again.

### Combined location and dive data

One female King Eider was tracked between 7 September 2003 and 11 January 2004 (127 days) using a satellite transmitter with a depth recorder installed. During this period, the bird used three distinct home range areas (Table 2, Fig. 4). At the Store Hellefiskebanke staging area, the minimum water depth is about 20 m. The bird spent about 5% of the time at the depth interval

1-20 m in the time frames 10:00 to 14:00 and 14:00 to 18:00. For this bottom-feeder, this is time spent swimming between the surface and the bottom. The overall maximum diving depth of 43 m was recorded at Store Hellefiskebanke. The total daily diving activity (time spent below 1 m ±SD) was 138 ±45 min, 99 ±16 min and 102 ± 22 min for the moulting area and the two subsequent staging areas, respectively, and thus tended to be highest in the moulting area. This King Eider showed a clear diurnal dive rhythm in all areas (p<0.001), preferring to dive during daylight. This pattern resulted in a short diving peak

**Table 2. Fixed-kernel home range in three staging areas for a female King Eider *Somateria spectabilis*.**

| Locality | No. of days | No. of locations | Kernel home range (km²)* | |
|---|---|---|---|---|
| | | | 95% area | 50% area |
| Moulting area | 29 | 44 | 256 | 50 |
| Staging A.2 | 17 | 40 | 97 | 15 |
| Staging A.3 | 72 | 90 | 621 | 54 |

\* Calculations of area of fixed-kernel home range with LSCV.

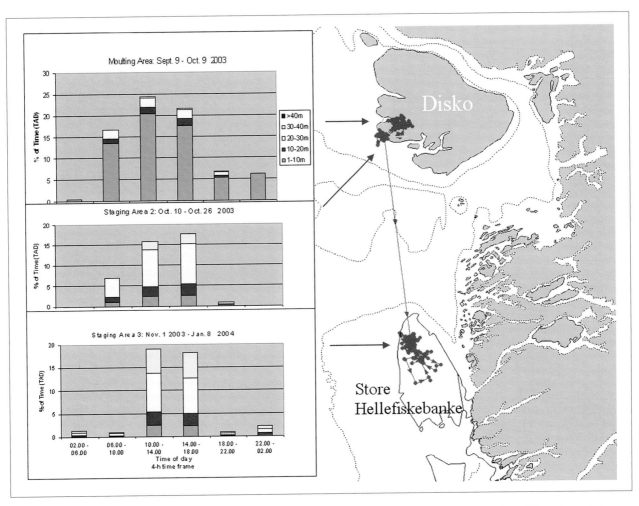

Fig. 4. PTT locations and track-line for a female King Eider *Somateria spectabilis* using three distinct staging areas from 7 September to 8 January, and diurnal diving behaviour in these three areas. The columns show the time spent in different depth intervals (Time At Depth, TAD) as a percentage of the time in each four-hour time frame and averaged for the staging period. The diving data covered 75%, 79% and 54% of the time spent in the three staging areas, respectively.

during the winter at Store Hellefiskebanke, when there is only a short period of twilight at this latitude (68°N).

## DISCUSSION

This satellite telemetry study has provided valuable information on migration routes and staging areas, and has clearly shown that the offshore area at Store Hellefiskebanke and adjacent coast are very important wintering habitat for King Eiders breeding in the eastern Canadian Arctic.

Although the sample size is small, it is striking how diverse the migration routes and moulting and staging areas are for the birds tracked from the East Bay breeding area. This diverse dispersal accords well with the lack of spatial genetic structure found among nesting and wintering King Eiders (Pearce *et al.* 2004). Based on stable isotope signatures, Mehl *et al.* (2004) found that female King Eiders breeding at the migratory divide in the central Arctic of the American continent are not strongly philopatric to wintering areas in eastern or western North America. Some females have been found to use completely different migration routes in different years.

While large flocks of King Eiders had previously been observed in the drift ice over Store Hellefiskebanke in March and April (Mosbech & Johnson 1999), this satellite telemetry study has shown that the first birds arrive in this offshore area in

October. Satellite tracking from the major moulting areas in West Greenland and a breeding area in central Canada indicates that about 50% of the King Eiders from these areas choose to stage for a period on Store Hellefiskebanke. Why do the birds choose this area in the drift ice north of the Open Water Area? Firstly, it is the largest continuous area of shallow water in West Greenland that provides appropriate foraging areas. Secondly, the dynamic drift-ice environment that is the usual condition on Store Hellefiskebanke from midwinter (January) may actually reduce energetic costs because the birds can roost on the ice and the ice dampens the waves and the wind. Mosbech & Johnson (1999) found that in March and April, the distribution of King Eiders during aerial surveys of the bank was not negatively correlated with heavy ice (up to 90%). However, new ice formation in calm weather, as seen in January 2004, may close the water surface and force the birds to move away. Ice conditions on the bank are dynamic, and usually the water surface will only be completely closed for a few days. The offshore drift-ice habitat seems to resemble the wintering habitat of Spectacled Eiders described by Petersen & Douglas (2004).

In 2004, most birds shifted to the coast in January and stayed there for several weeks, indicating the importance of the coastal part of the area as well. Satellite telemetry showed that the birds were not commuting between the coast and the offshore area.

Such information is important for planning and interpretation of surveys.

The diurnal diving activity that we found for a female is in accordance with earlier reports that King Eiders feed mainly by day (Cramp & Simmons 1977). We found less feeding activity at the moulting locality (138 min or 10% of a 24-hour period) than Frimer (1994) found during his land-based observations in the Disko moulting area in September. He found that King Eiders allocated 12% of the 24 hours to diving. Frimer found that most feeding took place at depths of between 10 and 25 m, while our bird spent most of its diving time at depths of between 1 and 10 m. At the two subsequent staging areas, this King Eider allocated less time to diving (99 min and 102 min, respectively, or about 7% of the 24 hours), and dived considerably deeper. This is very much like the King Eiders wintering in a fjord in northern Norway (70°N). Here, land-based observations have shown that flocks of King Eiders usually dived deeper than 20 m and were diving down to depths of 40 m (Bustnes & Lønne 1997, Systad *et al.* 2000). These birds allocated 102 min per day (November-April) to diving; a similar time to that spent by the female King Eider from this study in West Greenland. However, the Norwegian birds increased their diving time from 57 min on the shortest days in December to 161 min on the longest day in April. The reduced diving activity in December in northern Norway compared with our bird is probably due to there being less daylight in northern Norway, which lies at two degrees latitude further north.

One important point to be taken into account in the management of staging areas for King Eiders is that nearly all foraging takes place during daylight hours. Thus, disturbance during the few hours of daylight in midwinter could have a significant impact on foraging. Further analysis of location and diving data combined with data on body condition, stomach samples and benthos will provide precise descriptions of habitat quality, and has the potential to identify population bottlenecks.

## ACKNOWLEDGEMENTS

We thank the field teams at East Bay and Disko Island for their invaluable support in catching the birds. We thank Ebbe Bøgebjerg, NERI, for generously sharing his experience with net designs, Margaret R. Petersen and Daniel M. Mulcahy, Alaska Science Center, for helping us with implantation expertise, and Paul Howey, Microwave Telemetry, for solving all the technical problems and collaborating with us on the development of the PTTs with depth recorder. We were supported by Dancea (Danish Co-operation for Environment in the Arctic) and the North American Sea Duck Joint Venture. Avatangiisinut Pinngortitamullu Pisortaqarfik, The Nature Directorate, Greenland, granted us the necessary permits for the work in Greenland.

## REFERENCES

**Boertmann, D., Lyngs, P., Merkel, F. & Mosbech, A.** 2004. The significance of Southwest Greenland as winter quarters for seabirds. Bird Conservation International 14: 87-112.

**Britten, M.W., Kennedy, P.L. & Ambrose, S.** 1999. Performance and accuracy evaluation of small satellite transmitters. Journal of Wildlife Management 63: 1349-1358.

King Eider *Somateria spectabilis*. Photo: Anders Mosbech.

**Bustnes, J.O. & Lønne, O.J.** 1997. Habitat partitioning among wintering Common Eiders *Somateria mollissima* and King Eiders *Somateria spectabilis*. Ibis 139: 549-559.

**CAFF** 1997. Circumpolar Eider Conservation Strategy and Action Plan. Conservation of Arctic Flora and Fauna Report.

**Cramp, S. & Simmons, K.E.L.** (eds). 1977. The birds of the Western Palearctic. Vol. 1. Oxford University Press.

**Douglas, D.C.** 2003. PC-SAS Argos Filter V6.0 Software Documentation. United States Geological Survey, Alaska Biological Science Center, Anchorage, Alaska, USA.

**Frimer, O.** 1994. The behaviour of moulting King Eiders *Somateria spectabilis*. Wildfowl 45: 176-187.

**Frimer, O.** 1995. Adaptations by the King Eider *Somateria spectabilis* to its moulting habitat: review of a study at Disko, West Greenland. Dansk Ornitologisk Forenings Tidsskrift 89: 135-142.

**Gilchrist, G.** 2003. Studies on the Demography and Reproductive Ecology of Common and King Eiders, East Bay Nunavut. Banding Methods. Canadian Wildlife Service. Unpublished report.

**Gratto-Travor, C.L., Johnston, V.H. & Pepper, S.** 1998. Changes in shorebird and eider abundance in the Rasmussen Lowlands, NWT. Wilson Bulletin 110: 316-325.

**Hooge, P.N., Eichenlaub, W.M. & Solomon, E.K.** 1999. The animal movement program. U.S. Geological Survey, Alaska Biological Science Center. Available at: http://www.absc.usgs.gov/glba/gistools.

**Hooge, P.N., Eichenlaub, W.M. & Solomon, E.K.** 2004. Using GIS to analyze animal movements in the marine environment. U.S. Geological Survey, Alaska Biological Science Center. Unpublished report. Available at: http://www.absc.usgs.gov/glba/gistools.

Korschgen, C.E., Kenow, K.P., Gendron-Fitzpatrick, A., Green, W.L. & Dein, F.J. 1996. Implanting intra-abdominal radiotransmitters with external whip antennas in ducks. Journal of Wildlife Management 60: 132-137.

Lyngs, P. 2003. Migration and winter ranges of birds in Greenland - an analysis of ringing recoveries. Dansk Ornithologisk Forenings Tidsskrift 97(1): 1-167.

Mehl, K.R., Alisauskas, R.T., Hobson, K.A. & Kellett, D.K. 2004. To winter east or west? Heterogeneity in winter philopatry in a central-arctic population of King Eiders. Condor 106: 241.

Merkel, F.R., Mosbech, A., Boertmann, D. & Grøndahl, L. 2002. Winter seabird distribution and abundance off south-western Greenland, 1999. Polar Research 21(1): 17-36.

Mosbech A. & Boertmann, D. 1999. Distribution, abundance and reaction to aerial surveys of post-breeding king eiders (*Somateria spectabilis*) in western Greenland. Arctic 52: 188-203.

Mosbech A. & Johnson, S.R. 1999. Late Winter Distribution and Abundance of Sea-Associated Birds in Southwest Greenland, Davis Strait, and Southern Baffin Bay. Polar Research 18: 1-17.

Mosbech, A., Merkel, F.R., Flagstad, A. & Grøndahl, L. 2001. Satellitsporing af kongeederfugl i Vestgrønland. Identifikation af raste- og overvintringsområder (Satellite tracking of King Eiders in west Greenland. Identification of staging- and wintering areas). Technical Report No. 381. National Environmental Research Institute (NERI), Roskilde, Denmark.

Mosbech, A., Gilchrist, G., Merkel, F., Sonne, C., Flagstad, A. & Nyegaard, H. In press. Year-round movements of Common Eiders *Somateria mollissima borealis* breeding in Arctic Canada and West Greenland followed by satellite telemetry. ARDEA

Pearce, J.M., Talbot, S.L., Pierson, B.J., Petersen, M.R., Scribner, K.T., Dickson, D.L. & Mosbech, A. 2004. Lack of spatial genetic structure among nesting and wintering King Eiders. Condor 106: 229-240.

Petersen, M.R. & Douglas, D.C. 1995. Use of implanted satellite transmitters to locate Spectacled Eiders at sea. The Condor 97: 276-278.

Petersen, M.R. & Douglas, D.C. 2004. Winter ecology of Spectacled Eiders: Environmental characteristics and population change. The Condor 106: 79-94.

Petersen, M.R., Larned, W.W. & Douglas, D.C. 1999. At-sea distribution of Spectacled Eiders: A 120-year-old mystery resolved. Auk 116(4): 1009-1020.

Salomonsen, F. 1968. The moult migration. Wildfowl 19: 5-24.

Seaman, D.E. & Powell, R.A. 1996. An evaluation of the accuracy of kernel density estimators for home range analysis. Ecology 77(7): 2075-2085.

Systad, G.H., Bustnes, J.O. & Erikstad, K.E. 2000. Behavioral responses to decreasing day length in wintering sea ducks. The Auk: 33-40.

Worton, B.J. 1989. Kernel Methods for Estimating the Utilization Distribution in Home-Range Studies. Ecology 70(1): 164-168.

Shallow waters in Disko Bugt, West Greenland, July 1995: important areas in winter for King Eiders *Somateria spectabilis*. Photo: David Stroud.

# Cape Gannet *Morus capensis* movements in Africa

*H. Dieter Oschadleus[1] & Michael Brooks[2]*

*Avian Demography Unit, Department of Statistical Sciences, University of Cape Town, Rondebosch, 7701, South Africa.*
*(email: [1]dieter@adu.uct.ac.za, [2]mbrooks@adu.uct.ac.za)*

Oschadleus, H.D. & Brooks, M. 2006. Cape Gannet *Morus capensis* movements in Africa. *Waterbirds around the world.* Eds. G.C. Boere, C.A. Galbraith & D.A. Stroud. The Stationery Office, Edinburgh, UK. pp. 777-778.

Cape Gannets *Morus capensis* breed at only six coastal islands off Namibia and South Africa (Table 1, Fig. 1). They are the third most-ringed birds in southern Africa, with some 140 000 ringed since 1950 (Oschadleus & Underhill 1999). Most ringing records since 1975 have been captured electronically.

After breeding, gannets disperse around the African coast, to West Africa on the west coast and to the Gulf of Guinea and Mozambique on the east coast. However, there have been some unusual recoveries. On 18 October 1986, a ringed Cape Gannet was entangled with fishing line in Western Australia, and was released unharmed. It had been ringed on Bird Island, Algoa Bay, 7 860 km away. In October 1989 this individual was seen on an unoccupied Yellow-nosed Albatross *Diomedea chlorhynchos* nest on Amsterdam Island, in the southern Indian Ocean halfway between South Africa and Australia. It was seen again on several dates in the same season, and in the following season, on Amsterdam Island.

Two other unusual Cape Gannet recoveries have been reported to SAFRING. One was found in a rubbish dump in Murmansk, NW Russia, but the gannet was probably caught on a Russian trawler and the ring and leg later discarded. Similarly, a South African ringed bird was reported from the Philippine Islands, without further details, but presumably this ring was also dropped off by a trawler. Cape Gannets often forage around trawlers and may become entangled in their nets.

A total of 2 516 gannets have been recovered sick or dead (0.6%), and 21 700 have been recaptured (5.4%). Adults usually remain within 540 km of their breeding site but may move up to 3 300 km, while immature birds of under two years old migrate as far as 6 800 km (Table 2).

The Cape Gannet is a regular winter visitor as far as the Gulf of Guinea. Outside of South Africa and Namibia, there have been 103 recoveries from Angola, 14 from Congo, 11 from Gabon, 17 from Equatorial Guinea, 10 from Cameroon, two from Nigeria, and one from Western Sahara. The last record is of a fledgling ringed at Lambert's Bay in 1966 that had moved to Western (former Spanish) Sahara after only 51 days. On the east coast of Africa, it is a regular winter visitor to Kwazulu-Natal

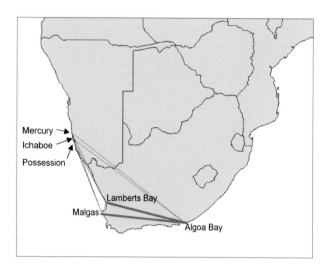

Fig. 1. The six breeding colonies of Cape Gannets *Morus capensis* in South Africa and Namibia, and known movements between the colonies.

**Table 2. Number of Cape Gannet *Morus capensis* recoveries by ringing age.**

| Area of recovery | Juv | Adult | Total |
|---|---|---|---|
| Angola | 33 | 68 | 103 |
| Gulf of Guinea | 12 | 44 | 56 |
| Mozambique | 20 | 17 | 37 |

**Table 3. Number of Cape Gannet *Morus capensis* recoveries by decade and area of recovery.**

| | 1950s | 1960s | 1970s | 1980s | 1990s |
|---|---|---|---|---|---|
| Angola | 64 | 19 | 0 | 6 | 14 |
| Gulf of Guinea | 50 | 4 | 0 | 0 | 2 |
| Mozambique | 13 | 7 | 0 | 9 | 8 |
| Totals | 127 | 30 | 0 | 15 | 24 |

**Table 1. Numbers of pulli and adult Cape Gannets *Morus capensis* ringed at breeding colonies 1975-2002, and all recoveries 1950-2004. Colonies are sorted in decreasing size (no. of pairs in 1995 from Rob Crawford *in litt.*).**

| Breeding site | Pulli | Adults | Recovered | No. of pairs in 1995 |
|---|---|---|---|---|
| Algoa Bay, Eastern Cape | 29 317 | 1 847 | 2 441 | 68 000 |
| Malgas, Western Cape | 21 480 | 3 827 | 5 483 | 58 000 |
| Ichaboe, Namibia | 7 621 | 742 | 471 | 28 000 |
| Lamberts Bay, Western Cape | 11 838 | 1 586 | 3 766 | 10 000 |
| Mercury, Namibia | 4 012 | 135 | 367 | 2 100 |
| Possession, Namibia | 2 300 | 215 | 186 | 800 |
| Total | 76 568 | 8 352 | 12 714 | 166 900 |

**Table 4. Number of Cape Gannet *Morus capensis* resighted or retrapped between breeding colonies.**

| Ringed at: | Colony moved to: | | | | | | |
|---|---|---|---|---|---|---|---|
| | Mercury | Ichaboe | Possession | Lamberts | Malgas | Algoa | Other* |
| Mercury | | 10 | | 8 | 11 | | |
| Ichaboe | 7 | | 3 | 31 | 22 | | |
| Possession | 3 | 18 | | 16 | 16 | | |
| Lamberts Bay | 1 | 6 | | | 291 | 5 | 6 |
| Malgas | 2 | 2 | 1 | 260 | | 3 | 6 |
| Algoa | 1 | 1 | | 34 | 56 | | 1 |

* birds resighted or retrapped at non-breeding locations

and Delagoa Bay, Mozambique. Recoveries along the east coast of Africa include 37 from Mozambique and one from Madagascar.

The number of recoveries reported declined after the 1950s (Table 3), indicating a possibly altered pattern of dispersal (Oatley 1988, Klages 1994). This cannot be explained by a decrease in ringing effort.

Most inter-colony movement occurred between the closest colonies: Malgas and Lambert's Bay (Table 4, Fig. 1). Some movement occurred between South African and Namibian colonies. The most isolated colony seems to be at Algoa Bay.

**REFERENCES**

Oatley, T.B. 1988. Change in winter movements of Cape Gannets. In: Macdonald, I.A.W. & Crawford, R.J.M. (eds). Long-term data series relating to southern Africa's renewable natural resources. South African National Sciencific Progress Report No. 157. CSIR, Pretoria, South Africa.

Klages, N.T.W. 1994. Dispersal and site fidelity of Cape Gannets *Morus capensis*. Ostrich 65(2): 218-224.

Oschadleus, H.D. & Underhill, L.G. 1999. SAFRING ringing totals over 50 years. Safring News 28: 11-13.

Cape Gannets *Morus capensis* at Lamberts Bay, western Cape. Photo: Dieter Oschadleus.
Inset: Displaying Cape Gannets *Morus capensis* at Lamberts Bay, western Cape. Photo: Dieter Oschadleus.

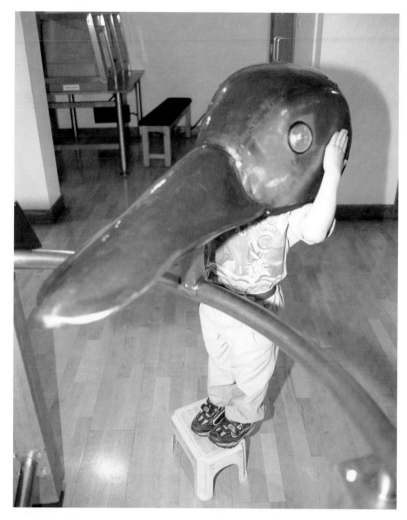

Seeing the world through duck eyes.  Photo: The Wildfowl & Wetlands Trust.

Education and awareness raising is a crucial element of any conservation programme.  Talking to schoolchildren at Shuangtaizi Hekou National Nature Reserve, Liaoning Province, China (Yellow Sea).  Photo: Mark Barter.

# Part 6.

## Conflict resolution

## Sections

# 6.1 Conflict resolution. Workshop Introduction

*Bruce Batt*

*Ducks Unlimited, Inc., One Waterfowl Way, Memphis, Tennessee 39120, USA.*

Batt, B. 2006. Conflict resolution. Workshop Introduction. *Waterbirds around the world.* Eds. G.C. Boere, C.A. Galbraith & D.A. Stroud. The Stationery Office, Edinburgh, UK. pp. 782-783.

"Farmer - what have you done with my grain?"
There are a growing number of examples from many countries, where there has been successful resolution of conflicts between goose populations and farmers. Protest banner (from 1989) in Nordrhein Westfalen, Germany, where goose shooting had been prohibited. Photo: David Stroud.

The conservation of waterbirds often comes into conflict with the advancement of economic, recreational, transportation and agricultural development both at broad landscape scales and at specific sites. This workshop covered several examples of the kinds of issues that are emerging as society advances.

Among the key points emerging from the papers were:

- Waterbird specialists must play key roles in the development of practical and sustainable solutions to most problems. It is critical to waterbird conservation that the best science available is applied to each situation.
- Problems can emerge unexpectedly in areas that may, even recently, have been thought to be of low threat to conservation interests. It is highly desirable to monitor all waterbird species, even the most common, to help ensure sensitivity to environmental changes when they occur in the future.
- After management actions have been implemented, it is important to follow through with adequate evaluation programs to encourage the continuation of satisfactory prac-

tices or to offer feed-back that provides guidance for improvements of future management programs. The case of the permanent inundation of the estuarine Cardiff Bay in the UK was reported by Burton.

- Competing alternative uses for limited habitats remain at the centre of most conflicts. With the habitats available to most species already generally much limited over what was historically available, it is critical that waterbird interests engage in these problems before significant investments have been made by economic interests.
- It is usually preferable to define mutually compatible uses of areas for both their natural values and for economic development, but these cases are often illusive to discover.
- It is critical to get all stakeholders involved in the resolution of most conflicts as mutual ownership of action plans is a highly desirable element that can lead to the successful results.
- The unusual problem of overabundant species has begun to emerge among a few species of waterbirds as described by Batt *et al..* Management experience of the current cases

will provide important guidance for similar issues when they arise in the future with other species, or in other regions.

- Non-native waterbirds introduced beyond natural ranges, especially Anatidae, may have closely related species that might be subject to genetic swamping and excessive competition to the detriment of indigenous species (as described by Henderson in relation to the genetic impacts of Ruddy Duck *Oxyura jamaicensis* on White-headed Ducks *O. leucocephala* in Europe). Introductions of non-native waterbirds should be prevented at the outset, but if - despite this - ecologically damaging species have become established, it is preferable to move quickly to remove or contain them before the problem grows to the point where little can be done.

- New industrial uses of intertidal and supratidal habitats are especially threatening as these areas are critical to many species of waterbird. Conflicts raised by intensive shellfisheries in the Dutch Wadden Sea are described by Ens, and as a consequence of intensive shrimp aquaculture by Schaeffer-Novelli *et al.*. (See also papers within the section on 'Declining waterbirds: problems, processes and sites'). These problems are emerging in both developed and developing countries.

- Two examples of apparently successful resolution of conflicts between hunting and the local protection of waterfowl populations are described by Stroud *et al.* and by Cope *et al.*

- The growth of wind farms is a broadly important issue for bird conservation and has recently emerged in offshore environments. As stressed by Fox & Petersen, it is highly desirable to implement extensive monitoring of the impacts on waterbirds as better knowledge is critical for the location and management of this industry in the future.

The severe physical disturbance of inter-tidal sediments following mechanised dredging for cockles in the Dutch Waddensea is clearly visible from the air. Ens (this volume, p. 806) summarises the consequences of this fishery for waterbirds. Following intervention by the European Court of Justice, these damaging practices have now ceased. Photo: Jaap de Vlas.

# Reducing waterbird mortality in severe cold weather: 25 years of statutory shooting suspensions in Britain

*David A. Stroud[1], John Harradine[2], Colin Shedden[3], Julian Hughes[4], Gwyn Williams[4], Jacquie A. Clark[5] & Nigel A. Clark[5]*

[1] *Joint Nature Conservation Committee, Monkstone House, City Road, Peterborough, PE1 1JY, UK. (email: David.Stroud@jncc.gov.uk)*

[2] *British Association for Shooting and Conservation, Marford Mill, Rossett, Wrexham, LL12 0HL, UK.*

[3] *British Association for Shooting and Conservation Scotland, Trochry, Dunkeld, Tayside, PH8 0DY, Scotland, UK.*

[4] *Royal Society for the Protection of Birds, The Lodge, Sandy, Bedfordshire, SG19 2DL, UK.*

[5] *British Trust for Ornithology, The Nunnery, Nunnery Place, Thetford, Norfolk, IP24 2PU, UK.*

Stroud, D.A., Harradine, J., Shedden, C., Hughes, J., Williams, G., Clark, J.A. & Clark, N.A. 2006. Reducing waterbird mortality in severe cold weather: 25 years of statutory shooting suspensions in Britain. *Waterbirds around the world.* Eds. G.C. Boere, C.A. Galbraith & D.A. Stroud. The Stationery Office, Edinburgh, UK. pp. 784-790.

## ABSTRACT

In periods of severe or particularly harsh winter weather in Britain, wildlife legislation enables the suspension of waterbird shooting so as to help reduce mortality from both direct and indirect causes. Following controversy over the imposition of shooting suspension in the severe weather of January 1979, a formal system of criteria to be operated under similar future circumstances was jointly agreed by the British government's nature conservation advisory body and non-governmental organizations representing shooting and conservation interests. These criteria have been progressively developed in the years since, with formal reviews following those winters when suspensions occurred so as to learn lessons and further refine good practice. We outline the evolution of the current system and summarize the last 25 winters, in particular focussing on those elements that have led to the effective operation of the system and lessons learnt in reducing unnecessary conflicts. There are some aspects of the British system that would be of wider applicability to other countries interested in developing a similar system. Finally, we review the recent pattern of severe midwinter weather and note the decreasing frequency of prolonged severe weather events consequent on currently changing climate.

## INTRODUCTION

For many species of bird, and especially for waterbirds, midwinter can be an ecological "bottle-neck" when they have particular difficulty obtaining enough food. They face reduced prospects for survival during winter (Goss-Custard *et al.* 1977, Clark 2002) and especially in periods of harsh weather (Dobinson & Richards 1964, Davidson & Evans 1982, Mitchell *et al.* 2000). In addition, there can be significant movements within Europe of waterbirds seeking milder conditions, and many move to Britain to escape from even colder conditions in continental Europe (Lack 1986, Ridgill & Fox 1990, Kirby 1995).

Lengthy spells of severe weather can result in changed behaviour, with birds becoming "tame" and reluctant to fly when approached in order to avoid using up remaining energy reserves. Under such circumstances, the conservation response should be to limit unnecessary disturbance to enable the conservation of remaining energetic reserves, and thus reduce mortality.

## EVOLUTION OF CRITERIA FOR SUSPENDING WATERBIRD SHOOTING

In Great Britain, the open season for waterbird shooting on inland sites finishes on 1 February, although shooting on the

Fig. 1. The British network of meteorological stations currently used to provide ground condition data for severe weather alerting (since 2001/02).

foreshore continues until 21 February (Section 2 (4) of the Wildlife and Countryside Act 1981). In periods of prolonged severe winter weather (usually when freezing is persistent), the relevant Secretary of State(s) have the power under Section 2 (6) of the Wildlife and Countryside Act to make a Protection Order temporarily suspending the shooting of waterbirds.

In January 1979, a ban on wildfowling (waterbird shooting) was imposed as a result of prolonged severe weather. There was considerable disagreement and confusion between interested parties over the calling of this ban due to the lack of universally accepted criteria and procedures. As a result, a government Working Group was established to devise criteria for future use, and proposals focused on the recording of frozen ground states at a network of coastal meteorological stations (Batten & Swift 1982). Since then, there have been progressive modifications to the system, as detailed by Stroud (1992).

The current guidelines, given below, have been agreed between the statutory conservation agencies (Joint Nature

**Table 1. Summary of past severe winter weather events in Great Britain (see Stroud 1992 for further detail).**

| Year | No. stations recording SoG | JNCC Day 5 trigger | Day 7/Voluntary restraint | Shooting suspension into force | Shooting suspension lifted | Unusual levels of waterbird mortality |
|---|---|---|---|---|---|---|
| 1980/81 | 13 | GB Day 5 on 16 February | | | | |
| 1981/82 | 13 | GB Day 5 on 12 December | 15 December (England & Wales) | 00:01 on 22 December / 00:01 on 23 December (Scotland) / 11 January (Scotland) / 00:01 on 13 January (England & Wales) | 5 January / 23:59 on 24 January / 23:59 on 22 January (England & Wales) | Mortality greatest in Scotland and least in several south and west coast estuaries. |
| 1982/83 | 13 | GB Day 5 on 12 February | Day 7 on 14 February | *Day 13 on 20 February* | | |
| 1983/84 | 13 | GB Day 5 on 24 January | 26 January | | | |
| 1984/85 | 13 | GB Day 5 on 6 January / GB Day 5 on 13 February | Day 7 on 15 February | 09:00 on 16 January | 23:59 on 29 January | Weather in Scotland not as severe as in south-east / Condition of birds in Scotland worse than in January. / High mortality (p. 14 JNCC Report 75). |
| 1985/86 | 23 | GB Day 5 on 9 January | | | | High mortality in south-east England, especially on the Wash and the Stour. |
| | | GB Day 5 on 9 February | Day 7 on 11 February | Day 14 on 18 February | | |
| 1986/87 | 23 | GB Day 5 on 11 January / GB Day 5 on 17 February | 13 January / Day 7 on 19 February | 09:00 on 21 January | 12:00 on 26 January | No large-scale mortality noted. |
| 1987/88 | 23 | None | | | | |
| 1988/89 | 23 | *(No data on file between 3-9 January and 14-20 February)* | | | | |
| 1989/90 | FILE LOST — NO DATA AVAILABLE | | | | | |
| 1990/91 | 23 | GB Day 5 on 6 January | 8 January | | | Heavy mortality of waders on the Wash by 18 February. |
| 1991/92 | 22 | GB Day 5 on 26 January | Day 7 on 28 January | | | |
| 1992/93 | 21 | England & Wales Day 5 on 1 January | | | | |
| 1993/94 | 24 | Scotland (and GB) Day 5 on 24 November | | 26 November (Scotland only) | | |
| 1994/95 | 23 | None | | | | |
| 1995/96 | 23 | Scotland Day 5 on 26 December / England & Wales (and GB) Day 5 on 29 December | Day 7 on 28 December | | | |
| | | England and Wales Day 5 on 31 January | Day 7 on 2 February. [Restraint called on 5 February (England & Wales)] | 09:00 on 10 February (England and Wales) | 20 February | Major mortality of waders in the Wash area. |
| | | GB Day 5 on 1 February | GB Day 5 on 3 February | | | |
| 1996/97 | 22 | Scotland Day 5 on 27 December / England and Wales Day 5 on 28 December | 31 December / Day 7 on 31 December | 09:00 on 10 January | 09:00 on 18 January | |
| 1997/98 | 22 | None | | | | |

**Table 1 (cont.). Summary of past severe winter weather events in Great Britain (see Stroud 1992 for further detail). (Continued)**

| Year | No. stations recording SoG | JNCC Day 5 trigger | Day 7/Voluntary restraint | Shooting suspension into force | Shooting suspension lifted | Unusual levels of waterbird mortality |
|---|---|---|---|---|---|---|
| 1998/99 | 22 | None | | | | |
| 1999/2000 | 24 | None | | | | |
| 2000/01 | 20 or less | Scotland Day 5 on 29 December<br>Scotland Day 5 on 15 January<br>England & Wales Day 5 on 19 January | Day 7 on 31 December<br>Day 7 on 17 January | | | None reported.<br>Little reported (cold but little wind).<br>Little reported (cold but little wind). |
| 2001/02 | 23 | Scotland Day 5 on 26 December (final Day 11 on 4 January) | 4 January | | | |
| 2002/03 | 23 | Scotland Day 5 on 7 January (final Day 8 on 10 January)<br>England & Wales Day 5 on 12 January and again 19 February | 10 January | | | None reported although wetlands heavily frozen in much of Scotland.<br>None reported. |
| 2003/04 | 23 | None | | | | None reported - very mild winter. |
| 2004/05 | 23 | None | | | | None reported - very mild winter. |

Conservation Committee (JNCC), English Nature, Countryside Council for Wales, and Scottish Natural Heritage), the Department of the Environment, Food and Rural Affairs (DEFRA), the Scottish Executive Environment and Rural Affairs Department (SEERAD), the National Assembly of Wales, and the principal non-governmental organizations involved in the monitoring and management of severe-weather suspensions: the Royal Society for the Protection of Birds (RSPB), Wildfowl & Wetlands Trust (WWT), British Trust for Ornithology (BTO), and British Association for Shooting and Conservation (BASC). A similar but separately organized system operates in Northern Ireland.

### Current criteria for suspending waterbird shooting

Under contract to JNCC, the UK Meteorological Office summarizes daily data on ground conditions at 23 meteorological stations throughout England, Scotland and Wales (Fig. 1). These stations are chosen to reflect the winter weather conditions around the whole British coast and because they are close to major estuaries and other centres of foreshore shooting, since waterbirds typically concentrate at the coast during severe weather.

Suspensions can occur either throughout Great Britain, in Scotland alone, or in England and Wales only. However, since the advent of devolved government in Britain in the mid-1990s, the system has operated effectively at only two scales, Scotland, and England and Wales. Although, in principle, simultaneous suspensions in these two areas would give a shooting suspension at the scale of Great Britain, this has not occurred since 1986/87.

### Current procedures in the event of a severe cold period

- When more than half of these stations (either throughout Great Britain, in Scotland alone, or in England and Wales) have recorded frozen conditions for five consecutive days, JNCC is alerted. Weather conditions are then monitored more closely during a "countdown period" prior to a statutory suspension being invoked.
- After seven days of frozen conditions, JNCC informs BASC who initiate a comparable information-gathering and condition-monitoring exercise of birds and habitat through regional staff and local contacts if severe weather looks likely to continue. Once alerted, BASC contacts all its member wildfowling clubs and shooting syndicates, calling for voluntary restraint in waterbird shooting in those parts of the country where appropriate (and warning of the possibility of a statutory suspension if conditions persist). Such voluntary measures continue up to the point of any statutory suspension or as considered necessary in the light of prevailing conditions and information, especially on the condition of birds and their habitats. When several periods of severe weather occur within a short time scale, voluntary restraints play a particularly important role because they allow populations to recover from stress. At this stage, waterbird shooters and others provide invaluable information on local conditions.
- With respect to the criteria applying to the "count-down period", short periods of thaw (one or two days with less than half the stations frozen) have no effect on the process that will trigger a statutory suspension, but three or more days of thaw have the effect of terminating the process. Such short periods of thaw are "neutral" in terms of counting

a) Stations used from 1980/1 - 1984/5        b) Stations used from 1985/6 - 2000/1

**Fig. 2.** Progressive development in numbers and range of the network of meteorological stations used to provide the initial alert for statutory shooting suspensions (after Stroud 1992).

days towards a suspension – that is they neither count towards, nor terminate, the process.

- During the alert stage (Day 7 onwards), regional representatives from relevant country agencies, RSPB and BASC liaise with one another to exchange information and pass this to JNCC for national collation. The BTO supplies JNCC with information from their observer networks. Particular attention is paid not only to the foreshore and the freezing of inland waters and feeding grounds, but also to the condition of birds, bird numbers, movements and behaviour, appearance of unusual species, significance of wind chill and snow cover, the last especially in Scotland. To aid review, information is encouraged to be reported on a standard proforma available on JNCC's web-site.

- On the thirteenth day after the start of the severe weather, if more than half the relevant meteorological stations are still frozen, a case is presented to the relevant Secretary of State(s) requesting a suspension of waterbird shooting due to the severe weather. Such suspensions can be instituted throughout Great Britain, or in Scotland alone, or in England and Wales, dependent on the extent of the severe weather.

- Once this Statutory Instrument has been signed, it comes into force at 09:00 hrs on the fifteenth day of severe weather.

- The two intervening days are used to publicize the impending suspension as widely as possible. BASC contacts all its wildfowling clubs and game shooting syndicates, issues press releases to newspaper, sporting magazine, radio and television editors, and institutes a 24-hour telephone information service in all regions of the country. Similarly DEFRA and SEERAD, as appropriate, issue press releases and place public notices of the suspension in an agreed selection of national and regional newspapers. Efforts are made to have such notices included on national and regional television and radio news, and weather programmes. A general call is made for other recreational users of the coasts to avoid disturbing waterbirds.

- Once the suspension comes into force, it prohibits the shooting of any bird on Schedule 2 Part 1 of the Wildlife and Countryside Act 1981[1]; in effect it introduces a temporary close season for shootable ducks, geese, waders, Common Coot *Fulica atra* and Common Moorhen *Gallinula chloropus*, for an initial period of 14 days. This applies throughout the specified country, affecting all inland and coastal waterfowl shooting. The species affected include the Eurasian Woodcock *Scolopax rusticola* and Common Snipe *Gallinago gallinago*, often encountered in non-wetland habitats, and so affects all those who shoot waterbirds, whether on the coast or inland.

- The suspension is examined after seven days: if the weather conditions have improved and the forecast is for a continua-

[1] Pink-footed Goose *Anser brachyrhynchus*, Greater White-fronted Goose *A. albifrons* (England and Wales only), Greylag Goose *A. anser*, Canada Goose *Branta canadensis*, Eurasian Wigeon *Anas penelope*, Gadwall *A. strepera*, Common Teal *A. crecca*, Mallard *A. platyrhynchos*, Northern Pintail *A. acuta*, Northern Shoveler *A. clypeata*, Common Pochard *Aythya ferina*, Tufted Duck *A. fuligula*, Greater Scaup *A. marila*, Common Goldeneye *Bucephala clangula*, Common Moorhen *Gallinula chloropus*, Common Coot *Fulica atra*, Eurasian Golden Plover *Pluvialis apricaria*, Common Snipe *Gallinago gallinago* and Eurasian Woodcock *Scolopax rusticola*.

tion of this improvement, then, in consideration with other factors, the lifting of the suspension can be recommended. However, if there has been no thaw and the weather is still severe, then the suspension continues for the full 14 days.

- Any lifting of the suspension before the full 14 days takes into consideration the need for a period of recovery for waterbirds after the end of the severe weather itself. In this event, DEFRA or SEERAD, and BASC undertake publicity campaigns as extensively as possible to provide information to the shooting community.

- There can be an extension of the suspension beyond 14 days, through a second Statutory Instrument, if weather is still severe and no improvement in conditions is forecast. The management of the second period of suspension is undertaken in the same manner as the first.

## 25 YEARS OF IMPLEMENTATION

Table 1 summarizes episodes of severe winter weather from 1980/81 to 2004/05, and the policy responses under this system. Overall the system has worked well, especially so in more recent years as there has been increasing familiarization of the criteria and their operation by all concerned.

### Lessons learnt

When the system was established in the early 1980s, the Secretary of State requested that there be a review of the operation of the system following each year when it came into effect, in order to learn lessons and further refine its operation. A number of important themes have emerged over the years, which we summarize below.

### 1. The importance of good communication

The need for good (clear and regular) communication has been repeatedly stressed, not only at a national scale between the staff in headquarters of collaborating government departments, agencies and non-governmental organizations, but also regionally and locally between the various interested parties. In particular, the need for clear communication with the shooting community – whose recreational activities are directly affected – is crucial, particularly through their representative body (BASC), but also via the media.

### 2. Value of data and information on condition of waterbirds

The interpretation of meteorological data is greatly aided by information on the physiological condition of waterbirds, and this is a very valuable adjunct to decision making. To this end, a standard form was developed in 1995 for field reporting of bird condition and ground conditions, and this has been disseminated especially to BASC regional contacts, nature reserve wardens and other networks, as well as being made available via JNCC's web-site (www.jncc.gov.uk).

### 3. Importance of review after implementation of a severe weather suspension to improve future planning

The establishment of consultative arrangements after each severe weather event has allowed progressive fine-tuning of the system. For example, the need for a greater number and spread of meteorological stations was highlighted in the 1980s (Fig. 2). However, not least from the perspective of clear communication

with the shooting community, the need for consistency of criteria and approaches has also been recognized. There are no doubt sophisticated elaborations of criteria that might be possible, but there is merit in having criteria that are intuitively and easily understood, and which remain constant from year to year.

### 4. The scale of shooting suspensions

The possibility of regional[2] suspensions of shooting has been discussed several times and always rejected, for two principal reasons. Firstly, problems of clearly communicating to shooters and police in which areas shooting is suspended and in which it is not would give considerable enforcement problems. Secondly, in a severe weather period, although ground conditions in some parts of the country may not be equally frozen, birds in areas with milder weather may have moved from colder regions and so be recovering their condition. From a waterbird management perspective, it makes conservation sense to consider policies towards severe-weather suspensions over as large an area as possible – at least at the scale of a whole country.

### 5. Importance of a full complement of sites to avoid ambiguity

Although the alerting system operated by the Meteorological Office operated well in the 1980s, by the mid-1990s, there were growing problems caused by the progressive automation of meteorological stations resulting in an abandonment of the visual observations of ground state needed to operate the alerting system. This resulted in the network in some years operating with less than a full complement of sites, and data being needed from regions without appropriate stations. Accordingly, in 2001, JNCC commissioned the Meteorological Office to undertake a modelling exercise so as to assess the potential for use of automatically collected data. The results (Ashcroft 2001) indicated that automatically collected data could be used, and such data were included from the winter of 2001/02 to supplement observations made at the remaining manned stations. The ability to operate an alert system based on a geographically balanced, full network of stations has removed an element of ambiguity that gave problems with decision making.

### 6. Reaching other sectors

Clearly, shooting is not the only source of potentially damaging disturbance for waterbirds in prolonged severe weather, although owing to the statutory basis under which it occurs, it is one of the most feasible to regulate in a responsive manner. A number of recreational and other activities can also significantly disturb waterbirds, notably dog-walking, horse-riding, anglers, water-based sports, low-flying aircraft and others (Davidson & Rothwell 1993, Madsen 1998). In publicity related to the operation of this system, it has been important to get clear messages to these other interests, so as to try and more widely reduce disturbance to waterbirds in poor energetic condition. Thus, for example, the BTO bans the capture and ringing of waterbirds except by individuals studying the effect of weather, who have to apply for a specific exemption.

## CONCLUSIONS AND FUTURE PROSPECTS

Overall, the system developed in the early 1980s has worked well. The criteria developed have been robust in identifying periods that most of those concerned would intuitively consider

---

[2] meaning a scale smaller than that of a single country.

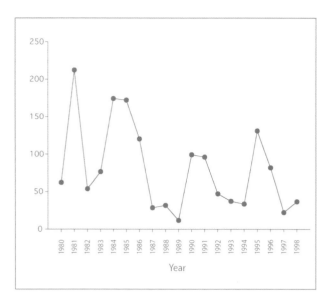

**Fig. 3.** Frost days at a an example meteorological station on the English east coast at the Wash (Terrington St Clement). Frost days are the total days when the temperature was below 0°C multiplied by the difference from zero on each day (from Clark 2002).

to be weather that is prolonged and severe. In no small measure, the success of the system has been due to the co-operation of the shooting community and the partnership approach adopted from the outset by involved organizations – itself a result of a long history of collaborative working between non-statutory and statutory bodies concerned with British waterbird conservation (Harrison 1973). The need to review the alerting system after each use has provided a formal means for exchanging differing perspectives and a trigger for developing enhancements (such as the increased size of the network of meteorological stations from 1985/86, and the consideration of proposals to use some different types of data from 2002/03). The close working

together of nature conservation and shooting organizations in the joint exchange of information has avoided a return to the damaging public conflicts of January 1979.

It is somewhat ironic then, that having developed a widely accepted alert system, current changes in climate seem set – in the medium term – to render this system redundant. The trend through the 1990s has been for progressively milder winters, with few extended periods of severe, cold weather. This is apparent both from local temperature records (Fig. 3) as well as nationally (Fig. 4). Projections undertaken by the UK Climate Impacts Programme suggest that Britain will experience very few periods of prolonged severe weather after 2030 (Fig. 4; Hulme & Jenkins 1998, Watkinson *et al.* 2004). Although reducing risks to wintering waterbirds associated with severe weather, the ecological consequences of such climate change will be highly uncertain, affecting as they will Arctic breeding areas, migratory flyways and over-wintering areas.

However, at least for the next decades, climate models predict occasional periods of severe weather. These have potential to have significant effects on waterbird populations as many of the birds will be naive, through not having experienced severe weather previously, and may therefore be less able to cope. Further, with a current change of winter distributions within Britain (with increasing concentrations now occurring on east coasts; Austin & Rehfisch 2005), a higher proportion of total populations will be likely to occur on those eastern coasts typically most severely affected by periods of prolonged severe weather. There is thus merit in maintaining the current system for the foreseeable future.

## ACKNOWLEDGEMENTS

The British system of suspending shooting in severe weather has evolved over the last 25 years. We are grateful to all those who have given inputs to the development of criteria and provided subsequent advice leading to the progressive "fine-tuning" of the

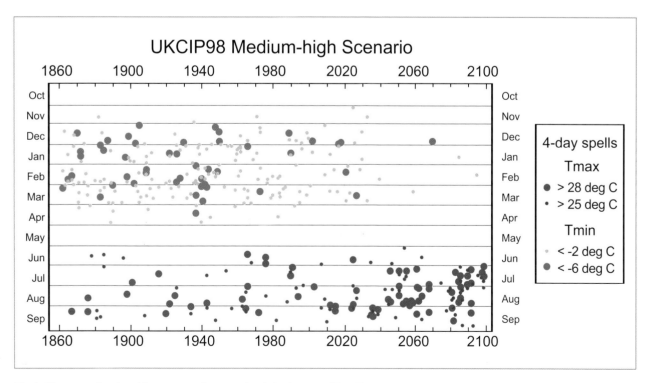

**Fig. 4.** The past, and projected future, seasonal pattern of periods of severe cold (and hot) weather in the UK. Data drawn from Hulme & Jenkins (1998).

current system, in particular to Leo Batten and John Swift for their initial work, and to the many individuals who have contributed to the Working Group since the 1970s.

## REFERENCES

**Ashcroft, J.** 2001. Identification of periods of severe weather for the JNCC winter weather monitoring scheme using automated observations. Unpublished Meteorological Office report to JNCC.

**Austin, G.E. & Rehfisch, M.M.** 2005. Shifting nonbreeding distributions of migratory fauna in relation to climatic change. Global Change Biology 11: 31-38.

**Batten, L.A. & Swift, J.A.** 1982. British criteria for calling a ban on wildfowling in severe weather. In: M. Smart & J.A. Swift (eds) Proceedings of the Second Technical Meeting on western Palearctic migratory bird management, Paris 1979. IWRB, Slimbridge, UK: 181-189.

**Clark, J.A.** 2002. Effects of severe weather on wintering waders. M.Phil. thesis, University of East Anglia, UK.

**Davidson, N.C. & Evans, P.R.** 1982. Mortality of Redshanks and Oystercatchers from starvation during severe weather. Bird Study 29: 183-188.

**Davidson, N.C. & Rothwell, P.** 1993. Disturbance to waterfowl on estuaries. Wader Study Group Bulletin 68, Special Issue.

**Dobinson, H.M. & Richards, A.J.** 1964. The effects of the severe winter of 1962/63 on birds in Britain. British Birds 57: 373-434.

**Goss-Custard, J.D., Jenyon, R.A., Jones, R.E., Newbery, P.E. & Williams, R. le B.** 1977. The ecology of the Wash. II. Seasonal variation in the feeding conditions of wading birds (Charadrii). Journal of Applied Ecology 14: 701-719.

**Harrison, J.** 1973. A Wealth of Wildfowl. A Survival Book, Corgi Books, London.

**Hulme, M. & Jenkins, G.J.** 1998. Climate change scenarios for the UK: scientific report. UKCIP Technical Report No. 1. Climate Research Unit, Norwich.

**Kirby, J.S.** 1995. Distribution and dynamics of wintering waders in Britain with particular reference to weather. PhD thesis, Open University, UK.

**Lack, P.** 1986. The Atlas of Wintering Birds in Britain and Ireland. T. & A.D. Poyser, Calton.

**Madsen, J.** 1998. Experimental refuges for migratory waterfowl in Danish wetlands. I. Baseline assessment of the disturbance effects of recreational activities. Journal of Applied Ecology 35: 386-397.

**Mitchell, P.I., Scott, I. & Evans, P.R.** 2000. Vulnerability to severe weather and regulation of body mass of Icelandic and British Redshanks *Tringa totanus*. Journal of Avian Biology 31: 511-521.

**Ridgill, S.C. & Fox, A.D.** 1990. Cold weather movements of waterfowl in western Europe. IWRB Special Publication 13, Slimbridge, UK.

**Stroud, J.M.** 1992. Statutory suspension of wildfowling in severe weather: review of past winter weather and actions. JNCC Report 75. JNCC, Peterborough, UK.

**Watkinson, A.R., Gill, J.A. & Hulme, M.** 2004. Flying in the face of climate change: a review of climate change, past, present and future. Ibis 146 (Supplement 1): 4-10.

Frozen inter-tidal areas give major problems for the waterbirds that usually feed in these areas, resulting in significant mortality and/or movements away from such areas. An 'ice-winter' in the Dutch Wadden Sea. Photo: Andy Brown.

# From conflict to coexistence: a case study of geese and agriculture in Scotland

*David R. Cope[1], Juliet A. Vickery[2] & J. Marcus Rowcliffe[3]*

[1]*The Macaulay Institute, Craigiebuckler, Aberdeen, UK. (email: d.cope@macaulay.ac.uk)*

[2]*British Trust for Ornithology, Thetford, Norfolk, UK.*

[3]*Institute of Zoology, Regent's Park, London, UK.*

Cope, D.R., Vickery, J.A. & Rowcliffe, J.M. 2006. From conflict to coexistence: a case study of geese and agriculture in Scotland. *Waterbirds around the world.* Eds. G.C. Boere, C.A. Galbraith & D.A. Stroud. The Stationery Office, Edinburgh, UK. pp. 791-794.

## ABSTRACT

This paper is a summary of: Cope, D.R., Vickery, J.A. & Rowcliffe, J.M. In press. From conflict to coexistence: a case study with geese and agriculture in Scotland. In: S.M. Thirgood, A. Rabinowitz & R. Woodroffe (eds) People and Wildlife: Conflict or Coexistence? Cambridge University Press, Cambridge.

Nine distinct populations of geese are found in Scotland, most of which are increasing in number due to increased legislative protection from shooting. They are concentrated in time and space, and increasingly feed on agricultural land, reducing yields in grass and cereal crops. Whilst geese are economically valuable for their recreational amenity, the farmers who suffered yield losses have not shared in these benefits in the past. This caused a conflict of interest between geese and farmers, which has threatened to destabilize the balance between the needs to conserve Scotland's fauna and the needs of farmers to run economic businesses that provide food for the nation. While culling, scaring, the provision of alternative feeding areas or compensatory payments were unlikely to solve this conflict in isolation, a co-ordinated stakeholder-driven approach to solve this conflict was initiated in the 1990s. This approach used payments to encourage farmers adversely affected by the presence of geese to redistribute geese into areas designated as undisturbed feeding refuges. Payments were directed towards farmers for positively managing the land for the benefit of geese, ensuring that Scotland met its international conservation obligations.

## INTRODUCTION

Scotland hosts six species of geese for all or part of the year, comprising nine distinct breeding populations (Table 1). Six of these populations breed in arctic regions (Greenland, Iceland, Svalbard or Russia) and winter in Scotland, making Scotland a vital part of several goose flyways. Many populations are protected under the 1979 European Union Birds Directive (Directive 79/409/EEC) and the 1981 Wildlife and Countryside Act in the UK. Most populations are increasing, largely as a result of hunting controls (Owen 1990). However, their ranges in Scotland remain very restricted in time and space (Table 1 and Fig. 1).

Agricultural damage caused by geese is of two broad types: (i) on grass, where the standing crop may be reduced and sward structure damaged, and (ii) on arable crops such as wheat and oilseed rape, where the yield may be reduced (Patton & Frame 1981, Patterson *et al.* 1989, Percival & Houston 1992). The conflict may be localized, but is often intense, with a small number of farmers incurring a large proportion of the damage, resulting in conflict "hot spots".

## MANAGING THE GOOSE-AGRICULTURE CONFLICT: POSSIBLE SOLUTIONS

A number of solutions to the goose-agriculture conflict have been suggested in recent years.

**Table 1. The size and trend of goose populations occurring in Scotland.**

| English name | Scientific name | Population size (1999-2001)[†] | Trend |
|---|---|---|---|
| Bean Goose* | *Anser fabalis* | 300[1,2] | Stable |
| Pink-footed Goose | *Anser brachyrhynchus* | 245 000[3] | Increasing |
| Greenland White-fronted Goose | *Anser albifrons flavirostris* | 20 660[1] | Increasing |
| Greylag Goose (Icelandic population) | *Anser anser* | 80 000[3] | Stable |
| Greylag Goose (Scottish population) | *Anser anser* | 6 500[1] | Increasing |
| Greylag Goose (naturalized population) | *Anser anser* | 21 000[1,4] | Increasing |
| Canada Goose* | *Branta canadensis* | 50 000[1,4] | Increasing |
| Barnacle Goose (Greenland population) | *Branta leucopsis* | 37 800[1] | Increasing |
| Barnacle Goose (Svalbard population) | *Branta leucopsis* | 21 000[5,6] | Increasing |

† Totals for the United Kingdom only.
* These species do not cause significant goose–agriculture conflict in Scotland, and are not considered in the text.
[1] The Wetland Bird Survey 1999-2000 (Musgrove *et al.* 2001).
[2] Scottish population is around 150 individuals (Musgrove *et al.* 2001).
[3] The 2000 census of Pink-footed Geese and Icelandic Greylag Geese (Hearn 2002). About 80% of Pink-footed Geese and over 90% of Greylag Geese were found in Scotland.
[4] Most naturalized Greylag Geese and Canada Geese are found outside Scotland.
[5] WWT Svalbard Barnacle Goose Project Report 2000-2001 (Griffin & Coath 2001).
[6] The wintering range of Svalbard Barnacle Geese covers both England and Scotland, with more than half using the Scottish range (Griffin & Coath 2001).

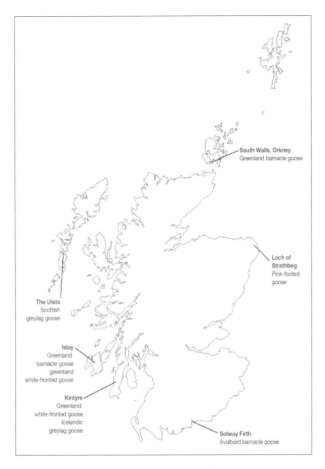

The Uists
Scottish
greylag goose

Islay
Greenland
barnacle goose
greenland
white-fronted goose

Kintyre
Greenland
white-fronted goose
Icelandic
greylag goose

South Walls, Orkney
Greenland barnacle goose

Loch of
Strathbeg
Pink-footed
goose

Solway Firth
Svalbard barnacle goose

Fig. 1. The main locations of wintering wild goose populations in Scotland.

## Culling

By culling, we here refer to systematic efforts to reduce population sizes. To be effective in resolving the conflict, this approach must reduce goose populations to levels at which little or no damage is incurred. Geese are relatively long-lived birds, and changes in survival rates therefore have a strong effect on population growth (Rowcliffe *et al.* 2000), as demonstrated by the heavy impact of hunting on goose populations in the past (Ebbinge 1991). Culling by encouraging existing wildfowling and lethal crop protection is being used to reduce "over-abundant" white goose (*Chen* spp.) populations in North America, through greatly liberalized legislation on bag limits, timing and methods of hunting (USFWS 2001). Owen (1990) estimated that an effective cull of Pink-footed Geese *Anser brachyrhynchus* and Greylag Geese *A. anser* in the UK would require 90 000 birds to be shot in each of the first five years and a maintenance cull of 40 000 each year thereafter. This would require a large number of highly active hunters, probably far more than are currently active in the UK where around 32 000 grey geese (*Anser* spp.) are shot annually.

The main arguments against culling are political. Most goose populations are considered "at risk" under the EU Birds Directive. Even though Member States can derogate from the protection rules to prevent serious damage to crops, shooting under the derogation is licensed only where it has been demonstrated that there is no other satisfactory solution. In effect, this means that numbers shot by farmers are kept to a minimum required for localized crop protection. Initiating a systematic cull would require demonstrating first that populations are excessively high, well beyond anything that could be considered

at risk in the long term, and second, that levels of damage are also unacceptably high. No such arguments can be made in the case of any European goose population.

## Scaring

A range of methods has been deployed for scaring geese off agricultural land, from the use of scarecrows or gas guns and barriers in or above fields (streamers on sticks or kites) to the employment of a full time human goose scarer (Vickery & Summers 1992). However, geese become habituated to most scaring techniques relatively quickly (Vickery & Summers 1992) and, since scaring is rarely co-ordinated between farms, it usually serves simply to move the problem elsewhere. Where trials have been carried out, co-ordinated scaring has proved extremely costly (Percival *et al.* 1997) and only effective in reducing damage levels when it is deployed alongside dedicated refuge areas for geese (Vickery & Summers 1992, Vickery & Gill 1999).

## Compensation schemes

Direct financial compensation for goose damage is a third option, but estimating damage is costly, complex and time-consuming (Owen 1990, Patterson 1991). Goose densities or dropping densities have been used as surrogates for actual yield losses, for example on Islay, but agreement on the timing and frequency of counts, and hence payment levels, were difficult to reach (NGF 1998a). Overall, direct compensation for losses has not proved effective in reducing goose-agriculture conflict, either in Britain (NGF 2000) or abroad (Van Eerden 1990).

## Management of reserves for geese

Alternative feeding areas or refuges can be established and managed to attract geese off agricultural land and reduce damage levels (Owen 1990, Percival 1993, Vickery *et al.* 1994). Such refuges have existed in Scotland for some time; for example, Caerlaverock National Nature Reserve in south-west Scotland was designated in 1957.

A great deal is known about how to optimize the design and management of grassland refuges (for a review, see Vickery & Gill 1999). Most species require fields of at least 5 ha, near traditional roost sites with minimal disturbance. The attractiveness of the fields can be greatly enhanced by managing the sward through cutting or grazing and application of fertilizer. However, even well-managed reserves are unlikely to attract and support the entire target population throughout the winter, and so agricultural damage is still likely to occur on land adjacent to refuges. Furthermore, on a local scale the areas required are large, and although they can be reduced by effective management (Vickery & Gill 1999), such management can be costly.

## MANAGING THE GOOSE-AGRICULTURE CONFLICT: A CO-ORDINATED APPROACH

From the preceding sections it is evident that: (i) on their own, neither culling, scaring, compensation nor reserves provides an adequate solution; (ii) the conflict is likely to escalate as goose populations increase; (iii) the problem is highly localized and very variable with respect to damage levels so solutions must be site specific; (iv) at the national level, there must also be a degree of commonality and equity across sites; and (v) because many of the species are migratory and protected by international laws, solutions must meet international conservation obligations.

The Islay Goose Management Scheme addresses the agricultural impacts of Greenland White-fronted Geese *Anser albifrons flavirostris* and the Greenland population of Barnacle Geese *Branta leucopsis*. Photo: Paul Marshall.

Other countries in Europe suffer from goose-agriculture conflict, and the most successful resolution of the conflict appears to be closely linked to the provision of a co-ordinated approach. A mixture of techniques has been used to reduce conflict, from uncoordinated shooting or non-lethal scaring (e.g. Poland, France, Romania), through regional co-ordination of compensation and management (e.g. Germany), to nationally co-ordinated schemes that include scaring, compensation and land management (e.g. The Netherlands, Sweden, Norway). Under the Dutch system, the legislation that regulates the hunting of geese also provides a public body that advises farmers on how to avoid damage. This public body also pays compensation to those farmers adversely affected by geese, with part of the funding coming from hunting license fees. However, compensation payments increased rapidly from 1977 to 1986, so other techniques were developed, such as providing reserves and changing crops away from those favoured by geese (Van Eerden 1990). A national policy was implemented in 1991 that encouraged the planting of less sensitive crops, the use of non-lethal scaring, compensation and dedicated waterfowl reserves (NGF 1998b). In this way, geese could be managed in reserve areas both by attracting them into the reserves through positive land management, and by moving them away from commercial farmland by scaring and planting crops unlikely to be damaged by geese. This co-ordinated approach inside and outside reserves, involving payments, appears to have helped considerably in reducing goose-farmer conflict in The Netherlands.

The approach in Scotland has been to develop a national framework with locally devolved schemes, ensuring a high degree of input from stakeholders at all levels. Local goose management schemes were launched in Scotland in the early 1990s. These local schemes used a combination of scaring, shooting and refuge management alongside payments to farmers (e.g. Cope *et al.* 2003), but initially were independent of one another and uncoordinated at a national level, with no forum for sharing experience. In 1997, the National Goose Forum (NGF) was formed to develop a National Policy Framework (NPF) for the management of geese and agriculture in Scotland (NGF 1997a). The aims of this policy were: (i) to meet the UK's nature conservation obligations; (ii) to minimize the economic losses to farmers; and (iii) to maximize the value for money of public expenditure (SOAEFD 1996). As well as advising ministers on this national policy, the NGF provided advice to local goose management groups, oversaw the monitoring of goose populations in Scotland, and co-ordinated research on geese and agriculture (NGF 1997b). Members included those with farming, conservation, wildfowling and government interests (NGF 1997b).

The NGF delivered the National Policy Framework in 2000 (NGF 2000), at which point government ministers approved the continuation of local goose management schemes. The National Goose Monitoring Review Group (NGMRG) replaced the NGF as the national co-ordinating organization, with the remit of assessing, on an annual basis, the proposals from local goose management groups for conformity to the guidelines set out in the NPF. These local groups develop proposals tailored to local needs, and are given the primary responsibility for administering schemes on the ground (SOAEFD 1996). Thus, the general parameters for goose management schemes are set at the national level, determined by constraints, while local groups ensure that the details match local needs.

## CONCLUSIONS

Scotland is an important part of the international flyway for several species of geese, especially for those species in which the entire breeding population spends the winter within Scotland. However, the success of international conservation action has, in many cases, brought about a conflict with local agricultural interests. In an attempt to reduce this goose-agriculture conflict, several options have been considered (culling, scaring, compensation schemes and alternative feeding areas), but the most effective way in which to move from a conflict situation to a coexistence situation has been to produce an integrated strategy.

The key strength of the strategy adopted for goose management in Scotland is its combination of top-down and bottom-up management whereby government ministers control the general parameters and local groups ensure that the details are tailored to local needs. This approach should be widely applicable to other cases of wildlife conflict. The clear definition of agricultural, conservation and budgetary goals at the national level has led to a marked reduction in perceived conflict without resorting to a strategy of extermination. At the same time, the fact that local stakeholders in conflict areas have strong input to the form of local schemes has been crucial to their widespread acceptance. This is perhaps best demonstrated by the fact that levels of interest in goose management schemes have increased, as has the geographic spread of proposed schemes.

## ACKNOWLEDGEMENTS

We are grateful to many people who supplied information: G. Banks, B. Bremner, G. Churchill, G. Dalby, J. Doherty,

L. Griffin, R. Hearn, E. Laurie, J. Love, M. MacKay, I. Patterson, E. Rees, A. Robertson, and F. Younger. N. Read, S. Gough and R. Hooper helped in the production of the manuscript. JAV's involvement was partly funded by the Joint Nature Conservation Committee.

## REFERENCES

Cope, D.R., Pettifor, R.A., Griffin, L.R. & Rowcliffe, J.M. 2003. Integrating farming and wildlife conservation: the Barnacle Goose Management Scheme. Biological Conservation 110: 113-122.

Ebbinge, B.S. 1991. The impact of hunting on mortality rates and spatial distribution of geese wintering in the western palearctic. Ardea 79: 197-210.

NGF 1997a. NGF3/97 Development of a National Policy Framework. www.scotland.gov.uk/nationalgoose-forum/MEETING1/NGF03_97.pdf.

NGF 1997b. NGF2/97 Terms of reference and membership. www.scotland.gov.uk/nationalgooseforum/MEETING1/NGF02_97.pdf.

NGF 1998a. NGF10/98 National Goose Forum: review of management techniques and habitat creation. www.scotland.gov.uk/nationalgooseforum/MEETING3/NGF10_98.pdf.

NGF 1998b. NGF14/98 Goose Management in Other European Countries. www.scotland.gov.uk/nationalgooseforum/MEETING4/NGF14_98.pdf.

NGF 2000. Policy Report and Recommendations of the National Goose Forum. www.scotland.gov.uk/national-gooseforum/ngf-00.asp.

Owen, M. 1990. The damage-conservation interface illustrated by geese. Ibis 132: 238-252.

Patterson, I.J. 1991. Conflict between geese and agriculture: does goose grazing cause damage to crops? Ardea 79: 179-186.

Patterson, I.J., Abdul Jalil, S. & East, M.L. 1989. Damage to winter cereals by greylag and pink-footed geese in north-east Scotland. Journal of Applied Ecology 26: 879-895.

Patton, D.L.H. & Frame, J. 1981. The effect of grazing in winter by wild geese on improved grasslands in West Scotland. Journal of Applied Ecology 18: 311-325.

Percival, S.M. 1993. The effects of reseeding, fertiliser application and disturbance on the use of grassland by barnacle geese, and the implications for refuge management. Journal of Applied Ecology 30: 437-443.

Percival, S.M. & Houston, D.C. 1992. The effect of winter grazing by barnacle geese on grassland yields on Islay. Journal of Applied Ecology 29: 35-40.

Percival, S.M., Halpin, Y. & Houston, D.C. 1997. Managing the distribution of barnacle geese on Islay, Scotland, through deliberate human disturbance. Biological Conservation 82: 273-277.

Rowcliffe, J.M., Pettifor, R.A. & Mitchell, C.R. 2000. Icelandic population of the greylag goose (*Anser anser*): the collation and statistical analysis of data and population viability analyses. Scottish Natural Heritage, Edinburgh.

SOAEFD 1996. Wild Geese and Agriculture in Scotland: A discussion paper. Scottish Office, Edinburgh.

USFWS 2001. Draft Environmental Impact Statement: Light Goose Management. U.S. Fish and Wildlife Service, Washington, D.C.

Van Eerden, M.R. 1990. The solution of goose damage problems in The Netherlands, with special reference to compensation schemes. Ibis 132: 253-261.

Vickery, J.A. & Gill, J.A. 1999. Managing grassland for wild geese in Britain: a review. Biological Conservation 89: 93-106.

Vickery, J.A. & Summers, R.W. 1992. Cost-effectiveness of scaring brent geese *Branta b. bernicla* from fields of arable crops by a human bird scarer. Crop Protection 11: 480-484.

Vickery, J.A., Sutherland, W.J. & Lane, S.J. 1994. The management of grass pasture for brent geese. Journal of Applied Ecology 31: 282-290.

In winter Scotland is host to over 80% of the Greenland population of Barnacle Geese *Branta leucopsis*, concentrated on the Inner Hebridean island of Islay. Photo: Paul Marshall.

# Case study of conflict resolution in the management of overabundant light geese in North America

*Bruce D.J. Batt[1], Paul R. Schmidt[2] & Steve Wendt[3]*

[1] *Ducks Unlimited, Inc., One Waterfowl Way, Memphis, Tennessee 39120, USA. (email: bbatt@ducks.org)*

[2] *U.S. Fish and Wildlife Service, 4401 North Fairfax Drive, Arlington, Virginia 22203, USA. (email: Paul_Schmidt@fws.gov)*

[3] *Canadian Wildlife Service, 351 St. Joseph Boulevard, Hull, Quebec, J8Y 3Z5, Canada. (email: Steve.Wendt@ec.gc.ca)*

Batt, B.D.J., Schmidt, P.R. & Wendt, S. 2006. Case study of conflict resolution in the management of overabundant light geese in North America. *Waterbirds around the world.* Eds. G.C. Boere, C.A. Galbraith & D.A. Stroud. The Stationery Office, Edinburgh, UK. pp. 795-800.

## ABSTRACT

During the decade of the 1990s, North American waterfowl managers detected extraordinary increases in populations of Lesser Snow Geese *Chen caerulescens caerulescens*, Greater Snow Geese *C. c. atlanticus* and Ross's Geese *C. rossii*. This led to more intensive study of available information by several teams of scientists who concluded initially that mid-continent Lesser Snow Geese were causing irreversible damage to their Arctic breeding habitats. They recommended that goose numbers should be reduced through proactive management programs to levels that could be sustained for the long term. Other reports concluded that Greater Snow Geese would soon be at similar levels and that Ross's Geese were also more abundant than ever previously recorded. Waterfowl population managers took actions to achieve the recommended objectives through the promulgation of management interventions that have now been in place for several years. We review several critical elements of how managers have responded to these conflicts with the mid-continent Lesser Snow Goose. These were: assure a strong science base existed to support management recommendations; consult fully with all stakeholders associated with the issue; develop clear resolve by management agencies to address the issue; communicate effectively with all stakeholders about the nature of the problem and the proposed management actions; implement management programs; and monitor the response of the targeted resource and adapt to information obtained from monitoring with additional or improved management practices.

## INTRODUCTION

The Lesser Snow Goose *Chen caerulescens caerulescens* is among the most well-studied of the world's waterfowl. In recent years, it has become sympatric throughout most of its range during breeding, migration and wintering periods in the mid-continent region of North America with the congeneric Ross's Goose *Chen rossii* (Fig. 1). Together, these species are generally referred to as 'light geese'.

A seminal publication by Cooke *et al.* (1995) summarized much of the basic biological information on the Lesser Snow Goose. Populations have grown rapidly during the past half century (Abraham *et al.* 1996). Researchers on Arctic and sub-Arctic breeding colonies started to detect changes in body condition and size (Cooch *et al.* 1991) as higher gosling mortality (Cooch *et al.* 1993, Williams *et al.* 1993) and degradation of habitats used by breeding geese (Jeffries *et al.* 1995) were observed as the goose populations grew. Despite these factors, the populations continued to grow as a result of increased adult survival (Francis *et al.* 1992). A variety of cause-and-effect rela-

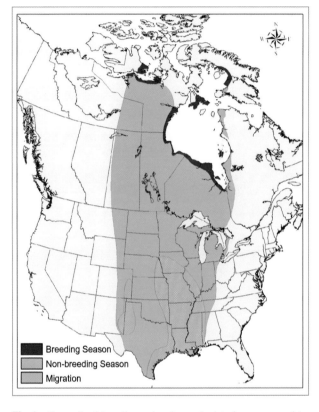

Fig. 1. Generalized breeding, migration and wintering areas used by mid-continent Ross's Geese *Chen rossii* and Lesser Snow Geese *Chen caerulescens caerulescens* in North America (modified from Ridgely *et al.* 2003).

tionships have been explored but the general consensus is that the birds' pre-adaptation to thrive on the vast agricultural landscapes of North America (Fig. 2) is the dominant factor that has resulted in the observed changes (Jeffries *et al.* 2003).

Abraham & Jeffries (1997) provide a variety of data describing population trends of Snow and Ross's Geese. Up-to-date population estimates from the mid-winter period are presented in Fig. 3.

During the mid 1990s, researchers from across the Canadian and U.S. Arctic regions observed similar patterns as populations continued to grow in most breeding colonies. Concern began to emerge that population growth may have been occurring at such a rate that overabundant geese may have been causing serious damage to fragile Arctic habitats and that the populations might be "out of control" (Ankney 1996). The upshot of this concern was the formation of the Arctic Goose Habitat Working Group (AGHWG) by the Arctic Goose Joint Venture (AGJV)

**Fig. 2.** Mid-continent Lesser Snow Geese *Chen caerulescens caerulescens* stage on agricultural lands during spring migration. Waste agricultural grains have been preserved by cold winter weather and snow cover since the previous year's harvest.

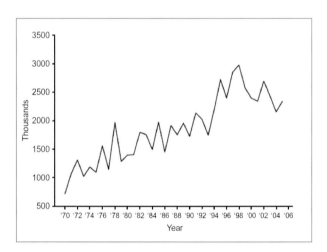

**Fig. 3.** Status and population trends of mid-continent light geese from 1970 - 2005 (U.S. Fish and Wildlife Service 2005).

**Fig. 4.** Geese have been excluded from this fenced area near La Perouse Bay on Hudson Bay, Manitoba, Canada. The grass and sedge vegetation from the surrounding land has been destroyed by feeding geese. High natural salinity of the subsoil has resulted in only the salt tolerant *Salicornia* sp. being able to survive. In time, further increased salinity will also remove the *Salicornia* and result in highly saline bare mineral soil from which there is no known mechanism that will allow recovery of the sward for decades into the future.

Management Board of the North American Waterfowl Management Plan (Anon. 1986). The Working Group engaged a broad cross-section of scientists, population managers and other interests with a stake in the future management of these geese to review the information available on population growth patterns. They were asked to decide if the burgeoning numbers of birds were a problem that should be corrected by management intervention.

The product of the group's work was a comprehensive report (Batt 1997) that concluded that the population was growing at such a rate that the birds threatened to become so abundant as to permanently destroy large tracts of their Arctic breeding habitats

(Fig. 4). The destruction was expanding rapidly and thought to threaten the integrity of vast areas of the Arctic that are used by a multitude of other resident and migratory species. This was considered to be an ecosystem in peril, and it was recommended that the population be brought under control by decreasing adult survival through significantly increased harvest by hunters.

Several recommendations called for: legalizing hunting practices that had previously been illegal; extending hunting seasons through the winter and spring months during which hunting had been prohibited for decades; and allowing very high harvest limits for individual hunters. The AGJV Management Board approved the report, and the management community was faced with trying to bring about management interventions that had never been attempted before in waterfowl conservation. These changes were certain to result in considerable conflict among scientists, managers, hunters, aboriginal Canadians, public officials, the general public and interest groups that are opposed to hunting for any reason. Changes to harvest regulations were accomplished, and the management program proceeded following an extensive conflict resolution process that is the subject of this paper.

## RESOLVING CONFLICTS IN NORTH AMERICAN SNOW GOOSE MANAGEMENT

At the onset, we believe that few truly extraordinary measures were undertaken to make dramatic changes to the previous approach to Snow Goose harvest management. Indeed, the authors feel that the main accomplishments came about as a result of patient and disciplined attention to fundamentally important features of conflict resolution that must be followed by others in many situations. The most extraordinary steps required were a result of the international scale at which various phases of the effort had to be accomplished. These steps are reflected in Fig. 5 and are explained below in more detail. Note that most of these are not separate and independent steps that were taken in sequence. Rather, each contributed to the success of all steps as there was always considerable feedback to earlier and subsequent steps as managers developed new information and experience at every step of the way.

### Science underpinnings

Wildlife management programs should be based on the best scientific information available. Managers are often faced with imperfect information, so it is simply their responsibility to use everything that is available to them to guide management decisions. This should be done in an open and transparent way, with peer review of the technical syntheses pertaining to the particular subject followed by consultation with all audiences with a stake in the actions that are ultimately undertaken.

With mid-continent light geese, there was a strong scientific record and extensive management experience on which to base the understanding of the threats that overabundant light geese posed to the Arctic ecosystems that they used heavily each year. The scientific literature was rich with information, and several members of the Working Group were considered to be among the most accomplished scientists that had extensively studied the birds and their habitats. This science was thoroughly and critically reviewed by the Group in the preparation of the Batt (1997) report, hereafter referred to as the Arctic Ecosystems in Peril report. In our view, this was the most critical step taken in the whole process, without which the additional actions, discussed below, would not have been warranted or successful.

### Involve stakeholders

Because so many segments of society have an interest in the proper management of the waterfowl resource, it was critical to

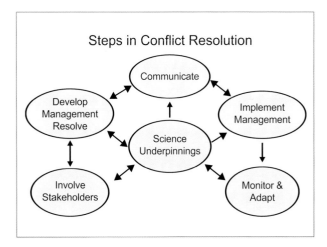

Fig. 5. The interaction of steps taken in the resolution of potential and actual conflicts as a result of dramatically changed management strategies applied to mid-continent light geese in North America.

get them involved in the review and development of recommendations from the outset. The 17 members of the Working Group had skills and perspectives that contributed to the synthesis of the science and the generation of management recommendations: seven were research scientists; six were waterfowl managers; and two represented non-government conservation organizations. Further, several of the individuals had additional experience and training that allowed them to cross readily between, and integrate the perspectives of, many different interests.

Once all the technical information was assimilated by the Working Group, they developed a series of specific recommendations (Arctic Goose Habitat Working Group 1997). These were presented to, and fully reviewed by, the Arctic Goose Joint Venture Management Board at two meetings in 1996 and 1997 and during extensive interim discussions and communications between meetings.

After the scientific report had been delivered to the Management Board, it was recognized that taking the recommendations to the point where they could be implemented would require considerable consultation with other interested entities. The following section describes steps taken to focus more closely on the nature of the management interventions that were needed and, at the same time, expand the breadth of stakeholder consultation and communications that were critical to success.

### Develop management resolve

Following approval of the report by the Management Board, it became the responsibility of the respective federal governments to begin the public decision-making process. At the same time, the lead federal agencies sought a wider review of the report and the recommendations through a Stakeholders' Committee (Appendix I) that was formed by the International Association of Fish and Wildlife Agencies (IAFWA) in the autumn of 1997. That group provided a series of recommendations that substantially supported the recommendations of the Working Group. They also provided an additional summary of concerns by participants that surfaced during the meetings held by the group.

The administrative flyways were all briefed by their representatives on the original Working Group or by one of the participants in the Stakeholders' Committee. This resulted in resolutions from each flyway in which they substantially endorsed the recommendations that were contained in the Arctic Ecosystems in Peril report. These resolutions were followed by a series of similar endorsements from such diverse national groups as The Audubon Society and The Ornithological Council.

## Communicate

Any major change in the management of an exploited natural resource that has traditional patterns of use and different ethical perspectives will be of great interest to resource "users." It was recognized from the onset of this initiative that there would be many interested parties that must be informed about the scientific underpinnings of any new management actions and would need assurance that all possible alternative courses of action were properly investigated.

Communications on this issue permeated every step taken by the AGJV Management Board and the Working Group. Initially, this took the form of dialogue between scientists and managers who were charged with making recommendations for future changes in management activities. The review of the Working Group report by the IAFWA Stakeholders' Committee, and the critical reviews of the flyway councils and the ornithological societies were other steps in communications with organizations that reflect their members' interests.

Additional communication forums were brought together by the Canadian Wildlife Service and U.S. Fish and Wildlife Service. For example, a series of workshops developed by the U.S. Fish and Wildlife Service was reported in Arnold (1998). There were numerous other formal and informal reports and communication items developed by the federal agencies in each country. Communication was a broadly pursued activity at many events throughout 1997, 1998 and 1999.

An essay by Robert Rockwell and colleagues (1997) in the winter 1997 issue of The Living Bird, the magazine of the Cornell Laboratory of Ornithology, was a singularly important first piece to be shared with the public. It was written by three leading Snow Goose research scientists and accurately described, in words and pictures, what was known about the overabundance of Snow Geese and the devastation in some Arctic habitats.

From this point, we only single out the following major items as we believe they had a major influence on establishing the issue in the media. Because of the accuracy of their content, they also helped immeasurably to ensure that the information that was promulgated did not contain a lot of errors that would be prone to proliferation.

The first major newspaper piece was published in the New York Times in February 1997 (Brody 1997). It was based on Rockwell *et al.* (1997), but included a broader sampling of information and opinions from a variety of involved parties. It also accurately reported on the science which was critical in helping to ensure that the central messages did not diverge from the solid science that served as the basis for the management recommendations. Because the New York Times is one of the world's leading newspapers, coverage in the Times helped put the Snow Goose issue into the mainstream of current news.

Following these two seminal items, there was a proliferation of national and regional newspaper, popular magazine, scientific society magazine, and radio and television stories about the plight of the mid-continent light geese. A detailed record was not maintained by the authors of this report, but each engaged in

between 200 and 300 interviews with the press during 1997 and 1998. Other individual members of the Working Group participated in a similar number of contacts by the press.

One of the most important communication items for the general scientific community was published in BioScience Magazine by Ben-Ari (1998). This piece was especially valuable because it was in a technical magazine with very high journalism standards that are constantly under scrutiny by the critical scientific community. It helped to reaffirm to a growing base of scientists that were aware of the issue that there was a strong scientific basis for management intervention.

One very valuable communication tool was a documentary video produced in 1998 by Ducks Unlimited entitled Snow Geese in Peril, with an accompanying book (Batt 1998a). Communications about this issue were going to be difficult because very few individuals would ever have the chance to visit the areas where the damage to the Arctic ecosystem was taking place. Video scenes came from several of the affected habitats that were used heavily by the geese and, through interviews with the principal scientists involved, the issue was brought fully illustrated in front of a multitude of audiences. The video was made available free on request to any interested party.

Finally, it was very important to inform public officials in the U.S. and Canada about the issue. This was done through several testimonials given in 1997 and 1998 by the authors to committees and elected officials of the U.S. and Canadian federal governments. Many other testimonials were provided to local, state and provincial governments by members of the Working Group or by individuals that became especially well-informed about the issue.

In summary, communication has been an integral component of the Snow Goose management program in North America - we believe to the extent that the program would have failed if it had not been done as fully as it was. Also, we reaffirm that all of the steps taken, including the extensive communications effort, had their grounding in the strong scientific basis that led to the recommendations for changes in light goose management strategies.

## Implement management

Both the Canadian Wildlife Service and the U.S. Fish and Wildlife Service promulgated changes in their management strategies for mid-continent light geese to come into effect during the 1997-1998 waterfowl hunting season. These actions were followed immediately by court actions pressed by groups in each country that did not agree with the new management programs. A thorough review of the background for these actions is beyond the scope of this paper. However, a legal challenge is a course of action that individuals or groups can take if they do not feel that the conflicts that they have with an issue have been adequately considered.

In each case, the challenge was towards the federal agency's legal authority to implement the new management strategies under the Migratory Bird Management Treaty of 1916 between the U.S. and Canadian governments. In each case, the presiding judge ruled that the agency did indeed have legal authority to implement management actions that were supported by the best science available.

In Canada, the court ruled that the scientific basis of the Arctic Ecosystems in Peril report did not adequately address the population status of the Ross's Goose, which would be affected by harvest that was directed at mid-continent Lesser Snow Geese. The Canadian Wildlife Service subsequently implemented regulations that would provide protection for Ross's Geese during the extended spring hunting period. Another working group was formed by the AGJV in 1999 to provide a complete review of the status and management of Ross's Geese (Moser 2001). This information has not yet been used to appeal the decision by the court to exclude Ross's Geese from the new management strategies.

In the U.S., the court also commented that it would rule in favor of any future challenge to the light goose management program if it was based on the need for an environmental impact statement (EIS) of the proposed management action. As a result, the U.S. Fish and Wildlife Service decided to delay implementation of the program until an EIS could be completed and approved.

This potential setback was overcome by the 1999 Arctic Tundra Habitat Emergency Conservation Act of the U.S. Congress (H.R. 2454-3), which authorized the U.S. Fish and Wildlife Service to implement the new management strategies until the EIS was completed. We believe this action was only possible because of two of the fundamental factors that are discussed above, namely: the strong scientific basis for the management actions; and the extensive and effective communication program that was implemented by the members of the AGJV. In short, the issue was so well understood by the policy makers and the public in general that it was broadly agreed that a change in the management of these birds was very desirable for the long-term sustenance of the Arctic ecosystems upon which the geese and other wildlife are dependent.

## Monitor and adapt

The Arctic Ecosystems in Peril report provided initial guidance for an evaluation program to monitor populations and key vital rates of the mid-continent light geese (Rusch & Caswell 1997). The Management Board subsequently assigned the AGJV Technical Committee the task of expanding this report into a more comprehensive monitoring program with detailed plans and initial budgets (AGJV Technical Committee 1998). This report was approved in October 1998 by the Management Board and has provided guidance for the subsequent monitoring of the effects of the new management actions.

The next step in this overall process is soon to unfold with an overall evaluation of what has been accomplished with the management actions that have been undertaken. It will also be critical to integrate information that has been developed through new research that was not available when this program started. Additionally, other syntheses of information about light geese and management alternatives have been developed since this management program started (Batt 1998b, Moser 2001, Johnson & Ankney 2003).

These evaluations will likely result in adjustments to the management strategies that are underway to reduce light geese to levels that can be sustained by their breeding habitats. When that occurs, most of the events and steps outlined in this paper to resolve or prevent future conflicts will be repeated to some extent, as managers seek to continually improve their approaches to managing light geese in North America.

## REFERENCES

**Abraham, K.F. & Jeffries, R.L.** 1997. High goose populations: causes, impacts and implications. In: B.D.J. Batt (ed) Arctic Ecosystems in Peril: report of the Arctic goose habitat working group. Arctic Goose Joint Venture Special Publication. U.S. Fish and Wildlife Service, Washington, D.C., and Canadian Wildlife Service, Ottawa, Ontario: 7-72.

**Abraham, K.F., Jeffries, R.L., Rockwell, R.F. & MacInnes, C.D.** 1996. Why are there so many white geese in North America? In: J. Ratti (ed) Proceedings of Ducks Unlimited's 7th International Waterfowl Symposium. Ducks Unlimited, Inc., Memphis, Tennessee: 79-92.

**Ankney, C.D.** 1996. An embarrassment of riches: too many gaggles of geese. Journal of Wildlife Management 60: 217-223.

**Anon.** 1986. The North American Waterfowl Management Plan: A Strategy for Cooperation. United States Department of the Interior and Canadian Wildlife Service.

**Arctic Goose Habitat Working Group** 1997. Conclusions and recommendations. In: B.D.J. Batt (ed) Arctic Ecosystems in Peril: Report of the Arctic Goose Habitat Working Group. Arctic Goose Joint Venture Special Publication. U.S. Fish and Wildlife Service, Washington, D.C., and Canadian Wildlife Service, Ottawa, Ontario: 117-120.

**Arctic Goose Joint Venture Technical Committee** 1998. Science needs for the management of increasing lesser snow goose populations. Technical Committee report to the Arctic Goose Joint Venture Management Board.

**Arnold, A.** 1998. Report: Mid-continent lesser snow goose workshops Central and Mississippi Flyways Fall 1997. U.S. Fish and Wildlife Service.

**Batt, B.D.J.** (ed). 1997. Arctic Ecosystems in Peril: report of the Arctic Goose Habitat Working Group. Arctic Goose Joint Venture Special Publication. U.S. Fish and Wildlife Service, Washington, D.C., and Canadian Wildlife Service, Ottawa, Ontario.

**Batt, B.D.J.** 1998a. Snow geese: grandeur and calamity on an Arctic landscape. Ducks Unlimited, Inc., Memphis, Tennessee.

**Batt, B.D.J.** (ed). 1998b. The greater snow goose: report of the Arctic Goose Habitat Working Group. Arctic Goose Joint Venture Special Publication. U.S. Fish and Wildlife Service, Washington, D.C., and Canadian Wildlife Service, Ottawa, Ontario.

**Ben-Ari, E.T.** 1998. A new wrinkle in wildlife management. BioScience, Washington, D.C. 48: 667-673.

**Brody, J.E.** 1997. Snow geese survive all too well, alarming conservationists. The New York Times: Science Times, 11 February 1997, C1-C2.

**Cooch, E.G., Lank, D.B., Rockwell, R.F. & Cooke, F.** 1991. Long-term decline in body size in a snow goose population: evidence of environmental degradation? Journal of Animal Ecology 60: 483-496.

**Cooch, E.G., Rockwell, R.F. & Lank, D.B.** 1993. Environmental change and the cost of philopatry: an example in the lesser snow goose. Oecologia 93: 128-138.

**Cooke, F., Rockwell, R.F. & Lank, D.B.** 1995. The Snow Geese of LaPerouse Bay. Oxford University Press, Oxford.

Francis, C.M., Richards, M.H., Cooke, F. & Rockwell, R.F. 1992. Long-term changes in survival rates of lesser snow geese. Ecology 73: 1346-1362.

Jeffries, R.L., Gadallah, F.L., Srivastava, D.R. & Wilson, D.J. 1995. Desertification and trophic cascades in arctic coastal ecosystems: a potential climatic change scenario? In: T.W. Callaghan (ed) Global Change and Arctic Terrestrial Ecosystems. Ecosystem Research Report No. 10. European Commission, Luxembourg: 201-206.

Jeffries, R.L., Rockwell, R.F. & Abraham, K.F. 2003. The embarrassment of riches: agricultural food subsidies, high goose numbers, and loss of Arctic wetlands – a continuing saga. Environmental Review 11: 193-232.

Johnson, M.A. & Ankney, C.D. (eds). 2003. Direct control and alternative harvest strategies for North American light geese: Report of the Direct Control and Alternative Harvest Measures Working Group. Arctic Goose Joint Venture Special Publication. U.S. Fish and Wildlife Service, Washington, D.C., and Canadian Wildlife Service, Ottawa, Ontario.

Moser, T.J. (ed). 2001. The status of Ross's geese. Arctic Goose Joint Venture Special Publication. U.S. Fish and Wildlife Service, Washington, D.C., and Canadian Wildlife Service, Ottawa, Ontario.

Ridgely, R.S., Allnutt, T.F., Brooks, T., McNichol, D.K., Mehlman, D.W., Young, B.E. & Zook, J.R. 2003. Digital distribution maps of the birds of the western hemisphere, version 1.0 NatureServe, Arlington, Virginia, USA.

Rockwell, R.F., Abraham, K.F. & Jeffries, R.L. 1997. The best laid plans: what happens when conservation efforts work too well? Living Bird. Brodock Press, Ithaca, New York. 16: 16-23.

Rusch, D.H. & Caswell, F.D. 1997. Evaluation of the Arctic goose management initiative. In: B.D.J. Batt (ed) Arctic Ecosystems in Peril: Report of the Arctic Goose Habitat Working Group. Arctic Goose Joint Venture Special Publication. U.S. Fish and Wildlife Service, Washington, D.C., and Canadian Wildlife Service, Ottawa, Ontario: 113-116.

U.S. Fish and Wildlife Service 2005. Waterfowl population status, 2005. U.S. Department of the Interior, Washington, D.C.

Williams, T.D., Cooch, E.G., Jeffries, R.L. & Cooke, F. 1993. Environmental degradation, food limitation and reproductive output: juvenile survival in lesser snow geese. Journal of Animal Ecology 62: 766-777.

## APPENDIX I

Agencies and organizations invited to be represented on the International Association of Fish and Wildlife Agencies Stakeholders' Committee

### Members
Mississippi Flyway Council
Inuvialuit Game Council (Canada First Nation)
National Audubon Society
Canadian Nature Federation
Manitoba Department of Natural Resources
World Wildlife Fund
Nunavut Wildlife Management Board

Pacific Flyway Council
Canadian Wildlife Federation
Atlantic Flyway Council
Government of Northwest Territories
National Waterfowl Council
The Humane Society of the United States
National Wildlife Federation

### Advisors
U.S. Fish and Wildlife Service (three individuals)
Ducks Unlimited
Canadian Wildlife Service

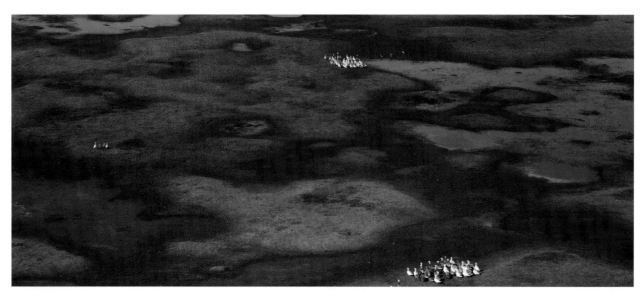

The ecosystem impact of over-abundant grazing geese is considerable, including where irreversible habitat damage has not occurred. At the world's largest goose colony, the Great Plain of the Koukdjuak on Baffin Island, vegetation is modified by geese everywhere over more than 20 000 square kilometres. Photo: Dale Humburg.

# Assessing the degree of habitat loss to marine birds from the development of offshore wind farms

*Anthony D. Fox & Ib Krag Petersen*

*Department of Wildlife Ecology and Biodiversity, National Environmental Research Institute, Kalø, Grenåvej 14, DK-8410 Rønde, Denmark. (email: tfo@dmu.dk)*

Fox, A.D. & Petersen, I.K. 2006. Assessing the degree of habitat loss to marine birds from the development of offshore wind farms. *Waterbirds around the world*. Eds. G.C. Boere, C.A. Galbraith & D.A. Stroud. The Stationery Office, Edinburgh, UK. pp. 801-804.

## ABSTRACT

Environmental impact assessment of offshore wind farms requires an assessment of waterbird habitat loss, both physical and as a result of behavioural avoidance. This paper briefly summarizes the aerial survey transect sampling methods and approach adopted to undertake such assessments at two marine wind farms constructed in Danish waters in 2003. At present, bird encounter rates per unit effort on track have been used to assess the "preferences" of bird species for wind farm and adjacent areas and to make a statistical comparison of abundance and distribution before and after construction. Preliminary results from the two case studies are presented. These results suggest that divers (Gaviidae), grebes (Podicipedidae), gannets (Sulidae), some seaducks (Anatidae) and auks (Alcidae) avoid wind farms after the erection of turbines, whilst some species of gulls (Laridae) and terns (Sternidae) show some preference for sites in which wind farms have been constructed compared to the previously undeveloped sites. A description of an improved application is given. This combines distance sampling and spatial modelling techniques currently being developed, and will provide more robust comparisons of waterbird density surfaces with respect to pre and post-construction development scenarios to support more effective environmental impact assessment in marine environments.

## INTRODUCTION

The dramatic development of offshore wind farms in inshore/nearshore marine waters around Europe in recent years has focussed attention on the hazards they present to waterbirds and other migratory birds that encounter these constructions. Direct impacts, such as result from direct collision, cause mortality that affect the demography of populations, but local effects (such as the extra energy costs incurred by avoidance flights or habitat loss) are more difficult to quantify. Habitat gain and loss as a result of the construction of wind turbines can be considered on two spatial and temporal scales. Firstly, long-term but small-scale change results from the physical loss of feeding substrate under foundations and anti-scour protection and the physical gain associated with the creation of these new substrates. However, since the area of foundations and anti-scour protection rarely exceeds 2% of the total sea area covered by a wind farm, this change in food availability is considered trivial in most instances. Secondly, effective habitat loss may result from behavioural displacement of foraging birds, the response to specific stimuli such as rotating turbines and/or the activity of maintenance vessels in the vicinity. In theory, if birds avoid coming closer that half the distance between adjacent turbines, the effective loss of habitat exceeds the entire area of the wind farm. In practice, birds may avoid going between the rows of turbines because of the confining visual effects, such that even at avoidance distances less than half the distance between turbines, net habitat loss equivalent to the size of the wind farm occurs. Since birds may habituate over time to unfamiliar constructions in their foraging distribution at sea, there may be a temporal component to their avoidance responses.

Environmental impact assessment of offshore wind farms requires a basic evaluation of the significance of such habitat loss. Indeed, assessment of the consequences at local and population/flyway level may be a foregone requirement, for example, under environmental criteria placed on construction. Hence, it is important to quantify habitat loss in a way that accounts for the spatial and temporal heterogeneity in bird distributions prior to and after construction. In this short account, we summarize the approach taken to assess effective habitat loss to foraging waterbirds based on experiences from two wind farms constructed in Danish inshore waters mainly during 2003. These are situated at Horns Rev (off the exposed west coast of Jutland in the North Sea) and Nysted (south of Rødsand in the brackish Baltic). Both projects have already been widely reported elsewhere (e.g. Christensen *et al.* 2004, Kahlert *et al.* 2004, Petersen *et al.* 2004), but are summarized here. We also discuss the current state of development of the necessary tools required for effective assessment of the degree of habitat loss to foraging birds offshore.

## METHODS

The strategic approach adopted in the study of the effects of the two Danish offshore wind farms has been to use aerial surveys to describe changes in bird abundance and distribution as a proxy measure of habitat loss. The problem associated with such assessments is the very large degree of spatial and temporal heterogeneity associated with bird distributions in dynamic media such as inshore marine waters. Benthic feeders (such as eiders *Somateria* spp. and scoters *Melanitta* spp. feeding on marine bivalve molluscs) may show relatively simple responses to factors such as water depth and substrate type that determine the nature and profitability of the benthos they feed upon. Nevertheless, temporal variation in the abundance of benthic feeders will be subject to temporal variation in spat settlement and age class distributions of their prey. Bird species preying on pelagic fish, such as divers (Gaviidae), grebes (Podicipedidae) and auks (Alcidae), are even less predictable, dependent upon temporal and spatial patterns of distribution and abundance of their highly mobile prey.

To enable a pre and post-construction comparison of the bird distribution and abundance in such heterogeneous systems, it is essential to survey and re-survey a sufficiently large geographical area with high temporal frequency. This BACI (before-after control-impact) type of design should encompass sampling bird

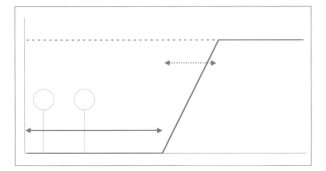

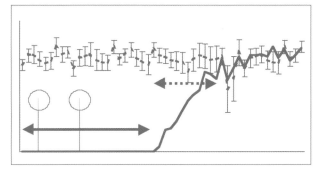

Fig. 1. Diagrammatic representation of theoretically constant bird densities along a transect prior to construction of offshore wind farms (broken line), compared with post construction (solid line). The features of interest are the extent of complete habitat loss (solid arrow) and the extent of reduced densities (broken arrow).

Fig. 2. Diagrammatic representation of theoretical modelled bird densities (with confidence intervals) along a transect sampled prior to construction of offshore wind farms (pecked line), compared with post construction (solid line). The features of interest are the extent of complete habitat loss (solid arrow), the extent of reduced densities (pecked arrow), and hence the difference in overall densities between the two samples.

densities within:

- the area physically affected by the construction area;
- an area around this where behavioural avoidance may also cause an effect (assumed to be a gradient of avoidance with increasing distance from the turbines); and
- a reference area where bird distributions are likely to be unaffected by the construction of the wind turbines.

Such sampling needs to be undertaken as frequently as necessary to characterize changes in temporal abundance throughout the annual cycle. In two-dimensional space, we may hypothesize complete bird avoidance within a specific distance of the turbines (Fig. 1). In this case, the objective is to measure the area of displaced birds, both in terms of defining the extent of areas of water without birds and areas of water with reduced densities relative to the baseline. The ideal objective for any sampling protocol is therefore to generate bird density surfaces over large areas of open sea using data:

- from as large a reference area as possible;
- sampled as simultaneously as possible;
- gathered with the greatest level of spatial precision possible;and
- using observation platforms that cause least disruption to the patterns of abundance and distribution of undisturbed birds.

For this reason, the Danish studies have adopted aerial survey using high-winged twin-engined aircraft to cover large areas of open marine waters as rapidly as possible using internationally agreed standardized data collection protocols (described in Camphuysen *et al*. 2004).

Initially, a very simple analytical approach has been adopted to analyse these transect count data, based on encounter rates of birds or bird clusters observed on transects per unit effort. This approach determines the relative number of birds of different species that would be susceptible to potential disturbance effects from the wind turbines based on encounter rate corrected for observation effort. The method assesses the relative importance of the wind farm area and the adjacent waters, generally a zone within 2 and 4 km of the outermost turbines of a wind farm (see methods in Petersen *et al*. 2004). The method describes the "preference" of bird species for the wind farm area and adjacent zones of differing extent immediately adjacent to the construc-

tion area. In doing so, we define the potential impact of loss of these areas relative to the preference shown by the species for the entire study area. In a typical analysis, species encounter rate was calculated for all pre-construction surveys combined, and compared with the data generated from post-construction surveys. For these zones, the preference of the most numerously occurring species is calculated using Jacob's selectivity index (Jacobs 1974). Jacob's selectivity index ($D$) varies between -1 (all birds present outside the area of interest) and +1 (all birds inside the area of interest), and is calculated as:

$$D = (r - p)/(r + p - 2rp)$$

where $r$ = the proportion of birds in the area of interest compared to the birds in the whole study area, and $p$ = the proportion of the survey effort in the area of interest compared to the total survey effort in the whole study area. The difference between the two proportions is tested as the difference between the observed number of birds in the area of interest and the number expected in this area, estimated from the share of the survey effort in relation to survey effort in the total area (one-sample $\chi^2$-test). Tests are made on the basis of number of observed clusters, rather than birds, because observations of individual birds fail to meet the statistical criteria of being independent. However, for some species a cluster can represent a wide range of number of individual birds, varying from 1 to 26 000 in the case of the Common Scoter *Melanitta nigra*, so the use of cluster data may appear unhelpful.

An alternative approach has been to compare the pre- and post-construction frequency distribution of birds at increasing distance intervals out from wind turbines. Using GIS and other tools to construct species cumulative percentage frequency distributions of bird numbers in successive 500 m distance intervals away from the wind turbines, it is possible to use non-parametric tests to compare pre- and post-construction distributions for significant displacement effects.

However, the ultimate aim has been to develop a more sophisticated suite of analytical tools to permit more robust comparisons of before/after densities of birds. The use of survey data collected at different distances from the observer aircraft provides transect counts of birds assigned to distance categories out from the transect track-lines. Such a line-transect count approach allows the use of Distance Sampling techniques

(Buckland *et al.* 2001) to generate bird densities, by modelling detectability functions to correct bird density estimates for the decline in detectability probability with increasing distance from the observer. The use of such techniques also enables the incorporation of factors and covariates (such as individual observer functions, differences in sea state and light conditions, etc.) into modelled densities of birds encountered. The ultimate objective for this project has been to develop spatial modelling techniques that use line-transect counts as samples and generalized additive models to construct bird density surfaces as a function of spatially explicit covariates (e.g. Hedley *et al.* 1999, Hedley & Buckland 2004, Clarke *et al.* 2004). This method offers an approach to the theoretical objectives established in Fig. 1 by constructing a modelled bird density surface with confidence intervals over extended areas of sea generated from aerial line-transect census data (see Fig. 2). For benthic feeding birds, the covariates used in the predictive-modelling exercise could include environmental factors such as water depth which determine profitability of shallow inshore waters (e.g. Common Scoters forage more in shallow water depths than would be expected by chance; see Fig. 17 in Petersen *et al.* 2004). In the fullness of time, other environmental covariates, such as bottom substrate type and bottom aspect can be incorporated to improve the effectiveness of such model estimates. For seabirds dependent on a more dynamic food base, such as pelagic fish, the challenges to generating density surfaces are considerably greater. However, incorporation of macro-environmental parameters, such as current, salinity and water temperature profiles (which are now routinely modelled throughout the water column around many European coasts) which correlate with prey abundance, offers some opportunities to generate bird density surfaces for these organisms as well.

At present, software to generate such modelled density surfaces is still being developed in collaboration with the Centre for Research into Ecological and Environmental Modelling at the University of St Andrews in Scotland, for implementation in the near future.

## RESULTS

Results from tests based on the numbers of bird clusters encountered have been used to compare pre-construction and post-construction distributions to look for changes in preference for the wind-farm area and surroundings between the two "treatments". Use of the Jacobs selectivity index has suggested changes in distribution of different species, both in terms of avoidance of, and attraction to, the structures, as outlined below (see also Christensen *et al.* 2004 and Petersen *et al.* 2004).

At both sites, analysis of the preference indices calculated for different species prior to construction confirmed that the majority of waterbirds avoided the wind farm area at both sites. Bird densities were generally low before any construction activities on the site, making comparisons after construction difficult, especially since at present there is only a single post-construction year available for comparisons.

At Horns Rev, divers, Northern Gannets *Sula bassana*, Common Scoters and Guillemots/Razorbills *Uria aalge/Alca torda* showed an increased avoidance of the wind farm area (and zones within 2 and 4 km of it) after the erection of the wind turbines. In contrast, Herring Gulls *Larus argentatus* showed a decreased avoidance of the wind farm area, while Great Black-

backed Gulls *L. marinus*, Little Gulls *L. minutus* and Arctic/Common Terns *Sterna paradisea/S. hirundo* showed a shift from avoidance before construction to a preference for the wind farm area after construction (Petersen *et al.* 2004).

At Nysted, Long-tailed Ducks *Clangula hyemalis* and Common Eiders *Somateria mollissima* showed a reduced preference for the wind farm area (and zones within 2 and 4 km of it) after the erection of the wind turbines. Herring Gulls showed a slight increase in preference for the wind farm area and the zones around it after construction (Kahlert *et al.* 2004).

## DISCUSSION

The bird studies being carried out at Nysted and Horns Rev during the period 1999-2006 were initiated under the terms and conditions placed upon the granting of permission to construct wind farms at the two sites by the Danish authorities. These studies have been carried out before, during and after construction of both wind farms. The installation of wind turbines was finished in autumn 2002 (Horns Rev) and summer 2003 (Nysted). However, the construction phase was too short to offer any opportunity to assess the effects of the physical construction of turbines on bird distribution. Construction activities coincided with periods of the year when fewest feeding birds were in the vicinity (by prior design), with the result that no assessment could be made of the disturbance effects of building work during that phase. Furthermore, the data reported here (for the period up to 2004) represent material gathered from one year or less into the initial operational phase of the wind farms. For this reason, it is not possible to quantify natural variation between years, seasons, species and sites and the possible habituation effects during the operational phase. Therefore, it must be emphasized that these results are to be considered as preliminary, and must await further compilation of data before firm conclusions can be drawn with respect to the impact on birds. The final environmental impact assessment for the two wind farms will be undertaken upon termination of the environmental monitoring programmes in 2006.

There remains considerable scope to improve on these methods and to test many of the assumptions associated with their use. In particular, distance sampling necessitates that all objects on the track-line are observed from the count platform, an assumption that has considerable bearing on the ability to generate unbiased density estimates. Studies to assess whether this assumption is met, using double-platform repeat counting, have been attempted, including the use of two aircraft and vertical photographic techniques to capture scenes of the distribution of birds on the sea surface to which count observers were exposed in the following aircraft. Such techniques proved so effective, and the imagery quality sufficient to enable automated computer identification and counting of bird "objects" on the photographs, that alternative methods of counting birds at sea have presented themselves. The use of geo-rectified vertical photography of large areas of sea surface, and subsequent computer based pattern recognition software to identify, position with great spatial accuracy and ultimately count birds on that surface, frees the need for distance sampling to generate bird densities, and offers some very exciting prospects for future developments in this field.

## ACKNOWLEDGEMENTS
We gratefully acknowledge the help and support of our NERI colleagues, especially the aerial survey observers, Ib Clausager,

Johnny Kahlert, Thomas Kjær and Mark Desholm. Our thanks also to David Borchers, Sharon Hedley and colleagues at St Andrews University for support with developing analytical techniques and to E2, Elsam and their staff for funding and support for the two Danish case studies reported here.

## REFERENCES

Buckland, S.T., Anderson, D.R., Burnham, K.P., Laake, J.L., Borchers, D.L. & Thomas, L. 2001. Introduction to Distance Sampling - Estimating Abundance of Biological Populations. University Press, Oxford.

Camphuysen, C.J., Fox, A.D., Leopold, M.F. & Petersen, I.K. 2004. Towards standardised seabirds at sea census techniques in connection with environmental impact assessments for offshore wind farms in the U.K. A comparison of ship and aerial sampling methods for marine birds, and their applicability to offshore wind farm assessments. Report to Collaborative Offshore Wind Research into the Environment (COWRIE), Crown Estate Commissioners, London. Available at: http://www.thecrownestate.co.uk/1352_bird_survey_phase1_final_04_05_06.pdf.

Christensen, T.K., Hounisen, J.P., Clausager, I. & Petersen, I.K. 2004. Visual and radar observations of birds in relation to collision risk at the Horns Rev offshore wind farm. Annual status report 2003. Report request. Commissioned by Elsam Engineering A/S. National Environmental Research Institute. Available at: http://www.hornsrev.dk/Miljoeforhold/miljoerapporter/Visual_radar_observations_2003_status_report.pdf.

Clarke, E.D., Spear, L.B., McCracken, M.L., Marques, F.F.C., Borchers, D.L., Buckland, S.T. & Ainley, D.G. 2004. Validating the use of generalized additive models and at-sea surveys to estimate size and temporal trends of seabird populations. Journal of Applied Ecology 40: 278-292.

Hedley, S.L. & Buckland, S.T. 2004. Spatial models for line transect sampling. Journal of Agricultural, Biological and Environmental Statistics 9: 181-199.

Hedley, S.L., Buckland, S.T. & Borchers, D.L. 1999. Spatial modelling from line transect data. Journal of Cetacean Research and Management 1: 255-264.

Jacobs, J. 1974. Quantitative measurements of food selection. Oecologia 14: 413-417.

Kahlert, J., Petersen, I.K., Fox, A.D., Desholm, M. & Clausager, I. 2004. Investigations of birds during construction and operation of Nysted offshore wind farm at Rødsand - Annual status report 2003. Report request. Commissioned by Energi E2 A/S. National Environmental Research Institute. Available at: http://uk.nystedhavmoellepark.dk/upload/pdf/Birds2003.pdf.

Petersen, I.K., Clausager, I. & Christensen, T.K. 2004. Bird numbers and distribution in the Horns Rev offshore wind farm area. Annual status report 2003. Report commissioned by Elsam Engineering A/S. National Environmental Research Institute. Available at: http://www.hornsrev.dk/Miljoeforhold/miljoerapporter/Bird_numbers_2003%20status_report.pdf.

The Nysted Offshore Wind Farm in the Danish part of the Baltic Sea consists of 72 turbines situated c. 11.5 km south of the island of Lolland and covering an area of 24 km². Water depth in the area is 6 - 9.5 m. The windfarm has a total power capacity of 165.6 MW, and is the world's largest offshore wind farm. (Photo provided by Energy E2). Photo: Ib Krag Petersen.

# The impact of the Cardiff Bay barrage on wintering waterbirds

*Niall H.K. Burton*

*British Trust for Ornithology, The Nunnery, Thetford, Norfolk, IP24 2PU, UK. (email: niall.burton@bto.org)*

Burton, N.H.K. 2006. The impact of the Cardiff Bay barrage on wintering waterbirds. *Waterbirds around the world*. Eds. G.C. Boere, C.A. Galbraith & D.A. Stroud. The Stationery Office, Edinburgh, UK. p. 805.

Cardiff Bay (51°27'N, 3°10'W), a 200 ha area of intertidal mudflats and saltmarsh at the mouth of the Severn Estuary in the UK, was enclosed by a barrage on 4 November 1999. The consequent inundation of the bay has created a freshwater lake that now forms the centre point for the redevelopment of Cardiff's former docklands.

This paper provides an overview of results from 14 years of monitoring which aimed to determine the impacts of this habitat loss on the waterbirds that formerly wintered in the bay. Peaks of 310 Shelduck *Tadorna tadorna*, 120 Oystercatcher *Haematopus ostralegus*, 790 Dunlin *Calidris alpina*, 120 Curlew *Numenius arquata* and 300 Redshank *Tringa totanus* occurred in the bay in the winter immediately before barrage-closure; both Dunlin and Redshank had declined in number over the 10 pre-barrage years.

Between 1989 and 2003, waterbird numbers were monitored both in the bay and neighbouring areas. The results of these counts were used to show how the waterbird community changed following closure and whether displaced birds were able to re-locate to neighbouring sites.

Impacts on the movements and survival of Redshank were also monitored through colour-ringing and radio-tracking. Prior to closure, individual Redshank were highly site-faithful to the bay both within and between winters (Burton 2000) and were thus seen as being particularly at risk from its loss. Over 450 Redshank were individually colour-ringed in the bay in the five years preceding closure. Twenty Redshank were additionally radio-tagged there in October 1999. Following closure, birds were also caught to look at changes in their body condition.

The inundation of the bay resulted in the loss of all of the mudflats, but left a fringe of saltmarsh. Although the new freshwater lake is used by some waterbirds, the overall numbers and diversity of species have been greatly reduced. The loss of species' diversity (from a mean of 26.5 to 22 waterbird species per year) has been due, primarily, to a loss of waders, which now only use the site as an occasional high tide roost.

Almost all the Shelduck, Oystercatcher, Dunlin, Curlew and Redshank that formerly used the bay were displaced by its inundation. Counts in the first winter following closure indicated that some displaced Shelduck, Oystercatcher and Curlew settled at adjacent sites within 4 km - the Rhymney Estuary and Orchard Ledges. However, these increases were not sustained in following winters. It was not possible to determine whether displaced Dunlin were able to settle elsewhere due to an ongoing decline of the local population (unpubl. data).

Observation of colour-ringed and radio-tagged birds supported the evidence from counts that most Redshank were also displaced to the Rhymney Estuary, though in the winter following closure, some displaced Redshank were also recorded at other sites up to 19 km away. The loss of birds from the bay could have accounted for the overall increase in numbers observed at Rhymney over the four winters subsequent to closure (Burton *et al.* 2006). Displaced colour-ringed birds using this area were seen on mudflats by the River Rhymney and Cardiff Heliport. Radio-tracking had shown that the Heliport mudflats were formerly used only at night (Burton & Armitage 2005), probably due to disturbance during the day from helicopters.

Although count data suggested that Redshank displaced from Cardiff Bay were able to settle at Rhymney, analysis of biometric data revealed that adult Redshank from the bay had difficulty in maintaining their body condition in the first winter following closure. Adults which were displaced from Cardiff Bay to Rhymney were significantly lighter than those that they joined (Burton *et al.* 2006).

Most significantly, the survival rate of adult Redshank displaced from Cardiff Bay declined between the two years prior to closure and the three following years. Given that there was no significant change in the annual survival rate of Rhymney-based Redshank over this time, it seems likely that this was a direct consequence of the birds' displacement (Burton *et al.* 2006).

The results of this study indicate that waterbirds may have difficulty in settling in new areas following habitat loss. Birds displaced by the inundation of Cardiff Bay only moved to the nearest available alternative sites. There was reduced survival in the population of displaced birds of at least one species. Initial increases in numbers at neighbouring sites were not sustained.

## ACKNOWLEDGEMENTS

The study was funded from 1989 by the Cardiff Bay Development Corporation and from 2000 by the Council of the City and County of Cardiff. Particular thanks are due to those BTO staff who helped with counts and Steve Dodd, Graham Couchman and Peter Ferns for their help in ringing activities.

## REFERENCES

Burton, N.H.K. 2000. Winter site-fidelity and survival of Redshank *Tringa totanus* at Cardiff, South Wales. Bird Study 47: 102–112.

Burton, N.H.K. & Armitage, M.J.S. 2005. Differences in the diurnal and nocturnal use of intertidal feeding grounds by Redshank *Tringa totanus*. Bird Study 52: 120-128.

Burton, N.H.K., Rehfisch, M.M., Clark, N.A. & Dodd, S.G. 2006. Impacts of sudden winter habitat loss on the body condition and survival of Redshank *Tringa totanus*. Journal of Applied Ecology 43: 464-473.

# The conflict between shellfisheries and migratory waterbirds in the Dutch Wadden Sea

*Bruno J. Ens*

*Alterra, PO Box 167, NL-1790 AD Den Burg (Texel), The Netherlands. (email: Bruno.Ens@sovon.nl)*

Ens, B.J. 2006. The conflict between shellfisheries and migratory waterbirds in the Dutch Wadden Sea. *Waterbirds around the world.* Eds. G.C. Boere, C.A. Galbraith & D.A. Stroud. The Stationery Office, Edinburgh, UK. pp. 806-811.

## ABSTRACT

At the end of the 1980s, the supply of nutrients (especially Phosphorus) to the Dutch Wadden Sea strongly declined. It seems likely that this decline in nutrients reduced the maximum shellfish stocks and the productivity of these stocks. Shellfish fishermen did not adapt to this reduced productivity, but attempted to deliver the same amount of shellfish to the market that they delivered during the 1980s. In this paper, I argue that this contributed to the mass mortality observed among Common Eiders *Somateria mollissima* and decline in numbers of wintering Eurasian Oystercatchers *Haematopus ostralegus* from 260 000 to 170 000. Two types of shellfisheries were involved: mussel culture and suction-dredging cockles. Mussel culture has the potential to increase the average stock of mussels in the sub-littoral part of the western Wadden Sea and probably did so by an estimated 15% in the 1990s. However, there is evidence suggesting that transport of mussels to culture lots in the southern part of The Netherlands increases during years of scarcity, thereby actually exacerbating the food shortage for the Common Eiders. During the period of declining productivity, the mussel farmers also increasingly exploited the inter-tidal mussel beds. This increasing exploitation contributed significantly to the decline of the inter-tidal mussel beds, which completely disappeared in 1990 and remained virtually absent for the next four years. The disappearance of the inter-tidal mussel beds is the primary reason for the decline in the number of wintering Eurasian Oystercatchers by an estimated 90 000 birds. Calculations indicate that the mechanized cockle fishery also contributed to this decline by reducing the carrying capacity for oystercatchers by an estimated 15 000 birds. The negative impacts of shellfish fishery on shellfish-eating birds occurred because insufficient quantities of shellfish were reserved for the birds.

## INTRODUCTION

The Dutch Wadden Sea is an internationally acclaimed natural area harbouring large stocks of mussels *Mytilus edulis* and cockles *Cerastoderma edule* which are an important source of food for several species of birds. The stocks of shellfish are also targeted by an intensive mechanized shellfish fishery. This paper reviews the impact of the shellfish fishery on shellfish-eating birds in the Dutch Wadden Sea. It does not consider bird species preying on the smaller sizes of shellfish, such as the Red Knot *Calidris canutus,* or bird species which do not prey on shellfish but whose habitat may be affected by the shellfish fishery. For those species, I refer the reader to Piersma & Koolhaas (1997), Piersma *et al.* (2001), van Gils *et al.* (2004), Leopold *et al.* (2004) and van Roomen *et al.* (2005). Instead, this paper focuses on those bird species that are in direct competition with the fishermen by feeding on the same large sizes of shellfish, i.e. the Eurasian Oystercatcher *Haematopus ostralegus* and the

Common Eider *Somateria mollissima.* Both species breed in the Wadden Sea, but numbers during winter are much higher due to the influx of large numbers of birds that breed elsewhere.

The large numbers of birds are among the natural values that give the Wadden Sea its high international importance. These high natural values receive protection from national legislation (since 1981) and international treaties, including the EU Birds Directive (since 1991) and the EU Habitats Directive (since 1996). Initially, the intense exploitation of shellfish by the mechanized fishery was not considered to be in conflict with proper protection of the birds and other natural values, but this situation changed around 1990 during a period with low shellfish stocks and high mortality of shellfish-eating birds (Steins 1999, Verbeeten 1999). It emerged that the existing legislation did not allow the Government to close areas for shellfish fishery to protect nature. In 1993, a new policy came into effect (the Sea and Coastal Fisheries Policy) that attempted to strike a balance between the interests of the fishermen and the interests of the conservationists, but the debate continued. Between 1993 and 2003, several amendments were made to the policy, but these failed to satisfy the conservationists. The evaluation of the Sea and Coastal Fisheries Policy in 2003 became entangled with another political hot potato: the extraction of gas from under the Wadden Sea. The Government set up a committee to provide advice on both the shellfish fishery and the gas extraction. This committee concluded that gas could be extracted without causing ecological damage, but that the current practices of the mechanized cockle fishery were not sustainable and that the current practices of the mechanized mussel fishery were perhaps not sustainable (Meijer *et al.* 2004). On the basis of this advice, the Government decided to close the Dutch Wadden Sea for mechanized cockle fishery from 1 January 2005 onwards. Remarkably, at the same time the Government issued one last permit for the cockle fishermen to fish in the autumn of 2004. This permit, together with many previous permits, was declared unlawful by the Raad van State because no proper assessment of the possibly significant negative effects on the ecosystem was provided. A recent ruling of the European Court of Justice (7 September 2004, case C-127/02) makes clear that such a proper assessment is required for any activity that does not directly contribute to the conservation of the area. Activities are only allowed when it can be proven that they do not significantly harm nature. This ruling may have important consequences for the mussel fishery that was allowed to continue under the new shellfish policy that came into effect in 2004 (LNV 2004). The Government asked J.M. Verschuuren to investigate if this new policy met with EU requirements. Verschuuren (2004) concluded that the new policy was an improvement over the old policy, but that many questions remained and that a final judgement could only be based on the actual permits.

Throughout this period of conflict and changing policies, mass mortality and declining numbers of shellfish-eating birds fuelled the debate on the impact of the shellfish fishery. Many studies were initiated, and this paper reviews the evidence that has emerged from these studies with regard to the contribution of both types of shellfish fishery to bird mortality and changes in bird numbers. The Sea and Coastal Fisheries Policy that came into effect in 1993 specifically aimed to minimize negative effects on shellfish-eating birds through a policy of food reservation: the shellfish fishery was stopped when shellfish stocks fell below a certain level. If the shellfish fishery contributed to the mass mortality and declining numbers of birds, it can be concluded that the policy of food reservation did not work and we must investigate why.

## METHODS

Ideally, the effect of the shellfish fishery should have been investigated on a strictly experimental basis. For various reasons, this proved to be impossible. Most of the research consisted of analysing and combining data sets collected for other reasons. In addition to statistical analyses of the data, mathematical models were developed and employed to investigate causal relationships. Additional data were collected as part of EVA II, a major evaluation study that ran from 1999 to 2003 (Ens *et al.* 2004). This material included analyses of historical records of mussel beds from fishermen and fishery inspectors, analyses of historical photographs for the occurrence of mussel beds, sampling the sediment to obtain recent estimates of silt content, sampling benthic invertebrates on fished and unfished cockle beds, measuring sediment, benthic fauna and bird densities in a fished and unfished control site, measuring cockle abundance in autumn to check the extrapolation procedure from the spring survey, and experiments on food selection by Common Eiders.

## RESULTS

### Decline in mussel production

Mussel culture was introduced in the Dutch Wadden Sea in 1951. Before that time, the only fishery of mussels was from wild beds. Once mussel culture became established, wild beds

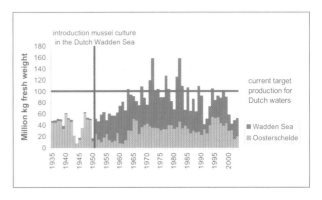

**Fig. 1.** Annual landings of mussels from Dutch coastal waters. A distinction is made between mussels landed from culture lots in the Wadden Sea and from culture lots in the Oosterschelde. The timing of the introduction of mussel culture in the Dutch Wadden Sea and the current target production are also indicated. The year 1953 refers to the season 1953/1954, and so on. From Ens *et al.* (2004).

were only fished for seed mussels. These seed mussels are subsequently transported to culture lots (located in both the Oosterschelde and the western Dutch Wadden Sea) where they are left to grow to marketable sizes. Mussel production from Dutch coastal waters almost doubled between 1951 and 1970 (Fig. 1). Between 1970 and 1985, the total landings fluctuated around 100 million kg fresh weight, and since that time, this has been the target production of the mussel farmers. However, production has declined since about 1985, and an all-time low was reached in the season of 1991/1992, when only 41 million kg of mussels were landed. Production has not exceeded 60 million kg in the four most recent years.

We have no data for fishing pressure on the wild sub-littoral stocks before 1990, but estimates are available from 1991 onwards (Table 1). In the period 1991-2001, there was only one year with good recruitment (1996) and one year with normal recruitment (1992). All other years were below normal. To calculate fishing pressure, we added the amount fished in the following spring to the amount

**Table 1.** Fishing pressure on wild mussel stocks in the sub-littoral part of the western Wadden Sea. For each year, the reconstructed wild stock in autumn, the amount fished in autumn and the amount fished in the following spring (all in million kg fresh weight) are indicated. The penultimate column gives the fishing pressure as a percentage of the initial stock. Basic data from Bult *et al.* (2004). The last column presents the index of recruitment of mussels in the sub-littoral parts of the western Wadden Sea (0 = absent, 1 = local, 2 = normal, 3 = good, 4 = very good). The index is assessed in the spring following the recruitment (van Stralen 2002).

| Year | Wild stock in autumn | Fished in autumn | Fished in following spring | Fished as % of initial stock | Index of recruitment |
|------|------|------|------|------|------|
| 1991 | 26 | 14 | 5 | 75% | 0.5 |
| 1992 | 56 | 25 | 23 | 84% | 2.0 |
| 1993 | 45 | 0 | 24 | 53% | 0.5 |
| 1994 | 56 | 17 | 19 | 64% | 1.0 |
| 1995 | 42 | 8 | 15 | 56% | 0.0 |
| 1996 | 78 | 18 | 29 | 60% | 3.0 |
| 1997 | 124 | 20 | 44 | 51% | 1.5 |
| 1998 | 41 | 0 | 18 | 44% | 1.0 |
| 1999 | 51 | 18 | 18 | 70% | 1.5 |
| 2000 | 14 | 0 | 4 | 28% | 0.5 |
| 2001 | 56 | 19 | 23 | 76% | |

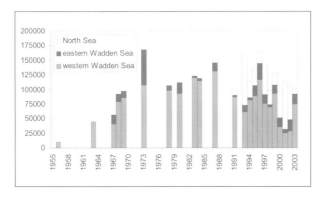

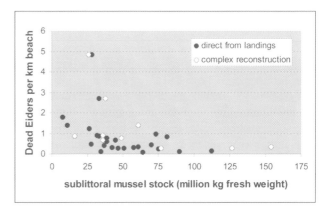

**Fig. 2.** Midwinter counts of the Common Eider *Somateria mollissima* (mostly in January) in the Wadden Sea (eastern and western parts) and adjacent North Sea coastal zone. Data before 1993 from literature; data thereafter from RIKZ and Alterra. From Ens *et al.* (2004).

fished in autumn and compared this with the initial stock in autumn. During winter, stocks decline due to mortality, but the calculation assumes that this is compensated for by the growth in early spring, before stocks are sampled. Fishing pressure was always high, averaging 60% for the years 1991-2001 (Table 1). This means that low landings indicate a shortage of mussels.

## Numbers, distribution and mass mortality of the Common Eider

Sub-littoral mussels have thin shells and a high flesh content, and this makes them a very profitable food item for Common Eiders (Ens & Kats 2004). Large stocks of sub-littoral mussels are only found in the western Dutch Wadden Sea, and this explains why the western Dutch Wadden Sea traditionally held the largest numbers of Common Eiders. However, since 1991, large numbers of eiders have also occurred in the North Sea Coastal Zone, where they feed on *Spisula* (Fig. 2). In the winters of 2000-2002, there were more eiders in the North Sea Coastal Zone than in the western Wadden Sea. During the 1980s, around 130 000 eiders wintered in Dutch coastal waters, but the numbers have decreased in recent years to around 110 000.

The periods with a changed distribution correspond to years with mass mortality, suggesting a link with the food supply (Camphuysen *et al.* 2002). Eider mortality (measured as the number of dead birds per km of beach) was regressed against estimates of different shellfish stocks. Long series of data were available for sub-littoral mussels stocks (using a back calculation from the landings) and littoral cockle stocks (assuming data from the Balgzand to be representative of the entire Wadden Sea). Short and more precise series of data were available for sub-littoral mussels, littoral mussels, sub-littoral cockles, littoral cockles and Spisula. In both analyses, a shortage of sub-littoral mussels correlated significantly with increased mortality in Common Eiders (Fig. 3). There was no effect of other shellfish stocks when the stock of (large) sub-littoral mussels was controlled for in the analysis (Ens & Kats 2004).

## Disappearance of inter-tidal mussel beds from the Wadden Sea

In 1990, the inter-tidal mussel beds virtually disappeared from the Dutch Wadden Sea, and it took more than a decade before they recovered (Fig. 4). According to Dankers *et al.* (2003), the area of inter-tidal beds fluctuated between 1 000 and 5 600 ha in

**Fig. 3.** Relationship between the mortality of Common Eiders *Somateria mollissima* (expressed in number of dead eiders per km of beach) and the stock of immature sub-littoral mussels in the Wadden Sea. When this stock was estimated by direct back-calculation from the landings (and the logarithm of the number of dead eiders was taken), the correlation was r=-0.57, N=25, P=0.003 (Ens & Kats 2004). The stock of half-grown and older sub-littoral mussels can also be reconstructed in a more complex fashion, yielding more precise estimates for a smaller number of years (Bult *et al.* 2004).

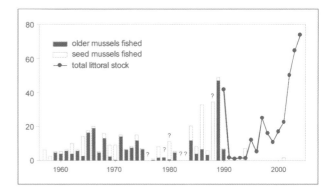

**Fig. 4.** Comparison of the amounts of mussels fished from the littoral zone (stacked bars) for the years 1957-2004 (Dankers *et al.* 2003) with the development of the littoral stock (solid line) for the years 1990-2004 (Ens *et al.* 2004).

the 1970s. Assuming 25 000 kg fresh weight per ha (Dankers *et al.* 2003), this amounts to stocks varying between 25 and 140 million kg fresh weight. Mussel farmers (pers. comm.) blame heavy storms in January and February 1990 for the disappearance of the inter-tidal mussel beds. While storms may cause extensive damage to mussel beds, it is unlikely that they are the prime cause of the complete disappearance in 1990 for the following reasons. Firstly, several years with unprecedented high fishing pressure preceded the disappearance of the littoral beds (Fig. 4). Secondly, an estimated 42 million kg fresh weight were left in the spring of 1990, i.e. after the two storms (Fig. 4). Thirdly, the extent of the fishery in 1990 is underestimated because Dankers *et al.* (2003) assumed that the littoral fishery was restricted to the eastern Dutch Wadden Sea. However, in 1990 stocks of littoral mussels were high on the flats of the Balgzand in the western Wadden Sea, and these were all removed by fishermen (Beukema 1993). Fourthly, the littoral beds recovered after the fishery on the littoral beds was stopped (Fig. 4). Thus, there can be no doubt that the fishery was a major factor in the disappearance of the inter-tidal beds in 1990.

Fig. 5. Numbers of Eurasian Oystercatchers *Haematopus ostralegus* wintering in the Dutch Wadden Sea (average per year from August until March) for the winters 1975/76 to 2002/03. Missing counts were imputed; see van Roomen *et al.* (2005).

## Decline of the Eurasian Oystercatcher population

Before the inter-tidal mussel beds disappeared in 1990, it was estimated that over half of the Eurasian Oystercatchers wintering in the Dutch Wadden Sea lived on mussels (Smit *et al.* 1998, Ens *et al.* 2004). Model calculations indicate that in the following decade, cockles were the main prey item (Rappoldt *et al.* 2003a). These same calculations indicate that the cockle stocks during the 1990s were of insufficient size to maintain the 260 000 oystercatchers that were present in the 1980s. Without the cockle fishery, the carrying capacity in the 1990s was estimated at about 145 000 oystercatchers. Although this estimate has a large margin of error, there can be no doubt that the prime cause of the decline in the number of wintering oystercatchers (Fig. 5) was the disappearance of the inter-tidal mussel beds. The cockle fishery may have contributed as well, because the carrying capacity in the 1990s with the cockle fishery was estimated to be 15 000 birds lower than the carrying capacity without the cockle fishery (Rappoldt *et al.* 2003a).

## DISCUSSION

### Unravelling the complex chain of events

According to Ens (2003), at least eight different hypotheses exist to explain the decline in mussel production that occurred around 1990. Of these, the hypothesis that the declining production was due to a decline in the eutrophication of Dutch coastal waters recently received support from a study by Brinkman & Smaal (2004). They showed that input of nutrients to the western Dutch Wadden Sea, especially Phosphorus and to a lesser extent Nitrogen, declined during the 1980s. Using the ecosystem model ECOWASP, Brinkman & Smaal calculated that the declining nutrient inputs must have caused a strong decline in benthic productivity. Comparing the 1980s with the 1990s, the maximum stocks of shellfish almost halved. The actual stock will often be lower than the maximum stock, e.g. because of recruitment failure in the preceding years, mortality due to storms or icy winters, and heavy predation by birds or fishermen. However, when the maximum stocks are reduced, we would expect the average stock and the minimum stock to be reduced as well.

Fishermen could have adapted to the declining productivity by reducing their catches, but they did not. In 1990, when cockle stocks were very low, cockle fishermen successfully contested the decision of the Government to close half of the tidal flats for the fishery. Similarly, mussel farmers based their target production on

the years when productivity was at a maximum, and retained this target production during the subsequent years of reduced productivity. As a result, fishing pressure on the wild sub-littoral stocks of mussels was very high during the 1990s, averaging 60% of the stock per year. By comparison, fishing pressure on the total stock of cockles was much lower during the 1990s, averaging less than 10% of the biomass (Kamermans *et al.* 2004). The difference in exploitation pressure between the cockle fishery and the mussel fishery can be explained by 25% of the tidal flats being permanently closed to cockle fishing, the closure of the fishery in years of scarcity, and the extreme variability of the cockle stocks, making it impossible to fish a high percentage in good years.

The difficulty that the mussel farmers experienced in maintaining their target production under conditions of declining eutrophication may explain why they intensified seed-fishing on inter-tidal beds. This intensified fishery was a major cause of the disappearance of the inter-tidal beds, although the possibility that storms also played some role cannot be excluded. In addition, recruitment of mussels was reduced in the early 1990s (Ens *et al.* 2004). However, this could have been a consequence of the low mussel stocks, rather than a cause. Mussel spat preferentially settle on or nearby old mussels, and the current exceptionally low recruitment of littoral mussels in The Wash in the UK is explained as a consequence of the over-fishing of littoral stocks in the early 1990s (Dare *et al.* 2004). Irrespective of these details, there is no doubt that the mussel fishery played an important role in the disappearance of the inter-tidal mussel beds in the Dutch Wadden Sea, which was the primary cause of the decline in the number of wintering oystercatchers.

The relationship between the mussel fishery and Common Eiders is more complicated. Fishing pressure on sub-littoral mussels was high, but this does not prove that the mussel fishery was responsible for low stocks and thus for high mortality among Common Eiders. Culture lots are located in areas where natural recruitment of mussels is low, but where they grow and survive well (Bult *et al.* 2004). Transport of mussels to areas where they grow and survive better will increase the mussel stock, while transport from the culture lots in the Wadden Sea to culture lots in the Oosterschelde or to auction will decrease the mussel stock in the Wadden Sea. In the 1990s, the net effect of these opposing effects was probably positive. It has been estimated that the sub-littoral stock in the western Dutch Wadden

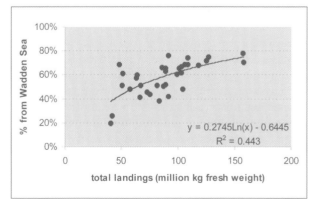

Fig. 6. Mussels landed from the Dutch Wadden Sea as a proportion of the total landings from Dutch waters, plotted against the total landings for the years 1970-2004. Each dot represents an entire season. Based on the data shown in Fig. 1.

**Table 2.** Estimates of the physiological food requirement and ecological food requirement of the Eurasian Oystercatcher *Haematopus ostralegus* (in kg wet flesh per bird per winter) at various locations with either mussels or cockles as the main winter food. The ratio between the ecological food requirement and the physiological food requirement is also given. The kg AFDM estimates of Goss-Custard *et al.* (2004) were transformed to kg wet flesh, assuming that 1 kg wet flesh corresponded to 0.1 g AFDM (Beukema & Cadée 1997).

| Study location | Prey species | Physiological food requirement | Ecological food requirement | Ratio | Source |
|---|---|---|---|---|---|
| Exe Estuary | mussel | 41 | 321 | 7.7 | Goss-Custard *et al.* (2004) |
| Bangor Flats | mussel | 41 | 263 | 6.4 | Goss-Custard *et al.* (2004) |
| Burry Inlet | cockle | 41 | 232 | 5.6 | Goss-Custard *et al.* (2004) |
| The Wash | cockle | 42 | 105 | 2.5 | Goss-Custard *et al.* (2004) |
| Baie de Somme | cockle | 35 | 174 | 5.0 | Goss-Custard *et al.* (2004) |
| Wadden Sea | cockle | 65 | 200 | 3.1 | Rappoldt *et al.* (2003a) |
| Oosterschelde | cockle | 60 | 150 | 2.5 | Rappoldt *et al.* (2003b) |

Sea was increased by an average of 15% during this period (Bult *et al.* 2004). However, if the transport of mussels from culture lots in the Wadden Sea to culture lots in the Oosterschelde is increased during years of scarcity, it is still possible that mussel culture actually decreases the stock during poor years. There is some evidence that this may actually happen, as the proportion of the landings that is obtained from the Wadden Sea is especially low during years of scarcity, i.e. when total landings are low (Fig. 6). A counter argument is that Bult *et al.* (2004) did not find a relationship between the amounts of mussels transported to the Oosterschelde and the total stock in the Wadden Sea on the basis of the reconstructed sub-littoral stocks. The problem with this argument is that the reconstruction assumes constant flows of mussels between culture lots in the Wadden Sea and Oosterschelde. Finally, apart from the possibility that the amounts transported increase during years of scarcity, there is also the possibility that sub-littoral stocks, like the littoral stocks, can be over-fished, thereby hampering recruitment.

### Policy of food reservation

The policy of food reservation that was part of the Sea and Coastal Fisheries Policy introduced in 1993 was specifically aimed at preventing additional food shortages for shellfish-eating birds in years of scarcity as a result of the shellfish fishery. Why did this policy fail? The simple answer is that insufficient amounts of food were reserved for the birds. A distinction must be made between the physiological food requirement and the ecological food requirement of a bird (Ens *et al.* 2004). The physiological food requirement is the total amount of food that an individual bird consumes during the winter to stay in good health. The ecological food requirement is the amount of food that must be present in the ecosystem at the start of winter so that the bird can satisfy its physiological food requirement during the course of winter. There are many reasons why the ecological food requirement is much higher than the physiological food requirement. In areas with high food stocks, interference between the birds sets a maximum limit to the level of exploitation. Furthermore, stocks cannot be exploited if shellfish size is too small, or stock density too low. Finally, even without bird predation, stocks decline in the course of winter due to mortality from other sources and individual shellfish losing body condition. The best data on the relationship between the physiological food requirement and the ecological food requirement are available for Eurasian Oystercatchers (Table 2). For

Oystercatcher populations that feed primarily on cockles, the ecological food requirement is between three and five times higher than the physiological food requirement. When mussels are the staple food, this ratio is even higher. Given the aim of the policy of food reservation, this policy should have been based on the ecological food requirement of the birds. Yet from its inception, the policy basically assumed that reserving food on the basis of the physiological food requirement would be sufficient. This assumption was criticized (Ens 2000), and some amendments were made following mass mortality of Common Eiders in the winters of 1999/2000 (Camphuysen *et al.* 2002) and 2001/2002 (Ens *et al.* 2002), making it more complicated but offering little improvement for the birds. In essence, policy makers continued to ignore the fact that a proper policy of food reservation should be based on the ecological food requirement. The new policy has abandoned food reservation as a management tool (LNV 2004). Whether this new policy offers sufficient protection for the birds remains to be seen.

### ACKNOWLEDGEMENTS

Without the persistent harassment and encouragement of Gerard Boere, this paper would not have been written.

### REFERENCES

Beukema, J.J. 1993. Increased mortality in alternative bivalve prey during a period when the tidal flats of the Dutch Wadden Sea were devoid of mussels. Netherlands Journal of Sea Research 31: 395-406.

Beukema, J.J. & Cadée, G.C. 1997. De voor winning beschikbare jaarlijkse schelpkalk-produktie door kokkels in de Nederlandse Waddenzee. Rijkswaterstaat, Directie Noord-Nederland, Leeuwarden, The Netherlands.

Brinkman, A.G. & Smaal, A.C. 2004. Onttrekking en natuurlijke produktie van schelpdieren in de Nederlandse Waddenzee in de periode 1976-1999. Alterra Report 888, Wageningen, The Netherlands.

Bult, T.P., van Stralen, M.R., Brummelhuis, E. & Baars, D. 2004. Eindrapport EVA II deelproject F4b (Evaluatie Schelpdiervisserij tweede fase): Mosselvisserij en -kweek in het sublitoraal van de Waddenzee. RIVO Report C049/04. RIVO, Yerseke, The Netherlands.

Camphuysen, C.J., Berrevoets, C.M., Cremers, H.J.W.M., Dekinga, A., Dekker, R., Ens, B.J., van der Have, T.M., Kats, R.K.H., Kuiken, T., Leopold, M.F., van der Meer, J. & Piersma, T. 2002. Mass mortality of common eiders (*Somateria mollissima*) in the Dutch Wadden Sea, winter 1999/2000: starvation in a commercially exploited wetland of international importance. Biological Conservation 106: 303-317.

Dankers, N.M.J.A., Meijboom, A., Cremer, J.S.M., Dijkman, E.M., Hermes, Y. & te Marvelde, L. 2003. Historische ontwikkeling van droogvallende mosselbanken in de Nederlandse Waddenzee. Alterra Report 876, Wageningen, The Netherlands.

Dare, P.J., Bell, M.C., Walker, P. & Bannister, R.C.A. 2004. Historical and current status of cockle and mussel stocks in The Wash. CEFAS Report, Lowestoft, UK.

Ens, B.J. 2000. Berekeningsmethodiek voedselreservering Waddenzee. Alterra Report 136, Wageningen, The Netherlands.

Ens, B.J. 2003. What we know and what we should know about mollusc fisheries and aquacultures in the Wadden Sea. In: W.J. Wolff, K. Essink, A. Kellerman & M.A. van Leeuwe (eds) Proceedings of the 10th International Scientific Wadden Sea Symposium, Ministerie van LNV, Den Haag, The Netherlands.

Ens, B.J. & Kats, R.K.H. 2004. Evaluatie van voedselreservering Eidereenden in de Waddenzee - rapportage in het kader van EVA II deelproject B2. Alterra Report 931, Wageningen, The Netherlands.

Ens, B.J., Borgsteede, F.H.M., Camphuysen, C.J., Dorrestein, G.M., Kats, R.K.H. & Leopold, M.F. 2002. Eidereendensterfte in de winter 2001/2002. Alterra Report 521, Wageningen, The Netherlands.

Ens, B.J., Smaal, A.C. & de Vlas, J. 2004. The effects of shellfish fishery on the ecosystems of the Dutch Wadden Sea and Oosterschelde. Final report on the second phase of the scientific evaluation of the Dutch shellfish fishery policy (EVA II). Alterra Report 1011; RIVO Report C056/04; RIKZ Report RKZ/2004.031. Alterra, Wageningen, The Netherlands.

Goss-Custard, J.D., Stillman, R.A., West, A.D., Caldow, R.W.G., Triplet, P., dit Durell, S.E.A.l.V. & McGrorty, S. 2004. When enough is not enough: shorebirds and shellfishing. Proceedings of the Royal Society of London, Series B - Biological Sciences 271: 233-237.

Kamermans, P., Bult, T., Kater, B.J., Baars, D., Kesteloo-Hendrikse, J.J., Perdon, J. & Schuiling, E. 2004. EVA II deelproject H4: Invloed van natuurlijke factoren en kokkelvisserij op de dynamiek van bestanden aan kokkels (*Cerastoderma edule*) en nonnen (*Macoma balthica*) in de Waddenzee, Ooster- en Westerschelde. RIVO Report C058/03, Yerseke, The Netherlands.

Leopold, M.F., Smit, C.J., Goedhart, P.W., van Roomen, M., van Winden, A.J. & van Turnhout, C. 2004. Langjarige trends in aantallen wadvogels, in relatie tot de kokkelvisserij en het gevoerde beleid in deze. Eindverslag EVA II (Evaluatie schelpdiervisserij tweede fase). Deelproject C2. Alterra Report 954; SOVON-onderzoeksrapport 2004/07. Alterra, Wageningen, The Netherlands.

LNV 2004. Ruimte voor een zilte oogst. Naar een omslag in de Nederlandse schelpdiercultuur. Beleidsbesluit Schelpdiervisserij 2005-2020. Ministerie LNV, Den Haag, The Netherlands.

Meijer, W., Lodders-Elfferich, P.C. & Hermans, L.M.L.H.A. 2004. Ruimte voor de Wadden. Eindrapport Adviesgroep Waddenzeebeleid. Adviesgroep Waddenzeebeleid, 's-Gravenhage, The Netherlands.

Piersma, T. & Koolhaas, A. 1997. Shorebirds, shellfish(eries) and sediments around Griend, western Wadden Sea, 1988 - 1996. NIOZ Report 1997 - 7. NIOZ, Den Burg, The Netherlands.

Piersma, T., Koolhaas, A., Dekinga, A., Beukema, J.J., Dekker, R. & Essink, K. 2001. Long-term indirect effects of mechanical cockle-dredging on intertidal bivalve stocks in the Wadden Sea. Journal of Applied Ecology 38: 976-990.

Rappoldt, C., Ens, B.J., Dijkman, E. & Bult, T. 2003a. Scholeksters en hun voedsel in de Waddenzee. Rapport voor deelproject B1 van EVA II, de tweede fase van het evaluatieonderzoek naar de effecten van schelpdiervisserij op natuurwaarden in de Waddenzee en Oosterschelde 1999-2003. Alterra Report 882, Wageningen, The Netherlands.

Rappoldt, C., Ens, B.J., Dijkman, E., Bult, T., Berrevoets, C.M. & Geurts van Kessel, J. 2003b. Scholeksters en hun voedsel in de Oosterschelde. Rapport voor deelproject D2 thema 1 van EVA II, de tweede fase van het evaluatieonderzoek naar de effecten van schelpdiervisserij op natuurwaarden in Waddenzee en Oosterschelde 1999-2003. Alterra Report 883, Wageningen, The Netherlands.

Smit, C.J., Dankers, N., Ens, B.J. & Meijboom, A. 1998. Birds, Mussels, Cockles and Shellfish Fishery in the Dutch Wadden Sea: How to Deal with Low Food Stocks for Eiders and Oystercatchers? Senckenbergiana maritima 29: 141-153.

Steins, N.A. 1999. Balancing fisheries and nature: Three case studies of fisheries co-management in the Dutch Wadden Sea. Centre for Coastal Zone Management.

van Gils, J.A., Piersma, T. & Spaans, B. 2004. Consequenties van schelpdiervisserij voor een kenmerkende predator, de kanoet *Calidris canutus*. Bijlage 2 bij Koninklijk NIOZ - intern rapport van Kraan et al. NIOZ, Den Burg, The Netherlands.

van Roomen, M., van Turnhout, C., van Winden, E., Koks, B., Goedhart, P.W., Leopold, M.F. & Smit, C.J. 2005. Trends van benthivore watervogels in de Nederlandse Waddenzee 1975-2002: grote verschillen tussen schelpdiereneters en wormeneters. Limosa 78: 21-38.

van Stralen, M.R. 2002. De ontwikkeling van mosselbestanden op droogvallende platen en in het sublitoraal van de Waddenzee vanaf 1955: een reconstructie op basis van gegevens uit de mosselzaadvisserij. MarinX Report 2001.10. MarinX, Scharendijke, The Netherlands.

Verbeeten, T.C.M. 1999. Wise use of the Wadden Sea? A study of policy-oriented learning (with a summary in English). Dissertation, University of Utrecht, The Netherlands.

Verschuuren, J.M. 2004. Juridische risicoanalyse 'Beleidsbesluit Schelpdiervisserij 2005-2020' met het oog op toetsing aan de Vogel- en Habitatrichtlijn. Rapport Centrum voor wetgevingsvraagstukken. Universiteit van Tilburg, Tilburg, The Netherlands.

# Managing shorebird flyways: shrimp aquaculture, shorebird populations and flyway integrity

*Yara Schaeffer-Novelli[1], Gilberto Cintrón-Molero[2] & Clemente Coelho, Jr.[3]*

*[1] BIOMA Lab, Associate Professor, Oceanographic Institute, University of São Paulo, Brazil. (email: novelliy@usp.br)*

*[2] U.S. Fish and Wildlife Service, Washington D.C., USA.*

*[3] BIOMA Lab Associate, Oceanographic Institute, University of São Paulo, Brazil.*

Schaeffer-Novelli, Y., Cintrón-Molero, G. & Coelho, C., Jr. 2006. Managing shorebird flyways: shrimp aquaculture, shorebird populations and flyway integrity. *Waterbirds around the world.* Eds. G.C. Boere, C.A. Galbraith & D.A. Stroud. The Stationery Office, Edinburgh, UK. pp. 812-816.

## ABSTRACT

Requirements for the conservation of shorebird habitat are changing as human use of coastal wetlands has shifted from traditional, low-level, resource-conservative patterns to intense "frontier-style" occupation and conversion. Within coastal wetlands, salt flats are being targeted for development because they are considered barren wastelands, are "non-mangrove", and are not protected by national legislation in most countries. In the Neotropics, the role of these wetlands as stopover sites for migratory shorebirds remains ignored or unknown by resource managers in most countries. We believe that increasing awareness is required to promote coordination efforts at regional and flyway level, to conserve these shorebird habitats and the potentially threatened migratory processes of these birds.

## INTRODUCTION

At a meeting of the International Wader Study Group (IWSG) in 2003, it was concluded that most species of shorebirds (waders) with known population trends were in decline all around the world, making this issue a matter of international conservation concern. Forty-eight percent of populations with known trends were found to be declining, in contrast to 16% which were increasing. The reasons for these declines were stated to be diverse and poorly understood (IWSG 2003). The IWSG was reluctant to state explicitly that there was a relationship between the decreasing shorebird populations and the considerable loss of coastal wetlands that had occurred as a result of recent human activities such as transformation of coastal wetlands for industrial aquaculture. Although the loss of mangroves and its resulting environmental effects have been well publicized and this awareness has triggered massive and effective conservation campaigns and conservation legislation, the loss of mangrove-associated salt flats remains unrecognized as a threat to coastal ecological processes including the long-distance migrations of shorebirds. Salt flats are extremely important components of stopover habitats for shorebirds in the Neotropics as elsewhere in the world. In this paper, we suggest that the declines of populations of shorebirds in the Western Hemisphere must be assessed in the context of the widespread loss of a naturally limited habitat (upper inter-tidal salt flats) and the exponential rate at which the remaining salt flats are being converted by a rapidly growing shrimp-farming industry on both the Pacific and Atlantic coasts of South America, as well as on the Pacific coast of Mexico and Central America. Salt flats are now, *de facto*, open-access areas into which anyone can encroach, or worse, are seen by governments as wastelands that should be reclaimed for the development of highly profitable activities.

Forty-nine species of shorebirds regularly breed in North America and undergo extraordinary migrations to wintering grounds as far south as the tip of South America (Tierra del Fuego). These birds migrate through some 13 countries in South America and seven in Central America. Many of these shorebird populations are showing significant decreases (Brown *et al.* 2001). Comprehensive management to ensure the survival of these species is made difficult by the fact that events occurring at migration stopover habitats are often unknown to resource managers and management agencies in the breeding grounds of the birds.

### Coastal wetlands: a resource of unknown extent

The extent of coastal wetlands in the Neotropics is poorly known. In general, it is estimated that coastal wetlands comprise less than 3% of the land surface of the Western Hemisphere (Bildstein *et al.* 1991). Large-scale development of coastal wetlands in the region is limited by physiographic and hydrological features to relatively few locations where tides and local hydrology act synergistically. Information on the extent of wetlands at a global scale has been found to be inadequate, but even the most basic information is not readily available for much of the Neotropics (Finlayson & Davidson 1999). Of even greater concern is that there is little agreement on what constitutes a wetland, and there are numerous gaps and inaccuracies in the information that is available. The resulting fundamental discrepancies in estimates of wetland cover and wetland type make the few existing estimates of dubious usefulness (Finlayson & Davidson 1999). Thus, too little information is available to make even an approximation of the current extent of coastal wetlands in the Neotropics, or to calculate the loss of habitat for migratory shorebirds on a regional basis.

Although salt flats are important elements of stopover habitats and constitute a significant feature of coastal seascapes in the Neotropics, they remain unrecognized as wetlands because they are frequently confused with dry, barren, non-tidal lands. The banded or zonal arrangement of associations inland from the sea or tidal channels is well recognized and described, but the hypersaline upper portions where high salinity is inimical to mangrove trees are mistakenly considered to be "bare" when, in fact, they maintain inconspicuous but important associations of epipelic (mud-living), tapetic (felt-forming) microorganisms. Although lacking above-ground vascular vegetation, the algal mats and bacterial films that grow on upper inter-tidal substrates are extraordinarily productive, and build up a complex and very rich trophic structure. Features such as salinas, albinas, coastal sabkhas or apicum-like structures are, in fact, productive marine depositional environments characterized by distinctive sediments (evaporitic mudflat facies, algal mats and mud-halite crusts) that reveal marine influence and origin (Gallaway & Hobday 1996). The sediment bacteria, including autotrophic cyanobacteria and chemo-autotrophs, are food sources for a diverse and rich invertebrate fauna, and this crustacean/molluscan-dominated assemblage in turn provides an abundant and reliable food source for shorebirds of the suborder Charadrii that use these "bare" flats as staging areas during their long-distance migrations. Plovers, sandpipers and some migratory waterfowl are the major and most conspicuous users of these habitats as food sources. Hypersaline flats are a dominant feature of low-gradient coastal landscapes where climatic and oceanographic conditions give rise to extreme aridity and prolonged droughts. Examples of coastlines dominated by salt flats are those of north-eastern Brazil on the Atlantic coast, and those of northern Peru (Tumbes), most of the Ecuadorian coast, Panama, the Gulf of Fonseca and western Mexico on the Pacific coast. These habitats, which are of high value for shorebirds, are not generally recognized as wetlands by resource managers; they have remained unreported in the few available wetland inventories, and remain unprotected by national legislation in most countries in the region.

### Industrial shrimp farming in the Western Hemisphere

Aquaculture is not a novel development in the Neotropics (the Incas practiced mariculture 500 years ago). However, shrimp farming on an industrial scale is a new development. This began in Ecuador in 1969 and has grown at a phenomenal rate of 10-30% per year in the last two decades, spreading rapidly to Peru, Panama, Mexico, Colombia and Central American countries during the 1980s. Industrial shrimp farming as practiced in the Western Hemisphere differs from that in Asia by being an export-oriented and industrial-scale activity since its establishment. This is significant because the impacts of industrialized activities, in terms of demand for conversion of natural wetlands and degradation of the surrounding areas, are greater than those of subsistence-level aquaculture. Industrial-scale aquaculture is characterized by extremely detrimental impacts in terms of demands for space, intensity of development and the magnitude of the transformation of the coastal landscape.

On a global scale, shrimp farming has transformed itself from a traditional, small-scale endeavor into a US$ 6 billion business with severe environmental repercussions for resources associated with coastal ecosystems. In 1995, aquaculture accounted for 30% of the total world shrimp production. If current trends continue, it will supply 50% of global demand by 2005 (the total world production of marine-farmed shrimps in 2001 was 1 270 875 MT). Much of the expansion required to meet the projected demand is expected to take place within Neotropical coastal wetlands, particularly in the remaining shorebird habitats in Central America, Mexico and Brazil. Brazil is projected to produce 160 000 MT by 2005: a 400% increase from the 2001 production level of 40 000 MT (Rocha 2004).

### METHODOLOGY

This paper was developed in an effort to evaluate a probable cause for the observed declines in shorebird populations in the Western Hemisphere despite increasing conservation efforts and increasing regulatory structures on the breeding grounds. We use the term "shorebird" to refer to birds of the Suborder Charadrii. The words "shrimp" and "prawn" are often used interchangeably in the literature. Here the term "shrimp" is used to refer to

**Table 1.** **Shrimp production in converted coastal wetlands (mangrove and salt-flat habitats) in Latin America in recent years.**

| Country | Marine farmed shrimp production (MT) | Coastal wetlands converted (ha) | Shrimp production ÷ coastal wetland area (MT/ha) |
|---|---|---|---|
| Ecuador (1996)[5] | 120 000 | 130 000 | 0.92 |
| Ecuador (1998)[1] | 130 000 | 200 000 | 0.65 |
| Ecuador (2001)[2] | 60 000 | 200 000 | 0.30 |
| Mexico (1998)[1] | 16 000 | 20 000 | 0.80 |
| Colombia (1998)[1] | 10 000 | 2 800 | 3.57 |
| Panama (1998)[1] | 7 500 | 5 500 | 1.36 |
| Peru (1996)[5] | 5 000 | 3 000 | 1.66 |
| Peru (1998)[1] | 6 000 | 3 200 | 1.88 |
| Nicaragua (1996)[5] | 3 000 | 4 000 | 0.75 |
| Nicaragua (1997)[6] | 4 000 | 5 000 | 0.80 |
| Brazil (1998)[1] | 4 000 | 4 000 | 1.00 |
| Brazil (2002)[2, 4] | 50 000-60 000 | 11 016 | 4.54-5.44 |
| Honduras (1996)[3] | 10 000 | 12 000 | 0.83 |
| Honduras (1998)[6] | 12 000 | 14 000 | 0.86 |

Sources: [1] Hinrischsen (1998); [2] FAO (2002); [3] Rosenberry (1996); [4] Rocha (2004); [5] World Bank *et al.* (2002); [6] Rodríguez & Windevoxhel (1998).

Peneaid or tropical marine shrimps. In the US market, "shrimp" is the usual name for marine shrimps, but the term "prawn" often refers to freshwater shrimps or to large saltwater shrimps.

Shrimp farms are preferably established on upper inter-tidal flats. Recent awareness of the need to conserve mangroves has driven most new pond construction into salt flats. Because of the lack of information on wetland transformation in the hemisphere, the rate at which coastal wetlands are being transformed was estimated indirectly from production and yield figures from various sources. For Latin America and the Caribbean, we used FAO shrimp aquaculture statistics for the period 1984-1995 (FAO 1997). For Brazil, we used a data set derived from various sources spanning the time period 1997-2003 (Hinrichsen 1998, World Bank *et al.* 2002, Rocha 2004, WRM 2004, FAO 2005). Because the reported yields per hectare for individual farms are highly variable, depending on farm management procedures, local conditions and the emergence of disease, we have chosen to use aggregate (country-level) production statistics to assess the space requirements of the industry. Estimates of the potential space requirements for pond complexes and the resulting annual loss of wetlands were based on three levels of aggregate yield: low yield (<1 MT/ha), medium yield (1-3 MT/ha) and high yield (>3 MT/ha). Yields lower than 0.5 MT/ha are considered to be below the profit threshold and were disregarded. Low yields reflect poor farm performance, unsuitability of environmental conditions or emergence of disease, whereas high yields reflect higher farm performance and adequate environmental subsidies but require larger investments and involve greater risks (Quarto 2004, WRM 2004).

### RESULTS

Shrimp production in Latin America was reported to be 146 000 MT in 1995, and the industry has shown a steady linear increase in production of approximately 10 000 MT per year since 1984 (FAO 2005). Production yields range from 0.65 to 4.50 MT/ha (Table 1). Based on reported production and production trend figures, the rate of conversion of salt-flat habitat is currently estimated to be in the range of about 4 000 ha/year (medium yield) to 10 000 ha/year (low yield). Medium yields are most likely to be the result of frequent disease outbreaks in all production areas, the large number of idle ponds (>20%) due to disease and environmental problems (such as El Niño events and other flood causes), and the need to clean and disinfect ponds regularly. Projections for the expansion of the industry in Brazil suggest that the rate of occupation of coastal wetlands (16 000 ha/year) will exceed by a factor of four the present estimate of the annual conversion rate based on recent production levels. This is because of the unrestricted growth of the industry in Brazil, driven by the current potential for expansion (availability of undeveloped salt flats) and government policies that support the occupation of up to 80% of tidal lands (Federal-level CONAMA Resolution No. 312/2002 and state-level subsidies).

The rate of occupation of coastal wetlands (mangrove/salt flat system) in Brazil is in an exponential growth phase ($Y = b_0 e^{.212}$; $r^2 = 0.984$). Making projections in aquaculture is particularly speculative because of the large number of factors that influence production and demand. However, applying the exponential model described above projects a requirement of salt flats ranging from 37 000 to 55 000 ha by the year 2010. The actual rate of occupation may be much greater than this because of land speculation and the tendency to seize the most accessible sites as rapidly as possible.

Brazil's plans for the development of aquaculture are extremely optimistic. Of Brazil's 16 coastal states, nine north-northeastern states have moderate salt flat/apicum development. The area of salt flats in north-eastern Brazil with potential for transformation into shrimp ponds has been estimated by the industry to be 350 000 ha, but the basis for this estimate is unknown. Government agencies have not carried out an inventory of coastal resources to assess the potential for sustainable expansion or for potential resource allocation. Although Brazil has a National Coastal Zone Management Plan (PNGC), this has yet to be implemented. New areas are being explored and opened up for production along the northern coastline of Brazil, where local governments consider that they have been left out of the "Blue Revolution" in aquaculture that has taken place elsewhere. The coast of north-central Brazil, between Belém (Pará State) and São Luiz (Maranhão State), stands out as one of the most spectacular areas in the Western Hemisphere, in terms of its importance for migratory shorebirds. This coastal segment contains the "Reentrâncias Maranhenses", a geomorphologically diverse landscape that comprises 2 680 911 ha, of which 1 775 036 ha have been designated as a Western Hemisphere Shorebird Reserve Network (WHSRN) site and a Ramsar site.

### DISCUSSION

Currently one of the greatest obstacles to the protection of shorebird habitat in the Western Hemisphere is the lack of explicit national legislation throughout the hemisphere to protect salt flats, even if these are ecologically a part of mangrove ecosystems and functional elements of coastal wetlands (Box 1). Regrettably, the returns brought by the "Pink Gold" economic growth in many of the hemisphere's developing nations have been invested in further exploitation of the remaining natural resources, rather than in increasing efforts to develop means to manage the residual coastal systems on a sustainable basis to ensure delivery of ecological services and food security for coastal populations.

The Neotropical Realm of Central America, the Caribbean and South America was, until recently, one of the least disturbed and most biologically rich of the Earth's biogeographical regions. Coastal wetlands, in particular, remained relatively undisturbed. The emergence of industrial-scale shrimp farming has now changed this because of its aggressive expansion and the fact that shrimp aquaculture in the region is embedded in a governance context which is extremely frail and generally incapable of developing strong policies to protect valuable resources. Regional and international funding and development agencies (the World Bank, the Interamerican Development Bank and the U.S. Agency for International Development in Central America) have fueled the growth of aquaculture despite its negative environmental and social impacts. This points towards the need for changes in the operational policies for development lending. Throughout the Neotropics, government and state-level policies support perverse subsidies and prescribed plans of actions that promote escalating coastal degradation in support of industrial-scale aquaculture and coastal development.

The impacts of shrimp monoculture on coastal wetlands are unambiguous. The occupation of coastal habitats takes place on a landscape scale, and involves extreme hydrological and topographical transformation. For instance, Ecuador lost half of its

## Box 1. Summary of findings and conclusions.

1) Aquaculture is a significant threat to shorebird populations on both the Atlantic and Pacific flyways in the Western Hemisphere. High rates of habitat conversion are taking place despite total ignorance of the extent of the remaining habitat.

2) Salt flats must be considered as an intrinsic part of coastal wetland ecosystems. They are ecologically important habitats that support migratory shorebirds as well as coastal processes which provide key services including maintenance of local fisheries that contribute to food security. Resource managers must consider coastal wetlands as a functional whole that includes all inter-tidal habitats such as mangroves, salt flats and mudflats.

3) Shorebird conservation is given little priority in most Western Hemisphere countries. High-value habitats such as salt flats are not considered to be wetlands and remain unreported in wetland inventories and unprotected by legislation in most countries. Salt flats are, *de facto*, open-access areas into which anyone can encroach, or worse, are seen by governments as wastelands that should be reclaimed for development of highly profitable activities.

4) Although the exact extent of the resource is unknown, it is being allocated without consideration of quantity, quality or ecological function. The role of these wetlands as stopover sites for migratory birds remains ignored or unknown by resource managers in the region.

5) Shorebird population levels should be seen as indicators of coastal wetland health. Decreasing populations are the result of transformation and degradation of habitats.

6) The greatest obstacle to the protection of shorebird habitat is the lack of national legislation throughout the Neotropical region to protect salt flats, even when these are a functional part of mangrove ecosystems.

7) Industrial aquaculture should be relocated away from ecologically important wetlands such as mangroves and salt flats.

8) Development organizations, such as the World Bank and the Interamerican Development Bank, must be alerted to the impacts of their lending policies on salt-flat conversion and migratory shorebirds. Shorebirds have the potential to be used as indicators of the functional integrity of coastal wetlands that is required to meet the "Millennium Development" (MD) goals and targets agreed by most countries in the region.

9) Unless extraordinary measures are taken, unrestricted free trade agreements within the region, operating without strict environmental safeguards, could fuel further degradation and destruction of stopover habitats for shorebirds.

10) Shorebird conservation must be seen as an essential component of coastal resource and biodiversity conservation to support integrated coastal zone management and sustainable fisheries.

mangrove forests in the last two decades (Lacerda *et al.* 2002) and 77% of its salt flats (c. 4 000 ha/year of c. 66 000 ha) in the last fifteen years (Southgate 1992). In Honduras, a significant increase in shrimp farming is destroying important coastal wetlands and polluting coastal waters. Even a Ramsar site (No. 1000) in Honduras has been invaded by shrimp farms (Lal 2002). The government continues to encourage further development, although it is estimated that over 280 km$^2$ of shrimp farms have been developed in a region which USAID has estimated could support a maximum of only 200 km$^2$ (NAWCC 1993). Whereas in most of the Western Hemisphere the growth of industrial aquaculture faces a number of constraints such as diminishing space (most salt flats being already occupied), frequent and severe outbreaks of disease and increasing local community awareness and resistance to further development, in north-eastern Brazil, investors have found favorable conditions that include resource availability (large areas for development) and government policies that subsidize occupation and transformation of salt flats.

The increasing proliferation of shrimp aquaculture is evident in satellite images of the coast of northern Peru, Ecuador, Central America (Gulf of Fonseca) and the northern and north-eastern coastal states of Brazil. International agreements such as the Ramsar Convention have proven unable to limit the large-scale conversion of salt flats despite resolutions expressing concern for such conversion (Ramsar Resolution VII. 21) and the pledge of Contracting Parties to conserve the ecological character of designated wetlands.

## CONCLUSION

Although the loss of mangrove ecosystems and resultant environmental effects have been well publicized, the potential impact of the loss and degradation of bare salt flats in the upper inter-tidal zone on shorebirds has been largely disregarded, even though this may threaten flyway phenomena at hemispheric level. The loss of these salt flats now constitutes the greatest threat to the conservation of entire populations of shorebirds in the region because of its scale and the high rates of conversion. Shorebirds have the potential to be used as indicators of the functional integrity of coastal wetlands within the region, and shorebird conservation must be seen as an integral part of coastal resource and biodiversity conservation to support sustainable fisheries.

Unless extraordinary measures are taken, unrestricted free trade agreements within the region, without strict environmental safeguards, could encourage further conversion and loss of stopover habitats for shorebirds on a regional scale. The loss or alteration of even small areas may be critical because of the degree to which migratory shorebirds concentrate at particular sites. Regrettably, shorebird conservation now has little priority for most countries in the Western Hemisphere. However, coastal wetlands, including mangroves and salt flats, are important productive units that support local fisheries, and are also a source of food for large segments of coastal communities. Furthermore, it is a requirement of the "Millennium Development" goals and targets agreed by most countries in the region that the ecological integrity of these coastal wetlands be safeguarded by 2015.

Shorebirds, because of their "flagship" status, could be used as indicators of the ecological integrity of these coastal systems, as well as a tool to promote shrimp production under more environmentally and socially acceptable conditions, if it were made possible to differentiate these products in the market (shrimps that were not grown in converted inter-tidal zones). Ironically, farmed shrimp is now sold in the USA as "turtle safe" because it is not trawled and does not endanger sea turtles, but consumers are unaware of how environmentally unfriendly these farmed shrimp are, particularly for shorebirds. We trust that increasing awareness will promote efforts at both regional and flyway level to conserve these important shorebird habitats and thereby help to safeguard migratory shorebird populations throughout the hemisphere.

## ACKNOWLEDGEMENTS

Many of the ideas presented here originated from a brain-storming workshop on the issue of shrimp farming, coastal environments and migratory bird conservation sponsored by the U.S. Fish and Wildlife Service, the U.S. Environmental Protection Agency and the BIOMA Laboratory at the University of São Paulo, Brazil. Significant contributions were made by officials in the Brazilian Federal Prosecutor Office while sharing their legal and environmental concerns regarding this topic. Dr Liette Vasseur (Universite de Moncton, Canada) provided valuable insights based on her experience in Asia. Wetlands International and Wetlands International/US supported this activity directly or indirectly by providing support to the authors to participate in the 27th Annual Meeting of the Waterbird Society's "Wetland Conservation and Aquaculture" Workshop held in Cuiabá, Brazil, in 2003. Drs Frank Rivera assisted with the statistical analysis of the data and Melanie Steinkamp made substantive contributions throughout the preparation of the manuscript. To our colleagues at the BIOMA Lab, we are grateful for their constant encouragement and enthusiastic support.

## REFERENCES

**Bildstein, L.B., Bancroft, G.T., Dugan, P.J., Gordon, D.H., Erwin, R.M., Nol, E., Payne, L.X. & Senner, S.E.** 1991. Approaches to the conservation of coastal wetlands in the Western Hemisphere. Wilson Bulletin 103 (2): 218-254.

**Brown, S., Hickey, C., Harrington, B. & Gill, R.** (eds). 2001. United States Shorebird Conservation Plan. Second Edition. Manomet Center for Conservation Sciences, Manomet, Massachussetts.

**FAO – United Nations Food and Agriculture Organization** 1997. Review of the state of World Aquaculture. FAO Fisheries Circular No. 886, Rev. 1. FAO, Rome.

**FAO – United Nations Food and Agriculture Organization** 2005. World Mangrove Atlas. In press. http://www.fao.org/forestry/foris/webview/forestry2.

**Finlayson, C.M. & Davidson, N.C.** (eds). 1999. Global review of wetland resources and priorities for wetland inven-tory: summary report. Report to the Ramsar Bureau from Wetlands International, Wageningen, The Netherlands, & the Environmental Research Institute of the Supervising Scientist, Jabiru, Australia. Wetlands International and the Ramsar Bureau.

**Gallaway, W.E. & Hobday, D.K.** 1996. Terrigenous clastic depositional systems. Springer-Verlag, Berlin.

**Hinrischsen, D.** 1998. Coastal waters of the world: trends, threats and strategies. Island Press.

**IWSG – International Wader Study Group** 2003. Waders are declining worldwide. Conclusions from the 2003 International Wader Study Group Conference, Cadiz, Spain. Wader Study Group Bulletin 101/102: 8-12.

**Lacerda, L.D., Conde, J.E., Kjerve, B., Álvarez-León, R., Alarcón, C. & Polanía, J.** 2002. American mangroves. In: L.D. Lacerda (ed) Mangrove Ecosystems, Function and Management. Springer-Verlag, Berlin.

**Lal, P.N.** 2002. Integrated and adaptive mangrove management framework – an action oriented option for the New Millennium. In: L.D. Lacerda (ed) Mangrove Ecosystems, Function and Management. Springer-Verlag, Berlin.

**NAWCC – North American Wetland Conservation Council** 1993. Wetland conservation in Central America. Report 93-3, North American Wetland Conservation Council (Canada). Ottawa, Canada.

**Quarto, A.** 2004. Shrimp farms not for the birds. Earth Island Institute, Autumn 2004, 19(3).

**Rocha, I.** 2004. Advantages and constraints of the Brazilian fishing industry. In: FAO Report of the Expert Consultation of International Fish Trade. Rio de Janeiro, Brazil, 3-5 December 2003. FAO Fisheries Report No. 744. FAO, Rome.

**Rodríguez, J.J. & Windevoxhel, N.J.** 1998. Análisis regional de la situación de la zona maritima costera centroameri-cana. IUCN 10/98, ENV-121, En, Es.

**Rosenberry, B.** 1996. World shrimp farming 1996. Shrimp News International, San Diego, California.

**Southgate, D.** 1992. Shrimp mariculture development in Ecuador: some policy issues. Working Paper No. 15. USAID EPAT/MUSIA – Research Training. University of Wisconsin, Madison, Wisconsin.

**World Bank, NACA, WWF & FAO** 2002. Shrimp farming and the environment. A World Bank, NACA, WWF and FAO Consortium Program "To analyze and share experiences on the better management of shrimp aquaculture in coastal areas". Synthesis report. Work in Progress for Public Discussion. Published by the Consortium.

**WRM – World Rainforest Movement** 2004. Brazil: mangrove ecosystems turned into shrimp aquaculture ponds. WRM Bulletin 84.

# Waterbirds and aviation: how to mediate between conservation and flight safety?

*Luit Buurma*

*Honorary Vice Chairman, International Bird Strike Committee, 'de Olmenhorst', Lisserweg 493, 2165 AS Lisserbroek, The Netherlands. (email: LuitBuurma@worldmail.nl)*

Buurma, L. 2006. Waterbirds and aviation: how to mediate between conservation and flight safety? *Waterbirds around the world.* Eds. G.C. Boere, C.A. Galbraith & D.A. Stroud. The Stationery Office, Edinburgh, UK. pp. 817-821.

## ABSTRACT

Waterbirds contribute disproportionately to the problem of collisions between aircraft and birds. World-wide, civil airlines suffer an annual loss of several billion US dollars. Certain waterbird species, especially some geese, have adapted very well to man-modified landscapes, even to the level of becoming pests. Furthermore, many airports have been located in relatively cheap wetland areas, asking for bird problems. The International Civil Aviation Organization has recently upgraded its recommendations on the prevention of bird strikes into standards. This paper briefly explores the phrasing of some of the new standards, and emphasizes the need to develop best practice, especially with respect to wildlife control in the vicinity of airports. It is a plea for the co-operation of good hunters and realistic scientists, and emphasises the need to focus on the study of bird migration and local flight behaviour near airports. In particular, studies of the evasive manoeuvring of birds in response to approaching aircraft, as well as to hunters, might help to mediate between conservation and flight safety.

## BIRD STRIKES: THE SIZE OF THE PROBLEM

Collisions between aircraft and birds have occurred ever since the first powered flights of man. However, only during the past decade has it become clear that the number of reported strikes is just the proverbial tip of the iceberg. Furthermore, quieter aircraft, increasing numbers of birds weighing over four pounds (1.8 kg) and tougher safety regulations could transform the bird strike problem into a major issue, especially where airports adjoin nature reserves, particularly wetland sites. Strategic alliances with local conservationists provide a solution.

The historical record of bird strikes in civil aviation world-wide documents the loss of 80 aircraft and 231 lives (Thorpe

Gulls taking of from the runway of Woensdrecht air force base, as regularly observed from the cockpit.

2003). Indicative of the huge number of military aircraft written-off is a recent overview by Richardson & West (2005) of 110 aircraft lost by Britain's Royal Air Force during the period 1923-2004. Sixty-three of the write-offs were in the UK, the others elsewhere. The majority of bird strikes, however, have not been recognized or reported.

The truth of the problem, as old as aviation itself, is now becoming clearer. A recent estimate of the world-wide costs due to collisions between large civil transport aircraft and birds amounts to US$ 1.0-1.5 billion annually (Allan 2003). Allan made his estimate with the help of two major U.S. carriers who could not be identified for commercial reasons. The basis of the estimate was a one-year data set of 1 326 "routine bird strikes" from only one company, and without major engine write-offs or hull losses. Consequently, Allan (2003) emphasises that his estimate is probably conservative. Costs due to delay and cancellation were about seven times higher than the costs of repairing damage. Updated estimates using a three-year data set from the same company show the estimate to be broadly consistent from year to year. Pilots report only 20% of the number of collisions based on comparisons with bird remains collected from the runway. Off-airport bird strikes might also be overlooked. In the case of damage to engines, recognizing and identifying bird remains may only be possible with microscopic or DNA analysis, further hampering data collection.

This paper explores some of the consequences of the new and much stronger, but as yet not very clearly explained, safety regulations ratified by the world community (ICAO 2003) that force the conservation movement to join the debate on planning and management of wetlands near airports.

## NEW ICAO STANDARDS ON PREVENTION OF BIRD STRIKES

The International Civil Aviation Organization (ICAO) was established in 1944 by 54 nations with the aim of assuring the safe, orderly and economic development of international air transport. This specialized agency of the United Nations now has 189 participating States, and has grown into a very influential regulator that also deals with environmental protection. The ICAO has recognized the need to raise awareness of the bird strike issue and to understand the true size and nature of the problem. In order to initiate an airport bird-control certification process, three recommendations of ICAO's Annex 14 were recently upgraded into standards (ICAO 2003). Chapter 9.5.1. of Aerodromes Volume I (modified on 27 November 2003) now reads as follows: "The bird strike hazard on, or in the vicinity of, an aerodrome shall be assessed through: a) the establishment of a national procedure for recording and reporting bird strikes to aircraft; and b) the collection of information from aircraft operators, airport personnel, etc., on the presence of birds on or around the aerodrome constituting a potential hazard to aircraft operations."

The ICAO realized, of course, that the bird strike problem would not be solved simply by order. Although there is an ICAO Bird Strike Information System (IBIS) to which reports of bird strikes should be forwarded, international reporting is not yet mandatory. It is left to the national authorities to develop their own procedures.

A small proportion of the bird corpses found on runways have been shown to be slipstream victims that did not hit the aircraft at all. A greater part of the killed birds grazed against the

Canada Goose *Branta candensis* family intruding into a Dutch airport.

A Common Goldeneye *Bucephala clangula* damaged the wing of this small airplane above California.

fuselage, only leaving a small smear of blood for those keen to find it, and a thud mostly passing unnoticed in the cockpit. Then, there is a whole array of incidents from a minuscule dent in the aircraft skin through a crack in a window to an obvious hole in the leading edge of the wing. In these cases, the aircraft is usually still perfectly able to fly, but when noticed in flight, the incident may create doubts about what to do or whether or not to turn back. Later on, it is very tempting to ignore a small dent in order to avoid the potential accumulation of delay costs. Ultimately, it is the engineer who signs off the aircraft as fit to fly, but this person might miss the incident. An internal cockpit or company dispute about what to do and whether or not to report the incident can be avoided by more refinement in the safety regulations. It is, of course, the task of the aviation industry to solve this, but the ICAO can help to create a platform for developing internationally agreed procedures.

The definition of a bird strike is simple: any physical contact between a bird and an aeroplane on the move. However, a majority of these strikes do not damage the fuselage or engine, while bird remains may be almost invisible to the non-specialist. Consequently, improving the prevention of bird strikes mostly results in an initial increase in the bird strike rate because of better reporting. The less diligent air companies and airports may show a low record of bird strikes, if judged superficially, until a serious accident alerts the aviation community. Openly reporting on bird strike statistics, especially occurrences, is a difficult as well as a delicate matter, often creating confusion if not undeserved blame.

Who is making the difference between "blame-free reporting" and "naming and blaming"? A few centimetres can make the difference between a blood smear and a fatal accident (seen from the human point of view; the birds will always die). Reporting procedures should therefore be depersonalised and dedicated to safety improvement only. Due to their stochastic nature, all bird strikes, occurrences as well as incidents (thus irrespective of damage), can and should be used in the analysis. Blameworthy human behaviour can easily be separated from the open debate on bird strike statistics.

Assessing the severity of the bird strike is the key for deciding what type of bird presence should be considered as a potential hazard to aircraft operations. Again, this cannot be answered by the ICAO. While the definition of the different classes of bird strikes can (and should) be solved globally, the evaluation of bird presence on and around the aerodrome needs the involvement of local bird expertise. Birds will always seek new ways for survival. They vary geographically in ecology and behaviour, not only between but also within species. Consequently, even local flight behaviours are very diverse as the birds try to adapt to the predictability of a certain airport and its environment. Understanding this behaviour implies the need for an interest in the life strategies of the birds, which often does not parallel the obvious safety obligation to harass or even kill them. Only when good hunters and responsible ornithologists are brought together might the gap between theory and practice be closed.

## LAW OF DIMINISHING RETURNS

Airport managers often tend to underestimate the difficulties that have to be faced when setting up a sound bird-control programme. This is partly understandable, as the law of diminishing returns is clearly applicable here. Making an airport unattractive for large concentrations of birds and scaring away flocks of birds that nevertheless visit the runway do not seem to require high skills, but predicting the emergence of new problems may require considerably larger sums of money. The cost effectiveness of these investments is not yet clear, but a wide variety of measures indicating state-of-the-art practice can be found in the industry guide "Sharing the Skies" (Transport Canada 2001).

However, the story does not end here. It does not require a great imagination to understand the risks involved in building an airport besides a bird sanctuary or flying at low altitude over a nearby area with a high concentration of birds. However, many airports have not been very well located with respect to local bird flight-lines. In the past, potential bird problems were often not considered because of economic priorities or lack of knowledge about local bird movements. With the considerable improvement in safety regulations, existing airports are now forced to reconsider their bird strike prevention policy. This certainly requires clear management commitment, not only because relatively high costs in relation to relatively low rewards might be involved, but also because the image of the airport is at stake with respect to safety and environmental responsibility.

With the recent change in ICAO regulations, countries are now required to contribute to an improvement in the general level of flight safety by re-evaluating their national procedures for prevention of bird strikes. The gap between current practice and state-of-the-art practice provides governments with the opportunity to allow their aviation sectors to choose between taking a role as a pioneer or fighting a rear-guard action. Ultimately, however, the overall safety level will be above, between or below an internationally agreed upper and lower threshold. As yet, nobody has succeeded in quantifying these levels very precisely. Consequently, no airport should relax. But safe and rich aerodromes might consider the possibility of "adopting" an unlucky and poor airport. Spending a dollar on bird strike prevention in Africa will certainly create more safety than spending a dollar in the USA or Western Europe. As passengers expect the same level of safety at both ends of their flight, they might appreciate such "safety help agreements" and credit in one way or another the donor airport and/or air carrier.

### FLIGHT SAFETY VERSUS NATURE CONSERVATION?

While expressing extreme concern for the future of many shorebird species, the Edinburgh Conference has also drawn attention to a number of conflict situations that have arisen because of the superabundance of some waterbird species, notably certain species of geese. Superabundance indicates that the ecosystem is out of balance as a result of human interference. While biodiversity as a whole is threatened, certain species turn into pests. The only way out of these human-induced problems is through a combination of applied and fundamental scientific research.

The most controversial issue in the debate is the application of the shotgun. A shot bird cannot, of course, collide with an aircraft anymore, but simply reducing bird numbers is only effective very locally and for a short period of time. Attempting to widen a culling zone beyond the periphery of the runway will create an empty space which attracts new birds. Moreover, these newcomers are not yet adapted to aircraft movements, and might pose a greater risk than the local population. Many bird

controllers agree that bird-scaring is more effective than killing. However, they also agree that shooting a flock member from time to time helps to reinforce the non-lethal scaring. Finding the balance between "zero tolerance" (at or near the runway) and "optimal scaring" (from intense scaring near the runway to mild scaring far away) is a delicate matter. Dolbeer *et al.* (2003) showed that the scaring effect of a very large shooting programme at John F. Kennedy International Airport, New York, was about four times more effective than the simple reduction in numbers of Laughing Gulls *Larus atricilla*. Wild birds cannot be controlled fully and consequently absolute rules do not exist. This may open up a complicated liability debate in the case of a serious bird strike. A more scientific evaluation of the effect of shooting and scaring is urgently needed. Modelling bird behaviour will help to judge the quality of the bird control programme.

The deeper philosophical challenge is how to deal with almost opposing forces: the wish to maximize profits by developing and exploiting natural resources versus bird conservation and the wish to secure wetlands from reclamation. Safety is a tangible field of mediation here. However, profit/safety dilemmas very often end up in conflicts between market-oriented and science-oriented groups. In the case of the bird strike issue, the key problem is how to deal with flocks of birds flying over the aerodrome from somewhere in the airport vicinity. It is relatively easy to monitor and predict the commuting flights of large gregarious birds such as wintering geese. However, the introduction of a warning system for flocks of swifts feeding on insects above the runways in summer, although scientifically feasible, will not be easy. Even hardliners in aviation are now beginning to understand that it is necessary to accept and pay for a model of local goose movements, but very few aviators see the need to develop and finance systems that will facilitate avoidance of the smaller bird species.

### LOCAL EXPERTISE WITH BIRD BEHAVIOUR IS CRUCIAL

Recent research shows that many birds successfully avoid aircraft. Given the frontal area of aircraft and the numbers of birds in the air, as determined by radar studies in The Netherlands, the number of bird strikes is much lower than expected. A research team led by Dr Tom Kelly in Ireland has very nicely described the flight performance of Rooks *Corvus frugilegus* and Wood Pigeons *Columba palumbus* in response to approaching aircraft (Kelly *et al.* 1999). The avoidance reactions explain why quieter aircraft hit more birds. Together, the Irish and Dutch observations strongly emphasise the need for more research on evasive behaviour. Can we stimulate the birds to start their escape manoeuvres earlier by giving them the appropriate signals, and can we determine the responses of different bird species according to their age class, condition and local experience, as well as the influence of different weather and environmental factors on the birds flying behaviour? Several observations indicate that the answer to these questions is at least partially yes.

To date, the aviation industry has not recognized the relevance of this work and the need to give it substantial support. Indeed, we have a long way to go before we can speak the language of birds in flight. The conservation problem may be a short-term trigger. The new standard 9.5.3. in Annex 14 reads as follows: "When a bird strike hazard is identified at an aerodrome, the appropriate authority shall take action to decrease the number of birds constituting a potential hazard to aircraft operations by adopting measures for discouraging their presence on, or in the vicinity of, an aerodrome."

Many countries have conflicting laws for aviation and bird conservation which present problems to the authority responsible for the management of a nature reserve in the vicinity of an airport. Decreasing the number of birds may be the exact opposite of the primary aim of the management authority. Understandably, this authority will question the supposed hazard caused by protected birds at the nearby airport if their threat to aircraft operations is not very clear. Simultaneously, at the airport, the bird control unit will tend to maintain a policy of zero tolerance. This might result in the bizarre situation in which ducks sitting on the airport side of a border ditch will be shot while their fellows on the other side may sleep peacefully. Draconian legal subtleties can be avoided by relying upon the third new standard 9.5.4.: "The appropriate authority shall take action to eliminate or to prevent the establishment of garbage disposal dumps or any such other source attracting bird activity on, or in the vicinity of, an aerodrome unless an appropriate aeronautical study indicates that they are unlikely to create conditions conducive to a bird hazard problem."

By focussing on garbage dumps, the ICAO apparently starts with an emphasis on birds that make a living from human waste. We could rank birds from nutrient-rich water bodies, heavily fertilized grassland and certain arable fields in the same category. It is possible that these individuals have adopted a way of life that makes them more accident prone, or their offspring find it easier to invade the airfield niche while showing less fear of aircraft. This effect has yet to be proven, and if it exists, it is certain that it will be only partially true.

## MODELLING LOCAL BIRD FLIGHT PATTERNS

Conservationists might be able to obtain support for their cause if they could conduct an aeronautical study which demonstrated that most bird species and individuals are unlikely to create a bird hazard problem. To formulate this more precisely: such a study might reveal that even at a fairly limited distance from the runway and aircraft flight paths, the flight activity of birds from a local source does not significantly exceed the average level of bird flight activity measured over a much larger area. It might also reveal that only certain individuals develop a dangerous flight behaviour which could be eliminated or selectively brought under control. However, in coastal zones and wetland regions in particular, local bird flight-lines may cover tens of kilometres, while bird migration may become intensified at certain times of the year, thus creating a danger that can only be coped with by adapting operations.

The type of study needed implies the application of sophisticated detection and tracking equipment such as radar (Buurma & Bruderer 1990, Walls 2005) or devices carried by individual birds. Monitoring the behaviour of the birds at very small scale (near departing and arriving aircraft) as well as at larger scales (local movements and migration) appears to be very promising. This type of research will not only bring safety-minded and conservation-minded people together on speaking terms, but will also stimulate the development of affordable warning systems to improve local bird control. Ultimately, these technical improvements might also enhance conservation by contributing to the understanding of bird mobility from local to global scale (Leshem *et al.* 2001).

## ACKNOWLEDGEMENTS

I would like to thank Richard Dolbeer, Derek Scott, John Thorpe, John Allan, Anastasios Anagnostopoulos and an anonymous reviewer for improvements of this text which remains a reflection of my personal views.

## REFERENCES

**Allan, J.** 2003. http://www.aphis.usda.gov/ws/nwrc/symposia/economics/.

**Buurma, L.S. & Bruderer, B.** 1990. The application of radar for bird strike prevention. Proceedings of the Bird Strike Committee Europe 20: 373-445, Helsinki.

**Dolbeer, R.A., Chipman, R.B., Gosser, A.L. & Barras, S.C.** 2003. Does shooting alter flight patterns of gulls: case study at John F. Kennedy International Airport. Proceedings of the International Bird Strike Committee 26, Vol. II: 547-562, Warsaw. http:// www.int-bird-strike.com.

**ICAO** 2003. Annex 14, Aerodromes Vol. I. http://www.icao.int.

**Kelly, T.C., O'Callaghan, M.J.A. & Bolger, R.** 1999. The avoidance behaviour shown by the rook (*Corvus frugilegus*) to commercial aircraft. Proceedings of the Second European Vertebrate Pest Management Conference, Braunschweig, Germany.

**Leshem, Y., Froneman, A., Mundy, P. & Shamir, H.** 2001. Wings over Africa. Proceedings of the international seminar on bird migration, research, conservation and flight safety, Tel-Aviv.

**Richardson, W.J. & West, T.** 2005. Serious birdstrike accidents to U.K. military aircraft, 1923 to 2004: numbers and circumstances. Proceedings of the 27th World Conference of the International Bird Strike Committee, Athens. http:// www.int-birdstrike.com.

**Thorpe, J.** 2003. Fatalities and destroyed civil aircraft due to bird strikes, 1912-2002. Proceedings of the 26th World Conference of the International Bird Strike Committee, Vol. I: 85-113, Warsaw. http:// www.int-birdstrike.com.

**Transport Canada** 2001. Sharing the Skies, An Aviation Industry Guide to the Management of Wildlife Hazards. http:// www.tc.gc.ca/aviation.

**Walls, R.** 2005. Monitoring avian movement using bird detection radar; impacts of nocturnal movement on flight safety at a military aerodrome. http:// www.int-bird-strike.com.

## POSTSCRIPT

The International Bird Strike Committee (IBSC) offers a platform for the exchange of local experiences and the development of global guidelines. Through the integration of theory and practice and the involvement of all relevant disciplines, best practices will emerge. Participation of representatives from aviation as well as the conservation side is encouraged at the world conferences. Further details and a large amount of "grey literature" can be found at http://www.int-birdstrike.com. Given the new ICAO policy, a number of controversial issues will be identified. Anyone wishing to discuss general bird strike matters and the constitutional consequences for IBSC is welcome to contact the author at luitbuurma@worldmail.nl.

# Recent measures to control Ruddy Ducks *Oxyura jamaicensis* in the United Kingdom

*Iain S. Henderson*

*Central Science Laboratory, York, YO41 1LZ, UK. (email: i.henderson@csl.gov.uk)*

Henderson, I.S. 2006. Recent measures to control Ruddy Ducks *Oxyura jamaicensis* in the United Kingdom. *Waterbirds around the world.* Eds. G.C. Boere, C.A. Galbraith & D.A. Stroud. The Stationery Office, Edinburgh, UK. pp. 822-825.

## ABSTRACT

The Ruddy Duck *Oxyura jamaicensis* is a native of the Americas, but was introduced to wildfowl collections in the UK in the 1940s. Following escapes, Ruddy Ducks became established in the UK, and by 2000, there was an estimated feral population of c. 6 000 birds. As the feral population in the UK increased, so did the number of records in mainland Europe. Hybridization in Spain between the globally-threatened White-headed Duck *Oxyura leucocephala* and Ruddy Ducks, presumably originating from the UK, was first recorded in 1991, and this is now regarded as the greatest threat to the long-term survival of the White-headed Duck. The UK Government began research into Ruddy Duck control in 1994, and further research was undertaken between 1999 and 2002 and in 2003/2004. A total of 4 332 Ruddy Ducks have been culled since 1999. Between February 2003 and February 2004, numbers nationally were reduced by almost 20%, and regional reductions of up to 70% have been achieved annually with limited manpower. Shooting, particularly of large winter flocks, has proved to be the most effective method of control. Modelling suggests that the UK population could be reduced to less than 50 birds within five years if eight full-time staff were available to carry out control in all seasons.

## INTRODUCTION

The Ruddy Duck *Oxyura jamaicensis* is a native of the Americas and is common in its native range, with a stable population of over 500 000 (Wetlands International 2002). However, since being introduced into wildfowl collections in the UK from North America in the 1950s, it has become established as an invasive, non-native species in Britain and is now beginning to colonize other north-west European countries. By January 2000, the UK population was estimated at c. 6 000 birds (WWT Wetlands Advisory Service 2002). In 1983, the first feral Ruddy Duck was recorded in Spain, raising concerns about the risk of hybridization with the globally-threatened White-headed Duck *Oxyura leucocephala*. Ruddy Ducks have been recorded annually in Spain since 1991, and the first Ruddy Duck x White-headed Duck hybrids were observed in the same year (Hughes *et al.* 1999). At least 139 Ruddy Ducks have been recorded in Spain since 1991, at a minimum of 43 different locations. Hybrids are fertile to the second and possibly third generation in the wild. Despite an active and well-organized control programme to cull any Ruddy Ducks present, 59 hybrids have been recorded (José Antonio Torres pers. comm.) on at least 23 sites (Hughes *et al.* 1999*).*

The numbers of White-headed Ducks in Spain have risen from 22 in 1977 to 2 600 in 2003, and Spain is the only region in which the White-headed Duck has expanded its breeding range and population size in recent years. There has been a major expansion of breeding sites eastwards and northwards

since 1980, from Andalucia to Valencia and Castilla-La Mancha (Ayala *et al.* 1994 and Torres & Moreno-Arroyo 2000, cited in Green & Hughes 2001), following protection of habitat and a ban on hunting. Breeding now occurs annually at over 20 sites (Torres 2003). The Council of Europe Species Action Plan for the White-headed Duck highlights hybridization with the Ruddy Duck as being of critical importance, and regards this as the most severe threat to the long-term survival of the White-headed Duck, particularly in Europe (Green & Hughes 1996).

Initial research into control of Ruddy Ducks in the UK in order to protect the White-headed Duck began in 1993, and further research took place in 1999-2002 and 2003/2004. The UK Government recognizes that eradication of Ruddy Ducks from the UK is the desired outcome (Morley 2003). As the UK holds an estimated 95% of the European feral population of Ruddy Ducks, control in other countries (including Spain) is likely to be futile unless eradication occurs in the UK.

## METHODS

### Introduction

In general terms, it is recognized that no eradication programme should begin unless a specific assessment study has shown that this is technically and financially feasible (European Commission 2004). Control of Ruddy Ducks in the UK has been viewed from the beginning as a three-phase process, with the first two phases addressing the issues surrounding the feasibility and cost of eradication.

Small-scale research was carried out between 1993 and 1996, concentrating on the feasibility of control. This work was carried out by the Wildfowl and Wetlands Trust (Hughes 1996), and involved testing different methods of control, namely shooting during the breeding season, shooting in winter, trapping females at the nest, trapping in winter, and egg-oiling. The results showed that shooting during the breeding season was the most effective method of control, followed by shooting in winter. Although trapping at the nest had a high intrinsic efficiency, the rate of control in terms of staff effort was very low. The report concluded that eradication was feasible, but that larger-scale control was required to obtain a better indication of the time-scale and costs involved.

### Regional control trials and control on major sites nationally

Research into large-scale control was undertaken between 1999 and 2004. This work concentrated on control by shooting in line with the results of the initial research, and was conducted by the Central Science Laboratory (CSL), an Executive Agency of the Department for Environment, Food and Rural Affairs (Defra). Four full-time and two part-time control staff were employed on the project. The principal aims of the research were to assess the feasibility and cost of reducing the UK population by over 95%, to reduce the breeding population on Anglesey, Wales, by a minimum of 70% within three years, and to conclude whether compulsory access to land would be necessary to ensure the success of any future national control strategy.

Access to all sites was by agreement in advance with site owners and tenants. The owners, tenants and principal users of all the known breeding, post-breeding and wintering sites for Ruddy Ducks within the trial areas were contacted and asked for permission to control Ruddy Ducks by shooting.

Control by shooting during the breeding season (1 March to 31 August) was carried out in two regions during this phase of research: the Western Midlands in England and the Island of Anglesey in Wales. Control of birds early in the breeding season, especially of adult females, is important in an eradication programme as it minimizes the numbers of young birds hatched and the total number of birds which must be killed. It is more efficient early in the season as by late May more cover is available for both sexes and the females begin to spend a large part of their time sitting on eggs and are thus more difficult to shoot. Most birds were shot from the bank with either a .223 rifle or a shotgun.

Control by shooting during the post-breeding and winter periods (defined as 1 September to 28 February) was carried out in all trial areas, including the Western Midlands and Anglesey. Ten visits were made to sites outside the trial areas in the winter of 2000/2001, and work was carried out at a range of sites nationally in the winter of 2003/2004. At this time of year, a high proportion of the UK population is found on a small number of sites (Fig. 1). For example, in January 2000, 83% of the UK population was recorded on only 25 sites, with 67% occurring on only ten sites. Thus access to these sites and the ability to carry out control effectively are critical to the feasibility of eradicating

Ruddy Ducks from the UK. Four to six Field Officers were usually involved, and the ducks were either herded towards guns on the bank by means of a boat or, on the larger waters, shot from the boats themselves. With very few exceptions, only shotguns were used for post-breeding and winter control.

## RESULTS
### Access
Agreement to control Ruddy Ducks by shooting was forthcoming from 58% of the landowners and tenants approached (at both breeding and wintering sites), with little variation between the two main trial areas of Anglesey and the Western Midlands. However, this proportion rose to 78% for major wintering sites nationally, which contain large flocks of Ruddy Ducks in the post-breeding and winter periods. Thus access to a relatively small number of sites gives access to a large proportion of the UK population.

### Breeding season control
A total of 249 control visits were made during the period April 1999 to March 2002, and a total of 793 Ruddy Ducks were shot (255 adult females, 398 adult males and 140 immature birds). This figure represents 30.1% of the total number of Ruddy Ducks killed during the period. However, this figure would have been higher had control operations in the 2001 breeding season not been severely curtailed as a result of an outbreak of foot and mouth disease in the UK.

The mean amount of time per staff member spent on site for each bird killed in the breeding season was 1.98 hours. On average, 47.3% of the Ruddy Ducks present were shot at each visit (range 0-100%). In over 85% of cases where at least one bird was shot, the staff input was four hours or less on site (Defra 2002).

### Post-breeding and winter control, September 1999 – March 2002
A total of 1 841 birds (727 adult males, 491 adult females and 623 immature birds) were shot on seventeen sites. This figure represents 69.9% of the total number culled between April 1999 and March 2002 (Defra 2002). Because of the range of sizes of post-breeding and wintering sites and the effect that this had on efficiency, data for sites of less than 1 sq. km in size ("small wintering sites") were analysed separately from data for sites greater than 1 sq. km in size ("large wintering sites").

Data from the 54 visits to thirteen small post-breeding and wintering sites showed that the average staff time on site per bird killed was 1.11 hours in these situations (1 107 birds shot in total). On average, 53.9% of the Ruddy Ducks present were shot per visit (range 8% to 92%).

Many of the major wintering sites used by Ruddy Ducks are large reservoirs ranging from 1 sq. km to 12 sq. km in extent. A total of 21 control visits were made to four water bodies of this size, although in one case shooting was limited to two bays and not permitted in the main body of water. A total of 651 Ruddy Ducks were shot on these sites. Data from these visits show that although a smaller proportion of the Ruddy Ducks was killed per visit (mean 18.7%, range 1% to 56%), the staff input, at 0.81 hours per bird shot, was lower than on the smaller sites.

The main wintering site in the Western Midlands is approximately 3.5 sq. km in extent. A total of 522 Ruddy Ducks were

**Mean of peak counts over three years**
- 46-99
- 100-249
- 250 +
- Control by shooting tested
- No control

Fig. 1. The major post-breeding and wintering sites for Ruddy Ducks *Oxyura jamaicensis* in the UK.

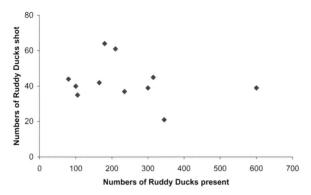

**Fig. 2.** Number of Ruddy Ducks *Oxyura jamaicensis* shot and number present per visit at a major wintering site in the Western Midlands: 1999-2002.

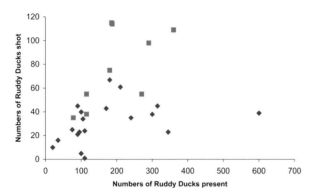

**Fig. 3.** Number of Ruddy Ducks *Oxyura jamaicensis* shot and number present per visit at larger wintering sites: 1999-2002 (blue diamonds) and 2003/04 (red squares).

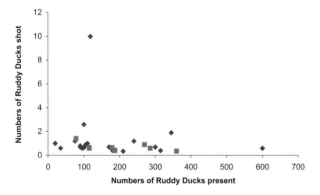

**Fig. 4.** Staff time per Ruddy Duck *Oxyura jamaicensis* shot at larger wintering sites: 1999-2002 (blue diamonds) and 2003/04 (red squares).

shot on 15 visits to this site during the September to February period. The results from this site showed that similar numbers of Ruddy Ducks were culled on each visit, regardless of numbers present (Fig. 2). Therefore as numbers were reduced, a larger proportion of those present was removed at each visit. Evidence from the 1999-2002 research suggested that at sites with high numbers of birds, the presence of more staff and the availability of more boats on the first few visits would allow a greater proportion of the birds present to be removed per visit (a maximum of four boats was available between 1999 and 2002). In order to test this, further research on large wintering sites was carried out in the winter of 2003/2004.

## Post-breeding and winter control, winter of 2003/2004

Three additional boats were bought in March 2003. Although of similar design to three of the boats used during the Regional Control Trials, these were slightly larger (14ft in length rather than 12ft) and had more powerful engines (20hp rather than 9.9hp). Thus, for the control operations on large wintering sites in 2003/2004, the CSL had a total of seven boats available: three 12ft aluminium boats with 10hp engines, three 14ft aluminium boats with 20hp engines, and one 12ft RHIB with a 25hp engine. In addition to the six staff used during the Regional Control Trials, a further three were trained in Ruddy Duck control and used on the large wintering sites in 2003/2004. One other member of staff was used to drive a boat on these sites. Thus, where operations during the period 1999-2002 typically involved three to four boats and five to seven staff, visits during the winter of 2003/2004 typically involved five to seven boats and up to ten staff.

Nine visits were made to five large wintering sites between December 2003 and February 2004. These five water bodies hold 70% of the Ruddy Ducks occurring on the ten most important wintering sites in the UK, and 30% of those on the forty most important wintering sites. A further sixteen visits were made to twelve small wintering sites between September 2003 and February 2004. The results of this further research show substantially increased efficiency on both larger and smaller wintering sites when compared with the results from the Regional Control Trials. There was a 58% increase in efficiency in terms of the proportion of Ruddy Ducks shot per visit on the large wintering sites (Fig. 3). This increase in efficiency was due principally to the availability of additional staff and, in particular, additional boats allowing better coverage of the waters bodies involved. There was also an 18% increase in the proportion of ducks shot per visit on the smaller sites. This was due principally to the refinement of site-specific methods for carrying out the control operations. Importantly, this increase in the proportion of birds shot was not at the cost of a large increase in staff time. On the large wintering sites there was a 55% reduction in the staff time on site per bird killed (Fig. 4), while on smaller wintering sites the comparable figure was 72%.

## CONCLUSIONS

The research on Ruddy Duck control in the UK since 1999 has shown that it is highly feasible to eradicate the species from the UK. A number of factors have led to this conclusion.

1   Ruddy Ducks are highly visible, particularly in the autumn and winter, when very large numbers of birds congregate on known traditional sites. For example, in January 2000, 83% of the UK population was recorded on only 25 sites, with 67% occurring on only ten sites. This makes control easier than if the birds were widely dispersed, and permits a more accurate estimation of the national population.
2   High quality data are available on the location, numbers and spread of Ruddy Ducks in the UK. There have been regular counts of Ruddy Ducks on many sites as part of the Wetland Bird Survey (WeBS) counts, and in recent years the number of sites for which these data are available has risen to over 1 500. These data, supplemented by data from County Bird Reports, allow better planning of an eradication programme.

3 In 2002, the Wildfowl and Wetlands Trust carried out a detailed analysis of all available WeBS data. This gave an estimated total UK population of almost 6 000 in January 2000 (WWT Wetlands Advisory Trust 2002), and an annual growth rate of between 6% and 7% in recent years (without control), compared to a mean annual rate of 24% in the years 1976-1996. Count data from 20 key wintering sites in February 2004 suggest that the national population now stands at around 5 000 following the recent control measures.

4 Several years of active control have allowed the development of a model which predicts the response of the Ruddy Duck population to further control (Smith *et al.* in press). This model suggests that eradication from the UK is feasible as part of a five-year control programme. The mean time predicted to reduce the population to less than 50 individuals (i.e. by over 99%) is five years.

5 Analysis of the WeBS data and experience of control since 1999 have shown that Ruddy Ducks move freely between sites in response to changes in weather conditions and during seasonal migrations. This makes access to all sites unnecessary, as it is highly likely that birds will occur at some time on sites where permission to carry out control has been granted. Ruddy Ducks move between sites in large numbers in response to changes in weather conditions in winter. During cold weather, birds move from smaller waters to larger ones, which are less likely to freeze over. Movement between sites also occurs as a result of the birds' mating strategy during the breeding season, when unattached males move between sites in search of females.

6 A range of control methods has been tested and the most effective identified. Shooting is the most effective method in all seasons, but trapping during the breeding season, trapping at the nest and egg-oiling are also effective on some sites. In the winter of 2003/2004, with additional staff and equipment available, it proved possible to cull between 20% and 60% of Ruddy Ducks per visit on the larger wintering sites. On smaller wintering sites, the mean proportion culled per visit rose to 59% (up to 220 birds) during the same period. On breeding sites, the mean proportion culled per visit was 47%.

7 Agreement has been obtained for access to a high proportion of sites. The owners of 37 of the 40 most important wintering sites in the UK have been approached, and 78% of these have given permission for Ruddy Ducks to be shot on their sites. As discussed above, the regular movement of this species between sites means that it is not necessary to secure access to all sites in order to meet the aims of the project.

8 The much reduced numbers of Ruddy Ducks on Anglesey during the 2000 breeding season allowed an assessment of the likely time requirements when dealing with very low numbers of birds. The count information from Anglesey suggests that reduced numbers of birds are not distributed across all the potential breeding sites. Rather, the birds appear to concentrate in the best breeding habitats in the area.

## REFERENCES

**Ayala, J.M., Matamala, J.J., Lopez, J.M. & Aquilar, F.J.** 1994. Distribución actual de la Malvasia en España. IWRB Threatened Wildlife Research Group Newsletter 6: 8-11.

**Defra (Department for Environment, Food and Rural Affairs)** 2002. UK Ruddy Duck Control Trial Final Report. www.defra.gov.uk

**European Commission** 2004. Alien species and nature conservation in the EU. The role of the LIFE program. Office for Official Publications of the European Communities.

**Green, A.J. & Hughes, B.** 1996. Action Plan for the White-headed Duck *Oxyura leucocephala*. In: B. Heredia, L. Rose & M. Painter (eds) Globally threatened birds in Europe: Action plans. Council of Europe Publishing, Strasbourg: 119-145.

**Green, A.J. & Hughes, B.** 2001. Birds of the Western Palearctic Update. Vol. 3, No. 2: 79-90. Oxford University Press, Oxford.

**Hughes, B.** 1996. The Feasibility of Control Measures for North American Ruddy Duck *Oxyura jamaicensis* in the United Kingdom. Wildfowl and Wetlands Trust report to the Department of the Environment.

**Hughes, B., Criado, J., Delany, S., Gallo-Orsi, U., Green, A.J., Grussu, M., Perennou, C. & Torres, J.A.** 1999. The status of the North American Ruddy Duck *Oxyura jamaicensis* in the Western Palearctic: towards an action plan for eradication, 1999-2002. Council of Europe Publication T-PVS/Birds (99) 9. Council of Europe Publishing, Strasbourg.

**Morley, E.** 2003. Parliamentary Statement on Ruddy Duck control by the Parliamentary Under-Secretary of State for Environment, Food and Rural Affairs. The Official Report (Hansard), House of Commons, London, 3 March 2003.

**Smith, G.C., Henderson, I.S., & Robertson, P.A.** 2005. A model of Ruddy Duck *Oxyura jamaicensis* eradication for the UK. Journal of Applied Ecology 42: 546-555.

**Torres, J.A.** 2003. La Población Española de la Malvasía Cabeciblanca (*Oxyura leucocephala*) Veinticinco Años Después del Mínimo de 1977. Oxyura, Volume XI, No. 1: 6-43.

**Torres, J.A. & Moreno-Arroyo, B.** 2000. Presensia de la Malvasia Canela (*Oxyura jamaicensis*) en España. Oxyura 10: 69-78.

**Wetlands International** 2002. Waterbird Population Estimates – Third Edition. Wetlands International Global Series No. 12, Wageningen, The Netherlands.

**WWT Wetlands Advisory Service** 2002. The Winter Status and Distribution of Ruddy Ducks in the UK, 1966/1967-1999/2000. Report to the Department for Environment, Food and Rural Affairs, March 2002.

# Resolving Double-crested Cormorant *Phalacrocorax auritus* conflicts in the United States: past, present, and future

*Shauna L. Hanisch[1] & Paul R. Schmidt[2]*

*[1] U.S. Fish and Wildlife Service, Division of Migratory Bird Management, 4401 N. Fairfax Drive, MS-MBSP-4107, Arlington, VA 22203, USA. (email: Shauna_Hanisch@fws.gov)*
*[2] U.S. Fish and Wildlife Service, Migratory Birds and State Programs, 1849 C St. NW, Room 3250, Washington, D.C. 20240, USA.*

Hanisch, S.L. & Schmidt, P.R. 2006. Resolving Double-crested Cormorant *Phalacrocorax auritus* conflicts in the United States: past, present, and future. *Waterbirds around the world.* Eds. G.C. Boere, C.A. Galbraith & D.A. Stroud. The Stationery Office, Edinburgh, UK. pp. 826-828.

## ABSTRACT

The Double-crested Cormorant *Phalacrocorax auritus* has been protected by the Migratory Bird Treaty Act since 1972, as a result of a bilateral treaty with Mexico. Since that time, the U.S. Fish and Wildlife Service has had authority for cormorant management and conservation. From the late 1970s to the present, Double-crested Cormorants experienced dramatic population growth. Management policies and practices to address resource conflicts associated with cormorants have evolved over the last 30+ years, culminating most recently in new regulations that were adopted following the development of an Environmental Impact Statement and considerable public involvement. The new regulations expand the authority of certain agencies to address conflicts between cormorants and aquacultural, recreational, and ecological resources. In this paper, we discuss the past and present of Double-crested Cormorant management and possible directions for the future.

## INTRODUCTION

Long a concern of commercial fishermen, the Double-crested Cormorant *Phalacrocorax auritus* was never so great a problem as after it underwent, in the mid- to late 1970s, a population explosion in parts of the eastern United States and Canada. In the Great Lakes (U.S. and Canadian), which experienced the most significant increases, the number of Double-crested Cormorant breeding pairs increased from 89 in 1970 to an estimated 115 000 in 2000. A combination of mostly anthropogenic factors influenced this population rebound: elimination of the use of organochlorine contaminants (e.g. DDT), expansion of commercial aquaculture, growth in the number of fish-stocked artificial water bodies, changes in fish populations in the Great Lakes and elsewhere, and legal protection of Double-crested Cormorants. On the one hand, the comeback of the cormorant, like that of the Bald Eagle *Haliaeetus leucocephalus* and Brown Pelican *Pelecanus occidentalis*, was a positive event signaling a healthier environment. On the other hand, by the 1980s increasing Double-crested Cormorant populations were raising concerns in a number of areas, namely in fishing hotspots in the Great Lakes. In time, commercial aquaculture producers, particularly commercial catfish farmers in the southern United States, were becoming increasingly concerned about the economic impacts caused by Double-crested Cormorant depredation.

## EARLY APPROACHES TO DAMAGE CONTROL

Protected under the Migratory Bird Treaty Act (MBTA) since 1972, Double-crested Cormorants cannot be lawfully killed unless the U.S. Fish and Wildlife Service (hereafter referred to as

the Service) provides authorization, either through the issuance of a permit or through special regulations (for example, a depredation order). In the case of addressing damages to resources such as aquaculture stock or sport fish, a "depredation permit" is the relevant permit. Policy on issuing these permits refers to "the nature of the crops or other interests being injured," indicating that depredation permits could be issued rather broadly (i.e. for damage to agricultural and any other interests). The Service's Migratory Bird Program focused on issuing permits in situations in which depredation either caused economic loss to a person's livelihood, or involved a threatened or endangered species (or one that was the focus of a restoration effort).

In 1990, formal guidance on the issuance of depredation permits for fish-eating birds (including cormorants) came in the form of Director's Order No. 27. This policy statement established internal Service policy stating that "kill permits for migratory, fish-eating birds preying on fish aquaculture and hatchery facilities" can be issued under certain circumstances, and then outlined those circumstances. Its objective was "to provide immediate, short-term relief to the aquaculture producers from the economic and resource losses occurring from fish-eating birds." The Director's Order is still in place (although it now exists as a Service Manual chapter) and continues to provide permit issuance guidance to Service Regions that do not fall under special regulations relevant to cormorants.

In 1998, in response to complaints from aquaculture producers about the depredation permit process, the Service developed regulations to create a "depredation order" for the protection of aquaculture stock from damage caused by Double-crested Cormorants. The order allows "landowners, operators, and tenants [and their agents] actually engaged in the production of commercial freshwater aquaculture stocks" in 13 States (12 south-eastern States and Minnesota) to take depredating Double-crested Cormorants without a depredation permit. This depredation order is one of five in existence for various bird species, all of which have the purpose of protecting some form of agricultural interest.

## DEVELOPMENT OF A NEW POLICY

The aquaculture depredation order, however, did not put an end to resource conflicts related to Double-crested Cormorants. The question that could not be avoided was what, if anything, should be done about Double-crested Cormorants and open water fisheries? For a long time, the answer was simple because there was limited scientific evidence that Double-crested Cormorants had actual impacts on fisheries. Eventually, studies emerged providing strong evidence that cormorant predation had negative

Double-crested Cormorant *Phalacrocorax auritus*. Photo: Stan Tekiela, USFWS.

impacts on recruitment of certain fisheries, for example, small-mouth bass in New York's eastern Lake Ontario (Ross & Johnson 1999, Schneider *et al.* 1999, Johnson *et al.* 2000, Lantry *et al.* 2002) and walleye in Oneida Lake (Van De Valk *et al.* 2002). In addition, evidence of natural resource impacts (for example, on vegetation and other bird species) was growing stronger and becoming a greater cause of concern among resource professionals (Bédard *et al.* 1995, Jarvie *et al.* 1999, Shieldcastle & Martin 1999). Thus, in 1999, the Service decided to re-examine its policy on Double-crested Cormorant management, perhaps even to develop a national cormorant management plan, and determined that this process would require the completion of an Environmental Impact Statement (EIS) under the National Environmental Policy Act.

In late 1999, the Service officially announced its intention to prepare an EIS, with the U.S. Department of Agriculture's Wildlife Services program (USDA/WS) as a formal cooperating agency. The purpose of the EIS was to provide a detailed explanation of the environmental (e.g. natural, economic, social, and cultural) consequences associated with various management options. The EIS process also gave the public the opportunity to be involved in the decision. To that end, the Service initiated a "scoping" period that allowed the public to help define the scope of the problem and possible solutions. This comment period lasted for over 100 days and included 12 public meetings around the nation (mostly in the eastern U.S.), culminating in publication of a draft EIS (DEIS) in December 2001.

The DEIS examined six management "alternatives" for addressing conflicts with Double-crested Cormorants: these consisted of a status quo option, an option allowing only non-lethal control, an option that would liberalize issuance of depredation permits, an option that would create a new depredation order to protect public resources, an option emphasizing regional population reduction, and an option that would authorize regulated hunting. These alternatives were analyzed with regard to their potential impacts on Double-crested Cormorant populations, fish, other birds, vegetation, federally-listed threatened and endangered species, and socio-economic issues such as aquaculture.

The purpose of the change in strategy would be threefold: (1) to reduce resource conflicts associated with Double-crested Cormorants in the contiguous United States, (2) to enhance the flexibility of natural resource agencies in dealing with Double-crested Cormorant conflicts, and (3) to ensure the conservation of viable Double-crested Cormorant populations. To that end, the Service selected its preferred alternative. This alternative

proposed to establish a "public resource depredation order" that would authorize certain resource agencies to take Double-crested Cormorants without a permit to protect public resources (e.g. fish, wildlife, and plants). In response to problems at fish hatcheries and continued problems at aquaculture facilities, the preferred alternative would also authorize take of Double-crested Cormorants at Federal and State hatcheries and allow USDA/WS officials to control Double-crested Cormorants at winter roost sites.

The DEIS was followed by a 100-day public comment period and 10 more public meetings from Portland, Oregon, to Burlington, Vermont. The Service received about 1 000 letters and/or emails on the DEIS with the range of comments running from "cormorants are being scapegoated and should be left alone" to "cormorants are a scourge and their populations should be greatly reduced." Overall, the greatest public support (c. 45%) was for the preferred alternative, with many who commented also supporting the regional population management elements of another alternative. The public comment period closed in late February 2002 and a year later, in March 2003, the Service published a draft of the new regulations (i.e. proposed rule) that would implement the preferred alternative. The proposed rule gave the public an opportunity to comment on the draft regulations. In 60 days of public comment, we received over 9 700 letters, faxes, and emails on the rule. About 85% of these comments were opposed to the rule and were part of mass letter campaigns sponsored by interest groups.

## THE FINAL OUTCOME AND OPTIONS FOR THE FUTURE

In August 2003, a final EIS was completed and shortly after that, in October 2003, the final rule and Record of Decision were published. The final rule made two important changes from the status quo that the Service believes are biologically justified and legally sound under the MBTA. First, it revised the 1998 aquaculture depredation order to specifically authorize take at Federal and State fish hatcheries and to give USDA/WS authority to take cormorants at winter roost sites. Second, it created a public resource depredation order to give State fish and wildlife agencies, USDA/WS, and Federally recognized Tribes in 24 States in the eastern U.S. the authority to control Double-crested Cormorants without a depredation permit when necessary to alleviate damages to publicly-owned natural resources such as fish, wildlife, and plants. Each depredation order has a number of terms and conditions which must be followed by participating agencies and individuals. These include limitations on allowable control techniques, requirements for obtaining landowner permission and abiding by all applicable State laws, disposal procedures, and measures to avoid take of ESA-protected species or any migratory birds other than Double-crested Cormorants. Additionally, there are requirements for reporting and evaluation and, in the case of certain activities under the public resource depredation order, advanced notification.

This approach is balanced and responsive in that it gives the on-the-ground resource management agencies more authority, while maintaining accountability (through reporting and record-keeping requirements and other terms and conditions) to ensure the conservation of healthy Double-crested Cormorant populations. The Service's role in implementation of the new regulations is largely one of coordination and oversight. It is the State fish and wildlife agencies and USDA/WS who will conduct most of the actual management activities. The Service will work to promote coordination among the action agencies, and will oversee control activities and gauge their population impacts at the regional and continental scales.

Some of the Service's partners, including USDA/WS, would have preferred a population management, even reduction, program to a localized damage control program. However, the analysis of the best available information on Double-crested Cormorants led us to conclude that there is currently insufficient justification for a large-scale population management strategy. In the final rule, the Service acknowledged that there is a need for more information about Double-crested Cormorants and their resource impacts, but that in weighing these deficiencies against the costs of taking no action, it concluded that it is prudent to move forward with the new regulations. The Service also stated in the final rule that if supported by biological evidence and appropriate monitoring resources, the Service would, in the future, consider a management approach that focuses on setting and achieving regional population goals. But until then, the strategy will continue to focus on alleviating localized damages.

Over the summer of 2004, control activities (including nest destruction, egg oiling, and shooting) authorized under the public resource depredation order were carried out in the states of Arkansas (193 birds killed and 95 nests destroyed), Michigan (1 424 birds killed and 3 114 nests oiled), New York (482 birds killed, 2 818 nests destroyed, and 11 450 nests oiled), and Vermont (208 birds killed and 1 458 nests oiled). State wildlife agencies and USDA/WS worked cooperatively with the Service to develop plans for implementing these actions, and carried out the work in a responsible and professional manner. It will take both time and new knowledge resulting from adaptive management efforts to tell how effectively the new regulations help resolve conflicts with cormorants.

Clearly, the process of addressing Double-crested Cormorant conflicts has been an evolving one in which the Service's policies shifted from a fairly narrow emphasis, mainly on private resource conflicts, to one that addressed, as the need to do so became increasingly apparent, a broader range of resource conflicts. The process has certainly not been without contention, as revealed by the fact that we received nearly 10 000 public comments on the proposed rule alone. In the Service's efforts to develop a balanced but effective wildlife damage management strategy, it has been accused of a range of evils, from being politically driven (either beholden to "the sport fishing industry" or "the animal rights wackos," depending on the individual's perspective) to initiating a war against fish-eating birds. As a public agency that seeks to conserve wildlife in the context of the diverse interests of all Americans, the Service must act in a manner that is well-balanced, responsive, and guided by the best available science. As times and issues related to cormorants and other abundant migratory bird species change, so too must the strategies used to address them.

## REFERENCES

**Bédard, J., Nadeau, A. & LePage, M.** 1995. Double-crested cormorant culling in the St. Lawrence River Estuary. Colonial Waterbirds 18 (Special Publication 1): 78-85.

**Jarvie, S., Blokpoel, H. & Chipperfield, T.** 1999. A geographic information system to monitor nest distributions of double-crested cormorants and black-crowned night herons at shared colony sites near Toronto, Canada. In: M.E. Tobin (ed) Symposium on Double-crested Cormorants: Population Status and Management Issues in the Midwest. USDA Technical Bulletin No. 1879: 121-130. Washington, D.C.

**Johnson, J.H., Ross, R.M. & McCullough, R.D.** 2000. Diet composition and fish consumption of double-crested cormorants from the Pigeon and Snake Island colonies of eastern Lake Ontario in 1999. In: New York State Department of Environmental Conservation Special Report. Albany, New York.

**Lantry, B.F., Eckert, T.H., Schneider, C.P. & Chrisman, J.R.** 2002. The relationship between the abundance of small-mouth bass and double-crested cormorants in the eastern basin of Lake Ontario. Journal of Great Lakes Research 28(2): 193-201.

**Ross, R.M. & Johnson, J.H.** 1999. Fish losses to double-crested cormorant predation in eastern Lake Ontario, 1992-97. In: M.E. Tobin (ed) Symposium on Double-crested Cormorants: Population Status and Management Issues in the Midwest. USDA Technical Bulletin No. 1879: 61-70. Washington, D.C.

**Schneider, C.P., Schiavone, A., Jr., Eckert, T.H., McCullough, R.D., Lantry, B.F., Einhouse, D.W., Chrisman, J.R., Adams, C.M., Johnson, J.H. & Ross, R.M.** 1999. Double-crested cormorant predation on smallmouth bass and other fishes of the eastern basin of Lake Ontario: overview, summary and recommendations in New York Department of Environmental Conservation Special Report. Albany, New York.

**Shieldcastle, M.C. & Martin, L.** 1999. Colonial waterbird nesting on West Sister Island National Wildlife Refuge and the arrival of double-crested cormorants. In: M.E. Tobin (ed) Symposium on Double-crested Cormorants: Population Status and Management Issues in the Midwest. USDA Technical Bulletin No. 1879: 115-120. Washington, D.C.

**Van De Valk, A.J., Adams, C.M., Rudstam, L.G., Forney, J.L., Brooking, T.E., Gerkin, M.A., Young, B.P. & Hooper, J.T.** 2002. Comparison of angler and cormorant harvest of walleye and yellow perch in Oneida Lake, NY. Transactions of the American Fisheries Society 131(1): 27-39.

Double-crested Cormorant *Phalacrocorax auritus*. Photo: Stan Tekiela, USFWS.

# Variation in the behavioural responses of Whooper Swans *Cygnus cygnus* to different types of human activity

*Eileen C. Rees[1], Jennifer H. Bruce[1] & George T. White[2]*

[1] *The Wildfowl & Wetlands Trust, Slimbridge, Gloucestershire, GL2 7BT, UK. (email: eileen.rees@wwt.org.uk)*
[2] *107 Hollows Avenue, Foxbar, Paisley, PA2 0RD, UK.*

Rees, E.C., Bruce, J.H. & White, G.T. 2006. Variation in the behavioural responses of Whooper Swans *Cygnus cygnus* to different types of human activity. *Waterbirds around the world*. Eds. G.C. Boere, C.A. Galbraith & D.A. Stroud. The Stationery Office, Edinburgh, UK. pp. 829-830.

The impact of human activity on bird populations has been studied and discussed extensively in recent years (Hill *et al.* 1997, Gill & Sutherland 2000, Nisbet 2000, Gill *et al.* 2001) but variation in the birds' response to disturbance is still poorly understood. Variation in the behaviour of wintering Whooper Swans *Cygnus cygnus*, wintering in and around the Black Cart Special Protection Area (SPA), near Glasgow (55°53'N 04°27'W), was analysed to:

- assess the effects of the different conditions and different types of disturbance on the swans, by testing whether the type and timing of disturbance, and location of swans, affected the distance at which the swans became alert;
- determine whether the swans become habituated to human activity, by testing whether their response to disturbance events diminishes over time;
- describe variation in the time taken for the swans to resume feeding following disturbance, to determine whether recovery rates are more rapid at times (e.g. late in the day) when pressure to resume feeding might be greater; and
- describe temporal and spatial factors affecting the time that

the swans spend feeding and being alert, to determine the landscape features (including the frequency and type of human activity) likely to influence the behaviour of the birds, with a view to advising on site management for the species in the wintering range.

This short note presents a summary of the results; they are presented in full in Rees *et al.* (2005).

Observations were made in winters 1997-98 to 1999-2000 inclusive at the Black Cart SPA in Scotland, which receives at least 1% of the Icelandic-breeding Whooper Swan population in winter. The site is semi-rural, consisting of mixed farmland interspersed with light industrial development, adjacent to Glasgow Airport and within two km of the Paisley conurbation (Fig. 1, Rees *et al.* 2005).

All fields and sections of river within the study area were visited at least two days a week to map the number and distribution of swans, and note the crop type in each field. The swans' behaviour and human activity at the site were monitored during three main periods each winter, in autumn (late October-early November), mid-winter (January) and spring (March). The data

Fig. 1. Whooper Swans *Cygnus cygnus* on the Black Cart Water, Scotland, with Rolls Royce factory in the background. Photo: Rebecca Woodward, WWT.

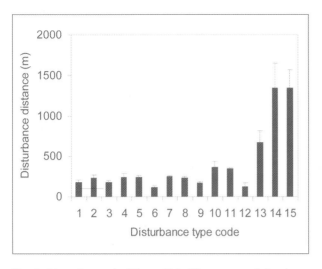

Fig. 2. Mean distance (± SE) at which different types of disturbance alerted the swans over the 3-year study. Note: 1 = car, 2 = van, 3 = tractor, 4 = other farm vehicle/lorry, 5 = construction vehicle, 6 = bicycle, 7 = pedestrian, 8 = pedestrian with dog, 9 = farm worker on foot, 10 = angler, 11 = wildfowler, 12 = cattle, 13 = bird scaring at airport, 14 = helicopter, 15 = aircraft. From (Rees *et al.* 2005).

were analysed using two-way and three-way ANOVAs in SPSS (version 11), and generalised linear modelling in GLIM (version 4).

Overall, the swans' feeding activity varied within and between years, and in relation to the feeding site, but there was less variation in the amount of time spent alert. Disturbance frequency resulting from human activity was lower with increasing flock size and with increased distance to the nearest road or track.

Distances that humans could approach before alerting the birds similarly varied with field characteristics (e.g., size and proximity to roads or tracks), and also with the type of disturbance involved. Helicopters and other aircraft alerted the swans at longer distances than ground-based disturbances (Fig. 2), but the proportion of birds alerted was lower. On the ground, anglers and wildfowlers alerted the swans at greater distances than other pedestrians. Similarly cars and bicycles were able to approach closer than other vehicles.

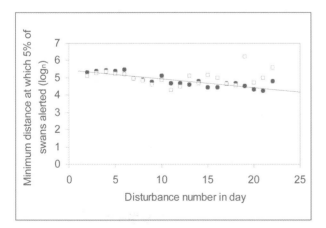

Fig. 3. Distance (log$_n$ transformed; open squares) at which Swans became alert in relation to the number of previous disturbances recorded in the day. The linear regression line is for fitted disturbance distance n values (closed circles; distance = 0.0545 x disturbance number + 5.46). From (Rees *et al.* 2005).

The distance at which >5% of the flock became alert because of human activity decreased with the number of previous incidents in the day (Fig. 3), indicating that swans become less sensitive to disturbance events if daily disturbance frequency is high, but there was no evidence that habituation to disturbance persisted over longer periods. The time taken for the birds to resume undisturbed behaviour varied with the duration of the disturbance event, which in turn depended on the type of disturbance involved, with pedestrians alerting the birds for longer periods than vehicles and aircraft. Recovery rates following disturbance were also associated with field size, flock size and the proportion of the flock alerted.

Feeding activity was influenced by a range of variables, including: year, season, field location, crop type and the number of days that the flock had used the field (32.9% of variance in the data explained by these variables), with disturbance factors explaining an additional 4.9% of variance in the proportion feeding per hour. Conversely, alert activity was influenced mainly by disturbance events.

The range of factors influencing the swans' feeding behaviour, and variability in their response to human activity, has implications for management programmes and for attempts to predict the effects of human activity on the birds at a local and wider scale.

Given the variation in feeding activity for undisturbed swans, and in their response to different types of disturbance under different conditions, information on factors affecting both disturbed and undisturbed behaviour is needed to determine whether changes in disturbance levels affect food intake for other species over a winter season. Factors influencing behaviour also may vary at different parts of the flyway, depending on changes in food availability, predation risks and energetic requirements. Determining variation in a species' response to human activity throughout the year and migratory range would be necessary for any assessment of the impact of disturbance at a population level.

## REFERENCES

Gill, J.A. & Sutherland, W.J. 2000. Predicting the consequences of human disturbance from behavioural decisions. In: L.M. Gosling & W.J. Sutherland (eds.), Behaviour and Conservation. Cambridge University Press, Cambridge: 51-64.

Gill, J.A., Norris, K., & Sutherland, W.J. 2001. Why behavioural responses may not reflect the population consequences of human disturbance. Biological Conservation 97: 265-268.

Hill, D., Hockin, D., Price, D., Tucker, G., Morris, R. & Treweek, J. 1997. Bird disturbance: improving the quality and utility of disturbance research. Journal of Applied Ecology 34: 275-288.

Nisbet, I.T.C. 2000. Disturbance, habituation and management of waterbird colonies – commentary. Waterbirds 23: 312-332.

Rees, E.C., Bruce, J.H. & White, G.T. 2005. Factors affecting the behavioural responses of whooper swans (*Cygnus c. cygnus*) to various human activities. Biological Conservation 121: 369-382.

## 6.2   Let the waterbirds do the talking. Workshop Introduction

*Christine Prietto*

*The Wetlands Centre, NSW Department of Education and Training, PO Box 292, Wallsend, NSW 2287 Australia.*
*(email: priettoclub@aapt.net.au)*

Prietto, C. 2006. Let the waterbirds do the talking. Workshop Introduction. *Waterbirds around the world.* Eds. G.C. Boere, C.A. Galbraith & D.A. Stroud.  The Stationery Office, Edinburgh, UK.  p. 831.

The launch of an educational booklet on the critically threatened Siberian Crane *Grus leucogeranus* at Fereydoon Kenar city in Mazandaran Province of I.R. Iran as part of the UNEP/GEF Siberian Crane Wetlands Project.  Communication, education and public awareness is an essential component to such programmes.  Photo:  Crawford Prentice.

---

Waterbirds, through their often charismatic behaviour, their international migrations, and association with 'untamed nature' have great potential to increase support for biodiversity conservation at all levels.

The processes of communication, education and public awareness (CEPA) are all invaluable complements to waterbird conservation but must be valued and funded accordingly. Conservation efforts may not realise their intended aims without CEPA.

The workshop was constructed to present a range of strategies, products and initiatives that deliver educational outcomes among various target audiences.  This range of examples, presented in the papers that follow was significantly broader than what is normally considered under the classification of communication, education and public awareness.

The ultimate aim of those working for the conservation of waterbirds and their wetland habitats is to increase support for biodiversity conservation across all sectors of society.  The CEPA workshop aimed to show that these processes produce real outcomes on their own but also add value to other conservation activity more generally.  However, CEPA strategies and products must be tailored to the framework and needs of the target audience: a high degree of targeting is necessary to ensure successful outcomes.

A number of the presentations and following papers summarise information on formal and community educational programs, community events, networks and partnerships.

All speakers emphasised the value of these initiatives in increasing support for conservation efforts and strongly underscored the need for adequate funding.

Participants agreed that there is a need for communication components to be fully integrated with management efforts. Even in a conference such as this it would have been good to have relevant CEPA papers slotted into other presentations.

# Shorebird Sister Schools Program — shorebird education in North America and beyond

*Hilary Chapman[1], Brad A. Andres[2] & Suzanne Fellows[2]*

[1] *USDA Forest Service, Monogahela National Forest, 200 Sycamore Street, Elkins, West Virginia, 26241, USA.*

2 *U.S. Fish and Wildlife Service, Migratory Bird Management, PO Box 25486, DFC, Denver, Colorado, 80225, USA.*
*(email: Brad_Andres@fws.gov)*

Chapman, H., Andres, B.A. & Fellows, S. 2006. Shorebird Sister Schools Program - shorebird education in North America and beyond. *Waterbirds around the world.* Eds. G.C. Boere, C.A. Galbraith & D.A. Stroud. The Stationery Office, Edinburgh, UK. p. 832.

The Shorebird Sister Schools Program (SSSP) uses the tool of environmental education to integrate shorebird conservation across geographic scales, cultural experiences, and shared ecologies (Andrew & Andres 2002). The linkage of students along the North American Pacific Coast migration route of the Western Sandpiper *Calidis mauri* was the major impetus for launching SSSP. Learning about sandpipers during their brief spring stopover in Kachemak Bay, Alaska, students questioned where the sandpipers spent the rest of the year. Educators responded by initiating an electronic network of 17 Pacific coast schools that tracked the progress of the spring Western Sandpiper migration, and the U.S. Fish and Wildlife service began developing an Arctic-nesting shorebirds curriculum. Growing from these local beginnings, SSSP has expanded to cover all Western Hemisphere, Central Pacific, and East Asian-Australasian flyways, and involves teachers, students, youth groups, nature center interpreters, and protected areas educators at sites that support breeding, migrating, or wintering shorebirds. Equally important is the involvement of professional biologists and amateur enthusiasts who share their research and observations with other participants. Their participation greatly enriches the experience and knowledge gained by students and educators.

The vision of the SSSP is to engage public participation in the conservation of shorebirds and their wetland, grassland, and shoreline ecosystems. Public participation begins with increasing understanding and awareness of local species and habitats, which participants gain through the primary components of the program; an educator's guide for school grades 2–12 (ages 7–18), a student's activity booklet, and a website. The website provides background shorebird information in English, Spanish, and Japanese (http://sssp.fws.gov). Field trips create first-hand awareness of shorebirds, their habitats, and their conservation issues, and information is provided to educators on how to conduct meaningful field trips. In the U.S.A., seven regional coordinators have committed, in conjunction with other professional duties, to develop materials and conduct workshops to familiarize teachers with the activities and resources of the program. These SSSP coordinators focus on "train the trainer" workshops rather than on making individual schoolroom visits. SSSP activities are communicated via professional education journals (Grafe 2004).

Sharing cultural experiences among SSSP participants has always paralleled the geographic linkages of shorebirds. E-mail and written letter exchanges expand the students' education beyond biology. In Japan, staff of the World Wide Fund for Nature (WWF) have translated and modified SSSP materials and have held workshops in Japan and South Korea (http://www.chidori.jp/education/). WWF has developed educational materials specific to the Yellow Sea, which is a critically important stopover site for many migratory shorebirds. Using efforts in Japan and the U.S.A. as a model, the Wetland Centre Australia developed a website, "Feathers, Flyways, and Friends", that contains information on East Asian-Australasian migratory shorebirds and has been translated into Chinese and Japanese (http://www.wetlands.org.au/shorebirds). Their "postcard program" invites children to use the blank side of the postcard to draw a picture about shorebirds and send it to another school. Within the Western Hemisphere, coordinators in Argentina and Mexico have dedicated time to promote and adapt concepts of the SSSP for use in Latin America (Streeter 2004); the educator's guide and student activity booklet have been translated into Spanish. A strong partnership, in which SSSP plays a central role, has been formed between biologists and educators at the Great Salt Lake, Utah, U.S.A., and Marismas Nacionales, Nayarit, Mexico.

Integration across taxonomic boundaries is accomplished in SSSP by developing activities that promote the general conservation of grassland, wetland, and beach ecosystems. Activities have also been designed to reach beyond biology: the educator's guide is correlated to the U.S.A. National Science Education Standards in science, geography, social studies, visual arts, language arts, and mathematics. Shorebird tracking projects, field trips, and other participatory activities engage students in real-life science - the successes, challenges, and setbacks. Students learn that habitats in their own community are part of a chain of healthy habitats critical to shorebirds and other migratory species. In keeping with the program's primary goal of flyway conservation, SSSP connects with researchers and managers through the U.S. Shorebird Conservation Plan Council (http://shorebirdplan.fws.gov). This linkage ensures that SSSP is integrated with shorebird conservation priorities, which in turn strengthens the program's relevance. The success of this education program is due to agency support, partner commitment, and participant enthusiasm. Cruise the super shorebird highway with Shorebird Sister Schools at: http://sssp.fws.gov. For further information, e-mail the National Shorebird Sister Schools Program Coordinator at: sssp@fws.gov.

## REFERENCES

**Andrew, J.M. & Andres, B.A.** 2002. Towards Integrated Bird Conservation – A U.S. Fish & Wildlife Service Perspective. In: K.C. Parsons, S.C. Brown, R.M. Erwin, H.A. Czech, J.C. Coulson, (eds) Waterbirds 25 (Special Publication) 2: 122–127.

**Grafe, D.** 2004. Activity: What can I eat with this beak? — How shorebirds share habitat. Journal of Marine Education 20: 22–24.

**Streeter, N.** 2004. Mi shorebird es su shorebird. Birdscapes (Spring-Summer): 30–31.

# Ten years of International Migratory Bird Day

*Jennifer Wheeler[1] & Susan Bonfield[2]*

[1] *U.S. Fish and Wildlife Service, Division of Migratory Bird Management, 4401 N. Fairfax Drive, Suite 634, Arlington, VA 22203, USA. (email: jennifer_a_wheeler@fws.gov)*
[2] *National Fish and Wildlife Foundation, PO Box 934, 998 Blue River Parkway, Silverthorne, CO 80498, USA.*

Wheeler, J. & Bonfield, S. 2006. Ten years of International Migratory Bird Day. *Waterbirds around the world.* Eds. G.C. Boere, C.A. Galbraith & D.A. Stroud. The Stationery Office, Edinburgh, UK. pp. 833-835.

## ABSTRACT

Public awareness and concern are crucial components of migratory bird conservation. Citizens who are enthusiastic about birds, informed about threats, and empowered to become involved in addressing those threats can make a tremendous contribution to maintaining healthy bird populations. In the Americas, a successful vehicle for public education on migratory birds is International Migratory Bird Day (IMBD), a day of recognition created to foster appreciation and stimulate conservation action. This paper describes how IMBD has grown from a good idea to a significant, annual occurrence marked by hundreds of public celebrations. It provides a brief history of IMBD, a review of the partnerships that sustain it, and a discussion of future directions for the program.

## INTRODUCTION

IMBD, held annually on the second Saturday in May, is an invitation to celebrate and support migratory bird conservation. Like any day of recognition, IMBD exists to focus attention on a valuable resource – the nearly 350 species of migratory birds that travel between nesting habitats in North America and wintering grounds in South and Central America, Mexico, the Caribbean, and the southern USA. IMBD was created in response to disturbing findings in the late 1980s that many of these bird species were in decline, facing a growing number of threats on their migration routes and in both their summer and winter habitats. Thus, IMBD, in addition to being a day to foster appreciation, was created as a call to action.

## A RETROSPECTIVE

The history of IMBD is one of growth – the event was launched with a tremendous amount of energy and has continued to gather momentum over time. Below are some of the highlights in the IMBD story:

### 1993

- Saturday 8 May 1993 marked the first annual IMBD. It was conceived to "provide a platform for the numerous conservation efforts already underway through the Partners In Flight – Aves de las Americas Program, as well as to inspire others into action."
- The Smithsonian Migratory Bird Center compiled The Migratory Bird Handbook, providing activists and educators with strategies, ideas, and resources.
- A Partners In Flight poster with art by Kendahl Jan Jubb was created for distribution.
- The IMBD was considered a glowing success, with 130 events in 39 states, two Canadian provinces, and several locations in Guatemala and Mexico.

International Migratory Bird Day has been a successful vehicle for public education on migratory birds in the Americas. Photo: Jennifer Wheeler.

### 1994

- An Organizer's Information and Media Packet was coordinated by Cornell Laboratory of Ornithology and the National Audubon Society, with a Latin American version produced by the Smithsonian Migratory Bird Center.
- A total of 2 300 packets were mailed by the IMBD date.
- An IMBD 1994 poster was created by Kendahl Jan Jubb, and depicted a wide variety of birds.
- Events tallied at about 100, in at least 30 states and three provinces. The apparent drop in numbers since 1993 was likely due to reporting, as those reports received indicated increases (e.g. the number of events doubled in Alaska).

### 1995

- Coordination moved to the U.S. Fish and Wildlife Service (USFWS) and National Fish and Wildlife Foundation (NFWF), with major sponsorship by Phillips Petroleum Company and others. For the first time, a contractor was hired as a coordinator.
- A new annual Organizer's Packet and an IMBD-specific tee-shirt were developed for distribution on an order basis, and over 30 000 free IMBD 1995 posters were distributed, again featuring art by Kendahl Jan Jubb.
- Promotional material touted "more than 400 events."
- The focus was put on the economic values of non-game birds and non-consumptive, bird-related recreation.

### 1996

- Two separate and expanded packets were produced: an Organizer's Packet and an Educator's Packet.

- Sales of IMBD products were initiated, including banners, tee-shirts, tote-bags, pins, and stickers, on top of distribution purely by sponsorship. Over 40 000 Partners In Flight posters were distributed, featuring art by Margo McNight.
- It was estimated that there were between 250 and 500 local events, and that "tens of thousands" of people were reached by IMBD activities.
- The focus was on the production of the Partners In Flight "Flight Plan".

### 1997

- The first formal products catalogue was produced, including promotional banners, tee-shirts, pins, patches and stickers. Products were distributed by the USFWS.
- The IMBD 1997 poster featured a montage of bird profiles created by Keith Hanson.
- The theme switched from "Sharing A Passion for Birds" to "Join the Flock" – encouraging measurable steps towards conservation. A concerted effort was made to offer the media "solutions."
- Substantial supplements were created for the nearly 1 500 Organizer's and Educator's Packets distributed.

### 1998

- A catalogue was published in full color; the theme was "Catch the Migration Sensation" and highlighted the importance of coastal beaches to neotropical migrants.
- The IMBD 1998 poster by artist John Sill depicted migrants on a Gulf Shore beach.
- IMBD went on-line via an American Birding Association web-site, which included data entry.
- Approximately 24 000 posters were distributed; about 500 contacts were compiled on the sales list.

### 1999

- IMBD highlighted the critical importance of wetlands to migratory birds.
- The IMBD 1999 poster illustrated wetland diversity through art by Carol Decker.
- Product sales were handled out of the American Birding Association's Sales Office.
- Events continued to number in the hundreds.

### 2000

- Art by Roger Tory Peterson featured on IMBD products. The theme was the recovery of an Endangered Species, the Peregrine Falcon.
- A USFWS web-site, including access to an Events Registry, went on-line.
- The first IMBD Distance Learning Program was provided by the National Conservation Training Center.
- A focused effort to tally IMBD activities supported an estimate of hundreds of thousands of people reached via at least 500 public events, countless private events, distance learning and media coverage.

### 2001

- The theme was the benefits of shade-grown coffee, resulting in many new connections and partnerships. The artist Terry Isaac was flown to Guatemala to produce original art for the IMBD 2001 poster.

- Product distribution moved to a NFWF contractor in Colorado Springs; on-line ordering via a NFWF web-site was established.
- A total of 25 000 catalogues were distributed.
- The poster and education piece were translated into Spanish for the first time.

### 2002

- IMBD turned 10 years old! The theme was "Celebrating Special Places for Birds," highlighting habitat conservation especially via the Important Bird Areas programs.
- The IMBD 2002 poster featured a popular print "Mystery of the Missing Migrants" by artist Charley Harper.
- Approximately 40 000 catalogues and 75 000 posters were distributed; about 1 500 contacts were now on the sales list.
- Data from the Events Registry indicated that IMBD was reaching a growing audience.

### PARTNERSHIPS

From its beginnings, IMBD has drawn on the ideas, talents and energies of many individuals and organizations. The principal responsibility for coordination has been shouldered by a few parties, but IMBD is an event that belongs to all who celebrate it.

IMBD's first and lasting affiliation is with Partners In Flight (PIF), recognized by the PIF logo on IMBD products. When PIF formed in 1990, education was identified as a critical element of bird conservation. Members of the PIF Information and Education Working Group and associated Task Group on Education and Outreach produced the first IMBD materials. IMBD is now considered the hallmark outreach event for PIF, and continues to be supported by partners through sponsorship, creation and review of products, promotion, coordination, and celebration. It is particularly effective when a geographic working group or partnering agency takes on local coordination, as has occurred in Colorado, Georgia, Nebraska, Georgia, and Utah, among others.

IMBD also owes much of its success to individuals and organizations not directly affiliated with PIF. For example, sponsors over the years have included Birder's World Magazine, BirdLife International, Canon, the Center for Conservation Research and Technology, Eagle Optics, Harcourt Brace, Mark Feldstein and Associates, Inc., Mill Pond Press, Phillips Corporation, Sanctuary Coffee, The Summit Foundation, Swift Optics, Thanksgiving Coffee, and the Wild Bird Feeding Institute/National Bird Feeding Society (with apologies to any omitted).

The American Zoo and Aquarium Association and its members have promoted and celebrated IMBD; a formal campaign in 2000 resulted in 100 facilities hosting activities, most of which continue to do so. Via an arrangement with Eagle Optics, IMBD catalogues are sent out with every order and taken to trade shows and festivals. The non-profit Kids for Saving Earth mails out catalogues supplemented with their poster. Schools and school systems have embraced IMBD; in 2001, a consortium of 23 school districts highlighted IMBD as part of their county-wide, internet-based project on migratory birds. IMBD has recently partnered with the Council for Environmental Education (Project WILD) to support a new middle-school based program, Flying WILD.

IMBD belongs to all who celebrate it, and IMBD coordinators are eager to develop new partnerships that advance its goals.

## FUTURE DIRECTIONS

By definition, IMBD is a single-day observance. In hindsight, perhaps it might have been easier to have International Migratory Bird Week or Month. Also, its annual date – the second Saturday in May – often conflicts with the timing of bird counts or surveys. However, these issues really are not limiting. Event planners are encouraged to schedule activities on the date or dates best suited to the presence of migrants in their area and are certainly not discouraged from celebrating IMBD on an alternative date. The date of IMBD has intentionally been left off IMBD products to avoid drawing attention to necessary or appropriate rescheduling. Moreover, for those skilled birders with commitments on the second Saturday in May, what better way to celebrate IMBD than to involve new enthusiasts in their activities?

More importantly, IMBD is a movement as well as a day of recognition. The materials and messages created for IMBD are useful year-round. And indeed, IMBD posters are distributed at bird walks and talks all summer long. As another example, IMBD-related educational materials, including the new Junior Birder packets, have been embraced by the Girl Scouts. Wild Bird Centers and Wild Birds Unlimited shops stock IMBD items. Public festivals will always be a core element of IMBD, but providing year-round resources for migratory bird educators is also an important aspect of the program.

How secure is IMBD's future financially and organization-ally? Sales of IMBD products provide income, and prices are set to recover the costs of production and some development. However, an objective of IMBD coordinators is to provide cele-brants, educators especially, with resources at the lowest price possible. Thus, it is likely that IMBD products development will always require sponsorship. "External" funding is also neces-sary to continue IMBD coordination, the bulk of which is performed under contract. However, IMBD itself has been embraced and institutionalized by many organizations. For example, the National Wildlife Refuge System holds IMBD as one of its primary observances. Many zoos and aquariums report IMBD as one of their most successful events. Festivals providing positive economic returns are unlikely to be cancelled. IMBD as an observance will persist as long as it is needed.

Has IMBD been effective? Those involved with IMBD at the time of its creation asked three questions of the program, the answers to which can help us decide if IMBD is achieving its goals.

### Does IMBD educate the public about migratory birds: their habitats, the challenges they face, and status of their populations?

Yes. The materials and messages crafted for IMBD each year always include conservation issues (i.e. they are not limited to natural history or ornithology topics). Given the increasing size of the audience reached, IMBD has certainly been an effective vehicle for education.

### Does it raise awareness of our biological and economic ties to Latin America?

Needs improvement. While IMBD materials and messages have traditionally focused on neotropical migrants, more could be done to connect northern audiences directly to individuals and organizations in Latin America. For example, some festivals highlight an adopted sister-city in the tropics. Alternatively, correspondence programs could be developed enabling students to communicate internationally. Also, it has been a challenge to provide affordable IMBD materials to Latin America to encourage them to celebrate IMBD. Additional sponsorship to support Latin American celebrants would be welcomed.

### Does it prompt the initiation of conservation projects or support existing ones?

We do not know. A primary purpose of IMBD is to stimulate the audience to engage in activities that provide real benefits to populations of wild birds. To this end, IMBD coordinators have striven to integrate suggestions for how people can support bird conservation through specific actions. Themes in recent years have promoted ongoing conservation projects (e.g. shade coffee campaigns, the IBA Programs). However, no evaluations have been conducted to determine if audiences have actually changed their behaviors as a result of exposure to IMBD activities. This question is at the heart of all environmental education programs, and researchers are invited to conduct studies as a means of answering it.

## ACKNOWLEDGEMENTS

The authors wish to acknowledge the sponsorship and support of the National Fish and Wildlife Foundation and the U.S. Fish and Wildlife Service. Special thanks to those individuals – Mary Deinlein and Terry Rich – who reviewed the manuscript.

Meet the heron. Photo: Jennifer Wheeler.

# Wetlands International's Communication, Education and Public Awareness Programme on wetlands for west Africa

*Mame Dagou Diop[1] & Charles Beye[1]*

[1] *Wetlands International, West Africa Programme, PO Box 8060, Dakar Yoff, Senegal. (email: dagouwet@sentoo.sn)*

Dagou Diop, M. & Beye, C. 2006. Wetlands International's Communication, Education and Public Awareness Programme on wetlands for west Africa. *Waterbirds around the world.* Eds. G.C. Boere, C.A. Galbraith & D.A. Stroud. The Stationery Office, Edinburgh, UK. pp. 836-837.

The Wetlands International West Africa Regional Programme established a Wetland Communication, Education and Public Awareness (CEPA) Programme as part of a sub-regional project between 1998 and 2003. At a sub-regional level it aims to improve knowledge of wetlands and their wise use within the general public, decision makers, the private sector and other target groups. This paper reports on activities carried out by the programme.

The Wetlands CEPA Strategy is a framework that supports the integration of various local, national, regional and international concerns on wetlands, including those of the Information Programme of the Ramsar Convention. It also aims to enable direct training policies that are applicable at different levels. The development of a draft Wetlands CEPA Strategy for West Africa was finalised after wide consultation with stakeholders through questionnaires and a regional workshop. During this process, partners were encouraged to define problems and solutions for adopting CEPA as a central instrument towards satisfying wetland conservation objectives.

Training course for protected area managers, Khartoum, Sudan. Wetlands International has organised a wide range of courses for protected area personnel in East and West Africa. Photo: Tim Dodman.

CEPA started in 2001 with the circulation at the regional level of a questionnaire to inventory and identify CEPA needs in West Africa and two Central African countries, Cameroon and Chad. A background document was developed after analyzing the questionnaire responses and subsequently adopted during a regional workshop held in September 2002 in Dakar. After consultation on regional priorities, an action framework was proposed and embodied in the strategy document.

Several opportunities were identified in the sub-region:

- the existence of educational and training institutions interested in the issue of wetlands and which already offer training opportunities on various themes (general knowledge of wetlands, development, conservation, management);
- the existence of proven expertise in this field, and networks and advisory groups offering skill and experience;
- the support of various international organizations for wetlands conservation and restoration (IUCN, Wetlands International, Birdlife International); and
- the involvement of local, national and regional associations in education and public awareness activities.

In order to supplement and strengthen these opportunities, the strategy needed to focus on two major objectives:

- enhance awareness of the values and functions of wetlands through education, awareness and training; and
- provide support and tools for the practical implementation of the communication, education and public awareness (CESP) activities at the national and local levels.

**Fig 1.** Booklet for students on wetlands and waterbird migration in Guinea-Bissau.

These are essential elements in the overall strategy to conserve wetland environments, and are a prerequisite to the adoption of wetland issues by local stakeholders, and to their effective involvement in the sustainable use of resources.

Within the framework of the draft strategy and related projects, a range of activities have already been carried out, including:

- publication of a bilingual newsletter on wetlands, "Fadama". This is intended as a forum for the interchange of knowledge of wetlands management and the conservation of wetlands wildlife, including its distribution and threats to the habitat;
- "Better Understanding our Wetlands" is a series of four publications which aims to raise awareness among NGO decision-makers and planners, administrative authorities, national aid organisations, donors and the national education sector to promote wetland related issues and environmentally-friendly decisions in development matters favourable to the preservation of these ecosystems and the sustainable use of their resources;
- development and publication of a "Wetland Games" manual for primary schools after a trial in Senegalese schools. The present manual is intended help teachers of elementary schools define and present environmental concepts to their pupils;
- publication of a waterbird exercise book and booklet on migration in Mali; and
- publication of CEPA booklets for students on wetlands and waterbird migration in Guinea-Bissau (Fig. 1).

In June 2004, a series of Conferences was held at the Department of Geography, Cheikh Anta Diop University (Dakar, Senegal) on "Waterbirds Biodiversity in Coastal Wetlands: Conservation, Monitoring and Management."

Field activities on Education and Public Awareness on wetlands have included:

- support of World Wetlands Day celebrations (conferences, field trips, competitions, TV and radio broadcast) in Burkina Faso, Côte d'Ivoire, The Gambia, Guinea, Guinea-Bissau, Ghana, Mauritania, Senegal, Sierra Leone and Nigeria;
- regular production of diverse CEPA materials including T-shirts, caps, posters and calendars; and
- creation of local clubs and site guardians to build awareness of wetlands and threatened species at key sites.

Although a sub-regional strategy is now available, a key challenge is raising funds for its implementation. Limited funds are a key obstacle to the implementation of CEPA by many environmental NGOs in the sub-region. Another challenge at the sub-regional level is the need to provide materials in many local languages to make them widely accessible, especially in rural communities.

Overall, some key actions are required for the continued sustainable operation of the programme:

- develop an implementation plan for the regional CEPA Strategy;
- establish a sub-regional CEPA Specialist Group to guide implementation and identify national needs;
- establish a framework for consultation on wetlands CEPA, especially between environmental and development NGOs; and
- enable CEPA to act through the development of a sub-regional funding mechanism to which partners across the region may apply for support to carry out CEPA activities.

Community environmental awareness meeting at Bouyou village, Lac Nanga, a coastal wetland in Congo. Photo: Tim Dodman.

# Wetland Link International (WLI): a global network for wetland centres

*Malcolm Whitehead*

*The Wildfowl & Wetlands Trust, London Wetland Centre, Queen Elizabeth's Walk, Barnes, London, SW13 9WT, UK.*

Whitehead, M. 2006. Wetland Link International (WLI): a global network for wetland centres. *Waterbirds around the world.* Eds. G.C. Boere, C.A. Galbraith & D.A. Stroud. The Stationery Office, Edinburgh, UK. pp. 838-840.

## ABSTRACT

The importance of wetland centres for connecting people to nature is discussed. Wetland centres are important vehicles for delivering CEPA (communication, education and public awareness) about wetlands. In this way, they assist countries to meet their commitments as Contracting Parties to the Ramsar Convention on Wetlands. The potential of wetland centres is increased when they are able to share ideas and expertise. Hence the need for a global umbrella network – WLI – or Wetland Link International. This paper outlines the objectives of WLI, the benefits of membership, and how to join.

## WHY HAVE WETLAND CENTRES? THE CONTEXT

Without wetlands, there is no water for life. Of the world's water, 97% is salty and oceanic. Of the remaining 3%, nearly all is frozen in polar regions or imprisoned underground. Most life – including human life – depends on 0.26% of global freshwater. This water is stored in wetlands: from lakes and lagoons to marshes, ponds, pools, fens, bogs and rivers.

Wetlands store water and carbon. They filter and clean water. They mitigate against the effects of storms and floods. They stabilize shorelines and prevent coastal erosion. They are the source of numerous products from food and fibre to fuel and pharmaceuticals. They are homes for a wealth of biodiversity. They reveal clues to historic and modern human cultures through archaeology. They are enormously productive and of immense economic, political, developmental and socio-cultural importance.

People need wetlands. Life needs wetlands. This is not always immediately apparent. City dwellers may not know or consider how their household water supply depends on local wetlands. Many people world-wide have to travel long distances for fresh, clean water. In some countries, access to water is a major health and security issue.

Wetlands disappear under development, drainage and pollution; underground aquifers recede with over-consumption; species are lost; the combination of extreme weather and diminishing wetlands causes major flooding, affecting countries as diverse as Bangladesh, China, the USA and the UK.

The solution depends on many things, but primarily on people. First, though, people must become aware and engaged with wetlands. They must be connected, concerned and competent to make informed decisions and take positive action for wetland environments.

This is where wetland centres come in.

## THE ROLE AND DIVERSITY OF WETLAND CENTRES – REAL VALUE FROM REAL LIFE

Wetlands are a great conduit – a "way in" – for exploring all sorts of topical environmental issues. These include basic ecological literacy, the conservation of species and habitats (biodiversity), and local/global water issues. Further, they are amphitheatres of experience where feelings, emotions and values are developed.

Wetland centres are prime vehicles for raising awareness, focusing experience and catalysing environmental action on behalf of wetlands.

There are several hundred wetland centres throughout the world. They range from embryonic, community-led initiatives in Lagos, Nigeria, to high-tech, multi-media interactive exhibits in Hong Kong's International Wetland Park. Many are managed by non-governmental organizations (NGOs) such as the Wildfowl & Wetlands Trust (WWT, with nine centres in the UK) and Worldwide Fund for Nature (WWF, with wetland centres including those at Karachi, Pakistan, and Mai Po, Hong Kong). Some are run by governments (e.g. Sungei Buloh Wetland Reserve in Singapore, managed by the government's National Parks Board). A few are managed by NGOs for governments (e.g. Kota Kinabalu City Bird Sanctuary in Sabah, Malaysia).

Wetland centres may operate in partnership with other sectors. The WWT's London Wetland Centre in the UK was developed by the WWT, Thames Water (a public water company) and Berkeley Homes (a private housing developer). The Point-a-Pierre Wildfowl Trust in Trinidad is sited within a major petrochemical complex (Petrotrin). The Soonabai Pirojsha Godrej Foundation Mangrove Project in India is a public charitable Trust linked to M/s Godrej & Boyce Mfg. Co. Ltd., a multi-product Indian corporate.

## WETLAND CENTRES – THE PEOPLE POTENTIAL

Wetland centres bring people and wildlife together for the benefit of both. They offer major opportunities for CEPA (communication, education and public awareness) about wetlands: their biodiversity, functions and values. Globally, wetland centres provide numerous learning programmes for formal (school and university) and non-formal (the general public – adults and youth) audiences. Many have education staff and volunteers. At The Wetland Centre at Shortlands in Australia, a successful schools programme is run in partnership with the State Government (New South Wales) Department of Education and Training.

Wetland centres provide amazing natural spectacles. They are wildlife havens, conservation centres, visitor attractions and eco-tourism venues operated as sites for public learning, access to green space, and biodiversity/heritage conservation. During the southern summer, over two million migratory shorebirds visit Australian wetlands on migration. Visitors to coastal wetland centres marvel at the diversity and sheer numbers. Most of the Svalbard population of the Barnacle Goose *Branta leucopsis* winters in and around the WWT wetland centre at Caerlaverock on the banks of Scotland's Solway Firth in the UK.

Cultural heritage is also a major feature of wetland centres. At the WWT Martin Mere centre in the UK, interpretation reveals the rich history of the mere through "biofacts" and arte-facts, from Pleistocene mammals to Neolithic wooden parth-ways and "bog bodies" buried in the mere in Roman times. The Pointe-a-Pierre Wildfowl Trust in Trinidad has an Amerindian Museum.

The sense of place engendered by immersion in a wetland centre can be a significant life experience leading to concern and care for the planet. Who could not be affected by the big skies of the WWT Welney centre in the fens of eastern England, the haunting peat bog landscapes associated with Peatland World in Ireland's Bog of Allen, the tropical coastal paradise of Cousin Island in the Seychelles, and the majesty of Chesapeake Bay around the Horsehead Wetland Centre in the eastern USA?

Wetland centres offer unparalleled close encounters and access to secret worlds. Hidden cameras bring the breeding dramas of seabird colonies to the comfort of the Scottish Seabird Centre; Denmark's Aqua Ferskvands Aqvarium is an inside-out aquarium with fresh views of grebes, otters and others; and at Het Zwin in Belgium, visitors can come eyeball to eyeball with a White Stork *Ciconia ciconia*. The Caneo Visitor Centre near Trieste in Italy provides an opportunity to stay in the middle of reed-beds and salt-marsh, while at Wye Marsh Wildlife Centre in Canada, visitors can canoe, ski cross-country, hike or snowshoe across the site during different seasons.

Connection to nature at wetland centres relieves stress and is spiritually uplifting. At the WWT's London Wetland Centre, yoga groups and "green" gym members escape the stresses of city life. Everyday, a host of urban dwellers walk, cycle and roller skate around the Costanera Sur Ecological Reserve on the edge of Buenos Aires in Argentina. The health benefits of being around nature are only beginning to be understood.

Wetland centres link local communities to "their" wetlands, encouraging ownership and stewardship. At Lake Elementeita in Kenya's Rift Valley, a group of local people have built an Education Centre to encourage local engagement and environ-mental action around this important site for flamingos.

Wetland centres may be a mixture of nature reserve, wilder-ness area, botanical garden, collection of captive animals, museum, science centre and cultural heritage site. They may be important wildlife and landscape features in the integrated management of urban water catchments. They are inclusive and offer access to all. In much of Europe, Australia and North America, they offer exposure to real life in safe surroundings. This is vital where people are increasingly alienated from nature through prescriptive school-based curricula, health and safety fears, litigious societies, and the dominance of virtual media

## POLICY AND PARTNERS – THE RAMSAR CONVEN-TION AND CEPA

The Ramsar Convention on Wetlands is an intergovernmental treaty providing the framework for countries to adopt local, regional and national actions and international co-operation for the conservation and wise use of wetlands and their resources. The Convention was launched at the Iranian town of Ramsar in 1971. Today, some 152 countries have joined Ramsar as Contracting Parties, and have designated nearly 1 400 sites world-wide as wetlands of international importance, totalling over 145 million hectares (Ramsar Convention 2004).

Ramsar Resolution VIII. 31 defines the CEPA Programme of the Convention. The vision of the Ramsar CEPA Programme is

"people working for the wise use of wetlands." The programme is underpinned by the following guiding principles (Ramsar Convention 2004b):

- Wetlands provide important goods and services which help sustain human life, conserve biological diversity, and combat the impacts of climate change and desertification. CEPA are the tools for placing people's social, political, economic and cultural realities within the context of the goods and services provided by wetland ecosystems.
- The Ramsar Convention seeks to motivate people to appre-ciate the values of wetlands so that they become advocates for wetland conservation and wise use and may act to become involved in relevant policy formulation, planning and management.
- The key actors in the implementation of the Ramsar Convention need effective CEPA tools and expertise to engage major stakeholders and to convey appropriate messages in order to mainstream the wise-use principle throughout society.
- Wise-use issues and concepts need to be communicated effectively to ensure participation of major stakeholders from different sectors and mainstreaming of the issues in sector plans and actions. This communication needs to operate laterally, across and between sectors, and also verti-cally from stakeholders to governments and back.
- Support for the CEPA Programme should be recognized by Parties to the Convention as an investment which will reduce conflicts over wetland resources, increase the number of advocates, actors and networks involved in the issues, and build an informed decision-making and public constituency. CEPA mobilizes actions directed at achieving the wise use of wetlands. CEPA should form a central part of imple-menting the Ramsar Convention by each Contracting Party.

Operational Objective 3.3 of the Ramsar CEPA Programme identifies Wetland Education Centres as key locations for promoting the principles of wetland conservation and wise use through CEPA activities. It seeks to establish wetland education centres at Ramsar and other wetland sites to provide Ramsar focal points for local and national CEPA activities.

The programme also identifies the Wetland Link International (WLI) network as a key organization to assist the Ramsar Contracting Parties in this area of work. It encourages participation in the Wetland Link International of the Wildfowl & Wetlands Trust, UK, as a mechanism for gaining access to global and national expertise in CEPA (Ramsar Convention 2002).

## WETLAND LINK INTERNATIONAL (WLI)

WLI is a global network of Wetland Education Centres. The network defines Wetland Education Centre as "any place where there is interaction between people and wildlife, and CEPA activity occurs in support of wetland conservation" (WWT 2004).

The WLI network embraces wetland nature and cultural heritage reserves with a diverse range of visitor facilities (e.g. centres run by the WWT), environmental education centres, field study centres, zoos and botanical gardens, interactive natural history museums, and a wide variety of site-based community projects and programmes.

WLI was founded in 1991 and developed from a range of wishes and desires. These included:

- the wish to reduce feelings of isolation of those involved with on-the-ground CEPA activities;
- the wish to share knowledge and practical expertise;
- the wish to raise the profile and status of CEPA activity as part of conservation and sustainability objectives;
- the desire to produce solutions.

WLI is co-ordinated by the Wildfowl & Wetlands Trust, the UK's largest NGO dedicated to international wetland conservation. The network is endorsed by the Ramsar Secretariat and supported by the HSBC Bank plc.

## WLI OBJECTIVES

WLI has the following objectives:

- To encourage and support the exchange of information and expertise internationally between those involved in wetland education programmes, particularly those operating from Wetland Education Centres, field study and environmental education centres, zoos and botanical gardens, and aquariums.
- To advocate for, and assist in, the development of new Wetland Education Centres and their associated programmes world-wide.
- To improve the effectiveness of operations at Wetland Education Centres by sharing expertise through training and exchange programmes.
- To lobby for the greater inclusion of CEPA programmes within wetlands and related conservation initiatives and instruments, and to support the development of frameworks for subsequent implementation at national, regional and global levels.

No-one knows how many wetland centres exist world-wide. A compilation of national Ramsar reports reveals several hundred, but if other categories are included (e.g. non-Ramsar sites, public aquariums, zoos), the number may be thousands. About 200 of these from six continents are included on the WLI database

## WLI MEMBERSHIP

WLI membership is site-based and open to any organization, group or individual who is planning, designing or operating a place or places that conform to the definition of a Wetland Education Centre above. Members may be governmental, non-governmental, professional, amateur, paid or voluntary. Details of specific Wetland Education Centres may be found in the "WLI World Global Directory" on the WLI web-site, or by emailing the WLI Co-ordinator. Benefits of membership include the following: WLI members become part of an international community of Wetland Education Centres.

- There is a WLI e-group to share ideas and expertise, from the design and planning of centres to specific programmes and events, such as World Wetlands Day.
- A quarterly E-newsletter will be sent to all WLI members and key contacts (e.g. Ramsar focal point) from 2005.

- All WLI members have access to advice, support and expertise from the WLI Co-ordinator and membership.
- There will be opportunities for training, meetings and staff exchange as the WLI Professional Development programme progresses.

WLI is keen to develop regional networks that assist with local, national and regional issues in wetland education. For example, a local network may be well suited to pool ideas and resources for events such as World Wetlands Day. National networks can be presented to governments as evidence that they (the governments as Contracting Parties to the Ramsar Convention) are "ticking the boxes" in terms of fulfilling their obligations to the Ramsar CEPA Programme.

Currently there is a WLI Australia, co-ordinated by The Wetlands Centre, Shortlands, and a WLI UK, co-ordinated by the Wildfowl & Wetlands Trust. A WLI-Asia network is in the development stage, with a preliminary meeting booked for mid-2005, and a WLI Europe-Africa is at the planning stage, with an intended launch in late 2005. Efforts will be made in the future to organize WLI regional representation on all continents.

## HOW TO JOIN WLI

Prospective members should email the WLI Co-ordinator, Malcolm.whitehead@wwt.org.uk, or write to: The WLI Co-ordinator, WWT London Wetland Centre, Queen Elizabeth's Walk, Barnes, London SW13 9WT, UK. Membership is free, but members will be asked to submit a WLI site profile for inclusion in the "WLI World Global Directory" on the WLI web-site (www.wli.org.uk).

## REFERENCES

**Ramsar Convention** 2006. www.ramsar.org. As at 24 July, 2006.

**Ramsar Convention** 2002. Resolution viii.31. The Convention's Programme on communication, education and public awareness (CEPA) 2003-2008. http://www.ramsar.org/key_res_viii_31_e.htm.

**WWT** 2004. Making a Splash – the potential and practice of wetland centres. Downloadable from www.wli.org.uk .

Wetland centres bring people and wildlife together for the benefit of both. Photo: The Wildfowl & Wetlands Trust.

# Birding in the United States: a demographic and economic analysis

*Genevieve Pullis La Rouche*

*Division of Federal Aid, U.S. Fish and Wildlife Service, Washington, D.C. 20240, USA. (email: genevieve_pullis@fws.gov)*

Pullis La Rouche, G. 2006. Birding in the United States: a demographic and economic analysis. *Waterbirds around the world.* Eds. G.C. Boere, C.A. Galbraith & D.A. Stroud. The Stationery Office, Edinburgh, UK. pp. 841-846.

## ABSTRACT

Bird-watchers are an untapped source of support for bird conservation. Data from the United States Fish and Wildlife Service's 2001 National Survey of Fishing, Hunting and Wildlife-Related Recreation provide socio-demographic and economic information about birders that can be used when planning outreach and building public backing for bird conservation plans. The Survey, conducted since 1955, is one of the oldest and most comprehensive continuing recreation studies. Conducted every five years, it was initially created to collect participation and expenditures of sportspersons, but was expanded in 1980 to include non-consumptive recreation – feeding, photographing and observing of wildlife. In August 2003, the Survey's first report on bird-watching was released as an Addendum to the 2001 Survey (Pullis La Rouche 2003). It revealed that in the United States 46 million people watched birds – nearly one in five adults – and they spent US$ 32 billion in retail sales thereby contributing US$ 85 billion in economic output and creating 863 405 jobs. The data also provide a wealth of information about the kind of birds being watched (47% of bird-watchers watch waterbirds), and trends in participation, avidity, and spending.

## INTRODUCTION

In January 2002 an unprecedented major media event unfolded in a Louisiana swamp. A team of top ornithologists set out to find the Ivory-billed Woodpecker *Campephilus principalis*, a bird last seen in the United States in 1943 and, until a recent credible sighting by a turkey hunter, considered extinct in the U.S. The expedition, funded by a corporate sponsor, received worldwide media attention including coverage by the New York Times, USA Today, and National Public Radio. This high-profile search for the Ivory-billed Woodpecker is just one indicator of the growing popularization of birds and birding. Other evidence abounds. A field guide, *Sibley's Guide to Birds*, became a New York Times bestseller. And a quick search of the internet yields numerous birding sites, some of which list hundreds of birding festivals held around the country each year.

This growing awareness of birding comes at an odd time; birds are in jeopardy. According to 35-year trend data (1966-2001) from the U.S. Geological Service, almost one-in-four bird species in the United States show "significant negative trend estimates" (Sauer *et al.* 2003). This decline is attributed primarily to the degradation and destruction of habitat resulting from human population growth and short-sighted environmental practices such as the razing of wetlands needed by migratory birds. Although there is a certain irony in people becoming enthusiastic about birds as they disappear, it also presents an opportunity: birders may be the economic and political force that can help save the birds. The following report provides up-to-date information so birders and policy makers can make informed decisions regarding the protection of birds and their habitats.

This report identifies who birders are, where they live, how avid they are, where they bird and what kinds of birds they watch. In addition to demographic information, this report also provides two kinds of economic measures. The first is an estimate of how much birders spend on their hobby and the economic impact of these expenditures. The second is the net economic value of birding, that is, the value of birding to society.

By understanding who birders are, they can be more easily educated about pressures facing birds and bird habitats. Conversely, by knowing who is likely *not* a birder, or who is potentially a birder, information can be more effectively tailored. The economic values presented here can be used by resource managers and policy makers to demonstrate the economic might of birders, the value of birding – and by extension, the value of birds. In fact, research shows that these kinds of values help wildlife managers make better decisions and illustrate the value of wildlife to American society (Loomis 2000).

All data presented here are from the wildlife-watching section of the 2001 National Survey of Fishing, Hunting, and Wildlife-Associated Recreation (FHWAR). It is the most comprehensive survey of wildlife recreation in the U.S. Overall, 15 300 detailed wildlife-watching interviews were completed with a response rate of 90 percent. The Survey focused on 2001 participation and expenditures by U.S. residents 16 years of age and older.

## BIRDERS

In 2001 there were 46 million bird-watchers or birders, 16 years of age and older, in the United States – a little over one in five people. What is a birder? The National Survey uses a conservative definition. To be counted as a birder, an individual must have either taken a trip a mile or more from home for the primary purpose of observing birds and/or closely observed or tried to identify birds around the home. So people who happened to notice birds while they were mowing the lawn or picnicking at the beach were not counted as birders. Trips to zoos and observing captive birds also did not count.

Backyard birding or watching birds around the home is the most common form of bird-watching. Eighty-eight percent (40 million) of birders are backyard birders. The more active form of birding, taking trips away from home, is less common with 40 percent (18 million) of birders partaking.

The average birder is 49 years old and more than likely has a better than average income and education. She is slightly more likely to be female, and highly likely to be white and married. There is also a good chance that this birder lives in the northern half of the country in a small city or town. Does this paint an accurate picture of a birder? Like all generalizations the description of an "average" birder does not reflect the variety of people who bird, with millions falling outside this box. The tables show in numbers and participation rates (the percentage of people who participate) birders by various demographic breakdowns.

**Table 1. Age distribution of the United States population and birders: 2001. (Population 16 years of age and older; numbers in thousands).**

| Age | US population | Number of birders | Participation rate |
|---|---|---|---|
| 16 and 17 | 7 709 | 1 043 | 14% |
| 18 to 24 | 22 234 | 1 894 | 9% |
| 25 to 34 | 5 333 | 5 990 | 17% |
| 35 to 44 | 4 057 | 10 414 | 24% |
| 45 to 54 | 40 541 | 10 541 | 26% |
| 55 to 64 | 25 601 | 7 177 | 28% |
| 65 plus | 36 823 | 8 893 | 24% |

**Table 2. Income distribution of the United States population and birders: 2001. (Population 16 years of age and older; numbers in thousands).**

| Income | US population | Number of birders | Participation rate |
|---|---|---|---|
| Less than $10 000 | 10 594 | 2 212 | 21% |
| $10 000 to $19 000 | 15 272 | 2 754 | 18% |
| $20 000 to $24 000 | 10 902 | 2 335 | 21% |
| $25 000 to $29 000 | 11 217 | 2 392 | 21% |
| $30 000 to $34 000 | 11 648 | 2 618 | 22% |
| $35 000 to $39 000 | 9 816 | 2 005 | 20% |
| $40 000 to $49 000 | 16 896 | 4 116 | 24% |
| $50 000 to $74 000 | 31 383 | 7 476 | 24% |
| $75 000 to $99 000 | 17 762 | 4 771 | 27% |
| $100 000 or more | 19 202 | 5 224 | 27% |

**Table 3. Educational distribution of the United States population and birders: 2001. (Population 16 years of age and older; numbers in thousands).**

| Education | US population | Number of birders | Participation rate |
|---|---|---|---|
| 11 years or less | 32 820 | 4 627 | 14% |
| 12 years | 73 719 | 13 933 | 19% |
| 1 to 3 years at college | 49 491 | 11 363 | 23% |
| 4 years at college | 34 803 | 8 922 | 26% |
| 5 years or more college | 1 646 | 7 107 | 33% |

**Table 4. Racial and ethnic distribution of the United States population and birders: 2001. (Population 16 years of age and older; numbers in thousands).**

| Race/ethnicity | US population | Number of birders | Participation rate |
|---|---|---|---|
| Hispanic | 21 910 | 1 880 | 9% |
| White | 181 129 | 43 026 | 24% |
| African-American | 21 708 | 1 243 | 6% |
| Native American | 1 486 | 321 | 22% |
| Asian | 7 141 | 436 | 6% |
| Other | 833 | 55 | 7% |

The tendency of birders to be middle-age or older is reflected in both the number of birders and participation rates. Looking at the different age breakdowns in Table 1, the greatest number of birders were in the 35 to 44 and 45 to 54 age groups. People aged 55 to 64 had the highest participation rates while the participation rate was particularly low for people aged 18 to 24. Birders who take trips away from home to pursue their hobby were on average slightly younger, at 45 years old compared to backyard birders who were on average 50 years old.

The higher the income and education level the more likely a person is to be a birder. Twenty-seven percent of people who live in households that earn US$ 75 000 or more were bird-watchers – 5 percent above the national average of 22 percent. Education, which is often highly correlated with income, shows the same trend. People with less than high school education participated at 14 percent – far below the national average – while people with five or more years of college had the highest participation rate at 33 percent. See Tables 2 and 3 for more information.

Unlike hunting and fishing where men were overwhelmingly in the majority, a slightly larger percent of birders were women – 54 percent in 2001. And most birders, 72 percent, were married.

Excepting Native American participation, birders are not a racially or ethnically diverse group. Ninety-four percent of birders identified themselves as white. The scarcity of minority birders is not just a reflection of their relatively low numbers in the population at large, it is also a function of low participation rates. The participation rates of African-Americans, Asians, and Hispanics were all 9 percent or lower while the rate for whites, 24 percent, was slightly above the 22 percent national average. Native Americans on the other hand had a participation rate (22 percent) on par with the national average. See Table 4.

The sparser populated an area, the more likely its residents were to watch birds. The participation rate for people living in small cities and rural areas was 28 percent – 6 percent above the national average. Whereas large metropolitan areas (1 million residents or more) had the greatest number of birders, their residents had the lowest participation rate, 18 percent. See Table 5.

When measured in terms of the percent of state residents participating, states in the northern half of the United States generally had higher levels of participation than did states in the southern half. While 44 percent of Montanans and 43 percent of Vermonters watched birds, only 14 percent of Californians and Texans did. See Table 6.

The participation rate was highest (30%) in the West North Central region of the United States. The New England states had the second highest participation rate at 27 percent with a close third going to the Rocky Mountain states (26 percent). The West South Central states had the lowest rate of 17 percent while the Pacific and South Atlantic states yielded slightly higher rates, both 19 percent. However, in terms of sheer numbers, the Pacific and South Atlantic states had the most resident birders – 7 million and 8 million respectively, while New England had the least, 3 million.

Bird-watching by state residents tells only part of the story. Many people travel out-of-state to watch birds and some states are natural birding destinations. Wyoming reaped the benefits of this tourism with a whopping 67 percent of their total birders coming from other states. The scenic northern states of New Hampshire, Vermont, Montana, and Alaska also attracted many birders – all had more than 40 percent of their total birders coming from other states. See Table 7.

**Table 5. Percentage of United States population who birded by residence: 2001. (Population 16 years of age and older; numbers in thousands).**

| Metropolitan Statistical Area | US population | Number of birders | Participation rate |
|---|---|---|---|
| 1 000 000 or more | 112 984 | 20 868 | 18% |
| 250 000 to 999 999 | 41 469 | 8 991 | 22% |
| 50 000 to 249 000 | 16 693 | 4 622 | 28% |
| Outside MSA | 41 151 | 11 470 | 28% |

**Table 6. Birding participation rates by state residents: 2001. (Population 16 years of age and older).**

| | | US average | 22% |
|---|---|---|---|
| Montana | 44% | Vermont | 43% |
| Wisconsin | 41% | Washington | 36% |
| Minnesota | 36% | Maine | 36% |
| Alaska | 36% | Kentucky | 35% |
| Oregon | 35% | New Hampshire | 34% |
| Wyoming | 34% | Iowa | 34% |
| South Dakota | 33% | Idaho | 29% |
| Indiana | 29% | New Mexico | 28% |
| Virginia | 28% | Utah | 27% |
| Oklahoma | 27% | Pennsylvania | 27% |
| Missouri | 26% | Colorado | 25% |
| Tennessee | 25% | Nebraska | 25% |
| Connecticut | 25% | West Virginia | 24% |
| Arkansas | 24% | Kansas | 24% |
| Michigan | 23% | Maryland | 22% |
| Arizona | 22% | Massachusetts | 22% |
| South Carolina | 20% | Ohio | 20% |
| Rhode Island | 19% | North Carolina | 18% |
| Illinois | 18% | New Jersey | 18% |
| Delaware | 18% | Mississippi | 18% |
| Alabama | 18% | North Dakota | 17% |
| New York | 17% | Florida | 16% |
| Louisiana | 16% | Georgia | 15% |
| Nevada | 15% | Texas | 14% |
| California | 14% | Hawaii | 9% |

## Where and what are they watching?

Backyard birding is the most prevalent form of birding with 88 percent of participants watching birds from the comfort of their homes. Forty percent of birders travel more than a mile from home to bird, visiting a variety of habitats on both private and public lands. Of the 18 million Americans who ventured away from home to watch birds, public land rather than private land was visited more frequently, although many visited both. Eighty-three percent of birders used public land such as parks and wildlife refuges, 42 percent used private land, and 31 percent visited both.

The most popular setting to observe birds was in the woods (73%), followed by lakes and streamside areas (69%) and brush-covered areas and fields (62% and 61%). Less popular sites were the ocean (27%) and manmade areas (31%) such as golf courses and cemeteries. See Table 8.

What kinds of birds are they looking at? Seventy-eight percent reported observing waterfowl, making them the most spied on

**Table 7. Birding by state residents and non-residents: 2001. (Population 16 years of age and older; numbers in thousands).**

| State | Total birders | Percent state residents | Percent non-residents |
|---|---|---|---|
| Alabama | 703 | 90 | 10 |
| Alaska | 321 | 51 | 49 |
| Arizona | 1 168 | 70 | 30 |
| Arkansas | 548 | 88 | 12 |
| California | 3 987 | 91 | 9 |
| Colorado | 1 077 | 74 | 26 |
| Connecticut | 732 | 88 | 12 |
| Delaware | 172 | 63 | 37 |
| Florida | 2 363 | 80 | 20 |
| Georgia | 1 063 | 84 | 16 |
| Hawaii | 164 | 48 | 52 |
| Idaho | 478 | 60 | 40 |
| Illinois | 1 815 | 90 | 10 |
| Indiana | 1 423 | 94 | 6 |
| Iowa | 813 | 93 | 7 |
| Kansas | 569 | 87 | 13 |
| Kentucky | 803 | 91 | 9 |
| Louisiana | 608 | 86 | 14 |
| Maine | 595 | 61 | 39 |
| Maryland | 1 068 | 82 | 18 |
| Massachusetts | 1 263 | 86 | 12 |
| Michigan | 1 961 | 88 | 12 |
| Minnesota | 1 471 | 90 | 10 |
| Mississippi | 437 | 88 | 12 |
| Missouri | 1 299 | 85 | 15 |
| Montana | 558 | 55 | 45 |
| Nebraska | 386 | 83 | 17 |
| Nevada | 343 | 63 | 37 |
| New Hampshire | 569 | 57 | 43 |
| New Jersey | 1 335 | 85 | 15 |
| New Mexico | 531 | 70 | 30 |
| New York | 2 802 | 88 | 12 |
| North Carolina | 1 296 | 80 | 20 |
| North Dakota | 134 | 60 | 40 |
| Ohio | 1 899 | 93 | 7 |
| Oklahoma | 760 | 91 | 19 |
| Oregon | 1 187 | 77 | 23 |
| Pennsylvania | 2 721 | 91 | 10 |
| Rhode Island | 193 | 76 | 25 |
| South Carolina | 742 | 84 | 16 |
| South Dakota | 271 | 68 | 32 |
| Tennessee | 1 420 | 76 | 24 |
| Vermont | 383 | 53 | 47 |
| Virginia | 1 818 | 86 | 14 |
| Washington | 1 877 | 86 | 14 |
| West Virginia | 428 | 80 | 20 |
| Wisconsin | 1 944 | 86 | 14 |
| Wyoming | 388 | 33 | 67 |

**Table 8. Sites visited by away-from-home birders: 2001. (Population 16 years of age and older; numbers in thousands).**

|                       | Number of birders | Percent |
|-----------------------|-------------------|---------|
| Total, all birders    | 18 342            | 100     |
| Woodland              | 13 405            | 73      |
| Lake and streamside   | 12 615            | 69      |
| Brush-covered areas   | 11 324            | 62      |
| Open field            | 11 184            | 61      |
| Marsh, wetland, swamp | 8 632             | 47      |
| Man-made areas        | 5 770             | 31      |
| Oceanside             | 4 921             | 27      |
| Other                 | 2 418             | 13      |

**Table 9. Percentage of birders\* who can identify birds by sight or sound and who kept birding life lists: 1980 and 2001.**

|                        | 1980 | 2001 |
|------------------------|------|------|
| 1-20 bird species      | 74%  | 74%  |
| 21-40 bird species     | 14%  | 13%  |
| 41 or more bird species| 5%   | 8%   |
| Kept birding life list | 4%   | 5%   |

\* In 1980, the question was asked of all wildlife-watchers (formerly called non-consumptive) and in 2001 the question was asked of only birders.

type of bird. Songbirds were also popular with 70 percent of birders watching them, followed in popularity by birds of prey (68%) and other waterbirds such as herons and shorebirds (56%).

### Birding trends

Is birding increasing? Despite recent popularization (high visibility within the media and popular culture and increased recognition of the sport within American homes) of birding, past FHWAR Survey results point to a more complicated story. A comparison of results from the 1991, 1996, and 2001 estimates show that bird-watching around the home has decreased rather than increased over that 10-year period (USFWS 1993, 1997, 2002). In 1991, 51.3 million people reported observing birds around their homes. In 1996 that number dropped to 42.2 million and in 2001 to 40.3 million. Because the 2001 Survey is the first time people were asked if they specifically watched birds on trips away from home, it cannot be said conclusively if this activity increased or decreased. However, in all three Surveys, people were asked if they observed, fed, or photographed birds away from home. These numbers indicate a net decrease in away-from home birding from 24.7 million in 1991 to 18.5 million in 2001 but a slight uptick from 1996 (17.7 million) to 2001.

### Avidity

All people identified as birders in this report said that they took an active interest in birds – defined as trying to closely observe or identify different species. But what is the extent of their interest? In order to determine their "avidity" the following factors were considered: the number of days spent bird-watching; the number of species they could identify; and if they kept a bird life list.

Presumably because of the relative ease of backyard birding, birders around the home spent nine times as many days watching birds as did people who traveled more than a mile from home to bird-watch. In 2001, the median number of days for backyard birders was 90 and for away-from-home birders it was 10.

Although birders are investing a fair amount of time pursuing their hobby, most do not appear to have advanced identification skills. Seventy-four percent of all birders could identify only between 1 to 20 different types of bird species, 13 percent could identify 21 to 40 birds and only 8 percent could identify more than 41 species. Skill levels are higher for birders who travel from home to bird-watch compared to backyard birders – 10 percent of away-from-home birders could identify 41 or more birds as opposed to 6 percent of backyard birders. Tallies of birds seen during a birder's life, sometimes called birding life lists, were kept by only 5 percent of birders. This was roughly the same for backyard birders and away-from-home birders alike.

### Avidity trends

If we can't say there are more birders can we say that birders are more knowledgeable about their hobby than in the past? In order to gauge birders' avidity and level of expertise, the 2001 Survey asked birders how many birds they can identify – a question last asked in the 1980 Survey (USFWS 1982). A comparison of responses shows that skill levels did not change much in that 20 year time period. For both years, the same percent, 74, was in the beginner category (1 to 20 species of birds) and roughly the same percent, 13 and 14, respectively, fell into the intermediate (21 to 40 birds) level. A slightly higher percentage of expert birders, however, (41 or more species) was found in the 2001 Survey, 8 percent versus 5 percent in the 1980 Survey. Yet another sign that the more things change the more they stay the same, almost the same portion, 4 and 5 percent, kept birding life lists. See Table 9.

### THE ECONOMICS OF BIRD-WATCHING
#### Measures of economic value

Putting a dollar figure on birding can appear a tricky business. How can dollars be used to value something as intangible as the enjoyment of birds and birding? Looked at from a practical perspective we live in a world of competing resources and dollars. Activities such as golfing and industries such as computer software are regularly described in terms of jobs generated and benefits to consumers. The same economic principles that guide the measure of golf and software apply also to birding.

Expenditures by recreationists and net economic values are two widely used but distinctly different measures of the economic value of wildlife-related recreation. Money spent for binoculars in a store or a sandwich in a deli on a trip has a ripple effect on the economy. It supplies money for salaries and jobs which in turn generates more sales and more jobs and tax revenue. This is economic output or impact, the direct and indirect impact of birders' expenditures and an example of one of two economic values presented in this paper. Economic impact numbers are useful indicators of the importance of birding to the local, regional, and national economies but do not measure the economic benefit to an individual or society because, theoretically, money not spent on birding (or golf, or software) would be spent on other activities, be it fishing or scuba diving. Money is just transferred from one group to another.

However, from the perspective of a given community or region, out-of-region residents spending money for birding represents real economic wealth.

Another economic concept is birding's economic benefit to individuals and society: the amount that people are willing to pay over and above what they actually spend to watch birds. This is known as net economic value, or consumer surplus, and is the appropriate economic measure of the benefit to individuals from participation in wildlife related recreation (Bishop 1984, Freeman 1993, Loomis *et al.* 1984, McCollum *et al.* 1992). The benefit to society is the summation of willingness to pay across all individuals. Net economic value is measured as participants' "willingness to pay" above what they actually spend to participate. The benefit to society is the summation of willingness to pay across all individuals.

**Table 10. Birders' expenditures for wildlife-watching: 2001. (Population 16 years of age and older; numbers in thousands of US dollars).**

| Expenditure item | Expenditure (thousands of US$) |
|---|---|
| **Total: all items** | 31 686 673 |
| **Total: trip-related expenditures** | 7 409 679 |
| Food | 2 646 224 |
| Lodging | 1 851 206 |
| Public transportation | 682 202 |
| Private transportation | 1 790 951 |
| Guide fees, pack trip or package fees | 110 374 |
| Private land use fees | 48 999 |
| Public land use fees | 108 414 |
| Boating costs | 135 381 |
| Heating and cooking fuel | 35 928 |
| **Total: equipment and other expenses** | **24 276 994** |
| Wildlife-watching equipment, total | 6 010 141 |
| Binoculars, spotting scopes | 471 264 |
| Cameras, video cameras, special lenses, and other photographic equipment | 1 431 807 |
| Film and developing | 837 868 |
| Bird food | 2 239 259 |
| Nest boxes, bird houses, feeders, baths | 628 060 |
| Daypacks, carrying cases and special clothing | 288 648 |
| Other wildlife-watching equipment (e.g. field guides, maps) | 113 235 |
| Auxiliary equipment, total | 523 700 |
| Tents, tarps | 163 999 |
| Frame packs and backpacking equipment | 121 217 |
| Other camping equipment | 238 835 |
| Other auxiliary equipment (such as blinds) | 117 267 |
| Special equipment, total | 11 158 302 |
| Off-the-road vehicles | 5 512 624 |
| Travel or tent trailers, pickups, campers, vans, motor homes | 4 657 752 |
| Boats, boat accessories | 946 688 |
| Other | 41 238 |
| Magazines | 297 780 |
| Land leasing and ownership | 4 197 666 |
| Membership dues and contributions | 808 101 |
| Plantings | 639 986 |

**Table 11. Economic impact of birders: 2001. (Population 16 years of age and older).**

| | |
|---|---|
| Retail sales (expenditures) | US$ 31 686 673 000 |
| Economic output | US$ 84 931 020 000 |
| Salaries and wages | US$ 24 882 676 000 |
| Jobs | 863 406 |
| State income taxes | US$ 4 889 380 000 |
| Federal income taxes | US$ 7 703 308 000 |

### Facts-at-a-glance

- 46 million birders
- US$ 32 billion in retail sales
- US$ 85 billion in overall economic output
- US$ 13 billion in State and Federal income taxes
- 863 406 jobs created

### Birders' expenditures and economic impact

Birders spent an estimated US$ 32 billion on wildlife-watching in 2001 (see Table 10). This estimate includes money spent for binoculars, field guides, bird food, bird houses, camping gear, and big-ticket items such as boats. It also includes travel-related costs such as food and transportation costs, guide fees, etc. When using the numbers in Table 10 it is important to know that these dollar figures represent the money birders spent for all wildlife-watching recreation – not just birding. The 2001 Survey collected expenditure data for people who fed, photographed, or observed wildlife. Expenditure data were not collected solely for birding. It is possible that people who watched birds in 2001 may have spent money on other types of wildlife-related recreation such as binoculars for whale-watching or gas for a moose-watching trip rather than only bird-watching. Therefore, these estimates for birding expenditures may be overestimates.

This US$ 32 billion that birders spent generated US$ 85 billion in economic benefits for the nation in 2001. This ripple effect on the economy also produced US$ 13 billion in tax revenues and 863 406 jobs. See Table 11.

The sheer magnitude of these numbers proves that birding is a major economic force, driving billions in spending around the country. On a local level, these economic impacts can be the life-blood of an economy. Towns such as Cape May, New Jersey, and Platte River, Nebraska, attract thousands of birding visitors a year generating millions of dollars – money that would likely otherwise be spent elsewhere.

**Table 12. Net economic values for wildlife-watching: 2001. (Population 16 years of age and older).**

| Net economic values | State residents | Non-residents |
|---|---|---|
| Net economic value per year | US$ 257 | US$ 488 |
| Standard error of the mean | 12 | 37 |
| 95 percent confidence interval | US$ 233-282 | US$ 415-561 |
| Net economic value per day of bird-watching | US$ 35 | US$ 134 |
| Standard error of the mean | 2 | 12 |
| 95 percent confidence interval | US$ 32-39 | US$ 110-158 |

## Estimated net economic values

As stated earlier, the willingness to pay above what is actually spent for an activity is known as net economic value. This number is derived here by using a survey technique called contingent valuation (Mitchell & Carson 1989). Respondents to the 2001 Survey were asked a series of contingent valuation (CV) questions to determine their net willingness to pay for a wildlife-watching trip. Please note that the data presented here are net economic values for wildlife-watching trips – not for bird-watching trips solely. However, since the vast majority of away-from-home wildlife-watchers are birders (84 percent), the values presented here are acceptable for use in valuing birding trips.

As seen in Table 12, the net economic value per year for a wildlife-watcher in their resident state is US$ 257 per year or US$ 35 per day. Wildlife-watchers who travel outside their state have a different demand curve (they generally take fewer trips and spend more money) and therefore have their own net economic values of US$ 488 per year and US$ 134 per day. When and how can these values be used? These numbers are appropriate for any project evaluation that seeks to quantify benefits and costs. They can be used to evaluate management decisions (actions) that increase or decrease participation rates. In a simple example, if a wildlife refuge changed its policies and allowed 100 more birders to visit per year, the total value to society due to this policy change would be US$ 25 700 (257 x 100) per year (assuming all visitors are state residents). This value, however, assumes that these 100 birders could and would watch birds only at this refuge and that they would take a certain number of trips to this refuge. In a more realistic example, if the refuge changed its policy and stayed open two more weeks a year and knew that 100 people visited each day during this period then the benefit to society could be estimated by multiplying the number of people by days (100 x 14) by the average value per day (US$ 35) for a total of US$ 49 000. If the refuge had data on the number of in-state and out-of-state visitors then the numbers could be adjusted to reflect their appropriate value.

Net economic values also can be used to evaluate management actions that have a negative affect on wildlife-watching. For example, if a wildlife sanctuary was slated for development and birders were no longer able to use the site, and if the sanctuary manger knew the number of days of birding over the whole year (e.g. 2 000 days) it is possible to develop a rough estimate of the loss from this closure. This estimate is accomplished by multiplying net economic value per day (US$ 35) by the days of participation (2 000) for a value of US$ 70 000 per year.

Two caveats exist to the examples above: (1) if bird-watchers can shift their birding to another location then the values are an over-estimate; and (2) if a loss of wildlife habitat causes an overall degradation in the number of birds and in the quality of birding then the values are an under-estimate.

## CONCLUSION

Back in Louisiana, the search for the Ivory-billed Woodpecker ended in disappointment. After an exhaustive two week search, none were found. Optimism, however, continues to prevail. In a group statement the expedition team said they think the bird may exist based on the availability of good quality habitat and other evidence. This optimism of always looking hopefully into the next tree is the esprit-de-corps of birders. As this report shows, birders come from many walks of life and watch a variety of birds in different settings. Their enthusiasm for birding also translates into spending, thereby contributing significantly to national and local economies. The high values birders place on their birding trips is a solid indicator of birding's benefit to society. While the numbers of birders may not have grown statistically, the power of a mobilized birding community and the willingness of mass media sources and the general public to give play to birding issues has an impact felt deeply in the economy and promotes the sustainability of bird habitats. Hopefully, the information in this paper will allow resource managers and policy makers to make informed management decisions when birds and birding are involved.

## ACKNOWLEDGMENTS

The author thanks Sylvia Cabrera, Richard Aiken, Grant La Rouche, John Charbonneau and Jim Caudill for reviewing earlier drafts of this paper.

## REFERENCES

**Bishop, R.C.** 1984. Economic Values Defined. In: Valuing Wildlife: Economic and Social Perspectives, D.F. Decker & G.R. Goff (eds), Westview Press, Boulder, Colorado.

**Freeman, A.M.** 1993. The Measurement of Environmental and Resource Values: Theory and Methods. Resources for the Future, Washington, D.C.

**Loomis, J.B.** 2000. Can Environmental Economic Valuations Techniques Aid Ecological Economics and Wildlife Conservation? Wildlife Society Bulletin 28:52-60.

**Loomis, J.B., Peterson, G.L. & Sorg, C.** 1984. A Field Guide to Wildlife Economic Analysis. Transactions of the Forty-ninth North American and Natural Resources Conference: 315-324.

**McCollum, D.W., Peterson, G.L. & Swanson, C.** 1992. A Managers Guide to Valuation of Nonmarket Resources: What do you really want to know? In: G.L. Peterson, C.S. Swanson, D.W. McCollum & M.H. Thomas (eds) Valuing Wildlife Resources in Alaska. Westview Press, Boulder, Colorado.

**Mitchell, C. & Carson, R.T.** 1989. Using Surveys to Value Public Goods: The Contingent Valuation Method. Resources for the Future. Washington, D.C.

**Pullis La Rouche, G.** 2003. Birding in the United States: a demographic and economic analysis. Addendum to the 2001 National Survey of Fishing, Hunting and Wildlife-Associated Recreation. Report 2001-1. U.S. Fish and Wildlife Service, Arlington, Virginia.

**Sauer, J.R., Hines, J.E. & Fallon, J.** 2003. The North American Breeding Bird Survey, Results and Analysis 1966—2002. Version 2003.1, USGS Patuxent Wildlife Research Center, Laurel, Maryland.

**U.S. Fish and Wildlife Service.** 1982. 1980 National Survey of Fishing, Hunting and Wildlife Associated Recreation. U.S. Fish and Wildlife Service, Arlington, Virginia.

**U.S. Fish and Wildlife Service** 1993. 1991 National Survey of Fishing, Hunting and Wildlife Associated Recreation. U.S. Fish and Wildlife Service, Arlington, Virginia.

**U.S. Fish and Wildlife Service** 1997. 1996 National Survey of Fishing, Hunting and Wildlife Associated Recreation. U.S. Fish and Wildlife Service, Arlington, Virginia.

**U.S. Fish and Wildlife Service** 2002. 2001 National Survey of Fishing, Hunting and Wildlife Associated Recreation. U.S. Fish and Wildlife Service, Arlington, Virginia.

# Wetlands as part of the natural heritage: the educational response

*Yu.L. Mazourov[1,2] & T.Yu. Zengina[2]*

[1]*Russian Heritage Institute, ul. Kosmonavtov 2, Moscow, 129366 Russia. (email: jmazurov@yandex.ru)*
[2]*Department for Nature Management, Faculty of Geography, Moscow State M.V. Lomonosov University, Lenin Hills, Moscow, 119992 Russia. (email: tzengina@mail.ru)*

Mazourov, Yu.L & Zengina, T.Yu. 2006. Wetlands as part of the natural heritage: the educational response. *Waterbirds around the world*. Eds. G.C. Boere, C.A. Galbraith & D.A. Stroud. The Stationery Office, Edinburgh, UK. p. 847.

Wetlands are not only a human resource but are also part of the natural heritage. Public awareness, through high quality environmental education, is needed to generate adequate protection of these areas. The *UN Decade of Education for Sustainable Development* is an opportunity for a radical 'greening' of educational curricula so that wetland studies are included. This paper explains the authors' experience of teaching wetland conservation issues as part of a course on heritage studies.

Wetlands have long been perceived as unimportant habitats or even as 'badlands'. It is only since the 20th century that their huge ecological importance has been highlighted, and conservation actions undertaken. However, this recognition is still not widespread among the general public, and the best way to change this situation is through education, notably by providing a new vision of wetlands as a special part of nature.

In Russia, wetlands are now seen as a natural resource, and the main reason for establishing nature reserves e.g. Zapovednik in the Volga River delta in 1919, was to save waterbirds, sturgeon and to provide clean drinking water. Gradually, this approach has been changing, as a result of academic research, to one of conserving biological and landscape diversity, e.g. the Great Arctic Reserve on the Taimyr Peninsula and other protected areas in Russia (Ebbinge *et al.* 2000). This has been largely due to changes in the global view of wetlands, (e.g. UNESCO, which seeks to encourage the identification, and preservation of world heritage sites as irreplaceable sources of life and inspiration). This is embodied in the 1972 UNESCO World Heritage Convention. The World Heritage List contains many wetlands of importance, e.g. Danube Delta in Romania, Everglades National Park in the USA, Greater St Lucia Wetland Park in South Africa, and the Tasmanian Wilderness in Australia. This list has contributed to a new vision for nature and wetlands as a common heritage, rather than just as a natural resource.

Unfortunately, this new recognition has been only by professionals in environmental studies and policy (Mazurov 2002, 2003). In 2003, the 57th Session of the United Nations General Assembly adopted Resolution 57/254 *United Nations Decade of Education for Sustainable Development*. This has helped academics make radical changes to the way they teach ecology to the general public and so to raise ecological culture and heritage awareness.

At Moscow State University, the basic course structure is multi-disciplinary and has been modified to incorporate a wetland theme into a one-term lecture course on heritage studies at the Faculty of Geography with an integrated module 'Wetlands as a natural heritage'. Students study wetland conservation, particularly in areas of natural heritage. Specific wetland issues are studied within the traditional courses of biology, ecology, etc. Students are being trained to work in research and planning institutions, state agencies, government bodies, committees, in secondary schools, private enterprises, and other organizations involved in analysis, assessment, training and decision-making in the fields of environmental and nature resource management. Students are being taught that wetlands must be considered as unique and important parts of the regional natural heritage, and wise use is essential for sustainable regional development to provide economic and environmental well-being.

In computer related courses such as 'Remote Sensing in Environmental Research', students learn the potential for ecological interpretation of remotely sensed images to assess wetland status. For example the waterlogged landscapes of Meshchera National Park are used as a demonstration and field study area. Peatlands which had been excavated between 1930 and 1990 are now flooded, and are important habitats for many rare species. Students determine conservation or restoration measures on the basis of the current ecological status of habitats. Students learn digital image processing methods and thematic interpretation of Earth Observation data so as to recommend further wetland restoration and wise use.

Post-graduate students participate in international wetland ecology research undertaken by Russian research institutes together with the ALTERRA-Green World Institute, DLO-Institute for Forestry and Nature Research (the Netherlands). Field research in the Kola Peninsula is an important component of the training and research for wetland studies. This area holds about 100 000 lakes and 21 000 rivers, with peatlands and swamps occupying 37% of the area.

Wetlands are important for nesting, staging, and wintering waterfowl, but industrial developments have brought significant environmental changes to many. The Lapland State Nature Biosphere Reserve, supporting 190 species of terrestrial and migratory waterbirds, is studied as an area mostly unaffected by anthropogenic changes, where students study habitats of species listed in the Russian Red Data Book,. Ecosystem changes are studied in areas exposed to industrial emissions from the Severonickel and Apatit Co. industrial plants, with students carrying out visual observations, satellite imagery, lichen and bryophyte identification, geobotanical and geochemical studies, and hydrological and hydrochemical measurements.

## REFERENCES

Ebbinge, B.S., Mazourov, Yu.L. & Tomkovich, P.S. (eds.) 2000. Heritage of the Russian Arctic: Research, conservation and international cooperation. Ecopros Publishers. Moscow.

Mazourov, Yu.L. 2002. Nature as a heritage: a Russian Arctic case study. Tamkang Review 32(3-4): 197-218.

Mazourov, Yu.L. 2003. Natural heritage of the Russian Arctic: perspectives and tools for preservation. In: Selected papers from The second meeting of The International Contact Forum on Habitat Conservation in the Barents Region: 17-20. Directorate for Nature Management, Trondheim, Norway.

# 6.3 Sustainable waterbird harvest. Workshop Introduction

*Niels Kanstrup*

*Danish Hunters' Association, Molsvej 34, DK-8410 Rønde, Denmark.*

Kanstrup, N. 2006. Sustainable waterbird harvest. Workshop Introduction. *Waterbirds around the world.* Eds. G.C. Boere, C.A. Galbraith & D.A. Stroud. The Stationery Office, Edinburgh, UK. p. 848.

Trapped ducks for sale at Fereydoon Kenar market, Iran. Increasing harvests of waterbirds by growing human populations in many parts of the world challenge waterbird sustainability. Photo: Crawford Prentice.

Waterbird harvest is widespread, long-standing and an important activity for local communities around the world. In many countries the harvest takes place as a primary food source, but sport or recreational hunting is also popular. Waterbird harvesting is a diverse activity and includes a huge variety of methods, and both formal and informal management systems.

Subsistence hunting of waterbirds has a history that stretches back to the dawn of man. In many remote regions (*e.g.* the arctic, central Siberian lowlands, tropical regions), waterbirds are still an important food resource. Local communities (including of indigenous peoples) in these areas have considerable cultural knowledge of trapping techniques, including how to locate species within the landscape, and have considerable emotional links to waterbird populations as an integral component of their environment.

At the same time, sustainable utilization at all levels is regarded as a cornerstone in the conservation of nature. Kanstrup reviews the different components of sustainability, whilst has both ecological and political aspects.

One of the major challenges for waterbird managers is to assess annual harvest levels and to ensure, through regulation, that these are sustainable for the populations concerned. In many countries there is a long tradition of detailed wildlife harvest management including programmes for bag surveys and monitoring of harvest levels. America has a long history of such regulation, and Padding *et al.* and Gobeil outline North American experiences, whilst Bregnballe *et al.* review Danish policies and practices. At the scale of single sites Mondain Monval summarise harvest levels in the Camargue, whilst Sorrenti similarly assesses take in the Po Delta.

In most countries, however, the management of waterbird harvests is poor or completely lacking, and very little information is available on the annual harvest and its impact on populations. In addition, international and flyway based co-ordination is lacking in many regions, and systems need to be developed in order to obtain reliable data on harvest rates in relation to population levels and trends. Despite this, various projects are underway to reduce unsustainable waterbird harvests.

The symposium provided an overview of current waterbird harvest activities and various methods applied; to identify harvest numbers and to review methods of collecting harvest data. It also explored aspects of traditional hunting, such as the use of toxic lead gun-shot that are now known to be unsustainable. Olivier and Kanstrup reviewed Danish and other experiences in moving towards eliminating lead gunshot from waterbird shooting.

Although there are examples of unsustainable harvest practices, there seems to be no reason to believe that harvesting/hunting should inherently be thus. On the contrary, the right to use natural resources can motivate local people – especially hunters – to get involved in conservation. Training, however, is a vital element.

To build capacity at all levels, the workshop concluded that more knowledge is needed in terms of (a) the direct impact of harvest (bag, products) and indirect impact (disturbance); (b) population status and trends at flyway, migration route and population level; (c) mankind and nature, in relation to the processes of sustainable development. To secure the conservation of flyways across borders and across continents world-wide, co-operation is needed at all levels – including that of the hunters.

# Estimating waterfowl harvest in North America

*Paul I. Padding[1], Jean-Francois Gobeil[2] & Cynthia Wentworth[3]*

[1]*U.S. Fish and Wildlife Service, 10815 Loblolly Pine Drive, Laurel, Maryland 20708, USA. (email: paul_padding@fws.gov)*

[2]*National Wildlife Research Centre, Canadian Wildlife Service, Ottawa, Ontario, K1A 0H3, Canada.*

[3]*U.S. Fish and Wildlife Service, 1011 E. Tudor Road, Anchorage, Alaska 99503, USA.*

Padding, P.I., Gobeil, J.-F. & Wentworth, C. 2006. Estimating waterfowl harvest in North America. *Waterbirds around the world.* Eds. G.C. Boere, C.A. Galbraith & D.A. Stroud. The Stationery Office, Edinburgh, UK. pp. 849-852.

## ABSTRACT

Most of the waterfowl harvested in North America are taken by sport hunters. The United States and Canada monitor the sport harvest through annual surveys of those hunters. Both countries employ sport harvest survey systems that consist of two major mail surveys: a questionnaire survey that asks a large sample of hunters to report their total harvest of ducks and geese for the year, and a parts collection survey that asks a smaller, separate sample of hunters to send in a wing from every duck and the tail feathers from every goose they harvest. The questionnaire survey gives estimates of total duck and goose harvest, whereas the parts collection survey provides estimates of the species, age and sex composition of the waterfowl harvest. These data are used to examine long-term trends in species-specific harvest and demographics that can yield vital information on the status of North American waterfowl populations. Subsistence harvest in Canada is estimated using indirect methods, but in Alaska an intensive specialized survey is used to estimate subsistence harvest.

## INTRODUCTION

Regulating the harvest of waterfowl to ensure that it is commensurate with population status is an important component of waterfowl management in North America. In order to establish appropriate waterfowl hunting regulations each year, both harvest and population size must be monitored (Geis *et al.* 1969, Smith *et al.* 1989). Most of the waterfowl harvest is monitored through surveys of hunters that are conducted annually.

The primary sources of waterfowl harvest in North America are sport hunting in Canada, the United States and Mexico, and subsistence hunting in Alaska and northern Canada. In this paper, we summarize the various methods used in North America to estimate the number of ducks and geese harvested by sport and subsistence hunters. We describe the sample frames of the various surveys, how those sample frames are obtained, and the survey methodologies and estimation procedures that are employed. Then we present the results of those efforts, and discuss how harvest estimates are used to help ensure that the harvest is sustainable.

## METHODS
### Estimating sport harvest in the United States

In the United States, sport hunters are required to purchase hunting licenses annually. Those hunting licenses are issued by the individual state governments, not by the federal government. The cooperative state-federal Migratory Bird Harvest Information Program uses the states' licensing systems to provide the sample frame for the federal migratory bird harvest survey system. Under this program, state wildlife agencies collect the name and address of each migratory bird hunter who purchases a hunting license. They also ask each of those migra-

tory bird hunters a series of general questions about the species they hunted and their hunting success the previous year. The state wildlife agencies then send those names and addresses to the U.S. Fish and Wildlife Service. Participation in this program is mandatory for migratory bird hunters; thus, the sample frame includes all licensed sport hunters who are legally authorized to hunt migratory game birds. This totals about 3 500 000 sport hunters each year.

The U.S. Fish and Wildlife Service selects samples of hunters from the name and address data that the state wildlife agencies provide. Hunters are stratified by state and by hunting activity and success in the previous year, and stratum-specific sampling rates are selected to increase precision and maximize sampling efficiency. For example, the small group of duck hunters who were very successful in the previous year is sampled at a high rate, the larger group of moderately successful duck hunters is sampled at a lower rate, and the very large group of hunters who rarely if ever hunt ducks is sampled at a very low rate.

At the beginning of the hunting season, each sampled hunter is mailed a hunting diary form and asked to record the date, location and number of ducks and geese taken for each day of waterfowl hunting. After the end of the hunting season, the U.S. Fish and Wildlife Service sends the sample hunters a postcard reminder asking them to complete and mail back their hunting diaries. This mailing is followed by two additional reminders to all sample hunters who still have not responded. Both of those reminder mailings include replacement diary forms.

Hunters' responses are used to estimate the mean number of ducks and geese harvested per hunter for each stratum, and the total harvests of ducks and geese are estimated by expanding the means by the number of active hunters in each stratum. About 60 000 hunters are selected annually for the waterfowl hunting diary survey. Participation is voluntary, and the response rate is 55-60%.

Some hunters are unable to identify to species all of the birds they harvest. Thus the survey described above does not ask participants to report their harvest by species. To obtain species-specific harvest estimates, the U.S. Fish and Wildlife Service selects another sample of waterfowl hunters annually, and asks those hunters to participate in the Waterfowl Parts Collection Survey. Hunters who agree to participate are given special postage-paid "wing envelopes", and are asked to send back a wing from every duck they shoot and the tail feathers of every goose they shoot throughout the hunting season.

Biologists identify the species, age and sex of each duck wing sample and the species and age of each goose tail sample. Thus, the survey yields estimates of the species composition of the duck and goose harvest. Results of this survey are combined with the results of the hunting diary survey to provide species-specific harvest estimates, as well as estimates of age and sex ratios (Martin & Carney 1977, Geissler 1990). The annual sample size for the Waterfowl Parts Collection Survey is about 90 000 duck wings and 20 000 goose tails (Padding *et al.* 2003).

## Estimating sport harvest in Canada

The Canadian waterfowl harvest survey system was established in 1967 (Cooch *et al.* 1978). All sport hunters who wish to hunt waterfowl in Canada must purchase the Canada Migratory Game Bird Hunting Permit, which was introduced in 1966. This is a national permit that is issued by the federal government, primarily at post offices throughout the country. The permit includes a stub on which the postmaster records the person's name and address, and whether or not that person purchased a permit and hunted the previous year. The postmaster then detaches the completed stub and sends it to the Canadian Wildlife Service. Thus, the sample frame for Canada's harvest survey system consists of all sport hunters who are legally authorized by the Canadian government to hunt migratory game birds. In recent years, this amounts to about 200 000 sport hunters each year.

The Canadian Wildlife Service selects samples of permit buyers, stratified by geographic survey zone, permit renewal status, past hunting success and county of residence (Cooch *et al.* 1978). The permit includes a hunting diary on which hunters are asked to note the date, location, and harvest for each of their hunts. Near the end of the migratory bird hunting season, each sampled hunter is mailed the Harvest Questionnaire Survey, which is a more detailed survey form. Hunters are asked to use their permit diaries to help them report their hunting activity and harvest accurately on the survey form. About two months after the first mailing, the Canadian Wildlife Service sends a second survey form to those who have not responded.

Estimates of mean and total duck and goose harvest are derived in much the same way as they are in the United States (Cooch *et al.* 1978). The Canadian Wildlife Service selects about 45 000 hunters annually for the Harvest Questionnaire Survey. Participation in the survey is voluntary, and the response rate is about 40%.

The Canadian Wildlife Service selects another sample of waterfowl hunters annually and asks those hunters to participate in the Species Composition Survey. This survey is conducted for the same purpose as the Waterfowl Parts Collection Survey in the United States, and employs similar methods. Likewise, Canada's analyses are similar to those used by the United States. The results of the Harvest Questionnaire Survey and the Species Composition Survey are combined to produce species-specific harvest estimates (Cooch *et al.* 1978). The annual sample size for Canada's Species Composition Survey is about 20 000 duck wings and 8 000 goose tails.

## Estimating subsistence harvest in Alaska

The sample frame for the Alaska Subsistence Harvest Survey consists of all households in the parts of Alaska in which subsistence harvesting of birds and eggs is a legal activity. There are about 26 000 such households. The sample frame is stratified by geographic region, by communities within regions, and by previous history of hunting activity for each household. About two thirds of the communities in each region are selected for sampling. In those communities, about 40% of the high-harvest households, 15% of the low-harvest households, and 10% of the no-harvest households are selected to participate in the survey.

The survey covers the subsistence harvest period, April-October, in three increments. Survey workers hand-deliver the first survey forms to sampled households in April, at which time the workers explain how the forms should be filled out. The survey form shows pictures of the various species of birds, and participants are asked to record how many birds and eggs of each species they take. Three months later, the survey workers visit the households again to retrieve the first survey forms and deliver the forms for the second period. Two months after that, the survey workers visit again to pick up forms and deliver the forms for the last period, and at the end of the final period they visit once more to collect the last survey forms.

The analyses used to estimate the harvest are similar to those used to estimate sport harvest in the United States and Canada, except that species-specific estimates are derived directly from household reports rather than from a wing survey. Participation in the survey is voluntary, and the response rate is about 66%.

## Sport harvest in Mexico

There are no annual estimates available for sport harvest in Mexico. However, a study by Kramer *et al.* (1995) gives a good indication of the magnitude and species composition of the annual waterfowl harvest in Mexico. From 1987 to 1992, Kramer *et al.* conducted a census of harvest in all the traditional waterfowl hunting areas of Mexico, visiting each major area in a different year. Then they applied area-specific correction factors to adjust for under-reporting by hunters. Finally, they summed the results for each area across years to obtain estimates of average annual harvest for all of Mexico.

## Subsistence harvest in Canada

The most recent comprehensive assessment of subsistence harvest in Canada was undertaken by Wendt & Dickson in 1994 (unpublished report). They reported harvest estimates for all areas where surveys had been conducted at some time during the previous 20 years. For areas where surveys had not been conducted, they derived indirect estimates of harvest. Their report gives estimates of total duck and goose harvest, but no species-specific estimates are available. The Canadian Wildlife Service is expecting to obtain up-to-date, direct estimates of subsistence harvest for most of Canada in the near future.

## RESULTS

Sport hunting accounts for by far the greatest proportion of the total duck and goose harvest in North America. Of the approximately 15 000 000 ducks harvested in 2002, about 14 000 000 were taken by sport hunters, primarily in the United States (Fig. 1). Similarly, of about 4 850 000 geese harvested in 2002, nearly 4 300 000 were taken by sport hunters in the United States and Canada (Fig. 2). Most of the waterfowl hunting and harvest in Canada occurs in the south-central part of the country (Quebec, Ontario, Manitoba, Saskatchewan and Alberta), whereas comparatively little sport hunting occurs along the coasts and in the far north (Table 1). Similarly, in the United States, about 70% of the waterfowl hunters are in the middle of the country (Mississippi Flyway and Central Flyway); thus most of the duck and goose harvest also occurs there, compared to the east (Atlantic Flyway) and west (Pacific Flyway) coasts (Table 1). In general, more ducks are harvested in southern states (e.g. Arkansas, Louisiana, Texas), whereas more geese are harvested in northern and mid-latitude states (Table 1).

**Table 1.** Estimated sport harvest of ducks and geese and number of waterfowl hunters in Canada and the United States during the 2001 hunting season.

| State/Province | Duck Harvest | Goose Harvest | Waterfowl Hunters |
|---|---|---|---|
| **Canada** | | | |
| Newfoundland | 50 200 | 5 600 | 8 700 |
| Prince Edward Island | 17 800 | 25 100 | 2 700 |
| Nova Scotia | 58 500 | 10 600 | 4 600 |
| New Brunswick | 41 700 | 5 600 | 4 700 |
| Quebec | 215 800 | 166 800 | 22 800 |
| Ontario | 364 500 | 149 900 | 42 000 |
| Manitoba | 168 300 | 128 000 | 13 500 |
| Saskatchewan | 153 500 | 323 300 | 17 600 |
| Alberta | 135 400 | 162 700 | 16 000 |
| British Columbia | 55 600 | 15 500 | 5 100 |
| Northwest Territories | 1 000 | 1 000 | 100 |
| Yukon Territory | 400 | 100 | 100 |
| **United States** | | | |
| Maine | 82 800 | 9 400 | 9 400 |
| Vermont | 27 000 | 5 900 | 3 800 |
| New Hampshire | 18 200 | 4 900 | 3 800 |
| Massachusetts | 31 800 | 12 200 | 6 800 |
| Connecticut | 17 900 | 15 139 | 4 400 |
| Rhode Island | 11 000 | 3 400 | 1 200 |
| New York | 195 900 | 104 400 | 31 100 |
| Pennsylvania | 129 400 | 129 700 | 42 100 |
| West Virginia | 6 500 | 7 300 | 1 700 |
| New Jersey | 82 200 | 75 600 | 9 600 |
| Delaware | 43 600 | 40 800 | 5 300 |
| Maryland | 160 200 | 95 400 | 24 800 |
| Virginia | 101 700 | 45 800 | 17 500 |
| North Carolina | 205 700 | 30 200 | 25 600 |
| South Carolina | 255 300 | 14 600 | 20 900 |
| Georgia | 95 600 | 11 100 | 20 400 |
| Florida | 145 800 | 600 | 14 000 |
| **Atlantic Flyway Total** | **1 610 500** | **606 400** | **242 400** |
| Minnesota | 648 000 | 238 900 | 128 500 |
| Wisconsin | 252 700 | 40 700 | 63 800 |
| Michigan | 281 400 | 134 900 | 53 300 |
| Iowa | 246 800 | 48 000 | 27 700 |
| Illinois | 448 700 | 76 800 | 47 000 |
| Indiana | 147 000 | 60 300 | 25 200 |
| Ohio | 121 700 | 78 200 | 30 400 |
| Missouri | 478 800 | 104 400 | 37 100 |
| Kentucky | 119 600 | 22 500 | 17 500 |
| Arkansas | 1 114 300 | 72 800 | 57 600 |
| Tennessee | 282 400 | 20 700 | 30 800 |
| Louisiana | 2 211 700 | 141 500 | 92 800 |
| Mississippi | 247 300 | 18 400 | 21 700 |
| Alabama | 148 100 | 5 500 | 15 800 |
| **Mississippi Flyway Total** | **6 748 400** | **1 063 600** | **648 900** |
| Montana* | 43 700 | 56 500 | 6 700 |
| North Dakota | 693 400 | 242 000 | 29 400 |
| South Dakota | 289 200 | 188 300 | 28 800 |
| Wyoming* | 43 600 | 51 600 | 7 800 |

(Cont)

| State/Province | Duck Harvest | Goose Harvest | Waterfowl Hunters |
|---|---|---|---|
| Nebraska | 223 400 | 64 800 | 28 100 |
| Colorado* | 115 113 | 104 500 | 24 000 |
| Kansas | 261 000 | 90 300 | 24 100 |
| New Mexico* | 32 100 | 5 000 | 3 600 |
| Oklahoma | 259 600 | 47 500 | 19 200 |
| Texas | 1 440 800 | 308 900 | 111 600 |
| **Central Flyway Total** | **3 401 800** | **1 159 500** | **283 000** |
| Washington | 340 600 | 59 700 | 30 000 |
| Oregon | 275 900 | 79 300 | 25 800 |
| Idaho | 198 600 | 53 200 | 19 800 |
| Montana* | 95 000 | 36 600 | 11 400 |
| Wyoming* | 5 900 | 1 900 | 800 |
| California | 948 600 | 90 800 | 65 000 |
| Nevada | 33 800 | 800 | 6 100 |
| Utah | 200 900 | 25 100 | 26 600 |
| Colorado* | 27 100 | 5 300 | 3 600 |
| Arizona | 42 700 | 2 800 | 5 100 |
| New Mexico* | 2 600 | 1 900 | 500 |
| **Pacific Flyway Total** | **2 171 700** | **357 400** | **194 800** |
| Alaska | 61 900 | 8 600 | 7 800 |

* Montana, Wyoming, Colorado, and New Mexico are transected by the Central/Pacific Flyway boundary and are therefore listed in both flyways. Estimates are partitioned into their respective flyways.

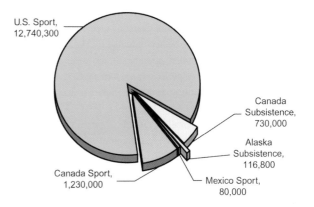

U.S. Sport, 12,740,300

Canada Subsistence, 730,000

Alaska Subsistence, 116,800

Canada Sport, 1,230,000

Mexico Sport, 80,000

**Fig. 1.** Distribution of the duck harvest in North America among sport and subsistence hunters during the 2002 waterfowl hunting season.

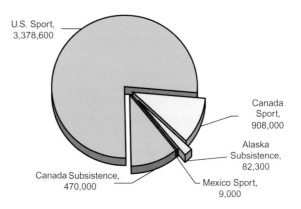

U.S. Sport, 3,378,600

Canada Sport, 908,000

Alaska Subsistence, 82,300

Canada Subsistence, 470,000

Mexico Sport, 9,000

**Fig. 2.** Distribution of the goose harvest in North America among sport and subsistence hunters during the 2002 waterfowl hunting season.

The annual sport harvest is comprised of 33 species of ducks and five species of geese. The species composition of the duck harvest during the 2002 hunting season was typical of recent years. More than 30% of all ducks harvested were Mallard *Anas platyrhynchos*, followed by Green-winged Teal *A. crecca*, Gadwall *A. strepera* and Wood Duck *Aix sponsa* at about 10% each. Ring-necked Duck *Aythya collaris* and Lesser Scaup *A. affinis* were the most commonly harvested diving-ducks. As with ducks, the species composition of the sport harvest of geese during the 2002 hunting season was typical of recent years. About 70% of all geese taken were Canada Geese *Branta canadensis*, followed by Snow Geese *Chen (Anser) caerulescens* at about 20%.

Although most of the waterfowl harvest in North America is due to sport hunting, there are some cases in which subsistence hunting is an important source of mortality, especially for some species of concern. For example, the Emperor Goose *Chen (Anser) canagicus* population numbers only about 75 000 birds. Sport hunting of this species is not allowed, and therefore the only harvest that occurs is subsistence harvest in Alaska. The estimated harvest is 3 200 birds per year, or about 4% of the population. Another species of concern is the Black Brant *Branta bernicla nigricans*, which has a population of about 120 000 birds. Of a total harvest of about 17 000, more than half are taken by subsistence hunters in Alaska. Only 2 000 are taken by sport hunters in the United States and Canada, whereas 5 000 are taken by sport hunters in Mexico.

## DISCUSSION

National sport harvest survey systems have been in place in the United States since 1952 and in Canada since 1967, and subsistence harvest surveys have been conducted in Alaska since 1985. These surveys have provided annual estimates over an extended period of time that enable biologists to evaluate long-term trends in hunter numbers, hunting pressure, harvest, and waterfowl population demographics (e.g. Trost *et al.* 1987). These data in turn help biologists to formulate models of population dynamics that are used to determine harvest management prescriptions for species such as Mallard, Northern Pintail *Anas acuta* and Canvasback *Aythya valisineria*.

Estimates of the annual harvest also help waterfowl managers assess the impacts of hunting regulations on harvest. For example, the results of the harvest surveys described above can be used to predict the effects of changes in season length and bag limits on total duck or goose harvest, or to predict the effects of changes in species-specific bag limits on individual species (Martin & Carney 1977). This helps managers determine the appropriate regulatory actions to take when harvest must be reduced or, if populations are expanding, when it can be allowed to increase.

The estimates of age and sex composition derived from wing surveys can also be valuable, particularly for showing long-term trends in productivity (e.g. Reynolds 1987, Miller 2000). Harvest age ratios can serve as an early warning system that helps identify declining species or populations. For example, age ratios (immature/adult) of Lesser Scaup harvested in the United States have been declining for the last 20 years (Padding *et al.* 2003), suggesting a gradual decline in productivity of the species.

During the same period, the North American breeding population of the species has also undergone a significant decrease (U.S. Fish and Wildlife Service 2003). As a result of these findings, several research efforts to determine the causes of the decline in the Lesser Scaup population are currently underway, and these are focusing on adult female survival and productivity.

## REFERENCES

**Cooch, F.G., Wendt, S., Smith, G.E.J. & Butler, G.** 1978. The Canada migratory game bird hunting permit and associated surveys. In: H. Boyd & G.H. Finney (eds) Migratory game bird hunters and hunting in Canada. Canadian Wildlife Service Report Series No. 43: 8-39.

**Geis, A.D, Martinson, R.K. & Anderson, D.R.** 1969. Establishing hunting regulations and allowable harvest of mallards in the United States. Journal of Wildlife Management 33: 848-859.

**Geissler, P.H.** 1990. Estimation of confidence intervals for federal waterfowl harvest surveys. Journal of Wildlife Management 54: 201-205.

**Kramer, G.W., Carrera, E. & Zaveleta, D.** 1995. Waterfowl harvest and hunter activity in Mexico. Transactions of the North American Wildlife & Natural Resources Conference 60: 243-250.

**Martin, E.M. & Carney, S.M.** 1977. Population ecology of the mallard. IV. A review of duck hunting regulations, activity, and success, with special reference to the mallard. U.S. Fish and Wildlife Service Resource Publication 130, Washington, D.C.

**Miller, M.W.** 2000. Modeling annual mallard production in the prairie-parkland region. Journal of Wildlife Management 64: 561-575.

**Padding, P.I., Martin, E.M. & Spriggs, H.L.** 2003. Age and sex composition of ducks and geese bagged in the 2002 hunting season in comparison with prior years. Administrative Report. U.S. Fish and Wildlife Service, Laurel, Maryland.

**Reynolds, R.E.** 1987. Breeding duck population, production and habitat surveys, 1979-85. Transactions of the North American Wildlife & Natural Resources Conference 52: 186-205.

**Smith, R.I., Blohm, R.J., Kelly, S.T., Reynolds, R.E. & Caswell, F.D.** 1989. Review of data bases for managing duck harvests. Transactions of the North American Wildlife & Natural Resources Conference 54: 537-544.

**Trost, R.E, Sharp, D.E, Kelly, S.T. & Caswell, F.D.** 1987. Duck harvests and proximate factors influencing hunting activity and success during the period of stabilized regulations. Transactions of the North American Wildlife & Natural Resources Conference 52: 216-232.

**U.S. Fish and Wildlife Service** 2003. Waterfowl population status, 2003. U.S. Department of the Interior, Washington, D.C.

**Wendt, J.S. & Dickson, K.M.** 1994. Estimated annual harvest of waterfowl in Canada by aboriginal people. Unpublished report of the Canadian Wildlife Service.

# Migratory bird harvest surveys in Canada

*Jean-François Gobeil*

*Canadian Wildlife Service, National Wildlife Research Centre, Ottawa, Ontario, K1A 0H3, Canada.*
*(email: jean-francois.gobeil@ec.gc.ca)*

Gobeil, J.-F. 2006. Migratory bird harvest surveys in Canada. *Waterbirds around the world.* Eds. G.C. Boere, C.A. Galbraith &
D.A. Stroud. The Stationery Office, Edinburgh, UK. p. 853.

In Canada, the Canadian Wildlife Service (CWS) of Environment
Canada is mandated to protect migratory birds under the Migratory
Birds Convention Act (MBC Act 1994). This Act and its regulations are the main domestic legal instruments used to implement
the Migratory Birds Convention, an international treaty signed
with the U.S. in 1916. The MBC Act 1994 and its regulations
confer powers to regulate migratory game bird hunting by
following guiding principles of conservation such as sustaining
healthy migratory bird populations while allowing activities such
as harvesting. Science-based management, which involves basing
management on sound scientific models, is implemented using a
variety of monitoring programs to evaluate and update the models.

For waterfowl, these monitoring programs include breeding
ground surveys to estimate population sizes and productivity,
banding programs to estimate survival rates and movements, and
harvest surveys to estimate the size of the harvest, and assess the
impacts of hunting regulations on populations. By combining
these data, CWS has the capacity to assess the status of all
migratory game birds found in Canada and adjust regulations
accordingly.

CWS introduced the Migratory Game Bird Hunting Permit
(MGBHP) in 1966 to obtain information about hunters. The
following year, a programme entitled the National Harvest
Survey (NHS) was initiated, consisting primarily of two annual
surveys sent to MGBHP purchasers: the Harvest Questionnaire
Survey (HQS) and the Species Composition Survey (SCS).

The HQS consists of a questionnaire mailed to approximately
44 000 hunters to estimate hunting activity and the annual harvest
of major groups of birds (e.g. ducks, geese) and other species
such as snipe and woodcock. The sample is random stratified;
hunters are selected based on permit renewal, region, and residency. Hunting activity data are provided as estimates of numbers
of active and successful hunters, and bag sizes. For ducks and
geese, specific data are also obtained about hunting locations and
the distribution of bags and hunting activity throughout the
season (provided by calendars in the questionnaire).

The SCS asks hunters to submit samples of each duck (one
wing) and goose (tail feathers and primaries) they harvest. A total
of 35 000 hunters are screened prior to each season, and 10 000
participate. The sample (random stratified) takes into account
previous responses to the HQS, permit renewal, and past participation. Annually, 25 000 samples are collected and species, age
and sex are identified with waterfowl experts confirming the identification. Identification cue cards and posters are used for
training and reference, and are being incorporated into an updated,
comprehensive Canadian identification guide.

Both the HQS and the SCS provide a wealth of data used
mainly for the revision of annual bag and possession limits, and
of season dates. However, there are other "indirect" uses of the

data such as the collection of tissue samples for genetic studies
and contaminant studies.

CWS also conducts additional "special" surveys such as the
Spring Snow Goose Survey. This survey has been running since
1999 to monitor the Spring Snow Goose Hunting Season, a
special conservation measure introduced to reduce Snow Goose
populations breeding in the Arctic.

Since the 1980s, CWS has also been conducting surveys in
Newfoundland and Labrador to monitor harvest and hunting of
sea ducks and murres. For these special surveys, methodologies
are adjusted based on their particular objectives and the desired
results.

The NHS is a large-scale survey and suffers from some limitations. There will always be errors or missing information, for
example due to mis-classification of hunters into survey strata,
misinterpretation of instructions by hunters, and unidentifiable
bird parts. For some species, identification keys are not yet reliable (e.g. scoters). Low participation rates in some areas result
in poor estimates at smaller spatial scales, an inevitable trade-off
between cost and precision. Furthermore, surveys do not take
into account native harvest, illegal hunting and losses from crip-
pling. Some of those pitfalls are currently being addressed.

Some species form a major portion of the total harvest,
resulting in a lot of information collected and their harvest being
estimated with good precision; other species are poorly sampled.
The different level of precision for different species is an
inherent property of the sampling procedure. The NHS is
redesigned periodically by reallocating the sampling effort,
which can generally achieve a reduction of 10-15% in the coefficient of variation (CV) of harvest estimates. Computer models
estimate the impact of reallocating survey effort under various
scenarios. The objective is to find the allocation that leads to the
greatest reduction in the total CV of the harvest for various
species and regions, while keeping survey costs the same.
Optimal allocations are then derived under all scenarios and the
appropriate scenario selected following discussions amongst
CWS biologists and managers, allowing for a conscious decision
on the optimal trade-off between precision at various scales and
for various species.

Despite their limitations, the National Harvest Survey and the
special surveys are valuable sources of data for monitoring and
managing migratory game birds in Canada and North America.
The data are relatively inexpensive to obtain compared with other
types of monitoring schemes such as banding. Periodic redesign
of the survey helps to maintain its efficiency, although there is a
trade-off between reallocating effort and maintaining consistency
over time. In some cases, special surveys may be a better
approach to deal with specific management issues, rather than reallocating resources within the long-term survey.

# Sustainable hunting of migratory waterbirds: the Danish approach

*Thomas Bregnballe[1], Henning Noer[1], Thomas Kjær Christensen[1], Preben Clausen[1], Tommy Asferg[1], A. D. Fox[1] & Simon Delany[2]*

[1] *National Environmental Research Institute, Department of Wildlife Ecology and Biodiversity, Grenåvej 14, DK-8410 Rønde, Denmark.*
[2] *Wetlands International, PO Box 471, 6700 AL Wageningen, The Netherlands.*

Bregnballe, T., Noer, H., Christensen, T.K., Clausen, P., Asferg, T., Fox, A.D. & Delany, S. 2006. Sustainable hunting of migratory waterbirds: the Danish approach. *Waterbirds around the world.* Eds. G.C. Boere, C.A. Galbraith & D.A. Stroud. The Stationery Office, Edinburgh, UK. pp. 854-860.

## ABSTRACT

The harvesting of migratory waterbirds continues unmodified on a large scale in many European countries despite increasing calls in several countries and at the EU level to ensure that the take is "sustainable". Despite widespread and common interest, there is neither consensus in Europe concerning an operational definition of "sustainable harvesting" nor consensus concerning the criteria that should be applied in determining sustainability. Around 700 000 wild waterbirds are killed annually in Denmark where the hunting of migratory waterbirds has a strong tradition. We applied simple assessments combining population trends and size of take to determine whether the current kill of quarry species in Denmark is sustainable or not. We present the national approach taken to determine sustainability and provide examples of how data on bag records and knowledge about specific population sizes have been used as case studies in Denmark.

## INTRODUCTION

Shooting of waterbirds is a widespread and legitimate recreational activity in many parts of the world, including Europe. Over the past century, its role in regulating the size and distribution of waterbird populations has been the focus of much debate, and this has affected the management of hunting in both the USA and Europe. As a result of increasing political unification, enhanced international co-operation and a vast improvement in our knowledge, the legislative management of bird species and hunting activities in Europe has grown increasingly international over the last 30 years. Starting with the Ramsar Convention on Wetlands (1971), followed by the EEC Directive on the Conservation of Wild Birds ("Birds Directive", 1979), the Convention on Migratory Species of Wild Animals (CMS, 1979) and the African-Eurasian Migratory Waterbird Agreement (AEWA, 1999), both international and national legislation have increasingly emphasised that the harvest of game animals must be "sustainable". As yet, however, there is no general consensus nor any internationally accepted operational definition of "sustainable harvesting" that can serve as a basis for the scientific assessment of the impact of hunting (see, for example, Sutherland 2001).

Denmark is an important staging and wintering area for migratory waterbirds, and has a strong tradition of waterbird hunting. There are open seasons for 29 species of waterbirds, many of which occur in concentrations that are internationally important according to the 1% criterion of the Ramsar Convention. The present Danish Game Act came into effect in 1994, both confirming international obligations and emphasising the sustainable management of hunting and game species, not only in an ecological sense, but also in an ethical sense (although

we here limit the discussion to ecological rather than ethical considerations).

Responsibility for establishing hunting seasons lies with the Danish Ministry of the Environment and the process of their revision is administered by the Forest and Nature Agency. Under the 1994 Game Act, hunting seasons can be revised at three-year intervals by Government Orders, increasing flexibility considerably over the previous arrangements when, more often than not, Parliament had to pass a new Game Act to change hunting seasons. On a three-year cycle, the National Environmental Research Institute (NERI) undertakes a scientific review of changes in the bags and population sizes and a re-assessment of the effects of hunting on each species. The available estimates of population size for a given species may, for example, indicate that numbers continue to decline, in which case NERI may recommend that the length of the open season be reduced (see Bregnballe *et al.* 2003 for an example of a detailed review). This recommendation is passed on to the Council for Wildlife Management, which is composed of representatives of stakeholders (including the Danish Hunters' Association and Danish Ornithological Society), and their main task is to discuss the options for adjusting current regulations, attempt to reach consensus and pass on their conclusions to the Forest and Nature Agency, i.e. the Minister of the Environment. Based on this and other advice, the Minister will thereafter announce the appropriate new local and national adjustments to the length of open seasons. For the species in decline, the change in the open season may or may not slow down the speed of decline.

It has been impractical to wait for international consensus on definitions of sustainability, and so NERI has had to establish operational pragmatic concepts on a "national" level. In this paper, we present this view of sustainability and use worked examples to exemplify how information on bag records and population trends is used to assess whether or not the take in Denmark is sustainable for three different species of waterbirds.

## METHODS

### What is sustainability?

Our basic concept of sustainability applied to exploitation is that a renewable resource must not be over-exploited, over-exploitation representing a state where the ability of a resource to renew itself and maintain current distribution and abundance is curtailed. In the long run, such over-exploitation will eventually exterminate the resource.

Much effort has been devoted to obtaining the population data necessary for assessing whether hunted populations are over-exploited (e.g. Sutherland 2001), often based upon information on trends in both reproduction and survival as well as abundance (e.g.

Williams & Nichols 2001). Sutherland (2001) argued that knowledge of growth rates should be provided as a basis for assessing sustainable takes. In the absence of such detailed data for most species, Madsen *et al.* (1996) defined sustainable exploitation by means of combining the size of the take and population trends, the basic idea being that as long as a population is stable or increasing, over short periods, current exploitation can be assessed as sustainable. While this obviously works for large and well-known populations, care has to be taken for small and vulnerable populations (Madsen *et al.* 1996). Since many of the waterbird populations hunted in Denmark are indeed stable or increasing, this definition reduces the task of assessing 29 different species considerably.

The initial definition, however, leaves open the interpretation of cases involving decreasing populations. Though not yet fully resolved, a decreasing population trend is not necessarily evidence of unsustainable hunting. For example, breeding numbers and output may be limited by available breeding habitat. If the extent of this breeding habitat is undergoing reduction, harvest is expected to contribute to the rate of population decrease, but also to reach a sustainable level eventually (though depending on the take), if the population in question stabilizes at a new level (Bregnballe *et al.* 2003). Basically, then, decreasing populations will have to be the focus of closer scrutiny before any assessment as to the sustainability of hunting can be made.

Classifying the hunting of a species as "not sustainable" does not necessarily result in recommending a ban on hunting, in particular if the population decline is moderate and the population continues to be large (see the example of Common Eider *Somateria mollissima* below). In the evaluations made at three-year intervals, we distinguish, as objectively as possible, between "sustainable", "probably sustainable", "probably not sustainable", "not sustainable" and "not possible to judge".

Compared to the Ramsar Convention and the EC Birds Directive, the Habitats Directive of 1992 (implemented 8-10 years later) introduced a new generation of Directives relating to nature conservation in Europe. Since the Habitats Directive does not concern birds, the legal status of the Birds Directive in Denmark was strengthened in 2001 by giving it the same status as the Habitats Directive by Government Order. This requires that an assessment of the conservation status of a given bird species be provided to the European Commission at regular (six-year) intervals. In order to ensure a unified treatment, Bregnballe *et al.* (2003) substituted the "simple" population trends used by Madsen *et al.* (1996) with an assessment of the conservation status of each individual species/population.

### Information base

In the north-western Palearctic, most flyway populations breed, stage and winter across several member (and non-member) states of the European Union. Data on population trends – vital to our assessment by the definitions given above – are provided by Wetlands International, based on indices generated from the annual mid-winter International Waterbird Census (e.g. Delany *et al.* 1999). For some species, we also use results from other surveys, e.g. those aimed at estimating the size of sub-populations of geese, and results from the monitoring of Danish breeding populations.

Data on Danish hunting are provided through bag return statistics. After each season, all holders of Danish hunting licenses are required to inform the Forest and Nature Agency of the size

and composition of their annual hunting bag. However, the following groups are pooled in these returns: geese (five species), dabbling ducks except Mallard *Anas platyrhynchos* (six species), diving ducks except Common Eider (nine species), snipes (two species) and gulls (three species). Between the mid-1970s and the early 1980s, about 95% of all licence holders reported their annual bags, but after two major changes in the reporting system, the number of respondents dropped, first to 78%, then recently to 58%. Although estimates of the national bag are corrected for this, maintenance of a higher return rate would clearly be preferable. Since 1982/83, hunters have also voluntarily submitted the wings of bagged waterbirds to NERI, enabling assessment of changes in the age and sex ratios of the bagged sample (Clausager 2004 and references therein). Data from this wing survey are used to estimate the species composition amongst the amalgamated groups "geese", "other dabbling ducks", "other diving ducks", "snipes" and "gulls". The proportion of hunters submitting wings, however, is relatively low, ranging from 3% of those bagging "other dabbling ducks" to 1% of those bagging geese. Because so few wings are received compared with the total bag, uncertainties amongst species in which fewer than 2 000 individuals are bagged are considerable. The wing survey also provides us with an opportunity to estimate the temporal and geographical distribution of the bag, as well as the age and sex composition.

### RESULTS

#### The bag of waterbirds in Denmark

The number of holders of hunting licences increased during the 1960s and 1970s, and has subsequently stabilized at 160 000 - 170 000 (Fig. 1), c. 3% of the total Danish population. The annual bag of waterbirds (excluding Mallard) declined from a maximum of 900 000 in the mid-1970s to 350 000 in the mid-1990s, and has changed little since then. The decline was partly caused by the protection in 1982 of divers, grebes, auks (alcids) and some species of waders, followed by the protection in 1994 of Eurasian Curlew *Numenius arquata*, Whimbrel *N. phaeopus*, Black-headed Gull *Larus ridibundus* and Common Gull *L. canus*. For species still subject to an open season, marked reductions in bag sizes have taken place for all species of diving ducks, Common Coot *Fulica atra*, snipes and gulls. The bags of Northern Pintail *Anas acuta* and Northern Shoveler *A. clypeata* have declined, but not those of Eurasian Wigeon *A. penelope* or

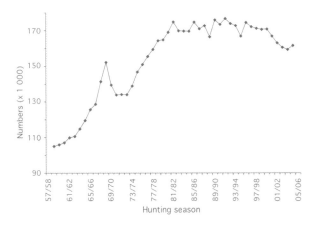

**Fig. 1.** Changes in the number of hunters holding a hunting licence in Denmark during the period 1969/70-2004/05.

**Table 1.** Conservation status, population trend, estimated annual bag (1999/2000-2003/04) and sustainability of hunting for 29 species of waterbirds for which there was an open season in Denmark in 2003/04. Conservation status, population trend (25 year trends up to and including 1996 or later) and sustainability of hunting were assessed by the National Environmental Research Institute in 2002 (Bregnballe *et al.* 2003). The estimated species composition of the bags of geese, ducks (except Mallard and Common Eider), snipes and gulls is somewhat uncertain and therefore given in brackets.

| Group/species/sub-population | Conservation status | Population trend | Estimated bag 1999/00-2003/04 | Sustainability of hunting |
|---|---|---|---|---|
| **Geese** | | | 18 000 – 29 000 | |
| Greylag Goose *Anser anser* | Favourable | Increasing | (> 12 000) | Sustainable |
| White-fronted Goose *Anser albifrons* | Favourable | Increasing | (< 300) | Sustainable |
| Bean Goose *Anser fabalis* | | | (< 400) | |
| Sub-population A (Finland) | Favourable | Increasing | | Sustainable |
| Sub-population B (Åsele Lapmark, Sweden) | Unfavourable and decreasing | Decreasing | | Local ban on hunting |
| Sub-population C (unknown origin) | Unknown | Stable-decreasing? | | Uncertain |
| Pink-footed Goose *Anser brachyrhynchus* | Favourable | Increasing | (> 2 000) | Sustainable |
| Canada Goose *Branta canadensis* | Favourable | Increasing | (> 1 200) | Sustainable |
| Mallard *Anas platyrhynchos* | Favourable | Increasing | 554 000 – 731 000[1] | Probably sustainable |
| **Other dabbling ducks** | | | 99 000 – 129 000 | |
| Northern Pintail *Anas acuta* | Favourable | Stable? | (3 200 – 7 100) | Sustainable |
| Eurasian Wigeon *Anas penelope* | Favourable | Increasing | (29 000 – 53 000) | Sustainable |
| Common Teal *Anas crecca* | Favourable | Increasing | (59 000 – 82 000) | Sustainable |
| Garganey *Anas querquedula* | Uncertain | Decreasing? | (100 – 400) | Sustainable |
| Northern Shoveler *Anas clypeata* | Favourable | Stable | (1 300 – 2 700) | Sustainable |
| Gadwall *Anas strepera* | Favourable | Increasing | (300 – 1 100) | Sustainable |
| Common Eider *Somateria mollissima* | Unfavourable and decreasing | Decreasing | 75 000 – 95 000 | Uncertain |
| **Other diving ducks** | | | 31 000 – 34 000 | |
| Common Pochard *Aythya ferina* | Favourable | Stable | (700 – 1 700) | Sustainable |
| Tufted Duck *Aythya fuligula* | Favourable | Stable | (3 300 – 4 400) | Sustainable |
| Greater Scaup *Aythya marila* | Favourable | Stable | (300 – 500) | Sustainable |
| Common Goldeneye *Bucephala clangula* | Favourable | Increasing | (11 000 – 18 000) | Sustainable |
| Long-tailed Duck *Clangula hyemalis* | Favourable | Stable? | (1 500 – 4 700) | Sustainable |
| Common Scoter *Melanitta nigra* | Favourable | Stable | (2 800 – 5 200) | Sustainable |
| Velvet Scoter *Melanitta fusca* | Favourable? | Unknown | (1 600 – 2 800) | Sustainable |
| Goosander *Mergus merganser* | | | (800 – 1 900) | |
| Flyway | Favourable | Stable-increasing | | Sustainable |
| Danish breeding population | Favourable but rare | Slowly increasing | | Local ban on hunting |
| Red-breasted Merganser *Mergus serrator* | Favourable | Increasing | (2 000 – 3 700) | Sustainable |
| Common Coot *Fulica atra* | Favourable | Increasing | 17 000 – 20 000 | Sustainable |
| **Snipes** | | | 15 000 – 24 000 | |
| Common Snipe *Gallinago gallinago* | Unfavourable | Unknown | (14 000 – 23 000) | Probably sustainable |
| Jack Snipe *Lymnocryptes minimus*[2] | Uncertain | Unknown | (1 100 – 3 500) | Uncertain |
| Eurasian Woodcock *Scolopax rusticola* | Favourable | Stable | 24 000 – 39 000 | Sustainable |
| **Gulls** | | | 28 000 – 36 000 | |
| Lesser Black-backed Gull *Larus fuscus* | | | (100 – 600) | |
| Baltic sub-population | Unfavourable and decreasing | Decreasing | | Not sustainable |
| Other sub-populations | Favourable | Increasing | | Sustainable |
| Herring Gull *Larus argentatus* | Favourable | Increasing | (19 000 – 25 000) | Sustainable |
| Great Black-backed Gull *Larus marinus* | Favourable | Increasing | (9 000 – 11 000) | Sustainable |

[1] The vast majority were released for shooting.
[2] Hunting of the species has been banned since 2004/05.

Common Teal *A. crecca*. The Mallard bag increased from 350 000 in the mid-1970s to 700 000 in the 1990s, concurrent with an increase in the release of Mallard for shooting, although the bag has recently decreased to 600 000. The bag of geese has more than doubled over the last 10 years, reaching 30 600 in 2004/05, mainly because of an increase in the take of Greylag Goose *Anser anser*. The bag of Eurasian Woodcock *Scolopax rusticola* has increased since the early 1970s. Table 1 gives the range of the estimated bags during the period 1999/2000 to 2003/04, together with population trends, for most of the 29 species of waterbirds for which there was an open season in 2003/04.

## Small and vulnerable populations: Bean Goose and other populations

The Bean Goose *Anser fabalis* occurs in Denmark during migration and winter. Information from phenology, recoveries and re-sightings of ringed birds suggests that the Taiga Bean Geese *A. f. fabalis* appearing in Denmark belong to at least three partly or entirely separated breeding populations (Madsen *et al.* 1996, Bregnballe *et al.* 2003). Sub-population "A" is large, and is composed of birds that breed in Finland and migrate to wintering areas in southern Sweden, south-eastern Denmark (Fig. 2) and The Netherlands. Sub-population "B" is small, breeds in central Sweden (Åsele Lapmark), and migrates to north-western Jutland (Thy; Fig. 2), with some birds continuing on to eastern England (Yare Valley) during the winter (Parslow-Otsu & Kjeldsen 1992). Sub-population "C" has unknown breeding origins and winters in north-eastern Jutland (Tjele near Viborg and Lille Vildmose; Fig. 2). These "C" birds have a different phenology from those occurring in north-western Jutland, and recovery and re-sighting data indicate that some of them winter in The Netherlands. A possible breeding area for the "C" birds is the border region between Norway, Finland and Russia. It is, however, puzzling that most birds ringed in northern Norway have been recovered in the same region as Finnish ringed birds, and that no Finnish and few Norwegian ringed birds have been recovered in the "C" bird region of Denmark (Fig. 2).

The Finnish breeding population (sub-population "A") increased during the 1970s and 1980s and probably stabilized thereafter (Nilsson *et al.* 1999). The conservation status of this population is therefore judged as favourable (Table 1). The two other sub-populations do not, however, appear to have a favourable conservation status. Winter counts in northern Jutland show a decline over the last 30-40 years from 3 000-4 000 birds to fewer than 1 500 birds at present. During the 1990s, mid-winter counts for northern Jutland and the Yare Valley combined have never exceeded 2 000 birds. Based on such pieces of information, we judged the conservation status of sub-population "B" as unfavourable-declining and of sub-population "C" as uncertain.

The change in the size of the Bean Goose bag in Denmark is not known in detail because the hunters do not distinguish between species when reporting their kill of geese. Furthermore, the number of goose wings received from hunters in relation to the total bag of geese has declined from 4-5% in the second half of the 1980s to 1% in the second half of the 1990s. A study of the species composition of the bag of geese in the 1960s suggested that c. 1 100 Bean Geese were bagged annually in Denmark. Based on the wing survey, it was estimated that the annual bag amounted to c. 500 in the early 1990s. It is unknown what proportion of these birds belonged to the different sub-populations. Uncertainty about the effects of hunting on sub-population "B" in the early 1990s led to a regional ban on Bean Goose hunting in parts of northern Jutland in 1994/95. This regional hunting ban probably led to a further decline in the annual bag of Bean Geese.

In 2002, we assessed the effect of hunting as sustainable for sub-population "A" and uncertain for sub-population "C". Based on the uncertainty of the effect on hunting on sub-population "C" and the unfavourable-declining conservation status of sub-population "B", we recommended that the regional hunting ban

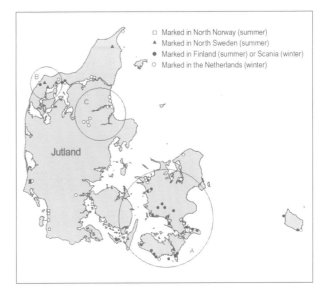

**Fig. 2.** Distribution of the three sub-populations of Taiga Bean Goose *Anser fabalis fabalis* in Denmark, based on ringing recoveries. Each sub-population has a different phenology, conservation status and breeding origin. Circle "A" indicates birds believed to belong to a population breeding in Finland and wintering mainly in southern Sweden (Scania). Circle "B" indicates birds from a small breeding population in northern Sweden. (In addition to the recoveries shown, neck-bands of 29 different individuals from the northern Swedish breeding range have been reported from this area). Circle "C" indicates a small population of unknown breeding origin which winters in north-east Jutland and apparently also in The Netherlands. Recoveries from outside these three areas indicate birds that were shot on migration or at staging areas that were used in the past. Map redrawn from Bregnballe *et al.* (2003) and updated with data from Bønløkke *et al.* (in press).

for Bean Goose (covering parts of northern Jutland) be expanded to include all areas in northern Jutland where the Bean Goose was known to occur. Following this recommendation, the Bean Goose was protected in Jutland by the 2004 Government Order.

Similar regional hunting bans have been used for a few other species of waterbirds in Denmark, e.g. hunting of gulls was banned south of latitude 55°40'N in order to increase the protection of the now threatened and declining nominate (Baltic) subspecies of the Lesser Black-backed Gull *Larus fuscus*. Also, as a result of representations to the Council for Wildlife Management, the Goosander *Mergus merganser* was protected south of 55°40'N in order to assist the establishment of a breeding population in Denmark (presently <30 pairs). Because of the problem of "look-alike species", the Red-breasted Merganser *M. serrator* was also protected within this area.

### Eurasian Wigeon

Eurasian Wigeon breeding in Scandinavia, Finland, Russia and Siberia occur in Denmark during August-November. Based on January counts, the estimated North-west European population of the Eurasian Wigeon increased three-fold between 1987 and 1996 (Delany *et al.* 1999), and subsequently declined to a lower level (Fig. 3). The decline in estimated population size was probably partly an effect of very poor breeding success in 1994 and in several of the subsequent years (Clausager 2004; Fig. 4).

The open season for Eurasian Wigeon is the same as that for all dabbling ducks in Denmark, i.e. 1 September – 31 December.

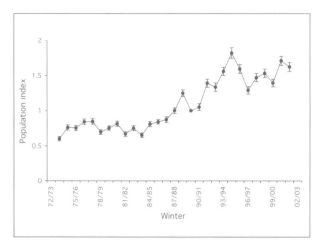

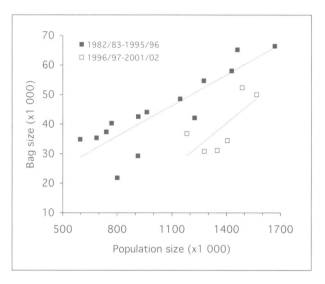

**Fig. 3.** Population trend of Eurasian Wigeon *Anas penelope* in North-west Europe during the period 1974-2002, estimated by Wetlands International from annual mid-winter counts (Wetlands International, unpubl. data). Points indicate index values ± SE using TRIM methods to estimate values (Pannekoek & van Strien 1998).

**Fig. 6.** Relationship between the annual bag of Eurasian Wigeon *Anas penelope* in Denmark and the estimated population size for North-west Europe during the periods 1982/83-1995/96 and 1996/97-2001/02.

The Danish bag of Eurasian Wigeon increased until 1995/96 (Fig. 5) simultaneously with an increase in the size of the population (Fig. 6). After 1995/96, the bag decreased markedly to a lower level than expected from the relationship between bag size and population size in the preceding years (Fig. 6). The seasons 2000/01 and 2001/02 had a higher bag than in former and subsequent years, probably because of a relatively high breeding success (Fig. 4).

Our interpretation in 2002 was that there had been no further decline in the size of the flyway population and that the species had a favourable conservation status. Furthermore, the take in Denmark in proportion to the size of the flyway was low in most seasons after 1995/96. Consequently, we judged the take in Denmark as sustainable.

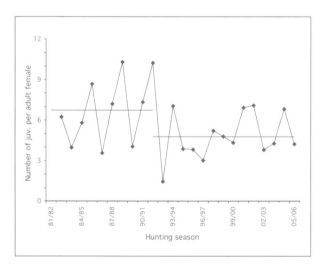

**Fig. 4.** Proportion of juveniles among Eurasian Wigeon *Anas penelope* bagged in Denmark during the hunting seasons 1982/83-2005/06. The proportion of juveniles is given as the number of juveniles of both sexes per adult female. The two solid horizontal lines give the means for the periods 1982/83-1991/92 and 1992/93-2005/06, respectively.

## Common Eider: first steps towards adaptive management?

Common Eiders breeding in Denmark, southern Norway, the west coast of Sweden and the Baltic moult, stage and winter in Danish waters. These populations all increased substantially throughout the twentieth century, but from the mid-1990s, the population trend was reversed, with overall peak numbers of at least 2 000 000 apparently decreasing by 30-50% in less than a decade (Desholm *et al.* 2002). This decline has been further aggravated by a change in the sex ratio over the same period from 60:40 (males to females) to 70:30 at present. The decline in the Baltic Sea/Wadden Sea flyway of Common Eiders is probably, to some extent, a result of the combined effects of avian cholera (causing mass mortality of incubating females), parasites and viral infections (causing low duckling survival), and poor feeding conditions in parts of the wintering area causing mass mortality, e.g. 25 000 Common Eiders were found dead in the Dutch-German part of the Wadden Sea in 1999/2000 (Desholm *et al.* 2002).

The annual bag in Denmark has partly reflected population trends, increasing to c. 140 000 in 1970, after which it fluctuated until the 1990s and then declined to 69 000 in 2004/05 (Fig. 7). It is likely, however, that the decline in annual bags reflects the declining interest of hunters in seaducks, as the number of hunters

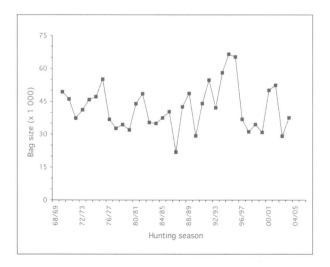

**Fig. 5.** Danish bag of Eurasian Wigeon *Anas penelope* during the period 1969/70-2003/04.

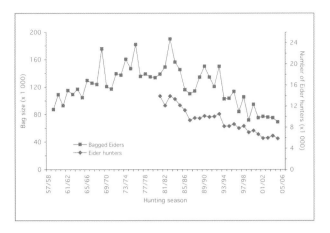

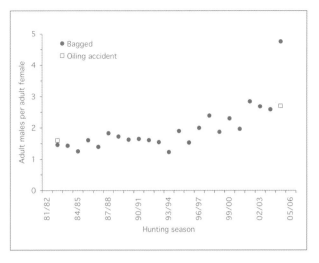

**Fig. 7.** Danish bag of Common Eider *Somateria mollissima* during the period 1958/59-2004/05, and the number of hunters that bagged Common Eiders during the period 1980/81- 2004/05.

bagging Common Eiders decreased from c. 14 000 in 1980 to 6 000 in 2001/02 (Fig. 7, Christensen 2005). For many years, the open season for eiders in Denmark was 1 October – 29 February, but since 1994, hunting in February has not been permitted in EU Special Protection Areas.

In 2002, we assessed the conservation status of the Baltic Sea/Wadden Sea population of the Common Eider as

Shooting seaducks from punts in the shallow waters around Denmark is highly traditional.   Photo: Niels Søndergaard

**Fig. 8.** Number of adult male Common Eiders *Somateria mollissima* per female based on the wing survey in 1982/83-2004/05 and on birds found dead during oiling accidents in 1982/83 and 2004/05.

unfavourable-declining and the effect of hunting as uncertain. Our interpretation of the available information was that the overall impact of hunting on the population had probably changed from reducing the rate of annual increase to potentially adding directly to the decline in breeding numbers. By 2002, the declines led NERI to consider means to limit the take, particularly of females. Consequently, we recommended differentiating between the two sexes, with the open season for females closing on 15 January and that for males on 15 February. At the same time, the open season for Common Scoter *Melanitta nigra*, Velvet Scoter *M. fusca* and Long-tailed Duck *Clangula hyemalis* was extended from 31 January to 15 February. This proposal was accepted, and although the data are still limited, they suggest a shifting sex ratio in the bag of eiders (see 2004/05 in Fig. 8), with the harvest of females being reduced by approximately 8 800 per year, of which 7 500 would belong to the Baltic population breeding to the east of Denmark.

## DISCUSSION
### Sustainability of hunting
Strategies for achieving and developing sustainable hunting differ widely. In general, researchers have sought to develop highly sophisticated systems of adaptive management based on collection of data, not only on population trends but also on reproduction and survival rates and habitat conditions, which coupled with advanced modelling lead to adaptive management through the introduction of bag limits and variations in annual open seasons. In our case, we have been forced by temporal and financial constraints to develop much more pragmatic systems based on the best information available.

Although most scientists would probably agree that improved data sets are always needed to inform changes in hunting regulation, we note that given an inventory of 29 huntable waterbird species, a considerable subset will always be scarcer, and that abundant species may be split into sub-populations, some of which may be small. By definition, these species and populations will be more vulnerable. The obvious solution – to protect them because they are of limited hunting interest – is often difficult because of "look-alike" issues; for example, it is hardly practicable to protect the Garganey *Anas querquedula* efficiently while maintaining an open season for the Common Teal. While over-exploitation of common and abundant species leaves time to carry out needed adjustments in case of population declines, the quest for sustainability may indeed be more challenging for scarce populations or sub-populations.

In our case, the continuing development of simple systems is based on the political desire for simplicity of management. So far, the specific objective for providing guidelines for Danish hunting management has been the desire for simple rules.

While the tools for assessing sustainability of hunting are undoubtedly in need of further refinement, we note that the need for assessing the impact of hunting on other aspects of waterbird populations based on factors other than population size are increasing. The recent demands for improved information relating to the timing of breeding seasons and the onset of spring migration under the Sustainable Hunting Initiative launched by the European Commission emphasise that hunting should not take place after birds commence their prenuptial migration. Combined with the demands for ethical sustainability, such new initiatives are likely to prolong the period necessary to harmonize general definitions of sustainability at international level.

### Improvement of the information base

Compared to many other countries, Denmark has a unique and fairly reliable system for monitoring its bag of migratory waterbirds. Nevertheless, challenges remain to improve the system: two major current problems are that the proportion of hunters reporting their bag has dropped to 58%, and that the estimated bag for most species is based on the wing survey, which is subject to bias. Steps have now been taken to ensure that reporting rates will increase again, but as long as wings are received from only 1-3% of the migratory waterbirds harvested, we face problems of scaling up from such samples. For example, the Eurasian Wigeon bag may be underestimated if the proportion of hunters contributing to the wing survey is low in that part of the country where most wigeon are bagged. This scaling-up problem could largely be avoided if hunters were required to report their entire bag at species level.

At present, it is possible for a few species to give a rough estimate of the proportion of the total bag in the flyway that is taken in Denmark. However, for most species we lack precise information on bag sizes along the remainder of the flyway. It would be useful if, for example, all Member States of the EU were obliged to publish their annual bag statistics, preferably within a year to permit effective feedback to flyway management.

With the present definition of sustainable hunting applied in Denmark, we rely heavily on the best available information from a variety of sources, such as estimates of population trends. It is therefore most unfortunate that trends have been updated only after a delay of several years because of insufficient resources for the International Waterbird Census, co-ordinated by Wetlands International. For a number of species, the available information on population size and geographical extent of populations and sub-populations is insufficient or unreliable. As a consequence, information on the conservation status of the populations we are harvesting may be outdated or inaccurate. We must continually strive to improve this situation, especially at the international level.

## ACKNOWLEDGEMENTS

We thank Ib Clausager for his long-term commitment in running the Danish wing survey. The estimation of waterbird trends would not be possible without the contribution, freely given every year, of thousands of voluntary waterbird counters.

## REFERENCES

**Bregnballe, T., Asferg, T., Clausager, I., Noer, H., Clausen, P. & Christensen, T.K.** 2003. Vildtbestande, jagt og jagttider i Danmark 2002. En biologisk vurdering af jagtens bæredygtighed som grundlag for jagttidsrevisionen 2003. NERI Technical Report No. 428, National Environmental Research Institute, Denmark. (Available electronically at: http://www2.dmu.dk/1_viden/2_Publikationer/ 3_fagrapporter/rapporter/FR428_2.pdf).

**Bønløkke, J., Madsen, J.J., Thorup, K., Pedersen, K.T., Bjerrum, M. & Rahbek, C.** In press. Dansk Trækfugleatlas. Forlaget Rhodos, Holtegaard, Humlebæk, Denmark.

**Christensen, T.K.** 2005. Factors affecting the bag size of the common eider *Somateria mollissima* in Denmark, 1980-2000. Wildlife Biology 11: 89-100.

**Clausager, I.** 2004. Vingeindsamling fra jagtsæsonen 2003/04. NERI Technical Report No. 504, National Environmental Research Institute, Denmark.

**Delany, S., Reyes, C., Hubert E., Pihl, S., Rees, E., Haanstra L. & van Strien, A.** 1999. Results from the International Waterbird Census in the Western Palearctic and Southwest Asia 1995 and 1996. Wetlands International Publication No. 54, Wetlands International, Wageningen, The Netherlands.

**Desholm, M., Christensen, T.K., Scheiffarth, G., Hario, M., Andersson, Å., Ens, B., Camphuysen, C.J., Nilsson, L., Waltho, C.M., Lorentsen, S.-H., Kuresoo, A., Kats, R.H.K., Fleet, D.M. & Fox, A.D.** 2002. Status of the Baltic/Wadden Sea population of the Common Eider *Somateria m. mollissima*. Wildfowl 53: 167-203.

**Madsen, J., Asferg, T., Clausager, I. & Noer, H.** 1996. Status og jagttider for danske vildtarter. Thematic Report No. 6, National Environmental Research Institute, Denmark.

**Nilsson, L., van den Bergh, L. & Madsen, J.** 1999. Taiga Bean Goose *Anser fabalis fabalis*. In: J. Madsen, G. Cracknell & T. Fox (eds) Goose Populations of the Western Palearctic. A Review of Status and Distribution. National Environmental Research Institute, Denmark, and Wetlands International, Wageningen, The Netherlands. Wetlands International Publication 48: 20-36.

**Pannekoek, J. & van Strien, A.** 1998. Trim 2.0 for Windows (Trends and Indices for Monitoring Data). Research Paper No. 9807. Statistics Netherlands, Voorburg.

**Parslow-Otsu, M. & Kjeldsen, J.P.** 1992. Laplandske sædgæs i Nordvestjylland. Dansk Ornitologisk Forenings Tidsskrift 86: 104-106.

**Sutherland, W.J.** 2001. Sustainable exploitation: A review of principles and methods. Wildlife Biology 7: 131-140.

**Williams, B.K. & Nichols, J.D.** 2001. Systems identification and the adaptive management of waterfowl in the United States. Wildlife Biology 7: 223-236.

# Non-toxic shot – Danish experiences

*Niels Kanstrup*

*Danish Hunters' Association, Molsvej 34, DK-8410 Rønde, Denmark. (email: nk@jaegerne.dk)*

Kanstrup, N. 2006. Non-toxic shot – Danish experiences. *Waterbirds around the world.* Eds. G.C. Boere, C.A. Galbraith & D.A. Stroud. The Stationery Office, Edinburgh, UK. p. 861.

Lead poisoning of waterbirds as a consequence hunters' use of lead shot is an issue which needs to be addressed internationally, since migratory waterbirds cross many borders during their migrations. Hence management practices - such as whether the use of lead shot is, or is not, permitted - in one country has consequences for the conservation of waterbirds in all countries on their flyways. The issue is also one of public relations and the image of hunting, and both hunters' and national and local government administrations can benefit from international co-operation and the exchange of knowledge and experience. To phase out lead shot, suitable alternatives must be available, and the research and development of alternatives and analysis of the market for their sale facilitated through international co-operation.

In Denmark, when the use of lead shot was first regulated in 1985, the hunters themselves initiated the use of alternative shot. The successful introduction of steel shot for clay pigeon shooting allayed the concerns of many hunters by showing that steel shot cartridges were not dangerous to fire and that the price of steel shot cartridges was still acceptable. Research by the Hunters Association also demonstrated that steel shot was just as effective as lead shot for killing birds.

Denmark enforced a total ban on the use of lead shot in 1996. However, this led to problems not for hunting in wetlands but in forests, since the use steel shot was unacceptable to foresters because of its hardness and the consequent risk of damage to machinery used in the timber industry from steel shot embedded in trees. This led to pressure to develop softer shot alternatives such as bismuth, tin and wolfram products. Five such alternatives have now been introduced and have proved to be popular, even though the prices of these cartridges are significantly higher than those of lead or steel shot.

Many Danish hunters were concerned the phasing out of lead shot would lead to the phasing out of hunting, but this has not been the case and the number of hunters and the annual bag has not changed significantly. In addition, the hunters' initial main concern, that there was increased risk of guns exploding or being damaged by steel shot, proved groundless.

The efficiency of alternative shot has been investigated in several scientific studies and more popular programmes, with results showing that efficiency is more related to hunters' experience and their shooting distances rather than to the performance of the cartridge; and in turn that the performance of the cartridge (its velocity generated, conformity etc.) is more critical than the shot material itself. Although lead is still regarded as an ideal shot material due to its ballistic qualities, there have been many examples of lead shot cartridges operating far less efficiently than cartridges containing alternative shot material.

Concerns by Danish hunters about the consequences of changing from lead to non-toxic shots have proved groundless. Photo: Else Ammentorp, Danmarks Jægerforbund/Danish Hunters Association.

The phasing out of lead shot has now led to more focus on the efficiency and effectiveness of hunting techniques. Steel shot has, to some extent, taught hunters to be more cautious, by shortening their shooting distances to quarry. This seems to have caused an increase in the efficiency of the hunting since shortening the quarry distance will markedly increase the probability of cleanly striking the birds.

Addressing the problems of lead poisoning of waterbirds caused by hunting with lead shot may seem a less important issue in many countries than addressing other pressures on wetland conservation such as safeguarding the future existence of ecosystems such as wetlands themselves. But maintaining and restoring the quality of wetlands, including reducing pollution levels such as from toxic lead, is an important component of their conservation. The Danish example of a total ban on lead for hunting has demonstrated that this can be achieved, and to inspire and motivate the process there is a clear need for a constructive dialogue at both national and international level between governments, nature conservationists and hunters – all of whom share the objective of maintaining wetlands for waterbirds. Such co-operation is a precondition for continuing the momentum and progress towards flyway-wide phasing out the use of lead shot in wetlands.

# The monitoring of hunting bags and hunting effort in the Camargue, France

*Jean-Yves Mondain-Monval[1], Pierre Defos du Rau[1,2], Nathalie Mathon[1], Anthony Olivier[1,3] & Laurent Desnouhes[1,3]*

[1] *Office National de la Chasse et de la Faune Sauvage, Le Sambuc, 13200 Arles, France. (email: j.y.mondain@oncfs.gouv.fr)*
[2] *Present address: ONCFS 10 bis Rte d'Ax. 31120 Portet/Garonne. France.*
[3] *Present address: Station Biologique de la Tour du Valat, Le Sambuc, 13200 Arles, France.*

Mondain-Monval, J-Y., Defos du Rau, P., Mathon, N., Olivier, A. & Desnouhes, L. 2006. The monitoring of hunting bags and hunting effort in the Camargue, France. *Waterbirds around the world*. Eds. G.C. Boere, C.A. Galbraith & D.A. Stroud. The Stationery Office, Edinburgh, UK. pp. 862-863.

The Camargue, in the Rhone river delta, is the most extensive wetland area in France, covering about 150 000 hectares of natural, semi-natural and agricultural habitats, and is a wetland of international importance. It is the most important wintering site in France for Anatidae species and for Coot *Fulica atra*. The numbers of ducks and coots in mid-winter amount, on average, to 10-20% of the numbers wintering in France. The Camargue is also one of the most important places for wildfowling in the country. Despite its ecological, cultural and economic impact on habitats, hunting activity has received little attention (Mathevet *et al*. 2002). Several research projects in the area aim to achieve a better understanding of population dynamics of game species, such as Teal *Anas crecca*, a very popular quarry species in Europe (Devineau 2003, Guillemain *et al*. 2002). However, precise data on mortality through hunting, recognised as vital information (Aebischer *et al*. 1999), is still missing. The aims of this work were to provide preliminary figures about the recent/latest hunting bag trend and composition, and to encourage hunters to set up an efficient monitoring scheme of their bag and hunting effort.

About 205 private hunting estates and 23 hunters' associations shoot on public land or extensive private estates. For many estate managers, there is a strong tradition of recording annual hunting bags. However, long-term data are not always available because of the high turnover of managers. Managers were contacted first at random, then by acquaintance, focusing on the most important in terms of annual bag or managed area. Therefore, this sample cannot be considered as truly randomly selected, although the intention in the medium-term is to sample most of the total hunted area throughout the Camargue. Bag statistics for about 50 estates were collected, covering very different periods of time (from one year, to 90 years). For 15 estates, bag data are available for a recent 12 year period. However, data from hunters' shooting on common/public land are totally missing as there is no organised scheme to collect this type of data.

Mallard *Anas platyrhynchos* and Teal amount to two-thirds of the Anatidae bag (Fig 1). The Mallard proportion has increased from 29% to 46% over the 1988 to 1999 period. The Simpson index for diversity (Fig. 2) shows a non significant tendency of decline ($R^2$=0,23 p=0.114 N=12), possibly due to increasing dominance of annually released mallards.

A TRIM index (Pannekoek & Van Strienen 1998) for raw bag data and an index adjusted to hunting effort were compared (Figs. 3 & 4) with a count index obtained from aerial counts (Tamisier 2003) to examine bag trends.

There was no significant linear relationship between the adjusted bag index and count index (Teal $R^2$=0.013 p=0.725 n=12; Mallard $R^2$=0.176 P=0.175 N=12).

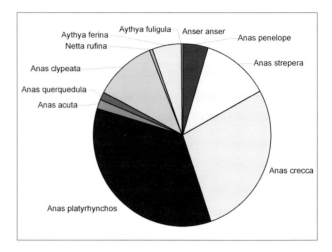

**Fig. 1.** Species composition of the bag sample of ducks between 1988-1999.

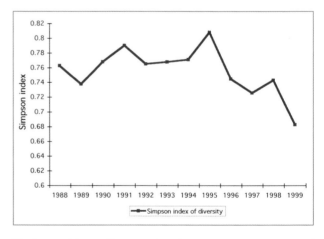

**Fig. 2.** Trends in the Simpson Index of diversity for the bag sample of ducks 1988-1999.

The main current technical challenges are that:

- a longer-term dataset seems necessary to reach more robust conclusions on trends, if any exist;
- raising awareness of the crucial importance of monitoring hunting effort as well as hunting bags for both individual hunters and estate managers is urgent;
- improving the representativeness of wildfowling areas in the analysis seems a necessary step but is likely to add major costs in data collection, as randomly sampled hunting managers might be reluctant to cooperate; and

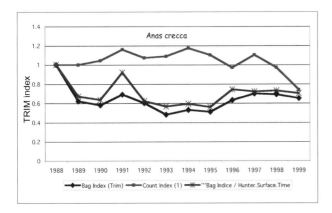

**Fig. 3.** Trends (TRIM index) in the bag and count indices for Teal *Anas crecca* 1988-1999.

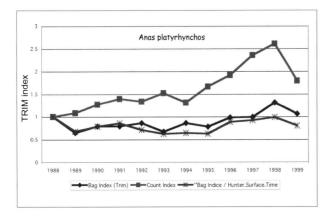

**Fig. 4.** Trends (TRIM index) in the bag and count indices for Mallard *Anas platyrhynchos* 1988-1999.

• hunting bag collection in this area is very time consuming, as hunters very rarely answer mailed questionnaires and often want to be met personally before participating.

It is therefore time to discuss opportunities, strategies and issues to increase monitoring effort and capacities; and the re-launching of a new monitoring program of hunting activity in the area.

If hunting statistics were to be collected at a broader scale, for example at a flyway level, it is absolutely vital to fully consider local, national and international hunting organisations as key partners for this type of survey.

## REFERENCES

**Aebischer, N.J., Potts, G.R. & Rehfisch, M.** 1999. Using ringing data to study the effect of hunting on bird populations. Ringing and Migration, 19 (suppl.): 67-81.

**Devineau, O.** 2003. Dynamique et gestion des populations exploitées: l'exemple de la Sarcelle d'hiver. Université de Montpellier II Sciences et technique du Languedoc. ENSA. Montpellier. Rapport de DEA. 26 pages & Annexes.

**Guillemain, M., Leray, G., Caizergues, A. & Schricke, V.** 2002. Dynamique de population de la sarcelle d'hiver (*Anas crecca*). ONCFS. Rapport scientifique 2002: 55-58.

**Mathevet, R. & Mesléard, F.** 2002. The origins and functioning of the private wildfowling lease system in a major Mediterranean wetland: the Camargue (Rhone delta, southern France). Land Use Policy 19(4): 277-286.

**Pannekoek, J. & Van Strienen, A.** 1998. TRIM 2.0 for Windows.

**Tamisier, A.** 2003. Anatidés et foulques en période hivernale. Revue d'écologie. 58(1): 27-35.

The natural (unmanaged) marshes in the Camargue support high densities of waterbirds.  Photo: Jean-Yves Mondain-Monval.

# Duck harvest in the Po delta, Italy

*Michele Sorrenti[1], Lorenzo Carnacina[2], Davide Radice[1], & Alessandro Costato[3].*

[1] *ACMA (Associazione Cacciatori Migratori Acquatici), settoriale della Federazione Italiana della Caccia via Messina 45, 20154, Milano, Italy. (email: acma_ricerche@yahoo.com)*

[2] *Ambito Territoriale di Caccia 4A3 Delta del Po, piazza Ciceruacchio, Porto Tolle, Italy.*

[3] *Provincia di Rovigo, Via della Pace, Rovigo, Italy.*

Sorrenti, M., Carnacina, L., Radice, D. & Costato, A. 2006. Duck harvest in the Po delta, Italy. *Waterbirds around the world.* Eds. G.C. Boere, C.A. Galbraith & D.A. Stroud. The Stationery Office, Edinburgh, UK. pp. 864-865.

Estimates of waterfowl hunting bags are the main research activity of the Associazione Cacciatori Migratori Acquatici (ACMA). These data are necessary for good species management, and are also a tool to provide an objective basis for public debate on hunting. The main objective is to create a monitoring scheme that allows the organisation to estimate, for each hunting season, the total bag in Italy (Sorrenti *et al.* 1999).

This short note provides the results obtained from public (ATC – Italian Hunting Association) and private (Aziende Faunistico Venatorie, AFV) shooting areas in the Po river delta, situated in the Rovigo district of the Veneto region, for the duck hunting season of 2002/03. This area is an important wintering site for many species, both at national and international level (Verza 2003, Baccetti *et al.* 2002).

The Rovigo District Administration worked with ACMA, in cooperation with the local hunting association, ATC Delta del Po, to estimate the waterfowl harvest in public shooting areas. ATC collected sheets compiled by waterfowl hunters and generalist hunters which gave the total number of hunters of each category and the total number of fixed hunting hides in the area. Rovigo District Administration provided reports of official bags from private shooting areas. A sample from the public area records were elaborated to expand the results to a wider area, using a Poisson distribution with 95% confidence interval.

The results from waterfowl hunters are provided in Table 1, and those of generalist hunters in Table 2. Table 3 reports the declared bag of the AFV. The total estimate of the duck harvest

**Table 1. Estimates of bag totals of waterfowl shot by specialized waterfowl hunters 2002/03 public area.**

| Species | n | Total species estimates | | | | | |
| | | 95% confidence interval | | | 95% confidence interval | | |
| | | Mean | Lower | Upper | Mean | Lower | Upper |
|---|---|---|---|---|---|---|---|
| Teal *Anas crecca* | 35 | 27 | 25 | 29 | 7 679 | 7 198 | 8 183 |
| Mallard *Anas platyrhynchos* | 35 | 25 | 24 | 27 | 7 122 | 6 659 | 7 607 |
| Wigeon *Anas penelope* | 35 | 23 | 22 | 25 | 6 524 | 6 082 | 6 990 |
| Pintail *Anas acuta* | 35 | | | | | | |
| Garganey *Anas querquedula* | 35 | 1 | 1 | 1 | 266 | 183 | 374 |
| Shoveler *Anas clypeata* | 35 | 3 | 2 | 4 | 840 | 686 | 1 017 |
| Gadwall *Anas strepera* | 35 | 6 | 6 | 7 | 1 801 | 1 572 | 2 053 |
| Pochard *Aythya ferina* | 35 | 12 | 11 | 13 | 3 407 | 3 090 | 3 748 |
| Tufted Duck *Aythya fuligula* | 35 | 3 | 3 | 4 | 937 | 774 | 1123 |
| Total | 35 | 106 | 103 | 110 | 29 972 | 29 015 | 30 952 |

**Table 2. Estimates of bag totals of waterfowl shot by generalist hunters 2002/03 public area.**

| Species | n | Total species estimates | | | | | |
| | | 95% confidence interval | | | 95% confidence interval | | |
| | | Mean | Lower | Upper | Mean | Lower | Upper |
|---|---|---|---|---|---|---|---|
| Teal *Anas crecca* | 16 | 2 | 1 | 2 | 675 | 445 | 982 |
| Mallard *Anas platyrhynchos* | 16 | 6 | 7 | 10 | 3 325 | 2 784 | 3 940 |
| Wigeon *Anas penelope* | 16 | 0 | 0 | 1 | 125 | 41 | 292 |
| Pintail *Anas acuta* | 16 | 0 | 0 | 0 | 0 | 0 | 92 |
| Garganey *Anas querquedula* | 16 | 0 | 0 | 0 | 0 | 0 | 92 |
| Shoveler *Anas clypeata* | 16 | 0 | 0 | 0 | 25 | 1 | 139 |
| Gadwall *Anas strepera* | 16 | 1 | 0 | 1 | 225 | 103 | 427 |
| Pochard *Aythya ferina* | 16 | 1 | 0 | 1 | 250 | 120 | 460 |
| Tufted Duck *Aythya fuligula* | 16 | 0 | 0 | 1 | 150 | 55 | 326 |
| Total | 16 | 12 | 10 | 14 | 4 775 | 4 122 | 5 502 |

in the Po delta is presented in Table 4 as a sum of the averages of Tables 1 and 2 and data from Table 3. However, the declared harvest of the AFV is considered an underestimation of the real numbers. A further 8 000-10 000 ducks should be added to the AFV declared bag, bringing the total duck harvest in this study area for the 2002/03 season to an estimated c. 70 000 birds. Based on the results from Table 4, the most common species of ducks shot were: Mallard *Anas plathyrhynchos (38%)*, Wigeon *Anas penelope (22%)*, Teal *Anas crecca (21%)*, Pochard *Aythya ferina* (6%) and Gadwall *Anas strepera* (3%).

**Table 3. The declared waterfowl hunting bag in private shooting areas (AFV) in 2002/03.**

| Species | Numbers |
|---|---|
| Teal *Anas crecca* | 4 667 |
| Mallard *Anas plathyrhynchos* | 12 665 |
| Wigeon *Anas penelope* | 6 880 |
| Pintail *Anas acuta* | 284 |
| Garganey *Anas querquedula* | 36 |
| Gadwall *Anas strepera* | 570 |
| Shoveler *Anas clypeata* | 1 029 |
| Pochard *Aythya ferina* | 101 |
| Tufted Duck *Aythya fuligula* | 6 |
| **Total** | **26 238** |

**Table 4. total waterfowl bag estimates 2002/03.**

| Species | Numbers |
|---|---|
| Teal *Anas crecca* | 13 021 |
| Mallard *Anas plathyrhynchos* | 23 112 |
| Wigeon *Anas penelope* | 13 529 |
| Pintail *Anas acuta* | 1 681 |
| Garganey *Anas querquedula* | 302 |
| Gadwall *Anas strepera* | 1 894 |
| Shoveler *Anas clypeata* | 2 596 |
| Pochard *Aythya ferina* | 3 758 |
| Tufted Duck *Aythya fuligula* | 1 093 |
| **Total** | **60 985** |

**REFERENCES**

**Verza E.** 2003 In: Piano Faunistico Venatorio Provinciale 2003-2007. Provincia di Rovigo Area Attività Produttive, Risorse Faunistiche e Vigilanza.

**Sorrenti, M., Fasoli, G. & Concialini A.** 1999. Italian waterfowl harvest: features from ACMA study. Proceedings of the International Union of Game Biologists XXIV Congress, Thessaloniki Greece.

**Baccetti, N., Dall'Antonia, P., Magagnoli, P., Melega, L., Serra, L., Soldatini, C. & Zenatello, M.** 2002. Risultati dei censimenti degli uccelli acquatici svernanti in Italia: distribuzione, stima e trend delle popolazioni nel 1991-2000. Biol. Cons. Fauna, 111; 1-240.

Mallards *Anas platyrhynchos* are the most commonly hunted waterbird in Italy's Po Delta. Photo: Else Ammentorp, Danmarks Jægerforbund/Danish Hunters Association.

# Considerations on the use of lead shot over wetlands

*Guy-Noël Olivier*

*OMPO Secretary General, 5, ave des Chasseurs 75017 Paris, France. (email: ompo@ompo.org)*

Olivier, G.-N. 2006. Considerations on the use of lead shot over wetlands. *Waterbirds around the world.* Eds. G.C. Boere, C.A. Galbraith & D.A. Stroud. The Stationery Office, Edinburgh, UK. pp. 866-867.

## ABSTRACT

OMPO (Migratory Birds of the Western Palearctic) was created some 20 years ago, and is committed to the conservation and sustainable use of Western Palearctic wetlands and the migratory waterbirds that inhabit them. OMPO has focussed its efforts on safeguarding wetlands from drainage and other detrimental activities within the framework of the Ramsar Convention on Wetlands, and has strong links with this Convention in Europe and Africa. OMPO was aware of the pollution caused by the use of lead shot in wetlands over 10 years ago, but at that time, the alternatives to lead shot were of poor quality and could not be recommended to hunters. Further studies on the effects of lead poisoning on waterbirds were conducted in France in the 1990s. These studies were financed by the hunting community and supervised by the Ministry of Environment, with the participation of OMPO. The conclusions, published in April 2001, reinforced the results of previous studies regarding the consequences of lead poisoning on reproductive success. OMPO is now strongly recommending to its network of partners throughout the Western Palearctic region that they abandon lead shot in hunting over wetlands and replace it with non-toxic substitutes. The additional mortality caused by lead poisoning is unacceptable for both conservationists and hunters, and is contrary to the long tradition of hunting to which OMPO is strongly attached.

## INTRODUCTION

OMPO (Migratory Birds of the Western Palearctic) was created some 20 years ago, and has committed itself to the conservation of migratory waterbird species inhabiting Palearctic wetlands for breeding, staging or wintering. OMPO is also committed to the principle of sustainable use of these renewable natural resources through the management of wetlands and bird populations. This avoids any waste of this international wealth.

In the past, OMPO was well aware of the damage caused by the intensive use of lead shot over wetlands and some of the consequences for wildlife (Bellrose 1959, Sanderson & Bellrose 1986, Roster 2002). Regrettably, however, this was by no means the only source of pollution having a negative impact on wetlands. Chemical residues and poisons of all kinds used in intensive agriculture and industry, as well as domestic garbage, were all going directly or indirectly into hydrological systems and consequently wetlands, where they were poisoning waterbirds and their predators.

The first studies of lead poisoning in waterbirds were conducted in the USA in 1959 (Bellrose 1959). In 1990, the results of French studies conducted in the Camargue were convincing for ornithologists but quite difficult to interpret for millions of hunters and still more so for the many millions of other polluters (Beck *et al.* 1995, Beck & Olivier 1998, Pain 1991a, 1991b, Pain *et al.* 1992). Furthermore, at that time, the alternatives to lead shot were of poor quality, and their efficiency

was so uncertain that they could not be recommended to hunters. This is why, from 1985, OMPO gave priority to fighting the causes of wetland loss, i.e. to making every possible effort to save wetlands from various types of drainage caused by agriculture, industry, expansion of urban areas and development of infrastructure.

The safeguarding of wetlands appeared to OMPO to be more efficient and essential than to reduce specific forms of pollution. An international conservationist NGO with a small staff and limited budget must make choices. Thanks to the stimulus provided by the international convention on wetlands signed in Ramsar, Iran, in 1971 (the Ramsar Convention on Wetlands), OMPO pressed ahead with its programme. Of the many projects subsequently carried out by OMPO, we give simply two examples:

1  The Ndiael Bowl, covering 10 000 hectares in the delta of the Senegal River, has been listed as a Wetland of International Importance under the Ramsar Convention since July 1977, but was drained in 1989 as a result of construction works. In 1991/1992, OMPO decided to restore the site to its former importance for birds. A feasibility study was carried out by the National Centre for Scientific Research (CNRS), and in 1994, work began on the digging of a 10 km long canal that would eventually replenish the site with water.

2  OMPO provided the financing for studies relating to the first three Ramsar sites in Latvia, including the renowned Lake Engure.

## LEAD POISONING IN WATERBIRDS AND A CALL FOR A BAN ON LEAD SHOT

In the 1990s, various scientific studies were conducted in France on lead pollution in wetlands and the possible consequences of direct or indirect lead poisoning affecting waterbirds. The purpose of these studies was to build upon previous studies undertaken in 1959 and 1990, to identify the collateral effects of this poisoning. These studies, conducted by the Laboratory of Chemistry and Toxicology at the National Veterinary School of Nantes, took over six years (Pinault 1996, Mézières 1999). They were financed by hunters' organizations and supervised by the Ministry of Environment, with the active co-operation of OMPO. The conclusions were made available in April 2001 (Baron 2001), and reinforced the results of previous studies concerning the consequences of the use of lead shot over wetlands and the ingestion of this poisonous heavy metal by birds, e.g.:

- death of birds that have ingested more than two pellets;
- weakness of contaminated birds and consequently increased predation;
- alteration of energy requirements and consequently a handicap for birds on migration;

- reduction in clutch size; and
- risk of eggshell and embryo malformations.

Most of these toxicological studies were conducted on species of ducks and swans. Thus, it appeared interesting to OMPO, the Office National de la Chasse et de la Faune sauvage (ONCFS), the Biological Station of Tour du Valat and the International Snipe Hunters' Club (CICB) to investigate if lead poisoning could have a similar effect on waders. Studies were conducted on two species: Common Snipe *Gallinago gallinago* (Beck *et al.* 1995, Veiga 1984) and Jack Snipe *Lymnocryptes minimus* (Beck & Olivier 1998, Veiga 1985). A sample of 269 Common Snipe revealed an ingestion rate of 15.6%, whereas a sample of 178 Jack Snipe revealed an ingestion rate of 6.5%. It was concluded that lead poisoning also affects waders and to a similar extent to that found in ducks, thus confirming previous studies.

A French Ministerial Order signed on 21 March 2002 by the Minister of Environment stipulated that from the opening day of the 2005 hunting season on migratory waterbirds, the use of lead shot would be forbidden in France on the following wetlands: coastal and inshore areas, permanent wetlands, rivers, canals, reservoirs, lakes, ponds and stretches of water.

For the past three years, OMPO has been associated, as a corresponding member, with the work undertaken by the Technical Committee of the African-Eurasian Waterbird Agreement (AEWA). OMPO used its influence to persuade the French Government to ratify the Agreement as quickly as possible, and this was achieved in July 2003, when a new hunting law including the ratification of the Agreement was approved by parliament. OMPO has also been accredited to promote the AEWA in those states covered by its network of partners, and to encourage them to join the Agreement.

OMPO is particularly sensitive to the need to promote sustainable hunting, as this provides a highly appreciated - and sometimes even essential - argument for the conservation of waterbirds, particularly in Africa and Eastern Europe where hunting is strongly anchored in local traditions. At the same time, OMPO is well aware of the negative impact of lead poisoning on waterbird populations as a result of the use of lead shot over wetlands. Therefore, in accordance with the Convention on the Conservation of European Wetlands and Natural Habitats (Bern Convention) and the AEWA, OMPO recommends to its international network of partners throughout the Western Palearctic region that consideration be given to abandoning the use of lead shot over wetlands.

Additional mortality of waterbirds due to all types of poisoning, including lead poisoning, is unacceptable for both conservationists and hunters. As the primary concern of hunters is to ensure that hunting opportunities persist into the future, it seems obvious that a decision should be made to abandon the use of lead shot so that the conservation status of those species that may be hunted remains in a favourable condition.

## CONCLUSION

It seems clear that the use of lead shot over wetlands should come to an end and appropriate substitutes used instead. This will take some time, given not only that it is an international political issue, but also that it requires the technical adaptation of guns and ammunition, especially in a number of countries located mostly in south-western Europe. It is in these countries, where hunters are strongly attached to their old traditions, that lead shot is most widely used and remains the most popular. OMPO is therefore making a strong recommendation to hunters to adopt a positive attitude in this regard, to avoid further wastage of a natural resource which is so valuable to them.

## REFERENCES

**Baron, P.** 2001. Suppression de l'utilisation de la grenaille de plomb de chasse dans les zones humides exposant les oiseaux d'eau au saturnisme. Rapport Inspection Générale de l'Environnement, Ministère de l'Aménagement du Territoire et de l'Environnement.

**Beck, N. & Olivier, G.-N.** 1998. Régime alimentaire de la bécassine sourde (*Lymnocryptes minimus*) en hivernage dans le nord de la France. Gibier Faune Sauvage, Game and Wildlife 15: 259-267.

**Beck, N., Granval, P. & Olivier, G.-N.** 1995. Techniques d'analyse du régime alimentaire animal diurne de bécassines des marais (*Gallinago gallinago*) du nord-ouest de la France. Gibier Faune Sauvage, Game and Wildlife 12: 1-20.

**Bellrose, F.C.** 1959. Lead poisoning as a mortality factor in waterfowl populations. Illinois Natural History Survey Bulletin 27, Art. 3.

**Mézières, M.** 1999. Effets de l'ingestion de plombs de chasse sur la reproduction du canard colvert (*Anas platyrhynchos*). Thèse Doct. Vét., Ecole nationale vétérinaire de Nantes.

**Pain, D.J.** 1991a. L'intoxication saturnine de l'avifaune: une synthèse des travaux français. Gibier Faune Sauvage, Game and Wildlife 8(1): 93-95.

**Pain, D.J.** 1991b. Why are lead-poisoned waterfowl rarely seen? The disappearance of waterfowl carcasses in the Camargue, France. Wildfowl 42: 118-122.

**Pain, D.J., Amiard-Triquet, C. & Sylvestre, C.** 1992. Tissue lead concentrations and shot ingestion in nine species of waterbirds from the Camargue (France). Ecotoxicology and Environmental Safety 24: 217-233.

**Pinault, L.** 1996. Evaluation de l'exposition au plomb des canards en France - Résultats d'une enquête conduite de 1992 à 1995 en 7 sites. Laboratoire de pharmacie et toxicologie, Ecole nationale vétérinaire de Nantes.

**Roster, T.** 2002. Lead poisoning in waterbirds through the ingestion of spent lead shot. AEWA Newsletter Special Edition No. 1, September 2002: 12.

**Sanderson, G.C. & Bellrose, F.C.** 1986. A review of the problem of lead poisoning in waterfowl. Illinois Natural History Survey. Special Publication No. 4.

**Veiga, J.** 1984. Régime alimentaire de la bécassine des marais (*Gallinago gallinago*) sur le bassin d'Arcachon (Gironde). Gibier Faune Sauvage, Game and Wildlife 1(2): 5-43.

**Veiga, J.** 1985. Contribution à l'étude du régime alimentaire de la bécassine sourde (*Lymnocryptes minimus*). Gibier Faune Sauvage, Game and Wildlife 2(1): 75-84.

# Harvesting status of migratory waterfowl in northern Iran: a case study from Gilan Province

*Behnam Balmaki[1] & Ahmad Barati[2]*

[1] *Department of Environmental Sciences, Azad University of Arak, Iran*

[2] *Department of Environmental Sciences, Higher Education Complex of Malayer, Iran. (email: abarati@basu.ac.ir)*

Balmaki, B. & Barati, A. 2006. Harvesting status of migratory waterfowl in northern Iran: a case study from Gilan Province. *Waterbirds around the world*. Eds. G.C. Boere, C.A. Galbraith & D.A. Stroud. The Stationery Office, Edinburgh, UK. pp. 868-869.

Commercial and recreational waterfowl hunting is a well established part of the culture of northern Iran and migratory waterbirds have an important role in the economic and social development of this area. This survey was carried out to determine the abundance and diversity of hunted waterfowl in Gilan province, northern Iran, from November 2001 to February 2002. The results showed that 393 693 individual birds from 49 species and eight families were harvested from the aquatic ecosystems of Gilan province during the study period (Table 1). Anatidae were the most abundantly hunted group of species.

Due to its ecology and geographical situation, northern Iran is an important key wintering area for waterbirds in the Middle-East (Mansori 1984). It contains diverse habitats which attract many different species. Gilan province (36°02'- 38°27'N and 48°30'-50°30'E) covers 14 711 km², has three Ramsar sites and numerous other aquatic ecosystems making this area a key site for wintering migratory waterbirds. The legal and illegal harvesting of these migratory waterbirds is an important source of income for the indigenous people of this state.

Surveys found that the main local markets for hunted birds are in the cities of Rashat, Anzali and Langrud. In order to determine the number of birds harvested, counting was carried out during the four months of November, December, January and February in these three cities. Each week data was collected on the diversity and numbers of species in the bird markets of these cities.

From November 2001 to February 2002 a total of 393 693 waterbirds were harvested. Comparison of the three main cities suggested that the harvesting rate in Anzali was the highest, about 39% of all hunted birds (Fig. 1). The highest number of birds was recorded in January, with a total of 160 514 birds (Fig. 2).

Commercial and recreational waterbird hunting is a well established part of the culture of northern Iran. It is recognized

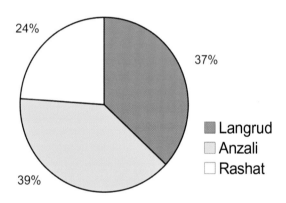

24%
37%
Langrud
Anzali
Rashat
39%

Fig. 1. Harvesting percentages in each location.

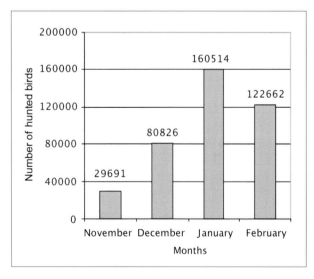

Fig. 2. Number of hunted waterfowl in different months (November 2001-February 2002)

Fig. 3. Hunted waterfowl for sale in Gilan Province, northern Iran.

**Table 1. Number of hunted individuals of each species in Gilan Province, northern Iran.**

| Species | | Number of Hunted Birds | | | |
|---|---|---|---|---|---|
| | | Feb.2002 | Jan.2002 | Dec.2001 | Nov.2001 |
| *Tachybaptus ruficollis* | Little Grebe | 63 | 130 | 86 | 95 |
| *Podiceps nigricollis* | Eared Grebe | 52 | 23 | 23 | 44 |
| *Podiceps cristatus* | Great Crested Grebe | 63 | 54 | 43 | 58 |
| *Phalacrocorax carbo* | Great Cormorant | 33 | 8 | 15 | 17 |
| *Phalacrocorax pygmaeus* | Pygmy Cormorant | 33 | 16 | 17 | 17 |
| *Anser anser* | Greylag Goose | 14 | 11 | 17 | 14 |
| *Tadorna ferruginea* | Ruddy Shelduck | 40 | 14 | 15 | 27 |
| *Tadorna tadorna* | Common Shelduck | 45 | 28 | 37 | 16 |
| *Anas platyrhynchos* | Mallard | 10 410 | 13 732 | 19 602 | 9 098 |
| *Anas crecca* | Teal | 54 681 | 75 465 | 40 910 | 15 659 |
| *Anas strepera* | Gadwall | 620 | 494 | 494 | 410 |
| *Anas penelope* | Wigeon | 149 | 127 | 173 | 14 |
| *Anas acuta* | Pintail | 55 | 46 | 38 | 6 |
| *Anas querquedula* | Garganey | 707 | 313 | 255 | 178 |
| *Anas clypeata* | Shoveler | 974 | 797 | 424 | 199 |
| *Netta rufina* | Red Crested Pochard | 149 | 538 | 258 | 217 |
| *Aythya ferina* | Eurasian Pochard | 585 | 508 | 707 | 226 |
| *Aythya nyroca* | Ferruginous Duck | 46 | 37 | 31 | 16 |
| *Aythya fuligula* | Tufted Duck | 86 | 118 | 126 | 15 |
| *Aythya marila* | Greater Scaup | 101 | 85 | 109 | 49 |
| *Gallinula chloropus* | Common Moorhen | 54 | 164 | 132 | 198 |
| *Porphyrio porphyrio* | Purple Swamphen | 56 | 80 | 76 | 107 |
| *Fulica atra* | Eurasian Coot | 52 682 | 66 550 | 16 439 | 2 581 |
| *Vanellus vanellus* | Northern Lapwing | 32 | 33 | 15 | 2 |
| Charadriidae | plovers and lapwings | 407 | 275 | 144 | 80 |
| Scolopacidae | sandpipers | 525 | 868 | 472 | 197 |
| Laridae | gull and terns | - | - | 168 | 151 |
| | **Total** | **122 662** | **160 514** | **80 826** | **29 691** |

as a legitimate activity within the context of sustainability but requires management. Harvesting of these species by recreational hunters is minimal. The management of commercial harvesting is achieved through the declaration of an annual waterbird hunting season with regulation of the length of each

Ruddy Shelduck *Tadorna ferruginea*. Photo: Anastasia Popovkina.

season, setting of daily opening and closing times and the setting of daily bag limits and total possession limits. Estimates of total waterbird populations are used to vary these parameters in order to restrict the harvest to sustainable levels (Balmaki 2002). The standard waterbird hunting season lasts three months but may be extended in 'good' years and reduced in 'bad' years.

Surveys showed that 83 Pygmy Cormorant *Phalacrocorax pygmaeus* and 130 Ferruginous Duck *Aythya nyroca* were hunted during this period. These species are listed as threatened in the IUCN Red List (BirdLife International 2000). The presence of these species in the bird markets indicates that management of the traditional harvest is extremely difficult due to cultural constraints in Gilan, and is not being fully implemented at present.

The most abundant group of harvested waterbird in this region was the Anatidae family with the Eurasian Coot *Fulica atra* the most popular prey for hunters.

### REFERENCES

**Balmaki, B**. 2002. Harvesting Rate on Migratory Waterfowls in Gilan. M.Sc thesis, University of Tarbiat Modarres, Iran.

**Mansori, J**. 1984. Survey on Migratory Waterbird Populations. Journal of Environmental Studies 12: 123-150.

**BirdLife International** 2000. Threatened birds of the world. Lynx Edicions and BirdLife International, Barcelona and Cambridge.

# Harvest of migratory geese *Chloephaga* spp. in Argentina: an overview of the present situation

*Daniel E. Blanco & Victoria M. de la Balze*

*Wetlands International, 25 de Mayo 758 10° I (1002) Buenos Aires, Argentina. (email: deblanco@wamani.apc.org)*

Blanco, D.E. & de la Balze, V.M. 2006. Harvest of migratory geese *Chloephaga* spp. in Argentina: an overview of the present situation. *Waterbirds around the world*. Eds. G.C. Boere, C.A. Galbraith & D.A. Stroud. The Stationery Office, Edinburgh, UK. pp. 870-873.

## ABSTRACT

Austral geese (*Chloephaga* spp.) are endemic to South America. Four species are migratory and occur in Argentina and Chile. One of these, the Ruddy-headed Goose *Chloephaga rubidiceps*, is endangered on the mainland of South America, where the population is estimated at only about 1 000 individuals. During the migration periods and in winter, austral geese are threatened by recreational hunting and hunting to control crop damage. Recreational hunting is a common activity in Argentina, and attracts many foreign hunters from Europe and North America. Despite the fact that large numbers of geese are killed each year, no information exists on the impact of this hunting on their populations. The aims of the present study were to make an assessment of the hunting of austral geese in Argentina, and to evaluate the potential consequences of hunting for the conservation of these species. The assessment was based on an intensive literature search, an analysis of current hunting regulations, questionnaires to waterfowl hunters, and interviews with wildlife authorities and key specialists. Issues addressed include the status of the geese, hunting practices, hunting regulations, and implications for conservation. The results are discussed in the context of the current situation, and monitoring and management needs are formulated in order to contribute to the conservation of migratory geese in southern South America.

## INTRODUCTION

The five species of austral geese (*Chloephaga* spp.) are endemic to South America. Four of the species occur on the mainland of southern South America (including Tierra del Fuego) and also have separate subspecies or populations in the Malvinas Falkland Islands (Canevari 1996). The mainland populations of the Upland Goose *Chloephaga picta*, Ashy-headed Goose *C. poliocephala* and Ruddy-headed Goose *C. rubidiceps* are migratory (Canevari 1996). Their breeding grounds are located in southern Patagonia and Tierra del Fuego (Argentina and Chile), while their wintering areas are in northern Patagonia and the southern pampas of Buenos Aires Province (Argentina).

The mainland and Tierra del Fuego population of the Ruddy-headed Goose has a very restricted distribution. Breeding pairs concentrate in the surroundings of Punta Arenas (southern Chile) and in the northern portion of Tierra del Fuego island (Madsen *et al.* 2003), while during the winter, the birds concentrate in a small area in southern Buenos Aires Province (Blanco *et al.* 2003a). This population has declined steeply since the 1950s, and is now considered in danger of extinction in both Argentina and Chile (García Fernández *et al.* 1997, Glade 1993, de la Balze & Blanco 2002). The size of this population is currently estimated at around 1 000 individuals (Madsen *et al.* 2003, Blanco *et al.* 2003b).

The available information suggests a decreasing trend not only for the Ruddy-headed Goose but also for the other two migratory species (Canevari 1996, Wetlands International 2002)

**Table 1.** Status of the subspecies (s) or populations (p) of three species of austral geese (*Chloephaga* spp.) on the mainland of South America.

| Species | Common name | Estimate | Trend |
|---|---|---|---|
| *Chloephaga picta picta (s)* | Upland Goose | D | DEC |
| *Chloephaga poliocephala (p)* | Ashy-headed Goose | C/D | DEC |
| *Chloephaga rubidiceps (p)* | Ruddy-headed Goose | 900-1 178 | DEC |

C = 25 000-100 000 individuals; D = 100 000-1 000 000 individuals; DEC = decreasing trend.

Sources: Wetlands International (2002), Blanco *et al.* (2003b).

(Table 1). Recent observations of reduced numbers both in mainland South America and in Tierra del Fuego (Blanco *et al.* 2003b, N. Loekemeyer pers. comm., J. Veiga pers. comm.) point in the same direction. Population declines appear to have been caused by the combined effects of various factors.

The hunting of austral geese is a common activity in Argentina and Chile, and is legally restricted to two species, the Upland Goose and Ashy-headed Goose (Canevari 1996, Servicio Agrícola y Ganadero 1999, Blanco *et al.* 2002). In Argentina, hunting affects goose populations during the autumn migration season and in winter, mainly in the northern portion of their ranges. The aims of the present study were to undertake an assessment of the hunting of austral geese in Argentina, including a review of the provincial regulations, and to consider the implications for conservation.

## STUDY AREA AND METHODS

Argentina is a federal country with 23 provincial jurisdictions. Provinces are responsible for the management of natural resources within their territories, including wildlife. This assessment was restricted to the provinces of Buenos Aires, Neuquén, Río Negro, Chubut, Santa Cruz and Tierra del Fuego, which encompass the main distribution of austral geese in Argentina (Fig. 1).

The assessment was based on the following sources of information: 1) an intensive search of the literature concerning the harvesting of austral geese; 2) an analysis of hunting regulations in each province; 3) questionnaires to waterfowl hunters; and 4) interviews with wildlife authorities and key specialists.

## RESULTS AND DISCUSSION

Waterfowl are hunted for recreation (sport hunting), as a subsistence harvest and for the control of crop damage (Ojasti 2000). Many South American species of waterfowl are threatened by intensive hunting because of insufficient regulations; most of the regulations that do exist relate to those species with a critical conservation status (Meneghetti *et al.* 1990).

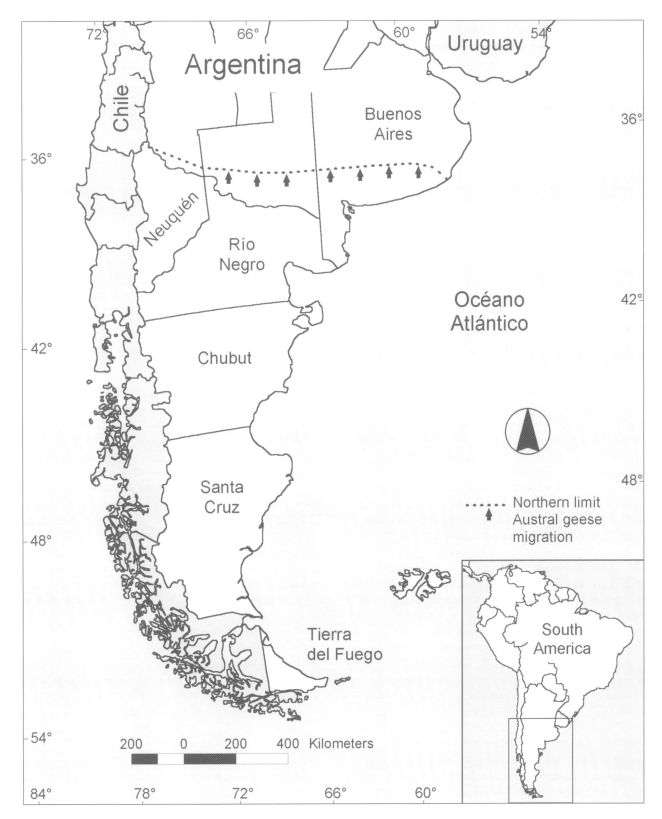

Fig. 1. The study area in southern Argentina, indicating provincial jurisdictions and the northern limit of austral goose migration.

Austral geese are amongst the most commonly hunted species of waterfowl in Argentina. The hunting of Upland and Ashy-headed Geese is permitted in various provinces, while the Ruddy-headed Goose is protected by national and provincial laws. However, the difficulty in distinguishing Ruddy-headed Geese from female Upland Geese poses a serious threat to the former species, as the geese form mixed flocks during migration and in winter.

**Sport hunting**

The hunting of austral geese is common in several provinces of Argentina, although local hunters generally prefer terrestrial game species such as the Spotted Nothura *Nothura maculosa* and European Hare *Lepus capensis* (Blanco *et al.* 2002). In Buenos Aires Province, for example, only about 18% of the hunters interviewed expressed a preference for waterfowl (Parisi 1998).

Goose hunting is permitted throughout the entire range of

**Table 2.** Hunting regulations and bag limits (geese per hunter per day) for the Upland Goose *Chloephaga picta* (CHLPI) and Ashy-headed Goose *C. poliocephala* (CHLPO) in Argentina.

| Province | Bag limits | | Season | Maximum |
| --- | --- | --- | --- | --- |
| | CHLPI | CHLPO | | per season |
| Buenos Aires | No limit | | Whole year | No limit |
| Río Negro | 12 | 12 | 1 May – 30 September | 48 |
| Neuquén | 6 | 6 | 1 May – 31 July | 24 / 36 |
| Chubut | 5 | 5 | 1 May – 31 July | ? |
| Santa Cruz | 2 | 0* | 1 April – 31 August | 2 |
| Tierra del Fuego | Prohibited | | —- | —- |

\* The hunting of Ashy-headed Geese is prohibited in Santa Cruz Province.

the geese, with the exception of Tierra del Fuego, and takes place mainly during the autumn migration and in winter. It is practised mainly by foreign hunters who consider the austral geese as overlooked game species. In recent years, goose hunting has become more popular not only in Buenos Aires (F. Moschione pers. comm.), but also in the Patagonian provinces (A. Contreras pers. comm.).

The limited information available suggests that the contribution of sport hunting to the total number of geese killed per year in Argentina varies between provinces. In Chubut Province, for example, about 80% of the goose harvest results from recreational hunting and only 20% from hunting to control the numbers of geese which utilize agricultural land in the river valleys as staging areas during their migrations (A. Contreras pers. comm.). Bag limits for Upland and Ashy-headed Geese also differ between provinces, ranging from "unlimited hunting" in Buenos Aires Province (a wintering area) to total prohibition in Tierra del Fuego (a breeding area) (Table 2).

### Hunting to control numbers

Hunting to control the numbers of geese is more common in the northern portion of their range than in the south. In northern Patagonia and the southern Pampas, geese have traditionally been persecuted by local farmers because they feed on crops (mainly wheat) and pastures during the migration seasons and in winter. In the past, geese were also considered to compete with sheep in southern Patagonia, where they were chased and killed by ranchers (N. Loekemeyer pers. comm.).

In 1931, austral geese were officially declared "agricultural pests" (Pergolani de Costa 1955), but the Ruddy-headed Goose was later excluded from the list of "pest species" because of its remarkable fall in numbers (Rumboll 1975). More recently, Tracanna & Ferreira (1984) and Martin *et al.* (1986) questioned the real magnitude of wheat losses caused by grazing geese, and pointed out that situations in which austral geese come into conflict with agriculture are relatively few. In some areas of Buenos Aires Province, where geese are still considered harmful by local farmers, aircraft are used to scare them away from wheat fields (R. Scoffield pers. comm.). Furthermore, some farmers welcome foreign hunters to kill as many geese as they want in return for a payment of just US$ 10 per hunter per day.

### Is sustainable harvest possible?

The hunting of austral geese in Argentina lacks an adequate regulatory framework to guarantee the sustainable use of the resource. In Buenos Aires Province, the hunting of Upland and

Ashy-headed Geese is allowed without limits throughout the whole year (Blanco *et al.* 2002). This decision, which is not based on population data, allows geese to be killed on a massive scale without any governmental control.

According to Zaccagnini (2002), a programme aimed at ensuring the sustainable use of waterfowl populations should include at least the following components: 1) biological (monitoring of populations and basic ecological research); 2) use/harvest (monitoring the harvest by working with hunters); 3) conservation and education (training and outreach materials such as brochures, field guides etc.); and 4) financial (fundraising for implementation of actions under components 1, 2 and 3.

Some of these components and activities are mentioned briefly in the provincial regulations, but are rarely put into practice. The main gaps that we identified if sustainable management of the resource is to be achieved are the lack of:

- accurate population estimates and trend data for the Upland Goose and Ashy-headed Goose;
- data on the geese hunted per season in each province (species, numbers, sex ratio, age composition);
- Specific actions to protect the Ruddy-headed Goose from illegal hunting;
- co-ordination between the provinces with respect to hunting regulations and the setting of bag limits within Patagonia;
- education/awareness campaigns directed at farmers, outfitters and hunters, with an emphasis on conservation of the Ruddy-headed Goose;
- funding support to keep the programme functioning.

Our main recommendations are as follows:

- organization of a National Austral Goose Monitoring Programme with the participation of the federal government and provinces, based on "survey stations" distributed throughout the migration and wintering ranges of the geese;
- organization of a harvest monitoring programme in each province involving the local hunting associations;
- prohibition of goose hunting within the main breeding and wintering areas of the Ruddy-headed Goose, as well as along its migration route (e.g. Chubut Province has recently prohibited goose hunting in the coastal departments along the migration route of the Ruddy-headed Goose);
- promotion of inter-provincial co-ordination concerning goose management and conservation within the framework of the Patagonian Wildlife Advisory Council (CARPFS).

## FINAL REMARKS

The conservation and management of migratory species which are shared by two or more countries require international co-operation. Furthermore, under a federal system of natural resource management such as that found in Argentina, co-ordination is required between provinces in their efforts to manage shared species such as the austral geese.

As in many other parts of the world, geese are considered simultaneously to be pests on agriculture and to be overlooked game species. In Argentina, austral geese are hunted without there being an adequate framework for the sustainable use of the resource. As in the case of the globally threatened Lesser White-fronted Goose *Anser erythropus*, the Ruddy-headed Goose is today seriously threatened by illegal hunting during the autumn migration season and in winter, as farmers and hunters do not distinguish it from other very similar goose species. Immediate action is required to bring the mainland population of the Ruddy-headed Goose to a favourable conservation status.

## ACKNOWLEDGEMENTS

This assessment is based on data compiled under the "Waterbird harvest in the Pampas wetlands" project funded by The Netherlands Ministry of Foreign Affairs (DGIS), as well as information gathered by the Ruddy-headed Goose Project funded by the Convention on the Conservation of Migratory Species of Wild Animals (CMS-UNEP). We would also like to give special thanks to Rosemary Scoffield, Flavio Moschione, Nora Loekemeyer, Luis Benegas, Jorge Veiga and Adrián Contreras for their valuable contributions.

## REFERENCES

**Blanco, D.E., Beltrán, J. & de la Balze, V.M.** 2002. La caza de aves acuáticas en la provincia de Buenos Aires: diagnóstico de la situación actual. In: D.E. Blanco, J. Beltrán & V.M. de la Balze (eds) Primer Taller sobre la Caza de Aves Acuáticas: Hacia una estrategia para el uso sustentable de los recursos de los humedales. Wetlands International, Buenos Aires: 5-25.

**Blanco, D.E., Zalba, S.M., Belenguer, C.J., Pugnali, G. & Rodríguez Goñi, H.** 2003a. Status and conservation of the ruddy-headed goose *Chloephaga rubidiceps* Sclater (Aves, Anatidae) in its wintering grounds (Province of Buenos Aires, Argentina). Revista Chilena de Historia Natural 76 (1): 47-55.

**Blanco, D.E., Zalba, S.M., de la Balze, V.M., Petracci, P.F. & Scorolli, A.** 2003b. Distribution and population status of the Ruddy-headed Goose: Preliminary results 2003. Workshop Measuring Waterbird Abundance. 27th Annual Meeting of the Waterbird Society, 24-27 September 2003. Cuiabá, Mato Grosso, Brazil.

**Canevari, P.** 1996. The austral geese (*Chloephaga* spp.) of Southern Argentina and Chile: a review of their current status. Gibier Faune Sauvage, Game and Wildlife 13: 355-366.

**De la Balze, V.M. & Blanco, D.E.** 2002. El cauquén colorado (*Chloephaga rubidiceps*): una especie amenazada por la caza de avutardas. In: D.E. Blanco, J. Beltrán & V.M. de la Balze (eds) Primer Taller sobre la Caza de Aves Acuáticas: Hacia una estrategia para el uso sustentable de los recursos de los humedales. Wetlands International, Buenos Aires: 119-122.

**García Fernández, J.J., Ojeda, R.A., Fraga, R.M., Díaz, G.B. & Baigún, R.J.** (compilers). 1997. Libro rojo de mamíferos y aves amenazados de la Argentina. FUCEMA-SAREM-AOP-APN.

**Glade, A.** (ed). 1993. Libro rojo de los vertebrados terrestres de Chile. Corporación Nacional Forestal, Santiago, Chile.

**Madsen, J., Matus, R., Blank, O.M., Benegas, L., Mateazzi, G. & Blanco, D.E.** 2003. Population status of the Ruddy-headed Goose (*Chloephaga rubidiceps*) in Tierra del Fuego and mainland Patagonia (Chile and Argentina). Ornitología Neotropical 14 (1): 15-28.

**Martin, S.I., Tracanna, N. & Summers, R.** 1986. Distribution and habitat use of sheldgeese populations wintering in Buenos Aires Province, Argentina. Wildfowl 37: 55-62.

**Menegheti, J.O., Rilla, F. & Burger, M.I.** 1990. Waterfowl in South America: their status, trends and distribution. In: G.V.T. Matthews (ed) Managing Waterfowl Populations. Proceedings of IWRB Symposium, Astrakhan 1989. IWRB Publication No. 12. Slimbridge, UK: 97-103.

**Ojasti, J.** 2000. Manejo de Fauna Silvestre Neotropical. In: F. Dallmeier (ed) SIMAB Series No. 5. Smithsonian Institution/MAB Program, Washington, D.C.

**Parisi, R.** 1998. La caza deportiva en la provincia de Buenos Aires, Argentina. Conociendo al cazador. Manejo de Fauna, Publicacion Técnica 9: 23-24.

**Pergolani de Costa, M.J.I.** 1955. Las avutardas. Especies que dañan a los cereales y las pasturas. IDIA 88: 1-9.

**Rumboll, M.** 1975. El cauquén de Cabeza Colorada (*Chloephaga rubidiceps*): Una nota de alarma. El Hornero 11: 315-316.

**Servicio Agrícola y Ganadero** 1999. Cartilla de Caza. SAG - Ministerio de Agricultura, Chile.

**Tracanna, N.A. & Ferreira, L.** 1984. Evaluación de los efectos sobre el rendimiento en grano de cultivos de trigo pastoreados por avutardas (*Chloephaga* sp.). Plan de estudios y control de avutardas. Unpublished report.

**Wetlands International** 2002. Waterbird Population Estimates - Third Edition. Wetlands International Global Series No. 12, Wageningen, The Netherlands.

**Zaccagnini, M.E.** 2002. Los patos en las arroceras del noreste de Argentina: ¿plagas o recursos para caza deportiva y turismo sostenible? In: D.E. Blanco, J. Beltrán & V.M. de la Balze (eds) Primer Taller sobre la Caza de Aves Acuáticas: Hacia una estrategia para el uso sustentable de los recursos de los humedales. Wetlands International, Buenos Aires: 35-57.

# The Wetlands International Waterbird Harvest Specialist Group: challenges and objectives

*Gilles Deplanque[1] & Tunde Ojei[2]*

[1]*ANCGE c/o OMPO, 5 avenue des Chasseurs, 75017 Paris, France. (email: gillesdeplanque@nordnet.fr)*
[2] *Capacity Building Officer, Wetlands International, PO Box 471, 6700 AA Wageningen, The Netherlands.*

Deplanque, G. & Ojei, T. 2006. The Wetlands International Waterbird Harvest Specialist Group: challenges and objectives. *Waterbirds around the world.* Eds. G.C. Boere, C.A. Galbraith & D.A. Stroud. The Stationery Office, Edinburgh, UK. pp. 874-875.

An IWRB "Hunting Research Group" was originally established in 1969, and was subsequently renamed the Wetlands International "Waterbird Hunting Specialist Group". However, for a number of reasons, not least the reluctance of the hunting world to provide information on the size and composition of hunting bags, since the mid-1990s the group found it increasingly difficult to operate effectively so as to contribute assessment of patterns of waterbird hunting in different parts of the world.

In 2001, Wetlands International and other relevant bodies including OMPO - Migratory Birds of Western Palearctic and other organisations concerned with waterbird harvesting reviewed the situation, and agreed to redevelop the Specialist Group. The Group has now been renamed the "Waterbird Harvest Specialist Group" (WHSG), in recognition of a widened scope that now covers other forms of waterbird harvest beyond direct hunting harvest. Its overall objectives are:

i.   to use waterbird harvest data to improve population estimates of waterbird species which are too widespread and dispersed for estimates to be made from site-based censuses such as the International Waterbird Census; and

ii.  to assess the hunting pressure on huntable waterbird populations, so as to established whether or not it is sustainable.

Concerning objective i., waterbird harvest data has already been used to improve the biogeographic population estimates for some waterbird species, notably for Jack Snipe *Lymnocryptes minimus* in Europe which has led to a major correction to previous underestimates in the latest editions of Wetlands International's *Waterbird Population Estimates*.

The Group's working basis is that sustainable use is the harvesting, whatever its nature, of a species with due consideration for its conservation status, whether its demographic trend is stable or increasing. To better understand and assess the extent of sustainability of waterbird harvests there is a need to combine and compare different parameters such as population estimate, productivity rate, natural mortality, hunting harvest assessment, other human harvest and other human causes of mortality.

The new Group held its first meeting during the Edinburgh Global Flyways Conference, and identified three initial challenges in developing its work. These are: defining the Group's scope of activity within the field of waterbird harvests; developing a strong global network with a good balance between developed and developing countries; and defining a strategy, objectives and priorities for developing work on the different aspects of the Group's scope.

## The Harvest Group's scope of activity

The Group's work will cover:

i.   Waterbird harvests by hunting and hunting trade exploitation;

ii.  Intentional non-hunting waterbird harvests for food or trade purposes; and

iii. Unintentional waterbird harvests (anthropogenic mortality) which are directly caused by other human activities such as marine oil pollution, all types of collisions (wires, land and air transportation, glass-facades of buildings, installation of wind turbines on migratory corridors etc.), various poisoning (hunting lead, agricultural pesticides or insecticides), proliferation and straying of pets, and introduced predators (especially cats).

The Harvest Group will not be dealing with indirect waterbird mortality or disappearance resulting from human activities such as wetland degradation, urbanisation and coastal development.

## Establishing a global network

A strong membership network of motivated and competent people in each of the three main areas of the Group's scope, and good regional spread of expertise and activity, will be crucial for the group to be meet its objectives. The initial membership of the Group was over 30 people from 21 countries and several continents, and this has now grown and widened following the discussions at the Global Flyways Conference. However, there remains a gap in good regional coverage, with most of the membership still being European-based.

## Defining a strategy, objectives and priorities

The Group recognises that there is a real need for better knowledge of hunting harvests on waterbird species. The majority of the Group's members have expertise in this aspect of waterbird harvest: many are members of hunting societies while others live in communities where waterbirds are hunted for food. Although waterbird hunting assessment will therefore be a strong priority for the Group, other harvest sectors will not be neglected.

Teal *Anas crecca* decoys. Photo: Else Ammentorp, Danmarks Jægerforbund/Danish Hunters Association.

## Waterbird hunting harvests

On the basis of available data, some countries monitor, or seek to monitor, the waterbird hunting harvests, but on the whole the effort is inconsistent: some countries have harvest monitoring schemes for all hunted waterbirds, but others monitoring only for particular species (e.g. Woodcock *Scolopax rusticola* or Mallard *Anas platyrhynchos*) or have data only by species group (e.g. geese, ducks, sea ducks, waders). In addition, the methods used for the monitoring also differ greatly between countries for technical, cultural or sometimes political reasons.

The Group identified the major potential for comparing the results of different monitoring methods as a way forwards to avoid long debates about the use and accuracy of different methodologies. For example, in France two different monitoring methods, exhaustive and statistical, have been applied simultaneously for Jack Snipe. Both methods provided the same result, with an estimate of a little less than 50 000 birds harvested annually. Such similarity is quite remarkable, and such comparisons suggest that at least in some cases, the results of different methods used in different countries may be comparable. This will be helpful in compiling multi-county harvest assessments, since some countries have long-established methods which they do not wish to change. It may also be helpful in recommending appropriate methodologies to countries which do not yet undertake harvest monitoring.

The key approach, regardless of what method is used, it to collect the data at the species level. This is essential so as to allow for comparisons between species, to use the results in improving waterbird population estimates, and to use the data in assessments of sustainable use.

### Intentional non-hunting harvests

This aspect of the group's work will focus on:

i. Estimates of seabird harvest from fishery activities (nets and long-lines); and
ii. An awareness campaign aimed at public authorities, through providing mortality or productivity decrease estimates resulting from lead-shot and lead-weights from fishing in wetlands; and recommending, without delay, further research effort on substitute materials.

### Unintentional harvests directly linked to human activities

Here the priority will be to assess the anthropogenic mortality of seabirds from oil-spills, both from shipwrecks, and from dumping of oil at sea which is believed to cause heavy annual mortality of seabirds, as the basis for encouraging the reinforcement of security norms and international controls, especially for degraded ships.

All those involved in waterbird harvest assessment worldwide are encouraged to join the WHSG, so as to strengthen and broaden its capacity to undertake its priority work.

As well as exploring direct harvests, the Harvest Specialist Group will also review unintentional waterbird mortality as a result of collisions with man-made structures such as wind-turbines. Photo: Tom Stroud.

## 6.4    Financing global flyway conservation: innovation, linkages, options. Workshop Introduction

*Randy Milton[1] & Trevor Swerdfager[2]*

*[1] Wetlands and Coastal Habitats Program, Department of Natural Resources, 136 Exhibition Street, Kentville, Nova Scotia, B4N 4E5, Canada.*

*[2] Director General, Canadian Wildlife Service, Ottawa, Ontario, K1A 0H3, Canada.*

Milton, R. & Swerdfager, T. 2006. Financing global flyway conservation: innovation, linkages, options. Workshop Introduction. *Waterbirds around the world.* Eds. G.C. Boere, C.A. Galbraith & D.A. Stroud. The Stationery Office, Edinburgh, UK. pp. 876-877.

It is rare for banks to directly raise awareness of waterbirds, but the States of Jersey have highlighted Light-bellied Brent Geese *Branta bernicla hrota* on their currency, providing a good return for migratory species conservation. Copyright: The States of Jersey.

Funding for migratory bird and flyway conservation is not expected to increase and new approaches are required to meet identified needs. Programs must become inclusive and collaborative, and be broadened through partnerships and networking to include working landscapes where goals can be integrated into general operating procedures of those who influence practices on the land. Financing global flyway conservation must become more than birds. Migratory flyways need to be internalized within the biodiversity and sustainable development context of human well-being and poverty reduction.

Programs for flyway conservation are multi-faceted and delivered by numerous organizations at different spatial scales. A commonality to all is a reliance on government directed and supported funding mechanisms that have bird or habitat conservation as their primary objectives. To respond to increasing and competing demands for limited human and fiscal resources, financing global flyway conservation must become more creative, innovative and inclusive.

Flyway based conservation programs in the North American (Swerdfager) and Asia-Pacific (Watkins & Mundkur) regions were presented alongside an examination of Global Environment Facility (Castro) supported programs. Symposium participants were challenged to identify and respond to the linkages and opportunities that exist between financing mechanisms and conservation's other "cost elements". These were interpreted to include multi-lateral agreements and conventions, regional and national supporting infrastructure, effective delivery mechanisms and evaluation processes. Speakers identified how these elements (globally or on a flyway basis) contribute to leverage financial and human resources from national and international (government, non-government and business) organizations in support of flyway conservation activities. This symposium explored innovative approaches, opportunities to expand conservation networks, options to refocus and enhance the delivery of conservation activities and access a wider range of funding mechanisms

Although based on different experiences, common themes emerged from the presentations and discussion. Central to the symposium is a recognition that migratory bird and flyway conservation have unmet financial needs. However, budgetary pressures in many developed countries will severely limit their ability to directly target additional fiscal resources to meet this need. Moreover, the increases in funding delivered by development agencies through bilateral and multilateral agreements during the 1980s and 1990s appear to have reached a stable plateau. The conservation community must apply the synergy that results from greater collaboration among governments, public and private agencies, businesses, and NGOs, through sharing of information and pooling of expertise and resources, and a combining of forces to support specific conservation finance mechanisms on-the-ground.

To achieve this synergy, changes must occur in how we 'package and deliver' conservation programs to include solid biological and socioeconomic planning and measurable objectives. This may require organizations to identify and incorporate new 'skill sets' into their program development mix. The base of support must broaden to be inclusive and less restrictive to participation by a sometimes diverse stakeholder community.

Flyway conservation initiatives have traditionally focussed on increasing the network of protected areas. Opportunities for new protected areas still exist, but there is also great potential to become actively involved with the 'working landscape'. Partnerships and networking to engage local communities will build local capacity, heighten awareness and knowledge, and influence how activities are undertaken in working landscapes. By building upon common interests and developing trust among engaging organizations, it is often possible to extend the influence of the project beyond the negotiating table. Program goals can become integrated into general operating procedures of

companies and government agencies, by becoming collaborative partners rather than competing interests.

The financing of global flyway conservation must move beyond seeking funds for migratory birds to become more inclusive of all birds and refocus to embrace the local dimension. A reassessment of program goals should seek to refine priorities in-line with key funding sources such as the GEF, World Bank, and national and international development agencies. The Convention on Biological Diversity (CBD) and World Summit on Sustainable Development have defined the key deliverables (human well being and poverty reduction) within which the financing of global flyway and migratory bird conservation could be structured.

Migratory flyways need to be internalized within the broader agendas of biodiversity conservation and issues of sustainable development. We must be able to bridge the needs of migratory birds by responding to the needs and aspirations of society for poverty alleviation, and sustainable development in a growing and diversified economy which includes biodiversity conservation as an integral component of production systems. We need to respond to the CBD and other conventions by shifting our focus to mainstream biodiversity conservation into developing projects which promote poverty alleviation — tackling the cause rather than the symptoms. By addressing the needs of people we will produce an environmental dividend in the conservation of migratory birds.

Male Wrybill *Anarhynchus frontalis* – one of several non-migratory waders which are globally threatened. Photo: Colin Galbraith.

# Conservation finance for waterbird flyways: key issues and emerging opportunities

*Gonzalo Castro*

*Head of Biodiversity Team, Global Environment Facility, 1818 H. Street NW, Washington, D.C. 20433, USA. (email: Gcastro@thegef.org)*

Castro, G. 2006. Conservation finance for waterbird flyways: key issues and emerging opportunities. *Waterbirds around the world*. Eds. G.C. Boere, C.A. Galbraith & D.A. Stroud. The Stationery Office, Edinburgh, UK. pp. 878-880.

## ABSTRACT

This paper includes data on trends in global financing for conservation, a discussion on the special conservation needs of migratory waterbirds, and a set of concrete recommendations for future financing of waterbird flyways. Trends in global financing for conservation show a large financing gap that is likely to grow as competing international societal demands for other issues including health, education, security, and poverty alleviation become more acute. In addition, the conservation financing needs of migratory species and their flyways present special challenges. Because migratory species represent a pure "global common," their conservation requires the concerted cooperation of the countries that host them throughout their life cycles. Furthermore, because the stopover sites used by migratory birds may not always coincide with national conservation priorities, many critical sites may be left out of national-level conservation efforts. There are successful examples of international financing of migratory flyways. Because of strong competition for resources with other priorities and the pressure to find sustainable financing sources, these examples cannot be extrapolated to all flyways. Instead, over the long term and to be successful, advocates for the conservation of migratory species need to develop strong scientific and political scenarios to find a space within the broader conservation and development processes that determine the configuration of land uses at any given location, and the political processes that support these decisions. In the long term, financing shortcomings can only be met through the mainstreaming of biodiversity conservation within economic sectors in production landscapes, as well as through the development of sustainable funding sources based on market approaches.

## INTRODUCTION

To be successful, conservation of nature cannot occur in a vacuum. Sustainable conservation requires continuous support from societies, the political processes responsible for allocating resources to economic priorities, and must be anchored on mainstreamed, market-based mechanisms that promote individual behaviours that are compatible with conservation.

Migratory species, however, present additional challenges to conservationists; their lives take place in habitats that are very often located in different countries, and thus their conservation depends on maintaining the integrity of each and every habitat or stopover needed for their survival. As with any chain, the strength of this migratory chain of stopovers is only as strong as its weakest link (Myers *et al.* 1987).

Further adding to the challenge of conserving migratory species, there is currently a large financial gap for conservation of biodiversity that is unlikely to be met in the short or mid-term through public funds, whether national or international.

In this paper, I review current funding trends for biodiversity conservation, discuss the unique conservation needs of migratory bird species and their flyways, and propose a set of principles that can enhance the availability of financial resources for the conservation of migratory species by placing their special needs in the context of current financing trends for conservation and environment.

## CURRENT FINANCING TRENDS FOR CONSERVATION AND ENVIRONMENT

Accurate information on conservation financing is largely unavailable, and its collection presents methodological challenges because of lack of standard definitions and methods of data collection and maintenance by funding bodies. Accurate data have only been compiled for the Latin American and Caribbean region, covering the period 1990-1998 (Castro & Locker 2000).

In that survey, the authors relied on questionnaires sent to 118 funding bodies, of which 65 responded. These responses, however, included all known major funding bodies and thus it is likely that the study captured most funding that was actually available during the period. From these sources, the total cumulative funding over the nine-year period was US$3.26 billion, representing 3 489 projects. The great majority of these funds (90%) was provided by multilateral and bilateral sources, followed by NGOs (5.8%) and private foundations (3.8%). Most funds were allocated to protected areas (36%), followed by biodiversity conservation within natural resources management (35%), policy (8%), research (5%), and capacity building (4%).

Over time, and when compared with a previous study that covered the period 1987-1989 (Abramovitz 1989, 1991), there

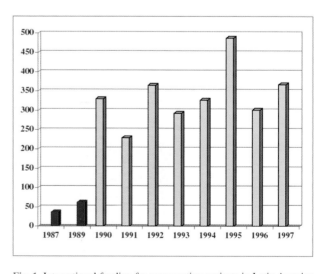

Fig. 1. International funding for conservation projects in Latin America and the Caribbean: 1987-1997. In millions of US dollars. Sources: Abramovitz 1989 (1987-1989); Castro & Locker 2000 (1990-1997).

was a significant jump in funding. Funding grew from an average of c. US$50 million per year in the late 1980s to c. US$350 million per year in the 1990s. Nevertheless, the trends during the 1990s remained flat and without a clear increase during the period (Fig. 1). These trends have continued until today, and are due to various reasons, primarily the emergence of new priorities for development assistance that are more focused on poverty alleviation and related issues (Lapham & Livermore 2003).

Global trends for development assistance confirm these results. The international community has refocused its efforts towards achieving the Millennium Development Goals, a set of priorities agreed at the 2002 United Nations Conference on Environment and Development (UNCED) in Johannesburg. These goals are the following:

- Reduce extreme poverty and hunger.
- Achieve universal primary education.
- Promote gender equality.
- Reduce infant mortality.
- Improve maternal health.
- Fight AIDS and other diseases.
- Promote sustainable development.
- Promote global development.

It is clear that most of these goals focus on social needs and poverty alleviation, legitimate societal priorities that compete with resource allocation for environment (goal 7) at national and international levels. Further complicating this difficult outlook for environmental financial resources, there is an overall shortage of funds for all development issues. Since the 1990s, the total amount of overseas development assistance (ODA) has remained constant in US dollar terms at about US$60 billion (Fig. 2), but when expressed as a percentage of GDP, it has decreased steadily over the last 15 years and it is still very far away from the target of 0.7% of GDP agreed in the 1970s (World Bank unpubl. data). Finally, new international priorities have emerged in the last few years, related to security and war, and these urgent issues have drained additional resources away from development funds.

The funding picture from international sources for waterbird flyway conservation is therefore bleak. As we have seen, most

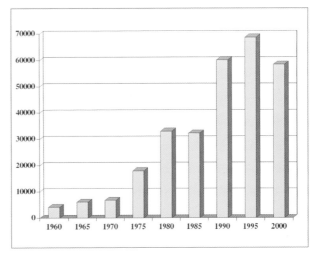

**Fig. 2.** Overseas development assistance (ODA) available world-wide: 1960-2000. In millions of US dollars.

current funding sources for development and environment are provided by multilateral and bilateral sources, but the magnitude of ODA since the early 1990s has not grown. Within this flat international funding picture, environment now competes with other social issues that receive higher priorities. Therefore, advocates for migratory species conservation face a total "pie" that has not grown, and a slice within it (environment) that is shrinking.

The picture is complicated even further by the fact that the financial needs of most other conservation issues, many of which are widely considered to be higher priorities, are not currently being adequately met. Even for an issue such as protected areas, commonly considered a top conservation priority and one that receives most conservation funds, current financial flows only cover about 30% of the needs (Brunner *et al.* 2004). How can migratory species receive the funding that not even top priority issues such as protected areas receive today?

## SPECIAL NEEDS OF MIGRATORY SPECIES

As has been documented earlier, the conservation needs of migratory species present special challenges to conservationists. An important characteristic of many migratory waterbirds is that they concentrate in large numbers during migration. This concentration means that very large proportions of entire populations can be found at key locations and at the same time, thus making them extremely vulnerable to local conditions during migration. Many species that migrate long distances rely on a series of these migratory stopover sites, and the loss of just one of these sites could result in catastrophic disruptions to their life cycles and even survival (Myers *et al.* 1987).

Migratory species conservation thus requires concerted international efforts, including the identification and protection of these key sites. Major challenges, however, emerge. Are all such sites well known? Do these sites always coincide with national conservation priorities? Where can the funding be found for sites that do not coincide with national priorities? Are all sites properly conserved and managed? Clearly, the conservation needs of migratory waterbirds present additional challenges to conservationists, over and above existing efforts to conserve biodiversity.

The Millennium Development Goals are increasingly driving international assistance and development policies. Photo: David Stroud.

## PERSPECTIVES AND RECOMMENDATIONS

Successful examples exist of conservation efforts that have addressed the challenges of conserving migratory waterbirds. Among them, the establishment of the Western Hemisphere Shorebird Reserve Network by J.P. Myers and collaborators in the mid-1980s represented a milestone that has been emulated in other parts of the world. Other efforts have included the establishment of international conservation agreements under the umbrella of the Convention on Migratory Species (CMS), and the support of several projects with funding provided by the Global Environment Facility and with the support of international NGOs (notably BirdLife International) and countries, to conserve migratory flyways in Africa, Europe and parts of Asia. These efforts, however, cannot be replicated on a scale that would satisfy the needs of all migratory flyways, because resources of such magnitude are simply not available. Furthermore, such approaches are not sustainable because in the absence of sustainable financing mechanisms, they are vulnerable to changes in international financing trends. Instead, these pilot experiences can simply be taken as experiments that have provided important lessons for future work in flyway conservation.

Clearly, these examples are not sufficient, and it is unlikely that they can be replicated at scales sufficiently large and in a timely manner to address all conservation needs of migratory waterbirds. Clearly, additional steps are required. The following is a list of four proposed steps:

1. Build public support. Over the long term, conservation can only succeed to the extent that societies understand its importance and exert pressure over policy-makers to allocate the necessary resources to achieve it. Bird migration is one of the most fascinating spectacles in nature. Therefore, advocates of migratory waterbird conservation must step up efforts to build public support, at all levels, and in all countries.

2. Strengthen the scientific basis of conservation decisions. To be credible, conservation needs to be based on solid scientific data. Information on flyways, stopovers, and resilience of migratory populations to disruptions are key elements to sharpen strategies for migratory waterbirds.

3. Support broader conservation efforts. The conservation of migratory waterbirds is just a "subset" of broader conservation efforts. Its long-term success in developing countries strongly depends upon the ability to achieve broader conservation goals in these countries, including building the necessary local capacity, institutions and policies that support conservation. Advocates of migratory waterbird conservation need to avoid the perception that they represent a "special interest group," but rather, support broader conservation efforts at national levels.

4. Bring conservation into the mainstream of broader development issues and utilize market-based mechanisms.

Conservation must be perceived as relevant to society's well-being. Given existing severe financial shortcomings, stand-alone conservation efforts will not succeed and will not attract sufficient funding to address this issue. Therefore, and in addition to continued efforts to increase overall funding for conservation at all levels, it is important to promote development actions that have the potential to generate conservation benefits. There are numerous examples of successful efforts of such "piggy-backing" or "mainstreaming". For example, coffee grown in the shade and certified as biodiversity friendly commands better prices in the international specialized markets, and provides direct economic incentives to local farmers to maintain forest cover in areas of high biodiversity. Market-based schemes of payments for environmental services have been successfully established in Costa Rica and other countries in Latin America.

In the case of migratory waterbirds, there are numerous opportunities for such "mainstreaming", for example: (i) with the tourism sector, given the strong overlap between migratory stopovers and coastal areas with high tourism potential; (ii) with the agricultural sector, when crops can be grown in ways that provide habitat for waterbirds, as in the case of rice; and (iii) with the infrastructure sector, finding ways to incorporate the conservation of migratory stopovers within broader regional development schemes.

As with most other conservation issues, there is no single-bullet solution that can address all challenges at the same time. Success will require sustained efforts, creativity, and the willingness to innovate and involve all sectors of society in the conservation of nature.

## REFERENCES

Abramovitz, J. 1989. A Survey of U.S.-Based Efforts to Research and Conserve Biological Diversity in Developing Countries. World Resources Institute, Washington, D.C.

Abramovitz, J. 1991. Investing in Biological Diversity: U.S. Research and Conservation Efforts in Developing Countries. World Resources Institute, Washington, D.C.

Brunner, A.G., Gullison, R.E. & Balmford, A. 2004. Financial Costs and Shortfalls of Managing and Expanding Protected-Area Systems in Developing Countries. Bioscience 54: 1119-1126.

Castro, G. & Locker, I. 2000. Mapping Conservation Investments: An Assessment of Biodiversity Funding in Latin America and the Caribbean. Biodiversity Support Program, Washington, D.C.

Lapham, N. & Livermore, R. 2003. Striking a Balance: Ensuring Conservation's Place on the International Biodiversity Assistance Agenda. Conservation International, Washington, D.C.

Myers, J.P., Morrison, R.I.G., Antas, P.Z., Harrington, B.A., Lovejoy, T.E., Salaberry, M., Senner, S.E. & Tarak, A. 1987. Conservation Strategy for Migratory Species. American Scientist 75: 19-26.

# Partnering to finance and deliver local flyway conservation in Nova Scotia, Canada

*G. Randy Milton[1], Glen J. Parsons[1] & Reginald Melanson[2]*

[1]*Nova Scotia Department of Natural Resources, 136 Exhibition Street, Kentville, Nova Scotia, B4N 4E5, Canada. (email: miltongr@gov.ns.ca)*

[2]*Environment Canada (Canadian Wildlife Service), 17 Waterfowl Lane, Sackville, New Brunswick, E4L 1G6 Canada.*

Milton, G.R., Parsons, G.J. & Melanson, R. 2006. Partnering to finance and deliver local flyway conservation in Nova Scotia, Canada. *Waterbirds around the world.* Eds. G.C. Boere, C.A. Galbraith & D.A. Stroud. The Stationery Office, Edinburgh, UK. pp. 881-882.

Nova Scotia's coastal waters support regional and global waterbird populations. With most of the province and its coastline in private ownership, the conservation of waterbird habitat is a shared responsibility. This paper examines different forms of partnering to help deliver flyway conservation activities at a local level.

Nova Scotia's coastal habitats, located in the North American Atlantic Flyway, support regionally and globally significant numbers of migrating, staging, and wintering waterbirds. However, approximately 75% of the province and 95% of its coastline is in private ownership. Provincial and federal governments have historically applied provisions under legislation (e.g. sanctuaries and management areas) or listed areas under international agreements (e.g. Ramsar Convention) to regulate or influence activities that may directly impact waterbirds or their habitats. Although the Southern Bight Minas Basin Ramsar site has overlapping designation with the Western Hemispheric Shorebird Reserve Network (WHSRN), it receives no legislated habitat protection.

Since 1989 the Eastern Habitat Joint Venture (EHJV) partnership has delivered the North American Waterfowl Management Plan (NAWMP) to reduce/ reverse wetland loss and to restore waterfowl populations in Eastern Canada. Government agencies on the EHJV Management Board in 2002 identified the partnership as the principle delivery mechanism for bird habitat conservation under the North American Bird Conservation Initiative (NABCI). This decision by the North American Wetlands Conservation Council (NAWCC-Canada) to support NABCI objectives provided an opportunity to address threats to the waterbirds and habitat of the Southern Bight Minas Basin Ramsar and WHSRN site.

The Southern Bight Minas Basin is located in the upper reaches of the Bay of Fundy. Beginning in late July, 50-95% of the world population of Semipalmated Sandpiper *Calidris pusilla* migrates south through the upper bay. To complete the non-stop 5 000 km transoceanic flight to wintering grounds in South and Central America, the birds depend upon high quality foraging and undisturbed resting (roosting) habitat. An estimated 400 000 Semipalmated Sandpipers and 10 000 Least Sandpipers *Calidris minutilla* stop in the Southern Bight to feed on the high densities of mud shrimp *Corophium volutator* exposed at low tide in the extensive mud flats. During high tide, shorebirds will roost on the upper beach in flocks numbering tens or hundreds of thousands - a key roosting area that is a popular tourism destination where public ownership is limited.

Major threats to the birds and habitat are bloodworm *Glycera dibranchiata* harvesting, agricultural impacts, cottage development and tourism and recreation. To address these threats, a multi-faceted conservation initiative builds upon a science base, legislation, and stewardship. Stewardship is the wise and ethical management of natural resources by stakeholders who share a common interest in the sustainable management of all resources that occur in the natural environment. Stewardship activities involving governments, landowners, interest groups and/or the general public are voluntary and promote cooperative partnerships.

Unregulated bloodworm harvesting was shown to occur at levels likely to exceed the population's replacement capacity, and the activity had a detrimental effect on populations of *Corophium*, the primary prey of most migrating shorebirds. The demand for bloodworms has led to conflicts between harvesters wishing to exploit the resource.

Research results presented to provincial and federal managers, harvesters, and the local community increased interest in the effects of bloodworm harvesting on the intertidal ecosystem. Uncertainties in federal and provincial legislative jurisdiction hampered introduction of regulatory controls on the industry, but efforts by the provincial government to work cooperatively with bloodworm harvesters yielded positive early results. Local harvesters formed an association and worked with the provincial government to develop conservation guidelines in the Ramsar/WHSRN site. Voluntary guidelines served a useful role for several years until conflict with outside harvesters resulted in active involvement by the federal government. Harvesters are now organized and regional representatives participate on a Marine Advisory Committee with federal and provincial counterparts to manage the resource and minimize impacts. In a period of ten years, an unregulated harvest moved to voluntary guidelines and a formal licensing and zoning system encompassing size restrictions allowing sexually mature worms to spawn.

Nova Scotia agriculture has declined in numbers but increased in the size of operations. For livestock producers, a limited landbase upon which to apply manure has predictable impacts on ground and surface water quality. Moreover, riparian areas and wetlands have been impacted by activities that have negatively affected wildlife habitat and water quality. High levels of nutrients flow into the Southern Bight from rivers draining the most intensively farmed agricultural regions in Nova Scotia.

The *Kings County Agricultural Landscape Habitat Conservation Project* is conserving wildlife habitats and improving water quality through partnerships with municipal governments, local conservation organizations and private landowners. This project forges alliances with new partners within the agricultural community, develops and distributes wildlife habitat information/education packages to a multitude of stakeholders, negotiates and signs binding habitat conservation agreements, and jointly funds habitat conservation projects (e.g. riparian fencing and watering ponds, small marsh restoration, and wetland wastewater treatment systems). This project is strongly supported by agricultural and wildlife communities; and builds upon conservation and biodiversity components using Best Management Practices within the recently signed federal/provincial Agricultural Policy Framework (APF) Implementation Agreement.

Cottages and recreational areas line many sensitive shorelines that serve as roost sites, and human recreational and development activity frequently disturbs roosting flocks, while shoreline integrity is compromised through lack of protection on privately owned beaches. With a focus on the Southern Bight Minas Basin, the *Bay of Fundy Shorebird Project* (BoFSP) was initiated in 2001 with four objectives to address concerns related to disturbance of roosting shorebirds:

- Inform coastal landowners and other users about shorebird ecology and the potential effects of human activities to wildlife;
- Develop and implement stewardship initiatives to conserve the habitat of migratory shorebirds & other coastal wildlife;
- Produce educational materials and establish interpretive facilities to promote shorebird conservation;
- Secure key shorebird roosting habitat, through purchase, conservation easements and agreements.

The BoFSP has strong stewardship, educational and public awareness components. In cooperation with the Nova Scotia Nature Trust, a program was begun to cultivate a community-based stewardship ethic: landowners were provided with material on shorebirds and the site's sensitivity, and how to assist in conservation that could include a stewardship agreement. Community meetings, interpretive programs and field tours extended the message to visitors. Project staff identified critical roosting sites and installed information signs at public

access points and, with consent of landowners, private lands close to active shorebird areas.

The BoFSP partnered with local community organizations to jointly finance and construct an interpretive facility to inform visitors and residents about migratory shorebirds. The structure and its information panels, video and brochure reinforce local awareness and inform tourists about the conservation ethics promoted by the program. A proactive approach was undertaken with the tourism industry by offering information intended to familiarize visitors with 'wildlife-friendly' practices.

The initiatives with the bloodworm harvesters, agricultural community and the BoFSP advance the goals established for the NAWMP and the Canadian Shorebird Conservation Plan. Multi-lateral (NAWMP, NABCI) and bilateral (APF) agreements and international conventions (Ramsar, WHSRN), regional (EHJV) and national (NAWCC) supporting infrastructure, effective partnerships (EHJV, BoFSP) and evaluation processes (research) contribute to leverage financial and human resources to deliver flyway conservation activities at the local level. The conservation community recognizes and promotes the synergy that results from

- greater collaboration among governments, public agencies and NGOs;
- the sharing of information and pooling of expertise and resources; and
- combining forces to deliver specific conservation activities on-the-ground.

## ACKNOWLEDGEMENTS
This work is being delivered through the Nova Scotia Eastern Habitat Joint Venture (EHJV) partnership with funding from Wildlife Habitat Canada, the North American Wetland Conservation Act, The Nature Conservancy, Nature Conservancy of Canada, Ducks Unlimited Canada, Environment Canada-Canadian Wildlife Service, Maritimes and North-East Pipelines and the Nova Scotia Department of Natural Resources.

A visitor reads the information panels at the interpretive pavilion overlooking the exposed mudflats of the Southern Bight Minas Basin Ramsar site, Nova Scotia, Canada. Photo: Randy Milton.

# 6.5 Building and sustaining capacity for waterbird conservation and research. Workshop Introduction

*Tim Dodman*

*Wetlands International, Hundland, Papa Westray, Orkney, KW17 2BU, UK.*

Dodman, T. 2006. Building and sustaining capacity for waterbird conservation and research. Workshop Introduction. *Waterbirds around the world*. Eds. G.C. Boere, C.A. Galbraith & D.A. Stroud. The Stationery Office, Edinburgh, UK. p. 883.

International collaborative projects greatly aid the transfer of skills and expertise. Training course participants counting Eurasian Cranes *Grus grus* at Lake Zharsor, Kazakhstan. Photo: Crawford Prentice.

Conserving migratory waterbirds depends not only on the commitment of many individuals but also on exchanges between networks of many different people. For conservation to be effective, these networks need to possess both practical ability and scientific know-how at all stages of migratory flyways. As there is a wide imbalance in capacity across flyways, it is thus important to develop and sustain capacity in areas where resources and experience are relatively low. This requires strategies and programmes that address training, institutional strengthening and network development.

The workshop reviewed capacity building strategies, many of which are summarised in the following papers which describe activities in west and east Africa, Central Asia and the Caucasus, and made the following recommendations:

Frameworks for establishing and implementing sub-regional strategies for capacity building need urgently to be developed. These should draw on the experiences of existing sub-regional initiatives in West Africa (Ndiaye), Central Asia (Solokha *et al.*), East Asia-Australasia and elsewhere.

Within such programmes, it is important to carry out a comprehensive training needs analysis, and to incorporate in these the requests for training and other aspects of capacity building, which will ensure a 'bottom-up' approach.

Training programmes for waterbird conservation and research should address the following main target groups:

- scientists, field workers and data managers;
- Government and local officials together with those involved with non-governmental organisations;

- Those managing wetlands or other protected areas; and
- community leaders and community groups.

They must in addition ensure the training of trainers, which is vital for execution of training.

Sub-regional training programmes should incorporate:

- academic training;
- practical training, for delivery through both regular, established courses and *ad hoc* initiatives in response to need and local situation;
- on-site field training; and
- the transfer of know-how through exchange.

These should be tailored according to needs of the target groups, to ensure that training programmes are appropriate.

In order to maximise partnerships and information exchange across the globe, it will be most cost-effective to develop transferable training modules, which may then be adapted for different levels or target groups.

Training materials in appropriate languages and formats, such as training manuals and tool-kits should be developed and disseminated.

Given that the need for training is widespread and long-term, exit strategies or self-supporting mechanisms need to be built into sub-regional training programmes to ensure their continuity.

This can include marketing training programmes, to raise funds for their execution and to gain strong local, national and international support.

# Building capacity in Africa through a regional training programme

*Abdoulaye Ndiaye, Tim Dodman & Cheikh H. Diagana*

*Wetlands International, West Africa Programme, PO Box 8060, Dakar-Yoff, Senegal. (email: ablaywet@sentoo.sn)*

Ndiaye, A., Dodman, T. & Diagana, C.H. 2006. Building capacity in Africa through a regional training programme. *Waterbirds around the world*. Eds. G.C. Boere, C.A. Galbraith & D.A. Stroud. The Stationery Office, Edinburgh, UK. p. 884.

This paper discusses the results of a training programme implemented after a training needs analysis had been carried out with all partners. The analysis identified the following targets: field technicians, administration officers, students and women's groups. During the implementation of the project, a large monitoring programme, waterfowl surveys, networking, exchange visits and some short courses and field projects were organised.

There has been a lack of expertise in the West Africa region on wetland issues. The impetus for training at the sub-regional level came from the strategy discussed at Djoudj National Park in Senegal (1996). From February 1998 to April 2001, several regional and national training courses were organized with a total of 492 participants. The following countries hosted at least one training course, either Regional or National: Burkina Faso, Niger, Togo, Cote d'Ivoire, The Gambia, Guinea Conakry, Nigeria, Congo Brazzaville, Liberia and Madagascar. The ten national training courses trained 220 participants and seven regional courses trained 140. A field exercise called a "trans-boundary training course" was successfully held in Ghana, as was a joint course with IUCN in Saint-Louis USA. A field project in Mali has also trained around 100 people. Due to the Ramsar Convention requirement, 12 people have been sent to the Netherlands for a qualification in Wetland Management Planning. As experience built up, support has ben offered to universities teaching wetlands issues to post graduate level in Ouagadougou (Burkina-Faso) and Dakar (Senegal).

Training started with data collection and management for the African Waterfowl Census (AfWC) coordinators, as until now census activities have often been not standardized. Women were the second target of training: the regional course gathered together women involved in wetland natural resources in a type of exchange visit. The third target was the decision makers (key stakeholders) mainly Deputy Ministers and General Secretaries at the ministries in charge of wetlands. A workshop was held to inform them about the need for a Wetland National Policy and the mechanisms for implementation, biodiversity programmes with wetland components, and the need to support the Ramsar convention and key partners.

There are still several challenges to over come as there is a big gap between different regions and their wetland knowledge. The problems faced were:

- Communications – it was very difficult to exchange information with some countries or even send an invitation for a workshop.
- Civil wars / rebellion are common in Africa and have disorganized the programme to some extent, particularly in Sierra Leone and Liberia.

- Lack of funding was also a big challenge as we had only one key donor. Other funding possibilities were explored mainly with stakeholders using the wetland resources, such as tour operators, hotel managers and hunting associations.
- Language barrier - the working languages are English and French, however interpreters have to be used frequently which are very costly.

Conservation of migratory waterbirds is integrally linked to the maintenance and protection of wetland areas along their flyways. Various international conventions and agreements such as the African-Eurasian Waterbird Agreement (AEWA) and the Ramsar Convention are integral in providing technical and legal standards and mechanisms for their coordination. However, for strategic conservation of site networks along flyways additional investment is needed to ensure that:

- Activities are coordinated
- International conventions and agreements are implemented
- Understanding of flyway site networks is improved
- Best practices are disseminated
- Communication and training networks are established.

The African Waterfowl Census network remains the most vital network within the continent. Building on this, other networks have been created liaising with wetlands endorsed by the Ramsar convention. The African Partnership, a new initiative, is also creating good linkages within the different institutions for a good programme on capacity development mainly on wetland. The key partners within the continent are the international scientific partners such as Birdlife International, IUCN, WWF, and others at national, local and international level.

Looking to the future, different courses should continue to be organized at all levels: the Wetland Management Course should be launched soon to meet the requirements of the West African Sub-region. The existing centres should be strengthened to develop liaison with projects, and the courses should be given a formal qualification status. The cost of language interpretation for courses is an issue, and either an adequate budget needs to be provided or courses should be with participants from one language zone only.

## ACKNOWLEDGEMENTS

We are grateful to all who have participated in the development of the training programme and its implementation. We acknowledge financial support from the Dutch Ministries mainly the DGIS and LNV. Countries hosting meetings have also played an important role in the success of the programme.

# Building capacity in Central Asia and the Caucasus to promote waterbird research and conservation

*Alexander Solokha[1], Ward Hagemeijer[2] & Taej Mundkur[3]*

[1] *Wetlands International - Russia Office, Nikoloyamskaya Ulitsa, 19, strn.3, Moscow 109240, Russia. (email: asolokha@wwf.ru)*

[2] *Wetlands International, Droevendaalsesteeg 3A, PO Box 7002, 6700 CA Wageningen, The Netherlands.*
*(email: ward.hagemeijer@wetlands.org)*

[3] *Wetlands International - South Asia Office, A-127, 2nd Floor, Defence Colony, New Delhi 110 024, India.*
*Contact address: Swarankit, Plot No 6, Kothrud Mahatma Housing Society, Kothrud Pune City 411 029 (Maharashtra State), India.*
*(email: taej.mundkur@wetlands.org)*

Solokha, A., Hagemeijer, W. & Mundkur, T. 2006. Building capacity in Central Asia and the Caucasus to promote waterbird research and conservation. *Waterbirds around the world.* Eds. G.C. Boere, C.A. Galbraith & D.A. Stroud. The Stationery Office, Edinburgh, UK. pp. 885-888.

## ABSTRACT

This paper gives an overview of conservation frameworks and expert institutions in Central Asia and the Caucasus. It describes how Wetlands International has contributed to capacity building at both regional and local level through promoting international conventions, developing a flyway action plan, strengthening the specialist network and other catalysing activities during the period 2001-2004. Although considerable progress has been made in improving co-operation and co-ordination, strengthening institutional capacity and raising awareness, there remains a need for better training courses and public education and awareness programmes to promote waterbird and wetland conservation at all levels. The establishment of a Wetland Training Centre would facilitate the development and implementation of appropriate training and education programmes across the region.

## INTRODUCTION

During the time of the USSR, waterbird research and protection in the republics of Central Asia and the Caucasus were supported and co-ordinated through implementation of government programmes. Scientists from various local academic institutions, universities and nature reserves conducted a broad range of studies on the ecology, distribution and migrations of waterbirds. Waterbird experts from leading scientific centres, primarily in Moscow and Leningrad (now St Petersburg), also made a major contribution to these studies. The exchange of information and co-operation between specialists and institutions were promoted through publications, regular conferences and missions. With the accession of the USSR to the Ramsar Convention on Wetlands in 1975, five wetlands in Central Asia and the Caucasus were designated as Wetlands of International Importance, or Ramsar sites, and another 49 sites from this region were identified as Wetlands of National Importance (Skokova & Vinogradov 1986).

Since the disintegration of the Soviet Union in 1991, there has been a substantial decrease in research and conservation activities relating to waterbirds and wetlands in the region. The main reasons for this were a lack of government funding, a shortage of specialists and a breakdown in the former links between people and organizations. However, the political changes that have occurred in the new independent countries have opened up new opportunities for co-operation with international organizations and sponsors. As a consequence, various local projects were developed and supported, including some on wetland and water-

bird conservation (Krever *et al.* 1998, Krever *et al.* 2001).

In general, however, research and conservation work on waterbirds and wetlands in Central Asia and the Caucasus remained at a low level until 2001-2002. With the exception of Turkmenistan and Azerbaijan, none of the countries in the region was involved in the regular mid-winter waterbird counts carried out within the framework of the International Waterbird Census organized by Wetlands International. This resulted in underestimation of many waterbird populations and a lack of contemporary information on their wintering habitats. The capacity of government agencies, non-governmental organizations and research institutes to carry out research and conservation

Chatkal State Nature Reserve, Uzbekistan is a biosphere reserve covering the southwestern end of the Chatkal'skiy Range in the western Tien-Shan Mountains. Photo: David Stroud.

activities relating to waterbirds and wetlands was very limited. In comparison with other regions of the Western Palearctic and Asia-Pacific, the level of co-operation and exchange of information within Central Asia and the Caucasus was very weak. The main inter-governmental treaties dealing with the conservation of wetlands and migratory waterbirds, primarily the Ramsar Convention on Wetlands and the African-Eurasian Migratory Waterbird Agreement (AEWA), were in need of much better representation in the region.

Training, networking and raising awareness were required in Central Asia and the Caucasus to build the capacity of local organizations and to improve efforts to conserve wetlands and waterbirds. This paper gives an overview of conservation frameworks and expert institutions in the region, and describes activities carried out by Wetlands International during the period 2001-2004 that have contributed to capacity building at both regional and local level.

## FOCAL AREA

In accordance with the majority of current political and geographical opinions, Central Asia is here taken to include the countries of Kazakhstan, Kyrgyzstan, Tajikistan, Turkmenistan and Uzbekistan; the Caucasus region is taken to include Armenia, Azerbaijan, Georgia and Russian territory (North Caucasus) extending north to the Astrakhan and Rostov administrative regions (*oblast*). The study area is therefore located within the southern and south-western parts of the former USSR.

The sub-region of Central Asia and the Caucasus has enormous importance for migratory waterbirds because it is located at a crossroads between migration routes extending from the Russian Arctic and Siberia towards southern Europe and Africa to the west and the Indian subcontinent to the east (Isakov & Shevareva 1968, Scott & Rose 1996). The region contains a number of very large wetlands including the coasts of the Sea of Azov, Black Sea and Caspian Sea, Issyk Kul and Lake Balkhash, as well as many other lakes and reservoirs. Several million waterbirds breed, migrate through or spend the winter here.

**Table 1. Accession to international conventions and agreements directly relevant to the conservation of waterbirds in Central Asia and the Caucasus (as at July 2006).**

| Country | International treaties | | | |
| | Biological Diversity | Ramsar | CMS | AEWA |
| --- | --- | --- | --- | --- |
| Armenia | + | + | | |
| Azerbaijan | + | + | (+) | |
| Georgia | + | + | + | + |
| Kazakhstan | + | | + | |
| Kyrgyzstan | + | + | | |
| Russia | + | + | (+) | |
| Tajikistan | + | + | + | |
| Turkmenistan | + | | (+) | |
| Uzbekistan | + | + | + | + |

Notes:
+ : Countries are Contracting Parties
(+) : Countries are not Contracting Parties to the CMS, but participate in the CMS Memoranda of Understanding, particularly in the MOUs on Siberian Crane *Grus leucogeranus* and Slender-billed Curlew *Numenius tenuirostris*.

## OVERVIEW OF FRAMEWORKS AND INSTITUTIONS INVOLVED IN THE CONSERVATION OF MIGRATORY WATERBIRDS

### International and regional conventions, agreements and other initiatives

There are four key inter-governmental treaties relevant to the conservation of migratory waterbirds in Central Asia and the Caucasus:

- Convention on Biological Diversity (CBD).
- Convention on Wetlands (Ramsar Convention).
- Convention on the Conservation of Migratory Species of Wild Animals (Bonn Convention or CMS).
- African-Eurasian Migratory Waterbird Agreement (AEWA; an agreement under the CMS).

As at the end of 2004, all countries in Central Asia and the Caucasus are Contracting Parties to the Convention on Biological Diversity; seven countries (all except Kazakhstan and Turkmenistan) are Contracting Parties to the Ramsar Convention; three countries, Georgia, Tajikistan and Uzbekistan, have signed the Convention on Migratory Species (CMS); and only Georgia and Uzbekistan are Contracting Parties to the African-Eurasian Migratory Waterbird Agreement (Table 1).

In addition to the above legally binding treaties, the Asia-Pacific Migratory Waterbird Conservation Strategy: 2001-2005, a non-legal co-operative initiative co-ordinated by Wetlands International, covers Russia and the Central Asian countries (including Azerbaijan), as well as the countries in South Asia. This Strategy promotes the establishment of a site network for the conservation of migratory waterbirds in the Central Asian Flyway.

The key conservation framework in the Central Asian region is the Regional Environment Action Plan (REAP), developed and implemented by the Interstate Sustainable Development Commission (ISDC) and other government and non-governmental organizations with the support of the Asian Development Bank and UNDP. In the field of biodiversity protection, REAP aims at establishing an ecological network in Central Asia (UNEP/GEF Central Asian Econet project), including a network of important wetlands.

### International non-governmental organizations

Working in collaboration with governments, conventions and with each other, various international non-governmental organizations (NGOs) promote waterbird and wetland conservation in Central Asia and the Caucasus. Side by side with Wetlands International, the following international NGOs are active in the region:

- BirdLife International
- International Crane Foundation (ICF)
- World Wide Fund for Nature (WWF)
- World Conservation Union (IUCN)
- Flora & Fauna International

### Governmental and inter-governmental organizations

The conservation of migratory waterbirds and their habitats is mainly the responsibility of national ministries or committees for the protection of either environment, nature, natural resources or forest. Issues relating to the protection and use of wetland resources can also be shared with other agencies, e.g. ministries of agriculture.

There are two key inter-governmental organizations responsible for conservation and wise use (including wetland and biodiversity issues) in Central Asia. These organizations are:

- Interstate Sustainable Development Commission (ISDC), with its Secretariat currently based in Ashgabat, Turkmenistan, until 2006; and
- Interstate Water Commission, with its Secretariat based in Tashkent, Uzbekistan.

These organizations are represented by government officials and have close links with each other.

### Local technical institutions and NGOs

There are many national educational, research and non-governmental organizations involved in the conservation of migratory waterbirds in Central Asia and the Caucasus. Universities, biological institutes of the National Academies of Sciences and research institutes (e.g. fishery research institutes), located in capitals and other big cities, work primarily with scientific and co-ordination issues at national and provincial level. Nature reserves and national parks are responsible for research and conservation of particular wetlands and their biodiversity, and thus play a critical role at site level. In the region under review, there are nearly 20 nature reserves and national parks working with wetlands and waterbirds, including such well known reserves as Astrakhansky NR in Russia, Sevan NP in Armenia, Kyzylagach NR in Azerbaijan, Naurzumsky NR in Kazakhstan, Issyk Kul NR in Kyrgyzstan, Tigrovaya Balka NR in Tajikistan and Turkmenbashi (formerly Krasnovodsky) NR in Turkmenistan. At national level, all technical organizations can co-operate with each other through state co-ordination programmes.

Among local NGOs involved in waterbird and wetland conservation, the science-oriented ornithological units deserve special mention. These have been established in many countries (Armenia, Azerbaijan, Russia, Kazakhstan), and work with support mainly from BirdLife International or its partners.

## WORKING TOWARDS INCREASING REGIONAL AND LOCAL CAPACITY

Capacity building in Central Asia and the Caucasus was promoted in 2001-2004 through organizing workshops and training courses, raising the awareness of stakeholders and the general public, and establishing a waterbird specialist network.

### Promoting wetland and waterbird conservation initiatives

Wetlands International monitors the status of collaboration between countries and international conventions dealing with wetlands and waterbirds, and promotes further accessions to these conventions. This promotion is being achieved through raising awareness of the importance of waterbirds and their wetland habitats and facilitating contacts between conventions and the responsible national agencies. For example, Wetlands International has been assisting the Government of Turkmenistan in joining the Ramsar Convention on Wetlands. It is anticipated that in 2005 the two remaining countries, Kazakhstan and Turkmenistan, will become Contracting Parties to this Convention.

Wetlands International promotes implementation of the Asia-Pacific Migratory Waterbird Conservation Strategy (APMWCS) in Russia and the Central Asian countries. The Russia Federation has participated in this initiative since 1996, and has nominated a total of ten sites to the Crane, Anatidae and Shorebird Site Networks along the East Asian-Australasian Flyways. Due to administrative reorganization over the last few years, the Russian Ministry of Natural Resources has been unable to send its representative to the annual meetings of the Asia-Pacific Migratory Waterbird Conservation Committee (APMWCC) and nominate new important sites to the site networks. Nevertheless, the Ministry has been kept informed of the outcome of meetings and has been encouraged to renew its active participation in the implementation of this initiative.

In the Central Asian region, a representative of the Scientific Information Centre (SIC) of the ISDC based in Ashgabat was invited to attend the APMWCC meetings in 2002-2004. With the assistance of the SIC ISDC, the APMWCS: 2001-2005 was translated into Russian to increase the awareness of decision-makers and the general public concerning waterbirds and the APMWCS, and thus promote implementation of this strategy in Russia and the Central Asian countries.

### Development of an Action Plan for the Central Asian Flyway

The development of an Action Plan throughout the Central Asian Flyway is one of the project goals. A draft document was presented at the first Central Asian (Central Asian-Indian) Flyway Workshop, which was organized in Tashkent, Uzbekistan, from 18-22 August 2001 in conjunction with a Central Asian Outreach workshop, and co-funded by the CMS. Official representatives from 15 Range States, as well as international experts and representatives of the relevant international conventions, participated in the meeting and contributed in reviewing the Action Plan and developing it further.

Both workshops were also important in terms of gathering general information along the flyway and identifying government agencies, NGOs and research institutions responsible for the conservation of waterbirds and their habitats in the range states. Official delegations were encouraged to strengthen co-operation in the region to promote waterbird and wetland research and conservation. During the period 2001-2004, the Action Plan was given further consideration at Ramsar COP8, CMS COP7 and AEWA MOP2. It is anticipated that the Action Plan will be finalized and approved at the second Central Asian Flyway workshop planned for 2005.

### Establishing co-operation at regional and local level

Useful relationships were established with the Interstate Sustainable Development Commission (ISDC) and its Scientific and Information Centre (SIC). Founded by the governments of all Central Asian countries and supported by international agencies, the ISDC co-ordinates environmental protection and sustainable development across the region. Currently the SIC ISDC assists in the implementation of the Asia-Pacific Migratory Waterbird Conservation Strategy: 2001-2005, and its representative is a member of the APMWCC. Wetlands International attended the regional workshop and ISDC meeting in February 2004 in Dushanbe, Tajikistan, to give a presentation on the activities of Wetlands International and to discuss issues relating to regional co-operation in the wise use and conservation of wetlands.

Wetlands International seeks to co-operate with WWF within the framework of the UNEP/GEF Central Asian Econet project. Officially endorsed by ISDC and included as a component in the Regional (Central Asian) Environmental Action Plan, the Econet project aims to establish a network of protected areas to secure conservation of biological diversity at all levels and promote sustainable development in the region. Wetlands International has developed a preliminary list of internationally important wetlands in the Central Asian region based mainly on the Ramsar criteria relating to migratory waterbirds. This list has been submitted to WWF for use in the establishment of the Central Asian ecological network. It is anticipated that incorporation of important wetlands in this project will provide additional emphasis and tools to strengthen wetland conservation and wise use in the region. The list of internationally important wetlands in Central Asia can serve as a basis for working with other organizations, such as ICF and CMS, to support the establishment of a site network along the Central Asian Flyway.

### Co-ordination of the IWC and strengthening a specialist network

The International Waterbird Census (IWC) is a long-term monitoring programme which is being run throughout the world under the co-ordination of Wetlands International. In addition to its considerable scientific value, the International Waterbird Census can serve as an important tool for strengthening communication and linkages between specialists and facilitating the building of organizational and personnel capacity. In 2003 and 2004, waterbird counts were carried out in Russia and most other countries in Central Asia and the Caucasus as part of the IWC, and nearly 50 professionals and amateurs were involved in this work. Training of field observers to increase their skills in waterbird identification and counting was included as part of the mid-winter surveys, and was provided by IWC national co-ordinators and Wetlands International staff.

The mid-winter census in Central Asia and the Caucasus often entailed visits to remote wetlands that were difficult of access. In order to travel to such wetlands, local teams of counters co-operated with the relevant local organizations. For example, in Uzbekistan, Azerbaijan and Krasnodar Province in Russia, the counters obtained logistic support from hunters' associations and nature reserves.

In November 2003, a Central Asian Co-ordination Workshop was organized at Issyk Kul, Kyrgyzstan, in collaboration with the State Forest Service of the Kyrgyz Republic. Nearly 30 participants from across the sub-region came together to review the status of co-operation in Central Asia and increase their professional skills in wetland study and survey techniques. A brief field course was specially organized to provide basic training for rangers from the Issyk Kul Nature Reserve. This workshop was very successful in building institutional capacity in the Central Asian region and promoting further co-operation and collaboration under the IWC and other wetland related projects.

In order to raise awareness of the needs of wetland and waterbird conservation in Russia, Central Asia and the Caucasus, the Russia Office of Wetlands International maintains a web-site in the Russian language, and this includes, in particular, information on the progress of the Central Asian Flyway project.

Several international collaborations have assisted the conservation in Central Asia and the Caucasus. Visit of AEWA's Technical Committee to Chatkal State Nature Reserve, Uzbekistan, 2003. Photo: David Stroud.

### CONCLUSION

This overview of work conducted in Central Asia and the Caucasus during the period 2001-2004 shows that some progress was achieved in developing co-operation and co-ordination, strengthening institutional capacity and raising awareness. A number of government agencies, research institutes and non-governmental organizations were involved in one way or another in waterbird and wetland research and conservation. A specialist network was significantly enhanced and strengthened through training and a concerted monitoring programme. However, there remains a need to enhance training courses and public education and awareness programmes to promote waterbird and wetland conservation at all levels. The establishment of a Wetland Training Centre would facilitate the development and implementation of appropriate training and education programmes across the region.

### ACKNOWLEDGEMENTS

This work has been made possible thanks to the project "Towards a Strategy for waterbird and wetland conservation in the Central Asian flyway", supported by the Dutch Ministry of Agriculture, Nature and Food Quality. The authors express their gratitude to Gerard Boere, Marcel Silvius, Simon Delany and Olga Anisimova (all from Wetlands International) who initiated this project in 2001.

### REFERENCES

Isakov, Y.A. & Shevareva, T.P. 1968. Interrelationship of waterfowl breeding and wintering areas in the Central Palaearctic. IUCN Publications New Series, No.12. Morges, Switzerland.

Krever, V., Pereladova, O., Williams, M. & Jungius, H. (eds). 1998. Biodiversity Conservation in Central Asia: An Analysis of Biodiversity and Current Threats and Initial Investment Portfolio. World Wide Fund for Nature.

Krever, V., Zazanashvili, N., Jungius, H., Williams, L. & Petelin, D. (eds). 2001. Biodiversity of the Caucasus Ecoregion: An Analysis of Biodiversity and Current Threats and Initial Investment Portfolio. World Wide Fund for Nature.

Scott, D.A. & Rose, P.M. 1996. Atlas of Anatidae Populations in Africa and Western Eurasia. Wetlands International Publication No. 41, Wetlands International, Wageningen, The Netherlands.

Skokova, N.N. & Vinogradov, V.G. 1986. Protection of water-bird habitats. Moscow. (In Russian).

# Building capacity in waterbird and wetland monitoring in eastern Africa

*Oliver Nasirwa[1,2], Mark O'Connell[2], Seb Buckton[2] & Tim Dodman[3]*

[1]*National Museums of Kenya, PO Box 40658-00100 GPO, Nairobi, Kenya. (email: onasirwa@africaonline.co.ke)*

[2]*Wildfowl & Wetlands Trust, Slimbridge, Gloucestershire, GL2 7BT, UK.*

[3]*Wetlands International, West Africa Programme, PO Box 8060, Dakar-Yoff, Senegal. (email: tim@timdodman.co.uk)*

Nasirwa, O., O'Connell, M., Buckton, S. & Dodman, T. 2006. Building capacity in waterbird and wetland monitoring in eastern Africa. *Waterbirds around the world*. Eds. G.C. Boere, C.A. Galbraith & D.A. Stroud. The Stationery Office, Edinburgh, UK. pp. 889-891.

## ABSTRACT

The wetlands of eastern Africa support internationally important assemblages of plants and animals, and are a vital source of livelihood and water for many societies. The combined human population of Burundi, Djibouti, Eritrea, Ethiopia, Kenya, Rwanda, Sudan, Tanzania and Uganda is estimated to be about 200 million. The region has an area of about 5.6 million $km^2$ of which only 4.5% is open water/wetlands. Wetland conversion to agriculture often provides only short-term benefits and can pose long-term problems. The ever-increasing human population density coupled with the scarce water resources in Africa have put African governments under increasing pressure to allow further exploitation and drainage of wetlands. Lack of sufficient up-to-date information to guide policy and development programmes for the respective Africa governments is considered as one of the causes for the continued loss and degradation of wetlands. To fill this information gap, it was recognized that a standardized system for monitoring wetland biodiversity and making the data and information available to governments and other stakeholders was required. In 2002, a project was implemented to build and maintain capacity in the monitoring of wetland biodiversity in eastern Africa and to provide the necessary information required for wetland conservation. This paper describes the capacity building process leading to: (1) the development of a wetlands database with query tools; (2) the provision of training in the use of the wetland monitoring database; (3) the launch of the Wetland Biodiversity Monitoring Scheme (WBMS) to provide data for use in wetland conservation and development of site management plans; and (4) training in the development of a wetland site management plan in each of the nine partner countries.

## INTRODUCTION

In terms of biodiversity, the wetlands of eastern Africa consist of a broad range of habitat types, from the vast Rift Valley lake systems to the Nile River and floodplains, papyrus and mangrove swamps, flooded forests and shallow coral reefs (Hughes & Hughes 1992). They support internationally important assemblages of plants and animals according to the Ramsar Convention criteria, and are a source of livelihood for many human populations. The combined human population of Burundi, Djibouti, Eritrea, Ethiopia, Kenya, Rwanda, Somalia, Sudan, Tanzania and Uganda is estimated to be about 200 million, on a landmass of about 5.6 million $km^2$. This landmass is covered by only about 4.5% of open water, and has a coastline of about 5 361 km (The World Fact Book 2002). The actual area covered by wetlands of all types in eastern Africa (and indeed in the whole of Africa) has yet to be quantified. According to Stevenson & Fraser (1999), a rough estimate of the area covered by wetlands in Africa is about 1.25 million $km^2$. More than 1.07 million $km^2$ are inland wetlands, with about 0.1 million $km^2$ described as marine/coastal wetlands and a further 0.05 million $km^2$ described as artificial wetlands (i.e. reservoirs, rice fields and sewage works). The average rate of loss of Africa's wetlands is estimated at 2% per year (OECD 1996). However, rates of loss of 9% to 15% per year have been recorded in specific catchment areas in Africa (Hollis 1993, Taylor *et al.* 1995).

In eastern Africa (and indeed throughout Africa), wetlands have been lost and degraded as a result of human activities. The main destructive activities include drainage, construction, pollution, siltation (due to soil erosion), and the introduction of alien species (Howard & Matindi 2003). Human population increase, rising poverty and, in recent years, extremes in climate have acted as the drivers of these changes and placed increasing pressure on wetlands and other renewable natural resources. Unlike in the developed world, many African government bodies are under growing pressure to allow further exploitation of wetland resources and to allow development and extensive drainage of wetlands, principally for agriculture. Although wetland drainage and cultivation can make a key contribution to food and livelihood security in the short term, in the long term there are concerns over the sustainability of this utilization and the maintenance of wetland benefits (Dixon & Wood 2003). The unregulated use of agrochemicals has also been a source of problems in recent years, and the construction of dams has resulted in new pressures on the biodiversity of many wetland sites. The loss or degradation of wetlands has serious consequences for the plants and animals that occur in wetland habitats. For example, migratory waterbirds depend on a chain of suitable stopover (wetland) sites to rest and feed. The loss of these stopover sites is among the major threats to migratory waterbirds (Nasirwa & Bennun 1999). Regardless, given the social, economic and cultural importance of wetlands for humans, it is in the best interest of all societies that they look after their wetlands and continue to benefit from wetland services and functions. This can best be achieved by incorporating a wetland biodiversity-monitoring programme into the management planning process for wetlands. The monitoring process would provide the necessary information to African governments and stakeholders. This information would guide the process of formulating appropriate policies and aid in the designing of development projects to be in harmony with efforts to conserve and utilize wetlands on a sustainable basis.

## DEVELOPMENT OF WETLAND AND WATERBIRD MONITORING IN EASTERN AFRICA

Biodiversity monitoring encompasses a wide variety of activities and has been defined in many different ways. Here we use the term "monitoring" to describe five key processes in relation to wetland data. They are Collection, Collation, Management,

Analysis and Dissemination. Biodiversity monitoring generates data that can be used both to assess status and underpin management planning. It is therefore a key process in the wise use of wetlands. Experience from many different parts of the world has demonstrated that named, "badged", and appropriately funded monitoring schemes are an extremely efficient way in which to assess trends in the biodiversity status of sites

Over the years, the eastern Africa region has benefited from considerable investment in training facilities focused on science-based nature/wildlife management. It also has a relatively extensive network of protected sites and a long history of inter-organizational collaboration for conservation. During the 1990s, there were a number of cornerstone meetings that clearly identified the capacity needs of African states in relation to management planning for wetlands, and how regional states might use these to fulfil requirements under international agreements. The IUCN Species Survival Commission also produced a comprehensive analysis of conservation needs in sub-Saharan Africa, as part of the Biodiversity Conservation Strategy Programme. In 1998, Wetlands International held a meeting in Dakar (Senegal) at which a number of requirements were identified for wetland biodiversity conservation in Africa. The inaugural meeting of the African-Eurasian Migratory Waterbird Agreement (AEWA, Bonn Convention) in Cape Town in 1999 also identified specific conservation and research needs as part of the AEWA Action Plan.

The eastern Africa region has a number of training facilities and programmes for training in relation to site management plans. It also has a waterbird monitoring scheme, the African Waterbird Census (AfWC) established in 1990 (Perennou 1991). Since the early 1990s, most countries in eastern Africa have participated in the AfWC and contributed data to it in varying degrees. During the period 1999-2001, seven countries submitted their data to Wetlands International. In this period 152 sites were surveyed and the average total number of waterbirds counted in the month of January was 1.6 million waterbirds of a total of 160 species (Dodman & Diagana 2003). The AfWC collects and disseminates information on waterbird populations, but has also collated basic information about wetland habitats. There have also been many independent initiatives by both governments and NGOs in relation to the collection or collation of biodiversity and land-use data at a variety of spatial and temporal scales.

Despite all these activities, at the end of the 1990s, there was still the need to standardize data collection and to make monitoring data more accessible through a regional database. There was also the need to focus the collection and use of data towards addressing specific regional and national pre-set goals. Immediately prior to the 10th Pan-African Ornithological Congress in 2000, the Wildfowl & Wetlands Trust (WWT) took part in a four-day roundtable discussion with African NGO partners and statutory agencies in Kampala, Uganda, at a development workshop organized by the Wetlands International – Africa Office. The result of the meeting was the submission of a bid to the UK Government's Darwin Initiative to develop and launch a dedicated wetland biodiversity monitoring scheme. This would both benefit from and enhance the work undertaken under the auspices of the AfWC and other programmes and fulfil the needs listed above. The bid was successful, and May 2002 saw the start of a three-year project involving WWT, Wetlands International and nine eastern Africa partner organizations. The project aimed to: (1) provide training in wetland monitoring and site management planning; (2) establish a "badged" wetland biodiversity monitoring scheme; (3) create a regional wetland monitoring database; and (4) make use of monitoring data for conservation.

## PROJECT OUTCOMES

### Training in wetland monitoring and site management planning

In November 2003, the project conducted a training course/workshop at the Kenya Wildlife Service Training Institute (KWSTI) in Naivasha, Kenya. Twenty-one participants took part in the training course/workshop: they were the national focal points and their counterparts (two from each country), as well as representatives from Wetlands International, WWT and KWSTI. The training course/workshop was tailored to set up a framework for monitoring and database management, and strengthen institutional and volunteer network capacity to collect wetland biodiversity data. Other aspects covered by the workshop included how to develop and implement standardized procedures for collecting wetland biodiversity data across the eastern African region. To guide the training course/workshop, the project produced a training manual. In September-October 2003, the project sponsored two trainees (the national focal points for Ethiopia and Sudan) to participate in the East Africa Wetlands Management Course (now renamed the International Course on African Wetland Management – ICAWM) held every year at the KWSTI. Apart from benefiting from the training in wetland management, trainees also developed a draft management plan for a wetland site in their own country as part of the course. Equipped with the skills to train others and a training manual, the national focal points now have tools to train others at national and site level.

### Wetland Biodiversity Monitoring Scheme for eastern Africa launched

On 18 November 2003, the project launched the Wetland Biodiversity Monitoring Scheme for eastern Africa (WBMS) in Nairobi, Kenya. WBMS is a collaboration between organizations in nine eastern Africa countries, to collect, manage, analyse and disseminate information on wetland biodiversity. The scheme has a regional secretariat based in Nairobi, Kenya, and nine national organizers. A network of volunteers is co-ordinated to collect data from a range of wetland sites, and the resultant data are stored and managed on the WBMS database. The scheme provides a framework for standardized monitoring of wetland biodiversity in the eastern Africa region. The aim of WBMS is to generate scientifically robust data to underpin the conservation, wise use and management of wetlands in eastern Africa. WBMS activities are planned and organized within the framework and network of the AfWC, and national focal points of WBMS are currently the National Co-ordinators of the AfWC. The WBMS Steering Group oversees the management of the range of core WBMS tasks, to guide the implementation of new WBMS developments, and to identify WBMS priorities. Members of the WBMS Steering Group are the national focal points from each participating country. Where appropriate, ex-officio members representing other relevant organizations such as Wetlands International and WWT also play a role in the Steering Group. The Steering Group meets at least once every year. So far the Steering Group has met twice during the project period. Most of the work carried out by the Steering Group is via email. A list-server to enhance quick communication between the Steering Group, collaborators and supporters of the project and scheme has been established. The project has also produced a brochure and developed a web-site to publicize and market the scheme.

## THE DATABASE

The project has provided each national focal point with computer hardware and software to improve storage, analysis and dissemination of wetland biodiversity data for use in wetland management planning and biodiversity conservation. The database is designed to ease data entry, and ensures that wetland biodiversity data are stored in a compatible and consistent format within the region. The hierarchical structure of the database enables storage of data to the level of sections of a site, but also to the level of combined sites, depending on how the data were collected. However, data collection is encouraged primarily at the site-section level to allow more robust use of the data for conservation purposes.

## THE WAY FORWARD

This year (2004/05), the project will sponsor another six candidates for the ICAWM course in October-November 2004. It is anticipated that through this course the project will deliver six more draft management plans. During the course of the year, it is projected that the WBMS database will be fully populated with the backlog of wetland and waterbird data from the AfWC. The next stages will be to encourage the use of these data for research, case work, public awareness and education, development of more site management planning, species management plans, site designation (under Ramsar etc.), and national reporting under conventions. Procedures on how to collect data on other parameters of wetland biodiversity are also among the next steps on the project calendar. The Steering Group is working on the terms of reference of its committee that will guide procedures for running WBMS after the project phase. The project is also developing a strategic work plan for WBMS and working on an exit strategy. The objective of the exit strategy is to establish WBMS as a fully-fledged wetland biodiversity monitoring scheme for eastern Africa.

## DISCUSSION AND CONCLUSIONS

There are differences among eastern African countries in the political and institutional set-up in which waterbird and wetland work is carried out. This presents a challenge in evaluating the level of training and training needs required at the regional level. For this reason, there is need for co-ordination and continuous re-evaluation and updating of the training manual as more information about wetlands is gathered. The establishment of the WBMS, WBMS Secretariat and Steering Group provided the structures needed to oversee the implementation of this work. Meanwhile, the database provides easier ways of handling data and hopefully this will enable focal points to elucidate wetland biodiversity trends in eastern Africa. The data exchange mechanism will allow bilateral and multilateral site or species management plans to be developed. This will enable adjacent countries to address issues affecting cross-border wetland sites.

The structures set up by this project (i.e. to improve communication at regional level and especially the formation of the Steering Group) should boost communication between key players and also work as a forum to discuss wetland issues at a regional level. This will build and strengthen the capacity of wetland biodiversity monitoring in eastern Africa, as well as encourage countries to

participate more regularly in the AfWC and other wetland-related initiatives at international level. The training in wetland management and the production of draft management plans are key to capacity building for wetland management at national level. The establishment of the Steering Group to co-ordinate the scheme secures the implementation of the WBMS Strategic Workplan as well as boosting the activities of the AfWC. These outcomes ensure an increase in wetland monitoring, training activities, implementation of management plans, and national reporting on wetland issues in the eastern Africa region. The challenges of WBMS will be fund-raising, increasing the wetland biodiversity parameters monitored, increasing coverage and ensuring ongoing training, implementation of management plans, and maintaining the database after the project phase. These issues are, however, being addressed by the exit strategy.

## REFERENCES

**Dixon, A.B. & Wood, A.P.** 2003. Wetland cultivation and hydrological management in eastern Africa: Matching community and hydrological needs through sustainable wetland use. Natural Resources Forum 27(2): 117-129.

**Dodman, T. & Diagana, C.H.** 2003. African Waterbird Census / Les Dénombrements d'Oiseaux d'Eau en Afrique 1999, 2000 & 2001. Wetlands International Global Series 16, Wageningen, The Netherlands.

**Hollis, G.E.** 1993. Goals and objectives of wetland restoration and rehabilitation. In: M. Moser, R.C. Prentice & J. van Vessem (eds) Waterfowl and Wetland Conservation in the 1990s: A Global Perspective. Proceedings of the IWRB Symposium, St. Petersburg, Florida, November 1992. IWRB Special Publication 26: 187-194.

**Howard, G.W. & Matindi, S.W.** 2003. Alien invasive species in Africa's wetlands. Some threats and solutions. IUCN Eastern Africa Regional Programme. Kul Graphics Ltd., Nairobi, Kenya.

**Hughes, R.H. & Hughes, J.S.** 1992. A Directory of African Wetlands. IUCN-The World Conservation Union, Gland, Switzerland, and Cambridge, UK, United Nations Environment Programme, Nairobi, Kenya, and World Conservation Monitoring Centre, Cambridge, UK.

**Nasirwa, O.O. & Bennun, L.A.** 1999. Migratory waterbirds and their conservation in Kenya. In: F. Ng'weno & P. Matiku (eds) Kenya and the African-Eurasian Waterbird Agreement. Proceedings of a workshop held at the National Museums of Kenya, 29 July 1999. Nature Kenya, Nairobi: 14-23.

**OECD** 1996. Guidelines for aid agencies for improved conservation and sustainable use of tropical and sub-tropical wetlands. OECD, Paris, France.

**Perennou, C.** 1991. African Waterfowl Census 1991 – Les Dénombrements Internationaux d'oiseaux d'eau en Afrique 1991. IWRB, Slimbridge, UK.

**Stevenson, N. & Frazier, S.** 1999. Review of wetland inventory information in Africa. Wetlands International – Africa, Europe, Middle East. Wageningen, The Netherlands.

**Taylor, R.D., Howard, G.W. & Begg, G.W.** 1995. Developing wetland inventories in Southern Africa: A review. Vegetation 118: 57-79.

**The World Fact Book** 2002. http://www.cia.gov/cia/publications/factbook/geos/

# The role and potential of the Central-Asian Scientific Information Centre of the Interstate Sustainable Development Commission (SIC ISDC) for studying wetlands and waterbirds

*Bakhar Tashlieva*

*International Fund for the Aral Sea Interstate Sustainable Development Commission Scientific-Information Centre, 15 Bitarap Turkmenistan St., Ashgabat, Turkmenistan 744000. (email: sic@online.tm)*

Tashlieva, B. 2006. The role and potential of the Central-Asian Scientific Information Centre of the Interstate Sustainable Development Commission (SIC ISDC) for studying wetlands and waterbirds. *Waterbirds around the world.* Eds. G.C. Boere, C.A. Galbraith & D.A. Stroud. The Stationery Office, Edinburgh, UK. p. 892.

The Central-Asian Scientific Information Centre of the Interstate Sustainable Development Commission (SIC ISDC) is one of various Central Asian organizations and initiatives which coordinates regional co-operation in the area of nature protection and sustainable development. These include the development of regional strategies (programs and action plans) on sustainable development; and the organization, coordination and management of related projects and action plans.

In June 2002, at the seventh meeting of the Asia Pacific Migratory Waterbird Conservation Committee, SIC ISDC made proposals regarding the development of a regional network of experts, cooperation with government departments and agencies, wide public access to information, training, and support for scientific research and monitoring.

During this time SIC ISDC were assisting Wetlands International in the implementation of the Asian Wetland Inventory, raising awareness of waterbird conservation issues, and capacity building in the Central Asian region. The SIC was also keen to assist Turkmenistan and other Central Asian countries becoming signatories to the Ramsar Convention.

Currently, SIC ISDC is mandated to support the development of a wide regional database on ecological issues and sustainable development within the region. Following a series of national seminars in all Central Asian countries on indicators for sustainable development for use in the integrated evaluation of the state of the environment, several indicators on environmental quality (water, land, air, biodiversity) and socio-economic conditions have been prepared and introduced in each Central Asian countries. During the seminars, issues of water resources and wetlands, in particular their biodiversity, were a priority. In the future SIC ISDC could play a role in supporting the coordination of the Asia-Pacific Migratory Waterbird Conservation Strategy in Central Asia.

SIC ISDC also coordinates activities of all conventions and international agreements in Central Asian countries. All these countries are signatories to the Convention on Biological Diversity (CBD), but currently only Uzbekistan, Tajikistan and Kyrgyzstan are signatories to the Ramsar Convention, although Kazakhstan and Turkmenistan are preparing to sign.

In Turkmenistan, wetlands occupy 20% of the total surface area and have extremely important economic, environmental and cultural values. Their role as water regime regulators and as habitats for flora and fauna and for animal species, especially waterbirds for hunting, are important.

Protection of these wetlands and their flora and fauna can only be achieved by a combination of far-sighted national policy in each Central Asian country combined with coordinated international efforts.

Establishing an effective decision-making system for environmental protection and sustainable development is of special importance. This requires good public relations and an understanding of the role of ecological factors in socio-economic planning. To create such a system, sound environmental information is an essential pre-requisite in the development of actions plans for environment protection and sustainable development.

Information requirements arise at all levels of society and the provision to the decision-making process with reliable information requires filling information gaps, and broad access to information. Each participant in sustainable development processes is simultaneously both a user and supplier of information.

In the provision of training on environment and sustainable development at all levels of management in Central Asian countries, international cooperation is also needed. Training should include technical aspects of collection, evaluation and transfer of data, as well as assistance to government bodies in the use of such information.

Governments also need to consider the support of governmental and non-governmental organizations so as to create effective and coordinated information exchange mechanisms at national and international levels, including data formats, forms of access, distribution and communication.

SIC ISDC has carried out an inventory of existing data on indicators/criteria of sustainable development, as stipulated by "Agenda 21" and priority ecological problems of REAP.

Regarding biological diversity, the geographical landscapes of Central Asia are very varied with low populations in the mountainous territories of Kyrgyzstan and Tajikistan steppes, and the deserts and semideserts of Kazakhstan, Turkmenistan and Uzbekistan. Rivers, valley floor, *tugai*, and oases contribute to maintaining the biodiversity of the region. The biological diversity of this arid belt, comprising more than a half of all species in Eurasia, including: 7 000 species of higher plants, 900 vertebrates, and 200 000 invertebrates. The region is an overlap of Asian and Mediterranean floras with a high index of endemism (up to 20% species of higher plants).

The extensive development of arable agriculture, use of toxic chemicals, salinization, overgrazing, deforestation and cutting of *tugai* vegetation in river floodplains are all resulting in environmental degradation and loss of biodiversity.

The implementation of sound environment and sustainable development policies will be essential to maintain genetic biological diversity for the benefit of future generations and their livelihoods.

On the final evening of the conference, conference participants acknowledged Gerard Boere's leadership in international waterbird conservation. He has been a major influence on the development of international structures for migratory waterbird conservation during the last three decades, initially through his research on migratory waders in the Dutch Waddensea; his activities to guide and promote non-governmental conservation and research organisations; his development and promotion of AEWA; effective involvement with several international biodiversity treaties (including the Ramsar, Bonn and Berne Conventions, as well as CAFF); work for the Dutch government to promote bilateral co-operation on waterbird and wetland conservation with Russia and Ukraine especially (notably in the arctic); and latterly his further strengthening of the international programmes and activities of Wetlands International. This photograph, taken on 7 April 2004, shows His Royal Highness The Prince of Wales discussing waterbird conservation matters with Gerard Boere. Photo: Dougie Barnett.

# Species index

The species index is based on the listing of waterbird species and populations of the fourth edition of Wetlands International's (2006) *Waterbird Population Estimates* (Wetlands International, Wageningen, The Netherlands. 239pp.). It has been supplemented by other bird species referred to in this volume. Non-avian species have not been indexed. The taxonomic sequence of families adopted in this index follows that of BirdLife International (www.birdlife.org/datazone/species/taxonomy.html). Sequencing of species within families for traditional waterbirds follows *Waterbird Population Estimates*.

Following the presentational style of *Waterbird Population Estimates*, IUCN Red-listed species are indicated by colour as follows:

**Black**  Species not known to have unfavourable conservation status

Red      Globally threatened species. IUCN threat status appears after the scientific name, using the following codes:
    CR      Critically Endangered
    EN      Endangered
    VU      Vulnerable

Green    Threatened species considered to be at a lower risk of extinction. IUCN threat status appears after the scientific name, using the following code:
    NT      Near Threatened
Also included are species in the following IUCN threat category:
    DD      Data Deficient

Blue     Extinct species

Page numbers relate to the first page of each paper within which the relevant species or population is mentioned. Page numbers in **bold** indicate photos of the species concerned within the indexed paper.

As well as indexing to species level, to aid further uses of the data contained within this volume, for 'traditional' waterbirds only, an attempt has been made to index to the level of populations/races using information on distributional limits in the third edition of *Waterbird Population Estimates* (2002). In many cases such allocations are obvious from the geographic context of the paper (or is specifically stated within), but it should be stressed that any such allocations are based on personal judgement only and should not be taken as definitive unless stated as such by the authors of the papers concerned.

| Species | English name | Subspecies/population | |
|---|---|---|---|
| *Dendrocygna viduata* | | W Africa | 226, 228, 725 |
| | | E & S Africa | 255 |
| | | Madagascar | 374 |
| | | Central & South America | 161 |
| *Dendrocygna autumnalis* | **Black-bellied Whistling Duck** | | 166 |
| | | *autumnalis* | 166 |
| | | *fulgens* | 166 |
| *Thalassornis leuconotus* | **White-backed Duck** | | 721 |
| | | *leuconotus,* W Africa | 721 |
| *Cygnus olor* | **Mute Swan** | | 264, 266, 267, 269, 277, 432, 476, **478**, **484**, 487, 519, 569, 680 |
| | | NW, C Europe | 478, 484, 487, 519 |
| | | Britain | 680 |
| | | W & Central Asia, Caspian | 264, 266, 267, 277 |
| | | East Asia | 432 |
| *Cygnus melanocoryphus* | **Black-necked Swan** | | 183, 186 |
| | | South America | 183, 186 |
| *Cygnus buccinator* | **Trumpeter Swan** | | 209, 635 |
| *Cygnus cygnus* | **Whooper Swan** | | 264, 266, 267, 269, **357**, 432, 484, 574, 663, 705, 743, 829 |
| | | Iceland (bre) | 574, 663, 705, 829 |
| | | N mainland Europe (bre) | 484, 574, 743 |
| | | Black Sea, E Mediterranean (non-bre) | 574 |
| | | Caspian, Central Asia (non-bre) | 264, 267, 269, 357, 574 |
| | | E Asia | 432 |
| *Cygnus columbianus* | **Tundra Swan "Whistling Swan"** | | 199, 264, 267, 269, 354, 398, 432, 448, 675, 680, 705, 743 |
| | | *columbianus,* E North America | 155 |
| | **"Bewick's Swan"** | *bewickii,* NW Europe (non-bre) | **155**, 354, **357**, 398, 675, 680, 705, 743 |
| | | *bewickii,* Caspian (non-bre) | 269, 357 |
| | | *jankowskii* | 432, **649** |
| *Coscoroba coscoroba* | **Coscoroba Swan** | S South America | 183, 186 |
| *Anser cygnoides* EN | **Swan Goose** | C & E Asia | 81, 269, 332, 357, 482, **649**, 690 |
| *Anser fabalis* | **Bean Goose "Taiga Bean Goose"** | | 267, 269, 354, 356, 357, 471, 484, 508, 514, 649, 680, 743, 791, 854 |
| | | *fabalis,* NW Europe (non-bre) | 514, 680, 791, 854 |
| | | *fabalis,* Central Asia (non-bre) | 269 |
| | **"Tundra Bean Goose"** | *rossicus* | 649, 680, 743, 791 |
| | | *middendorffi* | 357, 649 |
| | | *serrirostris* | 649 |
| *Anser brachyrhynchus* | **Pink-footed Goose** | | 98, 385, **508**, 675, 680, 784, 791, 854 |
| | | Greenland, Iceland (bre) | 675, 680, 784, 791 |
| | | Svalbard (bre) | 98, 385, 508, 854 |
| *Anser albifrons* | **Greater White-fronted Goose** | | 266, 267, 269, 354, 356, 366, 380, 432, 439, **446**, 448, **471**, 484, 496, 508, 545, 569, 619, 633, 637, 640, 6022, 649, 680, 697, 705, 743, 784, 791, 854 |
| | | *albifrons,* Baltic - North Sea | 354, 356, 508, 680, 705, 784, 854 |
| | | *albifrons,* Pannonic | 484 |
| | | *albifrons,* Pontic/Anatolian | 366, 496, 619 |

| Species | English name | Subspecies/population | |
|---------|-------------|----------------------|---|
| *Anser albifrons* | **Greenland White-fronted Goose** | *flavirostris* | **120**, **385**, **410**, **505**, **637**, **640**, 680, 697, **791** |
| | | *frontalis,* E Asia | 649 |
| | | *frontalis,* Pacific | 545 |
| *Anser erythropus  VU* | **Lesser White-fronted Goose** | | **29**, 265, 266, 267, 269, **283**, 285, 292, 332, 354, 356, 357, 370, 372, 380, 471, 602, 619, **629**, **633**, **635**, 643, 672, 689, 690, 697, 743 |
| | | N Europe, W Siberia (bre) | 266, 354, 356, 471, 602, 633, 689, 690, 743 |
| | | C & E Siberia | 269, 370, 372, 380, 629, 643, 690 |
| *Anser anser* | **Greylag Goose** | | 98, 266, 267, **269**, 277, 283, 354, 356, 357, 366, **373**, 432, **471**, 476, 484, **498**, 508, 514, 569, 582, 649, 680, 784, 791, 854, 868 |
| | | *anser,* Iceland (bre) | 498, 680, 791 |
| | | *anser,* NW Scotland | 498, 791 |
| | | *anser,* NW Europe (bre) | 354, 356, 373, 476, 508, 514, 854 |
| | | *anser,* C Europe (bre) | 484 |
| | | *rubrirostris,* Black Sea, Turkey | 366 |
| | | *rubrirostris,* Caspian, Iraq (non-bre) | 283, 868 |
| | | *rubrirostris,* E Asia (non-bre) | 649 |
| *Anser indicus* | **Bar-headed Goose** | C, S & SE Asia | 269, 292, 311, **432**, 649 |
| *Chen (Anser) caerulescens* | **"Lesser" Snow Goose** | | 157, 197, 199, **204**, 269, 412, 439, **446**, 448, **795**, 849 |
| | | *caerulescens,* E Asia | 649 |
| | | *caerulescens,* Hudson Bay (bre) | 795 |
| | | *caerulescens,* C Canadian Arctic (bre) | 795 |
| | | *caerulescens,* W North American Arctic | 795 |
| | | *caerulescens,* Wrangel Is (bre) | 649 |
| | **"Greater" Snow Goose** | *atlanticus* | 199, 448, 795 |
| *Chen (Anser) rossii* | **Ross's Goose** | North America | 199, 795 |
| *Chen (Anser) canagica  NT* | **Emperor Goose** | N Pacific | 649 |
| *Branta sandvicensis  VU* | **Hawaiian Goose, Nene** | Hawaii | 422 |
| *Branta canadensis* | **Canada Goose** | | 27, 157, 197, **199**, 439, 448, 476, 524, 569, 640, 649, 784, 791, **817**, 849, 854 |
| | | *canadensis/interior,* NE Canada (bre) "Atlantic" | 640 |
| | | *minima,* Cackling | 524 |
| *Branta leucopsis* | **Barnacle Goose** | | 269, 385, 439, 484, 508, 635, 637, **680**, 690, **791** |
| | | E Greenland (bre) | **680**, **791** |
| | | Svalbard (bre) | 385, 439, 680, 791, 838 |
| | | N Russia, E Baltic (bre) | 269, 484, 508 |
| *Branta bernicla* | **Brent Goose** | | 28, 158, 199, 269, 373, 385, 432, 448, 463, 505, 508, 517, 519, 524, 614, **649**, 680, 690, 705 |
| | **"Dark-bellied Brent Goose"** | *bernicla* | 373, 463, 508, **517**, 680, 705 |
| | **"Light-bellied Brent Goose"** | *hrota,* Svalbard, N Greenland (bre) | 28, 385, 680, 705 |
| | **"Light-bellied Brent Goose"** | *hrota,* Ireland (non-bre) | 28, 385, 505, **519**, **614**, 680, 705 |
| | **"Grey-bellied Brant"** | *hrota/nigricans,* western Canadian high Arctic (bre) | 385 |

| Species | English name | Subspecies/population | |
|---|---|---|---|
| *Branta bernicla* | **"Black Brant"** | *nigricans,* E Pacific (non-bre) | 158, 199, 448, 849 |
| | | *nigricans,* E Asia (non-bre) | 649 |
| *Branta ruficollis VU* | **Red-breasted Goose** | N C Russia to E Europe | 52, 266, 267, 269, 285, 332, 372, **496**, 569, 574, 582, **600**, 602, 619, 635, 672, 689, 690, 731 |
| *Chloephaga picta* | **Upland Goose, Magellan Goose** | | 195, 870 |
| | | *picta* | 870 |
| | | *leucoptera* | 870 |
| *Chloephaga poliocephala* | **Ashy-headed Goose** | South America | 195, 870 |
| *Chloephaga rubidiceps* | **Ruddy-headed Goose** | | 189, **195**, 870 |
| | | Tierra del Fuego (bre) | 189, 870 |
| | | Falkland/Malvinas Is | **195**, 870 |
| *Alopochen aegyptiaca* | **Egyptian Goose** | | 226, 228, 721, 725 |
| | | W Africa | 226, 228, 725 |
| | | E & S Africa | 721 |
| *Tadorna ferruginea* | **Ruddy Shelduck** | | 267, 269, 277, 285, 311, 357, 366, 432, **480, 662, 868** |
| | | Ethiopia | 480 |
| | | NW Africa | 480 |
| | | E Med, Black Sea, NE Africa | 366, 480 |
| | | W Asia, Caspian, Iran, Iraq | 267, 277, 480, 868 |
| | | S & SE Asia (non-bre) | 311, 480 |
| | | E Asia (non-bre) | 432, 480 |
| *Tadorna cana* | **Cape Shelduck, South African Shelduck** | S Africa | 218 |
| *Tadorna cristata CR* | **Crested Shelduck** | NE Asia | 332 |
| *Tadorna tadorna* | **Common Shelduck** | | 226, 267, 269, 366, 432, 705, 805, 868 |
| | | NW Europe (bre) | 705, 805 |
| | | Black Sea, Mediterranean | 226, 366 |
| | | Caspian, SW Asia (non-bre) | 267, 269, 868 |
| *Plectropterus gambensis* | **Spur-winged Goose** | | 226, 228, 725 |
| | | *gambensis,* W Africa | 226, 228, 725 |
| *Cairina moschata* | **Muscovy Duck** | C & S America | 166, 484 |
| *Cairina scutulata EN* | **White-winged Duck** | | 332 |
| *Sarkidiornis melanotos* | **Comb Duck** | | 226, 228, 257, 374 |
| | | *melanotos,* W Africa | 226, 228 |
| | | *melanotos,* Madagascar | 374 |
| *Nettapus coromandelianus* | **Cotton Pygmy-Goose** | | 305 |
| | | *coromandelianus,* South Asia | 305 |
| *Nettapus auritus* | **African Pygmy- Goose** | | 226, 228, 374 |
| | | W Africa | 226, 228 |
| | | Madagascar | 374 |
| *Aix sponsa* | **(American) Wood Duck** | | 484, 849 |
| *Aix galericulata* | **Mandarin Duck** | | 484, 690 |
| | | European non-native popn. | 484 |
| | | China (non-bre) | 690 |
| *Anas* spp. | **Domestic poultry** | | 427, 432 |
| *Anas penelope* | **Eurasian Wigeon** | | 98, 226, 267, 269, 303, 354, 356, 357, 366, 432, 459, 474, 476, 478, 484, 569, 574, 582, 705, 784, 854, 864, 868 |
| | | NW Europe (non-bre) | 98, 354, 356, 459, 474, 476, 478, 484, 569, 574, 705, 784, 854 |

| Species | English name | Subspecies/population | |
|---------|-------------|----------------------|---|
| *Anas penelope* | | Black Sea, Mediterranean (non-bre) | 226, 366, 569, 574, 864 |
| | | SW Asia, NE Africa (non-bre) | 267, 269, 569, 868 |
| | | South Asia (non-bre) | 303, 357 |
| | | E Asia (non-bre) | 432 |
| *Anas falcata NT* | **Falcated Duck** | C & E Asia | 269, 432 |
| *Anas strepera* | **Gadwall** | | 98, 266, 267, 269, 303, 357, 366, 432, 474, 476, 484, 490, 520, 582, 705, 784, 854, 864, 868 |
| | | *strepera*, NW Europe (bre) | 98, 474, 476, 484, 705, 784, 854 |
| | | *strepera*, C Europe, Black Sea, Mediterranean (non-bre) | 366, 520, 864 |
| | | *strepera*, SW Asia, NE Africa (non-bre) | 868, 266, 267, 269 |
| | | *strepera*, South Asia (non-bre) | 303, 357 |
| *Anas formosa VU* | **Baikal Teal** | E Asia | 81, 269, 332, 357, 366, 412, 432, 690 |
| *Anas crecca* | **Common Teal** | | 98, 226, 257, 266, 267, 269, 277, 287, 357, 373, 422, 432, 459, 474, 487, 496, 520, **569**, 574, 582, 697, 705, 784, 849, 854, 862, 864, 868, **874** |
| | | *crecca*, NW Europe (non-bre) | 98, 226, 373, 459, 474, 487, 520, 697, 705, 784,854, 862 |
| | | *crecca*, Black Sea, Mediterranean (non-bre) | 697, 864 |
| | | *crecca*, SW Asia, NE Africa (non-bre) | 266, 267, 269, 277, 287, 357, 496, 487, 697, 868 |
| | | *crecca*, E & SE Asia (non-bre) | 432 |
| | **"Green-winged Teal"** | *carolinensis* | 422, 474, 849 |
| *Anas capensis* | **Cape Teal** | | 453 |
| *Anas bernieri EN* | **Madagascar Teal, Bernier's Teal** | W Madagascar | 217, 218, 252 |
| *Anas gracilis* | **Grey Teal** | | 252 |
| *Anas platyrhynchos* | **Mallard** | | **98**, 154, 199, 267, 269, 277, 285, 287, **349**, 354, 356, **357**, 366, 370, 373, **412**, 418, **422**, 432, 439, 448, **474**, 476, 478, 484, 487, 496, 569, 574, 582, 675, 705, 582, 784, 849, 854, 862, **864**, 868, 874 |
| | | *platyrhynchos*, NW Europe (non-bre) | 354, 356, 357, 373, 418, **474**, 476, 478, 484, 569, 574, 675, 705, 784, 854, 862 |
| | | *platyrhynchos*, W Mediterranean (non-bre) | 487, 569, 574, 864 |
| | | *platyrhynchos*, Black Sea, E Mediterranean (non-bre) | 366, 496, 487, 569, 574 |
| | | *platyrhynchos*, SW Asia (non-bre) | 267, 269, 277, 285, 287, 370, 569, 574, 868 |
| | | *platyrhynchos*, E Asia (non-bre) | 432 |
| | | *platyrhynchos*, North America | 98, 199, 422, 439, 448, 582, 849 |
| | | *conboschas* | 154 |
| *Anas wyvilliana EN* | **Hawaiian Duck** | Hawaii | 422 |
| *Anas rubripes* | **American Black Duck** | | 199 |
| *Anas undulata* | **Yellow-billed Duck** | | 257, 457 |
| | | *undulata*, E Africa | 457 |
| *Anas poecilorhyncha* | **Spot-billed Duck** | | 432 |
| *Anas luzonica VU* | **Philippine Duck** | N Philippines | 332 |

| Species | English name | Subspecies/population | |
|---------|-------------|----------------------|---|
| *Anas acuta* | **Northern Pintail** | | 98, 157, 172, 197, 199, **226**, 228, 267, 269, 303, 354, 356, 357, 366, 422, 432, 448, 457, 474, 484, 490, 574, 582, 705, 725, 784, 849, 854, 864, 868 |
| | | NW Europe (non-bre) | 98, 226, 354, 356, 474, 484, 490, 574, 582, 705, 784, 854 |
| | | Black Sea, Mediterranean, W Africa (non-bre) | 228, 366, 582, 725, 864 |
| | | SW Asia, E & NE Africa (non-bre) | 267, 269, 357, 457, 582, 868 |
| | | South Asia (non-bre) | 303, 582 |
| | | E & SE Asia | 432, 582 |
| | | North America (bre) | 157, 172, 197, 199, 422, 448, 582, 849 |
| *Anas erythrorhyncha* | **Red-billed Duck** | | 218, 257 |
| | | E Africa | 218 |
| *Anas hottentota* | **Hottentot Teal** | | 255, 257, 374 |
| | | E Africa | 255 |
| | | Madagascar | 374 |
| *Anas querquedula* | **Garganey** | | 98, 226, 228, 266, 267, 269, 357, 366, 432, 457, 474, 520, 574, 582, 725, 854, 864, 868 |
| | | W Africa (non-bre) | 98, 226, 228, 474, 520, 574, 582, 725, 854, 864 |
| | | SW Asia, NE Africa (non-bre) | 266, 267, 269, 357, 366, 457, 582, 868 |
| | | South Asia (non-bre) | 582 |
| *Anas discors* | **Blue-winged Teal** | N, C & N South America | 172 |
| *Anas cyanoptera* | **Cinnamon Teal** | | 166, 448 |
| | | *septentrianalium* | 166, 448 |
| *Anas clypeata* | **Northern Shoveler** | | 98, 172, 226, 228, 266, 267, 269, 303, 357, 366, 370, 422, 432, 474, 484, 520, 582, 705, 725, 784, 854, 864, 868 |
| | | NW & C Europe (non-bre) | 98, 226, 474, 484, 520, 705, 784, 854 |
| | | Black Sea, Mediterranean, W Africa (non-bre) | 228, 366, 370, 725, 864 |
| | | SW Asia, NE & E Africa (non-bre) | 266, 267, 269, 357, 868 |
| | | South Asia (non-bre) | 303 |
| | | North America | 172, 422 |
| *Marmaronetta angustirostris VU* | **Marbled Teal** | | 269, 283, 285, 292, 332, 372, 602, 690, 731 |
| | | W Mediterranean, W Africa | 602 |
| | | E Mediterranean | 602 |
| | | SW Asia (non-bre) | 269, 283, 285, 292, 332, 372, 690, 731 |
| *Rhodonessa caryophyllacea CR* | **Pink-headed Duck** | NE India, Myanmar | 308, 332 |
| *Netta rufina* | **Red-crested Pochard** | | 267, 269, 277, 285, **303**, 366, 370, 379, 432, **503**, 520, 868 |
| | | C Europe & W Mediterranean | 379, 503, 520 |
| | | Black Sea, E Mediterranean (non-bre) | 366, 370 |
| | | C & SW Asia (non-bre) | 267, 269, 277, 285, 868 |
| | | South Asia (non-bre) | 303 |
| *Netta erythrophthalma* | **Southern Pochard** | | 721 |
| | | *brunnea* | 721 |
| *Aythya valisineria* | **Canvasback** | N America | 448, 853 |

| Species | English name | Subspecies/population | |
|---------|--------------|----------------------|---|
| *Aythya ferina* | **Common Pochard** | | 226, 264, 266, 267, 269, 277, 287, 356, 357, 366, 370, 373, 432, 474, 484, 487, 490, 496, 520, 582, 705, 784, 854, 864, 868 |
| | | NE & NW Europe (non-bre) | 226, 356, 373, 474, 484, 487, 705, 784, 854 |
| | | C Europe, Black Sea, Mediterranean (non-bre) | 366, 370, 496, 520, 864 |
| | | SW Asia (non-bre) | 264, 266, 267, 269, 277, 287, 357, 868 |
| *Aythya americana* | **Redhead** | N America | 412, 448 |
| *Aythya collaris* | **Ring-necked Duck** | N America | 172, 474, 849 |
| *Aythya baeri VU* | **Baer's Pochard** | C, E, SE & S Asia | 332, 357, 690 |
| *Aythya nyroca NT* | **Ferruginous Duck** | | 226, 228, 267, 269, **275**, 285, **292**, 354, 356, 366, 372, 484, 496, 602, 690, **700**, 733, 868 |
| | | N & W Africa (non-bre) | 226, 602 |
| | | E Europe, E Mediterranean, Black Sea (bre) | 366, 484, 496, 602, 733 |
| | | SW Asia & NE Africa (non-bre) | 267, 269, 275, 285, 292, 372, 690, 868 |
| | | S, E & SE Asia (non-bre) | 690 |
| *Aythya fuligula* | **Tufted Duck** | | 226, 264, 266, **267**, 269, 277, 354, 356, 357, 370, 372, 373, 432, 463, 474, 476, 478, 484, 487, 490, 496, 520, 582, 705, 784, 854, 864, 868 |
| | | NW Europe (non-bre) | 226, 354, 356, 373, 463, 474, 476, 478, 484, 487, 705, 784, 854 |
| | | C Europe, Black Sea, Mediterranean (non-bre) | 370, 496, 520, 864 |
| | | SW Asia, NE Africa (non-bre) | 264, 266, 267, 269, 277, 868 |
| | | E & SE Asia (non-bre) | 432 |
| *Aythya marila* | **Greater Scaup** | | 157, 197, 199, 264, 267, 269, 368, 432, 484, 705, 784, 854, 868 |
| | | *marila*, W Europe (non-bre) | 705, 784, 854 |
| | | *marila*, Black & Caspian Seas (non-bre) | 264, 269, 368, 868 |
| | | *mariloides*, North America | 157, 197 |
| *Aythya affinis* | **Lesser Scaup** | N & C America | 199, 439, 849 |
| *Somateria mollissima* | **Common Eider** | | 98, 412, 478, **512**, 569, 582, 705, 743, **756**, 758, 801, 806, 854 |
| | | *mollissima*, Britain, Ireland | **512**, 705, **756**, 758 |
| | | *mollissima*, Baltic, Wadden Sea | 98, 478, 801, 806, 854 |
| | | *mollissima*, Norway, NW Russia | 512, 743 |
| | | *faeroeensis*, Shetland, Orkney Is | 705 |
| | | *dresseri* | 756 |
| *Somateria spectabilis* | **King Eider** | | 269, 357, 512, 743, 758, **769** |
| | | N Europe, W Siberia (bre) | 512, 743, 758, 769 |
| | | E Canada, N Greenland (bre) | 769 |
| *Somateria fischeri* | **Spectacled Eider** | E Siberia, N & W Alaska | 690, 769 |
| *Polysticta stelleri VU* | **Steller's Eider** | | **120**, 512, 582, 602, 690, 743 |
| | | N Norway, SE Baltic (non-bre) | 120, 512, 582, 602, 743 |
| | | N Pacific (non-bre) | 690 |
| *Histrionicus histrionicus* | **Harlequin Duck** | | 269, 357 |
| | | *(pacificus)* | 269, 357 |

| Species | English name | Subspecies/population | |
|---|---|---|---|
| *Clangula hyemalis* | **Long-tailed Duck, Oldsquaw** | | 154, 267, 269, 354, 412, 432, 512, 705, 739, 801, 854 |
| | | Iceland, Greenland (bre) | 154 |
| | | W Siberia, N Europe (bre) | 269, 354, 512, 705, 739, 801, 854, · |
| *Melanitta nigra* | **Common Scoter, Black Scoter** | | 269, 432, 512, 705, 743, **750**, 754, 801, 854 |
| | | *nigra* | 512, 705, 743, 750, 754, 801, 854, |
| *Melanitta fusca* | **Velvet Scoter, White-winged Scoter** | | 267, 269, 357, 432, 484, 512, 705, 739, 854 |
| | | *fusca,* Baltic, W Europe (non-bre) | 267, 484, 512, 705, 739, 854 |
| | | *deglandi* | 269, 357 |
| *Bucephala clangula* | **Common Goldeneye** | | 266, 267, 269, 357, 368, 476, 478, 484, 487, 512, 520, 582, 705, 784, **817, 854** |
| | | *clangula,* NW, Central Europe (non-bre) | 476, 478, 484, 487, 512, 520, 705, 784, 854 |
| | | *clangula,* W Siberia (bre) | 266, 267, 269, 357, 368 |
| | | *americana* | 817 |
| *Lophodytes cucullatus* | **Hooded Merganser** | N America | 211 |
| *Mergellus albellus* | **Smew** | | 267, 269, 277, 357, 366, 368, 432, 484 |
| | | NW & C Europe (non-bre) | 484 |
| | | Black Sea, E Mediterranean (non-bre) | 366 |
| | | C & SW Asia (non-bre) | 267, 269, 277, 357, 368 |
| *Mergus serrator* | **Red-breasted Merganser** | | 154, **211,** 267, 269, 277, 368, 432, 478, 484, 512, 705, 854 |
| | | NW & C Europe (non-bre) | 154, 478, 484, 512, 705, 854 |
| | | SW & C Asia (non-bre) | 267, 269, 277, 368 |
| | | North America | **211** |
| *Mergus squamatus EN* | **Scaly-sided Merganser** | E & SE Asia | 81, 332, 690 |
| *Mergus merganser* | **Goosander, Common Merganser** | | 211, 264, 267, 269, 277, 354, 368, 432, 476, 478, 484, 487, 512, 705, 854 |
| | | *merganser,* NW & C Europe (non-bre) | 354, 476, 478, 484, 487, 512, 705, 854 |
| | | *merganser,* Caspian Sea (non-bre) | 264, 267, 269, 277, 368 |
| | | *americanus,* North America | 211 |
| *Oxyura jamaicensis* | **Ruddy Duck** | | 19, 172, 412, 822 |
| | | European non-native popn. | 19, 822 |
| | | *jamaicensis* | 172 |
| | | *(rubida)* | 412 |
| *Oxyura leucocephala EN* | **White-headed Duck** | | 19, 81, 267, 269, 275, 277, 283, 285, 292, 294, 332, 368, 370, 496, 602, 619, 690, 731, 822 |
| | | Spain, Morocco | 19, 81, 602, 690, 822 |
| | | E Mediterranean, SW Asia | 267, 269, 275, 277, 283, 285, 292, 294, 368, 370, 496, 619, 690, 731 |
| | | South Asia (non-bre) | 332, 619, 690 |
| *Oxyura maccoa* | **Maccoa Duck** | | 721 |
| | | E Africa | 721 |

| Species | English name | Subspecies/population | |
|---|---|---|---|
| **SPHENISCIDAE** | **PENGUINS** | | 257 |
| *Aptenedytes fosteri* | **Emperor Penguin** | | 412 |
| *Pygoscelis adalaiae* | **Adelie Penguin** | | 412 |
| *Eudyptes chrysocome VU* | **Rockhopper Penguin** | | 412 |
| *Spheniscus demersus VU* | **African Penguin** | | **224**, 257, 760 |
| *Spheniscus magellanicus NT* | **Magellanic Penguin** | | 189, **737** |
| | | | |
| **GAVIIDAE** | **DIVERS & LOONS** | | |
| *Gavia stellata* | **Red-throated Diver, Red-throated Loon** | | 432, 484, 739, 754 |
| | | NW Europe (non-bre) | 484, 739, 754 |
| *Gavia arctica* | **Black-throated Diver, Arctic Loon** | | 264, 356, 432, 582, 675, 739 |
| | | *arctica* | 264, 356, 582, 675, 739 |
| | | *(suschkini)* | 582 |
| *Gavia immer* | **Great Northern Diver, Common Loon** | | 206 |
| | | North America | 206 |
| | | | |
| **DIOMEDEIDAE** | **ALBATROSSES** | | 16, 50, 245 |
| *Phoebastria irrorata VU* | **Waved Albatross** | | 113 |
| *Phoebastria albatrus VU* | **Short-tailed Albatross** | | 113 |
| *Phoebastria nigripes EN* | **Black-footed Albatross** | | 113, 206, 412 |
| *Phoebastria immutabilis VU* | **Laysan Albatross** | | **13**, 412 |
| *Diomedea exulans VU* | **Wandering Albatross** | | **113** |
| *Diomedea antipodensis VU* | **Antipodean Albatross** | | **113** |
| *Diomedea amsterdamensis CR* | **Amsterdam Albatross** | | 113 |
| *Diomedea dabbenena EN* | **Tristan Albatross** | | 113 |
| *Diomedea sanfordi EN* | **Northern Royal Albatross** | | 16, 113, **737** |
| *Diomedea epomophora VU* | **Southern Royal Albatross** | | 113, **737** |
| *Diomedea immutabilis VU* | **Laysan Albatross** | See *Phoebastria immutabilis* | |
| *Diomedea nigripes EN* | **Black-footed Albatross** | See *Phoebastria nigripes* | |
| *Procellaria fusca EN* | **Sooty Albatross** | | 113 |
| *Procellaria palpebrata NT* | **Light-mantled Sooty Albatross** | | **113** |
| *Procellaria melanophrys EN* | **Black-browed Albatross** | | **7, 113**, 189 |
| *Procellaria impavida VU* | **Campbell Albatross** | | 113 |
| *Procellaria cauta NT* | **Shy Albatross** | | 113 |
| *Procellaria eremita CR* | **Chatham Albatross** | | 113 |
| *Procellaria salvini VU* | **Salvin's Albatross** | | 113 |
| *Procellaria chrysostoma VU* | **Grey-headed Albatross** | | 113 |
| *Thalassarche chlororhynchos EN* | **Atlantic Yellow-nosed Albatrosses** | | **113**, 777 |
| *Procellaria carteri EN* | **Indian Yellow-nosed Albatross** | | 113 |
| *Procellaria bulleri VU* | **Buller's Albatross** | | 113 |
| | | | |
| **PROCELLARIIDAE** | **FULMARS, PETRELS & SHEARWATERS** | | 161, 245 |
| *Macronectes giganteus VU* | **Southern Giant Petrel** | | **113** |
| *Macronectes halli NT* | **Northern Giant Petrel** | | 113 |
| *Fulmaris glacialis* | **Northern Fulmar** | | 765, 767 |
| *Pterodroma feae NT* | **Fea's Petrel** | | 602 |
| *Pterodroma maderia EN* | **Zeno's Petrel** | | 602 |
| *Procellaria aequinoctialis VU* | **White-chinned Petrel** | | 113 |
| *Procellaria conspicillata CR* | **Spectacled Petrel** | | 113 |
| *Procellaria westlandica VU* | **Westland Petrel** | | 113 |
| *Procellaria parkinsoni VU* | **Black Petrel** | | 113 |
| *Procellaria cinerea NT* | **Grey Petrel** | | 113 |
| *Puffinus pacificus* | **Wedge-tailed Shearwater** | | 432 |
| *Puffinus creatopus VU* | **Pink-footed Shearwater** | | 206 |

| Species | English name | Subspecies/population | |
|---------|--------------|----------------------|---|
| *Puffinus puffinus* | **Manx Shearwater** | | 765 |
| *Puffinus mauretanicus  CR* | **Balearic Shearwater** | | 602 |
| **HYDROBATIDAE** | **STORM-PETRELS** | | **161** |
| *Oceanodroma leucorhoa* | **Leach's Storm-Petrel** | | 206, 765 |
| *Hydrobates pelagicus* | **European Storm-petrel** | | 765 |
| **PODICIPEDIDAE** | **GREBES** | | **161, 245, 257** |
| *Tachybaptus ruficollis* | **Little Grebe** | | 366, 374, 432, 476, 484, 705, 868 |
| | | *ruficollis* | 366, 476, 484, 705 |
| | | *capensis*, Sub-Saharan Africa | 374 |
| | | *capensis*, SW, Central, S Asia | 868 |
| | | *poggei* | 432 |
| *Tachybaptus pelzelnii  VU* | **Madagascar (Little) Grebe** | Madagascar | 374 |
| *Podilymbus podiceps* | **Pied-billed Grebe** | | 172 |
| | | *antillarum* | 172 |
| *Podiceps grisegena* | **Red-necked Grebe** | | 266 |
| | | *grisegena*, Caspian (non-bre) | 266 |
| *Podiceps cristatus* | **Great Crested Grebe** | | 264, 277, 303, 311, 366, 432, 463, 484, 705, 868 |
| | | *cristatus*, N & W Europe (non-bre) | 463, 705 |
| | | *cristatus*, Black Sea, Mediterranean (non-bre) | 366 |
| | | *cristatus*, Caspian Sea (non-bre) | 264, 868 |
| | | *cristatus*, South Asia (non-bre) | 277, 303 |
| *Podiceps auritus* | **Slavonian Grebe, Horned Grebe** | | 264, 705, 739 |
| | | *auritus*, NW Europe (large billed) | 705, 739 |
| | | *auritus*, Caspian, S Asia (non-bre) | 264 |
| *Podiceps nigricollis* | **Black-necked Grebe, Eared Grebe** | | 158, 218, 264, 266, 277, 302, 412, 439, 519, 760, 868 |
| | | *nigricollis*, Europe, N Africa | 519, 760 |
| | | *nigricollis*, E Africa | 760 |
| | | *nigricollis*, SW & S Asia (non-bre) | 264, 266, 277, 302, 760, 868 |
| | | *gurneyi* | 218 |
| | | *californicus* | 158, 412, 439 |
| *Aechmophorus occidentalis* | **Western Grebe** | | 206, 209 |
| | | *occidentalis* | 206, 209 |
| **PHOENICOPTERIDAE** | **FLAMINGOS** | | **245, 257** |
| *Phoenicopterus roseus* | **Greater Flamingo** | | **234**, 239, **245**, 257, 264, 287, 296, 366, 374, 562, 672, 688, 725 |
| | | E Africa | **234**, 239, 374 |
| | | W Africa | 688, 725 |
| | | W Mediterranean | 688 |
| | | East Mediterranean | 366, 688 |
| | | South & Southwest Asia | 264, 287, 296, 562 |
| *Phoenicopterus ruber* | **Caribbean Flamingo** | | 172 |
| | | Bahamas, Cuba | 172 |
| *Phoenicopterus minor  NT* | **Lesser Flamingo** | | 217, 218, 230, **234**, 239, 257, 374 |
| | | W Africa | 234 |
| | | E Africa | 218, 230, **234**, 239 |
| | | S Africa | 234, 239 |
| | | S Asia | 234 |
| *Phoenicoparrus andinus  VU* | **Andean Flamingo** | South American Andes | 189 |

| Species | English name | Subspecies/population | |
|---------|--------------|----------------------|---|
| **CICONIIDAE** | **STORKS** | | **161, 257** |
| *Mycteria americana* | **Wood Stork** | | 161, 166, 189 |
| | | South America | 189 |
| | | Mexico, Caribbean, Central America | 161 |
| *Mycteria cinerea  VU* | **Milky Stork** | | 332 |
| *Mycteria ibis* | **Yellow-billed Stork** | | 239, 374 |
| | | Africa | 239 |
| | | Madagascar | 374 |
| *Anastomus oscitans* | **Asian Openbill** | S, SE Asia | 432, 457 |
| *Anastomus lamelligerus* | **African Openbill** | | 218, 257, 374 |
| | | *lamelligerus* | 218 |
| | | *madagascariensis* | 374 |
| *Ciconia nigra* | **Black Stork** | | 264, 277, 292, 356, 366, **608**, 725 |
| | | SW Europe (bre) | 608, 725 |
| | | C, E Europe (bre) | 356, 366, 608 |
| | | South Asia (non-bre) | 277, 292 |
| | | E Asia (non-bre) | 239 |
| *Ciconia abdimii* | **Abdim's Stork** | Africa | 218 |
| *Ciconia episcopus* | **Woolly-necked Stork** | | 721 |
| | | *microscelis* | 721 |
| *Ciconia stormi  EN* | **Storm's Stork** | SE Asia | 332 |
| *Ciconia ciconia* | **European White Stork** | | 257, 277, 366, **493**, 569, 590, 838 |
| | | *ciconia,* South Africa (bre) | 590 |
| | | *ciconia,* SW & W Europe (bre) | 493, 838 |
| | | *ciconia,* C & E Europe + Syria, Israel (bre) | 366, 493 |
| *Ciconia boyciana  EN* | **Oriental (White) Stork** | E Asia | 81, 320, 332, 690 |
| *Ephippiorhynchus asiaticus  NT* | **Black-necked Stork** | | 305, 308 |
| | | *asiaticus* | 305, 308 |
| *Jabiru mycteria* | **Jabiru** | | 161 |
| | | Central America, N South America | 161 |
| *Leptoptilos javanicus  VU* | **Lesser Adjutant** | S & SE Asia | 305, 332 |
| *Leptoptilos dubius  EN* | **Greater Adjutant** | | 332 |
| *Leptoptilos crumeniferus* | **Marabou (Stork)** | Africa | 218 |
| **THRESKIORNITHIDAE** | **IBISES & SPOONBILLS** | | **161, 217** |
| *Threskiornis aethiopicus* | **Sacred Ibis** | | 257, 721, 725 |
| | | Sub-Saharan Africa | 257, 721, 725 |
| *Threskiornis bernieri  EN* | **Madagascar Sacred Ibis** | | 374 |
| | | *bernieri* | 374 |
| *Threskiornis melanocephalus  NT* | **Black-headed Ibis** | | 690 |
| | | South Asia | 690 |
| | | SE Asia | 690 |
| | | E Asia | 690 |
| *Pseudibis davisoni  CR* | **White-shouldered Ibis** | | 332 |
| *Thaumatibis gigantea  CR* | **Giant Ibis** | Indochina | 332 |
| *Geronticus eremita  CR* | **Northern Bald Ibis, Waldrapp** | | 332, 633 |
| | | SW Asia | 332 |
| *Nipponia nippon  EN* | **Crested Ibis** | China | 332 |
| *Eudocimus albus* | **American White Ibis** | | 161 |
| | | Central & South America | 161 |
| *Plegadis falcinellus* | **Glossy Ibis** | | 172, 255, 283, 372, 374, 432, 721 |
| | | *falcinellus,* Sub-Saharan Africa (bre) | 255, 721 |
| | | *falcinellus,* Madagascar | 374 |
| | | *falcinellus,* SW Asia (bre) | 283, 372 |
| | | *falcinellus,* North & Central America, Caribbean | 172 |

| Species | English name | Subspecies/population | |
|---------|-------------|----------------------|--|
| *Platalea leucorodia* | **Eurasian Spoonbill** | | 218, 305, 432, 569, 725 |
| | | *leucorodia,* E Atlantic | 218 |
| | | *leucorodia,* C, SE Europe (bre) | 218 |
| | | *balsaci* | 218, 725 |
| | | *archeri* | 218 |
| | | *(major),* SW, S Asia (non-bre) | 305 |
| *Platalea minor  EN* | **Black-faced Spoonbill** | *minor* | 81, 332, 339, 432, 690 |
| *Platalea alba* | **African Spoonbill** | | 374, 721 |
| | | *alba* | 721 |
| | | Madagascar | 374 |
| *Ajaia ajaja, Platalea ajaja* | **Roseate Spoonbill** | | 161 |
| | | N Neotropics to S USA | 161 |
| | | | |
| ARDEIDAE | HERONS N EGRETS | | 161, 245, 812 |
| *Ardea cinerea* | **Grey Heron** | | 264, 266, 277, 366, 370, 374, 432, 476, 484, 487 |
| | | *cinerea,* W Europe, NW Africa (bre) | 476 |
| | | *cinerea,* C & E Europe (bre) | 366, 370, 484, 487 |
| | | *cinerea,* Central & SW Asia | 264, 266, 277 |
| | | *jouyi,* E, SE Asia | 432 |
| | | *firasa* | 374 |
| *Ardea herodias* | **Great Blue Heron** | | 172 |
| | | *occidentalis,* Caribbean | 172 |
| *Ardea alba (Casmerodius albus, Egretta alba)* | **Great (White) Egret** | | 161, 172, 266, 277, 366, 374, 484, 487, 721, 725 |
| | | *alba,* W, C & E Europe, Black Sea & E Mediterranean (bre) | 366, 484, 487 |
| | | *alba,* SW Asia (non-bre) | 266, 277 |
| | | *melanorhynchos* | 721, 725 |
| | | *egretta,* C2 | 161 |
| | | *egretta,* Caribbean | 172 |
| *Ardea (Mesophoyx) intermedia* | **Intermediate Egret** | | 721 |
| | | *brachyrhyncha* | 721 |
| *Ardea humbloti  EN* | **Madagascar Heron, Humblot's Heron** | Madagascar | 374 |
| *Ardea insignis  EN* | **White-bellied Heron** | S & SE Asia | 332 |
| *Ardea goliath* | **Goliath Heron** | | **453** |
| | | Sub-Saharan Africa | **453** |
| *Ardea purpurea* | **Purple Heron** | | 366, 374 |
| | | *purpurea,* C & E Europe, Black Sea, Mediterranean | 366 |
| | | *madagascariensis* | 374 |
| *Ardea (Bubulcus) ibis* | **Cattle Egret** | | 161, 172, 257, 374, 412 |
| | | *ibis,* S Africa | 257, 374 |
| | | *ibis,* Tropical Africa | 257 |
| | | *ibis,* North America | 412 |
| | | *ibis,* Central America | 161, |
| | | *ibis,* Caribbean | 172 |
| *Butorides virescens* | **Green Heron** | | 172 |
| | | *virescens,* Caribbean | 172 |
| *Butorides striata* | **Striated Heron, Green-backed Heron** | | 374 |
| | | *rutenbergi* | 374 |
| *Ardeola ralloides* | **Squacco Heron** | | 218, 366, 374 |
| | | *ralloides,* C & E Europe, Black Sea & E Mediterranean (bre) | 366 |
| | | *paludivaga* | 374 |

| Species | English name | Subspecies/population | |
|---|---|---|---|
| *Ardeola bacchus* | **Chinese Pond-Heron** | E, SE & S Asia | 432 |
| *Ardeola idae  EN* | **Madagascar Pond-Heron** | Madagascar | 218, 374, 457 |
| *Egretta ardesiaca* | **Black Heron** | Africa | 374, 457 |
| *Egretta tricolor* | **Tricolored Heron** | | 161, 172 |
| | | *ruficollis,* Central America | 161 |
| | | *ruficollis,* Caribbean | 172 |
| *Egretta caerulea* | **Little Blue Heron** | | 161, 172 |
| | | Central America | 161 |
| | | Caribbean | 172 |
| *Egretta thula* | **Snowy Egret** | | 161, 172 |
| | | *thula,* Central America | 161 |
| | | *thula,* Caribbean | 172 |
| *Egretta garzetta* | **Little Egret** | | 366, 374, 432, 705, 721 |
| | | *garzetta,* Sub-Saharan Africa (bre) | 721 |
| | | *garzetta,* W Europe, NW Africa | 705 |
| | | *garzetta,* C & E Europe, Black Sea, E Mediterranean (bre) | 366 |
| | | *garzetta,* E, SE Asia | 432 |
| | **Madagascar Reef Heron, Dimorphic Egret** | *dimorpha,* Madagascar | 374 |
| *Egretta eulophotes  VU* | **Chinese Egret, Swinhoe's Egret** | E, SE Asia | 332 |
| *Nyctanassa violaceus, Nycticorax violaceus* | **Yellow-crowned Night-Heron** | | 172 |
| | | *violacea,* North America | 172 |
| *Nycticorax nycticorax* | **Black-crowned Night-Heron** | | 161, 172, 366, 374, 418, 432, 446 |
| | | *nycticorax,* C & E Europe, Black Sea, E Mediterranean (bre) | 366, 446 |
| | | *nycticorax,* Sub-Saharan Africa, Madagascar (bre) | 374 |
| | | *nycticorax,* E, SE Asia | 432 |
| | | *nycticorax,* North America (bre) | 418 |
| | | *nycticorax,* Central America | 161 |
| | | *nycticorax,* Caribbean | 172 |
| *Gorsachius magnificus  EN* | **White-eared Night-Heron** | SE Asia | 332 |
| *Gorsachius goisagi  EN* | **Japanese Night-Heron** | E & SE Asia | 332 |
| *Botaurus lentiginosus* | **North American Bittern, American Bittern** | North America | 206 |
| *Botaurus stellaris* | **Eurasian Bittern, Great Bittern** | | 13, 264, 356, 484, 602, 705 |
| | | *stellaris,* W Europe, NW Africa (bre) | 13, 356, 602, 705 |
| | | *stellaris,* C & E Europe, Black Sea, E Mediterranean (bre) | 484, 602 |
| | | *stellaris,* W & Central Asia (bre) | 264 |
| *Ixobrychus exilis* | **Least Bittern** | | 172 |
| | | *exilis* | 172 |
| *Tigrisoma mexicanum* | **Bare-throated Tiger-Heron** | | 161, 166 |
| | | Colombia to Mexico | 161, 166 |
| *Tigrisoma fasciatum* | **Fasciated Tiger-Heron** | | 161 |
| | | *salmoni* | 161 |
| *Cochlearius cochlearia* | **Boat-billed Heron** | | 161 |
| | | *panamensis* | 161 |
| **PHAETHONTIDAE** | **TROPICBIRDS** | | **161, 245** |
| *Phaethon aethereus* | **Red-billed Tropicbird** | | **161, 735** |
| *Phaethon rubicauda* | **Red-tailed Tropicbird** | | 412, 735 |

| Species | English name | Subspecies/population | |
|---------|-------------|----------------------|---|
| **FREGATIDAE** | **FRIGATEBIRDS** | | 161, 245 |
| *Fregeta magnificens* | **Magnificent Frigatebird** | | 158, 161, 166, 177, 181 |
| *Fregata minor* | **Great Frigatebird** | | 161 |
| **SCOPIDAE** | **HAMERKOP** | | 245 |
| *Scopus umbretta* | **Hamerkop** | | 245 |
| | | *umbretta* | 245 |
| **BALAENICIPITIDAE** | **SHOEBILL** | | |
| *Balaeniceps rex  VU* | **Shoebill** | C Africa | 245, 457, **613** |
| **PELECANIDAE** | **PELICANS** | | 161, 245, 257, 412 |
| *Pelecanus onocrotalus* | **Great White Pelican** | | **217**, 218, 257, 283, 372, **725**, 760 |
| | | W Africa | **217**, 218, 725 |
| | | Europe, W Asia (bre) | 283, 372 |
| *Pelecanus philippensis  VU* | **Spot-billed Pelican** | | 305, 332 |
| | | South Asia | 305, 332 |
| | | SE Asia | 332 |
| | | Sumatra | 332 |
| *Pelecanus crispus  VU* | **Dalmatian Pelican** | | 266, 275, 277, 283, 285, 292, 303, 332, 370, 372, 496, 602, 690, 760 |
| | | Black Sea, Mediterranean (non-bre) | 370, 496, 602 |
| | | SW, S Asia (non-bre) | 266, 275, 277, 283, 285, 292, 303, 372, 690 |
| *Pelecanus erythrorhynchos* | **American White Pelican** | *North America* | 206, 412, 418, 422, **448** |
| *Pelecanus occidentalis* | **Brown Pelican** | | 158, 161, 166, 177, 181, 422, 826 |
| | | *carolinensis* | 158, 161 |
| | | *californicus* | 158, 161, 166, 422, 826 |
| | | *murphyi* | 177, 181 |
| *Pelecanus thagus* | **Peruvian (Brown) Pelican** | *thagus* | **157, 177** |
| **SULIDAE** | **GANNETS N BOOBIES** | | 161, 245 |
| *Sula (Morus) bassanus* | **Northern Gannet** | | **3, 752**, 765, 801 |
| *Morus capensis  VU* | **Cape Gannet** | | 257, 760, **777** |
| *Sula nebouxii* | **Blue-footed Booby** | | 158, 177, 181 |
| *Sula variegata* | **Peruvian Booby** | | **177,** 181 |
| *Sula dactylatra* | **Masked Booby** | | **181** |
| *Sula granti* | **Nazca Booby** | | 177 |
| *Sula sula* | **Red-footed Booby** | | 161, 177, **181** |
| *Sula leucogaster* | **Brown Booby** | | 158, 161, 177, 181 |
| **PHALACROCORACIDAE** | **CORMORANTS** | | 245, 412 |
| *Phalacrocorax auritus* | **Double-crested Cormorant** | | 206, 412, **418, 826** |
| *Phalacrocorax brasilianus (olivaceus)* | **Neotropic Cormorant** | *brasilianus* | 161, 166, 172, 181 |
| *Phalacrocorax carbo* | **Great Cormorant** | | 218, 266, 277, 366, 432, 476, 478, 484, 487, 496, 569, 574, 705, 721, 760, 765, 868 |
| | | *carbo,* NW Europe | 476, 705, 765 |
| | | *sinensis,* N, C Europe | 478, 484, 487 |
| | | *sinensis,* Black Sea, Mediterranean | 366, 496 |
| | | *sinensis,* SW Asia (non-bre) | 266, 277, 868 |
| | | *sinensis,* E, SE Asia (non-bre) | 432 |

| Species | English name | Subspecies/population | |
|---------|--------------|------------------------|---|
| *Phalacrocorax carbo* | **"White-breasted Cormorant"** | *lucidus,* C & E Africa | 218, 721 |
| | | *lucidus,* Coastal W Africa | 218, 725 |
| | | *lucidus,* S Africa | 218 |
| *Phalacrocorax capensis  NT* | **Cape Cormorant** | Southern Africa | 412, 760 |
| *Phalacrocorax nigrogularis  VU* | **Socotra Cormorant** | | 332, 735, 760 |
| | | Arabian coast | 332, 735, 760 |
| | | Gulf of Aden | 760 |
| *Phalacrocorax neglectus  EN* | **Bank Cormorant** | SW Africa | 760 |
| *Phalacrocorax penicillatus* | **Brandt's Cormorant** | W North America | 158, |
| *Phalacrocorax aristotelis* | **European Shag** | | 765 |
| | | *aristotelis* | 765 |
| *Phalacrocorax magellanicus* | **Rock Shag** | | 602 |
| | | S South America | 602 |
| *Phalacrocorax bougainvillii  NT* | **Guanay Cormorant** | | 181 |
| | | Peru, Chile | 181 |
| *Phalacrocorax africanus* | **Long-tailed Cormorant, Reed Cormorant** | | 257, 374, 457 |
| | | *africanus,* S, E Africa | 457 |
| | | *pictilis* | 374 |
| *Phalacrocorax coronatus  NT* | **Crowned Cormorant** | SW Africa | 412, 760 |
| *Phalacrocorax niger* | **Little Cormorant** | | 432 |
| *Phalacrocorax pygmeus* | **Pygmy Cormorant** | | 277, 283, 285, 366, 370, 372, 484, 496, 602, 690, 868 |
| | | SE Europe, Turkey | 366, 370, 484, 496, 602 |
| | | SW Asia (non-bre) | 277, 283, 285, 690, 868 |

| **ANHINGIDAE** | **DARTERS** | | **161, 245** |
|---------|--------------|------------------------|---|
| *Anhinga anhinga* | **Anhinga** | | 161 |
| | | *leucogaster* | 161 |
| *Anhinga rufa* | **African Darter** | | 245, 374, 725 |
| | | *rufa,* W Africa | 725 |
| | | *rufa,* S & E Africa | 245 |
| | | *vulsini* | 374 |

| **FALCONIDAE** | **FALCONS & CARACARAS** | | |
|---------|--------------|------------------------|---|
| *Falco naumanni  VU* | **Lesser Kestrel** | | 602, 690 |
| *Falco tinnunculus* | **Common Kestrel** | | 266 |
| *Falco sparverius* | **American Kestrel** | | 172 |
| *Falco eleonorae* | **Elenora's Falcon** | | 602 |
| *Falco columbarius* | **Merlin** | | 266 |
| *Falco subbuteo* | **Eurasian Hobby** | | 266 |
| *Falco biarmicus* | **Lanner Falcon** | | 602 |
| *Falco cherrug  EN* | **Saker Falcon** | | 432 |
| *Falco rusticolus* | **Gyrfalcon** | | 264, 602 |
| *Falco peregrinus* | **Peregrine** | | 356, 427, 432, 619, 833 |

| **ACCIPITRIDAE** | **OSPREY, KITES, HAWKS & EAGLES** | | **412** |
|---------|--------------|------------------------|---|
| *Pandion haliaetus* | **Osprey** | | 218, 264, 292, 356 |
| *Gampsonyx swainsonii* | **Pearl Kite** | | 166 |
| *Elanus leucurus* | **White-tailed Kite** | | 166 |
| *Milvus milvus  NT* | **Red Kite** | | 356, |
| *Milvus migrans* | **Black Kite** | | 264, 266, 374 |
| *Milvus aegyptius* | **Yellow-billed Kite** | | 721 |
| *Haliaeetus vocifer* | **African Fish Eagle** | | 245, 457 |
| *Haliaeetus vociferiodes  CR* | **Madagascar Fish Eagle** | | 374 |
| *Haliaeetus leucoryphus  VU* | **Pallas's Sea Eagle** | | 285, 292· |
| *Haliaeetus albicilla* | **White-tailed Eagle** | | 264, 266, 275, 277, 285, 356, 372, 484, 690 |

| Species | English name | Subspecies/population | |
|---|---|---|---|
| *Haliaeetus leucocephalus* | **Bald Eagle** | | 412, 602, 826 |
| *Haliaeetus fasciatus* | **Bald Eagle** | See *Haliaeetus leucocephalus* | |
| *Haliaeetus pelagicus VU* | **Steller's Sea Eagle** | | 690 |
| *Gypaetus barbatus* | **Bearded Vulture** | | 602 |
| *Aegypius monachus* | **Cinereous Vulture** | | 602 |
| *Circaetus gallicus* | **Short-toed Snake Eagle** | | 275 |
| *Circus aeruginosus* | **Marsh Harrier** | | 266, 520 |
| *Circus cyaneus* | **Hen Harrier** | | 266 |
| *Circus macrourus NT* | **Pallid Harrier** | | 266, 275, 457 |
| *Circus pygargus* | **Montagu's Harrier** | | 356 |
| *Accipiter gentilis* | **Northern Goshawk** | | 432, 602 |
| *Heterospizias meridionalis* | **Savannah Hawk** | | 166 |
| *Buteo buteo* | **Common Buzzard** | | 266, 432, 619 |
| *Aquila pomarina* | **Lesser Spotted Eagle** | | 356 |
| *Aquila marila VU* | **Greater Spotted Eagle** | See *Aquila clanga* | |
| *Aquila clanga VU* | **Greater Spotted Eagle** | | 264, 266, 356, 602, 690 |
| *Aquila rapax* | **Steppe Eagle** | | 275, 602 |
| *Aquila adalberti VU* | **Spanish Imperial Eagle** | | 602 |
| *Aquila heliaca VU* | **Imperial Eagle** | | 275, 690 |
| *Aquila chrysaetos* | **Golden Eagle** | | 264, 356 |
| **OTIDIDAE** | **BUSTARDS** | | |
| *Otis tarda VU* | **Great Bustard** | | 602, 690 |
| *Chlamydotis undulata VU* | **Houbara Bustard** | | 275, 294, 602 |
| *Tetrax tetrax NT* | **Little Bustard** | | 602, 690 |
| **EURYPYGIDAE** | **SUNBITTERN** | | 161 |
| *Eurypyga helias* | **Sunbittern** | | 161 |
| | | *major* | 161 |
| **RALLIDAE** | **RAILS, GALLINULES & COOTS** | | 161, 412 |
| *Coturnicops exquisitus VU* | **Swinhoe's Rail** | C & E Asia | 332, 690 |
| *Coturnicops noveboracensis* | **Yellow Rail** | | 206 |
| | | *noveboracensis* | 206 |
| *Laterallus jamaicensis NT* | **Black Rail** | | 172 |
| | | *jamaicensis* | 172 |
| *Gallirallus okinawae EN* | **Okinawa Rail** | Okinawa | 332 |
| *Rallus elegans* | **King Rail** | | 172 |
| | | *elegans* | 172 |
| *Rallus antarcticus VU* | **Austral Rail** | S South America | 189 |
| *Rallus aquaticus* | **Water Rail** | | 264, 368, 474, 487 |
| | | *aquaticus* | 264, 474, 487 |
| *Dryolimnas cuvieri* | **White-throated Rail** | | 374 |
| | | *cuvieri*, Madagascar | 350 |
| *Crex crex NT* | Corncrake | Sub-Saharan Africa (non-bre) | 13, 264, 266, 356, 372, 602, 690, 731 |
| *Aramidopsis plateni VU* | **Snoring Rail, Platen's Rail** | Sulawesi | 332 |
| *Gymnocrex rosenbergii VU* | **Bald-faced Rail, Bare-faced Rail, Blue-faced Rail** | Sulawesi & Peleng | 332 |
| *Gymnocrex talaudensis EN* | **Talaud Rail** | Talaud Is | 332 |
| *Amaurornis akool* | **Brown Crake** | | 432 |
| | | *coccineipes* | 432 |
| *Amaurornis flavirostra* | **Black Crake** | Sub-Saharan Africa | 255 |
| *Porzana parva* | **Little Crake** | | 368 |
| | | *parva* | 368 |
| *Porzana porzana* | **Spotted Crake** | | 356, 368, 474, 491 |
| | | Europe & W Asia (bre) | 356, 368, 474, 491 |

| Species | English name | Subspecies/population | |
|---------|--------------|----------------------|---|
| *Porzana carolina* | **Sora** | N America (bre) | 172 |
| *Pardirallus maculatus* | **Spotted Rail** | | 189 |
| | | *maculatus* | 189 |
| *Habroptila wallacii  VU* | **Invisible Rail** | Halmahera Is: N Moluccas | 332 |
| *Porphyrio porphyrio* | **Purple Swamphen** | | 368, 372, 432, 474, 602 |
| | | *porphyrio* | 602 |
| | | *caspius* | 368, 372 |
| *Porphyrio alleni* | **Allen's Gallinule** | Sub-Saharan Africa | 255 |
| *Porphyrio martinica* | **(American) Purple Gallinule** | N, C & N South America | 172 |
| *Gallinula chloropus* | **Common Moorhen, Common Gallinule** | | 172, 255, 366, 368, 374, 432, 439, 474, 476, 484, 784, 868 |
| | | *chloropus,* Europe, N Africa (bre) | 255, 218, 439, 474, 476, 484, 784 |
| | | *chloropus,* SW Asia (non-bre) | 366, 368, 868 |
| | | *pyrrhorrhoa* | 374 |
| | | *cachinnans* | 172 |
| *Gallinula angulata* | **Lesser Moorhen** | Sub-Saharan Africa | 218, 255 |
| *Fulica cristata* | **Red-knobbed Coot, Crested Coot** | | 602 |
| | | Morocco, Spain | 602 |
| *Fulica atra* | **Common Coot, Eurasian Coot** | | 218, 264, 266, 277, 303, 354, 366, 368, 372, 432, 474, 484, 496, 520, **582**, 705, 784, 862, 868 |
| | | *atra,* NW Europe (non-bre) | 354, 474, 484, 520, 705, 784, 862 |
| | | *atra,* Black Sea, Mediterranean (non-bre) | 366, 496 |
| | | *atra,* SW Asia (non-bre) | 264, 266, 277, 368, 372, 868 |
| | | *atra,* South Asia (non-bre) | 303, 582 |
| *Fulica alai  VU* | **Hawaiian Coot** | Hawaii | 422 |
| *Fulica americana* | **American Coot** | | 172, 412, **439** |
| **HELIORNITHIDAE** | **FINFOOTS** | | **161, 245** |
| *Podica senegalensis* | **African Finfoot** | | 245 |
| | | *senegalensis* | 245 |
| *Heliopais personatus  VU* | **Masked Finfoot** | S, SE Asia | 308, 332 |
| *Heliornis fulica* | **Sungrebe** | C America, N South America | 161 |
| **GRUIDAE** | **CRANES** | | **161, 245, 257, 412** |
| *Balearica pavonina  NT* | **Black Crowned Crane** | | 218, 453, **608** |
| | | *pavonina* | **608** |
| | | *ceciliae* | 608 |
| *Grus virgo* | **Demoiselle Crane** | | 266, **302**, 303 |
| | | W Central Asia (bre) | 266, 302, 303 |
| *Grus paradisea  VU* | **Blue Crane** | | 257 |
| | | South Africa | 257 |
| *Grus carunculatus  VU* | **Wattled Crane** | | 218, 613 |
| | | C-S Africa | 613, |
| *Grus leucogeranus  CR* | **Siberian Crane** | | 81, **269**, **287**, 292, **294**, **311**, **320**, 332, 368, 635, 672, 690, 697, **831**, 885 |
| | | Western | 690, 697 |
| | | Central | 690 |
| | | Eastern | 690 |
| *Grus canadensis* | **Sandhill Crane** | | 209, 412, 448 |
| | | *canadensis* | 412, 448 |
| | | *tabida* | 209, 448 |

| Species | English name | Subspecies/population | |
|---|---|---|---|
| *Grus antigone* VU | **Sarus Crane** | | 292, 308, 309, 332 |
| | | *antigone* | 292, 308, 309, 332 |
| | | *sharpii,* Indochina | 332 |
| | | *sharpii,* Myanmar | 332 |
| *Grus vipio* VU | **White-naped Crane** | | 320, 332, 690 |
| | | China (non-bre) | 320, 332, 690 |
| | | Korea, Japan (non-bre) | 320, 332 |
| *Grus grus* | **Common Crane, Eurasian Crane** | | 16, 264, 266, 277, 283, 302, 356, **883** |
| | | *grus,* NW Europe (bre) | 356 |
| | | *grus,* SW Asia, NE Africa (non-bre) | 277, 283 |
| | | *(lilfordi),* India (non-bre) | 302, |
| *Grus monacha* VU | **Hooded Crane** | | 320, 332, 690 |
| | | C China (non-bre) | 690 |
| *Grus americana* EN | **Whooping Crane** | | 206, 412, 635 |
| | | W C Canada (bre) | 206 |
| *Grus nigricollis* VU | **Black-necked Crane** | C & S Asia | 311, 332 |
| *Grus japonensis* EN | **Red-crowned Crane** | | 320, 332, 690 |
| | | E China (non-bre) | 690 |

| | | | |
|---|---|---|---|
| **BURHINIDAE** | **THICK-KNEES** | | 245, 643 |
| **HAEMATOPODIDAE** | **OYSTERCATCHERS** | | 161, 207, 245, 328, 643 |
| *Haematopus leucopodus* | **Magellanic Oystercatcher** | | 188 |
| | | S South America | 188 |
| *Haematopus ater* | **Blackish Oystercatcher** | | 188 |
| | | S South America | 188 |
| *Haematopus palliatus* | **American Oystercatcher** | | 188, 701 |
| | | *palliatus* | 701 |
| | | *(pitanay)* | 188 |
| *Haematopus moquini* NT | **African Black Oystercatcher** | SE Africa | 257, 668 |
| *Haematopus ostralegus* | **Eurasian Oystercatcher** | | 63, 88, 140, 264, 266, 296, 316, 319, 356, 364, 368, 398, 432, 476, 488, 569, 663, 705, 805, 806 |
| | | *ostralegus* | 140, 356, 398, 476, 488, 705, 805, 806 |
| | | *longipes* | 368 |
| | | *osculans* | 316, 319, 663 |

| | | | |
|---|---|---|---|
| **DROMADIDAE** | **CRAB PLOVER** | | 245, 643 |
| *Dromas ardeola* | **Crab Plover** | NW Indian Ocean | 245, **257**, 296, 374, 735 |

| | | | |
|---|---|---|---|
| **IBIDORHYNCHIDAE** | **IBISBILL** | | 643 |
| *Ibidorhyncha struthersii* | **Ibisbill** | Central Asia | 643 |

| | | | |
|---|---|---|---|
| **RECURVIROSTRIDAE** | **STILTS & AVOCETS** | | 161, 245, 643 |
| *Himantopus himantopus* | **Black-winged Stilt** | | 266, 287, 296, 305, 324, 366, 368, 374, 432, 663, 721 |
| | | *himantopus,* Sub-Saharan Africa | 721 |
| | | *himantopus,* Madagascar | 374 |
| | | *himantopus,* Central & E Europe, E Mediterranean (bre) | 366 |
| | | *himantopus,* SW Asia (non-bre) | 266, 287, 368 |
| | | *himantopus,* S Asia | 296, 305 |
| | | *himantopus,* E & SE Asia | 324, 663 |
| *Himantopus mexicanus* | **Black-necked Stilt** | | 172, 422 |
| | **"Hawaiian Stilt"** | *knudseni* | 422 |

| Species | English name | Subspecies/population | |
|---|---|---|---|
| *Recurvirostra avosetta* | **Pied Avocet** | | 140, 266, 287, 296, 275, 319, 356, 364, 366, 368, 432, 663, 705, 721, **729** |
| | | E Africa | 721 |
| | | W Europe (bre) | 140, 356, 705, 729 |
| | | Mediterranean & SE Europe (bre) | 366 |
| | | W, SW Asia & Eastern Africa | 287, 368 |
| | | Central & S Asia | 296, 275 |
| | | E Asia | 319, 663 |
| *Recurvirostra americana* | **American Avocet** | N & C America | 158, 172, **209** |
| CHARADRIIDAE | PLOVERS | | 161, 207, 245, 257, 316, 328, 376, 512, 643 |
| *Vanellus vanellus* | **Northern Lapwing** | | 63, 74, 98, 140, 266, 277, **285**, 354, 364, 366, 368, 398, 487, 582, 663, 705, 868 |
| | | Europe (bre) | 140, 354, 364, 398, 487, 705 |
| | | W Asia (bre) | 277, 366, 368, 868 |
| | | E, SE Asia (non-bre) | 663 |
| *Vanellus crassirostris* | **Long-toed Lapwing** | | **453**, 457 |
| | | *crassirostris*, E & C Africa | **453**, 457 |
| *Vanellus armatus* | **Blacksmith Lapwing** | S & E Africa | 239, 257 |
| *Vanellus spinosus* | **Spur-winged Lapwing** | | 218, 366 |
| | | Africa | 218 |
| | | SE Europe, Asia Minor | 366 |
| *Vanellus duvaucelli* | **River Lapwing** | S & SE Asia | 432 |
| *Vanellus malabaricus* | **Yellow-wattled Lapwing** | South Asia | 305 |
| *Vanellus lugubris* | **Lesser Black-winged Lapwing, Senegal Plover** | | 218 |
| *Vanellus coronatus* | **Crowned Lapwing** | | 218 |
| *Vanellus cinereus* | **Grey-headed Lapwing** | E, SE & S Asia | 305, 663, 690 |
| *Vanellus indicus* | **Red-wattled Lapwing** | | 264 |
| | | *indicus* | 305 |
| *Vanellus macropterus* CR | **Javanese Wattled Lapwing, Sunda Lapwing** | Java | 332 |
| *Vanellus gregarius* CR | **Sociable Lapwing** | | **29**, **88**, 269, 292, 332, 643, 690, 731 |
| | | SW Asia & NE Africa (non-bre) | 731 |
| *Vanellus chilensis* | **Southern Lapwing** | | 166 |
| | | *cayennensis* | 166 |
| *Pluvialis apricaria* | **Eurasian Golden Plover** | | 74, 140, 305, 356, 364, 368, 374, 398, 500, **675**, 705, 784 |
| | | *apricaria* | **675**, 705, 784 |
| | | *altifrons*, Iceland & Faeroes (bre) | 705, 784 |
| | | *altifrons*, N-Central Siberia (bre) | 500 |
| *Pluvialis fulva* | **Pacific Golden Plover** | | 305, 316, 324, 339, 343, 374, 535 |
| | | SW & S Asia, E Africa (non-bre) | 305, 374 |
| | | E, SE Asia Australia & Oceania (non-bre) | 316, 324, 339, 343 |
| *Pluvialis dominica* | **American Golden Plover** | Americas | 186, 189, 535, 682 |
| *Pluvialis squatarola* | **Grey Plover, Black-bellied Plover** | | 140, 166, 172, 296, 305, 316, 364, 368, 374, **376**, 663, 668, 675, 705 |
| | | *squatarola*, E Atlantic (non-bre) | 140, 364, 675, 705 |
| | | *squatarola*, SW Asia, E & S Africa (non-bre) | 368, 374 |
| | | *squatarola*, S Asia (non-bre) | 296, 305 |
| | | *squatarola*, E, SE Asia & Australia (non-bre) | 316, 663 |
| | | *squatarola*, Alaska (bre) | 172 |

| Species | English name | Subspecies/population | |
|---|---|---|---|
| *Charadrius hiaticula* | **Great Ringed Plover** | | 140, 316, 354, 364, 368, 374, 398, **705** |
| | | *hiaticula* | 705 |
| | | *tundrae* | 705 |
| *Charadrius semipalmatus* | **Semipalmated Plover** | Americas | **166**, 172, 181, 701 |
| *Charadrius placidus* | **Long-billed Plover** | E, SE & S Asia | 305, 643, 663, 690 |
| *Charadrius dubius* | **Little Ringed Plover** | | 266, 305, 324, 368, 398, 663 |
| | | *curonicus,* W, Central Europe, NW Africa (bre) | 398 |
| | | *curonicus,* E Europe, W Asia (bre) | 266, 368 |
| | | *curonicus,* C & E Asia | 324, 663 |
| | | *jerdoni* | 305 |
| *Charadrius wilsonia* | **Wilson's Plover** | | 166, 172, 181 |
| | | *wilsonia* | 166, 172, 181 |
| *Charadrius vociferus* | **Killdeer** | | 172 |
| | | *vociferous* | 172 |
| *Charadrius melodus* NT | **Piping Plover** | | 701 |
| *Charadrius thoracicus* VU | **Black-banded Plover, Madagascar Plover** | Madagascar | 250, 374 |
| *Charadrius pecuarius* | **Kittlitz's Plover** | | 218, 250, 374 |
| | | *pecuarius,* E, C & S Africa | 218 |
| | | *pecuarius,* Madagascar | 250, 374 |
| *Charadrius tricollaris* | **Three-banded Plover** | | 250, 374 |
| | | *tricollaris,* E & S Africa | 250 |
| | | *bifrontatus* | 374 |
| *Charadrius marginatus* | **White-fronted Plover** | | 250, 374 |
| | | *tenellus* | 250 |
| | | *mechowi,* Coastal E Africa | 374 |
| *Charadrius alexandrinus* | **Kentish Plover, Snowy Plover** | | 40, 287, 305, 319, 324, 364, 366, 368, 663 |
| | | *alexandrinus,* E Atlantic, W Mediterranean | 40, 364 |
| | | *alexandrinus,* Black Sea, E Mediterranean (bre) | 364, 366 |
| | | *alexandrinus,* SW Asia (bre) | 287, 305, 324, 368, 663 |
| | | *dealbatus* | 319 |
| *Charadrius pallidus* | **Chestnut-banded Plover** | | 218, 239 |
| | | *pallidus* | 218 |
| | | *venustus* | 239 |
| *Charadrius collaris* | **Collared Plover** | | 188 |
| | | *gracilis* | 188 |
| *Charadrius falklandicus* | **Two-banded Plover, Double-banded Plover** | | 188 |
| | | S South America | 188 |
| *Charadrius mongolus* | **Lesser Sandplover, Mongolian Plover** | | 296, 305, 311, 316, 339, 343, 374, 663 |
| | | *mongolus* | 316, 663 |
| | | *pamirensis* | 374 |
| | | *atrifrons* | 296, 305, 311, 343 |
| | | *stegmanni* | 663 |
| *Charadrius leschenaultii* | **Greater Sandplover** | | 287, 296, 368, 374 |
| | | *leschenaultii,* South Asia (non-bre) | 368, 287, 296 |
| | | *leschenaultii,* E Africa (non-bre) | 374 |
| *Charadrius asiaticus* | **Caspian Plover** | Central Asia (bre) | 218, 574 |
| *Charadrius veredus* | **Oriental Plover** | Central Asia (bre) | 663 |
| *Charadrius montanus* VU | **Mountain Plover** | N America | 668 |
| *Charadrius modestus* | **Rufous-chested Dotterel** | | 188, 189 |
| | | S South America | 188, 189 |
| *Anarhynchus frontalis* VU | **Wrybill** | New Zealand | **876** |

| Species | English name | Subspecies/population | |
|---|---|---|---|
| **ROSTRATULIDAE** | **PAINTED-SNIPES** | | 245, 643 |
| *Rostratula benghalensis* | **Greater Painted-Snipe** | | 245, 305, 324 |
| | | Africa | 245 |
| | | Asia | 264, 324 |
| | | | |
| **JACANIDAE** | **JACANAS** | | 245, 643 |
| *Actophilornis africanus* | **African Jacana** | Sub-Saharan Africa | 457, 721 |
| *Jacana jacana* | **Wattled Jacana** | | 166 |
| | | *hypomelaena* | 166 |
| | | | |
| **PEDIONOMIDAE** | **PLAINS-WANDERER** | | 643 |
| **THINOCORIDAE** | **SEEDSNIPES** | | 643 |
| **SCOLOPACIDAE** | **SNIPES, SANDPIPERS & PHALAROPES** | | 161, 207, 245, 316, 328, 643 |
| *Scolopax rusticola* | **Eurasian Woodcock** | | 368, 432, 457, 574, 582, 784, 854, 874 |
| | | Europe (bre) | 457, 582, 784, 854, 874 |
| | | W Asia (bre) | 368, 582 |
| *Scolopax mira* VU | **Ryukyu Woodcock, Amami Woodcock** | Ryuku Is | 332 |
| *Scolopax rochussenii* EN | **Moluccan Woodcock** | N Moluccas | 332 |
| *Scolopax minor* | **American Woodcock** | | 701 |
| *Lymnocryptes minimus* | **Jack Snipe** | | 305, 364, 368, 398, 487, 854, 866, 874 |
| | | Europe (bre) | 368, 398, 487, 854, 866, 874 |
| | | W Siberia (bre) | 305 |
| *Gallinago solitaria* | **Solitary Snipe** | | 368 |
| | | *solitaria* | 368 |
| *Gallinago nemoricola* VU | **Wood Snipe** | S & SE Asia | 332 |
| *Gallinago stenura* | **Pintail Snipe** | | 305 |
| | | S, SW Asia, E Africa (non-bre) | 305 |
| *Gallinago nigripennis* | **African Snipe** | | 218 |
| | | *aequatoralis* | 218 |
| *Gallinago media* NT | **Great Snipe** | | 356, 368, 457, 690 |
| | | Scandinavia (bre) | 356 |
| | | W Siberia, NE Europe (bre) | 368, 690 |
| *Gallinago gallinago* | **Common Snipe** | | **63**, 172, 305, 316, 324, 354, **355**, 364, 368, 432, 484, 487, 505, 520, **522**, 784, 854, 866 |
| | | *gallinago*, Europe (bre) | 354, 355, 484, 487, 520, 522, 784, 854, 866 |
| | | *gallinago*, W Siberia (bre) | 368 |
| | | *gallinago*, S Asia (non-bre) | 305 |
| | | *gallinago*, E & SE Asia (non-bre) | 316, 324, 432 |
| | | *faeroeensis* | **63**, 522, 784 |
| *Limnodromus griseus* | **Short-billed Dowitcher** | | **172**, 701 |
| | | *griseus* | 177, 701 |
| | | *hendersoni* | 177, 701 |
| | | *caurinus* | 701 |
| *Limnodromus scolopaceus* | **Long-billed Dowitcher** | N & C America (non-bre) | 166, 172, 316 |
| *Limnodromus semipalmatus* NT | **Asian Dowitcher** | C & E Asia (bre) | 296, 305, 319, 663, 690 |
| *Limosa limosa* NT | **Black-tailed Godwit** | | 28, 218, 266, 296, 305, 316, 364, 368, 432, 643, 663, 705 |
| | | *limosa*, W Europe (bre) | 28, 364, 643 |
| | | *limosa*, W Asia (bre) | 368 |
| | | *limosa*, S Asia (non-bre) | 296, 305 |
| | | *melanuroides* | 663 |
| | | *islandica* | 705 |

| Species | English name | Subspecies/population | |
|---------|--------------|----------------------|---|
| *Limosa haemastica* | **Hudsonian Godwit** | | 189, 524, 701 |
| | | Alaska (bre) | 524 |
| *Limosa lapponica* | **Bar-tailed Godwit** | | 74, 140, 296, 305, 316, 319, 328, 345, 364, 368, 376, 432, 505, **524**, 675, 705, 717 |
| | | *lapponica* | 140, 364, 675, 705 |
| | | *taymyrensis,* W, SW Africa (non-bre) | 140, 524 |
| | | *taymyrensis,* E Africa, SW, S Asia (non-bre) | 296, 305 |
| | | *menzbieri* & *(anadyrensis)* | 140, 524, 663, 717 |
| | | *baueri* | 524 |
| *Limosa fedoa* | **Marbled Godwit** | | **158**, 166, 711 |
| | | *fedoa,* SC Canada & NC USA (bre) | 711 |
| *Numenius minutus* | **Little Curlew** | N Siberia (bre) | **346**, 663 |
| *Numenius borealis* CR | **Eskimo Curlew** | N Canada (bre) | 207, 346, 316, 364, 368, 643 |
| *Numenius phaeopus* | **Whimbrel** | | 166, 181, 188, 305, 343, **363**, 374, 376, 398, 432, 500, 663, **682**, 717, 854 |
| | | *phaeopus,* NE Europe (bre) | 363, 364, 500, 854 |
| | | *phaeopus,* W Siberia (bre) | 368 |
| | | *islandicus* | 398 |
| | | *variegatus,* S Asia (non-bre) | **363**, 305, 717 |
| | | *variegatus,* E & SE Asia (non-bre) | 316, 339, 343, 663 |
| | | *hudsonicus* | 181, **682** |
| *Numenius tahitiensis* VU | **Bristle-thighed Curlew** | W Alaska (bre) | 127, 332 |
| *Numenius tenuirostris* CR | **Slender-billed Curlew** | Mediterranean basin (non-bre) | 127, 269, 332, **602**, 643, 690, 885 |
| *Numenius arquata* | **Eurasian Curlew** | | 140, 266, 296, 305, 319, 356, 364, 368, 398, 432, 663, 705, 805, 854 |
| | | *arquata* | 140, 356, 364, 398, 705, 854 |
| | | *orientalis,* SW Asia, E Africa (non-bre) | 368 |
| | | *orientalis,* S Asia (non-bre) | 305 |
| | | *orientalis,* E & SE Asia (non-bre) | 319, 663 |
| *Numenius madagascariensis* | **Far Eastern Curlew, Australian Curlew** | C & E Asia (bre) | 127, 316, 319, 328, 663, 690, 717 |
| *Numenius americanus* NT | **Long-billed Curlew** | | **701** |
| *Bartramia longicauda* | **Upland Sandpiper** | Americas | 166 |
| *Tringa erythropus* | **Spotted Redshank** | | 140, 296, 305, 316, 319, 332, 364, 368, 432, 500, 663 |
| | | Europe (bre) | 140, 364, 500 |
| | | W Siberia (bre) | 368 |
| | | S Asia (non-bre) | 296, 305 |
| | | E, SE Asia (non-bre) | 316, 663 |
| *Tringa totanus* | **Common Redshank** | | 40, 63, 140, 305, 339, 343, 364, 366, 368, 398, 432, 476, 535, 663, 705, 805 |
| | | *totanus,* E Atlantic (non-bre) | 40, 140, 364, 398, 476, 705 |
| | | *totanus,* E Europe (bre) | 366 |
| | | *ussuriensis,* SW Asia & E Africa (non-bre) | 368 |
| | | *ussuriensis,* S & SE Asia (non-bre) | 305, 339, 343, 663 |
| | | *robusta* | 506 |
| | | *britannica* | 476, 535, 705 |
| *Tringa stagnatilis* | **Marsh Sandpiper** | | 305, 339, 343, 345, 368, 663 |
| | | C & NE Europe (bre) | 305, 339, 345 |
| | | SE Europe & W Asia (bre) | 368 |
| | | S Asia (non-bre) | 305 |
| | | E, SE Asia, Oceania (non-bre) | 339, 343, 663 |

| Species | English name | Subspecies/population | |
|---------|-------------|----------------------|---|
| *Tringa nebularia* | **Common Greenshank** | | 140, 305, 316, 319, 324, 339, 343, 364, 366, 368, 374, 500, **675**, 717 |
| | | NW Europe (bre) | 140, 364, 500, **675** |
| | | NE Europe, W Asia (bre) | 366, 368 |
| | | South Asia (non-bre) | 305 |
| | | E, SE Asia, Australia (non-bre) | 316, 324, 339, 343, 717 |
| *Tringa guttifer*  EN | **Nordmann's Greenshank, Spotted Greenshank** | NE Asia (bre) | 81, 296, 305, 319, 332, 663 |
| *Tringa melanoleuca* | **Greater Yellowlegs** | Americas | 166 |
| *Tringa flavipes* | **Lesser Yellowlegs** | Americas | 166, 157 |
| *Tringa ochropus* | **Green Sandpiper** | | 305, 364, 432, 476, 484, 487 |
| | | Europe (bre) | 364, 476, 484, 487 |
| | | South Asia (non-bre) | 305 |
| *Tringa glareola* | **Wood Sandpiper** | | 257, 305, 316, 368, 500 |
| | | NW Europe (bre) | 500 |
| | | NE Europe, W Siberia (bre) | 368 |
| | | South Asia (non-bre) | 305 |
| | | E, SE Asia & Australia (non-bre) | 316 |
| *Xenus cinereus* | **Terek Sandpiper** | | 305, 316, 368, 374, 663 |
| | | SW Asia, E Africa (non-bre) | 368, 374 |
| | | India (non-bre) | 305 |
| | | E, SE Asia & Australia (non-bre) | 316, 663 |
| *Actitis hypoleucos* | **Common Sandpiper** | | **305**, 316, 364, 368, 374, 398 |
| | | N, W & C Europe (bre) | 364, 374, 398 |
| | | E Europe, W Asia (bre) | 368 |
| | | South Asia (non-bre) | 305 |
| | | E & SE Asia to Oceania (non-bre) | 316 |
| *Actitis macularius* | **Spotted Sandpiper** | | 181 |
| | | W North America (bre) | 181 |
| *Heteroscelus brevipes* | **Grey-tailed Tattler** | C & E Siberia (bre) | 316, 663, 717 |
| *Heteroscelus incana* | **Wandering Tattler** | N North America (bre) | 316, 701 |
| *Catoptrophorus semipalmatus* | **Willet** | | 166, **668** |
| *Prosobonia cancellata*  EN | **Tuamotu Sandpiper** | Tuamotu Archipelago | 643 |
| *Arenaria interpres* | **Ruddy Turnstone** | | 131, 140, 166, 172, **181**, 188, 266, **296**, 305, 316, 364, 368, 374, 376, 398, 432, 551, 590, 663, 705 |
| | | *interpres,* NE Canada, Greenland (bre) | 140, 364, 398, 551, 705 |
| | | *interpres,* SW Asia, E & S Africa (non-bre) | 368, 374, 376, 590 |
| | | *interpres,* South Asia (non-bre) | 296, 305 |
| | | *interpres,* Pacific & SE Asia (non-bre) | 166, 172, 316, 663 |
| | | *morinella* | 181, 188 |
| *Arenaria melanocephala* | **Black Turnstone** | Alaska (bre) | 172 |
| *Aphriza virgata* | **Surfbird** | Alaska, Yukon (bre) | 188, 701 |
| *Calidris tenuirostris* | **Great Knot** | | 296, 305, 316, 319, 328, 345, 524, 663 |
| | | SW & W S Asia (non-bre) | 296, 305 |
| | | SE Asia, Australia (non-bre) | 316, 345, 524, 663 |
| *Calidris canutus* | **Red Knot** | | 40, 63, **74**, 140, 166, 189, **207**, 296, 305, 316, 345, 364, 376, 432, 505, 524, **535**, 574, 643, 663, 668, 675, 705, 806 |
| | | *canutus* | 40, 74, 140, 376, 806 |
| | | *rogersi* | 74, 316, 345, 663 |
| | | *piersmai* | 74, 140 |
| | | *roselaari* | 74 |
| | | *islandica* | 74, 140, 364, 705, 806 |
| | | *rufa* | 40, **74**, 189, **207**, 505, **535**, 643, 668, 675 |

| Species | English name | Subspecies/population | |
|---------|--------------|-----------------------|---|
| *Calidris alba* | **Sanderling** | | 40, 140, 188, 296, 296, 316, 319, 364, 368, 374, 376, 432, **574**, 663, 682, 705 |
| | | E Atlantic (non-bre) | 40, 140, 364, 376, 574, 705 |
| | | SW Asia, E & S Africa (non-bre) | 368, 374 |
| | | S Asia (non-bre) | 296 |
| | | E & SE Asia, Australia, New Zealand (non-bre) | 316, 663 |
| | | N & S America (non-bre) | 188 |
| *Calidris pusilla* | **Semipalmated Sandpiper** | | 172, 881 |
| | | E North Canada (bre) | 881 |
| *Calidris mauri* | **Western Sandpiper** | Alaska, Chukotskiy (bre) | 107, 158, 166, 172, 181, 545, 832 |
| *Calidris ruficollis* | **Red-necked Stint** | NE Siberia (bre) | 131, 147, **316**, 432, 663 |
| *Calidris minuta* | **Little Stint** | | 218, 296, 305, 316, 364, 366, 368, 721 |
| | | Europe & West Africa (non-bre) | 364 |
| | | SW Asia, E & S Africa (non-bre) | 366, 368 |
| | | South Asia (non-bre) | 296, 305 |
| *Calidris temminckii* | **Temminck's Stint** | | 305, 316, 432 |
| | | SW Asia, E Africa (non-bre) | 305, 316 |
| *Calidris subminuta* | **Long-toed Stint** | Siberia (bre) | 316 |
| *Calidris minutilla* | **Least Sandpiper** | N North America (bre) | 158, 166, 172, 881 |
| *Calidris fuscicollis* | **White-rumped Sandpiper** | N North America (bre) | **186,** 189 |
| *Calidris bairdii* | **Baird's Sandpiper** | E Siberia, N North America (bre) | 188 |
| *Calidris melanotos* | **Pectoral Sandpiper** | E Siberia, N North America (bre) | 166 |
| *Calidris acuminata* | **Sharp-tailed Sandpiper** | C & E Siberia (bre) | 131, 316, 432, 663 |
| *Calidris ferruginea* | **Curlew Sandpiper** | | 131, 138, 140, 296, 305, 319, 328, 339, 343, 368, 374, 376, 432, 564, 663 |
| | | W Africa (non-bre) | 140 |
| | | E & S Africa (non-bre) | 138, 368, 374, 376, 564 |
| | | South Asia (non-bre) | 296, 305, 319, 339 |
| | | E, SE Asia & Australia (non-bre) | 328, 343, 432, 663 |
| *Calidris himantopus* | **Stilt Sandpiper** | N North America (bre) | 172 |
| *Calidris maritima* | **Purple Sandpiper** | | 364, 668 |
| | | *maritima,* E Atlantic (non-bre) | 364, 668 |
| *Calidris alpina* | **Dunlin** | | 28, 63, 81, 140, 147, 305, 316, 324, 328, 354, 356, 364, 368, 374, 398, 432, 488, 524, **535**, 541, 564, 663, **668, 675**, 705, 805 |
| | | *alpina* | 140, 541, 675, 705 |
| | | *centralis,* South Asia (non-bre) | 305 |
| | | *centralis,* SW Asia, NE Africa, E Mediterranean (non-bre) | 140, 368 |
| | | *schinzii,* Iceland (bre) | 140, 541, 705 |
| | | *schinzii,* Baltic (bre) | 140, 541 |
| | | *schinzii,* Britain & Ireland (bre) | 140, 541, **675** |
| | | *arctica* | 140, 541 |
| | | *sakhalina* | 663 |
| | | *actites* | 663 |
| | | *kistchinskii* | 663 |
| *Eurynorhynchus pygmeus EN* | **Spoon-billed Sandpiper** | E Siberia (bre) | 81, 128, 127, **147**, 296, 305, 316, 328, 332, **501, 641**, 643, 663 |
| *Limicola falcinellus* | **Broad-billed Sandpiper** | | 305, 368, 663 |
| | | *falcinellus* | 305, 368 |
| | | *sibirica* | 663 |

| Species | English name | Subspecies/population | |
|---|---|---|---|
| *Tryngites subruficollis  NT* | **Buff-breasted Sandpiper** | E Siberia, N North America (bre) | 127, 166, 189, 682 |
| *Philomachus pugnax* | **Ruff** | | **74**, 264, 266, 296, 305, 316, 354, 364, 366, 368, 432, 705, 721 |
| | | W Africa (non-bre) | 354, 364, 705 |
| | | E & S Africa (non-bre) | 366, 368, 721 |
| | | S Asia (non-bre) | 305, 316 |
| *Steganopus (Phalaropus) tricolor* | **Wilson's Phalarope** | North America (bre) | 158 |
| *Phalaropus lobatus* | **Red-necked Phalarope, Northern Phalarope** | | 158, 316, 368, 663, 701, 760 |
| | | NW Eurasia (bre) | 154, 368, 760 |
| | | North America (bre) | 158, 701 |
| | | NE Asia (bre) | 663 |
| *Phalaropus fulicarius* | **Grey Phalarope, Red Phalarope** | | 154, 316, 760 |
| | | Canada, Greenland, Iceland (bre) | 154, 316, 760 |
| | | Alaska, North Siberia (bre) | 316 |
| **GLAREOLIDAE** | **COURSERS & PRATINCOLES** | | 245, 643 |
| *Cursorius cursor* | **Cream-coloured Courser** | | 602 |
| | | *bogulubovi* | 602 |
| *Rhinoptilus bitorquatus  CR* | **Jerdon's Courser** | SE India | 332 |
| *Glareola pratincola* | **Collared Pratincole** | | 257, 303, 368 |
| | | *pratincola*, SW Asia (bre) | 303, 368 |
| *Glareola maldivarum* | **Oriental Pratincole** | | 319, 328, 663 |
| | | South Asia | 319, 328 |
| | | E-SE Asia, Australia | 663 |
| *Glareola nordmanni  NT* | **Black-winged Pratincole** | E Europe - Central Asia | 266, 275, 368, **600**, 643, 690 |
| *Glareola ocularis  VU* | **Madagascar Pratincole** | Madagascar | 218 |
| *Glareola lactea* | **Small Pratincole** | S & SE Asia | 305 |
| **LARIDAE** | **GULLS** | | 161, 245, 257, 765 |
| *Larus atlanticus  VU* | **Olrog's Gull** | SE South America | **186**, 189 |
| *Larus heermanni  NT* | **Heermann's Gull** | Pacific N & C America | 158, 206 |
| *Larus leucophthalmus  NT* | **White-eyed Gull** | Red Sea | 760 |
| *Larus hemprichii* | **Sooty Gull** | NW Indian Ocean, Red Sea | 735, 760 |
| *Larus canus* | **Common Gull, Mew Gull** | | 266, 368, 484, 569, 765, 854 |
| | | *canus* | 569, 765, 854 |
| | | *heinei* | 266, 368, 569 |
| *Larus audouinii  NT* | **Audouin's Gull** | Mediterranean (bre) | 602, 760 |
| *Larus delawarensis* | **Ring-billed Gull** | North America (bre) | 158, 206, 418 |
| *Larus marinus* | **Great Black-backed Gull** | | 765, 801, 854 |
| | | NW Atlantic | 765, 801, 854 |
| *Larus dominicanus* | **Kelp Gull** | | 760 |
| | | *vetula* | 760 |
| | | *melisandae* | 760 |
| *Larus occidentalis* | **Western Gull** | | 158 |
| *Larus thayeri* | **Thayer's Gull** | N Canada (bre) | 206 |
| *Larus argentatus* | **Herring Gull** | | 172, 206, 264, 368, 432, 484, 553, 569, 765, 801, 854 |
| | | *argentatus* | 484, 487, 801, 889 |
| | | *argenteus* | 765 |
| | | *mongolicus* | 264, 368 |
| | | *smithsonianus* | 172, 206 |
| *Larus heuglini* | **Heuglin's Gull** | | 760 |
| *Larus armenicus* | **Armenian Gull** | SE Europe, SW Asia | 731, 760 |
| *Larus cachinnans* | **Yellow-legged Gull** | | 266, 484, 553, 760 |
| | | *michahellis* | 484, 487 |
| | **Caspian Gull** | *cachinnans* | 266 |

| Species | English name | Subspecies/population | |
|---------|-------------|----------------------|---|
| *Larus fuscus* | **Lesser Black-backed Gull** | | 368, 760, 765, 854 |
| | | *fuscus* | 368, 760, 854 |
| | | *graellsii* | 760, 765 |
| *Larus ichthyaetus* | **Great Black-headed Gull, Pallas's Gull** | | 368, **432**, 520, 760 |
| | | E Europe, W Asia (bre) | 368, 520 |
| | | Central Asia (bre) | **432** |
| *Larus brunnicephalus* | **Brown-headed Gull** | Central Asia (bre) | 311, **432** |
| *Larus cirrocephalus* | **Grey-headed Gull** | | 218, 255, 457, 760 |
| | | *poiocephalus*, West Africa | 218, 737 |
| | | *poiocephalus*, C & E Africa | 218, 255, 457, 760 |
| | | *poiocephalus*, Coastal S Africa | 218, 760 |
| | | *poiocephalus*, Madagascar | 760 |
| *Larus hartlaubii* | **Hartlaub's Gull** | Southern Africa | 257, 760 |
| *Larus ridibundus* | **Common Black-headed Gull** | | 266, 267, 366, 368, 432, 457, 484, 490, 496, 569, **582**, 760, 765, 854 |
| | | West & Central Europe (bre) | 484, 582, 765, 854 |
| | | East Europe (bre) | 366, 490, 496, 582 |
| | | SW Asia, E Africa (non-bre) | 368, 457 |
| | | South Asia (non-bre) | 266, 267 |
| | | E & SE Asia (non-bre) | 432 |
| *Larus genei* | **Slender-billed Gull** | | 287, 302, 366, 368, 432, 760 |
| | | Black Sea, Mediterranean | 366 |
| | | W, SW & S Asia (bre) | 287, 302, 368 |
| *Larus philadelphia* | **Bonaparte's Gull** | North America | 206 |
| *Larus saundersi VU* | **Saunders's Gull** | NE Asia (bre) | 81, 332, 690 |
| *Larus melanocephalus* | **Mediterranean Gull** | Europe, SW Asia | 760, 765 |
| *Larus relictus VU* | **Relict Gull** | C Asia (bre) | 332, 432 |
| *Larus atricilla* | **Laughing Gull** | | 172, 181, 817 |
| | | *(megalopterus)* | 181, 817 |
| | | *atricilla* | 172 |
| *Larus pipixcan* | **Franklin's Gull** | Americas | **209**, 760 |
| *Larus minutus* | **Little Gull** | | 266, 368, 801 |
| | | N, C & E Europe (bre) | 801 |
| | | Black, Caspian & E Mediterranean Seas (non-bre) | 266, 368 |
| *Pagophila eburnean NT* | **Ivory Gull** | High Arctic | **29**, 206 |
| *Xema sabini* | **Sabine's Gull** | | 760 |
| *Creagrus furcatus* | **Swallow-tailed Gull** | Galapagos Is | 181 |
| *Rissa tridactyla* | **Black-legged Kittiwake** | | 10, 432, 743, **765**, 767 |
| | | *tridactyla*, East Atlantic (bre) | 10, 743, 765, 767 |
| *Rissa brevirostris VU* | **Red-legged Kittiwake** | North Pacific | 332 |
| *Sterna nilotica* | **Gull-billed Tern** | | 161, 172, 287, 457, 760 |
| | | *nilotica*, W Europe & W Africa (bre) | 457, 760 |
| | | *nilotica*, Black Sea, E Mediterranean (bre) | 760 |
| | | *nilotica*, SW Asia (non-bre) | 287, 760 |
| | | *vanrossemi* | 161 |
| | | *aranea* | 172 |
| *Sterna caspia* | **Caspian Tern** | | 218, 257, 356, 368, 374, 418, 582, 760 |
| | | Southern Africa (bre) | 257, 760 |
| | | Madagascar (bre) | 374, 760 |
| | | W Africa (bre) | 218, 760 |
| | | Europe (bre) | 356, 750, 760 |
| | | Caspian (bre) | 368, 582, 760 |

| Species | English name | Subspecies/population | |
|---|---|---|---|
| *Sterna (Thalasseus) bengalensis* | **Lesser Crested Tern** | | 305, 374, 760 |
| | | *emigrata* | 760 |
| | | *par* | 374, 760 |
| | | *bengalensis* | 305 |
| *Sterna (Thalasseus) sandvicensis* | **Sandwich Tern** | | 257, 368, 569, 760, 765 |
| | | *sandvicensis*, W Europe (bre) | 257, 569, 760, 765 |
| | | *sandvicensis*, Black Sea (bre) | 569, 760 |
| | | *sandvicensis*, Caspian (bre) | 368, 569 |
| *Sterna (Thalasseus) bernsteini  CR* | **Chinese Crested Tern** | E China (bre)  332 |
| *Sterna (Thalasseus) maxima* | **Royal Tern** | | 158, 172, 181, 218, 760 |
| | | *maxima*, W Atlantic (bre) | 172 |
| | | *maxima*, E Pacific (bre) | 158, 181 |
| | | *albididorsalis* | 218, 760 |
| *Sterna (Thalasseus) bergii* | **(Greater) Crested Tern, Swift Tern** | | 257, 305, 374, **760** |
| | | *bergii* | **760** |
| | | (*enigma*) | 374, 760 |
| | | *thalassina* | 760 |
| | | *velox*, Red Sea & NE Africa (bre) | 760 |
| | | *velox*, Persian Gulf & Indian Ocean (bre) | 305, 760 |
| *Sterna dougallii* | **Roseate Tern** | | 13, 218, 602, 760, 765 |
| | | *dougalli*, South Africa (bre) | 760 |
| | | *dougalli*, E Africa (bre) | 760 |
| | | *dougalli*, W Europe (bre) | 13, 602, 760, 765 |
| *Sterna hirundo* | **Common Tern** | | 189, 257, 266, **267**, 368, 374, **405**, 422, 432, 760, 765, 801 |
| | | *hirundo*, W Africa (bre) | 405, 422, 760 |
| | | *hirundo*, S, W Europe (bre) | 760, 765, 801 |
| | | *hirundo*, N, E Europe (bre) | 760 |
| | | *hirundo*, W Asia (bre) | 266, 267, 368, 760 |
| *Sterna paradisaea* | **Arctic Tern** | | 16, 154, 432, 760, 765, 801 |
| | | N Eurasia (bre) | 16, 154, 765, 801 |
| *Sterna vittata* | **Antarctic Tern** | | 760 |
| | | *vittata* | 760 |
| | | *tristanensis* | 760 |
| *Sterna forsteri* | **Forster's Tern** | | 206 |
| *Sterna albifrons* | **Little Tern** | | 264, 302, 356, 368, 432, **560**, 721, 760, 765 |
| | | *albifrons*, W Europe (bre) | 356, **560**, 760, 765 |
| | | *albifrons*, E Europe (bre) | 264, 721, 760 |
| | | *albifrons*, SW Asia (bre) | 302, 368 |
| | | *guineae* | 760 |
| *Sterna saundersi* | **Saunders's Tern** | N & W Indian Ocean, Red Sea | 374, 760 |
| *Sterna antillarum* | **Least Tern** | | 172 |
| | | *antillarum* | 172 |
| *Sterna balaenarum  NT* | **Damara Tern** | SW Africa (bre) | 760 |
| *Sterna repressa* | **White-cheeked Tern** | N & W Indian Ocean, Red Sea | 302, 735, 760 |
| *Sterna anaethetus* | **Bridled Tern** | | 161 |
| | | *nelsoni* | 161 |
| *Chlidonias hybrida* | **Whiskered Tern** | | 218, 457 |
| | | *hybrida*, E Europe, E Mediterranean (bre) | 457 |
| | | *sclateri*, Southern Africa | 218 |
| *Chlidonias leucopterus* | **White-winged (Black) Tern** | | 245, 264, 266, 302, 368, 432, 457 |
| | | Africa (non-br) | 245, 457 |
| | | Asia, Australasia | 302 |

| Species | English name | Subspecies/population | |
|---|---|---|---|
| *Chlidonias niger* | **Black Tern** | | 172, 206, 264, 356, 432, 760 |
| | | *niger* | 264, 356, 432, 760 |
| | | *surinamensis* | 172, 206 |
| *Anous stolidus* | **Brown Noddy** | | 161, 181 |
| | | *ridgwayi* | 161, 181 |
| *Anous minutus* | **Black Noddy** | | 181 |
| | | *americanus* | 181 |
| *Anous tenuirostris* | **Lesser Noddy** | | 218 |
| | | *tenuirostris* | 218 |
| *Gygis alba* | **White Tern** | | 161 |
| | | *alba* | 161 |
| *Larosterna inca  NT* | **Inca Tern** | Peru & Chile | 181 |
| *Rynchops niger* | **Black Skimmer** | | 161 |
| | | *niger,* Pacific North America | 161 |
| *Rynchops flavirostris  NT* | **African Skimmer** | | 457 |
| | | East & Southern Africa | 457 |
| *Rynchops albicollis  VU* | **Indian Skimmer** | S & SE Asia | 305, 308, 332 |

| | | | |
|---|---|---|---|
| **STERCORARIIDAE** | **SKUAS** | | **161, 765** |
| *Stercorarius skua* | **Great Skua** | | 765 |
| *Catharacta antarctica* | **Brown Skua** | | 412 |
| *Catharacta maccormicki* | **South Polar Skua** | | 432 |
| *Stercorarius pomarinus* | **Pomarine Skua** | | 368, 432 |
| *Stercorarius parasiticus* | **Arctic Skua** | | 368, 765 |

| | | | |
|---|---|---|---|
| **ALCIDAE** | **AUKS** | | **765** |
| *Uria aalge* | **Common Guillemot/Murre** | | **120**, 432, 752, **765**, **767**, 801 |
| *Uria lomvia* | **Brunnich's Guillemot/** | | 743 |
| | **Thick-billed Murre** | | |
| *Alca torda* | **Razorbill** | | 752, 765, 801 |
| *Pinguinus impennis  EX* | **Great Auk** | | 10 |
| *Cepphus grylle* | **Black Guillemot** | | 765 |
| *Cepphus grylle/carbo* | **Black/Spectacled Guillemot** | | 432 |
| *Synthliboramphus antiquus  EN* | **Marbled Murrelet** | | 206 |
| *Ptychoramphus aleuticus* | **Cassin's Auklet** | | 206 |
| *Fratercula arctica* | **Atlantic Puffin** | | 752, 765 |

| | | | |
|---|---|---|---|
| **PTEROCLIDIDAE** | **SANDGROUSE** | | |
| *Syrrhaptes paradoxus* | **Pallas's Sandgrouse** | | 275 |
| *Pterocles alchata* | **Pin-tailed Sandgrouse** | | 275 |

| | | | |
|---|---|---|---|
| **COLUMBIDAE** | **PIGEONS & DOVES** | | |
| *Columba eversmanni* | **Pale-backed Pigeon** | | 275 |
| *Columba palumbus* | **Wood Pigeon** | | 817 |
| *Columba trocaz* | **Madeira Laurel Pigeon** | | 602 |
| *Columba bollii* | **Dark-tailed Laurel Pigeon** | | 602 |
| *Columba junoniae* | **White-tailed Laurel Pigeon** | | 602 |
| *Streptopelia orientalis* | **Rufous Turtle Dove** | | 432 |
| *Streptopelia tranquebarica* | **Red Turtle Dove** | | 432 |
| *Streptopelia decaocto* | **Collared Dove** | | 432 |
| *Macropygia ruficeps* | **Little Cuckoo Dove** | | 432 |
| *Zenaida macroura* | **Mourning Dove** | | 172 |

| | | | |
|---|---|---|---|
| **STRIGIDAE** | **OWLS** | | |
| *Nyctea scandiaca* | **Snowy Owl** | | 264 |
| *Bubo bubo* | **Eurasian Eagle Owl** | | 264, 275, 356 |

| Species | English name | Subspecies/population |
|---|---|---|
| **ALCEDINIDAE** | **KINGFISHERS** | |
| *Alcedo atthis* | **Common Kingfisher** | 264, 476, 484, 487 |
| *Alcedo vintsiodes* | **Madagascar Malachite Kingfisher** | 374 |
| *Ceryle alcyon* | **Belted Kingfisher** | 172 |
| **PICIDAE** | **WOODPECKERS** | |
| *Dendrocopus medius* | **Middle Spotted Woodpecker** | 356 |
| *Dendrocopus major* | **Great Spotted Woodpecker** | 432, 602 |
| *Dendrocopus leucopterus* | **White-winged Woodpecker** | 275 |
| *Campephilus principalis  CR* | **Ivory-billed Woodpecker** | 841 |
| **TYRANNIDAE** | **TYRANT FLYCATCHERS** | |
| *Empidonax trailli* | **Willow Flycatcher** | 668 |
| **MALACONOTIDAE** | **HELMETSHRIKES & ALLIES** | |
| *Laniarius mufumbiri  NT* | **Papyrus Gonolek** | 457 |
| **LANIIDAE** | **SHRIKES** | |
| *Lanius ludovicianus* | **Loggerhead Shrike** | 214 |
| *Lanius excubitor* | **Great Grey Shrike** | 356 |
| **DICRURIDAE** | **DRONGOS** | |
| *Dicrurus macrocerus* | **Black Drongo** | 432 |
| **PARIDAE** | **TITS** | |
| *Parus major* | **Great Tit** | 398 |
| **CORVIDAE** | **CROWS** | |
| *Pica pica* | **Common Magpie** | 432 |
| *Corvus splendens* | **House Crow** | 432 |
| *Corvus frugilegus* | **Rook** | 817 |
| *Corvus brachyrhynchus* | **American Crow** | 418 |
| *Corvus corone* | **Carrion Crow** | 432 |
| *Corvus macrorhynchus* | **Large-billed Crow** | 432 |
| **HIRUNDINIDAE** | **SWALLOWS & MARTINS** | |
| *Riparia riparia* | **Sand Martin** | 264 |
| *Hirundo rustica* | **Barn Swallow** | 432 |
| **PYCNOTOTIDAE** | **BULBULS** | |
| *Pycnonotus goiaver* | **Yellow-vented Bulbul** | 432 |
| **SYLIVIDAE** | **WARBLERS** | |
| *Sylvia communis* | **Common Whitethroat** | 432 |
| *Phylloscopus collybita* | **Chiffchaff** | 668 |
| *Wilsonia pusilla* | **Wilson's Warbler** | 506 |
| *Megalurus pryeri  VU* | **Japanese Marsh Warbler** | 690 |
| *Acrocephalus schoenobaenus* | **Sedge Warbler** | 264 |
| *Acrocephalus paludicola  VU* | **Aquatic Warbler** | 264, 356, 602, 690 |
| *Chloropeta gracilirostris  VU* | **Papyrus Yellow Warbler** | 457 |
| **ZOSTEROPIDAE** | **WHITE-EYES** | |
| *Zosterops japonicus* | **Japanese White-eye** | 432 |
| **STURNIDAE** | **STARLINGS** | |
| *Sturnus vulgaris* | **Common Starling** | 432 |
| *Acridotheres tristis* | **Crested Mynah** | 432 |

| Species | English name | Subspecies/population | |
|---|---|---|---|
| **TURDIDAE** | THRUSHES | | |
| *Turdus pilaris* | **Fieldfare** | | 582 |
| *Turdus iliacus* | **Redwing** | | 505, **506**, 582 |
| *Turdus philomelos* | **Song Thrush** | | 582 |
| **MUSCICAPIDAE** | CHATS & OLD WORLD FLYCATCHERS | | |
| *Luscinia svecica* | **Bluethroat** | | 668 |
| *Copsychus saularis* | **Oriental Magpie Robin** | | 432 |
| **CINCLIDAE** | DIPPERS | | |
| *Cinclus cinclus* | **Dipper** | | 476, 484, 487 |
| **PASSERIDAE** | SPARROWS | | |
| *Passer domesticus* | **House Sparrow** | | 432 |
| *Passer montanus* | **Eurasian Tree Sparrow** | | 432 |
| **ESTRILDIDAE** | WAXBILLS, MUNIAS & ALLIES | | |
| *Lonchura striata* | **White-rumped Munia** | | 432 |
| *Lonchura punctulata* | **Scaly-breasted Munia** | | 432 |
| **MOTACILLIDAE** | PIPITS & WAGTAILS | | |
| *Motacilla flava* | **Yellow Wagtail** | | 432 |
| *Motacilla cinerea* | **Grey Wagtail** | | 264, 476, 484 |
| *Motacilla alba* | **White Wagtail** | | 432, 484 |
| **FRINGILLIDAE** | FINCHES | | |
| *Fringilla coelebs* | **Chaffinch** | | 582 |
| *Fringilla montifringilla* | **Brambling** | | 582 |
| *Fringilla teydea NT* | Blue Chaffinch | | 602 |
| *Loxia scotica DD* | Scottish Crossbill | | 602 |
| *Pyrrhula murina CR* | Azores Bullfinch | | 602 |
| *Carpodacus mexicanus* | **House Finch** | | 412, 418, 668 |
| **EMBERIZIDAE** | BUNTINGS | | |
| *Emberiza aureola NT* | Yellow-breasted Bunting | | 432 |
| *Emberiza schoeniclus* | **Reed Bunting** | | 484 |
| *Emberiza jankowskii VU* | Jankowski's Bunting | | 690 |
| *Emberiza spodocephala* | **Black-faced Bunting** | | 432 |
| *Sporophila palustris EN* | Marsh Seedeater | | **186** |
| *Sporophila cinnamomea VU* | Chestnut Seedeater | | 186 |
| *Sporophila zelichi CR* | Narosky's Seedeater | | 186 |
| **PARULIDAE** | NEW WORLD WARBLERS | | |
| *Geothlypis trichas* | **Common Yellowthroat** | | 206 |

David Stroud, co-editor.  Photo: David Sowter.

# Geographical index

Page numbers relate to the first page of each paper within which the relevant country or territory is mentioned. Page numbers in bold indicate illustrations of the places concerned within the indexed paper. Generally indexing has been undertaken to the level of countries, although a few major sites within countries have also been included, especially where these are the subject of several papers.

# Subject index

Page numbers relate to the first page of each paper within which a subject is mentioned. Page numbers in bold indicate relevant photos within the indexed paper.

Properly managed ecotourism has the potential to give significant economic inputs to protected and other areas in developing countries. Costa Rica.  Photo: David Stroud.

# Author index

Page numbers relate to the first page of each paper authored or co-authored by the relevant individual.